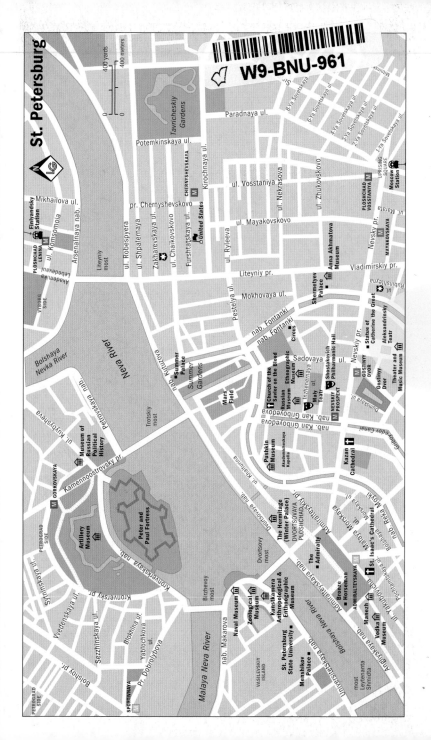

St. Petersburg

W9-BNU-961

0 400 yards
0 400 meters

Tavricheskiy Gardens

Paradnaya ul.

Potemkinskaya ul.

Mikhailova ul.

Finlyandsky Station

PLOSHCHAD LENINA Ⓜ

Akademika Lebedeva ul.

VYBORG SIDE

Arsenalnaya nab.

pr. Chernyshevskovo

CHERNYSHEVSKAYA Ⓜ

Kirochnaya ul.

ul. Vosstaniya

ul. Nekrasova

ul. Zhukovskovo

Liteyniy most

ul. Robespyera

ul. Shpalernaya

Zakharevskaya ul.

ul. Chaikovskovo

Furshtatskaya ul.

United States

ul. Mayakovskovo

ul. Ryleeva

8-ya Sovetskaya ul.
7-ya Sovetskaya ul.
6-ya Sovetskaya ul.
5-ya Sovetskaya ul.
4-ya Sovetskaya ul.
3-ya Sovetskaya ul.
2-ya Sovetskaya ul.
1-ya Sovetskaya ul.

UPRISING SQUARE

PLOSHCHAD VOSSTANIYA Ⓜ **Moscow Station**

Liteyniy pr.

Mokhovaya ul.

Pestelya ul.

nab. Fontanki

nab. Fontanki

Vladimirskiy pr.

Anna Akhmatova Museum

ul. Marata

MAYAKOVSKAYA Ⓜ

Nevsky pr.

Rubinshteyna

VLADIMIRSKAYA Ⓜ

Shermetyev Palace

Circus

Bolshaya Nevka River

Neva River

Trotskiy most

nab. Kutuzova

Summer Palace

Summer Gardens

Mars Field

Church of the Savior on the Blood

Russian Museum

Ethnographic Museum

Maly Teatr

Sadovaya ul.

Inzhenernaya ul.

Shostakovich Philharmonic Hall

Nevsky pr.

Statue of Catherine the Great

Aleksandrinsky Teatr

Theater and Music Museum

GOSTINIY DVOR Ⓜ

Gostiny Dvor

Dumskaya ul.

NEVSKIY PROSPEKT Ⓜ

nab. Kan Griboyedova

nab. Kan Griboyedova

Griboedov Canal

Pushkin Museum

Akademicheskaya Kapella

ul. Khalturina

Kazan Cathedral

Malaya Morskaya ul.

Bolshaya Morskaya ul.

Reka Moyki

nab. Reka Moyki

Museum of Russian Political History

GORKOVSKAYA Ⓜ

Kamenoostrovskiy pr.

ul. Kuybysheva

Petrogradskaya nab.

PETROGRAD SIDE

Artillery Museum

Peter and Paul Fortress

Kronverkskaya nab.

Birzhevoy most

Dvortsovaya nab.

The Hermitage (Winter Palace)

DVORTSOVAYA PLOSHCHAD

Dvortsoy most

The Admiralty

Admiralteyskaya nab.

Bronze Horseman

ADMIRALTEYSKAYA

St. Isaac's Cathedral

Manezh

Vodka Museum

Bolshaya Neva River

Konnogvardeyskaya nab.

Angliyskaya nab.

most Leytenanta Shmidta

ul. Yakubovicha

Neva River

Naval Museum

Zoological Museum

Kunstkamera Anthropological & Ethnographic Museum

St. Petersburg State University

Menshikov Palace

nab. Makarova

Universitetskaya nab.

Malaya Neva River

VASILYEVSKY ISLAND

SPORTIVNAYA Ⓜ

PETROGRAD SIDE

Sytninskaya ul.

Vvedenskiy pr.

Bolshoy pr.

Kronverkskiy pr.

Blokhina ul.

Yablochkova ul.

Sezzhinskaya ul.

Pr. Dobrolyubova

Bolshoy pr.

Pr. Dobrolyubova

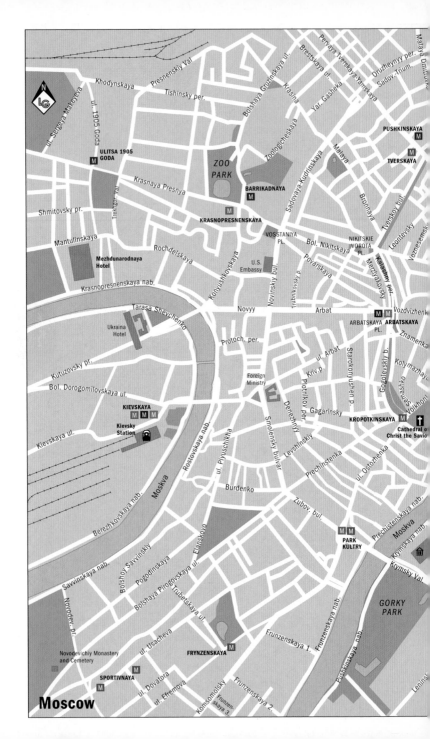

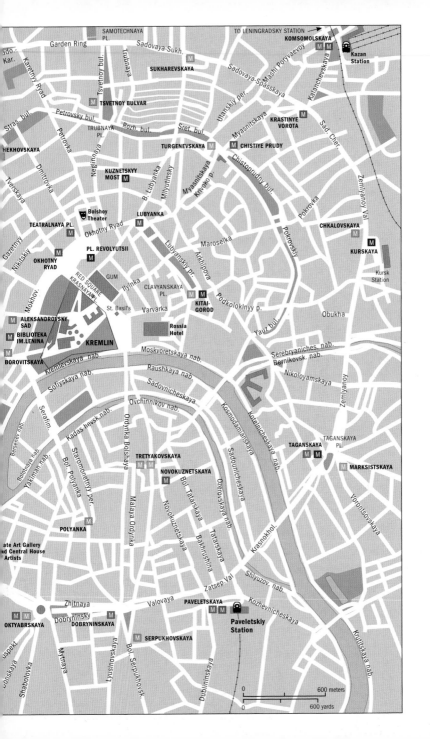

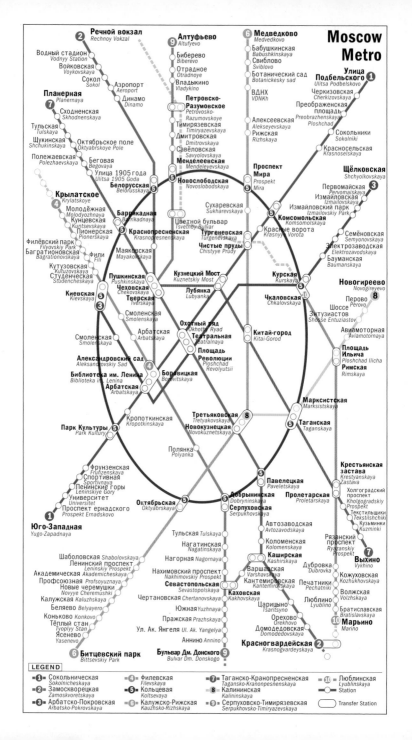

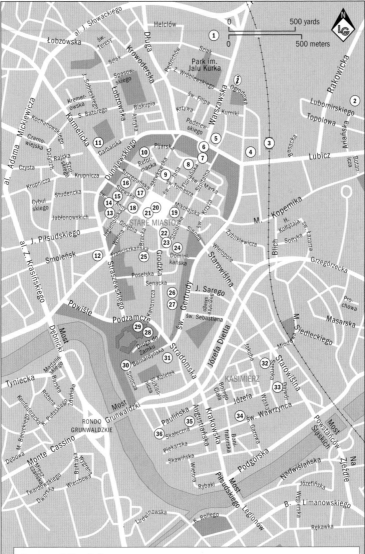

Central Kraków

Akademia Ekonomiczna, **2**
Almatur Office, **22**
Barbican, **6**
Bernardine Church, **31**
Bus Station, **4**
Carmelite Church, **11**
Cartoon Gallery, **9**
Collegium Maius, **14**
Corpus Christi Church, **34**
Czartoryski Art Museum, **8**

Dragon Statue, **30**
Filharmonia, **12**
Franciscan Church, **25**
Grunwald Memorial, **5**
History Museum of Kraków, **17**
Jewish Cemetery, **32**
Jewish Museum, **33**
Kraków Glowny Station, **3**
Monastery of the
  Reformed Franciscans, **10**
Pauline Church, **36**
Police Station, **18**
Politechnika Krakowska, **1**

St. Andrew's Church, **27**
St. Anne's Church, **15**
St. Catherine's Church, **35**
St. Florian's Gate, **7**
St. Mary's Church, **19**
St. Peter and Paul Church, **26**
Stary Teatr (Old Theater), **16**
Sukiennice (Cloth Hall), **20**
Town Hall, **21**
United States Embassy, **23**
University Museum, **13**
Wawel Castle, **28**
Wawel Cathedral, **29**

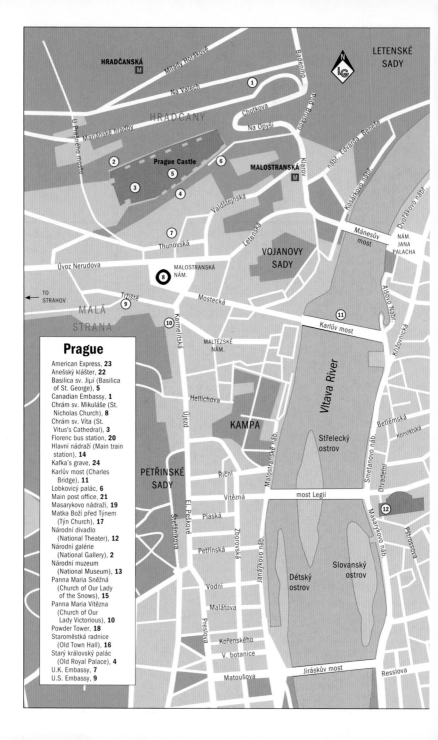

LETENSKÉ
SADY

HRADČANSKÁ Ⓜ Milady Horákové

Na Valech

Chotkova

HRADČANY Na Opyši

Badeniho

Pod Bruskou

Mariánské hradby

U prašného mostu

Prague Castle ⑥
Ⓝ ②
Ⓝ ⑤
③
④ MALOSTRANSKÁ Ⓜ

Klárov

nábř. Edvarda Beneše

Kosárkovo nábř.

Dvořákovo nábř.

Valdštejnská

NÁM.
JANA
PALACHA

Letenská

Mánesův
most

⑦
Thunovská

VOJANOVY
SADY

Úvoz Nerudova

MALOSTRANSKÁ
NÁM.
⑧

Alšovo nábř.

TO
STRAHOV
←

Tržiště
⑨

Mostecká

Karlův most
⑪

MALÁ
STRANA

⑩
Karmelitská

Křižovnická

MALTÉZSKÉ
NÁM.

Prague

American Express, **23**
Anešský klášter, **22**
Basilica sv. Jiųí (Basilica
   of St. George), **5**
Canadian Embassy, **1**
Chrám sv. Mikuláše (St.
   Nicholas Church), **8**
Chrám sv. Víta (St.
   Vitus's Cathedral), **3**
Florenc bus station, **20**
Hlavní nádraží (Main train
   station), **14**
Kafka's grave, **24**
Karlův most (Charles
   Bridge), **11**
Lobkovicý palác, **6**
Main post office, **21**
Masarykovo nádraží, **19**
Matka Boží před Týnem
   (Týn Church), **17**
Národní divadlo
   (National Theater), **12**
Národní galérie
   (National Gallery), **2**
Národní muzeum
   (National Museum), **13**
Panna Maria Sněžná
   (Church of Our Lady
   of the Snows), **15**
Panna Maria Vítězna
   (Church of Our
   Lady Victorious), **10**
Powder Tower, **18**
Staroměstská radnice
   (Old Town Hall), **16**
Starý královský palác
   (Old Royal Palace), **4**
U.K. Embassy, **7**
U.S. Embassy, **9**

Hellichova

KAMPA

Vltava River

Betlémská
Konviktská

Střelecký
ostrov

Smetanovo nábř.

Divadelní

PETŘINSKÉ
SADY

Říční

El. Peškové

Vítězná

most Legií

Masarykovo nábř.

⑫

Pštrossova

Štefánikova

Plaská

Petřínská

Zborovská

Janáčkovo nábř.

Slovanský
ostrov

Dětský
ostrov

Resslova

Vodní

Malátova

Preslova

Kořenského

V. botanice

Jiráskův most

Matoušova

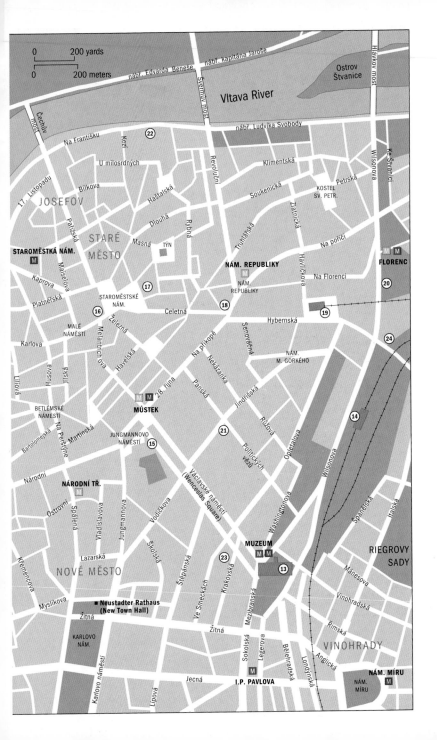

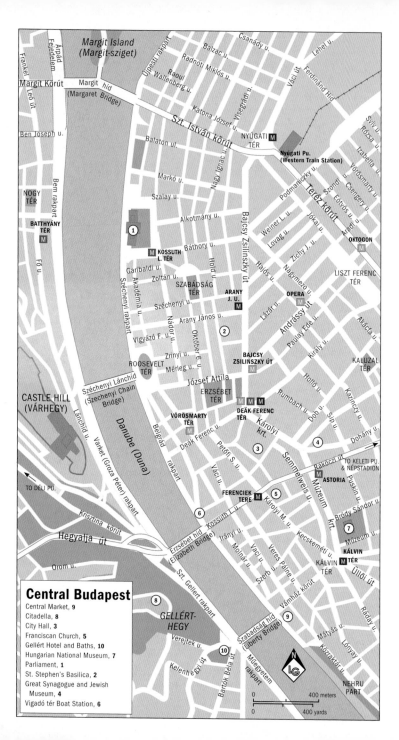

Central Budapest

Central Market, 9
Citadella, 8
City Hall, 3
Franciscan Church, 5
Gellért Hotel and Baths, 10
Hungarian National Museum, 7
Parliament, 1
St. Stephen's Basilica, 2
Great Synagogue and Jewish
  Museum, 4
Vigadó tér Boat Station, 6

LET'S GO

■ THE RESOURCE FOR THE INDEPENDENT TRAVELER

"The guides are aimed not only at young budget travelers but at the independent traveler; a sort of streetwise cookbook for traveling alone."

—*The New York Times*

"Unbeatable; good sight-seeing advice; up-to-date info on restaurants, hotels, and inns; a commitment to money-saving travel; and a wry style that brightens nearly every page."

—*The Washington Post*

"Lighthearted and sophisticated, informative and fun to read. [Let's Go] helps the novice traveler navigate like a knowledgeable old hand."

—*Atlanta Journal-Constitution*

"A world-wise traveling companion—always ready with friendly advice and helpful hints, all sprinkled with a bit of wit."

—*The Philadelphia Inquirer*

■ THE BEST TRAVEL BARGAINS IN YOUR PRICE RANGE

"All the dirt, dirt cheap."

—*People*

"Anything you need to know about budget traveling is detailed in this book."

—*The Chicago Sun-Times*

"Let's Go follows the creed that you don't have to toss your life's savings to the wind to travel—unless you want to."

—*The Salt Lake Tribune*

■ REAL ADVICE FOR REAL EXPERIENCES

"The writers seem to have experienced every rooster-packed bus and lunar-surfaced mattress about which they write."

—*The New York Times*

"Value-packed, unbeatable, accurate, and comprehensive."

—*The Los Angeles Times*

"[Let's Go's] devoted updaters really walk the walk (and thumb the ride, and trek the trail). Learn how to fish, haggle, find work—anywhere."

—*Food & Wine*

LET'S GO PUBLICATIONS

TRAVEL GUIDES

Australia 8th edition
Austria & Switzerland 12th edition
Brazil 1st edition
Britain & Ireland 2005
California 10th edition
Central America 9th edition
Chile 2nd edition
China 5th edition
Costa Rica 2nd edition
Eastern Europe 2005
Ecuador 1st edition **NEW TITLE**
Egypt 2nd edition
Europe 2005
France 2005
Germany 12th edition
Greece 2005
Hawaii 3rd edition
India & Nepal 8th edition
Ireland 2005
Israel 4th edition
Italy 2005
Japan 1st edition
Mexico 20th edition
Middle East 4th edition
Peru 1st edition **NEW TITLE**
Puerto Rico 1st edition
South Africa 5th edition
Southeast Asia 9th edition
Spain & Portugal 2005
Thailand 2nd edition
Turkey 5th edition
USA 2005
Vietnam 1st edition **NEW TITLE**
Western Europe 2005

ROADTRIP GUIDE

Roadtripping USA **NEW TITLE**

ADVENTURE GUIDES

Alaska 1st edition
New Zealand **NEW TITLE**
Pacific Northwest **NEW TITLE**
Southwest USA 3rd edition

CITY GUIDES

Amsterdam 3rd edition
Barcelona 3rd edition
Boston 4th edition
London 2005
New York City 15th Edition
Paris 13th Edition
Rome 12th edition
San Francisco 4th edition
Washington, D.C. 13th edition

POCKET CITY GUIDES

Amsterdam
Berlin
Boston
Chicago
London
New York City
Paris
San Francisco
Venice
Washington, D.C.

LET'S GO

EASTERN EUROPE

2005

SETH ROBINSON EDITOR
AMELIA ATLAS ASSOCIATE EDITOR
EMILY R. GEE ASSOCIATE EDITOR
ALEXANDRA C. STANEK ASSOCIATE EDITOR

RESEARCHER-WRITERS

CALUM DOCHERTY	**CLAY H. KAMINSKY**
ANDREA HALPERN	**AARON LITVIN**
DANIEL HEMEL	**HUNTER MAATS**
DIANA HRISTOVA	**LAUREN RIVERA**
NOAM KATZ	**ALKA R. TANDON**

JANE YAGER

WILL RIFFELMACHER MAP EDITOR
CHRISTINA ZAROULIS MANAGING EDITOR

ST. MARTIN'S PRESS ≋ NEW YORK

Maps by David Lindroth copyright © 2005 by St. Martin's Press.

HOW TO USE THIS BOOK

Hello, intrepid Reader, and welcome to ⬛Let's Go: Eastern Europe 2005. This year, our crack team of researchers and editors went to unprecedented lengths to bring you the best that this historic and culturally rich region has to offer. We worked tirelessly to completely revamp our coverage of major cities like Warsaw and Dubrovnik, breaking only to marinate in various rural hamlets and scour the shimmering coastlines of the Baltic, Black, and Adriatic Seas. Don't fear—our signature Trans-Siberian Railroad route still awaits your adventurous eyes, alongside several other outdoors itineraries for the rough and ready. So pack up and dig in—a wealth of nations, people and customs loom on the travel horizon.

GREETINGS. Inside the first pages of this book you'll find a comprehensive introduction to planning your trip. The first chapter, **Discover Eastern Europe,** provides an overview of travel in Eastern Europe and—for those who appreciate a bit of structure in their lives—lists some **suggested itineraries. Life and Times** gives a brief synopsis of the history and culture of the region, while the **Essentials** section outlines the practical information you'll need to prepare and execute your journey. **Alternatives to Tourism** offers a refreshing perspective on travel, and suggests diverse ways to deeply immerse yourself in the culture of your destination.

CHAPTER BY CHAPTER. Our chapters are divided by country, listed alphabetically from Albania to Ukraine. Each chapter begins with a detailed introduction to the country's history, culture, and practical travel information. Major cities are listed thereafter, and then smaller cities and hubs. Newly introduced ⬛tipboxes are peppered throughout the chapters, pointing out insider information that every travel savvy explorer should know. Keeping with *Let's Go* tradition, each of our chapters is jam-packed with hidden deals, extensively detailed maps, and **sidebars,** which provide in-depth looks at the lives, politics, and gems that would keep even locals on the edge of their seats. Our final chapter, **Gateway Cities,** is perfect for the meandering traveler who may end up in Berlin, Helsinki, Beijing, or Vienna.

PRICE DIVERSITY. We list establishments in order from best to worst. Our absolute favorites are denoted by the renowned *Let's Go* ⬛thumbpick. Since the best value doesn't always come at the cheapest price, we've also incorporated a scale from ❶ to ❺ for ranking food and accommodations (❶ being the cheapest), where each icon corresponds to a specific range. Tables at the begining of each chapter list country-specific price ranges, but be sure to check out the **master table** (p. ix), which will tell you what to expect in general.

LANGUAGES. From Albanian to Romani, languages can present an interesting challenge to those traveling in Eastern Europe. If making overwhelming hand gestures and speaking slowly and loudly seems to be producing few results, we've listed some key words and useful phrases in a variety of tongues, which you'll find in the **Language** section of each chapter and in the **Glossary** at the back of the book.

A NOTE TO OUR READERS. The information for this book was gathered by *Let's Go* researchers from May through August of 2004. Each listing is based on one researcher's opinion, formed during his or her visit at a particular time. Those traveling at other times may have different experiences since prices, dates, hours, and conditions are always subject to change. You are urged to check the facts presented in this book beforehand to avoid inconvenience and surprises.

CONTENTS

PRICE RANGES >> EASTERN EUROPE

Our researchers list establishments in order of value from best to worst; our favorites are denoted by the Let's Go thumbs-up (🖢). Since the best value is not always the cheapest price, however, we have also incorporated a system of price ranges, based on a rough expectation of what you will spend. For **accommodations,** we base our range on the cheapest price for which a single traveler can stay for one night. For **restaurants** and other dining establishments, we estimate the average amount a traveler will spend. The table below tells you what you will *typically* find in Eastern Europe at the corresponding price range; keep in mind that no system can allow for every individual establishment's quirks.

ACCOMMODATIONS	WHAT YOU'RE *LIKELY* TO FIND
❶	Camping; most dorm rooms, such as HI or other hostels or university dorm rooms. Expect bunk beds and a communal bath; you may have to provide or rent towels and sheets.
❷	Upper-end hostels or small hotels. You may have a private bathroom, or there may be a sink in your room and communal shower in the hall.
❸	A small room with a private bath. Should have decent amenities, such as phone and TV. Breakfast may be included in the price of the room.
❹	Similar to 3, but may have more amenities or be in a more touristed area.
❺	Large hotels or upscale chains. If it's a 5 and it doesn't have the perks you want, you've paid too much.

FOOD	WHAT YOU'RE *LIKELY* TO FIND
❶	Mostly street-corner stands, pizza places, or fast-food joints; some sit-down establishments in smaller towns.
❷	Sandwiches, appetizers at a bar, or low-priced entrees; likely a sit-down meal.
❸	Mid-priced entrees, possibly coming with a soup or salad. A tip may bump you up a couple dollars, since you'll probably have a waiter or waitress.
❹	A somewhat fancy restaurant. You'll probably have some specialized silverware. Few restaurants in this range have a dress code, but some may look down on t-shirt and jeans.
❺	Upscale restaurant, generally specializing in regional fare, with a decent wine list. Slacks and dress shirts may be expected.

RESEARCHER-WRITERS

Cal Docherty
Southern Poland and the Slovak Republic

A seasoned traveler, devoted soccer fan, and former resident of Scotland and Singapore, Cal was a true *Let's Go* trekker. He took his worldliness and charm to the streets and trails of Southern Poland and the Slovak Republic, befriending fellow travelers and uncovering the hippest hotspots during his travels. He sent back his invaluable research and colorful prose along with mesmerizing Slovak trinkets worth much more than their weight in postage.

Andrea Halpern
Czech Republic

With her "sentimental" Nalgenes in tow, Andrea made her way across the Czech Republic, tackling incomprehensible bus schedules and quenching her bottomless thirst for beer. An experienced world traveler and Boston native, she was ready for adventure at every cobblestone turn. Even near-sleepless nights in Prague and a hive-inducing hike along train tracks couldn't stop her from sending back inconceivably detailed notes. As Andrea would say, rock on.

Daniel Hemel
Estonia, Latvia, Lithuania, and Kaliningrad

A true budget traveler, Daniel watched every dime while exploring the Baltic region by train, bus, and bike. Daniel chilled with artists in Lithuania, visited the land of his ancestors in Latvia, scaled the sand dunes in Russia, and tackled the island transportation system in Estonia. He proved that it is possible to be a vegetarian in Eastern Europe. Thanks to Daniel, we now have greatly improved our coverage of the Jewish historical sites of the Baltic region.

Diana Hristova
Bulgaria

With the speed and efficiency that only a native could possess, Diana swept across the Bulgarian countryside, taking breathers only to party hard in Sofia and meditate in an array of magnificent monasteries. Despite computer troubles and the tantalizing distractions of the shimmering Black Sea Coast, the recent Harvard grad employed her eye for detail and turned in sparkling copy every week, all while "finding herself" in the process.

Noam Katz
Moldova and Romania

Noam had the experience of writing for *Let's Go: Alaska 2004* under his belt when he set off to explore the concrete-block cities, famed monasteries, and rural plains of Romania and Moldova. He survived the occasional less-than-wholesome meal, wrote detailed descriptions of Soviet-era kitsch, and seriously revamped our coverage of his first love: the great outdoors. Noam plans to spend early 2005 studying abroad before heading to law school in the fall.

Clay H. Kaminsky
Sarajevo

Taking a one week hiatus from his scholarly endeavors, Clay came out of *Let's Go* retirement to marvelously research the Balkan beauty of Sarajevo. A veritable *Let's Go: Eastern Europe* god, Clay explored Romania and Moldova in 2002, edited the book in 2003, and was the 2003-2004 Low Season Manager. Beloved by Roma and absinthe peddlers everywhere, Clay teamed up with the brilliant Inna Livitz to turn in spectacular copy at breakneck speed.

Aaron Litvin
Belarus and Ukraine

Whether perched atop medieval fortresses or eating hearty, exotic fare, Aaron sent back terrific writing and greatly improved our coverage. Aaron kept us amused with his ubiquitous sarcasm, and his eye for detail and fluency in Russian led him to produce consistently outstanding copy. Having spent spring in Japan and summer in Eastern Europe, he is headed for Brazil to conquer a third continent.

Hunter Maats
Russia

Hunter's language skills and new Eurotrash wardrobe allowed him to blend in with the locals. Fueled by a diet of bananas and *shasklyk*, Hunter attacked his ever-changing itinerary with cheerleader-like enthusiasm. He covered Moscow, Petersburg, and everything in between, and he added coverage of Nizhniy Novgorod to our book. From $16 pineapple juice to stiff-yet-sultry waitresses, Hunter found that legendary Soviet customer service lives on.

Lauren Rivera
Croatia and Slovenia

Having researched the Czech Republic for *Let's Go* in 2003, Lauren hit the road again, armed with an arsenal of adjectives and healthy dose of spontaneity. A student of sociology, she put her observation skills to work, tracking down the hottest nightspots and, of course, the hottest tourist bureau officials. From the Dalmatian Coast to the Julian Alps, Lauren made writing impeccable prose look easy, all while questing with fervent passion for the perfect salad.

Alka Tandon
Hungary

A fun-loving Michigan native with Great Lakes charm, Alka took Budapest by storm before venturing through Hungary's countryside. She left no local uninterrogated and no ice cream untasted on her trek through cobblestone towns, vast plains, and national parks. Though she missed her family, Alka never complained; instead, she responded to our endless requests with text so exquisite we were tempted to drop our day jobs and head to Hungary ourselves.

Jane Yager
Poland

Jane traipsed across virtually all 312,000 sq. km of Poland without missing a single step. Despite having to battle back from an ill-fated kebab incident, fight through hordes of schoolchildren and read "poignant" backpacker poetry, Jane consistently turned in sophisticated, witty copy that never ceased to impress. Now wielding a Polish lexicon, Jane must be content to sheath her pen and return to her Anthropology studies at Harvard's Divinity School. Dziękuję, Jane!

CONTRIBUTING WRITERS

Sherry Chen and Xiao Linda Liu

Beijing

Patrick Hosfield

Helsinki

Venu Aarre Nadella

Berlin

Barbara Richter

Vienna

Kate McIntyre

Editor, Let's Go: Austria and Switzerland

Veronique Hyland

Associate Editor, Let's Go: Austria and Switzerland

Shelley Jiang

Editor, Let's Go: China

Shelley Cheung

Associate Editor, Let's Go: China

Stuart Robinson

Editor, Let's Go: Europe

Marcel LaFlamme

Associate Editor, Let's Go: Europe

Katherine Thompson

Editor, Let's Go: Germany

Will Payne

Associate Editor, Let's Go: Germany

Mallory Greimann hails from Wellesley, MA. She is currently pursuing an undergraduate degree in economics at Harvard University.

Ian Hancock is the UN representative to the International Romani Union and a professor of linguistics and English at the University of Texas, Austin, where he directs the Romani Archives and Documentation Center. His books include *We Are the Romani People* and *A Handbook of Vlax Romani*.

ACKNOWLEDGMENTS

LET'S GO

TEAM EASTERN EUROPE THANKS: Christina, for love and merciless edits; our spectacular team of RWs, who roamed 16 countries and somehow found their way back; Josiah, for pod visits; C. Clayton, for TSR touch-ups; Vicki for constant help; Jesse, Handsome Jackson, the N. End, Harry Potter, the Olympics, and iPods for making everything reasonable.

SETH THANKS: Christina, for guidance and weekly meals; my RWs for their inimitable style; Alexandra for staying one step ahead; Molly for coffee breaks; Emily for desserts and Cyrillic; Will for Becherovka; Emma & Teresa for trust and another year of LG; Chris/Stu/John/Aaron for summer; Alex, for keeping me in line; Mom, Dad, and Kim for the visit and support; Nana and Papa, who made it all possible.

EMILY THANKS: Seth, for his humor and leadership, past and future; Molly, for her writing talents and good taste in acronyms; Alexandra, for fashion advice and getting it right; Will, for many adjectival suffixes; Cami, for being a great roomie and friend; Mom, Dad, and Michael, for their love and support; and Данилов Монастырь, for the bells.

AMELIA "MOLLY" THANKS: Seth, for being in all instances "the jam"; Emily, for keeping us out of the dark; Alexandra, for dance parties and winter colors; Rachel and Maya for Amaretto Wednesdays; Mom, Dad, and Will for giving me up for the summer; Tom, for Barcelona; the NYC gang for some great weekends; and, of course, 58, official and otherwise.

ALEXANDRA THANKS: Seth, our talented editor and welcoming friend; Molly, a gifted wordsmith, for late-night chats; Emily, for her dedication and perspective; Maya and Rachel, for a memorable summer; Mom, Dad, Andrew, Steven, grandma and the family for their support; Mather House, Kay, Leslie, and Zoey; Holworthy; Jonah, Sharon, and everyone in CA.

WILL THANKS: Seth and the rest of EEUR for their attention to detail, mapland for crazy tunes, and my family for all their support and encouragement.

Editor
Seth Robinson
Associate Editors
Amelia Atlas, Emily R. Gee, Alexandra C. Stanek
Managing Editor
Christina Zaroulis
Map Editor
Will Riffelmacher
Typesetter
Melissa Rudolph

Publishing Director
Emma Nothmann
Editor-in-Chief
Teresa Elsey
Production Manager
Adam R. Perlman
Cartography Manager
Elizabeth Halbert Peterson
Design Manager
Amelia Aos Showalter
Editorial Managers
Briana Cummings, Charlotte Douglas, Ella M. Steim, Joel August Steinhaus, Lauren Truesdell, Christina Zaroulis
Financial Manager
R. Kirkie Maswoswe
Marketing and Publicity Managers
Stef Levner, Leigh Pascavage
Personnel Manager
Jeremy Todd
Low-Season Manager
Clay H. Kaminsky
Production Associate
Victoria Esquivel-Korsiak
IT Director
Matthew DePetro
Web Manager
Rob Dubbin
Associate Web Manager
Patrick Swieskowski
Web Content Manager
Tor Krever
Research and Development Consultant
Jennifer O'Brien
Office Coordinators
Stephanie Brown, Elizabeth Peterson

Director of Advertising Sales
Elizabeth S. Sabin
Senior Advertising Associates
Jesse R. Loffler, Francisco A. Robles, Zoe M. Savitsky
Advertising Graphic Designer
Christa Lee-Chuvala

President
Ryan M. Geraghty
General Manager
Robert B. Rombauer
Assistant General Manager
Anne E. Chisholm

Eastern Europe

Railways of
Eastern Europe

Yaroslavl
Nizhny Novgorod
Kazan
Vladimir
Simbirsk
Tolyatti
Moscow
Samara
Ryazan
Penza
Volsk
Tula
RUSSIA
Saratov
Bryansk
KAZAKHSTAN
Voronezh
Povorino
Kursk
Konotop
Sumy
Volgograd
Kharkiv
Volga R.
Smila
Dnipropetrovsk
Astrakhan
UKRAINE
Donetsk
Rostov-na-Donu
Zaporizhya
Azov
Caspian Sea
Krivy Rih
Mariupol
Primorsko-Akhtarsk
Nikolayiv
Sea of Azov
Stavropol
Odesa
Dzhankoy
Yekaterinodar
Kerch
Grozny
CRIMEA
Yevpatoriya
Feodosiya
Tuapse
Sevastopol
Simferopol
Sochi
GEORGIA
Yalta
Black Sea
Batum
Tbilisi
ARMENIA
Sinop
Yerevan
TURKEY
AZERBAIJAN
Ankara

0   200 miles
0   200 kilometers

DISCOVER EASTERN EUROPE

Not much holds the amorphous region known as Eastern Europe together anymore. Countries that once lived on the same Bloc now have little in common and, in some cases, little to do with each other. The Baltics have lost touch with their Balkan cousins; Central Europe has shed its Soviet skin more quickly than her stepsiblings Belarus and Ukraine; and Russia has remained bold, unpredictable, and isolated from most of her neighbors. Regional unity—if it ever really existed in the first place—was forsaken at the hands of reborn nationalism and cultural pride; as well as increased integration into the global community. States like Latvia, independent for a mere 34 years throughout its entire history, finally have the opportunity to identify themselves as self-defining nations and people.

Perhaps all that *can* be said of the countries in the region is that after more than a decade of transformation, they're still changing—and still a haven for budget travelers. Undiscovered cities, pristine national parks, empty hostel beds, and cheap beer lure adventure-, culture-, and bargain-hunters to this varied expanse. Prague, St. Petersburg, Budapest, and Kraków will charm even the most jaded backpacker, while the jagged peaks of the Tatras, the dazzling beaches of the Dalmatian Coast, and the isolated marvels of Siberia will stagger even the most experienced outdoor adventurer.

The distances are great, and the bureaucracies often infuriating, but hitting the road here is always rewarding. Your senses will be bombarded and, more likely than not, your conceptions of rationality challenged: you can't use a bottle of vodka as a visa anywhere else in the world, let alone take the same train across seven time zones, riding the whole way with family pets. Should the absurdity of the post-Soviet world ever get you down, take comfort in knowing that for every stony border guard and badgering *babushka* (grandmotherly old women), there are countless locals willing to give you a bed, a shot of homemade liquor, and a ride to the next town. If you bring along flexibility, patience, and resilience, you'll have an incredible journey through one of the most geographically varied, historically rich, and culturally dynamic areas of the world.

FACTS AND FIGURES

POPULATION: 336 million.

OLDEST UNIVERSITY: Charles University in Prague, est. 1348.

FIRST SOVIET SATELLITE: The German Democratic Republic, June 5, 1945.

SEVENTH SOVIET SATELLITE: Sputnik, Oct. 4, 1957.

NUMBER OF ISLANDS IN ST. PETERSBURG: 101.

PER CAPITA BEER CONSUMPTION IN THE CZECH REPUBLIC: 160L per year.

WRITER OF THE 1944, 1977, AND 2000 RUSSIAN ANTHEMS: Sergei Mikhalkov, age 90; all to the same tune.

DISCOVER

WHEN TO GO

Summer is Eastern Europe's high season. What high season means, however, varies for each country and region. Prague, Kraków, and Budapest are swarmed with backpackers. In the countryside, "high season" simply means that hotels might actually have guests staying in them. Along the Adriatic, Baltic, and Black Sea coasts, things fill up as soon as it is warm enough to lounge on the beach, usually from June to September. In the Tatras, Julian Alps, and Transylvanian Alps, there is both a summer high season for hiking (July to August) and a winter high season for skiing (November to March). In the low season, you'll often be the only tourist in town. Although securing accommodations and strolling down the street will be easier in low season, high season brings with it an entire subculture of young backpackers. You decide whether that's a good thing. For a temperature chart, see p. 55. Major national holidays are listed in the introduction to each country. Festivals are detailed in city listings where appropriate; major festivals in each country are summarized on p. 56.

WHAT TO DO

Like a tracksuit-clad mafioso on a Moscow street corner, Eastern Europe has got what you need, encompassing both heavily backpacked cities and sleepy hamlets. Perhaps the only constant is the generally good, though rather strong, alcohol. For the best of the regional attractions—from absinthe to *żubrówka*—see the ■Let's Go Picks throughout this book.

THE GREAT OUTDOORS

Leave the urban bustle behind to explore the wonders of the Eastern European wilderness. From the rolling hills of Poland and the Czech Republic to stark Siberia, the untamed corners are a thrill-seeker's Eden. The **High Tatras, SLK** (p. 822) can compete with any mountain range in the world; head here for jagged peaks, Olympic-quality skiing, and heart-stopping hang-gliding. Isolated adventure awaits along the **Trans-Siberian Railroad, RUS** (p. 756), especially in the environs of the **Altaiskiy Krai** (p. 746) and **Lake Baikal** (p. 756), the deepest, oldest, and largest freshwater lake on Earth. Acres of giant, windswept dunes rise above the sparkling waters of the Baltic in **Nida, LIT** (p. 475), the darling of the **Curonian Spit** (p. 474 and 733). The seven-day **Trail of Eagles' Nests** (p. 559) runs through the heart of Poland's green uplands past limestone eruptions and castle ruins. Other outdoor wonderlands include: the lakes of **Mazury, POL** (p. 600); the spas of the **Julian Alps, SLN** (p. 853); the winding rivers of **South Bohemia, CZR** (p. 275); the deserted bison-land of **Białowieski National Park, POL** (p. 603); Dracula's mountainous **Transylvania, ROM** (p. 623); the rocky coastline of **Lahemaa National Park, EST** (p. 317); the untouched island of **Mljet National Park, CRO** (p. 223); and the sand dunes and ice-filled valleys of the **South Gobi Desert** (p. 773).

BEACH BUMMING

Most travelers don't come to Eastern Europe for its beaches, but they should: the region boasts enough surf and sand to accommodate lounging and sunning from June to August. The star of the Mediterranean is Croatia's **Dalmatian Coast** (p. 191). From the karstic cliffs near **Dubrovnik** (p. 216) to the isolated beaches of **Hvar** (p. 212) and **Vis** (p. 210), the azure waters of the Adriatic lap at the feet of this coastal god. **Albania** (p. 69), **Montenegro** (p. 790), and **Slovenia** (p. 840) also share room on the Adriatic. Spear-fishing and rock-climbing are only a few of the diversions in **Crimea, UKR** (p. 894), the starlet of the Black Sea. For more relaxed Crimean days, lounge with wealthy Russians on the pebbled beaches around **Yalta, UKR** (p. 899). **Bulgaria** (p. 113) and **Romania** (p. 605) have lovely Black Sea coastlines. Chillier waters await to the north in the Baltics, where you can bike for days along the deserted roads of the untouched **Estonian Islands** (p. 322) past windswept beaches and spinning windmills, or lounge on the white sands of **Jūrmala, LAT** (p. 435). More Baltic sands await near the **Tri-city Area, POL** (p. 589), the Curonian Spit near **Kaliningrad, RUS** (p. 732); and **Klaipėda, LIT** (p. 466). If you can't make it to the coast, Hungary has the answer: **Lake Balaton** (p. 389) is like a slice of sea in the middle of Hungarian plane.

EVIL EMPIRES

While most of the region is successfully rebuilding after communism's fall, Eastern Europe can't escape its past. Though not the most uplifting of the region's highlights, memorials of traumatic events of the past 100 years provide powerful travel experiences in Eastern Europe. The Resistance movement of Nazi-occupied **Odessa, UKR** (p. 888) hid itself underground during WWII; its headquarters is now one of Europe's most stirring war memorials. More sobering are Eastern Europe's many concentration camps. **Auschwitz-Birkenau, POL** (p. 540), the largest and most infamous of Nazi death camps, today houses a large museum on the Holocaust. The remains of smaller camps are in **Majdanek, POL** (p. 546), **Terezín, CZR** (p. 265), **Salaspils, LAT** (p. 435), and **Paneriai, LIT** (p. 455). Almost entirely destroyed by German bombers in WWII, reconstructed **Warsaw, POL** (p. 511) is a testament to the region's admirable ability to regroup and rebuild, even in the face of utter ruin. Meanwhile, **Sarajevo, BOS** (p. 102), still closed in by landmines, left over from the recent war with Serbia, reminds visitors how long regrouping and rebuilding take. The shadows of Joseph Stalin, Enver Hoxha, and Josip Broz Tito fall all over Eastern Europe, but **Moscow, RUS** (p. 665), **Minsk, BLR** (p. 87), **Bucharest, ROM** (p. 613), **Tirana, ALB** (p. 74), and **Niš, SMN** (p. 789) aren't bad places to start looking for them. You can see where WWII kicked off in **Gdańsk, POL** (p. 589) and then where the Big Three wound it down near Yalta in **Livadiya, UKR** (p. 904). Battles for independence were waged in **Cēsis, LAT** (p. 439), **Vis, CRO** (p. 210), and **Kaunas, LIT** (p. 458).

TOP TEN LIST

SIZE MATTERS

From mountains to microchips, Eastern Europe has got it in XL:

1 Biggest bust: of Lenin, in Ulan Ude, RUS (p. 761).

2 Biggest brick castle: Malbork, POL (p. 595).

3 Biggest bonfire: in Tallinn, EST (p. 316), at Grillfest in late June.

4 Biggest bell: the Tsar Bell in the Kremlin, Moscow, RUS (p. 676). Damaged by fire soon after construction, it has never rung.

5 Biggest cannon: next to the Tsar Bell in the Kremlin (p. 676). You guessed it—it has never been fired.

6 Biggest catacombs: in Odessa, UKR (p. 892). The serpentine tunnels were home to resistance fighters during WWII.

7 Deepest lake: Lake Baikal, RUS (p. 756). Fish live in such depths that they explode when brought to the surface.

8 Biggest square in Europe: Parade Square, Warsaw (p. 524).

9 Second biggest building: Parliamentary Palace, Bucharest, ROM (p. 619). Its promenade is 1m wider than Paris's Champs-Elysées.

10 Biggest country in the world: Covering a staggering 17,075,400 sq. km, Mother Russia (p. 652) reigns supreme.

RUINS AND RELICS

From Romans to Roma and Muslims to Magyars, Eastern Europe has been inhabited by scores of distinct peoples, who have left behind castles, palaces, churches, mosques, temples, and synagogues, overwhelming visitors with history and heritage. The widespread Roman empire certainly made its mark. Emperor Diocletian's Palace in **Split, CRO** (p. 203) harbors a haunting labyrinth, while Vespasian's gladiatorial amphitheater in **Pula, CRO** (p. 177) is now used for concerts. At the heels of Roman legions came legions of churches, cathedrals, and monasteries. **Belgrade, SMN's** beautiful **Saborna Crkva** (p. 785) is the headquarters of the Serbian Orthodox Church, while Wawel Cathedral, in **Kraków, POL** (p. 529) is a center of Catholicism. **Ohrid, MAC** (p. 486) is ground zero for church-gazing, with cathedrals and monasteries dating from AD 1037 to 2002. Cloister-lovers should head to **Bucovina, ROM** (p. 642), **Rila, BUL** (p. 129), and **Kyiv, UKR** (p. 873). The **Hill of Crosses, LIT** (p. 465) is a tribute to Christianity and the human spirit that you won't soon forget, and **Kutná Hora, CZR** (see sidebar, p. 266) has a chapel that will *really* haunt you forever. The Ottoman Turks influenced much of southeast Europe. Visit **Sarajevo, BOS** (p. 102) for its Gazi Husrev-Bey Mosque and an entire Turkish Quarter. Turkish influence is also apparent in the Old Bazaar in **Skopje, MAC** (p. 482) and the Et'hem Bey Mosque in **Tirana, ALB** (p. 74). Despite the catastrophic events of the 20th century, there is still a palpable Jewish presence in the Josefov region of **Prague, CZR** (p. 233) and the Kazimierz area of **Kraków, POL** (p. 529). The largest synagogue in Europe is in **Budapest, HUN** (p. 344). Non-religious locales are often as stunning as their ecclesiastical counterparts. Wawel Castle, one of Poland's "Eagles' Nests," and the best sight in the entire country, is in **Kraków** (p. 529). The world's largest brick castle is also in Poland, in **Malbork** (p. 595). Check out Dracula's alleged old haunt in **Bran, ROM** (p. 626). **Prague, CZR** (p. 233) and **Budapest, HUN** (p. 344) each have their own large castles overlooking the cities.

WRITER'S BLOC

Eastern Europeans love their poets and novelists—and, for that matter, their playwrights, song writers, and essayists—so much that they frequently elect them as presidents and prime ministers. The strongest doses of literary adoration are dispensed in Russia (p. 658). Sample it firsthand at the **Moscow literary museums** (p. 683) devoted to (among others): **Anton Chekhov, Fyodor Dostoevsky, Nikolai Gogol, Alexander Pushkin,** and **Leo Tolstoy.** Or, pay your respects to the graves of Gogol, Chekhov, and Mikhail Bulgakov at **Novodevichiy Cemetery** (p. 678). If that doesn't wear you out, venture on to **St. Petersburg, RUS** and stop by **Dostoevsky's grave** (p. 714) and the statue that inspired Pushkin's poem "The Bronze Horseman" (p. 710). Although it' not *quite* as vocal about its local talent as Russian cities are, **Prague, CZR** (p. 233) won't let you visit without appreciating Czech sons **Milan Kundera** and **Franz Kafka.** If you're a devout member of the literati, make a pilgrimage to Kafka's grave in the **New Jewish Cemetery** (p. 260). Or, stop by the wine-cottage "Bar Apertif Winifera" in **Gdańsk, POL** (p. 589) to see a haunt that inspired Nobel Laureate **Günter Grass.** While in Poland, it's difficult to miss statues and references to Romantic poet extraordinaire **Adam Mickiewicz;** swing by the museum devoted to him in **Warsaw, POL** (p. 511) or venture up to **Vilnius, LIT** to see his old apartment (p. 456). For a little philosophy, visit **Immanuel Kant's** grave in **Kaliningrad, RUS** (p. 732).

SO YOU WANT TO BE AN EXPAT

You've been on an Eastern European whirlwind tour, frantically climbing every mountain and touring every capital, determined to see it all before heading back to the real world. But then you encounter a place that is unpredictable and familiar, paved with cobblestones and history, and you can't bring yourself to leave—ever. Eastern Europe is bursting at the seams with settlement-worthy towns. **Prague, CZR** (p. 233) is Eastern Europe's expat capital; the number of Anglophone residents there today has elicited comparisons to 1920s Paris. If the hordes of Hemingway-wannabes frequenting Prague's cafes frighten you, head south to medieval **Český Krumlov, CZR** (p. 278), where mellower backpackers and locals relish their tight-knit community. The Backpack Guesthouse (p. 352) is home base to **Budapest, HUN's** (p. 344) English-speaking residents, who linger in Turkish baths. If walled cities are your thing, **Dubrovnik, CRO** (p. 216) just might seduce you. If canals are more your style, set up shop in **St. Petersburg, RUS** (p. 697), which you'll affectionately call "Pete's" as you stroll along the Neva. The most unlikely of the alluring locales is **Ulaanbaatar, MON** (p. 768), where you can get away from it all. Other cities that top the growing list include **Kraków, POL** (p. 529) and **Vilnius, LIT** (p. 446).

▨ LET'S GO PICKS

BEST SUNSHINE: Croatia's Dalmatian Coast (p. 191).

BEST MOONSHINE: Albanian *raki;* Bulgarian *rakiya;* Macedonian *rakija;* Bosnian, Croatian, and Serbian *šljivovica;* Slovenian *slivovka;* Hungarian *pálinka;* Romanian and Moldovan *palincă.* It's all the same: Balkan unity in a Coke bottle.

BEST PLACE TO WAKE UP WITH A HANGOVER: The beer-barrel beds at Prague's Na Vlachvoce Campsite (p. 233).

BEST EPIC JOURNEY: The Trans-Siberian Railroad (p. 739).

BEST PIZZA: At Pekara Kovaći Kod Mahira Pizza, Sarajevo, BOS (p. 106).

BEST-PRESERVED ROMAN AMPHITHEATER: In Pula, CRO (p. 181).

BEST-PRESERVED DICTATOR: Vladimir Ilyich Lenin in Moscow, RUS (p. 677).

BEST PLACE TO PLAY TOP GUN: High above Russia in a MiG (see sidebar, p. 676).

BEST PLACES WHERE NO ONE IS: Sf. Gheorghe, ROM (p. 649); Tuva, RUS (p. 751).

BEST PLACES TO TAKE A BATH: The thermal baths in Budapest, HUN (p. 362) and Karlovy Vary, CZR (p. 271); a *banya* in Moscow, RUS (p. 685).

BEST PLACE TO FEEL LIKE JAMES BOND: The KGB Museum, Moscow, RUS (p. 682).

BEST USE OF SULFUR: For dragon-slaying in Kraków, POL (p. 535).

BEST PLACE TO GET TANKED: The wine cellars in the Valley of Beautiful Women, HUN (p. 369).

BEST WAY TO EAT A GENIUS: Copernicus gingerbread in Toruń, POL (p. 579).

TASTIEST SCULPTURE: The white-chocolate Michael Jackson in Szentendre, Hungary's Marzipan Museum (p. 364).

MOST RANDOM STATUE: Frank Zappa Monument, Vilnius, LIT (p. 454).

BEST PLACE TO MEET BEAUTIFUL WOMEN: Eastern Europe.

BEST PLACES TO DANCE: At the Graduation Parade in Slovenia (see sidebar, p. 842); in Lava Tunnels in Eger, HUN (see sidebar, p. 370).

SUGGESTED ITINERARIES

DISCOVER

BEEN THERE, DONE THAT (52 DAYS)

CENTRAL EUROPE TOUR (48 DAYS)

BEEN THERE, DONE THAT (52 DAYS).

If you're looking to hit strictly the name-brand highlights of Eastern Europe, begin your journey on the pristine **Dalmation Coast, CRO** (p. 182; 5 days) where breath-taking beach sunsets melt into sizzling nights. After making your way up the coast, set your eyes upon the exquisite castles and cathedrals of **Ljubljana, SLO** (p. 798; 2 days). Head west to **Lake Balaton, HUN** (p. 365; 2 days) for an array of water-front activities before moving on to legendary **Budapest, HUN** (p. 325; 5 days). After adding your own touch to the city's timeless lore, catch a train to **Bratislava, SLK** (p. 756; 4 days) for a captivating look at the rapidly modernized medieval center. Perhaps the moment you've most been waiting for is your arrival in **Prague, CZR** (p. 221; 5 days), the crossroads of West and East for centuries. The city does more than live up to its name, though it's rivaled by nearby **Kraków, POL** (p. 497; 4 days). Head up to the revitalized and bustling streets of **Warsaw, POL** (p. 483; 4 days) before traveling to **Kyiv, UKR** (p. 825; 4 days) for an eastern look at an Eastern European city. **Vilnius, LIT** (p. 423; 4 days) will prove a striking contrast to your short-lived trip east, as expat-filled cafes complement historic districts and cobblestone streets. Stop by **Riga, LAT** (p. 400; 3 days) before venturing to **St. Petersburg, RUS** (p. 658; 5 days), where Commuist blocs have been eerily replaced by tourist filled squares and wild nights. End your trip in the heart of communist Eastern Europe, **Moscow, RUS** (p. 630; 5 days).

CENTRAL EUROPE TOUR (48 DAYS).

Prague, CZR (p. 233; 5 days), home to beer, absinthe, ghosts and *golems*, is an ideal beginning point. Backpackers' heaven **Český Krumlov, CZR** (p. 278; 2 days) is a maze of medieval streets. **Olomouc, CZR** (p. 297; 2 days) and **Brno, CZR** (p. 291; 2 days) are a study in contrasts: one drips with old-world charm, while the other is a bustling tech town. Both are stops on the way to **Vienna, AUS** (p. 927; 5 days). **Bratislava, SLK** shows a successful recovery from communism (p. 801; 3 days). Party on the beach in **Siófok, HUN** (p. 390; 2 days), the most vivacious Hungarian city outside of inexhaustible **Budapest, HUN** (p. 344; 5 days). Descend into the wine cellars of **Eger, HUN** (p. 367; 2 day) before going on to hike the Polish and Slovak Tatras (p. 822 and p. 551; 3 days). The gem of Poland is **Kraków, POL** (p. 529; 4 days); explore the city and visit the sobering Auschwitz death camp (p. 540; 1 day). **Warsaw, POL** (p. 511; 4 days) is sprawling, hectic, and doesn't forget its past. Take a break on the Baltic in the **Tri-city area, POL** (p. 589; 3 days). Finally, head to storied and sexy **Berlin, GER** (p. 919; 5 days), where East and West once met, then back to Prague.

DISCOVER

THE BLUE DANUBE (33 DAYS)

VIA BALTICA (35 DAYS)

THE BLUE DANUBE (33 DAYS).

Though it's not technically on the Danube, don't miss **Prague, CZR** (p. 233; 5 days), a dreamy and debaucherous paradise. In **Vienna, AUT** (p. 927; 5 days), revel in the home of some of history's greatest before floating down to **Bratislava, SLK** (p. 801; 3 days), an old-world city on the cutting edge. Disembark in **Sopron, HUN** (p. 381; 2 days) and **Pécs, HUN** (p. 403; 2 days) to see the remnants of empires (Austro-Hungarian and Ottoman, respectively), with a trip to boisterous, breath-taking **Budapest, HUN** (p. 344; 5 days) sandwiched in between. Then, set a course for **Novi Sad, SMN** (p. 787; 1 day), the city that's most glad to have you as a visitor. You probably won't hear air-raid sirens in **Belgrade, SMN** (p. 780; 3 days); a likelier nighttime sound is the thumping disco beat. Stop in **Timișoara, ROM** (p. 636; 1 day), site of revolution, before shoving off for **Bucharest, ROM** (p. 613; 4 days), home of 300,000 dogs and the world's second-largest building. Finally, drift to the **Danube Delta, ROM** (p. 649; 2 days), for solitude and fresh fish under the willow trees.

VIA BALTICA (35 DAYS).

Although not officially Baltic, **St. Petersburg, RUS** (p. 697; 6 days) is the alter-ego of the former USSR: more cultured and much less overwhelming. Multicultural **Helsinki, FIN** (p. 932; 3 days) is the epitome of chill, while **Tallinn, EST** (p. 309; 3 days) is surprisingly cosmopolitan. **Tartu, EST** (p. 330; 1 day) is the oldest city in the Baltics. Get muddy in **Pärnu, EST** (p. 318; 1 day) at one of the town's famous spas. The island of **Saaremaa, EST** (p. 322; 3 days) is more Estonian than Estonia itself, complete with windmills and beaches. **Rīga, LAT** (p. 426; 3 days) is decidedly more Soviet than its neighbors. **Klaipėda, LIT** (p. 466; 3 days) is the gateway to the Curonian Spit. Climb 90m sand dunes in **Nida, LIT** (p. 475; 1 day). Stop by serene, trendy **Kaunas, LIT** (p. 458; 2 days), on your way to **Vilnius, LIT** (p. 446; 3 days), now touted as the "New Prague." Missing Mother Russia? Head to **Kaliningrad, RUS** (p. 732; 2 days). **Gdańsk, POL** (p. 589; 2 days), takes you back to the 19th century, while the popular beaches of **Sopot, POL** (p. 595; 1 day) make a good stop.

BACK IN THE USSR (42 DAYS)

BACK IN THE USSR (42 DAYS).

Start where it all began, in **Moscow, RUS** (p. 665; 6 days). Glimpse Europe from **St. Petersburg, RUS** (p. 697; 7 days), Russia's "Window on Europe." Head to Europe

DISCOVER

proper—or EU at least—in **Tallinn, EST** (p. 309; 3 days). Continue the Baltic circuit with stops in historic **Rīga, LAT** (p. 426; 3 days) and in **Vilnius, LIT** (p. 446; 4 days), one of Europe's prettiest capitals. Prepare for a shock when you reach totalitarian but awesome **Minsk, BLR** (p. 87; 2 days). Play soldier at the WWII "hero-fortress" in **Brest, BLR** (p. 93; 1 day). Wander the streets of **Lviv, UKR** (p. 909; 3 days), the center of Ukrainian nationalism, before exploring **Kyiv, UKR** (p. 873; 4 days). Head down to the Black Sea, stopping in the port town of **Odessa, UKR** (p. 888; 3 days) on your way to the Ukrainian resort region **Crimea** (p. 894; 4 days), playground of the Soviets. Finish in **Chişinău, MOL** (p. 496; 2 days), where hope grows through cracks in the concrete.

VLADIVOSTOK OR BUST (41 DAYS).

Start your monumental journey in **St. Petersburg, RUS** (p. 697; 7 days) and then hit **Moscow** (p. 665; 7 days) to stock up on supplies and civilization, stopping in ancient **Novgorod** (p. 723; 2 days) on the way south. From Moscow, jaunt to the pilgrimage point of **Sergiyev Posad** (p. 687; 1 day). Put on the Golden Ring in **Yaroslavl** (p. 687; 4½hr.; 2 days), a flourishing city with the comforts of a capital. Your next stop on the Trans-Siberian, **Novosibirsk** (p. 744; 46hr.; 2 days), brings you to the heart of Asia. Continue on to **Irkutsk** (p. 753; 33hr.; 2 days), a former Siberian trading post where you can rest up before trekking to **Lake Baikal** (p. 756; 3 days), the world's oldest and deepest freshwater lake. **Ulan Ude** (p. 759; 8hr.; 2 days), the center of Russian Buddhism, is quite possibly Russia's most surreal city. If your enthusiasm for all things Russian is waning, head to **Ulaanbaatar, MON** (p. 768; 22hr.; 3 days) to sleep in a yurt, and end in **Beijing, CHI** (p. 937; 31hr.; 5 days). If you're ready to jump back on the Trans-Siberian, however, roll on to **Khabarovsk** (p. 762; 50hr.; 2 days), Russia's summer paradise. Then, explore **Vladivostok** (p. 763; 14hr.; 3 days), Russia's eastern terminus, open to foreigners since 1990.

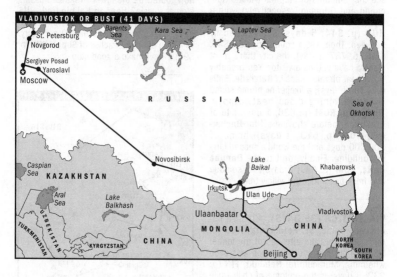

VLADIVOSTOK OR BUST (41 DAYS)

ESSENTIALS

FACTS FOR THE TRAVELER

ENTRANCE REQUIREMENTS
Passport (p. 9). Required of citizens of Australia, Canada, Ireland, New Zealand, the UK, and the US to enter all countries in Eastern Europe.
Visa and Letter of Invitation (p. 10). See the chart to determine if a visa and/or letter of invitation is required for travel to your destination country.
Inoculations (p. 21). Recommended up-to-date on DTaP (diphtheria, tetanus, and pertussis), Hepatitis A, Hepatitis B, MMR (measles, mumps, and rubella), Polio booster, and Typhoid.
Work Permit (p. 11). Required of foreigners planning to work in Eastern Europe.
Driving Permit (p. 41). If you plan to drive while in Eastern Europe, check to see if your destination country requires a driving permit.

EMBASSIES AND CONSULATES

Eastern European embassies and consulates abroad are listed in the **Documents and Formalities: Embassies and Consulates** section at the beginning of each country chapter. American, Australian, British, Canadian, Irish, and New Zealand embassies and consulates in Eastern European countries are listed in the **Practical Information** sections for the capitals of each country.

DOCUMENTS AND FORMALITIES

PASSPORTS

Citizens of Australia, Canada, Ireland, New Zealand, the UK, and the US need valid passports to enter any country in Eastern Europe and to re-enter their home countries. Many European countries will not allow entrance if the holder's passport expires within six months; returning home with an expired passport is illegal, and may result in a fine.

Citizens of Australia, Canada, Ireland, New Zealand, the UK, and the US can **apply for a passport** at any post office, passport office, or court of law. Any new passport or renewal applications must be filed well in advance of the departure date, although most passport offices offer rush services for a steep fee of $60.

Photocopy the page of your passport with your photo, as well as your visas, traveler's check serial numbers and any other important documents. Carry one set of copies in a safe place, apart from the originals, and leave another set at home. Consulates also recommend that you carry an expired passport or an official copy of your birth certificate.

If you lose your passport, immediately notify the local police and the nearest embassy or consulate of your native country. To expedite its replacement, you will need all information previously recorded and show ID and proof of citizenship. A replacement may take weeks, and may be valid only for a limited time. Any visas stamped in your old passport will be irretrievably lost. In an emergency, ask for temporary traveling papers that will permit you to re-enter your home country.

VISAS, INVITATIONS, AND WORK PERMITS

VISA REQUIREMENTS

	AUS	CAN	IRE	NZ	UK	US
ALBANIA	N	N	N	N	N	N
BELARUS	Y*	Y*	Y*	Y*	Y*	Y*
BOSNIA	N	N	N	N	N	N
BULGARIA	N¹	N¹	N	N¹	N	N¹
CROATIA	N	N	N	N	N	N
CZECH REPUBLIC	N	N	N	N	N	N
ESTONIA	N	N	N	N	N	N
HUNGARY	N	N	N	N	N	N
LATVIA	N	N	N	N	N	N
LITHUANIA	N	N	N	N	N	N
MACEDONIA	Y	Y	N	N	N	N
MOLDOVA	Y*	Y	Y	Y*	Y	Y
MONGOLIA	Y	Y	Y	Y	Y	N
POLAND	N	N	N	N	N	N
ROMANIA	Y	N	N¹	Y	N	N¹
RUSSIA	Y*	Y*	Y*	Y*	Y*	Y*
SERBIA AND MONT.	N	N	N	N	N	N
SLOVAK REPUBLIC	N	N	N	N	N	N¹
SLOVENIA	N	N	N	N	N	N
UKRAINE	Y*	Y	Y	Y*	Y	Y

Y	visa required	N	no visa required
1	visa required for stays longer than 30 days	*	invitation required

VISAS

Visas can be purchased from your destination country's consulate or embassy. In most cases, you will have to send a completed visa application (obtainable from the consulate), the required fee, and your passport. Private organizations within your own country may offer visa services as well. For more information on each country's visa requirements, see the **Documents and Formalities** section at the beginning of each country chapter. US citizens can take advantage of the **Center for International Business and Travel** (CIBT; ☎800-925-2428), which secures visas for travel to almost all countries for a variable service charge. Double-check on entrance requirements at the nearest embassy or consulate of your destination country for up-to-date info before departure. US citizens can also consult http://travel.state.gov/foreignentryreqs.html.

INVITATIONS

To obtain a visa, some countries acquire an invitation from a sponsoring individual or organization (for applicable countries, see the table on p. 10). Specialized travel agencies can arrange for those without private sponsors, as well as hotels at which you plan to stay. Many travel agencies will take care of visa processing (including letters of invitation). Two such establishments are **www.waytorussia.net** and Boston's **Info Travel** (☎617-566-2197; www.infortravel.com). For more agencies that specialize in countries of the former USSR, see **Russia Essentials: Visa and Entry Information**, p. 661. Requirements change rapidly, so always double-check with the relevant embassy.

WORK PERMITS

Admission as a visitor does not include the right to work, which is authorized only by a work permit. Entering to study requires a special visa. For more information, see **Alternatives to Tourism** (p. 59).

BORDER CROSSINGS

Outside European Union (EU) countries, many of the countries in Eastern Europe have strict visa requirements. Even for the new EU nations newly admitted in 2004, membership in the Schengen Agreement, which allows the free movement of EU citizens across borders, will only be granted after a two-year period of transition. To avoid delays and possible deportation, obtain visas for countries that require them ahead of time and carry all required paperwork, including passports and letters of invitation.

IDENTIFICATION

When you travel, always have at least two forms of identification on you, including at least one photo ID. A passport combined with a driver's license or birth certificate is usually adequate. Never carry all your IDs together; split them up in case of theft or loss, and keep photocopies in your luggage and at home.

STUDENT, TEACHER, AND YOUTH IDENTIFICATION

The **International Student Identity Card (ISIC),** the most accepted form of student ID, provides discounts on some sights, accommodations, food, and transport; access to a 24hr. emergency help line; and insurance benefits for US cardholders (see **Insurance**, p. 25). Applicants must be full-time secondary or post-secondary school students at least 12 years of age. Because of the proliferation of fake ISICs, some services (particularly airlines) require additional proof of student identity. For the emergency help line, call the operator of the country in which you are traveling and ask to make a reverse charge call to the number ☎44 20 8762 8110.

The **International Teacher Identity Card (ITIC)** offers teachers the same insurance coverage as the ISIC and similar but limited discounts. For travelers who are 25 years old or under but are not students, the **International Youth Travel Card (IYTC)** also offers many of the same benefits as the ISIC. Each of these identity cards costs US$22 or equivalent. They are valid roughly one year. Many student travel agencies (see p. 34) issue the cards; for a list of issuing agencies or more information, see the **International Student Travel Confederation (ISTC)** website (www.istc.org).

The **International Student Exchange Card (ISE)** is a similar identification card, available to students, faculty, and youth aged 12-26. The card provides discounts, medical benefits, and access to a 24hr. emergency help line, and allows you to purchase student airfares. The card costs US$25; call US ☎ 800-255-8000 for more info, or visit www.isecard.com.

CUSTOMS

EASTERN EUROPE AND THE EUROPEAN UNION. The idea of European unity has come a long way since 1958, when the European Economic Community (EEC) was created in order to promote solidarity and cooperation. Since then, the EEC has become the European Union (EU), with political, legal, and economic institutions spanning its Western European member states. What implications does this have for the traveler to Eastern Europe? Eight Eastern European nations joined the EU on May 1, 2004: the Czech Republic, Estonia, Hungary, Latvia, Lithuania, Poland, the Slovak Republic, and Slovenia. Estimates vary as to the date these countries will adopt the euro; the Baltics are currently aiming to fulfill the criteria set forth in the Maastricht Treaty as early as 2007, while the Czech Republic has set its target date for as late as 2010. Similarly, borders may not open to citizens of other EU member states for several years. For now, bring your passport and be prepared to exchange your currency. Much is changing quickly, so check before you go to see what progress has been made in your destination country regarding integration into the EU.

Upon entering any country, you must declare certain items from abroad and pay a duty on the value of those articles if they exceed the allowance established by that country's customs service. Note that goods and gifts purchased at **duty-free** shops abroad are not exempt from duty or sales tax; "duty-free" merely means that you need not pay a tax in the country of purchase. Duty-free allowances were abolished for travel between EU member states on July 1, 1999, but still exist for those arriving from outside the EU. Upon returning home, you must likewise declare all articles acquired abroad and pay a duty on the value of the articles in excess of your home country's allowance. In order to expedite your return, make a list of any valuables brought from home and register them with customs before traveling abroad, and keep receipts for all goods acquired abroad.

MONEY

CURRENCY AND EXCHANGE

A chart at the beginning of each country chapter lists the August 2005 exchange rates between local currency and Australian dollars (AUS$), Canadian dollars (CDN$), New Zealand dollars (NZ$), British pounds (UK£), US dollars (US$), and EU euros (EUR€). Check the currency converter on financial websites such as www.bloomberg.com and www.xe.com, or with a large newspaper for the latest exchange rates. As a general rule, it's cheaper to convert money abroad than at home. While currency exchange will probably be available in your arrival airport, it's wise to bring enough foreign currency to last the first 24 to 72 hours of a trip.

When changing money, go only to banks or exchange offices that have at most a 5% margin between their buy and sell prices. **Convert large sums** (unless the currency is depreciating rapidly), **but no more than you'll need** within that one country, since it may be difficult or impossible to change it back. Some countries, such as the Czech Republic, Russia, and the Slovak Republic, may require transaction receipts to reconvert local currency. Of foreign currencies, US$ or EUR€ are the most widely—and at times the only—foreign currencies accepted for exchange.

If you use **traveler's checks** or bills, carry some in small denominations (the equivalent of US$50 or less) for times when you are forced to exchange money at disadvantageous rates, but bring a range of denominations since charges may be levied per check cashed. In some countries of Eastern Europe US$ or EUR€ will be preferred to local currency. Although some establishments post prices in US$ or EUR€ due to high inflation and will insist that they don't accept anything else, avoid using Western money. Not only are such prices generally more expensive than those in the local currency, but Western currency may also attract thieves.

TRAVELER'S CHECKS

Traveler's checks are one of the safest and least troublesome means of carrying funds. American Express and Visa are the most recognized brands. Many banks and agencies sell them for a small commission. Check issuers provide refunds if the checks are lost or stolen, and many provide additional services, such as toll-free refund hotlines abroad, emergency message services, and stolen credit card assistance. It is best to get checks in either US$ or EUR€. They are readily accepted in Prague and similar urban centers, but unfortunately it is difficult—if not impossible—to cash these checks in Belarus, Bosnia, and Russia. Ask about toll-free refund hotlines and the location of refund centers when purchasing checks. Always carry emergency cash.

American Express: Cheques available with commission at select banks, AmEx offices, and online (www.americanexpress.com; US residents only). AmEx cardholders can also buy cheques by phone (☎800 721 9768). Available in Australian, British, Canadian, euro, Japanese, and US currencies. *Cheques for Two* can be signed by either of 2 people traveling together. In Eastern Europe, AmEx offices cash cheques commission-free (unless prohibited by national governments), but often at worse rates than banks. For purchase locations or more information, contact AmEx's service centers: in Australia ☎800 68 80 22, in New Zealand 0508 555 358, in the UK 0800 587 6023, in the US and Canada 800-221-7282; elsewhere, call the US collect at 1-801-964-6665.

Visa: Checks available (generally with commission) at banks worldwide. For the location of the nearest office, call Visa's service centers: in the UK ☎0800 51 58 84, in the US 800-227-6811; elsewhere, call the UK collect at 44 173 331 8949. Checks available in Canadian, Japanese, Euro, British, and US currencies.

Travelex/Thomas Cook: In Canada and the US ☎800-287-7362, in the UK (0)8 0062 2101; elsewhere, call UK collect ☎17 3331 8950. Travelex/Thomas Cook offices cash checks commission-free but are less common in Eastern Europe than American Express.

MONEY CARDS

Where they are accepted, **credit cards** often offer superior exchange rates—up to 5% better than the retail rate used by banks and other currency exchange establishments. Credit cards may also offer services such as insurance or emergency help, and are sometimes required to reserve hotel rooms or rental cars. **MasterCard** (a.k.a. EuroCard or Access in Europe; **MC**) and **Visa** (a.k.a. Carte Bleue or Barclaycard; **V**) are the most welcomed; **American Express (AmEx)** cards work at some ATMs and at AmEx offices and major airports.

ATM cards are relatively widespread in Eastern Europe, particularly in urban locations. Depending on the system that your home bank uses, you can most likely access your personal bank account from abroad. ATMs get the same wholesale exchange rate as credit cards, but there is often a limit on the amount of money you can withdraw per day (usually around US$500). There is typically also a surcharge of US$1-5 per withdrawal. While ATMs are generally easy to come by, particularly in cities, it can't hurt to carry a bit of extra cash if traveling in rural regions.

Debit cards are a form of purchasing power that are as convenient as credit cards but have a more immediate impact on your funds. A debit card can be used wherever its associated credit card company (usually MC or V) is accepted, yet the money is withdrawn directly from the holder's checking account. Debit cards often also function as ATM cards and can be used to withdraw cash from associated banks and ATMs throughout Eastern Europe. Ask your local bank about obtaining one.

The two major international money networks are **Cirrus** (US ☎ 800-424-7787; www.mastercard.com) and **Visa/PLUS** (www.visa.com). Most ATMs charge a transaction fee that is paid to the bank that owns the ATM.

E S S E N T I A L S

PIN NUMBERS AND ATMS. To use a cash or credit card to withdraw money from a cash machine (ATM) in Europe, you must have a four-digit **Personal Identification Number (PIN)**. If your PIN is longer than 4-digits, ask your bank whether you can just use the first 4, or whether you'll need a new one. **Credit cards** don't usually come with PINs, so if you intend to hit up ATMs in Europe with a credit card to get cash advances, call your credit card company before leaving to request one.

Travelers with alphabetic, rather than numerical, PINs may also be thrown off by the lack of letters on European cash machines. The following are the corresponding numbers to use: 1=QZ, 2=ABC, 3=DEF, 4=GHI, 5=JKL, 6=MNO, 7=PRS, 8=TUV, and 9=WXY. Note that if you mistakenly punch the wrong code into the machine 3 times, it will swallow your card for good.

GETTING MONEY FROM HOME

If you run out of money while traveling, the easiest and cheapest solution is to have someone back home make a deposit to your credit card or ATM card. The online **International Money Transfer Consumer Guide** (http://international-money-transfer-consumer-guide.info) may also be of help. Failing that, consider one of the following options.

It is possible to arrange a **bank money transfer,** which means asking a bank back home to **wire money** to a bank abroad. This is the cheapest way to transfer cash, but it's also the slowest, usually taking several days or more. Note that some banks may only release your funds in local currency, potentially sticking you with a poor exchange rate; inquire about this in advance. Money transfer services like **Western Union** are faster and more convenient than bank transfers—but also much pricier. Western Union has many locations worldwide. To find one, visit www.westernunion.com, or call in Australia ☎ 800 501 500, in Canada 800-235-0000, in the UK 0800 83 38 33, or in the US 800-325-6000. **American Express** and **Thomas Cook** offices also do money transfers.

US STATE DEPARTMENT (US CITIZENS ONLY)

In serious emergencies only, the US State Department will forward money within hours to the nearest consular office, which will then disburse it according to instructions for a US$15 fee. To use this service, you must contact the Overseas Citizens Service division of the US State Department (☎ 317-472-2328; nights, Sundays, and holidays 202-647-4000).

COSTS

The cost of your trip will vary considerably, depending on where you go, how you travel, and where you stay. The most significant expense will probably be your round-trip **airfare,** which can be much more expensive than a ticket to Western Europe (see **Getting to Eastern Europe: By Plane,** p. 37). Before you go, it's helpful to spend some time calculating a per-day **budget** that will meet your needs.

THE ART OF THE DEAL. bargaining in Eastern Europe is common. Prices are often not set in stone, and vendors and drivers will automatically quote you a price that is several times too high. Successful merchants enjoy the haggling (just remember they do this for a living and have the benefit of experience). The following tips and some finesse will help you impress even the most hardened hawkers:

1. Start low. Never feel guilty offering what seems to be a ridiculously low price. Your starting price should be no more than one-third to one-half the asking price

2. Use your poker face. The less your face betrays your interest in the item, the better. Coming back again and again to admire a trinket is a good way of ensuring that you pay a ridiculously high price. Never get too enthusiastic; point out flaws in workmanship and design while remaining respectful of the vendor's work. Be cool.

3. Know when to bargain. Most private transportation fares and items in open-air markets are fair game. Don't bargain on prepared or pre-packaged foods on the street or in restaurants. In some stores, signs will indicate whether "fixed prices" prevail. When in doubt, ask, "Is that your lowest price?" or whether discounts are given.

4. Never underestimate the power of peer pressure. Bargaining with more than one person at a time always leads to lower prices. Try having a friend discourage you from purchase—if you seem reluctant, the merchant will drop the price to interest you again.

5. Know when to turn away. Refuse any vendor or driver who bargains rudely; don't hesitate to move on to another vendor if one will not be reasonable. However, to start bargaining without an intention to buy is a major *faux pas.* Agreeing on a price and declining it is also poor form. Turn away slowly with a smile and "thank you" upon hearing a ridiculous price—the price may plummet.

Generally, a bare-bones day in Eastern Europe (camping or sleeping in hostels/guesthouses, buying food at supermarkets) will cost US$10-20; a slightly more comfortable day (sleeping in hostels/guesthouses and the occasional budget hotel, eating one meal a day at a restaurant, going out at night) will run about US$20-30. If you spend more than that you'll be living like royalty. But even these ranges vary throughout the region: expect to spend US$10-15 more per day in Slovenia and Croatia and US$5 less in Romania and Bulgaria. Also, don't forget to factor in emergency reserve funds (at least US$200) when planning how much money you'll need. Eastern Europe is the budget traveler's paradise. The price of a hostel in London equals that of a quality hotel in most of Eastern Europe, while local restaurants and transportation services charge a fraction of their western counterparts. Often the difference of a couple US$ or EUR€ in price means an improvement by leaps and bounds in quality

ESSENTIALS

TIPS FOR SAVING MONEY

Some simple ways include searching out opportunities for free entertainment, splitting accommodation and food costs with trustworthy fellow travelers, and buying food in supermarkets rather than eating out. Bring a **sleepsack** (see p. 26) to save on possible sheet charges in hostels, and do laundry in the sink (unless you're explicitly prohibited from doing so). That said, there's no need to go overboard. Though staying within your budget is important, doing so at the expense of your health or enjoyment could ruin an otherwise great travel experience.

SAFETY AND SECURITY

While many parts of Eastern Europe are considered safe for travel, safety considerations vary from country to country. The new EU members, in particular, have been working to improve tourist infrastructure in recent years, making parts of the region increasingly stable for travelers. The Czech Republic and Poland, for instance, are as safe as—if not safer than—Western Europe and are far removed from the situation in the Balkans. The legacy of the 1990s wars in the Balkans requires travelers to use precaution in some areas, as landmines plague less populated areas of the former Yugoslav states. Albania, Bosnia and Herzegovina, and the Kosovo region in Serbia continue to suffer from political instability and high crime rates. In most countries, however, crime is restricted primarily to pickpocketing on busy streets and public transportation. Travelers should exercise caution when taking night trains due to recent robberies. For concerns specific to individual regions, see the **Essentials: Health and Safety** section of each country chapter.

PERSONAL SAFETY

EXPLORING

To avoid unwanted attention, consider adopting the dress prevalent in the country where you are traveling. For women, skirts may be more appropriate than shorts and, for both men and women, it may be safer to avoid baggy jeans, sneakers, and sandals, as well as flashy, brightly colored clothing. Backpacks also make one stand out as a tourist; courier or **shoulder bags** are less likely to draw attention. Familiarize yourself with your surroundings before setting out, and carry yourself with confidence. As much as you may be tempted to "explore" in Bosnia, eastern Croatia, Kosovo and its environs, and the area of Macedonia bordering Kosovo: the countryside is littered with **landmines** and **unexploded ordnance (UXO).** While de-mining is underway, it will be years before all the mines are removed. UXOs are not a danger on paved roads or in major cities. Road shoulders and abandoned buildings are particularly likely to harbor UXOs.

SELF DEFENSE

There is no sure-fire way to avoid every threatening situation you might encounter while traveling, but a good self-defense course will give you concrete ways to react to unwanted advances. **Impact, Prepare, and Model Mugging** (☎ 800-345-5425) can refer you to local self-defense courses in the US. Visit www.impactsafety.org for a list of nearby chapters. Workshops (2-3hr.) start at US$50; full courses (20hr.) US$350-500.

DRIVING

If you are using a car, learn local driving signals and wear a seatbelt. Children under 40 lb. should ride only in specially designed carseats, available for a small fee from most car rental agencies. Study route maps before you hit the road, and, if you plan on spending a lot of time driving, consider bringing spare parts. Be sure to learn the local roadside assistance number. Park your vehicle in a garage or well-traveled area, and use a steering wheel locking device in larger cities. **Sleeping in your car** is one of the most dangerous (and often illegal) ways to get your rest. For info on the perils of **hitchhiking**, see p. 41. Countries in Eastern Europe usually require an International Driving Permit for foreigners intending to travel by car.

TERRORISM

As a result of the Sept. 11 attacks on the US, airports throughout the world have heightened security. Terrorist acts are rare in Eastern Europe, and potentially violent situations are confined to Russia, the Transdniester region of Moldova, and the Balkan states of Albania, Bosnia and Herzegovina, Macedonia, and Serbia and Montenegro. Terrorism in Russia has been blamed on the **Chechen separatists**, a largely Muslim ethnic group in the Russian Caucasus region. Their drawn-out fight for independence has attracted Muslim militants from around the world, and media outlets often report that Chechnya has been a recruiting ground for the terrorist group al-Qaeda. The US Department of State strongly warns against travel to Chechnya and surrounding areas.

LET'S (NOT) GO: TRAVEL ADVISORIES. Western governments have issued **travel warnings** against unnecessary travel to politically unstable or dangerous regions. In 2004, travel warnings were updated for the northern border regions of **Albania, Kosovo** and its environs, and **Macedonia.** As a result of incidents of violence targeted at foreigners, especially Westerners, travelers are cautioned against going to certain regions of **Bosnia and Herzegovina,** including Mostar, Medjugorje, Grude, Posusje, Livno, Tomislavgrad, Republika Srpska, and Siroki Brijeg. Other regional warnings have been issued as well: governments caution travelers to the **Transdniester** region of Moldova, **Eastern Slavonia** in Croatia, and the Presevo and Bujanovac areas of **Serbia and Montenegro.** They further warn against travel to the **Chechnya** province and bordering areas in Russia. Due to the regional unrest, *Let's Go* was unable to send researchers for the 2005 guide to Albania, Serbia and Montenegro, Macedonia, and, with the exception of Sarajevo, Bosnia and Herzegovina. The following government offices provide travel information and advisories by telephone, by fax, or via the web:

Australian Department of Foreign Affairs and Trade: ☎ 13 0055 5135; www.dfat.gov.au.

Canadian Department of Foreign Affairs and International Trade (DFAIT): In Canada and the US ☎ 800-267-6788, elsewhere 613-944-4000; www.dfait-maeci.gc.ca. Call for their free booklet, *Bon Voyage...But.*

Irish Department of Foreign Affairs: ☎ (0)1 478 0822; www.irlgov.ie/iveagh.

New Zealand Ministry of Foreign Affairs: ☎ (0)4 439 8000; www.mft.govt.nz/travel/index.html.

United Kingdom Foreign and Commonwealth Office: ☎ (0)20 7008 0232; www.fco.gov.uk.

US Department of State: ☎ 202-647-5225; http://travel.state.gov. For *A Safe Trip Abroad*, call ☎ 202-512-1800.

FINANCIAL SECURITY

PROTECTING YOUR VALUABLES. Never leave your belongings unattended; crime occurs in even the most demure-looking hostel or hotel. Bring your own padlock for hostel lockers, and don't ever store valuables in any locker. Be particularly

ESSENTIALS

careful on **buses** and **trains;** horror stories abound about determined thieves who strike while travelers are sleeping. Carry your backpack in front of you where you can see it. When traveling with others, sleep in shifts. When alone, use good judgment in selecting a train compartment: never stay in an empty one, and use a lock to secure your pack to the luggage rack. Try to sleep on top bunks with your luggage stored above you (if not in bed with you), and keep important documents and valuables on your person.

There are a few steps you can take to minimize the financial risk associated with traveling. First, **bring as little with you as possible.** Second, buy a few combination **padlocks** to secure your belongings either in your pack or in a hostel or train station locker. Third, **carry as little cash as possible.** Keep your traveler's checks and ATM/credit cards in a **money belt**—not a "fanny pack"—along with your passport and ID cards. Fourth, **keep a small cash reserve separate from your primary stash.** This should be about US$50 (US$ or euros are best) sewn into or stored in the depths of your pack, along with your traveler's check numbers and important photocopies.

CON ARTISTS AND PICKPOCKETS. In large cities like Prague, Budapest, and Warsaw, **con artists** often work in groups and may involve children. Beware of certain classics: sob stories that require money, rolls of bills "found" on the street, mustard spilled (or saliva spit) onto your shoulder to distract you while they snatch your bag. **Never let your passport and your bags out of your sight.** Beware of **pickpockets** in city crowds, especially on public transportation. Also, be alert in public telephone booths: If you must say your calling card number, do so very quietly; if you punch it in, make sure no one can look over your shoulder.

If you will be traveling with electronic devices, such as a laptop computer or a PDA, check whether your homeowner's insurance covers loss, theft, or damage when you travel. If not, you might consider purchasing a low-cost separate insurance policy. **Safeware** (☎US 800-800-1492; www.safeware.com) specializes in covering computers and charges $90 for 90-day comprehensive international travel coverage up to $4000.

DRUGS AND ALCOHOL

Remember that you are subject to the laws of the country in which you travel, not to those of your home country. Throughout Eastern Europe, recreational drugs—including marijuana—are illegal, and often carry a much heavier jail sentence than in the West. For more specific information on the drug laws of Eastern European countries, consult the website at the US State Department's Bureau for International Narcotics and Law Enforcement Affairs (www.state.gov/g/inl/). If you carry **prescription drugs** while you travel, bring a copy of the prescriptions themselves and a note from a doctor. Alcohol laws vary throughout the region; be familiar with local laws if this issue may affect you. The legal drinking age varies from 16 in Bulgaria to 21 in Belarus and Ukraine; most countries' legal age is 18.

HEALTH

Common sense is the simplest prescription for good health while traveling. Drink water to prevent dehydration. Since tap water quality in Eastern Europe is highly variable, in some countries you will need to buy bottled water or boil your own.

BEFORE YOU GO

In your **passport,** write the names of those you wish to be contacted in case of a medical emergency; also list any allergies or medical conditions you want doctors to be aware of. Matching a **prescription** to a foreign equivalent may not be safe or possible. Carry up-to-date, legible prescriptions or a statement from your doctor with the medication's trade name, manufacturer, chemical name, and dosage.

IMMUNIZATIONS AND PRECAUTIONS

For travel to Eastern Europe, the Center for Disease Control (CDC) recommends up to date vaccinations for **MMR** (measles, mumps, and rubella), **DTaP** or **Td** (diphtheria, tetanus, and pertussis), **OPV** (polio), **HbCV** (haemophilus influenza B), and **HBV** (hepatitis B), **Hepatitis A,** and **Typhoid.** Adults traveling to the CIS (Commonwealth of Independent States) should consider getting an additional dose of **polio** vaccine if they have not already had one during their adult years. The viral infection tickborne encephalitis occurs principally in Central Europe, so avoid wildlife areas where possible. Bulgaria requires documentation verifying that you are **HIV negative** in order to issue visas for periods longer than one month to study or work in the country. Belarus, Moldova, Russia, and Ukraine all require documentation to issue visas for periods longer than three months. The Slovak Republic and Hungary require documentation for persons staying longer than one year. Latvia and Lithuania require documentation for those seeking a residency permit. In addition, a **rabies** vaccine is recommended due to stray dogs in Eastern Europe, especially in Romania. For recommendations on immunizations, consult the CDC (see below) in the US or the equivalent in your home country.

USEFUL ORGANIZATIONS AND PUBLICATIONS

The US **Centers for Disease Control and Prevention (CDC;** ☎877-FYI-TRIP; fax 888-232-3299; www.cdc.gov/travel) maintains an international travelers' hotline and an informative website. The CDC's comprehensive booklet *Health Information for*

ESSENTIALS

International Travel (The Yellow Book), an annual rundown of disease, immunization, and general health advice, is free online or US$29-40 from the Public Health Foundation (☎877-252-1200; http://bookstore.phf.org). Consult the appropriate government agency of your home country for consular information sheets on health, entry requirements, and other issues abroad (see **Travel Advisories box,** p. 19). For quick information on health and other travel warnings, call the **Overseas Citizens Services** (M-F 8am-8pm; ☎888-407-4747, after hours 202-647-4000, from overseas 317-472-2328), or contact a passport agency, embassy, or consulate abroad. For information on medical evacuation services and travel insurance firms, see the US government website at http://travel.state.gov/medical.html or the **British Foreign and Commonwealth Office** (www.fco.gov.uk). For general health info, contact the **American Red Cross** (☎800-564-1234; www.redcross.org).

MEDICAL ASSISTANCE WHILE TRAVELING

The quality and availability of medical assistance varies greatly throughout Eastern Europe. In Westernized cities, like Prague and Budapest, there are generally English-speaking medical centers or hospitals for foreigners; the care there tends to be better than elsewhere in the region. In the countryside and in less-touristed countries such as Belarus and Moldova, English-speaking facilities are virtually impossible to find. In the event of an emergency, go to your embassy for aid and recommendations. Tourist offices sometimes have the names of local doctors who speak English. The quality of medical service varies from region to region, although few hospitals are maintained at Western standards. Less developed countries such as Macedonia and Belarus tend to provide only more rudimentary care. Private hospitals will generally have better facilities than the state-operated hospitals. For more specific information about healthcare, see the individual chapter for the country to which you are traveling.

If you are concerned about access to medical support while traveling, special support services are available. The *MedPass* from **GlobalCare, Inc.,** 6875 Shiloh Rd. E., Alpharetta, GA 30005, USA (☎800-860-1111; www.globalcare.net), provides 24hr. international medical assistance, support, and medical evacuation resources. The **International Association for Medical Assistance to Travelers (IAMAT;** US ☎716-754-4883, Canada 416-652-0137; www.iamat.org) has free membership and lists English-speaking doctors worldwide. If your **insurance** policy does not cover travel abroad, you may wish to purchase additional coverage. Those with medical conditions (diabetes, allergies to antibiotics, epilepsy, heart conditions) may want to obtain a stainless-steel **Medic Alert ID tag** (first year US$35, annually thereafter US$20), which identifies the condition and gives a 24hr. collect-call number. Contact the **Medic Alert Foundation,** 2323 Colorado Ave., Turlock, CA 95382, USA (☎888-633-4298, outside US ☎209-668-3333; www.medicalert.org).

ONCE IN EASTERN EUROPE

INSECT-BORNE DISEASES

Many diseases are transmitted by insects—mainly mosquitoes, fleas, ticks, and lice. Be aware of insects in wet or forested areas; wear long pants and long sleeves, tuck your pants into your socks, and buy a mosquito net. Use insect repellents such as DEET and spray your gear with permethrin.

Bubonic Plague: If headed to Mongolia via the Russian Far East, watch out for this bacterial infection. Transmitted by fleas, it may also be contracted by human contact. Symptoms include swollen lymph nodes, fever, chills, headache exhaustion and difficulty breathing. Lethal if not treated with antibiotics. Areas with poor sanitation present the greatest risk. Those in modern accommodations are at minimal risk.

Japanese Encephalitis: A mosquito-borne virus occurring in far eastern Russia. Symptoms include headache, fever, disorientation, coma, and tremors. Short-term travelers to this region don't need a vaccine, but those staying over 30 days are advised to get the 3-injection vaccination series. No treatment for the contracted illness exists.

Tickborne Encephalitis: A viral infection of the central nervous system transmitted by tick bites or by unpasteurized dairy products. Occurs in wooded areas of Belarus, Bosnia, Croatia, the Czech Republic, Estonia, Latvia, northern Russia, Serbia and Montenegro, the Slovak Republic, Slovenia, and less frequently in Bulgaria and Romania. Vaccination recommended for those traveling in these areas for more than 3 weeks during warm weather months. Risk of contraction low when precautions are taken.

Lyme Disease: A bacterial infection carried by ticks and marked by a circular bull's-eye rash of 2cm or more. Later symptoms include fever, headache, fatigue, and aches. Antibiotics are effective if administered early. Left untreated, Lyme disease can cause problems in joints, heart, and nervous system. Travelers spending time in wooded areas in Eastern Europe are more likely to be exposed to ticks. If you find a tick, grasp the head with tweezers as close to your skin as possible and apply slow, steady traction. Removing a tick within 36hr. reduces the risk of infection. Do not remove ticks by burning them or by coating them with nail polish remover or petroleum jelly.

FOOD- AND WATER-BORNE DISEASES

Prevention is the best cure: be sure that your food is properly cooked and the water you drink is clean. Peel fruits and vegetables and avoid tap water (including ice cubes and anything washed in tap water, like salad). Other culprits are raw shellfish, unpasteurized milk, and sauces containing raw eggs. Buy imported bottled water, or purify your own water by bringing it to a rolling boil or treating it with **iodine tablets.** Food- and water-borne diseases are the primary illnesses that affect travelers to Eastern Europe.

Cholera: An intestinal disease caused by a bacteria found in contaminated food. Symptoms include severe diarrhea, dehydration, vomiting, and muscle cramps. See a doctor immediately; if left untreated, it may be deadly, even within a few hours. Antibiotics are available, but the most important treatment is rehydration. The US no longer administers the cholera vaccine because of its inadequacy. Outbreaks of cholera are infrequent in Eastern Europe. The CDC maintains an active website monitoring regional outbreaks of cholera (www.cdc.gov/travel/diseases/cholera.html).

Hepatitis A: A viral infection of the liver caused by contaminated water, ice, shellfish, and unwashed produce. Symptoms include fatigue, fever, loss of appetite, nausea, dark urine, jaundice, vomiting, aches and pains, and light stools. The illness can range from mild symptoms over 1-2 weeks to a more severe illness lasting several months. Travelers are at risk of contracting the infection; the risk is highest in the countryside, but it may also be present in urban areas. Ask your doctor about the vaccine (Havrix or Vaqta) or an injection of immune globulin (IG; formerly called gamma globulin).

Typhoid Fever: Caused by the salmonella bacteria. Common in villages and rural areas in the developing regions of Eastern Europe. Though mostly transmitted through contaminated food and water, it may also be acquired by direct contact with another person. Early symptoms include fever, headaches, fatigue, loss of appetite, constipation, and a rash on the abdomen or chest. Antibiotics can treat typhoid, but a vaccination (70-90% effective) is recommended for all travelers to affected regions.

OTHER INFECTIOUS DISEASES

Diphtheria: The 1990s saw a massive diphtheria outbreak in the former Soviet Union, and travelers to this area are still at risk for this highly infectious disease. Early symptoms, including severe sore throat, swollen lymph nodes, and fever, can lead to paralysis, heart failure, and death. Be up-to-date on diphtheria vaccinations before traveling.

Hepatitis B: A viral infection of the liver transmitted via bodily fluids (i.e., sexual contact or needle sharing). Symptoms may not surface until years after initial infection; they include jaundice, loss of appetite, fever, and joint pain. A 3-shot vaccination sequence is recommended for health-care workers, sexually active travelers, and those planning to seek medical treatment abroad; it must begin 6 months before traveling. Chronic HBV is not particularly common in Eastern Europe, with the exception of Russia, where rates are slightly higher.

Rabies: Transmitted through the saliva of infected animals. Fatal if untreated. By the time symptoms (thirst and muscle spasms) appear, the disease is in its terminal stage. If you are bitten, wash the wound thoroughly, and seek immediate medical care. Try to have the animal located. Exposure is treated by a 28-day regimen of rabies vaccine and immune globin injections in a 5-shot series. A rabies vaccine (3 shots given over a 21-day period) is available but only semi-effective. Those who will be exposed to or handling wild animals should consider getting the vaccine.

Tuberculosis: Tuberculosis (TB) is on the rise throughout Eastern Europe. Symptoms include fever, persistent cough, and bloody phlegm. TB is usually transmitted by breathing air in an enclosed area with an infected person. If untreated, the disease is fatal. Usually it responds to antibiotics. If you think you are infected, tell your doctor you have been to Eastern Europe recently, as the recent return of TB indicates a drug-resistant strain that requires special treatment.

AIDS, HIV, AND STIS

For detailed information on **Acquired Immune Deficiency Syndrome (AIDS)** in Eastern Europe, call the **US Centers for Disease Control's** 24hr. traveler's hotline (☎ 877-394-8747), or contact the **Joint United Nations Programme on HIV/AIDS (UNAIDS)**, 20, ave. Appia, CH-1211 Geneva 27, Switzerland (☎ 41 22 791 3666; fax 22 791 4187). Note that several countries in Eastern Europe, including Belarus, Bulgaria, Hungary, Moldova, Russia, the Slovak Republic, and Ukraine, require documentation that you are HIV-negative if you are those planning an extended visit for work or study; some of these countries deny entrance to those who test HIV-positive. The US State Department (http://travel.state.gov/HIVtestingreqs.html) maintains a relatively current listing of HIV testing requirements in foreign countries.

Sexually transmitted infections (STIs) such as gonorrhea, chlamydia, HPV, syphilis, and herpes are more often caught than HIV and can be just as deadly. **Hepatitis** B and C can also be transmitted sexually (see p. 24). Though condoms help protect against STIs, oral or even tactile contact can lead to transmission.

WOMEN'S HEALTH

Women traveling in unsanitary conditions are vulnerable to **urinary tract** and **bladder infections,** common and very uncomfortable bacterial conditions that cause a burning sensation and painful urination. If symptoms persist, see a doctor.

Tampons and **pads** are sometimes hard to find in areas of Eastern Europe. It's advisable to take supplies along. **Reliable contraceptive devices** may also be difficult to find. Women on birth control pills should bring enough to allow for possible loss or extended stays. Condoms are increasingly available but usually expensive and variable in quality.

INSURANCE

Travel insurance covers four basic areas: medical/health problems, property loss, trip cancellation/interruption, and emergency evacuation. Though regular insurance policies may well extend to travel-related accidents, you may consider purchasing separate travel insurance if the cost of potential trip cancellation, interruption, or emergency medical evacuation is greater than you can absorb. Prices for travel insurance purchased separately generally run about US$50 per week for full coverage, while trip cancellation/interruption may be purchased separately at a rate of US$3-5 per day depending on length of stay.

Medical insurance (especially university policies) often covers costs incurred abroad; check with your provider. **US Medicare** generally does not cover foreign travel; **Canadian** provincial health insurance plans increasingly does not either. Check with the provincial Ministry of Health or Health Plan Headquarters for details. **Homeowners' insurance** (or your family's coverage) often covers theft during travel and loss of travel documents (passport, plane ticket, etc.) up to US$500.

ISIC and **ITIC** (see p. 11) provide basic insurance benefits to US cardholders, including US$100 per day of in-hospital sickness for up to 60 days and US$5000 of accident-related medical reimbursement (see www.isicus.com for details). Cardholders have access to a toll-free 24hr. helpline for medical, legal, and financial emergencies overseas. **American Express** (US ☎ 800-528-4800) grants most cardholders automatic collision and theft car rental insurance and ground travel accident coverage of US$100,000 on flight purchases made with the card.

STA (see p. 34) offers a range of **insurance plans** that can supplement your basic coverage. Other private insurance providers in the US and Canada include: Access America (☎ 800-284-8300; www.acessamerica.com), Berkely Group (☎ 800-323-3149; www.berkely.com); Globalcare Travel Insurance (☎ 800-821-2488; www.globalcare-cocco.com), Travel Assistance International (☎ 800-821-2828; www.europassistance.com), and Travel Guard (☎ 800-826-4919; www.travelguard.com). Columbus Direct (☎ 020 7375 0011; www.columbusdirect.co.uk) operates in the UK and AFTA (☎ 02 9264 3299; www.afta.com.au) in Australia.

PACKING

Pack lightly. Lay out only what you absolutely need, then take half the clothes and twice the money. If you plan on doing a lot of travel in the outdoors, see **Camping and the Outdoors,** p. 28.

Luggage: If you are covering a lot of ground by foot, a sturdy **frame backpack** is unbeatable. A suitcase or trunk is fine if you plan to stay in 1 or 2 cities and explore from there. Carrying a daypack (a small backpack or courier bag, never a fanny pack) is a must.

Clothing: Eastern European climate is highly variable from region to region, so be prepared for all kinds of weather. Women should bring a **head covering** for mosque and monastery visits.

Converters and adapters: Throughout Eastern Europe, electricity is 220 or 230V AC, enough to fry any 110V appliance. **Americans** and **Canadians** should buy an **adapter** (which changes the shape of the plug) and a **converter** (which changes the voltage; US$20). Don't make the mistake of using only an adapter (unless appliance instructions explicitly state otherwise). **Australians, Brits, Irish,** and **New Zealanders** (who use 230V at home) won't need a converter, but they will need a set of adapters to use anything electrical. Check out http://kropla.com/electric.htm for more info.

Other useful items: For safety purposes, you should bring a money belt and small padlock. For those planning to stay in hostels, some require that you either provide your own linen or rent sheets from them. Save cash by making your own **sleepsack:** fold a full-size sheet in half the long way, then sew it closed along the long side and one of the short sides. Basic **outdoors equipment** (plastic water bottle, compass, waterproof matches, pocketknife, sunglasses, sunscreen, hat) may also prove useful. A needle and thread can come in handy. Also consider bringing electrical tape for patching tears. If you're looking to cut costs and want to do laundry by hand, bring detergent, a small rubber ball to stop up the sink, and string for a makeshift clothes line. **Other things** you're liable to forget: an umbrella, an **alarm clock,** safety pins, rubber bands, a flashlight, earplugs, garbage bags, and a small calculator.

ACCOMMODATIONS

HOSTELS, HOTELS, AND PENSIONS

Hostels are generally laid out dorm-style, often with large single-sex rooms and bunk beds, though a small number do offer private rooms for families and couples. They sometimes have kitchens and utensils for your use, bike rentals, storage areas, transportation to airports, breakfast, and laundry facilities. There can be drawbacks: some hostels close during certain daytime "lockout" hours, have a curfew, don't accept reservations, impose a maximum stay, require a minimum stay, or, less frequently, require that you do chores. In Eastern Europe, a bed in any sort of hostel will usually cost you US$10-15.

For inexpensive **hotels,** singles in Eastern Europe cost US$20-35 per night, doubles US$30-60. You'll typically share a hall bathroom; a private bathroom will cost extra, as may hot showers. Smaller **guest houses** and **pensions** are often cheaper than hotels. Not all hotels take **reservations,** and few accept checks in foreign currency. After hostels, pensions are the most common budget accommodation in Eastern Europe. A cross between a hostel and a hotel, a pension is generally clean, safe and intimate and run by a family, similar to a bed and breakfast. They usually rent by the room but occasionally offer dorm-style accommodations. In Eastern Europe, a single room in a pension runs US$15-20.

HOSTELLING INTERNATIONAL

Joining the youth hostel association in your own country automatically grants you membership privileges in **Hostelling International (HI)**, a federation of national hosteling associations. HI hostels are scattered irregularly throughout Eastern Europe, but, if you will be spending time in the more touristed areas of Croatia, Hungary, and Poland, an HI card is a worthwhile investment. Hostels in Bulgaria, Croatia, the Czech Republic, Estonia, Hungary, Lithuania, Macedonia, Poland, Romania, Russia, Serbia and Montenegro, the Slovak Republic, and Slovenia accept reservations via the **International Booking Network** (☎ 202-783-6161; www.hihostels.com). HI's umbrella organization's web page (www.iyhf.org), which lists the web addresses and phone numbers of all national associations, can be a great place to begin researching hostels in a specific region. Other comprehensive hosteling websites include www.hostels.com and www.hostelplanet.com. **Guest memberships** are not valid in much of Eastern Europe, but it is a good idea to ask anyway. Most student travel agencies (see p. 34) sell HI cards.

ESSENTIALS

OTHER TYPES OF ACCOMMODATIONS

 A HOSTELER'S BILL OF RIGHTS. There are standard features we do not include in our hostel listings. Unless we state otherwise, expect that hostels have no lockout, no curfew, a kitchen, free hot showers, and no key deposit.

UNIVERSITY DORMS

Many **colleges** and **universities** open their residence halls to travelers when school is not in session; some even do so during term-time. Usually situated amid student centers, these dorms often prove to be invaluable sources on things to do in the

city. Finding a room may take a couple of phone calls and much planning in advance, but the hassle can be worth it. Rates tend to be low, and many offer free local calls. Tourist offices can often provide more information about this option.

PRIVATE ROOMS

An increasingly popular option in rural locations is to rent a room in a private home. Although it may seem dangerous, going home with an old woman from the train station or knocking on doors advertising private rooms (often marked by *zimmer frei*, *sobe*, etc.) is legitimate, generally reliable, and often preferable to staying in a hostel. Prices tend to be competitive with hostel and pension prices.

Home exchanges offer the traveler various types of homes (houses, apartments, condominiums, villas, and even castles), as well as the opportunity to experience local life from within and to cut down on accommodations fees. For more information, contact the following numbers: **HomeExchange.Com,** P.O. Box 30085, Santa Barbara, CA 93130, USA (☎800-877-8723; www.homeexchange.com). Includes listings from Bosnia and Herzegovina, Croatia, the Czech Republic, Hungary, Poland, Romania, Russia, and Serbia and Montenegro; **Intervac International Home Exchange** (www.intervac.com) has two offices in Eastern Europe. **Intervac Czech Republic,** Antonin and Lena Machackovi, Pod Stanici 25/603, 10/CSFR 10 200 Praha, CZR (☎2 71 96 16 47; antonin.machacek@iol.cz); **Intervac Poland,** Ewa and Stanisław Krupscy, ul. Mackiewicza 12, 31-213 Kraków, POL (☎12 415 18 18; intervac@york.edu.pl).

CAMPING AND THE OUTDOORS

Eastern Europe offers many opportunities for hiking, biking, mountain climbing, camping, trekking, and spelunking. Camping is one of the most authentic ways to experience the vacation culture of the region: Eastern Europeans tend to spend their vacations exploring the outdoors. There is very little English-language literature on outdoor opportunities and adventures available in the region. Undiscovered as the Eastern European wilderness is, however, it's surprisingly difficult to truly rough it. In most countries, camping within the boundaries of national parks is either illegal or heavily restricted; many areas require a camping permit. Check with the local tourist office or locals before setting up camp in an area that's not explicitly designated for camping. Alternatively, you can often stay in a **chata** located within the park interiors; these huts offer dorm-style rooms for US$5-10, running water (not always hot), and some sort of mess hall. **Organized campgrounds** that offer tent space and bungalows are often situated around the borders of parks. All campgrounds have running water; some offer restaurants and other facilities. Tent sites range from US$3-10 per person with a flat tent fee of US$5-10. Bungalow fees are usually US$5-10.

USEFUL PUBLICATIONS AND RESOURCES

For information about camping, hiking, and biking, write or call the publishers listed below to receive a free catalog. Travelers planning to camp extensively in Eastern Europe might consider buying an **International Camping Carnet.** Similar to a hostel membership card, it's required at some campgrounds and provides discounts at many others. It's available in North America from the **Family Campers and RVers Association** (www.fcrv.org); in the UK from **the Caravan Club;** Australians, Irish, and New Zealanders can obtain one from their national automobile associations. An excellent general resource for travelers planning on camping or spending time in the outdoors is the **Great Outdoor Recreation Pages** (www.gorp.com).

Automobile Association, Contact Centre, Car Ellison House, William Armstrong Dr., New-castle-upon-Tyne NE4 7YA, UK. (☎(0)870 600 0371; www.theaa.co.uk). Publishes *Caravan and Camping: Europe* (UK£9). They also offer European road atlases.

The Mountaineers Books, 1001 SW Klickitat Way, #201, Seattle, WA 98134, USA (☎800-553-4453; www.mountaineersbooks.org). Over 600 titles on hiking, biking, mountaineering, natural history, and conservation. Publishes *Trekking in Russia and Central Asia: A Traveler's Guide,* by Frith Maier (US$17).

WILDERNESS SAFETY

Stay warm, dry, and hydrated. Prepare yourself for an emergency by always packing raingear, a hat and mittens, a first-aid kit, high energy food, and extra water for any hike. Be sure to check all equipment before setting out. Wool or warm layers of synthetic materials designed for the outdoors make the best hiking apparel; never rely on cotton for warmth, as it is useless when wet. Check **weather forecasts** and pay attention to the skies when hiking. In parts of Eastern Europe there is a risk of **landmines** still buried in parks and the wilderness. To minimize the danger, stay on the beaten path and consider purchasing a local **landmine map.**

CAMPING AND HIKING EQUIPMENT

WHAT TO BUY...

Good camping equipment is both sturdy and light. North American suppliers tend to offer the most competitive prices.

Sleeping Bags: Most sleeping bags are rated by season; "summer" means 30-40°F (around 0°C) at night; "four-season" or "winter" often means below 0°F (-17°C). Bags are made of **down** (warm and light, but expensive, and miserable when wet) or of **synthetic** material (heavy, durable, and warm when wet). Prices range US$50-250 for a summer synthetic to US$200-300 for a good down winter bag. **Sleeping bag pads** include foam pads (US$10-30), air mattresses (US$15-50), and self-inflating mats (US$30-120). Bring a **stuff sack** to store your bag and keep it dry.

Tents: The best tents are free-standing (with their own frames and suspension systems), set up quickly, and only require staking in high winds. Low-profile dome tents are the best all-around. Worthy 2-person tents start at US$100, 4-person US$160. Make sure your tent has a rain fly and seal its seams with waterproofer. Other useful accessories include a **battery-operated lantern,** a plastic **groundcloth,** and a nylon **tarp.**

Backpacks: Internal-frame packs mold well to your back, keep a lower center of gravity, and flex adequately to allow you to hike difficult trails, while **external-frame packs** are more comfortable for long hikes over even terrain, as they carry weight higher and distribute it more evenly. Make sure your pack has a strong, padded hip-belt to transfer weight to your legs. There are models designed specifically for women. Any serious backpacking requires a pack of at least 4000 in³ (16,000cc), plus 500 in³ for sleeping bags in internal-frame packs. Sturdy backpacks cost anywhere from US$125 to 420—your pack is an area where it doesn't pay to economize. On your hunt for the perfect pack, fill up prospective models with something heavy, strap it on correctly, and walk around the store to get a sense of how the model distributes weight. Either buy a **rain cover** (US$10-20) or store all of your belongings in plastic bags inside your pack.

Boots: Be sure to wear hiking boots with good **ankle support.** They should fit snugly and comfortably over 1-2 pairs of **wool socks** and a pair of thin **liner socks.** Break in boots over several weeks before you go to spare yourself blisters.

Other Necessities: Synthetic layers, like those made of polypropylene or polyester, and a pile jacket will keep you warm even when wet. A **space blanket** (US$5-15) will help you to retain body heat and doubles as a groundcloth. Plastic **water bottles** are vital;

look for shatter- and leak-resistant models. Carry **water-purification tablets** for when you can't boil water. Although most campgrounds provide campfire sites, you may want to bring a small **metal grate** or **grill**. For those places (including virtually every organized campground in Europe) that forbid fires or the gathering of firewood, you'll need a **camp stove** (the classic Coleman starts at US$50) and a propane-filled **fuel bottle** to operate it. Also bring a **first-aid kit, pocketknife, insect repellent,** and **waterproof matches** or a **lighter.**

...AND WHERE TO BUY IT

The mail-order and online companies listed below offer lower prices than many retail stores, but a visit to a local camping or outdoors store will give you a good sense of the look and weight of certain items and allow you to check the fit of backpacks or boots.

Campmor, 28 Parkway, P.O. Box 700, Upper Saddle River, NJ 07458, USA (☎888-226-7667; www.campmor.com).

Discount Camping, 880 Main North Rd., Pooraka, South Australia 5095, AUS (☎(0)8 8262 3399; www.discountcamping.com.au).

Eastern Mountain Sports (EMS), 1 Vose Farm Rd., Peterborough, NH 03458, USA (☎888-463-6367; www.ems.com).

L.L. Bean, Freeport, ME 04033 (US and Canada ☎800-441-5713; UK ☎0800 891 297; elsewhere ☎207-552-3028; www.llbean.com).

Recreational Equipment, Inc. (REI), Sumner, WA 98352, USA (US and Canada ☎800-426-4840, elsewhere 253-891-2500; www.rei.com).

KEEPING IN TOUCH

The ease of communication varies widely from country to country. In Central European countries, such as Hungary, Poland, and the Czech Republic, postal and telephone systems are as reliable and efficient as in the US and Western Europe. Even the Russian mail system now offers relatively speedy delivery to the West. However, in Belarus, Bulgaria, and Ukraine—particularly outside the capital cities—postal services are less predictable and should not be depended upon. Phone cards can also be problematic throughout the region: double-check with your phone card carrier before departure in order to ensure that their service will allow you to call home. Keeping in touch can be troublesome, inefficient, and downright mind-boggling. For country-specific information, read **Essentials: Keeping in Touch** in each country chapter.

MAIL

SENDING MAIL FROM EASTERN EUROPE

Airmail is the best way to send mail home from Eastern Europe. **Aerogrammes,** printed sheets that fold into envelopes and travel via airmail, are generally available at post offices. Write *"par avion"* or "airmail" in the language of the country you are visiting (in Cyrillic if applicable) on the front. Most post offices will charge exorbitant fees or simply refuse to send aerogrammes with enclosures. Surface mail is by far the cheapest and slowest way to send mail. It takes one to three months to cross the Atlantic and two to four to cross the Pacific—good for items you won't need to see for a while, such as souvenirs or other articles you've acquired along the way that are weighing down your pack.

SENDING MAIL TO EASTERN EUROPE

Mark envelopes "airmail," *"par avion,"* or airmail in the language of the country that you are visiting, otherwise your letter or postcard will never arrive. If regular airmail is too slow, **Federal Express** (Australia ☎ 13 26 10, Canada and US 800-247-4747, New Zealand (0)800 73 33 39, UK (0)800 12 38 00; www.fedex.com) offers three-day service to most of Eastern Europe, though international rates are expensive. **Surface mail** is by far the cheapest way to send mail, though it is also the slowest. It takes one to three months to cross the Atlantic and two to four to cross the Pacific. **General delivery** (Poste Restante) averages seven days to Eastern Europe.

RECEIVING MAIL IN EASTERN EUROPE

For a country-by-country guide to what can and can't be sent to each country, consult the US Postal Service at http://pe.usps.gov/text/Imm/Immctry.html, which also tells you how mail is likely to be treated upon arrival in each country. There are several ways to arrange pick-up of letters sent to you by friends and relatives while you are in Eastern Europe.

GENERAL DELIVERY

Mail can be sent to Eastern Europe through **Poste Restante** (the international phrase for General Delivery) to almost any city or town with a post office. While *Poste Restante* is reliable in most countries, it is far less likely to reach its intended recipient in less developed nations. Addressing conventions for *Poste Restante* vary by country; *Let's Go* gives instructions in the **Essentials: Keeping in Touch** section at the beginning of each country's chapter. Be sure to include the street address of the post office on the third line lest mail never reaches the recipient. As a rule, it is best to use the **largest post office** in the area, as mail may be sent there regardless of what is written on the envelope. When possible, it is usually safer and quicker to send mail express or registered—this also ensures that mail will arrive in postally problematic countries. When picking up your mail, bring a passport for identification. There is often no surcharge; if there is, it usually does not exceed the cost of domestic postage. If the clerks insist that there is nothing for you, have them check under your first name as well.

AMERICAN EXPRESS

AmEx's travel offices will act as a mail service for cardholders if contacted in advance. Under this free **Client Letter Service,** they will hold mail for up to 30 days and forward upon request. Some offices will offer these services to non-cardholders (especially those who have purchased AmEx Travelers Cheques), but you must call ahead. *Let's Go* lists AmEx office locations in the Practical Information section of many large cities.

TELEPHONES

CALLING TO OR FROM EASTERN EUROPE

A **calling card** is probably cheapest and your best bet. Calls are either billed collect or to your account. You can often call collect without possessing a company's calling card, just by dialing their access number and following the instructions. **To obtain a calling card** from your national telecommunications service before leaving home, contact the appropriate company listed below. Be forewarned that not all calling card companies offer service in every Eastern European country. Before settling on a calling card plan, be sure to research your options in order to pick the one that best fits both your needs and your destination.

ESSENTIALS

PLACING INTERNATIONAL CALLS. The international dialing prefixes and country codes of Eastern European nations are listed at the beginning of each country chapter and on the inside of the back cover. To call Eastern Europe from home or to call home from Eastern Europe, dial:

1. The **international dialing prefix.** To dial out of out of Eastern Europe, use the international dialing prefixes listed at the beginning of each chapter and on the inside of the back cover; **Australia,** 0011; **Canada** or the **US,** 011; the **Republic of Ireland, New Zealand,** or the **UK,** 00. The international dialing prefix for each country in Eastern Europe can be found in the Facts and Figures table of every Essentials chapter.

2. The **country code** of the country you want to call. To call **Australia,** dial 61; **Canada** or the **US,** 1; the **Republic of Ireland,** 353; **New Zealand,** 64; the **UK,** 44; Eastern European nations, codes listed at the beginning of each country chapter and on the inside of the back cover.

3. The **city/area code.** *Let's Go* lists the city/area codes for cities and towns in Eastern Europe opposite the city or town name, next to a ☎. Omit initial digits in parentheses (e.g., (0)12 for Kraków), when calling from abroad.

4. The **local number.**

Let's Go has recently partnered with **ekit.com** to provide a calling card that offers a number of services, including email and voice messaging. Before purchasing any calling card, always be sure to compare rates with other cards, and to make sure it serves your needs (a local card is generally better for local calls, for instance). For more information, visit **www.letsgo.ekit.com.**

To call home with a calling card, contact the local operator for your service provider by dialing the access numbers listed in the **Essentials: Keeping in Touch** section at the beginning of each country chapter and on the inside of the back cover. Not all of these numbers are toll-free; in many countries, phones will require a coin or card deposit to call the operator. Wherever possible, use a calling card for international calls—the long-distance rates for national phone services are often exorbitant. Where available, locally purchased **prepaid phone cards** can be used for direct international calls, but they are still less cost-efficient than calling cards purchased through the service providers listed above. **In-room hotel calls** invariably include an arbitrary and sky-high surcharge, and will sometimes charge you for the call even if you use a calling card. You can usually make **direct international calls** from pay phones, but if you aren't using a calling card you may need to drop your coins as quickly as your words.

Placing a **collect call** through an international operator is even more expensive, but may be necessary in care of emergency. You can place collect calls through the service providers listed above even if you don't have one of their phone cards. To reach an English-speaking operator, you must dial the phone company access number for the country you're in.

COMPANY	TO OBTAIN A CARD, DIAL:
AT&T (US)	800-364-9292
Canada Direct	800-561-8868
Ireland Direct	800 40 00 00
MCI (US)	800-777-5000
New Zealand Direct	0800 000 000
Telstra Australia	13 22 00

CALLING WITHIN EASTERN EUROPE

The simplest way to call within the country is to use a coin-operated phone or to use **prepaid phone cards,** which are slowly phasing out coins in most Eastern European countries. Rates tend to be highest in the morning, lower in the evening, and lowest on Sunday and late at night.

TIME DIFFERENCES

A map with Eastern European time zones is on the inside back cover of this book—Vancouver, CAN and San Francisco, USA are GMT -8; New York, USA is GMT -5; Sydney, AUS is GMT +10; and Auckland, NZ is GMT +12. All Eastern European countries observe Daylight Saving Time.

GMT + 1			GMT +2			GMT + 3
Albania Bosnia	Croatia	Czech Rep.	Baltic States	Belarus	Bulgaria	European Russia
Hungary	Macedonia	Poland	Moldova	Romania	Ukraine	(Including Moscow and St. Petersburg)
Slovak Rep.	Slovenia	Serbia and Montenegro		Kaliningrad, Russia		

EMAIL AND INTERNET

The World Wide Web has made its way into Eastern Europe. Every major city now has some sort of Internet access, usually cybercafes. While it may be more difficult to find in smaller towns and the rural countryside, Internet access is often available in public libraries, hostels, and tourist offices. Rates are reasonable; 1hr. costs from US$1-3 on average, though rates fluctuate from country to country.

Though in some places it's possible to forge a remote link with your home server, in most cases this is a much slower (and thus more expensive) option than taking advantage of free web-based email accounts (e.g., www.hotmail.com and www.yahoo.com). Travelers with laptops can call an Internet service provider via a modem. Long-distance phone cards specifically intended for such calls can defray normally high phone charges; check with your long-distance phone provider to see if it offers this option. Internet cafes and the occasional free Internet terminal at a public library or university are listed in the Practical Information sections of major cities. For lists of additional cybercafes in Eastern Europe, check out www.cybercafes.com or www.netcafeguide.com.

GETTING TO EASTERN EUROPE

BY PLANE

When it comes to airfare, a little effort can save you a bundle. If your plans are flexible enough to deal with the restrictions, courier flights are the cheapest. Tickets bought from consolidators and standby seating are also good deals, but last-minute specials, airfare wars, and charter flights often beat these fares. Students, seniors, and those under 26 should never pay full price for a ticket.

AIRFARES

Airfares to Eastern Europe peak roughly between mid-June and early September (the high season); holidays are also expensive. The cheapest times to travel are November through mid-December and mid-January through March. Midweek (M-

Th mornings) round-trip flights run US$40-100 cheaper than weekend flights, but they are generally more crowded and less likely to permit frequent-flier upgrades. Not fixing a return date ("open return") or arriving in and departing from different cities ("open jaw") can be pricier than round-trip flights. Patching one-way flights together is the most expensive way to travel. For those willing to make the extra effort, the least expensive route is often to fly into London, Paris, Munich, or Milan and reach your destination by train or bus; it will often be necessary to connect from one of these cities regardless.

If your destination is only one stop on a more extensive globe-hop, consider a round-the-world (RTW) ticket. Tickets usually include at least five stops and are valid for about a year; prices range US$1200-5000. Try **Northwest Airlines/KLM** (US ☎800-447-4747; www.nwa.com) or **Star Alliance,** a consortium of 16 airlines including United Airlines (US ☎800-538-2929; www.staralliance.com). Round-trip commercial **fares** to the larger, more touristed cities (Budapest, Prague, Warsaw) from the US or Canadian east coast can usually be found, with some work, for US$600-800 in high season; from the UK, UK£150-180; from Australia, AUS$3000-4000; from New Zealand, NZ$3000-3500. Tickets to mid-range cities, including Bucharest, Moscow, Sofia, and Zagreb, generally cost about US$200 more, while Bratislava, Kyiv, Minsk, and the Baltic capitals can cost US$1000-1400/UK£400-600/AUS$4000-5000/NZ$5000-7000. Prices drop US$200-500 the rest of the year.

BUDGET AND STUDENT TRAVEL AGENCIES

While knowledgeable agents specializing in flights to Eastern Europe can make your life easy and help you save, they may not spend the time to find you the lowest possible fare—they get paid on commission. Travelers holding **ISIC** and **IYTC cards** qualify for big discounts from student travel agencies. Most flights from budget agencies are on major airlines, but in peak season some may sell seats on less reliable chartered aircraft.

CTS Travel, 30 Rathbone Pl., London W1T 1GQ, UK (☎0207 209 0630; www.ctstravel.co.uk). British student travel agency with offices in 39 countries including a US office, Empire State Building, 350 Fifth Ave., ste. 7813, New York, NY 10118 (☎877-287-6665; www.ctstravelusa.com).

STA Travel, 5900 Wilshire Blvd., ste. 900, Los Angeles, CA 90036, USA (24hr. reservations and info ☎800-781-4040; www.sta-travel.com). A student and youth travel organization with over 150 offices worldwide (check their website for a listing of all their offices), including US offices in Boston, Chicago, L.A., New York, San Francisco, Seattle, and Washington, D.C. Ticket booking, travel insurance, railpasses, and more. Walk-in offices are located throughout Australia (☎03 9349 4344), New Zealand (☎09 309 9723), and the UK (☎0870 1 600 599).

Travel CUTS (Canadian Universities Travel Services Limited), 187 College St., Toronto, ON M5T 1P7, CAN (☎416-979-2406; www.travelcuts.com). Offices across Canada and the US including Los Angeles, New York, Seattle, and San Francisco.

USIT, 19-21 Aston Quay, Dublin 2, IRE (☎01 602 1777; www.usitworld.com), Ireland's leading student/budget travel agency has 22 offices throughout Northern Ireland and the Republic of Ireland. Offers programs to work in North America.

Wasteels, Skoubogade 6, 1158 Copenhagen K., DEN (☎3314 4633; www.wasteels.com). A huge chain with 180 locations across Europe. Sells Wasteels BIJ tickets discounted 30-45% off regular fare, 2nd-class international point-to-point train tickets with unlimited stopovers for those under 26 (sold only in Europe).

FLIGHT PLANNING ON THE INTERNET. The Internet may be the budget traveler's dream when it comes to finding and booking bargain fares, but the array of options can be overwhelming. Many airline sites offer special last-minute deals on the Web: **STA** (www.sta-travel.com) and **StudentUniverse** (www.studentuniverse.com) provide quotes on student tickets, while **Orbitz** (www.orbitz.com), **Expedia** (www.expedia.com), and **Travelocity** (www.travelocity.com) offer full travel services. **Priceline** (www.priceline.com) lets you specify a price, and obligates you to buy any ticket that meets or beats it; **Hotwire** (www.hotwire.com) offers bargain fares, but won't reveal the airline or flight times until you buy. Other sites that compile deals for you include www.bestfares.com, www.flights.com, www.lowestfare.com, www.onetravel.com, and www.travelzoo.com. For those flying from within Europe, EasyJet (www.easyjet.com) offers inexpensive flights from London to Prague and Budapest. Increasingly, there are online tools available to help sift through multiple offers; **SideStep** (www.sidestep.com; download required) and **Booking Buddy** (www.bookingbuddy.com) let you enter your trip information once and search multiple sites. An indispensable resource on the Internet is the **Air Traveler's Handbook** (www.faqs.org/faqs/travel/air/handbook), a comprehensive listing of links to everything you need to know before you board a plane.

COMMERCIAL AIRLINES

The commercial airlines' lowest regular offer is the **APEX** (Advance Purchase Excursion) fare, which provides confirmed reservations and allows "open-jaw" tickets. Generally, reservations must be made one to three weeks ahead of departure. Book peak-season APEX fares early; by May you will have a hard time getting your desired departure date. Popular carriers to Eastern Europe include:

FROM NORTH AMERICA AND WESTERN EUROPE
The **Air Travel Advisory Bureau** in London (☎0870 737 0026; www.atab.co.uk) gives referrals to agencies and consolidators that offer discounted airfares from the UK.

Aer Lingus: Ireland ☎1 886 8844; www.aerlingus.ie. Return tickets from Dublin, Cork, and Shannon to Amsterdam, Bologna, Brussels, Copenhagen, Düsseldorf, Frankfurt, Lisbon, Madrid, Málaga, Milan, Munich, Nice, Paris, Rome, Vienna, and Zürich.

Air France: France ☎33 820 820 820, Canada and US ☎1 800-237-2747; www.airfrance.com. Covers much of Eastern Europe via Western Europe.

Austrian Airways: UK ☎800 843 0002; www.aua.com. Connects to many Eastern European cities via Vienna.

British Airways: UK ☎84 5773 3377, Canada and US ☎800-247-9297; www.britishairways.com. Flies into most large cities in Eastern Europe.

Delta Air Lines: US ☎800-241-1212, Canada ☎800-221-1212, UK ☎800 41 4767; www.delta.com. A more reliable US carrier serving Eastern Europe.

Finnair: ☎800-950-4768; www.us.finnair.com. Cheap round-trips from San Francisco, New York, and Toronto to Helsinki; connections throughout Europe.

KLM: ☎870 507 40 74; www.klm.com. Connects to a number of cities in Eastern Europe via Amsterdam.

Lufthansa: Canada ☎800-563-5954, US ☎800-645-3880; www.lufthansa.com. Has a wide variety of routes covering most of Eastern Europe.

SAS: UK ☎20 8990 7159; Canada and US ☎800-221-2350; www.scandinavian.net. Reliably connects to Baltic cities.

FROM AUSTRALIA AND NEW ZEALAND

Air New Zealand: ☎800 737 000; www.airnewzealand.com. Reasonable fares from Auckland to London and special sales at much lower prices.

Lufthansa: Australia ☎13 0065 5727, New Zealand ☎800 94 5220; www.lufthansa.com. Offers reliable flights that connect to a number of cities throughout Eastern Europe.

Qantas: Australia ☎13 13 13; New Zealand ☎9 357 8900; www.qantas.com. Flies from cities in Australia and New Zealand to London, where connecting flights are easy to find.

TICKET CONSOLIDATORS

Ticket consolidators buy unsold tickets in bulk from commercial airlines and sell them at discounted rates. Not all of them are reliable, so insist on a receipt that gives full details of restrictions, refunds, and tickets, and pay by credit card (in spite of the 2-5% fee) so you can stop payment if you never receive your tickets. For more info, see www.travel-library.com/air-travel/consolidators.html.

Travel Avenue (☎800-333-3335; www.travelavenue.com) searches for best available published fares and then uses several consolidators to attempt to beat that fare. **NOW Voyager,** 315 W. 49th St. Plaza Arcade, New York, NY 10019 (☎212-459-1616; www.nowvoyagertravel.com) arranges discounted flights, mostly from New York, to Barcelona, London, Madrid, Milan, Paris, and Rome. Other consolidators worth trying are **Rebel** (☎800-732-3588; www.rebeltours.com), **Cheap Tickets** (☎800-652-4327; www.cheaptickets.com). Yet more consolidators on the web include **Flights.com** (www.flights.com) and **TravelHUB** (www.travelhub.com). *Let's Go* does not endorse any of these agencies. As always, be cautious, and research companies before you hand over your credit card number. In London, **Lupus Travel**

(☎ 20 7306 3000; www.atab.co.uk) provides names of consolidators and discount flight specialists. From Australia and New Zealand, look for consolidator ads in the *Sydney Morning Herald* and other papers.

GETTING AROUND

Fares are either **single** (one-way) or **return** (round-trip). "Period returns" require you to return within a specific time frame; "day return" means you must return on the same day. Unless stated otherwise, *Let's Go* always lists single fares. Round-trip fares in Eastern Europe are usually less than double the one-way fare.

BY PLANE

 AIRLINE SAFETY. The airlines of the former Soviet Republics do not always meet safety standards, especially for internal flights. When flying within Eastern Europe, it's often safest to spend the few extra rubles and book a seat on a Western airline rather than a domestic carrier. When a foreign carrier is not an option, the *Official Airline Guide* (www.oag.com) and many travel agencies can tell you the type and age of aircraft on a particular route. The **International Airline Passengers Association** (US ☎ 800-821-4272; UK 020 8681 6555; www.iapa.com) provides region-specific safety information. The American **Federal Aviation Administration** (☎ 202-366-2220; www.faa.gov) reviews the airline authorities for countries whose airlines enter the US.

Flying across Eastern Europe on regularly scheduled flights can devour your budget, but if you're short on time (or flush with cash) you might consider it. Student travel agencies sell cheap tickets, and budget fares are often available in the spring and summer on popular routes. Consult budget travel agents and local newspapers for more info. A number of European airlines offer discount coupon packets. Most are available only as tack-ons for transatlantic passengers, but some are stand-alone offers. Most must be purchased before departure. **Europe by Air** (☎ 888-387-2479; www.europebyair.com) offers a *FlightPass* (US$99 per flight) that allows you to country-hop between over 150 European cities. SAS (☎ 800-221-2350; www.scandinavian.net) sells one-way coupons for travel within the Baltics and greater Europe. Most are available only to transatlantic **SAS** passengers, but some United and Lufthansa passengers also qualify. (US$65-225.)

BY TRAIN

Flying into a Western European city and then taking a train to Eastern Europe often proves to be the cheapest option. Many travelers fly into Milan to connect by train to the Balkans; Munich or Berlin to reach Poland, the Baltics, and Ukraine; and Vienna for the short train ride to the Czech and Slovak Republics and Hungary. Check out **transit visa** requirements if you plan on passing through other Eastern European countries en route to your final destination. Those touring the EU on their way to or from Eastern Europe might consider a **Eurailpass**—keep in mind that it is **not valid in Eastern Europe,** with the exception of Hungary. Trains in Eastern Europe are generally a reliable means of travel, as trains run both within countries and across national borders. Rail infrastructure is slightly weaker, however, in areas of the Balkans. No international trains travel to Albania, and Dubrovnik, Croatia is not connected by rail.

ESSENTIALS

Second-class seating on Eastern European trains is pleasant, and compartments, which fit two to six, are great places to meet fellow travelers. Trains, however, are not always safe in terms of personal safety, especially at night. For safety tips, see **Safety and Security,** p. 18. For long trips make sure you are on the correct car, as trains sometimes split at crossroads. Destinations listed in parentheses on Eastern European train schedules require a train switch, usually at the town listed immediately before the parenthesis. When traveling through Eastern Europe by train, you can either buy a **railpass,** which allows you unlimited travel within a particular region for a given period of time, or rely on buying individual **point-to-point tickets** as you go. Almost all countries give students or youths (under 26) discounts on domestic rail tickets, and many sell a student or youth card that provides 20-50% off all fares.

VISAS AND RESERVATIONS

Some Eastern European countries require **transit visas** for all travelers just passing through the country by train; for example, trains from Central Europe must pass through Belarus to reach the Baltics or Russia. Be aware that some domestic trains in Ukraine pass through Moldova, which requires a transit visa. To avoid getting detained in Minsk, Chişinău, or elsewhere, have your paperwork in order, or that your route works around countries with transit visas. For more information, consult the **Visa and Entry Info** section of each country.

Many train stations have different counters for domestic and international tickets, seat reservations, and information—check before lining up. Seat reservations (usually US$3-10) are only required on select trains (usually major international lines), but you are not guaranteed a seat without one. Reservations are available on major trains as much as two months in advance, and Europeans often reserve far ahead of time. The Moscow-St. Petersburg train is famous for selling out weeks in advance during the summer.

RAILPASSES

It may be tough to make your railpass pay for itself in Eastern Europe, where train fares are ridiculously cheap and buses are sometimes preferable. In general, it's better to buy **point-to-point tickets.** If you must purchase a pass, do so before you arrive in Europe, as most passes are available only to non-Europeans and are consequently difficult to find in Europe. Try **Rail Europe Group,** 44 South Broadway, White Plains, NY 10601, USA (☎800-438-7245, Canada 800-361-7245, UK 87 0584 8848; www.raileurope.com) or **Destination Europe Resources (DER),** 9501 W. Devon Ave. Rosemont, IL 60018, USA (☎800-782-2424; www.der.com).

MULTINATIONAL RAILPASSES

For those dead set on purchasing a multinational railpass, there are a few options. A **Eurailpass** is not one of them: it covers only Hungary in Eastern Europe. The **European East Pass** covers Austria, the Czech Republic, Hungary, Poland, and the Slovak Republic (5 days in 1 month 1st class US$226, 2nd class US$160). The **Balkan Flexipass** (5 days in 1 month US$152, under 26 US$90; 10- and 15-day passes also available) is valid for travel in Bulgaria, Greece, Macedonia, Romania, Serbia and Montenegro, and Turkey.

NATIONAL PASSES

Bulgarian Flexipass, Czech Flexipass, Hungarian Flexipass, Polrail Pass, and **Romanian Flexipass** are the only national passes available. These tend not to be as economical as point-to-point travel, but if you're spending a significant amount of time in one country, they can be a worthwhile investment. Another type of regional pass covers a specific area within a country or a round-trip from any border to a particular destination and back. Examples include the **Prague Excursion Pass,** which covers travel from any Czech border to Prague and back to any Czech border. (Round-trip must be completed within 7 days. 1st class US$55, 2nd US$40; under 26 US$45/35.) For more information, contact Rail Europe (see p. 39).

INTERRAIL PASSES

InterRail passes can only be purchased in Europe, by people who have lived in Europe for at least six months. There are eight InterRail zones, two of which serve Eastern European routes. **Zone D** includes the Czech and Slovak Republics, Croatia, Hungary, and Poland; **Zone H** Bulgaria, Macedonia, Romania, and Serbia and Montenegro. A pass may be purchased for up to three zones. The **Under 26 InterRail Card** allows either 21 consecutive days or one month of unlimited travel within one, two, three or all of the eight zones; the cost (UK£159-295) is determined by the number of zones the pass covers. The Over 26 InterRail Card provides 415. The new Child Pass (ages 4-11; UK£111-207) offers the same services. For info and ticket sales, contact **Student Travel Centre,** 24 Rupert St., 1st fl., London W1D 6DQ, UK (☎020 7434 1306; www.student-travel-centre.com). Tickets are also available from travel agents, at major train stations throughout Europe, or online. (☎17 3340 2001; www.railpassdirect.co.uk.)

EURODOMINO

Like the InterRail Pass, the Eurodomino pass (also known as the **Freedom Pass**) is available to anyone who has lived in Europe for at least six months; however, it is only valid in one country, which you designate when buying the pass. It is valid for three to eight days of travel over a one month period. It is available for 29 European countries, including Bulgaria, Croatia, the Czech Republic, Hungary, Macedonia, Poland, Romania, Serbia and Montenegro, the Slovak Republic, and Slovenia. Reservations for each country must be paid for separately. **Supplements** are included for many high-speed trains. The pass must be bought within your home country; each country has its own price for the pass. Ask your national rail company for more info. See www.railchoice.co.uk for information.

READING AND RESOURCES ON TRAIN TRAVEL.
Info on rail travel and railpasses: www.raileurope.com.
Point-to-point fares and schedules: www.raileurope.com/us/rail/fares_schedules/index.htm. Allows you to calculate whether buying a railpass will save you money.
European Railway Server: http://mercurio.iet.unipi.it/home.html. Links to rail servers throughout Europe.

BY BUS

All over Eastern Europe, buses reach rural areas inaccessible by train. In addition, long-distance bus networks may be more extensive, efficient, and sometimes more comfortable than train services. In the Balkans, air-conditioned buses run by private companies are a godsend. **Contiki Holidays,** 801 E. Katella Ave., 3rd fl., Anaheim, CA 92805, USA (☎888-266-8454; www.contiki.com) offers a variety of European vacation packages designed exclusively for 18- to 35-year-olds. For an average cost of $65 per day, tours include accommodations, transportation, guided sightseeing and some meals. **Eurolines,** 4 Cardiff Rd., Luton, Bedfordshire, L41 1PP, UK (☎990 14 32 19; www.eurolines.com), is Europe's largest coach operator, offering passes (UK£113-299) for unlimited 15-, 30-, or 60-day travel between 500 destinations in 25 countries, including many spots in Eastern Europe and Russia. It has offices in most countries in Eastern Europe; see website for details.

BY BOAT

Ferries in the **North** and **Baltic Seas** are reliable and comfortable. Those in the **Black Sea** are less predictable, and traveling between the coasts of Romania, Bulgaria, Ukraine, and Russia is no easy task. Those content with deck passage rarely need to book ahead, but should check in a few hours early and allow extra time to get to the port. **Polferries** (☎91 32 26 140; www.polferries.pl), in Poland, go from Świnoujście, Poland to **Ronne, DEN** (6hr.) and **Ystad, SWE** (7hr.) and from Gdańsk, Poland to **Oxelösund-Stockholm** (17hr.) and **Nynäshamn** (7hr.), both in Sweden. **Silja Line** (US ☎800-533-3755; www.silja.com) leaves Helsinki, FIN to **Rīga, LAT** (17hr., mid-June to Dec.), **St. Petersburg, RUS** (15hr., May 1 - Sept. 27), and **Tallinn, EST** (3hr., June to mid-Sept.). Also Turku, EST to **Stockholm, SWE** (12hr., Jan. to Sept.).

BY CAR

Public transportation is generally the best way to get around in Eastern Europe. and travelers unfamiliar with the region and its roads will likely find catching a bus or train more efficient than driving. Because car rental prices in Eastern Europe can be among the highest on the continent and gas (petrol) is not always readily available (particularly unleaded), travel by bus, train, and sometimes even by plane, can be a cheaper alternative to hitting the road. Roads are often poorly maintained and roadside assistance rarely exists, contributing to some of the highest driving fatality rates in the world. In recent years, a network of limited access highways has been expanding in Eastern Europe, such as an expressway linking Budapest to Vienna. On the whole, conditions worsen the farther east you travel. As driving gains popularity in Central Europe, however, support services for drivers have been on the rise in countries, like the Czech Republic, Hungary, and Poland. If you do choose to strike off on your own, know the laws of the countries in which you'll be driving and read up on local road conditions. For an informal primer on European road signs and conventions, check out www.travlang.com/signs. The **Association for Safe International Road Travel (ASIRT)**, 11769 Gainsborough Rd., Potomac, MD 20854, USA (☎ 301-983-5252; www.asirt.org), can provide more specific information about road conditions.

DRIVING PERMITS AND CAR INSURANCE

INTERNATIONAL DRIVING PERMIT (IDP)

If you plan to drive a car while in Eastern Europe, you should have an International Driving Permit (IDP), though certain countries allow travelers to drive with a valid American, British, or Canadian license for a limited number of months. It is useful to have one anyway, in case you're in an accident or stranded in a small town where the police do not speak English. Information on the IDP is printed in 10 languages, including German and Russian. An IDP, valid for one year, must be issued in your home country. The application requires one or two photos, a current local license, an additional form of identification, and a fee. To apply, contact your home country's automobile association or visit the **International Automobile Driver's Club** (www.driverlicense.net).

CAR INSURANCE

Most credit cards cover standard insurance. If you rent, lease, or borrow a car, you need an **International Insurance Certificate (green card)** to certify that you have liability insurance that applies abroad. You can get a green card at car dealers (for those leasing cars) or rental agencies, some travel agents, and some border crossings. Rental agencies in some countries may require you to purchase theft insurance.

BY BICYCLE

In most of Eastern Europe, bringing your own bike is not worthwhile. In many countries, especially Estonia, Poland, and Slovenia, **renting** a bike will allow you to see much more of the natural scenery. For more information, consult the **Practical Information** section of the city or town in which you will be traveling.

BY THUMB

Hitchhiking involves serious risks, including theft, assault, sexual harassment, and unsafe driving. If you do decide to hitch, consider where you are. Hitching remains relatively common in Eastern Europe, though Westerners are a definite target for theft. In Russia, the Baltics, Poland, and some other Eastern European countries, hitchhiking can be akin to hailing a taxi, and drivers will likely expect to be paid a sum at least equivalent to a bus ticket to your destination.

Let's Go never recommends hitchhiking as a safe means of transportation, and none of the information presented here is intended to do so.

ADDITIONAL INFORMATION

SPECIFIC CONCERNS

WOMEN TRAVELERS

Solo female travelers are still a relatively new phenomenon in Eastern Europe, particularly in public places like bars and restaurants. Women traveling alone may encounter quizzical stares. The attitudes that contribute to these surprised looks, when coupled with crime in urban areas, can make for dangerous situations. Hostels which offer single rooms that lock from the inside or religious organizations that provide rooms for only women offer female travelers the most security. Some communal showers in some hostels are safer than others; check before settling in. Hitchhiking is never safe for lone women, or even for two women traveling together. Choose train compartments occupied by women or couples; ask the conductor to put together a women-only compartment if there isn't one.

Generally, the less you look like a tourist, the better off you'll be. Dress conservatively, especially in rural areas. Wearing the clothes that are fashionable among local women will cut down on stares, and a *babushka*-style kerchief discourages even the most tenacious of catcallers. Some travelers report that wearing a wedding band or carrying pictures of a "husband" or "children" is extremely useful to help document marital status. In cities, you may be harassed no matter how you're dressed. Your best answer is no answer at all. Staring straight ahead will do a world of good that reactions usually don't achieve. The extremely persistent can sometimes be dissuaded by a firm, loud, and very public "Go away!" in the appropriate language. If need be, turn to an older woman for help; her stern rebukes should usually embarrass the most persistent harassers into silence.

Let's Go lists emergency numbers (including rape crisis lines) in the **Practical Information** of most major cities. Memorize the emergency numbers in places you visit, and consider carrying a whistle on your keychain. A self-defense course will not only prepare you for a potential attack but also heighten your awareness and boost your confidence (see **Self Defense,** p. 18). Make sure you are aware of the health concerns that women face when traveling (see **Women's Health,** p. 25, and the **Health and Safety** section at the beginning of each country's chapter).

GAY, LESBIAN, AND BISEXUAL TRAVELERS

Though the legality of homosexuality is not generally an issue in Eastern Europe, it is strongly stigmatized in the Balkans, much of the former Soviet Union and rural areas. Regardless of the legality, homophobic views persist and public displays of homosexuality give local authorities an excuse to be troublesome. Even within major cities, gay nightclubs and social centers are often hidden and frequently change location, though in such cities as Prague and Budapest, gay nightlife is gradually becoming more common. For coverage of the current legal and social climate in each country, consult the website of the **International Lesbian and Gay Association** (www.ilga.org). *Let's Go* lists local gay establishments. Word of mouth is often a great source for finding the latest hotspots. Listed below are contact organizations, mail-order bookstores, and publishers that offer materials addressing some specific concerns. **Out and About** (www.planetout.com) offers a biweekly newsletter addressing travel concerns and a comprehensive site addressing gay travel concerns. The online newspaper **365gay.com** also has a travel section (www.365gay.com/travel/travelchannel.htm).

Gay's the Word, 66 Marchmont St., London WC1N 1AB, UK (☎44 20 7278 7654; www.gaystheword.co.uk). The largest gay and lesbian bookshop in the UK, with both fiction and non-fiction titles. Mail-order service available.

Giovanni's Room, 1145 Pine St., Philadelphia, PA 19107, USA (☎215-923-2960; www.queerbooks.com). An international lesbian/feminist and gay bookstore with mail-order service (carries many of the publications listed on p. 43).

International Lesbian and Gay Association (ILGA), 81 rue Marché-au-Charbon, B-1000 Brussels, Belgium (☎32 2 502 2471; www.ilga.org). Provides political information, such as homosexuality laws of individual countries.

FURTHER READING: GLBT TRAVEL

Spartacus 2003-2004: International Gay Guide. Bruno Gmunder Verlag (US$33).

Damron Accommodations Guide, Damron City Guide, and *Damron Women's Traveller.* Damron Travel Guides (US$11-19). For info, call ☎800-462-6654 or visit www.damron.com.

Ferrari Guides' Gay Travel A to Z, Ferrari Guides' Men's Travel in Your Pocket, Ferrari Guides' Women's Travel in Your Pocket, and *Ferrari Guides' Inn Places.* Ferrari Publications (US$16-20).

The Gay Vacation Guide: The Best Trips and How to Plan Them, by Mark Chesnut. Kensington Books (US$15).

TRAVELERS WITH DISABILITIES

Unfortunately, Eastern Europe is largely inaccessible to disabled travelers. Ramps and other amenities are all but nonexistent in most countries. Contact your destination's consulate or tourist office for information, arrange transportation early, and inform airlines and hotels of any special accommodations required ahead of time. Guide-dog owners should inquire as to the specific quarantine policies of each destination. **Rail** is probably the most convenient form of travel for disabled travelers in Eastern Europe: some stations have ramps, and some trains have wheelchair lifts, special seating areas, and specially equipped toilets. Bulgaria, the Czech Republic, Hungary, Poland, and the Slovak Republic's rail systems all offer limited resources for wheelchair accessibility. Some major **car rental** agencies (Hertz, Avis, and National) also offer hand-controlled vehicles.

USEFUL ORGANIZATIONS AND AGENCIES

Accessible Journeys, 35 West Sellers Ave., Ridley Park, PA 19078, USA (☎800-846-4537; www.disabilitytravel.com). Designs tours for wheelchair users and slow walkers.

Directions Unlimited, 123 Green Ln., Bedford Hills, NY 10507, USA (☎800-533-5343). Books individual vacations for the physically disabled; not an info service.

Flying Wheels, 143 W. Bridge St., P.O. Box 382, Owatonna, MN 55060, USA (☎507-451-5005; www.flyingwheelstravel.com). Escorted trips to Europe.

Mobility International USA (MIUSA), P.O. Box 10767, Eugene, OR 97440, USA (☎541-343-1284; www.miusa.org). Books and other publications.

Society for Accessible Travel & Hospitality (SATH), 347 Fifth Ave., #610, New York, NY 10016, USA (☎212-447-7284; www.sath.org). An advocacy group that publishes free online travel information and the travel magazine *OPEN WORLD.*

MINORITY TRAVELERS

Minority travelers, especially those of African or Asian descent, will usually meet with more curiosity than hostility, especially outside big cities. Travelers with darker skin of any nationality may experience some prejudice, particularly in the Balkan region, where ethnic tensions run high. Anti-Muslim sentiment lingers in the Balkans from the conflicts that plagued the region throughout the 1990s. **Roma** (gypsies) also encounter substantial hostility in Eastern Europe. The ranks of **skinheads** are on the rise in Eastern Europe, and minority travelers, especially Jews and blacks, should regard them with caution. **Anti-Semitism** is still a problem in many countries, including Poland and the former Soviet Union; it is generally best to be discreet about your religion.

DIETARY CONCERNS

Vegetarian and **kosher** dining is often a challenge in Eastern Europe. Most of the national cuisines tend to be meat- (particularly pork-) heavy. **Markets** are often a good bet for fresh vegetables, fruit, cheese, and bread. The **North American Vegetarian Society,** P.O. Box 72, Dolgeville, NY 13329, USA (☎518-568-7970; www.navsonline.org), offers information and publications for vegetarian travelers. There are many resources on the web; try www.happycow.net for starters.

Travelers who keep kosher should contact synagogues in larger cities for information on kosher restaurants. A good resource is the *Jewish Travel Guide*, by Michael Zaidner (Vallentine Mitchell; US$17), which lists synagogues, kosher restaurants, and Jewish institutions in over 110 countries.

OTHER RESOURCES

USEFUL PUBLICATIONS

Central Europe Profiled, Barry Turner ed. St. Martin's Press, 2000. (US$18). A breakdown of the culture, politics, and economy of each country in Eastern Europe.

On Foot to the Golden Horn, by Jason Goodwin. Picador, 2000. (US$11). Join this fellow backpacker on a journey from Poland to Turkey.

The Great Railway Bazaar: By Train Through Asia, by Paul Theroux. Penguin Books, 1995. Travel-writer Theroux documents his adventures on the Trans-Siberian Railroad.

TRAVEL PUBLISHERS AND BOOKSTORES

Adventurous Traveler Bookstore, P.O. Box 2221, Williston, VT 05495, USA (☎800-282-3963; www.adventuroustraveler.com).

Globe Corner Bookstore, 28 Church St., Cambridge, MA 02138, USA (☎800-358-6013; www.globecorner.com). A wide variety of travel guides, and background reading.

Hunter Publishing, 470 W. Broadway, 2nd fl., South Boston, MA 02127, USA (☎617-269-0700; www.hunterpublishing.com). Extensive catalog of travel guides and adventure travel books.

Rand McNally, P.O. Box 7600, Chicago, IL 60680, USA (☎847-329-8100; www.randmcnally.com). Publishes road atlases.

THE WORLD WIDE WEB

Many countries' embassies maintain websites where you can check visa requirements and news related to your destination (see **Embassies and Consulates,** p. 9). For general information about travel check out the listings below.

THE ART OF BUDGET TRAVEL

■ **How to See the World:** www.artoftravel.com. Great travel tips, from cheap flights to self defense to local culture.

Robert Young Pelton's Dangerous Places: www.comebackalive.com/df. Helpful hints and amusing anecdotes for those going off (way off) the beaten path.

INFORMATION ON EASTERN EUROPE

■ **In Your Pocket:** www.inyourpocket.com. The online version of an excellent series of city and regional guides. The coverage of the Baltic states is particularly thorough.

CIA World Factbook: www.odci.gov/cia/publications/factbook/index.html. Tons of vital statistics on Eastern Europe's geography, government, economy, and people.

Foreign Language for Travelers: www.travlang.com. Provides free online translating dictionaries and lists of phrases in various European languages, including Czech, Hungarian, and Polish.

Geographia: www.geographia.com. Highlights, culture, and people of Eastern European countries.

PlanetRider: www.planetrider.com. A subjective list of links to the "best" websites covering the culture and tourist attractions of several countries, including the Czech Republic, Hungary, and Russia.

 WWW.LETSGO.COM Our freshly redesigned website features extensive content from our guides; community forums where travelers can connect with each other and ask questions or advice—as well as share stories and tips; and expanded resources to help you plan your trip. Visit us soon to browse by destination, find information about ordering our titles, and sign up for our e-newsletter!

LIFE AND TIMES

During the Cold War, Westerners imposed the name "Eastern Europe" on the Soviet satellites east of the Berlin Wall. The title has always been somewhat of a misnomer, capturing a political rather than geographical reality: Vienna lies farther east than Prague, Croatia sprawls along the Mediterranean, the geometric center of the European continent is in Lithuania, and most of Russia is, quite frankly, in Asia. To understand the remarkable complexity of Eastern Europe is to picture a map of the region a little over a decade ago: in 1989, there were a total of seven countries behind the Iron Curtain; today, 19 independent states comprise that same area. In the past decade, the region has undergone an astounding political and cultural transformation. While communism has fallen from power throughout most of Europe and the Soviet Union no longer exists, Eastern Europe continues to be defined by its historical legacy. The region is united by what it longs to leave behind—a history of political upheaval and foreign domination—and by what it now confronts—a more optimistic but similarly uncertain future. In the process of breaking from the communist mold and redefining themselves, these newly sovereign states have created another Europe, a Europe which some might consider backward, others more authentic, and still others simply distinct. As it looks to shed its troubled past, Eastern Europe must face an array of lingering political and economic problems; while many countries seek a coveted spot in the European Union, they must first tackle issues of domestic poverty and corruption. Yet even amidst such turmoil, Eastern Europe has become the *en vogue* destination for European students on holiday. While spirited travelers once ventured to Paris, London and Rome, today Prague, Budapest, and Dubrovnik equally entice and captivate the younger generation. Now more than ever, backpackers are digging in, dressing up, and breathing new life into this tumultuous, yet spectacular and rewarding region. Exactly what will emerge when all the smoke clears remains to be seen, but it's certain to be an exciting and diverse set of nations.

A HISTORY OF HALF THE WORLD IN FIVE PAGES

SLAVS (BEFORE AD 800)

With the exception of Albania, Hungary, Romania, and the Baltic countries, Eastern Europe is populated primarily by **Slavic** peoples, who constitute the largest ethnic and linguistic group in Europe. Originally believed to come from the Caucasus, the Slavs migrated to the Dnieper region in today's Ukraine during the 2nd or 3rd millennium BC. The movement of ancient tribes westward in the 5th and 6th centuries AD sparked the **Great Migration,** during which Slavs penetrated deeply into Europe, displacing Celts in the Czech and Slovak lands, Illyrians in the Balkans, Turks and Avars in Bulgaria, Vikings in Russia and western Ukraine, and Germanic tribes in Hungary. Poland, which was conquered in the 9th century AD, was the last to be settled by Slavs. Unlike other migrating tribes at this time, the Slavs were cultivators and settlers rather than pillagers. In the mid-9th century, Slavs in modern Ukraine established the first major civilization in Eastern Europe, **Kyivan Rus.**

Despite their shared roots, there has never been any natural unity between all the Slavic peoples that settled in these lands. The division of Christendom in 395 into the Roman Empire and the Byzantine Empire split the Slavs into two culturally distinct groups. The fault line between the two cultures ran directly through the Balkans: the Slovenes and Croats were yoked to Rome, while the Bulgarians, Macedonians, Romanians, and Serbs were loyal to Constantinople. Since the split, the political and social history of the western Slavs has been inextricably linked to Western Europe, while the history of the southern and eastern Slavs has been influenced far more by their eastern neighbors, especially the **Ottoman Turks.**

The non-Slavic lands in Eastern Europe were inhabited by a vast array of settlers and invaders. Estonia was invaded by **Vikings** and **Finns** in the 9th and 11th centuries respectively. Latvians and Lithuanians are of **Baltic** descent. All of the original non-Slavic areas, including Albania, Bulgaria, Hungary, and Romania were strongly influenced by Slavic neighbors and settlers. Romanians, Romanized descendants of the indigenous **Dacian** tribes, assimilated the Slavic migrants of the 6th century while the **Magyars,** who hailed from the area between the Baltics and the Ural Mountains, began invading Hungary in the 9th century. **Albanians** have managed to preserve their ancient Illyrian language, but the originally **Turkic** Bulgarians adopted a Slavic language and are now considered Slavs.

OTTOMANS AND HAPSBURGS (800-1914)

Beginning in the 8th century, several short-lived kingdoms emerged in Eastern Europe, such as the **Empire of Great Moravia,** which, in 830, consisted of Bohemia, Moravia, Hungary, and Slovakia. The **Hungarian Kingdom,** one of the few Eastern European empires to actually achieve longevity and greatness, first came to power in the late 9th century. With the exception of the year-long Tatar occupation in 1241, the kingdom kept growing for 700 years and eventually included Polish Silesia, Croatian Pannonia, and territories as far east as Romanian Wallachia and Bessarabia. The kingdom came to an end at the 1526 **Battle of Mohács,** at which the Ottomans defeated Louis II, king of Hungary and Bohemia. The Russians also came into their own by the end of the 15th century, when Ivan III finally threw off the Mongol yoke. The **Ottoman Empire** firmly established itself in southeastern Europe when it crushed the **Serbs** on June 28, 1389 at the **Battle of Kosovo.** This victory confirmed Constantinople's dominion over what are now Albania, Bosnia, Bulgaria, inland Croatia, Hungary, Macedonia, Moldova, Romania, and Serbia and Montenegro. The Ottoman infiltration of Europe was forever halted when Polish king **Jan III Sobieski** defeated Turkish forces at the **Siege of Vienna** in 1683. The loss marked the beginning of Ottoman decline, which was expedited by a series of losses to Russia from the 17th to the 19th century.

As the Ottoman Empire was floundering, the **Russian Empire** was rapidly expanding east to the Pacific and west into Poland and Ukraine. At the **first partition of Poland** in 1772, the Russians wrested control of Estonia and Lithuania from Sweden and eventually dissolved the **Polish-Lithuanian Commonwealth** (1569-1792), which had been one of the largest realms in Europe and the earliest democratic state of the modern period. Two years later, the **Treaty of Kuchuk Kainarji** between Russia and the Ottomans placed the Orthodox subjects of the Ottoman Empire under the control of the Russian tsar. The landmark treaty granted Russia the right to intervene in the Balkans to protect Christians under Muslim rule. By 1801, the Russians controlled Belarus, Estonia, Latvia, Lithuania, eastern Poland, and Ukraine, but further expansion was halted in the 19th century. The **1878 Congress of Berlin** marked the end of the **Russo-Turkish Wars;** in Eastern Europe, only Albania, Bulgaria, and Macedonia remained in the Ottoman sphere of influence. All other nations were either granted independence or ceded to the Russian and Austro-Hungarian Empires.

The colossal **Austrian Empire** ultimately swallowed most of Central and Eastern Europe. Although the Hapsburgs' rule in Austria dates back to the early 13th century, they did not come to dominate Central Europe until after the **Battle of Mohács,** when the Hungarian kingdom was split between Turkish and Austrian control. The Austrians acquired Bohemia, Moravia, Slovakia, and parts of Croatia, including Zagreb and Rijeka. After a series of Hungarian uprisings in 1699, the Turks relinquished the rest of Hungary to the Hapsburgs. The Hungarians remained restless subjects, however, and in 1867 the Austrians entered into a **dual monarchy** with the Hungarians creating the **Austro-Hungarian Empire,** in which Hungary was granted autonomy. From 1867 to 1918, Austria-Hungary controlled what are now the Czech and Slovak Republics, Bosnia, Croatia, Slovenia, and parts of Belarus, Poland, Romania, and Ukraine. By the 19th century, nearly all of Eastern Europe was controlled by either the Ottoman, Russian, or Austro-Hungarian Empires. Albania was created in 1913 following the **Balkan Wars.** Following **Napoleon's** brief dominion over Europe at the beginning of the 19th century, a wave of **Pan-Slavism,** or a belief in the unity of Slavic people, swept through the subordinated nations. Although it was confined to intellectual circles, it contributed to Europe's emerging **nationalism.**

DEATH OF THE GREAT EMPIRES (1914-1938)

World War I began with an attempt by the Serbs to free the South Slavs from the clutches of the Austro-Hungarian Empire. Serb nationalists of the illegal **Black Hand** movement believed that their cause would best be served by the death of **Archduke Franz Ferdinand d'Este,** heir to the Austro-Hungarian throne. On June 28, 1914, Bosnian Serb nationalist **Gavrilo Princip** assassinated Ferdinand and his wife Sophia in Sarajevo. Exactly one month later, Austria-Hungary declared war on Serbia. What started as an attempt to overthrow the Empire snowballed in the ensuing months into a series of war declarations by France, Germany, Russia, Great Britain, Montenegro, Serbia, and the Ottoman Empire as they sought to aid of their allies. Because they were controlled by the Austro-Hungarian and Ottoman Empires, most Eastern European nations fought alongside the **Central Powers.** The Baltic nations were controlled by both Germans and Russians and remained divided in their alliances between the **Allies** and Central Powers. The only nations to wholeheartedly support the Allies were Russia, Bosnia, Montenegro, and Serbia. Belarus and Ukraine became hotly contested battlegrounds between the Germans and the Russians and eventually fell to German wartime occupation.

As the war dragged on, Russia's participation became more tenuous. The Russians had entered the war because of their dual interests in the demise of the Ottoman and Austro-Hungarian Empires and the growth of strong, Russia-friendly Slavic nations throughout Eastern Europe. As catastrophic losses caused the death toll to skyrocket, the Russian people became increasingly frustrated with their inefficient government. Coupled with a crippled wartime economy, the tension finally erupted with the **Russian Revolution.** Riots began over food shortages in March 1917, leading to the Tsar's abdication. In November, the **Bolsheviks,** led by **Vladimir Ilyich Lenin,** took power and established Russia's Communist government. Russia's empire crumbled as nationalist independence movements emerged on the heels of the March 1917 revolution. American president Woodrow Wilson's **Fourteen Points,** which followed the 1919 **Treaty of Versailles** that ended World War I, argued for the self-determination of all nations under the yoke of the great empires. With support from the West, Estonia, Latvia, and Ukraine declared independence from Russia, and Lithuania declared independence from Germany. Poland, which had been partitioned by Prussia, Austria, and Russia, became one state for the first time since 1792.

While the Russian Empire disintegrated, the defeated Austria-Hungary was mercilessly dismantled by the victorious powers. The Czechs and Slovaks united to create **Czechoslovakia**. Romania's size doubled with the acquisition of Transylvania, Bessarabia, and Bucovina. Finally, in keeping with the vision of South Slav nationalism that had sparked the war, 1918 saw the creation of the **Kingdom of Serbs, Croats and Slovenes**, later known as **Yugoslavia**. In 1922 the **Union of Soviet Socialist Republics (USSR)** was declared. The **interwar period** was a turbulent time, as many states, independent for the first time in centuries (and in the case of Latvia, ever), struggled to establish their own governments, economies, and societies in a period made even more unstable by the global **Depression** of the 1930s.

"PEACE IN OUR TIME" (1938-1945)

Just two decades after WWI ravaged the continent, **World War II** rose out of its many lingering conflicts. **Adolf Hitler** was determined to reclaim the "Germanic" parts of Poland, Bohemia, and Moravia that Germany had lost in the Treaty of Versailles. He claimed that the 3 million Germans living in the Czechoslovak **Sudetenland** were being discriminated against by their government. Hoping to avoid another war, France and Britain ignored Hitler's glaringly aggressive moves against a sovereign country and adopted their infamous policy of **appeasement**. France and Britain sealed Czechoslovakia's fate by signing the **Munich Agreement** with Germany on September 30, 1938, which ordered all non-German inhabitants of the Sudetenland to vacate their homes within 24 hours and permitted the German army to invade. Upon his return from Munich, Britain's Prime Minister Neville Chamberlain mistakenly believed he had secured "peace in our time." Hitler, however, ignored the stipulations of the agreement and proceeded to annex the remainder of Czechoslovakia, which he turned into the **Bohemian-Moravian Protectorate** in March 1939. Hitler and Stalin shocked the world by signing the **Molotov-Ribbentrop Non-Aggression Pact** (Aug. 1939), forging an uneasy alliance between the two historical enemies. Secret clauses detailed a dual invasion of Poland, by which Germany would control the western two-thirds while the USSR would keep the eastern third. In September 1939, Hitler annexed Poland, sparking WWII.

Hitler had no intention of upholding the Pact, and in June 1941 he launched an offensive against the Soviet Union. An unsuccessful attempt to capture Moscow prompted the Soviets to join the Allied forces, led by Great Britain and the United States. The 1941 **Anglo-Soviet Agreement** was a turning point in the war, as were the Allies' decisive victories in 1942. Total war casualties for both civilians and military personnel are estimated at 50-60 million. Of these, the nations of Eastern Europe suffered the heaviest losses. The USSR lost 20 million of its citizens (10% of its population), more people than any other nation involved in the war. Yugoslavia also lost over 10% of its population. Poland lost nearly 6 million people, a staggering 20% of its pre-war population, only about 200,000 of which were military casualties. More than half of the 6 million estimated Jews murdered in **Nazi concentration camps** were Polish. Before World War II, Eastern Europe had been the geographical center of the world's Jewish population, but Hitler's **"final solution"** succeeded in almost entirely eliminating the Jewish communities of the Czech and Slovak Republics, Hungary, Yugoslavia, Lithuania, Moldova, Poland, and Ukraine through both genocide and forced emigration. Albania alone succeeded in sheltering its Jews from the Nazis.

THE RUSSIANS ARE COMING! (1945-1989)

The wartime alliance between the Soviet Union and the West had been an uneasy one. The West was opposed to the ideological expansion of communism, but Russia claimed it necessary in order to prevent another German threat to the Slavic nations. Plans for post-war division of power in Europe were sketched out as early as 1944 and were sealed at the **Yalta Conference** in February 1945. The Allies reluctantly agreed to recognize Eastern Europe as the Soviet sphere of influence. The institution of Communist governments in Albania, Bulgaria, Czechoslovakia, Hungary, Poland, Romania, and Yugoslavia from 1945 to 1949 established a ring of satellite People's Democracies in Eastern Europe. With the division of Germany between Capitalist West and communist East, the **Cold War** had begun.

The **Iron Curtain** first descended with the founding of the **Council for Mutual Economic Assistance (COMECON)**, in January 1949, an organization meant to facilitate and coordinate the economic growth of the Soviet Bloc; COMECOM was created in rejection of the 1948 **Marshall Plan,** which poured US dollars into the reconstruction of Western Europe. The West reacted to this alliance in April 1949 by creating the **North Atlantic Treaty Organization (NATO),** a military alliance meant to "keep the Americans in, the Russians out, and the Germans down." In typical Cold War fashion, the Eastern Bloc retaliated in 1955 with a similar alliance, the **Warsaw Pact.** The pact enabled the maintenance of Soviet military bases throughout Eastern Europe, and tightened the USSR's grip on its satellite countries. The only communist European country never to join the Warsaw Pact was **Yugoslavia** as former partisan **Josip Broz Tito** broke away from Moscow as early as 1948 and followed his own vision of combining communism with a market economy.

After Stalin's death in 1953, and **Nikita Khrushchev's** denunciation of him in the so-called **Secret Speech** of 1956, the Soviet Bloc was plagued by chaos. The 1950s saw the emergence of **National Communism,** or the belief that the attainment of ultimate communist goals should be dictated internally rather than by orders from Moscow. The presence of Russian troops in Eastern Europe, however, enabled Moscow to respond to rising nationalist movements with military force. Such was the case in 1956, when the Soviets violently suppressed the **Hungarian Revolution** and workers' strikes in Poland. The **Berlin Wall** was erected in 1961, creating a physical symbol of the economic, political, and ideological divide between East and West. The **Prague Spring** of 1968 witnessed another wave of violent suppression as the emerging Czechoslovakian dissidence movement demanded increased freedom and attention to human rights. Russia consistently used the Warsaw Pact to justify military occupation and the institution of martial law. Political repression coupled with the economic stagnancy of the Leonid Brezhnev years (1964-1982) increased unrest and disapproval for Moscow and its policies among the satellites.

BRAVE NEW WORLD (1989 ONWARD)

When **Mikhail Gorbachev** became Secretary General of the Communist Party in 1985, he began to dismantle the totalitarian aspects of the Communist regime through his policies of **glasnost** (openness) and **perestroika** (restructuring). The new freedom of political expression gave way to increasing displays of dissidence, which finally erupted in 1989 with a series of revolutions throughout Eastern Europe. The first occurred in June when the Poles voted the Communists out of office. In their place, they elected **Lech Wałęsa** and the **Solidarity Party** to create a new government. This Polish victory was swiftly followed by a new democratic constitution in **Hungary** in October, the crumbling of the **Berlin Wall** on November 9, the resignation of the **Bulgarian** communists on November 10, the **Velvet Revolution** in Czechoslovakia on November 17, and the televised execution of Romania's communist dictator, **Nicolae Ceauşescu,** on December 25. Almost all of the Warsaw Pact nations had successfully—and almost bloodlessly—broken away from the Soviet Union and begun the move toward democracy.

The **USSR** crumbled shortly after its Empire. Within the first five months of 1990, **Estonia, Latvia, Lithuania,** and **Ukraine** all declared independence from Moscow. In an attempt to keep the Soviet Union together, Gorbachev condoned military force against the rebellious Baltic republics. A bloody conflict erupted in Vilnius, Lithuania in January 1991. By September, the Soviet Union had dissolved and all of its constituent republics and satellite nations were fully independent. Belarus, Moldova, Russia, Ukraine, and the former Soviet republics of Central Asia formed the **Commonwealth of Independent States (CIS)** on December 8, 1991. Communism in Albania finally fell in March 1992.

Meanwhile, following Tito's death in 1980, **Yugoslavia** was slowly disintegrating. Economic inequality between its different republics caused to suppressed nationalist sentiments to resurface. Inspired by the developments in the rest of Eastern Europe, both **Slovenia** and **Croatia** declared independence on June 25, 1991; the Serb-controlled government responded with military force. **Macedonia** and **Bosnia and Herzegovina** followed suit by the end of the year. The conflict in Slovenia lasted only 10 days, but Croatia's attempts to secede resulted in a war involving Bosnia and Herzegovina, Croatia, Montenegro, and Serbia that continued until the signing of the US-negotiated **Dayton Peace Agreement** in November 1995. The only republics to remain in Yugoslavia were Serbia and Montenegro. Four years later, Serbia's ultra-nationalist leader **Slobodan Milošević** dragged the region into another military conflict in the Serbian province of **Kosovo.** In an effort to stop the ethnic cleansing of Kosovo's Albanian majority by the Serbian army, **NATO** launched an intensive air campaign, which led to Serbia's withdrawal from the region but ruined the country's economy in the process.

With the exception of the tumultuous Balkans, the former Soviet satellites are progressing, with varying degrees of success, toward democracy and market economies. In March 1999, the Czech Republic, Poland, and Hungary joined NATO. May 2002 saw the formation of the **NATO-Russia Council,** a strategic alliance between Russia and the organization originally established as a military alliance against it. Bulgaria, Estonia, Latvia, Lithuania, Romania, the Slovak Republic, and Slovenia were welcomed as new members of NATO in April 2004. The following month, the Czech Republic, Estonia, Hungary, Latvia, Lithuania, Poland, the Slovak Republic, and Slovenia became part of the **European Union (EU).** Bulgaria and Romania are expected to join in 2007.

PEOPLE AND CULTURE

THE PEOPLES OF EASTERN EUROPE

Eastern Europe's recent opening up to the world has increased diversity and exposure, but the region's population still remains fairly homogeneous. Most Eastern European countries are inhabited by Slavic peoples. After the Great Migration (see p. 46), the Slavs split into **West Slavs** (Czechs, Poles, and Slovaks), **South Slavs** (Bosniaks, Croats, Macedonians, Montenegrins, Serbs, and Slovenes) and **East Slavs** (Belarusians, Russians, and Ukrainians). These peoples swept West, and **Bulgarians,** originally of Turkic origin, were ethnically integrated into Slavic culture.

The non-Slavics inhabiting Central and Eastern Europe include Albanians, Estonians, Hungarians, Latvians, Lithuanians, and Romanians. **Latvians** and **Lithuanians** belong to the Baltic branch of the Indo-European family. The Balts originally included additional ethnic groups that are now extinct, such as the Prussians, the Curonians, and the Selonians. **Estonians,** who also occupy the Baltic Coast, form a branch of the Baltic Finns, descendants of the Finno-Ugric family who have been strongly Germanized. **Hungarians** constitute the "Ugric" part of the Finno-Ugric family. They separated from other Finno-Ugric tribes in the Urals and, at the end of the 9th century, migrated southwest to the Carpathian Basin, which they inhabit today. Hungarian minorities still live in Romanian Transylvania and the southern region of the Slovak Republic. **Romanians** are descendants of Dacians, and **Albanians** are descendants of the Illyrians, who together with Thracians were the earliest known inhabitants of the Balkan Peninsula.

There are significant **Jewish** communities living in Poland, the Czech Republic, Hungary, and Russia, though their numbers decreased dramatically after WWII as a result of Hitler's "final solution." Well-integrated into the society in most countries, Jewish people still face severe anti-Semitism in Russia, Belarus, and some rural parts of Eastern Europe. **Roma,** known as gypsies, came from northern India during the Middle Ages. They now live in small, tight-knit communities across Eastern Europe, particularly in the Czech and Slovak Republics, Bulgaria, Hungary, Romania, and Serbia and Montenegro. Anglophone **expats** flooded Eastern Europe after the fall of the Berlin Wall and created distinct cultures in Prague, Budapest, St. Petersburg, and elsewhere.

RELIGION

Christianity became Eastern Europe's main religion by the 10th century, and it remains the principal religion in the region today. The monks **Cyril and Methodius** brought Christianity to the Slavs (see **Languages** and **It's All Greek to Me,** p. 53), and most Belarusians, Bulgarians, Macedonians, Moldovans, Romanians, Russians, Serbs, and Ukrainians subscribe to the **Eastern Orthodox** faith. With the exception of the Baltic states, which have been influenced by German **Protestantism,** all other nations of Eastern Europe are predominantly **Roman Catholic.** Birthplace of the current Pope, John Paul II, Poland is one of the world's most devoutly Catholic countries. In the Czech Republic, which lies on the geographic boundary between Protestant and Catholic Europe, both Protestantism and Catholicism are common. In fact, religious dissent against Catholicism originated in the Czech lands in the 14th century, when **Jan Hus** (see p. 225) preached church reform, preceding Luther's **Protestant Reformation** by a full century. Christian faith nonetheless remained strong in Eastern Europe until the early 20th century. Then, the doctrine of communism, repression of churches, and the sense of hopelessness that followed the World Wars spread **atheism** across Eastern Europe. Most Eastern European countries, however, saw a Christian revival after the fall of communism in the early 1990s, and today religious faith in Eastern Europe is much stronger than it was just a few decades ago. **Islam** came to Europe with the Ottoman Empire and is the most practiced religion in Albania. There are significant Muslim Albanian populations in Bulgaria, Macedonia, and the Kosovo region of Serbia. **Judaism** constitutes another important minority religion, practiced mainly in the Czech Republic, Poland, Russia, and Hungary.

LANGUAGE

With the exception of Estonian and Hungarian, which are **Finno-Ugric** (though not mutually intelligible), all nations in Eastern Europe speak languages of **Indo-European** origin. Romanian, like French and Italian, belongs to the **Romance** branch, and Latvian and Lithuanian to the **Baltic** branch. **Albanian** is a unique language, the sole member of its Indo-European subgroup, while **Romani,** the language of the Roma (gypsies) is an Indian language related to Hindi. Belarusian, Bosnian, Bulgarian, Croatian, Czech, Macedonian, Polish, Serbian, Slovak, Slovenian, Russian, and Ukrainian are all **Slavic** languages. The **Cyrillic alphabet** is a script used in Belarus, Bulgaria, Macedonia, Serbia and Montenegro, Russia, and

IT'S ALL GREEK TO ME. When the Greek priest Constantine and his brother Methodius set off on a Christian mission to convert the Slavs in AD 863, they brought with them more than their religion. To succeed where others had failed, the brothers translated liturgical text into the language of the people, using an alphabet he invented. Based on their dialect, **Old Church Slavonic,** the new script was a smashing success among the people. Rome, however, was less than thrilled to hear that the Word of God was being spread in any language less dignified than Greek or Latin. The brothers were summoned to explain themselves before Pope Nicholas I, who died before they arrived in 868. While his successor Adrian II gave their mission his full blessing, Constantine fell ill and died before he could return to preach. Before he passed away, he adopted the name Cyril. **Cyrillic alphabet,** developed by Greek missionaries over a hundred years after Constantine's death, was credited to him by medieval Slavs and brought to Kyivan Rus in 988 with the Baptism of Kyiv. It was this script that facilitated Slavic unions in the name of religion and language and made the great empires of the Bulgarians and the Kyivan Rus possible.

Ukraine. For many centuries, Cyrillic was a source of unity for the Slavic nations who wrote in it, and its use (or non-use) still makes a political statement in some parts of the world. One of the major differences between the otherwise very similar Serbian and Croatian languages is that Croatian is written in the Latin alphabet, while Serbian is written in Cyrillic. Some republics of the former Soviet Union have begun replacing Cyrillic with their own scripts, a political gesture to emphasize their break with Moscow. For phrasebooks and glossaries of key Eastern European languages, see the **Glossary,** p. 944.

The Russian Cyrillic transliteration index is given below. Other languages include some additional letters and pronounce certain letters differently. Each country's **Language** section outlines these distinctions.

CYRILLIC	ENGLISH	PRONOUNCE	CYRILLIC	ENGLISH	PRONOUNCE
А а	a	ah; Prague	Р р	r	r; October **Revolution**
Б б	b	b; **Bosnia**	С с	s	s; **Serbia**
В в	v	v; **Volga**	Т т	t	t; **tank**
Г г	g	g; *glasnost*	У у	u	oo; **Budapest**
Д д	d	d; **Danube**	Ф ф	f	f; **Former** USSR
Е е	e, ye	yeh; **yellow**	Х х	kh	kh; Ger. *Bach*
Ё ё*	yo	yo; **yo!**	Ц ц	ts	ts; **Let's** Go
Ж ж	zh	zh; mira**ge**	Ч ч	ch	ch; **China**
З з	z	z; communi**sm**	Ш ш	sh	sh; dictator**ship**
И и	i	ee; **Eastern** Europe	Щ щ	shch	shch; Khru**shch**ev
Й й	y	y°	Ъ ъ	(hard)	(no sound)
К к	k	k; **Kremlin**	Ы ы	y	y; s**i**lver
Л л	l	l; **Lenin**	Ь ь	(soft)	(no sound)
М м	m	m; **Macedonia**	Э э	e	eh; **Estonia**
Н н	n	n; **Non**-Aggression Pact	Ю ю	yu	yoo; **Ukraine**
О о	o	o; **Croatia**	Я я	ya	yah; **yawn**
П п	p	p; **Poland**			

*Often printed without dots. ° Й creates dipthongs, altering the sounds of the vowels it follows: ой is pronounced "oy" (b**oy**), ай is "ai" (**I**ron Curtain), ей is "yay" (**yay**), and ий is "eey" (Hungar**y**).

FOOD

Although food specialities vary from region to region, Eastern Europe stands united in its love of **sausage**. There are endless varieties of packed meat products; the spiciest ones are from Hungary. Central European cuisine is characterized by lots of meat in sauces accompanied by cabbage and potatoes, whereas on the coasts, a lighter, seafood-based cuisine predominates. **Vegetarian** restaurants are rare, but they are becoming more common, especially in Central Europe. Restaurants specializing in the cuisine of other cultures and worldwide fast food chains are also popping up all over the region. Delicious **breads** are baked throughout the region, and always provide a welcome substitute for the region's heavy dishes. **Dairy products** are extremely popular throughout Eastern Europe. From spicy crumbling cheese (Russia's *monouri*) to cheese in trees (Romania's *brânză de copac*), Eastern Europe milks its resources for all they're worth. See the **Food and Drink** section of each chapter introduction for country-specific information.

ALCOHOLIC DELIGHTS

Beer, **vodka, absinthe, brandy,** and even wine abound in Eastern Europe, where alcohol is a regional pastime. Eastern Europe is perhaps best loved for its endless shelves of locally produced, throat-burning libations. Don't limit yourself to imported, far-away versions; drink these magic liquids straight from the source. The word's best hops are in the Czech Republic: world famous *Pilsner Urquell* is produced in Plzeň (p. 267) while České Budějovice (p. 275) brews the delectable *Budvar* (called Budweiser in the Czech Republic; *not* to be confused with the American brand). The best **beer** in the Czech Republic, Krušovice, is produced in Prague (p. 233); enjoy it along with a fiery glass of absinthe (see **Food and Drink,** p. 227). While it pales next to the Czechs' brews, the Polish *Żywiec*, concocted just south of Bielsko-Biała (p. 548), is the thing to try if you're looking for bitters in a bottle. Not-quite-alcoholic Ukrainian *kvas*, made from fermented beets or fruits, is sold from barrels on the streets of Kyiv (p. 873), even in pouring rain. In Karlovy Vary, CZR (p. 271), you can imbibe *becherovka*, an herb liquor purported to have "curative powers." For good vodka, head anywhere in Russia (p. 652). Better yet, head to the Latvian-Estonian or Belarusian-Polish borders, where vodka smuggling makes for very cheap inebriation. In the states that formerly comprised Yugoslavia, ask for a shot of *šljivovica*, fiery plum brandy that will knock you on your back. Hungary currently holds the crown for Eastern Europe's finest **wines**—don't miss famous Bull's Blood in Eger (p. 367), Aszú in Tokaj (see sidebar, p. 373), and the Balaton-flavored wines of Badacsony (p. 396). Croatia (p. 157) is also up-and-coming in the world of wines. Tiny Moldova once produced a whopping 20% of the wine in the USSR; the best is from Cricova (p. 500). The wines of twin cities Mělník, CZR and Melnik, BUL (p. 137) are so good, Churchill had them shipped to England, even during WWII. See the **Food and Drink** section of each chapter introduction for country-specific information.

GEOGRAPHY

LAND AND WATER

The vast majority of Eastern Europe consists of several low-altitude **plains.** The North and East European Plains span from Poland to the Baltic states, Belarus, Ukraine and European Russia. The Hungarian Plain covers the southern Slovak Republic and most of Hungary, whereas the Romanian Plain dominates southern Romania. Most of the Czech Republic sits on a plateau, the Bohemian Massif. The largest mountains in Eastern Europe are the **Carpathians,** which include the **Tatras,** running along the Polish-Slovak border. South of the lowlands lie Europe's highest mountain ranges, the **Alps** in Austria and Slovenia and the **Balkan Mountains** spanning from eastern Serbia to the Bulgarian Black Sea coast.

Europe's longest river is the **Volga** in Russia. The **Danube,** which flows through 11 countries and creates a natural border between Hungary and the Slovak Republic and between Bulgaria and Romania, is the region's most economically and historically important river. Other rivers include the **Dnieper** in Ukraine, the **Vltava** in the Czech Republic, and the **Oder** and **Wisła** in Poland. Eastern European rivers dump their water (and waste) into three seas: the **Baltic,** the **Adriatic,** and the **Black.** Whereas the Baltic coast is entirely composed of lowlands, the Adriatic is characterized by dramatic mountains, jagged peninsulas and miniature islands. **Lake Balaton,** in Hungary, is the largest (and most popular) lake in Europe west of Russia; **Lake Ladoga,** in northwestern Russia, is the largest in Europe (though not the largest in Russia—Lake Baikal, in Asia, the deepest lake in the world, is bigger).

CLIMATE

The sun shines on the Eastern Bloc, despite what Western anti-communist propaganda—television images of rainy Moscow and ice-cold Siberia—used to suggest. But don't get us wrong, it gets so cold in northern Siberia that your *Baltika* (a Russian brand of beer) will freeze in your hand. Eastern Europe, however, is so expansive that its climate is extremely varied. The **central regions,** such as Poland and the Czech and Slovak Republics, get warm summers (May-Sept.) and bitingly cold winters (Dec.-Feb.). **South** of these countries, toward the Mediterranean Sea, in Albania, Croatia, Macedonia, Serbia and Montenegro, and Slovenia summers become extremely hot and winters pleasantly mild. It gets just as hot along the Bulgarian, Romanian, Russian, and Ukrainian **Black Sea Coast.**

Avg Temp (hi/lo)	January		April		July		October	
	°C	°F	°C	°F	°C	°F	°C	°F
Belgrade, SMN	03/-03	38/27	17/08	63/46	27/16	81/61	18/08	64/46
Bratislava, SLK	02/-03	36/26	16/04	60/40	26/14	79/58	15/06	59/42
Bucharest, ROM	01/-06	34/22	16/04	64/42	28/16	83/60	18/06	64/42
Budapest, HUN	01/-04	34/24	16/06	61/43	26/15	79/59	16/07	61/44
Chişinău, MOL	00/-06	32/21	16/06	60/42	26/16	79/60	22/11	71/52
Kyiv, UKR	-04/-10	25/-14	14/05	57/41	25/15	77/59	13/06	55/43
Ljubljana, SLN	02/-04	35/25	15/04	59/40	26/14	79/59	16/06	61/43
Minsk, BLR	-04/-10	24/14	10/01	51/35	22/12	72/54	09/03	49/37
Moscow, RUS	-06/-12	21/11	09/01	49/34	22/13	71/55	07/01	45/33
Prague, CZR	01/-04	34/24	12/02	54/36	22/12	72/54	12/04	54/39
Rīga, LAT	-02/-05	29/22	09/02	48/35	21/13	69/56	10/05	50/41
Sarajevo, BOS	03/-04	38/26	15/05	59/41	26/13	80/56	16/06	62/43
Skopje, MAC	04/-04	39/25	18/05	65/41	30/14	86/58	19/06	66/43
Sofia, BUL	02/-05	36/23	15/04	59/40	26/13	78/56	16/06	61/42
Tallinn, EST	-02/-06	28/21	07/01	45/33	20/13	68/55	08/03	47/38
Tirana, ALB	12/02	54/36	18/8	64/46	31/17	88/63	23/10	73/50
Vilnius, LIT	-04/-09	25/16	06/02	51/34	22/12	71/54	10/03	50/38
Warsaw, POL	-01/-06	30/21	13/03	55/37	22/11	72/52	12/04	54/40
Zagreb, CRO	03/-02	37/28	16/08	61/46	26/16	79/61	15/08	59/47

LIFE AND TIMES

FESTIVALS IN EASTERN EUROPE

The following list is by no means exhaustive; it is meant to suggest highlights of Eastern European revelries in 2005.

COUNTRY	APR. – JUNE	JULY – AUG.	SEPT. – MAR.
BOSNIA	Apparitions' Anniversary June, Međugorje (p. 112)	Turkish Nights July, Sarajevo (p. 109) Sarajevo Film Festival Aug. (p. 109) Youth Theater Festival Aug., Međugorje (p. 112)	Sarajevan Winter Feb.-Mar. (p. 109)
BULGARIA	Rose Festival June, Kazanluk (see sidebar, p. 140)	Varna Summer July (p. 145) Int'l Jazz Festival Aug., Varna (p. 145) Int'l Jazz Festival Aug., Bansko (p. 135)	Arts Festival Apoloniya Aug.-Sept., Sozopol (p. 148) Love is Folly Film Fest. Aug.-Sept., Varna (p. 145)
CROATIA	Eurokaz Theater Fest. June, Zagreb (p. 174) Cest is d'Best June, Zagreb (p. 174) Int'l Children's Festival June-July, Šibenik (p. 200)	Biker Days Festival July, Pula (p. 182) Dubrovnik Summer Fest. July-Aug. (p. 222) Split Summer Festival July-Aug., Split (p. 208) Festival of Sword Dances July-Aug., Korčula (p. 216)	Int'l Puppet Festival Sept., Zagreb (p. 174) Marco Polo Festival Sept., Korčula (p. 216) International Jazz Days Oct., Zagreb (p. 174) Christmas Fair Dec., Zagreb (p. 174)
CZECH REPUBLIC	Prague Spring Festival May-June (p. 261) Five-Petal Rose Festival June, Č. Krumlov (p. 282) Prague Fringe Festival June (p. 261)	Int'l Film Festival July, Karlovy Vary (p. 275) International Music Fest Aug., Český Krumlov (p. 278)	Int'l Organ Festival Sept., Olomouc (p. 299) Jazz Goes to Town Oct., Hradec Králové (p. 289)
ESTONIA	Country Dance Festival June, Pärnu (p. 320) Jaanipaev June, Tallinn (p. 316) Grillfest June, Tallinn (p. 316) Old Town Days June, Tallinn (p. 316)	Beersummer July, Tallinn (p. 316) Freedom Parade Aug., Tartu (p. 333) White Lady Days Aug., Haapsalu (p. 321)	Dark Nights Film Festival Dec., Tallinn (p. 316) Student Jazz Festival Feb., Tallinn (p. 316)
HUNGARY	Sopron Festival Weeks June (p. 383) Bloomsday Festival June, Szombath. (p. 386) Danube Festival June, Budapest (p. 361)	Bartok Choral Comp. July, Debrecen (p. 410) Golden Shell Folklore July, Siófok (p. 393) Szeged Open Air Festival July-Aug. (p. 414) Sziget Rock Festival July, Budapest (p. 361) Haydn Festival July and Sept., Fertőd (p. 384)	Jazz Days Sept., Debrecen (p. 410) Eger Vintage Days Sept. (p. 371) Festival of Wine Songs Sept., Pécs (p. 407) Spring Festival Mar., Szombath. (p. 418) Budapest Spring Festival Mar. (p. 361)
LATVIA	Int'l Ballet Festival Apr., Rīga (p. 316) Int'l Ballooning Festival May, Sigulda (p. 438)	Opera Music Festival July, Sigulda (p. 438)	
LITHUANIA	Vilniaus Festivalis Vilnius, May (p. 456) Pažaislis Music Festival May-Sept., Kaunas (p. 463)	Thomas Mann Festival July, Nida (p. 475) Night Serenades July-Aug., Palanga (p. 473) Trakai Festival July-Aug. (p. 457)	Kaziukas Fair Mar., Vilnius (p. 443)

FESTIVALS IN EASTERN EUROPE

The following list is by no means exhaustive; it is meant to suggest highlights of Eastern European revelries in 2005.

COUNTRY	APR. – JUNE	JULY – AUG.	SEPT. – MAR.
MACEDONIA	Skopje Summer Festival June-July (p. 485)	Ohrid Summer Festival June-Aug. (p. 487) Struga Poetry Evenings Aug. (p. 488)	Skopje Jazz Festival Oct. (p. 485)
MOLDOVA			Chişinău City Days Oct. (p. 500)
POLAND	Int'l Short Film Fest. May, Kraków (p. 539) Probaltica May, Toruń (p. 580) Int'l Theater Festival June, Poznań (p. 576) Summer Jazz Days June, Warsaw (p. 526)	Street Theater July, Kraków (p. 539) InterFolk Aug., Kołobrzeg (p. 589) Highlander Folklore Aug., Zakopane (p. 554) Rock and Pop Music Aug., Sopot (p. 597)	Jazz Festival Mar., Poznań (p. 576)
ROMANIA	Int'l Folk Music Festival June, Timişoara (p. 637) Int'l Theater Festival June, Sibiu (p. 630)	Golden Stag Festival July, Braşov (p. 625) Medieval Festival July, Sighişoara (p. 628)	Int'l Chamber Music Sept., Braşov (p. 625)
RUSSIA	White Nights Festival June-July, St. Petersburg (See sidebar, p. 709)	Tun Pairam June, Abakan (p. 750)	Russian Winter Festival Dec.-Jan., Irkutsk (p. 756)
SERBIA AND MONTENEGRO	Mediterranean Festival June, Budva (p. 792)	Exit Festival July, Novi Sad (p. 789) BELEF July-Aug., Belgrade (p. 786) Golden Brass Summit Aug., Guča (p. 778)	BITEF Theater Festival Sept., Belgrade (p. 786)
SLOVAK REPUBLIC	Int'l Fest. of Ghosts and Spirits May, Bojnice (p. 812)	Fest. of Marian Devotion July, Levoča (p. 817)	Bratislava Music Fest. Sept.-Oct., (p. 808) Jazz Days Sept., Bratislava (p. 808)
SLOVENIA	Int'l Wine Fair Apr., Ljubljana (p. 851) Int'l Jazz Festival June, Ljubljana (p. 851) Lent Festival June-July, Maribor (p. 864)	Int'l Summer Festival July, Ljubljana (p. 851) Bled Days July (p. 855) Primorska Summer Fest. July, Piran (p. 860) No Borders Music Fest. Aug., Bled (p. 855)	Int'l Film Festival Nov., Ljubljana (p. 851) Kurent Carnival Feb., Ptuj (p. 864)
UKRAINE	Kyiv Days May (p. 885) Holiday of Humor Apr., Odessa (p. 894)	Int'l Film Festival July, Kyiv (p. 885)	Lviv City Days May (p. 915)

LIFE AND TIMES

The Plight of Eastern Europe's "Gypsy" Population

Throughout Central and Eastern Europe, there are between five and eight million Roma, or "gypsies," as they are popularly but inaccurately known. A diaspora people, the Roma are Europe's largest and most widespread ethnic population. Ultimately of non-European origin, having left India in response to 11th-century Islamic expansion, the Roma have remained the quintessential outsiders. Lacking a political territory, an economy, or any military strength, distanced from the non-Roma world by inherited cultural restrictions based on concepts of ritual pollution, and easily scapegoated for all of these reasons, the Roma today constitute a major human rights issue for European governments. A May 2001 editorial in *The Economist* stated that the Roma in Europe were "at the bottom of every socio-economic indicator: the poorest, the most unemployed, the least educated, the shortest-lived, the most welfare-dependent, the most imprisoned, and the most segregated." These issues are being taken very seriously by those countries hoping for membership into the EU.

The first Roma to cross into Europe from Asia Minor were enslaved under Ottoman rule in the Moldavian and Wallachian regions of Romania; in the mid-1800s the slaves were freed after more than five centuries of bondage and their descendents, the *Vlax* (Wallachian) Roma, are the largest single Roma group in the world. Following abolition, hundreds of thousands of them left Romania for Russia and elsewhere; an estimated two million of their descendents live in North and South America today.

Problems facing the Roma are numerous. They are no longer a homogeneous population; 700 years of separation by time and geography have led to great differences in (or even loss of) dialects of the ancestral language and sense of identity. The notion of constituting a single, unified people is only now being addressed by Roma activists, but compared with the much more immediate priorities of racism, health, employment, housing, and education, most Roma have little time to consider such academic issues. Nevertheless, self-determination is necessary if Roma populations are to cease living on the fringes of non-Roma society, living on handouts. The impetus must come from Roma populations' own leaders, with cooperation and guidance, but not management, by non-Romani governmental and non-governmental bodies. Several human rights organizations are, in fact, doing just that. The Open Society Institute has invested millions of dollars in training programs and in monitoring antigypsyism, while the Project on Ethnic Relations publishes a series of useful reports on Roma-related issues. The World Bank has made funds available for scholarships, and the creation of another education fund is underway. This fund utilizes the assets secreted in Swiss banks by the Nazis during the Holocaust, where Himmler's proposed "Final Solution to the Gypsy Question" ultimately led to the loss of over a million Roma lives.

A particular problem in taking Roma issues seriously is the existence of the widespread, fictional "gypsy" image. Since the mid-19th century, a literary stereotype has emerged, and for most people this remains their sole understanding of the Roma. This is being challenged now through education: a number of universities throughout Europe and North America now have Romani Studies programs, and international conferences on Roma issues are held annually. The distinct history of the Roma and their experiences under slavery and in the Holocaust are becoming better known. A number of websites exist to provide information (PATRIN and RADOC are just two), and several publishing houses now specialize in Roma-related literature (The University of Hertfordshire Press, L'Harmattan, and Wallada). A number of video documentaries are also available. Roma-led organizations, such as the Roma National Congress and the International Romani Union, push for human and civil rights and increasingly interact with representatives of national governments.

Despite having the shortest life expectancy and the highest infant mortality rate in Europe, Roma are its fastest-growing population; the same *Economist* report predicted that by 2060 they would outnumber Slovaks in the Slovak Republic. Clearly, coexistence is the only viable option.

Ian Hancock is director of the Romani Archives and Documentation Center at the University of Texas and author of We Are the Romani People *and* A Handbook of Vlax Romani.

ALTERNATIVES TO TOURISM

Let's Go believes that the connection between travelers and their destinations is important. We've watched the growth of the "ignorant tourist" stereotype with dismay, knowing that many travelers care passionately about the communities and environments they explore—but also knowing that even conscientious tourists can inadvertently damage natural wonders and harm cultural environments. With this "Alternatives to Tourism" chapter, *Let's Go* hopes to promote a better understanding of the countries of Eastern Europe and enhance your experience there.

In the developing world, there are many different options for those who seek to participate in Alternatives to Tourism. Opportunities for **volunteerism** abound, both with local and international organizations. You can also **study,** either by directly enrolling in a local university or by doing an independent research. *Let's Go* discourages **working** in the developing world due to high unemployment rates and weak economies, like some of those in Eastern Europe still struggling with the aftermath of communism.

As a volunteer in Eastern Europe, you can participate in projects from giving necessary aid to the struggling Roma population at a Bulgarian work camp to helping the conservation efforts of the Czech environmental movement *Hnuti Duha*, either on a short-term basis or as the main component of your trip. In this section, we recommend organizations that can help you find the opportunities that best suit your interests, whether you're looking to pitch in for a day or a year.

Studying at a college or language program is another way to immerse yourself in a the culture of a country. Study abroad programs provide an opportunity to look beneath the touristed veneer of such cities as Prague and St. Petersburg and to experience the life of post-communist Eastern Europe more authentically. From filmmaking to language-learning, these programs enable you to look at Eastern Europe from within.

 Start your search at ◼ **www.beyondtourism.com,** *Let's Go's* brand-new database of Alternatives to Tourism, where you can find exciting feature articles and helpful program listings divided by country, continent, and program type.

VOLUNTEERING

Volunteering can be an extremely fulfilling experience and is very common in Eastern Europe, particularly in the Balkans. Many volunteer services charge you a fee to participate. These fees can be surprisingly hefty (though they frequently cover airfare and most, if not all, living expenses). You may find it worthwhile to research a program before committing—talk to people who have previously participated and find out exactly what you're getting into, as living and working conditions vary greatly. Different programs are geared toward different ages and experience levels, so make sure you are not taking on too much or too little. The more informed you are and the more realistic expectations you have, the more enjoyable the program will be. Most people choose to go through a parent organization that takes care of logistical details and frequently provides a group environment and support system. Some of these organizations are religious, although there are rarely restrictions on who is eligible to participate.

GENERAL RESOURCES

Cross-Cultural Solutions, 2 Clinton Pl., New Rochelle, NY 10801 (☎800-380-4777; http://crossculturalsolutions.org). 2- to 12-week education and social service placements in **Russia** and many other countries. 17+. From US$2175.

Global Volunteer Network (www.volunteer.org.nz). Volunteer opportunities helping children in **Romania** and **Russia.** Program costs from US$600.

Global Volunteers, 375 E. Little Canada Rd., St. Paul, MN 55117, USA (☎800-487-1074; www.globalvolunteers.org). Volunteer opportunities in for short-term workers (1-3 weeks) in **Hungary, Poland, Romania,** and **Ukraine.** Programs focus on teaching and aiding children. From US$2000. Airfare not included.

COMMUNITY DEVELOPMENT

Aid to Russia and Moldova, P.O. Box 200, Bromley, Kent, BR1 1QF, UK (☎44 20 8460 6046). Humanitarian organization with projects focused on helping children in **Moldova, Russia,** and **Ukraine.**

Citizens Network for Foreign Affairs, 1111 19th St. NW #900, Washington, D.C. 20036 (☎1888-872-2632; www.cnfa.org). Help to develop marketing strategies for farmers in **Belarus, Moldova,** and **Russia.**

Habitat for Humanity International, 121 Habitat St., Americus, GA 31709, USA (☎229-924-6935, ext. 2551; www.habitat.org). Volunteers build houses in over 83 countries, including **Hungary, Macedonia, Poland, Romania,** and the **Slovak Republic.** From 2 weeks to 3 years. Short-term program about US$1350, plus airfare.

MAR-Bulgarian Youth Alliance for Development, P.O. Box 201, 1000 Sofia, Bulgaria (☎359 29 80 20 37; www.mar.bg). Places short-term volunteers (2-3 weeks) in Bulgarian work camps. Aid Roma population or foster environmental awareness.

Outreach Moldova, P.O. Box 8039, Dun Laoghaire, Co., Dublin, Ireland (☎353 1275 1842; www.outreachmoldova.org. This Irish charity accepts volunteers to work in an orphanage in **Moldova,** providing aid to disabled children.

Jewish Volunteer Corps, American Jewish World Service, 45 W. 36th St., New York, NY 10018 (☎800-889-7146). Places volunteers in NGOs as consultants.

Oxfam International, 274 Banbury Rd., ste. 20, Oxford, OX2 7DZ, UK (☎18 6531 1311; www.oxfam.org). Runs poverty relief campaigns, including one centered in **Sarajevo** at Hiseta 2 (☎66 81 33). The task force is mainly composed of Brits.

Peace Corps, Office of Volunteer Recruitment and Selection, 1111 20th St. NW, Washington, D.C. 20526, USA (☎800-424-8580; www.peacecorps.gov). Sends volunteers to developing nations, including **Bulgaria, Macedonia, Moldova, Romania, and Ukraine.** Typical assignments in Eastern Europe focus on business, education, or environmental issues. Must be a US citizen age 18+ willing to make a 2-yr. commitment. Bachelor's degree usually required.

Service Civil International Voluntary Service (SCI-IVS), SCI USA, 5474 Walnut Level Rd., Crozet, VA 22932, USA (☎206-350-6585; www.sci-ivs.org). Placement in work camps in Eastern Europe. 18+. US$175 for 2 weeks.

UNICEF, 333 E. 38th St., 6th fl., New York, NY 10016, USA (☎800-367-5437; www.unicef.org). UN organization, with offices throughout Eastern Europe, accepts volunteers for such projects as teaching and healthcare. By application. Undergraduate degree and work experience required.

Women's Action Vidra, Dr. V.D. Kecmanovia 27, Republic of Srpska, Bosnia and Herzegovina (☎387 51 303 685; www.vidra-bl.org). Volunteer in **Bosnia** to help women to gain independence by fostering critical skills.

CULTURAL EXCHANGE

Canada World Youth, 2330 Notre-Dame St. W., 3rd fl., Montréal, QC H3J 1N4, Canada (☎514-931-3526; www.cwy-jcm.org/en). Canadian residents only. Spend 3 months in Canada living with a Ukrainian citizen then travel with him or her to **Ukraine** for 3 months. Participate in volunteer activities in both countries. About CDN$2200.

Tahoe-Baikal Institute, P.O. Box 13587, South Lake Tahoe, CA 96151, USA (☎530-542-5599; www.tahoebaikal.org). Environmental exchange (typically 10 weeks). College students and young professionals spend 5 weeks at Lake Tahoe, CA and 5 weeks at Lake Baikal, **Russia.** AmeriCorps workers can receive a stipend with this program.

WorldTeach, 79 JFK St., Cambridge, MA, USA 02138 (☎800-483-2240; www.worldteach.org). Live with a family in **Poland** and teach English to high school students. $1500.

ENVIRONMENTAL WORK AND HISTORICAL PRESERVATION

Archaeological Institute of America, 656 Beacon St., Boston, MA 02215, USA (☎617-353-9361; www.archaeological.org). The *Archaeological Fieldwork Opportunities Bulletin,* available on the website, lists field sites throughout Europe including **Bulgaria, Moldova, Romania,** and **Russia.** Print edition US$20.

Brethren Volunteer Service, 1451 Dundee Ave., Elgin, Illinois, 60123 (☎800-323-8039, ext. 454; www.brethrenvolunteerservice.org). Volunteer for conservation efforts and public information campaigns with Hnuti Duha, a **Czech** environmental movement.

BTVC, 163 Balby Rd., Balby, Doncaster DN4 ORH (☎44 01302 572 224). Help monitor bear and wolf predator populations in the Tatras Mountains of the **Slovak Republic.**

Business Enterprises for Sustainable Travel (www.sustainabletravel.org). Supports travel that helps communities preserve natural and cultural resources. Has listings of local programs, innovative travel opportunities, and internships.

Earthwatch, 3 Clocktower Pl., ste. 100, P.O. Box 75, Maynard, MA 01754, USA (☎800-776-0188 or 978-461-0081; www.earthwatch.org). Arranges 1- to 3-week programs in the **Czech Republic, Estonia, Poland, Romania,** and **Russia** to promote conservation of natural resources. Programs average US$2000.

Eco-Centre Caput Insulae-Beli, Beli 4, 51559 Beli, Cres Island, Croatia (☎/fax 385 51 840 525; www.caput-insulae.com). Spend 2 weeks protecting the natural, cultural, and historical heritage of Cres Island, **Croatia.**

EcoVolunteer (www.ecovolunteer.org). Volunteer to preserve the wildlife of Eastern Europe in programs ranging from the conservation of Croatian vultures to Polish beavers. Programs in **Bulgaria, Croatia, Poland, Romania,** and **Russia.**

INEX—Association of Voluntary Service, Senovázné nám. 24, 116 47 Praha 1, Czech Republic (☎420 494 547 012; www.inexsda.cz/en/index.php). Ecological and historical preservation efforts in the **Czech Republic.**

World Wide Opportunities on Organic Farms (WWOOF), Main Office, P.O. Box 2675, Lewes BN7 1RB, England, UK (www.wwoof.org). Arranges volunteer work with organic and eco-conscious farms around the world.

HEALTH AND EDUCATION

Coalition for Psychotrauma and Peace, Gunduliceva 18, 32000 Vukovar, Croatia (☎385 32 441 975; www.cwwpp.org). Work for 1½-2yr. in education and health care related to long-term conflict stress in **Bosnia, Croatia,** and **Serbia and Montenegro.**

Downside Up, 15 Ozerkovsky per., Moscow 115184, RUS (☎/fax 951 00 79; www.downsideup.org). Bike 250km through the **Moscow** region to raise money for this organization that benefits Russian children with Downs Syndrome.

Kitezh Children's Community (http://atschool.eduweb.co.uk/ecoliza/files/kitezh.html). Teach English to **Russian** orphans in a rural setting. Young people taking a "gap year" between high school and college are especially welcome as volunteers.

Russian Orphan Opportunity Fund (ROOF), Voznesenskiy per. 8, 103 009, Moscow, Russia (☎/fax 7 095 229 5100; www.roofnet.org). Help Russian orphans gain vocational training, English-language proficiency, and computer literacy.

Doctors Without Borders, 333 7th Ave., 2nd fl., New York, NY 10001 (☎212-679-6800; www.doctorswithoutborders.org/volunteer). Medical and non-medical volunteer assignments wherever there is need.

HUMAN RIGHTS AND PEACE

Peacework, 209 Otey St., Blacksburg, VA 24060, USA (☎800-272-5519; www.peacework.org). Volunteer in the Czech Republic, Russia, and Ukraine for 1- to 3-week stints.

Volunteers for Peace, 1034 Tiffany Rd., Belmont., VT 05730, USA (☎802-259-2759; www.vfp.org). Arranges placement in work camps throughout Eastern Europe. Membership required for registration. Annual *International Workcamp Directory* US$20. 2-3 week programs average US$200-400.

European Roma Rights Center, H-1386 Budapest 62, P.O. Box 906/93, Hungary (fax 36 1 413 22 01; www.errc.org). Those of Romani origin may apply for a human rights advocacy internship in **Hungary** lasting 6 weeks to 6 months. Interns must be 18+.

REFUGEES

Balkan Sunflowers, Bregu i Diellit 2, Bl. 13 Apt. 32, Priština, Kosovo, Serbia and Montenegro (☎387 38 222 087; www.ddh.nl/org/balkansunflower). In **Albania, Kosovo,** and **Macedonia.** Programs generally last 6 weeks. Volunteers often work with children.

UNHCR (United Nations High Commission for Refugees), Case Postale 2500, CH-1211 Genève 2 Dépôt, Switzerland (☎22 739 8111; www.unhcr.ch), will gladly provide advice on how and where to help. **Sarajevo** office ☎66 61 60.

Firefly UK/Bosnia, 3 Bristo Pl., Edinburgh, Midlothian, EH1 1 EY, UK (☎44 79 56 98 38 85; www.fireflybosnia.org). Scottish organization that arranges summer camps in **Croatia** for refugees from Bosnian youth centers.

STUDYING ABROAD

Study abroad programs range from basic language lessons to university-level courses. To choose a program that best fits your needs, it is important to find out who participates in the program and what sort of accommodations are provided. Programs in which many students speak your language may allow you to feel comfortable in the community, but will limit your opportunities to practice or befriend other international students. Foreign study programs have multiplied rapidly in Eastern Europe. Most American undergraduates enroll in programs sponsored by US universities and many college study abroad offices can provide advice and information. Libraries and bookstores are helpful sources of current information on study abroad programs, as are **www.language-learning.net, www.studyabroad.com,** and **www.worldwide.edu.** If you are fluent in an Eastern European language, you may want to consider enrolling directly in a **foreign university.** This route is usually less expensive and more immersive than programs run by **American universities,** though it may be harder to get university credit for your adventures abroad. Contact the nearest consulate for a list of educational institutions in your country of choice. There are also several international and national fellowships available (e.g., Fulbright or Rotary) that fund stays abroad. Below are several organizations that run programs to Eastern European countries.

AMERICAN PROGRAMS

American Field Service (AFS), 71 W. 23rd St., 17th fl., New York, NY 10010 (☎212-807-8686; www.afs.org), with branches in over 50 countries. Offers summer-, semester-, and year-long homestay exchange programs for high school students and graduating seniors in the **Czech Republic, Hungary, Latvia, Russia,** and the **Slovak Republic.** Community service programs also offered for young adults 18+. Teaching programs available for current and retired teachers. Financial aid available.

American Institute for Foreign Study (AIFS), River Plaza, 9 West Broad St., Stamford, CT 06902 (☎800-727-2437; www.aifsabroad.com). Organizes programs for study in universities in the **Czech Republic, Poland,** and **Russia.** Financial aid and scholarships available. US$75 application fee.

Association for International Practical Training (AIPT), 10400 Little Patuxent Pkwy., Ste. 250, Columbia, MD 21044 (☎410-997-2200; www.aipt.org). 8- to 12-week and year-long programs in Eastern Europe for college students aged 18-30 who have completed 2 years of technical study as well as year-long programs for qualified professionals under 35. Scholarships available. US$75 application fee.

Council on International Educational Exchange (CIEE), 7 Custom House St., 3rd fl., Portland, ME 04101 (☎800-407-8839; www.ciee.org). Sponsors work, volunteer, and academic programs in the **Czech Republic, Hungary, Poland,** and **Russia.** Scholarships available.

NYU, Tisch School of the Arts, 721 Broadway, 12th fl., New York, NY 10003 (☎212-998-1500; www.specialprograms.tisch.nyu.edu). Spend the fall in **Prague** studying filmmaking and directing a film.

School for International Training, College Semester Abroad, Admissions, Kipling Rd., P.O. Box 676, Brattleboro, VT 05302 (☎800-257-7751; www.sit.edu). Semester- and year-long programs in the **Balkans, Czech Republic, Poland,** and **Russia.** Must have completed at least 1yr. of college with a 2.5 cumulative GPA. US$12,000-13,050. Financial aid available. Also runs the **Experiment in International Living** (☎800-345-2929; www.usexperiment.org). 5-week summer programs (US$5000) that offer high-school students cross-cultural homestays, community service, ecological adventure, and language training in **Poland.**

University Study Abroad Consortium, USAC/323, Reno, NV 89557 (☎775-784-6569; http://usac.unr.edu). Study Czech language and culture in **Prague** for the duration of a summer, semester, or year. Prices from $2780.

In most Eastern European countries, studying requires a special **student visa.** Applying for such a visa usually requires proof of admission to a university or program in your home country. For additional visa information, see **Essentials** (p. 9) or consult the **Consulates and Embassies** section at the beginning of each country chapter.

Youth for Understanding USA (YFU), 6400 Goldsboro Rd., ste. 100, Bethesda, MD 20817 (☎866-493-8872 or 240-235-2100; www.yfu.org). Places US high school students for a year, semester, or summer in **Estonia, Hungary, Latvia, Poland, Russia,** and **Ukraine.** US$75 application fee plus $500 enrollment deposit.

EASTERN EUROPEAN PROGRAMS

American University in Bulgaria, Blagoevgrad 2700, Bulgaria (☎359 73 888 218; www.aubg.bg). University in **Bulgaria** based on the American liberal arts model. Accepts international students.

Hungarian Dance Academy, Columbus u. 87, Budapest H-1145, Hungary (☎361 273 34 34; www.mtf.hu). Summer programs in **Hungary** for international students.

Liden & Denz Language Centre, Transportny per. 11 5th fl., 191119 St. Petersburg, Russia (☎7 812 325 22 41; www.lidenz.ch). Branch at Grusinski per. 3-181, ground fl., 123056 Moscow, Russia. Russian language classes and cultural excursions into **Moscow** and **St. Petersburg.**

Lithuanian Academy of Music, Gedimino Ave. 42, 2600 Vilnius, Lithuania (☎370 5 261 26 91; www.lma.lt). Classes in music, art, and theater in **Lithuania.** Offers music classes in English.

Lomonosov Moscow State University, A-812a, Main Building, Moscow State University, Leninskie Gory, Moscow 119992-GSP-2, Russia (☎7 035 939 35 10; www.msu.ru). Accepts international students for study in **Russia.**

Odessa Language Center, (☎380 482 345 058; www.studyrus.com). Spend a summer in the **Ukraine** learning Russian and taking courses on history and culture. P€240 for 2 weeks.

Ohrid Summer University, (☎389 02 37 55 70; www.euba.org.mk). Balkan studies and other summer programs in **Macedonia.**

The Prague Center for Further Education and Professional Development, Karmelitska 18, 180 00 Prague 1, Czech Republic (☎420 257 534 013; www.prague-center.cz/etlbar.html). Teaches courses on art, filmmaking, and design in **Prague.**

University of Bucharest, 36-46, M. Kogălniceanu Bd., Sector 5, 70709 Bucharest, Romania (☎40 21 307 73 00; www.unibuc.ro). Accepts international students for study in **Romania.**

University of West Bohemia, Univerzitni 8, 306 14 Plzen, Czech Republic (www.zcu.cz). An international student-friendly university centrally located in a **Czech** brewery city.

LANGUAGE SCHOOLS

Language schools are often independently run organizations or divisions of foreign universities that rarely offer college credit. Language schools are a good alternative to university study if you desire a deeper focus on the language or a slightly less rigorous course load. **American Councils for International Education,** 1776 Massachusetts Ave., NW, ste. 700, Washington, D.C., 20036, USA (☎202-833-7522; www.actr.org), offers summer, semester, and year-long college-level Russian-language programs throughout the former USSR. Programs in **Russia** range US$6000-16,000. Prices for programs in Central Europe vary depending on location and specifics, but are generally lower. **Languages Abroad,** 413 Ontario St., Toronto, ON Canada M5A 2V9 (☎800-219-9924; www.languagesabroad.com), has two- to eight-week language programs (US$1200-3000) in the **Czech Republic, Croatia, Hungary, ⸺nd,** and **Russia.** Participants lives in homes or university dorms. It also offers ⸺nteer and internship opportunities (18+), and language programs for corpo- ⸺xecutives (26+) and young multilinguals (10+).

WORKING

Let's Go urges you to use discretion if seeking work in Eastern Europe—travelers should not take jobs in developing countries that could otherwise be filled by locals in need of employment.

LOCAL CLASSIFIEDS

Eastern European capitals produce a weekly English-language publication, with which local organizations recruit foreign workers. All these newspapers are published weekly:

Bulgaria: The Sofia Echo (www.sofiaecho.com).

Czech Republic: The Prague Post (www.praguepost.com).

Estonia, Latvia, and Lithuania: The Baltic Times (www.baltictimes.com).

Hungary: The Budapest Sun (www.budapestsun.com).

Poland: The Warsaw Voice (www.warsawvoice.pl).

Russia: The Russia Journal (www.russiajournal.com).

Slovak Republic: The Slovak Spectator (www.slovakspectator.sk).

Ukraine: The Kyiv Post (www.kyivpost.com).

LONG-TERM WORK

Teaching jobs abroad are rarely well paid, although elite American or international schools usually offer competitive salaries. **Volunteering as a teacher** is a popular option. Volunteering teachers often get some sort of a daily stipend to help cover living expenses. In almost all cases, you must have at least a bachelor's degree to

A L T E R N A T I V E S
T O T O U R I S M

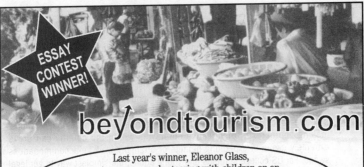

ESSAY CONTEST WINNER!

beyondtourism.com

Last year's winner, Eleanor Glass, spent a summer volunteering with children on an island off the Yucatan Peninsula. Read the rest of her story and find your own once-in-a-lifetime experience at **www.beyondtourism.com!**

"... I was discovering elements of life in Mexico that I had never even dreamt of. I regularly had meals at my students' houses, as their fisherman fathers would instruct them to invite the nice gringa to lunch after a lucky day's catch. Downtown, tourists wandered the streets and spent too much on cheap necklaces, while I played with a friend's baby niece, or took my new kitten to the local vet for her shots, or picked up tortillas at the tortilleria, or vegetables in the mercado. ... I was lucky that I found a great place to volunteer and a community to adopt me. ... Just being there, listening to stories, hearing the young men talk of cousins who had crossed the border, I know I went beyond tourism." - Eleanor Glass, 2004

LET'S GO

be a full-fledged teacher, though college undergraduates can sometimes obtain summer positions as tutors. There remains a demand for English instructors in Eastern Europe, though the market has been saturated in highly touristed countries, like Hungary and the Czech Republic. Many schools require teachers to have a **Teaching English as a Foreign Language (TEFL)** certificate. Those without the certificate are not necessarily excluded from teaching, but certified teachers often find higher-paying jobs. Placement agencies or university fellowship programs are the best resources for finding teaching jobs in Eastern Europe. You can also contact schools directly or try your luck once you get there. If you are going to do the latter, the best time of the year is several weeks before the school year starts in September. Taking on individual students as a **private English tutor** is a popular alternative to traditional teaching positions in Eastern Europe; contact schools about potential pupils to help you get started. The following organizations are extremely helpful in placing teachers:

Central Bureau for Educational Visits and Exchanges, 10 Spring Gardens, London SW1A 2BN, UK (www.britishcouncil.org/education/students). Places qualified British undergraduates and teachers in teaching positions in **Hungary, Russia,** and **Slovenia.**

International Schools Services (ISS), 15 Roszel Rd., P.O. Box 5910, Princeton, NJ 08543, USA (☎609-452-0990; www.iss.edu). Hires teachers for more than 200 overseas schools, including many in Eastern Europe. Candidates should have experience with teaching or international affairs. Bachelor's degree required. 2-yr. commitment.

Office of Overseas Schools, US Department of State, Room H328, SA-1, Washington, D.C. 20522, USA (☎202-261-8200; www.state.gov/m/a/os/). Keeps comprehensive lists of schools abroad and agencies that place Americans to teach abroad.

Petro-Teach, Westpost, P.O. Box 109, Lappeenranta 53101, Finland (www.petroteach.com). Places teachers from abroad in schools in St. Petersburg, **Russia** for a semester or for a full academic year. US$3000-5000.

VISAS. Though working in Eastern Europe is rewarding, it entails jumping through a whole new set of bureaucratic hoops. Most countries require a work permit as well as a visa or a permit for temporary residency. In some countries, to make it all the more confusing, a particular type of visa, often called a "visa with work permit," is required in addition to (not as a replacement for) a work permit. These visas are issued from the nearest consulate or embassy (see the **Embassies and Consulates** section of each country chapter). Applying for one will require that you present your work permit, which must be issued directly from the Labor Bureau in the country in question. Given these complications, making contact with prospective employers within the country can prove extremely useful in expediting permits or arranging work-for-accommodations swaps. For US college students and young adults, the simplest way to get legal permission to work abroad is through **Council Exchanges Work Abroad Programs,** which can help you obtain a 3- to 6-month work permit and/or visa and provide assistance finding jobs and housing (US$300-425).

AU PAIR WORK

Au pairs are typically women aged 18-27, who work as live-in nannies, caring for children and doing light housework in exchange for room, board, and a small spending allowance or stipend. In many countries, au pairs are required to be enrolled in college during their stay. While the au pair experience allows foreigners to get to know a country without the high expenses of traveling, the job often involves long hours and somewhat mediocre pay. Payment for au pairs varies with placement, and much of the au pair experience really does depend on the family for which you'll be working.

Svezhy Veter, 426000 Izhevsk P.O. Box 2040, Russia (☎7 341 24 50 037; www.sv-agency.udm.ru).

AuPairConnect, Max Global, Inc., 8370 W. Cheyenne Ave. #76, Las Vegas, NV 89129, USA (www.aupairconnect.com).

Childcare International, Ltd., Trafalgar House, Grenville Pl., London NW7 3SA, UK (☎44 20 8906 3116; www.childint.co.uk).

SHORT-TERM WORK

Traveling for long periods of time can get expensive; therefore, many travelers try their hand at odd jobs for a few weeks at a time to make some extra cash to carry them through another month or two of touring around. Obtaining a short-term paid position can prove problematic as unemployment continues to plague much of Eastern Europe. With a good number of qualified locals unable to find jobs, many local establishments are unlikely to hire foreigners, particularly those who are not fluent in the language. But with the necessary language skills and extra effort, work can still be found. Working in a hostel or restaurant and teaching English are the most common forms of employment among travelers to Eastern Europe. Opportunities tend to be more abundant in larger cities, but so do prospective workers, creating increased competition. Word-of-mouth is often the best resource when seeking a job; ask other backpackers and friendly hostel-owners for tips on locating an appropriate opportunity. Another popular option is to work several hours a day at a hostel in exchange for free or discounted room or board.

INTERNSHIPS

Internships, usually for college students, are a good way to segue into working abroad, although they are often unpaid or poorly paid (many say the experience, however, is well worth it). **Internships International,** 1612 Oberlin Rd., Raleigh, NC 27608, offers unpaid internships and connections to language schools in cities around the world, including Budapest, **Hungary.** Fee of US$1100 guarantees placement in an internship. (☎919-832-1575 Dec.-May, 207-443-3019 June-Nov.; www.internshipsinternational.org.)

FOR FURTHER READING ON ALTERNATIVES TO TOURISM

How to Live Your Dream of Volunteering Overseas, by Collins, DeZerega, and Heckscher. Penguin Books, 2002 (US$17).

International Dictionary of Volunteer Work, by Whetter and Pybus. Peterson's Guides and Vacation Work, 2000 (US$16).

Summer Jobs Abroad 2003, by James and Woodworth. Peterson's Guides and Vacation Work, 2003 (US$18).

International Jobs: Where They Are and How To Get Them, by Kocher and Segal. Perseus Books, 1999 (US$18).

Alternatives to the Peace Corps: A Directory of Third World and U.S. Volunteer Opportunities, by Joan Powell. Food First Books, 2000 (US$10).

Peterson's Study Abroad. Peterson's, 1999 (US$30).

WORLD TEACH
Volunteering in Poland

Sausages sizzle over an open bonfire while shots of homemade vodka pass through a dozen pairs of eager lips. Simple English and Polish phrases mingle precariously in the air while hand gestures and laughter compensate for the multitude of holes in my two-week-old Polish lexicon. This was the scene of my most memorable birthday party yet: an experience that was only possible because I chose to be a resident rather than a tourist in a foreign country.

In January 2004, posters started appearing around my college campus advertising a program called WorldTeach (see p. 61 for more info), which places volunteers in classroom settings around the world for either a summer or a full year. Eager to return to Europe after an incredible month in France during 2003, I chose Poland from among WorldTeach's five summer options. After applying and being accepted into the program, I journeyed half way around the world to live and teach in a small village in rural Poland.

My first experience in front of a classroom of Polish students (or any students for that matter) came rather abruptly, only five days after stepping off the airplane. I, along with the 12 other WorldTeach volunteers, received a lightning-quick orientation to living and working in Poland during our first four days, which we spent in a student dormitory at a school in Makow Mazowiecki. A former Peace Corps volunteer provided some useful teaching advice and information on differences between the Polish and American educational systems, but overall the theme of orientation was "be prepared for anything."

Upon arriving in Lyse, I was greeted by a well-organized, hospitable school director and a staff who maintained a bright and cheerful school environment. I taught a total of 40 students—two classes at the high school and three at the middle school—ranging 12 to 18 years in age. I tutored small groups for two hours at a time, five days a week. Because the students were on their summer holiday, the ambience in the classroom was somewhat out of the ordinary. On the one hand, the students were excited and attentive since it was their choice to be there. The sun-drenched fields outside, however, not only drew the concentration of my students away from their work, but also forced me to be more lenient than a term-time teacher usually would have been.

Because most of my students struggled with oral expression, classes tended to focus on general speaking exercises rather than specific points of grammar. Though all of the material and lesson planning was left entirely to my discretion, I had no knowledge of my students' prior English experience, so I had to quickly assess students' abilities and often modify lesson plans on the spot. Cultural differences also emerged quickly in lessons. Questions like "It's Saturday night, what are you up to?" did not prove the most practical conversational exercise for students who lived primarily on farms.

Since arriving in Poland barely able to count to 10 in Polish, I had often found the language barrier significant; it was not uncommon to feel lonely and isolated from native speakers. Yet it was these very nights that inspired me to open up my Polish grammar book before bed and remind myself that all learning takes time. With every new day I became more confident in my language skills, with which I made a close group of lasting friends and became able to participate in everyday life.

Having friends nearby who spoke English was also a great comfort. We would all congregate about once a week, and we traveled as a group at various points in the summer. While some days were frustrating, others opened my eyes to the charm and culture of the people and students with whom I worked. Even on the hardest days, I found my time in Poland to be exceptionally rewarding.

On one of my trips through other parts of Europe I visited the European Parliament in Brussels and also spent time in Berlin. It was on my way home from this trip that I had an important revelation: I had admired the architectural treasures of Brussels and marveled at the impressive infrastructure of Germany, but as our train brought us back into Poland at the end of the week, I felt that I was truly going home. Poland is a place that I have worked in, and explored by bike, train, foot, and plane. The rugged, untamed landscape flashing past my window was no longer unclaimed scenery; rather, in some small, impossible way, my new home.

Mallory Greimann hails from Wellesley, MA. She is currently pursuing an undergraduate degree in economics from Harvard University, and uses her spare time to sail on the Charles River.

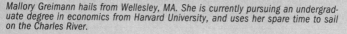

ALBANIA (SHQIPËRIA)

AUS$1 = 73.08 LEKË	100 LEKË = AUS$1.37	
CDN$1 = 77.26 LEKË	100 LEKË = CDN$1.29	
EUR€1 = 125.03 LEKË	100 LEKË = EUR€0.80	
NZ$1 = 69.93 LEKË	100 LEKË = NZ$1.49	
UK£1 = 187.22 LEKË	100 LEKË = UK£0.53	
US$1 = 102.39 LEKË	100 LEKË = US$0.98	

Proud, fierce, and defiant, Albania has played a part in every struggle between East and West. Since the days when national hero Skënderbeg rallied his forces and scattered the Turks, Albanians have taken pride in preserving their unique heritage. Today, Albania's mountainous terrain takes on an almost alien appearance—the result of communist dictator Enver Hoxha's "bunker-in-every-plot" defense campaign. Coverage of Albania was last updated in July of 2003.

HISTORY

ILLYRIA. Archaeological studies indicate that Albanians are descendants of the ancient **Illyrian tribes.** In 229 BC, the **Roman Empire** defeated Illyria—and established the province of Illyricum. In AD 395, the Roman Empire was divided, the Illyrian lands were partitioned, and the territory of modern Albania became part of the **Byzantine Empire.** The Illyrian lands were invaded by tribes of Huns, Visigoths, and Ostrogoths; not to be outdone, the Slavs arrived in the 6th to 8th centuries. However, the southern tribes of modern Albania preserved their tongue.

ISTANBUL IS CONSTANTINOPLE. The Albanian church was controlled from Rome until AD 732, when it began to fall under Constantinople's jurisdiction. Albania experienced its first religious fragmentation in 1054 when the Christian church split between the East and West. Northern Albania reverted to the control of the Roman pope, but the Byzantine Empire proved too weak to protect Albania from successive invasions. The hero **Skënderbeg** united the Albanian princes in the 1444 **League of Lezhë** and staved off the Turks for 25 years. Following his death, Albania became part of the **Ottoman Empire.**

FACTS AND FIGURES

OFFICIAL NAME: Republic of Albania

CAPITAL: Tirana (pop. 353,000)

POPULATION: 3.5 million (95% Albanian, 3% Greek, 2% other)

LANGUAGE: Albanian (Tosk)

CURRENCY: 1 lek = 100 qindarka

RELIGION: 70% Muslim, 20% Orthodox Christian, 10% Catholic

LAND AREA: 27,398km²

CLIMATE: Mild temperate

GEOGRAPHY: Mountainous, plains along the 362km coastline

BORDERS: Greece, Macedonia, Serbia and Montenegro

ECONOMY: 50% Agriculture, 25% Industry, 25% Services

GDP: US$4400 per capita

COUNTRY CODE: 355

INTERNATIONAL DIALING PREFIX: 00

Albania

LAND OF THE EAGLE. By the end of the 17th century, Albanians had begun calling themselves *shqiptarë*, "sons of eagles," and their country *Shqipëria*, "the land of the eagle." The **Albanian League** was founded in 1878 with the goal of unifying all the Albanian territories (Janinë, Kosovo, Monastir, Shkodër). When the Balkan states declared war on the Ottoman Empire in October 1912, Albania issued the **Vlorë Proclamation** of independence to protect itself from its Slavic neighbors. After the defeat of the Ottomans, the **conference of the Great Powers** agreed to recognize independent Albania. Ethnic divisions were ignored, however: Kosovo was given to Serbia and other regions to Greece and Macedonia.

LAND OF THE DICTATOR. During WWI, Albania's neighbors threatened to partition the country, but US President Wilson prevented this at the **Paris Peace Conference of 1918. Bishop Fan Noli** was elected prime minister in 1924 and began democratization. The process lasted only a few months, until **Ahmet Zog** overthrew the government. He crowned himself king in 1928, but his reign collapsed under WWII occupation. Until his death in 1985, communist **Enver Hoxha,** who had led the wartime resistance, formed and then rejected ties with Yugoslavia, the Soviet Union, and China, finally closing Albania's doors to foreigners entirely.

ALIA IACTA EST. Hoxha's successor, **Ramiz Alia,** faced growing opposition after the fall of communism in 1989. Seeking to preserve the regime, Alia restored religious freedom and endorsed the creation of political parties. The regime collapsed when it lost the March 1992 elections to the Democratic Party. Alia was succeeded by **Sali Berisha,** the first Democratic president of Albania since Bishop Noli.

TODAY. Following the 1997 financial collapse, general elections ushered the **Socialist Party** into power. In November 1998, Albania's new constitution was approved by referendum, but the **Democratic Party** boycotted the vote. July 2002 elected **Alfred Moisiu** president, marking an unprecedented consensus between the Socialists and the Democrats. Moisiu seeks to move toward integration with NATO and the EU. Though the economy has rebounded since 1997, Albania remains the second poorest country in Europe (after Moldova). The country's inadequate infrastructure makes large-scale tourism only a hope for the future.

PEOPLE AND CULTURE

LANGUAGE

Albanian (called *Shqip* by Albanians) is the sole surviving descendant of Illyrian. Two main dialects can be distinguished: **Geg** (or *Gheg*) in the north and **Tosk** in the south. *Tosk* is the official language of Albania. **Pronunciation** is phonetic. There are seven vowels: *i* (ee), *e* (eh), *a* (ah), *u* (oo), *ë* (uh), and *y* (u). A final *ë* is usually silent. Consonants are as in English, expect for: *ç* (ch as in "chips"); *th* (th as in "thin"); *dh* (th as in "this"); *gj* (j as in "jinx"); *j* (y as in "yellow"); *q* (ch as in "Charles"); *x* (dz), and *xh* (j as in "judge"). See **Glossary: Albanian,** p. 944, for a phrasebook. **Italian** is a common second language in Albania. Younger Albanians tend to speak some **English.** In **non-verbal communication,** Albanians nod to mean "no" and shake their heads to say "yes." Reply verbally with *po* (yes) and *jo* (no).

FOOD AND DRINK

ALBANIA	❶	❷	❸	❹	❺
FOOD	under 100 lekë	100-300 lekë	301-500 lekë	501-700 lekë	over 700 lekë

Albanian cuisine revolves around *mish* (meat) and *patate* (potatoes), which can often be ordered *më garniturë* (with vegetables), probably salted and oiled. The predominance of *djathë* (feta-like cheese) recalls Greek cuisine. *Kos*, yogurt, is served at most meals. Salads are a popular prelude to a meal and are often accompanied by *raki,* a potent brandy drunk in small sips.

CUSTOMS AND ETIQUETTE

Albanian **hospitality** is influenced by the *Kanun*—the legendary code of the medieval lawgiver Lek Dukagjini. *Kanun* overrides even revenge; a house will shelter and feed a man who has killed one of its members. You will be served coffee and *raki* and offered a smoke whenever you enter a home. It is polite to accept, but no offense is taken if a cigarette is refused. It is customary to remove your shoes upon crossing the threshold of a house. **Tipping** is uncommon outside of Tirana, where 10% is appropriate. Women **dress** more conservatively in Albania, though shorts and jeans are more common in larger cities.

THE ARTS

During the period of Turkish occupation, many Albanians rejected Ottoman cultural dominance and formed a group now known as the **Arbëresh**. These expats remained fiercely loyal to Albania and created a patriotic literature about exile and the homeland. During the 19th century, Arbëresh writer **Jeronim de Rada** spearheaded the nationalistic Association of Printing Letters in Albanian, and poet **Naim Frashëri** greatly enriched his native Tosk dialect, which later became the literary language. Twentieth-century poet Millosh Gjergj Nikolla (1911-38), called **Migjeni**, wrote about social awareness in his *Vargjet e lira* (Free Verse). Albania's most famous modern author is **Ismail Kadare**, whose works include *The General of the Dead Army* (1963) and *The Three-Arched Bridge* (1997).

ADDITIONAL RESOURCES

Balkan Ghosts: A Journey Through History, by Robert Kaplan (1994). A travel journal dealing with the political complexities of Albania and its neighbors.

Women Who Become Men: Albanian Sworn Virgins, by Antonia Young (1999). An examination of a unique social phenomenon (see **Sidebar**, p. 76).

NATIONAL HOLIDAYS IN 2005	
January 1 New Year's Day	**October 4** Ramadan begins
January 11 Republic Day	**November 3** Ramadan ends
February 22 Islamic New Year	**November 28** Independence Day
May 1 Labor Day	**November 29** Liberation Day
May 2 Prophet's Birthday	

ALBANIA ESSENTIALS

ENTRANCE REQUIREMENTS

Passport: Required of all travelers.

Visa: Not required of citizens of Australia, Canada, Ireland, or New Zealand, the UK, or the US for stays up to 90 days.

Letter of Invitation: Not required.

Inoculations: Recommended up-to-date on DTaP (diphtheria, tetanus, and pertussis), Hepatitis A, Hepatitis B, MMR (measles, mumps, and rubella), Polio booster, and Typhoid.

Work Permit: Required of all foreigners planning to work in Albania.

International Driving Permit: Required of all those planning to drive.

DOCUMENTS AND FORMALITIES

EMBASSIES AND CONSULATES

Embassies and consulates of other countries in Albania are all in **Tirana** (see p. 74). Albania's embassies and consulates abroad include:

Canada: 130 Albert St., Ste. 302, **Ottawa,** ON K1P 5G4 (☎613-236-4114; embassyre-publicofalbania@on.aivn.com).

Greece: 1 Rue Karachristou 115 21 **Athens** (☎210 723 4412; fax 723 1372).

Italy: 5 Via Asmara, 00 199 **Rome** (☎6 862 144 75; fax 862 160 05).

UK: 2nd fl., 24 Buckingham Gate, **London** SW1E 6LB (☎20 7828 8897; fax 7828 8869).

US: 2100 S St. NW, **Washington, D.C.** 20008 (☎202-223-4942; fax 628-7342).

VISA AND ENTRY INFORMATION

Citizens of Australia, Canada, Ireland, New Zealand, the UK, and the US may visit Albania visa-free for up to 90 days, though they must pay €10 for an **entry card** at the border. Upon payment, you will receive an exit card and proof of payment inside your passport; keep it with you to ensure that you will be permitted to leave without paying again. An extension for stays up to 180 days may be obtained by application at police stations.

GETTING AROUND

Commercial **flights** into Tirana are limited and expensive. **Adria Airways** runs regular flights from **Ljubljana,** SLN; **Alitalia** from **Rome; Austrian Airlines** from **Vienna;** and **Olympic Airways** from **Athens. Ferries** connect Durrës with Bari, ITA and Ancona, ITA daily in winter and twice daily in summer.

Trains, slow and uncomfortable, are the cheapest option. Trains run to Tirana, Vlorë, Pogradec, and Ballsh, but not to international destinations. There are no public **buses** in Albania, but private buses have stepped up to fill the public need. Many travelers prefer **microbuses.**

Taxis are often essential when other transport fails. Poor road conditions make driving unnecessarily dangerous and **carjackings** are frequent outside of Tirana. **Hitchhiking** is common (riders are expected to pay), but *Let's Go* does not recommend hitchhiking, especially in Albania.

TOURIST SERVICES AND MONEY

Albania has no real tourist infrastructure. There are **no ATMs** in the country, so bring hard currency. **Tirana Bank** gives Visa cash advances; **Banka e Kursimeve** gives MasterCard cash advances and cashes traveler's checks. **Inflation** is 6%; prices should remain pretty steady. **Normal business hours** are Monday-Friday 8am-3pm.

HEALTH AND SAFETY

 EMERGENCY NUMBERS: Police: ☎ 19 **Fire:** ☎ 18 **Ambulance:** ☎ 17

In case of **medical emergency,** get out of Albania. Albanian hospitals are relatively unequipped. Your embassy is your best resource. Don't count on finding **medical supplies** in Albania. Bring extra prescription medications with you, especially Cipro. Albanian **pharmacies** stock condoms, tampons, and sanitary products. Out-

ALBANIA

side Tirana, **armed crime** is common. Cars are frequent targets. **Street crime** is fairly common everywhere, so stay on well-lit streets and keep an eye on your money and passport. **Women** should not travel alone in Albania. **Minority** travelers will probably get stares but generally are not hassled. **Homosexuality** was legalized in Albania in 1995, though gay and lesbian travelers may still be treated with hostility.

ACCOMMODATIONS

ALBANIA	❶	❷	❸	❹	❺
ACCOM.	under 2000 lekë	2000-3500 lekë	3501-6000 lekë	6001-10,000 lekë	over 10,000 lekë

There are no **hostels** in Albania. **Hotels** are generally overpriced, but **pensions** and **guesthouses** are good options where available. **Private rooms** are the way to go in Gjirokastër, but they are nonexistent elsewhere.

KEEPING IN TOUCH

Mail can be received general delivery through **Poste Restante**. Address envelopes as follows: Molly (First name) ATLAS (LAST NAME), POSTE RESTANTE, Tiranë (city), ALBANIA. Only **AT&T Direct** (☎ 00 800 00 10) has an international access number in Albania. Call ☎ 12 for international directory assistance. **Internet access** has slow connections, but it's the most reliable option.

TIRANA (TIRANË) ☎ (0)4

Tirana (pop. 598,000) is a depressing blemish on an otherwise sublime landscape of forest-carpeted mountains and quilted farmland. The entire city looks like a disorganized construction zone, with open manholes and crumbling sidewalks and buildings. A vibrant younger population is trying to reclaim its soul, but for now Tirana remains decades behind other Balkan capitals.

⌨ TRANSPORTATION

Flights: Rinas Airport (☎ 362 137) is 26km northeast of town. A taxi to the center costs about €15—negotiate the price before getting in. Airport-bound microbuses (50 lekë) leave from the intersection of Rr. Mine Peza and Rr. Durrësit, but you should head out early to wait for the bus to fill (often 30-60min.). Book flights through **Skënderbeg Travel** (see p. 75) or **24 Hours,** Rr. Vaso Pasha 4/1 (☎ 271 149; virgin@ice_al.org). Open M-Sa 8am-8pm. Direct flights to **Rome, ITA** (round-trip US$330) and **Vienna, AUT** (round-trip US$465). MC/V.

Trains: At the north end of Bul. Zogu I. Domestic routes only. To: **Durrës** (1hr., 7 per day, 50 lekë); **Shkodër** (5hr., 2 per day, 120 lekë); **Vlorë** (7hr., 2 per day, 225 lekë).

Buses: There is no bus station, nor 1 central location from which all buses depart. To add to the confusion, locations from which buses depart change almost annually. Domestic travel is most easily accomplished by **microbuses**. The cost is equal to (or slightly less than) that of a bus and they run more frequently. Departures from Mine Peza, 1 block from the train station. Turn right with your back to the train station and walk until you see the minivans. Shout out your destination and the helpful old men will point you in the right direction.

Taxis: Congregate around every corner. There are no meters, and they seem to think 300 lekë is a fair price for anywhere in downtown Tirana. Counteroffer with 200, and they'll usually acquiesce. **Radio Taxi** (☎ 377 777) is the only official company in town.

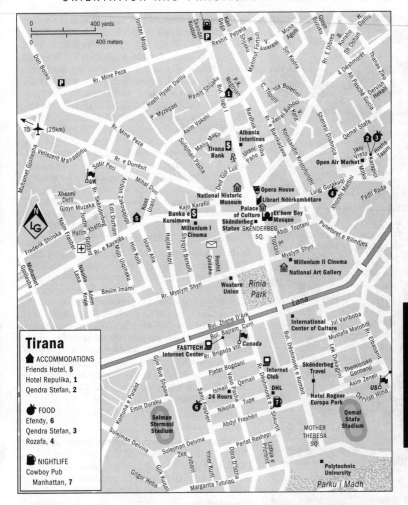

Tirana

🏠 ACCOMMODATIONS
Friends Hotel, **5**
Hotel Repulika, **1**
Qendra Stefan, **2**

🍎 FOOD
Efendy, **6**
Qendra Stefan, **3**
Rozafa, **4**

🍷 NIGHTLIFE
Cowboy Pub
Manhattan, **7**

ALBANIA

⊹ 🛈 ORIENTATION AND PRACTICAL INFORMATION

Street names, numbers, and bus stations seem to elude even locals. The city expands in all directions from **Sheshi Skënderbej** (Skënderbeg Square). From the square, the town's main thoroughfares are **Bul. Dëshmorët e Kombit,** extending south to the Polytechnic University, and **Bul. Zogu I,** stretching to the train station to the north. The **Lana River** runs east-west three blocks south of Skënderbeg Sq., bordered by **Bul. Zhane d'Ark** on the north bank and **Bul. Bajram Curi** on the south bank. Tirana's only map can be purchased at bookstores for a whopping 800 lekë.

Tourist Office: Skënderbeg Travel, Bul. Dëshmorët e Kombit (☎ 235 035; fax 235 050), in the lobby of the Hotel Rogner Europapark. English spoken. Arranges flights, accommodations, rental cars with drivers, ferry tickets, and guided excursions to local sights. Open M-F 8:30am-3pm. AmEx/V.

IN-RECENT NEWS

I'M A VIRGIN, I SWEAR!

There are few options for Albanian women who seek to break the boundaries of gender in their work and social life. Albanians still live according to the Kanun—a set of oral laws, which date from the 15th century and prescribe societal norms, including a strict separation of labor roles according to gender. Women were given almost all tasks in the home, while men were given responsibilities outside the home (including socializing in cafes and avenging blood feuds). Anthropologists have uncovered a practice among women from the northern mountainous regions of Albania in which they announced to society their intent to remain celibate, in order to be treated by family and community as honorary men.

Known as "sworn virgins," over 100 women have registered as honorary men since the mid-19th century. These "sworn virgins" are completely accepted as men in society: they take male names, others address and refer to them with male pronouns, and they sit on the "male" side at public gatherings. Some dress in traditionally male costume with a cap and trousers, while others prefer to wear women's clothing. They are allowed to socialize in public with men, work outside the home, and play the *gusle* (a traditionally male, stringed instrument), and could own and inherit property long before Albanian law afforded property rights to women.

Embassies and Consulates: Citizens of **Australia** should contact the embassy in Athens, GCE (☎30 210 645 0404; fax 642 0132) and register with the Canadian embassy in Tirana. **Canada,** Rr. Brigada VIII 2 (☎257 275; tirana@dfait-maeci.gc.ca). Open M-F 8am-5pm. **Greece,** Rr. Frederik Shiroka (☎223 959; grconstir@albnet.net). Citizens of **Ireland** should contact the embassy in Athens, GCE (☎30 210 723 2771). **Italy,** Rr. Lek Dukagjini 2 (☎234 045; ambittia@icc.al.eu.org). **Serbia and Montenegro,** Rr. Skënderbeg 8/3-II (☎223 042; ambatira@icc-al.org). **UK,** Rr. Skënderbeg 12 (☎234 973; fax 247 697). Open M-Tu and Th 8am-1pm and 2-5pm, W and F 8am-2pm. With your back to the front of the Skënderbeg Statue, turn left down Rr. e Kavajës and walk 800m. Turn right on Rr. Skënderbeg. **US,** Rr. Elbasanit 103 (☎247 285; fax 232 222). Take Bul. Dëshmorët e Kombit from Skënderbeg Sq. and turn left along the river. Turn right at the next bridge onto Elbasanit. Open M-F 8am-5pm.

Currency Exchange: Banka e Kursimeve, (☎374 361; fax 235 050), on Bul. Dëshmorët e Kombit in the lobby of the Hotel Rogner Europapark, exchanges currency for no commission, gives **MC cash advances** for 1% commission, and cashes **traveler's checks** for 1% commission. Open M-F 9am-4pm. **Tirana Bank,** Bul. Zogu I 55 (☎269 705; fax 269 707), 2 blocks up from Skënderbeg Sq. on the left, gives V **cash advances.** Open M-F 8:15am-3pm. **Western Union** offices exist on practically every corner. A centrally located one is at the corner of Rr. Myslym Shri and Rr. Dëshmorët e 4 Shkurtit, 1 block from the post office. Open M-F 8am-3pm, Sa 8am-1pm.

American Express: Pjeter Bogdani 23 (☎227 908; rezerium@albnet.net).

English-Language Bookstore: Librari Ndërkombëtare, Sami Frashëri 20/I (☎240 018), in the Palace of Culture in Skënderbeg Sq., sells an endless stock of books, city and country guides, and newspapers. Open M-Sa 8:30am-3pm, 5:30-10:30pm. V.

Pharmacy: Pharmacia N.7, Bul. Zogu I (☎222 241), next to Tirana Bank. Open daily 3pm-12:30am. **Pharmacia N.17,** (☎222 241), on the other side of the bank, does day shifts. Open daily 8am-4pm.

Hospitals: Most hospitals don't have emergency care. Try the **clinic** at Rr. e Kavajës 120 (☎223 906). Open daily 8am-noon and 3-7pm. Better yet, don't get sick in Albania.

Internet Access: Internet Club, Bul. Dëshmorët e 4 Shkurtit 7, across from the UNDP headquarters; walk through the iron gate, straight back, and down the stairs. 150 lekë per hr. Open 24hr. **FASTTECH Internet Center,** Rr. Brigada VIII 8 (☎251 947; info@fastech.com.al). 100 lekë per hr. Open daily 8am-11pm.

Post Office: On the corner of Rr. Dëshmorët e 4 Shkurtit, 1 block south of e Kavajës. (☎232 126). **Poste Restante** at window 16. **Western Union** at window 15a. Open M-F 7:30am-8pm. **Telephone office** is next door to the left. Open M-F 6am-10pm.

ACCOMMODATIONS

Private rooms, like most budget accommodations in Albania, are practically nonexistent, although the **American Express** office (see **Orientation and Practical Information,** p. 75) still claims to book them. Most hotels are modern or recently renovated, with air conditioning and hot water. Unfortunately, none can promise either when electricity is interrupted.

■ **Qendra Stefan** (Stephen Center), Rr. Hoxha Tahsin 1 (☎234 748; stephenc@icc-al.org). From the train station, walk to Skënderbeg Sq. and turn left onto Rr. Luigj Gurakuqi just before the mosque; it's 2 long blocks up on the left, just past the market. Ring the bell or ask in the restaurant. Run by American missionaries, these newly renovated rooms have comfortable furnishings with modern bathrooms and showers. Breakfast included. Reception M-F 8am-6pm. Outside of business hours call ahead. €30. ❸

Hotel Repulika, Bul. Zogu I 66 (☎222 400; fax 225 014), between the train station and Skënderbeg Sq. So ugly it's cool. Fluorescent turquoise door frames, 7m brownish-yellow ceilings, green carpets, and hardwood floors adorn large rooms with A/C and modern showers. Reception 24hr. Doubles and triples €30; 5-person suites €50. ❸

Friends Hotel, Rr. e Kavajës 86 (☎/fax 273 669), 4 blocks from Skënderbeg Sq. Ultra-chic modern hotel opened in 2003. Breakfast included. Reception 24hr. Small doubles with showers €40, larger doubles with bathtubs €50. ❹

FOOD

Cafes outnumber restaurants in the city, and tourists will have difficulty finding restaurants specializing exclusively in traditional Albanian fare. Fast-food joints abound, serving up local favorites like *suflaqe* (shaved meat wrapped in flatbread, like a *gyro*), *doner* (shaved meat topped with tomatoes and yogurt sauce), *shishqebap* (grilled skewered meat), *qofte* (spiced meat balls), and *byrek* (meat- or cheese-filled pastry). The proximity to Durrës and the Adriatic makes fresh seafood options available in most restaurants.

Many ask why a woman would cast off her sexuality to achieve social equality with a man. Yet, some sworn virgins have no part in the decision to renounce their womanhood, as parents without male descendents can declare at birth that a girl should be raised as a boy. Others are selected to carry on the name and legacy of a family that had lost a male heir to a blood feud or the rigors of mountain life. Often, becoming a sworn virgin is the only respectable way for a woman to refuse to marry a man to whom she was betrothed. Some women also adopt this status after widowhood or divorce as the way to remain independent.

Sworn virgins still exist and can occasionally be seen in cities and villages in and around Albania, although foreigners may not realize that the man they are meeting is anatomically a woman. Sworn virgins, although often misogynists, consider themselves women and pride themselves on their ability to be accepted as a man in society despite the handicap of female anatomy. Their existence has raised new questions regarding the role of socialization versus sex in gender identity. As long as the practice continues, sworn virgins will provide insight into what may be the earliest equal rights movement in history.

▓ **Rozafa,** Rr. Luigj Gurakuqi between the market and Rr. Barrikavdave (☎248 670). *The place to go for seafood.* Don't be deterred by the cheesy fast-food looking signs outside—the food here is remarkable. Try the *risoto fruta deti* (seafood risotto; 350 lekë) or the *bjata rosafa* (a plate of fried octopus, shrimp, squid, and fish; 700 lekë). Other seafood dishes 400-650 lekë. Open daily 10am-midnight. ❸

▓ **Qendra Stefan,** Rr. Hoxha Tahsin 1 (☎234 148). Breakfast options include omelettes (250-355 lekë), and pancakes (290-380 lekë), while lunch and dinner bring chicken (595-755 lekë), and sandwiches (290-490 lekë), all in the only smoke-free dining room in Tirana. Open M-Sa 8am-10pm. ❸

Efendy, Rr. Sami Frashëri 20 (☎246 624), serves up delicious Turkish and Ottoman specialties—suspiciously similar to Albanian specialties, just with different names. Try the *abanush* (miniature meatballs served over a hot tomato salsa; 900 lekë) and the rice pilaf with peanuts and currants (400 lekë). All entrees are accompanied by rosemary flatbread fresh from the oven. English menu. Open daily noon-midnight. ❺

◉ ♫ SIGHTS AND ENTERTAINMENT

Communism lives on in Tirana's stark architecture and gargantuan concrete city squares. Skënderbeg Square is no exception, adorned by the larger-than-life **statue** of the hero himself. The statue faces the enormous Socialist mosaic "Albania," adorning the front of the **National Historic Museum** (Muzek Historik Kombëtar), which offers a three-floor crash course in Albanian history from antiquity to modern times. (Open M-F 8am-1pm and 5-7pm, Sa 8am-1pm. 300 lekë, students 50 lekë. No cameras.) Next to the statue is the **Et'hem Bey Mosque,** built in 1793. The cantor on duty will offer to take you up into the dizzying minaret, and when you get to the top will ask you for a donation: 100-200 lekë is appropriate. Don't forget to remove your shoes before entering. Down Bul. Dëshmorët e Kombit on the left is the **National Art Gallery** (Galeria e Artere), displaying a permanent collection of iconography from the 13th to 19th centuries, plus an array of sculpted busts. (Open Tu-W and F-Su 9am-1pm and 5-8pm, Th 5-8pm. 100 lekë.)

The **Opera House** in Skënderbeg Sq. shows a program of opera, ballet, and classical music concerts. The program is posted to the left of the ticket office. (☎224 753. Open daily 9am-noon and 5-7pm.) For other cultural and artistic events, stop into the lobby of the Tirana International Hotel on Bul. Zogu I to pick up a free copy of the **Albanian Daily News,** an English daily with a program of cultural events on the back page. Outdoor cafes and bars overflow with young Tiranans south of the river between Bul. Dëshmorët e 4 Shkurtit and Rr. Sami Frashëri. The club of the moment is the **Cowboy Pub Manhattan,** Rr. Dëshmorët e 4 Shkurtit 7. Locals stand outside longingly trying to get a table after 8pm. (Open noon-2am.)

⟩ DAYTRIP FROM TIRANA

KRUJË

Skënderbeg's Krujë fortress is a 45km north of Tirana. Microbuses (1hr., 50 lekë) leave as soon as they fill from the corner where Mine Peza bends south. Avoid the ones going to Frushë Krujë; they'll leave you 16km from the action. The microbus makes a sharp left at the top of the hill in view of the castle. Get off there and follow the road to the castle. Skënderbeg Museum open Tu-W and F-Su 9am-1pm and 4-7pm, Th 9am-1pm. 200 lekë. No cameras. Ethnographic Museum open daily 9am-7pm. 100 lekë.

The restored ▓**castle of Krujë** embodies nationalism and hero-worship in the form of the **Skënderbeg Museum** (Muzeu Kombëtar Gjergj Kastrioti Skënderbeu), which tells Skënderbeg's story. Born Gjergj Kastrioti to a powerful family, the young

ALBANIA

Gjergj was given as a hostage to the Ottoman Sultan Murat. Schooled by the Turks, Kastrioti was given the name Iskënder (a form of Alexander) due to his excellent military skills, and later earned the rank of *bey* (governor), to become "Skënderbeg." In 1443, the Albanian hero abandoned the Ottomans, united the Albanian princes, and drove the Turks from Albania. The Turks attacked Krujë 24 times, and 24 times it withstood them. A daunting statue of the hero and his warrior-sister Donika Kastrioti adorns the lobby, and replicas of his helmet and sword are at the end of the second floor. One traditional Albanian house within the citadel has been converted into an excellent **Ethnographic Museum**, including a Turkish bath, an olive press, a spinning wheel, an iron and ceramic workshop, and a *raki* still.

DURRËS ☎(0)52

One of Albania's oldest cities, Durrës (pop. 85,000) provides the ancient charm lacking in 21st-century Tirana. The older section of the city feels like a small town, with quiet public squares, a bustling open-air market, and ancient ruins around every corner. The newer section of town, waterfront development stretching along the Adriatic coast, accommodates tourists flocking to the beaches.

The **train station,** Rr. Dëshmorëve 4 (☎235 86), sends trains to: **Pogradec** (6hr., 2 per day, 200 lekë); **Shkodër** (5hr., 2 per day, 135 lekë); **Tirana** (1hr., 9 per day, 50 lekë); **Vlorë** (6hr., 2 per day, 175 lekë). **Buses** leave from the lot adjacent to the train station to: **Sarandë** (7hr., 1 per day, 1000 lekë); **Shkodër** (5hr., 1 per day, 500 lekë); **Tirana** (1hr.; 1 per 5-30min., as they fill; 100 lekë). **Microbuses** to every destination can be caught farther up Rr. Dëshmorëve in front of the post office. They cost the same as large buses, leave more frequently, and are often quicker. **Ferries** leave for **Ancona, ITA** (19hr.; 4 per wk.; simple passage US$65-85, cabins US$70-140) and **Bari, ITA** (9hr.; July 17-Sept. 15 2-3 per day, Sept. 16-July 16 2 per day; simple passage €45-50, cabins €58-95). An **express ferry** also speeds for **Bari, ITA** (4hr., 1 per day, €70 simple passage only). Orange **public buses** (15 lekë) run every 5min. in summer, from the square in front of the post office to stops along the beachfront. **Taxis** lie are next to the buses in the same lot.

The **train** and **bus stations** lie on **Rr. Dëshmorëve,** the main street connecting the Old City with the beaches. Facing the buses, turn right and take the first left onto **Skënderbeg,** the street that runs down to the **ferry port** (1km). Take the second left to get to the **post office,** or continue farther up to get to the **Old City square** and shopping district. Tourist agencies selling **ferry tickets** *(bileta trageti)* are all along Skënderbeg and the port. For the only one that takes credit cards, take a left out of the train station onto Dëshmorëve, then take the second left just before Tirana Bank and walk one block to **Albtours,** Rr. Prokop Meksi. They also book flights and hotel rooms. (☎/fax 236 27; albtours@albaniaonline.net. Open M-Sa 8am-8pm. MC/V.) **Tirana Bank,** on Rr. e Dëshmorëve, just off the train and bus station square, **exchanges currency** and gives Visa **cash advances** for no commission. (☎247 66; fax 269 88. Open M-F 8am-2pm.) The **pharmacy, Farma Plus,** is opposite Albtours on Rr. Prokop Meksi. (Open daily 7am-9pm.) Log on at **Albania Online Marine Internet Center,** Rr. Prokop Meksi 4, just beyond the pharmacy. (☎254 65. 150 lekë per hr. Open daily 8:30am-11pm.) The **post office,** I Quemali 11, around the corner from Albtours, next to Hotel Durrës, offers **Western Union** services. Purchase **phone cards** (350-1100 lekë) inside for the public phones. (☎220 12. Open daily 7am-9pm.)

Hotel Florida ❶, Plazh Iliria 13, is a funky 500-room hotel along the waterfront. Take the orange public bus to the fourth stop. You'll see the turquoise-and-white hotel on the right. (☎/fax 600 30. Breakfast included. Reception 24hr. Singles 800-2350 lekë; doubles 1300-3160 lekë; triples 1600-4740 lekë; 4-person apartments 2500-6320 lekë.) **Hotel Pepeto ❸,** Mbriti Mynom 3, is just off the central square in the Old City. From the bus station, walk toward Albtours and go straight until you

ALBANIA

reach the square with the mosque. Just before the trees, turn left down the alley and follow it right—look for the Hotel sign on the pink building. Sparkling rooms with A/C and private bathrooms. (☎263 46. Breakfast and laundry included. Reception 24hr. Singles €30; doubles €40.)

The **open-air market** (open daily 7am-4pm) is in the block in front of Hotel Luli. The excellent **Supermarket Çameria,** Skënderbeg 4, is a block up Skënderbeg from the bus station. (☎225 83. Open 7:15am-11:30pm.) **Restaurant Piazza ❸,** Rr. Tavlantia 1, in the blue high rises to the right of the port, has the biggest seafood buffet (400 lekë per plate) in Albania. (☎069 209 4887. Open 10am-midnight.) Hotel Florida's **restaurant ❷,** Plazh Iliria 13, has stools and tables made of brightly painted tree trunks. (Meat and fish dishes 200-500 lekë. Open 10am-2:30am.)

SOUTHERN ALBANIA

The rugged mountains and dry, Mediterranean climate lend southern Albania a decidedly Greek feel. The same olive trees, the same hot, dry wind, and the same Greek ruins pepper the same spectacular, continuous coastline, but you'll find no crowds and no tourist infrastructure this side of the border. Instead you'll find a a neighbor's welcome here, but be prepared for death-defying bus rides along narrow, cart-path highways through the mountains.

GJIROKASTËR ☎(0)762

Breathtaking mountains, and an ominous stone citadel have inspired legends and great works of literature in the town of Gjirokastër. The birthplace of two of Albania's most famous sons—writer Ismail Kadare and dictator Enver Hoxha—the city has preserved an ancient feel in the older section that creeps up the hillside.

Roman ruins pepper the landscape of ancient Durrës. To get to the **Roman Amphitheater,** follow directions to the Hotel Pepeto (see above). Continue straight through the Old City square and turn right up the stairs just before entering the commercial district. The sprawling ruins appear on your left. (Open 9am-dusk. 200 lekë.) The **Archaeological Museum** is 500m down from the port in the opposite direction from the train station. Inside, you'll find an endless collection of Greek, Roman, Venetian, and Ottoman artifacts. English placards tell the history of the town. The **Citadel** above the city, built between the 6th and 13th centuries, has one central entrance. The gates open to a menacing arcade, spookily lit and flanked by enormous WWII guns captured from German and Italian invaders. To get to the **Ethnographic Museum,** walk uphill from the post office and take the first right; bear right at the iron gates past the small grocery store. If no one is there, have a neighbor call the caretaker at home (☎7206. Museum 200 lekë). The Ethnographic Museum sits on the foundation of **Enver Hoxha's birth house,** and has also suffered tribulations. Hoxha was born here in 1908. In 1916, the house burned to the ground and was not reconstructed until 1966. In 1997, when operating as the museum, a random grenade destroyed most of the artifacts and seriously damaged the structure. For an in-depth tour of the region, try contacting **Florenc Mene** (☎069 226 4941), a freelance tour guide; he will give you his perspective in flawless English.

Buses run daily to **Sarandë** (2hr., 7:30 and 9am, 200 lekë) and **Tirana** (7hr.; 5, 7, and 8am; 800 lekë). Street names exist in Gjirokastër, but no locals know them. Roads thwart the traveler by twisting into bizarre contortions and there are no maps of the town. One main road stretches from the corner near the bus stop past **Tirana Bank** (☎9705; fax 9707; open M-F 8:30am-3pm), at the bottom of the hill, which **exchanges currency** for no commission and gives V **cash advances,** and through the **market** (open daily 8am-1pm) to a traffic circle. At the traffic circle, the road that forks to the left of the **pharmacy** (Sopoti Farmaci; ☎7726; open M-F 8am-

10pm, Sa 8am-2pm, Su 4pm-10pm) continues at a daunting grade past the **post office** (☎/fax 2239; open M-Sa 8am-noon and 1:30-3:30pm) and **telephone office** (☎/fax 2239; open M-Sa 8am-3pm) on the right.

📖**Drago Kalemi ❸**, an unassuming man-about-town and former English teacher, renovated a 200-year-old Albanian house into a hotel adding 21st-century amenities like TV and central heating. The guest house is just down the street from Haxhi Kotoni (see below)—a taxi driver will know where to go. (☎3724; ☎/fax 7260. Simple breakfast included. Doubles €30.) **Haxhi Kotoni ❶** and his family used to run a small B&B at the top of the hill. Walk up the main road and take the first right at the post office, follow the road around to the right, then take the sharp left to cut back up the hill 20m on the right. Ask a taxi driver to take you to "HAHDJ-ee koh-TOH-nee"—he'll know where to go. Three doubles have private showers and 24hr. hot water. (Breakfast included. €10.) **Fantazia ❸** is the best place to catch the Gjirokastër breeze, a view of the city below, and delicious Italian food. From the Old Town crossroads, turn your back to the citadel and walk straight. Bear left up the ramp; Fantazia is 50m up on your left, on the far side. (☎6991. Pasta 250-420 lekë. Pizza 430-600 lekë. Open daily noon-midnight.)

SARANDË
☎(0)862

Warmed by Ionian breezes, the beach resort town of Sarandë (sah-RAHND) enjoys mild weather year-round. In the summer months, Albanians from across the country flock to its beaches and cafes. Yet beaches aren't Sarandë's only attraction; the UNESCO-protected Greek settlement of 📖**Butrint**, 24km south of Sarandë, is one of archaeology's best-kept secrets—layers of civilization, from the 6th century BC to the AD 19th century, rise from the soil. The best way to reach Butrint is by taxi (45min., round-trip €15 plus waiting time). There are no English signs, but the arrows lead you on a path through the ruins. To access the 19th-century Turkish fortress, take a free, 1min. ride on the ferry stationed across from the entrance to the ruins. (Entrance 700 lekë. Open daily 8:30am-dusk.)

Buses run to **Durrës** (7hr., 7:30 and 9am, 900 lekë); **Gjirokastër** (2hr., 6 and 8:15am, 200 lekë); Tirana (8hr., 5 per day, 1000 lekë). Facing the waterfront from the street in front of the bus station, there are four nameless main roads that run parallel to the water to the left, and three to the right. (The first is directly behind you.) To get to the port, walk downhill from the bus station and turn right just before the steps to the waterfront. Take the first left, walk one block and turn right, then follow the road to the intersection and turn left. **Albtours**, on the first street down to the left, runs English **tours** of Sarandë and Butrint, sells **ferry tickets** to **Corfu, GCE**, and books **private rooms ❶** (300 lekë), which are the best deal in town. (☎2447. Open M-Sa 8am-2pm and 4-10pm, Su 9am-noon and 6-10pm.)

On the fourth street down to the left, **Paradise's ❹** three-level, indoor-and-rooftop restaurant is also the site of an eponymous cafe, the center of the local singles scene. (☎3292. Meat and seafood dishes 560-920 lekë. Open 7am-midnight.) For a day and night party scene, head to **Corfu, GCE**, then catch the morning boat back. For more info on Corfu, see *Let's Go: Greece*.

ALBANIA

BELARUS (БЕЛАРУСЬ)

Still clinging to its Soviet past, Belarus is the unwanted stepchild of Mother Russia. A testament to the glory days of the Soviet Union, ubiquitous concrete highrises dominate Belarus's sprawling urban landscapes, while the untouched villages of the countryside call back to an earlier period of agricultural beauty and tranquility. For those willing to endure the difficulties of travel and yards of bureaucratic red tape, Belarus presents a unique look at a people in transition.

HISTORY

DIVIDED AND CONQUERED. Belarus was one of the first areas settled by the **Slavs,** and by AD 980 achieved statehood under the Polotsk principality; by the mid-1000s it was ruled by **Kyivan Rus,** the precursor of Russia and Ukraine. When the Mongols sacked Kyiv in 1240, they destroyed nascent Belarusian settlements and cleared the way for the **Duchy of Lithuania,** which ruled until the 1386 creation of the **Polish-Lithuanian Commonwealth.** Under the new empire, Belarus's sense of national identity grew, eventually leading to the 1648 Cossack rebellion. During the 1812 Franco-Russian War, Belarusians fought on both sides. In the late 18th century, the **First and Second Partitions of Poland** (see **Poland: History,** p. 502) handed the territory over to Russia.

MORE OF THE SAME. WWI brought heavy fighting to the region, so it was fitting that **Brest-Litovsk** (see p. 93) hosted the 1918 treaty that got Russia out of the war—and ceded Belarus to **Germany.** The treaty lasted only a few months, but it was long enough for Belarus to declare **independence.** The Poles and Bolsheviks later divided the region and Belarus became a charter member of the **USSR** in 1922.

FACTS AND FIGURES

OFFICIAL NAME: Republic of Belarus

CAPITAL: Minsk (pop. 1.8 million)

POPULATION: 10.3 million (81% Belarusian, 11.5% Russian, 7.5% other)

LANGUAGE: Belarusian, Russian

CURRENCY: 1 Belarusian ruble (BR) = 100 kopeks

RELIGION: 80% Orthodox Christian, 20% other

LAND AREA: 207,600km²

CLIMATE: Continental and maritime

GEOGRAPHY: Plains, marshes

BORDERS: Latvia, Lithuania, Poland, Russia, Ukraine

ECONOMY: 13% Agriculture, 42% Industry, 45% Services

GDP: US$8200 per capita

COUNTRY CODE: 375

INTERNATIONAL DIALING PREFIX: 8-10

Belarus

BACK FROM THE ASHES. The confrontation between Germany and Russia in **WWII** destroyed most of Minsk, and according to Belarus's government, killed 25% of the country's population. Belarus quickly recovered after the war and **Minsk,** the model Soviet city, was rebuilt in grand Stalinist style.

THE FALLOUT... The 1986 nuclear power plant explosion at **Chernobyl** spewed radioactive material across southern Belarus. The long-term effects of the country's contamination have surfaced in the form of childhood thyroid cancer.

...THEN THE FALL. Content with the communist system, Belarus grudgingly declared sovereignty on July 27, 1990 and independence on August 25, 1991. Despite adopting a new constitution on March 15, 1994, Belarus remains an authoritarian state. The fledgling republic has found a security blanket in the **Commonwealth of Independent States** (CIS), a pledge of devotion between 12 ex-Soviet states, including Russia and Ukraine (see also Russia: History, p. 656).

TODAY. President **Aleksandr Lukashenka** has garnered much criticism from the West as he has resorted to **suppressing the media** and **arresting dissenters** to maintain power. On December 8, 1999 Belarus and Russia signed an accord promising future economic integration and possibly political union. In June 2002, however, President Putin of Russia again halted the process, accusing Lukashenka of trying to resurrect the Soviet Union. In 2004 Belarus re-entered the international spotlight when the Council of Europe charged the country with **human rights violations** after a number of political opposition leaders had been abducted.

PEOPLE AND CULTURE

LANGUAGE

Most Belarusians speak **Russian** and very rarely Belarusian (see the **Cyrillic Alphabet**, p. 52, and **Glossary: Russian,** p. 958). The only important differences are that the Cyrillic letter "г," which is pronounced "g" in Russian, is transliterated as "h" in Belarusian ("г" is "g"), and that "i" is used instead of the Russian letter "и." The rarely seen letter "ў" is pronounced "w." *Let's Go* lists place names in Belarusian in deference to the official line, but in order to be understood, you'll have to replace "h" with a "g" sound ("Hrodna" is more commonly pronounced "Grodno").

FOOD AND DRINK

BELARUS	❶	❷	❸	❹	❺
FOOD	under US$2	US$2-5	US$6-10	US$11-20	over US$20

Belarusian cuisine consists of what farmers can either grow or fatten: potatoes, wheat, chicken, and pork. Local favorites include *draneki* (дранеки; potato pancakes). Most desserts involve fruit or honey. The favorite Belarusian drink is bread-based *kvas* (квас), which is sold at stores or from huge kegs on the street.

CUSTOMS AND ETIQUETTE

On **public transportation,** it's polite for women to give their seats to elderly or pregnant women. Men should yield seats to all women. Don't wear **shorts** in public. Visiting a museum in **sandals** is regarded as disrespectful. Locals claim that criminals spot tourists by their sloppy appearances. In restaurants, **tip** 5-10% if it isn't in the bill already. Don't tip taxi drivers. Bargain only at markets.

THE ARTS

Domination by myriad rulers put off Belarus's literary development until the 15th century, when **Frantsishek Skaryna** translated the Bible into Old Church Slavonic. Literature revived in the 18th century with the poet and songwriter **Jan Chachot** (writing in Polish) and later with **Vincent Dunin,** who founded the **New Belarusian Literature.** After the death of Stalin, prose and poetry were finally able to flourish. Today's major figures include poets **Pimen Pachanka** and **Arkady Kalyashov** and novelists **Yanka Bryl** and **Ivan Shamyakin.** Other figures include the female poet and writer **Volha Ipatova** and historian **Jan Zaprudnik.**

Until the 20th century, Belarusian **art** consisted of icon painting; in the 17th century, artists blended Orthodox **iconography** with Western European techniques. In the 1920s Belarusian fine art emerged with abstractionist **Kazimir Malevich** and sculptor **Ossip Zadkine.** Contemporary artists include Belarusian-French painter and sculptor **Pinchus Kremegne** and artist **Marc Chagall.**

HOLIDAYS AND FESTIVALS

NATIONAL HOLIDAYS IN 2005	
January 1 New Year's Day	**May 1** Labor Day
January 7 Orthodox Christmas	**May 9** Victory Day and Mother's Day
January 14 Old (Orthodox) New Year	**July 3** Independence Day
March 15 Constitution Day	**November 2** Dzyady (Remembrance Day)
May 1 Easter	**November 7** October Revolution Day

ADDITIONAL RESOURCES

Belarus: A Denationalized Nation, by David R. Marples (1999). A look at the history of modern Belarus with a focus on post-USSR economy and politics.

Colours of the Native Country: Stories by Belarusian Writers (1972). A collection of 19 short stories by Belarusian authors.

BELARUS ESSENTIALS

ENTRANCE REQUIREMENTS

Passport: Required of all travelers. Must be valid 3 months before intended stay.

Visa: Required of all travelers.

Letter of Invitation: Required of all travelers.

Inoculations: Recommended up-to-date on DTaP (diphtheria, tetanus, and pertussis), Hepatitis A, Hepatitis B, MMR (measles, mumps, and rubella), Polio booster, and Typhoid.

Medical Insurance Requirement: Travelers to Belarus must have an insurance certificate from an approved insurance company, valid within Belarus territory. Such a policy can be purchased at the Belarusian border.

International Driving Permit: Required of most foreigners planning to drive.

DOCUMENTS AND FORMALITIES

EMBASSIES AND CONSULATES

Embassies and consulates of other countries in Belarus are all in **Minsk** (see p. 87). Belarus's embassies and consulates abroad include:

Canada: 130 Albert St. Ste. 600, **Ottawa,** ON K1P 5G4 (☎203-233-9994; fax 233-8500).

UK: 6 Kensington Ct., **London,** W8 5DL (☎20 7937 3288, visa section 6641 0140; fax 7361 0005).

US: 1619 New Hampshire Ave. NW, **Washington D.C.** 20009 (☎202-986-1606; www.belarusembassy.org).

VISA AND ENTRY INFORMATION

To visit Belarus, you must secure an invitation, a visa, and medical insurance—an expensive and head-spinning process. If you have an acquaintance in Belarus who can provide you with an official invitation, you may obtain a single-entry (5-day service US$100, next business day US$180); double-entry (5-day processing US$200, next day US$380); triple entry (5-day service US$300, next day US$580); or multiple entry (5-day service $350). Obtain a visa at an embassy or consulate by submitting your passport, the application, a check or money order, and a recent professional passport photograph. **Belintourist** (www.belintourist.by), the country's official tourism office, offers visa support. Those without Belarusian friends can turn to **Alatan Tour** (www.alatantour.com) or **SMOK Travel** (www.smok-travel.com) for visa invitations and support services. Transit visas (US$40), valid for 48hr., are issued at a consulate and at the border. Belarus requires all foreign nationals to either have documentation of **medical insurance** issued by an approved company or to purchase insurance at the port of entry (US$1 for a one-day stay, US $15 for 30 days, US$28 for 60 days, and up to US$85 for a year).

 NO MORE STICKY FINGERS. While giving a *vzyat* (bribe) used to be a common and accepted practice, bribery is illegal in Belarus. Officials are rewarded for turning in those who to try to bribe them. The best way to prevent complications when passing through customs is to keep a low profile and avoid speaking Russian, which may provoke harsh questioning from officials.

GETTING AROUND

Belavia, Belarus's national airline flies into Minsk from many European capitals. **Lufthansa** has daily direct flights from Frankfurt. Minsk's airport, **Minsk-II,** recently installed technology enabling it to meet international safety guidelines. **Trains** and **buses** run between Minsk and most European capitals and to other cities in Belarus, the Baltic states, and the CIS. Local buses are often poorly maintained and crowded. Purchase tickets at kiosks or from the driver and punch them on board. **Taxis** may be poorly maintained; rates vary widely and drivers may overcharge. **Drivers** should enter Belarus from Western Europe via the E30 highway. US citizens may drive in Belarus for up to six months with a US license.

TOURIST SERVICES AND MONEY

Belinturist (Белитурист) is helpful and often the only resource. Hotel Belarus in Minsk has a private travel agency. The **Belarusian ruble** (BR) is the national currency and comes in denominations of 1, 5, 10, 20, 50, 100, 500, 1000, 5000, and 10,000. Currency is in the form of paper bills; there are no coins. Exchange rates from the euro and US$ are rising constantly. Monetary exchanges can be made in most banks and hotels in major cities, but currency other than Russian rubles, euros, or US$ is difficult to exchange. **Traveler's checks** are rarely accepted. **ATMs** can be found in hotels, train stations, and airports.

HEALTH AND SAFETY

 EMERGENCY NUMBERS: Police: ☎02 **Fire:** ☎01 **Ambulance:** ☎003

Medical care in Belarus is inadequate. There is a severe shortage of basic health supplies like antibiotics, vaccines, and anesthetics. In a medical emergency, try to get to a more developed country (an evacuation to the US costs up to US$50,000). Belarus was affected by the 1986 **Chernobyl** accident more than any other region. Avoid cheap **dairy products,** which may come from contaminated areas, and **mush-**

rooms and **berries,** which collect radioactivity. Drink **bottled water. Toilet paper** is available in most supermarkets, but not in most public toilets. **Condoms, medications,** and **feminine hygiene** supplies from the West are becoming available, but bring your own in case. In an emergency, your embassy is a better bet than the police. Stay clear of dodgy nightclubs, which may be run by the **mafia.** Belarus is ethnically homogenous, and people with dark skin may experience **discrimination. Homosexuality** is still looked down upon in Belarus; use discretion at all times.

ACCOMMODATIONS

BELARUS	❶	❷	❸	❹	❺
ACCOM.	under US$15	US$15-30	US$30-50	US$50-70	over US$75

Hotels are generally expensive and run-down. Keep receipts from hotels; you might have to show them to the authorities to avoid fines when leaving Belarus. *Babushki* (old women; literally "grandmother") sometimes offer **private rooms** at train stations, but foreigners can legally stay only in hotels. Camping facilities in Belarus are extremely limited, but camping is permitted in the countryside.

KEEPING IN TOUCH

Avoid the **mail** system; it is extremely unreliable. **Local calls** require tokens, sold at kiosks, or magnetic cards (1500BR and up), available at the post office and some hotels. Place **international calls** at the telephone office and pay up front in cash. (Calls to the US and Western Europe US$1-3 per min.) International access numbers include: **AT&T Direct** (☎8800 101), **MCI WorldPhone** (☎8800 104), **NZ Direct** (☎8800 641). Dialing from the **Gomel** and **Mogilev** regions requires the insertion of 10 after the first 8. **Email** is the easiest and cheapest way to communicate with the outside world. Internet cafes are rare; check the local post office for access.

MINSK (MIHCK) ☎(8)017

For a true Soviet city, skip Moscow and head straight to Minsk (pop. 1,800,000). Having been almost completely destroyed in WWII, the city was rebuilt in Stalinist style, with a broad central avenue and imposing gray concrete buildings. Though some may find it dreary, Minsk is serenely drab and safe compared to many other former Soviet capitals, due in large part to President Lukashenka's recent reforms.

▐ TRANSPORTATION

Flights: General Info ☎006. **Minsk-II** (☎279 13 00) is the main airport. Buses run to the central bus station (1hr., every hr., 2000BR). From the bus station, walk next door to the train station and cross the street to catch the Metro (M-blue: pl. Nezalezhnastsi; Незалежнасцi). Taxis should cost US$20 to the city center; don't pay above US$30 without a fight. To: **Moscow** (3 per day, $85); **Kaliningrad** (2 per day, $56); **Kiev** (M, W, F 1 per day, $68). If arriving at **Minsk-I** (☎222 54 76), located south of downtown, take bus #100 to the Metro (M-blue: Nezalezhnastsi; Незалежнасцi)

Trains: Chigunachny Vokzal (Чыгуначны Вокзал), Privakzalnaya pl. (info ☎005). M-blue: Nezalezhnastsi pl. (Незалежнасцi). Tickets sold on the 1st fl. of the train station, or purchase advance tickets at **Belinturist** (☎226 91 90). To: **Brest** (3-5hr., 8 per day, 15,000BR); **Hrodna** (6-9hr., 2-3 per day, 19,000BR); **Kyiv, UKR** (12hr., 9:07pm, 42,000BR); **Moscow, RUS** (10-11hr., 15 per day, 38,000BR); **St. Petersburg, RUS** (16hr., 2 per day, 41,350BR); **Vilnius, LIT** (4hr., 3 per day, 25,000BR).

BELARUS

Buses: Avtovakzal Tsentralny (Автовакзал Центральны), Babruyskaya vul. 6 (Бабруйская; ☎227 37 25, info 004). M-blue: pl. Nezalezhnastsi (Незалежнасці). Next to the train station. Buses run to: **Hrodna** (4-5hr., 2-3 per hr., 22,000BR); **Brest** (4½hr., 2 per day, 15,000BR); **Białystok, POL** (8hr., 2 per day, 38,000BR); **Vilnius, LIT** (4hr., 4 per day, 20,000BR). Buy tickets to non-CIS countries on the 2nd fl. Open M-F 5am-1am, Sa 5am-11pm, Su 5am-5pm.

Public Transportation: The **Metro, buses, trolleybuses,** and **trams** (250BR) run 5:30am-1am. The Metro consists of 2 lines, blue (#1) and red (#2), which meet at the center in Kastrytchinskaya and Kupalavskaya. Stops are announced in Belarusian but are sometimes posted in Russian on platforms. 10-day passes are available for the Metro (4450BR) and for all combinations of the other 3 forms of public transport The easiest solution is to pay 10,590BR for a 10-day pass for all forms of public transport.

Taxis: ☎081 or 087.

TIP   **TAXI, TAXI!**   Many taxis in Belarus do not have meters. To avoid getting ripped off, agree on a price beforehand. A ride shouldn't cost more than US$2 per 10min. If the driver pulls over on the way to "add oil" and look under the hood, be watchful: the meter may start to run considerably faster.

ORIENTATION AND PRACTICAL INFORMATION

The center of town lies in the 3km between northeastern **pl. Peramohi** (Перамоні) and southwestern **pl. Nezalezhnastsi** (Незалежнасці; Independence Square), with the city's main street, **pr. Frantsishka Skaryny** (Францішка Скарыны), connecting the two. **Pr. Masherava** (Машэрава), which turns into **vul. Lenina** (Леніна) after pl. Svabody, runs perpendicular to pr. F. Skaryny. The **Svislach River** divides the city, with most of the attractions located on the southwest bank. The **train station** sits behind **Privakzalnaya pl.** (Прівакзальная). To get to the center of town, walk up Leningradskaya vul. from the square and go left on Sverdlova (Свердлова) to reach pl. Nezalezhnastsi, then take a right and continue down pr. F. Skaryny.

Tourist Office: Belinturist (Белінтуріст), pr. Masherava 19 (☎226 90 56; www.belin-tourist.by), next to Gastsinitsa Yubileny. M-red: Nyamiha. Plane and train tickets sold on 1st fl. Provides visa support and extensions, airport transfers (US$15), hotel bookings, and guided tours of Minsk and outlying areas (from US$25). Open M-Sa 8am-1pm.

Passport Office: All foreigners must register their visas in Minsk. If you stay at a hotel, your visa will be registered there, which may require a small additional fee. If you are not staying at a hotel, you must register your visa at the **OVIR** (ОВИР), pr. Frantsishka Skaryny 48b, room 18 (☎231 91 74), located near the concert hall, 2 courtyards behind Frantsishka Skaryny 48; it's behind the building through the arch as you walk into the courtyard. M-blue: Yakuba Kolasa. Open Tu 10am-4pm, W and F 10am-1pm.

Embassies: Poland, Rumiancew 6 (☎288 23 21; fax 236 49 92). **Russia,** Staravilen-skaya vul. 48 (Старавіленская; ☎283 28 34, visas 222 49 85; fax 250 36 64). Open M-F 8:30am-1pm and 2-5:30pm. **UK,** vul. Karla Marksa 37 (Карла Маркса; ☎210 59 20; fax 229 23 11). Open M-F 9am-1pm and 2-5:30pm. **US,** Staravilenskaya vul. 46 (☎210 12 83; fax 234 78 53), next door to the Russian Embassy. Entrance on vul. Comunistichnaya. Open M-F 8:30am-5:30pm.

Currency Exchange: Look for the ubiquitous "Обмен Валюты" signs. Cash **AmEx Traveler's Cheques** at the **American Express** office, 40 pr. Frantsishka Skaryny. Open M-F 9am-6pm, Sa-Su 10am-4pm. **ATMs** can be found inside large stores, in the train station, and outside Hotel Yubileynaya, Masherava 19.

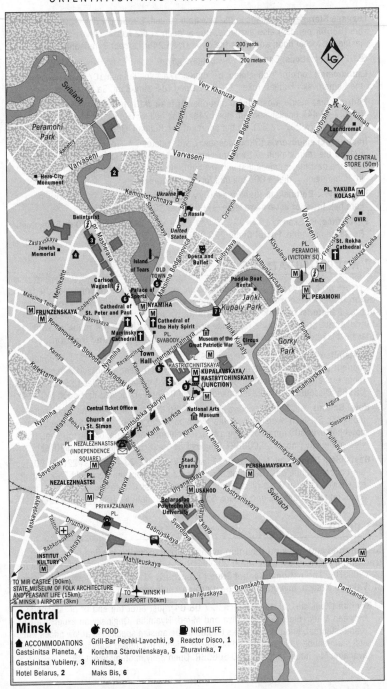

BELARUS

Central Minsk

🏕 FOOD

Grill-Bar Pechki-Lavochki, **9**
Korchma Starovilenskaya, **5**
Krinitsa, **8**
Maks Bis, **6**

■ NIGHTLIFE

Reactor Disco, **1**
Zhuravinka, **7**

♠ ACCOMMODATIONS

Gastsinitsa Planeta, **4**
Gastsinitsa Yubileny, **3**
Hotel Belarus, **2**

Luggage Storage: Downstairs in the new train station. 890BR per day. Soviet-style lockers (535BR per day) also available. Buy a token at the *kassa*, choose a combination inside the locker door, and close the door. Open 24hr., except 3-4am and 1-2pm.

GLBT Organizations: Check out www.belgays.gay.ru.

Laundromat: Look for "прачечная" or "химчистка." Vul. Kulman 10/17 (Кульман) near the Kamarovskiy Market. Token 1120BR. Open Tu-F 8am-8pm, Sa 8am-5pm.

Pharmacies: Inside most **Metro** stations. **Apteka #13,** pr. Frantsishka Skaryny 16 (☎227 48 44). English spoken. Open 24hr., ring bell for late-night service. **Nordin,** Kuybyshava 40 (☎237 32 67), on the corner of vul. Kulman. Open 24hr.

Hospital: Ekomedservis (Экомедсервис), vul. Talstoho 4 (Толстого; ☎207 74 74). Behind the train station exit on Druzhnaya vul. (Дружная). Take the 1st left and walk until the next major crossing at vul. Talstoho; the clinic is across the street to the right. In an emergency, dial ☎003 toll free for an **ambulance.**

Telephones: Beltelekom (Белтелеком), vul. Engelsa 14 (☎219 06 79; www.beltelecom.by). **Internet** access available. 1200BR per 30min. Open 24hr.

Post Office: Pr. Skaryny 10 (☎227 77 71). Open M-Sa 8am-8pm, Su 10am-5pm. **Poste Restante** available. **Postal Code:** 220 050.

ACCOMMODATIONS

There are no hostels or budget accommodations in Minsk. Old women at the train station offer private rooms, but foreigners should stick to hotels. Travel agencies such as **Belinturist** can take care of booking rooms, sometimes at a discount. The standard rate at Soviet-style high-rise hotels is about US$35 per night for tourists. Most hotels and rooms look the same, so choose by on price and location.

Gastsinitsa Yubileny, pr. Masherava 19 (☎226 90 24; fax 226 91 71). Yubileny is modern and centrally located, with a plush lobby and clean rooms. ATM outside; currency exchange in the lobby. Private bath. Breakfast included. Singles US$50; doubles US$65. Discounts available if booked through Belinturist, located next door. MC/V. ❹

Hotel Belarus, vul. Storozhevskaya 15 (☎209 76 93; www.hotel-belarus.com). Located along the Svislach riverside near the Nyamiha metro station, this grandiose 22-story hotel has over 500 rooms of varying size. Restaurant Panorama, on the top floor, has a view of the city (meals 30,000BR). Singles US$46-$86; doubles US$60-$90. ❹

Gastsinitsa Planeta, pr. Masherava 31 (☎226 78 53 or 223 78 55; fax 226 77 80), up the central avenue past Gastsinitsa Yubileny, across from the Peramohi Park. Though expensive, a stay at Gastsinitsa Planeta includes access to a casino, an outdoor cafe, a restaurant with dancing, and 2 bars. Singles US$89; doubles US$107. MC/V. ❺

FOOD

Restaurants and cafes on the main avenues are expensive, while meals at nearby traditional eateries are well under 20,000BR. Sidewalk food stands sells snacks for 500-2000BR. The national **Central Store** (Tsentralny Magazin; pr. Skaryny 23), near M: Yakuba Kolasa, has one of the best grocery selections in Minsk.

Krinitsa (Криница), ul. Lenina 2 (☎227 08 04), just after the end of pr. Masherava, between M-red/blue: Kupalavskaya and M-red: Nyamiha. Originally an expensive German restaurant, Krinitsa now offers traditional Belarusian specialties at low prices while still maintaining its high standard of service. Nightly live music starting 8pm. Set menu available M-F noon-4pm for 5600-6660BR. Open daily noon-midnight. ❷

Grill-Bar Pechki-Lavochki (Печки-Лавочки), Frantsishka Skaryny 22 (☎227 78 79). M-red/blue: pl. Kastrytch-itskaya. You can watch the chef prepare your food on the flaming grill. For an intriguingly inebriating experience, try the 42-proof "honey drink" with the "rabbit in beer" entree. Entrees 8000-25,000BR. Open daily 8am-midnight. ❸

Korchma Starovilenskaya (Корчма Старовиленская), Starovilenskaya 2. (☎289 37 54) M: Nyamiha. In the Old Town, this cosmopolitan eatery serves Belarusian and Italian dishes with South American wines. Entrees 13,000-24,000BR. Open daily 9am-11pm. ❸

Maks Bis (Макс Бис), pr. Masherava 1, next to the Metro exit and Na Nyamiha mall. M-red: Nyamiha. A fast-food version of Belarusian cuisine. Sandwiches 1700-3340BR, salads 610-2100BR. Open daily 8am-11pm. ❶

👁 🏛 SIGHTS AND MUSEUMS

INDEPENDENCE SQUARE. Formerly named Ploshchad Lenina, Independence Square (Площадь Незалежнасци; Ploshchad Nezalezhnastsi) is one of the main squares of Minsk, located at the end of pr. Skaryny. A statue of **St. Simon** slaying a dragon stands before the crimson church dedicated to the saint. *(Savetskaya 15. M-blue: Nezalezhnastsi. Just north of the train station.)*

WORLD WAR II MEMORIALS. A 40m **obelisk** in Ploshchad Peramohi (Victory Square) celebrates the defeat of the German army in WWII. *(M-red: pl. Peramohi; пл. Перамогі.)* North of Svislach Island stands the **Minsk Hero-City Monument.** The **Jewish Memorial** remembers the 5000 Jews murdered by the Nazis here in 1942. *(M-blue: Frunzenskaya; Фрунзенская).* Exit the Metro onto vul. Melnikayte; the memorial is on the left. Turn left on Masherova to find the Hero-City Monument.) The most recent memorial is the **"Island of Tears"** in the Svislach river, a manmade island dedicated to the fallen soldiers of the Soviet war in Afghanistan. *(M: Nyamiha.)*

STATE MUSEUM OF FOLK ARCHITECTURE AND PEASANT LIFE. The museum (Белорусский Государственный Музей Народой Архитектуры и Бута; Belorusskiy Gosudarstvennyy Muzey Narodnoy Arkhitektury i Byta) contains a collection of nail-less 17th-century houses and churches, including one featured in the work of Belarusian-born painter Marc Chagall. Guide (50,000BR) recommended. *(Near the village Azyatso (Азяцо). ☎506 53 81. M-blue: Institut Kultury. Take minibus #81 to Gorodishe and mention "muzey," pronounced MOO-zay, to the driver. Open Tu-Sa 10am-4:30pm. 10,000BR.)*

WHAT A DUMP

While certain venues attract a throng of tourists for beautiful artwork or serene landscape, the park outside the Yanki Kupala National Theater is famous for a striking reason: though known for its porcelain, the house's use of it has little to do with fanciful plates or rare tea-sets. Instead the park is home to the most intimate of hearths, which boasts its own, unique take on porcelain pageantry.

In the 19th century, wealthy residents of Minsk flaunted their power and prestige by building extravagant mansions throughout the city. According to local lore, one wealthy resident of Minsk developed a particularly strong dislike for another powerful citizen. In a clever show of contempt, he commissioned a scale model of his adversary's mansion right down to the windows and the shutters, and made the entire miniature house into a toilet.

The toilet house is located in the park next to the Yanki Kupala National Theater, across from pl. Kastrytchnitskaya, between pr. Skaryny and vul. Karla Marksa near M: red/blue Kupalavskaya/Kastrytchnitskaya. The house still functions as a regular public toilet (the windows are covered up from inside), with separate entrances for men and women. For a mere 250BR, you can enter the little mansion and pay your respects.

NATIONAL ART MUSEUM. The museum (Нацыянальны Мастацкі Музей Распублікі Беларусь; Natsyanalny Mastatski Muzey Raspubliki Belarus) exhibits Russian and Belarusian artwork. *(Pr. Lenina 20. M-red/blue: Kastrytchnitskaya.* ☎ *227 56 72. Open Su-M and W-Sa 11am-7pm. Ticket offices closes at 6:30pm. 5000BR.)*

MUSEUM OF THE GREAT PATRIOTIC WAR. Glorifying the heroic efforts of the Soviet Army during WWII, this museum (Музей Велікой Отечественной Войны; Muzey Velikoy Otechestvennoy Voyny) also paints at suitably grim and realistic picture of the war in which Belarus lost 25% of its population. *(Pr. Skaryny 25a. M-red/blue: Kastrytchnitskaya.* ☎ *227 56 11. Open Tu-Su 10am-6pm; ticket office closes at 5pm. 3000BR.)* Outside, behind the museum, is a display of tanks and planes. *(Free.)*

🎵🎭 ENTERTAINMENT AND NIGHTLIFE

Small bars line pl. Skaryny and vul. Karla Marksa. For more nightlife information, consult *What and Where in Minsk*, available at major hotels and tourist centers.

National Opera and Ballet Theater, vul. Paryzhskai Kamuny 1 (Парыжскай Камуны; ☎ 234 06 66). M-red: Nyamiha. Exit the Metro on Maksima Bagdanovica; the theater is on the right. With a variety of international plays and performances (1000-10,000BR), the theater has been the artistic highlight of Minsk since the 1930s. Opera season runs late Sept.-May. Purchase advance tickets from the Central Ticket Office, pr. Skaryny 13 (open M-F 9:30am-8pm, Sa 10am-7pm, Su noon-5pm) or at the theater. Open Tu-Su 11:30am-7:30pm; ticket office Tu-Su noon-3pm and 4-8pm. Opera 1000-6000BR.

Minsk Circus, pr. Frantsishka Skaryny 32 (☎ 227 22 45). M-blue: pl. Peramohi (Перамогі). Shows on M-F 7pm, Sa 3pm and 7pm, Su 11:30am, 3pm, 7pm. Perhaps the most entertaining of the Soviet legacies left in Minsk. Tickets 3000-14,500BR; under 5 free. Box office open daily 9am-8pm.

Reactor Disco, vul. Very Kharuzay, 29 (288 61 60). Up the street from M-blue: Pl. Yakuba Kolasa. Assorted music, from Brazilian techno to Russian ballads. Crazed atmosphere and occasional racy contests with audience participation. Cover 2000-12,000BR. Open daily noon-6am. Attached strip club, cover 20,000BR.

Zhuravinka Night Club (Журавинка), vul. Janki Kupaly 25 (Янкі Купалы; ☎ 206 68 86). M-red: Nyamiha or M-blue: Kastrychnitskaya. Part of a large entertainment complex that includes a casino. Cover starts at 20,000BR. Drinks 4000BR. Open daily 8:30pm-late.

🎿 DAYTRIP FROM MINSK

MIR CASTLE

Take a bus from Minsk to Mir (2hr., 5500BR), and ask the bus driver to drop you off at Mirski Zamak (Мирски Эамак). Open W-Su. Guided tours 10,000BR. Museum 5000BR.

Perched in the lonely countryside, **Mir Castle** (Мир) was the first Belarusian monument to appear on UNESCO's World Cultural Heritage list. Duke Ilich began building the Gothic-style castle in the early 16th century. The Radzivil family, taking over in 1568, preferred the ways of the Renaissance and finished the job accordingly. Despite its earthen ramparts and water moat, the castle was severely damaged several times by warfare, including by Napoleon's troops in 1812. Climb the tall and tortuous stairs for a glimpse into the castle's past: a small **museum**, located in one of the five towers, displays relics of yore, including weapons and traditionally embroidered garments. The tower affords a great view of the countryside through the shooting holes. Guided tours are recommended, as the true beauty of the castle is its rich history. Minsk's Belinturist and Vneshintourist offer reasonably priced group daytrips (see **Practical Information: Tourist Office**, p. 88)

BREST (БРЭСТ)   ☎(8)016

Located in the southwest corner of Belarus, near the Polish border, Brest's high-light is its historic fortress, which lies between the Bug and Mukhavets Rivers.

⬛🔌 TRANSPORTATION AND PRACTICAL INFORMATION. The **train station** (☎27 32 77), north of vul. Ardzhanikidze, is the main border crossing for trains run-ning between Moscow and Warsaw. **Trains** to: **Minsk** (4½hr., 12 per day, 20,000BR); **Kyiv**, UKR (15hr., odd-numbered days 11:58pm, 44,000BR); **Warsaw**, POL (4hr., 4 per day, 55,000BR). To get to the city center from the train station, face the tracks next to the departure hall, turn right and walk to the end of the platform, then go up the steps and turn left onto the bridge. Continue down the street and you will reach pl. Lenina. The **bus station** is on the corner of vul. Kuybyshava (Куйбушава) and vul. Mitskevicha (Міцкевіча; ☎23 81 42). From Pushkinskaya vul., take a left on Sovy-etskaya and turn right after the yellow church. **Buses** to: **Hrodna** (5hr., 8 per day, 21,000BR); **Minsk** (4½hr., 4 per day, 18,300BR); **Lviv**, UKR (8hr., 1 per day, 13,850BR); **Warsaw**, POL (7½hr., 2 per day, 20,000BR).

To get to the **Brest-Litovsk Fortress** from pl. Lenina, the main square, go down vul. Lenina away from the bridge, turn right on vul. Masherova, and walk 15min. You will pass a series of red signs decorated with images of historical figures. The travel agency at **Gastsinitsa Intourist**, vul. Masherava 15, speaks English and arranges English tours of the fortress. Tours start at US$25. There is an **ATM** at the train station. **Store luggage** in the train or bus stations (lockers 535BR, guarded 890BR). A 24hr. **pharmacy** (аптека), vul. Gogolya 32, lies at the intersection of vul. Lenina and vul. Gogolya.

🛏🍴 ACCOMMODATIONS AND FOOD. The rooms at **Gastsinitsa Intourist** ❹, vul. Masherava 15, are comfortable, though somewhat expensive. (☎20 05 10; fax 22 19 00. Singles 71,000BR; doubles 126,000BR.) **Gastsinitsa Vesta** ❸ (Веста), vul. Krupskoy 16 (Крупской), is clean and has its own restaurant. Walk about 200m through the park and take the a left on the first road. (☎23 71 69. Singles 60,000BR; doubles 105,000BR.) Bars, cafes, and restaurants line Sovetskaya vul. For a classy meal, try **Traktir "U Ozera"** ❷ (Трактиръ "У Озера;" Tavern by the Lake). From pl. Lenina, walk toward the bridge over the railroad. Take a left into the park and con-tinue straight until you see the pond on the right. English menu available. The *har-cho* (lamb soup, 5640BR) is a great appetizer, and "open flame" entrees (10-15,000BR) are a house specialty. (☎23 57 63. Open daily noon-11:30pm.) For fresh produce, head to the **market,** in the domed building behind the bus station.

🎭🎵 SIGHTS AND ENTERTAINMENT. The ⬛**Brest-Litovsk Fortress** (Крэпасць Брэст-Літовск; Krepasts Brest-Litovsk) garnered national fame for its legendary WWII holdout against the German army. When the surrounding area had been taken, a group of Soviet soldiers refused to leave the fortress and survived several months of intense bombing. The fortress was also the site of the 1918 signing of the Brest-Litovsk peace treaty in which Russia pledged an end to hostilities against Germany. The main **monument** consists of an obelisk next to an imposing bust carved into rock and an eternal flame on the grave of an unknown soldier. The names of the dead are etched into marble walls. Loudspeakers in the ruins behind the graves emit eerie, howling music. To the right of the monument, the **Museum of the Defense of the Brest Hero-Fortress** (Музей Абароны Брэсцкой Крэпасці-Героя; Muzey Abarony Brestskoy Krepastsi-Geroya) describes the history of the fortress and recounts the siege. The exhibit includes a copy of the rhyming Rus-sian phrase etched into a wall of the fortress: "We will die, but we won't leave the fortress." (☎20 03 65. Open Mar.-Oct. Tu-Su 9:30am-6pm; Nov.-Feb. Tu-Su 9:30am-5pm; closed last Tu of each month. Last entry 30min. before closing. 3000BR.)

BELARUS

To the left of the monument, behind the row of buildings, is the surprisingly intriguing **Archeological Museum of Brest** (Брест Областной Краеведческий Музей; Brestskiy Oblastnoy Krayevedcheskiy Muzey), founded in 1982. The museum contains at its center a 13th-century excavation of a group of wooden houses and two wooden streets; around the edges of the hall are photos of the excavation as well as artifacts and information about the middle ages. English brochures are available for 1500BR. (Open daily Apr.-Oct.; Nov.-Mar. W-Su 10am-6pm. 2100BR.) On the way to the fortress on the right side of the street is the **Railroad Museum** (Muzey Dzelezniy Darogiy Tehniki), pr. Masherava 2, which opened in 2002. Even if you don't enter, you can peer through the gate at the trains on display. (Open May.-Oct. 9am-6pm; Nov.-Apr. 9am-5pm. 5000BR.)

Those in Brest for the evening can see a symphony concert, drama, or musical at the **Brest Theater**, vul. Lenina 21, between pl. Lenina and pr. Masherava. Performances 7pm. (☎ 23 54 25. Ticket office open Tu-Su 2-7pm. Tickets 3000-6000BR.)

BOSNIA AND HERZEGOVINA
(BOSNA I HERCEGOVINA)

The mountainous centerpiece of the former Yugoslavia, Bosnia and Herzegovina has defied all odds to stand as an independent nation today. Bosnia's distinctiveness—and its troubles—spring from its diverse population of Muslim Bosniaks, Catholic Croats, and Orthodox Serbs. In Sarajevo, the country's cosmopolitan capital, these groups co-exist in peace, but ethnic hostilities continue in the countryside. The last decade devastated both the peoples of Bosnia and the country itself, which is marred with abandoned houses and gaping rooftops. The citizenry of Bosnia and Herzegovina, however, is optimistic, and reconstruction is beginning. Coverage of Sarajevo was updated in August of 2004; the rest of Bosnia and Herzegovina was last updated in July of 2003.

HISTORY

BYE BYE BYZANTIUM. Bosnia was part of the sprawling **Roman Empire.** After the empire fell, the region became a battleground of the Empire's Frankish and Byzantine successors. When the Byzantines lost control of the region in AD1180, and neither the Croatian nor the Serbian kingdoms could establish rule over the territory, Bosnia emerged as an independent nation. It remained free for more than 260 years, populated almost entirely by Christians.

FACTS AND FIGURES

OFFICIAL NAME: Bosnia and Herzegovina

CAPITAL: Sarajevo (pop. 387,000)

POPULATION: 4.2 million (48% Bosniak, 37% Serb, 14% Croat, 1% other)

LANGUAGE: Bosnian, Croatian, Serbian

CURRENCY: 1 convertible mark (marka; KM) = 100 convertible pfennigs

RELIGION: 43% Muslim, 30% Serbian Orthodox, 18% Catholic, 9% other

LAND AREA: 51,129km²

CLIMATE: Mild continental

GEOGRAPHY: Mountainous, plains in the north, 20km of coast

BORDERS: Croatia, Serbia and Montenegro

ECONOMY: 56% Services, 28% Industry, 16% Agriculture

GDP: US$1800 per capita

COUNTRY CODE: 387

INTERNATIONAL DIALING PREFIX: 00

SATISFIED BY SÜLEYMAN. In the late 14th century, the flourishing **Ottoman Empire** invaded the Balkans, and by 1463 it had swallowed Bosnia. Due in part to the organizational weaknesses of the established Churches (both Catholic and Orthodox), **Islam** gained more converts in Bosnia than in neighboring countries. Despite this religious diversity, Christians and Muslims lived in relative harmony and referred to themselves simply as Bosnians. During 400 years of Turkish rule, the region developed into a prosperous and autonomous province of the Empire.

POWDER KEG OF EUROPE. In 1878 the Western European powers took advantage of the Ottoman Empire's increasing weakness, and, at the **Congress of Berlin,** transferred Bosnia to **Austria-Hungary.** Although Austria-Hungary tried to modernize Bosnia, resentment toward Austrian rule sparked nationalistic sentiments throughout the nation and led to the establishment of a Bosnian Serb terrorist organization, the **Black Hand.** Austria-Hungary tightened its grip on Bosnia and annexed the country in 1908. As in other Balkan countries, increased repression and imported Russian ideology contributed to a desire for **South Slav** unity and sovereignty. On June 28, 1914, **Gavrilo Princip** a member of the Black Hand, assassinated the Austrian heir to the throne, **Archduke Franz Ferdinand,** triggering **WWI.**

TITO TIME. After the war, Pan-Slavism took on a concrete shape in the **Kingdom of Serbs, Croats, and Slovenes.** Bosnian Muslims, who fit neatly into none of these three nationalities, nevertheless had to choose one with which to register. When Hitler put an end to the kingdom by invading Yugoslavia in 1941, Bosnia was handed over to Croatia, an obedient satellite of Hitler's regime. The majority of Bosnians joined the pro-Allies Partisans led by **Josip Broz Tito** during **WWII.** In 1945, Bosnia joined its Slavic neighbors as one of the six constituent republics of **Yugoslavia.**

MASSACRE UNDER MILOŠEVIĆ. Nationalist sentiment was suppressed under Tito, but his death in 1980 triggered a revival. Tensions increased in 1986 with the rise of the Serb nationalist **Slobodan Milošević,** who sought to abolish the federation and create a unitary state under Serbian control; the collapse of the republic began in 1990. Following the 1991 secession of Slovenia and Croatia from the federation, Bosnia held a referendum on independence. To the outrage of Milošević, 70% of Bosnians, including much of the Serbian population, voted in favor of independence. The federal army and Serb militias quickly took control of 70% of Bosnian territory. Sarajevo suffered a brutal **siege** from May 2, 1992 to February 26, 1996. A United Nations force sent to deliver humanitarian assistance had little success in stopping the "ethnic cleansing" undertaken by both Serb and Croat forces.

PEACE AT LAST. The international community remained largely unaware of the conflict until footage of the "ethnic cleansing" of **Srebrenica,** documenting the first genocide in Europe since WWII, was broadcast on international television. The atrocities continued until the 1995 **Dayton Peace Accords.** Dayton brought a fragile peace, which UN peacekeeping forces have helped sustain to this day.

TODAY. The present-day government of Bosnia and Herzegovina consists of two bodies, the Muslim/Croat **Federation of Bosnia and Herzegovina** and the Serbian **Republika Srpska (RS).** A central government and a three-person rotating presidency connect the two entities. According to the Dayton constitution, the presidents must be a Croat, a Serb, and a Bosniak, elected by a popular vote for four-year terms. The offices are presently held by Serb **Boris Paravac,** Croat **Dragan Covic,** and Bosniak **Sulejman Tihic.** Today's Bosnia, however, resembles more of an international protectorate than an independent nation. High Representative **Paddy Ashdown,** a diplomat appointed by the UN Security Council to implement the Dayton Peace Accords, has the power to issue legal decrees and dismiss any member of the government. Bosnia will probably remain under direct international supervi-

Bosnia and Herzegovina

sion for at least another five years. The international community is optimistic about Bosnia's prospects for permanent stability and peace. Though the economy remains a substantial problem, as half the country is **unemployed** and **international aid** has been reduced, funds from tourism and investors are beginning to flow through the country once more, bringing hopes of a more prosperous future.

PEOPLE AND CULTURE

DEMOGRAPHICS AND RELIGION

Bosnia and Herzegovina's population is as diverse as they come. Although they have different traditions and label themselves differently, all Bosnians share a **South Slavic** origin and speak mutually intelligible languages. The predominately Muslim **Bosniak** group constitutes the largest minority with 44% of the population. **Serbs,** almost all of whom live in the Republika Srpska (RS), make up 31% of the population, while **Croats** comprise 17%. Bosnia's religious composition is the most complex in Eastern Europe. There are three large religious groups: Croats are **Catholic;** Serbs **Orthodox Christian;** and Bosniaks **Muslim.**

LANGUAGE

When in Bosnia, speak **Bosnian,** except in the RS, where **Serbian** prevails. In both districts, **Croatian** will be understood. The difference between the three languages is political rather than substantive, but never underestimate its importance; languages in the former Yugoslavia have become tools of nationalism. The languages do have certain distinctions. For example, coffee is *kava* in Croatian, *kafa* in Serbian, and *kahva* in Bosnian. See the guidelines for pronouncing Croatian (p. 160); for a phrasebook and glossary, see **Glossary: Croatian,** p. 947. Foreigners who try to speak a little Bosnian are few and far between; an effort to pronounce even a few sentences will endear you to locals. **English** and **German** are widely spoken, especially in Sarajevo; **Russian** may also be understood.

FOOD AND DRINK

BOSNIA	❶	❷	❸	❹	❺
FOOD	under 4KM	4-6KM	7-10KM	11-14KM	over 14KM

Bosnian cuisine has a mixed heritage, and it proudly shows its Central European, Mediterranean, and Middle Eastern influences. **Sausages** and patties are usually made from a mixture of beef, pork, and lamb. The national dish, *Bosnanki lonac*, a layered meat and vegetable stew, is served in the ceramic pot in which it is cooked. *Ćevap* (kebab) is omnipresent and well prepared. *Burek*, a stuffed pastry, is also popular; **vegetarians** should try cheese or spinach fillings. Baklava and *lokum* (Turkish delight) are popular sweets. Strong, Turkish-style **coffee** is drunk throughout the day. Festive occasions call for *šlivovica*, a potent plum brandy.

CUSTOMS AND ETIQUETTE

Tipping is not expected but feel free to add a gratuity for excellent service. At restaurants and cafes, the bill is never split; one person pays, and it is assumed that the other will pay next time. It is customary for the waiter or a man to open and pour a woman's drink. In **Muslim homes** and **mosques**, women should cover their head and shoulders, and everyone should remove his or her shoes at the door.

THE ARTS

HISTORY. The Balkans have shared literary and artistic traditions since the Middle Ages, but it is only in the recent past that Bosnia has come into its own in the artistic world. **Mak Dizdar** is celebrated as the nation's greatest poet. He revolutionized post-WWI poetry with his stark Modernist style and refusal to pander to Socialist Realism. Bosnian Serb **Ivo Andrić**, who won the 1961 Nobel Prize for Literature, is one of the few Bosnian writers to receive international acclaim. The sober compassion and beauty of his works are exemplified by *The Bridge on the Drina* and *The Travnik Chronicles*, which focus on delicate political issues.

CURRENT SCENE. Theatrical productions are common in Sarajevo, as entertainers follow in the footsteps of the Sarajevo War Theater, a group of playwrights and actors who performed almost 2000 productions during the four-year siege of Sarajevo. In the wake of the war, Bosnian authors have turned their energies to war memoirs and diaries. *Zlata's Diary*, by **Zlata Filipović**, an adolescent during the siege of Sarajevo, is a poignant account of growing up during the conflict. **Semezdin Mehmedinović** presents a darker, more mature picture of wartime in the internationally acclaimed *Sarajevo Blues*, a 1998 collection of prose and poetry. Up-and-comers like **Aleksandar Hemon** and **Meša Semilović** also contribute to a rich literary atmosphere. In 1993, several Bosnian artists organized the **Witnesses of Existence** exhibit in which language and national context were interpreted using shrapnel and bullets as media. The exhibit toured Italy and the US, but its creators were trapped in Sarajevo and unable to travel with it. Born in Sarajevo to a Croat father and a Serbian mother, **Goran Bregović** plays world-class rock music, heavily influenced by Balkan folk melodies. The recent picture *No Man's Land* (2001), directed by **Danis Tanovic,** won an Oscar for Best Foreign Film. Thousands flock to Bosnia for Sarajevo's innovative, annual **Jazz Fest and Film Festival.**

HOLIDAYS AND FESTIVALS

NATIONAL HOLIDAYS IN 2005	
January 1 New Year's Day (Catholic)	**May 1** Labor Day
January 7 Orthodox Christmas	**May 2** Prophet's Birthday
January 14 New Year's Day (Orthodox)	**October 4-November 2** Ramadan
February 22 Islamic New Year	**November 1** All Saints' Day (Catholic)
March 1 Independence Day	**November 25** National Day
May 1-2 Orthodox Easter Holiday	**December 25** Catholic Christmas

ADDITIONAL RESOURCES

Balkan Ghosts: A Journey Through History, by Robert Kaplan (1994). A travel journal dealing with the political complexities of Bosnia and Herzegovina and its neighbors.

Bosnia: A Short History, by Noel Malcolm (1996). A concise yet comprehensive account of the nation's troubled past.

The Balkans, by Misha Glenny (2000). An engaging survey of the history of the Balkans over the past century, with an emphasis on the recent fall of Yugoslavia.

The Bridge on the Drina, by Ivo Andrić (1959). A Nobel prize-winning novel of everyday life in Bosnia under the Ottomans.

No Man's Land, directed by Danis Tanović (2001). This black comedy about 2 soldiers, a Bosniak and a Serb, who find themselves trapped together in a mined trench between enemy lines, recently won Bosnia its 1st Academy Award.

Zlata's Diary, by Zlata Filipović (1995). A memoir of one teenager's struggle to live a normal life during the disintegration of Yugoslavia.

BOSNIA ESSENTIALS

ENTRANCE REQUIREMENTS
Passport: Required of all travelers.

Visa: Not required for stays under 90 days for citizens of Australia, Canada, Ireland, New Zealand, the UK, and the US.

Letter of Invitation: Not required.

Inoculations: Recommended up-to-date on DTaP (diphtheria, tetanus, and pertussis), Hepatitis A, Hepatitis B, MMR (measles, mumps, and rubella), Polio booster, and Typhoid.

Work Permit: Required of all foreigners planning to work.

International Driving Permit: Required of all those planning to drive.

DOCUMENTS AND FORMALITIES

EMBASSIES AND CONSULATES

Embassies and consulates of other countries in Bosnia and Herzegovina are all in **Sarajevo** (see p. 102). Bosnia's embassies and consulates abroad include:

Australia: 5 Beale Crescent, Deakin, ACT 2600 (☎61 2 6232 4646; www.bosnia.web-one.com.au).

Canada: 130 Albert St. Ste. 805, Ottawa, ON K1P 5G4 (☎1 613-236-0028; fax 236-1139).

UK: 5-7 Lexam Gardens, London W8 5JJ (☎44 20 7373 0867; fax 20 7373 0871).

US: 2109 E St., NW, Washington, D.C. 20037 (☎202 337-1500; www.bhembassy.org).

VISA AND ENTRY INFORMATION

Citizens of Australia, Canada, Ireland, New Zealand, the UK, and the US do not need visas for stays of up to 90 days. A valid passport is required to enter and leave the country. Occasionally travelers will encounter police checkpoints within the country. All foreigners must **register** with their hotel or with police within 24hr. of arrival. It is also wise to register with your embassy, and to keep your papers with you at all times.

GETTING AROUND

Commercial plane service into Sarajevo is limited and expensive. **Adria Airways** provides regular service from **Ljubljana, SLN; Austrian Airways** from **Vienna, AUT; Croatia Airlines** from **Zagreb, CRO; Lufthansa** from **Frankfurt, GER;** and **Malév** from **Budapest, HUN.** Travel agencies in Sarajevo can arrange and change flights, but most only accept cash.

Railways suffered in wartime and should not be considered an option. **Buses** run daily between Sarajevo and **Belgrade, SMN; Dubrovnik, CRO** (the most popular route into Bosnia); **Podogorica, SMN; Split, CRO;** and **Zagreb, CRO.** Buses are reliable, uncrowded, and clean, but road travel in the Balkans can be nerve-wracking. Avoid **driving** along the **Zone of Separation (ZOS)** between the Federation Bosnia and Herzegovina and the RS, as this area is rife with **landmines. Hitchhiking** is common, but *Let's Go* does not recommend it.

TOURIST SERVICES AND MONEY

Bosnia's tourist infrastructure is disorganized, but the scattered municipal **tourist offices** really know their stuff—when you can find one. The US Embassy's consular department also has useful info. Some independent tourist agencies exist, but most focus on arranging vacations for locals.

Introduced in 1998, the **convertible mark** (KM) is fixed to the euro at a rate of 1KM to €0.51. Bosnia also named the Croatian **kuna** an official currency in 1997; while not legal tender in Sarajevo, it is accepted in the western (Croatian) area of divided Mostar. The old Bosnian *dinar* is no longer valid. Change your money to euros before leaving, as the convertible mark is not so convertible outside Bosnia. Banks are the best places to exchange money; a few in Sarajevo cash traveler's checks. **Western Union** in Sarajevo has very helpful English-speaking staff. **ATMs** are also available in the capital. Bring euros along if you venture outside Sarajevo. Bosnian **business hours** are Monday through Friday 8am-4:30pm.

HEALTH AND SAFETY

 EMERGENCY NUMBERS: Police: ☎92 **Fire:** ☎93 **Ambulance:** ☎94

In Sarajevo, finding **medical assistance** and supplies is not a problem; your embassy is your best resource. UK citizens receive free medical care with a valid passport. Peacekeeping operations have brought English-speaking doctors, but not insurance; pay in cash. All drugs are sold at **pharmacies,** and basic hygiene products are sold at many drugstores. Bring your own supply of prescription medication. **Tampons** are hard to find; bring them with you. **Condoms** are available but expensive. If you have bad allergies, take along some antihistamines.

Outside Sarajevo, **do not set foot off the pavement.** Even in Sarajevo, de-mining experts recommend staying on paved roads and hard-topped surfaces. Do not pick up any objects off the ground. Hundreds of thousands of **landmines** and **unexploded ordnance** (UXOs) cover the country. Mine injuries occur daily. About 15% of landmine injuries occur on road shoulders, where farmers bring unexploded ordnance from their fields for troops to pick up. Should your car veer off the road, carefully retrace your tracks back to the pavement. Abandoned houses are also unsafe; many have been rigged with booby traps. Absolute caution is essential at all times. It is estimated that 30 years of intensive, full-time effort would be necessary to declare Bosnia "mine-free"—and even de-mining is not 100% fool-proof. For details, contact the **Bosnia and Herzegovina Mine Action Center** (see **Sarajevo: Local Services and Communications,** p. 104).

Women should take the usual precautions, but most likely will not encounter difficulties traveling in Bosnia. **Minority** travelers will probably get stares but generally are not hassled. **Homosexuality** is still treated with hostility, particularly outside Sarajevo.

 TRAVEL WARNING In June 2004, the US State Department renewed its Travel Warning for Bosnia. Specific threats include "localized political violence, landmines, and unexploded ordnance," and crime is rising, particularly in Sarajevo. Before visiting, contact the US Embassy in Sarajevo for recent updates, and consult http://travel.state.gov/travel_warnings.html for further information.

ACCOMMODATIONS AND CAMPING

BOSNIA	❶	❷	❸	❹	❺
ACCOM.	under 35KM	35-40KM	41-50KM	51-60KM	over 60KM

Accommodations options are still very limited in Bosnia and the only choice is usually a **hotel** or **pension. Private rooms** only exist in Sarajevo, and usually cost the same as cheaper pensions (30-50KM). **Camping** should be avoided due to the threat of landmines and UXOs; the only safe way to camp is through a specialized organization, such as **Green Visions.**

KEEPING IN TOUCH

Yellow-and-white "PTT" signs indicate post offices. **Mail service** is improving in efficiency. Mail to Europe takes three to five days, to North America seven to 10 days. Address mail to be held according to the following example: Clay (first

BOSNIA AND HERZEGOVINA

name) KAMINSKY (LAST NAME), *Post Restante*, Zmaja od Bosne 88, Sarajevo 71000 BOSNIA AND HERZEGOVINA. Telephone connections are troublesome and expensive; the best option is to call collect from the main Sarajevo post office. An international access number is available for **AT&T** (☎ 00 800 0010). **Faxes** can be sent from the post office; it's 3KM per page to Australia or the UK and 5KM to the US. **Internet access** is becoming widely available.

SARAJEVO ☎ (0)33

Sarajevo lives again. The enchanting charm of this "big village" (pop. 450,000), where Istanbul and Innsbruck seem to meet, makes it easy to forget the massive destruction it faced ten years ago. Reconstruction projects are healing the physical scars, but glimpses of the suffering this city faced during the brutal 1992-95 siege by Bosnian Serbs are unavoidable. The lively marketplace of the old Turkish Quarter, a burgeoning arts scene, and a revived nightlife all promise a return to the pre-war glory that won the city the 1984 Winter Olympics. As in 1984, visitors today are warmly welcomed by pension owners, shopkeepers, and taxi drivers.

■ INTERCITY TRANSPORTATION

Flights: Sarajevo Airport, Kurta Šorka 36 (☎ 463 596), 12km southwest of the city center. To: **Belgrade, SMN** (1 per day, 180KM); **Budapest, HUN** (1 per day, 340KM); **Istanbul, TUR** (4 per week, 190KM); **Ljubljana, SLN** (1 per day, 160KM); **Munich, GER** (1 per day, 700KM); **Vienna, AUT** (1 per day, 700KM); **Zagreb, CRO** (1 per day, 590KM). Ticket prices do not include the 60-80KM airport tax. Buy tickets at **Centrotrans,** Ferhadija 16 (☎ 211 282; fax 205 481). Open M-F 8:30am-8pm, Sa 8am-2pm. MC/V. For other ticket providers, see **Tourist and Financial Services,** p. 103.

Trains: Put Života 2 (☎ 655 330), next to the bus station. Open daily 5:30am-9pm. To: **Mostar** (2½hr., 1 per day, 9KM); **Budapest, HUN** (12½hr., 1 per day, 91.50KM); **Ljubljana, SLN** (7½hr., 1 per day, 65KM); **Zagreb, CRO** (9hr., 1 per day, 45KM).

Buses: Put Života 2 (☎ 213 100), behind the Holiday Inn at the corner with Halida Kajtaza. Tram #1 runs between the station and the center. Open daily 6am-10pm. Very little English spoken; the best place to book a ticket is at Centrotrans (see **Flights,** p. 102), at the bus station or in the city. Tickets there are 2KM cheaper than at the station. To: **Mostar** (3hr., 11-13 per day, 12KM); **Dubrovnik, CRO** (7hr., 1-2 per day, 44KM); **Frankfurt, GER** (22½hr., 1 per day, 198KM); **Ljubljana, SLN** (10hr., 3 per week, 74KM); **Munich, GER** (15hr., 1-2 per day, 110KM); **Skopje, MAC** (20hr., 2 per day, 82KM); **Split, CRO** (7hr., 5 per day, 34KM); **Zagreb, CRO** (7hr., 3 per day, 54KM). Add 2KM per bag (6KM per bag to Frankfurt). For destinations within **Serbia and Montenegro,** use the Lukavica bus station in **Srpsko Sarajevo** (Serbian Sarajevo). Take trolley #103 to **Dobrinja** from Austrijski trg to the end of the line (30min.). If you're planning to arrive at this station, be sure to change money before departing—there is no ATM and no way to change money within walking distance of the station. To: **Belgrade, SMN** (7½hr., 7 per day, 25KM); **Niš, SMN** (10hr., 2 per day, 29KM); **Novi Sad, SMN** (8hr., 3 per day, 24KM); **Podgorica, SMN** (6hr., 7 per day, 22KM).

■ ORIENTATION

Sarajevo's center is a series of easily navigable streets running parallel to the **Milijacka** river. They can be traversed end-to-end in less than 30min. **Maršala Tita** is the main street, running from the yellow Holiday Inn to the **Eternal Flame,** a 1945 war memorial. Address numbers increase west to east. At the Flame, Maršala Tita branches into **Ferhadija,** the city's main pedestrian thoroughfare, and **Mula Mustafe Bašeskije,** a heavily trafficked street with narrow sidewalks. Follow Ferhadija for 10min. to reach the cobblestoned streets of **Baščaršija** (Turkish Quarter). A walk in the opposite direction of the Flame down Maršala Tita leads to the stark **Zmaja od Bosne** (Dragon of Bosnia), called **"Sniper's Alley"** during the war—a nickname not used casually. **Alipašina** bisects Maršala Tita between the Holiday Inn and the Eternal Flame. Streets have changed names since the war, but street signs are up-to-date. **Maps** are available at the tourist bureau (free) or at bookstores (12KM).

>
> The Bosnia and Herzegovina Mine Action Center (see p. 104) estimates that over 10,000 locations throughout the country contain as many as 670,000 **landmines** and 650,000 **unexploded ordnance** devices. As a result, 1450 people have been killed or injured since 1996. To stay safe, attend a **mine risk education briefing,** and check out a map that highlights approximate danger zones.

⌷ LOCAL TRANSPORTATION

Public Transportation: Central Sarajevo is small enough to walk, but if you're in a rush, a great **tram** network loops west along Maršala Tita and back east along Obala Kulina Bana. Regular service begins between 5:10am and 6:25am and ends around midnight; exact time depends on the route (1.2KM from kiosks, 1.5KM on board). **Buses** use the same tickets and extend farther from the town center. A listing of the tram and bus lines is available at the tourist office (see below). Schedules are posted at kiosks, and most transportation arrives every 5-15min. Riding ticketless will earn you a 20KM fine.

Taxis: Taxis are cheap. If there isn't a meter, agree on a price beforehand. **Sarajevo Taxi** (☎ 15 15) is the biggest company (1KM plus 1KM per km; large bags 1-2KM each).

◪ PRACTICAL INFORMATION

TOURIST AND FINANCIAL SERVICES

There is a tourist office, ◪**Turistička Zajednica,** at Zelenih Beretki 22a. Bear right at the Eternal Flame Maršala Tita, turn right down Strossmajerova, then left on Zelenih Beretki. Super-helpful staff distributes free maps and provides info. (☎ 220 724; sightseeingsarajevo@europe.com. Open summer M-Sa 9am-8pm, Su 10am-2pm; winter M-Sa 9am-6pm, Su 10am-2pm.) Another one, **Sartour,** is at Mula Mustafe Bašeskije 63/3, just before the intersection with Kovaći; look for the info sign. It boasts one of the only three accredited guides in Sarajevo; guides conduct English and German private tours (2-2½hr.), with themes to fit all interests. (☎238 680; sartour@lsinter.net. 25KM per person, 3-15 persons 40KM; transportation available for a fee. Open daily May-Oct. 10am-8pm; Nov.-Apr. 10am-2pm. **Turistička Agencija Ljubičica** (see p. 105) offers daily "history and tolerance" tours (2½hr.; 25KM per person) that include the tunnel museum (see p. 109).

Budget Travel: Centrotrans, Ferhadija 16 (☎211 282; fax 205 481). Open M-F 8:30am-8pm, Sa 8am-2pm. **Kompas Tours,** Maršala Tita 8 (☎208 014; fax 208 015), past the intersection with Alipašina toward the Holiday Inn. Open M-F 8:30am-5:30pm and Sa 9am-2pm. Both book **flights** and accept credit cards.

Embassies: Citizens of **Australia** should contact the embassy in **Vienna, AUT,** Mattiellistr. 2 (☎43 1 512 85 80; fax 513 16 56). **Canada:** Grbavička 4 (☎222 033; fax 222 044). Open M-F 8:30am-5pm. **Croatia:** Skenderija 17 (☎442 591; fax 650 328). Open M-F 8:30am-4:30pm. Citizens of **New Zealand** should contact the embassy in

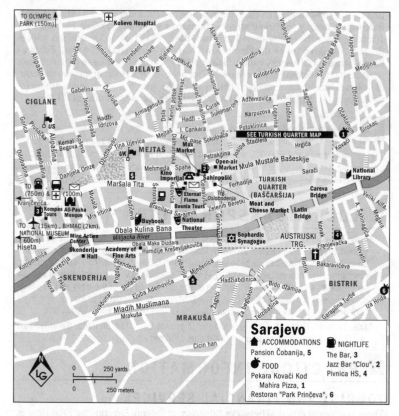

Sarajevo

ACCOMMODATIONS
Pansion Čobanija, 5

FOOD
Pekara Kovači Kod
Mahira Pizza, 1
Restoran "Park Prinčeva", 6

NIGHTLIFE
The Bar, 3
Jazz Bar "Clou", 2
Pivnica HS, 4

Rome, ITA, Via Zara 28 (☎6 440 29 28; fax 440 29 84). **Serbia and Montenegro:** Obala Marka Dizdara 3a (☎260 090; yugoamba@bih.net.ba). **UK:** Petrakijina 11 (☎208 229; fax 204 780). Open M-F 8:30am-5pm. **US:** Alipašina 43 (☎445 700; www.usembassy.ba). Open M-F 2-3:30pm, Tu and Th 8am-noon.

Currency Exchange: Central Profit Banka, Zelenih Beretki 24 (☎533 688; fax 532 406), cashes **traveler's checks** for 2% commission and **exchanges** euros for 0.5% commission, US$ and UK£ 1% commission. Open M-F 8am-7pm, Sa 8am-noon.

ATMs: ATMs are springing up everywhere. Look for the yellow-and-black **Raiffeisenbank** signs at 5 branches and 6 24hr. (MC/V) **ATMs** in the city. The most convenient locations are Ferhadija 9 and Maršala Tita 17. **Western Union** services are available at all Raiffeisenbank branches and at many other international banks.

LOCAL SERVICES

Bosnia and Herzegovina Mine Action Center (BHMAC): Zmaja od Bosne 8 (☎667 310; www.bhmac.org). Take tram #2, 3, or 5 from the Eternal Flame 6 stops to the Fakultat za Saobraćaja and turn right. Walk 200m and turn right through a parking lot, following the signs. Provides mine risk education briefings (to schedule, call, or email webmaster@bhmac.org 1 week in advance) and **maps** that highlight estimated landmine locations throughout the country. Open M-F 8am-4pm.

Luggage Storage: At the **bus station.** 3KM for up to 3hr., 0.50KM for each additional hour. Open daily 6am-10pm.

English-Language Bookstores: Šahinpašić, Mula Mustafe Bašeskije 1 (☎220 112), near the Eternal Flame, sells English classics, dictionaries, guidebooks, maps, and newspapers. Open M-Sa 8am-2pm and 4-10pm, Su 10am-2pm. **Buybook,** Radićeva 4 (☎716 450), toward Skenderija, has an excellent selection of music and English books. Open M-Sa 9am-10pm, Su 10am-6pm. MC/V.

24hr. Pharmacy: Baščaršija Apoteka, Obala Kulina Bana 40 (☎272 300) and **Novo Sarajevo,** Zmaja od Bosne 51 (☎713 830). MC/V.

Turkish Quarter

♠ ACCOMMODATIONS	♦ FOOD
Hostel Ljubičica, 4	Čevabdžinica Željo, 6
Pansion Baščaršija, 5	Dveri, 3
Sartour Accommodation, 1	■ NIGHTLIFE
	City Pub, 7
	Jazz Bar "Clou", 2

Emergency: Ambulance: ☎124. **Police:** ☎122. **Fire:** ☎125.

Hospital: Koševo University Medical Center, Bolnicka 25 (☎666 620). **State Hospital,** Kranjčevića 12 (☎285 100).

Telephones: In- and outside any post office. The most central is behind the Eternal Flame on Ferhadija. Open M-Sa 7am-8pm. Buy phone cards (5-60KM) at any post office. It is possible to dial internationally from the main branch between the bus and train stations. Directory info ☎1182, international directory info 1201.

Internet Access: Internet Café Gemini, Šenoina 16, just off Maršala Tita before the Eternal Flame. It's upstairs at the unmarked door on the left. 24 good connections. 2KM per hr. Open daily 24hr. **Internet Club Click,** Kundurdziluk 1, in Baščaršija (☎236 914). 3KM per hr. Open M-Sa 9am-11pm.

Post Office: Central Post Office, Put Života bb (☎723 433). Open Ma-Sa 7am-8pm. **Poste Restante** available. **Postal Code: 71000.**

ACCOMMODATIONS

Until recently, housing in Sarajevo was absurdly expensive, but prices are dropping rapidly as competition works its capitalist magic. You can find relatively cheap **private rooms** (30-50KM) all over town. **Turistička Agencija Ljubičica,** Mula Mustafe Bašeskije 65 (☎535 829; taljubic@bih.net.ba), boasts 550 beds in rooms and apartments in private houses. (In the city center singles 32KM, doubles 48KM. Within 1km of the center singles 22KM; doubles 32KM; apartments 30KM per person. Open daily June-Sept. 24hr.; Oct.-May 7am-11pm.) **Bosnia Tours,** Maršala Tita 54 (☎/fax 202 059), before the Eternal Flame, books rooms in family apartments along Maršala Tita. Call 2-3 days ahead. (Singles 40KM; doubles 70KM. Open M-F 9am-5pm, Sa 9am-2pm.) If you arrive late at night without prior arrangements, ask a taxi driver at the station for help—they often make deals with local families offering private rooms. The drivers might not speak English, but they'll understand "room" and "center" and will write down a price.

Pansion Baščaršija, Veliki Čurčiluk 41 (☎232 185, shuttle service mobile 061 177 950; heartofthebascarsija@hotmail.com). Walk down Ferhadija away from the Eternal Flame. Take a right onto Gazi Huzrev-Begova and your 3rd left onto Veliki Čurčiluk; the pension is 2 blocks up on the left. Built at the same time as the Gazi Huzrev-Bey Mosque, the 2 buildings share a backyard. Immaculate rooms and the best location. Free pick-up. Reception 24hr. Singles 60KM; doubles 100KM; triples 120KM. ❹

Sartour Accommodation, Mula Mustafe Bašeskije 63/3 (☎238 680; sartour@lsinter.net), just before Baščaršija's main square; look for the green-and-white info sign. Spotless and newly refurbished, with 43 beds. Within 5min. of the center. Hot water is occasionally elusive. Linen 6KM. Laundry 20KM. Reception 24hr. Lockout 11am-4pm, but a phone call will allow access. Dorm €13; private 1-6 bed room €15.❶

Hostel Ljubičica, Mula Mustafe Bašeskije 65 (☎535 829; www.hostellgubicica.com), The private room agency (see p. 105) has recently opened hostel accommodations in 3 locations. A little crowded, but clean and only a stone's throw from the Baščaršija. Open daily June-Sept. 24hr.; Oct.-May 7am-11pm. Laundry 10KM. In Baščaršija, dorm beds 20KM; doubles 48KM. Across the river, dorms 16KM per person. ❶

Pansion Čobanija, Čobanija 29 (☎441 749; fax 203 937). With your back to the Flame, take the 1st left onto Kulovica, which crosses the river and becomes Čobanija. The *pansion* is at the end of the street, 5min. from the center. Don't let the old exterior or the scorpion logo fool you; luxury and charm await within. Breakfast included. Reception 24hr. Best to reserve 5-7 days in advance. Singles 80KM; doubles 120KM. ❺

◻ FOOD

Sarajevan cuisine is quintessentially Balkan—meaty, cheesy, and greasy—but also has distinctive Middle Eastern influences. For an authentic Bosnian meal, scour the Turkish Quarter for *čevabdžinica* (kebab shops). Ethnic Albanians settling in Sarajevo brought with them *slastičarna* (sweet shops), now sprinkled throughout Baščaršija, which serve specialty sweets like *tufahija* (a cored and peeled apple filled with sweetened, crushed walnuts and topped with whipped cream), and *palačinka* (a crepe-like treat). The small **Max Market**, Mula Mustafe Bašeskije 3, is well-stocked and open 24hr. The large open-air market **Markale**, Mula Mustafe Bašeskije 11, sells fresh vegetables and baked goods. (Open M-Sa 8am-4pm, Su 8am-2pm.) Across the street and down is a **meat and cheese market**, Mula Mustafe Bašeskije 4a; enter also from Ferhadija 7. (Open M-Sa 7am-5pm, Su 7am-2pm.)

▩ **Restoran "Park Prinčeva,"** Iza Hrida 7 (☎061 222 708). Take a cab (5KM) up the hill, or, to work up an appetite, walk up Bistrik from Austrijski trg, follow it to the left before the overpass, cross the transit road, and take the next left onto Iza Hrida; there will be signs to guide you. Sit on the 30m-long balcony and enjoy Bosnian grill fare and the vibrant, romantic atmosphere. Live music. Entrees 10-20KM. Open daily 9am-11pm. ❹

▩ **Čevabdžinica Željo,** Kundurdžiluk 19 (☎447 000), in the Turkish Quarter. Named after a local soccer team, this restaurant brims with sporty patriotism and crowds of hungry locals. Follow their lead and order the *čevapčiči* (a gargantuan grilled pita pocket overflowing with little sausages, served with a side of fresh onions; 4KM) with *kajmak* (not quite butter, not quite cheese; 1KM). Open daily 8am-10pm. ❷

Pekara Kovaći Kod Mahira Pizza, Kovaći 57 (☎531 532). Walk straight up Kovaći from the far end of the Baščarčija. 200m up (vertically) on the left. One bite of this pizza, and you will understand how and why this pizzeria remained open through the siege. Only 1 size (about 25cm across) and 1 style (mushroom and beef bacon). Delivery is free if you can communicate where to bring the pizza. 5KM. Open daily 9am-midnight. ❷

Dveri, Prote Bakovića 12 (☎537 020). Walking up Ferhadija from the Baščaršija end, turn right at the 1st side street, then left into the small alley. Come here for Bosnian home-cooking. Feels like a warm Bosnian farmhouse and serves great homemade wine and spirits. The outdoor patio is torch-lit in the evenings and graced by live music on summer weekends. Entrees 7-15KM. Open M-Sa 11am-11pm. MC. ❸

◉ SIGHTS

TURKISH QUARTER (BAŠČARŠIJA). The centerpiece of the mosque-flanked Turkish Quarter is a traditional Turkish-style **bazaar:** squares interlaced with tiny streets are packed with shops, which offer an array of souvenirs from Bosnian carpets to copper coffee sets. Bargain aggressively and have someone who speaks Bosnian at your side if possible. The **Sebilj,** a wooden fountain in Baščaršija's main square, is notable more for its dynamic surroundings than for its beauty. Legend has it that once you sip the fountain water, you'll never leave the city—though the water is drinkable, better yet is the great Bosnian (a.k.a. Turkish) coffee available at the nearby cafes. *(Between the Eternal Flame and the National Library.)*

REMNANTS OF THE SIEGE. The pavement of Sarajevo's streets is littered with splash-shaped indentations created by exploding shells during the siege. After the war, some of the marks were filled in with red concrete and dubbed **"Sarajevo Roses,"** in memory of those killed on the spots. See several along **Maršala Tita,** between Alpanšina and the Eternal Flame. The glaring treeline in the hills above the city marks the war's front lines. Bosnians trapped in Sarajevo cut down all available wood for winter heating. Across the street from the Holiday Inn and next to the National Museum (see p. 108), the shattered tower of the **Parliament Building** is a stunning reminder how most of the city looked immediately following the war. By contrast, the now lively **Markale Market** (see p. 106) was the site of two of the most devastating massacres of the war. During the siege, the city's defenders built a **tunnel** under the runway of Butmir Airport to a city suburb. It became the city's lifeline, the only route by which food and arms were smuggled in and the wounded were evacuated. A section of the tunnel now serves as a museum (see p. 109).

CHURCHES, MOSQUES, AND SYNAGOGUES. The structures of various religions huddle together in Central Sarajevo, representing the mixture that once inspired Sarajevo's nickname, "The Jerusalem of Europe." That coexistence may not be as easy now, but Sarajevo remains a unique religious melting pot. The 16th-century **Gazi Husrev-Bey Mosque,** perhaps Sarajevo's most famous building, dominates the Turkish Quarter. Entering through the door on the left side of the mosque, you will encounter brightly colored Bosnian carpets and intricately laced designs. Prayer services occur between the irregular visiting hours and take place on the outdoor terrace in front of the birdcage fountain. *(18 Sarači. Ferhadija becomes Sarači as you walk away from the Flame. No shoes inside. Women must cover their heads and shoulders. Open daily 9am-noon, 2:30-4pm, 5:30-7pm. Admission 1KM. Headscarfs 3KM.)* The **Orthodox Cathedral,** built in 1871, is a beautiful but now mostly empty space, as much of the city's Serb community fled during the war. *(Trg Oslobođenje, off Ferhadija; enter from Zelenih Beretki 1. Open M-Sa 8am-5pm, Su 8:30am-1:30pm. Liturgy services Su 9:30am.)* The ancient Orthodox **Church of St. Michael the Archangel** is a dollhouse-sized church that guards a trove of medieval iconography on its interior balcony. *(Mula Mustafe Bašeskije 59. ☎ 536 704. Open Tu-Su 10am-3pm.)* Across the street, the **old synagogue** preserved an art collection among sand bags during the war. Now it houses a **Jewish Museum.** Though small, it's worth paying admission to get into the beautiful synagogue. *(Mula Mustafe Bašeskije 38. Open M-F and Su 10am-5pm. 2KM.)* The 1892 **Sephardic Synagogue** serves as the base for the Jewish Community Center's service organization. *(Hamdije Kreševljakovica 59. From the Orthodox Cathedral, walk to the river and cross over to the building directly opposite on the far bank. Enter around the block on Hamdije Kreševljakovica. ☎ 663 472. Open daily 9am-2pm. Services Sept.-June F 7:30pm. Tours on request.)*

BOSNIA AND HERZEGOVINA

ASSASSINATION SITE. On this spot **Gavrilo Princip** shot Austrian Archduke Franz Ferdinand and his wife Sofia on June 28, 1914, leading to Austria's declaration of war on Serbia and the subsequent maelstrom that spawned WWI. Princip, a Belgrade Serb, was part of the **Black Hand** terrorist group that fought Austrian rule (see **History, p.** 95). He was actually the third in a string of assassins who attacked within a matter of minutes. The first, carrying a rifle, lost his nerve and didn't shoot. The second threw a grenade that overshot the royal carriage and blew up the first assassin. Princip took no such chances and shot at near point-blank range. Following WWII, the bridge was renamed "Principov Most," in honor of Princip's brave act. During the recent war, the plaque that marked the historic spot with Princip's footprints was torn out, and following the war, the city reverted to *Latinska Ćuprija* (Latin Bridge), the bridge's old name. *(At the intersection of Obala Kulina Bana and Zelenih Beretki, the 3rd bridge when walking toward the center from the National Library. A new plaque on Zelenih Beretki marks the spot.)*

NATIONAL LIBRARY. The National Library exemplifies Sarajevo's recent tragedy. The 1896 Moorish building, once the most beautiful in the city, served as town hall until 1945, when it was converted into the university library. The besieging Serbs, attempting to demoralize the city, targeted civilian institutions early in the war; the library was firebombed on August 25, 1992, exactly 100 years after construction began. Almost the entire collection was lost to fire. Shortly after the war, the Austrian government paid for a new roof to prevent further damage. An EU effort to restore the structure to its former dignity began in November 2002 and is progressing slowly. *(From Maršala Tita, walk toward the river to Obala Kulina Bana and turn left.)*

ETERNAL FLAME. The Eternal Flame, where Maršala Tita splits into Ferhadija and Mula Mustafe Bašeskije, was lit in 1945 as a memorial to all Sarajevans who died in WWII. Its dedication to South-Slav unity now seems painfully ironic.

ACADEMY OF FINE ARTS. This is Sarajevo's most beautiful building. If you're interested in Sarajevo's current art scene, come here for rotating exhibits (Sept.-May) and a cafe full of art students sitting on plywood boxes near the river. *(Obala Maka Dizdara 3, on the river near Skenderija Hall. Cafe open M-F 11am-11pm, Sa-Su 5-11pm.)*

🏛 MUSEUMS

Many museums in Sarajevo found themselves homeless after the war. Contact the **Turistička Zajednica** (see **Tourist and Financial Services,** p. 103) to find out which museums may have recently reopened.

■ NATIONAL MUSEUM (ZEMALJSKI MUZEJ). Among the Balkans' best museums, the National Museum surrounds a botanical garden. Sail through the uninspiring collection of Roman stonework to find the impressive ethnographic and natural history exhibits. *(Zmaja od Bosne 3, near the intersection with Maršala Tita. From the Flame, take Maršala Tita toward bus station. ☎ 668 027. Open Tu-F and Su 10am-2pm. 5KM.)*

HISTORY MUSEUM (HISTORIJSKI MUZEJ). Check out Sarajevo Surrounded (Opkoljeno Sarajevo)—a small but striking exhibit on the recent siege of the city. A comprehensive collection of photographs, documents, and weaponry, donated by residents, comprises the majority of the collection. *(Zmaja od Bosne 5, next to the National Museum. ☎ 210 416. Open M-F 9am-2pm and 4-8pm, Sa-Su 9am-1pm. 1KM.)*

ART GALLERY OF BOSNIA AND HERZEGOVINA. This museum (Umjetnička Galerija Bosne i Hercegovine) has a phenomenal collection of 20th-century painting and sculpture from Sarajevo and the former Yugoslavia. *(Zelenih Beretki 8. Enter from the parking lot or from Buybook Art. ☎ 266 550. Open M-Sa noon-8pm. Free.)*

TUNNEL MUSEUM. Sarajevo's lifeline during the siege (see **History,** p. 96) surfaced in the cellar of Bajro and Edis Kolar, who have since opened up a restored 25m section of the tunnel as a museum. Visitors see a room of photos and memorabilia and watch a 20min. video on the tunnel's history before delving in. *(Tuneli 1. From the Ali-Pasha mosque, take tram #3 or 6 to Ilidža, the end of the line (30min.). From there, catch a taxi to the "tunel" (6KM). Ask your driver to pick you up 1hr. later.* ☎ *628 591; kolare@bih.net.ba. Open daily summer 9am-5pm; winter 9am-4pm. 5KM.)*

♫ 🏵 ENTERTAINMENT AND FESTIVALS

Sarajevo has begun a steady ascent to return to its former position as the cultural capital of the Balkans. For a monthly schedule of theater, opera, and ballet at the revived **National Theater,** Obala Kulina Bana 9, stop by the tourist office (see **Tourist and Financial Services,** p. 103) and pick up a **Program of Cultural Events.** From the Eternal Flame, walk down Maršala Tita to Kulovića and take a left; one block down on the left is Pozorišni trg (Theater Square). Enter on Branilaca Sarajeva. (☎ 221 682. Box office open daily 9am-noon and 4-7:30pm.) **Kino Imperijal,** Maršala Tita 56, shows English-language movies daily at 6pm and 8:15pm. (Tickets 4KM.)

Every summer, for the entire month of July, the Turkish Quarter hosts the **Baščaršija Noci** (Turkish Nights), featuring outdoor music, theater, and film. The festival is organized by the Sarajevo Art Center, Dalmatinska 2/1. (☎ 207 921; www.bascarsijskenoci.ba.) In August, locals turn up for the **Sarajevo Film Festival,** eight days of American blockbusters, contemporary European productions, and domestic films. (☎ 609 609; www.sff.ba. Box office open summer M-F 9am-6pm. 4-5KM per film.) Since 1984, Sarajevo has also held the annual festival of **Sarajevska Zima** (Sarajevan Winter; Feb. 7-Mar. 21), Maršala Tita 9, a celebration of culture and art that persisted even through the siege. (☎ 207 948; www.sarajevskazima.ba.)

🎷 NIGHTLIFE

In the warmer months, bars and cafes overflow with people every night. Popular music pumps from clubs along **Štrosmajerova,** steamy jazz rises out of basement bars, and traditional Turkish music resonates from all corners of **Baščaršija.**

🎵 **Jazz Bar "Clou,"** Mula Mustafe Bašeskije 5 (☎ 061 182 445), 2 blocks up from the Eternal Flame, on the left. Could be a speakeasy, except for the bright white sign outside. A club downstairs streams the best music selection in town into the open-air patio. The club begins to fill up around 11pm. Beer 3-4KM. Open daily 8:30pm-5am.

🎵 **Pivnica HS,** Franjevačka 15 (☎ 239 740). Follow Konak away from the Carevo Bridge, and bear left on Franjevačka. Run by the Sarajevsko Pivo brewery next door, this beer hall resembles a 19th-century Viennese cafe. Beer 7KM per L. Open daily 10am-11pm.

The Bar, Maršala Tita 5 (☎ 061 202 159). Draws international and local trendsetters to a shaded, open-air patio with platforms covered in cushions. Chill outside or dance inside to house. The Bar now also hosts occasional art exhibits and fashion shows. Beer 3-5KM. Cover F-Sa night 3KM. Open daily June-Aug. 9am-3am; Sept.-May 6pm-3am.

City Pub, Zelenih Beretki 22b (☎ 209 789). Don't even think about getting inside on a summer evening—young people with cheap tap beer (2-3KM) overflow from the pub, taking over the entire street. Live jazz W 2pm. Open Su-Th 10am-midnight; F-Sa the pub accommodates night owls until 3-4am. MC/V.

🔃 DAYTRIP FROM SARAJEVO

JAHORINA ☎(0)57

Buses run to Pale (30min., 5-6 per day, 3.50KM). From there, take a taxi to the top (15min., 20KM). In winter, daily buses run directly to and from Jahorina from the National Museum (see p. 108; round-trip 10KM).

Prior to 1990, Sarajevo was a popular winter destination, boasting world-class skiing; the mountain resorts of Jahorina and Bjelašnica hosted the 1984 Winter Olympics. Bjelašnica's winter wonderland was mostly destroyed in the 1990s war, but Jahorina was left virtually untouched. In winter, the resort once again attracts skiers; a full day of skiing costs less than 20KM. In summer, visitors hike across the mountain's 20km of ski trails and enjoy picnics near mountain springs. If you want to stay the night, try **Pansion Sport ❶**, Jahorina Poljice (☎270 444), 50m from the slopes. (Open year-round. English spoken. 65 beds in 24 rooms. Breakfast included. 40KM). **Hotel Bistrica** (☎270 020; www.oc-jahorina.com) **rents skis** (20KM).

MOSTAR ☎(0)36

Bosnia and Herzegovina's second-largest city, Mostar (MOH-stahr; pop. 120,000) spreads out on either side of the turquoise Neretva River. The 16th-century Turkish city takes its name from the *mostari*, the keepers of the famous Stari Most (Old Bridge), a 21m high bridge built without mortar in 1566. After the fall of the Ottoman Empire at the end of the 19th century, Mostar became defined by its capacity to bring Catholic, Muslim, and Orthodox citizens together peacefully. Although the recent civil war shattered that balance, destroyed much of the city, and left Mostar starkly divided, international assistance has been strongly invested in restoring the Old Bridge and constructing new housing. Coverage of Mostar was last updated in July of 2003.

⌷ TRANSPORTATION. The **bus station,** Trg Krndela bb (☎552 025), lies 50m from the river on the east bank in the northern part of the city. To reach the east side of Kujundžiluk, walk straight across Titova and take the next left onto M. Balorde, which becomes Fejića (15min.). For the west side, cross the bridge on Deset Hercegivaške Brigade. Before Hotel Ero, just past the bridge, turn left on Aleske Šantica, walk for 15min., and turn left onto Rade Bitange. **Buses** to: **Sarajevo** (3hr., 6 per day, 11KM); **Dubrovnik, CRO** (3hr., 2 per day, 21KM); **Split, CRO** (4hr., 3 per day, 17KM); **Zagreb, CRO** (9hr., 1 per day, 42KM). **Trains,** behind the bus station, go to **Sarajevo** (3hr., 2 per day, 9KM) and **Zagreb, CRO** (15hr., 1 per day, 58KM).

⌷🔃 ORIENTATION AND PRACTICAL INFORMATION. Mostar is large and sprawling with no compact downtown. The **Neretva River** divides the city from north to south, paralleled on the east by **Maršala Tita** and on the west by **Ante Starčevića,** which becomes bul. Hrvatskih Branitelja south of Šanski trg. The heart of the city is **Kujundžiluk,** the Old Town, named after the *kujundžije* (coppersmiths) who lived and worked here. It straddles the river near the southern end of the two main streets. In general, Bosniaks live to the east of Aleske Šantića, and Croats to the west. The division is anything but arbitrary; it reflects the old **front line** of the war. If you get lost, look up—the side with the enormous cross on the mountain is the Croat side. The **Tourist Information Center (TIC),** at the intersection of Rade Bitange and Onešcukova on the west side of Kujundžiluk, provides directions and info on accommodations and food and sells guidebooks with city **maps.** (☎/fax 580 833. Open daily 8am-5pm.) **Zagrebačka Banka,** Kardinala Stepinca bb, on the right side of Hotel Ero, **exchanges currency** for no commission, cashes **traveler's**

checks for 1.5% commission, and provides **Western Union** services. (☎/fax 312 120. Open M-F 8am-2:30pm, Sa 8am-noon.) There is a 24hr. (MC/V) **ATM** in front of the bank. A **24hr. pharmacy, Dežrna Apoteka,** Poslovnica 1 (☎551 035), is near Kujundžiluk; enter from Maršala Tita, next to #123. The **telephone office** (☎328 362; open M-F 7am-8pm, Sa 7am-7pm) is next to the **post office,** Ante Starčevića bb, around the corner from Hotel Ero, which **exchanges currency** for no commission and holds **Poste Restante.** (☎328 362. Open Apr.-Sept. M-F 7am-8pm, Sa 7am-7pm; Oct.-Mar. M-F 7am-7pm, Sa 7am-6pm.) **Postal Code:** 88101.

▐▐ ACCOMMODATIONS AND FOOD. Unless you plan to spend a pretty penny in one of Mostar's modern hotels, *pansions* are your best bet. A 5min. walk from Kujundžiluk, **Villa Ossa ❶,** Vukovića 40b, offers five spotless rooms with double beds, showers, and A/C. From the bus station, walk across the bridge and turn left just after Hotel Ero, at Zagrebačka Banka. Walk down Ante Starčevića and continue along bul. Hrvatskih (20min.); turn left at the third traffic light then bear right over the bridge at Restoran Oscar on Vokovića. A taxi from the bus station will cost you 10KM. (☎578 322. Reception 24hr. Check-out 10am. Reserve 2-3 days in advance. Singles 30KM; doubles 40KM.) Another option on the west side of the Old Town is the **Erna Puzić's pansion ❶,** Maršala Tita 189. (☎550 416. Singles 20KM; doubles 40KM; 3-person apartments 60KM.) The best places to dine are in Kujundžiluk. On the west side, try **◼Konoba Taurus ❹,** Kriva Ćuprija bb, a local favorite in a stone hut above a small branch of the Radobolja River. From Onešcukova, take the small stone steps down to your left. (☎212 617. Open daily 11am-11pm.) **Pozorišna Kafana ❸** (Theater Cafe), Braće Brkića 2, is in the National Theater (Narodno Kazalište) building on Maršala Tita. Enter on the right side through the square. Roman blinds, low-hanging paper lamps, and deep red table cloths add a sense of intrigue; tasty food completes the thrill. (☎551 113. Entrees 6-15KM. Vegetarian options available. Open daily 8am-midnight.)

◼◼ SIGHTS AND NIGHTLIFE. The famous **Stari Most** (Old Bridge) is both the symbol of Mostar and one of the most potent metaphors for the war in Bosnia. Built by the Turks in the 16th century, it connected the Muslim and Croat halves of the city through the fall of the Ottoman Empire and the two World Wars. On November 9, 1993, Bosnian Croat gunmen defied UNESCO protection and senselessly brought it down, inspiring an official Bosnian day of mourning. Restoration was completed in August, 2003, with the help of international funding, using many of the original *tenelija* stones were recovered from the river. The enchanting, cobblestone **Kujundžiluk** (Old Town) lies on both sides of the bridge. The most famous mosque in Mostar is the **Karadžozbeg Mosque,** built in 1557. From Kujundžiluk, walk north along the river on Ulica Braće Fejića for 5min. The minaret and other parts of the mosque were completely destroyed during the war, but the Turkish government paid to rebuild it in 2001. (Open daily 9am-8pm. Free.) The **Turkish House,** Bišćevića 13, features traditional Turkish arts and crafts and hand-carved wooden detailing in the ceiling and walls. (Open daily 8am-8pm. 2KM.) Much of Mostar has been rebuilt since the 1992-95 civil war, but along the old **front line,** visitors can see 3km of post-apocalyptic destruction juxtaposed with new yellow apartment buildings, starting at the Hotel Ero, running down Aleske Santića for a block, then moving away from the river to bul. Hrvatskih Braitelja, and continuing south.

When the sun goes down, make for **◼Havana,** Trg Republike 1, at the second bridge downstream from the bus station. Mostar's newest hotspot is perched on the roof of the *Gradsko Kupatilo* (City Bath). Check out the twinkling lights of the city or the sparkling eyes of the comely locals who flock here. (☎061 839 474. Open daily 9pm-3am.) Kick it with the artists at **Alternativni Institut,** Bunur bb, at the permanent footbridge 200m upstream from Stari Most. Tucked into the rocks on the east bank of the Neretva, this club got its start as a meeting place for artists to share their work. The founders began an underground magazine of poetry and art, and soon local musicians began showing up to entertain. (☎061 194 796; www.kolaps.org. Open daily 10am-3pm and 5pm-1am.)

▶ **DAYTRIP FROM MOSTAR: MEĐUGORJE.** On June 24, 1981, six teenagers from Međugorje (Meh-joo-GOHR-yeh; pop. 4000) reported that a vision of the Virgin Mary appeared and spoke to them while they were playing on a nearby hill. This apparition, which they claim has visited them daily ever since, has made the small mountain town a popular Catholic pilgrimage destination. Nearly 20 million visitors have passed through since 1981. At the heart of Međugorje is **St. James's Church.** Built in 1969, long before the visions, the church has been expanded to accommodate the pilgrims. (English Mass M-Sa 10am, Su and feast days noon.) The **tourist office,** left of the church, has info on the history of the visions and on Međugorje's festivals (☎651 988. Open daily 9am-6pm). Behind the church, an **open-air theater** holds multilingual **prayer services** daily 6-9pm. The children first saw the vision on the **Hill of Apparitions** in the hamlet of **Podbrdo,** a dusty 1.5km walk from the church. The rocky path uphill is marked by reliefs by Italian sculptor Carmelo Puzzolo depicting the mysteries of the rosary; a life-sized statue of Mary stands on top. Every year Međugorje celebrates the **Anniversary of the Apparitions** on June 25 and the massive **Youth Theater Festival,** which occurs from July 31 to Aug. 6. *(Two buses run daily from Mostar to Međugorje. The ride takes 45min. and costs 3KM. For a bus schedule, look on the door of the post office next to the station.)*

BULGARIA
(БЪЛГАРИЯ)

LEVA		
AUS$1 = 1.14LV	1LV = AUS$0.87	
CDN$1 = 1.21LV	1LV = CDN$0.82	
EUR€1 = 1.96LV	1LV = EUR€0.50	
NZ$1 = 1.04LV	1LV = NZ$0.95	
UK£1 = 2.93LV	1LV = UK£0.34	
US$1 = 1.59LV	1LV = US$0.62	

From the pine-covered slopes of the Rila, Pirin, and Rodopi mountains in the southwest to the beaches of the Black Sea, Bulgaria is blessed with a countryside rich in natural resources and steeped in ancient custom. The history of the Bulgarian people, however, is not as serene as the landscape: crumbling Greco-Thracian ruins and Soviet-style high-rises attest to centuries of turmoil and political struggle. Today, Bulgaria's flagging economy hinders the likelihood of its entering the EU. However, travelers still find rewarding vacations on the beautiful Bulgarian Black Sea Coast, in cosmopolitan Sofia, and in charming, traditional villages.

HISTORY

BULGARIA IS BORN. The ancient **Thracian tribes,** who occupied Bulgaria during the Bronze Age (c. 3500 BC), were gradually assimilated or expelled by Greek and Roman settlers. The Western Roman Empire crumbled in AD 476, and by the 7th century the Slavs had invaded the Balkan Peninsula. The late 7th century also brought the **Bulgars,** nomads from central Asia. The year 681 marks the birth of the Bulgarian state (the third oldest in Europe), when Byzantium recognized Bulgar control between the Balkans and the Danube.

FIRST AND SECOND BULGARIAN EMPIRES. Under **Boris I** and his son **Simeon I,** the Bulgars and Slavs integrated under a common language (Old Church Slavonic) and religion (Christianity). This **First Bulgarian Empire** saw vast artistic develop-

FACTS AND FIGURES

OFFICIAL NAME: Republic of Bulgaria

CAPITAL: Sofia (pop. 1.2 million)

POPULATION: 7.6 million

LANGUAGE: Bulgarian

CURRENCY: 1 lev (lv) = 100 stotinki

RELIGION: 84% Orthodox Christian, 12% Muslim, 2% Catholic, 2% other

LAND AREA: 110,910km²

CLIMATE: Temperate

GEOGRAPHY: Mountains and plains

BORDERS: Greece, Macedonia, Romania, Serbia and Montenegro, Turkey

ECONOMY: 43% Services, 31% Industry, 26% Agriculture

GDP: US$6600 per capita

COUNTRY CODE: 359

INTERNATIONAL DIALING PREFIX: 00

B U L G A R I A

ment and the construction of many sumptuous palaces. After Simeon I's death, however, the empire became weak from internal divisions and fell prey to Byzantine invasion. A revolt in 1185, led by the brothers **Ivan** and **Peter Asen** of Tŭrnovo, forced Constantinople to recognize the independence of the **Second Bulgarian Empire,** which came to extend from the Black Sea to the Aegean (and, after 1204, to the Adriatic) and was the leading power in the Balkans.

REVOLUTIONARY RUMBLINGS. Internal upheaval, wars with the Serbian and Hungarian kingdoms, and attacks by Mongols soon weakened the new empire, and by 1396 what remained of Bulgarian independence was lost to the Turks. For the next 500 years, Bulgaria suffered under the **"Turkish yoke."** During this period of repression, bandits known as **haiduti** kept the spirit of resistance alive. The **National Revival,** a period of Bulgarian cultural and educational awakening, was led by **Lyuben Karavelov** and **Vasil Levski,** who created the Bulgarian Secret Central Committee in Bucharest. The revolutionaries planned the **April Uprising,** which was so brutally suppressed by the Turks that it became known as the **Bulgarian Horrors.** A conference of European statesmen convened after the uprising and proposed reforms, which Turkey rejected. Russia declared war in response.

BOUNDARIES CHALLENGED. The **Russo-Turkish War** (1877-78) ended with the **Treaty of San Stefano** and the expansion of Bulgaria's boundaries to stretch from the Danube to the Aegean and to the Black Sea. Austria-Hungary and Britain, however, were unhappy with such a large Slavic state in the Russian sphere of influence. At the 1878 **Congress of Berlin** they redrew the boundaries to create a much smaller state that included less of Macedonia. Simmering tensions over the new borders erupted in the **First** and **Second Balkan Wars** in the 1910s. These resulted in a further loss of territory for Bulgaria, which surrendered its neutrality in **WWI** and sided with the Central Powers in the hope of recovering its losses. Unsuccessful, Bulgaria lost land in the 1919 **Treaty of Neuilly** at the end of the war. Though neutral at the start of **WWII,** a lust for Greek and Yugoslav territories caused **Boris III** (1918-1943) to join the Axis Powers in 1941, and in 1944 the Soviet Union declared war on Bulgaria. The **Fatherland Front,** an anti-German resistance group, led a successful coup d'état four days later, and the new prime minister sought an immediate armistice with the USSR. Elections in 1945 left Bulgaria a communist republic.

A NEW BULGARIA. Bulgaria saw nationalization under communist leader **Georgi Dimitrov** in the late 1940s, isolationism under **Vulko Chervenkov** in the 1950s, and rapid industrialization and alignment with the Soviet Union under **Todor Zhivkov** from 1962-89. With sociologist **Zhelyu Zhelev** as president and poet **Blaga Dimitrova** as vice-president, the new government embraced openness and pluralism and ended repression of ethnic Turks. The 1990s were not kind to Bulgaria. The country's first elections were won by reform communists of the Bulgarian Socialist Party. President Zhelev experienced political opposition that rendered Prime Minister **Andrei Lukanov's** cabinet impotent. A "government of national unity" took over to produce a new constitution. Currency troubles led to the resurgence of the BSP in 1994, but they only drove the economy farther into the ground. The leva fell from 71lv to the US dollar in April 1996 to 3000lv in February 1997. The **United Democratic Forces,** a coalition led by Prime Minister **Ivan Kostov,** managed to stabilize the economy. Under public scrutiny for instituting reforms that have incurred record unemployment, Kostov continued with his plans in the hopes that they will improve Bulgaria's chances of joining the **EU** in 2007.

TODAY. In 2001, the Bulgarian electorate brought the **Simeon II National Movement (SNM)** and the Bulgarian monarch to power as prime minister; current president Georgi Parvanov is a member of the **Bulgarian Socialist Party.** Despite

promises of economic revival, Bulgaria remains one of Europe's poorest countries. Though it acquired a US$450 million loan from the **World Bank,** Bulgaria may lose the US$150 million it has already received if it doesn't reform its legal system and privatize its state-owned tobacco monopoly. Bulgaria became a member of **NATO** in 2004.

PEOPLE AND CULTURE

LANGUAGE

 YES AND NO. Bulgarians shake their heads from side to side to indicate "yes" and up and down to indicate "no," the exact opposite of Brits and Yanks. For the uncoordinated, it's easier to just hold your head still and say *da* or *neh.*

Bulgarian is a South Slavic language. A few words are borrowed from Turkish and Greek, but most vocabulary is similar to Russian and other Slavic languages. **English** is spoken by urban young people and in tourist areas. **German** and **Russian** are often understood. Street names are in the process of changing; you may need both old and new names. Bulgarian transliteration is much the same as Russian (see **the Cyrillic Alphabet,** p. 52) except that "щ" is "*sht*" and "ъ" is "*ŭ*" (pronounced like the "u" in bug). For a phrasebook and glossary, see **Glossary: Bulgarian, p. 945.**

FOOD AND DRINK

BULGARIA	❶	❷	❸	❹	❺
FOOD	under 4lv	4-8lv	9-14lv	15-18lv	over 18lv

Restaurants average 6lv per meal, while food from **kiosks** is much cheaper (0.60-2.50lv). Kiosks sell *kebabcheta* (кебабчета; sausage burgers), sandwiches, pizzas, and *banitsa sus sirene* (баница със сирене; feta cheese-filled pastries). Try *shopska salata* (шопска салата), a mix of tomatoes, peppers, and cucumbers with feta cheese. *Tarator* (таратор), a cold soup made with yogurt, cucumber, garlic, and sometimes walnuts, is also tasty. Bulgaria enjoys **meat.** *Kavarma* (каварма), meat with onions, spices, and egg is slightly more expensive than *skara* (скара; grills). **Vegetarians** should request *iastia bez meso* (iahs-tea-ah bez meh-so) for meals without meat. Bulgarians are known for cheese and yogurt—the bacteria that makes yogurt from milk bears the scientific name *Lactobacillus bulgaricus*. *Ayran* (айран; yogurt with water and ice) and *boza* (боза; similar to beer, but sweet and thicker) are popular drinks that complement breakfast. Breads and meats are often plain-tasting; soups offer more flavor. Bulgaria exports mineral water and locals swear by its healing qualities. **Tap water** is generally safe to drink. Melnik (see p. 138) produces famous red **wine** and the northeast is known for excellent whites. On the Black Sea Coast, *Albenu* is a good sparkling wine. Bulgarians begin meals with *rakiya* (ракия; grape or plum brandy). Good Bulgarian **beers** include Kamenitza and Zagorka. The drinking age is 18.

CUSTOMS AND ETIQUETTE

Making the **"V" sign** signifies showing support for the opposition party; don't make it. Do not address someone by their first name until you have become friends. Always shake someone's hand when introduced. If invited to someone's home, it is a good idea to bring a **gift** of flowers, candy, or wine. Don't bring calla lilies or gladioli, they are usually only used for weddings or funerals. Giving postcards of your home town is a good way to thank someone or to say hello. Ask permission before taking someone's photograph. Avoid wearing baggy shorts or backpacks–you will stick out as a tourist. Button-down shirts and long pants are a safe bet.

Seat yourself at **restaurants** and ask for the *smetka* (сметка; bill) when you're done. It is customary to share tables in restaurants. *Nazdrave!* (Наздзаве!) means "Cheers!"—you're sure to hear this in bars. When clinking glasses (or beer mugs), make sure to look the person in the eye and call *Nazdrave!* loudly. While dining, rest your wrists on the table; do not put one hand in your lap. **Tipping** is not obligatory, but 10% doesn't hurt, especially in Sofia where waitstaff expect it. A 7-10% service charge will occasionally be added for you; always check the bill or the menu to see if it's listed. Restaurants and *mekhani* (механи; taverns) usually charge a small fee to use the restrooms.

THE ARTS

With Tsar Boris's conversion to Christianity came the first major epoch of Bulgarian literature, the **Old Bulgarian** period (AD 900-1200). Under the guidance of the first Slavic language school in Preslav, the translation of religious texts flourished. Bulgarian culture during this **Golden Age** was on pace to compete with that of the Byzantine capital of **Constantinople**, when conquest by the Byzantines stalled progress until the **Middle Bulgarian** period (13th-17th centuries).

Art and literature went into hibernation during the 500 years of Ottoman rule, but monasteries managed to preserve manuscript writing and iconography until the coming of the **National Revival** *(Vuzrazhdane)* in 1762. The Revival brought on a new romantic style of architecture, excellent examples of which can be seen in Plovdiv. The Revival also coincided with **Paisy of Hilendar's** romanticized *Istoria* *slavyanobulgarska* (Slavo-Bulgarian History), which helped sow the first seeds of nationalism. Using their works as a tool toward liberation, realists **L. Karavelov** and **V. Drumev** depicted small-town life, **Khristo Botev** wrote impassioned revolutionary poetry, and **Petko Slaveykov** and **Georgi Rakovski** drew on folklore to whip the populace into a revolutionary fervor. The works of poet **Ivan Vazov** span the gap from subjugation to liberation, recounting the struggle against the Turks. Meanwhile, brothers Dimitar and Zahari Zograf painted church walls and secular portraits (see **Plovdiv: Sights**, p. 131; **Bachkovo Monastery**, p. 134; **Rila Monastery**, p. 129; **Bansko: Sights**, p. 135; and **Troyan Monastery**, p. 154)

Several female poets have emerged in recent decades. **Petya Dubarova's** promising career was cut short by her early death in 1979. Her collection *Here I Am, in Perfect Leaf Today* was recently published in English. Bulgaria's most important 20th-century poet, **Elisaveta Bagryana**, skillfully fused the experimental and the traditional in her love poems. Young Bulgarian contemporary artists broke through the wall of communist-mandated art in the late 1980s and have jumped onto the postmodern bandwagon. These self-conscious works are edgy and surprising, from **Nikolai Alekseev's** surreal canvases to **George Kalenderov's** conceptual installations. Composer **Kiril Stefanov** blends classical music with tradional folk melodies; the multi-regional ensemble **Chor Angelite** performs an excellent blend of secular and sacred music.

HOLIDAYS AND FESTIVALS

NATIONAL HOLIDAYS IN 2005	
January 1 New Year's Day	**May 24** Education and Culture Day; Day of Slavic Heritage
March 1 Baba Marta (Spring Festival)	
March 3 Liberation Day (1878)	**June 5** Festival of the Roses (Kazaluk)
May 1 Easter	**September 6** Day of Union
May 1 Labor Day	**September 22** Independence Day
May 6 St. George's Day	**December 24-26** Christmas Holiday

Christmas and **New Year's** are holidays characterized by the two related Bulgarian customs of *koledouvane* and *sourvakari*. On Christmas, groups of people go from house to house and perform *koledouvane*, or caroling, while holding beautiful oak sticks called *koledarkas*. On New Year's, a group of *sourvakari* wish their neighbors well while holding decorated cornel rods called *sourvachka*. **Baba marta** (Spring Festival) celebrates the beginning of Spring. Bulgarians traditionally give each other *martenitzas*, small red and white tassels formed to look like a boy and a girl. These fertility charms are meant to be worn around the neck or pinned on until a stork is seen. The **Festival of the Roses** is celebrated in Kazanlŭk and Karlovo on the first Sunday in June (June 5, 2005), and revels in the beauty of one of Bulgaria's most famous exports. Carnivals, feasts, and folk dances abound.

ADDITIONAL RESOURCES

Balkan Ghosts: A Journey Through History, by Robert Kaplan (1994). Both an engaging travelogue and an accessible regional history.

Beyond Hitler's Grasp: The Heroic Rescue of Bulgaria's Jews, by Michael Bar Zohar (2001). An in-depth study of one of Bulgaria's proudest moments.

BULGARIA

BULGARIA ESSENTIALS

ENTRANCE REQUIREMENTS

Passport: Required of all travelers; must be valid for 3 months beyond stay.
Visa: Not required of citizens of Australia, Canada, New Zealand, and the US for up to 30 days; EU citizens do not need visas for up to 90 days.
Letter of Invitation: Not required for those who do not need a visa.
Inoculations: Recommended up-to-date on DTaP (diphtheria, tetanus, and pertussis), Hepatitis A, Hepatitis B, MMR (measles, mumps, and rubella), Polio booster, and Typhoid.
Work Permit: Required of all foreigners planning to work.

DOCUMENTS AND FORMALITIES

EMBASSIES AND CONSULATES

Embassies of other countries in Bulgaria are all in **Sofia** (see p. 121). Bulgaria's embassies and consulates abroad include:

Australian Consulate: 4 Carlotta Rd., Double Bay, Sydney, NSW 2028; Double Bay, NSW 1360 (☎2 9327 7581; www.users.bigpond.com/bulcgsyd).

Canada: 325 Stewart St., Ottawa, ON N1K 6K5 (☎613-789-3215; mailmn@storm.ca).

Greece: 15452 Athens 33 Stratigou Kallari St. (☎301 647 8106; fax 647 8130).

Ireland: 22 Bulington Rd. Dublin 4 (☎1 660 3293; fax 660 3915).

Turkey: Atatürk Bulvarı No: 124 Kavaklıdere, Ankara (☎312 467 1948; fax 467 25 74).

UK: 186-188 Queensgate, London SW7 5HL (☎20 7584 9400; www.bulgarianembassy.org.uk).

US: 1621 22nd St. NW, Washington, D.C. 20008 (☎202-387-0174; www.bulgaria-embassy.org).

VISA AND ENTRY INFORMATION

Citizens of Australia, Canada, New Zealand, and the US may visit Bulgaria visa-free for up to 30 days. Citizens of the EU may visit visa-free for up to 90 days. Anyone planning to stay more than 30 days must obtain a 90-day visa from their local embassy or consulate (see above). US citizens may obtain a visa for free, although they must pay a US$20 processing fee. For non-US citizens, single-entry visas are approx. US$50 for 10 business days processing; US$65 for priority processing; US$120 for multiple-entry visas. Transit visas are US$40 and are valid for 24hr; double transit (valid 24hr.) US$60. Prices include a border tax of approx. US$20; those not needing visas are required to pay the tax upon entering the country. The application requires a passport valid more than six months after return from Bulgaria, a passport photograph, an invitation (if not a US citizen), a copy of your green card (if applicable), proof of medical insurance, payment by cash or money order, and a self-addressed, stamped envelope. There is no express service for multiple-entry visas. If staying in a private residence, register your visa with police within 48 hours of entering Bulgaria; hotels and hostels will do this for you. A Bulgarian **border crossing** can take several hours, as there are three different checkpoints: passport control, customs, and police. Visas are difficult to purchase at the border. Crossing the border on bus or train is often a lengthy process. The border crossing into Turkey is particularly difficult. Enter from Romania at Ruse or Durankulac.

BULGARIA

Foreigner registration is required as of March 2002 in response to September 11. If you are staying in Bulgaria for more than 48 hours, you must register with the police. The hotel or hostel you are staying in will do this for you, and may ask for your passport, but should return it immediately. Keep the registration with your passport, and make sure you are re-registered every time you change accommodations. If you are staying with friends, register yourself with the **Bulgarian Registration Office;** see the consular section of your embassy for details.

GETTING AROUND

All **flights** to Sofia connect through England or Western Europe. Tickets to the capital may run over US$3000 during the summer months. Budget travelers might want to fly into a nearby capital—Athens, Istanbul, or Bucharest—and take a bus to Sofia. Bulgarian airports are on par with international standards.

Bulgarian **trains** run to **Greece, Hungary, Romania,** and **Turkey** and are better for transportation in the north; **Rila** is the main international train company. The train system is comprehensive but slow, crowded, and smoke-filled. Purse-slashing, pickpocketing, and pinching has been reported on more crowded lines. Buy tickets at the Ticket Center (Билетен Център; Bileten Tsentur) stations. There are three types of trains: express (експрес; *ekspres*), fast (бърз; *burz*), and slow (пътнически; *putnicheski*). Avoid *putnicheski* at all costs—they stop at anything that looks inhabited, even if only by goats. Arrive well in advance if you want a seat. Stations are poorly marked and often only in Cyrillic; watch closely for your destination, bring a map, and ask for help. First class (първа класа; *purva klasa*) is identical to second (втора класа; *vtora klasa*), and not worth the extra money. Store luggage at the "гардероб" *(garderob)*.

Buses are better for travel in eastern and western Bulgaria and are often faster than trains, but less frequent and comfortable. Buses head north from Ruse, to Istanbul from anywhere on the Black Sea Coast, and to Greece from Blagoevgrad. For long distances, **Group Travel** and **Etap** have modern buses with A/C and bathrooms for 50% more than trains. Some buses have set departure times; others leave when full. Grueling local buses stop everywhere. **Ferries** from Varna and Burgas make infrequent trips to **Istanbul, TUR** and **Odessa, UKR.**

Yellow **taxis** are everywhere in cities. Refuse to pay in US dollars and insist on a ride *sus apparata* (with meter). Ask the distance and price per kilometer. Don't try to bargain. Some taxi drivers fix the meters to acrue mileage faster than in reality. Tipping **taxi drivers** usually means rounding up to the nearest lev or half-lev. Urban roads are in fair condition. Rural roads are in poor repair; rocks and landslides pose a threat in mountainous areas. **Seatbelts** are mandatory in Bulgaria. **Motoroads** (www.motoroads.com) and travel agencies offer bike tours; stay alert when biking in urban areas as drivers ignore traffic signals. Hitchhiking is rare in Bulgaria because drivers rarely stop. Those who do get picked up report it's generally safe, but *Let's Go* does not recommend hitchhiking.

TOURIST SERVICES AND MONEY

Tourist offices and local **travel agencies** are generally knowledgeable and reserve private rooms; some mostly plan itineraries. Staffs are helpful and usually speak English, German, and some Russian. Big hotels often have an English-speaking receptionist and **maps** and make good resources.

The **lev** (**lv**; plural **leva**) is the standard monetary unit (1 lev = 100 stotinki), though sometimes US dollars or euros are accepted. **Inflation** is around 10.2%, so expect prices to change over the next year. Private banks and exchange bureaus exchange money, but bank rates are more reliable. The four largest **banks** are Bulbank, Biohim, Hebros, and OBB. **Traveler's checks** can only be cashed at banks (with the exception of a few change bureaus). Many banks also give **Visa cash advances. Credit cards** are rarely accepted. **ATMs** give the best exchange rates and are common throughout Bulgaria, usually accept MasterCard, Visa, Plus, and Cirrus and give the best rates. It is illegal to exchange currency on the street.

Businesses usually open at 9am and take a 1hr. lunch break between 11am and 2pm. Banks are usually open 8:30am to 4pm, but some close at 2pm. Stores close at 6 or 8pm; in tourist areas and big cities, shops may stay open as late as 10pm.

HEALTH AND SAFETY

 EMERGENCY NUMBERS: Police: ☎166 **Fire:** ☎160 **Emergency:** ☎150

While basic **medical supplies** are available in Bulgarian **hospitals,** specialized treatment is not. Emergency care is better in Sofia than in the rest of the country, but it's best to avoid hospitals entirely. Travelers are required to carry proof of insurance; most doctors expect cash payment. In the case of extreme emergency, air evacuation runs about US$50,000.

The sign "Аптека" (apteka) denotes a **pharmacy.** There is always a night-duty pharmacy in larger towns. *Analgin* is headache medicine; *analgin chinin* is for colds and flu; bandages are *sitoplast.* Foreign brands of *prezervatifs* (condoms) are safer. Prescription drugs are difficult to obtain—bring enough of your own. Fiber tablets are a must, as it's easy to get constipated on a Bulgarian diet. Public **bathrooms** (Ж for women, M for men) are often holes in the ground; pack toilet paper and hand sanitizer. Expect to pay 0.05-0.20lv. **Tampons** are widely available. Don't buy bottles of **alcohol** from street vendors, and be careful with homemade liquor—there have been cases of poisoning and contamination. Asthmatics, beware: most of Bulgaria's restaurants, taverns, and public transportation are heavily smoke-filled; buses are an exception. Be aware of petty **street crime,** especially pickpocketing and purse snatching. Also be wary of people posing as government officials; ask them to show ID. Accepting beverages from strangers may result in being drugged and robbed.

As long as they exercise the necessary precautions, it's generally fine for **women** to travel alone. Wear skirts and blouses to avoid unwanted attention; only young girls wear sneakers, tank tops, or shorts outside of big cities. Visitors with physical **disabilities** will confront many challenges in Bulgaria. There is much **discrimination** against **Roma** (gypsies), who are considered a nuisance at best and thieves at worst. While hate crimes are rare, persons of a foreign ethnicity might receive stares. The Bulgarian government has recently recognized **homosexuality,** but acceptance is slow in coming; it is prudent to avoid public displays of affection.

ACCOMMODATIONS AND CAMPING

BULGARIA	❶	❷	❸	❹	❺
ACCOM.	under 20lv	21-35lv	36-50lv	51-70lv	over 70lv

Bulgarian **hotels** are classed on a star system and licensed by the Government Committee on Tourism. Rooms in one-star hotels are nearly identical to rooms in two- and three-star hotels, but have no private bathrooms. All accommodations provide sheets and towels. Expect to pay US$9-50, though foreigners are sometimes charged higher prices. **Hostels** can be found in most major cities and run US$10-18 per bed. Almost all include free breakfast and many offer amenities such as Internet and laundry service. For a complete list of the hostels in Bulgaria see www.hostels.com/en/bg.ot.html. **Private rooms** are cheap and usually have all the amenities of a good hotel (US$6-12); if one has the language skills and persistence, they can be found in any small town. Outside major towns, most **campgrounds** provide spartan bungalows and tent space. Some are poorly maintained or unpredictable, so check before it's too late to stay elsewhere.

KEEPING IN TOUCH

The Bulgarian **mail** system moves slowly. "Създушна поща" on letters indicates **airmail**. It's better than ground transport mail, but postal workers may be reluctant to let you pay extra to have it sent by air. Sending a **letter** abroad costs 0.60lv to Europe, 0.90lv to the US, and 0.80-1.00lv to Australia or New Zealand; note that a Bulgarian return address is required. **Packages** must be unwrapped for inspection. Register important packages, and allow two weeks for it to arrive. Mail can be received general delivery through Poste Restante (писма до поискване), though it is unreliable. Address envelope as follows: Diana (first name), HRISTOVA (LAST NAME), POSTE RESTANTE, писма до поискване централна поща, Гурко 6 (post office address), София (city) 1000 (postal code), България (Bulgaria).

Making international **telephone** calls from Bulgaria can be a challenge. Pay phones are expensive; opt for the phone offices. If you must make an **international call** from a pay phone with a card, purchase the 400 unit, 20lv card. Units run out quickly on international calls, so talk fast or have multiple cards ready. There are two brands: **BulFon** (orange) and **Mobika** (blue), which work only at telephones of the same brand; BulFon is better and more prevalent. One minute costs 0.70lv to Australia, 0.30lv to the US, and 0.40lv to the UK. To **call collect,** call the international operator ☎ 01 23. The Bulgarian phrase for collect call is *za tyahna smetka* (за тяхна сметка). Pay phones rarely accept coins. Instead, use a phone card for **local calls.** You can also call from the post office, where a clerk assigns you a booth and you pay when finished. International access codes include: **AT&T** Direct (☎ 00-800-0010); **BT Payphones** (☎ 00-800-9727); and **MCI** (☎ 00-800-0001).

Internet cafes can be found throughout urban centers, cost approx. 1lv per hr., and are often open 24hr.

SOFIA (СОФИЯ)   ☎(0)2

A history of national submission has left Bulgaria a little unsure of its own identity, but Sofia resolves this crisis by adopting multiple personalities. Skateboarding ramps stand in front of the iron Soviet Army monument, while the Harry Potter craze and McDonald's make their presence known throughout the city. Yet neither communism nor globalization have robbed the city of its identity; with rich architecture and thriving cultural life, Sofia clings to its complicated individuality.

✈ INTERCITY TRANSPORTATION

Flights: Airport Sofia (International info ☎ 79 80 35). Bus #84 is to the right as you exit international arrivals. Buy tickets (0.50lv) at kiosks with a "Билети" (bileti) sign. Runs from the airport to Eagle Bridge (Орлов Мост), near Sofia University, a 10min. walk from the city center. Minibus #30 (in front of the international arrivals exit; 1lv) runs between the airport and pl. Sv. Nedelya along bul. Tsar Osvoboditel. The minibus has no specific stops; to ride, flag it down and request a stop. Taxis in front of the airport are expensive (up to 25lv), but taxis ordered from the **OK Supertrans taxi** desk inside the terminal or at an outside stand are significantly cheaper (5lv). Airlines include: **Air**

France, Suborna 5 (Съборна; ☎981 78 30; open M-F 9am-5:30pm); **British Airways,** Patriarkh Evtimiy 49 (Патриарх Евтимий; ☎954 70 00; open M-F 9am-5:30pm); **Lufthansa,** Suborna 9 (☎980 41 41; open M-F 9am-5pm).

Trains: Tsentralna Gara (Централна Гара; Central Train Station), Knyaginya Mariya Luiza St. (Мария Луиза; www.razpisanie.bdz.bg), a 1.6km walk from pl. Sveta Nedelya past the department store TSUM (ЦУМ) and the mosque. Trams #1 and 7 run between pl. Sveta Nedelya and the station; #9 and 12 head down Khristo Botev (Христо Ботев) and bul. Vitosha (Витоша). See website for up-to-date timetables. Info booth and tickets for northern Bulgaria are on the 1st fl. To: **Burgas** (5 per day, 9.60-17.90lv); **Plovdiv** (14 per day, 4.20-8.30lv); **Ruse** (4 per day, 8.80-16.70lv); **Varna** (6 per day, 12.00-21.50lv). Trip lengths depend on type of train (Пътнически, slow; Бърз, fast; Експрес, express). Train schedules change with the season, so call ahead. International tickets available at the **ticket office** (☎931 11 11). Open M-F 7am-7pm. International trips must be approved by border officers. To the left of the main entrance, **Rila Travel Bureau** (Рила; ☎932 33 46) sells tickets to: **Athens, GCE** via **Thessaloniki, GCE** (1 per day, 65-90lv); **Niš, SMN** (2 per day, 12lv); and **Budapest, HUN** via **Bucharest, ROM** (1 per day, 150lv). Open daily 6am-11pm.

Buses: Private buses, which leave from the parking lot across from the train station, are reasonably priced and usually fast. International bus companies are located next to the parking lot directly across from the entrance to the train station. **Group Travel** (☎931 81 23) sends buses to: **Burgas** (2 per day, 17lv); **Varna** (3 per day, 21lv); **Veliko Tŭrnovo** (4 per day, 11lv). **Matpu** offers service to **Skopje, MAC** (1 per day, 20lv). Buy tickets at kiosks labeled "Билетен Център" (Bileten Tsentŭr; Ticket Center; ☎ 900 21 00). Pay in lv. Arrive 30-45min. early for a guaranteed seat. Open daily 6am-11pm.

■ ORIENTATION

The city center, **pl. Sveta Nedelya** (Света Неделя), is a triangle formed by the Tsurkva (Church) Sv. Nedelya, the wide Sheraton Hotel, and the department store Tsentralen Universalen Magazin (TSUM). **Bul. Knyaginya Mariya Luiza** (Княгиня Мария Луиза) connects pl. Sveta Nedelya to the train station. Trams #1 and 7 run from the train station through pl. Sveta Nedelya to **bul. Vitosha** (Витоша), one of the main shopping and nightlife thoroughfares. Bul. Vitosha links pl. Sveta Nedelya to **pl. Bŭlgaria** and the huge, concrete **Natsionalen Dvorets na Kulturata** (Национален Дворец на Културата; **NDK, National Palace of Culture**). Historic **bul. Tsar Osvoboditel** (Цар Освободител; Tsar the Liberator) is on your right as you go down bul. Mariya Luiza, and heads to both **Sofia University** and the hottest spots for dancing and drinking. The free *Inside & Out Guide* (available at the Sheraton Hotel and at tourist centers) is a great English publication with loads of tourist info. *The Program (Programata*, Програмата; www.programata.bg) is a weekly city guide that offers listings of current events and more up-to-date information. Available in Bulgarian in most establishments and sometimes in English. **Maps** are available in the lobby of the Sheraton Hotel (open 24hr.) and the open-air book market at Slaveykov Sq. (Славейков) on Graf Ignatiev (Граф Игнатиев).

■ LOCAL TRANSPORTATION

Public Transportation: Trams, trolleybuses, and buses cost 0.50lv per ride, 2lv for 5 rides, day pass 2.20lv, 5-day pass 10lv. Buy tickets at kiosks with a "билети" (bileti) sign stuck to the window or from the driver; exact change only. Punch the tickets in the machines on board to avoid a 5lv fine. If you put your backpack on a seat, you may be required to buy a second ticket, or pay a 5lv fine for an "unticketed passenger." All transportation runs daily 5:30am-11:00pm; after 9pm service becomes less frequent.

Sofia

▲ ACCOMMODATIONS
Art-Hostel, 10
Hotel Sofia, 2
Hotel Stivan-Iskar, 1

● FOOD
Dani's Bistro, 8
Divaka, 9
Jimmy's, 7
Murphy's Irish Pub, 6

■ NIGHTLIFE
The Barn, 11
Dali, 3
My Mojito, 5
Spartacus, 4

BULGARIA

Taxis: While some travelers have terrible taxi tales, **Taxi-S-Express** (☎912 80), **OK Taxi** (☎973 21 21), and **INEX** (☎919 19) are reliable options. Always make sure that the company's name and phone number are listed on the side of the car. Instead of bargaining, simply insist that the driver turn on the meter. Drivers don't speak English, so learn how to pronounce the Bulgarian names for destinations. Fares are 0.40-0.45lv per km, and become slightly more expensive 10pm-6am.

🔢 PRACTICAL INFORMATION

TOURIST AND FINANCIAL SERVICES

🔲 **Tourist Office: Odysseia-In/Zig Zag Holidays,** bul. Stamboliyski 20-B (Стамболийски; ☎980 51 02; http://zigzag.dir.bg). From pl. Sv. Nedelya, go down Stamboliyski and take the 2nd right on Lavele; Odysseia is halfway down on the left. The staff arranges homestays in Bulgarian villages and outdoor excursions, including rock climbing, spelunking, biking, skiing, and snowshoeing. Consultation 5lv per session. Open daily high season 9am-6:30pm; low season M-Sa 9am-6:30pm.

Embassies: Australia, ul. Trakiya 37 (☎946 1334). **Canada,** ul. Assen Zlatarov 11 (☎943 37 04). **Macedonia,** ul. Joliot-Curie 17F (☎970 28 32; todmak@bgnet.bg). **Romania,** ul. Sitniakovo 4 (☎973 28 58; ambsofro@exco.net). **Serbia and Montenegro,** Veliko Tŭrnovo 3, (☎946 16 35; yembisof@tradel.net). Open M-F 9am-noon. **Turkey,** Vasil Levski bl. 80 (☎980 22 70). **UK,** ul. Moskovska 9 (Московска; ☎933 92 22). Register either by phone or in person upon arrival in Bulgaria. Open M-Th 8am-12:30pm and 2-5pm, F 9am-12pm. Citizens of **Ireland** or **New Zealand** should contact the UK embassy. **US,** ul. Sŭborna 1a (Съборна; ☎937 51 004), 3 blocks from pl. Sveta Nedelya behind the Sheraton. Open M-Th 8:30am-5pm, F 8:30am-1pm. Consular section at Kapitan Andreev 1 (Капитан Андреев; ☎963 20 22), behind the NDK. Open M-F 9am-5pm.

Currency Exchange: Bulbank (Булбанк; ☎923 21 11), pl. Sv. Nedelya 7, cashes **traveler's checks** (min. US$3 fee) and gives Visa **cash advances** (4% commission). Open M-F 8am-6pm.

American Express: D. Ignatiy 21, 2nd fl. (☎988 49 53), on the left past the post office heading toward Slaveykov Sq. Issues (1% commission) and cashes (3.5% commission) AmEx Traveler's Cheques. Open daily M-F 9am-6pm, Sa 9am-noon.

LOCAL AND EMERGENCY SERVICES

Luggage Storage: Downstairs at the central train station. 0.80lv per piece. Claim bags 30min. before departure. Open daily 6am-midnight.

Library: Biblioteka Slaveiykov, Slaveykov 4 (☎980 66 88, ext. 530) has an English library. Library cards 4lv. Open M-Tu, Th-F 9:30am-12:30pm and 1-6pm, W 1pm-6pm.

Cultural Center: Euro-Bulgarian Cultural Centre (**EBCC;** Евро-Български Културен Център), bul. Stamboliyski 17 (Стамболийски; ☎988 00 84; www.eubcc.bg). A knowledgeable, English-speaking staff answers all of your questions and provides info about Bulgarian culture. On your way out, check out the Arts Cinema, the bookstore Khelikan (Хеликон), and the art gallery. **Internet access** (open M-F 9am-10pm, Sa 10am-10pm, Su 11am-7pm) 1.20lv per hr. The office has a scanner and photocopier. Open M-F 9am-7pm, Sa 12:30pm-5:30pm.

24hr. Pharmacies: Apteka Sv. Nedelya, pl. Sv. Nedelya 5 (☎950 50 26), at Stamboliyski. **Apteka Vassil Levski,** bul. Vassil Levski 70 (☎ 986 17 55), around the corner from Popa.

Medical Assistance: State-owned hospitals offer foreigners free 24hr. emergency aid, but the staff may not speak English. **Pirogov Emergency Hospital,** bul. Gen. Totleben 21 (Ген. Тотлебен; ☎915 44 11), across from Hotel Rodina. Take trolley #5 or 19 from the center. The **Okruzhna Bolnitsa Hospital,** Mladost 1, ul. Dimitar Mollov 1, offers a ward for foreigners but is far from the city center. (☎975 90 00). For dog bites or emergency tetanus shots (9.20lv), go to the **First City Hospital,** bul. Patriarkh Evtimiy 37 (Патриарх Евтимий; ☎988 36 31).

Telephones: Telephone Center, ul. General Gurko 4. Take a right out of the post office on Vasil Levski and then a left on Gurko; it's a large white building 1 block down. Offers telephone, fax, photocopy, and telegram service. To make a call, go to windows 2 or 3; the staff will tell you from which booth to call. Local call or phone cards 0.09lv. Pay at window when finished. **Internet access** 0.80lv for 1hr., 1.40lv for 2hr., 2lv for 3hr. Fastest connections in town. Open 24hr.

Internet Access: Stargate, Pozitano 20 (Позитано), 30m west of Hostel Sofia. 1lv per hr. Open 24hr.

Post Office: General Gurko 6 (Гурко). Go down Suborna behind pl. Sv. Nedelya, then turn right on Lege (Леге) and left on Gurko; entrance to the right on ul. Vasil Levski (not bul.). Street is also known as Diakon Ignatiy (Дякон Игнатий). International mailing available at windows #6-8 in the 1st hall. **Poste Restante** at window #12; international money transfers at window #7 in the 2nd hall. Open M-Sa 7am-8:30pm, Su 8am-1pm. **Postal Code:** 1000.

█ ACCOMMODATIONS

Big hotels are rarely worth the exorbitant prices—smaller, privately owned hotels or hostels are better alternatives. If the hostels are full, private rooms are often the best options (available through Odysseia-In, see **Tourist Office,** p. 124).

■ **Hostel Sofia,** Pozitano 16 (Позитано; ☎989 85 82; www.hostelsofia.com). From pl. Sv. Nedelya, walk down Vitosha. Turn right on Pozitano. Walk 1 block; the hostel is on the right, above the Chinese restaurant. Sofia-savvy, English-speaking staff. Summer-camp atmosphere. Kitchen access, a balcony, and a living room with cable TV. Breakfast, laundry, and linen included. Shared hot shower and bathroom. Reception 24hr. Flexible check-out. €9 for 1st and 2nd nights, €8 3rd and following nights. ❶

Art-Hostel, ul. Angel Kŭnchev 21A (Ангел Кънчев; ☎987 05 45; www.art-hostel.com). From pl. Sv. Nedelya, walk down Vitosha and turn left on William Gladstone. Walk 2 blocks and turn right on Angel Kŭnchev. Part art gallery, part hostel, with 2 new dormitories, kitchen, bar, free Internet access, tea room, and garden. 2 shared showers and bathrooms. Linen included. Laundry 5lv. Reception 24hr. Free breakfast. €10 per night, €9 after 3rd, and €8 after 7th and following nights. ❶

Hotel Stivan-Iskar, ul. Iskar 11b (☎986 67 50; www.hoteliskar.com). Walk up bul. Mariya Luiza to ul. Ekzarh Iosif. Go right for 2 blocks, then right on Bacho Kiro and left on Iskar. Comfortable new rooms. Breakfast €2. Check-out noon. Doubles €25, with bath €37; 2-person apartments €50; 3-person €55. ❸

█ FOOD

From fast food to Bulgarian specialties, low-priced meals are easy to find. You won't have any trouble finding small cafes offering assorted snacks and drinks. Large markets, **Khali** (Хали) and **Women's Bazaar** (Женски Базар), are across bul. Mariya Luiza from the department store **TSUM** (ЦУМ).

■ **Dani's Bistro,** Angel Kŭnchev 18A (Ангел Кънчев; ☎987 45 48). Visit this quiet streetside cafe known for its friendly staff and savory fare. Try the chicken fettuccine (6.40lv) or the New Orleans chicken salad accompanied by a hearty helping of lightly toasted bread (8.80lv). Brownies 1.60lv. Delivery M-Sa. Open daily 10am-10pm. ❸

Divaka, ul. William Gladstone 54 (Уилям Гладстон; ☎989 95 43). Facing the McDonald's in Slaveykov Sq., go down the side street to the left. Stay to the right when the street forks; Divaka is on the left. So popular you might have to share a table with other patrons in the greenhouse dining area. The seemingly bottomless bowls of salad (1.50-3.50lv) and *sacheta*, sizzling heaps of veggies and meat cooked and served on an iron plate (6.50lv), are particularly tasty. Open 24hr. ❷

Murphy's Irish Pub, Kŭrnigradska 6 (Кърниградска; ☎980 28 70; www.jjmurphys.net). An international crowd bonds at this chain Irish pub, which feels quite un-Bulgarian. Flavorful meals include large portions of steak (12.90lv) and Leprechaun burger (6.90lv). Special "Irish breakfast" (2 meals in itself) comes with a drink (9.90lv). Live music on F nights. Open M-Th noon-12:30am, F-Sa noon-1:30am. ❷

Khali (Хали), Knyaginya Mariya Luiza 25, directly across from Banya Boshi Mosque. Within this modern, 3-fl. market are over 100 shops, restaurants, delis, cafes, and specialty shops. Choose from the extensive selection of pastries, sip on coffee, or sit down to lunch (1.5-3lv) upstairs in the food court. Open daily 7am-midnight. ❶

Jimmy's, Angel Kŭnchev 11 (Ангел Кънчев; www.jimmys.bg). Sofia's celebrated Jimmy's dishes out 30 flavors of gourmet ice cream (0.70lv per scoop) on crowded outdoor tables. Try Jimmy's alcoholic ice cream cocktails (0.90lv) like "Chocolate Kiss." Open M-Sa 7:30am-midnight, Su 10am-midnight. ❶

◉ SIGHTS

ST. ALEXANDER NEVSKY CATHEDRAL. The gold-domed Byzantine-style St. Alexander Nevsky Cathedral (Св. Александър Невски; Sv. Aleksandŭr Nevski.), erected from 1904 to 1912 in memory of the 200,000 Russians who died in the 1877-78 Russo-Turkish War, was named after the patron saint of the tsar-liberator. Housing over 400 frescoes by Russian and Bulgarian artists, it is the largest Orthodox church on the Balkan Peninsula. In a separate entrance to the left of the church, the **crypt** contains a spectacular array of painted icons and religious artifacts from the past 1500 years. The adjacent square has become a marketplace for religious, WWII, Soviet and Nazi souvenirs. *(In the center of pl. Alexander Nevsky. Open daily 7am-7pm; crypt open Tu-Su 10:30am-6:30pm. Cathedral free; crypt 4lv, students 2lv. Guided tours of the crypt 25lv for 5 or more people, 20lv for fewer than 5.)*

CATHEDRAL OF ST. NEDELYA. The focal point of pl. Sveta Nedelya and all of Sofia, the cathedral (Катедрален Храм Св. Неделя; Katedralen Khram Sv. Nedelya.) is a reconstruction of the 14th-century original, which was destroyed by a bomb in an attempted assassination of Boris III in 1925. The current frescoes date from 1975 but are already blackened with the soot of candles (0.10-2lv) lit by visitors and worshippers. The church has great acoustics and an imposing altar. Religious services held nightly. *(At the center of pl. Sveta Nedelya. Open daily 7am–6:30pm.)*

ST. NICHOLAS RUSSIAN CHURCH (СВ. НИКОЛАЙ; SV. NIKOLAI). Named for the patron saint of marriage, fish, and sailors, this 1913 church was built to appease a Russian diplomat unwilling to worship in Bulgarian churches. Richly hued patterns, elegant domes, icons by painters from the Novgorod school, and exquisite ornamentation make this building a sight to behold. *(Down bul. Tsar Osvoboditel from pl. Sv. Nedelya. Open daily 9am-10:30pm. Services W and Sa 5-7pm.)*

SYNAGOGUE OF SOFIA (СОФИЙСКА СИНАГОГА; SOFIYSKA SINAGOGA). Built upon a foundation of Jewish gravestones, Sofia's only synagogue opened for services in 1909. Modeled after the Sephardic synagogue in Vienna, Sofia's synagogue boasts a vast interior, the largest in the Balkans. Recent renovations repaired damage done by a stray Allied bomb from WWII, which miraculously didn't explode. A museum upstairs outlines the history of Jews in Bulgaria. *(On the corner of Ekzarh Iosif and George Washington. Walk to the gate on Ekzarh Iosif and ring the bell. Open M-F 9am-5pm. Weekly services F 7pm, Sa 10am. Synagogue 2lv, museum free. Donation requested for repairs.)*

BANYA BOSHI MOSQUE. Constructed in 1576 during the Ottoman occupation, this mosque escaped the fate suffered by the 26 others that once existed in Sofia. During the communist era, all mosques in Sofia except Banya Boshi were shut down or destroyed. *(Across from Khali Market on Mariya Luiza. Open daily 6am-midnight.)*

ST. GEORGE'S ROTUNDA (СВ. ГЕОРГИ; SV. GEORGI). Near a former Roman bath and the ruins of the ancient town of Serdica, the 4th-century rotunda is Sofia's oldest preserved building. St. George's itself is covered in 11th- to 14th-century murals. After it was converted from a bath to a church in the 5th century, it served as a house of worship under Bulgarians, Byzantines, and Turks. The beautiful original murals, which were covered by the Ottomans in an attempt to obscure the building's Christian past, have been restored and now adorn the functioning church and a museum, which showcases small art exhibits. *(In the courtyard enclosed by the Sheraton Hotel and the Presidency. Enter from bul. Tsar Osvoboditel or ul. Suborna. Open daily summer 8am-6pm; winter 8am-5pm. Services daily 9am.)*

CHURCH OF SEVEN SAINTS. Erected in 1528 at the request of Sultan Süleyman the Great, this former mosque earned the moniker "Black Mosque" for its dark granite composition. Today, this building is a church that honors the seven saints who created the Cyrillic alphabet. *(On Graf Ignatiev. Open daily 8am-7pm.)*

ST. SOFIA CHURCH (СВ. СОФИЯ; SV. SOFIYA). The oldest Eastern-Orthodox church in Sofia, this church lent it's name to the city in the 14th century. During the 19th century, while the church was used as Sofia's main mosque, a series of earthquakes repeatedly destroyed the minarets. Amazingly, the 5th-century floor **mosaic** survived. *(On pl. Alexander Nevsky. Open daily 7am-7pm.)*

BOYANA CHURCH (БОЯНСКА ЦЪРКВА; BOYANSKA TSURKVA). Set in the woods of the suburb Boyana, this UNESCO heritage site boasts some of the most striking religious artwork in the country. The church houses murals dating back to 1259 and an array of pre-Italian Renaissance paintings. Ask the curator to show you the scribbles on the murals left by pastors in the 17th and 18th centuries. *(Take bus #64 from Hladilnika, or a taxi from the center (4-5lv). 15min. walk from the National History Museum. Open daily 9:30am-6pm. 10lv, students 5lv. Tour 5lv.)*

BUL. TSAR OSVOBODITEL (ЦАР ОСВОБОДИТЕЛ). As you stroll down bul. Tsar Osvoboditel, keep in mind that your boots are stepping on the first paved street in Sofia, weighted down on either end by the House of Parliament and the Royal Palace. The 1884 National Assembly provides the backdrop for a dramatic equestrian statue of the tsar *osvoboditel* (liberator) himself, Russian Tsar Aleksandr II.

THEATERS. Rakovski (Раковски) is Bulgaria's theater hub, with six theaters in a 1km stretch. A left on Rakovski leads to the columns of the **National Opera House,** built in 1950. *(Rakovski 59, main entrance at Vrabcha 1 (Врабча). ☎ 987 13 66 , for group visits ☎ 981 15 67. Shows Tu-Sa 6pm. Box office open M-Tu 9:30am-2pm and 2:30-6:30pm, W-F 8:30am-7:30pm, Sa 10:30am-6:30pm, Su 10am-6pm. 5-20lv.)*

NATIONAL PALACE OF CULTURE. This monolith was erected by the Communist government in 1981 to celebrate the country's 1300th birthday. The Palace of Culture (Национален Дворец на Културата; Natsionalen Dvorets na Kulturata) houses a number of restaurants, cinemas (screening both local and recent American movies), theaters (tickets 3-10lv), and concert halls. *(In Yuzhen Park. From pl. Sv. Nedelya, take bul. Vitosha to bul. Patriarkh Evtimiy and enter the park. The Palace is at its far end. www.ndk.bg. Open daily 10am-7pm; box office open daily 9am-7pm.)*

BULGARIA

🏛 MUSEUMS

NATIONAL HISTORY MUSEUM. Once the secret lair of former Bulgarian dictator Todor Yivkov, the fortress-like Natural History Museum (Национален Исторически Музей; Natsionalen Istoricheski Muzey) now traces the evolution of Bulgarian culture since prehistoric times and houses some of the country's most precious archaeological treasures. The 30min. ride is worth the trip. English captions. *(Residence Boyana, Palace 1. Take minibus #21, trolley #2, or bus #63 or 111 to Boyana. ☎955 42 80. Open daily 9:30am-5:30pm. 10lv, students 5lv. Tour 10lv.)*

NATIONAL MUSEUM OF ETHNOGRAPHY. Founded after the 1878 liberation (see **History,** p. 113), the museum (Национален Етнографски Музуй; Natsionalen Etnografski Muzey) covers the past 400 years of Bulgarian folk history. *(In the Royal Palace on bul. Tsar Osvoboditel. Open Tu-Su 10am-6pm. 4lv, students 2lv. Guided tour for groups of 5 or more 15lv, for fewer than 5 10lv.)*

NATIONAL ART GALLERY. Displaying Bulgaria's most prized traditional and contemporary art, the National Gallery (Национална Художествена Галерия; Natsionalna Khudozhestvena Galeriya) showcases an array of ornamental exhibits and works in a variety of mediums. *(In the Royal Palace on bul. Tsar Osvoboditel. Open Tu-Su 10:30am-6:30pm. 4lv, students 2lv. Guided tours in English 20lv for up to 5 people, 25lv for 5 people or more.)*

🎵 ENTERTAINMENT

To get the latest schedule of events and nightlife, purchase the English language newspaper the **Sofia Echo** (2.40lv) from a kiosk. In the Culture Shock section is entertainment information, including restaurants, sightseeing, concerts, nightlife and movie listings. For more info, consult the Cyrillic guide called the **"Program"** (Програмата; in English at www.programata.bg). Sofia's **Beer Fest** takes place in late summer for one week. Each night of the week, different bands light up the crowd with traditional Bulgarian music, as well as pop and jazz. Fish and chips (1.50lv) compliment your beer (0.80lv). The event takes place in Alexander Batemberg Square, which also houses the three-week stint of open-air performances called **Opera in the Square.** Concerts are regularly staged outside the **National Palace of Culture.** Also, catch the traditional **Sofia Music Week** festival during the first week of June in Bulgaria Hall.

🎭 NIGHTLIFE

Nightlife centers on **bul. Vitosha** or Sofia University at the intersection of **Vasil Levski** and **Tsar Osvoboditel.** Young people often meet at **Popa,** the irreverent nickname for Patriarkh Evtimiy's monument, where bul. Patriarkh Evtimiy intersects with Vasil Levski and **Graf Ignatiev.** The city is more dangerous at night, so stay vigilant and try not to attract undue attention.

🏠 **My Mojito,** Ivan Vazov 12 (Иван Вазов; ☎088 776 27 01). Walk down Rakovski from Slaveykov Sq. toward the National Assembly. Take a right on Ivan Vasov. Mojito is on the corner with 6 Septemvri. A younger crowd flocks to My Mojito, where students party to deafeningly loud music until morning hours. Mojito (5lv). Most crowded for the Retro Party every Th. Open daily 8pm-late, DJ starts at 10pm. Cover 3lv F and Sa.

Spartacus, in the underpass in front of Sofia University. Layered with plush red velvet, this 2-story club seduces Sofia's flashiest trendsetters with a night of drinking and dancing. Dress flashily to get in. Open W-Sa 10pm-5am. Cover 3lv.

Dali (☎846 51 29), behind the university on Krakra. Attracts a more mature and affluent crowd, pulsating with high-energy latin music and its patrons' dizzying dance moves. Call ☎943 40 04 to reserve a table. Cover 3lv. Open daily 8pm-5am.

The Barn (Хамбара; Khambara), 22 6-September. Go down Graf Ignatiev, hang a right at 6-September, walk a ½ block. #22 is on the right. Turn into the alleyway behind the pizza parlor and walk through the unmarked wooden door. If the door is closed, knock hard. Once touted as the most exclusive club in Sofia, the Barn has opened its doors to the public but retains its selective admittance policy and haughty attitude. Inside, mellow out to New Age beats and savor the candlelit, cave-like ambience. Open 8pm-late.

◢ DAYTRIP FROM SOFIA

VITOSHA NATIONAL PARK (ПРИРОДЕН ПАРК ВИТОША)

Take tram #9 from the intersection of Khristo Botev and Makedonya to Hladilnika Station, the last stop. From there, you can take bus #122 to the Simeonovo lift, which goes up to Hija Aleko (Хижа Алеко) or bus #22 to the Dragalevtsi lift, which goes up to Bai Krustjo and Goli Vrkh stations. Bring bug spray.

Although it lies just next to Sofia, Vitosha National Park mutes the din of the neighboring metropolis. The park shelters a monastery, a stone river, and a waterfall, but **Mount Vitosha,** rising 2290m to its peak, Cherni Vrŭkh (Черни Връх), dominates this natural sanctuary. Established in 1934 by the Ministry of Environment and Water, this verdant haven is traversed by Bulgarians and foreign tourists. Conquering the mountain by trekking the marked trails from Aleko hut is the most popular activity, followed by winter-time skiing and snowboarding on Vitosha's scenic slopes. Pick up English maps and brochures from the **Information Center,** a 5min. walk uphill between Restaurant Vodenitsata and Vodenicharski Mehani. Paths at the top of the mountain are marked on the map, but there are few trail markers; even the most experienced hikers need a tour guide. The most direct, difficult path starts at the lift station by the bus station. Ride the **Dragalevtsi chairlift** (0.80lv) to either the Bai Krustjo station or the higher Goli Vrkh station. Other exploration opportunities include **hikes** to the **peak,** the **Dragalevtsi Monastery, Boyanna Waterfall,** and **Peat Branishte Reserve.** The paths are dotted with well-marked **campsites** and shelters. For a taste of Bulgarian folk culture and the traditional *nestinari* dance, try **Restaurant Vodenitsata** ❸, by the chairlift, set next to its picturesque waterwheel. (☎967 10 58. Entrees 8-18lv. Open daily noon-midnight.)

RILA MONASTERY (РИЛСКИ МАНАСТИР) ☎(0)7054

Holy Ivan of Rila built Rila Monastery (Rilski Manastir) in the 10th century as a refuge from the lascivious outside world. It sheltered the arts of icon-painting and manuscript-copying during the Byzantine and Ottoman occupations, remaining an oasis of Bulgarian culture during five centuries of foreign rule. Rila Monastery is a pleasant hideaway from the noise and heat of the city.

☲◪ TRANSPORTATION AND PRACTICAL INFORMATION. Take **tram** #5 from in front of Hostel Sofia to Ovcha Kŭpel Station (Овча Къпел) to make the bus to Rila Town (2hr., 1 per day, 10.20am, 5lv). From there, you can hop on a **bus** to the monastery (30min., 3 per day, 1.50lv). Staying the night s recommended, as there are few buses back to Sofia. There is an **ATM** on the storefront opposite the bus station in Rila Town. Blue Mobika **telephones** are by the shops behind the monastery; phone cards are available in the souvenir shop.

◪◻ACCOMMODATIONS AND FOOD. Hotel Tsarev Vrŭkh ❸ (Царев Връх). From behind the monastery, the hotel is 100m down the path that passes through the outdoor dining area of Restaurant Rila. It features private baths, telephones, a restaurant, and a wine cellar. The reception also organizes sightseeing trips. (☎/fax 22 80. Hot water 6pm-midnight and 6-10am. US$22. Breakfast US$2.) Inquire at room #170 in the monastery about staying in a heated **monastic cell ❷**, but be prepared for bare rooms and no shower. (☎ 22 08. Monastery doors close at 9:30pm, ring the bell if you're out later than that. Cells US$15.) **Camping Bor ❶** is tucked away at the base of the mountains with clean but bare campsites and bungalows. Walk down the left-most road behind the monastery and take a right across the bridge at the triangular intersection, then take a left and follow the signs. (3lv per person, 2lv per tent; 2-bed bungalows 20lv. 3lv per car. Student groups 10% off.) Behind the monastery are several cafes and a minimart. Try the monks' homemade bread (0.50lv) or slice into a chicken steak (5lv) at **Restaurant Rila ❶**, a *mekhani* (механи; Bulgarian folk restaurant) in which the waiters wear traditional dress. (☎ 048 890 418. Entrees 2.50-12lv. Open daily 8am-midnight.)

◙ SIGHTS. The original 10th-century monastery was destroyed. Today's monastery was built between 1834 and 1837; only a brick tower remains from the 14th-century structure. The monastery's vibrant murals were painted by brothers Dimitar and Zahari Zograf—"Zograf" actually means "mural painter"—who were famous for their work at the Troyan and Bachkovo monasteries (see **Daytrip from Plovdiv**, p. 134). The 1200 frescoes on the central chapel form a brilliantly colored outdoor art display. The iconostasis is also one of the largest and most ornate in Bulgaria. Inside lies the grave of Bulgaria's last tsar, Boris III. (Open daily 6am-10pm. Backpacks, cameras, shorts, and sleeveless shirts not permitted. Admission free.) The **museum** in the far right corner of the monastery displays weapons, embroidery, illuminated texts, and icons. The exhibit includes a wooden cross that took 12 years to carve and left its creator, the monk Rafail, blind. The cross is carved with miniature figures that depict scenes from the Bible and the lives of the saints. (Open daily 8:30am-4:30pm. English tours 15lv. 5lv, students 3lv.)

◪ HIKING. Maps and hiking routes through **Rila National Park** are on signs outside the monastery. Alternatively, look in the **Manastirski Padarŭtsi** (Манастирски Падаръци) alcove, just outside the monastery's back entry, for a Cyrillic map of the paths (6lv). Incredible views—particularly at **Seventh Lake** (Седемте Езера; Sedemte Ezera) and **Malovitsa** (Мальовица)—and welcoming huts *(hizhi)* await within the park. Expect to pay around US$2 for a spot (not necessarily a bed) to sleep. Follow the **yellow markings** to the **Khizha Sedemte Ezera** (Хижа Седемте Езера; Seventh Lake Hut; 6½hr.). The **blue** trail leads to **Khizha Malovitsa** (Мальовица; 7hr.). **Red** leads to the highest hut in the Balkans (6hr.).

Don't miss the short hike (1hr.) to the **cave** where Holy Ivan lived and prayed for years. To reach it, walk down the road behind the monastery. After the triangular intersection, head left up the path through the field. Follow the signs for the grave (гроб; grob), which point the way to the church where Ivan was originally buried. Behind the church is the entrance to the cave. It's believed that passing through will purify your soul. Enter at the bottom and crawl through the dark winding passages. A flashlight or lighter is helpful. According to legend, this part of the journey represents the journey out of the womb. Emerge at the top for a symbolic rebirth—unless you have sinned too much, in which case, legend holds that rocks will fall on you. Next, continue uphill 40m to the spring and cleanse yourself near the shrine to St. Ivan. You're now ready to enter the chapel guilt-free.

SOUTHERN MOUNTAINS

The Rila, Pirin, and Rodopi mountains sheltered Bulgaria's cultural and political dissidents throughout 500 years of Turkish rule. During this era, local monks chose to preserve their culture in secret by copying manuscripts in remote monasteries. Other dissidents, like the *haiduti* outlaws, took an activist approach, using mountain hideouts to launch attacks against unwanted visitors. The region now wholeheartedly celebrates its folk culture and welcomes newcomers. Its strongly rooted traditions and natural lushness now harbor such tourist attractions as wine tasting in Melnik and hiking near Bansko.

PLOVDIV (ПЛОВДИВ) ☎(0)32

Although Plovdiv (pop. 376,000) is significantly smaller than Sofia, Bulgaria's second largest city, is widely regarded as its cultural capital. Founded around 600 BC as Philipopolis (in honor of Philip II of Macedonia), the city's long history includes centuries of trade fairs and arts festivals that enthrall visitors to this day.

▐ TRANSPORTATION

Trains: The main train **station** is on bul. Khristo Botev (Христо Ботев). Trains to: **Burgas** (5hr., 6 per day, 4.70-6.70lv); **Sofia** (2½hr., 14 per day, 2.90-4.20lv); **Varna** (5½hr., 3 per day, 5.90-8.40lv). Most trains from Sofia to **Burgas** or **Istanbul, TUR** stop in Plovdiv. Only the **Rila station,** bul. Khristo Botev 31a (☎64 31 20), sells international train tickets. Open M-F 8am-7:30pm, Sa 8am-2pm.

Buses: Matpu (Матпу; ☎63 26 33). Walk down the block to the right of Hotel Trimontsium (Тримонциум); Matpu is on your left. To: **Ohrid, MAC** (2 per day, 28lv) and **Thessaloniki, GCE** (2 per day, 40lv). Open daily 8am-5pm. There are 3 additional stations:

Sever (Север; North; ☎95 37 05), at the intersection of Dimitr Stambolov (Димитър Стамболов) and Pobeda (Победа), north of bul. Bŭlgaria. Bul. Ruski becomes Pobeda when it crosses the river. Take bus #12 from the intersection of Ruski and Gladston (Гладстон). Buses to: **Koprivshtitsa** (2hr., 4:30pm, 5.50lv); **Pleven** (4hr., 3pm, 10.50lv); **Ruse** (5hr., 8am, 13lv).

Yug (Юг; South; ☎62 69 37), bul. Khristo Botev 47, across from the train station. Open 5:30am-9pm. Buses service South Bulgaria and go to: **Asenovgrad** (30min., every 30min., 0.80lv); **Blagoevgrad** (4hr., 1 per day, 7lv); **Sofia** (2hr., every 30min., 8lv); **Istanbul, TUR** (5 per day, 20lv, students 18lv). Private firms inside the station send buses to: **Burgas** (10lv) and **Varna** (15lv).

Rodopi (Родопи; ☎77 76 07), behind the train station through the underpass beneath the trains. Service to the **Rodopi Mountains.** To: **Smolyan** (1hr., 5 per day, 5.50lv). Open 5am-7pm.

✦ ▐ ORIENTATION AND PRACTICAL INFORMATION

Although the center is clearly defined, Plodiv's streets are poorly marked; an up-to-date **map** is essential. Street vendors sell good Cyrillic maps (3lv). Running past the train station, the east-west thoroughfare **bul. Khristo Botev** (Христо Ботев) marks the town's southern edge. With your back to the train station, turn left on Khristo Botev to get to **bul. Ruski** (Руски); a right turn on Ruski takes you across the river and to bus station Sever. Khristo Botev also intersects with **bul. Tsar Boris III Obedinitel** (Цар Борис III Обединител), which runs to the **Maritsa River** (Марица), at the northern end of **Stariya Grad** (Стария Град; Old Town). The pedestrian way **Kayaz Alexander** connects to the central square. In the middle of town, bul. Tsar Boris III Obedinitel runs along the east side of **pl. Tsentralen** (Централен). To get to the center from the train station, take bus #2, 20, or 26 (0.40lv) or cross under bul. Khristo Botev and take **ul. Ivan Vazov** (Иван Вазов).

Currency Exchange: Bulbank (Булбанк; ☎60 16 17), ul. Ivan Vazov 4, on the right when facing Hotel Trimontium. Cashes **traveler's checks** for 0.2% commission, min. US$1 fee. Open M-F 8:30am-4:30pm.

ATM: MC/V ATM in front of Bulbank. MC ATM outside the post office on pl. Tsentralen.

Luggage Storage: In the train station. 0.80lv per bag. Open 24hr. with breaks.

24hr. Pharmacy: Apteka 47 Tunela (Аптека Тунела), bul. Tsar Boris III Obedinitel 62 (☎27 07 93). From pl. Tsentralen, follow bul. Tsar Boris III through the tunnel.

Telephones: In the post office. Open daily 6am-11pm. **Fax** (☎/fax 65 02 70) available daily M-F 7am-8pm.

Internet Access: Speed, Kryaz Aleksandr 12, on the left before the mosque. Newly wired; modern atmosphere. 1lv per 1hr., 2lv per 3hr., 30min. minimum. Open 24hr.

Post Office: Pl. Tsentralen. **Poste Restante** in the room to the left of the entrance across from the park. Open M-Sa 7am-7pm, Su 7-11am. **Postal Code:** 4000.

⌐ ACCOMMODATIONS

In Plovdiv, higher prices don't always mean higher quality. Prices triple during trade fairs (the first weeks of May and the end of September.). In summer months, especially July and August, call ahead, as budget hotels are often full.

▨ **Bed and Breakfast Queen Mary Elizabeth,** ul. Gustav Vaigand 7 (☎62 93 06). From Ruski, turn left onto Gustav Vaigand. It's on the right side, 100m down. Clean and friendly, the "Queen" rolls out the red carpet for weary guests. English-speaking owner is very helpful. Shared bathrooms. Free laundry. Reception 24hr. 15lv per person. ❶

Hostel Plovdiv Bulgaria Inn (Найден Геров), ul. Naiden Gerov 13 (☎63 84 67; www.pbihostel.com). Cozy rooms look out on the pedestrian zone, and fellow travelers provide company. €10 per bed. ❶

Hotel Bulgaria, Patriarch Evtimii 13 (☎63 35 99; www.hotelbulgaria.net), at the intersection with Knyaz Aleksandr. Great location in Plovdiv's pedestrian center. Immaculate rooms with TV, A/C, and private bath. Reception 24hr. Check-out noon. Singles €35. ❹

Hotel Phoenix (Феникс), Silivriya 18A (Силиврия; ☎69 36 75). From Rodopi bus station, head away from the train tracks on Dimitr Talev (Димитър Талев) for 15min. After crossing Nikola Vaptsarov (Никола Вапцаров), take the 2nd right; it's 200m down on the right. Small doubles (40lv) with private bath, A/C, and TV. Reception 8am-11pm. ❷

◖ FOOD

Plovdiv has an array of Bulgarian restaurants with pleasant outdoor dining areas. On the way to the hostel Turisticheski Dom, the **Monday Market** (понеделник пазар; ponedelnik pazar), in pl. Vuzrazhdane, sells fruit and veggies (2-3lv per kg). Get there early for the freshest produce. An array of equally delectable cafes line the pedestrian street Knyaz Aleksandr. Walking down Knyaz Aleksandr, take a right at Hotel Bulgaria, followed by another right to get to **Zlatna Krusha** ❶ (Златна Круша), Otetz Paisii 30 (☎27 05 05). There you can fuel up on deep-dish pizza (3.50-5.50lv) or tortellini bolognese (5lv) on the shaded balcony. Open daily 11am-midnight. **Diana** ❷ (Даяна), Dondukov 3, is nestled at the base of Plovdiv's most central hill, at the entrance of a defunct bomb shelter. Try the excellent mushroom appetizers (5lv) or take a stab at the skewered meats (6-11lv), served tableside straight off the sword. (☎62 30 27, deliveries 65 05 05. Open 24hr.)

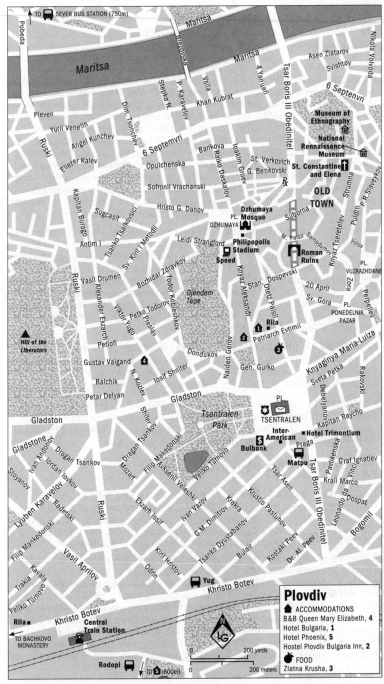

Plovdiv

▲ ACCOMMODATIONS
B&B Queen Mary Elizabeth, 4
Hotel Bulgaria, 1
Hotel Phoenix, 5
Hostel Plovdiv Bulgaria Inn, 2

♦ FOOD
Zlatna Krusha, 3

⊙ SIGHTS

Most of Plovdiv's treasures are on Staria Grad's **Trimontsium** (three hills).

ROMAN RUINS. A 2nd-century Roman ⊠**Amphitheater** (Античен Театър; Antichen Teatŭr), one of the best-preserved in the world, looms over the city. It serves as a popular performing arts venue, hosting the **Festival of the Arts** in the summer and early fall and the annual **Opera Festival** in June. Most festival tickets are available at the opera box office on the ground floor of the Inter-American building on pl. Tsentralen. Movies are often screened here; keep an eye out for schedules. *(Take a right off Knyaz Aleksandr onto Suborna and another right up the steps along Mitropolit Paisii. Continue uphill until you reach another small set of steps next to the music academy. At the top, walk past the cafes to the theater. Open daily 9am-7pm. 3lv.)* **Philipopolis Stadium,** which once seated 30,000 spectators, now consists of just the poorly preserved bottom 10-15 rows, still accessible to the public. The gladiators' entrance remains intact— some locals claim that lion bones were found inside. A cafe inside serves visitors. *(Follow Knyaz Aleksandr to the end; the stadium is underneath pl. Dzhumaya. Free.)*

MUSEUMS. The **Museum of Ethnography** (Етнографски Музей; Etnografski Muzey) displays artifacts from Bulgaria's past, such as clothes, musical instruments, and tools in a quintessential National Revival building. One display features the *kukerski maksi,* masks used to ward off evil spirits during the Christmas season. *(At the end of Suborna.* ☎ *62 56 54. English captions. Open Tu-Th and Sa-Su 9am-noon and 2-5pm, F 9am-noon. 3lv, students 2lv.)* Each room in the **National Renaissance Museum** details a different stage in Bulgarian history through the 1800s. *(Tsanko Lavrenov 1 (Цанко Лавренов). Turn right at the end of Suborna and head through the Turkish Gate.* ☎ *62 33 78. Open M-Sa 9am-5pm. 2lv, students 0.40lv.)*

CHURCH OF ST. CONSTANTINE AND ELENA. Built in the 4th century, this is the oldest Orthodox church in Plovdiv. During its 1832 renovation, Bulgarian artist Zahari Zografwas embellished the church with stunning murals and icons. *(On Suborna, before the Museum of Ethnography. Open daily 9am-6pm. Free.)*

OTHER SIGHTS. Take an evening stroll up the Hill of the Liberators for a view of Plovdiv. The **Dzhumaya Mosque** (Джумая; Dzhumaya Dzhamiya), pl. Dzhumaya's namesake, holds beautiful wall mosaics and the impressive throne of the sultan. *(Go past pl. Dzhumaya and turn right to reach the main entrance. Free.)*

⚡ DAYTRIP FROM PLOVDIV

BACHKOVO MONASTERY (БАЧКОВСКИ МАНАСТИР)

Buses (25min., every 30min., 0.80lv) and trains (25min., 17 per day, 0.80lv) run from Yug station to Asenovgrad. From the Asenovgrad bus station, catch a bus to Luki (Лъки) for the monastery (20min., 4 per day, 0.60lv). Exit at the 3rd stop (after the 2 tunnels). Follow the cobblestones up the incline. Open daily 7am-8pm. Free. English tour 10lv.

Bulgaria's second-largest monastery is in the Rodopi Mountains, 28km south of Plovdiv. Bachkovo Monastery (Bachkovski Manastir) was built in 1083 by Georgian brothers Grigory and Abazy Bakuriani, and is known for its original architecture and fine murals. An oasis of Bulgarian culture, history, and literature during the 500 years of Turkish rule, Bachkovo today draws crowds to its phenomenal art exhibits. The main church is home to the **icon of the Virgin Mary and Child** (икона Света Богородица; ikona Sveta Bogoroditsa), which is said to have miraculous healing powers. When the Turks plundered the monastery, the monks hid the icon in the mountains. It was rediscovered by an unsuspecting shepherd centuries later. Next door, the brightly colored paintings of famed National Revival artist Zahari Zograf (see **The Arts,** p. 116) decorate the 12th-century **Church of Archangels.** Ask to be let into the **Trapezaria** (old dining room; 3lv) across the courtyard. Along the roads leading uphill from the monastery, there are small shrines and paths labeled with yellow and white markings. The hills makes for a pleasant, unchallenging hike and has picnic areas and breathtaking mountain vistas.

BANSKO (БАНСКО)   ☎(0)7443

A great destination for nature enthusiasts, Bansko (pop. 10,000) is surrounded by countless lakes and the Pirin Mountains, whose highest peak is the 2914m Mount Vihren. While the mountain range around Bansko hosts hiking, skiing, and breathtaking views, the cobblestone streets and taverns below come alive during the town's annual **International Jazz Festival** in mid-August.

日2 TRANSPORTATION AND PRACTICAL INFORMATION. Take a **bus** from **Blagoevgrad** (1hr., 12 per day, 4lv) or **Sofia's** Ovcha Kupel station (3hr., 8 per day, 6lv). For a **taxi,** call ☎47 43. From Bansko's bus station, turn left on Patriarkh Evtimiy (Патриарх Евтимий). Take a right at the tiny pl. Makedoniya (Македония), marked by the stairways leading under the street and the "Bansko Skiing Centre" sign; veer left on **Todor Aleksandrov** (Тодор Александров), which leads to fountain-filled **pl. Vaptsarov** (Вапцаров). Continue on **ul. Pirin** (Пирин), in the upper right corner of pl. Vaptsarov as you enter the square from Todor Aleksandrov, to the 2nd square, **pl. Vŭzrazhdane** (Възраждану).

You can get a **map** from a newsstand on pl. Vaptsarov (3lv) or from the **Tourist Information Center,** to the left before pl. Vaptsarov. (☎80 76. Open M-F 9am-2pm and 3-7pm, Sa 10am-2pm and 3-6pm.) **Bulgarian Post Bank,** Khristo Botev 1 (Христо Ботев), **exchanges currency** and gives V **cash advances** for 5% commission. (☎81 24. Open M-F 8:30am-5pm.) **Luggage storage** (0.50lv) is available in the bus station. A **pharmacy** is at Tsar Simeon 73, near Todor Aleksandrov. (☎47 00. Open daily 8am-midnight.) **Internet access** (1lv per hr.) is located one block below the pl. Vaptsarov. **Telephones** (open daily 8:30am-9pm) are inside the **post office,** Tsar Simeon 69. (Open M-F 7:30am-noon and 1-5pm.) **Postal Code:** 2770.

日 ACCOMMODATIONS AND FOOD. Locals rent **private rooms** (8-10lv), but it's possible to find other cheap accommodations. **☑Tourist Home Tepikh ❶** (Тепих), Khristo Botev 2 (Христо Ботев), offers pleasant rooms right on pl. Vaptsarov. (☎23 10. Bed in singles 12lv; in doubles 10lvl; in triples 9lv.) **Hotel Mir ❷** (Мир), Neofit Rilski 28 (Неофит Рилски), offers spacious rooms, spotless bathrooms, hot water, cable TV, and a sauna. From pl. Vaptsarov with your back to ul. Todor Aleksandrov, take a left on Tsar Simeon and turn right on ul. Bŭlgaria. Go straight, turn left on Rilski after the playground. (☎83 01; www.mir.domino.bg. Breakfast included. Singles 30lv; doubles 50lv.) **Hotel Glazne ❹** (Глазне) has luxurious facilities, including a pool, fitness room, and sauna. Feel pampered in rooms with phones, TV, fridges, and balconies. (☎80 24; www.glazne.bansico.bg. Breakfast included. Apr.14-Dec.19 M-F doubles 68lv, Sa-Su 88lv; Dec.20-Apr.14 and Sept. 21-Dec. 14 daily 58lv; Dec. 15-Apr. 13 M-F 82lv, Sa-Su 98lv.)

Mekhani (механи; taverns) abound in Bansko, and most serve their own unique versions of dried meat. Try **Dŭdo Pene ❷** (Дъдо Пене), Aleksandr Buynov 1 (Александър Буйнов), a rugged restaurant that greets you at the door with a line of shepherd bells. Try *file Diadke* (fillet Diadke; 6.17lv), the house specialty. (☎83 48; www.dedopene.com. Entrees 2.20-7lv. Live folk music F-Sa after 8pm. Open daily 9am-late.)

BABA MARTA

egend has it that when one of
he first Bulgarian khans was
away at war, he was supposed to
send word of the outcome home
through a pigeon. A white thread
ied around its leg meant victory,
while a red one signaled defeat.
After a victorious turn of events,
he khan sent a pigeon bearing
he appropriate white thread. Dur-
ng the trip, however, the pigeon
was wounded and drops of blood
colored the thread red, thus delivering the wrong message.

Ever since, the holiday of Baba
Marta, which is celebrated annually on March 1st, and the surrounding exchange of *martenitsi*
have been an undying tradition.
The *martenitsa* is made from
white and red thread and ranges
in form from simple to more complex designs. Traditionally, it is
worn as a brooch pinned on the
left side of the shirt above the
heart and can be as intricate as
two miniature people delicately
holding hands. At its simplest, it
s a bracelet of two interwoven
hreads, worn around the wrist.

Martenitsi are sold on every
street corner throughout February
and are exchanged on the day of
Baba Marta. Family and friends
rade them to bring good health
and protect loved ones from evil.
Traditionally the *martenitsa* is
worn until you see a stork or a
blossoming tree, both of which
are symbols of the coming spring.
When such an event occurs, the
wearer ties *martenitsa* to a blossoming tree for fertility.

🅾 **SIGHTS.** Bansko's most interesting sight
◼**Nikola Vaptsarov House-Museum** (Къща-Музей
Никола Вапцаров; Kŭshta-Muzey Nikola Vaptsarov), on the corner of pl. Demokratsia and Vaptsarov,
recounts the life and work of the 20th-century poet
who died in the struggle against fascism. Ticket
includes admission to the **House of Poetry and Art**
(Дом на Поезията и Изкуството; Dom Na Poyez-
iyata i Izkustvoto), which exhibits images of the
National Revival movement and photographs of the
region. (☎83 03. Open M-F 8am-noon and 2-6pm. Taped
English tours 1lv. Museum 2lv, students 1lv.) Also
worth a visit is the 1835 **Holy Trinity Church** (Църква
Света Троица; Tsŭrkva Sveta Troitsa), on pl.
Vuzrazhdane, at the corner of Neofit Rilski. The church
is a product of Turkish rule. According to legend, the
local Turkish governor dreamt of an icon that Bansko's resilient faithful had carefully hidden beneath
pl. Vuzrazhdane. He was convinced by the townspeople that it was a sign from God to build an Orthodox
church where the icon was hidden. An Islamic crescent was added next to the cross on the church door,
making the building a symbol of both faiths. (Open
daily 8am-6pm. Free; large groups 1lv per person.) Next
door to the church is the **Neofit Rilski House-Museum**
(Къща-Музей Неофит Рилски; Kŭshta-Muzey
Neofit Rilski), home to one of the National Revival
movement's forefathers, who later became Father
Superior at Rila Monastery (p. 129). The founder of
the Rila School for church singing, Rilski also taught
painter Zahari Zograf. (☎82 72. Open daily 9am-noon
and 2-5pm. Taped English tours 1lv. Museum 2lv, students 1lv.) Also in the vicinity of the church, down
Yanel Sandanski from pl. Vuzrazhdane on the left, is the
1749 former convent, home to an **icon collection,**
including an icon once considered sacrilegious.
Why? The angels portrayed are female. (☎82 73. Open
M-Sa 9am-noon and 2-5pm. 1lv.)

🅽 **HIKING.** Hiking routes are marked with signs of
different colors. Ask at the tourist office for info on
mountain guides, accommodations, and transportation. Kiosks in Bankso sell **maps** that cover the town
and mountain routes, and suggested hiking itineraries in detail. Many trails start at **Khizha Vikhren** (Хижа
Вихрен; Vikhren Hut). From town, take any street
leading to the Glazne (Глазне) River. At the river,
follow the Glazne road upstream and out of town to
the entrance of **Pirin National Park** (Народен Парк
Пирин; Naroden Park Pirin). The hut can be
accessed by hiking (5hr.) or driving. The route,
marked with a yellow line on white background,

runs past **Khizhen Bŭnderitsa** (Хижен Бъндерица; Bŭnderitsa Hut) and **baykushe-vata mura** (байкушевата мура), a 1300-year-old fir tree that has lived as long as the Bulgarian state.

Four trails begin at the hut and lead over a rocky peak. After 10min., the red and green trails branch off and cross the river. The **red trail** leads up Vikhren Peak (2914m) to **Khizha Yavorov** (Хижа Яворов; Javor's Hut; 1740m). The **green trail** scales Todorin Peak (Тодорин) to **Khizha Demyanitsa** (Демяница; 6hr.). **Khizha Bezbog** (Безбог), which is becoming increasingly popular as a ski resort, is another 8hr. away. A **lift** connects it to **hizha Gotse Delchev** (Гоце Делчев), which is 2hr. by foot from the village of Dobrinishte (Добринище). There, you can catch a **bus** to **Bansko** or **Razlog**, which makes this an excellent three-day hike. The **blue trail** goes in the other direction and is much shorter, reaching **Sini vraha** in only 4hr. You'll have plenty of time to turn back or to continue on the **yellow trail** to chalet **Yanel Sandanski** (5hr.). Mountain **huts** scattered throughout the park provide the barest of accommodations for the lowest of prices (US$4-5). Cooked meals are available at select huts; if you are staying in remote huts, bring your own food.

MELNIK (МЕЛНИК) ☎(0)7437

Bulgaria's smallest town, Melnik (pop. 250), and its exquisite National Revival houses, sit in a sandstone gorge where life goes on as it has for centuries. While the whitewashed walls of the town's houses are enough to charm any visitor, Melnik is best known for what it keeps concealed below: barrels of delicious wine.

Even Winston Churchill had his favorite wine shipped all the way from Melnik during WWII. Travelers can see the famous wine in its original storage place at ▓ **Kordopulova Kŭshta** (Кордопулова Къща), the biggest National Revival house in Bulgaria. Built in 1754, the house also contains the largest wine cellar in Melnik—the caves inside the sandstone hill took a full 12 years to carve and can store up to 300 tons of wine. Stop by for a relaxing afternoon and a free glass of wine. To get to the house, follow the main road uphill, take the right fork, and go left up the steep stone path. (☎265. Open daily 10am-9pm. 2lv. Wine bottles 3.50-7lv.) Next door, Mitko Manolev's **wine-tasting cellar** (Изба за Дегустация на Вино; Izba za Degustatsiya na Vino) is a 200-year-old establishment that boasts naturally cool caverns and serves spectacular Melnik wine straight from the barrel. (☎234. Open daily 9am-9pm. Glass 0.50lv, bottle 3lv.)

Melnik is an ideal base for several good day **hikes**. Unfortunately, all paths are poorly marked with orange-and-white lines painted on trees and rocks. A plateau with a beautiful vista of Melnik and the surrounding "sand pyramids" awaits 15min. up the path to the left of Sv. Nikola Church. The trail begins opposite Hotel Vinarna. A 5km hike takes you to the 13th-century **Rozhen Monastery** (Роженски Манастир; Rozhenski Manastir). The monastery houses impressive 16th-century murals and 17th-century stained glass, and provides magnificent views of the countryside. Buses leave daily from Melnik's main street for Sandanski (40min., 5 per day, 1.70lv) and Sofia (3½hr., 1 per day via earliest bus to Sandanski, 8lv). The **post office** is up main street on the left. (Open M-F 7:30am-noon and 1-4:30pm.) For **private rooms ❶** look for "rooms to sleep" (Стаи зи Нощувка) signs all over town (8-20lv). **Uzunova Kŭshta ❶** (Узунова Къща) rooms have fridges and private baths. (20lv per person). **Mecheva Kŭsta ❷** (Мечева Куста), past the river on the left side of the main street's right fork, is a traditional restaurant with mouth-watering food. (☎339. Entrees 3.50-10lv. Open 8am-11:30pm.) A **mini-market** (мини маркет) is on the left side of the main street as you head uphill. (Open daily 7am-10pm.)

VALLEY OF ROSES (РОЗОВА ДОЛИНА)

Between the Stara Planina and Sredna Gora mountain ranges await opportunities to retrace the paths of Bulgarian revolutionaries, sniff 250 varieties of roses, and slurp water-buffalo yogurt. While Shipka Town lies in the shadow of the Freedom Monument and the pivotal battle it commemorates, Kazanlŭk blooms yearly with its Rose Festival, where visitors can celebrate with a shot or two of rose brandy.

KOPRIVSHTITSA (КОПРИВЩИЦА) ☎(0)7184

Todor Kableshkov's 1876 "letter of blood," urging rebellion against Ottoman rule, incited the War of Liberation in this little village, tucked away in the Sredna Gora Mountains along the Topolka River. Today, Koprivshtitsa is home to Bulgaria's most popular folk festival and over 250 National Revival structures.

▐▘▌ TRANSPORTATION AND PRACTICAL INFORMATION. A bus runs from the train station to town (15min., 6 per day timed to meet trains, 1lv). **Trains** go to **Plovdiv** (3½hr., 5 per day, 2.60-3.20lv) via **Karlovo** and **Sofia** (2hr., 3 per day, 5lv). **Private buses** also go to **Plovdiv** (2½hr., 1 per day, 5.50lv) and **Sofia** (2hr., 4 per day, 5.50lv). The **bus station** posts bus and train schedules in Bulgarian; the tourist office (see below) has the schedules English.

To reach the **main square** from the bus station, walk left 200m on the road that runs next to the river. The English-speaking staff at the **tourist office,** on 20 April (Април) in the main square, rents **mountain bikes** (3lv per hr.) and offers an invaluable **map** (2lv) of the town. (☎21 91; koprivshtiza@hotmail.com. Open daily 10am-6pm.) **Currency exchange** and **ATM** service are available at **State Savings Bank** (ДСК; DSK) next to the bus stop on Hadzhi Nencho 68. (☎21 42. Open M-F 8am-4pm.) **Pharmacy Apteka Lyusi** (Аптека Люси), Lyuben Karavelov 2 (Любен Каравелов), is on your left after the park ends on the road directly in front of the tourist office. (☎20 06. Open M-Sa 9am-noon and 3-6pm.) Across the street is the town's **medical clinic** (Амбулатория; Ambulatoriya), Lyuben Karavelov 3. (☎048 920 341. Open M-F 8am-noon and 3-5pm.) The **post office** at Lyuben Karavelov 14 has **telephones.** (Open M-F 7:30am-noon and 1-4pm.) **Postal Code:** 2077.

▐▘▌ ACCOMMODATIONS AND FOOD. There are many hotels and **private rooms** in Koprivshtitsa. Check with the tourist office. (€10-12 for a room in the center. Call ahead during festivals.) A great budget option is **Hotel Trayanova Kŭshta ❶** (Траянова Къща), ul. Gerenilogo 5 (Гepeнилого). Turn right from the tourist office and continue past Restaurant Byaloto Konche (Бялото Конче); the house is on the first left. This hotel has homey rooms with private baths. (☎30 57. Breakfast included. BulFon telephones available. Reception 24hr. Check-out noon. 30-36lv.) **Bonchova Kŭshta ❶** (Бончова Къща), ul. Tumangelova Cheta 1 (Тумангелова Чета), has freshly renovated rooms. With your back to the tourist office, follow the road past the park and pharmacy until you reach an arched stone bridge, then turn left. (☎26 14. Breakfast included. Reception 24hr. Check-out noon. Singles 25lv; doubles 40lv.) **Hotel Kalina ❸** (Калина), ul. Palaveev 35 (Палавеев), offers luxurious rooms with TV and minibar. With your back to the main square, cross the bridge and take a left; Kalina is on the right. (Breakfast included. Reception 24hr. Check-out noon. Singles 36lv; doubles 50lv.)

It's easy to find great Bulgarian food at any *mekhana* (механа; tavern). **Mekhana "20 April" ❶** (20 Април) is in the main square. The attentive staff serves scrumptious *sirene po trakiyski* (сирене по тракийски; fried and stewed cheese) for a mere 3.30lv. (☎048 916 430. Entrees 3-5lv. Open 8am-midnight.) **Stravnnopriemnitsa**

"Dedo Liben" ❷ (Сранноприемнца "Дедо Либен"), across the square and just over the bridge, offers traditional Bulgarian cuisine and a rich selection of wines. (☎ 07 184. Entrees 3-30lv. Open daily 11am-midnight.)

◙ SIGHTS. The wonderfully preserved **National Revival houses,** the homes of the town's first settlers, are an important part of Bulgaria's heritage. Many have enclosed verandas and delicate woodwork, and six (see **History,** p. 113) have been turned into **museums** of history and ethnography. The 1831 **Georgi Benkovski Museum-House** (Георги Бенковски) immortalizes the life of the leader of the "Flying Troop," a cavalry unit that fought in the revolution. From the post office, walk across the bridge and up the cobblestone road; take a right at the top on ul. Petko Kŭlev (Петко Кълев) and go straight for 5min. The museum is downstairs on the right. (☎ 20 30. Open M and W-Su 9:30am-5:30pm.)

The **Dimcho Debelyanov Museum-House** (Димчо Дебелянов) is the birthplace of Debelyanov, one of Bulgaria's best lyric poets (see **The Arts,** p. 116), who was killed in WWI. There are originals of his works on the first floor and a photographic history on the second. (☎ 20 77. Open Tu-Su 9:30am-5:30pm.) The house of the merchant **Lyutovata** (Лютовата) boasts spectacular wall decorations and a collection of fine Bulgarian carpets. (☎ 21 38. Open M and W-Su 9:30am-5:30pm.) Tickets are available at any of the houses or at the shop (Купчийница; Kupchiynitsa), next to the tourist office. (Open W-Su 9:30am-5:30pm. English tours 15lv. Admission to all 6 houses 5lv, students 3lv. One museum 3lv.)

KAZANLŬK (КАЗАНЛЪК)   ☎ (0)431

In the first week of June, Kazanlŭk (pop. 56,000) hosts the annual Rose Festival (see sidebar, p. 140) with traditional song-and-dance troupes and comedians. Arrive after the festivities and you'll only see a few rose bushes against a quintessential Bulgarian metropolitan background. But during the festival, the lack of budget accommodations could potentially wreak havoc on the pockets of frugal travelers.

▐▟ TRANSPORTATION AND PRACTICAL INFORMATION. Trains go to: **Burgas** (3½hr., 2 per day, 2.20-2.80lv); **Ruse** (3hr., 5 per day, 7.30lv); **Sofia** (3½hr., 3 per day, 6.50-8lv); **Varna** (3½hr., 4 per day, 8.50lv). The bus station is across from the train station. **Buses** go to: **Burgas** (4hr., 2 per day, 8lv); **Pleven** (3½hr., 3 per day, 11lv); **Plovdiv** (2hr., 4 per day, 6lv); **Sofia** (3½hr., 7 per day, 5-7lv); **Veliko Tŭrnovo** (3½hr., 4 per day, 6lv).

To reach the city center from the train station, go left 100m and turn right on ul. Rozova Dolina (Розова Долина). The road leads to the main square, **pl. Sevtopolis** (Севтополис). The main street, **23ti Pekhoten Shipchenski Polk** (23ти Пехотен Шипченски Полк), runs perpendicular to ul. Rozova Dolina. The **tourist office** is on pl. Sevtopolis, across from Hotel Kazanlŭk. (☎ 628 17. Open M-F 8:30am-4:30pm.) **Bulbank** (Булбанк), Sevtopolis 11, to the right down 23ti Pekhoten Shipchenski, when your back is to the main square, **exchanges currency** and cashes **traveler's checks** for 1% commission. (☎ 647 77. Open M-F 8:30am-4pm.) MC/V **ATMs** stand on 23ti Pekhoten Shipchenski near the post office and in front of Bulbank. **Luggage storage** (0.80lv per day) is at the train station. (Open within 15min. of train arrivals or departures.) A **pharmacy** is on 23ti Pekhoten Shipchenski, across from Bulbank. (☎ 269 40. Open daily 8am-8:30pm.) The **post office,** also on 23ti Pekhoten Shipchenski, sells Bulfon and Mobika phone cards, offers **Poste Restante** (in the room to the left after the stairs by the row of yellow mailboxes), and provides **telephone** and fax (☎ 6 38 40) services. (Post office open M-F 8:30am-6:30pm, Sa 8:30am-12:30pm. Telephones and fax open daily 7am-9:30pm.) **Postal Code:** 6100.

BULGARIA

ROSE FESTIVAL

Each year in Kazanlŭk and Korlovo, people gather to celebrate the prominent history of Bulgarian rose harvesting. The Rose Valley, which stretches from the Balkan Range to the Sredna Gora Mountains, is the region from which the prized Damask rose is cultivated. While there are over 5000 species of rose, only the Damask rose produces the liquid gold known as rose oil. Native to Tunisia, this rose was introduced to the area by the Turks in the 15th century. With superlative climatic conditions that retain the roses' aroma, the Rose Valley churns out some of the world's most sought-after fragrances, vital to perfume companies worldwide.

To thank Mother Nature for this wonderfully lucrative flower, local harvesters stage a celebratory festival from May 30 to June 1 every year. Dating back to 1903, the ritualistic folk singing and dancing processions celebrate both the rose pickers and the flower's natural splendor. While the masked folk dancers are charming in their own right, the crowning of the Queen Rose most convincingly celebrates the beauty of the rose. Meanwhile, the beauty contest features the region's most gorgeous women. Later, casual observers are draped with rose wreaths and goaded into drinking puckering rose brandy. If booze isn't your thing, get a sugar high from the sweet selection of rose jams.

ACCOMMODATIONS AND FOOD. For a bed during the Rose Festival, call at least one month in advance. The cheapest and most traditional lodging in town is tucked away in the vine-covered cobblestone walls of **Hadji Eminova Kŭshta ❶**, on ul. Nikola Petkov 22. This 19th-century guesthouse exudes a Renaissance ambience rarely found outside a mountainside village. While the thick foliage and prominent walls insulate patrons from the bustle of the city, its *mekhana* creates a buzz of its own when the nightly tunes heat up. (☎ 625 95. Doubles 20lv.) **Hotel Palas ❸**, ul. Petko Stainov 9 (Петко Стайнов), offers massages (1hr. upper-body 10lv), a sauna, a solarium (4lv per 10min.), and a pool. Facing away from pl. Sevtopolis, go right on 23ti Pekhoten Shipchenski. Turn left at ul. Petko Staynov. Palas (☎ 6 21 61; info@hotel-palas.com. Breakfast included. Singles 70lv; doubles 88lv.) The best meals in town are offered at the *mekhana* **Hadji Eminova Kŭshta ❶**, which serves up authentic Bulgarian fare. Fill up on the grilled chicken breast in French wine sauce (6lv). (Entrees 3lv-8lv. Open daily 10:30am-midnight.) The **restaurant ❷** at Hotel Palas offers a outstanding lunch menu. (Entrees 120-130lv. Open daily 7:30am-11:30pm.) For superb pizza and pasta, head to **New York Pizza ❶**, on Seovtopolis under Hotel Kazanluk. (☎ 62 464. Open daily 10am-1am.)

SIGHTS. While best known for its roses, Kazanlŭk harbors sights that maintain the town's spirit during the low season. Kazanlŭk's foremost museum, the **Iskra Art Gallery and Historical Museum** (Художествена Галерия и Исторически Музей Искра; Khudozhestvena Galeriya i Istoricheski Muzey Iskra), St. Kiril i Metodii 9, features pieces by Bulgaria's most famous artists, and tools, pottery, and other items from Thracian and Roman times. From Hotel Kazanlŭk, stand across pl. Svetopolis with your back to the hotel. Proceed one block to the right and the museum will be on the right at the next intersection. (☎ 637 62. Open May 15-Oct. 14 M-F 9am-6pm; Oct. 15-May 14 M-F 9am-5:30pm. 2lv, students 1lv.) With your back to the steps of the museum, walk right one block and, when you get to the large, concrete building that says "Ресторант Капитал" on the front, take another right on Stara Reka (Стара Река). Head down the street, cross the small bridge, and go up the stone steps to reach the **Thracian Tomb** (Тракийска Гробница; Trakiyska Grobnitsa), located inside a city park. While the original 3rd-century BC tomb is sealed off, a replica of the tomb's interior, complete with frescoes from the

Soviet era, lies 20m away. (☎647 50. Open daily 9am-6pm. 2lv, students 1lv.) If you are just passing through Kazanlŭk and don't have the time to visit the Rose Museum (see below), check out the **Ethnographic Complex of Kulata** (Етнографски Комплекс Кулата; Etnografski Kompleks Kulata), located next to the Hadji Eminova Kushta, on Nikola Petrov, to see a village house and a city dwelling from the Revival years. At the end of your visit you'll be treated to a shot of genuine rose liquor and a sample of rose jam. Be sure to stop by the museum's garden courtyard. Its distillery demonstrates the traditional method for making rose oil and liquor. (☎217 33. Open daily 9am-5:30pm. 3lv, students 1.50lv.) To get to the **Rose Museum and Gardens** (Музей на Розата; Muzey na Rozata), a 30min. walk from pl. Sevtopolis to bul. Osvobozhdeniye (Освобождение), head out of the center on General Skobelev (Генерал Скобелев), opposite Hotel Kazanlŭk, bearing right when Skobelev forks. Proceed on Osvobozhdnie. Alternatively, catch bus #5 or 6 across from Hotel Kazanlŭk (15min., every 30min., 0.40lv) and ask to get off at the *muzey* (MOO-zey). The museum teaches visitors everything they ever wanted to know about producing rose oil. (☎640 57. Open daily May-Oct. 9am-5pm. 2lv, students 1lv. English tours 5lv.) To glimpse the flowers from which all this rosiness springs, head next door to the **Scientific Research Institute for Roses, Aromatic, and Medicinal Plants** (Институт по Розата и Етеричномаслените Култури; Institut po Rosata i Eterichnomaclenite), home to experimental gardens that grow 250 varieties of roses. (☎620 39. Open daily 8am-5pm.)

▶ DAYTRIP FROM KAZANLŬK

SHIPKA (ШИПКА)   ☎(0)4324

From Kazanlŭk, take city bus #6 from the train station or the bus stop opposite Hotel Kazanlŭk to the end of the line (25min., 1 per hr., 0.40lv). To reach Shipka Pass and the monument, take an intercity bus from Kazanlŭk to Gabrovo, Pleven, or Veliko Tŭrnovo, and get off at the pass (30min., 6 per day, 1.50lv). Alternatively, hike up the trail behind the Nativity Church in Shipka Town (1½hr.); make sure to wear pants.

At the Rose Valley's northern edge lies the small town of Shipka, shaded by the legendary **Shipchenski Prokhod** (Шипченски Проход; Shipka Pass), site of the bloody battle that lasted an entire winter and ultimately liberated Bulgaria from the Turks in 1878 (see **History,** p. 113). Built in honor of the Russian and Bulgarian soldiers who lost their lives here, the golden domes of the Russian Orthodox **Nativity Memorial Church** are visible from almost every point in town. With your back to the bus stop, turn left at the end of the adjacent building, then left out of the little square on Khristo Patrev (Христо Патрев). Continue for 10min. to the concrete steps leading up to the church on the right. (Open daily May-Aug. 8:30am-7pm; Sept.-Apr. 8:30am-5pm. English tours 3lv. 2lv, students 1lv.) From the center of Shipka Pass, follow the road toward the looming **Monument to Freedom** (Паметник на Свободата; Pametnik na Svobodata), and climb the 912 stone steps to the ridge above the pass. A lion looking to the east guards the entrance, symbolizing Bulgaria's gratitude to Russia. Many of the manuscript fragments inside the monument are taken from Ivan Vazov's legendary poem "Shipka" (see **The Arts,** p. 116), which most Bulgarian students learn by heart. Climb to the top of the monument for a stunning view of the valley and the Balkan Mountains. (Open daily June-Aug. 9am-5pm; Sept.-May 9am-4:30pm. English tour 3lv. 2lv.) Be sure to try the water-buffalo yogurt (1.30lv per 0.25kg, 1.90lv per 0.50kg), a treat found only at the pass.

BLACK SEA COAST (ЧЕРНО МОРЕ)

Bulgaria's most popular destination for foreigners and natives alike, the Black Sea Coast (Cherno More) is covered with centuries-old fishing villages, secluded bays, energetic seaside towns, and plastic resorts. In Varna, the folk traditions of the past often clash with luxury resorts and bronzed German tourists, but more secluded beaches and tiny villages lie only slightly off the beaten track.

VARNA (ВАРНА)   ☎(0)52

In 600 BC, Varna (pop. 760,000), then called Odessos, was a thriving Greek town. By the time the Romans arrived, the city had become a cosmopolitan center, and it remains Bulgaria's seaside commercial and cultural hub. Thanks to a history of conquest and reconquest, its museums house some of the country's best exhibits.

▐ TRANSPORTATION

Trains: Near the commercial harbor. To: **Gorna Oryahovitsa** (4hr., 5 per day, 8lv); **Plovdiv** (7hr., 3 per day, 8-11lv); **Ruse** (4hr., 2 per day, 7lv); **Shumen** (1½hr., 8 per day, 4lv); **Sofia** (8hr., 6 per day, 13.50lv). **Rila**, ul. Preslav 13 (☎63 23 47), sells tickets to **Budapest, HUN** (27hr.; Tu, F, Su 5:30pm; 121lv) and **Istanbul, TUR** (12hr.; 1 per day; 38lv, with bed 58lv) via **Staru Zagora**. Open M-F 8am-6:30pm, Sa 8am-3pm.

Buses: Ul. Vladislav Varenchik (Владислав Варенчик). To reach the bus station, take city bus #1, 22, 40, or 41 from either the train station or the north side of the cathedral, opposite the post office, or walk 30min. on Preslav from pl. Nezavisimost to Varenchik. Buses are the best way to and from **Burgas** (2½hr., 5 per day, 7lv). Ticket office open daily 6am-7pm. Private buses leave for **Sofia** from the bus station (6hr., 16 per day, 19lv). **Group Travel** (☎50 49 59), behind the public bus station, sells international bus tickets from Sofia to **Budapest, HUN** (13-16hr.; M-Tu and Th-F 4:30pm; 100lv) and **Prague, CZR** (24hr., 10am, 100lv). Buy tickets in advance. Open daily 7am-5pm.

Black Sea Coast of Bulgaria

Minibuses: At the private station **Mladost** (Младост). Cross the busy street in front of the station. Walk between the concrete apartment buildings. The private station is a block down on the left; the minibuses are parked in front. To: **Balchik** (40min., 1 per hr. 6:30am-7pm, 2.50lv) and **Burgas** (2hr.; 7:30am, 1 per hr. 9am-5pm, 5:30pm; 6lv).

Public Transportation: Buses cost 0.50lv; pay on board. Bus stops are marked with small black signs displaying the bus number.

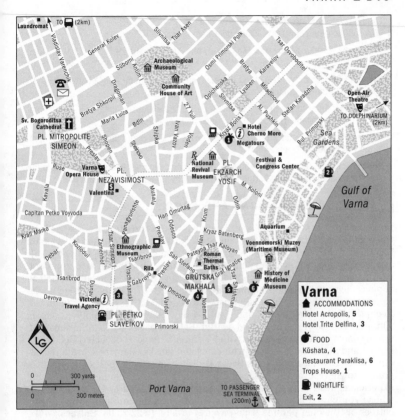

Varna

🏠 ACCOMMODATIONS

Hotel Acropolis, 5

Hotel Trite Delfina, 3

🍴 FOOD

Kūshata, 4

Restaurant Paraklisa, 6

Trops House, 1

🌙 NIGHTLIFE

Exit, 2

ORIENTATION AND PRACTICAL INFORMATION

All major sights fall within a 30min. walk of one another. To get to the central **pl. Nezavisimost** (пл. Независимост) from the train station, take **Tsar Simeon I** (Цар Симеон I). Varna's main pedestrian artery, **bul. Knyaz Boris I** (Княз Борис I), starts at pl. Nezavisimost, and **ul. Slivnitsa** connects it to the sea garden's main entrance. **Preslav** (Преслав) heads from pl. Nezavisimost to the **Sv. Bogoroditsa Cathedral.** To reach the beach from the train station, go right on **Primorski** (Приморски).

Tourist Office: There is no official tourist office in Varna. Try **Megatours,** Slivnitsa 33 (☎61 27 61), in the Hotel Cherno More. Offers **American Express** services and sells **city maps** (4lv). English spoken. Open M-F 8:45am-6:30pm, Sa 8:45am-2pm.

Currency Exchange: Bulgarian Post Bank, Knyaz Boris I 3 (☎68 69 00), in the main square, cashes **traveler's checks** (US$5 commission) and gives V **cash advances** for 4% commission, with a US$5 min.). Open M-F 8:30am-5pm.

ATMs: Outside the Valentina shopping complex next to Bulgarian Post Bank (see above). There are more MC/V ATMs on ul. Slivnitsa, on the stretch from Hotel Cherno More to the port, and in front of banks on Maria Luiza between Varenchik and Dragoman.

Luggage Storage: At the train station, by the end of track #8. 2lv per bag. Open daily 6am-10:50pm.

Laundromat: Byalata Pantera (Бялата Пантера), zh. Kyuri 28 (ж. Кюри). Wash 2lv. Dry 1.50lv. Detergent 0.50lv. Open daily 8am-9pm.

Pharmacy: Apteka Khaneman (Ханеман), bul. Kryaz Boris I 29 (☎60 71 97). Open daily 9am-7pm.

Hospital: Polyclinic Sv. Klementina (Клементина), bul. Sŭborni 40 (Съборни; ☎60 38 02), next to the post office.

Telephones: Enter to the right of the main post office entrance. Open daily 7am-11pm. **Fax** services available (fax 60 00 81). Open daily 7am-9pm.

Internet Access: Bulstar 2000, Preslov 35 (☎63 32 70). 8am-10pm 1lv per hr.; 10pm-8am 0.80lv per hr. Open 24hr.

Post Office: Bul. Sŭborni 49 (Съборни), behind the cathedral. **Poste Restante** is in the central room at window #12. Open M-Sa 7am-7pm, Su 8am-noon. **Postal Code:** 9000.

■ ☐ ACCOMMODATIONS AND FOOD

Victorina Tourist Agency, ul. Tsar Simeon I 36, offers **private rooms.** (☎60 35 41. Open daily Apr.-May 10am-6pm; June-Sept. 7am-9pm. Singles from 22lv.) **Astra Tour,** near track #6 at the train station, finds private rooms for €8. (☎60 58 61; astratur@yahoo.com. Open summer daily 6am-10pm.) Locals also approach backpackers at the train station and offer lodging for 8-10lv. **Hotel Trite Delfina** (Трите Делфина; Three Dolphins) ❸, ul. Gabrovo 27, boasts well-kept, spacious rooms with cable TV and private baths. (☎60 09 11. Breakfast included. Reception 24hr. Check-out noon. Call 3-4 days ahead. Singles 50lv; doubles 60lv.) Tucked away in Varna's old quarter, **Hotel Acropolis** ❸, Tsar Shishman 13, offers simple but roomy doubles with TV and A/C. (☎60 31 08. 55lv.) Bul. Knyaz Boris I and ul. Slivnitsa swarm with cafes and kiosks. Many beachside restaurants serve fresh seafood. **Trops House** ❶ dishes up the cheapest cafeteria-style grub in town. (Entrees 1-4lv. Open daily 8am-11pm.) For a more elegant dining experience, head over to ▨**Restaurant Paraklisa** (Параклиса) ❸, Primorski 47, where you can challenge your tastebuds by mixing and matching various entrees, as the chef permits ½ and even ¼ orders. (☎22 23 95. Entrees 7-16lv. Open M-Sa 11am-10pm.) ▨**Kŭshata** (Къщата) ❷, 8 Noemvri 7, serves up some of Varna's tastiest meals in traditional Bulgarian style. (☎60 28 79. Entrees 3-12lv. Open daily 9am-midnight.)

◉ SIGHTS

The well-preserved ▨**Roman Thermal Baths** (Римски Терми; Rimski Termi), the largest ancient complex in Bulgaria, stand on San Stefano in the old quarter, **Grŭtska Makhala.** (Гръцка Махала. Open Tu-Su 10am-5pm. 3lv, students 2lv.) Two buildings display 19th-century folk crafts from Bulgaria's historic National Revival period (see **History,** p. 113). The **Ethnographic Museum** (Етнографски Музей; Etnografski Muzey) is at Panagyurishte 22. (Панагюрище; ☎63 05 88. Open summer Tu-Su 10am-5pm; winter Tu-F 10am-5pm. 4lv, students 2lv.) The **National Revival Museum** is just off pl. Ekzarkh Yosif (Екзазх Йосиф). It houses the first Bulgarian school and Orthodox church in Varna. (Open daily 8am-5pm. Free.) The **Archaeological Museum** (Археологически Музей; Arkheologicheski Muzey), in the park on Maria Luiza, traces the country's history from the Stone Age, with ancient objects and the world's oldest golden artifacts. (Open summer Tu-Su 10am-5pm; winter Tu-Sa 10am-5pm. English tours 20lv. English booklet 6lv. Museum 4lv.)

🎵 🎭 ENTERTAINMENT AND NIGHTLIFE

Hidden among the fountains and trees in the seaside gardens is a vine-covered **open-air theater** (☎61 28 03; open M-F 11am-8pm; tickets 5-7lv), home of the biannual **International Ballet Festival** (May-Oct.). Buy tickets at the gate or at the Festival and Congress Center (see below). The pink **Opera House**, on the main square, has weekly performances and sells theater tickets. (Opera ☎22 33 88. 10-20lv. Open M-F 10:30am-2pm and 2-7pm. Theater ☎60 07 99. 6lv. Open M-F 10am-1pm and 2-8pm, Sa 10am-1pm and 4-6pm.) In late August, Varna holds an **International Jazz Festival**. The chamber music festival **Varna Summer** (Варненско Лято; Varnensko Lyato) runs from around June 21 to July 28; tickets are available at the Opera House. The **Festival and Congress Center,** with cafes, Internet access, and a cinema (tickets 3lv), is popular with younger crowds. From late August to early September, the international **Love is Folly** film festival takes place at the complex.

Beaches are cramped in summer but make for an enjoyable afternoon. The sands stretch north from the train station and are separated from bul. Primorski by the seaside gardens. Dedicated beachgoers should consider purchasing an umbrella (7lv) rather than renting one (3lv). In summer, a long strip of discos and bars rock the beach. Crowds pack the outdoor disco **Exit**. Take Slivnitsa to its end at the sea garden, proceed down the steps, and head left. Hip-hop reigns, but don't expect any bumping and grinding. (Drinks 1-5lv. Cover F-Sa 2lv. Open daily 10pm-5am.)

🔺 DAYTRIPS FROM VARNA

BALCHIK (БАЛЧИК)

Minibuses (40min., every hr. 6:30am-7:30pm, 2.50lv) run from Varna's private bus station, Mladost. From Balchik's bus station, walk downhill on the main street, Cherno More (Черно Море), to pl. Nezavisimost; from there continue downhill on Cherno More to reach pl. Ribarski. Ul. Primorska is on the other side of the plaza and runs along the shore.

For a break from Varna's crowded boardwalks, visit Balchik (BAHL-chik), a fishing village with houses carved into the chalky cliffs, where life moves at a pleasantly lethargic pace. Picturesque Balchik has the conveniences of a resort, but without the resort prices and crowds. The **public beach** is small—arrive early to secure a spot. Entrance is free and you can rent chairs (3lv) and umbrellas (2lv). The best sands lie sheltered by Romanian Queen Maria's **Summer Palace**, built in the 1920s when Romania controlled the area. To reach the palace from pl. Ribarski (Рибарски), turn right and walk along Primorska (Приморска) or the beach boardwalk (20min.). You can sit on Maria's marble throne or explore the garden, which boasts the largest cactus collection in the Balkans. Maria so loved Balchik that she left her heart here—in a small chapel on the palace grounds. (Open daily 8am-8pm. Tours 15lv. English booklet 3lv. Palace 5lv, students 1lv.)

For an epidermal treat, visit the **mud baths** of Tuzlata, 6km north of Balchik. Take a taxi from pl. Ribarski (4lv) and ask for the sanatorium. Although the spa has seen better days, you can still get a great *gryazni banya* (грязни баня; grand bath). Women enter on the right, men on the left. Get naked and rub mud all over yourself, then sit in the sun while it dries. (Open summer daily 8:30am-7pm. 3lv.) **Tourist Agency Chaika** (Чайка), on pl. Ribarski 2, sells **maps** of Balchik (2lv) and arranges private rooms. (☎720 53; www.bgtur.hit.bg. 10-15lv. Open daily summer 8am-8pm.) Seafood restaurants line the beach.

ALADZHA MONASTERY (АЛАДЖА МАНАСТИР)

Bus #29 travels to the monastery from the train station, but only in the early morning and late afternoon (20min., 2 per day, 0.80lv). Alternatively, ask a minibus headed to Balchik to stop at the Golden Sands Resort. From there take a taxi to the monastery (5lv). Be sure not to miss the last bus back, which leaves at 6:30pm. Monastery ☎35 54 60. Open daily 9am-6pm. In an effort to preserve its treasures, the chapel is open only by appointment with the curator. Museum, monastery, and catacombs 3lv; students 2lv.

Known as the rock *(skalen)* monastery, Aladzha, 14km from Varna, was carved from the side of a mountain during the 13th and 14th centuries. Now primarily a tourist attraction, the monastery has two levels in the 40m white limestone cliff. Organ music resonates throughout the **chapel,** which boasts incredible biblical frescoes and a breathtaking view of the sea. A **museum** exhibits medieval paintings and gives historical info about the monastery and surrounding **Golden Sands National Park** (Народен Парк "Златни Пясъци;" Naroden Park "Zlatni Pyasŭtsi"). Northeast along the forest trail (800m), past the museum, the **catacombs,** a group of caves once inhabited by hermits, offer a look into the life of 14th-century monks.

BURGAS (БУРГАС) ☎(0)56

Bulgaria's main industrial port, Burgas (BOOR-ghas; pop. 230,000) is best known for the hulking freight ships that dominate its almost-pristine bays. Though less popular among tourists than Varna, Burgas is vibrant at night and serves as an ideal base from which to explore the coast. The city is best enjoyed with a stroll along the beach or a sunset visit to the seaside gardens.

⚏🔀 TRANSPORTATION AND PRACTICAL INFORMATION. Trains run to: **Plovdiv** (5hr., 4 per day, 8lv); **Sofia** (6-8hr., 5 per day, 9lv) via **Plovdiv** or **Karlovo;** and **Varna** (5hr., 4 per day, 5.30-10.70lv) via **Karnobat.** To the left as you face the train station, **minibuses** go to the resorts, including **Akhtopol** (2hr., 5 per day, 6.20lv); **Nesebŭr** (40min.; every 20min. 6:20am-8:40pm, 10pm; 3lv); **Primorsko** (50min., 11 per day, 3lv); **Sozopol** (40min., every 30min. 6am-9:30pm, 2.40lv); and **Varna** (2hr., 15 per day, 7lv).

The Burgas **train** and **bus stations** are near the port at **pl. Garov** (пл. Гаров). **Aleksandrovska** (Александровска), the main pedestrian drag, begins across the street and extends through **Troykata Square** (Тройката) to **ul. San Stefano** (Сан Стефано). **Bulbank,** across the street from Hotel Bulgaria (see below) on Aleksandrovska, cashes **traveler's checks** for 1.5% commission, exhanges currency, and has a MC/V **ATM.** (Open M-F 8:30am-4pm.) Other **ATMs** are across from McDonald's, farther up Aleksandrovska. If heading to **Istanbul,** make sure to obtain a visa from the **Turkish Consulate,** Demokratsiya 38 (Думокрация). From the train station, take a right down bul. Bulair and follow it as it turns into Demokratsiya. Just behind the consulate, you can purchase tickets to Istanbul. Find **Internet access** at **Lio,** Alexandra Bogoridi 29, at the intersection with Slavianska. (Open 24hr. 1lv per hr.) To get to the new **post office,** walk through Troykata Sq. to the end of Aleksandrovska and turn right on San Stefano. It's one block down on the left, with **telephones** inside. (Open M 7:30am-noon and 1-7pm, Tu-F 7:30am-7pm, Sa 8am-noon and 1-5pm. Phones open daily 7am-10pm.) **Poste Restante** is left of the old post office's main entrance. Walk down Aleksandrovska, go right at the train station, and then make a right on Tsar Retur. The old post office will be on your left. (Open M-F 7:30am-8pm, Sa 8am-noon and 1-5pm, Su 8am-1pm.) **Postal Code:** 8000.

🛏🍴 ACCOMMODATIONS AND FOOD. For overnight stays, **private rooms** are the most convenient. You can secure private rooms at **Primorets Tourist Burgas.** Take a right out of the train station; it's across the street. (☎84 27 27. Open daily 7am-7pm. 11lv.) Otherwise, check into **Hotel Mirage ❸** (Мираж; Mirazh), Lermontov 48. From the station, go up Aleksandrovska, take a right on Bogoridi (Богориди), pass Hotel Bulgaria, and take the second left on Lermontov. This drab hotel offers basic yet well-kept rooms. (☎84 56 57. Shared bathrooms. TV 4lv. Reception 24hr. Check-out noon. Doubles and triples 40lv.) For authentic Bulgarian fare at break-neck speed, head to **BMS,** Aleksandrovska 20. Vegetable marrow with yogurt (тиквичи с кисело мляко; tikvichi s kiselo mlyako; 18lv) is a summer favorite. (Open daily 8am-10pm.) Be sure to also take advantage of the **seaside vendors** hawking cheap food. **Bacardi Club,** Aleksandrovska 51, is a dance club with modern decor and a lively crowd. (☎82 76 29. Open 24hr.)

AROUND BURGAS

Heading south from Burgas, you'll come across an array of beautiful seaside points, from the pristine hamlets of Kiten and Sinemorets to the thriving artistic and cultural center of Sozopol. Primorsko, Bulgaria's biggest youth center, lies only a short bus ride away. Just north of Burgas, Nesebŭr offers both crowded beaches and a smorgasbord of ancient relics within the Byzantine gates of its Old City. All of these towns make good daytrips from Burgas, but those interested in a longer stay can rent private rooms from the locals.

NESEBŬR (НЕСЕБЪР)   ☎(0)554

Nesebŭr (neh-SEH-buhr; pop. 10,000), a beach town with cultural flair, lies atop the peninsula at the south end of **Sunny Beach.** Don't expect a respite from the summer crowds, however, as this might be the most popular town in Bulgaria. A walk through the ancient **Stariya Grad** (Old Town) begins with the AD 300 stone **fortress walls.** The Byzantine **gate** and **port** date from AD 500. The **Archaeological Museum** (Археологически Музей; Arkheologicheski Muzey), to the right of the town gate, exhibits ancient ceramics and artifacts, like stone anchors from 1200 BC. The museum sells a **map** (0.50lv) of Old Nesebŭr's sights in Bulgarian and German. (☎460 18. Open M-F 9am-1pm and 1:30-7pm, Sa-Su 9am-1pm and 2-6pm. English tours 5lv per group. Museum 2.50lv, students 1.20lv.) The 13th-century **Church of Christ the Almighty** (Христос Пантократор; Khristos Pantokrator), in the main square, doubles as an art gallery in summer. (☎450 00. Open daily 9am-9pm.) The UNESCO-protected **Temple of John the Baptist** (Йоан Кръстител; Yoan Krŭstitel), now an art gallery, dates from the 10th century. To reach the church, walk on Mitropolitska from the center; the church is on the left. (Open daily 10am-10pm. Free.) After a day of sightseeing, cool off with a dip in the **beach's** shallow waters.

Buses to and from **Burgas** (40min., every 40min. 6am-9pm, 2.40lv) stop at the Old Nesebŭr port and at the gate leading to town. Minibuses heading for Sunny Beach also make the trip from Burgas (30min., every 30-40min., 2.40lv) but only stop in **New Nesebŭr.** Take a **city bus** (10min., every 10min., 0.50lv) from there, or head left with your back to the bus station to get to Stariya Grad (15min.).

SOZOPOL (СОЗОПОЛ)   ☎(0)5514

Thirty-four kilometers south of Burgas, Sozopol (soh-ZOH-pohl), settled in 610 BC, is Bulgaria's oldest Black Sea town. Once the resort of choice for Bulgaria's artistic community, it still serves as a haven for the creative set. Take a **boat cruise** around Sozopol from the seaport (behind the bus station) to get a closer look at the two adjacent islands, **St. Peter** and **St. Ivan.** The boats leave twice per day (7 and 8:15pm, 6lv). The entrance to the public beach is in the park across from the bus station. To explore some of Sozopol's less-crowded **beaches,** rent a **motorbike** near the New Town beach and cruise along the shoreline (10lv per hr.). Awaken your inner child on the **trampoline** (1lv per 10min.), get a massage (22lv), or take a ride on an **oversized rubber banana** pulled by a motorboat (6lv per person; min. 4 riders). **Biohim Bank,** Apoloniya 17, cashes **traveler's checks** for 1% commission and US$2 min. There is an **ATM** outside. (☎224 85. Open M-F 8:30am-6:30pm.) Farther down is the **pharmacy.** (Open daily 8am-midnight.) One block over, **medical assistance** is available at Meditsinski Tsentŭr. (Медицински Център; ☎244 25. Open daily 8am-10pm.) A few buildings past the bank, you'll find the **Internet Club.** (☎220 82. 1.50lv per hr. 8am-midnight; 1lv per hr. midnight-8am. Open 24hr.)

Imperial Tour, Ropotamo 5 (☎/fax 224 63; imperialtour@abv.bg), arranges **private rooms** and trips to Istanbul (Tu and F 10:20pm; 60lv). After taking the left fork into New Town on Republikanska, walk until the road runs into a pedestrian street. Head down the blocked street and the office will be on the left. (Open daily 9am-10pm. Singles 10-12lv.) If you plan to spend the night, the aptly-named **Hotel Sozopol ❷,** ul. Industrialna 9a, proves an affordable alternative to private accommodations with simple, clean rooms. (☎223 62. Check-out noon. Double 20lv). A traditional *mekhana,* ▩**Restaurant "Viaturna Melnitsa" ❶,** ul. Morski Skali 27, boasts delectable meals, gorgeous views, and live folk music. (☎228 44. Open daily 10am-midnight.) With a panoramic view of Sozopol's cliff-enclosed bay, **Orfei ❷** (Орфеи) offers an encyclopedic list of seafood specialities including lobster rolls (4lv) and grilled Danube herring (7.50lv). Walking into Old Town, take the rightmost fork along the seacoast. (☎224 41. Open daily 10am-midnight.) Start your night off at the waterfront **Tequila Bar,** behind the bus station, then get down to the beat of techno, hip-hop, and folk on the biggest dance floor in town at **Disco Club Teodora.** It's located past the food market to the right of the bus station. (Drinks 1-8lv. Cover 2lv. Open daily 10pm-sunrise.) During the first 10 days of September, Bulgarian artists take over the town for the **Arts Festival Apoloniya.**

Minibuses run from **Burgas** (45min., every 30min. 6am-9:30pm, 2.40lv) and **Primorsko** (20min., every hr. 9am-8pm, 2-3lv). Go on Apoloniya (Аполония) to reach the Old Town. To get to the New Town, turn right from the bus station and bear left when the road, Republikanska (Републиканска), forks.

PRIMORSKO (ПРИМОРСКО) ☎(0)550

Young Bulgarians know Primorsko (pree-MOHR-skoh) as the site of the **International Youth Center ❸** (ММЦ, or Международни Младежки Център; Mezhdunarodni Mladezhki Tsentŭr). Once a compound for the best Communist Pioneers, the Youth Center now has the feel of an aged summer camp. The complex and its five hotels have numerous sports facilities, restaurants, and conference halls. (☎301 27. July-Aug. singles €20; June and Sept. €12.) In the oak forest between the beach and the complex you can play tennis, basketball, handball, or table tennis. (2lv per hr. Open daily 8am-8pm.) For a free **map,** head to the info office in room #1 of the building to the right of Hotel Druzhba, located at the complex. (☎301 01. Open daily May-Oct. 8am-5pm.) Back in the city center, a 30min. walk from the complex, **Hotel Koral ❹,** Stzandzha 25, offers clean, comfortable rooms with A/C, TV, and included breakfast. (☎322 30. Doubles 58lv.) On Cherno More, across the street from the Spektar Palace Hotel, you can rent **bikes** (3lv per hr.). At the **beach,** you can lie under an umbrella (3lv) or rent a paddleboat (vodno kolelo; 8lv per hr.). To the left when facing the beach there is an **open-air theater** and a **cinema.** For nightlife, try the Egyptian-themed **Luxor Disco Club,** where you can sweat to the hip-hop and techno or get drenched on the waterslide. (Drinks 2-3lv. Cover 3lv.)

Minibuses run from **Burgas** (1hr., every 40-50min. 6am-8pm, 3.40lv) and **Sozopol** (20min., every hr., 2-3lv). All lines stop at Primorsko's main street, **ul. Cherno More** (Черно Море). To reach the main complex of the ММЦ (International Youth Center) from the Primorsko bus station, take a right facing away from the station and head out of town. Turn left at the open intersection. Cross the bridge over **Dyavolka Reka** (Дяволка Река; Devil's River) and go for 15min. A cab costs 4-5lv.

SINEMORETS (СИНЕМОРЕЦ) ☎(0)550

With warm waters, few tourists, and a beautiful beach nestled below a high grassy bluff, Sinemorets, a tiny village of 400 inhabitants only 10km north of Turkey, is the last remaining gem on Bulgaria's commercialized coast. The best hotel and restaurant are at **Complex Domingo ❸** (К-С Доминго), on the road to the beach; signs point the way from the town center. The bright rooms have balconies with distant seaside views, tiled floors, and private baths. (☎660 93; www.casadomingo.info. July-Aug. €42; June and Sept. €15.) Domingo's **patio restaurant ❷** features a renowned poolside grill, which has become famous for its stuffed-pork specialties. (Entrees 1.40-13lv. Open daily 7am-midnight.) Walking toward the beach, **Restaurant Zafo ❸** rents **bicycles** (1lv per hr.) and **motorbikes** (12lv per hr.) and offers cramped two-bed bungalows ❶. (☎661 41. Doubles 24lv, with bath 34lv.)

Minibuses run to **Akhtopol** (4 per day, 0.50lv). Buses go to **Burgas** (2hr.; 3 per day; 5.40lv) and **Tsarevo** (45min., 3 per day, 1.60lv). To get to the beach from the minibus stop, turn right at the 1st street after a trio of cafes, then take the 1st left. After Complex Domingo, turn right on the road going downhill and continue 10min.

NORTHERN BULGARIA

From the ancient ruins of Bulgaria's first capitals at Pliska and Veliki Preslav to the war memorial in Pleven, the region between the Danube River and the Balkan Mountains is most notable for its historic relics.

VELIKO TŬRNOVO (ВЕЛИКО ТЪРНОВО) ☎(062)

Perched on the slopes above the Yantra River, 5000-year-old Veliko Tŭrnovo (Veh-LEEK-oh TURN-oh-voh), was Bulgaria's capital from 1185 to 1393, and was home to Bulgaria's greatest kings—Petur, Asen I, Kaloyan, and Asen II. Tapping into its glorious legacy, Bulgarian revolutionaries wrote Bulgaria's first constitution here in 1879. Veliko Tŭrnovo's cozy balconies provide an amazing view of the fortress ruins and the sparkling river, lifting the spirits of even the most jaded traveler.

▐ TRANSPORTATION

Trains: All trains north head to nearby **Gorna Oryakhovitsa** (Горна Оряховица; 20min., 10 per day, 0.60lv), where connecting trains are scheduled to meet them. Trains run from Gorna Oryahovitsa to: **Burgas** (6hr., 5 per day, 6.40lv); **Pleven** (1½hr., 16 per day, 3.30lv); **Ruse** (2½hr., 8 per day, 3.50lv); **Sofia** (5hr., 9 per day, 8.30lv); **Tryavna** (1hr., 9 per day, 1.90lv); **Varna** (4hr., 4 per day, 7.30lv). You can also take a **bus** to the Gorna train station (see **Buses**, below). To: **Gabrovo** (1½hr., 6 per day, 2lv).

Buses: Station on Nikola Gabrovsky (Никола Габровски), 5 stops from the center on bus #10 (0.40lv), heading to the right when facing the post office. Buses run to: **Gabrovo** (40min., 13 per day, 3lv) and **Stara Zagora** (3hr., 7 per day, 6lv). **Minibuses** and buses connect V. Tŭrnovo with Gorna. Minibuses run between the intersection of Nikola Gabrovsky and ul. Bŭlgaria in V. Tŭrnovo to Gorna's train station (20min., every 30min., 1lv). Buses #10 and 14 go from V. Tŭrnovo's bus station to Gorna's train station (30min.; before noon every 30min., after noon every 1hr.; 1.40lv). **Etap**, a private daily bus service to most major cities, is located in Hotel Etur (☎63 05 64). Walk down Khristo Botev and turn left on Aleksandŭr Stamboliyski; Etur is a tall tower. Runs buses to **Sofia** (3hr., 11 per day, 11lv) and **Varna** (3hr., 8 per day, 11lv). Open 24hr.

⚡ ORIENTATION

Veliko Tŭrnovo is spread along a loop of the Yantra River, with its central square, **pl. Mayka Bulgaria** (Майка България), located on the outside bank. Through the center, the main drag follows the river east, changing its name as it goes: it begins as **bul. Vasil Levski**, becomes **Nezavisimost** (Независимост), turns into **Stefan Stambolov** (Стефан Стамболов), **V. Dzhandzhiyata** (В. Джанджията), **Nikola Pikolo** (Никола Пиколо) and **Mitropolska** (Митрополска) as it reaches the ruins of **Tsarevets Krepost** (Царевец Крепост). The other key street, **Khristo Botev** (Хзисто Ботев), intersects Nezavisimost at pl. Mayka Bulgaria. With your back to the **train station,** go uphill along the river to the left for 10min. and then cross the bridge, which leads to **Aleksandŭr Stamboliyski** (Александър Стамболийски). Turn right on Khristo Botev (Христо Ботев). You can also take almost any of the buses (0.40lv, timed to meet trains) from the station; ask the driver *"za tsentura?"* ("to the center?").

🛈 PRACTICAL INFORMATION

Tourist Office: Khristo Botev 5 (☎622 148), on the left just after pl. Mayka Bulgaria. English spoken. **Maps** 3lv. Open M-F 9am-noon and 1-6pm.

Currency Exchange: Biokhim Bank (Биохим), Rafayel Mihailov 4 (Рафаел Михайлов; ☎62 39 55). Facing away from the post office, walk right on Nezavisimost; the bank is on the 1st street to your left. Cashes **traveler's checks** for 1% commission. Open M-F 8:30am-4:30pm.

ATM: On Khristo Botev, opposite La Scalla Pizzeria.

Luggage Storage: At the train station. 0.80lv per day. Luggage must be claimed at least 30min. prior to departure of train.

24hr. Pharmacy: Ul. Vasil Levski 29 (Васил Левски; ☎60 04 33).

Hospital: St. Cherkezov Regional Hospital (Св. Черкезов), Nish 1 (Ниш; ☎268 42), off Nikola Gabrovsky.

Telephones: At the post office (fax 62 98 77). BulFon and Mobikom cards sold. Open daily 7am-10pm. You can send international **faxes** for 1.08lv per min. plus 0.75 lv per page; 0.60lv per page received. Open M-F 7:30am-9pm, Sa 8am-noon and 1-7pm.

Internet Access: Bezdnata (Бездната), Khristo Botev 3 (☎60 21 18), on the street behind Bar Poltava, off pl. Mayka Bulgaria. Look for the submarine decor (noon-10pm 0.80lv per hr., 10pm-noon 0.50lv per hr.). Open 24hr.

Post Office: Pl. Maika Bulgaria. **Poste Restante** is down the stairs, 30m left of the main entrance. Open M-F 7am-7pm, Sa 8am-noon and 1-4:30pm. **Postal Code:** 5000.

🏠 ACCOMMODATIONS

Rooms in Veliko Tŭrnovo are plentiful, and if you wear a backpack for over five seconds in public, you'll be approached by locals offering **private rooms** (8-20lv).

🛏 **Hotel Comfort,** Panayot Tipografov 5 (Панайот Типографов; ☎287 28). With your back to the post office, head right up Nezavisimost, which becomes Stambolov. Veer left on Rakovski (Раковски), the cobblestone street that splits off the main road. After all the souvenir shops, turn left at the small square and continue straight; the hotel is on the left. Clean rooms, beautiful private bathrooms, and amazing views of Tsarevets. Reception 24hr. Check-out noon. Singles €25; doubles €30. ❸

Hostel Trapezitsa (HI; Трапезица), Stefan Stambolov 79 (☎622 061). From the center, walk on Nezavisimost to the post office and follow the street to the right (5min.). Clean sheets and private bathrooms. Request a room with a view. Reception 24hr. Check-out 11am. Doubles 20lv; 3- to 4-bed dorms 17lv. ISIC discounts available. ❶

Elida Guest House (Елида), Reservoarska 3 (☎323 29). Walking toward Hotel Comfort, look for the green sign on the left side of the street. Peacefully situated in Veliko's historic Samovodska Charshia Sq., this guest house offers unadorned rooms at a bargain rate. Check-out noon. Singles 15lv; doubles 30lv. ❶

🍴 FOOD

A large **open-air market** sells fresh fruit and veggies (0.60-2.50lv per kg) daily from dawn to dusk at the corner of Bulgaria and Nikola Gabrovsky, while multiple *mekhana* (механа; tavern) make use of the balconies overlooking the river.

Starata Mekhana (Старата Механа), Stefan Stambolov (☎638 878). The savory aroma of Bulgarian cuisine lures patrons off the street to pop in and jockey for a spot at 1 of the 2 tables overlooking the beautiful vista. Try the heavenly chicken stew (3.50lv). Entrees 2-9lv. Open daily noon-midnight. Closed Su in winter. ❷

Shtastlivetsa Pasta and Pizza (Щастливеца), Stefan Stambolov 79 (☎60 06 56), next door to the Trapezitsa Hotel. A seemingly infinite number of options are packed into the 2 different Italian and Bulgarian menus. Try Bulgarian *kavarma* (meat casserole; 5.90lv) served in a traditional pot. Entrees 2-9.50lv. Open daily 10am-11pm. ❷

La Scalla Pizzaria, Khristo Botev 14 (☎63 58 11). Take your pick from an assortment of sizzling hand-tossed pizzas and hungrily watch your pie sear to a crisp under the flames of the open-fire oven. Entrees 2.15-5lv. Open daily until 1am, last orders at midnight. ❶

👁 SIGHTS

The ruins of ◪**Tsarevets** (Царевец), a fortress that once housed the royal palace and a cathedral, stretch across a hilltop outside the city. Nikola Pikolo leads to the gates, where the *kasa* (каса; ticket counter) stands. (Open 8am-7pm. 4lv.) Climb uphill to the beautiful **Church of the Ascension** (Църква Възнесениегосподне; Tsŭrkva Vŭzneseniegospodne), restored in 1981 for the 1300th anniversary of Bulgaria. (Open 7am-6:30pm.) **The National Revival Museum** (Музей на Възраждането; Muzey na Vŭzrazhdaneto) exhibits relics from the National Revival movement, including the first Bulgarian Parliament chamber (see **History**, p. 113) and the first Bulgarian constitution. From the center, follow Nezavisimost until it becomes Nikola Pikolo, then veer right on ul. Ivan Vazov (Иван Вазов). It's a light blue building, set off from the street. (☎298 21. Open M and W-Su 8am-6pm. 4lv.) Go left, down the stairs, and around to the back to reach the **Museum of the Second Bulgarian Kingdom** (Музей Второто Българско Царство; Muzey Vtoroto Bŭlgarsko Tsarstvo). Ring the bell if the door is locked. Medieval crafts from Tŭrnovo and religious frescoes trace the region's history from the Stone Age to the Middle Ages. (Open Tu-Su 8am-noon and 1-6pm. 4lv. English tours 8lv.)

🎭 🎦 ENTERTAINMENT AND NIGHTLIFE

On summer evenings there's often a ◪**sound and light show** above Tsarevets Hill— huge projectors light up the ruins for an unforgettable sight. (Show starts between 9:45 and 10pm.) Check at **Interhotel Veliko Tŭrnovo** (☎60 10 00), off Khristo Botev, for dates. **Scream Club**, on Nezavisimost (Независимост), attracts a stream of Turnovo's sleekest night owls. (Open M-Sa 10pm-5am. Cover M-Th 1lv, F-Sa 2lv.)

BULGARIA

DAYTRIPS FROM VELIKO TŬRNOVO

ETŬRA (ЕТЪРА)

Buses from Veliko Tŭrnovo (45min., 13 per day, 3lv) and Kazanlŭk (40min., 5 per day, 2lv) stop in Gabrovo. From the bus station, turn right at the end of the building, and make another right to reach the center. Take trolley #32 or 36 or bus #1 from the center to the last stop, Bolshevik (20min., 0.40lv). Then, take bus #7 or 8 and ask to be dropped off at Etŭra (10min., 4 per day, 0.40lv). Buses are rare on weekends; take a taxi (☎126; 3lv) from Bolshevik. All buses stop by Hotel-Restaurant Etŭra, which is white with wood trim.

Midway between Kazanlŭk and Veliko Tŭrnovo sits a small village where blacksmiths still pound goatbells by hand and no traditional crafts have been lost. If you want to experience Bulgaria's past and see the best Revival architecture in the country, visit Etura, an **outdoor ethnographic museum**, 8km south of Gabrovo. Sixteen of the houses have been turned into workshops, where craftsmen make woodcarvings, metalwork, jewelry, icons, musical instruments, herbal medicines, and pottery just as they've done for centuries. At the **Vŭzrozhdenska Mekhana ❷** (Възрожденска), try the lamb *à la* St. George (8.20lv). (☎80 18 31; www.tourinfo.bg/etar. Open daily May-Sept. 9am-6pm; Oct.-Apr. 9am-4:30pm. 6lv, students 4lv. English tours 7lv.) If you decide to stay the night, head to posh **Hotel Eŭtra ❷**, beautifully nestled between the foothill of the mountain and the stream. (☎066 801 831; http://etar.hit.bg. Breakfast included. Singles 48lv; doubles 78lv.)

TRYAVNA (ТРЯВНА)   ☎(0)677

Take a train from Veliko Tŭrnovo (1hr., 9 per day, 1.90lv) or a minibus from Gabrovo (45min., every 30min., 1.50lv). From the train station, go right 50m to the bus station. From the back of the bus station, turn right on Angel Kŭnchev (Ангел Кънчев) and follow it 10min. to the center. At the a tree-lined square, turn right at the yellow building and follow Angel Kŭnchev to pl. Kapitan Dyado Nikola (Капитан Дядо Никола) and the site.

A center of woodcarving, icon-painting, and unique architecture, Tryavna is itself a museum of National Revival arts (see **The Arts**, p. 116). Works of the 17th-century Tryavna School of Woodworking and Icon Painting endure as reminders of the settlement's greatest years. The **Church of the Archangel Michael** (Църквата Св. Архангел Михаил; Tsŭrkvata Sv. Arkhangel Mikhail), Angel Kŭnchev 9, which dates back to the Middle Ages, stands across the street and a little way down from the post office. It holds the treasured **Tsar's Crucifix** (Царският Кръст; Tsarskiyat Krŭst), a wooden relic on which 12 scenes from the Gospels are carved—ask the priest to remove it from its locked case for you. (Open daily 7am-6:30pm.) To the left when facing the church, the **Museum of the School** (Музей Школа; Muzey Shkola) stands at pl. Kapitan Dyado Nikola 7, the only preserved National Revival square in Bulgaria. The museum displays a comprehensive collection of art, both modern and classical, from around the world. (☎20 39. Open daily Apr.-Sept. 9am-6pm; Oct.-Mar. 8am-noon and 1-5pm. 2lv, students 1lv. English tours 5lv.) To find the **Museum of the Tryavna School of Icon Painting** (Музей Тревненска Иконописна; Muzey Trevnenska Ikonopisna), turn right out of the old square when your back is to the Museum of Old School and cross the small bridge. Take a left on Slaveikov (Славеиков), the next street, then take the first right. Continue uphill over the railroad tracks. Take a left on Breza (Бреза), and after the buildings, head up the stairs on the right through the woods; the museum is on the right. It has icon-making tools and over 160 icons. (Open daily May-Sept. 10am-6pm; Oct.-Apr. 10am-4pm. English captions. 2lv, students 1lv.) For more active recreation, **Stara Planina**, Angel Kŭnchev 22 (☎677 22 47), provides routes for daytrips, and gives info about the area. (Open M-F 9am-noon and 2-5pm.) The brand-new **Complex Zograf** ❸ (Зограф), ul. Slavikov 1 (Славецков) boasts luxurious rooms with spotless baths. Take the bridge leading out of the old square; the hotel is at its end. (☎49 70. Breakfast included. Check-out noon. Singles €24; doubles €40.) With your back to the old square's Museum of the Old School, take the street in the upper left-hand corner of the square to its end and turn right on Kaleto (Калето) to get to **Restaurant Pri Maystora** ❶ (При Майстора). Try the veal, pork, and cheese in the form of a pyramid (6lv) or the *shopska salad* (1.80lv). Maistora has creative versions of traditional dishes. (☎32 40. Open daily 11am-3pm and 6pm-midnight.)

PLEVEN (ПЛЕВЕН)   ☎(0)64

Bulgaria's final liberation from Turkish rule took place in Pleven after a war that lasted five months and claimed over 25,000 lives. Roughly 200 memorials commemorate the Russo-Turkish war of 1877. Still, an afternoon in the verdant main square may make visitors forget the town's gloomy history.

🚊🕎 TRANSPORTATION AND PRACTICAL INFORMATION. Trains go to: **Veliko Tŭrnovo** via **Gorna Oryahovitsa** (2hr., 14 per day, 3.50-5.75lv); **Ruse** (3½hr., 4 per day, 5.30-9.15lv); **Sofia** (3hr., 3 per day, 5-8.50lv). **Buses** run to **Ruse** (3hr., 4 per day, 6-8lv) and **Sofia** (2½hr., 18 per day, 8lv).

Pleven's focal points are its two spacious squares, **pl. Vŭzrazhdane** (Възраждане; Revival) and **pl. Svoboda** (Свобода; Freedom). **Ul. Vasil Levski** (Васил Левски) connects the two. From the train station, go through the park and walk down **bul. Danail Popov** (Данаил Попов), which runs perpendicular to the front of the train station and becomes Osvobozhdenie (Освобождение; Liberation). It eventually intersects with **pl. Svoboda** (10min.). Kiosks on Vasil Levski sell excellent English **maps** (4lv). There is no tourist office in town. **Bulgarian Post Bank** (Българска Пощенска Банка), bul. Danail Popov 18, **exchanges currency.** (☎89 09 90. Open M-F 8am-5pm.) **Biokhim Bank** (Биохим), ul. Kosta Khadzhipakev 1 (**Коста Хаджипакев**), is on the right behind the market as you head up Osvobozhdenie to pl. Svoboda. The bank cashes **traveler's checks** for 1% commission. (☎80 02 20. Open M-F 8:30am-4:30pm.) **Store luggage** at the train station. (0.80lv. Open 24hr., except 8:15-8:45am, 8:15-8:45pm, and 11:30pm-midnight.) **Pharmacies** abound. The **Diagnostic Consulting Center,** San Stefano 1 (☎281 04), to the right when facing the post office, provides **medical assistance.** (Open M-F 7:30am-6:30pm.) **Internet access** is available at **Lik** (Лик), bul. Danail Popov 2, near the park in front of the train station. (1lv per hr. Open 24hr.) The **post office,** at pl. Vŭzrazhdane, left from Osvobozhdenie, has **telephones** inside and an **ATM** out front. (Open M-F 7am-7:30pm. Telephones open daily 7am-1:45pm and 2-9:50pm.) **Postal Code:** 5800.

🏠🍴 ACCOMMODATIONS AND FOOD. There is a very limited selection of budget accommodations in Pleven. **Rostov na Don** ❹ (Ростов на Дон), Osvobozhdenie 2, on the left as you enter pl. Svoboda, is a tower hotel with TV, phone, and private bath. (☎80 10 95. Reception 24hr. Check-out noon. Singles €55; doubles €80. MC/V, 5% surcharge.) **Hotel Pleven** ❸, pl. Republika 2 (Република), is to the left of the train station when facing the park. Despite the drab, haunted-house feel, private baths and comfy beds make this proletarian compound the only deal in town. (☎830 181. Reception 24hr. Check-out noon. Singles US$25.) To the right of Vasil Levski, a cluster of *mekhani* serve up national cuisine. Walk to the end of Vasil Levski toward the train station and listen for the music. Buy fruits and vegetables (0.3-3lv per kg) at the **open-air market** on Osvobozhdenie before Rostov-na-Don.

THE LOCAL STORY

CAN I GET A HAND HERE?

While the average tourist comes to gawk at the enormity of the Troyan Monastery, many locals visit to see the icon it has housed for nearly 300 years. The icon of the Three-Handed Virgin emerges during an annual celebration held on August 15, when devout followers transport it to a local chapel. It is believed that the prayers of the faithful will be answered after they kiss the hand of the virgin.

The icon's story supposedly started back in the 8th century, when John of Damascus was accused by a Syrian King of painting icons. As punishment, he was sentenced to have his hand chopped off. Before being sent to the butcher, he prayed to the Holy Virgin, promising that he would cast a third silver hand on her icon if she healed his amputated appendage. The day after he was relieved of his hand, it miraculously reappeared. Following up on his end of the bargain, he tacked on the third silver hand.

Later, in the 17th century, the icon made its home at the monastery. When a monk was transporting the icon to Romania, he made a pit stop at Troyan. But after saddling up to continue onward, his horse refused to move. This was seen by the monks as a divine omen designating Troyan monastery as the icon's home. From this moment on, the three-handed virgin has bestowed her miracles on the sleepy village of Oreshka.

◎ **SIGHTS.** Of all of Pleven's sights, the **Panorama** (Панорама), depicting the third Russo-Turkish Battle of Pleven and the liberation of Bulgaria (see **History**, p. 113), attracts the most attention. From the center, take bus #1 (7min., 0.40lv) away from the train and bus stations and ask for the Panorama. Get off, take a left, and follow the winding road to the top of the hill. You can also take a cab from the center for 1-2lv. (Admission ☎302 51. Open daily 9am-noon and 12:30-6pm. English tours Tu-W. Admission 6lv, students with ISIC 2lv.) Down the path from the main entrance of the Panorama is the old battlefield, now **Park Skobelev** (Парк Скобелев). Soldiers' graves and guns remind visitors of the price Bulgarians paid for their freedom. Built in 1834, **St. Nicholas's Church** (Св. Николай; Sv. Nikolai), on Vasil Levski between the Museum of the Liberation of Pleven (see below) and the train station, was sunk 2m to comply with Ottoman laws that no church be higher than local mosques. (☎837 208. Open daily 8:30am-6:30pm.) The **Museum of the Liberation of Pleven** (Музей Освобождението на Плевен; Muzey Osvobozhdenieto na Pleven), across from the post office, gives a detailed history of the Battle of Pleven. (Open Tu-Sa 9am-noon and 12:30-5pm. 3lv, students with ISIC 1lv.) The **Historical Museum** (Исторически Музей; Istoricheski Muzey), Sv. Zaimov 3 (Св. Заимов), stretches across two floors in several buildings, taking you through archaeology and National Revival exhibits. Exit pl. Vuzrazhdane past the post office onto ul. San Stefano. Take the second right onto Zaimov. The museum is the black dome on the left. (☎822 623. Open Tu-Sa 9am-noon and 1-5pm. 3lv, students with ISIC 1lv.) Named after a famous Bulgarian caricaturist, the **Iliya Beshkov Art Gallery** (Художествена Галерия "Илия Бешков"; Khudozhestvena Galeriya "Iliya Beshkov"), bul. Skobolev 1 (Скоболев), opposite the Historical Museum, exhibits Bulgaria's best painters. (☎80 20 91. Open M-F 9am-5pm. Knock if door is locked. Free.) Now an **art gallery**, the Old Public Bathhouse, Doyran 75 (Дойран), a white building with red brick stripes on pl. Vuzrazhdane, displays Bulgarian and international paintings. On the third floor, look for pieces by Picasso and Dalí. (☎383 42. English tours available. Open Tu-Sa 10:30am-6:30pm. Free.)

▶ **DAYTRIP FROM PLEVEN: TROYAN MONASTERY.** In the tiny mountain village of **Oreshka** (Орешка), the Troyan Monastery (Троянски Манастир; Troyansky Manastir) was an integral part of the 19th-century independence movement, hiding revolutionary leader Vasil Levski (see **History,** p. 113). The largest monastery in the Balkans, it has many murals by master artist **Zahari Zograf** (see **The Arts,** p. 116). His work *Last Judgment,* depicting Death leading damned souls to hell, welcomes you at the church entrance. The **Three-Handed Holy Virgin,** the church's oldest icon, is believed to work miracles. (See sidebar, p. 154. Dress modestly. Open daily summer 7:30am-7:30pm; winter 7:30am-6pm. English tours 5lv. Church 3lv.) If you decide to stay the night, you can sleep in a **monastic cell ❷.** (Private bathrooms. Summer 20lv; winter 24lv.) Across the street, the **Manastirska Bara Restaurant ❷** (Манастирска Бара) serves tasty Bulgarian fare (entrees 2.50-8.50lv) above a bubbling brook and is open daily 8:30am to midnight. *(Buses run from Pleven to Troyan (1½hr., 2 per day, 4lv). Troyan can also be reached from Pleven via Lovech (40min, 1 per hr. 7am-6pm, 2.80lv). From Lovech, take a bus to Troyan (50min., 1 per hr., 2lv). In Troyan, catch the bus to the monastery outside the station—30min., every hr., 0.80lv).*

SHUMEN (ШУМЕН)   ☎ (0)54

Shumen (pop. 106,400) is notable for its proximity to archaeological sites at Preslav, Pliska, and Madara. The city is mainly an industrial center—its name literally means "noisy." Climb up to the huge cement **"Soviet Man"** monument for a view of the town. It can be reached by **train** from: **Ruse** (3hr., 1 per day, 5-8lv); **Sofia** (6hr., 4 per day, 10-15lv); and **Varna** (1½hr., 8 per day, 3-5lv). **Negima Travel** (☎644 17), in a kiosk next to the bus station and opposite the train station, sends **buses** to **Sofia** (6hr., 2 per day, 17lv) and **Varna** (1hr., 2 per day, 6lv). Everything you need in Shumen is located between the cobblestone **Tsar Osvoboditel** (Цар Освободител) and **bul. Slavyanski** (Славянски), the town's main pedestrian drag. To get to the origin of these two streets from the train station, take bus #1, 4, or 10 (0.40lv) and get off at Hotel Shumen; this is pl. Oborishte (Оборище). Khristo Botev heads uphill from the square and becomes Slavyanski at pl. Osvobozhdenie (Освобождение).

With bare rooms, private baths, and an inconvenient location, **Hotel Orbita ❷,** in Kyoshkovete Park (Кйошковете Парк), at the western end of town near the Shumen Brewery (Шуменско Пиво), is the cheapest place in town. Take bus #1, 4, or 10 from the train station to the last stop. With your back to the stop, take the road to your left for 5min. to reach the park entrance. Walk down the paved path, and head up another path in the park to the right. The hotel will be at the end, next to a small zoo. (☎523 98. Singles 30lv; doubles 40lv.) On nights or weekends, take a **Tikko Cab.** (☎800 161. Taxis from the center 1-1.5lv.) **Hotel Shumen ❹,** 1 Oborishte Sq., indulges guests with luxurious rooms and a host of amenities. (☎80 00 03. Breakfast included. Check-out noon. Singles €65; doubles €90.) Restaurants and vendors line ul. Slavyanski and Khristo Botev. Within the revival walls of its well-shaded garden, 📷 **Veliki Preslav ❶,** Tsar Osvoboditel 142, serves up the best home cooking in town. The chicken stew (6lv) is delicious. (☎80 03 06. English menu. Entrees 3-8lv. Open M-F 10am-midnight, Sa-Su 11am-midnight.)

The **tourist office** inside Hotel Shumen arranges **private rooms** (10-15lv), sells maps (3lv), and provides info. (☎553 13. Open M-F 9am-6pm.) You can also buy maps (2lv) from kiosks on bul. Slavyanski. **BulBank,** Slavyanski 64, cashes **traveler's checks** for 2% commission with a US$1 minimum. (☎80 06 97. Open M-F 8:45am-4:30pm.) There's an **ATM** at the United Bulgarian Bank on Tsar Osvoboditel. **Pharmacy Siana** is outside Hotel Shumen. (☎500 11. Open M-F 8:30am-7:30pm, Sa-Su 9am-6pm.) **Icon Internet,** ul. Tsar Petur 4, next to hi. Kristal. (☎80 06 97; www.icon.bg. 1.20lv per hr. Open daily 9am-midnight.) **The post office,** at the beginning of Slavyanski in pl. Osvobozhdenie, has **telephones** and fax inside. (Post office open daily M-F 7:30am-5pm; telephone and fax 7am-10pm.) **Postal Code:** 9700.

BULGARIA

🗷 DAYTRIP FROM SHUMEN: VELIKI PRESLAV (ВЕЛИКИ ПРЕСЛАВ).
Veliki Preslav (Veh-LEEK-ee PREHS-lav) was the second capital of the Bulgarian
Kingdom (AD 893-972) and is now an archaeological site from Bulgaria's Golden
Age. The **Archaeological Museum** (Археологически Музей; Arkheologicheski
Muzey) exhibits artifacts found in the area and shows three short films in English
about the town's history. Ask the curator to unlock the safe to see the museum's
most valuable treasure: a 10th-century gold necklace believed to have belonged to
Peter, son of King Simeon. The **ruins** are down the road from the museum through
a stone gate. Be sure to view the remains of the **Golden Temple** (AD 908) and its well
preserved floor mosaic. Parts of the city's fortress wall and the **King's Palace** still
stand. (*Buses run to Preslav, 18km south of Shumen—45min., 7 per day, 1.20-2.30lv—via
Kochov (Кочово). To get to the museum, face the bus station, then walk to the left up the main
street. Take a left on the road just before the plaza with big stone statues and a church. Staying
to the left, pass the food market (пазар; pazar) to reach the park. Enter the park, walk past the
statue of a man and woman, and bear right at the next intersection. Walk to the parking lot, then
take a sharp left on a paved path after about 20min.* ☎ 538 26 30; preslavcap@yahoo.com.
*Open Apr.-Sept. M-F 8am-6pm, Sa-Su 9am-7pm; Oct.-May daily 9am-5pm. 3lv, students 1.50lv.
English guide 2lv. Film 1.50lv.*)

CROATIA (HRVATSKA)

AUS$1 = 4.30KN	1KN = AUS$0.23
CDN$1 = 4.64KN	1KN = CDN$0.22
EUR€1 = 7.38KN	1KN = EUR€0.14
NZ$1 = 3.94KN	1KN = NZ$0.25
UK£1 = 11.16KN	1KN = UK£0.09
US$1 = 6.11KN	1KN = US$0.16

KUNA

Croatia is a land of unearthly beauty, endowed with thick forests, barren mountains, sun-kissed beaches, and crystal-clear waters. Positioned at the convergence of the Mediterranean, the Alps, and the Pannonian plain, it is situated in the middle of dangerous political divides—between the 9th-century Frankish and Byzantine empires, the 11th-century Catholic and Orthodox Churches, Christian Europe and the Islamic Ottoman Empire during the 15th through 19th centuries, and its own fractious ethnic groups in the past decade. Achieving full independence for the first time in 800 years after the devastating 1991-95 war, Croatia is finally at peace.

HISTORY

101 DALMATIANS. Today's Croatia has its roots in the Roman province of **Dalmatia,** with its capital at **Salona** (now **Split,** see p. 203). Emperor **Diocletian** (AD 284-305) hailed from this city, where his palace still stands. The Slavic ancestors of Croatia's present inhabitants settled the region in the 6th and 7th centuries, partly expelling and partly assimilating the indigenous Illyrian population. Over the next two centuries, they slowly accepted **Catholicism.** In the 9th century, an independent Croatian state was consolidated by **King Tomislav** (910-28), who earned papal recognition for his country. King Zvonimir was crowned by Pope Gregory in 1076, decisively strengthening Croatia's orientation toward Catholic Europe.

UNDER THE HUNGARIAN YOKE. In 1102, the Croatian Kingdom entered into a dynastic union with Hungary. While Croatia originally maintained its sovereignty, it was soon stripped of both its independence and its territory, effectively disap-

FACTS AND FIGURES

OFFICIAL NAME: Republic of Croatia

CAPITAL: Zagreb (pop. 779,000)

POPULATION: 4.4 million (89% Croat, 4% Serb, 1% Bosniak, 6% other)

LANGUAGE: Croatian

CURRENCY: 1 kuna (kn) = 100 lipa

RELIGION: 88% Catholic, 4% Orthodox, 1% Muslim, 7% other

LAND AREA: 56,542km²

CLIMATE: Mediterranean and temperate

GEOGRAPHY: Mountainous coast; numerous islands; lowlands in the north

BORDERS: Bosnia and Herzegovina, Hungary, Serbia and Montenegro, Slovenia

ECONOMY: 58% Services, 33% Industry, 9% Agriculture

GDP: US$9800 per capita

COUNTRY CODE: 385

INTERNATIONAL DIALING PREFIX: 00

pearing for 800 years. Following Hungary's defeat in 1526, the **Austrian Hapsburgs** took over what remained of Croatia and turned it into a buffer zone against the Ottomans. Orthodox Christians from the Ottoman-controlled area migrated to the region, laying a foundation for the Serbian minority in Croatia. Desperate for autonomy, the Croats, led by **Josip Jelačić,** sided with the Austrians and demanded self-government when Hungary revolted in 1848.

BITTERSWEET UNION. As part of Austria-Hungary, Croatian troops fought with the Germans during **WWI.** After Austria-Hungary's defeat, the Croats declared **independence** on December 1, 1918, and announced their incorporation into the **Kingdom of the Serbs, Croats, and Slovenes** under Serbian King Alexander I. The Croats preferred a federation, but the government became centralized in Belgrade. In 1934, Alexander was assassinated by Croatian nationalists from the **Ustaše** (Insurgents), a terrorist organization demanding the complete independence of Croatia.

FASCISM. The Ustaše finally achieved Croatia's "independence" in 1941 in the form of a fascist puppet state. The ruthless regime sought to eliminate the country's Jewish and Serbian populations, killing more than 350,000 people in massacres and concentration camps. Croatia's support of the Axis powers during **WWII** would become the principle reason behind the international community's reluctance to support Croatian independence in the 1990s. The majority of Croats, however, joined the communist-led **Partisan** resistance early on in the war. The Partisans, led by **Josip Broz Tito,** demanded the creation of a federal Yugoslav state. In 1945, the **Socialist Federal Republic of Yugoslavia** declared its independence as communist regimes took power across Eastern Europe.

TITO AND NOTHING ELSE. Tito, Yugoslavia's first president, placed all industry and natural resources under state control and suppressed ethnic rivalries. In 1948, Yugoslavia broke from Moscow control, remaining communist, and began trading with the West. Despite these improvements, the Croats were upset over growing numbers of Serbian nationals in the government. In 1971, the Croatian leadership demanded greater autonomy within Yugoslavia, which led to its dismissal and replacement. After Tito's 1980 death, Yugoslavia descended into confusion.

A COSTLY FREEDOM. A rotating presidency established upon Tito's death was unable to curb the tide of nationalism. In April 1990, Croatian nationalist **Franjo Tudjman** was elected President of Croatia, and on June 25, 1991, Croatia declared **independence.** Tensions soon escalated between Croats and the large Serbian minority. Claiming to protect Serbian nationals, the Serb-controlled **Yugoslav National Army** invaded Croatia. In a few months, it drove out hundreds of thousands of Croats from **Eastern Slavonia** and shelled Vukovar, Zagreb, and Dubrovnik. Meanwhile, the Serbian minority declared its own independent republic, **Serbian Krajina,** around Knin in central Croatia. Not until the senseless destruction of Dubrovnik did international political leadership realize that Croatia was indeed occupied. On January 15, 1992, the European Community recognized Croatia's independence, and a UN military force was brought in to keep further fighting at bay. In May 1995, Croatia, frustrated with its lack of control over its territory, seized Krajina, expelling over 150,000 Serbs. Their own experience did not stop the Croatian leadership from making claims on Bosnia and Herzegovina, sending troops, and participating in massacres of Bosnian Serbs and Muslims. The 1995 **Dayton Peace Accords,** negotiated by American Richard Holbrooke, established a ceasefire in Bosnia and Herzegovina and stabilized the situation in the disputed areas of Croatia.

Croatia

TODAY. Croatia is a **parliamentary democracy** with extensive executive powers invested in the president, who is elected by popular vote for a five-year term. The **Sabor** acts as a parliament; deputies are elected for four years. For better or worse, **Franjo Tudjman** led Croatia as President from 1991 until his death in December 1999. During his eight-year tenure, Tudjman and his nationalist **Democratic Party** (Hrvatska Demokraticka Zajednica; HDZ) established Croatia as a sovereign state, but their corruption, abuse of power, and censorship of the media also isolated the country from the West. The 2000 elections transferred power to the democratically inclined left, headed by a reformed communist **Social Democratic Party (SDP).** A pro-Western liberal, **Stipe Mesić,** became President and immediately began accession talks with the EU and NATO. With an economy dependent upon tourism, Croatia suffered severely from the recent war. **Unemployment** rates skyrocketed to over 20%. The country's hopes for recovery were halted by the Kosovo crisis in 1999, which once again discouraged Western tourists from travel to the Balkans. Economic reforms have met with strong resistance from both parliament and the public, further hindering growth and reconstruction. As the political situation continues to calm, Croatia has now focused its resources on rebuilding the nation's infrastructure to support Croatia's booming tourism industry.

PEOPLE AND CULTURE

DEMOGRAPHICS AND RELIGION

Croatia retains a significant **Serbian** minority (4%) despite an exodus as the war ended in 1995. Tensions between Serbs and Croats still run high, but outbreaks of violence are now rare. Both communities remain relatively closed to the other, and the Serbian population suffers from stigmatization and unemployment. Croatia's **Bosniak** minority (1%) also suffers discrimination, but to a much milder extent than the Serbian population. Nearly 100% of the ethnically Croat population is **Catholic.** Serbs remaining in the country after the massive exodus of 1995 belong to the **Serbian Orthodox** Church, while the Bosniak minority practices **Islam.**

LANGUAGE

Croats speak **Croatian,** a South Slavic language, written in Roman characters, recently distinguished from Serbo-Croatian. Only a few expressions differ from Serbian, but be careful not to use the Serbian ones in Croatia—you'll make few friends. Words are pronounced exactly as they are written: *č* and *ć* are both "ch" (only a Croat can tell them apart), and *š* is "sh." The letter *r* is rolled, except in the absence of a vowel, in which case it makes an "ur" sound as in "Brrrr!" The letter *j* is equivalent to "y," so *jučer* (yesterday) is pronounced "yucher." Street designations on maps often differ from those on signs by "-va" or "-a" because of grammatical declensions (see p. 168). The most useful phrase to learn is *"Može?"* which means, literally, "Is it possible?" and serves as an all purpose phrase, whether asking to take a brochure or asking for the bill *(račun).* For the differences between Bosnian, Croatian, and Serbian, see **Serbia and Montenegro: Language** (p. 777). **German and Italian** are common second languages among adults. Most Croatians under 30 speak some **English.** For a phrasebook and glossary, see **Glossary: Croatian,** p. 947.

FOOD AND DRINK

CROATIA	❶	❷	❸	❹	❺
FOOD	under 40kn	41-70kn	71-110kn	111-190kn	over 190kn

Croatian cuisine is defined by the country's varied geography. In continental Croatia around and east of Zagreb, heavy meals featuring meat and creamy sauces dominate. *Purica s mlincima* (turkey with pasta) is the regional dish near Zagreb. Also popular is the spicy Slavonian *kulen,* which is considered one of the world's best **sausages** by panel of German men who decide such things. *Pašticada* (slow-cooked meat) is another excellent option. On the coast, textures and flavors change with the presence of **seafood** and Italian influence. Don't miss out on *lignje* (squid) or *Dalmatinski pršut* (Dalmatian smoked ham). The **oysters** from Ston Bay have received a number of awards at international competitions. If your budget does not allow for such treats, *slane sardele* (salted sardines) are a tasty substitute. Croatia offers excellent **wines;** price is usually the best indicator of quality. Mix red wine with tap water to get the popular *bevanda,* and white with carbonated water to get *gemišt. Šljivovica* is a hard-hitting plum brandy found in many small towns. *Karlovačko* and *Ožujsko* are the two most popular beers.

CUSTOMS AND ETIQUETTE

Tipping is not expected, although it is appropriate to round up when paying; in some cases, the establishment will do it for you—check your change. Fancy restaurants often add a hefty service charge. **Bargaining** is reserved for very informal transactions, such as hiring a boat for a day or renting a private room directly from an owner. If a price is posted, they usually mean it. If you wear **shorts** and **sandals,** you'll stick out as a tourist in the cities, but will blend in along the coast. Though southern Croatia tends to be of a beach-oriented mentality, remember that this land of skin and shorts is also quite Catholic. Avoid jumping from the beach to the cathedral without a change of clothes (long pants or skirts and close-toed shoes). Croats have few qualms about **drinking** and **smoking,** but abstain in buses, trains, and other marked areas. When you clink glasses with someone before drinking, look them in the eye, even if there are a dozen people at the table. Otherwise, local superstition holds you will have seven years bad luck.

THE ARTS

Croatian texts first emerged during the 9th century, but for the next 600 years literature consisted almost entirely of translations from other European languages. In southern Dalmatia, Dubrovnik was the only independent part of Croatia after 1102 and produced literature that had a lasting impact on Croatian culture. After the city's 1667 devastation by an earthquake, the nexus of Croatian literature shifted north. The 16th-century dramatist **Martin Držić** and the 17th-century poet **Ivan Gundulić** raided Italy for literary models, combining them with traditions from back home. During Austrian and Hungarian repressions of the Croatian language, **Ljudevit Gaj** led the movement to reform and codify Croatian vernacular. **August Šenoa,** Croatia's dominant 19th-century literary figure, played a key part in the formation of a literary public and in completing the work that Gaj had begun.

Croatian prose sparkled in the late 20th century. **Dubravka Ugrešić's** personal, reflective novels, which discuss nostalgia and the revision of history, have become instant best-sellers. The novelist **Slavenka Drakulić** is more popular abroad than at home. Croatian visual arts have also come into their own recently. Characterized by the rejection of conventional and "civilized" depictions, **naïve art** presides as the most popular painting style. This movement, begun by **Krsto Hegedušić** (1901-1971), is highly influenced by folk traditions. It eliminates perspective and uses only vivid colors. Croatia's most famous modern sculptor and architect, **Ivan Meštrović** (see **Split: Museums,** p. 206), has achieved fame outside Croatia. His wooden religious sculptures can be seen at London's Tate Gallery and New York City's Metropolitan Museum of Art. **Vinko Bresan** is Croatia's recent contribution to the film scene. His 1996 comedy, *How the War Started on My Island (Kako je poceo rat na mom otoku)*, won multiple awards and is enormously popular both at home and abroad.

HOLIDAYS AND FESTIVALS

NATIONAL HOLIDAYS IN 2005

January 1 New Year's Day	**August 5** National Thanksgiving Day
January 6 Epiphany	**August 15** Assumption of the Blessed Virgin Mary
March 26-27 Easter Holiday	
May 1 May Day	**November 1** All Saints' Day
May 30 Independence Day	**December 25-26** Christmas
June 22 Anti-Fascist Struggle Day	

Croatian summer brings out the country's best with a large number of festivals. Some highlights are below, but check each city's festivals and entertainment section for a full picture. Stores may close on holidays, but buses and trains still run. In late June, Zagreb holds its own version of Woodstock, **Cest Is D'Best.** An easygoing philosophy keeps revelers on city streets out all night (see p. 174). The **Dubrovnik Summer Festival** (Dubrovački Ljetni) spans a period of 45 days from mid-July to mid-August. Open-air concerts and theatrical performances make it the event of the summer in Dubrovnik (see p. 216). In July and August, Korčula (see p. 214) becomes sword-dance central with the **Festival of Sword Dances** (Festival Viteških Igara). The Moreška, Moštra, and Kumpanija sword dances are performed all over the island. Featuring everything from a children's demolition derby to puppet performances, the **International Children's Festival** taking place in the last week of June and the first week of July, is an annual highlight in Šibenik (see p. 199).

ADDITIONAL RESOURCES

GENERAL HISTORY

Croatia: A Nation Forged in War, by Marcus Tanner (1998). A British journalist's powerful, if somewhat pro-Croat, take on the nation's troubled history.

The Balkans, by Misha Glenny (2000). An engaging survey of the history of the Balkans over the past century, with a special emphasis on the recent fall of Yugoslavia.

FICTION, NONFICTION, AND FILM

Balkan Ghosts: A Journey Through History, by Robert Kaplan (1994). A travel narrative guiding the reader through the political complexities of Croatia and its neighbors.

Black Lamb and Grey Falcon, by Rebecca West (1941). Written just before WWII, this classic weaves history and personal experience into a captivating narrative.

How We Survived Communism and Even Laughed, by Slavenka Drakulic (1993). A series of perceptive essays on everyday life before and after the Balkan conflict.

How the War Started on My Island, directed by Vinko Bresan (1996). This unusually comedic film about recent Balkan violence was hugely successful.

CROATIA ESSENTIALS

ENTRANCE REQUIREMENTS

Passport: Required of all travelers.

Visa: Not required for stays under 90 days for citizens of Australia, Canada, Ireland, New Zealand, the UK, and the US.

Letter of Invitation: Not required.

Inoculations: Recommended up-to-date on DTaP (diphtheria, tetanus, and pertussis), Hepatitis A, Hepatitis B, MMR (measles, mumps, and rubella), Polio booster, and Typhoid.

Work Permit: Required of all foreigners planning to work.

International Driving Permit: Required of all those planning to drive.

DOCUMENTS AND FORMALITIES

EMBASSIES AND CONSULATES

Embassies of other countries in Croatia are all in **Zagreb** (see p. 166). There is no Croatian embassy in Ireland. Croatia's embassies and consulates abroad include:

Australia: 14 Jindalee Crescent, O'Malley ACT 2606, Canberra (☎2 6286 6988; croemb@dynamite.com.au).

Canada: 229 Chapel Street, Ottawa, ON K1N 7Y6 (☎613-562-7820; www.croatiaemb.net).

New Zealand Consulate: 291 Lincoln Rd., Henderson (☎9 836 5581; cro-consulate@xtra.co.nz). Mail to: P.O. Box 83-200, Edmonton, Auckland.

UK: 21 Conway St., London W1P 5HL (☎20 7387 2022; amboffice@croatianembassy.co.uk).

US: 2343 Massachusetts Ave. NW, Washington, D.C. 20008 (☎202-588-5899; www.croatiaemb.org).

VISA AND ENTRY INFORMATION

Citizens of Australia, Canada, Ireland, New Zealand, the UK, and the US do not need **visas** for stays of up to 90 days. All visitors must **register** with the police within 48hr. of arrival—hotels, campsites, and accommodation agencies should automatically register you, but those staying with friends or in private rooms must do so themselves to avoid fines or expulsion. Police may check foreigners' passports anywhere and at any time. There is no entry fee. The most direct way of entering or exiting Croatia is by a bus or train between Zagreb and a neighboring capital.

GETTING AROUND

BY PLANE AND TRAIN

Croatia Airlines flies from many cities, including **Chicago, Frankfurt, London, Paris,** Zagreb, Dubrovnik, and Split. Rijeka, Zadar, and Pula also have tiny international airports. **Trains** (www.hznet.hr.) run to Zagreb from **Budapest, HUN, Ljubljana, SLN, Venice, ITA,** and **Vienna, AUT,** and continue on to other Croatian destinations. Due to the 1991-1995 war, trains are *very* slow and nonexistent south of Split. *Odlazak* means departures, *dolazak* arrivals.

BY BUS

Buses (www.akz.hr) are the best option for domestic travel, running faster and farther than trains at comparable prices. Tickets are cheaper if you buy them on board, bypassing the 2kn service charge at station kiosks. In theory, luggage must be stowed (3kn), but this is only enforced on the most crowded lines.

BY BOAT

If you're on the coast, take a **Jadrolinija ferry** (www.jadrolinija.hr). Boats sail the Rijeka-Split-Dubrovnik route, stopping at islands on the way. Fer-

ily Chronicle

IN RECENT NEWS

WATCH YOUR STEP

In addition to residual ethnic tensions and tens of thousands of displaced persons, remnants of the recent war between Croatia and Serbia literally linger in the land. During the four-year conflict (1991-1995), hundreds of thousands of **landmines** were planted across Croatia. These small explosive devices, hidden in the ground and invisible to the naked eye, detonate when even a small amount of pressure is applied, causing a powerful explosion. Since the beginning of the war, it is estimated that there have been nearly 2000 casualties in Croatia due to landmines.

Though great strides have been made in clearing these mines, the situation remains severe. Croatia and Bosnia and Herzegovina together are estimated to have the most serious landmine problem in the world.

One of the greatest difficulties of removing the mines is not only the high cost, but finding them, since there are no precise records of where they were planted. Consequently, it is a dangerous process involving workers, de-mining machines, explosive-sensitive dogs, and a risky dose of guesswork.

Croatia expects to be mine-free by March of 2009. Until then, the most touristed parts of the country are generally safe. However, watch for local mine warnings, particularly in **Eastern Slavonia** and the **Krajina,** and stick to paths when hiking.

ries also go to **Ancona, ITA** from Split and Zadar and to **Bari, ITA** from Split and Dubrovnik. Though slower than buses and trains, ferries are more comfortable. A basic ticket provides only a place on the deck. Cheap beds sell out fast, so buy tickets in advance. If the agency only sells basic tickets, you'll need to *run* to get a bed.

BY CAR AND BY BIKE

Anyone over 18 can rent a **car** in larger cities (350-400kn per day), but downtown parking and gas are expensive. Rural roads are in bad condition, and those traveling through the Krajina region and other conflict areas should be cautious of off-road **land-mines.** Traveling by car can get especially expensive when island-hopping—Jadrolinija charges a huge amount for decking your wheels. **Moped** and **bicycle rentals** (50-80kn per day) are a good and cheap option in resort or urban areas.

TOURIST SERVICES AND MONEY

Even the smallest towns have a branch of the excellent and resourceful **state-run tourist board** *(turistička zajednica).* Their staff speak English, almost always Italian, and often German and French, and give out amazing free maps and booklets. Private accommodations are handled by private agencies *(turistička/ putnička agencija).* The largest is the ubiquitous **Atlas.** Local outfits are generally cheaper. Most tourist offices, hotels, and transportation stations exchange currency and traveler's checks; banks have the best rates. Croatia's monetary unit, the **kuna** (kn), which is divided into 100 lipa, is extremely difficult to exchange abroad, except in Bosnia, Hungary and Slovenia. Inflation hovers around 2%, so prices should stay relatively constant over the next year. Most banks give MasterCard and Visa cash advances, and credit cards are widely accepted. ATMs are everywhere. Public offices are typically open M-F 8:30am-4:30pm; banks M-F 8am-7pm, Sa 7am-noon; grocery stores M-F 7am-8pm, Sa 7am-3pm.

HEALTH AND SAFETY

 EMERGENCY NUMBERS: Police: ☎92 **Fire:** ☎93 **Ambulance:** ☎94

Pharmacies are well stocked with Western products, including tampons, sanitary napkins *(sanitami ulosci),* and condoms *(prezervativ).* UK citizens receive free medical care with a valid passport. Tap water is normally chlorinated, and while relatively safe, may cause mild abdominal upsets. **Bottled water** is readily available. Travel to the former conflict area of the **Slavonia** and **Krajina regions** remains dangerous due to **unexploded landmines.** If you choose to visit these regions, do not stray from known safe roads and areas. Croatians are friendly toward foreigners and sometimes a little too friendly to **female** travelers; go out in public with a companion to ward off unwanted displays of machismo. **Disabled travelers** should contact *Savez Organizacija Invalida Hrvatske* (☎1 369 4502), in Zagreb. Croatians are *slowly* beginning to accept **homosexuality;** discretion is best.

ACCOMMODATIONS AND CAMPING

CROATIA	❶	❷	
ACCOM.	under 100kn	100-150kn	
CROATIA	❸	❹	❺
ACCOM.	151-210kn	211-360kn	over 360kn

HOSTELS AND HOTELS

For info on the country's six youth hostels (in Zagreb, Pula, Zadar, Dubrovnik, Šibenik, and Punat), contact the Croatian Youth Hostel Association, Savska 5, 10000 Zagreb (☎1 482 92 94; www.hfhs.hr/front/index.php?jezik=en). **Hotels** in Croatia are wildly expensive—a cheap overnight stay in a Zagreb hotel will run you at least US$80. If you opt for a hotel, call a few days in advance, especially in summer along the coast.

PRIVATE ROOMS

Apart from hostels, private rooms are the only budget accommodations options. Look for *sobe* signs, especially near transportation stations. English is rarely spoken by room owners. Agencies generally charge 30-50% more if you stay fewer than three nights. All accommodations are subject to a tourist tax of 5-10kn (one reason the police require foreigners to register).

CAMPING

Croatia is one of the top camping destinations in Europe—33% of travelers stay in campgrounds. Facilities usually meet Western standards concerning space and utilities and prices are among the

With your nightly rate, you get to see how people live among marble alleyways of Dalmatia and postcard-perfect islands. You get to experience the smells of *real* Croatian cooking (no, people don't really eat pizza and risotto for every meal), the religious undercurrent of the country as shown through the icons that adorn the walls of its homes, and how everybody, even grandmas, watches soccer when a Slavic team is playing. If you share a language with your host, you might hear stories of what it is like to live though three empires, communism, fascism, and a bloody civil war. On a lighter note, you get restaurant tips and laundry access.

Throughout my time here, I was consistently impressed by the hospitality with which my hosts received me. That said, there are a few **tips** for making your experience as safe and comfortable as possible: The safest rooms are those which are listed with a certified travel agency, like Atlas, and those which are registered with the local tourist authorities. Often, these are identified by a shiny blue placard with the word "SOBE" in capital letters (beware of counterfeits). When in a city, ask to see where the room is on a map before negotiating: the lower the price, the more remote the location. Be sure to check out the room before making any kind of deal and to set a price before settling in. If the first option doesn't work out, in the land of *sobe* there are always more rooms.

—Lauren Rivera, 2005

cheapest along the Mediterranean. Camping outside of designated areas is illegal. For more info, contact the **Croatian Camping Union**, HR-52440 Poreč, Pionirska 1 (☎52 451 324; www.camping.hr).

KEEPING IN TOUCH

The **Croatian Post** is reliable. Mail from the US arrives within one week. Mail addressed to **Poste Restante** will be held for 30 days at the main post office. Address envelopes as follows: Lauren (first name) RIVERA (LAST NAME), POSTE RESTANTE, Pt. Republike 28 (post office street address), 20000 (postal code), Dubrovnik (city), CROATIA. *Avionski* and *zrakoplovom* both mean "airmail."

Post offices usually have **public phones;** pay after you talk. All phones on the street require a *telekarta* (phone card), sold at newsstands and post offices. Fifty "impulses" cost 23kn (1 impulse equals 3min. domestic, 36sec. international; 50% discount 10pm-7am, Sundays, and holidays). Calls to the US and Europe are expensive (20kn per min). International access numbers include: **AT&T Direct** (☎0800 22 01 11); **BT Direct** (☎0800 22 10 44); **Canada Direct** (☎0800 22 01 01); **MCI WorldPhone** (☎0800 22 01 12). For the **international operator,** dial ☎901. Most towns, no matter how small, have at least one **Internet** cafe. Connections on the islands are slower and less reliable than those on the mainland.

ZAGREB
☎(0)1

Though many visitors treat it as little more than a stop-over en route to the Croatian coast, exploring Zagreb is a perfect introduction to Croatia as a whole. Throughout the city's magnificent churches, diverse museums, and lively outdoor cafes, locals—not visitors—dominate the scene. Despite its spacious Austro-Hungarian boulevards and its vast public parks, the city maintains a distinctive small-town feel. At dusk, the bustle of daily activity calms into an enchanted stillness, broken only by nightclub music and the laughter of evening revels. Rapid post-war renovations have transformed the city into a thriving cultural center, attracting international festivals and conventions. Hold back from the tourist route for a few days and follow the lead of the *Zagrebčani* by relaxing and enjoying their city.

◼ INTERCITY TRANSPORTATION

Flights: The **international airport** (☎626 52 22) is about 30min. from city center. **Buses** (☎615 79 92) run between the main bus station and the airport (every 30min. daily 5:30am-7:30pm; 25kn). **Taxis** from behind the Croatia Airlines office to the center should cost no more than 250kn. **Croatia Airlines,** Zrinjevac 17 (toll free ☎080 07 77, reservations 481 96 33, flight info 487 27 27; www.croatiaairlines.hr), flies to **Dubrovnik** (4 per day); **Split** (3 per day); **Zadar** (2 per day). Their international flights to the Balkan region include **Sarajevo, BOS** and **Skopje, MAC.** There are no flights from Zagreb to Belgrade, SMN. Also inquire here to book flights on other airlines. Open M-F 8am-5pm, Sa 8am-2pm. **Airport lost and found** ☎456 22 29.

Trains: Glavni Kolodvor (Main Station), Trg Kralja Tomislava 12 (☎060 333 444, international info 378 25 32; www.hznet.hr). From the bus station, take tram #2, 6, or 8 to the 3rd stop ("Glavni Kolodvor"). To: **Rijeka** (3hr., 3 per day, 102kn); **Split** (9hr., 2 per day, 149kn); **Belgrade, SMN** (6½hr., 3 per day, 130kn); **Budapest, HUN** (7hr., 4 per day, 224kn); **Ljubljana, SLN** (2½hr., 4 per day, 106kn); **Skopje, MAC** (16½hr., 1 per day, 264kn); **Venice, ITA** (7hr., 2 per day, 320kn); **Vienna, AUT** (6½hr., 2 per day, 355kn); **Zurich, SWI** (8hr., 1 per day, 647kn). There are trains to **Dubrovnik** or **Sarajevo, BOS.** AmEx/MC/V.

CROATIA

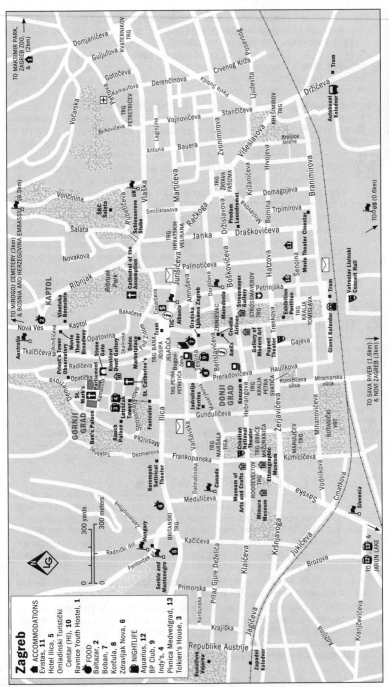

Zagreb

▲ ACCOMMODATIONS
Evistas, **11**
Hotel Ilica, **5**
Omladinski Turistički
Centar (HI), **10**
Ravnice Youth Hostel, **1**

🍴 FOOD
Baltazar, **2**
Boban, **7**
Korčula, **8**
Zdravljak Nova, **6**

🍸 NIGHTLIFE
Aquarius, **12**
BP Club, **9**
Indy's, **4**
Pivnica Medvedgrad, **13**
Tolkien's House, **3**

CROATIA

Buses: Autobusni Kolodvor (Bus Station), Držićeva bb (☎060 313 333; www.akz.hr). Info, tickets, and luggage storage on the 2nd fl. To: **Dubrovnik** (11hr., 17 per day, 185kn); **Pula** (4½hr., 18 per day, 107-146kn); **Rijeka** (3½hr., 27 per day, 115kn); **Split** (6½-8½hr., 29 per day, 120kn); **Belgrade, SMN** (6½hr., 4 per day, 188kn); **Frankfurt, GER** (15hr., 2 per day, 630kn); **Ljubljana, SLN** (2½hr., 2 per day, 115kn); **Sarajevo, BOS** (8½hr., 3 per day, 220kn); **Skopje, MAC** (13hr., 1 per day, 325kn); **Vienna, AUT** (8hr., 2 per day, 250kn).

Ferries: Jadrolinija, in the Marko Polo Travel Agency, Masarykova 24 (☎481 52 16; www.jadrolinija.hr). Reserves tickets for travel along the Dalmatian coast to **Dubrovnik, Rijeka, Split, Zadar,** and the islands and to **Ancona** and **Bari, ITA.** Pick up one of their helpful schedules if you plan on taking any ferries later in your trip. Open M-F 8am-4pm.

Finding your way around Zagreb can be tricky. Many street names appear differently on street signs than on maps and in addresses because of grammatical declensions. The root of the name remains the same, but the ending changes. For example, a street sign may show ul. Ljudevita Gaja, but addresses and maps usually list the street as Gajeva. In general, the case declension from proper street name to an address or map changes the ending from -a to -ova or -eva and from -e to -ina. In addition, "bb" after a street name means buildings on the street are not numbered. Furthermore, street names sometimes change from block to block. Names themselves change frequently and are made even more confusing when a street sign, or a map, is just wrong. When exploring the city, try to rely on landmarks, and count streets when necessary.

■ ORIENTATION

Unlike the city's sprawling outskirts, the center of Zagreb is easily walkable. To the north, historic **Gornji Grad** (Upper Town) is composed of the **Kaptol** and **Gradec** hills. While Kaptol has retained its name, Gradec, where most of the historic sites are located, is referred to simply as **Gornji Grad.** The central **Donji Grad** (Lower Town) is home to most of the museums, squares and parks. The **Sava River** separates these neighborhoods from the modern residential area **Novi Zagreb** (New Zagreb). Both Gornji and Donji Grad are bustling centers of activity. The winding streets of Gornji Grad tend to be more peaceful. Most shopping is located around the city's central square, **Trg bana Josipa Jelačića,** and on **Ilica,** the commercial artery that runs through the square.

▐ LOCAL TRANSPORTATION

Trams: www.zet.hr. Organized by number (1-17), trams are often sweltering in the summer and packed year-round but do cover the entire city. Buy tickets at any newsstand (6.5kn) or from the driver (8kn). Day pass 18kn. Punch them in boxes near the doors—an unpunched ticket is as good as no ticket. 150kn fine for riding ticketless; checks are frequent. Midnight-4am trams run about every 30min., and tickets cost 20% more. Pick up a tram route map at the TIC (see **Tourist and Financial Services,** p. 169).

Buses: (☎660 04 46). Beyond the city center, buses pick up where the trams stop. All the same rules and fares apply as for trams. Also organized numerically.

Taxis: Cabs congregate at the stand on Gajeva south of Teslina, at the corner of Trg b. Jelačića and Bakačeva, and in front of major hotels and the main bus and train stations. Rates are generally fair, averaging 25kn to start plus 7kn per km, plus 5kn for luggage, but prices increase 20% 10pm-5am, Su and holidays. **Radio Taxi** (☎668 25 05) is fairly reliable, but operators speak little English.

🔢 PRACTICAL INFORMATION

TOURIST AND FINANCIAL SERVICES

Tourist Office: Tourist Information Center (TIC), Trg b. Jelačića 11 (☎481 40 51; www.zagreb-touristinfo.hr). The friendly, resourceful staff will supply you with **free maps** and pamphlets. Ask for the invaluable, free *Zagreb Info A-Z* pamphlet, also available on the website; it contains listings of everything you might need, from hotels and restaurants to cinemas and embassies. Also request the free *Zagreb in Your Pocket* for similarly detailed listings with humorous commentary. Pick up a **Zagreb Card** (valid 3 days; 60kn), which covers all bus and tram rides and provides great discounts in restaurants and museums. Open M-F 9am-9pm, Sa 9am-5pm, Su 9am-2pm.

Embassies: Albania, Jurišićeva 2a (☎481 06 79). Open M-F 8am-4pm. **Australia,** Centar Kaptol, Nova Ves 11, 3rd fl. (☎489 12 00, emergency 098 41 47 29). Open M-F 8:30am-4:20pm. **Bosnia and Herzegovina,** Torbarova 9 (☎468 37 61). Open M-F 8am-4pm. Consular department, Pavla Hatza 3 (☎481 94 18; fax 481 94 20). **Canada,** Prilaz Gjure Deželića 4 (☎488 12 00; fax 488 12 30). Open M-F 8am-4pm. **Hungary,** Pantovčak 255-257 (☎489 09 00; www.hungemb.hr). Open M-F 8am-4pm. **Macedonia,** Petrinjska 29/1 (☎492 29 02). Open M-F 8am-4pm. **New Zealand** (consulate), Trg S. Radića 3 (☎615 13 82). Open M-F 8:30am-4pm. **Serbia and Montenegro,** Pantovčak 254 (☎457 90 67). Open M-F 8am-4pm. **Slovenia,** Savska 41 (☎631 10 14). Open M-F 8am-4pm. **UK,** Lučića 4 (☎600 91 00, www.britishembassy.gov.uk/croatia). Open M-Th 8:30am-5pm, F 8:30am-2pm. **US,** Thomas Jefferson 2 (☎61 22 00; www.usembassy.hr). Open M-F 8am-4:30pm.

Currency Exchange: Zagrebačka Banka, Trg b. Jelačića 10 (☎610 40 00). Open M-F 7am-8:30pm, Sa 7:30am-noon. Cashes **traveler's checks** (1.5% commission). Banks and hotels throughout the city offer similar rates. **Western Union** service available at **Splitska Banka,** Trg N. Š. Zrinkog 16 (☎487 33 02). Open M-F 8am-7pm, Sa 8am-noon. **ATMs** (bankomat) can be found at the bus and train stations and city center.

American Express: Zrinjevac 17 (☎487 30 64, lost cards 612 44 00). Open M-F 8am-7pm, Sa 8am-noon.

LOCAL SERVICES

Luggage Storage: At the train station, 10kn per piece per day. At the bus station, 2nd fl., 1.20kn per bag per hr., 2.30kn for bags over 15kg. Both open 24hr.

English-Language Bookstore: Algoritam, Gajeva 1 (☎481 86 72; fax 481 74 97), next to Hotel Dubrovnik. Carries international newspapers, magazines, and music on the ground fl. The basement holds Croatian phrase books, English fiction and classics, travel guides. Books 50-400kn. Open M-F 8:30am-9pm, Sa 8:30am-3pm. AmEx/MC/V.

Laundromat: Predom, Draškovićeva 31 (☎461 29 90). 2-day service 2-30kn per item; next day 50% more. No English. No self-service. Open M-F 6am-9pm, Sa 8am-4pm.

Swimming Pool: ŠRC Šalata, Schlosserove stube 2 (☎461 72 55). From the intersection of Vlaška and Draškovićeva, cross the square and head up the stairs; follow the smell of chlorine. M-F 20kn, Sa-Su 30kn; discounts after 4pm. Changing rooms and lockers are underneath the cafe. Open M-F 1:30-6pm, Sa-Su 11am-7pm.

EMERGENCY AND COMMUNICATIONS

Police: Department for Foreign Visitors, Petrinjska 30 (☎456 36 23, after hours 456 31 11). Room 103 on the 2nd fl. of the central police station. To **register,** bring your passport and use form #14. Open M-F 8am-4pm.

Pharmacy: Gradska Liekarna Zagreb, Zrinjevac 20 (☎487 38 73). Open M-F 7am-8pm, Sa 7am-2:30pm. **24hr. service** available at Ilica 43 (☎484 84 50). AmEx/D/MC.

Medical Services: Hospital REBRO, Kišpatićeva 12 (☎238 88 88). Open 24hr.

Telephones: Pay phones are scattered throughout the city, but they only take prepaid cards, not coins. Buy a **phone card** (telekarta; 25-200 units, about 13-70kn) from any news kiosk, or call from the **post office** and pay afterwards.

Internet Access: Charlie Net, Gajeva 4 (☎488 02 33), through the courtyard and on the right. Friendly, English-speaking staff. Great connections. 16kn per hr., 12kn per hr. with ISIC. Open M-Sa 8am-10pm. **Art Net Club,** Preradovićeva 25 (☎455 84 71). 18kn per hr. Features photo exhibits, TV, bar, and live music (Sept.-Nov.). Open M-Sa 9am-9pm. **Sublink Cyber Cafe,** Teslina 12 (☎481 13 29). Through the courtyard, upstairs, and to the left. Dark but modern interior. 15kn per hr. 10% ISIC discount if you sign up for free membership beforehand. Open M-Sa 9am-10pm, Su 3-10pm.

Post Office: Branimirova 4 (☎484 03 45), next to the train station. From Branimirova, turn left up the stairs. **Poste Restante** on 2nd fl. (desk #3). Desk #1 **exchanges currency** and cashes **traveler's checks** for 1.5% commission. Open 24hr. **Central Post Office:** Jurišićeva 4 (☎481 10 90). Open M-F 7am-9pm, Sa 8am-6pm, Su 8am-2pm. **Postal Code:** 10000.

ACCOMMODATIONS

Cheap accommodations are scarce in Zagreb; fortunately, so are budget travelers. If a hostel is full or you would prefer something a little less like summer camp, try a **private room** at **Evistas.** From the train station, take a right on Branimirova, a quick left onto Petrinjska, and then a right onto Augusta Šenoe. This friendly travel agency can register you and reserve beds in private rooms or hotels, even at the height of festival season. (☎483 95 46; evistas@zg.hinet.hr. Open M-F 9am-1:45pm and 3-8pm, Sa 9:30am-5pm. Singles 185kn; doubles 264kn; apartments 390-750kn. Minimum 2 day stay for apartments; 20% more for 1 night only; 30% more during festivals; under 26 10% off. 7kn tax.) Foreigners entering Croatia and staying in private accommodations must **register** with the police (see **Emergency and Communications,** p. 169) within 48hr. of arrival. Hostels and hotels will register you automatically. Check out *Zagreb in Your Pocket,* available at the TIC (see p. 169), for a more extensive listing of accommodations.

Ravnice Youth Hostel, 1. Ravnice 38d (☎233 23 25; www.ravnice-youth-hostel.hr). Take tram #11 or 12 from Trg b. Jelačića, #4 from the train station, or #7 from the bus station to Dubrava or Dubec. About 20min. from the center. The unmarked Ravnice stop is 1 block past football stadium "Dinamo," and is the 2nd-to-last tram stop. Family-run hostel is ideal for budget travelers. Kitchen, Internet (16kn per hr.), and laundry facilities (15kn). Reception 9am-noon and 5-8pm. Check-out noon. 99kn. AmEx/MC/V. ❶

Hotel Ilica, Ilica 102 (☎377 75 22; www.hotel-ilica.hr). Walk down Ilica from Trg b. Jelačića, past Trg Britanki. From the train station, take tram #6 toward Črnomerec and get off the 2nd time it stops on Ilica. All rooms in this small hostel have TV, Internet, and phones. Breakfast and parking included. English spoken. Reception 24hr. Check-out noon. Call ahead. Singles 399kn; doubles 449-599kn; 3-person apartments 849kn. ❺

Omladinski Turistički Centar (HI), Petrinjska 77 (☎484 12 61; www.hfhs.hr). With your back to the train station, walk right on Branimirova; Petrinjska will be on your left. Despite the noise, graffiti, and less-than-clean communal bathrooms, nothing beats the central location and great prices. The grocery store to the left as you leave sells giant sandwiches (10-15kn). Reception 24hr. Check-in 2pm-1am. Check-out 9am. 6-bed dorm 80kn; singles 158kn, with bath 218kn; doubles 211kn/286kn. ❶

◨ FOOD

Zagrebčani adore meat, and restaurant menus reflect their carnivorous tastes, offering local specialities like *štruca*, grilled veal scallop stuffed with Dalmatian ham, mushrooms, and cheese. Behind Trg b. Jelačića in Gornji Grad, along ul. Pod Zidom lies Zagreb's liveliest open-air market, **Dolac**. Here you can find great deals—go upstairs for vegetables and fruit, or head downstairs for cheese, meat, pasta, fish, and more. (Open M-Sa 6am-3pm, Su 6am-1pm.) There are grocery stores throughout the city, including a **Konzum** at the corner of Preradovićeva and Hebrangova. (Open M-F 7am-8pm, Sa 7am-3pm. AmEx/MC/V.) For a shopping mall experience, head to the train station and take the escalator to your right down to the **Importanne Centar**, Starčevićev trg bb. You'll find over 125 shops, several large grocery stores, a disco, and even bowling. (☎457 70 76. Open M-Sa 9am-9pm, cigarettes and newspapers available 24hr.) For a list of the best restaurants and pubs, pick up the free *Zagreb Info A-Z* or consult *Zagreb in Your Pocket.*

▨ **Baltazar,** Nova Ves 4 (☎466 68 24). Kaptol becomes Nova Ves about 7min. past the Cathedral. Big sausages and steaks dominate the menu at this relaxed outdoor cafe; vegetarians and chicken-lovers beware. The *pljeskavica sa kajmakom* (seasoned hamburger with cheese; 50kn) is delicious. Open daily noon-midnight. AmEx/MC/V. ❷

Zdravljak Nova, Ilica 72/1 (☎484 71 19). Go into the passageway, enter the building on the right, and walk up 1 flight into a world of peace, love, and tofu. This combined health store and restaurant serves up Asian-influenced vegan cuisine, like the nutritious Tao and Zen plates, a refreshing alternative to Croatian chunks of meat. Entrees 39-75kn. Open M-Sa noon-10pm. AmEx/DC/MC/V. ❷

Korčula, Teslina 17 (☎487 21 59). From Trg b. Jelačića, go down Gajeva to Teslina; the restaurant will be directly in front of you. Named after the Adriatic island, Korčula brings a taste of the sea to inland Zagreb with Dalmatian seafood specialties. The *crni rižoto* (black risotto; 70kn) is an excellent squid dish, colored with its ink. Entrees 50-350kn. Restaurant open daily 10am-11pm; bar 8am-11pm. AmEx/MC/V. ❸

Pod Gričkim Topom, Zakmardijeve stube 5 (☎483 36 07). With your back to the Lotrščak Tower gift shop, head down the stairs on the far left from the funicular station into the restaurant's serene hillside garden. Locally dubbed "Marko's Place" for the exuberant personality of its multilingual leading waiter, this restaurant features a wonderful atmosphere and a delicious selection of meats and fish. Entrees 55-105kn. Open daily 11am-midnight, July 20-Aug. 15 5pm-midnight. AmEx/MC/V. ❷

Restaurant Boban, Gajeva 9 (☎481 15 49). If you've had your fill of meaty fare and heavy sauces, this bright, subterranean restaurant serves a dazzling array of delicious pastas (28-55kn) and fresh salads (29-35kn). The upbeat cafe upstairs is the perfect spot to relax over a cappuccino (9kn) and a book on a rainy day. (Restaurant open daily 10am-11pm; cafe 7am-11pm.) ❶

Pivnica Vallis Aurea, Tomičeva 4 (☎483 13 05). From the bottom of the funicular, walk down the hill toward Ilica; the restaurant is on the left. Hungarian-influenced dishes from Croatia's eastern region will widen your culinary horizons. Quick service and large portions leave you satiated and happy for hours. If you're feeling adventurous, try the grilled ox tongue (19kn). Entrees 25-50kn. Open M-Sa 9am-11pm. AmEx/MC/V. ❶

CROATIA

◎ SIGHTS

The best way to see Zagreb is on foot. A short walk up any of the streets behind Trg b. Jelačića leads to **Gornji Grad,** where you can wander through winding cobblestone streets and visit most sights in a single day. To give your weary feet a rest, hop on the **funicular,** an entertaining but peculiarly inefficient way of getting up the short hill. (Open 6:30am-9pm. 3kn, with Zagreb Card free.) Walk down Ilica from Trg b. Jelačića; the funicular is on the right. The free and informative *Zagreb: City Walks,* available at the TIC (see **Tourist and Financial Services,** p. 169), provides a number of additional sightseeing routes that can be done by foot.

▧**CATHEDRAL OF THE ASSUMPTION (KATEDRALA MARIJINA UZNESENJA).** Known simply as "the Cathedral," the church's first incarnation was built in 1217. After being destroyed by the Tatars and rebuilt, remodeled, and restored multiple times, it gained its current appearance between 1880 and 1902, when the distinctive neo-Gothic towers were added. Exterior renovations began in 1990 and continue to this day. The Cathedral's interior is breathtaking. *(Kaptol 1. Services M-Sa at 7, 8, 9am; Su 7, 8, 9, 10, 11:30am. Open daily 10am-5pm. Free.)*

ST. MARK'S CHURCH (CRKVA SV. MARKA). Even if you're hopelessly lost in Gornji Grad, St. Mark's bright roof will help orient you. The mosaic of colored tiles depicts the coat of arms of Croatia, Dalmatia, and Slavonia on the left side and that of Zagreb on the right. This sparkling display contrasts the dark stone interior, but if you squint you can make out the newly restored frescoes on the walls. *(From the top of the funicular, turn right and then left onto Cirilometodska; the church is straight ahead. Entrance to the left. Open daily 7am-1:30pm and 5:30-7pm. Free.)*

LOTRŠČAK TOWER (KULA LOTRŠČAK). This 13th-century tower, constructed to protect the city after Tatar attacks had nearly destroyed it, is marked by a 19th-century addition—a peculiar staircase that winds up halfway on the outside, and halfway on the inside. The view offers a panorama of Zagreb. The cannon near the top of the tower has been fired at noon every day since 1877. If you go a few minutes before noon, you can meet the cannoneer. *(At the corner of Strossmayerovo and Dverce, right at the top of the funicular. Open May-Sept. Tu-Su 11am-8pm. 10kn, students 5kn.)*

ST. CATHERINE'S CHURCH (CRKVA SV. KATRINSKI). Built by Jesuits between 1620 and 1632, St. Catherine's modest facade does nothing to prepare you for the elegance of its interior. Decorated with the gifts of Croatian nobles, the church's crowning feature is the intricate pink and white stucco on the vault, the walls of the chapel, and the shrine—all fashioned by the Italian master Anton Joseph Quadrio. The unstained windows let light bounce off the sculptures with gold leaf and delicate pink designs and illuminate the frescoes along the far wall. *(Katarinin trg bb. From the top of the funicular, the 1st church on your right. Open M-F and Su 7am-11pm, Sa 7am-6:30pm. Services M-F 6pm, Sa 6:30pm, Su 11am. Free.)*

MIROGOJ CEMETERY. Set at the edge of the city, this beautiful cemetery is so big you wonder if its population rivals that of Zagreb itself. Wander through the serene park composed of cypress trees, wide avenues, and endless rows of elaborate gravestones. Beyond the ivy-colored walls and grand mausoleum at the entrance you'll find the massive dark granite grave of Croatia's first president, Franjo Tudjman, who died of cancer in the fall of 1999. *(Take a bus from Kaptol in front of the Cathedral. 8min., every 15min. Photography not allowed. Open M-F 6am-8pm, Su 7:30am-6pm. Free.)*

RIBNJAK PARK. Spacious and tree-covered Ribnjak Park offers the chance for a peaceful walk without leaving the city. A light breeze and ample shade make for a refreshing getaway on hot summer days. Come to enjoy an inexpensive picnic or to watch the Zagreb's canine population play in the grass. *(Behind the Cathedral. From Trg b. Jelačića, turn down Jurišićeva, then right on Palmotićeva. The entrance is on the left.)*

MAKSIMIR PARK AND THE ZAGREB ZOO. Covered in gentle meadows, lakes, and tall oaks, Maksimir Park is one of the largest parks in southeast Europe—so big, in fact, that hundreds of critters reside comfortably in the **Zagreb Zoo** within the park's borders. Chill with penguins and hang out with monkeys—the multifarious species and hordes of excited children will make you feel like a kid again. *(From Trg b. Jelačića, take tram #11 or 12 to Dubrava or Dubec. Get off at the 7th stop, Bukovačka. Continue walking down the road; the park entrance is on the left. Park open daily sunrise to sunset. Zoo open daily 9am-5pm. Ticket office closes 4pm. 20kn, children 10kn.)*

🏛 MUSEUMS

While you may not find many famous masterpieces in Zagreb, there are plenty of interesting collections and exhibits to occupy the art lover for a few days. For a complete list of museums, consult the free monthly *Zagreb: Events and Performances*, available at the TIC (see **Tourist and Financial Services,** p. 169). It also lists galleries, performances, festivals, concerts, sporting events, and films. Many of the museums lie in Donji Grad below Ilica. Trams #12, 13, 14, and 17 all reach the Museum of Arts and Crafts, the Mimara, and the Ethnographic Museum.

🖼 MUSEUM OF ARTS AND CRAFTS (MUZEJ ZA UMJETNOST I OBRT). Though its name recalls summer-camp fun, this museum has an eclectic mix of elaborate works from the 15th century onward. From timepieces to antique furniture, glass to graphic art, each room holds a surprise. Complementing the golden altar pieces on the first floor is an impressive collection of 19th-century world Judaica on the second floor. The exhibit on Croatian photography from the 1850s to the 1930s, located in the second floor atrium, is small but fascinating. *(Trg Maršala Tita 10. ☎ 482 69 22. Open Tu-F 10am-6pm, Sa-Su 10am-1pm. 20kn, students 10kn.)*

KLOVIČEVI DVORI GALLERY (GALERIJA KLOVIĆEVI DVORI). Situated in a beautifully converted 17th-century monastery, this gallery's exhibits change monthly and usually feature Croatian artists. Regardless of the exhibit, the building itself makes your visit worthwhile. After visiting the gallery, enjoy a coffee (7kn) in the elegant central courtyard. *(Jesuitski trg 4, immediately to the left of St. Catherine's. ☎ 485 19 26. Open Tu-Su 11am-7pm. 20kn, students 10kn.)*

GALLERY OF MODERN ART (MODERNA GALERIJA). This attractive gallery features rotating exhibitions of Croatia's best artists. With a collection of 9500 paintings, sculptures, watercolors, drawings, and prints, this gallery is a great way to explore the budding modern art scene. *(Hebrangova 1, across from the Strossmayer Gallery. ☎ 492 23 68. Open Tu-Sa 10am-6pm, Su 10am-1pm. Prices vary with each exhibition.)*

MIMARA MUSEUM (MUZEJ MIMARA). A vast and varied collection from prehistoric Egyptian art to a handful of lesser known works by famed European masters including Raphael, Velasquez, Renoir, Manet, Rubens, and Rembrandt, although little background or English info is provided. *(Rooseveltov trg 5. ☎ 482 81 00. Open Tu-W and F-Sa 10am-5pm, Th 10am-7pm, Su 10am-2pm. 20kn, students 15kn.)*

STROSSMAYER GALLERY (STROSSMAYER GALERIJA STARIH MAJSTORA). Go up two flights in the stately Croatian Academy of Arts and Sciences. Founded by Bishop Josip Juraj Strossmayer in 1884, the permanent collection includes paintings from Flemish, Dutch, French, and Italian schools from the Renaissance through Baroque periods. Pick up a guide at the entrance. *(Zrinjskog trg 11. ☎489 51 17. Open Tu 10am-1pm and 5-7pm, W-Su 10am-1pm. 10kn, students 5kn.)*

ETHNOGRAPHIC MUSEUM (ETHNOGRAFSKI MUZEJ). This small museum offers a unique look at the traditional culture of Croatia, with rotating exhibits focusing on diverse regions. It also includes an eclectic mix of traditional costumes and etchings of local architecture. Don't miss the "Cultures of the World in Three Rooms" gallery. *(Mažuranićev trg 14, across the street from the Mimara. ☎482 62 20. No English info. Open Tu-F 10am-6pm, Sa-Su 10am-1pm. 20kn, students 10kn; Th free.)*

🎭 🌿 ENTERTAINMENT AND FESTIVALS

If visual arts aren't your cup of tea, fear not—performance is Zagreb's middle name. As always, the latest schedules and contact info can be found in the monthly *Zagreb: Events and Performances*, available for free at the TIC. Classical music lovers should seek out **Vatroslav Lisinski Concert Hall,** Trg Stjepana Radića 4, about two blocks behind the train station, home to the Zagreb Philharmonic and visiting orchestras from abroad, jazz and blues performances, and solo artists. (☎612 11 66. Tickets 50-300kn, student discounts available. Office open M-F 9am-8pm, Sa 9am-2pm.) The **Croatian National Theater** (Hrvatsko Narodno Kazalište), Trg Maršala Tita 15 (☎482 85 32), puts on dramas, ballets, and operas. At **Jarun Lake** you can find "Theater on the Water" during the summer months, and the nearby **Sports and Recreation Center** hosts **Jarunfest,** a series of musical theater, ensemble, and operetta performances in late June and early July. From April to October, the **Arts Pavilion** in Zrinjevac Park holds weekly Promenade Concerts, varied performances from tango to jazz. **SRČ Šalata** (see **Local Services,** p. 169), hosts many rock concerts. Jazz fans should head for **BP Club** (see **Nightlife,** p. 174) and remember International Jazz Days in October. If you're in the mood for a recent American movie, **cinemas** abound in Zagreb and tickets are cheap (15-29kn). The largest and most popular are **Cinestar,** Branimirova 29 (☎468 66 00; www.blitz-cinestar.hr), in the Branimirova Shopping Center and **Broadway 3,** Nova Ves 11 (☎466 76 86; www.broadway-kina.com), in the Centar Kaptol.

Zagreb hosts an impressive array of festivals. Each year kicks off with a **blues festival** in January. In the beginning of June, streets burst with performances for the annual Zagreb street festival **Cest is d'Best** ("The Streets are the Best"), and the **Eurokaz Avant-Garde Theaters Festival.** Throughout June, the Kerempuh Satirical Theater (Ilica 31) hosts **Satire Days,** with various satirical plays in Croatian running almost daily. Folklore fetishists will flock to Zagreb in mid-July 2005 for the 39th **International Folklore Festival,** the premier gathering of European folk dancers and singing groups. The huge **International Puppet Festival** occurs at the beginning of September, and the end of October sees Zagreb's **International Jazz Days.** Every year, mid-December is filled with the colorful **Christmas Fair.** For up-to-date, detailed info and schedules, check out www.zagreb-touristinfo.hr.

🎵 NIGHTLIFE

The lively outdoor **cafes** lining the street **Tkalčićeva,** in Gornji Grad, attract young people from all over the city, and each tends to have its own unique atmosphere and high-energy music. **Opatovina,** a parallel street, hosts a slightly older and quieter group. Most of the cafes in Donji Grad are indistinguishable but pleasant. Many **discos** are open all week, except in the beginning of August, when nearly the entire city goes on holiday. The best discos lie outside the center. For a complete listing of all discos and nightclubs in Zagreb, consult *Zagreb Info A-Z* or *Zagreb in Your Pocket* for a local perspective on selected spots.

■ **Aquarius,** on Lake Jarun (☎364 02 31). Take tram #17 from the center and get off on Srednjaci at the 3rd unmarked stop after Studenski dom "S. Radić" (15min.). Cross the street and take one of the paths—they all lead to the lake. At the lake, walk along the boardwalk to the left; Aquarius is the last building. This popular lakeside cafe and night-club offers something for everyone. Boogie in- or outside, or take a late-night dip in the artificial lake. Drinks 15-45kn. Live jazz on some Tu, funk W, Latin Th, house Su, and a mix on weekends. Cover 30kn. Cafe open daily 9am-9pm; club open Tu-Su 10pm-4am.

■ **Pivnica Medvedgrad,** Savska 56 (☎617 71 19). Take tram #13, 14, or 17 from Trg b. Jelačića to the corner of Avenija Vukovar and Savska. The best (and cheapest) beer in town. This microbrewery's long, wooden tables, dim lights, and homemade beer (18kn per L) attract crowds of students and suits. When the munchies kick in, try the whole-grain bread and *čevapčici* (small sausages served with raw onion; 22kn), or nibble on some *perec* (large, soft pretzels; 2kn). Open M-Sa 10am-midnight, Su noon-midnight.

Indy's, Vranicanijeva 4 (☎485 20 53). From St. Mark's, go down Cirilometodska and right on Vsanicanijeva. One of Zagreb's hippest nightspots, Indy's has the most extensive cock-tail menu in town. Enjoy a creatively named Martian Sex Monster (30kn) on the outdoor terrace or a Test Tube Baby (20kn) in the green-lit cave interior. Open daily 9am-11pm.

BP Club, Teslina 7 (☎481 44 44). Head for the right side of the courtyard, then down the yellow stairs. The venue for jazz (also blues, trance, and U2), BP keeps it cool year-round. Live music Sept.-Apr. Outdoor seating in summer. Open daily 5pm-2am.

Tolkien's House, Vsanicanijeva 8, a few doors down from Indy's. Indulge your question-able hobbit fetish at this quirky Irish pub, festooned with memorabilia from J.R.R. Tolk-ien's fantasy books. Tolkienana aside, the Irish music and the pints of Guinness (27kn) make this a great place to relax. Drinks 13-32kn. Open M-Sa 9am-11pm, Su 10am-11pm. For even more Tolkien-themed decor, visit its sister establishment down the street, **Fantasy Club in Tolkien's Pub,** Katarinin trg 3. Open M-Sa 8am-midnight.

⚡ DAYTRIPS FROM ZAGREB

Defining the crests of Zagreb's surrounding hilltops are the 56 mysterious **castles** of Hrvatsko Zagorje (the region north of Zagreb), formerly owned and constructed by warring Croatian nobles. They now lie in various states of disrepair, waiting to be conquered with cameras instead of cannons. Trakošćan is in the best shape and is one of the most popular. Consult *Zagreb and Surroundings,* available at the TIC in Zagreb (see **Tourist and Financial Services,** p. 169) to explore the others.

TRAKOŠĆAN

From the Zagreb bus station, take a bus to Varaždin (1¾hr., 20 per day, 50kn), and change to a local bus (1hr. 25min.; M-F 11 per day, Sa-Su 7 per day; 26kn). Leave early in order to make the connection and still have plenty of time at the castle. The last bus back from Trakošćan to Varaždin leaves M-F around 9pm, Sa-Su around 5pm. ☎42 79 62 81. Open daily Apr.-Oct. 9am-6pm; Nov.- Mar. 9am-3pm. Free guided tours in English for groups only; reservations necessary. 20kn, students 10kn. English booklet 20kn.

The fairy-tale white walls of ■**Trakošćan** rise high above the surrounding forests and rolling hills. Built as a defense tower in the 13th century, it passed in 1584 to the Drašković nobility, who enlarged and refurbished it, retaining the castle until

WWII. Today, stately family portraits, elaborate tapestries, and collections of fire-arms and armor from the 15th-19th centuries are on display in the castle's pre-served interior. Leave time to wander around the quiet lake and to hike through the hills, if only to escape the crowds of Croatian school-children. The restaurant at the bottom of the hill is absurdly overpriced, so bring a sandwich, get a hot dog or hamburger (25kn) at the cafe, or be prepared to lighten that wallet.

PLITVICE LAKES NATIONAL PARK

Buses run from Zagreb (2½ hr., every 30min., 70kn) and Zadar (2½hr., every 45min., 72kn). Ask the bus driver to let you off at one of the park entrances. Tourist office ☎ 75 20 15 or 75 10 13; www.np-plitvicka-jezera.hr. Park open daily 7am-7pm. July-Aug. 95kn, students 55kn; May-June and July-Oct. 75kn/45kn; Nov.-Apr. 45/22kn. MC/V. Tourist centers at each of the 3 park entrances sell tickets, and offer maps and a comprehensive guide. Most buses stop near tourist center #2. To get to the center, walk toward the pedestrian overpass. (If you're coming on a bus from Zagreb, you'll need to cross the road.) Head up the stairs and follow the path on the left downhill. Store your luggage at the center while you explore the lakes.

Plitvice Lakes National Park lies in the Krajina region, where Croatia's bloody war for independence began. Throughout the conflict (1991-95), the Serbians holding the area planted **landmines** in the ground. There are still landmines in the surrounding area. Under no circumstances should you leave the road or the marked paths. Don't let this warning stop you from visiting the natural wonder of the Plitvice lakes; just be cautious about where you walk.

Though it's a bit of a trip from either Zagreb or Zadar, ◼**Plitvice Lakes National Park** (Nacionalni Park Plitcicka Jezera) is definitely worth the transportation hassle. Some 30,000 hectares of forested hills, dappled with 16 lakes and hundreds of waterfalls, make this pocket of paradise one of Croatia's most spectacular sights. Declared a national park in 1949, Plitvice was added to the UNESCO World Heri-tage list in 1979 for the unique evolution of its lakes and waterfalls, which formed through the interaction of water and petrified vegetation. A system of wooden pathways hovering just above the iridescent blue surface of the lakes winds around the many waterfalls. Two bus routes (every 20min.) help you get around the park, while one boat runs on the largest of the lakes (every 30min.). Though most tourists circulate around the four lower lakes (Donja Jezera) to snap pictures of Plitvice's famous 78m waterfall, **Veliki Slap** (follow trail F, 2-3hr.), the true adventurer explores the hidden falls of the 12 upper lakes, **Gornja Jezera** (4hr.). Although easily done as a daytrip, if you find yourself awestruck by the heavenly beauty and can't bring yourself to leave, the private accommodation service across from tourist center #2 will find you a room. (Singles 150kn; doubles 220-300kn. Open daily noon-9pm.)

ISTRIA

The Istrian Peninsula lies on the northern part of the Adriatic Coast, where the Mediterranean kisses the foot of the Alps. Influenced throughout history by its rather pushy neighbor, the region seems almost more Italian than Croatian. Today, the mosaics of Poreč, ruins of Roman Pula, unspoiled 19th-century Rovinj, and the clear waters of the Adriatic lend this area a touch of paradise.

CROATIA

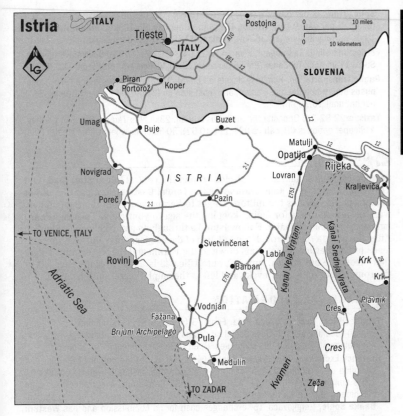

Istria

ITALY
Trieste
ITALY
Postojna
0   10 miles
0   10 kilometers
SLOVENIA
Piran
Portorož   Koper
Umag
Buje
Buzet
Matulji
Opatija
Rijeka
Novigrad
Lovran
Kraljevica
ISTRIA
Poreč
Pazin
TO VENICE, ITALY
Svetvinčenat
Labin
Krk
Rovinj
Barban
Krk
Adriatic Sea
Plavnik
Fažana
Vodnjan
Cres
Brijuni Archipelago
Pula
Cres
Medulin
TO ZADAR
Kanal Vela Vratam
Kanal Srednja Vrata
Kvarneri
Zeča

PULA   ☎ (0)52

At the threshold of Pula's old center, an enormous billboard welcomes visitors to the "3000-year-old town." Pula's Roman amphitheater, which has been an entertainment stage since ancient times, has featured everything from gladiatorial combat to rock concerts. Despite the tourist crowds, Pula (pop. 65,000) maintains its laid-back character. Relax on the rocky coast, mingle in outdoor cafes, and soak in the vibrant culture of one of Istria's richest destinations.

▮ TRANSPORTATION

Trains: Kolodvorska 5 (☎54 17 83). Ticket window open daily 8am-4pm. To: **Rijeka** (2½hr., 4 per day, 47kn); **Zagreb** (7hr., 4 per day, 112-125kn); **Ljubljana, SLN** (7½hr., 3 per day, 127kn).

Buses: Trg Istarske Brigade bb (☎50 29 97), off Ulica 43 Istarske Divizije. Ticket office open M-Sa 4:30am-8:30pm; tickets can also be purchased on board. To: **Dubrovnik** (15hr., 1 per day, 408kn); **Poreč** (1½hr., 8-14 per day, 43kn); **Rijeka** (2½hr., 14-21 per day, 53kn); **Rovinj** (1hr., 12-23 per day, 25kn); **Šibenik** (9hr., 3 per day, 238kn);

CROATIA

Split (10hr., 3 per day, 287kn); **Zagreb** (5-6hr., 15 per day, 136kn); **Koper, SLN** (3¼hr., 2 per day, 93kn); **Trieste, ITA** (3hr., 4 per day, 85-103kn); **Milan, ITA** (8½hr., 1 per day only in summer, 365kn); **Venice, ITA** (6hr., 1 per day, 170kn).

Ferries: Jadrolinija Jadroagent, Riva 14 (☎21 04 31; fax 21 17 99). Open M-F 8am-4pm, Sa-Su 11am-4pm. To: **Zadar** (8hr., 5 per wk., 112kn); **Venice, ITA** (6hr., 2 per wk., 365kn).

Public Transportation: Purchase tickets on board (10kn) or at newsstands (8kn). Local **buses** depart from the bus station, and most stop on Giardini (M-Sa every 20min., Su 1 per hr.; until 10:30pm).

Taxis: ☎22 32 28. Opposite the main bus station. 23kn plus 7kn per km; 3kn per bag. A cheaper option is **Citycab** (☎091 111 10 52). 30-50kn anywhere within greater Pula.

◢ ORIENTATION

Sergijevaca, Pula's main street, circles around the central hill in **Stari Grad** (Old Town) and turns into **Kandlerova** after the **Forum. Castropola,** a parallel street higher up, also circles the hilltop. To get to Sergijevaca from the **train station,** walk on Kolodvorska for 5min., keeping the sea to your right. Turn right onto **Istarska** at the **amphitheater.** Follow Istarska through its name change to **Giardini.** After the park, a right through the tall **Arch of the Sergians** (Slavoluk Sergijevaca) leads to Sergijevaca, which runs down to the Forum and the waterfront. To get there from the **bus station,** turn left onto Ulica 43 Istarske Divizije, veer left at the roundabout onto Flavijevska and left at the amphitheater onto Istarska.

◢ PRACTICAL INFORMATION

Tourist Office: Tourism Office Pula, Forum 3 (☎21 29 87; www.pulainfo.hr). Friendly English-speaking staff provides useful **city maps;** info on accommodations, events, and entertainment. Ferry and bus schedules. Open M-Sa 8am-midnight, Su 10am-6pm.

Currency Exchange: Zagrebačka Banka (☎21 47 44), at the corner of Giardini and Laginjina ul., exchanges cash for no commission and cashes **traveler's checks** for 1.5% commission. Open M-F 7:30am-7pm, Sa 8am-noon. A currency exchange machine is outside **Raiffeisen Bank,** ul. 43 Istarske Divizije, next to the bus station. **Banka Sonic,** Sergijevaca 16, exchanges cash for no commission and has **Western Union** services. Open M-F 8am-6pm, Sa 8am-noon. **ATMs** common in the city center.

American Express: Atlas Travel Agency, Starih Statuta 1 (☎39 30 40; fax 21 40 94). AmEx moneygram service and lost card replacement. Open Apr.-Oct. M-Sa 8am-2pm and 5:30-8pm, Su 9am-noon and 6-8pm; Nov.-Mar. M-F 8am-2pm and 5:30-8pm.

Luggage Storage: At the bus station. 1.2kn per hr., over 15kg 2.2kn per hr. Open M-F 5:30-9:30am, 10am-6pm, 6:30-11:30pm; Sa 5am-11pm; Su 5:30am-11pm.

English-Language Bookstore: Algoritam, off Sergijevaca toward the post office, stocks recent fiction and travel guides. Books 50-140kn. Open M-F 9am-9pm, Sa 9am-2pm.

Police: Trg Republike 2 (☎53 21 11).

24hr. Pharmacy: Ljekarna Centar, Giardini 15 (☎22 25 44). AmEx/MC/V.

Hospital: Clinical Hospital Center, Zagrebačka 34 (☎21 44 33). Open 24hr.

Internet Access: Multimedijalni Centar Linka, Istarska 30, 1 block from the amphitheater, offers fast connections in a hip bar. 25kn per hr. Open M-Sa 8am-midnight. **Cyber Café,** Flanatička 14 (☎21 53 45), is a small but chic cafe with 4 computers. Facing away from the Arch of the Sergians, walk up Flanatička past the market area. 25kn per hr. Open daily 7am-9pm.

Post Office: Danteov trg 4 (☎21 59 55; fax 21 89 11). Go left for mail and right for **Poste Restante** (open M-F 7am-10pm, Sa 7am-2pm, Su 8am-noon) and **telephones.** Open M-F 7am-8pm, Sa 7am-2pm, Su 8am-noon. **Postal Code:** 52100.

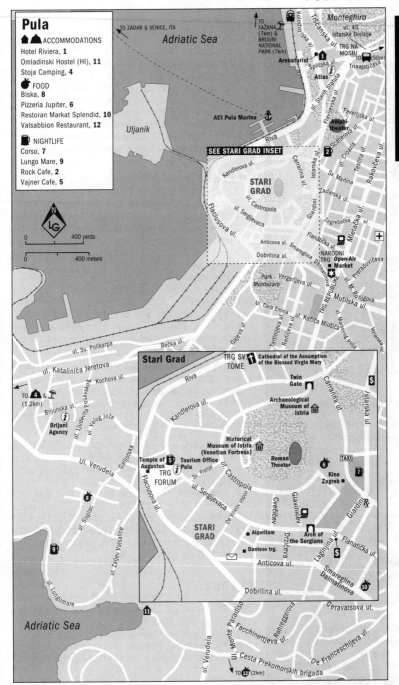

Pula

ACCOMMODATIONS
Hotel Riviera, **1**
Omladinski Hostel (HI), **11**
Stoja Camping, **4**

FOOD
Biska, **8**
Pizzeria Jupiter, **6**
Restoran Markat Splendid, **10**
Valsabbion Restaurant, **12**

NIGHTLIFE
Corso, **7**
Lungo Mare, **9**
Rock Cafe, **2**
Vajner Cafe, **5**

Adriatic Sea

TO ZADAR & VENICE, ITA

Monteghiro
ul. 43. Istarske Divizije

TO FAŽANA (7km) & BRIJUNI NATIONAL PARK (7km)

Aronaturist
Atlas
Splitska ul.
ul. Starih Statuta
Flavijevska ul.
Faverijska ul.
Scalierova ul.
Tešlina ul.
ul. Croazia
Sv. Martina
Rakovčeva ul.

TRG NA MOSTU
Trešćanska ul.
Koloborska ul.

Amphi-theater

Zadarska ul.
Zagrebačka ul.
Mletačka ul.

NARODNI TRG Open-Air Market
Flanatička ul.
Smareglina Dalmatinova
Anticova ul.
Dobrilina ul.

ACI Pula Marina

Uljanik

SEE STARI GRAD INSET

Kandlerova ul.
Cararina ul.
Istarska ul.
Flaciusova ul.

STARI GRAD
ul. Castropola
ul. Sergijevaca
Giardini

Riva

Park - Montezaro
Vergerijeva ul.
Mutilska ul.
ul. M. Benigova
ul. Preradovičeva
ul. Cara Emina
ul. Kačiča Miošiča
TRG REPUBLIK
Gajeva ul.
Tartinijeva ul.
Radičeva ul.
ul. Mesarsko polja
Vinjanska ul.

TO (50m)
Trinajstičeva

0   400 yards
0   400 meters

ul. Sv. Polikarpa
Bečka ul.
ul. Katalinića Jeretova

TO 4 & (1.2km)
Brijunska ul.
Brijuni Agency

Kochova ul.
ul. Ljudevita Posavskog
ul. Velog Jože

Ul. Verudela
Gajjotska
Flaciusova ul.
ul. Sergijevaca

Stari Grad

Riva
Kandlerova ul.

TRG SV TOME
Cathedral of the Assumption of the Blessed Virgin Mary

Twin Gate

Archaeological Museum of Istria

Historical Museum of Istria (Venetian Fortress)

Roman Theater

Temple of Augustus
Tourism Office Pula
TRG FORUM
Sv. Franje
ul. Castropola

Cvebičev
Glavinčev
Držićeva

Algoritam
Danteov trg.
Anticova ul.

Arch of the Sergians

Kino Zagreb
TAXI

Cararina ul.
Istarska ul.
Giardini
Laginina ul.
Flanatička ul.
Smareglina Dalmatinova

STARI GRAD

Dobrilina ul.
Geravaisova ul.

ul. Slaplac
Ul. Zaljev Valsaline

Adriatic Sea

ul. Lungomare
ul. Verudela
ul. Monte Paradiso
Facchinettjeva ul.
Renneggerova
Ul. Cesta Prekomorskih brigada
De Franceschijeva ul.

TO (2km)

THE BIG SPLURGE

THE BRIJUNI ARCHIPELAGO

Although costly to access, the Brijuni Archipelago, just a short bus and ferry ride from Pula, is one of Croatia's most fascinating and beautiful regions. It has animals for the kids, ruins for the historians, and politics for the governmentally inclined. The archipelago's largest island, Veli Brijun, accessible only by guided tour, was once home to a Roman resort and a Venetian colony.

More recently, the island hosted former Yugoslav president Josip Broz Tito's opulent residence. The tour begins with a mini-trolley ride through a safari park inhabited by curiosities, including a pair of elephants given to Tito by Indira Gandhi. The tour continues on foot though a gallery of photos of Tito in all his publicity-grubbing glory. It's worth the steep 25kn per hour (100kn per day) to explore the island's deserted beaches by bike (rentals on the far side of Hotel Neptune).

The only way to see Veli Brijun is with a guided tour by the Brijuni Agency, Brijunska 10 (☎52 58 83; www.np-brijuni.hr), in Fazana. To get to the agency, take a local bus (20min.; M-Sa 1 per hr., Su 1 every 2-3hr.; 12kn) from Ulica 43 Istarske Divizije in Pula, and get off at the supermarket. Cross the street and walk to the water. It is 1 block to the right. Tours run daily 11:30am; call 1 day ahead. Tours in English. Round-trip ferry and 4hr. tour 80kn. Open daily 8am-7pm.

ACCOMMODATIONS

Several agencies help tourists locate private rooms. The tourist office can help find the best deals. **Arenaturist,** Splitska 1, inside Hotel Riviera, arranges private rooms throughout Pula. (☎52 94 00; www.arenaturist.hr. 50% more for 1 night, 25% for 2-3 nights. Registration 10kn. July 12-Aug. 23 singles 114-150kn; doubles 180-250kn; June 28-July 11 and Aug. 24-30 90-120kn/140-190kn; June 7-27 and Aug. 31-Sept. 6 75-110kn/120-150kn. Open M-Sa 8am-8pm, Su 8am-1pm.)

Omladinski Hostel (HI), Zaljev Valsaline 4 (☎39 11 33; www.hfhs.hr). From the bus station, catch bus #2 toward "Veruda" at the far end of the station. After 10min., the bus turns onto Verudela. Get off at the 1st stop on Verudela. Follow the HI signs and go downhill. A trek from the center, this beachside getaway attracts a mix of families, teenage tour groups, and backpackers. Private cove, diving school, bar, table tennis, shared showers. Internet access 1kn per min. Simple breakfast included. Reception 8am-10pm. Call ahead. Dorms July-Aug. 100kn; June and Sept. 84kn; May and Oct. 79kn; Apr. and Nov. 74kn. Camping July-Aug. 65kn; Sept.-June 40kn. 10kn additional per night without HI membership. Registration fee 10kn. Tax 4.5-7kn. ●

Hotel Riviera, Splitska 1 (☎21 11 66; fax 21 91 17), across the park from the amphitheater by the waterfront. This old, elegant yellow hotel has kind staff, large rooms, views of the waterfront, and a wonderful terrace. June-Aug. singles 313-416kn; doubles 481-686kn. Sept.-May. 219-277kn/365-481kn. ●

Stoja Camping (☎52 94 00, reservations 22 20 43; fax 38 77 48). From Giardini, take bus #1 to Stoja to the end. Within walking distance of town (20min), surrounded by beaches. Showers, bathroom, sports facilities, restaurant, and grocery. Camping April-May 22 and Sept. 4-Nov.6 26.25kn; May 23-June 26 and Aug. 28-Sept. 4 35.35kn; June 26-July 10 47.25kn; July 10-31 and Aug 21-28 51kn; Aug. 1-21 52.50kn. Tents Apr.-June and Sept.-Nov. 16-40kn, with electricity 34-64kn; July-Aug. 65kn/90kn. ●

FOOD

Fresh fish, meat, and cheese are available in the market building. (Fish market open M-Sa 7am-1:30pm, Su 7am-noon; meat and cheese markets open M-Sa 7-noon, Su 7am-2pm.) **Puljanka** grocery store has several branches throughout the town, including one at

Sergijevaca 4. (Open M-F 6am-8pm, Sa 8am-1:30pm, Su 7am-noon.) Buffets and fast-food restaurants line **Sergijevaca**. There is an open-air fruit and vegetable **market** at Trg Narodni, off Flanatička. (Open daily 6am-2pm.)

🦪 **Biska,** Sisplac 15, (☎38 73 33). From the center, take bus #2 to the 1st stop on Veruda. Backtrack on Verduda, past Tomasinjeva ul., and turn left on Sisplac. This small terrace cafe, set in residential Veruda, serves large portions of delicious seafood and pasta dishes. Huge bowls of freshly-made soups (10-15kn) and grilled calamari (38kn) attract a dedicated local following. Entrees 25-75kn. Open June-Sept. M-Sa 9am-11pm, Su 2-11pm; Oct.-May M-Sa 9am-10pm, Su 2-10pm. ❶

🦪 **Valsabbion,** Pješčana uvala IX/26, (☎21 80 33. www.valsabbion.net). Take bus #2 from Giardini, toward the hostel. After getting off, turn left down the hill and walk along Prekomorskih Brigada (5min.), then go right on the first unnamed road leading to Veruda Marina. Walk along the marina until you round the tip of the peninsula (20min.); Valsabbion will be on the right, 100m past the marina. A "slow food" restaurant in a sea of "fast food" establishments, Valsabbion tenderly prepares every dish (entrees 95-150kn) from scratch, which makes for long waits and excellent food. ❹

Pizzeria Jupiter, Castropola 42 (☎21 43 33). Walk behind the bus station along Carrarina ul., past the Archaeological Museum. Curve sharply to the left up the ramp; it is on the left. Lauded by Pulians young and old, this is the perfect spot for a bite before amphitheater concerts. Pizza 20-39kn. Open M-F 9am-11pm, Sa-Su 1-11pm. AmEx. ❶

Restoran Markat Splendid, Trg Privoga Svibvija 5 (☎22 32 84), across from the far side of the market building at Narodni trg. A Croatian version of the school-lunch lady fills trays with inexpensive delights in this cafeteria-style eatery. Meat, fish, soups, vegetarian fare, sausages, and salads 6-30kn. Open M-F 9:30am-9pm, Sa-Su 9:30am-4pm. ❶

📷 SIGHTS

AMPHITHEATER. Completed in the AD first century during the reign of Roman Emperor Vespasian, the arena was used for gladiatorial combat until sport killing was outlawed in the 4th century. Today, it houses entertainment of a different sort: concerts, from opera to heavy metal. An underground system of passages, constructed as a drainage system, now house a **museum** of Istrian history. *(From the bus station, take a left on ul. 43 Istarske Divizije and another on Flavijevska ul., which becomes Istarska. Open daily 8am-9pm; low season 8am-4pm. 16kn, students 8kn. English booklet 30kn.)*

ARCH OF THE SERGIANS (SLAVOLUK OBITELJI SERGII). The sturdy stone arch was built in 29 BC for three local members of the Sergii family, one of whom commanded a Roman battalion at the battle of Actium between Mark Antony and Octavian. It is now a gateway to Sergijevaca, Pula's main street. *(From the amphitheater, follow Istarska left as it turns into Giardini. The arch is on the right.)*

THE FORUM. The Forum, at the end of Sergijevaca, was the central gathering place for political, religious, and economic debates in Roman days. Today, the original cobblestones lie buried safely 1.2m beneath the ground and the square is used primarily for cafe lounging and gazing at the nearby Temple of Augustus.

TEMPLE OF AUGUSTUS (AUGUSTOV HRAM). This remarkably preserved temple, constructed between 2 BC and AD 14, was dedicated to Roman Emperor Octavian Augustus. Until the early Middle Ages, two similar temples stood nearby; the larger was destroyed, but the rear wall of the smaller Temple of Diana now serves as the facade of the City Hall from which Pula has been governed since 1296. The

Temple of Augustus houses a small **museum** with pieces of Roman statues and stone sculptures from the AD 1st and 2nd centuries. (*At the Forum.* ☎ *21 86 89. Open M-F 9:30am-1:30pm and 4-9pm, Sa-Su 9:30am-1:30pm. 4kn, students 2kn.*)

OTHER SIGHTS. Up the hill from Castropola, the **Venetian Fortress** has guarded Pula since Roman times, but in 2002 it became the **Historical Museum of Istria**, a small maritime and military history exhibit. (*Open summer daily 8am-8pm; winter 9am-5pm. 10kn.*) On the nearby hilltop stand the remains of a **Roman Theater.** Farther down is the **Twin Gate** (Dvojna vrata). If ancient history excites you, you'll be ecstatic about the **Archaeological Museum of Istria** (Arheološki Muzej Istre), Carrarina 3, up the hill from the Twin Gate. The museum offers an overview of Istria's history, with an emphasis on Roman stone artifacts from the 2nd century BC to the AD 6th century. (☎ *21 86 09. Open May-Sept. M-F 9am-8pm, Su 10am-3pm; Oct.-Apr. M-F 9am-2pm. 12kn, students 6kn. English guidebook 30kn.*) Near the waterfront, off Trg Sv. Tome, the **Cathedral of the Assumption of the Blessed Virgin Mary,** constructed in the AD 4th century, is in remarkably good shape.

❊ ◑ FESTIVALS AND BEACHES

Amphitheater shows are the impressive highlight of a trip to Pula. Open seating allows you to sit or stand wherever you can climb. Tickets (150-800kn) are available at the theater from the booking agency, **Lira Intersound** (☎ 21 78 01; open M-F 8am-3pm), or from tourist agencies. If the cost of a ticket is out of your budget, you can listen to world-class music while enjoying the striking backdrop of the ruins for free by sitting in one of the surrounding gardens. The only drawback is that you won't actually see the performer. Agencies also sell tickets (150kn) to the popular **Biker Days Festival,** which takes place during the first week of August. Exhibitions at this chrome-and-leather celebration have included female mud wrestling. Movie buffs can enjoy the **Pula Film Festival** (www.pulafilmfestival.com), which occurs in mid-July. The **International Accordion School** hits town in the second half of July, offering a series of concerts and classes. If you prefer punk to polka, the annual **Festival "Monte Paradiso,"** turns an old army barracks into a stage and mosh pit in the first weekend in August. **Kino Zagreb,** Giardini 1, the only permanent cinema in Pula, mostly shows Hollywood movies with Croatian subtitles. (Screenings nightly 7 and 9pm. 15-20kn, midnight special 12kn.)

You wouldn't guess it when looking at the shipyards, but Pula is lined with private coves and **beaches.** To scope out the perfect spot, start by taking bus #1 to Stoja Campground. Facing the sea, walk left down the coastline. Rock shelves line the sea from the campground to the hostel. A pleasant pebble beach curves in front of a hostel, which offers **paddle boats** (40kn per hr.) and **scuba diving** (30min. novice dive 200kn). For quieter, less crowded beaches, head to the neighboring town of **Fazana.**

◧ NIGHTLIFE

Lungo Mare, Cortanova Ujula bb (☎ 39 10 84). Take bus #2 or 7 from Giardini, get off at Verud, go right on Verudela to Hotel Pula, and go down to the sea. Cafe by day, raging club by night, this outdoor chameleon blasts music in its own cove. 1L *Favorit* 25kn. On the beach and along the road, hundreds of young Pulans gather for raucous Croatian **tailgates** most Th-Sa summer nights. Bring your own booze. Open daily 10am-4am.

Corso, Giardini 3 (☎ 53 51 47). Occupying a prime people-watching spot in the Old Town, this chic cafe/bar is often filled with trendy young Pulians sipping *bijela kava* (latte; 9kn) by day and cocktails (20-40kn) by night. Open daily 8am-midnight.

Rock Cafe, Scalierova 8 (☎21 09 75). Not to be confused with the "harder" worldwide chain, this oak bar with pool tables has a terrace. 0.5L *Pivo Točeno* (draft) 10kn. Open M-Sa noon-3pm and 6pm-midnight, Su 6pm-midnight.

Vajner Cafe, Forum 2 (☎21 65 02). Inside, modern art jives with Roman-style frescoes on the walls and a bank vault next to the bar. Outside, tables provide views of the Temple of Augustus. *Dupli* cappuccino 9kn. Mixed drinks 30kn. Open daily 8am-11pm.

POREČ ☎(0)52

A stone's throw away from Slovenia and Italy, Poreč sits on a tiny peninsula jutting into the azure Adriatic. The town is brimming with gorgeous Gothic and Romanesque houses, unique 6th-century Byzantine mosaics, Roman ruins, and, unfortunately, throngs of tourists. Nevertheless, this foreign influx gives the town a kind of internationally festive flair, and Poreč proves a fun stop as you island-hop down the coast.

☐ TRANSPORTATION. The **bus station,** ul. K. Hoguesa 2 (☎43 21 53), sends buses to **Pula** (1hr., 8 per day, 36kn); **Rijeka** (2hr., 5 per day, 59kn); **Rovinj** (1hr., 6 per day, 27kn); **Zagreb** (6hr., 4 per day, 159kn); **Koper, SLN** (30min., 3 per day, 52kn); **Ljubljana, SLN** (5hr.; Aug. 3 per day, June-July and Sept. 2 per day, Oct.-May 1 per day; 121kn); **Portoroz, SLO** (1.5hr, 2-3 per day, 41kn); **Trieste, ITA** (2hr., 3 per day, 59kn).

■ ☑ ORIENTATION AND PRACTICAL INFORMATION. Poreč is easy to navigate. The main pedestrian walkway, **Decumanus,** begins at **Trg Slobode** and runs through **Stari Grad** (Old Town), which is lined with shops, cafes, and restaurants. To reach the central Trg Slobode, turn left out of the bus station, walk down the street, and take a right onto the pedestrian Milanovića. The **tourist office,** Zagrebačka 9, is up the road and to the right from Trg Slobode and should be your first stop for **free maps,** accommodation info, bus schedules, and pamphlets galore. It also has one computer with **free Internet access** (limit 15min.), but the connection is temperamental and you'll need to be prepared to wait. (☎45 12 93; www.istra.com/porec. Open May-Oct. M-Sa 8am-10pm, Su 9am-1pm and 4-10pm; Nov.-Apr. daily 8am-4:30pm.) **Zagrebačka Banka,** Obala M. Tita bb, by the sea, **exchanges cash** for no commission, cashes **traveler's checks** for 1.5% commission, and provides **Western Union** services. (☎45 11 66. Open M-F 7:30am-7pm, Sa 8am-noon.) There is a MC **ATM** and a **currency exchange** machine outside. Other MC/V ATMs are available throughout the Old Town. **Luggage storage** is available at the bus station. (Open daily 5-9am, 9:30am-5:30pm, and 6-9pm; 15kg 5kn, 15kg 10 kn). The **pharmacy** is at Trg Slobode 13. (☎43 23 62. Open daily July-Sept. 7:30am-10pm; Oct.-June M-Sa 7:30am-8pm.) The **tourist office** (see above) provides **Internet access.** Connections at **Cybermac,** around the corner, are slow and expensive. (☎42 70 75; 25kn per 30min., 42kn per hr.; open M-Sa 8am-midnight, Su 10am-midnight). The **post office,** Pino Brudicin 1, is opposite the church. (☎43 18 08. Open M-F 8am-noon and 7-10pm, Sa 8am-1pm.) **Postal Code:** 52440.

▐ ☐ ACCOMMODATIONS AND FOOD. Accommodations in Poreč are abundant but expensive, particularly if you're staying less than three nights. Nearly every fifth building in Poreč books private rooms, but ask the tourist office for recommendations. **Eurotours,** Nikole Tesle 12, has comparably decent rates and a huge stock of rooms, ranging from the city center to the hinterlands of Poreč. (☎45 15 11; eurotours@pu.hinet.hr. Open daily June-Aug. 7:30am-10pm; Sept.-May 8am-2pm and 5-9pm. Singles 100-200kn; doubles 160-250kn; apartments 160-280kn. 50% more for stays under 3 nights, 30% more for under 4. Registration fee 15kn. Tourist tax 4.5-7kn.) **Hotel Poreč ❺**, R. Končara 1, has modern and clean rooms with TV, fridges, and telephones. (☎ 45 18 11; www.hotelporec.com. July-Sept. 12 singles 365-448kn, doubles 578-684kn; Sept. 13-June 243-266kn/364-410kn. 20% more for stays under 3 nights. Tourist tax 4.5-7kn. AmEx/MC/V.) Both of the following **camping grounds** offer a range of services (grocery stores, restaurants, laundromats, and sports facilities) and are accessible by the same bus from the station (25min., 9 per day, 12kn). The large **Lanterna Camp ❶** is 13km to the north and has a 3km beach. (☎40 45 00. Open Mar.-Oct. 20-40kn per person, 41.50kn per tent, with electricity 51kn.) Save on your laundry bill at the nudist camp and apartment village **Solaris ❶**. (☎40 40 00. Open Mar.-Oct. Camping 41.60kn per person, 58.50-77.30kn per tent or car. Apartments 353-405kn.)

Ulixes ❷, Decumanus 2, peaceful and away from the main tourist strip, offers a daily replenished selection of fresh meat and seafood, like the house specialty, sea devil fish (95kn). The beautiful outdoor terrace overlooks the stone walls of Stari Grad. (☎45 11 32. Entrees 60-110kn. Open daily noon-3pm and 6pm-midnight.) While it doesn't have Ulixes's atmosphere, **Gostionica Istra ❷**, Milanovića 30, by the bus station, sells delicious fish, meat, and pasta dishes. (☎43 46 36. Entrees 25-80kn. Open daily noon-10pm.) **Nono ❶**, down the street from the tourist office on Zagrebačka 4, serves a variety of massive pizzas. (☎45 30 88. Pizza 25-45kn. Open daily noon-midnight.) Perched atop the tower, **Caffe Torne Rotunda** provides a post-card-perfect view of Poreč's tiled rooftops and bright ocean. (Macchiato 8kn. Open daily 10am-1am.) **Konzum supermarket** is at Zagrebačka 2, next to the church at Trg Slobode. (☎45 24 29. Open daily 7am-10pm.)

🅖 **SIGHTS.** From Trg Slobode, walk down to the **Pentagonal Tower** (Peterokunta Kula), built in 1447 as a city gate. Continuing down Decumanus, turn right on Sv. Eleuterija to find the 6th-century ▨**St. Euphrasius' Basilica** (Eufrazijeva Bazilika), which was placed on UNESCO's World Heritage list in 1997 for its preserved **mosaics**. Across from the basilica entrance stands the octagonal baptistry and **belltower**, which you can climb for a view of the tiled roofs of Poreč. (Services held Su 7:30, 11am, 7pm; M-Sa 7:30am and 7pm. Open daily 9am-7pm. Basilica free. Belltower 10kn.) Don't miss the **museum,** to the right of the basilica entrance. Housed in the ancient bishop's palace, the museum displays fragments of the intricate floor mosaics from the original chapel floor, as well as other historical treasures. (☎091 521 78 62. Open daily 10am-3pm and 4-7pm. 10kn.) Returning to Decumanus, head down through Trg Marator and toward the right to the pile of stones and columns on the left side that was once the Roman **Temple of Neptune,** constructed around the AD 1st century. A stroll left along Obala m. Tita, next to the ocean, brings you to the **Round Tower,** a 15th-century defensive structure.

🅲🅙 **BEACHES AND ENTERTAINMENT. Beaches** in Poreč, as along most of the Istrian coast, are steep and rocky but offer convenient tanning shelves cut into the shoreline. The best sites near town are south of the marina. Hop on the passing **mini-train** (9am-11pm every 35min., 15kn), or face the sea on Obala m. Tita, turn left, and head along the coast for about 15min. to reach the **Blue Lagoon** (Plava Laguna). Walk another 10min. to get to the **Green Lagoon** (Zelena Laguna). Or, from the bus station, go straight to the Green Lagoon (10min., 7 per day, 9kn). These resorts offer **waterslides, tennis,** and **minigolf,** most of which are open to non-guests. To escape the crowds, continue past the Green Lagoon toward the marina (30min.). A ferry (every 30min. 7am-1am, round-trip 15kn at kiosk nearby) leaves from the marina for the less popular, quieter **Saint Nicholas Island** (Sveti Nikola), just across the harbor. The trip is worth it if you're looking for a secluded rock shelf. However, if it's a scenic beach you crave, stick to the mainland. To see more of the coast, rent a **bike** (15kn per hr.) from **Ivona**, Prvomajska 2, a block up from the tourist office and across Trg J. Rakovca. (☎43 40 46. Open M-Sa 8am-1pm and 4-7pm, Su 8am-1pm.) Ask for a free bike map. Its two marked trails take you through more than 50km of olive groves, forests, vineyards, and medieval villages.

■ **NIGHTLIFE.** Any beach that has a name also has a hotel complex and a disco, invariably frequented by (mostly German) tourists of all ages. To dance with a young and more local crowd, take a 10min. walk south down the beach past the marina to the open-air, Roman-columned **Colonia Iulia Parentium.** (☎51 89 41. Open daily June 4-Sept. 4 9pm-4am.) **Club No. 1,** Trg Marafor 10, the coolest of a cluster of little bars and cafes at the end of Decumanus, stays lively throughout the week with wild cocktails and a dance floor inside. (Cocktails 35-45kn. Open daily 6pm-4am.) Say hello to the cardboard cut-out of Humphrey Bogart on your way to **Bar Casablanca,** Eufrazijeva 4. Outdoor seating lines the narrow street in the shadow of nighttime crowds, while smoky portraits hanging on the bar's interior pay homage to the man himself. (☎45 31 31. Beer 8-20kn. Open daily 9am-1am.)

ROVINJ ☎(0)52

Purported to be one of the healthiest places in the world at the beginning of the 19th century, Rovinj (ro-VEEN; pop. 15,000) was the favorite summer resort of Austro-Hungarian emperors. Vacationers still bask in the town's unspoiled beauty. Once Istria's most important fishing settlement and a fortress for the Venetian Navy, Rovinj's crystal-clear waves provide a pleasant setting for a quiet getaway.

▐ TRANSPORTATION

With no train station, Rovinj sends **buses** to **Poreč** (1hr., 7-10 per day, 27kn); **Pula** (1hr., 2 per hr., 25kn); **Rijeka** (3½hr., 8-11 per day, 90kn); **Zagreb** (5-6hr., 9 per day, 150kn); **Belgrade, SMN** (13hr., 2 per day, 325kn); **Ljubljana, SLN** (5hr., high season 1 per day, 146kn); **Skopje, MAC** (420kn, M and F 1 per day, 23hr.); **Trieste, ITA** (2½hr., 2-3 per day, 90kn). **Bikes** are available at **Bike Planet,** Trg na Lokvi 3, across the street from the bus station. (☎81 11 61. 20kn per hr., 70kn per day. Open M-Sa 8:30am-12:30pm and 5-8pm.) The tourist office (see below) has **free maps** for suggested bike routes 22-60km in length.

▟ ▟ ORIENTATION AND PRACTICAL INFORMATION

Turn left out of the bus station and walk down Nazora toward the marina or up on Karera to **Stari Grad.** Street signs and numbers are often difficult to find or non-existent, but the town is small enough that you cannot stay lost for long.

Tourist Office: Turistička Zajednica Rovinj, Pino Budičin 12 (☎81 15 66; www.tzgrovinj.hr). From the station, walk down Nazora to the sea and follow the waterfront on the right for 10min. Rovinj's official tourist agency provides a free brochure packed with valuable info. Open daily June 16-Sept. 8am-9pm; Oct.-June 15 8am-4pm. **Globotours,** Rismondo 2, offers **free maps**. Open daily 9am-8pm.

Currency Exchange: Istarska Banka (☎81 32 33) on Aldo Negri , cashes all major **traveler's checks, exchanges currency** for no commission, and offers **Western Union** services. Open M-F 7:30am-7pm, Sa 7:30am-noon.

ATMs: In front of Privredna Banka, N. Quarantaotto 48, on the right off Nazora just before the waterfront. Open 24hr. ATMs are also in the town center near Stari Grad.

Luggage Storage: ☎81 14 53. In the bus station on M. Benussi. Ask for the *garderoba* service at the ticket counter. 10kn, over 30kg 15kn. Open 6:30am-8:30pm.

Pharmacy: Gradska Ljekama (☎81 35 89). With your back to the bus station, turn right on M. Benussi. Open M-F 7:30am-9pm, Sa 8am-4pm, Su 9am-noon. AmEx/MC/V.

Internet Access: Tourist Agency Planet, Svetog Križa 1 (☎84 04 94). A small store past the tourist office and right after Veli Jože (see p. 186), has 2 terminals. 4kn per 10min. Open M-Sa 10am-1pm and 6-10pm, Su 6-10pm. If they're full, **Caffe Bar "Aurora,"** Prolaz M. Maretic 8 (☎83 03 33), has more computers but is farther from the center. From the bus station, walk up Carducci, past the small church on the right and turn left on Lorenzetto. The cafe is set back from the road on your right, across the park. Before you email, try an Istra bitter vodka (10kn) to get those creative juices flowing. 30kn per hr. Open daily 9am-9pm.

Post Office: ☎81 14 66. Go right from the bus station. **Poste Restante** and **telephones** available. Open M-F 7am-9pm, Sa 8am-noon, 6-9pm. **Postal Code:** 52210.

⌂⌂ ACCOMMODATIONS AND FOOD

As usual, your best bet for a budget room is to search for a **private room.** Across the street from the bus station, friendly **Natale,** Carducci 4, offers decent prices and high-quality double rooms in and around the center. Call ahead in the summer. It also **exchanges currency** and cashes **traveler's checks** for no commission. (☎81 33 65; www.rovinj.com. Doubles 180-200kn; 2-person apartments 230-300kn. Prices double for only 1 night; 50% more for 2; 30% more for 3. Registration 20kn. Open July-Aug. M-Sa 7:30am-9:30pm, Su 9am-9:30pm; Sept.-June M-Sa 7:30am-8pm, Su 8am-8pm.) For solo travelers, **Globotours,** Rismondo 2, offers a modest selection of single rooms. (Singles 120-180kn; doubles 180-260kn. Open daily 9am-8pm.) The sprawling **Hotel Monte Mulini** ❸, A. Smareglia bb, offers clean but worn rooms. Facing the sea at the end of Nazora, walk to the left all the way past the marina and go up the stone steps on your left. (☎81 15 12; fax 81 58 82. Breakfast included. July 31-Aug. 20 singles 255-293kn; doubles 438-512kn; July 17-30 237-275kn/401-476kn; June 26-July 16 and Aug. 21- Sept. 3 226-264kn/379-454kn; May 29-June 25 and Sept.4-Sept. 10 189-227kn/306-381kn; May 15-228 and Sept. 11-Oct. 1 160-197kn/248-323kn. Breakfast and dinner included. AmEx/MC/V.) For those with tents, **Camping Polari** ❶, 2.5km east of town, also has a supermarket and several bars. To get there, take one of the frequent buses (6min., 9kn) from the bus station. (☎80 15 01; fax 81 13 95. July-Aug. 100kn per person, June 85kn per person.)

Don't miss the seafood hot spot ▨**Veli Jože** ❸, Svetog Križa 3, at the end of the marina past the tourist office. Enjoy some of the best food around amid funky maritime artifacts, including a primitive deep-sea diving suit. Prices vary by season, but you can usually get first-rate fish for 250kn per kg. (☎81 63 37. Open M-Su noon-2am. AmEx/MC/V.) For a great deal and filling meal, head across the street to **Stella di Mare** ❷, S. Croche 4, with its terrace overlooking the ocean and huge pizzas. (Pizzas and pastas 25-65kn. Seafood 40-120kn. Open daily 10am-11pm. AmEx/MC/V.) Buy **groceries** at Nazora 6, between the bus station and the sea. (Open M-Sa 6:30am-8pm, Su 7-noon.) There is an **open-air market** on Trg Valdibora with fruit, vegetables, cheese, and homemade liquor, which you can sample for free. (Open daily 6am-10pm.)

◉ SIGHTS

Although Rovinj has been surrounded by walls since the 7th century, only three of the original seven gates—**St. Benedict's, Holy Cross,** and the **Portico**—survive today. When entering the Old Town, you'll probably walk through the **Balbijer Arch** (Balbijer luk), a Baroque structure built on the site of the 17th-century outer gate, just off Trg Maršala Tita. Narrow streets and old houses packed on the tiny peninsula lead uphill to the 18th-century **St. Euphemia's Church** (Crkva Sv. Eufemije), built when

Rovinj was a fortress under the Venetian Navy. During Roman Emperor Dio-cletian's reign, Euphemia and other Christians were imprisoned and tortured for refusing to deny their faith. The 15-year-old martyr survived the torture wheel, but not the pack of lions. Amazingly, the beasts left her body intact and her fellow Christians encapsulated it in a **sarcophagus.** The vessel made its way to Constanti-nople but disappeared in 800—only to float mysteriously back to Rovinj later that year. Today, Euphemia is the patron saint of Rovinj, and her sarcophagus, behind the right altar, is often visited by locals, particularly on St. Euphemia's Day (Sept. 16). The rickety stairs up to the **belltower** (61m) lead visitors to a majestic view of the city and sea (10kn). During the summer, the lawn outside hosts many classical music performances that comprise part of Rovinj's seasonal celebrations. (Church free. Open M-Sa 10am-2pm and 4-6pm, Su 4-6pm. Services Su 10:30am and 7pm.)

The **City Museum of Rovinj,** Trg Maršala Tita 11, has changing displays, including local modern art, archaeological exhibits, and three millennia worth of local paint-ings. (Open Tu-Sa 9am-noon and 7-10pm; low season Tu-Sa 10am-1pm. 15kn.) Boats anchored in the harbor are eager to take off on trips to the 22 nearby **islands** (around 50kn) or to the strikingly beautiful **Lim Fjord** (around 50kn), a flooded can-yon that separates Rovinj from Poreč. You can buy tickets at the tourist office or from boat owners. Prices and departure times vary by boat.

🎵 🍷 ENTERTAINMENT AND NIGHTLIFE

For the best beaches in the area, take a ferry to **Red Island** (Crveni Otok; 10min., 17 per day, 20kn). Nude sunbathing is permitted. On the mainland, reach natural rock shelves by walking left past the marina for 30min. and cutting through **Golden Cape** (Zlatni vrt). Alternatively, join locals on the patios cut into the peninsula for sunset seating. Ferries from the marina also go to beaches on **Katarina Island** (7min., 1 per hr. 5:45am-midnight, 10kn). At night, Rovinj's cafe culture springs to life. Most of the action takes place along the marina. Recline in the neo-colonial decadence of 🗺**Zanzi Bar's** palmetto bushes and garden torches, next to the tourist office on the marina. This new bar attracts international trendsters with its array of cocktails (20-50kn) and swanky decor. (Open daily 8am-1am.) **Bar Sax Cafe,** Ribarski Prolaz 4, in an alley off the marina, hosts lively patrons inside and out. There's a bar but no sax. (Mixed drinks 25-35kn, .5L *Favorit* 14kn. Open daily 8am-3am.)

For three days in the last week of August, Rovinj looks to the sky for **Rovinjska noć** (Rovinj Night), its famous annual night of fireworks. On the second Sunday of August, international artists come to display their work at the traditional open-air art festival, **Grisia,** held on the street of the same name. **Kanfanar** (July 25th), a folk festival dedicated to St. Jacob, features traditional Istrian music played on the tra-ditional *mih* (bagpipes) and the *roženice* (flute), and a healthy spread of regional cuisine—wine, cheese, and the famous Istrian olive oil.

GULF OF KVARNER

Blessed with long summers and gentle sea breezes, the islands just off the coast of mainland Croatia are natural tourist attractions. While larger Krk tends to bear the brunt of the tourist invasion, Rab, which is farther south and a greater distance from the mainland, is greener, less visited, and definitely merits the longer trip.

RIJEKA   ☎(0)51

A typical sprawling Croatian port town, Rijeka (ree-YEH-kah) is a functional trans-portation hub but not exactly the prettiest stop in Croatia. It earns its keep by pro-viding access to the islands in the Gulf of Kvarner and the Dalmatian coast.

CROATIA

There is a **train station** located at Kralja Tomislava 1 (☎211 11 11; info desk open daily 7am-6:45pm). Trains run to: **Split** (7hr., 2 per day, 150kn) via **Ogulin; Zagreb** (3½hr., 7 per day, 102-117kn); **Berlin, GER** (11¾hr., 3 per day, 983kn); **Budapest, HUN** (9hr., 1 per day, 326kn); **Ljubljana, SLN** (2½hr., 4 per day, 83kn); **Vienna, AUT** (9hr., 1 per day, 430kn). **Buses**, Žabica 1, down Krešimirova, to the right of the train station (☎33 88 11. Open daily 5:30am-9pm). Buses run to: **Dubrovnik** (12hr., 3 per day, 430kn); **Krk Town** (1½hr., 13 per day, 38kn); Pula (2½hr., 1 per hr., 57kn); **Split** (8hr., 12 per day, 220kn); **Zagreb** (4hr., 1 per hr., 110kn); **Ljubljana, SLN** (3hr., 2 per day, 106kn); **Sarajevo, BOS** (13hr., 3 per week, 231kn); **Trieste, ITA** (2hr., 4 per day, 58kn). For ferry tickets, Riva 16, face the sea from the bus station and go left to Jadrolinija (☎66 61 00. Open M and W-F 7am-8pm, Tu and Sa 7am-6pm.) Ferries run to: **Dubrovnik** (18-24hr.; June-Sept. 5 per week, Oct.-May 2 per week; 233kn); **Hvar** (10-15hr., 9 per week, 187kn); **Korčula** (15-18hr., 8 per week, 210kn); **Sobra** (21hr., 2 per week, 233kn); **Split** (12hr., 7 per week, 169kn); **Zadar** (6hr., 4 per week, 115kn). All prices listed are for July; June 15% less, Sept.-May 35% less.

Free maps are available at the bus station, next to the ticket counter. For more detailed information, head to the **tourist office,** Korzo 33. From the stations, turn right onto Trpimirova, cross the street, and continue right down the pedestrian street Korzo. (☎33 58 82, www.tz-rijeka.hr. Open June 15-Sept.15 M-Sa 8am-8pm, Su 8am-2pm, closed Su Sept.16-June 14). The train station has a bank, which **exchanges currency** and cashes **traveler's checks** for no commission, and it also has an AmEx/MC/V **ATM.** (☎21 33 18. Open M-Sa 8am-8pm, Su 8am-12:30pm.) **Luggage storage** is in the train station (10kn per day. Open 9am-11am, 11:30am-6:30pm, and 7-9pm) and in the bus station (9kn, backpacks 10kn; open daily 5:30am-10:30pm), along with a **24hr. restaurant,** an overpriced **grocery store,** and **currency exchange.**

If you need to stay in Rijeka, the closest hotel to the train and bus stations that offers reasonable rates is **Prenoćište Rijeka ❸,** 1. Maja 34/1. With your back to the train station, turn right on Krešimirova and left on Alessandra Manzonia. As you continue up the hill for 5min., the road becomes 1. Maja. Look for a small white sign on the right. A concrete monster from the outside, the hotel has convenient but worn rooms with balconies and less-than-clean shared bathrooms. (☎55 12 46; www.zug.hr. Reception 24hr. Singles 200kn, with bath 280kn; doubles 270kn/ 550kn. AmEx/MC.) **Viktorija ❶,** Manzoni 1a, on the left as you head to the hotel, serves a good selection of grilled specialties (29-85kn) and pizza. (☎33 74 16. Open M-Sa 7am-11pm, Su noon-11pm.) A large, reasonably-priced **supermarket** is in the building next door, to the right of the train station. (Open daily 6am-10pm.)

KRK ISLAND: KRK TOWN ☎(0)51

Croatia's largest island, Krk is only a short ride across the Krk Bridge. Its mountains and valleys are most stunning toward its southern end, in the town of Baška. While Baška reels in a large catch of tourists, Krk Town remains more peaceful. Both towns' hiking trails and hidden coves lend them an undiscovered feel.

▮ TRANSPORTATION. Krk Island's main inter-island transport hub and the gateway to the rest of Croatia make it an excellent base for visits to the rest of the island. Buses run from Rijeka to **Krk Town** (1½hr., 10-16 per day, 37kn), and most continue to **Baška** (40min., 5-9 per day, 19kn). Jadrolinija operates a **ferry** between Baška and Lopar on the northern tip of Rab Island (1hr., 4 per day, 31kn, car 140kn, bike 30kn; June-Aug. only). The **bus station** (☎22 11 11) is at Šetalište Sv. Bernardina 1. Walk left along the sea to Stari Grad and its main square, **Vela placa.** The tourist and travel agency **Autotrans,** Šetalište Sv. Bernardina 3, next to the bus station, **exchanges currency** and cashes **traveler's checks** for no commission. (☎22 26 61; fax 22 21 10. Open M-Sa 8am-9pm, Su 9am-1:30pm.)

🔳🖪 ORIENTATION AND PRACTICAL INFORMATION. Ereste Bank, on Trg b. Josipa Jelačića, up and left of Vela pl., offers **Western Union** services and has a MC/V **ATM.** (Open M-F 8am-8pm, Sa 8am-noon.) Another ATM is outside the **supermarket** on Šetalište Sv. Bernardina bb, behind the bus station. (Open daily 7am-9pm.) There's a **pharmacy** at Vela pl. 3. (☎22 11 33. Open M-F 7:30am-9pm, Sa 7am-1pm and 6-8pm, Su 9am-noon. AmEx/MC/V.) **KRK Sistemi,** on the second floor of the bus station, provides **Internet access.** The entrance is on the opposite side of the building from where the buses depart. (10kn per 20min. Open daily June-Sept. 9am-2pm and 6-11pm; Oct.-May 9am-8pm.) The **post office,** Trg b. Josipa Jelačića bb, gives MC **cash advances** and has **telephones** outside. (☎22 11 25. Open M-F 7am-8pm, Sa 7am-2pm.) **Postal Code:** 51500.

🖪🖪 ACCOMMODATIONS AND FOOD. Autotrans (see above) books private rooms. (July-Aug. singles 85-115kn, doubles 128-219kn, low season 70kn/117-146kn. 30% surcharge on stays under 4 days. Registration 10kn. Tourist tax 4.5-7.5kn.) *Sobe* and *apartman* signs line Slavka Nikoliča and Plavnička, but before you climb the hill, be forewarned that many owners deal only through agencies. The tree-covered **Autocamp Ježevac ❶,** Plavnička bb, is a 7min. walk from the bus station away from Stari Grad with the sea to the left. (☎ 22 10 81; www.jezevac@zlatni-otok.hr. July 19-Aug. 28 33.50kn per person, 23kn per tent, 20kn per car. June 28-July 18 32kn/22kn/19kn. Apr.-June 27 and Aug. 30-Oct.15 24.50kn/16.50kn/16kn. Registration 8kn. Daily tax 4.5-7kn.) Although touristy at first glance, **Galeb ❷,** Obala hrvatske mornarice bb, serves delicious Adriatic standards, including the fabulous *pureći odrezak* (turkey with rice, curry, and pineapple; 65kn), on a terrace overlooking the marina. Its salad bar is a rare sight in Croatia. (Meat entrees 35-80kn. Vegetarian dishes 30-40kn. Open daily 9am-midnight.)

🔳 SIGHTS. This drowsy town's main attraction is its 14th-century fortification, **Kamplin,** which is visible at the **South Town Gate** (Mala Vrata), the entrance to Stari Grad on the marina. The waters around Krk Town offer more excitement than the town itself. **Fun Diving Krk,** Lukobran 8, leads underwater expeditions throughout the year. (☎/fax 22 25 63. Dives 170-300kn; daytrip dives 285kn, with equipment 430kn; full-day snorkel trip 100kn. Equipment rental 10-80kn per piece. Open daily 8am-1pm and 2-7pm.) The town's **beach** is next to the diving center. Less populated, cleaner beaches are farther away, in **Autocamp Ježevac** (see above).

RAB ISLAND: RAB TOWN   ☎(0)51

Even after centries of Byzantine, Venetian, and Hungarian rule, Rab still boasts ruins from the original Roman city, constructed under Emperor Augustus during the first century BC. If the whitewashed stone houses and the scent of rosemary from backyard gardens don't seduce you, the island's thriving nightlife and beautiful beaches will. Unlike rocky-shored Krk, Rab is blessed with long stretches of sandy coastline, so you can leave your shoes at home.

🔳 TRANSPORTATION. Getting to and from Rab can be difficult, particularly in the low season, so plan ahead, consult tourist agencies, and be prepared for frustration. If you're traveling during the summer months (mid-June to September), it's easiest to take the **Jadrolinija ferry** between **Rijeka** (1½hr., 4 per week, 90kn) and **Novalja** (35min., 4 per week, 35kn) via Rab. Alternatively, a ferry runs between **Baška,** on Krk, and **Lopar,** on the northern tip of Rab Island (June-Sept. only, 1hr., 2-5 per day, 31kn). From the drop-off, walk 10min. down the road to the bus stop to catch the bus to Rab Town (30min., 5-11 per day, 15kn). Check the bus and ferry schedules beforehand, as they tend to be poorly timed. From Rab, buses go to **Rijeka** (3hr., 2-3 per day, 96kn) and **Zagreb** (5½hr., M-Sa 4 per day, 157kn). If you're planning to continue your journey south along the coast by land, catch a Zagreb- or Rijeka-bound bus to **Živi Bunari** (45min., 5 per day, 37kn). Tell the driver your destination, and he'll drop you off on the *magistrala* (highway) where southbound buses stop. To ensure that there will be a southbound bus to your destination there to pick you up, have the Rab ticket office check the schedule. The only buses guaranteed to come are those serving major cities, like Split and Zadar. (Office open M-Sa 5:45am-12:45pm, 1:15-4pm, and 4:30-7:45pm, Su 10:30am-5pm.)

■ ⁊ ORIENTATION AND PRACTICAL INFORMATION. Rab Town is the island's historical center and main destination. The peninsular **Stari Grad** is organized around three parallel streets: **Gornja** (Upper), **Srednja** (Middle), and **Donja** (Lower). To reach them from the **bus station** (☎72 41 89), turn left on Mali Palit, walk downhill, then turn right and walk along the waterfront. The **ferry stop** is at the far right side of the marina, at the tip of Stari Grad. The friendly, English-speaking staff at the **tourist office, Turistička Zajednica**, Trg M. Arbae, across from the ferry stop, provides **free maps** of the area and deciphers tricky ferry schedules. There is also a **branch** to the right and around the corner from the bus station at Mali Palit. (☎77 11 11; www.tzg-rab.hr. Both open daily 8am-10pm.) **Ereste Bank**, also on Mali Palit, **exchanges currency** for no commission. It also has **Western Union** services and cashes **traveler's checks** for 1.5% commission. (Open M-F 8am-noon and 6-8pm, Sa 8am-noon.) There is a 24hr. (AmEx/MC/V) **ATM** outside the bank and another off Trg Sv. Kristofora. The **pharmacy** is next to the bus station. (☎/fax 72 54 01. Open M-Sa 8am-9pm, Su 9-11:30am. AmEx/MC/V.) **Internet access** is available at **Digital X**, Donja 4. (☎77 70 10. 0.50kn per min. Open M-Sa 10am-2pm and 6pm-1am, Su 6pm-1am.) Go toward the water from the tourist office at Mali Palit to find the **post office**, Palit bb, which has **Poste Restante**, gives MC **cash advances**, **exchanges currency**, and cashes **traveler's checks** for a 1.5% commission. **Telephones** inside. (Open M-F 7am-9pm, Sa 8am-noon and 6-9pm.) **Postal Code:** 51280.

⁊❑ ACCOMMODATIONS AND FOOD. Katurbo, M. de Dominisa 5, on the waterfront one block from the bus station toward the center, arranges **private rooms.** (☎72 44 95; www.katurbo.hr. Open daily July-Aug. 8am-9pm; Sept.-June 8am-1pm and 4-9pm. July-Aug. singles 60-100kn, doubles 120-200kn; Sept.-May 50-70kn/100-140kn. 30% more for stays under 3 nights. Tourist tax 7kn. Also rents **bikes,** 20kn per hr.) **Hotel Istra ❹**, M. de Dominisa bb, is a reasonably priced, modern hotel that sits just off the waterfront. (☎72 41 34; fax 72 40 50. Breakfast included. Reception 24hr. July 24-Aug. 20 320kn; July 3-23 and Aug. 21-27 266kn; June 19-July 2 and Aug. 28- Sept. 10 236kn; April 1-June 18 and Sept.11-Nov. 1 190kn.) In nearby Banjol, **Camping Padova ❶** has its own sandy beach and is often packed. To get there, take the bus heading toward Barbat (10min., 7 per day, 8kn) or walk left along the shore for 2km. (☎72 43 55; fax 72 45 39. July 12-Aug. 22 36.20kn per person, 26.20kn per tent, 7kn tax per day; June 21-July 11 and Aug. 23-Sept. 1 30kn/23.90kn/7kn; Apr. 1-June 20 and Sept. 2-Oct. 15 23.10kn/17.70kn/5.50kn. Registration 4.50kn.) **▧St. Maria ❷**, Dinka Dokule 6, a narrow extension of the street Srednja Ulica, specializes in such Hungarian titillations as *gulaš* (goulash; 50kn) and *punjena paprika* (stuffed bell pepper; 45kn), served either in the elegant medieval courtyard or indoors amid nautical decor. (☎72 41 96. Entrees 50-90kn. Open daily 10am-2pm and 5pm-midnight.) **Buffet Harpun ❶**, on a quiet stretch of Donja bb, treats you to friendly service and tasty fish and meat specialties. (☎82 27 43. Entrees 30-70kn. Open daily 10am-midnight.) A **supermarket,** Dalit 88, is next door to the post office. (Open daily 6am-10pm.)

◙ **SIGHTS.** The best way to see the sights of Rab is to stroll along scenic Gornja Ulica to the end of the peninsula. Walking down Gornja takes you from the remains of St. John's Church (Crkva Sv. Jvana), a Roman basilica, to the ruins of the Church of the Holy Cross (Crkva Sv. Križa). Its icon of Jesus is said to have wept. Farther down, Gornja leads to Trg Slobode and to St. Justine's Church (Crkva Sv. Justine), which houses a museum dedicated to Christian art. (Open daily 10am-12:30pm and 7:30-10pm. 5kn. Services Su 7:30 and 10am.) For an aerial view of the town, climb the steep ladders to the top of the bell tower of the 13th-century St. Mary's Church (Crkva Sv. Marije), and peek into the nuns' lush garden. (Open daily 10am-1pm and 7:30-10pm. 5kn.) The 12th-century Virgin Mary Cathedral (Katedrala Djevice Marije) and the nearby 14th-century St. Anthony's Monastery (Samostan Sv. Antuna), farther down Gornja, complete the tour of the historical quarter. For more info, pick up a free pamphlet from the tourist office.

◪ ◙ **BEACHES AND NIGHTLIFE.** Beaches aren't difficult to find. Komrčar, a park and cemetery, lies along the base of Stari Grad peninsula and offers shade as well as a rock beach. To reach the sandy beach aptly named Sahara, take a bus to San Marino (25min., 9 per day, 15kn) and ask someone to point you in the right direction. Signs mark the trail to this bathing suit-optional beach (20min.). Escape the crowds and the kids by exploring the beautifully clear rocky beaches on the western tip of the island. Taxi boats run hourly to Frkanj (20min, round-trip 20kn), which has its own nudist colony, while buses run a bit farther out to the secluded coves of the Suha Punta peninsula (4 per day, 20min., 14kn). Other beaches include Supetarska Draga, Kampor, and Barbat, all of which can be reached by bus and 30min. walk or on bicycle (20kn per hr., 60kn per 5hr.) rented from a local outfit (ask at the tourist office for a map). In general, sand beaches are on the north side of the island, rocky beaches on the west, pebble beaches on the east.

Cafes abound in Rab. The most popular spot among local youth is the street cafe and club **Le Journal,** on Donja just off Kristofor trg. Hipsters gather here to throw back a few heavy-hitting "Le Journal" cocktails (20-25kn) and hear the latest underground music. (Open nightly 7pm-2am.) Closer to the waterfront, **San Antonio,** Trg Municipium Arbae, throws a fine fiesta, with two bars and an open dance floor inside. (☎ 72 11 45. Coffee 5-10kn. Mixed drinks 30-45kn. DJs spin F-Sa. Open daily 8am-4:30am.) The **Grand Restaurant,** just past Trg Sv. Kristofora, is restaurant by day, cafe by night. It hosts live cover bands and an older crowd on its outdoor terrace. (Open daily 8am-midnight.)

DALMATIAN COAST

A seascape of unfathomable beauty set against dramatic backdrop of sun-drenched mountains, the Dalmatian Coast has become synonymous with heavenly vistas and unparalleled tranquility. Stunning blue waters delicately wash onto endless stretches of rocky beach, and even during the busiest travel seasons, many parts of the coast remain the perfect refuge from the bustle of urban Europe. With more than 1100 islands (only 66 are inhabited), Dalmatia is Croatia's largest archipelago, and boasts the cleanest and clearest waters in the Mediterranean.

ZADAR   ☎(0)23

Zadar (pop. 77,000), the administrative center of northern Dalmatia, hides its many scars well. Allied attacks destroyed Zadar during WWII and the recent war (1991-1995) shattered much of what had been rebuilt. Residents have restored their

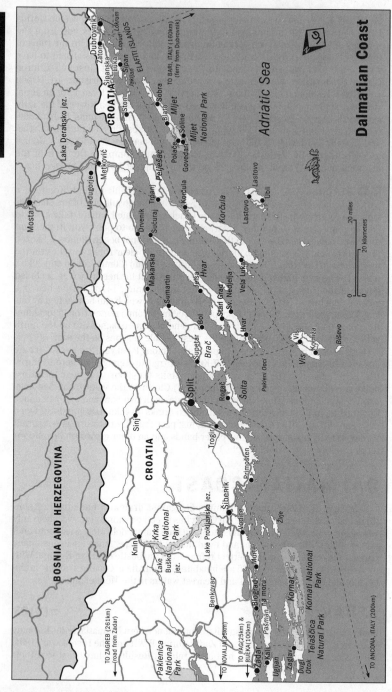

CROATIA

Dalmatian Coast

Adriatic Sea

CROATIA

BOSNIA AND HERZEGOVINA

Dubrovnik
Zaton
Šipanska Luka
Lokrum
Lopud Šipan
ELAFITI ISLANDS
TO BARI, ITALY (160km)
(ferry from Dubrovnik)
Ston
Janjina
Sobra
Blato
Mljet
Polače
Soline
Goveđari
Mljet
National Park
Pelješac
Trpanj
Korčula
Korčula
Lastovo
Ubli
Lastovo
Drvenik
Sućuraj
Makarska
Jelsa
Hvar
Sv. Nedjelja
Vela Luka
Sumartin
Bol
Stari Grad
Hvar
Superar
Brač
Vis
Komiža
Vis
Biševo
Split
Rogač
Šolta
Pakleni Otoci
Trogir
Primošten
Sinj
CROATIA
Šibenik
Vodice
Žirje
Krka
National
Park
Lake Prokljansko jez.
Knin
Lake
Buško
jez.
Murter
Betina
Benkovac
Biograd na moru
Pašman
Kornat
Kornati National
Park
Kornati National
Natural Park
TO ZAGREB (261km)
(road from Zadar)
TO NOVALJA (35km)
TO PAG (25km) &
RIJEKA (100km)
Zadar
Kali
Ugljan
Zaglav
Dugi
Otok
Telašćica
Paklenica
National
Park
TO ANCONA, ITALY (200km)

Mostar
Međugorje
Metković
Lake Deransko jez.

20 miles
20 kilometers

homes yet again and the city now stands beautifully rejuvenated. With the extraordinary Kornati Islands just a boat ride away and a history so well preserved that Roman ruins serve as city benches, Zadar is the quintessential Dalmatian city.

⌨ TRANSPORTATION

Trains: Ante Starčevića 4 (☎31 92 12). To **Zagreb** (5-7hr., 3 per day, 90-130kn). Info office open M-F 7:40-10:30am and 11:30am-3:40pm. Closed holidays.

Buses: Ante Starčevića 2 (☎221 10 35, schedule info 21 15 55). More reliable than trains. To: **Dubrovnik** (8hr., 9 per day, 155-207kn); **Rijeka** (4½hr., 1 per hr., 129kn); **Split** (3hr., 2 per hr., 77-80kn); **Zagreb** (5hr., 1 per hr., 103-117kn); **Ljubljana, SLN** (8hr., 1 per day, 207kn); **Sarajevo, BOS** (6hr., 1 per day, 197kn); **Trieste, ITA** (7hr., 2 per day, 150kn).

Ferries: Depart from Liburnska Obala, 5min. up the peninsula from the pedestrian bridge. **Jadrolinija** (☎25 48 00; fax 25 03 51) has ferry info and sells tickets. The branch at the tip of the peninsula handles ferries operating beyond the local islands of Dugi Otok and Ugljan. Open M 7am-11pm, Tu 7am-9pm and 11:30pm-12:30am, W 6am-8pm, Th 7am-9pm, F 6am-12:35am, Sa 6:30am-9pm, Su 6am-1pm and 3:30-11pm. To: **Dubrovnik** (16hr., 3-5 per week, 157kn); **Korčula** (12hr., 4 per week, 119kn); **Rijeka** (7hr., 4 per week, 97kn); **Split** (6hr., 4 per week, 97kn); **Ancona, ITA** (8hr., 3-5 per week, 306kn).

Public Transportation: Schedules for buses (M-Sa every 15-20min., Su and holidays 1 per hr. 5:30am-11pm) are posted at the main bus station and at most stops. Station names are rarely posted at each stop; ask for help. Buy tickets from the driver (6kn) or any kiosk (round-trip 10kn) and validate on board.

✳❓ ORIENTATION AND PRACTICAL INFORMATION

Most of the city's businesses and sights are scattered along **Široka,** the main street in **Stari Grad.** The **bus** and **train stations** are at Ante Starčevića 1. To get to Široka from there, with your back to the main entrance, go through the pedestrian underpass and continue straight until you hit **Zrinsko-Frankopanska.** Follow this street (and the signs to the "Centar") all the way to the water, then walk along the left side of the harbor to the first gate of Stari Grad. Široka branches off **Narodni trg** to the right after you pass through the gate. Alternatively, hop on bus #2 or #4 to Poluotok. Facing the water, head right to the main gate opposite the footbridge.

Tourist Office: Tourist Board Zadar, M. Klaića bb (☎31 61 66; tzg-zadar@zd.tel.hr). Go straight along the road from the main gate to the far corner of Narodni trg. Offers free detailed **maps** and a helpful info booklet about Zadar. Open daily 8am-8pm.

Currency Exchange: Nosa Banka, Trg Sv. Stošije 3 (☎29 09 59), on Široka, exchanges currency for no commission and cashes **traveler's checks** for 1.5% commission. Also has **Western Union** services. Open M-F 8am-8pm, Sa 8am-noon.

Luggage Storage: At the bus station; follow the *garderoba* signs. 1.20kn per hr.; over 15kg 2.20kn per hr. Open daily 7am-9pm. Closer to Stari Grad, **Bagul Garderoba,** opposite the local Jadrolinija office on the waterfront, also stores luggage. 3kn per hr., 15kn for full day. Open M-F and Su 7am-8pm, Sa 7am-3pm.

Pharmacy: Ljekarna Center, Barakovića 2 (☎21 33 74). Open M-F 7am-8pm, Sa 8am-noon.

Internet Access: Gradska Knjižnica Zadar (Zadar City Library), Stjepana Radića 116 (☎31 57 72). Cross over the pedestrian bridge and continue 2 blocks; the library is on your left. 10kn per hr., 10kn min. Open M-F 8am-7pm, Sa 8am-1pm. The quick connections and central location of **Netcafe,** S. Ljubavća 6, are worth the extra kunas (25kn per hr.). To get there, take M. Klaića off Narodni Trg (see **Tourist Office**), turn left on Kovačka, and take the 2nd right on S. Ljubavća. Open daily 7am-10pm.

CROATIA

Post Office: Nikole Matafara 1 (☎25 05 06), off Široka, has **telephones** inside and gives MC **cash advances. Poste Restante** at the main post office, Kralja Držislava 1 (☎31 60 23). Open M-Sa 7am-7pm. **Postal Code:** 23000.

▮ ACCOMMODATIONS

Zadar has a youth hostel, but it's far from Stari Grad and you may ultimately end up spending a good deal on bus tickets. If you're a party animal, your best option might be a **private room** in the center of town. Occasionally, *sobe* (room) signs crop up on the waterfront, but a more reliable option is the **Aquarius Travel Agency,** inside the main gate at Nova Vrata bb. From the bus station, take bus #2 or 4 to Poluotok. Facing the water, go right and head to the second city entrance on your right across from the footbridge. (☎/fax 21 29 19; www.jureskoaaquarius.com. Open daily 7am-10pm. Singles 100-150kn; 2-person apartments 250-300kn. Tax 5.50-7kn.)

Omladinski Hostel Zadar, Obala Kneza Trpimira 76 (☎33 11 45; www.hfhs.hr), on the waterfront at the outskirts of town. From the station, take bus #5 heading to Puntamika (15min., 6kn) or bus #8 to Diklo (20min., 6kn), ask the driver to let you off at the 1st stop after Autocamp Borik. Walk left toward the marina. This huge harborside complex has plenty of dorm rooms along with a bar and sports facilities. Breakfast included. Reception 8am-10pm. Check-out 10am. Call ahead. July 1-Aug. 29 97kn; June and Aug. 30-Sept. 19 86kn; May and Sept. 20-Oct. 10 81kn; Nov.-Apr.7 1kn. Tourist tax 5.5-7.5kn. Non-HI members 11.5kn extra per night. ❶

Autocamp Borik, Gustavo Matoša bb (☎33 20 74; fax 33 20 65), on the beach. Follow directions to Hostel Zadar and look for large signs on the right. Ample, clean sites, but the trees don't quite block the road noise. July-Aug. 52.5kn per person, 60kn per tent, 75kn per car. Tax 7.50kn. May-June and Sept. 37.5kn/45kn/52kn/50kn/5.50kn. ❶

▮ FOOD

The **Konzum supermarket** has several branches, including Široka 10 and J. Štrossmayerova 6. (Both open M-Sa 6:30am-10pm, Su 7am-8pm.) A **market** on Zlatarska, below Narodni trg and past the cinema, sells produce, meat, cheese, and bread; it also doubles as a densely packed flea market. (Open daily 6am-2pm.)

Foša, Kralja Dmitra Zvonimira 2 (☎31 44 21), named after the inlet upon which it sits outside the city walls. Grills up sizable portions of fresh fish (45-160kn) and meat (55-75kn) on a wide patio overlooking the bay. The atmosphere is romantic after sundown. Open M-Sa 11am-midnight, Su 5pm-midnight. ❷

Restaurant Dva Ribara (Two Fishermen), Blaža Jurjeva 3 (☎21 34 45), off Plemića Borelli, is a local favorite. In addition to the ubiquitous Croatian standards, this mythical duo offers leafy salads, vegetarian plates (30-38kn), and a colorful array of pizzas (30-50kn). Open daily 10:30am-midnight. ❶

Gostionica Zlati Vrtič, Borelli 12 (☎21 10 76), serves meat (45-75kn) and fish dishes (50-120kn) in a pebbled courtyard. You can watch the cook's culinary performance over the old-fashioned, open-air grill. Open daily 7am-11pm. ❷

▮ SIGHTS

The most storied area in Zadar is the ancient **Forum,** a wide-open square ornamented with haphazardly arranged stone relics, located on Široka in the center of the peninsula. In the evenings, watch out for the kiddies driving around the ruins in their rented mini play-cars. Built in Byzantine style at the beginning of the 9th century, **St. Donat's Church** (Crkva Sv. Donata) sits atop the ruins of an ancient Roman temple; the ruins are still visible from inside. Today, the building remains one of only three circular Catholic churches in the world. Although no longer a place of worship, it is still used by Zadarians for the occasional high school graduation. (Open daily 9am-2pm and 4-8pm. 5kn.) **St. Mary's Church** (Crkva Sv. Marija), Trg Opatice Čike 1, across the square and toward the water from St. Donat's, is a more traditional place of worship. It houses the fabulous **Permanent Exhibition of Religious Art** (Stalna Izložba Crkvene Umjetnosti). Its gold and silver busts, reliquaries, and crosses are regarded as some of Croatia's most precious artifacts—shrewd nuns keep a close watch over visitors. (☎21 15 45. Buy tickets to the left of the church. Open M-Sa 10am-1pm and 6-8pm, Su 10am-1pm. 20kn, students 10kn.) Next to St. Mary's stands the **Archeological Museum** (Arheološki Muzej), which documents the epochal history of Zadar with aerial photographs of towns and archaeological sites, beautiful medieval stonework, and innumerable shards of prehistoric pottery. (☎25 05 16. Open M-F 9am-1pm and 6-9:30pm, Sa 9am-1pm. 10kn, students 5kn.) Though smaller, the **National Museum** (Narodni Muzej Zadar) offers a more accessible and entertaining view of the city's history. Scale models of Zadar chronicle the city's development through the centuries. From St. Mary's, follow the same street to the other side of peninsula; the museum is on the right. (☎25 18 51. Open M-Tu and Th-F 9am-2pm, W 9am-2pm and 5-7pm. 5kn, students 3kn.) Though it may strain your pocketbook, consider taking a guided boat tour of **Kornati National Park.** The going rate for a full daytrip (8:30am-6:30pm) is 250kn and includes breakfast, lunch, and mixed drinks. Each of the dozen or so agencies offer essentially the same tour for the same price. Either book directly through the many kiosks that line the waterfront and try to talk the price down or consult the tourist office (see **Orientation and Practical Information,** p. 193) for additional details. These tours are the only way to venture into the unique park: it's home to 365 islands, almost completely uninhabited, and the famous saltwater **Silver Lake.**

ENTERTAINMENT AND NIGHTLIFE

Kino Pobjeda, on Jurja Dalmatinca just off Narodni trg, shows mainstream English-language movies with Croatian subtitles in an enormous theater. (Screenings daily 6:30-11pm. 12-25kn. Later screenings are more expensive.) For a taste of high culture, Zadar hosts classical and medieval music concerts in beautiful St. Donat's Cathedral every night in July. Contact the tourist office for details. Although Zadar is an early-to-bed, early-to-rise kind of town, you can always find a late-night party at **Central Kavana,** Široka 3, the trendiest and liveliest venue around. CK is a kaleidoscope of funky lights and decor, including hanging blue bicycles, orange TVs, and sewing machines. Live music on weekends ranges from jazz to reggae. Internet access 30kn per hr. (Mixed drinks 20-35kn. ☎21 10 41. Open M-Th 7:30am-midnight, F-Su 7:30am-1am.) Perfect for a casual sunset drink, **Caffe Bar Forum,** on Široka at the Forum, has comfortable chairs and outdoor seating overlooking the ruins. (0.33L *Karlovačko* 13kn. Open daily 7:30am-midnight.) For a loud twenty-something scene, check out the cafes along **Varoška,** just off of Špire Brusine.

PAG ISLAND

Pag draws together a strange mix of barren expanses and lush green coastline. Pag Town is made up of low white buildings set dramatically on one side of an artificial isthmus wedged between the mountains. Novalja, the "Beverly Hills of Croatia," attracts celebrities looking to soak up some sun during the summer months. Often overlooked by tourists, Pag retains an authentic Croatian flair.

PAG TOWN ☎(0)23

While Pag Town's moon-like terrain appears harsh in the daytime sun, it gains an unearthly beauty as dusk falls. The town and its traditions have been left largely unaltered by the tourist economy, making it a pleasant change from the Miami Beach-like coast. *Paška čipka*, the famous local lace, is still sold straight from the skilled hands of its elderly makers. With smaller crowds and a relaxed lifestyle, Pag's residents are among the friendliest you'll find anywhere along the Adriatic.

TRANSPORTATION. Pag Town has a **bus stop**, but no station. Buses run to: **Zadar** (1hr., 3 per day, 30kn); **Rijeka** (4hr., 2 per day, 125kn); **Zagreb** (6hr., 6 per day, 146kn). If you're on a southbound bus from smaller towns along the coast, you'll need to ask the driver to drop you off at Prizna. Walk 2km down to the water and catch a **ferry** to Zigljen on Pag Island. Buses to Pag Town meet the incoming ferries.

ORIENTATION AND PRACTICAL INFORMATION. To reach the center from the bus stop, face the sea and walk left along the waterfront. Turn left on Vela ul. to get to the main square, **Trg Kralja Krešimira IV.** Pag's center is miniscule, so getting around is easy. For those without internal compasses, **free maps** are available at the **tourist office**, Katine bb, on the waterfront past Vela ul. by the pedestrian bridge. (☎/fax 61 13 01. Open daily 7am-9pm.) **Erste Bank**, Vela ul. bb, on the way to the main square, has an **ATM** outside. (Open M-F 8am-noon and 6-9pm, Sa 8am-noon.) There's a **pharmacy**, S. Radića bb, on the waterfront one block beyond the tourist office. (☎61 10 43. Open M-Sa 7:30am-1pm and 5-9pm.) **Buša**, Kraljaz-vronmir 5, just beyond the right side of the main square, has **Internet access.** (25kn per hr. Open daily 9am-1pm and 7-11pm.) The **post office,** two streets behind the bus stop at A.B. Šimića, **exchanges currency** and cashes **traveler's checks** for no commission. **Telephones** inside. (☎61 10 33. Open M-Sa 7am-9pm.) **Postal Code:** 23250.

ACCOMMODATIONS AND FOOD. Accommodations in Pag are limited, particularly for solo travelers. Apartments are more readily available than rooms but are also much more costly. The helpful staff at **Mediteran ❷**, Vladimira Nazora 12, opposite the bus station, will try their best to find you a private room or apartment. (☎61 12 38; www.mediteran-pag.com. Rooms 120-150kn per person.) Those with tents can head down to **Autocamp Šimuni ❶**, which offers some of the best **camping** beaches on the island, although it's a long way to either Pag Town or Novalja. To get there from the town, grab a Zagreb-bound bus; ask the driver to let you off at Šimuni (20min., 5 per day), then follow the signs downhill. (☎69 74 40. July-Aug. 98kn per person; May-June and Sept. 58kn per person. Tourist tax 5kn.) If convenience is your priority, the pricey **Hotel Pagus ❺** offers clean and spacious waterfront rooms next door to the bus station. (☎61 13 20; hotelpagus@coning.hr. Doubles July 24-Aug. 8 680kn, July 3-24 610kn, June 19-July 3 and Aug. 21-28 500kn, June 2-19 and Aug. 28-Sept. 4 480kn, June 5-12 and Sept. 4-11 290kn. 30% more for stays less than three nights. Breakfast included. AmEx/MC/V.)

Follow the locals to **Na Tale ❷**, S. Radića 2, next to the pharmacy, and eat well amid boisterous Croatian families. Choose from pasta and risotto (25-65kn), *Kotlet sa žara* (grilled cutlet; 44kn), and many other tasty entrees. (☎61 11 94. Veggie plates 36kn. Meat entrees 45-82kn. Open daily 8am-11pm.) Hidden one road behind the main square, the terrace restaurant **Tamaris ❸**, Križevaćka bb, serves up the local favorite *Paška pletenica* (meat Pag-style; 60kn), in addition to typical island seafood fare. (☎61 22 77. Open daily 6:30am-11pm. AmEx.) For groceries, stop by **Minimarket Golija,** across from the post office. (Open M-Sa 7am-9pm, Su 7am-12pm.) The **produce market** is in front of Tamaris. (Open daily 6am-10pm)

CROATIA

ENTERTAINMENT AND NIGHTLIFE. Every year, during the last weekend of July, Pag's main square hosts the town's **summer carnival**. Locals dress up in the traditional costume *Paška Naškja*. Women sport triangular headdresses, fashioned from Pag lace, and perform the two-by-two folk dance *Paška Kolo*. On the last day, watch the ceremonial "Burning of Marco"—the burning of a sealed coffin symbolizing the year's sins. If you can't find your own spot of sand among the reclining bodies on the **beach**, try the pebbly **Gradska Plaža** (Town Beach), right across the bridge from Stari Grad. For more secluded tanning spots, walk farther down the coast. Alternatively, follow the waterfront past Hotel Pagus to reach the beaches on the opposite side of the bay, or if it's sand you're craving, take a day-trip to the famed **Zrće**, near Novalja.

Bars and cafes line the waterfront between the bus stop and the tourist office. Join a young and laid-back crowd at **Kamerlengo**, Jadrulićeva Br. 1. *Karlovačko* and *Ožujsko* (12kn per 0.5L) complement the soothing lighting and the mellow dance music. (Open daily 8am-1am.) Most cafes close around 1am, but fear not: the party continues across the bridge at the newly renovated **disco**, at the historic warehouse V Magazin. The 500-year-old party zone comes complete with ancient stone walls, disco balls, themed raves, and all of the party-goers of Pag Island. Just past the disco, on the water, the open-air, thatch-roofed **Cafe del Sol** is a great place to watch night fall over the mountains. (Mixed drinks 17-38kn. Open daily 8am-1am.)

NOVALJA ☎ (0)53

With its famous Croatians and equally famous sandy beaches, this modern summer resort stands in contrast to more modest Pag. Although less typically Dalmatian in architecture and character than some of its neighboring Adriatic towns, Novalja's posh yet peaceful feel makes it an old favorite of Croatians and an up-and-coming destination for foreigners.

TRANSPORTATION. The **bus station**, Slatinska ul., sends buses to: **Pag Town** (40min., 5 per day, 20kn); **Rijeka** (3hr., 2 per day, 100kn); **Zadar** (1½hr., 5 per day, 52kn) **via Pag Town**; **Zagreb** (5hr., 3 per day, 135kn). Mid-June through September, a Jadrolinija **catamaran** runs from Novalja to **Rijeka** (2hr., 4 per week, 100kn) with a stop at **Rab Town** (30min., 35kn). A small **boat** runs from Lun, on the northern tip of the island, to Rab Town (1hr., 1 per day, 35-40kn), but you'll need to catch a **taxi** (☎ 886 13 66) to Lun (20min.).

ORIENTATION AND PRACTICAL INFORMATION. To reach the town center from the bus station, face the main road and walk left on **Slatinska** through its name change to **Petra Krešimira IV** and continue to **Trg Loža**. Along the way, **Kompas,** Slatinska bb, offers info about excursions and books rooms and apartments. Farther down the road and across the street, the incredibly helpful **Tourist Office of Novalja** has **free maps**, info booklets, and ferry and bus schedules. (☎/fax 66 14 04. Open daily 7am-11pm.) **Exchange currency** and cash **traveler's checks** for no commission at **Croatia Osiguranje,** just past Trg Loža on Krešimira IV. (☎ 66 26 62. Open daily 7:30am-10:30pm.) A 24hr. (AmEx/MC/V) **ATM** stands next door, in front of **Ereste Bank.** (☎ 66 13 21. Open M-F 8am-noon and 6-9pm, Sa 8am-noon.) There is a **pharmacy** at Dalmatinska 1, off Krešimira IV. (☎ 66 13 70. Open M-Sa 8am-1pm and 5-9pm, Su 10am-noon and 7-8pm.) For **Internet access,** head to **Cafe La Paloma,** off the main square and across from the vegetable market on Trg Bazilike. (☎ 66 19 60. 20kn per hr. Open daily July-Aug. 7am-11pm; May, June, and Sept. 7am-1pm, 5-11pm) The **post office** is around the corner from Ereste Bank, facing the water. There are **telephones** inside. (☎ 66 11 18. Open M-F 7am-9pm, Sa 8am-noon and 6-9pm.) **Postal Code:** 53291.

▶◉ ACCOMMODATIONS AND FOOD. There are two hotels in Novalja, but you can save money by shopping around for **private rooms** or **apartments.** "Sobe" signs are abundant along Slatinska, from the bus station to the main square. If you're having trouble finding accommodations, travel agency **Kompas,** Slatinka bb, can help out, but will cost about 20kn more than if you find a room on your own. (☎66 12 15; www.navajlija-kompas.hr. Singles and doubles June 26-Aug. 18 190kn, Aug. 19-June 25 146kn. Open daily in summer 8am-10pm.) One of the best values in town, **Pansion Maria ❷,** Krešimira IV, has comfortable rooms with big beds, balconies, and private baths. If you're a light sleeper, ask for a room toward the back—those facing the road tend to be somewhat noisy. From the bus station, face the main road and walk left 5min. (☎66 13 73. Breakfast 25kn. Singles 100kn; doubles 160kn. 30% more for stays under 3 nights.) Campers can head to **Autocamp Straško ❶,** which has its own rock beach and nude camping area. The truly adventurous can participate in activities from aerobics to minigolf in their birthday suits. Bring your own tent; leave your inhibitions. From the main bus station, with your back to the playground, turn left on Zeleni Put, and turn left again at the reception sign 500m down. (☎66 12 26; www.turistdd.hr. July-Aug. 42.50kn per person, 38.80kn per car, 31.20kn per tent; May-June 29.70kn/25.90kn/33kn; Sept. 28.20kn/25.10kn/21.30kn. Tax 4.50-7kn, registration 5kn.) **Hotel Loža ❺,** along the shore by Trg Loža only seconds from the nighttime action, is more upscale and clothing-friendly. (☎66 13 26; fax 66 13 04. Breakfast included. Doubles July 24-Aug. 13 475-600kn, July 3-23 and Aug. 14-20 548-569kn, June 19-July 7 and Aug. 21-Sept. 3 360-443kn, June 5-18 and Sept. 4-10 315-378kn, Sept. 11-June 4 253-315kn. AmEx/MC/V.)

Restaurants in Novalja tend to be excellent. A local favorite, the charming **Bistro Stefani ❷,** opposite the tourist office, serves up a delectable grilled turkey breast with stuffed with four cheeses (55kn), and other Pag-style house specialties. (☎66 16 97. Entrees 25-80kn. Open daily 7am-midnight. AmEx/DC.) Through town past the post office along Braće Radic on your right, **Starac I More ❷** (Old Man and the Sea) puts you in the mood for fresh seafood (50-140kn) aboard their wooden "ship-deck." It also serves pasta (50-70kn) and risotto. (☎66 24 23. Open daily noon-midnight. AmEx/MC/V.) For cheap and tasty brick-oven pizza (18-45kn), large salads (30-49kn), and freshly baked bread, head to **Moby Dick ❶,** across the street and to the right from the tourist office on Krešimira IV. (☎66 24 88. Open daily 10am-1am.) There is an open-air **fruit and vegetable market** in the center of town on Trg Bazilike, above Trg Loža. (Open daily 7am-10pm.)

▶◉ ENTERTAINMENT AND NIGHTLIFE. June 13 is **Novalja/St. Anton's Day,** which honors the town's patron saint. Local dancers perform to the *mih,* a sheepskin bagpipe-like instrument unique to Dalmatia. **Zrće** is the most famous **beach** near Novalja; take advantage of **paddle boating, kayaking, parasailing,** and the **Blato,** a natural mineral spa. In July and August a minivan and trolley run from the front of the bus station to **Zrće** (4km) and other beaches. (10 per day, 9kn.) Otherwise, get there by renting a **bicycle** (20kn per hr., 90kn per day) or **scooter** next to Hotel Loža. Walk left along the water from the bus station to reach the sandy beach, **Plaža Lokunje,** or head farther along the coast to **Straško** (15min., entrance fee 10kn per person if you are not staying at the campsite). In July and August, people go out every night, starting at midnight. Head to ▣**Cocomo,** opposite the tourist office at Krešimira IV 9, a chic Caribbean-themed bar and disco that keeps the night alive. (Drinks 15-35kn. Open daily 8am-5am.) Out on Zrće, **Kalypso** (www.novalja.com/kalypso) nearly owns the beach. The thatched-roof venue is a combination disco, bar, volleyball court, and massive party house. Things get pumping around midnight and don't stop until the sun comes up. (Beer 5-15kn. Open 24hr.)

ŠIBENIK ☎(0)22

Facing the magnificent bay of Šibenicka Luka at the mouth of the Krka River, Šibenik (pop. 40,000) slips under the average tourist's radar. The few who venture here are rewarded with a town of nightlife-loving locals, winding medieval streets, and one of the most beautiful cathedrals on the Adriatic.

⌷ TRANSPORTATION. The **bus station** is at Drage bb. (☎21 20 87. Open daily 6:30am-9pm.) Buses go to: **Dubrovnik** (6hr., 8 per day, 167kn); **Split** (1½hr., every 30min. 5am-11:30pm, 43-53kn); **Zadar** (1½hr., 20 per day, 40kn); **Zagreb** (6hr., 14 per day, 124kn); and **Ljubljana, SLN** (7hr., 1 per day, 204kn).

◪ ⯑ ORIENTATION AND PRACTICAL INFORMATION. While much of new Šibenik sprawls across the hills rising from the harbor, **Gorica Grad** (Old Town) is packed tightly on a steep face overlooking the water. To get to Gorica Grad from the **bus station,** face the water and walk right along the waterfront (5min.). Gorica Grad's confusing maze of alleyways is cut by **Kralja Tomislava,** which runs diagonally uphill from the waterfront at the base of **St. Jacob's Cathedral.** This road leads up to the main traffic artery, **Kralja Zvonimira,** which serves as a border between the Old and New Towns. **Vladimira Nazora** goes uphill from the water near the bus station and connects with Kralja Zvonimira.

The **tourist office,** Obala Dr. Franje Tudmana 5, is on the waterfront between the bus station and Gorica Grad, past Vladimira Nazora. The enthusiastic staff provides **free maps** and info about excursions. (☎21 44 11; www.summernet.hr. Open daily May-Sept. 8am-8pm; Oct.-Apr. M-F 9am-2pm.) **Jadranska Banka,** on Trg Kralja Državislava, **exchanges currency** for 1% commission, cashes **traveler's checks** for no commission, and has a 24hr. **ATM** outside. (☎33 33 88. Open M-F 7:30am-8pm, Sa 7am-12:30pm.) There is also a MC/V **ATM** on the far side of Kralja Zvonimira, diagonally opposite Trg Poljana. **Luggage storage** is available at the bus station. (1.20kn per day, bags over 15kg 2.20kn. Open daily 6am-10pm.) The main **pharmacy, Ljekarna Varoš,** is at Kralja Zvonimira 20. (☎21 22 49. Open M-F 7am-8pm, Sa 7am-2pm.) Check email at the funky **Da Noi Internet Club,** Trg Jurja Barakovića 3, the third street on your left after Pizzeria Kike (see below) off Kralja Tomislava; signs point the way. Connections are slow but are the only option in town. (0.5L Karlovaćko 15kn. 24kn per hr. Open M-Th 8:30am-11pm, F-Sa 9am-1am, Su 3-11pm.) The **post office,** Vladimira Nazora 5, has **telephones.** (☎21 49 90. Open M-Sa 7am-8pm, Su 7am-2pm.) **Postal Code:** 22000.

⌷⌷ ACCOMMODATIONS AND FOOD. Private rooms are the best option in town. To find one, try **Cromovens Travel Agency,** Trg Republike Hrvatske, by the cathedral. (☎21 25 15; www.cromovens.hr. Singles 100-180kn; doubles 150-220kn. Prices are highest late June-Aug. Open M-F 8:30am-3:30pm and 5-8pm, Sa 9am-2pm). For a prime location on the waterfront near the cathedral, **Hotel Jadran ❺,** Rivijera bb, offers spacious rooms with A/C, satellite TV, and private showers. Some have sea views. (☎21 81 55, www.rivijera.hr. Breakfast included. July-Aug. singles 390kn; doubles 640kn; June and Sept. 350/586kn; low season 300/500kn. Tax 3.50-6kn.) Campers should make their way to **Autocamp Solaris ❶,** on the Zablaće peninsula across the bay, where **beaches** abound. Take a local bus from the station to Solaris (10min., every 2hr. 8am-10pm, 8kn) and ask the driver to drop you off at the camp. (☎36 40 00; www.solaris.hr. July-Aug. 29kn per person, 64kn per tent or car; tax 6kn. May-June and Sept.-Oct. 28kn/52kn/4kn.)

Thre are few food options. If you can't stand the thought of another pizza or pile of fries, head to **Steak House No. 4 ❷,** Trg Dinka Zavorivića, up from Zagrebaćka ul. and hidden behind the church. It offers a light, fresh mozzarella salad (25kn) or hearty meat and vegetable entrees for 50-150kn. (☎21 75 17. Open daily 8am-1am.) The peppy folks at **Pizzeria Kike** (kee-keh) ❶, Durija Sižgorića 3, serve pizza (27-50kn) in a quiet courtyard off Kralja Tomislava. (☎33 01 41. Open M-Sa 7am-11pm, Su 3-11pm.) A huge **Kerum Supermarket** is at Kralja Tomislava 8. (Open M-Sa 6:30am-8pm, Su 7am-1pm.)

◉🗗 SIGHTS AND ENTERTAINMENT. The Gothic-Renaissance **Cathedral of St. Jacob** (Katedrala Sveti Jakova) is Šibenik's pride. This massive masterpiece, made entirely of white stone by sculptor **Juraj Dalmatinac,** has a view of Gorica Grad. Dalmatinac, a Zadar native, took over construction of the cathedral in 1432, but it was completed only in 1536 by his pupil, Nikola Firentinac. The intricate dome designed by Firentinac and the frieze of 71 heads on the exterior walls of the apses are striking examples of their incredible artistic talent. (Open daily May-Oct. 8am-7pm. Services daily 9am and 7:30pm. Additional services Su 9:30 and 11am.) For a spectacular view of the town, harbor, outlying islands, and distant Kornati, climb up to the crumbling **St. Ana Fortress** above Gorica Grad. (Open 24hr. Free.)

Šibenik has no seaside sand, but a short bus ride to **Zablaće** (10min., 1 per hr. 7am-8pm, 8kn), across the harbor, takes you to a number of **pebble beaches.** Daily boat excursions to **Kornati** (see **Zadar: Sights,** p. 194) are available from the nearby town of **Murter,** which is accessible by bus (15min., 8 per day, 14kn). Contact the **Kornata Agency,** Rudina 1 in Murter, one day in advance. (☎43 54 47. Open daily 8am-10pm. Excursions daily 9am-6pm. 250kn per person, including lunch, drink, and park ticket.) A number of travel agencies in Šibenik offer similar packages but for 20-70kn more per person. The cultural event of the year is the **International Children's Festival,** held during the last week of June and the first week of July. The line-up includes a kiddie demolition derby, a nightly program of children's films, puppet performances, and children's theater. International performers headline during the first week, while dancers and local comedians take over the second. Contact the tourist office for schedules and prices.

�◨ NIGHTLIFE. Welcome to one of the best nightspots on the Dalmatian Coast. For the wildest dance club on this stretch, take a nighttime excursion to ▨**Aurora.** Take a Split-bound bus (12-16kn) to **Primošten,** 35min. south of Šibenik, follow the stream of partyers back up the hill to the main highway, and turn right. (15-20min. from the bus stop). Fliers advertise Aurora's special weekend events that feature house and techno DJ masters from around the world. When in need of revival after hours of dancing, an in-house pizzeria and chill-out room await you. Although the Aurora and its dedicated following stay up all night, the last bus back to Šibenik leaves at 12:30am; bus service resumes at 6am, (☎57 08 36. www.auroraclub.hr. Open Th-Sa 8pm-6am. Call ahead for event schedule.) Back in town, Šibenik parties every night of the week, and the party happens in **Dolac,** a neighborhood by the waterfront. Facing the water from Gorica Grad, turn right and walk along the harbor, past the cathedral and straight into the crowds and the competing beats. In July and August, it can feel like Croatian Mardi Gras. For techno and a spot above the crowds, try **Domald,** Obala Prvoboraca 3. (0.5L Guinness 40kn. Tu live music, DJs Th-Sa. Open daily 7am-late.)

TROGIR ☎(0)21

Trogir (pop. 1500), a tiny island between the mainland and the much larger Otok Čiovo, is a sheltered spot along the coast. Perfect for a daytrip or short excursion from Split, the town's medieval buildings crowd winding streets while palmed promenades open onto parks and the blue sea. Now a popular hangout for sailors

CROATIA

exploring Dalmatia, Trogir has been an attractive and coveted destination throughout history. As early as the 13th century, Renaissance artists ventured here and stayed, building countless churches. In 1997, Trogir earned a coveted place on the UNESCO World Heritage List.

TRANSPORTATION. The **bus station** (☎88 14 05) is on the mainland. Many **buses** from **Rijeka, Zadar,** and **Zagreb** stop at Trogir on their way south to **Split** (30min., 22kn); buses stop in front of the station, so make sure to wait outside. You can also take local bus #37 from Trogir to Split and back (30-45min., 2-3 per hr., 18kn). All the buses that pass through Trogir heading north stop in Šibenik (45min., 31kn). There are **no ferries** to or from Trogir. To check **bus schedules** and find out about ferries to other towns, head across the Čiovski bridge to **Atlas,** Obala kralja Zvonimira 10. The staff clears up bus confusion and sells tickets for boats and flights to and from **Split.** (☎88 42 79 or 88 13 74; fax 88 47 44. Open M-Sa 8am-9pm, Su 8am-noon and 5-8pm; low season M-Sa 8am-7pm, Su 8am-noon.)

ORIENTATION AND PRACTICAL INFORMATION. The town spills from the mainland across short bridges to two islands. **Stari Grad** (Old Town) is on the small island of Trogir; behind it lies Čiovo, which has the town's best beaches, accessible by the Čiovski bridge. The main street, **Gradska ulica,** is a short walk from the bus station across the tiny bridge, to the left of the stone **North Gate,** and to the right of the post office. Gradska leads past the central square, **Trg Ivana Pavla,** to the Čiovski bridge.

The gracious staff at the **tourist office, Turistička Zajednica Grada Trogir,** Trg Ivana Pavla 2, give out **free maps** of the city. (☎/fax 88 14 12. Open M-Sa 8am-9pm, Su 8am-noon and 5-7pm.) **Zagrebačka Banka,** Gradska Vrata 4, just past the North Gate, **exchanges currency** for no commission and cashes **traveler's checks** for 2% commission. (Open M and W 8am-2pm, Tu and Th 1-7pm, F 2-7pm, Sa 8am-noon.) There is a MC/V **ATM** outside the bank and an AmEx/MC/V **ATM** at Gradska 15, near the tourist office. The main **pharmacy** is at Gradska 23. (☎88 15 35. Open M-F 7:30am-9pm, Sa 7:30am-1pm and 6-9pm, Su 8am-noon. AmEx/MC/V.) **Internet access** is available at **Online Club,** Matije Gupa 4, past Zagrebačka; follow the signs and look for the smiley faces on the walls. (20kn per hr. Open daily 9am-1pm and 5-9pm.) **Cafe Bar Online Club,** at ACI Marina across the Čiovski bridge and to the right along the waterfront, is also wired. (24kn per hr. Open daily 7am-midnight.) **Telephones** are inside the **post office,** B. Jurjeva Trogiranina 1. The post office also gives MC **cash advances,** exchanges cash for 1.5% commission, and cashes **traveler's checks** for no commission. It also provides **Western Union** services. (☎88 14 52. Open M-Sa 7am-8pm, Su 8am-1pm.) **Postal Code:** 21220.

ACCOMMODATIONS AND FOOD. The best deals in the center of town are **private rooms,** arranged by **Čipko ❷,** Gradska 41, opposite the cathedral, through a stone archway and to the back. (☎/fax 88 15 54. Open daily 8am-8pm. July-Aug. singles 200kn, doubles 330kn; tax 7.50kn. May-June and Sept. 150kn/250kn/ 5.50kn.) To get to beachside **Hotel Saldun ❶,** Sv. Andrije 1, cross the Čiovski Bridge and walk straight on Pt. Balana, which winds up the hill; keep to the right and Saldun will be at the top (about 10min.). Half of the small rooms have balconies overlooking the harbor; all have clean, shared bathrooms. (☎80 60 53. Breakfast 28kn. Reception 24hr. Call ahead. 76kn per person. Tax 6kn.) **Vila Sikaa ❺,** Obala Kralja Zvonimira 13, sits on the water just across the Čiovski Bridge. It's worth the cash to bask in this lap of luxury. The modern rooms have full amenities. (☎88 12 23; www.vila-sikaa.hr. Breakfast included. Reception 24hr. Reserve 10 days ahead. July-Aug. singles 470kn; doubles 500-600kn; Sept.-June 420kn/450-550kn.)

CROATIA

Stari Grad is filled with tourist-oriented eateries of similar price and quality. For something different, head over the Čiovski Bridge and take a right to find **Bistro Lučica ❷**, Kralja Tomislava bb. A favorite among the marina crowd, this bistro grills seafood and meat delights (25-180kn) on the outdoor barbecue and plays country favorites in the background. (☎88 56 33. Open M-F 9am-midnight, Sa-Su 4pm-midnight. AmEx/MC/V.) The small **Čiovka Supermarket**, Obala v. Bakarvića 11, carries groceries. (Open M-Sa 5:30am-9pm, Su 6:30am-8pm.) An enormous **Konzum** supermarket stands on A. Stepincal, at the end of the bridge opposite the North Gate by the bus station. (Open M-Sa, 7am-9pm, Su 7am-7pm.) There is also a fruit, vegetable, and meat **market** across the bridge from the bus station. (Open M-Sa 7am-3pm, Su 10am-2pm.)

🔲🔲 **SIGHTS AND NIGHTLIFE.** A statue of Trogir's patron, St. Ivan Orsini, tops the **North Gate,** a beautiful Renaissance arch that forms the entrance to Stari Grad. Most sights, including the **Cathedral of St. Lawrence** (Crkva Sv. Lovre; ☎88 14 26), are in **Trg Ivana Pavla,** at the center of the old quarter. This Romanesque basilica was begun in 1213 but was not completed until 1598. Croatian Master Radovan chiseled its famous entrance in 1240. Inside the cathedral is a small **treasury** and the Renaissance **Chapel of St. John of Trogir,** a work built between 1461 and 1497 chiefly under the guidance of Florentine architect Nikola Firentinac. Check out the accompanying **belltower** for a panoramic view of tiny Trogir; watch your step, as the tower is a popular hangout for birds. The cathedral is currently being restored, and, although restoration was scheduled to be completed in 2001, the actual date of completion remains anyone's guess. (Open daily 9am-noon and 4:30-7:30pm. Chapel free. Treasury 5kn. Tower 5kn.) For other examples of Trogir's spectacular tradition of stone-carving, visit the **City Museum of Trogir,** housed in two buildings. The first, at Gradska 49, near the cathedral, exhibits photographs and documents outlining the city's fascinating past and miscellany, like a giant wooden chicken taken as a war trophy from a Turkish ship at the 1571 Battle of Lepanto. The **lapidary,** through the arch directly in front of the North Gate, features stone sculptures by Firentinac and others. (☎88 14 06. Open M-Sa 9am-1pm and 5-9pm. 10kn, students 5kn. The museum occasionally closes due to traveling events, so call ahead to check it will be open.) If it's religious art you crave, head to **Kairos,** a collection in the convent of St. Nicholas, Gradska 2, past Trg Ivana Pavla. The centerpiece of the exhibition is a 3rd-century BC Greek relief of a figure symbolizing Kairos, god of the "fleeting moment." Be sure to step outside the city walls and admire the intricate lattice-work on the belltower of the monastery. (☎88 16 31. Open M-Sa 8am-12:30pm and 3-7:30pm. 10kn, students 5kn.) At the tip of the island are the remains of the **Fortress of Kamerlengo.** Built in 1380 by Genoans to defend the city, it now it serves as Trogir's only **cinema,** showing Hollywood flicks beneath the night sky in summer. (Open M-Sa 9am-11pm. Fortress 10kn, students free. Movies 20-25kn.) Trogir celebrates the summer with almost daily music and dance performances around town; pick up a free schedule from the tourist office.

The rocky **beach** starts below Hotel Saldun, across the Čiovski Bridge and on the other side of the hill. The beach then winds around the larger island. Generic cafes line Gradska and the waterfront, but there is only one **Big Daddy,** Obala b. Berislavića 14. Enjoy 0.33L bottles of *Zlatorog* (10kn) while you rock on swing chairs. (Cocktails 25-60kn. Open daily 8am-3am.) For a bit of gender balance, its partner in crime **Big Mummy,** next door, offers an identical menu and hours. On weekend nights, all the action goes down on this stretch. For cake, coffee, and a cathedral view, try **Radovan,** Trg Ivana Pavla 2, which has seating on the quiet terrace. (☎88 23 80. 0.5L *Karlovačko* 12kn. Coffee 5kn. Pastries 5-10kn. Gelato 3-8kn. Open daily 7am-midnight.)

SPLIT ☎(0)21

Metropolitan and bustling Split (pop. 200,000), is by no means a typical Dalmatian town. Croatia's second-largest city, it is more a cultural center than a beach resort, boasting a wider variety of activities and nightlife than any of its neighbors. Stari Grad, wedged between a high mountain range and a palm-lined waterfront, is framed by a luxurious palace where Roman emperor Diocletian spent his summers. In the 7th century, the local Illyrian population fled to the palace to escape the attacks of marauding Slavs and built a town, incorporating the walls and arches of the palace into their houses and public squares. The result is perhaps Europe's most puzzling architecture and surely one of its most interesting.

▐ TRANSPORTATION

Flights: Split Airport (☎20 35 06; fax 20 35 07) sends planes to domestic and international destinations. A bus (30kn) runs between the airport and the waterfront near the catamaran dock, Gat. Sv. Nikole, 1½hr. before each departure. **Croatia Airlines,** Obala hrvatskog narodng preporoda 9 (☎36 29 97), flies through Split Airport. Airport open M-F 8am-8pm, Sa 9am-noon.

Trains: Obala Kneza Domagoja bb (☎33 85 25, info 33 34 44). Due to the destruction of railways during the recent war, trains are very inefficient; use buses. Trains do not run south of Split. Ticket office open daily 6am-10pm. To: **Rijeka** (12hr., 2 per day, 147kn) via **Oguli; Zadar** (6½hr., 1 per day, 68kn) via **Knin; Zagreb** (7½hr., 4 per day, 143kn); **Budapest, HUN** (16hr., 1 per day, 434kn) and **Ljubljana, SLN** (12hr., 2 per week, 213kn). 25% discount with ISIC or Euro26 card.

Buses: Obala Kneza Domagoja 12 (☎33 84 83, schedule info 060 32 73 27). Domestic tickets sold inside at main counter, international tickets (međunarodni karte) in the small office to the right. Open daily 5am-11pm. To: **Dubrovnik** (4½hr., 17 per day, 125kn); **Rijeka** (7hr., 13 per day, 220kn); **Zadar** (3½hr., 2 per hr., 125kn); **Zagreb** (8hr., 2 per hr., 140kn); **Ljubljana, SLN** (11hr., 1 per day, 260kn); **Sarajevo, BOS** (7½hr., 6 per day, 142kn). Buses to **Trogir** (30min.; 3 per hr.; 18kn, round-trip 25kn) leave from the **local bus station** on Domovinskog rata, an extension of Zagrebačka.

Ferries: Obala Kneza Domagoja bb (☎33 83 33; fax 33 82 22). To: **Dubrovnik** (8hr., 5 per week, 97kn); **Korčula** (6hr., 6 per week, 32kn); **Rijeka** (10½hr., 5 per week, 140kn); **Ancona, ITA** (10hr., 4 per week, 274kn); **Bari, ITA** (25hr., 3 per week, 274kn). 25% discount with Euro26 card.

Public Transportation: Buy tickets (8kn) from the driver and punch them on board. Buses run all night but are few and far between after midnight.

Taxis: Many wait in front of Diocletian's Palace on Obala hrvatskog narodnog preporoda and at the bus station/ferry terminal. Average fare 18kn, plus 9kn per km. **Radio Taxi** (☎970 47 53 43).

▟ ORIENTATION

The **train** and **bus stations** lie on **Obala Kneza Domagoja** across from Gat Sv. Petra, where the ferries arrive. With your back to the stations, follow Obala Kneza Domagoja, often referred to as **Riva**, to the right along the water until it runs into **Obala hrvatskog narodnog preporoda,** which runs roughly east to west. Behind this boulevard, opposite the water, lies **Stari Grad** (Old Town), centered on the main square, **Narodni trg,** and packed inside the walls of **Diocletian's Palace** (Dioklecijanova Palača). To reach Stari Grad from the local bus station, go right on **Domovinskog Rata,** which becomes **Livanjska** and then **Zagreba⁻ka.** Go right on **Kralja Zvonimira** at the end of Zagrebačka and follow it to the harbor.

CROATIA

⚡ PRACTICAL INFORMATION

Tourist Offices: Turistički Biro, Obala hrvatskog narodnog preporoda 12 (☎/fax 34 71 00), sells **maps** of Split (15-30kn). Open M-F 8am-9pm, Sa 8am-10pm. **Tourist Information Center (TIC),** Peristil bb (☎34 56 06), beside the cathedral, hands out free, detailed maps of Stari Grad and brochures. Both sell the **Splitcard** (35kn, valid 72hr., free if you stay in a city-registered hotel for 3 nights or more), which is good for freebies and discounts at museums, theaters, hotels, restaurants, and shops.

Consulates: UK (☎34 60 07, emergency 091 455 53 26; open M-F 9am-1pm). **Italy,** and **Germany** all share a building, Obala hrvatskog narodnog preporoda 10, above Zagrebačka Bank. UK consulate is on the 3rd fl.

Currency Exchange: Splitska Banka, Obala hrvatskog narodnog preporoda 10 (☎34 74 23), **exchanges currency** for no commission and cashes **traveler's checks** for 2% commission. **Western Union** available. Open M-F 8am-8pm, Sa 8am-noon.

American Express: Atlas Travel Agency, Trg Braće Radić 6 (☎098 24 47 23). Open M-Sa 8am-8pm, Su 8am-noon and 6-9pm.

Luggage Storage: At the bus station kiosk marked **Garderoba.** 2.50kn per hr. Also at the train station, Obala Kneza Domagoja 6. 10kn per day. Both open daily 6am-10pm.

English-Language Bookstore: International Bookshop, Obala hrvatskog narodnog preporoda 21 (☎34 16 26). Satisfies your cravings for *Vogue, Newsweek,* and other foreign-language magazines and newspapers. Open M-Sa 8am-8pm, Su 8am-12:30pm. For a more substantial read, **Algoritam,** Bajamotijeva ul. 2, has a decent selection of novels and nonfiction in English. Books 50-150kn. Open M-F 8am-8:30pm, Sa 8am-1pm. **Žute Stranice** (see below) offers a broader array of options.

Police: Trg Hrvatske Bratske Zajednice 9 (☎30 71 11). From Stari Grad, take Kralja Zvonimira and bear right onto Pojišanka; the station is on the right.

Pharmacy: Marmontova 2 (☎34 57 38). Open M-F 7am-8pm, Sa 7am-1pm. AmEx/MC/V.

Hospital: Klinička Bolnica Split, Spinčiceva 1 (☎55 61 11). From Stari Grad, follow Kralja Zvonimira until it runs into Poljička. Turn right onto Pt. Iza Nove Bolnice; the hospital is on the right. Cash only.

Internet Access: Žute Stranice, Obala Kneza Domagoja 1 (☎33 85 48). Friendly Aussie proprietor Steve hooks you up for 30kn per hr., sells used English-language paperbacks, and gives advice on getting around. Open daily 7am-9pm. In the center of Stari Grad, **Cyber Caffe Mriža,** Kružićeva 3 has cheaper but somewhat slower connections (☎32 13 20.) 20kn per hr. Open M-F 9am-9pm, Sa 9am-2pm.

Post Office: Ul. Kralja Tomislava 9 (☎36 14 21). Mail through the main doors; **Telephones** and **fax** through the doors to the left. Also **exchanges currency** for 1.5% commission. Open M-F 7am-8pm, Sa 7am-1pm. **Poste Restante** at Hercegovačka 1 (☎38 33 65). Take Zagrebačka from Stari Grad to Domovinskog Rata and go left onto Pt. Stinica (20min.). Take a right onto Hercegovačka. Open M-Sa 7am-8pm. Buses #5, 9, 10, and 13 run here from the market; ask the driver where to get off. **Postal Code:** 21000.

🏠 ACCOMMODATIONS

For a city its size, Split has a paltry selection of accommodations—especially budget ones—because many hotels are still recovering from the war. Two of the largest hotels closed recently, although some are attempting to reopen them. The Croatian Youth Hostel Association has plans for a place in Split, but the process may take a few years. **Daluma Travel Agency,** Obala Kneza Domagoja 1, near the bus and train stations, can help find **private rooms.** (☎33 84 84; www.tel.hr/daluma-

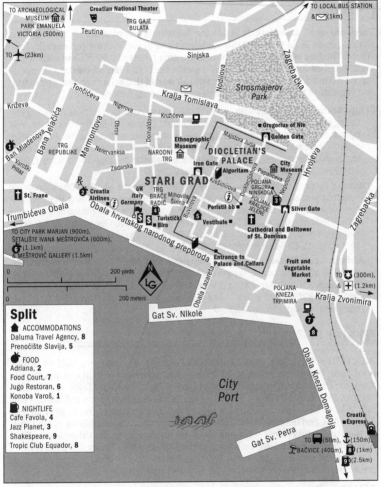

Split

🏠 ACCOMMODATIONS
Daluma Travel Agency, **8**
Prenoćište Slavija, **5**

🍴 FOOD
Adriana, **2**
Food Court, **7**
Jugo Restoran, **6**
Konoba Varoš, **1**

🎵 NIGHTLIFE
Cafe Favola, **4**
Jazz Planet, **3**
Shakespeare, **9**
Tropic Club Equador, **8**

travel. Open M-F 7am-9pm, Sa 8am-2pm. May-Oct. singles 150kn, with bath 200kn; doubles 240kn/300kn. Nov.-Apr. singles 100-120kn; doubles 200kn.) If affordability is a priority, consider staying with people who advertise at the bus station and ferry landing, offering rooms at substantially lower rates than agencies. It is advisable to take a look at any room before striking a deal—rooms are of varying quality. Moreover, Split is a sprawling city, and particularly low prices may indicate long bus rides into town. The recently renovated **Prenoćište Slavija** ❹, Buvinova 2, in the middle of Stari Grad, has 70 beds in clean, high-ceilinged rooms, all with private bath. It's right next to some of the hippest (and loudest) cafes in town. Follow Obala hrvatskog narodnog preporoda to Trg Braće Radića and head right, then right again on Mihovilova Širina. Signs lead up the stairs. (☎34 70 53; fax 59 15 58. Breakfast included. Reception 24hr. Check-out 11am. Singles 320-400kn; doubles 460-55kn; triples 610-700kn; quads 700-800kn. Tax 5.50-7kn. Registration 6kn.)

🍴 FOOD

There are small **supermarkets** inside the Jadrolinija complex across from the bus station (open M-Sa 6am-9pm, Su 7am-9pm) and at Svačićeva 4 (open daily 7am-10pm). The **food court ❶**, Obala Kneza Domagoja 1, between Stari Grad and the stations, has fast food and custom-made sandwiches. (8-15kn. Open daily 8am-midnight.) Across Kralja Zvonimira is an **open-air market** that sells everything from fruit and vegetables to clothing and cigarettes. (Open daily 6am-8pm.)

🍴 **Jugo Restoran,** Uvala Baluni bb (☎34 12 12). Facing the water on Obala hrvatskog narodnog preporoda, walk right along the waterfront (10min.) to Branimirova Obala. Veer right at the fork near the marina; signs to the restaurant lead up the hill. This modern restaurant, boasting one of the best views in Split, seduces local celebrities with excellent seafood, brick-oven pizza, and homemade Slavonian sausage. Large menu. Entrees 30-200kn. Open daily 9am-midnight. AmEx/MC/V. ❷

Konoba Varoš, Ban Mladenova 7 (☎39 61 38). Facing the water on Obala hrvatskog narodnog preporoda, head right on Varoški Prilaz and then left on Ban Mladenova. A true Dalmatian feast, prepared and served in a den adorned with fishing nets and wine racks. Stick with pasta (35-53kn) or prepare your taste buds for something different—steamed octopus (75kn), ostrich steak (80kn), or calves' hearts (42kn). Open M-F 9am-midnight, Sa-Su noon-midnight. ❷

Adriana, Obala Hrvatskog narodnog preporoda 8 (☎34 00 00). Always packed, this sprawling terrace restaurant stands out among the plethora of waterfront cafes because of ambience and quality. Serves a wide array of hearty Croatian fare ranging from fish dishes (45-320kn) and grilled meats (50-75kn) to enormous pizzas (30-40kn). Open daily 8am-midnight. AmEx/MC/V. ❷

📷 SIGHTS

DIOCLETIAN'S PALACE (DIOKLECIJANOVA PALAČA). The eastern half of Split's Stari Grad occupies the one-time fortress and summer residence of the Roman Emperor Diocletian. The colossal stone palace, built between AD 395 and 410, has seen its fair share of empires—and refugees. Having first protected Roman royalty, it later served as sanctuary for Galla Placidia, daughter of Byzantine Emperor Theodosius, and her son Valentinius III, who were dodging the blades of usurpers. In the 7th century, local residents used the fortress to protect themselves from Slavic raids, and they later built their city within its walls. Today, it's a museum of classical and medieval architecture. *(Across from the taxis on Obala hrvatskog narodnog preporoda. Go the right and down into the cool, dark corridor.)*

CELLARS. The city's haunting cellars are located near the entrance to the palace. Nearly two millennia ago, the dark stone passages served as the floor for the emperor's apartments. The central hall runs from Obala hrvatskog narodnog preporoda to the Peristyle and holds booths that sell local crafts. The hall on the left houses an interactive station that gives a wealth of history about the palace and city while entertaining visitors with Renaissance music. Some archaeological finds are displayed in hallways to the left of the entrance. The airier right side is used as a gallery that houses rotating exhibits by local artists, authors, and filmmakers. Every year the palace becomes more complete as more rooms (some right under local residences) are excavated. *(Cellars open M-F 9am-9pm, Sa-Su 10am-6pm. 8kn.)*

CATHEDRAL. The cathedral on the right side of the Peristyle is one of architecture's great ironies: it's one of the oldest Catholic cathedrals in the world but was originally the mausoleum of Diocletian, who was known for his violent persecution of Christians. It was consecrated in the 7th century when Diocletian's body was removed and replaced with St. Domnius's remains. The small, circular interior, which contains intricately wrought stonework, leaves almost no room for the tourists who come to wonder at the magnificent inner door and altar. The cathedral **treasury,** upstairs and to the right, displays 15th-century ecclesiastical garments, delicate 13th-century books, and many silver busts and goblets. Construction began on the adjoining **Belltower of St. Domnius** (Zvonik Sv. Duje), in the 13th century. It took 300 years to complete. The view is incredible, but take a buddy—the climb up the 186 steps can be a bit unnerving. *(Cathedral and tower open daily 8:30am-9:30pm. Tower and treasury 5kn.)*

OTHER SIGHTS IN STARI GRAD. Stari Grad is framed on its eastern side by the **Silver Gate** (Srebrna Vrata), which leads to the main open-air market. Outside the north **Golden Gate** (Zlatna Vrata) stands Ivan Meštrović's portrayal of **Gregorius of Nin** (Grgur Ninski), the 10th-century Slavic champion of commoners. The western **Iron Gate** (Željezna Vrata) leads to Narodni trg. Medieval architecture dominates this side of town, where many of the houses are crumbling with age and occasionally drop their stones. **Park Emanuela Victoria,** off Zrinsko-Frankopanska en route to the Archaeological Museum (see p. 207), is a great locale for a daytime stroll.

🏛 MUSEUMS

▧ MEŠTROVIĆ GALLERY (GALERIJA IVANA MEŠTROVIĆA). The gallery has a comprehensive collection of works by famed Croatian sculptor **Ivan Meštrović** (see **The Arts,** p. 161), and tremendous views of the ocean. The entrance fee includes the **gallery,** housed in a stately villa that the artist built for himself, and the 17th-century **Kaštelet,** decorated with wood carvings depicting New Testament scenes. While all of Meštrović's works are dazzlingly intricate, his marble Roman Pietà (ground floor) and agonized Job (first floor) are particularly impressive. *(Šetalište Ivana Meštrovica 46. A 25min. walk along the waterfront, or take bus #12 from the stop across from Trg Franje Tudjmana. ☎34 08 00. Open June-Aug. Su 9am-2pm, Tu-Sa 9am-1pm and 5-8pm; Sept.-May Su 10am-2pm, Tu-Sa 10am-4pm. 15kn, students 10kn. English booklet 20kn.)*

ARCHAEOLOGICAL MUSEUM (ARHEOLOŠKI MUZEJ). One of the oldest museums in Croatia, this venerable institution makes fascinating shards of pottery and has well-written English descriptions. The beautiful garden is filled with an impressive hodgepodge of Roman statuary and finds from Solana, a nearby ancient town. *(Zrinsko-Frankopanska 25. From the waterfront, follow Marmontova to Trg Gaje Bulata, turn left on Teutina, and take the 1st right, which leads to Zrinsko-Frankopanska. ☎31 87 21. Open Tu-F 9am-noon and 5-8pm, Sa-Su 9am-1pm. 10kn, students 5kn.)*

CITY MUSEUM (MUZEJ GRADA SPLITA). Houses a minimal selection of artifacts but tells the history of Split in detail. Set beside a scenic stone courtyard, the 15th-century building was designed by **Dalmatinac,** architect of Šibenik's Cathedral. *(Papalićeva 1. From the Golden Gate, enter Stari Grad and turn left on Papalićeva. ☎34 49 17. www.mgst.net. Placards in English. Open Tu-F 9am-9pm, Sa-Su 10am-1pm. 10kn, students 5kn.)*

ETHNOGRAPHIC MUSEUM (ETNOGRAFSKI MUZEJ). This museum displays artifacts of Croatia's domestic and ceremonial life in times past. Interesting if you enjoy intricate old clothing. *(Narodni trg 1. ☎34 41 64; www.et-mu-st.com. Open M-F 9am-2pm, 5-8pm, Sa 10am-1pm. 10kn, students 5kn.)*

CROATIA

🔊 BEACHES AND ENTERTAINMENT

The rocky cliffs, wide green hills, and pebbly beaches on the west end of Split's peninsula make up 100-year-old **City Park Marjan**, a great expanse for walking or jogging. From Obala hrvatskog narodnog preporoda, face the water and head right (15min.). Paths are indicated on the map; you can find your own way, but watch for signs marking trails that lead to private lands. The closest beach to downtown Split is crowded **Bačvice**, a favorite among nocturnal local skinny-dippers; Bačvice is the starting point of a strip of bars along the waterfront that make up the heart of Split's colorful nightlife. In early May, Split honors its patron saint, St. Domnius, with festivities in Stari Grad, which include Dalmatian *klapa* singers, folk dancing, and many games of bingo. From mid-July to mid-August, Split hosts an annual **Summer Festival.** The region's best artists and international guests perform ballets, operas, plays, and classical concerts in the town's churches and ruins. (Info and ticket reservations ☎34 49 99. Tickets 754-215kn.) A three-day **Folk Concert** is held in the open-air stage in Zvončac every summer at the beginning of July.

💬 NIGHTLIFE

Tropic Club Equador, Kupalište Bačvice bb (☎32 35 71. www.tropic-club-equador.com). Just past Bačvice beach (see above). 2nd level of the club complex. Dancing the rumba under the stars on the Latin-themed terrace bar might be easier after you've sipped a few decadent tropical cocktails (27-47kn). Open daily 9am-1am.

Shakespeare, Cujetna 1 (☎51 94 92). Follow the waterfront past Tropic Club Equador for another 20min. The Bard might turn over in his grave now that 2 floors of raging techno bear his name. Cover 30kn. Open Th-Su 11pm-late.

Jazz Planet, Grgura Ninskoga 3 (☎34 76 99). Hidden on a tiny but lively square opposite the City Museum, Jazz Planet has comfy chairs outside and a mellow blue color scheme inside that mixes well with jazz and beer. Occasional live music. 0.5L Guinness 25kn, 0.25L *Bavaria* 14kn. Open Su-Th 1pm-midnight, F-Sa 8am-2am.

Cafe Favola, Trg Braće Radić 1. (☎34 48 48), is a chic, laid-back bar that lures both locals and tourists with views of one of the city's quieter but most beautiful squares. Prošek 10kn. Open daily 7am-midnight.

BRAČ ISLAND: BOL ☎(0)21

Central Dalmatia's largest island, Brač (pop. 1500) is an ocean-lover's paradise. Most visitors come here for Zlatni rat, a peninsula just a short walk from the town center; it packs the crowds on its white pebble beach that juts out into emerald waters. Brač (BRACH) has more to offer than location: churches, galleries, lively nightlife, and water sports will keep you busy for as long as you choose to stay.

☐ TRANSPORTATION. The **ferry** from **Split** docks at Supetar (1hr.; July-Aug. 13 per day, Sept.-June 7 per day; 25kn). From there, take a well timed **bus** to Bol (1hr., 5 per day, 15kn). The last bus back to the ferry leaves at 5:50pm; the last ferry to Split leaves June-Aug. at 8:30pm and Sept.-May at 7:30pm. Alternatively, a **catamaran** runs directly to Bol from **Split**. (☎63 56 38. 40min. M-Sa leaves from Bol 6:30am, from Split 4pm; Su 7:30am/4pm. 22kn. Buy tickets on board.)

🔳🛈 ORIENTATION AND PRACTICAL INFORMATION. Bol is organized around a waterfront of many names: at the bus stop and marina, the waterfront is called **Obala Vladimira Nazora.** Left of the bus station (facing the water) it becomes

Riva, then **Frane Radića**, then **Porat bolskih pomorca.** To the right it's **Put Zlatnog Rata.** Facing the sea on the far side of the small marina, walk 5min. to the left of the bus station to reach the **tourist office,** Porat bolskih pomorca bb. It dispenses a free Bol guide and a large selection of **free maps.** (☎63 56 38; www.bol.hr. Open M-Sa 8:30am-2pm and 5-9pm, Su 9am-1pm.) Facing the water, walk right from the bus station to reach the walkway, Put Zlatni Rata, which leads to the larger hotels, Zlatni rat, and other small beaches along the way. **Zagrebačka banka,** Uz Pjacu 4, uphill from Frane Radića, **exchanges currency** for no commission and cashes **traveler's checks** for 1.5% commission. (☎63 57 63. Open M-W and F 8am-2pm, Th 8am-1pm, Sa 8am-noon.) A 24hr. **ATM** sits outside of **Splitska Banka,** Radića 16. **Adria Tours,** Obala Vladimira Nazora 28, to the right of the bus station facing the water, **rents scooters** (120kn per half-day, 200kn per day) and **cars** (400-500kn per day including mileage). The Adria office also books rooms and organizes excursions (70-190kn) to nearby islands. There's a **pharmacy** and **medical clinic** at Porat bolskih pomorca bb. (☎63 51 12. Open M-Sa 7:30am-9pm, Su 8am-noon.) **M@3X** (www.orca-sport.com/caffe), on Rudina a few doors down from Aqvarius (see **Nightlife,** p. 210) has fast and cheap **Internet access.** (25kn for first hr., 20kn per hr. thereafter. Open daily 10am-1pm and 4-9pm.) The **post office,** Uz Pjacu 5, has **telephones** outside. (☎63 56 78; fax 63 52 53. Open M-Sa 7am-9pm.) **Postal Code:** 21420.

⌂⌂ ACCOMMODATIONS AND FOOD. The cheapest option is to call one of the local residence numbers listed in the tourist office's booklet and arrange a **private room,** which generally saves 10-20% off agency prices. If the locals are all at the beach, **Adria Tours** (see above) will find you a room. (☎63 59 66; www.adria-bol.hr. Open daily 8am-9pm. July-Aug. 60-115kn per person; singles 105-170kn. Tax 10kn. 20% surcharge for stays under 4 nights.) For a **hotel room,** going through an agency can save you 10-15% off the price at the desk. Adria Tours offers special deals on local hotel rooms from 250kn. The extravagant **Hotel Kaštil ❺,** Frane Radica 1, is housed in a baroque manor that once served as a silk and silver trading post, and has small but spotless rooms with striking views of Hvar Island. All rooms have TVs, A/C, phones, and bathrooms. Breakfast buffet included. (☎63 59 95; www.kastil.hr. July 18-Aug. 21 singles 620kn, doubles 899kn; July 4-17 and Aug. 22-28 503/713kn; June 20-July 3 and Aug. 29-Sept. 11 433/620kn; May 30-June 19 and Sept. 12-Sept. 25 364/511kn; Mar.1-May 22 and Sept.26-Oct. 29 287/402kn. There are five **campgrounds** around Bol; the largest is **Kito ❶,** Bračka bb, on the main road into town. (☎63 55 51. Open May-Sept. 44kn per person, tent included.)

Konoba Gušt ❷, Frane Radića 14, offers shady respite among hanging fishing gear, quirky photos, and local diners, and serves an array of fresh seafood. (☎63 59 11. Entrees 40-150kn. Open daily noon-2am.) Drawing flocks of locals and tourists to its hearty portions and picture perfect terrace view, **Taverna Riva ❸** serves savory fish and meat, such as grilled tuna (75kn), alongside traditional Croatian pastas and risottos. (☎63 52 36; www-riva-bol.com. Entrees 42-160kn, 10kn cover. Open 11am-3pm, 6-11pm. AmEx/MC/V.) If you're tired of bringing picnic lunches to the beach, the cafeteria **Plaža Zlatni Rat ❶,** under the pines off the famous pebble beach, is the answer to paper bags and pâté. (☎63 52 22. Salads and grilled specialties 20-50kn. Open daily 8am-6pm.) **Pizzeria Topolino ❶,** Riva 2, on the waterfront in the town center, has tasty pizza and pasta (25-50kn), traditional Croatian meat dishes (55-75kn), and an impressive selection of salads. (☎63 57 67. Open daily 8am-2am.) **Supermarket KERUM,** on Uz Pjacu up the hill from the post office, has 10-12kn sandwiches. (☎71 83 00. Open M-Sa 6am-10pm, Su 6:30am-10pm.)

◙⌐ SIGHTS AND ENTERTAINMENT. The **free map** distributed by the tourist office (see **Orientation and Practical Information,** p. 208) shows all the town's sights, the most important of which is the 1475 **Dominican Monastery,** located on the eastern tip of Bol. Facing the water, walk left for 15min, beyond the tourist office. The highlight of the monastery is Tintoretto's altar painting of the **Madonna with Child.** Apparently concerned they'd need a refund, the monks kept the masterpiece's invoice, which is on display in the **museum,** among other artifacts of local history. (☎ 77 80 00. Museum and monastery open daily 10am-noon and 5-7pm. 10kn. Dress appropriately.) The **Dešković Gallery,** on Porat bolskih pomorca, behind the pharmacy, exhibits contemporary Croatian art in a small, 17th-century Baroque mansion. (Open daily 5-10pm. 5kn.) More art comes to town during **Bol Cultural Summer** (Bolsko Kulturno Ljeto), which runs throughout July and August, and features a variety of classical and folk music concerts. (Tickets free-20kn, depending on event.) The English-speaking staff at **Big Blue Sport,** Podan Glavice 2, on the way to Zlatni rat, organizes an array of watersports including **scuba diving** and **windsurfing.** Back on land, they also offer beach volleyball and rent **bikes.** (☎ 098 21 24 19; www.big-blue-sport.hr. One-day dive with equipment rental 350kn, half-day 275kn, night dive 300kn. 8hr. windsurfing course 800kn; rentals 360kn per day, 280kn per half day. Beach volleyball 50kn per hr. Bikes 15kn per hr., 70kn per day. Open daily 9am-7pm.) If you crave velocity, **waterskiing** (200kn, with lesson 300kn) and **banana boat rides** (40kn per person, 3 person min.) are available through **Diving Center Bol,** 50m down the waterfront from Big Blue Sport. (☎ 63 53 67; www.nautic-center-bol.com. Open 9am-6pm. Walk-ins welcome). **Boat rentals** are available through Adria Tours (see **Accommodations and Food,** p. 209) and along the waterfront past the bus station. The **outdoor cinema** opposite the bus station, has nightly showings, weather permitting. (Shows 8:30-11pm. 15-18kn.)

NIGHTLIFE. Bol's awe-inspiring natural beauty shines even brighter once the sun goes down. Soak in the calm sea under the clear night sky near one of the small piers along Put Zlatnog Rata, or head to the center of town for a surprisingly lively night scene. ▨ **Varadero,** at the base of Hotel Kaštil, has the hippest terrace in town, complete with wicker couches, tiki torches, and ambient techno. It's the perfect place to start the morning with a frothy cappuccino (9kn) or cap off the night with a delicious cocktail. (Mixed drinks 35-50kn. Open daily 9am-1pm.) Join a friendly crowd of vacationing Croatian youths and a live DJ at **Aqvarius,** which starts at Rudina 26 and spills over across the street to an outdoor terrace on Radića 8, overlooking the beach. Sip on fruity cocktails like a "Woo Woo" (vodka, peach liqueur, and blueberry juice; 25kn) while rocking to mellow tunes in a swing chair. (☎ 63 58 03. Open daily May-Sept. 9am-1am; Oct.-Apr. Su-Th 9am-11pm, F-Sa 9am-midnight.) **Pivnica Moby Dick,** Loža 13, is uphill from the tourist office and has a perfect view of the sunset over the harbor. (☎ 63 52 81. Mixed drinks 25-60kn, 0.3L *Ožujsko* 12kn. Pizza 25-55kn. Entrees 35-70kn. Live music daily in summer. Open 5pm-2am.)

VIS ISLAND: KOMIŽA ☎(0)21

A bit farther from the mainland than Dalmatia's most popular islands, Vis's relative isolation—until 1989 it served as a Yugoslav military base—has preserved its natural beauty and slow pace of life. Residents continue to fish, grow olives, and make wine as they have for centuries. Vis offers stunning natural attractions, from boat rides through the blue grotto on nearby Biševo to scuba diving in sunken ships.

PRACTICAL INFORMATION AND ORIENTATION. A ferry runs to Vis Town from Split (2½hr., June-Sept. 1-2 per day, 34kn). There is also a Semmarina catamaran (1 per day, 26kn) that makes the trip more quickly every morning. Buses (30min., 7 per day, 15kn) to Komiža meet the ferry. Komiža is tiny enough that you can't get lost. The bus stops on Hrvatskih Mučenika, a few

CROATIA

steps from Riva (the waterfront). A right turn on Riva leads to Ribarska and to the beach, while a left takes you to most services and sights. To get to the tourist office, Riva 1, face the water and walk left along the waterfront until the end of the harbor. (☎71 34 55; tzg-komiza@st.hinet.hr. Open July-Aug. M-Sa 8am-9pm; Sept.-June M-Sa 8am-9pm, Su 9am-noon.)

On your way you'll pass the bus station and the tourist agency **Darlić and Darlić**, Riva 13. Mother Darlić, brother Darlić, or sister Darlić will arrange private rooms (see p. 211), and rent scooters (300kn per day). You can also make quick connections to the Internet with their computer. (☎71 72 05; www.darlic-travel.hr. 30kn per 15min. Open daily in summer 8am-9pm; winter 8am-1pm.) **Splitska Banka**, Trg Kralja Tomislava 10, on the waterfront, exchanges currency for no commission and traveler's checks for 2% commission, and offers Western Union services. (☎71 82 88. Open M-F 8am-noon and 6-8pm, Sa 8am-noon.) There is a 24hr. **ATM** on Riva 2, next to Travel Agent Komiža. The **pharmacy,** San Pedro 11, is the only tricky place to find; from the waterfront, turn on Hrvatskih Mučenika, then take the second left. When the street curves to the left, curve with it and then walk up a ramp that leads behind a long white building; the pharmacy is at the end of the ramp and up the stairs. (☎71 34 45. Open M-F 8am-1pm and 7-8pm, Sa 8:30-10:30am.) The **post office,** Hrvatskih Mučenika 8, next to the bus station, **exchanges currency,** cashes **traveler's checks** for 1.5% commission, and gives MC **cash advances.** There are telephones inside. (☎71 30 20; fax 71 35 98. Open M-F 8am-2pm, Sa 8am-1pm) **Postal Code:** 21485.

🖩🖵 ACCOMMODATIONS AND FOOD. The only budget option is a private room through **Darlić and Darlić** (p. 210). They'll do their best to find a bed, but call ahead during high season. (July 15-Aug. 19 singles 90-130kn; doubles 130-180kn. July 1-10 and Aug. 19-Sept. 10 65-105kn/90-150kn. June and Sept. 60-80kn/75-105kn. 30% surcharge for stays under 3 nights. Tourist tax 3.50-6kn.) The one hotel in town is the **Hotel Biševo ➍**, Ribarska 96. Turn right as you face the water from anywhere in town and keep walking; it's next to the beach. Small, modern rooms offer TVs, phones, and fridges. (☎71 30 95; fax 71 30 98. Breakfast included. July 17-Aug. 21 singles 335kn; doubles 500kn. June 26-July 17 and Aug. 21-Sept. 4 270kn/440kn. May 29-June 6 and Sept. 4-26 210/340kn. Oct.-May 175kn/290kn. Tourist tax July-Aug. 6kn; June and Sept. 4.5kn; Oct.-May 3.5kn. 15-30kn extra for balcony and seaside view.) Don't miss local favorite **🖾Konoba Bako ➌**, Gundulićeva 1, on the way to Hotel Biševo (see above) from the bus station. In its own little cove, Konoba Bako delights patrons with wonderful food and a waterfront setup. (☎71 37 42. Entrees 50-200kn, 10kn per person cover. Open daily 11am-2am.) For similar Croatian seaside cuisine, try **Riblji Restoran Komiža ➋**, on the water next to Darlić and Darlić. (Entrees 50-85kn. Open daily 7am-midnight. AmEx.) **Studenac**, a small supermarket, is at Trg Kralja Tomislava 11. (Open M-Sa 7am-midnight.)

🖾 SIGHTS. St. Nicholas Church (Crkva Sv. Nikole), called *muster* (monastery) by the locals, overlooks Komiža. To get there, follow any side street uphill from the waterfront. Built as part of a Benedictine monastery in the 12th century, it now holds services every Sunday, which is the only time you'll be able to get inside to take a look. Right on the beach sits the **Pirates' Church** (Gusarica). According to legend, pirates stole a Madonna from this church, but were soon caught in a storm so fierce that only the Blessed Virgin made it back to shore. (Open daily morning and evening during summer.) Several agencies run daytrips to neighboring islands; try the excursions organized by **tourist agency Darlić & Darlić** (see above). Trips include the incredible **Blue Cave** on Biševo Island (2 per day; full-day 95kn, half-day 80kn); and **St. Andrew,** which entails fishing with a local fisherman and then cooking up your catch (1 per day, 230kn). If you'd rather spend three to four days exploring and treasure-hunting with local fishermen, inquire at the tourist office (see p. 210). Gain a whole new appreciation for the art of rope-tying at the **Fisherman's Museum** (Ribarski muzej), on Riva next to the tourist office. Though the museum lacks English placards, the enthusiastic seaman/curator will give you the low-down. (Open M-Sa 10am-noon and 7-10pm, Su 7-10pm. 10kn, children 5kn.)

BEACHES AND NIGHTLIFE. Komiža's scenic **pebble beach** is small and crowded, but Vis Island boasts some of the best diving in the Adriatic. Both **Issa Diving Center,** Ribarska 91 (☎71 36 51; www.diving.hr/idc), on your left before the beach, and **Manta Diving Center** (☎71 72 62; manta@st.tel.hr) at the far end of the beach offer 30min. intro dives (300kn) and advanced dives to sunken shipwrecks. (Shore dive 125kn, boat dive 250kn. Walk-ins welcome). Komiža's nightlife recently suffered the loss of Voga Disco Bar, Croatia's first disco, established in 1969, but fun times can still be had at the countless cafe-bars along the waterfront. Enjoy the town's lazy, easygoing nightlife at **Cafe Bane,** Škor 8, in a small square beside other cafe-bars, which has a stock of swing-chairs. (0.33L *Ožujsko* 9kn. Open daily 7am-1am.)

HVAR ISLAND ☎(0)21

This narrow, 88km-long island affords breathtaking views of the mainland mountains from its high, rugged hills. A favorite summer getaway for chic urbanites, the town plays host to sun-worshippers from mid-July through August. Fortunately, the nearby Pakleni Otoci (Hellish Islands) provide enough beach for everyone. Many resort hotels actually guarantee the weather—if the temperature dips too low, rooms are on the house.

TRANSPORTATION. Ferries make the trip from **Split** to Hvar's Stari Grad (2hr.; June 21-Sept. 9 M-Th 3 per day, F-Su 5 per day; 32kn, with car 216kn). From there, **buses** scheduled around the ferry take passengers to Hvar Town (15min., 7 per day, 15kn). Alternatively, head straight from Split to Hvar Town: there's a fast **catamaran** in the morning (1hr., 1 per day, 32kn) in addition to a regular ferry (2hr., 2 per day, 32kn). A bus runs to Hvar Town from **Jelsa** (40min.; M-Sa 6 per day, Su 5 per day; 19kn), from which **taxi boats** run every morning at 9am to Bol on Brač Island (40-50kn each way). To reach the **bus station,** walk through Trg Sv. Stjepana from the marina and then left of the church; the station is on your left. **Jadrolinija,** Riva bb, on the left tip of the waterfront, sells ferry tickets. (☎74 11 32; fax 74 10 36. Open M-Sa 5:30am-1pm and 3-8pm; Su 8-9am, noon-1pm, 3-4pm. Opening hours may vary according to ferry schedule.) Pelegrini Tours, Riva bb, runs a catamaran between Hvar and **Komiža** for day trips during the summer (1hr., 1 per day, 100kn). Pelegrini also **rents cars** (500kn per day) in summer. (☎74 27 43; pelegrini@inet.hr. Open M, W, F-Sa 7:15am-1pm and 5-8pm, Tu and Th 8:30am-1pm and 5-8pm.)

ORIENTATION AND PRACTICAL INFORMATION. Hvar Town has virtually no street names and even fewer signs. The main square, **Trg Sv. Stjepana,** directly below the bus station by the waterfront, is the one place graced with a name. Facing the sea from the main square, take a left along the waterfront to reach the **tourist office, bank,** and **ferry terminal;** a right leads to the major hotels and beaches. The tourist office, **Turistička Zajednica,** Trg Sv. Stjepana 16, is on the corner of the main square closest to the water. The smiling staff has detailed **maps** of the island (20kn) and bus schedules. (☎74 10 59; www.tzhvar.hr. Open M-F 8am-8pm, Sa-Su 8am-1pm and 4-8pm; daily low season 8:30am-noon.) **Splitska Banka,** Riva 4, offers **Western Union** services, **exchanges currency** for no commission, and

CROATIA

cashes **traveler's checks** for 2% commission. (Open M-F 8am-noon and 6-8pm, Sa 8-noon.) There's an **ATM** outside the bank and an AmEx/MC **ATM** across the harbor in front of **Privredna Banka Zagreb**. A well-stocked **pharmacy** is at Trg Sv. Stjepana. (☎74 10 02. Open M-F 8am-9pm, Sa 8am-1pm and 4-8pm, Su 9am-noon.). The most convenient **Internet access** is at **Internet Club Luka Rent**. From Trg Sv. Stjepana, turn left at the waterfront and take the second left after the post office. (☎74 29 46; www.lukarent.com. 30kn per hr.) Alternatively, there's **Cima**, Dolac bb. From the bus station, veer left away from Trg Sv. Stjepana, cross the street and look for a blue sign with dolphins. (☎71 87 52. 30kn per hr. Open daily 9am-2pm and 5-11pm.) The **post office** is on Riva just past Splitska Banka, and has **telephones** and **Poste Restante**. (☎74 24 13. Open M-Sa 7am-9pm.) **Postal Code:** 21450.

▮▯ ACCOMMODATIONS AND FOOD. As in other Croatian resort towns, the only budget accommodations are **private rooms,** and even these are expensive. **Pelegrini Tours** (see p. 214) can make arrangements. (July 31-Aug. 28 singles 200-250kn, doubles 300-350kn; July 3-31 and Aug. 28-Sept. 11 175/277kn; May 1-July 3 and Sept. 12-Oct. 2 153/219kn; low season 102/146kn. Tax and registration 4.5-7kn. 30% surcharge for stays under 3 nights.) If they can't help, check with the tourist office. Settle the price with your host upon arrival. Ask the tourist office about the going rate, then bargain around that. Many locals hang around the bus station offering rooms for less, and some even make the trip to Stari Grad to meet ferries and offer you a ride. If all else fails, look for *sobe* (room) signs down the waterfront from the main square. However, if resort-style luxury is more your taste, the newly renovated **Hotel Adriatic ❺** (☎74 10 24; fax 74 28 66) has spacious rooms with views of the marina. From the ferry stop, facing the water, turn right and follow the bay as it curves. (July 16-Aug. 31 singles 630kn; doubles 750kn; July 1-15 and Sept. 1-15 450/570kn; June 375/443kn; Oct.-May 345/413kn. Taxes 4.50-7kn. 30% more for stays less than 3 days. Breakfast, lunch, and dinner included. AmEx/MC/V.)

Overpriced pizza and pasta restaurants line the waterfront and the square. For a cheaper and better meal, head one block up the steps leading from the main square to the fortress to visit ▧**Luna ❷.** On the gorgeous rooftop terrace, you'll dine on excellent fish, poultry, and meat standards. Don't miss the gazpacho (20kn) on a hot day. (☎74 86 95. Entrees 50-120kn. Open daily noon-3pm and 6pm-midnight). For a splurge, **Macando ❹,** one street above Luna, transforms a marble alleyway into a seafood connoisseur's dream. Elegant ambience and gourmet fish dishes (70-240kn), such as lobster risotto (140kn) keep this upscale bistro consistently packed. (☎74 28 50. Open daily 6pm-midnight). For a more casual meal, dine with the spirited local crowd under hanging lanterns and grapevines at **Alviz ❷,** opposite the bus station. Hearty grilled meats (40-85kn) alongside vegetable lasagna (38kn) and delicious salads (20-35kn) satisfy carnivores and vegetarians alike. (☎74 27 97. Open daily 6pm-midnight.) There's a small **open-air market,** between the bus station and the main square, which sells primarily fruit and vegetables. (Open daily 7am-8pm.) The **Studenac supermarket,** on Trg Sv. Stjepana is small but well stocked. (Open M-Sa 7am-8pm, Su 8am-noon.)

◪ SIGHTS. The stairs to the right of the square (as you face the sea) lead to a 13th-century **Venetian fortress**. Although Turkish attacks weakened the fortress, the lightning bolt that struck the gunpowder room proved even more devastating. (Open daily 8am-midnight. 10kn.) Inside, you'll find a tiny **marine archaeological collection** (hidraorheološka zbirka) displaying Greek and Byzantine relics from ship-wrecked boats. (Open daily 10am-4pm. Free.) The **Gallery Arsenal,** up the stairs next to the tourist office, is worth a look. It features rotating exhibits by local artists. (☎74 10 09. Open daily 10am-noon and 8-11pm. 10kn) Between tanning sessions, stop by the **Last Supper Collection** in the **Franciscan monastery,** down Riva past the ferry terminal, which includes the another famous *Last Supper*, an oil-painting by Matteo Ignoli. (☎74 11 23. Open M-Sa 10am-noon and 5-6pm. 10kn.)

FESTIVALS AND NIGHTLIFE. During the **Days of Theater** in the last two weeks of May, Hvar celebrates the stage above the Arsenal in one of Europe's oldest **community theaters,** dating from 1612. The Franciscan monastery and the theater host outdoor drama performances during the **Hvar Summer Festival.** (Mid-June to early Oct. Performances 30-50kn.) For 10 days each September, the monastery hosts the **Shakespeare Days Festival,** which includes performances and workshops dedicated to the Bard. Inquire at the tourist office (see **Orientation and Practical Information,** p. 212) for more info.

The most crowded bars line the waterfront. For something smaller and more intimate, head to **Caffe Bar Jazz,** Burak bb, on a side street uphill from Splitska Banka. The bar's funky footstools, Technicolor interior, inexpensive drinks, and local flavor help revive the sun-weary psyche for a nocturnal second wind. (Vodka and juice 15kn. Open daily 8pm-2am.) For an authentic taste of Dalmatia, ■**Konoba Katarina,** Groda bb, on the steps to the fortress, offers delicious homemade sweet and dry wines in a wood-panelled cellar. Samples abound, and the decadent dessert wine *prosek* is so good, you might be tempted to take a bottle home. (35-70kn. Open daily 10am-1pm and 6pm-midnight). At the end of Riva past the Jadrolinija office, ■**Carpe Diem** has loud live DJs and the best outdoor terrace on the waterfront, always busy with hip and hot twenty-somethings. Jumpstart a vigorous day of sunbathing with a delicious cappuccino (25kn) or fruit smoothie. (Mixed drinks 35-75kn, beer 25-30kn. Open daily 9am-2am.) Walk all the way around to the opposite side of the marina and up the garden path on your right to get to the local **disco,** which has dancing indoors and outside around a big fountain. (Open daily 10pm-5am.) Earlier in the evenings, this same space functions as an **open-air cinema.** Look for posters advertising what's playing. (Tickets 15-20kn.)

BEACHES AND ISLANDS. To enjoy some of the Adriatic's clearest waters, you'll have to brave the loud, crowded, gravel **beaches.** Quieter beaches as well as terraced rock sunbathing and swimming areas are a 20min. walk to the left down the waterfront. Or, head to Jevolim, Ždrilca, and Palmižana, known collectively as the **Hellish Islands** (Pakleni Otoci). The last is home to **Palmižana beach,** which has waterside restaurants, rocks for tanning, sparse sand, and an area frequented by nude bathers at the far tip of the cove. **Taxi boats** run between the islands. (Every 30min. 10am-6:30pm, round-trip 20-40kn.) Back on the mainland, the family staff at the **Jurgovan diving center,** on the beach below Hotel Amfora, offers diving and rentals. (☎74 24 90; www.divecenter-hvar.com. Dives 200-250kn. Motorboats 200-400kn per day. Snorkel equipment 40kn per day. Kayaks 20kn per hr. Open daily 10am-6pm.)

KORČULA ISLAND ☎(0)20

Korčula (KOHR-choo-lah) got its name from the Greek words *kerkyra melaina* (black woods) because of the dark macchia thickets and woods that cover the island. Korčula Town (pop. 4000) faces the stunning mountains of the Croatian mainland, just a short ferry trip away. Weekly sword dances in the summer, a superb music scene, and friendly locals combine to create the small town's unique atmosphere. A healthy crop of tourists has also made it significantly more developed than its neighbors Vis and Mljet.

TRANSPORTATION. Korčula is one of the few islands served by buses (which board a ferry to the island). The **bus station** is at Porat bb. (☎71 12 16. Ticket window open M-Sa 6:30-9am, 9:30am-4pm, and 4:30-7pm, Su 2-7pm.) **Buses** run to:

Dubrovnik (3½hr., 1 per day, 77kn); **Split** (5hr., 1 per day, 90kn); **Zagreb** (11-13hr., 1 per day, 209kn) via Knin or Zadar; **Sarajevo, BOS** (6½hr., 4 per week., 145kn). For **ferry info** and tickets, check the **Jadrolinija** office, 20m toward Stari Grad from the ferry landing. (☎71 54 10; fax 71 11 01. Open M-F 8am-8pm, Sa-Su 8am-1pm.) **Ferries** run from Korčula Town to: **Dubrovnik** (3½hr., 5 per week, 67kn); **Hvar** (3hr., 1-2 per day, 67kn); **Split** (4½hr., 1 per day, 82kn). Ferries arrive in Korčula Town or in Vela Luka on the opposite side of the island. A bus meets ferries for the latter and transports you to Korčula Town (1hr., 5 per day, 26kn). For a **taxi**, call ☎71 54 52.

■ ⁊ **ORIENTATION AND PRACTICAL INFORMATION.** The town is situated beside the sea on the end of the island. **Stari Grad** (Old Town) was built on a small oval peninsula, and its streets are arranged in a herringbone pattern. Outside the city walls, medieval, Baroque, and modern houses blend together, tapering off into hotels farther down the coastline. Street addresses are rare, but the town is small and easily navigable. The **tourist office, Turistička Zajednica,** is on the opposite side of the peninsula from the bus and ferry terminals. To get there, face the water and walk left, following the main street as it curves away from the marina. Then head right along the water toward the peninsula to Hotel Korčula; the office is just before the hotel in a glass building. (Open M-Sa 8am-3pm and 4pm-8pm, Su 9am-1pm.) **Splitska Banka,** in front of the stairs to Stari Grad, **exchanges currency** for no commission, cashes **traveler's checks** for 2% commission, gives **cash advances,** and offers **Western Union** services. (☎71 10 52. Open M-F 7:30am-7:30pm, Sa 7:30-11am.) There is a 24hr. (MC/V) **ATM** outside Splitska Banka and another around the corner toward Stari Grad. The **pharmacy,** Trg Kralja Tomislava bb, is at the foot of the Stari Grad stairs. (☎71 10 57. Open M-F 7am-8pm, Sa 7am-noon and 6-8pm, Su 9-11am. AmEx/MC/V.) For **Internet** access, your best bet is **Tino Computers,** Pr. Tri Sulara 9, before Stari Grad, on a little street heading away from the marina. (☎71 60 93. 25kn per hr., 10kn min. Open M-Sa 8am-noon and 5-9pm, Su 5-11pm.) **Rent-a-Đir,** next door to Marko Polo, rents **cars** (400kn per day, 100kn deposit), **scooters** (200-250kn per day, 50kn deposit), and **boats.** (400kn per day. ☎71 19 08. Open daily 8am-10pm.) The **rental kiosk** in front of the Hotel Park (see below) **exchanges currency,** cashes **traveler's checks** for 1.5% commission, and has **telephones** in- and outside. (☎71 11 32. Open M-F 7am-9pm, Sa 8am-8pm.) **Postal Code:** 20260.

⁊ ⁊ **ACCOMMODATIONS AND FOOD. Private rooms** are the only budget accommodations available. **Marko Polo ❶,** Biline 5, on the waterfront where the ferries dock, will arrange one for you. (☎71 54 00; www.korcula.com. Open daily 8am-9pm. July 12-Aug. 23 singles 188kn; doubles 263kn; triples 330kn. May 17-July 11 and Aug. 24-Sept. 30 150kn/210kn/285kn. Oct.-May 16 105kn/150kn/210kn. 30% more for stays under 3 nights.) Or, look for *sobe* (room) signs uphill from the bus station away from Stari Grad or on the road to Hotel Park (see below). While not exactly budget, **Hotel Park ❸** offers simple, functional rooms near the beach, some with balconies and marina views. From the bus station, walk away from Stari Grad along the waterfront and follow the signs. (☎72 60 04; fax 71 17 46. Breakfast included. Jan. and May singles 319-395kn; doubles 456-608kn. June and Sept. 319-395kn/608-760kn. July and Aug. 532-628kn/760-912kn. Camping is available farther out at **Autocamp Kalac ❶,** with a sandy beach and nice views of the mainland across the water. (☎71 11 82; fax 71 17 46. Reception open daily 7am-10pm. 36kn per person, 30kn per tent, 23kn per car. Tourist tax 7.5kn.) A bus runs to the camp from the station (10min., 1 per hr., 8kn).

At ▨**Adio Mare ❷,** Marko Polo bb, next to Marco Polo's house, local specialties like *korčulanska pasticada* (beef stewed in vegetables and plum sauce with dumplings, 70kn) or *Ražnjic Adio Mare* (mixed meats skewered with apples, onions, and bacon; 60kn) draw crowds. (☎71 12 53. Entrees 40-80kn. Open M-Sa

5:30pm-midnight, Su 6pm-midnight.) Up the double staircase to the right of the tourist office, **Pizzeria Agava ❶**, Cvit. Bokšic 6, caters to hungry local youths. (Pizzas 29-41kn. Pasta 26-36kn. Open daily 9am-2pm and 6pm-2am.) For a late-night snack, have a hamburger (16kn), salad (15-20kn), or beer (12-15kn) at **Fast Food Tri Sulara ❶**, down the street from Olea. (Open M-Sa 6:30am-2am, Su 6:30am-10pm.) Restaurants in Korčula are expensive and tourist-driven. If you don't mind paying for the view, there are a string of nearly identical *konoba* overlooking the bay down the road from Gaudi (see p. 216) that serve the usual assortment of seafood and pasta. The frugal should try **Kozum supermarket** (open M-Sa 6:30am-9pm, Su 7am-9pm), by the bus station and next to Marko Polo (see p. 215); and the open-air **produce market** to the right of the Stari Grad stairs. (Open daily 6am-9pm.)

◉ **SIGHTS.** Korčula's grandest tribute to its patron, **St. Mark's Cathedral** (Katedrala Sv. Marka), roosts at the highest point of the Stari Grad peninsula. Planning began in the 14th century, inspired by the founding of the Korčula Bishopric, but construction wasn't completed until 1525. The Gothic-Renaissance cathedral is complemented by the older **bell tower**. (Open daily 9am-9pm. Services M-Sa 6:30pm and Su 7, 9:30am and 6:30pm. Appropriate dress required) The **Abbey Treasury of St. Mark** (Opatska Riznica Sv. Marka), next to the cathedral, houses an extensive collection of 12th-century manuscripts, Renaissance and Baroque drawings, religious robes, and coins from all periods. (Open M-Sa 9am-5pm, 10kn.) The **Town Museum** (Gradski Muzej) sits opposite the treasury in the Renaissance Gabrielis Palace. Four floors display nearly five millennia of Korčula's culture, including everything from 5000-year-old knives to a 19th-century wedding dress. (Open M-Sa 9:30am-6pm. 10kn, students 5kn.)

🎭 🎟 **ENTERTAINMENT AND NIGHTLIFE. Carnival celebrations,** including weekly masked balls *(maškare)*, are held from Epiphany to Ash Wednesday. All events are free. The ◼**Festival of Sword Dances** (Festival Viteških Igara) takes place every July and August. The Moreška, Moštra, and Kumpanija sword dances are performed throughout the island. In the city of Korčula, dancers perform the Moreška every Monday and Thursday evening. Tickets (60kn) are available at major tourist agencies (www.moreska.hr). To save money, come for the free shows at the end of July that take place on **St. Theodore's Day** and **Day of Korčula Town.** Ask at the tourist office for details. The first two weeks of September are dedicated to the **Marco Polo Festival.** Events include folk entertainment and a grand reconstruction of the famous 1298 naval battle in the Pelješac channel between Korčula and the mainland in which *Signore* Polo and the forces of Venetian Korčula clashed with Genoa's navy.

While tourists stick to Stari Grad in the evenings, the late-night cafe happens at **Olea,** just off the marina on Prolaz Tri Sulara between the bus station and Stari Grad. (Mixed drinks 25-40kn. Open M-Sa 7am-2am, Su 9am-2am.) For a club-like atmosphere, try **Gaudi.** The cafe outside has gorgeous views, but the real action happens inside the stone cocoon of sound and colored lights behind it. Go up the ramp to the right of the steps that lead to Stari Grad (toward the canon) and it will be on your left. (Beer 12-18kn. Nightclub open daily 11pm-3am.)

DUBROVNIK ☎ (0)20

Countless epithets have been used to describe Dubrovnik, including "the pearl of the Adriatic" and "the city of stone and light." Although it would be hard for any location to live up to such adulation, a stroll through the winding lanes of the Old Town reveals why this Venetian city merits such praise. Though ravaged by war in 1991 and 92, Dubrovnik is miraculously scarless; only close inspection reveals bul-

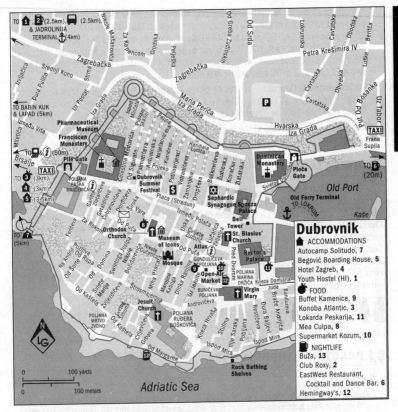

Dubrovnik

♠ ACCOMMODATIONS
Autocamp Solitudo, **7**
Begović Boarding House, **5**
Hotel Zagreb, **4**
Youth Hostel (HI), **1**

🍴 FOOD
Buffet Kamenice, **9**
Konoba Atlantic, **3**
Lokarda Peskarija, **11**
Mea Culpa, **8**
Supermarket Kozum, **10**

🍸 NIGHTLIFE
Buža, **13**
Club Roxy, **2**
EastWest Restaurant,
Cocktail and Dance Bar, **6**
Hemingway's, **12**

let holes and burned hillsides. Instead, Dubrovnik is defined by its Mediterranean grace. Azure waters, golden sunsets, and the Italian marble of the central plaza have made this ancient port a popular tourist destination for decades.

▣ TRANSPORTATION

Flights: Dubrovnik Airport Ćilipi (☎ 77 33 77) serves national and European destinations. Bus to airport from main station 30kn. **Croatia Airlines,** Brsalje 9 (☎ 41 37 76). Open M-F 8am-4pm, Sa 9am-noon.

Buses: Pt. Republike 19 (☎ 35 70 88). To: **Rijeka** (12hr., 4 per day, 345kn); **Split** (4½hr., 16 per day, 125kn); **Zadar** (8hr., 8 per day, 220kn); **Zagreb** (11hr., 8 per day, 180kn); **Frankfurt, GER** (27hr., 2 per wk., 800kn); **Ljubljana, SLN** (14hr., 1 per day, 380kn); **Međugorje, BOS** (2½hr., 1 per day, 77kn); **Mostar, BOS** (3hr., 2 per day, 77kn); **Sarajevo, BOS** (6hr., 1 per day, 157kn); **Trieste, ITA** (15hr., 1 per day, 340kn). To get to Stari Grad, face opposite the bus station and turn left onto Ante Starčevića. Follow this road uphill to the Pile Gate (25min.). Local buses running to Stari Grad make several stops along Ante Starčevića before reaching Pile.

Ferries: Jadrolinija, Obala S. Radića 40 (☎ 41 80 00; fax 41 81 11; www.jadrolinija.tel.hr/jadrolinija). Open M-Tu and Th 8am-8pm, W and F 8am-8pm and 9-11pm, Sa 8am-2pm and 7-8pm, Su 8-10am and 7-8:30pm. The ferry terminal is opposite the

Jadrolinija office. Face away from the bus station and head left; when the road forks, bear right (5min.). To: **Korčula** (3½hr., 4 per week., 67kn); **Rijeka** (22hr., 4 per week., 195kn); **Sobra** (2hr., 1-2 per day, 30kn); **Split** (8hr., 1 per day, 97kn); **Zadar** (16hr., 1 per week., 157kn); **Bari, ITA** (9hr., 5 per week., 315kn). To reach Stari Grad, start with your back to the ferry dock, walk left 50m along Gruška obala to the bus stop and take bus #1a, 1b, or 3 to Pile Gate (the last stop).

Public Transportation: ☎35 70 20. All buses except #5, 7, and 8 go to Stari Grad's Pile Gate. Tickets 8kn at kiosks, 10kn from the driver. Exact change required except on buses #1a and 1b. The driver checks everyone's ticket upon boarding.

Taxis: ☎35 70 44. In front of the bus station, the ferry terminal, and Pile Gate. 25kn plus 8kn per km. 50kn from the bus station to Stari Grad.

ORIENTATION

The walled **Stari Grad** (Old Town) is the city's cultural, historical, and commercial center. Its main street, called both **Placa** and **Stradun,** runs from the **Pile Gate,** the official entrance to Stari Grad, to the **Old Port** at the opposite tip of the peninsula. Outside the city walls, the main traffic arteries, **Pt. Republike** and **Ante Starčevića,** sandwich the **bus station** from the front and rear, respectively, merge into Ante Starčevića, and end at the Pile Gate. The new **ferry terminal** in Gruž is a 15 min. bus ride from Stari Grad. Dubrovnik has no train station. To the west of Stari Grad, two hilly peninsulas—**Babin Kuk** and **Lapad**—are home to modern settlements, sand beaches, and numerous hotels.

Do not explore the beautiful bare mountains rising above Dubrovnik—these peaks may still harbor concealed **landmines.**

PRACTICAL INFORMATION

Tourist Offices:

Tourist Board, Ante Starčevića 7 (☎42 75 91; ured.pile@tzdubrovnik.hr). From the bus stop at Pile Gate, take Ante Starčevića away from Stari Grad; the office is on your left. Distributes **free maps** and offers inexpensive **Internet access** (5kn per 15min.). Ask for the free Dubrovnik *City Guide.* Open daily June-Sept. M-Sa 8am-8pm; Oct.-May 8am-3pm.

Turistička Zajednica Grada Dubrovnika, Cvijete Zuzorić 1/2, 2nd fl. (☎32 38 87; www.tzdubrovnik.hr). From the end of Placa, turn right between St. Blasius's Church and Cafe Gradska Kavana, and take the 1st right. The English-speaking staff hands out the invaluable *City Guide* (free). Open June-Aug. M-F 8am-4pm, Sa 9am-3pm, Su 9am-noon; Sept.-May M-F 8am-4pm.

Turistički Informativni Centar (TIC), Placa bb (☎42 63 54; fax 42 63 55), next to the fountain at the head of Placa. Arranges private rooms, **exchanges currency** for 2% commission, and sells **maps** (20kn). Open daily June-Aug. 9am-8pm; Sept.-May 9am-7pm.

Budget Travel: Atlas, Lučarica 1 (☎0800 44 22 22; www.atlas-croatia.com), next to St. Blasius' Church at the end of Placa. The friendly, English-speaking staff arranges accommodations, sells plane and ferry tickets (student discounted airfares with Euro 26 card), **exchanges currency** for 1% commission, and cashes and sells **AmEx Traveler's Cheques.** Organizes expensive but convenient tours to: **Elafiti Islands** (2 per week, 240kn); **Mljet National Park** (3 per week, 360kn); **Neretva River Delta** (2 per week, 370kn with lunch); **Mostar, BOS** (2 per week, 290kn). **Branches** at Sv. Đurđa 1 (☎44 25 74; fax 44 25 70). near the Pile Gate, and at Gruška Obala (☎41 80 01; fax 41 83 30), near the ferry terminal. All open June-Aug. M-Sa 8am-9pm, Su 8am-1pm; Sept.-May M-Sa 8am-7pm, except the Pile Gate branch, which is closed Su throughout the year. AmEx/MC/V.

Currency Exchange: Dubrovačka Banka, Placa 16 (☎32 10 46). Don't be fooled by the loaves of plastic bread in the window—this centrally located bank exchanges currency for no commission, cashes for 1% commission **traveler's checks,** and offers **Western Union** services. **ATM** located outside. Open M-F 7:30am-9pm, Sa 7:30am-8pm. **Branch** next to the bus station, Pt. Republike 9 (☎35 63 33). Open M-F 7:30am-8pm, Sa 7:30am-1pm.

Luggage Storage: At the bus station kiosk marked *Garderoba.* 15kn per day. Open daily 4:50am-9pm.

Pharmacy: Ljekarna Mala Braća, Placa 2 (☎32 14 11), inside the Franciscan monastery just within Pile Gate. The oldest working pharmacy in Europe. Open daily 8am-8pm. **Night service** (8pm-8am) at either Ljekarna Gruž, Gruška Obala bb (☎41 89 90), the ferry terminal, or Ljekarna Kod Zvonika, Placa 1 (☎32 11 33). AmEx/MC/V.

Internet Access: See **Tourist Board** (above)

Post Office: Široka 8 (☎32 34 27), in Stari Grad. Has a number of public **telephones.** Open M-F 8am-7pm, Sa 8am-2pm. **Postal Code:** 20108.

ACCOMMODATIONS

Dubrovnik offers accommodations in the city center, beachside in Lapad, as well as near the ferry terminal. Due to lingering damage from the war and the subsequent refugee situation, however, the city's hotel scene currently leaves something to be desired—establishments tend to be either exorbitantly expensive or somewhat rundown. Consequently, for two or more people, a **private room** or **apartment** tends to be the most comfortable and least expensive option as well as the best way to assure that you get your desired location. Arrange one through the TIC, or **Atlas** (singles 100-150kn; doubles 120-375kn). For potentially cheaper rooms, try your luck with the locals holding *sobe* signs who hover around the bus and ferry terminals. They may start by asking absurd prices but tend to drop to reasonable rates with some bargaining (doubles 100-150kn). Be sure to agree on a price and ask to see the room before settling down anywhere.

Begović Boarding House, Primorska 17 (☎43 51 91; fax 45 27 52). From the bus station, take bus #6 toward Dubrava; tell the driver to let you off at Post Office Lapad. Facing the pedestrian walkway, turn right at the intersection. Go left at the fork, and take the 1st right onto Primorska. Call ahead and the hospitable owner, Sado, will pick you up at the bus or ferry terminal; look for him holding a small sign. A cozy villa with 10 spacious doubles, kitchenettes, TVs, and a terrace view shaded by fig trees. Social atmosphere. If the house is full, Sado will gladly arrange a place with one of his neighbors down the road. Doubles 110-120kn per person; triples 80-100kn per person. ❶

Youth Hostel (HI), B. Josipa Jelačića 15/17 (☎42 32 41; www.hfhs.hr). With your back to the bus station, turn left onto Ante Starčevića. Walk along the road for 10min., turn right at ul. Pera Rudenjaka, and left at the end of the street onto b. Josipa Jelačića. Look for a concealed HI sign on the left immediately after #17. From the ferries, take bus #12 in the direction of Pile to the stop after the bus station. Small but clean doubles, quads, and 6-person dorms. Breakfast 5kn. Check-out 10am. Curfew 2am. July-Aug. 26 110kn; June and Aug. 27-Sept.20, 95kn; May and Sept. 21-Oct., 85kn; Nov.-Apr., 75kn. 10kn extra without HI membership. ❶

Hotel Zagreb, Šetalište Kralja Zvonimira 27 (☎43 61 46; fax 43 60 06). Follow directions to Post Office Labad (see **Begović Boarding House,** above). Walk through the 1st intersection and turn left onto the pedestrian walkway Šetalište Kralja Zvonimira. The hotel is on the left. Near the beach and an array of cafes. Wonderful veranda, clean rooms with hardwood floors, bath, TV, and phone. Breakfast included. Reception 24hr. Singles 225-300kn; doubles 350-640kn. Tourist tax 5.50-7kn. AmEx/MC/V. ❸

CROATIA

Autocamp Solitudo, Iva Dulčića 39, Babin Kuk (☎44 86 86; sales.department@babinkuk.com). From the bus station, take bus #6 toward Dubrava and ask the driver to let you off at Autocamp. Follow the signs downhill. 5km from Stari Grad. New campground equipped with clean bathrooms, small grocery store, cafe, laundry facilities, and access to a long and uncrowded beach. Reception 7am-10pm, July-Aug. 24hr. 31kn per person, 65kn per tent or car. AmEx/MC/V. ❶

🍴 FOOD

Most establishments have seafood-oriented menus, risotto, and pasta. **Prijeko,** the first street parallel to Placa on the left when coming from Pile Gate, is lined with cookie-cutter *konobi* (taverns), which cater almost exclusively to tourists. The **open-air market,** on Gundulićeva Poljana, sits behind St. Blasius' Church. (Open daily 7am-8pm.) **Kozum,** facing the market, offers a modest array of groceries at extraordinarily low prices by Old Town standards. (Open daily 7am-8pm. AmEx/MC/V.) For a wider selection including fresh produce, check out **Kerum supermarket,** Kralja Tomislava 7, in Lapad. With your back to Post Office Lapad, turn left toward the white shopping center. Kerum is on the ground floor of the mall, at the back. (Open M-Sa 7am-10pm, Su 8am-9pm.)

🦑 **Lokarda Peskarija,** Na Ponti bb (☎32 47 50). From the bell tower at the end of Placa, turn right on Pred Dvorom and take the 1st left out of the city walls. This charming outdoor cafe is truly one of Dubrovnik's hidden gems. Tucked behind the Old Port, it offers the freshest and, surprisingly, least expensive seafood in the Old Town. Large, steaming pots of mouthwatering risotto, filled to the brim with shellfish, are sure to delight even the pickiest of palettes. Seafood 30-35kn. Open daily 8am-midnight. ❷

Konoba Atlantic, Kardinala Stopinga 42 (☎098 185 96 25). Take bus #6 to Post Office Labad and walk straight on the walkway; take a right on the staircase before Hotel Kompas, which takes you to Kardinala Stopinga. This tiny, family-run restaurant above the beach is worth the walk. Homemade bread, some of the best pasta in Croatia (49-260kn), and a wide range of seafood (48-120kn). Open daily noon-11pm. ❷

Mea Culpa, Za Rokum 3 (☎32 34 30). This lively pizzeria tucked in the back alleys of the Old Town serves Dubrovnik's freshest Italian fare. Latin for "I'm guilty," Mea Culpa lives up to its name in indulgence. Portions are massive: a pizza or calzone feeds two. Don't fret if the prospect of finishing your meal is daunting; the staff will happily wrap it up in a take-home box. Pizza 20-35kn, pasta 35kn. Open daily 8am-midnight. ❶

Buffet Kamenice, Gundulićeva poljana 8 (☎32 36 82). Stari Grad's best greasy spoon, Kamenice specializes in shellfish (38kn) and other edible aquatic creatures under a large umbrella beside the market. For breakfast, try one of their fluffy omelettes (20-30kn). Open M-Sa 7am-10pm, Su 10am-10pm. ❶

👁 SIGHTS

Stari Grad is packed with churches, museums, palaces, and fortresses—every angle is an eyeful. The most popular sights are those along the broad Placa, but much of Dubrovnik's history is off the beaten path.

🏰 **CITY WALLS (GRADSKE ZIDINE).** Providing stunning views of orange tiled roofs set against the sapphire blue backdrop of the Adriatic, a climb atop the city walls is the highlight of any trip to Dubrovnik. Originally constructed in the 8th century, the walls consist of nearly 2000m of limestone (25m tall at points), averaging 1.5m thick, which connect four round towers, two corner towers, three fortresses, 12 forts, five bastions, two land gates, and two port gates. The fortifications took their present form in the 13th century when, after liberation from Venetian rule,

CROATIA

the city needed stronger defenses to guard against potential Turkish attacks. Once you've seen the sunset from the top of the walls, you may never be able to leave the city. *(Entrances to walls are through the Pile Gate on the left and at the old port. Open daily May-Oct. 9am-7pm; Nov.-Apr. 10am-3pm. 30kn, children under 5 15kn.)*

FRANCISCAN MONASTERY AND PHARMACEUTICAL MUSEUM. Masterly stonework encases this 14th-century monastery (Franjevački Samostan). The southern portal that opens on the Placa includes a Pietà relief by the Petrović brothers, the only relic from the original Franciscan church. The cloister was built in 1360 by Mihoje Brajkov. No two capitals of the colonnade are the same. Take a gander at the gardens and check out the glass-encased shell holes, one of the few reminders of this city's war-torn past. The monastery also houses the oldest working pharmacy in Europe, established in 1317. The small museum holds displays of elegant medicinal containers, historical tools, and collections of religious icons and gold and silver jewelry. *(Placa 2. ☎42 63 45. On the left side of Placa, just inside Pile Gate next to the entrance to the city walls. Appropriate dress recommended for those visiting the chapel. Open daily 9am-6pm. 10kn, children 5kn).*

CATHEDRAL OF THE ASSUMPTION OF THE VIRGIN MARY. This Baroque cathedral (Riznica Katedrale) was erected after the previous Romanesque cathedral was destroyed in the 1667 earthquake. In 1981, the foundation of a 7th-century Byzantine cathedral was found beneath the cathedral floor, necessitating considerable revision of Dubrovnik's history. The cathedral **treasury** houses religious relics collected by Richard the Lionheart, Roman refugees, and a few centuries of fishermen. Crusaders in the 12th century brought back a silver casket from Jerusalem that contains 2000-year-old cloth material allegedly worn by Jesus. *(Kneza Damjana Jude 1. From Pile Gate, follow Placa to the Bell Tower and turn right to Poljana Marina Držića. Cathedral open daily 6:30am-8pm. Treasury open M-Sa 8am-5:30pm, Su 11am-5:30pm. 7kn, children 5kn.)*

ORTHODOX CHURCH AND MUSEUM OF ICONS. Around 2000 Serbs live in Dubrovnik—only a third of the pre-war population—and their church stands as a symbol of Dubrovnik's continued ethnic and religious tolerance. The museum (Pravoslavna Crkva i Muzej Ikona) houses a variety of 15th- to 19th-century icons gathered by local families. Traditionally, each Serbian household is protected by a specific saint and any member of the family traveling abroad collects icons depicting that saint. *(Od Puča 8. From Pile Gate, walk 100m down Placa and turn right onto Široka, the widest side street. Turn left down Od Puča. Church open daily 8am-noon and 5-7pm. Museum open M-Sa 9am-1pm. 10kn.)*

MOSQUE (DŽAMIJA). This former apartment serves Dubrovnik's 4000 Bosnian Muslims. The beautifully carpeted room upstairs is divided in two: one half contains an Islamic school for children and the other is used for prayer. A small anteroom serves as a social center for the Bosnian community. Members are glad to let tourists in as long as you take off your shoes. *(Miha Pracata 3. From Pile Gate, walk down Placa and take the 8th street on the right, M. Pracata. The mosque is marked by a small sign on the left side of the street. Open daily 10am-1pm and 8-9pm.)*

SEPHARDIC SYNAGOGUE (SINAGOGA). Round off your tour with a visit to the second-oldest Sephardic synagogue in Europe (the oldest one is in Prague). The city's 46 Jews have their offices inside. Most of Dubrovnik's Jewish archives were lost during the Nazi occupation, but a number of families risked their lives to hide much of the synagogue's interior in their own homes. *(Žudioska 5. From the Bell Tower, walk toward Pile gate and take the 3rd right onto Žudioska. Open M-F 9am-1pm. Museum 10kn.)*

BEACHES AND FESTIVALS

One of the most beautiful beaches in Dubrovnik actually lies just beyond the city walls. From the **bell tower,** turn left onto Svetog Dominika, bear right after the footbridge, and continue along Frana Supila. Descend the stairs next to the post office to discover a pristine **pebble beach** with spectacular views of Lokrum Island. Although privately owned, the *bajne* is free and open to the public. Alternatively, for sand, palms, and crowds, hop on bus #6 toward Dubrava and ask to get off at Post Office Lapad. Go through the intersection to the pedestrian boulevard and follow the bikinis. For a surreal seaside experience, take a swim in the cove at the foot of the wreckage of the old **Hotel Libertas,** still marked on most maps. The hotel was damaged during the war and then abandoned. You can also continue on the path to the beach below Hotel Bellevue. Walk along Starčevića (10min.), then take a left after the hotel. Another option is the nearby island of **Lokrum,** which features a **nude beach.** Ferries run daily from the Old Port (20min.; 9am and every 30 min. 10am-6pm; round-trip 35kn, children 15kn). To get to the nude beach, follow the main path from the ferry stop that traces the perimeter of the island. Veer left at the restaurant and follow the "FKK" signs. For those who prefer to stay clothed, there is a smaller beach adjacent to the boat dock as well as a gorgeous **nature preserve** worth exploring. The **Dubrovnik Summer Festival** (Dubrovački Ljetni Festival; mid-July to mid-Aug.) transforms the city into a cultural mecca and lively party scene. (☎32 34 00; www.dubrovnik-festival.hr.)

NIGHTLIFE

Young hipsters and cafe loungers congregate in **Stari Grad. Šetalište Kralja Zvonimira,** near Begović Boarding House (see **Accommodations,** p. 219), is also a budding spot for cafes, bars, and evening strolls by the nearby sea.

EastWest Cocktail and Dance Bar, Frana Supila bb (☎41 22 20). Nightlife newcomer EastWest lives up to its motto of "Welcome to Heaven." Situated on a private beach with spectacular ocean views, this lounge epitomizes luxury. The dressed-to-impress clientele relaxes on the bar's plush white couches, while hipsters congregate in the sand "living room," complete with leather sofas on the beach. Those craving complete relaxation after a long day or night out can recline on one of their decadent beachside canopy beds. Cocktails 33-78kn, beer 12-30kn. Open daily 8am-3am.

Hemingway's, Pred Dvorum bb. This small yet swanky bar, facing Poljana M. Držića, has the most extensive cocktail menu in the Old Town. Creatively named specialities such as Kick in the Balls (40kn), She is Paying (48kn), and the "XXL" Viagra (serves 3-6 people, 168kn) are sure to inspire. With gorgeous views of the Rector's Palace, the bell tower, and cathedral, and a patio with cushioned thrones, Hemingway's is the perfect place to sit back and take in Dubrovnik's beauty. Open daily 10am-1am.

Buža, Sv. Margarita. From the open air market (see p. 220), walk up the stairs toward the monastery. Veer left and follow the signs marked "Cold drinks" along Od Margarite. Hidden on a bed of boulders under the city walls, this laid-back watering hole perched above the Adriatic has the most spectacular sunsets. Beer 17-22kn. Open 9am-late.

Club Roxy, B. Josipa Jelačića 11. Only a short stumble away from the HI hostel, the Roxy's hanging motorcycles and hot-rod paraphernalia beckon a relaxed, local crowd looking to avoid the downtown crunch. 0.5L domestic draft 15kn, 0.33L Guinness 18kn, coffee 6kn. Open daily 8am-late.

⚡ DAYTRIPS FROM DUBROVNIK

LOPUD ISLAND

A ferry (50min., summer M-Sa 4 per day and Su 1 per day, round-trip 22kn) runs to Lopud and the Elafiti Islands during the summer months. The beach is on the opposite side of the island from the village. From the dock, face the water, walk around to the left for 5min., and turn left onto the road between the high wall and the palm park. Follow signs for the beach and "Konoba Barbara." Continue up and over the hill for 20min. Keep right at the fork and follow the stairs down to the beach.

Less than one hour from Dubrovnik, Lopud is an enchanting island. The tiny village, dotted with white buildings, chapels, and parks, stretches along the island's waterfront *(obala)*. Currently under renovation, **Dordič Mayneri** remains among the most beautiful parks in Croatia. Signs from Kavana Dubrava on the waterfront point to the **museum,** which is the meeting place for **tours** (Th 9am) of the church, museum, and monastery. A 15min. stroll along the waterfront leads to a gazebo with a breathtaking view of the white cliffs and a dark blue sea. A short walk in the other direction brings you to the abandoned **monastery.** Though slated for reconstruction and development, its current semi-ruined state makes for wonderful exploring. Be careful, though, as many of the floors have fallen in. The **beach, Plaža Šunj,** has that special quality that most of the Dalmatian Coast lacks: sand. **Warning:** beautiful as it is, parts of Lopud are still rife with **landmines.** Stick to the paved paths and the beach, and do not wander off into the wilderness.

MLJET NATIONAL PARK

Take a ferry, run by Atlantagent, Obala S. Radića 26 (☎ 41 90 44), behind the Jadrolinija office. The ferry (1½hr., June-Sept. 1 per day, round-trip 90kn) leaves in the morning, drops passengers in Pomena, and returns in the evening. In winter, the Jadrolinija ferry drops passengers on the eastern side of the island in Sobra (2hr., 2 per day, 32kn). The bus meets the ferry in Sobra and travels to its western end, Pomena (1hr., 12kn). ☎ 74 40 58; www.np-mljet.hr. Park entrances are in Polače and Pomena. High season 65kn, students 45kn. Atlas and other travel agencies offer 1-day excursions to the park. Private rooms (75-100kn) available in Sobra or Pomena; inquire at the cafe or look for signs.

Mljet's relative isolation and small population make it an ideal location for a national park. The saltwater **Large** and **Small Lakes** (Veliko and Malo Jezero), created by the rising sea level 10,000 years ago, are the most unique formations on the island. Every 6hr. the direction of flow between the lakes changes with the tides, so the water is constantly cleansed. In the center of Veliko Jezero sits the **Island of St. Maria** (Sv. Marija), home to a beautiful, white-stone **Benedictine monastery,** built in the 12th century and abandoned 700 years later when Napoleon conquered the area. Today, it houses a restaurant and a church.

If you plan on spending the night, **Polače** is worth a stop for its **Roman ruins** and **Christian basilica,** once part of the second-largest Roman city in Croatia. Unfortunately, most of the city is now underwater. Get off at Polače (which also has a tourist office), walk 2km to Pristanište, to the park's info center, and jump on the boat to St. Maria (5min., 1 per hr.). To return, take the boat to Mali Most (2min.) and walk another 3km to Pomena. When you get tired, a minivan run by park management will give you a ride; if you miss it, catch one of the Atlas-operated buses.

CZECH REPUBLIC
(ČESKÁ REPUBLIKA)

AUS$1 = 18.52Kč	10Kč = AUS$0.54
CDN$1 = 19.97Kč	10Kč = CDN$0.50
EUR€1 = 31.75Kč	10Kč = EUR€0.32
NZ$1 = 16.97Kč	10Kč = NZ$0.59
UK£1 = 49.04Kč	10Kč = UK£0.21
US$1 = 26.30Kč	10Kč = US$0.38

From the Holy Roman Empire through the USSR, the Czechs have long stood at a crossroads of international affairs. Unlike many of their neighbors, the citizens of this small, landlocked country have rarely resisted as armies marched across their borders, often choosing to fight with words instead of weapons; as a result, Czech towns and cities are among the best-preserved and most beautiful in Europe. Today, the Czechs face a different kind of invasion, as enamored tourists sweep in to savor the magnificent capital, the welcoming locals, and the world's best beers.

HISTORY

FROM GOLDEN AGE TO DARK AGE. According to legend, Father Čech climbed Říp mountain near present-day Prague, and, seeing how good it was, ordered the land settled. Textbooks, however, trace the civilization back to the first-century Celtic Boii. By the 6th century, Slavs had settled in the region and by the 11th century, the Czechs were united under the **Přemyslid Dynasty. Wenceslas** (Václav), legendary patron saint and king of Bohemia, was one of the dynasty's earliest rulers. In 1114, the Holy Roman Empire invited the Czech kings to join as electors.

FACTS AND FIGURES

OFFICIAL NAME: Czech Republic

CAPITAL: Prague (pop. 1.2 million)

POPULATION: 10.3 million (81% Czech, 13% Moravian, 3% Slovak, 3% other)

LANGUAGE: Czech

CURRENCY: 1 crown (koruna; Kč) = 100 hellers *(haleru)*

RELIGION: 40% non-religious, 39% Catholic, 5% Protestant, 16% other

LAND AREA: 78,864km²

CLIMATE: Temperate

GEOGRAPHY: Plateaus, mountains, and rolling hills

BORDERS: Austria, Germany, Poland, Slovak Republic

ECONOMY: 65% Services, 31% Industry, 8% Agriculture

GDP: US$15,300 per capita

COUNTRY CODE: 420

INTERNATIONAL DIALING PREFIX: 00

The reign of Holy Roman Emperor **Charles (Karel) IV** (1346-1378) was a Golden Era. His feats included the promotion of Prague to an Archbishopric and the founding of Charles University, the first university in Central Europe, in 1348. Unfortunately, Charles's eldest legitimate son, Václav "the Lazy," was unable to attain the golden heights of his father. During his reign, **Jan Hus** (1369-1415) was burned at the stake for his protests against the corruption of the Catholic church. In response to the execution, the proto-Protestant **Hussite movement** organized the **First Defenestration of Prague** in 1419—protestors threw the royalist mayor out the window of the Council House. The strategy had some merit: two centuries later, the **Second Defenestration of Prague** set off the **Thirty Years' War** (1618-1648) as Protestant dissidents launched two royal regents out of a castle window, only to have them saved by a pile of manure. The Protestants' eventual defeat was sealed when they suffered an early, harsh blow in the **Battle of White Mountain** in November 1620. Their loss led to the absorption of Czech territory into the **Austrian Empire** and three centuries of oppression.

CZECHMATE. The **nationalism** that engulfed Europe during the 19th century invigorated the Bohemian peoples. The sentiment was crushed, however, in the imperial backlash that followed the **1848 revolutions.** While **WWI** did little to increase harmony among the nationalities of the Hapsburg Empire, mutual malcontent united the Czechs and Slovaks. In the postwar confusion, **Edvard Beneš** and **Tomáš Garrigue Masaryk** convinced the victorious Allies to legitimize a new state joining Bohemia, Moravia, and Slovakia into **Czechoslovakia.** This **First Republic** was a new golden era for the Czechs. The country enjoyed remarkable economic prosperity but was torn apart when Hitler exploited the Allies' **appeasement** policy. The infamous **Munich Agreement** (1938) handed the Sudetenland to Germany. The following year, Hitler annexed the entire country.

UN-CRUSHED VELVET. Following the Allied liberation, the communists won the 1946 elections, seizing permanent power in 1948. In 1968, Communist Party Secretary **Alexander Dubček** sought to reform the country's nationalized economy and ease political oppression during the **Prague Spring.** The Soviets invaded immediately. **Gustáv Husák** became president in 1971, ushering in 18 years of repression under his regime. Czech intellectuals protested his human rights violations with

TOP TEN: CZECH REPUBLIC

1 Best hostel: the Buena Vista Backpackers' Hostel, Karlovy Vary (p. 272 and p. 273).

2 Best castle: Telč Castle (p. 301).

3 Best beer: straight from the barrel at the Pilsner Urquell brewery in Plžen (p. 270).

4 Prague's best-kept secret: Troja Chateau, Prague (p. 259).

5 Best place to be drunk: Charles Bridge, Prague, provided you don't fall off (p. 251).

6 Best city: Olomouc, like a smaller Prague without the tourists (p. 297).

7 Best restaurant: Radost FX, Prague (p. 264).

8 Best place to pretend you're a knight in shining armor: Karlstejn Castle (p. 267).

9 Best place to get lost in the woods: hiking in Jičín (p. 285).

10 Best place to meet up: Jan Hus Statue, Prague (p. 251).

the nonviolent **Charter 77** movement. Its leaders were persecuted and imprisoned, but nonetheless fostered increasing dissidence. Communism's demise in Hungary and Poland and the fall of the Berlin Wall in 1989 prompted Czechoslovakia's **Velvet Revolution**, named for the almost bloodless transition from communism to a multi-party state system. The Communist regime's violent suppression of a peaceful demonstration outraged the nation, which retaliated with a strike. Within days the communists resigned, and **Václav Havel**, long-imprisoned playwright and leader of both Charter 77 and the Velvet Revolution, became president. Slovak pleas for independence grew stronger and, after much debate, the Czech and Slovak nations separated on January 1, 1993.

TODAY. The Czech Republic is a **parliamentary democracy** with political power residing principally in the hands of a prime minister. A president is elected by Parliament to a five-year term and retains symbolic powers. Appointed by the president, the prime minister is typically a leader of the majority party. The country enjoyed a rapid revival after communism but has recently experienced economic stagnation and rising unemployment. In 1997, the economic policies of Prime Minister **Václav Klaus** resulted in a tremendous depreciation of the koruna's value, and the 1998 elections allowed **Miloš Zeman,** leader of the **Social Democrats,** to form the first left-wing government since 1989. **Vladimir Spidla** replaced Zeman as head of the Social Democrats and, in June 2002, the party topped the polls, making Spidla prime minister. Yet having won only 70 of 200 seats in Parliament, the Social Democrats were forced to ally with a number of centrist parties in order to form a tiny 101-seat majority. Playwright and former dissident **Václav Havel,** re-elected to the presidency in 1998 by a single vote, remained the country's official head of state until the 2003 presidential election. Unruffled by former economic catastrophes, Czech citizens elected Václav Klaus, former Prime Minister and opponent of Havel, to the presidency. In 2004, the young and relatively unknown Social Democrat **Stanislav Gross** succeeded Spidla as prime minister.

The Czech Republic joined **NATO** in March 1999 and was admitted to the **EU** in May 2004. Some concern lingers over Czech policies toward the Roma (gypsies), who suffer high poverty and unemployment, and over a shaky record in European relations. In 2000, the Czech Republic and Austria disagreed over a Czech nuclear power plant near the countries' shared border, and in 2002 Germany objected strongly to Czech refusal to revoke the **Benes Decree**, which legalized the confiscation of property from the millions of German civilians expelled from the country after WWII. In August 2002, the country suffered a major economic setback due to **severe flooding.** Much of the western half of the country was affected, causing damage to roads, railway lines, and landmarks.

PEOPLE AND CULTURE
LANGUAGE

Czech is a Western Slavic language, closely related to Slovak and Polish. **English** is widely understood among young people, and **German** can be useful, especially in South Bohemia because of its proximity to the German and Austrian borders. In eastern regions, you're more likely to encounter **Polish. Russian** is often understood, but tread carefully as the language is not always welcome. The trick to good pronunciation is to pronounce every letter. Stress is always placed on the first syllable. When there is a diacritical over a vowel—*á, é, í, ó, ú, ů,* and *ý*—this means you hold the vowel sound longer, without placing emphasis on it. *"C"* is pronounced "ts"; *"g"* is always hard, as in "good"; *"ch,"* considered one letter, is a cross between "h" and "k" but "h" is a comprehensible approximation; *"j"* is "y"; *"r"* is slightly rolled; and *"w"* is "v." The letter *"ě"* softens the preceding consonant: for instance, *"mě"* is "mnye," as in *město* (MNYEH-stoh). Similarly, all other diacritics soften the consonant: *"č"* is "ch," *"ř"* is "rzh," and *"š"* is "sh." For phrasebook and glossary, see **Glossary: Czech,** p. 949.

FOOD AND DRINK

CZECH	❶	❷	❸	❹	❺
FOOD	under 80Kč	80-110Kč	111-150Kč	151-200Kč	over 200Kč

Loving Czech cuisine starts with learning to pronounce *knedlíky* (KNED-lee-kee). These thick loaves of dough, feebly known in English as dumplings, are a staple. Meat, however, lies at the heart of almost all main dishes; the **national meal** (known as *vepřo-knedlo-zelo*) is *vepřové* (roast pork), *knedlíky*, and *zelí* (sauerkraut). If you're in a hurry, grab *párky* (frankfurters) or *sýr* (cheese) at a food stand. **Vegetarian** restaurants serving *bez masa* (meatless) specialties are uncommon outside Prague, and traditional restaurants serve little more than *smaženy sýr* (fried cheese) and *saláty* (salads). Ask for *káva espresso* rather than just *káva:* the Czech brew may be unappealing to a Western palate. *Jablkový závin* (apple strudel) and *ovocné knedlíky* (fruit dumplings) are favorite sweets, but the most beloved is *koláč*—a tart filled with poppy-seed or sweet cheese. Moravian **wines** are of high quality. They're typically drunk at a *vinárna* (wine bar) that also serves a variety of spirits, including *slivovice* (plum brandy) and *becherovka* (herbal bitter), the **national drink.** However, local brews, like *Plzeňský Prazdroj* (Pilsner Urquell), *Budvar*, and *Krušovice*, dominate the drinking scene.

CUSTOMS AND ETIQUETTE

Firmly established customs govern wining and dining. When beer is served, wait until all raise the common *"na zdraví"* ("to your health") toast before drinking, and always look into the eyes of the individual with whom you are toasting. Similarly, before biting into a saucy *knedlík*, wish everyone "dobrou chut" ("to your health"). The official **tipping** rate given in guidebooks and generally used by tourists is 10%. However, this rate is not the one used by locals. Czechs don't consider tipping a necessity. If they are satisfied with the service, 5% is considered sufficient, and 10% would signal excellent service. People often leave nothing if they are unimpressed. While not tipping may seem stingy to travelers from the US and Western Europe, where 10-20% is considered normal, in the Czech Republic the tip is completely at your discretion.

THE ARTS

LITERATURE. The Czech Republic is a highly literate country where writers hold a privileged position as important social and political commentators. From the first Czechoslovak president, **T.G. Masaryk,** to the recently retired **Václav Havel,** literary figures have proven to be the nation's most powerful citizens. The Hapsburgs repressed Czech literature during the 18th century, but the 19th century saw a literary renaissance. In 1836, **Karel Hynek Mácha** penned his celebrated epic *May (Máj)*, considered a lyric masterpiece. The founding of the literary journal *Máj*—named after Mácha's poem—in 1856 marked the beginning of the **National Revival,** during which nationalist literary output exploded. One of its brightest stars, **Bozena Němcová,** introduced the novel to modern Czech literature with *Granny (Babička;* 1855). The 20th century saw the creation of **Jaroslav Hašek's** satire, *The Good Soldier Švejk (Dobrý voják Švejk;* 1921-23), which became a classic commentary on life under Hapsburg rule. While he wrote in German, **Franz Kafka's** work is pervaded by the dark circumstances of his position as a German-speaking Jew in his native Prague. **Jaroslav Seifert** and **Vítězslav Nezval** explored Poetism and Surrealism, producing image-rich meditations. In 1984, Seifert became the first Czech author to receive a **Nobel Prize.**

FINE ARTS AND ARCHITECTURE. Marie Čerminová Toyen, a notable Surrealist, immigrated to Paris in the 1920s to work closely with André Breton. One of the most important Czech artists of the 20th century, **Alfons Mucha** also worked in Paris and helped develop the **Art Nouveau** painting style. **Josef Čapek** was a Cubist and caricaturist best known for his satire of Hitler's ascent to power.

While few Czech architects have become household names, the country itself is rife with architectural treasures. Both **Český Krumlov** (see p. 278) and **Kutná Hora** (see sidebar, p. 266) have been declared protected cultural monuments by UNESCO for their medieval buildings and winding streets. Within **Prague** (see p. 233), architectural styles intermingle, juxtaposing the 1000-year-old **Prague Castle** (see p. 257) with daring examples of Art Nouveau and Cubism.

MUSIC AND FILM. The 19th-century National Revival brought out the best in Czech music. The nation's most celebrated composers, **Antonín Dvořák, Leoš Janáček,** and **Bedřich Smetana,** are renowned for transforming Czech folk tunes into symphonies and operas. Dvořák's *Symphony No. 9, From the New World,* combining Czech folk tradition with the author's experience of America, is probably the most famous Czech masterpiece. Among Czechs, however, Smetana's symphonic poem *My Country (Má vlast)* remains more popular.

The Czech Republic has been successful in the **film** industry. In 1966, director **Jiří Menzel's** *Closely Watched Trains (Ostře sledované vlaky)* won the Academy Award for Best Foreign Film. Director **Miloš Forman** immigrated to the US in 1968 and exploded into the film industry with the acclaimed *One Flew Over the Cuckoo's Nest* (1975). His 1984 film *Amadeus* won eight Oscars.

TODAY. The Czech literary tradition remains strong today. The country's best known author of the present day is **Milan Kundera,** whose philosophical novel *The Unbearable Lightness of Being,* set against the backdrop of communist Prague, met with international acclaim. His late 20th-century novels, as well as those of writer **Josef Škvorecký,** continue to be popular both at home and abroad. The country's recent president, **Václav Havel,** is a well-known playwright with several revered dramas to his name. Film has become an increasingly popular medium in the Czech Republic, and **Karlovy Vary** (see p. 271) hosts a major film festivals. In 1997, an Oscar traveled to the Czech Republic for Jan Svěrák's film **Kolya.**

HOLIDAYS AND FESTIVALS

The Czech Republic hosts a number of internationally renowned festivals. While this provides a feast of activities for the traveler, if you are planning to attend any major festivals, reserve a room and your tickets well in advance.

Classical musicians and world-class orchestras descend on **Prague** (see p. 261) for the **Spring Festival** held from mid-May to early June. Held each June, the **Five-Petaled Rose Festival,** a boisterous medieval festival in Český Krumlov (see p. 278) features music, dance, and a jousting tournament. **Masopust,** the Moravian version of Mardi Gras, is celebrated in villages across the Czech Republic from Epiphany to Ash Wednesday. Revelers dressed in animal masks feast, dance, and sing until Lent begins.

NATIONAL HOLIDAYS IN 2005

January 1 New Year's Day	**September 28** Czech Statehood Day
March 27-28 Easter Holiday	**October 28** Independence Day
May 1 May Day	**November 17** Struggle for Freedom and Democracy Day
May 8 Liberation Day	**December 24-26** Christmas
July 5 Cyril and Methodius Day	
July 6 Jan Hus Day	

ADDITIONAL RESOURCES

GENERAL HISTORY

The Coasts of Bohemia, by Derek Sayer (2000). Weaving together politics and culture, Sayer's lively narrative is scholarly but accessible.

Prague in Black and Gold, by Paul Dementz (1998). A comprehensive yet engaging account of the complicated past of Central Europe.

FICTION AND TRAVEL BOOKS

The Garden Party, by Václav Havel (1993). A collection of the former Czech president's renowned dramas.

Prague: A Traveler's Literary Companion, by Paul Wilson, ed. (1995). A series of essays and short stories by various Czech authors illuminating the historical and literary significance of Prague's monuments and cityscapes.

The Unbearable Lightness of Being, by Milan Kundera (1984). This lyrical novel about two couples has become a classic of high Modernism, and is one of the most famous works to emerge from the Czech Republic.

FILM

Kolya, directed by Jan Svěrák (1996). The Academy Award-winning story of a Czech musician who finds himself in charge of his stepson after his wife leaves the country.

Closely Watched Trains, directed by Jiří Menzel (1966). Another Oscar-winner, this film recounts the lives and loves of Czech railway employees during WWII.

CZECH ESSENTIALS

ENTRANCE REQUIREMENTS

Passport: Required of all travelers.
Visa: Not required for stays under 90 days for citizens of Australia, Canada, Ireland, New Zealand, and the US. Not required for stays under 180 days for citizens of the UK.
Letter of Invitation: Not required.
Inoculations: Recommended up-to-date on DTaP (diphtheria, tetanus, and pertussis), Hepatitis A, Hepatitis B, MMR (measles, mumps, and rubella), Polio booster, and Typhoid.
Work Permit: Required of all foreigners planning to work.
International Driving Permit: Required of all those planning to drive.

DOCUMENTS AND FORMALITIES

EMBASSIES AND CONSULATES

Embassies and consulates of other countries in the Czech Republic are in **Prague** (see p. 233). The Czech Republic's embassies and consulates abroad include:

Australia: 8 Culgoa Circuit, O'Malley, Canberra, ACT 2606 (☎02 6290 1386; canberra@embassy.mzv.cz).

Canada: 251 Cooper St., Ottawa, ON K2P 0G2 (☎613-562-3875; ottawa@embassy.mzv.cz).

Ireland: 57 Northumberland Rd., Ballsbridge, Dublin 4 (☎01 668 1135; **New Zealand:** See Australian embassy).

UK: Embassy: 26 Kensington Palace Gardens, London W8 4QY (☎020 7243 1115; www.czechembassy.org.uk).

US: Embassy: 3900 Spring of Freedom St. NW, Washington, D.C. 20008 (☎202-274-9100; www.mzv.cz/washington).

VISA AND ENTRY INFORMATION

Citizens of Australia, Canada, Ireland, New Zealand, and the US may visit visa-free for up to 90 days, and UK citizens for up to 180 days. Visas are available at those countries' embassies or consulates. You cannot obtain a Czech visa at the border. Processing takes seven to 10 days when submitted by mail; five days when submitted in person. With the application, you must submit your passport; one photograph (two if applying to the Czech consulate in Los Angeles) glued—not stapled—to the application; a self-addressed, stamped envelope (certified or overnight mail); and a cashier's check or money order.

GETTING AROUND

Air Canada, Air France, American Airlines, British Airways, ČSA, Delta, KLM, Lufthansa, and **SAS** are among the major carriers with flights into Prague.

The easiest and cheapest way to travel between cities in the Czech Republic is by **train**. **Eastrail** is accepted in the Czech Republic, but **Eurail** is not. The fastest international trains are *EuroCity* and *InterCity* (*expresní;* marked in blue on schedules). *Rychlík* trains are fast domestic trains, (*zrychlený vlak;* marked in red on schedules). Avoid slow *osobní* trains, marked in white. *Odjezdy* (departures) are printed on yellow posters, *příjezdy* (arrivals) on white. Seat reservations (*místenka;* 10Kč) are recommended on express and international trains and for first-class seating.

Czech **buses** are efficient and convenient, but their schedules can be confusing (see sidebar, p. 238). For travel in the countryside, they're a quicker and cheaper option than trains. **ČSAD** runs national and international bus lines, and many European companies offer international service. Consult the timetables or buy your own bus schedule (25Kč) from kiosks.

Roads are well-kept and **roadside assistance** is usually available. In addition to an International Driving Permit, US citizens must have a **US driver's license. Taxis** are a safe way to travel, but may overcharge you, especially in Prague. Negotiate the fare beforehand, as notoriously exorbitant fees arise from cabbies "estimating" the fare. Phoning a taxi service is generally more affordable than flagging a cab on the street. Though common in the Czech Republic, *Let's Go* does not recommend hitchhiking.

TOURIST SERVICES AND MONEY

Municipal tourist offices in major cities provide info on sights and events, distribute lists of hostels and hotels, and often book rooms. **CKM**, a national student tourist agency, is helpful for young travelers, booking hostel beds and issuing ISICs and HI cards. Most bookstores sell a national hiking map collection, *Soubor turistických map*, with an English key.

The Czech unit of currency is the **koruna** (crown, **Kč,** plural *koruny*). **Inflation** is around 2.2%. **Banks** offer good exchange rates. **Komerční banka** is a common bank chain. **ATMs** are everywhere—look for the abundant *"Bankomat"* signs—and offer the best exchange rates. **Traveler's checks** can be exchanged almost everywhere, though rarely without commission. MasterCard and Visa are accepted at most establishments, but many hostels and budget establishments remain wary of plastic.

 VAT'S THE WAY THE COOKIE CRUMBLES. Czech-bound travelers may be shocked to discover that the **value added tax (VAT)** rate on Czech goods skyrocketed from 5% to **22%** in January 2004. This increase is expected to generate nearly 11 million Kč in revenues—a healthy boost for the Czech government, but a kick in the teeth for budget travelers. Mercifully, food and lodging do not fall under this VAT increase and remain at the 5% rate. The supply costs for restaurants and hotels, however, have risen because of the new VAT rate and many have had to raise their prices slightly to accommodate this change. The prices listed in this book reflect the new 2004 VAT rate.

HEALTH AND SAFETY

 EMERGENCY NUMBERS: Police: ☎ 158 **Fire:** ☎ 150 **Ambulance:** ☎ 155

Medical facilities in the Czech Republic are of high quality, especially in Prague, and major foreign insurance policies are accepted. *Lékárna* (pharmacies) and supermarkets carry international brands of *náplast* (bandages), *tampóny* (tampons), and *kondomy* (condoms). For prescription drugs and aspirin, look for proper pharmacies (marked with a green cross). Petty **crime** has increased dramatically since 1989; beware of pickpockets prowling among the crowds in Prague's main squares and tourist attractions.

Women traveling alone should experience few problems in the Czech Republic. However, caution should be exercised while riding public transportation, especially after dark. **Minorities** should not encounter too much trouble. **Homosexuality** is legal in the Czech Republic and gay nightlife is taking off, but displays of homosexual affection are not common; travelers should expect to encounter stares and are advised to remain cautious in public situations.

ACCOMMODATIONS AND CAMPING

CZECH ACCOM.	❶	❷	❸	❹	❺
	under 320Kč	320-500Kč	501-800Kč	801-1200Kč	over 1200Kč

Hostels and **university dorms** are the cheapest option in July and August; two- to four-bed dorms cost 250-400Kč. Hostels are clean and safe throughout the country. **Pensions** are the next most affordable option at 600-800Kč, including breakfast. **Hotels** tend to be more luxurious and expensive than hostels or pensions, with prices from 1000Kč. From June to September reserve at least a month ahead in Prague and a week ahead in Český Krumlov, and Brno. If you can't keep a reservation, call to cancel so that some weary backpacker won't be sleeping on the street—at some point, that weary backpacker might be you. **Private homes** are not nearly as popular (or as cheap) as in the rest of Eastern Europe. Scan train stations for *"Zimmer frei"* signs. As quality varies, do not pay in advance. There are many **campgrounds** strewn about the country; however, most are open only from mid-May to September.

KEEPING IN TOUCH

The **postal system** is reliable and efficient. A postcard to the US costs 12Kč, to Europe 9Kč. When sending by **airmail**, stress that you want it to go on a plane (*letecky*). Go to the customs office to send packages heavier than 2kg abroad. **Poste Restante** is generally available. Address envelopes as follows: Andrea (first name) HALPERN (LAST NAME), POSTE RESTANTE, Jindřišská 14 (post office street address), 110 00 (postal code) Praha (city), CZECH REPUBLIC.

Card-operated **phones** (175Kč per 50 units; 320Kč per 100 units) are simpler to use than coin phones. You can purchase phone **cards** (telefonní karta) at most *Tábaks* and *Trafika* (convenience stores). To make domestic calls, simply dial the entire number. City codes no longer exist in the Czech Republic and dialing zero is no longer necessary. To make an international call to the Czech Republic, simply dial the country code followed by the entire phone number. Calls run 8Kč per min. to Australia, Canada, the UK, or the US; and 12Kč per min. to New Zealand. Dial ☎ 1181 for English info, ☎ 0800 12 34 56 for the international operator.

International access codes include: **AT&T** (☎00 420 00 101); **British Telecom** (☎00 420 04412); **Canada Direct** (☎00 420 00 151); **MCI** (☎00 420 00112); **Sprint** (☎00 420 87 187); and **Telstra** Australia (☎00 420 061 01).

Internet access is readily available throughout the Czech Republic. Internet cafes offer fast connections for about 1.50Kč per min.

PRAGUE (PRAHA)

From the nobility of Prague Castle to the pastel facades of the Old Town Square, Prague (pop. 1,200,000) is a city on the cusp of the divine. King of Bohemia and Holy Roman Emperor, Charles IV foresaw a royal seat worthy of his rank and refashioned Prague into a city of soaring cathedrals and lavish palaces. Its maze of shady alleys and supposedly demon-haunted houses lend it a dark and dreamy atmosphere. Even in the 21st century, an ethereal magic hangs over the city, captivating the imaginations of writers, artists, and tourists alike.

The magic has been well tested in recent years. Since the lifting of the Iron Curtain, hordes of outsiders have flooded the venerable capital. In summer, most locals leave for the countryside and the foreigner-to-resident ratio soars above nine-to-one. Beer runs cheaper than water in these tourist-filled streets, but look elsewhere to find the city's true spirit. Walk a few blocks from any of the major sights and you'll be lost in the labyrinthine cobblestone alleys. But even in the hyper-touristed Old Town, Prague's majesty gleams: the Charles Bridge, packed so tightly in summer that the only way off is to jump, is still breathtaking at sunrise and eerie in a fog.

■ INTERCITY TRANSPORTATION

Flights: Ruzyně Airport (☎220 111 111), 20km northwest of the city. Bus #119 runs between the airport and Metro A: Dejvická (5am-midnight; 12Kč, 6Kč per bag). Buy tickets in kiosks or machines but not on board. An **airport bus** run by **Cedaz** (☎220 114 296; 20-45min., every 30min., 5:30am-9:30pm) collects travelers outside Metro stations at Nám. Republiky (90Kč) and Dejvická (60Kč). **Taxis** to **Ruzyně** can be expensive but may be the only option at night. Try to settle on a price before starting (400-600Kč). Airlines include: **Air France,** Václavské nám. 57 (☎221 662 662); **British Airways,** Ruzyně Airport (☎222 114 444); **Czech Airlines** (ČSA), V Celnici 5 (☎239 007 007); **Delta,** Národní třída 32 (☎224 946 733); **KLM,** Na Příkopě 21 (☎233 090 933); **Lufthansa,** Ruzyně Airport (☎220 114 456); **Swissair,** Pařížská 11 (☎221 990 444).

Trains: (☎221 111 122, international info 224 615 249; www.vlak.cz.) International spoken on international info line and attempted at station info offices. Prague has 4 main terminals. **Hlavní nádraží** (☎224 615 786; Metro C: Hlavní nádraží) and **Nádraží Holešovice** (☎224 624 632; Metro C: Nádraží Holešovice) are the largest and cover most international service. Domestic trains leave from **Masarykovo nádraží** (☎840 112 113, 221 111 122; Metro B: Nám. Republiky), and from **Smíchovské nádraží** (☎972 226 150; Metro B: Smíchovské nádraží). International trains run to: **Berlin, GER** (5hr., 5 per day, 1400Kč); **Bratislava, SLK** (4½-5½hr., 6 per day, 576Kč); **Budapest, HUN** (7-9hr., 4 per day, 1400Kč); **Kraków, POL** (7-8hr., 4 per day, 874Kč); **Moscow, RUS** (31hr., 1 per day, 3000Kč); **Munich, GER** (7hr., 5 per day, 1650Kč); **Vienna, AUT** (4½hr., 6 per day, 925Kč); **Warsaw, POL** (9½hr., 3 per day, 1290Kč). **BIJ Wasteels** (☎224 641 954; fax 224 221 872; www.wasteels.cz), on the 2nd fl. of Hlavní nádraží, to the right of the stairs, sells discounted international tickets to those under 26, books sleeping cars, and also sells bus tickets. Open M-F 9am-7pm, Sa 9am-4pm. Wasteels tickets are also available from the **Czech Railways Travel Agency** (☎224 239 464; fax 224 223 600) at Nádraží Holešovice. Open M-F 9am-5pm, Sa-Su 8am-4pm.

Buses: (☎900 149 044; www.vlak-bus.cz) Open daily 6am-9pm. The state-run **ČSAD** (Česká státní automobilová doprava; Czech national bus transport; ☎257 319 016) has several bus terminals. The biggest is **Florenc**, Křižíkova 4 (☎900 149 044). Metro B or C: Florenc. Info office open daily 6am-9pm. Buy tickets in advance. To: **Berlin, GER** (7hr., 1 per day, 850Kč); **Budapest, HUN** (8hr., 1 per day, 1550Kč); **Paris, FRA** (14hr., 3 per day, 2200Kč); **Sofia, BUL** (24hr., 5 per day, 1600Kč); **Vienna, AUT** (5hr., 1 per day, 600Kč). 10% ISIC discount. The **Tourbus** office (☎224 218 680; www.euro-lines.cz), on the main fl. of the terminal, sells tickets for **Eurolines** and airport buses. Open M-F 7am-7pm, Sa 8am-7pm, Su 9am-7pm.

✈ ORIENTATION

Shouldering the river **Vltava**, greater Prague is a mess of suburbs and maze-like streets. Fortunately, nearly everything of interest to travelers lies within the compact downtown. The Vltava runs south-northeast through central Prague, separating **Staré Město** (Old Town) and **Nové Město** (New Town) from **Malá Strana** (Lesser Side). On the right bank of the river, the Old Town's **Staroměstské náměstí** (Old Town Square) is Prague's focal point. From the square, the elegant **Pařížská ulice** (Paris Street) leads north into **Josefov**, the old Jewish ghetto in which only six synagogues and the Old Jewish Cemetery remain. Lying just south of the Old Town, the more modern **Nové Město** houses **Václavské náměstí** (Wenceslas Square), the administrative and commercial core of the city. To the west of Staroměstské nám., the picturesque **Karlův most** (Charles Bridge) spans the Vltava, connecting the Old Town with **Malostranské náměstí** (Lesser Town Square). **Pražský Hrad** (Prague Castle) looks over Malostranské nám. from **Hradčany** hill. Prague's **train station, Hlavní nádraží,** and **Florenc bus station** lie northeast of Václavské nám. All train and bus terminals are on or near the **Metro** system. To get to Staroměstské nám., take the Metro A line to Staroměstská and go down Kaprova away from the river. Kiosks and bookstores sell an indexed *plán města* (map), which is essential for newcomers to the city.

▐ LOCAL TRANSPORTATION

Public Transportation: Prague's **Metro, tram,** and **bus** services are excellent and share the same ticket system. Buy tickets at newsstands, *tabák* kiosks, machines in stations, or DP (*Dopravní podnik;* transport authority) kiosks. The DP offices (☎222 646 350; open daily 7am-6pm), near the Jungmannovo nám. exit of the Můstek Metro stop and the 24hr. tourist office in Old Town Hall, sell **multi-day passes** valid for the entire network (1-day 70Kč, 3-day 200Kč, 1-week 250Kč, 15-day 280Kč). 8Kč tickets good for 1 15min. ride or 4 stops on the Metro. 12Kč ticket valid for 1hr., in which you can travel with unlimited bus, tram, and Metro connections, as long as all travel is in the same direction. Large bags, bikes, and baby carriages 6Kč; babies travel free. Validate tickets in machines above the escalators to avoid the 400Kč fines issued by plainclothes inspectors who roam the transport lines. The 3 **Metro** lines run daily 5am-midnight: A is green on maps, B is yellow, and C is red. **Night trams** #51-58 and **buses** #502-514 and 601 run after the last Metro and cover the same areas as day trams and buses (every 30min. 12:30-4:30am); look for dark blue signs with white letters at bus stops. For the most up-to-date information, contact the DP (☎296 191 817; www.dpp.cz).

Taxis: Radiotaxi (☎272 731 848) or **AAA** (☎140 14). 30Kč flat rate plus 22Kč per km and 4Kč per min. waiting. You can hail a cab anywhere on the street, but call ahead to avoid getting ripped off. To sidestep the taxi scams that run rampant through the city, always ask for a receipt (*"Prosím, dejte mi paragon"*) with distance traveled and price paid. If the driver doesn't comply, you aren't obligated to pay. Many drivers speak enough English to collect their money, though few can hold a conversation.

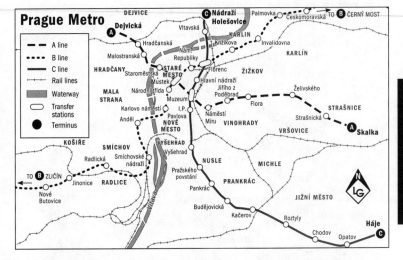

Prague Metro

- – – A line
- ∙∙∙∙ B line
- —— C line
- +–+– Rail lines
- Waterway
- Transfer stations
- ● Terminus

Car Rental: Hertz, at the airport. (☎233 326 714; www.hertz.cz/en.) Must have a 1-year-old driver's license and major credit card. 21+. Cars from 1880Kč per day for the first 5 days with unlimited mileage. Open daily 8am-10pm. **Branch** at Karlovo nám. 28 (☎222 231 010). Open daily 8am-10pm.

🛈 PRACTICAL INFORMATION

TOURIST AND FINANCIAL SERVICES

Tourist Office: The green "i"s around Prague mark the myriad tourist agencies that book rooms and sell **maps,** bus tickets, and guidebooks. The main **Pražská Informační Služba** (PIS; Prague Information Service; ☎12 444; www.pis.cz), in the Old Town Hall, sells maps (25-199Kč) and tickets for shows and public transport. Open Apr.-Oct. M 11am-6pm, Tu-Su 9am-6pm; Nov.-Mar. M 11am-5pm, Tu-Su 9am-5pm. **Branches** at Na příkopě 20 and Hlavní nádraží (summer M-F 9am-7pm, Sa-Su 9am-5pm; low season M-F 9am-6pm, Sa 9am-3pm), and in the tower by the Malá Strana side of the Charles Bridge. (Open daily Apr.-Oct. 10am-6pm.)

Budget Travel:

CKM, Mánesova 77 (☎222 721 595; www.ckm-praha.cz). Metro A: Jiřího z Poděbrad. Sells budget air tickets to those under 26. Also books accommodations in Prague from 250Kč. Open M-Th 10am-6pm, F 10am-4pm.

GTS, Ve smečkách 27 (☎222 211 204; www.gtsint.cz). Metro A or C: Muzeum. Offers student discounts on airline tickets (225Kč-2500Kč within Europe). Open M-F 8am-10pm, Sa 10am-4pm.

Lesser Travel, Karmelitská 24 (☎257 534 130; www.airtickets.cz). Offers student airfares. Open M-F 10am-5pm.

Passport Office: Foreigner police headquarters are at Olšanská 2 (☎974 811 111). Metro A: Flora. From the Metro, turn right on Jičínská with the cemetery on your right and go right again on Olšanská. Or, take tram #9 from Václavské nám. toward Spojovací and get off at Olšanská. To get a **visa extension,** get a 90Kč stamp inside, line up at doors #2-12, and prepare to wait up to 2hr. Little English spoken. Open M-Tu and Th 7:30-11:30am and 12:15-3:00pm, W 8:00am-12:15pm and 1-5pm, F 7:30-11:30am.

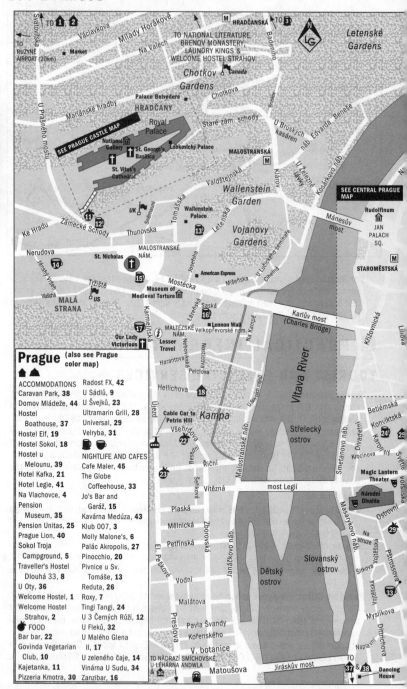

Prague (also see Prague color map)

ACCOMMODATIONS
Caravan Park, **38**
Domov Mládeže, **44**
Hostel
  Boathouse, **37**
Hostel Elf, **19**
Hostel Sokol, **18**
Hostel u
  Melounu, **39**
Hotel Kafka, **21**
Hotel Legie, **41**
Na Vlachovce, **4**
Pension
  Museum, **35**
Pension Unitas, **25**
Prague Lion, **40**
Sokol Troja
  Campground, **5**
Traveller's Hostel
  Dlouhá 33, **8**
U Oty, **36**
Welcome Hostel, **1**
Welcome Hostel
  Strahov, **2**
⚫ FOOD
Bar bar, **22**
Govinda Vegetarian
  Club, **10**
Kajetanka, **11**
Pizzeria Kmotra, **30**

Radost FX, **42**
U Sádlů, **9**
U Švejků, **23**
Ultramarin Grill, **28**
Universal, **29**
Velryba, **31**

NIGHTLIFE AND CAFES
Cafe Maler, **45**
The Globe
  Coffeehouse, **33**
Jo's Bar and
  Garáž, **15**
Kavárna Medúza, **43**
Klub 007, **3**
Molly Malone's, **6**
Palác Akropolis, **27**
Pinocchio, **20**
Pivnice u Sv.
  Tomáše, **13**
Reduta, **26**
Roxy, **7**
Tingi Tangi, **24**
U 3 Černých Růží, **12**
U Fleků, **32**
U Malého Glena
  II, **17**
U zeleného čaje, **14**
Vinárna U Sudu, **34**
Zanzibar, **16**

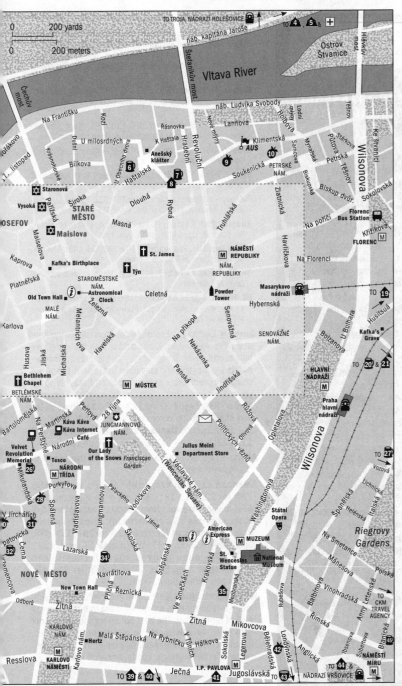

0 200 yards
0 200 meters

TO TROJA, NÁDRAŽÍ HOLEŠOVICE

náb. kapitána Jaroše

Štefánikův most

Ostrov
Štvanice

Čechův most

Vltava River

Na Františku

náb. Ludvíka Svobody

Lannova

Klimentská
AUS

PETRSKÉ
NÁM.

Soukenická

Staronová

Anežský klášter

Vysoká

Široka

STARÉ
MĚSTO

OSEFOV

Maiselova

Dlouhá

Rybná

Masná

Truhlářská

Na poříčí

Florenc
Bus Station

FLORENC

Kaprova

Kafka's Birthplace

St. James

NÁMĚSTÍ
REPUBLIKY

NÁM.
REPUBLIKY

Na Florenci

Platnéřská

Týn

Old Town Hall

STAROMĚSTSKÉ
NÁM.
Astronomical
Clock

Celetná

Powder
Tower

Masarykovo
nádraží

TO 19

MALÉ
NÁM.

Hybernská

Karlova

Melantrichova

Na příkopě

SENOVÁŽNÉ
NÁM.

Kafka's
Grave

Husova

Bethlehem
Chapel

Havelská

Panská

Jindřišská

HLAVNÍ
NÁDRAŽÍ

TO 20 & 21

BETLÉMSKÉ
NÁM.

MŮSTEK

Praha
hlavní
nádraží

28 října

Káva Káva
Káva Internet
Café

JUNGMANNOVO
NÁM.

Politických vězňů

Velvet
Revolution
Memorial

Tesco

NÁRODNÍ

Národní

Our Lady
of the Snows

Franciscan
Garden

Julius Meinl
Department Store

NÁRODNÍ
TŘÍDA

TO 27

Purkyňova

Vozová

V Jirchářích

Spálená

American
Express

Riegrovy
Gardens

Černá

Lazarská

GTS

MUZEUM

St.
Wenceslas
Statue

National
Museum

NOVÉ MĚSTO

New Town Hall

Na Smetance

TO
CKM
TRAVEL
AGENCY

Odborů

Žitná

Mikovcova

KARLOVO
NÁM.

Hertz

Žitná

I.P. PAVLOVA

NÁMĚSTÍ
MÍRU

Resslova

KARLOVO
NÁMĚSTÍ

Ječná

Jugoslávská

TO 39 & 40

TO 43

TO 44 &
NÁDRAŽÍ VRŠOVICE

CZECH TRANSPORT, DIGITAL STYLE

Though it may sound simple, catching intercity transport in the Czech Republic is a tricky endeavor. Finding a route that runs between two cities is only a quarter of the battle—tracking down the right bus or train at the station is the real test. As I discovered my first day in transit, Czech bus and train stations are littered with posted schedules, each a maze of numbers, hammers, sickles, and circles that bear a closer resemblance to target practice than an intelligible course from point A to point B.

But there is a quick and easy way of getting to your destination that bypasses scrutinizing schedules and anxiously asking directions. The answer is the Internet. Unless you're clairvoyant, fluent in Czech, or both, the public transit system's website is an invaluable tool for successfully navigating the country.

Log onto www.vlak.cz, which is in Czech only. Enter your departure city in the box marked "odkud," your destination city in the box below marked "kam," your desired departure date (with the day first and then the month) and departure time (using military time), and click "vyhledat." Like magic, all the up-to-date bus and train information for your chosen time and route will appear.

Once you've decided which train or bus to take, click on the route number located next to the

Embassies and Consulates:

Australia, Klimentska 10 (☎296 578 350; www.embassy.gov.au/cz.html) and **New Zealand,** Dykova 19 (☎222 514 672) have consulates, but citizens should contact the UK embassy in an emergency. Australian consulate open M-Th 8:30-5pm, F 8:30-2pm.

Canada, Mickiewiczova 6 (☎272 101 800; www.canada.cz). Metro A: Hradčanská. Open M-F 8:30am-12:30pm and 1:30-4:30pm.

Germany, Vlašská 19 (☎257 113 111; www.germanembassy.cz). Metro A: Malostranská. Open M-F 9am-noon.

Hungary, Badeniho 1 (☎233 324 454). Metro A: Hradčanská. Open M-W, F 9am-noon.

Ireland, Tržiště 13 (☎257 530 061). Metro A: Malostranská. Open M-F 9:30am-12:30pm and 2:30-4:30pm.

Poland, Valdštejnské nám. 8 (☎257 530 388; www.ambpol.cz). Metro A: Malostranská. Open M-F 8am-4pm.

Russia, Pod Kaštany 1 (☎233 374 100). Metro A: Hradčanská. Open M,W, and F 9am-1pm.

Slovak Republic, Pod Hradební 1 (☎233 321 442). Metro A: Dejvická. Open M-F 8:30am-noon.

UK, Thunovská 14 (☎257 402 111). Metro A: Malostranská. Open M-F 9am-noon.

US, Tržiště 15 (☎257 530 663, after-hours emergency ☎253 12 00; www.usembassy.cz). Metro A: Malostranská. Open M-F 8am-4:30pm.

Currency Exchange: Exchange counters are everywhere and rates vary wildly. Don't bother with the expensive hotels, and never change money on the streets. **Chequepoints** are plentiful and stay open until about 11pm, but charge unpredictable commissions and may try to rip you off, so know your math. Try bargaining. **Komerční banka,** Na příkopě 33 (☎222 432 111), buys notes and checks for 2% commission. Open M-W 9am-6pm, Th-F 9am-5pm. **E Banka,** Václavské nám. 43 (☎222 115 222; www.ebanka.cz). Open M-F 8am-7pm.

ATMs: ATMs are ubiquitous; look for the plentiful "*Bankomat*" signs.

American Express: Václavské nám. 56 (☎222 800 224; fax 222 211 131). Metro A or C: Muzeum. AmEx **ATM** outside. Western Union services available. MC/V **cash advances** (3% commission). Open daily 9am-7pm. **Branches** at Mostecká 12 (☎257 313 638; open daily 9:30am-7:30pm), Celetná 17 (☎/fax 222 481 205; open daily 8:30am-7:15pm), and Staroměstské nám. 5 (☎224 818 388; fax 224 818 389; open daily 9am-7:30pm).

Work Opportunities: Unless you're near-fluent in Czech, many establishments will be reluctant to hire you on as a short-term worker. The best option for short-term work is to place advertisements on bulletin boards in cafes, Internet cafes, laundromats, or even in the local newspaper offering language, sports, or music lessons.

LOCAL SERVICES

Luggage Storage: Lockers in train and bus stations take two 5Kč coins. 30Kč fee for forgetting the locker number or combination. For storage over 24hr., use the luggage offices to the left in the basement of **Hlavní nádraží** (15Kč per day, bags over 15kg 30Kč. Open 24hr. with breaks 5:30-6am, 11-11:30am, and 5:30-6pm) or along the stairs at **Florenc.** (30Kč per day; 100Kč for lost ticket. Open daily 5am-11pm.)

English-Language Bookstores:

The Globe Bookstore, Pštrossova 6 (☎224 934 203; www.globebookstore.cz). Metro B: Národní třída. Exit Metro left on Spálená, make the first right on Ostrovní, then the third left on Pštrossova. A haven for English speakers, this bookstore and coffeehouse sells a wide variety of new and used books and periodicals, and offers **Internet access** (1.5Kč per min.). Doubles as a café serving up fruit smoothies (55-70Kč) and brunch late into the afternoon—perfect after a day of sleeping off an alcohol-induced fog. Open daily 10am-midnight.

Anagram Bookshop, Týn 4 (☎224 895 735; www.anagram.cz). Metro A: Staroměstská. Behind Týn Church in the Ungelt passageway. One of few bookstores to sell academic English textbooks as well as traditional fiction. Trade-ins for used books great for lightening your load. Open M-Sa 10am-8pm, Su 10am-7pm.

Big Ben Bookshop, Malá Štupartská 5 (☎224 826 565; www.bigbenbookshop.com). Metro A: Staroměstská. Near St. James's church. Open M-F 9am-6:30pm, Sa 10am-5pm, Su noon-5pm.

The different lengths of telephone numbers, ranging from 4 to 9 digits, can be confusing. Prague is continuously updating its phone system and modified all numbers in Sept. 2002, adding a 2 before most land lines and removing the 0 for mobile numbers. Updated numbers have 9 digits; if a number has fewer than 9, it is either an information or emergency line or is missing its city area code. The city area code is the first three digits of a number, usually a 2 followed by a number from 10 to 35. The numbers listed here reflect the most recent changes, but call the city's telephone info line for any updates (☎141 11).

Laundromat: Laundry Kings, Dejvická 16 (☎233 343 743). Metro A: Hradčanská. Exit metro to Dejvická, cross the street, and turn left. Travelers flock here at night to watch CNN and pick each other up. Bulletin board for apartment-seekers, English teachers, and "friends." Internet access 55Kč per 30min. Wash 70Kč per 6kg; dry 15Kč per 8min. (usually takes 25min.; use

bus or train icon and write i down. When buses or trains rol through stations, they tend to dis play only their route number anc final destination, so this info is a key way of finding out whick coach to actually board.

With these facts in hand arrive at the station (abou 20min. early, just to be safe) and simply check the station's main schedule—usually locatec near the entrance to the statior information office—to find the platform from which your bus departs. Now, with this bit of vir tual help, you can impress you fellow travelers and breathe a sigh of relief, knowing you'll ge to Litomysl even though you're on a bus labeled "Libec."

If you're without Interne access, here's a rough guide tc deciphering the hieroglyphics you'll encounter on the schedule crossed mallets indicate service: that operate only on weekdays The number 6 indicates Saturda service. A "K" or an "L" accompa nied by a number corresponds tc notes at the bottom of the sched ule which detail periods of time during which the bus does not rur as scheduled. Also, check the arrival time at your destination: i you see a vertical or zig-zaggec line running through it, this means that the service is express anc passes through but does not stop at that destination. Good luck!

—*Lauren Rivera*

the spinner to save on drying). Soap 30Kč. Full-service 50Kč more and takes 24hr. Dry cleaning 41-225Kč (M-F 7am-7pm, Sa 8am-noon). Beer 20Kč. Open M-F 6am-10pm, Sa-Su 8am-10pm. **Laundromat/Internet Cafe,** Korunní 14 (☎222 510 180). Metro A: Nám. Míru. Kill two birds with one stone. Wash and dry 70Kč each. Soap 75Kč. Internet 30Kč per 15min. Open daily 8am-8pm.

Praha Bike, Dlouhá 24 (☎732 388 880; www.prahabike.cz). Bike rental includes helmet, lock, and map. Student discount available. City rides at 11:30am, 2:30pm, and 6pm. 420Kč for 2 hr. rental, 460Kč for 3hr.

Central Prague (also see Prague color map)

🏠 ACCOMMODATIONS	U Rozvarilů, 9
Apple Hostel, 9	U Špirků, 17
Dům U Krále Jiřího, 25	Vinárna v Zátiší, 30
Hotel Junior, 29	
Hostel Dlouha, 5	🍺🍷 NIGHTLIFE & CAFES
Hostel Týn, 8	Bakeshop Praha, 6
Ritchie's Hostel, 18	Bugsy's Bar, 7
Traveller's Hostel Husova 3, 24	Cafe Ebel, 12, 23
U Lilie, 19	Cafe Marquis de Sade, 15
🍴 FOOD	Jazz Club Železná, 16
Cafe Bambus, 2	Karlovy Lázně, 22
Country Life, 21	Kavárna Imperial, 10
Jáchymka, 11	Kozička, 3
Klub architektů, 31	Le Chateau, 14
Picante, 4	Paneria, 28
Pizza Express, 27	U staré paní, 26
Roma Due, 20	Ungelt, 13
	Umě, 1

EMERGENCY AND COMMUNICATIONS

24hr. Pharmacy: U Lékárna Anděla, Štefánikova 6 (☎257 320 918, after-hours 257 320 194). Metro B: Anděl. With your back to the Anděl metro station, turn left and follow Nádražní until it becomes Štefánikova. Open M-F 7am-7pm, Sa 8am-1pm. For after-hours service, press the button marked "Pohotovost" to the left of the main door.

Medical Services: Na Homolce (Hospital for Foreigners), Roentgenova 2 (☎257 272 146, after hours 257 211 111; www.homolka.cz). Bus #168 and 184. Major foreign insurance plans and credit cards accepted. **American Medical Center,** Janovského 48 (☎220 807 756, after hours 220 877 973; www.amcenters.com). Major foreign insurance policies accepted. **Canadian Medical Center,** Veleslavínská 30 (☎235 360 133, after hours 724 300 301; www.cmc.praha.cz). BUPA and MEDEX insurance accepted.

Telephones: Virtually everywhere. Card phones are the most common and convenient. Phone cards are sold at kiosks, post offices, and some exchange establishments for 175Kč per 50 units and 350Kč per 100 units; don't let kiosks rip you off. Coins also accepted (local calls from 4Kč per min.).

Internet Access: Prague is an Internet nirvana. Jump on the web in libraries, hostels, posh cafes, and trendy bars. **Národní třída** is home to several lab-like cybercafes.

🖥**Bohemia Bagel,** Masna 2 (☎224 812 560; www.bohemiabagel.cz). Metro A: Staroměstská. An expat favorite, this cafe serves up excellent bagel sandwiches (65-145Kč) to complement its speedy Internet. 1.8Kč per min. Open M-F 7am-midnight, Sa-Su 8am-midnight. **Branch** at Újezd 16. Open daily 9am-midnight.

Cafe Net, Havelská 27. Metro A: Staroměstská. See directions to U Špirků restaurant (**Staré Město Restaurants,** p. 247), then go through the arch to the left. Friendly staff, funky decor, and a full bar make writing home most enjoyable. 20Kč per 15min. Open daily 10am-10pm.

Káva Káva Káva, Národní třída 37 (☎224 228 862). Metro B: Národní třída. Across the street from Tesco, to the right and through the arch on your left. A cute cafe that provides Internet (2Kč per min. 7-10am and 6-10pm, 2.5Kč per min. 10am-6pm) and sells pricey espresso (45Kč) in a lovely, warm atmosphere. Open M-F 7am-10pm, Sa-Su 9am-8pm. AmEx/MC/V.

Internet Cafe, Národní třída 25 (☎776 555 666). Metro B: Národní třída. Across from Tesco inside the Pasáž paláce Metro. Blacklighting and arcade games make for a dubious atmosphere, but the Internet is fast and cheap. 1Kč per min. Open daily 10am-midnight. **Branch** at Liliová 18, near the Charles Bridge. Open M-F 9am-11pm, Sa-Su 10am-11pm.

Post Office: Jindřišská 14 (☎221 131 445). Metro A or B: Můstek. **Poste Restante** available. Take a number from the kiosks in the main hallway and wait for your number to be called. Internet 1Kč per min. Tellers close at 7pm. Open daily 2am-midnight. **Postal Code:** 110 00.

CZECH REPUBLIC

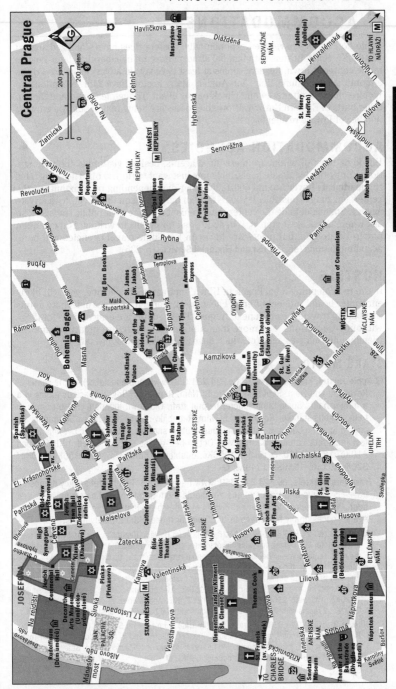

Central Prague

N

0   200 meters
0   200 yards

Havlíčkova
Dlážděná
Masarykovo nádraží
SENOVÁŽNÉ NÁM.
Jubilee (Jubilejní)
Jeruzalémská
TO HLAVNÍ NÁDRAŽÍ
U Půjčovny
Růžová

V. Celnici
Zlatnická
Na Poříčí
Trubližská
Truhlářská
NÁMĚSTÍ REPUBLIKY
NÁM. REPUBLIKY
Hybernská
St. Henry (sv. Jindřich)
Jindřišská

Revoluční
Kotva Department Store
Králodvorská
U Obecního Domu
Municipal House (Obecní dům)
Powder Tower (Prašná brána)
Senovážná
Nekázanka
Panská
Na Příkopě
Mucha Museum
V Cípu
Museum of Communism

Benediktská
Rybná
Rybná
Templova
Big Ben Bookshop
St. James (sv. Jakub)
Jakubská
American Express
Celetná
OVOCNÝ TRH
Estates Theatre (Stavovské divadlo)
Havířská
MŮSTEK
VÁCLAVSKÉ NÁM.

Rámová
Malá Štupartská
House of the Golden Ring
TÝN Anagram
Štupartská
Týn Church (Panna Marie před Týnem)
Provaznická
Na můstku
Rytířská

Bohemia Bagel
Masná
Dlouhá
Golz-Kinský Palace
Týnská
Kamzíková
Karolinum (Charles University)
Železná
St. Gall (sv. Havel)
Havelská Uličká

Kozí
Masná
Dlouhá
V Kolkovně

Spanish (Španělská)
Vězeňská
Dušní
St. Salvátor (sv. Salvátor)
Image Theater
American Express
Pařížská
Jan Hus Statue
STAROMĚSTSKÉ NÁM.
Astronomical Clock
Old Town Hall (Staroměstská radnice)
Melantrichova
Michalská
Kožná

El. Krásnohorské
Dušní
Church (sv. Duch)
Kostečná
Maisel (Maiselova)
Maiselova
Cathedral of St. Nicholas (sv. Mikuláš)
Kafka Museum
Platnéřská
MARIÁNSKÉ NÁM.
Linhartská
MALÉ NÁM.
Hlavsova
Jilská

Pařížská
Brehová
High Synagogue
Old-New (Staronová)
Josefská
Joseph Town Hall (Židovská radnice)
Žatecká
Říše loustek Theater
Valentínská
Husova
St. Giles (sv. Jiljí)
Zlatá
Czech Museum of Fine Arts
Jilská

U Starého
JOSEFOV
Jewish Ceremonial Hall
Klaus (Klausová)
Pinkas (Pinkasová)
STAROMĚSTSKÁ
Kaprova
Seminářská
Husova
Řetězová
Zlatá
Anenská
ANENSKÉ NÁM.
Bethlehem Chapel (Betlémská kaple)
BETLÉMSKÉ NÁM.

Na reidiší
Decorative Arts Museum (Uměleckoprůmyslové)
Cemetery
Široká
17. listopadu
Valentinská
Thomas Cook
Kanova
Liliová
Stříbrná
Náprstek Museum
Boršov

Dvořákovo
Rudolfinum (Dům umělců)
JAN PALACHA SQ.
Alšovo náb.
Veleslavínova
Klementinum and sv. Kliment (St. Clement Church)
Křižovnícka
St. Francis (sv. František)
TO CHARLES BRIDGE
Smetana Museum
Na Zábradlí
Theatre at the Balustrade (Divadlo na zábradlí)
Náprstkova
Karolíny Světlé

Mánesův most
Dvořákovo náb.

⌐ ACCOMMODATIONS

While hotel prices have risen exponentially, hostel prices have stabilized around 300-600Kč. Small hostels with familial atmospheres are cheaper than large hostels in the center of town. Reserve rooms at least two days in advance and as early as a month ahead in June, July, and August. Many hostels have 24hr. reception and require check-in after 2pm and check-out by 10am. Though less common than in other parts of Eastern Europe, affordable rooms are being rented out by a growing number of Prague residents.

ACCOMMODATION AGENCIES

Hawkers, most of whom are mere hired agents, besiege visitors at the train station. Many offer legitimate deals, but some just want to rip you off. The going rates for **apartments** hover around 600-1200Kč per day, depending on proximity to the center; haggling is possible. If you're wary of bargaining on the street, try a private agency. Staying outside the center is convenient if you're near public transport, so ask where the nearest stop is. If in doubt, ask for details in writing. You can often pay in US dollars, but prices are lower in Kč. Some travel agencies will book accommodations (see **Tourist and Financial Services,** p. 235).

HOSTELS

If you're schlepping a backpack in Hlavní nádraží or Holešovice, you will likely encounter hostel runners offering cheap beds. Many hostels are university dorms that take in travelers from June to August. These rooms are easy options for those without reservations. For more than a mere bed, there are plenty of smaller, friendlier alternatives, most of which have an English-speaking staff.

STARÉ MĚSTO

▨ **Apple Hostel,** Krádlodvorská 16 (☎224 231 050; www.applehostel.cz), at the corner of Revoluční and Nám. Republiky. Metro B: Nám. Republiky. Bright, spacious rooms in a a former bank. Social atmosphere, helpful staff, Old Town location, and proximity to train and bus stations. Rooms facing Nám. Republiky can be a bit noisy. Bathrooms are large and clean but have communal, push-button showers. Internet 1Kč per min. Breakfast included. Laundry 120Kč. Mar.-Oct. 4-bed dorms 450Kč, 5-bed 440Kč, 8-bed 410Kč, 12-bed 360Kč; singles 1950Kč; doubles 1240Kč. Nov.-Feb. 350Kč/340Kč/320Kč/300Kč/1950Kč/1240Kč. ❷

Travellers' Hostels, (☎224 826 662; www.travellers.cz). This hostel agency rounds up travelers at bus and train stations and herds them to one of its hostels for beds and beer. Price varies by location but always includes breakfast. Due to high turnover, the agency occasionally has space in Old Town for those without reservations.

Dlouhá 33 (☎224 826 662; fax 224 826 665). Metro B: Nám. Republiky. Exit the Metro and walk toward Hotel City Center, following Revoluční toward the river. Go left on Dlouhá; the hostel is on the right. Large rooms, unbeatable location, and a terrace bar make up for the peeling paint. In the same building as the Roxy Club, but with soundproofing. The only Traveller's Hostel open year-round, it has social dorms and more private renovated apartments. Book 2-3 weeks in advance in summer. Internet 1Kč per min. Laundry 150Kč. 10-bed dorm 370Kč, 6-bed 430Kč; singles 1120Kč, with bath 1300Kč; doubles 620Kč/720Kč. Apartments: 2- or 3-bed 2100Kč, 4-bed 2400Kč; 2 rooms with 4 beds 2500Kč; 2 rooms with 5-6 beds 3000Kč. 40Kč ISIC discount. ❷

Husova 3 (☎222 220 078). Metro B: Národní třída. Turn right on Spálená (which turns into Na Perštýně after Národní), and then Husova. Smaller, quieter, and in the middle of the Old Town, with bright rooms, gingham sheets, and heavenly pillows. Breakfast included. Satellite TV. Open July-Aug. 4- to 5-bed dorms 450Kč; doubles 620Kč. ❷

Hostel Týn, Týnská 19 (☎224 828 519; www.hostel-tyn.web2001.cz). Metro A: Staroměstská. From Staroměstské nám., head down Dlouhá, bear right at Masná, and take another right on Týnská. A quiet getaway in the center of Old Town, Týn boasts immaculate facilities and a friendly staff. 5-bed dorms 400Kč; doubles 1100Kč. ❷

Ritchie's Hostel, Karlova 9 (☎222 221 229; www.praguehostel.net). Metro A: Staroměstská, down Karlova from the Charles Bridge, past the small square. Enter through the souvenir shop. Ritchie's location in the heart of Old Town is enticing and its newly renovated rooms are basic but bright. Bathrooms sparkle. Internet 30Kč per 20min. 6-bed dorm 390Kč, 500Kč with bathroom; doubles 1890Kč/2000Kč. 10% discount for cash payment. MC/V. ❷

NOVÉ MĚSTO

▨ Pension Unitas Art Prison Hostel/Cloister Inn, Bartolomějská 9 (☎224 221 802; fax 224 217 555; www.unitas.cz). Metro B: Národní třída. Cross Národní, head up Na Perštýně away from Tesco and turn left on Bartolomějská. Once home to a communist jail, the "pink prison" today offers clean and pleasant dorms. A bargain, despite communal bathrooms. The upstairs offers hotel rooms in renovated cells. The bright decor makes it hard to imagine what Havel's cell must have looked like when he was incarcerated here. Breakfast buffet included. Reception 24hr. Reservations at least 3 weeks in advance advised; via fax or email preferred. Dorm 270Kč per person. Mar.-Oct. singles 1100Kč; doubles 1400Kč; triples 1800Kč; quads 2100Kč. Nov.-Mar. 1000Kč/1200Kč/1500Kč/1800Kč. MC/V. Hostel ❶/hotel ❹

Hostel u Melounu (At the Watermelon), Ke Karlovu 7 (☎224 918 322; www.hostelumelounu.cz). Metro C: IP Pavlova. With your back to the Metro, turn left on Sokolská, make an immediate right on Na Bojišti, and turn left at the street's end on Ke Karlovu. A beautiful respite, this former hospital provides the ideal environment in which to recuperate from the city's frenetic pace. Bar and private garden. Provides a list of the top 5 clubs, bars, and restaurants in Nové Město, but the grounds are so peaceful you won't want to leave. Breakfast included. Laundry 100Kč. Internet 1Kč per min. Dorms 380Kč; singles 550Kč; doubles 450Kč. 30Kč ISIC discount. AmEx/MC/V. ❷

Hostel Advantage, Sokolská 11-13 (☎224 914 062; www.advantagehostel.cz). Metro C: IP Pavlova. From the Metro, take the stairs on the left, leading to Ječná, cross the street, make a left onto Sokolska, and the hostel will be 100m down on your right. In the heart of Nové Město, this beautifully maintained hostel has simple rooms in a homey atmosphere. Breakfast included. Reserve at least 1 week in advance. Dorm 400Kč; double 500Kč. 10% ISIC discount. ❷

Prague Lion, Na Bojišti 26 (☎296 180 018; www.praguelion.com). Metro C: IP Pavlova. With your back to the Metro, turn left on Sokolská and make an immediate right on Na Bojišti. Good location, extremely welcoming staff, and clean rooms, but on the pricey side. Internet 1Kč per min. Breakfast included. Check-in 2pm. Check-out 10am. Singles 1250Kč; doubles 1400Kč; triples 1750Kč; quads 2100Kč. Prices lower Sept.-May. ❺

Hotel Junior, Senovážné nám. 21 (☎224 231 754; euroagentur@euroagentur.cz). Metro B: Nám. Republiky. Follow Revoluční toward the Powder Tower, go left on Senovážná at the tower, then left again to Senovážné nám. Immaculate white rooms in a social hostel. Down a beer while bowling (daily 4pm-3am) and reward yourself with a bite at the downstairs pizzeria. Breakfast included. Check-in 2pm. Reservations recommended 1-2 weeks in advance. June-Aug. dorms 550Kč; Sept.-May 450Kč. 100Kč ISIC discount. ❸

MALÁ STRANA

Hostel Sokol, Nosticova 2 (☎257 007 397). Metro A: Malostranská. From the Metro, take tram #12 or 22 to Hellichova; or walk from Malostranské nám. down Karmelitská about 300m. Take a left on Hellichova, then the last left on Nosticova, and watch for signs. Reception on the 3rd fl. Located in the Malá Strana sports club, this quiet but institutional hostel offers large, clean rooms. While the peaceful location adjacent to a park is appealing, the three flights of cracked, peeling stairs are not. Rooftop terrace and communal kitchen. Safes and lockers available. Breakfast not included but a special rate is offered at neighboring Bohemia Bagel. Reception 24hr. Check-out 10am. Weekend rooms are often unavailable due to athletic competitions at affiliated Sokol gymnasium. Dorms Oct.-May 340Kč, June-Sept. 350Kč; doubles 660Kč/900Kč. ●

VINOHRADY

Hostel Elf, Husitská 11 (☎222 540 963; fax 222 540 927; www.hostelelf.com). From Metro C: Hlavni nadrazi, turn left through the park, then cross the tram tracks and turn right, then immediately left. Cross the large street and turn left onto Husitská. The hostel is 100m down on your left. In walking distance of the main train and bus stations and Stare Mesto, this establishment provides spacious rooms, a fully equipped kitchen, and bright orange decor. A highly social atmosphere and nearby train tracks make it less than ideal for those seeking peace and quiet. Dorms don't have keys, but lockers are provided (bring your own lock). Breakfast included. Laundry 150Kč. 9-bed dorms 290Kč; singles 700Kč, 1000Kč with private bath; doubles 840Kč/1200Kč. ●

Domov Mládeže, Dykova 20 (☎222 511 777; www.dhotels.cz). From Metro A: Jiřího z Poděbrad, follow Vinohradská toward the huge clock, then go right on Nitranská and make the third left on Dykova, which isn't sign-posted. 100 beds in the tree-lined Vinohrady mansion district; so peaceful you might forget you're in Prague. Breakfast included. Reserve 1-2 weeks in advance. 2- to 7-person dorms 370-480Kč; doubles 940-1360Kč. 10% ISIC discount. ❷

OUTSIDE THE CENTER

▨ **Hostel Boathouse,** Lodnická 1 (☎241 770 051; www.aa.cz/boathouse). Take tram #21 from Národní třída south toward Sídliště. Get off at Černý Kůň (20min.), go down the ramp from the tram, turn left toward the Vltava, and follow the yellow hostel signs. Věra runs one of the most highly praised staffs in all of Europe, and even manages to remember almost every guest's name. A young, energetic crowd and 70 beds make this hostel the perfect fusion of nurturing home and summer camp. The Boathouse serves meals (hot dinner 120Kč) and offers board games, Internet access, satellite TV, and laundry service (150Kč per load). Call ahead; if they're full, Věra might let you sleep in the hall. Breakfast included. Email reservations preferred. 3- to 5-bed dorms above a working boathouse 340Kč; 8-bed dorm 320Kč. ●

▨ **Penzion v podzámčí,** V podzámčí 27 (☎241 444 609; www.sleepinprague.com). From Metro C: Budějovická, take bus #192. Request that the driver stop at Nad Rybníky. The hostel is up the hill behind the bus stop. The friendly staff provides homey service, including laundry (100Kč per load). Communal kitchen, satellite TV, comfy beds, and amazing hot chocolate. Highway-side rooms can be noisy. Internet access 100Kč per hr. Breakfast 40Kč. Reserve in advance. Sept.-June dorms 310Kč; doubles 690Kč; triples 960Kč; July-Aug. 330Kč/790Kč/1080Kč. 30Kč student discount. ●

Welcome Hostel, Zíkova 13 (☎224 320 202; www.bed.cz). Metro A: Dejvická. Exit the Metro on Šolinova and go left on Zíkova. An incredible bargain: an entire room in a spacious, convenient university dorm for the price of an Old Town bed. Proximity to airport shuttle; they can book you at their sister hostel (see below) if they're full. Check-in 2pm. Check-out 9:30am. Singles 400Kč; doubles 540Kč. 10% off with ISIC. ❷

Welcome Hostel at Strahov Complex, Vaníčkova 7 (☎224 320 202; www.bed.cz). Take bus #149 or 217 from Metro A: Dejvická to Koleje Strahov (15min.) and cross the street to reach the hostel reception, located in Block 3. Right by an enormous stadium,

Strahov is 10 concrete blocks of bright blue high-rise dormitories. Rooms are basic but clean and only 10min. by foot from Prague Castle. Not convenient but sufficient. Open July-Sept. Singles 300Kč; doubles 440Kč. 10% ISIC discount. ❶

HOTELS AND PENSIONS

As tourists colonize Prague, hotels are upgrading their services and their prices; budget hotels are now scarce. Call several months ahead to book a room for the summer and confirm by fax with a credit card. For something out of the ordinary, try the admirably renovated prison cells at the Cloister Inn (see p. 243).

STARÉ MĚSTO

▨ **Dům U Krále Jiřího,** Liliová 10 (☎222 220 925; www.kinggeorge.cz). Metro A: Staroměstská. Exit at Nám. Jana Palacha. Walk down Křížovnická toward Charles Bridge and go left on Karlova; Liliová is the 1st street on the right. Enter through restaurant. Capturing the antique character of the Old Town, Krále Jiřího offers gorgeous rooms with private bath. Buffet breakfast included. Reception daily 7am-11pm. Mar.-Oct. singles 1800Kč; doubles 3100Kč; triples 4300Kč; apartments 3100Kč-6550Kč. 300Kč discount Jan.-Feb. and Nov.-Dec. ❺

U Lilie, Liliová 15 (☎222 220 432; www.pensionulilie.cz). Metro A: Staroměstská. Follow the directions to Dům U Krále Jiřího. U Lilie boasts a lovely courtyard; satellite TV, telephone, and minibar in every room. Breakfast included. Singles with shower 1850Kč; doubles 2150Kč, with bath 2800Kč. No credit cards. ❺

NOVÉ MĚSTO

▨ **Pension Museum,** Mezibranská 15 (☎296 325 186; www.pension-museum.cz). Metro C: Muzeum. From the Metro, go right on Mezibranská and walk up the hill. It's on the right-hand side. Ultra-modern B&B near Wenceslas Sq. Beautiful courtyard leads to elegant rooms with TV and spacious bath. Welcoming staff speak English, French, and German. Decadent breakfast buffet included. Reserve at least a month in advance. Singles Apr.-Dec. 2240Kč, Jan.-Mar.1450Kč; doubles 2650Kč/1800Kč; apartments 2750Kč-4450Kč/1790Kč.-3180Kč. AmEx/MC/V. ❺

Hotel Legie, Sokolská 33 (☎224 266 231, reservations 224 266 240; www.legie.cz). Metro C: IP Pavlova. From the Metro, turn left on Ječná; the hotel is across the street. The unattractive Soviet facade of this high-rise hotel hides sparkling rooms with private showers, phone, and cable TV; some afford great views of Prague Castle. Breakfast included. Apr.-Oct. and Jan. singles 2500Kč; doubles 3000Kč; triples 3900Kč. Feb. and Nov.-Dec. 1800Kč/2100Kč/2800Kč. AmEx/MC/V. ❺

OUTSIDE THE CENTER

Hotel Kafka, Cimburkova 24 (☎/fax 222 781 333, reservations 224 225 769), in Žižkov near the TV tower. From Metro C: Hlavní nádraží, take tram #5 toward Harfa, #9 toward Spojovací, or #26 toward Nádraží Hostivař; get off at Husinecká. Head uphill along Seifertova 3 blocks and go left on Cimburkova. Spotless, comfortable hotel located in a residential neighborhood. Phone and TV in every room. Breakfast included. Singles Apr.-Oct. 1700Kč, Nov.-Mar. 1000Kč; doubles 2300Kč/1300Kč; triples 3200Kč/1700Kč; quads 3500Kč/2200Kč. MC/V for 5% commission. ❺

B&B U Oty (Ota's House), Radlická 188 (☎257 215 323; www.bbuoty.cz). Metro B: Radlická. Exit the Metro up the stairs to the left, go right past Bistro Kavos on Radlická, and walk 400m. Though not very convenient for reaching the city center, Ota—the quirky yet charming proprietor—offers spacious, well-furnished, clean rooms in his home at an affordable price. Best for groups of 2 or more due to the deserted walk to and from the Metro station along a poorly lit highway. Reserve in advance. Breakfast included. Laundry free after 3 nights. Kitchen facilities. Singles 700Kč; doubles 770Kč; triples 990Kč; quads 1300Kč. 100Kč extra if staying only 1 night. ❸

☀ CAMPING

Campsites have taken over both the outskirts and the centrally located Vltava islands. Reserve bungalows in advance. Tents are generally available without prior notice. Tourist offices sell a guide (15Kč) to campsites near the city.

Sokol Troja, Trojská 171 (☎/fax 233 542 908). Prague's largest campground, north of the center in the Troja district. From Metro C: Nádraží Holešovice, take bus #112 to Kazanka, the 4th stop. A unique camping experience—pitch a tent and admire the beautiful houses of one of Prague's wealthiest neighborhoods. Sparkling bathing facilities. If the grounds are full, at least 4 similar establishments line the same road. July-Aug. tents 90-180Kč plus 130Kč per person; Oct.-June 70-150Kč. Private rooms available. July-Aug. singles 320Kč, doubles 640Kč; Oct.-June 290Kč/580Kč. ❶

Caravan Park, Císařská louka 599 (☎025 40 925), on the Císařská louka peninsula. Metro B: Smíchovské nádraží, then any of the 300-numbered buses to Lihovar. Go left on the shaded path as you head to the river (1km). Or, a ferry leaves on every hr. until about 10pm from the landing, 1 block from Smíchovské nádraží (10Kč). Small, tranquil campground on the banks of the Vltava. Clean facilities, friendly staff, and convenient cafe. Currency exchange on premises. 95Kč per person, 90-140Kč per tent. Local tax 15Kč per person, plus 5% national tax. Children and students exempt from local tax. ❶

Na Vlachovce, Zenklova 217 (☎284 692 035; r.terc@worldonline.cz). Take bus #102 or 175 from Nádraží Holešovice to Okrouhlická. Cross the street and continue up the hill. Enter through the restaurant. If you've ever felt like crawling into a barrel of Czech beer, try these bungalow beds in tiny 2-person barrels. Great view of Prague. Breakfast included. Reserve 1 week ahead. If the barrels (200Kč) invoke claustrophobia, the attached pension has singles (500Kč) and doubles (975Kč). ❶

◐ FOOD

The nearer you are to the center, the more you'll pay. In less-touristed areas, you can have pork, cabbage, dumplings, and a beer for 75Kč. Always bring cash and check the bill, as you'll pay for everything the waiter brings, including ketchup and bread, and some restaurants try to massage bills higher than they should. For lunch, *hotová jídla* (prepared meals) are cheapest. Though vegetarian establishments are quickly multiplying, veggie options at traditional Czech restaurants often remain limited to fried cheese, Balkan cheese salad (similar to Greek salad), and cabbage. For fresher alternatives, head to the **daily market** at the intersection of Havelská and Melantrichova in Staré Město.

STARÉ MĚSTO RESTAURANTS

▨ **Jáchymka,** Jáchymova 4. (☎224 819 621). Walk up Pařížská and take a right on Jáchymova. A favorite among locals, Jáchymka serves heaping portions of traditional cuisine in a lively, casual atmosphere. Try the goulash with dumplings (95Kč) or a massive meat *escalope* (98-195Kč). For those who prefer lighter fare, salmon with pasta and vegetables (128Kč) will also satisfy. Open daily 11am-11pm. MC/V. ❷

▨ **Klub architektů,** Betlémské nám. 52A (☎224 401 214; www.klubarchitektu.com). Metro B: Národní třída. Take Spálená until it becomes Na Perštýně, then turn left on Betlémské nám. Walk through the gate immediately on your right and descend underground. A 12th-century cellar with sleek table settings and copper pulley lamps. Meat dishes (160-190Kč), like the delicious pork steak, are tantalizing. Veggie options 120-150Kč. The fruit dumpling dessert (100Kč) is divine. Open daily 11:30am-midnight. Kitchen closes at 11pm. AmEx/MC/V. ❸

Country Life, Melantrichova 15 (☎224 213 366; www.countrylife.cz). Metro A: Staroměstská. See directions to U Špirků (see below). After days of Czech dumplings and fried cheese, Country Life's salad bar is the perfect antidote for any veggie cravings you may have. Attached to an organic gourmet grocery store, it's always packed at lunchtime with locals looking for a quick bite before heading back to work. Pay by weight for a mix of greens (19.90Kč per 100g) and a variety of delicious, light, dairy-free dishes. Open M-Th 9am-8:30pm, F 9am-4pm and Su 11am-8:30pm. ❷

Vinárna v Zátiší, Liliová 1 (☎222 221 155), on the corner of Liliová and Náprstkova. As you walk into the frescoed entrance hall of this elegant restaurant, the massive crystal chandelier hints at what is to come. With all the dressings of a gourmet establishment, Vinarná distinguishes itself with creative regional specialties like crisp Bohemian duckling with red cabbage and fresh herb dumplings. Fine Moravian wines. 3-course lunch menu 795Kč. Bohemian evening tasting menu 1175Kč. Reservations recommended. Open daily noon-3pm and 5:30-11pm. AmEx/MC/V. ❺

Cafe Bambus, Benediktská 12 (☎224 828 110; www.bambus.cz). Metro B: Nám. Republiky. See directions to Hostel Dlouhá 33 (see **Accommodations,** p. 242) and take a left on Benediktská. Step out of the tourist jungle into this African oasis where masks, statuettes, and crocodiles adorn the walls. Asian and international cuisine with Czech flavors (55-228Kč); sweet and savory Czech pancakes (55-75Kč). Open M-Th 10am-1am, F 10am-2am, Sa 11am-2am, Su 11am-11pm. ❷

U Špirků, Kožná ulička 12 (☎224 238 420). Metro A: Staroměstská. With your back to the astronomical clock, go through the archway down Melantrichova and take the 1st left on Kožná. Sit next to hungry locals and devour huge portions of well-prepared Czech food for reasonable prices. Salads 25-40Kč; pork, steak, potatoes, and cabbage 105Kč. Additional 20Kč and 10% service charge. Open daily 11am-midnight. ❷

NOVÉ MĚSTO RESTAURANTS

🟦 **Radost FX,** Bělehradská 120 (☎224 254 776; www.radostfx.cz). Metro C: IP Pavlova. Locals and expats agree that Radost has the best vegetarian food in town. Offering a range of healthy yet hearty entrees, including pizzas, salads, sandwiches, pastas, and stir-fries (105-195Kč), Radost satisfies even the staunchest of carnivores. A cafe, lounge, art gallery, and nightclub in one, Radost boasts one of the hippest atmospheres in the city. Brunch Sa-Su (95-140Kč). Italian night Su 5pm-2am. Open daily 11am-late (at least 3am on weekdays and 5am on weekends). ❸

🟦 **Universal,** V jirchářích 6 (☎224 934 416). Metro B: Národní třída. Follow the directions to Velryba (see p. 248), but head right around the church to V jirchářích. A fusion of Mediterranean, French, and Asian flavors, Universal offers huge, fresh salads (119-17Kč) in a bright and spacious dining room. Imaginative entrees (115-329Kč) go brilliantly with a glass or two of Moravian wine (50Kč for a small carafe, 100Kč for a large carafe). Scrumptious Sunday brunch buffet (135Kč). Open M-Sa 11:30am-1am, Su 11am-midnight. MC/V for bills higher than 500Kč. ❸

U Sádlů, Klimentská 2 (☎224 813 874; www.usadlu.cz). Metro B: Nám. Republiky. From the square, take Revoluční toward the river and right on Klimentská. A descent into the candlelit entry reveals a medieval dining dungeon. The armor by the bar suggests that portions are bountiful enough to sustain a full day of knight-errantry—or sightseeing. Call for reservations. The staff can help you order traditional meals (105-235Kč) from the Czech-only menu. Open M-Sa 11am–1am, Su noon-midnight. AmEx/MC/V. ❸

Ultramarin Grill, Ostrovni 32 (☎224 932 249; www.ultramarin.cz). Metro B: Narodni Trida. With your back to the Metro, turn left and immediately right; Ultramarin will be on your left. This classy copper- and wood-filled bar and restaurant provides a chic alternative to the more touristed options in Staré Město. An open grill, woven mat chairs, and occasional live music explain why this place is a favorite with locals. The chef specializes in steak, duck, and lamb (100-165), making the menu a carnivore's dream come true. Krusovice on tap. Open daily 10am-11pm. AmEx/MC/V.

Velryba (The Whale), Opatovická 24 (☎224 932 391; www.kavarnavelryba.cz). Metro B: Národní třída. Cross the tram tracks and follow narrow Ostrovní, then take a left on Opatovická. Enjoy a cheap Czech or Italian pasta dish (62-145Kč) among a diverse crowd of locals, expats, suits, and tourists, or slip back to the plush cafe for coffee (espresso 22Kč) or wine. Open daily 11am-midnight. Cafe and gallery open daily 11am-9pm. ❷

Pizzeria Kmotra, V jirchářích 12 (☎224 945 809). Metro B: Národní třída. Follow the directions to Universal. It may look quiet from the outside, but descend into the cellar of this lively pizzeria and you'll find droves of diners devouring huge salads, pizzas, and pastas (85-140Kč). Open daily 11am-midnight. AmEx/MC/V. ❷

Govinda Vegetarian Club, Soukenická 27 (☎224 816 631). Metro B: Nám. Republiky. Walk down Revoluční, away from the Obecní Dum, and turn right on Soukenická. Hindu gods gaze upon customers eating delicious vegetarian stews. Set menu includes stew, rice, salad, and chutney. Small portions 80Kč, large 90Kč. Open M-F 11am-5pm. ❶

U Rozvarilů, Na Poříčí 26. Metro B: Nám. Republiky. Exit the station on Na Poříčí and take a sharp right around the church. Quality dining doesn't come cheaper—Czech regulars gorge themselves on traditional meals like meat with cream sauce (42Kč) and potato dumplings (13-15Kč). The stainless steel decor of this cafeteria-style establishment may feel sterile, but the jovial company and hearty food make perfect antidotes. Open M-F 7:30am-8:30pm, Sa 8am-6pm, Su 10am-6pm. AmEx/MC/V. ❶

MALÁ STRANA RESTAURANTS

Bar bar, Všehrdova 17 (☎257 313 246). Metro A: Malostranská. Follow the tram tracks from the Metro station down Letenská, through Malostranské nám., and down Karmelitská. Take the left on Všehrdova after the museum. The diverse selection of meats, cheeses, and veggie dishes (45-125Kč), as well as delicious sweet and savory Czech-style filled pancakes (48-89Kč), will please every palate. Funky atmosphere for whisky-drinking (from 65Kč) and jazz. Open Su-Th noon-midnight, F-Sa noon-2am. MC/V. ❶

U Švejků, Újezd 22 (☎257 313 244; www.usvejku.cz). Metro A: Malostranská. From the Metro, head down Klárov and right on Letenská. Bear left through Malostranské nám. and follow Karmelitská until it becomes Újezd. Converted to a restaurant in 1993, this former inn dates back to 1618. After a few beers (or a massive 1L brew), try to dance with the accordionist (plays after 7pm). The restaurant was named for Svejk, of Hašek's novel *The Good Soldier Svejk*, so murals of the cartoon hero cover the walls. Few vegetarian options. Entrees 118-148Kč. Open daily 11am-midnight. AmEx/MC/V. ❸

Kajetanka, Hradčanské nám. (☎257 533 735). Metro A: Malostranská. Exit the Metro and walk down Letenská, through Malostranské nám. Climb Nerudova until it curves around to Ke Hradu. Kajetanka is at the foot of the castle about 100m uphill. This cafe survives because its outdoor terrace offers a spectacular view over the red-tiled roofs of Prague. Salads and meat dishes (119-369Kč) aren't special, but the hordes of tourists don't seem to mind. Open daily Apr.-Sept. 10am-8pm; Oct.-Mar. 10am-6pm. ❹

LATE-NIGHT EATING

4:45am. Charles Bridge. Discos are still pumping ferociously, but all you can hear is your stomach. Rather than catching a bus, grab a *párek v·rohlíku* (hot dog) or a *smažený sýr* (cheese sandwich) on Václavské nám., or a gyro on Spálená. Make a morning of it with Prague's developing late-night cuisine. A great option for hungry hipsters is **Radost FX** (see **Nové Město Restaurants,** p. 247).

Roma Due, Lillová 18 (☎ 777 268 145). Metro A: Staroměstská or Night Tram 51: Staroměstská. From the Charles Bridge, take the 2nd right off Karlova on Lillová. Perfect for capping off a night out in Malá Strana or Karlovy Lázně. Even for the humorously inebriated, hay rides in the wagon above the bar are not permitted. Pasta (89-155Kč) until 10pm; pizza (89-175Kč) until 5am. Open 24hr. ❸

Picante, Revoluční 4. (☎ 222 322 022). Metro B: Nám. Republiky or Night Tram 52: Nám. Republiky. At the corner of Revoluční and Nám. Republiky. Tex-Mex restaurant serves up a spicy and healthy solution to the late-night munchies. Made-to-order quesadillas, tostadas, burritos, tacos, and fresh chips and salsa (49-179Kč). Open 24hr. ❶

Pizza Express, Na mustku 1 (☎ 224 229 500). Metro A or B: Můstek or Night Tram 51: Můstek. 100m from Můstek, across from the Prague Tourist Center. Fast-food pizza, falafel, salads, and pastries 39-79Kč. Open Tu-Su 24hr. ❶

SUPERMARKETS

The basements of Czech department stores have food halls and supermarkets. *Potraviny* (delis) and vegetable stands can be found on most street corners.

Tesco, Národní třída 26 (☎ 222 003 111). Right next to Metro B: Národní třída. Open M-F 8am-9pm, Sa 9am-8pm, Su 10am-8pm.

Kotva department store (☎ 283 088 320), at the corner of Revoluční and Nám. Republiky. Metro B: Nám. Republiky. Two-floor supermarket with fresh cheese and deli counters. Open M-F 7am-8pm, Sa 8am-7pm, Su 10am-8pm.

Julius Meinl department store (☎ 816 193 938; www.julius-meinl.cz), Václavské nám., at the intersection with Jindřišská. Metro A or B: Můstek. Open M-Sa 8am-9pm, Su 10am-9pm.

☕ CAFES

When Prague journalists are bored, they churn out yet another "Whatever happened to cafe life?" feature. The answer: it turned into *čajovna* (tea house) culture. Tea is all the rage, and many tea houses double as bars or clubs in the evening. Java junkies shouldn't fret: quality coffeehouses still abound. For those who desire email and fiction, rather than just sugar, with their coffee, see the **Globe Bookstore** (p. 239).

█ Cafe Ebel, Týn 2 (☎ 603 441 434; www.ebelcoffee.cz). Metro A or B: Staroměstská. From Old Town Square, follow Týnska, go right on Týn, then take an immediate left under the Ungelt arches. Relax in a plush chair on the terrace while sipping the best coffee in town. The "Jumbo" latte is so big you could bathe in it (85Kč). Friendly, English-speaking staff. Sandwiches and salads (60-100Kč). Continental breakfast (bread, yogurt, muesli, cheese, jam, and a latte; 160Kč) is a filling and affordable way to start the day. **Branch** at Retezova 9. Open daily 9am-10pm. AmEx/MC/V.

█ Bakeshop Praha, Kozí 1. (☎ 222 316 823; info@bakeshop.cz). From Old Town Square, follow Dlouhá to the intersection of Kozí. American-style bakery and cafe serving mouthwatering breads, pastries, salads, sandwiches, quiches, and a multitude of espresso and tea-based drinks. Chocolate-chip cookies like Mom makes (25Kč). For a bite of heaven, try the caramel brownies (18Kč). The fresh-squeezed orange juice is an island of nutrition in Praha's sea of indulgence (85Kč). 10% extra if you eat in. **Branch** at Lázenska 19, off Mostécka in Malá Strana. Open daily 7am-7pm.

U zeleného čaje, Nerudova 19 (☎ 225 730 027). Metro A: Malostranská. Follow Letenská to Malostranské nám. Stay right of the church and head down Nerudova. This adorable shop at the foot of Prague Castle takes tea to new heights. Choose from over 60 varieties of fragrant tea and creative tea-based drinks that will please the senses and calm the mind. To add a little kick, try an alcoholic tea cocktail like the Boiling Communist (35Kč) or Himalayan Tiger (49Kč). Sandwiches 25-59Kč. Open daily 11am-10pm.

Kavárna Imperial, Na Poříčí 15 (☎222 316 012; www.hotelimperial.cz). Metro B: Nám. Republiky. Lofty ceilings and mosaic tiles lend a refined atmosphere to this pillared cafe. Ella Fitzgerald accompanies Louis Armstrong on the horn as you consume a delicious ice cream sundae (57-91Kč). For 1943Kč, you can disturb the courtly air by purchasing a "bowl of yesterday's doughnuts that you can throw at other customers" (provided you're of legal age and passably sober). Live jazz, swing, and dixie F-Sa 9pm. Open M-Sa 9am-midnight, Su 9am-11pm.

Paneria, Dlouhá 50 (☎224 827 401; www.paneria.cz), on the corner of Revolucní and Dlouhá, serves up fresh French-style pastries (10-22Kč) and rolls (3Kč) for very reasonable prices. If the chocolate eclairs (8Kč) don't tempt you, the friendly Czech staff and colorful decor should. Open daily 7am-8pm.

U Malého Glena, Karmelitská 23 (☎257 531 717; www.malyglen.cz). From Metro A: Malostranská, take tram #12 to Malostranské nám., or walk down Letenská. This cafe, with the motto, "Eat, Drink, Drink Some More," has consumption down to a science. Entrees include salads (85-125Kč), sandwiches (95-125Kč), and baked potatoes (120-165Kč). After 9pm, the Maker's Mark basement bar downstairs has jazz or blues (cover 100-150Kč). Kitchen closes at midnight. Open daily 10am-2am. AmEx/MC/V.

Kavárna Medúza, Belgická 17 (☎222 515 107). Metro A: Nám. Míru. Head down Rumunská, and turn left at Belgická. An authentic taste of Prague cafe culture. Mismatched lamps, musty sofas, and murky mirrors mark this antiquated coffee shop, frequented by locals. Excellent espresso 23Kč. Open M-F 11am-1am, Sa-Su noon-1am.

◉ SIGHTS

One of the only major Central European cities unscathed by WWII, Prague is a well-preserved combination of labyrinthine alleys and Baroque buildings. You can easily find respite from the throngs of tourists by heading beyond Staroměstské nám., the Charles Bridge, and Václavské nám to Namesti miru, Vinohrady, and the southern part of Nové Město. While there are few places in the center left untouched by tourists, the masses have overlooked many of the city's most authentic and beautiful areas. To see a Prague not entirely made up of crystal and souvenir shops, try visiting a suburban sight, heading north of Staré Město, or exploring any of the city's beautiful gardens. Best traveled by foot, central Prague—Staré Město, Nové Město, Malá Strana, and Hradčany—is compact enough to be traversed in one day, but deserves more. Don't leave the city without strolling through the synagogues of Josefov, exploring the heights of Vyšehrad, or meandering through the streets of Malá Strana.

LITTLE GREEN MEN. Crossing Prague's streets provides an interesting puzzle for foreigners. There are stoplights with designated crossing areas for pedestrians, but the lights seem eternally stuck on the "don't walk" signal, a red man standing still. Indeed, one can easily wait five minutes for the walking green man to light up, only to have to race across the street before the red man reappears. Prague's crossings seem intended for sprinters instead of ordinary folk, but you won't see any jaywalkers. Drivers are unlikely to stop, and jaywalking is generally not acceptable. So instead, join the Czech crowd on the street corner and begin your wait for that elusive little green man.

STARÉ MĚSTO

Settled in the 10th century, Staré Město (Old Town) is a maze of narrow streets and alleys. Eight magnificent towers enclose **Old Town Square** (Staroměstské nám.) in the heart of Old Town. The vast stone plaza fills with blacksmiths, painters, carriages, and ice cream vendors in summer. As soon as the sun sets, the labyrinth of narrow roads and alleys fills with a younger crowd seeking midnight revelry at Staré Město's jazz clubs and bars.

CHARLES BRIDGE (KARLŮV MOST). This Baroque footbridge has become one of Prague's most treasured landmarks. Charles IV built the 520m bridge to replace the wooden Judith, the only bridge crossing the Vltava, which washed away in a 1342 flood. Defense towers border the bridge on each side; the smaller *Malostranská mostecká věž* (Malá Strana Bridge Tower) dates from the 12th century as part of Judith's original fortification, while the taller *Staroměstská mostecká věž* (Old Town Bridge Tower) was erected in the 15th century. Both towers offer splendid views of the river and of Prague's most precious sites. Over the years, the bridge has been decorated with 16 Baroque statues, but don't be fooled—they are replicas. The originals are locked away in local museums, safe from tourists and pigeons alike. *(Open daily 10am-10pm. 40Kč, students 30Kč.)* According to local legend, it was on this bridge that the hapless St. Jan Nepomuk, was tied in goatskin and thrown off the bridge for concealing the extramarital secrets of his queen from a suspicious King Wenceslas IV. The King tried every torturous trick in the book, but they all failed to loosen Jan's lips; finally, the King ordered that he be drowned. A halo of five gold stars appeared as Jan plunged into the icy water. The right-hand rail, from which Jan was supposedly tossed, is now marked with a cross and five stars between the fifth and sixth statues. Place one finger on each star and make a wish. *(The best way to reach Charles Bridge is on foot. Nearest Metro stops A: Malostranská on the Malá Strana side and A: Staroměstská on the Old Town side.)*

OLD TOWN HALL (STAROMĚSTSKÁ RADNICE). Next to the grassy knoll in Old Town Square, Old Town Hall is the multi-faceted building with the trim blown off the front. Partially demolished by the Nazis in the final days of WWII, the original pink facade now juts out from the tower. Prague's Old Town Hall has long been a witness to violence—crosses in front of it mark the spot where 27 Protestant leaders were executed on June 21, 1621 for staging a rebellion against the Catholic Hapsburgs. Crowds throng on the hour to watch the **astronomical clock** chime as the skeletal Death empties his hourglass and a procession of apostles marches by. The clock is such a masterpiece that legend says the clock-maker **Hanuš's** eyes were put out so he couldn't design another, making Prague's truly unique. The clock's operation stops for the night at 9pm. Inside the hall, you can climb (or take the lift) to the top of the tower to take in the view, which includes Týn Church. *(Metro A: Staroměstská; Metro A or B: Můstek. In Staroměstské nám. Open summer M 10am-7pm, Tu-F 9am-7pm, Sa-Su 9am-6pm. Clock tower open daily 10am-6pm; enter through 3rd fl. of Old Town Hall. 50Kč, students 40Kč.)*

JAN HUS STATUE. Burned at the stake in 1415 for his invocations against the indulgences of the Catholic Church (see **History,** p. 224), Jan Hus now stands as a symbol of Czech nationalism. Today this massive statue in the heart of Old Town Square serves mostly as a meeting place. *(In the center of Staroměstské nám.)*

TÝN CHURCH (CHRÁM MATKY BOŽÍ PŘED TÝNEM). Across from Old Town Hall, the spires of the Gothic Týn Church rise above a mass of medieval homes. Although the church is open only for mass, you can catch a glimpse of its amazing Baroque gold-and-black interior from the entrance. Buried inside the church's hallowed halls is famous astronomer Tycho Brahe, whose overindulgence at one of Emperor Rudolf's lavish dinner parties cost him his life. Since it was deemed most improper to leave the table before the Emperor, poor Tycho had to remain in his chair while his bladder filled and finally burst. *(In Staroměstské nám.; enter to the left of Cafe Italia. Mass W-F 6pm, Sa 8am, Su 11am and 9pm. Free.)*

ST. JAMES'S CHURCH (KOSTEL SV. JAKUBA). Creamy marble, pastel paintings, and ornate sculptures are a feast for the eyes, but think twice before touching anything. Legend has it that 500 years ago a thief tried to pilfer a gem from the Virgin Mary of Suffering, whereupon the figure came to life, seized his arm, and wrenched it off. Taking pity on the bleeding soul, the monks invited him to join their order. He accepted and remained pious, but his story warns that Mary protects the church. *(Metro B: Staroměstská. On Malá Štupartská, off Staroměstské nám. behind Týn Church. Open M-Sa 10am-noon and 2–3:45pm. Su mass 8, 9, and 10:30am.)*

POWDER TOWER AND MUNICIPAL HOUSE (PRAŠNÁ BRÁNA, OBECNÍDÚM). The contrasting designs of the Gothic Powder Tower and the Art Nouveau Municipal House make a fitting entrance to Staré Město. Though the Powder Tower was rendered a useless fortification by the establishment of Nové Město, you can still climb the winding tower to appreciate the expansive views from its topmost lookout. *(Metro B: Nám. Republiky. Open daily July-Aug. 10am-10pm; Apr.-June and Sept.-Oct. 10am-6pm. Top of tower 40Kč, students 30Kč.)* Next door, on the former site of the royal court, the Municipal House captures the opulence of Prague's 19th-century cafe culture. The new Czechoslovak state proclaimed its independence here on October 28, 1918. On the same spot, Czech culture continues to thrive with lavish coffeehouses (latte 50Kč), concerts (50-350Kč), art exhibitions (admission 150Kč), and salons adorned with the work of Czech artist Alfons Mucha. *(Nám. Republiky 5. Metro B: Nám. Republiky. www.obecni-dum.cz. Open daily 10am-6pm. Guided tours Sa noon and 2pm, 150Kč.)*

JAN PALACH SQUARE (NÁMĚSTÍ JANA PALACHA). Down river from the Charles Bridge, Jan Palach Square offers a peaceful view of the Vltava and Prague Castle. Originally called Red Army Square in honor of the Russians who liberated Prague in 1945, the square was renamed in 1990. It now honors one of the Red Army's great opponents, the late Jan Palach, who burned himself to death on Václavské nám. to protest the 1968 Soviet invasion. On the river banks, stone lions guard the entrance to the Rudolfinum, a famous concert hall that hosts the annual classical music *Pražské jaro* (Prague Spring; see **Entertainment,** p. 261). Across the tram tracks from the Rudolfinum, the main building of the Faculty of Arts of **Charles University** (Filozofická fakulta Univerzity Karlovy) shelters a statue of Jan Palach by its outside wall. The stunning view of the castle from the faculty classrooms has kept many a daydreaming student awake throughout the years. A beautiful path from Jan Palach Square hugs the Vltava, but you can also cruise the river in paddle boats, which are for rent just under the Mánesů for 80Kč per hr. *(Metro A: Staroměstská. Just off the Metro exit on Křížovnická.)*

BETHLEHEM CHAPEL (BETLÉMSKÁ KAPLE). Although the current chapel is a 1950s reconstruction, its unadorned walls and accessible pulpit help you imagine how Jan Hus achieved such a powerful following at the turn of the 14th century. Today the church is largely a living monument to the great Czech hero—the first floor contains the original pulpit from which Hus preached as well as frescoes depicting his death, while the second floor contains a more formal historical exhibit documenting his life and work. *(Metro A or B: Můstek. From the Metro, walk down Národní třída toward the river and turn right on Na Perštýně; the chapel is in Betlémské nám., which will appear on your left. Open Tu-Su 9am-6:30pm. 35Kč, students 20Kč.)*

CHURCH OF ST. NICHOLAS. While smaller and less impressive than its brother cathedral across the Vltava, this church is still worth a visit, if only for the magnificent crystal chandelier in the center, complete with a giant iron cross. The ceiling frescoes are also noteworthy. *(Metro A: Staroměstská. Next to the Kafka Museum. Open M noon-4pm, Tu-Sa 10am-4pm, Su noon-3pm. Su Mass 10:30am. Free.)*

GOLTZ-KINSKÝ PALACE. The flowery 14th-century Goltz-Kinský Palace is the finest of Prague's Rococo buildings. On February 21, 1948, Klement Gottwald made the palace the official birthplace of Soviet communism when he stood on its balcony and declared communism victorious. *(At the corner of Staroměstské nám. and Dlouhá, next to Týn Church. Open Tu-F 10am-6pm; closes early in summer for daily concerts.)*

NOVÉ MĚSTO

Nové Město (New Town) has become the commercial core of Prague and has embraced the global ties that such growth seems to entail. There's little else new in Nové Město, which Charles IV established in 1348 (see **History**, p. 224) as a separate municipality. Today, visitors can experience the fruits and perils of modernization with a walk in historic Wenceslas Square. Name-brand clothing stores and fast-food joints dominate the boulevard, but a simple stroll through the tranquil Franciscan Gardens will remind you of Prague's natural beauty.

WENCESLAS SQUARE (VÁCLAVSKÉ NÁMĚSTÍ). More a boulevard than a square, Wenceslas Square owes its name to the equestrian statue of 10th-century Czech ruler and patron St. Wenceslas (Václav) that stands in front of the National Museum. At his feet in solemn prayer kneel smaller statues of the country's other patron saints: St. Ludmila, St. Agnes, St. Prokop, and St. Adalbert (Vojtěch). The perfectionist sculptor Josef Václav Myslbek completed the statue after 25 years of deliberation. Others gasped at its 1912 unveiling, but poor Myslbek just mumbled, "It could have been bigger." The inscription under St. Wenceslas reads, "Do not let us and our descendants perish." The Czech nation seems to have taken these words to heart as many historical events have taken place in the square: a new Czechoslovak state was proclaimed in 1918, Jan Palach set himself on fire to protest the 1968 Soviet invasion, and proclamations against the Communist regime were voiced in 1989. The square sweeps down from the statue past department stores, posh hotels, trashy casinos, and Art Nouveau architecture. The boulevard has become far more commercial in recent years, but the view of the statue from the Můstek stop remains hypnotic at full moon. *(Metro A or B: Můstek serves the bottom of the square; Metro A or C: Muzeum serves the top of the square by the statue and the museum.)*

FRANCISCAN GARDEN (FRANTIŠKÁNSKÁ ZAHRADA). Amazingly, the Franciscans have maintained this bastion of serenity in the heart of Prague's commercial district. An ideal escape from Wenceslas Sq., the rose garden provides a perfect spot to relax or relax. *(Metro A or B: Můstek. Enter through the arch to the left of the intersection of Jungmannova and Národní, behind the Jungmannova statue. Open daily Apr. 15-Sept. 14 7am-10pm; Sept. 15-Oct. 14 7am-8pm; Oct. 15-Apr. 14 8am-7pm. Free.)*

CHURCH OF OUR LADY OF THE SNOWS (KOSTEL PANNY MARIE SNĚŽNÉ). Founded by Charles IV in 1347, this church was meant to be the largest in Prague. The Gothic walls are, indeed, higher than those of any other house of worship, but there wasn't enough in the coffers to complete the building. The result: extraordinarily high ceilings in a church of strikingly short length. Yet, as the saying goes, length doesn't matter—the effect of the massive gold altar in such a short space is breathtaking. *(Metro A or B: Můstek. From the bottom of Wenceslas Sq., turn left on Jungmannovo nám.; the entrance is behind the statue.)*

THE DANCING HOUSE (TANČÍCÍ DŮM). Built by American architect Frank Gehry, of Guggenheim-Bilbao fame, in cooperation with Slovenian architect Vladimir Milunic, the building—known as "Fred and Ginger" to Western visitors and as the "Dancing House" to Czechs—is one of Prague's most controversial landmarks. Its nicknames derive from the building's undulating glass wall and paired cone and cube, which evoke a dancing couple. It opened in 1996 next to President Havel's former apartment building amid a stretch of remarkable Art Nouveau buildings. Since its unveiling, the Dancing House has frequently been called an eyesore to the Prague skyline, yet some claim that it is a shining example of postmodern design. *(Metro B: Karlovo nám. Exit to Karlovo nám. and head down Resslova toward the river. It's at the corner of Resslova and Rašínovo nábřeží.)*

VELVET REVOLUTION MEMORIAL. Under Národní's arcades stands a memorial to the hundreds of Czech citizens beaten on November 17, 1989. Police attacked a march organized by students at the Film Faculty of Charles University (FAMU) to mourn the Nazi execution of nine Czech students some 50 years earlier. The simple yet moving plaque depicts a wall of hands. The inscription—*Máme holé ruce* ("Our hands are empty")—was the protesters' cry as they were beaten by the police. Visitors place flowers in the fingers of the memorial in remembrance. At the nearby **Magic Lantern Theater** (Laterna magika divadlo; Národní 4), Revolutionary leader Havel once plotted to overthrow the old regime. *(Metro B: Národní třída. Exit the Metro and head down Spálená; go left on Národní. The memorial is in the arcade across from the Black Theater.)*

JOSEFOV

Metro A: Staroměstská. From the Metro, walk down Maiselova, which is parallel to Kaprova. ☎ 222 325 172; www.jewishmuseum.cz. Synagogues and museum open Apr.-Oct. Su-F 9am-6pm, Nov.-Mar. 9am-4:30pm. Closed Jewish holidays. Admission to all synagogues except Staronová Synagogue 300Kč, students 200Kč. Staronová Synagogue 200Kč/140Kč. Buy tickets at any of the synagogues. A head covering is required for men at most sites; kippahs provided at the door.

Prague's historic Jewish neighborhood and the oldest Jewish settlement in Central Europe, Josefov lies north of Staroměstské nám., along Maiselova and several side streets. Its cultural wealth lies in five well-preserved synagogues, all that remains of this former Jewish ghetto. In reaction to the Pope's 1179 decree that all good Christians avoid contact with Jews, Prague's citizens constructed a 4m wall surrounding the area. The gates were opened in 1784, but the walls didn't come down until 1848, when the city's Jews were first granted limited civil rights. The closed neighborhood bred exotic legends, many of which surrounded the famed **Rabbi Loew ben Bezalel** (1512-1609), who, according to legend, created the golem—a creature made from mud that came to life to protect Prague's Jews. Rabbi Loew lived at Široká 90, now a private residence. The century following 1848 proved devastating for Prague's Jews. The open quarter quickly became a disease-racked slum. In an ill-conceived attempt to turn Prague into a small Paris (evident in today's Pařížská), devoid of all less desirable neighborhoods, the whole quarter, save the synagogues, was demolished. Then, most infamously, the Nazis rose to power and deported most of Prague's Jews to Terezín (see **Terezín**, p. 265) and the death camps. Ironically, Hitler's decision to create a "museum of an extinct race" led to the preservation of Josefov's old Jewish cemetery and synagogues.

PINKAS SYNAGOGUE (PINKASOVA SYNAGOGA). Some 80,000 names line the walls of Pinkas Synagogue in requiem for the Czech Jews persecuted during the Holocaust. This incredibly moving display reminds visitors of the tremendous horror and loss that Hitler's Nazis dealt to the community. Upstairs, drawings by children interred at the Terezín camp further memorialize the inhumanity of Hitler's Nazi armies. *(On Široká, between Žatecká and Listopadu 17.)*

OLD JEWISH CEMETERY (STARÝ ŽIDOVSKÝ HŘBITOV). This cemetery remains Josefov's most popular attraction. Between the 14th and 18th centuries, 20,000 graves were dug in 12 layers. Striking clusters of tombstones are visible today because older stones were lifted from underneath other layers. Rabbi Loew is buried by the wall opposite the entrance—you'll recognize his grave by the pebbles and coins placed on his tomb. *(At the corner of Široká and Žatecká.)*

SPANISH SYNAGOGUE (ŠPANĚLSKÁ SYNAGOGA). The youngest and most ornate synagogue in Josefov, the Spanish Synagogue was built in 1868 and modeled after Granada's Alhambra. True to its Moorish inspiration, the stunning interior of this small synagogue is lined with intricate patterns of gold lattice. Today it also displays a history of Czech Jews from the 18th century to the present. *(On the corner of Široká and Dušní.)*

MAISEL SYNAGOGUE (MAISELOVA SYNAGOGA). This synagogue displays treasures from the extensive collections of the Jewish Museum, which were only returned to the city's Jewish community in 1994. Its exhibits render an excellent history of the Jews in Bohemia and Moravia, including Prague's ghetto and the events that took place within it. *(Maiselova, between Široká and Jáchymova.)*

KLAUS SYNAGOGUE (KLAUSOVÁ SYNAGOGA). More educational than eye-catching, the Klaus Synagogue gives a brief introduction to the holidays, ceremonies, and traditions of Judaism. *(Next to Ceremony Hall on Červená, just off Maiselova.)*

CEREMONIAL HALL (OBŘADNÍ DÚM). An informative complement to the Old Jewish Cemetery, Ceremonial Hall (originally for the Jewish Burial Society) houses exhibits devoted to the themes of Jewish illness and death customs, Jewish cemeteries in Bohemia and Moravia, and the activities of the Prague Burial Society. The turreted stone exterior of the building is interesting on its own. *(On Červená, just off Maiselova.)*

OLD-NEW SYNAGOGUE (STARONOVÁ SYNAGOGA). The oldest operating synagogue in Europe and the earliest Gothic structure in Prague, the tiny Old-New Synagogue is still the religious center of Prague's Jewish community. Behind the iron gates fly the tattered remnants of the Star of David flag flown by the congregation in 1357, when Charles IV first allowed them to display their own municipal emblem. Prague's Jews were the first to adopt the Star of David as their official symbol. *(On the corner of Maiselova and Pařížská. Entrance fee not included in price of museum ticket. Open in summer Su-Th 9:30am-6pm, F 9:30am-5pm. Services F and Sa at 8pm reserved for practicing members of the Jewish community. 200Kč, students 140Kč.)*

JEWISH TOWN HALL (ŽIDOVSKÁ RADNICE). Once the administrative center of Josefov, the Jewish Town Hall was one of the few Jewish administrative centers in Europe to survive WWII. The small Hebrew clock at the top of the Rococo town hall runs counter-clockwise. On the other side of the building, a statue of Moses by František Bílek was hidden from the Nazis during the war. *(Next to the Old-New Synagogue, on the corner of Maiselova and Červená. The building is permanently closed to the public.)*

MALÁ STRANA

The hangout of criminals and counter-revolutionaries for nearly a century, the cobblestoned streets of Malá Strana have become the most prized real estate on the Vltava. Urbanites dream of flats overlooking St. Nicholas's Cathedral, while affluent foreigners sip beer in the former hangout of Jaroslav Hašek and his bum-bling soldier Švejk (see **The Arts**, p. 228). Malá Strana seems to have realized the vision of its 13th-century designer, King Přemysl Otakar II, who dreamed of a powerful economic and cultural quarter. In the 15th century, the Austrian nobility built great churches and palaces here. Now carefully restored, Malá Strana is home to some of Prague's most impressive architecture.

▨ PETŘÍN HILL AND GARDENS (PETŘÍNSKÉ SADY). Petřín Gardens, on the hill beside Malá Strana, provide a tranquil retreat from Prague's urban bustle and offer spectacular views of the city. Although the climb to the garden's peak is steep, the beauty of its forested footpaths is well worth the trek. For a more relaxed ascent, take a cable car to the top from just above the intersection of Vítězná and Újezd. *(Look for Lanovka Dráha signs. Daily, every 10-15min, 9am-11pm; 12Kč.)* It stops once along the way to deposit visitors at Nebozízek, Prague's most scenic cafe. *(☎ 257 315 329; www.nebozizek.cz. Entrees 240-360Kč. Open daily 11am-11pm.)* A plethora of delights awaits you at the summit: lush rose gardens, a small Eiffel Tower *(Open daily 10am-10pm; 50Kč, students 40Kč)*, the city's observatory, the Church of St. Lawrence, and a befuddling maze of mirrors at Bludiště that will leave you in stitches. Ever seen yourself with a forehead as tall as your torso? *(☎ 257 315 272. Open daily 10am-9:30pm. 40Kč, students 30Kč.)* Just east of the park is Strahov Stadium, the world's largest, covering the space of 10 soccer fields.

▨ WALLENSTEIN GARDEN (VALDŠTEJNSKÁ ZAHRADA). This tranquil, 17th-century Baroque garden is enclosed by old buildings that glow on sunny afternoons. General Albrecht Wallenstein, owner of the famous Prague palace of the same name and hero of Schiller's grim plays (the *Wallenstein* cycle), held parties here among Vredeman de Vries's classical bronze statues. When the works were plundered by Swedish troops in the waning hours of the Thirty Years' War, Wallenstein replaced the original casts with duplicates. Frescoes inside the arcaded patio depict episodes from Virgil's *Aeneid*. *(Letenská 10. Metro A: Malostranská. Exit the Metro and turn right on Letenská. The garden will be on the right. Open daily Apr.-Oct. 10am-6pm. Free.)*

ST. NICHOLAS'S CATHEDRAL (CHRÁM SV. MIKULÁŠE). The towering dome of the Baroque St. Nicholas's Cathedral, Malá Strana's centerpiece, is one of Prague's most discernible landmarks. The father-son team of Kristof and Kilián Ignaz Dienzenhofer, who also built the Church of St. Nicholas in Staré Město (see p. 253) and the Břevnov Monastery (see **Outer Prague**, p. 259) near Hradčany, constructed St. Nicholas's as their crowning achievement. Pricey and tourist-frequented classical music concerts take place here each night. *(Metro A: Malostranská. Follow Letenská from the Metro to Malostranské nám. ☎ 257 534 215. Open daily 9am-4:45pm. 50Kč, students 25Kč. Concert tickets 390Kč/290Kč.)*

JOHN LENNON WALL. Hroznová, a tiny street on Kampa Island, is home to the infamous John Lennon Wall. The mural, a crumbling memorial to John Lennon, became controversial and well-known when Communist authorities attempted to suppress it. In summer 1998, the wall was whitewashed and it is now covered with an unimpressive portrait of Lennon amidst a multitude of anti-war messages and tourist graffiti. *(Metro A: Malostranská. From the Metro, walk down U Lužického semináře to the Charles Bridge. Descend the stairs leading to Na Kampě and take the first right on Hroznová. Stay close to the wall and bear right over the bridge on Velkopřerovské nám.)*

CHURCH OF OUR LADY VICTORIOUS (KOSTEL PANNY MARIE VÍTĚZNÉ). Not known for its exterior, the modest Church of Our Lady Victorious contains the famous polished-wax statue of the **Infant Jesus of Prague,** rumored to perform miracles for the faithful. According to legend, the statue arrived in the arms of a 16th-century Spanish noblewoman who married into Bohemian royalty; mysteriously, the plague bypassed Prague shortly thereafter. In 1628, the Carmelite abbey gained custody of the statue and allowed pilgrims to pray to it; the public has been enamored ever since. Six times a year the statue is redressed in one of over 75 costumes by the nuns of a nearby convent. The museum displays a few of the spectacular robes and crowns. *(Metro A: Malostranská. Follow Letecká through Malostranské nám. and continue on Karmelitská. ☎ 257 533 646. Open daily 8:30am-7pm. Mass in 5 languages; call for schedule. Museum open M-Sa 9:30am-5:30pm, Su 1-6pm. Free.)*

PRAGUE CASTLE (PRAŽSKÝ HRAD)

Take tram #22 or 23 from the center, get off at "Pražský Hrad," and go down U Prašného Mostu past the Royal Gardens and into the Second Courtyard. Or, hike up picturesque Nerudova street or climb the Staré Zámecké Schody (Old Castle Stairs) from Malostranské nám. ☎ 224 373 368; www.hrad.cz. Open daily Apr.-Oct. 9am-5pm; Nov.-Mar. 9am-4pm. Ticket office opposite St. Vitus's Cathedral, inside the castle walls. 1-day ticket gains access to St. Vitus's Cathedral, the Royal Crypt, Cathedral Tower, Old Royal Palace, Powder Tower, Golden Lane, and Basilica of St. George. 350Kč, students 175Kč.

Prague Castle has been the seat of the Bohemian government since it was erected over 1000 years ago. Over the last century, liberal presidents, Nazi despots, and Communist officials have all held court here. After the declaration of independent Czechoslovakia in 1918, first President Tomáš Garrigue Masaryk invited renowned Slovenian architect Josip Plečnik to rebuild his new residence, which had suffered from centuries of Hapsburg neglect. Plečnik not only restored all the castle's buildings and redesigned its gardens, but added fountains, columns, and embellishments characteristic of his style. Arrive on the hour to catch the changing of the guard, which takes place daily 5am-midnight.

HRADČANY SQUARE AND FIRST CASTLE COURTYARD. Outside the Castle gates at Hradčany Sq. lies the **Šternberg Palace,** home to the National Gallery's collection of European Old Masters, including works by Rembrandt, El Greco, Goya, and Rubens. *(☎ 230 090 570. Open Tu-Su 10am-6pm. 150Kč, students 70Kč.)* The Baroque **Matthias Gate** (Matyášská brána), inside the First Castle Courtyard, is the castle's official entrance. Plečnik designed the two spear-like wooden flagpoles next to it.

SECOND CASTLE COURTYARD AND ROYAL GARDEN (KRÁLOVSKÁ ZAHRADA). After passing through Matthias Gate, turn left in the Second Castle Courtyard for access to the lush Royal Garden. Recently opened to the public after years as a private paradise for only the highest Communist officials, the serene Royal Garden offers a respite in the midst of one of the city's most popular tourist attractions. Past the tulip beds, the trickling **Singing Fountain** spouts its watery, harp-like tune before the **Royal Summer Palace.** Place your head under the fountain to hear the chiming water. *(Royal Garden open Apr.-Oct. 24hr.)*

THIRD CASTLE COURTYARD. In the Third Castle Courtyard stands Prague Castle's centerpiece, the colossal **St. Vitus's Cathedral,** which was completed in 1929, some 600 years after construction began. Right of the high altar stands the silver **tomb of St. Jan Nepomuk.** A statue of an angel holds a silvered tongue that many believed belonged to Jan, whose tongue was reputedly silvered after he was thrown into the Vltava by King Charles IV (see **Charles Bridge,** p. 251). It remains on display, though the story was officially proven false in 1961. The walls of **St. Wenceslas's Chapel** are lined with precious stones and paintings telling the saint's story. In an adjoining but inaccessible room, the real crown jewels of the Bohemian kings are sealed behind a door with seven locks, the keys to which are in the hands of seven different religious and secular Czech leaders. Attack the 287 steps that spiral up to the roof of the **Great South Tower** for one of the city's best views. Alternatively, head under-

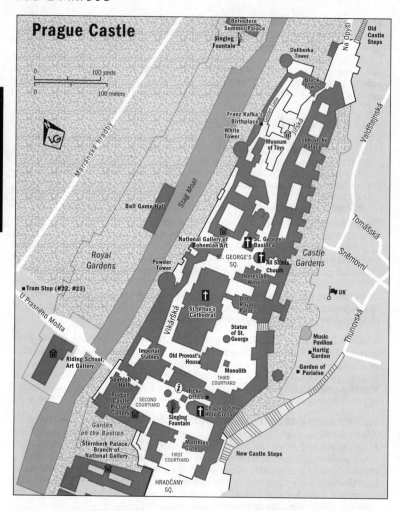

Prague Castle

0 ——— 100 yards
0 ——— 100 meters

Belvedere Summer Palace
Singing Fountain
Daliborka Tower
Na Opyši
Old Castle Steps
Black Tower
Franz Kafka's Birthplace
White Tower
Golden Lane
Jiřská
Museum of Toys
Lobkovický Palace
Valdštejnská
Mariánské hradby
Stag Moat
Ball Game Hall
Tomášská
National Gallery of Bohemian Art
St. George's Basilica
Royal Gardens
Powder Tower
ST. GEORGE'S SQ.
All Saints Church
Castle Gardens
Sněmovní
Theresian Wing
Tram Stop (#22, #23)
Vikářská
St. Vitus's Cathedral
Old Royal Palace
UK
Thunovská
U Prasného Mosta
Statue of St. George
Music Pavilion
Hartig Garden
Imperial Stables
Old Provost's House
Monolith
Garden of Paridise
Riding School; Art Gallery
THIRD COURTYARD
Spanish Hall
Ticket Office
Prague Castle Picture Gallery
SECOND COURTYARD
Chapel of the Holy Cross
Garden on the Bastion
Singing Fountain
Šternberk Palace; Branch of National Gallery
Matthias Gate
New Castle Steps
FIRST COURTYARD
HRADČANY SQ.

ground to the **Royal Crypt** to visit Emperor Charles IV's tomb. All four of Charles's wives are buried together in the grave to his left, along with a handful of other Czech kings. To the right of St. Vitus's, the **Old Royal Palace** (Starý královský palác) houses the lengthy **Vladislav Hall,** where jousting competitions were once held.

ST. GEORGE'S SQUARE. Across the courtyard from the Old Royal Palace stands the Romanesque **St. George's Basilica** (Bazilika sv. Jiří) and its adjacent convent. Built in AD 921, the simple yet elegantly designed basilica enshrines the tomb of St. Ludmila, complete with skeleton on display. A mason who stole Ludmila's thighbone supposedly activated a vicious curse that killed three people before the mason's son restored the bone to the grave. The convent next door houses the **National Gallery of Bohemian Art,** which displays art ranging from the Gothic to the Baroque. In the medieval galleries, Master Theodorik's ecclesiastical portraits, the relief from *Matka Boží před Týnem*, and the so-called Kapucínský *Cycle of Christ and the Apostles* stand out; upstairs, Michael Leopold Willmann's paintings warrant a visit. *(Open Tu-Su 10am-6pm. 100Kč, students 50Kč.)*

JIŘSKÁ STREET. Jiřská begins to the right of the basilica. Halfway down, the tiny, colorful, and extremely crowded **Golden Lane** (Zlatá ulička) heads off to the right. Alchemists who once worked here attempting to create gold inspired the street's name. **Franz Kafka** lived at #22, where today a herd of cramped souvenir shops feed off of his fame. Upstairs a hallway displays replicas of the Bohemian court's armory; visitors are sometimes permitted to shoot the crossbow for 50Kč. Back on Jiřská, the **Lobkovický Palace** has a replica of Bohemia's coronation jewels and a history of the Czech lands. *(Open Tu-Su 9am-4:30pm. 40Kč, students 20Kč.)* Across the street from the Palace is the **Museum of Toys** (Muzeum hraček), the personal toy collection owned by cartoonist and filmmaker Ivan Steiger. *(☎ 224 372 294. Open daily 9:30am-5:30pm. 50Kč, students 30Kč.)* The **Old Castle Steps** (Staré zámecké schody) at the end of the street descend to Malostranská.

OUTER PRAGUE

If you have more than two days in Prague, you may have a chance to explore the green fields, majestic churches, and panoramic vistas of the city's outskirts, all hidden from the touring hordes.

▨ **TROJA.** Located a beautiful neighborhood, Troja is the site of French architect J. B. Mathey's masterly **chateau,** one of the city's best-kept secrets. The colossal palace, overlooking the Vltava, includes a terraced garden, oval staircase, and magnificent collection of 19th-century Czech artwork. Strap on a pair of leather slippers provided at the door and enjoy Mathey's aesthetic wonder. It's hard to tell what's more beautiful—the famous landscapes and moving portraits that line the palace walls, or the intricate frescoes featuring royal, mythical, and religious figures that adorn the ceilings. Don't miss the **Main Hall,** Prague's answer to the Sistine Chapel, covered from floor to ceiling in magnificent frescoes. *(Take bus #112 from Metro C: Nádraží Holešovice to Zoologická Zahrada. Open Apr.-Oct. Tu-Su 10am-6pm; Nov.-Mar. Sa-Su 10am-5pm. 140Kč, students 70Kč.)* If you fancy more wild pursuits, venture next door to the **Prague Zoo.** *(Open daily 9am-7pm. Apr.-Sept. 80Kč, students 50Kč; Oct.-Mar. 50Kč/30Kč.)*

PRAGUE MARKET (PRAŽSKCTRZNICE). An old-school Eastern European market remains Prague's best place to haggle over clothing, fresh produce, jewelry, and everything else. Rows of stalls and Czechs of all ages make this a truly authentic shopping experience. *(Take tram #3 or 14 from Nám. Republiky to Vozovna Kobylisy; get off at Pražskátrznice. Open M-F 8am-6pm, Sa 8am-1pm.)*

BŘEVNOV MONASTERY. The oldest monastery in Bohemia was founded in AD 993 by King Boleslav II and St. Adalbert, who were both guided by a divine dream to build a monastery atop a bubbling stream. **St. Margaret's Church** (Bazilika sv. Markéty), a Benedictine chapel, awaits you inside the complex. Beneath the altar rests the tomb of the vegetarian St. Vintíř. Czechs claim that on one particular diplomatic excursion, St. Vintíř dined with a German king who, being a fanatical hunter, served up a main course of pheasant slain by his own hand. The saint prayed for deliverance from the embarrassment of having to decline the king's offering, whereupon the main course sprang to life and flew out the window. The monastery's green bell tower and red roof were the only parts of the original Romanesque structure that were spared when the Dientzenhofers, Prague's leading father-son architects, redesigned the complex in a High Baroque style. Pack a lunch and take a stroll along the stream leading to the small pond to the right of the church. Guided tours (in Czech only) are essential as they allow you to access the monks' quarters and the crypt. *(Metro A: Malostranská. Take a 15min. ride uphill on tram #22 to Břevnovský klášter. Facing uphill, cross the road to the right. Entrance is on the left, under the statue of the monk. Church open only for mass; M-Sa 7am and 6pm, Su 7:30, 9am, 6pm. Tours Sa-Su 10am, 2, 4pm. 50Kč, students 30Kč.)*

NEW JEWISH CEMETERY. Although less visited than the more central Old Jewish Cemetery, the New Jewish Cemetery is one of Central Europe's largest burial grounds. Enigmatic author Franz Kafka is interred here. Obtain a map and, if you're male, a mandatory head covering from the attendant before entering the cemetery. *(Metro A: Želivského. Open Apr.-Sept. Su-Th 9am-5pm, F 9am-2pm; Oct.-Mar. Su-Th 9am-4pm, F 9am-1pm. Closed Jewish holidays. Free.)*

🏛 MUSEUMS

Prague's magnificence is not in its museums; if the weather's good, you may want to stick to the streets. On one of the many rainy days, however, peruse some of its interesting and quirky collections. Keep your eyes open for special exhibits, listed on poster boards around town, and check out the work of local artists at the private galleries off Národní třída and Staroměstské nám. Most museums are closed on Mondays.

🖼 MUCHA MUSEUM. This is the only collection devoted entirely to the work of Alfons Mucha, the Czech Republic's most celebrated artist, who gained his fame in Paris for his poster series of "la divine Sarah," Sarah Bernhardt, Paris's most famous actress. It was through this series that Mucha pioneered the Art Nouveau movement. Be sure to see the collection of Czech and Parisian posters, including the famous "Gismonda" which revolutionized poster design, as well as Mucha's panel paintings. *(Panská 7. Metro A or B: Můstek. Head up Václavské nám. toward the St. Wenceslas statue. Hang a left on Jindřišská and turn left again on Panská. ☎ 224 215 409; www.mucha.cz. Open daily 10am-6pm. 120Kč, students 60Kč.)*

CITY GALLERY PRAGUE: HOUSE OF THE GOLDEN RING. This refreshingly homey gallery (Dům u zlatého prstenu) houses a collection of 20th-century Czech art, emphasizing installations and technological art. This museum is a four-floor maze of modern art, each with a separate theme, ranging from Cubism to post-modernism. Surrealism fans will love the second-floor exhibit "In the Distorted Mirror," while those with more traditional tastes will enjoy the first-floor collection "Dream, Myth, and Ideal" and the basement collection of Czech art from the 1990s. *(Týnská 6. Metro A: Staroměstská. Behind Týn Church in Old Town Sq. ☎ 222 327 677; www.citygalleryprague.cz. Open Tu-Su 10am-6pm. Top 3 floors 60Kč, students 30Kč; entire museum 70Kč. First Tu of each month free.)*

MUSEUM OF MEDIEVAL TORTURE INSTRUMENTS. This is not a museum for the weak of stomach. The collection includes numerous pain-inducing devices, such as the Head Crusher, thumbscrews, iron gag, and the Masks of Shame and Infamy. The highly detailed explanations are guaranteed to nauseate. *(Mostécka 21. Metro A: Malostranská. Follow Letenská from the Metro and turn left on Mostécka. ☎ 608 889 361; torture@post.cz. Open daily 10am-8pm. 120Kč.)*

MUSEUM OF COMMUNISM. This new gallery is committed to exposing the flaws of the communist system that suppressed the Czech people from 1948 to 1989. The exhibition is divided into three parts: the dream (the origins of communism); the reality (the impact of communism on the Czech people); and the nightmare (the despair that led to the Velvet Revolution). A model factory and an interrogation office send you behind the Iron Curtain. *(Na Příkopě 10. Metro A: Můstek. Exit the Metro and turn right on Na Příkopě; enter through Casino. ☎224 212 966. Open daily 9am-9pm. 180Kč, students 140Kč.)*

NATIONAL GALLERY (NÁRODNÍ GALERIE). The National Gallery runs nine museums in different locations throughout Prague; the notable **Šternberský palác** and **Klášter sv. Jiří** are within the **Prague Castle** complex (see p. 257). All museums carry a pamphlet describing the collections of the other galleries, most of which are in suburban Prague and not worth the trek. The **Trade Fair Palace and the Gallery of Modern Art** (Veletržní palác a Galerie moderního umění) display the National Gallery's impressive collection of 20th-century Czech and European art. The seven-story functionalist building is almost as stunning as the art inside. *(Dukelských hrdinů 47. Metro C: Holešovice. Tram #5, 12, or 17 to Veletržní. ☎224 301 024. Open Tu-Su 10am-6pm. 150Kč, students 70Kč.)*

CZECH MUSEUM OF FINE ARTS (ČESKÉ MUZEUM VÝTVARNÝCH UMĚNÍ). Moved in 2003 from its location at the House of the Black Madonna, the museum, an architectural monument of the Romanesque period, features both classical and modern works. The first two floors are devoted to a history of Czech Cubism, while the downstairs gallery exhibits works of Western European Modernists. *(Husova 19-21. Metro A: Staroměstská. Follow Karlova down from Charles Bridge. Turn right on Husova. ☎222 220 218. Open Tu-Su 10am-6pm. 50Kč, students 20Kč.)*

MONUMENT TO NATIONAL LITERATURE (PAMÁTNÍK NÁRODNÍHO PÍSEMNICTVÍ). Part of the Strahov Monastery, the star attraction here is the **Strahov Library,** with its magnificent **Theological and Philosophical Halls.** The frescoed, vaulted ceilings of the Baroque reading rooms were intended to spur monks to the peaks of erudition. *(Strahovské nádvoří 1. Metro A: Hradčanská. From the Metro, take tram #25 toward Bílá Hora to Malovanka. Turn around, follow the tram tracks, then turn right on Strahovská through an arch, into the park. The museum is inside the monastery on the left. ☎220 516 671. Open daily 9am-noon and 1-5pm. 70Kč, students 50Kč.)*

NATIONAL MUSEUM (NÁRODNÍ MUZEUM). With a commanding view over all of Wenceslas Square, the National Museum provides a wonderful starting place for a tour of Nové Město. While the paleontological and anthropological exhibitions inside the museum are less than thrilling, the impressive exterior is worth a stop. *(At the head of Wenceslas Square. Metro A or C: Muzeum. Open May-Sept. 10am-6pm; Oct.-Apr. 9am-5pm. Closed first Tu of each month.)*

RUDOLFINUM. The Czech Philharmonic Orchestra shares this space with one of Prague's oldest galleries. Rotating exhibits, as well as an elegant cafe, fill the huge Art Nouveau interior. *(Alšovo náb. 12. ☎224 893 205; galerie.rudolfinum@telecom.cz. Open July-May Tu-Su 10am-6pm. 100Kč, students 50Kč.)*

🎦 ENTERTAINMENT

For a list of current concerts and performances, consult *The Prague Post, The Pill, Threshold,* or *Do města-Downtown* (the latter three are free and distributed at many cafes and restaurants). Most performances begin at 7pm; unsold tickets are sometimes available 30min. before show time. The majority of Prague's theaters close in July and August, but the selection is extensive during the rest of the year—particularly in mid-May and early June when the **Prague Spring Festival** draws musicians from around the world. Tickets (400-3500Kč) may sell out up to a year in advance. Try **Bohemia Ticket International,** Malé nám. 13, next to Čedok.

(☎224 227 832; www.ticketsbi.cz. Open M-F 9am-5pm, Sa 9am-2pm.) Early June ushers in the **Prague Fringe Festival** (www.praguefringe.cz) which—much like its Scottish namesake—stages cutting-edge performances of international theater. **Národní divadlo**, **Stavovské divadlo**, and **Státní opera** (see below) all stage operas; while performances tend to fluctuate in quality, the staggeringly low prices do not. **Cinemas** showing English-language blockbusters abound. Prices depend on the movie's popularity; ask at a tourist office for a list of current films. The **Kino Cafebar** shows Czech films with English subtitles, as do many theaters in town. Look for a sign posted on the ticket booth. (Karlovo nám. 19. ☎224 915 765. Tickets around 100Kč.)

Říše loutek, (Marionette Theater), Žatecká 1 (☎224 819 322; www.mozart.cz). Metro A: Staroměstská. On the corner of Žatecká and Mariánské nám. The world's oldest marionette theater is a cultural staple of the Czech Republic. The humorous version of Mozart's *Don Giovanni* amazes audiences with the agility and spunk of its lifelike puppets. The marionette cast springs to life as the curtains rise, and a delightfully drunken Mozart marionette interacts with the audience during interludes. June-July performances M-Tu and Th-Su 8pm. Box office open daily 10am-8pm. 490Kč, students 390Kč.

Národní divadlo (National Theater), Národní třída 2/4 (☎224 901 448; www.narodni-divadlo.cz). Metro B: Národní třída. One of Prague's most beautiful venues, the National Theater features drama, opera, and ballet. Box office open daily 10am-6pm and 30min. before performances. Tickets 30-1000Kč. MC/V.

Stavovské divadlo (Estates Theater), Ovocný trg 1 (☎224 921 528). Metro A or B: Můstek. Left on the pedestrian Na Příkopě. Box office to the right of the theater, on the right side of the street. Once the site of *Don Giovanni's* 1787 premiere, this Baroque-style theater mainly features classical performances, opera, and ballet. Use the Národní divadlo box office (see above) or turn up 30min. before the show.

Black Theatre Image, Pařížská 4 (☎222 314 448; www.imagetheatre.cz). Metro A: Staroměstská. From the Metro, walk down Křížovnická toward Josefov. Turn right on Široká and continue straight until you hit Pařížská. Features silent, black-light performances incorporating aspects of drama, music, and dance. Shows daily 8pm. Box office open daily 9am-8pm. 400Kč.

Státní opera (State Opera), Wilsonova 4 (☎224 227 266; www.opera.cz). Metro A or C: Muzeum. Box office open M-F 10am-5:30pm, Sa-Su 10am-noon and 1-5:30pm and 1hr. prior to performances. Tickets 50-600Kč.

▧ NIGHTLIFE

The most authentic way to experience Prague at night is through an alcoholic haze. With some of the best beers in the world on tap, pubs and beer halls are understandably the city's favorite places for nighttime pleasures. These days, however, authentic pub experiences are often restricted to the suburbs and outlying Metro stops; in central Prague, Irish pubs and American sports bars are cropping up everywhere, charging high prices for foreign beers. You may have to look a bit harder for them, but a few trusty Czech pubs remain scattered throughout Staré Město and Malá Strana.

Prague is not a clubbing city, although there are enough dance clubs pumping out techno to satisfy those craving the Euro-club scene. More popular among Czechs are the city's many jazz and rock clubs, which host excellent local and international acts. Otherwise, you can always retreat to the Charles Bridge to sing along with aspiring Brit-pop guitarists. Whichever way you indulge in Prague nightlife, swig a few pints of *pivo*, grab some 4am snacks (see **Late-Night Eating**, p. 248), and forgo the night bus for the morning Metro.

BEER HALLS AND WINE CELLARS

■ **Vinárna U Sudu,** Vodičkova 10 (☎222 232 207). Metro A: Můstek. Cross Václavské nám. to Vodičkova and follow it as it curves left. Undiscovered by tourists, this Moravian wine bar looks plain from its 1st fl. entrance, but beneath the facade sprawls a labyrinth of catacombs and cavernous cellars, where the carafes of smooth red wine (125Kč) go down frighteningly fast. Whether you choose to isolate yourself in one of the many cellars or challenge locals to a match of foosball, the wine and atmosphere are sure to leave you smiling. Open M-Th 1pm-2am, F-Sa 1pm-3am, Su 3pm-1am.

U Fleků, Křemencova 11 (☎224 934 019; www.ufleku.cz). Metro B: Národní třída. Hang a right on Spálená, away from Národní, then turn right on Myslíkova and right again on Křemencova. Prague's oldest beer hall, founded in 1499. Live brass bands play "Roll out the Barrel" nightly. Huge outdoor terrace is perfect for warm summer nights. Home-brewed beer 49Kč. Open daily 9am-11pm. Beer museum tours M-Sa 10am-5pm; 50kč.

Pivnice u Sv. Tomáše, Letenská 12 (☎257 531 835; www.pivnice-sv-tomas.cz). Metro A: Malostranská. Go downhill on Letenská. The mighty dungeons echo with boisterous revelry. Sing drunken ballads with beer in one hand and meat off the roasting spit in the other. (Roasting spit meats must be ordered a day in advance, 350-400Kč.) Beer 40Kč. Live brass band 7-11pm. Kitchen closes 10pm. Open daily 11:30am-midnight. MC/V.

BARS

■ **Kozička,** Kozí 1 (☎224 818 308; www.kozicka.cz). Metro A: Staroměstská. Take Dlouhá from the square's northeast corner, then bear left on Kozí. The giant cellar bar is always packed—you'll know why after your first *Krušovice* (30Kč). Great if you're looking for a Czechmate. Open M-F noon-4am, Sa 6pm-4am, Su 6pm-3am. MC/V.

■ **Cafe Marquis de Sade,** Melnicka 5. Metro B: Nám. Republiky. From the Metro, go down U Obecního Domu to the right of the Obecního Dum. Take a right on Rybna, a left on Jakubská, and a left on Melnicka. This spacious bar soothes the senses with rich red velvet walls. Ascend the wrought-iron staircase to the loft, knock back a "shot de fuck up" (80Kč), and scope out the crowd below. Open daily 2pm-2am.

Le Chateau, Jakubská 2 (☎222 316 328). Metro B: Nám. Republiky. From the Metro, walk through the Powder Tower to Celetná, then take a right on Templová. On the corner of Templová and Jakubská. Non-stop techno-rock keeps the place pumping until the wee hours. Open M-Th noon-3am, F noon-4am, Sa 4pm-4am, Su 4pm-2am.

Zanzibar, Saská 6 (☎312 246 876). Metro A: Malostranská. From the square, head down Mostecká toward the Charles Bridge, turn right on Lázeňská, and left on Saská. The tastiest, priciest, and most exotic mixed drinks this side of the Vltava (80-190č). Cuban cigars 29-169Kč. Open daily 5pm-3am.

Bugsy's, Pařížská 10 (☎224 810 287; www.bugsybar.cz). Sophisticated, 21st-century, American-style speakeasy serving the tastiest mixed drinks in town. Cocktail menu so thick it's hardcover (cocktails 95-1490Kč). Fresh mojitos and fig shots go down like water. For something even more exotic, try the bar's off-the-menu tropical secret Shu Shu (ingredients strictly classified). When the upscale munchies hit, sushi awaits. Live jazz M nights at 9pm. Open daily 7pm-2am. AmEx/MC/V.

U 3 Černých Ruží, Zámecká 5. Metro A: Malostranská. Take tram #12, 22, or 23 to Malostranské nám and turn right, then left on Zamecka. At the foot of the New Castle Steps. A small, quirky bar that pours endless pints at low prices (Budvar 18Kč) for a thirsty local crowd. If you can still stand after sitting in one of the not so comfy armchairs, a moonlit walk to the castle makes a fabulous end to the night. Open 11am-midnight.

Umě, Dlouhá 10. Metro B: Nám. Republiky. Just down the street from Roxy. A laid-back bar full of Czech students swigging Pilsner Urquell (22Kč). Occasional live music starts up around 8:30pm. If the amateur acts get too loud, you can retreat to the sagging sofas in the back. Open daily 11am-midnight.

CZECH REPUBLIC

Molly Malone's, U obecního dvora 4 (☎224 818 851; www.mollymalones.cz). Metro A: Staroměstská. Turn right on Křižonvická, away from the Charles Bridge. After Nám. Jana Palacha, turn right on Široká, which becomes Vězeňská; turn left at its end. Grab 3 friends, 4 pints of Guinness (80Kč), and head for the loft. Irish and British newspapers Su. Live music Th 9pm-midnight. Open Su-Th 11am-1am, F-Sa 11am-2am.

Jo's Bar and Garáž, Malostranské nám. 7. Metro A: Malostranská. If you can't bear the idea that the people at the next table might not speak English, Jo's Bar is the perfect spot for you. Foosball, darts, card games, and a dance floor downstairs. Some of Prague's best DJs spin acid jazz, techno, house, and dance. Long Island Iced Tea 115Kč. Beer 40Kč. Open daily 11am-2am. AmEx/MC/V.

CLUBS AND DISCOS

■ **Radost FX,** Bělehradská 120 (☎224 254 776; www.radostfx.cz). Metro C: IP Pavlova. Although heavily touristed, Radost remains the gem of Prague nightlife, playing only the hippest techno, jungle, and house music from internationally renowned DJs. The spacious, ventilated chill-out room is perfect for taking a break from the dance floor and watching the throngs of trendy clubbers strut their stuff. Creative drinks (Frozen Sex with an Alien 140Kč.) will expand your clubbing horizons. Also serves brunch (see **Nové Město Restaurants,** p. 247). Cover 100-200Kč. Open M-Sa 10pm-5am.

Roxy, Dlouhá 33 (☎224 826 296; www.roxy.cz). Metro B: Nám. Republiky. Walk up Revoluční to the river; go left on Dlouhá. Hip locals and informed tourists come to this converted theater for experimental DJs and theme nights. Watch out for swooping butterflies from the balcony above. Beer 30Kč. Cover Tu and Th-Sa 100-350Kč. Open M-Tu and Th-Sa 9pm-late. ·

Karlovy Lázně, Novotného Lávka 1 (☎222 220 502). An irresistible location beneath the Charles Bridge. The teenagers and early 20-somethings in line at the door stare eagerly at televisions broadcasting from inside this heaving 4-story complex. Different rooms play R&B, techno, oldies, and pop music every night. Cover 120Kč, 50Kč before 10pm and after 4am. Open daily 9pm-5am.

Palác Akropolis, Kubelíkova 27 (☎296 330 911; www.palacakropolis.cz). Metro A: Jiřího z Poděbrad. Take Slavíkova and turn right on Kubelíkova. Less touristed than other clubs, Akropolis features live bands that run the musical gamut from hardcore house to reggae several times per week. Top Czech act Psí Vojáci is an occasional visitor. Packed dance floor gets steamy in summer. Open daily 10pm-5am.

Klub 007, Chaloupeckého 7 (☎257 211 439; www.klub007strahov.cz). Metro A: Dejvicka. From Dejvicka take bus #217 to Stadion Strahov and walk uphill on Chaloupeckého for 450m. For a truly local experience, make the hike out to 007. A favorite with local university students, this club is better for musical appreciation than dancing. Hard core, punk, and reggae alternate nights. No cover. Open M-Sa 7pm-2am.

JAZZ CLUBS

U staré paní (The Old Lady's Place), Michalská 9 (☎603 551 680; www.jazzinprague.com). Metro A or B: Můstek. Walk down Na můstku at the end of Václavské nám. through its name change to Melantrichova. Turn left on Havelská and right on Michalská. Showcases some of the finest jazz vocalists in Prague in a tiny, yet swank, downstairs venue. Performances every night 9pm-midnight. Cover 150Kč, includes 1 drink. Open daily 7pm-2am. AmEx/MC/V.

Ungelt, Týn 2 (☎224 895 748; www.jazzblues.cz). Metro A or B: Staroměstská. From Old Town Sq., follow Týnska and take a right on Týn. Two-floor music room and bar in a subterranean vault. Jazz a la B.B. King. Live concerts daily 9pm-midnight. Cover 200Kč, students 150Kč or listen from the pub for free. Open daily 8pm-midnight.

Reduta, Národní 20. (☎224 933 487; www.redutajazzclub.cz) Metro A: Národní třída. Exit on Spálená, take a left on Národní, and go through the façade of the Louvre cafe. This classic jazz venue is an old haunt of Presidents Clinton and Havel, as photos attest. Cover 200Kč. Open daily 9pm-midnight.

U Malého Glena II, Karmelitská 23 (☎257 531 717; www.malyglen.cz). The cellar club of U Malého Glena (see **Cafes,** p. 250) hosts smoky jazz, throaty blues, and Stan the Man's nightly funk. Su jam sessions feature local amateurs straining or entertaining the crowd. Beer 30Kč. Cover 100-150Kč. Call ahead for weekend tables. Shows start at 9:30pm. Open daily 8pm-2am. AmEx/MC/V.

GLBT PRAGUE

Prague's gay and lesbian scene is developing fast and in many directions: transvestite shows, stripteases, discos, bars, cafes, restaurants, and hotels aimed at gay and lesbian travelers can be easily found. At any of the places listed below, you can pick up a copy of the monthly *Amigo* (www.amigo.cz; 69Kč), an English-heavy guide to gay life in the Czech Republic, or *Gayčko* (60Kč), a glossier magazine mostly in Czech. Check out www.praguegayguide.net for a comprehensive list of attractions.

Cafe Maler, Blanická 28 (☎222 013 116). Metro A: Náměstí Míru. Exit the Metro and take a right on Korunní and then the 1st left on Blanická. The club is on the right, just after the intersection with Vinohradská. This classy glass- and bamboo-filled cafe turns into Prague's only lesbian club at night. While the evening crowd is mostly female, men are always welcome. Club open M-Th 6:30pm-late, F-Sa 7pm-late.

Tingl Tangl, Karolíny Světlé 12 (☎777 322 121; www.tingi-tangi.cz). Metro B: Národní třída. Exit the Metro and take a right on Spálená, a left on Národní, and a right on Karolíny Světlé; under the arch to the left. Draws crowds to its cabarets, where magnificent drag queens lip-sync on stage. Shows after midnight. Women welcome. Cover 120Kč. Open W and F-Sa 10pm-5am.

Pinocchio, Seifertova 3 (☎222 710 776). Metro C: Hlavní Nádraží. Take tram #5, 9, 26, or 55 uphill; exit tram at Husinecka and walk downhill. Complex includes poker machines, strip shows, video arcades, and pension rooms. Beer 25Kč. Open daily 3pm-6am.

▟ DAYTRIPS FROM PRAGUE

When you're in the city, it's easy to forget that there are places worth visiting outside Prague. But even if you're only spending a few days in the capital, take the time to explore the towns and sights in the surrounding Bohemian hills. A day spent wandering through the resplendent castles of Karlštejn or exploring the former concentration camp of Terezín will give you a richer experience and a more complete understanding of the Czech Republic's diverse history.

TEREZÍN (THERESIENSTADT)

Buses from Florenc (1hr., 15 per day, 61Kč). Exit at the Terezín stop by the tourist office. You can also catch a train from Hlavní Masarykovo to the station 2km outside town. Ask for directions, as there are no street signs or signposts. Trains are more reliable on weekends. 500m right of the bus stop, the museum sells tickets to Terezín's sights. ☎416 782 576; www.pamatnik-terezin.cz. Open daily Apr.-Sept. 9am-6pm; Oct.-Mar. 9am-5:30pm. Ticket to museum, barracks, and fortress 180Kč; students 160Kč. Crematorium and graveyard open Apr.-Oct. Su-F 10am-5pm; Nov.-Mar. Su-F 10am-4pm. Free.

The fortress town of Terezín (Theresienstadt) was built in the 1780s by Hapsburg Emperor Josef II to safeguard the northern frontier. In 1940, Hitler's Gestapo set up a prison in the Small Fortress, and in 1941 the town itself became a concentra-

BONE-CHILLING CHAPEL

n and around Prague, you will ind churches of stone, brick, iron, glass—and one of bones. Kutnà Hora, a small, picturesque village hr. from Prague, is both famous and infamous for its ossuary, a chapel filled with artistic and religious creations made entirely rom parts of human skeletons. he village was originally formed around silver mines; its more morbid side only came out when the Plague and a superstition about he holiness of the village's graveyard combined to leave the cemetery overflowing with corpses. The Cistercian Order built a chapel in order to house the extra remains, and in a fit of whim (or possibly nsanity), one monk began designing flowers from pelvises and crania. He never finished the ossuary, but the artist František Rint eventually completed the project in 1870, decorating the chapel from floor to ceiling with the bones of over 40,000 people.

rains run from Hlavni Nadrazi 1hr., 1 per hr., round-trip 12Kč). A 1km. walk from the rain station. From the train station, turn right, then left, left again on the highway. After 500m, turn right at the church. he ossuary is at the end of the road. Open daily Apr.-Sept. 8am-5pm; Oct. 9am-noon and 1-5pm; Nov.-Mar. 9am-noon and 1-4pm. 5Kč, students 20Kč. Cameras 0Kč, video 60Kč.

tion camp. By 1942, the entire pre-war civilian population had been evacuated, and the town became a way station for over 140,000 Jews awaiting transfer farther east. Terezín was one of Hitler's most successful propaganda ploys: the camp was intended to paint a false portrait of ghetto life in order to receive Red Cross delegations. Sparkling clean bathrooms and sleeping facilities were created purely for show. The large park that dominates the town square was built to create an illusion of aesthetic and athletic opportunities for residents, yet, except for publicity stunts, Jews were not allowed to enter it. Nazi films described the area as a "self-governed" settlement, where Jews were allowed to educate their children, partake in arts and recreation, and live a "fulfilling" life. In reality, overcrowding, malnourishment, and death chambers killed over 30,000 people in the camp. Since the war, Terezín has been repopulated, and life goes on in the former concentration camp. Supermarkets occupy former Nazi offices and families now live in the barracks. The population, however, has yet to reach its pre-war levels, when the town numbered over 4000—by the last census, there were fewer than 2000 residents.

TOWN AND CEMETERY. To walk the eerily quiet streets of Terezín is to confront its ghosts. Every building here was used to house and monitor Jews during the war. The former school has been converted into a **museum** of ghetto life, displaying documents that place Terezín in the wider context of WWII. The museum's most moving exhibits are dedicated to the rich artistic life that emerged among the Jews in response to the horrors of persecution—the second floor features original paintings, music, theater, and poetry by children and adults imprisoned in Terezín. East of the marketplace, the **Magdeburg Barracks** explain the lives of Jews within their prison walls. Outside the walls lie Terezín's **Cemetery and Crematorium,** where Nazis disposed of the remains of the executed. *(Open Apr.-Sept. Su-F 10am-5pm; Nov.-Mar. Su-F 10am-4pm. Free.)*

SMALL FORTRESS. The Small Fortress sits across the river, much of it left bare and untouched for visitors to explore freely. Permanent exhibitions chart the town's development from 1780 to 1939 and the story of the fortress during WWII. Above the entrance lies the ironic epitaph of the Nazi concentration camps: *"Arbeit macht frei"* (Work shall set you free). The true horror of this phrase comes alive in the dim underground passage to the excavation site, where those imprisoned here were buried after being literally worked to death. Liberators uncovered mass graves after the war and transferred many of the bodies to the memorial cemetery. *(160Kč, students 130Kč for fortress alone. Open daily Apr.-Oct. 8am-6pm; Nov.-Mar. 8am-4:30pm. Closed Dec. 24-26 and Jan. 1.)*

KARLŠTEJN

Trains from Hlavní nádraží (55min., 1 per hr., 46Kč). Head right from the station and take the 1st left over the Berounka River. Turn right after the bridge, go left at the fork, and walk through the village (25min., mainly uphill). ☎311 681 617; www.hradkarl-stejn.cz. Open July-Aug. Tu-Su 9am-noon and 1-6pm; Sept. and May-June 9am-noon and 1-5pm; Oct. and Apr. 9am-noon and 1-4pm; Nov.-Mar. 9am-noon and 1-3pm. Great Tower open July-Oct. only. Castle tour mandatory. Czech tour 120Kč, students 60Kč; English tour 200Kč/100Kč. 7-8 tours per day. Chapel tours July-Nov. by reservation only. Call ☎274 008 154 or email rezervace@stc.npu.cz. Open Tu-Su 9am-5pm. Chapel tour 300Kč, students 100Kč. MC/V.

Karlštejn is Bohemia's gem, a walled and turreted **fortress** built by Emperor Charles IV in the 14th century. The castle is unique in that it was never meant to be an administrative residence but was always intended as a storehouse for crown jewels and holy relics. Charles originally banned women from entering the castle but soon changed his mind when his wife snuck inside dressed as a castle guard and spent the night. He later built a secret passage that allowed him to go directly from his bedroom to the queen's chambers. Karlštejn's most striking feature is its imposing exterior, as many of its original interior decorations were stolen during wars. Only the **Chapel of the Holy Cross** (excluded from the basic tour) managed to escape the plunder and is decorated with over 2000 precious stones and 129 apocalyptic paintings by medieval artist **Master Theodorik.** The castle's surroundings are as impressive as the castle itself, so take some time to walk along the Berounka River or venture into the surrounding forest. But beware: obscure trail markers may lead you astray.

WEST BOHEMIA

Bursting at the seams with healing waters of all sorts, West Bohemia is an oasis. Over the centuries, emperors and intellectuals alike soaked in the waters of Karlovy Vary (*Carlsbad* in German). Today, tourists still flock to the town's bubbling springs and wander through its colonnades, but they come seeking beer, including one of the world's finest brews, *Pilsner Urquell.*

PLZEŇ   ☎377

Tell Czechs you're going to Plzeň (PIL-zenyuh; pop. 175,000), and they may advise you to spend your time elsewhere, thinking back to the days when the presence of the Škoda car company made this city one of Bohemia's most polluted areas. Efforts to clean up the city, however, have left its beautiful architecture and gardens looking fresh and new. But it is the world-famous beer, not the architecture, that lures so many to Plzeň. Between the Pilsner Brewery, Brewery Museum, and the countless beer halls, Plzeň is a beer-lover's utopia.

◪ TRANSPORTATION

Trains: ☎377 322 079. On Sirková between Americká and Koterovská. To: **Prague** (1¾hr., 12 per day, 140Kč) and **Český Krumlov** (3hr., 3 per day, 140-200Kč) via **České Budějovice.** Domestic tickets on the 1st level; international tickets on the 2nd. Open M-F 3:15am-2am, Sa 2:45am-2am, Su 3:30am-12:30am.

CZECH REPUBLIC

Buses: Husova 58 (☎377 237 237). Many Euroline buses pass through en route to **Prague** (2hr., 16 per day, 70-80Kč) from **France, Germany, the Netherlands,** and **Switzerland.** To **Karlovy Vary** (45min., up to 16 per day, 65-80Kč). Open M-F 5am-10:30pm, Sa 5am-8pm, Su 5am-10:30pm.

Public Transportation: Tram #1 goes to the train and bus stations, Nám. Republiky, and Pension AMOR. Tram #4 runs north-south along Sady Pětatřicátníků. Get tickets (12Kč, backpacks 4Kč) from any *tabák* or from machines at the tram stops and punch them on board by pressing hard on the orange box. 200-1000Kč fine for riding ticketless. **Trams** stop running on their normal schedule at 11:45pm; night trams, labeled with an N followed by the number of the tram, take over, with service every hr.

Taxis: Radio Taxi (☎377 377 377). Taxis stalk the stations and Nám. Republiky.

■*■* ☎ ORIENTATION AND PRACTICAL INFORMATION

Nám. Republiky (Republic Sq.), the main square, from which the city's sights branch out, lies amid a grid of parks and streets. Restaurants and cafes are clustered outside the square. The nightlife is concentrated around the square and **Smetanovy sady.** From the **train station,** turn right on **Sirková** and enter the pedestrian underpass. When you emerge from the Americk exit, continue down Sirková (300m). Turn left on **Pražská,** then right at the fork to reach Nám. Republiky. From the **bus station,** turn left on **Husova.** After it becomes Smetanovy sady, turn left on **Bedřicha Smetany** and follow it to the square (15min.).

Tourist Office: Městské Informační Středisko (MIS), Nám. Republiky 41 (☎378 035 330; www.icpilsen.cz), offers **free maps,** books rooms (from 179Kč), and sells phone cards (150-350Kč). **Internet access** 2Kč per min. Open daily Apr.-Sept. 9am-6pm; Oct.-Mar. M-F 10am-5pm, Sa-Su 10am-3:30pm.

Budget Travel: GTS Int, Pražská 12 (☎377 328 621; www.gtsint.cz), arranges plane and train tickets. Open M-F 8am-5pm.

Currency Exchange: Plzeňská Banka, Nám. Republiky 16 (☎377 235 354), cashes **traveler's checks** for 2.5% commission. Open M-F 8:30am-4:30pm. A **24hr. currency exchange** machine sits in **ČSOB,** Americká 60, near the train station.

ATM: There are MC/V machines scattered all over Nám. Republiky.

Luggage Storage: On the 1st fl. of the train station behind the staircase, on the left. 12Kč, bags over 15kg 23Kč. Lost tickets 30Kč. Lockers 30Kč per day (24hr. limit). Open daily 7am-11:15am, 11:35am-7pm.

Emergency: ☎155.

Pharmacy: Lekarna U Bílého Jenorožce, Nám. Republiky, near the corner of Prešovská and Bedřicha Smetany. Open M-F 7am-6pm, Sa 7am-noon.

Internet Access: Internet Kavarna Arena, Františkánská 10 (☎377 220 402). Ring bell to enter. 0.90Kč per min. Open M-F 9am-10pm, Sa-Su 10am-10pm.

Post Office: Solní 20 (☎377 211 543). **Poste Restante** available. Open M-F 7am-7pm, Sa 8am-1pm, Su 8am-noon. **Postal Code: 301 01.**

▐ ACCOMMODATIONS

There aren't many budget accommodations in Plzeň, as the tourist industry mainly caters to older German travelers. **MIS** (see **Tourist Office,** p. 268) and **CKM,** Dominikánská 1 (☎603 298 570), both book **private rooms** (from 179Kč; 10-15min. walk from main square). **Pensions** range from 300 to 900Kč.

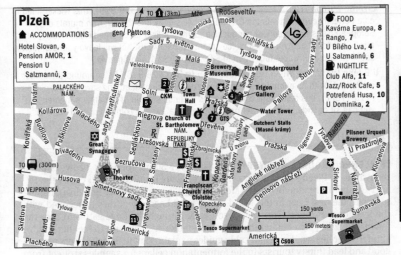

Plzeň

♠ ACCOMMODATIONS
Hotel Slovan, 9
Pension AMOR, 1
Pension U
  Salzmannů, 3

● FOOD
Kavárna Europa, 8
Rango, 7
U Bílého Lva, 4
U Salzmannů, 6

▮ NIGHTLIFE
Club Alfa, 11
Jazz/Rock Cafe, 1
Potrefená Husa, 10
U Dominika, 2

█ **Hotel Slovan,** Smetanovy sady 1 (☎377 227 256; http://hotelslovan.pilsen.cz), at the corner of Jungmannova and Smetanovy Sady. A sweeping, Neo-Renaissance stairway leads guests to simple but beautifully furnished rooms with leather paneled doors, soft beds, and shared bathrooms. Luxury rooms include private bathrooms. All rooms include breakfast. Breakfast buffet 120Kč, dinner 190Kč. Reception 24hr. Singles 620Kč, luxury 1450Kč; doubles 990Kč/2100Kč; extra bed 370Kč/550Kč. MC/V. ❸

Pension U Salzmannů, Pražská 8 (☎377 235 855; www.usalzmannu.cz.) Attached to the eponymous, well-known restaurant, this pension has an unbeatable location for reasonable prices. Rooms are basic but well-equipped, with private bath, telephones, and TV. Breakfast included. Singles start at 550Kč, doubles at 700Kč; extra bed 300Kč. ❸

Pension AMOR, Stikova 14 (☎377 529 986). From the train station, take the pedestrian underpass to the Tramvaj Bolevec exit and then take tram #1 toward Bolevec 8 stops and exit at Plaská (the 2nd to last stop). Cross the street away from the apartment complex and backtrack on Plaská. Take a left on Stikova. The 2 sparkling rooms, each with private bathroom, are maintained by warm and welcoming owners. Kitchen and lounge for guests. 450Kč, 500Kč with breakfast. ❷

◳ FOOD

Every meal in Plzeň should include a glass of *Pilsner Urquell*, a smooth, golden beer, or its dark, stronger brother, *Purkmistr*. If you can't decide, have a *Řezané*, a Czech black and tan, which mixes the two varieties. For groceries, try **Tesco**, Sirkova 47. (Open M-W 7am-7pm, Th-F 7am-8pm, Sa-Su 8am-6pm.)

█ **Rango,** Pražská 10 (☎732 99 69). If you need a break from sausage, cabbage, and dumplings, this candle-lit, 16th-century vaulted cellar may do the trick. A selection of fine wines (bottles from 190Kč), international specialties (95-210Kč), and mouthwatering Italian desserts (50Kč) should satisfy any craving. A salad and pasta (65-180Kč) menu caters to vegetarians. Open M-F 11am-11pm, Sa-Su noon-11pm. MC/V. ❹

U Salzmannů, Pražská 8 (☎377 235 855). Walk through the original Renaissance portal to the city's oldest beer hall, where hearty Czech pub fare has yet to grow old. The fillet of beef with dumplings and cranberries in cream sauce (84Kč) is exceptional. Entrees 72-155Kč. Beer 20Kč. Open M-Sa 11am-11pm, Su 11am-10pm. MC/V. ❸

Kavárna Europa (Euro Café), Nám. Republiky 12 (☎377 329 999). This wicker-filled cafe perfectly complements the Czech Republic's entry into the EU, with murals of other European cities and excellent cappuccino (29Kč). A light lunch (sandwiches 55Kč, salads 50Kč) followed by a delicious ice cream sundae (45-60Kč) will leave your stomach satisfied and your wallet full. Open M-F 9am-8pm, Sa 10am-6pm. ❶

U Bílého Lva (At the White Lion), Pražská 15 (☎377 226 998). Enter around the corner on Perlová. With its animal-skin decor and extensive menu featuring savory meat dishes (115-170Kč), this restaurant could pass as a hunter's cabin. If the antlers frighten you, you can sit outside on the tamer patio. Open M-Sa 11am-11pm, Su noon-10pm. ❷

⚙ SIGHTS

🍺 PILSNER URQUELL BREWERY. In 1842, over 30 independent brewers plied their trade in Plzeň's beer cellars. They eventually formed a union called the Pilsner Urquell Burghers' Brewery (Měščanský Pivovar Plzenský Prazdroj), hoping to create the best beer in the world. Many would agree that they succeeded with the legendary *Pilsner Urquell*. As you walk through the huge gate and spot the famous Prazdroj sign behind the billowing smoke, it's hard not to feel like you've entered beer heaven. Knowledgeable guides explain what makes the beers taste so good and lead thirsty tourists to the fermentation cellars for samples straight from the barrel. The cellars can get chilly, so bring a sweater. *(300m from Staré Město over the Radbuza River, where Pražská becomes U Prazdroje; cross the street and take the pedestrian overpass. ☎ 377 062 888; www.beerworld.cz. 70min. tours daily June-Aug. 12:30 and 2pm; Sept.-May 12:30pm. 120Kč, students 60Kč.)* After the tour, head to Na spilce, the on-site beer house, where Pilsner pours forth at 20Kč per pint. *(Open M-Th and Sa 11am-10pm, F 11am-11pm, Su 11am-9pm.)*

REPUBLIC SQUARE (NÁMĚSTÍ REPUBLIKY). Imperial dwellings loom over this marketplace, but none overshadow the country's tallest belfry, that of the **Church of St. Bartholomew** (Kostel sv. Bartoloměje). Inside, Gothic statues and altars bow to the stunning 14th-century statue Plzeňská Madona. *(Open Apr.-Sept. W-Sa 10am-4pm; Oct.-Dec. W-F 10am-4pm. 20Kč, students 10Kč.)* Tourists can climb 60m to the tower's observation deck for a dazzling—if dizzying—view of town. *(Open daily 10am-6pm. 30Kč, students 20Kč.)* The square's other architectural attraction is Plzeň's Renaissance town hall, topped by a golden clock. *(Nám. Republiky 39.)*

WATER TOWER COMPLEX. Head down Pražská from the square to reach the **water tower** (vodárenská věž), which once stored the crystal-clear water needed for fine beer. *(Pražská 19.)* A 40min. tour of the tower and **Plzeň's underground** (Plzeňské podzemí) winds through the cellars where the town's burghers used to brew their beers. *(Perlová 4. ☎377 225 214. Open June-Sept. Tu-Su 9am-5pm; Apr.-May and Oct.-Nov. W-Sa 9am-5pm. Tours 30-40min., every 30min. Last tour leaves 4:20pm. 45Kč, students 30Kč.)* The **Trigon Gallery** next door features a small collection of early 20th-century art which includes works by painter Frantisek Kupka. *(Pražská 19. ☎377 325 471. Open M-F 10am-5pm, Sa 10am-noon. 10Kč, students 5Kč.)*

GREAT SYNAGOGUE. Built in 1892 by Plzeň's once considerable and prosperous Jewish community, this temple is the third largest in the world. During the Holocaust, Plzeň's Jews were forced to flee, and today fewer than 50 remain in the city. A captivating exhibit displays photos taken over the past fifty years of Jewish sights and people. *(From the southern end of Nám. Republiky, go down Prešovská to Sady Pětatřicátníků and turn left; the synagogue is on the right. Open Apr.-Sept. Su-F 10am-6pm; Oct. Su-F 10am-5pm; Nov. Su-F 10am-4pm. 35Kč, students 15Kč.)*

OTHER SIGHTS. The sprawling **Brewery Museum** displays all things beer, from medieval taps to a coaster collection. Learn about the history of brewing through miniature brewing plants, reconstructed malt houses, chemical laboratories, and simulated pub environments. The zaniest room, "the room of curiosities," showcases steins of all sizes and a statue of Shakespeare's famous drunk, Sir John Falstaff. You can even buy a souvenir glass (from 55Kč) to sample the beer. *(Veleslavínova 6. From the square, go down Pražská and turn left on Perlová, which ends at Veleslavínova. ☎ 377 235 574; fax 377 224 955. Open daily Apr.-Sept. 10am-6pm; Jan.-Mar. 10am-4pm. Free English text available. 100Kč, students 50Kč.)* The black iron gate of the **Franciscan Church and Cloister** (Františkánský kostel a klášter) leads to a quiet garden with statues and several ice cream vendors. Inside, the highlight is the 15th-century **Chapel of St. Barbara**, which is covered with brilliant frescoes. *(Enter at Františkánská 11, south of Nám. Republiky. Open M and W 9-11:45am and 2-5pm, Tu and Th-F 9-11:45am. 30Kč, students 15Kč.)* At the edge of the Old Town, you can stroll and relax in the **Kopecký gardens** (Kopeckého sady) while brass bands perform. *(Františkánská runs into the park south of Nám. Republiky.)*

NIGHTLIFE

Thanks to students from the University of West Bohemia, Plzeň abounds with bars and late-night clubs. Things heat up around 9:30pm.

Jazz/Rock Cafe, Sedláčova 18 (www.jazzrockcafe.cz). From the square, go down Solní and take the first left on Sedláčova. Lined with photos of past acts, this underground cellar cafe earns its name with quality music in a relaxed atmosphere. Beer 26Kč. Live music Sept.-June every W. Open M-F 10pm-4am, Sa 6pm-4am, Su 4pm-2am.

Potrefená Husa (☎377 320 832), on the corner of Kopeckého sady and Martinska. With its hip young Czech crowd, snazzy red wallpaper, and expensive cocktails (martini 100Kč), this classy bar has become one of Plzeň's hottest night spots. The scene picks up early here. While casual dress is acceptable, jeans may mark you as a tourist. Open M-F 9pm-1am, Sa-Su 11-1am.

U Dominika, Dominikánská 3 (☎377 223 226), off Nám. Republiky. Filled with boisterous locals, patrons of this popular bar partake mainly in foosball, not dancing, though techno plays regardless. The upstairs pub offers a quieter setting, with less chatter and jazz. Open M-Th 11am-midnight, F 11am-1am, Sa 4pm-1am, Su 4pm-midnight.

Club Alfa (☎197 227 070), at intersection of Americká and Jungmannova. Teens and twenty-somethings sweat the night away to techno-pop in this beautiful Renaissance ballroom, while the statue of a king looks on disapprovingly. Bowling 11am-closing, 150Kč per hr. Cover F-Sa 20Kč. Open M-Th and Su 7:30pm-5am, F-Sa 7:30pm-6am.

KARLOVY VARY
☎353

From the bus station, Karlovy Vary (pop. 60,000) doesn't look like much, but a stroll into the spa district reveals why Johann Sebastian Bach, Peter the Great, Sigmund Freud, and even Karl Marx frequented salons here. Along the serene, willow-lined Teplá is a row of ornate pastel buildings. The town now hosts mostly older Germans and Russians seeking the springs' therapeutic powers.

TRANSPORTATION. The **train station** (☎353 913 145) is northwest of the center and has few connections. To: **Prague** via **Chomutov** (4hr. plus 1-2hr. layover in Chomutov, 4-5 per day, 280Kč) and **Berlin, GER** (6-8hr., 1 per day, 1300Kč). Buses are more convenient. The **bus station** (☎353 504 516), on Západní, is closer to town and sends buses to: **Plzeň** (1hr. 40min., 10 per day, 80Kč) and **Prague** (2½hr., 10 per day, 120Kč). Buy tickets on board. Local **buses** pass through the main city

THE HIDDEN DEAL

THE BUENA VISTA BACKPACKERS' HOSTEL

ust when you thought budget ravel meant endless nights in rowded dorm rooms, ⍰ Buena Vista Backpacker's Hostel opens up a new world of comfort at prices lower than typical spa-district entrees. The hostel, in one of Karlovy Vary's most beautiful residential neighborhoods, is the epitome of luxury. Each dorm is a self-contained apartment complete with spacious private bath; living, dining, and wardrobe areas; storage room; and a fully equipped kitchen. Beds, though bunked, rival the softness of expensive hotel beds. And with every small touch taken care of, from thick towels to hangers, you won't even know you're not at home. Downstairs, a cafe and bar quell late-night hunger pangs, and a pool table and sauna are a perfect way to unwind after a long day. The staff will gladly arrange other entertainment, ranging from spa treatments and theater tickets to paintball.

Moravská 42. ☎ 353 239 002; www.premium-hotels.com/ buenavista. Take bus #2, 8, 11, or 13 from the bus stand 4 stops to Na Vyhlídce. Continue walking, veer right at the fork to the market, and go downhill then uphill. The hostel is at the end of the street. Linens included. Pool 20Kč per game; ping pong 30Kč per game. Sauna 150Kč per hr. 4- to 6-bed dorms 248Kč. ❶

---

stop on **Varšavská** (10Kč) and run from 4am-10pm. Night buses are infrequent so hailing a cab is advisable. **Taxis** line the main bus stop (Varšavská) and the front of the train station. **Centrum Taxi**, Zeyerova 9 (☎ 353 223 000), has 24hr. service.

🔢 🔢 **ORIENTATION AND PRACTICAL INFORMATION.** Karlovy Vary sits at the confluence of two rivers. The commercial district lies below the **Ohře River**, and **T.G. Masaryka** leads to the **Teplá River**. The spa district, called **Kolonáda** (Colonnade), begins at **Hotel Thermal**, from which **Mlýnská nábřeží** winds through the town's hot springs, changing its name to **Lázeňská, Tržiště**, and **Stará Louka** before ending at the **Grandhotel Pupp**. To reach the spa district from the **train station**, take bus #11 or 13 to the last stop. It's 15min. downhill on foot. Cross the street and go right on **Nákladní**. Take the first left and cross **Ostrovský most** at the highway. Follow the Teplá to T.G. Masaryka, which leads to Hotel Thermal. To get to the center from the **bus station**, turn left and take the left fork of the pedestrian underpass, toward Lázně. Turn right at the next fork, following the sign for the supermarket, and go straight up the stairs to reach T.G. Masaryka, which runs parallel to **Dr. Davida Bechera,** the other main street.

Komerční banka, Tržiště 11, **exchanges currency** for 2% commission and has a MC/V **ATM** outside. (☎ 353 222 205. Open M-F 9am-noon and 1-5pm.) Pick up **maps** (39-69Kč), theater tickets (100-500Kč), and *Promenada* (15Kč), a monthly booklet with event schedules, at the **Infocentrum tourist office,** Lázeňská 1. (☎ 353 224 097; www.karlovyvary.cz. Open Jan.-Oct. M-F 8am-6pm, Sa-Su 10am-4pm; Nov.-Dec. M-F 7am-5pm.) **Luggage storage** at the train station. (10Kč per day, bags over 15kg 20Kč. Lockers 5Kč.) **Centralni Lekarna,** Dr. D. Bechera 3 (☎ 353 230 886), is a **pharmacy** (open M-F 8am-6pm, Sa 8am-noon), and the **hospital,** Bezrucová 19 (☎ 353 115 111), is northwest of the spa district. Surf the **Internet** at **Cafe Bistro Atrium** (☎ 173 181 312), in the Atrium Shopping Center, across the river from the Garden Colonnade. (Open daily 10am-8pm. 30Kč per 15min.) The **post office,** T.G. Masaryka 1, offers **Western Union** services. (☎ 353 161 107. Open M-F 7:30am-7pm, Sa 8am-1pm, Su 8am-noon.) **Postal Code:** 360 01.

🔢🔢 **ACCOMMODATIONS AND FOOD.** Budget accommodations are hard to come by in Karlovy Vary. For festival time in July, most rooms are booked four to five months in advance. **Infocentrum** (see **Orientation and Practical Information,** p. 272) books rooms (from 400Kč). Private agencies can also help you out. **City Info,** at the kiosk at T.G. Masaryka

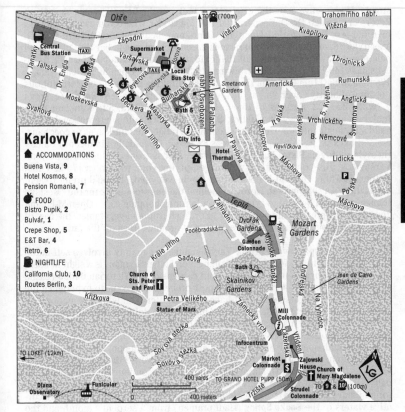

Karlovy Vary

🏠 ACCOMMODATIONS
Buena Vista, 9
Hotel Kosmos, 8
Pension Romania, 7

🍴 FOOD
Bistro Pupik, 2
Bulvár, 1
Crepe Shop, 5
E&T Bar, 4
Retro, 6

🎵 NIGHTLIFE
California Club, 10
Routes Berlin, 3

CZECH REPUBLIC

9, offers singles in pensions from 630Kč and hotel doubles from 950Kč. (☎353 223 351. Open daily 10am-6pm.) A quick bus ride out of the spa district will save you quite a few crowns.

One of the best values in the Czech Republic, ■ **Buena Vista Backpackers' Hostel ❶** (see sidebar, p. 272) aims to please. For luxurious, modern rooms and an exceptional location, head to **Pension Romania ❹**, Zahradní 49, next to the post office on the corner of Zahradní and T.G. Masaryka. All rooms come with baths, TVs, telephones, safes, and fridges. (☎353 222 822; www.romania.cz. Breakfast included. Singles 900Kč, student singles 715Kč; doubles 1480Kč, with view of river 1630Kč; triples 1900Kč. Oct.-Mar. 15-30% discount.) Nearby, **Hotel Kosmos ❹**, Zahradní 39, offers clean, simple rooms overlooking the Teplá with private baths, TVs, and fridges. (☎353 225 476; www.hotelkosmos.cz. Breakfast included. Singles 750Kč, newer rooms 950Kč, deluxe suites 1180Kč; doubles 950Kč/1150Kč/1750Kč. Oct.-Apr. 100Kč discount.)

Meals in the spa district are expensive, but the ambiance and food may be worth the extra money; cheaper options hide in the commercial district. Karlovy Vary is known for its sweet *oplatky* (wafers, around 6Kč), which are almost as enjoyable as the soothing spa waters. You can watch them being made at the kiosk next to City Info, on T.G. Masaryka, or get them from any of the vendors who line the streets. If you crave something sweeter, check out the **Dobrotky crepe shop** ❶ on Zeyerova between Dr. D. Bechera and T.G. Masaryka, where you can design your own dessert for 14-25Kč. (Open M-F 9am-7pm, Sa 10am-noon.) **Retro** ❸, T.G. Masaryka 18, entrance on Bulharská, is an old-school music bar that pleases all palates—meaty Czech cuisine (79-189Kč) for the carnivores and the biggest, freshest salads (49-119Kč) for the herbivores. (☎353 100 710. Open M-Th 10am-1am, F 10am-3am, Sa 11am-3am, Su 11am-1am.) Faithful regulars dine on scrumptious portions of hearty Czech fare at the lovely outdoor terrace at **E&T Bar** ❸, Zeyerova 3. (☎353 226 022. Entrees 75-155Kč. Open M-Sa 9am-2am, Su 10am-2am.) The funkiest cafe in Karlovy Vary, **Bulvár** ❹, Bélehradská 9, offers international dishes amid an eclectic interior where the decorations range from birdcages to coat hangers and oxcarts. (☎353 585 199. Entrees 89-189Kč. Open daily 11am-2am.) Cafeteria-style dining at **Bistro Pupik** ❶, Horova 2, across from the local bus stop on Varšavská, fills your stomach without emptying your wallet. (☎173 223 450. Entrees 50-75Kč. Open M-F 7:30am-7pm, Sa-Su 8am-5pm.) If you'd prefer to self-cater, there's a **supermarket,** Horova 1, behind the bus stop. Look for the "Městská tržnice" sign and be sure to bring a 5Kč coin for a shopping cart. (Open M-F 6am-7pm, Sa 7am-5pm, Su 9am-5pm. MC/V.) For fresh fruit and vegetables, the row of **stalls on Varšavská** provides a good selection of produce fresh off the farm.

◪ **SIGHTS.** A spa town, Karlovy Vary's sightseeing mainly involves self-indulgence in all its various forms. Just strolling along Mlýnské nábř. is a sight in itself. The **spa district** begins with the manicured gardens of the Victorian **Bath 5** (Lázně 5), Smetanovy sady 1, across from the post office. If you want to experience the healing properties of spa life first-hand, Bath 5 offers the widest selection and most affordable treatments in town. Among these delights are thermal baths (355Kč), underwater massages (495Kč), and paraffin hand treatments (255Kč) that are sure to soothe even the weariest of travelers. (☎353 222 536; www.spa5.cz. Pool and sauna open M-F 8am-9pm, Sa 8am-6pm, Su 10am-6pm. 90Kč. Treatments M-F 7am-3pm; select treatments Sa 7am-noon. Reserve 1-2 days in advance. MC/V.) Cross the bridge on T.G. Masaryka, turn right, and continue along the river. The path crosses back over the Teplá and leads through the **Dvořák Gardens** to the Victorian **Garden Colonnade** (Sadová kolonáda). Here you can sip the supposedly curative waters of the **Snake Spring** (Hadí pramen) from a serpent's mouth and the **Garden Spring** (Sadový pramen, 105-300Kč) from a marble peasant woman. Bring your own cup or buy a porcelain one from the kiosks. During the summer months, the Colonnade also hosts free outdoor **concerts** daily 2-3:30pm. **Bath 3**, at Mlýnské nábř. 5, offers massages to complement the healing springs. (☎353 225 641; www.lazneIII.cz. Neck and shoulder massage 455Kč; full body 735Kč. Treatments daily 7-11:30am and noon-3pm. Pool and sauna open M-F 3-7pm, Sa 1-6pm. 90Kč.) Next door, the Greek-inspired **Mill Colonnade** (Mlýnská kolonáda) shelters five separate springs with waters that tend to have a less pungent taste than that of its neighbors. Farther along, the former **market** *(tržiště)* appears by the white **Market Colonnade** (Tržní kolonáda), where two springs bubble to the surface. Across the street, the **Zawojski House,** now the Živnostenská Banka, is a 20th-century Art Nouveau building. The best way to see the building's ornate gilding is to cross the river. The modernist **Strudel Colonnade** (Vřídelní kolonáda), a massive iron and glass building, looms next door. Inside is the **Strudel Spring** (Vřídlo pramen), which spouts 30L of water per second at 72°C. (Open daily 6am-7pm.)

At the end of Stará Louka sits **Grandhotel Pupp.** Founded in 1774 by Johann Georg Pupp, the impressive Grandhotel was the largest in 19th-century Bohemia. From the right side of the hotel, follow the narrow walkway Mariánská to the funicular, which leads to the **Diana Observatory,** and a breathtaking view of the city and surrounding forest. (Funicular runs every 15min. June-Sept. 9:15am-6:45pm;

Apr.-May and Oct. 9:15am-5:45pm; Feb.-Mar. and Nov.-Dec. 9:15am-4:15pm. 30Kč, round-trip 50Kč. Tower open daily 9am-7pm. 10Kč.) To return to town, you can either take the funicular back down or wind your way through the wooded paths of Petra Velikého, which ends at a statue of **Karl Marx.** The stern likeness commemorates Marx's visits to the bourgeois spa between 1874 and 1876. He apparently needed to experience the luxuries of wealth before he could denounce it in good conscience. Around the corner on Krále Jiřího, the turquoise-and-gold Russian Orthodox **Church of Saints Peter and Paul,** built in the 19th century, has inspiring painted domes, icons, and an enormous chandelier.

🗗🎫 **ENTERTAINMENT AND NIGHTLIFE.** Cultural activities abound in Karlovy Vary. *Promenáda,* a brochure available at the tourist office (15Kč; see p. 272), lists the month's concerts and performances; it includes info for Karlovy Vary's **International Film Festival,** held in July, which screens independent films from all over the globe. If you plan to attend, buy a pass to see five films per day inside **Hotel Thermal,** the festival's center. Tickets go quickly, so get to the box office early. You can also buy tickets from the kiosks lining Mlýnské nábř. Otherwise, try your luck at purchasing remainders 1hr. before each showing. The town's hotels and pensions fill up months in advance, so reserve early or camp outside of town.

Like its restaurants, Karlovy Vary's nightlife is geared toward older tourists. Though clubs are sparse, expensive cafes abound. **Routes Berlin,** Jaltská 7 (☎353 233 792), off D. Bechera, attracts Karlovy Vary's hippest crowd to its seductive red interior. (Beer from 15Kč, mixed drinks 35-70Kč. Open daily noon-midnight. The bar occasionally hosts live DJs to mix things up.) It's a steep hike up Kolmá from behind the Church of Mary Magdalene to **California Club,** Tyrsova 2 (☎173 222 087), but the club's late hours and hot dancing make it worth the trek. (Beer from 15Kč. Open daily 1pm-5am.)

SOUTH BOHEMIA

Truly a rustic Eden, South Bohemia's hills make the region a favorite among Czech cyclists and hikers, who flock to the countryside to traipse through castles, observe wildlife in virgin forests, and guzzle Budvar from the source.

ČESKÉ BUDĚJOVICE   ☎38

České Budějovice (CHES-kay BOOD-eh-yoh-vay-tsay), located deep in the heart of the Bohemian countryside, is a great base for exploring the surrounding region. It lacks the small-town charm of Český Krumlov but boasts a beautiful town square and plenty of beer, as the city is home to the great Budvar brewery. Every other building houses a pub where the brews flow freely—a good thing—as it may take a stein or two before you can pronounce České Budějovice.

▟ TRANSPORTATION

Trains: Nádražní 12 (☎387 854 490). To: **Brno** (4½hr., 3 per day, 274Kč); **Český Krumlov** (50min., 8 per day, 46Kč); **Plzeň** (2hr., 10 per day, 162Kč); **Prague** (2½hr., 12 per day, 204Kč); **Milan, ITA** (2330Kč); **Munich, GER** (1494Kč); **Rome, ITA** (3201Kč). Info office open daily 6:30am-6:30pm. Ticket booths open daily 3:45am-midnight.

Buses: (☎386 354 444). On Žižkova, around the bend from the train station. To: **Brno** (4½hr., 6 per day, 200Kč); **Český Krumlov** (50min., 25 per day, 25Kč); **Plzeň** (2¾hr, 1 per day, 110-140Kč); **Prague** (2½hr., 10 per day, 120-144Kč); **Milan, ITA** (14hr., 2 per week, 2030Kč); **Munich, GER** (4½hr., 3 per week, 1000 Kč). Info office open M-F 5:30-10:15am and 10:45am-6:30pm, Sa 8am-noon, Su 8-11:30am.

Public Transportation: Explore České Budějovice by **bus** and **trolleybus** (info ☎386 358 116). Buy tickets (8Kč for 1 bus, 12Kč for transfer) at kiosks, *tabáks*, or machines by the bus stands (provided you have change). Punch them on board.

Taxis: Taxi-Budějovice (☎800 141 516).

✚🛈 ORIENTATION AND PRACTICAL INFORMATION

Staré Město (Old Town) centers around the gigantic **Nám. Přemysla Otakara II.** From the train station, turn right on **Nádražní** and hang a left at the first crosswalk on the pedestrian **Lannova třída.** This stretch of road, which becomes **Kanovnická** after the canal, meets the northeast corner of Nám. Otakara II. The **bus station** is on **Žižkova.** To get to the center turn left on Žižkova and then right on **Jeronýmova.** Go left on Lannova třída, which leads to the center.

Tourist Office: Turistické Informační Centrum (TIC), Nám. Otakara II 2 (☎386 801 413; www.c-budejovice.cz). Friendly English-speaking staff provides **free maps,** books private rooms, and organizes tours. Open M-F 8:30am-6pm, Sa 8:30am-5pm, Su 10am-noon and 12:30-4pm.

Currency Exchange: Komerční Banka, Krajinská 15 (☎387 741 147), off Nám. Otakara II. Cashes **traveler's checks** for 2% commission. Open M-F 8am-5pm.

ATMs: MC/V machines line Nám. Otakara II.

Luggage Storage: Along the right wall of the **train station.** 12Kč per day, bags over 15kg 45Kč per day. Open daily 5:15am-8:30pm. Lockers 12Kč per day. Make sure to set the combination on the inside of the locker door before you shut it.

English-Language Bookstore: Omikron, Nám. Otakara II 25 (☎077 46 68 34 57). Small selection of books, maps, and newspapers. Open M-Sa 8am-6pm, Su 8am-noon.

Emergency: ☎387 878 90. **Children:** ☎387 878 625.

Pharmacy: Nám. Otakara II 26 (☎386 353 063). Open M-F 7am-6pm, Sa 8am-1pm.

Hospital: Nemocnice, B. Nemcove 54 (☎387 871 111).

Internet Access: X-Files@Internet Cafe, Senovážné Nám. 6 (☎386 350 404). Fast access 1Kč per min. Open M-F 10am-10pm, Sa-Su 4-8pm. **Babylon Cafe and Cocktail Bar,** Nám. Otakara II 30, 5th fl. (☎728 190 461; www.cafeinternet.cz), next to Orient. This restaurant and Internet cafe lets you grab a decent espresso (40Kč) while you surf the web. 1Kč per min. Open M-F 10am-8pm, Sa 1-9pm, Su 1-10pm.

Post Office: Senovážné nám. 1 (☎387 734 122), south of Lannova as it enters Staré Město. The large pink and peach building. **Poste Restante** available at window #12 and 13. Take a number from the machine on the right of the entrance for the service you need; wait to be called. Open M-F 7am-7pm, Sa-Su 8am-noon. **Postal Code:** 37001.

🏠 ACCOMMODATIONS

Accommodations don't come cheap. If price is a priority, look beyond Staré Město. **Private rooms** are the best option, as they are neither too expensive nor too far from the center (usually a 10-15 minute walk); **TIC** (see p. 276) has a big book of listings (from 240Kč). To get to the **AT Penzion ❸,** Dukelská 15, head right on Dr. Stejskala from Nám. Otakara II. Turn left at the first intersection and follow Široká, veering right on Dukelská. Penzion is on left, three blocks down. Private baths, well furnished rooms, and friendly family management make this residential pension well worth the extra crowns. (☎387 312 529; fax 387 651 598. Breakfast 50Kč. Book in advance during summer months. Singles 500Kč; doubles 800Kč.) To get to the **Penzion U Výstaviště ❶,** U Výstaviště 17. Take bus #1 from the bus station trolleybus stop five stops to U Parku and follow the street to the right behind the bus stop (200m). Fall asleep under the cloud-patterned sheets behind the cloud-patterned doors of this friendly, quiet pension. (☎387 240 148 or 602 840 906. Call ahead. Communal kitchen and TV. Check-in by 9pm. 250Kč for the 1st night, 200Kč thereafter.)

◘ FOOD

The main streets of Nám. Otakara II and their offshoots shelter numerous restaurants; most have terraces and hearty fare, as well as the requisite Budvar or Pilsner Urquell on tap. Get groceries at **Večerka,** Palachého 10. (Enter on Hroznova. Open M-F 7am-8pm, Sa 7am-1pm, Su 8am-8pm.) **Dr. Stejskala,** off Nám. Otakara II, has a fruit and vegetable store, a butcher, and a bakery.

Malý Pivovar, Vilke Karla IV 8-10 (☎386 360 471), under the Malý Pivovar Hotel, just off Nám. Otakara II. An official Budvar restaurant, this classy brewhouse offers hearty portions of Czech and regional specialties. Pour beer (25Kč) from the tap and relax in one of the massive wooden booths. English menu. Entrees 86-175Kč. Open M-Th 10:30am-8:30pm, F-Sa 10:30am-11pm, Su 10:30am-9pm. MC/V (200Kč min.). ❸

Česká Rychta, Nám. Otakara II 30, under Grand Hotel Zvon. A Pilsner Urquell original restaurant serving delicious cordon bleu steaks, and other meats to accompany your brew of choice (68-265Kč). Dine in the wooden interior amid beer-guzzling merriment or people-watch on the patio overlooking Nám. Otakara II. Open M-Th 10am-11pm, F-Sa 10am-midnight, Su 11am-10pm. ❸

Zeleninovy Bar (Vegetable Bar), Nám. Otakara II 27 (☎721 61 183), next to the pharmacy, at back of the building off the courtyard. This tiny, cafeteria-style restaurant is a great budget option and a haven for vegetarians. A bowl filled with your choice of fresh veggies, sauces, and tofu or meat runs 30-60Kč. Open M-F 11am-6pm. ❶

Restaurant Rio, Hradební 14 (☎386 350 572), off ul. Černé věže. Despite the Brazilian name, this restaurant serves cheap Czech cuisine on an alleyway terrace. Entrees 45-85Kč. Open M-Th 10am-11pm, F 10am-11pm, Sa 4-11pm, Su 4-10pm. ❶

◉ SIGHTS

To reach the city's biggest attraction, the **Budvar Brewery,** Karoliny Světlé 4, catch bus #2 from the center, going toward Borek and Točna, and get off at Budvar. The inner workings of the functioning brewery are intriguing, but beware of the strong fumes. Try to book a tour in advance, though those who show up early often get in. English guidebooks make it easy to join non-English groups. (☎387 705 341. Tours Su-Th and Sa 9am-4pm. Tasting tours in Czech 70Kč; English tours: M-Th 92Kč, students 70Kč; Sa-Su 122Kč/100Kč.)

Encased by colorful Renaissance and Baroque architecture, **Nám. Otakara II,** encompassing over one hectare of cobblestone, is Central Europe's largest square. The square's colorful, early 18th-century Baroque **town hall** (*radnice*) rises a full story above the square's other buildings. The ornate **Samson's Fountain** (*Samsonova kašna*) from 1726 stands in the center of the square, making it a great orientation point. Samson's right eye looks across the square to the 72m **Black Tower** (Černá věž). It's free to climb up, but it costs 20Kč to get to the balcony after the climb. The steep stairs can be treacherous, but the views are worth the trek. (☎386 352 508. Open daily July-Aug. 10am-6pm; Apr.-June and Sept.-Oct. Su, Tu-Sa 10am-6pm. Last climb 5:45pm.) The tower once served as a belfry for the neighboring 17th-century Baroque **Cathedral of St. Nicholas** (Chrám sv. Mikuláše). Choral and orchestral concerts now make use of the cathedral's acoustics—check the posted schedules. (Open daily 7am-6pm.)

České Budějovice's other famous place of worship is the **Church of the Sacrifice of the Virgin Mary,** located in historic Piaristické Nám. The cobbled square and small courtyard garden offer a respite from the more touristed main square. (☎387 311 263. Open M-Th and Sa 10am-noon and 2-4pm, Su 2-4pm.) Next door is the **Museum of Motorcycles.** The exhibit showcases over 100 motorcycles, racing trophies, and motorcycle paraphernalia from the early 1900s to today. (☎723 247 104. Open Su, Tu-Sa 10am-6pm. 40Kč, students 20Kč.)

■ NIGHTLIFE

České Budějovice is more of a pubbing than clubbing town. Bars line the cobblestone streets of the town center, but the hidden pubs on the upper floors of the buildings overlooking Nám. Otakara II, such as Club Zeppelin, are the best way to taste the local scene. Watch for signs underneath the porticos of the square. Posters around town also advertise summertime open-air **concerts** around the lakes, including the Emmy Destinn International Music Festival in late August.

■ **Restaurant Heaven Club Zeppelin,** Nám. Otakara II 38, 3rd fl. (☎386 352 681). A youthful crowd chills to classic and alternative rock in this small, lively bar. Great view over Nám. Otakara II. Budvar 25Kč. Open M-Th 11am-1am, F 11am-late, Sa 6pm-late.

K2, Sokolsky ostrov 1 (☎706 54 891). From MotorCycles Legend Pub, go down the small covered alley on the left of the fork. Cross river and turn right through the small park. Entrance is straight ahead; it is signposted. A cave-like dance club with theme nights and cheap tequila. Techno and oldies Tu and Th. Cover 30-60Kč, depending on the night. Free with ISIC before 10pm. Open M-Tu and Th-Sa 9pm-2am.

MotorCycles Legend Pub, Radniční 9 (☎386 354 945). For the leather-clad, bleached-blond, tattooed crowd. A steak and beer joint where bikers and teenaged tourists congregate beneath skeleton lampshades. Open M-Sa 5pm-3am, Su 5pm-midnight.

ČESKÝ KRUMLOV

This once-hidden gem of the Czech Republic has finally been discovered—some might say besieged—by tourists seeking refuge from Prague's hectic pace and overcrowded streets. Český Krumlov (TSCHES-kee KRUM-lov) won't disappoint those who wander its medieval streets, raft down the meandering Vltava, and explore the enormous 13th-century castle. This UNESCO-protected town, with its countryside charm and beautiful surrounding hills, can be explored for days. Apart from hiking, horseback riding, and kayaking, the town lures visitors with affordable accommodations and burgeoning nightlife.

▛ TRANSPORTATION

Trains run from Nádražní 31 (☎387 551 111), 2km uphill from the center, to **České Budějovice** (1hr., 8 per day; 46Kč) and **Prague** (2½hr., 8 per day; 224Kč). A bus runs from the station to the center of town (5Kč). **Buses** run from Kaplická 439 (☎380 715 415) to **České Budějovice** (30min., 33 per day M-F, 14 per day Sa-Su; 26Kč) and **Prague** (3hr., 9 per day M-F, 6 per day Sa-Su; 130-145Kč). For **taxis** call **Krumlov Taxi** (☎380 712 712) or catch one in Nám. Svornosti.

◪ ▧ ORIENTATION AND PRACTICAL INFORMATION

The curves of the **Vltava River** cradle the central square, **Náměstí Svornosti.** The main **bus station** is on **Kaplická,** east of the square. From the bus station, take the path behind the terminal to the right of stops #20-25. Go downhill once it intersects with

Kaplická. At the light, cross the highway and go straight on **Horní,** which leads into the square. If you get off at the **Špičák** stop north of town, it's an easy downhill walk to the center. From Špičák, take the overpass, walk through **Budějovice Gate,** and follow **Latrán** past the castle and over the Vltava. It becomes **Radniční** as it enters Staré Město and leads to Nám. Svornosti.

Tourist Office: Nám. Svornosti 2 (☎380 704 622; www.ckrumlov.cz/infocentrum). Books accommodations, sells trail **maps** (50-90Kč), and rents audio guides (500Kč deposit; 1hr. 100Kč, students 80Kč; 2hr. 150Kč/100Kč; 3hr. 180Kč/120Kč). Open Apr.-Oct. M-F 9am-7pm, Sa-Su 9am-1pm and 2pm-7pm.

Currency Exchange: Bank SMW, Panská 22 (☎380 712 221), cashes **traveler's checks** for 0.75% commission (min. 100Kč). Changes cash for 1.5% commission (min. 30Kč). Open M, W, F 8:30am-5pm, Tu and Th 8:30am-4pm.

ATM: MC/V ATM on the left side of Horní just before Nám. Svornosti.

Luggage Storage: At the **train station,** across from the ticket booths. 15Kč per day, over 15kg 20Kč per day. Open daily 6am-9pm.

Laundromat: Lobo, Latrán 73 (☎380 713 153), part of the Lobo Pension. Wash 100Kč, dry 10Kč per 10min. Detergent and fabric softener included. Open daily 9am-6:30pm.

Emergency: ☎380 717 646.

Pharmacy: Nám. Svornosti 16 (☎380 711 787). Open M-F 8am-noon, 1-4pm.

Hospital: Horní Braná, Hřbitovní 424 (☎380 761 911), behind the bus station.

Telephones: Card-operated phones around the corner from the Post Office on Pivovarská and just past Krumlov House. Buy cards inside or at local *tábaks*.

Internet Access: At the **tourist office.** No chairs. 5Kč per 5min. 10Kč minimum. **Internet Café,** Zámek 57 (☎380 712 219), in the same building as the castle tourist office (see **Sights,** p. 280). 1Kč per min. Open daily 9am-8pm.

Post Office: Latrán 193 (☎380 716 610). **Poste Restante** at window #2 on the right. Open M-F 7am-6pm, Sa 8am-noon. **Postal Code:** 38101.

ACCOMMODATIONS

Krumlov's stellar hostels offer the best beds in town. They fill up fast in summer, so make reservations at least four days in advance. **Private rooms** abound; look for *Zimmer frei* signs on ul. Parkán or contact the **tourist office** (See **Practical Information,** p. 279. Pensions from 300Kč per person, including breakfast; private doubles 800Kč; camping from 50Kč per person).

Krumlov House, Rooseveltova 68 (☎380 711 935; www.krumlovhostel.com). From Nám. Svornosti, turn left on Rooseveltova, and follow the signs. A backpacker's Shangri-La, this former bakery is now a legendary hostel with a huge kitchen, comfortable living room, funky staircase, and laid-back atmosphere. English-speaking staff will arrange everything from massages to horseback riding. Laundry 150Kč per load. 100Kč key deposit. 7-bed dorms 250Kč; doubles 600Kč; suites 750Kč. ❶

Hostel 99, Vežni 99 (☎380 712 812; www.hostel99.com). From Nám. Svornosti, head down Radniční until it changes to Latrán; continue to the 13th-century red-and-yellow gate, then turn right on Vežni. Neighboring Hospoda 99 provides a gypsy band and jazz nights. The outdoor terrace, overlooking town, hosts barbecues and "free keg Wednesdays." Internet access 30Kč per 30min., 50Kč per hr. Laundry service 200Kč. Checkout 11am. Attic beds 250Kč; 4- to 10-bed dorms 300-390Kč; doubles 700Kč. ❶

Travellers' Hostel, Soukenická 43 (☎380 711 345; www.travellers.cz). Take Panská from Nám. Svornosti and go right on Soukenická. One of the most social hostels in Krumlov. An unbeatable location, spacious dorms, and lots of amenities make this offshoot of the

Travellers' chain a great deal. The youthful guests make good use of the kitchen, lounge, satellite TV, pool table, and foosball. Lively bar on 1st fl. is a popular hub for backpackers in the city. Internet access 1.50Kč per min. Breakfast included. Laundry 150Kč per load. 4- to 8-bed dorms 300Kč, students 270Kč, 7th night free; doubles 380Kč. MC/V. ●

Hostel Merlin, Kájovská 59 (☎602 432 747; www.ckrumlov.cz/nahradbach). From the Nám. Svornosti, drift left on Kájovská. Merlin is just before the bridge. The most peaceful hostel in the center of town with a caring staff. Full of modern rooms and remodeled bathrooms. Free Internet. Communal kitchen. Laundry 10Kč for detergent, 50Kč to wash, 40Kč to dry. 5-bed dorms 250Kč; doubles 500Kč; triples 750Kč. ●

⬛ FOOD

While many restaurants pander to tourists, a few manage quality and distinction in their cuisine. Český Krumlov is home to the oldest cuisine in Bohemia, so medieval-style food abounds. To do your own cooking, the central supermarket in town is **NOVA Potraviny,** at Linecká 49. (Open M-Sa 7am-6pm, Su 8am-6pm.)

⬛ U dwau Maryi (Two Marys), Parkán 104 (☎380 717 228). From Nám. Svornosti, turn right on Radniční and take the 2nd right on Parkán. Overlooking the castle, this riverfront restaurant serves large platters of medieval Bohemian fare. An outdoor patio and intimate dining room provide a peaceful atmosphere. Inventive vegetarian options. Potato dumplings with poppy seed and sugar 72Kč. Finish with a glass of delicious but potent mead (30-45Kč). Entrees 54-120Kč. Open daily Apr.-Oct. 11am-11pm. ●

Na louži, Kájovská 66 (☎337 711 280). From the square, go down Na louži opposite the tourist office and hang a right on Kájovská. Sizable portions of great Czech cooking in a small wooden dining room with antique beer ads. A favorite of locals and tourists alike. Entrees 59-160Kč, vegetarian 62-81Kč. Open daily 10am-10pm. ●

Krčma v Šatlavske, Horní 157 (☎380 713 344), on the corner of Šatlavská and Masná, just off the square (follow the signs from Horní). A roaring fire prepares the banquet for your medieval feast. Period music, waiters in medieval dress, and occasional performances by musketeers and fencers make this candle-lit restaurant an entertaining experience. Grilled meat 95-210Kč. Open daily noon-midnight. Reservations recommended. ❷

Barbakán, Kaplická 26 (☎337 712 679). Savor the best meat dishes in town while dining on the patio overlooking the river or inside the 13th-century battlement. Grill service can be slow. Entrees 85-195Kč. Open daily June-Sept. 11am-midnight; Oct.-May 3-11pm. AmEx/MC/V. ❷

◉ SIGHTS

Towering above Krumlov since the 1200s, the **castle** has been home to a succession of Bohemian and Bavarian noble families. Follow Radniční across the river to the castle's main entrance on Latrán. The stairs on the left lead into the stone courtyards. There is a beautiful Baroque **garden** and sparkling Renaissance frescoes above the castle. (Garden open daily June-Aug. 8am-7pm; May and Sept. 8am-6pm; Apr. and Oct. 8am-5pm.) Two one-hour tours take you into the castle: **Route 1** covers the older Baroque rooms and the **Schwarzenberg chambers** before concluding in the festive excess of **Masquerade Hall. Route 2** gives the history of the Schwarzenberg family and showcases their 19th-century Renaissance suites. Enter through the third stone courtyard, just after the moat with the bears. (☎380 704 721. Open June-Aug. Su, Tu-Sa 9am-noon and 1-6pm; Apr.-May and Sept.-Oct. 9am-noon and 1-5pm. Last tour 1hr. before closing. Route 1: Czech tour 90Kč, students 50Kč; English tour 150Kč/80Kč. Route 2: Czech tour 70Kč/40Kč; English tour 140Kč/70Kč. MC/V.) Tours of the **Mansion Baroque Theater** cover the rest of the structure. The majority of the tour is narrative, so tours in English are recom-

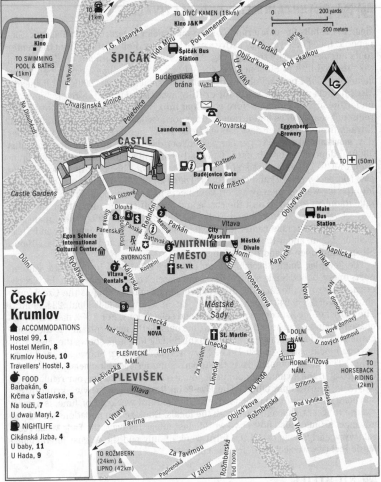

Český Krumlov

🏠 ACCOMMODATIONS
Hostel 99, **1**
Hostel Merlin, **8**
Krumlov House, **10**
Travellers' Hostel, **3**

🍴 FOOD
Barbakán, **6**
Krčma v Šatlavske, **5**
Na louži, **7**
U dwau Maryi, **2**

🍺 NIGHTLIFE
Cikánská Jizba, **4**
U baby, **11**
U Hada, **9**

mended. (Open May-Oct. 10-11am and 1-4pm. Czech tour 100Kč, students 50Kč; English tour 180Kč/90Kč.) From the **castle tower,** you can take in a fine view of the town. (Open daily June-Aug. Tu-Su 9am-5:30pm; May and Sept. 9am-4:30pm; Oct. and Apr. 9:30am-4:30pm. 30Kč, students 20Kč.) Hardier souls should wander among the eerie melodies and distorted sculptures of the **crypt.** (Open June-Aug. daily 10am-5pm. 20Kč, students 10Kč.) Less creepy, though no less controversial, the 🖼 **Egon Schiele International Cultural Center,** Široká 70-72, highlights the work of Austrian painter Egon Schiele (1890-1918), who set up shop here in 1911. The citizens ran him out of town, however, when he started painting burghers' daughters in the nude. The infamous nudes now share wall space with top-notch exhibits from other prominent 20th-century artists. 2005 exhibits include artists Milan Knízak and Emil Orlik. Check out the website for full listings in English. (☎ 380 704 011; www.schieleartcentrum.cz. Open daily 10am-6pm. 180Kč, students 105Kč.)

CZECH REPUBLIC

🎵 🎆 ENTERTAINMENT AND FESTIVALS

Head to the hills for an afternoon of **horseback riding** at **Jezdecký klub Slupenec,** Slupenec 1. Rides take you high above Český Krumlov. Follow Horní from the center to its intersection with the highway. At the second light, turn left on Křížová and take the red trail to Slupenec. (☎380 711 052; www.jk-slupenec.cz. Open Tu-Su 9am-6pm. 250Kč per hr. Full-day trip with refreshments from 2000Kč. Call ahead.) Most hostels rent inner tubes for drifting away the day on the river. Jump out under the arched bridge before you float into Budějovice. **Vltava,** Kájovská 62, rents boats and bikes and arranges transport. (☎380 711 988; www.ckvltava.cz. Kayaks from 390Kč per day; canoes from 640Kč per day; rafts from 960Kč per day; **mountain bikes** 200Kč per 6hr., 320Kč per day, 300Kč after the first day, plus 3000Kč deposit or credit card. Open all year daily 9am-noon and 12:30-6pm. AmEx/MC/V.) If you're not up for a dip in the Vltava, check out the town's **indoor pool** (*plavecky bazen*) and **steam baths** (*para*). For 20Kč per hr., you can plunge into the icy waters, then sweat off your beers in a steam room. From the center, take Radniční to Latrán past the castle and post office, and turn left on the highway Chvalšinská, then right on Fialková. The pool is just after the stream and across from the tennis center. (20Kč deposit. Pool open Su 1-9pm; Tu and Th 7-8:30am, 2-5pm, and 6-10pm; W and F 6-8:30am, 1:30-4pm, and 6-10pm; Sa 1-10pm. Steam baths open W and F-Sa 6-9pm.)

The **Revolving South Bohemia Theater** (*Otáčivé Hlediště*), in the castle garden, hosts opera, ballet, Shakespeare plays, and classic comedies. Sitting in the bleachers as they rotate to face the different sets is as entertaining as the Czech-only shows. (☎386 356 643. Open June-Sept. Tu-Su. Shows 8:30-9:30pm, 224-390Kč.) The tourist office lists current showings and sells tickets. For a 30% discount, purchase remainders an hour before showtime outside the main entrance to the castle gardens. **Kino J&K,** Highway 159 next to the Špičák bus stop, shows the latest Hollywood blockbusters. (☎380 711 892; www.kina.365dni.cz. Shows at 6 and 8pm. 60Kč.) The same company runs the town's summer **open-air cinema.** Follow the directions to the swimming pool until you see the **Letni Kino** on your right. (Open July-Aug. Shows 8pm 60Kč.) The **Five-Petal Rose Festival** (www.ckrumlov.cz/slavnosti), Krumlov's raucous medieval gig the third weekend of June, is a great excuse to wear tights and joust with the locals. Book accommodations months in advance. Krumlov also hosts two world-class music festivals: the **Early Music Festival** (www.earlymusic.cz) in the third week of July and the August **International Music Fest** (www.czechmusicfestival.com).

🌙 NIGHTLIFE

Party animals enjoy the city's full array of bars and cafes, many of which line Rybářská. You'll find most of the city in a slumber on weekdays, though the fun picks up early Friday evening and lasts all weekend long.

Cikánská Jizba (Gypsy Bar), Dlouhá 31 (☎380 717 585), first left off Radniční. Packed on weekends, this bar and restaurant serves interesting Roma cuisine (entrees 45-150Kč) and cheap beer (18Kč). Locals and tourists are willing to stand to hear bands you haven't heard of but will soon love. Open M-Th 11am-10pm, F-Sa 11am-midnight.

U Hada (Snake Bar), Rybářská 37 (☎777 607 576). Live snakes slither in their tank beneath the bar, feasting on mice, while the crowd searches for drinks, lost in the smoky haze. The cellar bar's small size doesn't stop locals and tourists from dancing the night away. 0.5L beer 22Kč. Open M-Th 7pm-3am, F-Sa 7pm-4am, Su 7pm-2am.

U baby (Granny's), Rooseveltova 66 (☎721 983 577), next to Krumlov House (see p. 279). Pronounced "oo BAH-bee." As the drinks flow in this medieval bar, the locals grow less gruff, joining the nearby hostel-goers as they jam to Creedence and the Grateful Dead. Beer 15-22Kč. Open M 5-10pm, Tu-Th 3-10pm, F 3-11pm, Sa 6-11pm.

⚑ OUTDOOR ACTIVITIES

Local firms rent mountain bikes (see **Entertainment and Festivals,** p. 282). There are two challenging but beautiful routes that begin in Český Krumlov. The first is a 70km loop along the banks of the Vltava; the second a shorter, hillier trip. Check the weather before heading out, as sudden summer rains are common.

LONG ROUTE (70KM)

For a ride along the Vltava, turn right on the bridge from Vltava Travel. Cross the river, turn left on Linecká, and then turn right as it crosses the river again to intersect Po vodě. At the highway intersection, turn right on Května, cross the river, and follow the signs to **Rožmberk** (24km). This winds through the towns of **Větřní** and **Záton,** which is so small that only the church perched atop the hill reveals you're in a town. Following the banks of the river until the pale fortress on the left, you will see Rožmberk, seat of the mighty **Rožmberk Castle,** around the bend. (☎380 749 838. Open June-Aug. Tu-Su 9am-5:15pm; May and Sept. Tu-Su 9am-4pm; Apr. and Oct. Sa-Su 9am-4pm. Tours every hr. Czech tour 60Kč, students 35Kč. Call ahead for English tour; 120Kč/70Kč.) **Lipno** lies another 18km upstream, and the "up" part of "upstream" becomes particularly clear here. Look for the ancient **Cistercian monastery** at **Vyšší Brod.** More pleasant than Lipno, **Frymburk** sits along the lake shore 8km west. The Swiss-like town comes complete with a waterside church. From here, a road leads back to Český Krumlov; the next 22km are mostly downhill. If you can't make it this far, head back the way you came: there's no alternate route. Travelers daunted by the hills can take a **bus** from Krumlov to Rožmberk (22Kč) or Lipno (35Kč) from the main bus station. Bikes are not allowed on buses.

SHORTER ROUTE (40KM)

This route heads north through hillside meadows. Take Horní across the river to where it intersects the highway. Turn left at the light and follow the highway as it veers left across the river. At the sign toward Budějovice, turn right and head uphill, turning toward **Srnín;** two gas stations and a supermarket point the way. When the road splits near a factory, turn right and into the meadow. From here, you'll whiz through Srnín, following the signs to **Zlatá Koruna** (Crown of Thorns). The descent ends in front of the 1263 **monastery,** where a tour winds through massive courts, halls, a convent, a church (which supposedly housed a piece of Jesus's crown of thorns in its altar), and the Czech Republic's second-largest library. Over the course of its tumultuous history, the local order of monks was abolished several times before being stripped of its property in 1785. Since then, the building has been a pencil factory and an under-appreciated tourist attraction. (☎380 743 123. Open June-Aug. Tu-Su 8am-noon and 1-5pm; Apr.-May and Sept.-Oct. 9am-noon and 1-4pm. English tours min. 5 people, 50min; last tour 45min. before closing. 55Kč, students 25Kč.) From here, walk your bike back uphill. At the T-junction, go straight toward **Křemže.**

After entering **Třísov,** take the second right (by the village notice board) and cross the rail line just below the station. Continuing down this stone path toward the river (10min.), you'll reach the river bank. The stone path becomes a sidewalk and leads to a metal bridge. If you cross the bridge and head left without crossing the second metal bridge, you'll find the 1349 ruins of the castle **Dívčí kámen** up the steps on the right. Getting out of Dívčí kámen can be brutal. Though the area is quiet, as a precaution it's a good idea to always lock your bike. Once out of Třísov the trip home is mostly downhill.

CZECH PARADISE (ČESKÝ RÁJ)

Centuries of volcanic activity, erosion, and the like have carved Český Ráj into a fairytale landscape. Picturesque valleys, towering rock towns, and dense forests typify what Czechs affectionately call their "Bohemian Paradise." A state nature preserve since 1951, Český Ráj offers spectacular views, stellar climbing, and a vast network of trails perfect for hikers.

JIČÍN
☎ 433

With attractive Renaissance and Baroque buildings lining its streets, Jičín's (EE-chin) architectural beauty remains second only to that of its sister city, Prague. Visitors flock to Český Ráj's gateway village. Its convenient location, just minutes from the park, makes it an ideal base camp for nature lovers.

⊏ TRANSPORTATION. Trains run from **Prague** (3hr., 5 per day, 70Kč), but usually require a stopover. **Buses** from Cerny Most in **Prague** (1½hr., 8 per day, 77Kč) are the best means of transportation to Jičín. Schedules in Jičín change frequently, so double check them at the station or online at www.vlak.cz.

⊡⊠ ORIENTATION AND PRACTICAL INFORMATION. Valdštejnovo náměstí (Wallenstein Square) is the center of town. It meets **Žižkovo náměstí** through Valdice Gate. Shops, cafes, and restaurants line **Husova,** which stretches out from Valdštejnovo nám. Just off Husova, **Šafaříkova** leads to the **bus station.** The **train station,** Dělnická 297, is a 5min. walk from the bus station. From the bus station, bear left on Riegrova and turn right at **Dělnická.** (☎ 493 503 483. Office open M-F 5:30am-5:50pm, Sa 7:15am-6pm, Su 7:15am-7:10pm) The **tourist office,** Valdštejnovo nám. 1, sells **city maps** (39-69Kč) and maps of various hiking areas in Český Ráj. It also organizes river rafting, rock climbing, mountain biking, and hiking excursions. No English is spoken, German language helps. (☎ 493 534 390; www.jicin.org. Open June-Aug. M-Sa 9am-5pm, Su 9am-noon and 4-6pm; Jan.-May and Sept.-Dec. M-F 9am-5pm, Sa 9-11:30am.)

   GE Capital Bank, Žižkovo nám. 4, **exchanges currency** for 2% commission. (☎ 493 544 281. Open M and W 8am-noon and 1-5pm, Tu and Th-F 8am-noon and 1-4pm.) An **ATM** sits next to the tourist office. ATMs are also plentiful along Husova and Valdštejnovo nám. The **police station** is at Balbínova 27. (☎ 974 520 251, **emergency** 158. Open M and W 8am-5pm; reception daily 7am-3:30pm.) A **pharmacy** is at Tylova 812, just off Žižkovo nám. (Open M-F 8am-5pm, Sa 8am-noon.) **Telephones** are in the main square and along Husova. **Internet Cafe Jičín,** Husova 1058, just past the traffic circle, has great rates. (☎ 608 710 123; cafe.jcşseznam.cz. 1Kč per min., students 45Kč per hr. Open M-F 8am-10pm, Sa-Su 6-10pm.) The **post office** is at Šafaříkova 141. (☎ 711 498 306. Open M-F 8am-6pm, Sa 8am-noon.) **Postal Code:** 506 01.

⌐▢ ACCOMMODATIONS AND FOOD. Brand new ▨ **Hotel Jičín ❹,** Havlíčkova 21, just off Žižkovo nám., is a perfect place to rest weary feet after a strenuous day of hiking. The luxurious rooms are bright, clean, modern, and equipped with TV and private baths. (☎ 493 544 250; www.hotel-jicin.cz. Breakfast included. Singles 1010Kč; doubles 1320Kč; triples 1830Kč; quads 2240Kč. Discounts for large groups or extended stays. AmEx/MC/V.) Well-located, **Hotel Paříž ❷,** Žižkovo nám. 3, offers spacious rooms with TV, private baths, and 1970s revival decor—swivel chairs, orange lamps, and tablecloths to match. It also houses a buffet-style restaurant. To access both the hotel and restaurant, enter through the unmarked double doors to the right of Trefa market. (☎493 532 750. Doubles 550-750Kč.) A 10min. walk from the center, the 11-story **Hotel Start ❶** towers above the trees at Revoluční 863. Follow Žižkovo nám. and take Havlíčkova until it becomes Revoluční. A Czech version of Club Med, Hotel Start offers dining, swimming, water slides, bowling, tennis, and an outdoor track. The rooms are basic but clean, and many have excellent views of the countryside. Sore hikers can enjoy a massage or a dip in the hot tub next door. (☎433 523 810; www.hotelstartjc.cz. Breakfast included. Dorms 240Kč; singles 690Kč, with bath 990Kč; doubles 990Kč/1190Kč; triples 1200Kč/1490Kč. AmEx/MC/V.) The cheapest beds in town at **Motel Rumcajs ❶**, Koněva 331, which has both rooms and **camping.** From Valdštejnovo nám., take Nerudova to B. Němcové and turn right. Head through Komenského nám., then bear left on Kollárova, which becomes Koněva. The motel is on your right (25min.). Don't be turned off by the broken-down cars at the attached service garage—the rooms are clean and comfortable. (☎493 531 078. Doubles 280Kč; triples 465Kč; quads 620Kč. Camping 35Kč per person, 35-55Kč per tent.)

Most of Jičín's restaurants have decent food at affordable prices. The best of the lot is **U Dělové Koule ❷**, in Hotel Jičín, which serves generous portions of Czech and international cuisine in a cozy, relaxed atmosphere. To refuel after hitting the trails, try the outstanding chicken "old world Czech style" (89Kč) with raisins, almonds, and apples. Plenty of vegetarian options are available. (☎493 544 252. Entrees 89-249Kč. Open M-Sa 11am-11pm, Su 11am-10pm. AmEx/MC/V.) For a more elegant meal, **Restaurant Lucie ❷**, Fügnerova 197, bathes its trendy clientele in candlelight, offering an international menu. (☎433 531 192. Entrees 80-195Kč; desserts 30-45Kč. Reservations required. Open M-Th 10am-10pm, F-Sa 10am-11pm. AmEx/MC/V.) Grab **groceries** at **Trefa Market**, Žižkovo nám. 1, next to Hotel Paříž. (Open M-F 7am-8pm, Sa-Su 7:30am-7pm.)

🖸📷 **SIGHTS AND ENTERTAINMENT.** The entrance to the main square is **Valdice Gate.** Ascending the gate's tower via its steep, creaky stairs provides a view of the town. (Open Apr.-May and Sept. Th-Su 2-5pm; June-Aug. daily 9am-5pm. 15Kč, students 10Kč.) Next door, the **Church of St. James,** constructed between 1627 and 1634, boasts a magnificent painted dome. (Open daily 9am-5pm.) The wooden doors in the arcade to the right of the church lead to an Italian-designed **chateau,** which houses a museum dedicated to archaeological finds from the Jičín region. The Renaissance, Outdoor Life, Prussian-Austrian War, and WWI rooms are worth a peek. (Open M-F 8am-4pm. 50Kč, children and students 30Kč.) The main square draws crowds to its **open-air markets,** but, for those who prefer to stay in, Hotel Start (see p. 284) offers **bowling.** (210Kč per hr. Open M-Th 4pm-1am, F-Sa 1pm-3am, Su 1pm-1am.) **Sport-Plus** recreation center next door has swimming, squash, and aerobics facilities open to the public. (☎493 533 462; www.sport-jicin.cz. Swimming 50Kč per hr., students 30Kč. Sauna 60Kč/50Kč per 75min. Open M-F 2-9pm, Sa 10am-9pm, Su 10am-8pm.)

🏔📷 **HIKING AND OUTDOOR ACTIVITIES.** Numerous trails cross **Český Ráj National Preserve.** There are four main trails for **hiking** and one for **cycling.** Red signs mark the long **Golden Trail,** which connects Prachovské skály (Prachovské Rocks) to Hrubá Skála (Rough Rock). Green, blue, and yellow signs guide hikers to sights other vistas, including **Pechova vyhl,** which offers a magnificent panorama of the rocks. All trails cross each other, and many connect in loops, creating circular hikes of different distances, ranging 2-12km. **Triangle signs,** in the color of their respective trail, denote vistas off the main trails. None of these hiking trails are

CZECH REPUBLIC

open to cyclists. The main cycling route is marked by blue dots. It follows the road before veering off into the wilderness and only connects with the red trail once, near the rock castle. The trail conditions are generally good, and off-road bikes are only necessary if it has rained recently.

To hike in **Prachovské skály,** catch a bus headed toward Pařežká skály or Jinolice from stand #14 at Jičín station and take it to the Prachov/Český Ráj stop (15min., several per day, 10Kč). The posted schedules are often incorrect, so the best way to find your bus time is to ask the information office at the end of the station. The staffers don't speak English, but if you say your destination and make it clear that you don't speak Czech, they will write down the platform number and time of your bus. Check the return schedule with the ticket office at the head of the trail before you set out because buses back to town run less frequently than those headed to the park. Buses often run behind, so you should be prepared to wait. You can also walk to and from the park along the relatively easy 6km trail, beginning at the Motel Rumcajs (see p. 284). The **ticket office** sells **trail guides** at the base of the rocks. Because signs on the trail are often unclear, a **map** is very helpful in preventing you from getting eternally lost. From the bus station, head uphill past the outdoor cafe and follow the red trail. Trails wind through Prachovské skály's massive, pillar-like sandstone formations, the ruins of the 14th-century **castle** Pařez and the natural, **rock-lined pond** Pelíšek. (Open daily 8am-5pm. Park entrance 45Kč, students 20Kč.)

To get to **Hrubá Skála,** take a train from Jičín toward Turnov (45min., 12 per day, 43Kč round-trip). Get off at Hrubá Skála station and follow the signs to the blue trail, which leads behind the train station to the right, over the tracks, and uphill through the village to the castle. This small town surrounds a hilltop **castle** and hotel (admission 25Kč), where hikers can enjoy some of the best views of the famous **Trosky sandstone rocks.** For the same view without the comforts of a hotel patio, take an offshoot of the blue trail leading to the right just after the village. A left up a set of wooden stairs will bring you to the yellow trail. Go left and follow the yellow markers up the steep steps to a yellow triangle denoting a vista. If panoramic views bore you, the climbers scaling the vertical rocks are sure to entertain. The roadside trails tend to be more level than those in Prachovské skály but offer similarly extraordinary views. The red trail leads from the castle up to the ruins of **Valdštejnský hrad** (Wallenstein Castle), a contested commodity during the Hussite Wars of the 15th century. A peek through the archers' window evokes romantic visions. The red and blue trails are open to cyclists, but the yellow is not, and only the blue is ideal for biking.

EAST BOHEMIA

From the fertile lowlands of the Elbe to the mountain ranges that create a natural border with Poland, oft-overlooked East Bohemia has skiing, sightseeing, and swimming opportunities to spare. Under Hapsburg rule, the Czech language was kept alive among the people of East Bohemia. Consequently, within these villages many 19th-century Czech intellectuals and nationalists were born. Today, Hradec Králové, the region's administrative and cultural center, combines marvelously preserved medieval buildings with a lively urban pace.

HRADEC KRÁLOVÉ   ☎ 49

At the confluence of the Elbe and the Orlice Rivers, Hradec Králové (HRA-dets KRAH-lo-veh), literally "Queens' Castle," once served as a depository for royal widows, but now caters to a much younger crowd. Cyclists and university students rule the boulevards of this town, one of the most active areas in the Czech

Republic. Bicycles are so popular that the town developed special roads for them. Hradec Králové prides itself on its ability to entertain, scheduling numerous cultural events, festivals, and outdoor activities throughout the year.

TRANSPORTATION

Trains: Riegrovo nám. 914 (☎495 537 555). To: **Prague** (2hr., every hr. 5am-8pm, 222Kč). Open daily 3am-11:30pm; info center open daily 6am-7pm.

Buses: Operate out of the train station. Buy tickets on board. To: **Prague** (2hr., every hr., 72-80Kč). **Public bus** tickets (9-11Kč) are sold at kiosks and at the station. Validate your ticket in the red boxes on board by pulling the black lever towards you.

Taxis: Sprint Taxis (☎551 51 51) congregate in front of the train station.

ORIENTATION AND PRACTICAL INFORMATION

Hradec Králové feels like two separate towns separated by the **Labe** (Elbe) River. On the west side, the pedestrian-only **Čelakovského** is a favorite local drag along the shop-infested **Nové Město** (New Town). The east side is home to the churches and cafes of **Staré Město** (Old Town). The **train** and **bus stations** are next to each other, on the edge of Nové Město away from the river. To get to **Velké náměstí** (Great Square) from the stations, take a right on Puskinova and then a left on **Gočárova třída.** Follow Gočárova through Nové Město to the river, cross the bridge, and continue one block. When you hit **Čs. armády,** head left and then turn right on **V kopečku,** which leads to Velké nám. Alternatively, buses #1-3 and 5-17 go to the center from the train station.

Tourist Office: Information Center, Gočárova třída 1225 (☎495 534 485; www.ic-hk.cz). English-speaking staff arranges accommodations and sells tickets to events in town. **Free maps** and info on town festivals, which run throughout the year; the most famous are in June and Oct. Open June-Aug. M-F 8am-6pm, Sa 10am-4pm; Sept.-May M-F 8am-6pm. 2nd **location** at Velké nám. 165 (☎495 534 482), next to Pension Pod Věží. Internet 40Kč per hr. Open M-F 8am-noon and 12:30-4:30pm, Sa-Su 10am-4pm.

Budget Travel: GTS, Čelakovského 623 (☎495 515 825; www.gtsint.cz), several doors down from the pharmacy. Discounted airline and bus tickets for students. Open M-F 8:30am-5:30pm.

Currency Exchange: Komerční Banka, Čelakovského 642 (☎495 815 550), at Masarykovo nám. Charges 2% commission. **ATM** inside. Open M-F 8:30am-5pm.

Luggage storage: At train station. Bags less than 15kg 20Kč; 15kg and up 30Kč. Lockers 5Kč. Open 24hr.; breaks 10:45-11:15am, 1:25-1:40pm, and 6:30-7pm.

English-Language Bookstore: Skippy Bookstore, Střelecká 748 (☎495 522 779; www.skippy.cz). Small English section. Enter at the corner of Střelecká and Gočárova. Open M-F 8am-6pm, Sa 8am-noon. MC/V.

Police: Haškova, near the train station. **Emergency:** ☎158. Open 24hr.

Pharmacy: Centrální lékárna, Masarykovo nám. 637 (☎495 511 614), across from Komerční Banka (see above). Open M-F 7am-6pm, Sa 8am-noon.

Hospital: ☎495 837 211. On Sokolská, south of Old Town.

Internet Access: Jowin Digital, Gočárova 1261 (☎495 536 595; www.jowin.cz), across from the tourist office on the 2nd fl. 1Kč per min.; 60Kč per hr. Free coffee with 1hr. Internet time. Open M-F 9am-6pm.

Post Office: (☎495 540 733), on Riegrovo nám., next to the train station. Get a ticket from the machine in the waiting area. Send packages at window #6. Card **telephones** in front; cards can be purchased inside. Open M-F 7am-7pm, Sa 7am-1pm, Su 8am-noon. **Postal Code:** 500 02.

■ ⬤ ACCOMMODATIONS AND FOOD

You won't find budget accommodations in the center of Old Town. Inexpensive options are plentiful around the university, just a short walk south of the center. The best rooms for your buck are at **Hotel Dům ❶**, Heyrovského 1177, a 10min. walk from Staré Město. From the train station, take bus # 1, 9, 21, or 28 to Heyrovského, cross Sokolská, and take the first right on Heyrovského. Clean, cheap rooms have fridges, desks, and shared balconies. (☎495 511 175; www.hotelovydum.cz. Reception 24hr. Singles 240Kč; doubles 340Kč. Check-out 9am.) Farther outside the center is **Hotel Garni ❷**, Na Kotli 1147. All its rooms have bath. It also offers more basic hostel-style accommodations in the summer. Take bus #1, 9, or 28 from the station to Hotel Garni; it's to the right of the bus stop. (☎495 763 600. Breakfast included. Reception 24hr. Dorm singles 500Kč. Apartments with TV, fridges, and telephones singles 690Kč; doubles 1260Kč. Hostel beds July 15-Sept. 15, 250Kč. Discounts for HI members 80-200Kč.) If location is your top priority, brand-new **Penzion Pod Věží ❹**, Velké nám. 165, offers massive, luxurious rooms equipped with TV, phones, private baths, and minibars. Rooms facing the front have great views of Velké náměstí. (☎495 514 932; www.pod-vezi.cz. Breakfast included. Singles 1110Kč; doubles 1490Kč. 10% discount for cash payment. AmEx/MC/V.)

Staré Město boasts many pubs and restaurants offering traditional Czech cuisine. In Nové Město, **Pivnice Gobi ❶**, Karla IV 522, is an underground hangout with inexpensive meals but a menu limited to sausages, frankfurters, and fried cheese. This student haven features pool, darts, foosball, and a big-screen TV. (☎495 511 003; www.gobişbar-oasa.cz. Entrees 30-158Kč. Open M-Th 2pm-1am, F-Sa 5pm-3am.) The best lunch option is **Jídelna Praha ❶**, Gočárova 1229, a cafeteria-style local favorite serving large portions of high-quality food. (☎495 561 897. Entrees 38-48Kč. Open M-F 6:30am-4pm, Sa 8am-noon.) For lighter fare, **Atlanta ❸**, Švehlova 504, has a sprawling outdoor patio, which dominates Masarykovo nám. in summer. It offers a huge array of salads, pastas, and vegetarian options (59-159Kč) alongside the usual meat and dumplings. (☎495 515 431. Open M-Th 8am-midnight, F 8am-1am, Sa 9am-1am, Su 10am-11pm. MC/V.) The giant supermarket **Tesco**, Nám. 28 října 1610, sells groceries. (☎495 072 111. Open M-F 7am-8pm, Sa 7am-7pm, Su 8am-6pm.)

⬤ 🎵 SIGHTS AND ENTERTAINMENT

Most sights in Hradec Králové are on **Velké nám.**, the center of Staré Město. Here, the 1307 **Church of the Holy Spirit** (Kostel Svatého Ducha) attests to the town's royal past with priceless items, like a 1406 tin baptismal font (one of the oldest in Bohemia) and tower bells affectionately named Eagle and Beggar. (Open M-Sa 10-11am and 2:30-3:30pm, Su 2-3:30pm. Free.) Climb up the 71m **White Tower** (Bílá věž) beside the church to see Bohemia's second-largest bell. You may feel your inner clappermeister stirring, but the bell-ringing is reserved for eight burly men who have been assigned to perform the honor on special occasions only. (Open daily 9am-noon and 1-5pm. 15Kč, students 10Kč.) In the middle of the square, the excellent **Gallery of Modern Art** (Galerie moderního umění), #139, showcases 20th-century Czech painting and sculpture. The floors lead you chronologically through Czech takes on Impressionism, Cubism, Expressionism, and more recent trends, showcasing artists, like Emil Filla and Josef Váchal. The first floor gallery's collection of František Bílek's wood sculptures is a highlight. (☎495 514 893. Open Tu-Su 9am-noon and 1-6pm. Permanent collection 25Kč, students 10Kč., exhibitions 15Kč/5Kč.) Walk across the square from the museum to the **Church of the Assumption of the Virgin Mary** (Kostel Nanebevzetí Panny Marie), constructed by Jesuits from 1654 to 1666. Prussian soldiers destroyed its interior in 1792, but 19th- and 20th-century renovations have revived this Baroque beauty. (Open daily 10am-5pm. 20Kč, students 10Kč. Peek in through the window for free.)

Fish lovers can find peace at the **Ohří Aquarium,** Baarova 1663. From Velké nám., cross the Elbe River on Gočárova and bear left on to V. Lipkách. After you cross Střelecká, Baarova will be on the left. Walk across the tropical rain forest bridge or through the tank while 40 species of fish swim above and therapeutic music plays in the background. (☎495 534 555. Open Tu-Su 9am-6pm. 60Kč, students 40Kč.) A stroll through the lush **Jiraskovy Sady** city gardens is a relaxing way to cap off a long day of sightseeing, or simply to escape the city's cyclists. Enter at the intersection of Komenského and Rokycanova. (Open daily Apr.-Sept. 6am-9pm, Sa-Su 8am-9pm; Oct.-Mar. M-F 6am-7pm, Sa-Su 8am-7pm.)

In late October, Hradec Králové's largest festival, **Jazz Goes to Town** (www.jazzgoestotown.com), features musicians from all over the world. The action takes place at the Aldis Center, Eliščino náb. 357 (☎495 052 111), and at pubs all over town. You can buy tickets at the tourist office. For more information call ☎495 411 140. The **Theater Festival of European Regions** (www.klicperovodivadlo.cz) is usually held in the last two weeks of June. Classic and modern plays are performed daily all over town by professional groups from the Czech Republic and nearby regions. Schedules and tickets are available at the tourist office by calling ☎495 514 876. **Hogo Fogo Bar,** 19 Eliščino náb., is a relaxing pub where the students flock when night falls. (☎495 515 592. Beer 17Kč. Open M-Th 1pm-1am, F 1pm-3am, Sa 4pm-3am, Su 4pm-1am.)

LITOMYŠL

One of the Czech Republic's rural gems, Litomyšl (LIT-ohm-shil) has been greatly ignored by non-Czech tourists. A lack of attraction does not explain this oversight, as this tiny town is home to a magnificent chateau and enchanting architecture. While you can easily cover the town in a day, the relaxed village atmosphere and lack of tourists may seduce you into staying longer.

▐ TRANSPORTATION

Trains: Nádražni 510 (☎461 612 203). The station is inconvenient, and most trains require a connection. To: **Hradec Králové** (2hr., several per day, 88Kč).

Buses: Mařákova 1078 (☎461 613 352). To: **Hrádec Kralové** (1hr., 12 per day, 52Kč).

Taxis: Taxi Dańsa (☎602 411 844). There aren't many taxis in town, so call ahead.

▐ ▐ ORIENTATION AND PRACTICAL INFORMATION

Litomyšl's tiny center is dominated by the banana-shaped **Smetanovo náměstí** (Smetana Square). A series of small, uphill paths lead to the chateau and gardens that make up the town's cultural core. Almost everything of interest is either on the main square or on one of its side streets. To reach the center from the bus station, turn left on Mařákova and follow it over the river to Tyršova. Turn left and then bear left again at Braunerovo nám. to get to Smetanovo nám.

Tourist Office: Smetanovo nám. 72 (☎461 612 161; www.litomysl.cz). Provides free **maps** of the town center and accommodations listings. Sells phonecards. English spoken. Open M-F 9am-7pm, Sa-Su 9am-3pm.

Currency Exchange: Komerční banka, Smetanovo nám. 31, cashes **traveler's checks** for 2% commission and has an **ATM.** Open M-F 8:30am-4:30pm.

Pharmacy: Lekarná U andela Strázce, Smetanovo nám. Open M-F 7:30am-5:30pm, Sa 8am-noon.

Hospital: Nemocnice, J.E. Purkyně 652 (☎461 655 111), south of the center, off Mařákova.

Internet Access: At the **tourist office** (see above). Speedy connections for 1Kč per min., but there are only 5 terminals.

Post Office: Smetanovo nám. 15 (☎461 654 372). Open M-F 8am-6pm, Sa 8am-noon. **Postal Code:** 570 01.

■ ◖ ACCOMMODATIONS AND FOOD

While Litomyšl does not have much to offer in terms of budget accommodations, it is too small and untouristed a location to have sky-high prices. If saving crowns is your priority, you will have to venture about 10min. outside the center. Camping is the cheapest option (from 50Kč). Inquire at the tourist office for details. If you prefer something more central, ▥**Pension Kraus ❷,** Havlíčkova 444, although relatively more expensive, is still the best deal around. From the main square, walk to the northernmost end and continue down Havlíčkova; it's on the right. This beautiful pension provides bright, spacious rooms in a peaceful atmosphere, complete with a summer garden. Soft beds, satellite TV, and sparkling, private bathrooms complement the well-furnished settings. (☎461 614 823; www.pension-kraus.cz. Breakfast buffet 100Kč. Singles 500Kč; doubles 800Kč. AmEx/MC/V.) Outside the center, the **Pedagogical School ❷,** Strakovská 1071, provides basic rooms in a university boarding house. It has clean, comfortable beds, shared bathrooms, and communal kitchenettes. From the bus station, turn left on Mařákova and then make a right on Strakovská, which is the local highway. Continue for 600m; the school is on the right. (☎461 654 612; novotna@vospspgs.lit.cz. Open June-Sept. Doubles 400Kč; triples 600Kč.)

Litomyšl's restaurant selection is not huge, but its portions are large and its prices low. Most menus are limited to Czech cuisine, so vegetarians may be stuck with fried cheese. The majority of the town's restaurants are scattered along the main square and the uphill paths to the chateau. Overlooking a serene cobbled square, **Restaurace Pod Klásterem ❷,** B. Nemcove 158, is always packed with locals enjoying massive platters of grilled meats and lighter pastas. The lovely, geranium-filled outdoor terrace is the perfect place to indulge in a delicious ice cream sundae. (☎602 712 703. Entrees 90-120Kč. Open M-Th 11am-11pm, F-Sa 11am-1am, Su 11am-10pm.) Located in the pristine gardens and overshadowed by a massive church, **Klasterni sklipek ❷,** in Klasterni Zahrady, has arguably the best location and ambiance in town. (☎724 063 040. Entrees 50-145Kč. Open daily June-Aug. 10am-11pm and Nov.-Mar. 9am-7pm; Apr.-May and Sept.-Oct. M-F 9am-7pm, Sa-Su 9am-10pm. AmEx/MC/V.) **Supermarket Kubik ❶,** Smetanovo nám. 72, carries groceries. (Open daily 7am-8pm.)

◉ ♫ SIGHTS AND ENTERTAINMENT

The town's highlight is the magnificent UNESCO-protected ▥**chateau,** which overlooks the center from its hilltop perch. Built between 1568 and 1581 by Vratislav of Perštejn, the chateau was intended to relieve the homesickness of the supreme chancellor's wife, Marie Manrique de Lara of the Spanish Mendoza family, who desperately missed the Renaissance architecture of her home country. The elegant arcades are adorned with thousands of *sgrafitti*, each of which, like snowflakes, have wholly unique geometrical shapes. Tours wind through the chateau's salons and parlors, but the main attraction is the 1797 wooden **theater**. To get here from the square, ascend Váchalova, take a right, and hang a quick left up the covered stairs. (☎461 611 066. Open May-Aug. Tu-Su 9am-noon and 1-5pm; Sept. Tu-Su 9am-noon and 1-4pm; Apr. and Oct. Sa-Su 9am-noon and 1-5pm. Tour 1 covers the theater and state rooms. Tour 2 starts in the chapel and travels through the many banquet rooms. Both tours last 50min. Tour 60Kč, students 30Kč. English tours 120Kč. Free English info available on Czech tours.) Visitors can also stroll through the birthplace of "Bartered Bride" composer **Bedřich Smetana**, situated in the castle brewery. While the exhibit is tiny, seeing Smetana's cradle while his compositions play in the background is a must for any music lover. (See chateau opening hours. 20Kč, students 10Kč.) The surrounding **castle gardens** make a lovely break after a tour. (Open M-Sa 5am-10pm, Su 8am-8pm. Free.) Opposite the chateau, locals lounge among the garden statues of **Klášterní Zahrady.** (Open daily 8am-11pm. Free.) Two blocks away, on Terezy Novákové 75, lies the **Portmoneum House.** Its interior was vibrantly decorated by experimental painter **Josef Váchal** in the 1920s. (☎461 612 020. Open May-Sept. Tu-Su 9am-noon and 1-5pm. 40Kč, students 20Kč. Ring the bell to enter.) During the last weeks of June, the chateau courtyard houses the **Smetana Opera Festival,** which occurs June 17-27, 2005. (☎461 616 070. Tickets 80-1200Kč.)

MORAVIA

Winemaking Moravia forms the easternmost third of the Czech Republic. Home of the country's finest folk music and two leading universities, it is also the birthplace of a number of Eastern European notables, including Czechoslovakia's first president Tomáš G. Masaryk, psychoanalyst Sigmund Freud, and chemist Johann Gregor Mendel, avatar of modern genetics. Tourists have yet to weaken Brno's cosmopolitan vigor or disrupt Olomouc's cobblestoned charm. Outside the city, the low hills of the South Moravian countryside harbor the remarkable chateau of Kroměříž and the architectural pearls of Telč.

BRNO ☎(0)5

The Czech Republic's second-largest city, Brno (berh-NO; pop. 388,900) has been an international marketplace since the 13th century. Today, emissaries of global corporations compete for space and sales among local produce stands. The result is a dynamic and spirited city where historic churches soften the glare of the clubs lining some of its streets.

⊏ TRANSPORTATION

Trains: Nádražní (☎541 171 111). To: **Prague** (3hr., 16 per day, 294Kč); **Bratislava, SLK** (2hr., 8 per day, 250Kč); **Budapest, HUN** (4hr., 2 per day, 945Kč); **Vienna, AUT** (1½hr., 1 per day, 536Kč).

Buses: ☎543 217 733. On the corner of Zvonařka and Plotní. To: **Prague** (2½hr., several per day, 112-167Kč) and **Vienna, AUT** (2½hr., 2 per day, 250Kč).

Public Transportation: Tram, trolley, and bus tickets at a *tábak* or any kiosk. 8Kč for 10min., 13Kč for 40min.; 24hr. pass 50Kč. Luggage requires an extra ticket; 4Kč for 10min., 6Kč for 40min. 400-800Kč fine for riding ticketless; ticket checks are common. Bus routes #90 and above run all night; trams and all other buses run daily 5am-11pm.

Taxis: Impulse Taxi (☎542 216 666). Taxis line Starobrněnská and Husova.

✴🛈 ORIENTATION AND PRACTICAL INFORMATION

Everything in central Brno is accessible by foot. Its main streets radiate from **Nám. Svobody** (Freedom Square). From the **train station** entrance, cross the tram lines on **Nádražní**, turn left, walk 15m, and then turn right on **Masarykova**, which leads to Nám. Svobody. From the bus station, facing the main schedule board, ascend the stairs at the leftmost corner of the station. Go straight on the pedestrian overpass and follow the foot path, which runs aside **Plotní**. Pass **Tesco** and take the pedestrian underpass to the train station. When you resurface, with your back to the train station, go left on Nádražní; Masarykova is on the right.

Tourist Office: Kulturní a informační centrum města Brna, Radnická 8 (☎542 211 090; fax 542 210 758), inside the town hall. From Nám. Svobody, go down Masarykova, turn right on Průchodní, and then right on Radnická. **Free maps** of the city center. Sells maps of the entire city (29-79Kč). Open M-F 8am-6pm, Sa-Su 9am-5pm.

Budget Travel: GTS International, Vachova 4 (☎542 221 996; fax 542 221 001). English spoken. ISIC 250Kč. Open M-F 9am-6pm, Sa 9am-noon.

Currency Exchange: Komerční banka, Kobližná 3 (☎521 271 11), just off Nám. Svobody. Gives V **cash advances,** cashes **traveler's checks** for 2% commission (min. 50Kč) on the 2nd fl., and has an AmEx/MC/V **ATM.** Open M-F 8am-5pm.

Luggage Storage: At the train station. 17Kč per 15kg bag per day, 26Kč per 15-20kg bag, 9Kč per 5kg thereafter. Lockers 10Kč per day. Open 24hr.

English-Language Bookstore: Barvic a Novotny, Česká 13 (☎542 215 040; www.barvic-novotny.cz). Broad selection of fiction on 2nd fl. Open M-Sa 8am-7pm, Su 10am-7pm.

Laundromat: Kavarna Pradelna, Hybešova 45. Take tram #1 or 2 from the train station to "Hybešova" and it's 25m ahead on the left. Wash 60Kč, dry 40Kč, detergent 35Kč. Offers the best **Internet** rates in town. M-F 30Kč per hr., Sa-Su 20Kč per hr. Open M-F 10am-midnight, Sa 2pm-midnight, Su 2-10pm.

Pharmacy: Kobližná 7 (☎542 212 110). Open M-F 7am-10pm, Sa 8am-1pm. AmEx/MC/V.

Hospital: Urazova Nemocnice, Ponávka 6 (☎532 260 111). From Nám. Svobody, take Kobližná to Malinovského nám. Continue on Malinovského nám. to Celi (300m) and take a left on Ponávka.

Internet Access: Internet Center Cafe, Masarykova 2/24. 52 computers with fast connections in the town center. 40Kč per hr. Open M-F 8am-midnight, Sa-Su 9am-11pm.

Post Office: Poštovská 3/5 (☎542 153 622). **Poste Restante** at corner entrance. Open M-F 7am-7pm, Sa 8am-noon. **Postal Code:** 601 00.

🏠 ACCOMMODATIONS

Brno's hotel scene is geared toward business suits, so it's no great surprise that one of the city's budget hotels was recently replaced by the "Moulin Rouge Erotic Night Club Disco." Though few and far between, budget options are available, especially in the summer. Student dormitories, transformed into hostels from July to September, are the best deal in town. During the low season, the local tourist office (see **Orientation and Practical Information,** p. 292) can arrange **private rooms** (from 500Kč).

🏨 **Hotel Astorka,** Novobranská 3 (☎542 510 370; astorka@jamu.cz). With your back to the train station, cross the tram tracks, turn right, and make an immediate left up a set of stairs. At the top, turn right on Novobranská and cross Orli. Centrally located, brand-

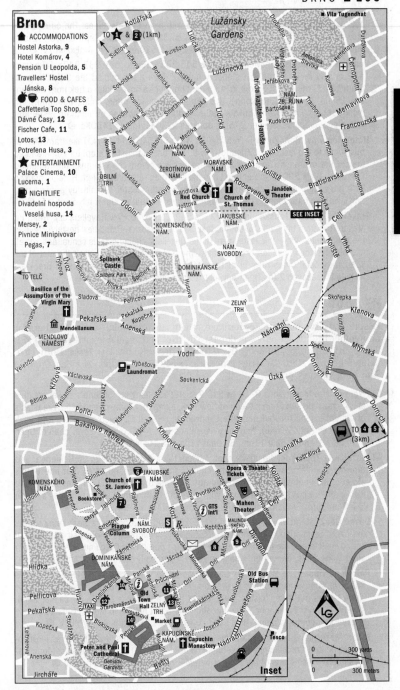

CZECH REPUBLIC

Brno

🏠 ACCOMMODATIONS
Hostel Astorka, **9**
Hotel Komárov, **4**
Pension U Leopolda, **5**
Travellers' Hostel
Jánska, **8**

🍴 FOOD & CAFES
Caffetteria Top Shop, **6**
Dávné Časy, **12**
Fischer Cafe, **11**
Lotos, **13**
Potrefena Husa, **3**

⭐ ENTERTAINMENT
Palace Cinema, **10**
Lucerna, **1**

🍺 NIGHTLIFE
Divadelní hospoda
Veselá husa, **14**
Mersey, **2**
Pivnice Minipivovar
Pegas, **7**

TO 🏠 & 🍺(1km)

Lužánsky Gardens

■ Vila Tugendhat

Kotlářská
Šušilova
Tučkova
Sokolská
Kounicova
Závodní
Pekářenská
Veveří
Arna
Nováka
Jaselská
Botanická
Cíhlářská
Bureśova
Smetanova
Antonínská
Slováková
Mášova
Meríka
Lidická
Lužanecká
Antonína
Slavíka
Kuneśova
Drobného
Vrchlického
sady
Drobného
Jeřábkova
Třída kapitána Jaroše
Traubova
Bartošova
Kudelova
NÁM.
28. ŘÍJNA
Merhavitova
Francouzska
Hellertova
Durďákova
Čornopolní
Stará
Příční
Přikop
JANÁČKOVO
NÁM.
ŽEROTÍNOVO
NÁM.
MORAVSKÉ
NÁM.
Milady Horákové
Koliště
Roosevellova
OBILNÍ
TRH
Mareśova
Brandlova
Joštova
Red Church
Church of
St. Thomas
Janáček
Theater
Bratislavská
Komenrza
Porářská
Koliště
Vlhká
Údolní
Husova
JAKUBSKÉ
NÁM.
KOMENSKÉHO
NÁM.
NÁM.
SVOBODY
SEE INSET
Cejl

TO TELČ
Úvoz
Trýbova
Pellcova
Šilingrovo
Spilberk Castle
Spilberk Park
Hlídka
Šilberk
DOMINIKÁNSKÉ
NÁM.
ZELNÝ
TRH
Skořepka
Křenova

Basilica of the
Assumption of the
Virgin Mary
Sladová
Pellcova
Pekařská
Pekařská
Kopečná
Anenská
Husova
Nádražní
Rumiśtě
MENDLOVO
NÁMĚSTÍ
Mendelianum
Pivovarská
Veletrzní
Bělidla
Křtová
Ypsilantino
Zahradnická
Václavská
Hybešova
Laundromat
Nové sady
Beznova
Vodní
Soukenická
Úzká
Trnitá
Spařená
Domych
Plotní
Domych
Poříčí
Bakalovo nábřeží
Nádvorní
Náplavka
Křidlovická
Zvonařka
Kosť'alova
Rosická
Plotní
Uhelná
TO 🏠 🏠
(3km)

Inset

KOMENSKÉHO
NÁM.
Opletalova
Solniční
Česká
JAKUBSKÉ
NÁM.
Church of
St. James
Jezuitská
Mozarlova
Rašinova
Jakubská
Opera & Theater
Tickets
Údolní
Besední
Skřita
Střední
Veselá
Panénská
Bookstore
Plague
Column
NÁM.
SVOBODY
Bárvařská
Dvořákova
Roosevellova
Sukova
GTS
Int'l
Mahen
Theater
Za Divadlem
Kozí
Postovská
Koblížná
MALINOV-
SKÉHO
NÁM.
Orlí
Divadelní
HlídKa
DOMINIKÁNSKÉ
NÁM.
Pellcova
Pekařská
Kopečná
Letherova
Anenská
Jircháře
Dominikánská
Husova
Studaná
Biskupská
Petrská
Mečová
Zámečnická
Jánská
Minoritská
Panská
Radnická
Starobrněnská
Peroutkova
Průchodní
Masařská
Orlí
Josefská
Novobranská
Benesová
TAXI
Old Town
Hall
ZELNÝ
TRH
Market
Františkánská
Old Bus
Station
KAPUCÍNSKÉ
NÁM.
Muchní
Capuchin
Monastery
Nádražní
Baśty
Peter and Paul
Cathedral
Denisovi
Gardens
Tesco

0   300 yards
0   300 meters

N

new Astorka boasts clean rooms that come with a host of amenities. The outdoor terrace and restaurant cap it all off. Reception on 3rd fl. Open July-Sept. Singles 520Kč; doubles 1040Kč; triples 1560Kč. Students 260Kč/520Kč/780Kč. AmEx/MC/V. ❶

Pension U Leopolda, Jeneweinova 49 (☎545 233 036; fax 545 233 949). Take tram #12 or bus #A12 to the last stop, "Komárov." Take a left behind the *tábak* huts on Studnicni. At the end of Studnicni, turn right on Jeneweinova. Quite a trek from the center (15min. by public transport), this suburban pension offers small, beautifully furnished rooms with TV and private baths. Ground floor houses an intimate restaurant with a cozy fireplace. Singles 775Kč; doubles 1250Kč; triples 1450Kč. ❸

Hotel Komárov, Brati Zurku 5 (☎545 233 197; fax 545 234 187). Take tram #12 or bus #A12 to the last stop, "Komárov." With your back to the bus stop, turn right and go toward the overpass. Take the 2nd-to-the-last left before the overpass on unmarked Pompova. Walk 200m, go right on Lomena, and then take the 1st left. Hotel is marked by a large sign. A high-rise dormitory well outside the center (20min. by public transport), with no-frills doubles (390Kč) with showers and baths. Open July-Sept. 15. ❷

Travellers' Hostel Jánska, Jánska 22. (☎542 213 573; www.travellers.cz). Head up Masarykova from the train station and take a right on Jánska. Brand-new hostel located in the town center. While this installment of the Travellers' chain hostel is central and social, it is also lacking in comfort or personality. The building is a school during the rest of the year. The hostel offers rows of rusty metal beds with rock-hard mattresses. Breakfast included. Reception 24hr. Open July-Aug. 15-bed dorms 290Kč. MC/V. ❶

▐ FOOD

Despite the city's marketplace heritage, street-side pizza joints and coffee bars far outnumber traditional *párek* peddlers. The fruit and vegetable **market** (open M-F 9am-6pm) still thrives on Zelný trg. (strawberries 19Kč per kg). **Tesco,** Dornych 4, behind the train station, carries groceries. (☎543 543 111. Open M-F 8am-9pm, Sa 8am-7pm, Su 9am-7pm.)

▨ **Fischer Cafe,** Masarykova 8/10 (☎542 221 880). A hangout for Brno's jet-setters, this sleek, chic cafe serves up a touch of New York, along with some phenomenal breakfasts of omelettes and toasted baguette sandwiches (53-98Kč), ingenious pasta and fresh fish entrees (113-216Kč), and massive salads (90-147Kč). 20Kč cover charge. Open M-Th 8am-10pm, F 8am-11pm, Sa 9am-11pm, Su 10am-8pm. ❸

▨ **Caffetteria Top Shop,** Jakubské nám. 4. From Nám. Svobody, head up Rašínova, and turn right on Jakubské. A refreshing change from the generic cafes that line Brno's streets, this charming cafe offers top-notch coffee drinks (27-61Kč). Revive yourself with a superb hot chocolate mixed with anything from orange syrup to Bailey's. Open M-F 9am-8pm, Sa 9am-noon. ❶

Dávné Časy, Starobrněská 20 (☎544 215 292), up Starobrněnská from Zelný trh. As the Czech inscription at the door reads, forget your problems and revisit the world of heroic knights and medieval feasts. Dig into huge portions of Czech cuisine (79-189Kč) amid stone walls, armor, and dungeon gates. Open daily 11am-11pm. AmEx/V. ❸

Potrefena Husa (The Messed-Up Goose), Moravské nám. 8 (☎452 213 177). Follow Rašinova from Nám. Svobody to the corner of Joštova. This popular Czech brewhouse chain serves pub fare, pastas, and salads (59-195Kč) in a trendy yet casual atmosphere. TVs over the monochrome bar show the latest news and sports. Outside terrace is good for people-watching. Beer 20Kč. Open daily 11am-1am. AmEx/MC/V. ❷

Lotos, Masarykova 14. Perfect for late-night hunger pangs, this tiny cafe serves inexpensive Asian and Czech-inspired vegetarian dishes (25-75Kč) and traditional fast-food staples into the wee hours of the morn. Open M-F 8am-3am, Sa-Su 9am-2am. ❶

👁 SIGHTS

Most of Brno's sights center on Nám. Svobody.

▧ PETER AND PAUL CATHEDRAL. Brno was allegedly saved from the Swedish siege of 1645 in one day. The attacking general promised to retreat if his army didn't capture the city by noon, so when the townsfolk learned of his claim, they rang the bells one hour early and the Swedes slunk away. The bells have been striking noon at 11am ever since. Although the Swedes burnt the cathedral (Biskupská katedrála sv. Petra a Pavla) as they retreated, some of it was left intact, and the remains of the earliest Romanesque church on Petrov are still visible in the current cathedral's crypt. *(On Petrov Hill. Climb Petrska from Zelný trh. Cathedral open M-Sa 8:15am-6:15. Su 7am-6pm. Chapel, tower, and crypt open M-Sa 11am-6pm. Su 1-6pm. Cathedral and chapel free. Tower 25Kč, students 20Kč. Crypt 25Kč/10Kč.)*

▧ ŠPILBERK CASTLE (HRAD ŠPILBERK). Once home to Czech kings and a mighty Hapsburg fortress, Špilberk has had an illustrious past. After a brief stint as the city's fortress against the Swedes, the castle served as a prison for convicted criminals, and for Czech, Hungarian, Italian, and Polish revolutionaries during the 18th and 19th centuries. The gruesome torture methods employed here earned the castle a reputation for being the cruelest prison in Hapsburg Europe. During WWII, the Nazis kept their political and racial prisoners here. The corridors now contain extensive **galleries** detailing the prison's history, and the art, architecture, and social history of Brno. For a taste of prison life, trek through the moat's tomb-like **encasements,** where the most dangerous criminals were imprisoned. The memorial to those who lost their lives here, in the final cell of the prison museum, is particularly moving. *(Take Zámečnická from Nám. Svobody through Dominikánské nám. and go right on Panenská. Cross Husova and follow the path uphill. ☎542 123 611; muzeum.brno@spilberk.cz. Open May-Sept. Tu-Su 9am-6pm; Apr. and Oct. Tu-Su 9am-5pm; Nov.-Mar. W-Su 9am-5pm. Call ahead to reserve an English tour. Castle 80Kč, students 40Kč; castle tower 20Kč/10Kč.)*

CAPUCHIN MONASTERY CRYPT (HROBKA KAPUCÍNSKÉHO KLÁŠTERA). If bones and bodies catch your fancy, you'll love this morbid resting place. The monks at this crypt developed an innovative burial method in which a series of air ducts allowed bodies to dry out naturally. As a result, the crypt preserved more than 100 18th-century monks and nobles. The displayed results now enlighten the living: the crypt opens with the Latin inscription, "Remember death!" and ends with the dead monks' dark reminder: "What you are, we were. What we are, you will be." *(Left of Masarykova from the train station. ☎542 221 207. Open May-Sept. M-Sa 9am-noon and 2-4:30pm, Su 11-11:45am and 2-4:30pm. English brochures 40Kč, students 20Kč.)*

AROUND MENDEL SQUARE (MENDLOVO NÁMĚSTÍ). In the heart of Old Brno sits the beautiful Gothic **Basilica of the Assumption of the Virgin Mary** (Bazilika Nanebevzetí Panny Marie). Its intricate golden altar displays the 13th-century **Black Madonna,** the country's oldest wooden icon, which purportedly held off the Swedes in 1645. *(From Špilberk, walk downhill on Pelicova and take the stairs to Sladová. Go left on Úvoz to Mendlovo nám. Open Su, Tu, Th-F 5:45-7:15pm.)* The Augustinian monastery next door was home to **Johann Gregor Mendel,** father of modern genetics. The newly renovated and expanded **Mendelianum,** Mendlovo nám. 1a, features slide shows, audio presentations, and exhibits documenting the his life and experiments. After watching the interactive **video** on how Mendel's pea plants led him to the theory of inherited genotypes, you can explore the garden that houses the foundation of his greenhouse and a recreated version of his pea garden. The barley grown is used by the brewery next door where, by tasting the beer, you fully appreciate Mendel's work. (☎543 424 043. Open May-Oct. Tu-Su 10am-6pm; Nov.-Apr. W-Su 10am-6pm. English info book 200Kč. Monastery 80Kč, students 40Kč.)

OLD TOWN HALL (STARÁ RADNICE). Brno's Old Town Hall facade is the subject of a range of legends. Its crooked Gothic portal supposedly took on its shape after the carver blew his commission on too much Moravian wine. As for the dismayed stone face looking out on Mecova from the back of the hall, rumor has it that it's the petrified head of a burgher, who met his doom there after siding with the Hussites in 1424. The most famous tale involves the stuffed "dragon" hanging from the ceiling in the passageway. Legend claims that the dragon perished after devouring an ox carcass that had been stuffed with quicklime. As thirst began to overwhelm him, he downed a whole river and his belly burst. Actually, the dragon is an Amazonian crocodile Archduke Matyáš gave Brno to garner favor among the burghers. (Radnická 8, just off Zelný trh. Open daily Apr.-Oct. 9am-5pm. Last entrance 4:30pm. 20Kč, students 10Kč.)

AROUND NÁMĚSTÍ SVOBODY. The partially gold **Plague Column** (Morový sloup) in the square has successfully warded off infections for the last 300 years. North of Nám. Svobody, along Rašínova, the **Church of St. James** (Kostel sv. Jakuba) was built for Brno's medieval Flemish and German communities. On the way back to the square, walk left along Koblížná and turn left on Rooseveltova for a game of comparative architecture. On the right is the grand **Mahen Theater** (Mahenovo divadlo), built by the Viennese duo Helmer and Fellner in the 19th century. Two blocks down, the 1960s **Janáček Theater** (Janáčkovo divadlo) is Brno's **opera house.**

🎭 🎟 ENTERTAINMENT AND NIGHTLIFE

The Old Town Hall hosts frequent summer **concerts;** buy tickets (100-600Kč) at the tourist office (see **Orientation and Practical Information,** p. 292). **Theater** and **opera** tickets available at Dvořákova 11. (☎542 321 285. Open July-Aug. M-F 8am-noon and 12:45-3pm; Sept.-June M-F 8am-noon and 1-4:30pm.) **Cinemas** playing western and Czech flicks abound (80-140Kč). **Palace,** Mecova 2 (☎543 560 111; www.palacecinemas.cz) features American blockbusters and mainstream Czech films. **Lucerna,** Minská 19 (☎542 747 070), shows British and American independent films. Look for posters advertising **techno raves,** Brno's hottest summer entertainment. While it's surprisingly easier to find a beer hall than a wine cellar in the heart of wine-producing Moravia, there is an occasional *vinárna* (bottles 80-150Kč).

Divadelní hospoda Veselá husa (Merry Goose Theatrical Pub), Zelný trh 9 (☎542 211 630), just behind the theater. This pub's artsy crowd gathers after experimental performances in the attached Merry Goose Theater. Performances start between 7:30 and 8pm and last 1-3hr. *Pilsner* 23Kč. Open M-F 11am-1am, Sa-Su 3pm-1am.

Pivnice Minipivovar Pegas, Jakubská 4 (☎542 210 104). This modern microbrewery on the 1st fl. of Hotel Pegas has a young, loyal following that tosses back homemade brews. Pints 16Kč. Open M-Sa 9am-midnight, Su 10am-10pm. MC/V.

Mersey, Minská 15 (☎541 240 623; www.mersey.cz). Take tram #3 or 11 from Česká to Tábor and continue down Minská. This rock club-disco-pub hosts live bands and DJs playing funk, disco, and rock depending on the night. Easygoing atmosphere. Large crowds gather for theme events, like U2 and James Bond nights. Beer 25Kč. Internet access 30Kč per hr. Occasional cover. F-Sa 30Kč. Open M-Sa 8pm-late.

KROMĚŘÍŽ   ☎(0)634

The small town of Kroměříž (KROHM-yer-sheesh) is a pleasant Czech village, but the only thing that makes it worth visiting is its commanding UNESCO-protected chateau. Midway between Olomouc and Brno, Kroměříž is a good candidate for a daytrip, though it is also easy, if not cheap, to spend the night. Founded in 1260 by Bishop Bruno of Schaumburk, the countryside castle, set in the heart of Moravia, was completely lost to Swedish arson during the Thirty Years' War. To replace what was lost, Bishop Karel II of Lichtenstein-Kastelkorn reconstructed the castle in Baroque style in the second half of the 17th century. Designed by Filiberto Lucchese, the stunning **Archbishop's Chateau** (Arcibiskupský zámek), just off the main square, is the town's major attraction. (☎573 502 011; www.azz.cz. Open July-Aug. Tu-Su 9am-6pm; May-June and Sept. Tu-Su 9am-5pm; Apr. and Oct. Sa-Su 9am-5pm. 80Kč, students 50Kč. 90min. English tours 80Kč/50Kč. Free English info with Czech tours.) The chateau complex includes a **tower,** the only remaining relic of the original castle (40Kč, students 20Kč), and a **painting gallery** (30Kč, students 15Kč), which highlights a number of Van Dycks and a magnificent Titian. Just outside the castle walls, the **Chateau Garden** (Podzámecká Zahrada), provides relaxing walks on gravel paths, which wind past a small pond and afford great views of the massive building from the rear. (Open daily 6:30am-8pm. Free.)

The **bus** and **train stations** are next door to each other on Nádražni, a short walk from the center. Trains are infrequent and inconvenient, usually requiring multiple changes. Buses (☎573 331 257), which also often require changes, run to **Brno** (2hr., 9 per day, 70Kč) and **Olomouc** (1¼hr., 12 per day, 37Kč). **Taxis** (☎573 334 430) line up outside the stations. The center of town is very compact and spirals outward from **Velké nám.,** the main square. From the stations, go left on Nádražni; left on Holínská, which leads over the river; right on Komenského nám.; and then left on Vodní, which leads to Velké nám. The **tourist office,** Velké nám. 50, has **free maps** of the center and arranges accommodations. (☎573 331 473; www.mesto-kromeriz.cz. Open M-F 8:30am-5pm, Sa-Su 9am-1pm.) Just down the block, **Česká Spořitelna,** Velké nám. 43, exchanges **traveler's checks** for a 2% commission and has an **ATM.** (☎573 319 111. Open M and W 9am-12:30pm and 1:30-5pm, Tu and Th-F 9am-12:30pm and 1:30-4pm.) The central **pharmacy** is **U Zlatého Lva,** Velké nám. 49. (☎063 425 579. Open M and W-Th 7:30am-12:30pm and 1:30-3pm, Tu 7:30am-12:30pm and 2-5pm, F 7:30am-12:30pm and 1:30-2:30pm.) The town's **Internet access** is limited, but you can get decent connections at **UM@xe,** Velké nám. 39, for 1Kč per min. (☎573 331 532. Open M-F 10am-10pm, Sa 1-10pm, Su 1-9pm.) The **post office** is at Velké nám. 11. (Open M-F 8am-noon and 1-5pm.) **Postal Code:** 767 01.

Pensions and hotels are plentiful, though most come at a hefty price. **Penzion Mensik ❸,** Velké nám. 107, is a good central option, with bright, simple rooms overlooking the main square. (☎602 569 863. Singles 650Kč; doubles 1300Kč.) A few doors down, **Pizzeria Bohemia ❶,** Velké nám. 113, serves up a large selection of fresh pizzas (50-110Kč) on its terrace. (☎606 319 173. Open daily 11am-9pm.) Find **groceries** at **Potraviny Ambrož,** Vodní 27. (☎573 337 646. Open M-F 6am-6pm, Sa 7am-noon.)

OLOMOUC

Today, Olomouc (OH-lo-mohts; pop. 103,372) is the echo of Prague before it was engulfed by hordes of tourists. The historic capital of Northern Moravia, Olomouc embodies the best aspects of the Czech Republic. By day, locals enjoy the Baroque architecture and cobblestone paths of the rebuilt town center. By night, students from the local university keep the clubs thumping until dawn.

⌐ TRANSPORTATION

Trains: Jeremenkova 23 (☎585 785 490). To: **Brno** (1½hr., 7-8 per day, 120Kč) and **Prague** (3½hr., 19 per day, 294Kč).

Buses: Rolsberská 66 (☎585 313 848). To: **Brno** (1½hr., 10 per day, 75-85Kč) and **Prague** (4½hr., 3 per day, 310Kč). Info office open M-F 6am-6pm, Sa-Su 6am-2pm.

CZECH REPUBLIC

Public Transportation: Buy tickets (6Kč) for the **trams** and **buses** at kiosks by the station and machines at each stop.

Taxis: Eurotaxi (☎ 603 449 541). Taxis congregate in front of the train station and at the intersection of Riegrova and Národních hridinů.

ORIENTATION

Olomouc's Staré Město (Old Town) forms a triangle, in the center of which is the enormous **Horní náměstí** (Upper Square). Behind the *radnice* (town hall), **Dolní nám.** (Lower Square) connects with Horní nám. **Masarykova třída** leads west from the train and bus stations to the town center, though not before changing its name to **1. máje** and then **Denišova**. Trams or buses marked "X" shuttle between the **train station** and the center (5 stops, 6Kč per ticket). Get off at Koruna, in front of the gigantic **Prior** department store, then follow **28. října** to Horní nám. Alternatively, trams #1-6 stop just outside the center. Get off at **Nám. Hridinů** and follow **Riegrova** to the center. From the **bus station**, just beyond the train station, take the pedestrian passageway beneath Jeremenkova to reach trams #4 and 5, which run to the center.

PRACTICAL INFORMATION

Tourist Office: Horní nám. (☎ 685 513 385; www.olomoucko.cz), in town hall. Free **maps** of the town center. Detailed city maps (49-59Kč). Books hotels, hostels, and private rooms. English spoken. Open daily Mar.-Nov. 9am-7pm; Dec.-Feb. 9am-5pm.

Budget Travel: CKM, Denišova 4 (☎ 585 222 148; zajezdy@ckmolomouc.cz). Sells ISICs (250Kč) and train tickets. Open M-F 9am-5:30pm, Sa 9am-noon.

Currency Exchange: Komerční banka, Svobody 14 (☎ 585 509 111) and Denišova 47 (☎ 585 509 169), cashes most **traveler's checks** for 1% commission and gives MC **cash advances** for 2% commission; Denišova gives AmEx/MC cash advances for 2% commission. Svobody branch open M-F 8am-7pm. Denišova branch open M and W-Th 8:30am-12:30pm and 1:30-5pm, Tu and F 8:30am-12:30pm and 1:30-4pm.

Luggage Storage: At the train station. 10Kč per day per piece under 15kg, 20Kč per piece over 15kg. 24hr. lockers 5Kč. Bus station lockers 5Kč.

English Bookstore: Votobia, Riegrova 33 (☎ 685 223 99). A few shelves of English titles in the back of the store. Open M-F 8:30am-6pm, Sa 9am-noon.

Pharmacy: Lekarná, on the corner of Ostružnická and Horní nám., behind the town hall. Open M-F 7:30am-6pm, Sa 8am-noon.

Hospital: Fakultni Nemocnice, IP Pavlova 6 (☎ 585 851 111; fax 585 413 841), southwest of the center off Albertova.

Internet Access: Internet u Dominika, Slovenská 12 (☎ 777 181 857), has great connections and the most terminals. 1Kč per min. Open M-F 9am-9pm, Sa-Su 10am-9pm.

Post Office: Horní nám. 27. Open M-F 7:30am-7pm, Sa-Su 8am-noon. **Postal Code:** 771 27.

ACCOMMODATIONS

The cheapest beds (from 230Kč) pop up in summer when **Palacký University dorms ❶** open to tourists; most are opposite the Botanical Gardens, on the other side of 17. Listopadu, a 15min. walk from the center. The tourist office has info on arranging these accommodations and private rooms (from 360Kč).

Poet's Corner Hostel, Sokolská 1 (☎ 777 570 730; www.hostelolomouc.com), steps from the center. From the train or bus station, take trams #4-7 to Nám. Hridinů and walk 2 blocks continuing in the same direction to Sokolská. Or, from Horní nám., walk down 28. října 2 blocks; go left on Sokolska. Run by 2 charming Australians, this apartment feels more like a home than a hostel. Rooms are spacious, brightly decorated, and clean. Kitchen, laundry (100Kč), and bike rental (100Kč per day) available. 7-person dorm Sept.-June 250Kč, July-Aug. 300Kč; doubles 800Kč; triples 1000Kč. ❶

Pension na Hradbách, Hrnčířská 3 (☎585 233 243; nahradback@quick.cz). From Horní nám., head down Školní, go straight along Purkrabská, and turn right on Hrnčířská. A small, homey pension on one of the quietest streets of the town center. Call ahead. Singles with private bath and TV 600Kč; doubles 800Kč; triples 900Kč. ❸

Penzion Best, Na Strelnici 48 (☎/fax 585 231 450). Take tram #1 or 4-7 to Nám. Hridinů, then hop on bus #17, 18, or 22 to Na Strelnici. Continue in the same direction until the hotel appears on your right (5min.). Although a bit out of the way, Best is an excellent deal (as its name implies), as all rooms have bathrooms and TVs. Breakfast 40Kč. Singles 500Kč; doubles 750Kč. AmEx/MC/V. ❷

FOOD

With cuisine from Czech to Chinese, Olomouc makes food easy to find. Numerous restaurants line both Horní nám. and Dolní nám, serving various types of fare for 50-150Kč. You can grab groceries at **Supermarket Delvita,** 8. května 24, in the basement of Prior department store, at the corner of 28. října. (☎685 535 135. Open M-F 7am-8pm, Sa 7am-2pm.)

▓ **Čajovna Dřevená Panenka** (Wooden Doll Teahouse), Hrnčířská 12. (☎585 233 858), across the street from Pension na Hradbách (see above). This labyrinthine, multi-story teahouse is a mecca for relaxation. Smoke a water pipe in a secluded enclave (75Kč), sip one of over 70 varieties of tea (35-65Kč), or enjoy freshly made couscous (45Kč), all in a peaceful, incense-filled atmosphere. "Secret" tea blend Yogi Yogi will open up new worlds for spiced chai lovers. Open M-F 11am-11pm, Sa-Su 3-11pm. ❶

▓ **Hanácká Hospoda,** Dolní nám. 38 (☎777 721 171). This large restaurant is always packed with locals, and it's easy to see why. Serves up the very best of Czech food, like beer-braised duck with cabbage and dumplings (169Kč), in an atmosphere that exudes Moravian countryside comfort. Open daily 10am-midnight. AmEx/MC/V. ❷

Café 87, Denisova 47 (☎724 210 159). Owner Vera runs a remarkable cafe, with welcoming, English-speaking waitstaff, info about events around town, and Internet access in back (1Kč per min.). Relax with a cup of java (20Kč) and a slice of decadent chocolate pie (25Kč) on a comfortable sofas. Quiches and sandwiches (25-40Kč) satisfy mid-afternoon hunger pangs. Open M-F 6:30am-10pm, Sa-Su 8am-10pm. ❶

Cafe Caesar, Horní nám. (☎685 229 287), in the town hall. Named after Caesar, the supposed founder of Olomouc, this Italian restaurant serves up dishes that could have fed (and protected) his armies. Tourists and locals enjoy the garlicky pizzas (30 varieties; 25-110Kč) and plates of pasta (47-113Kč). Huge outdoor terrace good for people-watching. Open M-Sa 9am-1am, Su 9am-midnight. AmEx/MC/V. ❷

U Kejklire (The Juggler), Michalská 2 (☎543 590 799), behind the town hall. Elegant restaurant that serves hefty portions of meats, steak (100-138Kč) and vegetables (26-49Kč). Open M-Sa 9am-11pm, Su 10am-10pm. MC/V. ❸

SIGHTS

The massive 1378 **town hall** (radnice) and its spired clock tower dominate the town center; the tourist office arranges trips to the top. (Daily at 11am and 3pm. 15Kč.) An amusing **astronomical clock** is set in the town hall's north side. In 1955, communist clockmakers replaced the mechanical saints with archetypes of "the people."

Since then, the masses strike the hour with their hammers and sickles in show of socialist spirit. (Chimes daily at noon.) The 35m black and gold **Trinity Column** (Sloup Nejsvětější Trojice) soars higher than any other Baroque sculpture in the country. One of Europe's largest Baroque organs bellows each Sunday in the **Church of St. Maurice** (Chram sv. Mořice), 28. října. It also stars in Olomouc's **International Organ Festival** each September.

Returning to Horní nám., take Mahlerova to the intimate **Jan Sarkander Chapel** (Kaple sv. Jana Sarkandra), which, with its awesome frescoes, honors a Catholic priest tortured to death by Protestants in 1620 after he refused to divulge a confessor's secret. (Open daily 10am-noon and 1-5pm. Free.) On Mahlerova, turn left on Univerzitní, and then right on Denišova. The **Museum of National History and Arts** (Vlastivědné Muzeum), Nám. Republiky 5, tells the history of the astrological clock and displays 16th- to 19th-century time pieces. There is a zoological exhibit on the first floor. (☎685 515 111; www.vmo.cz. Open Apr.-Sept. Su-Tu 9am-6pm; Oct.-Mar. Su-W 10am-5pm. 40Kč, students 20Kč.)

From Nám. Republiky, continue away from the center on 1. máje and then climb Dómská, on the left, to reach Václavské nám. Let the spires of **St. Wenceslas Cathedral** (Metropolitní Kostel sv. Václava), reminiscent of Paris's Notre Dame, lead the way. The church interior is in excellent condition, having been reworked virtually every century since it was damaged by fire in 1265. Its delicate wall designs will impress even the most jaded travelers. The crypt exhibits the gold-encased skull of St. Pauline (Sv. Pavlína), Olomouc's protectress. (Open Su 11am-5pm, W 9am-4pm, Tu and Th-Sa 9am-5pm. Free. Donation requested.) Next door to the cathedral, the walls of the wondrous **Přemysl Palace** (Přemyslovský palác) are covered in 15th- and 16th- century frescoes. (☎685 230 915. Open Apr.-Sept. Tu-Su 10am-6pm. 15Kč, students 5Kč. W free.) Across the square sits the former **Capitular Deaconry** (bývalé Kapitulní děkanství), where an 11-year-old Mozart composed his *Symphony in F Major*. Continue away from the center on 1. máje and go right on Kosinova to reach the path that runs through **Bezrucovy sady**, the city park. Stroll through the forested paths and take a left past the statues. Go over the footbridge and along the tennis courts to reach the **Botanical Garden** across the stream. The highlight of the manicured grounds is the rosarium, which fills with blossoms in summer. (Bezrucovy sady open dawn to dusk. Free. Botanical gardens open Apr. Tu-Su 9:30am-4pm; May-Sept. 9:30am-6pm. 20Kč, students 15Kč.)

■ NIGHTLIFE

Exit Discoteque, Holická 8, is the Czech Republic's largest outdoor club and Olomouc's wildest. From Horní nám., walk to Dolní nám., then follow Kateřinská 400m to 17 Listopadu. Turn left, then take a right on Wittgensteinova; follow it across the bridge (200m). The club is on the right. The loud techno and spotlights emanating from the building draw clubbers like moths to a flame. Eight bars ensure that you'll never wait for a drink. The terraces are perfect for sipping a cocktail while watching youthful clubbers on the dance floor below. (☎585 230 573. Cover 50-60Kč. Open June-Sept. F-Sa 9pm-5am.) The popular **Depo No. 9,** Nám. Republiky 1, pours *Staropramen* (20Kč) in three underground rooms with metallic decor and comfy seats. In the wee hours, the basement becomes Olomouc's most happening student dance club, with frequent live rock performances. (☎585 221 273; www.depo9.cz. Occasional cover 50-100Kč. Open M-Th 10am-2am, F 10am-6am, Sa 7pm-6am, Su 7pm-midnight.) Closer to town is **Barumba,** Mlýnská 4, which churns out techno and beer. Follow Pavelčákova out of Horní nám.; go left on Mlýnská. (☎585 208 425; www.barumba.cz. Beer 14Kč. Cover men 30-60Kč, women free. Open M-Th 7pm-3am, F-Sa 9pm-6am.) If you're looking for a more low-key spot to have a drink or two, head next door to **The Crack,** an upscale Irish pub set in the renovated cellar of the old town brewery. (☎520 842 829. Open M-Th 11am-midnight, F 11am-2am, Sa 4pm-2am, Su 4pm-1am.) For a unique experience, **Vinárna Letka,** Legionářská 6, an old Soviet airplane converted into a bar, is just the thing. The decor is tacky and the crowd touristy, but the opportunity to pretend the Cold War never ended is not to be missed. (Open M-Th 9pm-6am, F-Sa 9pm-7am.)

TELČ ☎(0)66

The tiny town of Telč (TELCH; pop. 6000) has an Italian aura that stems from a trip **Zachariáš of Hradec,** the town's ruler, made to Genoa, Italy, in 1546. He was so enamored with the new Renaissance style that he brought back a battalion of Italian artists and craftsmen to spruce up his humble Moravian castle and town. With a cobblestone footbridge and a square flanked by arcades of peach-painted gables, it is easy to see why UNESCO named the gingerbread town of Telč a World Heritage Monument.

The highlight of Telč's many attractions is its breathtaking **castle,** a monument from the town's glory days as a water fortress. Arguably the most magnificent castle in the country, both inside and out, the overwhelming stone building, complete with courtyard garden and lily pond, houses an amazingly well-kept interior. There are two options for viewing the castle—tour A and tour B, both 45min. Tour A goes through the Renaissance hallways, past tapestries and exotic hunting trophies, through the old chapel, and beneath extravagant ceilings. Tour B leads through the rooms decorated in the 18th and 19th centuries, untouched since the Czech state seized control of the castle in 1945. The free English information sheets are extremely helpful. (☎567 243 821; www.zamek-telc.cz. Open May-Aug. Tu-Su 9am-noon and 1-5pm; Apr. and Sept.-Oct. Tu-Su 9am-noon and 1-4pm. 70Kč, students 35Kč. English tours 140Kč.) In the courtyard, a **museum** displays examples of Telč's folklore. (Same hours as castle. 20Kč, students 10Kč.) The **gallery** is a memorial to artist **Jan Zrzavý** (1890-1977), who trained as a neo-Impressionist, dabbled in Cubism, and produced religious paintings. (Open Su and Tu-F 9am-noon and 1-4pm, Sa 9am-1pm. 30Kč, students 15Kč.) Beside the castle grounds stands the town's 13th-century **tower.** If you can bear the winding stairs and unstable ledges, the climb to the top offers a stunning view of Telč. (☎604 985 3398. Open June-Aug. Tu-Sa 10-11:30am and 12:30-6pm, Su 1-6pm; May and Sept. Sa-Su 1-5pm. 15Kč, students 10Kč.) Those not fond of heights can stroll through the quiet **park** at the castle's edge, where the stone walls meet the river. (Open daily dawn-dusk. Free.)

The **bus station** (☎567 302 477), which provides the only viable means of intercity transport, is on Slavíčkova, a 5min. walk from the main square. Buses run to **Prague** (3hr., 7 per day, 100Kč) and **Brno** (2hr., 8 per day, 88Kč). **Taxis** line the main square (☎602 517 775). The town center forms a peninsula jutting into two conjoining rivers, with **Nám. Zachariáše Hradce,** the oblong main square, in the middle. To reach it from the bus station, follow the walkway and turn right on Tyršova, then left on Masarykovo. Enter the square through the archway on the right. The **tourist office** Nám. Zachariáše Hradce 10, in the town hall, sells **maps** (30-79Kč) and has **Internet access** (1Kč per min.) and accommodations listings. (☎567 112 407; www.telc-etc.cz. Open M-F 8am-6pm, Sa-Su 10am-6pm.) Across the street, **Česká Spořitelna,** Nám. Zachariáše Hradce 62, exchanges **traveler's checks** and has an **ATM.** (Open M and W-Th 9am-12:30pm and 1:30-5pm, Tu and F 9am-12:30pm.) The **pharmacy** is on Masarykovo, just before the intersection with Tyršova. (☎567 213 579. Open M-F 7:30am-5pm, Sa 8-11am. MC/V.) The **post office** is around the corner on Tyršova. (☎567 243 212. Open M-F 8-11am and 1-6pm, Sa 8-10am.) **Postal Code:** 588 56.

While Telč has a curiously large amount of hostels and pensions, the central ones tend fill quickly in July and August. The only truly budget digs are **campgrounds** ❶ outside of town, available through the tourist office (see above; 80-100Kč), but the town's diminutive size means that you can get a private room with bath for 350Kč. The best deal is **Privát U Šeniglů** ❹, Nám. Zachariáše Hradce 11, which offers clean, well-kept doubles with private baths, skylights, and kitschy decor for a decent price. (☎ 567 243 406. 300Kč per person.) Unfortunately, Telč's restaurant selection is smaller. The main square has a few touristy **pizza parlors and cafes** where you can get a decent meal for 100Kč, but the only other food you'll find is in the **grocery store, Horacké Potraviny,** Nám. Zachariáše Hradce 65. (Open M-F 7am-6pm, Sa 7am-noon.)

ESTONIA (EESTI)

KROONIS		
AUS$1 = 9.11EEK	1EEK = AUS$0.11
CDN$1 = 9.68EEK	1EEK = CDN$0.10
EUR€1 = 15.65EEK	1EEK = EUR€0.06
NZ$1 = 8.33EEK	1EEK = NZ$0.12
UK£1 = 23.39EEK	1EEK = UK£0.04
US$1 = 12.78EEK	1EEK = US$0.08

Happy to sever its Soviet bonds, Estonia has been quick to revive its historical and cultural ties to its Nordic neighbors, and Finnish tourism and investment are revitalizing the nation. The wealth that has accumulated in Tallinn, however, belies the poverty that still lurks outside of big cities, as well as the chagrin of the ethnically Russian minority over Estonia's European leanings. Still, having overcome successive centuries of domination by the Danes, Swedes, and Russians, Estonians are now proud to take their place as members of modern Europe.

HISTORY

THOR, BJÖRN, ETC. Ninth-century **Vikings** were the first to impose themselves on the Finno-Ugric people who had settled the area before. In 1219, King Valdemar II of **Denmark** conquered northern Estonia. Shortly thereafter, Livonia, now southern Estonia and northern Latvia, fell to German knights of the **Teutonic Order,** who purchased the rest of Estonia in 1346.

TERRIBLE IVAN AND SWEDISH KINGS. German domination continued until the emergence of Russian Tsar Ivan IV (the Terrible), who, in the **Livonian War** of 1558, crushed many of the tiny feudal states that had developed in the region. In an attempt to oust Ivan, the defeated states searched for foreign assistance: northern Estonia capitulated to Sweden in 1629, while Livonia joined the Polish-Lithuanian Commonwealth. During the **Swedish Interlude** (1629-1710), **Tartu University** (p. 332) and a number of Estonian-language schools were established.

FACTS AND FIGURES

OFFICIAL NAME: Republic of Estonia

CAPITAL: Tallinn (pop. 409,516)

POPULATION: 1.4 million (65% Estonian, 28% Russian, 3% Belarusian, 4% other)

LANGUAGES: Estonian (official), Russian

CURRENCY: 1 Estonian kroon (EEK) = 100 senti

RELIGION: 65% Evangelical Lutheran, 19% Russian and Estonian Orthodox Christian, 15% Baptist

LAND AREA: 45,226km^2

CLIMATE: Maritime

GEOGRAPHY: Lowlands; 1520 islands

BORDERS: Latvia, Russia

ECONOMY: 66% Services, 29% Industry, 5% Agriculture

GDP: US$10,900 per capita

COUNTRY CODE: 372

INTERNATIONAL DIALING PREFIX: 00

THE RUSSIANS INVADE. The Russians invaded once more and the 1721 **Peace of Nystad** concluded the Great Northern War, handing the Baltics to Peter the Great. Russian rule reinforced the power of the nobility and serfs lost all rights until Estonian serfdom was finally abolished by **Tsar Alexander I** in 1819, 45 years earlier than in Mother Russia herself. In 1881, reactionary **Tsar Alexander III** attempted to Russify Estonia, prompting a nationalistic backlash, led by **Konstantin Päts.** The backlash peaked in a bid for independence during the Russian Revolution of 1905.

WAR. At the outbreak of **WWI**, Estonians were caught in a tough spot. Most of the Estonian-German population sympathized with Prussia, but had to fight in the Russian army. The **1917 Russian Revolution** spurred Estonian nationalism, but by the time the state declared **independence** in 1918 it was already under German occupation. After WWI, the country prospered until the **Depression** of the 1930s, which allowed extreme right-wing parties, led by veterans from the war for liberation, to gain public support. The circumstances drove President **Konstantin Päts** to proclaim a state of emergency in 1934. Päts's tenure was cut short by the Soviets, who occupied Estonia in 1940 under the **Nazi-Soviet Non-Aggression Pact.** Päts and other Estonian leaders, as well as a significant portion of the Estonian population, were arrested, deported, or killed. When **Hitler** reneged on the pact, he annexed Estonia, stationing German troops there from 1941 to 1944. When the Red Army returned, thousands of Estonians fled and thousands more died trying to escape as Estonia became part of the **USSR.**

SOVIET ESTONIA AND ITS FALL. The 1950s saw extreme repression and Russification under **Soviet rule,** when internal purges removed the few native Estonians left in the ruling elite. It was not until *glasnost* and *perestroika* in the 1980s (see **Russia: History,** p. 652) that Estonians won enough freedom to establish a political renaissance. In 1988, the **Popular Front** emerged in opposition to the communist government, pushing a resolution on independence through the Estonian legislature. Nationalists won a legislative majority in the 1990 elections and successfully declared independence after the failed 1991 coup in the Soviet Union.

ESTONIA'S RISING STAR. The 1992 general election, Estonia's first after declaring independence, saw the rejection of the government of **Edgar Savisaar,** who had founded the Popular Front in the twilight of Soviet rule. Savisaar's regime was replaced by a coalition of parties committed to radical economic reform, a trend which has continued to the present day under **Lennart Meri.** The government has managed to privatize most industries, lower trade barriers, and add a balanced budget amendment to its constitution. Its success in eliminating the old planned economy made the country the darling of Western investors.

TODAY. Estonia is a **parliamentary democracy,** with a much weaker presidency than most other post-Soviet states. **Prime Minister, Juham Parts,** who was elected in March 2003, currently presides over the **Riigikogu** (Parliament). The ruling coalition consists of pro-business **Res Publica,** center-left **People's Union,** and center-right **Reform Party.** Under the second Estonian **President Arnold Rüütel,** elected in September 2001, the state made **NATO** and **EU** ascension its top priorities. Estonia joined both organizations in spring 2004. After independence, relations with **Russia** grew troubled, when the Estonian government tried to deny citizenship to those unable to speak Estonian. However, in 1998, citizenship was automatically extended to the children of Russian speakers born in Estonia.

PEOPLE AND CULTURE

LANGUAGE

Estonian is a **Finno-Ugric** language, closely related to **Finnish.** Estonians speak the best **English** in the Baltic states; most young people know at least a few phrases. Many also know **Finnish** or **Swedish,** but **German** is more common among the older set and in the resort towns. **Russian** used to be mandatory, but Estonians in secluded areas are likely to have forgotten much of it since few Russians live there. For a phrasebook and glossary, see **Glossary: Estonian, p. 951.**

FOOD AND DRINK

ESTONIA	❶	❷	❸	❹	❺
FOOD	under 50EEK	51-80EEK	81-100EEK	101-140EEK	over 140EEK

Most inexpensive Estonian cuisine is fried and doused with **sour cream.** Estonian specialties include *schnitzel* (a breaded and fried pork fillet), *seljanka* meat stew, and *pelmenid* dumplings, as well as smoked fish. Bread is usually dark and dense. If you visit the islands, try picking up some *Hiiumaa leib.* A loaf of this **black bread** easily weighs a kilo. **Pancakes** with cheese curd and berries are a delicious and common dessert. The national brew *Saku* is excellent, as is the darker *Saku Tume.* Local beers, like *Saaremaa* in Kuressaare, are less consistent. The Estonian brand of carbonated **mineral water,** *Värska*, is particularly salty.

CUSTOMS AND ETIQUETTE

Tipping is becoming increasingly common; foreigners are expected to tip 5-10% in restaurants. Expect to be bought a drink if you talk with someone awhile; repay the favor in kind. If you're invited to a meal in someone's home, bring a **gift** for the hostess (an odd number of flowers is customary). **Handshaking** is a form of greeting. **Shops** sometimes close for a break between noon and 3pm.

THE ARTS

LITERATURE. The oldest book in Estonian is the **Wanradt-Koell Lutheran Catechism** (1535), but true literature didn't appear until the Estophile period (1750-1840) centuries later. The most notable publication of this period was **Anton Thor Helle's** 1739 translation of the Bible. Folklore provided the basis for **Friedrich Reinhold Kreutzwald's** *Kalevipoeg* (1857-61), an epic that became the rallying point of Estonian national rebirth in the Romantic period. Toward the end of the century, the Neo-Romantic nationalist **Noor-Eesti** (Young Estonia) movement appeared, led by the poet **Gustav Suits** and the writer **Friedebert Tuglas. Anton Tammsaare's** prose evolved from the Noor-Eesti approach toward Realism. His *Truth and Justice* (*Tõde ja õigus;* 1926-33), is essential to the Estonian canon, and Tammsaare has been praised as Estonia's foremost writer. The strictures of the official Soviet style of **Socialist Realism** sent many authors abroad or into temporary exile in Siberia, but under Khrushchev's thaw in the early 1960s, Modernism arose via the work of **Artur Alliksaar, Lydia Koidula,** and **Juhan Viidng.** Frequent Nobel nominee **Jaan Kross** managed to criticize the realities of Soviet life despite USSR censors in *The Tsar's Madman* (1978). In the same year, **Aimée Beekman** addressed plight of women in *The Possibility of Choice.*

FINE ARTS. The first Estonian art school was founded at **Tartu University** (p. 332) in 1803. The first nationally conscious Estonian art emerged at the close of the 19th century with painters **Johann Köler** and **Amandus Adamson** and sculptor **August Weizenberg.** The Neo-Impressionist paintings of **Konrad Mägi** and the landscapes of **Nikolai Triik** moved increasingly toward abstraction at the end of the 19th century, while the later painting of the 1920s and 1930s was heavily influenced by European trends, including Cubism and the principles of the German *Bauhaus.*

CURRENT SCENE. In the last decade, several Estonian writers have been nominated for the Nobel Prize. Among them are poet and essayist **Jaan Kapinski** and novelist **Emil Tode,** whose 1993 *Border State (Piiririik)* was internationally acclaimed as a great postmodern text. **Aarne Ruben** has attracted the public's attention with *The Volta Works Whistles Mournfully (Volta annab Kaeblikku vilet;* 2001). The most Estonian popular writer today is **Andrus Kivirähk,** best known for his humorous *Memoirs of Ivan Orav (Ivan Orava mälestused).* Popular contemporary Estonian **composers** include **Arvo Pärt,** known for *Tabula rasa* (1977) and *St. James's Passion* (1992), pieces reminiscent of medieval compositions; **Veljo Tormis,** who revived the **runic,** an ancient chanting-style of choral singing; and **Alo Mattisen,** whose pop-rock songs became pro-independence anthems. Conductors and musical groups from around the world are drawn to Pärnu, the so-called "summer capital" of Estonia. An updated list of Estonia's cultural events is on www.kultuuriinfo.ee.

HOLIDAYS AND FESTIVALS

NATIONAL HOLIDAYS IN 2005	
January 1 New Year's Day	**June 23** Victory Day
February 24 Independence Day	**June 24** Jaanipäev (St. John's Day, Mid-
March 25 Good Friday	summer)
March 27-28 Easter Holiday	**August 20** Restoration of Independence
May 1 Labor Day	**December 25** Christmas
May 30 Pentecost	**December 26** Boxing Day

ESTONIA

ADDITIONAL RESOURCES

Baltic Revolution: Estonia, Latvia, Lithuania and the Path to Independence, by Anatol Lieven (1994). Provides a solid background in Baltic history.

Estonia: Independence and European Integration, by David Smith (2001). Examines Estonia's recent past and EU prospects.

Border State, by Emil Tode (1993). A look at tensions between East and West as played out in post-communist Estonia.

The Tsar's Madman, by Jaan Kross (1978). A historical novel about a 19th-century Baltic nobleman. Arguably the best Estonian fiction available.

ESTONIA ESSENTIALS

ENTRANCE REQUIREMENTS
Passport: Required of all travelers.
Visa: Not required for citizens of Australia, Canada, Ireland, New Zealand, the UK, and the US for stays under 90 days.
Letter of Invitation: Not required.
Inoculations: Recommended up-to-date on DTaP (diphtheria, tetanus, and pertussis), Hepatitis A, Hepatitis B, MMR (measles, mumps, and rubella), Polio booster, and Typhoid.
Work Permit: Required of all foreigners planning to work.
International Driving Permit: Required of all those planning to drive.

DOCUMENTS AND FORMALITIES

EMBASSIES AND CONSULATES

Embassies of other countries in Estonia are all in **Tallinn** (see p. 309). Estonia's embassies and consulates abroad include:

Australia: Consulate: 86 Louisa Rd., Birchgrove, NSW 2041 (☎61 2 9810 7468; eestikon@ozemail.com.au).

Canada: 260 Dalhousie St., ste. 210, Ottawa, ON K1N 7E4 (☎1 416 461-0764; www.estemb.ca).

Finland: Itäinen Puistotie 10, 00140 Helsinki (☎358 9 622 02 60; www.estemb.fi).

Germany: Hildebrandstraße 5, 10785 Berlin (☎49 30 254 606 00; www.estemb.de).

Sweden: Tyrgatan 3/3a, 11427 Stockholm (☎46 8 5451 2280; www.estemb.se).

UK: 16 Hyde Park Gate, London SW7 5DG (☎44 20 7589 3428; www.estonia.gov.uk).

US: 2131 Massachusetts Ave., NW, Washington, D.C. 20008 (☎1 202 588-0101; www.estemb.org).

VISA AND ENTRY INFORMATION

Citizens of Australia, Canada, Ireland, New Zealand, the UK, and the US can visit Estonia visa-free for up to 90 days in a six month period. Visa **extensions** are not granted. For more info, consult **www.vm.ee/eng.** The easiest means of crossing the **border** is from Tallinn to Moscow, St. Petersburg, or Rīga.

ESTONIA

GETTING AROUND

BY PLANE, BY TRAIN, AND BY FERRY

Several international airlines offer flights to Tallinn; try **SAS** or **AirBaltic.** If you're coming from another Baltic state or **Russia,** trains may be even cheaper than **ferries,** which also connect to **Finland, Sweden,** and **Germany,** but expect more red tape when crossing the border.

BY BUS

Domestically, buses are much cheaper and more efficient than trains. It's even possible to ride buses from the mainland to island towns (via ferry) for less than the price of the ferry ride. During the school year (Sept. to late June), students receive half-price bus tickets. Internationally, buses can be a painfully slow choice as clearing the border may take hours.

BY CAR, BY TAXI, AND THUMB

Although **road conditions** in Estonia are fair and steadily improving, the availability of **roadside assistance** remains poor. For info concerning speed limits and license requirements, check out the **Estonian National Road Administration** (www.mnt.ee). **Taxis** (about 7EEK per km.) are a safe means of transportation. *Let's Go* does not recommend **hitchhiking.** Those who do hitchhike should stretch out an open hand.

TOURIST SERVICES AND MONEY

Most towns have well-equipped tourist offices with English-speaking staff. Booths marked with a green "i" sell maps and give away brochures. The unit of currency is the **kroon (EEK),** divided into 100 **senti.** The kroon is pegged to the euro at €1=15.64EEK. **Inflation** is around 3.7%, so exchange rates should be relatively stable. Many restaurants and shops accept **MasterCard** and **Visa.** When purchasing an item, cash is not usually passed between hands, but is instead put in a small tray.

HEALTH AND SAFETY

 EMERGENCY NUMBERS: Police: ☎110. **Fire** and **Ambulance:** ☎112

Medical services for foreigners are few and far between, and usually require cash payments. There are two kinds of **pharmacies** (both called "apteek"). Some only stock prescription medication, but most are well-equipped Scandinavian chains that stock just about everything (except medication). Try grocery stores for **toiletries.** Public **toilets** *(tasuline),* marked by "N" or a triangle pointing up for women and "M" or a triangle pointing down for men, usually cost 3EEK and include a very limited supply of toilet paper. While Tallinn's tap water is generally safe to drink, **bottled water** is worth the extra money and is necessary in the rest of the country. The petty **crime** rate is low.

Women should not have a problem traveling alone, though you might want to dress conservatively. **Minorities** in Estonia are rare; they receive stares but generally experience little discrimination. For English-speaking help in an emergency, contact your embassy. **Homosexuality** is legal in Estonia and relatively tolerated.

ACCOMMODATIONS AND CAMPING

ESTONIA	❶	❷	❸	❹	❺
ACCOM.	under 200EEK	201-400EEK	401-550EEK	551-600EEK	over 600EEK

Each **tourist office** has accommodations listings for its town and can often arrange a bed for visitors. There is little distinction between **hotels, hostels,** and **guesthouses;** some upscale hotels still have hall toilets and showers. The word *vöörastemaja* (guesthouse) in a place's name usually implies that it's less expensive. Many hotels provide laundry services for an extra charge. Some hostels are part of larger hotels, so be sure to ask for the cheaper rooms. **Homestays** are common and inexpensive. For info on HI hostels around Estonia, contact the **Estonian Youth Hostel Association,** Narva Mantee 16-25, 10121, Tallinn (☎372 6461 455; www.baltichostels.net). **Camping** is the best way to experience Estonia's islands and unique selection of fauna and flora. Camping outside designated areas is illegal and a threat to wildlife. **Farm stays** are gaining in popularity. For more info visit **Rural Tourism,** www.maaturism.ee.

KEEPING IN TOUCH

Mail can be received general delivery through **Poste Restante.** Address envelopes as follows: Daniel (first name) HEMEL (LAST NAME), POSTE RESTANTE, Narva mnt. 1 (post office address), 0001 (postal code) Tallinn (city), ESTONIA. An airmail letter costs 7.50EEK to Europe and the CIS, and 8EEK to the rest of the world. Postcards cost 6EEK/7EEK. **Telephones** take digital cards, available at any kiosk. Cards come in various denominations (min. 50EEK). Calls to the Baltic states cost 5EEK per min., to Russia 10EEK. Pre-paid phone cards can get you rates of US$0.30 to US$0.50 per min. to phone the US. Otherwise, expect to pay US$1-4 per min. International access codes include: **AT&T** (☎0 800 12 001); **Canada Direct** (☎0 800 12 011); and **MCI** (☎0 800 12 122). **Internet access,** which is common, usually costs 30-60EEK per hr.

PHONE MAYHEM. The phone system in Estonia proves that the universe tends toward chaos. Tallinn numbers all begin with the number 6 and have 7 digits. Numbers in smaller towns, however, often have only 5 digits. Tallinn, unlike other Estonian cities, has no city code; to call Tallinn from outside Estonia on the digital system, dial Estonia's country code (372) and then the number. To call any city besides Tallinn from outside the country, dial the country code, the city code, and then the number. The 0 listed in parentheses before each city code need only be dialed when placing calls within Estonia.

TALLINN ☎(0)

Medieval buildings, German spires, and Danish towers loom over Tallinn (pop. 370,792), the self-proclaimed "Heart of Northern Europe." The capital's bustling shops and cosmopolitan youth point to Estonia's successful economic liberalization. Unfortunately, invading tourists sometimes give Old Town a theme-park feel.

ESTONIA

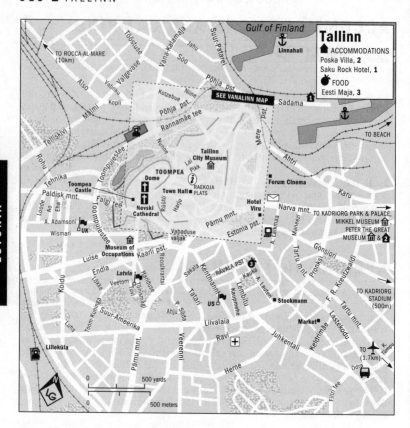

▐▀ TRANSPORTATION

Flights: Tallinn Airport, Lennujaama 2 (☎605 88 88, 24hr. info 605 88 87; www.tallinn-airport.ee). Bus #2 runs between the airport and the intersection of Gonsiori and Laikmaa, 300m southeast of the Old Town. Airlines include: **Estonian Air,** Lennujaama tee 13 (☎640 11 01; www.estonian-air.ee); **Finnair,** Roosikrantsi 2 (☎611 09 50; www.finnair.ee); **LOT,** Lembitu 14 (☎646 60 51; loteesti@hot.ee); **SAS,** Rävala pst. 2 (☎666 30 30; www.scandinavian.net). **Copterline** (☎610 18 18; www.copterline.com) runs a **helicopter** service to **Helsinki, FIN** (18min.; 1 per hr. 8:30am-9:30pm; €69). Open daily 9am-7pm.

Trains: Toompuiestee 35 (☎615 68 51; www.evrekspress.ee). Book ahead for international routes. (Open odd-numbered days 9am-7:30pm, even days 9am-11pm. To: **Moscow, RUS** (14½hr.; 1 per day; 515EEK, sleeper car 723EEK); **St. Petersburg, RUS** (10hr., 1 per day on even days, 390EEK); **Parnu** (2½hr., 2 per day, 40EEK); **Tartu** (3-5½hr., 2-3 per day, 70EEK). Domestic tickets on the 1st fl. or on the train.

Buses: Lastekodu 46 (☎680 09 00), 1.5km southeast of Vanalinn. Trams #2 and 4 run between Hotel Viru and the station, "Bussijaam." Open daily 6:30am-11:30pm; ticket office open daily 6:30am-9:15pm. International schedules www.eurolines.ee; domestic schedules www.bussireisid.ee. Buses run to: **Haapsalu** (1½-2½hr., 1-2 per hr., 45-65EEK); **Pärnu** (2½hr., 36 per day, 55-105EEK); **Tartu** (2½-3hr., 2-3 per hr., 65-85EEK); **Berlin, GER** (27hr., 1 per week, 1360EEK); **Kaliningrad, RUS** (15hr., 1 per day, 300EEK); **Rīga, LAT** (5-6hr., 5 per day, 200EEK); **Vilnius, LIT** (10½hr., 2 per day, 370EEK); **St. Petersburg, RUS** (8-10½hr., 5 per day, around 200EEK); **Moscow, RUS** (18½hr.; Tu, Th-F, Su; 500-900EEK). 10% ISIC discount.

Ferries: ☎631 85 50. At the end of Sadama. Boats, hydrofoils, and catamarans cross to **Helsinki, FIN. Eckerö Line,** Terminal B. (☎631 86 06; www.eckeroline.ee. 3½hr.; 1 per day; 220EEK, students 150EEK. MC/V.) **Viking,** Terminal A. (☎666 39 66; www.vikingline.ee. 3hr.; 2 per day; Su-Th 235EEK, students 165EEK; F-Sa 315EEK/250EEK.) **SeaWind,** Terminal D. (☎611 66 99; www.seawind.fi. 3½hr., 3 per day, 265EEK.) **Nordic Jet Line,** Terminal C. (☎613 70 00; www.njl.info. 1½hr., 6 per day, 295-595EEK. MC/V.) **Silja Line,** Terminal D. (☎611 66 61; www.silja.ee. 1½hr.; 5 per day; 250-530EEK, students 200-480EEK. MC/V.) **Tallink,** Terminals A and D. (☎640 98 08; www.tallink.ee. 3¼hr.; 3 per day; 315-345EEK, students 284-310EEK. Express ferries 1½hr.; 7 per day; 235-425EEK, students 212-384EEK. MC/V.)

Public Transportation: Buses, trams, minibuses, and **trolleys** run 6am-midnight. Buy tickets *(talong)* from kiosks (10EEK) or from drivers (15EEK). Validate them in the metal boxes on board. 600EEK fine for riding ticketless or for not validating your ticket.

Taxi: Klubi Takso (☎142 00) 5.50-7EEK per km, minimum 35EEK. Call ahead to avoid the 8-50EEK "waiting fee."

Bike rental: CityBike, Narva mnt. 120b, inside Comfort Hotel Oru (☎511 18 19; www.citybike.ee). 35EEK per hr. Rent for 24hr. (225EEK) and get free delivery anywhere in Tallinn. Open daily 11am-8pm.

✦ ORIENTATION

Even locals lose their way along the winding medieval streets of Tallinn's **Vanalinn** (Old Town), an egg-shaped maze ringed by five main streets: **Rannamäe tee, Mere pst., Pärnu mnt., Kaarli pst.,** and **Toompuies tee.** The best entrance to Vanalinn is through the 15th-century **Viru ärarad,** across from Hotel Viru, Tallinn's central landmark. **Viru,** the main thoroughfare, leads directly to **Raekoja plats** (Town Hall Square), the scenic center of Old Town. It has two sections: **All-linn,** or Lower Town, and **Toompea,** a rocky, fortified hill.

WI-FI? WHY NOT?

Estonia has a tradition of technological innovation that has distinguished it from its Baltic neighbors. Maybe Estonia's technological strength is due to the proximity of Finland's mobile-phone powerhouse, Nokia. Or maybe Estonia's relatively small population allows technological change to spread more quickly. Whatever the reason, the result is a godsend for the cyber-savvy budget traveler.

Estonia is the most Internet-friendly country in the Baltics. The World Wide Web has so pervaded the Estonian lifestyle that most Estonians under the age of 25 have no need for a checkbook—they pay all of their bills over the Internet.

For travelers, the biggest benefit of Estonia's Internet-euphoria is the abundance of free Internet options all over the country. Nearly every single area in Estonia, from the island of Hiumaa to the crowded streets of Tallinn's Old Town, has free wireless Internet (the WiFi/802.11b standard). All you need is a laptop and a wireless card to take advantage of this generosity.

WiFi, the company that has put together this communications venture, has set up well over a hundred free access points throughout Estonia. For more information on the unplugged Baltics, check out www.wifi.ee.

🖪 PRACTICAL INFORMATION

TOURIST AND FINANCIAL SERVICES

Tourist Office: Tourist Information Center (TIC), Kullassepa 4/Niguliste 2 (☎645 77 77; www.tourism.tallinn.ee). Sells city **maps** and the invaluable *Tallinn in Your Pocket* (35EEK), provides transportation schedules, and helps plan trips to other Estonian cities. Open July-Aug. M-F 9am-8pm, Sa-Su 10am-6pm; Sept. M-F 9am-6pm, Sa-Su 10am-5pm; Oct.-Apr. M-F 9am-5pm, Sa 10am-3pm; May-June M-F 9am-7pm, Sa-Su 10am-5pm. Branch at Sadama 25, in Ferry Terminal A (☎/fax 631 83 21). Open daily 8am-4:30pm.

Embassies: For a complete list, check www.vm.ee or consult *Tallinn This Week* (free at most hotels). **Canada,** Toom-kooli 13 (☎627 33 11; tallinn@canada.ee). Open M, W, F 9am-noon. **Finland,** Kohtu 4 (☎610 32 00; www.finland.ee). Open M-F 9am-noon. **Latvia,** Tõnismägi 10 (☎627 78 50; embassy.estonia@mfa.gov.lv). Open M-F 10am-noon. **Lithuania,** Uus 15 (☎631 40 30; www.hot.ee/lietambasada). Open M-Tu and Th 9-10:30am, F 9-10am. **Russia,** Pikk 19 (☎646 41 75; www.estonia.mid.ru). Open M-F 9am-5pm. **UK,** Wismari 6 (☎667 47 00; www.britishembassy.ee). Open M-F 10am-noon and 2-4:30pm. **US,** Kentmanni 20 (☎668 81 00; emergency 509 21 29; www.usemb.ee). Open M-F 9am-noon and 2-5pm.

Currency Exchange: Located throughout the city, though banks have better rates than hotels and private exchange bureaus. **ATMs** are located throughout the city.

American Express: Suur-Karja 15 (☎626 62 11; www.estravel.ee). Books hotels and tours, sells airline, ferry, and rail tickets, and provides visa services. Open June-Aug. M-F 9am-6pm, Sa 10am-5pm; Sept.-May M-F 9am-6pm, Sa 10am-3pm.

LOCAL AND EMERGENCY SERVICES

Luggage Storage: At the bus station. 10EEK per day. Open daily 6:30am-11:30pm. At the train station. 15-30EEK. Open even-numbered days 9am-10pm, odd days 9am-5pm.

English-Language Bookstore: Apollo Raamatumaja, Viru 23 (☎654 84 85; www.apollo.ee), stocks an impressive selection of guides, bestsellers, and classics. Open M-F 10am-8pm, Sa 10am-7pm, Su 11am-4pm.

Laundromat: Seebimull, Livalaia 7 (☎643 33 33). Follow Parnu mnt. south from the Old Town and then go left. Open M-F 8am-10pm, Sa 9am-7pm, Su 10am-4pm.

Pharmacy: Raeapteek, Raekoja plats 11 (☎631 48 30), has been in business since 1422 and features an adjoining **mini-museum**. Open M-F 9am-7pm, Sa 9am-5pm.

Hospital: Tallinn Central Hospital, Ravi 18 (☎602 70 00, 24hr. info 620 70 15).

Medical Assistance: Tallinn First Aid Hotline (☎697 11 45). The local emergency number is 112; operators speak English.

Internet Access: Central Library, Estonia pst. 8, 2nd fl. (☎683 09 00). Free for 15min. without membership. Open M-F 11am-7pm, Sa 10am-5pm.

Post Office: Narva mnt. 1 (☎661 66 16), opposite Hotel Viru. **Poste Restante** in basement. Open M-F 7:30am-8pm, Sa 8am-6pm, Su 9am-3pm. **Postal Code:** 10101.

🖪 ACCOMMODATIONS

Tallinn's hostels fill quickly in summer; it's wise to book in advance. ◼ **Rasastra,** Mere pst. 4 (☎661 62 91; www.bedbreakfast.ee), finds **private rooms** in central Tallinn and anywhere else in the Baltics. (Open daily 9:30am-6pm. In Tallinn singles 275EEK; doubles 500EEK; triples 650EEK. Breakfast 30-50EEK.)

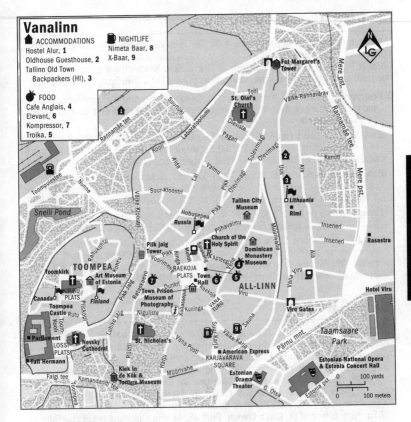

Vanalinn

🛏 ACCOMMODATIONS
Hostel Alur, **1**
Oldhouse Guesthouse, **2**
Tallinn Old Town
  Backpackers (HI), **3**

🍺 NIGHTLIFE
Nimeta Baar, **8**
X-Baar, **9**

🍴 FOOD
Cafe Anglais, **4**
Elevant, **6**
Kompressor, **7**
Troika, **5**

ESTONIA

🏅**Tallinn Old Town Backpackers (HI),** Uus 14 (☎051 711 337; www.balticbackpackers.com). Knock on the windows to be let in. Clean, safe hostel with incredible perks. Fun staff leads group pub crawls and organizes daytrips. Internet 5EEK per 20min. Linen 25EEK. Dorms 225EEK, with HI card 200EEK. ❷

🏅**Poska Villa,** Poska 15 (☎601 36 01; www.hot.ee/poskavilla). From Vanalinn, follow Gonsiori; make a left on Laulupeo, which becomes Poska; it's the small green house. Charming B&B in a quiet residential neighborhood close to Kadriog Park and Palace. Private baths. Breakfast included. Singles 650EEK; doubles 760-980EEK. MC/V. ❺

Saku Rock Hotel, Sadama 25a (☎680 66 00; www.sakurockhotel.ee). Sparkling new hotel next to Ferry Terminal D pays tribute to Estonia's popular national brew. Rooms with satellite TV, private bath, and free beer. Free Internet. Doubles 986EEK. MC/V. ❹

Oldhouse Guesthouse, Uus 22/1 (☎641 14 64; www.oldhouse.ee). Immaculate rooms in a quiet, homey atmosphere. Shared kitchen and hallway bathrooms. Book up to 2 weeks in advance summer. Reception daily 8am-11pm. 6-bed dorms 290EEK; singles 450-550EEK; doubles 650EEK; quads 1300EEK; luxury 2-person apartments in the Old Town 950-1900EEK. 10% discount with ISIC. ❷

Hostel Alur, Rannamäe 3 (☎6311531; www.alurhostel.com), next to train station and just steps away from Old Town. Clean, 6-8 bed dorms. Reception 24hr. 250EEK. ❶

🗂 FOOD

A **Rimi** supermarket is at Aia 7. (☎644 38 55. Open daily 8am-10pm.) Well-stocked **Stockmann supermarket** is on the corner of Liivalaia and A. Lauteri. (☎63 39 59 Open M-F 9am-10pm, Sa-Su 9am-9pm.) The **market,** Keldrimäe 9, is on the right as you take Lastekodu toward the bus station. (Open M-Sa 7am-5pm, Su 7am-4pm.)

▨ **Kompressor,** Rataskaevu 3 (☎646 42 10). Choose from incredible Estonian pancakes and giant portions of meat, fish, and veggie fillings (35-45EEK). Open F-Sa noon-10pm, Su 11am-10pm. ❶

Eesti Maja, Lauteri 1 (☎645 52 82; www.eestimaja.ee), at the corner with Rävala pst. This cellar kitchen serves traditional Estonian favorites like blood pudding and sauerkraut stew. Entrees 45EEK-165EEK. Open daily 11am-11pm. ❷

Cafe Anglais, Raekoja plats 14 (☎644 21 60). Brilliant sandwiches (75-80EEK) accompany spectacular views of the Town Square from this 2nd fl. art gallery and cafe. Live piano music M-Sa 8-11pm. Open daily 11am-11pm. MC/V. ❷

Elevant, Vene 5 (☎631 31 32). Tasty Indian fare with many vegetarian options. Entrees 84-278EEK. Lunch specials M-F noon-4pm around 100EEK. Open daily noon-11pm. ❸

Troika, Raekoja plats 15 (☎627 62 45). An extravagant Russian restaurant, Troika dishes up an array of delicacies, including the always-hard-to-find stroganoff of bear meat (495EEK). The less adventurous can enjoy the outstanding pot roast (95EEK). Live music daily 7-10pm. Open daily 10am-11pm. MC/V. ❹

👁 SIGHTS

LOWER TOWN (ALL-LINN). Tallinn's 14th-century **town hall** is the oldest in Europe, and contains several rooms decorated in classic medieval style. The hall features a **tower** with one of the world's tallest toilets (77m), built so that guards could relieve themselves without descending the winding, narrow steps. *(Raekoja Plats. ☎645 79 00. Open July-Aug. M-Sa 10am-4pm. Ask for booklet with English translations of display captions. Tower open daily May 15-Aug. 31 11am-6pm. Town hall 30EEK, students 20EEK; tower 25EEK/15EEK.)* The other dominant feature of the All-linn skyline is the 123.7m high tower of **St. Olaf's Church,** Pikk 48. As you climb up, tread carefully to avoid the fate of the architect, who fell from the tower to his death. Also beware of lightning: a bolt struck the tower in 1820, reducing it nearly 20m to its present height. The top offers a great view of the Old Town—so great that the KGB used it as an observation post to spy on locals. *(☎641 22 41; www.oleviste.ee. Open daily Apr.-Oct. 10am-6pm. Church free; tower 25EEK, students 10EEK. Services M and F 6:30pm, Su 10am and noon.)* On the south side of the Old Town is **St. Nicholas Church** (Niguliste Kirkko), Niguliste 3. The Soviets destroyed the original 13th-century Gothic building when they bombed Tallinn in 1944, but restored it years later so it could house part of the **Art Museum of Estonia** (see **Museums,** p. 316) collection. Don't miss the 15th-century "Dance Macabre" by Bernt Notke, in the back right corner of the church. *(☎631 43 27. Open W-Su 10am-5pm. Last entrance 4:30pm. Organ concerts Sa-Su 4-4:30pm. Museum 35EEK, students 20EEK.)* The **Church of the Holy Spirit,** at the intersection of Pikk and Pühavaimu, is notable for its intricate, 17th-century wooden clock and its former minister, Jakob Koell, who wrote the first book in the Estonian language in 1525. *(☎646 44 30. Open May-Sept. M-Sa 10am-4pm; Oct.-Apr. M-Sa 10am-2pm. 10EEK, students 5EEK.)*

TOOMPEA. The **Castle Square** (Lossi plats) is home to the **Alexander Nevsky Cathedral,** named for the 13th-century Russian warrior who conquered much of Estonia. *(Services 9am and 6pm. Open daily 8am-8pm.)* **Toompea Castle,** the present seat of the Estonian **Parliament** (Riigikogu), also faces the square, but is closed to visitors.

Directly behind it, a fluttering Estonian flag tops **Tall Hermann** (Pikk Hermann), Tallinn's tallest tower and most impressive medieval fortification. Follow Toom-Kooli north one block to get to the Lutheran Church of **Toomkirik,** Toom-Kooli 6, whose 13th-century spires tower over Toompea. As you walk in, you'll have to step on the tomb of Johann Thume, who asked to be buried at the church's entrance. *(☎ 644 41 40. Services Su 10am. Open Tu-Su 9am-5pm.)* To get to **Kiek in de Kök,** a 1483 tower, walk on Toompea away from Lossi plats and turn left on Komandandi tee. Its name, which means "peep in the kitchen," comes from the views it provides through the windows of neighboring houses. There is a haunting **torture museum** inside the tower. (☎ 644 66 86. Open Mar.-Oct. Tu-Su 10:30am-6pm; Nov.-Feb. Tu-Su 11am-5pm. 15EEK, students 7EEK.) Follow Toompea south just beyond the Old Town to reach **St. Charles' Church** (Kaarli Kirik), Toompuiestee 4, at the intersection with Kaarli pst. The highlight of the 19th-century limestone behemoth is Johann Köler's "Come to Me" mural, which the master painter finished in just 10 days. As you leave, look up to see the largest organ in Estonia. (☎ 611 91 00. Open M-F 10am-2pm. Services Su 10am. Donations accepted.)

KADRIORG. Quiet paths, shady trees, and fountains adorn **Kadriorg Park.** Its jewel, ▨ **Kadriorg Palace,** was designed by architect Niccolo Michetti (architect of Peterhof in St. Petersburg) as a summer palace for Tsar Peter the Great. *(Weizenbergi 37. ☎ 606 64 00. Open May-Sept. Tu-Su 10am-5pm; Oct.-Apr. W-Su 10am-5pm. 45EEK, students 35EEK.)* Its collection of 17th-century Dutch and Flemish art includes two paintings by Pieter Brueghel the Younger. The only Rembrandts in the Baltics are at the nearby **Mikkel Museum;** they include the Dutch master's 1621 sketch of himself. *(Weizenbergi 28. ☎ 601 34 30; www.ekm.ee. Open W-Su 11am-6pm. 15EEK, students 5EEK. Joint ticket with Kadriorg Palace 55EEK/30EEK.)* Cross the flower garden to see the **President's Palace,** in a pink building. Admission is strictly reserved for heads of state. To reach Kadriorg Park from Old Town, follow Narva mnt. and veer right on Weizenbergi when it splits from Narva mnt. Trams #1 and 3 also run to Kadriorg. *(Flower garden open daily May-Aug. 9am-10pm; Sept.-Oct. 9am-9pm. Free.)* Behind the park is the **Song Festival Grounds,** where 20% of the country gathered in 1989 to sing the once-banned national anthem.

ROCCA-AL-MARE. This peninsula, 10km west of central Tallinn, includes a popular **Zoo** (Loomaaed), Paldiski mnt. 145, best-known for housing the endangered Bactrian red deer and wild yak. *(☎ 694 33 00; www.tallinnzoo.ee. Open daily 9am-9pm. Ticket office closes at 7pm. Elephant house open Tu-Sa 9am-8pm. 39EEK, students 23EEK.)* The peninsula's main attraction is the **Estonian Open Air Museum,** a park with 68 buildings transplanted from the countryside, including the 1699 **Sutlepa Chapel.** *(☎ 654 91 00. Museum and chapel open daily May-Oct. 10am-6pm. Park and restaurant open daily May-Sept. 10am-8pm; Oct. 10am-4pm; Nov.-Apr. 10am-5pm. 28EEK, students 12EEK; last Tu of each month free. Folk song and dance performances May-Sept. 15 Sa-Su 11am. English tours Sa-Su noon. Bikes 35EEK per hr., 65EEK per 2hr.)*

🏛 MUSEUMS

▨ **MUSEUM OF OCCUPATION AND OF THE FIGHT FOR FREEDOM.** This brand-new collection at the southeastern edge of the Old Town documents Estonia's experience under Soviet and German rule. *(Toompea 8. ☎ 6680 250; www.okupatsioon.ee. Open Tu-Sa 11am-6pm. Donations accepted.)*

▨ **ESTONIAN HISTORY MUSEUM (EESTI AJALOOMUUSEUM).** Soviet archaeologists in the early 1950s tried to dispel the notion that bourgeois Danes and Germans founded medieval Tallinn. Now the museum's **Great Guild** branch restores the Scandinavian warriors and Teutonic Knights to their rightful places in history. Well-organized exhibits on Estonia up to the 19th century. *(Pikk 17. ☎641 16 30; www.eam.ee. Open M-Tu and Th-Su 10am-6pm. 10EEK, students 8EEK. Free last Sa of each month.)* Where it leaves off, the Maarjamäe Loss branch picks up. This restored palace east of the city documents modern Estonian history, with jarring photos of Tallinn and Pärnu residents cheering the arrival of Nazi "liberators" in 1941. *(Pirita 56. From Kadriog Park, follow Pirita along the bay 1km. ☎601 45 99. Open W-Su 11am-6pm. 10EEK, students 8EEK; free last Sa of each month.)*

TALLINN CITY MUSEUM (TALLINNA LINNAMUUSEUM). Exhibits on Tallinn characters, such as Old Thomas, the dutiful town watchman, and Johann von Uexkyll, the infamous serf-beating nobleman. *(Vene 17. ☎644 65 53; www.linnamuuseum.ee. Open Mar.-Oct. M and W-Su 10:30am-5:30pm; Nov.-Feb. 11am-4:30pm. Museum 25EEK, students 10EEK. All captions in English and Estonian. English tours available.)*

PETER I (THE GREAT) HOUSE MUSEUM. This simple residence (Peeter I Majamuuseum), where Peter stayed before a palace in Tallinn was completed, houses many original furnishings, as well as an imprint of Peter's extremely large hand. *(Mäekalda 2, near Kadriorg Park. ☎601 31 36; www.linnamuuseum.ee/peeter1maja. Open May 15-Sept. W-Su 10:30am-5:30pm. 10EEK, students 5EEK.)*

KNIGHTHOOD HOUSE (ART MUSEUM OF ESTONIA). This gallery (Eesti Kunstimuuseum Ruutelkonna Hoonies) houses remarkable cityscapes of early 18th-century Tallinn and provocative sketches by Estonia's early 20th-century avant garde. Much of the collection will move to a new branch behind Kadriog Palace, most likely by summer 2005. *(Kiriku plats 1. ☎644 14 78; www.ekm.ee. Open W-Su 11am-6pm; last admission 5:30pm. 20EEK, students 5EEK.)*

TOWN PRISON MUSEUM OF PHOTOGRAPHY (RAEVANGLA-FOTOMUUSEUM). A 14th-century jail seems like a gloomy location for a picture gallery until you consider the dismal lives many of Estonia's most talented photographers lived. *(Raekoja 4/6, behind the town hall. ☎644 87 67; www.linnamuuseum.ee. Open Mar.-Oct. M-Tu and Th-Su 10:30am-5pm; Nov.-Feb. M and Th-Su 11am-5pm. 10EEK, students 5EEK.)*

DOMINICAN MONASTERY MUSEUM (DOMINIIKLASTE KLOOSTRI MUUSEUM). To enter, you need to buy a copper coin (45EEK, students 30EEK), which you'll have to hammer into an amulet. Keep it, since it's a lifetime pass to this peaceful courtyard cloistered from the Old Town bustle. *(Vene 16. ☎644 46 06. www.kloostri.ee. Open daily May 12-Sept. 23 9:30am-6pm; winter by appointment only.)*

🎵 🌿 ENTERTAINMENT AND FESTIVALS

Tallinn This Week, free at tourist offices, lists performances. The **Estonia Concert Hall** and the **Estonian National Opera**, both at Estonia pst. 4, hold performances of opera, ballet, musicals, and chamber music. (Concert hall ☎614 77 60; www.concert.ee. Tickets 30-150EEK. Box office open M-F noon-7pm, Sa noon-5pm, Su 1hr. before curtain. Opera ☎626 02 60; www.opera.ee. Tickets 30-270EEK. Box office open daily noon-7pm.) The **Forum Cinema** at Coca-Cola Plaza, Hobujaama 5, shows Hollywood films in English. (☎11 82. Tickets 110EEK.) There is a **beach** at Pirita (buses #1, 1a, 8, 34, or 38 from the post office). In early June, chefs from nearby countries face off during **Grillfest** (www.grillfest.ee). During **Old Town Days,** held the first weekend of June, the city hosts open-air concerts, fashion shows, singing, and skits. **Jaanipaev** (Midsummer's Day), June 23-24th, is an pagan celebration featuring bonfires and barbecues. Celebrate the power of barley during **Beersummer** (www.ollesummer.ee), July 6-10, 2005. In late February, the **Student Jazz Festival** brings prodigies from all over northern Europe. In the midst of December, the international **Dark Nights Film Festival** (www.poff.ee) showcases cinematic talent.

◨ NIGHTLIFE

▨ **Karja Kelder,** Vaike-Karja 1 (☎644 10 08; www.karjakelder.ee). This former cellar brewery, established in 1832, claims to have the city's widest selection of beers, with over 50 on the menu. Beer 30EEK per 0.5L. (Live music F-Sa night. Open Sept.-June Su-Th 11am-2am, F-Sa 11am-4am; July-Aug. M and Su 11am-midnight, Tu-Th 11am-1am, F-Sa 11am-3am. MC/V.)

Beer House, Dukri 5, (☎627 65 20; www.beerhouse.ee). The only on-site microbrewery in Tallinn, Beer House is an ultimate beer experience. Wander the 1st fl. to see the vats where the 2-week brewing process takes place, or head upstairs to the sauna (300EEK per hr. for up to 6 people; reserve in advance) and disco. Live music F-Sa 10pm. House beer 30-40EEK per 0.5L; 15EEK noon-2pm. Open Su-Th 9am-midnight, F-Sa 9am-2am.)

Nimeta Baar, (The Pub with No Name), Suur-Karja 4/6 (☎641 15 15. www.nimetabaar.ee), is the best place to meet jolly, rugby-loving expats. Beer 32EEK. 2-for-1 beers at Happy Hour (6-7pm). Open Su-Th 11am-2am, F-Sa 11am-4am. MC/V. With cushy couches and a big dance floor, **Nimega Baar** (The Pub with a Name), Suur-Karja 13 (☎620 92 99. www.jjj-bars.com), has a more local crowd than its nameless counterpart. Beer 32EEK. Open M-Th 11am-2am, F-Sa 11am-4am, Su noon-2am. MC/V.

X-Baar, Sauna 1 (☎620 92 66). Marked by a rainbow flag spray-painted outside, X has a relaxed atmosphere and a small dance floor. Largely gay clientele, though straight women are known to stop by. Live DJ F and Sa. Beer 30EEK. Open daily 2pm-1am.

COASTAL ESTONIA

East of Tallinn, vast Lahemaa National Park shelters pristine coastline, dense forests, and historic villages. To the west, hip Pärnu and quiet Haapsalu offer beaches and mudbaths and serve as a gateway to the Estonian islands.

LAHEMAA NATIONAL PARK ☎(0)232

Founded in 1971, Lahemaa was the USSR's first national park. Today, it's one of Europe's largest, protecting numerous animals and over 838 unique plant species. **Palmse Manor** is among the best-restored estates in Lahemaa. The manor grounds include gardens, stables, a pond, and streams. The former servants' quarters now house an **Old Cars Museum.** (Kodanik Kirsi Erahobiklubi; ☎688 88. Manor open daily May-Sept. 10am-7pm; Oct.-Apr. 10am-3pm. 25EEK, students 15EEK. Car museum open daily May-Aug. 10am-7pm; Sept. 10am-5pm. 20EEK/10EEK.) The **famine stones,** 1km past the tourist office, were piled up by serfs picking rocks from the fields in preparation for plowing. Next to Lainela Puhkemajaad, the **Kásmús Maritime Museum,** Kásmús Merekööl 3, introduces visitors to the history of the surrounding fishing village. Ask the proprietor, Aarne Vaik, for a tour. (☎381 36. Open daily 9am-9pm. Free.) On the far side of the Puhkemajaad Neemetee, a path through the woods opens to a rocky beach where the **stone hill** grants wishes to those who contribute a new rock to the pile. The fishing huts on the cape are part of an **open-air museum.** (Open daily 24hr.) As you continue around the cape and cross the river, white stripes on the trees mark a short trail running

ESTONIA

through the forest and back to town. The harbor visible is **Vergi**, connected to the cape by a land bridge 2.5km farther along the road. In early July, every other year, the **Vihula Folklore Festival** summons storytellers from around the world. The biannual **Lahemaa Bagpipe Music Festival** draws bagpipers from across Lahemaa.

As Lahemaa is very large and public transportation is infrequent, your best bet for visiting is to rent a car in Tallinn. The most convenient base for exploring the park is **Palmse**, home to the **Lahemaa National Park Visitor Center**, which offers help in booking rooms and navigating the park. (☎955 55; info@lahemaa.ee. English spoken. Open daily May-Aug. 9am-7pm; Sept. 9am-5pm; Oct.-Apr. M-F 9am-5pm.) From Tallinn, take the **Rakvere bus** to Viitna (1hr.; 28 per day; 15-45EEK, ISIC discount). From there, catch a bus to Palmse Mõis or walk the 7km road. Call the visitor center for the bus schedule from Viitna to Palmse Mõis, as there are only four buses per week and visitors have been known to hitchhike from Viitna. *Let's Go* does not recommend hitchhiking. For direct access to the **coast** and the **Palmse Manor House**, inquire at the Tallinn station about buses to **Võsu** (3 per week). **Rent bikes** at the Park Hotel Restaurant (100EEK per day). **Postal Code:** 45202.

Near Palmse, the best bet is the **Ojaäärse Hostel ❶**. From Viitna, take the road to Palmse and turn right about 500m before the visitor center. (Singles 100EEK.) Situated a scenic 8km hike from Võsu in the village of Käsmu, **Lainela Puhkemajaad ❶**, toward the end of Neema, offers small, tidy rooms, a basketball court, tennis courts, and a sauna. (☎/fax 381 33. Singles 170EEK; doubles 340EEK. Campsites 40EEK per person.) In Viitna proper, the lakeside **campground ❶** is 400m past the bus stop, through the wooden arch on the right. Campsites and rooms in log cabins are available. (☎936 51. Campsites 20EEK per person. Doubles 180EEK.) In the wilds of Palmse Mõis, **Park Hotel Restaurant ❷** has fresh salads for 20EEK and *schnitzel* for 70EEK. (☎236 26. Open daily 11am-10pm.) The **tavern ❷** in Viitna, opposite the bus stop, has dishes for 50-100EEK. (☎586 81. Open daily 8am-11pm.)

PÄRNU   ☎(0)44

Known as the summer capital of Estonia, Pärnu (PAER-noo; pop. 45,000) lives up to its name, as Estonians and cosmopolitan Europeans flock to its beaches in July and August. The city is also famous for its curative mud baths.

▐ TRANSPORTATION

Trains: The station is 3km east of the center, near the corner of Riia and Raja; take bus #15 or 40 to Raeküla Rdtj (6EEK). To: **Tallinn** (3hr.; 2 per day; 40EEK, with ISIC 32EEK). Trains are not the best way to get to Pärnu.

Buses: Ringi 3 (☎720 02, Eurolines 278 41; fax 417 55). To: **Haapsalu** (2½hr., 1-2 per day, 90EEK); **Kuressaare** (2½hr., 5 per day, 90EEK); **Tallinn** (2hr., 42 per day, 55-80EEK); **Tartu** (2½hr., 21 per day, 90-100EEK); **Rīga, LAT** (3½hr., 6-8 per day, 110-150EEK). ISIC discounts available for domestic fares.

Taxis: Pärnu Takso (☎412 40) and E-Takso (☎311 11). 6-7EEK per km.

Bike Rental: Rattapood, Ringi 14a. M-F 10am-6pm, Sa 10am-3pm. 40EEK per hr.; 150EEK per day.

▄▐ ORIENTATION AND PRACTICAL INFORMATION

The **River Pärnu** neatly bisects the city. The town center stretches from **Tallinn Gate** to the bus station on **Ringi**. The main street is **Rüütli**. A short walk down **Nikolai** and **Supeluse** from the center of town leads to the **mud baths** and **Ranna pst.**, which runs along the **beach**. Be sure not to confuse the two streets **Aia** and **Aisa**.

Tourist Info Center: Rüütli 16 (☎730 00; www.parnu.ee). From the bus station, follow Ringi away from Pikk and hang a right on Ruutli. **Free maps.** Open May 15-Sept. 15 M-F 9am-6pm, Sa 9am-4pm, Su 10am-3pm; Sept. 16-May 14 M-F 9am-5pm. When it's closed, head to the 24hr. reception desk at **Best Western Hotel Pärnu,** Rüütli 44 (☎78 911; hotparnu@www.ee). Instead of turning right on Ruutli to the TIC, head left. The TIC and many hotels sell *Pärnu In Your Pocket* (25EEK).

Currency Exchange: Krediidipank (☎447 3600), Rüütli 47, has better rates than its competitors. Cashes **traveler's checks** for 1% commission or 25EEK (whichever is higher). Open M-F 9am-5pm, Sa 9am-2pm. 24hr. (MC/V) **ATMs** line Rüütli.

American Express: Estravel, Kuninga 34 (☎737 71; www.estravel.ee), on the street parallel to Rüütli. Open M-F 9am-6pm, Sa 10am-3pm.

Luggage Storage: At **Cargobus,** along the bus station platforms. 6-25EEK per day. Open M-F 8am-7:30pm, Sa 8am-1pm and 1:45-5pm, Su 9am-1pm and 1:45-5pm.

Hospital: Pärnu Hospital, Sillutise 6 (☎731 01; www.ph.ee).

Internet Access: Rüütli Internetipunkt, Rüütli 25 (☎315 52). The entrance is through the courtyard in the yellow building. 13 fast connections. 25EEK per hr. Open M-F 10am-9pm, Sa-Su 10am-6pm.

Post Office: Akadeemia 7 (☎711 11). The west end of Rüütli. Open M-F 8am-6pm, Sa 9am-3pm. **Postal Code:** 80010.

ACCOMMODATIONS

Rooms at hotels and guesthouses fill quickly, so reserve far in advance. **Tanni-Vakoma Majutusbüroo,** Hommiku 5, behind the bus station, rents **private rooms.** The office can be reached by phone year-round. (☎310 70; tanni@online.ee. Office open May-Aug. M-F 10am-8pm, Sa 10am-3pm. 200EEK and up.)

Hostel Lõuna, Lõuna 2 (☎309 43; www.hot.ee/hostellouna). From the bus station, walk down Ringi, turn right on Rüütli. Go 500m, then turn left on Akadeemia. It's at the end of the street, on the left. Bright, comfortable rooms with shared but clean baths near the beach and the city center. Reception 24hr. Dorms 250EEK. ❷

Külalistemaja Delfine, Supeluse 22 (☎269 00; www.delfine.ee). From the bus station, turn left on Ringi. Go left on Pühavaimu and bear right onto Supeluse. Cheery rooms with private baths, TVs, and phones. To stay here in summer, try to reserve in Feb. or Mar. Sauna 150EEK per hr. Breakfast included. June 15-Aug. 15 singles 600EEK, doubles 890EEK, triples 1050EEK; May-June 14 and Aug. 16-Sept. 30 550EEK/800EEK/950EEK; Oct.-Apr. 30 490EEK/550EEK/700EEK. MC/V. ❹

Kalevi Pansionaat, Ranna pst. 2 (☎257 99). From the bus station, turn left on Ringi, left on Pühavaimu, and continue on Supeluse. Bear left at the fork and take a left onto Ranna pst. Kalevi is on the left (350m). Steps from the beach. Some rooms have views of a local soccer stadium. 2-3 bed dorm rooms 250EEK per person. 4-5 bed family rooms with private bath 900EEK. Staff speaks limited English. ❷

FOOD

A **market** *(turg)* is on the corner of Sepa and Karja. (Open M-F 8am-6pm, Sa 8am-4pm, Su 9am-3pm.) **Georg ❶,** Rüütli 43, is a cafeteria-style eatery packed with locals enjoying Estonian cuisine. (☎311 10. Open summer M-F 7:30am-10pm, Sa-Su 9am-10pm; winter M-F 7:30am-7:30pm, Sa-Su 9am-5pm.) **Kadri Kohvik ❷,** Nikolai 12, around the corner from the TIC, serves hearty fare. (☎45 334. Entrees 25-48EEK. Open M-F 7:30am-8pm; Sa-Su 9am-5pm.) **Trahter Postipoiss ❸,** Vee 12, has authentic

Russian cuisine; service can be brusque. There is a buffet (95EEK) each night starting at 5pm. (☎648 64; www.restaurant.ee. Entrees 45-175EEK. Live music and dancing F-Sa from 9pm. Open Su-Th noon-midnight, F-Sa noon-2am. MC/V.)

👁 SIGHTS

The 18th-century **Elizabeth's Church,** on Nikolai between Kuninga and Louna, was named after the reigning Russian empress. J.H. Wulburn, the architect who planned its maroon spire (with a peacock atop the weathervane), also designed the spire of St. Peter's Church in Riga. Catherine the Great one-upped her predecessor with the construction of the Russian Orthodox **Catherine Church** (Ekateriina kirik), Vee 8, at the corner of Uus and Vee, one block north of Rüütli. (☎431 98. Open M-F 11am-6pm, Sa-Su 9am-6pm. Services Sa 8:30am and 6pm, Su 9am and 5pm. Cameras 50EEK.) The interior, which shimmers with icons, is even more astonishing than the imposing silver-and-green spires.

Take a stroll down **Kuninga,** named for King Gustav II of Sweden. On the east end, at the corner with Ringi, set in a pleasant public park, is the **statue of Lydia Koidula** (1843-1885), the Estonian poet who wrote the now-famous anthem, "My Fatherland is My Beloved." But it was in love that Koidula deserted her fatherland—marrying a German from Riga and moving with him to Russia. At the opposite end of Kuninga stands the **Tallinn Gate,** a relic from the 17th-century days when walls surrounded the Swedish-controlled city.

For the less pious, the **Museum of New Art,** Esplanaadi 10, also known as the **Chaplin Center** (in honor of the silent film star), hosts the **12th Annual Nude Art Exhibition** from June to Aug. 2005. (☎307 72; www.chaplin.ee. Open daily 9am-9pm. 15EEK, students 10EEK.) On the white sand **beach,** swings and trampolines are set up on the sand, and a free waterslide is open from June to August. Women can bathe nude on the right side of the beach. **Mudravilla,** Ranna pst. 1, by the beach, offers mud bath treatments (head-to-toe 150EEK, localized therapy 100EEK). Add 60EEK for a medical examination beforehand. (☎442 5525; www.mudaravila.ee).

🎟 NIGHTLIFE

Head to the Swedish-owned **Veerev Olu** (The Rolling Beer), Uus 3a, in a courtyard behind the TIC, for live rock and folk Sa 9:30pm-1am. (☎534 03 149. 0.5L *A. Le Coq Premium* 20EEK. Entrees 17-35EEK. Open M-Sa 11am-1am, Su noon-1am.) You'll find live jazz (F 8 or 9pm) and "happy jazz" (vodka, pineapple juice and lemon soda; 40EEK) at **Jazz Cafe,** Ringi 11. (☎044 27546; www.abijoon.ee.) Try *Saku* (1L 20EEK), Estonia's national brew, at **Tallinna Väravad,** Vana-Tallinna 1, atop the Tallinn Gate. (☎450 73. Open daily 11am-11pm.) Pärnu's most famous disco is **Sunset Club,** Ranna pst. 3. (☎306 70. Cover M-Th and Su after midnight 50EEK, F-Sa 100EEK. Open summer M-Th and Su 10pm-4am, F-Sa 10pm-6am.)

❋ FESTIVALS

The ⚑**Estonian Country Dance Festival** takes place in mid-June at Sassi Horse Farm, near Pärnu. It ends with a line dance that stretches the length of Rüütli. (☎500 70; www.noorusemaja.ee.) The end of June is the beginning of festival season, starting with **Hello, Pärnu Summer!** (☎764 91). The **Pärnu David Oistrakh Festival,** which runs from late June to early July, draws international musicians and conductors. (☎665 40; www.oistfest.ee.) The **International Film Festival,** in early July, has documentaries and anthropological films. (☎307 72; www.chaplin.ee.) Artists from around the world come to the **Pärnu Jazz Festival** during late June and early July.

The **Watergate Festival,** broadcast throughout Estonia, brings every water sport and activity imaginable to Pärnu in mid-July. (☎919 66; www.watergate.ee. 40-90EEK per day; 340EEK for the entire festival, including admission to Sunset Club.)

HAAPSALU ☎(0)47

Haapsalu (HAHP-sah-lu; pop. 12,000) is the gateway to the Estonian islands. Historically, its location was too strategic for its own good; the Soviets planted a military base there and cut the city off from the outside world.

⌂❷ TRANSPORTATION AND PRACTICAL INFORMATION. The **bus station,** Raudtee 2, has a 216m long platform. (☎347 91. Ticket office open daily 5am-1pm and 2-7pm.) Buses go to: **Kärdla** (3hr., 3 per day, 65EEK); **Pärnu** (2-3hr., 2 per day, 75EEK); **Tallinn** (1½-2hr., 24 per day, 40-65EEK). ISIC discounts are available. **Taxis** (☎335 00) charge 6EEK per km. To reach the center from the bus station, walk down Jaama and turn left on Posti. Rent **bikes** at Rattad Vabatog, Karja 22, for 100EEK per day. (☎472 9846. Open M-F 10am-6pm, Sa 10am-3pm.) At the **Tourist Information Center,** Posti 37, the friendly, English-speaking staff provide **maps** and city directories and books rooms in Haapsalu and on the islands for a 10EEK fee. (☎332 48; www.haapsalu.ee. Open May 15-Sept. 15 M-F 9am-6pm, Sa-Su 10am-3pm; Sept. 16-May 14 M-F 9am-5pm.) A smaller branch is outside the castle entrance. (Open daily 10am-6pm). You can **exchange currency** at **Hansapank,** Posti 41, which also has a **24hr. ATM.** (☎472 0200. Open M-F 8am-6pm, Sa 9am-2pm.) The **post office,** Nurme 2, is around the corner from the TIC. (☎472 0400. Open M-F 7:30am-6pm, Sa 9am-3pm.) **Postal Code:** 50901.

⌂❐ ACCOMMODATIONS AND FOOD. From the bus station, walking away from the train tracks, turn left at the traffic circle onto Kalda, left onto Lahe, and left onto Suur-Lilva to reach the **Bergfeldt Mud Cure Resort ❹,** which offers seaside **singles** (590EEK) and **doubles** (790EEK) with TV and private showers. (Breakfast included. 30min. mud treatment 200EEK; physician consultation 120EEK. Package deals available for mud-treatment patients.) **Ungru Majutus ❶,** Ungru 4-3, boasts cozy private rooms (200EEK per person). Cross the tracks behind the bus station, take a left on Kiltsi. Turn right on Ungru tee and continue 1.5km. (☎473 5843; ungrukodu@hot.ee. Open May-Oct. Call in advance.) Take Lahe toward Bergfeldt, then turn right on Wiedemanni to reach the **Sport Hostel ❶,** Wiedemanni 15, which offers spartan private rooms (120EEK) with shared baths and a common kitchen. (☎473 5140; haapsalu@spordibaasid.ee. Reception M-F 1-9pm.) Overlooking the south wall of the castle, **Restoran Central ❹,** Karja 21, has medieval cuisine. (☎35595; centraal@hot.ee. Entrees 35-140EEK. Open Su-Th noon-11pm, F-Sa noon-2am. MC/V). **Pizza Grande ❷,** Karja 6, flips pizzas (32-37EEK) across from the castle. Free delivery to anywhere in Haapsalu. (☎473 7200; www.hot.ee/pizzagrande. Open daily 11am-11pm.) **Sinine Kangur ❷,** Karja 16, has Chinese cuisine. (Entrees 29-39EEK. Open daily 11am-11pm.) **Lemmik,** Jaama 11, has groceries. (Open daily 8am-9pm.) Dance until sunrise at **Africa,** Tallinna mnt. 1/Posti 43, in the shopping center. Its restaurant (entrees 60-150EEL) is open daily 11am-midnight; the space next door is Haapsalu's most hopping disco. (☎905 07. Cover 100EEK. Open F-Sa 10pm-4am.) The party starts early at **Gambrino,** Kalda 1, at the corner with Posti. Happy hour runs from noon-2pm. (1L *A. Le Coq* 20-30EEK.)

◧❀ SIGHTS AND FESTIVALS. Head to the 13th-century **Bishop's Castle** (Piiskopilinnus) in the center of town. Inside the castle is a tiny **museum** and the **Dome Church.** On the full moon of February and August, watch for the White Lady of Haapsalu, who was imprisoned in the castle. **White Lady Days** festivities occur in

ESTONIA

August. (☎473 7076. Open May 15-Sept. 15 Tu-Su 10am-6pm. 15EEK, students 5EEK. In low season, call ☎473 5516 or e-mail kk@haapsalu.ee to arrange a visit.) **Africa Beach,** northeast of the castle, features views of Haapsalu Bay. The best swimming is on the western edge of town at Paralepa Beach.

Early August brings the **Augustibluus Blues Festival,** Estonia's only blues festival. (☎056 489 01 66; www.haapsalu.ee/augustibluus.) Since blues is a uniquely American musical form, the organizers of Augustibluus feature American cars at the same time in the **American Beauty Automobile Festival.** The **Only Girls in Jazz** festival brings female jazz musicians to Haapsalu. (☎050 977 95; www.kuursaal.ee.) In mid-July, the **String Music Festival** (☎050 324 68) spotlights Pyotr Tchaikovsky, who spent a summer in Haapsalu in 1867.

ESTONIAN ISLANDS

Many Estonians say the country's 1521 islands offer a glimpse of the way life used to be. Afraid the islands would become an escape route out of the USSR, the Soviets isolated the region, shielding it from outside influence. Today, the islands are a top holiday destination for vacationing foreigners and Estonians.

SAAREMAA

Meteorite craters, bubbling springs, rugged coasts, and formidable cliffs attest to the natural beauty of Saaremaa (SAH-reh-mah; pop. 38,760), Estonia's largest and most popular island. Come summer, young Estonians from the mainland arrive in droves to party beachside. As distances are long and buses infrequent, the best way to see the entire island is to rent a car in Kuressaare. Ambitious travelers can take in all the major sights by bike. Though you'll log 100-150km of cycling each day, Saaremaa's terrain is flat.

KURESSAARE   ☎(0)45

Kuressaare (KOO-rehs-sah-re; pop. 15,820), on Saaremaa's southern coast, is the island's largest town. The local accent and folklore distinguish it from the mainland, but the town's distinct character is slipping away as posh hotels and multinational chain stores invade.

■ **TRANSPORTATION. Buses** run from **Tallinn** via **Haapsalu** (4-6hr., 9-11 per day, 100-160 EEK) and from **Tartu** via **Parnu** (6hr., 3-5 per day, 180-194EEK). **Flights** depart from **Tallinn** to **Kuressaare** (45min., 1-2 per day, 160-385EEK). See www.avies.ee for info. You can call the **bus station** (☎45 31476) in advance to be picked up at the Triigi **ferry** terminal and taken south to Kuressaare. Request that the bus stop at the Triigi port. Those who take the morning ferry from **Sõru** on Hiiumaa to Triigi need to find a ride in order to reach Kuressaare by nightfall. *Let's Go* does not recommend hitchhiking. Getting off Saaremaa can be difficult. For help planning your departure, go to the **bus station** (open daily 7am-7:30pm) or Kuressaare's TIC. If you're headed back to **Tallinn,** book your bus ticket one day in advance, or take one of the faster minibuses. If you're traveling by car, you must reserve a spot on the ferry in advance by contacting the Sõru booking office (☎46 95205; open daily 8am-1pm and 4-7pm) or **AS Saaremaa Laevakompanii** (☎45 24444; www.laevakompanii.ee). **Taxis** run from the town hall, the bus station, and Smuuli pst. (☎533 33. 6EEK per km.) The cheapest **car rental** rates are at Metra, Aia 25, behind the hospital. (☎45 39361; www.metra.ee. Open daily 8am-6pm. From 400EEK per day.) Call at least one

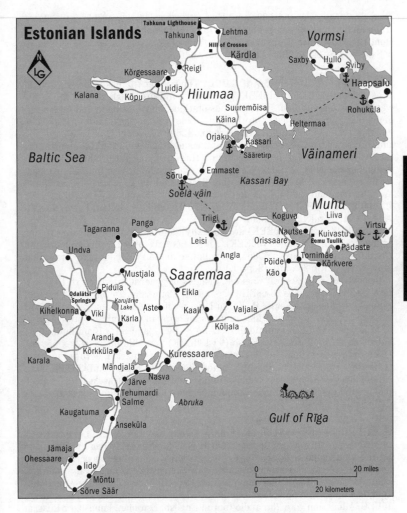

Estonian Islands

ESTONIA

week in advance. Rent **bikes** from Bivarix, Tallinna 26. Call in advance, or show up early, as they sometimes sell out. Helmets are available upon request. (☎571 18; bivarix@bivarix.ee. 135EEK per day. Open M-F 10am-6pm, Sa 10am-2pm.)

ORIENTATION AND PRACTICAL INFORMATION. The town is centered on narrow **Raekoja pl.** (Town Hall Square). The **Tourist Information Center (TIC),** Tallinna 2, inside the town hall, offers car rental advice and **free maps.** (☎331 20; www.visitestonia.com. Open May-Sept. 15 M-F 9am-7pm, Sa 9am-5pm, Su 10am-3pm; Sept. 16-Apr. M-F 9am-5pm.) **Eesti Ühispank,** Kauba 2, **exchanges currency,** cashes **traveler's checks,** and gives MC/V **cash advances.** (☎215 00; fax 215 33. Open M-Sa 9am-5:30pm, Sa 9am-2pm.) **24hr. ATMs** are abundant in Kuressaare. **Store luggage** outside the bus station. (3-5EEK per day. Open M-F 7:15am-2pm and 2:30-

8pm, Sa 7:15am-2pm and 2:30-6pm.) Free **Internet access** is available at the **library**, Tallinna 8. (Open July-Aug. M-F 11am-7pm; Sept.-June M-F 10am-7pm, Su 10am-4pm.) The **post office**, Torni 1, is on the corner of Komandandi. (☎240 80. Open M-F 8am-6pm, Sa 8:30am-3pm.) **Postal Code:** 93801.

ACCOMMODATIONS AND FOOD. The staff at **TIC** make same-day bookings at local B&Bs for a 10EEK fee. Family-run ⚑**Transvaali 28 B&B ❷**, Transvaali 28, is a great deal. From the bus station, follow Tallinna and take a left immediately past the TIC onto Raekoja. Bear left on Kaevu and turn left one block after the windmill. All three rooms (250EEK) include private bath, TV, and breakfast. (☎45 333 34; www.saaremaa.ee/transvaali28.) From the station, follow Põhja past Tallinna, turn left on Hariduse, and turn right on Kingu to reach **Sug Hostel ❶**, Kingu 6. A dorm during the academic year, Sug offers clean, basic rooms with Internet access and fitness facilities. (☎543 88. Open June-Aug. Bed in quad 120-145EEK; in double 150-175EEK; singles 210-250EEK. 15% discount Su-W.) Follow Tallinna toward the TIC and turn left on Torni to reach **Arabella ❸**, Torni 12. The unadvertised economy rooms (singles 350EEK; doubles 590EEK; triples 790EEK) are virtually identical to the renovated rooms (singles 500EEK; doubles 790EEK). All rooms have phones, private bath, and breakfast included. (☎45 55885; www.hot.ee/arabell. Discounts for two-night stays. Rates drop 20% after Sept. 1.)

Õuemaja ❶, Uus 20A, off Raekoja, dishes out generous portions of Estonian fare. (☎334 23. Entrees 20-68EEK. Open M-W 10am-9pm, Th-Sa 10am-10pm, Su noon-7pm.) **Pannkoogikohvik ❶**, Kohtu 1, serves hearty "hot pots" (28-35EEK) of noodles, cheese, meat and fish, and has an array of vegetarian options. (☎45 33575. Open M-F 8:15am-midnight; F-Sa 8:15am-2am; Su 9:15am-midnight). **Vanalinna ❺**, Kauba 8, serves fish (99-130EEK) and wild boar. (☎/fax 553 09. Open daily noon-10pm. MC/V.) **John Bull Pub ❷**, Lossipark 4, across the moat from the castle, may be the only place that serves *Saku* (0.5L 25EEK) in a school bus. (☎45 39988. Open daily 11am-last customer). **Raekeskus**, Raekoja 10, just behind the TIC, is a huge shopping center with a large supermarket. (Open daily 9am-10pm. MC/V.)

SIGHTS AND FESTIVALS. Follow Tallina and merge onto Lossi to reach the massive, 13th-century **Bishopric Castle** (Piiskopilinnus). When the Bishop of Saare-Lääne served as judge at the castle, convicts were thrown to a pack of hungry lions. The eclectic **Saaremaa Museum** inside the castle has medieval weaponry, stuffed swans, and local contemporary art. (☎563 07. Open daily May-Aug. 10am-7pm; last admission 6pm; Sept.-Apr. W-Su 11am-6pm. Admission 30EEK, students 15EEK. Admission with 2hr. audio tour in English, Estonian, Finnish, or Russian 60EEEK.) Test your **archery** skills outside, or rent a **boat** and paddle around the moat. (Archery daily 10am-5pm. 4 arrows 15EEK, 15min. 60EEK. Boats daily 11am-8pm; 15min. 30EEK, 30min. 50EEK, 1hr. 75EEK.) Inside the 1670 **town hall** *(raekoja)*, a gallery presents rotating exhibits of Estonian artwork, and the second floor has a recently reinstalled, 17th-century ceiling painting brought back from Tallinn. The biblical painting, whose creator remains anonymous, was discovered in an old house in Kuressaare after WWII. (☎332 66. Hours vary.) Kuressaare's most popular **beach** is directly behind the castle. On weekends in July, there's **live music** in the park around the castle. (Sa brass band, Su orchestra. Shows 6pm.) In late July, **Õlletoober**, a beer festival, peps up Leisi, while an **Opera Festival** takes over Kuressaare. At the end of June and beginning of July is the **Saaremaa Waltz Festival**, which features Finnish-style dancing and a deluge of tourists from Helsinki.

WEST SAAREMAA

Follow Rte. 78 from Kuressaare 30km toward **Kihelkonna** to reach the **Mikhli Farm Museum**, where you can climb inside a working windmill, which spins only on very gusty days. (☎45 46613. Open daily May-Sept. 10am-6pm. 15EEK, students 10EEK). One kilometer down the road, hang a left to reach the 13th-century **Kihelkonna Church.** Although there's a sign indicating that visitors can't enter the late 19th-century tower, the attendant will let you climb to the top, but you must pledge not to ring the bell. (☎45 46558. Open daily 10am-5pm). Backtrack along Rte. 102, crossing Rte. 78, and continue 8km along a bumpy dirt path to reach **Pidula Fish Farm ❸** (Pidula Veskitiigi Forellipüük), where the pond is swarming with trout. Cast a line, reel in your catch, and pay 100EEK per kg. They'll gut (extra 5EEK), salt (15EEK), and grill (40EEK) for you as well. You can also **rent your own island ❷**, in the center of the pond, where there's a one-room cabin. (☎45 46613; www.pidulakalakasvatus.ee. No running water. Reserve in advance. 350EEK per night.) It's another 7km to Rte. 101, where you'll hang a left toward **Mustjala**. The town **church**, 2km down the road, is a popular concert venue. Next door is a grocer, **Mustjala Kauplus.** (Open daily 9am-8pm. MC/V.) The road becomes unpaved; continue toward **Ninase** (4km), where a **windmill** decorated as a peasant greets you. In another 4km, you'll reach a fork, where a wooden sign reads "Kurli Talu." Sovietphiles: bear left to roam through an **abandoned Red Army training facility.** Head straight to the fishing village of **Tagaranna,** which offers views of the **Panga cliffs** on your right. The infamous 16th-century child sacrifice site has been immortalized on the back of the 100EEK note. From Tagaranna, it's 40km back to Kuressaare.

SOUTHWEST SAAREMAA

Fifty kilometers from Kuressaare down the narrow **Sõrve Peninsula,** Southwest Saaremaa's southernmost tip affords glimpses of Latvia, 25km south across the Baltic. Riding out of Kuressaare, you'll pass a string of sandy **beaches** 8-12km out of town; you won't find a private place to bathe in the sun, as locals line the shores on summer weekends. At Tehumardi (17km from Kuressaare), a giant concrete sword and rows of **memorials** mark the location of a 1944 WWII battle. Your last chance to stock up on bottled water and snacks is 4km farther at **Salme Kauplus** (open daily 8am-10pm), which also has a 24hr. (MC/V) **ATM** outside. After another 15km, the road is paved only sporadically.

MUHU

You can reach Muhu Island from the mainland via the Virtsu-Koivastu **ferry** route (30min.; 10-12 per day; 35EEK, students 10EEEK; cars 55-80EEK); motorists should reserve a spot with the Kuressaare booking office in advance. **Buses** run frequently from **Kuressaare** to Muhu. If you want to bike, bear in mind that you can't rent a bike once you leave Saaremaa. It's an ambitious but manageable 55km ride from Kuressaare to Väikese Väine Tamm, the 1896 causeway that connects Saaremaa to Muhu. After you cross, watch on your left for **Eeme Tuulik,** a windmill. (Open W-Su 10am-6pm. 5EEK, students 3EEK.) Buy 🌾**fresh bread** (23EEK) made from the flour it grinds. Past the windmill, go left toward Nautse; in 700m, you'll reach the Laasu **ostrich farm.** You can visit the birds and buy a giant egg (300EEK), which can be cracked open only with a drill or a hatchet. (☎452 81 48; www.jaanal-ind.ee) About 1km down the dirt path, turn left on the paved road to **Koguva** (4km), a well-preserved 19th-century fishing village and open air museum. (Open daily summer 10am-7pm; winter 10am-5pm.)

Vanatoa Tunsmitalu ❷ offers bright rooms in a stone longhouse with shared bath/sauna. (Breakfast included. 275EEK per person.) The adjacent **restaurant** ❹ (☎488 84) serves *solyanka* (40EEK), a thick Russian soup, and oven-baked eel in tartar sauce (180EEK). There's **bus** service (2 per day) here from Kuressaare and Koivastu. It's 6km back to Rte. 10, where you'll turn left toward Liiva; on your right after 5km, you'll see the 13th-century **Muhu Katariina Church.** Portions of the early-Gothic church's 13th-century murals are still visible through the layers of whitewash with which they were plastered during the Reformation. The trapezoidal tombstones are from the pagans who took refuge here when mainland Estonia was converted to Roman Catholicism. (Open daily 10am-6pm.) Next to the church, **Aki Kõrts** ❶ offers tiny, windowless cabins, a shared bath, and a common kitchen. (☎459 81 04. Laundry 25EEK per load. Cabins 2-person 250EEK, 4-person 500EEK.) Just down the road on your left, you'll find the well-stocked supermarket **Liiva Pood** (open daily 8am-10pm), with a 24hr. (MC/V) **ATM.** It's 65km back to Kuressaare; after 49km, you'll see a well-signed turn-off on the left to the Kaali meteorite **crater field** (Kaali meteoriidikraatrite rühm). A tranquil green pond now sits where 4,000 years ago, a 1,000-ton mass fell.

HIIUMAA

By restricting access to the island of Hiiumaa (HEE-you-ma; pop. 11,497) for 50 years, the Soviets unwittingly preserved many rare plant and animal species, and the island's traditional way of life. Locals still speak of the ghosts, giants, trolls, and devils of ancient legends.

More than two-thirds of all the plant species native to Estonia exist only on Hiiumaa. Due to this biodiversity, much of the island now belongs to the **West Estonian Islands Biosphere Reserve.** Hiking and camping are permitted and encouraged; just be sure to pick up info at the tourist office about off-limits regions. Motor vehicles are not allowed within 20m of the seashore and campfires and smoking are prohibited in some areas due to dry conditions.

KÄRDLA ☎(0)46

The Swedish settlers who stumbled across this sleepy spot on Hiiumaa's north coast named it "Kärrdal," meaning "lovely valley." Home to many more creeks and trees than houses, Kärdla (pop. 4118) is hardly an urban center, but with easy access to the beach and bike rentals, the town remains the capital of Hiiumaa.

🖃⑦ TRANSPORTATION AND PRACTICAL INFORMATION. Tiit Reisid, at Kärdla's **bus station,** Sadama 13, will help you navigate Hiiumaa's horrendous public transit system. (☎320 77; hiiumaa@tiitreisid.ee. Open M-F 7am-7pm, Sa-Su 7am-9am, 11am-3pm, 4am-7pm.) From Kärla, **buses** run west to **Kõrgessaare** and **Kõpu** (2-3 per day; 15-30EEK) and south to **Käina** (3-4 per day). A **ferry** runs from Hiiumaa's southern town of **Sõru** to **Triigi** on Saaremaa (1hr.; 20EEK, students 10EEK, bikes 15EEK, cars 70EEK). Bus fare to Kärdla from **Tallinn** includes a ferry **ticket** from **Rohükla** (on the mainland) to **Heltermaa,** Hiiumaa's easternmost port. For a **taxi,** call ☎314 47.

The island's **Tourist Information Center,** Hiiu 1, in **Keskväljak,** the main square, sells **maps** (5-40EEK) and the handy *Lighthouse Tour* guide (20EEK), available in English. (☎222 32; www.hiiumaa.ee. Open May-Sept. M-F 9am-6pm, Sa-Su 10am-3pm; Oct.-Apr. M-F 10am-4pm.) **Eesti Ühispank,** Keskväljak 7, **exchanges currency,** cashes **traveler's checks,** and has an **ATM.** (☎320 40; fax 320 47. Open M-F 9am-

4pm.) Rent **bikes** (150EEK per day) from **Kerttu Sport,** Sadama 15, across the bridge past the bus station. (☎321 30; fax 320 76. Open M-F 10am-6pm, Sa 10am-3pm.) The **pharmacy, Keskväljaku Apteek,** Põllu 1, is just off the main square. (☎321 37. Open M-F 9am-6pm, Sa 10am-2pm. MC/V.) Free **Internet access** is available at the cultural center, Rookopli 18 (☎321 82; open M-F noon-6pm, Su 10am-1pm), but you must reserve in advance. The **post office,** Keskväljak 3, is on the main square. (☎320 13. Open M-F 8am-5:30pm, Sa 8:30am-1pm.) **Postal Code:** 92412.

ACCOMMODATIONS AND FOOD. Every room at **Padu Hotel ❸,** Heltermaa 22, has a balcony, private bath, TV, phone, and Internet. It's a short walk from Kardla's main crossroads. Head toward Heltermaa and you'll see the hotel on the left. By bus, ask the driver to let you off at the Padu stop and backtrack 100m. (☎46 330 37; www.paduhotel.ee. Breakfast included. Singles 390EEK; doubles 650EEK; apartment with kitchen 750EEK, with sauna 850EEK. Reserve ahead. Prices drop 100EEK Sept.-Apr. MC/V.) **Eesti Posti Hostel ❷,** Posti 13, 5min. from the town center and close to the beach, has comfortable private rooms, shared baths, a kitchen, and a common room. Follow Uus from the center and turn right on Posti. (☎918 71. Sauna 25EEK per hr. Call ahead. Rooms May-Sept. 200EEK; Oct.-Apr. 150EEK.) The bubbly, English-speaking owner of **Nõmme Puhkemaja ❷,** Nõmme 30, offers one single (200EEK) and two doubles (400EEK) in a cozy cottage with shared bath, kitchen, and common room. From the main crossroads, head toward Korgessaare for 300m, turn left on Metsa and right on Nomme. (☎313 38; nommepm@hot.ee. Call ahead.)

Restoran Priiankru ❷, Sadama 4, just past the bus station, serves huge pizzas and hot meals. (☎225 85. Entrees 35-180EEK. Open daily 10am-10pm.) **Arteesia Kohvik ❶,** Keskväljak 5, has generous portions of meat and seafood. (☎321 73. Entrees 30-65EEK. Open M-Th 9am-11pm, F-Sa 9am-midnight, Su 11am-10pm.) It's above the small grocer **Toidukauplus.** (Open daily 9am-11pm.) Both Toidukauplus and **Konsum,** KesvAljak 1 (open daily 9am-9pm), stock the unskimmed Hiiumaa yogurt, ⨳**Anno** (7.20EEK per 500g).

SIGHTS. **Rannapark,** at the end of Lubjaahju, is a shallow **beach** with walking trails and a 14-hole miniature golf course. (Golf 20EEK. Open 10am-10pm.) The **Pikas Majas** (Long House) branch of the **Hiiumaa Museum,** Vabrikuväljak 8, was once home to cloth factory director Robert Eginhard von Unguru-Sternberg. (☎320 91. Open June-Aug. Tu-Sa 10am-5pm; Sept.-May M-F 10am-5pm, Sa 10am-2pm. English descriptions. 10EEK, students 5EEK.) Follow Rookopoli to the main crossroads to see a **memorial** to the Soviet soldiers who defeated the Germans in WWII. Nicknamed "Kivi Jüri" by the locals, it is jokingly called the last Russian soldier remaining on Hiiumaa. Turn left toward Heltermaa and, after 3km, bear left toward the airport to reach **Paluküla Church.** Built in 1820, it was a landmark for sailors—and later target practice for Soviet soldiers. You'll see hundreds of rusty bullet shells.

BIKING TO KÖPU. Heading west out of Kärdla toward Kõrgessaare, you encounter the spooky **Hill of Crosses** (Ristimägi) on your left after about 4km. The crosses, which seem to emerge from the surrounding forest, were placed here to commemorate the Hiiumaa Swedes who were deported to Ukraine by Catherine the Great in 1781. However, local folklore has it that the crosses are a result of two wedding parties who met on this spot but fought because the road was too narrow for both to pass. The bride of one couple and the groom of the other were killed in the squabble, but the families made the best of it and married the remaining bride and groom to each other.

ESTONIA

About 2km past the Hill of Crosses, a right turn leads to the **Tahkuna Lighthouse** (11km), built in Paris in 1874. After 4km, the road is unpaved. The lighthouse consistently failed to warn ships about the coast's shallow waters, but no one seemed to mind, since salvaging loot and rescuing passengers was quite profitable. On your left, before you reach the lighthouse, you'll find the **Tahkuna Defense Structures**, remnants of the gun pits and ammo bunkers built by locals and Soviet soldiers during WWII. If you want to explore the crumbling remains, bring a flashlight. Just past the lighthouse is the **Tahkuna Kivilaburint** (Tahkuna Labyrinth), built by the Hiiumaa Royal Association of Temperate Bee-Lovers in 1997. Legend has it that mariners who landed on Hiiumaa because of bad weather would enter the labyrinth, and by the time they emerged, the weather would have improved enough to complete their voyage. Near the lighthouse is a **bell** memorializing the children lost in the 1994 sinking of the ocean liner *Estonia.*

On the way back to the main road, detour to the **Mihkli Farm Museum,** off the lighthouse road, on a plot of land that's been cultivated since 1564. The museum has been popular ever since hosting a television show, **Farm,** in which several contestants from all over the Baltics had to live in 200-year-old farm conditions. Say hi to Yoshu, the resident goat. (☎320 91. Open daily May 15-Sept. 15. 10am-6pm. 10EEK, students 5EEK.)

Go back to the main road and turn right, heading toward Kõrgessaare. Down 7km, you'll see **Reigi Church,** built between 1800 and 1802 by Count Ungern Sternberg in memory of his son, Gustav Dietrich Otto. The nobleman scolded his son for accruing massive gambling debts; Gustav committed suicide soon after. After a few kilometers, turn right into Kõrgessaare, where you can take a break at excellent **Restoran Viinaköök ❸,** Sadama 2, in an old whiskey distillery. "Edgar's piggy-wiggy fillet" (90EEK) sounds too cute to eat, but this pork fillet, served with fried potatoes, vegetables, and mushroom sauce, is delectable. (☎933 37. Entrees 52-140EEK. Open daily noon-10pm.) Continue 20km past Kõrgessaare to reach Western Hiiumaa's most impressive site, the 16th-century **Kõpu Lighthouse.** The ticket office houses a **cafe** with **Internet access** (15EEK per 30min.). It hosts **concerts** every Friday in July at 9pm. Climb the lighthouse's narrow staircase to see how far you've come. (20EEK. Open daily 9am-10pm.)

KÄINA ☎(0)46

Käina (pop. 2500), southwest of Suuremõisa, is Hiiumaa's second most populous area and an excellent base for exploring the island's southern tip. From Vetsi Tall on Kassari, it's about 5km to Puulaiu Matkamaja and another 4km to Käina.

📧🔌 **TRANSPORTATION AND PRACTICAL INFORMATION.** The main **bus stop** in town is located at Hiiu mnt. 11, outside Tondilossi in the center of Käina. Buses (☎320 77; fax 320 65) run daily to **Haapsalu** and **Sõru,** where a ferry connects to **Saaremaa.** Local buses also go to **Kärdla** (25-30min., 3 per day). The morning bus from Käina (6:25am) makes a loop around **Kassari.** The best place for **tourist info** is the **cultural center,** Maë 2, which also has free **Internet access.** (☎362 31. Open M-F 10am-5pm, Sa 10am-2pm.) **Hansapank** and an **ATM** are on the first floor. (Open daily 8:30am-12:30pm and 1-4:30pm.)

🛏️🍴 **ACCOMMODATIONS AND FOOD.** From Käina's center, head 2km toward Emmaste on Hiiu mnt. and hang a left toward Kassari. After another 2km stretch, you'll be at **Puulaiu Matkamaja ❶,** where the friendly, English-speaking owner offers beautiful beachside cabins (130-180EEK per person) and tent space (no rentals; 50EEK per person), as well as bikes (100EEK/day) and boats (20EEK/hr). (☎291 70. Breakfast 40EEK. Call in advance.) **Tondilossi öömaja ❶,** Hiiu mnt. 11, in Käina center, has private rooms (230EEK) with shared bath. (☎363 37;

kylvi.rannu@mail.ee. Breakfast included. Open M-F 11:30am-6pm, Sa 10am-6pm.)
The family-run **pub ❶** next door serves hearty fare. (Entrees 25-38EEK.) Ask for a
room with a balcony at luxurious **Hotell Lillia ❺**, Hiiu mnt. 22. Rooms have private
bath and TV. (☎361 46; www.hot.ee/liiliahotell. Breakfast included. May-Sept. singles 700EEK, doubles 800EEK, triples 1000EEK; low season 500/600/1000. By reservation only Nov.-Feb.) The hotel's popular **restaurant ❸** offers steak with
chocolate sauce (140EEK), but locals prefer the shrimp and herb omelettes
(35EEK). Vegetarian options available. (☎361 46. Open daily 11am-11pm.)

◙ **SIGHTS.** Turn right on Hiiu mnt. toward the **Rudulf Tobias House-Museum** (R.
Tobiase Maja-Muuseum), Hiiu mnt. 33. The famous Estonian composer, who was
born here in 1873, started writing music when he was six years old. Captions are in
Estonian and Russian only, but the staff gives tours in English. (☎463 6586. Open
daily May 15-Sept. 15 11am-5pm. 10EEK, students 5EEK. Call in advance during
winter.) To pay for his son's piano, Tobias's father worked to build the organ at
Käina Church on the other side of town. A German tracer bullet destroyed the
house of worship during WWII; reconstruction projects are underway. To get to
the church, follow Hiiu through Käina past Lillia.

▨ **BIKING TO SUUREMÕISA AND KASSARI. Pühalepa Church,** in Suuremõisa,
contains the graves of the Baltic-German Count Ungern-Sternberg's family. The
Count wanted to acquire the entire island, but his shipping business was cut short
when he killed an employee and was banished to Siberia. From the church parking
lot, take a right onto a gravel road to the mysterious **Contract Stones** (Põhilise leppe
kivid). Some believe the stones were placed here in the 6th century to mark the
grave of a Swedish king, while others think sailors stacked the boulders as a symbol of their devotion to God. From the stones, head back to the highway and take
the next right onto an oak-lined alley. After about 200m, on the left, is the
Suuremõisa Palace. (☎943 91. Open July-Aug. M-F noon-6pm, Sa-Su 10am-3pm;
Sept.-June M-F 8am-4pm. 10EEK, students 5EEK.)

The ride to ▧**Kassari** (kah-SAH-ree; pop. 286), a tiny village on its own island
southeast of Käina, passes through some fantastic forest scenery. Roads from the
east and the west feed into Kassari; a circular ride allows you to see all the sights.
Follow Hiiu mnt. in the direction of Emmaste to reach the **Rudulf Tobias House
Museum** (R. Tobiase Maja-Muuseum), Hiiu mnt. 33, in the house where the composer and organist was born in 1873. (☎46 36586. Open daily May 15-Sept. 15
11am-5pm. 10EEK, students 5EEK.) If you enter Kassari from the west, the **Hiiumaa Museum,** in the middle of the island, is about a 7km ride from the turn to Kassari village. From the turn to Kassari, go about 6km and take a left at the signs for
the museum. The exhibit chronicles the history and wildlife of the island. (☎971
21. English captions. Open May 15-Sept. 15 daily 10am-5:30pm. 10EEK, students
5EEK.) Backtrack to the main road, head straight and veer right, and follow the
road to the most beautiful of the island's sights, **Sääretirp,** a 1.3m wide sandbar
lined with strawberry and juniper bushes. Legend holds that this 3km peninsula is
the remains of an ancient bridge between Hiiumaa and Saaremaa. Supposedly, a
giant named Leiger built the link so his brother Suur Tõll could visit.

INLAND ESTONIA

All roads inland from Tallinn lead to Tartu, the intellectual, historic, and nationalistic heart of Estonia. However, the countryside should not be overlooked. Visitors
can immerse themselves in the mystical town of Otepää or daytrip to Viljandi to
see the mountains and the medieval castle that protects the town.

TARTU
☎ (0)27

Tartu (pop. 110,000) bills itself as "the city of good thoughts," a fitting moniker for the intellectual capital of Estonia. It boasts a rich array of museums, a broad selection of performing arts events, and the top university in the country. Even as posh hotels and glittering casinos spring up in Tartu, it remains a college town.

▚ TRANSPORTATION

Trains: Vaksali 6 (☎615 68 51; www.edel.ee), at the intersection with Kuperjanovi, 1.5km from the city center. Although the station itself is closed, a few trains to **Tallinn** (2½-3hr., 3 per day, 70EEK).

Buses: Inter-city station, Turu 2 (☎477 227), on the corner of Riia and Turu, 300m southeast of Raekoja plats along Vabaduse. To: **Pärnu** (4hr., 20 per day, 50-95EEK); **Tallinn** (2-3hr., 46 per day, 50-80EEK); **Rīga, LAT** (5hr., 1 per day, 190EEK); **St. Petersburg, RUS** (9hr., 1 per day, 160EEK). 30-50% ISIC/ITIC discount on some routes. Info office open daily 8am-8pm. A complete bus schedule is available at ▨ www.bussireisid.ee; international connections schedule at www.eurolines.ee.

Public Transportation: Bus tickets 8EEK from kiosks, 10EEK on board. Buses #5 and 6 go from the train station to Raekoja plats and the bus station. Bus #4 travels up and down Võru. Buses #2 and 22 travel away from the river on Riia; #6, 7, and 21 head toward it; #3, 8, and 11 go both ways. Bus routes converge at the Kaubamaja on Riia.

Taxis: Barclay Taksod (☎420 420) or **Rivaal** (☎422 222). 10-15EEK base fare plus 6EEK per km; 25-35EEK min. fare.

✳ ❼ ORIENTATION AND PRACTICAL INFORMATION

From the bus station, take **Turu** along the river, cross **Riia,** and after three blocks go left on **Raekoja plats** to reach the **tourist office,** Raekoja plats 14 (☎442 111; www.tartu.ee). From the train station, get there by following **Kuperjanovi** two blocks; turn left on **Valikraavi** and follow it as it curves right. When it ends at **Kuuni,** take a left and turn right on **Raekoja plats.** The office arranges guides, rental cars, and **private rooms** (180EEK; 15EEK booking fee, outside Tartu 25EEK). It offers a **free map** of Tartu and free **Internet access** on one computer. (Open June-Aug. M-F 9am-5pm, Sa 10am-3pm; Sept.-May M-F 9am-6pm, Sa-Su 10am-3pm.)

Currency Exchange: Hansapank, Ülikooli 1 (☎447 230), cashes AmEx and Thomas Cook **traveler's checks** for 1% commission. **24hr. ATM** inside. Open M-F 9am-4pm.

American Express: Estravel, Vallikraavi 2 (☎440 300; www.estravel.ee). Open M-F 9am-6pm, Sa 10am-3pm.

Luggage Storage: In the bus station. 4-12EEK per bag per day. Open M-Sa 6am-9pm, Su 7am-9pm.

24hr. Pharmacy: Raekoja Apteek (☎433 528), on the Toomemägi side of Town Hall.

Internet Access: ZumZum, Küüni 2, below the ground-floor cafe. 8 quick connections for 25EEK per hr. **Elion,** Küüni 5b (www.elion.ee), in the glass building. 20EEK per hr. Open M-F 9am-7pm, Sa 10am-5pm. Free Internet at the **Tourist Info Center** and the **Estonian National Museum** (see p. 333). If you have your own laptop, use free wireless connections in the town square, **Wilde Irish Pub,** or anywhere with the **wifi.ee** sign.

Post Office: Vanemuise 7 (☎410 600). Open M-F 8am-7pm, Sa 9am-4pm. **Postal Code:** 51003.

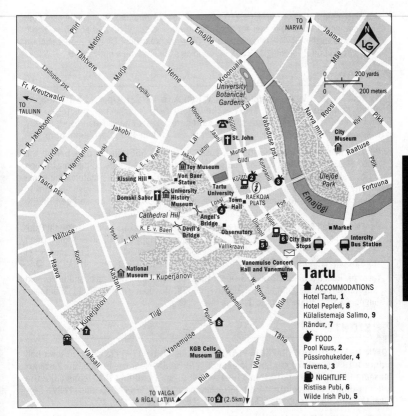

Tartu

♠ ACCOMMODATIONS
Hotel Tartu, 1
Hotel Pepleri, 8
Külalistemaja Salimo, 9
Rändur, 7

🍎 FOOD
Pool Kuus, 2
Püssirohukelder, 4
Taverna, 3

🍸 NIGHTLIFE
Ristiisa Pubi, 6
Wilde Irish Pub, 5

ESTONIA

🏠 ACCOMMODATIONS

Hostel Pepleri, Pepleri 14 (☎427 608; janikah@ut.ee). From the bus station, walk down Vabaduse pst. toward town, take a left on Vanemuise, then turn left on Pepleri. These Tartu University dorms are more luxurious than many upmarket hotels, with private showers, full kitchens, and satellite TV. Self-service laundry 20EEK (bring your own detergent), dryer 10EEK. Singles 250EEK; doubles 400EEK. ❷

Hotel Tartu, Soola 3 (☎314 300; www.tartuhotell.ee), across the parking lot from the intercity bus station. More charming inside than its Soviet-style exterior suggests. Comfy rooms feature private baths, telephones, and satellite TV. Singles 696-895EEK; doubles 995EEK; triples 1200EEK. 15% ISIC discount; 10% off for online bookings. Breakfast included. ❹ Space is always available in the **youth rooms,** so it's unlikely you'll have roommates. Common baths. 3 beds per room. Breakfast not included. 300EEK. ❷

Rändur, Kuperjanovi 66 (☎427 190; randur66@hot.ee), opposite the train station. Quality varies: the shared-bath single (300EEK) and double (400EEK) on the 1st fl. are nicer than the identically priced rooms upstairs. Doubles with private bath 500EEK.

Külalistemaja Salimo, Kopli 1 (☎470 888; salimo@khk.tartu.ee), 3km southeast of the bus station off Võru. Take bus #4 from Riia to Alasi. Cross Võru, and go left on Kopli. The rooms in this Soviet-style hostel are bright and spacious. Every 2 rooms share a bath. Reception 24hr. Singles 200EEK; doubles 400EEK; triples 600EEK. ●

◗ FOOD

Tartu Kaubamaja, a large **supermarket,** is at Riia 2. (☎476 231. Open M-F 10am-8pm, Sa 10am-6pm, Su 11am-5pm. MC/V.) The indoor *turg* (market), opposite the bus station on the corner of Vabaduse and Vanemuise, sells cheap fresh food, primarily meat and fish. (Open M-F 7:30am-5:30pm, Sa 7:30am-4pm, Su 7:30am-3pm.)

▨ **Püssirohukelder** (Gunpowder Cellar), Lossi 28 (☎333 555), in the park behind the Town Hall. Look for the 2 cannons outside. Catherine the Great ordered the construction of this storehouse to fortify Tartu. The "student menu" (35-48EEK) features the same hearty Estonian fare at significantly lower prices. Live music (Tu-Sa, usually from 9-10pm) often ends with table-top dancing. 0.5L *Gunpowder Red* house beer 25EEK. Open M-Th noon-2am, F-Sa noon-3am, Su noon-midnight. MC/V. ●

Pool Kuus (Half Past Five), Rüütli 1 (☎441 175), just off Raekoja plats. Traditional Estonian fare and Mexican food. 1L Saku is 25EEK during happy hour (5:30-8:30pm). Don't be too excited if the wall clocks say the hour of glee has arrived—all are permanently set to 5:30pm. Entrees 30-75EEK. 10% ISIC discount. Open daily 11am-4am. MC/V. ●

Taverna, Raekoja plats 20 (☎423 001). Large portions of meat, pasta, and pizza, and vegetarian options. Entrees 39-79EEK. 7.5% ISIC discount. Open M-Th 11:30am-midnight, F-Sa 11:30am-1am, Su 1-11pm. MC/V. ●

◉ SIGHTS

TOWN HALL SQUARE (RAEKOJA PLATS). In front of the 1775 Dutch-style **town hall** stands a 1998 statue of students kissing in a fountain. Near the bridge, the **Tartu Art Museum** (Tartu Kunstimuuseum) hosts exhibits in a building that leans (like the student population) a little to the left. *(Raekoja plats 18. ☎441 080. Open W-Su 11am-6pm. Museum 10EEK, students 5EEK; F free. Call ahead for a guided tour, 100EEK.)*

TARTU UNIVERSITY (TARTU ÜLIKOO). In 1632, the Swedish King Gustavus Adolfus II established the first university in Estonia (Academia Gustaviana) on this spot. It became Tartu University in 1919, when Estonia achieved independence from Russia. Russian, German, and Jewish students outnumbered ethnic Estonians at the school until the country gained independence following WWI. The **main building** of the University, featured on the back of the 2EEK bank note, includes an **assembly hall** that hosted concerts conducted by Liszt and Schumann. The **student lock-up** *(kartser)* in the attic was used until 1892 to detain students for breaking school rules. You can still see drawings and inscriptions on the walls. Tartu was the only university in the Russian empire allowed to have fraternities after the Great Northern War, and it used the privilege well: in 1870, the **Estonian National Awakening** began here with the founding of the Estonian Student Association (Eesti Üliõpilaste Selts). The Association's members were so central to Estonia's struggle for independence that the Estonian flag bears the frat's colors: blue, black, and white. *(Ülikooli 18. With the town hall behind you, follow Ülikooli right. ☎375 384. Open M-F 11am-5pm. Assembly Hall 10EEK, students 5EEK; student lock-up 5EEK/4EEK.)*

CATHEDRAL HILL (TOOMEMÄGI). The hill's central site is the once-majestic 15th-century **Domski Sabor** (Dome Cathedral; a.k.a. **Cathedral of St. Peter and Paul**), which is now in ruins. A sign warns: "Be cautious! The building is liable to fall down." An adjoining building houses the **Tartu University History Museum** (Museum

Historicum Universitatis Tartuensis), featuring an array of intriguing displays, among them a replica of the interior of a 1980s university dorm room, strewn with Russian rock posters, empty beer cans, and, inexplicably, a dead fish. Some captions are in English. *(Lossi 25. ☎375 674; www.ut.ee/ream. Open W-Su 11am-5pm. English or German tours 120EEK. 20EEK, students 5EEK.)* Near the church are two 17th-century Swedish cannons. **Kissing Hill** (Musumägi), once part of a prison tower, is the site of an ancient pagan sacrificial stone. Each April, the university choirs compete on the two bridges that lead to the east hump of Toomemägi. Women crowd onto the wooden **Angel's Bridge** (Inglisild), while men stand on the concrete **Devil's Bridge** (Kuradisild). Cathedral Hill is also littered with **statues.** Embryologist Karl Ernst von Baer, who graces the 2EEK banknote, is at the peak, awaiting the biology students who douse him with champagne annually.

OTHER SIGHTS. Don't miss the **Estonian National Museum** (Eesti Rahva Muuseum), which charts the evolution of Estonian culture from the Stone Age to the Soviet era. Among the USSR's strangest dictates: an order cracking down on the cultivation of tomatoes and roses, which were considered "elements of the bourgeois past." *(☎421 251. Open W-Su 11am-6pm. Permanent exhibit 12EEK, students 8EEK; with admission to temporary display 20EEK, students 14EEK; F free.)* Let your inner child loose at the **Tartu Toy Museum** (Tartu Manguasjamuuseum). Estonian ladies commonly played with dolls in the early 20th century, and you can too in the museum's massive **play room.** *(Lutsu 8. ☎746 1777, play room 736 1554; m.muudrum@neti.ee. Facing the Town Hall, turn right on Ruutli and hang a left on Lutsu. Open W-Su 11am-6; play room open W-Su 11am-4pm. 15EEK, students 10EEK. Play room 5EEK.)* The **KGB Cells Museum** (KGB Kongide muuseum) is housed in the Soviet spy agency's former South Estonian headquarters; prisoners in the tiny basement pens received just 200g of bread and a half-liter of cold soup once every three days. *(Riia 15b. ☎461 717; www.tartu.ee/linnamuuseum. Open Tu-Sa 11am-4pm. 5EEK, students 3EEK.)* The **Tartu City Museum** (Tartu Linnamuuseum) displays the table on which the 1920 Peace Treaty of Tartu was signed with the USSR, granting Estonia independence. *(Narva mnt. 23. ☎461 911; www.tartu.ee/linnamuuseum. English captions. Open Tu-Su 11am-6pm. Tours 120EEK. 20EEK, students 5EEK.)* **Tartu University Botanical Gardens** includes a greenhouse featuring an impressive collection of cacti and other plants not indigenous to Estonia. *(Lai 40. Open daily 7am-7pm. Greenhouse open daily 10am-5pm. Greenhouse 10EEK, students 5EEK.)*

🎵 🎭 ENTERTAINMENT AND FESTIVALS

For listings of cultural events in Tartu, go to http://kultuuriaken.tartu.ee. The **Vanemuise Concert Hall** (Vanemuise Kontserdimaja), Vanemuise 6 (☎377 530; www.vkm.ee), has classical concerts. The 1870 theater **Vanemuine,** Vanemuise 6 (☎440 165; www.vanemuine.ee), holds theater performances and operas, including some in English. **Eesti Suve Teater** (Summer Theater; ☎427 471) hosts performances in July and August in and outside the medieval church on Cathedral Hill. The second week of February brings the **Tartu Maraton,** which features a 63km cross-country ski race and non-competitive 31 and 16km group jaunts. (☎421 644; tartumaraton@tartumaraton.ee.) Everyone makes a port call during the **Hanseatic Days** in mid-June, when the Middle Ages return with craft fairs and folk dancing in Raekoja plats (www.tartu.ee/hansa). The **Freedom Parade,** a smaller version of Berlin's Love Parade, sets off on the second-to-last weekend August.

🎷 NIGHTLIFE

A bronze Oscar Wilde meets his Estonian counterpart Eduard Wilde outside the ⊠**Wilde Irish Pub,** Vallikraavi 4. The pub serves Irish and Estonian dishes (49-170EEK) and a variety of brews. A digital billboard registers every order of *Saku.*

ESTONIA

(☎309 764; www.wilde.ee. Vegetarian options. Tu karaoke, F-Sa live music 9 or 10pm-late. Open Su-Tu noon-midnight, W-Th noon-1am, F-Sa noon-3am. MC/V.) **Ristiisa Pubi** (Godfather Pub), Küüni 7, is just down the street from Raekoja plats. Crowds mob the outdoor terrace on summer nights, but inside, you're part of the family. It offers cheap Cuban cigars (from 25EEK) and a cocktail list as extensive as Al Capone's police record. (☎303 970; ristiisapubi@hot.ee. 0.5L *Saku* 25EEK. Th 10pm live music. Open Su-Tu 11am-midnight, W-Th 11am-1am, F-Sa 11am-3am.

▶ DAYTRIPS FROM TARTU

VILJANDI   ☎(0)43

Buses arrive from Tartu (1¼hr.; 20 per day; 30-50EEK; ISIC discount). The Tourist Info Center, Vabaduse Plats 6 (☎304 42; viljandi@visitestonia.com), gives out free maps, provides pamphlets with a walking tour, and has free Internet access. Open May 15-Sept. 15 M-F 9am-6pm, Sa-Su 10am-3pm; Sept. 16-May 14 M-F 10am-5pm, Sa 10am-2pm. To get to the castle from the bus station, take a left on Tallinna, and go through Vabaduse plats (the main square) toward the river. The road becomes Tasuja pst.; follow it to its end. The path just to your left leads to the castle. St. John's Church ☎330 00; viljandi.jaani@eelk.ee. Open daily May 15-Sept.15 10am-5pm; Sept. 15-May 15 M-F noon-1pm. Free. Museum ☎433 3316; www.muuseum.viljandimaa.ee. Open W-Su 10am-6pm. 20EEK, students 15EEK.

The town of Viljandi is along the road connecting Tartu and Parnu; almost all the main sites can be seen in a couple of hours, making it an ideal diversion. Its imposing **Order's Castle** (Ordulinnuse varemed), constructed by the Knights of the Sword in the 13th century, was once one of the largest in the Baltics, spanning three hilltops connected by bridges. Although the castle is now in ruins, the remainder offers a panorama of **Viljandi Lake** (Viljandi järv), the largest lake in the region. Around the back is the candy-colored 1879 **suspension footbridge** *(rippsild)*, which leads to town. In the central castle park is the 15th-century **St. John's Church** (Jaani kirik), Pikk 6. Its organ was shipped north to Poltsamaa when Soviet authorities converted the church into a granary in the mid-1950. Its replacement is used for concerts each Saturday at 2pm. In the center of town, the **Viljandi Museum**, Kindval Laidoneri plats 10, sports a collection of stuffed lynx and wolves and first-ever model of an Ericsson phone, dating from 1892. The 158-step staircase leading to the **lake** passes the statue of a **runner;** the names of past winners of hilly Viljandi's annual 15k foot-race are engraved on the nearby pillars.

OTEPÄÄ   ☎(0)76

Otepää (pop. 4800), the highest town in Estonia (152m), becomes a mecca for skiers in winter. In summer, it's ideal for cyclists and hikers. **Pühajärve** (Holy Lake) is famous for being conducive to deep meditation. Follow Pühajärve tee south from the town center and go left after 1km onto Mae to reach Otepää's **Energy Column** (Energiasammas), a 4m high wooden pole at a site selected by psychics for its positive vibe. Head back to Pühajärve tee and continue another 2.5km to reach Pühajärve, blessed by the Dalai Lama in 1991.

Downhill skiers head to **Vaike-Munamae Skiing and Snowboarding Centre** (☎521 4040; www.munakas.ee), 4km from the center of town. At a height of 70m and with its longest run just 500m, it's no Matterhorn, but it just might be the best skiing in the Baltics. Take a **taxi** (about 25EEK from the bus station) to get there. (Open Oct.-Apr. M-F noon-8pm, Sa and holidays 10am-8pm, Su 10am-5pm. Ski rental M-F 250EEK per day, Sa-Su 70EEK per day; snowboards 300EEK/90EEK; lift ticket 80EEK/200EEK, free with rental.) **O'Boy Snowtubing Park** is off Valga mountain, just south of the center. (☎52 150 40; www.snowtubing.ee. Open late Oct. to late Apr. 250EEK per day; M-F 50EEK per hr., Sa-Su 100EEK per hr.) **Karupesa Hotel** is right by the **Tehvandi Olympic Center** (☎766 5600; www.tehvandi.ee), where Estonia's national ski-jumping team trains; they'll make way for amateurs. Beneath Karupesa, you can rent cross-country skis (150EEK per day) at **Fansport** (☎050 77 537; www.fansport.ee. Bikes 200EEK per day. Reserve in advance.) The **TIC** offers a free guide to the region's skiing opportunities. **Club Tartu Marathon** has the area's longest cross-country track (63km), which opens to tourists in the second week of February. (☎742 1644; www.tartumaraton.ee.) Rent **waterbikes, rowboats,** and **canoes** (80EEK per hr.) at the lake's **beach.**

Buses run from **Tartu** (1hr.; 15 per day; 30EEK, 5EEK ISIC discount). The last bus from Otepää to Tartu leaves at 7:10pm on weekends, but as late as 10pm on other days. The **tourist office**, Lipuväljak 13 (☎612 00; otepaa@visitestonia.com), next to the bus station, offers a small **guidebook** with **maps** (10EEK). The office has free guides to **hiking, biking,** and **cross-country skiing.** (Open May 15-Sept. 15 M-F 9am-6pm, Sa-Su 10am-3pm; Sept. 16-May 14 M-F 9am-5pm, Sa 10am-3pm.) **Hansapank** (M-F 9am-5pm), on Lipuvaljak, **exchanges currency,** cashes Thomas Cook and AmEx **traveler's checks** for 1% commission, and has a 24hr. (MC/V) **ATM** outside. The **post office** is at Lipuvaljak 24. (☎767 9385; otepaapost@hot.ee. Open M-F 8am-6pm, Sa 8am-3pm.) **Postal Code:** 67405.

The TIC offers an extensive list of accommodations. Your best bet is **O-Maja ❶**, Parna 4, steps away from the center of town. From the TIC, turn left on Puhajarve tee and right on Parna. Enter from the backyard. It has bright, clean rooms with private baths. (☎501 4114; www.kite.ee/majutus. Breakfast 25EEK. Singles 200EEK; doubles 400EEK.) Follow Puhajarve tee south 2km from the center and turn left on Kolga tee to reach **Valge Kroon Guesthouse ❸**. The pleasant rooms have private baths. (☎766 284; www.valgekroon.ee. Breakfast included. Summer M-Th 500EEK, F-Su 600EEK; winter M-Th 600EEK, F-Su 700EEK.) Farther down Puhajarve tee, turn left on Tamme to reach the **Tamme Guesthouse ❷**, Tamme 6. It has cramped, three-bed dorms and more comfortable doubles with private baths. (☎766 3474; www.hot.ee/tammekylalistemaja. Dorms 250EEK; singles 400EEK; doubles 600EEK.) Otepää's small number of restaurants, pubs and nightclubs center on Lipuvaljak and Puhajarve within sight of the tourist office. Locals pack **Edgari Trahter ❶**, Lipuvaljak 3, which serves up cheap but hearty fare. (Entrees 15-55EEK. Open M-Sa 9am-10pm, Su 10am-10pm.) **Rae Kohvik ❶**, Lipuvaljak 15, in the same building as the TIC, offers an all-Estonian menu. (☎767 9565. Entrees 20-50EEK. Open M-F 7:30am-9pm, Sa-Su 7:30am-midnight. MC/V.)

ESTONIA

HUNGARY
(MAGYARORSZÁG)

FORINTS		
AUS$1 = 143.66FT	1000FT = AUS$6.95
CDN$1 = 152.80FT	1000FT = CDN$6.54
EUR€1 = 246.86FT	1000FT = EUR€4.05
NZ$1 = 131.54FT	1000FT = NZ$7.60
UK£1 = 368.49FT	1000FT = UK£2.71
US$1 = 201.84FT	1000FT = US$4.94

Communism was a mere blip in Hungary's 1000-year history of repression and renewal, and today the nation embraces its new-found capitalist identity. A must-see destination in Eastern Europe, hip and vibrant Budapest remains Hungary's social, economic, and political capital. Be sure to venture beyond this Westernized cultural center to the charming cobblestone towns and luscious wine valleys nestled in Hungary's northern hills, the cowboy plain in the South, and the luxurious beach resorts in the East. Otherwise, you'll have seen the heart of Hungary, but missed its soul entirely.

HISTORY

THE MIGHTY MAGYARS. In the 3rd century BC, **Celtic tribes** invaded what is now Hungary. They were followed by the **Romans,** who founded the provinces of Pannonia and Dacia, which they held until the AD 5th century. The **Magyars,** Central Asian warriors, arrived in AD 896. Led by **Prince Árpád,** they conquered the middle Danube. Árpád's descendant, **Stephen I,** was made king on Christmas Day, 1000. Canonized in 1083, Stephen is considered the founder of modern Hungary.

FACTS AND FIGURES

OFFICIAL NAME: Republic of Hungary

CAPITAL: Budapest (pop. 1.9 million)

POPULATION: 10.3 million (90% Magyar, 4% Roma, 3% German, 2% Serb, 1% other)

LANGUAGES: Hungarian (Magyar)

CURRENCY: 1 forint (Ft) = 100 Fillérs

RELIGIONS: 67.5% Roman Catholic, 20% Calvinist, 5% Lutheran, 7.5% atheist and other

LAND AREA: 92,340km²

CLIMATE: Continental

GEOGRAPHY: Mostly plains; hills and low mountains on Slovak border

BORDERS: Austria, Croatia, Romania, Serbia and Montenegro, Slovak Republic, Slovenia, Ukraine

ECONOMY: 62% Service, 34% Industry, 4% Agriculture

GDP: US$13,300 per capita

COUNTRY CODE: 36

INTERNATIONAL DIALING PREFIX: 00

THOSE GOLDEN YEARS. As Hungary grew stronger, the nobles forced the king to sign the **Golden Bull** (1222), which granted rights to the people and restricted monarchical power. Then, a devastating Mongolian invasion swept through, and by 1301 the Árpáds' reign ended. Leadership changed in the 13th and 14th centuries, and Hungary entered a **Golden Age** of economic and military prowess.

ONLY THE GOOD DIE YOUNG. Royal infighting weakened the country and tarnished its golden hue. In the mid-15th century, throne contenders imprisoned Mátyás Hunyadi, known as **Matthias Corvinus** (1458-1490). Nobles freed and coronated Corvinus, who reigned during Hungary's renaissance. He supported education and cultivated a huge library, but later rulers undid most of his reforms. The peasant **rebellion** in 1514 was unsuccessful, but its repercussions lingered for centuries. The **Turks** conquered the Hungarians at **Mohács** in 1526.

EMPIRE FALLS. Conflict among the Protestants, Ottomans, and Holy Roman Empire plagued Hungary for the next 150 years, until the Austrian **Hapsburgs** took over in the early 17th century. A war of independence began in 1848, led in spirit by young poets **Sándor Petőfi** and **Lajos Kossuth**. They convinced the **Diet** (Parliament) to pass reforms known as the **April Laws**. Kossuth's state held out for a year, but in 1849, Hapsburg Emperor Franz Josef I regained Budapest with the support of Russia's Tsar Nicholas I. Though heavily repressed, Hungary, led by **Ferenc Deák,** did make some headway, as the nation was granted its own government in the **Compromise of 1867.** Thus, the **dual monarchy** of the **Austro-Hungarian Empire** was born. Magyarization provoked opposition among Romanians, Serbs, Croats, and Slovaks. These divisions erupted in WWI and resulted in the permanent dissolution of the Austro-Hungarian Empire. After the war, Hungary lost two-thirds of its territory to the Allies in the 1920 **Treaty of Trianon.**

APOCALYPSE NOW. As the empire collapsed, a democratic revolution emerged in 1918 and was replaced in less than six months by the communist Hungarian Republic of Councils under Bolshevik **Béla Kun.** Counter-revolutionary forces eventually took control and brutally punished those involved with the communist administration. **Admiral Miklós Horthy** settled in for a rather paradoxical 24 years of dictatorial control (1920-1944) over a (hardly) democratic government. A tentative alliance with Hitler in **WWII** led to Nazi occupation and the near-total destruction of Budapest during the two-month Soviet siege of 1945. Two-thirds of Hungary's **Jews,** whose pre-war population numbered close to one million, were murdered in the Holocaust. Nearly all survivors fled the country.

COME ON RISE UP. In 1949 Hungary became a people's Republic under **Mátyás Rákosi.** Rákosi tied Hungary to the **USSR;** the country often served as a "workshop" for Soviet industry. Rákosi lost control in the violent **1956 Uprising,** in Budapest, in which **Imre Nagy** declared a neutral, non-Warsaw Pact government. Soviet troops crushed the revolt and executed Nagy and his supporters.

FIGHT FOR YOUR RIGHTS. Over the next three decades, Nagy's replacement, **János Kádár,** oversaw the partial opening of borders and a rising standard of living. Inflation halted progress in the 1980s, but democratic reformers in the Communist Party pushed Kádár aside in 1988; they sought freedom and a market economy. Hungary broke free of the Soviet orbit in 1989, and in 1990 power was transferred to the Hungarian Democratic Forum in the first free elections. Slow progress, inflation, and unemployment eroded the Forum's popularity. In 1998, right-of-center **Viktor Orban** succeeded socialist **Gyula Horn** as Prime Minister.

TODAY. Hungary has come a long way since communism. Its government is led by a **president** who serves a five-year term as commander-in-chief of the armed forces but has authority over little else. The **National Assembly** elects the president, the **prime minister,** and the **cabinet ministers,** who comprise the Council of Ministers. Members are elected to Parliament every four years. Since 2000, **Ferenc Mádl** has been president. **Péter Medgyessy** was prime minister from 2002 to 2004. Four **parties** participate regularly in parliament: the Hungarian Democratic Forum, the Hungarian Civic Alliance, the Alliance of Free Democrats, and the Hungarian Socialist Party. After 1994, Hungary recouped economic and social stability as its borders opened to the West. Today, wage problems and inflation are of diminishing concern, and Hungary has managed to stem unemployment and stabilize GDP growth. The country is politically stable and entered the **European Union (EU)** on May 1, 2004. Though Hungary is ruled internally by a Socialist-Liberal coalition, the conservative opposition won the majority of Hungary's seats in the recent European parliamentary elections.

PEOPLE AND CULTURE

LANGUAGE

Hungarian, a **Finno-ugric** language, is distantly related to Turkish, Estonian, and Finnish. After Hungarian and **German, English** is Hungary's third language. Almost all young people know some English. *"Hello"* is often used as an informal greeting. Coincidentally, *"Szia!"* (sounds like "see ya!") is another greeting—friends will often cry: "Hello, see ya!" A few starters for pronunciation: *"c"* is pronounced "ts" as in "pots," *"cs"* is "ch" as in "which," *"gy"* is "dy" as in *"adieu,"* *"ly"* is "y" as in "yak," *"s"* is "sh" as in "shard," *"sz"* is "s" as in "sell," *"zs"* is "zh" as in "fusion," and *"a"* is "a" as in "paw." The first syllable is always stressed. For a phrasebook and glossary, see **Glossary: Hungarian,** p. 951.

FOOD AND DRINK

HUNGARY	❶	❷	❸	❹	❺
FOOD	under 400Ft	400-800Ft	801-1300Ft	1301-2800Ft	over 2800Ft

Hungarian food is more flavorful than many of its Eastern European culinary cohorts, with many spicy meat dishes. **Paprika,** Hungary's chief agricultural export, colors most dishes red. In Hungarian restaurants *(vendéglő* or *étterem),* meals often begin with *halászlé,* a spicy fish stew. Or, try *gyümölcsleves,* a cold fruit soup with whipped cream. The Hungarian national dish is *bográcsgulyás,* a soup of beef, onions, green pepper, tomatoes, potatoes, dumplings, and plenty of paprika. *Borjúpaprikás* is veal with paprika and potato-dumpling pasta. For **Vegetarians** there is tasty *rántott sajt* (fried cheese) and *gombapörkölt* (mushroom stew). Delicious Hungarian fruits and vegetables abound in summer. Vegetarians should also look for *salata* (salad) and *sajt* (cheese), as these will be the only options in many small-town restaurants. *Túrós rétes* is a chewy pastry filled with sweet cottage cheese, while *Somlói galuska* is a rich, rum-soaked sponge cake of chocolate, nuts, and cream. The Austrians stole the recipe for *rétes* and called it "strudel," but this concoction is as Hungarian as can be.

Hungary produces an array of fine wines (see sidebar, p. 373). The northeastern towns of Eger and Tokaj produce famous red and white wines, respectively. *Sör* (Hungarian **beer**) ranges from first-rate to acceptable. Lighter beers include *Dreher Pils, Szalon Sör,* and licensed versions of *Steffl, Gold Fassl, Gösser,* and *Amstel.* Hungary also produces *pálinka,* which resembles brandy. Among the best-tasting are *barackpálinka* (like apricot schnapps) and *körtepálinka* (pear brandy). *Unicum,* advertised as the national drink, is an **herbal liqueur** that was used by the Hapsburgs to cure digestive ailments.

CUSTOMS AND ETIQUETTE

Rounding up the bill as a **tip** is standard for everyone from waiters to cab drivers to hairdressers. Check the bill: gratuity may be included. Waiters expect foreigners to tip 15%, but locals never give more than 10%. When the waiter brings the bill, pay immediately. Hand your tip to your server. At meals, **toasts** are common and should be returned. *Egészségünkre* (ay-gash-ay-goonk-gre; "to our health") is a useful word. Bargaining over open-air-market goods and taxi fares is appropriate. **Clothing** is westernized—jeans, skirts, and t-shirts are the norm. In cities, women often dress in tight or revealing attire. Religious sites may require covered knees and shoulders. **Smoking** seems to be the national pastime.

THE ARTS

LITERATURE. The writers who lived through the Revolution of 1848 greatly impacted the country's literature. The Populist, anti-Romantic **Sándor Petőfi** fueled nationalistic rhetoric that drove the revolution. **Ferenc Kazinczy** promoted national literature in the Hungarian language instead of Latin. **Mór Jókai's** nationalism and down-to-earth tone endeared him to 19th-century readers. Hungarian literature gained focus with the founding of the *Nyugat* literary journal in 1908, and with the work of avant-garde poet and artist **Lajos Kassák,** whose subject matter was working-class life. **Attila József,** an influential poet, integrated politics and art when he merged Freudian thought with Marxism. After WWII, communists forced Magyar writers to adopt Socialist Realism, but a new generation developed individual styles more freely.

HUNGARY

FINE ARTS AND MUSIC. The growth of fine arts in Hungary was significantly influenced by artistic evolution in the rest of Europe. Yet, Hungary was sure to add its own character. Renaissance and medieval frescoes on buildings were the most widely practiced art forms, later giving birth to historical painting and portraiture. The 20th century saw **Lajos Kassák** and **László Moholy-Nagy** emerge as avant-garde painters, and **Miklós Jancsó** and **István Szabó** stand as pioneers in Hungarian **film.** One staple of Hungarian culture is **folk dancing. Csárdás,** the national dance, includes a women's circle and men's boot-slapping dances. All begin with a slow section *(lassú)* and end in a fast section *(friss).* Dancers don embroidered costumes and perform music in double time.

Hungary has gained the most international acclaim for its **music.** The greatest piano virtuoso of his time, **Ferenc Liszt** (1811-1886), is the most prolific musician in Hungary's history. His contributions range from advancing piano composition technique to inventing the symphonic poem. Though he spoke German, not Hungarian, his heritage shines through in his Hungarian Rhapsodies, 19 pieces based on Hungarian folk music. Similarly, **Béla Bartók** (1881-1945) was noted for his use of folk material to create music that expressed a strong sense of nationalism. His most famous works include string quartets and the *Concerto for Orchestra.*

CURRENT SCENE. In 2002, **Imre Kertész** won Hungary's first Nobel Prize in Literature for his work drawing on experiences as a teen in Nazi concentration camps. Less concerned with historical issues than with the postmodern exploration of words, the work of **Péter Esterházy** marks a new cultural movement in Hungarian literature. In the architectural arena, organic influences are a new source of inspiration. **Imre Makovecz's** pavilion at the Seville Expo won him international acclaim in 1992. **Roma** music has gained increasing popularity.

HOLIDAYS AND FESTIVALS

NATIONAL HOLIDAYS IN 2005	
January 1 New Year's Day	**August 20** Constitution Day
March 15 National Day	**October 23** Republic Day
April 11-12 Easter holiday	**November 1** All Saints' Day
May 1 Labor Day	**December 25-26** Christmas
May 30-31 Pentecost	

Europe's largest rock festival, **Sziget (Pepsi Island) Festival,** hits Budapest each August, featuring rollicking crowds and international superstar acts. Eger's fabulous **World Festival of Wine Songs** celebration of kicks off in late September, bringing together boisterous choruses and world-famous vintages.

ADDITIONAL RESOURCES

GENERAL HISTORY

A History of Hungary, ed. by Peter Sugar, Peter Hanak, and Tibor Frank (1994). More exhaustive than most books of its kind in its treatment of Hungarian history.

A History of Modern Hungary 1867-1994, by Jorg K. Hoensch (1996). Provides a brief summary of Hungarian history.

FICTION AND NONFICTION

The Bridge at Andau, by James Michener (1988). A gripping account of the 1956 Uprising when the Hungarians fled from the Russians into Austria.

Embers, by Sándor Márai (1942). This recently rediscovered masterpiece depicts the reunion of two old men who were boyhood friends.

Fateless, by Imre Kertész (1975). Kertész's Nobel Prize-winning work based on his experiences as a 15-year-old in Auschwitz and Buchenwald.

The Melancholy of Rebirth: Essays from Post-Communist Central Europe 1989-1994, by György Konrád (1995). Humorous and depressing views of communism in Hungary.

HUNGARY ESSENTIALS

ENTRANCE REQUIREMENTS

Passport: Required for all travelers.

Visa: Not required for stays under 90 days for citizens of Australia, Canada, Ireland, New Zealand, the UK, and the US.

Letter of Invitation: Not required for citizens of Australia, Canda, Ireland, New Zealand, the UK, and the US.

Inoculations: Recommended up-to-date on DTaP (diphtheria, tetanus, and pertussis), Hepatitis A, Hepatitis B, MMR (measles, mumps, and rubella), Polio booster, and Typhoid.

Work Permit: Required of all foreigners planning to work in Hungary.

Driving Permit: Required for all those planning to drive in Hungary.

DOCUMENTS AND FORMALITIES

EMBASSIES AND CONSULATES

Embassies and consulates of foreign countries in Hungary are all in **Budapest** (see p. 349). Hungary's embassies and consulates abroad include:

Australia: 17 Beale Crescent, Deakin, ACT 2600 (☎2 6282 3226; fax 6285 3012).

Austria: Bankgasse 4-6, A-1010 Vienna (☎378 03 00; kom@huembvie.at).

Canada: 299 Waverley St., Ottawa, ON K2P 0V9 (☎613-230-2717; www.docuweb.ca/Hungary). **Consulate:** 121 E. Bloor St., # 1115, Toronto, ON, M4W 3M5 (☎416-923-8981; fax 923-2732).

Ireland: 2 Fitzwilliam Pl., Dublin 2 (☎1 661 2902; http://www.kum.hu/dublin)

New Zealand: The Embassy in Australia covers New Zealand. **Consulate-General:** 37 Abbott St., Wellington 6004 (☎4 973 7507; www.hungarianconsulate.co.nz).

UK: 35 Eaton Pl., London SW1X 8BY (☎020 7201 3440; www.huemblon.org.uk).

US: 3910 Shoemaker St. NW, Washington, D.C. 20008 (☎202-364-8218; www.hungaryemb.org). **Consulate:** 223 East 52nd St., New York, NY 10022 (☎212-752-0661; http://www.kum.hu/newyork/).

VISA AND ENTRY INFORMATION

Citizens of Australia, Canada, Ireland, New Zealand, the UK, and the US can visit Hungary without **visas** for up to 90 days, assuming they carry a passport, which does not expire within six months of the trip's end, and intend not to work. If you do need a visa, consult your embassy. There is no fee for crossing a Hungarian **border.** In general, border officials are efficient; plan on 30min. crossing time.

GETTING AROUND

Hungary's **national airline, Malév,** flies to the Hungary area from London, New York, and other major cities. Many international airlines arrive in Budapest.

Most **trains** (*vonat*) pass through Budapest, and are generally reliable and inexpensive. Several types of **Eurail passes** are valid in Hungary. Check schedules and fares at ⌨**www.elvira.hu.** *Személyvonat* trains have many local stops and are excruciatingly slow; *gyorsvonat* trains, listed in red on schedules, move much faster for the same price. Large towns are connected by blue *expressz* lines; these air-conditioned *InterCity* trains are fastest. A *pótjegy* (seat reservation) is required on trains labeled "R," and violators face a hefty fine. A basic vocabulary will help you navigate: *érkezés* (arrival), *indulás* (departure), *vágány* (track), and *állomás* or *pályaudvar* (station, abbreviated *pu*). The *peron* (platform) is rarely indicated until the train approaches the station, and will be announced in Hungarian. Many stations are not marked; ask the conductor what time the train will arrive (point at your watch and say the town's name).

Buses, which are cheap and clean but crowded, are best for travel between outer provincial centers. Purchase tickets on board, and arrive early for a seat. In larger cities, buy tickets at the kiosk, and they will be punched when you get on. There's a fine if you're caught without a ticket. A ferry runs down the Danube from Vienna to Budapest. For more info, contact **Utinform** (☎322 36 00).

Taxi prices should not exceed the following: 6am-10pm base fare 200Ft, 240Ft per km, 60Ft per min. waiting; 10pm-6am maximum rates are 300Ft/280Ft/70Ft. Beware of taxi scams. Before getting in, check that the meter is working and ask how much the ride will cost. Taxis ordered by phone charge less than those hailed on the street. To **drive** in Hungary, carry your **International Driving Permit** and your registration and insurance papers. Drinking and driving is illegal. For info on road conditions, contact ☎117 11 73 in Budapest, elsewhere 322 22 38. Emergency phones are every 2km on Hungarian motorways. For 24hr. English assistance, contact the **Magyar Autóklub** (**MAK;** in Budapest ☎252 80 00, elsewhere ☎088). Biking terrain varies. The northeast is topographically varied; the south is flat. Roads are usually well paved. *Let's Go* does not recommend **hitchhiking.**

TOURIST SERVICES AND MONEY

Tourinform has branches in most cities and is a useful first-stop **tourist service.** Tourinform doesn't make reservations but will find vacancies, especially in university dorms and private *panzió*. Agencies also stocks maps and provide abundant local information; employees generally speak **English** and German. Most **IBUSZ** offices throughout the country book private rooms, exchange money, and sell train tickets, but they are generally better at assisting in travel plans than at providing info. Pick up *Tourist Information: Hungary* and the monthly entertainment guides *Programme in Hungary* and *Budapest Panorama* (all free and in English). Local agencies may be staffed only by Hungarian- and German-speakers, but they are generally very helpful and offer unique local tips.

The national currency is the **forint (Ft),** which is divided into 100 **fillérs,** which have mostly disappeared from circulation. Hungary has a **Value Added Tax** Rate (VAT) of 25%. **Inflation** hovers around 5.3%, so expect price increases. Currency exchange machines are slow but offer good rates, and Banks, such as **OTP Bank** and **Postabank,** offer the best exchange rates for traveler's checks. Never change money on the street, and avoid extended-hour exchange offices, which have poor rates. Watch for scams: the maximum legal commission for cash-to-cash exchange is 1%. **ATMs** are common; major **credit cards** are accepted in many establishments. Standard business hours in Budapest are Monday to Thursday 9am-4pm, Friday 9am-1pm. Businesses generally close on holidays.

HEALTH AND SAFETY

 EMERGENCY NUMBERS: Police: ☎ 107 **Fire:** ☎ 105 **Ambulance:** ☎ 104.

In Budapest, **medical assistance** is easily obtained. Embassies have lists of Anglophone doctors, and most hospitals have English-speaking doctors on staff. Outside Budapest, try to bring a Hungarian speaker to the hospital with you. **Tourist insurance** is valid—and necessary—for many medical services. In an emergency, call ☎ **112. Tap water** is usually clean; the water in Tokaj is poorly purified. Buy **bottled water** at most food stores. Public bathrooms vary in cleanliness: pack soap, towel, and 30Ft for the attendant. Carry **toilet paper,** as many hostels do not provide it, and you get a single square in public restrooms. Gentlemen should look for *Férfi,* and ladies for *Nõi* signs. Many **pharmacies** (gyógyszertár) stock Western brands, tampons, and condoms. 24hr. pharmacies are common.

Violent **crime** is low, but in Budapest and other large cities, foreign tourists are targets for petty thieves and pickpockets. Check prices before getting in taxis or ordering food or drinks. In an emergency, your embassy will likely be more helpful than the **police.** Lone **women,** the elderly, and families with children all travel in Hungary. **Minorities** are generally accepted, though dark-skinned travelers may encounter prejudice. Though homosexuality has been legal since 1961, **GLBT** travelers may face serious discrimination, especially outside Budapest.

ACCOMMODATIONS

Tourism is developing rapidly, and rising prices make hostels attractive. Hostels are usually large enough to accommodate summer crowds, and HI cards are often useful. Many hostels can be booked through Express (☎ 266 32 77), a student travel agency, or through local tourist offices. From June to August, many university dorms become hostels. These may be the cheapest options in smaller towns, as hostels are less common outside Budapest. Locations change annually; inquire at Tourinform and call ahead. Guesthouses and pensions *(panzió)* are more common than hotels in small towns. Private rooms booked through tourist agencies are sometimes a cheaper option. Singles are scarce—it's worth finding a roommate, as solo travelers must often pay for doubles. Check prices: agencies may try to rent you their most expensive rooms. Outside Budapest, the best offices are region-specific (e.g., Eger Tourist in Eger). They will often make advance reservations for your next stop. After staying a few nights, make arrangements directly with the owner to save your agency's 20-30% commission.

Over 300 **campgrounds** are sprinkled throughout Hungary. Most open from May to September and charge for unfilled spaces in their bungalows. For more information, consult *Camping Hungary,* a booklet available in most tourist offices, or contact Tourinform in Budapest (see **Tourist And Financial Services,** p. 348).

KEEPING IN TOUCH

Hungarian **mail** is usually reliable; airmail *(légiposta)* takes one week to 10 days to the US and Europe. Mailing a letter costs about 36Ft domestically and 140-150Ft internationally. Those without permanent addresses can receive mail through

HUNGARY

Poste Restante. Use Global Priority mail, as it is reliable. Address envelopes: Alka (first name) TANDON (last name), POSTE RESTANTE, Városház u. 18 (post office address), 1052 (postal code) Budapest (city), Hungary.

For **intercity calls,** wait for the tone and dial slowly; "06" goes before the phone code. **International calls** require red or blue phones. The blue phones tend to cut off calls after 3-9min. Phones often require *telefonkártya* (phone cards). The best ones for international calls are **Neophone,** available at the post office, and **Micronet,** available at Fotex stores. Calls to Australia, Canada, and Ireland cost 45-50Ft per min., to the US 35Ft per min., to the UK 39Ft per min. Make direct calls from Budapest's phone office. International access numbers include: **AT&T Direct** (☎06 800 01111); **Australia Direct** (☎06 800 06111); **BT Direct** (☎0800 89 0036); **Canada Direct** (☎06 800 01211); **MCI WorldPhone** (☎06 800 01411); **NZ Direct** (☎06 800 06411); and **Sprint** (☎06 800 01877).

Internet is readily available in major cities. The Hungarian keyboard differs significantly from English-language keyboards. After logging on, click the "Hu" icon at the bottom right corner of the screen to switch the setting to "Angol." Look for free Internet access at hostels. Most Internet cafes charge 150-300Ft per hr.

BUDAPEST   ☎(06)1

A vibrant mix of East and West, medieval and modern, Budapest (pop. 1.9 million) is one of the most unique and exhilarating cities in Europe. While other parts of Hungary seem uninterested in adopting the hectic pace of contemporary Western life, Budapest has steamrolled into the nucleus of the very chic, earning the name "Paris of the East." Once two cities, Budapest was born in 1872 with the union of Buda and Pest. It became the Hapsburg Empire's number-two city. Although it was ravaged by WWII, proud Hungarians rebuilt their city from rubble and restored its majesty. It was through the same pride that Budapest weathered the Soviet invasion. Indeed, even 40 years of communism couldn't kill the Maygar spirit. That spirit still resonates through the streets today as this exciting and lively city reassumes its place as a major European capital.

■ INTERCITY TRANSPORTATION

Flights: Ferihegy Airport (☎296 9696, departures 296 7000, arrivals 296 8000). **Malév** (Hungarian Airlines; reservations ☎235 3888). To the center, take **bus #93** (20min., every 15min. 4:55am-11:20pm, 150Ft), then take M3 to Kőbánya-Kispest (15min. to Deák tér, in downtown Budapest). To catch this bus, turn right from Terminal A or left from B and find the "BKV Plusz Reptér Busz" sign. Purchase tickets from the kiosk in Terminal B or the machines outside Terminal A. Alternatively, take the **Airport Minibus** (☎296 8555) to hotels or hostels. Service runs 24hr.; call 1 day in advance for flights leaving Budapest. One-way 2100Ft.

Trains: For a complete listing of Hungarian rail schedules, go to the useful www.mav.hu. (International ☎461 5500, domestic 461 5400.) The main stations—**Keleti pu., Nyugati pu.,** and **Déli pu.**—are also Metro stops. Train stations are favorite haunts of thieves and pickpockets, so be careful. Most international trains arrive at and depart from Keleti pu. To: **Belgrade, SMN** (7hr., 2 per day, 6605Ft); **Berlin, GER** (12-15hr.; 2 per day; 26367Ft, 1500Ft reservation fee); **Bucharest, ROM** (14hr., 5 per day, 16000Ft); **Prague, CZR** (8hr., 4 per day, 11700Ft); **Vienna, AUT** (3hr.; 17 per day; 6000Ft, 700Ft reservation fee); **Warsaw, POL** (11hr.; 2 per day; 13899Ft, 2000Ft reservation fee). The daily **Orient Express** stops on its way from **Paris, FRA** to **Istanbul, TUR.** Trains depart from Budapest to almost all destinations in the country. Check

HUNGARY

www.elvira.hu for schedules and some prices or ask at the info booths in the stations. For **student discounts,** show your ISIC and tell the clerk "diák." On domestic trains an ISIC is technically invalid, but ask anyway.

International Ticket Office: Keleti pu. Open daily 8am-7pm; info desk 24hr. Nyugati pu. Open daily 5am-9pm.

MÁV Hungarian Railways, VI, Andrássy út 35 (☎461 5500; www.mav.hu). Branch offices at all train stations. Sells domestic and international tickets. Check the website for prices. Often 30-40% off international fares with ISIC. Open M-F 9am-5pm.

Carlson Wagonlit Travel, V, Dorottya u. 3 (☎483-3384; agent@carlsonwagonlit.hu), off Vörösmarty tér. Open M-Th 9am-5pm, F 9am-3:30pm. AmEx/MC/V.

Buses: Most buses to Western Europe depart at **Volánbusz main station,** V, Erzsébet tér (☎117 2966, international tickets 485-2100; www.volanbusz.hu). M1, 2, or 3: Deák tér. Buses to closer countries depart from **Népstadion,** Hungária körút 48/52. (☎252 1896. Cashier open 5:30am-6pm.) M2: Népstadion. To: **Berlin, GER** (14½hr., 5 per week, 19,900Ft); **Prague, CZR** (8hr., 4 per week, 6990Ft); **Vienna, AUT** (3-3½hr., 5 per day, 5790Ft). Buses to the Danube Bend depart outside **Árpád híd** Metro station.

🞧 ORIENTATION

Budapest was originally Buda and Pest, two cities separated by the **Danube River** (Duna). The modern capital preserves the distinctive character of each. On the west side, **Buda's** tree-lined streets wind through the cobblestone **Castle District** on the way to the hilltop citadel. On the east side, grid-like avenues, shopping boulevards, and the Parliament spread over the commercial center of **Pest.** In contrast to Buda's backroads, Pest's layout is intricate but easily navigable with the efficient transportation system and a good map. Three main bridges tie Budapest together: **Széchenyi Lánchíd** connects **Roosevelt tér** to the **Várhegy** (Castle Hill) cable car. To the south, **Erzsébet híd** runs from near **Petőfi tér** to the St. Gellért monument at **Gellért-hegy** (Gellért Hill). Farther along the **Danube, Szabadság híd** links **Fővám tér** to the south end of Gellért-hegy. Finally, **Petőfi híd** and **Lágymányosi híd,** farther south, also connect Buda and Pest. Budapest's tram and transportation hub sits north of the Castle District at **Moszkva tér,** and the HEV commuter railway, which heads north through **Óbuda** to **Szentendre** (see **Local Transportation,** p. 345), starts at **Batthyány tér,** which lies opposite the Parliament, one Metro stop past the Danube in Buda. Budapest's **Metro** is the oldest on the Continent. Its three lines (the yellow M1, red M2, and blue M3) converge at **Deák tér,** by the international bus terminal at **Erzsébet tér.** Deák tér is at the center of Pest's concentric boulevards and radiating avenues. Two blocks toward the river is **Vörösmarty tér.** The pedestrian shopping zone **Váci u.** is to the right, facing the statue of Mihály Vörösmarty. The zone ends at the central market, housed in a building with a roof of multi-colored tiles. **Addresses** in Budapest begin with a Roman numeral representing one of the city's **23 districts.** Central Buda is I; central Pest is V. The middle two digits of postal codes indicate the district.

🞏 LOCAL TRANSPORTATION

Commuter Trains: The **HÉV commuter railway** station is across the river from Parliament, 1 Metro stop past the Danube in Buda. Trains head to **Szentendre** (45min., daily every 15min. 5am-9pm, 268Ft). Purchase tickets at the station for transport beyond city limits or face a hefty fine. On the list of stops, those within city limits are in a different color. Békásmegyer is the last stop within city limits. For travel within the city, a simple transportation ticket or pass will work.

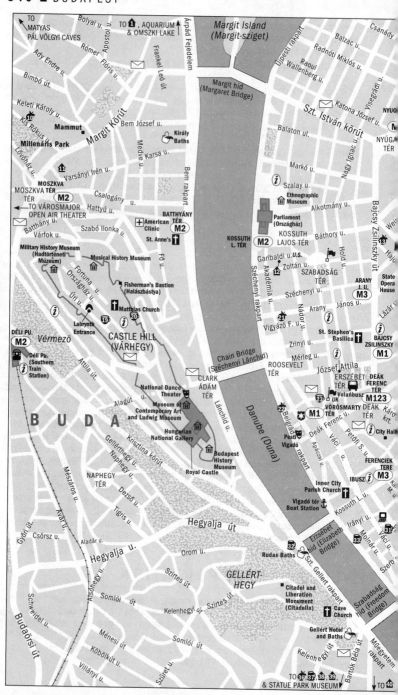

TO MATYAS PÁL VÖLGYI CAVES

Bolyai u.

TO, AQUARIUM & OMSZKI LAKE

Margit Island (Margit-sziget)

Csanády

Ady Endre u.

Rómer Flóris u.

Apostol u.

Frankel Leó út

Árpád Fejedelem

Balzac u.

Radnóti Miklós u.

Raoul Wallenberg u.

Bimbó út.

Margit híd (Margaret Bridge)

Keleti Károly u.

Katona József u.

NYUG

Kis Rókus

Mammut

Szt. István körút

Margit Körút

Bem József u.

Király Baths

Balaton ul.

Nagy Ignác u.

Visegrádi u.

M

NYÚGA TÉR

Millenáris Park

Medve u.

Karsa u.

Lövőház u.

Varsányi Irén u.

Markó u.

Bajcsy Zsilinszky út

Wei

MOSZKVA TÉR

MOSZKVA TÉR M2

TO VÁROSMAJOR OPEN AIR THEATER

Csalogány u.

Bem rakpart

Hattyú u.

BATTHYÁNY TÉR

Szalay u.

Ethnographic Museum

Alkotmány u.

Hajó

13

Batthány u.

Szabó Ilonka u.

American Clinic M2

St. Anne's

Parliament (Országház)

KOSSUTH LAJOS TÉR

Báthory u.

Várfok u.

Military History Museum (Hadtörténeti Múzeum)

Musical History Museum

Fő u.

KOSSUTH L. TÉR M2

Garibaldi u.

U.S.

Hold u.

State Opera House

Fortuna u.

Országház u.

Fisherman's Bastion (Halászbástya)

Akadémia u.

Zoltán u.

SZABADSÁG TÉR

ARANY J. U. M3

Úri u.

Matthias Church

Széchenyi rakpart

Széchenyi u.

Arany János u.

DÉLI PU. M2

Labrynth Entrance

19

20

Vigyázó F. u.

Nádor u.

St. Stephen's Basilica

BAJCSY ZSILINSZKY M1

Déli Pu. (Southern Train Station)

Vérmező

CASTLE HILL (VÁRHEGY)

Zrinyi u.

Mérleg u.

ROOSEVELT TÉR

Lázár u.

Attila út

Chain Bridge (Széchenyi Lánchíd)

József Attila

ERSZÉBET TÉR

DEÁK FERENC TÉR

M123

DEÁK FERENC TÉR

Alagút

CLARK ÁDÁM TÉR

Volánbusz

UK

23

Károly krt.

Mészáros u.

B U D A

National Dance Theater

Museum of Contemporary Art and Ludwig Museum

Lánchíd u.

Danube (Duna)

M1

Belgrád rakpart

VÖRÖSMARTY TÉR

22

Deák Ferenc u.

Váci u.

City Hall

Krisztina körút

Gellérthegy u.

Naphegy u.

Hungarian National Gallery

Pesti Vigadó

Apáczai u.

Petőfi u.

FERENCIEK TERE M3

NAPHEGY TÉR

Dezső u.

Budapest History Museum

Royal Castle

Inner City Parish Church

Kossuth L.u.

IBUSZ

Tigris u.

Vigadó tér Boat Station

Irányi u.

31

33

Molnár u.

Avár U.

Hegyalja út

Erzsébet híd (Elizabeth Bridge)

Szerb

Csörsz u.

Aladár u.

Orom u.

32

Szirtes út

Rudas Baths

Szt. Gellert rakpart

Győri út

Hegyalja u.

GELLÉRT-HEGY

Szirtes út

Szabadság híd (Freedom Bridge)

Somlói út

Citadel and Liberation Monument (Citadella)

Schweidel u.

Budaörsi út.

Alsóhegy u.

Kelenhegyi út

Cave Church

Szirtes út

Ménesi út

Somlói út

Gellért Hotel and Baths

Kőbölkút u.

Villányi út.

Szüret u.

Kelenhegyi út

Műegyetem rakpart

TO 36, 37, 38, 39 & STATUE PARK MUSEUM

Bartók Béla út

40

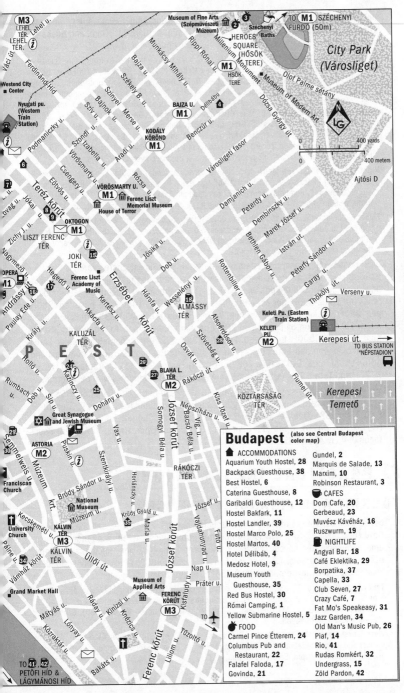

HUNGARY

Public Transportation: Budapest's public transport is inexpensive, convenient, and easy to navigate. The **Metro** and **trams** run every few min. 4:30am-11:30pm, and **buses** are always on time (schedules posted at stops). Many buses run all night.

Budapest Public Transport (BKV; ☎80 406 686; www.bkv.hu) has info in Hungarian. Open M-F 7am-3pm. All public transport uses the same **tickets** (140Ft, 10 tickets 1200Ft, 20 tickets 2350Ft; no transfers), sold in Metro stations, *Trafik* shops, and kiosks. Punch them in orange boxes at Metro gates and on buses and trams. A ticket is valid for a single trip on only 1 metro line. (105Ft ticket (*metrószakaszjegy*) valid for 3 Metro stops; 160Ft ticket (*metrószakaszállójegy*) valid 5 Metro stops with transfer. Consider buying a **pass.** (Day-pass 1150Ft, 3-day 2200Ft, 1-week 2700Ft, 2-week 3350Ft, 1-month 5200Ft. Unlimited public transportation and other perks available with the Budapest Card; see **Tourist and Financial Services,** p. 348.) Monthly passes require a transport ID card (100Ft), so bring a photo. Budapest transport tickets are good on HÉV suburban trains within city limits. Otherwise, purchase separate HÉV tickets.

Night Transportation: The Metro discontinues service around 11:30pm, but gates may lock at 10:30pm. All Metro stops post the 1st and last trains by the tracks. Buses and trams stop at 11pm. Buses with numbers ending in "É" run midnight-5am. Buses #7É and 78É follow the M2 route, #6É follows the 4/6 tram line, and bus #14É and 50É run the same route as M3.

Fines: Riding ticketless hits you with a fee of 2000Ft if you can pay on the spot and much more if you need to pay by mail. Inspectors, who wear red armbands, prowl Deák tér. They generally wait at the top of escalators. Punch a new ticket when switching lines. They also issue fines for losing the cover sheet to the 10-ticket packet.

Taxis: Because the transport system in Budapest is so efficient, there's rarely a need for a taxi. Beware of scams; check for a yellow license plate and running meter. Before getting in, ask how much the ride usually costs. Prices should not exceed: 6am-10pm base fare 200Ft plus 200Ft per km and 50Ft per min. waiting; 10pm-6am base fare 280Ft plus 280Ft per km and 70Ft per min. waiting. **Budataxi** (☎233 3333) has very good rates—135Ft per km by phone and 200Ft per km on the street. To the airport: 3500Ft from Pest and 4000Ft from Buda. **Főtaxi** (☎222 2222) has competitive rates—140Ft per km by phone and 160Ft per km on the street. To the airport: 3500Ft from Pest and 4000Ft from Buda. **6x6 Taxi** (☎266 6666), **City Taxi** (☎211 1111), **Rádió Taxi** (☎377 7777), and **Tele 5 Taxi** (☎355 5555) are also reliable companies with decent rates.

Car Rental: There are several reliable rental agencies in Budapest. Cars from US$40-50 per day. Credit card required. Few agencies rent to those under 21. **Avis,** V, Szervita tér 8 (☎318-4859). Open M-Sa 7am-6pm, Su 8am-noon. **Budget,** I, Krisztina krt. 41-43 (☎/fax 214 0420). Open M-F 8am-8pm, Sa-Su 8am-6pm. **Hertz,** V, Apáczai Csere János u. 4 (☎266 4361). Open daily 7am-7pm.

◪ PRACTICAL INFORMATION

TOURIST AND FINANCIAL SERVICES

Tourist Offices: Tourist offices, Metro stations, and travel agencies sell the **Budapest Card** (Budapest Kártya). It includes unlimited public transport, entrance to most museums, reduced rates on car rental and the airport minibus, and discounts at shops, baths, and restaurants. (2-day card 4350Ft, 3-day 5400Ft.) Pick up ▨ *Budapest in Your Pocket* (www.inyourpocket.com; 750Ft), an up-to-date city guide.

Tourinform, V, Sütő u. 2 (☎317 9800; www.hungary.com), off Deák tér behind McDonald's. M1, 2, or 3: Deák tér. Open daily 8am-8pm. **Branches** at VI, Liszt Ferenc tér 11 (☎322 4098; liszt@budapestinfo.hu). M1: Oktogon, and VI, Nyugati Pályaudvar (☎302-8580). Outstanding event and tour information.

Vista Travel Center: Visitor's Center, Paulay Ede 7 (☎429 9950; incoming@vista.hu). Arranges tours and accommodations, and has **luggage storage.** Go in the morning before it gets crowded. Open M-F 9am-6:30pm, Sa 9am-2:30pm.

Budapest Public Transport

Legend:
- M1 (yellow) line
- M2 (red) line
- M3 (blue) line
- Rail lines
- Transfer stations
- End stops
- Major Tram Line
- HÉV Commuter Rail (green)
- Tram Terminal
- Train Station
- Bus Station

HUNGARY

IBUSZ, V, Ferenciek tere 10 (☎485 2700). M3: Ferenciek tere. Books cheap tickets and sightseeing tours (3hr. tour 6400Ft, with Budapest Card 4350Ft); finds rooms (see **Accommodations,** p. 351); and **exchanges currency.** Open M-F 9am-5pm. Sa 9am-1pm for currency exchange only. **Western Union** available. AmEx/MC/V for some services.

Malév Airlines, XII, Váci u. 26, (☎235 3222; centrum@malev.hu). M1: Vörösmarty tér. Youth discounts for those under 24. Open M-F 8:30am-7pm, Sa-Su 10am-6pm.

Embassies and Consulates:

Australia, XII, Királyhágó tér 8/9 (☎457 9777; www.australia.hu). M2: Déli pu., then bus #21 or tram #59 to Királyhágó tér. Open M-F 9am-noon.

Austria, VI, Benczúr u. 16 (☎351-6700). M1: Bajza u. Open M-F 8-10am.

Canada, XII, Budakeszi út 32 (☎392 3360). Take bus #158 from Moszkva tér to the last stop. Entrance at Zugligeti út 51-53. Open M-Th 8:30-10:30am and 2-3:30pm.

Croatia, VI, Munkácsy M. u. 15 (☎354 1315). M1: Bajza u. Open M-Tu and Th-F 1-3pm.

Ireland, V, Szabadság tér 7 (☎302 9600), in Bank Center. M3: Arany J. u. Walk down Bank u. toward the river. Open M-F 9:30am-12:30pm and 2:30-4:30pm.

New Zealand, VI, Teréz krt. 38, 4th fl. (☎428 2208). M3: Nyugati pu. Open M-F 11am-4pm by appointment only.

Romania, XIV, Thököly út 72 (☎384 0271; roembbud@mail.datanet.hu). Open M-F 7:30am-noon.

Serbia and Montenegro, VI, Dózsa György út 92/b (☎322 9838). M1: Hősök tere. Open M-F 10am-1pm.

Slovak Republic, XIV Stéfania u. 22-24 (☎460-9010). Open M-F 8am-noon.

Slovenia, II, Cseppkő u. 68 (☎438 5600). M2: Moszkva tér. Open M-F 9am-noon.

UK, V, Harmincad u. 6 (☎266 2888; fax 266 0907), near the intersection with Vörösmarty tér. M1: Vörösmarty tér. Open M-F 9:30am-12:30pm and 2:30-4:30pm.

Ukraine, XII, Nográdi u. 8 (☎355 2443). Open M-W and F 9am-noon. By appointment only.

US, V, Szabadság tér 12 (☎475 4400, after hours 475 4703; fax 475 4764). M2: Kossuth tér. Walk 2 blocks down Akadémia and turn on Zoltán. Open M-Th 1-4pm, F 9am-noon and 1-4pm.

Currency Exchange: Banks have the best rates. Avoid the steep premiums at the airport, train stations, and small exchange shops. **Citibank,** V, Vörösmarty tér 4 (☎374 5000; fax 374 5100). M1: Vörösmarty tér. Cashes **traveler's checks** for no commission and provides MC/V **cash advances. Budapest Bank,** V, Váci u. 1/3 (☎328 3155; fax 267 3040). M1: Vörösmarty tér. Offers credit card **cash advances,** cashes **traveler's checks** into US currency for 3.5% commission, and has great exchange rates. Open M-F 8:30am-5pm, Sa 9am-2pm. Omnipresent **OTP** and **K&H** banks also have good rates.

American Express: V, Deák Ferenc u. 10 (☎235 4330; amex.retail.bud@aexp.com). M1, 2, or 3: Deák tér. Open M-F 9am-5:30pm, Sa 9am-2pm. Cardholders can have mail delivered here. Other services include tourist info and free maps.

LOCAL SERVICES

Luggage Storage: Keleti pu., lockers across from international cashier (240Ft, large bags 480Ft). **Nyugati pu.,** in the waiting room near the ticket windows. 240Ft per day, large bags 480Ft. Open 24hr. **Déli pu.** charges 150Ft, large bags 300Ft. Lockers 200Ft per day. Open daily 3:30am-11:30pm. The **Volánbusz** station has small lockers (90Ft per day). Open M and F-Sa 6am-8pm, Tu-Th and Su 6am-7pm. **Vista Travel Center** (see **Tourist Offices,** p. 348) has lockers big enough to hold a sizable pack. 100Ft per hr.

English-Language Bookstores: Libri Könyvpalota, VII, Rákóczi u. 12 (☎/fax 267-4843) is the best choice. A multilevel bookstore, it has 1 floor of up-to-date English titles. Open M-F 10am-7:30pm, Sa 10am-3pm. M2: Astoria. MC/V. **Bestsellers,** V, Október 6 u. 11 (☎312 1295; www.bestsellers.hu), off Arany János u. M1, 2, or 3: Deák tér or M3: Arany János. Carries a wide variety of English and French media. Open M-F 9am-6:30pm, Sa 10am-5pm, Su 10am-4pm.

Gay Hotline: GayGuide.net Budapest (☎0630 932 3334; www.budapest.gayguide.net). This volunteer organization posts an online guide and runs a hotline (daily 4-8pm) with info and reservations at gay- and lesbian-friendly lodgings. See also **Gay Budapest,** p. 364.

EMERGENCY AND COMMUNICATIONS

Tourist Police: V, Vigadó u. 6 (☎463-9165). M1: Vörösmarty tér. Walk toward the river from the Metro to reach the station. Tourists can report stolen and lost items, and other police matters. Tourist Police often can't do very much. Beware of people pretending to be Tourist Police who may demand your passport. Open 24hr.

Pharmacies: II, Frankel Leó út 22 (☎212 4406). III, Szentendrei út 2/a (☎388 6528). IV, Pozsonyi u. 19 (☎379-3008). VI, Teréz krt. 41 (☎311 4439). Open 24hr. VII, Rákóczi út 39 (☎314 3695). Open M-F 7:30am-8pm, Sa 7:30am-2pm; no after-hours service. VIII, Üllöi út 121 (☎215 3900). Look for a tan-and-white sign with *Gyógyszertár, Apotheke,* or *Pharmacie* in the window. After-hours service 100-200Ft.

Medical Assistance: Ambulance, ☎104. **Falck (SOS) KFT,** II, Kapy út 49/b (☎200 0100). Ambulance service US$120. **American Clinic,** I, Hattyú u. 14 (☎224 9090; www.americanclinics.com), accepts walk-ins, but calling a day ahead is helpful. Open

M 8:30am-7pm, Tu-W 10am-6pm, Th 11:30am-6pm, F 10am-6pm. You will be charged for physician's time plus tests. Direct insurance billing available. 24hr. emergency ☎224 9090. The US embassy also maintains a list of English-speaking doctors.

Telephones: Domestic operator and info ☎198; international operator 190, info 199. Most phones use **phone cards,** available at kiosks and Metro stations. 50-unit card 800Ft, 120-unit card 1800Ft.

Internet Access: Cyber cafes litter the city, but access can be expensive and long waits are common. Internet access is available at many hostels.

Ami Internet Coffee, V, Váci u. 40 (☎267 1644; www.amicoffee.hu). M3: Ferenciek ter. Lounge with drinks. 200Ft per 15min., 700Ft per hr. Open daily 9am-midnight.

Libri Könyvpalota, VII, Rákóczi út 12 (☎267 4843; www.libri.hu). M2: Astoria. Reserve ahead. Sells drinks. 250Ft per 30min., 400Ft per hr. Open M-F 10am-7:30pm, Sa 10am-3pm.

Net Club, II, Frankel Leó út 11 (☎212 3999; www.net-klub.hu). HEV. Margit hid. On the Buda side. 290Ft per 30min., 500Ft per hr. Open daily 10am-midnight.

Post Office: V, Városház u. 18 (☎318 4811). **Poste Restante** (Postán Mar) in office around the right side of the building. Open M-F 8am-8pm, Sa 8am-2pm. Branches at Nyugati pu.; VI, Teréz krt. 105/107; Keleti pu.; VIII, Baross tér 11/c; and elsewhere. Open M-F 7am-9pm, Sa 8am-2pm. **Postal Code:** Depends on the district—postal codes are 1XX2, where XX is the district number (1052 for post office listed above).

⚑ ACCOMMODATIONS

Tourists fill the city in July and August; phone first or store luggage while looking for a bed. If you book a room, call again the night before to confirm, as hostels can "misplace" your reservation. Tourists arriving at Keleti pu. enter a feeding frenzy as hostel solicitors jostle each other for guests. Don't be drawn in by promises of rides or discounts: some hostel-hawkers may stretch the truth.

ACCOMMODATION AGENCIES

Private rooms ❸ (3000Ft-5000Ft; prices decrease with longer stays) are slightly more expensive than hostels, but offer what most hostels can't: peace, quiet, and private showers. Accommodation agencies are everywhere. For cheaper rooms, be there when they open and haggle. Before accepting a room, be sure the hostel is easily accessible by public transport. Bring cash. **IBUSZ,** V, Ferenciek tere 10, at M3: Ferenciek tere, books comparatively cheap rooms. (Doubles 5000-10,000Ft; triples 6500-12,000Ft. 1800Ft fee for stays fewer than 4 nights.) They also rent central Pest apartments with kitchen and bath. (1-bedroom flat from 8000Ft, 2-bedroom from 12,000Ft). Make reservations by email or fax. (☎485-2700; accommodation@ibusz.hu. Open M-F 8:15am-5pm.) There's a branch at VIII, Keleti pu. (☎342 9572. Open M-F 8am-6pm.) **Best Hotel Service,** V, Sütö u. 2, at M1, 2, or 3: Deák tér, is in the courtyard. It is accessible by bus #7 from Keleti pu. The service handles hotel, apartment, and hostel reservations, car rentals, and city tours. (☎318 4848. Rooms 6000Ft and up. Open daily 8am-8pm.)

HOSTELS AND HOTELS

From the quiet hotel to the lively hostel, Budapest has accommodations to fit every visitor's preference. Some of the city's most exciting social centers, hostels are often full of backpackers in summer and are a great place to make friends. Many university dorms become hostels in summer. The **Hungarian Youth Hostels Association,** which operates from Keleti pu., runs many hostels. Their staff wear Hostelling International t-shirts and will—along with legions of competitors—accost you as you get off the train. Many provide free transport.

BUDA

■ **Backpack Guesthouse,** XI, Takács Menyhért u. 33 (☎209 8406; backpackguest@hotmail.com), 12min. from central Pest. From Keleti pu., take bus #7 or 7a toward Buda. Get off at Tétényi u. and walk back under the bridge to a sharp left turn. Take the 3rd right at Hamzsabégi út. With creatively-themed rooms, a huge common room with movies, and a kitchen full of amateur cooks, this cozy neighborhood house will make you feel at home. The backyard features a gazebo, which you can rent out at night, and a slew of hammocks. The 49E night bus gets you home after the trams stop. Internet 10Ft per min. Laundry 1500Ft. Reception 24hr. Reserve ahead; reconfirm the night before. Dorms 2200Ft; doubles 6600Ft; mattress in gazebo 1800Ft. ❷

Hostel Martos, XI, Stoczek u. 5/7 (☎209 4883; reception@hotel.martos.bme.hu). From Keleti pu., take bus #7 to Móricz Zsigmond Körtér and go 300m toward the river on Bartók Béla út. Turn right on Bertalan Lajos and take the 3rd right on Stoczek u. Cheap, clean student-run hostel with kitchen on each floor. It expands in summer, but there are rooms available year-round. A short walk to the outdoor clubs along the river. Free Internet and satellite TV. Laundry 60Ft per hr., free to guests who stay a few days. Check-out 10am. Reserve a few days in advance. Singles 4000Ft; doubles 5000Ft, with shower 8000Ft; triples 7500Ft; 2- to 4-bed apartments with bath 15,000Ft. ❸

PEST

■ **Red Bus Hostel,** V, Semmelweis u. 14 (☎/fax 266 0136; www.redbusbudapest.hu). A fabulous value in downtown Pest. New, very clean, spacious dorms, large common room, kitchen, and info desk. Free luggage storage. Internet 12Ft per min. Simple breakfast included. Laundry 1200Ft. Reception 24hr. Check-out 10am. Dorms 2900Ft; singles 6500-7500Ft; doubles 7500Ft; triples 10,500Ft. ❷

Aquarium Youth Hostel, VII, Alsóerdősor u. 12 (☎322 0502; aquarium@budapesthostels.com). Unmarked by signs. Ring the buzzer with the hostel symbol on it. Close to Keleti pu., and near Metro, trams, and buses. Run by a hospitable staff, this small, fun-loving hostel is decorated with an underwater theme. Free Internet and kitchen. Laundry 1200Ft. Reception 24hr. Dorms 2600Ft; doubles 8500Ft. ❷

Medosz Hotel, VI, Jókai tér 9 (☎374 3001; info@medoszhotel.hu), a 5min. walk from Oktogon shopping center and the Opera House. Spacious and sunny rooms in central Pest. English-speaking staff arranges sightseeing tours. Breakfast included. Reserve ahead. Singles 8000-10,500Ft; doubles 10,500-13,000Ft; triples 10,500-15,500Ft; apartments 17,500-20,000Ft. 10% student or HI discount. MC/V. ❸

Yellow Submarine Hostel, VI, Teréz Körút 56, 3rd fl. (☎331 9896; www.yellowsubmarinehostel.com), across from Nyugati pu. A great place to crash after a hard day's night. Known as a party hostel. Large dorms with bunk beds and lockers. Doubles and triples in nearby apartments. Internet access 10Ft per min. Breakfast included for dorms. Laundry 1500Ft. Check-out 9am. Dorms 2800Ft; singles 7500Ft; doubles 8000-9000Ft; triples 9900-10,500Ft; quads 13,200Ft. 10% HI discount. MC/V. ❷

Hostel Marco Polo, VII, Nyár u. 6 (☎413 2555; www.marcopolohostel.com). M2: Astoria or Blaha Lujza tér. Has a luxury-hotel feel and more privacy than other hostels, as dorm bunk beds are in separate compartments blocked off by curtains. Courtyard patio and basement restaurant and bar. Internet access 300Ft per hr. Laundry 600Ft. Reception 24hr. July-Aug. reserve ahead. Dorms 5000Ft; singles 13,750Ft; doubles 18,900Ft; triples 21,000Ft; quads 26000Ft. 10% HI and ISIC discount. ❸

Hotel Délibáb, VI, Délibáb u. 35 (☎342 9301; info@hoteldelibab.hu). Take M1: Hősök tere. This century-old neo-renaissance house is in a quiet neighborhood just outside Heroes Square. Its well-decorated rooms are a great base for exploring the museums and baths in the city's east end. Breakfast included. Laundry available. Singles 12,750-16,500Ft; doubles 14,750-19,000Ft; extra bed 3750Ft. MC/V. ❹

Best Hostel, VI, Podmaniczky u. 27, 1st fl. (☎332 4934; www.besthostel.hu). Take a left out of Nyugati pu.; it's the 1st street you come to. Ring bell #33 in the building on the corner. This quiet hostel has large dorms with wooden floors, common room, and kitchen. For the benefit of people who want to get up early, lights must be out in dorms by 11pm. No smoking or drinking allowed. Internet 10Ft per min. Breakfast included. Laundry 1000Ft. Dorms 3000Ft; doubles 8400Ft; triples 10800Ft. 10% HI discount. ❷

Museum Youth Guesthouse, VIII, Mikszáth Kálmán tér 4, 1st fl. (☎318 9508; museumgh@freemail.hu). M3: Kálvin tér. Take the left exit onto Baross u.; at the fork, take the left branch, Peviezky u. At the square, go to the right corner and ring buzzer at gate #4. Offers a convenient location and lofted beds that create a sense of privacy. English spoken. Free Internet, kitchen, and luggage storage. Locker deposit 500Ft. Laundry 1200Ft. Reception 24hr. Check-out 11am. Reserve ahead. Dorms 2600Ft. ❷

SUMMER HOSTELS, GUEST HOUSES, CAMPING

Many **university dorms** moonlight as hostels in July and August. Most are clustered around Móricz Zsigmond Körtér in District XI. All have kitchens, luggage storage, and TV in the common room. For a home-away-from-home feel, stay in a **guest house** or **apartment.** Only slightly more expensive (about 1500Ft extra per person) than a hostel bed, guesthouses offer privacy, peace, and perks like private bathrooms and TV. Owners often allow guests to use the kitchen or laundry machine. Provided with keys, guests can come and go as they please. While Budapest's nearest **campgrounds** are a bit out of the way, they can be peaceful and rewarding alternatives to staying in the bustling hub of the city. Situated in the lofty hills of Buda or on the Danube itself, campgrounds offer beautiful views of the city and great access to hiking trails.

Garibaldi Guesthouse, V, Garibaldi u. 5 (☎302 3456; garibaldiguest@hotmail.com). M2: Kossuth tér. Head away from Parliament along Nádor u. and take the first right on Garibaldi u. Welcoming and comfortable, the guesthouse is a block from the Danube and Parliament building. Spacious and beautifully furnished rooms range from singles to quads. Most have TV, kitchenettes, and showers. Sheets and towels included. Owner has rooms throughout the city, including near Astoria and Nyugati pu. Dorms 3000-4000Ft; singles 6500-7000Ft; doubles 8000Ft, apartments 6000-10,000Ft per person. Prices decrease with longer stays, big groups, and off-season dates. ❸

Hostel Bakfark, II, Bakfark u. 1/3 (☎413 2062). M2: Moszkva tér. Walk along Margit krt. and take the 1st right after Mammut. Though across the river from the action, these are among the most comfortable dorms in town, with lofts instead of bunks. Check-out 10am. Call ahead. Open June 15-Aug. 28. Dorms 3300-3500Ft. 10% HI discount. ❸

Római Camping, III, Szentendrei út 189 (☎388 7167). M2: Batthyány tér, then take the HÉV to Római fürdő, cross the street, and go toward the river. Complex indulges its guests with grocery store and restaurants, swimming pool, and a park. **Római Strandfürdő,** next door, is a waterpark (1400Ft, children 1200Ft) with pools and slides. Bungalows ranked by amenities. Complex guarded. Communal showers and kitchen. Breakfast 880Ft. Laundry 800Ft. 990Ft, children 590Ft. Tents 1950Ft per person; bungalows 1690-15,000Ft. Electricity 600Ft. Tourist tax 3%. 10% HI discount. ❶

Caterina Guesthouse and Hostel, III, Teréz krt. 30, apt. #28, ring code: #48 (☎269-5990; www.caterinahostel.hu). M1: Oktogon. Or trams #4 or 6. Prime location in central Pest. Newly renovated, sunny, and spacious rooms. Fresh linens and in-room TV. Transport to airport 1800Ft. English spoken. Laundry 1200Ft. Reception 24hr. Check-out 10am. Lockout 10am-1pm for cleaning. Reserve by fax or email. Dorms 2300Ft; doubles 6000Ft; triples 9000Ft. ❷

Hostel Landler, XI, Bartók Béla út 17 (☎463 3621). Take bus #7 or 7A across the river to Gellért. Cheerful, antiquated building with natural light. Free transport from bus or train station. Laundry available. Check-out 9am. Open July-Sept. 5. Singles 5850Ft; triples 11,700Ft; quads 15,600Ft. Prices will increase in 2005. 10% HI discount. ❸

◘ HUNGARY?

Explore the cafeterias beneath "Önkiszolgáló Étterem" signs for something cheap (300-500Ft) or seek out a neighborhood *kifőzés* (kiosk) or *vendéglő* (vendor). Corner markets stock the basics, and many have 24hr. windows. The king of them all, the █**Grand Market Hall,** IX, Fövam tér 1/3, next to Szabadság híd (M3: Kálvin tér), built in 1897, boasts 10,000 sq. m of stalls. You'll find produce, baked goods, meat, and every souvenir imaginable. (☎217 6067. Open M 6am-5pm, Tu-F 6am-6pm, Sa 6am-2pm.) Try **lángos,** Hungarian-style fried dough with cheese and sour cream toppings. For ethnic restaurants, try the upper floors of **Mammut Plaza** (see **Entertainment,** p. 361), just outside of the Moszkva tér Metro stop in Buda, or the **West End Plaza,** accessible from the Nyugati Metro stop in Pest.

███ **Columbus Pub and Restaurant,** V, Danube (☎266 9013), on the promenade below the Chain Bridge. If you've neglected the beautiful Danube during your stay, enjoy a meal on this moored ship. A great view to go along with the fine selection of Hungarian food, beer, and drinks. (Entrees 1200-3000Ft.) Open daily 11am-midnight. AmEx/MC/V. ❸

███ **Govinda,** V, Vigyázó Ferenc u. 4 (☎269 1625). A vegetarian Indian restaurant, complete with yoga classes and a store selling meditation books and incense. The best deals are the meals (big plate 1600Ft, small plate 1250Ft, student plate 620Ft) which include vegetables, rice, and soup. English menu available. Yoga classes (500Ft) Sept.-June M 5-6:30pm. Open M-Sa noon-9pm. ❷

███ **Gundel,** XIV, Allatkerti út 2 (☎468 4040). Hungary's most famous restaurant, Gundel has served its delicate cuisine to Queen Elizabeth II and Pope John Paul II. There are 7-course meals (13,000-17,500Ft), and sandwiches outside for those who want to just say they've been there (400-600Ft). Goose Liver (6110Ft). Su brunch buffet 11:30am-3pm 4900Ft. Open daily noon-3:15pm and 6:30-11:15pm. AmEx/MC/V. ❺

Falafel Faloda, VI, Paulay Ede u. 53 (☎351 1243; www.falafel.hu). M1: Opera. Cross Andrássy, continue on Nagymező, and go left on Paulay Ede. Healthy fast food at its best: patrons order personalized falafels. Choose from toppings like tahini and fresh vegetables. Falafel 540Ft. Salads 530-640Ft. Open M-F 10am-8pm, Sa 10am-6pm. ❷

Robinson Mediterranean-Style Restaurant and Cafe, XIV, Városliget tó (☎422 0222; fax 422 0072), floats on a docked boat in the scenic City Park. The open-air dining area overlooks the castle and lake. Dishes up enchanting Mediterranean fare (albeit a bit slowly). Serves favorites like liver (2150Ft) and paprika veal (2600Ft). Vegetarian options available. Entrees 1800-5800Ft. Open daily noon-midnight. ❹

Marquis de Salade, VI, Hajós u. 43 (☎302 4086). M3: Arany János. At the corner of Bajcsy-Zsilinszky út, 2 blocks from the Metro. Huge menu with dishes from Azerbaijan and Russia. Try the popular Jalancs Dolma, a vegetarian dish of savory veggies stuffed with rice. Entrees 1800-3500Ft. Open daily noon-midnight. ❹

Carmel Pince Étterem, VII, Kazinczy út 31 (☎342 4585). M2: Astoria. In the old Jewish quarter near Dohány Synagogue. Serves up generous Jewish-Hungarian delicacies. Not kosher. Entrees 1000-3000Ft. Live *klezmer* music second Su of each month. Cover 2000Ft. Open daily noon-11pm. 10% student discount. AmEx/MC/V. ❸

Marxim, II, Kis Rókus u. 23 (☎316 0231; www.extra.hu/marxim). M2: Moszkva tér. Walk along Margit krt., then turn left after passing Mammut. Hip locals unite at this tongue-in-cheek, red-colored, communist-themed pizzeria. Great pizzas 590-1290Ft. Open M-F noon-1am, Sa noon-2am, Su 6pm-1am. ❷

▐ CAFES

The former haunts of the literary, intellectual, and cultural elite as well as political dissidents, Budapest's cafes boast rich histories. The current "hip" cafes, frequented by expats and yuppies, are at Ferenc Liszt tér (M1: Oktogon). Each cafe has a large summer patio—come early to grab a great people-watching post.

▨ Dom Cafe, I, Szentháromság tér, behind the Castle Hill Church. If you're thirsty after climbing the hill, reward yourself with a coffee or beer (both from 360 Ft) at this cafe, which boasts amazing views of the Danube and Pest. Open daily 10am-10pm.

Gerbeaud, V, Vörösmarty tér 7 (☎429 9020). M1: Vörösmarty tér. Hungary's most famous cafe and dessert shop has served its homemade layer cakes (620Ft) and ice cream (250Ft) since 1858. The desserts taste and smell delicious. Large terrace sprawls over the end of Vörösmarty tér. Open daily 9am-9pm.

Muvész Kávéház, VI, Andrássy út 29 (☎352 1337). M1: Opera. Across from the Opera. Before or after a show, stop in for a slice of sinful cake (320Ft) and cappuccino (300Ft) at the polished stone tables. Open daily 9am-11:45pm.

Ruszwurm, I, Szentháromság 7 (☎375 5284), off the square on Várhegy in the Castle District. This tiny cafe has been at it since 1827, when it prepared sweets for the Hapsburgs. Pastries and cakes (170-460Ft) sometimes made right behind the counter. Coffee and espresso from 300Ft. Ice cream 100Ft. Open daily 9am-8pm.

Faust Wine Cellar, I, Hess András tér 1-3 (☎488 6873). Enter the Hilton in the Castle District, head left and descend into the 13th-century cellar. Sit at the patio, which is atop a high cliff. An overwhelming array of excellent Hungarian vintages served with cheese and salami. 300-4500Ft per glass. Open daily 4-11pm.

◉ SIGHTS

In 1896, on the verge of its Golden Age and its 1000th birthday, Hungary constructed Budapest's most prominent sights. Works included **Heroes' Square** (Hősök tere), **Liberty Bridge** (Szabadság híd), **Vajdahunyad Castle** (Vajdahunyad vár), and continental Europe's first **Metro;** they are damaged by time, war, and communist occupation. Consider **Absolute Walking and Biking Tours.** The basic tour (3½hr.; 4000Ft, under 27 3500Ft) meets daily June through August at 9:30am and 1:30pm, on the steps of the yellow church in Deák tér, and at 10am and 2pm, in Heroes' Square.

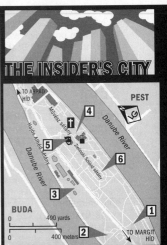

THE INSIDER'S CITY

MARGIT ISLAND

In the middle of the Danube River, between Buda and Pest, Margit Island is a secluded refuge, which mixes history and leisure. It is covered with Flintstone-esque vehicles and Hungarian lovers holding hands, but the island is big enough to make it feel like your own. Below are some highlights you won't want to miss.

1 Lounge by the fountain with Speedo-clad Hungarians, jump on the trampolines (200Ft per 5min.), and grab a snack.

2 Rent a pedal car (1800Ft per hr.).

3 Splash in the pools and scream down the slides at Palatinus Strandfürdo.

4 Walk through the statue park, where Hungary's cultural icons are immortalized, and visit the convent ruins.

5 Pay to see a show at the theater or just listen as the music carries across the island.

6 Walk through the rose gardens and enter the small zoo.

Low-season tours, September through May, leave at 10:30am from Deák tér and 11am from Heroes' Square. Choose from tours that focus on everything from communism to pubbing. (☎211 8861; www.absolutetours.com. Specialized tours 3½-5½hr. 4000-5000Ft.) **Boat tours** leave from Vigadó tér piers 6-7. **The Danube Legend,** which runs in the evening, costs 4200Ft. The **Duna Bella,** a daytime boat, costs 2600Ft for the 1hr. tour and 3600Ft for the 2hr. tour.

BUDA

CASTLE HILL (VÁRHEGY)

M1, 2, or 3: Deák tér, then take bus #16. Alternatively, take the Metro to M2: Moszkva tér and walk up to the hill on Várfok u. Bécsi kapu marks the castle entrance. Or take an elevator (600Ft) up the hill, but know that it doesn't take passengers back down.

Towering above the Danube, the castle district has been razed and rebuilt three times over 800 years, most recently in 1945 when the Red Army destroyed most of Castle Hill. Today, its winding, touristed streets are cluttered with art galleries, souvenir shops, and cafes that give way to breathtaking panoramic views.

The Castle (Vár) was built in the mid-13th century, shortly after the Mongols destroyed the city. Centuries later, **Matthias Corvinus** (see History, p. 336) chose Buda for the site of his Renaissance palace, but restless Turks seized the castle in 1541. Nearly a century and a half later, Hapsburg forces leveled the castle to oust the Ottomans. A reconstruction was completed just in time to be decimated by the Germans in 1945. The Hungarians cemented it together once more, only to face the Red menace. Today, its bullet holes are reminders of the 1956 Uprising (see History, p. 336). The castle recently underwent extensive restoration. Bombings during WWII unearthed artifacts from the original castle; they are now housed in the **Budapest History Museum** (Budapesti Történeti) in the Royal Palace (Budavári palota). For a description of Castle Hill museums, see p. 361.

Castle Hill

The **Gothic Matthias Church** (Mátyás Templom), with its multi-colored roof, is one of Budapest's most photographed buildings. The intricate columns and ceiling are impressive. When the Ottoman armies seized Buda in 1541, the church was converted into a mosque overnight. In 1688, the Hapsburgs defeated the Turks, sacked the city, and reconverted the building. Ascend the staircase to reach the **Museum of Ecclesiastical Art,** which houses a replica of the St. Stephen's Crown of Hungary. (*I, Szentháromság tér 2. Open M-Sa 9am-5pm, Su 1-5pm. High mass daily 7, 8:30am, 6pm; Su and holidays 10am and noon. Church and museum 550Ft, students 270Ft.*)

Castle Labyrinths (Budvári Labirintus) were created naturally by thermal springs, and the caverns beneath the Castle extend 1200m underground. Once used as shelter by prehistoric humans, they were more recently used as Cold War shelters and military barricades. The vastly dark and damp expanse has been converted into a series of chambers that walk the line between museum and haunted house. All the artifacts, like the 3m rock with a Coke bottle imprint, are fictitious but play a part in Hungarian lore. Although these exhibits may teach you a bit about Hungarian anthropology, the visit may be more fitting for a good laugh rather than scaring your friends. There's no minotaur in the center, but children under 14 and people with heart conditions are advised not to participate in the spooky experience. *(Úri u. 9. ☎ 212 0207; www.labirintus.com. Open daily 9:30am-7:30pm. Labyrinth lit with oil lamps 6-7:30pm. 1200Ft, students 1000Ft.)*

OTHER SIGHTS IN BUDA

Less industrialized than Pest, older Buda tumbles down from the Castle and Gellert Hills on the east bank of the Danube and sprawls into Budapest's main residential areas. With great parks, lush hills, and islands, Buda abounds with beautiful views of the city and great opportunities to learn about its history.

▓ **GELLÉRT HILL (GELLÉRTHEGY).** In the 11th century, the Pope sent Bishop Gellért to the coronation of King Stephen, the first Christian Hungarian monarch, to help convert the Magyars (see **History,** p. 336). Unconvinced, the pagans revolted and hurled the bishop to his death from atop the hill that now bears his name. The Soviets closed off **St. Ivan's Cave Church** (Szikla Templom), on the south side of the hill, with a concrete wall in the 1960s, and the church did not reopen until 1990. *(Masses daily 11am, 5:30 and 8pm. Additional Su mass at 9:30am.)* Atop Gellért Hill, the **Liberation Monument** (Szabadság Szobor), a bronze statue of a woman raising a palm branch, commemorates the liberation of Budapest after WWII. Later marked by communism, the statue was only recently stripped of its Soviet Star. The adjoining **Citadel** was built as a symbol of Hapsburg power after the failed 1848 Revolution. Inside, you'll find an exhibit about the history of the hill and unobstructed views of the city. The view from the hilltop is fabulous at night, when the Danube and its bridges shimmer in black and gold. A short way down from the Citadel, the **statue of St. Gellért,** complete with glistening waterfall, overlooks Erzsébet híd. Walk down the hill via the bus route and turn right at the St. Gellért Étterem. At the base sits the **Gellért Hotel and Baths** (see **Baths,** p. 362), Budapest's most famous Turkish bath. *(XI. Tram #18 or 19, or bus #7, to Hotel Gellért. Follow Szabó Verjték u. to Jubileumi Park, and continue on the paths to the summit. Or, take bus #27, get off at Búsuló Juhász, and walk 5min. to the peak. Citadel 400Ft.)*

MARGIT ISLAND (MARGITSZIGET). Off-limits to private cars, Margit Island offers garden pathways and shaded terraces. It is named after King Béla IV's daughter, whom he vowed to rear as a nun if the nation survived the 1241 Mongol invasion. Though decimated, Hungary survived, and poor Margit was confined to the island convent. **Palatinus Strandfürdő,** on Borsodi Beach, has pools and waterslides. *(Open May-Aug. 8am-7pm; Sept. 10am-6pm, weather permitting. 1400Ft, children 1200Ft.)* You can **rent bikes** or **bike-trolleys,** cars that you pedal with your feet. *(400-1700Ft per 30min., 600-2700Ft per hr. Prices slightly lower at Margit híd, but selection is slimmer than at Bringóhintó, on the far side of the island.)* **Golf carts** allow you to putter about the island (2500Ft per 30min.). **Szabadtéri Szinpad** (☎340 4796), the theater in the center, hosts concerts. See the sidebar, p. 355 for a walking tour. *(M3: Nyugati pu. Take tram #4 or 6 or the HÉV from Batthyány tér to Margit híd.)*

THE SANDWICH OF DEATH

The descent into the Matyas Caves, situated in the depths of the Buda Hills, is met by overwhelming darkness and absolute silence. The air is so cold—hovering at a chilly 10°C—that you would be able to see your breath as clearly as a bellowing chimney—that is, if you could see.

What brings travelers so deep into the silent depths is the opportunity to partake in caving, the unforgettable experience of snaking through the underground labyrinthine caves. Yet what brings visitors to these particular caves is the "Sandwich of Death," the finale of the journey. Equipped only with a helmet and flashlight, spelunkers venture through the path that descends 220m to sea level and back up again, inching past heart-stopping 40m drops and squeezing through crevices barely large enough to fit your helmet. The climactic sandwich isn't quite as dangerous as it sounds—it's a 12m stomach-crawl through two slabs of limestone.

Caving is not for the claustrophobic. That being said, the experience certainly isn't only for the rough-and-ready. Guides judge the skill level of their groups, and choose the difficulty of the path accordingly.

Follow directions to the Pal Volgyi Caves (see right). Call ahead (☎28 49 69) to reserve a spot and check tour times. 2100 Ft.

PÁL-VÖLGYI CAVES. Smaller but similar to the Aggtelek caves (p. 371), these caverns introduce novices to the underground terrain. Descend the 40m ladder for a 1hr. tour of the caves, which were formed by the thermal springs that now source the baths in the city. Wear warm clothing, as the caves are 10°C. For spelunking or a more challenging cave visit, see the sidebar, p. 358. *(Bus #86 from Batthyány tér to Kolosi tér, walk back up the street and make the 1st right to get to the bus station. From there, catch bus #65 to the caves. ☎325 9505. Open Tu-Su 10am-4pm. Tours every hr. 700Ft, students 500Ft. Tour that also visits Szemlőhegy Cave 900Ft/ 600Ft.)*

PEST

Buda and Pest complement each other perfectly. Though downtown Pest dates back to medieval times, its feel, unlike Buda's, is decidedly modern. Pest is Budapest's commercial and administrative center and holds many of the city's most interesting sites. Its streets were constructed in the 19th century; today, they run past shops, cafes, restaurants, and Hungary's biggest corporations.

■**PARLIAMENT (ORSZÁGHÁZ).** On the outside, Budapest's palatial Parliament looks more like a Cathedral than a government building. It was modeled after the UK parliament, right down to the riverside location. Standing 96m tall, a number symbolizing the date of Hungary's millennial anniversary, architect Steindl Imre's masterpiece is one of Europe's most beautiful buildings. Upon construction, the neo-Gothic building was one of the most technologically advanced of its time. Lit by gas lamps, the electricity needed to power the massive 692-room structure was more than that needed for the rest of the city. Home to the **Hungarian crown jewels**, the gold and marble interior is stunningly ornate. *(M2: Kossuth Lajos tér. ☎317 9800. English tours M-F 10am, noon, 2, 2:30, 5, and 6pm; min. 5 people; Sa-Su 10am only. Ask the guard to let you in and purchase tickets at gate X. Ticket office opens 8am. Entrance with mandatory tour 2000Ft, students 1035Ft. Free with EU passport.)*

GREAT SYNAGOGUE (ZSINAGÓGA). The largest synagogue in Europe and the second largest in the world, the 1859 Great Synagogue was designed to hold 3000 congregants. Renovations began in 1990 and are nearly complete. Beside the synagogue lies the last **ghetto** established in WWII. 80,000 Jews were imprisoned and 10,000 died in the final two months of the war. Today, the 2500 people whose bodies could be identified are buried here; the rest lie in a common grave in the Jewish Cemetery. In the garden sits the **Tree of Life,** an enormous metal tree honoring Holocaust victims. Each leaf bears the name of a Hungarian family whose members perished, and names can be added upon request. Next to it are four granite memorials honoring "righteous Gentiles," non-Jews who aided Jews during the War. While tours are not required, the English-speaking guides give excellent tours. *(VII. M2: Astoria. At the corner of Dohány u. and Wesselényi u. Open May-Oct. M-Th 10am-5pm, F 10am-1pm, Su 10am-2pm; Nov.-Apr. M-Th 10am-3pm, F 10am-1pm, Su 10am-1pm. Services F 6pm. Admissions often start at 10:30am. Covered shoulders required. Tours M-Th 10:30am-3:30pm on the half-hour, F and Su 10:30, 11:30am, 12:30pm. Tours 1900Ft, students 1600Ft. Admission includes admission to the Jewish Museum, see p. 360.)*

ST. STEPHEN'S BASILICA (SZ. ISTVÁN BAZILIKA). Though the city's largest church was seriously damaged in WWII, its spectacular interior still attracts tourists and worshippers. The 360° balcony of the Panorama Tower, Pest's highest vantage point, offers an amazing view. Don't miss **St. Stephen's mummified hand,** one of Hungary's most revered religious relics. A 100Ft offering in the box lights the hand for 2min. *(V. M1, 2, or 3: Deák tér. Open May-Oct. M-Sa 9am-5pm; Nov.-Apr. M-Sa 10am-4pm. Mass M-Sa 7, 8am, 6pm; Su 8:30, 10am (High mass), noon, 6pm. Church free. See the relic M-Sa 9am-5pm, Su 1-4pm. 200Ft, students 150Ft. Tower open daily June-Aug. 9:30am-6pm; Sept.-Oct. 10am-5:30pm; Apr.-May 10am-4:30pm. Tower 500Ft, students 400Ft.)*

ANDRÁSSY ÚT AND HEROES' SQUARE (HŐSÖK TERE). Built in 1872, the elegant balconies and gated gardens of Hungary's grandest boulevard are reminiscent of Budapest's Golden Age. Perhaps the most vivid reminder of this era is the Neo-Renaissance **Hungarian National Opera House** (Magyar Állami Operaház), whose walls are adorned with magnificent paintings. *(Andrássy út 22. M1: Opera. ☎ 332 8197. 1hr. English tours daily 3 and 4pm. 2000Ft, students 1000Ft. 20% off with Budapest Card. See Entertainment p. 361 for show info.)* The **House of Terror** (see p. 360), home of both Nazi and Soviet police headquarters, lies along it. Andrássy út's most majestic stretch is near Heroes' Square, where the **Millennium Monument** (Millenniumi emlékmű) dominates the street. The structure, built for the city's millennial anniversary, commemorates the nation's most prominent leaders. The seven horsemen at the base represent the Magyar tribes who settled the Carpathian Basin. Archangel Gabriel, atop the statue, holds the Hungarian crown to St. Stephen. On either side are the **Museum of Fine Arts** and the **Museum of Modern Art,** respectively. *(VI. Andrássy út stretches along M1 from Bajcsy-Zsilnszky út to Hősök tere.)*

CITY PARK (VÁROSLIGET). The shaded paths of City Park are perfect for lazy strolls by the lake. Balloon vendors and hot dog stands herald a small **amusement park,** a permanent **circus,** and a **zoo. Vajdahunyad Castle** sits in the center. Created for the 1896 millennium celebration, the castle's facade is a beautiful collage of Hungarian architecture through the ages. The only part you can visit is the **Magyar Agricultural Museum,** which has exhibits on rural life. *(Open Su and Tu-F 10am-5pm, Sa 10am-6pm. 400-1200Ft.)* Outside the castle broods the hooded statue of Anonymous, King Béla IV's scribe and the country's first historian, who recorded everything about medieval Hungary but his own name. Across the castle moat lies the **Bridge of Love.** Legend says that if sweethearts kiss below the bridge, they'll marry within three years. Those already married can kiss to secure eternal love. Be sure to take a dunk in the **Széchenyi baths** (p. 362) before leaving. *(XIV. M1: Széchenyi Fürdő. Zoo ☎ 343 6075. Open May-Aug. M-Th 9am-6pm, F-Su 9am-7pm; daily Sept.-Oct. 9am-5pm; Nov.-Feb. 9am-4pm. 1300Ft, children 900Ft, students 1000Ft. Park ☎ 363-8310. Open May-June M-F 11am-7pm, Sa-Su 10am-8pm.; daily July-Aug. 10am-8pm. 300Ft.)*

🏛 MUSEUMS

The beautiful buildings that house Budapest's eclectic museums are delightful. Thoughtful patrons can find backroom gems that a see-the-sights plan would surely miss. Museums attract relatively little attention here—you'll have space to enjoy paintings and artifacts that would be mobbed in other capitals.

🖼 MUSEUM OF FINE ARTS (SZÉPMŰVÉSZETI MÚZEUM). This magnificent building has an extensive collection of European art. In addition to countless paintings by world-famous artists, the museum houses a precious stone collection, a pottery display, and many sculptures. *(XIV. Hősök tere. M1: Hősök tere. ☎ 469 7100, English ☎ 069 036 9300. Open Tu-Su 10am-5:30pm. Free English tours Tu-F 11am. Museum 900Ft, students 500Ft. Cameras 300Ft, video 1500Ft.)*

🖼 NATIONAL MUSEUM (NEMZETI MÚZEUM). An extensive exhibition chronicles the history of Hungary. The exhibit extends from the neolithic era through the 21st century. In one room, a cheery Stalin reaches out to guide you to rooms devoted to Soviet propaganda, while past exhibits have included current events information, often regarding the EU. Descriptions have English translations and historical maps. *(VIII. Múzeum krt. 14/16. M3: Kálvin tér. ☎ 338 2122; www.mng.hu. Open Mar.-Oct. 15 Tu-Su 10am-6pm; Oct. 16- Feb. 28 Tu-Su 10am-5pm. 800Ft, students 400Ft.)*

🖼 STATUE PARK MUSEUM (SZOBORPARK MÚZEUM). Encircled by a brick wall so that locals can avoid seeing the faces of their oppressors, this park houses a collection of communist statues, often scary and imposing, gathered from Budapest's parks and squares after the collapse of Soviet rule. There are no captions beside the statues, but the indispensable English guidebook (1000Ft) explains the facts. *(XXII. On the corner of Balatoni út and Szabadkai út. Take express bus #7 from Keleti pu. to Étele tér, then take the Volán bus from terminal #2 to Diósd (15min., every 15 min.). ☎ 424 7500; www.szoborpark.hu. Open daily Mar.-Nov. 10am-dusk, weather permitting; Dec.-Feb. Sa-Su and holidays only. 600Ft, students 400Ft.)*

HOUSE OF TERROR (TERROR HÁZA). This museum is housed in the former headquarters of the Hungarian Nazi Party and later the Soviet secret police. The city's most technologically advanced museum, it has a series of strikingly realistic and comprehensive exhibits explained by the headset you receive upon entrance. For further explanation, pick up a summary, available in each of the rooms, which details the horrific history of the Hungarian Holocaust. Perhaps the most appalling part of the tour is the elevator ride during which a former Nazi soldier explains on video clip how he killed Jews. The basement, a series of actual torture chambers and prison cells, is equally horrifying. *(VI. Andrássy út 60. M1: Vörösmarty u. ☎ 374 2600; www.terrorhaza.hu. Open Tu-Su 10am-6pm. 3000Ft, students 1500Ft.)*

MUSEUM OF APPLIED ARTS (IPARMŰVÉSZETI MÚZEUM). This collection of handcrafted pieces—including Tiffany glass, furniture, metalwork, and ceramics—deserves careful examination. Excellent temporary exhibits highlight specific crafts, while videos show artists at work. Built for the 1896 millennium celebration, the building's Hungarian Art Nouveau architecture is as detailed, interesting, and important as the pieces within. *(IX. Üllői út 33-37. M3: Ferenc krt. ☎ 456 5100. Open daily 10am-6pm. 1-2hr. guided tours, under 6 people 2500Ft total, 6-25 people 200Ft each. English pamphlet 100Ft. Museum 600Ft, students 300Ft.)*

JEWISH MUSEUM (ZSIDÓ MÚZEUM). The first Jewish people arrived in Budapest with the Romans during the 1st century. Then confined to Buda, they moved to central Pest in 1873 when Joseph II gave them free settlement in Hungary. The beautiful Jewish museum, beside the Synagogue, celebrates the rich Jewish presence in the region, with exhibits ranging from commemoration of Holocaust victims to celebration of the customs and holidays which have helped Jewish people survive oppression. The museum is also the birthplace of Theodor Herzl (1860-1904), founder of the Zionist nation. Admission includes entrance to the Great Synagogue. *(VII. See p. 358. M2: Astoria. Open May-Oct. M-Th 10am-5pm, F 10am-1pm, Su 10am-2pm; Nov.-Apr. M-F 10am-3pm, F 10am-1pm, Su 10am-1pm. Tours M-Th 10:30am-3:30pm every 30min., F and Su 10:30, 11:30am, 12:30pm. Tours 1900Ft, students 1700Ft. Museum 600Ft, with ISIC 200Ft.)*

BUDA CASTLE. Leveled by Soviets and Nazis, the palace now houses several fine museums. You will not be able to traverse all of them in one day. *(I. Szent György tér 2. M1, 2, or 3: Deák tér, then take bus #16 across the Danube to the top of Castle Hill. ☎375 7533.)* **Wing A** houses the **Museum of Contemporary Art** (Kortárs Művészeti Múzeum) and the smaller **Ludwig Museum,** both devoted to Picasso, Warhol, Lichtenstein, and other big names in modern art. The highlight is the impressive collection of works by Eastern European artists, many of whom were oppressed under Soviet rule. *(☎375 9175; www.ludwigmuseum.hu. Open Tu-Su 10am-6pm. 600Ft, students 300Ft. Cameras 1200Ft, video 2000Ft.)* **Wings B-D** hold the huge **Hungarian National Gallery** (Magyar Nemzeti Galéria), a definitive collection of the best in Hungarian painting and sculpture. Organized chronologically from Medieval and Renaissance art to a spectacular 20th-century sculpture exhibit, its treasures include works by realist Mihály Munkácsy and impressionist Pál Mersei, gold medieval altarpieces, and many depictions of national tragedies. *(☎375 7533. Open Tu-Su 10am-6pm. English tour by appointment. Museum free.)* **Wing E** houses the well-organized **Budapest History Museum** (Budapesti Történeti Múzeum), a collection of artifacts found in Budapest from the Middle Ages to today, including weapons, tombstones, and glassware. *(☎375 7533. English info. Open Mar.-Nov. M and W-Su 10am-6pm; Nov.-Mar. 10am-4pm. 800Ft, students 400Ft.)*

🎵 ENTERTAINMENT

Budapest's cultural life flourishes with a series of performance events (for more info on festivals, visit **IBUSZ,** see p. 349). In August, Óbudai Island hosts the week-long **Sziget (Pepsi Island) Festival,** Europe's largest open-air rock festival. (☎372 0650. Call for ticket prices.) Hungary's largest cultural festival, the **Budapest Spring Festival** (☎486 3311) showcases Hungary's premier musicians and actors in the last two weeks of March. The **Danube Festival** in late June celebrates the building of the Chain Bridge that links Buda and Pest. Highlights include traditional Hungarian folk dancing and contemporary dance acts, which end in a fireworks display. Racing enthusiasts zoom into the suburb of Mogyoró each August to attend the **Formula 1 Hungarian Grand Prix** (☎317 2811; www.hungaroring.hu). Prices for most performance events are reasonable; check the **Music Mix 33 Ticket Service,** V, Ferenciek tér 10. (☎317 7736; www.musicmix.hu. Open M-F 9am-5pm.) Free guides available at tourist offices and hotels detail everything from festivals to art showings. The "Style" section of the *Budapest Sun* (www.budapestsun.com; 300Ft) has 10-day listings and an English-language film reviews. Movie theaters abound, especially in malls. (Tickets 600-1200Ft). **Westend City Center,** next to Nyugati Pu. on the city's west end, is Budapest's biggest shopping mall, stocking everything from clothes to electronics. (M3: Nyugati Pu. ☎238 7777; info@westend.hu. Open M-F 7am-midnight, Sa-Su 10am-6pm.) The five levels of **Mammut,** in central Buda, are packed with Western boutiques. (M2: Moszkva tér. 345 8020; www.mammut.hu. Open M-Sa 10am-9pm, Su 10am-6pm.)

HUNGARY

■ **State Opera House** (Magyar Állami Operaház), VI, Andrássy út 22 (☎331 2550, box office 353 0170). M1: Opera. One of Europe's leading performance centers hosts operettas, ballets, and orchestra concerts. While some shows sell out a yr. ahead of time, many have seats available the day of the performance. Tickets 800-8700Ft. Box office open M-Sa 11am-7pm, Su 4-7pm. Closes at 5pm on non-performance days.

National Dance Theater (Nemzeti Táncszínház), Szinház u. 1-3, I (☎201 4407, box office 375 8649; www.nemzetitancszinhaz.hu), on Castle Hill. The theater hosts a variety of shows, but the Hungarian folklore shows are most popular. Most shows 7pm.

Városmajor Open-Air Theater, XII, Városmajor (☎375 5922). M1: Moszkva tér. Walk up the big stairs, right on Várfok u., left on Csaba u., right on Maros u., and left on Szamos u. Performances in this lovely open-air theater include a diverse selection of musicals, operas, and ballets. Open June 27-Aug. 18. Box office open W-Su 3-6pm.

Millenáris Park, II, Lövőház u. 39 (☎438 5335, box office 438 5312; www.millenaris.hu). M2: Moszkva ter. This hidden park has three indoor theaters, an outdoor theater, and a projection screen in the lawn which broadcasts live sports. While occasional art shows take place outside, the theaters host acts ranging from jazz performances to ballets and movie screenings. Call or visit the box office, just inside the theater, for details and program listings. Tickets 400-1600Ft. Park open daily 6am-2am.

Pesti Vigadó (Pest Concert Hall), V, Vigadó tér 2 (☎318 9167; fax 375 6222). On the Danube near Vörösmarty tér. A beautiful building houses orchestra and opera performances. Shows feature flashy costumes and lots of vibrato. Hosts operettas every other night. Box office open M-Sa 10am-6pm.

◨ BATHS

Experiencing Budapest's thermal baths is a must. Flowing up from underground springs, the medicinal baths are frequented by locals and tourists alike for their supposed healing powers. Many bathe in the nude, but baths are separated by gender and suits are required in pools. Most are clean and strictly enforce rules.

■ **Széchenyi**, XIV, Állatkerti u. 11/14 (☎321 0310). M1: Hősök tere. In the center of City Park, this is one of the biggest and most luxurious bath complexes in Europe, with 3 swimming pools and 12 thermal baths. Massage, spa, and a variety of medical treatments available. Play on floating chessboards in the outdoor pool or lounge in the sun. Open daily May-Sept. 6am-7pm; Oct.-Apr. M-F 6am-7pm, Sa-Su 6am-5pm. 1900Ft. 900Ft returned if you leave within 2hr., 500Ft within 3hr., and 200Ft within 4hr.; keep your original receipt. 15min. massage 2400Ft.

Gellért, XI, Kelenhegyi út 4/6 (☎466 6166). Bus #7 or tram #47 or 49 to Hotel Gellért, at the base of Gellért-hegy. Known as one of the most elegant baths in Budapest, Gellért's boasts a rooftop sun-deck, wave pool, and a la carte spa options, including mud baths and "Thai massage" (11000Ft, call for reservations). Baths and pools open M-F 6am-7pm, Sa-Su 6am-5pm. Thermal bath and pool 2900Ft. 15min. massage 2400Ft, pedicure 1300Ft, foot massage 800Ft. MC/V.

Király, I, Fő u. 84 (☎202 3688). M2: Batthány tér. Basic baths in a building featuring Turkish architecture. Almost 500 years old, these baths have remained authentic and have no swimming pools. Here, bathing is a truly relaxing experience. Women only M, W, F 7am-6pm; men only Tu, Th, Sa 9am-8pm. Call ahead first, as the days often switch. 1000Ft. 15min. massage in private room 1500Ft, 30min. 2200Ft.

Rudas, XI, Döbrentei tér 9 (☎356 1322). Take bus #7 to the 1st stop in Buda. On the river under a dome built by Turks 400 years ago, this is the gorgeous bath you see in the brochures. Age hasn't altered the dome, the bathing chamber, or the "men-only" rule. The main swimming pool and 4 smaller ones, each of a different temperature, allow women. Open M-F 6am-6pm, Sa 6am-1pm. Baths 1000Ft. Pool 700Ft.

NIGHTLIFE

On any night in Budapest, you can experience an amazing variety of scenes, from lively all-night outdoor parties to thumping discos to elegant clubs. Despite throbbing crowds in the clubs and pubs, the streets themselves are surprisingly empty. The chic cafes in VI, **Ferencz Liszt tér** (M2: Oktogon) are the newest retreat for Budapest's youth. In summer, the scene moves to outdoor venues, the biggest of which are along the Danube, where great views and cheap drinks abound. Outdoor venues open from late April to mid-September. Ask Tourinform for entertainment guides that will get you to the most happening scenes.

> **NIGHTLIFE SCAM.** There have been reports of a mafia-organized scam involving a Hungarian woman who approaches foreign men and suggest that they buy her a drink. The bill, accompanied by imposing men, can be US$1000 for a single drink. If he claims not to have money, they have an ATM in the bar. The US embassy has advised against patronizing certain establishments in the Váci u. area. Check prices before ordering at places you are not sure about. For a current list of establishments about which complaints have been filed, check the US embassy's list at www.usembassy.hu/conseng/announcements.html#advisory. If you face this situation, call the police. You'll probably still have to pay, but get a receipt to complain formally at the Consumer Bureau.

PUBS

Old Man's Music Pub, VII, Akácfa u. 13 (☎322 7645; www.oldmans.hu). M2: Blaha Lujza tér. Popular with locals, expats, and tourists, this underground institution features live blues and jazz every evening at 11pm—check the schedule and arrive early as it gets very crowded very quickly. Relax in the pub (open 3pm-3am) or hit the small and crowded dance floor (11pm-late). Count your change. Open M-Sa 3pm-4:30am.

Fat Mo's Speakeasy, V, Nyári Pál u. 11 (☎267 3199). M3: Kálvin tér. "Spitting prohibited" in this bar, which celebrates Prohibition speakeasies. Come for 14 varieties of draft beer (450-1000Ft) and stay for live jazz and blues (Su-Th 9-11pm). Th-Sa DJ after midnight. No cover. Open M-W noon-2am, Th-F noon-4am, Sa 6pm-4am, Su 6pm-2am.

Crazy Café, VI, Jókai u. 30 (☎302 4003). M3: Nyugati pu. The place to start a long night out. With 30 kinds of whiskey (shots 450-890Ft), 8 kinds of tequila (690Ft), and 17 kinds of vodka (590-690Ft), the scene at this underground, vaguely jungle-themed bar has been known to get hot and rowdy. Karaoke Su-Tu. Open daily 11am-1am.

Borpatika (Wine Bar), XI, Bertalan L. út 26 (☎204 2644). Take tram #47 or 49 from Deák tér to Bertalan Lajos. This tavern lures adult patrons to its boisterous happy hour. Open daily 8am-midnight.

SUMMER VENUES

 Zöld Pardon, XI, on the Buda side of Petőfi Bridge. If you're wondering where everyone is on seemingly quiet weeknights, wonder no more. 3 large screens project the funny goings-on on the giant dance floor—make yourself seen in this bar which easily holds 1000. Multiple bars, including one on a fake island. Snack bar to satisfy late-night cravings. Beer 250-400Ft. Open daily 9am-6am.

Rio, XI, on the Buda side of Petőfi Bridge. Budapest's young and raucous convene at Rio, where ravers dance the night away. Open daily 9am-6am.

Rudas Romkért, XI, Döbrentei tér 9, just over Szabadság Bridge. Take the bus #7 to the 1st stop in Buda. Upscale and trendy, this beer garden is packed with twenty-somethings. Beer 350-800Ft. Open M-F noon-3am, Sa 6pm-5am, Su 6pm-3am.

CLUBS

■ **Undergrass,** VI, Ferencz Liszt tér 10 (☎322 0830). M1: Oktogon. Tram #4 or 6. The hottest club in Pest's trendiest area. Behind the bank vault door, the underground bar has little seating, but most patrons are happy to stand. The soundproof door allows bar talk while the disco spins funk and pop. Cover F 300Ft, Sa 1000Ft. Open F-Sa 10pm-4am.

Piaf, VI, Nagymező u. 25 (☎312 3823). A much-loved after-hours spot and the final destination for many. Guests are admitted into the red velvet lounge after knocking on an inconspicuous door and meeting the approval of the club's matron. Cover 800Ft, includes 1 beer. Open Su-Th 10pm-6am, F-Sa 10pm-7am; don't come before 1am.

Club Seven, VII, Akácfa u. 7 (☎478 9030). M2: Blaha Lujza tér. Upscale but crowded local favorite that plays funk, jazz, soul, or disco every night of the week. Cover Sa-Su men 2000Ft, women free. Open daily 6pm-5am, casino open 10pm-5am.

Jazz Garden, V, Veres Pálné u. 44a (☎266 7364). This joint has live jazz every night, 2 dining rooms, and a full bar. Descend the stairs into the brick layered "garden" terrace, complete with lanterns, low-hanging vines, and a stage. The next room is more sophisticated. Beer 500-550. Performances at 9pm. Open daily 6pm-midnight.

GLBT BUDAPEST

An underground world for decades, GLBT Budapest is only beginning to appear in the mainstream. Still, it's safer to be discreet. If you run into problems or are looking for info on gay venues or accommodations, contact the **gay hotline** (☎0630 932 33 34; budapest@gayguide.net), and take advantage of the knowledgeable staff. The website **www.budapest.gayguide.net** has up-to-date info on what's hot. **Na Végre** is a free monthly digest with an English section with entertainment listings. It can be found at most of the establishments below, which are either gay-friendly or have gay clientele.

Café Eklektika, V, Semmelweis u. 21 (☎266 3054). Lesbian-owned and operated, this cafe is centrally located and hosts special events. Dance classes (Th and Su 6pm, 500Ft) with prize-winning instructors and women's parties (2nd Sa of each month). Open M-F 10am-1am, Sa-Su 5pm-1am.

Angyal (Angel) Bar, VII, Szövetség u. 33 (☎351 6490). M2: Blaha L. tér. 1st gay bar in Budapest. Huge 3-level disco, cafe, and bar packed weekends. F-Sa drag shows. Cover 1000Ft. Open F-Sa 10pm-5am.

Capella, V, Belgrád rakpart 23 (☎318 6231; www.extra.hu/capellacafe). Very popular, this 3-level cafe has reopened after renovations. Attracts a gay, lesbian, and mixed crowd.

▶ DAYTRIPS FROM BUDAPEST

SZENTENDRE   ☎(0)26

HÉV travels from Batthyány tér (45min., every 20min., 374Ft). Buses run from the Árpád híd Metro station (30min., every 20-40min., 240Ft). Boats (☎484 4000) leave from pier below Vigadó tér (1½hr.; 2 per day; 950Ft, students 713Ft). HÉV, train, and bus stations are a 10min. walk from Fő tér, the main square. Descend stairs past the end of the HÉV tracks, go through the underpass, and head up Kossuth út. At fork in road, bear right on Dumtsa Jenő út. From ferry station, turn left on Czóbel sétány and left on Dunakorzó u.

To glimpse Hungary's rural past without straying far from Budapest, head to ■**Szentendre,** where cobblestone streets and masterful art abound in a city known for its relaxing, pleasant pace. The streets are packed with tourists, but the museums and art galleries, which host a variety of unique exhibits, remain uncramped.

Start your visit by climbing **Church Hill** (Templomdomb), above the town center in Fő tér, to visit the 13th-century **Catholic Church** (Plébánia-templom), one of the few medieval churches left in Hungary, which boasts the best view in town. The sundial on the wall inside the church is one of the oldest in the country. (Open Tu-Su 10am-4pm. Services Su 7am. Free.)

The **Czóbel Museum,** Templom tér 1, left of the church, displays the work of Béla Czóbel, Hungary's foremost post-Impressionist painter, including his "Venus of Szentendre." Admission includes access to the adjoining exhibit of works by the Szentendre Artists' Colony. (☎312 721. Open Tu-Su 10am-6pm. English captions. 400Ft, students 200Ft.) Szentendre's most popular museum, the **Margit Kovács Museum,** Vastagh György út 1, exhibits whimsical ceramic sculptures by the 20th-century Budapest artist. (☎310 244, ext. 114; fax 310 790. Open daily Mar.-Oct. 10am-6pm; Nov. 9am-5pm; Dec.-Feb. Tu-Su 10am-5pm. 600Ft, students 300Ft.) The ▧**National Wine Museum** (Nemzeti Bormúzuem), Bogdányi u. 10, is a cellar exhibit of wines from Hungary's eight wine-making regions. A wine tasting (1600Ft) includes 10 samples, Hungarian appetizers, and admission to the exhibition. (☎/ fax 317 054. Exhibit 100Ft. Open daily 10am-10pm.) The edible exhibits of the ▧**Szabó Marzipan Museum and Confectionery,** Dumtsa Jenő út 7, are made entirely of marzipan. Watch the artists work; then look at more intricate creations, including scenes from fairytales, historical figures, and a 80kg statue of Michael Jackson, which is made of white chocolate. To indulge your sweet tooth, head downstairs to the gift shop or adjoining cafe. (☎311 931. Open daily May-Sept. 10am-7pm; Oct.-Apr. 10am-6pm. 350Ft.)

Get info and **maps** from **Tourinform,** Dumsta Jenő út 22. (☎317 965; www.szentendre.hu. Open Mar. 16-Nov. 2 M-F 9am-4:30pm, Sa-Su 10am-2pm; Nov. 3-Mar. 15 M-F 9:30am-4:30pm.) ▧**Nostalgia Cafe ❷,** Bogdányi u. 2, owned by internationally recognized opera-singers, sometimes host concerts in the outdoor courtyard. Try the "Special Nostalgia Coffee," made with orange liqueur, chocolate bits, and whipped cream. (☎311 660. Pastry or coffee from 300Ft. Open daily 10am-10pm.) If you stay overnight, **Ilona Panzió ❸,** Rákóczi Ferenc út 11, rents rooms with private baths. (☎313 599. Breakfast included. Call ahead. Doubles 6600Ft; triples 8000Ft.) Popular **Pap-szigeti Camping ❷** sits 2km north of the center on its own island in the Danube, near a small but popular beach. (☎310 697; fax 313 777. Call ahead. Open May-Oct. 15. Tent sites 2100Ft. 2-person caravan 3600Ft, each additional person 1000Ft. Pension rooms with shower doubles 5500Ft; triples 6500Ft; quads 7500Ft.)

ESZTERGOM ☎(0)33

Trains run from Budapest (1½hr., 22 per day, 436Ft). Catch a bus from Szentendre (1½hr., 1 per hr., 476Ft) or Visegrád (45min., 1 per hr., 316Ft). Boats (☎484 4000) also hail from Budapest (4hr.; 3 per day; 1200Ft, students 900Ft); Szentendre (2¾hr.; 2 per day; 980Ft, students 490Ft); and Visegrád (1½hr.; 2 per day; 700Ft, students 525Ft). The train station is an easy 10min. walk from town. Facing away from the station, go left on the main street. Follow the street around the bend, and then turn right at Kiss János Altábornagy út. From the bus station, walk up Simor János u. toward the market.

One thousand years of religious history have earned Esztergom the nickname "the Hungarian Rome," as pilgrims still flock to its winding streets. The birthplace of Saint-King Stephen and the site of the first Royal Court of Hungary, the cathedral remains central to Catholicism in Hungary. For info, visit **Grantours,** Széchenyi tér 25, at the edge of Rákóczi tér, which also sells maps. (☎417 052; grantour@mail.holop.hu. Open July-Aug. M-F 8am-6pm, Sa 9am-noon; Sept.-June M-F 8am-4pm, Sa 9am-noon.) Named the **Basilica of Esztergom,** the Neoclassical cathedral, Hungary's largest, was consecrated in honor of St. Adalbert in 1856. The red marble **Bakócz Chapel,** to the nave's left, is a Renaissance masterpiece. Dismantled

HUNGARY

during Turkish occupation, the chapel was reassembled from 1600 pieces. (Open daily Mar.-Oct. 9am-4pm; Nov.-Dec. M-F 11am-3:30pm, Sa-Su 10am-3:30pm. English guidebook 100Ft. Chapel free.) Its **treasury** houses religious iconography, ornate relics, and textiles spanning a millennium. A jewel-studded cross served as the 13th-century **Coronation Oath Cross** (Koronázási Eskükereszt) on which Hungary's rulers pledged their oaths until 1916. (Open Tu-Su 9am-4:30pm. 400Ft, students 200Ft.) Ascend the interminable staircases to the cathedral ⬛**cupola** (200Ft) for an incredible echo and the best view of the Danube Bend. On clear days, you can see the Slovak Low Tatras. The **crypt** below the cathedral holds the remains of Hungary's archbishops. (Open Tu-Su 9am-4:45pm. 100Ft.) The **museum** surrounding the cathedral was built atop the ruins of the 972 **castle** where St. Stephen was born. An architecture-lover's dream, the museum exhibits excavated fragments of the castle. Look through a glass floor onto an excavation site. The exhibit has helpful English captions. (☎415 986. Free. Open Tu-Su 10am-4:45pm). **Csülök Csárda** ❷, Batthyány út 9, serves fine cuisine, adding creative variations to the usual repertoire of roasts and stews. Try the mushroom soup with sour cream (790Ft) or the fillet of catfish with garlic (1590Ft). Vegetarian options are available. (☎412 420. Entrees 480-1800Ft. Open daily noon-10pm.)

SZÉKESFEHÉRVÁR   ☎(0)22

Take the train from Budapest (1hr., 21 per day, 594Ft). To get to the center from the train station, walk down Deák Ferenc u. Turn left on the Budai út and then right on Varkörút. Buses also run from Budapest (1hr., 4 per day, 478Ft). From the bus station (☎311 057), on Piac tér, veer left of terminal #2 and take a right on Liszt Ferenc u., which becomes Városház tér.

Géza, St. Stephen's father, established Székesfehérvár in AD 972, making it **Hungary's oldest town.** Today, those traveling from Budapest to Balaton stop in this friendly, unpretentious city to visit the extraordinary ⬛**Bory Castle** (Bory-vár). Take bus #32 from the train station to Vágújhelyi u., walk down the hill, and turn left on Bory tér. Not your typical Hungarian castle (partly because it remains intact), it was built over the course of nearly 40 summers, beginning in the 1920s. Architect and sculptor Jenő Bory constructed this mansion by hand in honor of his wife, his art, and his country's history. This beautiful palace resembles a fairytale castle: it is endowed with towers, terraced gardens, crooked paths, winding staircases, and stone chambers. Bory decorated every inch of this eccentric retreat and erected a chapel for his wife as the ultimate "monument to marital love." The small museum displays dozens of Bory's sculptures as well as paintings by the architect and his wife. Today his grandson and his family live in the castle and care for the museum. (☎305 570. Open daily 9am-5pm. 400Ft, students 200Ft.) Many explore Székesfehérvár's cobblestone streets. Pick up a walking tour guidebook and **free maps** at **Tourinform,** Városház tér 1 (☎312 818; fax 502 772). In the center, the **King St. Stephen Museum** (Szent István Király Múzeum), Fő u. 6, houses an archaeology exhibit that showcases fantastic Roman artifacts. (☎315 583. Open Apr. 29-Oct. Tu-Su 10am-4pm; Mar. 4-Apr. 28 Tu-Su 10am-2pm. 260Ft, students 120Ft.) The **Budenz House: Ybl Collection** (Budenz-ház: Ybl Gyűjtemény), Arany János út 12, includes exquisite 18th- to 20th-century Hungarian art and furniture. Learn more about Miklós Ybl, one of Budapest's preeminent architects, through the display of family portraits and medals on the second floor of the building. (☎313 027. Open Tu-Su 10am-4pm. 260Ft, students 120Ft.)

   Match Supermarket, Palotai u. 1-3, inside Alba Shopping Plaza, sells the basics. (Open M-Sa 7am-9pm, Su 8am-6pm.) Straddling pedestrian Fo u., **Korzó Söröző** ❸ serves Hungarian dishes like liver soup and goulash on one side, and beers and spirits on the other. (☎312 373 Entrees 700-3200Ft. Open daily 10am-midnight). If you're spending the night in Székesfehérvár, the newly renovated **Szent Gellért Tanulmányi Ház ❹**, Mátyás Király krt 1, is a 10min. walk from the city center. It offers rooms, and less-expensive dorms. (☎510 810; szentgellert@axelero.hu. Dorms 2300Ft. Singles 8800Ft; doubles 10,900Ft; triples 17,400Ft. Tax 300Ft.)

NORTHERN HUNGARY

Hungary's northern upland is dominated by a series of low mountain ranges running northeast from the Danube Bend along the Slovak border. The mountain villages delight in local custom and opportunity to explore. The charming, historic towns of Eger and Tokaj are home to world-famous wineries, while Bükk and Aggtelek National Parks beckon hikers with scenic trails and stunning caves.

EGER   ☎(06)36

The Ottomans captured Eger Castle in 1557, but Captain István Dobó's victorious stand against the sieging Turks four years prior is still hailed as a miracle. The legendary key to his triumph: the strengthening powers of *Egri Bikavér* (Bull's Blood) wine. The region's legacy of powerful wines continues in the spirted cellars of the Valley of Beautiful Women. Though Eger (EGG-air, pop. 57,000) is a good daytrip from Budapest, its cobblestone streets, culinary delicacies, and infectious friendliness inspire many visitors to extend their stay.

TRANSPORTATION

Trains: Vasút u. (☎314 264). To: **Budapest** (2hr.; 21 per day, 6 direct; 1036-1242Ft); **Szeged** (4½hr., 12 per day, 3050Ft). Non-direct trains run to **Keleti station** via **Füzesabony.**

Buses: Barkóczy u. (☎511 706; www.agriavolan.hu). To: **Aggtelek** (3½hr., 1 per day at 8:45am, 1309Ft); **Budapest** (2hr., 15-20 per day, 1360Ft); **Debrecen** (3hr., 5-6 per day, 1296Ft); **Szilvásvárad** (45min., 4 per day, 316Ft).

Taxis: City Taxi ☎555 555.

ORIENTATION AND PRACTICAL INFORMATION

The **train station** lies on the outskirts of town. To walk to the **Dobó tér,** the main square and town center, from the train station (20min.), head straight and take a right on Deák Ferenc út, a right on Kossuth Lajos u., and a left on Tokaj u. To get to the center from the bus station, turn right on **Barkóczy u.** from terminal #10 and right again at the next main street, **Bródy u.** Follow the stairs to the end of the street and turn right on **Széchenyi u.;** a left down **Érsek u.** leads to Dobó tér. Most sights are within a 10min. walk of the square.

Tourist Office: Tourinform, Bajcsy-Zsilinszky u. 9 (☎517 715; www.tourinform.hu/eger). Free **maps.** Open June-Sept. M-F 9am-7pm, Sa-Su 10am-6pm; Oct.-May M-F 9am-5pm, Sa 9am-1pm.

Bank: OTP, Széchenyi u. 2 (☎310 866; fax 313 554), gives AmEx/MC/V **cash advances** and cashes **AmEx Traveler's Cheques** for no commission. A MC/V **ATM** stands outside. Open M-Tu and Th 7:45am-5pm, W 7:45am-6pm, F 7:45am-4pm; currency desk open M-Tu and Th 7:45am-2:45pm, W 7:45am-4:30pm, F 7:45am-noon. A 24hr. **currency exchange** machine is opposite the church on Dobó tér.

Luggage Storage: Available at the bus station.

HUNGARY

English-Language Bookstore: City Press, next to the Széchenyi u. Post Office, carries English-language newspapers.

Pharmacy: Zalár Patika, Zalár Jósef u. (☎310 191), stocks Western products. Open daily 7:30am-8pm. MC/V.

Hospital: Knézich Károly u. 1-3 (☎411 414). Open M-Th 7am-6pm, F 7am-4pm. Call number in an emergency on weekends.

Internet: Broadway Cafe, Kossuth Lajos u. 3 (☎517 220), has several computers in relative privacy. **Bar,** with small dining area inside and patio outside, is located under the Eger Cathedral. 250Ft. per hr. Open M-Sa noon-11pm, Su 3pm-11pm.

Post Office: Széchenyi u. 22 (☎313 232). Open M-F 8am-8pm, Sa 8am-2pm. **Poste Restante** available. **Telephones** outside. **Postal Code: 3300.**

⛰ ACCOMMODATIONS

Accommodations are plentiful within Eger's central city. **Private rooms** (around 3000Ft) are a welcoming option. Look for *Zimmer frei* or *szoba eladó* signs outside the main square, particularly near the castle on Almagyar u. and Mekcsey István u. **Eger Tourist ❷,** Bajcsy-Zsilinszky u. 9, arranges private rooms. (☎517 000; fax 510 270. Open M-F 9am-5pm. Rooms around 3000Ft.)

Lukács Vendégház, Bárány u. 10 (☎/fax 411 567), next to Eger Castle. With its own garden, outdoor seating area, and spacious rooms, this guesthouse provides comfort without the cost. 1- to 4-person rooms 2500-4000Ft. ❶

Hotel Minaret, Knézich K. u. 4, (☎/fax 410 233), is centrally located. Indulge in the beauty center, massage center, tanning salon, swimming pool, and underwater gym. All rooms include satellite TV. Singles 87,000Ft; doubles 14,900Ft; triples 2,500Ft; quads 31,300Ft. Prices about 1000Ft lower Nov.-Mar. ❹

Autós Caravan Camping, Rákóczi u. 79 (☎/fax 410 558), 20min. north of the center by bus #5, 11, or 12. Get off at the Shell station and follow the signs. Call ahead, or reserve bungalows or camp space through Eger Tourist. Open Apr. 15-Oct. 15. 500Ft per person, 300Ft per tent. ❶

🍴 FOOD

Piaccsarnok market is hidden just off Széchenyi u.—go right on Árva Köz; it's on the right at Katona J. tér. (Open M-F 6am-5pm, Sa 6am-1pm, Su 6-10am.) **Hossó ABC supermarket** is across the street. (Open M-F 6am-7pm, Sa 6am-1pm. Su 6am-11am. AmEx/MC/V.)

▧ Dobos, Széchenyi u. 6, offers a mouthwatering selection of decadent pastries and desserts (170-350 Ft). Indulge your sweet tooth with a marzipan snail or rose (280Ft), delicious ice cream (110Ft), or other creative confections. Open daily 9:30am-9pm. ❶

Kulacs Csárda Borozó (☎/fax 515 516), in the Valley of Nice Women. Hungarian cuisine in a vine-draped courtyard. Try the house specialty, boar stew, before walking across the street to the cellars. Meals 950-2000Ft. Open M and W-Su noon-11pm. ❸

Bajor Sörház, Bajcsy-Zsilinsky u. 19 (☎316 312), off Dobó tér, to the right of the church. Sells unique "Hungarian standards" such as cold brains, ham knuckles, and liver. Other less daring yet authentic options are also available. English menu. Entrees 850-2950Ft. Open daily 11:30am-10pm. AmEx/MC/V. ❸

Gyros Étterem Sörözö, Széchenyi u. 10 (☎413 781), serves gyros (450-950Ft) and roasts (850-1800Ft) in a well-cared-for setting with a patio. Open daily 9am-10pm. ❷

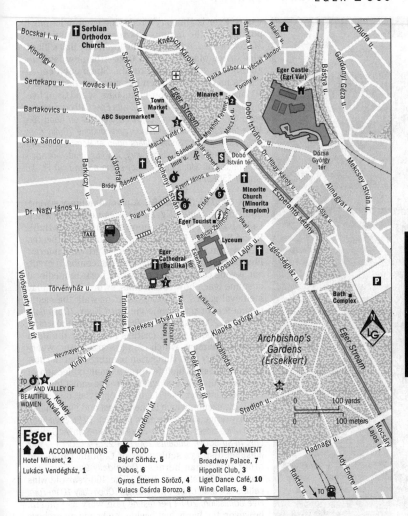

Eger

▲▲ ACCOMMODATIONS	● FOOD	★ ENTERTAINMENT
Hotel Minaret, **2**	Bajor Sörház, **5**	Broadway Palace, **7**
Lukács Vendégház, **1**	Dobos, **6**	Hippolit Club, **3**
	Gyros Étterem Söröző, **4**	Liget Dance Café, **10**
	Kulacs Csárda Borozo, **8**	Wine Cellars, **9**

👁 SIGHTS

■ VALLEY OF BEAUTIFUL WOMEN (SZÉPASSZONY-VÖLGY). After exploring Eger's sights by day, spend the evening in the wine cellars of the Valley of Beautiful Women. Following WWII, cheap land allowed hundreds of wine cellars to sprout on this volcanic hillside. Most are little more than a tunnel and a few tables and benches, but each has its own personality: some are hushed while others burst with Hungarian and Roma sing-alongs. Subdued in the afternoon, the valley springs to life at night when its 25 cellars open their doors to host both serious wine tasters and those who stay around to chat with friends. They are in a row, so hop in and out to experience their different ambiences and sample their famous

LIVING LARGE IN THE LAVA TUNNELS

Walking around Eger, one doesn't see neon signs advertising posh dance clubs or tacky discos. It would make sense that this quiet little town, full of history and abundant wine, wouldn't need these modern diversions. However, the town is crawling with them—or more accurately, crawling on them. What most tourists would never guess is that below Eger is a labyrinth of passages. Eger is formed on a 120km bed of lava through which these tunnels have been carved. A few of them now have been converted to nightclubs, obscured to the world above except for small, barely marked entrances.

One of the most popular of these dens lies under the Eger Cathedral, where blaspheming youths dance the night away, leaving the club only a couple of hours before the church above opens for morning services. The entrance to Broadway Palace is on Kossuth L. u. on the left side of the Cathedral. (Cover 400-600Ft. Open W and F-Sa 10pm-4am.)

Another popular underground spot is Liget Dance Café, Érsekkert (☎42 77 54), under Excalibur restaurant in the Archbishop's Gardens. (Cover 600Ft. Open F-Sa 10pm-6am.) Hippolit Club and Restaurant, Katona tér 2, is more expensive and classier. (☎41 10 31. Dancing starts around 11pm. Open M-F noon-midnight, F-Sa noon-4am.)

wines. Eger is Hungary's red wine capital; its most popular are the famous *Bikavér* and the sweeter *Medok* or *Medina*. Sample the legendary **Bull's Blood wine** or **red wine mixed with Coke**—the new favorite among the younger generation. Since each cellar makes its own wine, each has a unique taste. After 10pm some become after-hours bars, with DJs or live music. *(Start out on Széchenyi u. with Eger Cathedral on the right. Go right on Kossuth Lajos u., then left on Kapu Tér. Make the 1st right on Telekessy u. and continue 20min. until Szépasszony-völgy. Some cellars open at 9am, but all are quiet until night. Closing times vary. July-Aug. some are open until midnight. Most tastes free, some around 50 Ft. 1L around 350Ft.)*

EGER CASTLE (EGRI VÁR). A pivotal military stronghold in the 1500s, Eger castle gained fame when Dobo Ivan, supposedly empowered by famous Bull's Blood Wine, led Hungarian troops to an unexpected victory against Ottoman invaders. Egri Vár's interior includes subterranean barracks, catacombs, a crypt, and a wine cellar. In the courtyard, hosts in medieval costume teach how to use stilts, sword fight, or play medieval games. Hike the tower or walk the castle perimeter for panoramic views of Eger. *(Open daily 8am-8pm. 200Ft, students 100Ft.)* An additional ticket buys admission to the castle's museums: the **Dobó István Vármúzeum**, which displays armor and weaponry; a **gallery** with Hungarian paintings; and the **dungeon exhibition**, which features a small collection of torture equipment that will inspire the sadist but horrify more innocent hearts. If you only visit one, go to the Vármúzeum, which is the biggest and has English descriptions. *(Museums open Mar.-Oct. Tu-Su 9am-5pm; ticket office closes at 4:20pm. Nov.-Feb. 9am-3pm. All 3 museums Tu-Su 500Ft, students 250Ft; M 250Ft/120Ft.)* A **wax museum** displays sculptures of Captain Dobó and other Hungarian heroes. *(Open daily 9am-6pm. Wax museum 350Ft, students 250Ft.)* The 400-year-old **wine cellars** are also open for tastings. *(Open daily 10am-7pm. Free admission; 200Ft per tasting.)* Be wary as you sip, however: the bar is just beside the hands-on archery exhibit of longbows with real arrows. *(☎312 744, info 432 813; www.div.iif.hu. Underground passages open M only. English tour 500Ft.)*

LYCEUM. The ceiling fresco in the 20,000 volume **Diocesan Library** on the first floor of the Rococo Lyceum portrays the Council of Trent, the meeting that established the edicts of the Counter-Reformation. Built in the late 18th century, the Rococo Lyceum, home to a college, is one of the most beautiful Baroque buildings in Hungary. Upstairs, an **astronomical museum** has 18th-century telescopes and instruments in its **Specula Observatory.** A marble line in the museum floor represents the meridian; when the sun strikes it through a pin-hole aperture in the south wall, it is astronomical noon. Two floors up, a **"camera obscura,"** made of a mirror and lenses, projects a live picture of the surrounding town onto a table, giving a god-like view of the city below. *(At the corner of Kossuth Lajos u. and Eszterházy tér. Open Apr.-Sept. Tu-Su 9:30am-3:30pm; Oct.-Mar. 9:30am-1pm, Sa-Su 9:30am-1:30pm. Library, museum, and camera obscura 450Ft; students 300Ft.)*

EGER CATHEDRAL. The only Neoclassical building in Eger, the 1887 cathedral, was designed to be the largest in Hungary. The soaring architecture, soft pastel hues, and intricately painted domes create a brighter feel than that of most Baroque interiors. **Organ Concerts** (30min.) are held from May to mid-October. *(On Eszterházy tér just off Széchenyi u. Concerts M-Sa 11:30am, Su 12:45pm. 400Ft. Church entrance is free when concerts are not in progress.)*

OTHER SIGHTS. The Ottomans' northernmost possession in Hungary, the **Minaret,** Knézich K. u., was used to call Muslim villagers to prayer. Its 97-step staircase might induce a touch of vertigo, but the view from top rewards the effort. *(Open Apr.-Oct. M-Su 10am-6pm. 100Ft.)* Below the high-vault ceilings of the 1758 pink marble **Minorite Church** hang intricate still-life paintings and detailed sculptures. *(In Dobó tér. ☎516 613. Open Apr.-Oct. Tu-Su 9am-6pm. Services Su 9am. Free.)* The 18th-century **Serbian Orthodox Church** (Szerb Ortodox Templom), on Vitkovics u. at the center's north end, drips with gilt decoration. Follow Széchenyi u. from the center for roughly 10min. and enter at #30. *(Open daily 10am-4pm.)*

🎵 🎭 ENTERTAINMENT AND NIGHTLIFE

While Eger's popular **bath complex** offers a desperately needed respite from the summer heat, it is garnered fame for the supposedly curative effects of its Turkish thermal bath water. Fed by Artesian wells 3km away, the unique water is prescribed by local doctors as therapy for chronic diseases. The complex also includes swimming pools. From Dobó tér, take Jókai u. to Kossuth Lajos u. and continue on Egészségház u. Make a left on Klapka György u. and cross the stream. (☎311 585. Open May-Sept. M-F 6am-7pm, Sa-Su 8:30am-7pm; daily Oct.-Apr. 9am-7pm. 500Ft, students 350Ft.) While Eger may seem quiet by day, the town livens in the evening. After drinking in the valley, check out one of the **underground discos** (see sidebar, p. 370).

Eger hosts free musical evenings on Small Dobó tér nightly at 6pm. From late July to mid-August, the town celebrates its cultural heritage during the **Baroque Festival.** Nightly music and opera performances take place in and around the city. Buy tickets at the venue. (☎410 324.) An international folk dance festival, **Eger Vintage Days,** takes place in early September. Tourinform (see **Orientation and Practical Information,** p. 367) provides festival schedules.

🗓 DAYTRIPS FROM EGER

🖿 BARADLA CAVES   ☎(06)48

The bus leaves Eger daily at 8:45am and arrives in Aggtelek at 11:25am. Returning bus leaves from the same stop at 3pm. Another bus leaves Miskolc at 9:15am, arrives in Aggtelek around 11am, and heads back from the same stop at 5pm. To get to the cave from the bus, cross the street and go down the path to the caves; the park entrance is on the right. ☎/fax 350 006. 1hr. Hungarian tours daily 10am, 1 and 3pm; in high season also 5pm. 1400Ft, students 700Ft. Tours of the main branch of the cave (5hr., 7km, 3000Ft) can be arranged by Tourinform. Call ahead ☎503 000. Open daily 8am-6pm. If you choose to do the long hike, plan to stay overnight as you will miss the bus back.

Straddling the Slovak-Hungary border, Aggtelek National Park is home to Hungary's fantastic Baradla Caves. Over 200,000 visitors enter this forest of dripping stalactites, stalagmites, and imposing stone formations each year. A UNESCO World Heritage site and a worthwhile daytrip from Eger or Miskolc, the limestone caves were formed 200 million years ago and span over 25 km. A chamber with perfect acoustics was converted into an auditorium, and tours take a dramatic pause here for a sound and light show. Concerts are given regularly (around 1500Ft; schedules available through Tourinform). Another chamber houses an Iron Age cemetery where 13 people are buried, and many ceremonies, including weddings, take place in the caves. The numerous tours vary in length. There are 1hr. basic and Bat Ranch tours (1400Ft, students 700Ft), but cave-lovers may embark on a five-hour guided hike (3000Ft). The temperature is 10°C year-round, so be sure to bring a jacket. A scenic picnic spot up the stairs to the left of the ticket window overlooks the Slovak countryside. Beside the ticket booth, **Barlang Vendéglo** (☎343 177) offers reasonably priced Hungarian favorites (entrees 750-2300Ft) in a pleasant outdoor setting. **Baradla Hostel ❶** (☎503 005), next to the park, is an excellent base from which to explore the caves and take hikes in the nearby region. (1600Ft, students 1300Ft; cottage singles 3000Ft; doubles 3600Ft; triples 4500Ft; quads 4800Ft. Camping 700Ft, students 350Ft.)

LILLAFÜRED
☎(06)36

While a traveler can cover it in a day, Lillafüred may be more relaxing as an overnight getaway. From Eger, hop on a bus bound for Miskolc (1½hr., 2 per hr., 737Ft). When you get to Búza tér, take bus #1, 1a, or 101 to Diósgyőr (150Ft). From the stop in Diósgyőr catch bus #5 to Lillafüred and get off at Palotasszallo, the first stop after the lake. Together the buses take about 45min. Neptune Rental rents rowboats. 250Ft per 30min.; pedal boats 300Ft, children 200Ft. For a trail map, inquire at hotels. Take the Scenic Forest Train (schedule ☎370 345, or see schedule at station; 300Ft) for a closer view of the forest and Hungarian villages on your way back to Miskolc. The train takes slightly more than 30min. From last stop, cross the street and walk left 100m to the bus stop. Take bus #1 or 101, but not 101b, back to Búza tér. Stalactite Cave (☎334 130) open daily Apr. 16-Oct. 15 9am-5pm, last tour at 4pm; Oct. 16-Apr. 15 9am-4pm, last tour at 3pm. Lime Cave (☎334 130) open daily Apr. 16-Oct. 10am-3:30pm, last tour 3pm. At both caves, tours start on the hr. and last 20-30min. Adults 500Ft, students and children 350Ft.

Close to Eger and Miskolc, Lillafüred (pop. 200) is an ideal base from which to explore the Bükk Mountains and National Park. The mountains' excellent lookouts, varied rock surfaces, and winding cave system make for exciting **hikes**, which range from 5-36 km. **Row** and **pedal boats** are available on Lake Hámori at **Neptune Rentals**, across from Hotel Palota. The **Szent István Stalactite Cave,** smaller but similar to the Aggtelek's Baradla Caves, has a 170m area where visitors can examine stalactites. The cave's unique climate, 10°C with 97% humidity, supposedly has a curative effect on respiratory diseases. The **Lime Tuff Anna Cave** is beneath Hotel Palota. The cave, which harbors calcium-covered plans, is adjacent to a waterfall and river and surrounded by hanging flower gardens.

If traipsing through the great outdoors gives you an appetite, stop by the **King Matthias Restaurant ❷** in the basement of Hotel Palota. With a Renaissance ambience, Matthias serves generous portions of wild game, fruit, and potatoes. Cutlery is available, but it is customary to eat as the king did—with your hands. (☎331 411. Entrees 800-6000Ft. Call ahead. Open daily noon-11pm.) Several small shops and stands sell hot dogs, hamburgers, and other snacks. The dominant structure in Lillafüred is the **Hotel Palota ④**. Built between 1927 and 1930, this castle-like hotel overlooks Lake Hámori and the Bükk Mountains. With a luxurious lobby area and beautiful gardens, this hotel is a self-indulgent splurge. Call ahead, as the hotel is often booked. (☎331 411; reserve@hotelpalota.hunguesthotels.hu. Breakfast included. Rooms 19,500-31,000Ft in high season.) For a less expensive option, walk up the road to **Étterem és Panzió ②**. (☎379 299. Breakfast included. Singles 4300Ft; doubles 6600Ft; quads 13,200Ft.)

TOKAJ ☎(06)47

Called home to "the wine of kings and the king of wines" by French King Louis XIV, Tokaj (tohk-OY; pop. 5100) has had an illustrious reputation for producing fine wines since the 12th century. While Eger is known for its reds, wine-cellar-filled Tokaj produces only whites. If Tokaj gives the wine its name (Tokaji Fehérbor), the wine gives Tokaj its flavor: the scent of its rich grapes drifts through the town's streets and into the surrounding rivers and vine-covered hills. A popular base for hiking and canoeing, the town lies at the foot of the Kopasz mountains, bordered by the volcanic Zemplen hills to the north and the Tisza and Bodrog rivers to the south.

⬛▮ TRANSPORTATION AND PRACTICAL INFORMATION. The **train station**, Baross G. u. 18, (☎352 020; www.elvira.hu), sends trains to: **Debrecen** (2hr., 8 per day, 802Ft) via **Nyíregyháza** and **Miskolc** (1hr., 10 per day, 700Ft). **Buses** from the train station serve local towns.

To get to the center, take a left from the train station entrance and follow the tracks, then turn left on **Bajcsy-Zsilinszky u.** Bear left as the road forks by Hotel Tokaj. Bajcsy-Zsilinszky u. becomes **Rákóczi u.** after the Tisza bridge, then **Bethlen Gábor u.** after **Kossuth tér.** The staff at **Tourinform**, Serház u. 1, on the right side of Rákóczi u. as you walk into town, arranges accommodations and can set you up with a horse, canoe, or rafting tour. (☎352 259; tokaj@tourinform.hu. Open daily June 15-Sept. 15 9am-6pm; Sept. 16-June 14 M-F 9am-4pm.) **Exchange currency,** cash **traveler's checks,** and get MC/V **cash advances** at **OTP,** Rákóczi u. 35. (☎352 523. Open M-Th 7:45am-3:30pm, F 7:45am-2pm.) A MC/V **ATM** sits outside. **Luggage storage** is available at the train station. **Paracelsus Pharmacy** (in a building labeled Gyógyszertár) is on Kossuth tér.; ring after hours for emergencies. (Open M-F 8am-5pm, Sa 8am-4pm, Su 8am-noon and 12:30-4:30pm.) There is a **medical center** labeled Szakorvosi Rendelő on Bethlen G. u.

WINES OF TOKAJ

Tokaj's wines are admired by connoisseurs, imitated by foreign wine makers, and exported around the world. When visiting the Tokaj region, you have the opportunity to sample these wines for much less than you'd pay for them outside Hungary.

Furmint is a basic dry white wine, with a fruity, intensely aromatic character. The most common of Tokaj's wines, it complements seafood and poultry.

Hárslevelu is made from a traditional thin-skinned grape. Served chilled, this dry, young, fresh wine particularly enhances a fish or shellfish entree. It can also be enjoyed as an aperitif.

Aszú grapes, which ripen more quickly than others grapes from the same bunch, makes the most famous of Tokaj's wines: a very sweet dessert wine. Its sweetness is measured in *puttonyos*. **Eszeneia,** which means "essence," is a true delicacy, and is made from the first juices of Aszú grapes. It should be drunk alone or accompanied by a great cigar.

The years 1972, 1975, 1983, 1988, 1993, and 1999 are considered good vintages of wines from the Tokaj region. It is best to sample wines in order from the driest to sweetest; when dry wines follow sweet wines, they taste unpleasantly bitter and acidic.

4, with doctors available 8am-7pm. An **ambulance service** (☎104) can take you to the nearest hospital in Miskolc. **Internet Café Tokaj**, Bajcsy-Zsilinszky 34, provides **Internet access**. (☎353 137. Open 10am-10pm.) There are **telephones** in the **post office**, Rákóczi u. 24 and in the center of town. (☎353 647. Open M-F 8am-5pm, Sa 8am-noon.) **Postal Code:** 3910.

▓▓ ACCOMMODATIONS AND FOOD. You can check for rooms at **Tourinform**, but *Zimmer frei* and *Szoba Kiadó* (rooms available) signs abound—your best bet is to walk along Rákóczi u. (Singles 2000-3000Ft; doubles 4000-6000Ft.) Don't be afraid to bargain, but beware: your host may talk you into sampling—and buying—expensive homemade wine. **Lux Panzió ❸**, Serház u. 14, provides sunny rooms with pink-infused interiors. Turn right on Vároháza-köz from Rákóczi u., just after OTP. Ask for the double with the private shower—it's the same price as those that share. (☎352 145. Breakfast 600Ft. Reception 8am-10pm. Doubles 4900Ft; triples with TV 6500Ft. Tax 125Ft.) The convenient **Makk Marci Panzió ❸**, Liget Köz 1, on the main street in the center, boasts a prime location just steps from some of the town's best wine cellars. (☎352 336; fax 353 088. Breakfast included. Reception 24hr. Singles 4800Ft; doubles 7500Ft; triples 10,640Ft; quads 12,300Ft. Tax 125Ft. AmEx/MC/V.) If you'd rather camp out, cross the Tisza and take your second left to reach **Vizisport Centrum Youth Hostel ❶**, which provides campground and bungalows with a view of the Tisza. (☎352 645. Free Internet. First night 1400Ft., additional nights 1200Ft.) Keep going and you'll reach **Tiszavirag Camping ❶**, a peaceful campground with waterfront campsites and small bungalows. (☎352 012. Camping 700Ft per person; bungalow 1400Ft per person.)

The **MaxiCoop** supermarket is on Kossuth tér. (Open M-F 6am-6pm, Sa 6am-1pm, Su 7-11am.) **ABC Coop**, on Rákóczi u., is a little more expensive but offers more vegetarian foods. (Open M-F 6:30am-6:30pm, Sa 6:30am-1pm, Su 7-11am.) Enjoy Hungarian favorites in a pleasant dining room and garden setting at **Toldi Fogadó ❷**, Hajdú Köz 2, at Rákóczi u. (☎353 403. English menu available. Entrees 690-1800Ft. Open daily 11am-10pm.) **Makk Marci Pizzeria Étterem ❷**, connected to Makk Marci Panzió (see above), serves homemade pizza with a variety of vegetables or meat cooked under the cheese. (Pizzas 430-1800Ft, spaghetti 440-580Ft. Open daily 8am-8pm.) **Taverna ❷** is on Hősök tér, across the street from the Tisza bridge, burrowed into the hill. Its skinny rooms make it feel like a wine cellar. (☎352 346. Entrees 650-800Ft. Open Tu-Su noon-midnight. M groups only.)

◙⚑ SIGHTS AND ENTERTAINMENT. Signs saying *"Bor Pince"* herald **private wine cellars.** Owners are generally pleased to let visitors sample their wares (about 1000Ft for 5 or 6 0.1L samples). Ring the bell if a cellar is closed. Cellars on the main road are usually more touristy—on the side streets you'll find higher-quality wines and homier atmospheres. For an authentic wine-tasting experience head to the 1.5km long tunnel cellar of **▨Rákóczi Pince**, Kossuth tér 15. Five hundred years worth of wine making magic chill in the 10°C cellar. In 1526, János Szapolyai was elected king of Hungary in this subterranean hall. Wine tastings and tours of the cellar and hall are arranged on the hour, but can be preempted by tour groups. Individual tours can be arranged at any time; English-speaking guides are available at no extra cost. Call ahead. (☎352 408; fax 352 741. Open 10am-7pm. 2000Ft for 1hr. tour and 6-glass tasting. AmEx/MC/V.) The young, family-run **Tokaji Hímesudvar Winery**, Bem u. 2, produces phenomenal *Aszú* wines—their 1993 *5 puttonyos* received national awards. The Várhelyi family happily guides you through the history of the region and the subtleties of the Tokaj wines. Their 1999 *6 puttonyos Aszú* is indescribably sweet. To get to the royal hunting lodge where the cellar is located, take the road to the left of the church in Kossuth tér and follow the signs. (☎352 416. Open daily 10am-9pm, in winter 10am-6pm. Tastings 2000Ft for 6 wines.) The **Tóth Family Cellar,** Óvár út 40, produces five exceptional whites, including a 1988 *6 puttonyos Aszú.* Take the street that begins opposite Tourinform on Rákóczi u. You will be guided into a thoroughly authentic mold-infested cellar. (6 glasses 600Ft, 1L of *6 puttonyos* 4000Ft. Open daily 9am-7pm.) See sidebar, p. 373.

When you want a break from tasting, venture to the **Tokaj Museum,** down Rákóczi u., built in 1790. The stairs inside are original, and the frescoes on the walls are refurbished replicas. The rooms are filled with a wide collection of artifacts representing Tokaj's rich history and culture. After viewing an impressive collection of Catholic iconography, visit the attic, which houses a large display of wine-making instruments. (☎352 636. Open Tu-Su 10am-4pm. 400Ft, students 200Ft.) From the museum, continue down Rákóczi u. until it meets Josef Attila u. and turn right. You'll come to the largest structure in Tokaj, the **synagogue,** which sits forlorn and boarded up. Once a landmark to a thriving pre-war Jewish population, the synagogue will likely be converted to a cinema or youth center.

Outdoor recreation in Tokaj is almost as popular as wine. The steep vineyard slopes make for challenging hikes, and the slow-flowing Tisza and Bodrog are always filled with paddleboats. **Vízisport Centrum** (☎352 645) rents bikes (1000Ft per day) and canoes (500Ft per person per day, 2-4 person canoes available) and arranges horseback riding. (1800Ft per hr., 2500Ft with trainer; call 1 day ahead.) Take the first left over the bridge. **Spori Sport** also rents canoes. Take the first right after the Tisza bridge and follow the road 500m. (☎481 716; fax 506 304. 2-seater 900Ft per day, 4-seater 1500Ft per day.) The best place to canoe is up the Bodrog River. Paddle upstream, and you will be rewarded with a pleasant float back to town. Tourinform (p. 374) gives advice about **hikes.** While the red and blue trails are easy to follow, the green is steep and poorly marked. **Halihó Sörkert,** a hamburger joint by day (5-10pm), is a hotspot at night. Crowds begin to arrive around 8:30pm. (Open daily 5pm-2am.) **Murphy's Műhely Söröző,** Rákóczi u. 30/32, is an Irish pub that packs in students for an after-dinner round. (Beer 80-130Ft. Pool 60Ft per game. Open daily 2pm-2am.)

VISEGRÁD ☎(0)26

Seat of the royal court in medieval times, Visegrád (VEE-sheh-grad) has literally turned to ruins. The town was destroyed when the Turks invaded in 1544, but it was partly rebuilt when Germans resettled the region in the 18th century. Today, visitors stop in Visegrád to wander around the ruins of the royal palace and castle and look at the excavation exhibits inside. Although the town is a good daytrip from Budapest, its beautiful mountain trails and spectacular views of the Danube draw hikers and bikers for longer stays.

▐▊ TRANSPORTATION AND PRACTICAL INFORMATION. Buses depart from Budapest at Árpád híd, M3 (1½hr., 30 per day, 421Ft) and will drop you at any of Visegrád's 4 stops. Get off at the first stop to hike up to the citadel or check out the tower; stay on until the third stop to go into the town center. **Ferries** leave from the **Budapest pier** below Vigadó tér (3½hr.; 2 per day; 1050Ft, students 788Ft) and stop in front of the town center.

Buses stop along Harangvirag u., which runs parallel to the river. The town's main road, Fő út., is a pedestrian street behind Harangvirag u. **Visegrád Tours,** Rév út 15, across the street from the river at the third bus stop, provides accommodations info and hiking maps. (☎398 160; fax 397 597. Open daily Apr.-Oct. 8am-6pm;

Nov.-Mar. M-F 10am-4pm.) There's an **ATM** at Fő út. 34, and a **post office** (open M-F 8am-4pm) across the street. The **pharmacy**, Fő út. 79, stocks Western products. (☎398 255. Open M-F 8am-5pm. Ring bell on door after hours).

ACCOMMODATIONS AND FOOD. Visegrád's cheapest accommodations are **private rooms** outside the town center. Search for *Zimmer Frei* signs on the south side of Fő út. and on Nagy Lajos út. **Matyas Tanya ❸**, Fő út. 47, has sunny rooms in a comfortable guesthouse. (☎398 309. Breakfast included. Reserve ahead. Doubles 7900-8500Ft; triples 10000-12000Ft. Tax 300Ft.) The rooms at **Hotel Visegrád ❹**, Rév út 15, boast balconies overlooking the castle and the Danube. (☎397 034; hotelvisegrad@visegradtours.hu. Breakfast included. Doubles 10000Ft; triples 14000Ft. Tax 300Ft.) On weekends, food stalls line Fő út selling *langos* (150-300Ft), *gyros* (600-1000Ft), and a variety of fried foods. For something more filling, head to **Don Vito Pizzeria ❷**, Fő út. 83, where friendly waiters serve brick-oven pizza. (☎397 230. Live jazz Sa-Su 9pm. Pizza 300-1400Ft. Pasta 800-1100Ft. Open daily noon-midnight.) **Gulyás Csárda ❸**, Nagy Lajos út 4, prepares five excellent Hungarian dishes; you'll smell the garlic from the garden outside. (☎398 329. Entrees 1050-2050Ft. Open daily noon-10pm.) On a sunny day, the grassy banks of the Danube provide a perfect picnic spot. Pick up supplies at **CBA Élelmiszer supermarket**, across from Visegrád Tours at the end of Rév út. (Open M 7am-6pm, Tu-F 7am-7pm, Sa 7am-3pm, Su 7am-noon. AmEx/MC.)

SIGHTS AND ENTERTAINMENT. The 13th-century **citadel** is Visegrád's main attraction. Perched above the Danube, this former Roman outpost is the highest vantage point for miles and provides a panorama of the Danube bend. Heading north on Fő út., go right on Salamontorony u. and follow the path. It has a **wax museum** where medieval torture techniques now petrify wax victims. (Open daily Mar. 15-Oct. 15 10am-5pm; Oct. 16-Mar. 14 Sa-Su 10am-5pm. 750Ft, students 350Ft.) Named for a king imprisoned here in the 13th century, the Romanesque **Solomon's Tower** (Alsóvár Salamon Torony), on the path to the citadel, gives a view of the medieval district. Inside, the **King Matthias Museum** displays artifacts from the palace ruins. (☎398 026. Open May-Oct. Tu-Su 9am-5pm; last admission 4:30pm. Free.) Considered a myth until archaeologists uncovered it in 1934, King Matthias's **Royal Palace** (Királyi Palota) sprawls above Fő út. The remains alone make the visit worthwhile, but there is also an impressive exhibit with a reconstruction of the castle as it was in 1259. (☎398 026; fax 398 252. Open Tu-Su 9am-5pm; last admission 4:30pm. Limited English info provided. Free.) In the second weekend of July, parades, jousting tournaments, concerts, and a market overtake the grounds for the **Visegrád Palace Games**. Contact the **Visegrád Cultural Center** (☎398 128; muvelodesihaz@visegrad.hu). **Nyári Bobpálya** hosts a popular, if frightening, toboggan slide. From the citadel, go left up Panorama út. (☎397 397. Open daily Apr.-Aug. 9am-6pm; Sept.-Oct. 10am-5pm; Nov.-Feb. 11am-4pm, Mar. 11am-5pm. M-F 280Ft, children 230Ft, Sa-Su 320Ft/250Ft.) If you'd rather hike, pick up a map (400Ft) from Visegrád Tours or the Solomon's Tower ticket office. Visegrád Tours also rents bikes. (1500Ft per day.)

SZILVÁSVÁRAD   ☎(06)36

Renowned for its carriages, prized Lipizzaner horses, and national park, Szilvás-várad (SEEL-vahsh-vah-rahd; pop. 1900) has much to be proud of. At the foot of the Bükk Mountains, this small town hosts famous horseraces and attracts hikers and vacationing families with winding mountain trails and scenic beauty.

E2 TRANSPORTATION AND PRACTICAL INFORMATION. Trains run to **Eger** (1hr., 7 per day, 324Ft). **Buses** are generally the most convenient transport; they go to **Eger** (45min., every 30min.-1hr., 316Ft) and **Aggtelek** (1¾hr., 9:20am, 744Ft). The bus stops just outside the park entrance. The *Zimmer Frei* rooms lie to either side of the park—look for direction signs posted right outside the park entrance.

The main street, **Egri út,** extends from the **Szilvásvárad-Szalajkavölgy train station** and bends sharply. **Szalajka u.** leads to the national park. Farther north, Egri út becomes **Miskolci út.** There's no **tourist office,** so get info and a basic map at the **Eger Tourinform** (see p. 367) before heading out. The women at **Hegyi Camping** provide a wealth of info about the area and sell maps. **Hiking maps** are posted throughout the park. **Free maps** of the mountains are available at the **bike shop,** on Szalajka u., just past the stop sign at the park entrance. (☎335 2695. Open daily 9am-10pm.) A small **bank** is to the left of the bus stop on Egri út. (☎354 105. Open M-F 8am-noon and 12:30-4pm.) There is an **ATM** at Nagy ABC (see below). There's a **pharmacy, Magyar Korona,** Egri út 4. (☎355 128. Open M-Th 8am-noon and 1-4pm, F 8am-1:30pm.) A **post office** is on Szilvásvárad-Park u. (Open M-F 8am-4pm.) **Postal Code:** 3348.

[] ACCOMMODATIONS AND FOOD. Although you can visit Szilvásvárad as a daytrip from Eger, many stay the night. **Private rooms** are cheapest (from 2000Ft), but prices rise 1000-1500Ft during the Lipicai Festival. **Hegyi Camping ❷,** Egri út 36a, has great views of the valley. (☎355 207. Open Apr. 15-Oct. 15. Tents 1-person 1100Ft, students 650Ft; 2-person 2400Ft/1300Ft, additional persons 1100Ft/650Ft; bungalows with bath doubles 4200Ft; triples 5000Ft; quads 5800Ft.) If camping isn't your style, try **Éden Panzió ❹,** Jókai ut 5/A, to reinvigorate your aching bones in the sauna. (☎564 008. Singles 7000Ft; doubles 10,000Ft; extra bed 2000Ft.)

After the booth on Szalajka u., there is a row of restaurants with indoor and patio seating. **Csobogó Étterem ❷** has a patio next to a waterfall. (Meals 600-2000Ft. Open daily noon-8pm.) **Fenyo Vendéglo ❷,** 3348 Szilvásvárad u., offers typical Hungarian and vegetarian dishes. (☎564 015. Open daily noon-8pm.) For trail food, go to **Nagy ABC,** Egri út 6. (Open M-F 6am-6pm, Sa 6am-1pm, Su 8am-noon.)

[] ENTERTAINMENT AND OUTDOOR ACTIVITIES. From leisurely biking in the Szalajka Valley to arduous hikes through the mountains, Bükki National Park offers a variety of outdoor opportunities. The arena on Szalajka u., just off the park entrance, hosts weekend **horseshows** (800Ft). You can learn to drive a carriage, brandish a whip, or ride a steed. In early July, the arena hosts the hugely popular **Lipicai Festival** (call Lipicai Stables or Hegyi Camping for info). The event draws carriage drivers from across the globe for a three-day competition. **Lipicai Stables,** the stud farm for Szilvásvárad's Lipizzaner breed, is at the heart of the town's horse tradition. For a glimpse of the famous horses, head away from the park on Egri út, turn left on Enyves u., and follow the signs to the farm. (☎355 155. Open daily 8:30am-noon and 2-4pm. 300Ft.)

Shaded walks through the **Bükk Mountains** and the **Szalajka Valley** are beautiful but not always tranquil—in May and June they are swarming with school groups and picnicking families. The lazy trailside stream transforms into the most dramatic of the park's attractions at the **Fátyol Waterfall.** It takes 45min. to get here by walking at a leisurely pace by the green trail, or 15min. by the open-air train, which departs from park entrance. (7 per day 9:25am-4:10pm; 220Ft, students 110Ft. Trains only leave when there are enough passengers.) A 30min. hike past the waterfall on the green trail leads to **Istálóskő Cave,** home to a Stone Age cult. After the brook, the paved trails ends, though more adventurous hikers can

HUNGARY

explore the rugged terrain that sets off at 45° angles from the path. **Millennium Lookout Tower,** built in 2000, offers a spectacular view of the town and surrounding countryside. (Open daily 10am-9pm.) Avoid the crowds by **renting a bike** (800Ft 1st hr., 200Ft per hr. thereafter), at Szalajka u., just past the stop sign at the park entrance. Pick up a tourist guide before hitting the trails. The shop can also arrange other outdoor activities, such as climbing excursions (900Ft, children 800Ft) in the nearby trees at **Adventure Forest.** (☎352 695. Open daily 10am-7pm.) While Szilvásvárad is a quiet town at night, locals do stop into **Sörbár,** at Éden Panzió (see p. 377), for a drink or two.

WESTERN TRANSDANUBIA

During the Cold War, authorities discouraged people from entering the pastoral region of Western Transdanubia, as they believed capitalist Austria and Tito's Yugoslavia were too close for comfort. Thus, a region that had always been a bit behind the times—electricity didn't arrive until 1950—fell even farther beyond modernity's reach, leaving much of the countryside unchanged. The rolling hills and stretches of farmland are perfect for leisurely strolls, bicycle rides, and hiking in summer, and holiday fairs lighten up town streets in winter.

GYŐR
☎(0)96

The streets of Győr (DJUR; pop. 130,000) wind peacefully around illustrious museums and stunning 17th- and 18th-century architecture. The large population that lives within the Old Town brings life to the storybook beauty of its streets. Parks, pedestrian passageways, and a popular water park prove that recreation and relaxation reign in one of Hungary's most soothing cities. Győr is a must-see if you're making your way from Budapest to Vienna.

■7 TRANSPORTATION AND PRACTICAL INFORMATION. The **train station,** Révai út 4-6 (domestic ☎311 613, international 523 366), lies 3min. from the city center; as you exit the station, turn right. Turn left just before the underpass and cross the street to get to the pedestrian **Baross Gábor út.** Trains run to: **Budapest** (2½hr., 26 per day, 1284-1646Ft); **Sopron** (1-1½hr., 16 per day, 726Ft); **Vienna, AUT** (2hr., 13 per day, 4450Ft). The **bus station,** Hunyadi út 9 (☎317 711), is connected to the train station. Buses head to Budapest (2½hr., 1 per hr., 1300Ft).

 Tourinform (☎311 771), Árpád út 32, provides accommodations info and **free maps.** (Open June-Aug. M-F 8am-8pm, Sa-Su 9am-6pm.) **IBUSZ** (☎311 700), Kazinczy út 3, has accommodations info. (Open Apr.-Aug. M-F 8am-5pm, Sa 9am-1pm; Sept.-Mar M-F 8am-4pm. AmEx/MC/V.) **OTP Bank,** Teleki L. út 51, at the corner of Bajcsy-Zsilinszky út, has good **exchange** rates. (MC/V **ATM** and currency exchange machine outside. Open M 7:45am-6pm, Tu-Th 7:45am-5pm, F 7:45am-4pm.) The **Postabank** desk in the post office cashes **AmEx Traveler's Cheques** for no commission. **Luggage storage** is at the train station. (260Ft per day. Open 3am-midnight.) A **pharmacy, Aranyhajó Patika** (☎328 881), can be found at Jedlik Á. út 16. A sign in the window lists pharmacies with emergency hours. (Open M-F 7am-6pm, Sa 7am-2pm.) If you need **medical assistance** (☎418 244), go to Vasvári P. u. 2. (Open M-F 8am-5pm.) **Different Internet Cafe & Club** (☎516 810; www.different.hu), Liszt Ferenc út 20, is in a courtyard. The entrance is on Pálffy u. (250Ft per 30min. Open M-W 8am-3pm, Th 8am-5pm, F 8am-noon. Ring bell if door is shut.) The **post office** (☎314 324) is at Bajcsy-Zsilinszky út 46. (Open M-F 8am-6pm. **Poste Restante** available.) **Postal Code:** 9021.

⌐⌐ ACCOMMODATIONS AND FOOD. Accommodations may overflow in summer, so it's smart to make reservations before arriving. **Tourinform** (p. 378) can help you find a *panzió* or hotel room and will make reservations for you if you call ahead. They also keep a list of the **campsites** around the city. **IBUSZ** (p. 378) can also arrange accommodations, with rooms starting at 4200Ft. ◙**Katalin's Kert ❸**, Sarkantyú köz 3, off Bécsi Kapu tér, is hidden in a quaint courtyard. Its huge, modern rooms include TVs and showers. A restaurant downstairs has live music most nights. (☎/fax 452 088. Breakfast included. Singles 7100Ft; doubles 9100Ft; triples 12500Ft. Tax 300Ft per person.) **Széchenyi István Főiskola Egyetem ❷**, Hédevári út 3, is across the Moscow-Dune River. Follow Czuczor Gergely út, which runs parallel to Baross Gábor út, across the bridge. Hang a left on Káloczy tér, and continue to the parking lot. The entrance is to the left, at K4; after 9pm, enter at K3. Its modern buildings offer standard dorm rooms with private showers and shared hall bathrooms. (☎503 400. Reception 24hr. Check-out 9am. Open July-Aug. Doubles 3500Ft; triples 3000Ft. Tax 300Ft per person.)

Matróz Restaurant ❷, is at Dunakapu tér 3, off Jedlik Ányos. This local favorite fries up mouthwatering fish, turkey, and pork dishes. The food is fancier than the folksy decor or dwarf-sized wooden chairs might lead you to believe. (☎336 208. Entrees 550-1390Ft. Open Su-Th 9am-10pm, F-Sa 9am-11pm.) **Teátrum Étterem ❷**, Schweidel út 7, is an upscale eatery with medium-scale prices. Enjoy the air-conditioned, nicely-lit dining area. (☎310 640. Entrees 600-1990Ft. English menu available. Open daily noon-11pm.) **John Bull Pub ❸**, Aradi út 3, is a delicious respite from Hungarian food. This restaurant by day and pub by night has Italian options, lava-stone grilled meat, and salads (330-580Ft). Choose between tables on the street and a US Civil War-themed interior. (☎618 320. Entrees 780-2350Ft. 0.5L Guinness 800Ft. Open daily 10am-midnight.) **Kaiser's supermarket** sprawls across the corner of Arany János út and Aradi út. (Open M 7:30am-7pm, Tu-F 6:30am-7pm, Sa 6:30am-3pm.)

◙ SIGHTS. Head uphill on Czuczor Gergely út, parallel to Baross Gábor u., and then take a left at Gutenberg tér to reach **Chapter Hill** (Káptalandomb), the oldest sector of Győr. Overlooking the junction of three rivers—the Danube, the Rába, and the Rábca—the hill is covered in monuments, which call attention to Győr's rich history as a cultural crossroads. The striking 1731 **Ark of the Covenant statue** (Frigyláda Szobor) was bankrolled by taxes King Charles III levied on his impoverished mercenaries. The **Episcopal Cathedral** (Székesegyház), at the top of the hill, has been under constant construction since 1030. Its exterior is now a medley of Romanesque, Gothic, and Neoclassical styles. Gilded cherubim perch above the magnificent frescoes that illuminate the Baroque interior. Seeking refuge from Oliver Cromwell's forces in the 1650s, a priest brought the miraculous **Weeping Madonna of Győr** to the Cathedral from Ireland. On St. Patrick's Day in 1697, the image reportedly wept blood and tears for the persecuted Irish Catholics. The painting is left of the main altar. The Hédeváry chapel, inside the cathedral, holds the **Herm of King St. Ladislas,** a medieval bust of one of Hungary's first saint-kings. It also contains the **tomb of Baron Vilmas Apor,** a Győr martyr revered for his anti-Nazi and anti-communist stance. (Open daily 8am-noon and 2-6pm. Free.) In the alley directly behind the cathedral, the **Diocesan Library and Treasury** (Egyházmegyei Kincstár), Káptalandomb 26, displays 14th-century gold and silver religious artifacts. A priceless 19th-century gold reliquary contains about 30 saints' fingernail clippings and the blood-stained shirt of Bishop Apor. (☎311 153. English captions. Open Tu-Su 10am-4pm. 300Ft, students 150Ft.)

The **Imre Patkó Collection** (Patkó Imre Gyűjtemény), Széchenyi tér 4 (enter on Stelczera út), has two floors of modern Hungarian art and one floor of 16th-century Asian and African works. The museum is housed in the **Iron Log House** (Vas-

HUNGARY

tuskós ház), a centuries-old former inn for traveling craftsmen. (☎310 588. Open Tu-Su 10am-6pm. 240Ft, students 120Ft.) Down Kenyér Köz from Széchenyi tér, the **Margit Kovács Museum** (Kovács Margit Gyűjtemény), Apáci út 1, displays the Győr artist's expressive ceramic sculptures and tiles. (☎326 739. Open Mar.-Oct. Tu-Su 10am-6pm; Nov.-Feb. Tu-Su 10am-5pm. 400Ft, students 200Ft.)

🎭🎵 **ENTERTAINMENT AND NIGHTLIFE.** In summer, locals delight in splashing in the water and basking in the sun. Across the river, thermal springs supply a large **water park** (*fürdő*), Cziráky tér 1. Sprawling over a beautiful outdoor and indoor complex, the park has a waterslide, two outdoor swimming pools, two thermal baths, and a spa. From Bécsi kapu tér, walk over the bridge to the island and take the first right on the other side. (Open daily 8am-10pm. 950Ft, students 600Ft; after 3pm 700Ft/500Ft.) Győr flits away June and July at **Győri Nyár,** a festival of concerts, drama, and the city's famous ballet. Schedules are at Tourinform (see **Practical Information,** p. 375); buy tickets at the box office on Baross Gábor út. or at the venue. The **Győr National Theater** (Nemzeti Színház), Czuczor Gergely u. 7 (☎314 800; fax 326 999), has a lineup of opera, rock, musicals, and plays; buy tickets at the theater box office. (Theater open Mar. 17-June 25 and Aug. 23-Sept. 22 M-F 9am-1pm and 2-4pm. Tickets 2000-3000Ft.) If you're looking to shop, head to **Skala Shopping Center,** above Kaiser's Supermarket (see **Accomodations and Food p. 379**).

At night, music and young people spill out from cellar bars onto Győr's streets. 🍺**Komédiás Biergarten,** Czuczor Gergely u. 30, has a decorated patio that invites laughing and drinking. (☎527 217. Beer 290-460Ft. Open M-Sa 11am-midnight.) If you're wistful for the Emerald Isle, **Dublin Gate Irish Pub,** Bécsi kapu tér 8, taps a lively young crowd and lots of beer. (☎528 466. 0.5L Guinness 900Ft. Open daily 3pm-last customer.) Győr's bold and beautiful head to **The 20th Century,** Schweidel út 25. (Beer 250-480Ft. Mixed drinks 400-1250Ft. Open M-Sa 9am-midnight, Su 5pm-midnight.) Try **Patio Belvárosi Kavéház,** Baross Gábor út 12. Popular with locals for beer (300-660Ft), wine, and desserts (150-500Ft), it's a great place for a mellow evening. (☎310 096. Open daily 11am-midnight.)

🔾 **DAYTRIP FROM GYŐR: ARCHABBEY OF PANNONHALMA.** Visible from Győr on a clear day, the hilltop 🏛**Archabbey of Pannonhalma** (Pannonhalmi Főapátság) has seen a millennium of destruction and rebuilding since the Benedictine order established it in 996. Now a UNESCO World Heritage Site, it is home to some of the most valuable ecclesiastical treasures and diverse architecture in the world. About 60 monks live in the abbey, which also houses a 13th-century basilica, an opulent 360,000-volume library, a small art gallery of religious iconography, and one of the finest boys' schools in Hungary. Its treasures include a 1055 deed founding the Benedictine abbey in Tihany, the oldest document with Hungarian writing, and a charter from 1001 establishing the Archabbey of Pannonhalma and bearing St. Stephen's signature. Unfortunately, these charters are in the archives and only reproductions are on display. There is also a famous **mosaic** of the Madonna created from naturally bright stones. While the large library, still in use by students, is now wired with electric lights, one of its most interesting features is its natural lighting by a series of large windows and mirrors. Although renovations in honor of the Pope's visit in 1996 left the abbey halls looking spiffy, Hungary's oldest graffiti is still visible: a soldier defending the hill against the Turks "was here" in 1578. You can hear **Gregorian chant** at the Sunday 10am mass and at classical music concerts, which take place frequently in the halls of the abbey; inquire at **Pax Tourist.** (*Take the bus from stand #11. 45min., 7 per day, 347Ft. Ask the driver if the bus is going to Pannonhalma vár. If so, get off at the huge gates. If not, the uphill walk from Pannonhalma takes 20min. From the bus stop, face the abbey, walk left, and turn right up the hill just after Borpince. The abbey can only be visited by guided tour. Hungarian tours Tu-Su 9am-5pm on the* *hr. English tours Mar. 21-Nov. 11 Tu-Su 11am and 1pm. Hungarian tour 1000Ft, students 500Ft; English tour 1200Ft. Tickets at Pax Tourist, Vár 1. ☎570 191; pax@osb.hu. Leaving the abbey, take a left and head down the hill; the ticket office is on the right side. AmEx/MC/V.)*

SOPRON   ☎(0)99

At first glance, Sopron (SHO-pron; pop. 54,000) appears to have moved away from its traditions and cultural history. Lined with brand-name boutiques and mouth-watering dessert shops, its facade is efficient and industrious. But the city's alley-ways reveal the older town it hides. The winding cobblestone sidestreets of Inner Town are home to museums, monuments, beautiful churches, and 4th-century ruins from the Roman city Scarbantia. Though many stop here en route to Vienna, its vibrant culture warrants a trip in its own right.

▐ TRANSPORTATION

Trains: Budapest (3-4hr., 14 per day, 2725Ft); **Győr** (1½hr., 14 per day, 802Ft); **Szombathely** (1¼hr., 16 per day, 594 Ft); **Vienna, AUT** (1-2hr., 1 per hr., 3060Ft).

Buses: Lackner Kristóf u. 9 (☎311 040). To: **Budapest** (4hr., 5 per day, 2370Ft) and **Győr** (2hr., 1 per hr., 1010Ft).

✈ ▟ ORIENTATION AND PRACTICAL INFORMATION

Belváros (Inner Town), the historic center, is a 1km-long horseshoe bound by three main streets: **Ógabona tér, Várkerület u.,** and **Széchenyi tér.** At the end farthest from the train station, museums and notable buildings line **Fő tér.** To get to the center from the **train station,** veer to the left following **Mátyás Király u.,** which leads to Széchenyi tér and becomes Várkerület u. as it curves around the Inner Town. The **bus station** is 5min. from the center. Exit the station and turn right on **Lackner Kristóf u.;** turn left at Ógabona tér to reach Várkerület near Fő tér.

Tourist Office: Tourinform, Előkapu út 11 (☎/fax 338 892), off of Várkerület u.; when the road splits, stick to the inner road to get to the office. **Free maps** and accommodations info. Open May-Oct. M-F 10am-7pm, Sa 10am-6pm; Nov.-Apr. M-F 10am-4pm. Closed daily for lunch 1:30-2:15pm.

Currency Exchange: OTP, Várkerület u. 96A, offers good exchange rates and cashes **traveler's checks.** There's a 24hr. (MC/V) **ATM** and a **currency exchange** machine outside. Open M 7:45am-6pm, Tu-Th 7:45am-5pm, F 7:45am-4pm.

Luggage Storage: At the train station. 120Ft per 6hr. 240Ft per day.

Pharmacy: There are 5 pharmacies: Deák tér 35, Magyar út 6, Mátyás király út 23, and 2 on Várkerület u. A sign in the window of each lists emergency services available.

Medical Assistance: Győri u. 15 (☎312 120). Open M-F 9am-5pm.

Internet Access: ISE, Új u. 3 (☎310 252), in the center of Belváros. 200Ft per 30min., 400Ft per hr.; students 150Ft/200Ft. Open M 1pm-7pm; Tu-F 11am-7pm, Sa 10am-4pm.

Post Office: Széchenyi tér 7/10 (☎313 100), outside Belváros. Open M-F 8am-7pm, Sa 8am-noon. **Telephones** are inside. Open M-F 8am-4pm. **Postal Code:** 9400.

▐ ACCOMMODATIONS

Ciklámen Tourist, Ógabona tér 8, can set you up with a **private room.** (☎312 040; fax 314 183. Singles from 4200Ft; doubles from 5000Ft. Open M-F 8am-4:30pm, Sa 8am-1pm.) **Tourinform** (See **Orientation and Practical Information**) has a list of all the accommodations in the area and can check on room availability.

Ringhofer Panzió, Balfi út 52 (☎325 022; fax 326 081). From Széchenyi tér, go down Várkerület u. Turn right on Ikva-híd u. and right again on Balfi út. Large rooms with clean showers, TVs, and refrigerators. Bike rental 1000Ft per day. Breakfast 600Ft. Reception 24hr. Check-out 10am. Doubles 5000Ft; triples 8500Ft. Tax 300Ft. ❸

Wieden Panzió, Sas tér 13 (☎523 222; www.wieden.hu), just 5min. from the center. English-speaking staff offers advice on outdoor daytrips and even lends bikes for free. Breakfast included. Singles 5400-6600Ft; doubles 7900-9900Ft; triples 11,300-12,500Ft; 4-person apartments 12,500-15,900Ft. AmEx/MC/V. ❸

Vakácio Vendégház, Rákóczi Ferenc u. 39 (☎933 8502; fax 506 779), across from the shaded Erzsébet Park. 15min. walk from town. One of the least expensive options in town. Modest rooms with bunk beds. Huge common room with TV and a coffee machine. Bathrooms in the hall. Reception 24hr. 2000Ft. 10% HI discount. ❶

Ózon Camping, Erdei Malom köz 3 (☎331 144). Take bus #10B. The beautiful grounds offer scenic views of Hungary and Austria. Swimming pool on site. Tennis, fishing, and horseback riding 2km away. Sauna 2800Ft per hr. Breakfast 350-400Ft. Reception 24hr. Open Apr. 15-Oct. 15. Tents 560Ft, plus 1020Ft per person; 1- to 2-person bungalows 2100-2970Ft, 3- to 4-person 3600-5100Ft. MC/V. ❶

■ FOOD

The large **Smatch supermarket** at Várkerület u. 100/102 stocks groceries. (Open M-F 6:30am-8pm, Sa 6:30am-6pm. MC/V.)

Várkerület Restaurant, Várkerület u. 83 (☎319 286), near Széchenyi tér. Spices up a traditional Hungarian menu with its own "house-proud dishes." The efficient staff brings meaty entrees (680-1800Ft) and vegetarian dishes (690-1180Ft) to dining room and beer garden tables. Open M-Sa 9am-1am, Su 11am-1am. ❷

Fórum Pizzeria, Szt. György út 3 (☎340 231). In a quiet courtyard, this Italian eatery provides a refreshing break from Hungarian fare. Choose from among 41 pizza options (650-1190Ft), 18 different pastas (550-1100Ft), and a salad bar (350-480Ft). Dine in the candle-lit dining room or on the summer terrace. Open daily 11am-10pm. ❷

Pince Csárda, Széchenyi tér 5 (☎349 276; fax 240 008). An array of chicken, venison, and veal dishes. Vegetarian options. Comfy canvas seats. English menu available. Entrees 890-1690Ft. Open M-Th 11am-11pm, F-Sa 11am-midnight, Su 11am-4pm. ❷

◉ SIGHTS

Most of Sopron's sights are downtown. You can purchase a ▨**museum pass** (2000Ft, students 1000Ft), allowing access to nine of Sopron's museums, including all of those listed below. Once you've visited five museums, the pass pays for itself. Passes are available at the **Storno-Collection ticket office,** Fő tér 8. (☎311 327. Open Tu-Su 10am-6pm.)

▨**FIRE-WATCH TOWER (TUZTORONY).** Built from the remains of a town wall during Roman times, the tower, which a fire destroyed in 1676, stands rebuilt as the symbol of Sopron. During reconstruction, a balcony was added from which guards could signal the position of fires with flags during the day and lanterns at night. Squeeze up the staircase to the balcony for a view of the surrounding hills. *(At Fő tér 6, to the left before the passage under the tower. Open Apr. and Sept.-Oct. Tu-Su 10am-6pm; May-Aug. Tu-Su 10am-8pm. 500Ft, students 250Ft. Binoculars 400Ft.)*

▨**FABRICIUS HOUSE.** Originally the site of an ancient Roman bath, the Fabricius House today boasts a well-organized **archaeological museum** with artifacts of the area's inhabitants dating back to the Bronze Age. Jewelry, urns, pottery, tools, and tombstones are among its holdings. The English info next to each display is extremely helpful. The underground **Roman Lapidarium** (Római Kőtár) houses tombs and statues that date back to Sopron's origins as the Roman colony of Scarbantia. There is also a museum showing 12th century artifacts of regional furniture. English info sheets are given in each room. *(Fő tér 6. Open Jan.-Mar. and Oct.-Dec. 10am-2pm; Apr.-Sept. Tu-Su 10am-6pm. Archaeological Museum and Lapidarium 500Ft, students 250Ft. Furniture exhibit 500Ft/250Ft.)*

BENEDICTINE CHURCH (BENCÉS TEMPLOM). Built in the 13th century by a herder whose goats stumbled upon a cache of gold, the Benedictine Church was the site of coronations for three monarchs. Since 1997, it has been under restoration to become a votive church to thank God for Hungary's liberation from communism. *(On Fő tér. Open daily 10am-noon and 2-5pm. Holy Mass M-F 8am, Su 9:30am.)*

TRINITY COLUMN. The most prominent sight on Fő tér and one of Europe's first corkscrew column sculptures, Trinity was commissioned by Éva Katalin Thököly to commemorate the Great Plague of 1695-1701. *(Just outside the church.)*

OLD SYNAGOGUE (KÖZÉPKORI Ó-ZSINAGÓGA). This synagogue, one of few to survive the Holocaust, is now a museum depicting the daily life of the local Jewish community before it was expelled from Sopron in 1526. Built around 1300, it has a stone Torah ark, women's prayer room, and ritual bath well. An English info sheet is provided. *(Új út 22. Open May-Oct. Tu-Su 10am-6pm. 400Ft, students 200Ft.)*

🔪 🌿 OUTDOOR ACTIVITIES AND FESTIVALS

Sopron is a good base for outdoor enthusiasts. Bike trails begin just north of the center, leading to **Lake Fertő-Hanság National Park** (a UNESCO World Heritage Site), and Fertőd, 30km away (see p. 384). Bike maps are free at Tourinform (see **Orientation and Practical Information**, p. 381), which also lists **bike rental** shops (rentals about 2000Ft per day). For info on cultural events, pick up a free copy of the monthly *Ünnepi Hetek* (Sopron Program) from the Festival Bureau (see below) or Tourinform. During the **Sopron Festival Weeks** (late June to mid-July), the town hosts opera, ballet, and concerts. Some are set in the **Fertőrákos Quarry**, 10km away, reachable by hourly buses from the terminal. (Quarry 300Ft, students 150Ft. Concerts 3000-8000Ft.) Buy tickets for all events from the **Festival Bureau**, Liszt Ferenc u. 1 (☎517 517), on Széchenyi tér, opposite the post office. (Open M-F 9am-5pm, Sa 9am-noon.) **Cinema City** at Sopron Plaza shows both Hungarian- and English-language films (490-950Ft).

🄿 NIGHTLIFE

Cézár Pince, Hátsókapu 2 (☎311 337), near Fő tér. You may never want to leave this classy bar, converted from a spacious 17th-century home. Eat on the vine-draped patio. Wine 600-950Ft, 0.5L *Gösser* 290Ft. Open M-Sa 11am-midnight, Su 1-11pm.

Goac Pont, Várkerület u. 22 (☎524 018). Sopron youth pack the place so tight that it's hard to appreciate the eclectic decor, complete with painted waves, a sombrero, sewing machine, and *Gone With the Wind* poster. Beer 250-380Ft, mixed drinks 700-1400Ft. Open Su-M and W-Th 6pm-1am, F-Sa 6pm-2am.

Dancing Cafe, Selmeci u. 15-17, 2 streets after the bus station when coming from town. One of Sopron's best clubs, Dancing Cafe features a different themed party each weekend night. Beer 250-350Ft, shots 200-500Ft. Open F-Sa 10pm-4am.

HUNGARY

⮊ DAYTRIP FROM SOPRON

FERTŐD
☎ (0)99

Buses leave from platform #11 in Sopron (45min., every 30min.-1hr., 338Ft). Get off at the 3-way intersection in Fertőd. From the bus stop, walk in the direction of the bus to the castle. ☎537 640. Palace open Mar. 16-Sept. 30 Tu-Su 10am-6pm; Oct. 1-Mar. 15 F-Su 10am-4pm. Tours (1hr.) summer 2 per hr.; low season variable. Last tour 1hr. before closing. Call ahead to request a tour in English. 1000Ft, students 600Ft. MC/V.

Twenty-seven kilometers east of Sopron, Fertőd (FER-tewd) is home to the magnificent **Eszterházy Palace,** Joseph Haydn 2. The 126-room palace, with its bright yellow Baroque facade and manicured gardens, has been dubbed the "Hungarian Versailles." Prince Miklós Eszterházy ordered its construction in 1766 to host his Bacchic feasts and operas. The tour explains the marble floors, the painted ceilings, and the cleverly concealed door in the prince's bedroom. Ask for the English info sheet. The palace was used as a stable and then a hospital during WWII; government funding helped restore it after the 1957 revolution. **Joseph Hadyn** lived here for almost 30 years as Eszterházy's composer. A small exhibit inside recounts his life. ▤**Concerts** celebrating his work are held in the castle's small concert hall, where he himself conducted, during the semiannual **Haydn Festival,** in mid-July and the first week of September. (Concerts 7pm. Reserve ahead. 5000-8000Ft.) On weekends, when the festival is not going on, less-expensive performances (2500-4000Ft) are held. To reserve tickets to any of the concerts, call or visit the box office, in the right wing of the palace. (☎537 645. Open daily 11am-6pm.) **Gránátos Étterem ❷,** Joseph Haydn u. 1, just across the street, offers Hungarian entrees (850-1790Ft) and desserts. (☎370 944. Open daily 9am-10pm. English menu available.)

Fertőd is part of **Fertő-Hanság National Park,** a UNESCO World Heritage Site. Straddling the Austro-Hungarian border, Lake Fertő, in the park's center, is one of Europe's most diverse water habitats, while the surrounding swampland is home to over 200 species of birds. For preservation purposes, some parts of the park can only be visited with a certified guide, but bike and hiking trails are scattered throughout the park. Pick up a **map** from **Tourinform Fertőd,** Joseph Haydn 3, just behind the palace (☎370 544; fertod@tourinform.hu; open Apr.-June Tu-F 10am-5pm, Sa 10am-4pm), or **Park Information,** Sarród u. 4 (☎537 620; fehnpi@ktm.x400gw.itb.hu). The trails begin 2km from the Palace; follow Sarród u., the street perpendicular to the bus stop. **Water sports,** including waterskiing, sailing, and swimming, take place on the lake. The paved bike path around it is also popular. Bike rental info is available at the Park Information office.

SZOMBATHELY
☎ (06)94

A major crossroads between Transdanubia and Austria, Szombathely (SOM-bahthay; pop. 80,000) hides 2000-year-old ruins of Roman Savaria beneath the cover of modern storefronts and Baroque buildings. Though it's one of the oldest towns in Hungary, Szombathely's modern restaurants, lively cafes, and year-round festivals make it a pleasant stop for travelers crossing the border, or for those looking to hike in the beautiful Őrség National Park.

⊏ TRANSPORTATION. Trains (☎311 420) run to: **Budapest** (3¾hr., 18 per day, 2130Ft; InterCity 2¾hr., 15 per day, 3195Ft plus 400Ft reservation fee); **Győr** (2hr., 19 per day, 1010Ft; InterCity 1¼hr., 10 per day, 1641Ft plus 400Ft reservation fee); **Keszthely** (2½hr., 11 per day, 1475Ft); **Vienna, AUT** (4hr., 17 per day). Buy tickets in the **train station** or at Király út 8/a. (Schedules at www.elvira.hu. Open M-F 8am-

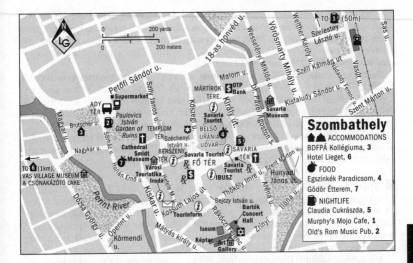

Szombathely

▲▲ ACCOMMODATIONS
BDFPÁ Kollégiuma, 3
Hotel Lieget, 6

🍴 FOOD
Egszínkék Paradicsom, 4
Gödör Étterem, 7

🎵 NIGHTLIFE
Claudia Cukrászda, 5
Murphy's Mojo Cafe, 1
Old's Rom Music Pub, 2

5pm, Sa 8am-noon.) **Buses** (☎312 054; www.volanbusz.hu.) run to: **Budapest** (3½hr., 6 per day, 2360Ft); **Győr** (2½hr., 8 per day, 1100Ft); **Keszthely** (2½hr., 6 per day, 947Ft); **Sopron** (2hr., 5 per day, 842Ft).

⬛🛈 ORIENTATION AND PRACTICAL INFORMATION. Szombathely is formed from several interconnected squares, the largest of which is **Fő tér,** home to the main **tourist offices, Savaria,** and **Tourinform.** From the train station, turn left and then right on Széll Kálmán út. Follow this until you reach Mártírok tere. Turn left on Király u., which ends in **Savaria tér.** The **bus station** sits on the opposite side of the center; turn left on the street parallel to the station and follow it into town (5min.). Cross Kiskar u. and then head straight to the pedestrian Belsikátor, which ends in Fő tér.

Tourinform, Kossuth Lajos u., on the edge of Fő tér, has a helpful staff, which offers **free maps** and helps book rooms. (☎514 451. Open M-F 9am-5pm.) **Savaria Tourist** provides info, books rooms, and gives out **free maps** at three locations: Király u. 1 (☎509 485; fax 509 486), Mártírok tere 1 (☎511 435), and Berzsenyi tér 2 (☎511 446; fax 511 445). All locations **exchange currency.** (Open M-F 8:30am-4:30pm, Sa 8am-noon.) **OTP Bank,** Fő tér 4, exchanges currency and has a MC/V **ATM** outside. (Open M 7:45am-6pm, Tu-Th 7:45am-5pm, F 7:45am-4pm.) A **pharmacy** is at Fő tér 9. (☎312 466. Open M-F 8am-6pm, Sa 8am-1pm.) For special attention, see the **doctor,** Wesselényi Miklós út 4 (☎317 127). The best **Internet** rates are at **Szombathelyi Siker Könyvitár,** Ady tér 40, behind the bus station. (300Ft per hr. Membership for 700Ft, students 350Ft. M-Th free for members. Open M-F 9am-5pm.) The **post office,** Kossuth Lajos u. 18, has **Poste Restante.** (☎311 584. Open M-F 8am-6pm, Sa 8am-noon.) **Postal Code:** 9700.

🛏🍴 ACCOMMODATIONS AND FOOD. To book a **private room,** visit **Savaria Tourist** (see **Orientation and Practical Information,** p. 385; doubles from 3500Ft) or **IBUSZ,** Fő tér 44. (☎314 141; szombath@iroda.ibusz.hu. Open M-F 8am-5pm, Sa 9am-1pm. Singles from 5000Ft; doubles from 5200Ft.) **Berzsenyi Dániel Főiskola Pável Ágoston Kollégiuma ❶,** Ady tér 3/A, books clean singles in two buildings near the bus station. (☎313 591. Check-out 9am. Singles 1400Ft.) **Hotel Liget ❸**, Szent István park 15, accessible by bus 2c or 2a from the bus or train station, offers spacious rooms in St. Stephan's Park, within easy reach of the city center and the Vas Village Museum. (☎509 323; hliget@ax.hu. Reception 24hr. Singles 5000-6990Ft; doubles 6000-8900Ft; triples 11990-13990Ft.)

Most restaurants line Fő tér's pedestrian walkway. **Smatch supermarkets** are at Fő tér 17 (open M-F 7am-7:30pm, Sa 7am-4pm; MC/V) and behind the bus station (open M-F 6am-7pm, Sa 7am-3pm; MC/V). ⚅**Gödör Étterem ❸**, Hollán Ernő 10/12, dishes up huge portions of Hungarian specialties ordered from an amusing menu. (☎510 078. Entrees 650-2490Ft. Open M-Th 11am-11pm, F-Sa 11am-midnight, Su 11am-3pm.) **Égszínkék Paradicsom ❷** (Sky-blue Paradise), Belső Uránia udvar, serves up heavenly pasta (480-890Ft) by candlelight. Walk through the archway at Kőszegi u. 2 off Fő tér. (☎480 890. Open daily 11am-11pm.)

🟦 **SIGHTS.** The ⚅**Vas Village Museum** (Vasi Múzeum Falu) displays authentic 200-year-old farmhouses moved from villages throughout the region. Inside the 13 farmhouses are collections of pottery, kitchenware, and regional farming tools. A church and cemetery were recently added to the village. From Ady tér, walk 10min. down Nagykar u. which becomes Gagarin u., cross Bartók Béla, the main street, then go up Árpád u. to the end. (Open Apr.-Nov. Tu-Su 10am-5pm. 500Ft, students 250Ft. English brochure 80Ft.) Szombathely is the proud home of Hungary's third-largest **cathedral**, built in 1797 in Baroque and Neoclassical styles. The chapel to its right is the only portion of the original building that still stands today. It is still under restoration to repair WWII damage. To the right of the cathedral, the **Paulovics István Garden of Ruins** (Paulovics Romkert), Templom tér 1, was once the center of the Roman colony of Savaria. From Fő tér, go left on Széchenyi út, right on Szily János út, and straight to Templom tér. (☎313 369. Open Mar.-Dec. 15 Tu-Su 9am-5pm. 360Ft, students 180Ft. English brochure 20Ft.) The **Smidt Museum**, Hollán Ernő u. 2, shows off Dr. Lajos Smidt's obsessive collection of just about anything he could get his hands on: weapons, watches, old money, clothing, clocks, tableware, Roman artifacts, ancient maps, and Franz Liszt's pocket watch. From Fő tér, walk through Belsikátor u. to Hollán E. u. (☎311 038. No English info. Open Mar.-Dec. 20 Tu-Su 10am-5pm; Jan. 8-Feb. 28 Tu-F 10am-5pm. 460Ft, students 230Ft.)

🎭🎵 **ENTERTAINMENT AND NIGHTLIFE.** In the evening, laze on the banks of the beautiful **Csókanázótó Lake** or rent a boat and paddle on its waters (500-1000Ft per hr.). Szombathely's active spirit has brought a range of new activities to the region, including golf, tennis, rock climbing, and the ever-popular paintball. In early June, the **Savaria Dance Competition** tangos into town, while the **Savaria Historical Carnival,** held in Fő tér at the end of August, brings the city's medieval history to life with historical reenactments and an open-air market. The **Bartók Seminar and Festival,** in the middle of July, attracts musicians and music lovers from around the world. The seminars are for participants only, but the concerts are open to all. The two-week **Spring Festival** in March celebrates music and the performing arts. One of the most curious festivals in Hungary takes place in mid-June, when Szombathely celebrates the **Bloomsday Festival,** in honor of Leopold Bloom, the character from Irish author James Joyce's *Ulysses.*

Nightlife in Szombathely centers around **Fő tér.** The square hosts summer concerts and ice cream stands that stay open late into the night. Enjoy a gooey pastry (160-320Ft) or an ice-cream concoction (330-700Ft) at the charming and cozy **Claudia Cukrászda,** Savaria tér 1. (☎313 375. Open daily 9am-8pm.) The younger element flocks to **Murphy's Mojo Cafe,** Semmelweis Ignác út 28. Enjoy beer (380-

510Ft), Serbian food, and friendly conversation in a dining room filled with collector's items. (☎315 891. English menu available. Open daily 4:30pm-midnight.) **Old's Rom Music Pub,** Ady tér, is a favorite among the dancing crowd. (Open Su-Th 9am-midnight, F-Sa 11am-2am. Cover 700Ft on Sa.)

🢂 DAYTRIP FROM SZOMBATHELY

ŐRSÉG NATIONAL PARK

Entrance is in Őriszentpéter. Take the bus from Ady tér in Szombathely (1½-2hr., 8 per day, 752Ft) and take a right out of the bus station. From the center, take a right on Városszer u. and walk for 1km until you reach the park information building. Here you'll find maps (650Ft), as well as hiking and camping advice. Open M-Th 8am-noon and 1-4pm, F 8am-2pm, Sa 10am-4pm. Before leaving Szombathely, ask at Tourinform for the free "Camping in Hungary" map.

Located near the Slovenian border, the Őrség National Park provides a mixture of hiking and culture. The trails reveal stunning views of the Slovenian and Hungarian hillsides, and the towns in the area, virtually unchanged over centuries, provide a glimpse into what settlement was like following the Hungarian conquest in the 10th and 11th centuries. You may want to stop in the village of **Szalafő,** 4 km from Őriszentpéter, where the **Pityerszer Rural Museum** displays typical "encircled" cottages. (Open Tu-Su 10am-6pm.) **Magyarszombatfa,** 7km south of Őriszentpéter, is known for its ceramics. In the nearby town of **Pankasz,** check out the famous wooden belfry, which even has wooden headstones in its cemetery. Local buses run between the towns; check schedules posted on the bus stops. The park, popular for its variety of plants and animals, is home to **rare birds** like black storks and honey buzzards, and 500 species of **butterflies**—more than anywhere else in Hungary. For help locating wildlife, pick up an English guide from the park information building before setting off.

In the center of Őriszentpéter, on Városszer u., is a **pharmacy, Encián Gyógyszertár.** (☎428 006. Open M-F 7:30am-5pm, Sa 8am-noon.) Be sure to stock up, as the nearest 24hr. pharmacy is in Körmend. Across the street, in the building labeled **Iparcikkek,** you can buy camping supplies. (☎548 015. Open M-F 7:30am-noon and 1-4:30pm, Sa 7:30am-noon.) An **ABC supermarket** is also in the center. (Open M-F 6am-5:30pm, Sa 6am-1pm, Su 7am-11am.) If you want one last big meal before heading into the hills, fill up on fried Hungarian food at **Centrum Étterem ❷.** (Entrees 300-1200Ft. Open M-F 6am-10pm, Sa-Su 7am-10pm.) **Őrségi Camping ❶,** Városszer u. 57, in Őriszentpéter, is a good campsite. (☎428 046. Open June 5-Aug. 25.) Employees can suggest hiking routes. If you have time, visit the **Árpádkori Műemlék Templom,** the small 12th-century church 100m from the park info building. Guarded by the statue of King Stephan I, Hungary's first Christian king, it was a fortress during Turkish invasions. (Mass Su 8:30am.)

KŐSZEG ☎(36)94

Nestled at the foot of the Kőszeg mountains, the quiet town of Kőszeg charms visitors with its beautiful churches, historical monuments, and country cottages. Just a mile from the Austrian border, the town was built as defense against Austria's repeated attempts at expansion, but became famous in 1536 when, under the leadership of Miklós Jurisich, it rejected the Turks, and managed to deflect their march on Vienna. The castle, which withstood the siege, enchants visitors with tales of victory and panoramic views of the Austrian countryside.

⬛🔢 TRANSPORTATION AND PRACTICAL INFORMATION. The **bus station,** Liszt Ferenc 16 (☎360 180), is a block from the town center. Buses to: **Szombathely** (30min., 8-10 per day, 188Ft) and **Sopron** (1¼hr, 10 per day, 676Ft). The **train station,** krt 2 (☎360 053), is 1km south of town. Trains to: **Szombathely** (30min., 15 per day, 162Ft) and **Sopron** (1-2hr., 12 per day, 756Ft). Várkör u. encircles the town. The two main squares, **Fő tér** and **Jurisich tér** lie on the south end, while the **castle** *(vár)* sits in the north. To get to the center from the bus station, go right out of the station onto **Kossuth Lajos u.,** which leads to Fő tér. From the train station, follow **Rákóczi Ferenc ut.** to get to Fő tér. **Tourinform,** Jurisics tér 7, has free maps and helps find accommodations. (☎563 121. Open M-Sa 9am-5pm.) The **OTP bank,** Kossuth L. u. 8, has an **ATM** and **currency exchange** machine. (Open M 7:45am-5pm, Tu-Th 7:45am-3pm, F 7:45am-12:30pm.) The **pharmacy,** Kossuth L. u. 12, has Western products. (☎360 066. Open M-F 8am-6pm, Sa 8am-2pm.) A **post office** is at Várkör u. 65. (☎360 094. Open M-F 8am-4pm, Sa 8am-noon.) **Postal Code: 9732.**

⬛⬛ ACCOMMODATIONS AND FOOD. Savaria Tourist, Várkör u. 57, arranges **private rooms.** (☎563 048; tompasav@matavnet.hu. Singles from 4000Ft; doubles from 5500Ft. Open M-F 8am-4pm, Sa 8am-noon.) Most restaurants in town has guest rooms upstairs, although the cheaper rooms generally lie outside Várkör u. **Kóbor Macskához Pension ❸,** Várkör u. 100, offers clean doubles and triples, with views of the belltower of St. Imre Church. (☎362 273; dr.doros-zlay@netquick.hu. Breakfast 600Ft. Reception 24hr. Doubles 5300Ft; triples 6800Ft.) In the heart of town, **Hotel Aranystrucc ❹,** Várkör u. 124, provides luxu-rious, well-furnished rooms. Note the bells of nearby Church of Jesus' Heart toll once each quarter hour. (☎360 323. Doubles 9500Ft; triples 12000Ft. Reception 24hr.). You can set up camp at **Gyöngyvirág Camping ❶,** Bajcsy-Zsilinszky u. 6, on the shore of peaceful Gyöngyös River. (☎360 454; fax 364 574. 500Ft per adult, 300Ft per child, 300Ft per tent, 300Ft per car.) ⬛**Pizzeria de Rocco ❷,** Várkör u. 55, bakes delicious pizza in its wood oven. Enjoy a view of the castle from the terraced patio or relax to jazz in the dining room. (☎362 379. Pizza 400-1350Ft. Salads 550-650Ft. Open M-Sa noon-midnight, Su noon-10pm.) Revert to the Mid-dle Ages in the time-warped dining room of **Bécsikapu Étterem ❷,** Rajnis u. 5, where you can feast on game dishes fit for a king. (☎563 122; www.bec-sikapu.hu. Entrees 690-1850Ft. Open daily 11am-10pm.) The modern **Portré Res-taurant ❸,** Fő tér 7, serves a variety of Mediterranean and Hungarian dishes. (☎363 170. Entrees 890-2190Ft. Coffee 200-390Ft. Open daily 8am-10pm.) Pick up groceries and snacks at **Match supermarket,** Várkör u. 20 (Open M-F 6am-7pm, Sa 6am-4pm. MC/V.)

⬛ SIGHTS. The most imposing of Kőszeg's sights is **Jurisich Castle** (Vár), con-structed in Gothic style during the late 13th century. It was at this castle that 4000 people fought the Turkish siege of 1532, which the Turks eventually lost because of internal revolt. The last contingent left the outskirts of town at 11am on Aug. 30, 1532. Since then, the town church bells have tolled daily at 11am as a reminder of the remarkable victory. The castle, now open to visitors, houses the **Jurisich Miklos Museum,** in memory of the man who lead the Hungarian forces. The museum dis-plays artifacts from the blockade and other historical documents important to the town, but the most interesting part is the long hallway which connects the rooms where you'll find paintings of the town during various stages of its history. The views from the **belltower,** just beside the museum, offer a panorama of the city and nearby hills. (☎360 240. Castle open Tu-Su 10am-5pm. 120Ft, students 80Ft, chil-dren 80Ft. Museum 460Ft/230Ft/150Ft.)

The 1894 **Church of Jesus' Heart** (Jézus Szíve Plébánia templom) dominates Fő tér. The colorful mosaic walls and columns complement the intricate stained glass windows behind the altar. (Open daily 9am-6pm. Free. Mass Su 10am.) Branching off Fő tér, Városház u. leads onto Jurisics tér, which is surrounded by multiple monuments. To enter the square, you'll pass under **Heroes' Gate** (Hősi kapu), built on the 400th anniversary of the Turkish blockade. A highlight of Jurisics tér is the patriotically striped **Town Hall** (Városház), Jurisics tér 8, which has served the town since the 15th century. The **Pharmacy Museum** (Apotéka), Jurisics tér 11, houses instruments and medicine from old pharmacies in the region. Check out the special collection of medicinal herbs on the second floor. (☎360 337. Open Tu-Su 10am-5pm. 360Ft, students 180Ft, children 100Ft. English brochure 80Ft). The highlight of **St. James Church** (Szent Jakab templom), in the center of the square, is the beautiful Gothic wooden Madonna sculpture near the altar. (Open daily 9am-6pm. Free.) The smaller **St. Henry's Church** has a beautiful Gothic altar. (Open daily 9am-6pm. Free.) The **synagogue ruins** stand on the corner of Várkör u. and Gyöngyös u. Though you can't go past the gates, the Hebrew inscription over the main entrance is worth a look.

🎭🎵 **ENTERTAINMENT AND NIGHTLIFE.** Kőszeg is a quiet town, day and night. The serene **Chernel Kert** (Chernel Park) offers shaded walks at the base of the tree-covered Kőszeg mountains. You can also begin hikes from here—pick up maps and info at **Tourinform** (p. 388). To get to the park, follow Várkör u. past Fő tér, keeping the Church of Jesus' Heart to your left. Go a left on Hunyadi u. and continue to the end of the road. For something a little more upbeat, join the locals at **Ciao Amico,** where you can enjoy pizza (420-950Ft) and beer (220-750Ft) at the bar or try your luck in the adjoining casino and arcade. (☎349 952. Bar, arcade, and casino open 24hr.; pizzeria daily noon-midnight.) In mid-June, the town's biggest festival, the **Ost-West Fesztival,** features open-air performances of folk music and dance in the town's main squares and the castle courtyard. For exact dates and tickets (900-2000Ft), contact Tourinform.

LAKE BALATON

Surrounded by the volcanic wine hills of Badacsony and Tihany, the shaded parks of Balatonfüred, and the sandy of Keszthely, Lake Balaton is one of Central Europe's most beautiful and popular vacation spots. The area became a playground for the European elite when the railroad linked the lake's surrounding towns in the 1860s. Frequented by nature lovers, history buffs, and party-goers, it attracts young and old, the rich and the budget-conscious, with its incomparable vistas, beautiful weather, and boisterous nightlife. Teeming with fish, the lake is also the source of the region's distinct cuisine, which is complemented by white wines from the hills in the north.

Storms roll in over Lake Balaton in less than 15min., raising dangerous white-caps on the usually placid lake. Yellow lights on top of tall buildings at Siófok's harbor give **weather warnings.** If the light flashes once per 2 sec., stay within 500m of shore; 1 flash per sec. means swimmers must return to shore. Don't worry too much about storms spoiling your vacation: most last fewer than 30min.

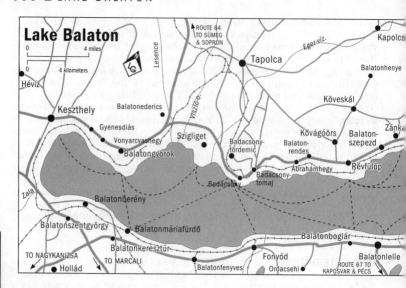

Lake Balaton

SIÓFOK ☎ (06)84

There are more tourist offices per sq. km in Siófok than any other Hungarian city—its population grows ten-fold in summer with vacationers. The lake provides ample excuse for the bikinis, beer, and bacchanalia that rule this summer capital. Students, families, elderly people, and everyone in between take in the sun and party together.

▐ TRANSPORTATION

Trains: To: **Budapest** (2½hr.; 20 per day; 1094Ft, plus 400Ft reservation fee); **Keszthely** (3-5hr., 15 per day, 1666-2106Ft); **Pécs** (4-8hr., 1 per day, 1493Ft). Siófok is a stop on the Budapest lines to: **Ljubljana, SLN; Split, CRO; Venice, ITA; Zagreb, CRO.**

Buses: To: **Budapest** (1½hr., 9 per day, 1320Ft) and **Pécs** (3hr., 4 per day, 2456Ft).

Ferries: The quickest way to north Balaton is the hourly **MAHART ferry**, 10min. from the train station in the *Strand* center. To: **Balatonfüred** (1hr.; 6-9 per day; 800 Ft, students 400Ft) and **Tihany** (1¼hr.; 6-9 per day; 1000Ft, students 500Ft).

▟ ▐ ORIENTATION AND PRACTICAL INFORMATION

Siófok's excellent transport services to other parts of the lake make it an ideal base from which to explore the region. The **train** and **bus stations** straddle Kálmán Imre sétány, near the center of town. The main street, **Fő út,** runs parallel to the tracks in front of the station. **FA Canal** connects the lake to the Danube and divides the town. The eastern **Gold Coast** (Arany-part), to the right as you face the water, is home to older, larger hotels, while the **Silver Coast** (Ezüst-part), to your left, has newer and slightly cheaper accommodations. Both are a 20-30min. walk from the city center, which sits between them. The Silver Coast conveniently has its own train station, **Balatonszéplak felső.**

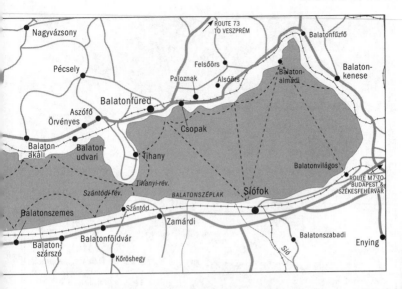

Tourist Offices: Tourinform, Fő út at Szabadság tér (☎315 355; www.siofok.com), in the water tower opposite the train station. English-speaking staff finds rooms and offers **free maps.** Open June 15-Sept. 15 M-F 8am-8pm, Sa-Su 9am-6pm; Sept. 16-June 14 M-F 9am-4pm. **IBUSZ,** Fő út 61, 2nd fl. (☎510 720; fax 315 213), changes currency for no commission and books private rooms. Open M-F 8am-8pm, Sa 9am-1pm.

Currency Exchange: OTP, Szabadság tér 10 (☎310 455), exchanges currency for no commission. A MC/V **ATM** is outside. Open M 7:45am-6pm, Tu-Th 7:45am-5pm, F 7:45am-4pm. **Postabank,** Fő út 174-6 (☎310 400), exchanges currency and cashes **traveler's checks** for no commission. A MC/V **ATM** and currency exchange machine outside. Open M 8am-5pm, Tu-Th 8am-4pm, F 8am-3pm.

Luggage Storage: Available at the train station. Small bags 240Ft for 24hr., 120Ft for 6hr.; large bags 480Ft/240Ft.

Emergency: Police, Sió u. 14 (☎310 700). **Coast Guard:** ☎310 990.

24hr. Pharmacy: Régi Pharmacy, Fő út 202 (☎310 041). Open M-F 8am-7pm, Sa 8am-2pm; ring bell after hours. Extra 200Ft per item after hours. AmEx/MC/V.

Internet Access: Net Game Pont, (☎776 670) Fő út 45, 100Ft per 15min., 300Ft per hr. Open daily 10am-10pm.

Post Office: Fő út 186 (☎310 210). **Poste Restante** available; go upstairs and left. Open M-F 8am-7pm, Sa 8am-noon. **Telephones** and ATM outside. **Postal Code:** 8600.

ACCOMMODATIONS

Because Balaton is frequented by affluent Western tourists, sojourns in the lake country have grown increasingly expensive. Expect prices to be slightly higher than in Budapest. Several agencies offer **private rooms.** Your best bets are **Tourinform** (see above), which finds rooms and negotiates rates with hotels (doubles 6000-15,000Ft), and **IBUSZ** (doubles 6000Ft; tourist tax 150-300Ft per night; 30% surcharge for fewer than 4 nights). If you'd rather bargain on your own, knock on

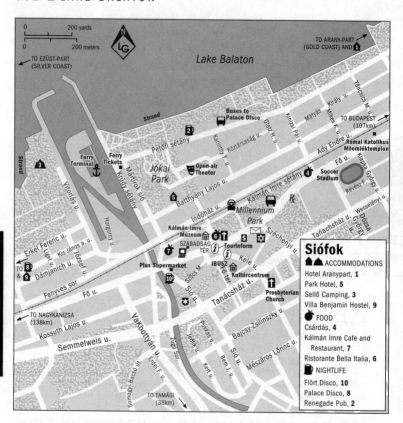

doors with *Panzió* and *Zimmer frei* signs on streets close to the water. Start hunting on **Erkel Ferenc u.,** on the far side of the canal, and **Szent László u.,** to the left as you leave the train station.

Park Hotel, Batthány u. 7 (☎310 539), near the main *strand*, 5min. from the center. Spacious rooms have high-vaulted ceilings. All rooms have A/C, and many have cable TV and jacuzzis. Reception 24hr. Doubles July-Aug. 10,000-15,000Ft; Sept.-June 8000-10,000Ft; triples 12,000-18,000Ft; 4-person apartments 15,000-25,000Ft. MC/V. ❹

Villa Benjamin Youth Hostel, Siófoki u. 9 (☎350 704). Get off at the Balatonszéplak felső station if arriving by bus or train, 1 stop after Siófok when coming from Budapest. Located on the Silver Coast. 25min. from central Siófok but next to the Palace Disco and near plenty of places to eat. Garden rooms, with a beach bungalow feel, are simple but pleasant and have a closet, table, and sink. Kitchen and picnic areas. Singles 2500Ft; doubles 5000Ft; triples 7500Ft; 4- to 6-person apartments 14,000-21,000Ft; 8- to 10-person house 28,000-35,000Ft. ❷

Sellő Camping, Kikötő u. 3 (☎550 367; www.balatonihajozas.hu), next to the marina. Cheapest accommodation in the town center. On a sandy beach on the canal, this campground is well-maintained, with recently renovated bathroom facilities. July-Aug. 1250Ft per person, 1140Ft per tent; Apr.-June and Sept. 1030Ft/840Ft. Tax 300Ft. ❶

Hotel Aranypart, Beszédes J. sétány 82, (☎519 450; www.aranypart.hu). Take bus #2 from city center to the front of the hotel. On the Gold Coast beach. Views are beautiful. Spacious rooms with full baths. Restaurant, coffee shop, and safe in lobby. Sauna and tennis courts. Rooms have radio, TV, and freezer. Breakfast included. Singles 7000-13000Ft; doubles 8750-14750Ft. Extra bed 3750Ft. Tourist tax 200Ft. MC/V. ❹

🍴 FOOD

In the Lake region, many restaurants serve a combination of Hungarian and Italian food. Grab supplies for the beach at **Plus Supermarket,** Fő út 156-160. (Open M-F 7am-8pm, Sa 7am-3pm, Su 8am-noon. MC/V.) If you're staying on the Silver Coast, **CBA Supermarket** is open daily 7am-10pm. The *Strand* kiosks off snack foods, with *lángos* (200-300Ft), hamburgers (300Ft), and pizza (500Ft).

■ **Kálmán Imre Cafe and Restaurant,** Kálmán Imre sétány 13 (☎310 651), at the far end of Kálmán Imre sétány. On the corner of Fő tér, on the left as you exit the train station. Offers a variety of local foods, including many fish dishes, on a pleasant covered patio. Entrees 790-2790Ft. On your way out, grab something sweet (120-450Ft) from the pastry display in the corner of the restaurant. Open daily 10am-10pm. ❸

Csárdás, Fő út 105 (☎310 642). Proximity to the lake makes Csárdás's tasty local dishes ideal for an after-beach meal. Lit terrace has a romantic atmosphere. Live gypsy music Th-Sa 6pm. Entrees 800-2500Ft. Open daily noon-10pm. AmEx/MC/V. ❷

Ristorante Bella Italia, Szabadság tér 1 (☎310 826). The statue-flanked restaurant dishes out enticing entrees with speed and stellar service. Enjoy a cold glass of their fresh squeezed orange juice (159Ft) on the roomy terrace. Pizza and pasta 530-1900Ft. Open daily 9am-midnight. ❷

🎭 ENTERTAINMENT

Though Siofok's other daytime attractions are entertaining, none compare to the **strand,** a series of park-like lawns running to the shoreline. There are public and private sections; entrance to a private area costs around 200-400Ft, though with public spaces available, it seems unnecessary to pay. The largest private beach lies to the right of town as you face the water. (700Ft, children 350Ft. Open M-F 8am-3am.) Most sections of the beach rent an assortment of water vehicles, including paddleboats and kayaks (200-400Ft per hr.). The young often gather in the "party cafes" that line the streets before heading out to beach parties.

For a taste of culture beyond the beach-bum variety, check out the operettas (in German and Hungarian) held nightly in the **Kultúrcentrum,** Fő tér 2. Tourinform (see **Tourist Offices,** p. 391) sells tickets (1200-4000Ft). In early July, week-long **Golden Shell International Folklore Festival** (☎504 262) celebrates folk music and dancing. The **Kálmán Imre Múzeum,** Kálmán Imre sétány, next to the train station, displays the local composer's piano and playbills. The second floor hosts art exhibitions. (Open Apr.-Oct. Tu-Su 9am-5pm; Nov.-Mar. Tu-Su 9am-4pm. 250Ft.) **Római Katolikus Műemléktemplom,** Fő út 57, holds organ concerts (900Ft, students 600Ft) Saturdays at 8pm.

🌙 NIGHTLIFE

At nightfall, excessive displays of skin, drunkenness, and debauchery move from Siofok's beaches to its bars. **Nightclubs** line the lakefront; many feature semi-nude dancers and sexy murals. Disco lovers hop on *Discoschiff,* the **disco boat** (☎310 050). DJs, live pop, and ABBA keep the party alive. (Cover 1400Ft, under 191200Ft. Departs from the ferry dock daily July-Aug. at 9pm.)

▓ **Renegade Pub,** Petőfi sétány 3 (www.renegade-pub.com), in the center of the *strand*. This bar and dance club is full by 11pm. Feast your eyes on the beautiful people dancing on tables to the latest Euro-pop hits. If you aren't in the mood to be shoulder-to-shoulder, there is a large patio in back. Enough beer (320-530Ft; 0.5L Carlsberg 750Ft) and liquor (500-700Ft) to float you home. Open daily June-Aug. 8pm-5am.

▓ **Palace Disco,** Deák Ferenc sétány 2 (☎082 045), on the Silver Coast. Free buses depart every hr. from behind the water tower. You must purchase a ticket to the club or show a club stamp to ride. The open-air party complex—discos, bars, restaurants (pizza 800-950Ft), and an "erotic bar"—is surrounded by a well-lit courtyard with yet another dance floor. Mixed drinks 980-1750Ft, beer from 600Ft. Cover 1500-2500Ft. There are often specials, like all-you-can-drink beer and sangria, 11pm-3am. Disco open daily May to mid-Sept. 10pm-5am. Pizzeria open daily 11am-5am.

Flört Disco, Sió u. 4 (☎333 303; www.flort.hu). Follow the spotlights to this 2-story hotspot in the center of town. Admire yourself and the young crowd shaking to house music on the mirrored walls. Beer 650-850Ft. Cover 1500-3000Ft; Tourinform often has fliers for a 300Ft discount. Open daily mid-June to late Aug. 10pm-6am.

BALATONFÜRED ☎(06)87

Across the lake from Siófok, Balatonfüred (BAL-a-ton-FEWR-ed; pop. 13,500) is its quieter counterpart. With sandy beaches, a central park with volcanic springs, and a convenient location near Tihany and Badacsony, this friendly town is the best way to experience the lake while avoiding Siófok's crassness and debauchery. Cheap yet central accommodations make it easy to enjoy the bountiful outdoor activities and savory fresh seafood that make Balaton famous.

▐ TRANSPORTATION

Trains: To: **Badacsony** (55min., 2 per hr., 468Ft); **Budapest** (2½hr., 1 per hr., 1923Ft); **Győr** (4hr., 20 per day, 1844-2602Ft); **Keszthely** (2hr., 12 per day, 698Ft); **Pécs** (4-8hr., 13 per day, 2762Ft).

Buses: Express buses *(gyorsjárat)* go to: **Budapest** (1½hr., 9 per day, 1320Ft); **Keszthely** (1½hr., 9 per day, 700Ft); **Pécs** (3hr., 4 per day, 2456Ft).

Ferries: The quickest way to south Balaton is the hourly **MAHART ferry** (10min.), which leaves from the main pier. To: **Siófok** (1hr.; 6-9 per day; 1000Ft, students 500Ft); **Tihany** (15min.; 6-9 per day; 200Ft, students 100Ft).

▓▐ ORIENTATION AND PRACTICAL INFORMATION

The **train** and **bus stations** are next to each other, 10min. from the town center. To get to town, take a left on **Horváth Mihály u.,** a right on **Jókai Mór u.,** and walk toward the lake. Jókai Mór u. runs perpendicular to the water from the upper part of town to the ferry dock. To the right of the ferry dock, **Záconyi Ferenc u.** is home to the tourist office, many restaurants, and the central market. To the left, **Tagore sétány** takes you through the town park and brings you to the main *strand* (beach). In **Gyógy tér,** above the park, you can fill up your water bottles with sulfuric-smelling **volcanic spring water** under the **Well House Pavilion.** On **Petőfi Sándor u.,** which runs through the main part of town, you will find the **Tourinform** office, the bank, and a large supermarket.

The **City Tourist Bureau,** left of the ferry dock on Záconyi Ferenc u., has free info and maps and arranges accommodations. (Open July-Aug. M-F 9am-5pm.) **Tourinform,** Petőfi Sándor u. 68, has an English-speaking staff that suggests private rooms and supplies **free maps** and info. (☎580 480; www.balatonfured.hu. Open July-Aug. M-F 9am-7pm, Sa 9am-6pm, Su 9am-1pm; Sept.-June M-F 9am-4pm.) **OTP**, Petőfi Sándor u. 8, **exchanges currency** for no commission and has **Western Union**. A MC/V **ATM** is outside. (☎581 070. Open M 7:45am-5pm, Tu-F 7:45am-4pm.) **Krisztina Pharmacy**, on Csokonai u., has 24hr. emergency service. (Open M-F 9am-1pm and 2-6pm. AmEx/MC/V.) **Internet access** is expensive; the cheapest is at **NEToybe Eszpresszo**, Horváth M. u. 3, one street past Petőfi Sándor u. when walking up Jókai Mór u. (☎342 235. 120Ft per 10min. Open M-F 6am-10pm, Sa 10am-midnight, Su 10am-10pm.) There's a **post office** on Zsigmond u. (Open M-F 8am-noon and 12:30-4pm.) The main post office, Kossuth L. u. 19, is 15min. from the beach. (Open M-F 8am-6pm, Sa 8am-noon.) **Postal Code: 8230.**

█ ACCOMMODATIONS

Accommodations in Balatonfüred are surprisingly cheap, convenient, and comfortable. Almost every house on Petőfi Sándor u. offers private rooms, which start at about 5000Ft; look for *Zimmer frei* signs. The City Tourist Bureau and Tourinform can also find great deals on accommodations.

▨ **Ifjúsági Szálláshely-Jugendherberge-Youth Hostel**, Hősök tere 1 (☎/fax 342 651). 25min. walk from town center but easily accessible by bus. Bus #4 conveniently runs from the hostel to the main *strand*. The cheapest accommodations in town. Clean dorms, a common room with TV, and free laundry. Breakfast 360Ft, lunch 720Ft, dinner 490Ft. Dorms 2460Ft, 2 or more nights 2000Ft, 4 nights 1800Ft. Tax 300Ft. ❶

Hotel Aranyhíd, Aranyhíd sétány 2 (☎342 058; fax 340 481), across from the main *strand*. Though the outside of the building masks its luxury, this hotel, right next to the beach, boasts large apartments with kitchenettes, bathrooms, phones, TVs, and balconies. Ask for a room overlooking the water—it's the same price. July-Aug. singles 8500Ft; doubles 13,000Ft; triples 16,000Ft. May-June 7000Ft/10,500Ft/13,000Ft. Apr. and Sept.-Oct. 5700Ft/8000Ft/11,000Ft. Tax 300Ft per person. ❹

Camping Füred, Széchenyi u. 24 (☎580 241; fax 342 341), on the shore to the right of town when facing the water. At this luxurious campsite, bungalows are pricey but small tents are reasonably priced. 4- to 6-person bungalows 17,490-22,490Ft. Tents July 7-Aug. 24 2850Ft plus 1300Ft per person; June 20-July 6 and Aug. 25-Sept. 2300Ft plus 1050Ft per person; May 19-June 19 and Sept. 1-14 2000Ft plus 800Ft per person, Apr. 12-May 18 and Sept. 15-Oct. 15 1750Ft plus 600Ft per person. ❷

Hotel Árkád, Gyógy tér 1 (☎342 277; fax 343 457). Newly renovated. Unbeatable location and beach view. Open June-Sept. Singles 3300Ft; doubles 4600Ft; triples 5800Ft; quads 7200Ft. Tax (for foreigners) 100Ft. Call ahead; prices and dates will change. ❸

▐ FOOD

The local diet is based largely on seafood from the lake. Stock up on food, snacks, and beach supplies at the **Silbergold ABC Supermarket**, on Tagore sétány (Open daily 8am-8pm.) Restaurants and cafes line this beach promenade.

▨ **Halászkert Étterem**, Zákonyi u. 3 (☎343 039). Serves dozens of the region's famous fish dishes, including Balaton pike perch (1350Ft) and *halászlé* (700Ft). The patio overlooks the fishing docks. Entrees 480-1850Ft. Open daily 11am-10pm. ❷

Borcsa Restaurant (☎580-070), next to the entrance to Esterházy Strand on Tagore sétány. Decorated with a ship theme, this restaurant, just off the harbor, offers a variety of fish and game dishes. The 2 terraces and beautiful dining room are filled with wicker furniture. Many vegetarian options. Entrees 780-2800Ft. ❸

Brázay Kert, (☎321 633), at the entrance to Brázay Strand on Aranyhíd sétány, offers a gypsy roast (890Ft). Or, satiate your desire for hamburgers (490Ft) and pizza (790Ft) at wooden tables set amid trees. Lounge on the private beach (250Ft, children 150Ft) behind the restaurant. Open daily 8am-10pm. ❷

🎵 🎭 ENTERTAINMENT AND NIGHTLIFE

Balatonfüred is a city visited mainly for its *strands* (beaches) and water sports. The most popular destination is the main beach, **Esterházy Strand,** on Tagore sétány. A walk through the park from the ferry dock reveals sandy beaches and many forms of entertainment for adults and kids: there is a a giant slide (100Ft per ride), a water castle (500Ft), paddleboats (1500Ft per hr.), kayaks (700Ft per hr.), a trampoline (250Ft per 5min.), and minigolf (400Ft per round, children 300Ft). If you leave the park and return, you'll pay the entrance fee again, so bring everything you will need during your visit. (Beach ☎343 817. Admission 330Ft, children 190Ft. Lockers 230Ft.) Should lazing about make you hungry, countless restaurants and a mini-**ABC supermarket** are close to the beach. **Kisfaludy Strand,** on Aranyhíd sétány, is a quieter beach next door. Although it offers fewer water activities, its larger, less-shaded beach allows more room to swim and tan. (☎342 916. Open 8:30am-7pm. 290Ft, children 180Ft.) Also popular is **Oszi Go-Kart,** at the corner of Munkácsy Mihály u. and Kosztolányi Dezső u. (☎309 898 843. Open daily 10am-8pm. Five rounds 1000Ft, 15 rounds 2000Ft.) Bikes available at **Rent-a-Bike,** across from Esterházy Strand on Deák Ferenc u. (☎480 671. Open daily 9am-7pm. 350Ft per hr., 2400Ft per day, 12,000Ft per week.) There are **souvenir markets** on Jókai Mór u., off Petőfi Sándor u. (Open 9am-9pm.)

The tourist season kicks off with the **Sail Unfurling Ceremony** in mid-May. For the rest of the summer, sailing competitions abound. The **Anna-ball,** in late July, is Balatonfüred's most famous event. The only ball held out of season in Hungary, it attracts both foreign and domestic guests. In mid-August, winemakers set up tents on Tagore sétány for **Balatonfüred Wine Weeks.** At night, folk-dancing ensembles perform, and on the last day, there is a day of celebration complete with fireworks. Call Balatonfüred Tourinform (p. 394) for info and tickets.

While you won't find the same throngs of party-goers as in Siófok, the cafes and bars along the beach attract small crowds. **Borház-Weinhaus,** on Blaha L. u., patronized by young and old both day and night, has slot machines. A dance floor opens on Saturday nights. (Beer 220-690Ft, wine 600-700Ft per L. Open 8am-late.) On Saturday nights, **Átruim Music Club,** across the street, throbs as local DJs spin. (☎343 229. Open daily 10pm-5am. Cover before midnight 1500Ft, after midnight 2000-2500Ft.)

🔺 DAYTRIPS FROM BALATONFÜRED

BADACSONY   ☎(06)87

Trains run from Balatonfüred (55min., 2 per hr., 312Ft). You can also get to Badacsony by bus from Keszthely (1hr., 7-8 per day, 340Ft).

Though four resort towns lie at the foot of the volcanic Badacsony Mountain (Badacsonyhegy), ◾**Badacsony** and Badacsonytomaj (BAHD-uh-chohn TOH-mai) are the most popular and lie about 2km apart. The towns' main draw is the **wine cellars,** on the southern face of the hill, where you can sample a vintage or purchase it by the 1L plastic jug (from 500Ft). Unlike those in Eger and Tokaj, the local wine cellars sit just beside the vineyards on the hill. Each offers a different variety of the region's popular *Oraszrizling* and *Kéknyelü* (Blue Stalk) wines. For a free map and brochures about the cellars, head to **Tourinform Badacsony**, Park u. 6 (☎431 046). A walk uphill yields views of Balaton and the vineyards, but it's steep and can take 20-30min. Alternatively, the Jeeps waiting in front of the post office will take a group of up to six to the top of the hill for 3600Ft. The paved road ends at **Kisfaludy Ház ❸**, which serves Hungarian dishes and regional wines on a patio with a stunning view of the lake. (☎431 016. Entrees 1090-2700Ft. Open daily 11am-10pm.) Surrounded by vineyards, the cellar **Szent Orbán Borhány ❸**, Kisfaludy S. u. 5, serves special Hungarian beef sirloin (2800Ft) and other game dishes. Their **wine tasting** (260-560Ft) is popular. (☎431 382. Entrees 1200-3500Ft. Open daily noon-10pm.) Two less pricey cellars sit on cobblestone Hegyalja u., which is part of the yellow-cross hiking trail. (Samples from 55Ft.)

If the round of samples hasn't done you in, head farther uphill to try one of Badacsony's pleasantly shaded but somewhat challenging hikes. Pick up a hiking map from Tourinform (450Ft). A short trek on the red trail leads to **Rose Rock** (Rózsa-kő), where legend has it that any couple who sits facing away from the water will be married within a year. An hour's hike farther up the rocky stairs brings you to **Kisfaludy Lookout Tower** (Kisfaludy kilátó), which is free to climb and offers a gorgeous view of Lake Balaton. Walk to the right when facing the Rose Rock, and follow the **Hegyteto trail**. For those willing to make a day of it, the **stone gate** (kőkapu), a cliff-side basalt formation, awaits farther along the trail. Although Badacsony's **beach** (open daily 8am-9pm; 250Ft, students 100Ft) is small and grassy, the lively **marketplace** around it creates a carnival-like atmosphere. If you end up staying the night, **Egry Fogadó ❶**, Római út 1 in Badacsony-tomaj, rents cheap rooms. (☎471 057. Call ahead for July and Aug. weekends. June 20-Aug. 20 2000Ft; Apr. 15-June 19 and Aug. 20-Oct. 15 1400Ft.)

VESZPRÉM

Buses (☎423 815) run from Balatonfüred (18 per day, 20min., 188Ft). Trains (☎329 999) also run into town (10 per day, 2½hr., 1094Ft). From the bus station (Jutasi u. 4) or train station (Jutasi u. 34), follow Jutasi u. and make a right on Budapest u. A right on Buhim u. takes you to the Hero's Gate entrance to Castle Hill.

Known as the "City of Queens," Veszprém has a regal air for a reason: it was part of the royal estate for centuries. More romantic than other famous neighborhoods near Lake Balaton, Veszprém's Castle District is known for preserved Baroque buildings and royal churches, cozy cafes along winding cobblestone roads, and hidden vistas with fantastic views of the valley below. The **Fire Tower**, left of the **Hero's Gate** entrance, was once used as a watch tower. Its balcony now offers visitors a bird's-eye view of town. (Open daily 10am-6pm. 300Ft, students 200Ft.) Abstract paintings of Jesus, saints, and famous kings are displayed along the walls of the **Piarist Church**, Vár u. 8. (Open daily Mar.-Aug. 10am-6pm; Sept.-Oct. 10am-5pm. Free.) Farther down Var u., 10th-century **St. Michael's Cathedral** is famous for its stained glass windows and royal artifacts, including a bone from the corpse of Gizella, Hungary's first queen. (Open daily Mar.-Aug. 10am-6pm.; Sept.-Oct. 10am-5pm. Mass Sa 7pm; Su 9 and 11:30am, 7pm. Free.) The current **Archbishop's Palace**, Vár u. 33, has been the seat of the Archbishop of Veszprém since 1993. Beautiful frescoes adorn the dining hall, where windows reveal a panoramic view of the valley. In an adjacent room, portraits of successive archbishops are displayed beside Herend stoves. (Open Mar.-Aug. Tu-Su 10am-6pm, Sept.-Oct. Tu-Su 10am-5pm. 500Ft, students 250Ft.) Across the street, the **Gizella Museum** houses ecclesiastical relics and a golden cloak that belonged to Bishop Albert Vetesi. (Open daily Mar.-Aug. 10am-6pm; Sept.-Oct. 10am-5pm. 300Ft, stu-

HUNGARY

dents 150Ft.) A short walk to the end of Var u. leads to a cliff that provides an incomparable view of the valley. Statues of the first Hungarian royal couple, St. István I and Queen Gizella, look down on the town.

After seeing the sights, head down the hill to **Elefant Bisztró ❷**, Óváros tér 6, where you can watch colorful fish swim in the Bisztró's tank while enjoying a variety of Italian foods. (☎334 1217. Pizzas 750-890Ft. Salads 790-890Ft. Pasta 890-1290Ft. Open M-Sa 9am-10pm, Su 10am-10pm. AmEx/MC/V.) **Tourinform,** Vár u. 4, located under the entrance to Castle Hill, provides **free maps** of the district, and can help find accommodations in the area.

TIHANY PENINSULA ☎(06)87

A possible daytrip from Balatonfüred and a terrific destination for simple hikes, the beautiful Tihany (TEE-hahn-yuh) Peninsula is known as the pearl of Balaton. It is heavily touristed, but Tihany retains a historical weight and outdoorsy charm, making this little gem seem more mature than its hard-partying peers.

▤ TRANSPORTATION. Buses are the most convenient transport, running to **Balatonfüred** (15min., every 45min., 127Ft), and **Badascony** (1hr., 6 per day, 346Ft). **Trains** run to **Badascony** (1hr., 17 per day, 312Ft), **Veszprém** (2-4hr., 15 per day, 1094-1656Ft) and **Székesfehérvár,** (1½hr., 15 per day, 594Ft), but the train station is at the edge of the peninsula, so you'll have to hike or take the bus from town to get there. The bus stops at Kossuth u., in front of the abbey.

▦ ▨ ORIENTATION AND PRACTICAL INFORMATION. The main road, **Kossuth u.,** spans the peninsula and runs through town, just below the abbey. There are five main bus stops on the peninsula. Get off at the first stop to hit the beach; otherwise, stay on until the bus stops in front of the abbey. The **red trail** runs beside the abbey stop; to start your hike, follow the red arrows. To find accommodations, head down Kossuth u., make a left on **Kiss u.** and a right on **Csokonai u.,** where many houses rent **private rooms. Tourinform,** below the abbey, arranges accommodations and has maps of the town and of hiking trails. (☎438 804; tihany@tourinform.hu. Open M-F 9am-7pm.) **Rent-a-bike** is at Kossuth u. 32 (☎938 560. Open daily 10am-6pm. Half-day 1650Ft, full-day 2600Ft). There's a **pharmacy** at Kossuth u. 10 (☎448 480; open M-F 8am-noon and 1-6pm, Sa-Su 8am-noon) and an **ATM** just up the hill at Kossuth u. 12. The **post office,** Kossuth u. 37, is adjacent to **Mini Market Elelmiszer,** which sells snacks and drinks. (Post office open M-F 8am-4pm. Market open daily 8am-8pm.) **Postal Code:** 8237.

▣ ▢ ACCOMMODATIONS AND FOOD. The most abundant accommodations are private rooms, indicated by *Zimmer frei* signs along Csokonai u. Most are reasonably priced (starting at 4000Ft) and have views of the valley and lake. **Kantas Pension ❸,** Csokonai u. 49, has good-sized doubles with balconies overlooking the valley. (☎448 072; kantaspension@axelero.hu. Breakfast included. Doubles 8250-10,250Ft; 2 nights 7750-9750Ft, 3 or more 7250-9250Ft.) If you'd rather stay closer to the water, **Hotel Panorama ❹,** Lepke sor 9-11, offers luxurious doubles and triples across from the *strand*. (☎538 220. Breakfast included. Doubles 11,900-16,900Ft; triples 18,900-20,900Ft. Tax 300Ft.)

The food stalls around the beach and by the abbey will hold you over with fried fast food. If you'd rather sit down, try ▨**Echo Étterem ❸,** Visszhang u. 23, along the green and red hiking trails. This beautiful restaurant serves typical Hungarian dishes atop a cliff overlooking Balaton. Ask for a spot on the roof for a great view of the lake. (☎448 460. Entrees 1200-2500Ft. Open daily Mar.-Nov. 10am-10pm.) At the base of Echo Hill, **Pál-tál Csárda ❸** offers a variety of fish and poultry dishes, including *halászlé* soup and roasted trout, on a lovely vine-covered patio. The entrees are big enough to feed multiple people. (Entrees 1300-3000Ft. English menu available. Open daily Mar.-June 10am-10pm. AmEx/MC/V.) Just outside the exit of the abbey museum, **Rege Kávézó ❷** dishes out delectable pastries while customers enjoy panoramic views of the lake. (☎448 280. Pastries 350-520Ft. Coffee 350-950Ft. Ice cream 450-1050Ft. Open daily 10am-6pm.)

◪◩ SIGHTS AND HIKING. The small but magnificent **Benedictine Abbey** (Bencés Apátság) presides over the hillside. Its pastel frescoes, intricate Baroque altars, and views of the lake draw over a million visitors each year. The church's foundation letter, scripted in 1055, is the oldest written document in the modern Hungarian language. A copy is on display inside the church, while the original is in the archives at the abbey in Pannonhalma (p. 380). The András I crypt (I. András kriptája) contains the remains of King András I, one of Hungary's earliest kings and the abbey's founder. To the right of the crypt, the ◪**Tihany Museum,** an 18th-century former monastery, exhibits an odd combination of contemporary art and Roman archaeological finds, all on display in the subterranean lapidarium. (Abbey, crypt, and museum open daily Mar.-Oct. 9am-6pm. Mass M-F 7:30am; Sa 7:30pm; Su 7:30 and 10am, 7:30pm. Church, crypt, and museum 400Ft, students 200Ft; families 650Ft; Su free.) To the left of the church rises **Echo Hill.** On a calm day, if you stand on the Echo Hill's stone pedestal and holler, your yell will echo off the church wall. Follow the *"strand"* signs along the promenade behind the church and descend to the beach, where you can rent paddleboats (1500Ft per hr.) and play beach volleyball, ping-pong, and pool beside the lake. (Open daily 9am-5pm. 380Ft, children 200Ft, students 250Ft.) If you'd rather tan, walk along the shore toward the mainland, where you can rent beach chairs (400Ft per hr.).

With beautiful clearings, winding mountain paths, and steep inclines, Tihany was made for hikers. **Hiking** across the peninsula through hills, forests, farms, and marshes takes only an hour or two. For an even shorter hike, take the **red cross trail** around Belső-tó Lake and turn right on the **red line trail** on the opposite side. The path will take you to the summit of Kiserdő Tető (Top of Little Wood), from which you can see Belső-tó and Külső-tó, Tihany's other interior lake. The ◪**green line trail,** covering the eastern slope of Óvár, snakes past Barátlakások (the Hermits' Place), where you can see cells and a chapel hollowed out of the rocks by 11th-century Greek Orthodox ascetics. Buy a **map** for 350Ft by the abbey before you start your hike or pick up a free copy at Tourinform. If you'd rather stick to the paved roads, bikes are a great option for exploring the hillside.

KESZTHELY ☎(06)83

Sitting at the lake's west tip, Keszthely (KEST-hay) was once the toy-town of the powerful Festetics family. Though their palace continues to be the main attraction, the city that sprung up around the gates has a charm of its own. Street cafes and souvenir shops dot the promenade, while the beach draws a crowd with its waterslide and rows of food stands. The healing thermal spring in nearby Heviz attracts both locals and tourists. Though the center of Keszthely has a less of a resort feel than other Balaton towns, its streets are just as crowded.

▐ TRANSPORTATION. The **train station** is on Kazinczy u. InterCity trains run to **Budapest** (3hr., 13 per day, 1556Ft plus 400Ft reservation fee), while slow trains *(személyvonat)* go to: **Balatonfüred** (2-3hr., 12 per day, 698Ft); **Pécs** (3-5hr., 10 per day, 1844Ft); **Siófok** (1½-2hr., 19 per day, 630-1070Ft); **Szombathely** (3hr., 1 per day,

1084Ft). The **bus terminal** is next to the train station. Buses beat trains for local travel to **Balatonfüred** (1½hr., 9 per day, 810Ft) and **Pécs** (4hr., 5 per day, 1486Ft). Some buses leave from the terminal while others use stops at either Fő tér or Georgikán u. Each departure is marked with an "F" or a "G" to indicate which stop it uses; check the schedule. In summer, **ferries** run to **Badacsony** (1¾hr.; May 28-Aug. per day, July-Sept. 4 per day; 900Ft, students 450Ft) from the end of the dock.

█ █ ORIENTATION AND PRACTICAL INFORMATION. The main street, **Kossuth Lajos u.**, runs parallel to the shore, from **Festetics Palace** (Festetics Kastély) to the center at **Fő tér**. To reach the main square from the train station, walk straight up **Mártirok u.** to its end at Kossuth Lajos u., and turn right to reach Fő tér (10min.). The main **beach** *(strand)*, is to the right as you exit the stations. If you're coming from the pier, head straight and follow Erzsébet kir. u. to get to Fő tér.

Tourinform, Kossuth Lajos u. 28, off Fő tér, distributes **free maps** and info and will help you find a room. (☎/fax 314 144. Open July-Aug. M-F 9am-8pm, Sa-Su 9am-6pm; Oct.-June M-F 9am-5pm, Sa 9am-1pm.) **IBUSZ**, Fő tér 6/8, exchanges currency and books **private rooms** for 16% commission. (☎314 320. Open June-Aug. M-Th 8:30am-5:30pm, F 8:30am-4:30pm; Sept.-May M-F 8:30am-4pm.) **OTP Bank,** at the corner of Kossuth L. u. and Helikon u., **exchanges currency** and cashes **traveler's checks** for no commission. There's a 24hr. (MC/V) **ATM** and currency exchange machine outside. (Open M 7:45am-5pm, Tu-F 7:45am-4pm.) **Luggage storage** is at the train station. (120Ft for 6hr., 240Ft for 24hr. Open 3:30am-11:30pm.) The **Ezüstsirály Patika pharmacy,** Sopron u. 2, is on call 24hr. (☎314 549). Walk through the palace gates on Kossuth L. u. and out the next set of gates; it's immediately on your left. (Open M-Th 7:30am-5pm, F 7:30am-3pm.) **Internet access** is available at **Micronet Internet Kávézó,** Nádor u. 13. Walking down Kossuth L. u. from the palace, take the first right. (☎314 009. 5Ft per min. Open daily 9am-9pm.) Card-operated **telephones** are outside the **post office,** Kossuth L. u. 48. (☎515 960. **Poste Restante** and **Western Union** available. Open M-F 8am-6pm, Sa 8am-noon.) **Postal Code:** 8360.

█ █ ACCOMMODATIONS AND FOOD. Homes with *Zimmer frei* signs abound near the *strand*, off Fő tér on Erzsébet Királyné u., and near Castrum Camping on **Ady Endre** u. Head up Kossuth L. u. and turn right on Szalasztó u. before the palace entrance; Ady Endre is a few streets down on the right. Expect to pay 3000-4000Ft. **IBUSZ** (see above) books central, private doubles with showers (from 5000Ft) and, for longer stays, apartments with kitchens (from 7000Ft). To avoid finder's fees, try the folks at **Tourinform** (see above), who offer a few private rooms near the center from 3000Ft. ▨ **Kiss-Máte Panzió ❸**, Katona J. u. 27, offers spacious rooms near the castle, plus a large common kitchen, free laundry, and access to a tennis court and swimming pool. (☎319 072. Doubles 6000Ft; triples 8000Ft; quads 10000Ft.) Near the main market (Piac), **Szabó Lakás ❷**, Arany János 23, offers newly furnished rooms, with kitchen and cable TV. (☎312 504; jutka.szabo@axelero.hu. 3000Ft per person.) **Castrum Camping ❶**, Móra F. u. 48, boasts large sites with full amenities: tennis courts, beach access, a restaurant, a swimming pool, and close proximity to the most happening nightspots. (☎312 120. 900Ft, children 700Ft. July-Aug. 600Ft per tent, with electricity 750Ft; Sept.-June 480Ft per tent. Tax 250Ft.)

There has been a **fruit and flower market** on Piac tér since medieval times. At its center, the **supermarket, Smatch** sells everything you could possibly need. (Open M-F 6:30am-6:30pm, Sa 6:20am-2pm. MC/V.) Most restaurants around Fő tér and on Kossuth L. u. are overpriced, but there are more reasonable options farther from the center. **Corso Restaurant ❸**, Erzsébet Királyné u. 23, closer to the *strand* in the Abbázia Club Hotel, draws on Balaton's fish stock for its concoctions. (☎312 596. Entrees 800-2800Ft. Pizza from 690Ft. Live music nightly from 6pm. Open M-Sa

7am-10pm. MC/V.) Just outside the palace, **Kolostor Restaurant ❷**, Katona J. u. 2/c, offers a variety of game and seafood dishes on a covered balcony overlooking the palace gardens. (Entrees 600-1350Ft. Open 11:30am-9pm.) **Donatello ❷**, Balaton u. 1/A, serves pizza and pasta in a sun-drenched courtyard. (☎315 989. Pasta 410-880Ft. Pizza 440-1080Ft. Open daily noon-11pm.) For a snack that will hold you over until your next meal, follow the smell of baked goods (100-150Ft) wafting from **Helyben Sült Finompékáruk ❶**, on the corner of Kossuth L. u. and Balaton u. (Open M-F 6am-6pm, Sa 6am-noon.)

◧ ☐ SIGHTS AND ENTERTAINMENT. Keszthely's pride is the ▧**Helikon Palace Museum** (Helikon Kastélymúzeum) in the **Festetics Palace**. From Fő tér, follow Kossuth L. u. past Tourinform. Built by one of the most powerful Austro-Hungarian families of the 18th century, the storybook Baroque palace boasts fanciful architecture and lush gardens. The site of Hungarian literary events hosted by György Festetics (1755-1819), the palace was named "Helikon" after Helicon Hill, the mythical Greek home of the nine muses. Of the 360 rooms, visitors may only enter those in the **central wing**, but if the mirrored halls and extravagantly furnished chambers aren't captivating enough, take a peek in the 90,000-volume, wood-paneled **Helikon Library,** just past the entrance. The arms collection with weapons spanning 1000 years and the exhibit of the Festetics's elaborate porcelain pieces are also worth a look. To find out all the details, rent an audio guide (500Ft) or pick up an English guidebook (700Ft). Sporadic English translations are available. The interesting "Trophies of Four Continents" exhibit, through a door in the back courtyard features the exotic prizes of famous hunters. The **English park** around the museum provides photo-worthy panoramas for afternoon promenades. (Open Tu-Su 9am-4:30pm. 1500Ft, students 700Ft. Cameras 800Ft, video 1600Ft.) Popular chamber music **concerts** are held frequently in the mirrored ballroom; reserve tickets two weeks ahead by calling the ticket office. (☎312 192. 1000-5500Ft.) In summer, the palace holds individualized **candlelit tours** through the castle. (Th-Sa 10pm. English tours upon request. Call the ticket office to reserve, or buy tickets at the door at 9pm. 2500Ft, reservation fee 500Ft.) The 1896 pastel green tower of the **Church of Our Lady** on Fő tér conceals the main structure, which dates from 1386 and is a shining example of Gothic architecture. Spectacular stained glass and 14th-century paintings adorn the dark sanctuary. (Open M-Sa 8am-7pm. Su 11am-7pm. Free.)

Keszthely boasts many sandy beaches, and families throng to the main *strand*. From the center, walk down Erzsébet u. as it curves right into Vörösmarty u. Go through the park on the left after the train tracks to reach the beach. This arcade-lined strip draws many to its shores with its volleyball nets, giant slide, paddleboats, and kayaks. (Open daily May 15-Sept. 15 8:30am-7pm. May 15-June 350Ft, children 240Ft. July-Sept. 15 440Ft/300Ft.) After 7pm the beach becomes a free promenade, and while the town streets are quiet, the beach bars are lively.

◤ DAYTRIPS FROM KESZTHELY

HÉVÍZ ☎(06)83

Buses leave from Keszthely's Fő tér (15min., every 30min., 82Ft) and from Sümeg (55min., every 1-2hr., 410Ft). A visit to Hévíz can be combined with a trip to Sümeg.

Six kilometers outside Keszthely, Hévíz is home to the world's largest ▧**thermal lake.** Surrounded by trees, covered in gigantic lilies, and concealed by a slight mist, the sulfurous and slightly radioactive water is rumored to have miraculous healing

HUNGARY

powers. With waters naturally heated to a soothing 26-33°C (77-91°F), you too can seek longevity alongside the algae. The 44,550 sq. m lake is large and very deep, yet the spring that fills it pumps so fast that the water is replaced every 28hr. To bathe in these legendary waters, head to the **Fin-de-Siècle bathhouse,** Dr. Schülhof Vilmos sétány 1, across from the bus station. Look for the sign that reads "Tó Fürdő." Unique because of its natural setting, the house sits on stilts above the center of the scenic lake. A personal specialist recommends treatment for persistent aches or pains. Massages and pedicures are also available. (☎501 700; fax 540 144. Open daily in summer 8:30am-5pm; in winter 9am-4pm. Type A ticket 900Ft for 3hr.; 700Ft extra if you exceed 3hr. Type B ticket 1600Ft; 600Ft returned if you leave within 3hr., 400Ft within 4hr., 200Ft within 5hr. Tube rental 300Ft. Massages 2900-6800Ft.) Grab a snack at one of the cafeterias or restaurants in the park, or dine at **Grill Garden Restaurant ❸,** Kölesal u. 4, on the opposite side of the bus station from the bath. The log-cabin restaurant serves delicious Hungarian dishes. (☎343 970. English menu available. Entrees 690-1390Ft. Open daily 10am-11pm.)

SÜMEG   ☎(06)87

Buses run from Hévíz (1hr., 1 per hr., 410Ft) and Keszthely (1¼hr., 1 per hr., 226Ft). From the station, cross Petőfi Sándor u. to Kossuth L. u., the main street. To reach the castle, take a right on Vak Bottyán u. off Kossuth L. u. Bear right at Szent István tér and continue up the street. Turn left onto Városoldal u. and walk until you see the path. From there, it's a 5min. walk to the castle. Easily combined with Hévíz as a daytrip.

Though only a little farther inland than its coast-hugging neighbors, Sümeg feels worlds away. This cobblestone town doesn't attract the same racy crowds that frequent most of Balaton's resorts. It's frequented by families and schoolchildren, eager to get a glimpse of the medieval era. Trek up the stone path to visit Sümeg's **castle** (vár), one of Hungary's largest and best-preserved strongholds, which is perched 270m above the town. Built as a last defense against the Mongols, the 13th-century fortress also resisted the Turks, standing until the Hapsburg army burned it down in 1713. The most impressive view of the castle is from a distance—be sure to look out the window of the bus as it approaches Sümeg to see the castle looming over the city. If the trek up to the castle seems too steep, Jeeps waiting at the bottom of the hill can take you up to the ticket counter for 350Ft per person. The atmosphere inside the castle is kitschy, with magic shows, pony rides, archery ranges, and costumed characters performing to mandolins. (☎352 737. Open daily May-Oct. 8am-8pm. 1500Ft, students 800Ft.) The **museum** inside displays medieval armor; it may be a bit disappointing if you've been to the Helikon Palace Museum in Keszthely. There is also the requisite **torture chamber,** but the waiting line may prove to be more torturous than the instruments themselves. Walk the circumference of the castle and check out the panorama of the surrounding countryside. As you leave the castle, be sure to stop at the tournament stadium at the bottom of the hill, where you can watch swordfighting, archery, and a horseshow, followed by lunch or dinner in an old-fashioned tavern. (Shows 6:30pm. 5000Ft, students 4000Ft. Ticket includes entrance to the castle.)

The **Church of the Ascension,** at the corner of Deák F. u. and Széchenyi G. u., is a Sümeg must-see. Follow Deák F. u. downhill from the intersection across from the OTP bank on Kossuth L. u. The church's mundane exterior conceals a frescoed marvel known to locals as the "Hungarian Sistine Chapel." While this comparison may be a slight exaggeration, you can't help but be impressed by Franz Anton Maulbertsch's 1757 Rococo masterpiece covering the ceilings and walls of the church. Maulbertsch left his signature on the work by painting himself—he's the one on the left side of the first fresco on the right when you enter the church. The platter of cheese he's holding is curiously a symbol of humility. (Open M-F 9am-noon and 1-6pm, Sa 10am-noon and 2-5pm, Su 2-5pm. Free.) **Ferences Templom,** on Szent István tér on the way up to the castle, is also a pleasant stop. Its frescoed ceiling, though not as famous, has vivid colors. (Open daily 7am-6pm. Free.) Across the street, **Scotti Udvarház ❷,** Szent István tér 1, serves pastas (760-990Ft), pizzas (480-1400Ft), and Hungarian dishes in a courtyard with ivy overhangings. Ask to try some water from the spring shooting up right in the middle of the restaurant. (☎350 997. Open daily 10am-midnight.) If you're looking for a place to stay, **Hotel Kapitány ❸,** Tóth Tivadar u. 19, just outside the tournament stadium, provides spacious and luxurious rooms in a complex outfitted with a swimming pool, tennis courts, and sauna. (☎550 217. Singles 7000Ft; doubles 84000Ft; triples 11000Ft. Breakfast included.)

SOUTHERN TRANSDANUBIA

Framed by the Danube to the west, the Dráva to the south, and Lake Balaton to the north, Southern Transdanubia is known for its mild climate, rolling hills, and sunflower fields. Once the southernmost portion of the Roman Pannonia, the region is filled with historical memorials and palaces, weathered castles, and ancient burial grounds. The people of Southern Transdanubia are as diverse as the sights: the Germans, Serbs, Bosnians, and Croats who call the region home have added flavor to the food and culture west of the Danube.

PÉCS ☎(06)72

Pécs (PAYCH; pop. 180,000) is the most popular town in southern Hungary. Some travelers merely pass through on journeys between Budapest and Croatia, but those that visit Pécs are certainly rewarded for their efforts. Nestled at the base of the Mecsek mountains, Pécs has a warm climate, incomparable vistas, and captivating architecture. Its monuments reveal a 2000-year-old legacy of Roman, Ottoman, and Hapsburg occupation, while the famous Zsolnay porcelain, produced in a factory just outside the city, adorns many of the town's buildings. Evenings bring out a more festive side of Pécs, as its university students infuse local bars and clubs with youthful energy.

⌐ TRANSPORTATION

Trains: Take bus #30, 32, or 33 from the center or walk 20min. from Széchenyi tér down Jókai u. To **Budapest** (2½hr., 16 per day, 1918-2338FT). 4 trains leave daily for the **Lake Balaton** towns; get tickets at the MÁV office in the station (☎215 003; www.elvira.hu) or at Jókai u. 4 (☎212 734). Both open M-F 9am-5pm.

Buses: ☎215 215; www.agria.hu. To: **Budapest** (4½hr., 5 per day, 2088Ft); **Keszthely** (4hr., 3 per day, 1506Ft); **Szeged** (4½hr., 7 per day, 2100Ft).

Public Transportation: Bus tickets cost 125Ft at kiosks and 135Ft on the bus.

Taxis: Volán and Euro are reputable companies. Be wary of other cabs, as they may scam you. Base fare 100Ft plus 150Ft per km.

✳ ⑦ ORIENTATION AND PRACTICAL INFORMATION

Conveniently, north and south correspond to uphill and downhill. Inconveniently, it seems you're always walking uphill. Tourists descend upon the historic **Belváros** (inner city), a rectangle bound by the ruins of the city wall. The center is **Széchenyi**

HUNGARY

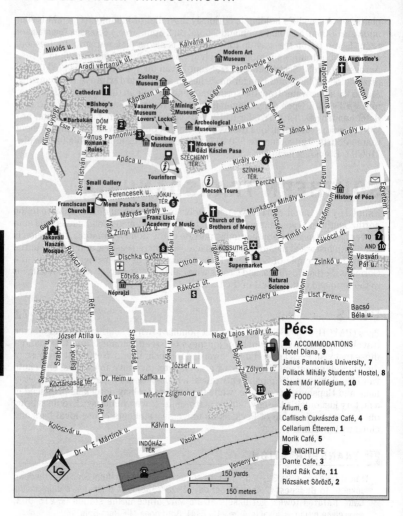

Pécs

🏠 ACCOMMODATIONS
Hotel Diana, **9**
Janus Pannonius University, **7**
Pollack Mihály Students' Hostel, **8**
Szent Mór Kollégium, **10**

🍴 FOOD
Áfium, **6**
Caflisch Cukrászda Café, **4**
Cellarium Étterem, **1**
Morik Café, **5**

🍺 NIGHTLIFE
Dante Cafe, **3**
Hard Rák Cafe, **11**
Rózsaket Söröző, **2**

tér, where most tourist offices are located. Both the train and bus stations are south of the center but within walking distance. It takes less than 20min. to cross Belváros going downhill, but be wary of the steep incline.

Tourist Offices: Tourinform, Széchenyi tér 9 (☎511 232; fax 213 315), offers **free small maps,** large maps for 300Ft, phone cards, and stamps. Open M-F 8am-6pm, Sa-Su 9am-3pm. **Mecsek Tours,** Széchenyi tér 1 (☎513 370; fax 513-373), arranges travel, sells phone cards, **exchanges currency,** books rooms, and has an **ATM** outside. Open M-F 8:30am-4:30pm.

Currency Exchange: OTP Bank, Rákóczi út 44 (☎502 900), cashes **traveler's checks** and **exchanges currency** for no commission. Open M 7:45am-6pm, Tu-Th 7:45am-5pm, F 7:45am-4pm. A 24hr. (MC/V) **ATM** is outside.

24hr. Pharmacy: Zsolnay Gyógyszertár, Zsolnay V. u. 8 (☎/fax 516 760). Open M-F 7:30am-7:30pm, Sa 7:30am-1:30pm. After hours, ring bell for service and be prepared to pay 100Ft extra per item.

Internet Access: Matrix Internet Café, Király u. 15. (☎214 487). 5Ft per min. Open 9am-11pm. **Tourinform** (see above) also has computer access for 100Ft per hr. 25Ft for 15min. or fewer. Open M-F 9am-5pm.

Post Office: Jókai Mór u. 10 (☎506 000). 2nd fl. office has so many services there's an info desk to guide you. Open M-F 7am-7pm, Sa 8am-12pm. **Postal Code:** 7621.

■ ACCOMMODATIONS

Dorms are the cheapest option, and they're more comfortable in Pécs than in many other towns. **Private rooms** are a decent budget option, though they normally start around 3000Ft. Pécs's efficient bus system makes cheaper rooms outside of town almost as convenient. Call ahead in summer and on weekends.

▓ **Pollack Mihály Students' Hostel,** Jókai u. 8 (☎315 846). Ideally located in the center of town, this former university dorm has spotless bedrooms and bathrooms, kitchen facilities, and a lounge. Call a few days ahead to reserve. Dorms 1800Ft. ❶

Hotel Diana, Timár u. 4a (☎/fax 333 373), just off Kossuth tér in the center of town. This hotel offers luxurious rooms with wooden floors and cable TV. Singles 7000Ft; doubles 10000Ft; 4-person apartments 12,000-16,000Ft. A/C 1000Ft extra. MC/V. ❹

Szent Mór Kollégium, 48-as tér 4 (☎503 610). Take bus #21 from the main bus terminal to 48-as tér, or walk up the hill to Rákóczi út and turn right. This gorgeous old university wing houses spiffy triples (1700Ft). Laundry by request. Reception 24hr. Check-out 10am. Curfew midnight. Ring the bell after 10pm. Open July-Aug. ❶

Janus Pannonius University, Universitas u. 2 (☎311 966; fax 324 473). Take bus #21 from the main bus terminal to 48-as tér, or walk up the hill to Rákóczi út and turn right. The dorm is to the right, behind McDonald's. Bathrooms in suites. 24hr. reception. Check-out 9am. Open June-Sept. Call ahead. 3-bed dorms 1800Ft. ❶

▐ FOOD

Because of the town's steep incline, many of its restaurants, cafes, and bars lie under the city streets in eclectic cellars. These subterranean vaults are among the city's biggest attractions; most serve Hungarian and Mediterranean dishes with an array of wines. Reservations are necessary at more popular restaurants on weekend nights, but a walk down Király u., Apáca u., or Ferences u. will yield a variety of tasty options. **Interspar,** Bajcsy-Zsilinszky u. 11, inside Árkád Shopping Mall, has a wide variety of food, a salad bar, a deli, and a bakery. (Open M-Th and Sa 7am-9pm, F 7am-10pm, Su 8am-7pm.)

▓ **Cellarium Étterem,** Hunyadi út 2 (☎314 453). Descend the cellar steps to indulge in a variety of traditional Hungarian dishes. Don't be frightened by the waiters' prisoner costumes or the newspaper menus, they're just part of the decor. Live Hungarian music on weekends. Entrees 950-3200Ft. AmEx/MC/V. ❸

▓ **Áfium,** Irgalmasok u. 2 (☎514 434). Underground restaurant furnished with relics, from radios to sewing machines. Italian and Hungarian menu. Vegetarian options. Entrees 990-2800Ft. Open M-Sa 11am-1am, Su 11am-midnight. ❸

Morik Café, Jókai tér, allows you to pick your own type of coffee and have it specially brewed. The 2 dozen options include Costa Rican, Guatemalan, Hawaiian, and Ugandan specialties. Enjoy your pick on the patio overlooking Jókai tér or stick close to the rich aroma inside the wooden shop. Coffee 195Ft, cappuccino 270Ft. ❶

Caflisch Cukrászda Café, Király u. 32 (☎310 391). Sink your sweet tooth into pastries (from 100Ft) and sundaes (300-650Ft) at one of the town's best cafes. Check out the Herend china espresso machine. Open M-Th 9am-10pm, F-Sa 8am-11pm, Su 8am-10pm. ❶

👁 SIGHTS

MOSQUE OF GHAZI KASSIM (GÁZI KHASIM PASA DZSÁMIJA). Nicknamed the "Mosque Church," the green-domed building is a former Turkish mosque. Today it serves as a Christian church, though it still retains some of its Turkish flavor. Verses from the Koran decorate the walls, and an ablution basin, where the faithful washed their feet before entering the mosque, now serves as a baptismal font. The largest structure from the Ottoman occupation still standing in Hungary, the church intertwines its rich Christian and Muslim traditions, making it a fitting symbol for the diverse city. (*Széchenyi tér. ☎321 976. Open Apr. 16-Oct. 14 M-Sa 10am-4pm, Su 12:30-4pm; Oct. 15-Apr. 15 10am-noon, Su closed except for services. Masses Su 9:30, 10:30, 11:30am. Admission free but donations are welcome.*)

CATHEDRAL AND BISHOP'S PALACE. Perched atop the Pécs hilltop, the 4th-century neo-Romanesque Cathedral and adjoining Bishop's Palace make the hill a perfect respite from bustling city and tourist life. Inside the cathedral, a small museum displays medieval stone carvings and detailed religious wall paintings, while the crypt that once housed the tomb of the first Bishop of Pécs is now a venue for music festivals. (*On Dóm tér. From Széchenyi tér, walk left on Janus Pannonius u., take the 1st right, and then go left on Káptalan to Dóm tér. ☎513 030. Palace not open to the public. Cathedral open M-F 9am-5pm, Sa 9am-2pm, Su 1-5pm. 700Ft, students 350Ft. Masses M-Sa 6pm; Su 8, 9:30, 11am and 6pm.*)

SYNAGOGUE. The stunning 1869 synagogue has paintings covering the ceiling and incredible replica of the Ark of the Covenant. However, because the city's Jewish population now numbers a mere 140, services are no longer held here. Visitors are given a pamphlet with detailed information on Jewish traditions and the effect of WWII on the local Jewish community. (*On Kossuth tér. Walk downhill from Széchenyi tér on Irgalmasok u. Open Mar.-Oct. Su-F 10-11:30am and noon-1pm. 300Ft, 200Ft.*)

ROMAN RUINS. Once a mass burial site for Roman Pécs (Sopianae), the 4th-century Christian mausoleum near the cathedral has become the largest excavated burial grounds in Hungary. Over 100 corpses have been uncovered from the area, and a chilling crypt with well-preserved Roman Christian paintings sits underneath the ruins. (*Cross Janus Pannonius from the cathedral or walk 5min. from Széchenyi tér. Open Apr.-Oct. Tu-Su 10am-6pm; Nov.-Mar. 10am-4pm. 300Ft, students 150Ft.*)

🏛 MUSEUMS

🔲 ZSOLNAY MUSEUM. A family workshop has hand-crafted the intricate, colorful, and world-famous Zsolnay porcelain since the 1800s. The famous porcelain adorns many central Pécs buildings: the Zsolnay Well, Széchenyi tér 1, sports a rare Eosin glaze; the windows of County Hall, Jókai u. 10, are framed by detailed tiles; Vilmos Zsolnay's Shop, Király u. 1, has decorative tiles; and Pecs National Theater, Színáz tér, houses Zsolnay sculptures and reliefs. (*Museum is at Káptalan u. 2. Walk up Szepessy I. u. behind the Mosque Church and go left at Káptalan u. ☎324 822. Open Tu-Sa 10am-6pm, Su 10am-4pm. 600Ft, students 300Ft. Cameras 400Ft, video 800Ft.*)

■ **VASARELY MUSEUM.** One of Hungary's most important 20th-century artists, Pécs' Viktor Vasarely (1908-97) is best known as the pioneer of Op-Art and geometric abstraction. The house in which he was born has been converted to a museum and now displays some of his most important works, along with works by other 20th-century artists. *(Káptalan u. 3, next to the Zsolnay.* ☎*324 822, ext. 21. Open Apr.-Oct. Tu-Su 10am-6pm. 500Ft, students 250Ft. Cameras 400Ft, video 800Ft.)*

CSONTVÁRY MUSEUM. This museum displays the works of Tivadar Csontváry Kosztka (1853-1919), a local artist who won international acclaim during 20 years of work. The exhibit highlights Csontváry's interest in nature. His mastery of luminous expressionism earned him the nickname "the Hungarian Van Gogh." *(Janus Pannonius u. 11.* ☎*310 544. Open Tu-Sa 10am-6pm. 500Ft, students 250Ft.)*

MINING MUSEUM (MECSEKI BÁNYÁSZATI MÚZEUM). The largest underground exhibit in Hungary, this hands-on labyrinth is in the same courtyard as the Vasarely Museum. The museum, designed to give guests a feel for what mines were really like, explains the coal mining process, which once drove the city's economy. *(Káptalan u. 3. Open Tu-Su 10am-6pm. 400Ft, students 200Ft.)*

▧ 🎭 FESTIVALS AND NIGHTLIFE

Programs run in the main square from June through late August. The activities range from theater performances to markets with handmade goods. Festivals in Pécs are abundant in September. Choir music and wine pleasantly mingle at Pécs's ▧**World Festival of Wine Songs** late in the month. For info, contact Pécsi Férfikar Alapitvány, Színház tér 2 (☎/fax 211 606). Other festivals include the **Gastronomic Pleasures of the Pécs Region,** the **Pécs City Festival,** and the **Mediterranean Autumn Festival.** Pécs has a lively **nightlife.** Destinations range from mellow coffee shops to raging clubs. Hit the crowded, colorful bars near Széchenyi tér, especially on the first two blocks of Király u. Clubs are close to the train station and pack in a vivacious crowd.

■ **Dante Cafe,** Janus Pannonius u. 11 (☎210 661), in the Csontváry Museum building and the courtyard behind it. Originally founded to finance the Pécs literary magazine *Szép Literaturari Ajándék,* it now hosts an artsy clientele and a large crowd of Hungarian youth. Beer 290-390Ft. Open daily 10am-1am, later on weekends.

Hard Rák Cafe, Ipar u. 7 (☎502 557), 10min. from the main town. Turn left at the corner of Bajcsy-Zsilinszky u. The name refers to the music, not the American restaurant chain. Local teens and young adults swarm the entrance of this cavernous club, which boasts a fine line-up of drinks and live musical acts. Live rock performances in summer F-Sa nights. Cover Th-Sa 500Ft. Open M-Sa 7pm-6am.

Rózsakert Söröző, Janus Pannonius u. 8/10 (☎310 862). Locals come here to enjoy the evening zephyr, live Hungarian gypsy music, and a lantern-adorned terrace. 0.5L Gold Fassl 260Ft. Open daily noon-midnight.

THE GREAT PLAIN (NAGYALFÖLD)

Romanticized in tales of cowboys and bandits, the grasslands of Nagyalföld stretch southeast of Budapest, covering almost half of Hungary. This tough region is home to arid Debrecen, fertile Szeged, and the vineyards of Kecskemét, which rise out of the flat soil like Nagyalföld's legendary mirages.

DEBRECEN
☎(06)52

Protected by the mythical phoenix and dubbed the festival capital of Hungary, Debrecen (DE-bre-tsen; pop. 210,000), the second largest city in Hungary, has survived over 30 devastating fires. Fortunately, recent reconstructions have bestowed wide boulevards and lush parks upon the city, including Nagyerdei Park, the "Great Forest." Today, the ultra-modern city is filled with the active and outspoken: Debrecen is the center of Hungarian Protestantism and is famed for its Reformed College, one of the country's oldest and largest universities. The student population fills the streets by day and the pubs by night.

⊏ TRANSPORTATION

Trains: ☎326 777. Petőfi tér. To: **Budapest** (3hr., 13 per day, 2000Ft; InterCity 2½hr., 8 per day, 2192Ft); **Eger** (3hr., 6 per day, 1323Ft) via **Füzesabony; Miskolc** (2½-3hr., 5 per day, 1096Ft); **Szeged** (3½hr., 7 per day, 2040Ft) via **Cegléd.**

Buses: (☎413 999; www.agriavolan.hu.) At the intersection of Nyugati u. and Széchenyi u. To: **Eger** (2½hr., 4 per day, 1392Ft); **Kecskemét** (5½hr., 1 per day, 2390Ft); **Miskolc** (2hr., every 30min.-1hr., 994Ft); **Szeged** (4-5½hr., 4 per day, 2390Ft); **Tokaj** (2hr., 2 per day, 894Ft).

Public Transportation: The most convenient way to navigate the city. Tram #1 runs from the train station through Kálvin tér, loops around the park past the university, and heads back to Kálvin tér. Ticket checks are frequent and fines are menacing (2000-5000Ft); buy tickets (130Ft) or day passes (450Ft) from the kiosk by the train station or tickets (150Ft) from the driver. Prices change frequently. Once on board, validate your ticket in a blue puncher. Trams stop only while inbound; to return to the town center, ride the loop. Get off at Varashaza for tourist offices and most other necessities.

Taxis: City Taxi ☎555 555. **FőTaxi Rt** ☎444 555.

✳ ⑦ ORIENTATION AND PRACTICAL INFORMATION

Debrecen is a big city, but has a small and easily navigable center 15min. from the train station. With your back to the station, head down **Petőfi tér,** which becomes **Piac u.,** a main street perpendicular to the station. Piac u. ends in **Kálvin tér,** where the huge yellow **Nagytemplom** (Great Church) presides over the center. Debrecen's other hub lies 3km farther along Piac u., which becomes **Péterfia u.** at Kálvin tér. The street runs north to **Nagyerdei Park** and **Kossuth Lajos Tudományegyetem** (KLTE; Kossuth Lajos University). Trams and buses run from the train station through Kálvin tér. to Nagyerdi Park; check with the info desk in the station for schedules and prices. The **bus station** is 10min. from the center. From the station, go right on **Széchenyi,** then left on Piac u., which opens into Kálvin tér.

Tourist Office: Tourinform, Piac u. 20 (☎412 250; tourinform@ph.debrecen.hu), above Széchenyi u., under the cream-colored building on the right side of Kálvin tér just after Kossuth u. Free maps and info on hostels, food, and daytrips. Open M-F 9am-5pm.

Currency Exchange: Banks abound on Piac u. **OTP,** Hatvan u. 2/4 (☎506 500), exchanges currency, gives MC **cash advances,** accepts most **traveler's checks,** and has a 24hr. (MC/V) **ATM.** Open M 7:45am-5pm, T-F 7:45am-4pm.

Luggage Storage: Available at the train station. (120Ft per 6hr., large bags 240Ft; 240Ft/480Ft per day.) After 10pm, luggage can be stored at the info desk, counter #9.

Emergency: ☎104.

Pharmacy: Nap Patika Pharmacy, Hatvan u. 1 (☎413 115). Open M-F 8:30am-6pm, Sa 8am-1pm. **Arany Egyszarvú,** Kossuth u. 8 (☎530 707). Open M-F 8:30am-6pm.

Medical Assistance: Emergency room (☎414 333), at the intersection of Erzsébet u. and Szoboszlói u. Look for the blue-and-white "Mentők, orvosi ügyelet" sign.

Internet: DataNet Cafe, Kossuth u. 8 (☎536 724; www.datanetcafe.hu). 8Ft per min. Open daily 9am-midnight.

Post Office: Hatvan u. 5-7 (☎412 111). Open M-F 7am-7pm, Sa 8am-1pm. Postal Code: 4025

▶ ACCOMMODATIONS

IBUSZ, on Széchenyi u. near Piac u., arranges centrally located private rooms (☎415 5155; fax 410 756. Open M-F 8am-5pm, Sa 8am-1pm. Doubles 4000Ft; triples 6000Ft. AmEx/MC/V.) The staff at Tourinform (See **Orientation and Practical Information**, p. 408) can also arrange rooms. In July and August, many **university dorms ❶** rent rooms (1300-2000Ft); ask at Tourinform since many dorms book only groups. Reserve rooms early during festival season.

Stop Panzió, Batthány u. 18 (☎420 301). From Kossuth u., turn right on Batthány u. At the Stop Hotel sign, go down the left side of the building to the back to find the entrance. Near the center. Bright rooms with TV and private bath look onto courtyard. Breakfast 900Ft. Reception 24hr. Check-out 11am. Doubles 5900Ft; triples 7900Ft. ❸

Kölcsey Kollégiuma, Blaháné u. 15 (☎502 780). From Kossuth u. go left on Újházi and right on Blaháné. The rooms are tiny and bathrooms are shared, but the dorm is cheap and well-located. Open mid-June to Aug. Singles 1300Ft. Tax 400Ft. ❶

Centrum Panzió, Péterfia u. 37/a (☎416 193), is comfortable and air-conditioned. Large, well-decorated rooms. Peaceful floral garden with lounge chairs, swings, and a shower. The owners offer horse rides with a trainer. Breakfast 900Ft. Singles 6500Ft; doubles 14950Ft; apartments 12,190-19,090Ft. Tax 15%. ❹

▶ FOOD

The **Match Supermarket** at the Debrecen Plaza, Péterfia u. 18, is well-stocked with fresh fruits and vegetables. (Open M-F 7am-9pm, Sa 6am-9pm, Su 7am-8pm.) **Heliker,** across from McDonald's, on Piac u., offers a smaller selection of snacks. (Open M-F 6:30am-7:30pm, Sa 6:30am-2pm, Su 7am-11am.)

Csokonai Söröző, Kossuth u. 21 (☎410 802), in a posh, candle-lit cellar. Peruse the user-friendly menu to pick out your meal from this outstanding local eatery. Entrees 580-1900Ft. Veggie soups and salads 450-800Ft. Open daily noon-11pm. ❷

Pompeji Cafe-Ristorante, Batthyány u. 4, (☎220 760). An Italian restaurant with Hungarian flavor. Try the French onion soup (480Ft), the chicken breast "a la Pompeji" (1100Ft), or, for something spicy, the Vesuvian roast (870Ft). On your way out, be sure to grab a slice of cake from **Batthyány Cukrászda** (100-200Ft). ❸

Aranybika Étterem, Piac u. 11-15 (☎533 408). To the left of the Aranyibika Hotel, on the corner of Piac u. and Bajcsy-Zsilinszky u. Plush leather chairs, stained-glass windows, and chandeliers make this restaurant ideal for a relaxing meal. Large dining room and plentiful patio seating. Entrees 1000-2800Ft. Open daily 10am-midnight. ❷

◉ SIGHTS

GREAT CHURCH. Hungary's largest Protestant church, built in 1836, looms over Kálvin tér. With a commanding yellow facade, white pillars, and twin spires, the Great Church (Nagytemplóm), is the sight most often depicted in photos of the town. The bell tower offers a great view of Debrecen, but beware: the narrow wooden stairs get steeper and more rickety as you climb. Hear the huge organ in action every Friday at noon. (☎*412 694. Open Apr.-Oct. M-F 9am-4pm, Sa 9am-noon, Su noon-4pm; Nov.-Mar. M-F 10am-noon, Su 1-3pm. 200Ft, students 100Ft. Concerts 1hr. Free.)*

REFORMÁTUS KOLLÉGIUM. Established in 1538 as a center for Protestant education, it housed the government of Hungary twice, and today it is home to Calvinist schools and a collection of religious art. The highlight, though, is the 650,000-volume library on the second floor. The impressive collection includes copies of the Bible in 214 different languages, dating as far back as the 16th century. *(Kálvin tér 16, behind the church. ☎414 744. Open Tu-Sa 9am-5pm, Su 9am-1pm. 200Ft, students 100Ft. English info 300Ft.)*

DÉRI MUSEUM. The Déri Museum displays a cultural collection ranging from local tinware to Japanese lacquerware. Awe-inspiring murals by Hungarian artist **Mihály Munkácsy** depicting Jesus's trial and crucifixion are displayed upstairs. Spot the artist's self-portrait in *Ecce Homo*, next to the arch. Coming from Kossuth tér, steer left of the Great Church and turn left on to Múzeum u.; the museum is on the right, flanked by the sculpture garden. *(☎417 577. Open Nov.-Mar. Tu-Su 10am-4pm; Apr.-Oct. Tu-Su 10am-6pm. English guide 200Ft. Museum 580Ft, students 290Ft; special exhibits 300Ft/150Ft. No cameras.)*

🎵 📷 ENTERTAINMENT AND NIGHTLIFE

Debrecen is enlivened by the energy of the city's young population. Much of the city's youth congregates in **Nagyerdei Park**, where bars, tattoo salons, paddle boats, and young men lounging in tank tops abound. There is also a zoo and an **amusement park** for children. At the park's **municipal thermal bath**, you can soak in the steamy baths with locals. (☎514 100; fax 346 883. Thermal bath open daily 7am-8:30pm. 840Ft, children 660Ft. Sauna open daily Sept.-May 10am-10pm. 650Ft per 2hr. Swimming pool open M-F 7am-6:30pm. 350Ft, students 310Ft. Zoo open M-F 9am-6pm. 300Ft, children 250Ft. Amusement park 200Ft; rides 100Ft each. Paddleboats 900Ft per hr., rowboats 850Ft per hr.)

The festival season officially runs from June to August. At the end of June there is the **Vekeri-tó Rock Festival** with Hungarian bands at a park 10km away. Camp out, or take the free bus from town. In July of even-numbered years, the **Béla Bartók International Choral Competition** attracts choirs from around the world. The festival season culminates with the popular **Flower Carnival** parade, in which floats are made entirely of flowers, on August 20. Starting on the fourth Friday in September, **Jazz Days** bring well-known musicians and bands to town.

At night, head to the smoky **El Tornado**, Pallagi u. 2, in Nagyerdei Park. This pub, with swinging doors, country music, and cowboy memorabilia, will transport you back to the Wild West. (☎340 590. 0.5L *Borsodi* 250Ft. Open daily 6pm-4am.) **Yes Jazz Bár**, Kálvin tér 4, isn't a mellow jazz bar, but rather a rock-and-roll hotspot for local teens. (Gösser 300Ft, Heineken 320Ft. Karaoke F-Sa night. Open M-F 3pm-4am, Sa-Su 5pm-4am.) Across the street is **Civis Gösser Söröző**, Kálvin tér 8-12, with an older crowd. (Open M-Sa 10am-midnight, Su 4pm-midnight.) Go right after the last building on the right side of Kálvin tér and enter through the Civis Étterem. The nine air-conditioned theaters of **Cinema City**, Péterfia u. 18 (☎456 111), on the 2nd floor of Debrecen Plaza, offers refuge from the summer heat and has movies in English. (890-990Ft. Last showing 10:45pm.)

SZEGED ☎ (06)62

The artistic capital of the Great Plain, Szeged (SAY-ged; pop. 166,000) has an easy-going charm that has prompted some to describe it as a Mediterranean town on the Tisza. After an 1879 flood practically wiped out the city, streets were laid out in orderly curves punctuated by large, stately squares. The result is a quiet, cosmopolitan atmosphere that closely resembles Europe's seaside cities. The colorful Art Nouveau buildings that surround Szeged's sidestreets and plazas reflect the city's vibrant festival culture and swinging social scene.

⌐ TRANSPORTATION

Trains: Szeged pu. (☎421 821; www.elvira.hu), on Indóház tér on the west bank of the Tisza. International ticket office on 2nd fl. Open daily 6am-5:45pm. To: **Budapest** (2½hr., 11 per day, 1780Ft); **Debrecen** (3-4hr., 9 per day, 2220Ft) via **Cegléd; Kecskemét** (1¼hr., 11 per day, 880Ft).

Buses: (☎551 166), on Mars tér. To reach the bus station, continue 2 more stops from the train stop at Széchenyi tér to the corner of Pacsirta u. and Kossuth L. út. Continue in the same direction as the tram, turning left on Pacsirta u., and walk 2 blocks to reach Mars tér. From the station, cross the street at the lights and follow Mikszáth Kálmán u. toward the Tisza. This intersects Széchenyi tér after becoming Károlyi u. To: **Budapest** (3½hr., 10 per day, 1880Ft); **Debrecen** (5¼hr., 2-4 per day, 2450Ft); **Eger** (5hr., 2 per day, 2260Ft); **Győr** (6hr., 2 per day, 2670Ft); **Kecskemét** (1¾hr., 10-14 per day, 947Ft); **Pécs** (4½hr., 7 per day, 2100Ft).

Public Transportation: Tram #1 connects the train station with Széchenyi tér (4-5 stops). Otherwise it's a 20min. walk. Tickets from kiosks 110Ft; from the driver 150Ft. Fine for riding without a ticket is a painful 2000Ft.

Taxis: ☎444 444, 490 490, or 480 480. 200Ft base fare plus 200Ft per km; students approximately 150Ft per km with no base fare. Taxis are better here than in other cities, but it is still best to clarify the price before getting in.

✦▮ ORIENTATION AND PRACTICAL INFORMATION

Szeged is divided by the **Tisza River,** with the city center on the west bank and the parks and residences of **Újszeged** (New Szeged) on the east. The center forms a semicircle against the river, bounded by **Tisza Lajos krt.** and centered on **Széchenyi tér,** the main square. Across **Híd u.** (Bridge St.) from Széchenyi, shops and cafes line the pedestrian **Klauzál tér.** Large multilingual **maps** are sold in kiosks.

Tourist Office: Tourinform, Dugonics tér 2 (☎488 690; szeged@tourinform.hu), in a courtyard on Somogyi u. Offers free maps and accommodations info. Open M-F 9am-6pm, Sa 9am-1pm. **Branch** at Széchenyi tér. Open daily June-Sept. 9am-8:30pm.

Currency Exchange: OTP, Klauzál tér 5 (☎480 380), cashes **traveler's checks** for no commission and gives MC/V **cash advances.** 24hr. money changer outside. Open M 7:45am-5pm, Tu-F 7:45am-4pm. **Budapest Bank Ltd.,** Klauzál tér 4 (☎485 585), doubles as a **Western Union** and has a 24hr. (MC/V) **ATM** outside. Open M-F 8am-5pm.

Luggage Storage: At the train station. 4am-4pm 150Ft per bag, 4am-11pm 200Ft. Open daily 4am-11pm.

24hr. Pharmacy: Kígyó Richter Referenciapatika, Klauzál tér 3 (☎547 174). Ring bell outside for after-hours service. Open M-Sa 7am-10pm, Su 7am-8pm.

Medical Assistance: Kossuth Lajos sgt. 15/17 (☎474 374). From the Town Hall, walk up the center of Széchenyi tér, turn left on Vörösmarty u., and continue as it becomes Kossuth Lajos sgt. The **medical center** is at the intersection with Szilágyi u. Open M-F 5:30am-7:30pm, Sa 7:30am-M 7:30am. Ring bell after hours.

Internet Access: Cyber Arena, Híd u. 1 (☎422 815), has Internet and phones with cheap international rates. 8am-midnight 6Ft per min., midnight-8am 3.6Ft per min. Open 24hr. **Matrix Internet Cafe,** Kárász u. 5 (☎423 830), plays techno and trance under dim lights. 10am-10pm 6Ft per min., 10pm-10am 5Ft per min. Open 24hr.

Post Office: Széchenyi tér 1 (☎476 276), at intersection with Híd u. Open M-F 8am-7pm, Sa 8am-1pm. **Western Union** and **Poste Restante** available. **Postal Code:** 6720.

ACCOMMODATIONS

Tourinform (see **Orientation and Practical Information,** p. 411) has info on **pensions, hotels, hostels, and campsites.** (Singles 1100-9000Ft; doubles 3000-12000Ft; triples 4600-14,500Ft; quads 4600-15000Ft.) **IBUSZ,** Oroszlán u. 3, will hook you up with a private room in a flat. (☎/fax 471 177. Open M-F 9am-6pm, Sa 10am-1pm. 3000-3500Ft; additional 30% for stays fewer than 4 nights). **University dorms** are generally the cheapest option, but they are only available in July and August.

Hotel Tisza, Széchenyi tér 3 (☎478 278; www.tiszahotel.hu). In the historic center of town, this elegant 1886 hotel was once frequented by the artistic elite: Béla Bartók performed in its concert hall and its restaurant was a favorite among Hungarian literary figures. Today, it offers spacious, intricately decorated rooms. Breakfast included. 24hr. reception. Check-out 10am. Singles 7900Ft., with shower and sink 10,800Ft; doubles 10,900Ft/13,800Ft; triples 14,900Ft. ❹

Familia Panzió, Szentháromság u. 71 (☎441 122; fax 441 616), a few minutes from the train station. This clean and comfortable family-run pension is a 15min. walk from the center, but buses and trams run by regularly. Many rooms have wood paneling. Breakfast 600Ft. Singles with bath 5500Ft; doubles 4000-8000Ft, with bath 5400-7700Ft; triples 8000-11,000Ft; quads 9000-12,000Ft. ❸

Loránd Eötvös Kollégium, Tisza Lajos krt. 103 (☎544 124; eotvos@petra.hos.u-szeged.hu). Heading out of town, the hostel is to the left of Hero's Gate. The entrance is hidden from the street, to the left of the restaurant. Cheap, centrally located dorms with mosquito-proof screens and clean bathrooms. Well-lit and pleasant. Laundry service included. Call ahead to reserve. Open July-Aug. Singles 1000Ft; doubles 2100Ft. ❶

Teleki Blanka Kollégium, Semmelweis u. 5 (☎546 088). University dorm rooms, mostly quads, are separated by clean shared bathrooms. Bring toilet paper. 2000Ft. ❶

FOOD

Not only is Szeged the paprika capital of Hungary, it is also home to Hungary's finest lunchmeats, especially salami, and is the best place for *halászlé* (spicy soup made with fresh Tisza fish). Keep in mind that it is taboo to order water with your soup, as it dilutes the paprika flavor; wine and beer are better complements anyway. The 24hr. **ABC market** on Mars tér, near the corner of Londoni krt. and Mikszáth Kálmán u., provides late-night sustenance. The daily **open-air market,** with meat and fruits, is behind the bus station.

Roosevelt téri Halászcsárda, Roosevelt tér 14 (☎424 111), next to the river. Aromatic waves of paprika wash over you here. Savor the famously spicy *szegedi halászlé* or any of the *hallé* (fish soup) dishes, heated with green paprika. View of Belvárosi híd. Vegetarian options. Entrees 500-2500Ft. Open daily 11am-11pm. MC/V. ❷

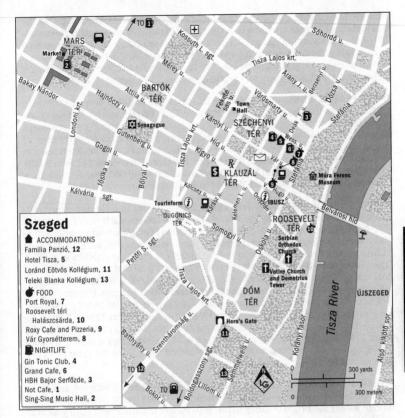

Szeged

🏠 ACCOMMODATIONS
Familia Panzió, **12**
Hotel Tisza, **5**
Loránd Eötvös Kollégium, **11**
Teleki Blanka Kollégium, **13**

🍴 FOOD
Port Royal, **7**
Roosevelt téri
  Halászcsárda, **10**
Roxy Cafe and Pizzeria, **9**
Vár Gyorsétterem, **8**

🎵 NIGHTLIFE
Gin Tonic Club, **4**
Grand Cafe, **6**
HBH Bajor Serfőzde, **3**
Not Cafe, **1**
Sing-Sing Music Hall, **2**

Port Royal, Stefánia 4 (☎547 988), to the right of the Móra Ferenc Museum. This ship-themed restaurant specializes in "lava rock grilling," a process in which gravy is steamed with meat. Great vegetarian options. Live jazz almost every night; outdoor performances in summer. Entrees 600-2450Ft. Open Su-Th 11am-midnight; F-Sa 11am-2am. Bar open Su-Th 11am-11pm; F-Sa 11am-midnight. ❸

Vár Gyorsétterem, Vár u. 4, provides the speed of fast-food prices without the compromise in taste. A large, sit-down restaurant with an exhaustive menu, including spaghetti (450Ft), pizza (470-1350Ft), hamburgers (550Ft), and gyros (470-620Ft). Down a quick beer (190-330Ft) at the bar while you wait. Open M-Tu and Th 7am-11pm; W 7am-midnight; F 7am-2am; Sa 10am-2am, Su 10am-11pm. ❷

Roxy Cafe and Pizzeria, Deák Ferenc u. 24 (☎423 496). Serves pizza (600-980Ft) and pasta (550-700Ft) to Szeged's hippest students. A perfect post-party, pre-hangover stop. Open M-Th 10am-midnight, F 10am-2am, Sa noon-2am, Su noon-midnight. ❷

🅖 SIGHTS

🕍 **SYNAGOGUE (ZSINAGÓGA).** Perhaps the most beautiful in Hungary, this 1903 synagogue is an awesome display of craftmanship and classical style, with Moorish altars and gardens, Romanesque columns, Gothic domes, and Baroque facades. The cupola, a brilliant amalgam of blue stained glass, sheds light on the vestibule walls, which are lined with the names of the 3100 congregation members killed in concentration camps. Today's small Jewish community still worships here. (Jósika u. 8. From Széchenyi tér, walk away from the river along Híd u. through Bartók tér; turn left on Jósika. Synagogue is on the left. Open Su-F 10am-noon and 1-5pm. Closed to visitors on holy days, though worshippers are welcome at services. 250Ft, students 100Ft.)

MÓRA FERENC MUSEUM. Exhibits in this riverside museum describe Szeged's history and its love-hate relationship with the Tisza River. Displays feature everything from anthropological excavations to modern city plans. The permanent exhibit "They Called Themselves Avars" showcases artifacts from the Age of Migration, including two corpses buried in a double grave. The museum reflects the great pride Szeged residents take in their heritage. (Roosevelt tér 1/3. From Széchenyi tér, turn right on Vár u., which brings you to Roosevelt tér. ☎ 549 040. Open July-Sept. Tu-Su 10am-6pm; Oct.-June 10am-5pm. 400Ft, children 200Ft, students with ISIC free.)

VOTIVE CHURCH (FOGADALMI TEMPLOM). This unusual neo-Romanesque red-brick church pierces the skyline with its dual 91m towers, each with four clocks. The fourth largest church in Hungary, it houses a 9040-pipe organ that is sometimes used for afternoon concerts. Inside, you'll find Janos Fádrusz's masterpiece "Christ on the Cross," which won several awards at the Paris Exhibition in 1900. The 12th-century **Demetrius Tower** (Dömötör Torony) is all that remains of the original church that stood on this site. On the walls surrounding the church, in bright colors laden with gold, is the **National Pantheon**, which portrays Hungary's great political, literary, and artistic figures. (From Széchenyi tér, turn left on Híd u., then right on Oskola u., which leads to Dóm tér. Open M-W and F-Sa 8am-5:30pm, Th noon-5:30pm, Su noon-5:30pm. Mass daily 7am and 6pm. Su mass 8:30am, 10am, 11:30am, 6pm. Guided tours 11am and 2pm; free with admission. English-speaking guides available. Entrance 400Ft, Su free. Call for group tours and organ concert times. Climb the tower for 600Ft. Tower open briefly M-F 2:30pm, Sa-Su 1pm.)

OTHER SIGHTS. The yellow **Town Hall** (Városháza), reshingled with red-and-green ceramic tiles after the devastating 1879 flood, overlooks grassy Széchenyi tér. The bridge joining the bright building to the drab former tax office next door was built so Hapsburg Emperor Franz Joseph wouldn't have to take the stairs. (Széchenyi tér 10.) The 1778 **Serbian Orthodox Church** (Palánki Szerb Templom) features impressive artwork. The iconostasis holds 80 gilt-framed paintings, while the ceiling fresco of God creating the Earth is covered with stars. (Somogyi u. 3a. ☎ 325 278. Opened by request.) **Hero's Gate** (Hősök Kapuja), actually a short tunnel, was erected in 1936 as a memorial to the soldiers who died in WWI. Two plaster soldiers guard the gate while a mural of Jesus guiding soldiers during battle decorates the tunnel's underside. (Start at Dóm tér and head away from the center to reach the gate, in the adjacent Aradi Vértanuk tér.)

🎵 ENTERTAINMENT

The **Szeged Open Air Festival,** from early July to late August, is Hungary's largest outdoor performance event. International troupes perform folk dances, operas, and musicals in the amphitheater, Deák u. 28/30, with the church as a backdrop. Buy tickets (1500-12,000Ft) at Tourinform (see **Orientation and Practical Information,** p. 411) or Kelemen u. 7. (☎716 717; www.szabadterijatekok.szeged.hu. Open M-F 10am-5pm.) Other festivals fill the streets from early spring to late autumn. The five-day mid-July **beer festival,** the **wine festival,** and the **jazz jamboree** are all popular. Swimming pools and baths line the **Partfürdő Strand;** from Szeged, cross the Belváros bridge and walk left along the river. Most of these places are open daily and charge 300-600Ft admission. Over the bridge to the left is a beach and swimming area. **Bike paths** line the streets, and you can **kayak** on the Tisza River. To rent equipment, contact **Vizisporttelep** at Felső-Tisza part 4 (☎425 574).

■ NIGHTLIFE

Grand Cafe, Deák Ferenc u. 18, 3rd fl. (☎420 578). Start your night at this sophisticated cafe, which screens 3 art films each evening. Sip on coffee or red wine as you watch a film (450Ft), or stay in the intimate coffee shop and relax to mellow jazz. Films daily 5, 7, 9pm. Open Sept.-July M-F 3pm-midnight, Sa-Su 5pm-midnight.

Gin Tonic Club, Wesselényi u. 1 (☎026-298), in the Tisza Hotel building. Trendy and well-decorated underground vault where the stylish get drunk and get down. Beer 250-520Ft. F DJ, Sa live music. Cover F 600Ft, Sa 400Ft. Open F-Sa 8pm-4am.

HBH Bajor Serfőzde (Beer House), Deák Ferenc u. 4 (☎420 394), in the city center. A major sponsor of the annual beer festival, this pub is a no-nonsense brewhouse with great snacks. Open M-Th 11:30am-11pm, F-Sa 11:30am-midnight, Su 11:30am-4pm.

Sing-Sing Music Hall (www.sing.hu), on Mars tér, C Pavilion. DJ turns popular beats for a ready-to-rave crowd. 0.5L Amstel 500Ft. Cover around 500Ft. Open daily 11pm-dawn.

Not Cafe, Római Körút u. 38 (☎702 255). An eclectic crowd frequents this popular joint. F-Sa go-go boys. Cover F-Sa. Cafe open daily 2-9pm, disco open daily 9pm-late.

HORTOBÁGY   ☎(0)52

Europe's largest open pasture region, Hungary's central plain is home to some of the continent's most ancient species of cattle, birds, and fish. Much of the land is part of **Hortobágy National Park,** which is a UNESCO World Heritage Site. A long-standing inspiration to Hungarian artists, the peaceful expanse sprawls over 72 sq. mi. of Hungary's central plain, making it the largest continuous natural grassland in Europe. It is home to ancient indigenous animals like the Hungarian gray long-horn cattle, spiral-horned "Racka" sheep, and Nonius horses. The park is also a birdwatcher's paradise, as over 330 species of birds travel through each year. **Walks, hikes,** and **cycling tours** are possible with admission. Most **trails** are clearly marked and info boards are in a variety of languages. (Open daily Apr. 15-Oct. 15 9am-5pm; Oct. 15-Dec. 10am-4pm. 800Ft per day, students 200Ft per day. English guided tours 3300Ft.) For info, contact the Hortobágy or Debrecen Tourinform. In town, the famous **Nine-Hole Bridge** (Kilene-lyuku hid) is an enduring symbol of the plain. Built in 1827 and named for its nine arches, the white stone bridge connected Budapest to Debrecen and served as an important military and postal route. No longer a residence for weary travelers, the white-stone **Hortobágy Csarda** (see below) was built in 1699, and, with its trademark arching windows, embodies plains architecture. The **Pasztormuzeum** across the street displays a wide variety of traditional tools and costumes, most notably the heavy cloaks of the shepherds. (Open daily 9am-6pm. 250Ft, children 150Ft.)

Search for **private rooms** at Tourinform. **Puszta Camping ❶,** behind Tourinform, offers spacious bungalows on the Puszta River. (☎369 300. Bungalows 1250Ft per person. Electricity 450Ft. Tax 250Ft.) The luxurious **Hortobágy Club Hotel ❹** has swimming pools and a horse stable. Enter across from the ticket counter by the park gate. (☎369 020; www.hortobagyhotel.hu. Singles 12000Ft; doubles 16000Ft. Breakfast included.) **Hortobágy Fogado ❸,** 1 Kossuth u., offers spacious rooms with TV and private bath. (☎369 137. Singles 3500Ft; doubles 6000Ft; triples 9000Ft; quads 1200Ft.) If you're hungry, head downstairs to the regal **Fogado Étterem ❷.** Try the hearty goulash soup (500 Ft). The famous **Hortobágy Csarda ❸,** Petófi tér 2,

HUNGARY

is across from Tourinform. The traditional restaurant has a view of the Nine-Hole Bridge and serves local dishes. (☎369 139. Entrees 700-200Ft. Open daily mid-Feb. to Oct. 9am-9pm). Buy food at **ABC Coop,** Kossuth u. 6, before hitting the trails. (Open M-F 5:30am-6pm, Sa 7am-1pm, Su 7am-11am.)

Trains run to **Tsizafüred** (45min., 1 per day, 372Ft.), **Debrecen** (1hr., 10 per day, 386Ft.), **Füzesbony** (1¼hr., 7 per day, 594Ft.), and **Eger** (2hr., 2 per day, 698Ft). The **train station,** Kossuth u. 10, is 5min. from town. Follow **Kossuth u.** with your back to the station. To reach the park, follow Kossuth u. through town and go right on Route 33 (45min.). Take the first right after crossing the Nine-Hole Bridge and follow the road until it ends. Turn right and continue ¾ mi. to the circular drive. The **ticket stand** and park entrance are on the left. **Tourinform,** Peófi tér 1, shares a building with **Pasztomuzeum,** which sells **maps** (200Ft) and books rooms. (☎589 321. Open daily 8am-4pm.) The **post office,** Kossuth u. 2, has an **ATM** and **currency exchange;** there's a telephone outside. (☎369 001. Open M-F 8am-noon and 12:20-4pm.) Across the street, the **pharmacy, Fekete Gólya Gyógyszertar,** Kossuth u. 3, has Western products. (☎369 141. Open M-F 10am-noon, Sa 3-5pm).

KECSKEMÉT   ☎(06)76

Surrounded by vineyards, fruit groves, and dusty *puszta* (plains), Kecskemét (KETCH-keh-mate; pop. 110,000) lures tourists with a park-like central square, famous *barackpálinka* (apricot brandy), and the musical genius of native composer Zoltán Kodály (1882-1967). It resembles other large Hungarian towns, but it hosts many festivals and is an excellent base from which to visit Bugacpuszta.

▊ TRANSPORTATION. The **train station** is on Kodály Zoltán tér, at the end of Rákóczi út. To: **Budapest** (2hr., 15 per day, 926Ft, InterCity 1263Ft); **Pécs** (5hr., 13 per day, 2326Ft) via **Kiskunfélegyháza; Szeged** (1¼hr., 14 per day, 678Ft). **Buses** run from the **bus station,** just around the corner from the train station on Kodály Zoltán tér, to: **Budapest** (1½hr., 26 per day, 894Ft); **Debrecen** (5hr., 1 per day, 2390Ft); **Pécs** (5hr., 3 per day, 1992Ft); **Szeged** (1¾hr., 13 per day, 947Ft). The **Volán** bus terminal is a block away from Kossuth tér; turn right from the terminal on Sík S. Timetables are posted at most stops. Buses stop running around 10pm. Tickets are 105Ft from kiosks; 150Ft from drivers. Prices change frequently.

▊▊ ORIENTATION AND PRACTICAL INFORMATION. Most sights are within walking distance. The town lies around a loosely connected string of squares. The largest, **Szabadság tér** (Liberty Square), is ringed by three satellite squares, **Kossuth tér, Kálvin tér,** and **Széchenyi tér.** To get to Szabadság from the train or bus station, go left as you exit the station, then straight, and go right on Rákóczi út. as the road turns. Follow the street for 10min. The staff at **Tourinform,** Kossuth tér 1, has **free maps,** arranges accommodations, and provides info on events. (Open July-Aug. M-F 9am-8pm, Sa-Su 9am-6pm; Sept.-June M-F 8am-6pm, Sa 9am-1pm). **OTP,** Szabadság tér 1/a, at Arany János u., **exchanges currency** at good rates and cashes **traveler's checks** for no commission. (Open M 7:45am-5pm, Tu-F 7:45am-4pm.) 24hr. MC/V ATM outside. The **pharmacy, Mátyás Király Gyógyszertár,** Szabadság tér 1, is across from the bank. (Open M-F 7:30am-8pm, Sa 8am-4pm, Su 8am-2pm). There's a **post office,** Kálvin tér 10/12. (Open M-F 8am-7pm, Sa 8am-12pm.) **Postal Code:** 6000.

▊▊ ACCOMMODATIONS AND FOOD. Dorm rooms and pensions are generally the best deals in town. **Hotel Pálma ❸,** Arany János u. 3, in the heart of the city, has rooms with full baths and showy decor. (☎321 045. Singles 5450Ft, 1st-class 7050Ft; doubles 8300Ft/9600Ft; triples 9750Ft/11550Ft; quads 11600Ft.) **Tanitóképző Kollégiuma** (Teachers' College) ❶, Piaristák tere 4, 5min. from Kossuth tér,

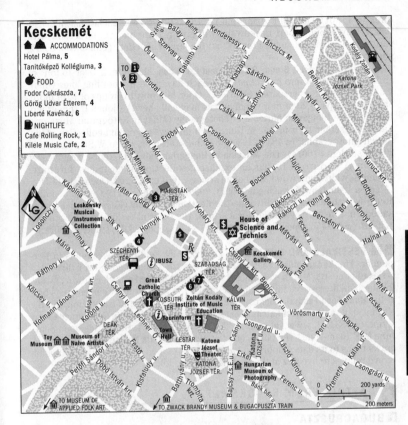

Kecskemét

▲▲ ACCOMMODATIONS
Hotel Pálma, **5**
Tanitóképző Kollégiuma, **3**

🍎 FOOD
Fodor Cukrászda, **7**
Görög Udvar Étterem, **4**
Liberté Kavéház, **6**

■ NIGHTLIFE
Cafe Rolling Rock, **1**
Kilele Music Cafe, **2**

HUNGARY

rents good-sized triples and quads on a per person basis. (☎486 977. Call 1-2 days ahead. 1600Ft.) Kecskemét is famous for its apricot *barackpálinka* (brandy), made from pure apricot distillate. 🌑**Liberté Kavéház ❷**, Szabadság tér 2 (☎480 350), has Hungarian specialties in a plush, quiet atmosphere. (Entrees 590-2090Ft. Open Su-Th 11am-11pm, F-Sa 11am-2am). Try **Fodor Cukrászda ❶** for dessert (100-450Ft) or ice cream (80Ft). **Görög Udvar Étterem ❸**, Hornyik J. 1, sells souvlaki, gyros, and veggie pitas in a Greek-style setting. (Entrees 750-2200Ft. Open daily 11am-11pm.) The **Coop Supermarket**, Deák tér 6, has a drugstore and cafe. (☎481 711. Market open M-F 6:30am-7pm, Sa 6am-1pm.)

🅖 🏛 **SIGHTS AND MUSEUMS.** The salmon-colored **town hall**, Kossuth tér 1, dominates Kecskemét's main square. (☎513 524. Tours every hr. on the hr. M-Th 9am-4pm, F-Sa 9am-1pm. 300Ft.) Beside it, the **Big Catholic Church**, the largest Baroque cathedral on the Great Plain, has marble columns and an interior of elaborate frescoes. (Open daily 7:30am-6pm.) From the entrance on the right of the church, climb the tower for a good view. (Open daily July-Aug. 10am-10pm; Sept.-June 10am-8pm. 200Ft, students 100Ft.) In the middle of the square, you can purchase Hungarian arts and souvenirs at the stalls. The cupola-topped **Synagogue**, Rákóczi u. 2, is no longer used for worship, but boasts 15 fake Michelangelo sculptures. (☎487 611. Open M-F 10am-4pm.) At the **Leskowsky Musical Instrument Collection,** Zimay u. 6/a, Albert Leskowsky will give a 1hr. concert and lesson with various musical instruments drawn from the large collection. (Call ahead. 500Ft, students 300Ft.)

At the ■ **Zwack Fruit Brandy Distillery and Exhibition,** Matkói u. 2, over 15 tons of apricots are turned into *barackpálinka* each day. Tour the bottling lines where the famous brandy is prepared. (☎487-711. Open M-F only to groups of 10 or more, Sa-Su to groups of 20 or more. Individuals may call ahead or join a F 1pm group. 1350Ft.) The **Hungarian Museum of Photography** (Magyar Fotográfiai Múzeum), Katona József tér 12, is unique in Hungary. It displays a poignant collection of historical photographs. (☎483 221; www.c3.hu/~fotomuz. Open W-Su 10am-4pm. 200Ft, students 100Ft). The **Museum of Hungarian Folk Art** (Népi Iparmüvészet Múzeuma), Serfözö u. 19, has an extensive collection of costumes, furniture, ceramics, whips, and wood and bone carvings. (☎/fax 327 203. Open Jan. 15-Dec. 14 Tu-Sa 10am-5pm. English guide 50Ft. 200Ft, students 100Ft.) Once a boarding house with a casino and ballroom, the **Kecskemét Gallery** (Kecskeméti Képtár), Rákóczi u. 1, features works by local artists. The colorful building is an attraction in itself. (☎480-776. Open Tu-Sa 10am-5pm, Su 1:30-5pm. 260Ft, students 130Ft.)

■■■ **FESTIVALS AND NIGHTLIFE.** Festivals are held most weekends in Kecskemét. The **Kodaly Music Festival** remembers the famous composer through a series of concerts. March welcomes the **Kecskemét Spring Festival,** featuring music, theater, and literary readings. In late summer, the food industry serves up its best at the **Hírös Food Festival.** Shakespeare may lose something in translation, but the elegant stage at the **József Katona Theater** (Színház), Katona tér 5, lends grace to any script. (☎483 283; www.katonaj.hu. Tickets from 1300Ft. Box office open Sept.-June M-F 10am-7pm.) The city is quiet at night, but **Cafe Rolling Rock,** Jókai u. 44, draws teens to its dance floor and bar. (☎506 190. Open W-Sa 6pm-1am.) An adult crowd relaxes to live jazz at the **Kilele Music Cafe,** Jókai 3.

■ **DAYTRIP FROM KECSKEMÉT**

■ **BUGACPUSZTA**

Buses (45min., 3 per day, 463Ft). Trains (45min., 3 per day, 412Ft). Pick up info before leaving Kecskemét. The train leads to the village of Bugac, not the puszta 5km away. Get off buses at the second-last stop, just after the bus takes a left at the entrance to Bugacpuszta. From the stop, walk down the road (15-20min.) to the entrance. Take the carriage to the museum and stables (2000Ft) or continue down the path 15min (1000Ft, students and children 500Ft). Or, buy a package (4500Ft) including admission, carriage ride, and a full lunch at Bugaci Karikás Csárda. Daily horseshow 1:15pm. Park open daily May-Oct. 10am-5pm.

A traveler on the Great Plain hears many legends about local cowboys, and Bugacpuszta is the place to take in the traditions and culture of Hungary's "Wild Wild East." Don't be fooled by the appearance of these cowboys, who may look less than macho with their flowing linen pants and feathered hats. These plainsmen ride without saddles: they stand up as the horses gallop at full speed, sometimes holding brimming pints of wine steadily in hand as they ride.

Bugacpuszta is the most touristed part of the **Kiskunság National Park** and the second largest *puszta* (plain) in Hungary. The 11am bus from Budapest is ideal, as it arrives in Bugac in time to visit the museum, see the stables, and grab a snack before the show. With admission, you can visit the **Shepherd's Museum,** which displays a teepee, musical instruments, and stuffed animals from the *puszta.* Then, head to the stables to see the pigs, sheep, and horses. Be sure to nab seats to the horseshow. The 30min. performance is action-packed: cowboys round up wild horses and crack their whips in synchronization. In an impressive trick, a cowboy stands with each foot on a different galloping horse and holds the reins of three others.

Take your time getting back to the entrance; the next bus won't come until 4pm. Once there, consider the **Bugaci Karikás Csárda ❸**, Nagybugac 135, which serves a range of traditional Hungarian dishes. (☎575 112; fax 575 114. Entrees 1000-2000Ft.) Some spend the night here in a luxurious *puszta* farmhouse. (Breakfast included. Doubles 9000Ft.) While activities in Bugac are focused on seeing horses not riding, there are opportunities to take the reins yourself. **Táltos Reiterpension,** Nagybugac 135, offers **horseback riding** for 2000Ft per hr. in the *puszta* or 1800Ft per hr. around their property. On the main road from the park, turn right and walk 150m. (☎372 633; fax 372 580. Open daily 9am-5pm.)

HUNGARY

LATVIA (LATVIJA)

Latvia has been caught for hundreds of years in the political struggles between Germany, Russia, Sweden, Lithuania, and Poland. The country has been conquered and reconquered so many times that the year 2004 was only the 35th year of Latvian independence—ever. However, national pride abounds, from patriotically renamed streets draped with crimson-and-white flags, to a rediscovery of native holidays predating even the Christian invasions. Rīga, Latvia's only large city, is a Westernized capital luring more and more international companies. The rest of the country is mostly a provincial expanse of green hills and quiet towns.

HISTORY

INVASION. Like its Baltic sisters, Latvia has consistently struggled under the yoke of foreign rule. The Germans arrived in the late 12th century to convert the locals to Christianity. In 1237, the Teutonic Knights established the **Confederation of Livonia,** which ruled over the territory for nearly 300 years. The confederation collapsed when Russian Tsar **Ivan IV** (the Terrible) invaded, beginning the 25-year **Livonian War** (1558-83) and a half-century of partition.

SWEDISH INTERLUDE. The 1629 **Truce of Altmark** brought a long period of relative stability and freedom known as the **Swedish Interlude,** achieved by ceding control of eastern Livonia (present-day Latvia and Estonia) to the Poles and giving Rīga and the northern regions to Sweden. Sweden, however, was forced to cede the Livonian territories to **Peter the Great** under the 1721 Peace of Nystad, and with the third partition of Poland in 1795 the entire country fell under Russian control. The

FACTS AND FIGURES

OFFICIAL NAME: Republic of Latvia

CAPITAL: Rīga (pop. 874,000)

POPULATION: 2.3 million (58% Latvian, 30% Russian, 4% Belarusian, 3% Polish 3% Ukrainian, and 3% other)

LANGUAGES: Latvian or Lettish (official), Russian

CURRENCY: 1 Lat = 100 santimi

RELIGION: 55% Lutheran, 25% Roman Catholic, 9% Russian Orthodox, 6% Old Believer, 5% Jewish

LAND AREA: 64,589km^2

CLIMATE: Maritime

GEOGRAPHY: Low plains

BORDERS: Belarus, Estonia, Lithuania, Russia

ECONOMY: 70% Services, 25% Industry, 5% Agriculture

GDP: US$8300 per capita

COUNTRY CODE: 371

INTERNATIONAL DIALING PREFIX: 00

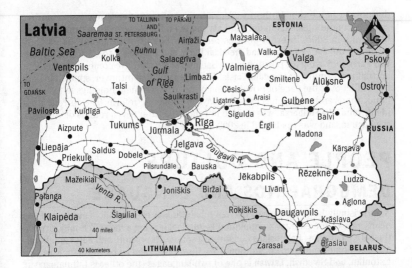

Latvian peasantry, which became prosperous after the **abolition of serfdom** in 1861, continued to struggle for freedom from the Russian empire during the 19th century. **Nationalism** flared with particular strength during the Russian Revolution of 1905.

THE WAR YEARS. Reacting to the Bolshevik coup of November 1917, the **Latvian People's Council** proclaimed independence on November 18, 1918, establishing a government in Rīga led by **Kārlis Ulmanis.** The **Constitution of 1922** created a republic governed by a president and a unicameral parliament, but the large number of political parties in the legislature, or **Saeima,** kept the political situation unstable. Ulmanis encountered problems when German elements within Latvia became sympathetic to the Nazi party, and in 1934 he declared a state of emergency. Under the **Nazi-Soviet Nonaggression Pact,** Latvia fell under Soviet control in 1939. However, Germany reneged on the Pact and occupied Latvia in 1941, only to be driven back in 1945 by the Red Army, which annexed its smaller neighbor.

SUPREMELY SOVIET. Latvia entered the **Soviet Union** as one of its wealthiest and most industrialized regions. Under Soviet rule, the state was torn by radical economic restructuring, political repression, and the Russification of its national culture. Some 35,000 Latvians, including many members of the intelligentsia, were deported to Russia during the first year of the occupation, as immigrants poured in from the rest of the USSR. Foreigners soon dominated local politics, and within four decades ethnic Latvians accounted for only half the population.

FREE AT LAST. Under *glasnost* and *perestroika* (see **Russia: History,** p. 652), Latvians protested en masse against the Communist regime and created the **Popular Front** in 1988. Faced with competition, the Communists were trounced in the 1990 elections. On May 4, 1990, the new legislature declared independence, but Soviet intervention sparked violent clashes in Rīga in 1991. Following the failed Moscow coup in August, the Latvian legislature reasserted independence. Soon after, the world recognized the legislature's sovereignty.

TODAY. Along with its two Baltic sisters, Latvia solidified its relationship with the West by becoming a member of the **European Union** in April 2004 and a member of **NATO** in May 2004. Latvian relations with both **Russia** and with the large Russian diaspora at home remain thorny. Tensions have flared over a new law requiring schools conduct lessons mainly in Latvian, even for Russian-speaking children, beginning in 2005. Internal politics remain turbulent, with numerous parties, including the **For Fatherland and Freedom Party,** the **People's Party,** and the **Latvian Way Party,** jockeying for position in the Saeima. **Coalitions** have come and gone. The current prime minister is **Indulis Emsis.** The rapid political turnover, spurred in part by conflict over the pace of privatization of large government holdings in telecommunications and energy, has caused delays in economic reform. The current president, **Vaira Vike-Freiberga,** was elected in June 1999, after seven rounds of voting in the Saeima, and was re-elected in 2003.

PEOPLE AND CULTURE

DEMOGRAPHICS AND LANGUAGE

A surprisingly large number of Latvian inhabitants aren't actually **Latvian.** In fact, nearly 30% of the country's population is **Russian,** leaving a mere 57% majority for the native Latvians. **Belarusians** constitute a sparse 4% portion, and **Poles** and **Ukrainians** combined make up an additional 5%. Heavily influenced by German, Russian, Estonian, and Swedish, **Latvian** is one of two languages (the other is Lithuanian) in the Baltic language group. Life, however, proceeds bilingually. **Russian** acceptable and widespread in Rīga; it is still spoken in the countryside but its popularity is waning. Many young Latvians study **English;** the older set knows some **German.** For a phrasebook and glossary, **see Glossary: Latvian,** p. 953.

FOOD AND DRINK

LATVIA	❶	❷	❸	❹	❺
FOOD	under 2Ls	2-3Ls	4-5Ls	6-7Ls	over 7Ls

Latvian food is heavy and starchy—and therefore delicious. Cities offer foreign and **vegetarian** cuisine. Tasty national specialties include *maizes zupa* (bread soup made from cornbread, currants, and cream), and the warming *Rīgas* (or *Melnais*) *balzams* (a black liquor). Dark rye bread is a staple. Try *speķa rauši,* a warm pastry, or *biezpienmaize,* bread with sweet curds. Dark-colored *kaņepju sviests* (hemp butter) is good but too diluted for "medicinal" purposes. Latvian beer, primarily from the Aldaris brewery, is great, particularly *Porteris.*

CUSTOMS AND ETIQUETTE

Restaurant customers should **tip** 5-10%. Expect to be bought a drink if you talk with someone for a while; repay the favor in kind. If you're invited to a meal in someone's home, bring a **gift** for the hostess (an odd number of flowers is customary). **Handshaking** is expected when meeting new people or greeting a friend. **Shops** sometimes close for a break between noon and 3pm.

THE ARTS

The mid-19th century brought a national awakening as the country asserted its literary independence in works such as *Lāčplēsis (Bearslayer),* **Andrējs Pumpurs's** 1888 national epic. Realism and social protest became important in the **New Move-**

ment in the late 19th century. Writer **Jānis Rainis** used folk imagery to critique contemporary problems. **Aleksandrs Čaks** detailed everyday life and gave a haunting account of WWI. Many Latvian writers turned to psychological detail in the 20th century. **Anslavs Eglītis** reveled in intensifying human traits to the point of absurdity. Following WWII the Soviets imposed **Socialist Realism,** mandating that texts promote revolutionary ideals. **Jānis Medenis,** exiled to a Siberian labor camp, longed for a free Latvia in his poetry. **Mārtiņš Zīverts** is regarded as the best 20th-century Latvian dramatist. Using folk tradition in their late 19th-century works, **Jazeps Vītols** and **Andrejs Jurjans** became the country's first composers.

The **contemporary art** scene in Latvia owes much of its growth to the pioneers of Latvian history. **Miervaldis Polis** has begun to enjoy international acclaim for his hyper-realist art and is best known for *A Golden Man.* The **International Chamber Choir Festival,** held each September in Rīga, commemorates the ever-present choral appreciation and religious allusions of Latvian music. **Rīga** is the **Art Nouveau** capital of Europe, with blocks upon blocks of buildings designed with this style.

HOLIDAYS

NATIONAL HOLIDAYS IN 2005

January 1 New Year's Day	**June 24** St. John's Day
March 25 Good Friday	**November 18** Independence Day
March 27-28 Easter Holiday	**December 25** Christmas
May 1 Labor Day	**December 26** Boxing Day
June 23 Ligo Day	**December 31** New Year's Eve

ADDITIONAL RESOURCES

Baltic Revolution: Estonia, Latvia, Lithuania and the Path to Independence, by Anatol Lieven (1994). A solid background to 20th-century Baltic history.

Historical Dictionary of Latvia, by Andrejs Plakans (1997). A detailed survey of Latvia's history, and an analytical view of its present situation.

Latvia in Transition, by Juris Dreifelds (1996). An excellent look at the early years of Latvian independence.

The Testimony of Lives: Narrative and Memory in Post-Soviet Latvia, by Vieda Skultans (1998). Eloquently examines the recent difficulties experienced by Latvians.

LATVIA ESSENTIALS

ENTRANCE REQUIREMENTS

Passport: Required of all travelers.

Visa: Not required for stays under 90 days for citizens of Australia, Canada, Ireland, New Zealand, the UK, and the US.

Letter of Invitation: Not required.

Inoculations: Recommended up-to-date on DTaP (diphtheria, tetanus, and pertussis), Hepatitis A, Hepatitis B, MMR (measles, mumps, and rubella), Polio booster, and Typhoid.

Work Permit: Required of all foreigners planning to work in Latvia.

International Driving Permit: Required of all those planning to drive.

DOCUMENTS AND FORMALITIES

EMBASSIES AND CONSULATES

Embassies of other countries in Latvia are all in **Rīga** (see p. 427). Latvia's embassies and consulates abroad include:

Australia: Honorary Consulate: 38 Longstaff St., East Ivanhoe, Victoria 3079; P.O. Box 23 Kew, VIC 3101 (☎61 3 949 969 20; latcon@ozemail.com.au).

Canada: 280 Albert St., ste. 300, Ottawa, ON K1P 5G8 (☎1 613-238-6014; latvia-embassy@magmacom.com).

UK: 45 Nottingham Pl., London W1M 3FE (☎44 020 7312 0040; embassy@embassy-oflatvia.co.uk).

US: 4325 17th St. NW, Washington, D.C. 20011 (☎1 202-726-8213; www.latvia-usa.org).

VISA AND ENTRY INFORMATION

Citizens of Australia, Canada, Ireland, New Zealand, the UK, and the US can visit Latvia **visa-free** for up to 90 days. If you are staying longer, apply to the Department of Citizenship and Immigration (see **Rīga: Passport Office,** p. 427) for temporary residency. The best way to enter Latvia is by plane, train, or bus to the capital.

GETTING AROUND

Airlines **flying** to Latvia use the **Rīga** airport. **Air Baltic, SAS, Finnair, Lufthansa,** and others make the hop to Rīga from their hubs. **Trains** link Latvia to **Berlin, GER; Lviv, UKR; Moscow, RUS; Odessa, UKR; St. Petersburg, RUS; Tallinn, EST;** and **Vilnius, LIT. Trains** are cheap and efficient, but stations aren't well marked, so make sure to always have a map. The **commuter rail** system renders the entire country a suburb of Rīga. For daytrips from Rīga, you're best off taking the **electric train;** as a rule, a crowded train is more comfortable than a crowded bus.

Ferries go to **Kiel** and **Lübeck, GER** and **Stockholm, SWE,** but are slow and expensive. Latvia's efficient long-distance **buses** reach **Berlin, GER; Kyiv, UKR; Moscow, RUS; Prague, CZR; Tallinn, EST; Vilnius, LIT;** and **Warsaw, POL.** Buses, usually adorned with the driver's collection of icons and stuffed animals, are quicker than trains for travel within Latvia. Beware of the standing-room-only long-distance jaunt.

Road conditions in Latvia are improving after several years of deterioration. Urban and rural road conditions are generally fair. For more info, consult the **Latvian Road Administration** (www.lad.lv). Taxis are considered safe. Taxi stands in front of hotels charge higher rates. **Hitchhiking** is common, but drivers may ask for pay at least comparable to bus fare. *Let's Go* does not recommend hitchhiking.

TOURIST SERVICES AND MONEY

Look for the green "i" marking official **tourist offices,** which are rather scarce. Private tourist offices such as **Patricia** (see p. 427) are much more helpful. The Latvian currency unit is the **Lat (Ls),** which divides into 100 santīmi. **Inflation** averages around 2%. There are many MC/V **ATMs** in Rīga, and at least one or two in larger towns. Larger businesses, restaurants, and hotels accustomed to Westerners accept **MasterCard** and **Visa. Traveler's checks** are harder to use, but both AmEx and Thomas Cook checks can be converted in Rīga. It's often difficult to exchange non-Baltic currencies other than US dollars or euros.

HEALTH AND SAFETY

 EMERGENCY NUMBERS: Police: ☎02 **Fire:** ☎01 **Ambulance:** ☎03

Latvia was hot-listed by the World Health Organization for its periodic outbreaks of incurable varieties of **tuberculosis,** though none have been reported since 2000. As a precaution, drink **bottled water** (available at grocery stores and kiosks; it is often carbonated) or boil tap water before drinking. **Medical facilities** do not meet Western standards. **Pharmacies** carry tampons, condoms, and band-aids. **Restrooms** are marked with an upward-pointing triangle for women, downward for men.

Foreigners in Rīga may be targets for petty theft and street assaults. **Pickpocketing** is a problem, especially in crowded areas. At nights, beware of drunken crowds around bars and casinos. Both men and women should avoid walking alone at night. If you feel threatened, *"Ej prom"* (EY prawm) means "go away;" *"Lasies prom"* (LAH-see-oos PRAWM) says it more offensively; and *"Lasies lapās"* (LAH-see-oos LAH-pahs; "go to the leaves"), is even ruder. You are more likely to find advice in English from your **consulate** than from the police.

Women should not experience many difficulties in Latvia, even when traveling alone. After dark in Rīga, it is best to be cautious and take a cab home. **Minorities** in Latvia are rare; they receive stares but generally experience little discrimination. **Homosexuality** is legal, but public displays of affection are not tolerated and may result in violence. Safe options include **gay and lesbian clubs,** which advertise themselves as such freely in Rīga. Expect less tolerance outside the city. You can call the Latvian Gay and Lesbian Hotline at ☎959 2229.

ACCOMMODATIONS AND CAMPING

LATVIA	❶	❷	❸	❹	❺
ACCOM.	under 8Ls	8-14Ls	15-19Ls	20-24Ls	over 24Ls

There is one HI hostel in Rīga and a scattering of **hostels** around the beaches. Contact the **Latvian Youth Hostel Association,** Aldaru 8, Rīga LV-1050 (☎921 8560; www.hostellinglatvia.com), for more info. **College dormitories** are often the cheapest option, but are only open to travelers in the summer. Rīga's array of **hotels** satisfy any budget. Most small towns outside the capital have only one hotel (if any) in the budget range; expect to pay 3-15Ls per night. **Camping** isn't very popular. Campgrounds exist in the countryside, but camping beyond marked areas is prohibited.

KEEPING IN TOUCH

Ask for *gaisa pastu* to send something by **airmail.** The standard rate for a letter to Europe is 0.30Ls, to anywhere else 0.40Ls; for a postcard 0.20Ls/0.30Ls. **Mail** can be received general delivery through **Poste Restante.** Address envelopes: Daniel (first name) HEMEL (LAST NAME), POSTE RESTANTE, Stacijas laukums 1 (post office address), LV-1050 (postal code), Rīga (city), LATVIA.

Most **telephones** take **cards** (2, 3, 5, or 10Ls denominations) from post offices, telephone offices, kiosks, and state stores. If a number is six digits dial a 2 before it; if it's seven, you needn't dial anything before it. To call abroad from an analog phone, dial 1, then 00, then the country code. If it's digital, dial 00, then the country code. Phone offices and *Rīga in Your Pocket* have the latest info on changes to the phone system. **International calls** can be made from telephone offices or booths. International access codes include **AT&T Direct** (☎800 2 288) and **MCI World-Phone** (☎800 8888). **Internet access** is readily available and averages 0.5Ls per hour.

RĪGA ☎8(2)

Although ethnic Latvians are outnumbered by Russians in their capital city, Rīga (pop. 756,000) is the unrivaled center of the country's cultural and economic life. Founded in 1201 by the German Bishop Albert, Rīga is an architectural treasure: medieval church spires dominate the Old Town, while early 20th-century Art Nouveau masterpieces line city's newer streets. For its 800th anniversary in 2001, Rīga renovated many of its signature sites, making it more vibrant than ever.

The phone code in Rīga is 2 for all 6-digit numbers; there is no phone code for 7-digit numbers. Dial ☎116 for a Latvian operator and 115 for an international operator. Still confused? Call ☎800 80 08 for info or 118, 722 22 22, or 777 07 77 for directory services.

■ INTERCITY TRANSPORTATION

Flights: Lidosta Rīga (Rīga Airport; ☎720 70 09), southwest of Vecrīga. The easiest way to get to Old Town is to take a bus (30min., about every 15min., 0.20Ls) from 13-jan-vara iela, at the far right side of the airport parking lot. Bus #22 goes to the south edge of Old Town, and #22a stops by the Orthodox Cathedral. A taxi to Vecrīga is 6Ls. **Air Baltic** (☎720 77 77; www.airbaltic.lv) flies to many European cities, not just Baltic capitals. **Finnair** (☎720 70 10; www.finnair.com) flies to **Helsinki, FIN. Lufthansa** (☎750 77 11; www.lufthansa.com) flies to **Frankfurt** and **Munich, GER.**

Trains: Centrālā Stacija (Central Station), Stacijas laukums (☎583 30 95), is next to the bus station south of the Old Town; head toward the clock tower. Long-distance trains depart from the larger of the 2 buildings. Most *perons* (platforms) have 2 *cels* (tracks). Open daily 4:30am-midnight. The info center at the train station charges 0.10Ls per question. To: **Moscow, RUS** (18hr., 1 per day, 25Ls); **St. Petersburg, RUS** (14hr., 1 per day, 22-33Ls); **Vilnius, LIT** (8hr., 2 per day on odd-numbered days, 9-11Ls). **Baltic Express** also goes to **Berlin, GER** and **Warsaw, POL.**

Buses: Autoosta (Bus Station), Prāgas 1 (☎900 00 09; www.autoosta.lv). From the train station, face Old Town and go left 100m. Across the canal from the central market. Calls 0.24Ls per min. Open daily 5am-midnight. To: **Kaliningrad, RUS** (9-10hr., 2 per day, 6Ls); **Kaunas, LIT** (5-6hr., 2 per day, 5.20Ls); **Klaipėda, LIT** (6hr., 1 per day, 5.20Ls); **Minsk, BLR** (12hr., 1 per day, 7Ls); **Tallinn, EST** (4-6hr., 8 per day, 7-8.50Ls); **Tartu, EST** (4hr., 1 per day, 7.50Ls); **Vilnius, LIT** (5hr., 4-6 per day, 4.50-6Ls). **Ecolines** (☎721 45 12; www.ecolines.lv) books buses to **Moscow** (12½hr., 2 per day) and **Prague, CZR** (25½hr.; 1 per week; 36Ls, students 24Ls). Book other international destinations through **Eurolines** (☎721 40 80; www.eurolines.lv).

⊞ ORIENTATION

The city is divided in half by **Brīvības iela**, which leads from the outskirts to the **Freedom Monument** in the center and continues through **Vecrīga** (Old Rīga) as **Kaļķu iela**. To reach Vecrīga from the **train station**, turn left on Marijas iela and right on one of the small streets beyond the canal, or just head toward the towering spires. **K. Valdemāra iela** cuts through Vecrīga roughly parallel to Brīvības; from the river, it passes the National Theater on the left and the Art Museum on its right. The semi-circular **Elizabetes iela** surrounds Vecrīga and its adjoining parks. The witty, info-packed *Rīga In Your Pocket* (1.20Ls), available at kiosks and travel agencies, has **maps** and up-to-date listings. The similar *Rīga This Week* is free at most major hotels and at the **Tourist Information Center (TIC)**.

⊟ LOCAL TRANSPORTATION

Trains: Suburban trains, running as far as the border with Estonia at **Valka/Valga**, leave from the smaller building of the train station. The Lugaži line includes **Cēsis** and **Sigulda**. Buy same-day tickets in the halls or advance tickets in the **booking office** (☎583 33 97) on the right. Purchase tickets on board for a 0.30Ls surcharge.

Public Transportation: Buses, trams, and **trolleybuses** run daily 5:30am-midnight. Buy tickets on board from the ticket collector (0.20Ls).

Taxis: Private taxis have a green light in the windshield. **Taxi Rīga** (☎800 10 10) charges 0.30Ls per km during the day, 0.40Ls per km midnight-6am.

⚡ PRACTICAL INFORMATION

TOURIST AND FINANCIAL SERVICES

Tourist Office: TIC, Ratslaukums 6 (☎703 79 00; www.rigatourism.com), next to the House of Blackheads and the Occupation Museum. Sells **maps,** hands out *Rīga This Week* and **free maps,** and gives helpful advice in English, German, Latvian, and Russian. Open daily summer 9am-7pm; low season 10am-6pm. **Branch,** Prāgas 1 (☎722 05 55), at the intercity bus station. Open M-F 9am-7pm, Sa-Su 10am-7pm. Most hotels and travel agencies sell the **Rīga Card,** which provides restaurant and museum discounts and free rides on trams and trolleys. However, unless you cram all of Rīga's museums into 1-2 days, the card is probably not worthwhile. (☎/fax 721 72 17. 1-day card 8Ls, 2-day 12Ls, 3-day 16Ls.)

Embassies and Consulates: Australia, Alberta iela 13 (☎733 63 83; acr@latnet.lv). Open Tu 10am-noon and Th 3-5pm. **Canada,** Baznicas 20/22. (☎781 39 45; riga@dfait-maeci.qc.ca). Open Tu and Th 10am-1pm. **Estonia,** Skolas iela 13 (☎781 20 20; www.estemb.lv). Open M-Tu and Th-F 10am-1pm. **Ireland,** Brīvības iela 54. (☎702 52 59; fax 702 52 60). Entrance on Blaumana. Open M-Tu and Th-F 10am-noon. In an emergency, citizens can call or stop by M-Tu and Th-F 10am-6pm. **Lithuania,** Rūpniecības iela 24 (☎732 15 19; fax 732 15 89). Open M-F 9:30am-12:30pm. **Russia,** Antonijas iela 2 (☎733 21 51; fax 783 02 09), entrance on Kalpaka bul. Open M-F 8:30am-5:30pm. **UK,** Alunāna iela 5 (☎777 47 00; www.britain.lv). Open M-F 9:30am-noon. **US,** Raiņa bul. 7 (☎703 62 00; www.usembassy.lv). Open M-Tu and Th 9-11:30am. US citizen services Tu-Th 2-4pm. In an emergency, citizens can stop by M and F 9-11:30am and 2-4pm or call an officer at ☎920 57 08.

Currency Exchange: At any kiosk labeled **"valutos maiņa."** **Unibanka,** Pils iela 23 and Valnu iela 11 (☎800 80 09; www.unibanka.lv), gives MC/V **cash advances** and cashes **AmEx and Thomas Cook Traveler's Checks** with no commission. Open M-F 9am-5pm. **Marika 24hr. currency exchange** desks are at Basteja bul. 14, Brīvības 30 and at almost all of Rīga's casinos. **Latvia Tours,** Kaļķu iela 8 (☎708 50 01; www.latviatours.lv), has an **AmEx representative.** Open M-F 9am-7pm.

LOCAL SERVICES AND COMMUNICATIONS

Luggage Storage: At the **bus station,** near Eurolines office. 0.20Ls per 10kg for 2hr. Open daily 6:30am-10:30pm. At the **airport,** left of the exit. Arrange drop-off or retrieval using the red phone. 0.60Lt per day. Open M-Tu, Th, Sa 4:30am-midnight; W, F, Su 5:30am-midnight.

English-Language Bookstore: Globuss, Vaļņuiela 26 (☎722 69 57). English-language classics and office supplies. Open M-Sa 8am-8pm, Su 8am-7pm. MC/V.

GLBT Organizations: Check out www.gay.lv.

Laundromat: Nivala, Akas iela 4 (☎728 13 46), between Ģertūdes iela and Lāčplēša iela. Self-service 3.40Ls per load. 1-day laundry service 4.90Ls. Open 24hr.

24hr. Pharmacy: Vecpilsetas Aptieka, Audeju 20 (☎721 33 40).

Telephones: Brīvības iela 19 (☎701 87 38). MC/V **ATM.** Open M-F 7am-11pm, Sa-Su 8am-10pm. 2nd location at the post office by the train station. Open 24hr.

Internet Access: Internet cafes dot the Old Town. The best is **Elik,** Kaļķu iela 11 (☎722 70 79; www.elikkafe.lv), in the center, which has 47 computers. 0.50Ls per hr., 1Ls per 3hr., 3Ls per half-day (8am-10pm), 4Ls per day. Full selection of drinks, beer, and snacks. Open 24hr. There's a **branch** at A. Čaka iela 26 (☎728 45 06).

Post Office: Stacijas laukums 1 (☎701 88 04; www.riga.post.lv), near the train station. **Poste Restante** at window #9. Open M-F 8am-8pm, Sa 8am-6pm, Su 8am-4pm. **Branches** at Brīvības 19 (☎701 87 38; open M-F 7am-10pm, Sa-Su 8am-10pm) and Aspazijas bul. 24 (☎701 88 56; open M-F 8am-8pm, Sa 8am-6pm, Su 8am-4pm). **Postal Code:** LV-1050.

▌ ACCOMMODATIONS

Lovers express their affection quite publicly along Rīga's streets in summertime. You can tell them to get a room, but they probably can't find one. Travelers should make reservations months in advance, especially in summer. For a homestay (20Ls) or an apartment (30-50Ls), try **Patricia,** Elizabetes iela 22. (☎728 48 68; tourism@parks.lv. Open M-F 9am-6pm, Sa-Su 11am-4pm.)

Radi un Draugi, Marstalu 1/3 (☎782 0200; www.draugi.lv). Head along Audeju toward the heart of Old Town. Unbeatable location and cozy rooms. Book reservations in advance. Breakfast included. Singles 35Ls; doubles 44Ls; triples 53Ls. MC/V. ❹

Krisjanis and Gertrude, K. Barona iela 39/1 (☎750 6603; kg@mail.teliamtc.lv). Press buzzer on Gertudes iela; staff will let you up to 3rd fl. reception. Charming B&B within walking distance of Old Town. Friendly, English-speaking staff. The economy single (20Ls) with private bath down the hall is a bargain. All other rooms have private bath attached. Singles 27-30Ls; doubles 35-40Ls; triples 45Ls. ❸

Viktorija, A. Čaka iela 55 (☎701 41 11; www.hotel-viktorija.lv). This 3-star hotel offers 1st-rate, renovated rooms with bathrooms and TVs. Breakfast included. Unrenovated (and unadvertised) economy rooms have TVs but shared bathrooms. Economy singles 12Ls, 3-star 30Ls; doubles 17Ls/40Ls. AmEx/MC/V. ❹

LU Dienesta Viesnicas, Basteja bul. 10 (☎721 62 21; bastejahotel@inbox.lv). From the bus station, cross under the railroad tracks and take the pedestrian tunnel. Bear right on Aspazijas bul., which becomes Basteja bul. Enter through the Europcar Internet office. Ask for one of the student rooms, which have shared baths but are larger, nicer, and cheaper than other rooms. Singles without bath 10Ls, with bath 20Ls, student room 8Ls; doubles 16Ls/30Ls/12Ls; triples with bath 45Ls. ❷

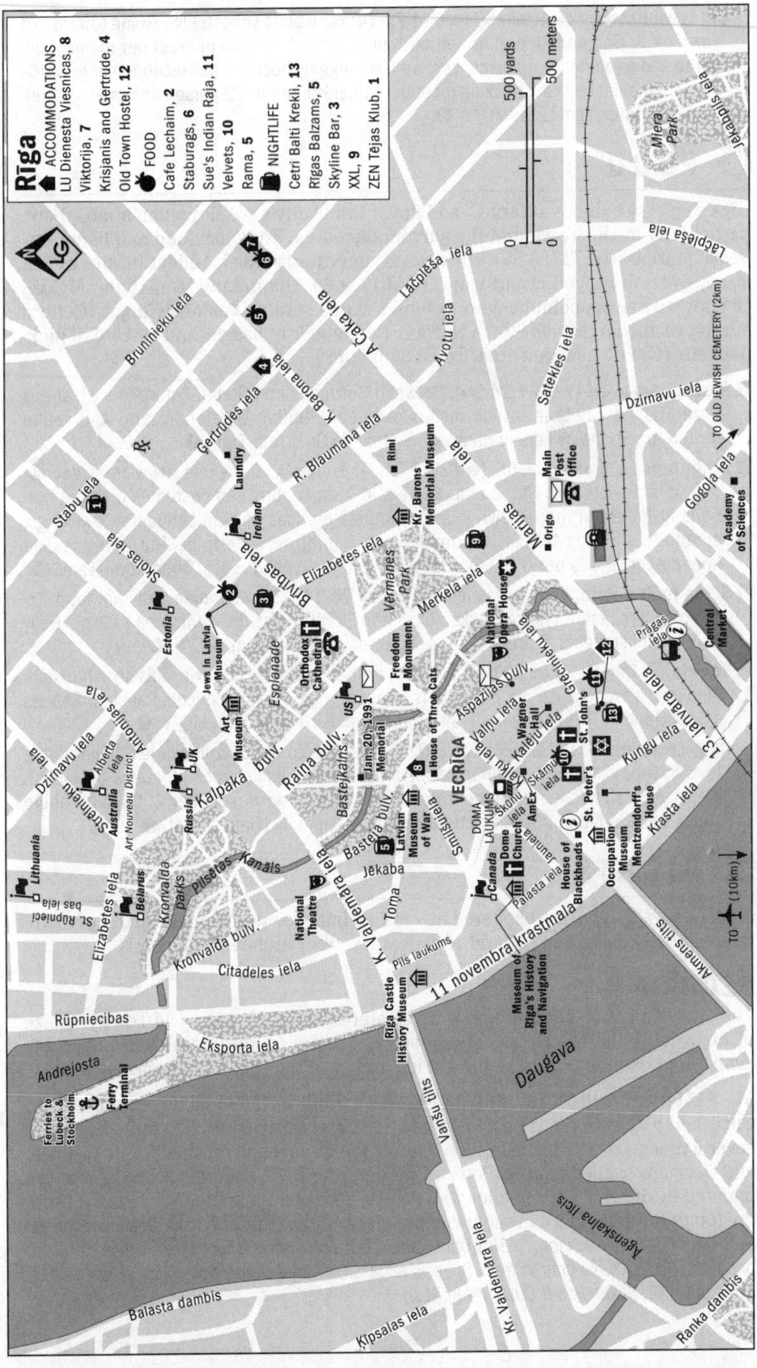

Rīga
ACCOMMODATIONS
LU Dienesta Viesnicas, 8
Viktorija, 7
Krisjanis and Gertrude, 4
Old Town Hostel, 12
FOOD
Cafe Lechaim, 2
Staburags, 6
Sue's Indian Raja, 11
Velvets, 10
Rama, 5
NIGHTLIFE
Cetri Balti Krekli, 13
Rīgas Balzams, 5
Skyline Bar, 3
XXL, 9
ZEN Tējas Klub, 1
500 yards
500 meters
Miera Park
Jēkabpils iela
Lāčplēša iela
Satekles iela
Dzirnavu iela
TO OLD JEWISH CEMETERY (2km)
Gogoļa iela
Academy of Sciences
Central Market
Prāgas iela
13. janvāra iela
Main Post Office
Origo
Marijas iela
Avotu iela
A. Čaka iela
K. Barona iela
R. Blaumaņa iela
Rimi
Kr. Barons Memorial Museum
Bruninieku iela
Ģertrūdes iela
Laundry
Stabu iela
Skolas iela
Ireland
Brīvības iela
Elizabetes iela
Vērmanes Park
Merķeļa iela
National Opera House
Estonia
Jews in Latvia Museum
Esplanade
Orthodox Cathedral
Freedom Monument
House of Three Cats
Aspazijas bulv.
Grēcinieku iela
St. John's
Wagner Hall
Valņu iela
Kaļķu iela
Kungu iela
Krasta iela
Mentzendorff's House
Occupation Museum
House of Blackheads
St. Peter's
Skārņu iela
AmEx
Šķūņu iela
Dome Church
DOMA LAUKUMS
VECRĪGA
Smilšu iela
Latvian Museum of War
Jan. 20, 1991 Memorial
Bastejkalns
Raiņa bulv.
US
Art Museum
Antonijas iela
Alberta iela
Dzirnavu iela
Strēlnieku iela
Australia
Art Nouveau District
Russia
UK
Kalpaka bulv.
Basteja bulv.
Pilsētas Kanāls
Kronvalda parks
Lithuania
Belarus
St. Rūpniecības iela
Elizabetes iela
National Theatre
Jēkaba
Torņa
Canada
Palasta iela
Jauniela
K. Valdemāra iela
Kronvalda bulv.
Citadeles iela
Pils laukums
Rīga Castle History Museum
11 novembra krastmala
Museum of Rīga's History and Navigation
TO (10km)
Akmens tilts
Rūpniecības
Eksporta iela
Andrejosta
Ferry Terminal
Ferries to Lubeck & Stockholm
Daugava
Vanšu tilts
Āgenskalna līcis
Kr. Valdemāra iela
Balasta dambis
Ķīpsalas iela
Ranka dambis

LATVIA

Old Town Hostel, Kaleju iela 50 (☎614 72 14; www.oldtownhostel.lv). Going toward Old Town on K. Barona/Adeju, turn left on Kaleju. With 4-12 backpackers per room, you'll get to know your fellow travelers very well. No luggage lockers; ask receptionist to watch your valuables. English-speaking reception. Check-in noon. 12-person dorms 9Ls, 8-person 10Ls, 4-person 12Ls. MC/V. ❷

◘ FOOD

Rīga's diverse culinary offerings add flavor to the city's cosmopolitan atmosphere, particularly in Old Town and the surrounding area. For 24hr. food and liquor, try **Nelda,** Marijas 5 (☎722 93 55). The central supermarket **Rimi,** Audēju 16, stocks just about everything you could want. (☎701 80 20. Open daily 8am-10pm. MC/V.) Occupying five zeppelin hangars behind the bus station, **Centrālais Tirgus** (Central Market) is the largest market in Europe. Remember to haggle, and beware of pickpockets. (Open Su-M 8am-4pm, Tu-Sa 8am-5pm.)

▨ **Rama,** Barona 56 (☎ 727 24 90). Between Gertrudes and Stabu. Eat well for 1L at this Hare Krishna cafeteria, which dishes out hearty Indian vegetarian fare. And you're invited to join the owners in meditation. Open M-Sa 11am-7pm. ❶

▨ **Staburags,** A. Čaka iela 55 (☎729 97 87). Follow A. Čaka iela away from Vecrīga until it intersects with Stabu iela. Servers in 19th-century serf costumes dish out portions fit for a tsar. Impressive interior features replicas of rural Lithuanian dwellings, complete with log tables, windmills, and miniature waterfalls. The unprocessed house beer (0.7Ls per 0.5L) is a favorite. Entrees 1.80-7.30Lt. Open noon-1am. ❷

▨ **Sue's Indian Raja,** Vecpilsetas iela 3 (☎721 26 14). Serves Indian and Thai food. Try the crowd-pleasing chicken tikka (5Ls) and don't forget the garlic *naan* (2Ls). Belly dancing most nights. Entrees 3-11Ls. Open daily noon-11pm. MC/V. ❹

Velvets, Skārņu iela 9 (☎721 50 75), just off Kaļķu iela in Old Town. This stylish restaurant serves French-inspired cuisine. Its beautiful outdoor terrace feels Parisian. Entrees 2-7Ls. Open M-Th 10am-2am, F-Sa 10am-4am, Su 11am-2am. MC/V. ❸

Cafe Lechaim, Skolas iela 6 (☎728 02 35), at the corner of Dzirnavu iela beneath the Jews in Latvia Museum. Popular among local Jews for its fish menu (entrees 0.65-3Ls). Rīga's only all-Kosher restaurant closed for renovation in summer 2004 but should spring back to life in 2005. Open Su-Th 10am-10pm, F 10am-sunset. ❷

◉ SIGHTS

Most of Rīga's sights are clustered in Vecrīga, but even the "modern" parts of town, which mostly date from the mid-19th century, offer architectural pearls.

VECRĪGA

The city's most famous landmarks are clustered in tiny Vecrīga (Old Town) a maze of crowded cobblestone streets mostly off-limits to automobiles. But Vecrīga hasn't kept capitalism out, as the golden arches at the eastern entrance attest.

ST. PETER'S CHURCH (SV. PĒTERA BAZNĪCA). Built in 1209 by Livs, who accepted Christianity, the church is best known for its 15th-century spire. The spire has fallen several times since its birth. In 1666 it fell to the ground and crushed locals to death, and Germans shelled it on St. Peter's Day, June 29, 1941. According to local lore, it's haunted by the ghost of a soldier who guarded the church in the 18th century. From the top of the spire you can see the entire city and the Gulf of Rīga. *(Open summer Tu-Su 10am-6pm; low season Tu-Su 10am-5pm. Staff sometimes shuts ticket office for lunch break 12:50-2:30pm. Church free. Spire is accessible via elevator. Spire 2Ls, students 1Ls. Exhibits 0.50Ls. Cameras 0.50Ls, video 3Ls.)*

RĪGA DOME CATHEDRAL. The Latvian Ministry of Culture closed this church, also known as St. Mary's Cathedral, in 2004, ruling that emergency action was necessary to preserve the large, early 13th-century structure. Tourists can still walk through the Cross-Vaulted Gallery of the Rīga Dome, an outdoor museum in the cathedral's courtyard. On display are a Salaspils stone head and a statue of Bishop Albert, the German missionary who founded Rīga in 1201. The original 1897 statue was moved to St. Petersburg during WWII and mysteriously disappeared. This 2001 replica commemorates Rīga's 800th anniversary. *(Gallery open May-Oct. 10am-5pm. English captions. 0.5Lt, students 0.2Lt.)*

HOUSE OF THE BLACKHEADS (MELNGALVJU NAMS). Originally erected in 1334, the building was purchased in 1687 by the Blackheads, a group of bachelor merchants. They adopted the quirky name to honor their patron saint, dark-skinned St. Maurice. Portraits and statues of him can be found inside. The intricate cream-pink second-floor assembly hall, open to the public, is also used for official state functions. The building was severely damaged during WWII and demolished by the Soviets in 1948, but was rebuilt for Rīga's 800th birthday. The basement houses a museum. *(Rātslaukums 7, in the town square by the Occupation Museum. ☎ 704 43 00; melngalv@rcc.lv. Open Tu-Su 10am-5pm. Tours in English, French, German, or Russian 5Ls. House and museum 1Ls, students and children 0.50Ls. Cameras 1Ls.)*

LATVIAN RIFLEMEN MONUMENT (LATVIEŠU STRĒLNIEKU LAUKUMS). A reminder of Latvia's Soviet past, this granite statue is a Socialist Realist work depicting three soldiers guarding the square. The monument honors the team that served as Lenin's bodyguards during and after the Revolution.

RĪGA CASTLE. In 1487, locals destroyed the castle on the banks of the Daugava when rebelling against their rulers, the Livonian Knights. The Livonians forced city-dwellers to rebuild the structure in 1515. It has been expanded since then and served as the presidential residence of Karlis Ulmanis during the country's brief period of independence between the world wars. Inside the castle is the **History Museum of Latvia.** The museum is incomprehensible to those who can't read Latvian. *(Pils laukums 3, off Valdemāra iela. ☎ 722 30 04. Open W-Su 11am-5pm. English, German, and Russian tours 5Ls. Museum 0.70Ls, students 0.40Ls.)*

POWDER TOWER. The German fraternity Rubonia once held its wild and crazy parties inside this 14th-century fortress, which has nine cannonballs still

THE LOCAL STORY

BEARING IT ALL

Before the late 19th century, two versions of the Lacplesis the Bearslayer legend circulated through the Latvian countryside. According to one story, the hero was the offspring of a dubiously amorous relationship between a man and a she-bear. Another version claimed that after Lacplesis's human parents abandoned him, he was reared by a genial bear. Whatever the truth, Lacplesis acquired extraordinary physical strength and two furry ears.

When Lacplesis confronted the monstrous, three-headed Black Knight in fierce combat, the knight cut off one of Lacplesis's ears. Neither fighter, however, got the last laugh—both combatants drowned in the Daugava River.

In 1888, Latvian writer Andrejs Pumpurs published an enormously popular epic recounting Lacplesis's valor, thereby changing the legend forever. The bard portrayed Lacplesis as a historically accurate figure who fought valiantly against the Teutonic Knights. Decades later, as Latvia struggled for independence from Russia, Lacplesis served as a compelling inspiration. Today numerous monuments document the bear-warrior's importance in Latvian history and lore. Yet the monuments, which can be found both at the Freedom Monument and in Majori's central square render the hero with a covered head, all in an effort to keep the legend historically accurate while paying homage to the lore.

lodged in its walls (curiously enough on the side facing the city). No toga parties take place here anymore: the tower now houses **Latvian Museum of War** (Latvijas Kara Muzejs). A long, belligerent history is jammed into four floors. Two sections are particularly captivating: the second floor displays Latvia's post-WWI effort to win independence from Russian and Baltic German armies, and the fourth-floor exhibit details the fall of communism. These are also the only two sections with English captions. *(Smilšu iela 20. ☎ 722 81 47. Open May-Sept. W-Su 10am-6pm; Oct.-Apr. W-Su 10am-5pm. Tours in English 3Ls. Museum 0.50Ls, students 0.25Ls. Cameras 2Ls.)*

NEW RĪGA

FREEDOM MONUMENT (BRĪVĪBAS PIEMINEKLIS). Recently renovated, this beloved monument depicts Liberty raising her arms skyward as three gold stars appear to levitate above her fingertips. Dedicated in 1935, during Latvia's brief period of independence, the monument—affectionately known as Milda—survived the subsequent Russian occupation by masquerading as a Soviet symbol. Mighty Milda raises up the three main regions of Latvia (Kurzeme, Latgale, and Vidzeme), but the Soviets claimed it represented Mother Russia supporting the three Baltic states. Two steadfast guards protect her honor daily 9am-6pm; the changing of the guard occurs on the hour. *(At the corner of Raiņa bul. and Brīvības iela.)*

BASTEJKALNS. Rīga's central park, surrounded by the old city moat (Pilsētas kanāls), houses ruins of the old city walls. Five red stone slabs around the canal stand as memorials of January 20, 1991, when Soviet special forces stormed the Interior Ministry on Raiņa bul. At the north end of Bastejkalns, on K. Valdemāra iela, is the **National Theater.** It was here that Latvia first declared independence on November 18, 1918. *(Kronvalda bul. 2. ☎ 732 27 59. Open daily 10am-7pm.)*

ESPLANADE. The park east of Bastejkals is home to Rīga's Byzantine **Orthodox Cathedral** (Pareizticigo Katedrāle), built between 1876 and 1884. Soviets closed the church in 1961 and revamped it as a "house of atheism," containing a cafe, lecture hall, library, and planetarium. Restoration is underway. *(Brīvības iela 23. ☎ 721 29 01. Services M-F 8am and 5pm; Sa-Su 7, 10am, 5pm. Open daily 7am-6pm. Donation requested.)*

ART NOUVEAU (JUGENDSTIL). The newer areas of Rīga showcase fantastic examples of Art Nouveau architecture. Figure-entwined buildings dot the city, with the largest grouping on Alberta iela. Works by the renowned architect **Mikhail Eisenstein,** father of Russian filmmaker Sergei Eisenstein, are at #2, 2a, 4, 6, 8, and 13. Others are at Elizabetes iela 10b and Strēlnieku iela 4a. Particularly spectacular are the gorgeous cream-colored building at Alberta iela 13 and the 1905 blue-and-white Stockholm School of Economics at Strēlnieku iela 4a.

JEWISH RĪGA

Jews were barred from Rīga until the 18th century. By 1935, the more than 40,000 Jews who lived in the city comprised about 10% of Rīga's total population. About 150 Jews remained at the end of WWII. Many returned during Soviet times, but thousands left after the fall of communism. Today, 10,000-15,000 Jews reside here.

JEWS IN LATVIA MUSEUM. Funded largely by non-Jewish German philanthropists, this museum contains photos and biographical information on the Rīga's most famous Jewish residents. Exhibits also tell the story of local Christians who sheltered Jews from Nazi persecution. *(Skolas 6, 3rd fl., at the intersection with Dzimavu. ☎ 728 34 84; ebreji.latvija@apollo.lv. Open Su-Th noon-5pm.)*

OLD JEWISH CEMETERY. Before the graveyard was established in 1725, local Jews had to cart their dead all the way to Poland for burial. Much of the cemetery was destroyed by Nazi soldiers and Latvian Nazi-sympathizers on July 4, 1941. The Nazis later it as a mass grave for the ghetto. The Soviets converted the site into a public **park**. A **monument** was erected here after the fall of communism. Most of the Hebrew inscriptions on the graves have worn away. *(2/4 Liksnas iela.)*

BIĶERNIEKI FOREST. Erected in 2001 by the German War Graves Commission, this beautiful, powerful memorial commemorates the Jews who were murdered here between 1941 and 1944. A central altar is inscribed with Job's words, "O earth, do not cover my blood, and let there be no resting place for my cry." Around the altar, rocks jut out of the ground, representing the cities from which Jews were taken. *(Take tram #14 from Brīvības to "Keguma"; do not get off at "Bikernicku." Walk straight 1km, and you will see a white gate leading to the memorial. The memorial extends into the woods on the left side of the road, 600m closer to the tram stop.)*

🏛 MUSEUMS

▌OCCUPATION MUSEUM (OKUPĀCIJAS MUZEJS). This compelling museum guides visitors through Latvia's tortured history, under the Soviets, then the Nazis, and then the Soviets again. It takes at least an hour to make your way through the gripping displays. The exhibits include a recreation of gulag barracks and movies and photographs about the terror of the Checka and KGB. The museum offers a sobering account of Latvian Nazi sympathizers' role in the slaughter of the country's Jewish population. *(Strēlnieku laukums 1, in the black building behind the Latvian Riflemen Monument. ☎721 27 15; www.occupationmuseum.lv. Open daily May-Sept. 11am-6pm; Oct.-Apr. Tu-Su 11am-5pm. Free; donations welcome.)*

MUSEUM OF BARRICADES OF 1991. Old Rīga morphed into a medieval fortress in January 1991, when locals built makeshift walls to defend the city center from Soviet special forces. Yet that didn't stop Red Army special forces from firing on protesters. A 40min. English-language video at this tiny three-room exhibit includes jarring footage taken by a Latvian TV crew during the gunfight. *(Follow Jauniela from Doma laukums; knock on door #1 on the 2nd fl. ☎721 35 25; www.barikades.ru. Open M-F 10am-5pm, Sa 11am-5pm. Free.)*

STATE MUSEUM OF ART (VALSTS MĀKSLAS MUZEJS). The building, which opened in 1905, is as interesting as the art within it. The museum showcases 18th- to 20th-century works by Latvian artists and a large collection of Russian art. Don't miss Nicholas Roerich's Himalayan landscapes on the first floor. The early 20th-century painter was fascinated by the Orient because he believed that Slavic civilization had originated in the Far East. *(Valdemāra iela 10a, near the Elizabetes iela intersection. ☎732 32 04; www.vmm.lv. Open Apr.-Oct. M, W, F-Su 11am-5pm, Th 11am-7pm; Oct.-Apr. M and W-Su 11am-5pm. English audio-guides 1L. Museum 0.50Ls, students 0.40Ls.)*

MUSEUM OF RĪGA'S HISTORY AND NAVIGATION. A dazzling collection of 500,000 items fills this history museum (Rīgas Vēstures un Kugnie-cības Muzejs), established in 1773. The museum helped preserve Latvian culture when the country was a part of the USSR and the Soviets attempted to repress national identity. Don't miss the giant statue of Latvia's patron saint, St. Christopher, on the top floor. *(Palasta iela 4, next to Dome Cathedral. ☎721 13 58; http://vip.latnet.lv/museums/riga. Open May-Sept. W-Su 10am-5pm; Oct.-Apr. 11am-5pm. English, German, and Russian tours 3Ls; students 2Ls. Museum 1.20Ls/0.40Ls.)*

OPEN-AIR ETHNOGRAPHIC MUSEUM (ETNOGRĀFISKAIS BRĪVDABAS MUZEJS).
Nearly 100 18th- and 19th-century buildings from all over Latvia are gathered
here, complete with artisans churning out traditional wares from wooden spoons
to pottery. *(Brīvības 440. Bus #1 from Merķela iela to "Brīvdabas Muzejs."* ☎ *799 41 06. Open
daily May-Oct. 10am-5pm. Tours 8Ls, students 5Ls. Call ahead. Museum 1Ls/0.25Ls.)*

RĪGA MOTOR MUSEUM (RĪGAS MOTORMUZEJS). A wax figure of Stalin sits in
the seat of his armored ZIS-1155 at this bizarre museum, which boasts a collection of the despots' automobiles. Particularly noteworthy is the 1966 Rolls Royce
Silver Shadow that Brezhnev crashed in 1980; see the bureaucrat gasp after dent-
ing his wheels. A treat for car-lovers and Soviet-philes. *(6 S. Eizensteina iela. Take
tram #14 from Brivibas iela to Gailezers Hospital. Cross the street and follow Gailezera iela
over the river 400m. Go right at the T-intersection.* ☎ *709 71 70. Some English captions. 1L,
students 0.50Ls.)*

🎭🌿 ENTERTAINMENT AND FESTIVALS

Rīga offers the best array of music and performance art in the Baltics. Theaters
close from mid-June through August, but the **Opera House** hosts summer events.
The **Latvian National Opera** (☎ 707 705; www.opera.lv) performs in the Opera House,
Aspazijas bul. 3. Richard Wagner once presided as director. The **Latvian Symphony
Orchestra** (☎ 722 48 50) has frequent concerts in the Great and Small Guilds off Filharmonija laukums. Smaller ensembles perform throughout the summer in **Wagner
Hall** (Vāgnera zāle), Vāgnera iela 4 (☎ 721 08 17). The topnotch **Rīga Ballet** carries
on the dance tradition of native star Mikhail Baryshnikov. The **ticket offices**, Teātra
10/12 (☎ 722 57 47; open daily 10am-7pm), and Amatu iela 6 (☎ 721 37 98), on the
first floor of the Great Guild, serve most local concerts. In 2005, check out the **10th
Annual International Ballet Festival** in late April.

🌙 NIGHTLIFE

Nightlife is centered on **Vecrīga**, where 24hr. casinos and *diskotekas* are multiplying. For a mellower evening, join Rīgans in their beer gardens.

🍸 **Skyline Bar**, Elizabetes iela 55, 26th fl. (☎ 777 22 22), in Reval Hotel Latvija. Arrive by
    8pm for a coveted "Vecrīga seat" with a view of the Old Town. Lively atmosphere and a
    well-stocked bar. Guinness and other foreign beers on tap (1-2.50Ls). Mixed drinks 3-
    4.50Ls. Snacks 2-6Ls. Open Su-Th 3pm-2am, F-Sa 3pm-3am. MC/V.

Cetri Balti Krekli (Four White Shirts), Vecpilsētas iela 12 (☎ 721 38 85; www. krekli.lv),
    off Kaleju. Hidden from the Old Town's crowds, this is the current "it" place. Latvians
    come well-dressed and ready to party. Live music F-Sa. No sneakers. Cover Tu-Th 1-2Ls,
    F-Sa 3-4Ls. Open Su-Th noon-2am, F-Sa noon-late. MC/V.

Rīgas Balzams, Torņa iela 4 (☎ 721 44 94), in Old Town, 100m east of the Powder
    Tower. For a truly Latvian experience, try the national liquor *(balsam)* with honey and
    egg yolk (2.30Ls). Don't go shot-for-shot with the locals at this hopping bar unless you
    are prepared to lose. Open Su-Th 11am-midnight, F-Sa 11am-1am. MC/V.

ZEN Tējas Klub, Stabu iela 6 (☎ 731 65 21; www.zen.lv). Follow Brivibas east from Old
    Town. Turn left on Stabu and go 1½ blocks down. Slip off your shoes to enjoy the privi-
    lege of sipping ZEN's black tea (1.20Lt), which promises to elongate your life and shield
    against cancer. In contrast to eardrum-piercing discos, this teahouse is the place to
    relax. Flavored waterpipes 5-8Ls. Open daily 2pm-2am. MC/V.

XXL, A. Kalniņa iela 4 (☎728 22 76; www.xxl.lv), off K. Barona iela. Buzz to be let in. A peculiar name for a gay club with a svelte clientele. Well-stocked bar and extensive lineup of red-hot events, including go-go dancing and live jazz. Male striptease Th and Su (men only). Stop by for a schedule. Th and Su (cover women 10Ls). Cover Tu-Su 1-5Ls, for women Th and Su 10Ls. Open daily 6pm-6am.

▶ DAYTRIPS FROM RĪGA

▩ RUNDĀLE PALACE

The palace is 10km west of Bauska. From Rīga, take the bus (1hr., about every 30min., 1.25Ls) to Bauska. From there, take a bus (15min., 7-9 per day, 0.20Ls) or taxi (3Ls) to Rundāles. Buses are infrequent; ask the palace staff for schedules. ☎621 97; *www.rpm.apollo.lv. Gardens, palace, and exhibit open daily May-Oct. 10am-6pm; Nov.-Apr. 10am-5pm. 1.50Ls, students 1L. Other exhibits 0.1-0.5Ls. Cameras 1L.*

The Rundāle Palace long served as a countryside retreat for local nobility. A Russian empress, Anna Ioanova, built the palace as a gift to one of her advisers, Ernst Johann von Bühren, a Baltic German noble. The palace was designed by Italian architect Bartolomeo Rastrelli, who also designed St. Petersburg's Winter Palace, and required the work of 15,000 laborers and artisans. Construction began in 1730 but stalled after Anna's death in 1740. It was finished under Catherine the Great in 1767. Accordingly, images of Catherine's life adorn the majestic interior; you can trace her growth—in power and in girth. Among the palace's 138 gilded rooms is the **Gold Room** (Selta Zāle), which contains the throne, murals, and soldiers' graffiti from 1812. The upstairs exhibit describes the palace's 1971-2002 restoration.

SALASPILS MEMORIAL

Electric trains run to Dārziņi (20min., 14 per day, 0.22Ls). Make sure the train stops at Dārziņi before leaving Rīga. Do not take the train to "Salaspils." Last train back to Rīga departs around 10pm. In the woods behind the Dārziņi station, you'll find a paved pathway. Turn right and continue 1km. Take a left after the soccer field.

The Salaspils Memorial marks the remains of the Kurtenhof concentration camp, where an estimated 100,000 people were killed by the Nazis. As is the case at other Soviet-era Holocaust memorials, Communist officials omitted any references to religion and referred to the dead obliquely as "victims of the Fascist terror." A huge concrete wall marks where the camp entrance once stood. The inscription over the entrance reads, "Here the innocent walked the way of death. How many unfinished words, how many unlived years were cut short by a bullet." Four sculptures—Motherhood, Solidarity, The Humiliated, and The Unbroken—watch over the Way of the Suffering, the circular path connecting barrack foundations.

JŪRMALA   ☎(8)77

According to legend, a shipwrecked soldier was bitten by a snake. But after he drank from an odd-smelling stream of water, he was revitalized, and later he spread the word about the region's mystical healing powers. Jūrmala (YOUR-mala; pop. 60,000), a resort region composed of 14 small towns, still draws Latvians to its many sanitaria, but its main attraction is the stunning 32km sandy beach.

▐▶ TRANSPORTATION AND PRACTICAL INFORMATION. A commuter rail (30min.; every 30min; 5am-11:30pm; 0.50Ls, 0.30Ls more if purchased on the train) runs from **Rīga.** Ride the Tukums-bound line to **Majori station** (☎583 03 15). **Public**

LATVIA

buses (0.18Ls), **microbuses** (0.20-0.30Ls), and **commuter trains** connect Jurmala's towns. Rent a **bicycle** along the beach (1.50Ls per hr.) or at Juras iela 24. (☎911 90 91. 6Ls per day. Open 10am-7pm.)

From the train station in **Majori,** follow the pedestrian boulevard Jomas iela east 100m to reach the **Tourism Information Center,** Jomas iela 42 (☎642 76; www.jurmala.lv). The English-speaking staff distributes **free maps** and brochures and sells guides. *Rīga In Your Pocket* (1.20Ls) includes a map of Jurmala. The free *Jurmala Visitor's Guide* offers more extensive regional info. The town immediately to the west of Majori is **Dubulti,** where there is a post office at 16 Strelnieku pr. (☎776 24 30. Open M-F 8am-5pm, Sa 8am-4pm.) To the east of Majori lies **Dzintari.** You can get there by following Jomas iela past the TIC and continuing for 1km. Along the way, you'll pass a **pharmacy, Majori Aptieka,** Jomas 41 (☎776 44 13; open daily 9am-8pm) and an **Internet** cafe, **Digitorklubs,** Jomas 62 (☎781 1411; open daily 10am-9pm). MC/V **ATMs** abound on Jomas iela. There is one outside Hansabanka, Jomas 37 (☎781 1482). For the **24hr. currency exchange** at the eastern end of Jomas, head toward Turaidas 1. Free coffee with transaction of more than 50Ls.

⌐⌐ ACCOMMODATIONS AND FOOD. The **TIC** books reservations at local hotels and hostels from 6Ls per night. There's no service charge, and TIC can usually provide better rates. **Hotel Majori ❺,** Jomas iela 29, across from the train station. The rooms aren't huge, but they all come with private bath and shower, TV and fridge, and breakfast in its restaurant or in your room. The staff is friendly and speaks English. (☎776 13 80; www.majori.lv. Singles 33L; doubles 48L. MC/V.) **Elina ❸,** Lienes 43, has bright, clean doubles (25Ls) with private baths above a pleasant cafe. Heading east on Jomas, turn right on J. Prieskana iela; it's 200m down on the right. (☎776 16 65; www.elinahotel.lv. Cash only). From the Dzintara rail station, walk 30m with tracks to your left to reach **Dzintars ❷,** Edinburgas iela 15. It's on a noisy street but has good prices and friendly, English-speaking staff. (☎775 15 82; orthos@apollo.net. Doubles 13Ls, with bath 17Ls.)

Cafes line Jomas iela, particularly in summertime, when practically every inch of open space in town becomes a beer garden. For spectacular seafood just steps away from the shore, head to **▨Jurus Zakis ❸,** Vienibas 1 (☎775 3005), in Bulduri. Follow Dzintari eastward from Jomas. After 2km, Dzintari becomes Bulduru. Continue 1km to Vienibas and turn left. (Entrees 2.40-4Ls. Open daily noon-11pm. MC/V.) **Sue's Asia ❹,** Jomas 74 (☎775 59 00), has Indian, Thai, and Chinese cuisine. (Entrees 3-10Ls. Open M-Th noon-11pm, F-Su noon-midnight. MC/V.) After a hearty Russian meal at **Slavu ❹,** Jomas 57 (☎776 14 01), head upstairs to the dance club, which has live DJs on some weekend evenings. (Entrees 4-12Ls. Restaurant open daily 11am-2am; nightclub 9pm-6am. MC/V.)

◙ SIGHTS. Jūrmala's main attraction is its beach. Powder-fine sand, warm waters, and festive boardwalks have drawn crowds since the late 19th century. A **statue of Lacplesis the Bear Slayer** (see sidebar, p. 431) across from the Majori train station. **Janis Pliekshans** (1865-1929), known by the pen name **Rainis,** was exiled by the tsar for participating in the 1905 Russian Revolution. The poet and playwright returned to Majori after Latvia gained independence. From 1927 to 1929 he lived in the two-story cottage at J. Plieksana iela 5-7, which now hosts the **Rainis and Aspazija Memorial Summer House** (☎776 4295). From the TIC, follow Jomas east 400m and turn left. (Open W-Su 10am-6pm; closed last F of each month. 0.5Ls, students 0.3Ls. Tour 0.2Ls.) Rainis's wife, Elza Rozenberg (1865-1943), who adopted the name **Aspazija,** was a significant writer herself. After her husband's death, she lived at Meierovica prospekts 20 in Dubulti, now the **Aspazija House** (☎776 9445), which includes a public library. The house is 1km west of the TIC. Follow Jomas away from Majori until it merges into Meierovica. (Open M 2-7pm, Tu-Th and Sa 11am-5pm. 0.3Ls, students 0.1Ls; Th free.)

Take a left on Turaidas and head toward the beach to reach the **Dzintari Concert Hall,** Turaidas 1. (☎776 2086. Tickets 776 2005.) US and Soviet diplomats met here in 1986 for negotiations over the USSR's occupation of Latvia. The open-air stage hosts a stream of summertime performances, including **chamber music concerts** and an international youth **singing contest** in July. Posters across town advertise the monthly line-up of cultural events, which take place daily in high season.

INLAND LATVIA

Latvia's longest river flows past the medieval castles of Cēsis and Sigulda. The lush Gauja Valley offers a wealth of opportunities for outdoor activities.

SIGULDA   ☎ (8)29

Situated in the Gaujas Valley National Park, Sigulda couldn't feel more removed from hectic Rīga. The Knights of the Sword, the Germanic crusaders who Christianized much of Latvia in the 13th century, staked their base here. This picturesque town is still home to dramatic castle ruins and hiking and biking trails.

🖅🛈 TRANSPORTATION AND PRACTICAL INFORMATION. Trains from **Rīga** run on the Rīga-Lugaži commuter rail line (1hr., 9 per day, 0.71Ls). **Buses** from **Rīga** (2hr., 6-8 per day, 0.80Ls) go the **bus station,** Raiņa iela 3. (☎721 06. Open daily 6am-8pm. Ticket office open M-Sa 8am-1:30pm and 2-5:30pm.) Buses to Cēsis may stop on the south edge of Sigulda along Highway A2; backtrack toward Rīga and turn right on Gātes to reach the center. To explore Sigulda, rent a **bike** at **Tridens,** Cēsu iela 15. Follow Raina from the bus station and turn left just before the tourist center onto Cēsu. (☎964 48 00. 1Ls per hr., 5Ls per day. Open daily 10am-8pm.)

From the **bus** and **train stations,** Raiņa iela runs 1km north to the **Gauja National Park Visitor Centre,** Baznicas 3, which has knowledgeable, English-speaking staff and **free maps** of Sigulda. (☎797 13 45; www.gnp.gov.lv. Open M 9am-5:30pm, Tu-Su 9am-7pm.) They also sell essential maps of the park (1.20Ls). Follow Raina as it turns into Gauja iela, crosses the river, curves right and becomes Turaidas iela (P8). The **Turaidas Museum Reserve,** 3km after the bridge, is reached by bus #12 (1 per hr., 0.20Ls) from the station. A **cable car** (5min.; 2 per hr. 7:25am-6:25pm; 1Ls, children 0.75Ls) runs from the Sigulda side of Gaujas to Krimulda Castle. **Exchange money,** cash Thomas Cook or AmEx **traveler's checks,** and get **Western Union** services at **Latvijas Krajbanka,** Pils iela 1. (Open M-F 9am-5pm, Sa 9am-1pm.) Next door is a **pharmacy, Centra Aptieka,** Pils iela 3. (☎797 09 10. Open M-F 7:30am-9:30pm, Sa 9am-8pm, Su 9am-6pm. MC/V.) For **Internet access,** open the door in the pharmacy marked "If..." and go to the second floor. (Open daily 10am-10pm.) Across the street is the **post office,** Pils iela 2. (☎797 21 77. Open M 8am-6pm, Tu-F 8am-5pm, Sa 8am-2pm.) **Telephones** are outside. **Postal Code:** LV-2150.

🖅🛈 ACCOMMODATIONS AND FOOD. The GNP Visitors Centre helps locate campsites and private rooms; if you're looking for the latter, they'll most likely send you to **🏠Viesu Nams Livonija ❶,** P. Brieža iela 55. Only 200m from the bus and train stations, it offers pleasant rooms with private baths (singles 14Ls; doubles 16-20Ls) and spacious shared-bath singles (7Ls). Cross the train tracks along the paved pathway in front of the stoplight and head straight; hang a left on Brieza.

(☎797 30 66; hotel.livonija@lis.lv. Kitchen, common room, and sauna. Breakfast 1Ls.) **Hotel Sigulda ❺**, Pils iela 6, in the center of town near the bus station, was recently renovated. (☎722 63; www.hotelsigulda.lv. Breakfast included. Pool and sauna 2Ls per hr. Singles 24Ls; doubles 30Ls, lux 36-46Ls. Reserve ahead. MC/V.)

🗾Pilsmuižas Restorāns ❹, Pils iela 16, generous portions of Latvian food. Try the pork chop with red bilberry jam (5.04Ls). The restaurant is in the 19th-century Pilseta Dome. (☎797 14 25. Entrees 3-12Ls. 10% service charge. Open daily noon-2am. MC/V.) **Trīs Draugi ❶** (Three Friends), Pils iela 9, is a Soviet-style cafeteria but the staff is friendly and the deep-fried fare is tasty. (☎797 37 21. Entrees under 1L. Open daily 8am-10pm. MC/V.) It shares space with a **bar** that has Latvian beers on tap. (Beer 0.60Ls per 0.5L. Open daily 11am-2am.) **T-Market**, a large grocery store, is nearby at Paegles iela 3. (☎797 14 63. Open M-Sa 8am-10pm, Su 9am-8pm. MC/V.)

◎ 🎭 SIGHTS AND ENTERTAINMENT. From Sigulda, cross the river and follow **Turaidas** 1.5km until you reach the turn-off for **Gutman's Cave** (Gūtmaņa Ala), inscribed with coats of arms and scribblings dating from the 16th century. Farther down the path is **Turaida Castle** (Turaidas Pils). Inside, a **museum** chronicles the saga of Kaupo, chieftain of the Livs, a pagan group that maintained a castle here in the late 12th century. Kaupo converted to Christianity in 1203 and plundered his tribe's fortress. (Tower open daily 9am-8pm; museum open May-Oct. 10am-6pm; Nov.-Apr. 10am-5pm. Info in English, German, and Russian. Admission with the ticket you bought at the reserve entrance.) Kaupo went on to build the **Krimulda Evangelical Lutheran Church** in 1205; follow the signs from the museum reserve 7km down P7. The church will celebrate its 800th anniversary with concerts and theatrical performances July 24-31, 2005. (Doors usually open. Services F 5 and 9pm, Sa 6pm, Su 2pm). Left of Victora ala, climb 366 steps to the scant ruins of 13th-century **Krimulda Castle** (Krimuldas Pilsdrupas), also accessible by cable car. On the Sigulda side of the river, on a ridge behind GNP headquarters is the 19th-century **Pilsetas Dome** (Castle Dome), the "new" castle-palace where the Russian Prince Kropotkin once lived. The immense ruins of the once glorious **Siguldas Castle** (Siguldas Pilsdrupas) are behind the palace. Constructed between 1207 and 1226, the castle was destroyed in the Great Northern War (1700-1721) between Russia and Sweden. The castle forms the backdrop for the **Opera Festival** (☎727 79 00; www.lmuza.lv/sigulda) in late July.

🎿 OUTDOOR ACTIVITIES. The **Ligatne Nature Trail** (Ligatne dabas takas; 41km round-trip from Sigulda) takes visitors on a 5.5km loop past captive **bears, elk, deer,** and **hares.** To get to the trailhead, follow Auskeja/Darza iela east from the town and turn right toward Vildoga (9km) at the fork. At the Vildoga bus stop, veer left and, after another 5km, hang a left on the main road. Turn left 3km down, at the cafe. After another 2km, take another left at the signs for the trail. A **branch** of the **GNP Information Center** at the site will give you a **free map** of the trail. (Open M 9am-5:30pm, Tu-Su 9am-7pm. Entrance to the trail is 1Ls; students 0.5Ls.)

An Olympic-sized **bobsled run** plummets from Sveices iela 13. You can take the plunge year-round; in summer, you'll be on wheels. (☎739 44; fax 790 16 67. 3Ls. Open Sa-Su 10am-8pm.) To go **bungee jumping,** go up to the cable car, sign a release, and battle gravity. (☎725 31; fax 722 53. 15Ls for the first jump, 13Ls thereafter. Open Sa-Su 6:30pm-last customer.) Watching jumpers from the bridge is a popular activity on weekend evenings. The **International Ballooning Festival** floats out of town in late May. Go left off Gaujas iela before you cross the river to reach **Makars Tourism Agency**, Peldu 1, which rents **tents** (2-4Ls per day) and arranges **canoe** and **rafting trips** starting at 4Ls for 1hr. (☎924 49 48; www.makars.lv.)

CĒSIS   ☎(8)41

Quiet Cēsis (TSEH-siss; pop. 17,500) is famous for sprawling medieval ruins and its local brew, Cēsu. The country's second-oldest city (after Rīga), it recently restored its landmark castle for its 800th anniversary in 2006. Crusading Germans arrived in 1209 over the next three decades built the famous ◪Cēsis Castle, which hasn't fared so well over time. When Russia's **Ivan the Terrible** laid siege in 1577, its defenders chose to fill the cellars with gunpowder and blow themselves up rather than surrender. The castle was later rebuilt, but in 1703, an attack by **Peter the Great** left it in tatters. Follow Rīgas iela south from the town 5km; merge onto P20 and go left after 1km. A Baltic German nobleman constructed a **new wing** as his personal estate in the late 18th century; it now houses a **history museum.** Museum admission includes access to the new castle's **tower,** with its views of the Gauja Valley, and the old castle's recently reopened **ruins.** Put on a helmet, grab a candle, and climb the narrow medieval staircases. (☎412 26 15. No English captions. Open May 15-Sept. Tu-Su 10am-5pm; Nov.-May 14 W-Su 10am-5pm. English, German, or Russian tours 10Ls.) Ivan also destroyed the nearby **Araisi Castle,** but those ruins haven't been thoroughly restored. The castle, on the near shore of Lake Araisi, is part of the **Open-Air Archaeological Museum.** Steps away from the Araisi castle is a reconstruction of a **Latgale settlement** that stood on the site from the 9th to 12th centuries. The Latgales were a short tribe, so watch your head as you enter the huts. To the right is a small **stone age reed dwelling,** modeled after what archaeologists believe once stood here. (☎419 7288. English captions. Open daily Apr. 15-Dec. 10am-6pm. 0.80Ls, students 0.40Ls.)

Cēsis is reached by infrequent **trains** from **Rīga** via **Sigulda** (1½-2hr.; 2 per day; about 1Ls, 0.21Ls extra with a bike). **Buses** from **Rīga** (2hr., 6am-9pm 1-2 per hr., 1.30Ls) are more convenient. Call ahead if you want to reserve a **bike** (5Ls per day) at **Cēsu Tourism Inventory,** Lencu iela 6 (☎942 32 70). It is a 2-3hr. ride to Sigulda each way. **Public transportation** consists of two **buses** (0.20Ls): bus #9 runs west to the Gauja River while bus #11 runs east along **Jana Poruka iela** and down **Lapsu iela. Raunas iela** heads to the town center from the station and opens onto the main square, **Vienības laukums. Rīgas iela** and **Valnu iela** go downhill at the square's south end and meet at **Līvu laukums,** the original 13th-century heart of the town. **Lenču iela,** which leads from Vienības laukums, travels to Cēsis Castle (Cēsu Pils). The English-speaking staff at the **Tourist Information Center,** Pils laukums 1, across from the castle arranges **private rooms** in the region (0.50Ls booking fee) or elsewhere in Latvia (1L) and has **free maps** and fast **Internet access.** (☎412 18 15; www.cesis.lv. 0.50Ls per hr. Open May 15-Sept. 15 M-F 9am-6pm, Sa-Su 10am-5pm.) **Exchange currency** at **Unibanka,** Raunas iela 8, which cashes **traveler's checks** and gives MC/V **cash advances.** (☎220 31. Open M-F 9am-5pm.) There are 24hr. **ATMs** on Rigas iela. Ask the cashier at the **bus** and **train station** (☎412 27 62) to **store luggage.** The **post office** is at Raunas iela 13, at the corner of Vienības laukums. (☎227 88. Open M-F 8am-6pm, Sa 8am-4pm.) **Postal Code:** LV-4100.

Hotel Cēsis ❺, Vienības laukums 1, is luxurious, with huge beds and sparkling private baths. (☎412 0122; www.danlat-group.lv. English spoken. Breakfast included. Singles 30Ls; doubles 42Ls. Sept.-May 25% off. MC/V.) The hotel's lively **Cafe Popular ❷** serves superb Latvian food by the kilo. (☎412 23 92. Entrees 1-2Ls. Open Su-Th 11am-11pm, F-Sa 11am-midnight. MC/V.) **Putniņkrogs ❶,** Saules iela 23, isn't bad for 70s-style Soviet accommodations, with small beds and lots of concrete. Follow Vaives iela away from town and turn right on Saules iela. (☎412 02 90. 5Ls per person.) **Restoran Alexis ❺,** Vienības laukums 1, in hotel Hotel Cēsis, serves elk roast (8.10Ls) and other Latvian and international dishes. (☎412 23 92. Entrees 4-9Ls. Open M-Sa 7-10:30am and noon-9pm, Su 7-10:30am. MC/V.) **Madara '89,** Raunas 15, is a supermarket. (Open daily 8am-10pm.)

LITHUANIA (LIETUVA)

LITAI

AUS$1 = 2.01LT	1LT = AUS$0.50
CDN$1 = 2.14LT	1LT = CDN$0.47
EUR€1 = 3.45LT	1LT = EUR€0.29
NZ$1 = 1.86LT	1LT = NZ$0.54
UK£1 = 5.16LT	1LT = UK£0.19
US$1 = 2.82LT	1LT = US$0.35

Lithuania's small size belies is historical role as a large power in Eastern Europe and its importance, in more recent history, as the first Baltic nation to declare independence from the USSR in 1990. Lithuania has become more Western with every passing year and, in 2004, became one of the newest members of the European Union and NATO. Its spectacular capital, Vilnius, welcomes hordes of tourists into Europe's largest old town. In the other corner of the country, the mighty Baltic Sea washes up against Palanga and the towering dunes of the Curonian Spit.

HISTORY

PAGAN AND PROUD OF IT. The Baltic people settled in the region at the beginning of the Christian era. The Lithuanian tribes united under **Mindaugas**, who accepted **Christianity** in AD 1251 and was named the country's first Grand Duke by Pope Innocent IV. Mindaugas reverted to paganism and was assassinated in 1263. In the 14th century, Lithuanian territory quickly swelled, swallowing modern Belarus and northern Ukraine, as **Grand Duke Gediminas** consolidated power.

UNION. Jogaila, Gediminas's grandson, married the 12-year-old Polish Princess Jadwiga and became Władisław II Jagiełło, King of Poland, in 1385. With this union, Jogaila introduced **Roman Catholicism** to Lithuania, converting the nobility. Turning his attention to Poland, Jogaila delegated control of Lithuania to **Vytautas Didysis** (the Great), most famous for his defeat of the Teutonic Knights (see **Trakai**, p. 457). Together, they expanded their empire until Vytautas's death in 1430, at which point Lithuanian territory included present-day Belarus and Ukraine,

FACTS AND FIGURES

OFFICIAL NAME: Republic of Lithuania

CAPITAL: Vilnius (pop. 580,000)

POPULATION: 3.6 million (81% Lithuanian, 9% Russian, 7% Polish, 3% other)

LANGUAGES: Lithuanian (official), Polish, Russian

CURRENCY: 1 Litas = 100 centas

RELIGION: 72% Roman Catholic, 2% Russian Orthodox, Evangelical Lutheran

LAND AREA: 65,200km²

CLIMATE: Maritime and continental

GEOGRAPHY: Lowlands with numerous lakes

BORDERS: Belarus, Latvia, Poland, Russia (Kaliningrad)

ECONOMY: 66% Services, 27% Industry, 7% Agriculture

GDP: US$8400 per capita

COUNTRY CODE: 370

INTERNATIONAL DIALING PREFIX: 00

stretching from the Baltics to the Black Sea, from Vilnius to a mere 160km away from Moscow. Lithuania solidified its ties to Poland with the 1569 **Union of Lublin,** which created the **Commonwealth of Two Peoples** (or Polish-Lithuanian Commonwealth), heralding a period of prosperity and cultural development. Along with the alliance came further class division, as the nobility became steeped in Polish culture while the peasantry held on to the old language and customs.

DECLINE AND FALL. In the 18th century the growing power of Russia and Prussia led to the three **Partitions of Poland** (see **Poland: History,** p. 502), which ceded most of Lithuania to Russia. By 1815, Russia had complete control of the territory. Nationalist uprisings in Poland in 1830-31 and 1863 provoked intensified campaigns of **Russification** in Lithuania. German troops returned to Lithuania in 1915, 500 years after the defeat of the Teutonic knights. They left at the end of 1918, only to have the Soviets try to regain hold of the country. The Lithuanians expelled the Red Army in 1919 and declared **independence,** but during the confusion Poland took **Vilnius**—the population of the city being predominantly Polish—and refused to release it. A dispute also arose with Germany over the port of **Klaipėda,** a predominantly German city that was Lithuania's only viable harbor on the Baltic.

STUCK IN THE MIDDLE AGAIN. Deprived of its capital and primary port, Lithuania's independence was short-lived. A parliamentary democracy collapsed in 1926 in a coup, as dictator **Antanas Smetona** banned opposition parties. Whatever autonomy remained disappeared with the 1939 **Nazi-Soviet Non-Aggression Pact** and subsequent treaties, which invited the Soviets to invade. In June 1941, the Soviets began deporting Lithuanians and exiling them to remote regions of the USSR. Some 35,000 people were displaced. Nazi occupation caused even greater devastation, as Lithuania lost another 250,000 citizens, including most of its Jewish population.

POLITICAL FREE-FOR-ALL. The Soviets returned in 1944, opposed by Lithuanian guerrilla fighters—at their height 40,000 strong—into the early 1950s. It was not until the 1960s that **Antanas Sniečkus** managed to solidify Soviet rule, though resistance persisted through the stagnation of the 1970s and 1980s, as the republic generated more *samizdat* ("self-made" dissident publications) per capita than any other region in the Soviet bloc. **Mikhail Gorbachev's** democratic reforms fell on dangerously fertile ground, and on March 1, 1990, Lithuania shocked the world when it seceded from the USSR. Moscow retaliated, futilely attempting to disconnect the region's oil and gas resources. In what has come to be known as the "Lithuanian massacre," the Soviets launched an assault on Vilnius's radio and TV center hoping to crush the independence movement, leaving 14 dead. Only in the wake of the failed Soviet *putsch* of August 1991 did Lithuania achieve independence.

TODAY. Although still poor relative to the rest of Central Europe, Lithuania got off to an early start on economic reforms, and has been labeled by investors as one of Eastern Europe's economic "tigers." Having joined both the **EU** and **NATO** in the spring of 2004, Lithuania is attempting to break from its Russia-dominated past. Russia is Lithuania's neighbor to the west; Russia's isolated **Kaliningrad** region is now an island in a sea of NATO states, a fact that is causing both Russia and Lithuania unease. Prime Minister **Algirdas Brazauskas,** elected to the position in 2001, is a former communist who nonetheless has made NATO and EU membership political priorities. President **Rolandas Paksas,** who was elected 2003, made history by being the first modern European head of state to be impeached. He was dismissed in April 2004. In a special election in June 2004, Lithuanians put former **President Valdas Adamkus** back in office. Adamkus immigrated to the United States in 1949 and returned to his native country after Lithuania gained independence.

PEOPLE AND CULTURE

LANGUAGE

Lithuanian is one of only two Baltic languages (Latvian is the other). All "r"s are trilled. **Polish** is helpful in the south and **German** on the coast. **Russian** is understood in most places, although it is not as prominent as in Latvia. Most Lithuanians understand basic English phrases. If someone seems to sneeze at you, he's might be saying *ačiu* (ah-choo; thank you). For a phrasebook and glossary, see **Glossary: Lithuanian,** p. 953.

FOOD AND DRINK

LITHUANIA	❶	❷	❸	❹	❺
FOOD	under 8Lt	8-17Lt	18-30Lt	31-40Lt	over 40Lt

Lithuanian cuisine is heavy and sometimes greasy. Keeping a **vegetarian** or **kosher** diet is difficult. Restaurants serve various types of *blynai* (pancakes) with *mėsa* (meat) or *varske* (cheese). *Cepelinai* are heavy, potato-dough missiles of meat, cheese, and mushrooms; *saltibarščiai* is a beet and cucumber soup prevalent in the east; *karbonadas* is breaded pork fillet; and *koldunai* are meat dumplings. Good Lithuanian **beer** flows freely. *Kalnapis* is popular in Vilnius and most of Lithuania, *Baltijos* reigns supreme around Klaipėda, and the award-winning *Utenos* is everywhere. Lithuanian **vodka** *(degtinė)* is also very popular.

CUSTOMS AND ETIQUETTE

Reserve informal greetings for those you know personally. Say *"laba diena"* (good day) whenever you enter a shop to ensure good feelings. In polite company, you can never say *"prašau"* too many times (both "please" and "you're welcome"). **Handshakes** are the norm for men; women get handshakes and perhaps a peck on the cheek. Lithuanians usually **tip** 10%. When eating at someone's home or going to the doctor, bring a gift of flowers or chocolates. Feel free to **smoke** anywhere.

THE ARTS

The earliest Lithuanian writings were the *Chronicles of the Grand Duchy of Lithuania*, written in an East Slavic dialect. The first book in Lithuanian, a Lutheran catechism, was printed in 1547. The year 1706 saw the appearance of secular literature with the publication of *Aesop's Fables*. A Lithuanian translation of the **New Testament** was published in 1701 and a Lithuanian Bible in 1727. After 1864, many writers violated the tsarist ban on publishing Lithuanian works in Latin letters (as opposed to Cyrillic), seeking to overthrow Russian political and Polish cultural control. Known for both dramatic and lyric poetry, "the poet-prophet of the Lithuanian renaissance" was **Jonas Mačiulis** (a.k.a. Maironis), whose 1895 *Voices of Spring (Pavasario balsai)* launched modern Lithuanian poetry. During the inter-war period, ex-priest **Vincas Mykolaitis-Putinas** pioneered the modern Lithuanian novel with *In the Shadows of the Altars (Altorių sesėly)*. After the WWII, Soviet rule gagged and shackled Lithuanian writers; however, the poetry of **Alfonsas Nyka-Niliunas** and the novels of **Marius Katiliskis** flouted propagandistic Soviet Socialist Realism. *Pre-Dawn Highways*, by **Bronius Radzevicius,** is considered the strongest work of the late Soviet period.

Both Lithuanian **music** and **painting** have been heavily influenced by the traditional folk culture. Much of the visual arts' development has centered around the **Vilnius Drawing School,** founded in 1866. Painter **Mikalojus Čiurlionis** was one of the major figures in this artistic school (see **Kaunas,** p. 458). One of the major independent filmmakers of this century has been the Lithuanian-American artist **Jonas Mekas,** who is perhaps best known for his 1976 film *Lost Lost Lost*—an account of his arrival in New York and his contact with New York art-house figures like Allen Ginsberg and Frank O'Hara.

HOLIDAYS AND FESTIVALS

Since the 19th century, craftsmen from around Eastern Europe have gathered to display their wares each March in Vilnius at the **Kaziukas Fair.**

NATIONAL HOLIDAYS IN 2005

January 1 New Year's Day and Flag Day	**July 6** Statehood Day
February 16 Independence Day	**August 15** Feast of the Assumption
March 11 Restoration of Independence	**November 1** All Saints' Day
March 27-28 Easter Holiday	**December 25-6** Christmas
May 1 Labor Day	

ADDITIONAL RESOURCES

GENERAL HISTORY

The Baltic Revolution: Estonia, Latvia, Lithuania and the Path to Independence, by Anatol Lieven (1993). Contrasts the Baltic states' respective histories.

The Jews of Lithuania, by Masha Greenbaum (1995). A must for anyone interested in Lithuania's rich Jewish history.

FICTION, NONFICTION, AND FILM

The Issa Valley, by Czesław Miłosz (1998). This Nobel Laureate poet (see **Poland: Fiction and Nonfiction,** p. 507) describes his childhood in the Vilnius of imperial Russia.

Native Realm, also by Miłosz (1968). In this phenomenal autobiography, Miłosz reflects upon the history of his home city and all of Eastern Europe.

There Is No Ithaca: Idylls of Semeniskiai and Reminiscences, by Jonas Mekas (1996). A series of reflections from a Lithuanian who left the country to become an underground New York filmmaker.

Reminiscences of a Journey to Lithuania, directed by Jonas Mekas (1971-1972). A film diary of Mekas's first trip to his country of birth after 25 years of exile.

LITHUANIA ESSENTIALS

ENTRANCE REQUIREMENTS

Passport: Required of all travelers.

Visa: Not required for citizens of Australia, Canada, Ireland, New Zealand, the UK, and the US.

Letter of Invitation: Not required.

Inoculations: Recommended up-to-date on DTaP (diphtheria, tetanus, and pertussis), Hepatitis A, Hepatitis B, MMR (measles, mumps, and rubella), Polio booster, and Typhoid.

Work Permit: Required for all foreigners planning to work.

International Driving Permit: Required of all those planning to drive.

DOCUMENTS AND FORMALITIES

EMBASSIES AND CONSULATES

Embassies of other countries in Lithuania are all in **Vilnius** (see p. 448). Lithuania's embassies and consulates abroad include:

Australia: Honorary Consulate: 40B Fiddens Wharf Rd., Killara NSW 2071 (☎61 2 949 825 71).

Canada: 130 Albert St., ste. 204, Ottawa, ON K1P 5G4 (☎1 613-567-5458; www.lithuanianembassy.ca).

New Zealand Honorary Consulate: 28 Heather St., Parnell (☎9 379 6639; saul@f1rst.co.nz).

UK and Ireland: 84 Gloucester Pl., London W1U 6AU (☎44 20 7486 6401; http://amb.urm.lt/jk).

US: 2622 16th St. NW, Washington, D.C. 20009 (☎1 202 234-5860; www.ltembassyus.org).

VISA AND ENTRY INFORMATION

Citizens of Australia, Canada, Ireland, New Zealand, the UK, and the US can visit Lithuania **visa-free** for up to 90 days. "Special Visas" (€60), for temporary residence and valid for up to one year, can be purchased from the Migration Department of the Ministry of the Interior. Avoid crossing through Belarus to enter or exit Lithuania: not only do you need to obtain visa (US$100) for Belarus in advance, but guards may hassle you at the border.

GETTING AROUND

Finnair, LOT, Lufthansa, SAS, and other airlines **fly** into Vilnius. **Trains** are more popular for international and long-distance travel. Two major lines cross Lithuania: one runs north-south from **Latvia** through **Šiauliai** and **Kaunas** to **Poland;** the other runs east-west from **Belarus** through **Vilnius** and Kaunas to **Kaliningrad,** branching out around Vilnius and **Klaipėda.** Domestic **buses** are faster, more common, and only a bit more expensive than trains, which are often crowded. Whenever possible, try to catch an **express bus** to your destination; such buses are normally marked with an asterisk or an "E" on the timetable. They are typically direct and can be up to twice as fast. Vilnius, Kaunas, and Klaipėda are easily reached by train or bus from **Belarus, Estonia, Latvia, Poland,** and **Russia. Ferries** connect Klaipėda with **Arhus** and **Aabenra, DEN; Kiel** and **Mukran, GER;** and **Ahus** and **Karlshamn, SWE.**

As of March 2002, all travelers planning to drive in Lithuania must purchase a **Liability Insurance Policy** at the Lithuanian border (79Lt for the 15-day min.). **US** citizens may drive with an American driver's license for up to three months; all other motorists must have an **International Driving Permit.** Inexpensive **taxis** are in most cities. Agree on a price before getting in. **Hitchhiking** is common. Many drivers charge a fee comparable to local bus or train fares. Locals line up along major roads leaving large cities. *Let's Go* does not recommend hitchhiking.

TOURIST SERVICES AND MONEY

Major cities have official **tourist offices. Litinterp** is generally the most helpful organization for travel info. It reserves accommodations and rent cars, usually without a surcharge. Kaunas, Klaipėda, Nida, Palanga, and Vilnius each have an edition of the *In Your Pocket* series, available at kiosks and some hotels. The unit of **currency** is the **Lita** (1Lt=100 centas), plural Litai. Since February 2002, the Lita has been fixed to the euro at €1 = 3.4528Lt. Prices are stable, with inflation hovering at just under 1%. Except in Vilnius, exchange bureaus near the train station usually have poorer rates than banks. Most banks cash **traveler's checks** for 2-3% commission. **Visa cash advances** can usually be obtained with minimum hassle. **Vilniaus Bankas,** with outlets in major cities, accepts major credit cards and traveler's checks for a small commission. If you're planning on traveling off the touristed path, be aware that most places catering to locals don't take credit cards. **ATMs** are readily available in most cities, though almost none accept AmEx.

LITHUANIA

HEALTH AND SAFETY

 EMERGENCY NUMBERS: Police: ☎02 **Fire:** ☎01 **Ambulance:** ☎03

Well-stocked **pharmacies** are common and carry most medical supplies, tampons, condoms, and toiletries. Drink bottled mineral water, and **boil tap water** for 10min. before drinking. A triangle pointing downward indicates men's **restrooms;** an upward-pointing triangle indicates women's bathrooms. Many restrooms are nothing but a hole in the ground, so carry your own toilet paper. Lithuania's **crime rate** is generally low. Vilnius is one of the safer capitals in Europe, although street crime does occur on occasion. Lithuanian **police** are generally helpful but understaffed, so your best bet for assistance in English is still your **consulate.**

Women traveling alone will be noticed but shouldn't encounter too much difficulty. Skirts, blouses, and heels are far more common than jeans, shorts, tank tops, or sneakers. **Minorities** traveling to Lithuania may encounter unwanted attention or discrimination, though most is directed toward Roma (gypsies). Lithuania has made little effort to provide services or facilities for **disabled** travelers. **Homosexuality** is legal but not always tolerated. Lithuania has the most nightclubs, hotlines, and services for gays and lesbians in the Baltics (see **Vilnius: Practical Information,** p. 448).

ACCOMMODATIONS AND CAMPING

LITHUANIA	❶	❷	❸	❹	❺
ACCOM.	under 30Lt	31-80Lt	81-130Lt	131-180Lt	over 180Lt

Lithuania has several youth **hostels.** HI membership is nominally required, but an LJNN guest card (10.50Lt at any of the hostels) will suffice. The head office is in Vilnius (see **Vilnius: Practical Information,** p. 448). Their *Hostel Guide* is a handy booklet with info on bike and car rentals, hotel reservations, and maps. **Hotels** across the price spectrum abound in Vilnius and most major towns. **Litinterp,** with offices in Vilnius, Kaunas, and Klaipėda, assists in finding homestays or apartments for rent. **Camping** is gaining popularity, but it is restricted by law to marked campgrounds; the law is well-enforced, particularly along the Curonian Spit.

KEEPING IN TOUCH

Airmail (*oro pastu*) **letters** abroad cost 1.70Lt (postcards 1.20Lt) and take about one week to reach the US. **Poste Restante** is available. Address envelope as follows: Daniel (first name) HEMEL (LAST NAME), POSTE RESTANTE, Laisves al. 102 (post office address), LT-3000 (postal code) Kaunas (city), LITHUANIA. There are two kinds of public **phones:** rectangular ones take magnetic strip cards and rounded ones take chip cards. Phone cards (8-30Lt) are sold at phone offices and kiosks. Calls to **Estonia** and **Latvia** cost 1.65Lt per min.; **Europe** 5.80Lt; and the **US** 7.32Lt. **Internet access** is widely available. International access numbers include: **AT&T Direct** (☎8 800 90028); **Canada Direct** (☎8 800 90004); **Sprint** (☎8 800 95877).

VILNIUS
☎(8)5

According to legend, Grand Duke Gendiminas dreamt of an iron wolf howling atop the hill where the Higher Castle now stands; the apparition convinced him to build a city on the site in 1323. Since its founding, Vilnius has suffered a series of foreign occupations: Russia, France and Germany have all conquered the city. WWII left the city in shambles, and a half-century of Soviet occupation stifled recovery. Nonetheless, Vilnius is experiencing cultural and economic revival. Vilnius embraces tourists with signs in English and luxury hotels, but some outlying areas, remain mired in the poverty resulting from Soviet rule.

⚏ TRANSPORTATION

Flights: Vilnius Airport (Vilniaus oro uostas), Rodūnės Kelias 2 (info ☎230 6666), 5km south of town. Take Bus #1 or 2 to reach the Old Town: bus #1 stops outside Geležinko Stotis train station; on Bus #2, get off at Lukiskiu, on Gendimino, the main street. Airlines include: **Austrian Airlines** (☎ 231 3137; www.austrianairlines.lt); **Czech Airlines** (☎215 1504; www.czech-airlines.com) **Finnair** (☎232 9339 www.finnair.com); **Lithuanian Airlines** (☎252 5555; www.lal.lt); **LOT** (☎273 9020; www.lot.com); **Lufthansa** (☎230 6031; www.lufthansa.com); **SAS** (☎239 6000; www.scandinavian.net).

Trains: Geležinkelio Stotis, Geležinkelio 16 (☎233 0086, reservations for Western Europe 269 37 22; www.litrail.lt). Entering the station, domestic tickets are sold to the left and international to the right. Tickets for trains originating outside of Lithuania can be bought no earlier than 3hr. and no later than 5min. before departure. Open daily 6-11am and noon-6pm. Most international trains pass through Belarus, which requires a Belarusian visa (see **Belarus: Essentials,** p. 85). To: **Berlin, GER** (22hr., 1 per day, 317Lt); **Kaliningrad, RUS** (7hr., 14 per day, 70Lt); **Minsk, BLR** (5½hr., 2 per day, 57Lt); **Moscow, RUS** (17hr., 3 per day, 128Lt); **Rīga, LAT** (7½hr., 1 per day, 72Lt); **St. Petersburg, RUS** (18hr., 3 per day, 110Lt); **Warsaw, POL** (8hr., 2 per day, 115Lt).

Buses: Autobusų Stotis, Sodų 22 (☎290 1661, reservations 216 2977), opposite the train station. **Eurolines Baltic International** (EBI; ☎215 1377; www.eurolines.lt) offers routes to **Minsk, BLR** (5 hr. 3 per day, 22Lt); **Riga, LAT** (5 hr., 4 per day, 40Lt); **St. Petersburg, RUS** (18hr., 4 per day, 44Lt); **Tallinn, EST** (10 hr., 2 per day, 90Lt); **Warsaw, POL** (9-10hr., 3 per day, 97Lt); and other Western European destinations. Buy tickets in EBI kiosks to the right of the main entrance to the bus station. English spoken. Open daily 6am-10pm.

Public Transportation: Buses and **trolleys** link downtown with the train and bus stations and the suburbs. All lines run daily 6am-midnight. Buy tickets at any kiosk (0.80Lt) or from the driver (1Lt); get them punched on board to avoid the 20Lt fine—tickets (5Lt) are checked more often than you'd expect. Monthly passes are available for students.

Taxis: Locals say that **Ekipažas** (☎1446) is the cheapest and most reliable service. **Vilnius** drivers are notorious for overcharging foreigners who hail cabs from the side of the street. If you're at a cafe or restaurant, ask your server to call for a cab, as the fare will likely be half the rate you would have paid if you tried to hail one yourself.

⚏ ORIENTATION

The train and bus stations are located side-by-side on **Geležinkelio.** With the stations behind you, walk right, passing McDonald's on your left and continuing 250m until you reach the base of a hill with an overpass on your right; turn left onto **Aušros Vartų,** which leads through the **Aušros Vartai** (Gates of Dawn) into **Senamiestis** (Old Town). Aušros Vartų becomes **Didžioji** and then **Pilies** before reaching the base of Gediminas Hill. Here, the Gediminas Tower of Higher Castle presides over **Arkikatedros Aikštė** (Cathedral Sq.) and the banks of **Neris.** Beyond Gediminas Hill to the east, the small **Vilnia River** winds north to the bigger **Neris River.** The commercial artery, **Gedimino,** leads west from the square in front of the Cathedral.

ⓘ PRACTICAL INFORMATION

TOURIST AND FINANCIAL SERVICES

Tourist Offices: Tourist Information Center (TIC) maintains 3 branches with courteous and knowledgeable staffers who speak fluent English. All offer excellent free maps as well as train and bus schedules. When *Let's Go* visited in 2004, the hours of operation for 2005 were not finalized. Main office at Didžioji 31 (☎262 6470; www.vilnius.lt), at the northeast corner of the Town Hall. **Branches** at Vilniaus 22 (☎262 96 60; fax 262 81 69), 50m north of the Radvilai Palace, and at Geležinkelio 16 (☎269 2091), in a kiosk inside the train station, to the left after passing through the main entrance.

Kelvita Tourism Agency, Geležinkelio 16 (☎210 6130; fax 210 6131), in a kiosk inside the train station at window #30. German and English spoken. Service may not be courteous, but turnaround is quick for visas for Belarus, Russia, and Ukraine. American visas 440Lt for 24hr. wait or 320Lt for 8-day wait. Citizens of other English-speaking countries pay roughly 20% less. Open M-F 8am-6pm, Sa 10am-4pm.

Embassies and Consulates:

Australia (consulate), Vilniaus 23 (☎212 3369; aust.con.vilnius@post.omnitel.net). Visas M, W, F 11am-2pm.

Belarus, Mindaugo 13 (☎266 2211; bpl@post.5ci.lt). Visas, Muitinės 41 (☎13 22 55; fax 33 06 26). Open M-Th 8am-noon and 1-4pm, F 8am-noon and 1-3pm.

Canada, Gedimino pr. 64 (☎249 0950; vilnius@canada.lt). Visas M, W, F 9am-noon. Open 8:30am-noon and 1-7pm.

Estonia, Mickevičiaus 4a (☎278 0200; www.estemb.lt). Visa applications accepted Tu-Th 10am-noon; visas issued Tu-Th 2-3:30pm.

Latvia, MK Čiurlionio 76 (☎213 1260; lietuva@latvia.balt.net). Visas M-F 9am-noon and 3-4pm.

Russia, Latvių 53/54 (☎272 1763; rusemb@rusemb.lt). Visas M-F 8am-noon.

UK, Antakalnio 2 (☎12 2070, emergency mobile 370 698 37 097; www.britain.lt). Visas M-F 8:30-11:30am. Open M-Th 8:30am-5pm, F 8:30am-4pm.

US, Akmenų 6 (☎266 5500; www.usembassy.lt). Visas M-Th 8:30-11:30am. US citizen services open M-Tu and Th 2-4:30pm and F 9-11:30am and 2-4pm. Closed last W of each month.

Currency Exchange: Most currency kiosks exchange British pounds, euros, Latvian lats, Swedish crowns, Swiss francs, and US dollars. **Pabex Bankas** Geležinkelio 6 (☎233 0763), to the left with the train station at your back, doesn't have the best rates, but it's open 24hr. and changes several currencies that aren't accepted at many other banks.

Vilniaus Bankas, Vokiečių 9 (☎/fax 62 78 69), gives MC/V **cash advances** at no commission and cashes AmEx and Thomas Cooke traveler's checks. Open M-F 8am-6pm. **Bankas Snoras,** A. Vivulskio 7 (☎16 27 70; fax 31 01 55), has the best rates, cashes traveler's checks, and gives Visa cash advances for 2% commission. Look for blue-and-white kiosks throughout town. Open M-F 8am-7pm, Sa 9am-2pm.

LOCAL SERVICES

Luggage Storage: The storage center in the bus station near the main entrance charges 3Lt per bag per day. Open M-F 5:30am-9pm, Sa-Su 7am-9pm. A better option is the self-service, electronic facility beneath the train station. Take the stairs down from the ground fl. and turn right. Place your bag in an open locker, then insert 2Lt into the nearby machine. Save the receipt: you will need the PIN to retrieve your baggage. Rates are lower the longer you store your bag. Open 24hr.

English-Language Bookstore: Oxford Centre, Trakų 20 (☎261 0416). Open M-F 10:30am-6pm, Sa 10:30am-3pm.

LITHUANIA

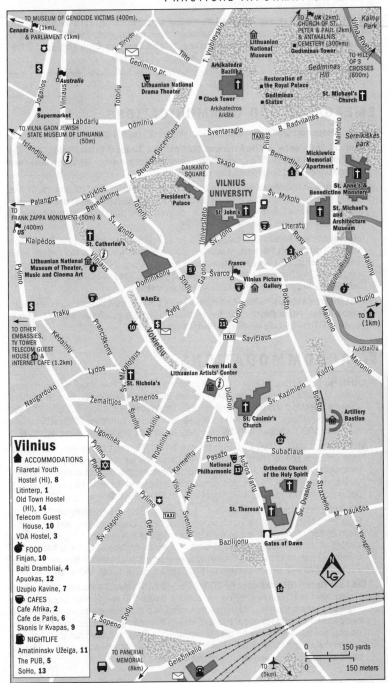

TO MUSEUM OF GENOCIDE VICTIMS (400m),
Canada (1km),
& PARLIAMENT (1km)

TO UK (2km),
CHURCH OF ST.
PETER & PAUL (2km)
& ANTAKALNIS
CEMETERY (300m)

Kalnų
Park

Vilna River

K. Sirvydo

Gedimino pr.

Tilto

T. Vrublevskio

Lithuanian
National
Museum

Gediminas Tower

TO HILL
OF 3
CROSSES
(600m)

Australia

Lithuanian National
Drama Theater

Arkikatedra
Bazilika

Clock Tower
Arkikatedros
Aikštė

Restoration of
the Royal Palace

Gediminas
Statue

Gediminas
Hill

St. Michael's
Church

Supermarket

Labdarių

Totorių

Odminių

TO VILNA GAON JEWISH
STATE MUSEUM OF LITHUANIA
(50m)

Islandijos

Šventaragio

B. Radvilaitės

Maironio

Sereikiškės
park

Jogailos
Vilniaus
Pylimo

TAXI

Pilies

Bernardinų

Patangos

Liejyklos

L. Stuokos-Gucevičiaus

Skapo

DAUKANTO
SQUARE

Mickiewicz
Memorial
Apartment

Benediktinų

President's
Palace

VILNIUS
UNIVERSITY

Šv. Mykolo

St. Anne's &
Benedictine Monstery

TO
FRANK ZAPPA MONUMENT (50m) &
US (400m)

Totorių

Šv. Ignoto

St. John's

Universiteto

Šv. Jono

Literatų
Rusų

St. Michael's
and
Architecture
Museum

Klaipėdos

St. Catherine's

Latako

Vilniaus

Lithuanian National
Museum of Theater,
Music and Cinema Art

Dominikonų

France

Švarco

Vilnius Picture
Gallery

Vilnia River

Malūnų

Traku

AmEx

Stiklių

Žydų

Gaono

Bokšto

Užupio
TO
(1km)

TO OTHER
EMBASSIES,
TV TOWER
TELECOM GUEST
HOUSE &
INTERNET CAFE (1.2km)

Kėdainių

Pranciškonų

Vokiečių

Didžioji

Savičiaus

TAXI

Aukštaičių

Maironio

Naugarduko

Lydos

Šv. Mikalojaus

Žemaitijos

Ašmenos

St. Nichola's

Mėsinių

Rudninkų

Town Hall &
Lithuanian Artists' Center

Didžioji

Šv. Kazimiero

Kūdrų

Bokšto

Artillery
Bastion

Ligoninės

Šiaulių

Etmonų

St. Casimir's
Church

Subačiaus

A. Strazdelio

Vilnius

🏠 ACCOMMODATIONS
Filaretai Youth
Hostel (HI), **8**
Litinterp, **1**
Old Town Hostel
(HI), **14**
Telecom Guest
House, **10**
VDA Hostel, **3**

🍎 FOOD
Finjan, **10**
Balti Drambliai, **4**
Apuokas, **12**
Uzupio Kavine, **7**

☕ CAFES
Cafe Afrika, **2**
Cafe de Paris, **6**
Skonis Ir Kvapas, **9**

🎵 NIGHTLIFE
Amatininskv Užeiga, **11**
The PUB, **5**
SoHo, **13**

Pylimo

Pilaioji

Karmelitų

Vilų

Arklių

Pasažo

National
Philharmonic

Aušros Vartų

Orthodox Church
of the Holy Spirit

Šv. Dvasios

M. Daukšos

K.Vanagėlio

Šv. Stepono

Gėlių

Šventųjų

TAXI

St. Theresa's

Bazilijonu

Gates of Dawn

F. Šopeno

Sodų

TO PANERIAI
MEMORIAL
(8km)

Geležinkelio

TO
(5km)

N

LG

0 — 150 yards
0 — 150 meters

LITHUANIA

GLBT Services: Gay and Lesbian Information Line, (☎233 3031; www.gay.lt). Info about organizations, events, and accommodations for gay men. The **Lithuanian Gay and Lesbian Homepage** (www.gayline.lt) and **The Gay Club** (☎998 50 09; vgc@takas.lt) list gay and lesbian establishments in Lithuania.

Laundromat: Nearly all hostels and hotels in Vilnius offer full-service laundry, often even if you are not staying there (10-30Lt).

EMERGENCY AND COMMUNICATIONS

24hr. Pharmacy: Gedimino Vaistinė, Gedimino pr. 27 (☎261 0135).

Medical Assistance: Baltic-American Medical and Surgical Clinic, Antakalnio 124 (☎234 2020 or 210 5757; www.baclinic.com). Accepts major American insurance plans. Open 7am-11pm; doctors on call 24hr.

Telephones: Public **phone kiosks** are omnipresent in Vilnius. Except for emergency and toll-free lines, you must buy a phone card to call; buy one from almost any street vendor. To call within Lithuania, buy a 50min. domestic card (9Lt) or an international card (20Lt). See www.ntel.lt for more information.

Internet Access: Klubas Lux, Svitrigailos 5 (☎233 3788), just north of the intersection with A. Vivulsikio on the western edge of town, offers the best rates and fastest terminals. 2Lt per hr., 8Lt for all-night access 9pm-8am. Open 24hr. **Collegium,** Pilies 22 (☎261 83 34). Turn right into courtyard across from Sv. Jono, then make an immediate left. 8Lt per hr., students with ID 6Lt. Open 8am-midnight.

Post Office: Centrinis Paštas, Gedimino 7 (☎262 5468; www.post.lt), west of Arkikatedros Aikštė. **Poste Restante** at the window labeled "iki pareikalavimo;" 0.50Lt fee. Open M-F 7am-7pm, Sa 9am-4pm. **Postal Code:** LT-2000

⌂ ACCOMMODATIONS

Litinterp, Bernardinų 7/2 (☎212 3850; www.litinterp.lt). This travel agency places guests in B&Bs in the Old Town or in its own beautiful, spacious rooms with spotless showers. Breakfast included. English spoken. Reception M-F 8:30am-5:30pm, Sa 9am-3pm. Reservations recommended. Singles with shared bathroom 80Lt, with private bathroom 100Lt; doubles 140-160Lt; triples 180-210Lt. 5% ISIC discount. MC/V. ❸

VDA Hostel, Lataĸo 2 (☎212 0102; fax 210 5444). For most of the year, this Soviet-style concrete artifice offers both dorms for Lithuanian art students and private rooms for tourists. July 15-Sept. 20 the dorms are transformed into low-cost accommodations. Staff speaks minimal English, but guests prize the central location. Shared shower. 5-person dorms 18Lt; singles 43Lt; doubles 78Lt; triples 99Lt. ❶

Telecom Guest House, A. Vivulskio 13a (☎264 4861; www.telecomguesthouse.lt). From the city center, follow Traku, which turns into J. Basanaviciaus. Just before the green-domed church, turn left on Algirido, then right on A. Vivulskio; the guest house is located on a courtyard. The beautiful room with private bathrooms make its hard-to-find location well worth the search. English spoken at reception. Breakfast included. Singles 220Lt, singles with shared bathroom 75Lt; doubles 260Lt/120Lt. MC/V. ❸

Old Town Hostel (HI), Aušros Vartų 20-15a (☎262 5357; www.balticbackpackers.com), tucked away in a courtyard 100m south of the Gates of Dawn. A great place to meet English-speaking travelers. Backpackers stuffed into 8-person rooms complain about being locked out midday and the lack of lockers for stowing valuables. Free coffee and Internet access, but the line for the lone computer is often long. Communal kitchen and 3 shared (but sometimes cold) showers. Reservations recommended. Dorms 34Lt, HI members 32Lt; 2-3 person apartments for 60Lt. MC/V. ❷

Filaretai Youth Hostel (HI), Filaretų 17 (☎ 15 4627; www.filaretaihostel.lt). Walk east on Užupio across the Vilina River. Where road forks, bear left onto Kriviwų; at next fork, bear right onto Filaretų; hostel is in a courtyard on your right. The 1km hike from Old Town is pleasant by day but is dark and desolate at night. Young clientele. Friendly staff. Luggage storage 3Lt. Kitchen, common room, and Internet. Bikes free. Linen 5Lt. Laundry 10Lt. Curfew 1am. Reservations recommended June-Sept. and weekends. Triples and quads 28Lt; 5- to 6-bed dorms 24Lt. Non-members 3Lt fee. MC/V. ❶

🖸 FOOD

Vilnius's inexpensive restaurants dish out regional cuisine, but locals often flock to pizzerias, such as the rapidly expanding **Cili Pica** (www.cili.lt), which has locations across the city. The several **Iki** supermarkets (www.iki.lt) on the outskirts of Vilnius have local and Western food brands. One convenient location is Sodu 22, opposite the bus station. (Open daily 8am-10pm.) There are seven Ikiukas (literally "little Iki") minimarts inside the city, including branches at Uzupio 7, Pylmio 21 and A. Vivulskio 15. (Open daily 8am-11pm.) For an authentic Lithuanian shopping experience, visit **Turgus Dirbu,** a sprawling indoor marketplace at the corner of Pylmio and Bazilijonų. Walk south out of the Old City through the Gates of Dawn; go right on Bazlijonu and continue for 250m. (Open Tu-Sa 7am-7pm, Su 7am-5pm.)

🖾 **Finjan,** Vokiečių 18 (☎ 261 2104). With friendly Israeli servers, an Iranian chef, and seductive belly dancers (Th-Sa nights), recently-renovated Finjan is one of the hottest spots in town. The hummus (10Lt) is spectacular. While vegetarians eat cheaply, carnivores devour mounds of meat (up to 110Lt). English menu. Open daily 11am-midnight. MC/V. ❸

Balti Drambliai (White Elephant), Vilniaus 41 (☎ 262 0875). Balti Drambliai remains one of the only establishments offering a decent range of options for vegetarians. English menu. Vegetable curry with spinach and paneer (8Lt) is flavorful, but portion sizes are anemic and service is sluggish. Less-than-inspiring live music. MC/V. ❷

Apuokas, Subaciaus 7. Though just steps away from tourist-filled Ausros Vartu, Apuokas is decidedly off the beaten track. Hard rock blares in the background as black-clad patrons enjoy name-brand beers (3Lt for 500mL) at ridiculously low prices. The food is good and hearty, but the menu is not translated into English. Open 11am-11pm. ❷

Uzupio Kavine, Uzupio 2 (☎ 212 2138), may be the only true beer garden in town. The city's mayor and many of Vilnius's top artists are among the cafe's patrons. The picturesque location overlooks the Vilnia River and more than makes up for the lethargic service. Vegetarian baked goods with cheese and wine sauce (12Lt) win raves from locals. Entrees 8-25Lt. English menu. Open 10am-11pm. MC/V. ❸

🖸 CAFES

Cafe de Paris, Didzioji 1 (☎ 261 1021). By day, homesick expats flow in from the adjacent French Embassy to enjoy authentic crepes (2.50-9Lt) in cozy environs. But on Wednesday nights, when live DJs rock the house, Cafe de Paris is said to host the hottest party in town. Lithuanian pop stars and French tourists groove on the microscopic dance floor. Open daily 10am-10pm.

Skonis Ir Kvapas, Trakć 8 (☎ 212 2803). Tucked away in a quiet courtyard near the heart of the Old City, this charming cafe offers fan-shaped menu of exotic teas (3-5Lt a pot). The name means "taste and smell," and, accordingly, servers will let you sniff your tea before ordering. Breakfast (6-10Lt) available all day. Dinner entrees (16-25Lt) are pricey and small. English menu. Open M-F 8:30am-11pm, Sa-Su 9:30am-11pm. MC/V.

LITHUANIA

Cafe Afrika, Pilies 28 (☎ 868 23 7793). This centrally-located establishment continues to attract students and counter-culture types. English menu features quirky dish titles, including a politically-incorrect beef soup spiced with chili named "Where's Pinochet?" (10Lt). Entrees (12-20Lt) and desserts (6-10Lt). Open daily 10am-11pm. MC/V.

◎ SIGHTS

SENAMIESTIS AND BEYOND

HIGHER CASTLE MUSEUM AND GEDIMINAS TOWER. Behind the cathedral (see below), a winding path leads to the top of the hill which has been crowned by a castle since 200 BC and is the present site of a majestic 15th-century Gothic structure. The Higher Castle Museum (Aukštutines Pilies Mziejus) details the history of the city and displays old maps and scale models of the castle. Its main attraction, however, is the magnificent view of Senamiestis and Gedimino. *(Castle Hill, Arsenalo 5. ☎ 61 74 53. Open daily Mar.-Oct. 10am-7pm; Nov.-Feb. Tu-Su 11am-5pm. 4Lt, students 2Lt.)*

CATHEDRAL SQUARE (ARKIKATEDROS AIKŠTĖ). The church that stood here in the 13th-century was converted to a shrine to Perkunas, a pagan god, after King Mindaugas failed to convert Lithuania to Christianity. After the nation embraced Catholicism in the 15th century, the site became home to a Gothic **cathedral** that, through renovations, has taken on a decidedly Neoclassical character. The remains of Casmir, Lithuania's patron saint, lie on the cathedral's southern side. The free-standing bell tower west of the cathedral dates back to the 16th century, although the six bells inside were donated in 2002. The Soviets converted the cathedral into an art gallery. *(At the end of Pilies and Universiteto. ☎ 261 11 27. Open M-Sa 7am-1pm and 2:30-8pm, Su 7am-2pm.)* The **statue** of Grand Duke Gediminas, founder of Vilnius (see History, p. 440), was erected in 1994. To the east of the cathedral is the **Royal Palace,** which the city is hoping to rebuild in time for the 2009 millennial celebration of the first mention of Lithuania in written records.

TOWN HALL SQUARE (ROTUŠĖS AIKŠTĖ). Located on Didžioji, Town Hall Square is an ancient marketplace dominated by the columns of the 18th-century **town hall**, now home to the **Lithuanian Artists' Center** (Lietuvos Menininkv Rumai), with exhibits of local work. When US President George W. Bush visited in 2002, he said that "anyone who would choose Lithuania as an enemy has also made an enemy of the United States of America." His words were immortalized in an engraving at the northeast corner of the hall. *(Didžioji 31. ☎ 61 0619. Open M-F 9am-6pm.)* Don't miss Lithuania's oldest church, the **Church of St. Nicholas** (Šv. Mikalojaus Bažnyčia), which was recently renovated. It was built in 1320 by German merchants while Lithuania was still a pagan nation. Vilnius' Russian Orthodox worshippers fill the church on Sunday mornings. *(Didžioji 12. ☎ 261 8559. Open daily 10am-6pm.)*

CHURCH OF ST. ANNE. This house of worship's Gothic exterior may be the image most frequently featured on postcards from Vilnius. Napoleon, arriving in the city triumphantly in the summer of 1812, supposedly said he wanted to carry the church back to Paris on the palm of his hand. *(Maironio 8, at the end of Bernardinu.)*

CHURCH OF ST. PETER AND PAUL. According to local lore, Italian stucco-workers built the ornate Baroque interior of the church (Šv. Apaštalv Petro ir Povilo Bažnyčia) in the late 17th-century after the Polish architect who designed the church decided that Lithuanian sculptors were inferior. Note the chandelier styled like a sailing ship. *(Antakalnio 1. Take tram #2, 3, or 4 from Senamiestis. Alternately, head to the northeast edge of the Old City, where the Neris and Vilnia Rivers intersect, and follow T. Kosciuskos 2km until you reach the church. ☎ 234 0229.)*

ANTAKALNIS CEMETERY (ANTAKALINO KAPINES). This stunning graveyard 3km outside the Old Town is a resting place for Lithuania's national heroes and artistic luminaries. *(Facing the Church of St. Peter and Paul, bear right onto Antakalnio and continue 150m until the road forks. Bear right onto Sapiegos and continue 400m; at the archway, turn right onto Jurates. Make the first left onto Kuoso; then make the first right onto Kariu Kapu.)*

VILNIUS UNIVERSITY (VILNIAUS UNIVERSITETAS). This Jesuit college, home to 14,000 students, dates back to the late-16th century, when it figured prominently in the Counter-Reformation. Distinguished alums include 19th-century bard Adam Mickiewicz and Polish poet Czeslaw Milosz, a Nobel Laureate in literature. **St. John's Church** (Šv. Jonų Bažnyčia), Šv. Jono 12, off Pilies, served as a science museum under Soviet rule. The 17th-century Astronomical Observatory, once rivaled in importance only by Greenwich and the Sorbonne, sits through the arches opposite St. John's. With more than 5,000,000 volumes, the **university library** remains Lithuania's largest. *(Universiteto 3. ☎ 261 1795.)* The nearby **Church of the Holy Spirit** (Šventosios Dvasios Bažnyčia), a gold-and-marble Baroque masterpiece, was last rebuilt in 1770. *(Dominikonų 8, near the corner of Pilies and Šv. Jono. ☎ 62 9595.)*

ST. CASIMIR'S CHURCH (ŠV. KAZIMIERO BAŽNYČIA). Named after the country's patron saint and topped with a golden crown to indicate Casimir's royal bloodline, this is Vilnius's oldest Baroque church. Built by the Jesuits in 1604, the church has endured a painful history: Napoleon used it to store grain, tsarist authorities of the Russian Orthodox faith seized it from Catholics in 1841, invading Germans declared it a Lutheran house of worship in WWI, and the Soviets converted the church into a monument to atheism. The church returned to Catholicism in 1989. Free English-language information pamphlet available inside. *(Didžioji 34. ☎ 222 1715. Open M-Sa 4-6:30pm, Su 9am-1pm.)*

GATES OF DAWN (AUŠROS VARTAI). The Gates of Dawn, the only surviving portal of the city walls, have guarded Senamiestis since the 16th century. The gates are a pilgrimage site for Eastern European Catholics, and it is common practice for locals to cross themselves before passing through. After entering the Old City, pass through a door to the right and climb the stairs; the gold-laced **portrait of the Virgin Mary** housed on the second floor is said to have miraculous powers. When the chapel was built in 1671, the canvas reportedly served to resuscitate a child who fell from a window. Karol Woytyla sought to visit the Gates when he was archbishop of Kracóv, but was blocked by Soviet authorities; he sent his skullcap instead, and—after being anointed as Pope John Paul II—finally visited Vilnius in 1993. *(Free. Open daily 9am-6pm.)* The highly decorated **St. Theresa's Church** (Šv. Teresės Bažnyčia) was built between 1633 and 1652 to honor a Carmelite mystic. **The Church of the Holy Spirit** (Šv. Dvasios Bažnyčia) is the seat of Lithuania's Russian Orthodox archbishop. It is the resting place of St. Antonius, Ivan, and Eustachius, martyred in 1347 by pagan militants. *(Aušros Vartų 10. ☎ 212 7765.)*

PARLIAMENT. In January 1991, the world watched as Lithuanians raised barricades to protect their parliament from the Soviet army. President Ladsbergis later said that all of the deputies expected to give their lives on the night of the Soviet invasion. East of the building, a section of the barricade remains as a memorial. Crosses, flowers, and photographs honor those who perished at the TV Tower (see below). An impromptu memorial remembers civilian victims of the ongoing conflict in Chechnya. *(Gedimino 53, just before the Neris River.)*

LITHUANIA

HILL OF THREE CROSSES (TRJIŲ KRŽIŲ KALNAS). From the northeast edge of the Old City, cross the Arsenalo bridge and immediately turn right up a winding path. Where the road diverges in front of an amphitheater, go right to reach the crosses and catch a breathtaking view of the area. In the 13th century, pagans crucified Franciscan monks on the hill. Four centuries later, locals erected crosses to commemorate the martyrs; however, in 1950, Stalin dismantled the monuments. They were rebuilt in 1989 to both memorialize the martyred monks and pay homage to the Lithuanians who were deported to Siberia under the Soviet regime.

TV TOWER (TELEVIZIJOS BOKŠTAS). Stretching to a height of 326.47m, the infamous tower is visible from the city center. Its current character as a popular tourist destination with a revolving platform and restaurant belies the tragic events of the site's past. Fourteen unarmed civilians were killed here on Jan. 13, 1991 as the Red Army forced the station off the air. Crosses and memorials surround the spot today, and the neighborhood's streets have been renamed in honor of the 14 victims. *(Sausio 13-Osios 10. Take tram #11 14 stops from Skalvija on Žaliasis Bridge's south end toward Pašilaičai. ☎ 245 8877. Open daily 10am-9pm. 1½hr. tours on the hr. 15Lt, children 6Lt.)*

FRANK ZAPPA MONUMENT. Though the rock musician never visited Vilnius, his anti-authority message struck a chord among a population buckling under Soviet oppression. Today, he is immortalized through a bust of his head elevated on a 3m pole in a parking lot. Perhaps the most random monument in Eastern Europe, it was installed in 1995 after the Museum of Theater, Music, and Cinema Art (see Museums, p. 455) turned it away. *(Off Pylimo between Kalinausko 1 and 3.)*

JEWISH VILNIUS

Vilnius, known in Yiddish as "Vilna," was once called "Jerusalem of the North," and served as a center of Jewish learning and culture. It was a stronghold of the "Mitnagdim," the scholarly rabbis who resisted the Chasidic movement in the 18th century. Jews accounted for 100,000 of the city's 230,000 population at the outbreak of WWII. Only 6,000 remained when the Red Army retook the city in 1944.

▨ VILNA GAON JEWISH STATE MUSEUM OF LITHUANIA. Named for the 18th-century Talmudic scholar Elijah Ben Shlomo Zalman (known as the *gaon*, or genius), this two-site museum seeks to preserve Vilnius's Jewish heritage and commemorate the Holocaust, in which 95% of Vilnius's Jews perished. **The Green House** has a jarring exhibit on the elite Nazi Einsatzkommando's extermination of the city's Jews. The museum also provides an honest account of Lithuanian fighters' persecution of their Jewish neighbors on the eve of the German invasion. The last room includes a tribute to Sempo Sugihara, "the Japanese Schindler," a diplomat who helped 4000 Jews escape from Poland and Lithuania. *(Pamėnkalnio 12. ☎ 262 0730; www.jmuseum.lt. English and Hebrew captions. Open M-Th 9am-5pm, F 9am-4pm. Donation requested.)* The **Tarbut Gymnasium** contains a display on the city's lost synagogues and pays homage to the 550,000 Jews—many of Lithuanian descent—who fought for the US Army in WWII. The **Gallery of the Righteous** (Teisuoliu Galerija) honors Lithuanians who sheltered Jews during WWII. Exhibits have English captions. *(Pylimo 4. ☎ 261 7917. Open M-Th 10am-5pm, F 10am-4pm. 4Lt, students 2Lt.)*

VILNIUS CHORAL SYNAGOGUE (SINAGOGA). Vilnius was once home to more than 100 Jewish houses of worship, including the majestic Great Synagogue, which Napoleon likened to Notre Dame. The Vilnius Choral Synagogue, built in 1903, is the only Jewish holy site that was not destroyed in WWII. Recently, it has fallen on hard times, partially due to security concerns. The synagogue was closed in 2004. If you find it shuttered, head to Tarbut Gymnasium (see p. 454), which displays photographs of the synagogue's ornate interior. *(Pylimo 39.)*

PANERIAIMEMORIAL (PANERIŲ MEMORIALAS). Hidden at the end of a desolate dirt road 8km southwest of the Old City, this stirring forest is where Nazis executed 100,000 Lithuanians, including 70,000 Jews. The Gestapo found that the oil pits the Soviets had drilled were convenient for executing Lithuania's Jews en masse. Inscriptions at the memorial are in Hebrew, Lithuanian, and Russian. You can reach the memorial by rail (10min.); most trains bound for Trakai and Kaunas from Geležinkelio Stotis, Vilnius's main station, will make their first stop in Panerai. Inquire about tickets (0.90Lt) at the windows to the left of the central entrance of the station. *(From Panerai's small yellow station house, turn right on Agrastu, continuing for 2km until you reach the memorial at a dead end. Return to Vilnius by train or cross the pedestrian bridge near the Paerai station to reach a highway and #8 bus stop.)* There is a museum with English captions. *(Agrastv 17. ☎ 260 2001. Open M and W-F 11am-5pm. Free.)*

CHABAD LUBAVITCH CENTER. This Jewish cultural center provides kosher meals (8Lt) for travelers, but call or e-mail well in advance. The only resident rabbi in Lithuania, American-born Sholom Ber Krinsky, coordinates community service and aids Jews visiting Vilnius for genealogical research. *(Šaltinių 12. ☎ 215 0387; www.jewish.lt. Open daily 9am-6pm.)*

🏛 MUSEUMS

MUSEUM OF GENOCIDE VICTIMS (GENOCIDO AUKŲ MUZIEJUS). The horrors of the Soviet regime are highlighted at the former KGB headquarters, which also served as a Gestapo outpost during WWII. The remains of some 706 former prisoners are still stored inside. The meticulously preserved execution room, isolation cells, and torture chambers are as chilling as the museum's seeming disregard for the building's Nazi past. A must-see site for travelers interested in Vilnius' tragic past. *(Aukv 2a. ☎ 262 2449. Open Tu-Sa 10am-5pm, Su 10am-3pm. Captions in English and Lithuanian. Museum 2Lt, students with ISIC card 1Lt from Sept.-May. Audio tour in English 8Lt)*

LITHUANIAN NATIONAL MUSEUM (LIETUVOS NACIONALINIS MUZIEJUS). The permanent display details traditional Lithuanian life, with an emphasis on rural areas around the time of the emancipation of the serfs. The fascinating exhibit on Napoleon's 1812 conquest of Vilnius and his soldiers' retreat through the city is slated to end mid-2005. *(Arsenalo 1, behind the Gedimino Tower. Enter Arsenalo 3 through the courtyard. ☎ 262 94 26; www.lnm.lt. English captions. Open W-Su 10am-6pm. 4Lt, students 2Lt.)*

VILNIUS PICTURE GALLERY (VILNIAUS PAVEIKSIŲ GALERIJA). Housed in the beautifully restored 16th-century Chodkeviciai Palace, this museum displays late 18th- and early 19th-century works, including an interesting Neoclassical room, from the Vilnius Art School, which was shut down by the tsarist government in 1831. *(Didžioji 4. ☎ 212 4258. Open Tu-Sa noon-6pm, Su noon-5pm. 5Lt, students 2.50Lt.)*

MUSEUM OF APPLIED ART (TAIKOMOSIOS DALIĖS MUZIEJUS). The museum holds over 270 pieces of gold, silver, and jeweled religious objects. The treasure was hidden in the Cathedral walls on the eve of the Russian invasion in 1655 and was only rediscovered in 1985. *(Arsenalo 3a, next to the National Museum. ☎ 212 1813; www.tdm.lt. Open Tu-Su 11am-6pm. 8Lt, students 4Lt.)*

MICKIEWICZ MEMORIAL APARTMENT. The Lithuanian-Polish poet Adam Mickiewicz (see **Poland: The Arts**, p. 506) lived in this apartment (Mickevičiaus Memorialinis Butas) for three months in 1822; his possessions remain. Although he wrote in Polish, Lithuanians cherish Mickiewicz for penning their national epic, *Pan Tadeusz*. The Baltic bard's words ring true to all the European nations whose authority over Vilnius proved ephemeral: "Lithuania...Only he who has lost you can know how much you are cherished." (*Bemardinv 11.* ☎ *279 1879. Open Tu-F 10am-5pm, Sa-Su 10am-2pm. English captions. 2Lt.*)

LITHUANIAN NATIONAL MUSEUM OF THEATER, MUSIC, AND CINEMA ART. This museum (Lietuvos Teatro, Muzikos Ir Kino Muziejus) chronicles the esoteric history of Lithuanian performing arts over the past 200 years. Its collections include musical instruments, clothing, and even shoes worn by famous Lithuanian thespians and cinematographers. (*Vilniaus 41.* ☎ *262 2406. Open Tu-F noon-6pm, Sa 11am-4pm. Few English captions. 4Lt, students 2Lt.*)

🎵 ENTERTAINMENT

Check *Vilnius in Your Pocket* or the Lithuanian-language morning paper *Lietuvos Rytas* for event listings, or pick up a free copy of *Exploring Vilnius*, distributed by hotels and **TIC** branches (see **Practical Information**, p. 448). TIC also has info on obtaining tickets. English-language movies are shown at **Lietuva Cinema,** Pylimo 17 (☎ 262 34 22), which has "seats for lovers" (two seats not separated by an arm rest). Catch a flick at **Coca-Cola Plaza,** Savanoriu 7 (☎ 265 1625; www.forumcinemas.lt). **Kino Centras Skalvija,** Goštauto 2/5 (☎ 268 5832), is the best independent film theater. *Lietuvos Rytas* and www.kinas.lt list locations and showtimes.

Lithuanian National Philharmonic (Lietuvos Naciolinė Filharmonija), Aušros Vartų 5 (☎ 266 5233; www.filharmonija.lt). Tickets 4Lt and up. Most performances W-Sa 7pm, Su noon. It also organizes the **Vilniaus Festivalis,** a month of concerts beginning in late May. Box office open Tu-Sa 10am-7pm, Su 10am-1pm. MC/V.

Opera and Ballet Theater (Operos ir Baleto Teatras), Vienuolio 1 (☎ 262 0727; www.opera.lt). Housed in a building of pure 70s Soviet concrete. Box office open Sept.-June M-F 10am-7pm, Sa 10am-6pm, Su 11am-3pm.

Lithuanian National Drama Theater (Lietuvos Nacionalinis Dramos Teatras), Gedimino 4 (☎ 262 9771; www.teatras.lt). Look for 3 muses carved in black stone. Most performances in Lithuanian, with occasional shows in English. Dance performances and an annual summer drama festival. Box office open Tu-Sa 10am-6pm.

🎭 NIGHTLIFE

The Vilnius bar and club circuit is vibrant and diverse, but also small. If you linger long in town, you'll begin to recognize names and faces. Look to the **Lithuanian Gay and Lesbian Homepage** or the **Gay Club** (see **GLBT Services,** p. 450) for the latest in Vilnius's gay nightlife scene.

🍹 **SoHo,** Aušros Vartų 7 (☎ 212 1210), next to the Filharmonija. This new bar's bright interior and music-filled courtyard make it great for drinks with friends. The Mexican food may be the best in town. Finger-painting on W; student battles-of-the-bands on Tu, live music F-Sa at 8pm. English menu. Open Su-W 11am-midnight, Th-Sa 11am-2am.

Broadway (Broadvejus), Mėsiniu 4 (☎210 7208; brodvejus.lt), in the Old Town. Extraordinarily popular with the Vilnius teenie-bopper crowd, though even the club's most diehard patrons complain of the uninspired playlist and crowded dance floor. No sneakers. 10Lt cover includes 2 drinks. Open M noon-3am, Tu noon-4am, W-Sa noon-5am. MC/V.

The PUB (Prie Universiteto Baras), Dominikonų 9 (☎261 8393; www.pub.lt). Frequented by students from the nearby Vilnius University, this late-night pub hangout proves that good English food is not always an oxymoron. Still, fish and chips (12Lt) is hardly the main attraction; the dungeon-like basement hosts Vilnius' wildest dance parties. Open Su-Th 11am-2am, F-Sa 11am-5am. MC/V.

Amatininskv Užeiga, Didžioji 19, #2 (☎261 7968). This bar remains lively even after the rest of town shuts down. Artsy types discuss poetry about the meaning of life while drinking themselves silly on cheap beer (3Lt per 0.5L). Service is notoriously slow, but patrons praise the staff. English menu. Open M-F 8am-5am, Sa-Su 11am-5am.

☒ DAYTRIPS FROM VILNIUS

TRAKAI CASTLE   ☎528

Buses run to Trakai, 28km west of Vilnius (30min., about 1 per hr. 6:45am-9:30pm, 2.90Lt). Last bus back departs at 11:30pm. Be sure to check the bus schedule for changes. Bus station (☎900 016 61) open daily 4am-midnight. The castle is 3km north of the bus station. Facing Lake Totoriskia, turn right from the train station and follow Vytauto g. Within 100m, you will reach a map of the area in front of Su Saule Fotostudija. The Tourist Information Center, Vytauto 69 (☎285 1934; www.trakai.lt), 1km from the bus station offers free maps and English-language guides. Open M 8:30am-noon and 12:45-4:15pm, Tu-F 8:30am-noon and 12:45-5:30pm, Sa 9am-noon and 12:45-3pm. Castle and museum open daily 10am-7pm. 8Lt, students with ISIC 4Lt. 1hr. tours 40Lt/20Lt. English captions in most places. The best way to see Lake Gavle is by paddleboat. Rental stands are just beyond the castle's footbridge; some charge 15Lt per hr., but you may be able to bargain down to 12Lt per hr. or 6Lt for 30min.

Trakai's red-brick **Insular Castle** served as home to the dukes who ruled Lithuania and Poland in the late medieval era. Following the defeat of the Teutonic Order at the Battle of Grunwald in 1410, Trakai became the capital of the Grand Duchy of Lithuania (see **History**, p. 440). In 1665, the Russians accomplished what the Germans could not, plundering the town and razing the castle. Perhaps out of guilt, the Soviets began restoring the castle in 1955. The original stone foundations are visible, but unfortunately the castle now looks like a 20th-century creation. Tickets are valid for both the 30m brick watchtower and the **City and Castle History Museum.** Actors dressed as knights sword fight in the courtyard. English captions accompany the medieval displays but not the exhibits on the modern era. Turn right before the drawbridge to try your hand at crossbow (1 arrow 1Lt), slingshot (10 arrows 5Lt), or pistol (5 shots 1Lt). In July and August, the castle is a dramatic backdrop for concerts at the **Trakai Festival** (☎262 07 27; www.trakaifestival.lt).

Outside the castle, stop by the **Karaite Ethnographic Museum,** Karaimų 22 (☎225 5286). Trakai is home to a dwindling community of Karaites, a breakaway sect of Judaism which sprung up in the Byzantine Empire during the 8th century. In the 10th century, Karaites migrated to the Crimean Peninsula. In 1398, Vytautas granted the Karaites religious freedom and brought a small group to Trakai to serve as his bodyguards. Captions are in English. (Open W-Sa 10am-6pm. 2Lt, students 1Lt.) North 50m is the **Kenesa,** Karaimų 30, a Karaite house of worship. You can borrow a copy of an English pamphlet. (Open Th-Sa, 11am-6pm.) Try traditional Karaite fare at ☒**Kybnlar,** Karaimu 29 (☎285 5179; kybynlar@takas.lt), across from the museum. The house beer (3.50Lt for 0.5L mug) is especially good. MC/V.

EUROPOS PARKAS

Take the #5 trolleybus (departs 3-10 times per hr.) from the train station to the 3rd stop after the Neris River. Then, at the adjacent bus stop (next to the kiosk) change to the #36 bus (leaves every 10-20min.) and continue to the last stop, which will drop you off about 3km away (30min. walk) from the park. There are also public transportation "minibuses" which run 4-7 times daily and leave from the same location as the #36 bus, but go directly to the park. Last minibus leaves the park at 5:50pm M-F and 4:45pm Sa-Su, but be sure to check the bus schedule as times may change. ☎237 7077; www.europospar-kas.lt. Park includes a restaurant, post office, and gift shop. Open daily 9am-sunset. Guided tours in Russian, English, or Lithuanian 50Lt. Park 10Lt, students 8Lt.

In 1989, the French National Geographic Institute made a rather earth-shattering calculation: the geographical center of continental Europe does not lie in Budapest, Kraków, or even Prague. Rather, Europe's center is in a remote forest outside of Vilnius. In light of this discovery, **Gintaras Karosas,** a Lithuanian sculptor and artist, had the idea to build a sculpture park. By the time the USSR fell and Lithuania achieved its independence, Karosas's park had become a reality. It is his poignant sculpture, reminiscent of the equator line in Ecuador, or the Prime Meridian line in Greenwich, that commemorates the center of Europe. The park also gives the distance to all of Europe's capitals, and there are about 90 outdoor sculptures spread over an area of 55 hectares in a forest. Particularly impressive is the **TV sculpture**—certified by the Guinness Book of World Records as the largest structure made from television sets—along with a fallen statue of Lenin at the center. There's also a wire-frame chair, a 6m pyramidal rock, and numerous other unique sculptures.

INLAND LITHUANIA

While flashier Vilnius has historically attracted foreign attention and investment, inland Lithuania has always been the bedrock of the nation. Today, Kaunas sets the standard of Lithuanian culture, while in the north, Šiauliai and its Hill of Crosses has become a symbol of resistance to communist rule.

KAUNAS   ☎37

For two glorious decades from 1920 to 1939, Kaunas (KOW-nas; pop. 420,000) was capital of independent Lithuania while Vilnius languished under Polish rule. In that period, Kaunas became the center of the country's intellectual life; its wealth of museums and monuments is the legacy of Kaunas's brief moment in the sun. In many ways, Kaunas offers a more authentic glimpse at Lithuanian culture than Vilnius does: while the modern capital city is the product of an eclectic blend of foreign influences, Kaunas is a more homogeneous city, consistently charming travelers with cobblestone streets and well-preserved 15th-century architecture.

▐ TRANSPORTATION

Trains: MK Čiurlionio 16 (☎29 22 60; www.litrail.lt), at the end of Vytauto, where it intersects with MK Čiurlionio. Open 24hr. To: **Vilnius** (2hr., 12 per day, 9.80Lt) and **Rīga, LAT** (5hr., 1 per day, 25Lt). Schedule varies for other connections, including **Kaliningrad, RUS; Tallinn, EST;** and **Warsaw, POL.** All international trains run through Vilnius.

Buses: Vytauto 24/26 (☎40 90 60, international reservations 32 22 22; fax 40 90 72). Open daily 4:30am-10pm. To: **Klaipėda** (2½-6hr., 9 per day, 26-30Lt); **Palanga** (2½-6½hr., 7 per day, 32Lt); **Šiauliai** (2½-3½hr., 11 per day, 19Lt); **Vilnius** (1½hr., every 30min., 11-12Lt). For bus schedules or advance tickets, visit **EuroLines,** Laisvės 36 (☎20 98 36; www.kautra.lt). Open M-F 9am-1pm and 2-6pm.

Hydrofoils: Raudondvario 107 (☎26 13 48), in the town of Vilijampolė, across the Neris. Take bus #7 from the train or bus station, or #10 or 11 from the stop at the west end of Laisvės. Get off at Kedainių, the 3rd stop across the river. In summer, Raketa hydrofoils splash to **Nida** via **Nemunas** (4hr., 1 per day, 59Lt).

Public Transportation: Bus and tram tickets are available from kiosks (0.6Lt) or from the driver (0.7Lt). Bus #7 runs parallel to Laisvės, never more than a block away from the main street. The best way to get around the city is by one of the **maršrutinis taksis vans** (1Lt, 2Lt at night) that zip along bus routes. Tell the driver where you want to get off.

Taxis: State Taxi Co. (☎23 66 66). From 1Lt per km. **Private Taxi** (☎23 98 80). Typically 0.9-1.5Lt per km, though rates vary.

ORIENTATION

Kaunas stands at the confluence of the Nemunas and Neris rivers, with **Senamiestis** (Old Town) in the west. In the center, vibrant **Naujamiestis** (New Town) is bisected by **Laisvės,** a pedestrian boulevard. The train and bus stations stand 300m apart along **Vytauto,** a bustling thoroughfare that defines the eastern edge of the New Town. Two blocks north of **Rambyes Park,** Vytauto forms an intersection with **Laisvės,** the tree-lined pedestrian boulevard flanked by upmarket clothiers and classy hotels. Laisvės's most prominent feature, the **Church of St. Michael the Archangel,** visible throughout much of Kaunas, helps travelers across the city find their bearings. Laisvės forks about 2km west of the church. The right fork, heavily congested **Šv. Gertrūdos,** leads to the **Kaunas Castle** and **Santakos park,** which overlook the **Neris River.** The left fork, narrow cobblestone **Vilniaus**—named such because it once ran all the way to Lithuania's largest city—now carries travelers through the Old Town to **Rotušės Square,** the site of Kaunas's oldest architectural gems. *Kaunas in Your Pocket* (8Lt), which includes helpful maps and information on restaurants, hotels, and sights, is available at Litinterp (see **Accommodations,** p. 460), the tourist office, and at most kiosks where magazines are sold.

PRACTICAL INFORMATION

Tourist Office: Tourist Information Center (TIC), Laisvės 36, 1.5km from train station (☎40 84 10; http://turinfo.lt). Helpful English-speaking staff provides free maps of Kaunas and arranges excursions. Open M-F 9am-6pm, Sa-Su 9am-12:15pm and 1-6pm.

Currency Exchange: Look for *Valiutos Keitykla* signs on Laisvės and Vilniaus. **Lietuvos Taupomasis Bankas,** Laisvės 82 (☎20 66 36), gives MC **cash advances** and cashes AmEx/MC/Thomas Cook **traveler's checks.** Open M-F 8am-4pm. **Hotel Taioji Neris,** K. Donelaičio 27, has a **24hr. currency exchange. ATMs** are everywhere.

Luggage Storage: In a tunnel under the train station. 1Lt per bag. Open daily 8:30am-2:15pm, 3-8pm, and 8:30pm-8am.

English-Language Bookstore: Centrinis Knygynas, Laisvės 81 (☎22 95 72; fax 22 31 01), stocks classics and best-sellers. Open M-F 10am-7pm, Sa 10am-5pm.

GLBT Organizations: Kaunas Organization for Sexual Equality (☎70 57 37; robejona@takas.lt) has info on gay clubs and events.

24hr. Pharmacy: Vaistinė Lucerna, Vytauto 2 (☎32 44 44).

Telephones: To the right as you enter the post office. Open M-F 7am-7pm, Sa 7am-5pm. Also throughout the city.

Internet Access: Kavinė Internetas, Vilniaus 24 (☎40 74 27). English spoken. 5Lt per hr. Open daily 10am-midnight. **Syla,** E. Ozeskienes 5, has the cheapest rates in town. 2Lt per hr., 10pm-10am 8Lt per hr. Open 24hr.

Post Office: Laisvės 102 (☎32 42 86). **Poste Restante** at window #11; 0.50Lt per package. Open M-F 7am-7pm, Sa 7am-5pm. **Postal Code:** LT-3000.

ACCOMMODATIONS

Accommodations in Kaunas don't come cheap. The best option for the budget-conscious is to arrange a **private room** through ▨**Litinterp,** Gedimino 28. Most of Litinterp's rooms and apartments have excellent locations, either in Senamiestis or on Laisvės. (☎22 87 18, after-hours 20 53 12; www.litinterp.lt. Open M-F 8:30am-5:30pm, Sa 9:30am-3pm. Singles 80-120Lt; doubles 140-160Lt; triples 180-210Lt.)

▨ **Minotel,** Vl. Kuzmos 8 (☎20 37 59; www.minotel.lt). This quiet hotel in the heart of Senamiestis has cheerful new rooms with baths, minibars, safes, phones, and TVs. A remarkably good deal when contrasted with comparable but more expensive accommodations. Breakfast included. Reception 7am-10pm. Singles 160Lt; doubles 240Lt. 20% discount F-Su, 10% discount for stays of 3 or more days. ❹

Apple Economy Hotel, M. Valanciaus 19 (☎32 14 04; www.applehotel.lt). Following Sv. Getrudos west toward Kaunas Castle, turn left onto M. Valanciaus. It's in a courtyard just beyond Pilies. True to the hotel's theme, the friendly, English-speaking staff places apples in each of the 14 cozy rooms. All but 2 come with private baths. Request a room with WC. Singles and doubles 145-160Lt. ❸

Metropolis, S. Daukanto 21 (☎20 59 92; metropolis@takiojineris.com), just off Laisvės in the center of town. Charmless Soviet-era rooms come with TV and bath. The room prices include breakfast at a restaurant 500m away; you can save 15Lt by telling the staff you'll forego the morning meal. Singles 70Lt; doubles 100Lt; triples 135Lt. ❷

FOOD

▨ **Žalias Ratas,** Laisvės 36b (☎20 00 71). Follow the narrow alley to the left of the TIC to reach this cozy, thatch-roofed cottage where the friendly staff dressed as Lithuanian peasants serves authentic regional cuisine (entrees 5-28Lt). The famous cold beat soup is only served before 3pm, so stop in for lunch. Live music in summer Th-Sa 8pm, low season F-Sa 8pm. English menu. Open daily 11am-midnight. MC/V. ❸

Miesto Sodas, Laisvės 93 (☎42 44 24). The eclectic menu at this popular restaurant includes a number of vegetarian options and takes an ambitious foray into East Asian fare. Watch out for surcharges (soy sauce 1Lt). Entrees 7-16Lt. Live music daily 6-9pm. Open daily 11am-midnight. MC/V. ❷

Arbatinė, Laisvės 100 (☎32 37 32). This vegan cafe attracts locals with freshly baked pastries (1-2Lt). Entrees 5-6Lt. Open M-F 8:30am-8pm, Sa 10am-6pm. ❶

SIGHTS

Sights in Kaunas cluster around the two ends of Laisvės, the city's main pedestrian boulevard. St. Michael's Church and Unity Sq. lie at one end, while Senamiestis and its cathedral, town hall, and smaller attractions are at the opposite end. The Ninth Fort and Pažaislis Monastery and Church lie outside the city.

UNITY SQUARE (VIENYBĖS AIKŠTĖ). On the south side, Vytauto Didžiojo University and the older Kaunas Technological University draw a student population of more than 16,000. Across the street, in an outdoor shrine to Lithuanian statehood, busts of famous political and literary figures flank a corridor leading from the **Freedom Monument** (Laisvės paminklas) to an eternal flame commemorating those who

Kaunas

🏠 ACCOMMODATIONS
Apple Enonomy Hotel, 1
Litinterp, 11
Metropolis, 9
Minotel, 3

🍎 FOOD
Arbatinė, 7
Miesto Sodas, 6
Žalias Ratas, 10

🍴 NIGHTLIFE

Avilys, 5
B.O., 4
Siena, 8
Skliautai, 2

0   300 yards
0   300 meters

VILIJAMPOLĖ

Santakos
Parkas

SENAMIESTIS

TO NINTH FORT
(3km)
& GHETTO
MONUMENT (10m)

Nemunas

Neris

Santakos g.

Vandens
Muziejaus
Daugirdo g.
Papilio g.
Karaliaus dvaro

ROTUŠĖS
AIKŠTĖ

Kauno
Castle
Ruins

Perkūnas
House

Vytautas
Church

Aleksoto
Bridge

Town Hall
Aleksoto

Kuzmos g.

Naugardo g.
Minties g.

Kumelių g.

Raguvos g.
Kumelių g.

Valančiaus g.

M.
Valančiaus g.

Kauno dvaro

Kaunas
Cathedral

M. Daukšos g.

Zamenhofo g.
A. Mapu g.

Kumpių g.
Nemuno g.

Palangos g.

J. Jablonskio g.

Šaukliu

Skriaudžiu g.

Karaliaus

Veiverių g.

Dariaus ir
Girėno g.

Antakalnio g.

H. ir O. Minkovskiu g.

Birštono g.

Druskininkų g.

Smalininkų g.

Pivotu g.
Šilutės g.

Trimito g.
I. Kanto g.

Nemuno
Salos
Park

Kęstučio g.

Mairono g.

Mindaugo pr.

Vilniaus g.

Gimnazijos g.

J. Gruodžio g.
Laisvės al.

D. Poškos g.

J. Žikaro g.

Savanorių pr.

A. Mackevičiaus g.

Benediktinių g.

Levu takas

Jonavos g.

Vyšnių g.

Žilibėro g.

Turženų g.
Paserinų g.

Skliaunų g.

Šatrijos g.

Telšių g.

Žaliakalnio g.

Pakrantės
takas

P. Kalpoko g.

Vaišviu g.

Kaunas
Philharmonic

Sapiegos g.
Yasario 16 g.

Musical
Theater

Centrinis
Knygynas

Academic
Drama Theater

S.Daukanto g.

Vytautas the
Great War
Museum

Eternal Flame &
Freedom Monument

Devil Museum

M.K. Čiurlionis
Museum

VIENYBĖS
AIKŠTĖ

Vytautas Didžiojo
University

Romura ■

Spaustuvininku g.

A. Mickevičiaus g.

M. Žilinskis
Dailes Galerija

Gedimino g.

St. Michael
the Archangel

Kaunas
Technological
University

Vašionkiu

Astronomijos g.

Aukštaičiu g.

Aušros g.

Žemaičiu g.

Christ's
Resurrection
Church

V. Putvinskio g.

K. Donelaičio g.

Kaunakiemio g.

Karo
Ligoninės g.

Griunvaldo g.

Miško g.
Bažnyčios g.

Museum of Exiles and
Political Prisoners

TAXI

Vytauto pr.

Ramybės
Park

Totoriu g.

Krėvos g.

Traku g.

NEPRIKLAUSOMYBĖS
AIKŠTĖ

Parodos g.

Radasty g.

Tupiliu g.

Vaidaužio g.

AŽUOLYNAS
PARK

Sugihara House
and Museum

Vaižganto g.

Margio g.

K. Bugos g.

MK Čiurlionio g.

Perkuno alėja

K. Petrausko g.

Vydūno alėja

Aukštaičiu g.

P. Vitkausko g.

Aušros g.

Lietuviu g.

Minties ratas g.
Geliu alėja

Sporto g.

V. Kudirkos g.

Rabalienu pl.

Radastu g.

TO JEWISH
CEMETARY
(100m)

Prancuzu g.

TO PAZAISLIS
MONASTERY AND
CHURCH (10km)

Ažuolynas

LITHUANIA

died in the liberation struggle of 1918-20. These symbols of nationhood disappeared during Soviet occupation, but Lithuanians rebuilt the square when the country's Soviet-era rulers broke away from the Moscow-based Communist Party in 1989. On a hill behind the Čiurlionis Museum (see **Museums,** p. 463) stands the enormous **Christ's Resurrection Church.** Construction began in 1932, but the structure languished for half a century due to the Soviet doctrine of atheism. It now belongs to the Catholic Church, which has yet to complete the project.

ST. MICHAEL THE ARCHANGEL CHURCH. Originally built for the tsar's Russian Orthodox troops at the end of the 19th century, this breathtaking neo-Byzantine church became a Catholic house of worship in the 1990s. Its striking blue domes can be seen throughout the city, but its exterior needs restoration. Outside, the detailed **Statue of Man** by Petras Mozuras reaches with outstretched arms. *(Nepriklausomybės aikštė 14, at the east end of Laisvės opposite Senamiestis. ☎ 22 66 76. Open M-F 9am-3pm, Sa-Su 8:30am-2pm. Services M-F noon, Sa 10am, Su 10am and noon. Free.)*

KAUNAS CATHEDRAL (KAUNO ARKIKATEDRA BAŽNYČIA). Lithuania's largest Gothic church, Kaunas Cathedral is thought to have been built around the 1408-13 Christianization of Low Lithuania. The breathtaking interior reflects Renaissance and Baroque influences, although several damaging fires over the years have necessitated a series of repairs. Inside, look to the right of the altar for the neo-Gothic **Chapel of St. John the Baptist.** In the chapel lies the tomb of Maironis, the priest from Kaunas whose poetry was key in Lithuania's 19th-century National Awakening (see **History,** p. 440); however, tourists are not welcome in the chapel. *(Vilniaus 26, inside the medieval city walls. ☎ 22 75 46. Open daily 7am-7pm. Free.)*

OLD TOWN SQUARE (ROTUŠĖS AIKŠTĖ). Just past the cathedral, the **town hall,** a stylistic melange constructed in stages from 1542 to 1771, presides over Old Town Square. Today, it is primarily used for weddings. Behind and to the left of the town hall stands a **statue of Maironis.** His hand hides his clerical collar, a ploy that duped the atheist Soviets into allowing the city to erect a statue of a priest. On the south side of the square is the **St. Francis Church and Jesuit Monastery,** which has changed hands several times since construction began 1666. It was converted into an Orthodox house of worship in the mid-19th century, but under the Soviet regime, the sanctuary served as a sports hall. The Jesuits regained control in 1990. Follow Aleksoto toward the river to reach the 15th-century **Perkūnas House** (Perkūnas namas), built for Hanseatic merchants on the site of a temple to Perkūnas, god of thunder. Its late-Gothic exterior resembles Vilnius's Church of St. Anne. While not nearly as well know as the latter structure, Perkunas House likely predates the Church of St. Anne by as many as 100 years. *(Open M-F 8am-5pm.)* At the end of the street is the **Gothic Vytautas Church** (Vytauto bažnyčia), also built in the early 1400s. According to legend, when Vytautas's army was defeated by the Tatars in 1398, the Lithuanian leader pledged to erect a church in the Virgin Mary's honor if his life was spared. *(☎ 20 38 54. Open for prayer M-F 6pm, Sa 10am and 6pm; Su 10am, noon, 6pm.)*

KAUNAS CASTLE. Up A. Jaksto, from northwest corner of Old Town Square, the Neris and Nemunas rivers meet at Santakos Parkas, a popular spot for young lovers on summer evenings. Turn left onto Pilies to reach the remains of Kaunas Castle. Teutonic knights destroyed the 13th-century castle in 1361. Later, flooding from the Neris river reduced the castle to shambles. To the south, along Papilio, is the **Church of the Holy Trinity.** Its seminary remained remarkably active under Soviet rule until 1963, when it became a dance studio. Farther west is the 15th-century Gothic **Church of St. George,** which is undergoing restoration.

NINTH FORT (IX FORTAS). The tsar's troops finished building this defensive installation in 1913 to protect Russia from an impending German invasion. Ironically, the fort eventually facilitated the mass murder of Kaunas's residents. During WWII, the Nazis killed 50,000 people, including 30,000 Jews, in the surrounding fields. Begin your visit at the architecturally innovative **new museum,** which houses the ticket book for both parts of the site and features an extensive display on the deportation of Lithuanians to Siberia during Stalin's rule. Inside the fort, the **old museum** contains Cell no. 5, where tourists can see inscriptions carved by French Jews who were held there before being executed in May 1944. Past the fort, an enormous Soviet-era sculpture commemorates "the victims of fascism," as the Holocaust dead were called in communist jargon. To your right as you approach the sculpture is a plaque, placed there by the city of Munich, which bears the inscription "in sorrow and shame, and appalled by the silence of the bystanders." *(Žemaičiv 73. ☎37 77 50. Hail microbus #46 along Lavies or 101 along Donelaico. 15 min., 2-5 per hr., 1Lt. Ask to stop at IX Fortas. An underpass beside of the highway leads to the site. Most Telsai-bound buses from the main station stop in front of the fort. 20 min., 1Lt. To return, take any passing microbus except #2, or wait for the buses, which come every 20min., in front of the new museum. Open W-Su 10am-6pm. Each museum 2Lt, students 1Lt. Cameras 20Lt. A tunnel connecting the prison with the barracks can be explored with a guide for 10Lt.)*

JEWISH KAUNAS. Kovno, as the city is known in Yiddish, was home to 37,000 Jews on the eve of WWII. Most were slaughtered at the Ninth Fort. Just 2500 Jews remained when the Soviets arrived in 1944. The Slobodka district, now known as Vilijampole, north of the Neris, traditionally served as home to the city's Jews. Little remains of the WWII ghetto except for a small **monument** to its former residents. To get to the monument, cross the Jurbarko bridge and turn right at the end. At the first fork, bear left onto Linkuvos and continue 50m to the intersection of Ariogalos and Krisciukaicio. The **Choral Synagogue** is renowned for its gold-trimmed *bimah* (altar). Inside is a memorial to Jewish soldiers who died fighting for Lithuanian independence between 1918 and 1920. Kaunas's remaining Jewish community cannot support a rabbi, but the synagogue opens briefly each day when congregants gather for prayer. *(E. Ozeskienes 17. ☎20 68 80 or 8 614 0 31 00. Open Su-F 5pm-5:30pm, Sa 10am-noon.)* The **cemetery** (senosios zydu kapines), located 2km from the city center, suffered utter neglect after the near-total extermination of Kaunas's Jewish community during WWII and is overgrown with vegetation. *(Go east down Parados east. Turn left on K. Petrauskro and continue 750m, then turn right onto Radvilenu. The cemetery is 500m down the road, at the intersection with J. Basanaviciaus.)*

PAŽAISLIS MONASTERY AND CHURCH. This vibrant, fresco-filled, Baroque complex sits on the right bank of the Nemunas 10km east of central Kaunas. Originally designed by three Florentine masters in the 17th century, the church was used as a KGB-run "psychiatric hospital" and then as a resort. The monastery was returned to the Catholic Church in 1990. The much-touted **Pažaislis Music Festival** (late-May to Sept.), featuring numerous classical music concerts, is held here, as are other **musical performances.** *(Kauno juros 31. Take tram #5 or 9 from the train station to the end of the line; the church is 1km down the road past a small beach. ☎75 64 85. Open Tu-Su 11am-6pm, but hours may vary, so call ahead. Free tour after 11am mass.)*

 MUSEUMS

🖾 **DEVIL MUSEUM (VELNIŲ MUZIEJUS).** According to Lithuanian folklore, the devil was a guardian figure until the advent of Christianity, when he transformed into an evil creature whose hapless attempts to deceive humanity were doomed to

LITHUANIA

fail. Painter Antanas Žmuidzinavičiaus (1876-1966) claims his longevity stemmed from his obsession with the devil. Over the course of his life, he amassed more than 260 images of the satanic figure. This museum, formerly known as the A. Žmuidzinavičiaus Art Collection, preserves and expands his collection. Most notable is "The Division of Lithuania," at the far left corner as you enter the third floor gallery, which depicts a satanic Stalin chasing a horned Hitler across skull-covered Lithuania. (V. Putvinskio 64. ☎ 22 15 87. Open Tu-Su 10am-5pm. 5Lt, students 2.50Lt.)

MUSEUM OF EXILES AND POLITICAL PRISONERS. This museum (Rezistencijos ir Tremties Muziejus) contains a collection of photographs and artifacts from the resistance to Soviet rule and has an exhibit on the life of Siberian exiles. The curator was an exile herself for 10 years and gives tours in Lithuanian, Russian, and German. (Vytauto 46, near Ramybės Park and a short walk from St. Michael's. ☎ 32 31 79. Open W-Sa 10am-4pm. English brochure free. Donation requested.)

VYTAUTAS THE GREAT WAR MUSEUM (VYTAUTO DIDŽIOJO KARO MUZIEJUS). Named after the 15th-century Lithuanian ruler, who conquered much of Eastern Europe and built a Lithuanian empire, this museum houses all sorts of weapons. It holds the airplane *Lituanica*, in which two Lithuanian-Americans, Steponas Darius and Stasys Girėnas (both featured on the 10Lt banknote), attempted to fly nonstop from New York to Kaunas in 1933. They crashed in Germany but were lauded as heroes and brought worldwide recognition to Lithuania. Another exhibit follows Napoleon's journey through the Baltics en route to his ill-fated Russian campaign. (Donelaičio 64, in Unity Sq. behind 2 soccer-playing lions. ☎ 32 09 39. Open Mar. 15-Oct. 15 Su and W-Sa 10am-6pm; Oct. 16-Mar. 14 W-Su 9am-5pm. 2Lt, students 1Lt.)

M.K. ČIURLIONIS MUSEUM (M.K. ČIURLIONIS MUZIEJUS). The works of painter and composer Mikalojus Konstantinas Ciurlionis (1875-1911) reflect Symbolist and Surrealist influences. His symphonies—both musical and visual—draw upon Lithuania's folk art tradition. This museum houses Ciurlionis's extensive portfolio. It has displays on Lithuanian cross-making and other folk art. (Putvinskio 55, in Unity Sq. ☎ 22 97 38. English captions. Open Tu-Su 11am-6pm. 5Lt, students 2.50Lt.)

SUGIHARA HOUSE AND FOUNDATION. Chiune Sugihara, the so-called "Japanese Schindler" served as Tokyo's consul in Kaunas at the beginning of WWII. In violation of government orders, Sugihara issued more than 6000 visas allowing Polish and Lithuanian Jews to travel to Kobe, Japan in 1940. The museum, at his former home, features powerful tributes from Jews who escaped death because of Sugihara's courage. (Valzganto 30, at the eastern edge of Naujamiestis. From Vytauto, follow Totoriu east to a mosque. Turn right, then left onto V. M. Putino. Climb the green staircase, then turn right and continue 100m to find the museum behind the Japanese Studies Center. ☎ 33 28 81. English captions. Open M-F 10am-5pm, Sa-Su 11am-6pm. Free.)

🎵 🍷 ENTERTAINMENT AND NIGHTLIFE

The **Musical Theater** (Muzikinis Teatras), Laisvės 91, performs operettas. (☎ 22 71 13. Box office open Tu-Su 10am-1pm and 3-6pm.) The **Academic Drama Theater** (Akademinis Dramos Teatras), Laisvės 71, stages dances and plays in Lithuanian and Russian. (☎ 22 40 64; www.dramosteatras.lt. Box office open daily 10am-7pm.) The **Kaunas Philharmonic,** Sapiegos 5, has classical concerts. (☎ 22 25 58. Box office open daily 2-6pm. Schedule posted at box office.) Cinemas with American films, usually in English, dot Laisvės, including **Laisvė**, Laisvės 46a (☎ 20 52 03).

🍷 **B.O.,** Multines 9 (☎ 20 65 42). This vivacious Old Town bar overcomes its unfortunate name to attract a fun, college-student crowd. Live music Th 9pm. Open M-F 10am-2am, Sa 3pm-2am, Su 3pm-midnight.

Siena (Wall), Laisvės 93 (☎42 44 24; www.siena.lt), beneath Miesto Sodas. The spacious dance floor fills quickly as local bands play and house DJs spin. Live jazz Su. Open W-Th 9pm-2am, F-Sa 9pm-4am.

Skliautai, Rotušės 26a (☎20 68 43). This cozy, smoke-filled tavern, located in a courtyard alongside Old Town's central square, pays homage to Kaunas's heyday as the capital of Lithuania with photo-lined walls. Cheap beer leaves patrons cheerfully tipsy. Live jazz W-Th 7pm. Open daily 10am-midnight. MC/V.

Avilys, Vilniaus 34 (☎20 34 76; www.avilys.lt). This cavernous Old Town cellar has Tibetan teas (4Lt) and photos from the Dalai Lama's 2001 visit. 2 excellent house microbrews on tap. Open M-Th 11am-midnight, F-Sa noon-2am, Su noon-midnight.

⚑ DAYTRIP FROM KAUNAS

ŠIAULIAI AND HILL OF THE CROSSES

The most direct route to the Hill of the Crosses (Kryžių Kalna) is by bus. Routes that run from Kaunas or Vilnius to Riga often let passengers off nearby; backtrack a few feet to the trailhead and turn left onto the 2km paved path leading to the hill. An alternate route is to take a bus (12 per day, 2½hr., 19.60Lt) to the bus station in the nearby town of Šiauliai (shoo-LAY), Tilzes 109 (☎52 50 58). Luggage storage (1Lt per bag each day) is available at bus station (☎52 33 93. Open M-F 6am-7pm, Sa 6am-6pm, Su 8am-4pm.) From the bus station, transfer to a Domantai-bound bus, at platform #2, which stops at Kryžių Kalna (8 per day, last returning shuttle at 5:20pm). You can also reach the Hill of Crosses by bike. The Šiauliai Tourist Information Center (Šiauliu Turizmo Informacijos Centras), Vilniaus 213, (☎52 31 10; tic@siauliai.net), rents bicycles (3Lt, each additional hr. 2Lt) and offers has free maps. To get to the TIC from the bus station, turn left on Tilzes and continue 100m to Vilniaus, then turn left and continue 50m. Once you have your bike, return to the intersection of Vilniaus and Tilzes and turn left; follow the road out of town 10km until you reach a brown sign marked "Kryžių Kalna." Turn right and continue 2km to the Hill of the Crosses. Note that these are busy roads, and TIC does not rent helmets.

Tucked away in the countryside, 12km outside the town of Šiauliai, is the **Hill of the Crosses.** The famous site attracts thousands of visitors each year, including throngs of Catholics who make the pilgrimage to the remote location on Easter. Pope John Paul II visited in 1993. Some say the hill's history reaches back to the Middle Ages, when—according to one legend—Lithuanians built a fort there to hold back Teutonic knights. Others speculate that the hill held significance for pagans or early Christians. In the 19th century, crosses dotted the hill as a memorial to those killed in the Lithuanian struggle for independence from tsarist rule. After the Soviet Union seized the country in WWII, Lithuanians planted crosses on the site to mourn loved ones who had been sent off to Siberian prison camps. Soviet authorities responded by burning the crosses, but Lithuanians persisted in replacing the symbols. Today, the hill is a dense forest of wooden crucifixes. Travelers can add to the collection by planting a cross of their own. Vendors sell wooden crosses at the parking lot. On your trip down the Hill back to town, turn left to visit **Broliu Svetaini ❷** (☎98 27 273), which serves up authentic Lithuanian fare, including pancakes, and has great views from its dining room. (5-9Lt. Open daily 11am-11pm.) The most popular attraction within the city of Šiauliai is the tall cathedral, known as the **Church of St. Peter and Paul** from 1625 until it became the seat of the local bishop in 1997. From the bus station, turn left on Tilzes and continue 400m. Once inside, notice the gunports, which line the balcony level; they are vestiges of the church's use as a defensive installation. If you decide to spend the night, the bargain **Youth Hostel ❶**, Rygos 36, offers beds in doubles (15Lt) with shared bath and kitchen. From the cathedral, follow Tilzes 500m toward Hill of the Crosses; turn right on Aukstoji. (☎41 523 992; romaspp@takas.lt.)

COASTAL LITHUANIA

Walk along Lithuania's luscious Baltic beaches and you'll see why Germany, Russia, and Latvia have all coveted—and, at various points in the 20th century, controlled—these shores. Dance the night away in Palanga's glittering discos, shed your swimsuit and bathe on Smiltyne's bawdy beaches, and climb the sand dunes that extend from Nida to the Russian border. The coast is an extraordinarily tourist-friendly region in summer. Outside Klaipėda, which bustles year-round, winter traveling in these parts could be bleak.

KLAIPĖDA ☎(8)46

Teutonic Knights and Prussian dukes kept the Klaipėda, formerly known as Memel, in German hands from 1252 until 1919, except during brief periods of Swedish and Russian rule. France gained control of the city after WWI but promptly surrendered it to newly independent Lithuania. Yet the local population remained largely German, a fact Hitler used as a pretext to storm Klaipėda's shores in 1939. While most Germans left town when the Soviets arrived in 1945, their legacy lingers: Klaipėda is birthplace of Lithuania's most popular beer, *Svyturus*. Microbreweries along the coast heartily reward the tourists who trek here.

▌ TRANSPORTATION

Trains: Geležinkelio stotis, Priestoties 1 (☎31 36 77). To: **Kaunas** (4hr., 1 per day, 27Lt) and **Vilnius** (5-6½hr., 3 per day, 36Lt). Station open daily 5:30am-10:30pm. *Kassa* (ticket booth) open daily 6am-9:45pm.

Buses: Autobusų stotis, Butkų Juzės 9 (☎41 15 47, reservations 41 15 40). To: **Kaunas** (3hr., 14 per day, 28Lt); **Palanga** (30-40min., 23 per day, 2.50-3Lt); **Šiauliai** (2½-3hr., 6 per day, 21Lt); **Vilnius** (4-5hr., 10-14 per day, 41Lt); **Kaliningrad, RUS** (4hr., 3 per day, 25Lt); **Rīga, LAT** (6hr., 2 per day, 35Lt). Station open daily 3:30am-midnight.

Ferries: Old Port Ferry Terminal, Žvejų 8 (☎31 42 17, info 31 11 17). Ferries to **Smiltynė** (10min.; every 30min. 5am-3am; 2Lt, students 1.50Lt, return trip 0.75Lt). Microbuses in Smiltynė connect to **Juodkrantė** (30min., 5Lt) and **Nida** (1hr., 7Lt).

Public Transportation: City buses (0.80Lt) and the wonderfully convenient **maršrutinis taksis** (route taxis; 6am-11pm 1.50Lt, 11pm-6am 2Lt) run all over town. #8 travels from the train station down H. Manto through Taikos.

Taxis: ☎006. Standard fare 1.20Lt per km. The cabs of several **private companies** roam the streets and charge 1-1.50Lt per km.

▌▐ ORIENTATION AND PRACTICAL INFORMATION

The **Danė River** divides the city into south **Senamiestis** (Old Town) and north **Naujamiestis** (New Town). **Kuršių Marios** (Curonian Lagoon) to the west cuts off **Smiltynė,** Klaipėda's Kuršių Nerija (Curonian Spit) quarter. **H. Manto,** the main artery, becomes **Tiltų,** as it crosses the river into Senamiestis, and **Taikos,** as it enters the more modern part of the city. All of mainland Klaipėda lies close to the **bus** and **train stations,** which are separated by **Priestoties.** Facing away from the bus station, turn right on **Butkų Juzės** and then left on **S. Nėries.** Follow S. Nėries away from the train station to its end, then take a right on S. Daukanto to reach the heart of the city. As you exit the ferry at **Old Castle Port,** turn left on **Žvejų** with the river behind you. From Žvejų, make any right after crossing Pilies to reach Senamiestis.

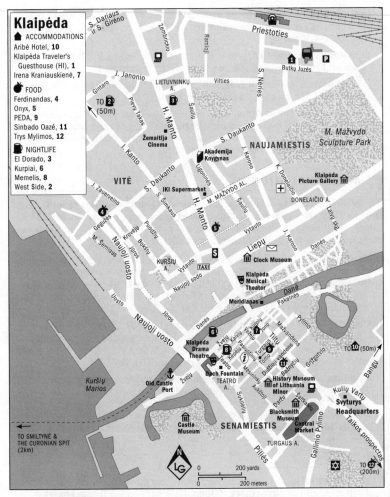

Klaipėda

⌂ ACCOMMODATIONS
Aribė Hotel, **10**
Klaipėda Traveler's
Guesthouse (HI), **1**
Irena Kraniauskienė, **7**

🍎 FOOD
Ferdinandas, **4**
Onyx, **5**
PEDA, **9**
Sinbado Oazé, **11**
Trys Mylimos, **12**

▮ NIGHTLIFE
El Dorado, **3**
Kurpiai, **6**
Memelis, **8**
West $ide, **2**

LITHUANIA

Tourist Offices: Tourist Information Center (TIC), Turgaus 7 (☎41 21 86; www.klaipeda.lt). Follow H. Manto south as it becomes Tiltu; take the 6th right after crossing the Dae River; the office is on your right. Offers **free maps** and a valuable **free guidebook,** "Exploring Klaipėda" (also available online at www.exploringvilnius.lt). The TIC and the Traveller's Guesthouse sell the *In Your Pocket* guide to Kaunas/Klaipėda (8Lt), which has info on Palanga and Neringa. Some local hotels distribute the guide free of charge. The guide comes in English and German. Open M-F 9am-7pm, Sa-Su 9am-4pm. **Litinterp,** S. Šimkaus 21/4 (☎31 14 90; klaipeda@litinterp.lt), arranges **private rooms:** Klaipėda (see p. 466), Nida (see p. 475), and Palanga (see p. 471). Call ahead. English spoken. Open M-F 8:30am-5:30pm, Sa 9:30am-3:30pm.

Currency Exchange: Hansabankas, Taikos 22 (☎48 46 37), cashes AmEx and Thomas Cook **traveler's check** and offers **Western Union** services. Branch at Turgaus 6, next to the Tourist Info Center. **ATMs** and currency exchange kiosks are everywhere.

Luggage Storage: Lockers in the train station. 2Lt per 24hr. Open daily 5:30am-10:30pm. Luggage racks at the bus station. 1.50Lt per 24hr. Open daily 3:30-11:30am and 12:30-8:30pm.

Bookstore: Akademija Knygynas, S. Daukanto 16 (☎31 08 20; www.akademija@takas.lt), has an English selection. Open M-F 10am-7pm, Su 10am-5pm. MC/V.

Internet Access: Infolinka, H. Manto 46 (☎ 21 04 42), has fast connections. 2Lt per hr. Open M-F 8am-midnight, Sa-Su 11am-midnight.

Post Office: Central Post Office, Liepų 16 (☎31 50 22; fax 41 11 68). Houses a 48-bell **carillon** (one of the largest musical instruments in the country), which rings Sa-Su at noon. **Poste Restante** at window #4. Also offers **Western Union** services. Open M-F 8am-7pm, Sa 9am-4pm. **Postal Code:** LT-5800.

ACCOMMODATIONS

The ever-obliging folks at **Litinterp,** S. Šimkaus 21/4, arrange **private rooms** for rent from local families. Litinterp also runs a **guest house** near M. Mažvydo. (☎31 14 90; klaipeda@litinterp.lt. Open M-F 8:30am-5:30pm, Sa 9:30am-3:30pm. Breakfast included. Singles from 70Lt; doubles from 120Lt. MC/V.)

▧ **Ms. Irena Kraniauskienė,** Kurpių 2-8 (☎67 31 71 88; jolita@klaipeda.lt). A retired elementary school teacher, Irena keeps her Old Town apartment sparkling-clean and lets travelers stay in her 2 spare rooms (60Lt). For an additional 10Lt, she'll stuff your belly full of *bliny* (pancakes). Be extra nice to her and she may offer you a home-cooked, Lithuanian-style lunch. Free coffee and tea. ❷

▧ **Klaipėda Traveler's Guesthouse (HI),** Butkų Juzės 7-4 (☎21 18 79; oldtown@takas.lt.), 50m from the bus station. A joy for the weary traveler, equipped with spacious dorms and hot showers. Make yourself a cup of tea, check your email (free), and chat with other backpackers. Laundry 12Lt. 34Lt, HI members 32Lt. ❷

Aribė Hotel, Bangų 17a (☎49 09 40; vitetur@klaipeda.omnitel.net). Heading away from the Danė River on Tiltų, go left on Kulių Vartų and again on Bangų. Reserve 1 week ahead for this small hotel a short walk from the center. Rooms have bath, phone, TV, and Internet. Breakfast included or 10Lt less per night without it. Laundry 3.50Lt per kg. Singles 140Lt; doubles 180Lt; suite 260Lt. Sept.-May Sa-Su 20Lt discount. MC/V. ❹

FOOD

The **central market** is on Turgaus aikštė; follow Tiltų through Senamiestis and take a sharp right at the first rotary. (Open daily 8am-6pm.) **Iki supermarket,** M. Mažvyado 7/11, is within walking distance of Senamiestis. (Open daily 8am-10pm.) The largest Iki in the Baltics lies farther away on Taikos. If you still needs supplies, try the monstrous mall **Hyper Maxima,** Taikos 61—the name says it all. Follow H. Manto 4km as it becomes Tiltų and then Taikos. (Open daily 8am-midnight.)

Trys Mylimos, Taikos 23 (☎41 14 79), 500m southeast of the Old Town. If you're hungry, head to this traditional Lithuanian beer hall, which dishes out gargantuan portions of deep-fried regional cuisine. Locals love it. Entrees 6-16Lt. Live music F-Sa 8-11pm. English menu. Open daily 11am-midnight. MC/V. ❷

PEDA, Targaus 10 (☎41 07 10). Most art museums wouldn't dare let you bring food inside, but that's where this charming cafe/gallery is different. Admire the works of Lithuanian metal sculptor Vytautas Karčiauskas while sipping coffee (2Lt) or enjoying a delicious entree (10-16Lt). Open M-Sa 10am-midnight. MC/V. ❷

Ferdinandas, Naujoji uosto 10 (☎31 36 84), at S. Daukanto. The Old Believers, a Russian Orthodox sect, came to Lithuania in 1650 to flee persecution. Leaders kept fastidious notes on their cuisine, and this restaurant recreates their recipes. Hearty Russian entrees 5-30Lt. Try *kvas* (fermented bread drink; 2Lt). Hefty portions. Open M-F 10am-midnight, Sa-Su noon-midnight. MC/V. ❸

Sinbado Oazé, Didzioji Vandeus 20 (☎ 21 17 86). Phenomenal falafel (8Lt) at this offshoot of the popular Vilnius restaurant Finjan. English menu. Open 11am-midnight. ❷

Onyx, Manto 4 (☎41 19 95). Stylish young locals flock to this hip New Town hangout, known for its extraordinarily generous portions and all-day breakfast menu (omelettes 5Lt). The place to go if you're bar-hopping or if you're just hungry. English menu. Open M-F 8:30am-midnight, Sa 10am-midnight, Su 11am-midnight. ❷

🔍 🏛 SIGHTS AND MUSEUMS

MAINLAND KLAIPĖDA

You could never guess that the lush, cheery **M. Mažvydo Sculpture Park** (M. Mažvydo Skulptūrų Parkas), between Liepų and S. Daukanto, was once the town's central burial ground. When Soviet authorities demolished the cemetery in 1977, townspeople saved some of intricately crafted crosses from the graves, which are now displayed at the **Blacksmith Museum** (Kalvystes muziejus), Saltkalviu 2. (☎41 05 26; www.mlimuziejus.lt. Open Tu-Sa 10am-6pm. 2Lt, students 1Lt.) Sculptures by Lithuanian artists and exhibits by international artists await you at the **Klaipėda Picture Gallery** (Paveikslų galerija), Liepų 33, across the park heading away from the bus station. (☎41 04 12. Most info in Lithuanian. Open Su noon-5pm, Tu-Sa noon-6pm. 4Lt, students 2Lt.) Exiting the gallery, continue right down Liepų to the **Clock Museum** (Laikrodžių Muziejus), Liepų 12. Its bizarre collection has every conceivable kind of time-keeping device, from Chinese candle clocks to a modern watch-pen. It also hosts occasional classical concerts; call or stop by for a schedule. The "common ticket" (9Lt, students 4.50Lt) grants admission both here and at Palanga's Amber Museum (see p. 472). (☎41 04 17. Open Tu-Su noon-6pm. Museum 4Lt, students 2Lt.)

The 1857 **Klaipėda Drama Theater** (Klaipėdos Dramos Teatras), Teatro aikštė, on the other side of H. Manto, is famous as one of Wagner's favorite haunts and infamous as the site where Hitler personally proclaimed the town's incorporation into the *Reich* in 1939. (Tickets ☎31 44 53. Box office open Tu-Su 11am-2pm and 4-7pm.) In front, the **Simon Dach Fountain** spouts water over Klaipėda's symbol, a statue of Ännchen von Tharau. The original statue disappeared in WWII. Some say it was removed by the Nazis, who didn't want the statue's back to face Hitler during his speech. The copy standing today was erected by German expatriates in 1989. The **History Museum of Lithuania Minor** (Mažosios Lietuvos Istorijos Muziejus) features ancient relics and vivid photos of Klaipėda's more recent German past. No English captions. (☎41 05 24. Open W-Su 10am-6pm. 2Lt, students 1Lt. W free.) In 2003, the History Museum opened the **Klaipėda Castle Museum,** Pilies 4, a separate exhibit featuring the remains of the 13th-century castle and displaying an archaeological history of the area. **Aukštoji,** near the history museum, is one of the best-preserved areas of Senamiestis, lined with the exposed-timber *Fachwerk* buildings for which prewar Klaipėda was famous. Past the central market, Aukstoji leads into **Sinagogu,** once the heart of Klaipėda's Jewish Quarter. On the eve of Hitler's invasion, Jews accounted for 17 percent of Klaipėda's population; today, just 300 remain. The historic **Jewish cemetery** lies 150m away from the market. The gray and blue building next to the cemetery is home to the **Klaipėda Jewish Society,** Ziedu 3. (☎49 37 58. Shabbat services Sa 10am. Open M-Sa 10am-3pm.)

SMILTYNĖ

As you get off the ferry (see **Transportation,** p. 466), make a right on Smiltynės and follow it along the river 200m to the **Tourist Information Center (TIC),** Smiltynės 11. (☎40 22 56; www.nerija.lt. Open M-Th 8am-4pm, F 8am-3pm.) Buses from the ferry terminal (1Lt) carry passengers straight to the **Lithuanian Sea Museum** (see below), and horse-drawn buggies charge 10Lt to make the trek. Yet the best way to see Smiltynė is to walk the 1km from the ferry terminal to the northern end of the Spit. Flanking the TIC on both sides is the three-house **Kuršių Nerija National Park Museum of Nature** (Kušrių Nerijos Nacionalinis Parkas Gamtos Muziejus), Smiltynės 9-12. The museum details the Spit's prominence as a site for tracking migratory birds. (Open June-Aug. Tu-Su 11am-6pm; May and Sept. Tu-Su 11am-5pm. 2Lt, students 1Lt, with ISIC free.) Just down the road, four ships sit on pillars in the **Garden of Veteran Fishing Boats** (Žvejybos Laivai-veteranai). The nearby **Fishermen's Village** (Ethnografinė Pajūrio Žvejo Sodyba) is a reconstruction of a 17th-century settlement. (Open 24hr. Free.) Go to the end of Smiltynės for the main attraction, the **Lithuanian Sea Museum** (Lietuvos Jūrų Muziejus), Smiltynės 3. It is housed in an 1860s fortress that once guarded Klaipėda's bustling port. Baltic seals and sea lions now frolic in the moat. (☎49 07 54; www.juru.muziejus.lt. Open June-Aug. Tu-Su 10:30am-6:30pm; Sept. W-Su 10:30am-6:30pm; Oct.-May Sa-Su 10:30am-5pm. 8Lt, students 4Lt. Cameras 5Lt.) Don't miss the highly amusing **sea lion show,** in which the gargantuan aquatic mammal sinks shots at a basketball hoop. (Shows 15min. at 11:15am, 1:15, 3:15pm. 3Lt.) Dolphins leap, paint, and dance at the museum's **Dolphinarium.** (Shows 40min. at noon, 2, and 4pm. Rows 1-6 get soaked. 12Lt, students 6Lt. Cameras 5Lt.) If you're not wet yet, follow the forest paths 500m from the Fishermen's Village to the **beaches** along the Spit's western coast. To the left is a 1.5km-long public bathing area for G-rated fun. Straight ahead is the **women's beach** (clothing optional), and south is a **coed nude beach.** Lines separate the areas, but bathers in the latter section don't always respect the boundaries.

🎵 🎭 ENTERTAINMENT AND NIGHTLIFE

The **Klaipėda Musical Theater** (Muzikinis teatras), Danės 19, hosts operas and other musical events. (☎41 05 56. Performances F 7pm, Sa-Su 6pm. Ticket office open Tu-Su 11am-2pm and 3-6pm. Season Oct.-May; brief series mid-Aug.) The **Žemaitija Cinema,** H. Manto 31, shows Hollywood films with Lithuanian subtitles. (☎31 40 90; www.zemaitojskinas.lt. 10Lt. MC/V.) The best bar hopping is along H. Manto.

　　Kurpiai, Kurpių 1a (☎41 05 55; www.jazz.lt), in the middle of Senamiestis. This superb jazz club is a mix between a traditional tavern and a jazz museum, attracting groups from Lithuania and well beyond. Live music nightly, usually starting at 9:30pm. Cover F-Sa 5-10Lt. Open Su-Th noon-1am, F-Sa noon-3am. MC/V.

　　Memelis, Žvejų 4 (☎40 30 40; www.memelis.lt), on the river across the street from the ferry port. It's a tough call between the 2 lines of "Memelio": Sviesusis (light beer) and Juodasis (dark beer), brewed in 2 large vats behind the bar. Try them both (4.70Lt per 0.5L). Upstairs, talented DJs spin as young Klaipėdans dance. No cover. Open M 11am-midnight, Tu-W 11am-2am, Th 11am-3am, F-Sa 11am-4am, Su noon-midnight. MC/V.

　　El Dorado, Lietuvniku 2 (☎ 41 20 59). Billed as an Italian-style bar, this joint's Age of Aquarius decor fashions a unique flavor of funkiness. Cheap beer (0.5L 3-4Lt). Open daily 8:30am-3am. MC/V.

　　West Side, I. Kanto 44 (☎41 15 85). Statues of cowboys and Native Americans crowd this hopping New Town restaurant and bar. Well-prepared American food (entrees 14-29Lt) will cure any traveler from the US suffering a bout of homesickness. Live music F-Sa starting at 9pm. Open M-Th noon-1am, F-Sa noon-2am, Su noon-midnight. MC/V.

PALANGA
☎ (8)460

Teutonic Knights repeatedly failed in their attempts to invade Palanga in the late Middle Ages. Today, the only folks invading this seaside town are tourists, who, on some summer weekends, outnumber the town's 20,000 permanent residents five to one. In the late 17th century, Jan Sobieski, King of Poland and Grand Duke of Lithuania, invited English merchants to build a harbor along Palanga's shallow shores. Rampaging Swedes destroyed the merchants' efforts in 1701, but Palanga still warmly welcomes English-speakers to its beaches: almost all street signs and menus are translated. Enjoy a swim in the chilly Baltic and dance the night away as street performers jam on J. Basnavicaus, Palanga's lively pedestrian boulevard.

⬛ TRANSPORTATION

Palanga is a short ride away from **Klaipėda.** Buses depart from both cities every 30min. until around 11:30pm (20min., 2.50Lt). The **bus station** (☎ 533 33) also sends buses to: **Kaunas** (3hr., 10 per day, 32Lt); **Klaipėda** (30min., every 30min., 2.50Lt); **Šiauliai** (2½-3hr., 7 per day, 19Lt); **Vilnius** (4hr., 11 per day, 43Lt); **Rīga, LAT** (5-6hr., 2 per day, 32Lt). Speedier **microbuses** also head to Klaipėda (20min., as they fill, 3Lt).

⬛⬛ ORIENTATION AND PRACTICAL INFORMATION

Palanga's main streets are **Vytauto,** which runs parallel to the beach and passes the bus station, and **J. Basanavičiaus,** which is perpendicular to Vytauto and becomes a boardwalk. The Gothic-style **Church of the Assumption,** built in 1907, across the street from the bus station, is a good point of reference near the center of town.

Tourist Office: Kretingos 1 (☎ 488 11; palangaturinfo@is.lt), adjacent to the bus station *kasa.* Gives out **free maps** and books **private rooms** with no service charge. Open daily 9am-1pm and 2-6pm.

Currency Exchange: Hansabankas, Juratés 15/2 (☎ 412 12), **exchanges currency,** cashes AmEx/MC/Thomas Cook **traveler's checks,** and gives MC **cash advances. Western Union** services are available inside. **24hr. ATM** outside. Open M-F 8am-6pm, Sa 9am-1pm. **Vilniaus Bankas,** Vytauto 61 (☎ 491 40), also exchanges currency. Open M-F 8am-5pm.

Luggage Storage: Racks in the bus station, just to the right of the ticket counter. 1Lt. Open daily 7am-1pm and 2-10pm.

24hr. Pharmacy: Vaistinė, Gintaro 41 (☎ 494 06).

Internet Access: Klubo Kaimynas, along J. Basanaviciaus just west of the intersection with S. Daukanto. 3Lt per hr. Open 24hr.

Post Office: Vytauto 53 (☎ 488 71). **Poste Restante** at window #1. **Western Union** services available. Open M-F 9am-6:30pm, Sa 9am-4pm. **Postal Code:** LT-5720.

⬛ ACCOMMODATIONS

Hotel prices rise considerably in the peak months of July and August. In the low-season, you'll pay a pittance for luxurious digs near the beach. Arrange a **private room** (from 25Lt per night) through the TIC. **Palanga Welcome Host,** Vytauto 21 (☎ 487 23; svetingas@service.lt), also arranges rooms. The staff speaks limited English, but you can browse a catalog with English listings and pictures. Study it closely, and you'll find prices much lower than those printed in the agency's thinner pamphlet (doubles June €15-20, July €20-25, Aug. €25-30). **Litinterp** in Klaipėda (see **Orientation and Practical Information,** p. 466) offers pricier private rooms in Palanga. (Singles 90-120Lt; doubles 140-180Lt.)

Ražė, Vytauto 74/2 (☎482 65; palturas@is.lt). Not to be confused with the bar of the same name 1 block away. Lovely private rooms with showers, refrigerator, and TV close to the city center. English-speaking staff. June 1-Sept. 15 singles 100Lt, doubles 140Lt, triples 160Lt; low season 60Lt/60Lt/80Lt. ❸

Egle, Kestucio 15/S. Daukanto 31 (☎51 466; www.eglehotel.lt). Bright, clean rooms with TV, fridge, and private bath. 500m from the shore. English spoken. Prices triple at peak times. May 31-Sept. 21 singles 140Lt; doubles 180Lt; triples 180Lt. Sept. 20-May 30 40Lt/60Lt/80Lt. MC/V. ❸

Mėguva, Valančiaus 1 (☎488 39), just west of the Church of the Assumption. Charmless but clean rooms with private baths and TVs in a run-down yet centrally located facility. June singles 50Lt; doubles 80Lt. July-Aug. 60Lt/120Lt. Sept.-May 40Lt/60Lt. ❷

Alanga Hotel, S. Nėries 14 (☎492 15; www.alanga.lt). Follow Valanciaus from the church. Spacious, modern bathrooms and candy on your pillow. Brightly colored rooms with TV, phone, and minibar. Breakfast 20Lt, children 12Lt. Book well in advance. Doubles 120-160Lt. MC/V. ❸

■ FOOD

The Palangan pedestrian will have no trouble finding food. **Vytauto** and **J. Basanavičiaus** are lined with cafes and restaurants offering outdoor seating and blaring music. Innumerable street vendors sell *čeburekai* (meat-filled pastries; around 3Lt). There are several supermarkets right in the center of town, including **Prekybos Centras,** J. Basanavičiaus 23. (Open daily 9am-2am.) The most popular local beer is HBH Vilkmerges, brewed just 7km outside Palanga. The town is divided between adherents of the dark and light varieties. You'll find both on tap (0.5L 3.50Lt) at **Dvitaktis** ❷ (Vytauto 80), a thatch-roofed lean-to that also offers a small menu of mostly Lithuanian entrees (6-22Lt).

Vila Aldona, J. Basanavičiaus 24 (☎403 13), offers delicious European cuisine. Be sure to sit outside among the flowers and fountain in the garden. Entrees 6-32Lt. MC/V. ❸

Senoji Dorė, J. Basanavičiaus 5 (☎534 55). A typical Palangan restaurant serving Lithuanian cuisine amid nautical decorations. Entrees 12-27Lt. Live music most nights 7pm-midnight. Open daily 10am-midnight. ❸

Lašas, J. Basanavičiaus 29 (☎513 89). Dig your jaws into shark (22-27Lt). Landlubbers rave about the steaks (8-45Lt). Live music nightly in the summer. Open Su-Th 10am-2am, F-Sa 10am-last customer. ❷

Monika, J. Basanavičiaus 12 (☎525 60). Monika has earned a name for itself as one of the most popular places on J. Basanavičiaus for its Lithuanian and Italian fare, namely its large selection of pizzas. Try the potato *bliny,* which make a good meal for just 8Lt. Entrees 5-25Lt. Open daily 10am-midnight. MC/V. ❷

◎ SIGHTS

Palanga's pride and joy is the world's first **Amber Museum** (Gintaro muziejus), which showcases the fossilized resin known as "Baltic Gold." It hosts a collection of 15,000 "inclusions," pieces of amber with primeval flora and fauna trapped inside. (☎513 19. English captions. Open June-Aug. Su 10am-7pm, Tu-Sa 10am-8pm; daily Sept.-May 11am-4:30pm; ticket office closes 1hr. before closing in summer and 30min. in winter. 5Lt, students 2.50Lt.) The museum is housed in the 1897 palace of Count Tiškevičius. The surrounding estate grounds are now home to the **Palanga Botanical Gardens.** Through the main entrance to the gardens, on the corner of Vytauto and S. Dariaus ir S. Girėno, is one of the nation's most famous sculptures, **Eglė,** Queen of the Serpents. According to local lore, a serpent thrust himself on Egle and forced her to marry him. When she did, he morphed into a charming prince. Egle's brothers then slaughtered her husband, and in despair, she turned herself into a tree. Inside the garden, along a forest path behind the Amber Museum, stands **Birutė Hill.** In another legend of betrothal, Duke Kestutis kidnapped the virgin Birute, made her his wife, and brought her to Trakai, where she gave birth to the famous Lithuanian warrior Vytautas. Archaeologists recently found the remains of a 14th-century pagan temple on the site; a 19th-century **chapel** stands atop the hill today. Less than 1km south of the Botanical Gardens, along tree-lined Vytauto, is a 1m high black marble marker pointing toward the **Holocaust Mass Graves** (Holokausto Auku Kapai). Follow the path into the woods, bear left at the fork, and continue 500m. Palanga's Jewish community was among the first to be exterminated by the Nazi Einsatzgruppe A in June 1944.

Toward the center of town, you will find the **Dr. Jonas Šliūpas Memorial Gardens and House,** Vytauto 23a. Sliupas, a physician, newspaper editor and politician, spent much of his life in the US and played a leading role in the Union of Lithuanian Socialists in America at the beginning of the 20th century. Captions in Lithuanian only. (Open daily in summer noon-7pm; low season 11am-5pm. 2Lt, students 1Lt; W free.) Just a bit farther north on Vytauto, turn left onto Kęstučio to reach the **Antanas Mončys House-Museum,** S. Daukanto 16. The sculptor left Lithuania in 1944 and didn't return for 45 years. As specified in Mončys's will, visitors may touch any of his works. (☎493 66. Open June-Aug. W-Su 2-9pm; Tu noon-5pm; Sept.-May Th-Su noon-5pm. 4Lt, students 2Lt, with ISIC 1.50Lt.)

🎵 🌿 ENTERTAINMENT AND FESTIVALS

The beach is the hallmark of any Palanga excursion, as summer visitors flock here for fun in the sun. Palanga is also part amusement park. Play **minigolf** (small course 10Lt, large course 15Lt) next to Ritos Virtuvė on J. Basanavičiaus or ride the **bumper boats** (5Lt per 3min.), next to Cafe Dviese, J. Basanavičiaus 22. The **Summer Theater** (Vasaraos Estrada) at Vytauto 43 hosts **concerts** by the Lithuanian National Philharmonic and the Klaipėda Philharmonic, as well as visiting performers. (☎522 10. Box office open daily 3-9pm.) Many cafes on J. Basanavičiaus and Vytauto feature live bands, some of which are quite good, and dancing at night. **Kinoteatras Naglis,** Vytauto 82, shows Hollywood flicks (8Lt) with Lithuanian subtitles. Many congregate on the pier to watch the **sunset.**

The **choir festival** opens at the end of May. The opening of the **summer season** takes place the first week of June, with theater, fireworks, and a giant feast. **Night Serenades,** evenings of classical music, are held every night from the last week of July to the first week of August at the Amber Museum and Botanical Gardens (see Sights, p. 472). On the first weekend of August for the **Cup of Palanga,** a massive canine exhibition held in the town stadium at Sporto 1.

🔊 NIGHTLIFE

Palanga has no shortage of nightlife, as almost everyone here is on vacation and almost every restaurant morphs into a club at dusk. The night scene centers around J. Basanavičiaus, where you'll experience auditory overload as dozens of street musicians battle for attention. **Arnėniski Šašlykai,** J. Basanavičiaus 27, is a restaurant by day and a club by night, featuring a popular house band. (Live music every night 8pm-midnight. Open daily 11am-last customer.) **Kupeta**, S. Dariaus ir Gireno 13 (☎400 14; www.feliksas.lt), just north of the Botanical Gardens, makes good use of the large courtyard it shares with an art gallery. The bar hosts a steady stream of impressive local bands and an international youth boxing competition in late June. (Occasional cover 5-10Lt. Open daily 9am-midnight.)

⚑ DAYTRIP FROM PALANGA

SOVIET MISSILE BASE AT PLOKSTINE RESERVATION

Go to Plungė from Klaipėda by bus (1hr., about 6 per day, 10Lt) or train (1hr., 2 per day, 6.40-8.30Lt). From there, board a minibus to the tiny town of Plateliai and ask the driver to let you off at Militarizmo Expozicija. You will be dropped off at a trailhead 5km from the site. Take the path and head left at the T-intersection. Tours daily June-Aug. every 2hr. 10am-6pm. Some guides speak Lithuanian only. 4Lt, students 2Lt. To arrange an English-language tour in any season (20Lt), contact the Zematijia National Park Information Center. (☎8281 49231; znp@plunge.omnitel.net. Open M-Sa 9am-noon and 1-5pm.) The Klaipėda Traveler's Guesthouse (see p. 468) also arranges excursions to the base. Email in advance. 25Lt per person.

Tucked away in the **Plokstine Reservation** inside **Zematijia National Park** lies one of the most remarkable sites in Lithuania: the remains of a **Soviet missile base.** Attempting to keep pace with US, which had begun to develop underground military installations, Soviet leader Nikita Krushchev ordered the construction of this site in September 1960. Lithuania was the ideal location for such a facility, as missiles fired here could have reached as far as Turkey and Spain. The base was put on high-alert during the Czechoslovak revolution of 1968. The Soviets abandoned the site in 1978 after signing the SALT accords with the US but left much of the infrastructure in place. Locals looted the facility for scrap metal during the lean years of the 1980s; as a result, much of the site is falling apart, and only one of the four silos is open to tourists. Peer down the 30m hole that once held warheads five times the strength of the atomic bomb dropped on Hiroshima. Walk through the underground tunnels where Soviet soldiers awaited orders to fire. The structure is deteriorating so quickly that it may be too dangerous within a few years.

CURONIAN SPIT (NERINGA)

A product of the glaciers of the last Ice Age, the Curonian Spit is a great sandbar lined with majestic dunes and criss-crossed by lush forests. It is bordered by the Baltic Sea to the west and the beautifully calm Curonian Lagoon to the east. The Kuršių Nerija National Park is devoted to preserving this pristine region. Outside of the major towns (Nida and Juodkrantė) lie endless kilometers of untouched waterfront ripe for exploration. Rent a bike in Klaipėda, take the ferry to Smiltynė, and keep pedaling until you're hot and ready for a dip in the chilly Baltic.

WITCHES' HILL

Goblins, devils, and amused mortals frolic on ⚑**Witches' Hill** (Raganų Kalnas) in Juodkrantė. Set aside an hour to wander the worn trail—the path loops back to the beginning—through the dense, magical wood lined with over 100 mythical wooden sculptures in high Lithuanian folk-art style. Visitors can mingle with the gnomes by frolicking on a seesaw, sliding down a giant tongue, or getting in a saddle 2m off the ground. Don't miss the chance to join a game of cards between the devil and a witch; they've left two seats free for you. Take a detour through the forest and head toward the sound of crashing water to find the **beach** on the Baltic side of the Spit. While Juodkrantė is always a site of mirth and ritual, Witches Hill is especially popular on **Midsummer's Eve** and **St. John's Day** (June 23-24, 2004). Buses run hourly along the Nida-Klaipeda (via Smiltynė) route and stop in the center of town. (30min., 5Lt to Nida. 15min., 3Lt to Smiltynė.)

NIDA ☎(8)469

Settlers have lived in this section of the Curonian Spit since the late-14th century, but their villages have been buried by shifting dunes on several occasions. Now, 50,000 tourists arrive in tiny Nida (pop. 1,550) each summer. Hike a couple of kilometers south from town, however, and you'll find yourself all alone in a dune-filled desert. Don't go too far, though: just 4km south of Nida's center, a militarized border separates Lithuania from the Russian region of Kaliningrad.

The ■**Drifting Dunes of Parnidis** rise high above Nida, though they sink 30cm each year. Walk south along the beach or down forest paths to reach the peak of the tallest sand dune, marked by the remains of an immense sundial. It was smashed by a storm in 1999. On the far side of the dunes lies the **Valley of Silence**, used by Prussia—the Spit's former owner—as a prison camp for French soldiers in the early 1870s. The **wooden houses** clustered along Lotmiško, the narrow lane leading back to town, are classified as historic monuments; dozens more are buried under the sand. From the town center, go 500m north on Pamario to the **Parish Church of Nidden**. Residents of the Spit raised funds from fellow Lutherans in Germany to build the Gothic-style church in 1887. Soviet authorities left it standing but looted the wooden pews to fuel a sauna. The handful of Nida's remaining Lutherans share the house of worship with local Catholics. Open daily 10am-6pm. Just 100m farther, the **Neringa Museum of History** (Neringos Istorijos Muziejus), Pamario 53, presents a thought-provoking exhibit on the occupations of Neringa inhabitants. (☎511 62. Open Tu-Su 10am-6pm. 2Lt, students 0.50Lt.) Bear right on Skruzdynės and climb the second wooden staircase on the left to reach the renovated **Thomas Mann House** (Thomo Manno Namelis) at #17. The German Nobel laureate built this cottage in 1930 and wrote *Joseph and His Brothers* here. Mann, a vocal opponent of Hitler, emigrated to the US in 1936. (☎522 60. Open daily June-Aug. 10am-6pm; Sept.-May Tu-Sa 11am-5pm. 2Lt, students 0.50Lt.) The **Thomas Mann Cultural Center** puts on classical concerts for the mid-July **Thomas Mann Festival.**

Buses run from the **bus station**, Naglių 18e (☎524 72), to **Klaipeda/Smiltynė** (45min., about 1 per hr., 7Lt); **Kaunas** (4½hr., 1 per day, 40Lt); and **Kaliningrad, RUS** (2½-4hr., 2 per day, 63Lt). You can also reach Nida from Kaliningrad by buying a ticket to Klaipeda and asking the driver to let you off at Nida (3hr., 2 per day, 155R). Buses to Smiltynė leave Nida hourly from 6am to 10pm. From the water, **Taikos** runs inland. Perpendicular to it, **Naglių** eventually becomes **Pamario.** The **Tourist Information Center (TIC)**, Taikos 4, opposite the station arranges private rooms (5Lt fee) and has **free maps**, transport info, and free **Internet access.** English spoken. (☎523 45; www.neringainfo.lt. Open June-Aug. M-F 10am-7pm, Sa 10am-6pm, Su 10am-3pm; low season M-F 9am-1pm and 2-6pm, Sa-Su 10am-3pm). **Hansabankas,** Taikos 5, **exchanges currency**, cashes **traveler's checks**, gives MC/V **cash advances**, and has **Western Union** services. (☎522 41. Open M-Th 8am-4pm, F 8am-3:30pm.) The **post office**, Taikos 13, is up the road. (☎526 47. Open M-F 9am-noon and 1-5:30pm, Sa 9am-1pm.) The adjacent **telephone office** has card phones. (☎520 07. Open daily May-Sept. 9am-10pm; Oct.-Apr. 9am-5:45pm.) **Postal Code:** LT-5872.

The **TIC** arranges **private rooms** (40-50Lt) and is the best option for inexpensive accommodations. **Litinterp ❸** in Klaipeda offers pricier rooms. (See **Klaipeda: Orientation and Practical Information,** p. 466. Singles 90-120Lt; doubles 140-180Lt.) If you are in the market for a hotel, try **Urbo Kalnas ❸**, Taikos 32, on a pine-covered hill 1km above town; it rents large rooms with clean, hot showers, TVs, and fridges.

LITHUANIA

(☎524 28; urbokalnas@is.lt. Breakfast 15Lt. July 1-Aug. 29 singles 109Lt; doubles 139Lt. Low season 60Lt/90Lt.) **Kempingas** (Camping) ❶, Taikos 45a (☎370 682 41150; www.kempingas.lt), just past Urbo Kalnas, offers a taste of the outdoor experience but with showers, flushing toilets, and an adjacent Chinese restaurant. (15Lt per person plus 10Lt per site. If you're traveling without wilderness gear, rent a tent for 10Lt and a sleeping bag for 5Lt.) The regional specialty is *rūkyta žuvis* (smoked fish), served with bread. Stop by **Fischbrotchen** ❶, in a yellow hut next to the bus station, for a 3.50Lt herring sandwich. (Open daily 11am-8pm.) **Seklyčia** ❸, at the end of Lotmiško, serves outstanding Lithuanian dishes and some vegetarian options. *Shashlyk* and *bliny* are the cheapest meals. English menu. (☎500 00. Entrees 15-85Lt. Open daily 9am-midnight.) **Ešerinė** ❸, Naglių 2, is a wacky collection of thatched-roofed, glass-walled huts with wonderful views of the dunes. English menu. (☎527 57. Entrees 14-40Lt. Open daily 10am-midnight.) Nida's largest **grocery store** is **Kuršis**, Naglių 29. (Open daily 8am-10pm.) It has a **cafe** that serves a great breakfast for early risers. (Open daily 8am-midnight. MC/V.)

MACEDONIA
(МАКЕДОНИЈА)

 For brevity's sake, *Let's Go* uses the name "Macedonia" to refer to the **Former Yugoslav Republic of Macedonia (FYROM)** throughout this chapter. The United Nations, the European Union, and the US, however, have recognized it under the name FYROM, because of diplomatic tensions between Macedonia and Greece, which has a northern province of the same name. When traveling in Macedonia, it is appropriate to call it by that name, but those traveling south to Greece should be certain to speak of it as "FEE-rum" to avoid hostility.

Years of UN- and Greek-enforced trade embargoes and unrest among the country's large, underprivileged Albanian minority have damaged Macedonia's economy, and the country is only slowly recovering. Despite its problems, Macedonia's historical and geographical treasures remain intact, accessible, and welcoming, particularly the spectacular mountain basin that is home to Lake Ohrid. Coverage of Macedonia was last updated in July of 2003.

HISTORY

ALEXANDER THE GREAT. Archaeological findings show evidence of civilization in Macedonia between 7000 and 3500 BC. In the first millennium BC, Thracians, Illyrians, and Celts settled on the Balkan Peninsula. Greek culture seeped into the

FACTS AND FIGURES

OFFICIAL NAME: The Former Yugoslav Republic of Macedonia (FYROM)

CAPITAL: Skopje (pop. 399,000)

POPULATION: 2 million (67% Macedonian, 23% Albanian, 4% Turkish, 2% Roma, 2% Serb, 2% other)

LANGUAGE: Macedonian, Albanian

CURRENCY: 1 denar (den) = 100 deni

RELIGION: 67% Orthodox, 30% Muslim, 3% other

LAND AREA: 24,856km²

CLIMATE: Mild temperate

GEOGRAPHY: Mountainous, large lakes in the south

BORDERS: Albania, Bulgaria, Greece, Serbia and Montenegro

ECONOMY: 40% Services, 40% Industry, 20% Agriculture

GDP: US$5000 per capita

COUNTRY CODE: 389

INTERNATIONAL DIALING PREFIX: 00

MACEDONIA

Macedonia

area, then known as **Paeonia,** and **King Philip II** of Macedon joined Paeonia with his kingdom in 358 BC. Under his son **Alexander the Great,** their kingdom would stretch to India. Macedon was defeated by Rome in the First and Second **Macedonian Wars** and was made the first foreign province of the **Roman Empire** in AD 146.

A MELTING POT. When the Roman Empire split in the 4th century, these early Macedonians fell under the Byzantine thumb. From the 7th to 14th centuries, the **Byzantines** and **Bulgarians** periodically warred over the territory. Serbian control, which began in 1331, ended with the 1389 **Battle of Kosovo Polje;** over the next 70 years the territory was absorbed into the **Ottoman Empire.** A mixture of Greek, Turkish, and Slavic ancestry has laid the foundation for contemporary conflict in Macedonia. The Christian culture brought by the Byzantines competed with the traditions of the Serbs and later with the religion of the Ottoman Turks.

MACEDONIA FOR EVERYONE ELSE. In the 19th century, South Slavs began agitating for independence. Russia forced the Ottoman Empire to reinstate Bulgaria (then including Macedonia) in 1878, but Austria-Hungary, Britain, France, and Prussia restored the land to the Ottomans. In reaction, the **International Macedonian Revolutionary Organization (IMRO)** was created in 1893 under the leadership of **Goce Delchev,** with the slogan "Macedonia for Macedonians." Twelve years later, during the **First Balkan War,** Macedonian territory was again contested. After the Ottoman defeat, Bulgarian troops turned on their Serbian and Greek allies, initiating the **Second Balkan War,** and most of the future Republic of Macedonia fell to Serbia. In 1941, Macedonia was partitioned again, this time among the **Axis powers.**

MACEDONIA, TAKE TWO. After **WWII,** Macedonia became a constituent republic of **Yugoslavia.** Under Yugoslav leader **Josip Broz Tito,** Macedonian language, literature, and culture flourished. The Archbishopric of Ohrid was restored in 1958, signifying a break with the Serbian Church. After Tito's death, nationalist pressures culminated when Macedonia declared **independence** on December 19, 1991.

TODAY. President **Kiro Gligorov** led the nascent country until 1999. In 1995, Greece, which originally contended that the new nation's name, currency, flag, and constitution all implied pretensions to the Greek province of the same name, lifted its trade embargoes. During the Kosovo crisis (1998-99), Macedonia was inundated with Albanian refugees. **Boris Trajkovski,** who called the attention of the West to Macedonia's refugee problem, became president in 1999. Though tensions ran high, he managed to avert a Macedonian repeat of the Kosovo crisis by backing a deal under which Albanian fighters laid down their arms; in return, they got a constitution that guarantees Macedonia's Albanian minority (23%) more rights and protections. When Trajkovski was killed in a February 2004 plane crash, **Branko Crvenkovski,** prime minister from 1992 to 1998, succeeded him as president and promised to continue Trajkovski's legacy of smoothing ethnic tensions.

PEOPLE AND CULTURE

LANGUAGE

Macedonian is a South Slavic language, related to Bulgarian and Serbian and written in a **Cyrillic** alphabet (see **The Cyrillic Alphabet,** p. 52) similar to Russian's, though "ц" is transliterated c (still pronounced "ts"). and "x" is h. There are additional letters, including "j," pronounced "y" (as in "yellow"), "џ" (dzh), "ѕ" (dz), "љ" (lj), and "њ" (nj). **Russian, Serbian,** and **Croatian** are widely understood, though **English** is the second language of choice. Older Macedonians may reverse the Western style of **head movements** for "yes" and "no;" confirm everything with words ("da" and "neh"). For more information on language, see **Glossary: Macedonian,** p. 954.

FOOD AND DRINK

MACEDONIA	❶	❷	❸	❹	❺
FOOD	under 200MKD	200-450MKD	451-600MKD	601-750MKD	over 750MKD

Macedonian food shows strong Serbian and Greek influences. Sesame seeds are the name of the game. Kiosks sell **grilled meats** (скара; skara), especially small hamburgers (плескавица; pleskavica; 50den), *chebab* (чебаб; kebab), and *bureks* (бурек; pastries stuffed with veggies, feta cheese, or meat; 30-35dn). *Chorba* (чорба; a thick soup) is a popular **main dish,** as are *mushkalica* (мушкалица; a stew of meat, peppers, onions, and tomatoes) and *ujavica* (уjавица; a rolled pork dish). Wash your food down with a shot of fiery **rakija** (ракиjа; grape or plum brandy). You can buy fruits and vegetables at a *pazar* (пазар; **open-air market**).

CUSTOMS AND ETIQUETTE

Small **tips** are appreciated (10% will be perceived as generous). In crowded restaurants, you'll share a table with locals. **Women** dress stylishly, even on mundane occassions. Tank tops and short skirts are not permitted in Orthodox churches. People are often unwilling to wait in line to buy tickets or to board a bus and instead push their way to the front.

THE ARTS

Little was written in Macedonian until the 19th century, when brothers **Konstantin and Dimitar Miladinov** began writing lyric poems, laying the foundation for modern Macedonian literature, which came into its own with the 1944 codification of the

MACEDONIA

literary language. After the 1995 lifting of the Greek trade embargo, a wealth of works poured forth such as **Ante Popovski's** collection *Providenija (Providence)*, **Sande Stojcevski's** *A Gate in the Cloud,* and **Petre Andreevski's** collection of short stories *Site Lica Na Smrtta (All the Faces of Death).* Among Macedonia's best **visual artists** are painters **Dimitar Pandilov** and **Vangel Kodzhoman.** *Before the Rain,* a film by **Milcho Manchevski,** earned an Academy Award nomination in 1995.

HOLIDAYS AND FESTIVALS

NATIONAL HOLIDAYS IN 2005

January 1 New Year's Day	**May 1** Labor Day
January 6-7 Orthodox Christmas	**May 24** St. Cyril and Methodius Day
January 14 Orthodox New Year	**August 2** Ilinden Day
April 29 - May 1 Easter Holiday	**September 8** Republic Day

ADDITIONAL RESOURCES

Balkan Ghosts: A Journey Through History, by Robert Kaplan (1994). A travel journal dealing with the political complexities of Macedonia and its neighbors.

Macedonia and Greece: The Struggle to Define a New Balkan Nation, by John Shea (1997). A candid look at the history of Macedonia and its recent dispute with Greece.

Before the Rain, directed by Milcho Manchevski (1995). A powerful film about love and ethnic strife in Macedonia, set to a phenomenal soundtrack.

MACEDONIA ESSENTIALS

ENTRANCE REQUIREMENTS
Passport: Required of all travelers.
Visa: Required of citizens of Australia and Canada.
Letter of Invitation: Not required.
Inoculations: Recommended up-to-date on DTaP (diphtheria, tetanus, and pertussis), Hepatitis A, Hepatitis B, MMR (measles, mumps, and rubella), Polio booster, and Typhoid.
Work Permit: Required of all foreigners planning to work.
International Driving Permit: Required of all those planning to drive.

DOCUMENTS AND FORMALITIES

EMBASSIES AND CONSULATES

Embassies and consulates of other countries in Macedonia are all in **Skopje** (see p. 482). Macedonia's embassies and consulates abroad include:

Australia: Perpetual Bldg., 10 Rudd St., Canberra, ACT 2601 (☎ 2 6249 8000; fax 6249 8088).

Canada: 130 Albert St., Ottawa, ON K1M 5G4 (☎ 613-234-3882; www3.sympatico.ca/emb.macedonia.ottawa).

Greece: Marathonoudromou 13, P. Psychico, 154 52 Athens (☎301 67 49 585; lormak@matrix.kapatel.gr).

UK: 25 James St., London W1U 1DU (☎20 7935 2823, consular dept. 7935 3842; mkuk@btinternet.com).

US: 3050 K St. NW, ste. 210, Washington, D.C. 20007 (☎202-337-3063; rmacedonia@aol.com).

VISA AND ENTRY INFORMATION

Citizens of Ireland, New Zealand, the UK, and the US may visit Macedonia visa-free for up to three months. **Visas** are required for citizens of Australia and Canada. In all cases, a valid passport is required. Macedonia no longer issues visas at the border. Australians and Canadians should contact their embassies to acquire a visa. With the exception of border crossings, immediate border areas are **military restricted zones.** Travelers must **register** with the police within 72hr. of arrival; accommodations will usually do it for you. You will receive an entry/exit card upon arrival in Macedonia; present the exit portion when you leave the country.

GETTING AROUND

Both **Skopje** and **Ohrid** have airports. There are flights from Ohrid to Greece. **Adria Airways** provides regular service from **Ljubljana, SLN; Austrian Airlines** from **Vienna, AUT;** and **Croatia Airlines** from **Zagreb, CRO.** Buses and trains travel around the country with comparable speed and comfort, but buses are usually more frequent. Nearly all international travel must be done through Skopje. Due to political tensions, there are no bus or train connections from Ohrid to Greece—to cross, you will have to walk the border or backtrack to Skopje. Macedonia's **highways** are in good shape, but its **secondary roads** are poorly maintained and poorly lit. In former conflict areas, many secondary roads were mined, so **only drive on paved roads.**

TOURIST SERVICES AND MONEY

Tourist offices don't exist outside of Skopje, where the office is helpful but underfunded. Around Lake Ohrid, private travel agencies, such as **Putnik,** are your best bet for tourist info. A few **ATMs** exist, concentrated in Skopje and Ohrid. **Stopanska Banka** is the best option for all financial services. **Inflation** is 3%, so prices should be relatively steady. Typical **business hours** are Monday through Friday 8am-8pm; banks Monday through Friday 8am-7pm, Saturday 8am-noon.

HEALTH AND SAFETY

 EMERGENCY NUMBERS: Police: ☎92 **Fire:** ☎93 **Ambulance:** ☎94

Macedonian **medical care** isn't up to Western standards. If you are seriously ill, the Faculty of Medicine at **Skopje University** and the **Military Hospital** are your best options. The US Embassy in Skopje has a list of **medical specialists.** Credit cards are accepted at hospitals. UK citizens receive free medical care with a valid passport. Basic **medicines** are available in Macedonian **pharmacies** (аптека; apteka). *Analgin cafetin* is aspirin, and *arbid* is cold medicine; bandages are *flexogal.* Other useful expressions include: *treska* (тзеска; fever), *glavobolka* (главоболка; headache), and *stomakot* (стомакот; stomachache). **Feminine hygiene products** are widely available.

MACEDONIA

Travelers should avoid the area near the **Kosovo border.** If you do go, travel by day and **stay on the pavement** to minimize the risk posed by **landmines** and **unexploded ordnance. Women** should take the usual precautions, but they shouldn't have any difficulties in Macedonia. **Minority** travelers may get stares but should encounter no real trouble. **Homosexuality** became legal in Macedonia in 1997, but there remains a widespread lack of tolerance; discretion is best.

ACCOMMODATIONS AND CAMPING

MACEDONIA	❶	❷	❸	❹	❺
ACCOM.	under 1300MKD	1300-2000MKD	2001-3000MKD	3001-4000MKD	over 4000MKD

The **hostel** in Skopje is phenomenal, but it is the only one in the country. **Hotels** are overpriced but often the only option. **Pensions** and **motels** are more reasonable. **Private rooms,** relatively unavailable elsewhere, are the best choice in Ohrid. **Camping** facilities exist around Lake Ohrid, but they are generally run-down.

KEEPING IN TOUCH

Mail can be received through **Poste Restante.** Address envelopes as follows: EMILY (First name) GEE (LAST NAME), POSTE RESTANTE, Nikola Karev 2 (post office address), 1000 (postal code) Скопје (city), МАКЕДОНИЈА. International access numbers include: **AT&T Direct** (☎00 800 4288); **Canada Direct** (☎00 800 4277); **MCI WorldPhone** (☎00 800 4266). **Internet access** is fast and ubiquitous.

SKOPJE (СКОПЈЕ) ☎(0)2

Skopje (pop. 453,000) gets a bad rap for being a smoggy commercial center—a reputation only partially deserved. In the busy capital, brimming with internationals involved in development and refugee programs, a burgeoning arts scene is beginning to give Skopje its soul back after 10 years of struggling to survive. The disastrous 1969 earthquake that destroyed 90% of the city spared the Old Bazaar; ancient mosques and churches still rise above an otherwise concrete cityscape.

> **!** There are **landmines** in Skopje's immediate vicinity, particularly to the northwest along the Kosovo border. Stay on paved roads.

TRANSPORTATION

Flights: Skopje Airport (☎3165 156), 20km east of the center. Taxis 800-1200dn. **Austrian Airlines** and **Lufthansa: Inex,** 27 Mart 12 (☎3128 177; inex1@mt.net.mk). Open M-F 8am-6pm, Sa 9am-2pm. **British Airways: Kompturs Ltd,** Dimitrija Chupovski 1 (☎3214 250; bakompturs@mol.com.mk). Open M-F 9am-5pm, Sa 10am-2pm.

Trains: (☎3234 255), 1km southeast of the center. To: **Belgrade, SMN** (9hr., 2 per day, €30); **Ljubljana, SLN** (19hr., 1 per day, 2814den); **Niš, SMN** (5hr., 2 per day, €15); **Thessaloniki, GCE** (Солун; 4½hr., 2 per day, €12). All fares are half price with **ISIC.**

Buses: (☎3166 254). At the end of Kamen Most pedestrian bridge on the Old Bazaar side. Open daily 4:30am-midnight. To: **Ohrid** (3½hr., 10 per day., 350den); **Belgrade, SMN** (8hr., 9 per day, 940den); **Sofia, BUL** (8hr., 4 per day, 670den). Buy **international tickets** at Tourist Agency "Vior 2," Do Kameniot Most (☎/fax 3222 126), across the street from the bus station along the river. Open daily 5:30am-10pm.

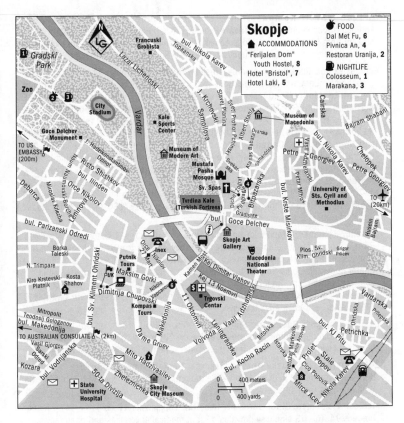

Skopje

🍎 FOOD
Dal Met Fu, 6
Pivnica An, 4
Restoran Uranija, 2

🏠 ACCOMMODATIONS
"Ferijalen Dom"
Youth Hostel, 8
Hotel "Bristol", 7
Hotel Laki, 5

🌙 NIGHTLIFE
Colosseum, 1
Marakana, 3

Public Transportation: Buy **bus tickets** from kiosks and travel agencies (20den) or from the driver (30den). Bus route maps don't exist, and buses are not well-labeled.

Taxis: Radiotaxi Vodno (☎9191). **Radiotaxi Vardar** (☎9195). 50den for the first 2.5km, then 15den per km. Make sure the meter is on. No ride should exceed 100den.

✦ 🛈 ORIENTATION AND PRACTICAL INFORMATION

Many sights lie along a small stretch of the **Vardar River** (Вардар) and on **Samoilova** (Самоилова), the street on the western edge of the **Old Bazaar** (Стара Чаршија; Stara Charshija). The **Trgovski Centar** (Трговски Центар; Central Shopping Center) is on the river next to **Ploshtad Makedonija** (Плоштад Македонија; Macedonia Square). Bookstores and kiosks sell **city maps** (200-250den). Streets have been renamed many times in an attempt to forget the city's Yugoslavian past.

Tourist Office: Skopje National Tourist Office Tourist Information Center (TIC) (☎3116 854; gocebo@mt.net.mk), around the corner from the bus station, opposite the entrance to the Old Bazaar. Provides **maps** (200den) and a guide to cultural events. Open M-F 8am-7pm, Sa 8am-4pm. If the door is locked, check the 1st cafe on the right.

Budget Travel: Kompas Tours, Dimitrija Chupovski 10 (☎3132 280; kompas@mol.com.mk), books **private rooms** (€5-20), **hotels** (€60), and **flights.** Walk straight from the pedestrian bridge across Macedonia Sq. At the end of the pedestrian zone, turn left onto Dimitrija Chupovski. Open M-F 8am-8pm, Sa 9am-2pm.

Embassies and Consulates: Albania, Hristijan Todorovski Karpoš 94/A (☎3614 636; ambshqip@mt.net.mk). Open M-F 8am-4pm, consular section 10am-noon. **Australian Consulate,** Motiva Londonska 11b (☎3061 114; motiva@mt.net.mk). Open M-F 8:15am-4:15pm, F 8:15am-2pm. **Bosnia and Herzegovina,** Mile Popjordanov 56b (☎3086 216; fax 3086 221). **Bulgaria,** ul. Zlatko Shnajder 3, 1000 (☎3116 320; fax 3116 139). **Croatia,** Mitropolit Teodosij Gologanov 59/II-4 (☎3127 350; velhr-skp@mpt.com.mk). **Canada,** Mitropolit Teodosij Gologanov 44 (☎3125 228; dfaitmk@unet.com.mk). Open M-F 8am-4pm. Citizens of **New Zealand** should contact the UK embassy. **Serbia and Montenegro,** Pitu Guli 8 (☎3129 298; fax 3129 427). **Slovenia,** Vodnjanska 42, (☎3176 663; fvsk@mzz-dkp.gov.si). **UK,** Dimitrija Chupovski 4/26. (☎3299 299; britishembassyskopje@fco.gov.uk). Open M-Th 9:45am-noon and 2-4:30pm, F 8:45am-noon. **US,** bul. Ilinden bb (☎3116 180; http://usembassy mpt.com.mk). Open M and W-F 2-4pm.

Currency Exchange: Stopanska Banka (Стопанска Банка), 11 Oktomvri bb (☎3295 344), in the Trgovski Centar, **exchanges currency,** cashes **traveler's checks,** and has commission-free **Visa cash advances.** A Visa ATM is on the left as you enter Trgovski Centar from Macedonia Sq.; the **exchange office** is down the 1st alley on the left in the courtyard on the left. Open M-F 7am-7pm, Sa 7:30am-1:30pm. At the entrance to the Trgovski Centar is **Komercijalna Banka** (Комерцијална Банка; ☎3165 906) with a MC **ATM** outside. MC **cash advances** inside. Open M-F 7am-7pm, Sa 7am-1pm.

English-Language Bookstore: Matica (Матица; ☎3221 138), on bul. Sv. Kliment Ohridski around the corner from the UK embassy. **City maps** (200-250den). 10% off all purchases with a discount card from the register. Open M-F 8am-9pm, Sa 8am-4pm.

24hr. Pharmacy: Gradska Apteka "Trgovski Centar" (Градска Аптека "Трговски Центар"), on the 1st fl. of the Trgovski Centar. English spoken. Open M-F 7am-9pm, Sa 8am-8pm, Su 8am-4pm. AmEx/V.

Medical Assistance: State University Hospital, Vodnjanska 17 (☎3147 147). **Ambulance** ☎94. The **US embassy** provides a list of medical specialists and pharmacies.

Internet Access: Internet Club Cyberia, Dimitrija Chupovski 24b (☎3298 060), next to the UK embassy. 60den per hr. Open daily 9am-2am.

Post Offices: Orce Nikolov bb (☎3141 141). Cross the pedestrian bridge from the bus station, turn right, and look for the cement fortress with yellow "Птт" signs. Open M-Sa 7am-7:30pm. **Main post office,** Nikola Karev 2, adjacent to the train station (☎3162 102). **Poste Restante** at window 22. Open M-Sa 7am-8pm. **Postal Code:** 1000.

♜ ACCOMMODATIONS

Generations of aid workers have taught hotels the laws of supply and demand—most hotels are overpriced. Taxi drivers at bus or train stations offer to take you to a **private room ❶** (800-1200den)—bargain hard. Decor at ▨**"Ferijalen Dom" Youth Hostel Skopje (HI) ❷,** Prolet 25 (Пролет), is Austin-Powers groovy, with turquoise hallways and studded leather doors. From the train station, go left toward the center on bul. KJ Pitu; turn left onto Prolet before the field. (☎3144 849; ferijalen@hotmail.com. Breakfast included. Reception 24hr. Call 1-2 days ahead. Singles 1580den, with ISIC/HI 1270den; doubles 2200/1780den.) **Hotel Laki ❸,** Leninova 79, offers A/C and competitive prices. (☎3128 120; fax 3116 827. Breakfast included.

Reception 24hr. Free transport from train and bus stations. Singles €25; doubles €40; apartments €35 per person.) **Hotel "Bristol" ❸**, bul. Makedonija 1, opposite the City Museum, has big rooms with comfy beds. (☎3237 502; fax 3166 556. Breakfast included. Reception 24hr. Singles 2660den; doubles 4380den. AmEx/MC/V.)

◖ FOOD

You'll find terrific dishes in the **Old Bazaar. Pivnica An** (Пивница Ан) ❷ is not your average *pivnica* (beer hall)—the food is as spectacular as the setting, a restored 1472 Turkish Inn. Enter the bazaar from the river and take the second right after the TIC; take the first left down the alley, follow it right, and go left down the stairs to the courtyard. (☎3212 111; www.pivnicaan.com.mk. English menu. Entrees 190-450den. Open daily 9am-midnight.) A sprawling cafe, **Dal Met Fu** ❷ (Дал Мет ау), pl. Makedonija bb (пл. Ьакедщниоф), is the best place to people-watch. (☎3112 482. Pizza 179-319den. Fresh pasta 194-245den. Grilled meat 330-420den. Vegetarian options. Open daily 8am-midnight.) Try the Krushevo Grill (Лрушево Грил; 400den) at **Restoran Uranija** ❷ (Ресторан Ураниja), in Gradski Park, past the stadium. (☎3121 014; fax 3118 030. Open Su-Th 9am-midnight, F-Sa 9am-1am. MC/V.)

◉ SIGHTS

Skopje is a beautiful old city, though it was brutally defaced by the 1963 earthquake, communist-era construction, and years of neglect. Most sights are easily reached on foot. To reach **Samoilova** (Самоилова), the main sightseeing drag, walk left out of the bus station and up the stairs to cross the walkway over bul. Goce Delchev. Across the walkway lies the **Old Bazaar** (Стара Чаршиоа; Stara Charshija), with its blend of Macedonian, Albanian, and Ottoman influences. Across from the TIC is the 15th-century **Daut Pasha Turkish Bath.** Since its 1948 restoration, the **Skopje Art Gallery** has filled the space with a permanent exhibit of over 1000 works from the late 19th century through the 1980s. (☎3133 102. Open Tu-Su 10am-9pm. 100den.)

Farther up Samoilova is the **Sveti Spas** church (Свути Спас; Holy Salvation), Makarija Frchkovski 8. In the courtyard is the sarcophagus of national hero **Goce Delchev** (see **History,** p. 477). Take the second right off Samoilova coming from the TIC. The submerged church is the legacy of prohibitions against churches taller than mosques. (☎3116 381. Open Tu-F 9am-5pm, Sa-Su 9am-3pm. English-guide 300den. Entrance 60den.) **Tvrdina Kale** (Твҏдина Кале; Turkish Fortress) is at the top of the hill. (Open 7am-11pm.) Cross back over Samoilova to the left and take a right onto Dvarska (Дваҏска) to reach the **Museum of Macedonia** (Музей на Македонска; Muzey na Makedonska. ☎3116 044; musmk@mpt.com.mk. Open Tu-F 8am-4pm, Sa 9am-3pm, Su and holidays 9am-1pm. 50den.)

♫ ▣ ENTERTAINMENT AND NIGHTLIFE

The **Skopje Summer Festival** (Скопско Лето; Skopsko Leto), lasts from mid-June to mid-July. Check with the TIC for a program. In mid-October, the city hosts the **Skopje Jazz Festival.** In May, the **Macedonian National Theater** (MNT), Kej Dimitar Vlahov bb, hosts Opera Evenings. A cinema in the Trgovski Centar, **Kino Millennium** (Кино Милениум), shows English-language movies with Macedonian subtitles (150den). **Colosseum,** at the end of the line of clubs around the corner right from the Trgovski Centar, is the best club for Eurodance. (Drinks 120-150den. DJs Th-Su; cover 200den. Open daily 9pm-3am.) Back toward the stadium in Gradski Park is **Marakana.** The best kind of rock club—smoky, dark, and loud—this place jams with local bands. (☎3221 548. Live music Th-Sa. Open daily 9pm-3am.)

MACEDONIA

LAKE OHRID

Rocky Lake Ohrid is perhaps Macedonia's greatest natural treasure. Unspoiled by overdevelopment, its clean spring water (visibility 22-25m) has been flowing for four million years. Wreathed with glorious green mountains, its shores are dotted with hundreds of small churches and monasteries, interspersed with grassy and sandy beaches. Tourists aren't the only ones attracted to the limpid water; eels and trout thrive in Lake Ohrid and are favorite culinary specialties.

OHRID (ОХРИД)   ☎(0)46

Ohrid (pop. 42,000) is Macedonia's premier summer resort and possibly its most beautiful town. The breezy lakeshore is lined with cafes facing the Albanian coast, while ancient Orthodox churches and monasteries dot cobblestone streets and forest paths. Ohrid has seen Roman, Slavic, and Ottoman rule and served as the Bulgarian capital in the late 10th and 11th centuries. Thanks to UNESCO's protection, the architectural legacy of Yugoslav socialism is scarcely visible.

E TRANSPORTATION. The **bus station** (☎260 339; open daily 4am-10pm) sends buses to: **Bitola** (2hr., 1 per hr., 270den); **Skopje** (3½hr., 10 per day, 350den); **Struga** (30min., 4 per hr., 40den); **Sveti Naum** (1hr., 7 per day, 20den); **Istanbul, TUR** (11hr., 1 per day, 3100den). **Ferries** leave from the dock in the city center for **Sveti Naum** (1½hr., 10am, 250den).

■■ ORIENTATION AND PRACTICAL INFORMATION. Ohrid stretches along the northeast corner of Lake Ohrid. **Makedonski Prosvetiteli** (Македонски Просветители), runs perpendicular to the lake from the pier where the ferries dock to **Bulevar Turistichka** (Туристичка), the other major transit road, which parallels the shore and is the outer boundary of the city center. Parallel to Makedonski Prosvetiteli on the west (Old Town) side, Kliment Ohridski stretches from a rose garden at the waterfront to **Ploshtad Krushevska Republika** (Плоштад Крушевска Република; Krushevo Republic Square). Along the water on the west side of Makedonski Prosvetiteli, Kosta Abrashevik (Коста Абрашевик) wraps along the water, as does Kej Marshal Tito (Кео Маршал Тито), on the east side. In the Old Town, nameless streets wind haphazardly; the new town exemplifies perfect socialist angularity. To get to the center from the bus station, exit left out of the ticket office and walk to the end of the driveway. Turn right onto Partizanska (Партизанска), and left after 20m onto Makedonski Prosvetiteli; follow it until you reach the rose garden at the lake. Turn around, and diagonally in front of you to the left stretches Kliment Ohridski. The Old Town creeps up the hill to your left.

Otex Tours, Partizanska bb, in the bus station building, sells **maps** for 150den. (☎261 244; biteli@yahoo.com. Open M-Sa 8am-8pm.) **Putnik,** Partizanska 4, sells an English guide (400den; see **Accommodations and Food,** p. 487). **Ohridska Banka** (Охридска Банка), Makedonski Prosvetiteli 19, on the corner of bul. Turistichka, **exchanges currency** for 0.2-0.5% commission, cashes **traveler's checks** for 0.55% commission, and has **Western Union** services. (☎231 400; fax 231 007. Open M-F 7am-5pm, Sa 7am-1pm.) Across the street, **Tutunska Banka** (Тутунска Банка) offers MC **cash advances** for 2% commission (☎257 350). Walking up Kliment Ohridski from the rose garden, a MC **ATM** is on the first wall on the right behind a sea of cafe tables. A Visa **ATM** is 50m up on the same side just after the "Fast Food" restaurant. There are several **Internet** cafes on the third floor of the white building at the corner of Makedonski Prosvetiteli and Partizanska (Kliment

Ohridski 238/II). **Palnet** is open 24hr. (☎253 650. 60den per hr. International calls 15den per min.) The **post office** is on Makedonski Partizanksa between Dimitar Vlahov and Partizanska. (☎265 171. Open M-Sa 7am-8pm.) **Poste Restante** is at window 4. **Postal Code:** 6000.

▐▐ ACCOMMODATIONS AND FOOD. Putnik, Partizanska 4, across from the bus station, books **private rooms ❶** (singles 300den; doubles 600den) and hotels. (☎/fax 252 020. 2000-4000den. Open daily 8am-6pm.) People at the bus station also offer private rooms (300-800den), but be sure you know the exact location. ▐**Motel Amsterdam ❷,** Goce Delchev 235A (Гоце Делчев), 1km from Ploshtad Krushevo Republike, is clean and homey, with balconies overlooking the lawn. (☎250 990. Reception 24hr. Singles 1300den; doubles 1800den.) A 5km taxi ride (100den) from the bus station, **Hotel Park ❸,** Naum Ohridski 5-7, offers rooms with balconies and newly renovated bathrooms. (☎261 521; fax 260 061. Breakfast included. Reception 24hr. Singles €44; doubles €68. MC/V.) ▐**Ohrid Fish Restaurant ❷** (Охридска Пастрмка Рибен Ресторан; Ohridska Pastrmka Riben Restoran), on the water to the right of the rose garden, serves the best of the lake's specialties. (☎263 827. Fish dishes 300-500den and 1200-1600den per kg, grilled meat dishes 150-350den. Open daily 7am-1am.) **Restoran Dalga ❷** (Ресторан Далга), Kosta Abrashevik 7, cooks up Macedonian cuisine on a breezy patio. Try the *uvijachi* (pork rolled with cheese, mushrooms, and ham; 300den) or other meat dishes. (260-450den. ☎255 999. Open daily 10am-1am.) For some pizza you can't refuse, stop into **Pizzeria Cosa Nostra ❶,** Kosta Abrashevik 50. (☎230 240. Small pizzas 110-200den; large 200-280den; pizza *sendvich* 150den. Open M-F 10am-midnight, Sa-Su 10am-10pm. MC.) Fruits and veggies are sold in the **town market** (Градско Пазариште; Gradsko Pazarishte), off Ploshtad Krushevska Republika, between Goce Delchev and Turistichka (daily 7am-8pm). At night, Marshal Tito and Kliment Ohridski fill up with vendors selling cotton candy (10den), corn on the cob (10den), and fast food (pizza and calzones 60den; burgers 100den; french fries 50den).

▐▐ SIGHTS AND ENTERTAINMENT. Start a tour of Ohrid's monasteries at **Sveta Sofija** (Света Соꙁрија), the town's oldest church. Take Kliment Ohridski to the water and go right on Kosta Abrashevik; it's 300m up on the right. The 11th- to 14th-century frescoes were restored in 1957. They had been whitewashed under Ottoman rule, when the church served as a mosque. (Open Tu-Su 9am-noon and 5-8pm. English guidebooks 200den. Admission 100den, students 30den.) Walk around the back of the church, turn right, and climb the steps to your left. Turn left on Kocho Racin (Кочо Рацин), and follow the path to get to the **Church of St. John "Kaneo" Bogoslav** (Sveti Jovan Bogoslav-Kaneo; Свети Јован Богослав-Канео), overlooking the lake. (Open daily 9am-2pm and 4-8pm. 100den, students 50den.) Take the steps around to the left and follow the stone path up to the **Monastery of St. Clement and Panteleimon at Plaoshnik** (Св. Клинентовиот Манастир Светите Климент и Пантелејмон На Плаошник; Sv. Klimentoviot Manastir Svetite Kliment i Pantelejmon Na Plaoshnik), Ohrid's newest monastery church. (Open daily 8am-8pm. Free.) Continue up the path to the left of the sheltered walkway to reach **Ohrid Fortress** (Охридската Тврдина; Ohridskata Tvrdina). It took its present form during the rule of Samuel (976-1014) and is referred to as Samuel's Fortress (Самуилова Тврдина; Samuilova Tvrdina). Enter through the gate and climb the stairs for great views. (Open 24hr. Free.) Exit through the gate of the fortress and turn left. When the road opens to a five-way intersection, go straight and bear left to reach the 1295 **St. Clement's Church of the Holy Mother of God.** (Свети Климент Света Богородица; Sveti Kliment Sveta Bogorodica.

MACEDONIA

Open Tu-Su 9am-1pm and 4-8pm. 100den, students 30den.) From the five-way intersection, go left down the hill. On the right is the **Classical Theater** (Античкиот Театар; Antichkiot Teatar), built 2000 years ago, excavated in 1977, and reconstructed in 2001. Better-preserved seats sport engraved names of ancient season ticket holders. Along with Sv. Sofija, the theater hosts classical music concerts during the **Ohrid Summer Festival.** (Охридско Лето; Ohridsko Leto. Info ☎9865. Occurs mid-June to mid-Aug.)

NIGHTLIFE AND BEACHES. If you've had your fill of Eurobeats, walk down the waterfront to the left on Marshal Tito and waddle in to the moody, dark, and sleek the **Duck Cafe,** Jane Sandanski 1. (☎250 009. Live music some weekends. Beer 60-100den. Mixed drinks 80-120den. Cigarettes 80den. Open daily 9am-midnight.) If you never tire of Eurobeats, head to **Aquarius,** Kosta Abrashevik 30. A cafe by day, it has tables jam-packed with trendy locals. At night, the club gets trendier and more crowded. (☎263 030. Beer 100-120den. Mixed drinks 100-150den. Open daily in summer 10am-2am; low season 10am-midnight.) Good **beaches** are on the lake's eastern side, starting at Hotel Park (see **Accommodations and Food,** p. 487). They get even better farther away, around Lagadin. **Water-taxis** wait on the shores of the town center. The trip to **Gorica I** costs 300den, and 400den to **Gorica II** and **III**—you can either pay it all yourself or wait for the boat to fill up.

STRUGA (СТРУГА) ☎(0)46

Fifteen kilometers northwest of Ohrid, Struga is considered by some to be a poor man's Ohrid. But cheaper accommodations, proximity to good beaches, and the mesmerizing blue water of the **Crni Drim River** (Црни Дрим) make it a destination unto itself. Every August, poets from around the world compete at **Struga Poetry Evenings** (Струшки Вечери на Поезијата; Strushki Vecheri na Poezijata). The festival commemorates Struga's favorite sons, Konstantin and Dimitar Miladinov (see **The Arts,** p. 479). The **House of the Miladinov Brothers,** Bracha Miladinovi 5 (Брача Миладинови), around the corner from Hotel Beograd, houses a library of the poetry of winners of past Poetry Evenings. (☎786 270. Open M-F 7am-3pm.) The **Nikola Nezlobinski Natural History Museum** (Народен Музео Др Никола Незлобински Природњачка Изложба; Naroden Muzey Dr. Nikola Nezlobinski Prirodnjachka Izlozhba), Bore Hadzhieski bb (Боре Хаџиески), displays species past and present. Turn left from Hotel Beograd, and left before the bridge. Hop on the traffic street to your left and follow it 400m; it will be on your right. No translation is needed to appreciate a meter-long *letnica* trout (16.5kg—the largest ever caught) or a two-headed calf. (Open M-F 7am-7pm, Sa 7am-8pm.)

🛏**Hotel Beograd ❶,** at the intersection of Marshal Tito and the river, delivers old-school charm, rooms with sofas, private balconies, and a staff of informal tour guides. (☎781 342; fax 782 126. Reception 24hr. Singles 750den; doubles 1160den. MC/V.) Taste the best of Struga at **Klimetica ❷** (Клинетица), Goce Delchev 90 (Гоце Делчев). With your back to the Hotel Beograd, walk right and turn left down the first street; it's down 50m on the left. Try the *Leskovica Mushkalica* (Лесковица Мушкалица; thick pork stew of tomatoes, peppers, and onions) for 250den. (☎788 178. Entrees 120-1200den. Open daily 10am-midnight.)

Buses run to and from Ohrid (30min., 4 per hr., 40den) from the bus station and from the yellow and red bus stops around town. When coming from Ohrid, stay on the bus after the bus-station stop; it will take you into the center. Buses also run to **Skopje** (3hr., 6 per day, 240den); **Belgrade SMN** (11hr., 1 per day, 1260den); **Istanbul, TUR** (13hr., 1 per day, 3100den); **Sofia, BUL** (6hr., 1 per day, 1300den). The **bus station** is on Partizanska (Партизанска), which runs along the waterfront perpendicular to the river. **Marshal Tito** (Маршал Тито), the main pedestrian zone, runs parallel to Partizanska along the west side of the river 500m downstream. **Proleterski Brigadi** (Пролетерски Бригади) borders the pedestrian zone to the west, running parallel to the river. At the intersection of Marshal Tito and Proleterski Brigadi, **Stopanska Banka** (Стопанска Банка), Marshal Tito 54, **exchanges currency** for 0.5% commission, cashes **traveler's checks** for 0.55% commission and offers V **cash advances** for no commission, up to 20,000den. (☎781 801; fax 781 365. Open M-F 7am-7pm, Sa 7:30am-1:30pm.) **Internet Klub "Saly"** is on the second floor of the old mall along Marshal Tito across from Hotel Beograd. (☎784 070; psaliv@hotmail.com. 60den per hr. Open daily 10am-midnight.) The **post office**, J.N.A. bb (J.H. A.), is across the river from the Hotel Beograd on the street that extends from the end of Marshal Tito. (☎781 548. Open M-Sa 7am-8pm.) **Postal Code:** 6330.

MOLDOVA

MOLDOVAN LEI		
AUS$1 = 8.39LEI	10 LEI = AUS$1.19	
CDN$1 =9.01 LEI	10 LEI = CDN$1.11	
EUR€1 = 14.27LEI	10 LEI = EUR€.70	
NZ$1 =7.62LEI	10 LEI = NZ$1.31	
UK£1 = 21.70LEI	10 LEI = UK£.46	
US$1 = 11.87LEI	10 LEI = US$.84	

Moldova was once part of the Romanian province of Moldavia, but it gained independence in 1991, after enduring 45 years of Soviet rule. Today, Moldova is struggling to overcome poverty and political instability, especially in the breakaway region of Transdniester. Moldova's scenery is often beautiful: rolling hills grace the countryside while unspoiled greenery is common, even in the capital city of Chișinău. Not many tourists stumble upon this tiny country in their travels—if you do, look past the Soviet bleakness and discover the spirit of the Moldovan people.

HISTORY

Russia and Romania dominate Moldovan history, as both countries have long competed for the regions of **Bessarabia** and **Transdniester.** Bessarabia has been controlled by Scythia (1000 BC), Kyivan Rus (AD 10th and 12th centuries), Galician princes (early 13th century), and the Tatars (1241-1300s). The region enjoyed temporary prosperity after its annexation by **Moldavia,** part of modern-day Romania, until it was captured by the **Turks.** In the 15th century, **Ștefan cel Mare** (Stephen the Great) expanded Moldavia's frontiers, pushing back the Poles to the north and the Turks to the south. Seeing this success, Russia cast its eye on the small but prosperous state. Beginning in 1711, Russia invaded five times, and the **Treaty of Bucharest** legitimized its claim in 1812.

Attempts to impose Russian culture on the region had little effect on the largely illiterate peasants who were culturally aligned with Romania. The birth of the Romanian state in 1881 fueled nationalism that erupted in a Moldovan unification

FACTS AND FIGURES

OFFICIAL NAME: Republic of Moldova

CAPITAL: Chișinau (pop. 708,000)

POPULATION: 4.5 million (64.5% Moldovan/Romanian, 14% Ukrainian, 13% Russian, 2% Bulgarian, 6.5% Gagauz and other)

LANGUAGE: Moldovan (much like Romanian), Russian, Gagauz (Turkish dialect)

CURRENCY: 1 leu (plural lei) = 100 bani

RELIGION: 98% Eastern Orthodox, 1.5% Jewish, 0.5% other

LAND AREA: 33,843 km^2

CLIMATE: Moderate winters, warm summers

GEOGRAPHY: Rolling steppes

BORDERS: Romania, Ukraine

ECONOMY: 49% Service, 28% Agriculture, 23% Industry

GDP: US$541 per capita

COUNTRY CODE: 373

INTERNATIONAL DIALING PREFIX: 8-10

MOLDOVA

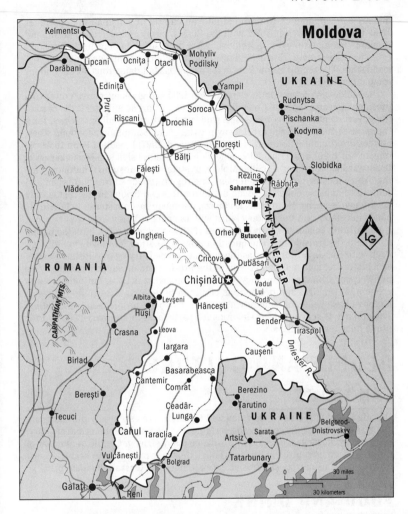

movement during the **Russian Revolution of 1905.** In 1917, Bessarabia renounced Russian rule and declared autonomy. The Bolsheviks invaded but Romanian forces drove them out. Moldova joined Romania in 1918 despite Russia's refusal to acknowledge the cession. In 1939, the Soviets invaded again. During **WWII,** Romania won Bessarabia back and deported most of its Jews to Auschwitz to make room for Romanian peasants. After the Axis defeat, the Russians invaded again and integrated the region into the USSR as the **Moldovan Soviet Socialist Republic.**

Nationalism grew as the USSR faltered in the 1980s; in 1991, the **Republic of Moldova** declared independence. A powerful nationalist movement reinstated the Latin alphabet and adopted Romania's national hymn. This alarmed the country's large Russian minority, who feared reunification with Romania. Russian nationalists in the **Transdniester** region, between the Dniester river and Ukraine,

MOLDOVA

declared independence from the Moldovan capital of Chişinău in September 1990. **Civil war** followed in 1992, with the Russian army aiding Transdniester and Romania backing the rest of Moldova. After a ceasefire in July 1992, Transdniester won autonomy. However, Transdniester is not an internationally recognized state. The region is now known for its porous but dangerous border and for rampant smuggling.

The Moldovan constitution was ratified in 1994 and gives executive power to a president and an appointed Council of Ministers. The prime minister is the head of the government, which consists of a **parliament** with 104 members elected for a four-year term. Due to the breakaway province and continuing economic woes, politics are fraught with internal strife. On May 8, 1997, President **Petru Lucinschi** (elected in 1996) and Transdniester leader **Igor Smirnov** signed a **Memorandum of Understanding,** affirming a united Moldovan state with substantial autonomy for the Transdniester region. Nonetheless, the region remained firmly Russian and refused to acknowledge Moldovan authority. Russian troops in the region only heightened tensions. Meanwhile, **Ion Sturza,** elected prime minister in 1999, had his hands full stabilizing an economy laden with rampant inflation.

In 2001, the **Communist Party of Moldova (PRCM)** took control of both the parliament and the presidency. The question now is whether Moldova should align itself with Russia or Romania, as the current regime is trying to reinstate **Russian** as a state language and undo many of the pro-Romanian reforms passed by its predecessor. Moldova's currency stabilized somewhat in 2004, but inflation was around 15% in 2003 and projections continue to be high. After mild recovery, Moldova has seen economic downturn, and its social problems are escalating. The country is scheduled for elections for parliament in February 2005 and for prime minister in April 2005.

PEOPLE AND CULTURE

LANGUAGE

Despite a few differences, **Moldovan** and **Romanian** are essentially the same language. About 60% of the country speaks Moldovan. For a phrasebook and glossary, see **Glossary: Romanian,** p. 956. You'll still see many signs in Cyrillic, a remnant of the area's former control by Russia. Though they may prefer not to hear it, almost everyone in Chişinău speaks **Russian,** so also check out **Glossary: Russian** (p. 958).

FOOD AND DRINK

MOLDOVA	❶	❷	❸	❹	❺
FOOD	under 20 lei	20-30 lei	31-40 lei	41-50 lei	over 50 lei

Moldovan **cuisine** is a combination of bland Russian dishes, Romanian *mamaliga* (cornmeal), and tasty Turkish kebabs, similar to what one might find in the Moldavia region of Romania. Uniquely Moldovan dishes, like bean and sausage salad and noodles with poppy seeds and cheese, are found in the countryside. Meat dishes are common first and second courses. **Vegetarian** diets are rare, and those with eating restrictions will have difficulty explaining their needs to meat-loving locals. **Wine** is an integral part of Moldovan life; the country has some of the most fertile vineyards in Europe. Its most famous wine comes from **Cricova** (p. 500).

CUSTOMS AND ETIQUETTE

You're unlikely to find many English speakers in Moldova. Moldovan customs are rooted in Romanian culture. Moldovan women do not shake hands, but it is considered impolite for men not to do so. Due to their great wine tradition, not finishing your glass of wine is considered an insult. Shoes worn outdoors should be removed before entering someone's home. **Bargaining** is always appropriate, except at restaurants and large hotels. A tip of 10% or less is expected at restaurants, and is never included in the bill. Wear pants and closed-toed shoes to avoid looking like a tourist. For more info on etiquette, see **Romania: Customs and Etiquette**, p. 608.

THE ARTS

Moldovan **literature**, like its history, is inextricably linked with that of Romania (see **Romania: The Arts**, p. 608). During the Soviet era, art in Moldova suffered under the yoke of **Socialist Realism**. One notable writer of this period was **Andrei Lupan,** who managed to enliven the otherwise bland praise for the Communist regime. **Ion Druta** explored the psyche of Moldova's rural population in his 1963 novel *Ballad of the Steppes (Balade de cîmpie)*. Though Lupan and Druta wrote in Moldovan, much of their work was published only in Russian by the Soviet-controlled press. Sovietization also reduced Moldova's **folk arts:** the state went to great lengths to preserve its native culture, but these efforts were negated by an economic program that eradicated much of the traditional lifestyle. Moldovan **architecture** is exemplified by the many **churches** built by Ştefan cel Mare in the 15th century.

The Moldovan National Opera and Ballet Theater reaps the benefits of Russian-trained ballet dancers like the talented soloist **Cristina Terentiev.** Fine art galleries in Chişinău feature some young Moldovan talent. Check out the **Holti Gallery,** Str. Columna 128 (☎ 24 37 03), or **L Gallery,** Str. Bucuresti 64 (☎ 22 19 75).

HOLIDAYS AND FESTIVALS

NATIONAL HOLIDAYS IN 2005	
January 1 New Year's Day	**May 1** Labor Day
January 7-8 Christmas (Orthodox)	**May 9** Victory and Commemoration Day
March 1 Marţişor (Moldova Day)	**August 27** Independence Day
March 8 International Women's Day	**August 31** National Language Day
April 11-12 Easter Holiday	**October 14** City Day

The vast majority of Moldovans are Orthodox Christian, so holidays are centered on the Eastern Orthodox calendar. Moldova also periodically celebrates international music and performance festivals. These include **Maria Bieşu Invites** (a week of opera and ballet featuring foreign guests), **Ukraine Culture Days,** and **Russian Culture Days. Marţişor,** or National Moldova Day, heralds the coming of spring. On March 1st, Moldovans give each other snowdrop flowers, symbols of serenity. The **Marţişor Music Festival** was started in 1967 and occurs in March.

ADDITIONAL RESOURCES

Moldova and the Transdniester Republic, by Nicholas Dima (2001). Part of the East European Monographs series, with several good offerings on Moldovan history.

Playing the Moldovans at Tennis, by Tony Hawks (2001). A British comedian tries to win a bet in which he must beat the entire Moldovan national soccer team at tennis.

Studies in Moldovan, by Donald Dyer (1996). The broadest historical and cultural overview of modern Moldova.

The Gypsy Camp Vanishes Into the Heavens, directed by Emil Loteanu (1976). Moldova's most internationally acclaimed film, *Gypsy Camp* is a romantic and cultural tale amazingly produced in the dark, oppressive Communist era.

MOLDOVA ESSENTIALS

ENTRANCE REQUIREMENTS
Passport: Required of all travelers.
Visa: Required of all travelers.
Letter of Invitation: Required of citizens of Australia and New Zealand.
Inoculations: Recommended up-to-date on DTaP (diphtheria, tetanus, and pertussis), Hepatitis A, Hepatitis B, MMR (measles, mumps, and rubella), Polio booster, and Typhoid.
Work Permit: Required of all foreigners planning to work.
International Driving Permit: Required of all foreigners planning to drive.

DOCUMENTS AND FORMALITIES

EMBASSIES AND CONSULATES

The UK and US embassies in Moldova are in **Chişinău** (see p. 497).

Belgium: 175 Ave. Emile Max, 1030 Brussels (☎02 732 93 00; ambassademoldavie@brutele.be). Accredited for the **EU.**

US: 2101 S St. NW, Washington, D.C. 20008 (☎202 667 1130; www.moldovaembassy.org). Provides visa assistance for citizens of the US, the **EU,** and **Canada**.

VISA AND ENTRY INFORMATION

Moldova is updating its visa and entry laws; check with your embassy for the most up-to-date information. Citizens of Australia and New Zealand need both **visas and invitations** to travel in Moldova; citizens of Canada, the EU, and the US just need visas for travel of duration greater than three months. Single-entry visas cost US$85 (valid 1 month); multiple-entry travel visas US$95-165 (depending on length of stay); transit visas US$65 for single-entry, US$85 for double-entry. There is also a **processing fee.** In all cases, passports must be valid two months after departure from Moldova. Regular service takes seven business days; **rush service** costs extra, depending on the visa type. Costs are lower for those born in Moldova. To apply, submit an application, an invitation (if applicable), your passport, a photo, an envelope, and the fee by money order or company check to the appropriate Moldovan embassy or consulate. Invitations can be obtained from acquaintances in Moldova or from a private organization such as **MoldovaTUR** (see **Chişinău: Practical Information,** p. 497), which issues invitations after you book a hotel room. All foreigners in Moldova must **register** with the police within three days of arrival. Also **register your valuables** to avoid customs duties upon exit. Some international buses to and from Odessa pass through Moldova's unstable breakaway **Transdniester Republic** (see p. 491). You will pass through an additional passport control at the

Transdniester/Moldovan border, where you will be given a slip of paper or passport stamp. The guards at the Transdniester/Ukrainian border demand to see this official Moldovan seal and will not let you pass without it.

GETTING AROUND

Chişinău International Airport (☎ 2 52 60 60, flight info 2 52 54 12). **Air Moldova** (☎ 2 52 55 02, reservations 2 52 50 02) is the national airline. Other airlines that service Moldova include: **Moldavian Airlines** (☎ 2 52 93 56, reservations 2 52 96 44); **Tarom,** the Romanian national airline (☎ 22 27 26 18); **CarpatAir** (☎ 40 256 30 69 33, reservations 20 27 01); and **Tyrolean Airlines** (☎ 43 0 512 2222, ext. 0, reservations 5 1789). **Trains** are extremely inefficient. The **Iaşi, ROM**-Chişinău train trip sometimes takes much more time in border controls and rail-gauge changing than in motion. There are direct train and bus connections from Chişinău to: **Bucharest, ROM; Kyiv, UKR; Odessa, UKR.** Internally, trains from Chişinău go to **Ocnita, Tighina,** and **Ungheni.** If you do decide to take the train, opt for first class. **Buses** are crowded and old but provide a much cheaper and more comfortable way of getting in, out, and around.

Taxis in Moldova are generally overpriced and drivers will often charge more if they recognize you as a foreigner. If you do take a taxi, be sure to only ride in officially marked cars. **Rental cars,** though they do exist, are rare. **Gas** stations and repair facilities are relatively uncommon. If you are driving in Moldova, stop for fuel whenever you see a gas station. **Biking** in Moldova can be hazardous, especially in cities where many manhole covers have been removed. **Hitchhiking** is dangerous, and *Let's Go* strongly discourages this practice.

TOURIST SERVICES AND MONEY

MoldovaTUR is the main tourist office. Its employees usually speak English. In general, though, there are few resources for tourists. Do not confuse **Moldovan lei** with the eponymous Romanian currency. Moldovan lei are fully convertible (1 leu = 100 bani). Current inflation is 8-10%, so prices will rise over the next year. **Bringing cash is necessary** since few places outside Chişinău take traveler's checks or give cash advances. **ATMs** are common in the capital. AmEx and MC are the most widely accepted credit cards, but they are only taken in banks and large hotels. Normal business hours in Moldova are Monday to Friday 8am-5pm. Some banks are also open Saturday. Most businesses are closed on national holidays. The **Value Added Tax** (VAT) in Moldova is 20%.

HEALTH AND SAFETY

 EMERGENCY NUMBERS: Police: ☎ 902 **Fire:** ☎ 901 **Ambulance:** ☎ 903

Medical facilities exist, but they may not provide the standard of care that Westerners expect. In an emergency, contact your embassy, which can provide info about local medical facilities. If you decide to go to a hospital, you will be expected to pay with **cash.** Bring your own antibiotics, syringes, bandages, and the like. **Pharmacies** are generally equipped with Western products. The **Farmacia Felicia** chain is open 24hr. Carrying **toilet paper** and **insect repellent** is a good idea. The **water** is not safe to drink. Boil water for 10min. or drink imported bottled water. Beware of unclean food, especially from street vendors. **Cholera** and **diphtheria** are problems; talk with your doctor before going.

Streets are poorly lit at night; take a taxi from a reputable company if you're out at night. Manhole covers have been scavenged for scrap metal, so random holes litter the streets. This makes biking and driving unsafe. Do not walk after dark unless accompanied by a local. **Avoid traveling through the Transdniester region,** as violence and illegal activity are rampant; foreign embassies can do little to help travelers in this region. **Women** should dress conservatively; stay away from tank tops, shorts, and sneakers. It is generally okay for women to travel alone in Moldova, but do not stay out after dark. Moldovans harbor **prejudice** against Roma (gypsies) and others with dark skin. Others of foreign **ethnicities** may receive suspicious looks, and **anti-Semitic** attitudes are prevalent. **Homophobia** persists. Discretion is strongly advised.

ACCOMMODATIONS

MOLDOVA	❶	❷	❸	❹	❺
ACCOM.	under 70 lei	70-140 lei	141-210 lei	211-280 lei	over 280 lei

There are no **hostels** in Moldova. **Homestays** are the cheapest option. You should have no problem finding quality **hotels** for under US$15. It is common to rent by the bed rather than by the room. Reservations are only needed in summer.

KEEPING IN TOUCH

Letters abroad cost 3.60-3.90 lei; **postcards** cost 2 lei. International delivery can take three weeks or more. Address **Poste Restante** envelopes as follows: Alexandra (first name) STANEK (LAST NAME), POSTE RESTANTE, Bd. Ştefan cel Mare 134 (post office address), 2001 (postal code) Chişinău (city), MOLDOVA. Moldova's **country code** is ☎373. There are **no international access numbers** in Moldova; collect calls also remain impossible. Most local phones use Moldtelecom cards (from 12 lei), available at the post office and from kiosks. For an **international operator,** dial ☎819. For domestic calls, use ☎813. **To call internationally,** dial 8, wait for the tone, then dial 10, the country code, and the number. When calling Moldova from other former Soviet republics, you need only to dial the city code, not the country code. Foreign calling cards do not call out of Moldova. **Internet access** is cheap (8-10 lei per hr.) and widely available in Chişinău.

CHIŞINĂU (КИШИНЁВ) ☎(8)2

Once "the greenest city in the USSR," Chişinău (KEE-shee-nau; pop. 677,000) will surprise you. The capital of Europe's second-poorest nation, the city may seem like the end of the line, but in the former USSR, it remains a hub of the southwest. Having emerged from Soviet rule, the city is marked by a fascinating blend of Russian and Romanian cultures that rewards the rare tourist who ventures this far.

▐ TRANSPORTATION

Flights: The **airport** (☎52 54 12) has daily flights to **Budapest, HUN** and **Bucharest** and **Timisoara, ROM** and less frequent flights to **Vienna** and **Paris.** It is 12km from downtown; take *marshrutka* (minibus) #165 to the corner of Ismail and Bd. Ştefan cel Mare (2 lei). Taxis start at US$10; try to bargain to US$5. **Voiaj Travel,** Bd. Negruzzi 7 (☎54 64 64), arranges flights. Open M-F 8am-8pm, Sa 9am-6pm, Su 9am-5pm.

MOLDOVA

Trains: Gara Feroviară (☎25 27 33), in the southwest corner. Buy international tickets at the office to the left. Long-distance trains may have sleeper cars only. Open 24hr. To: **Bucharest, ROM** (12½hr., 1 per day, 275 lei); **Iaşi, ROM** (6hr., 1 per day, 90 lei); **Kyiv, UKR** (12-18hr., 3 per day, 270 lei); **Moscow, RUS** (27-33hr., 2 per day, 322-510 lei); **Odessa, UKR** (5hr., 2 per day, 33 lei); **St. Petersburg, RUS** (37hr., 1 per day, 560 lei).

Buses: Autogara Chişinău, Str. Mitropolit Varlaam 58 (☎54 21 85, reservations 27 14 76), near the market. Ticket office open daily 9:30am-6:30pm. To: **Bucharest, ROM** via **Braşov** (10-12hr., 7 per day, 175 lei); **Iaşi, ROM** (5hr., 8 per day, 45 lei); **Kyiv, UKR** (12hr., 4 per day, 76 lei); **Moscow, RUS** (34hr., 3 per day, 330 lei); **Odessa, UKR** (5hr., 8 per day, 34 lei); **St. Petersburg, RUS** (34hr., 1 per day, 426 lei). Minibuses leave for domestic destinations from around the perimeter.

Public Transportation: Chişinău has an extensive **trolley** (0.75 lei) and **bus** (1-1.50 lei) system. (Runs daily 6am-10pm; departs every 15min.) **Marshrutki,** privately run shared vans, follow the same routes and are a quick alternative (2 lei). Flag them down anywhere on their route. Many run until 11pm, some until 2am. **Taxis** (☎907 or 908) are a gamble. Negotiate the price beforehand; a fair price around the center is 20 lei.

✈ 🛈 ORIENTATION AND PRACTICAL INFORMATION

Chişinău is easy to navigate due to its grid layout. From the train station, go past the fountain and take a right on the main street, **Bd. Gagarina.** At the circle in front of the Hotel Cosmos, bear left for **Bd. Negruzzi,** which climbs a hill and curves to the right to become **Bd. Ştefan cel Mare şi Sfint** (Stephen the Great and Saintly). From there, a right on **Str. Tighina** leads to the bus station and **Piaţa Centrala,** the open-air market. Go straight down Bd. Ştefan cel Mare to get to the main square, **Piaţa Marii Adunari Naţională.** A walkway that becomes **Bd. Renaşterii** heads through the center of the park to the right of the square. The park is flanked by **Str. Puşkin** and **Str. Bănulescu Bodoni.** Trolleybuses #1, 4, 5, 8, and 22 run from the train station to the center; #1, 4, 5, 8, 18, 22, and 28 run along Bd. Ştefan cel Mare.

Tourist Office: MoldovaTUR, Bd. Ştefan cel Mare 4 (☎54 03 01; www.ipm.md/mtur), in Hotel Naţional. Arranges tours (US$15-20 per hr.) and sells plane and train tickets. Provides free (but at times misleading) city **maps** and sells better ones (15 lei). Open in summer M-F 8:30am-6:30pm, Sa 9am-3pm; low season M-F 8:30am-5pm.

Embassies: Romania, Str. Bucureşti 66/1 (☎22 81 26; ambrom@ch.moldpac.md). **Russia,** Bd. Ştefan cel Mare 151 (☎/fax 23 26 00). **Ukraine,** Str. Sfatul Ţarii 55 (☎58 21 51; fax 58 51 08). Open M-F 9am-6pm. **UK,** Str. Nicolae Iorga 18 (☎23 89 91; octavian@be.moldline.net). Open M-Th 9am-5:30pm, F 9am-3pm. **US,** Str. Alexei Mateevici 103 (☎23 37 72). Open M-F 9am-6pm. Citizens of other countries should contact their embassies in **Bucharest, ROM** (see **Embassies and Consulates,** p. 497).

Currency Exchange: Look for "Shimb valutar" signs. **Victoria Bank,** Str. 31 Augusta 141 (☎23 30 65), cashes AmEx/MC **traveler's checks** for 1.5% commission. Open M-F 9am-1pm and 2-4pm. **ATMs** are scattered along Bd. Ştefan cel Mare.

English-Language Bookstore: Oxford University Press, Str. Mihai Eminescu 64 (☎22 89 87). Books 35-200 lei. Open M-F 10am-6pm, Sa 10am-3pm.

24hr. Pharmacy: Farmacia Felicia, Bd. Ştefan cel Mare 128 (☎22 37 25).

Hospitals: Str. Puşkin 51 (☎22 32 66) and Toma Ciorba 1 (☎21 06 93) treat foreigners. Cash only. Try to bring your own medical supplies, such as syringes and bandages.

Telephones and Internet: Moldtelecom, Str. Vlaicu Pircalab 52 (☎27 69 63). Across from the post office. Pay in advance for international calls. Internet 8 lei per hr.

Post Office: Bd. Ştefan cel Mare 134, opposite city hall. Mail packages from the **branch** next to the train station. Open M-Sa 8am-7pm, Su 8am-6pm. **Postal Code:** 2001.

IN RECENT NEWS

FALLING APART

Moldova's Russian-backed break-away republic of Transdniester is famous for its renegade govern-ment and frightening border crossings. However, Transdni-ester, which is autonomous but not internationally recognized, is not the only Moldovan region clamoring for independence.

The Gagauz, a people that speaks a Turkic language, are clustered in southern Moldova and are the country's second-most vocal ethnic minority. Unlike the rebels in Transdniester, the residents of the Gagauz-Yeri lack the backing of a major power, so they have pursued a more moder-ate and peaceful course in their quest for independence. They have fought no wars and have made no claims to being a sepa-rate country, but political pres-sure on the central Moldovan government since the mid-1990s has led to the creation of an autonomous zone in the south, granting the Gagauz cultural rights and powers. There is even a Gagauz-language university.

The main Gagauz center is the town of Comrat. There isn't much to do there, but if you're curious, it is a relatively easy trip, and much safer than Transdniester. The town is a few hours by bus (L10-20) from Chişinau's central station. The locals have a reputa-tion for friendliness, but may be surprised at the sight of a West-ern-dressed person this far off the beaten path.

ACCOMMODATIONS AND FOOD

Budget rooms are hard to find: **hostels** don't exist, and **hotels** are expensive. All hotels have a 9 lei **visa registration fee.** The best value is probably **Coopertiva Adresa,** Bd. Negruzzi 1, across from Hotel Cosmos, which rents **private apartments.** All have TV and baths with hot water; ask for something central. The friendly staff also arranges **homestays,** guided tours, and daytrips. Reception doesn't always speak English, but they will call someone who does. (☎27 46 98; www.adresa.mdl.net. Open 24hr. Apartments €15-45 per night.) The hotel **Turist ❹,** Bd. Renaşterii 13, has prices and quality that vary wildly. (☎22 06 37; fax 22 05 12. Reserve ahead in summer. Singles 240-360 lei; doubles 550-700 lei; suites 1300-1800 lei.) **Hotel Zarea ❷,** Str. Anton Pann 4, has clean rooms with TV, shared baths, and year-round hot water. From Bd. Bodoni, turn left onto Str. Alexandru cel Bun. Anton Pann is the first right. If you don't want to share, pay by room. (☎22 76 25; fax 22 06 58. No English spoken. Beds 95 lei; private rooms with bath 289 lei.)

The public market is in **Piaţa Centrala,** near the bus station. (Open daily 6am-6pm.) For a big grocery selection, try **Supermarket #1,** Str. Puşkin 32 (☎22 42 81. Open daily 9am-11pm.) For late-night groceries, try 24hr. **Fidesco,** Bd. Ştefan cel Mare 6, next to Hotel Naţional, and on Bd. Bodini, near Hotel Turist. The dining room at **Orasul Vechi ❷** ("Old City"), Str. Armenească 24, has an indoor porch and an array of neo-Realist paintings. The Russian-influenced menu specializes in meat dishes. (☎50 40 79. Entrees 20-100 lei. Bottles of wine 60-250 lei. Live folk music most nights. Open daily noon-midnight.) **Restaurant La Taifas ❷,** Str. Bucureşti 67 (entrance on Str. Puşkin), is famous for traditional decor and Moldovan fare. (☎22 76 92. Entrees 20-95 lei. Bottle of Cricova wine 45-55 lei. Live folk music nightly. Open daily 8am-midnight.) Homesick Brits head to **Robin ❹,** Str. Alexandru cel Bun 83, a pub. (☎24 11 27. Entrees 48-65 lei. Beer 8-45 lei, mixed drinks 35-60 lei. Live Celtic and British music daily 8-10pm. Open daily 11am-midnight.)

SIGHTS AND MUSEUMS

The ◪**National History Museum of Moldova** (Muzeul Naţional de Istorie a Moldovei), Str. 31 Augusta 1989, is comprehensive. Archaeological and historical exhibits explore the ancient Moldovan kingdom of Bessarabia in a lovely 18th-century middle-school

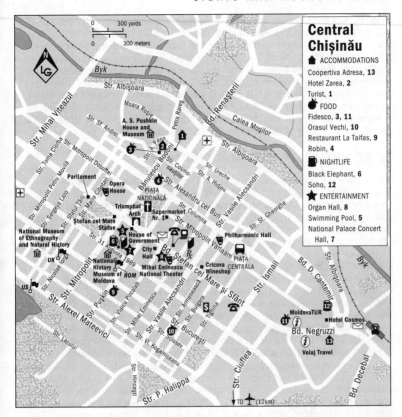

Central Chişinău

🏠 ACCOMMODATIONS
Coopertiva Adresa, **13**
Hotel Zarea, **2**
Turist, **1**

🍎 FOOD
Fidesco, **3, 11**
Orasul Vechi, **10**
Restaurant La Taifas, **9**
Robin, **4**

🍸 NIGHTLIFE
Black Elephant, **6**
Soho, **12**

⭐ ENTERTAINMENT
Organ Hall, **8**
Swimming Pool, **5**
National Palace Concert Hall, **7**

building. The standout section is devoted to WWII and includes a full-scale battle-field recreation. Some English info is available. (☎ 24 04 26. Open Apr.-Oct. M-Th and Sa-Su 10am-6pm; Nov.-Mar. M-Th and Sa-Su 10am-4:30pm. Last entrance 1hr. before closing. Foreigners US$1, students $0.50.) The **National Museum of Ethnography and Natural History** (Muzeul Naţional de Ethnographie şi Istorie Naturală), Str. Kogălniceanu 82, traces the endangered and extinct of the country's natural and cultural life. Murals cover the walls. Don't miss the full relief model of the country or the mammoth and dinosaur skeletons. (☎ 24 40 02. Open Tu-Su 10am-5pm. Call ahead to arrange an English tour, 10 lei. Foreigners US$1, students US$0.50. Cameras US$0.50.)

For the Moldovan take on Russian Pushkin-mania, visit the **A. S. Pushkin House and Museum** (Casa-Muzeul A.S. Puşkin), Str. Anton Pann 10. Pushkin was exiled to Chişinău from 1810 to 1823 for writing poems that offended the Russian tsar. He wrote his novel in verse *Eugene Onegin*, the opening pages of which are set in the city, while living in this building. (☎ 29 26 86. Open Tu-Su 10am-4pm. Call ahead for a 1hr. English tour, 100 lei. Museum 20 lei, students 2 lei.) At the intersection of Bd. Ştefan cel Mare and Str. Puşkin is **Piaţa Marii Adunari Naţională,** Chişinău's main square. In a line stand the **House of Government;** the **Triumphal Arch,** built in 1841 to commemorate a victory over the Ottoman Empire; the reconstructed **Bell Tower,** the original of which housed bells made entirely from the melted guns of Turkish

MOLDOVA

soldiers; and the **Orthodox Cathedral** (Catedrala Naşterea Domnului Clopotniţa), which boasts striking frescoes. In 1962, the Communist regime leveled the original bell tower and shortened the cathedral for standing slightly taller than the flag atop the government building. The cross- and sword-wielding statue of **Stephen the Great and Saintly** (Ştefan cel Mare şi Sfînt) marks the corner of the nearby park. Chişinău resident Alexandru Piă Mădeală sculpted the monument from 1923 to 1928. During WWII, it was twice seized and transported to Romania. At the entrance to the park 18m away, a plaque marks where it stood during the communist era, when it was displaced by a statue of Lenin. Busts of famous local literati line the "Alley of Classics" leading to the fountain in the park's center.

🎵 🎭 ENTERTAINMENT AND NIGHTLIFE

On October 14, Moldovans converge on the city for **Chişinău City Days.** Called *Hram*, Chişinău's biggest festival hosts outdoor rock concerts and countless street vendors, who sell traditional crafts, food, and drinks. To cool off on a hot summer day, try the very clean, if crowded, 50m outdoor **swimming pool** (Bazinul) outside the Centru Sportiv at Str. 31 Augusta 1989 #78. Walk up the alley opposite the National History Museum. (☎ 24 42 21. Pool 20 lei per hr. **Tennis court** 60 lei per hr. **Sauna** 100 lei per hr., up to 7 people. Reserve sauna in advance. Open daily 6am-10pm.) The **Organ Hall** (Sala cu Orgă), Bd. Ştefan cel Mare 81, holds concerts from September to June in an elegant turn-of-the-century hall. (☎ 22 54 04. Box office open M-Sa 11am-5pm, until 6pm on concert days. Tickets 5-20 lei.) The **Opera,** Bd. Ştefan cel Mare 152, hosts occasional touring troupes (☎ 24 51 04). The **Philharmonic,** Str. Mitropolitina Varlaam 78, is near the Oxford Press bookstore (☎ 22 27 34.) The **National Palace,** Str. Puşkin 21, hosts folk and pop concerts. (☎ 21 35 44.) If you don't have time to tour the Cricova Vineyards, stop by the **Cricova Wineshop,** Bd. Ştefan cel Mare 126. (☎ 22 27 75. Open M-F 10am-7pm, Sa-Su 10am-2pm.)

Chişinău has reasonably exciting nightlife. Elegant bars line Bd. 31 Augusta 1989, between Puşkin and Bodoni. For a more lively scene, the nearby **Black Elephant,** Str. 31 Augusta 1989 #78a, entrance off Bd. Bodoni, may be Moldova's coolest club, with live rock from 9pm. (☎ 23 47 15; www.freetime.md/slon. Internet 7 lei per hr. Billiards 5-10 lei. Cover 20-25 lei. Open daily 3pm-last customer.) Visit **Haus,** Str. Alexandru cel Bun 81, which features DJ-spun house music. (Cover 20 lei. Drinks from 10 lei. Open daily 10pm-late.) Check out the giant floor at **Soho,** Str. Negruzzi 2/4 on the second floor, in back of Hotel Cosmo. Throngs of college students dance to mostly house and pop. (☎ 27 59 94. Beer 8 lei per 0.5L. Tu-Su strip club on 3rd fl. Cover 10-40 lei. Open Th-Su 10pm-4am.)

🔁 DAYTRIPS FROM CHIŞINĂU

CRICOVA. The **Cricova Vineyards, Wine Factory, and Cellars,** producers of the famed Moldovan wine, are located in an old rock quarry north of Chişinău. Tiny Moldova once produced a staggering 20% of the wine in the USSR, including the delicious and controversial "Soviet Champagne." You can buy wine from the barrel for 30 lei per 700mL. View their extensive wine collection, housed in a huge maze of underground tunnels, or drive in the old mine. Cricova prefers groups, but you can badger the factory or tourist agency for an individual **tour.** If you have a car, call the factory to arrange your visit. Otherwise, arrange a tour at MoldovaTUR (See **Orientation and Practical Information,** p. 497), badgering if necessary. *(You must have a private car to take the factory and cellar tours. Open M-F 8am-4pm. ☎ 44 12 04. Tours 140 lei; tour, wine tasting, and a few bottles of wine 320 lei.)*

VADUL LUI VODĂ. A sandy **beach** about 12km northeast of Chișinău, this relaxing riverside park on the banks of the Dniester is packed with bikini-clad Moldovans on hot summer days. Some locals avoid the water, which is a bit murky. Work on your tan, rent a **rowboat** (20 lei per hr.), or grab an ice cream at one of the numerous cafes. *(From behind the bus station, on Str. Bulgara, take any marshrutki marked "Vadul lui Vodă" 45min., leaves when full, 4 lei. They can be a bit inconsistent; be patient. Or take a taxi, about 80 lei. To return, take any marshrutka marked "Chișinău"; last bus leaves at 9pm.)*

POLAND (POLSKA)

AUS$1 = 2.55Ł	1Zł = AUS$0.39
CDN$1 = 2.75ZŁ	1Zł = CDN$0.36
EUR€1 = 4.38ZŁ	1Zł = EUR€0.22
NZ$1 = 2.34ZŁ	1Zł = NZ$0.42
UK£1 = 6.64ZŁ	1Zł = UK£0.15
US$1 = 3.63ZŁ	1Zł = US$0.27

Poles consider their homeland the last Western country on the threshold of the East, and as such, it has long been the site of international skirmishes. It is easy to forget that from 1795 to 1918 Poland simply did not exist, and that its short spell of independence thereafter was brutally dissolved. Ravaged by WWII and viciously suppressed by Stalin and the USSR, Poland has finally been given freedom and self-rule, and its residents are not letting the opportunity slip by. The most prosperous of the "Baltic tigers," Poland now has a rapidly increasing GDP and membership in NATO. It became a member of the European Union in May 2004.

HISTORY

THE NASCENT STATE. In AD 966, **Prince Mieszko I** united many tribes that had been occupying modern Poland since 800, but the union wasn't complete until his son, **Bolesław Chrobry** (the Brave), was crowned Poland's first king in 1025. The conglomeration of states was devastated by the Mongols in 1241, but recovered by the 14th century, when it became more prosperous—particularly under **King Kazimierz III Wielki** (Casimir III the Great)—and exhibited unprecedented religious and political tolerance. Poland thus became a refuge for Jews expelled from Western Europe.

PROSPERITY. After Casimir III's death in 1370, Poland had great difficulty with the **Teutonic Knights,** who took East Prussia and cut off the Baltic. To combat them, in 1386 Polish nobles allied with the Lithuanians by marrying Casimir's only child, Princess Jadwiga, to the powerful Grand Duke of Lithuania, **Jogaila.** The duke was

FACTS AND FIGURES

OFFICIAL NAME: Republic of Poland

CAPITAL: Warsaw (pop. 1.6 million)

POPULATION: 38.6 million (97.5% Polish, 1.5% German, 0.5% Ukrainian, 0.5% Belarusian)

LANGUAGE: Polish

CURRENCY: 1 złoty (zł) = 100 groszy

RELIGION: 95% Roman Catholic (75% practicing), 5% Eastern Orthodox, Protestant, and other

LAND AREA: 312,685 km²

CLIMATE: Harsh winters, wet summers

GEOGRAPHY: Plains, southern mountains

BORDERS: Belarus, Czech Republic, Germany, Lithuania, Russia, Slovak Republic, and Ukraine

ECONOMY: 61% service, 35% industry, 4% agriculture

GDP: US$9500 per capita

COUNTRY CODE: 48

INTERNATIONAL DIALING PREFIX: 00

Poland

crowned King Wladyslaw II Jagiełło of Poland. The new **Polish Commonwealth** lasted 187 years and defeated the Teutonic Order in 1410. Poland became a center of learning in 1394 with the establishment of Kraków's **Jagiellonian University** (see **Sights,** p. 536). In the 16th century, under King Zygmunt I Stary (Sigmund the Old), the **Renaissance** reached Poland. The knowledge and spirit of the age found fertile ground at Jagiellonian University. Here, Mikołaj Kopernik, an astronomer from Toruń known by his Latin name, **Copernicus,** developed the revolutionary **heliocentric model of the solar system.**

DELUGE. Poland and Lithuania drew even closer with the 1569 **Union of Lublin,** which established the **Polish-Lithuanian Commonwealth** with an elected king, a customs union, and a shared legislature, but with separate territories, laws, and armies. **King Zygmunt III Waza** moved the capital from Kraków to Warsaw. He and his successors embroiled the state in wars with Sweden, Turkey, and Muscovy throughout the 17th century. Poland only survived this devastating period, known as the **"Deluge,"** because of great military commanders like **Jan Zamoyski** and **Stanislaw Zolkiewski.** During the wars, Poles demonstrated perseverence in the defense of **Częstochowa,** the holy resting place of the Black Madonna icon, where a small force of monks and villagers threw off an invading Swedish army of 9000 (see **Częstochowa**, p. 557). Yet divisive nobles, separate Polish and Lithuanian administrations, and a weakened monarch hobbled the Polish state.

THE THREE PARTITIONS. To oppose Russian influence and maintain the primacy of Catholicism, nationalist Poles formed the **Confederation of Bar** against the king in 1768. The resulting civil war threw Poland into anarchy. While France and Turkey aided the confederates, Russia backed the monarchy. Fearful of losing its influence, Russia supported Prussian ruler Frederick the Great's schemes to shrink Polish lands. In the **First Partition of Poland** (1772), Russia, Prussia, and Austria each claimed sizable chunks.

In 1788, Polish noblemen called a meeting of the *Sejm;* this "Great Sejm" produced a constitution calling for a parliamentary monarchy. Signed on May 3, 1791, the constitution was the second of its kind in the world. It established Catholicism as the national religion, set up a plan for political elections, and provided for a standing army. The prospect of a newly powerful state made Russia and Prussia very nervous. They incited the **Second Partition of Poland** (1793). The government capitulated; many patriots fled abroad. The following year, **Tadeusz Kościuszko** led an uprising against Russian rule. He ended up in prison, and Poland was divided again in the **Third Partition** (1795). With this final partition, Poland **ceased to exist** for 123 years, during which Russia attempted to crush all traces of Polish nationalism. Poland didn't regain independence until 1918, when **Marshal Józef Piłsudski** pushed back the Red Army. A delegation led by **Roman Dmowski** worked **Polish statehood** into the Treaty of Versailles one year later.

WWII AND THE RISE OF COMMUNISM. The 1939 **Nazi-Soviet Non-Aggression Pact** rendered Poland's defense treaties obsolete. Nazi and Soviet forces then attacked simultaneously. Germany occupied the western two-thirds of the country, while the USSR got the rest. **Concentration camps** were erected throughout Poland, and over six million Poles, including three million Jews, were killed during **WWII**. In April 1943, a small group of Jews organized the **Warsaw Ghetto Uprising**, valiantly rebelling against the Nazis. Though the revolt was brutally put down, the uprising was one of the most remarkable acts of courage during the **Holocaust**. When Red tanks rolled in, they "liberated" Warsaw with little opposition and inaugurated 45 years of **communism**. The first years brought mass migrations, political crackdown, and social unrest that led to the 1946 Jewish **pogrom** (religious massacre). The country grudgingly submitted, but **strikes** broke out in 1956, 1968, and 1970; all were violently quashed.

SOLIDARITY. In 1978 **Karol Wojtyła** became the first Polish Pope, taking the name **John Paul II**. His visit to Poland the next year helped to unite Catholic Poles and was an impetus for the 1980 birth of **Solidarność (Solidarity)**, the first independent workers' union in Eastern Europe. Led by **Lech Wałęsa**, an electrician from Gdańsk, Solidarity's anti-communist activities resulted in the declaration of **martial law** in 1981. Wałęsa was jailed and released only after Solidarność was officially disbanded and outlawed by the government in 1982.

In 1989, Poland spearheaded the peaceful fall of Soviet authority in Eastern Europe. **Tadeusz Mazowiecki** was sworn in as Eastern Europe's first non-Communist premier in 40 years. In December 1990, Wałęsa became the first elected president of post-communist Poland. The government opted to swallow the bitter pill of capitalism all in one gulp by eliminating subsidies, freezing wages, and devaluing the currency. This threw the economy into **recession** and produced the first true unemployment in 45 years, but Poland has rebounded toward stability.

ALEKSANDER ATTRACTS. In Poland's tightly contested 1995 presidential election, Lech Wałęsa—former leader of Solidarity—lost to **Aleksander Kwaś niewski**. A 1980s communist, Kwaśniewski was elected on a platform of moderately paced privatization and stronger ties with the West. Following Kwaśniewski's election, however, the **Solidarity Electoral Action Party (AWS)** saw success in local elections, marked by the ascendance of **Jerzy Buzek** to the post of prime minister in 1997.

TODAY. The Solidarity-Freedom Union government fell in 2000, and Kwaśńiewski was reelected in a landslide. A **NATO** member since 1999, Poland has improved its military and was a leading player in the war in Iraq. In 2003, Poland voted to accept their invitation into the **EU,** which they joined in May 2004. The same month, Kwaśniewski appointed **Marek Belka,** the former finance minister, to replace Leszek Miller as **Prime Minister.** Though initially denied by Parliament, Belka gained approval in June 2004.

PEOPLE AND CULTURE

LANGUAGE

Polish varies little across the country (see **Glossary: Polish,** p. 954). The two exceptions are in the region of **Kaszuby,** where the distinctive Germanized dialect is sometimes classified as a separate language, and in **Karpaty,** where the highlander accent is thick. In western Poland and Mazury, **German** is the most common foreign language, although many Poles in big cities speak **English.** Most can understand other Slavic languages if they're spoken slowly. The older generation may speak **Russian.** Polish uses some letters not in the Latin alphabet: *"ł"* sounds like "w;" *"ą"* is a nasal "on;" *"ę"* is a nasal "en." *"Ó"* and *"u"* are equivalent to "oo." *"Ż"* and *"rz"* are like the "s" in "pleasure;" *"w"* sounds like "v." Some consonantal clusters are easier to say than they seem: *"sz"* is "sh;" *"cz"* is "ch;" and *"ch"* and *"h"* sound like the English "h." *"C"* sounds like "ts;" *"dż"* is "dg" as in "fridge;" *"dź"* is "j" as in "Jeep;" *"ć"* or *"ci"* is "chyi;" and *"zi"* or *"ź"* is "zhy." One more thing: "no" means "yes" in Polish.

RELIGION

Poland is one of the most **Catholic** countries in the world and the Church enjoys immense respect and political power. Polish Catholicism has been bol-

TOP TEN: POLAND

1 Best reason to see more of Poland than just Kraków: the colorful and charming city of Wrocław (p. 559).

2 Best drink: Polish vodka, especially Białystok's Żubrowka, which has a blade of grass from Białowiecki in each bottle (p. 506).

3 Best castle: Warsaw's funky Ujazdowski Castle (p. 524).

4 Best place to bicycle, sail, fish, hike, and take in the breathtaking scenery: Mazury lakes region (p. 600).

5 Best student nightlife: Nowowieskiego Street, Poznań (p. 576).

6 Best souvenir: Polish poster art (p. 525).

7 Best pierogi: Pierogarnia, Kraków (p. 533).

8 Best bar: Łódź Kaliska (p. 572).

9 Best way to see sacred art: Lublin Museum of Religious Art, housed in a tower (p. 545).

10 Best use of red bricks: (tie) Toruń Old Town (p. 579), Malbork Castle (p. 595).

POLAND

stered since 1978 by the election of the Polish Pope John Paul II, the first non-Italian pope since the 1600s. **Protestant** groups are generally confined to German-border areas. Only traces of the rich pre-war **Jewish** culture are still apparent.

FOOD AND DRINK

POLAND	❶	❷	❸	❹	❺
FOOD	under 8zł	8-17zł	18-30zł	31-45zł	over 45zł

Polish cuisine blends French, Italian, and Slavic traditions. Meals begin with **soup,** usually *barszcz* (beet or rye), *chłodnik* (cold beets with buttermilk and eggs), *ogórkowa* (sour cucumbers), *kapuśniak* (cabbage), or *rosól* (chicken). **Main courses** include *gołąbki* (cabbage rolls with meat and rice), *kotlet schabowy* (pork cutlet), *naleśniki* (crepes filled with cheese or jam), and *pierogi* (dumplings). Poland bathes in **beer, vodka,** and **spiced liquor.** *Żywiec* is the most popular beer. *EB* is its gentler brother; *EB Czerwone* is a darker variety. Even those who dislike beer will enjoy sweet ◨**piwo z sokiem,** beer with raspberry syrup. *Wyborowa, Żytnia,* and *Polonez,* are popular *Wódka* (vodka) brands while *Belweder* (Belvedere) is Poland's main alcoholic export. *Żubrówka* vodka comes with a blade of grass from Woliński, where bison roam. It's often mixed with apple juice *(z sokem jabłkowym)*. *Miód* and *krupnik* (mead) are beloved by the gentry; grandmas make *nalewka na porzeczce* (black currant vodka).

CUSTOMS AND ETIQUETTE

In restaurants, tell the server how much change you want and leave the rest as a **tip** (10-15%). In taxis, just leave the change. If you say "thank you" after receiving the bill, the waiter will assume you don't want change. In any establishment, say *"dzien dobry"* as you enter, and *"do widzenia"* when you leave. Your waiter will often say *"smacznego"* when he serves you food; reply with *"dziękuję."* When arriving as a guest, bring a female host an odd number of flowers. Smoking is often prohibited indoors. Always give up your seat to an elderly person, woman, or child.

THE ARTS

HISTORY

The course of Polish **literature** changed when the nation adopted Roman Christianity. Poland's medieval texts, mostly religious works, were written in Latin. Self-taught 16th-century author **Mikolaj Rej** was the first to write consistently in Polish and is the father of Polish literature. Loss of statehood in 1795 paved the way for **Romanticism,** which held nationalism as an ideal. The writers of this great period— **Adam Mickiewicz, Juliusz Słowacki,** and **Zygmunt Krasiński**—depict Poland as a noble martyr. Lithuanian-born Mickiewicz's *Pan Tadeusz* is still considered the country's primary epic.

The early 20th-century **Młoda Polska** (Young Poland) movement was laden with pessimism. **Stanisław Wyspiański's** mystery-filled *Wesele* (The Wedding), a dramatic work, addressed many problems that defined Poland in the era. In the years following WWII, many Polish writers published abroad. Nobel Laureate poet **Czesław Miłosz** penned *Zniewolony Umysł* (The Captive Mind), a commentary on communist control of thought in the mid-1950s. In response to attempts to enforce **Socialist Realism,** the "thaw" brought an explosion of new work addressing life under communism. The **Generation of '68** ushered in a wave of works depicting life at an historical crossroads. In 1996 **Wisława Szymborska** became the second Polish writer in 16 years to receive the Nobel Prize.

Polish **music** is defined by the 19th-century work of **Frédéric Chopin** (Fryderyk Szopen), a master composer and the first of many acclaimed Polish instrumentalists (among them pianist **Artur Rubinstein**). Polish **films** have consistently drawn recognition. **Andrzej Wajda** explored his country's conflicts in *A Generation* and *Man of Marble*. He received an honorary Oscar in 2000 for his work. Directors **Roman Polański** and **Krzysztof Kieślowski** have achieved international recognition, the latter for his trilogy *Three Colors: Red, White, and Blue*. The controversial Polański won the 2003 Oscar for Best Director for his film *The Pianist*, set in the Warsaw ghetto during WWII.

CURRENT SCENE

Poland is a jazz hotbed. The **Gdynia Summer Jazz Days** festival hits town every July (see p. 597), and performances occur regularly in Kraków (see **Festivals and Entertainment,** p. 538). Popular contemporary composers include **Witold Lutoslawski** and **Krzysztof Penderecki.** Poland's art history has often been rocky and dissolute, but Kraków is emerging as Poland's contemporary fine arts leader. Galleries abound in the city center, and the Kraków Academy of Fine Arts harbors some of Europe's finest young talents.

HOLIDAYS AND FESTIVALS

NATIONAL HOLIDAYS IN 2005

January 1 New Year's Day	**August 15** Assumption Day
March 27-28 Easter Holiday	**November 1** All Saints' Day
May 1 May Day	**November 11** Independence Day
May 3 Constitution Day	**December 25-26** Christmas
May 26 Corpus Christi	

Festivals are tied to Catholic holidays, though folk tradition adds variety. Businesses close on holidays like **Corpus Christi** (May 26) and **Assumption Day** (August 15), which are not as widely observed elsewhere.

ADDITIONAL RESOURCES

GENERAL HISTORY

Heart of Europe: A Short History of Poland, by Norman Davies (1986). An easy read that provides a good sense of Polish history.

The Polish Way: A Thousand Year History, by Adam Zamoyski (1993). Focuses on the quirks and intricacies of Poland's past.

FICTION AND NONFICTION

Pan Tadeusz, by Adam Mickiewicz (ed. 1992). A classic by one of the founding fathers of Polish literature (see **The Arts,** p. 506).

Poems New and Collected, by Wisława Szymborska (ed. 2000). The haunting, human poetry that won Szymborska the 1996 Nobel Prize for Literature.

Treblinka, by Jean-Francois Steiner (1994). A compelling historical fiction about the uprising in one of Poland's most infamous death camps.

Mila 18, by Leon Uris (1976). A gripping novel about the Warsaw Ghetto by the celebrated American author.

FILM

The Pianist, directed by Roman Polański (2002). About Warsaw ghetto life during WWII.

Three Colors: Red, White, and Blue, directed by Krzysztof Kieślowski. A well-known, internationally acclaimed trilogy that explores the human experience.

POLAND ESSENTIALS

ENTRANCE REQUIREMENTS
Passport: Required for all travelers.
Visa: Not required for stays under 90 days for citizens of Australia, Canada, Ireland, New Zealand, the US, and the UK.
Letter of Invitation: Not required of most travelers.
Inoculations: Recommended up-to-date on DTaP (diptheria, tetanus, and pertussis), Hepatitis A, Hepatitis B, MMR (measles, mumps, and rubella), Polio booster, and Typhoid.
Work Permit: Required for all foreigners planning to work in Poland.
Driving Permit: Required for all those planning to drive.

DOCUMENTS AND FORMALITIES

EMBASSIES AND CONSULATES

Embassies and consulates of other countries in Poland are in **Warsaw** and **Kraków.** Poland's embassies and consulates abroad include:

Australia: 7 Turrana St., Yarralumla, Canberra, ACT 2600 (☎02 6273 1208; www.poland.org.au).

Canada: 443 Daly Ave., Ottawa, ON, K1N 6H3 (☎613-789-0468; www.polishembassy.ca).

Germany: Lassenstr. 19-21, 14193 Berlin (☎030 223 130; www.botschaft-polen.de).

Ireland: 5 Ailesbury Rd., Ballsbridge, Dublin 4 (☎01 283 0855; www.polishembassy.ie).

New Zealand: 17 Upland Rd., Kelburn, Wellington (☎04 475 9453; polishembassy@xtra.co.nz).

UK: 47 Portland Pl., London W1B 1JH (☎087 0774 2700; www.polishembassy.org.uk).

US: 2640 16th St. NW, Washington, D.C. 20009 (☎202 234 3800; www.polandembassy.org).

VISA AND ENTRY INFORMATION

Most travelers can go to Poland **visa-free** for 90 days. Single-entry visas cost US$60, students US$45; multiple-entry visas cost US$100, students US$75; 2-day transit visas cost US$20, students US$15. Applications require a passport, two photos, and payment by money order, certified check, or cash. Regular service takes four days with a US$10 surcharge; 24hr. rush service costs an extra US$35. To extend your stay, apply in the city where you are staying to the branch of the

regional government *(voi vodine)* or to the **Ministry of Internal Affairs,** ul. Ŝ
Batorego 5, Warsaw 02-591 (☎ 022 621 02 51; fax 849 74 94). **Passports** ɪ
valid for at least three months before the scheduled departure date from
and have at least one blank page.

GETTING AROUND

Warsaw's **Okęcie Airport** is modern. **LOT,** the national airline, flies to major cities.
   It's usually better to take a **train** than a bus, as buses are slow and uncomfortable. For a **timetable,** see **www.pkp.pl.** *Odjazdy* (departures) are in yellow, *przyjazdy* (arrivals) in white. *InterCity* and *ekspresowy* (express) trains are listed
in red with an "IC" or "Ex" in front of the train number. *Pośpieszny* (direct; in
red) are almost as fast and a bit cheaper. Low-priced *Osobowy* (in black) are
the slowest and have no restrooms. If you see a boxed R on the schedule, ask
the clerk for a *miejscówka* (reservation). Students and seniors buy *ulgowy*
(half-price) tickets instead of *normalny* tickets. Beware: **foreign travelers are
not eligible for discounts** on domestic buses and trains. **Eurail** is not valid in
Poland. **Wasteels** tickets and **Eurotrain** passes, sold at Almatur and Orbis, get
40% off international train fares for those under 26. Buy tickets in advance or
wait in long lines. Stations are not announced and can be poorly marked. Theft
often occurs on overnight trains; sleep in shifts with a friend (see **Safety and
Security,** p. 510).
   PKS buses are cheapest and fastest for short trips. There are *pośpieszny* (direct;
in red) and *osobowy* (slow; in black). In the countryside, PKS markers (yellow
steering wheels that look like upside-down Mercedes-Benz symbols) indicate
stops. Buses have no luggage compartments. **Polski Express,** a private company,
offers more luxurious service, but does not run to all cities.
   Ferries run throughout the Baltic area. For **taxis,** either arrange the price
before getting in or be sure the driver turns on the meter. The going rate is 1.50-
3zł per km. Arrange cabs by phone if possible. **Rental cars** are readily available in
Warsaw and Kraków. Though legal, **hitchhiking** is rare and sometimes dangerous
for foreigners. Hand-waving is the accepted sign. *Let's Go* does not recommend
hitchhiking.

TOURIST SERVICES AND MONEY

City-specific **tourist offices** are the most helpful. Almost all provide free info in
English and help arrange accommodations. Most have good free maps and sell
more detailed ones. **Orbis,** the state-sponsored travel bureau, operates hotels in
most cities and sells transportation tickets. **Almatur,** the student travel organization, offers ISICs, arranges dorm stays, and sells discounted transportation tickets. The state-sponsored **PTTK** and **IT** (Informacji Turystycznej) bureaus, in nearly
every city, are helpful for basic traveling needs. Try the *Polish Pages*, a free guide
available at hotels and tourist agencies.
   The Polish currency is based on the **złoty** (plural: złotych; 1 złoty=100 groszy).
Inflation is around 2.5%, so prices should be reasonably stable. **Kantors** (except
those at the airport and train stations) offer better exchange rates than banks.
Bank PKO SA and **Bank Pekao** have decent exchange rates; they cash **traveler's
checks** and give **cash advances. ATMs** *(bankomat)* are common, and are all in
English; **MasterCard** and **Visa** are widely accepted at ATMs. Budget accommodations rarely accept **credit cards,** but some restaurants and upscale hotels do. **Normal
business** hours in Poland are 8am-4pm.

POLAND

HEALTH AND SAFETY

 EMERGENCY NUMBERS: Police: ☎997 Fire: ☎998 Ambulance: ☎999

Medical clinics in major cities have private, English-speaking doctors, but they may not be up to Western standards. Expect to pay 50zł per visit. Avoid state hospitals. In an emergency, go to your embassy. **Pharmacies** are well stocked, and some stay open 24hr. **Public restrooms** are marked with a triangle for men and a circle for women. They range from pristine to squalid; They cost up to 0.70zł; soap, towels, and toilet paper may cost extra. **Tap water** is theoretically drinkable, but **bottled mineral water** will spare you from some unpleasant metals and chemicals.

Crime rates are low, but tourists are sometimes targeted. Watch for muggings and **pickpockets,** especially on trains. **Women** traveling alone should take usual precautions. Travelers of unfamiliar ethnicities may receive attention. Those with darker skin may encounter **discrimination.** There may be lingering prejudice against Jews despite great efforts on the part of the government. **Homosexuality** is legal and a frequent topic of media debate, although it remains fairly underground. Discretion is advised.

ACCOMMODATIONS AND CAMPING

POLAND	❶	❷	❸	❹	❺
ACCOM.	under 45zł	45-65zł	66-80zł	81-120zł	over 120zł

Hostels *(schroniska młodzieżowe)* abound and cost 15-40zł. They are often booked solid by tour groups; call at least a week ahead. **PTSM** is the national hostel organization. Dom Wycieczkowy and Dom Turystyczny hostels, which are geared toward adults, cost around 50zł. **University dorms** become budget housing in July and August; these are an especially good option in Kraków. The **Almatur** office in Warsaw arranges stays throughout Poland. PTTK runs several **hotels** called Dom Turysty, which have multi-bed rooms and budget singles and doubles. Hotels generally cost 80-150zł. **Pensions** are often the best deal: the owner's service more than makes up for the small sacrifice in privacy. **Private rooms** *(wolne pokoje)* are available most places, but be careful what you agree to. **Homestays** can be a great way to meet locals. Find them at the tourist office. Private rooms should cost 20-60zł. Campsites average 10-15zł per person, 20zł with a car. They may rent **Bungalows;** a bed costs 20-30zł. *Polska Mapa Campingów,* available at tourist offices, lists **campsites.** Almatur runs a number of sites in summer; ask them for a list. Only camp in campsites or risk a night in jail.

KEEPING IN TOUCH

Mail is admirably efficient. Airmail *(lotnicza)* takes two to five days to Western Europe and seven to 10 days to Australia, New Zealand, and the US. Mail can be received via **Poste Restante.** Address the envelope as follows: Jane (first name) YAGER (LAST NAME), POSTE RESTANTE, ul. Długa 22/25 (post office address), 80-800 (postal code) Gdańsk (city), POLAND. Letters cost about 2.20zł. To pick up Poste Restante, pay a fee (1.10zł) or show your passport.

Card telephones are standard. Cards are sold at post offices, Telekomunikacja Polska offices, and kiosks. Before using a card, break off its perforated corner. Some Telekomunikacja Polska offices also offer **Internet access.** To make a **collect call,** hand the clerk a sheet with the name of the city or country and the number plus "*Rozmowa 'R'*" International access codes include: **AT&T Direct** (☎00 800 111 11 11); **Australia Direct** (☎00 800 611 11 61); **BT Direct** (☎00 800 89 0036); **Canada Direct** (☎00 800 111 41 18); **MCI WorldPhone** (☎00 800 111 21 22); **Sprint** (☎00 800 111 31 15); **Telkom SA WorldCall** (☎00 800 271 11 27). Poland is **wired.** Most mid-sized towns have at least one Internet cafe and larger cities have several. The cost is about 3-8zł per hr.

WARSAW (WARSZAWA) ☎(0)22

Resilient Warsaw rebuilt itself from rubble at the end of World War II, when two-thirds of the population were killed and 83% of the city destroyed. Having weathered the further blow of a half-century of communist rule, Warsaw has now sprung to life as a dynamic center of business, politics, and culture. With Poland's recent accession into the European Union, things are moving even faster in the busy, youthful capital. A proud survivor and an unabashed striver, underrated Warsaw is a city on the rise.

■ INTERCITY TRANSPORTATION

Flights: Port Lotniczy Warszawa-Okęcie ("Terminal 1"), ul. Żwirki i Wigury (info desk ☎650 41 00, reservations 0801 300 952). Take bus #175 to the city center (after 10:40pm, bus #611); buy tickets at the *Ruch* kiosk. Open M-F 6am-10pm. In the arrivals hall is the **IT** (Informacji Turystyczna) office (see **Tourist Offices,** p. 515). Open M-F 8am-8pm. Airlines include: **Aeroflot,** al. Jerozolimskie 29 (☎621 16 11; open M-F 8am 4pm); **Air France,** ul. Krucza 21 (☎584 99 00, open M-F 9am-4pm; at the airport ☎846 03 03, open M-Sa 5am-7pm, Su 7:30am-7pm); **American Airlines,** ul. Ujazdowskie 20, (☎625 30 20; open M-F 9am-6pm); **British Airways,** ul. Krucza 49, off al. Jerozolimskie (☎529 90 00, M-F 9am-5pm; at the airport ☎650 45 03, open daily 6am-4:30pm); **Delta,** ul. Królewska 11 (☎827 84 61; open M-F 9am-5pm); **KLM,** (☎622 80 00; open M-F 8am-4pm) at the airport; **LOT,** al. Jerozolimskie 65/79 (☎577 99 53; open M-F 8am-7pm, Sa 9am-3pm) in the Marriott; **Lufthansa,** (☎338 13 00; www.lufthansa.pl; open M-F 9am-5pm); **Swiss Air,** (☎650 45 25; open M-Su 5:30am-6pm) at the airport.

Trains: There are 3 train stations; the most convenient is **Warszawa Centralna,** al. Jerozolimskie 54 (☎94 36; www.pkp.pl). Most trains also stop at **Warszawa Zachodnia (Western Station),** ul. Towarowo 1, and **Warszawa Wschodnia,** ul. Lubelska 1, in Praga. Warszawa Centralna has cafes, a 24hr. **pharmacy, ATMs, luggage storage,** and a **post office.** On the main level, international counters are to the left and domestic are to the right. Write down where and when you want to go, along with *"Który peron?"* ("Which platform?"). Yellow signs list departures *(odjazdy);* white signs arrivals *(przyjazdy).* To: **Gdańsk** (4hr., 12 per day, 43-117zł); **Kraków** (2½-5hr., 10 per day, 55-101zł); **Łódź** (1½-2hr., 10 per day, 27-40zł); **Lublin** (2½hr., 11 per day, 19-92zł); **Poznań** (2½-3hr., 15 per day, 42-114zł); **Szczecin** (5½hr., 5 per day, 47-117zł); **Toruń** (2½-4½hr., 7 per day, 35-105zł); **Wrocław** (4½hr., 9 per day, 45-125zł); **Berlin, GER** (6hr., 4 per day, 160zł); **Budapest, HUN** (11hr., 2 per day, 280zł); **Prague, CZR** (9-11hr., 2 per day, 270-310zł); **St. Petersburg, RUS** (27-30hr., 2 per day, 300zł).

Buses: Both PKS and Polski Express buses run out of Warsaw.

Polski Express, al. Jana Pawła II (☎620 03 20), in a kiosk next to Warszawa Centralna. A private company that is faster and nicer than PKS. Domestic trips only. To: **Białystok** (3½hr., 4 per day, 32zł); **Częstochowa** (5½hr., 2 per day, 46zł); **Gdańsk** (6hr., 2 per day, 68zł); **Kraków** (8hr., 2 per day, 60zł); **Łódź** (2½hr., 7 per day, 30zł); **Lublin** (3hr., 8 per day, 34zł); **Wrocław** (6hr., 3 per day, 65zł); **Toruń** (4hr., 15 per day, 46zł). Kiosk open daily 6:30am-10pm.

POLAND

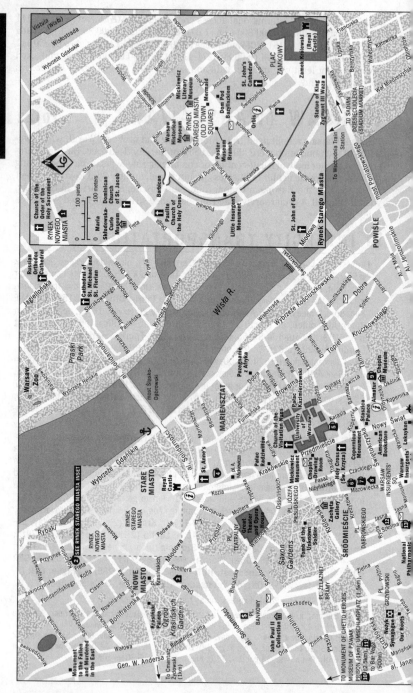

POLAND

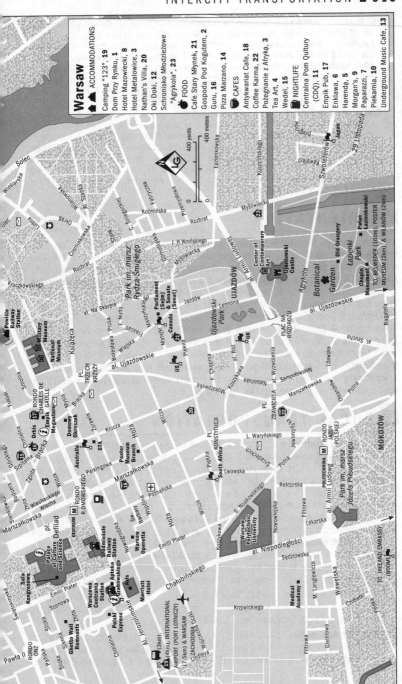

Warsaw

▲ ♠ ACCOMMODATIONS
Camping "123", 19
Dom Przy Rynku, 1
Hotel Mazowiecki, 8
Hotel Metalowiec, 3
Nathan's Villa, 20
Oki Doki, 12
Schronisko Młodzieżowe "Agrykola", 23

♦ FOOD
Cafe Stary Młynek, 21
Gospoda Pod Kogutem, 2
Guru, 16
Pizza Marzano, 14

♦ CAFES
Antykwariat Cafe, 18
Coffee Karma, 22
Pożegnanie z Afryką, 3
Tea Art, 4
Wedel, 15

■ NIGHTLIFE
Centralna Pom Qultury (CDQ), 11
Empik Pub, 17
Enklawa, 6
Harenda, 5
Morgan's, 9
Paparazzi, 7
Piekarnia, 10
Underground Music Cafe, 13

POLAND

PKS Warszawa Zachodnia, al. Jerozolimskie 144 (☎822 48 11, domestic info 94 33, international info 823 55 70; www.pks.pl), same building as Warszawa Zachodnia train station. Cross to the far side of al. Jerozolimskie and take bus #127, 130, 508, 517, or E5 to the center. To: **Białystok** (4hr., 5 per day, 25zł); **Częstochowa** (4½hr., 2 per day, 30zł); **Gdańsk** (7hr., 2 per day, 50zł); **Kazimierz Dolny** (3½hr., 8 per day, 22zł); **Kraków** (6hr., 4 per day, 38zł); **Lublin** (3hr., 20 per day, 25zł); **Toruń** (4½hr., 11 per day, 35zł); **Wrocław** (9½hr., 3 per day, 43zł); **Kaliningrad, RUS** (8½hr., 1 per day, 40zł); **Kyiv, UKR** (14½hr., 1 per day, 155zł); **Minsk, BLR** (10½hr., 1 per day, 55zł); **Vilnius, LIT** (9½hr., 3 per day, 115zł). Open daily 6am-9:30pm.

Centrum Podróży AURA, al. Jerozolimskie 144 (☎ 823 55 70; www.aura.pl), at the Zachodnia station. Open M-F 9am-6pm, Sa 9am-2pm.) Also at al. Jerozolimskie 54 (☎628 62 53), at Warszawa Centralna. International buses to: **Amsterdam, NED** (23hr., 1 per day, 300-330zł); **Minsk, BLR** (12hr., 1 per day, 55zł); **Geneva, SWI** (27hr., 1 per day, 370-400zł); **London, GBR** (28hr., 1-5 per day, 300-450zł); **Paris, FRA** (25hr., 1-3 per day, 300-450zł); **Prague, CZR** (11½hr.; 3 per wk., M, W, F; 100zł); **Rome, ITA** (29hr., 1 per day, 360-380zł). A few buses leave from **Warszawa Station** on Zieleniecka, on the other side of the river. Take bus #101 or 509 or tram #7, 8, 12, or 25 from the center.

⚅ ORIENTATION

The main part of Warsaw lies west of the **Wisła River.** Though the city is large, its grid layout and efficient public transport make it easy to navigate and explore. The main east-west thoroughfare is **al. Jerozolimskie.** It is intersected by several north-south avenues, including **ul. Marszałkowska,** a major tram route. **Warszawa Centralna** is at the intersection of al. Jerozolimskie and **al. Jana Pawła II.** The gargantuan **Pałac Kultury i Nauki** (Palace of Culture and Science) looms nearby, above **pl. Defilad** (Parade Square); its clock tower is visible throughout the center. The northern boundary of pl. Defilad is **ul. Świętokrzyska,** another large east-west thoroughfare. Intersecting al. Jerozolimskie east of the city center, the **Trakt Królewski** (Royal Way) takes different names as it runs north-south. Going north it first becomes **Nowy Świat** (New World Street) and then **ul. Krakówskie Przedmieście** as it leads into **Stare Miasto** (Old Town). Going south, the road becomes **al. Ujazdowskie** as it runs past embassy row, palaces, and **Łazienki Park.**

▄ LOCAL TRANSPORTATION

Public Transportation: ☎94 84; www.ztm.waw.pl. Warsaw's public transit system is excellent. Day **trams** and **buses** 2.40zł, with ISIC 1.20zł; day pass 7.20zł/3.70zł; weekly pass 26zł/12zł. Large baggage needs its own ticket. Punch the ticket in the machines on board or face a 84zł fine. Bus, tram, and subway lines share the same tickets and prices. It's wise to keep a supply of tickets because many corner stores and bright green *Ruch* booths that sell tickets are only open during the day; it can be hard to find a place to buy tickets at night. **Bus #175 goes from the airport** to Stare Miasto by way of Warszawa Centralna and ul. Nowy Świat. Watch out for pickpockets. There are also 2 **sightseeing bus routes:** #180 (M-F) and #100 (Sa-Su). Purchase an all-day ticket and you can hop on and off the bus. Warsaw's **Metro** has only 1 line; it connects the southern border of town and is not particularly convenient for tourists. With the exception of limited night buses, urban transport runs daily 4:30am-11pm.

Taxis: Try **MPT Radio Taxi** (☎919), **Euro Taxi** (☎96 62), or **Halo Taxi** (☎96 23). Overcharging is a problem; ask a Polish speaker to arrange pickup. Cabs with phone numbers on top are best. 5-6zł base fare, 1.80-3zł per km.

Car Rental: Avis (☎/fax 630 73 16), at the Marriott. Open daily 8am-6pm. Airport office (☎650 48 72) open daily 7am-10pm. From 317zł per day. **Budget** (☎630 72 80), at the Marriott and the airport (☎650 40 62). From 377zł per day. Open daily 8am-8pm.

🔃 PRACTICAL INFORMATION

TOURIST AND FINANCIAL SERVICES

Tourist Offices: Informacji Turystyczna (IT), al. Jerozolimskie 54 (☎94 31; www.warsawtour.pl), inside the central train station. English-speaking staff is informative. Provides **maps** (some free, some 4zł) and arranges accommodations. *Warsaw Insider* (6zł), the expat weekly, is sold in kiosks outside the office. Open daily May-Sept. 8am-8pm; Oct.-Apr. 8am-6pm. **Branches:** ul. Krakówskie Przedmieście 89, opposite pl. Zamkowy. Open daily May-Sept. 9am-8pm; Oct.-Apr. 9am-6pm. At the PKS bus station at the Western Station *(Dworzec Zachodnia)*. Open daily 9am-5pm. In the airport. Open daily May-Sept. 8am-8pm; Oct.-Apr. 8am-6pm.

Budget Travel: Almatur, ul. Kopernika 23 (☎826 35 12). Offers discounted plane tickets. ISIC 44zł. Open M-F 9am-7pm, Sa 10am-3pm. MC/V. **Orbis**, ul. Bracka 16 (☎827 07 30; fax 827 76 05), entrance on al. Jerozolimskie. Sells plane, train, ferry, and international bus tickets. Open M-F 8am-6pm, Sa 9am-3pm. **Branch** at ul. Świętokrzyska 23/25 (☎831 82 99; orbis.bis@pbp.com.pl). Open M-F 9am-6pm, Sa 10am-3pm. **STA**, ul. Krucza 41/43 (☎622 62 64; www.eria.pl). Open daily 10am-6pm.

Embassies: Most are near ul. Ujazdowskie. **Australia**, ul. Nowogrodzka 11 (☎521 34 44; fax 627 35 00). Open M-Tu and Th 9am-1pm and 2-4pm, W and F 9am-1pm. **Belarus**, ul. Ateńska 67 (☎617 32 12, visas 617 39 54). Open M-F 8am-4pm. **Canada**, al. Matejki 1/5 (☎584 31 00). Open M-F 10am-noon and 1-3pm. **Czech Republic**, ul. Koszykova 18 (☎628 72 21; warsaw@embassy.mzv.cz). Open M-F 8am-4pm. **Germany**, ul. Dabrowiecka 30 (☎617 30 11). Open M-F 8am-5pm. **Ireland**, ul. Humanska 10 (☎849 66 33). Open M-F 9am-1pm. **Lithuania**, ul. Szucha 5 (☎625 35 68). Open M-F 9am-noon. **Russia**, ul. Belwederska 49 (☎621 34 53; fax 625 30 16). Open M-F 9am-6pm. **Ukraine**, al. Szucha 7 (☎625 01 27). Open M-F 8am-noon. **UK**, ul. Emilii Plater 28 2nd fl. (☎625 30 30). Open M-F 10:30am-4:30pm. **US**, al. Ujazdowskie 29/31 (☎628 30 41; www.usinfo.pl). Open M and W-F 9am-noon, Tu 9am-3pm.

Currency Exchange: Except at tourist sights, *kantors* have the best rates for exchanging currency and traveler's checks. 24hr. **currency exchange** at Warszawa Centralna or at Al. Jerozolimskie 61. Many 24hr. *kantors* offer worse rates at night. **Bank PKO SA**, pl. Bankowy 2 (☎635 05 00), in the blue glass skyscraper, or ul. Grójecka 1/3 (☎658 82 17), in Hotel Sobieski, cashes AmEx/V **traveler's checks** for 1-2% commission and gives MC/V **cash advances**. All branches open M-F 8am-6pm, Sa 10am-2pm. 24hr. **ATMs**, called *bankomat*, accept Cirrus, Maestro, and Plus. **Western Union** in American Express (see below). **Branches** at many locations in major banks. Try **Bank Zachodni**, al. Jerozolimskie 91 (☎629 27 58). Open M-F 8am-6pm.

American Express: Al. Jerozolimskie 65/79 (☎630 69 52). Offers **Western Union** services. Open M-F 9am-7pm, Sa 10am-6pm. **Branch** at ul. Sienna 39 (☎581 51 53). Open M-F 9am-6pm.

LOCAL SERVICES

Luggage Storage (Kasa Bagażowa): At Warszawa Centralna train station. 6zł per item per day, plus 2.25zł per 50zł of declared value if you want insurance. Open 24hr. Storage also available in Zachodnia Station. 5zł for a large pack. Open daily 7am-7pm.

English-Language Bookstores: American Bookstore (Księgarnia Ameryańska), ul. Nowy Świat 61 (☎827 48 52; american@americanbookstore.pl). Good but pricey selection. Open M-Sa 10am-7pm, Su 10am-6pm. **Empik Megastore**, ul. Nowy Świat 15-17 (☎627 06 50). Great selection of maps. Open M-Sa 9am-10pm, Su 11am-5pm.

GLBT: Lambada, (☎628 52 22) in English and Polish. Tu gay Catholic, W lesbian, F gay. Open Tu-W 6-9pm and F 4-10pm. Other info can be found at www.queercity.pl.

Laundromat: Ul. Karmelicka 17 (☎831 73 17). Take bus #180 or 516 north from ul. Marszałkowska and get off at ul. Anielewicza; backtrack 1 block to ul. Karmelicka. Detergent 3zł. Wash and dry 26.60zł. Open M-F 9am-5pm, Sa 9am-1pm.

EMERGENCY AND COMMUNICATIONS

24hr. Pharmacy: Apteka Grabowskiego "21" (☎825 69 86), upstairs at Warszawa Centralna.

Medical Services: Centrum Medyczne LIM, al. Jerozolimskie 65/79, 9th fl. (24hr. **emergency line** ☎458 70 00, 24hr. **ambulance** 430 30 30; www.cm-lim.com.pl), at the Marriott. English-speaking doctors. 85zł. Open M-F 7am-9pm, Sa 8am-8pm, Su 9am-1pm. **Branch** at ul. Domaniewski 41 (☎458 70 00). Open M-F 7am-9pm, Sa 8am-8pm. **Central Emergency Station,** ul. Hoża 56 (☎999) has a 24hr. ambulance.

Telephones: Phones are at the post office and scattered throughout the city. Most only accept cards, available at the post office and many kiosks. Ask for a *karta telefoniczna.* Directory assistance ☎913.

Internet Access: ▧ **Simple Internet Cafe,** at the corner of al. Jerozolimskie and ul. Marszałkowska, has the best hourly rates and English-speaking staff. Open daily 24hr., rates vary from 1zł per hr. late at night to 4zł per hr. midday. Several 24hr. internet cafes line the bowels of the Central train station.

Post Office: Main branch, ul. Świętokrzyska 31/33 (☎827 00 52). Take a number at the entrance. For stamps and letters push "D;" packages "F." For **Poste Restante,** inquire at window #42. Open 24hr. *Kantor* open daily 7am-10pm. Most other branches open 8am-8pm. **Postal Code:** 00 001.

▮ ACCOMMODATIONS

Warsaw accommodations are improving rapidly, but demand still overwhelms supply, so reserve in advance. Conveniently located mid-range hotels are particularly hard to come by. **IT** (see **Tourist Offices,** p. 515) can get you a **university dorm ❶** (25-30zł) room if you're traveling between July and September. They also maintain a list of accommodations, including private rooms, and can help with reservations.

HOSTELS

▧ **Nathan's Villa,** ul. Piękna 24/26 (☎622 29 46; www.nathansvilla.com). From the center, take any train south on ul. Marszałkowska to Płac Konstytucji. Go left on ul. Piękna; the hostel will be on your left. Conveniently located, Nathan's has fabulous facilities and services. Bright colors and brand-new furniture make the rooms look like an Art Deco showroom. Fun-loving, English-speaking staff. Internet. Breakfast included. Laundry. 24hr. reception. Flexible check-out. Dorms 45-60zł; rooms 120-140zł. MC/V. ❷

Oki Doki, pl. Dąbrowskiego 3 (☎826 51 12; www.okidoki.pl). From the center, take any tram north on Marszałkowska to Świętokrzyska. Walk 1 block north on Marszałkowska and turn right on Rysia. Each room of this incredible hostel was designed by a different Warsaw artist, and has its own unique name, theme, and rotating photography exhibits. Dining room serves beer (5zł), coffee and breakfast. Free Internet. Laundry service 10zł. 24hr. reception. Check-in 3pm. Check-out 11am. Book ahead. Dorms 45-60zł; single room 110zł; doubles 135zł, with bathroom 185zł. Prices lower Sept.-Apr. MC/V. ❷

Dom Przy Rynku, Rynek Nowego Miasta 4 (☎831 50 33; www.cityhostel.net). Take bus #175 from the center to Franciszkańska. Turn right on Franciszkańska, then take a right into the *rynek* (main square); the hostel will be downhill on your left. In the summer this school for disadvantaged children makes money for supplies and furniture by converting into a hostel. Amazing location, TVs, and kitchenette. Reception 24hr. Flexible lockout 10am-4pm. Open late June to late Aug. 2- to 4-bed dorms 45zł. ❷

Schronisko Młodzieżowe "Agrykola," ul. Myśliwiecka 9 (☎622 91 10; www.hotelagrykola.pl), near Łazienki Park and Ujazdowski Castle. From Warszawa Centralno, take bus #151 or, from Marszałkowska, take bus #107, 420, or 520 to Rozbrat. From the bus stop, walk downstairs to the corner of ul. Myśliwiecka and al. Armii Ludowej. Serene locale. In-line skate rental for the track next door (6zł per hr.). Bath, TV, and free breakfast in the hotel rooms, but not in the hostel dorms. Dorms 47zł; singles 270zł; hotel doubles 320zł. MC/V. ❶

HOTELS AND CAMPING

Hotel Mazowiecki, ul. Mazowiecka 10 (☎827 23 65; www.mazowiecki.com.pl), just north of ul. Świętokrzyska between Marszałkowska and Nowy Świat. In the middle of the hottest nightlife in town. Rooms with renovated bathrooms are attractive; other rooms more basic. Breakfast included. Check-in 2pm. Check-out noon. Singles 150zł, with bath 198zł; doubles 200zł/248zł. Weekend discount 20%. ❺

Hotel Metalowiec, ul. Długa 29 (☎831 40 20). Take bus #175 from the center of town to ul. Dluga and turn left. Great location near Stare Miasto with quaint, slightly shabby little rooms. Reception 24hr. Check-in 2pm. Check-out 10am. Singles 75zł; doubles 114zł; quads with bath 206zł. ❸

Camping "123," ul. Bitwy Warszawskiej 15/17 (☎823 37 48). From Warszawa Centralna, take bus #127, 130, 508, or 517 to Zachodnia bus station. Cross to the far side of Al. Jerozolimskie and walk west on the pedestrian path to the corner of Bitwy Warszawskiego; turn left. The campground will be on your right. Close to the city center, yet secluded by a buffer of trees and parkland, this tranquil campground also boasts access to a swimming pool (14zł per day) and tennis courts. Guarded 24hr. Open May-Sept. 10zł per person, 10zł per tent, 10zł per vehicle. Electricity 10zł. Spartan 4-person bungalows: singles 40zł; doubles 70zł; triples 100zł; quads 120zł. ❶

◧ FOOD

The local street food of choice is the **kebab turecki,** a pita stuffed with spicy meat, cabbage and pickles (5-10zł). Excellent versions can be had at **Kebab Bar,** ul. Nowy Świat 31, and **Kebab Tureck,** ul. Marszałkowska 81. **Bakery stands** offer delicious treats: follow the smell of fresh baking and the word *domowe* (homemade). Be attentive to how clean all street food appears. In spring and summer, farmers from the surrounding countryside sell **fresh produce** on Warsaw streets. 24hr. **grocery stores** include **MarcPol** by the central train station and **Albert** on ul. Marszałkowska in the Galleria Centrum. Those eager to cook for themselves will delight in **Domowy Okruszek** Ul. Bracka 3, south of al. Jerozolimskie, which sells ready-to-cook dishes like *naleśniki* (pancakes) and *pierogi* (dumplings) for 15-20zł per kilo. (☎628 70 77. Open M-Sa 10am-6pm, Su 10am-3pm.) The most elusive of Warsaw culinary experiences is the **food bus,** a mysterious former school bus that has been known to serve cheap, delicious Polish food in front of the Palace of Culture between midnight and 3am on Friday and Saturday nights.

Gospoda Pod Kogutem, ul. Freta 48 (☎635 82 82; http://gospoda.pod.kogutem.iport.pl). A rare treat in touristy Stare Miasto: generous portions of delectable local food. Enjoy the barn-themed interior or sit outside along ul. Freta. Try the kiełbasa appetizer. Beer 6zł. Entrees 15-40zł. Open daily 11am-midnight. MC/V. ❷

Guru, ul. Bracka 18 (☎827 27 88). Some of the best vegetarian food in Warsaw, and only a stone's throw from Nowy Świat. Guru specializes in light Indian food with a dash of Polish influence. Live music on weekends. Entrees 15-25zł. Open M-Sa 10am-10pm, Su noon-10pm. AmEx/MC/V. ❷

Pizza Marzano, ul. Nowy Świat 42 (☎826 21 33). This trustworthy local chain cooks up a score of richly flavored pizzas (15-25zł), Polish spiced meats and savory appetizers. Open Su-Th 11am-11pm, F-Sa 11am-midnight. AmEx/MC/V. ❷

Bar Vega, ul. Jana Pawła II 36c (☎654 41 11), near the former Ghetto. With sunny decor and New Age music, Bar Vega serves a full vegetarian meal for about the price of a coffee on Nowy Świat (8-10zł). The inexplicably cheap cafeteria-style offerings include both Indian dishes and vegetarian versions of Polish favorites. Open daily noon-8pm. ❶

Cafe Stary Młynek, al. Ujazdowskie 6 (☎622 92 64), close to Ujazdowskie Park. Located in the cellar of a renovated old mill, this restaurant combines traditional Polish cooking with spare yet comfortable modern decor. Friendly waitstaff speak English, and with prices at 10-25 zł, sampling a wide range of small dishes here is a great way to get to know Polish cuisine. Open M-F 10am–10pm, Sa noon–11pm, Su noon–9pm. ❷

Bar Mleczny, ul. Nowy Świat 5. Get a true Soviet experience as you wait in a long line for ridiculously cheap "rations." Try one of the hearty, meat-heavy *danie* (main courses 3-5zł). Locals praise this subsidized, communist-era "milk bar" as one of the best of its dying breed. If you don't speak Polish, master your pointing skills. Open M-F 8am-8pm, Sa-Su 9am-5pm. ❶

🄲 CAFES

Pożegnanie z Afryką (Out of Africa), ul. Freta 4/6, ul. Ostrobranmska 75c, and ul. Dobra 56/66 (ul. Dobra: ☎552 74 12). This Polish chain of cafes brews consistently incredible coffee (8-15zł). It is worth the wait for 1 of 4 indoor tables. In warm weather, enjoy the sidewalk seating and the iced coffee (8zł). Open daily 10am-9pm.

Antykwariat Cafe, ul. Żurawia 45 (☎629 99 29). Antykwariat is a series of 4 handsome rooms with book-lined walls and engravings of pre-war Warsaw. The "Antiquarian" mesmerizes patrons with delicate cups of coffee (5-17zł) and tea (5zł) served with a wrapped chocolate. Also serves beer, wine, and desserts. Plush chairs and outdoor seating invite lingering. Open M-F 11am-11pm, Sa-Su 1-11pm.

Coffee Karma, pl. Zbawiciela 3/5 (☎875 87 05). This student hangout has it all: great coffee (6-11zł) and smoothies (7–10zł); laid-back, English-speaking staff; and sidewalk seating with a view of impressive Zbawiciela Church. While you're in the area, check out the delectable crepes at the stand around the corner and the Soviet monumental art on nearby ul. Marszałkowska. Open M-F 7:30am-10pm, Sa 9am-10pm, Su 10am-10pm.

Tea Art, ul. Bednarska 28/30 (☎826 24 16). Find refuge from the dreary Warsaw rain at this mellow cellar cafe just outside Stare Miasto, serving an encyclopedic selection of teas (small pot 8zł, large pot 14zł). Scrumptious desserts (6-12zł) include *szarlotka* (apple tart) and ginger cake. The fetching young staff is eager to speak English. Romantic lighting makes it a better place for chatting than reading. Open daily 11am-10pm.

Wedel, ul. Szpitalna 17 (☎827 29 16). The stained-glass grandeur of this chocolate-themed cafe offers a rare glimpse of pre-war Warsaw and serves heart-melting hot chocolate (8zł). The Emil Wedel house, built in 1893 for the Polish chocolate tycoon, was one of the few buildings to survive WWII, and its 1st floor now houses an elegant dessert cafe (6-11zł). The adjacent Wedel Chocolate company store has a diorama of elves making chocolate. Open M-Sa 10am-10pm, Su noon-5pm. AmEx/MC/V.

💿 SIGHTS

At first glance, Warsaw offers two strains of architecture: impeccably restored historical facades and Soviet-era concrete blocks. However, from cutting-edge art installations in rebuilt castles to the sobering stillness of the Jewish Cemetery, many of Warsaw's most compelling and rewarding sights are not as simple as they appear. The tourist bus routes #100 and 180 are convenient; they begin at pl. Zamkowy and run along pl. Teatralny, ul. Marszałkowska, al. Ujazdowskie, Łazienki Park, and back up the Royal Way, then loop through Praga before returning to pl. Zamkowy.

STARE AND NOWE MIASTO

Warsaw's reconstruction shows its finest face in the cobblestoned streets and colorful facades of *Stare Miasto* (Old Town), so well restored that it has been recognized as a UNESCO World Heritage site. The brick red Royal Castle on pl. Zamkowy anchors the neighborhood, and the reconstructed fortifications of the Barbican mark the old city walls. Just north, the *rynek* (square) of *Nowe Miasto* (New Town) hosts music and dance performances. Both areas were rebuilt using large fragments of the original buildings. *(Take bus #175 or E3 from the center to Miodowa.)*

STATUE OF ZYGMUNT III WAZA. Constructed in 1644 by Władisław IV to honor his father, the king who moved the capital from Kraków to Warsaw, the statue stood for 300 years before being destroyed in WWII. Rebuilt in 1949, Zygmunt and his cross continue to guard the entrance to Stare Miasto. *(Above pl. Zamkowy in front of the Royal Castle.)*

ST. JOHN'S CATHEDRAL. Decimated in the 1944 Uprising, Warsaw's oldest church (Katedra Św. Jana) was rebuilt in the Vistulan Gothic style, with pure white walls trimmed with brick vaulting. Documents from the 1339 case against the Order of Teutonic Knights, who had broken a pact, are hidden within. Its **crypts** hold the dukes of Mazovia and such famous Poles as Nobel Laureate Henryk Sienkiewicz and Gabriel Narutowicz, the first president of independent Poland. A side altar contains the tomb of Cardinal Stefan Wyszyński, premier of Poland from 1948 to 1981. *(On ul. Świętojańska and pl. Zamkowy. Open daily 10am-1pm and 3-5:30pm. Entrance to crypts 1zł.)*

OLD TOWN SQUARE. A stone plaque at the entrance commemorates the reconstruction of the square (Rynek Starego Miasta.), finished in 1954. The square bustles with sidewalk cafes and an art market, but the statue of the **Warsaw Mermaid** (Warszawa Syrenka) still marks the center. According to legend, a greedy merchant kidnapped the mermaid from the Wisła River, but local fishermen rescued her from captivity. In return, she swore to defend the city; she now protects Warsaw with her shield and raised sword. On the square's southeast side at #1/3, **Dom Pod Bazyliszkiem** immortalizes the Stare Miasto Basilisk, a reptile famous for its fatal breath and a stare that instantly killed all those who crossed its path. *(On ul. Swiętojanska.)*

BARBICAN. With its restoration near completion, the Barbican is a rare example of 16th-century Polish fortifications. Today, it is a popular spot to duck out of the traffic for a rest or to listen to the street performers who cluster here. The **Little Insur-**

gent Monument, facing ul. Podwale on the outside of the wall, honors the youngest soldiers of the 1944 Uprising. Around the Barbican are the crumbling walls that once enclosed Stare Miasto. *(Follow ul. Nowomiejska from the Rynek in Stare Miasto.)*

NOWE MIASTO. The Barbican opens onto ul. Freta, the edge of Nowe Miasto. The "New Town," established at the beginning of the 15th century, had its own separate town hall until 1791. Mostly destroyed during WWII, its 18th- and 19th-century buildings have enjoyed an expensive facelift. The great physicist and chemist **Maria Skłodowska-Curie,** winner of two Nobel prizes, was born at ul. Freta 16 in 1867 (see **Museums,** p. 526). Ul. Freta leads to New Town Square (Rynek Nowego Miasta), the site of the **Church of the Holy Sacrament,** founded in 1688 to commemorate King Jan III Sobieski's 1683 victory over the Turks. Its interior is only a ghost of its past glory, but the Baroque dome still inspires awe. *(Open daily dawn-dusk.)*

TRAKT KRÓLEWSKI

The 4km Trakt Królewski (Royal Way) begins at pl. Zamkowy at the entrance to Stare Miasto. From ul. Krakówskie Przedmieście, Trakt Królewski becomes ul. Nowy Świat (New World Street). The Royal Way, so named because it leads to Poland's former capital of Kraków, is lined with palaces, churches, and convents built when the royal family moved to Warsaw. The name New World Street dates to the mid-17th century, when a new settlement of working-class people was started here. It was not until the 18th century that the aristocracy started moving in and sprucing the place up with ornate manors and residences. Today, there's nothing working-class about it—it's the most fashionable street in town.

PL. ZAMKOWY. On the left as you leave pl. Zamkowy headed south, **St. Anne's Church** (Kościół św. Anny), with its striking gilded interior, dates from the 15th century but was rebuilt in the Baroque style. *(Open daily dawn-dusk.)* Farther down the street, a monument to poet **Adam Mickiewicz** gazes west toward pl. Piłsudskiego. In the square surrounding the statue, a computer kiosk offers free online tourist information.

CRAZY FOR CHOPIN. The next stretch of the Trakt is a requisite pilgrimage sight for fans of Frédéric Chopin (see **The Arts,** p. 506). Chopin spent his childhood near ul. Krakówskie Przedmieście and gave his first public concert in **Pałac Radziwiłłów,** ul. Krakówskie Przedmieście 46/48. The building, now the Polish presidential mansion (not open to the public), is guarded by four stone lions and at least as many military police. A block down the road and set back from the street behind a grove of trees, the **Church of the Visitation Nuns** (Kościół Wizytówek) once resounded with the romantic ivory pounding of the mop-topped composer. *(Open daily dawn-1pm and 3pm-dusk.)* Before he left for France in 1830, Chopin wrote many of his best-known compositions in **Pałac Czapskich.** The palace now houses the **Academy of Fine Arts** and **Chopin's Drawing Room,** a room from the Chopins' home that has been long preserved. *(Enter through the gate at ul. Krakówskie Przedmiescie 5. ☎826 62 51, ext. 267. Open M-F 10am-2pm. 3zł, students 2zł.)* Chopin died abroad at the age of 39 and was buried in Paris, but his heart belongs to Poland: the organ now rests in an urn in the left nave of the **Holy Cross Church** (Kościół św. Krzyża). Nobel Prize-winning author **Władysław Reymont** left his heart here, too. *(ul. Krakówskie Przedmiescie 3. Open daily dawn-dusk.)*

UNIVERSITY OF WARSAW. Opposite Kościół św. Krzyża, a complex of rebuilt palaces belongs to the **University of Warsaw** (Uniwersytet Warszawski), founded in 1816. **Pałac Kazimierzowski,** at the end of the alley connecting the main entrance to the university, once housed the School of Knighthood. The university has a history of political activism. Founded on Enlightenment principles, it was closed in 1831 by the Russian tsar as punishment for its contribution to the November Uprising. Upon its reopening in 1869, all courses were taught in Russian; its Polish students boycotted. Professors taught in private apartments during WWII bombings, lending the University of Warsaw the name the "Flying University." Many of its professors and administrators were sent to Majdanek death camp. In 1968, protests against censorship led to police violence, the dissolution of university departments, and a wave of communist-led anti-Semitism that forced nearly all of the remaining Jews from Poland. The **Copernicus Monument** and **Pałac Staszica,** home of the Polish Academy of Sciences, mark the end of ul. Krakówskie Przedmieście and the beginning of ul. Nowy Świat.

ŁAZIENKI PARK

The palaces and their park were built in the 18th century for Stanisław August Poniatowski, Poland's last king, but peacocks and squirrels rule the meandering paths and hillside gardens today. Rose bushes and benches ring the **Chopin Monument.** A nearby amphitheater hosts free **Chopin concerts** (Mar.-Oct. Su noon and 4pm). The Neoclassical palace outbuildings host rotating exhibits of contemporary Polish art. The tranquil 1822 **Temple of Diana** (Świątynia Diany) perches above a wooded pond. *(Park borders al. Ujazdowskie and Trakt Królewski. Take bus #100 from Marszalkowska, #116, 180 or 195 from ul. Nowy Swiat, or #119 from the city center to Bagatela. Open daily dawn-dusk.)*

PAŁAC ŁAZIENKOWSKI. Farther into the park is the striking Neoclassical Pałac Łazienkowski, also called the **Palace on Water** (Pałac na Wodzie) or **Palace on the Isle** (Pałac na Wyspie). Surrounded by water, peacocks, and leafy boughs, this breathtaking building was the creation of King Stanisław August and his beloved architect Dominik Merlini. Displays of period furnishings and picture-window views of the park come with the building's rather pricey admission. Be sure to pause before entering to put protective slippers over your shoes (available to the left of the entry), which you must take off and on at several points in the tour as directed by the signs that are only in Polish. *(Open Tu-Su 9am-4pm. 12zł, students 9zł. Guided English tour 66zł.)*

OTHER SIGHTS. Warsaw University's enchanting **Botanical Garden** (Ogród Botaniczny) welcomes visitors with a fragrant path lined by lilac trees. Student gardeners tend to this perpetual work-in-progress, which exhibits native and foreign plants. Highlights include the butterfly garden, alpine garden, and medicinal plants. *(☎553 05 11. Open Apr.-Aug. M-F 9am-8pm, Sa-Su 10am-8pm; daily Sept. 10am-7pm; Oct. 10am-6pm. 4.5zł, students 2.5zł.)* The **Old Orangery** (Stara Pomarańczarnia) houses the rich 1788 Stanisławowski Theater and the Gallery of Polish Sculpture (Galeria Rzeźby Polskiej), which exhibits work from the 1500s to 1939. (Open only by special appointment.) The **New Orangery** (Nowa Pomarańczarnia) is home to one of Warsaw's most expensive and renowned restaurants. **Belweder,** an 1818 palace just south of Łazienki, was built for the Russian tsar and was Józef Piłsudski's home. Now a residence for visiting heads of state, Belweder is closed to the public. Just north of Łazienki along al. Ujazdowskie is the **Ujazdowski Castle** (see **Museums,** p. 524), built in 1637 for King Zygmunt III Waza. Continue toward the center along al. Ujazdowskie and go right on ul. Matejki to reach the **Sejm** (Parliament) and the **Senate building.** *(Both closed to the public.)*

THE FORMER WARSAW GHETTO

Still referred to as the Ghetto, the modern Muranów (walled) neighborhood, north of the center, displays few vestiges of the nearly 400,000 Jews who comprised one-third of the city's pre-war population. The Nazis razed the entire area in 1943 fol-

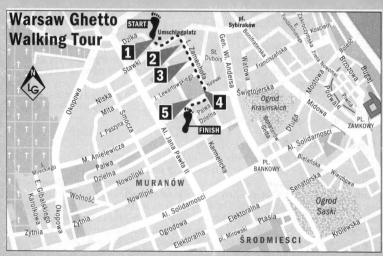

Warsaw Ghetto Walking Tour

START

While many visitors to the Warsaw Ghetto explore the Nożyk Synagogue, remnants of the Wall, and the cemetery, few take the time to witness many of the other, less visible sites scattered throughout the ghetto. Though few traces remain of the former Warsaw Ghetto, a series of monuments honors the heroes of the 1943 Ghetto Uprising and marks some of the most important sites of the tragic final years of a Jewish community that once numbered hundreds of thousands. This tour begins at the corner of ul. Dzika and ul. Stawki.

TIME: 1hr.

DISTANCE: Half Mile

WHEN TO GO: Mid-morning

STARTING POINT: Umschlagplatz, NE corner of intersection of ul. Dzika and ul. Stawki

FINISH POINT: Monument to the Relief Council for Jews

1 UMSCHLAGPLATZ. In 1942 and 1943, the Nazis gathered the Warsaw Ghetto Jews at the Umschlagplatz (Trans-shipment Square) for transport to death camps. The monument at this former railway platform bears the Polish, Hebrew, and Yiddish inscription of Job 16:18, "O earth, cover not thou my blood, and let my cry never be laid to rest."

2 ROUTE RECALLING MARTYRDOM AND STRUGGLE OF THE JEWS, UL. ZAMENHOFA. A series of black stone blocks, which commemorate leaders of the Ghetto Uprising, marks the path from the Umschlagplatz to the Monument to the Heroes of the Ghetto. Follow the blocks along ul. Zamenhofa, named for Ludwik Zamenhof, the Warsaw Jew who invented Esperanto.

3 COMMAND BUNKER OF UPRISING LEADERS, CORNER OF UL. MILA AND UL. DUBOIS. Where a command bunker at ul. Mila 18 once housed the headquarters of ŻOB, the Jewish fighting organization, a mound of dirt and a small monument commemorate Mordechaj Anielewicz and Arie Wilner, the ŻOB leaders who committed suicide when the Nazis discovered the bunker.

4 MONUMENT TO THE HEROES OF THE GHETTO UPRISING, ZAMENHOFA BETWEEN UL. LEWARTSKIEGO AND UL. ANIELWICZA. Facing a park as ul. Zamenhof approaches ul. Anielewicza, named in honor of Mordechaj Anielewicz, the Monument to the Heroes of the Ghetto pays homage to the leaders of the Ghetto Uprising. The monument was carved in 1948 from stone originally ordered by the Nazis for a Third Reich victory monument.

5 MONUMENT TO THE RELIEF COUNCIL FOR JEWS. The remnants of Poland's Jewish community erected the nearby red sandstone Monument to the Relief Council for Jews in 1946 to commemorate the efforts of the Poles who worked to rescue Polish Jews from the Holocaust.

lowing the Ghetto Uprising and the deportation of Ghetto residents to death camps. Soviet-era concrete block housing now fills much of the former Ghetto. The building next to the Nożyk Synagogue (see p. 523) houses **Our Roots,** ul. Twarda 6 (☎/fax 620 05 56), a Jewish travel agency that arranges English tours of Jewish Warsaw, Auschwitz, Treblinka, and Majdanek. It can also help with genealogical research. *(Open M-F 10am-5pm, but call before coming as hours may be irregular. Tours US$25 per person, min. 3 people.)*

JEWISH CEMETERY. Perhaps the most haunting testament to the near-total annihilation of Jewish Warsaw is this final resting place of 250,000 Polish Jews. The 19th-century cemetery (Cmentarz Żydowski) sadly lies in disrepair as most of the those buried here have no descendents to care for their graves. Notable figures buried here include Rabbi Szlomo Lipszyc (d. 1839), actress Ester Kamińska (d. 1925), and Ludwik Zamenhof (d. 1917), the creator of Esperanto. *(Ul. Okopowa 49/51, in the western corner of Muranów. From the center of town, follow al. Jana Pawła II north to Anielewicza and take a left. Alternatively, take tram #22 from the center to Cm. Żydowski. ☎ 838 26 22; www.jewishcem.waw.pl. Open Apr.-Oct. M-Th 10am-5pm, F 9am-1pm, Su 11am-4pm; Nov.-Mar. cemetery closes at dusk. Closed Jewish holidays. 4zł.)* Nearby, the **Monument of Common Martyrdom of Jews and Poles,** ul. Gibalskiego 2, marks the site of mass graves from WWII. *(Follow the street south of the cemetery to Gibalskiego, then turn left before the Nissenbaum building.)*

NOŻYK SYNAGOGUE. This restored synagogue is a living artifact of Warsaw's Jewish life. Used as a stable by the Wehrmacht, it was the only synagogue to survive the war. Today it serves as the spiritual home for the few hundred observant Jews who remain in Warsaw and also hosts meetings for Jewish student groups. There's a small kosher store in the basement. *(Ul. Twarda 6. From the center, take any tram along ul. Jana Pawła II to Rondo Onz. Turn right on Twarda and left at the Jewish Theater (Teatr Żydowski). ☎ 620 43 24. Open Su-F 10am-7pm. Closed on Jewish holidays. 5zł. Morning and evening prayer daily.)*

GHETTO WALL. Early in the occupation of Warsaw, the Nazis built a wall around the entire neighborhood, confining the Jews to the Ghetto until the Nazis liquidated the entire area in 1943 following the uprising. A small section of the original ghetto wall still stands between two buildings on ul. Sienna and ul. Złota, west of al. Jana Pawła II, near Warszawa Centralna station. Enter at ul. Sienna 55; the wall is on the left.

JANUSZ KORCZAK MEMORIAL. Physician and writer Janusz Korczak, revered by Jews and Christians alike, oversaw two orphanages in the years before WWII, one Catholic and one Jewish. He is known for his heart-wrenching courage during the liquidation of the Warsaw Ghetto. The Nazis gathered the children of his Jewish orphanage and, though several friends offered to help him escape, he chose to remain with the 200 children; he shepherded them to Umschplagplatz and died with them in Treblinka. Of his actions Korczak said, "You do not leave a sick child in the night, and you do not leave children at a time like this." The monument stands in front of the site of his Jewish orphanage. *(Ul. Jaktorowska 6, just west of ul. Towarowa and south of al. Solidarnosci.)*

COMMERCIAL DISTRICT

PALACE OF CULTURE AND SCIENCE. Warsaw's commercial district (next to the train station, southwest of Stare Miasto) is dominated by the 70-story Stalinist Gothic Palace (Pałac Kultury i Nauki, PKiN), Poland's tallest structure. First named the Joseph Stalin Palace, the building has been dubbed "The Wedding

Cake" for of its multi-tiered architecture. A 1955 "gift" from the Soviet Union, the Palace houses 3000 offices, exhibition facilities, theaters, a shopping center, cafes, and two museums. (☎656 60 00. *Open daily 9am-midnight. Observation deck on 33rd fl. 18zł, students 12zł; after 9pm, 20zł.)* Statues surround its periphery. Below lies **pl. Defilad** (Parade Sq.), Europe's largest square. It's bigger than Moscow's Red Square, but skating rink, gardens, and art exhibits overtake much of the open space. *(On ul. Marszałkowska.)*

OTHER SIGHTS. Warsaw Insurgents' Square (pl. Powstańców Warszawy) is marked by a large memorial. On August 1, 1944, the insurgents of the Warsaw Uprising began their heroic, though doomed, battle against the Germans here. *(On ul. Świętokrzyska, between ul. Marszałkowska and Krakówskie Przedmieście.)* Interesting **neighborhood walks** include the daily **outdoor flower market** on al. Jana Pawla II; the park- and gallery-dotted hillside **Mariensztat** neighborhood (between Stare Miasto and the University of Warsaw, east of ul. Krakówskie Przedmiescie); and the **Praga** suburb, which retains much of its pre-war architecture and is home to both the city zoo and Warsaw's only Orthodox church. *(To get to Praga, cross the al. Solidarności bridge. Orthodox Church of St. Mary Magdalena at the corner of al. Solidarności and al. Jagiellonska. Zoo north on al. Jagiellonska.)*

MUSEUMS

■ **ROYAL CASTLE.** In the Middle Ages, the castle (Zamek Królewski) was home to the Dukes of Mazovia. In the late 16th century, it replaced Kraków's Wawel as the official royal residence; later it became the presidential palace, and in September 1939 it was burned down and plundered by the Nazis. Following its destruction, many Varsovians risked their lives hiding the castle's priceless works. Some of the treasures were retrieved after WWII, but it took 40 years—and countless contributions from Poles, expats, and dignitaries worldwide—to restore this symbol of national pride. There are two routes for viewing: Route 1 snakes through the parliament chambers and apartments while Route 2 hits the King's apartments, throne rooms, and the spectacular Marble Cabinet and Ballroom. Each takes about 30min. *(Pl. Zamkowy 4. ☎657 21 70; www.zamek-krolewski.art.pl. Tickets and guides at the kasa inside the courtyard. Route 1 open M 11am-4pm, Tu-Sa 10am-4pm. 10zł, students 5zł. Route 2 open M 11am-6pm, Tu-Sa 10am-6pm. 15zł, students 8zł. Highlights tour Su 11am-6pm; free. English tour M-Sa; 70zł per group.)*

■ **CENTER OF CONTEMPORARY ART AT UJAZDOWSKI CASTLE.** The center (Centrum Sztuki Współczesniej) is a hub of Polish avant-garde culture. "Nowe jest stare" (what is new is old) is etched on a museum wall; indeed, this reconstructed 17th-century castle, its winding cellars now home to cutting-edge art installations, speaks volumes to the interplay between the contrasts that infuse contemporary Polish art. The castle offers a panoramic view of Łazienki Park, and the "Laboratorium" outbuilding hosts exhibits. Even the grounds are art: look for inscriptions on the marble benches outside the museum. Ujazdowski Castle is also home to Kino-Lab, which screens films, and the innovative Artistic Kitchen restaurant. *(Al. Ujazdowskie 6. Take the same buses as to Łazienki, but get off at pl. Na Rozdrożu; the museum is past the overpass. ☎628 12 71; www.csw.art.pl. Open Tu-Th and Sa-Su 11am-5pm, F 11am-9pm. 3.5zł, students 2.5zł.)*

WILANÓW. 30min. south of the city, this extraordinary residence is Warsaw's answer to Versailles. In 1677, King Jan III Sobieski bought the sleepy village of Milanowo and rebuilt the existing mansion as a palace. In 1805, Duke Stanisław Kostka Potocki opened Wilanów to visitors, founding one of Poland's first public museums. Since then, Pałac Wilanówski has served as a museum and as a residence for high-ranking guests of the state. Inside are frescoed rooms, countless portraits, and extravagant royal apartments. The French-influenced gardens form strict patterns and feature an array of elegant topiary creations. Inside, the Old Orangery houses a collection of European porcelain, some of which is over 400 years old. *(Take bus #180 from ul. Krakówskie Przedmiesce, #516 or 519 from ul. Marszalkowska south to Wilanów, or #116 south along the Royal Way. From the bus stop, cross the highway and follow signs for the Palac. ☎842 07 95. Open May 15-Sept. 15 M and W-Su 9:30am-4:30pm; Sept. 16-May 14 M and W-Su 9:30am-4pm. Free Thursday. 20zł, students 10zł; free Th. English tour 25zł. Admission includes a Polish-language tour, but it's better to explore on your own, letting the English captions be your guide. Gardens open M and W-F 9:30am-dusk. 4.5zł, students 2.5zł. Orangery open M and W-F Su 9:30am-3:30pm.)*

WARSAW HISTORICAL MUSEUM. The tiny entrance belies the size of this massive museum (Muzeum Historyczne Miasta Warszawy), which occupies an entire side of the *rynek*. Clothing, utensils, and reconstructed interiors of workshops offer glimpses of daily life throughout the city's 700-year history. *(Rynek Starego Miasta 42. ☎635 16 25. Excellent English-language film about WWII-era Warsaw Tu-Sa noon. Open Tu and Th 11am-6pm, W and F 10am-3:30pm, Sa-Su 10:30am-4:30pm. 5zł, students 2.50zł; Su Free.)*

POSTER MUSEUM. Polish artists have been producing stunning poster art for over a century, and the rotating exhibitions at this museum (Muzeum Plakatu), one of few in the world dedicated to this art form, are well worth the trip to Wilanów. The museum also hosts the International Poster Biennale in summers of even-numbered years. Phone ahead, since the museum often closes between exhibitions. The museum store sells prints for 10.50zł. *(Ul. Stanislawa Potockiego 10/16, by Pałac Wilanowski. Gallery branches at ul. Hoża 40 and Stary Rynek 23 focus on selling prints over exhibiting work. ☎842 48 48; fax 842 26 06. Open Tu-Su 10am-4pm. 8zł, students 5zł; W free.)*

NATIONAL MUSEUM. Poland's largest museum (Muzeum Narodowe) was looted by the Nazis in WWII but has since rebuilt an impressive collection of Polish and European art, from ancient statuary to 20th century paintings. Notable permanent collections include 18th-century Polish miniature paintings and a rare collection of 8th-14th century sacred art from the Nubian kingdom of present-day Sudan. Eclectic range of temporary exhibits, from Chinese traditional instruments to German Romantic paintings. *(Al. Jerozolimskie 3. ☎629 30 93, English tours 629 50 60; www.mnw.art.pl. Open Tu-W and F 10am-5pm; Th and Sa-Su 10am-6pm. Permanent exhibits 11zł, students 6zł; special exhibits 15zł, students 8zł. English tour 50zł; call one wk. in advance. AmEx/MC/V.)*

ZACHĘTA GALLERY. This state-funded gallery is housed in one of the few buildings left standing after WWII. It is dedicated to controversial art; displays feature photography, and many rotating exhibits have works by 20th-century Polish photographers. *(Pl. Malachowskiego 3. Buses #100 toward pl. Zamkowy and #160 toward Targowek from the center both stop at Zachęta. ☎827 58 54; www.zacheta-gallery.waw.pl. Open Tu-Su 10am-6pm. 10zł, students 7zł; Tu free. Guided tour in Polish 40zł, in English 60zł; call 2 days in advance.)*

MUSEUM OF PAWIAK PRISON. Built in the 1830s as a prison for common criminals, Pawiak (Muzeum Więzienia Pawiaka) later served as Gestapo headquarters under the Nazis. From 1939 to 1944, over 100,000 Poles were imprisoned and tortured here. One room has been converted into a museum, which exhibits a moving display of photographs and artifacts. A dead tree outside bears the names of some of the 30,000 prisoners killed at Pawiak during the war. *(Ul. Dzielna 24/26. ☎/fax 831 13 17. Open Su 10am-4pm, W 9am-5pm, Th and Sa 9am-4pm, F 10am-5pm. Donation requested.)*

POLISH MILITARY MUSEUM. This museum could equip its own army with its collection of Polish weaponry and uniforms, old planes, and tanks. *(Al. Jerozolimskie 3, in the same building as the National Museum. ☎ 629 52 71. Open May 15-Sept. 30 W-Su 11am-5pm; Oct. 1-May 14 W-Su 10am-4pm. Guided tours in English 20zł. 5zł, students 3zł.)*

FRÉDÉRIC CHOPIN MUSEUM. A small but fascinating collection of original letters, scores, paintings, and keepsakes, including the composer's last piano; his first published piece, the *Polonaise in G Minor* (penned at the ripe old age of seven); and his last composition, *Mazurka in F Minor*. The museum (Muzeum Fryderyka Chopina) also hosts the International Chopin Festival, with concerts on selected days in July and August. *(ul. Okólnik 1, in Ostrogski Castle. Enter from ul. Tamka. ☎ 827 54 71. Open May-Sept. M, W, F 10am-5pm, Th noon-6pm, Sa-Su 10am-2pm. Oct.-Apr. M-W and F-Sa 10am-2pm, Th noon-6pm. 8zł, students 4zł. Audioguide 4zł. Concerts 30zł, students 15zł.)*

MARIA SKŁODOWSKA-CURIE MUSEUM. Founded in 1967, on the 100th anniversary of the two-time Nobel Prize Laureate's birth, the exhibit (Muzeum Marii Skłodowskiej-Curie) chronicles Maria Skłodowska's life in Poland, immigration to France, and marriage to scientist Pierre Curie, with whom she discovered radium, polonium (named after Poland), and marital bliss. *(Ul. Freta 16, in Skłodowska's former house. ☎ 831 80 92. Open Su 10am-2pm, Tu-Sa 10am-4pm. 6zł, students 3zł.)*

JOHN PAUL II COLLECTION. This is not a museum about the Pope but a collection of paintings amassed by the Carroll-Porczynski family and donated to the city of Warsaw in honor of Poland's favorite son. Artists displayed here include Dalí, Goya, Picasso, Rembrandt, Rubens, Titian, Van Gogh, and others. *(Pl. Bankowy 1, in the Old Stock Exchange building. Enter from ul. Elektoralna. ☎ 620 21 81. Open May-Oct. Su, Tu-Sa 10am-5pm; Nov.-Apr. 10am-4pm. 8zł, students 4zł. Polish tour 1zł per person.)*

ADAM MICKIEWICZ MUSEUM OF LITERATURE. Old sketches, letters, books, a shrine room, and Mickiewicz's original inkpot recall the world of Poland's national poet. *(Rynek Starego Miasta 20. ☎ 831 40 61. Open M-Tu and F 10am-3pm, W-Th 11am-6pm, Su 11am-5pm. 5zł, students 4zł. Su free.)*

🎭 ENTERTAINMENT

Warsaw boasts an array of live music and free outdoor concerts abound in summer. Classical music performances are rarely sold out; standby tickets for major performances run as low as 10zł. Inquire at the **Warsaw Music Society** (Warszawskie Towarzystwo Muzyczne), ul. Morskie Oko 2 (☎ 849 56 51). Take tram #4, 18, 19, 35, or 36 to Morskie Oko from ul. Marszałkowska. The **Warsaw Chamber Opera** (Warszawska Opera Kameralna), al. Solidarności 76B (☎ 831 22 40), hosts a **Mozart Festival** in early summer. Nearby Łazienki Park has free Sunday performances at the **Chopin Monument** (Pomnik Chopina; concerts May-Oct. Su noon and 4pm.) The **National Philharmonic** (Filharmonia Narodowa), ul. Jasna 5 (☎ 551 71 28), gives regular concerts but is closed in summer. The first week of June brings the **International Festival of Sacred Music**, with performances at Warsaw's historic churches. Jazz, rock, and blues fans have quite a few options, especially in summer when Stare Miasto erupts with music. **Sala Kongresowa** (☎ 620 49 80), in the Pałac Kultury, hosts jazz and rock concerts with famous international bands. In June, watch for **Warsaw Summer Jazz Days** (☎ 620 12 19; www.adamiakjazz.pl). For tickets to rock concerts, call **Empik Megastore** (☎ 625 12 19).

Teatr Wielki, pl. Teatralny 1 (☎ 826 32 88; www.teatrwielki.pl), the main opera and ballet hall, has regular performances. (Tickets 10-100zł. AmEx/MC/V.) **Teatr Dramatyczny** (☎ 620 21 02), in the Pałac Kultury, has a stage for big productions and a studio theater playing more avant-garde works. **Teatr Żydowski** (☎620 70 25), pl. Grzybowski 12/16, is a Jewish theater with shows mostly in Yiddish. **Kinoteka** (☎826 1961), in the Pałac Kultury, shows Hollywood blockbusters in a Stalinist setting. **Kino Lab**, ul. Ujazdowskie 6 (☎628 12 71), features independent films. See **Center for Contemporary Art** (p. 524).

NIGHTLIFE

Warsaw's night scene is accessible, exuberant, and rapidly changing. New bars and clubs are emerging at fever pace, so check *Aktivist* (Polish) or *Warsaw in Your Pocket* for the latest listings. Many locals linger at cafes very late. Move on to bars as midnight approaches, and don't hit the clubs until the wee hours. Over the past few years, there has been an explosion of **gay clubs.** Though many have become raucous places of interest for the "mixed" crowd, many more remain secluded and discreet. For the latest info, call the gay and lesbian **hotline** (see **GLBT Organizations**, p. 516). Kiosks sell *Gazeta Wyborcza*, a magazine that lists some gay-oriented info.

BARS

Morgan's, ul. Okólnik 1 (☎826 81 38; www.morganspub.com), under the Chopin Museum. Ollie Morgan is a Warsaw institution, and so is the chummy Irish bar he's been running for 14 years. He says he pours the best Guinness (0.5L 15zł) in Poland, but his son Thomas down in Kraków may beg to differ. Live music on weekends. Regulars praise the Indian food at "curry night" (Tu and Th). Open M-F 9am-late, Sa-Su 10am-late.

Jezioro Łabędzie (Swan Lake), ul. Moliera 4/6 (☎826 65 99), between Ogród Saski and Stare Miasto. Gracefully hip, "Swan Lake" draws beautiful people with international DJs, upscale cuisine, and an innovative drink menu. House specialty drinks (10-30zł) feature local ingredients like mead vodka and rowanberry-infused vodka. Garden seating in back. Open M-Th 11am-2am, F 11am-4am, Sa 1pm-4am, Su 3pm-4am.

Paparazzi, ul. Mazowiecka 12 (☎828-42-19). The Brit who runs Paparazzi has a mission: to bring an international menu of high-quality, properly mixed drinks to discerning Varsovians. The mojito (15zł) is a masterpiece. Stylish patrons emulate the classic movie stars whose black-and-white portraits adorn the walls, and flush entrepreneurs in designer suits look on. Open M-F noon-1am, Sa-Su 4pm-1am. AmEx/MC/V.

Harendą, ul. Krakówskie Przedmieśćie 4/6 (☎826 29 00), at Hotel Harenda. Enter from ul. Karasia. The ranch-like interior is all sturdy wood. Huge outdoor beer garden is popular with students. Beer 6-10zł. Live music Tu and Th (cover 10-15zł). Disco F 10pm, Sa 9pm. Longest Happy Hour in Poland F-Sa 9am-5pm, all day Su. Open daily 9am-3am.

Empik Pub, ul. Nowy Świat 15/17 (☎625 10 86), in the basement and gardens outside. Empik Megastore. Hosts local rock and country bands. An ordinary rock venue six nights a week, Empik really shines at its quirky Thursday "shanty night," a rollicking nautical sing-a-long. The self-proclaimed "hairiest man in Poland" hosts this beer-soaked must see event. Beer 9zł. Live music Tu-Sa 10pm-1am. Open M-Sa 9am-late.

NIGHTCLUBS

Piekarnia, ul. Młocińska 11 (☎636 49 79). Take the #22 tram to Rondo Babka and backtrack on ul. Okopowa. Make a right on Powiązkowska, right on Burakowa, and right on Młocińska. The unmarked club will be down the road on your left. Night owls flock to Piekarnia, where the so-hip-it-hurts scene really picks up around 4am. The selective bouncer, packed dance floor, and progressive house music, often from top DJs, make this the hottest spot in Warsaw. Cover F 20zł, Sa 25zł. Open F-Sa 10pm-late.

Enklawa, ul. Masowiecki 12 (☎827 31 51). An elite crowd of expats, locals, students, and young professionals forks over hefty cover charges for a spot on the large, sexually charged dance floor. Come late to chat in English and take in hip-hop and techno. Check out the plasma video screens in the bathrooms. Cover Th men 10zł, women 5zł; F-Sa before 11pm 20zł, after 30zł. Open Su-Th 9pm-3am, F-Sa 9pm-4am. AmEx/MC/V.

Underground Music Cafe, ul. Marszałkowska 126/134 (☎826 70 48), behind the large McDonald's; walk down the steps. Boisterous students crowd the small, smoky floor for familiar chart hits. M-Tu and Sa house; W and Sa hip-hop; Th 70s and 80s. Beer 8.50zł. Cover W and F 10zł, students 5zł; Sa 20zł/10zł; Th 10zł; Su-Tu free.

Centralna Dom Qultury (CDQ), ul. Burokowska 12 (☎636 55 00; www.cdq.art.pl), around the corner from Piekarnia. Look for the Auto Electrix sign at the entrance. Rootsy and alternative, CDQ attracts a student crowd for indie pop, drum-and-bass, punk, and folk/gypsy. Call for details. Cover F-Sa 15zł. Open F-Sa and some weekdays 10pm-late.

▶ DAYTRIP FROM WARSAW

ŻELAZOWA WOLA

It's best to take the 9:30am PKS bus (1½-2 hr.) that leaves from Zachodnia (Western) station. To reach Zachodnia from central Warsaw, take local bus #130, 517, 127, 508, or 523 east on Al. Jerozilimiskie. From Warszawa Zachodnia (see p. 511), take the bus (9.1zł) headed to Wyszogród. Żelazowa Wola (53 km west of Warsaw) is a stop, but warn the driver that you're getting off here. The last return bus leaves at 4:30pm. Alternatively, trains (1hr.) leave from Warszawa Centralna (every 30min., 8.50zł) to Sochaczew. The #6 Sochaczew city bus heads to Żelazowa Wola (M-F every hr., Sa-Su every other hr.; 3zł. ☎46 863 33 00; fax 863 40 76. Open May-Sept. Tu-Su 9:30am-5:30pm; Oct.-Apr. Tu-Su 9:30am-4pm. English audio tour 20zl. 12zl, students 6zl. Park only 4zl/2zl.)

Etudes and waltzes still echo through the air of Żelazowa Wola on Sunday afternoons. First-rate musicians perform Chopin's masterpieces outside this **museum,** housed in the home where he was born. Twice each Sunday, the enchanting gardens of Żelazowa Wola host **free Chopin concerts** (May-Sept. 11am and 3pm), and locals gather on garden benches to listen. The gardens are well-groomed near the museum, but charmingly overgrown as their paths ramble past ponds, a stream, and a black marble obelisk commemorating Chopin's birth. The **museum** is respectable but lacks original furniture and features little more than rooms devoted to Chopin's parents, his birth certificate, and the cover page of his first published piece. Concerts in the gardens, however, are well worth the visit. The schedule of performances is posted throughout Warsaw and at the Chopin Museum (see p. 526). Grab a bite near the museum entrance at **Restauracja "Pod Wierzbami" ❸** (☎46 863 32 43; entrees 25zł) or at one of the snack bars across the street from the entrance, or pack a lunch and eat on a garden bench.

LESSER POLAND (MAŁOPOLSKA)

Małopolska, strewn with gentle hills and medieval castle ruins, stretches from the Kraków-Częstochowa Uplands in the west to Lublin in the east. Kraków, which suffered only minimal damage during WWII, remains Poland's cultural and social center. Lublin, with its many universities, is a hub of intellectual life. The surrounding landscape is home to some of the most beautiful and most horrific of mankind's creations: the artistry of the Wieliczka salt caves and the serenity of the castle at Pieskowa Skała contrast the remnants of the Auschwitz-Birkenau and Majdanek concentration camps.

KRAKÓW   ☎(0)12

Although Kraków (KRAH-koof; pop 745,500) only recently emerged as a trendy, international hotspot, it has long been Poland's most beloved city. The regal architecture, rich cafe culture, and palpable sense of history that now attract throngs of foreign visitors to Kraków have drawn Polish kings, artists, and scholars for centuries. Miraculously, Kraków, unlike most Polish cities, emerged from WWII and years of socialist planning nearly unscathed. The maze-like Old Town and the old Jewish quarter of Kazimierz hide scores of museums, galleries, cellar pubs, and clubs, with the city's 100,000 students adding to the spirited nightlife. Still, the city's gloss and glamour can't completely hide the scars of the 20th century: the Auschwitz-Birkenau Nazi death camps that lies just 70km outside the city is a sobering reminder of the atrocities committed in the not-so-distant past. But as the beloved child of Poland, now cast into the international spotlight, Kraków continues to bewitch visitors as it has for centuries.

◪ INTERCITY TRANSPORTATION

Flights: Balice Airport (John Paul II International Airport), ul. Kapitana Medweckiego 1 (☎411 19 55; airport@lotnisko-balice.pl), 18km from the center. Connect to the main train station by bus #192 (40min.) or 208 (1hr.). A taxi to the center costs 30-50zł. Carriers include **Austrian Airlines, British Airways, LOT,** and **Swissair.** Open 24hr.

Trains: Kraków Główny, pl. Kolejowy 1 (☎624 54 39, info 624 15 35; www.pkp.pl). Ticket office often 24hr. To: **Gdańsk** (destination "Gdynia;" 7-10hr., 4 per day, 52-100zł); **Poznań** (6-8hr., 4 per day, 46-70zł); **Warsaw** (4½-5hr., 10 per day, 45-70zł); **Zakopane** (3-5hr., 4 per day, 30zł); **Bratislava, SLK** (8hr., 1 per day, 167zł); **Budapest, HUN** (11hr., 1 per day, 227zł); **Kyiv, UKR** (22hr., 21 per day, 149zł); **Odessa, UKR** (21hr., 1 per day, 182zł); **Prague, CZR** (9hr., 2 per day, 226zł); **Vienna, AUT** (8½hr., 2 per day, 183zł). *Let's Go* does not recommend traveling on night trains.

Buses: ul. Worcella (☎93 16), across from Kraków Główny. Open 5am-11pm. To: **Bielsko-Biała** (2½-3½hr., 15 per day, 13zł); **Łódź** (6½hr., 1 per day, 31zł); **Warsaw** (6hr., 3 per day, 40zł); **Wrocław** (6½hr., 2 per day, 35zł); **Zakopane** (2hr., 33 per day, 10zł). **Sindbad** (☎421 02 40) in the main hall, sells international tickets. Open M-F 8am-5:30pm, Sa 9am-2pm. To: **Prague, CZR** (9hr., 2 per week, 98zł) and **Vienna, AUT** (9hr., 7 per week, 115zł).

▰ ORIENTATION

The heart of the city is the huge **Rynek Główny** (Main Marketplace), in the center of **Stare Miasto** (Old Town). Stare Miasto is encircled by the **Planty** gardens and, a bit farther out, a ring of roads that includes **Basztowa, Dunajewskiego, Podwale,** and **Westerplatte.** South of Rynek Główny looms the celebrated **Wawel Castle** (see **Sights,** p. 534). The **Wisła River** (VEE-swah) snakes past the castle and borders the old Jewish district of **Kazimierz.** The **bus** and **train** stations sit northeast of Old Town. A large, well-marked (and well-kiosked) underpass cuts beneath the road ring and into the Planty gardens; from there a number of paths lead into the *rynek* (10min.). Turn left from the train station or right from the bus station to reach the underpass.

▣ LOCAL TRANSPORTATION

Public Transportation: Buy **bus** and **tram** tickets at Ruch kiosks (2.40zł) or from the driver (2.90zł) and punch them on board. Large backpacks need their own tickets. Night buses (after 11pm) 4zł. Day pass 9zł; week 22zł. 200zł fine if you're caught ticketless, 44zł if your bag is. Foreigners are fined frequently—be sure your ticket is in order. Student fare (1.20zł) for Poles only (though a good accent has been known to work).

Taxis: Reliable taxi companies include: **Barbakan Taxi** (☎96 61, toll-free 0800 400 400); **Euro Taxi** (☎96 64); **Express Taxi** (☎96 29, toll-free 0800 111 111); **Radio Taxi** (☎919, toll-free 0800 500 919); **Wawel Taxi** (☎96 66).

Bicycle Rental: Kraków is a bicycle-friendly city and is one of few places in Poland where bikes are available for rent. **Jordan Travel Agency,** ul. Długa 9 (☎421 21 25), and **Sport MG,** ul. Topolowa 6 (☎430 40 21) both rent bicycles.

🛈 PRACTICAL INFORMATION

TOURIST AND FINANCIAL SERVICES

Tourist Office: MCI, Rynek Główny 1/3 (☎421 77 06; www.mcit.pl). The knowledge-able, multilingual staff sells maps, the handy guide *Kraków in Your Pocket* (5zł, English 10zł), and the cultural guide *Karnet* (3zł; www.karnet.krakow.2000.pl). Open May-Sept. M-F 9am-7pm, Sa 9am-1pm; Oct.-Apr. M-F 9am-5pm, Sa 9am-1pm.

Budget Travel: Orbis, Rynek Główny 41 (☎422 40 35; www.orbis.krakow.pl). Sells train tickets and arranges trips to Wieliczka and Auschwitz (115zł, both 220zł). Also **cashes traveler's checks** and **exchanges currency.** Open M-F 9am-7pm, Sa 9am-3pm. **Alma-tur,** ul. Zwierzyniecka 15 (☎422 46 68; www.almatur.pl), sells **ISICs** (M-F 10am-5pm). English spoken. Open M-F 9am-6pm, Sa 10:30am-2pm. Other **travel agencies** abound in **Rynek Główny.**

Consulates: UK, Św. Anny 9, 4th fl. (☎421 70 30; ukconsul@bci.krakow.pl). Open M-F 9am-2pm. **US,** ul. Stolarska 9 (☎424 51 00; www.usconsulate.krakow.pl). Open M-F 8:30am-5pm.

Currency Exchange: *Kantory* (exchange kiosks) have widely varying rates. Avoid those around the train station, and check rates carefully around Rynek Główny. **Bank PKO SA,** Rynek Główny 31 (☎422 60 22), cashes **traveler's checks** for 1-2% commission (10zł min.) and gives MC/V **cash advances.** Open M-F 8am-6pm, Sa 9am-2pm. **ATMs,** found all over the city, offer the best rates.

American Express: ul. św. Marka 25 (☎423 12 02; www.americanexpress.pl). Directs those seeking help with traveler's cheques to the Warsaw office. Open M-F 9am-5pm.

Western Union: Bank BPH, Rynek Główny 47. Many other banks require those receiving money from abroad to change it into złotys at an unfavorable rate. Open M-F 8am-6pm.

LOCAL SERVICES

Luggage Storage: At the train station. 1% of value per day plus 3.90zł for the 1st day and 2zł for each additional day. Lockers near the exit. Lockers also available at bus sta-tion. Small 4zł, large 8zł. Open 24hr.

English-Language Bookstore: Szawal, ul. Krupnicza 3 (☎0605 609 799). Cheap selec-tion of English classics. Open M-F 10am-7pm, Sa 10am-2pm.

Laundromat: Ul. Piastowska 47 (☎622 31 81), in the basement of **Hotel Piast.** Take tram #4, 13, or 14 to WKS Wawel and turn left on ul. Piastowska. Wash 15zł, dry 15zł, detergent 3zł. Open Tu and Th 11am-4pm, Sa 11am-2pm. **Betty Clean,** ul. Długa 17 (☎632 67 87), past the end of ul. Sławkowska. More cleaners than laundromat. Shirt 8.50zł, pants 12zł, nun's habit 25zł. Open M-F 8am-7:30pm, Sa 8am-2pm.

EMERGENCY AND COMMUNICATIONS

Pharmacy: Apteka Pod Zółtym Tygrysem, Szczepańska 1 (☎422 92 93), just off Rynek Główny. Posts a list of 24hr. pharmacies. Open M-F 8am-8pm, Sa 8am-3pm.

POLAND

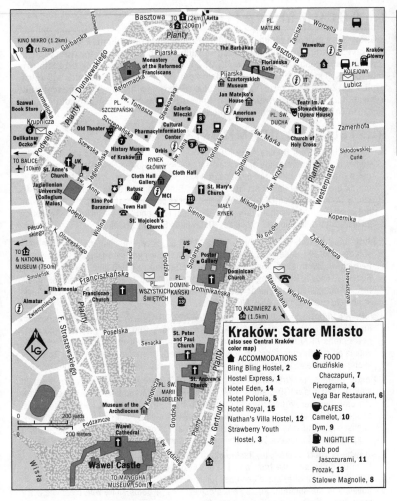

Kraków: Stare Miasto
(also see Central Kraków color map)

ACCOMMODATIONS
Bling Bling Hostel, 2
Hostel Express, 1
Hotel Eden, 14
Hotel Polonia, 5
Hotel Royal, 15
Nathan's Villa Hostel, 12
Strawberry Youth
 Hostel, 3

FOOD
Gruzińskie
 Chaczapuri, 7
Pierogarnia, 4
Vega Bar Restaurant, 6

CAFES
Camelot, 10
Dym, 9

NIGHTLIFE
Klub pod
 Jaszczurami, 11
Prozak, 13
Stalowe Magnolie, 8

Medical Assistance: Medicover, ul. Krótka 1 (☎430 00 34). English-speaking staff. Ambulance services available. Open M-F 8am-8pm, Sa 9am-2pm.

Telephones: At the post office and throughout the city. **Telekomunikacja Polska,** ul. Wielpole 2 (☎421 64 57; www.telekomunikacja.pl), sells phone cards. Open M-F 9am-7pm, Sa 10am-2pm.

Internet Access: Enter Internet Cafe, ul. Basztowa 23 (☎429 42 25). 8am-11am 2zł per hr., 1.5zł per 30min., 1zł per 15min.; 11am-11pm, 3zł/2.50zł/1.50zł. **Internet Point,** ul. Sławkowska 12, 3rd fl. (☎422 22 64; www.kafejka.eco.pl). 2zł per hr. Open M-F 8am-8pm. **Klub Garinet,** ul. Floriańska 18 (☎423 22 33). 3zł per hr. Open daily 10am-midnight. **Telekomunikacja Polska** offers **free Internet access.**

Post Office: ul. Westerplatte 20 (☎422 24 97). **Poste Restante** at counter #1. Open M-F 7:30am-8:30pm, Sa 8am-2pm, Su 9am-11am. **Postal Code:** 31-075.

⚑ ACCOMMODATIONS

Kraków has a growing range of affordable hotels and conveniently located hostels, but travelers still outnumber beds during high season. Call ahead for reservations. **Travel Agency Jordan,** ul. Dluga 9 (☎421 21 25; www.jordan.krakow.pl) arranges private rooms. (Open M-F 8am-6pm, Sa 9am-2pm. Singles 65-100zł; doubles 130-160zł; triples 180-240zł. AmEx/MC/V.) Locals also rent rooms that vary in price and quality; watch for signs at the train station. **University dorms** open up in July and August; *Kraków in Your Pocket* has a complete list.

HOSTELS AND DORMITORIES

▨ **Mama's Hostel,** ul. Bracka 4 (☎429 59 40; www.mamashostel.com.pl). Ul. Bracka begins on the southern side of the main square (Rynek Glówny), and Mama's is ½ block down Bracka on the left. The most central Kraków hostel, freshly painted Mama's pulls out all the stops for its guests. Housed in a 15th-century building, Mama's boasts 46 sturdy wooden beds and 4 bathrooms, and, unlike some of Kraków hostels, free-flowing hot water. Beautiful kitchen. Breakfast, storage, linen, and laundry included. Reception 24hr. Flexible check-in and check-out. Dorm beds 50zł. MC/V. ❷

▨ **Bling Bling Hostel,** ul. Pędzichow 7 (☎634 05 32; www.blingbling.pl). From the train station, take the underpass to ul. Basztowa and turn right onto Dluga. Bear right on Pędzichow. Warm staff, homey kitchen, and attention to detail give it a familial feel. Recently renovated building with new wooden beds and sparkling bathrooms. Breakfast, storage, linen, and laundry included. Free Internet. Reception 24hr. Flexible check-in and checkout. Dorms 45zł. MC/V. ❶

Nathan's Villa Hostel, ul. sw. Agnieszki 1 (☎422 35 45; www.nathansvilla.com). From Kraków Glówny, take tram #10 toward Wawel and get off at the 3rd stop. The party never stops at Kraków's most social hostel, where a staff of amateur models leads guests on nightly pub- and club-crawls. Book ahead. Breakfast is served until 2pm. Full kitchen. Breakfast, storage, linen, and laundry included. Reception 24hr. 50-60zł. ❷

Hostel Express, ul. Wroclawska 91 (☎633 88 62; www.express91.pl). From the train station, take bus #130 5 stops. Walk toward Raclawicka and take a sharp right; follow the path between Wroclawska and the train tracks to the end. Spacious bungalows, spotless baths, kitchens, and laundry (7zł per load). Noisy train stop nearby. Friendly, English-speaking staff. Breakfast 9zł. Sheets and storage included. Reception 24hr. Check-in 3pm. Check-out 10am. Quiet hours 10pm-6am. Dorms 29-35zł. MC/V. ❶

Strawberry Youth Hostel, ul. Raclawicka 9 (☎294 53 63; www.strawberryhostel.com). From train station, take tram #4, 13, or 24 to the 5th stop at Królewska Street. Turn right on Nowowiejska, which becomes Raclawicka. This well-kept student dorm opens to travelers in the summer. Rooms are mostly triples. 4 baths shine with cleanliness. TV room and kitchen. Free coffee and tea. Open July-Aug. Dorms 40zł. ❶

HOTELS

Hotel Polonia, ul. Basztowa 25 (☎422 12 33; www.hotel-polonia.com.pl), across from the train station, 5min. from Rynek Glówny. Elegant exterior, modern rooms, and great location. Highlights include see-through bathtubs in the suites. Breakfast 17zł, included for rooms with bath. Reception 24hr. Check-in 2pm. Check-out noon. Singles 99zł, with bath 268zł; doubles 119zł/319zł; triples 139zł/380zł; suites 484zł. MC/V. ❹

Hotel Royal, ul. sw Gertrudy 26-29 (☎421 58 49; www.royal.com.pl). From the train station, take tram #10 toward Lagiewniki and get off at Wawel. In the Planty gardens in Wawel's shadow. Spotless rooms, some with TV, phone, and bathroom. Check-in 4pm. Check-out 3pm. 2-star singles 160-210zł, 1-star singles 180-190zł; doubles 220-295zł/240-260zł; triples 360zł; quads 400zł. Apartments 400-600zł. AmEx/MC/V. ❺

Hotel Eden, ul. Ciemna 15 (430 65 65; www.hoteleden.pl). From Rynek Główny, follow ul. Sienna, which becomes ul. Starowislna near Kazimierz. Bear right on Dajwór, then turn right onto Ciemna. In a restored 15th-century building, Eden offers the only *mikvah* (Jewish ritual bath) in Poland, Kosher meals, and tours of Kazimierz. Rooms include bath, telephone, and satellite TV. Internet and Kosher breakfast included. Wheelchair accessible. Singles 200zł; doubles 280zł; triples 370zł; suites 450zł. AmEx/MC/V. ❺

◖ FOOD

While Warsaw turns its attention to international cuisine, Kraków remains solidly rooted in local culinary tradition. The restaurants and cafes on and around the *rynek* satisfy both the locals and the huge tourist population. Grocery stores surround the bus and train stations and dot the center. Two 24hr. **grocery stores, Delikatesy Oczko,** ul. Podwale 4, and **Avita,** Plac Kleparski 5, off ul. Bracka, are near the *rynek*. Plac Nowy, in the **Kazimierz district** (see p. 537), boasts an **open-air market** with fresh fruits and vegetables. (Open M-F 6am-8pm, Sa 7am-1pm.) Alternatively, head toward Rynek Kelaprski, next to Pl. Matejki, to find a food and **flea market.** (Open M-F 7am-8pm, Sa 7am-6pm, Su 7am-3pm.)

⊠ **Pierogarnia,** ul. Szpitalnia 30/32 (☎422 74 95). By the counter in this miniscule dumpling outpost, a window reveals a cook rolling dough and shaping delicious pastries. *Pierogi* range from classic cheese-and-potato *ruskie* to the more daring groats and liver. Also serves excellent *golabki* (cabbage rolls; 6zł) and 8 Polish fruit juices, including cherry and black currant (4zł). *Pierogi* 5.90zł-6.90zł. Open daily 10am-9pm. ❶

⊠ **Navara,** ul. Podbrzezie 2 (☎431 19 42), facing the Tempel Synagogue. The bagel returns to its birthplace in triumph at tiny Navara. Here, Nava and Tamara, an American-Polish couple, serve some of the best bagels east of New York and a variety of fresh spreads (1.30zł, 4-5zł with cream cheese or hummus). Open Tu-Su 10am-7pm. ❶

Gruzinskie Chaczapuri, ul. Slawkowska 19. This casual Georgian restaurant derives its name from *chaczapuri* (bread stuffed with sheep's cheese; 5zł). Other fresh, richly spiced specialities include grilled meats (5zł) and veggie-filled lavash (6-8zł). Open daily 9am-midnight. ❶

Vega Bar Restaurant, ul. Krupnicza 22 (☎430 08 46). Fresh flowers set the mood for munching on delightful, largely vegetarian cuisine (2-5zł). The cheese and soy *kotlety* (cutlet) will please every carnivore while the

ON THE MENU

THE ORIGINAL

According to legend, a Jewish Viennese baker concocted the first bagel in 1683 as a gift to Polish king Jan Sobieski to thank Sobieski for routing Turkish invaders. The bread (the story goes) was shaped like a stirrup "beugal" in honor of Sobieski's heroic horsemanship. The historical record, however, first spots the bagel in Kraków in 1610: community regulations decreed that bagels be given to pregnant women for easy childbirth, and to teething babies. Whatever the bagel's origins, it thrived in Poland, especially in the Kraków region. A 1915 chronicle of the Kazimierz neighborhood recalls that the smell of freshly baked bagels often wafted through the streets, especially near the Tempel Synagogue, where a tiny shop called Pan Bejgul (Mr. Bagel) stood at the end of Podbrzezie Street.

In Kraków today, street vendors hawk the Polish descendent of the original bagel, a crisp ring of bread known as *obwarzank* for less than a złoty. The smell of baking bagels, meanwhile, has returned to Podbrzezie St. Navara, facing the Tempel Synagogue at Podbrzezie 2, opened in 2001. Run by an American expat chef, Navara is currently the only shop in Poland that sells fresh bagels as they have evolved among Polish Jewish immigrants to North America: soft and chewy, with cream cheese spreads.

fasola z grzybami (beans with mushrooms) is a great spin on a Polish favorite. 36 varieties of tea (2.50zł). Open daily 9am-9pm. MC/V. **Branch** at ul. sw. Gertrudy 7 (☎422 34 94). Open daily 9am-9pm. MC/V. ❶

Fabryka Pizzy, ul. Józefa 34 (☎433 80 80). The wildly popular Kazimierz pizza place lives up to its hype. Excellent pizzas (12-20zł) and fabulous bread sticks and calzone (5-8zł). Open M-Th and Su 11am-11pm, F-Sa noon-midnight. ❷

Restauracja Samoobslugowa "Polakowski," ul. Miodowa 39 (☎421 21 17). The menu, prices, and cafeteria service of a milk bar meet upscale country decor and quality ingredients. Full meals 10-15zł, soups 4zł. Open daily 9am-10pm. ❷

◪ CAFES

▨ **Dym** (Smoke), ul. sw. Jana 5 (☎429 66 61). A hub for sophisticated locals, Dym earns high praise for it unbeatable coffee (4.50zł), though many enjoy the relaxed atmosphere over beer (5.50zł). The cheesecake (4zł) is divine. Smoke-colored interior also hosts art exhibitions. Open daily 10am-midnight. ❶

▨ **Camelot,** ul. sw. Tomasza 17 (☎421 01 23). One of Old Town's legends. Full of paintings and photos, soothing jazz, and the occasional 17th-century document. Sandwiches 3-6zł. Salads 19-21zł. Breakfast 9zł. Coffee 6-11zł. Music, readings, or cabaret (25zł) happens F 9pm, downstairs at Loch Camelot. Open daily 9am-midnight. ❶

Les Couleurs, ul. Estery 10 (☎429 42 70). Begin your day at this Parisian cafe with buttery croissants (4zł), fresh-squeezed juice (9zł), and international newspapers. By afternoon the back patio fills with laid-back coffee drinkers (4.5zł) and Kazimierz regulars nurse beer (Żywiec 6zł) at the bar. Lively late at night. Also a hub of information about arts and cultural events around Kazimierz. Open daily 7am-2am. ❶

Massolit Books Café, ul. Felicjanek 4 (☎432 41 50). A fantastic bookstore and good cafe. Impressive selection of English books. Peruse your newest find at one of the tiny cafe's 4 coveted tables while sipping coffee (4zł) or sampling a decadent dessert like banana cake (5zł). Open daily 10am-8pm, F-Sa 10am-10pm. ❶

Cafe Manggha, ul. M. Konopnickiej 26 (☎267 27 03; www.manggha.krakow.pl), in the Center for Japanese Arts. Not cheap, but the view, like the ice cream topped with green tea (9zł), is exquisite. Japanese teas 6-7zł. The best place in Poland to splurge on sushi (17-23zł). Open Tu-Su 10am-6pm. ❸

◎ SIGHTS

WAWEL CASTLE AND CATHEDRAL

Tourist Service Office (BOT) ☎422 64 64; www.wawel.krakow.pl. Open Tu-Sa 9am-3pm, Su 10am-3pm. Apr.-Oct. M free admission to State Rooms, Treasury and Armory, Oriental Art, and Lost Wawel. Wawel open daily May-Sept. 6am-8pm; Oct.-Apr. 6am-5pm. English info and tickets to all buildings except the cathedral at the main kasa. Open M 9:15-11:45am, Tu and F 9:15am-3:45pm, W-Th and Sa 9:15am-2:45pm, Su 9:45am-2:45pm. Only 10 tickets become available every 10min., so you may have to wait. Tickets often sell out, especially in summer, so it's advisable to buy tickets early in the morning.

▨ **WAWEL CASTLE (ZAMEK WAWELSKI).** An extraordinary architectural work, the Wawel Castle and Cathedral complex—arguably the best sight in Poland—lies at the heart of the country's history. Begun in the 10th century but remodeled in the 1500s, the castle contains 71 chambers and a magnificent sequence of 16th-century tapestries. Walk through the **Dziedziniec** (Courtyard) and take in the beautiful architecture. The royal family's treasures can be seen in the **Komnaty** (State Rooms) while the **Apartamenty** (Royal Private Apartments) showcase the royal lifestyle. The Skarbiec (Treasury and Armory) features swords, spears, ostentatious armor, and ancient guns. The star of the collection is **Szczerbiec,** the coronation sword used from 1230 to 1734. **The Lost Wawel** exhibit winds through archaeological digs, tracing Wawel Hill's evolution from the Stone Age. You can also visit the **Oriental Collection** of Chinese and Japanese porcelain, the spoils of Polish victory. *(Open Apr.-Oct. M 9:30am-noon, Tu and F 9:30am-4pm, W-Th and Sa 9:30am-3pm, Su 10am-3pm.; Nov.-Mar. Tu-Sa 9:30am-3pm, Su 10am-3pm. Royal Private Apartments closed M. Oriental Collection closed M. Lost Wawel Exhibit closed Tu Nov.-Mar. Museum is divided into Royal Private Apartments; Oriental Collection; Lost Wawel Exhibit; and State Rooms, Crown Treasury, and Armory. Admission to each 12zł, students 7zł.)*

WAWEL CATHEDRAL (KATEDRA WAWELSKA). On Wawel Hill, beside the castle, the Wawel Cathedral witnessed coronations of the kings who were later buried here. As you enter, look for the miraculous **crucifix of St. Jadwiga.** Legend has it that the young Polish queen asked it whether she should marry King Ladislaus Jagiełło of Lithuania (who now rests here), and the crucifix spoke, advising her to marry. Along with the union of the couple came the unification of their respective countries in 1386. In 1997, Jadwiga was canonized by John Paul II who, back when he was Archbishop Karol Wojtyla, was a member of the clergy here. On display are St. Jadwiga's apple and scepter and the **sarcophagus** of King Kazimierz Jagiellończyk, which was crafted by Wit Stwosz, who also designed the altar (see p. 536) in St. Mary's Church. *(Cathedral open May-Sept. M-Sa 9am-5pm; Oct.-Apr. 9am-3pm; Su and holy days 12:15-5:15pm. Buy cathedral tickets at the kasa across from the entrance. 8zl, students 4zl.)*

CATHEDRAL SIGHTS. The ascent to **Sigismund's Bell** (Dwon Zygmunta) affords a great view of Kraków. Make a wish and touch the bell's heart for good luck or a good spouse. Outside the Lipskich chapel, stairs lead to the **crypt** of poets Juliusz Słowacki and Adam Mickiewicz. Through the Czartoryskich Chapel, enter the maze that contains the elaborately carved sarcophagi of royals and acclaimed military leaders, including heroic generals Józef Piłsudski, Tadeusz Kościuszko, and Stanisław Poniatowski. The small **Cathedral Museum** (Muzeum Katedralne) boasts selections from the cathedral treasury, including exquisite textiles and a gold rose.

DRAGON'S DEN. Home to Kraków's **◪Erstwhile Menace,** the dragon's den is in the southwest corner of the complex. Legend has it that the dragon held the people of Kraków in terror until a clever young shepherd set a fake sheep full of sulfur outside its cave. Upon devouring the trap, the reptile became so thirsty that it drank water from the Wisła until it burst. Enjoy the legendary cave, or skip the den altogether and walk down to the path that borders the castle walls to the real treat, a statue of the fire-breathing dragon. *(Open daily Apr.-Oct. 10am-5pm. 3zł.)*

STARE MIASTO

At the center of Stare Miasto spreads **Rynek Główny,** and at the heart of the *rynek* stands the **Sukiennice** (Cloth Hall). Surrounded by multicolored row houses and cafes, it's a convenient center for exploring the nearby sights.

▨ JAGIELLONIAN UNIVERSITY (UNIWERSYTET JAGIELLOŃSKI). Established in 1364, Collegium Maius of Kraków's Jagiellonian University is the second oldest institution of higher learning in Eastern Europe (after Prague's Charles University). Among its celebrated alumni are astronomer **Mikołaj Kopernik (Copernicus)** and painter Jan Matejko. The Collegium became a museum in 1964 and now boasts an extensive collection of historical scientific instruments. Highlights include the oldest known globe showing the Americas (look for them near Madagascar) and an 11th-century Arabian astrolabe. *(Ul. Jagiellonska 15. ☎ 422 05 49. English tour daily 1pm. Open M-F 10am-3pm, Sa 11am-2pm. Guided visits only; tours begin every 20min. 16zł, students 12zł; Sa free.)*

◪ ST. MARY'S CHURCH (KOŚCIÓŁ MARIACKI). Deep blues and golds accent the black marble columns of the church's interior. Look down from the exquisite, star-flecked ceiling and notice a 500-year-old wooden altar, carved by Wit Stwosz, which portrays the joy and suffering of St. Mary. This gorgeous artifact, the oldest Gothic altar in the world, barely survived WWII. Dismantled by the Nazis, it was rediscovered by Allied forces at the war's end and reassembled. Every hour, the blaring Hejnał trumpet calls from the taller of St. Mary's two towers and cuts off abruptly to recall the near-destruction of Kraków in 1241, when the invading Tatars shot down the trumpeter as he attempted to warn the city. The opposing towers also stand as monuments to ancient sibling rivalry. The larger tower, according to legend, was the careful work of one brother, while the other brother built the smaller and less elaborate tower. The architect of the smaller tower murdered his brother out of jealousy. However, overwhelmed with guilt, he mounted his own tower, publicly confessed to the murder, and stabbed himself with the same knife. The murder weapon is on display in the Cloth Hall. Both towers are now historic sites. Visitors can climb the towers for a panorama. *(At the corner of the rynek closest to the train station. Open daily 11:30am-6pm. Icon unveiled daily M-F 11:50am-6pm, Su and holidays 2-6pm. No photography. Covered shoulders and knees expected. Altar 4zł, students 2zł. Video camera 5zł. Wieża Mariacka Open Tu, Th, Sa 9am-11am and 2-6pm. 5zł. Other tower open daily 10am-1:15pm, 2-5pm. 4zł, students 2.50zł.)*

ROYAL ROAD (DROGA KRÓLEWSKA). In medieval times, royals traversed this route on the way to coronations in Wawel. The road starts at **St. Florian's Church** (Kociół św. Florian), crosses Plac Matejki, passes the **Academy of Fine Arts** (Akademia Sztuk Pięknych), and crosses ul. Basztowa to the Barbakan. It then goes through Floriańska Gate, the old city entrance and the only remnant of the city's medieval fortifications. Inside the city walls the road runs down ul. Floriańska, past the *rynek* and along ul. Grodzka, which ends with **Wawel** in sight. From the church to Wawel, the walking tour is composed of 27 sights, including 10 churches and 6 museums. A **map** marking all the points can be found before Floriańska Gate. At the foot of Wawel, visitors to the **Museum of the Archdiocese** (Muzeum Archidiecezjalne) can admire the rooms where Karol Wojtyla lived as Archbishop of Kraków (1951-67) before becoming Pope John Paul II. The museum's collection of sacred art covers seven centuries and includes remarkable 13th-century pieces. *(Ul. Kanonicza 19/21. ☎ 421 89 63; muzeumkra@diecezja.krakow.pl. Open Tu-F 10am-4pm, Sa-Su 10am-3pm. 5zł, students 3zł.)*

CLOTH HALL (SUKIENNICE). In the *rynek*, the yellow Cloth Hall remains as profit-oriented today as when the cloth merchants used it. The ground floor is lined with wooden stalls hawking crafts. Upstairs, the Cloth Hall Gallery houses 18th- and 19th-century sculptures and paintings. Of the many pastoral and military depictions, the most striking and famous are Jan Matejko's *Hold Pruski*, Józef Chełmoński's *Four in Hand*, and Henryk Siemiradzki's *Nero's Torches*. During the academic year, students cruise the area between the Cloth Hall and St. Mary's and near the statue of Adam Mickiewicz, Poland's most celebrated poet. *(☎ 422 11 66. Open Tu and F-Sa 10am-7pm, W-Th 10am-4pm, Su 10am-3pm. 7zł, students 4zł; Th free.)*

CZARTORYSKICH MUSEUM. This branch of the National Museum displays **Leonardo da Vinci's** *Lady with an Ermine* and **Rembrandt's** *Landscape with a Merciful Samaritan.* Da Vinci's piece harbors several secrets: historians have debated whether the lady portrayed is Beatrice d'Este, the Duchess of Milan, or Cecilia Gallerani, the Duke of Milan's 16-year-old mistress. Also debatable are the painting's authenticity and where it spent the centuries preceding its 1800 purchase by Polish prince Adam Czartoryski. Read letters written by Copernicus, peer into a Turkish ceremonial tent captured at the Battle of Vienna, or witness the national spirit of Jan Matejko's *Poland Enchained*. (*Ul. sw. Jana 19, parallel to ul. Florianska.* ☎ *422 55 66. Open Tu and Th 10am-4pm, W and F 11am-7pm, Sa-Su 10am-3pm; closed 3rd Su of each month. Cameras without flash 15zł, 20zł plakietka deposit. 8zł, students 5zł, Su usually free.*)

OTHER SIGHTS. The main branch of the **National Museum** has permanent exhibits of armory and 20th-century art, and hosts acclaimed temporary exhibits. (*Al. 3 Maja 1. Take tram #15 to Cracovia.* ☎ *634 33 77; www.muz-nar.krakow.pl. Open Tu and Th 9am-3:30pm, W and F 11am-6pm, Sa-Su 10am-3:30pm. Permanent exhibit 8zł, students 5zł; temporary 5zł/3zł. MC/V.*) The **History Museum of Kraków,** another branch of the National Museum, displays ceiling frescoes and centuries-old documents from Kraków, including a 15th-century map of the city and religious and military artifacts. (*Rynek Główny 35.* ☎ *422 99 22. Open W and F-Su 9am-3:30pm, Th 9am-6pm; closed 2nd weekend of each month. 4zł, students 3zł; Sa free.*) The **Franciscan Church** is decorated with vibrant colors and Stanisław Wyspiański's amazing stained-glass window *God the Father.* (*Pl. Wszystkich Świętych 5.* ☎ *422 53 76; www.semkrak.franciszkanie.pl. Open daily until 7:30pm. Free English tours available; donations encouraged.*) Kraków's center of Japanese art, **Manggha,** is across the river from Wawel. The modern building houses Japanese cloth, armor, and sculpture. (*Ul. M. Konopnickiej 26.* ☎ *267 27 03; www.manggha.krakow.pl. Open Tu-Su 10am-6pm; closed 3rd Su of each month. 5zł, students 3zł.*) Both a store and gallery, **Galeria Autorska Andrzeja Mleczki** is a satirical, funky, and fun glimpse into Polish politics. (*Ul. św. Jana 14. Open M-F 11am-7pm, Sa 11am-4pm; June-Sept. also open Su 11am-4pm.*) For an even funkier experience, visit the **Poster Gallery** and view hundreds of Kraków-printed *plakaty.* (*ul. Stolarska 8.* ☎ *421 26 40. Open M-F 11am-6pm, Sa 11am-2pm. AmEx/MC/V.*)

KAZIMIERZ: THE OLD JEWISH QUARTER

Southeast of the rynek and Wawel. The 15min. walk from the rynek leads down ul. Sienna past St. Mary's Church. Eventually, ul. Sienna turns into Starowislna. After 1km, turn right on Miodowa and take the 1st left onto ul. Szeroka.

South of Stare Miasto lies Kazimierz, Kraków's 600-year-old Jewish quarter. Founded in 1335, Kazimierz was originally a separate town and was not linked to Małopolska's capital until 1495, when King Jan Olbrecht moved Kraków's Jews there in order to remove them from the city proper. On the eve of WWII, 68,000 Jews lived in the Kraków area—40,000 of them in Kazimierz. Occupying Nazis forced most of them out. The 15,000 remaining were resettled in the overcrowded Podgórze ghetto in 1941. All were deported by March 1943, many to nearby Płaszów and Auschwitz-Birkenau. While only about 100 practicing Jews now live here, modern Kazimierz is a focal point for Poland's 5000 Jews. The district, with its cafes and bars, is both a favorite haunt of Kraków's artists and intellectuals and the center of a resurgence of Central European Jewish culture. The **Jarden Bookstore** organizes guided **tours,** including a 2hr. tour of Kazimierz and the Płaszów concentration camp that traces the sites shown in the film *Schindler's List.* Płaszów, in the south of Kraków, was destroyed by the Nazis on their retreat and is now an overgrown field. (*ul. Szeroka 2.* ☎ *421 11 66; www.jarden.pl. Open M-F 9am-6pm, Sa-Su 10am-6pm. Kazimierz tour 35zł, 3 people min.; with ghetto 45zł. Schindler's List tours 65zł. Car tour of Auschwitz-Birkenau 110zł, students 95zł. 20% student discount. AmEx/MC/V.*)

POLAND

OLD SYNAGOGUE (STARA SYNAGOGA). Poland's oldest example of Jewish religious architecture, the Old Synagogue houses a **museum** depicting local Jewish history, tradition, and art. Sacred art and nostalgic pre-WWII photos are counterposed with WWII-era documents of segregation and deportation. *(Ul. Szeroka 24. ☎ 422 09 62; fax 431 05 45. Open Apr.-Oct. M 10am-2pm, W-Th and Sa-Su 9am-3:30pm, F 10am-5pm; Nov.-Mar. M 10am-2pm, W-Th and Sa-Su 9am-3:30pm, F 10am-5pm. 6zł, students 4zł, M free.)*

REMUH SYNAGOGUE AND CEMETERY. Rabbi Moses Isserles, a great legal scholar better known as the **Remuh,** founded this tiny synagogue in 1553 in honor of his wife, who had died in the plague of 1551-52. The Remuh, now buried under a tree to the left of the cemetery's entrance, is believed to have caused strong winds to rise up and cover the cemetery with sand, protecting it from 19th century Austrian invaders. Although the Nazis used the cemetery as a garbage dump, many of the gravestones remained buried through WWII. While the Nazis destroyed most Jewish cemeteries, the sands protected Kazimierz's from total destruction. Much of the cemetery has been painstakingly reconstructed in the past half-century. *(Ul. Szeroka 40. Open M-F and Su 9am-6pm. Services F at sundown and Sa morning. 5zł, students 2zł.)*

ISAAC'S SYNAGOGUE (SYNAGOGA IZAAKA). Renovation continues on this gorgeous 17th-century Baroque synagogue. The main room shows two historical documentaries while a smaller room features seven others, including *Ghetto Uprising.* Haunting stills are scattered throughout the synagogue. *(Ul. Kupa 18. ☎ 430 55 77; fax 602 144 262. Open Su-F 9am-7pm. Closed Jewish holidays. 7zł, students 6zł.)*

GALICIA JEWISH MUSEUM. Galicia, a region that includes much of southern Poland, was once the heart of Ashkenazi Jewish culture. In this unconventional museum, photojournalist Chris Schwarz uses contemporary photography to document the past and present Jewish life of Galicia and to pose difficult questions about the future of Jewish culture in this region. A spare converted warehouse houses the museum, a cafe, and a bookstore. *(Ul. Dajwór 18. ☎ 421 68 42; www.galicjamuseum.org. Open daily 9am-8pm. 6zl, students 4zl.)*

OTHER SIGHTS. In 2000, restoration was completed on the ornate gold-trimmed and stained-glass interior of the **Tempel Synagogue,** ul. Miodowa 24. *(Open Su-F 10am-6pm. 5zl, students 2zl.)* The **New Jewish Cemetery,** ul. Miodowa 55, created in 1800, houses tombstones of many of 19th-century Kraków's prominent citizens and memorializes families killed in the Holocaust. Head coverings required. *(Open Su-F 8am-4pm. Free.)*

CENTER FOR JEWISH CULTURE. The center organizes cultural events, arranges heritage tours, and aims to preserve the current Jewish culture in Kazimierz. Free temporary exhibits are across from the info desk. *(Rabina Meiselsa 17, just off pl. Nowy. ☎ 430 64 49; www.judaica.pl. Open M-F 10am-6pm, Sa-Su 10am-2pm. Closed Jewish holidays.)*

🎵 🎋 ENTERTAINMENT AND FESTIVALS

MCI (see p. 515) has brochures on cultural events. The **Cultural Information Center,** ul. św. **Jana 2** (☎421 77 87; fax 421 77 31), sells the monthly guide *Karnet* (3zł; www.karnet.krakow2000.pl) and directs visitors to box offices. (Open M-F 10am-6pm, Sa 10am-4pm.) The city jumps with jazz. Check out **U Muniaka** and **Harris Piano Jazz Bar,** Rynek Główny 28. (☎421 57 41. Open daily 9am-3am, shows

9pm-midnight.) Take in the talent at **Indigo,** ul. Floriańska 26 (☎429 17 43; www.nottwo.com). Classical music lovers will relish the **Sala Filharmonia** (Philharmonic Hall), ul. Zwierzyniecka 1. (☎675 02 00 025; www.filharmonia.krakow.pl. Box office open Tu-F 2-8pm, Sa-Su 1hr. before performance; closed June 9-Sept. 20.) The **opera** (www.opera.krakow.pl) performs at the **J. Słowacki Theater,** pl. św. Ducha 1. (☎422 40 22; www.slowacki.krakow.pl. Box office open M-Sa 11am-2pm and 3-7pm, Su 2hr. before performance. Tickets 30-50zł, students 25-30zł.) The **Stary Teatr** has a few stages that host movies, plays, and exhibits. (Booking office at ul. Jagielloska 1. ☎422 40 40; www.stary-teatr.krakow.pl. Order tickets at www.ebilet.pl. Open Tu-Sa 10am-1pm and 5-7pm, Su 5-7pm. Tickets 30-50zł, students 20-30zł.) Enjoy a relaxing evening at **Kino Pod Baranami,** Rynek Główny 27. (☎423 07 68; www.grafitikom.pl. Tickets M 9.90zł, Tu-Th 14zł, students 12zł; F-Su 15zł/13zł.) Catch a European flick at **Kino Mikro,** ul. Lea 5. (☎634 28 97; www.apollofilm.pl. Open daily 30min. before 1st showing. M-F 10zł, Sa-Su 12zł.)

Notable festivals include the **International Short Film Festival** (late May), **Wianki** (the Floating of Wreaths on the Wisła; June), **Festival of Jewish Culture** (early July), the **Street Theater Festival** (early July), and the **Jazz Festival** (late July).

▓ NIGHTLIFE

Kraków in Your Pocket has up-to-date info on the *rynek* and beyond, and on the hottest club and pub scenes. Most dance clubs are in the Old Town, while bohemian pubs and cafes cluster in Kazimierz. For more info, see www.puby.krakow.pl. Be advised that Kraków's night establishments have a high turnover rate. For tips on Kraków's **gay nightlife,** see http://gayeuro.com/krakow.

▓ **Stalowe Magnolie,** ul. św Jana 15 (☎422 60 84; fax 422 84 72). Scarlet lights illuminate this decadent jazz club and student hangout. Outstanding live jazz Tu-Th; contemporary rock Sa-Su. Pass through the bar, then chat and chill out on the comfy, king-sized beds. Beer 6-10zł, mixed drinks 14-25zł. Open daily 6pm-3am.

▓ **Alchemia,** ul. Estery 5 (☎292 09 70). Candles twinkle in the charismatically shabby bar, where patrons sip beer (Żywiec 6zł) and linger until dawn. Frequented by students, artists, and young Brits, this quintessential Kazimierz bar masquerades by day as a smoky cafe. Occasional live music and film screenings. Open M-Sa 11am-4am, Su 10am-4am.

Prozak, ul. Dominikańska 6 (☎429 11 28; www.prozak.pl). With more dance floors, bars, and intimate nooks than you'll be able to count, Prozak is the hottest club in town. Hipster students, porn star lookalikes, and fashionable foreigners lounge beneath mood lighting and on low-slung couches. Pass on the pricey, undersized mixed drinks (12-22zł) for pints of beer (7zł). Cover F-Sa about 10zł. Open daily 4pm-2am.

Propaganda, ul. Miodowa 20. Despite the candles and wobbly tables, Propaganda's take on bohemia has a punk rock feel. Decor mixes posters of Stalin with guitars of Polish rockers, some of whom have been known to tend bar here. Open daily 2pm-late.

Faust, Rynek Główny 6 (☎423 83 00). Sell your soul in this underground labyrinth, where a raucous, friendly crowd sits at massive wooden tables and dances unabashedly to pop hits of the past 30 years. Occasional techno, *klezmer,* and metal nights. Beer 4-6zł. Disco W-Sa. Cover F-Sa 5zł. Open Su-Th noon-1am, F-Sa noon-4am.

Klub pod Jaszczurami (Club under the Lizards), Rynek Główny 8 (☎292 22 02). A students-only cafe by day and thumping club party by night. Familiar tunes fill the dark dance floors as smoke wafts above tables of chatting 20-somethings. Beer 5.50zł. Open Su-Th 10am-1am, F-Sa 10am-late.

⚡ DAYTRIPS FROM KRAKÓW

AUSCHWITZ-BIRKENAU

Buses (1½-2hr., 5 per day, 8zł; get off at Muzeum Oświęcim) run to the town of Oświęcim from Kraków's central bus station. The bus back to Kraków leaves from a different stop across from the parking lot. Trains run from Kraków Płaszów. Tourist offices in Kraków organize trips that include transportation and guides. From outside the Oświęcim train station, buses #2-5, 8-9, and 24-29 drop visitors off at the Muzeum Oświęcim stop. Turn right as you exit the station, go 1 block, and turn left onto ul. Więźniów Oświęcimia; the Auschwitz camp is 1.6km down the road.

An estimated 1.5 million people—mostly Jews—were murdered, and thousands more suffered unthinkable horrors in the infamous Nazi concentration camps at **Auschwitz** (Oświęcim) and **Birkenau** (Brzezinka). As the largest and most brutally efficient of the camps, their names are synonymous with the Nazi death machine. In 1979, the complexes were added to the UNESCO World Heritage List.

AUSCHWITZ I. In 1940, the first and smaller of the two death camps was built on the ground of a Polish Army garrison. Originally consisting of 20 buildings, the camp grew as prisoners were used to construct additional barracks. In 1942, Auschwitz became the center of extermination of Jews, Roma, and other "inferior" peoples. The eerily tidy rows of red brick buildings seems almost peaceful until the bitter irony of the inscription on the camp's gate—*Arbeit Macht Freig* (Work Shall Set You Free)—sinks in. The chilling walk through the infamous camp confronts visitors with an up-close look at the horrifying realities of the Holocaust. The barracks that once incarcerated Jews and political prisoners now showcase the ghostly remnants of those murdered in the camp: a myriad of suitcases, shoes, eyeglasses, and even hair provides a terrifyingly personal look at the Nazis' atrocities. The lynching post and gas chamber also remain on the grounds. At 11am and 1pm, the building through which visitors enter shows a 15min. English-language film (2zł) with footage recorded by the Soviet Army when it liberated the camp on January 27, 1945. Children under 14 are strongly advised not to visit the museum. *(☎843 20 22; www.um.oswiecim.pl. Open daily June-Aug. 8am-7pm; May and Sept. 8am-6pm; Apr. and Oct. 8am-5pm; Mar. and Nov.-Dec. 15 8am-4pm; Dec. 16-Feb. 8am-3pm. Free. Polish tour daily 11am, 1, 3pm. English tour daily 11:30am. Both tours 3½hr., 25zł. Film and bus included. English guidebook 3zł.)*

AUSCHWITZ II-BIRKENAU. Konzentrationlager Auschwitz II-Birkenau was built when the massive influx of condemned prisoners being brought to Auschwitz motivated the Nazis to pursue a more "efficient" means of killing. Little is left now of the 300 barracks that spanned the 425-acre camp; the Nazis attempted to conceal their genocide by destroying the camp before it was liberated on January 27, 1945. The reconstructed railroad tracks run beneath the still-looming watchtower, gliding past the faceless rows and selection barracks where individuals were chosen for work or death. The tracks end between piles of rubber, former gas chambers, and crematoria, the final stop for countless victims sent to the camps. Beyond the ruins, a memorial pays tribute to those who died in the Auschwitz system and is a place for quiet reflection. Near the monument is a pond, gray from the ashes deposited there more than half a century ago. *(Birkenau is 3km from Auschwitz I. Turn right from the parking lot and follow the sign to a road on the left that turns into a bridge and curves back. Enter the watch tower to hear a commentary on the history, layout, and use of the grounds. Open Apr. 15-Oct. A 2zł shuttle runs every hr. 11:30am-5:30pm from the Auschwitz parking lot.)*

A PRISONER'S SACRIFICE. It is difficult to visit the concentration camps at Auschwitz and Birkenau without hearing the story of the priest Makaymilian Kolbe— prisoner 16670— who sacrificed his own life while imprisoned here. When another man was handed the brutal sentence of death by starvation, Kolbe willingly took the man's place and submitted himself to a torture even more ghastly than he and other prisoners were already enduring. Amazingly, he maintained his strength and staved off death for two weeks - but this triumph of will and faith was cut short by Nazi guards who, frustrated with his incredible endurance, executed him by lethal injection. After his death, Kolbe became a strong symbol of faith in the face of persecution within the Catholic Church. Indeed, in 1971 he became the first Nazi victim to be proclaimed blessed by the Catholic Church and was canonized by Pope John Paul II in 1982. Franciszek Gajowniczek, the man whom Kolbe replaced, survived through liberation and lived to the fiftieth anniversary of the end of World War Two. He died in 1995. Visitors can see Kolbe's starvation cell (#18), located in Barrack II of Auschwitz I. A tribute to the priest lies inside.

AUSCHWITZ JEWISH CENTER AND SYNAGOGUE. The center is adjacent to the town's only surviving synagogue. The knowledgeable staff speaks English. Geared toward those interested in exploring their Jewish ancestry, the center provides guidance for those seeking Jewish roots in Oświęcim. The exhibits focus on pre-war Jewish life in the town. Oświęcim offers study and research opportunities, discussion groups, and video testimonials of Auschwitz survivors. Guides for Auschwitz are available for hire. *(Pl. Ks. Jana Skarbka 5. From the train station take bus #1, 3-6, 8, or 28 to the town center, get off at the stop after the bridge, and backtrack, taking the 1st right and then a left to pl. Ks. Jana Skarbka. Alternatively, take a taxi, which costs about 17zł. ☎ 844 70 02; www.ajcf.pl. Open daily Apr.-Sept. 8:30am-8pm; Oct.-Mar. Su-F 8:30am-6pm.)*

WIELICZKA

Ul. Daniłowicza 10. Many hotels and companies, including Orbis, organize trips to the mine. The cheapest way to go is to take one of the frequent minibuses that leave from the road between the train and bus stations. (The 30min. "Lux-Bus" runs every 15min. 2zł.) In Wieliczka, follow the old path of the tracks and then the "do kopalni" signs. ☎ 278 73 02; www.kopalnia.pl. Open daily Apr.-Oct. 7:30am-7:30pm; Nov.-Mar. 8am-4pm. Closed holidays. Admission with tours only. Polish tours 32zł, students 18zł. English tours July-Aug. 5 per day; June and Sept.-Oct. 3 per day; Nov.-May 2 per day. Foreign-language tour 47zł, students under 25 36zł; Nov.-Feb. 20% off. Photo or video 9zł. Wheelchair accessible. MC/V.

Thirteen kilometers southeast of Kraków and 100m below the tiny town of Wieliczka lies the 700-year-old ⛏**Wieliczka Salt Mine.** Follow the footsteps of Goethe, one of the attraction's first tourists, and see how miners and artists transformed the salt deposits into a maze of chambers full of sculptures and carvings. Though salt has not been manually excavated here since July 1996, the mine still exports 20,000 tons of salt per year through natural processes. In 1978, UNESCO, citing the mine's beauty and part in Polish history, declared it one of the 12 most priceless monuments in the world. Amazingly, the mine once provided a third of Poland's GDP, and with the sheer number of tourists in high season, it still plays its economic part. The 2hr. tour meanders past spectacular underground lakes and sculptures of beloved Poles, like Copernicus and Pope John Paul II. The most impressive sight is **St. Kinga's Chapel,** with an altar, chandeliers, and religious relics. At the end of the tour, take the lift 120m back to the surface or go to the **underground museum**, "Muzeum Żup Krakowskich," which gives a more detailed history of the mines and features 14 additional chambers (1hr. tours 8zł, students 4zł; M free). Bring a sweater—the mine is chilly.

LUBLIN   ☎0(81)

Lublin (LOO-bleen; pop. 400,000) lulls visitors with its stunning skyline and quiet streets. The birthplace of many revolutionary movements, Małopolska's former capital was the center of the Polish Reformation and Counter-Reformation in the 16th and 17th centuries. Its Polish Catholic University was the country's only independent institution of higher learning in the communist era. Lublin is now home to five universities, and bustling student life offers a lively counterpoint to the city's embattled history.

▐ TRANSPORTATION

Trains: Pl. Dworcowy 1 (☎94 36). To: **Częstochowa** (6hr., 1 per day, 43zł); **Gdańsk** (7hr., 2 per day, 48zł); **Kraków** (4hr., 4 per day, 43zł); **Poznań** (10hr., 3 per day, 48zł); **Toruń** (8hr., 3 per day, 46zł); **Warsaw** (3hr., 14 per day, 32zł); **Wrocław** (9½hr., 3 per day, 48zł); **Berlin, GER** (13hr., 1 per day, 158-234zł).

Buses: Ul. Tysiąclecia 4 (☎776 649, info 934). To: **Kraków** (6hr., 4 per day, 42zł); **Warsaw** (2¼hr., 25 per day, 41zł); **Wrocław** (8hr., 20 per day, 46zł). **Polski Express** (☎620 03 30; www.polskiexpress.pl) runs buses to: **Kraków** (6hr., 1 per day, 43zł); **Warsaw** (3hr., 8 per day, 34zł); **Wrocław** (8hr., 1 per day, 42zł).

Public Transportation: Buy tickets for buses and trolleys at kiosks. 10min. ride 1.70zł; students 1zł; 30min. ride 1.90zł/1.40zł.

▐▐ ORIENTATION AND PRACTICAL INFORMATION

The city's main drag, **ul. Krakówskie Przedmieście**, connects **Stare Miasto** (Old Town) in east Lublin to the **Katolicki Uniwersytet Lubelski** (KUL; Catholic University of Lublin) and **Uniwersytet Marii Curie-Skłodowskiej** (Maria Curie-Sklodowska University) in the west. It passes the urban oasis of the **Ogród Saski** (Saxon Garden) and becomes **al. Racławickie**. Take bus #5, 10, or 13 into town from the bus station. On foot from the castle, climb **ul. Zamkowa**, which runs up to Stare Miasto. Changing names several times to become **ul. Grodzka** and then **ul. Bramowa**, ul. Zamkowa runs through the *rynek*, emerges through **Brama Krakówska** (Kraków Gate), and intersects ul. Krakówskie Przedmieście. From the train station, take trolley #150 or bus #13 to the city center.

Tourist Office: IT, ul. Jezuicka 1/3 (☎532 44 12; itlublin@onet.pl), near the Kraków Gate. Sells maps (5zł) and has train and bus info. Open May-Aug. M-Sa 9am-6pm, Su 10am-3pm; Sept.-Apr. M-F 9am-5pm, Sa-Su 10am-3pm. **Orbis**, ul. Narutowicza 31/33 (☎532 22 56), books tours and transportation. Open M-F 9am-6pm, Sa 9am-2pm.

Currency Exchange: Bank PKO S.A., ul. Królewska 1 (☎532 10 16; fax 532 60 69) cashes **traveler's checks** for 1.5% commission and offers MC/V **cash advances.** Open M-F 8am-6pm, Sa 10am-2pm. **ATMs** are all over town.

English-Language Bookstore: Empik, ul. Krakówskie Przedmieście 59 (☎/fax 534 30 99). Classics and contemporary favorites 25-40zł. Open M-F 9am-7pm, Sa 10am-5pm, Su 11am-4pm.

Emergency: ☎999. **Police:** ☎997.

POLAND

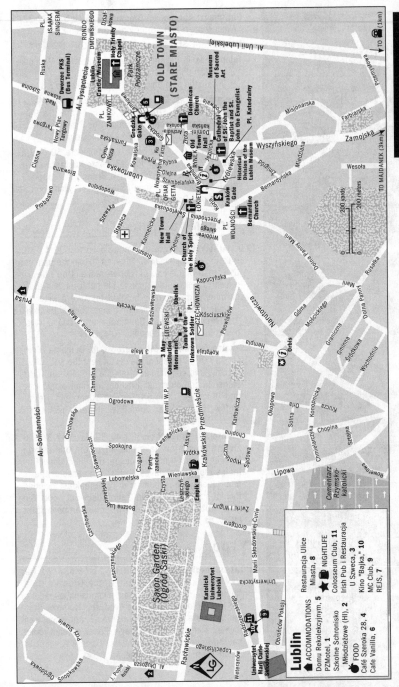

TO 🚉 (1km)

TO MAJDANEK (3km)

Lublin

▲ ACCOMMODATIONS
Domu Rekolekcyjnym, **5**
PZMotel, **1**
Szkolne Schronisko
Młodzieżowe (HI), **2**

◆ FOOD
Café Szeroka 28, **4**
Cafe Vanilla, **6**

Restauracja Ulice
Miasta, **8**
★ 🍸 NIGHTLIFE
Colosseum Club, **11**
Irish Pub i Restauracja
U Szweca, **3**
Kino "Bajka," **10**
MC Club, **9**
REJS, **7**

THE LOCAL STORY

DEVIL'S PAW

n the 17th century, the powerful _ublin Tribunal tried cases that ₁ad originated throughout ²oland. The rich often traveled to ₃ourt a few days ahead of their tri- ₄ls to bribe the corrupt judges. ₅uch was the case of a greedy ₁erchant who sued a poor widow ⱀver an inheritance in 1637. When the judges ruled in the mer- ₃hant's favor, the widow swore ⱀublicly that "devils would have ⱀassed a more just sentence."

That evening at nightfall, a car- ₁age drove up to the town gates. ₁ group of finely dressed gentle- ₁en, horns and tails visible ⱀeneath their robes, stepped from ₁he carriage and reconvened the ₃ourt. The devils retried the case ₁hrough the night, ultimately rul- ₁g in the widow's favor. When ⱀne of the devils announced the ᵣuling, the figure of Jesus hanging ⱀn the courtroom crucifix turned ₁is head away in shame that the ₁evils' judgment had been more ᵤst than the people's. The lead ₁evil then pressed his paw into ₁he judges' table to certify his rul- ₁g, the widow went home with ₁er inheritance, and the devils ₓped off in their carriage.

Today the table imprinted with ₓhat is said to be the devil's paw ₓits in the Lublin Museum, and ₁e abashed crucifix hangs in the ₃hapel of the Holy Sacrament in ₁he Cathedral of St. John.

Pharmacy: Apteka, ul. Bramowa 2/8 (☎535 32 32). Window open 24hr. Store open daily 8am-8pm.

Hospital: Ul. Staszica 16 (☎532 45 20).

Telephones: Inside and outside the post office. Most take only Polish phone cards. Purchase a card from the tellers inside the post office or at most kiosks around town.

Internet Access: Gonet Internet Cafe, ul. Grodzka 21 (☎532 81 18). Open Su-F 10am-10pm, Sa 9am-10pm. **Enzo Internet,** ul. Krakówskie Przedmieście 57 (☎534 75 25), upstairs. M-Sa 9am-10pm.

Post Office: Ul. Krakówskie Przedmieście 50 (☎/fax 532 20 71). Fax at window #3. **Poste Restante** at window #2. Open daily 7am-9pm. **Branch** at Grodzka 7. Open M-F 9am-4pm. June 15th-Aug. 31. also open Sa 11am-6pm. **Postal Code:** 20-950.

▊ ACCOMMODATIONS

▧ **Domu Rekolekcyjnym,** ul. Podwale 15 (☎532 41 38). Buzz the doorbell marked "director." From the train station, take bus #1 to ul. Lubartowska. Don't be surprised to see friendly nuns in full habit tending to the gardens and preparing breakfasts. All are welcome, though unmarried co-eds can't share rooms. Breakfast 7zł. Flexible check-out. Quiet hours after 10pm. No set prices for rooms, but usually 20-40zł. ❶

Szkolne Schronisko Młodzieżowe, ul. Długosza 6 (☎/fax 533 06 28), west of the center near the KUL. Clean, friendly, and communal. A favorite of Polish university students, and often full. Kitchen, open-air picnic area, and TV lounge. Linen 6zł. Lockout 10am-5pm. Flexible curfew 10pm. 10-bed dorm 24zł, students 18zł; triples 84zł/69zł. ❶

PZMotel, ul. Prusa 8 (☎533 42 32; fax 747 84 93). From train station, take bus #1 to the bus station. Nothing special from the outside, but the quality of the rooms more than makes up for the unassuming exterior. Squeaky-clean rooms with TVs. Breakfast included. Reception 24hr. Check-in 2pm. Check-out noon. Singles 140zł; doubles 180zł; 2-person apartment 350zł. MC/V. ❹

🍴 FOOD

▧ **Café Szeroka 28,** ul. Grodzka 21 (☎534 61 09; www.szeroka28.of.pl), close to the Grodzka Gate. Named after the address where a charismatic leader of the Hasidic movement once lived, this homey restaurant and cafe hosts live _klezmer_ music and occasional theater events on its tiny stage. Period-themed rooms pay homage to Lublin's history. Open M-Th and Su 11am-11pm, F-Sa 11am-late. MC/V. ❸

Cafe Vanilla, ul. Krakowskie Przedmiescie 12. Children flock to Cafe Vanilla on weekend afternoons for its architectural ice cream desserts (13-19zł). Adults hold sway the rest of the week in the plush rose interior and at the sidewalk seats in the heart of pedestrian *Krakowskie Przedmieście*. On the menu of crepes, salads, and traditional Polish dishes, the spinach *naleśniki* (12zł) is a standout. The French delicacies give way to drinking as night falls. *Żywiec* 6zł, coffee 6-12zł. Open daily 10am-11pm. AmEx/MC/V. ❶

Restauracja Ulice Miasta, pl. Łokietka 3 (☎534 05 92; www.ulicemiasta.com.pl), in the shadow of the Historical Museum. Betrays a touristy-looking beer garden with delicately prepared "country cuisine" (7-16zł) and dishes such as "the gamekeepers' money bag" (23zł) and venison with cherries (42zł). Open daily 10am-midnight. AmEx/MC/V. ❸

🔵 🌸 SIGHTS AND FESTIVALS

The ochre facades of **ul. Krakówskie Przedmieście** lead into medieval Stare Miasto. Pl. Litewski showcases an **obelisk** commemorating the 1569 union of Poland and Lithuania and a **Tomb of the Unknown Soldier.** Pl. Łokietka, east of pl. Litewski, is home to the 1827 **New Town Hall** (Nowy Ratusz), the seat of Lublin's government. To the right begins ul. Królewska, which runs down around the corner to the grand **Cathedral of St. John the Baptist and St. John the Evangelist** (1586-1596). Ul. Krakówskie Przedmieście runs through pl. Łokietka to the fortified **Kraków Gate,** which houses the **Historical Division of the Lublin Museum** (Oddział Historyczny Muzeum Lubelskiego), pl. Łokietka 3. Exhibits highlight town history in WWII and from 1585 to present. (☎532 60 01. Open Su 9am-5pm, W-Sa 9am-4pm. 2zł, students 1.50zł.) A great view awaits atop the spiral staircase.

Across the gate, ul. Bramowa leads to the *rynek* (market square) and the nearby Renaissance houses. In the *rynek*'s center stands the 18th-century **Old Town Hall** (Stary Ratusz), which also boasts a local history museum in its winding cellars. (Open Su 8am-5pm, W-Sa 8am-4pm. 3.50zł, students 2.50zł). A walk along ul. Grodzka leads through the 15th-century **Grodzka Gate** to ul. Zamkowa, which runs to **Lublin Castle** (Zamek Lubelski). Most of the structure was built in the 14th-century by King Kazimierz Wielki. During the Nazi occupation, the castle functioned as a Gestapo jail. Inside, the permanent collection at the **Lublin Museum** includes wood-carved folk art of the Lublin region, artifacts from nearby archaeological digs, and an exhaustive collection of armaments and military paintings. Temporary exhibits showcase the work of 20th-century Polish painters. The Lublin Museum also houses the famed **Devil's Pawprint** (see sidebar, p. 544). The Russo-Byzantine frescoes in the attached **Holy Trinity Chapel** are truly stunning. The panels, with gold figures depicting various biblical scenes against a midnight-blue background, were completed in 1418. (☎532 50 01, ext. 35. Museum open Su 9am-5pm, W-F 9am-4pm, Sa 10am-5pm. 6.50zł, students 4.50zł. Chapel open Su 9am-4:30pm, M-Sa 9am-3:30pm. 6.50zł, students 4.50zł. Video cameras 4zł.)

The **Archdiocesan Museum of Sacred Art** (Muzeum Archidiecezjalne Sztuki Sakralnej) occupies the 17th-century **Trinitarska Tower** beside the Cathedral. Medieval sacred music wafts through the rafters of this vertical museum as you climb past statues of saints, cherubs, and roosters. A side gallery halfway up the tower holds a 16th-century Madonna, and a panoramic view of Lublin awaits at the top of the tower. (☎743 73 92. Open daily Mar. 25-Nov. 15 10am-5pm. 5zł, students 3zł.)

Poles have a well established tradition of visiting the graves of their deceased loved ones in addition to attending mass on Sundays. They often bring votive flowers and candles and sit for hours praying for and talking with the deceased. After dusk, the flickering votive candles of **Cmentarz Rzymskokatolicki,** Lublin's oldest cemetery, make for an especially stirring experience.

Festivals abound in Lublin. June brings a month-long festival called **Uncover Lublin: Lublin Days** (*Odkryjmy Lublin: Dni Lublin*). The city hosts musical performances and art exhibits. Schedules are available in the tourist office. For more info visit **Nowy Ratusz**, pl. Łokietka 1 (☎444 55 55; www.ym.lublin.pl).

🎵 NIGHTLIFE

Lublin's ample nightlife concentrates in three spots. At the clubs near the intersections of ul. M.C. Skłodowsiej, ul. Akademicka, and ul. Radziszewskiego, students dance and drink well into the morning. An older and tamer crowd convenes at the sidewalk cafes along ul. Krakowskie Przedmieście, while the scenes mingle at the beer gardens that line the Old Town. Travelers can catch Hollywood blockbusters at **Kino "Bajka,"** ul. Radziszewskiego 8 (☎/fax 533 88 72; films start 9:30am-10:15pm; 14zł, students 10zł).

MC Club, ul. MC Skłodowskiej 5 (☎743 65 16; www.mcclub.pl). The hottest club in Lublin winds through the underbelly of the city philharmonium. In one room, DJs spin hip-hop every night; other rooms alternate house with techno for the student crowd. Beer 5zł, mixed drinks 10zł. Cover F-Sa 10zł, Su and Tu-Th 5zł. Open Tu-Su 6pm-3am.

Colosseum Club, Radziszewskiego 8 (☎534 43 00). This booty-shakin' students' favorite will give you ample opportunity to polish up on your English. Huge bar and disco. Mostly techno and pop, although 1 or 2 polka-inspired Polish tunes occasionally slip into the mix. *Hevelius* 4.50zl. Cover varies; usually F-Sa men 10zł, women 5zł. Open daily 8pm-late.

REJS, ul. Krakówskie Przedmieście 55 (☎534 90 37), named after the Polish film of the same name. Funky art student hangout in an intimate cellar that serves Greek and Polish food. *Żywiec* 4.50zł. Open M-F 10am-midnight, Sa-Su noon-midnight.

Irish Pub i Restautracja U Szweca, ul. Grodzka 18 (☎532 82 84). Still lively when the other Stare Miasto beer gardens are closing up for the night, this student outpost makes a halfhearted effort at Irish pub decor yet remains a bastion of pub spirit. *Żywiec* 5zł; Beamish Stout 10zł. Open Su-Th noon-midnight, F-Sa noon-1am. MC/V.

◆ DAYTRIPS FROM LUBLIN

MAJDANEK

*Take bus #28 from the train station, trolley #153 or 156 from al. Racławickie, or trolley #156 from ul. Królewska. Or walk the 4km from Lublin on Królewska, which becomes Wyszyńskiego, Zamojska, Fabryczna, and ultimately the **Droga Męczenników Majdanka** (Road of the Martyrs of Majdanek; 30min). ☎744 26 48; www.majdanek.pl. Open May-Sept. Tu-Su 8am-6pm; Mar.-Apr. and Oct.-Nov. Tu-Su 8am-3pm. Free. Children under 14 not permitted. Tours in Polish 60zł; in English, German, and Russian 100zł per group. Detailed English guide available at the ticket office (7zł); maps free.*

During WWII, the Nazis used Lublin as their eastern base and built a concentration camp in the suburb of Majdanek. About 235,000 died here. Many Warsaw Ghetto residents and Polish political prisoners were sent to Majdanek, which had the highest death rate of any concentration camp. Living conditions were extraordinarily harsh: fed bread made with sawdust, more died from malnutrition and starvation than outright execution. **Majdanek State Museum** was founded in 1944 after the Soviet liberation of Lublin. Since the Nazis didn't have time to destroy the camp, the original structures stand untouched, including the gas chambers, crematorium, prisoners' barracks, watchtowers, guardhouses, and electrified barbwire perimeter. On November 3, the camp holds a memorial service commemorating the day in 1943 when over 18,400 Jews were executed in the largest single mass execution of the Holocaust.

A visit to Majdanek begins in the info building, where a 25min. documentary includes footage taken by the camp's liberators. (Last showing 2:30pm. 3zł. Available in English. Min. 5 people. If you have fewer than 5 people, you can buy the remaining tickets.) Walking through the camp takes 1½-2hr. and the guided tour is worthwhile. It begins with the gas chambers; signs explain Nazi methods of extermination and experimentation. Guardhouses #43-45 contain historical exhibitions, including prisoners' clothes, instruments of torture, and samples of human hair and fabric. An astounding 730kg of human hair was exported to Germany and made into fabric. Exhibits of prisoners' artwork, confiscated religious articles, and photographs of prisoners and camp officials document daily life at Majdanek. Majdanek had the highest percentage of children in any concentration camp, and the collection of toys taken from the children's camp is an especially sobering sight. At the end of the main path, the intact crematorium ovens sit next to the concrete dome of the mausoleum, which stands as a giant open-air urn with a massive mound of ash and human bone. The chilling inscription reads, "Let our fate be a warning for you."

KAZIMIERZ DOLNY

Take the PKS bus from the Lublin bus station to Kazimierz Dolny (1½ hr., 8 per day, 8.10zł). Remember that the last bus back to Lublin leaves Kazimierz around 7pm.

In summer, schoolchildren swarm Kazimierz Dolny's attractive *rynek* to devour bread in the shape of roosters, a local specialty. Tourists visit galleries and dine in garden-side restaurants. The real highlight, however, lies outside of town. A network of hiking trails spreads into the surrounding hills and provides unparalleled views of the Wisła valley. Visit the **tourist office, PTTK**, Rynek 27, for info and 5zł **biking and trail maps**. (☎881 00 46; www.kazimierz-dolny.pl. Open May-Oct. 14 M-F 8am-5:30pm, Sa-Su 10am-5:30pm; Oct. 15-Apr. M-F 8am-4pm, Sa-Su 10am-2:30pm.) Uphill from the *rynek* off ul. Zamkowa, the **castle** (*zamek*) and the restored **watch-tower** (*baszta*) mark the start of two hiking routes (blue and red) and offer panoramas of the town and river. Both were built by Kazimierz the Great in the 14th century, but the castle was destroyed by the Swedes in the 1700s. (Open daily May-Sept. 10am-5pm; Oct.-Apr. Tu-Su 10am-3pm. Admission to both 2.20zł, students 1.60zł.) To the right as you approach the castle on ul. Zamkowa, the hilltop on **Góra Krzyzowa** (Mountain of Crosses) is a scenic picnic spot. (Open daily 10am-5pm, 1zł.) The **Jewish Cemetery,** destroyed when Nazis paved the courtyard of their local headquarters with its tombstones, was reclaimed in 1984 when the powerful "Wailing Wall" was fashioned from 600 of the original tombstones. A symbolic crack is designed into the wall. (2km from the *rynek*. Walk southeast on ul. Senatorska and right on ul. Czerniawy. Free.)

The **folk music festival** that takes over Kazimierz in June is the largest and best folk music gathering in Poland. In mid-summer, Kazimierz hosts the **Lato Filmow film festival** (www.latofilmow.pl). Both the boat bars along the Wisła and the restaurants in town draw patrons with their views of the river. Among the latter, a good choice is **Pod Wietrzną Górą ❷**, ul. Krakówska 1, which serves traditional Polish cuisine. (☎881 06 40. Entrees 15-28zł. Open daily 9am-late. MC/V.)

THE CARPATHIANS (KARPATY)

Once home to only the reclusive and culturally distinct Górale (Highlander) peoples, the Carpathians now lure millions every year to their superb hiking and skiing trails. Zakopane, the heart of the region, gives visitors a taste of local life and provides easy access to excellent trails. The ancient town of Bielsko-Biała preserves medieval Poland against a stunning backdrop of mountain scenery.

POLAND

BIELSKO-BIAŁA ☎ (0)33

Bielsko-Biała (BYEL-skoh BYAH-wah; pop. 180,000) is a composite of two separate towns. Now divided only by the dwindling river *Biała*, the cities were once divided politically. Bielsko spent centuries as part of Bohemia whereas Biała was part of Poland. Though Austrian rule brought the towns together, they were not officially united until 1951. Today, Bielsko-Biala, once nicknamed "Little Vienna," is home to medieval buildings and bustling cobblestone streets.

▐ TRANSPORTATION

Trains: Ul. Warszawska 2 (☎ 94 36). To: **Gdynia** (8½hr., 2 per day, 52-86zł); **Kraków** (1½-2½hr., 4 per day, 11.50-15zł); **Warsaw** (3½-4hr., 5 per day, 43-86zł); **Wrocław** (4-6hr., 3 per day, 25-39zł); **Zakopane** (4hr., 1 per day, 25zł); **Żywiec** (1-1½hr., 21 per day, 5.70zł); **Bratislava, SLK** (6hr.; 1 per day; 131zł, students 99zł).

Buses: Ul. Warszawska 7 (☎ 812 28 25). An overpass connects the bus and train stations. To: **Kraków** (2½hr., 21 per day, 12-15zł); **Oświęcim** (Auschwitz; 1hr., 13 per day, 6.60zł); **Zakopane** (3½hr., 2 per day, 17-19zł); **Żywiec** (50min., 22 per day, 4.60-5.50zł). Bus connections can be unreliable.

Taxis: MPT Taxi ☎ 919.

✦ ▐ ORIENTATION AND PRACTICAL INFORMATION

Bielsko-Biała's centers correspond to the centers of the once separate towns. Biała's more Western-feeling rynek, in the east, is filled with restaurants, shops, and beer gardens. The somewhat larger Bielsko retains a more relaxed atmosphere of quiet cafes and pubs. A 10min. walk along the pedestrian artery ul. 11-go Listopada connects the two city hearts. To get to Biała's center, turn left out of the train station down ul. 3-go Maja. At Hotel Prezydent, go down the long stairs that empty onto ul. 11-go Listopada. To reach Bielsko's rynek, go a bit farther on ul. 3-go Maja and then right up Wzgórze.

Tourist Office: Miejskie Centrum Informacji Turystyczne, pl. Ratuszowy 4 (☎ 819 00 50; www.it.bielsko.pl). From 11-go Listopada, turn right up ul. Ramszowa. Sells **maps** (4-7zł) and **guides** to the city, and helps find rooms. Open M-F 8am-6pm, Sa 8am-4pm.

Currency Exchange: Bank PKO SA, ul. 11-go Listopada 15 (☎ 816 52 31). Exchanges currency, cashes traveler's checks for 1.5% commission (min. 10zł), and has MC/V cash advances. Open M-F 8am-6pm, Sa 9am-1pm.

Emergency: ☎ 999. **Ambulance:** ☎ 812 34 12.

Pharmacy: Apteka Pod Korona, ul. Cechowa 4 (☎ 812 48 93), at the intersection with ul. 11-go Listopada. Open M-F 8am-8pm, Sa 8am-2pm.

Telephones: Inside and across the street from the post office.

Internet Access: Interplay, ul. 11-go Listopada 46 (☎ 507 45 15). 2zł per 30min., 3zł per hr.; 10pm-6am 16zł per hr.

Post Office: Ul. 3-go Maja 2 (☎/fax 822 89 83). Open M-F 9am-8pm. **Poste Restante** at *kasa* #9 (open 7-11:30am and noon-8pm). **Postal Code:** 43-300.

▐ ACCOMMODATIONS

There are few budget options near the main attractions. A better bet is to brave the lengthy bus rides to the surrounding areas and find accommodations there.

TTK Dom Wycieczkowy, ul. Krasińskiego 38 (☎812 30 19). From the bus station, turn right on ul. Piastowska. Peaceful location, comfortable rooms, and shared baths. Linen included. Check-in 2pm. Check-out 10am. Lockout 10am-2pm. Curfew 10pm. Singles with sinks 46zł; doubles with baths 76zł; triples 81zł, with baths 114zł. MC/V. ❷

Schronisko Młodzieżowe "Bolka i Lolka," ul. Starobielska 10 (☎/fax 816 74 66). Go through the bus station to reach ul. Traugutta. Turn left, make a right onto ul. Żeromskiego, a right on ul. Juliusza Słowackiego, and a left on Kresowa. Reception on the 3rd floor. Named after 2 Bielsko-Biała cartoon heroes, this bare-neoclassicist hostel is run by a friendly staff. Check-out 10am. Curfew 10pm. Dorms 12-24zł. ❶

Papuga Park Hotel, ul. Zapora 3 (☎818 58 60; www.papuga.pl). Take bus #16. Expensive and far from the Old City, but idyllic surroundings, large rooms, and baths warrant the price. Breakfast included. Tennis courts on grounds. Check-in 2pm. Check-out noon. Singles 218-288zł; doubles 278-348zł; triples 428zł; quads 488zł. AmEx/MC/V. ❺

🍴 FOOD

Grocery stores, bakeries, butcher shops, and bars abound on the central **ul. 11-go Listopada.** Actual restaurants are hard to find, and authentic Polish fare is elusive as Westernized locals devour pizza and burgers. Silesia has few regional dishes other than *Kluski Śląskie*, a boiled potato and flour mixture served with anything from fruit to meat. **Savia,** ul. 11-go Listopada 38 (☎812 35 44), stocks groceries. (Open M-F 6:30am-9pm, Sa 6:30am-8:30pm, Su 8am-4pm. MC/V.)

Bar Muzyczny "Nirvana," ul. Cechowa 18 (☎003 811 02 44), off 11-go Listopada. A veggie heaven, Nirvana is a delicious break from Poland's limited selection of meatless fare. Try soy creations that mimic regional favorites like *bigos* (7.50zł) and *fasolka po bretońsku* (7zł). Entrees 6.50-15zł. *Petry zestaw*, with soup, entree, and dessert (15zł). Open M-Sa 11am-11pm, Su 1-11pm. AmEx/MC/V. ❷

Pod Jemiolami, ul. Cechowa 6 (☎815 08 97), near the corner of ul. 11-go Listopada and 3-go Maja; go downstairs. Cozy, traditionally decorated bistro features various Polish dishes. Entrees 10-20zł. Open daily 9am-10pm. MC/V. ❷

Magnum Steak Pub, ul. Ratusowa 3 (☎816 53 39), off ul. 11-go Listopada. The easy-going atmosphere invites you to pull up a chair and devour a hearty steak (16-26zł) with an ice-cold beer (4-11zł). Open M-F noon-2am, Sa-Su noon-4am. AmEx/MC/V.❸

Morago, 11-go Listopada 32 (☎811 89 46). Situated on one of the town's main streets, this ice cream eatery will leave you blissfully breathless. M-Sa 11am-9pm. Cash only. ❶

Restauracia "Pirat," ul. Komorowicka 7 (☎816 68 46), off ul. 11-go Listopada. This seaworthy restaurant serves up tantalizing fish and poultry dishes with fries, soup, and salad included. Entrees 7.90-16zł. 10% student discount. Open daily 11am-9pm. ❷

👁 SIGHTS

CASTLE. Bielsko's 14th-century castle looms above pl. Chrobrego. It offers a "history tour" of Bielsko-Biała from prehistoric to modern times, a modest armory, and an impressive collection of art. Works include 17th-19th-century European paintings and several pieces by preeminent artists of the *Young Poland (Młodej Polski)* Movement. The last room contains modern surrealist art as well as works by local artists. (*Ul. Wzgórze 16.* ☎816 86 86; *www.muzeum.bielsko.pl. Open Tu and Sa 10am-3pm, W and Th 10am-6pm, F 11am-7pm, Su 10am-4pm. Guided tour 15zł, call ahead. Castle 7zł, students 4zł.*)

MUSEUMS. Travel a bit off the beaten path to experience **Dom Tkacza,** an 18th-century weaver's home. To reach this historic house, follow Wzgórze from the castle past the small *rynek.* From ul. Cieszyriskiego turn right on Piwowarska, then left onto Jana Sobieskiego. This house-museum offers a glimpse into the textile industry that put Bielsko-Biała on the map. (☎811 71 76; *www.muzeum.bielsko.pl. Open Feb.-Sept. Tu 9am-5pm, W and F 9am-3pm, Th 10am-6pm, Sa 10am-3pm; Oct.-Jan. Tu 9am-5pm, W and F 9am-3pm, Th 9am-5pm, Sa 10am-3pm. 2zł, students 1zł.)* Remnants of Bielsko-Biała's cloth trade and the city inhabitants' everyday lives are on display at **Muzeum Techniki.** Display items range from old kitchen appliances to washers and even vacuums. *(Ul. Sukiennicza 7. ☎812 23 67; www.muzeum.bielsko.pl. Open Feb.-Sept. Tu-W 9am-3pm, Th 10am-5pm, Sa 10am-3pm, F and Su 10am-6pm; Oct.-Jan. Tu-W 9am-3pm, Th 10am-5pm, F 9am-5pm, Sa 10am-3pm, Su 10am-6pm. 5zl, students 3zl.)*

CHURCHES. Visible from most of Bielsko-Biała, **St. Nicholas's Cathedral** (Katedra św. Mikołaja) was promoted from provincial status a few years ago when the Pope made the parish a bishop. Austrian influence is apparent in every pore of the beautiful chapel. Pay special attention both to the intricate steeple and to the depictions of the apostles on the elaborate door. Once inside, look up at the eye-capturing Last Supper mural. *(Pl. Mikolaja 19. Follow directions to Bielsko's rynek and turn left on ul. Koscielna. M-Sa 9am-5pm, Su service varies.)* Built in 1782, the **Lutheran Church** (Kościół Ewangelicko-Augsburski) features Poland's only **statue of Martin Luther.** *(Pl. Lutra 8. Follow directions to the castle, but go straight through pl. Chrobrego. ☎812 74 71. Open M-F 9am-noon and 2-6pm, Sa 9-11am, Su afternoon service.)*

BEER. Twenty-one kilometers south of Bielsko-Biała lies the quiet town of Żywiec (ZHI-vyets), home to Poland's best-known, hardest-hitting namesake. Once you arrive in town, the best way to get to the brewery is to take bus #1 or 5 from the train station. Buy tickets at the kiosk next to the bus stop (2zł, students 1zł). **Trans-Trade Żywiec,** ul. Browarna 90, Poland's own factory of bottled miracles, is the second stop after the bridge. Call ahead (☎861 99 03) and ask to speak to Master Duda to arrange a free tour (min. 15 people) of the brewery, or attach yourself to a group scheduled to visit. Next door **Żywiecka Pub,** ul. Browarna 88, a *piwiarnia* (beer-garden), sells possibly the cheapest, freshest beer (3zł per 0.5L) in Poland. Drink at the pub or buy beer at the gift shop. *(☎861 96 17. Open Su-Th 11am-11pm, F-Sa 11am-midnight.)*

🎵 🎭 ENTERTAINMENT AND NIGHTLIFE

The Żywiec flows freely in Bielsko-Biała. Settle into a quiet cafe or mellow beer-garden in Biała or dance the night away at one of the many establishments that line ul. Wygórze and ul. Podcienie near Bielsko's *rynek.*

Galeria Wygórze, ul. Wygórze 6 (☎812 27 05). Uphill from the castle, this pub and gallery combo showcases works of local artists—adding to the mellow and relaxed atmosphere—and invites locals of mixed ages to chat endlessly over drinks. Beer 4.50zł. Tea 2.50zł. Salsa night F 7pm. Open daily 11am-3am. ❶

Grawitacja Kawiarnia (Gravity Cafe), ul. Wzgórze 5 (www.pogodzinach.net). The joke on this establishment's name hits you when you walk in to find tables, chairs, bikes, and even a saxophone stuck to the ceiling. Low-key atmosphere draws coffee-bound dreamers to read by candlelight, while others join the surreal atmosphere with a cold beer (5zł). 18+. Open daily 5pm-midnight. ❶

Bazyliszek Pub and Gallery, ul. Wygórze 8 (☎812 23 03), across from Grawitacja Cafe. Artwork adorns the walls, and the artists themselves may be around, enjoying a beer (4.50zł) or live jazz. Open M-F 2-10pm, Sa-Su 4pm-midnight. ❶

ZAKOPANE   ☎(0)18

Zakopane (zah-ko-PAH-neh; pop. 28,000) is set in a valley surrounded by jagged Tatran peaks and alpine meadows. During the high season (June-Sept. and Dec.-Feb.), the heavily touristed city swells to over 100,000. Though Zakopane draws many visitors to its trails and slopes, guests can also explore the town's native Highlander culture, which endures in the region's everday life.

▐ TRANSPORTATION

Trains: Ul. Chramcówki 35 (☎201 45 04). To: **Częstochowa** (4hr., 3 per day, 42zł); **Kraków** (3-4hr., 19 per day, 20zł); **Poznań** (11hr., 2 per day, 49zł); **Warsaw** (8hr., 8 per day, 46-80zł).

Buses: Ul. Kościuszki 25 (☎201 46 03). To: **Bielsko-Biała** (3½hr., 2 per day, 16zł); **Kraków** (2-2½hr., 22 per day, 8zł); **Warsaw** (8½hr., 2 per day, 53zł). An **express bus** runs to **Kraków** (2hr., 15 per day, 10zł); buses leave from the "express" stop on ul. Kościuszki, 50m toward ul. Krupówki from the bus station.

Taxis: Interradio Taxi ☎96 21. **Radio Taxi** ☎919. **Zielone Taxi** ☎96 62.

Bike Rental: Sukces, ul. Nowotarska 39 (☎200 02 31) and ul. Sienkiewicza 39 (☎201 48 44), rents bikes (20zł per 4hr., 35zł per day), skis, and snowboards (35-50zł). Open daily July-Aug. 10am-5pm; June and Sept. Sa-Su. Call Oct.-May.

✦ 🛈 ORIENTATION AND PRACTICAL INFORMATION

The main drag in town is ul. Kościuszki, where you'll find most of the city's shopping, eating, and nighttime activity. The **bus station** sits on the intersection of **ul. Kościuszki** and **ul. Jagiellońska** and faces the **train station**. The town center is 15min. down ul. Kościuszki, which intersects **ul. Krupówki**. The **Tatras** spread around Zakopane.

Tourist Offices: Tourist Agency Redykołka, ul. Kościeliska 1 (☎201 32 53; www.tatra-tours.pl). Arranges private rooms for 10% commission, runs tours (4hr., 320zł per group) around Zakopane and organizes out-of-town excursions. Open M-F 9am-5pm, Sa 9am-1pm. **Centrum Informacji Turystycznej (CIT),** ul. Kościuszki 17 (☎201 22 11), provides regional info on topics from dining to hiking. Sells maps (4-7zł) and guides (11-28zł), offers help in locating a room, and books rafting trips on the Dunajec (see **Daytrip From Zakopane,** p. 556). Open daily 8am-8pm. **Sinus,** ul. Zaruskiego 5 (☎201 34 48; www.sinus.zakopane.pl), organizes guided trips around the Tatras (120zł) and rock-climbing and parasailing excursions. Open M-F 9am-5pm, Sa 9am-1pm.

Currency Exchange: Bank PKO SA, ul. Krupówki 71 (☎201 40 48), cashes **traveler's checks** for 1.5% commission (min. 10zł) and gives AmEx/MC/V **cash advances.** Open M-F 8am-7pm, Sa 8am-2pm. **Bank BPH,** ul. Krupówki 19 (☎080 132 13 21; www.bph-pbk.pl), offers **Western Union** services. AmEx/MC/V **ATMs** line ul. Krupówki.

Luggage Storage: At the train station. 4zł per day, plus 0.45zł per 50zł declared value. Lockers also in the train station. Small 4zł per day, large 8zł per day. Open daily 7am-1pm and 1:30-9pm. At the bus station. 3zł per day. Open daily 8am-7pm.

Police: ul. Jagiellońska 32 (☎201 32 11).

Pharmacy: ul. Krupówki 39 (☎206 33 31). Open M-Sa 8am-6pm.

Medical Assistance: Ambulance ☎992. **Mountain Rescue Service,** ul. Piłsudskiego 63a (☎206 34 44). **Samodzielny Publiczny Zakład Opieki Zdrowotnej** (Independent Public Enterprise of Healthcare), ul. Kamieniec 10 (☎/fax 201 53 51). Emergency room and ambulance service.

POLAND

Telephones: Telekomunikacja Polska, ul. Zaruskiego 1 (☎ 020 21 22; www.telekomuni-kacjapolska.pl). Open M-F 8am-5pm, Sa 9am-1pm.

Internet Access: Widmo Internet Cafe, ul. Gen. Galicy 8 (☎ 206 43 77; cafewidmo@wp.pl), offers fair rates. 1zł per 10min., 4zł per hr.; 10pm-7am 15zł. Open M-F 7:30am-midnight, Sa-Su 9am-midnight.

Post Office: ul. Krupówki 20 (☎ 206 38 58). **Poste Restante** at *kasa* #10. Open M-F 8am-8pm, Sa 8am-2pm, Su 10am-noon. **Postal Code:** 34-500.

ACCOMMODATIONS

Lodgings in Zakopane are not difficult to find, and reservations are generally unneccessary. While peak season (June-Sept. and Dec.-Feb.) sees an influx of tourists and a steep hike in prices, more **private rooms** (30-50zł) become available. Solicitors sell lodgings outside bus and train stations. Ul. Chramocówki has many *noclegi, Zimmer frei,* and *pokój* (room) signs. Hikers and skiers often stay in *schroniska* (mountain huts), but these fill quickly, so call two to three weeks ahead during high season.

Schronisko Morskie Oko (☎ 207 76 09; www.morskieoko.lapinska.prv.pl), perched above Zakopane on Morskie Oko. From the bus station, take the bus to Palenice Białczanśka (45min., 11 per day, 4zł) or a direct minibus from opposite the station (20min., 5zł). Hike the remaining distance on a paved road to the hostel (1-2hr.) or catch a horse-drawn wagon from the parking lot (30zł up, 15zł down). Situated right on the most scenic path, this immensely popular hostel is ideal for hikers. Linen 7zł. Reception 8:30am-9pm. Check-in noon. Check-out 10am. Quiet hours 10pm-6am. Reserve 2 months ahead in high season. June 15-Oct. 3- to 6-bed dorms 41zł, 8- to 12-bed dorms 32zł. Nov.-June 14 33zł/22zł. ●

Hotel Kasprowy Wierch, ul. Krupówki 50B (☎ 201 27 38; www.wierch.com). This hotel is clean, spacious, and nestled perfectly in the town center. The staff is remarkably friendly and the atmosphere is lively. Reception 24hr. Check-out noon. Singles 180zł; doubles 200zł; triples 300zł. MC/V. ❸

Camping Pod Krokwią, ul. Żeromskiego (☎ 201 22 56; www.mati.com.pl/camp). Views of the Tatras, well-kept grounds, friendly staff, and proximity to the hiking center of Kuźnice are perfect for outdoor fanatics. Reception 24hr. Check-out noon. Open July-Aug. 7zł per tent, large 9zł; camper 20zł. Bungalow 12-20zł; bed in house 30zł; room 35-40zł; 4- to 6-person apartments with kitchen and TV 140-200zł. MC/V. ●

FOOD

Restaurants run the gamut from famous Western chains to traditional mountain eateries. Highlanders sell the local specialty, *oscypek* (smoked goat cheese; 1-18zł), carved in delightful designs. If your Westernized palate doesn't agree with the warm beer and wine, try the local favorite *herbate ceperska* (25ml vodka with 50ml tea). For a respite, try the **Delikatesy** grocery store, ul. Krupówki 41. (☎ 201 25 83. Open M-Sa 7am-8pm. MC/V.) Alternatively, check out **Super Sam,** ul. Kościuszki 3. (☎ 200 19 10. Open 24hr.; low season M-Sa 24hr., Su 6pm-7am. AmEx/MC/V.)

Czarny Staw, ul. Krupówki 2 (☎ 201 38 52). Locals and tourists alike clamor to find seats at this traditional restaurant, where the fusion of Western and Polish tastes creates an eclectic and savory dining experience. Wine and beer accompany the delicious meal. Entrees 12-22zł. Open 10am-midnight. MC/V. ❸

Pizzeria Restauracja "Adamo," ul. Nowotarska 10d (☎201 52 90), has both Polish dishes and pizza in a setting that exudes the Italian/Polish cultural mix. *Danie dnia* (daily special; 11am-3pm; 13-16zł) includes soup, entree, coffee, and dessert. Entrees 5-31zł. Pizza 7.50-22zł. Open daily 11am-midnight. AmEx/MC/V. ❷

Bakowa-Zohylina, ul. Piłsudskiego 28a (☎206 63 16; www.zohylina.pl), serves traditional dishes like goulash (17zł) and the region's favorite, *pstrąg* (trout; 25zł). Dine in the mountain lodge atmosphere complete with animal pelts, an open hearth, and waiters in traditional dress, or sit in the garden for a view of Krokiew Mountain. Second location on ul. Piłsudskiego. Entrees 13-28zł. Open daily 1pm-midnight. MC/V. ❸

Bar Mleczny, ul. Weteranów Wojny 2 (☎206 62 57), off Krupówki. The homey atmosphere of this tiny "milk bar" matches its tasty cooking. For a true taste of Polish cuisine, try the *pierogi ruskie* (dumplings with potatoes and cheese; 5zł) or the scrumptious *omlet* (pancake with berries and whipped cream; 5.50zł). Entrees 3-10zł. Open daily 9am-8pm. ❶

POLAND

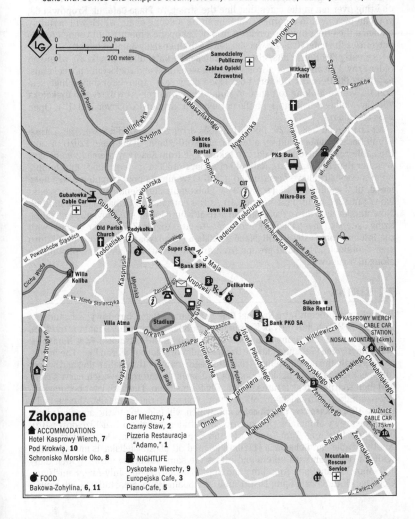

Zakopane

🏠 ACCOMMODATIONS
Hotel Kasprowy Wierch, **7**
Pod Krokwią, **10**
Schronisko Morskie Oko, **8**

🍎 FOOD
Bakowa-Zohylina, **6, 11**

Bar Mleczny, **4**
Czarny Staw, **2**
Pizzeria Restauracja
"Adamo," **1**

🎵 NIGHTLIFE
Dyskoteka Wierchy, **9**
Europejska Cafe, **3**
Piano-Cafe, **5**

◐ ♫ SIGHTS AND ENTERTAINMENT

Zakopane is primarily an outdoors destination, but you will see both the colorful Highlander and the modern tourist meander through the town's streets, as there are a variety of vibrant things to see and do. There are seven houses along ul. Kościeliska designed by architect and artist **Jan Witkiewicz**, the most famous of which was occupied by the Polish writer **Stanisław Ignacy Witkiewicz** in the 1930s. Stop by the **Tytus Chałubiński Tatra Museum** (Muzeum Tatrzańskie), ul. Krupówki 10, for an in-depth look at the geography and ecology of the Tatras. The museum also has exhibits displaying the interiors of a traditional Highlander house and regional devices and costumes. (☎201 52 05. Open Tu-Sa 9am-5pm, Su 9am-3pm. English info.)

In the evening **ul. Krupówki** fills with locals and tourists enjoying ice cream or chatting over tea in the cafes that line the street. At **Piano-Cafe**, ul. Krupówki 63, you can burrow into a corner couch or sit on a swing chair, which will certainly enhance the effect of your drinks. A mix of Zakopane's mature and young crowds patronizes the cafe. (0.5L Żywiec 4zł, tea 2.5zł. Open daily 3pm-midnight.) To experience early 80s Polish hits, check out **Europejska Cafe**, ul. Krupówki 37, where an older crowd unwinds over a frosty beer on weekdays and rocks out on weekends. (☎201 22 00. Beer 5zł. Dessert 4-6zł. Open daily 8am-11pm, later during high season.) If you're looking to dance to pop with a younger crowd, try the **Dyskoteka Wierchy**, Małkoszyńskiego 1, on the corner of ul. Krupówki. (Cover 10zł. 18+. Open F-Sa 9am-3am.)

Air-Taxi (☎060 228 75 28; fax 201 37 95) arranges **paragliding** over the Tatras. Climb **Nosal Mountain** and try a **tandem jump** (10-20min. flying time; 120zł) or take the cable car to the top and dare to take a dive from **Kasprowy Wierch** (30min.-3hr., weather dependent; 300zł). **Natural hot springs** (1600m underground) that bubble up at a cozy 30°C have been turned into the swimming pool complex **Basen Antalowka**, ul. Jagiellońska 18. (☎206 39 34. Open daily July-Sept. 8am-8pm. Day pass 9am-5pm 12zł, night pass 5-8pm 6zł.) At the entrance to Onbatówka, behind ul. Nowotarska, step into a daily **open-air market** where locals sell souvenirs and tantalizing *oscypek* (sheep cheese). From mid- to late-August, Zakopane resounds with the **International Festival of Highlander Folklore** (Międzynardowy Festival Folkloro ziem Górskich). Highland groups from around the world dance and play music along ul. Krupówki.

♦ HIKING

Poland's magnificent **Tatra National Park** (Tatrzański Park Narodowy; 3zł, students 1.50zł; see Polish and Slovak Tatras map, p. 822) is Zakopane's main attraction. Before heading out, consult a good map, such as the **Tatrzański Park Narodowy: Mapa Turystyczna** (7zł), and choose trails as calm or rigorous as you like. The best—and certainly the most popular—place to begin many of the challenging and scenic hikes is **Kuźnice.** Take ul. Jagiellońska and walk up the road, which curves right and then sharply left as it turns into ul. Chałubińskiego. The path later becomes ul. Przewodników Tatrzańskich; follow it until you reach the trailheads. Alternatively, try the 1987m **Kasprowy Wierch cable car,** which will take you to the amazing views atop Kasprowy Mountain. (Round-trip 28zł, students 18zł; up 18zł/13zł; down 10zł/5zł. Open July-Aug. 7am-7pm; June and Sept. 7:30am-4pm; Oct. 7:30am-3pm.) Another cable car, **Gubałówka** (1120m), located off ul. Kościeliska, is more popular with tourists than with hikers and offers the same dramatic views. (Open daily Jan.-Mar. 7:30am-9pm; Apr.-June and Sept. 8:30am-7:20pm; July-Aug. 8am-10pm; Oct.-Dec. 15th 8:30am-6pm; Dec. 15th-31st 7:30am-10pm. 8zł, students 5zł; round-trip 14zł/10zł.) Or get to the trailheads and cable car by taking a *"mikro-bus"* Sheep, huts, and fast-food restaurants populate the slopes. Walk down to Zakopane (30min.), or take the blue, black, or red trail to **Butorowy Wierch** (30min.) and descend via the chairlift. (Open daily May-Sept. 9am-6pm; Mar.-Apr. and Oct. 9am-5pm; Jan.-Feb. and Nov. 9am-4pm; Dec. 9am-3pm. 5zł, round-trip 9zł.)

⛰VALLEY OF THE FIVE POLISH TARNS

Called the Dolina Pięciu Stawów Polskich, this hike is perfect if you have time for only one trail. It covers all the major highlights in the nearby Tatras. An intense full-day hike takes you past five lakes between sharp peaks: Wielki ("enormous"), Czarny ("black"), Przedni ("front"), Zadni ("rear"), and Mały ("small"). Start this beautiful and rewarding hike at **Kuźnice** and follow the yellow trail through **Dolina Jaworzynka** (Jaworzynka Valley) until you reach the steep blue trail, which leads to **Hala Gasienicowa** and the nearby mountain hut **Schronisko Murowaniedc.** (☎ 0165 126 33; www.murowaniec.pttk.pl. Dorms 24-30zl). From the mountain shelter, the trail continues to **Czarny,** a tranquil lake which mirrors the tallest peaks of the Tatras. Continue on the blue trail to **Zawrat Peak,** where you'll have to use mountain chains and natural holds. Once you cross Zawrat, breathtaking views of the valley and its lakes await, along with Przedni and a *schronisko,* where you can refuel or spend the night. (☎207 76 07. Linen 5zl. Beds 21-25zl.) Those ready to go on can take the blue trail (2hr.) to **Morskie Oko** and the popular *schronisko,* which rests on its shores facing the impressive Rysy. Take a microbus back to Zakopane (10zl) or hike backward or onward (see Morskie Oko, p. 555). A **shorter version** of the hike (4-6hr.) begins at Palenica Białczańska. Head toward Morskie Oko, as described above. The green trail breaks off to the right, leads past the crashing Mickiewicza Waterfalls, and ends on a small bridge near the *schronisko* of the Five Polish Tarns, merging into the blue trail. Follow the blue trail to the majestic Morskie Oko Lake.

SEA EYE (MORSKIE OKO)

Glacial Morskie Oko Lake, surrounded by dramatic peaks, dazzles herds of tourists every summer. Take a bus from the PKS station to Palenica Białczańska. (45min., 11 per day, 4zl.) Alternatively, take a private microbus from across the street. (30-40min., 5zl.) A 9km paved road leads to the lake, which is fabled to connect to the Baltic Sea. Alternatively, take the green trail to the blue trail (4hr.) for an astounding view of Morskie Oko. *(Hike is 1406m. Takes 5-6hr.)*

STRAŻYSKA VALLEY (DOLINA STRAŻYSKA)

This trail is pleasant and easy to navigate. Walk down ul. Koscieliska and head left on ul. Kasprusie, which becomes ul. Strązyska, to the entrance to the **Tatras National Park** (30-45min.). Follow the lush forested path along streams until it ends at the dramatic **Siklawica waterfall.** Take the path to your right to **Mt. Sarnia Skala.** The peak offers unspoiled views of Zakopane and Mt. Giewont. *(Trail takes 4-5hr.)*

GIEWONT

This popular trail traverses Giewont, a mountain whose silhouette resembles a man lying down. Legend dictates that the mountain is a sleeping prince, and if the town of Zakopane is in trouble, he will awaken and defend it. To remind tourists and locals of Highlander faith, a priest placed an enormous cross on the peak. The moderately difficult blue trail (7km, 3hr.) leads to the summit. The path becomes much rockier toward **Hala Kondratowa** (☎0 165 152 14). Here a variety of fast-food restaurants and local stalls await weary travelers. The trail wraps around the ridge of Giewont's peak and leads to the tricky final ascent; here, chains and footholds

ne summit offers a striking view of Zakopane and the icy peaks
m the peak, take the yellow trail to Kondracka Kopa to reach the
eturn to Zakopane on the red trail to Strążyska Polina. For a **shorter**
the red trail from Strążyska Polina (2½hr.) and continue on the blue
uźnice (2½-3hr.) or on the yellow trail that leads to the Czerwone
. *(Trail begins at Kuznice. Hike is 1894m. Takes 6½hr.)*

.D PEAKS (CZERWONE WIERCHY)

This less rocky range is full of mild dips and ascents, during which the trail crosses
between the Polish and Slovak border. Three of the **Red Peaks** that follow
Kasprowy Wierch have trails that allow tired tourists to return to Zakopane, while
the last peak, Ciemniak, continues to **Schronisko na Hali Ornak** (☎ 165 705 10; 3hr.).
It passes through **Kościeliska Valley** and ends in **Kiry** (4hr.). For a direct descent, follow the red trail to its end at **Kiry** (3hr.). The heights of the ridge are known as "Red
Peaks" because native plants blossom throughout the area each autumn, coloring
the rocks. *(Take a right onto the red trail at the top of Kasprowy Wierch. Hike is 2122m and
takes a full day.)*

⬛ DAYTRIP FROM ZAKOPANE

DUNAJEC GORGE

*Take the bus (1-2hr., 10zł) toward Szczawnica and get off at Kąty. Depart early to make
the best use of the day—the 1st bus leaves Zakopane at 9am. Buses run from Szczawnica
(where the trip ends) back to Zakopane (1.5hr., 12zł). A better way to reach the gorge is
to arrive by microbus (13zł) and experience the rafting trip by scheduling an outing
through a tourist agency (see p. 551). Many packages include trips to Dunajec Castle.
Rafting tickets 40zł plus a 2zł entrance fee.*

Both residents and tourists embrace rafting along the Dunajec in **Pieniński National
Park** (☎ 262 56 01; fax 262 56 03). The calm and beautiful ride traces the steep peaks
and rolling forests dividing Poland from the Slovak Republic to the east. To complement the scenery, the guides sport traditional Highlander garb. Travelers
shouldn't expect death-defying rafting—the smooth ride is virtually splashless. Yet
the waters afford unparalleled views of Trzy Korony (Three Crowns Peak) and
Dunajec Castle. Unaccompanied rafting is not permitted. Visits to the 13th-century
castle are best arranged through tourist agencies in Zakopane. Legend has it that a
man drowned his unfaithful wife in the castle well; if you shout into the well, an
unfaithful lover will go bald.

The end of the 2hr. excursion leaves you in the town of Szczawnica. While Szczawnica is armed with souvenir stands and crowded bars, those seeking to savor
the outdoors can rent bikes to tour the city or take leisurely rides near the river.
Rent bikes at ul. Pienińska 6, a left turn from the raft drop-off point. (☎ 262 12 46.
4zł per hr., 20zł per day. Open daily 8am-9pm.) To ride along the Polish riverside
walkway, you must cross into the Slovak Republic. Alternatively, walkers can
follow the pathway that runs along the river for splendid views of the hills along
the border. Those wishing to wander off the path can take the chair lift (9am-
7.30pm, 10zł) and explore mountain paths with views of Szczawnica.

SILESIA (ŚLĄSK)

Poles have long treasured Silesia for the rough-hewn beauty of its limestone crags,
pine forests, and medieval castles. The region's industrial lowlands bear scars
from the uncontrolled Five-Year Plans of the communist era, but the mountains

remain pristine and lightly touristed. From the cultural hubs of Wrocław and Częstochowa, hiking and bicycle trails fan out into Karkonosze National Park and the Jura Uplands.

CZĘSTOCHOWA ☎(0)34

In 1382, a haggard traveler arrived in Częstochowa (chen-sto-HO-va) weary from her tribulations and scarred from a scuffle with Hussite thieves. The visitor, a Byzantine icon painting in the prime of her life at only 800 years old, found refuge atop the hill of Jasna Góra and entrusted herself to the care of the monks living there. Since she moved in, the city has been defined by little other than her presence. As the most sacred of Polish icons, she draws millions of Catholic pilgrims every year. They, and other visitors, flock to the city to catch a glimpse of her, the Black Madonna .

TRANSPORTATION AND PRACTICAL INFORMATION. Trains run to **Częstochowa Główna PKP,** ul. Piłsudskiego 38 (☎366 47 89; fax 366 47 63). To: **Gdynia** (7¼- 9½hr., 6 per day, 50zł); **Kraków** (2-2½hr., 6 per day, 25-28zł); **Łódź** (2hr., 8 per day, 31zł); **Poznań** (6hr., 3 per day, 42zł); **Warsaw** (3hr., 10 per day, 38zł); **Wrocław** (3-4hr., 4 per day, 32zł); **Zakopane** (7hr., 3 per day, 40zł). **Buses** go to **PKS,** ul. Wolności 45/49 (☎361 53 37). Left on ul. Wolności from train station. To: **Kraków** (3-3½hr., 7 per day, 12-24zł); **Łódź** (3hr., 8 per day, 17-24zł); **Lublin** (7hr., 1 per day, 46zł); **Warsaw** (3½-5hr., 6 per day, 33-37zł); **Wrocław** (4hr., 5 per day, 20-25zł); and **Zakopane** (5hr., 2 per day, 35zł). **Tram** and **bus** tickets cost 2zł per person and per backpack, students 1zł. 1-day pass 7zł, students 3.50zł. Stops on al. Najświętszej Marii Panny appear on bus schedules as Aleja I, II, and III. For taxi service, call **Auto Radio** (☎96 29) or **Carex** (☎96 26). The meter starts at 4zł. 2zł per km. The **train** and **bus stations** lie across the post office parking lot from each other and are between al. Wolności and ul. Piłsudskiego, by the town center. **Al. Najświętszej Marii Panny (NMP)** links them to **Jasna Góra,** whose spire is visible from almost anywhere in town. From either station, go right on al. Wolności to get to al. NMP. Take a left to reach Jasna Góra.

The **tourist office, MCI,** al. NMP 65 (☎368 22 50; www.czestochowa.um.pl), provides **free maps.** (Open M-F 9am-5pm, Sa-Su 9am-2pm.) **Bank Pekao S.A.,** ul. M. Kopernika 17/19 (☎365 50 60), cashes **traveler's checks** for 1% commission (min. 10zł) and gives MC/V **cash advances.** 24hr. **ATM** outside. Open M-F 8am-6pm, Sa 10am-2pm. **Punkt Medyczny Jasna Góra,** (☎377 72 45), at the monastery, can provides medical assistance. Open daily 6am-7:30pm, in winter 8am-4:30pm. **Ambulance** ☎999. **Post Office:** ul. Orzechowskiego 7 (☎324 29 59), between the bus and train stations. **Poste Restante** available at kasa 9. Open M-F 7am-9pm, Sa 8am-8pm. **Postal Code:** 42-200.

ACCOMMODATIONS AND FOOD. Reservations are recommended year-round, but are a must for May and August when pilgrims descend en masse. **Internat TZN** ❶, ul. Jasnogórska 84/96, is a youth hostel, but it's only open during July and August. (☎324 31 21. 15zł.) Many pilgrims use the quiet, immaculate rooms at **Dom Pielgrzyma im. Jana Pawla II** (The Pilgrim's House) ❶, ul. Wyszyńskiego 1, as a home base. From the train or bus station, take any bus to the end of al. NMP and cross through the Jasna Góra. Dom Pielgrzyma is at the exact opposite side of the monastery from al. NMP, near the monastery gates. (☎377 75 64. Quiet hours 10pm-5:30am. Check-in 3pm-10pm. Check-out 9am. Lockout 9am-3pm. Curfew 10pm. Dorms 22zł; singles 90zł; doubles 120zł; triples 105zł. MC/V.) Częstochowa's restaurants and ice cream stands keep both pilgrims and locals well-fed. The gigantic **Supermarket Billa,** in the red building across from the bus station, is a good place to stock up on supplies. (Open M-F 8am-9pm, Sa 8am-8pm, Su 9am-4pm.) With a garden facing neo-Byzantine Biegańskiego Square and a cool stone interior, tranquil **Cafe Skrzynka ❷**, ul. Dąbrowskiego 1, specializes in dessert and dinner crepes (6-18zł). Extensive coffee (5-10zł) and mixed drink (9-16zł) menu. (☎324 30 98. Open daily 8am-10pm.) **Pod Gruszką** (Under the Pear) ❶, al. NMP 37, serves coffee, tea, and hot chocolate (3-4zł) in a tree-shaded courtyard. (☎365 44 90. Open M-Th 10am-10pm, F-Sa 10am-midnight, Su 4pm-10pm.) Attached to the Dom Pielgrzyma, **Restauracja and Bar Dom Pielgrzyma**, ul. Wyszynkiego 1 ❶, is a devout variation on the milk bar that serves up hearty *pierogi* and *kotlets* (3-6zł). Beet and *flaki* soups (2-5zł). (☎377 75 64. Open daily 7am-8pm.)

◙ SIGHTS. The **Paulite Monastery** (Klasztor Paulinów), on top of **Jasna Góra** (Bright Mountain), is one of the world's largest pilgrimage sites. Founded in 1382, the monastery exterior, which resembles a Baroque fortress, belies its sanctity. Jasna Góra welcomes masses of pilgrims who come to see the reportedly miraculous **Black Madonna** (Czarna Madonna). The ornate 15th-century **Basilica** houses the icon inside the small **Chapel of Our Lady** (Kaplica Matki Bożej). Countless crutches, medallions, and rosaries strung up on the chapel walls attest to the pilgrims' faith in the painting's healing powers, while several jewel-encrusted robes crafted by devotees decorate the Madonna herself. The icon is veiled and revealed several times a day, with solemn festivities. (Chapel open daily 5am-9:30pm. Icon revealed Sept.-May M-F 6am-noon, 3-7pm, and 9-9:15pm; Sa-Su and holidays 6am-1pm, 3-7pm, and 9-9:15pm. June-Aug. M-F 6am-noon and 1-9:15pm; Sa-Su and holidays 2-9:15pm. Free, but donation encouraged.)

A PILGRIM'S PRAYER. Several of the rooms in the monastery are open for prayer, not for sightseeing. Visitors to Jasna Góra who are not on pilgrimage should be mindful of the sign posted at one of the entrances to the monastery: "This is a holy place; come here as a pilgrim."

The monastery also houses several small museums, all of which are free to the public (donation requested). The **Skarbiec** contains art donated by kings, nobility, clergy, and pilgrims. (Open daily June-Aug. 9am-5pm; Sept.-May 9am-4pm.) The **Arsenal** documents Jasna Góra's embattled history with jewel-encrusted batons, medieval swords, and other military artifacts dating from the Middle Ages to WWII. (Open daily in summer 9am-5pm; low season 9am-4pm.) The **Museum of the 600th Anniversary** (Muzeum Sześćsetlecia), assembled in 1982 to commemorate the anniversary of the icon's arrival at Jasna Góra, highlights the work and history of the Paulite Fathers, as well that of **Lech Wałęsa**, whose Nobel Prize rests here. The museum also protects the Monastery's 1382 founding document, an array of musical instruments used by the monks, and delicate rosaries crafted by concentration camp prisoners. (Open daily 9am-5pm.) The **Knight's Hall** (Sala Rycerska), which was once used to host parliamentary meetings, now features paintings of the major events of the monastery's turbulent history. Ascend the dizzying staircase of the *baszta* (tower) for excellent views. (Suggested donation 2zł. Tower open daily April-Nov. 8am-4pm.) The largest crowds converge on the monastery on May 3 (Feast of Our Lady Queen of Poland), July 16 (Feast of Our Lady of Scapulars), August 15 (Feast of the Assumption), August 26 (Feast of Our Lady of Częstochowa), September 8 (Feast of the Birth of Our Lady), and September 12 (Feast of the Name Mary). The grounds of the monastery also teem with pilgrims every Sunday, when the 11 daily masses include Latin Mass.

🔋 DAYTRIP FROM CZĘSTOCHOWA

TRAIL OF EAGLES' NESTS.

From Częstochowa, take bus #58 or 67 to Olsztyn-Rynek (30min.; 10 per day; 3zł, students 1.50zł) from ul. Piłsudskiego, across from the Częstochowa train station. Castle tower open daily 8am-8pm. 2zł, students 1zł.

Crags of Jurassic limestone erupt from green hills along the narrow 100km strip of land known as the **Kraków-Częstochowa Uplands** (Jura Krakówska-Częstochowska). These breathtaking extensions were incorporated into the fortifications of 12th-century castles built in the area, whose perches high on the rocky cliffs alongside the nests of eagle owls earned them the name "eagles' nests." As artillery grew stronger, the defensive walls grew less effective, and the fortifications proved no match for the invading Swedes. By the end of the 17th-century, the fortresses had badly deteriorated. Today, only a few, including Wawel Castle in Kraków (see p. 534), remain whole. The ruins of the rest lie along the uplands, waiting to be discovered.

The two biggest attractions on the trail, the **Olsztyn Castle** and the **Pieskowa Skała Castle**, are half-day trips from Częstochowa and Kraków, respectively. Constructed in the 12th and 13th centuries, the castle that currently stands in the pastoral town of Olsztyn has lost much of its former glory. In 1655, the Swedish army ransacked the complex and, a century later, the locals took bricks from the castle to rebuild the town church. The preserved sections are in the upper castle. Look for signs of the two famous castle ghosts: a young bride who got lost in the dungeon and Maćko Borkowic, who was starved to death in the circular tower for his rebellion against King Casimir the Great. The lack of formal paths surrounding the sprawling ruins and rock caves invites exploration. A night climb allows for a great view of the illuminated spire of Jasna Góra. A **hiking trail** that runs along the entire 100km takes about seven days. The Eagles' Nests trail is also a rewarding, if somewhat challenging, **bicycle route.** Kraków or Częstochowa branches of **PTTK** can provide maps. The trail is marked by red blazes, and maps are posted along the way. The route leads through many small towns that offer tourist info, food, and accommodations.

WROCŁAW   ☎(0)71

Wrocław (VROTS-wahv), the capital of Dolny Śląsk (Lower Silesia), is a graceful city of Gothic spires and stone bridges, islands and gardens. Beneath the tranquil *rynek*, however, lie centuries of turmoil. Passed among competing powers for centuries, Wrocław (Breslau in German) became Festung Breslau in WWII, when it was one of the last Nazi battlegrounds en route to Berlin. Though the rejuvenated city already captivates visitors, Wrocław has plans for expansion.

🚅 TRANSPORTATION

Trains: Wrocław Główny, ul. Piłsudskiego 105 (☎367 58 82). **24hr. currency exchange** inside. International ticketing at counter #20. MC/V. To: **Częstochowa** (4hr., 7 per day, 34zł); **Gdynia** (6½hr., 6 per day, 48zł); **Jelenia Góra** (3¼hr., 14 per day, 17zł); **Kołobrzeg** (6½hr., 3 per day, 66zł); **Kraków** (4½-5hr., 14 per day, 40-61zł); **Łódź** (6¼hr., 6 per day, 39zł); **Lublin** (8hr., 3 per day, 48zł); **Poznań** (3¼hr., 25 per day, 32zł); **Szczecin** (5½hr., 8 per day, 44zł); **Warsaw** (4¼hr., 12 per day, 44-89zł); **Berlin, GER** (6¼hr., 2 per day, 185zł); **Bratislava, SLK** (7½hr., 10:30pm, 167zł); **Dresden, GER** (4½hr., 4 per day, 160zł); **Prague, CZR** (5¼hr., 2 per day, 140zł).

Buses: Station at ul. Sucha 1 (☎361 22 99), behind the trains. Open daily 5am-11pm. To: **Częstochowa** (4¼hr., 10 per day, 23zł); **Gdańsk** (8hr., 1 per day, 55zł); **Jelenia Góra** (2hr., 28 per day, 24zł); **Karpacz** (3hr., 4 per day, 29zł); **Kraków** (6 hr., 2 per day, 30zł); **Łódź** (5hr., 3 per day, 31zł); **Lublin** (8hr., 24 per day, 46zł); **Poznań** (4hr., 4 per day, 26zł); **Warsaw** (6hr., 7 per day, 52zł).

Public Transportation: Tram and **bus** tickets cost 2zł per person, 1zł per student, and 2zł per backpack. 1-day pass 6.60zł, students 3.30zł; 10-day pass 24zł/12zł. Express buses (marked by letters) 2.40zł. Night buses 3zł/1.50zł. Most lines run 5am-midnight.

Taxis: ☎72 55 55. The trip from the train station to the *rynek* should cost around 12zł.

■ 🛈 ORIENTATION AND PRACTICAL INFORMATION

The political and social heart of Wrocław is the *rynek* (square). From the **train** and **bus stations,** turn left on **ul. Piłsudskiego,** take a right on **ul. Świdnicka,** and go past **pl. Kościuszki,** over the **Fosa River,** through the pedestrian underpass beneath Kazimierza Wielkiego, and into the *rynek*.

Tourist Office: IT, Rynek 14 (☎344 31 11; www.dolnyslask.info.pl). **Maps** 6-16zł. Open M-F 10am-9pm, Sa 10am-5pm, Su 11am-4pm. AmEx/MC/V. **Centrum Informacji Kulturalnej,** Rynek-Ratusz 24 (☎342 22 91; www.okis.pl). The cultural branch of the IT, specializing in info for events and festivals. Open M-F 10am-6pm, Sa 9am-2pm.

Currency Exchange: Bank Pekao SA, ul. Oławska 2 (☎371 61 24), cashes **traveler's checks** for 1.5% commission (min. 10zł) and gives MC/V **cash advances.** Open M-F 8am-6pm, Sa 9am-2pm.

Western Union, available at **Biuro Podróży,** ul. Kościuszki 27 (☎344 81 88). Open M-F 10am-4pm, Sa 10am-5pm.

Luggage Storage: Lockers in the **train station** (4-8zł per day). Also in the kiosk in the back of the **bus station.** 5.50zł per day plus 1zł per 50zł value. Open daily 6am-10pm.

English-Language Bookstore: Empik Megastore, Rynek 50 (☎343 39 72). Sells foreign books and newspapers. Open M-Sa 9am-9pm, Su 11am-7pm. MC/V.

Ambulance: ☎999.

Pharmacy: Apteka Podwójnym Złotym Orłem, Rynek 42/43 (☎343 44 28).

Hospital: Szpital Im. Babińskiego, pl. 1-go Maja 8 (☎341 00 00).

Internet Access: Internet Klub Navig@tor Podziemia, ul. Kuźnicza 11/13 (☎343 70 69). 2zł per 30min., 3zł per hr. Open daily 9am-10pm.

Post Office: Ul. Małachowskiego 1 (☎344 77 78), to the right of the train station. **Poste Restante** at window #22. **Telephones** inside and outside. Open M-F 6am-8pm, Sa-Su 8am-3pm. 2nd location at Rynek 28. Open 6:30am-8:30pm. **Postal Code:** 50-900.

🏠 ACCOMMODATIONS

Rooms are plentiful in Wrocław, but reserve ahead for reasonable accommodations near the center of town. Check with the tourist office for info and to make reservations in **student dorms ❶,** which rent rooms July through August (20-50zł).

Youth Hostel "Młodzieżowy Dom Kultury im. Kopernika" (HI), ul. Kołłątaja 20 (☎343 88 56), opposite the train station. A cheerful hostel plastered with student artwork. Kitchen and exquisite shared bathrooms. Sheets 7zł. Lockout 10am-5pm. Curfew 10pm. Call ahead. Dorms 22zł; doubles 58zł. Discount for stays over 1 night. ❶

POLAND

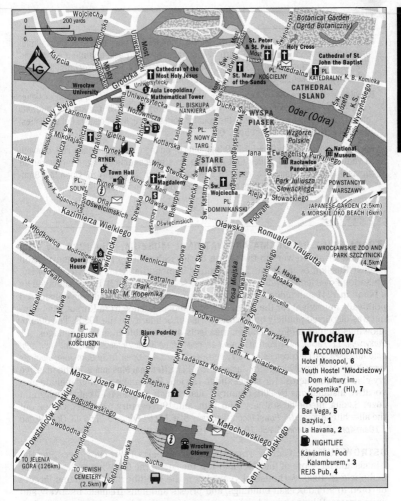

Wrocław

🏠 ACCOMMODATIONS
Hotel Monopol, **6**
Youth Hostel "Młodzieżowy
    Dom Kultury im.
    Kopernika" (HI), **7**
🍎 FOOD
Bar Vega, **5**
Bazylia, **1**
La Havana, **2**
🍷 NIGHTLIFE
Kawiarnia "Pod
    Kalamburem," **3**
REJS Pub, **4**

Hotel Monopol, ul. Modrzejewskiej 2 (☎343 70 40; www.orbis.pl). From the train station, take tram "K" to Kazimierza Wielkiego. The glamour has faded from this once wild and trendy hotel, but modern amenities, like satellite TVs, telephones, and attentive service, make the Monopol an excellent value. Price includes a princely breakfast buffet in the red-carpeted former ballroom. Check-in and check-out 2pm. Singles 115zł, with bath 180zł; doubles 260zł/290zł; triples with bath 310zł. AmEx/MC/V. ❹

Dizzy Daisy Hostel, ul. Górnickiego 22 (☎321 00 14; www.hostel.pl), near Ostrów Tumski. From the center of town, take tram #8, 9, 17, or 32 along Katarzyny Piaskowa across the river and along Sienkiewicza to Wyszyńskiego. Walk 3 blocks farther on Sienkiewicza to Górnickiego. In summer, this university dorm, on the outskirts of town, becomes a friendly hostel with international sensibilities and free Internet access. No curfew. Reception 24hr. Open July-Aug. Dorms 30zł. ❶

POLAND

🎦 FOOD

La Havana, ul. Kuźnicza 12 (☎343 20 72). Dig into layers of irony and tasty Cuban-influenced Polish food (entrees 10-20zł) in the company of a packed student crowd and images of Che and Castro. Large tropical mixed drinks 12-18zł. Reservations recommended on weekends. Open Su-Th 11am-11:30pm, F-Sa noon-1am. ❷

Bazylia, ul. Kuźnicza 42 (☎375 20 65). Wrapped under the glass facade and designer curtains of a businessman's bistro, Bazylia is a pure Polish milk bar serving students cheap, nourishing meals. Order at the counter from the long list of classic Polish dishes. Open M-F 7am-7pm, Sa 8am-5pm. ❶

Bar Vega, Sukiennice 1/2 (☎344 39 34), directly on the *rynek*. Vegetarian milk bar with a verdant interior and prices that defy the laws of economics. Vegan menu served upstairs. Try the Ukrainian *barszcz* (3.50zł) or an Indian *samosa* (4zł). Open M-F 8am-7pm, Sa-Su 9am-5pm. Upstairs open M-F noon-6pm, Sa noon-5pm. ❶

🔯 SIGHTS

▨ **RACŁAWICE PANORAMA AND NATIONAL MUSEUM.** The 120m by 15m **Panorama** wraps viewers in the action of the 18th-century peasant insurrection against Russian occupation. This painting depicts the legendary victory of the underdog Poles led by Tadeusz Kościuszko (see **History**, p. 502). It was damaged by a bomb in 1944 and hidden in a monastery for safekeeping. As it was considered politically imprudent for the Poles to glorify independence from Russia, the painting was displayed publicly only with the rise of Solidarity in the 1980s. The 30min. showings include audio narration; headsets are available in eight languages. *(Ul. Purkyniego 11. Facing away from the town hall, bear left on Kuźnicza for 2 blocks and then right onto Kotlarska, which becomes ul. Purkyniego. ☎344 23 44. Open Tu-Su 9am-4pm; viewings every 30min. 9:30am-3:30pm. 19zł, students 15zł.)* The **National Museum** is in the massive ivy-clad building across the street and to the left. Permanent exhibits include provocative installations by 20th-century Polish artists Magdalena Abakanowicz and Józef Szajna, medieval statuary, and 18th- and 19th-century paintings. Check out the all-white atrium. *(Pl. Powstańców Warszawy 5. ☎372 51 50; fax 343 56 43. Open W and F 10am-4pm, Th 9am-4pm, Sa-Su 10am-6pm. 15zl, students 10zl.)*

OSTRÓW TUMSKI. Ostrów Tumski, the oldest part of Wrocław, occupies the islands and far shore of the Oder and was the site of the founding of the Wrocław bishopric in 1000. A thousand years later, the neighborhood remains largely devoted to archdiocesan buildings, and priests and nuns frequent its lovely and quiet streets. Biking and pedestrian paths connect the islands. A statue of St. Jadwiga, the patron saint of Silesia, guards **Most Piaskowy** (Sand Bridge), the oldest bridge in Wrocław. The sky-piercing spires of the 13th-century **Cathedral of St. John the Baptist** (Katedra Św. Jana Chrzciciela) dominate Ostrów Tumski's skyline. Inside, light filters in through stained-glass windows, shrouding the Gothic interior with shadows. Climb the tower for a view of the surrounding churches. *(Open M-Sa 10am-5:30pm, Su 2-4pm. 4zł, students 3zł. Donation suggested.)* Nearby, the Church of **St. Mary of the Sands** (Najświętszej Marii Panny) houses a 14th-century icon of Our Lady of Victory that medieval knights carried into battle. To the right of the nave is an incredible chapel where the altar has been adorned with thousands of children's toys. Ask a priest to hit the switch and try not to gape as the toy village comes to life. *(Open daily 10am-6pm. Donation suggested.)* From Cathedral Square, go north on Kapitulna to reach the enchanting **Botanical Garden**. Sculptures of over-sized acorns and pine cones are scattered throughout, and students from the nearby university study on benches and tables facing the stream, which winds through the garden. *(Open daily 8am-6pm. 5zł, students 3zł.)*

WROCŁAW UNIVERSITY (UNIWERSYTET WROCŁAWSKI). This center of Wrocław's cultural life houses a number of architectural gems. **Aula Leopoldina**, an 18th-century frescoed lecture hall, is the most impressive. *(Pl. Uniwersytecka 1, on the 2nd fl. ☎375 26 18. Open M-Tu and Th-Su 10am-3pm. 4zł, students 2zł.)* Climb the **Mathematical Tower** for a sweeping view of the city. *(4zł, students 2zł.)* The breathtaking 17th-century **Cathedral of the Most Holy Jesus** (Kościól Najświętszego im. Jezusa), built on the site of the Piast castle, retains much of its original interior. The colonialist, 18th-century sculptures on the vaults depict the Christianization of African, American, and Asian indigenous people. *(Open to tourists M-Sa 11am-3:30pm. Suggested donation 2zł.)*

AROUND THE RYNEK. The *rynek* and its Gothic **Town Hall** are the heart of the city. Ul. Świdnicka, which borders one side of the *rynek*, is a street so beautiful that the Germans tried to deface it during WWII. Inside the town hall is the **Museum of Urban Art** (Muzeum Sztuki Mieszczańskiej), with both old and contemporary art in an ancient building. Check out the silver, including an amazing scepter, and then enjoy the sights and sounds from a horse-drawn carriage. *(☎374 16 90. Open W-Sa 11am-5pm, Su 10am-6pm. Museum 6zł, students 4zł. Carriage (☎398 84 00) 5zł.)*

JEWISH CEMETERY (CMENTARZ ŻYDOWSKI). The Jewish Cemetery, one of the best-preserved in Poland, holds the remains of German socialist Ferdinand Lasalle, the families of physicist Max Born and chemist Fritz Haber, and the wife of writer Thomas Mann. A walk around this shaded enclave reveals fragments of Jewish tombstones dating from the 12th and 13th centuries. *(Ul. Ślężna 37/39. From the stops along ul. Kołłątaja and ul. Piotra Skargi, take tram #9 and get off at Ślężna. ☎791 59 04. Guided tours Su noon. Open daily Apr.-Oct. 8am-6pm. 5zł, students 3zł.)* The oldest Jewish tombstone in Poland, dated 1203 and discovered at the site of the now-vanished Wroclaw Old Jewish Cemetery, is on display at the **Archaeology Museum** on ul. Cieszynskiego.

🎵 🎭 ENTERTAINMENT AND NIGHTLIFE

For event info, pick up *City Magazine* or *Co jest grane?* (What's Going On?). Visit **Centrum Informacji Kulturalnej** (see **Orientation and Practical Information**, p. 560) for info on Wroclaw's world-famous experimental theater. At **☒REJS Pub**, ul. Kotlarska 32a, students and locals down cheap beer and admire the bear above the bar. *(☎343 19 42. Beer 4.50zl. Open M-Sa 9:30am-late, Su 11am-late.)* Hang with art students at **Kawiarnia "Pod Kalamburem,"** ul. Kuźnicza 29a, in the university quarter. The Art Nouveau building includes a bar, cafe, and cinema. Readings and film screenings make it a cultural and intellectual hub. *(☎372 35 71. Beer and mixed drinks 3-15zl. Open M-Th 1pm-midnight, F-Sa 1pm-late, Su 4pm-midnight.)* In summer, join backpackers and students next door on the multi-level patio of unpretentious **Kalogródek**, ul. Kuźnicza 29b, for darts, foosball and beer. *(☎372 35 71. Open M-Th 10am-11pm, F-Sa 10am-late, Su 3-11pm.)* The best Wrocław cafe is the tiny, second-floor **Siedem Kotów** (Seven Cats), ul. Kielbasnicza 2. Seven Cats offers an encyclopedic array of teas, delicious homemade cakes, and a surfeit of charm. *(☎341 94 40. Open daily 11am-11pm.)*

POL

...and without visiting Karpacz is like eating herring without vodka: you ...ut it's inadvisable. Surrounding mountains throw long shadows over ...ested valleys, and the beauty of the landscape is stunning, even within ...self.

⌐⁊ TRANSPORTATION AND PRACTICAL INFORMATION. Most **buses** to Karpacz originate in, or at least pass through, **Jelenia Góra**. There is no bus station in town. Ul. 3-go Maja is the main thoroughfare for buses—eight stops dot the way to **Karpacz Górny**, the top of town, on their way to and from Jelenia Góra (45min., every 30min.-1hr., 5.20-5.80zł). Catch any bus to ride between stops within Karpacz (2.20zł). The poorly marked stops are named for local landmarks. Buses to Jelenia Góra go to either the train station or the bus station. For a more whimsical ride, try the open-air **trolley** (daily 10am-6pm; 4-8zł, depending on number of stops), adorned with stuffed animals, that runs more frequently than the bus. A scenic **bicycle path** also traverses the 28km from Jelenia Góra to Karpacz; maps are available at the Jelenia Góra tourist info office.

Karpacz is a vertical town: most of its restaurants and sights meander uphill along a single road, **ul. 3-go Maja.** Poorly marked side streets provide steeply sloped shortcuts. Uphill from Biały Jar, the road changes names to **Karkonoska.** Get off incoming buses at **Karpacz Bacchus** and go downhill to the Karpacz **tourist office,** ul. 3-go Maja 25a. They **exchange currency,** sell **maps,** and reserve rooms. Ask about biking, skiing, rock climbing, horseback riding, and camping. (☎761 86 05; www.karpacz.pl. Open July-Aug. M-F 9am-5pm, Sa 9am-4pm, Su 10am-2pm; Sept.-June closed Su.) Hotel Orbis Skalny, ul. Obrońców Pokoju 5, **rents bicycles.** (☎752 70 00. Open daily 7am-9pm. 10zł per 3hr., 18zł per 6hr., 25z per 12hr.) **Szkoła Górska,** ul. Karkonosak 2 (☎761 97 11), near Biały Jar, has rock climbing lessons, equipment, and excursions. Call ahead to make arrangements. **Bank Zachodni,** ul. 3-go Maja 43, cashes **traveler's checks** for 30zł commission. (☎/fax 753 81 20. Open M-F 9am-5pm.) It also has a Visa **ATM** and **Western Union** services. There's a **pharmacy, K-Med,** at ul. 3-go Maja 33. (☎761 86 69. Open M-F 9am-7pm, Sa 9am-5pm, Su 9am-1pm.) The **post office** is at ul. 3-go Maja 23. (☎761 92 20; fax 761 95 85. Open M-F 8am-6pm, Sa 9:30am-3pm.) **Postal Code:** 58-540.

⌐⁊ ACCOMMODATIONS AND FOOD. Reservations are not necessary. **Private pensions** (25-70zł) proliferate, especially on Kościelna just downhill from Karpacz Bacchus. Unfortunately, some are open only part of the year—inquire at the tourist office. As a general rule, the better deals are farther uphill. **Hotel Karpacz ❸,** ul. 3-go Maja 11/13 (☎/fax 761 97 28), has comfortably large rooms with TVs, baths, and a generous, inclusive breakfast buffet. (Buffet open 9-11am. Check-in noon-3pm. Check-out noon. Singles 80zł; doubles 120zł; triples 180zł.) **D.W. Szczyt ❶,** ul. Na Śnieżkę 6 (☎761 93 60), is at the uphill end of town just a few steps away from Świątynia Wang (see **Sights and Outdoor Activities,** below). Take the bus to Karpacz Wang, since the uphill hike from the center of town (1hr.) is impossible with luggage. If the amazing view doesn't leave you breathless, the great prices will—as will the 200m haul from the bus stop. Call the tourist office to make reservations. (Singles 25zł; doubles 50zł; triples 75zł; quads 100zł.) **Schronisko Smotnia ❶,** beside the stunning Mały Staw alpine lake, a 2hr. hike along the blue trail from town, offers perhaps the most secluded accommodations in Karpacz. There's a restaurant, ski rental, and a mountain rescue service. Call the tourist office to reserve. (Dorms 19-29zł; singles 31zł; doubles 58zł.)

Food in Karpacz is unpretentious, filling, and appealing after a long day of hiking or skiing. Green-roofed **Karczma Śląska ❷**, ul. Rybacka 1, just off ul. 3-go Maja, specializes in mouth-watering pork (8zł), great prices, and yard art. Pool tables (2zł per game) can be found at the restaurant's "Bar Oscar." (☎761 96 33. Open daily noon-10pm.) **Pizzeria Verde ❷**, ul. 3-go Maja 48, serves pizzas (small 7.50-18.50zł, large 8.50-19.50zł) and the best cappuccino (6zł) in town. (☎761 81 94. Open M-Sa 1pm-9pm.) **Afrika Pub ❷**, ul. Kostytucji 3-Maja 30, features an inexplicable camouflage-and-tiki theme that nearly overshadows the Arabian music, grilled kebabs (8.50zł), and 5L beer cylinders (45zł). There's no menu, but the day's offerings are posted on paper plates stapled to the wood carvings around the terrace. (☎761 95 82; www.gebirge.pl. Open daily May-Sept. 11am-2am.) The grocery store **Delikatesy**, ul. 3-go Maja 29, has everything you could need for a picnic in the mountains. (☎761 92 59. Open M-Sa 8:30am-9pm, Su 10am-6pm.) The **open-air produce market**, in the alley beside ul. 3-go Maja 45, stocks some of the best food in town. Marked by a "Warzywa Owoce" sign. (Open daily dawn-dusk.)

◉ 🅰 SIGHTS AND OUTDOOR ACTIVITIES. The uphill hike to **Wang Chapel** (Świątynia Wang), ul. Śnieżki 8, takes hours from the center of town but is worth the effort. Follow ul. 3-go Maja and side streets marked by a blue blaze. Alternatively, take the bus to Karpacz Wang and follow the signs. This Viking church was built in Norway at the turn of the 12th century. In the 1800s, it sorely needed a restoration that no one could afford, so Kaiser Friedrich Wilhelm III of Prussia sent it to Karpacz for the Lutheran community to enjoy. Dragons, lions, and intricate plant carvings adorn the building. (☎752 82 91. Open Apr. 15-Oct. 31 M-Sa 9am-6pm, Su 11:30am-6pm; Nov.-Apr. 14 closes 1hr. earlier. Occasionally closed for weddings. 4zł, students 3zł. Cameras 3zł.)

Hikers aim for the crown of **Śnieżka** (Mt. Snow; 1602m), the highest peak in Poland. The border between Poland and the Czech Republic runs across the summit. Śnieżka and the trails lie within **Karkonosze National Park** (4zł, students 2zł; 3-day pass 8zł/4zł). All the park's trails lead to **Pod Śnieżka** (1394m), the last stop under the peak. To get there as quickly and painlessly as possible, take the Kopa chairlift, ul. Turystczna 4. Follow the black trail from Hotel Biały Jar until you see the lift on the left. (☎761 86 19. Takes 2-3hr. Lift runs daily June-Aug. 8:30am-5:30pm; Sept.-May 8am-4pm. Before 1pm 17zł, students 14zł; round-trip 22zł/18zł. After 1pm 15zł/10zł; round-trip 18zł/13zł.) If you want to hike up, there are several possible routes:

Blue Trail (3hr.). The easiest way to reach Pod Śnieżka is to take the blue-blazed path from Świątynia Wang. This stone-paved road is also suited to vigorous biking. Follow the blue route to **Polana** (1080m, 1hr.), then hike up to scenic **Mały Staw** (Small Lake; 1hr.). From there, it's 35min. to **Spalona Strażnica**, then 30min. to **Pod Śnieżka**.

Yellow Trail (2½hr.). From Polana (see above), endurance hikers should continue along the yellow route to another petrified protrusion at **Słonecznik** (Sunflower; 35min.). This stretch, along a rocky stream bed, is a challenging, vertical haul not for the weak of ankle. Turning left here takes you to the real trail, which leads to **Pod Śnieżka** (1hr.).

Red Trail (2½hr.). The scenic red trail begins behind Hotel Biały Jar's parking lot. It travels along the Czech ridge to **Spalona Strażnica**, where it meets the yellow trail (see above). Once you emerge above the tree line, it's a difficult hike up to **Pod Śnieżka**.

Black Trail (2¼hr.). The most physically challenging and least scenic of the trails, the black trail heads up from behind Hotel Biały Jar's parking lot. After splitting from the red trail, it shoots straight up the ski slopes in an exhausting trek to the top.

From Pod Śnieżka, two trails lead to Śnieżka. The black **Zygzag** goes straight up the north side; look for the rubble path (20-30min.). The blue trail, **Jubilee Way**, winds around the peak (45min.). If incredible views of the Polish and Czech Sudety aren't

o to the **observatory**. (Open daily June-Aug. 9am-5pm; Sept.-May 9am-
...dents 1zł.) Winter brings snow and skiers. Lift and equipment rental
...ily available. (☎761 86 19; www.kopa.com.pl. 1-day pass 50zł, students
...iy pass 85zł/70zł. Ski rental 50zł, snowboard 45zł.) The longest lift is
...iong and leads to the Kopa peak. Back in town, be terrified by **CRiS**
...va, ul. Parkowa 10, the alpine slide, uphill from Pizzeria Verdi. (☎761 90 98;
...kolorowa.pl. 6zł per person per ride. 5 rides 20zł, 10 rides 35zł. Open daily
9am-8pm, weather permitting.)

JELENIA GÓRA   ☎(0)75

In Poland's southwest corner, the land buckles along the Czech border to form the
magnificent Sudety Mountains. The crisp air and mineral springs in the Jelenia
Góra (Deer Mountain) valley have provided tranquility for generations of city
dwellers, including Goethe and Henryk Sienkiewicz. At the foot of the Sudety's
Karkonosze range, the attractive town of Jelenia Góra provides a convenient base
for exploring the hiking, skiing, and bicycling trails that weave through the region.

▐ TRANSPORTATION. Buses to and from Jelenia Góra are generally faster and
more frequent than trains. The **bus station,** ul. Obrońców Pokoju 2 (☎642 21 00), is
a 5min. walk from the center of town. Buses run to: **Karpacz** (45min., 25 per day,
5.20-5.80zł); **Szklarska Poręba** (30min., 10 per day, 5zł); **Wrocław** (2hr., 12 per day, 14-
24zł). Connections to most major cities can be made in Wrocław. The **train station,**
ul. 1-go Maja 77 (☎94 36), is a 10min. walk from town. (Open 3am-12:15am.) Trains
run to: **Kraków** (8hr., 1 per day, 40zł); **Poznań** (6-7hr., 1 per day, 35zł); **Szklarska
Poręba** (40min., 7 per day, 6.30zł); **Warsaw** (9hr.; June-Aug. 3 per day, Sept.-May 2 per
day; 41.70zł); **Wrocław** (4-5hr., 7 per day, 15.52zł). **City buses** (☎764 87 36) connect
Jelenia Góra with other towns in the Jelenia Góra valley, including **Cieplice** and
Sobieszów. Tickets 1.80-2.50zł, Arrange pickup with **Radio Taxi** (☎919 or 767 55 55).

▦ ▪ ORIENTATION AND PRACTICAL INFORMATION. Stare Miasto (Old
Town) is encircled by one road, called **ul. Podwale** in the north, **Plac Wyszyńskiego** in
the west, **Plac Niepodległości** in the southwest, **ul. Bankowa** in the southeast, and **ul.
Pijarska** in the northeast. To get to the center of town from the bus station, make a
left onto **Obrońców Pokoju,** cross ul. Podwale, and continue along the sidewalks
that lead toward the visible tower of the town hall into the *rynek*. To get to the
center of town from the train station, turn right onto ul. 1-go Maja. Bear slightly
right at the first large intersection and follow ul. 1-go Maja directly to Stare Miasto.
IT, ul. Grodzka 16, can be tricky to find. Located at the end of Grodzka near ul.
Podwale, the office is marked by a small door on the side of the building facing the
Old Town. The friendly staff sells **maps** (4-6zł), including maps of hiking and biking
trails, and provides information about **bike rentals.** (☎/fax 767 69 35; www.jeleniag-
ora.pl. Open M-F 9am-6pm, Sa 10am-2pm; July-Sept. M-F 9am-6pm, Sa-Su 10am-
2pm.) **Luggage storage** is available at the train station. (7zł per day. Open 6am-
7:30pm.) **Bank Zachodni,** ul. Bankowa 5, gives Visa **cash advances** and cashes **AmEx
Traveler's Cheques** for a 0.5% commission. The bank also has **Western Union** services. (☎752 54 07. Open M-F 8am-5pm, Sa 8am-1pm.) **24hr. ATMs** line ul. Bankowa.
Emergency medical services (☎752 31 54) are available at 21 ul. Wolnosci Polskiej.
The local **pharmacy** is **Apteka pod Jelenium,** ul. 1-go Maja 30. (☎752 21 36. Open M-F
8am-7pm, Sa 8am-3pm.) **Cafe Internet,** ul. Konopnickiej 1, first floor, offers **Internet
access** and free coffee and tea. (☎764 74 15. Open daily 3-10pm. 3zł per hr.) **Telephones** are outside the main **post office,** ul. Pocztowa 9/10. From the train station,
walk along ul. 1-go Maja. It's on the left. (☎752 43 90. Open M-F 7am-9pm, Sa 8am-
3pm, Su 9-11am.) **Postal Code: 58-500.**

🛏️🍴 ACCOMMODATIONS AND FOOD. If you're visiting both Karpacz and Jelenia Góra, consider staying in Karpacz, where hotels are cheaper and more plentiful. That said, a little splurge goes a long way in Jelenia Góra. **Hotel Europa ❹**, ul.1-go Maja 16/18, rewards those willing to look beyond its garish hall decor with a great price and a central location. Spacious single rooms feature sparkling bathrooms, separate sitting rooms, and spectacular views. Price includes posh, multi-course breakfast. (☎649 55 00. Check-in and check-out noon. Singles 120zł; doubles 170zł; suites 240zł. 20% weekend discount.) **PTSM Bartek (HI) ❶**, ul. Bartka Zwycięzcy 10, near the train station, has the cheapest beds in town. From the center of town, head toward the train station on ul. 1-go Maja, turn right on ul. Kochanskiego, and turn right on Bartka Zwycięzcy. A rough-hewn log cabin, the no-frills Bartek draws throngs of Polish scout groups, so book ahead for a spot in its dorms. (☎752 57 46. Reception 7-10am and 5-9pm. Lockout 10am-5pm. Dorms 15zł.) A more adventurous hostel option is the **Schronisko Na Zamku Chojnik ❶**, which offers rustic but decent dorm accommodations inside the ruins of Chojnik Castle. (See **Sights**, below.) The hostel sometimes closes when no guests are expected, so be sure to phone ahead. (☎755 35 36. Open May-Sept. Dorms 25zł.)

Head to **Kurna Chata ❶** ul. Konopnickiej 1, to sample *Dolnoslaskie* regional dishes (6-10zł) amid ceramic cows and throbbing techno. (Open M-Sa 10am-late, Su noon-midnight.) **Karczma Staropolska ❶**, ul. 1-go Maja 35, serves tavern favorites like grilled *pierogi* (5.90zł) and 4-6zł soups. (☎752 23 50. Dinner 8.70-13.70zł. Open daily 7am-10pm.) **Pożegnanie z Afryką ❶**, ul. Grodzka 2, has the best coffee in town (4-7zł) and a view of the *rynek*. (Open M-F 10am-6pm, Sa 10am-5pm.)

🔷 SIGHTS. The **Town Hall** building (Ratusz) and **St. Anne's Cathedral** tower over the handsome, earth-toned *rynek* (Plac Ratuszowy). Beautiful views of the Sudety abound; you can get a particularly good look from the smaller side streets. Medieval **Chojnik Castle** (Zamek Chojnik) stands guard over the Jelenia Góra Valley from a mountain-top perch (627m). To get there, take bus #7 or 9 from the ul. Wolnosci stop (follow ul. Długa out of the *rynek* and onto Wolnosci) to Sobieszów (30min.), then hike 45min. into **Karkonosze National Park** (day pass 4zł, students 2zł) and up to the castle. Two trails lead to the castle: the red trail is a relatively mild hike, while the black trail will have you scrambling over boulders. You can also bike the red trail from Jelenia Góra. The ruins of the castle, destroyed in the 17th century, include a **tower** with a stunning view of the Polish and Czech Sudety. If you spend the night at the castle, you may catch a glimpse of Chojnik's most famous ghost, a princess of the castle who, bored with her suitors, proclaimed that she would marry the knight who could ride a horse around the castle ramparts. When one knight finally succeeded, he revealed that he was already married and refused her hand. The lovesick princess threw herself over the castle walls to her death. The castle stages a **jousting tournament** each September. (☎090 252 157. Open daily June-Aug. 10am-5pm; Sept.-May Tu-Su 10am-4pm. 3zł.)

GREATER POLAND (WIELKOPOLSKA)

A train ride through the lowlands reveals green fields, rolling hills, and woodlands. Except for a trio of urban centers—sophisticated Poznań, Copernicus's birthplace of Toruń, and oft-neglected Łódź—Wielkopolska is as serene as it is genteel.

ŁÓDŹ   ☎(0)42

Łódź (WOODGE; pop. 813,000), Poland's second-largest city, is overshadowed by international Warsaw to the northeast and picturesque Toruń to the north. This largely working-class industrial town doesn't have many attractions that

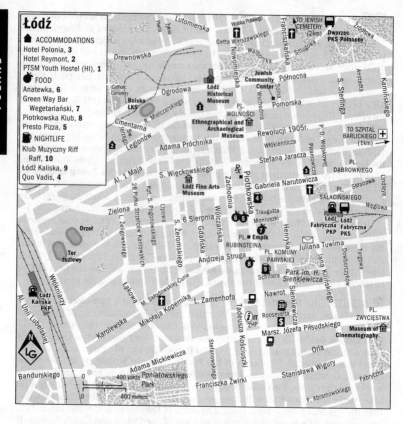

Łódź

🏠 **ACCOMMODATIONS**
Hotel Polonia, 3
Hotel Reymont, 2
PTSM Youth Hostel (HI), 1

🍴 **FOOD**
Anatewka, 6
Green Way Bar
   Wegetariański, 7
Piotrkowska Klub, 8
Presto Pizza, 5

🎵 **NIGHTLIFE**
Klub Muzyczny Riff
   Raff, 10
Łódź Kaliska, 9
Quo Vadis, 4

are easily placed on a postcard, but after strolling down ul. Piotrkowska—bustling by day and raucous by night—you'll understand why Varsovians come here to party hard. Beneath the soot and the graffiti, Łódź has many surprises and a charisma all its own.

⌨ TRANSPORTATION

Trains: There are two main train stations in town. **Łódź Fabryczna,** pl. B. Sałacińkiego 1 (☎664 54 67). To: **Białystok** (4½hr., 1 per day, 42zł); **Kraków** (3¼hr., 3 per day, 41zł); **Warsaw** (2hr., 17 per day, 28zł). **Łódź Kaliska,** al. Unii 1 (☎41 02). To: **Częstochowa** (2hr., 8 per day, 31zł); **Gdańsk** (7½hr., 4 per day, 45zł); **Kraków** (3¼hr., 3 per day, 41zł); **Warsaw** (2hr., 3 per day, 28zł); **Wrocław** (3¾hr., 5 per day, 39zł).

Buses: **Łódź Fabryczna PKS,** pl. B. Sałacinskiego 1 (☎631 97 06), is attached to the Fabryczna train station. **Polski Express** buses (☎620 03 30; www.polskiexpress.pl.) also leave from here. To: **Częstochowa** (2¼hr., 5 per day, 24zł); **Kraków** (5hr., 3 per day, 31zł); **Warsaw** (2½hr., 5 per day, 24zł). **Biuro Turystyczne PKS,** pl. B. Sałacinskiego 1, (☎631 92 30; www.pks.lodz.pl), provides international info. Open M-F 7am-6pm, Sa 9am-1pm.

Public Transportation: Trams and buses run throughout the city 4am-11pm (10min. 1.50zł, 30min. 2.20zł, 1hr. 3.40zł; students 0.75zł/1.10zł/1.65zł). Prices double at night. 1-day pass (8.80zł, students 4.40zł) and 7-day pass (35zł/17.50zł) available. A few late-night buses, designated by numbers over 100, run from 11pm-4am.

■✻ ⁊ ORIENTATION AND PRACTICAL INFORMATION

Ul. Piotrkowska is the 3km main thoroughfare. Its pedestrian-only section stretches from **al. Pomorska** to **al. Marsz. Józefa Piłsudskiego.** From **Łódź Fabryczna,** cross under ul. Jana Kilińskiego and head toward Łódźki Dom Kultury, one of the large buildings just across the way. Continue on ul. Traugutta to ul. Piotrkowska. From **Łódź Kaliska,** cross under al. Włókniarzy via the tunnel; the second exit on the left leads to the tram stop. Take tram #12 or 14 toward Stoki and get off at Piotrkowska.

Tourist Office: IT, al. Kościuszki 88 (☎638 59 55; cit@uml.lodz.pl). **Free maps,** brochures, and accommodations info. Open M-F 8:30am-6pm, Sa 9am-1pm.

Currency Exchange: Pekao SA, al. Piłsudskiego 12 (☎636 62 44), cashes **traveler's checks** for 1.5% commission (min. 10zł) and gives MC/V **cash advances.** Open M-F 8am-6pm, Sa 10am-2pm.

Luggage Storage: Locked storage rooms in Łódź Fabryczna and Łódź Kaliska. 4zł per item per day. Open daily 5am-10pm. **Key lockers** next to the ticket counter. 8zł per 24hr.; 4zł for small items. After 72hr. bags are removed and placed in storage room.

English-Language Bookstore: Empik, ul. Piotrkowska 81 (☎631 19 98). Classic fiction, maps, and magazines. Open M-Sa 9am-9pm, Su 11am-7pm. MC/V.

Pharmacy: Apteka Pod Białym Orłem, ul. Piotrkowska 46 (☎/fax 630 00 68). One of the oldest pharmacies in Łódź. Open M-F 8am-8pm, Sa 10am-3pm.

Hospital: Szpital Barlickiego, ul. Kopcińskiego 22 (☎678 92 88). Many doctors speak English. **Medicover,** al. Marszałka Piłsudskiego 3 (☎639 66 66). 24hr. **emergency line** ☎96 77).

Internet Access: Łódź is wired; Internet cafes dot the alleys off ul. Piotrkowska. **Gralnia Internet Cafe,** ul. Piotrkowska 143 (☎637 18 49; www.caffe.com.pl), above Club Social Latino. Ask about their "Meganoc" option. 1zł per 15min., 1.50zł per 30min., 2zł per hr. Open 24hr. **Meganet Caffe,** al. Piłsudskiego 3 (☎636 33 76; biuro@meganetcaffe.pl). Follow the signs in the alley to the right of the Silver Screen complex. 0.70zł per 20 min., 2.10zł per hour. Open daily 8am-midnight.

THE LOCAL STORY

THE ŁÓDŹ GHETTO

In February 1940, the Nazis established Europe's largest Jewish ghetto in Łódź. To confine and isolate the city's 230,000 Jews to a 4.3 sq. km area, the Nazis drove out non-Jewish residents with warnings of infectious diseases; ordered all of the city's Jews into the cramped district and, with the rapid building of a wall around the area, announced that the ghetto was "closed."

With the Nazis claiming that residents of the ghetto must work in exchange for their meager rations of food, the overcrowded ghetto became a massive textile factory: young girls even hand stitched the emblems on Nazi officers' uniforms. Conditions worsened when 20,000 Jews plus 5000 Roma joined the original ghetto residents. In 1942, deportations of the elderly, the infirm and children began. Until 1944 though, Łódź managed to escape the total liquidation that had been the fate of other ghettos.

In August 1944, with the Red Army approaching, Heinrich Himmler deported the ghetto's 70,000 remaining residents to Auschwitz and Majdanek. Eight hundred Jews remained as a cleaning crew, but as the Russians were about to capture Łódź, the Nazis decided to execute those that remained. The Russians' swift advance interrupted the execution, and the 800 were saved. Of those deported, 20,000 survived—the highest number of survivors of any European ghetto.

POLAND

Post Office: ul. Tuwima 38 (☎ 633 94 52; fax 632 82 08). Take a ticket as you enter: "A/B" for stamps, "C" for international packages, "D" for fax services. **Telephones** are inside. **Poste Restante** at window #19. Open M-F 7am-8pm, Sa 8:30am-3:30pm. **Postal Code:** 90-001.

ACCOMMODATIONS

IT (see Tourist Office, p. 569) maintains a list of private rooms and, in summer, rooms in university dorms. Beds in three-bed shared rooms begin at 25zł, while singles with bath will run you 45-65zl. Call from the train station and they'll make arrangements (☎/fax 638 59 55).

PTSM Youth Hostel (HI), ul. Legionów 27 (☎ 630 66 80; www.youthhostellodz.w.pl). Take tram #4 toward Helenówek from Fabryczna station to pl. Wolności; walk on Legionów past Zachodnia. Clean and quiet with lounge areas in the dorms. Free locked storage until 10pm. Linen 5zł. Reception 6am-11pm. Check-in 3pm. Check-out 10am. Flexible curfew 11pm. Dorms 30zł; one bathless single 45zł, singles with bath and TV 65zł; doubles with TV 80zł; triples with TV 120zł. ❶

Hotel Reymont, ul. Legionów 81 (☎ 633 80 23; www.hotelreymont.com), 4 blocks down from PTSM Youth Hostel. From pl. Wolnośći, take bus 43 along ul. Legionów. Well-maintained Art Deco hotel in a relatively scrubbed neighborhood. A single bed in a double (110-130zł) is a good value, especially considering the free breakfast and the bathroom, phone, radio, cable TV, microwave, and refrigerator in every room. Singles 160-198zł; doubles 210-258zł. 25% off Sa-Su. MC/V. ❺

Hotel Polonia, ul. Narutowicza 38 (☎ 632 87 73). From Fabryczna, take tram #1, 4, or 5 to Narutowicza. If you don't mind the rattling of trams at 5am, the Hotel Polonia offers decent rooms a short walk from the station. Request a room that doesn't face the street. Continental breakfast 15zł. Check-in 2-10pm. Check-out 10am. Singles 75zł, with bath 125-175zł; doubles with bath 140-270zł. 10% off Sa-Su. AmEx/MC/V. ❷

FOOD

Although Łódź has witnessed the same explosion in culinary diversity as Warsaw, prices remain affordable and portions large. Most restaurants line ul. Piotrkowska.

Anatewka, ul. 6 Sierpnia 2/4 (☎ 630 36 35). Meals start with complimentary matzo at quietly elegant Anatewka, where Ashkenazi Jewish cuisine is served on lace tablecloths under 19th-century Yiddish etchings. Lovingly prepared dishes (16-30zł) include goose liver and duck with apples. Call ahead F and Sa. Open daily 11am-11pm. ❸

Green Way Bar Wegetariański, ul. Piotrkowska 80 (☎ 632 08 52). The pursuit of health is a tall order in sooty, hard-drinking Łódź, but Green Way rises to the task with aplomb. Berry and yogurt *koktajly* (1.5-3zł), rich coffee (3.5-4.5zł), and fresh *naleśniki* (crepes) with fruit (6.5zł). Late in the day, the staff at this vegetarian oasis dish out *pakoras* (7.3zł) and veggie versions of traditional Polish favorites. Open daily 10am-9pm. ❷

Presto Pizza, ul. Piotrkowska 67 (☎ 630 88 83), in the alley across from Hotel Grand. Tests culinary limits with some of its wood-oven pies, including the "San Francisco," topped with pineapples, ham, curry, and bananas. A *mała* (small) pizza is frightfully large. Pizzas 8-19zł. Open M-Sa 11am-midnight, Su 11am-11pm. MC/V. ❷

Piotrkowska Klub, ul. Piotrkowska 97 (☎ 630 65 73). With fresh flowers on the tables and a double-decker terrace, Art Nouveau Piotrkowska Klub will make you feel like a star of old "HollyŁódź." Serves Polish standards such as *pierogi* (6.50-7.50zł) and *placki ziemniaczane* (potato pancakes; 6zł). Becomes a busy beer garden at night, with soccer games playing on the television inside. Open daily 11am-late. ❷

⊙ SIGHTS

JEWISH CEMETERY (CMENTARZ ŻYDOWSKI). The most stirring and beautiful sight in Łódź, the sprawling Jewish cemetery, established in 1892, is the largest in Europe. There are more than 200,000 graves and 180,000 tombstones, some quite elaborately engraved. Especially noteworthy is the colossal Poznański family crypt with its gold-mosaic ceiling. Near the entrance to the cemetery is a memorial to the Jews killed in the Łódź ghetto. Signs lead the way to the **Ghetto Fields** (Pole Ghettowe), which are lined with the faintly marked graves of Jews who died there. The cemetery is difficult to find and its gates are often locked even during hours when it is supposedly open, so the best way to see it is to contact the helpful and English-speaking tourist information bureau ahead of time for assistance. *(Take tram #1 from ul. Kilinskiego or #6 from ul. Kościuszki or Zachnodnia north to the last stop (20min.). Continue up the street, make a left onto ul. Zmienna, and head to the small gate on your right. It is better to try this entrance than the main gate on ul. Bracka, which is usually locked. ☎656 70 19. Open May-Sept. M-F and Su 9am-5pm; Oct.-Apr. M-F and Su 9am-3pm. Closed on Jewish holidays. 4zł; free for those visiting the graves of relatives.)* In the center of town, the **Jewish Community Center** (Gmina Wyznaniowa Żydowska) has info on those buried in the cemetery. *(Ul. Pomorska 18. ☎633 51 56. Open M-F 10am-2pm. Services daily. English spoken.)* The British Council office in pl. Wolnosci also has information about the Lódz Ghetto and the Jewish Cemetery.

POZNAŃSKI PALACE AND SCHEIBLER PALACE. Pre-war Łódź, a hub of European industry, thrived at the intersection of Polish, Jewish and German culture. In the late 19th century, factory magnates Izrael Poznański and Karol Scheibler competed fiercely for dominance of the city's lucrative textile industry. Striving to outdo one another, Jewish Poznański and German Scheibler each built lavish residences adjacent to their factories. The intact interiors of the two palaces are now home to Łódź's most interesting museums: the Historical Museum occupies the Poznański Palace, and the Scheibler Palace holds the Museum of Cinematography.

ŁÓDŹ HISTORICAL MUSEUM. Preserving the Poznański family home's Gilded Age splendor, this museum boasts an ornate Neo-Baroque palace ballroom, gorgeously furnished living rooms, and exhibits on Łódź's famous sons and daughters, including pianist Artur Rubinstein and writers Jerzy Koscinski and Władysław Reymont. Factory walls and workers' quarters are visible outside the palace. *(Ul. Ogrodowa 15. Take tram #4 toward Helenówek or #6 toward Strykowskar to the intersection of ul. Nowomiejska and ul. Północna. Turn left on Północna, which becomes Ogrodowa. ☎654 00 82. Open Tu and Th 10am-4pm, W 2-6pm, F-Su 10am-2pm. 7zł, students 4zł. W free.)*

MUSEUM OF CINEMATOGRAPHY (MUZEUM KINOMATOGRAFII). International film giants Andrzej Wajda, Krzysztof Kieślowski, and Roman Polański all got their start at Łódź's famous film school—the city, sometimes called "HollyŁódź," has its own "Avenue of the Stars" on ul. Piotrkowska. Contributing to this tradition, the museum has acquired props and sets from recent Polish films and rebuilt them in and around the building. With neo-Baroque cherubs lolling on the ceilings and Venetian mosaics underfoot, the style of Scheibler Palace is best described as Industrial Magnate Eclectic. Museum highlights include a massive 1900 animation machine called the *fotoplastikon* and the animation sets on the second floor. *(Pl. Zwycięstwa 1, behind a park off Piłsudskiego. ☎674 09 57; www.kinomuzeum.lodz.art.pl. Open Sept.-June Tu 9am-5pm, W and F-Su 9am-4pm, Th 11am-6pm; July-Aug. Tu-W and F-Su 10am-4pm. 4zł, students 3zł. Su free.)*

POLAND

🎵 🏙 ENTERTAINMENT AND NIGHTLIFE

Łódź prides itself on its extraordinary nightlife. Spectacular clubs and beer gardens abound; Ul. Piotrkowska turns into publand a little after 9pm.

■ **Łódź Kaliska,** ul. Piotrkowska 102 (☎630 69 55; www.lodzkaliska.pl). This local legend—bar, club, and offbeat art space—has such a cult following that people drive from Warsaw to drink here for the night. This epic institution boasts a tilted bar, subtly offbeat chairs interspersed among the regular chairs at the 1st fl. tables, and bathroom tiles that reproduce in miniature paintings on the walls. On the top 2 floors of 3-story Kaliska, patrons dance with abandon to the most eclectic playlist of music in town. Possibly the best bar in all of Poland. Beer 7zł. Open daily noon-3am. Disco F-Sa.

Quo Vadis, ul. Piotrkowska 65 (☎632 19 19). Named for the Nobel Prize-winning 1896 novel by Henryk Sienkewicz, Quo Vadis offers a Polish epic of a different sort: the house specialty drink is a towering 5L glass of beer (39zł). Open daily 10am-late.

Klub Muzyczny Riff Raff, ul. Roosevelta 9 (☎607 289 211). Pub/club Riff Raff blends foosball, rock, and beer with flickering fluorescent lighting to create an atmosphere as appealingly gritty as Łódź itself. Free concerts every Th; live DJ and dancing every F and Sa after 8pm. 18+. Cover F-Sa 5-10zł. Open daily 4pm-late.

POZNAŃ
☎(0)61

Influenced by the Prussians and the Germans, Poznań (POZ-nan; pop. 590,000) buzzes with economic efficiency, especially during its many international trade fairs. Yet the city's cosmopolitan flare is by no mean limited to the business world—music, art, and theater thrive just below Poznań's all-professional surface.

🚌 TRANSPORTATION

Trains: Ul. Dworcowa 1 (☎866 12 12). Open 24hr. To: **Częstochowa** (5hr., 3 per day, 43zł); **Gdynia** (4½hr., 7 per day, 44zł); **Gniezno** (1hr., 26 per day, 11zł); **Kołobrzeg** (4hr., 6 per day, 42zł); **Kraków** (5hr., 10 per day, 45-79zł); **Łódź** (5hr., 4 per day, 41zł); **Szczecin** (3hr., 14 per day, 36zł); **Toruń** (2½hr., 4 per day, 31zł); **Warsaw** (3hr., 23 per day, 57-87zł); **Wrocław** (2hr., 25 per day, 31-59zł); **Zakopane** (6hr., 3 per day, 49zł); **Berlin, GER** (3½hr., 7 per day, 138zł).

Buses: Dworzec, Ul. Towarowa 17/19 (☎833 15 11). To: **Gniezno** (1½hr., 54 per day, 9.80zł); **Jelenia Góra** (5½hr., 2 per day, 30-40zł); **Kraków** (9¾hr., 1 per day, 47zł); **Łódź** (4½hr., 4 per day, 34-38zł); **Malbork** (5½hr., 1 per day, 45zł); **Szczecin** (4¼hr., 1 per day, 33zł); **Warsaw** (4¼hr., 1 per day, 38zł); **Wrocław** (3½hr., 4 per day, 22-28zł).

Public Transportation: Tickets cost 1.20zł for 10min.; 2.40zł for 30min. Prices double 11pm-4am. Students half-price. Large baggage needs its own ticket.

Taxi: Radio Taxi (☎919).

✳ 🛈 ORIENTATION AND PRACTICAL INFORMATION

Poznań is a huge city, but almost everything you'll want can be found in **Stare Miasto** (Old Town). The **train station,** Poznań Główny, is on **ul. Dworcowa** in Stare Miasto's corner. The **bus station** is on **ul. Towarowa.** To get to the **Stary Rynek** (Old Market), exit the train station, climb the stairs, turn left onto the bridge, and turn right on **ul. Roosevelta.** After several blocks, turn right on **ul. Św. Marcin.** Continue

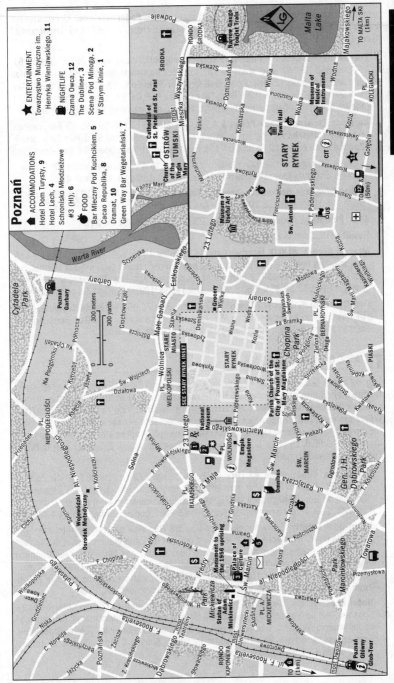

Poznań

ACCOMMODATIONS
Hotel Dom Turysty, 9
Hotel Lech, 4
Schronisko Młodzieżowe #3 (HI), 6

FOOD
Bar Mleczny Pod Kuchcikiem, 5
Cacao Republika, 8
Dramat, 10
Green Way Bar Wegetariański, 7

ENTERTAINMENT
Towarzystwo Muzyczne im. Henryka Wieniawskiego, 11

NIGHTLIFE
Czarna Owca, 12
The Dubliner, 3
Scena Pod Minogą, 2
W Starym Kinie, 1

to **al. Marcinkowskiego,** go left, and turn right on **ul. Paderewskiego.** Alternatively, catch any **tram** going to the right along Św. Marcin from the end of ul. Dworcowa. Get off at ul. Marcinkowskiego.

Tourist Offices: Centrum Informacji Turystycznej (CIT), Stary Rynek 59/60 (☎852 61 56; fax 855 33 79), sells **maps** (6-7zł), provides free maps and accommodation info, and arranges tours (220zł). Open June-Aug. M-F 9am-6pm, Sa 10am-4pm; Sept.-May M-F 9am-5pm, Sa 10am-2pm. **Glob-Tour** (☎/fax 866 06 67) is on ul. Dworcowa 1 in the train station. Offers tourist info, maps (6-8zł), and **currency exchange.** Open 24hr.

Currency Exchange: Bank Pekao S.A., ul. Św. Marcin 52/56 (☎855 85 58), cashes **traveler's checks** for 1% commission. Open M-F 8am-6pm, Sa 10am-2pm. **Bank Zachodni,** ul. Fredry 12 (☎853 04 16), has **Western Union.** Open M-F 8am-6pm.

Luggage Storage: At the train station. 2zł plus 0.15% of declared value. Open 24hr. Lockers also available at the train and bus stations. Large bin 8zł, small 4zł.

English-Language Bookstore: Omnibus Bookstore, ul. Św. Marcin 39 (☎853 61 82). Open M-F 10am-7pm, Sa 10am-4pm. AmEx/MC/V.

24hr. Pharmacy: Apteka Centralna, ul. 23 Lutego 18 (☎852 26 25).

Hospital: Ul. Szkolna 8/12 (☎999).

Internet Access: ▓**KLIK Internet Cafe,** ul. Szkolna 15 (☎609 276 072). Serving coffee, tea, and beer in a chic interior, KLIK would draw patrons even without Internet. 5zł per hr., students with ISIC 3.50zł per hr. Open daily 9am-late. **Pięterko,** ul. Nowowiejskiego 7 (☎662 38 45). 2.50zł per hr. Open M-Sa 10am-midnight, Su noon-midnight.

Post Office: Ul. Kościuszki 77 (☎853 67 43; fax 869 74 08). For **Poste Restante,** go to windows #6 or 7 upstairs. Open M-F 7am-9pm, Sa 8am-6pm, Su 9am-5pm. **Branch** next to the train station open 6am-10pm. **Postal Code:** 61-890.

▐ ACCOMMODATIONS

During trade fairs (all year except July-August and December), businesspeople fill the city. Some prices rise 10% while others double. Finding a decently priced room without calling ahead is virtually impossible. The enthusiastic staff at ▓**Przemysław ❶,** ul. Głogowska 16, rents comfortable **private rooms** near the center. (☎866 35 60; przemyslaw@przemyslaw.com.pl. Singles 42zł, during fairs 68zł; doubles 64zł/96zł. Open M-F 8am-6pm, Sa 10am-2pm. Open 2hr. later during fairs. July-Aug. closed some Sa.)

Schronisko Młodzieżowe #3 (HI), ul. Berwińskiego 2/3 (☎/fax 866 40 40), off ul. Głogowska. From train station, turn left on ul. Roosevelta, which becomes Głogowska. Go right on Berwińskiego (3rd stoplight). Outside the center of town and short on frills, but has clean 2- to 10-bed rooms. Reception 5-9pm. Curfew 10pm. Dorms 24-30zł. ❶

Hotel Dom Turysty, Stary Rynek 91 (☎852 88 93; www.domturysty-hotel.com.pl). Entrance on ul. Wroniecka. The threadbare oriental rugs and grand piano at this former nobleman's residence give an air of classic Central European faded grandeur. Dormitories in the former servants' quarters. Breakfast included with rooms, 10zł with dorms. Check-in noon. Check-out 10am. Dorms 50zł; singles with bath 150zł; doubles 150zł, with bath 250zł; triples with bath 300zł. Sa-Su 20% discount. MC/V. ❷

Hotel Lech, ul. Św. Marcin 74 (☎853 01 51; www.hotel-lech.poznan.pl). Recently opened, this lime-green hotel on busy Św. Marcin has airy, modern rooms. Communications amenities cater to business travelers: all rooms have satellite TV, telephone, Internet access, and bath. Breakfast buffet included. Singles €34; doubles €52; triples €71; suites €54. Sa-Su 20% discount. MC/V. ❺

⬛ FOOD

Along ul. Wielka there are several **24hr. grocery stores.** In summer, enjoy the fruits of local farms at the **open-air market** in pl. Wielkopolski, off ul. 23 Lutego.

Bar Mleczny Pod Kuchcikiem, ul. Św. Marcin 75 (☎853 60 94). The traditional Polish food is so scrumptious that this milk bar earned the "Dobre bo Polskie" (Good because it's Polish) stamp of approval. Go early, as lunch food runs short with the onslaught of ravenous students. Entrees 3-5zł. Open M-F 8am-8pm, Sa 8am-5pm, Su 10am-5pm. ❶

Dramat, Stary Rynek 41 (☎856 09 36). A rarity among the many overpriced, under-flavored Stary Rynek restaurants that coast on their prime location, Dramat serves good *naleśniki* (crepes) at reasonable prices. Breakfast 9.50zł; main course *naleśniki* 7.50zł. Beer 5.50-6.50zł. Open daily 10am-midnight, bar 2pm-midnight. ❶

Green Way Bar Wegetariański, ul. Taczaka 2 (☎853 69 12). Branch at ul. Zeylanda 3 (☎843 40 27). A rainbow of juice and smoothie pitchers lines the counter at this vegetarian favorite, where the servings are generous and the friendly staff make *naleśniki* to order. Rotating menu of soy dishes, vegetarian lasagnas, and hearty pastas and salads. Main dishes 5-9zł. Open M-F 11am-7pm, Sa noon-7pm, Su noon-5pm. ❶

Cacao Republika, ul. Zamkowa 7 (☎855 43 78). Stylish cafe just off the *rynek* crafts 15 kinds of hot chocolate (5-8zł) as well as masterly cakes. Romantic upstairs is strewn with plush red couches and low tables. Open M-Sa 10am-midnight, Su 10am-10pm. ❶

👁 SIGHTS

Ostentatious 15th-century merchant houses, notable for their rainbow paint jobs, line **Stary Rynek.** The houses surround the **Old Town Hall;** the multicolored gem faithfully restored after WWII is the finest secular Renaissance structure north of the Alps. Every day at noon a crowd gathers outside the clock tower to watch two **mechanical billy goats** emerge from a door above the clock and butt heads a dozen times. According to legend, the cook, hired to prepare a celebratory feast upon completion of the clock in 1511, burnt the venison that was to be served to the governor of Poznań Province. Frantic, the cook stole two goats to cook instead, but the goats exposed his ruse when they escaped to the clock tower and began butting heads in front of the guests. The museum within the town hall recalls Wielkopolska's history from the 13th century on, but the most captivating sights are the carved and painted ceilings. (☎852 56 13. Open M-Sa 10am-4pm, Su 10am-3pm. 5.50zł, students 3.50zł. Sa free.) The vast galleries of the **National Museum** (Muzeum Narodowe), ul. Marcinkowskiego 9, contain a marvelous collection of 13th- to 19th-century Western European paintings and modern Polish art. (☎856 80 00; fax 851 58 98. Open Tu 10am-6pm, W 9am-5pm, Th and Su 10am-4pm, F-Sa 10am-5pm. 10zł, students 6zł. Sa free.) One of the National's daughter museums is the ⬛**Museum of Musical Instruments** (Muzeum Instrumentów Muzycznych), Stary Rynek 45, which displays antique and foreign instruments, as well as the Chopin room, featuring a piano that once belonged Poland's famous son. (☎852 08 57. Open Tu-Sa 11am-5pm, Su 11am-4pm. 5.50zł, students 3.50zł. Sa free.) Its sister museum , the **Museum of Useful Art,** ul. Góra Przemysława 1, on the hill by Stary Rynek, features 13th- to 18th-century swords and other utilities. (☎852 20 35. Open Su 10am-3pm, Tu-W and F-Sa 10am-4pm. 3.50zł, students 2.20zł. Sa free.)

Within the striking rose exterior of the **Parish Church of the City of Poznań of St. Mary Magdalene,** at the end of ul. Świętosławska off Stary Rynek, sculpted ceilings and columns spiral heavenwards into an illusory dome. (Free concerts Sa

POLAND

12:15pm.) One stop from Old Town on the #1, 4, 8 or 16 trams in **Ostrów Tumski** stands the **Cathedral of St. Peter and St. Paul** (Katedra Piotra i Pawła), the first Polish cathedral. The original 10th-century church is said to have been the site of Poland's symbolic baptism. In its ornate **Gold Chapel** (Kaplica Złota) are the tombs of two Piast family members: Prince Mieszko I (d. 992) and his oldest son, Bolesław the Brave (d. 1025), Poland's first king. (Cathedral open M-Sa 9am-6pm, Su 1:15pm-6:30pm. Golden Chapel 2zł.) **Pl. Mickiewicza** commemorates the 1956 clash over food prices between workers and government troops, resulting in 76 deaths. Two stark crosses knotted together with steel cable are emblazoned with the dates of five of Poland's other communist-era worker uprisings. A recording tells the story from a console in front of the monument. (In several languages. Free.) In summer, escape to **Malta Lake** (Jezioro Maltańskie). Take tram #1, 4, 8 or 16 along Małe Garbary/Estrowskiego to Rondo Środka. From the southeast corner of the roundabout, catch the train that runs along the lake. (Runs daily 10am-6pm, every hr. on the hr.; M-F on the half-hour. 4.20zł, students 2.70zł). On the other side of the lake is **Malta Ski**, ul. Wiankowa 2, Poznań's year-round artificial ski slope. They also rent mountain bikes and roller skates. (☎855 74 27; www.maltaski.com.pl. Open daily 10am-8pm.) If skiing's not your style, watch world-class rowers practice on the lake.

🎵 🌿 ENTERTAINMENT AND FESTIVALS

Poznań's music and theater scene is lively but fickle. The monthly *Poznański Informator Kulturalny, Sportowy i Turystyczny* (IKST) is an English supplement on cultural events. (3.90zł. Sold at bookstores and some kiosks.) The **Towarzystwo Muzyczne im. Henryka Wieniawskiego** (Music Society), ul. Świętosławska 7, provides classical concert info. (☎852 26 42; fax 852 89 91. English spoken. Open M-F 9am-5pm. Ring the bell.) It also hosts the huge **International Theater Festival** at Malta Lake in late June and early July. Other festivals include the **Jazz Festival**, in early March; the **International Blues Festival**, in late May and early June; and a **folk art festival**, in July. For tickets and info on these and other cultural events, contact **Centrum Informacji Miejskiej**, ul. Ratajczka 44, next to the Empik Megastore. (☎94 31. Open M-F 10am-7pm, Sa-Su 10am-5pm.) Poznań's many cutting-edge and experimental artistic performances and film screenings are concentrated in the venues along ul. Nowowieskiego. For current listings, check the free monthly Mapa guide (www.czyli.info).

🍸 NIGHTLIFE

Bars and cafes surround the *rynek*, and dance clubs dot the Old Town. A more avant-garde scene thrives on ul. Nowowieskiego.

🎬 **W Starym Kinie**, ul. Nowowieskiego 8 (☎852 22 41; www.wstarymkinie.iq.pl). An antique film projector on the bar and a gregarious crowd welcome patrons to the magical "Old Cinema." Relax in old movie theater seats at the bar downstairs; head upstairs to take in one of the frequent film screenings, rock and jazz concerts, and innovative DJ sets. Beer 6.50zł. Tu movie night, W "Classic Vinyl," F Disko Inferno. 18+. Open M-Sa 10am-1am, Su 6pm-midnight.

Czarna Owca (Black Ewe), ul. Jaskółcza 13 (☎853 07 92; www.czarnaowca.pl). A Poznań institution. Wagon wheels festoon the sturdy bar upstairs. The dance floor hosts one of the most hedonistic parties in town. Beer 4.5-6zł. F house, garage, and hip-hop, Sa rock and pop. Open M-F noon-2am, Sa 6pm-3am, Su 6pm-midnight.

Scena Pod Minogą, ul. Nowowieskiego 8 (☎852 79 22). Neighboring W Starym Kinie is a tough act to follow, but exuberant Pod Minogą, a student dance favorite, holds its own. Rooms wind through 2 floors of a rambling house. Frequent live Polish hip-hop performances. Beer 4-6zł. 18+. Open M-Sa 10am-3am, Su 4pm-midnight.

The Dubliner, al. Niepodległości 80/82 (☎851 01 69). A warm, inviting pub full of warm, inviting spirits, tucked into a castle cellar. Guinness 12zł, cider 10zł. Live rock F-Sa 9am-1pm. May-Sept. concerts are held on back patio. Open daily 2pm-late.

TORUŃ ☎(0)56

Toruń (pop. 210,000; est. 1233), extols itself as the birthplace of Mikołaj Kopernik, a.k.a. Copernicus. Even before the local genius came to fame, the mercantile medieval city was known far and wide: it was called "beautiful red Toruń" for its impressive brick and stone structures. Today, parishioners pray in 500-year-old churches and children scramble through the ruins of a Teutonic castle, while visitors stroll through the city's cobblestone streets and linger along the riverwalk.

▐ TRANSPORTATION

Trains: Toruń Główny, ul. Kujawska 1 (☎94 36). International *kasa* sells Wasteels and InterRail. Open M-F 7am-5pm, Sa-Su 7am-2pm. To: **Gdańsk** (3¼hr., 7 per day, 36zł); **Gniezno** (1½hr., 5 per day, 15zł); **Łódź** (2¾hr., 4 per day, 32zł); **Poznań** (2¼hr., 5 per day, 31zł); **Szczecin** (4½hr., 1 per day, 36zł); **Warsaw** (2¾hr., 6 per day, 37zł).

Buses: Dworzec PKS, ul. Dąbrowskiego 26 (☎655 53 33). To: **Białystok** (8½hr., 1 per day, 52zł); **Gdańsk** (3½hr., 2 per day, 31zł); **Kołobrzeg** (7hr., 2 per day, 40zł); **Łódź** (3¼hr., 6 per day, 27zł); **Szczecin** (6½hr., 1 per day, 44zł); **Warsaw** (4hr., 9 per day, 36zł); **Berlin, GER** (9½hr., 1 per day, 120zł). **Polski Express** (☎22 620 03 30) runs buses from the Ruch Kiosk north of pl. Teatralny to: **Kołobrzeg** (6¾hr.; 1 per day; 44zł, students 27zł); **Łódź** (3hr.; 1 per day; 29-31zł, students 19-21zł); **Szczecin** (5¼hr.; 2 per day; 52zł, students 33zł); **Warsaw** (3½hr.; 15 per day; 34-37zł, students 21-23zł).

Public Transportation: (☎655 52 00). Tickets 1.80zł at kiosks, 2.30zł from drivers. Luggage needs its own ticket.

Taxis: ☎91 91, wheelchair-accessible transport 91 96. 4.30zł plus 1.60zł per km.

✦ ▐ ORIENTATION AND PRACTICAL INFORMATION

The tourist office and most sights are in and around **Rynek Staromiejski** (Old Town Square). To get to the *rynek* from the train station, take bus #22 or 27 across the **Wisła (Vistula) River** to Plac Rapackiego. Head through the park, with the river on your right, to find the square. On foot, take **ul. Kujawska** left from the train station, turn right onto **al. Jana Pawła II,** and hike over the Wisła. **Pl. Rapackiego** is on the right, after **ul. Kopernika.** From the bus station, walk through the park and take a left on **ul. Uniwersytecka.** Continue along the street and turn right on **Wały Gen. Sikorskiego.** At **pl. Teatralny,** turn left onto **ul. Chełmińska,** which leads to **Rynek Staromiejski. Ul. Szeroka** and **ul. Królowej Jadwigi** run to **Rynek Nowomiejski** (New Town Square).

Tourist Offices: IT, Rynek Staromiejski 25 (☎621 09 31; www.it.torun.pl). Has some **free maps,** including map of bus and tram system, and sells others (5.50-7zł). Open May-Dec. M and Sa 9am-4pm, Tu-F 9am-6pm, Su 9am-1pm; Sept.-Apr. closed Su.

Currency Exchange: Bank PKO, ul. Kopernika 38 (☎610 47 15), gives Visa **cash advances.** Open M-F 8am-6pm. **ATMs** line ul. Szeroka.

English-Language Bookstores: Polanglo, ul. Wielkie Garbary 19 (☎/fax 621 12 22; www.polanglo.pl). Good English fiction collection. Open M-F 8am-6pm, Sa 10am-2pm.

Pharmacy: Apteka Panaceum, ul. Odrodzenia 1 (☎622 41 59), off ul. Chełmińska, is open later than most. Open M-F 8am-10pm, Sa 8am-3pm, Su 10am-2pm. MC/V.

Medical Assistance: Szpital Bielany, ul. Św. Józefa 53/59 (☎610 11 00). Take bus #11. **Nasz Lekarz** has registration at ul. Szeroka 25 (☎622 61 89). Physicians' offices are around the corner at ul. Szczytna. 1.50zł per visit. Open M-F 8am-8pm, Sa 8am-2pm. After-hours **emergency** (☎999).

Internet Access: Jeremi Internet Cafe, Rynek Staromiejski 33, 1st fl. (☎602 350 652; www.jeremi.pl). Ring the buzzer. 3zł per hr. Open 24hr.

Post Office: Rynek Staromiejski 15 (☎621 91 00). **Telephones** inside. **Poste Restante** at window #9. Open M-F 8am-8pm, Sa 8am-3pm. Branch at train station open M-Sa 6:30am-8:30pm. **Postal Code:** 87-100.

ACCOMMODATIONS

There are a number of reasonably priced accommodations in the Old Town, but vacancies fill up fast, so call ahead. **IT** (see above) can help arrange rooms in hostels and in Mikolaj Kopernik University dorms in July and August. (Singles 45zł; doubles 60zł; triples 62zł.)

Hotel Kopernik, ul. Wola Zamkowa 16 (☎652 25 73). From Rynek Staromiejski, follow ul. Szeroka, go right onto ul. Św. Jakuba, and left onto ul. Wola Zamkowa. At the edge of the Old Town beside the Teutonic Knights' Castle, Kopernik has complimentary mineral water, fluffy towels, and satellite TV. Sausage-heavy breakfast buffet (10zł). Check-in and check-out 2pm. Singles 76zł, with bath 115 zł; doubles 136zł/180zł. MC/V. ❸

PTTK Dom Turystyczny, ul. Legionów 24 (☎/fax 622 38 55). Take bus #10 from the train station to Dekerta, then backtrack toward town on Legionów. Close to the bus station. Sunny, well-maintained rooms and clean, ample communal bathrooms make this student-filled dorm worth the trek from town. A favorite of Polish school groups, so be sure to book ahead. Check-in 2pm. Check-out noon. Dorms 25-30zł; singles 70zł; doubles 80zł; triples 99zł; quads 120zł; quints 150zł. ❶

Hotel "Gotyk," ul. Piekary 20 (☎658 40 00; gotyk@ic.torun.pl). Although the Gothic portal and burgundy walls may send you back a few centuries, the modern amenities will ease your return. The hotel staff escorts you to radiant rooms with carved bedsteads and Internet access. Breakfast included. Reception 24hr. Check-in and check-out 2pm. Singles 170zł; doubles 250-300zł; apartments 300-350zł. AmEx/MC/V. ❺

FOOD

Toruń still offers its centuries-old treat: **gingerbread** *(pierniki)*. Toruń's tradition of ginger-cakes dates to the 14th century, but the original cakes, tough and unsweetened, were considered a medicine rather than a snack. Toruń kept its gingerbread recipe a secret for centuries, and even today many gingerbread-makers guard their recipes closely. When selecting gingerbread, bear in mind that the intricately designed breads in the shapes of historical figures and buildings are made from the old recipes and are more decorative than edible. The smaller breads in simpler shapes are the soft, sweetened, modern form of gingerbread. Apart from gingerbread, Toruń's culinary offerings are relatively modest. **Supersam,** ul. Chełmińska 22, is a **24hr. grocery store. Targowisko Miejskie,** composed of an international bazaar and a farmer's market, sprawls on ul. Chełmińska. (Open daily 8am-4pm.)

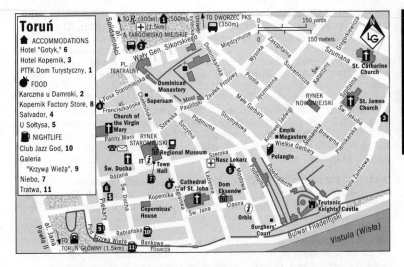

Toruń

🏠 ACCOMMODATIONS
Hotel "Gotyk," **6**
Hotel Kopernik, **3**
PTTK Dom Turystyczny, **1**

🍴 FOOD
Karczma u Damroki, **2**
Kopernik Factory Store, **8**
Salvador, **4**
U Sołtysa, **5**

🍸 NIGHTLIFE
Club Jazz God, **10**
Galeria
  "Krzywą Wieżą", **9**
Niebo, **7**
Tratwa, **11**

POLAND

Kopernik Factory Store, ul. Żeglarska 25 (☎ 621 05 61), and Rynek Staromiejski 6 (☎ 622 88 32). Collect gingerbread likenesses of your favorite Polish kings, saints, and astronomers. Among the sweetened, modern gingerbread offerings, highlights include heart-shaped, chocolate-covered *katarzynki* and gingerbread-filled boxes in the shapes of Toruń's most beautiful buildings. From 0.70zł for a small taste to 26zł for top-of-the-line historical figures. Sold by weight (about 12zł per kg) or pre-packaged. Open M-F 9am-7pm, Sa-Su 10am-2pm. MC/V. ❷

Karczma u Damroki, al. Solidarności 1 (☎ 622 36 60), in a Kashubian farmhouse in the Ethnographic Park. In medieval times, a *karczma* was an eatery and watering hole for knights and peasants alike. Karczma u Damroki draws on studies of local food culture to recreate traditional dishes with accuracy. Entrees 18-33zł. Open daily 10am-1am. ❸

Salvador, ul. Franciszkańska 20 (☎ 501 50 51 94), in a flatiron building on the edge of Old Town. Delivers tea (5-6zł per pot), coffee (cappuccino 3.50zł), and alcohol to students and professors from the nearby university. Open daily 10am-midnight. ❶

U Sołtysa, ul. Mostowa 17 (☎ 652 26 56, ext. 21). Polish inn focusing on cuisine of the Pomorze (Pomerania) region. Plum dumplings (10zł), sour soup (6zł), and pea-and-cabbage salad (7zł) complement rich entrees (10-35zł). Specializes in traditional drinks, including curd, apple *kvass*, and *siwucha* vodka. Open daily noon-midnight. MC/V. ❷

🄶 SIGHTS

An astounding number of attractions are packed into Toruń's ramparts, particularly in the 13th-century **Stare Miasto** (Old Town), built by the Teutonic Knights.

COPERNICUS'S HOUSE (DOM KOPERNIKA). The birthplace of astronomer Mikołaj Kopernik (1473-1543) has been meticulously restored and showcases astronomical instruments, Kopernik family documents, and other artifacts that paint a picture of the scientific, medical, and cultural life of 16th-century Toruń. An interesting sound and light show centered on a miniature model of the city (c. 1550) plays every 30min. Choose from eight languages, including English. (*Ul. Kopernika 15/17.* ☎ 622 70 38, ext.13. Open Su, W, F 10am-4pm; Tu, Th, Sa noon-6pm. 7zł, students 5zł. Sound and light show 8zł/5zł. Both 12zł/8zł.)

TOWN HALL (RATUSZ). One of Europe's finest examples of burgher architecture in Europe, this 14th-century building dominates the Old Town Square. The wings house 12 halls, 52 rooms, and 356 windows, while the 42m clock tower offers a grand view of the city. The town hall now contains the **Regional Museum** (Muzeum Okręgowe). Its exhibits include a famous 16th-century portrait of Kopernik and artifacts from Toruń's numerous craft guilds, including some 15th-century ginger-bread tins. *(Rynek Staromiejski 1.* ☎ *622 70 38. Museum open May-Aug. Tu-W and Sa noon-6pm, Th and Su 10am-4pm; Sept.-Apr. Tu-Su 10am-4pm. 6zł, students 4zł; Su free. Medieval tower open May-Sept. Tu-Su. 6zł/4zł.)* Outside, it's impossible to miss the statue of Kopernik watching over the city. Another local "hero," the Raftsman ringed by gold frogs, also flanks the Ratusz. Legend has it that his flute charmed animals, delivering the city from a pesky frog plague, and he was rewarded with marriage to the mayor's daughter.

TEUTONIC STRUCTURES. The 13th-century **Teutonic Knights' Castle** survived two centuries before the burghers burned it to the ground in a 1454 revolt. The remains of the building house a booth where you can try your hand at archery (4zł). The 14th-century **toilet tower** served as indoor plumbing and as a kind of fecal defense, shooting more than just the cannons in the enemy's direction. *(Ul. Przedzamcze.* ☎ *622 70 39. Open daily 9am-8pm. 1zl, students 0.50zł.)* The nearby **Burghers' Court,** at the end of ul. Podmurna, was built in 1489 from bricks of the destroyed Teutonic castle and served as a medieval social and sporting center. Across town, to the right as you face the river, stands the **Krzywą Wieżą** (Leaning Tower), built in 1271 by a knight as punishment for breaking the Order's rule of celibacy. The assumption was that the tower's "deviation" would remind the knight of his own. The less imaginative credit the shifting, sandy ground beneath. Either way, the 15m tower doesn't lean enough to scare away entrepreneurs, who have opened up a bar (see p. 581) and cafe inside. *(Ul. Krzywą Wieżą 17.)*

CHURCHES. The **Cathedral of St. John the Baptist and St. John the Evangelist** (Bazylika Katedralna pw. Św. Janów) is the most impressive of the many Gothic churches in the region. Built between the 13th- and 15th-century, it mixes Gothic, Baroque, and Rococo elements. A 14th-century polychrome in the chancel depicts the cathedral's burgher patrons, Old Testament scenes, and the Last Judgment. In 1473, the baby Kopernik was baptized in the **baptismal font.** The tower holds the Tuba Dei, the second-largest and oldest bell in Poland. *(At the corner of ul. Żeglarska and Św. Jana. Open April-Oct. M-Sa 8:30am-5:30pm, Su 2-5:30pm. 2zł, students 1zł. Tower 6zł/4zł.)* The **Church of the Virgin Mary** (Kościół Św. Marii), with its slender stained-glass windows, is less ornate than many Polish churches. The chancel holds the mausoleum of Swedish queen Anna Wazówna. *(On ul. Panny Marii. Open M-Sa around 8am-5pm. Recorded audio/visual info, 2zł.)*

❀ 🍷 FESTIVALS AND NIGHTLIFE

In May, Toruń hosts **Probaltica,** the Baltic celebration of chamber music and arts, and the "Kontakt" **International Theater Festival.** On June 20, the town celebrates the annual **Gingerbread Day.** In June and July, during the **Music and Architecture Festival,** classical concerts are held in different historical buildings each weekend. July and August usher in the annual **Summer Street Theater** series, which stages weekly performances in July and August. Check **IT** (see **Tourist Offices,** p. 577) for more info.

🏠 **Niebo,** Rynek Staromiejski 1 (☎621 03 27). Niebo (heaven) may be an odd name for a subterranean cafe, but this Gothic cellar beneath the Old Town Hall proves itself worthy with celestial *szarlotka* and summer outdoor seating. Run by a local singer-songwriter,

Nieba hosts live jazz and cabaret shows. Open Su-Th noon-midnight, F-Sa noon-2am. Be sure to check out the adjacent pub **Piwnica pod Aniołem** (Cellar Beneath the Angels; ☎658 54 82). Beer 4-5zł. Open M-F 10am-1am, Sa-Su 10am-4am.

Club Jazz God, ul. Rabiańska 17 (☎652 21 308; www.jazzgod.torun.com.pl). With live jazz on Su, this stone cellar pays homage to its namesake. During the rest of the week, it's a lively student hangout. M reggae, Tu heavy metal and hard rock, W-Sa disco. The party starts around 8:30pm. Open M-Th and Su 5pm-2am, F-Sa 5pm-4am.

Galeria "Krzywą Wieżą," ul. Pod Krzywąwieżą 1/3 (☎622 70 39), on the 1st fl. of the Leaning Tower. A must in summer. A terrace precariously attached to the ramparts offers views across the Wisła. Beer 4.50-6zł. Open M-F 1pm-1am, Sa-Su 10am-2am.

Tratwa, ul. Flisacza 7. The best of the bars alongside the Wisła, Tratwa occupies the former municipal gasworks, just outside the Monastery Gate. Hemmed by lush vines, the patio hosts frequent rock and reggae concerts and grills sausage and fish (10-15zł) on the open barbecue. Beer (5-6zł). Open Su-Th noon-2am, F-Sa noon-4am.

POMORZE

Pomorze encompasses the murky swamps and windswept dunes of the Baltic Coast. Centuries ago, fishermen battled the elements to build villages here. A few hamlets grew into large ports, such as Szczecin on the Odra River. Other towns, like Świnoujście, are building around their shoreline assets. Woliński National Park, with its hiking trails and native European bison, extends from the beaches of Międzyzdroje.

SZCZECIN   ☎(0)91

Szczecin (SHCHEH-cheen; pop. 420,000) is strategically situated at the mouth of the Odra River, the site of centuries of power plays at the hands of Sweden, Prussia, and finally Poland. Today, the city is a major transportation hub with railways and waterways that sprawl out from the center. Only a few kilometers from the German border, Szczecin is a popular destination for western visitors seeking bargain shopping and cut-rate medical services, as the ubiquitous "24hr. Dentistry" billboards attest.

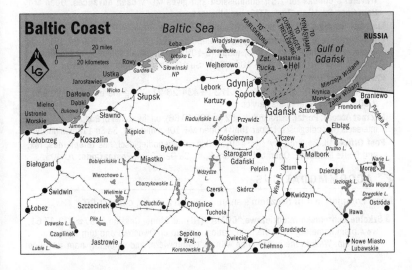

TRANSPORTATION

Trains: The **train station**, ul. Kolumba 1 (☎94 36), is at the end of ul. 3-go Maja. Trains to: **Gdańsk** (3¾hr., 4 per day, 44zł); **Kołobrzeg** (3hr., 3 per day, 34zł); **Kraków** (8¼hr., 5 per day, 50zł); **Lublin** (8½hr., 1 per day, 52zł); **Łódź** (7¾hr., 2 per day, 47zł); **Poznań** (2½hr., 13 per day, 36zł); **Świnoüjście** (2½hr., 18 per day, 26zł); **Toruń** (4½hr., 2 per day, 43zł); **Warsaw** (6hr., 6 per day, 49-93zł); **Wrocław** (7¾hr., 8 per day, 44zł); **Zakopane** (14¼hr., 1 per day, 53zł); **Berlin, GER** (2hr., 1 per day, 119zł); **Bratislava, SLK** (13hr., 1 per day, 232zł). Buy international tickets at *kasa* #15.

Buses: The **bus station** is on pl. Tobrucki, 2min. from the train station. To: **Jelenia Góra** (7hr., 1 per day, 52zł); **Kołobrzeg** (3hr., 3 per day, 25zł); **Międzyzdroje** (2hr., 10 per day, 19zł); **Świnoüjście** (2½hr., 3 per day, 18zł); **Toruń** (6½hr., 1 per day, 44zł); **Warsaw** (9hr., 1 per day, 58zł). Tickets for international transportation are available at **Euro Ster** in the bus station (☎489 38 78; www.e-bilety.pl.). Open M-F 9am-5pm.

Public Transportation: Numerous **tram** and **bus** lines run along major roads. 1.90zł per 20min., 2.90zł per hr., 3.80zł per 2hr.; prices double after 11pm. Students half-price. Day pass 8.70zł.

Taxis: Express-Taxi ☎96 25.

ORIENTATION AND PRACTICAL INFORMATION

The city center is uphill from the stations, which lie by the river. To reach the center from the train station, turn left and uphill onto **ul. Dworcowa**. Go right onto ul. 3-go Maja, which runs into **al. Niepodległości**, the main north-south thoroughfare, as it crosses **pl. Brama Portowa**. The **castle** and oldest part of town lie northeast of the center: from al. Niepodległości, turn right on ul. Małopolska.

Tourist Office: CIT, al. Niepodległości 1 (☎434 04 40; fax 433 84 20), provides **free maps** and info. Open M-F 9am-5pm; July-Aug. also Sa 10am-2pm. CIT has a 2nd location (☎489 16 30; fax 434 02 86), in the castle, specializing in cultural events and sights. Open daily 10am-6pm.

Currency Exchange: Bank Pekao SA, pl. Żołnierza Polskiego 16 (☎440 06 23), cashes **traveler's checks** for 1.5% commission and gives MC/V **cash advances.** Open M-F 8am-6pm, Sa 10am-2pm. **ATMs** are all over town.

Luggage Storage: In the train station. Lockers 4zł, large 8zł.

English-Language Bookstore: Empik, al. Niepodległości 60, 3rd fl. (☎489 39 35), sells international guidebooks, books, **maps** (5-10zł), and a small selection of modern fiction. Open M-F 10am-8pm, Sa 10am-6pm, Su 10:30am-4:30pm. AmEx/MC/V.

Emergency: ☎999.

24hr. Pharmacy: Ul. Więckowskiego 1/2 (☎434 26 27). Ring the bell midnight-8am. 2.50zł extra for after-hours service.

Internet Access: Portal, ul. Kaszubska 52 (☎488 40 66), on the corner of *Bogurodzicy*, which intersects Niepodległości. 1zł per 15min. Open M-F 10am-midnight, Sa-Su 11am-midnight.

Post Office: Ul. Bogurodzicy 1 (☎440 14 21), off Niepodległości, has **telephones, fax,** and **Poste Restante.** Open M-F 7:30am-8pm, Sa 9am-2pm. **Postal Code:** 70-405.

ACCOMMODATIONS

For a complete list of Szczecin's summer youth hostels, contact **CIT.**

▧ **Szkolne Schronisko Młodzieżowe "CUMA" (HI),** ul. Monte Cassino 19a (☎422 47 61; www.ptsm.home.pl). From the train station, pick up ul. Owocowa and turn right onto ul. 3-go Maja. Walk to the intersection with ul. Narutowicza, and catch city tram #1. Ride to Piotra Skargi, then backtrack and follow the signs with the HI symbol. Nestled in a leafy neighborhood, CUMA's outstanding facilities and services aim to please. Flexible 11pm curfew. Dorms 14-18zł; doubles from 44zł. 25% HI discount. AmEx/MC/V. ❶

Pocztylion, ul. Dworcowa 20 (☎440 12 11), between the stations and the center, in the old post office building. Its handsome, red-brick building is also home to the "Klub Poczta" dance club. Have the guard let you through—a far easier task if you've reserved ahead. Located in Building A on the 3rd fl. Rooms are spacious and come with gigantic fridges. Singles 42zł; doubles 84zł; triples 126zł. ❶

Hotelik Elka-Sen, al. 3-go Maja 1a (☎433 56 04). From the train station, go up ul. Dworcowa to ul. 3-go Maja and turn left. This popular, central hotel has well-kept rooms in an unassuming exterior. Rooms have baths and satellite TV. Breakfast included. Singles 110zł; doubles 165zł; triples 195zł. Sa-Su 10% discount. AmEx/MC/V. ❹

🖸 FOOD

Szczecin's restaurants, many of them aimed at foreign visitors, are among the most culinarily diverse—and high-priced—in Poland. For groceries, try **Extra**, at ul. Niepodległości 27. (Open M-Sa 7am-9pm, Su 10am-6pm. MC/V.)

Jazz Cafe Brama, pl. Hołdu Pruskiego 1 (☎804 62 95). Wedged beneath the arch of King's Gate, Brama has the best location in Szczecin. It is a genial spot for a quiet drink, with an atmosphere somewhere between a bar-like cafe and a cafe-like bar. Beer 5-7zł. Cappuccino 6zł. Open M-Th 10am-midnight, F-Sa noon-2am, Su noon-midnight. ❶

Brasserie Margot, ul. Księcia Mściwoja 8 (☎488 34 81). Earnest, French cuisine in the cellar of the Old Town Hall, with a smattering of Polish classics. Entrees 26-33zł, salads 7-16zł. Open daily noon-11pm. MC/V. ❸

Haga Holland Kitchen, ul. Sienna 10 (☎812 17 59). Plump Dutch pancakes (9.50-20zł) bear every conceivable topping, sweet or savory, meal or snack, at this subterranean respite from the bargain-shopping bustle of Szczecin. Open daily July-Aug. 11am-11pm; Sept.-June M-Th and Su 11am-10pm, F-Sa 11am-11pm. ❷

Bombay, ul. Partyzanow 1 (☎488 49 32; www.india.pl). Westward-looking Bombay caters to foreign visitors with sumptuous silk trimmings, enthusiastic customer service, and some of the most authentic Indian food in Poland. Enjoy spicy dishes in the hushed privacy of pillow-strewn booths. Entrees 25-45zł. Open daily noon-10pm. ❹

🖸 SIGHTS

Walks through the city usually start at the **Port Gate** (Brama Portowa), in pl. Zwycięztwa off al. Niepodległości. The gate bears an inscription commemorating Emperor Friedrich Wilhelm I and a panorama of 18th-century Szczecin. Viadus, god of the Odra, leans against a jug, from which the river's waters flow. Two blocks north, a right turn at pl. Żołnierza Polskiego leads to the Baroque **Pomeranian Parliament,** ul. Staromłyńska 27/28, on the corner. A sight not to be missed is ⬛**Muzeum Morskie,** on ul. Wały Chrobrego, which contains an impressive display of model ships, from 15th-century galleons to modern chemical tankers. It has a well-designed exhibit on the archaeology and history of Szczecin, including beehives, peasant life exhibits, and out-of-place reproductions of Greek statuaries. Reproductions of West African villages and Vietnamese Buddhist altars demonstrate the prowess of Polish anthropologists. (☎431 52 55. Open Tu-F 10am-5pm, Sa-Su 10am-4pm.) The best area for walking is the raised **riverfront promenade.** Across Żołnierza Polskiego and to the left lies another of the city's grand gates, **Brama Królewska** (Kings' Gate). The **old town hall** (ratusz), ul. Mściwoja 8, dates from 1450 and has been extensively restored since WWII. Today, the building houses the **Museum of** the **History of the City of Szczecin.** Check out the giant 19th-century music box masquerading as a mirror and the vodka bottle from 1615. (☎431 52 55. Open Tu-F 10am-5pm, Sa-Su 10am-4pm.) Uphill from the old town hall, the **Pomeranian Knights' Castle,** ul. Korsarzy 34, first constructed in the 14th century, was the stronghold of powerful princes in the 16th and 17th centuries. Rebuilt after WWII, the castle now hosts theaters, the city opera, museums, and beer gardens. Castle attractions include the gold-encrusted sarcophagi of 16th-century dukes and the ugly, hospital-green, concrete **bell tower.** Visitors can ascend the tower's staggering heights for a view of the small bell, which is swathed in chain-link fence and decorated with a lively graffiti exchange between local anarchists and Satanists. (☎434 73 91. Castle sights open daily 10am-6pm. Knights' crypt 6zł, students 3zł. Bell tower 6zł/3zł.)

ŚWINOÚJŚCIE ☎(0)91

A tiny slip of Polish seaside, Świnoújście has one of the best Baltic beaches. The white sand, girded by parkland and protected dunes, sprawls from the German border to a breakwater that hails from the city's 19th-century heyday as the health resort of Swinemunde. From the ferry terminal, the beach is a 10min. walk down any of the streets perpendicular to the harbor. Try ul. B. Chrobrego for a lovely stroll through **Park Zdrojowy Kurpark.** While at the beach, walk to **Stawa Młyny,** the windmill-shaped lighthouse where local fishermen gather to cast for the fish, served in beachside fry shacks. Working your way back to town along the footpaths that edge the Świna Causeway, you will come across the **Western Fort** (Fort Zachodni). These fortifications were built in 1843, expanded in WWII, and housed the Soviet Army until 1962. Now in a state of disrepair, the fort includes a collection of WWII German army memorabilia. (Open daily 10am-6pm. 5zł, students 3zł.) On Wednesday through Saturday nights, the **Redutta Association** hosts concerts ranging from jazz to opera. Across the Świna Causeway, a 10min. walk from the bus station, is **Gerard's Artillery Fort** (Fort Gerharda). Take ul. Dworcowa to ul. Barlickiego and turn left onto ul. Artyleryjska. Next door to the fort is the 68m **Laterna Morska,** the tallest lighthouse on the Balti. Inside is a small museum detailing the history of the Świnoújście forts (Open daily 10am-6pm. 5zł, students 3zł.)

The train station (ul. Dworcowa 1; ☎94 36) and bus station (ul. Dworcowa 3; ☎321 53 29) are across the Świna Causeway from the city center and beaches. The 5min. journey on a city ferry (24hr.) is free for pedestrians and runs every 15-40min. **Trains** run to: **Kraków** (9¾hr., 1 per day, 53zł); **Międzyzdroje** (20min., 19 per day, 3.80zł); **Poznań** (5¼hr., 5 per day, 45zł); **Szczecin** (2½hr., 18 per day, 26zł); **Warsaw** (7½hr., 2 per day, 50zł); **Wrocław** (10hr., 5 per day, 47zł). **Buses** run to **Gdańsk/ Gdynia** (8¼hr., 2 per day, 47zł); **Kołobrzeg** (3hr., 3 per day, 21zł); **Międzyzdroje** (20min., 44-65 per day, 3.60zł); **Sopot** (5¼hr., 2 per day, 47zł); **Szczecin** (3hr., 2 per day, 18zł). The international **ferry** terminal is 100m from the stations. Ferries go to **Copenhagen, DEN** and **Ystad, SWE.** For a taxi, call **Hallo Taxi,** ☎321 36 36, or **Radio Taxi,** ☎321 22 22. City buses (2zł) run throughout the town from 6am to 11pm, with many departing from the ferry dock.

IT, Wybreże Władysława IV, has **free maps,** arranges accommodations in private rooms, and provides info about the town. (☎/fax 322 49 99; www.swinoujscie.pl. Open M-F 9am-5pm; June-Sept. also Sa-Su 10am-3pm.) **ATMs** dot the city center. **Bank Pekao,** ul. Piłsudskiego 4, cashes **AmEx Traveler's Cheques,** gives MC/V **cash advances, exchanges currency,** and has an ATM outside. (☎321 57 33; fax 321 58 24. Open M-F 9am-5pm, Sa 10am-2pm.) **Luggage** lockers (4-8zł) are at the train station and the international ferry terminal. The **pharmacy, Apteka Morska,** is at ul. Bohaterów Września 81-82. (☎321 99 07. Open M-F 8am-7pm, Sa 9am-5pm.) The **hospital, Szpital Miejsk,** is at ul. Żeromskiego 22 (☎321 34 13). Check email at **Kawiarnia**

Internetowa "Jazz," at ul. Monte Cassino 35. (☎321 03 09. 4zł per hr. Open daily 9:30am-10pm.) The **post office** is in the city center at ul. Piłsudskiego 1. (☎321 26 01. Open M-F 8am-8pm, Sa 8am-1pm.) **Postal Code:** 72-600.

Reserve ahead in July and August, when singles are hard to come by and hotels require week-long stays. Otherwise, head straight to **IT**, where they keep an up-to-date list of available rooms. For basic budget accommodations, ask about available private rooms (*wolne pokoje*; 30-50zł). An excellent choice among private rooms is the house with the well-tended rose garden at **ul. Słowackiego 25a**, behind the Monster Museum. There are no set prices or reservations, but ring the bell. Rooms include TV, private bathrooms, and comfortable beds for 40-60zł per person. **Dom Wypoczynkowy "SAS" ❶**, ul. Nowowieskiego 1, is the least expensive option near the beach. Rooms are simple yet clean, and have shared baths. It's very popular with Polish families on holiday, so be sure to book ahead. (☎327 09 99; fax 321 14 41. Check-in and check-out noon. Doubles 76zł.) The massive hunk of Soviet-era concrete that houses the HI hostel, **Schronisko Szkolne Młodzezone ❶**, ul. Gdyńska 26, lies west of the center of town. From the ferry dock, turn left on ul. Wybrzeże Władisława, which becomes ul. Dazińskiego, and follow the plentiful signs with the HI emblem. The dorms, communal bathrooms, and full kitchen are clean but aging. (☎327 06 13. Reception open daily 6-10am and 5-10pm. Dorms 18-24zł.) The unusual Internet cafe "Alf," beside the hostel's reception, is decorated with stuffed likenesses of its namesake. (Open daily 10am-late. 3zł per hr.) **Restauracja, Jazz Club, and Cafe Centralna ❷**, ul. Armii Krajowej 3, is the unlikely outpost of bohemian culture in Świnoüjście. Dim and smoky by night with B movies flickering on the wall, Centralna is reborn each morning as a garden-side cafe with strawberry plants and excellent breakfasts. (☎/fax 321 26 40. Vegetarian and seafood entrees 10-31zł. Breakfast 12-21zł. Beer 4-5zł. Live concerts F-Sa. Open daily 10am-midnight.) For beachside fare, head to the ultra-casual **fried fish stands** along the streets next to the beach. The fish is generally excellent, but remember that listed prices are per 100g, not per fish. Most bars and clubs in Świnoüjście cater to locals, as the town's tourists tend to be elderly. Salty **Albatros**, ul. Żeromskiego 1, is a classic beach-town disco and beer garden playing pop hits, R&B, and classic rock. Party too hard and you might end up sleeping on the beach across the street. (☎691 35 88 76. Disco cover 10zł. Open 24hr.)

WOLIN ISLAND: MIĘDZYDROJE ☎(0)91

Within its mere 265 square km, Wolin Island cradles glacial lakes, sweeping sea bluffs, and a bison preserve. The largest of the island's resort towns, Międzyzdroje (myen-dzi-ZDROY-eh), lures visitors with a gorgeous stretch of coast and access to the hiking and cycling trails of pristine Woliński National Park. With a base in Międzyzdroje, intrepid visitors can explore the island's many hidden corners, from the scattered ruins of forts and churches to windswept marshes and the open-air museum in tiny Wolin.

TRANSPORTATION. Trains run to: **Kraków** (9¼hr., 2 per day, 52zł); **Poznań** (5hr., 5 per day, 42zł); **Świnoüjście** (20min., 19 per day, 3.80zł); **Szczecin** (2hr., 18 per day, 26zł); **Warsaw** (7hr., 2 per day, 50zł); **Wrocław** (9½hr., 5 per day, 47zł). **Buses** run to: **Kołobrzeg** (3hr., 9 per day, 21zł); **Świnoüjście** (20min., 44-65 per day, 3.60zł); **Szczecin** (2hr., 2 per day, 18zł); **Warsaw** (8hr., 1 per day, 36zł). Buses also frequently travel to points along the hiking trails, including the towns of **Kołczewo, Wolin,** and **Wisełka** (10-30min., 6zł).

ORIENTATION AND PRACTICAL INFORMATION. To reach the center from the **train station,** walk downhill and go left on ul. Norwida. The **PKS bus stop** is on Niepodległości in front of the Muzeum WPN, near the corner of ul. Kolejowa. Pedestrian **Plac Neptuna,** at the intersection of Niepodległości and Kolejowa, harbors many restaurants and shops. Several blocks north, the beach promenade along Bohaterów Warzsawy and Promenada Gwiazd bustles with fried fish stands, cotton candy, and a new pier. **PTTK**, ul. Kolejowa 2, sells **maps** (1-8zł) and provides info about the park and accommodations. Its map of the city and park (4.50zł) is useful for ventures in the woods. (☎328 04 62; fax 328 00 86. Open M-F 7am-4pm.) The *kantor* with the town's best **currency exchange** rates is at ul. Niepodległości 2A. (Open M-F 9am-6pm, Sa 9am-3pm, Su 10am-1pm.) There is an **ATM** outside the Polino Hotel at ul. Zwycięstwa 1. **Luggage storage** is at the train station. (Open daily 7am-9:30pm. 5zł.) A **pharmacy** is at ul. Zwycięstwa 9. (☎328 00 90. Open M-F 8am-7pm.) Use the web at **Internet Cafe**, ul. Norwida 17. (☎328 71 35. 3zł per hr. Open daily 10am-late.) The **post office** is at ul. Gryfa Pomorskiego 7. (☎328 01 40. Open M-F 8am-8pm, Sa 8am-1pm.) **Postal Code:** 72-500.

⌂⌂ ACCOMMODATIONS AND FOOD. Watch for *"wolne pokoje"* (available rooms) signs, particularly along ul. Gryfa Pomorskiego. Call ahead in July and August. Alternatively, talk to **PTTK**, ul. Kolejowa 2, which arranges private rooms (32-35zł, 40-45zł with bath) and runs the tidy **PTTK Hotel Dom Turysty ❶**, in the same building as the office. Quirky rooms are variously outfitted with old radios and tropical-themed lanterns. (☎328 03 82. June-Aug. singles 30zł, with bath 55zł; doubles 60zł/110zł; triples 90zł/165zł. Sept.-May singles 25zł/40zł; doubles 50zł/80zł; triples 75zł/120zł.) To get to **Camping Gromada ❶**, ul. Bohaterów Warszawy 1, continue down Kolejowa as it becomes ul. Gryfa Pomorskiego. Take the right fork to ul. Mickiewicza and turn right. (☎328 23 54. Reception open daily 8am-10pm. Campground open May-Sept. 1- to 4-person cabins with baths 30-59zł per person. Tents 8zł per person.)

    Bistro Bar Pieróg ❶, ul. Krasickiego 3, is a local favorite, with exemplary dumplings, hearty soups, and shark jaws decorating the walls. (☎328 04 23. Entrees 3-15zł. Open daily 9am-midnight; low season 9am-9pm.) The curious decor at **Dolce Vita ❷**, pl. Neptuna 2, involves bouquets of uncooked spaghetti. The eatery serves generous portions of pizza and pasta. It opens its pleasant terrace in summer. (☎328 17 70. Entrees 8-30zł. Open daily 10am-midnight. MC/V.) Cheery **Restauracja Cafeteria Centrum ❷**, pl. Neptuna 7/9, dishes up meaty *naleśniki* (6-10zł), superb coffee drinks (4-8zł) and breakfasts. (☎328 15 56. Open daily 10am-late.) To grab some food on the run, head to the 24hr. convenience store, **Sklep Smakasz**, ul. Norwida 4. For **nightlife**, young locals go to beachfront **Klub Scena**, ul. Promenada Gwiazd. Beware that most of the tables facing the dance floor are reserved for local VIPs, who may not take kindly to usurpers. (☎328 71 44. Beer 3zł. F-Sa 10zł cover. Open daily 9pm-late.)

◨ HIKING. Although Międzyzdroje draws crowds as a prime beach resort, the true accolades belong to adjacent **▨Woliński National Park**, whose wilds encompass much of *Wyspa Wolin* (Wolin Island) and shelter a dramatic stretch of coastline. The park is immaculately kept, with **hiking and bicycling trails** marked on trees and stones. The black and red trails begin at the end of **Promenada Gwiazd**, and the green at the end of **ul. Leśna**. The blue trail begins on **ul. Cmentarna** near the train station. These hikes are not very strenuous—don't expect Tatras trailblazing. Rent a **bike** at friendly **Willa 5**, ul. Bohaterów Warszawy 16. (☎328 26 10. 5zł per hr. ID required. Open daily 8am-8pm.)

    Black Trail. The most demanding trail immediately climbs the seaside cliffs to **Góra Kawcza** (61m), a lookout point with a breathtaking view of the Baltic. Look closely and you just might glimpse one of the park's famed eagles *(bieliki)*. Just after Kawcza Góra, the trail hits a closed military area; backtrack a few steps and follow the trail into the woods. It eventually intersects the green trail and returns to Międzyzdroje.

Red Trail. Sea breezes keep hikers refreshed along the red trail, which starts at the beach in Międzyzdroje and follows a 15km stretch of coastline beneath the cliffs. Just 2km from the pier, the crowds disappear and the beach alternates between rocky and sandy. The trail passes under the highest of the Baltic's cliffs at **Góra Gosan** (93m), then turns back into the woods and passes the lakeside town of Wisełka, the Kikut lighthouse, and another scenic cliff at **Strażnica** (74m) before intersecting the green trail.

Green Trail. Rent a bike to check out the green trail, which has an extensive set of **bike paths.** There are long stretches of less-rewarding territory between the highlights, but the 15km route heads into the heavily forested heart of the park past glacial lakes. 1.2km from the trailhead is the popular **bison preserve** *(rezerwat żubrów).* (☎328 07 37. Open May-Sept. Tu-Su 10am-6pm; Nov.-Apr. Tu-Su 8am-4pm. 3zł, students 2zł.) The trail passes the villages of Warnowo (7km), Kołczewo (7km), and **Lake Czajcze.** The green trail ends where it hits the red trail, 3km past Kołczewo.

Blue Trail. The longest trail winds all the way from Międzyzdroje to Szczecin. At 74.5km long, the blue trail is more conducive to bicycling than hiking. The tame stretch near Międzyzdroje heads south along the edge of Woliński Park, passing ruins, nature preserves and lookout points, and leaves the island through the small town of Wolin.

KOŁOBRZEG ☎(0)94

In 2005, the "Pearl of the Baltic" celebrates its 750th anniversary. In its three-quarters of a millennium, the one-time salt trading village of Kołobrzeg (koh-WOH-bzheg) has weathered occupations by Russians, Swedes, and even Napoleon; been leveled to rubble in WWII; and found glory as Poland's hottest vacation destination. The famed salt springs and crisp sea air of Kołobrzeg make the city a popular health resort, while less health-conscious visitors come to bake on beaches and imbibe the nightlife.

▐ TRANSPORTATION. The **train** and **bus** stations are on ul. Kolejowa. The train *kasa* (☎352 35 76) is open daily 5am-9pm. Trains run to: **Gdynia** (3½hr., 8 per day, 39zł); **Kraków** (11½hr., 5 per day, 51zł); **Łódź** (8hr., 2 per day, 48zł); **Poznań** (6hr., 5 per day, 40zł); **Szczecin** (3½hr., 3 per day, 21zł); **Warsaw** (8hr., 9 per day, 49-83zł). The bus *kasa* (☎352 39 28) is open daily 7am-10pm. Buses run to: **Gdańsk** (6hr., 1 per day, 40zł); **Gdynia** (5hr., 2 per day, 35zł); **Poznań** (5hr., 4 per day, 45zł); **Świnoújście** (3hr., 7 per day, 22zł); **Szczecin** (3hr., 2 per day, 25zł); **Warsaw** (11hr., 5 per day, 65zł). Buy **local bus** tickets (1.80zł) at kiosks or from the driver.

▐▐ ORIENTATION AND PRACTICAL INFORMATION. Most of Kołobrzeg's sights lie near the town center or along the beach. To get to town from the train station, walk down **ul. Dworcowa,** which intersects **ul. Armii Krajowej,** the major east-west thoroughfare. Turn left down Armii Krajowej to reach the center. Getting to the **beach** can be tough, as a tangle of train tracks separates it from the city. Turn left out of the train station (right out of bus station) and walk down **ul. Kolejowa.** The overpass that leads to the beach is on the left. Walk down **ul. Norwida** until it ends, then take any of the paths through the woods to the beach.

The **tourist office IT,** ul. Dworcowa 1, has free maps and info, and arranges accommodations. (☎352 79 39; www.kolobrzeg.turystyka.pl. Open daily June-Aug. 7am-7pm; Sept.-May M-F 7am-3pm.) **Bank PKO SA,** ul. Źródlana 5, gives MC/V **cash advances** and cashes **traveler's checks** for 1.5% commission. (☎354 68 50. Open M-F 9am-5pm.) **Bank Zachodni WBK,** ul. Emilii Gierczak 44-45, has **Western Union** services and a **24hr. ATM.** (☎352 33 62. Open M-F 9am-5pm.) **Luggage storage** is available in the back of the train station. (4zł, plus 0.45zł per 50zł declared value, 250zł min. declared value. Open daily 6am-10pm.) The **pharmacy** *(apteka)* is at ul. Mariacka 14, near St. Mary's. (☎/fax 354 27 50. Open M-F 8am-6pm, Sa 8am-2pm. Posts a list of addresses for pharmacies open 9pm-8am.) For a **hospital**, go to **Szpital Pogotowie Ratunkowe**, ul. Łopuskiego 3 (☎352 82 61.). **M@trix**, ul. Armii Krajowej 24/7, has **Internet access.** (☎354 43 30. 3zł per 15min., 4zł per 30min., 6zł per hr. Beer and coffee 4-5zł. Open daily 10am-11pm.) The **post office** is at ul. Armii Krajowej 1. For **Poste Restante**, enter the room to the left of the entrance. **Currency exchange** (open M-F 8am-1pm and 2-8pm) and a **telephone** office are inside. (☎354 43 02. Open M-F 7:30am-8pm, Sa 9am-8pm, Su 9am-1pm.) **Postal Code:** 78-100.

▌ ACCOMMODATIONS. In July and August, cheap rooms are hard to come by without a reservation. The best options are **private rooms** (15-50zł) arranged through the helpful IT office. Avoid like the plague the aggressive locals who congregate near the station wielding "wolne pokoje" signs, as decent private accommodations in Kołobrzeg are generally not those that berate travelers into accepting them. The **▌Hotelik Milenium ❷**, ul. Łopuskiego 38, attached to a new sports complex, offers the best budget accommodations in town. To reach the futuristic "Hala Milenium," which houses the hotel, follow Dworcowa from the train station until it ends at Łopuskiego. Turn right on Łopuskiego and cross the two canals. Airy rooms are outfitted in matching light-wood decor and include bathrooms and satellite TV. (☎355 13 03. Singles 50zł; doubles 100zł. Breakfast 15zł.) **Pensionat Górnik ❸**, ul. Kościuszki 3, one block from the beach and three from the train station, has rooms with balconies and a crew of manic maids that will probably keep it looking good for years to come. All rooms include breakfast, satellite TVs, and phones. (☎352 60 05; www.nat.pl. Singles 70zł; doubles 140zł; apartments 320zł. MC/V.) Sleep on cots at no-frills **Schronisko PTSM ❶**, ul. Śliwiń skiego 1. Follow directions for Hotelik Milenium, but continue on Łopuskiego until you reach Śliwińskiego; turn right onto Śliwińskiego. (☎/fax 352 27 69. Kitchenette available. Lockout 10am-5pm. Curfew 10pm. Dorms 14zł, students 11zł.)

▢ FOOD. Fried fish stands *(smażalnia ryb)* border the beach, and decent restaurants line the streets near the town hall. Try the large **Delikatesy**, which sits at ul. Warzyńskiego 2. (Open M-Sa 8am-midnight, Su 10am-midnight. MC/V.) A delightful and hidden milk bar, **▌Jadłodajnia Całoroczna ❷**, ul. Budowlana 28, is just outside the square. From ul. Armii Krajowej, turn right down Budowlana. Follow the alley at Budlowana 28 to the canal. Eating here is likely to require Polish-language skills; the most accessible option is the daily *zestawy*, a meal that begins with a huge bowl of soup and continues through meaty stews and a fruit dessert. (☎352 69 12. Entrees 12-15zł. Open M-F 10am-7pm, Sa-Su 10am-5pm.) **Restauracja Fregata ❶**, ul. Dworcowa 12, has a deck-side view of the post office and a glitzy decor; the traditional Polish meals at this disco/restaurant are top-notch. (☎352 37 87. Entrees 12-20zł. Open M noon-10pm, Tu-Su noon-2am. MC/V.) Tuscany may be a long way from the Baltic, but the vine-laden interior and extensive wine list of **Bar Pod Winogronami ❸**, ul. Towarowa 16, bring it a bit closer. Most entrees feature tenderly prepared seafood, but for 35zł, the daring might sample the sirloin wrapped in hay. (☎354 73 36; winogrona@wp.pl. Entrees 25-45zł. Open M-F noon-midnight, Sa-Su 11am-midnight. AmEx/MC/V.)

◑ SIGHTS. Most of Kołobrzeg's buildings were razed during WWII. The city has launched an impressive reconstruction program around the old town hall, though highrise Soviet-era concrete block housing is still visible. Built between the 14th and 16th centuries, **St. Mary's Basilica**, on the corner of ul. Katedralna and ul. Armii Kratowej, is an anomaly of Gothic architecture. The interior was torched during WWII, but its five-aisle structure remains. A towering iron candelabra from 1327 is a highlight.

From March 4-18, 1945, fierce battles raged between the Poles and the Nazis over Kołobrzeg. On the day of their triumph, the Poles vowed that the city would forever remain on Polish soil. The Poles then threw a wedding ring into the Baltic during a ceremony that has become known as Poland's **Marriage to the Sea** (Zaślubiny z Morzem). A **monument,** ul. Morska 1, commemorates these nautical nuptials. On the same corner, the 1745 lighthouse **Latarnia Morska** affords postcard views across the Baltic. (Open daily July-Aug. 10am-sunset; Sept.-June 10am-5pm. 3zł.)

Muzeum Oręża Polskiego, ul. Emilii Gierczak 5, features an array of Polish and international military uniforms and weaponry. Wander outside to see authentic military vehicles, scattered oddly throughout a rose garden. (☎352 52 53. Open M-Tu and Th-Su 9:30am-5pm, W 9:30am-6pm; 6zł, students 3zł; W noon-6pm free. Only outdoor exhibit open W noon-6pm.) The heart of the reconstructed old town is the neo-Gothic **town hall,** pl. Ratuszowy, built in 1829 on the site of Kołobrzeg's original Gothic hall. Cellars of the 15th-century building remain. The building now houses the **Gallery of Modern Art** (Galeria Sztuki Współczesniej), which hosts rotating exhibits of international modern paintings and drawings. Not to be missed is the gift shop, which sells an exquisite collection of paintings and sculptures (from 25zł), all by Polish artists and artisans. (☎352 43 48. Open Tu-Su 10am-6pm. Price varies with exhibit; about 8zł, students 6zł.)

ENTERTAINMENT AND FESTIVALS. Though most visitors come to Kołobrzeg for its healing springs and stretches of sand, the fun doesn't stop with beach and brine. August brings **InterFolk,** an international dance festival, to the streets of the city. From June to August, St. Mary's comes alive with the sound of music during **Music in the Cathedral.** (Muzyka w Katedrze. Shows Th 8pm. 10zł, students 8zł.) Kołobrzeg's nightlife centers on the beach cafes, but if you're in the mood for a memorable glimpse into Polish vacation life, head to **Port Jachtowy,** ul. Warzelnicza 1. In this old fortification, two beer gardens and a smoked fish stand welcome vacationing families. Be aware that the fish is served cold, which is what some might call an acquired taste. Nightly cover bands regale the multigenerational crowd with Polish folk songs and pop hits. Locals will encourage you to drink your fill. (☎354 43 01. Beer 6zł. Open daily June-Sept. 10am-late.)

TRI-CITY AREA (TRÓJMIASTO)

World-class beaches, a flurry of cultural life, and stunning Hanseatic architecture have made the portside Tri-city area (pop. 465,000) Poland's summer playground of choice. The three cities on the Baltic make a study in contrasts: the restored splendor of old Gdańsk conceals a turbulent millennium of history. Sopot basks in beachfront glitz, while the capitalist bustle of trade-rich Gdynia fuels the area's economy. Great public transportation makes it possible to find a bed in one city and explore the others.

GDAŃSK   ☎(0)58

At the mouth of the Wisła and Motława Rivers, Gdańsk (gh-DA-insk) has flourished for more than a millennium as a crossroads of art and commerce. As the free city of Danzig, it was treasured by Poles as the "gateway to the sea" during Poland's foreign occupation in the 18th and 19th centuries. The city's success was threatened by WWII—it was the site of the first war casualties and of Germany's last stand—but it was quick to rebound. By the early 1980s, Gdańsk found itself in the international spotlight as the birthplace of Lech Wałęsa's Solidarity. Restored to its former splendor for the 1997 city millennium celebration, Gdańsk is once again a captivating, must-see Baltic city.

POLAND

⌐ TRANSPORTATION

Trains: Gdańsk Główny, ul. Podwale Grodzkie 1 (☎94 36). To: **Białystok** (7½hr., 2 per day, 46zł); **Częstochowa** (8hr., 5 per day, 49zł); **Kołobrzeg** (2¾hr., 8 per day, 41zł); **Kraków** (7hr., 9 per day, 42zł); **Łódź** (8hr., 2 per day, 42zł); **Lublin** (8hr., 2 per day, 42zł); **Malbork** (50min., 36 per day, 15-30zł); **Mikołajki** (5hr., 1 per day, 37zł); **Poznań** (4½hr., 7 per day, 42-73zł); **Szczecin** (5¾hr., 5 per day, 45zł); **Toruń** (3¼hr., 7 per day, 36zł); **Warsaw** (4hr., 18 per day, 46-79zł); **Wrocław** (6-7hr., 6 per day, 47-80zł). **SKM** (Fast City Trains; ☎628 57 78) run to **Gdynia** (35min.; 4zł, students 2zł) and **Sopot** (20min.; 2.80zł/1.40zł) every 10min. during the day and less frequently at night. Buy tickets downstairs. Punch your ticket in a *kasownik* machine before boarding.

Buses: Ul. 3-go Maja 12 (☎302 15 32), behind the train station, connected by an underground passageway. To: **Białystok** (9hr., 2 per day, 51zł); **Częstochowa** (7½hr., 1 per day, 55zł); **Kołobrzeg** (6hr., 1 per day, 47zł); **Kraków** (10¾hr., 1 per day, 65zł); **Łódź** (8hr., 4 per day, 44zł); **Malbork** (1hr., 8 per day, 9.40-13zł); **Toruń** (2½hr., 4 per day, 31zł); **Warsaw** (5¾hr., 7 per day, 55zł); **Kaliningrad, RUS** (6-7hr., 2 per day, 28zł). Comfortable **Polski Express** buses run to **Warsaw** (4½hr., 2 per day, 45zł).

Ferries: Żegluga Gdańska (☎301 49 26; www.zegluga.gda.pl) runs ferries (May-Sept.) to domestic destinations, departing from the Green Gate (Zielona Brama). To: **Gdynia** (2hr.; 2 per day; 39zł, students 28zł); **Hel** (1½-3hr.; 2 per day; 46zł, students 32zł); **Sopot** (1hr.; 5 per day; 33zł, students 22zł); **Westerplatte** (50min.; 9 per day; round-trip 34zł, students 18zł). **Polferries**, ul. Przemysłowa 1 (☎343 18 87), in Gdańsk-Brzeźno, sends ferries to **Nynäshamn, SWE** (19hr.; 3 per wk.; 495-580zł, students 410-480zł). **DFDS Seaways**, ul. Sucharskiego 70 (☎340 50 00), sails to **Copenhagen, DEN** (17¼hr.; 4 per wk.; 190-495zł) via **Trelleborg, DEN**.

Public Transportation: Gdańsk has an extensive **bus** and **tram** system. 10min. 1.10zł; 30min. 2.20zł, 45min. 2.70zł, 1hr. 3.30zł, day pass 6.20zł. **Night buses** 30min., 3.30zł; night pass 5.50zł. Bags over 60cm need their own tickets.

Taxis: To avoid paying inflated tourist rates for taxis, book a cab by phone or over the Internet at state-run **MPT** (☎96 33; www.artusmpt.gda.pl).

▣ ▊ ORIENTATION AND PRACTICAL INFORMATION

While Gdańsk technically sits on the Baltic Coast, its center is 5km inland. From the **Gdańsk Główny** train and bus stations, the center lies just a few blocks south-east, bordered on the west by **Wały Jagiellońskie** and on the east by the **Motława River**. Take the underpass in front of the station, go right, and turn left on **ul. Hewe-liusza**. Turn right on **ul. Rajska** and follow the signs to **Główne Miasto** (Main Town), turning left on **ul. Długa**. Długa becomes **Długi Targ** as it widens near the Motława. Gdańsk has several suburbs, all north of Główne Miasto.

Tourist Offices: PTTK Gdańsk, ul. Długa 45 (☎301 91 51; www.pttk-gdansk.com.pl), in Główne Miasto, has free **maps**. Tour guides (☎301 60 96) available daily May-Sept. 12:30pm. Open May-Sept. M-F 9am-6pm, Sa-Su 9am-3pm; Oct.-Apr. M-F 9am-6pm.

Budget Travel: Almatur, ul. Długi Targ 11, 2nd fl. (☎301 29 31; www.almatur.gda.pl), in Główne Miasto. Sells **ISIC cards** (52zł), offers hostel info, and books international air and ferry tickets. Open M-F 10am-5pm, Sa 10am-2pm.

Currency Exchange: Bank Pekao SA, ul. Garncarska 31 (☎801 365 365) cashes **trav-eler's checks** for 1% commission and provides MC/V **cash advances** for no commis-sion. Open M-F 9am-5pm and the 1st and last Sa of each month 10am-2pm.

Luggage Storage: In the train station. Locked room downstairs (4zł plus 0.50zł per 50zł declared value; open 24hr.) or lockers upstairs (small 4zł, large 8zł). Lockers in bus sta-tion (small 4zł, large 8zł).

POLAND

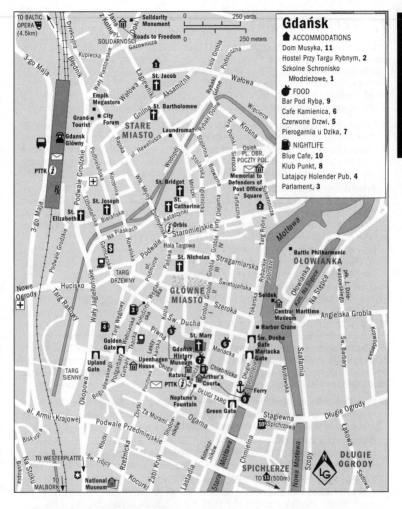

Gdańsk

▲ ACCOMMODATIONS
Dom Musyka, **11**
Hostel Przy Targu Rybnym, **2**
Szkolne Schronisko
  Młodzieżowe, **1**

● FOOD
Bar Pod Rybą, **9**
Cafe Kamienica, **6**
Czerwone Drzwi, **5**
Pierogarnia u Dzika, **7**

NIGHTLIFE
Blue Cafe, **10**
Klub Punkt, **8**
Latający Holender Pub, **4**
Parlament, **3**

English-Language Bookstore: Empik, ul. Podwale Grodzkie 8 (☎301 62 88, ext. 115). Sells maps and *Gdańsk in Your Pocket* (5zł). Open M-Sa 9am-9pm, Su 11am-8pm.

24hr. Pharmacy: Apteka Plus (☎763 10 74), at the train station. Ring bell at night.

Medical Assistance: Private doctors, ul. Podbielańska 16 (☎301 51 68). Sign says "Lekarze Specjaliści." 50zł per visit. Open daily 7am-7pm. For **emergency care,** go to **Szpital Specjalistyczny im. M. Kopernika,** ul. Nowe Ogrody 5 (☎302 30 31).

Internet Access: Jazz'n'Java, ul. Tkacka 17/18 (☎305 36 16; www.cafe.jnj.pl), in the Old Town. 3zł per 30min., 5zł per hr. Open daily 10am-10pm.

Post Office: Ul. Długa 23/28 (☎301 88 53). **Exchanges currency** and has **fax** service. Open M-F 8am-8pm, Sa 9am-3pm. For **Poste Restante,** use the entrance on ul. Pocztowa. **Telephones** inside. **Postal Code:** 80-801.

POLAND

▌ ACCOMMODATIONS

Gdańsk has limited accommodations; it's best to reserve ahead. In July or August you can stay in a **university dorm**. Consult **PTTK** for info. Otherwise, **private rooms** (20-80zł) can be arranged through **PTTK** or **Grand-Tourist** (Biuro Podróży i Zakwaterowania), ul. Podwale Grodzkie 8, connected to the train station. (☎301 26 34; www.grand-tourist.pl. Singles 43-60zł, doubles 75-100zł; 2-person apartments 160-170zł, 3-person 220zł, 4-person 250zł. Open daily July-Aug. 8am-8pm; Sept.-June M-Sa 10am-6pm.)

▨ **Hostel Przy Targu Rybnym,** ul. Grodzka 21 (☎301 56 27; www.gdanskhostel.com), off Targ Rybny, along the waterfront south of Podwale Staromieskie and across from the *baszta* (tower). At Poland's wackiest hostel, guests enjoy the chummy common room and free bowls of fresh strawberries, Internet access, laundry, coffee, and tea. Free bicycle and kayak use. 24hr. reception. Dorms 40zł; doubles 120-140zł; quads 250zł. ❷

Szkolne Schronisko Młodzieżowe, ul. Wałowa 21 (☎301 23 13). From the train station, follow ul. Karmelicka; turn left on ul. Rajska and right on ul. Wałowa. Full kitchen and common room set the facilities a cut above the most HI hostels, but the living is as clean as the rooms: there's a smoking and drinking ban and a midnight curfew. Reception 8am-10pm. Dorms 12-25zł; singles 25-30zł; doubles 50-60zł. ❶

Dom Musyka, ul. Łąkowa 1/2 (☎300 92 60). From the train station, take the #8, 13 or 63 trams to the Łąkowa stop. Dom Musyka is on the corner of Łąkowa and Podwale Przedmiejskie, behind the gate of the yellow building. Just across the Motława from the Old Town, recently renovated Musyka offers large, sunny rooms just a block away from the river. Singles 120zł; doubles 180-200zł; suites 300zł. ❹

▐ FOOD

For fresh produce, try **Hala Targowa,** on ul. Pańska, in the shadows of Kościół św. Katarzyny, just off Podwale Staromiejskie. (Open M-F 9am-6pm; 1st and last Sa of each month 9am-3pm.) If open-air markets aren't your bag, head to **Esta,** ul. Podwale Staromiejskie 109/112, in Targ Drzewny. (Open M-Sa 10am-10pm, Su noon-10pm.)

▨ **Cafe Kamienica,** ul. Mariacka 37/39, in St. Mary's shadow. Sink into the sofas of the upstairs lounge for tea, or enjoy a languid breakfast on the stone-walled terrace. Tea 4zł. Light entrees 12-19zł. Open June-Sept. 9am-midnight; Oct.-May 10am-10pm. ❷

Pierogarnia u Dzika (Wild Boar Pierogi Bar), ul. Piwna 59/60 (☎305 26 76). Locals swear by these *pierogi* (10-20zł) stuffed with everything from caviar to strawberries. The 35-piece mixed platter (50zł) is terrific for large groups. Open daily 10am-10pm. ❸

Bar Pod Rybą (Bar Under the Fish), Długi Targ 35/38/1 (☎305 13 07), serves huge baked potatoes with surprisingly addictive fillings (6-15zł) that run the global gamut from chicken *shawarma* to chili (4-7.50zł). The Hungarian sausage topping is not to be missed. Open daily July-Aug. 11am-10pm; Sept.-June 11am-7pm. AmEx/MC/V. ❶

Czerwone Drzwi, ul. Piwna 52 (☎301 57 64). A red door marks the entrance to the 19th-century burgher house, home to Gdańsk's most elegant cafe. Masterful Polish and international dishes. Entrees 17-32zł. Open daily noon-11pm. MC/V. ❷

◉ SIGHTS

▨ **NATIONAL MUSEUM.** Housed amidst the vaulted chambers of a former Franciscan monastery, this museum displays a large collection of 16th- to 20th-century art and furniture. The jewel of the museum, Hans Memling's "Last Judgment" altar triptych, has a checkered history. In 1473, it was intercepted by Gdańsk pirates en route to England. In 1807, Napoleon carted it off to the Louvre, from where Germans nabbed it in 1815. Gdańsk reclaimed it two years later. The 20th century saw it ricochet between the Nazis and the Soviets before coming to rest in Gdańsk in 1956. (Ul. Toruńska 1, off Podwale Przedmiejskie. ☎ 301 70 61; www.muzeum.narodowe.gda.pl. Open June to mid-Sept. Tu-F 9am-4pm, Sa-Su 10am-5pm; mid-Sept. to May Tu-Su 9am-4pm. 8zł, students 4zł.)

■ ROADS TO FREEDOM. In the Gdańsk Shipyard where the Solidarity (Solidarność) movement was born, a powerful permanent exhibit documents the rise of the Eastern Bloc's first trade union. This moving multimedia journey through postwar Poland begins with the early struggle against communist rule in the 1950s and documents the censorship, secret police, and propaganda that marked Polish life during the communist era. Slides, films, and photographs trace the changing fortunes of Solidarity through the strikes of 1980 and the brutal period of martial law to the sweeping victory of 1989. (Ul. Doki 1, in the Shipyard. ☎ 308 42 80. Open Tu-Su 10am-4pm. 5zl, students 3zl. W free.)

DŁUGI TARG (LONG MARKET). The handsome main square, Długi Targ is the heart of the painstakingly restored Główne Miasto. Gdańsk's characteristic row houses, adorned with dragon's head gutter spouts, line the surrounding cobblestone ul. Mariacka, ul. Chlebnicka, and ul. Św. Ducha. The stone Upland Gate and the elegant blue-gray Golden Gate, emblazoned with gold leaf moldings and the shields of Poland, Prussia, and Germany, mark the entrance to ul. Długa. The 14th-century **Ratusz** (Town Hall), ul. Długa 47, houses a branch of the **Gdańsk History Museum.** Baroque paintings adorn the ceiling of the museum's fantastic Red Chamber. Exhibits span Gdańsk's long history, from the first mention of the city to the rubble of Gdańsk right after WWII. Nearby, the 16th-century facade of **Arthur's Court** (Dwór Artusa), Długi Targ 43/44, now houses a second branch of the History Museum. The palace faces Neptune's Fountain, where the sea god stands astride a giant shell. Inspired by the court of Britain's legendary king, the 16th-century palace was fully restored in 1997, and its Renaissance interior and spiral staircase merit a visit. Closer to the city gates, the History Museum's 3rd branch, Rococo Upenhagen House (Dom Uphagena), ul. Dluga 12, is an 18th-century merchant's home. (Town Hall ☎ 301 48 71, Arthur's Court 301 43 59, Upenhagen House 301 23 71. Open June-Sept. M 10am-3pm, Tu-Sa 10am-6pm, Su 11am-6pm; Oct.-May Tu-Sa 10am-4pm, Su 11am-4pm. Each branch 6zł, students 3zł, combined ticket 12zł/6zł. W free.)

CHURCHES. The largest brick church in Poland and one of the largest in the world, gothic **St. Mary's** (Kościół Mariacki) holds 25,000. Don't miss the gigantic 1464 astronomical clock—legend has it that the king had the clockmaker's eyes put out so he could not create another. Climb the 405 steps for a panoramic view that the clockmaker never saw. (Open June-Aug. M-Sa 9am-5:30pm, Su 1-5:30pm; low-season hours vary. 3zł, students 1.50zł.) In the foreground on ul. Wielkie Młyny, the 13th-century **St. Nicholas's Church** (Kościół św. Mikołaja) is the only church in Gdańsk not gutted in WWII. Behind it is the 12th-century **St. Catherine's Church** (Kościół św. Katarzyny). It is the final resting place of astronomer **Jan Heweliusz** and preserves a cemetery dating from 997. Sixty-six steps above, the baroque **Tower Clocks Museum** displays a 49-bell carillon which has rung on the hour since the 50th anniversary of the outbreak of WWII. (☎ 305 64 92. Museum open June-Sept. Tu-Su 10am-5pm. Cemetery 1zł., museum 4zł. W free.)

NAUTICAL SIGHTS. The **Central Maritime Museum** (Centralne Muzeum Morskie) spans both banks of the Motława, including a main museum, the medieval **Żuraw** (Harbor Crane), and the ship **Sołdek.** The crane, an oft-photographed symbol of the city, towers over the riverside promenade **Długie Pobrzeże.** An exhibit beside the crane displays traditional boats of Asia, Africa, and South America, while the main museum offers an exhaustive tour through the colorful history of maritime

Poland. *(To reach the Sołdek, take the shuttle boat or walk from the end of Długi Targ, cross 2 bridges, and bear left. ☎301 86 11. Open daily June-Aug. 10am-6pm; Sept.-May Tu-Su 9:30am-4pm. English guide 15zł per group; call ahead. Crane 5zł, students 3zł. Museum 5zł/3zł. Sołdek 4zł/2.50zł. Shuttle boat round-trip 3zł/1.50zł. All museums and shuttle boat 12zł/7zł.)*

MAIN TOWN. The flags of Solidarity fly at the **Solidarity Monument**, on pl. Solidarności, at the end of ul. Wały Piastowskie. The **Memorial to the Defenders of Post Office Square** (Obrońców Poczty) recognizes the postal workers who bravely defended Gdańsk against the Germans in one of the first battles of WWII. On September 1, 1939, postal employees resisted the German army until the building was engulfed in flames. Those who survived the blaze were later executed or sent to concentration camps. A museum inside the reconstructed functioning post office also documents the controversial establishment of a Polish postal service in occupied Gdańsk in 1920. *(From Podwale Staromiejskie, go north on Olejarna and turn right at Urzad Pocztowy Gdańsk 1. ☎301 76 11. Open M and W-F 10am-4pm, Sa-Su 10:30am-2pm. 3zł, students 2zł.)*

WESTERPLATTE. When Germany attacked Poland, the little island fort guarding the entrance to Gdańsk's harbor gained unfortunate distinction as the first target of WWII. Outnumbered 20 to one, the Polish troops held out for a week until a lack of food and munitions forced them to surrender. **Guardhouse #1** has been turned into a museum with an exhibit recounting the fateful battle. *(☎343 69 72. Open May-Sept. 9am-6pm. 2zł, students 1.50zł. English booklet 6zł.)* The path beyond the exhibit passes the bunker ruins and the massive **Memorial to the Defenders of the Coast.** Follow the spiral path for a closer look at the monument and a glimpse of the shipyard and the sea. Below the monument, letters spell "Nigdy Wiecej Wojny" (Never More War). *(From the train station, take bus #106 or 606 south to the last stop. The bus stop is to the right of the station entrance in front of KFC. Żegluga Gdańska also runs a ferry—50min.; every hr. 10am-6pm; round-trip 34zł, students 18zł. ☎301 49 26. Board by the Green Gate (Zielona Brama) at the end of Długi Targ.)*

🎭 ENTERTAINMENT

Of the three cities that line this stretch of the Baltic, Gdańsk offers the most mainstream entertainment. The **Baltic Philharmonic,** ul. Ołowianka 1 (☎305 20 40), performs free riverside concerts in summer. Opera-lovers can check out the **Baltic Opera** (Opera Bałtycka), al. Zwycięstwa 15 (☎341 46 42). Tickets to the Philharmonic and the Opera cost from 8zł to 40zł. The **Church of the Blessed Virgin Mary** has organ concerts (20zł, students 10zł) every Friday at 8:15pm in July and August. Special summer events include a **Street Theater Festival** (July), a **Shakespeare Festival** (Aug.), and the **International Organ Music Festival** (Aug.), at nearby Oliwa. The first two weeks in August also welcome the immense **Dominican Fair,** a centuries-old trading party.

🍷 NIGHTLIFE

When the sun goes down, the crowds turn to the party spots of Długi Targ. Gdańsk tends more toward pubs than clubs, but the dance scene is picking up. *City* lists events in the Tri-city area, and *Gdańsk in Your Pocket* offers updated club listings.

Klub Punkt, ul. Chlebnicka 2 (☎302 18 11). At the intersection of Eastern Bloc debauchery and carnival haunted house, casually bohemian Klub Punkt stands apart from the tame crowd of Gdańsk bars. Open Su-Th 4pm-1am, F-Sa 4pm-3am.

Latający Holender Pub, ul. Wały Jagiellońskie 2/4 (☎802 03 63), near the end of ul. Długa. A hot-air balloon crashes through the ceiling of this affable den of oddities, where an easygoing student crowd packs onto velvet couches beneath an array of flying machines. Beer and mixed drinks 4-22zł. Open daily noon-midnight.

Blue Cafe, ul. Chmielna 103/104 (☎346 38 61), across the 1st bridge at the end of Długi Targ, to the right. Hip-hop and R&B (Th) draw overflow weekend crowds to the illuminated floor of the exuberant dance club. Blue doubles as a mellow coffee lounge by day, while evening sees occasional live rock. Beer 5-12zł. Open daily 11am-late. MC/V.

Parlament, ul. Św. Ducha 2 (☎302 13 65). This popular club entices a wild young crowd with a mile-long bar, fog machine, and maze of voyeuristic balconies overlooking the dance floor. Beer 5.50zł. 18+. Cover F-Sa after 10pm 10zł. Open Tu-Sa 6pm-late.

▶ DAYTRIP FROM GDAŃSK

MALBORK ☎(0)55

Both trains (40-60min.; 36 per day; 9.80zł, express 32zł) and buses (1hr., 8 per day, 9.40-13zł) run from Gdańsk to Malbork. From the station, turn right on ul. Dworcowa, then left at the fork. Go around the corner to the roundabout and cross to the street across the way, ul. Kościuszki. Follow it, then veer right on ul. Piastowska, where signs for the castle appear. ☎647 08 00; www.zamek.malbork.com.pl. Castle open May-Sept. Tu-Su 9am-7pm; Oct.-Apr. Tu-Su 9am-3pm. Courtyards, terraces, and moats open daily May-Sept. Tu-Su 9am-8pm; Oct.-Apr. Tu-Su 9am-4pm. Castle 23zł, students 14zł. 3hr. Polish tour included. English booklet 7zł. English-speaking guide 150zł. Grounds 6zł/4zł. Sound and light show May 15-Oct. 15 10pm, 10zł/5zł. Kasa open 8:30am-7:30pm. AmEx/MC/V.

The largest brick castle in the world, ◨**Malbork** is a stunning feat of restoration and a rich lens onto the turbulent history of the surrounding region. The **Teutonic Knights** built Malbork as their headquarters in the 1300s. The Teutons first came to the region in 1230 at the request of Polish Duke Konrad Mazowiecki to assist the nation in its struggle against the Prussians. The Teutons double-crossed the Poles, however, establishing their own state in 1309. In their heyday, the celibate order of warrior-monks marauded across the region, forcibly converting Lithuanians to Christianity and hunting bison in the forest surrounding Malbork. The knights' vows of poverty fell by the wayside, and while the Poles won several 15th-century battles against the order, it was the lavish lifestyle of the Teutonic Knights that lost them Malbork. In 1457, the Teutons had to turn over the castle to mercenary knights for outstanding debts, and the mercenaries promptly sold the castle to the Poles. The castle became part of Prussia after the first partition of Poland in 1772. It was under German control in WWII, when it housed a POW camp (Stalag XXB). Soviet bombing razed the castle at the war's end, but one of the world's largest works of reconstruction pieced the bricks of Malbork back together beginning in 1961. The most beautiful rooms in the castle are the unfurnished **Grand Master's Chambers,** notable for columns in the shape of palm trees. The tour winds through the **High, Middle,** and **Low Castles** and visits the treasures of the **amber collection** and **weapons collection.** Keep an eye out for the **castle ghost,** Hans von Endorf, who has wandered Malbork's halls since he killed his brother the Grand Master in 1330 and killed himself out of guilt. An **IT tourist office** is outside the castle at Piastowska 15. (☎273 49 90. Open May-Sept. M-F 10am-6pm, Sa-Su 10am-2pm.) If you need to stay the night, consult IT or look for the ubiquitous signs advertising **private rooms** (20-60zł).

SOPOT ☎(0)58

Poland's premier resort town, magnetic Sopot (pop. 50,000) draws throngs of visitors to its sandy beaches. Restaurants, shops, and street musicians dot Sopot's graceful pedestrian promenade, ul. Bohaterów Monte Cassino, and the longest wooden pier in Europe rewards seaside amblers with spectacular Baltic views.

POLAND

TRANSPORTATION. The **commuter rail (SKM)** connects Sopot to **Gdańsk** (20min.; 2.80zł, students 1.40zł) and **Gdynia** (15min.; 2.80zł/1.40zł) and runs daily 4:30am-1am. Trains leave from platform #1 every 10min. during the day and every hour at night. Stamp your ticket in the box before boarding or risk heavy fines. **PKP trains** run to: **Białystok** (7¾hr., 2 per day, 47zł); **Kołobrzeg** (2hr., 3 per day, 36zł); **Kraków** (7hr., 3 per day, 48zł); **Lublin** (6hr., 2 per day, 46zł); **Łódź** (6hr., 4 per day, 46zł); **Malbork** (1hr., 34 per day, 13zł); **Poznań** (4½hr., 5 per day, 41zł); **Szczecin** (5hr., 4 per day, 41zł); **Toruń** (3½hr., 6 per day, 37zł); **Warsaw** (4¼hr., 21 per day, 47-81zł); **Wrocław** (6-7hr., 5 per day, 47-81zł); **Berlin, GER** (9¾hr., 1 per day, 264zł). **Ferries** (☎551 12 93) leave from the end of the pier and go to **Gdańsk** (1hr.; 1 per day; round-trip 46zł, students 32zł); **Gdynia** (35min., 4 per day, 45zł/34zł); **Hel** (1½hr., 4 per day, 45zł/31zł); **Westerplatte** (35min., 2 per day, 34zł/22zł). For a **taxi,** call the state-run company **MPT** or order a taxi over the Internet through their website. (☎96 33; www.artusmpt.gda.pl. Base fare 5zł plus 2zł per km.)

ORIENTATION AND PRACTICAL INFORMATION. Ul. Dworcowa begins at the train station and heads left to the pedestrian **ul. Bohaterów Monte Cassino,** which runs toward the pier *(molo)*. Almost everything lies on or near ul. Bohaterów Monte Cassino. The **tourist office IT,** ul. Dworcowa 4, across from the train station, sells **maps** (4-5zł) of the area. (☎550 37 83; www.sopot.pl. Open daily June-Aug. 8:30am-7:30pm; Sept.-May 8am-4pm.) An **accommodations office** is in the same building. (☎551 26 17. Open daily June-Sept. 15. 10am-5pm; Sept. 16-May M-F 10am-3pm.) **PKO Bank Polski,** ul. Monte Cassino 32/34, exchanges currency, gives MC/V **cash advances,** cashes **traveler's checks** for 1.5% commission (min. 10zł), and has a MC/V **ATM.** (☎666 85 67. Open M-F 8am-7pm, Sa 9am-1pm.) A **24hr. pharmacy, Apteka pod Orlem,** is at ul. Monte Cassino 37. (☎551 10 18.) Head to **NetCave,** ul. Pułaskiego 7a, for **Internet access.** (3zł per 30min., 5zł per hr.; students 1zł/4zł. Open daily noon-10pm.) The **post office,** ul. Kościuszki 2, has **telephones.** (☎551 17 84. Open M-F 8am-8pm, Sa 9am-3pm.) **Postal Code:** 81-701.

ACCOMMODATIONS AND FOOD. Sopot is one of Poland's most popular and expensive resort towns, so reservations are a must in summer. Consider renting a **private room;** visit **IT** for help. (June-Aug. singles 46zł; doubles 78zł; triples 90zł; Sept.-May 39zł/62zł/90zł.) If your złotys are fluttering away like a flock of seagulls, stay in Gdańsk. The five-building ◙**Hotel Wojskowy Dom Wypoczynkowy (WDW) ❶,** ul. Kilińskiego 12, off ul. Grunwaldzka, in the building marked "Meduza," offers the cheapest sea views in Sopot. The pastel rooms have well-kept bathrooms and TV, and the premises include tennis courts. (☎551 06 85; www.wdw.sopot.pl. Breakfast included. Check-in 2pm. Check-out noon. Reserve a month ahead July-Aug. Singles 100-158zł; doubles 200-230zł; triples 290-300zł; apartments 270-350zł. "Tourist Class" rooms without bath or breakfast 30zł. Oct.-May 10-15zł discount.) The best midrange beachside option is **Hotel Amber ❸,** ul. Grunwaldzka 45, a small, modern hotel with bath, TV, and phone in each of its tidy rooms. (☎550 00 42. Check-in and check-out noon. Singles 240zł.) Find camping at **Kemping nr. 19 ❶,** ul. Zamkowa Góra 25. Take the commuter rail (3min., every 10-20min., 1.25zł) to Sopot-Kamienny Potok, then go down the stairs and turn right. Nr. 19 is a well-groomed and friendly campground. (☎550 04 45. Parking 7zł. Open May-Sept. 10zł per person, 4-9zł per tent; 4-person bungalows 90-130zł.) **Ul. Monte Cassino** is riddled with fashionable cafes and inexpensive food stands. A small **24hr. grocery,** Delikatesy, ul. Monte Cassino 60 (☎551 57 62), is steps away from the pier. **Błękitny Pudel ❷** (Blue Poodle) is at ul. Monte Cassino 44. The garden of this quirky cafe is lovely in summer, while the interior, chock-full of tapestried chairs and curiosities, is as charismatic as the food. (☎551 16 72.

Entrees 12-26zł. *Pierogi* 18zł. Open daily July-Aug. 10am-1am; Sept.-June noon-1am.) Local institution **Przystań ❶**, al. Wojska Polskiego 11, along the beach, serves seafood, grilled and fried, in an unbeatable location with a view of Hel. (☎550 02 41; www.barprzystan.pl. Fresh fish 3.90-6.50zł per 100g. *Hevelius* 5zł. Open daily 11am-11pm.) **Baola ❸**, ul. Grunwaldzka 27, is a dreamy French-inflected bistro with clouds painted on the ceiling, an artfully overgrown garden, and a sophisticated menu. (☎550 27 32. Entrees 15-60zł. MC/V.)

🔲 🎭 ENTERTAINMENT AND FESTIVALS. Sopot's popularity stems from its vast **beach**, which has white sands and endless recreational opportunities, from waterslides to outdoor theater. The most popular sands lie at the end of ul. Monte Cassino, where the 1827 wooden **pier**, ul. Chopina 10, the longest of its kind in Europe, extends 512m into the sea. (☎551 00 02. M-F 2.50zł, Sa-Su 3.30zł.) The flurry of **cafes, pubs,** and **discos** along ul. Monte Cassino bears testament to Sopot's status as one of the hardest-partying towns in Poland. **Galeria Kiński,** ul. Kościuszki 10, to the right when coming from the station, is a smoky tribute to actor Klaus Kiński, born upstairs. Don't miss the scarlet-walled upstairs lounge or the stylish balcony. (☎802 56 38. Beer 5zł. Open daily 11am-3am.) Not to be confused with the popular Polish restaurant chain of the same name, **Sfinks,** ul. Powstańców Warszawy 18, is one of the country's hottest clubs. Artsy decor, strong liquors, and a lively crowd make a potent mix. (Open daily 10pm-late.)

Opera Leśna (Forest Opera), ul. Moniuszki 12, is an open-air theater with some of the best acoustics in Europe. Its rock and pop music festival, the **International Song Festival,** (☎555 84 00) dominates the area in mid-August. For tickets or info, call the theater or contact **IT** (see p. 596). **Teatr Atelier,** ul. Franciszka Mamuszki 2, stages independent theater on its beachside stage. (☎555 14 84. Tickets 24-34zł. IT has a show schedule.)

GDYNIA ☎(0)58

Young Gdynia (gh-DIN-ya; pop. 253,500) is in no hurry to grow up. Happy to sink its teeth into modern business, it leaves history to nearby Gdańsk. A once-sleepy fishing village that became trading hub when the Treaty of Versailles rendered it the only port city in Poland, Gdynia continues to be the home of Poland's wealthiest residents. Few tourists venture to Gdynia, but an evening stroll through this waterfront metropolis reveals thriving cafes, dynamic nightlife, and the best restaurants in the Tri-city area.

🚍 TRANSPORTATION

Trains: pl. Konstytucji (☎628 53 08). To: **Białystok** (8hr., 2 per day, 49zł); **Hel** (2hr., 20 per day, 12zł); **Kołobrzeg** (2¼hr., 8 per day, 38zł); **Kraków** (7¼hr., 9 per day, 51-76zł); **Lublin** (6¼hr., 2 per day, 48zł); **Łódź** (6¼hr., 5 per day, 48zł); **Malbork** (1¼hr., 35 per day, 15zł); **Poznań** (4¾hr., 9 per day, 43zł); **Szczecin** (5¼hr., 5 per day, 43zł); **Toruń** (3¾hr., 8 per day, 39zł); **Warsaw** (4½hr., 18 per day, 46-81zł); **Wrocław** (6-7hr., 5 per day, 50-83zł); **Berlin, GER** (10hr., 1 per day, 266zł); **Prague, CZR** (7hr., 1 per day, 277zł). SKM commuter trains *(kolejka)* are the easiest way to get to **Gdańsk** (35min.; 4zł, students 2zł) and **Sopot** (15min.; 2.80zł/1.40zł). They depart every 10min. from platform #1. Punch your ticket in a yellow *kasownik* box or risk fines.

Buses: ☎620 77 47. To: **Hel** (2hr., 26 per day, 10zł); **Kołobrzeg** (5hr., 2 per day, 34zł), **Łódź** (8¾hr., 2 per day, 43zł); **Świnoujście** (8hr., 2 per day, 47zł); **Toruń** (4¼hr., 2 per day, 34zł). **Polski Express** heads to **Warsaw** (6½hr., 2 per day, 37zł). Buy tickets at the PKS *kasa* or Orbis (see **Orientation and Practical Information,** p. 598).

POLAND

Ferries: Żegluga Gdańska (☎620 26 42; www.zegluga.gda.pl), runs domestic ferries. Boats depart from al. Zjednoczenia 2, on Skwer Kościuszki. To: **Gdańsk** (1½hr.; 2 per day; 39zł, students 28zł); **Hel** (25min.-1¼hr., 9 per day, 33zł/22zł); **Sopot** (15-30min., 4 per day, 20zł/12zł); **Westerplatte** (1½hr., 1 per day, 33zł/22zł). **Stena Line,** ul. Kwiatkowskiego 60 (☎660 92 00; fax 660 92 09), sends ferries to **Karlskrona, SWE** (11hr., 1-2 per day, 200-325zł/150-240zł).

Public Transportation: 2zł, students 1zł.

⊞ 🛈 ORIENTATION AND PRACTICAL INFORMATION

The train and bus stations are adjacent to one another. Any of the roads running away from the train station on your right will take you toward the waterfront; **ul. 10-go Lutego,** farthest to the right, takes you directly to the fountain-filled main square, **Skwer Kościuszki,** and then down **al. Zjednoczenia** to the pier. If you end up on **ul. Jana Kolna, ul. Wójta Radtkiego,** or **ul. Starowiejska,** take a right and walk until you can take a left on ul. 10-go Lutego. To shop, explore **ul. Świętojańska,** which intersects ul. 10-go Lutego at the top of Skwer Kościuszki. The **beach** is to the right of the pier.

Tourist Office: IT, pl. Konstytucji 1 (☎628 54 66; www.gdynia.pl), in the train station, sells **maps** (5-9zł) and has an accommodations list. Open May-Sept. M-F 8am-6pm, Sa 9am-4pm, Su 9am-3pm; Oct.-Apr. M-F 10am-5pm, Sa 10am-4pm. **Branch** (☎620 77 11) at the end of the pier. Open May-Sept. Sa 10am-5pm, Su 10am-4pm.

Budget Travel: Orbis, ul. 10-go Lutego 12 (☎661 42 50; orbis.gdynia@pop.com.pl). Sells budget plane, train, bus, and ferry tickets, and arranges hotel stays. Open July-Aug. M-F 9am-5pm, Sa 10am-3pm; Sept.-June M-F 9am-5pm, Sa 10am-2pm.

Currency Exchange: Bank Pekao, ul. 10-go Lutego 30 (☎621 70 31). **Exchanges currency,** gives MC/V **cash advances,** and cashes **AmEx Traveler's Cheques** for 1.5% commission (10zł min.).

Luggage Storage: In the main hall of the bus/train station. 2zł, plus 1% declared value.

English-Language Bookstore: Księgarnia Językowa, ul. Świętojańska 14 (☎61 25 61). Open M-F 10am-6pm, Sa 10am-3pm.

24hr. Pharmacy: Apteka Pod Gryfem, ul. Starowiejska 34 (☎620 19 82).

Medical Assistance: Medicover, ul. Obrońców Wybrzeża 12 (☎661 60 39). Private service with English-speaking doctors. Appointments 80zł. Open M-F 7:30am-8pm.

Telephones: Outside the post office (see below).

Internet Access: TOMNet, ul. Świętojańska 69. 1zł per 15min. Open daily 9am-10pm.

Post Office: Ul. 10-go Lutego 10 (☎620 82 72), near Skwer Kościuszki. Open M-F 7am-8pm, Sa 9am-3pm. For **Poste Restante** go to window #28. **Postal Code:** 81-301.

⌂ ACCOMMODATIONS

Cheap rooms are hard to come by in the city center; look for **private rooms. Turus,** ul. Starowiejska 47, opposite the train station, arranges accommodations in the Kamienna Góra, Orłowo, and Wszgórze neighborhoods. (☎621 82 65; fax 620 92 87. Singles 40-60zł; doubles 60-100zł. Open M-F 8am-6pm, Sa 10am-6pm.)

Dom Studencki Marynarza, ul. Beniowskiego 24/24a (☎621 68 01). Exit the train station to ul. Śląska, which becomes ul. Morska north of the station. Take any bus north to the Stocznia SKM-Morska stop. Backtrack and take a right on ul. G. Denhoffa, then another right on ul. Kapitańska. Near the gray apartment buildings, look for a staircase and path that will take you up the hill to ul. Beniowskiego. Worth the trek from town for suites with kitchens, baths, and TVs. Private rooms open year-round: large rooms 60zł, smaller rooms 50zł. Discounts for extended stays. Dorms (24zł) open July-Aug. ●

Schronisko Młodzieżowe (HI), ul. Energetyków 13a (☎627 10 05). From the train station, bear right to ul. Jana z Kolna. Take bus #128, 150, 152, or 182 2 stops to Energetyków. Backtrack 20m and turn left onto Energetyków. Next to the shipyard, this new hostel has great rooms. Linen 4zł. Lockout 10am-5pm. Curfew 10pm. Dorms 22zł. ●

Dom Marynarza, Piłsudskiego 1 (☎622 00 25). An anchor marks the entrance to this former health resort. Tucked into the wooded slope of Kamienna Góra, Marynarza is just 100m from the sea—and close to the center of Gdynia despite its secluded surroundings. Freshly painted rooms include TVs, telephones, and breakfast, with upscale service sensibilities. Reception 24hr. Check-in 2pm. Check-out noon. Singles 150zł; doubles 190zł; suites with sea view 300zł. AmEx/MC/V. ❺

▐ FOOD

Hala Targowa, an extensive market, stretches between ul. Jana z Kolna and ul. Wójta Radtkiego. For a full sensory experience, try the pungent **Hala Rybna** (Hall of Fish; open M-F 9am-6pm, Sa 8am-3pm), on ul. Jana z Kolna near the bus station.

CK, ul. Świętojańska 49 (☎699 05 51). This burly, Czech-themed den of wild game, pickles, and macho ceramic pans is one of the worthiest splurges in the Tri-city. Specialties include heaping portions of rabbit and pheasant dishes (40-55zł) served alongside free-flowing Czech beer. Entrees 35-60zł. Open daily noon-11pm. AmEx/MC/V. ❹

Bistro Kwadrans, Skwer Kościuszki 20 (☎620 15 92). This aromatic milk bar smells like an Italian pizzeria and follows through with cheap pizza (4.50-13zł) and Polish fare (8-12zł). Open M-F 9am-10pm, Sa 10am-10pm, Su noon-10pm. ●

Kawiarnia Artystyczna Cyganeria, ul. 3 Maja 27 (☎699 90 15), off ul. 10-go Lutego. Excellent coffee (4-12zł) and a mildly countercultural atmosphere, with pictures of aardvarks on the menu, students smoking on red velvet couches, and posters for retro dance parties. Alcoholic milkshakes 7.50-11zł. Quintessentially Polish burritos 10-12zł. Open M-F 10am-1am, Sa 10am-2:30am, Su 3pm-1am. ❷

Green Way, ul. Abrahama 24 (☎620 12 53), near ul. 10-go Lutego. Vegetarian mecca with pumpkin-orange walls, cozy upstairs seating, and black currant smoothies (8zł). Favorites include daily stews (5.10zł). Open M-Sa 11am-9pm, Su noon-8pm. ●

Paczus, ul. Świętojańska 18. This tiny corner stand sells one thing only: *pączek*, the jelly-filled Polish doughnut of choice. Crisp glaze and high-quality jams make for some of the best *pączki* (1-2zł) in the country. Open M-Sa 8am-7pm, Su 10am-6pm. ●

◎ ▐ SIGHTS AND ENTERTAINMENT

Both hedonists and nautical history aficionados will be pleased by the city's massive pier off Skwer Kościuszki, where naval artifacts, marine biology, drinking, and dancing are all given their due. Ship tours replace history museums in this coastal city; the highlight is the destroyer **Błyskawica** ("Lightning"), the only Polish naval ship built before WWII. Sailors guide tourists through exhibits on Polish naval history. (☎626 37 27. Open Tu-Su 10am-12:30pm and 2-4:30pm. 4zł, students 2zł.) The 1909 sailboat **Dar Pomorza** (Gift of Pomerania), once known as the "fastest and most beautiful ship of the seas," served as a school at sea for the Polish navy between 1930 and 1981, and took first honors at the Cutty Sark Tall Ships Race.

(☎620 23 71. Open daily 9am-4:30pm. 5zł, students 3zł; June-Aug. Sa free.) At the end of the pier, the vast **Muzeum Oceanograficzne i Akwarium Morskie** (Museum of Oceanography and Aquarium) reels in schoolchildren with reef sharks, sea anemones, and a scale model of the Baltic seafloor. (☎621 70 21; www.mir.gdynia.pl/akw. Open daily May-Aug. 9am-7pm; Sept.-Apr. 10am-5pm. 10zł, students 6zł.) Upland, the forested hill **Kamienna Góra** makes an excellent observation point for those willing to scale its steps. Follow the signs from pl. Grunwaldzki. Atop the summit, a towering steel cross dedicated to the **Defenders of Pomerania** (Obrońców Pomorza) overlooks the Gdańsk Bay and the Hel Peninsula.

Gdynia Musical Theater (Teatr Muzyczny w Gdyni), pl. Grunwaldzki 1 (☎621 60 24), puts on productions and hosts concerts during the **Gdynia Summer Jazz Days** festival in mid-July. Consult IT for a schedule (see **Orientation and Practical Information,** p. 598). Toward the end of July, Gdynia is invaded by a fleet of nearly 100 ships and their crews from around the world. These vessels come as part of the annual **Cutty Sark Tall Ships Race.** Check out the ships and climb aboard a few of them for a tour. For info, contact IT or the **Gdynia Marina,** pl. Zjednoczenia 13a.

Gdynia's nightlife is steadily expanding beyond quayside beer gardens. The most intimate pub is ⊠**Cafe Strych** (Attic), pl. Kaszubski 7B, a bewitching 100-year-old fisherman's hut with antique radios and furniture. It's at the end of ul. Jana z Kolna. (☎620 30 38. Live piano Tu-F and Su 7-10pm Live rock M 7-10pm, Sa 7-11pm. Open daily June-Aug. 4pm-1am; Sept.-May Tu-Su noon-midnight.) Off-beat **Desdemona,** ul. Abrahama 37, is an Art Nouveau cafe with a bar attitude. Murals adorn the slate-blue walls, and the copper-plated bar serves beer (4.50-8.50zł), coffee (4-7zł), and mixed drinks (9.50-14.50zł). (☎661 87 22. W film screenings. Open Su-Th noon-1am, F-Sa noon-3am.)

MAZURY

A train ride through the rolling hills of Mazury reveals an achingly beautiful landscape of pine groves, poppy fields, and glassy lakes. East of Pomorze, the region called the "land of a thousand lakes" actually cradles more than 4000 lakes. The two largest, Śniardwy and Mamry, each cover more than 100 sq. km. Small towns like Mikołajki greet visitors with quiet shores and less-traveled waters to canoe, kayak, and sail.

MIKOŁAJKI (0)87

Serene Mikołajki is a gateway to Poland's largest lake, Lake Śniardwy. In the center of the lakeside town, a statue of a crowned fish leaps from a fountain. Legend has it that the residents of Mikołajki were bullied by a giant whitefish named **Król Sielaw,** who broke their nets and capsized boats until a fisherman caught him in a steel net. Król Sielaw said that if he were spared, Lake Mikołajskie would always be full of fish. Król Sielaw kept his word and, to show their appreciation, the fishermen tied him to the **bridge on ul. Kolejowa,** where he resides to this day.

🖪🔽 **TRANSPORTATION AND PRACTICAL INFORMATION.** Mikołajki is poorly connected to the rest of the country. If you can't find direct service, make connections in nearby Olsztyn. **Trains,** ul. Kolejowa 1 (☎421 62 38), go to: **Białystok** (3¾hr., 1 per day, 20zł); **Gdynia** (5½hr., 1 per day, 41zł); **Olsztyn** (2¼hr., 4 per day, 13zł). **Buses** go to: **Lublin** (8¼hr., 1 per day, 68zł); **Olsztyn** (2hr., 5 per day, 14zł); **Warsaw** (4-5hr., 5 per day, 58zł).

To reach the center from the train station, turn right on **ul. Kolejowa** and go left on ul. 3-go Maja, which will lead you to pl. **Wolności,** the center of town. The **bus stop** is at the intersection of ul. Kolejowa and ul. 3-go Maja, at the Protestant church. To get to the **lake,** take any right from pl. Wolności. **Al. Kasztanowa** and **al. Spacerowa,** pedestrian streets bordering the lake, bustle with restaurants and cafes. In the center, the **IT office,** pl. Wolności 3, provides visitors with **maps** (5zł) and info about accommodations and cultural events. (☎421 68 50; www.mikolajki.pl. Open daily July-Aug. 10am-6pm; June and Sept. Sa-Su 10am-6pm.) **Bank PKO BP,** pl. Wolności 7, cashes **traveler's checks** for 1.5% commission and provides MC/V cash advances. (☎421 69 36. Open M-Sa 9am-4pm, Su 10am-1pm.) A **pharmacy** sits in the alley behind ul. 3-go Maja 3. (☎421 63 16. Open daily 8am-7pm. MC/V.) Surf the **Internet** at **Usługi Informatyczne "Andernet,"** ul. Szkolna 4d, off ul. Kolejowa. (☎/fax 421 50 07. 4zł per 30min., 6zł per hr. Open daily 11am-9pm.) The **post office,** ul. 3-go Maja 8, has **telephones** outside. (Open May-Sept. M-F 8am-8pm, Sa 8am-2pm; Oct.-Apr. M-F 9am-5pm, Sa 8am-2pm.) **Postal Code:** 11-730.

🏠🍴 ACCOMMODATIONS AND FOOD. Yellow street signs point the way to **private rooms** and pensions. The best budget private rooms lay along ul. Kajki. Decent lakeside accommodations run 40-50zł per person. **Pensjonat Mikołajki ❷,** ul. Kajki 18, is a family-run business providing guests with stellar service and an amazing location on the banks of Lake Mikołajskie. From pl. Wolności, continue down ul. 3-go Maja until it turns into ul. Kajki. Ask about kayak and bike rentals. (☎421 64 37; www.pensjonatmikolajki.prv.pl. Singles July-Aug. 60zł, with lake view 100zł; doubles 140zł/160zł. Low-season discount 25zł.) Nearby **Noclegi ❶,** ul. Kajka 8, offers attentive service and gleaming rooms. (☎421 63 62. Doubles and triples with bath 40zł per person.) For local fish in a rustic garden sprinkled with plastic gnomes, head to open-air **Czarna Perła** (Black Pearl) ❷, ul. Okrężna 7a. Their specialty is *okonie na konie,* small and tasty Mazury lake fish (15zł). Fishing nets, pool tables, and foosball complete the vaguely pirate-themed experience. (Open daily May-Sept. 11am-late. Entrees 12-15zł. Beer 4zł.) **Restauracja Spizarnia ❷,** pl. Handlowy 14, serves traditional meals and pizzas amid animal pelts, dried flowers, and paper lanterns. (☎421 52 18. Entrees 8-16zł. Fish 6-10zł per 100g. Pizza 8-15zł. Breakfast 5-10zł. Open daily 10am-10pm. AmEx/MC/V.)

Tawerna pod Złamanym, ul. Kowalska 3, boasts the best lake view in town from its upstairs terrace and hosts all-night house and techno dance parties Jul.-Aug. Beer 4zł. (☎421 60 40. Tawerna open daily 8am-late. Dance parties F and Sa 9pm-dawn.)

🏞🎣 SIGHTS AND OUTDOOR ACTIVITIES. Żeglarska Mazurska (☎421 41 02), on the lakeshore on al. Żeglarska, offers excursions on Lake Śniardwy and ferry service to various Mazurian cities for 17-62zł. For those seeking lakeside adventure, **Wioska Żeglarska Mikołajki,** farther down the shore at ul. Kowalska 3, above Tawerna Pod Złamanym Pagatem, rents yachts. Although law prevents anyone without a Polish sailing license from renting a sailing craft, you can charter a skippered boat or settle for a kayak. (☎421 60 40. Sailboats 150-300zł per day. Kayaks 10zł per hr.) Rent bicycles in the 24hr. parking lot at ul. Orzyszowa 2. (☎888 107 776. 4zł per hr., 30zł per day). The **Museum of the Reformation** (Muzeum Reformacjii), pl. Kościelny 4, traces the history of Mikołajki's Protestant church and the effects of the Reformation through a collection of hymnals, some dating back as far as 1680. (☎321 68 10. Open daily 9am-5pm. 4zł.) Just uphill is the **Kościół,** Sw. Trójcy (Church of the Holy Trinity), one of the few Protestant churches in Poland. (☎421 62 93. Services Su 10:30am.)

PODLASIE

Poland extends maximum environmental protection to this small, northeastern region, often called "the green lungs of Poland." Poland's few Russian Orthodox villages dot wide-open fields which are interrupted only by the meandering Bug and Narew rivers. Białowieża Forest, once the favorite hunting ground of Polish kings, is now a national park and the domain of the scarce European bison.

BIAŁYSTOK   ☎(0)85

Most tourists know Białystok as a gateway to the natural wonders of Podlasie. Though much of the city is an unsightly jumble of Soviet-era concrete high-rises, the attentive visitor will find a town at the crossroads of Polish, Russian, and Tartar cultures. While Poland's accession to the EU has ended Białystok's once-roaring trade in used Kalashnikovs from Belarus and Ukraine, the town's atmosphere remains palpably eastern.

▣ **TRANSPORTATION.** The **train station**, Białystok Główny (☎94 36), is on ul. Kolejowa 9. Trains run to: **Gdynia** (7¾hr., 2 per day, 47zł); **Kraków** (5hr., 2 per day, 80zł); **Łódź** (4½hr., 1 per day, 41zł); **Olsztyn** (6hr., 5 per day, 24zł); **Szczecin** (13¾hr., 1 per day, 53zł); **Warsaw** (2hr., 21 per day, 34-62zł). The **bus station** (☎94 16) is toward town across the tracks on Bohaterów Monte Cassino 10. Buses run to: **Gdańsk** (9hr., 2 per day, 51zł); **Lublin** (6hr., 2 per day, 34zł); **Olsztyn** (4½hr., 3 per day, 31zł); **Warsaw** (3½hr., 7 per day, 25zł); **Wrocław** (12¾hr., 1 per day, 58zł); **Minsk, BLR** (8hr., 1 per day, 50zł). Comfortable **Polski Express** buses run to **Warsaw** (4hr., 4 per day, 28zł). Local buses cost 1.80zł, students 0.90zł. For a **taxi**, call ☎96 63.

▣▣ **ORIENTATION AND PRACTICAL INFORMATION.** The city center and most sights lie along a spine defined by **ul. Lipowa.** To reach the center from the stations, catch city bus #2, 4, 10, or 21S from the far side of ul. Bohaterów Monte Cassino. The **tourist office IT,** ul. Sienkiewicza 3 (☎653 79 50; www.city.bialystok.pl), inside Holiday Travel, sells **maps** (6-8zł) and has info about Białystok and the national parks. (Open M-F 9am-6pm, Sa 10am-2pm.) **PKO BP SA I Oddział,** ul. Rynek Kościuszki 16 (☎678 61 00), **exchanges currency,** has a 24hr. **ATM,** cashes **traveler's checks** for 1.5% commission, and gives MC/V **cash advances.** (Open M-W and F 8am-7pm, Th 10am-5pm, Sa 8am-2pm.) **Luggage storage** is available in the tunnel below the bus station. (3zł per day, 4zł for 2 days. Open daily 6am-5pm.) Lockers (4zł small, 8zł large) are in the **train station.** In an **emergency,** dial ☎999. A **pharmacy** (☎653 79 49) is at ul. Sienkiewicza 5. (Open M-F 8am-8pm, Sa 8am-3pm, Su 9am-2pm.) For **Internet access,** head to **Cybernet,** ul. Grochowa 2 (☎742 18 18; cyber.net@interia.pl), near ul. Lipowa. (2.50zł per 30min. Open daily 9am-midnight.) The **post office,** ul. Kolejowa 15 (☎652 61 91), has **telephone** and **fax** services. For **Poste Restante,** go to window #4. (Open daily 7am-6pm.) **Postal Code:** 15-900.

▣▣ **ACCOMMODATIONS AND FOOD.** Białystok's few budget options rarely fill up. **Szkolne Schronisko Młodzieżowe "Podlasie" ❶** is at al. Piłsudskiego 7b. From the bus station, turn left onto ul. Bohaterów Monte Cassino and take a right on ul. św. Rocha. Take the roundabout to al. Piłsudskiego, then follow the signs. Primary-color decor and curiously undersized tables and chairs give this friendly, impeccably clean hostel a nursery-school feel. The eager staff are a treasure trove of information about Podlasie, and the homey kitchen is a highlight. (☎652 42 50; www.ssm.bialystok.ids.pl. Linen 5zł. Dorms 25zł, under 26 21zł. With ISIC or Euro 26 card 19zł/23zł.) **Dom Turysty "Rubin" ❷** is at ul. Warszawska 7. From the train station take city bus #2, 21, or 21S to Warszawska. In a yellow neo-Baroque building festooned with stone cherubs, the Rubin offers clean rooms with TVs and a faint trace of the opulence of 19th-century Białystok. Small canteen offers drinks and snacks. (☎743 55 48; fax 743 62 71. Check-in 2pm. Check-out noon. Singles and doubles 70zł, with bath 120zł; triples 90zł/150zł.)

Restauracja Arsenał ❸, ul. Mickiewicza 2, in a wing of the Branicki Palace, serves excellent upscale traditional Polish cuisine and has gracious service to match. (☎742 85 67. Entrees 17-35zł. Salads 8-12zł. Open M-F and Su noon-11pm, Sa noon-3am. MC/V.) **Hocus Pocus ❶**, ul. Kilińskiego 12, takes pride in gale-force air conditioning that has the hanging lanterns swaying. A better reason to visit is the tasty range of pizzas, salads, and sandwiches. (☎741 63 48. Entrees 9-18zł. Open M-Sa 10am-11pm, Su noon-11pm.) **Asko Herbaty Świąty ❶**, ul. Kilińskiego 8, is a combination shop and teahouse with over 100 types of tea stacked up the walls in red bins. (☎741 72 96. Pots of tea 5.50-14zł. Coffee 4-9zł. Open M-Sa 10am-8pm, Su noon-8pm.)

🄶 **SIGHTS.** From ul. Lipowa, take a right onto ul. Sienkiewicza to get to the gardens of **Branicki Palace** (Pałac Branickich). A pretender to the Polish throne, Hetman Jan Klemens Branicki set out in the 18th century to establish a palace that would compare to Versailles. Though Branicki fell a bit short of his goal, the formal gardens and Baroque palace are an impressive feat of hubris. One of the best views of the garden is from the second-floor **Dzierżyński Balcony,** where Felix Dzierżyński proclaimed the creation of the Polish Soviet Republic in 1920. (Garden open daily Apr.-Sept. 6am-10pm; Oct.-Mar. 6am-6pm. Free. Palace open daily 9am-4pm. 2zł.) The **Military Museum** (Muzeum Wojska), ul. Kilińskiego 7, off ul. Lipowa, displays artifacts from the city's embattled history, including the original declaration of the 1944 Białystok ghetto uprising and a series of silver eagles showing the evolution of Poland's national symbol. (☎741 54 48. Open Tu-Su 9:30am-5pm. 4zł, students 2zł.) Down ul. Malmada, in a small triangular park, is a statue of the city's most famous son, Ludwig Zamenhoff, inventor of the international language **Esperanto.**

🄽 **NIGHTLIFE.** The large student population in Białystok makes for some decent nightlife, though more sophisticated venues are hard to come by. Gazela Magazyn has detailed info and is available free in most bars. **Metro**, ul. Białówny 9, has the telltale fluorescent lights and overgrown bouncers of the hottest disco in a small town. (☎732 41 54. Cover after 10pm 10zł. Open Tu-Sa 2pm-4am.) **Kino Polana Cinema Garden,** ul. Legionowa 10, has packed a large bar, double-decker seating, a movie screen, and a milk bar into a single building, which looks like an airplane hangar fused to a barn. Occasional film screenings and live music spice up nightly dance parties. (Entrees 6-12zł. Żubr 4.50zł. Open daily 9am-2am.)

BIAŁOWIESKI NATIONAL PARK

Białowieża Primeval Forest (Puszcza Białowieska), Europe's last remaining primeval forest, is a sprawling natural treasury of centuries-old oak trees, European bison, and 11,000 species of flora and fauna. Once the hunting ground of Polish kings and the former residence of Tsar Nicholas I, the park has been named a UNESCO World Heritage site and attracts visitors from around the world. Bordering Białowieża is the park's main attraction, the **Strict Preserve** (Obszar Ochrony Ścisłej) where 300 bison roam freely. The last wild bison were killed in 1919, but captive-bred Lithuanian bison were introduced to the park in 1929 and have thrived since. Only **guided tours** can enter this section of the park. Although you will be lucky to see any large mammals, the well-guided tour winds deeply through parts of the preserve and will leave you with a sound understanding of the forest's complex ecology and biodiversity. Another highlight is the show preserve of the tarpan, a genetically recreated wild horse that once roamed much of Europe but became extinct in the 19th century. (Open daily 9am-5pm. 5zł, students 3zł.) Just inside the park, the **Park Museum** (Muzeum Przyodniczo-Leśne) has exhibits on the park and an observatory tower. (☎681 22 75. Open daily 9am-4pm. 5zł, students 3zł.) To guarantee a view of the bison, head to the small **bison preserve** (Rezerwat Pokazowy Żubrów), 2km from the entrance, where bison and other animals are kept in tighter quarters. It is accessible via the yellow trail (2hr.), which leads from the PTTK office. (Bison preserve open daily 10am-5pm. 4zł, students 3zł.) The yellow, red, green, and blue trails offer great biking and walking paths.

Direct **buses** run from Białystok to **Białowieża** (3hr., 2 per day, 18zł). The last return bus from Białowieża is at 5:20pm. Don't get off at the main bus stop in front of the Orthodox church; wait and exit at the next stop. In the gateway of the park entrance, **PTTK,** ul. Kolejowa 17, arranges guides to enter the preserve. The price for the English-speaking guide is 150zł, so it's a good idea to get there early and hang around until a few more tourists show up. (☎681 26 24; www.pttk.bialow-ieza.pl. **Maps** 10-12zł. Open daily 8am-4pm. AmEx/MC/V.) Most travelers who visit the park stay overnight in the town of Białowieża. Either IT in Białystok or PTTK in Białowieża can arrange accommodations. Ask about a stay in the **eco-tourist farm,** which also rents bikes. (Bikes 5zł per hr., 13zł per 3hr. Rooms 17-45zł.) After a day of hikes, enjoy Polish fare at **Unikat ❸,** ul. Gen. Waszkiewicza 39. (☎681 27 74. Entrees 20zł. Open daily 8am-10pm.)

ROMANIA (ROMÂNIA)

Devastated by Nicolae Ceauşescu's lengthy reign, modern Romania is in a state of economic transition. Some of its citizens are eager to Westernize, but others choose traditional lives in the countryside. The resulting state of flux, combined with a largely undeserved reputation for poverty and crime, discourages travelers. But those who dismiss Romania do themselves an injustice—the country is rich in history, rustic beauty, and hospitality. Romania's fascinating legacy draws visitors to Dracula's dark castle, in a region where buildings are still crooked, and to the Bucovina monasteries, famous for their colorful frescoes. Meanwhile, new Romania is in evidence in Bucharest, where tourists explore the remnants of Ceauşescu's rule, and in the heavily touristed Black Sea Coast, where resort towns draw throngs of summer vacationers anxious to explore the rapidly changing country.

HISTORY

GROWING PAINS. Ancient Romania was inhabited by Dacian tribes, and trading cities grew up along the Black Sea Coast in the 7th Century BC. The first Romanian state, **Wallachia,** was established in the early AD 1300s. The second, **Moldavia,** was founded east of the Carpathians in 1349. The fledgling states constantly defended against the **Ottoman Turks,** who controlled Transylvania and other nearby lands. Moldavia's **Ştefan cel Mare** (Stephen the Great; 1457-1504) was most successful in warding off the attacks. During his 47-year rule, he built 42 beautiful monasteries and churches, one for each of his victorious battles (see **Bucovina Monasteries,** p. 642). However, successful resistance died with Ştefan, and Moldavia and Wallachia became Turkish provinces.

FACTS AND FIGURES

OFFICIAL NAME: Romania

CAPITAL: Bucharest (pop. 2.3 million)

POPULATION: 22.4 million

LANGUAGES: Romanian, Hungarian, German

CURRENCY: 1 leu (L) = 100 bani

RELIGIONS: 87% Eastern Orthodox, 7% Protestant, 6% Catholic

LAND AREA: 230,340km²

CLIMATE: Temperate and continental

GEOGRAPHY: Mountains and plains

BORDERS: Bulgaria, Hungary, Moldova, Serbia and Montenegro, Ukraine

ECONOMY: 40% Agriculture, 35% Service, 25% Industry

GDP: US$7600 per capita

COUNTRY CODE: 40

INTERNATIONAL DIALING PREFIX: 00

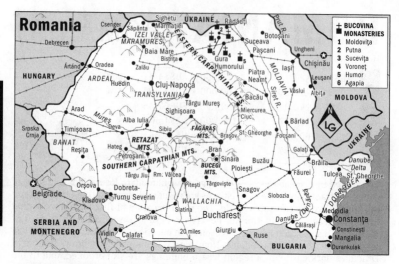

TURMOIL. For the next 400 years Austria-Hungary, Russia, Turkey, and Poland-Lithuania fought for the region. **Mihai Viteazul** (Michael the Brave) tried to create a unified state in 1599, but Polish, Hungarian, and Ottoman attacks left the country decimated. Moldavia and Wallachia united in 1859. **King Carol I** reduced corruption, built railroads, and strengthened the army that won Romania its independence in 1877. After Austria-Hungary's defeat in **WWI,** Romania gained Transylvania, Bucovina, and Bessarabia (now Moldova). The doubled population was more diverse, and ethnic tensions resulted. Under the 1941 **Nazi-Soviet Non-Aggression Pact,** Romania lost its new territory to the Axis powers. Hoping the Nazis would preserve an independent Romania, dictator **General Ion Antonescu** supported Germany in WWII. In 1944, **King Mihai** orchestrated a coup and surrendered to the Allies, but the bid was unsuccessful. The Soviets moved in and proclaimed the **Romanian People's Republic** in 1947.

YOU SAY YOU WANT A REVOLUTION. The government violently suppressed opposition in the postwar era. Over 200,000 died in the 1950s **purges,** and farmers were forced to collectivize. In 1965, **Nicolae Ceauşescu** took control of the Communist Party. He won praise in the West for attempting to distance Romania from Moscow, but his ruthless domestic policies deprived his citizens of basic needs. By the late 1980s Ceauşescu had transformed Romania into a police state. When the dreaded **Securitate** (Secret Police) arrested a popular priest, a violent protest erupted in **Timişoara** (p. 636), and soon Romania was in a state of full-scale revolt. The 1989 **revolution** was as ruthless as Ceauşescu himself. In December, clashes in Bucharest brought thousands of protesters to the streets. Ceauşescu was arrested, tried, and executed—on TV—all on Christmas Day. The enthusiasm following these December days didn't last, as **Ion Iliescu's National Salvation Front,** composed largely of former communists, seized power and won the 1990 elections. Despite moderate reforms, Iliescu provoked international condemnation for using violence and terror tactics to repress student demonstrations. Revolution, it seemed, had changed little.

TODAY. The 1991 constitution stipulates an elected **president** who serves a four-year term and nominates a **prime minister.** Members of **Parliament** are elected to four-year terms. In November 1996, **Emil Constantinescu** succeeded Iliescu in the country's first democratic transfer of power. Constantinescu's **Romanian Democratic Coalition (RDC)** promised reforms but focused more on disputes among its member parties. Iliescu won back the presidency in 2000. Romania is scheduled to join the **EU** in 2007 but faces several roadblocks. The country joined **NATO** in May 2004 and has amended its constitution and taken other steps toward democracy. Elections were held in November 2004.

PEOPLE AND CULTURE

LANGUAGE

Romanian is a Romance language. Those familiar with French, Italian, Portuguese, or Spanish should be able to decipher many words. Romanian differs from other Romance tongues in its Slavic-influenced vocabulary. **German** and **Hungarian** are widely spoken in Transylvania. Throughout the country, **French** is a common second language for the older generation; **English** for the younger. Avoid **Russian,** which is often understood but disliked. Spoken Romanian is like Italian but has three additional vowels: *"ă"* (pronounced like "u" in "fun") and the phonetically interchangeable *"â"* and *"î"* ("i" in "silver"). The other two characters peculiar to Romanian are *"ş"* ("sh" in "shiver") and *"ţ"* ("ts" in "tsar"). At the end of a word, *"i"* is dropped, but *"ii"* sounds like "ee" in "cheese." *"Ci"* is like "chea" in "cheat," and "ce" sounds like "che" in "ches olms." *"Chi"* is pronounced like "kee" in "keen," and *"che"* like "ke" in "kept." *"G"* before *"e"* or *"i"* sounds like "j" as in judge and *"gh"* before those vowels is like "g" in girl. For a phrasebook and glossary, see **Glossary: Romanian,** p. 956.

FOOD AND DRINK

ROMANIA	❶	❷	❸	❹	❺
FOOD	under L70,000	L70,000-110,000	L111,000-150,000	L151,000-200,000	over L200,000

A complete **Romanian meal** includes an appetizer, soup, fish, an entree, and dessert. Lunch includes **soup,** called *supă* or *ciorbă* (the former has noodles or dumplings, the latter is saltier, with vegetables), an entree (typically grilled meat), and dessert. Soups can be very tasty; try *ciorbă de perişoare* (with vegetables and ground meatballs) or *supă cu găluşte* (with fluffy dumplings). **Pork** comes in several varieties; *muşchi* and *cotlet* are of the highest quality. Common entrees include *mici* (rolls of fried meat), *sarmale* (stuffed cabbage), and *mămăligă* (polenta). **Beef** and **lamb** are other common meats. *Clătite* (crepes), *papanaşi* (doughnuts with jam and sour cream), and *torts* (creamy cakes) are all fantastic. *Ingheţată* (ice cream) is cheap and good, while the delicious *mere în aluat* (doughnuts with apples) and sugary *gogoşi* (fried doughnuts) are delectable. In the west, you'll find as much **Hungarian food** as Romanian. Some restaurants charge by weight rather than by portion. It's difficult to predict how many grams you will receive. *Garnituri,* the extras that come with a meal, are usually charged separately. This means you're paying for everything, even a bit of butter or a dollop of mustard. Pork rules in Romania, so keeping **kosher** is difficult, but it's possible with planning. Local **drinks** include *ţuică,* a brandy distilled from plums and apples, and *palincă,* a stronger version of *ţuică* that approaches 70% alcohol. A delicious liqueur called *vişnată* is made from wild cherries.

ROMANIA

ROMANIA

CUSTOMS AND ETIQUETTE

It is customary to give inexact change for purchases, rounding up to the nearest L500. Restaurants usually round up to the nearest L500 or give candy instead of L100s. Locals generally don't **tip,** but foreigners are expected to tip 5-10% in nice restaurants with good service. Hotel porters and helpful concierges are generally tipped modestly. Some tip **taxis,** but doing so is unnecessary. In all cases, tipping too much is inappropriate. **Bargain** over taxi fare and accommodations if there is no posted rate. Try for one third off in open-air markets. Romanians take pride in their **hospitality.** Most will be eager to help and offer to show you around or invite you to their homes. Bring your hostess an odd number of flowers; even-numbered bouquets are only brought to graves. Pack for a climate that resembles the Northeast US. Romanians **dress** well, and shorts are rare. For those over 30 and anyone in rural areas, men should wear pants and closed-toed shoes, and women should wear dresses.

THE ARTS

The first sign of **literary** activity came with the poet **Ovid,** who wrote his last works in exile near Constanţa. The literary resurgence in the late 1700s is credited largely to the **Văcărescu family:** grandfather **Ienăchiţă** wrote the first Romanian grammar, father **Alecu** wrote love poetry, and son **Iancu** is considered the master of Romanian poetry. **Grigore Alexandrescu's** 19th-century French-inspired fables and satires are also famous. The next generation of writers, clustered around the literary magazine *Junimea,* penned the Romanian classics. From this generation, **Ion Creangă's** most important work, *Aminitiri din Copilărie* (Memories of My Childhood), depicts village life. **Mihai Eminescu,** the father of modern Romanian poetry, wrote in the **Romantic** style. In the 20th century, **Nicolae Iorga** set a new standard for poetry, drama, and history.

The end of WWII brought the strictures of **Socialist Realism. Geo Bogza** and **Mihail Beniuc** were prominent adherents, composing works glorifying the worker. Some sought freedom in other lands and languages—absurdist dramatist **Eugen Ionescu** (Eugène Ionesco; 1909-1994), religious scholar **Mircea Eliade** (1907-1986), and Dada-founder **Tristan Tzara** (1896-1963) are the best-known. Contemporary artists include composer **George Enescu** (1881-1955) and painter **Nicolae Grigorescu** (1838-1907), who studied art in France before immortalizing the Romanian countryside. Famous **Constantin Brâncuşi** (1876-1957) is considered one of the greatest Modernist sculptors; some of his best work stand outside in Târgu Jiu. Bucharest's **National Art Museum** houses works by these artists.

Folk music is popular **today,** and glassware and decorated Easter eggs are fine crafts that continue to thrive. Edgy, realist Romanian **cinema** is gaining international recognition, especially through the popular **Film Festival Cottbus.** The attention has helped produce many films. In music, opera singer **Angela Gheorghiu** and pianist **Radu Lupu** are quickly gaining international fame.

HOLIDAYS AND FESTIVALS

NATIONAL HOLIDAYS IN 2005	
January 1-2 New Year's Holiday	**May 1** Labor Day
January 6 Epiphany	**December 1** National Unity Day
March 1 Mărţişor	(or Romania Day)
April 11-12 Easter Holiday	**December 25-26** Christmas

Romania Day, December 1, commemorates the day in 1918 that Transylvania became a part of Romania. For **Mărţişor,** March 1, locals wear *porte-boneurs* (good-luck charms) and give snow-drop flowers to friends and lovers.

ADDITIONAL RESOURCES

GENERAL HISTORY

Balkan Ghosts: A Journey Through History, by Robert Kaplan (1994). A deeply engaging travel narrative and an informative regional history. Also see Kaplan's 2001 tome **Eastward to Tartary,** which examines similar themes on a broader scale.

Dracula, Prince of Many Faces: His Life and Times, by Radu R. Florescu (1990). Debunks cultural myths and tells the real story of Vlad Ţepeş.

FICTION, NONFICTION, AND FILM

Dracula, by Bram Stoker (1897). The horror novel that launched a national obsession.

Red Rats (Şobolanii Roşii), directed by Florin Codre (1991). Exposes Romanian disillusionment about the revolution of 1989.

Taste of Romania: Its Cookery and Glimpses of its History, Folklore, Art and Poetry, by Nicolae Klepper (1999). Primer on Romanian culture, with insight on the local proclivity for larded pork.

Vampire Nation, by Thomas Sipos (2001). A novel connecting communism and vampirism in Romania.

ROMANIAN ESSENTIALS

ENTRANCE REQUIREMENTS

Passport: Required of all travelers.

Visa: Required of citizens of Australia and New Zealand. Required of citizens of Ireland for stays over 30 days.

Letter of Invitation: Not required for citizens of Australia, Canada, Ireland, New Zealand, the UK, and the US.

Inoculations: Recommended up-to-date on DTaP (diphtheria, tetanus, and pertussis), Hepatitis A, Hepatitis B, MMR (measles, mumps, and rubella), Polio booster, and Typhoid.

Work Permit: Required of all foreigners planning to work in Romania.

Driving Permit: Required for all those planning to drive in Romania.

DOCUMENTS AND FORMALITIES

EMBASSIES AND CONSULATES

Embassies and consulates of other countries in Romania are all in **Bucharest** (see p. 616). Romania's embassies and consulates abroad include:

Australia: 4 Dalman Crescent, O'Malley, ACT 2606 (☎26 286 2343; www.roembau.org).

Canada: 655 Rideau St., Ottawa, ON K1N 6A3 (☎613 789 4037; www.cyberus.ca/~romania).

Ireland: 47 Ailesbury Rd., Ballsbridge, Dublin 4 (☎01 269 2852; romemb@iol.ie).

UK: 4 Palace Green, London W8 4QD (☎0207 937 9666; www.roemb.co.uk).

US: 1607 23rd St. NW, Washington, D.C. 20008 (☎202 332 4848; www.roembus.org).

VISA AND ENTRY INFORMATION

Romanian **visa** info changes frequently; check with your embassy or consulate for the most accurate and specific info. Citizens of Canada, the UK, and the US can visit Romania for up to 90 days without a visa while citizens of Ireland may visit for up to 30 days without visas. Citizens of Australia and New Zealand need visas. In all cases, passports are required and must be valid six months after the date of departure. A visa application requires a passport, one application form per visa, a recent photograph, and the application fee. For Americans, a single entry visa costs US$35; multiple-entry US$70. Visas are not available at the border. Romanian embassies estimate 30-day processing time for some visas. Apply early to allow the bureaucratic process to run its slow, frustrating course. **Visa extensions** and related services are available at police headquarters in large cities or at **Bucharest's passport office,** Str. Luigi Cazzavillan 11. Long lines are common at the border. Bags are rarely searched, but customs officials are strict about visa laws. Beware of tax scams.

GETTING AROUND

Many **airlines** fly into Bucharest. **TAROM** (Romanian Airlines) recently updated its fleet; it flies directly from Bucharest to **New York** and major European and Middle Eastern cities (☎ 21 201 4000; www.tarom.ro.) Though recently improved, Bucharest's **Otopeni International Airport** is not completely modern.

Trains are better than buses for **international** travel. To buy tickets to the national railway, go to the ⬛CFR (Che-Fe-Re) office in larger towns. You must buy international tickets in advance. Train stations sell tickets 1hr. in advance. The English-language timetable *Mersul Trenurilor* (hardcopy L12,000; online at www.cfr.ro) is very useful. There are four types of trains: *InterCity* (indicated by an "IC" on timetables and at train stations); *rapid* (in green); *accelerat* (red); and *personal* (black). International trains (blue) are indicated with an "i." *InterCity* trains stop only at major cities. *Rapid* trains are the next fastest; *accelerat* trains start with "1" and are slower and dirtier. The sluggish and decrepit *personal* trains stop at every station. The difference between **first class** (*clasa întâi;* clah-sa un-toy; 6 people per compartment) and **second class** (*clasa doua;* 8 people) is small, except on *personal* trains. In an **overnight train,** shell out for a *vagon de dormit* (sleeping carriage), and buy both compartment tickets if you don't want to share.

Traveling to Romania by **bus** is often cheaper than entering by plane or train. Tourist agencies may sell timetables and tickets, but buying tickets from the carrier saves commission and is often cheaper. Use the slow **local bus system** only when trains are unavailable. Local buses are slightly cheaper but are just as packed and poorly ventilated. Minibuses are a good option for short distances because they are often cheap, fast, and clean. Rates are posted inside.

In the Danube Delta, **boats** are the best mode of transport. A ferry runs down the new European riverway from **Rotterdam, NED** to Constanţa, and in the Black Sea between **Istanbul, TUR** and Constanţa.

Be wary of **taxis;** only use cars that post a company name, phone number, and rate per kilometer. Be sure the driver uses the meter. Your ride should cost no more than L6000 per km plus a L7000 flat fee. If you wish to drive a **car,** you must bring an **International Driving Permit;** make sure you are insured and have your registration papers. **MyBike** (www.mybike.ro) provides excellent info on **biking** in Romania. *Let's Go* does not recommend **hitchhiking.** Hitchhikers stand on the side of the road and put out their palm, as if waving. Drivers generally expect a **payment** similar to the price of a train or bus ticket for the distance traveled. In some places, hitchhiking is the only way to get around.

TOURIST SERVICES AND MONEY

Romania has limited **resources for tourists,** but the National Tourist Office is still useful. Check its website at www.romaniatourism.com. Most tourist offices are intended for Romanians traveling abroad, and much of the country has poor resources for foreign travelers. It can help to walk into the most expensive hotel in town and pretend to be important. **Cluj-Napoca,** however, is a welcome relief with its many tourist offices.

The Romanian **currency** is the **leu,** plural lei (abbreviated **L**). Banknotes are issued in amounts of L10,000, L50,000, L100,000, and L500,000; coins come in amounts of 100L, 500L, and 1000L. Pay in lei and save hard currency for emergencies. **Inflation** rates have been very high (around 34%) but are dropping (projections are around 10%); prices quoted in lei will likely change over the year. Romania has a **Value Added Tax Rate (VAT)** of 19%. **ATMs** generally accept MasterCard and sometimes Visa, and are the best way to get money. ATMs are found everywhere but the smallest towns, usually operate 24hr., and occasionally run out of cash. Many locals carry US dollars, so **private exchange bureaus,** which often offer better exchange rates than **banks,** are everywhere and deal in common foreign currencies. However, few take **credit cards** or **traveler's checks.** Walk around and compare rates before exchanging money. Most banks will cash traveler's checks in US dollars, then exchange them for lei, with high fees. **American Express Traveler's Cheques** are most useful. Never change money on the street, as it is illegal; those who attempt to are generally cheated or scammed. Normal business hours are 9am-5pm.

HEALTH AND SAFETY

EMERGENCY NUMBERS:
Police: ☎955 Fire: ☎981 Emergency: ☎961

If possible, avoid Romanian **hospitals,** as they are often not up to Western standards. Pack a first-aid kit. Go to a private doctor for medical emergencies; your embassy can recommend a good one. Some **American medical clinics** in Bucharest have English-speaking doctors; pay in **cash.** *Farmacies* (pharmacies) stock basic medical supplies. *Antinevralgic* is for headaches; *aspirină* or *piramidon* for colds and the flu; and *saprosan* for diarrhea. *Prezervatives* (condoms), *tampoane* (tampons), and

ON THE MENU

ROMANIAN MOONSHINE

If you're tired of basic local plum brandy, commonly served in restaurants and touted as the major local drink, you may want to branch out and try the stronger version, *palinca*. This locally produced moonshine, widely available—but never in stores—is a triple-distilled version of tamer *tuica*. The alcohol content of *Palinca* often exceeds 60%.

In towns, *palinca* is usually sold in produce markets along with all the other wholesome farm goods, and in the countryside it is sold everywhere. It is commonly dispensed in old plastic drinking water bottles with labels removed. It has a light-yellow color, and its smell is perhaps less strong than one would imagine. Prices vary, but L100,000 per liter is usually fair.

As with any home-brew, a lot of caution is in order. Watch to see if a vendor's product is popular. If other locals are safely drinking it, chances are you can too. In any event, drink *palinca* sparingly and in moderation. It goes down easily and disorients its drinker quite quickly. For a real taste of the local culture, a sample of *palinca* is an eye-opening experience.

şerveţele igienice (sanitary napkins) are available at all drugstores and many kiosks. Most **public restrooms** lack soap, towels, and toilet paper, and many on trains and in stations smell rank. Attendants may charge L1000-1500 for a single square of toilet paper. Pick up a roll at a drug store and carry it with you. You can find relief at most restaurants, even if you're not a patron. Beware of **stray dogs,** common everywhere including major cities, as they bite frequently and often carry **rabies.** Water quality in Romania is less contaminated than it once was. Still, avoid untreated **tap water** and do not use **ice cubes;** boil water before drinking it or drink imported **bottled water.** Beware of water-contaminated ice and vendor food.

Violent **crime** is not a major concern, but petty **crime** against tourists is common. Be especially careful on public transport and night trains. Beware of con artists dressed as policemen who ask for your passport or wallet. If someone shows a badge and claims to be a plainclothes policeman, he is probably lying and trying to scam you. When in doubt, ask the officer to escort you to the nearest police station. Pickpocketing, money exchange, and taxi scams are very prevalent. Many scammers speak good English and German, so don't be fooled. The **drinking age,** which is 18, is not enforced. If you smoke marijuana, be prepared to spend the next seven years in a Romanian prison. Other **drug laws** are also strictly enforced. Single **female travelers** shouldn't go out alone after dark and should say they are traveling with a male. Tank tops, shorts, and sneakers may attract attention. **Minorities,** and especially those with dark skin, may encounter unwanted attention or discrimination. Practitioners of **religions** other than Orthodox Christianity may feel uncomfortable in the province of Moldavia. **Homosexuality** is now legal, but homosexual public displays of affection could get you arrested. Many Romanians hold conservative attitudes toward sexuality, which may translate into harassment of **GLBT** travelers. Still, women who walk arm-in-arm will not draw any attention.

ACCOMMODATIONS AND CAMPING

ROMANIA	❶	❷	❸	❹	❺
ACCOM.	under L400,000	L400,000-700,000	L701,000-1,000,000	L1,001,000-2,000,000	over L2,000,000

Hostels are often fairly pleasant, but few are accredited. Some have perks like free beer and breakfast. While some **hotels** charge foreigners 50-100% more, lodging is still inexpensive (US$7-20). Reservations are helpful in July and August, but you can usually get by without them. **Guesthouses** and **pensions** are simple and comfortable but rare. In summer, many towns rent low-priced rooms in **university dorms,** but these may be hard to locate if you don't speak Romanian. Consult the tourist office. **Private rooms** and **homestays** are a great option, but hosts rarely speak English. Renting a room "together" means sharing a bed. Rooms run US$7-12 in the countryside and US$15-20 in cities. Look at the room and fix a price before accepting. **Campgrounds** can be crowded and have frightening bathrooms. Still, **bungalows** are often full in summer; reserve far ahead. Hotels and hostels often provide the best **information for tourists.**

KEEPING IN TOUCH

At the post office, request *par avion* for **airmail,** which takes two weeks for delivery. A postcard to the US costs L22,000; a letter L27,000. **Mail** can be received through **Poste Restante.** However, you may run into problems picking up your package. Address envelopes as follows: Noam (first name) KATZ (LAST NAME), POSTE RESTANTE, Str. Nicolae Iorga 1 (post office address), 500057 (postal code) Braşov (city), ROMANIA. Major cities have **UPS,** and **Federal Express.** Most public phones are orange and accept **phone cards,** but the archaic blue phones take L500 coins. Buy phone cards at telephone offices, Metro stops, and some post offices and kiosks. Only buy cards sealed in plastic wrap. Rates run around L12,000 per min. to neighboring countries, L16,000 per min. to most of Europe, and L20,000 per min. to the US. Phones operate in English if you press "i." At an analog phone, dial ☎971 for international calls. You may need to make a phone call *prin comandă* (with the help of the operator) at the telephone office; this takes longer and costs more. There are **no toll-free calls** in Romania—you even need a phone card to call the police, an ambulance, or the operator. People with European cell phones can avoid roaming charges by buying a **SIM card** at **Connex, Dialog,** or **CosmoRom.** General info ☎931, operator ☎930. International access codes include: **AT&T Direct** (☎01 800 42 88); **Canada Direct** (☎01 800 50 00); **MCI WorldPhone** (☎01 800 18 00); and **Sprint** (☎01 800 08 770). **Internet** cafes are common in cities and cost L12,000-L22,000 per hr.

BUCHAREST (BUCUREŞTI) ☎(0)21

Once a fabled beauty on the Orient Express, Bucharest (pop. 2,040,000) is now infamous for its heavy-handed transformation under dictator Nicolae Ceauşescu. During his 25-year reign, Ceauşescu nearly ruined the city's splendor by replacing historic neighborhoods, grand boulevards, and Ottoman ruins with concrete blocks, wide highways, and communist monuments. Still, gems are scattered amid the concrete. Adults remember and probably participated in the 1989 revolution; all citizens have since endured a mix of communist nostalgia and break-neck capitalism, tempered by an unshakable vein of Christian Orthodoxy. Though Bucharest is no longer the "Little Paris" *(Micul Paris)* it once was, life here is fascinating, frustrating, and anything but boring.

◤ INTERCITY TRANSPORTATION

Flights: Otopeni Airport (☎204 10 00). Avoid taxis outside the terminal; they are notorious for scamming travelers. Call a cab (see **Taxis,** p. 616) or buy a bus ticket (L40,000, for 2 trips) at the little kiosk in the corner. Bus #783 runs from the airport to Pţa. Unirii (45min., 2-4 per hr.). It departs from the level beneath the international arrivals hall. **Băneasa Airport** (☎231 42 57), accessible from Pta. Romană by bus #131, 135, or 305, and from Gara de Nord by bus #205 or 783, handles domestic flights. Buy tickets at **TAROM,** Spl. Independenţei 17 (☎337 04 00). Open M-F 9am-7pm, Sa 9am-1pm.

Trains: Gara de Nord (☎223 08 80, info 95 21). M1: Gara de Nord. To: **Braşov** (4hr., 12 per day, L160,000); **Cluj-Napoca** (10hr., 5 per day, L272,000); **Constanţa** (3hr., 6 per day, L186,000); **Iaşi** (7hr., 4 per day, L272,000); **Sighişoara** (6hr., 7 per day, L203,000); **Timişoara** (9hr., 8 per day, L314,000); **Budapest, HUN** (14hr., 5 per day, L2,000,000); **Chişinău, MOL** (13hr., 1 per day, L650,000); **Kraków, POL** (27hr., 1 per day, L2,500,000); **Prague, CZR** (36hr., 1 per day, L3,200,000); **Sofia, BUL** (13hr., 2 per day, L1,300,000). ◤**CFR,** Str. Domniţa Anastasia 10-14 (☎313 26 43; www.cfr.ro) books domestic tickets. Open M-F 7:30am-7:30pm, Sa 8am-noon. **Wasteels** (☎222 78 44; www.wasteelstravel.ro), inside Gara de Nord, books international tickets. Open M-F 8am-6pm, Sa 8am-2pm.

Buses: There are 7 official bus stations in Bucharest; each serves a different sector of the city and buses to the destinations in that sector's direction. **Filaret,** Cuţitul de Argint 2 (☎335 11 40). M2: Tineretului. Buses are the best way to reach **Athens, GCE,** and **Istanbul, TUR.** To Athens, your best bet is **Ager Agency** (☎336 67 83; €65). To Istan-

ROMANIA

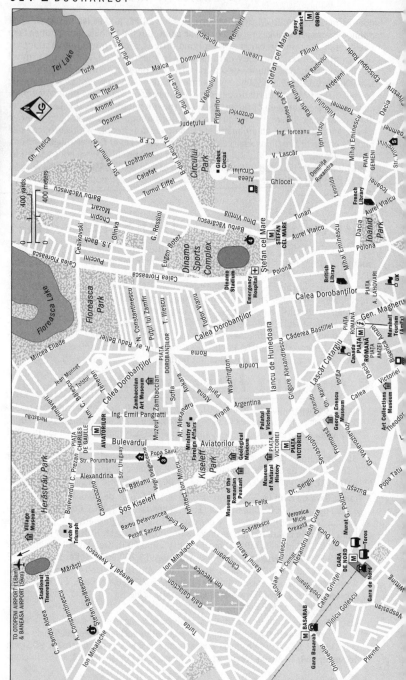

ROMANIA

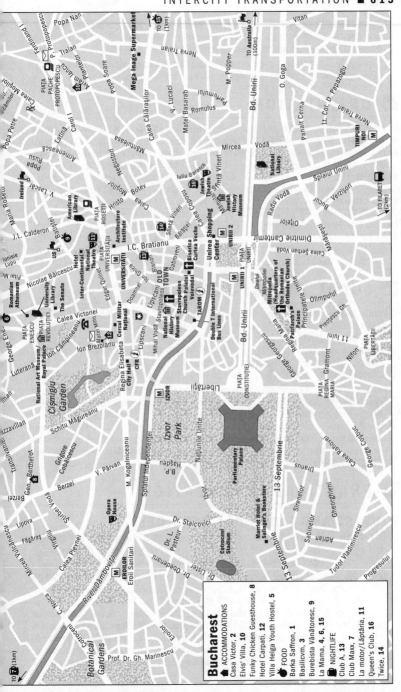

Bucharest

▲ ACCOMMODATIONS
Casa Victor, **2**
Elvis's Villa, **10**
Funky Chicken Guesthouse, **8**
Hotel Carpati, **12**
Villa Helga Youth Hostel, **5**
🍴 FOOD
Barka Saffron, **1**
Basilicvm, **3**
Burebista Vânătoresc, **9**
La Mama, **4, 6, 15**
🎵 NIGHTLIFE
Club A, **13**
Club Maxx, **7**
La motor/Lăptăria, **11**
Queen's Club, **16**
Twice, **14**

bul, try **Toros** (☎223 18 98; 1 per day) or **Murat** (☎224 92 93; 2 per day) from outside Gara de Nord. (Both L1,250,000.) **Double T**, Calea Victoriei 2 (☎313 36 42), or **Eurolines Touring**, Str. Ankara 6 (☎230 03 70; fax 315 01 66), go to Western Europe.

Microbuses: Comfortable, air-conditioned **Maxi-Taxi** leaves from outside Gara de Nord to domestic destinations near Bucharest for about half the price of trains.

■ ORIENTATION

Bucharest's main street changes its name from **Str. Lascăr** to **Bd. General Magheru** to **Bd. Nicolae Bălcescu** to **Bd. I.C. Brătianu** as it runs north-south through the city's four main squares: **Piaţa Victoriei, Piaţa Romană, Piaţa Universităţii,** and **Piaţa Unirii.** Another main drag slightly to the west is **Calea Victoriei**, which runs through **Piaţa Revoluţiei.** The **Metro** M1 line forms a diamond that encloses the city center. The M3 passes horizontally along the bottom of this diamond, while M2 pierces it vertically, stopping at the main squares. To reach the center from Gara de Nord, take M1 to Pţa. Victoriei, then change to M2 in the direction of Depoul IMGB. Go one stop to Pţa. Romana, two stops to Pţa. Universităţii, or three stops to Pţa. Unirii. It's a 15min. walk between each square. **Maps** are sold throughout Bucharest. The Amco Press series (L100,000) sets the standard. The ever-helpful *Bucharest In Your Pocket* (free) is available at hostels, museums, bookstores, and hotels.

◠ LOCAL TRANSPORTATION

Public Transportation: Buses, trolleys, and **trams** cost L8000 and run daily 5:30am-11:30pm. Validate tickets by sliding them into the small boxes to avoid a L300,000 fine. The transportation system is invaluable, but figuring out how it works is a chore. **Express buses** take only magnetic cards (L40,000 for 2 trips). Tickets are sold at kiosks. Pickpocketing is a problem during peak hours. The **Metro** offers reliable, less-crowded service. (L16,000 for 2 trips, L50,000 for 10. Open daily 5am-11:30pm.

Taxis: Taxi drivers in Bucharest are frequently dishonest; many will cheerfully attempt to charge you 10 times the regular fare, especially from airports, train stations, and major hotels. Rate are around L7000-9000 base fee and an equal amount per km. Only use taxis that have a company name, phone number, and rate posted. Make sure the driver uses the meter. Rare is the driver who speaks English, so carry directions to your hotel or hostel, written in Romanian. Reliable companies include **Meridien** (☎94 44), **ChrisTaxi** (☎94 61), and **Taxi2000** (☎94 94).

◪ PRACTICAL INFORMATION

TOURIST AND FINANCIAL SERVICES

Tourist Office: The information booth in the Gara de Nord is useful, but hotels and hostels are generally the best source of info. The staff of **Elvis' Villa** (see p. 618) organizes activities for its guests, including guided tours of Dracula's tomb (L270,000).

Embassies and Consulates: Australia, Bd. Unirii 74, 5th fl. (☎320 98 26; fax 320 98 23). M2: Pţa. Unirii, then bus #104, 123, or 124 to Lucian Blaga. Open M-Th 9:30am-12:30pm. **Bulgaria,** Str. Rabat 5 (☎230 21 50; fax 230 76 54). **Canada,** Str. Nicolae Iorga 36 (☎307 50 63). Check before going as the embassy is moving to Sos. Pavel Kisileff. M2: Pţa. Romană. Open M-Th 8am-2pm. **Hungary,** Str. Jean-Louis Calderon 63-65 (☎311 15 42; www.hungaryemb.ines.ro). **Ireland,** Str. Vasile Lascăr 42-44, 6th fl. (☎210 89 48; fax 211 43 84). M2: Pţa. Romană. Open M-F 10am-noon. **Moldova,** Al. Alexandru 40 (☎230 04 74; moldova@customers.digiro.net). Citizens of **New Zealand**

Bucharest Metro

Legend:
- M1: Eroilor - Dristor
- M2: Depou IMGB - Pipera
- M3: Industriilor - Pantelimon
- M4: Gara de Nord - 1 Mai
- ○ Transfer Station
- ● Terminus
- Street
- Water

should contact the UK embassy. **Serbia and Montenegro,** Calea Dorobanţilor 34 (☎211 98 71; ambiug@ines.ro). **UK,** Str. Jules Michelet 24 (☎312 03 03; fax 312 02 29). M2: Pţa. Romană. Open M-Th 8:30am-1pm and 2-5pm, F 8:30am-1:30pm. **Ukraine,** Calea Dorobantilor 16 (☎211 69 86; fax 211 69 49). **US,** Str. Tudor Arghezi 7-9 (☎210 40 42, ext. 403; after hours 210 01 49; fax 210 03 95). M2: Pţa. Universi-tăţii. A block behind Hotel Intercontinental. Open M-Th 8am-noon and 1-5pm.

Currency Exchange: Exchange agencies and **ATMs** are everywhere. Stock up before heading to remote areas, but don't exchange more than you'll need—many won't buy lei back. **Banca Comercială Romana** (☎315 82 99; www.bcr.com), in Pţa. Victoriei and Pţa. Universităţii, has good rates and exchanges **AmEx Travelers Cheques** for 1.5% commission. Open M-F 8:30am-5:30pm, Sa 8:30am-12:30pm. Changing money on the street is illegal and almost always a scam.

American Express: Marshall Tourism, Bd. Magheru 43, 1st fl. #1 (☎212 97 87). M2: Pţa. Romana. Books hotels and flights only. Open M-F 9am-1pm and 2-5pm.

LOCAL AND EMERGENCY SERVICES

Luggage Storage: Gara de Nord. L25,000, large bags L50,000. Open 24hr.

English-Language Bookstore: Salingers, Calea 13 Septembrie 90 (☎403 35 34), in the Mariott. Open M-Sa noon-9pm, Su 10am-9pm.

GLBT Organization: Accept Bucharest, Str. Lirei 10 (☎252 16 37; www.accept-romania.ro). News on gay rights in Romania, social info, and useful links.

Laundry: Public laundromats are rare. Your best bet is your hotel or hostel.

Pharmacies: They are everywhere. **Sensiblu** (☎203 90 09) is a reputable chain. Some open 24hr.

Medical Assistance: Spitalul de Urgenţă (Emergency Hospital), Calea Floreasca 8 (☎230 01 06). M1: Ştefan cel Mare. Open 24hr.

Telephones: Public pay phones are orange and take official pre-paid phone cards, which come in L80,000, L100,000, and L160,000 denominations. These work for domestic calls and are a simple if expensive way to place international calls. You need a phone card to make all calls, even to emergency numbers. Place collect calls at **Romtelecom,** Calea Victoriei 35 (☎313 36 35). M2: Pţa. Universităţii. In the back of the tallest building on the street. Open 24hr. Internet cafes often have relatively cheap overseas rates.

Internet Access: Internet cafes are everywhere. **Try P-C Net Café,** Calea Victoriei 136 (☎315 51 86). M2: Pţa. Romană. Fax, photocopying, printing, and international phones. Open 24hr. Internet rates M-F 6am-11pm L40,000 per hr., M-F 11pm-6am and Sa-Su L30,000 per hr. L10,000 minimum. International calls from L10,000 per min.

Post Office: The Central Post Office, Str. Matei Millo 10 (☎315 90 30). M2: Pţa. Universităţii. Go down Bd. Regina Elisabeta, turn right on Calea Victoriei, left on Str. Mille Constantin, right on Str. Oteteleşanu Ion, and left on Matei Millo. **Poste Restante** is on the right, just before Hotel Carpaţi. Open M-F 7:30am-8pm, Sa 7:30am-2pm. Branches are all over the city. **Postal Code:** 010144.

⌂ ACCOMMODATIONS

Bucharest doesn't have many private rooms; its hotels and hostels are more expensive than in other Romanian cities. The established hostels are fairly cheap, very international, and comfortable. Beware of people at Gara du Nord who claim to work for hostels—often they are con-artists and will scam you.

▣ **Elvis' Villa,** Str. Avram Iancu 5 (☎312 16 53; www.elvisvilla.ro). M2: Pţa. Universităţii. From Gara de Nord, take trolleybus #85 to Calea Moşilor. From Otopeni, take bus #783 to Pţa. Universităţii; change to any trolleybus going east on Bd. Carol I and get off at Calea Moşilor. Continue on Bd. Carol I and go right on Str. Sf. Ştefan. At the playground, turn left on Str. Avram Iancu. A newer hostel in a historic neighborhood, Elvis' boasts 4 clean and bright dorms with A/C, fat mattresses, and an international clientele. Internet €2 per 2hr. Spartan breakfast and laundry service included. €10 per day. ❶

Villa Helga Youth Hostel (HI), Str. Salcâcmilor 2 (☎610 22 14). M2: Pţa. Romană. Take bus #86, 79, or 133 2 stops from Pţa. Romană or 6 stops from Gara de Nord to Pţa. Gemeni. Go 1 block on Bd. Dacia and take a right on Str. Viitorului. Romania's first hostel. Pleasant and homey, with a relaxed atmosphere, book exchange, and friendly staff. Internet L30,000 per hr. Breakfast, kitchen, and laundry available. Call ahead in summer. €10 per day, €60 per week; singles €14; doubles from €12 per person. ❶

Funky Chicken Guesthouse, Str. General Berthelot 63 (☎312 14 25), from Gara de Nord, go right on Calea Griuiţei, right on Str. Berzei, and take the 3rd left. Run by the owner of Villa Helga. Bucharest's newest, cheapest, and best-located hostel. 36-bed dorms for a building filled with contemporary paintings. The neighborhood is near the train station and can be dodgy. Kitchen and laundry included. Dorms €8 per day. ❶

Casa Victor, Str. Emanoil Porumbaru 44 (☎222 57 23; fax 222 94 36). M2: Pţa. Aviatorilor. Lovely rooms in a small building in a pleasant, restaurant-filled neighborhood. Cable TV, Internet, A/C, and sauna. Breakfast included. Transportation to and from airport (€12) or train station (€6). Singles €40-55; doubles €70; apartments €80-90. ❹

Hotel Carpati, Str. Malei Millo 16 (☎ 315 01 40; fax 312 18 57). M2: Universităţii. From Pta. Universităţii, walk or take a bus down Bd. Regina Elizabeta until Str. I. Brezoianu. Turn right; the hotel is at the second corner. This budget hotel boasts a central location, clean rooms, and a professional staff. Modest breakfast included. Singles €14, with bath €20; doubles €24/€45. ❷

▢ FOOD

Food in Bucharest is cheap, plentiful and delicious. Staples include meat, cheese, flowers, fresh fruits, and vegetables. Look for them at an **open air markets;** try the one at **Piata Amzei,** near Pta. Romana. In addition to its countless corner shops, Bucharest has many first-rate **supermarkets. La Fourmi,** in the basement of the **Unirea Shopping Center,** is an outstanding option. (Open daily 8am-8pm.) **Mega Image,** at the corner of Câlea Calaraşilor and Traian, is one of the best in town. (Open M-Sa 8:30am-9:30pm, Su 8:30am-6pm. MC/V.)

R O M A N I A

▨ **La Mama**, Str. Barbu Văcărescu 3 (☎212 40 86; www.lamama.ro). M1: Ştefan cel Mare. Branches, Str. Del Veche 51 (☎320 52 13). M1: Pţa. Muncii. Str. Episcopiei 9 (☎312 97 97). M2: Pţa. Universităţii. Living up to its motto "like at mom's house," this well-known restaurant serves traditional cuisine in a pleasant atmosphere. No jeans or shorts. Call ahead. Entrees L70,000-95,000. Open daily 10am-2am. ❷

Burebista Vânătoresc, Str. Batistei 14 (☎211 89 29). M2: Pţa. Universităţii. Make a right off Bd. Nicolae Bălcescu. This hunting-themed restaurant has both taxidermy and live folk music. The cuisine centers on wild game; you can even order bear while sitting on a bear-skin rug. Entrees L100,000-230,000. Open daily noon-midnight. ❸

Barka Saffron (Saffron Boat), Str. Sănătescu 1 (☎224 10 04), at the intersection with Bd. Ion Mihalache. M2: Aviatorilor. Delicious Indian and Thai cuisine. A bit out of the way. Vegetarian options. Entrees L80,000-220,000. Open daily noon-last customer. ❷

Basilicvm, Str. Popa Savu 7 (☎222 67 79). M2: Aviatorilor, serves Italian food in a well-decorated building with a lovely terrace. Refined setting, praiseworthy food, and attentive service round out the deal. Don't miss the weekend lunch special: 50% off everything. Entrees L150,000-350,000. Open daily 11am-1am. MC/V. ❹

◉ SIGHTS

▨ **PARLIAMENTARY PALACE (PALATUL PARLAMENTULUI).** With 16 levels and 1100 rooms totaling 330,000 sq. m, the Parliamentary Palace is the **world's second-largest building,** after the Pentagon in Washington, D.C. Starting in 1984, 20,000 laborers and 700 architects struggled to construct the so-called **House of the People** (Casa Poporuli). It was completed in 1989, just in time for Ceauşescu's execution. It now houses Romania's **Parliament.** Extending eastward from the Parliamentary Palace is **Bd. Unirii,** a mammoth gray scar that was intentionally built 1m wider than Paris's Champs Elysées. Ceauşescu dreamed of recreating Bucharest in the image of a perfect socialist capital, with the road and palace as centerpieces. In constructing this Civic Center (Centru Civic), the dictator sacrificed 5 sq. km of Bucharest's historic center, demolishing over 9000 19th-century houses and displacing more than 40,000 Romanians. (*M1 or 3: Izvor. Visitors' entrance is on the south side of the building. Open daily 10am-4pm. English tours L100,000, students L50,000. Cameras L90,000.*)

HISTORIC NEIGHBORHOODS. In northern Bucharest, the peaceful, tree-lined side streets between Pţa. Victoriei and Pţa. Dorobanţilor M2: Victoriei are full of beautiful villas from pre-Ceauşescu Bucharest. What remains of Bucharest's **old center** lies near Str. Lipscani and Str. Gabroveni. The narrow, curving avenues contain the city's oldest church, **Biserica Curtea Veche,** where Romanian kings were crowned for centuries. Nearby are the ruins of **Palatul Voievoda**, a palace erected by Vlad Ţepeş (a.k.a. Vlad the Impaler). During his aesthetic assault, Ceauşescu inexplicably spared **Dealul Mitropoliei**, the hill southwest of Pţa. Unirii. Atop the hill is the **Catedrala Mitropoliei**, the **Romanian Orthodox Church** headquarters. Next door, **Palatul Patriarhiei**, once the Communist Parliament building, is now owned by the church; it hosts religious concerts. Pope John Paul II stayed here in 1999. *(M1, 2, or 3: Pta. Unirii. Up Aleea Dealul Mitropoliei.)*

SIGHTS OF THE REVOLUTION. Crosses and plaques throughout the city commemorate the *eroii revoluţiei Române* "heroes of the revolution" and the year 1989. The first shots of the Revolution were fired at **Piaţa Revoluţiei** on December 21, 1989. In the square are the **University Library**, the **National Art Museum**, and the **Senate Building** (former Communist Party Headquarters) where Ceauşescu delivered his final speech. Afterwards, he fled by helicopter from the roof but he didn't get far (see **History**, p. 605). A white marble triangle with the inscription "Glorie martirilor noştri" (glory to our martyrs) commemorates the rioters who overthrew the dictator. *(M2: Pta. Universitatii. Turn right on Bd. Regina Elisabeta and then take a right on Calea Victoriei.)* **Piaţa Universităţii** overlooks memorials to victims of the revolution and the 1990 protests. Crosses line Bd. Nicolae Bălcescu—the **black cross** lies where the first victim died. In June 1990, the *piaţa* was again the site of student riots. Ceauşescu's replacement, Ion Iliescu, bused in over 10,000 miners to suppress the protesters, and 21 students died. Iliescu was later elected president, but anti-Iliescu graffiti persists on the walls of **Bucharest University** and the **Architecture Institute**. *(M2: Pţa. Universităţii.)*

HERĂSTRĂU PARK. This immense, 1km sq. park, north of downtown, surrounds a lake of the same name; its diversions include rowboat rentals (10am-8pm, L50,000 per hr.), ferry rides (L40,000), and roller coasters. At the southern end of the park on Şos. Kiseleff, the **Arcul de Triumf** commemorates Romania's reunification in 1918 and honors those who died in World War I. Climb to the top for a view of the city. *(Bus #131 or 331 from Pta. Romana. M2: Aviatorilor.)*

CIŞMIGIU GARDENS. One of Bucharest's oldest parks, the Cişmigiu Gardens are the tree-filled eye of central Bucharest's gray modernity. Cobblestone walkways and a small lake (boat rentals L50,000 per hr.) are pleasing finds. Along with Herăstrău Park, these gardens are a focal point of the city's social life in summer. *(M2: Pţa. Universităţii. Bus #61 or 336. Open 24hr.)*

🏛 MUSEUMS

■ **VILLAGE MUSEUM (MUZEUL SATULUI).** This open-air museum is a replica village. It contains about 100 houses from the 18th and 19th centuries and churches, mills, and a sunflower-oil factory, all carted in from rural Romania. Festivals with musicians in traditional garb take place most weekends in spring and summer. Plaques describe each structure in Romanian, but pick up an English guide in (L10,000) in the bookstore. *(Şos. Kiseleff 28-30. M2: Aviatorilor. ☎ 222 91 06. Open Tu-Su 9am-6pm. L40,000, students L15,000.)*

NATIONAL ART MUSEUM (MUZEUL NAŢIONAL DE ARTĂ AL ROMÂNIEI). The renovated two-wing museum was constructed in the 1930s as a royal residence. The **European exhibit** presents an overview of European art history and boasts a selection of works by **Rembrandt, Monet**, and **El Greco**. The highlight, however, is the ■ **Romanian section**, which houses an extensive collection of medieval, modern, and contemporary art, including pieces by Romania's most famous painter, Nicolae Grigorescu, and sculptor, Constantin Brâncuşi. *(Calea Victoriei 49-53, in Pta. Revolutiei. M2: Pta. Universitatii. ☎313 30 30. Open summer W-Su 11am-7pm; winter W-Su 10am-6pm. L80,000 for 1 gallery, L120,000 for 2; students L60,000/L40,000.)*

NATIONAL HISTORY MUSEUM (MUZEUL NAȚIONAL DE ISTORIE AL ROMÂNIEI). The museum allows a thorough look at Romanian history from its Dacian roots to the present. Check out Romania's crown jewels and the replica of Trajan's Column, which depicts the ancient Roman conquest of Dacia under Emperor Trajan. Follow the panels counter-clockwise around the gallery. English Guidebooks (L30,000) available. *(Calea Victoriei 12. M2: Pța. Universității. ☎311 33 56. Open summer W-Su 10am-6pm; winter W-Su 9am-5pm. L31,000, students L15,500.)*

MUSEUM OF THE ROMANIAN PEASANT (MUZEUL ȚĂRANULUI ROMÂN). The museum takes an ethnographic look at life from the perspective of Romanian peasants in the not-so-distant past. It is similar in theme to the Village Museum, but much more technically detailed and somewhat less engaging. The windmill, waterwheel, and reconstructed peasant's cabin are the museum's most impressive pieces. Tours are expensive (L500,000), but the younger curators often speak English and are usually happy to show you around. Don't miss the collection of communist memorabilia, tucked away downstairs near the restrooms. On display is one of the few remaining publicly exhibited portraits of Nicolae Ceauşescu. *(Şos. Kiseleff 3. M2 or 3: Pța. Victoriei or bus #300. ☎212 96 61. Open Tu-Su 10am-6pm; last admission 5pm. L60,000, students 20,000.)*

🎭 ENTERTAINMENT

Bucharest is an exciting city and hosts many festivals and rock concerts in summer. Check local guides, like the Romanian language "B 24 FUN" pamphlet, for upcoming events. Performers run the gamut from rising local bands to established acts. Cinemas show a variety of foreign films (around L50,000-L100,000), mostly from the US, with Romanian subtitles. Movies are often released later here than in the West. Try the **Hollywood Multiplex** in the **Bucuresti Mall** (see below). Fans of the classical arts will appreciate the **opera, symphony orchestra**, and **theater**, which are world class and dirt cheap; seasons run October to June. (Tickets usually L10,000-150,000.) Buy tickets at theater box offices; they go on sale the Saturday two weeks before the performance. Whatever is left is sold at half-price 1hr. before showtime.

Soccer, or **football**, is Romania's favorite sport. The season is August to early June; major games are played at the **Dinamo** stadium (M1: Ştefan cel Mare). Shopping isn't Bucharest's main attraction, but the city has many stores and boutiques. For traditional souvenirs and handicrafts, try museum gift shops. Stores at the **Village Museum** and the **Peasant Museum** are good bets; both sell Romania's famous carpets. The **Unirea Shopping Center** sells all the basics. (M2: Unirii. Open M-Sa 9am-9pm, Su 9am-3pm.) The large **Bucuresti Mall**, Calea Vita 55-59, is a modern center with well-known boutiques. (M2: Unrii.)

🎭 **Atheneul Român**, Str. Franklin I (☎315 00 25). M2: Pța. Universității. In Pța. Enescu, near the Senate Building. The Athenaeum hosts Bucharest's classical concerts; the excellent performances are shockingly inexpensive. The opulent, recently-renovated interior sparkles, and the resident orchestra is outstanding. Tickets from L100,000.

🎭 **Opera Română**, Bd. Mihail Kogălniceanu 70-72 (☎313 18 57; www.operanb.ro). M1 or 3: Eroilor. Bus #61 or 336. The Romanian National Opera. The orchestra and vocalists will satisfy even the harshest critics, and the prices are fantastic—tickets start at L30,000. Box office open daily 10am-7pm, with a 1pm lunch break.

Teatrul Naţional I.L. Cargiale, Bd. Nicolae Bălcescu 2 (☎314 71 17). M2: Pţa. Universităţii. Romania's National Theater stages a wide variety of dramatic productions, usually in Romanian. Box office open daily noon-7pm. Tickets 30,000L-100,000L.

☒ NIGHTLIFE

Bucharest has countless bars, pubs, and watering holes. The club scene is a city highlight. Check out *Şapte Seri*, the club guide, available around the city, or *Bucharest in Your Pocket*. Venues are all over town, but they are concentrated in the old town center and in the student district by M1: Semănătoarea. Bring cab fare and directions to your hotel, written in Romanian, as public transit shuts down by midnight. Travel in groups and don't bring more money than you need. The listings below are a cross-section of different genres. For info on **GLBT nightlife,** consult the helpful staff of **Accept** (see p. 618).

☒ **Twice,** Str. Sfânta Vineri 4. (☎313 55 92) M2: Pţa. Universităţii. 2 clubs in 1. Head upstairs for disco or to the basement for house under fluorescent lighting. Barely-clad women gyrate atop the bar while art galleries supply a sophisticated feel amid the debauchery. The ground floor is an open-air terrace. Men L100,000, women free. Open daily 9pm-5am.

La motor/Lăptăria, Bd. Bălcescu 2 (☎315 85 08), on top of the National Theater. M2: Pţa. Universităţii. La motor, on the terrace between the 3rd and 4th fl., becomes indoor Lăptăria in the winter. In summer, congregations of students chill out on the picnic-style tables sipping beer (L30,000) from the cabana-style bar. Free open-air concerts or films in summer every night at 9:30pm. Open daily noon-2am.

Club A, Str. Blănari 14 (☎315 68 53; www.cluba.ro). M2: Pţa. Universităţii. Walk down Bd. Brătianu and take the 3rd right just after a store that says *Reparaţii Incălţăminte.* A Bucharest institution, where the young groove to Western pop and dance music. A great place to get your game on. Cheap drinks: cocktails from L25,000. F-Sa cover: men L50,000, women L20,000. Open daily 8pm-5am.

Club Maxx, Str. Independenţei 290 (☎223 00 39). M1: Grozăveşti. Giant room with 2 bars, house and hip-hop, and raucous university students. Crowded all week. The Str.'s thriving night scene is an alternative to the city center. L30,000, students free.

Queen's Club, Str. Iuliu Barasch 12-14 (☎0722 642 891; www.queen-s-club.ro.), near the Jewish Theater. M1 and M2: Unirii. Head up Calea Coposu, and turn right onto Iuliu Barasch. Romania's 1st GLBT-only nightspot; straight friends and gawkers not welcome. Membership card: L100,000. Open Th 9pm-5am, F-Sa 11pm-5am, Su 10pm-5am.

WALLACHIA (ŢARA ROMÂNEASCĂ)

Known simply as "The Romanian Land," Wallachia is the heart of the country and the seat of its capital. One of Romania's three historical regions—Wallachia, Transylvania, and Moldavia—it is a giant field of sunflowers rolling from the Carpathians to the Black Sea and broken only by Bucharest.

SINAIA   ☎(0)244

Long Romania's preeminent mountain resort and the summer home to its monarchs, Sinaia is on the dividing line between Wallachia and Transylvania. Many stop for a few hours en route to Bucharest. **Sinaia Monastery,** Str. Mânăstirii, was the region's first settlement and has a 17th-century chapel and prayer hall. Go up Str. Octavian Goga and take the road that loops to the right. The museum contains a 1688 Bible, the first complete translation into Romanian. (Open dawn-dusk. Free.) To reach the castles, follow the road that circles the monastery; continue straight on the cobblestone path through the wooded park. Fields of wildflowers surround **Peleş Castle** (Castelul Peleş), a Bohemian-Bavarian fantasia opened in 1883 under Carol I (see **History**, p. 605). The palace is known for its fairytale facade of decorative wood, rough stones, white columns, and tall spires. Its interior astounds with opulence and exquisite detail. Its **Hall of Honor** has intricately carved walls and a retractable stained-glass ceiling. (Open Tu 11am-5pm, W-Su 9am-5pm. English tours. L100,000, students L50,000.) Down the road is the stylistically different 1902 **Pelişor Castle** (Little Peleş). Queen Maria, decorated in Art Nouveau style. Her own work adorns the walls. (Open W noon-5pm, Th-Su 9am-5pm. English tours. L80,000; students L30,000.)

Telecabină, behind Hotel New Montana on Bd. Carol I, has cars to the **Bucegi Mountains,** where you can hike and ski. The car goes to Cota 1400—the number indicates the altitude. A second car heads to Cota 2000, above the treeline in a striking alpine meadow. (Open 8:30am-5:00pm. Cable car one-way L70,000; round-trip L120,000.) The **yellow stripe trail** is a moderate 4hr. climb past **Babele** (2200m) to **Omu** (2505m), the range's highest peak. You can spend the night at **Cabana Omu ❶**. Meals (L40,000-70,000) are available 7am-9pm. (Open May-Dec. Dorms L100,000; doubles L240,000.) Serious hikers can trek 6hr. to **Bran Castle** (see **Daytrips from Braşov,** p. 626); consult the tourist office first.

It's often best to do as the Romanians do and stay in **private villas.** In summer, locals offering rooms mob the train station. Some of the best budget accommodations are actually 3000 ft. above town, at the Cota 2000 station. With a bar and restaurant, **Cabana Miorița ❶** is the luxury queen of the mountain cabin system. (Bed in 12-person room L150,000; in smaller room L350,000; private doubles L600,000; triples L700,000.) For traditional fare including a wild game menu, head to **Restaurant Bucegi ❷,** adjacent to the Hotel Sinaia, near the top of the stairs from the train station. (Entrees L60,000-100,000. Open daily 11am-11pm.) Kiosks and small stores selling essentials litter Bd. Carol I. You may find *brânză de copac* (about L130,000 per kg), a "tree cheese" of Dacian origin. It is equal parts cow's and sheep's milk; its rind is the fresh bark of fir trees. Grab a few beers at the British-style pub, **Old Nick,** Bd. Carol I 22, next to the Hotel New Montana. (☎31 54 12. Open daily 9:30am-late)

Trains (☎31 00 40) run from Sinaia to: **Braşov** (1hr., 22 per day, L92,000); **Bucharest** (2hr., 19 per day, L175,000); **Cluj-Napoca** (5hr., 5 per day, L310,000). From the station, take the stairs across the street to Bd. Carol I, the main drag. Go left to reach the center. The **tourist office,** Bd. Carol I 8, has info and **maps.** (☎31 15 51. Open M-F 8am-4pm, Sa-Su 8am-2pm.) **Banca Comercială Română,** Bd. Carol I 49, cashes **traveler's checks.** (Open M-F 8:30am-5:30pm, Sa 8:30am-12:30pm.) An **ATM** is out front. A **pharmacy, Farmacia Regală,** is at Bd. Carol I 22. (☎31 10 29. Open daily 8am-9pm.) The **post office** (☎31 41 71), **telephone office** (☎31 10 80), and train **info booth** are at Bd. Carol I 33. (Post office open M-F 7am-8pm, Sa 8am-noon; telephones M-F 8am-8pm, Sa 10am-6pm.)

TRANSYLVANIA (TRANSILVANIA)

Though the name evokes images of a dark, evil land of black magic and vampires, Transylvania, with a long history of Saxon settlement dating back to the 12th and 13th centuries, is a relatively Westernized region. Its green hills and mountains gently descend from the rugged Carpathians in the south to the Hungarian Plain in the northwest. The vampire legends do, however, take root in the region's remarkable architecture: Transylvanian buildings are tilted, jagged, and more sternly Gothic than anywhere else in Europe.

ARDEAL

Ardeal is the largest, most mountainous, and most canonically Transylvanian of the Transylvanian regions—Ardeal, Banat, and Maramureş. Look for vestiges of medieval cities and vampire lore. Much of the wilderness in this region remains untamed, making for excellent hiking in the Făgăraş Mountains.

BRAŞOV   ☎(0)268

The historic center of Braşov (BRAH-shohv; pop. 353,000), known as Kronstadt to the Saxons, is a kaleidoscopic mish-mash of 800-year-old buildings. This small Transylvanian city, a regional transport hub, is home to prominent churches, delectable restaurants, and a mellow main square which hosts open-air concerts in summer. Its location at the foot of the Carpathians makes it the natural base camp for excursions to Poiana Braşov's ski slopes, Bran Castle, and the ruins at Râşnov. Braşov is no secret, however, and you'll undoubtedly run into fellow tourists.

TRANSPORTATION. Trains go from Braşov to: **Bucharest** (3-4hr., 13 per day, L195,000); **Cluj-Napoca** (5-6hr., 5 per day, L300,000); **Iaşi** (9-10hr., 1 per day, L272,000); **Sibiu** (4hr., 7 per day, L145,000). Buy tickets at **CFR**, Bd. 15 Noiembrie 43. (☎47 70 18. Open M-F 8am-7pm, Sa 10am-1pm.) Braşov has two main **bus stations:** Autogară 1, next to the train station, is the main intercity and international depot; Autogară 2, commonly called "Gara Bartolomeu," runs **buses** to **Râşnov** and **Bran.** To get there, take bus #16 or 38 from the center of town. Buy tickets (L8,000 per ride) for city buses at kiosks around the center.

ORIENTATION AND PRACTICAL INFORMATION. The city is divided into the picturesque old town, wedged in a valley between two tall mountains, and the communist-era section, which sprawls out on the plains. The old town consists of two districts. The old Saxon center, called Kronstadt, lies at the mouth of the valley and centers on **Piaţa Sfantului** and **Biserica Neagră** (Black Church). **Schei**, the old Romanian district, is farther back up the valley and centered on less spectacular **Pta. Unirii.** To get to the old town from the **train station** or from **Autogară 1,** take bus #4 in the direction of Pţa. Unirii. On foot, cross the street in front of the train station and head down **Bd. Victoriei.** Turn right on **Str. Mihai Kogălniceanu,** then bear right on **Bd. 15 Noiembrie,** which becomes **Bd. Eroilor. Str. Republicii** and **Str. Mureşenilor** branch off 1km apart, both converging on Pţa. Sfantului. Taxi fare from the train station to the old town should not exceed L50,000.

Maps (L40,000) are sold at *librarie* (bookstores) around town. **Banca Comercială Română,** Pţa. Sfatului 14, cashes **AmEx Traveler's Cheques** for 1.5% commission. (☎47 71 09. Open M-F 8:30am-5pm, Sa 9am-noon.) An **ATM** is in front of the bank; others line Str. Republicii. A **pharmacy, Aurofarm,** is at Str. Republicii 27. (☎14 35 60. Open daily 7:30am-midnight.) The **telephone office** is at Bd. Eroilor 23. (☎40 42 91. Open M-F 7am-9pm, Sa-Su 7am-8pm.) You can find 24hr. **Internet access** at Contrast Internet, Str. M. Weiss 11. Watch out, as the cafe may move down the street. (L10,000-L15,000 per hr.) The **post office,** Nicolae Iorga 1, across the park from Bd. Eroilor, also provides **Western Union** services. (Open M-F 7am-8pm, Sa 8am-1pm.) **Postal Code:** 500057.

ACCOMMODATIONS AND FOOD. The market for **private rooms** is booming. During high season, opportunists spend their days tourist-hunting in the train station. Look at the room and agree on a price (about €8-10) before you accept. For a sure thing, head to ◼**Kismet Dao Villa Hostel ❶,** Str. Democraţiei 2b, formerly known as Elvis's Villa Hostel. From Pţa. Unirii, walk up Str. Bâlea and turn right. Comfortable, well-decorated, and the area's only hostel, Kismet Dao has fabulous views of the surrounding hills. Free perks include breakfast, laundry service, a drink per day, and 1hr. of Internet access at a nearby cafe. (☎51 42 96. Dorms Apr.-Dec. €10, Jan.-Mar. €8; doubles €25.) For Romanian hospitality in spacious doubles or dorm-style rooms, try **Eugene Junior ❶**, Str. Neagoe Basarab 1, off Bd. 15 Noiembrie close to the center. (☎0722 54 25 81; ejrr68@yahoo.com. Call ahead. Room €10, negotiable.) At **Casa Beke ❶**, Str. Cerbului 32, a kind Hungarian family rents out four rooms on a pleasant side street near the main square. Follow Str. Republicii to Pţa. Sfatului and go left on Str. Apollonia Hirscher, then turn right. (Room €10, negotiable.)

Bella Muzica ❶, Str. G Bariţiu 2, is across Pţa. Sfatului from Str. Mureşenilor. Make your way through the music store downstairs to a candle-lit wine cellar. Bella offers an eclectic Romanian-Hungarian-Mexican menu, from traditional bean soup to goulash to fajitas. Free shots of *palincă*, Romanian plum moonshine, complete the meal. (☎47 69 46. Entrees L65,000-200,000. Open daily noon-midnight.) Another standout is the elegant **Taverna ❸**, Str. Politehnicii 6. From Pţa. Sfatului, walk up Str. Republicii and go right. Taverna serves Romanian, Hungarian and Italian fare. (☎47 46 18; www.taverna.ro. Dress nicely. Entrees L90,000-300,000. Open daily noon-midnight. MC/V.)

◨ SIGHTS. The area surrounding Pţa. Sfatului is perfect for a stroll, as is Str. Republicii, the main pedestrian drag. Jagged and aging, Romania's largest Gothic cathedral looms above the main square along Str. Gh. Bariţiu. Built in the 14th century, the **Black Church** (Biserica Neagră) became Lutheran during the Reformation and earned its name in 1689 when it was charred by the **Great Fire**, which destroyed most of Braşov. Inside is a renowned collection of 119 Anatolian carpets, compliments of 17th- and 18th-century German merchants. (Open M-Sa 10am-5pm. No cameras. L30,000, students L15,000. Organ concerts mid-June to mid-July Tu 6pm; mid-July to Aug. Tu, Th, Sa 6pm. L20,000.) The **summit of Mt. Tâmpa** boasts the best view of Braşov. Follow the red triangle markings to hike to the top (1½hr.). *Telecabine* (cable cars) can also carry you there. From Pţa. Sfatului, walk down Apollonia Hirscher, make a left on Str. Castelui, a right on Suişul Castelui, and head up the stairs to the white building. (Car runs M 9:30am-noon and 5-5:45pm, Tu-Su 9:30am-5:45pm. Round-trip L40,000.) Follow the blue stripe trail on the right (15min.) to reach the peak and the viewing platform. Pţa. Unirii is home to both **St. Nicholas Church** (Biserică Sfântu Nicolae), built in 1495 and filled with religious murals, and **Romania's First School** (Prima Şcoală Românească), which contains the first Romanian books printed in the Latin alphabet. (Church open daily 8am-7pm. Free. School open daily 9am-5pm. L20,000.) The **Braşov History Museum** (Muzeul de Istorie) is in the yellow building in the center of Pţa. Sfatului. (Open daily 10am-6pm. L21,000, students L10,500. Cameras L100,000.)

◨▒ ENTERTAINMENT AND FESTIVALS. Operas are low in cost but high in vocal talent. The **Opera House**, Str. Biserica Română 51, is a red building 3km north of the Old Town, near the university. Buy tickets at the box office on Str. Republicii 4. (☎41 59 90, tickets 47 18 89. Open late Aug. to mid-June M-F 10am-5pm, Sa 10am-1pm. L50,000-200,000.) The box office also sells tickets for the symphony orchestra and the summer **International Chamber Music Festival**, held in the first week of September. In the third week of each July, Pţa. Sfatului hosts the **Golden Stag Festival** (Cerbul de Aur), which brings Romanian and international musicians. **Saloon**, Str. Mureşenilor 13, is a tourist favorite by day (decent pizza L90,000) and by night, when it offers a selection of imported beers and mixed drinks. Try "Sex in the Forest," Romania's version of "Sex on the Beach." On Friday and Saturday

ROMANIA

nights, the saloon opens its basement lounge, which is filled with leather sofas. (☎41 77 05. Open daily 10am-2am.) **Opium,** Str. Republicii 2, bills itself as a "chill out cafe" and gives off the vibe of an exotic pleasure den. (☎39 78 87. Beer from L35,000. Open daily 10am-late. No opium served.) **Club Blitz,** Bd. Mihail Kogălniceanu 13, near the train station, features a dance floor, tasty frozen drinks, and house music from the resident DJ. (☎47 77 80. Open daily 11pm-5am.)

🏛 DAYTRIPS FROM BRAŞOV

BRAN CASTLE AND RASNOV FORTRESS ☎(0)268

From Braşov, take a taxi or city bus #5 or 9 to Autogara 2 ("Gara Bartolomeu"). From there, catch an intercity bus to Bran (45min., every 30min. 7am-6pm, L20,000). Get off when you see the souvenir market or the "Cabana Bran Castle—500m" sign. Backtrack along the road; the castle will be on the right amid souvenir shops. Castle and village open M 11am-6pm, Tu-Su 9am-6pm. L90,000, students L40,000. The same buses that go to Bran usually stop in Râşnov (25min.). From the bus stop, follow Str. Republicii past an open-air market. Go right and then left through an arch. Fortress is 10min. uphill. Open daily 10am-8pm. L35,000, students L20,000. Cameras L25,000. English info L25,000.

Ever since Bram Stoker's novel identified **Bran Castle** with bloodthirsty **Count Dracula,** castle and legend have been linked in the popular imagination. The history of this small castle, however, is more complicated than fables suggest. Though under Hungarian control at the time, the fortress was built by the residents of Bran on their own coin (1377-1382). The castle was meant to guard against the seemingly imminent invasion by the Turkish Empire and to serve as a tollbooth along the trade route through Wallachia and Transylvania. In the early 15th century, the Hungarian king gave the castle to Wallachian *voivod* (local governor) Mircea the Old, who was the grandfather of Vlad Ţepeş—the historical model of the vampire/count. During his own reign as *voivod*, it is likely that **Vlad the Impaler** ruled over Bran Castle. One of the only undisputed facts is that he was imprisoned here for two months in 1462 by the Hungarian king. Administered by Wallachia for almost 500 years, the castle became property of the city of Braşov when serfdom was abolished in 1848. It was then used as a summer residence for the royal family until it became a museum in 1956. The restored castle now contains furnished royal rooms from the Middle Ages to the 20th century. The dozens of stands selling Dracula paraphernalia, from toy stakes to "blood wine," have become part of the attraction.

For an authentic and less-crowded castle experience, head to **Râşnov.** The recently renovated fortress, constructed after the first Tatar invasion in 1241, offers a striking view of the surrounding countryside. Its original weakness was its lack of an internal water supply. Imported artisans designed spectacularly deep well. Try not to be shocked by the medieval skeleton, now on display after being discovered by archaeologists several years ago.

POIANA BRAŞOV ☎(0)268

From Braşov, take city bus #20 (25min., 2-3 per hr. 7am-10pm, L8,000) from Livada Postei, which is the western end of Bd. Eroilor. A taxi from town costs no more than US$6.

If Sinaia is Romania's long-standing summer alpine resort, Poiana Braşov (www.poiana-brasov.ro) is its newer winter counterpart. Tourist agencies and hotels abound, but there is little else in the small mountain town, where the main attraction is **skiing.** The 12 runs and multiple snowboarding trails range in difficulty. **Lifts** transport skiers up the slopes. (A ride costs up on the lift costs 6 points. About L10,000 per point.) **Equipment rental** is at the base, and **instructors** are multilingual. For a place to stay, try **Satul de Vacanta ❹** (☎26 25 35), which rents out well-equipped cabins. (4-person cabins from L5,000,000.) For a cheaper deal, stay in Braşov. In summer, popular activities include horseback riding and hiking.

SIGHIŞOARA ☎(0)265

Sighişoara (see-ghee-SHWAH-rah; pop. 39,000) is worthy of its title as Pearl of Transylvania. The area has been settled for close to 4000 years, and the city remains surrounded by its 15th-century citadel. The tiny old city, set atop a steep hill, and marked by gilded steeples, an aged clock tower, and irregularly tiled roofs, is this birthplace of Vlad Ţepeş, the "real" Dracula.

⌨ TRANSPORTATION. Trains run to: **Alba Iulia** (2hr., 3 per day, L166,000); **Braşov** (2hr., 11 per day, L170,000); **Bucharest** (5hr., 8 per day, L305,000); **Cluj-Napoca** (3½hr., 8 per day, L260,000); **Oradea** (6hr., 3 per day, L330,000).

⚑ 🖉 ORIENTATION AND PRACTICAL INFORMATION. It's hard to get lost in Sighişoara. To reach the center from the train station, take a right on to Str. Libertăţii, then left on Str. Gării. Veer left at the cemetery, turn right through the church courtyard, cross the pedestrian bridge over the river **Târana Mare,** and take a left onto **Str. Morii.** A right at the fork leads to **Str. O. Goga** and the **Citadel** *(cetatea);* a left leads to the main street, **Str. 1 Decembrie 1918.** Taking a right leads to the center of the modern town—in the shadow of the clock tower—and Str. Oberth. The statue of Romulus and Remus marks the center of town. If all else fails, aim for the clock tower, a highly visible landmark.

Maps (L80,000-L100,000), which are not necessary in a town this compact, are widely available at bookstores. There are **ATMs** throughout the town. **Banca Română Pentru Dezvoltare,** Str. Oberth 20, in the center, has an ATM and **Western Union** services. (Open M-Th 8am-1pm and 2-2:30pm, Sa 8am-1:30pm.) The train station has **luggage storage.** (Open 24hr. L30,000.) **Farmacia Genţiana** is at Str. Oberth 22. (Open M-F 7:30am-8pm, Sa 8am-7pm.) **Elsig Internet,** Str. Libertăţii 44, across from the train station, has **Internet access.** (☎77 12 69. L15,000 per hr., minimum L5000. Open daily 9am-11pm.) There are several net cafes in the old town as well. Both the **post office** (open M-F 7am-6pm) and the **telephone office** (open M-F 10am-6pm) are at Str. Oberth 16. **Postal Code:** 545400.

THE LOCAL STORY

SON OF A...

Yes, Dracula did exist—sort of. He was not the ruler of Transylvania but of Wallachia; he was not a count, but a *voivod* (a local governor or "prince"); and he was not a vampire. Still, the truth about Vlad Tepes (1431-1476) is enough to make anyone lock the lid to his coffin at night.

Dracula's story begins with his father, Vlad Basarab, who was nicknamed ▪Dragul (dragon) for his skill with arms. Dragul sent his son, Dragula (son of the dragon) to the Ottoman Empire as a hostage in 1442, when he was age 10. During his six years held hostage, Vlad learned what was to become his preferred method of torture: impalement. Victims of impalement—which involved inserting a large wooden stake through the victim's body without piercing the vital organs—usually begged for a swift death throughout the slow, agonizing process.

Vlad the Impaler earned his title during his reign as *voivod*. In addition to murderers, thieves, liars, and political rivals, he killed the old, the destitute, and the crippled. His crowning achievement was in turning the Turks' gruesome practice against them. In 1462, the invading Turks turned tail at Wallachia's border, which had been decorated with 20,000 of their impaled countrymen. As his terror tactics became infamous, the son of the dragon was renamed the son of the devil, Vlad Dracula.

ACCOMMODATIONS AND FOOD. Private rooms (US$8-12) are available in the Old City. People offer them on the street or at the station. Check out the room and negotiate the price before agreeing to anything. Formerly known as Elvis' Villa Hostel, **Nathan's Villa Hostel ❶**, Str. Libertății 8, a right turn out of the train station, is the place to stay in Sighișoara. This hostel is equipped: free beer, cigarettes, and laundry. Ask the charismatic American owner to make his famous punch, and watch out for the occasional pig roasted on a spit. (☎77 25 46. Dorms €8.) **Hotel Chic ❶**, directly across from the train station, has a clean, communal bathroom. The staff doesn't speak much English, but one of the kids playing video games next door at Elsig Internet should be able to translate for you. (☎77 59 01. Singles L400,000; doubles L500,000-600,000.) If you'd rather stay in Old Town proper, HI-affiliated **Berg Hostel ❶**, Str. Bastionului 4, in the square near the clock tower, is a reasonable choice. The cellar bar-Internet cafe is a popular hangout. (☎77 22 34. Beds from €7.50.)

Restaurant Rustic ❶, Str. 1 Decembrie 5, serves excellent Romanian food in a brick and wood-paneled dining room beneath old liquor ads and classic movie posters. It turns into a bar at night. (☎0723 08 54 94. Entrees L50,000-200,000. Open M-F 9:30am-1am, Sa-Su 9:30am-dawn.) In the Citadel, try **Casa Vlad Dracul ❷**, Str. Cositorarilor 5, under the big metal dragon sign. It really is Vlad's house—he was born here in 1431 and lived here until 1436. The traditional meals and medieval decor are truly worth the extra lei. (☎77 15 96. Entrees L100,000-250,000. Open daily 10am-midnight.) **Pizzeria Perla ❶**, Str. 1 Decembrie 1, serves tasty pizzas to in a classy interior. (Pizzas L60,000-120,000. Open daily 9am-late). **Grocery stores** line Str. 1 Decembrie 1918.

SIGHTS AND FESTIVALS. The **Citadel**, built by Saxons in 1191, is now a tiny medieval city-within-a-city. Enter through the **Clock Tower** (Turnul cu Ceas), off Str. O. Goga. Climb to the top to see the clock's mechanism and painted figurines representing the days of the week. The deck above provides an expansive view of the area. Plaques state the exact direction and distance to major cities around the world. (Open M 10am-4:30pm, Tu-F 9am-6:30pm, Sa-Su 9am-4:30pm. L36,000, students L20,500.) To the left as you leave the tower, the **Museum of Medieval Armory** offers a small exhibit on Vlad Țepeș and weapons from all over the world. (L20,000, students L10,200.) Underneath the clock tower, the **Torture Museum** houses a very small collection of pain-inflicting instruments and shackles, as well as diagrams on how to use them. (Armory and Torture Museum open Tu-Su 10am-3:30pm. L10,200.) Across the square, the Lutheran **Monastary Church** features antique Anatolian rugs donated by passing German merchants and memorials to local ethnic Germans, who fought and died in the two World Wars. Organ concerts are held here Friday afternoons. A left up Str. Școlii reveals the long, tunnel-enclosed **stairway,** built in 1642 to help children get to school. At the top is the magnificent Gothic **Biserica din Deal** (Church on the Hill). Its frescoes reflect Orthodox influences. They were painted in the 15th century, whitewashed in the 18th, and restored in the 20th. A trip to the **crypt** is always exciting. Its hilltop location affords moving views. (Open daily 10am-6pm. L20,000. No cameras.)

The second weekend in July brings the **Medieval Festival** to Sighișoara. The **Folk Art Festival** arrives in late August.

SIBIU ☎(0)269

The ancient capital of Transylvania and the seat of the ruling Brukenthal family during the Austro-Hungarian period, Sibiu (SEE-bee-oo; pop. 170,000) remains a town of medieval monuments and colorful, ornate houses. The appeal of the unhurried town lies in its proximity to the Făgăraş Mountains and to some of the best hiking in the country. It is an idyllic spot to relax for a couple days—if you can stand the summer heat.

TRANSPORTATION. Trains run to: **Braşov** (3½hr., 7 per day, L145,000); **Bucharest** (6hr., 4 per day, L222,000); **Cluj-Napoca** (4hr., 1 per day, L186,000); **Timişoara** (6hr., 1 per day, L222,000). **CFR,** Str. N. Bălcescu 6, past Hotel Împăratul Romanilor from Pţa. Mare, sells tickets. (Open M-F 7:30am-7:30pm, Sa 9am-1pm.) **Buses** run to: **Alba Iulia** (1½hr., 9 per day, L80,000); **Bucharest** (5hr., 5 per day, L200,000); **Cluj-Napoca** (3½hr., 9 per day, L110,000); **Timişoara** (5½hr., 2 per day, L200,000). **Microbuses** are a cheap, fast option. They run to **Braşov** (3hr., 4 per day, L130,000) and **Sighişoara** (2½hr., 4 per day, L100,000). Their station is beside the train station; incoming microbuses can drop off in Pţa. Unirii.

ORIENTATION AND PRACTICAL INFORMATION. When facing away from the train station, two roads lead toward the center; follow **Str. General Magheru,** the one on the left. When you reach the small square with a statue of Nicolaus Olahus, you can either take the left fork or bear right on **Str. Avram Iancu.** Either will lead to the main square of the old town, **Piaţa Mare.** To the right, through the tunnels, is **Piaţa Mică.** To reach **Piaţa Unirii,** the modern main square, proceed straight through Pţa. Mare and down **Str. Nicolae Bălcescu,** or take bus #5 from the train station (L16,000 for 2 trips).

Libraria Friedrich Schiller, Pţa. Mare 7, sells city and hiking **maps** (L50,000-100,000) and has a **tourist office.** (☎21 11 10. Open M-F 9am-noon and 1-5pm, Sa 10am-1pm.) **IDM Exchange,** Pţa. Mică 9, cashes **traveler's checks** for no commission and **exchanges currency.** (Open M-F 9am-5pm, Sa 9am-2pm.) MC/V **ATMs** are on Str. Bălcescu, on Calea Dumărăvii, and in Pţa. Unirii. **Farmacia Farmasib** is at Str. Bălcescu 53. (☎21 78 97. Open daily 7am-10pm. Open 24hr. for emergencies.) The **telephone office** is at Str. Bălcescu 11-13. (Open M-F 10am-6pm.) For **Internet,** try **Power Net,** Str. Brukenthal 3. (Open M-Sa 9am-10pm.) The **post office,** Str. Metropoliei 14, has **Western Union.** From Pţa. Mare, go down Str. S. Brukenthall and left on Str. Metropoliei. (Open M-F 7am-8pm, Sa 8am-1pm.) Postal Code:

ACCOMMODATIONS AND FOOD. Brand-new **Hotel Ela ❶** is a short walk away but is worth it for the thick mattresses, well-decorated rooms, and private toilets. From Pţa. Mare, proceed through the clock tower, across Pţa. Mica, and down a hill. Continue on Str. Ocnei and make a right on Str. Novâ. (☎21 51 97. Breakfast L150,000. Dorms L300,000; singles L500,000; doubles L700,000; triples L900,000. Book ahead.) **Hotel Bulevard ❸,** Pţa. Unirii 10, offers Western-style rooms with TVs, fridges, and private baths. The receptionists sell maps and speak good English. (☎21 60 60. Breakfast included. Singles L917,000; doubles L1,050,000.) To reach **Hotel Pensiune Leu ❶** (Lion), Str. Moş Ion Roată 6, walk along Str. S. Brukenthall from Pţa. Mare until it ends and continue down the staircase on the right. Follow the road, looping back onto Str. Moş Ion Roată. The hotel attracts guests with clean rooms, laundry service, hot showers, and a full bar. (☎21 83 92. Reception 24hr. Dorms L300,000; singles L400,000; doubles L600,000.) For essential supplies, stop at **Supermarket Alcomsib,** next to the phone office on Str. Bălcescu. (Open M-F 7:30am-9pm, Sa 8am-9pm, Su 8am-2pm.) For good and cheap Romanian food, walk 1km past the market to **Kon-Tiki ❶,** Str. Tudor Vladimescu 10. Don't be fooled by the no-frills decor: the ridiculously good *ciorbă de burtă* (cow's belly soup) is a local favorite. (☎22 03 50. Entrees L24,000-60,000. Open M-F 10am-10pm, Su noon-10pm.) More convenient is the traditional **Crama Ileanu ❶,** Pţa. Teatrului 2, downhill and to the left from Pţa. Unirii, off a side street called

Str. Berariei. Both the interior and exterior are bedecked with carved wood. (☎43 43 43. Entrees L60,000-150,000. Open daily noon-2am.) To reach the **open-air market,** follow the directions to Hotel Pensiune Leu, but continue straight instead of looping back to Str. Moş Ion Roată. (Open dawn-dusk; meat and dairy section open M-F 7am-8pm, Sa 7am-6pm, Su 7am-1:30pm.)

◙ ▓ **SIGHTS AND FESTIVALS.** The town square boasts a number of historically and architecturally significant buildings, many under renovation, including an 18th-century neo-Romanesque **Catholic church.** The main museum is **Muzeul Brukenthall,** Pţa. Mare 7-9. There is a history section and an 18th-century noble residence, which houses an art gallery. Works range from medieval to contemporary, with an emphasis on northern European schools. (☎21 76 91. Open Tu-Su 9am-6pm. L50,000, students L20,000.) The biggest attraction lies just outside of town. The ▓Astra Museum, in a forest preserve south of the center, rivals Bucharest's Village Museum for the country's finest open-air exhibits. From Pţa. Unirii, it's a 4km hike along Calea Dumbravii. Alternatively, take trolleybus #1 to the cemetery, then the tram into the forest (pay with local bus tickets), or take a taxi (L40,000). At 96,000 sq. km, the museum occupies a fair bit of local forest and displays a large collection of buildings from across the country. Blow on the 1.4m horn in the **instrument maker's residence.** The museum's 17th-century **Orthodox church** is still active, though it's currently under renovation. (☎21 17 58. English tours L150,000 per hr. Open M-F 10am-6pm, Sa-Su 10am-7pm. L60,000; students L30,000.) The **International Theater Festival,** in the first week of June, attracts groups from around the world. **Summer Fest** rages June 15-September 15 near Pţa. Unirii with free open-air concerts Thursday and Friday nights. The **Medieval Festival** occurs in late August.

◪ **HIKING.** The **Făgăraş Mountains** extend about 70km from the Olt Valley to the Piatra Craiului mountains, with a sharp ridge running east-west above the treeline. The tallest peaks, **Moldoveanu** and **Negoiu** (both 2500m), are often snow-capped year-round. Wildflower-strewn meadows, cloud-shrouded summits, and superb views of Wallachian plains and Transylvanian hills have earned the Făgăraş special status among Romanian hikers. While the Carpathians have many hiking trails, the Făgăraş's ruggedness and isolation make it an attraction. For food, shelter, and basic supplies, **cabanas** dot the area. Most are in the lowlands (500m), where facilities are more posh, or the middle uplands (1500m); few are above the treeline (2000m). Some offer sleeping sacks (L75,000-150,000); others have doubles with baths (L150,000-300,000).

The mountains are crossed by numerous trails. A popular option is a three-day, two-night excursion from Sibiu. Take a train to **Avrig,** about 16km (4hr. hike) from **Cabana Poiana Neamţului** (☎0744 57 39 06), a road-accessible town at the foot of the mountains. Taxis are rare in Avrig, so many traverse this stretch by private car. *Let's Go* does not recommend hitchhiking. If walking, follow the red cross markings from the train station. Continue up the mountains on the same trail (3hr.) as it separates from the road and spend the night at **Cabana Bircaci ❶** (☎0744 85 81 40). Then, take the blue dot trail to glacial **Lake Avrig** (elevation 2011m; 3hr.), and connect there with the red stripe to the **Puha Saddle** (Şaua Puha). For experienced hikers, **Custura Sărăţii** (1hr. east of the Puha Saddle) is the ridge trail's most spectacular and difficult portion. For 2hr. you'll cling to rocks on a path sometimes less than 30cm wide, with drops on either side (an alternate path avoids this route). Stay the night at 1546m **Cabana Negoiu ❶,** a 2hr. descent onto the blue cross trail. Then, exit the mountains via the blue triangle trail (1½hr.) and walk (4hr.) or catch a bus to **Porumbaco de Jos,** where trains return to Sibiu. Alternatively, enter the range by taking the train from Sibiu to **Ucea** (1½hr., 4 per day, L25,000) and take a bus to the base camp **Victoria** (25min., 7 per day, L20,000).

The prize for the serious hiker is to cross the entire Făgăraş ridge, which takes 7-10 days from west to east, with the wind at your back. **Libreria Friedrich Schiller** in Sibiu sells maps and guides (L70,000-200,000). Hiking season lasts from July to mid-September, but the mountains are never crowded. Temperatures can be cold year-round. Pack a sleeping bag, head lamp, warm clothing, hiking boots, and plenty of iodine tablets to purify water. You can buy food at the cabanas as you go. Call **SC Salişte-Bâlea SA** (☎21 17 03) in Sibiu to make reservations for Cabana Bâlea Cascada. In an emergency or for help planning a trip, contact the mountain-rescue organization **Salvamont,** Nicolae Balcescu 9 (☎21 64 77).

ALBA IULIA   ☎(0)258

Known as Apulum to the Romans and Alba to locals, Alba Iulia (AHL-bah YOO-lee-ah; pop. 72,000) is one of Romania's oldest cities, and much of its allure stems from its rich history: it was the capital of Romania in the early 1600s; Transylvanian delegates voted to join Romania here in 1918; and King Ferdinand I was coronated here in 1922. Virtually all of its important sights are in or next to its central **citadel** *(cetatea)*. The fortress, the size of a neighborhood, was built in shape of a star to emulate those built for Louis XIV. The current fortifications rest atop ruins which date at least as far back as Roman times. There are six numbered gates and two major approaches to the citadel. From the west, **Bd. Transilveniei** runs into a pedestrian plaza opposite gate 6. From the east, **Str. Mihai Viteazul** winds its way through gates 1 and 2, across the moat and up to gate 3, which grants access to the citadel proper (Citadel open 24hr. Free.) While in the Citadel, check out the equestrian statue of **Mihai Viteazul,** who reigned from 1593 to 1601. Directly behind Mihai and near gate 6 is the **Roman Catholic Cathedral.** Its 14th-century architecture reflects significant Western influence. Across the street, the Orthodox **Coronation Church,** built for Ferdinand I between 1921 and 1922, is a synthesis of traditional Romanian styles. The **Unification Museum** (Muzeul Naţional al Unirii), near the statue, is one of the country's most comprehensive national history museums. At **Unification Hall** (Sala Unirii), across the street, see where Aurel Lazar drafted the Transylvanian declaration of self-determination in October 1918, a move which paved the way for the union of December 1. The hall and museum are in ornate 19th-century military buildings. (Hall and museum open Tu-Su 10am-6pm. Each L20,000, students L10,000. English pamphlet L10,000.)

Most daily **trains** running in this area stop in Alba. Destinations include: **Bucharest** (6hr., 4 per day, L355,000); **Cluj-Napoca** (2hr., 5 per day, L150,000); **Sighişoara** (1¾hr., 4 per day, L165,000). The **bus station** is next to the train station, but stick to trains. To go to the citadel's west side, take bus #3 to Bd. Transilveniei; for the east, take bus #4 to the Romtelecom office on Str. Ardealului. Buy tickets (L8000) on board. A **taxi** should cost about L40,000. **Banca Comercială Română,** Bd. Transilvaniei 25, cashes **AmEx Traveler's Cheques** for 1.5% commission. (☎83 45 22. Open M-F 8:30am-5pm, Sa 8:30am-12:30pm.) **Store Luggage** in the train station. (L30,000. Open 24hr.) The **pharmacy, Farmacia Gelafarm,** is at Str. Iuliu Maniu 8. (☎81 87 66. Open M-F 7am-8pm, Sa 8am-6pm, Su 8am-2pm.) The **telephone office,** on Str. Ardealului, has a MC/V **ATM.** Use **Internet** at **Easy PC.** From Str. Ardealului, go left on Motilor; it's behind the green building. (L15,000 per hr. Open 8am-10pm.) The **post office,** near the telephone office, has **Western Union** services. (Open M-F 10am-6pm.) **Postal Code:** 510097.

Pensiune Flamingo ❷, Str. Mihai Viteazul 6, to the right of gate #1, has comfortable rooms in a family atmosphere. (☎81 63 54. Enter through the bar after 11pm. Singles L600,000; doubles L600,000, with bath L1,000,000; triples L900,000.) Farther from the Citadel but a step up in luxury, **Hotel Transilvania ❸,** Pţa. Iuliu Maniu 22, off Str. Ardealului, has pleasant rooms with TV, phones, and baths. (☎81 20 52.

Singles L900,000; doubles L1,050,000; apartments L1,500,000. V.) On the east, your best bet for Romanian food is **Restaurant Transilvania** ❶, attached to the hotel. The dining room is spacious and the *sarmale* (L69,000) are luscious. (☎81 11 95. Entrees L50,000-100,000. Open daily 7am-11pm.) On the west, **Pizzeria Roberta** ❶, Bd. Transilvaniei 23, next to the bank, is a local favorite. (Pizza and pasta L40,000-100,000. Open daily 9am-10:30pm.)

CLUJ-NAPOCA   ☎(0)264

Cluj-Napoca (KLOOZH nah-POH-kah; pop. 400,000) is Transylvania's unofficial capital and its undisputed student center. Its name reflects its rich heritage: it's been known as Napoca by the Romans, Klausenburg by the Germans, and Kolozs-vár by the Hungarians. Perhaps Romania's most important city after Bucharest, it is a hub of trade, transport, culture, and finance, yet it sports a city center compact enough to be easily managed on foot. It is also the gateway to regional mountains and caving opportunities.

TRANSPORTATION. **International Airport Cluj-Napoca** (☎416 702) has flights to Bucharest, as well as regional flights to Austria, Germany, Hungary, and Italy. The best way to reach the airport from the center is by **taxi** (about L160,000). For info and reservations, contact **TAROM** (☎43 26 69) or **Carpatair** (☎416 016). **CFR** is at Pţa. Mihai Viteazul 11. (Domestic ☎42 30 01, international 534 009. Open M-F 7am-7pm.) **Trains** run to: **Bucharest** (8-13hr., 9 per day, L400,000) via **Braşov** (5-7hr., L300,000); **Oradea** (3hr., 4 per day, L204,000); **Sibiu** (4hr., 2 per day, L204,000); **Sighetu Marmatiei** (5-7hr., 2 per day, L204,000); **Timişoara** (6hr., 3 per day, L255,000); **Budapest, HUN** (6½-7hr.; 2 per day; L1,130,000, 26 and under L870,000). **Local buses** and **trams** run 5am-10pm; buy tickets (L19,000 for 2 trips) at **RATUC** kiosks.

ORIENTATION AND PRACTICAL INFORMATION. From the **train station**, walk right to reach the intercity **bus station**, Str. Giordano Bruno 3. Trolleys #3-4 and 9 go from the train station to the main square, **Piaţa Unirii.** On foot, head down **Str. Horea,** which changes to **Bd. Regele Ferdinand.** Pţa. Unirii is on the right at its end. **Continental Tours,** Str. Napoca 1, in the Continental Hotel building off Pta. Unirii, distributes the free, useful pamphlet *Cluj-Napoca: What, Where, When.* It books plane tickets and arranges tours. (☎59 39 77. Open M-F 9am-6pm.) **Banca Transilvania,** Bd. Eroilor 36 (☎19 88 33), **exchanges currency** off Pţa. Avram Iancu, cashes **traveler's checks** for no commission, and has **Western Union** services. (Open M-F 9am-6pm, Sa 9:30am-12:30pm.) MC/V **ATMs** line Bd. Ferdinand. **Farmacia Clematis** is at Pţa. Unirii 10. (☎19 13 63. Open daily 8am-10pm.) For **Internet access,** go to **Net Zone Internet Cafe,** Pţa. Muzeului 5. (☎19 26 28. 7am-10pm L12,000 per hr.; 10pm-7am L6,000 per hr. Open 24hr.) **Telephone offices** (open M-F 10am-6pm) are behind the **post office,** Bd. Ferdinand 33. (Open M-F 7am-8pm, Sa 8am-1pm.) A second post office, Str. Aurel Vlaicu 3 (☎43 11 21), has **Poste Restante.** (Open Tu and Th 8am-1pm.) **Postal Code:** 400110.

ACCOMMODATIONS AND FOOD. **Retro Youth Hostel** ❶, Str. Potaissa 13, near the university, has a wonderful staff. (☎45 04 52; www.retro.ro. 30min. Internet included. Breakfast €2. Laundry service €2. Dorms €10. MC/V.) **Hotel Continental** ❸, Str. Napoca 1, on the corner of Pta. Unirii, has beautiful rooms. (☎591 441. Singles €17, with bath €50; doubles €25/€65. MC/V.) Central **Hotel Vladeasa** ❷, Bd. Regele Ferdinand 20, has simple rooms with private showers. (☎19 44 29. Breakfast included. Singles L750,000; doubles L1,000,000.)

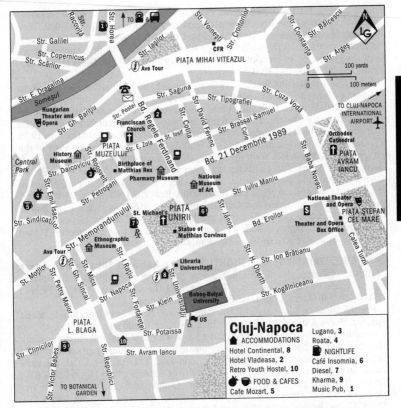

ROMANIA

Cluj-Napoca
ACCOMMODATIONS
Hotel Continental, **8**
Hotel Vladeasa, **2**
Retro Youth Hostel, **10**
FOOD & CAFES
Cafe Mozart, **5**

Lugano, **3**
Roata, **4**
NIGHTLIFE
Café Insomnia, **6**
Diesel, **7**
Kharma, **9**
Music Pub, **1**

Cluj loves its desserts—**pastry shops** are everywhere. ▣**Cafe Mozart ❶**, Str. Pavlov 7, has a Viennese atmosphere. Sample fine pastries in an alcohol- and smoke-free setting, and be sure to try their flavored coffee infusions. Background music is, naturally, by the classical masters. (☎ 19 19 97. Desserts L40,000-80,000. Open daily 9am-10pm.) **Roata ❶**, Str. Alexandru Ciura 6a, off Str. Emil Isac, is a traditional Romanian restaurant. The lack of an English menu may be inconvenient, but the food is authentic and delicious. (☎ 19 20 22. Entrees L60,000-200,000. Open Su-M 1pm-midnight, Tu-Sa noon-midnight. MC/V.) **Lugano ❷**, Str. Clemencasu 2, at the corner with Str. Rooseveldt, near Pta. Unirii, cooks up delectable Italian fare in a polished, modern environment. The courtyard terrace is also pleasant, and the bar is well-stocked. (Entrees L100,000-200,000. Open daily 11am-1pm. MC/V.)

▣ **SIGHTS.** Begin at **Piața Unirii**, where the 80m Gothic steeple of the Catholic **Church of St. Michael** (Biserica Sf. Mihail) pierces the skyline. It boasts some of the country's largest and most exquisite stained-glass windows. The church shares the square with an awesome yet controversial equestrian **statue** of Hungarian King Matthias Corvinus. The mayor has attempted to overshadow it with six even taller Romanian flags. To the right when facing the statue, **Bánffy Palace**, Pta. Unirii 30, houses the **National Museum of Art** (Muzeul National de Artb), which specializes in Romanian works. Don't miss the rooms devoted to painter **Nicolae Grig-**

orescu, famous for his depictions of peasant life. (☎19 69 53. Open W-Su noon-7pm. L20,000, students L10,000; with temporary exhibits L30,000/L15,000.) The **Pharmacy Museum** (Muzeul Farmacia), Pţa. Unirii 28, where Bd. Ferdinand intersects the square, is in the 1573 building which housed Cluj's first chemist shop. Visit the recreation of an apothecary's laboratory. (☎19 75 67. Open M-Sa 10am-4pm. L20,500, students L10,500.)

From Pţa. Unirii, head up Str. Regele Ferdinand and turn left on Str. E. Zola to reach Pţa. Muzeului. There, visit the **History Museum** (Muzeul de Istorie), Str. Constantin Daicoviciu 2, which showcases an impressive collection dating from the Bronze Age to the present. The contemporary displays, which include a model of a flying machine, built by a local professor in 1896, are on the second floor. (☎19 56 77. Open Tu-Su 10am-4pm. L20,400, students L10,200.) For a dazzling view of the city, head to **Cetăţuie Hill.** Walk up Str. Regele Ferdinand from Pţa. Unirii, turn left onto Str. Dragalina, and climb the stairs on your right. The **Central Park** (Parcul Barnutiv) is a good place to picnic. To get there, walk up Str. Regele Ferdinand from Pţa. Unirii and take a left on Str. Bariţiu. Bear right when Str. Bariţiu intersects Str. Emil Isac. (Open Apr.-Oct. M-F 9am-9pm, Sa-Su 9am-10pm.) The **Botanical Garden** (Grădina Botanică), Str. Republicii 42, off Str. Napoca, has over 12,000 plant species. Highlights include a Japanese garden and exotic greenhouse. (Open daily 9am-7pm; lily pad exhibit closes 6pm. L15,000. Map L10,000.)

🎭🎵 **ENTERTAINMENT AND NIGHTLIFE.** The **National Theater and Opera** (Teatrul Naţional şi Opera Română), in Pţa. Ştefan cel Mare, imitates the Garnier Opera House of Paris. The box office is across the street. (☎59 53 63. Tickets L30,000-80,000. Open Tu-Su 11am-5pm; closed in summer.)

For the latest on Cluj's nightlife, pick up the free *Şapte Seri* from hotels. **Music Pub,** Str. Horea 5, in an old wine cellar near the river, would be a good place to plot a revolution. As is, it's ideal for kicking back with students and cheap alcohol. Shoot pool in the back. (☎43 25 17. Live music F-Sa 9 or 10pm. Open summer daily 6pm-3am; low season M-Sa 9am-4am, Su noon-4am.) Off Pţa. Unirii, **Café Insomnia** caters to coffee-shop philosophers. If you tire of espresso, beer (from L18,000) is on tap. It mostly plays jazz, blues, and oldies, and piano performances are frequent. (☎19 43 12. Open daily 10am-1am.) If clubs are more your thing, **Diesel,** Pţa. Unirii 17, has hosted some of Romania's most popular bands. (☎19 84 41. Open daily 9am-3am.) For a dance scene, head to **Kharma,** Str. Lucian Blaga 1-3, which has intense house on weekends and a relaxed scene during the week. (Beer L24,000. Open daily 9am-4am.)

ORADEA
☎(0)259

Oradea (oh-RAHD-yah; pop. 223,000) is an important transportation hub and modern commercial center that is almost as Hungarian as it is Romanian. For many visitors, Oradea serves as a base to explore the surrounding Bihor County—a wellspring of waterfalls, rivers, caves, and mountains. The city's 19th-century squares lend Oradea an urbane charm.

🚆 **TRANSPORTATION. CFR** is at Calea Republicii 2, off Pţa. Ferdinand. **Trains** go to: **Braşov** (7hr., 4 per day, L300,000); **Bucharest** (10-11hr., 3 per day, L373,000); **Cluj-Napoca** (2½hr., 10 per day, L200,000); **Sighişoara** (7hr., 3 per day, L340,000); **Timişoara** (4hr., 5 per day, L180,000); **Budapest, HUN** (6hr., 3 per day, L1,000,000.)

🧭 **ORIENTATION AND PRACTICAL INFORMATION.** From the train station, take tram #1 toward **Piaţa Independenţei.** Get off before crossing the river and hang a right to reach the city's two main squares, **Piaţa Ferdinand** and **Piaţa Unirii,** which is across the bridge. On foot, make a left out of the station and head down **Calea Republicii**. Maps (L80,000) and helpful info are available at **Lucon Tour,** Str. General Traian Mosoiu, in Pţa. Unirii. (☎43 66 13. Open summer M-F 8am-6pm, Sa 9am-2pm; low season M-F 8am-5pm.) **HVB Bank,** in Pţa. Unirii, cashes **AmEx Traveler's Cheques** for 1.5% commission. (☎40 67 00. Open M-F 9am-4pm.) **Farmacia Christiana** is past the bank. (☎23 45 48. Open M-F 8am-8pm, Sa 8am-2pm.) The **telephone office,** Str. R. Ciorogariu 12, is off Calea Republicii. (Open M-F 10am-6pm.) For **Internet access,** head to **Game Star,** Str. M. Eminescu 4, off Calea Republicii from Pţa. Ferdinand. (☎47 60 90. L12,000 per hr. Open 24hr.) **Salvamont** (☎47 16 74; salvamontbihor@yahoo.com), the mountain safety organization, can help you plan outdoor trips in the region. The **post office,** which offers **Western Union** services, is next to the telephone office. (Open M-F 7am-8pm, Sa 8am-1pm.) **Postal Code:** 410017.

🏠🍴 ACCOMMODATIONS AND FOOD. Though parts of the exterior could use some paint, **Hotel Astoria ❶,** Str. Teatrului 47, is clean, well-run, and in a golden location. (☎23 05 08. Breakfast included. Reception 24hr. Singles L275,000; doubles with shower L550,000, with bath L650,000.) **Gobé Csárda ❷,** Str. Dobrogeanu Gherea 26, is on the far side of the Old Citadel. While the hostel is well-kept, neighboring farm animals can get noisy at times. Breakfast is included. The owner organizes extreme sports, from kayaking to skiing in the surrounding mountains. (☎41 35 13. Private bathrooms. Singles €10-20; doubles €25-30.) Elegant **Capitolium ❷,** Str. Avram Iancu 8, past Pţa. Unirii, specializes in Hungarian cuisine and satisfying pizzas. (☎23 05 51. Pizzas L40,000-80,000. Entrees L70,000-L150,000. Open 11am-11pm.) Another good option is the restaurant/pub **Taverna ❶,** Str. M. Eminescu 2. (Entrees L60,000-100,000.)

📷🎶 SIGHTS AND NIGHTLIFE. Every inch of the **Moon Church** (Biserica cu Lună), in Pţa. Unirii, is covered with frescoes. The 18th-century structure was named for its black and gold globe, which rotates every 28 days with the moon. The entire city is dotted with churches, many of them Roman Catholic, testament to the large Hungarian population. The **Black Vulture Palace** (Palatul Vulturul Negru), on the other side of the square, was questionably colored lime-green during its 1907-09 construction. Inside, a tunnel decorated with stained glass functions as a shopping mall. Running down from **Pta. Ferdinand** is the pedestrian portion of Calea Republicii, lined with attractive, well-preserved 19th-century buildings, which house up-and-coming cafes and shops. East of the central squares, the **Old Citadel** is a worth seeing. In the 13th century, the Tatars destroyed Oradea's 12th-century fortress—along with the rest of the city. Rebuilt, conquered, and rebuilt repeatedly, the Old Citadel now exemplifies 17th-century Vauban style, as it was built in the shape of a five-pointed star and encircled by a deep moat. The local art faculty has turned it into an open-air sculpture garden. To get there, face the river while standing in Pta. Unirii, make a right, and link up with Calea Clujului. After a few blocks you should see the ruins to the right. In the park (Parcul Palatului Baroc) next to the train station, the **Museum of the Oradea Area** (Muzeul Ţării Crişurilor), Bd. Dacia 1-3, is a Baroque palace built between 1762 and 1777 as a residence for the region's Roman Catholic bishop. Its 120 rooms are supposedly modeled after those in Vienna's Belvedere Palace. (Open Su, W, F 10am-6pm; Tu, Th, Sa 10am-3pm. L31,000, students L15,500.) The same architect built the neighboring **Roman Catholic Cathedral** (Catedrala Romano-Catolică), Str. Şirul Canonicilor 19.

At night, head down to the **Black Vulture Palace,** on Pta. Unirii, where an array of bars and clubs plays host to the area's young and fashionable. At the center of it all is **Heat Club,** a labyrinth of underground rooms with an intense trance and rave scene. (Open daily 9pm-late. Covers weekend L50,000.)

BANAT

Romania's westernmost province, Banat was heavily influenced by its Austrian and Hungarian rulers. Lying squarely on the plains beyond the Carpathian mountains, its geography ensures hot, dry summers which contrast with the cooler weather in the surrounding mountains. Today, its population is more ethnically diverse than the rest of Romania, and its chicken *paprikash* is second to none.

TIMIŞOARA   ☎(0)256

In 1989, 105 years after becoming the first European city with electric street lamps, Timişoara (tee-mee-SHWAH-rah; pop. 334,000) ignited the revolution that left Romanian communism in cinders. As the nation's westernmost city, geographically and ideologically, it remains a hotbed of political activity today.

ᐸ TRANSPORTATION. To reach Timişoara by train, get off at **Timişoara Nord. CFR** is at Str. Măchieşor 3. (☎22 05 34. Open M-F 10am-6pm.) **Trains** run to: **Alba Iulia** (4½hr., 2 per day, L225,000); **Braşov** (9hr., 1 per day, L310,000); **Bucharest** (8hr., 5 per day, L485,000); **Cluj-Napoca** (7hr., 4 per day, L265,000); **Oradea** (3½hr., 3 per day, L180,000); **Sibiu** (7hr., 1 per day, L255,000); **Belgrade, SMN** (4hr., 1 per day, L280,000); **Budapest, HUN** (5hr., 3 per day, L1,000,000).

ᐳᐸ ORIENTATION AND PRACTICAL INFORMATION. The train station is less than 2km west of the city center. Step out of the station and turn left. Alternatively, take tram #1, 8, or 11, heading straight ahead, or trolley-bus #11 or 14, heading left, to the center of town (2 trips L17,000; buy tickets at kiosks). Get off after crossing the river, when you see **Piaţa Victoriei,** the city's main square, with its multicolored cathedral. The old center itself is compact and circular, originally built within fortifications, which are now mostly gone.

    Banc Post, Bd. Mihai Eminescu, off Piaţa Victoriei, has **Western Union** services. (Open M-F 8:30am-1pm and 1:30-5pm.) **Librăria Mihai Eminescu,** in Pţa. Victoriei, sells **maps.** (L60,000-100,000. Open M-F 9am-7pm, Sa 9am-1pm.) There's a **Sensiblu pharmacy** where Bd. Eminescu hits Pţa. Victoriei. (☎40 61 53. Open daily 8am-10pm.) **Vlad Pharmacy,** (☎20 18 89), Str. Lazar 8, near the hospital, is open 24hr. Seek **medical assistance** at **Spitalul Clinic Municipal,** Str. G. Dima 5 (☎43 36 12). In an emergency, turn right after your center. The **telephone office** is off Mihai Eminescu 2, past Banc Post. (Open M-F 10am-6pm.) For **Internet,** try **Java Coffee House,** Str. Pacha 4, just below Pta. Unirii, which doubles as a stylish cafe. (L500 per min. Open 24hr.) The **post office,** Str. Craiului 1, is off Bd. Republicii and Pţa. Victoriei. (Open M-F 8am-7pm.) **Postal Code:** 300005.

ᐳᐸ ACCOMMODATIONS AND FOOD. The rooms at **Hotel Cina Banatul ❸,** Str. Republicii 2, are centrally located, clean and comfortable. All rooms have TVs, fridges, and private baths. (☎49 01 30. Breakfast included. Singles L1,000,000; doubles L1,300,000; triples L1,500,000. MC/V.) Central **Hotel Nord ❷,** Str. gen dragalina 47, has comfortable rooms with TV, private sink and toilet, and fridges. It's the yellow and pink building just across the street from the station. (☎112 308. Breakfast included. Singles €17; doubles €24; suites €42.)

    There are a number of good restaurants with outdoor tables on Pţa. Victoriei. **Harold's ❷,** Aleea Studenţilor 17, is a genteel, sit-down oasis in the midst of the student district, fast-food desert. It serves excellent Chinese, Mexican, and Romanian cuisine in a lovely courtyard. Try the Szechuan beef. To get there when standing by the Aleea Studentilor taxi stand, face the Pret a Manger and go left and left

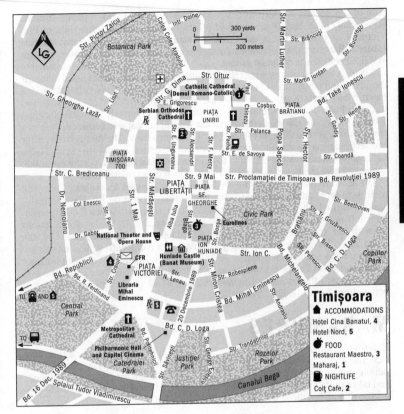

Timișoara

▲ ACCOMMODATIONS
Hotel Cina Banatul, **4**
Hotel Nord, **5**

🍴 FOOD
Restaurant Maestro, **3**
Maharaj, **1**

🍷 NIGHTLIFE
Colț Cafe, **2**

again after the first dorm. Its door is hidden to the right among the *shawarma* stands. (☎ 19 63 35. Entrees L70,000-L200,000. Open daily 11:30am-midnight.) For the best Indian fare outside Bucharest, head to **Maharaj,** at the northeast corner of Pta. Unirii. The tandoori specials are excellent. (☎ 43 78 45. Entrees L80,000-175,000. Open daily 11am-11pm.) **Restaurant Maestro ❸**, Str. Bolyai János 3, off Str. Lucian Blaga, serves scrumptious Romanian cuisine in an elegant, outdoor setting and an equally pleasant vaulted basement dining room. (☎ 29 38 61. Entrees L100,000-300,000. Open daily 9am-late.)

📷 🎭 **SIGHTS AND ENTERTAINMENT. Piața Victoriei** is flanked by the **Opera House** to the north and the **Metropolitan Cathedral** to the south; a statue of Romulus and Remus graces its center. Toward the church, a New Age sculpture commemorates the victims of the 1989 Revolution. The cathedral itself is a spectacular blend of Byzantine and Moldavian folk styles, capped by 13 green and gold spires. This Orthodox church contains sculpted chandeliers, 8000kg bells, and a display of religious artifacts in its museum downstairs. (Open daily 6:30am-8pm. Services M-F 7:30am and 6pm; Su 7, 10am, 6pm. Museum open W-Su 10am-3pm. L5000, students free.) The **Park of Roses** (Parcul Rozelor), to the south, has white benches surrounded by roses. Free concerts are held often. On the other side of the square, a white Neoclassical building houses the **National Theater.** (Open daily Sept.-May 10am-1pm and 5-7pm.) In the square to the right of Pța. Victoriei, as you face the opera, the old **Huniade Castle** houses the **Banat Museum** (Muzeul Banatului), which traces Timișoara's history from ancient times through WWII. Check out the **sculpture garden.** (Open Tu-Su 10am-4:30pm. L20,000, students L10,000.) A natural history wing (L20,000, students L10,000) houses usual dinosaur dioramas and a significant **butterfly collection.** Outside, you'll see original antique electric **lamp posts.** North of Victoriei, the increasingly gentrified old city stretches out until **Piața Unirii.** Its fountain spouts water said to remedy stomach ailments. West of the square sits the **Serbian Orthodox Church;** the **Catholic Cathedral,** built in a *fin de siecle* revival style, presides over the eastern flank. The first archway after the vestibule has a parabolic shape and perfect acoustics. In June, the annual **International Folk Music Festival** comes to town. The **Botanical Gardens,** northwest of Pța. Unirii and near the hospital, deserve a visit. (Open dawn to dusk. Free.)

At night, the place to be is the student district, **Complex Studențesc.** From the main square, head down Bd. I.C. Brătianu, make a right on Bd. Michelangelo, and cross the bridge. At Pța. Leonardo da Vinci, turn onto Aleea F.C. Ripensia. Veer left onto the busy Aleea Studenților. **Gulliver,** Str. Al. Studenților 1, has an open-air bar, two dance floors, and a lively student crowd. (Drinks from L30,000. Open 24hr.) Two doors down, **Happy Club** earns its name with a pleasant terrace and an intense scene on weekends. (☎29 52 99. Open 10am-late.) Another hot spot is the smoky **Colț Cafe,** Str. Ungureanu 10, near Pța. Unirii. Head out of the plaza on Str. Lazar until the corner of Ungureanu. (☎22 93 85. Shots from L30,000, coffee concoctions from L40,000. Open 24hr.)

MARAMUREȘ

Entering Maramureș (mah-rah-MOO-resh) is much like stepping into a time capsule: life here proceeds the same as it did 50 or 100 years ago. The population is famous for its loyalty to traditional dress, especially during feasts and holidays, and takes pride in its ancient Dacian roots. Few visitors venture to the poorly connected region, but those who do are richly rewarded.

SIGHETU MARMAȚIEI ☎(0)262

Just across the Tisa River from Ukraine, Sighetu Marmației is Maramureș's cultural center. Proximity to local villages, timeless beauty, and tranquil isolation make a trip to "Sighet" a must.

🖫🛈 TRANSPORTATION AND PRACTICAL INFORMATION. CFR is at Pța. Libertății 25. (Open daily 7am-2pm.) Trains run to: **Bucharest** (15hr., 1 per day, L400,000); **Cluj-Napoca** (6½hr., 2 per day, L200,000); **Sighișoara** (10hr., 1 per day, L440,000); **Timișoara** (13hr., 1 per day, L400,000).

Head straight out of the train station and bear right slightly down **Str. Iuliu Maniu.** At the dead end (about 1km), go left on **Str. 22 Decembrie 1989** to reach **Piața Libertății,** the main square. For info, try the tourist agency **MTMM,** Piața Libertății 21, opposite the Hotel Tisa in the main square. (☎31 25 52. Open M-F 9am-5pm). **BCR,** Str. Iuliu Maniu 32, cashes **AmEx Traveler's Cheques** at 1.5% commission. (Open M-F 8:30am-5:30pm, Sa 8:30am-12:30pm.) **Farmacia Minerva** is at Pța. Libertății 23. (☎31 19 77. Open M-F 8am-8pm, Sa 8am-3pm, Su 9am-1pm.) Use **Internet** at **Cafe Internet,** Str. Corneliu Ceposu 5, off Str. Bogdan Vodă. (☎31 22 21. L15,000 per hr. Open daily 7am-4pm.) The **post office** is at Str. Bogdan Vodă 2. (Open M-F 7am-8pm, Sa 8am-1pm.) **Postal Code:** 435500.

ACCOMMODATIONS AND FOOD. The best value is to stay in a **private villa** (€8-12), which you can rent from waiting proprietors at the train station. Alternatively, ask the staff at **MTMM** to book a room in a rural B&B in an adjoining village. **Hotel Tisa ❷**, Pța. Libertății 21, is a Western-style hotel with tourist info at the front desk. (☎31 26 45. Breakfast included. Singles L700,000; doubles L900,000.) The wildly popular **Perla Sigheteana ❷**, Str. Avram Iancu 65a, offers comfortable doubles and views in a new building at the edge of town, on the way to Săpânța. (☎31 06 13. Doubles L1,000,000. Call ahead. MC/V.) In town, a number of respectable cafes and pizzerias surround the main square. For tasty Romanian food and a beautiful view, try **Restaurant Perla Sigheteană ❷**, inside the eponymous hotel. (☎31 06 13. Entrees L50,000-150,000. Open daily 7am-midnight.) The **market,** one block up from the main square off Str. Vasile Alecsandri, sells fresh fruits and vegetables.

SIGHTS. Sighet's ▧**Memorial Museum** (Muzeul Memorialui), Str. Copusu 4, south of the main square, is unique and sobering. In the period after WWII, the building was the top-secret political prison of the Communist regime. The cells once imprisoned former leaders, famous intellectuals, and high-ranking Catholic clergy, and now contain different exhibits, from a re-creation of the prison's torture chamber to pictures, sculptures, and paintings of Nicolae Ceaușescu. Admission fee includes an in-depth English tour. (☎31 68 48. Open daily Apr.-Oct. 9:30am-6:30pm; Nov.-Mar. Tu-Su 9:30am-4:30pm. L40,000.) **Casa Elie Wiesel,** the light-blue house on Str. Drogoș Vodă, one block up from Str. Traian, on the corner of Str. Tudor Vladimirescu, is the childhood residence of the 1986 Nobel Peace Prize winner, best known for his literary work, *Night.* Wiesel, a Transylvanian Jew, spent WWII in concentration camps after Maramureș was swallowed by Nazi-sympathizing Hungary in the Vienna Dictum of 1940. The museum contains a Star of David-shaped monument in the courtyard, many samples of Wiesel's writings, displays about the fate of the region's Jews, and a few rooms restored to their pre-WWII appearance. (Open M-F 9am-5pm. L20,000, students L10,000. Cameras L20,000.) The **Maramureș Museum** has two branches: an **ethnographic wing,** Str. Bogdan Voda 1, opposite the post office; and an **open-air village museum,** at the end of Bogdan Voda. Follow the signs from Str. Bogdan Voda just before the little bridge. Displays put the region in historical context. You can borrow a book with English explanations. (Ethnographic wing open Tu-Su 10am-6pm. Village open daily 10am-7pm. Each L20,000.)

DAYTRIPS FROM SIGHETU MARMAȚIEI. For an alternative outlook on death, head to ▧**Sapânta**, site of the world-famous **Merry Cemetery** (Cimitirul Vesel). The cemetery, near the local church, is a sea of colorfully painted wooden grave markers depicting scenes from the life of the deceased and engraved with witty poems—often in first person—using archaisms and slang. Starting in 1935, local artisan Stan Ion Patras, drawing on rich traditions of folk art and woodworking, began carving these unique headstones; the tradition continues today. The crosses and markers have attracted worldwide attention and have been displayed in many foreign galleries. Despite its fame, this tiny village maintains a traditional lifestyle; its inhabitants sport straw hats, traditional dress, and head scarves. *(Buses run from Sighet's train station: 40min; M-F 7 per day, Sa-Su 1 per day; L40,000. Though hitchhiking from Str. Avram Iancu at the western edge of Sighet is also very common, you can make the round-trip for less than L300,000 by taxi. Let's Go does not recommend hitchhiking. Once in Sapânta, take a left off the road from Sighet onto the only other paved road, and go up 200 yards. Cemetery open daily dawn-dusk. L30,000.)*

Those seeking a glimpse of Romanian country life should head to the **Izei Valley.** Here, horse carts outnumber automobiles, traditional dress is the norm, and beautiful architectural elements, such as ornately carved wooden gateposts and churches, abound. Visitors soak up the mountain-town atmosphere along with the comfortable hospitality and authentic meals. The valley is defined by a series of small villages. At its mouth, 5km from Sighet, is **Vadu Izei**, the commercial hub. **Leud,** another village, is home to the **Church of the Valley** (Biscerica de Lemn), which is on the main street and marked by its wooden steeple; it is a perfect example of wooden church architecture and is sometimes called the "cathedral in wood." The 1365 **Church on the Hill**, east along the dirt road that juts off just north of the village council building, is the oldest of its kind. Cross the small river and ascend the hill; follow signs for the small museum (L10,000) near the church. The churches are often locked; ask around, and locals will find a key. At the far end of the valley, the old mining center of **Borsa** is a gateway to the Rodna mountains; a small ski area lies to its east. In the nearby Viseu river valley, the town of **Viseu de Sus** sometimes arranges rides on a restored cog railway. For info, inquire in Sighet. Food and lodgings are available at the ubiquitous B&Bs in the villages for €10-20 per person. Book rooms through the **MTMM tourist agency** (see p. 639) or look for signs, knock on doors, and arrange them on the spot. *(Transportation within the Izei Valley is variable. Buses, which stop in front of the train station, run from Sighet to various villages within the valley about 6-8 times per day each weekday in the summer. Buses 30min.-2hr., L40,000. Rental cars can be arranged through the Hotel Tisa (p. 639) for an alarming €50 per day. They can also arrange cars with drivers, which can be curiously cheaper, from €30 per day. They sell maps of the area for L70,000. Hitchhikers commonly stand in front of the Astra supermarket in Sighet, on Str. Bogdan Voda, a few blocks from the central square where buses also stop. Let's Go does not recommend hitchhiking. The best information on all towns described below can be obtained in Sighet.)*

MOLDAVIA (MOLDOVA)

Eastern Romania once included the entire Moldovan territory, but the Bessarabian section now comprises the independent Republic of Moldova. Romanian Moldavia, which extends from the Carpathians to the Prut River, is vastly starker than Ardeal but more developed than Maramureş. Travelers visit the hills of Bucovina, renowned for their masterfully painted monasteries.

IAŞI ☎(0)232

Iaşi (YAHSH; pop. 340,000) is a city of bustling streets, fast-food joints, and dance clubs. Yet Moldavia's capital is the most peaceful of Romania's big cities. Neoclassical homes and palaces that hosted late 19th century intellectuals are remarkably well-preserved and will delight any architecture connoisseur.

▐ TRANSPORTATION. The **train station**, Iaşi Nord, is on Str. Silvestru. To: **Braşov** (6hr., 1 per day, L272,000); **Bucharest** (7½hr., 6 per day, L372,000); **Cluj-Napoca** (9hr., 4 per day, L272,000); **Constanţa** (8hr., 1 per day, L272,000); **Sighetu Marmaţiei** (13hr., 3 per day, L272,000) via **Salva; Suceava** (2hr., 4 per day, L166,000); **Timişoara** (17hr., 3 per day, L373,000). **CFR** is at Pţa. Unirii 9/11. (☎14 52 69. Open M-F 8am-8pm.) The **bus station**, Str. Moara de Foc 15 (☎14 65 87), behind the health club, sends buses to: **Braşov** (8hr., 1 per day, L230,000) and **Chişinău, MOL** (5hr., 4 per day, L150,000).

▐▐ ORIENTATION AND PRACTICAL INFORMATION. Standing in the parking lot with the **train station** behind you, cross the street and walk up **Str. Gării** to the right of the **Vama Veche** (Old Customs Tower). Follow Str. Gării to the next major intersection, where the tram tracks curve right. These tracks follow **Str.**

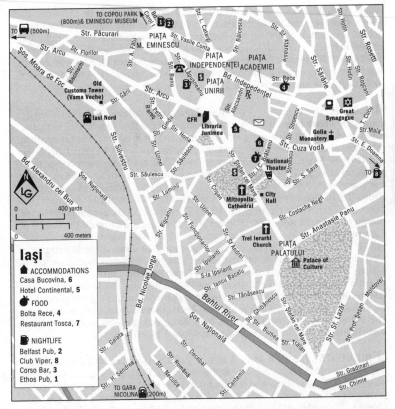

ROMANIA

Iaşi

⌂ ACCOMMODATIONS
Casa Bucovina, **6**
Hotel Continental, **5**

🍴 FOOD
Bolta Rece, **4**
Restaurant Tosca, **7**

🍷 NIGHTLIFE
Belfast Pub, **2**
Club Viper, **8**
Corso Bar, **3**
Ethos Pub, **1**

Arcu, which intersects with the main square, **Piaţa Unirii,** before changing its name to **Str. Cuza Vodă.** Here, **Str. Ştefan cel Mare** branches to the right. The center is also accessible by trams #3, 6, and 7 (2 trips L14,000) opposite the Vama Veche. **Banca Comercială Română,** Str. Ştefan cel Mare 8a, cashes **AmEx Traveler's Cheques** for 1.5% commission. (☎21 17 38. Open M-F 8am-2pm and 2:30-5pm, Sa 8am-12:30pm.) **ATMs** are ubiquitous. **Luggage storage** is available at the train station. (Small bags L30,000 per day, large L60,000.) **Libraria Junimea,** Pţa. Unirii 4, sells **maps.** (☎41 27 12. L70,000. Open M-F 8:30am-8pm, Sa 9am-4pm, Su 9am-2pm.) The **pharmacy, Sf. Paraschiva** (☎31 60 29), at the top of Pţa. Unirii near Bd. Independentei, has a 24hr. window. The **telephone** office, Str. Lăpuşneanu 14, is off the main square. (☎24 55 15. Open M-F 10am-6pm.) For **Internet access,** try **St@r Net,** Str. Sarariei 14. (☎27 61 71. Open 24hr.) The **post office,** Str. Cuza Vodă 10, in a neoclassical building, has **Poste Restante** at window #6. (☎21 22 22. Open M-F 8am-7pm, Sa 8am-1pm.) To pick up packages from overseas, head to Poste 13, behind the telephone office on Str. Banu. (Open M-F 9am-5pm.) **Postal Code:** 700037.

🏠🍴 ACCOMMODATIONS AND FOOD. Casa Bucovina ❶, Str. Cuza Vodă 30-32, has clean, adequate rooms. (☎31 44 93. Doubles L400,000, with bath L700,000.) **Hotel Continental ❷,** Str. Cuza Vodă 4, has a convenient location and quality rooms with TV, phone, and private bath. (☎21 18 46. Breakfast included. Singles

L630,000; doubles L930,000.) Established in 1786, ▨**Bolta Rece ❶**, Str. Rece 10, serves excellent traditional dishes. From Pța. Unirii, take Str. Cuza Vodă past Hotel Continental; go left on Str. Brătianu. At Bd. Independenței, go right and immediately left on Str. M. Eminescu, then left on Str. Rece. (☎21 22 55. Entrees L40,000-90,000. Open daily 8am-midnight.) **Restaurant Tosca ❶**, Str. Brătianu 30, near the theater, serves Romanian-influenced Italian dishes. (☎21 66 64. Entrees L40,000-130,000. Open daily 11am-11pm.)

◙ **SIGHTS.** The massive, neo-Gothic ▨**Palace of Culture** (Palatul Culturii), marked by a **clock tower,** which plays the anthem of the 1859 founding of Romania, contains historical, polytechnic, ethnographic, and art museums. The art museum contains splendid 19th-century paintings by such masters as Nicolae Grigorescu and Theodor Aman, while the history museum explores Moldavian heritage from prehistory through WWI. The polytechnic museum has an exhibit on music boxes and player pianos, and the ethnography section displays artifacts of peasant life. (Open Tu-Su 10am-5pm. Each museum L15,000, students L10,000. Combined ticket L50,000/L30,000. Cameras L100,000.) The exterior of the gorgeous **Trei Ierarhi church,** on the right side of Str. Ștefan cel Mare as you walk toward the Palace of Culture, is covered in intricate carvings—the Moldavian, Romanian, and Turkish symbols date to 1637. Though invading Tatars melted down the gold exterior in 1650, the interior retains its original sheen. (Church open daily 9am-noon and 3-5:30pm. L10,000, students L5000.) To get to **Copou Park,** Bd. Carol I, ride tram #1 or 13 from Pța. Unirii or take a stroll from Pța. Eminescu. Inside the park is the famous **Mihai Eminescu Linden,** the tree that shaded Romania's great poet as he worked (see **The Arts,** p. 608). The adjacent **Eminescu Museum,** one of a dozen museums in Iași devoted to literary figures, exhibits dozens of portraits of the poet and some of his documents. (Open Tu-Su 10am-5pm. L10,000.)

▨ **NIGHTLIFE.** The night scene is concentrated on the **Iulius Mall.** From the center, walk down Bd. Ștefan cel Mare and go left at Str. Costache Negri. At **Club Viper,** pool (L80,000), gambling, and bowling (L250,000 per hr.) are replaced by disco parties on the weekend. (Beer L50,000. Cover men L50,000. Open F-Sa 10pm-late.) Closer to the center, on the way to Copou park, the **Casa Studenților** houses drinking establishments, including **Belfast** (☎0788 508 076, open 1pm-1am) and **Ethos** (☎0741 080 272, open 1pm-1am). For a cafe atmosphere, try **Corso,** Str. Lapusneanu 11, just off Pța. Unirii. (☎27 61 43. Beer from L30,000. Open 9am-1am.)

BUCOVINA MONASTERIES

Hidden in rural Romania, Bucovina's painted monasteries are a source of national pride. Built 500 years ago by Ștefan cel Mare—rumor has it that he built one after every victory over the Turks—the exquisite structures meld Moldavian and Byzantine architecture. They served as isolated outposts against Turkish and Tatar marauders, acquiring massive walls and towers over the years. After repression under communism, the churches are again active.

SUCEAVA ☎(0)230

The capital of Moldavia under Ștefan cel Mare, Suceava (soo-CHYAH-vah) is the biggest town in monastery country and a good base for exploration. But it has more than just proximity to offer the monastery-seeker: you'll find intriguing museums, Ștefan's citadel, and yet more religious sites.

TRANSPORTATION. Gara Suceava Nord is the main station, and sends trains to: **Braşov** (8hr., 1 per day, L300,000); **Bucharest** (6hr., 8 per day, L410,000); **Cluj-Napoca** (6hr., 4 per day, L250,000); **Gura Humorului** (1hr., 10 per day, L25,000-70,000); **Iaşi** (2hr., 8 per day, L80,000-160,000); **Sighetu Marmaţiei** (14hr., 3 per day, L222,000) via **Salva**. Buy tickets at CFR, Str. N. Bălcescu 4. (☎21 43 35. Open M-F 7:30am-7pm.) The bus station (☎52 43 40), at the intersection of Str. N. Bălcescu and Str. V. Alecsandri, sends buses to: **Bucharest** (8hr., 4 per day, L226,000); **Cluj-Napoca** (7hr., 1 per day, L185,000); **Constanţa** (9hr., 2 per day, L300,000); **Gura Humorului** (1hr., 10 per day, L30,000); **Iaşi** (3hr., 4 per day, L100,000); **Chişinău, MOL** (3hr., 5 per day, L210,000).

ORIENTATION AND PRACTICAL INFORMATION. From the train station, take any of the **Maxi taxis** (L70,000) waiting outside to reach the center, **Piaţa 22 Decembrie.** As you walk up the square, to your right runs Str. Nicolae Bălcescu, and to the left, under the colonnade, is walkway Aleea Ion Grămadă (10min., L7000). **Str. Stefan cel Mare** crosses in front of the concrete communist-era theater on the square. **Bilco Agenţia de Turism,** Str. N. Bălcescu 2, organizes car tours to the monasteries. (☎52 24 60. €40-50 per car; max. 4 passengers. Open M-F 9am-6pm, Sa 9am-2pm.) **Luggage storage** is at the train station. (L30,000 per day. Open 24hr.) **Raiffeisen Bank,** Str. N. Bălescu 2, cashes **AmEx Travelers Cheques** for a 1.25% commission, offers **Western Union** services, and has a **24hr. ATM.** (☎52 25 06. Open M-F 8:30am-6:30pm, Sa 9am-1pm.) **Librăria Alexandria,** Aleea Ion Grămadă 5, in the main square, sells **maps.** (L70,000. Open M-F 7am-7:30pm, Sa 9am-6pm.) There is a pharmacy, **Farmacia Centrală,** Str. N. Bălcescu 2b. (☎21 72 85. Open daily 7am-9pm.) **Internet access** is in the tower in Pţa. 22 Decembrie, Bd. Ana Ipătescu 7. (☎52 30 44. L25,000 per hr. Open daily 9am-11pm.) To get to the **post office,** Str. Dimitrie Onciul 1, take a right off Str. N. Bălescu after passing the Banc Post building. (Open M-F 7am-8pm, Sa 8am-2pm.) **Postal Code:** 720005.

ACCOMMODATIONS AND FOOD. Despite its remote location, budget travelers flock to the new ⊠**Class Hostel ❶,** Str. Aurel Vlaicu 195, for its spacious rooms, comfortable beds, friendly atmosphere, and vegetarian cooking. The staff arranges car tours of the monasteries. (☎78 23 28. Breakfast €2; dinner €4. Dorms €10. MC/V.) **Villa Alice ❷,** Str. Simion Florea Marian 1b, left off Str. Nicolae Bălcescu in front of Cinema Modern (follow the signs), offers beautiful private rooms in a quiet neighborhood. (☎52 22 54. Breakfast L100,000. Singles L700,000; doubles L900,000. MC/V.) You can buy a variety of food at the impressive **produce market,** Pţa. Agroalimentara on Str. Petru Rareş, off the end of the pedestrian side of Str. Ştefan cel Mare. (Open daily dawn-dusk.) **Latino ❷,** Curtea Domnească 9, left off the pedestrian side of Str. Ştefan cel Mare, serves Italian dishes. (☎52 36 27. Entrees L100,000-250,000. Open daily 9am-11pm. MC/V.) **Pub Chagall ❷,** on the corner of Str. N. Bălescu and Str. Ştefan cel Mare, dishes up Romanian food in an atmospheric cellar. (Entrees L70,000-120,000. Beer from L25,000. Open daily 11am-11pm.)

SIGHTS AND ENTERTAINMENT. The mammoth equestrian **statue** of Ştefan cel Mare is visible from Pţa. 22 Decembrie, across Bd. Ana Ipătescu, next to the ancient **Citadel of the Throne** (Cetatea de Scaun). The citadel was built in 1388 by Petru Muşat I, who moved Moldavia's capital to Suceava; it was refortified by his great-great-grandson, Ştefan cel Mare, and withstood the 1476 siege by Mehmet II, conqueror of Constantinople. The citadel is only about a 10min. walk through the park in the valley, but take a taxi (5min., L30,000) since the park isn't safe. (Open daily summer 8am-8pm; winter 9am-5pm. L30,000, students L15,000.)

The adjacent **Bucovina Village Museum** (Muzeul Satului din Bucovina) displays 18th- through 20th-century houses from the region. (Open Tu-Su 8am-6pm. L12,000, students L5000. Cameras L30,000.) **Mânăstirea Sf. Ioan cel Nou** (Monastery of St. John the New), completed in 1522 by Ştefan's son Bogdan III, holds beneath its colorful tiled roof the body of St. John, martyred in 1330 for refusing to join the Zoroastrian faith. In late June, his silver casket is opened and the faithful may kiss his bones. Back near the center, 1535 frescoes decorate **Biserica Sf. Dumitru**, Str. Curtea Domnească.

Cinema Modern is at Str. Dragoş Vodă 1, down Str. N. Bălcescu. Films in English run four times per day. (Open daily; last show 7pm. L35,000.) The best **nightlife** is at the **Citadel**, where two terraces serve food and drinks. (Entrees L50,000-100,000. Open daily 8am-10:30pm.) **Club V**, Str. N. Bălcescu 2, is a pool hall with cheap drinks and relaxed atmosphere. Enter through the back.

GURA HUMORULUI   ☎(0)230

In walking distance of Humor and Voroneţ and closest to the other monasteries, Gura Humorului (GOO-rah hoo-MOHR-oo-loo-ee) is an ideal base.

The English-speaking proprietors of ☒**Pensiunea Casa Ella ❶**, Str. Cetăţii 7, off Bd. Bucovina, make travelers feel at home with pleasant rooms, soft beds, and good cooking. (☎23 29 61. Meals L75,000-150,000. Singles L450,000; doubles L550,000.) A step up in luxury is **Vila Fabian ❷**, Str. Câmpului 30, opposite Str. Voroneţ from Dispecerat de Cazare. Rooms are spacious and have TVs. Tea is served in a shady garden. (☎23 23 87. Breakfast €3. Singles €15; doubles €25.) Cheap and popular with the locals, **Nadianca ❶** serves traditional dishes near the arboreal Dendrological Park. From Pţa. Republicii, head down Bd. Bucovina and go right at Str. Parcului. Go right on Str. Mihai Eminescu and left on Str. Primăverii. Take the first right—on the left side, the restaurant is in the big, unmarked building. (☎0745 29 56 13. Entrees L40,000-90,000. Open daily 7am-midnight.) If you need of earthly pleasures after a day of monasteries, **VIP Dance Club**, Str. Sf. Gavril 12, left off Str. Mânăstirea Humorului, is the only option. (Beer from L20,000. Bar open M-F 10am-late, Sa noon-4am, Su 2pm-3am. Disco opens at 8pm.)

Trains, which stop at the station, called **Gura Humorului Oras**, on Bd. Castanilor, run to: **Bucharest** (6hr., 1 per day, L300,000); **Cluj-Napoca** (5hr., 4 per day, L200,000); **Iaşi** (3hr., 4 per day, L190,000); **Sighetu Marmatiei** (12hr., 2 per day, L160,000) via **Salva; Suceava** (1hr., 9 per day, L25,000-70,000); **Timişoara** (14hr., 3 per day, L400,000). To reach the center from the train station, go straight down the tree-lined street to the main road, **Str. Ştefan cel Mare**, and make a right. The road crosses a river and runs into **Piaţa Republicii**, the main square. Get **tourist info** at ☒**Dispecerat de Cazare**, where Str. Câmpului ends at Str. Voroneţ. It's about 1km away from the train station; follow signs to Voroneţ monastery. Turn left on Str. Ştefan cel Mare and left on Str. Câmpului. A friendly couple arranges car tours of local sights: monasteries, a pottery workshop, and a nearby underground salt mine that features a tennis court as well as two chapels. If it's closed, ask at Vila Fabian across the street. (☎/fax 23 38 63. Tours €30-35 per car per day.) There is an **ATM** at **Raiffeisen Bank**, Pţa. Republicii 16, which also offers **Western Union** services and cashes AmEx/MC **traveler's checks** for 0.5% commission. (☎23 13 65. Open M-F 8:30am-6:30pm.) Buy monastery **maps** at **Librăria Alexandria**, Bd. Bucovina 5. (☎23 50 97. Open M-F 7am-7pm, Sa 8am-5pm. MC/V.) The **pharmacy, Farmica Delia**, is at Bd. Bucovina 4. (☎23 15 55. Open M-F 8am-9pm, Sa 8am-8pm, Su 8am-2pm.) For **Internet**, try **Internet Cafe**, Bd. Bucovina 9. (Open daily 8am-midnight. L25,000 per hr.) The **post office** is at Str. Ştefan cel Mare 1. (Open M-F 8am-7pm, Sa 8am-noon.) **Postal Code:** 725300.

MONASTERIES AND CONVENTS

Many visit Bucovina just for the painted monasteries. Their bucolic setting is charming but makes them hard to reach. Voroneţ and Humor are easily accessible by public transportation; getting to Moldoviţa and Putna is harder; reaching the others is virtually impossible. Hitchhiking is possible, but *Let's Go* does not recommend it. Car tours, much more efficient than public transport, involve hiring a car and a driver, who probably won't speak English, to shuttle you around for a day. Tours cost €40-60 per car; arrange them in Gura Humorului or Suceava. Monasteries don't give tours but some sell booklets (L70,000).

VORONEŢ. In 1488, it took Ştefan cel Mare precisely three months, three weeks, and three days to erect Voroneţ. But it was Petru Rareş, his illegitimate son, who, in 1524, added the frescoes that have earned it the title "Sistine Chapel of the East." The rich **Voroneţ Blue** pigment, which changes shades depending on the humidity, still baffles art historians. Some believe the paint's secret ingredient to be finely crushed powder from the gemstone lapis lazuli, but many locals insist that divine intervention is the key ingredient. The west wall depicts the **Last Judgment**, but a vivid clarity of composition makes Voroneţ's version a masterpiece. The figures are arranged in five tiers and crossed by a river of fire from Hell—the damned wear the faces of Turks and Tatars. In 2003, restorations began on the frescoes. *(The monastery is accessible by bus from Gura Humorului: 15min., 3 per day M-F Sept. 15-June 15, L10,000. On foot, take Str. Ştefan cel Mare away from the center of town; following the signs, head left on Cartierul Voroneţ; the monastery is a scenic 5km down the road. A cab should be L50,000-60,000 one-way. Open daily 8am-8pm. L40,000, students L20,000. Cameras L60,000.)*

HUMOR. Founded in 1530 by landowner Teodor Bubuiog during the reign of Petru Rareş, Humor was one of the first monasteries to be painted in the Byzantine style. The exterior walls are covered in frescoes of Jesse's Tree, the Last Judgment, and the Siege of Constantinople, among other religious and historical scenes. The paintings are notable for their marvelous pink hue. The secret room *(tainiţa)* was the first of its kind—it was filled with the monastery's valuables and paved over when the region was threatened with invasion. The tower, built in 1641, provides a slightly tricky climb but a wonderful view. *(About 5km from Gura Humorului, this monastery is a painless walk or cab ride away. L50,000-60,000. When facing the Best Western hotel at the center of town, bear left down Str. Mânbstirea Humorului and follow the signs. Occasional shared vans ply the route. L10,000. Open daily dawn-dusk. L40,000, students L20,000. Cameras L80,000.)*

MOLDOVIŢA. Moldoviţa's frescoes are among the best-preserved of all the monasteries. Though it was destroyed shortly after Alexandru cel Bun (Alexander the Good) constructed it in 1402-1410, Petru Rareş rebuilt the monastery in 1532-1537. It is known for the painting of the monumental **Siege of Constantinople** that decorates its southern wall; in it, heroic Christians resist the inevitable onslaught of the Turks who took the city in 1452. Paintings on the north wall have been almost entirely washed away due to the wind. The doorway to the church was incorporated into the portrayal of the Last Judgment—visitors enter ambiguously, between heaven and hell. The museum houses the throne of Prince Petru and remnants from Alexandru's original church. The small doors at the entrance were designed to keep out mounted enemies. *(From Gura Humorului, take a train to Vama—20min., 9 per day, L39,000—then to Vatra Moldovitei—45min., 3 per day, L24,000. If you want to return the same day, take the earliest train out of Gura Humorului at about 6:40am. Open daily 7am-9pm. L40,000, students L20,000.)*

SUCEVIŢA. Suceviţa, the newest of the monasteries at 407 years young, looks like a fortress from the outside. During attacks, the population took refuge inside Suceviţa's incredibly thick walls. Its south wall presents a genealogy of Jesus, Moses receiving the 10 commandments, and a procession that includes the philosophers Pythagoras, Socrates, Aristotle, and Solon. Plato, supposedly the first scholar to ponder the meaning of death, carries a casket atop his head. While most of the monastery is painted emerald green, the west wall remains incomplete—it is said that the artist fell to his death from a scaffold and his ghost prevents completion. A museum displays a tapestry containing 10,000 pearls woven by the daughter of Ieremia Movila, the monastery's builder. *(Suceviţa lies 32km north of Moldoviţa. Public transportation is unavailable, but many car tours run out of Gura Humorului and Suceava. Hitchhiking from Moldoviţa is common, but Let's Go does not recommend it. Open daily 8am-8pm. L40,000, students L20,000.)*

PUTNA. Ştefan cel Mare's first creation and final resting place, the immaculately white 1469 Putna Monastery was not completely rebuilt until 1982. Only one of the original towers has survived the ravages of fires, earthquakes, and attacks. No original frescoes are left, but Putna's high arching, blank white walls remain touchingly austere. Dozens of rosebushes provide a touch of color. The church contains the marble-canopied **tomb** of Ştefan cel Mare. The king left Putna's location up to God; climbing a nearby hill, he shot an arrow into the air. A slice of the oak that it struck is on display at the museum. Take your first right in the direction of town from the monastery to climb **Dealul Crucii** (Hill of the Cross), Ştefan's shooting point, for fantastic a view. Two hills are marked with crosses—Ştefan's is the smaller one. *(Trains run from Suceava directly to Putna, 75km to the northwest. 2½hr., 4 per day, L31,000. The monastery is 1km from the train station. Turn right as you exit the platform and then left at the 1st intersection. Monastery open daily 6am-8pm. Free. Museum open daily 9am-8pm. L40,000, students L5000.)*

AGAPIA. All of Agapia's paintings are by **Nicolae Grigorescu,** the 19th-century Neoclassical master on the shortlist of Romania's greatest artists. After winning a nationwide contest, he spent 1858-1861 producing icons, canvasses, and a famous altar screen for the 14th-century church. Grigorescu, who studied at the Barbison school in Paris, is most well known for his scenes of peasant life, and Agapia is one of his only forays into religious art. Today, Agapia houses an Orthodox high school for girls. *(Trains run from Suceava, with a connection in Pascani, to Târgu Neamt, 9km from the monastery: 1½hr., 4 per day, L55,000. Try to take a morning trains out—otherwise, the ride back to Suceava will entail a long midnight wait at Pascani. From the station at Targu Neamt, walk the 1-2km down Str. Cuza Voda to the bus station, which has buses to the monastery. 20min., 5 per day, L16,000. L30,000, students L10,000.)*

BLACK SEA COAST (DOBROGEA)

Controlled at different times by Greeks, Romans, and Ottoman Turks, the land between the Danube and the Black Sea has endured a turbulent history that has made it Romania's most ethnically diverse region. The stunning coastline stretches south, while the interior valleys hold Romania's best vineyards. Summer crowds pack the area and make prices steep. If you tire of resort crowds, take refuge in the delta to the north, where the Danube meets the Black Sea.

CONSTANŢA   ☎(0)241

Once the Greek port of Tomis, Constanţa (con-STAN-tsa; pop. 500,000) has been the prize of various empires for over 2500 years. Romania's second-largest city is a commercial port, military base, and cultural center. While its inhabitants are tanner and more relaxed than their inland counterparts, Constanţa is more than a haven for beach bums. The city is a lively urban anchor for nearby resorts, and old Tomis still charms visitors with its ancient ruins.

TRANSPORTATION. Constanţa is north of most of the resorts. **CFR** is on Str. Petru Rareş off Pţa. Ovidiu. (Open M-Sa 7:30am-8:30pm, Su 8:30am-10:30pm.) **Trains** head to: **Braşov** (7hr., 4 per day, L340,000); **Bucharest** (3½hr., 7 per day, L280,000); **Cluj-Napoca** (12hr., 2 per day, L550,000); **Costineşti** (40min., 14 per day, L20,000); **Iaşi** (8hr., 2 per day, L290,000); **Mangalia** (1¼hr., 14 per day, L30,000); **Neptun** (50min., 14 per day, L25,000). Buy tickets in advance in summer. **Buses** and **microbuses** leave for **Mangalia,** stopping at various resorts on the way, from the parking lot next to the train station (20-40min., every 5-10min., L15,000-26,000). Local buses #23E and #41 run from the train station to **Mamaia.** (L20,000. Buy tickets on board.) Northbound buses leave from **Autogara Tomis Nord** (from the train station, go 5 stops on bus #100 or 9 on bus #43 and head left) to **Tulcea** (1½hr., 25 per day, L140,000). **Ferries** travel along the coast to **international destinations** as far as **Istanbul** (2 days, 1-2 per week; €50).

ORIENTATION AND PRACTICAL INFORMATION. To reach the center from the train station, take bus #2, 5, 40, or 43 to the intersection of **Bd. Tomis** and **Bd. Ferdinand.** Buy tickets (L10,000 per trip) in *Bilete RATC* kiosks. Validate your ticket on the bus, or risk a L500,000 fine. **Trans Danubius Tourist Office,** Bd. Ferdinand 36, provides **maps.** (☎61 58 36. Open M-Sa 9am-8pm, Su 9am-2pm.) **Banca Comercială Română,** Str. Traian 1, cashes AmEx/MC **traveler's checks** for 1.5% commission. (☎61 95 00. Open M-F 8:30am-5:30pm, Sa 8:30am-12:30pm.) **Luggage storage** is at the train station. (L32,000 per day; big bags L64,000. Open 24hr.) The **pharmacy** is at Bd. Tomis 80. (☎61 19 83. Open 24hr.) There is a **telephone office** on the corner of Bd. Tomis and Str. Ştefan cel Mare. (Open daily 7am-10pm.) For 24hr. **Internet access,** try the cafe opposite the post office. (L20,000 per hr., midnight-8am L55,000 for 8hr.) The **post office,** which offers **Western Union** services, is at Bd. Tomis 79-81. (Open M-F 7am-7pm, Sa 8am-1pm.) **Postal Code:** 900669.

Black Sea Coast of Romania

ACCOMMODATIONS AND FOOD. It is difficult to find a cheap bed in Constanţa; in high season, call ahead for reservations. You may find better deals in nearby Mamaia (p. 649), an easy commute away. **Hotel Tineretului ❷,** Bd. Tomis 20-26, has comfortable doubles with private baths. Facing the sea, follow Bd. Tomis to the right toward Pţa. Ovidiu. (☎61 35 90. Doubles L800,000.) **Hotel Sport ❸,** Str. Cuza Vodă 2, near the beach, has pleasant singles (L750,000) and doubles (L930,000) with striking views. Take Bd. Ferdinand to the water and go left on Str. Cuza Vodă. Getting a room here can be essentially impossible. (☎61 75 58. Breakfast included.) **Hotel Corna ❹**, Bd. Mamaia 201, has rooms with fat mattresses, A/C, TV, fridges, and lovely balconies. (☎55 55 75. Breakfast included. English reception 24hr. Doubles L1,500,000.) Fast-food joints and pizzerias line Str. Ştefan cel Mare, a tourist-trodden walkway parallel to Bd. Ferdinand. At the corner of Bd. Ferdinand and Bd. Tomis, the **Grand Supermarket** has groceries. (Open 24hr.) The fantastic seafood at ◪**On Plonge ❶** is wildly popular. With the sea to your left, follow the coast to the blue-and-white structure on the Marina. Dine on the dock or inside amid water-themed mosaics. (☎60 19 05. Entrees L50,000-250,000. Open daily 10am-1am.) The **Irish Pub ❸**, Str. Ştefan cel Mare 1, has beach views and is far more upscale than the name suggests. Try the beef marinated in Guinness (L170,000) or stick with seafood. (☎55 04 00; www.irishpub.ro. Entrees L100,000-350,000. Beer L40,000-55,000. Open daily 10am-1am.) **La Scoica ❶**, Str. Aprodul Purice 5, has a funky, aquarium-filled interior. It's known as a pizzeria but also serves pasta, fish, and meat dishes. (☎61 41 64. Entrees L70,000-320,000. Open 24hr.)

🄶 **SIGHTS.** Head straight down Bd. Ferdinand to reach **Tomis,** the Old Town. Make a right at Bd. Tomis to reach **Pţa. Ovidiu.** In the square's center stands the **Statue of Ovid,** who wrote here while in exile. He was ostensibly exiled for writing *The Art of Love,* although the real reason was more likely his practice of that art with Emperor Augustus's daughter. The epitaph on the statue is Ovid's own verse: "Here lies Ovid. The singer of delicate loves, killed by his own talent. Oh, passerby, if you have ever loved, pray for him to rest in peace." The poet's actual resting place is not under the statue, but somewhere in the Black Sea. The nearby **Museum of National and Archaeological History** (Muzeul de Istorie Naţională şi Arheologie), Pţa. Ovidiu 2, is famous for its collection of "heathen" statuettes, mostly of Greek deities, hidden in the 4th century when Christianity became the Roman Empire's official religion. Check out the collection of long-stemmed pipes. (☎61 87 63. Open daily summer 9am-8pm; low season W-Su 9am-5pm. L20,000, students L10,000.) Behind the museum is the **Edificial Roman Mosiac.** When it was built in the 4th century AD, this Roman port contained the **world's largest floor mosaic,** which covers 2000 sq. meters. After a 6th century earthquake, the site was too expensive to rebuild and was converted to a garbage dump, ironically preserving the ruins until their rediscovery in 1959. Though incomplete and faded, the remaining 700m sq. of mosaic are still quite impressive. (English placards. Open daily summer 9am-8pm; low season W-Su 9am-5pm. L40,000.)

The crescent atop its minaret visible from Pţa. Ovidiu, **Moscheia Carol I** is one of the few remaining vestiges of Turkish domination. Dating from 1823 and rebuilt in 1910 by Romanian King Carol I, this **mosque** combines Byzantine, Romanian, and Turkish architecture. On its floor lies one of the world's largest **Oriental carpets** (144m sq.), an 18th-century Turkish piece presented by the Sultan himself. Climb the 140 stairs of the **minaret** for a wonderful view of the city and coastline. Women must cover their heads. (Open daily June-Sept. 9:30am-9:30pm; Oct.-May services only. L30,000, students L15,000.) Also on Str. Arheipiscopei is the gold-domed **Cathedral of Sf. Petru şi Pavel,** which has traditional Wallachian architecture and striking porch frescoes. The **Naval History Museum** (Muzeul Marinei Române), Str. Traian 53, dazzles with its instruments, uniforms, and models. Its most precious piece is the 700-year-old trunk boat, carved from a single tree. (☎61 90 35. Open Tu-Su 10am-6pm. L30,000, students L15,000.) The **archaeological park,** opposite Trans Danubius on Bd. Ferdinand, offers respite among Greek amphorae and Roman sarcophagi.

■ NIGHTLIFE. In summer, much of Constanţa's social life leaks into nearby resorts, especially Mamaia. **Club New Orleans,** Str. Siretului 76, does its namesake proud with four levels of bars. Music varies from house to Latin to rock. (☎60 95 57. Drinks from L50,000. Open M-F noon-2am, Sa-Su 6pm-last customer.) **Megalos Pub** is across the street from La Scoica on Str. Aprodul Purice. Experience hip-hop and house amidst a Stone-Age decor. (Beer L30,000-100,000; M-W tequila L25,000. Tu rock. Open daily 9pm-last customer.)

▶ DAYTRIP FROM CONSTANŢA: DANUBE DELTA (DELTA DUNARII).
Here the mighty Danube, the 2850km river of nine countries and four capitals, pours into the Black Sea with savage beauty. The youngest region of the European continent, the Delta is home to over 200 species of birds, 1150 species of plants, and considerably fewer humans. An internationally recognized wildlife habitat, the wetlands are ideal for fishing and photo-safaris. The region is very far off the tourist track and can be sampled in a day-long or overnight trip from Constanţa or Bucharest. From the train or bus station in Tulcea (TOOL-chuh), face the river and turn right to get to the **Tourist Information Office,** where you can pick up maps and info. (☎0240 519 130; tourisminfo_tulcea@yahoo.com.) At the docks, you can hire a small **boat** (around L1,000,000) to take you on a tour route through the Delta; stock up on explanatory literature beforehand. Inquire in the major hotels around town, as many organize river expeditions.

The best way to experience the Delta is by taking a ferry to a town downstream. Visit **Sfântu Gheorghe,** a tiny fishing village on an island at the very tip of the southern branch, which has only two public telephones, a lighthouse, about 300 houses, and a fantastic stretch of beach. The sand streets don't even have names. Ferries depart from Tulcea in the red and white building behind the bus lot. (5hr. Ferries depart 1:30pm M and W-F, return 6am Tu, Th-F, Su. L150,000.) A tractor shuttles visitors back and forth from the docks to the most popular beach, which is 3km to the right down the marsh-lined main road. You may be offered **private rooms** at the dock; for a sure bet and good home-cooking, stay with "Tanti" **Tina Cazacu ❶,** house #240. Walk down the street marked by the church and make the first right. "Aunt" Tina offers comfortable, rustic rooms and serves the daily catch. Get a Romanian-speaker to call ahead, and she'll meet you at the dock. (☎54 68 22. Lunch and dinner included. L400,000.) After a day at the beach, head to **Zorile ❶,** a market, restaurant, and pool hall located toward the docks from the telephone and post office. Zorile also arranges tours. (☎0745 175 155. Open daily 7am-1pm and 5pm-midnight. Tour 3-5hr.; L150,000-300,000.) (*Minibuses head to Tulcea from Constanta's Autogara Tomis Nord—1¾hr., 25 per day 9am-7pm, L140,000— and from Bucharest's Gara de Nord—4 hr., 15 per day 5am-5pm, L300,000.*)

BLACK SEA RESORTS ☎(0)241

The coast south of Constanţa is lined with sandy beaches and 70s-style tourist resorts. **Mamaia** is closest to Constanţa and remains perpetually over-crowded. **Costineşti** is especially popular with young Romanians, while **Neptun** has the most luxurious amenities. **Mangalia** is the farthest from the city, and the least touristed. Resorts are open late June through early Sept. and on May 1, which is a school holiday. Peak season hits July 1 to August 15, bringing with it heavy crowds and high prices. Reserve rooms well ahead.

MAMAIA

The all-purpose behemoth of Romanian resorts, crowded Mamaia makes for a quick beach holiday and is easily accessible. Of all the Black Sea resorts, it sports the widest array of watersports and nightlife options (all are on the main pedestrian strip.) To reserve rooms in advance, call the **Dispecerat de Cazare** (☎555 555). Lakeside **Hotel Saguna ❷**, behind the reddish Hotel Piccadilly, offers small, basic rooms with shared bath. (☎ 831 956. Singles L650,000; doubles L1,000,000.) The **Hanul Piratilor** (Pirate's Inn) ❷ has a bungalow colony. (☎ 831 702. Bungalows from €20.) Toward the northern end of the strip, past the **nude beach**, there are several **campgrounds** (around L150,000). Produce stands, pastry kiosks, fast-food joints, and the occasional sit-down restaurant dot the area, but for serious dining it's best to head back to Constanţa. Soak up rays on the wonderful beach, or check out **Aqua Magic**, a full-scale water park on Bd. Mamaia, next to Hotel Perla. Visitors enjoy inner tubes, waterslides (like the "Space Bowl" and the "Black Hole"), and, of course, island bars. (Open daily 9am-8pm. L300,000, L150,000 if you're under 1.5m tall.) To reach Mamaia from **Constanţa**, take the #23E and #41 from the train station. (20 min; L20,000.)

COSTINEŞTI

Costineşti (coh-stee-NEHSHT) is the coast's undisputed hot spot. Crowded with young Romanians, it offers loud fun at low prices. Many indulge in Costineşti's **lake** by renting **boats** and **hydrobikes**. Hot running water is not a sure thing, so check at your hotel or villa. From the main street, head right at the **boardwalk**. You'll find several **night clubs** and **Albatros ❷**, which offers villa rooms near the sea with fridges, showers, and hot water. Reception is just past the lake and has "Albatros" written on the wall. (July 15-Aug. 14 doubles L700,000, June 30-July 14 and Aug. 15-Sept. 1 L480,000.) **Hotel Azur ❸**, farther along, offers comfortable, modern rooms with private showers and hot water. (☎73 40 14. Doubles L1,050,000; 4-person apartments L1,500,000.) **Cheap meals** abound near the train station, on the main street, and on the terraces overlooking the coast. A swankier option is the traditional **Restaurant Rustic Poieniţa ❶**, on the right before the lake. (☎73 40 21. Entrees L55,000-190,000. Open 24hr.) Follow the main street to **Disco Ring,** where Romanian youth groove on the outdoor dance floor, which has smoke machines and multicolored lights. (Open daily noon-6pm and 9pm-6am. Cover L25,000 after 9pm.) If you are arriving by **train,** get off at "Costineşti Tabără," make a right facing the station to reach the beach, and take a left to **Str. Tineretului**, the main street. Trains go to **Constanţa** (40min., 14 per day, L12,000) and **Neptun** (10min., 14 per day, L11,000). The makeshift **bus** station is at the red benches in front of the Internet cafe on the main street. Check in Constanţa to be sure your bus is stopping in Costineşti. Return buses depart for **Constanţa** (30min., 22 per day, L30,000).

NEPTUN

Neptun is well-known for its carriage rides and tasty cuisine. Its two fresh-water lakes are ingeniously named Neptun I and Neptun II; they're sandwiched between the main road and the pristine **beach**. Straddle an oversized rubber banana (L80,000 per 15min.) for a motorboat-pulled joyride around the sea. You can also explore the area on **jetskis** (L600,000 per 10min.) or **waterskis** (L100,000 per 30min). The three branches of **Dispecerat de Cazare** in Neptun help tourists find rooms for low prices. Try the 24hr. location in Hotel Apollo, near the bank. Call ahead. (☎70 13 00. Open May-Sept. Hotel singles L130,000-1,050,000. 10% commission.) From the post office on the main street, walk 300m and go left on the street that leads to Jupiter to reach **Campe Zodiac ❶**, the cheapest place to spend the night and one of the coast's better campgrounds. (Sites L120,000; tent rental L30,000.) ▧**Restaurant Insula ❷**, on a deck overlooking Lake Neptun I, has truly excellent seafood. It's toward the beach on the street marked by Hotel Dobregea. (☎70 13 06. Entrees L100,000-1,000,000. Open daily 8am-2am. MC/V.) **Disco Why**

Not, in the shopping center across the street and to the right with your back to the bank, attracts vacationers with house and pop music. (Beer L50,000. Cover L15,000. Open daily 10pm-last customer. **Trains** go to **Constanţa** (50min., 14 per day, L25,000) and **Costineşti** (10min., 14 per day, L11,000). The train station is near the **tourist booth,** which offers English info. A right at the fork gets you to the main street. Most **minibuses** (30min., 22 per day, L40,000) operate through Mangalia; you may have to go to Managlia to return to Constanţa. Practical services are available on the nameless main street.

MANGALIA, 2 MAI, AND VAMA VECHE

The beginning and end of resort minibus routes, Mangalia is a base to explore the southern coast. Beyond most tourists' reach, the town has pristine beaches. The adventurous venture far from civilization by bike or foot. To get here from Bulgaria, cross the Romanian border at Durankulak, BUL, by foot or private car (about €5). Customs are slow; it's often quicker to walk the 3.5km.

From in front of the Mangalia train station, **minibuses** go to **2 Mai** (10min., every 15min. in summer 5am-9pm, L15,000) and **Vama Veche** (15min., every 20min. in summer 5am-9pm, L16,000). An **ATM** stands on the left side of **Casa Rosemarie** (see below). While at the beach, **store luggage** (L30,000) at the train station. The **post office** (open M-Sa 7:30am-7:30pm), to the left when facing the train station, through the traffic circle and past the archaeology museum, has **telephones** and **fax.** With *cazare* signs in hand, locals swarm at the Mangalia train station, and offer inexpensive **private rooms** (a negotiable L300,000). Mangalia's most illustrious hotel, **Hotel President ❺,** 6 Teilor str, boasts sparkling rooms, incredible views, and organized beach excursions. (☎241 755 861; www.hpresident.com. Breakfast included. Singles L1,700,000; doubles L2,700,000.) The north end of 2 Mai's beach has a **campground ❶,** which includes sink, shower, and toilet. (☎722 731 724. L80,000.) At the beach's south end, you can camp for free at the **nude beach.** A few kilometers from the Bulgarian border, at Vama Veche, camp for free on the beach or arrange **private rooms** at **Dispecerat de Cazare.** (☎722 889 087; www.vamavecheholidays.ro. Open June-Sept. Rooms L200,000-1,000,000.) Back in Mangalia at **Casa Rosemarie ❷,** you can choose from a variety of salads and entrees, including giant burritos (L198,000). Walk 1km to the left when facing the train station, past the archaeology museum. (☎724 319 564. Entrees L70,000-250,000. Open daily 10am-11pm.)

RUSSIA (РОССИЯ)

RUSSIA

Fourteen years after the fall of the USSR, mammoth Russia struggles to redefine itself. Cosmopolitan Moscow gobbles down hyper-capitalism, majestic St. Petersburg struggles not to become a ghost capital, and provincial towns seem frozen in time. Russia is in many ways the ideal destination for a budget traveler—inexpensive with good public transportation and hundreds of monasteries, fortresses, and churches. While communism's legacy endures through present-day bureaucratic nightmares, Russia offers a mixture of opulent tsarist palaces, fossilized Soviet edifices, and a profusion of theaters and museums, bearing witness to one of the richest cultural heritages on Earth.

HISTORY

EARLY SETTLERS. The earliest recorded settlers of European Russia were the Scandinavian **Varangians,** or **Rus,** in the AD 9th century. In the 862, several tribes appointed **Ryurik** as their leader, and the center of power moved to **Kyiv. Volodymyr the Great** laid the foundations of **Kyivan Rus** by converting to **Orthodox Christianity** in 988. Following the death of Volodymyr in 1015, the Kyivan state was increasingly strained by clan wars and declining trade.

TATAR CONTROL. European Russia was in no position to resist the march of the Mongol **Golden Horde,** which arrived in 1223. Despite myths to the contrary, the Mongol conquest was not particularly violent and most of the subjected city-states were able to carry on as before. Mongol influence on the culture of the Varangian and East Slavic tribes was minimal, but this period saw increasing contact between Russia and Western and Central Europe, and the emergence of **Muscovy**

FACTS AND FIGURES

OFFICIAL NAME: Russian Federation

CAPITAL: Moscow (pop. 9.3 million)

POPULATION: 145 million (Russian 81.5%, Tatar 4%, Ukrainian 3%, Chuvash 1%, Bashkir 1%, Belarusian 1%, Moldovan 0.5%, other 8%)

LANGUAGE: Russian

CURRENCY: 1 ruble (R) = 100 kopeks

RELIGION: 74% unaffiliated, 16% Russian Orthodox Christian, 10% Muslim

LAND AREA: 16,995,800km²

CLIMATE: Temperate to subarctic

GEOGRAPHY: Western plains, Ural Mountains, Siberian plateau

BORDERS: Belarus, China, Estonia, Finland, Georgia, Kazakhstan, Latvia, Lithuania, Mongolia, Poland, Ukraine, others

ECONOMY: 61% Services, 28% Industry, 11% Agriculture

GDP: US$8800 per capita

COUNTRY CODE: 7

INTERNATIONAL DIALING PREFIX: 8-10

Western Russia

(today's Moscow) as a commercial center. Eventually the Mongol Khanate fell victim to wars between competing local rulers, permitting Muscovy, **Lithuania, Novgorod,** and the **Volga Bulgar Region** (later Kazan) to become powerful states.

IVANS AND BORIS AND BOYARS, OH MY! Duke of Muscovy **Ivan III** (1462-1505) filled the void left by the departure of the Mongols and began a drive to unify all East Slavic lands—parts of present-day Belarus, Russia, and Ukraine—under his rule. His grandson **Ivan IV (the Terrible)** was the first ruler to take the title "tsar." Ivan's second son, **Fyodor I,** proved too weak to rule alone. His brother-in-law **Boris Godunov** secretly ruled in his stead. When Fyodor died childless in 1598, Boris became tsar. Conspiring against Godunov, the Russian **boyars** (nobles) brought forward a pretender named Dmitry who claimed Fyodor I had been his father.

TOP TEN: RUSSIA

1 Best all-nighter: St. Petersburg during White Nights (see sidebar, p. 709).

2 Best museum: the Hermitage, St. Petersburg (p. 708).

3 Best beach: Curonian Spit, (p. 738).

4 Best bunker: Tunnel Night Club, St. Petersburg (p. 720).

5 Best place to be a spy: KGB Museum, Moscow (p. 682).

6 Best tree sap: the Amber Room in Catherine's Palace, Tsarskoye Selo (p. 722).

7 Best night at the opera: Bolshoy Theater, Moscow (p. 685).

8 Best tourist office: Nizhnegorodskiy Hospitality Center, Nizhniy Novgorod (p. 694).

9 Best underground art: Metro stations, Moscow.

10 Best train ride: Trans-Siberian Railroad (p. 739).

After Godunov's mysterious death, the *boyars* crowned this **"False Dmitry"** tsar. Unprecedented instability followed until **Mikhail Romanov** ascended to the throne in 1613, ushering in the dynasty that ruled until the Bolshevik Revolution of 1917.

PETER THE (DEBATABLY) GREAT. Mikhail's grandson **Peter the Great,** whose reign began in 1682, dragged Russia reluctantly westward, inciting the East-West schizophrenia that has plagued its national identity ever since. Peter created a **Westernized** elite, expanded Russia's borders to the Baltic Sea, and built European-style St. Petersburg in the middle of a Finnish swamp. Thousands of workers died in the process, but Peter left Russia with a modernized military and administrative structure when he died in 1725.

ENLIGHTENED ABSOLUTISM. The nobility, jockeying for power, gained political advantage until the reign of **Catherine the Great** (1762-96). The meek, homely daughter of an impoverished Prussian aristocrat, Catherine came to Russia to marry heir to the throne **Peter III,** whom she promptly overthrew. Catherine established a stable regime, extended the empire, and partook of certain **Enlightenment** trends, but she also unharnessed landowners' power over their serfs. This spurred the 1773 **Pugachov rebellion,** a peasant revolt that Catherine quickly trampled.

FRENCH INVASION. In June 1812, **Napoleon** launched a campaign to conquer Russia. The invasion failed as the Russians burned their crops and villages in retreat, leaving the French to face the winter without supplies. **Victory** over "the Corsican" brought prestige and new contact with Western Europe but led to internal strife. Russian officers returning from the West, inspired by the republican ideals of France, attempted the **Decembrist coup** on December 14, 1825. Russia's loss to the West in the **Crimean War** (1853-1856) spurred reforms, including **emancipation of the serfs** in 1861. **Alexander II,** "The Great Emancipator," was assassinated by populists shortly thereafter, hours before he was to introduce Russia's first constitution.

WAR AND PEACE. The famine, peasant unrest, terrorism, and strikes of the late 1800s culminated in the failed **1905 Revolution.** Coupled with the humiliating loss of the **Russo-Japanese War,** the uprising forced **Tsar Nicholas II** to establish a legislative body, the **Duma.** WWI, stalemate with the Duma, and fermenting revolution led him to abdicate the throne in March 1917. Vladimir Ilyich Ulyanov, a.k.a. **Lenin,** leader of the Bolsheviks, steered the coup of October 1917; a few well-placed words to **Aleksandr Kerensky,** leader of the provisional government, and a menacing ring around the Winter Palace turned the nation Red. A **Civil War** followed the October Revolution, but the communists won and the **Union of Soviet Socialist Republics (USSR)** was established in 1922. Iosev Dzhugashvili, better known as **Josef Stalin,** emerged triumphant from the infighting, which followed Lenin's death in 1924, and proceeded to eliminate his rivals in the **Great Purges,** killing and imprisoning millions of Russians and ethnic minorities. Stalin forced **collectivization** of Soviet farms and filled **Siberian gulags** (labor camps) with "political" prisoners.

MORE WAR. Stalin was able to find an ally only in **Adolf Hitler,** with whom he concluded the **Molotov-Ribbentrop Non-Aggression Pact**—more of a stalling tactic than an actual alliance—in August 1939. Later that year the USSR helped Germany in its attack on Poland, and the Red Army subsequently occupied the Baltics. When the Nazi-Soviet alliance finally soured, Stalin brought the USSR into **WWII** unprepared—he had executed most of his top generals in the Purges. Yet Hitler, who didn't learn from Napoleon's mistakes, invaded Russia and was defeated by the long winter combined with the tactics of military commander **Georgy Zhukov.** The **Battle of Stalingrad** (today **Volgograd**), in which 1.1 million Russian troops are thought to have been killed, broke the German advance and turned the tide of the war on the Eastern Front. In 1945, the Soviets took **Berlin** and gained status as a postwar superpower. Stalin, feeling abandoned by the Allies—as Russia had been left to defend the Eastern Front on its own and suffered more casualties than all other participating nations combined—reneged on previous agreements made at the **Yalta Conference** and refused to allow free elections in the nations of Eastern Europe. The USSR left its victorious Red Army in Eastern Europe as far west as East Germany, and the **Iron Curtain** descended on the continent.

BEHIND THE CURTAIN. In 1949, the Soviet Union formed the Council for Mutual Economic Assistance, or **COMECON,** which reduced the Eastern European nations to satellites of the Party's headquarters in Moscow. After Stalin's death in 1953, **Nikita Khrushchev** emerged as the new leader of the Soviet Union. In 1955 the Warsaw Pact drew Eastern Europe into a military alliance with the USSR to counterbalance the **North Atlantic Treaty Organization (NATO)** in the West. In the 1956 **"Secret Speech,"** Khrushchev denounced the terrors of the Stalinist period. He also inaugurated the space race with the US, putting the 84kg **Sputnik,** the first satellite, into orbit in 1957. A brief political and cultural "thaw" followed, lasting until 1964, when Khrushchev was ousted by **Leonid Brezhnev.** The Brezhnev regime remained in power until 1983, overseeing a period of economic stagnation and political repression. Internal dissent was quashed as well, as in the case of exiled physicist **Andrei Sakharov,** the reluctant father of the Soviet H-Bomb, who had become a staunch advocate of disarmament. The short but brutal regimes of **Yuri Andropov** and **Konstantin Chernenko** followed Brezhnev in quick succession. While the Party elites aged and weakened at home, the army became frustrated with its losses in the war against the anti-communist Muslim guerillas in **Afghanistan.** The geriatric regime finally gave way to 56-year-old firebrand **Mikhail Gorbachev** in 1985. Political and economic reform began slowly, with **glasnost** (openness) and **perestroika** (rebuilding). While Gorbachev intended to help Russia regain superpower status, the country gradually turned into a bewildering hodgepodge of near-anarchy, economic crisis, and cynicism. Gorbachev became the architect of his own demise, despite his popularity abroad (and 1990 Nobel Peace Prize). Discontent with reforms, coupled with a failed right-wing coup in August 1991, led to Gorbachev's resignation and the **dissolution of the Soviet Union** on December 25, 1991.

THE PARTY IS OVER. With the collapse of the USSR, **Boris Yeltsin,** named President of the Russian Republic in June 1991, assumed power. The constitution ratified in December 1993 gave the president sweeping powers, but Yeltsin was still powerless to institute lasting reforms. Those economic policies he did attempt came crashing down in August 1998, when the pyramid schemes Russia had played with its natural resources and bond sales were halted abruptly. The ruble was devalued in an attempt to lessen the country's foreign debt. As a result, **inflation** skyrocketed, hitting 84% by the end of 1998. In December of 1991, Russia banded together with many of the other former Soviet republics to create the **Commonwealth of Independent States (CIS),** but the largely symbolic organization has only begun to act as a common economic area. Only Belarus dreams of reunifying with Russia (see **Belarus: Today,** p. 83), and most of the former republics have drifted along their own trajectories.

TODAY. Yeltsin's resignation on January 1, 2000 marked the first-ever voluntary transfer of power by a Russian leader—Soviet leaders had maintained the tsarist tradition of either being forced from office or leaving in a casket. He passed on the presidency to his prime minister, ex-KGB official **Vladimir Putin.** Putin's government has encouraged economic growth and helped stabilize the ruble. In March 2004, Putin appointed a new prime minister, **Mikhail Fradkov,** and won reelection with a supposed 71% of the vote, supported by Russians satisfied with the stability he has created. The road to democracy remains a bumpy one, however. Putin's domestic reform policies often seem more authoritarian than democratic. In response to the Russian military campaign in the separatist province of **Chechnya,** Chechen rebels—including a suicide bomber who blew herself up in central Moscow in December 2003—have killed numerous Russian civilians.

PEOPLE AND CULTURE

LANGUAGE

Take time to familiarize yourself with the **Cyrillic** alphabet (p. 52). It's not as difficult as it might look and it will make getting around much easier. Once you get the hang of the alphabet, you can pronounce just about any Russian word, though you will probably sound like an idiot. Although more and more people are speaking **English,** come equipped with at least a few helpful Russian phrases. Note that улица (ulitsa; abbreviated ul./ул.) means "street," переулок (pereulok; per./пер.) means "lane," проспект (prospekt; pr./пр.) means "avenue," площадь (ploshchad; pl./пл.) means "square," and бульвар (bulvar; bul./бул.) is "boulevard." Кремль (kreml; fortress); рынок (rynok; market square); гостиница (gostinitsa; hotel); собор (sobor; cathedral); and церков (tserkov; church) are also good words to know. Also helpful is the all-purpose можно (MOHZH-nuh) which means literally "Is it possible?" and figuratively almost anything. For a phrasebook and glossary, see **Glossary: Russian, p. 958**.

DEMOGRAPHICS AND RELIGION

The **atheist** program of the communists discouraged the open expression of religious faith. But with the fall of the USSR, **Russian Orthodoxy,** headed by **Patriarch Aleksey II,** has emerged from hiding and is now winning converts. Despite the Patriarch's claim that the Orthodox Church does not seek state status, the Russian state has favored the Orthodox Church by making it difficult for other religious groups to own property or worship in public. Adherents to Orthodoxy in Russia are predominantly Slavic. Russia is home to over 85 ethnic groups. Most Tatar and Turkish groups in Russia, such a the **Turkmen** of the Caspian Sea region and the **Tatars** around Kazan, are **Muslim; Asiatic Inuits** practice animism and Mongolian-speaking groups, such as the **Buryat,** are **Buddhist.**

FOOD AND DRINK

RUSSIA	❶	❷	❸	❹	❺
FOOD	under 70R	70-150R	151-300R	301-500R	over 500R

Russian cuisine is a medley of dishes both delectable and unusual; tasty *borscht* (борщ; beet soup) can come in the same meal as *salo* (pig fat). The largest meal of the day, *obed* (обед; **lunch**), is eaten at midday and includes: *salat* (салат; salad), usually cucumbers and tomatoes or beets and potatoes with mayonnaise or sour cream; *sup* (суп; soup); and *kuritsa* (куритса; chicken) or *myaso* (мясо; meat), often called *kotlyety* (котлеты; cutlets) or *bifshteks* (бифштекс; beefsteaks). Other common foods include *shchi* (щи; cabbage soup) and *bliny* (блины; pancakes). Ordering a number of *zakuski* (закуски; small **appetizers**) instead of a main dish can save money. Common **desserts** include *morozhenoye* (мороженое; ice cream) or *tort* (торт; cake) with *kofe* (кофе; coffee) or *chai* (чай; tea), which Russians drink constantly. On the streets, you'll see a lot of *shashlyk* (шашлык; barbecued meat on a stick) and *kvas* (квас), a slightly alcoholic dark-brown drink made of fermented rye. Kiosks often carry **alcohol;** imported cans of beer are safe (though warm), but beware of Russian labels—you have no way of knowing what's really in the bottle. *Russky Standart* and *Flagman* are the best **vodkas;** the much-touted *Stolichnaya* is mostly made for export. Among local **beers,** *Baltika* (Балтика; numbered 1 through 7 according to brew and alcohol content) is the most popular and arguably the best. *Baltika* 1 is the weakest (10.5%), *Baltika* 7 the strongest (14%). *Baltikas* 4 and 6 are dark; the rest are lagers. Numbers 3 and 4 are the most popular; 7 is extreme.

CUSTOMS AND ETIQUETTE

Certain actions common in the US may be offensive in Russia. **Whistling** in public is disrespectful, while the "ok" sign may viewed as a **vulgar gesture.** Going through a row or aisle with your back to those you are passing is offensive. Don't praise Petersburg while in Moscow or vice versa—there is a longstanding **rivalry** between the two cities. Decades of collective lifestyle forced people very close together; as a result, the notion of **personal space** is almost nonexistent in Russia. People pack tightly in lines and on buses. When boarding a bus, tram, or Metro car, forceful shoving may be required. On **public transportation,** it's polite for women to give their seats to elderly or pregnant women and women with children. For men, it's gallant to yield seats to all women. Most establishments, even train ticket offices and restaurants, close for a **lunch break** sometime between noon and 3pm. Places tend to close at least 30min. earlier than they claim. "24hr." stores often take a lunch or "technical" break and one day off each week. Visiting a museum in **shorts** and **sandals** is disrespectful. **Women** should wear skirts and cover their heads when visiting Orthodox churches. Many locals say that criminals spot foreigners by their sloppy appearances, so dress up and don't smile when stared at. Russians do wear blue jeans but never wear shorts.

While **dining out,** despite what your mother may have told you, don't put your hands in your lap while eating; put your wrists on the edge of the table. Keep the fork in your left hand and the knife in your right. If, as a guest, you are served **vodka** and do not wish to drink it, in order to avoid offending your hosts, invent a medical excuse or say you will have to drive later. In restaurants in St. Petersburg and Moscow (but nowhere else) a 5-10% **tip** is becoming customary.

THE ARTS

LITERATURE. Ever since Catherine the Great exiled **Alexander Radishchev,** whose *Journey from St. Petersburg to Moscow* documented the dehumanizing nature of serfdom, Russian literature and politics have been bound together. The country's most beloved literary figure, **Alexander Pushkin,** was a Decembrist sympathizer but ultimately chose aesthetics over politics. His novel in verse, *Eugene Onegin,* was a biting take on the his own earlier Romanticism. The 1840s saw a turn, under the goading of **Vissarion Belinsky,** toward Realism. While the **absurdist** works of **Nikolai Gogol** were hardly Realist, they were read as masterful social commentary in his own time. His great novel *Dead Souls* exposed the corruption of Russian society. **Fyodor Dostoyevsky's** psychologically penetrating novels, such as *Crime and Punishment* and *The Brothers Karamazov,* remain classics in Russia and abroad. The same can be said for the sweeping epics of **Leo (Lev) Tolstoy,** who wrote *Anna Karenina* and *War and Peace.* The 1890s saw the rise of **Maksim Gorky,** whose "tramp period" fictions explored the dregs of Russian society and foreshadowed his position as the literary figurehead of the Bolshevik Revolution. **Realism's** last great voice belonged to **Anton Chekhov,** whose dramas and short stories distilled the power of his verbose predecessors.

With the beginning of the 20th century, literature entered its **Silver Age,** with many poets emulating French **symbolism. Alexander Blok** tinted his verse with mystic and apocalyptic hues. Symbolism was soon challenged, however, by the **Acmeist** movement, which prized elegance and clarity over the metaphysical vagueness of the Symbolists. Among the members of the Acmeist moment, **Anna Akhmatova** became known for her haunting, melancholic love verses, and later for *Requiem,* her memorial to the victims of Stalin's purges. Competing with the Acmeists, the **Futurists** embraced industrialization and technology in their verse, with such poets as **Vladimir Mayakovsky** urging that Pushkin be "thrown from the steamship of modernity" as a superfluous relic of the past.

In the 1920s the state mandated **Socialist Realism,** a coerced glorification of socialism. Along with political opponents, the regime targeted the intelligentsia in the Great Purges. **Boris Pasternak** was internally exiled for his Civil War epic *Doctor Zhivago.* Acmeist poet **Osip Mandelstam** composed many of his works in exile before dying in a Siberian *gulag.* The political "thaw" of the early 1960s allowed **Joseph Brodsky** to publish his verse and **Alexander Solzhenitsyn** to publish his novel *One Day in the Life of Ivan Denisovich,* detailing life in a labor camp. **Leonid Brezhnev,** however, plunged the arts into an ice age, from which it has yet to fully recover.

MUSIC AND DANCE. Mikhail Glinka began the modern Russian musical tradition, fusing folk melodies with the European harmonic system. His **ballets** *A Life for the Tsar* (1836) and the Pushkin-inspired *Ruslan and Lyudmila* (1842) remain in the repertoire of opera companies today. **Pyotr Tchaikovsky,** closest to Belinsky's Western-minded school, tempered native melodies with European convention. His *Piano Concerto No. 1 in B Flat Minor* (1874-5) and *Symphony No. 6 "Pathetique"* (1893) are highly regarded, as are his ballets, including *Swan Lake* (1895) and *The Nutcracker* (1892). The work of **Nikolai Rimsky-Korsakov,** best known for the symphonic suite *Scheherazade* (1888), in contrast, was bombastically Slavophilic. The early 20th century brought revolutionary ferment and artistic experimentation. This period saw the collaboration of composers **Igor Stravinsky** and **Sergei Diaghilev,** impresario of the Paris-based **Ballets Russes.** It was for Diaghilev's company that Stravinsky wrote his three greatest ballets: *The Firebird* (1910), *Petrushka* (1911), and *The Rite of Spring* (1913). *The Rite of Spring* was so unconventional that it caused a riot in the theater during its Paris premiere. The revolution of 1917 imposed ideological restrictions on such great composers as **Dmitri Shostakovich.** Despite repeated falls from official favor, Shostakovich maintained his stylistic integrity, often satirizing the unwitting Soviet authorities in his famous symphonies. His contemporary **Sergei Prokofiev** enjoyed more consistent official favor, composing a variety of excellent pieces from *Peter and the Wolf* (1936) to symphonies, concertos, and scores for Eisenstein's films. Virtuoso pianist and composer **Sergei Rachmaninov** fused the traditional romanticism of the Westernizer school with a unique lyricism, producing lasting works, including *Rhapsody on a Theme of Paganini* (1934).

ARCHITECTURE, FINE ARTS, AND FILM. St. Basil's Cathedral (the onion-domed building; see p. 676) epitomizes the splendor that is Russian architecture. This style of architecture dates back to the 11th century, when church construction began to follow a general design: a Greek cross, with all four arms equal in length; high walls with almost no openings; a sharply sloped roof; and a plethora of **domes** to top it all off. The period following the revolution saw the **fine arts** gain in prominence Russian music and literature had long enjoyed, with artists **Wassily Kandinsky,** Belarusian-born **Marc Chagall,** and neo-Primitivist **Natalya Goncharova** gaining international acclaim. Kandinsky, of Russian and Mongolian ancestry, is acknowledged as one of the pioneers of **Abstraction.** He was convinced as a child that each color had its own "internal life." Soviet-period artists, confined by the strictures of **Socialist Realism,** were limited to painting canvases with such bland titles as "The Tractor Drivers' Supper." Among the filmmakers of the young Soviet Union was **Sergei Eisenstein,** whom some consider the greatest **filmmaker** ever.

CURRENT SCENE. With the collapse of the Soviet Union, Russia has seen a rebirth of many artists. Modern architecture has assumed a more traditional Russian **folk** character. Writers such as **Dmitry Prigov, Victor Pelevin,** and **Lev Rubenstein** can now publish freely, but the fabric of their work has changed little. Russian filmmakers agree that lack of money has prevented the production of new masterpieces, and an esteemed look at nature and **post-communist** life continues to dominate the plots.

HOLIDAYS AND FESTIVALS

NATIONAL HOLIDAYS IN 2005	
January 1-2 New Year's Holiday	**May 1-2** Labor Day
January 7 Orthodox Christmas	**May 9** Victory Day
January 14 Orthodox New Year	**June 12** Independence Day
February 23 Defenders of the Motherland Day	**November 7** Accord and Reconciliation Day
May 1-2 Orthodox Easter Holiday	**December 12** Constitution Day

During **White Nights,** St. Petersburg celebrates the beautiful sun-filled June nights with musical performances, concerts, fireworks, and other festivities. Maslyanitsa (Butter Festival) is a farewell to winter, occurring in the spring just before Lent, during which people cook delectable dishes, including many, many pancakes.

ADDITIONAL RESOURCES

GENERAL HISTORY

The Icon and the Axe, by James Billington (1966). A classic study of Russian culture.

A People's Tragedy, by Orlando Figes (1996). An amazing overview of the late imperial period, the Russian revolution, and the Civil War.

The Russian Revolution, by Richard Pipes (1990). Remains the authoritative history of the revolutionary era by the foremost authority on Russian history.

FICTION AND NONFICTION

■ **Casino Moscow,** by Matthew Brzezinski (2002). A *Wall Street Journal* reporter's account of his days covering the reality of newly capitalist Russia.

■ **A Day in the Life of Ivan Denisovich,** by Aleksandr Solzhenitsyn (1963). A morally forceful account of life in the *gulag* under the Stalinist regime.

■ **Lenin's Tomb** and **Resurrection,** both by David Remnick (1993 and 1997). The books chronicle the fall of the Soviet Union and post-Soviet life.

RUSSIA ESSENTIALS

ENTRANCE REQUIREMENTS

Passport: Required of all travelers.

Visa: Required of all travelers.

Letter of Invitation: Required of all travelers.

Inoculations: Recommended up-to-date on DTaP (diphtheria, tetanus, and pertussis), Hepatitis A, Hepatitis B, MMR (measles, mumps, and rubella), Polio booster, and Typhoid.

Work Permit: Required for all foreigners planning to work in Russia.

International Driving Permit: Required for all those planning to drive.

DOCUMENTS AND FORMALITIES

EMBASSIES AND CONSULATES

Embassies of other countries in Russia are all in **Moscow** (see p. 665). Russia's embassies and consulates abroad include:

Australia: 78 Canberra Ave., Griffith, ACT 2603 (☎61 02 6295 9033; www.australia.mid.ru).

Canada: 285 Charlotte St., Ottawa, ON K1N 8L5 (☎1 613-235-4341; www.rusembcanada.mid.ru).

China: 100600, Beijing, Dongzhimennei Beizhong str., 4 (☎86 10 6532-2051; www.russia.org.cn/eng).

Ireland: 184-186 Orwell Rd., Rathgar, Dublin 14 (☎353 1 492 2048; www.ireland.mid.ru).

Mongolia: Enkhtayvany Gudamzh, A-6, C.P.O. Box 661, Ulaanbaatar (☎976 11 327 851; embassy_ru@mongol.net).

New Zealand: 57 Messines Rd., Karori, Wellington 6005 (☎64 04 476 61 13; www.rus.co.nz).

UK: 13 Kensington Palace Gardens, London W8 4QX (☎44 020-7229-26-66; www.great-britain.mid.ru).

US: 2650 Wisconsin Ave., N.W., Washington, D.C. 20007 (☎1 202-298-5700; www.russianembassy.org).

RUSSIA

VISA AND ENTRY INFORMATION

Citizens of Australia, Canada, Ireland, New Zealand, the UK, and the US all require a visa to enter Russia. Several types of visas exist. The **standard tourist** visa is valid for 30 days. All Russian visas require an **invitation** stating the traveler's itinerary and dates of travel. They are notoriously difficult to get without a Russian connection; the easiest way is to go through a travel agency.

GETTING A VISA ON YOUR OWN. If you have an invitation from an authorized travel agency and want to get the visa on your own, apply for the visa in person or by mail at a Russian embassy or consulate. Submit your original invitation; your passport; two completed applications; two passport-sized photographs; a cover letter stating your name, dates of arrival and departure, cities you plan to visit in Russia, date of birth, and passport number; and a money order or certified check (single-entry 30-day visas: 6-10 business day processing US$100, 3 business days US$150, next business day US$200, same day US$300; double-entry visas add US$50, except on 6-10 day processing; multiple-entry add US$150, except on 6- to 10-day processing; prices change constantly, so check with the embassy). If you have even tentative plans to visit a city, add it to your visa.

TRAVEL AGENCIES. Travel agencies that advertise discounted tickets to Russia often are also able to provide invitations and visas to Russia (from US$150), but they require at least three weeks notice. HOFA and Red Bear Tours (see below) require that you book accommodations with them.

Host Families Association (HOFA), 5-25 Tavricheskaya ul., 193015 St. Petersburg, RUS (☎812 275 19 92; www.hofa.us). Arranges homestays in the former Soviet Union. Visa invitations (€30, non-guests €50) available for Russia, Ukraine, and Belarus. Single rooms with breakfast start at €30. Discounts for stays over 7 days; €5 discount per day Oct.-Feb. Arranges Russian tutors, theater tickets, meals, and airport pickup.

Info Travel, 387 Harvard St., Brookline, MA 02446, USA (☎617-566-2197; www.infor-travel.com). Invitations and visas to Russia start at US$175. Also provides visas and invitations throughout the CIS.

Red Bear Tours/Russian Passport, 401 St. Kilda Rd., ste. 11, Melbourne 3004, AUS (☎9867 3888; www.travelcentre.com.au). Invitations to Russia and the Central Asian Republics. Also sells rail tickets for the Trans-Siberian, Trans-Manchurian, Trans-Mongolian, and Silk routes. Arranges tours.

VISAtoRUSSIA.com, 309A Peters St. Atlanta, GA 30313, USA (☎404-837-0099; www.visatorussia.com). Russian visa invitations from US$30. Also provides visas and invitations throughout the CIS.

Russia House, 1800 Connecticut Ave., NW, Washington, D.C. 20009, USA (☎202-986-6010; www.russiahouse.org). Branch, 44 Bolshaya Nikitskaya, Moscow 121854, RUS (☎7 095 290 34 59). Invitations and visas to Russia start at US$250.

ENTERING RUSSIA. The best way to cross the border is to **fly** directly into Moscow or St. Petersburg. Another available option is to take a **train** or **bus** into one of the major cities. This option, while easy, can also be frustrating. Expect long delays and red tape. Russian law dictates that all visitors must **register** their visas within three days of arrival. Many hotels will register your visa for you, as should the organizations listed above, but can only do so if you fly into a city where they are represented. Some travel agencies in Moscow and St. Petersburg (see **Tourist and Financial Services,** p. 663 and 705) will also register your visa for approximately US$30. As a last resort, or if you enter the country somewhere other than the two major cities, you'll have to head to the central OVIR (ОВИР) office, called UVIR

(УВИР) in Moscow, to register. Many travelers skip this purgatory, but it is the law and taking care of it will leave one less thing over which bribe-seeking authorities can hassle you—typical fines for visa non-registration are US$150. While in Russia, have your **passport** on you at all times. Police may ask to see your passport.

 BEFORE YOU GO See **Essentials: Safety and Security,** p. 18 for info on how to find the latest travel advisories. The US State Department has issued a travel advisory regarding bringing Global Positioning Systems (GPS), cellular phones, and other radio transmission devices into Russia. Regardless of whether you intend to use it, you cannot bring a **cell phone** into Russia without prior permission from a Russian service provider and proper documentation.

GETTING AROUND

BY PLANE

Most major international carriers fly into **Sheremetyevo-2,** Moscow's international airport, or **Pulkovo-2** in St. Petersburg. **Aeroflot,** Frunzenskaya Naberezhnaya 4 (☎ 095 245-3851; www.aeroflot.ru) is the most popular carrier. The majority of domestic routes are served by Soviet-model planes, many of which are in disrepair and have a poor safety record.

BY TRAIN OR BUS

In a perfect world, everyone would fly into St. Petersburg or Moscow, skipping customs officials who tear packs apart and demand bribes, and avoiding Belarus entirely. But it's not a perfect world, and you'll likely find yourself on a eastbound **train.** If that train is passing through **Belarus** you will need to obtain US$100 transit visa before your trip. **Domestically,** trains are generally the best option. Weekend or holiday trains between St. Petersburg and Moscow sometimes sell out a week in advance. If you plan far enough ahead, you'll have your choice of four **classes.** The best class is *lyuks* (люкс; lux), with two beds, while the second-class *kupeyniy* (купетний) has four bunks. The next class down is *platskartnyy* (плакартный), an open car with 52 shorter, harder bunks. Aim for places 1-33. Places 34-37 are next to the unnaturally foul bathroom, while places 38-52 are on the side of the car and get uncomfortably hot during the summer. **Women traveling alone** can try to buy out a *lyuks* compartment for security, or can travel *platskartnyy* with the regular folk and depend on the crowds to shame potential antagonists into silence. *Platskartnyy* is also a good idea on the theft-ridden St. Petersburg-Moscow line, as you are less likely to be targeted there. The fourth class, *obshchiy* (общий), may be devoid of crooks, but you'll be traveling alongside livestock.

Buses, slightly less expensive than trains, are better for shorter distances. However, they are often crowded and overbooked. Don't be shy about ejecting people who try to sit in your seat.

BY BOAT

Cruise ships stop in the main Russian ports: St. Petersburg, Murmansk, and Vladivostok. They usually allow travelers less than 48hr. in the city. In December 2002, a regular ferry route opened between Kaliningrad and St. Petersburg, which operates one to two times per week. Kaliningrad ferries also go to **Poland** and **Germany.** Ferries also traverse St. Petersburg-**Estonia,** Khabarovsk-**China,** Novorossiysk-**Georgia,** Sochi-**Turkey,** Sochi-Georgia, Vladivostok-**Japan,** and Vladivostok-**Korea** routes. A river cruise runs between Moscow and St. Petersburg.

ON THE ROAD

The combination of highly variable road conditions, aggressive **drivers,** and weather can create an interesting driving experience in Russia. Police officers may pull you over seemingly without provocation, and gasoline can be difficult to find. Even so, armed with patience and a sense of humor, driving through Russia can turn out to be a positive experience. **Biking** is relatively rare in Russia, but motorists are generally polite to bikers. Hailing a **taxi** is indistinguishable from **hitchhiking,** and should be treated with equal caution. Most drivers who stop will be private citizens trying to make a little extra cash (despite the recent restriction on this illegal activity). Those seeking a ride should stand off the curb and hold out a hand into the street, palm down. When a car stops, riders tell the driver the destination before getting in; he will either refuse altogether or ask "*Skolko?*" (Сколько?; How much?), leading to protracted negotiations. Non-Russian speakers will get ripped off unless they manage a firm agreement on the price. If the driver agrees without asking for a price, you must ask (sign language works too). **Never get into a car that has more than one person in it.** *Let's Go* does not recommend hitchhiking.

TOURIST SERVICES AND MONEY

There are two types of **tourist** office: those that arrange tours only and those that offer general travel services. The latter are especially eager to assist, particularly with visa registration. While Western-style tourist offices are not very common, big hotels are often home to tourist agencies with English-speaking staff. For accurate maps, the best bet is to buy one at a kiosk on the street. For trekking and adventure travel, consult **Wild Russia** (see **St. Petersburg: Tourist and Financial Services,** p. 705), which plans guided excursions to wilderness destinations.

 PAYING IN RUSSIA Due to the fluctuating value of the Russian ruble, some establishments list their prices in US dollars or euros. For this reason, some prices in this book may appear in US$, but be prepared to pay in rubles.

The **ruble (R)** was redenominated in 1998, losing three zeros, and the old currency has been phased out. Government regulations require that you show your **passport** when you exchange money. Find an *obmen valyuty* (обмен валюты; currency exchange), hand over your currency—most will only exchange US dollars and euros—and receive your rubles. With **inflation** running at around 12%, expect prices quoted in rubles and **exchange rates** to undergo frequent, significant changes. **Do not exchange money on the street. Banks** offer the best combination of good rates and security. You'll have no problem changing rubles back at the end of your trip (just keep exchange receipts), but it's best not to exchange large sums at once, as the rate is unstable. **ATMs** (*bankomat;* банкомат), linked to all major networks and credit cards, can be found in most cities. Banks, large restaurants, ATMs, and currency exchanges often accept major **credit cards,** especially Visa. Main branches of banks will usually accept **traveler's checks** and give cash advances on credit cards. Although you'll have to pay in rubles, it's wise to keep a small amount (US$20 or less) of dollars on hand. Be aware that most establishments do not accept crumpled, torn, or written-on bills of any denomination. Russians are also wary of old US money; bring the new bills.

Normal business hours are 9am-5pm. Banks and many businesses are closed on national holidays.

HEALTH AND SAFETY

 EMERGENCY NUMBERS: Police: ☎02 Fire: ☎01 Emergency: ☎03

In a **medical emergency,** either leave the country or go to the European Medical Centers or American Medical Centers in St. Petersburg or Moscow. These clinics have Western doctors who speak **English.**

Russian **bottled water** is often mineral water; you may prefer to boil or filter your own, or buy imported bottled water at a supermarket. **Water is drinkable** in much of Russia, but not in Moscow and St. Petersburg. Men's **toilets** are marked with an "M," women's with a "Ж." The 0.5-5R charge for public toilets generally gets you a hole in the ground and a piece of toilet paper; carry your own. **Pharmacies** abound and offer a range of Western medicine and hygiene products; look for the "апртека" signs.

Crimes against foreigners are on the rise, particularly in Moscow and St. Petersburg. Although it is often tough to blend in (especially with a huge pack on your back), try not to flaunt your nationality. Reports of **mafia** warfare are scaring off tourists, but unless you bring a shop for them to blow up, you are unlikely to be a target. Due to the violence in the northern Caucasus, avoid the **Dagestan** and **Chechnya** regions. It is extremely unwise to take pictures of anything **military** or to do anything that might attract the attention of a man in uniform—doing something suspicious provides an excuse to detain you or extort money.

The concept of **sexual harassment** hasn't yet reached Russia. Local men will try to pick up women and will get away with offensive language and actions. The routine starts with an innocent-sounding *"Devushka..."* (young lady). Just say *"nyet"* (no) or simply walk away. Women in Russia generally wear skirts or dresses rather than pants. The authorities on the Metro will frequently stop and question **dark-skinned** individuals, who also often receive rude treatment in shops and restaurants. Homosexuality is now officially legal, but **GLBT travelers** are commonly discriminated against, except at the gay clubs in Moscow and St. Petersburg.

ACCOMMODATIONS AND CAMPING

RUSSIA	❶	❷	❸	❹	❺
ACCOM.	under 400R	401-700R	701-1200R	1201-2000R	over 2000R

The only **hostels** in Russia are in St. Petersburg and Moscow, and even those average US$18-25 per night. Reserve well in advance. The hostels that do exist, though, are often English-speaking and amenity-filled.

Russian **hotels** offer several classes of rooms. "Lux," usually two-room doubles with TV, phone, fridge, and bath, are the most expensive. "Polu-lux" rooms are singles or doubles with TV, phone, and bath. The lowest priced rooms are *bez udobstv* (без удобств), which means a room with a sink. Expect to pay 300-450R for a single in a budget hotel. Many establishments accept only cash. In many hotels, **hot water**—sometimes all water—is only turned on for a few hours each day. Reservations are not necessary in smaller towns, but they may help you get on the good side of management, which is often inexplicably suspicious of backpackers.

University dorms offer cheap, livable rooms; some accept foreign students for US$5-10 per night. Don't expect sparkling bathrooms or reliable hot water. Make arrangements through an educational institute from home. In larger cities, **private rooms** and **apartments** can be found for reasonable prices (around 200R per night).

At major train stations, there are usually women with **private rooms** for rent—bargain with them. **Homestays,** which can be arranged through tourist offices, are often the cheapest (50-100R per night) and best option in the countryside.

KEEPING IN TOUCH

Mail service is more reliable leaving the country than coming in. Letters to the US and other destinations take one to three weeks. Domestic mail usually reaches its destination. From abroad, the best way to send letters to Russia is to have friends take them there. Airmail is *avia* (авиа). Send your mail "заказное" (certified; 40R) to reduce the chance of it being lost. Letters to the US cost 16R; postcards 11R. **Poste Restante** is "Письмо До Востребования" (Pismo Do Vostrebovaniya). Address envelopes as follows: MAATS (LAST NAME), Hunter (first name), 103 009 (postal code), Москва (city), Письмо До Востребования, RUSSIA.

Most **public telephones** take **phonecards,** which are good for both local and intercity calls. A 30-unit card costs 85R and is worth around 10min. of international airtime. Cards are sold at central telephone offices, Metro stations, and newspaper kiosks. When you are purchasing phonecards, the attendant will often ask, "На улице?" (Na ulitse; On the street?) to find out whether you want a card for the phones in the station/office or for outdoor public phones. For five-digit numbers, insert a "2" between the dialing code and the phone number. Make direct **international calls** from telephone offices in St. Petersburg and Moscow by first dialing ☎ 079. Calls to Europe run US$1-1.50 per min.; to Australia and the US about US$1.50-2. To make international calls from **Kaliningrad** or the rest of Russia, telephone offices must call through St. Petersburg or Moscow, making the prices go through the roof. International access codes include: **AT&T,** which varies by region, see www.att.com for specific info; **MCI:** Moscow ☎ 960 2222, elsewhere 747 3322; **Sprint:** Moscow ☎ 747 3324, elsewhere dial 8095 before this number; **Canada Direct:** Moscow ☎ 755 5045, elsewhere 810 800 110 1012.

Email is your best bet for keeping in touch while in Russia. Internet cafes are common throughout St. Petersburg and Moscow, but aren't as popular outside these cities. When all else fails, check the post office. Rates for Internet access vary from 20-70R per hour, depending on location and time of day.

MOSCOW (МОСКВА) ☎ (8)095

Like few other cities on Earth, Moscow (pop. 9 million) has an audacious sense of its role as a focal point of world history. Change happens quickly here; Western visitors may feel like they're balancing on a tightrope held tensely between the cosmopolitan and the underworld. When communism swept through, it leveled most of the domes and left behind dust, pain, and countless statues of Lenin. Yet, on the 16th-century side streets, it's still possible to glimpse the same quiet, golden domes that Napoleon saw after conquering the city in 1812. Now that residents are speaking out and rebuilding, Moscow is recreating itself as one of the world's most urbane capitals and embracing innovation with the same sense of enterprise that helped it command and then survive history's most ambitious social experiment.

✈ INTERCITY TRANSPORTATION

Flights: Moscow has many airports. The 2 principal airports are Sheremetyevo (Шереметьево; www.sheremetyevo-airport.ru) and Domodedovo (Домодедово; www.domodedovo.ru). **Sheremetyevo-1** (☎ 578 23 72) and **Sheremetyevo-2** (☎ 956 46

RUSSIA

66) can be reached by taking bus #551 or 851 or minibuses #48 or 49 from M2: Rechnoy Vokzal or bus #517 from M8: Planyornaya (Планёрная; 10R). **Domodedovo** (☎933 66 66), bus #405 to M2: Domodedovskaya. **Bykovo** (Быково; ☎558 47 38). The bus to and from Tsentralnyy Aerovokzal runs 6:35am-6:35pm. **Vnukovo** (Внуково; ☎436 28 13), take bus #611 to M1: Yugo-Zapadnaya. Buy tickets at the *kassa* (касса) at the **Tsentralnyy Aerovokzal** (Центральный Аэровокзал; Central Airport Station), Leningradskiy pr. 37, corpus 6 (☎941 99 99), 2 stops on almost any tram or trolley from M2: Aeroport (the sign on the front of the bus says Центральный Аэровокзал; Tsentralnyy Aerovokzal). **Taxis** to the center of town are grossly overpriced; bargain down to no more than US$30. **Yellow Taxi** (☎940 88 88) has fixed prices. Cars outside the departure area charge US$15-20. Agree on a price before getting in.

Air France, ul. Koroviy Val 7 (Коровий Вал; ☎937 38 39; fax 937 38 38). M5: Dobryninskaya (Добрынинская). Open M-F 9am-6pm. Branch at Sheremetyevo-2, 2nd fl. (☎578 52 37). Open M-F 6:15am-4:15pm.

British Airways, 1-ya Tverskaya-Yamskaya ul. 23 (1-я Тверская-Ямская; ☎363 25 25; www.britishairways.com). M2: Mayakovskaya (Маяковская). Open M-F 10am-7pm, Sa 10am-2pm.

Delta, 11 Gogolevskiy bul., 2nd fl. (Гоголевский; ☎937 90 90; www.delta.com). M1: Kropotkinskaya (Кропоткинская). Open M-F 9am-6pm. Customer service by phone Sa 9am-1pm.

Finnair, Kropotkinskiy per. 7 (Кропоткинский; ☎933 00 56; www.finnair.com). M1 or 5: Park Kultury (Парк Культуры). Open M-F 9am-5pm. Branch at Sheremetyevo-2 (☎/fax 956 46 23).

Lufthansa, Olimpiyskiy pr. 18/1 (Олимпийский; ☎737 64 00; www.lufthansa.ru), in Hotel Renaissance. M5 or 6: Prospekt Mira (Проспект Мира). Open M-F 9am-6pm and Sa 10am-3pm.

Trains: Moscow has 8 train stations arranged around the circle (M5) line.

Belorusskiy Vokzal (Белорусский), pl. Tverskoi Zastavy 7 (☎973 81 91). M5: Belorusskaya (Белорусская). To: **Kaliningrad** (22hr., 2 per day, 1400R); **Berlin, GER** (27hr., 1 per day, 3500R); **Brest, BLR** (15hr., 3-4 per day, 1250R); **Minsk, BLR** (10hr., 3-4 per day, 750R); **Prague, CZR** (35hr., 1 per day, 2860R); **Vilnius, LIT** (16hr., 1-2 per day, 1950R); **Warsaw, POL** (21hr., 2 per day, 2520R).

Kazanskiy Vokzal (Казанский), Komsomolskaya pl. 2 (Комсомольская; ☎264 31 81). M5: Komsomolskaya. Opposite Leningradskiy Vokzal. To: **Kazan** (12hr., 2 per day, 600R) and **Rostovna-Donu** (20hr., 1-2 per day, 1200R).

Kievskiy Vokzal (Киевский), pl. Kievskogo Vokzala 2 (Киевского Вокзала; ☎240 11 15). M3 or 5: Kievskaya (Киевская). To: **Kyiv, UKR** (14hr., 4 per day, 950R); **Lviv, UKR** (26hr., 2 per day, 1100R); **Odessa, UKR** (25-28hr., 1-2 per day, 1100R).

Kurskiy Vokzal (Курский), ul. Zemlyanoy Val 29/1 (Земляной Вал; ☎917 31 52). M3: Kurskaya (Курская). To: **Sochi** (28hr., 1 per day, 1800R); **Sevastopol, UKR** (26hr., 1-2 per day, 1100R), and the **Caucasus.**

Leningradskiy Vokzal (Ленинградский), Komsomolskaya pl. 3 (☎262 91 43). M1 or 5: Komsomolskaya. To: **St. Petersburg** (8hr., 10-15 per day, 700R); **Helsinki, FIN** (13hr., 1 per day, 2720R); **Tallinn, EST** (14hr., 1 per day, 1550R).

Paveletskiy Vokzal (Павелецкий), Paveletskaya pl. 1 (Павелецкая; ☎235 05 22). M2: Paveletskaya. To: **Astrakhan** (30hr., 1-2 per day, 1450R) and **Volgograd** (20-30hr., 2-4 per day, 800R). Also to: **Armenia; Azerbaijan; Crimea, UKR; Georgia;** eastern **Ukraine.**

Rizhskiy Vokzal (Рижский), Prospekt Mira 79/3 (☎631 15 88). M6: Rizhskaya (Рижская). To: **Rīga, LAT** (16hr., 2 per day, 2050R). Also to **Estonia.**

Yaroslavskiy Vokzal (Ярославский), Komsomolskaya pl. 5a (☎921 08 17). M1 or 5: Komsomolskaya. To: **Novosibirsk** (48hr., every other day, 1900R). Trains also head to **Siberia** and the **Far East.** The starting point for the legendary **Trans-Siberian Railroad** (see p. 739).

Train Tickets: Tickets for long trips within Russia can be bought at the **Tsentralnoye Zheleznodorozhnoye Agenstvo** (Центральное Железнодорожное Агенство; Central Train Agency; ☎266 93 33; www.mza.ru), to the right of Yaroslavskiy Vokzal (see p. 666). Your ticket will have your name and seat on it and tell you at which station (вокзал; vokzal) to catch your train. A Cyrillic schedule of trains, destinations, departure times, and *vokzal* names is posted on both sides of the hall. (*Kassa* open M-F 7am-8pm, Sa-Su 7am-5pm.) 24hr. service is available at the stations. If you plan to take the **Trans-Siberian Railroad** (see p. 739), check out Traveller's Guest House, Hostel Sherstone, Hostel Tramp, or G&R Hostel Asia (see **Accommodations**, p. 672). They explain how the Trans-Siberian works and arrange special tickets that allows you to get on and off the train at all major cities along the way. For shorter lines, try the 2nd location at Malyy Kharitonevskiy per. 6 (Малый Харитоневский; ☎262 06 04). M1 or 6: Turgenevskaya/Chistyye Prudy (Тургеневская/Чистые Пруды). Take a right off ul. Myasnitskaya (Мясницкая); it's the building on the right. Open daily 8am-1pm and 2-7pm.

✦ ORIENTATION

A series of concentric rings radiates from the **Kremlin** (Кремль; Kreml) and **Red Square** (Красная площадь; Krasnaya ploshchad). The outermost street, the **Moscow Ring** (Московское Кольцо; Moskovskoye Koltso), marks the city limits, but most sights lie within the much smaller **Garden Ring** (Садовное Кольцо; Sadovnoe Koltso). The tree-lined **Boulevard Ring**, made up of 10 short, wide boulevards, makes an incomplete circle within the center. **Tverskaya ulitsa** (Тверская), considered Moscow's main street, begins just north of Red Square and continues northwest along the green line of the Metro. The **Arbat** (Арбат) and **Novyy Arbat** (Новый Арбат), Moscow's hippest and most commercialized streets respectively, lie west of the Kremlin. **Zamoskvareche** (Замоскварече) and **Krymskiy Val** (Крымский Вал), the neighborhoods directly across the **Moscow River** to the south of Red Square, are home to numerous pubs, museums, mansions, and monasteries. To the east of Red Square is the 9th-century **Kitai-Gorod** (Китай-Город) neighborhood, packed with towering churches and bustling commercial thoroughfares. English and Cyrillic **maps** (35-60R) are sold at kiosks and bookstores all over the city. See this book's color insert for maps of the Metro and the city center.

☐ LOCAL TRANSPORTATION

Public Transportation: The **Metro** (Метро) is fast, clean, and efficient—a masterpiece of urban planning. A station serving more than 1 line may have more than 1 name. The M5 is known as the circle line (кольцевая линия; koltsevaya liniya). Trains run daily 6am-1am, but catch one by 12:30am to be safe. Rush hours are 8-10am and 5-7pm. Buy fare cards (10R; 5 trips 45R, 10 trips 75R) from *kassy* (singular *kassa*) in stations. Buy **bus** and **trolleybus** tickets at kiosks labeled "проездные билеты" (proyyezdnye bilety), and from the driver (10R). Punch your ticket when you board or risk a 100R fine. Buses run 24hr. Monthly passes (единые билеты; yedinyye bilety), valid for bus, trolleybus, tram, and Metro, are sold at Metro *kassy* after the 18th of the preceding month (500R).

Taxis and Hitchhiking: Most taxis do not use meters and tend to overcharge. To order a taxi, call the central bureau ☎927 00 00, which is open 24hr. Hailing a car on the street is common and always cheaper. Moscovites hold an arm out horizontally (no thumb extended); when the driver stops, they tell him their destination and haggle over the price. Within town, a ride to almost anywhere is 100R; shorter trips cost around 50R. Be aware that even if you hail a car marked "taxi," you may still have to haggle, as many drivers use taxi markings simply to attract riders. Catching a car doesn't guarantee safety; never get into a taxi or car with more than 1 person already in it. *Let's Go* does not recommend hitchhiking.

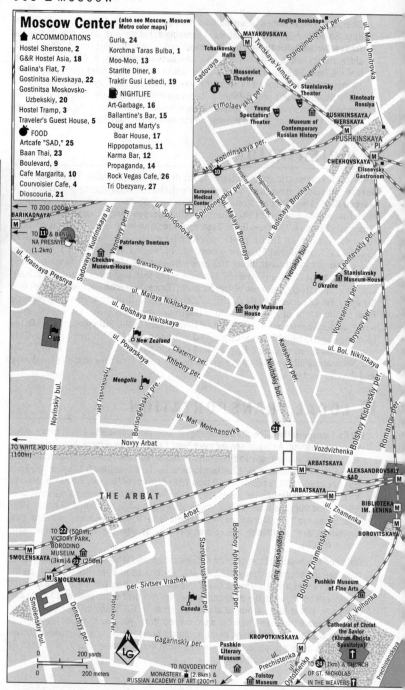

Moscow Center (also see Moscow, Moscow Metro color maps)

▲ ACCOMMODATIONS
Hostel Sherstone, **2**
G&R Hostel Asia, **18**
Galina's Flat, **7**
Gostinitsa Kievskaya, **22**
Gostinitsa Moskovsko-
  Uzbekskiy, **20**
Hostel Tramp, **3**
Traveler's Guest House, **5**

● FOOD
Artcafe "SAD," **25**
Baan Thai, **23**
Boulevard, **9**
Cafe Margarita, **10**
Courvoisier Cafe, **4**
Dioscouria, **21**

Guria, **24**
Korchma Taras Bulba, **1**
Moo-Moo, **13**
Starlite Diner, **8**
Traktir Gusi Lebedi, **19**

◨ NIGHTLIFE
Art-Garbage, **16**
Ballantine's Bar, **15**
Doug and Marty's
  Boar House, **17**
Hippopotamus, **11**
Karma Bar, **12**
Propaganda, **14**
Rock Vegas Cafe, **26**
Tri Obezyany, **27**

RUSSIA

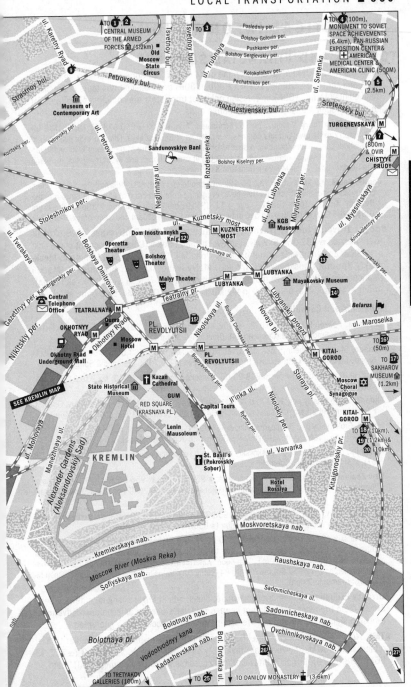

ul. Karetny Ryad

TO **1** **2**
CENTRAL MUSEUM
OF THE ARMED
FORCES 🏛 (1.2km)

TO **3**

Tsvetnoy bul.

Tsvetnoy bul.

Old
Moscow
State
Circus

9

Strastnoy bul.

Petrovskiy bul.

ul. Trubnaya

Posledniy per.

Bolshoy Golovin per.

Pushkarev per.

Bolshoy Sergievskiy per.

Kolokolnikov per.

Pechatnikov per.

TO **4** (100m),
MONUMENT TO SOVIET
SPACE ACHIEVEMENTS
(6.4km), PAN-RUSSIAN
EXPOSITION CENTER&
✚ AMERICAN
MEDICAL CENTER &
AMERICAN CLINIC (500M)

ul. Sretenka

TO **5**
(2.5km)

Museum of
Contemporary Art 🏛

Rozhdestvenskiy bul.

Sretenskiy bul.

Petrovskiy per.

ul. Petrovka

Kozitskiy per.

Neglinnaya ul.

Sandunovskiye Bani

ul. Rozdestvenka

Bolshoy Kiselnyy per.

TURGENEVSKAYA Ⓜ

TO **7**
(800m)
& OVIR

CHISTYYE
PRUDY ✉ Ⓜ

Stoleshnikov per.

ul. Bolshaya Dmitrovka

ul. Kuznetskiy most

Ⓜ KUZNETSKIY
MOST

ul. Bol. Lubyanka

Milyutinskiy per.

KGB 🏛
Museum

ul. Myasnitskaya

Krivokolennyy per.

Armyanskiy per.

ul. Tverskaya

Dom Inostrannykh
Knig **12**

Pyshechnaya ul.

13

Operetta
Theater

Bolshoy
Theater

Malyy Theater

Teatralny pr.

Ⓜ LUBYANKA

LUBYANKA
Ⓜ

🏛 Mayakovsky Museum

14

Belarus ⚑

Kamergerskiy per.

Gazetnyy per.

Central
Telephone
Office ✉

TEATRALNAYA Ⓜ

Duma

OKHOTNYY
RYAD Ⓜ

Okhotny Ryad

Okhotny Ryad
Underground Mall

PL.
REVOLYUTSII

15

Nikolskaya ul.

Bolshoy Cherkasskiy per.

Lubyanskiy proezd

Novaya pl.

ul. Maroseika

TO **16**
(50m)

TO **17**
SAKHAROV
MUSEUM 🏛
(1.2km)

Nikitskiy per.

ul. Mokhovaya

Moskva
Hotel

Ⓜ

PL.
REVOLYUTSII Ⓜ

Bogoyavlenskiy per.

Staraya pl.

KITAI-
GOROD Ⓜ

Moscow ✡
Choral
Synagogue

SEE KREMLIN MAP

State Historical
Museum 🏛

Kazan ✝
Cathedral

GUM

RED SQUARE
(KRASNAYA PL.)

Capital Tours ■

Il'inka ul.

Nikolskiy per.

Rybnyy per.

KITAI-
GOROD Ⓜ

TO **18** (10km),
19 (1.2km)&
20 (10km)

Manezhnaya ul.

Alexander Gardens
(Aleksandrovskiy Sad)

KREMLIN

Lenin
Mausoleum

St. Basil's
(Pokrovskiy
Sobor) ✝

ul. Varvarka

Kitaigorodskiy pr.

Hotel
Rossiya

Kremlevskaya nab.

Moskvoretskaya nab.

Raushskaya nab.

Moscow River (Moskva Reka)

Sofiyskaya nab.

Sadovnicheskaya ul.

Sadovnicheskaya nab.

nab.

Bolotnaya pl.

Vodootvodnyy kana

Kadashevskaya nab.

Bolotnaya nab.

Bol. Ordynka ul.

Ovchinnikovskaya nab.

26

TO **27**

TO TRETYAKOV
GALLERIES (100m)

TO **25**

TO DANILOV MONASTERY ✝ (3.6km)

RUSSIA

🔢 PRACTICAL INFORMATION

TOURIST AND FINANCIAL SERVICES

Tours: The folks with loudspeakers on the north end of Red Square offer walking tours of the area (1hr.; every 30min. 10am-12:30pm; 8OR) and excellent bus tours of the city's main sights (1½hr., 150R). In Russian only, but translators are sometimes available for an extra charge. Many hostels also arrange tours.

Patriarshy Dom Tours, Vspolnyy per. 6 (Вспольньй; from the US ☎650 678 70 76; fax 795 09 27; http://russiatravel-pdtours.netfirms.com). M5 or 7: Barrikadnaya. Offers a wide selection of English language tours including a special behind the scenes tour of the former KGB headquarters ($18). A schedule of their tours is available at various hotels and expat hangouts, including the Starlite diner. Open M-F 9am-6pm and Sa 11am-5pm.

Capital Tours, Ilyinka ul. 4 (☎232 24 42; www.capitaltours.ru). M3: Ploschad Revolutsii. Offers 3hr. bus tours of the city center; they cover everything from Cathedral of Christ the Saviour to the Bolshoy Theater. Tours (US$20, age 4-11 US$10) daily at 11am and 2:30pm. 3hr. tours (US$37/US$20) of the Kremlin and armory M-W and F-Su 10:30am and 3pm. AmEx/MC/V.

Budget Travel: Student Travel Agency Russia (STAR), Baltiyskaya ul. 9, 3rd fl. (Балтийская; ☎797 95 55; www.startravel.ru). M2: Sokol (Сокол). Discount plane tickets, ISICs, and worldwide hostel booking. Open M-F 10am-7pm, Sa 11am-4pm. **Moskovskiy Sputnik** (Московский Спутник), Malyy Ivanovskiy per. 6, corpus 2 (Малый Ивановский; ☎925 92 78; mows@mowsput.ru). M6 or 7: Kitai Gorod (Китай Город). Arranges visas, ISICs, and travel in the Moscow region. Open M-F 9am-6pm. MC/V.

Embassies and Consulates:

Australia, Podkolokolniy per. 10/2. (☎956 60 70; fax 956 61 62). M6: Kitai Gorod (Китай Город). M3: Smolenskaya (Смоленская). Open M-F 9:30am-12:30pm.

Canada, Starokonyushennyy per. 23 (Староконюшенный; ☎105 60 00; fax 232 99 50). M1: Kropotkinskaya or M4: Arbatskaya (Арбатская). Open M-F 8:30am-1pm and 2-5pm.

China, ul. Druzhby 6 (Дружбы; ☎938 20 06, consular section 143 15 40; fax 938 21 82). M1: Universitet (Университет). Open M-F 8:30am-noon and 3-6pm.

Finland, Kropotkinskiy per. 15/17 (☎787 41 74; fax 247 07 45). M1 or 5: Park Kultury. Open M-F 9am-1pm and 2-5pm. Consular section (☎247 31 25) open M-F 10am-noon and 2-4pm.

Ireland, Grokholskiy per. 5 (Грохольский; ☎937 59 11, consular section ☎937 59 02; fax 975 20 66). M5 or 6: Prospekt Mira. Open M-F 9:30am-1pm and 2:30-5:30pm.

Mongolia, consulate at Spasopeskovskiy per. 7/1 (Спасопесковский; ☎244 78 67; fax 244 78 67). M3: Smolenskaya. Open M-F 10am-1pm.

New Zealand, Povarskaya ul. 44 (Поварская; ☎956 35 79; fax 956 35 83). M7: Barikadnaya (Барикадная). Open M-F 9am-5:30pm. Consular section (☎956 26 42) open M-F 9:30-10:30am and 4-5pm.

UK, Smolenskaya nab. 10 (Смоленская; ☎956 72 00; fax 956 74 80). M3: Smolenskaya. Open M-F 9am-1pm and 2-5pm. Consular section (☎956 72 50) open M-F 8am-noon.

US, Novinskiy 19/23 (Новинский; ☎728 50 00; www.usembassy.ru). M5: Krasnoprenenskaya (Краснопресненская). Flash a US passport to cut the long lines. Open M-F 9am-6pm. Consular section (☎728 55 60) open M-F 9am-noon. **American Citizen Services** (☎728 55 77, after-hours emergency 728 50 00; fax 728 50 84) connects citizens to various organizations. Open M-F 9-10:30am and 2-4pm.

Currency Exchange: Banks are everywhere; check ads in English-language newspapers. Except main branches, most do not change **traveler's checks** or issue **cash advances;** a posted sign or sticker stating "We accept traveler's checks" is no guarantee.

ATMs: Nearly every bank and hotel has an ATM that allows withdrawals in either US$ or rubles. Indoor ATMs, however, are invariably safer. **Alphabank,** Varvarka 3 (☎777 33 66 or 788 88 78). M6 or 7: Kitay Gorod. Accessible 24hr. by inserting an ATM card.

American Express: Ul. Usacheva 33 (☎933 84 00). M1: Sportivnaya. Exit to the front of the train, turn right, and then turn right again after the Global USA shop onto Usacheva. Open M-F 9am-6pm.

LOCAL SERVICES

English-Language Bookstores: Angliya British Bookshop, Vorotnikovskiy per. 6 (Воротниковский; ☎299 77 66; www.anglophile.ru). M2: Mayakovskaya. Large selection includes travel guides, phrasebooks, translated Russian literature, and English and American fiction. Open M-F 10am-7pm, Sa 10am-6pm, Su 11am-5pm. ISIC discount. AmEx/MC/V. **Dom Inostrannykh Knig** (Дом Иностранных Книг; House of Foreign Books), ul. Kuznetskiy most 18 (☎928 20 21). M7: Kuznetsky Most. English-language fiction and a modest selection of works in several other European languages. Open M-Sa 10am-8pm. MC/V.

English-Language Press: The *Moscow Tribune* and the more widely read *Moscow Times* (www.themoscowtimes.com) have foreign and national articles for travelers and weekend sections listing upcoming events, English-language movies, housing, and job opportunities. *Where* magazine (www.whererussia.com), publishes monthly shopping, dining, and entertainment listings and has excellent maps. *Element* magazine comes out weekly with interviews, articles, and descriptions of clubs. An "alternative" paper, *The eXile* (www.exile.ru), is one of the funniest and most irreverent papers on earth, but is not for the meek. Nightlife section is indispensably candid, though undeniably crude.

EMERGENCY AND COMMUNICATIONS

Emergencies: Fire: ☎01. **Police:** ☎02. **Ambulance:** ☎03. **Lost property:** Metro ☎222 20 85, other transport 298 32 41. **Lost documents:** ☎200 99 57. **Lost credit cards:** ☎956 35 56. 24hr. free **crisis line** for English speakers: ☎244 34 49. **International Medical Clinic:** ☎280 71 71.

24hr. Pharmacies: Look for "круглосуточно" (kruglosutochno; open around the clock) signs. Tverskaya ul. 25 (☎299 24 59). M2: Tverskaya/Mayakovskaya. Ul. Zemlyanoy Val 25 (☎917 12 85). M5: Kurskaya. Kutozovskiy Prospekt 24 (Кутозовский; ☎249 19 37). M4: Kutuzovskaya (Кутузовская).

Medical Assistance: American Medical Center (AMC), Prospekt Mira 26 (☎933 77 00; fax 933 77 01). M5 or 6: Prospekt Mira. From the Metro, turn left on Grokholskiy per. US$120 per visit. Membership US$50 per yr. Open 24hr. AmEx/MC/V. **American Clinic,** Grokholskiy per. 31 (☎937 57 57; www.klinik.ru). M5 or 6: Prospekt Mira. See directions for AMC. American board-certified doctors; family and internal medicine services. Consultations US$100, house calls US$150. Open 24hr. MC/V. **European Medical Center,** Spiridoniyevskiy Per. 5/1 (☎933 65 55; www.emcmos.ru), M2, 7 or 9: Pushkinskaya. Offers psychiatric, pediatric, gynecological, and dental care and medical evaluations. Consultations €120. Open 24hr.

Telephones: Moscow Central Telegraph (see **Post Offices,** p. 672). To call abroad, go to the 2nd hall with telephones. Pre-pay at the counter, or buy a prepaid phonecard (which works only in the telegraph office). Collect and calling card calls not available. Calls to the US 9-20R per min., to Europe 12-35R per min. **Local calls** require new phone cards, available at some Metro stops and kiosks. Directory assistance ☎09.

Internet Access: Timeonline (☎363 00 60), on the bottom level of the Okhotnyy Ryad mall, near Red Square. M1: Okhotnyy Ryad. At night, enter through the Metro underpass. 30-75R per hr. Open 24hr. **Cafemax** (☎787 68 58; www.cafemax.ru). Massive, modern Internet cafe has 3 locations: Ul. Pyatnitskaya 25/1m (M2: Novokuznetskaya), Akademika Khokhlova 3 (M1: Universitet), and ul Novoslobodskaya 3 (M9: Novoslobodskaya). 70R per hr. Open 24hr.

RUSSIA

Post Offices: Moscow Central Telegraph, Tverskaya ul. 7, uphill from the Kremlin. M1: Okhotnyy Ryad. Look for the globe and the digital clock. **International mail** at window #23. **Faxes** at #11-12. **Telegram** service available. Open M-F 8am-2pm and 3-8pm, Sa-Su 7am-2pm and 3-7pm. **Poste Restante** at window #24. Bring packages unwrapped; they will be wrapped and mailed for you. **Postal Code:** 103 009.

█ ACCOMMODATIONS

As Russia's capital and the starting point for the TSR, Moscow attracts hostelers in droves. However, those willing to negotiate the difficulties of receptionists with limited English will often find better deals in standard Soviet hotels. Slowly but surely, hotels are being renovated, and affordably priced rooms are disappearing.

█ Galina's Flat, ul. Chaplygina 8, #35 (Чаплыгина; ☎921 60 38; galinas.flat@mtu-net.ru). M1: Chistyye Prudy. Head down Chistoprudnyy bul., take a left on Kharitonevskiy per., then a right on Chaplygina. Go into the courtyard at #8, curve right, and enter the building with the "Уникум" sign; on the 5th fl. Superb location. Galina and her cats provide real Russian hospitality. Book in advance. Kitchen access. Breakfast 50R. Airport transfers US$30. 5-bed dorms US$10; singles US$18; doubles US$25. ❷

Traveler's Guest House (TGH), Bolshaya Pereslavskaya ul. 50, 10th fl. (Болшая Переславская; ☎631 40 59; www.tgh.ru). M5 or 6: Prospekt Mira. Take the 2nd right across from Prospekt Mira 61, walk to the end of the *pereulok,* and go left on B. Pereyaslavskaya. Friendly English-speaking staff. Kitchen access. Internet 1R per min. Luggage storage 10R. Laundry service 130R per 3kg. Breakfast included. Visa invitations (US$50, guests US$30). Airport transport US$40. Check-out 11am. Dorms US$23; singles US$45; doubles US$55, with bath US$60. US$1-2 HI discount. MC/V. ❹

Gostinitsa Moskovsko-Uzbekskiy, Zelenodolskaya ul. 3/2 (Зеленодольская; ☎378 33 92 or 378 21 77; hotel@caravan.ru). M7: Ryazanskiy Prospekt (Рязанский). Take the Metro exit toward the back car of the outbound train. A "Гостиница" sign will be visible on top of the hotel to your left. Offers a wide range of rooms. Even the least refurbished are safe and clean. Singles 650-930R; doubles 1000-1500R. 500R key deposit. ❷

G&R Hostel Asia, Zelenodolskaya ul. 3/2 (Зеленодольская; ☎378 00 01; www.hostels.ru), 5th fl. of the Gostinitsa Moskovsko-Uzbekskiy. M7: Ryazanskiy Prospekt (Рязанский). Clean rooms. Helpful staff. Internet access 2R per min. Visa invitations €35. Reception 8am-midnight. Tranportation from airport €35, to airport €30. Dorms €18; singles €25; doubles €40; triples €54. €1 HI discount. 10th day free. MC/V. ❸

Gostinitsa Kievskaya (Гостиница Киевская), Kievskaya ul. 2 (☎240 14 44). M3, 4, or 5: Kievskaya. Beside the train station and a good market. Simple, comfy rooms with phone and TV. Book singles in advance. Singles 860R, with bath 1300-1650R; doubles 900R/1450-1650R; suites 1650-2100R. 30% added to 1st night reservation. ❷

Hostel Sherstone, Gostinichny proezd 8 (Гостиничны; ☎797 80 75), 3rd fl. of Hotel Sherstone. M9: Vladykino. Turn left from the Metro. Walk along the railway to overpass, then take a left and pass the post office. Reception in room 324; open 8am-midnight. Private showers. Visa support €30. Internet 2R per min. Breakfast included. Dorms €17; singles €35; doubles €22. €1 discount for HI and EURO under-26 youth card. ❸

Hostel Tramp, Selskohozyaistvennaya ul. 17/2 (☎187 54 33; www.hostelling.ru). M6: Botanicheskiy Sad. From the Metro station go left on ul. Vilgelma Pika and walk to Gostinitsa Turist. The hostel is in Gostina building #7; reception is in room #524. The hostel has limited dorm spaces. Singles and doubles are clean and simple with private baths. Breakfast included. Airport pickup US$35. 3hr. walking tour for 1-3 people US$25. Dorms US$22-25; singles US$45; doubles US$50. 10% off for HI or ISIC members. ❸

⊡ FOOD

Restaurants in Moscow can be very expensive compared to those in the rest of Russia. Some higher-priced establishments offer business lunch (бизнес ланч) specials (US$4-8), available noon-3pm. Russians tend to eat late in the evening; to avoid crowds, eat earlier. Kiosks at every corner offer cheap alternatives such as whole rotisserie chickens (110R) and the ubiquitous *shawarma* (35-50R). For fresh produce, head to Moscow's **markets**. Impromptu markets spring up around Metro stations; some of the best are at Turgenyevskaya and Kuznetsky most. Vendors arrive around 10am and leave by 8pm. Grocery stores are everywhere; look for "продукти" (produkty) signs. **Eliseevskiy Gastronom** (Елисеевский), Tverskaya ul. 14 (☎209 07 60), Moscow's most famous supermarket, has slightly marked up prices and decadent decor. (Open daily 11am-8pm.) Sadko's **Foodland**, 6 Bolshaya Dorogmilovskaya (M3: Kievskaya), is open 24hr. **Ramstore**, a 24hr. discount food giant, is everywhere. Try Leningradskiy pr. 79 (☎771 75 96; M2: Sokol) or Komsololskaya pl. 6 (☎207 31 65; M1 or 5: Komsololskaya).

RUSSIAN RESTAURANTS AND CAFES

▨ **Cafe Margarita** (Кафе Маргарита), Malaya Bronnaya ul. 28 (Малая Вронная; ☎299 65 34), at the intersection with Malyy Kozikhinskiy per. (Малый Козихинский). M2: Mayakovskaya. Go left on Bolshaya Sadovaya and left on Malaya Bronaya. Superb Russian cafe-restaurant popular with locals. Entrees 250-450R. Open daily 1pm-midnight. ➍

▨ **Artcafe "SAD"** (Арткафе "САД"), B. Tolmachevskiy per. 3 (Толмачевский; ☎239 91 15), across from ul. Krymskiy Val. M2, 6 or 8: Tretyakovskaya. Romantic atmosphere. Great service, but little English spoken. Entrees 150-360R. Open 10am-midnight. ➌

Courvoisier Cafe, Malaya Sukharevskaya pl. 8, bldg. 1 (Малая Сухаревкая; ☎924 82 42). M6: Sukharevskaya. Rub elbows with the Moscow elite while enjoying tasty entrees (220-350R). Breakfast 5-11:30am. Open 24hr. MC/V. ➌

Moo-Moo (My-My), Koroviy Val 1 (☎237 29 00; M5 Dobryninskaya), ul. Arbat 45/42 (☎241 13 64; M3: Smolenskaya). Look for the chain's signature cow statue outside. Moo-moo's many locations offer cheap, tasty European and Russian home cooking, served cafeteria-style. Pelmeni 46R. Pork cutlets 54R. Open daily 9am-11pm. ➊

Traktir Gusi Lebedi (Трактир Гуси Лебеди), Nikolayamskaya ul. 28/60 (☎502 99 08). M5 or 7: Taganskaya. Walk down Zemlyanoy Val and go left on Nikolayamskaya. Modeled on a hunting lodge. Waitresses wear cartridge belts, but, as far as we know, they're not actually packing heat. Entrees 160-395R. Open daily 11am-midnight. MC/V. ➌

INTERNATIONAL RESTAURANTS AND CAFES

▨ **Boulevard,** ul. Petrovka 30/7 (☎209 68 87). M2, 7 or 9: Pushkinskaya. Boasting French-inspired cuisine, Boulevard has survived the fickle New Russians by dint of its consistently high-quality food. Venison medallions with a pepper and vanilla reduction US$45. Wildfowl with foie gras, French mushrooms, and risotto US$26. 10% off before 4pm. Th live harp, F French singers. Open daily noon-midnight. AmEx/DC/MC/V. ➎

▨ **Korchma Taras Bulba** (Корчма Тарас Бульба), Sadovaya-Samotechnaya ul. 13 (☎200 00 56; www.tarasbulba.ru). M9: Tsvetnoy Bulvar (Цветной Бульвар). From the Metro, turn left and walk up Tsvetnoy Bulvar. Any place with a 24hr. feedback hotline obviously takes service seriously. Delicious Ukrainian specialities. English language menu available. Entrees 140-400R. Open 24hr. MC/V. ➌

Baan Thai, Bolshaya Dorogomilovskaya 11 (☎240 05 97; www.baanthai.ru). M3, 4, or 5: Kievskaya. Authentic but pricey Thai cuisine. *Baa mee phad* (garlic noodle stir-fry) 180R. Open daily noon-midnight. AmEx/MC/V. ➍

Guria (Гуриа), Komsomolskiy pr. 7/3 (Комсомольский; ☎246 03 78), opposite St. Nicholas of the Weavers. M1 or 5: Park Kultury. Tasty Georgian fare for some of the city's lowest prices; convenient to Gorky Park and the art galleries. Extensive menu includes vegetarian options. Entrees 80-250R. Open daily noon-midnight. ❷

Dioscouria, Merzlyakovskiy per. 2 (Мерзликовский). M4: Arbatskaya. Good Georgian eats close to the city center. Entrees 100-280R. Open daily 11am-midnight. ❷

Starlite Diner, Bolshaya Sadovaya 16 (☎290 96 38). M2: Mayakovskaya. Walk down Bolshaya Sadovaya toward the Mayakovskiy statue. Tasty and authentic American diner serves cheeseburgers with fries (250R) and delicious milkshakes (190R). Packed with expats on weekends. Entrees 350-599R. Breakfast all day. Open 24hr. AmEx/MC/V. ❸

◎ SIGHTS

Moscow's sights reflect the city's interrupted history: because St. Petersburg was the tsar's seat for 200 years, there are 16th-century churches and Soviet-era museums, but little in between. Though there are no grand palaces, Moscow's museums contain the very best of Russian art. Eighty percent of Moscow's pre-revolutionary splendor was torn down by the Soviet regime, but the capital still packs in plenty of sights. For info on guided tours, see **Practical Information,** p. 670.

THE KREMLIN

Enter through Borovitskaya gate tower in the southwest corner if you're going to the Armory; otherwise, enter between the kassy. Buy tickets at the kassa in Alexander Gardens. ☎ 202 37 76; www.kremlin.museum.ru. M1, 3, 4 or 9: Aleksandrovskiy Sad. Open M-W and F-Su 10am-5pm; last entrance 4:30pm. Audio guides 150R. English-speaking guides offer tours, sometimes at outrageous prices; haggle away. Entrance to the Kremlin territory and all cathedrals 300R. Cameras 50R. Large bags not allowed in the Kremlin. The bag check (60R, cameras 30R) is in the Alexander Gardens, under the arch (see map).

The Kremlin (Кремль; Kreml) is Moscow's historical center and the birthplace of much of Russian history and religion. It was here that Napoleon simmered while Moscow burned and here that the Congress of People's Deputies dissolved itself in 1991, breaking up the USSR. Much of the triangular complex is closed to tourists; the watchful police will blow whistles if you stray into a forbidden zone.

■**ARMORY MUSEUM AND DIAMOND FUND.** The most beautiful treasures of the Russian state can be found in the nine rooms of the Armory and Diamond Fund (Оружейная Палата и Выставка Алмазного Фонда; Oruzheynaya Palata i Vystavka Almaznogo Fonda.). Room 2, on the second floor, holds the legendary Fabergé Eggs and the royal silver. Room 6 holds pieces of the royal wardrobe. The thrones of Ivan the Terrible and Elizabeth stand imposingly next to the hats of Peter the Great and Vladimir Monomakh in Room #7. The **Diamond Fund,** in an annex of the Armory, has still more glitter, including a 190-carat diamond given to Catherine the Great by Gregory Orlov, a "special friend." Among the emerald necklaces and ruby rings of the tsars are Soviet-era finds, including the world's largest chunks of **platinum.** *(To the left as you enter the Kremlin by the Armory entrance. ☎ 229 20 36. Open M-W and F-Su. Armory 350R, students 175R. Cameras 50R. The Armory lets in groups for 1½hr. visits at 10am, noon, 2:30, 4:30pm. The Diamond Fund lets in groups every 20min. 10am-1pm and 2-6pm. 350R, students 250R. Buy tickets early in the day, as group size is limited. Bags and cameras must be checked before entering the Diamond Fund.)*

CATHEDRAL SQUARE (СОБОРНАЯ ПЛОЩАДЬ; SOBORNAYA PLOSHCHAD). From the Armory, go with the flow to Cathedral Square, home of the most famous golden domes in Russia. The first church to the left, **Annunciation Cathedral**

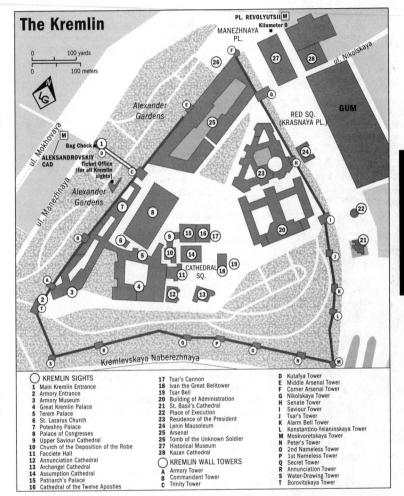

The Kremlin

0 — 100 yards
0 — 100 meters

PL. REVOLYUTSII [M]
Kilometer 0
MANEZHNAYA PL.

Alexander Gardens

Bag Check
ALEKSANDROVSKIY CAD
Ticket Office (for all Kremlin sights)

ul. Mokhovaya [M]

ul. Manezhnaya

Alexander Gardens

RED SQ. (KRASNAYA PL.)

GUM

ul. Nikolskaya

CATHEDRAL SQ.

Kremlevskaya Naberezhnaya

RUSSIA

○ KREMLIN SIGHTS

1 Main Kremlin Entrance
2 Armory Entrance
3 Armory Museum
4 Great Kremlin Palace
5 Terem Palace
6 St. Lazarus Church
7 Poteshny Palace
8 Palace of Congresses
9 Upper Saviour Cathedral
10 Church of the Deposition of the Robe
11 Facciete Hall
12 Annunciation Cathedral
13 Archangel Cathedral
14 Assumption Cathedral
15 Patriarch's Palace
16 Cathedral of the Twelve Apostles
17 Tsar's Cannon
18 Ivan the Great Belltower
19 Tsar Bell
20 Building of Administration
21 St. Basil's Cathedral
22 Place of Execution
23 Residence of the President
24 Lenin Mausoleum
25 Arsenal
26 Tomb of the Unknown Soldier
27 Historical Museum
28 Kazan Cathedral

○ KREMLIN WALL TOWERS

A Armory Tower
B Commandant Tower
C Trinity Tower
D Kutafya Tower
E Middle Arsenal Tower
F Corner Arsenal Tower
G Nikolskaya Tower
H Senate Tower
I Saviour Tower
J Tsar's Tower
K Alarm Bell Tower
L Konstantino-Yelaninskaya Tower
M Moskvoretskaya Tower
N Peter's Tower
O 2nd Nameless Tower
P 1st Nameless Tower
Q Secret Tower
R Annunciation Tower
S Water-Drawing Tower
T Borovitskaya Tower

(Благовещунский Собор; Blagoveshchenskiy Sobor), guards the loveliest iconostasis in the country, with luminous icons by Andrei Rublyov and Theophanes the Greek. Originally only three-domed, the cathedral was enlarged and gilded by Ivan the Terrible. The second entrance is also his; Ivan's seven marriages made him ineligible to enter the church; he was forced to stand on the porch during services as penance. Across the way, the square **Archangel Cathedral** (Архангельский Собор; Arkhangelskiy Sobor), gleaming with vivid icons, colorful frescoes, and metallic coffins, is the final resting place of many tsars who ruled before Peter the Great. Ivans III (the Great) and IV (the Terrible) rest beside the iconostasis; Mikhail Romanov is by the front right column. The center of Cathedral Square is **Assumption Cathedral** (Успенский Собор; Uspenskiy Sobor), one the oldest religious buildings in Russia, dating from the 15th century. Napoleon

THE BIG SPLURGE

RUSSIA FROM ABOVE

Rich adrenaline junkies of the world unite: Zhukovsky Military Air Base offers 30min. of flying at supersonic speeds in stratospheric skies. US$3500-10,000 gets you a custom-designed package featuring a flight in a fighter jet, plus arrangements for everything from visas to ejector seat training. Whether you go for a classic Cold War-era MiG, or the cutting edge SU-47 "Berkut," your view of the Earth is certain to amaze. Jet-setters should check out www.flymig.com.

A more affordable option is the Serpuchov Sporting Aviation Club at Drakino Aerodome. For just US$2.50 per min., you can take to the skies in one of the club's 52 light aircraft. But consider yourself warned: Drakino is the training site for the Russian Federation's national aerobatics team, so the pilot will be disappointed if you don't try (at no extra cost) a spin, chandelle, or loop-the-loop. Let's Go does not accept responsibility for loss of life or lunch. Only joking—the aircrafts all appear well-maintained, and are safer than crossing a Moscow street, at the very least.

Serpukhovskiy Aviatsionnyy Spoivnyy Klub ROSTO. ☎ 967 728 574. To reach Drakino Airfield, take an elektrychka *from Kurskiy Vokzal (2hr., 41R) and a taxi from the station at Serpukhov to the aerodome near Drakino (100-150R).*

---

used it as a stable in 1812. To the right of Uspenskiy Sobor stands **Ivan the Great Belltower** (Колокольная Ивана Великого; Kolokolnaya Ivana Velikogo), which holds rotating exhibitions. The tower is visible over 30km away.

OTHER KREMLIN SIGHTS. Directly behind the bell tower is the **Tsar Bell** (Царь-колокол; Tsar-kolokol). The world's largest bell, it has never rung—an 11½-ton piece broke off after a 1737 fire. Behind Assumption Cathedral stands the **Patriarch's Palace** (Патриарший Дворец; Patriarshiy Dvorets), site of the **Museum of 17th-Century Russian Applied Art and Life** and the **Cathedral of the Twelve Apostles** (Собор Двенадцати Апостолов; Sobor Dvenadtsati Apostolov). To the left of Assumption Cathedral and next to the Patriarch's Palace is the small **Church of the Deposition of the Robe.** The only other building inside the Kremlin you can enter is the **Kremlin Palace of Congresses,** a square, white monster built by Khrushchev in 1961 for Communist Party Congresses. The giant bas-relief of Lenin that once dominated has been removed, and the space is used as a **theater** for the Kremlin Ballet Company and other performances.

RED SQUARE

Red Square (Красная Площадь; Krasnaya Ploshchad) has been the site of everything from a giant farmer's market to public hangings. On one side of the 700m long square is the **Kremlin;** on the other is **GUM,** once the world's largest purveyor of Soviet "consumer goods," now an upscale mall. **St. Basil's Cathedral,** the **State Historical Museum,** the **Lenin Mausoleum,** and **Kazan Cathedral** flank the square. You can buy a combined ticket (230R, students 115R) for St. Basil's Cathedral and the State Historical museum at either location.

ST. BASIL'S CATHEDRAL. There is nothing more symbolic of Moscow—or Russia—than the colorful onion domes of St. Basil's Cathedral (Собор Василия Блаженного; Sobor Vasiliya Blazhennogo). Commissioned by Ivan the Terrible to celebrate his 1552 victory over the Tatars in Kazan, it was completed in 1561. The cathedral bears the name of a holy fool, Vasily (Basil in English), who correctly predicted that Ivan would murder his own son. The labyrinthine interior, unusual for Orthodox churches, is filled with both decorative and religious frescoes. *(M3: Ploshchad Revolyutsii (Площадь Революции). Buy tickets from the kassa to the left of the entrance, then proceed upstairs.* ☎ 298 33 04. Open daily 11am-6pm; kassa closes 5:30pm. 100R, students 50R. Cameras 100R, video 130R. Tours 350R. Services Su 10am.)

LENIN'S TOMB (МАВЗОЛЕЙ В.И. ЛЕНИНА; MAVZOLEY V.I. LENINA). Lenin's likeness can be seen in bronze all over the city, but here he appears eerily in the flesh. In the glory days, this squat red structure was guarded fiercely and the wait to enter took hours. Today's line is still long and the guards are still stone-faced, but visitors exude curiosity, not reverence. Entrance includes access to the Kremlin wall, where Stalin, Brezhnev, Andropov, Gagarin, and John Reed (author of *Ten Days That Shook the World*) are buried. *(Open Tu-Th and Sa-Su 10am-1pm. Free. No cameras or cellphones allowed. Check them at the bag check in the Alexander Gardens.)*

STATE DEPARTMENT STORE GUM. Built in the 19th century, GUM (Государазствунный Унивузсальный Магазин (ГУМ); Gosudarstvennyy Universalnyy Magazin) was designed to hold 1000 stores. Its arched, wrought-iron and glass roofs resemble a Victorian train station. During Soviet rule, GUM's 1000 empty stores were a depressing sight. Today, it's depressing only to those (almost everyone) who can't afford the designer goods. The renovated complex is an upscale arcade of boutiques and restaurants. *(M3: Ploshchad Revolyutsii. From the Metro, turn left, then left again at the gate to Red Sq. ☎929 33 81. Open daily 10am-10pm.)*

STATE HISTORICAL MUSEUM. The comprehensive collection traces Russian history from the Neanderthals through Kyivan Rus to modern Russia. The museum (Государственный Исторический Музей; Gosudarstvennyy Istoricheskiy Muzey) provides printed info in English to help visitors make sense of its vastness. *(Krasnaya pl. 1/2. M1: Okhotnyy Ryad. Entrance by Red Sq. ☎292 37 31. Open M and W-Sa 10am-6pm, Su 11am-8pm; kassa closes 1hr. earlier; closed 1st M of each month. 150R, students 75R. Cameras 60R, video 100R. Audio guides 50R plus 200R deposit.)*

KAZAN CATHEDRAL (КАЗАНСКИЙ СОБОР; KAZANSKIY SOBOR). The bright pink-and-green Kazan Cathedral was rebuilt and reopened for services after being demolished in 1936 to make way for the May 1 parades. *(M3: Ploshchad Revolyutsii. Opposite the State Historical Museum, just to the left of the main entrance to Red Sq. No flash photography. Open daily 8am-8pm. Services M-Sa 9am and 5pm; Su 7am, 10am, 5pm. Free.)*

NORTH OF RED SQUARE

AREAS FOR WALKING. Just outside the main gate to Red Sq. is an elaborate gold circle marking **Kilometer 0,** the spot from which all distances from Moscow are measured. But don't be fooled by this tourist attraction—the real Kilometer 0 lies below the Lenin Mausoleum. Around the corner, the **Alexander Gardens** (Александровский Сад; Aleksandrovskiy Sad) are a respite from the urban bustle of central Moscow. At the north end of the gardens is the **Tomb of the Unknown Soldier** (Могила Неизвестного Солдата; Mogila Neizvestnogo Soldata), where an **eternal flame** burns in memory of the catastrophic losses suffered in WWII.

AREAS FOR SHOPPING. Bordering Red Sq. are two other major squares. On the west side is **Manezh Square** (Манежная Площадь; Manezhnaya Ploshchad), only recently converted into a pedestrian area. The Manezh, which formerly served as the Kremlin stables and an exhibition hall, burned down in March 2004. The famous **Moscow Hotel,** slated to be demolished in late 2004 and rebuilt, separates Manezh Square from the older, smaller **Revolution Square** (Площадь Революции; Ploshchad Revolyutsii). The squares are connected in the north by **Okhotnyy Ryad** (Охотный Ряд; Hunters' Row), once a market for game. The glass domes on Manezh Sq. allow sunlight in the ritzy underground mall, **Okhotnyy Ryad,** full of new trends and New Russians. Across Okhotnyy Ryad from the Moscow Hotel is the **Duma,** the lower house of Parliament, and across from Revolution Sq. is **Theater Square** (Театральная Площадь; Teatralnaya Ploshchad), home of the **Bolshoy and**

Malyy Theaters (see **Entertainment,** p. 684). Lined with posh hotels, chic stores, government buildings, and the homes of Moscow's richest, **Tverskaya Street** is the closest the city has to a main street. *(Open daily 11am-10pm. Enter directly from the square or through the underpass.)*

RELIGIOUS SIGHTS

If the grime and bedlam get to you, escape to one of Moscow's houses of worship. Before the Revolution, the city had more than 1000 churches. Today, there are less than 100, though many are being restored. No visitor should wear shorts. Women should cover their heads with scarves and wear long skirts.

CATHEDRAL OF CHRIST THE SAVIOR. No one should leave Moscow without visiting the city's most controversial landmark: the gold-domed Cathedral of Christ the Savior (Храм Христа Спасителя; Khram Khrista Spasitelya). Though Nicholas I built a cathedral on this spot to commemorate Russia's victory over Napoleon, Stalin had it demolished in 1934 in order to erect a "Palace of the Soviets," which was intended to be the tallest building in the world. The ground proved too soft for such a weight, and after Stalin's death Khrushchev abandoned the project, converting the site into an outdoor swimming pool. The pool was closed in the early 1990s when it was discovered that vapor from the heated water was damaging paintings at the nearby Pushkin Museum. A controversy erupted over what was to become of the site; the Orthodox Church and Moscow's mayor finally won out and raised funds to build the US$250 million cathedral in just five years, completing it in 2000. *(Volkhonka 15, between ul. Volkhonka (Волхонка) and the Moscow River. M1: Kropotkinskaya. ☎ 202 47 17; www.xxc.ru. Open daily 10am-5pm. Cathedral free; donations welcome. Service schedule varies, but morning services are frequently at 8am, evening services at 5 or 6pm. Group tour 80R, students 40R. Individual tour 950R.)*

NOVODEVICHY MONASTERY AND CEMETERY. Moscow's most famous monastery (Новодевичий Монастырь; Novodevichiy Monastyr) is hard to miss thanks to its high brick walls, golden domes, and tourist buses. In the center of Novodevichy (no-vo-DEV-ich-ee), the **Smolensk Cathedral** (Смоленский Собор; Smolenskiy Sobor) shows off icons and frescoes. As you exit the gates, turn right and follow the exterior wall back around to the cemetery (кладбище; kladbishche), a pilgrimage site that holds the graves of such famous figures as Bulgakov, Chekhov, Gogol, Mayakovsky, Shostakovich, and Stanislavsky. *(M1: Sportivnaya. Take the Metro exit that does not lead to the stadium, turn right, and walk several blocks. ☎ 246 85 26. Open M and W-Su 10am-5:30pm; kassa closes 4:45pm; closed 1st M of each month. Cathedral closed on humid days; call in advance. English tours 300R. Grounds 40R, students 20R. Smolensk Cathedral and special exhibits each 93R/53R. Cemetery open daily in summer 9am-7pm; low season 9am-6pm; 30R. Helpful English maps of cemetery 5R. Buy tickets at the small kiosk to the right of the entrance. Cameras 60R, video 160R.)*

DANILOV MONASTERY (ДАНИЛОВ МОНАСТЫРЬ; DANILOV MONASTYR). Founded in 1282, the monastery has historically been as much a fortress as a house of worship. During the Stalinist Terror, the monks were all shot and the monastery fell into ruin. It has since been restored to its former glory and is now home to the Patriarch, head of the Russian Orthodox Church. The only thing missing from this perfect picture of ecclesiastical renewal are the bells. During the Revolution, they were sold to an American industrialist, who in turn donated them to Harvard University. Harvard has agreed to return them if the Orthodox Church will pay to move them and have a replica set built. The Church has agreed, and collection boxes for this purpose line the monastery walls. *(M9: Tulskaya (Тульская). From the* *square, follow the trolley tracks down Danilovsky val., away from the gray buildings and McDonalds, past a small park. Open daily 6:30am-7pm. Services M-F 6, 7am, 5pm; Sa-Su 6:30, 9am, 5pm. Museum open W and Su 11am-1pm and 1:30-4pm.)*

MOSCOW CHORAL SYNAGOGUE. Constructed in the 1870s, the Moscow Choral Synagogue provides a break from the city's ubiquitous onion domes. Although it functioned during Soviet rule, all but the bravest Jews were scared off by KGB agents. Today, more than 200,000 Jews live in Moscow, and services are increasingly well attended. The graffiti occasionally sprayed on the building and the metal detectors at the door are a sad reminder that anti-Semitism in Russia is not at all dead. A **cafe** in the courtyard serves kosher food. *(Bolshoy Spasoglinishchevskiy per. 10 (Большой Спасоглинищевский). M6 or 7: Kitai-Gorod. Go north on Solyanskiy Proyezd (Солянский Проезд) and take the 1st left. ☎924 24 24 . Open daily 8am-10pm. M-F services 8:30am and 8pm, Sa-Su 9am and 9pm. Cafe open M-F 2-9pm.)*

CHURCH OF ST. NICHOLAS IN THE WEAVERS. The red-brown and green trim gives St. Nicholas's (Церковь Николы в Хамовниках; Tserkov Nikoly v Khamovnikakh) the appearance of a giant Christmas ornament. Its name is derived from its location in the former cloth-making district. Enter off ul. Lva Tolstogo (Льва Толстого) for a view of the vivid interior. *(At the corner of Komsomolsky pr. M1 or 5: Park Kultury. Open daily 8am-8pm. Services M-Sa 8am and 5pm; Su 7, 10am, 5pm.)*

AREAS TO EXPLORE

MOSCOW METRO (МОСКОВСКОЕ МЕТРО). Most cities put their marble above ground and their cement below—but Moscow is not most cities. The Metro is worth a tour of its own. All of the stations are unique, and those inside the circle line are elaborately decorated, with mosaics, sculptures, stained glass, and chandeliers. Notable is the Baroque elegance of **Komsomolskaya** (Косомолская) and the stained glass of **Novoslobodskaya** (Новослободская). Perhaps the most memorable are the bronze statues representing archetypes of the revolution, from farmer to factory worker, in the **Ploshchad Revolutsii** (Площадь Револуции) station.

THE ARBAT (АРБАТ). Now a commercial pedestrian shopping arcade, the Arbat was once a showpiece of *glasnost* and a haven for political radicals, Hare Krishnas, and *metallisty* (heavy metal rockers). Old flavor lingers in the streets in the form of performers and guitar-playing teenagers, though today the Arbat is mostly populated by pricey souvenir stalls and shops. Intersecting but nearly parallel runs the bigger, newer, and uglier **Novyy Arbat,** lined with gray high-rises, foreign businesses, and massive stores. *(M3: Arbatskaya or Smolenskaya.)*

PUSHKIN SQUARE (ПУШКИНСКАЯ ПЛОЩАДЬ; PUSHKINSKAYA PLOSHCHAD). Pushkinskaya has inherited the Arbat's penchant for political fervor. During the Cold War's thaw, dissidents came here to protest and voice their visions of a democratic Russia. Today, missionaries evangelize while unknown politicians hand out petitions. Follow ul. Bolshaya Bronnaya downhill, turn right, and follow ul. Malaya Bronnaya to **Patriarch's Pond** (Патриарший Пруд; Patriarshiy Prud). This area is popular with artsy students and domino-playing old men. *(M7: Pushkinskaya.)*

PAN-RUSSIAN EXPOSITION CENTER. The enormous center (Всероссийский Выставочный Центр; Vserossiyskiy Vystavochniy Tsentr) has changed a great deal since its conception. Formerly the Exhibition of Soviet Economic Achievements (VDNKh), this World's Fair-like park, filled with pavilions, has become a giant shopping mecca. *(M6: VDNKh (ВДНХ). Exiting the Metro to "ВВЦ," go left down the kiosk-flanked pathway and cross the street. Most shops open 10am-7pm.)*

PARKS

VICTORY PARK (ПАРК ПОБЕДЫ; PARK POBEDY). Victory Park is a popular gathering point. Its museum (see p. 682) was built as a monument to WWII, or the Great Patriotic War. The main square showcases stones, each inscribed with a year that the Soviet troops fought in the war (1941-45). The gold-domed **Church of St. George the Victorious** (Храм Георгия Победаносного; Khram Georgiya Pobedanosnogo) commemorates the 27 million Russians who died in battle. *(M4: Kutuzovskaya. Past the Triumphal Arch. Services daily 9am, Sa also 5pm.)*

KOLOMENSKOYE SUMMER RESIDENCE (КОЛОМЕНСКОЕ). The tsars' summer residence sits on a wooded slope above the Moscow River. The centerpieces of the grounds are the cone-shaped, 16th-century **Assumption Cathedral** (Успенский Собор; Uspenskiy Sobor) and the seven blue-and-gold cupolas of the nearby **Church of Our Lady of Kazan** (Церковь Казанской Богоматери; Tserkov Kazanskoy Bogomateri). The most notable of the park's several small museums is Peter the Great's 1702 **log cabin,** where he lived for 2½ months before moving to St. Petersburg. *(☎ 112 81 74, tours 115 86 45; www.museum.ru/kolomen. Pr. Andropova 39. M2: Kolomenskaya; follow the exit signs to "к музею Коломенское." Exiting the Metro, walk down the kiosk-lined path that points from a tall gray building and follow the leftmost path up the hill for 10min. Map with English key available at stands to the right of the entrance. Grounds open daily Apr.-Oct. 7am-10pm; Nov.-Mar. 9am-9pm. Free. Museums open Tu-Su 10am-6pm; kassa closes at 5pm. Each museum 90R, students 45R. Cameras 10R.)*

IZMAILOVSKIY PARK (ИЗМАЙЛОВСКИЙ ПАРК). Your one-stop shop for souvenirs from Soviet kitsch to lacquer boxes, Izmailovsky Park and its colossal art market, **Vernisazh** (Вернисаж), are best visited on late Sunday afternoons, when vendors want to go home and are willing to make a deal. Compare prices and bargain hard, as the first set of nesting dolls (матрёшка; matryoshka) you see will not be the last. The market is crowded, so beware of pickpockets. *(M3: Izmaylovskiy Park (Измайловский Парк). Go left and follow the crowd. Open daily 8am-6pm.)*

GORKY PARK (ПАРК ГОРКОГО; PARK GORKOGO). Established in 1928, the park gained fame in the West through Martin Cruz Smith's novel (of the same name) and the film it inspired. In summer, out-of-towners and young Muscovites relax and ride the roller coaster at Moscow's main amusement park. In winter, paths are flooded to create a park-wide ice rink. Those seeking an American-style amusement park will be disappointed, as ice cream kiosks outnumber attractions. Still, the park's main draw is its rides, which include a giant ferris wheel, a mediocre roller coaster and an original Buran spacecraft. It's a fun place to mingle with delighted children, teenage couples, and a menagerie of "pet" (caged) animals. *(M1 or 5: Park Kultury or M5 or 6: Oktyabrskaya. From the Park Kultury stop, cross Krymskiy Most (Крымский Мост). From Oktyabrskaya, walk downhill on Krymskiy Val. Open daily Apr.-Sept. 9am-midnight; Oct.-Mar. 10am-10pm. Park admission free. Most rides 80-160R. Ice rink open Nov.-Apr. M-F 40R, ages 7-12 15R; Sa-Su 50R/15R.)*

KRASNAYA PRESNYA AND ZOOPARK (КРАСНАЯ ПРЕСНЯ И ЗООПАРК). One of the cleanest of the city's serene green areas, **Krasnaya Presnya** attracts readers and small children with its scattered wooden playgrounds and quiet benches. *(M7: Ulitsa 1905 goda (Улица 1905 года). Exit to ul. Krasnaya Presnya and cross it. The park is along ul. 1905 goda.)* The action is livelier a few blocks down ul. Krasnaya Presnya at the **Zoopark.** Going to the zoo used to be like watching calves raised for veal, until Mayor Luzhkov directed his energy and fundraising talents toward improving the animals' quality of life. *(Main entrance across from M7: Barrikadnaya. ☎ 255 53 75. Open Tu-Su 10am-8pm; kassa closes 6:30pm. 80R, students and children free. Cameras free, video 25R.)*

🏛 MUSEUMS

Moscow's museum scene remains the most patriotic and least Westernized part of the city. Some proudly display Russian art while others pay homage to the nation's historical and literary past.

ART GALLERIES

STATE TRETYAKOV GALLERY. This gallery (Государственная Третьяковская Галерея; Gosudarstvennaya Tretyakovskaya Galereya) is a veritable treasure chest of national art. Nineteenth-century portraits and landscapes comprise most of the collection, although it contains works by early 20th-century artists as well. A magnificent collection of icons includes works by Andrei Rublyov and Theophanes the Greek. *(Lavrushinskiy per. 10 (Лаврушинский). M8: Tretyakovskaya (Третьяковская). Exit the Metro, turn left and then left again; a right on Bolshoy Tolmachevsky per. Walk 2 blocks and turn right on Lavrushinskiy per. ☎ 230 77 88; www.tretyakov.ru. Open Tu-Su 10am-7:30pm; kassa closes 6:30pm. 225R, students 130R. Audio guides 250R. Tours in English ☎ 238 13 78; 640R.)*

NEW TRETYAKOV GALLERY. Where the State Tretyakov leaves off, this gallery (Новая Третьяковская Галерея; Novaya Tretyakovskaya Galereya) picks up. The collection starts on the third floor with early 20th-century art and moves through the Neo-Primitivist, Futurist, Suprematist, Cubist, and Social Realist schools. The second floor holds temporary exhibits that draw huge crowds; it's best to go on weekday mornings. Behind the gallery to the right lies a graveyard for Soviet statues. Once the main dumping ground for decapitated Lenins and Stalins, it now contains plaques (with English captions) to ease your journey among sculptures of Gandhi, Einstein, Niels Bohr, and Soviet secret police founder Dzerzhinsky. *(Ul. Krymskiy Val 10 (Крымский Вал). M5: Oktyabraskaya. From the Metro, walk toward the big intersection at Kaluzhskaya pl. (Калужская пл.); turn right on ul. Krymskiy Val. ☎ 238 13 78. Open Tu-Su 10am-7:30pm; kassa closes 6:30pm. 225R, students 130R. Cameras 30R. Tours in English ☎ 238 20 54; 640R.)*

PUSHKIN MUSEUM OF FINE ARTS. The Pushkin (Музей Изобразительных Искусств им. А.С. Пушкина; Muzey Izobrazitelnykh Iskusstv im. A.S. Pushkina), Moscow's most significant non-Russian art collection, was founded in 1912 by the father of poet Marina Tsvetaeva. The museum boasts major Egyptian, Classical, and European Renaissance works and a superb collection of modern painting including Van Gogh and Picasso. *(Ul. Volkhonka 12 (Волхонка). M1: Kropotkinskaya. ☎ 203 95 78. Open Tu-Su 10am-7pm; kassa closes at 6pm. 190R, students 60R. Audio guide 250R, deposit 200R.)* The smaller building to the left of the main entrance houses the Pushkin **Museum of Private Collections** (Музей Личныч Коллеций; Muzey Lichnych Kolletsiy), with artwork by Kandinsky, Rodchenko and Stepanov. *(Beside the main building of the Pushkin Museum of Fine Arts, opposite the Church of Christ the Savior. M1: Kropotkinskaya. ☎ 203 15 46; www.museum.ru/gmii. Open Tu-Su 10am-7pm; kassa closes 6pm. 60R.)*

MUSEUM OF CONTEMPORARY ART. The museum (Музей Соврумунного Искусства; Muzey Sovremennogo Iskusstva) contains a large collection of works in various media by Russian and international artists, including Zurab Tsereteli, Miró, Alexander Calder, and N. B. Hogans. Several of Tsereteli's larger sculptures stand in the courtyard. *(Petrovka 25 (Петровка). M9: Chekhovskaya. Walk down Strastnoy bul. and go right on Petrovka. ☎ 200 66 95. Open M and Sa-Su noon-7pm, W-F noon-8pm; kassa closes 1hr. earlier. Tours 350R. Museum 150R, students 75R.)*

EXHIBITION HALL OF THE RUSSIAN ACADEMY OF ART. This 60-room gallery displays work from Moscow's elite art academy. Media include paintings, sculptures, mosaics, and costume designs. The paintings and sculptures of academy president Zurab Tsereteli, who created the monument to Peter the Great, occupy two floors. Don't miss his prolific work. *(Ul. Prechistenka 19 (Пречистенка). M1: Kropotkinskaya. From the Pushkin Literary Museum, go 2 blocks to the left. ☎ 201 47 71. Open Tu-Sa noon-8pm, Su noon-7pm; last admission 1hr. before closing. 120R.)*

CENTRAL HOUSE OF ARTISTS. Part art museum, part gallery, and part pricey gift shop, this house (Центральный Дом Художникаж; Tsentralnyy Dom Khudozhnika) attracts browsers and serious collectors alike with cutting-edge exhibits from young new names and opportunities to acquire older artists' work. *(Ul. Krymskiy Val 10. In the same building as the State Tretyakov Gallery (see above). M1 or 5: Park Kultury. ☎ 238 96 34; www.cha.ru. Open Tu-Su 11am-8pm; kassa closes 7pm.)*

HISTORICAL MUSEUMS

KGB MUSEUM (МУЗЕЙ КГБ; MUZEY KGB). This museum documents the history and strategies of Russian secret intelligence from the reign of Ivan the Terrible to the present. Enjoy the guide's intriguing anecdotes and the opportunity to quiz a current intelligence agent. Today, it is a training center for the FSB, one of the four agencies replacing the KGB, so it is only open for pre-arranged tours. *(Lubyanka ul. 12 (Лубянка). M1: Lubyanka. Behind the concrete behemoth that towers over the northeast side of the Sq. Patriarshy. Dom Tours (see p. 670) leads 2hr. group tours of the museum periodically. US$18. Private tours can be arranged at an additional cost.)*

MUSEUM OF CONTEMPORARY RUSSIAN HISTORY. Housed in the former Moscow English Club mansion, the gallery (Центральный Музей Современной Истории России; Tsentralnyy Muzey Sovremennoy Istorii Rossii) thoroughly covers Russian history from the late 19th century to the present. *(Tverskaya ul. 21. M7: Pushkinskaya. Walk 1 block uphill on Tverskaya. ☎ 299 67 24. Open Tu-Sa 10am-6pm, Su 10am-5pm; last admission 30min. before closing; closed last F of each month. 100R. Cameras 100R, video 250R. Tours in English 3500R per group of 25 or fewer.)*

CENTRAL MUSEUM OF THE ARMED FORCES. The museum (Центральный Музей Вооруженных Сил; Tsentralnyy Muzey Vooruzhennykh Sil) exhibits a large collection of weapons, uniforms, and artwork from the time of Peter the Great to modern day. Don't miss the big outdoor display of tanks and planes behind the museum. *(Ul. Sovetskoy Armii 2 (Советской Армии). M5: Novoslobodskaya. Walk down Seleznyovskaya ul. (Селезнёвская) to the rotary (10min.). Turn left after the theater and bear right at the fork. ☎ 281 63 03. Open W-Su 10am-5pm. 30R, students 10R. Cameras 50R, video 100R. Call ahead for an English tour, 300R.)*

MUSEUM OF THE GREAT PATRIOTIC WAR. This impressive collection (Музей Отечественной Войны; Muzey Otechestvennoy Voyny) is one of Mayor Luzhkov's grandest completed projects, built to immortalize those who died fighting against Germany in WWII. After the Hall of Memory and Sorrow (where 2.6 million pendants of bronze "weep" for 27 million Russian casualties), though, the emphasis shifts from death to glory. *(Pl. Pobedy. M3: Kutuzovskaya. Behind the tall black WWII monument obelisk in Victory Park. ☎ 142 38 75. Open Tu-Su 10am-5pm; closed last Th of each month. 80R, students 40R. Cameras 15R, video 20R.)* In the park, behind the museum to the left (as you face it), is the **Exposition of War Technology** (Экспозиция Военной Техники; Ekspozitsiya Voyennoy Tekhniki), a large outdoor display of aircraft, tanks, and weaponry. *(Open Tu-Su 10am-5pm; closed last Th of each month.)*

COSMONAUT MUSEUM (УЗЕЙ РОСМОНАВТИКИ; MUZEY KOSMONAVTIKI). The tall, aesthetically challenged obelisk stands atop the museum is the **Monument to Soviet Space Achievements.** Inside the museum is a fascinating collection on Sputnik and life in space. The 15min. movie answers an age-old question: yes, Russian cosmonauts do eat freeze-dried *borshch*. *(Pr. Mira 111. M6: VDNKh. ☎ 283 79 14. Open Tu-Su 10am-6pm; closed last F of each month. 40R, students 20R. Cameras 40R, video 75R.)*

BATTLE OF BORODINO PANORAMA MUSEUM. The popular blue cylindrical museum (Музей Панорама Бородинкая Битва; Muzey Panorama Borodinkaya), guarded by an equestrian statue of General Kutuzov, features a 360-degree panorama of the bloody August 1812 battle against Napoleon at Borodino. *(See p. 652. Kutuzovsky pr. 38. M3: Kutuzovskaya. Walk 10min. down Kutuzovsky pr. toward the Triumphal Arch. Open Sa-Th 10am-6pm. Kassa closes 4:45pm and takes a break 2-2:30pm. 45R, students 20R. Cameras 20R, video 50R. Call ahead ☎ 148 19 27 for tours in English; 300R.)*

ANDREI SAKHAROV MUSEUM. This diminutive two-story complex commemorates the Russian nuclear scientist and patron saint of anti-Soviet ideologues. Sakharov, a Nobel laureate, was placed under house arrest by the Soviet regime. The museum (Музей и Общественный Центр Имени Андрея Сахарова; Muzey i Obshchestvennyy Tsentr Imeni Andreya Sakharova) has exhibits on Stalinist purges, life in the gulag, and the pursuit of human rights. *(Ul. Zemlyanoy Val. 57, ctr. 6. M10: Chkalovskaya (Чкаловская). Proceed to the main street, turn left, and walk 1½ blocks. ☎ 923 44 01; www.sakharov-center.ru. Exhibit captions in Russian. Open Tu-Su 11am-7pm. Free.)*

HOUSES OF THE LITERARY AND FAMOUS

Russians take immense pride in their literary history. They preserve authors' houses in their original state, even down to half-full teacups on the mantelpiece. Each is guarded by a team of fiercely loyal *babushki* who often outnumber visitors to the museum in their trust. Plaques on buildings mark where writers, artists, and philosophers lived and worked.

◼ PUSHKIN LITERARY MUSEUM. Fifteen rooms in this beautiful, modern building lead you through the key points in Pushkin's life and work, setting them in historical context. The museum (Литературный Музей Пушкина; Literaturnyy Muzey Pushkina) displays portraits and Pushkin's personal possessions. *(Ul. Prechistenka 12/2 (Пречистерка). M1: Kropotkinskaya. Entrance on Khrushchyovskiy per. (Хрущёвский). ☎ 201 56 74. Open Tu-Su 11am-7pm; kassa closes 6pm; closed last F of each month. 25R. Cameras 40R, video 150R.)*

◼ MAYAKOVSKY MUSEUM. This four-story work of Futurist Art illustrates the biography of the Revolution's greatest poet. Mayakovsky lived in a communal apartment on the fourth floor of this building from 1919 to 1930 (when he shot himself). His room is preserved at the top of the building, and the rest of the museum (Музей им. В. В. Маяковского; Muzey im. V.V. Mayakovskogo) was built around it as a poetic reminder. *(Lubyanskiy pr. 3/6 (Лубянский). M1: Lubyanka. Enter from ul. Myasnitskaya, at the bust of Mayakovsky surrounded by huge metal shards near the corner onto Lubyansky pr. ☎ 921 93 87. Open M-Tu and F-Su 10am-6pm, Th 1-9pm; closed last F of each month. 60R. Call ahead for tours in English; 600R.)*

TOLSTOY MUSEUM (МУЗЕЙ ТОЛСТОГО; MUZEY TOLSTOGO). This yellow-and white-building in the neighborhood of Tolstoy's first Moscow residence displays original texts, paintings, and letters related to Tolstoy's masterpieces. *(Ul. Prechis-*

tenka 11 (Пречистенка). M1: Kropotkinskaya. ☎ *202 21 90. Open Tu-Su 11am-7pm; kassa closes 6pm; closed last F of each month. 100R, students 15R. Exhibits have captions in English. Cameras 50R, video 200R.)*

GORKY MUSEUM-HOUSE (МУЗЕЙ-ДОМ ГОРКОГО; MUZEY-DOM GORKOGO).

This museum is a pilgrimage site as much for its architectural interest as for its collection of Maksim Gorky's possessions. Designed by F. O. Shekhtel in 1900, it's one of the best examples of Art Nouveau in Moscow. *(Malaya Nikitskaya ul. 6/2 (Малая Никитская). M3: Arbatskaya. From the Metro, cross Novyy Arbat and turn right on Merzlyakovskiy per. (Мерзляковский пер.) Cross the small park to reach ul. Malaya Nikitskaya.* ☎ *290 51 30. Open W-Su 10am-6pm; closed last Th of each month. Exhibit captions in English. Free, but donations requested. Cameras 50R. Group tours 500R.)*

STANISLAVSKY MUSEUM-HOUSE.
The venerated theater director held lessons and performances in his home, which is now a museum (Музей-дом Станиславского; Muzey-dom Stanislavskogo) that displays a collection of the costumes used in his theatrical productions. English info provides explanations. *(Leontyevsky per. 6. M7: Pushkinskaya. From Tverskaya ul., turn right on Leontyevsky per. Enter in back and ring the doorbell.* ☎ *229 24 42. Open Tu and F 2-7pm, Th and Sa-Su 11am-5pm; kassa closes 1hr. earlier; closed last Th of each month. 50R. Cameras 20R per photo. Tours 600R. Concerts Sept.-June. Call* ☎ *299 11 92 for more info.)*

LEO TOLSTOY ESTATE.
The celebrated author lived here during the winters of 1882-1901. Each room has been laid out exactly as it would have been with the original possessions of Tolstoy and his family. *(Ul. Lva Tolstogo 21. M1 or 5: Park Kultury. Exiting the Metro, walk down Komsomolsky pr. toward the colorful Church of St. Nicholas of the Weavers; turn right at the corner on ul. Lva Tolstogo.* ☎ *246 94 44. Open Tu-Sa 10am-5pm, winter 10am-3:30pm; kassa closes 30min. earlier; closed last F of each month. Exhibits in English. 150R, students 50R. Cameras 30R, video 50R.)*

DOSTOEVSKY HOUSE-MUSEUM.
This museum (Дом-Музей Достоевского; Dom-Muzey Dostoyevskogo) in Dostoevsky's childhood home displays some of the family's original furniture and photographs. The tour ends with the author's fountain pen. *(Ul. Dostoyevskogo 2. M5: Novoslobodskaya. From ul. Seleznevskaya (Селезневская), take a left at the trolley tracks onto Dostoyevskiy per. and follow the tracks onto ul. Dostoyevskogo; the museum is on the left.* ☎ *281 10 85. Open May-Sept. W-F 2-8pm, Th and Sa-Su 11am-6pm; Oct.-Apr. W-F 2-6pm, Th and Sa-Su 11am-6pm. Closed last day of each month. 50R, students 10R. Cameras 50R, video 100R.)*

CHEKHOV HOUSE-MUSEUM (МУЗЕЙ-ДОМ ЧЕХОВА; MUZEY-DOM CHEKHOVA).

Chekhov lived here with a baffling number of relatives from 1886 to 1890, writing, receiving patients, and thinking. *(Sadovaya-Kudrinskaya ul. 6 (Садовая-Кудринская) M7: Barrikadnaya. Exiting the Metro, turn left on ul. Barrikadnaya, and left again on Sadovaya-Kudrinskaya.* ☎ *291 61 54. English captions. Open Th and Sa-Su 11am-5pm, W and F 2-7pm; kassa closes 1hr. earlier; closed last day of each month. 15R, students 8R.)*

🎭 ENTERTAINMENT

PERFORMING ARTS

From September through June Moscow boasts some of the world's best **theater**, **ballet**, and **opera**, as well as excellent **orchestras**. Most of the performance venues are in the northern part of the city center. If you buy **tickets** far in advance and don't demand front row center, you can attend quite cheaply (US$5). Tickets can often be purchased from the *kassa* located inside the theater, which is usually open from noon until curtain. Kiosks around the city sell tickets and programs for the next two months (40R). For concerts, be warned that the acoustics of the Bolshoy's beautiful, new second theater are considered a failure by many. During July and August, Russian companies are on tour, and the only folks playing in Moscow are touring productions from other cities, which, with the exception of those from St. Petersburg, tend to be of lesser quality.

Bolshoy Theater (Большой Театр), Teatralnaya pl. 1 (Театральная; ☎250 73 17; www.bolshoi.ru). M2: Teatralnaya. Home to the opera and world-renowned ballet company. *Kassa* open M-W and F-Su 11am-3pm and 4-7pm, Th 11am-3pm and 4-9pm. Performances daily Sept.-June noon, 2 and 7pm. Tickets 250-3500R. MC/V.

Malyy Theater (Малый Театр), Teatralnaya pl. 1/6 (☎923 26 21). M2: Teatralnaya. Just right of the Bolshoy as you face it. Moscow's premier dramatic theater. Affiliate at Bolshaya Ordynka 69 (☎237 31 81). *Kassa* open daily 10am-8pm, closes 1hr. earlier on non-performance days. Performances daily Sept.-June 7pm. Tickets 100-400R.

Tchaikovsky Concert Hall, ul. Bolshaya Nikitskaya 13 (232 53 53). M2: Mayakovskaya. Classical music performances by premier international artists and orchestras. *Kassa*, Triumphalnaya pl. 4/31, open daily noon-3pm and 4-7pm. Tickets (150-1500R) go on sale 1-10 days in advance.

Moscow Operetta Theater, ul. Bolshaya Dmitrovka 6 (Большая Дмитровка; ☎292 12 37; www.operetta.org.ru), left of the Bolshoy. Famous operettas staged year-round. *Kassa* open M-Th noon-3pm and 4-7pm, F-Su noon-3pm and 4-6pm. Performances M-Th 7pm, F-Su 6pm, with additional daytime performances. Tickets 100-500R.

Old Moscow State Circus, Tsvetnoy Bulvar 13 (Цветной Бульвар; ☎200 10 60). M9: Tsvetnoy Bulvar. Turn right and walk half a block; the circus is on the right. Animal acts in the 1st half and glittery acrobatics in the 2nd. Buy tickets 2-3 days in advance. *Kassa* open M and W-Su 11am-2pm and 2-7pm and Tu 12:30pm-1:30pm. Performances M and W-Su 7pm, Sa 2:30pm and occasionally 1pm. Tickets 100-450R.

BANYAS

For info on the *banya* experience, see sidebar, p. 712.

Sandunovskiye Bani (Сандуновские Бани), a.k.a. Nomernye Bani (Номерные Бани), ul. Neglinnaya 14 (Неглинная; ☎925 46 31; www.sanduny.ru). M7: Kuznetsky Most. Enter on Zvonarskiy per. (Звонарский). Moscow's oldest *banya* features high ceilings, cavernous rooms, and classical statues. A session is 2hr. 1st class 500R, 2nd class 700R, but worth every ruble. Or, ask for the 3rd class (800R). Open M and W-Su 8am-10pm.

Bani Na Presnye (Бани На Пресне), Stolyarnyy per. 7 (Столярный; ☎255 53 06). M7: ul. 1905 Goda. Stolyarnyy per. is the 1st right on ul. Presnenskiy Val (Пресненский Вал) from the Sq. Large, sparsely decorated *banya* gets crowded on weekends. 2hr. sessions 600R. Open daily 8am-10pm.

⧉ NIGHTLIFE

Moscow's nightlife, the most Bacchanalian experience this side of the Volga, is varied, expensive, and dangerous. Steer clear of the drunken brawls common outside nightclubs. Some clubs enjoy flaunting their high cover charges and face-control policies, while some elite establishments even have club-cards, denying access to those passing through the city. Several more sedate venues draw bohemians and absinthe-seeking students with cheap prices. Check the *Moscow Times*'s Friday pull-out section, *Element,* or the *eXile*'s irreverent nightlife section (www.exile.ru) for excellent synopses of the week's events, and up-to-date reviews of clubs. Those looking for something more tame can head to the **American Cinema,** 2 pl. Yevropy (☎941 86 41; M3: Kievskaya), inside the Radisson SAS Slavyanskaya Hotel, or **Dome Cinema,** Olympiisky pr. 18/1, (☎931 98 73), M5 or 6: Prospekt Mira. Both theaters offer films in the original English.

CLUBS

■ Propaganda (Пропаганда), Bolshoy Zlatoustinskiy per. 7 (Большой Златоустинский; ☎924 57 32). M6 or 7: Kitai Gorod. Exiting the Metro, walk down ul. Maroseyka and take a left on Bolshoy Zlatoustinsky per. A Moscow spot where you can pulsate to house music without feeling like you're in a meat market. Th is the most popular night. Beer 70R, *sangria* 120R per 0.5L. Sa-Su cover 100R. Open daily noon-6am.

Karma Bar, Pushechnaya ul. 3 (☎924 56 33; www.karma-bar.ru). M1 or 7: Kuznetzky Most. With your back to the Metro, walk through the arch on your left and turn right on Pushechnaya ul. Crowd-pleasing dance music emanates from this hip club. English-speaking waitstaff. Beer 100-140R per 0.33L, vodka 80-150R, mixed drinks 180R. Su hip-hop. Cover F-Sa men 200R, women 100R. Open Th-Su 7pm-6am.

Art-Garbage, Starosadskiy per. 5 (☎928 87 45; www.art-garbage.ru). M6 or 7: Kitay Gorod. Art gallery, restaurant, and club, Art-Garbage is refreshingly more laid-back than many of the chic and trendy Moscow establishments. Vodka tonic 90R. Cover M 200R, W 150R. Disco M-Su 10pm-6am. Open 24hr.

Hippopotamus (Гиппопотам), Mantulinskaya ul. 5/1 (Мантулинсая; ☎256 23 46). M7: ul. 1905 Goda. Cross and continue down Tryokhgornyy Val (Трёхгорный Вал). After the park, go right on Shmitovskiy per. (Шмитовский), then take the 1st left onto ul. 1905 Goda. Take the next right on Mantulinskaya; entrance is around back. The hip-hop, R&B, and soul reels in a diverse group of clubbers. Beer US$2-3, mixed drinks US$2-5. W Arabian night. Th Latin/rock night, with live band and "rock" dance lessons from 1am. Club cards give reduced cover, but usually not exclusive access. Cover men US$8, women US$4. Open W-Su 10pm-6am.

Ballantine's Bar, Nikolskaya ul. 17 (Никольская; ☎928 46 92). M3: Ploshchad Revolyutsii. Follow the signs to Nikolskaya ul. away from Red Sq. Great dance music and a lively student crowd. Beer 65R-165R. Live DJ Th-Sa at 10pm; occasional live music. Cover F-Sa 100R; concerts up to 500R. Open daily 11am-6am. MC/V.

EXPAT HANGOUTS

■ Doug and Marty's Boar House, Zemlyanoy Val 26 (☎917 01 50). M3: Kurskaya. Opposite the train station. Curiously emulating "American" culture, Doug and Marty's packs in a rowdy crowd every weekend. Happy hour 6-9pm. 50% discount on food noon-8pm. Entrees 190R-450R. Beer 90-145R. Billiards 50R per game. Cover men 150R, women 100R. Open 24hr. AmEx/MC/V.

Rock Vegas Cafe, Pyatnitskaya 29/8 (☎959 53 33). M2, 6 or 8: Tretyakovskaya. Next to the Pizza Hut. A mix of ex-pats and local students frequent jazz, blues, and rock concerts F-Sa. Beer 90-160R. Tu latin night, W jazz, Th 70s-80s, F-Sa live gigs (cover men 150R, women 100R), Su hip-hop. Open daily noon-6am.

GLBT NIGHTLIFE

Tri Obezyany (Three Monkeys), ul. Sadovnicheskaya 71/2 (☎953 09 09). M2 or 5: Paveletskaya. Moscow's premier gay club, offering everything from disco to *travesty* (drag) shows. Open daily 9pm-9am.

▶ DAYTRIP FROM MOSCOW

SERGIYEV POSAD (СЕРГИЕВ ПОСАД)

Take the Elektrichki (commuter rail) from Yaroslavskiy Vokzal (1½-2hr., every 20-50min., round-trip 61R). Departure times are listed outside the prigorodnaya kassa (пригородная касса; suburban cashier). Alternatively, purchase a train ticket (31R) and return via the bus leaving from outside the Sergiyev Posad station (1-3hr., every 10min., 40R). Buses back to Moscow go to Yaroslavskiy Vokzal or VDNKh. Turn right toward the gold domes and follow the road to the city (10-15min.). Monastery open 9am-6pm. English tours 500R. Museums open W-Su 10am-5:30pm. Monastery free. Museum 160R, students 80R. Cameras 100R.

Russia's famous pilgrimage point, Sergiyev Posad (pop. 200,000), attracts believers to the several churches clustered around its main sight, **St. Sergius's Trinity Monastery** (Свято-Троицкая Сергиева Лавра; Svyato-Troitskaya Sergieva Lavra). During Soviet times, Sergiyev Posad was called Zagorsk, and many locals still use the name. After decades of state-propagated atheism, this stunning monastery, founded in the 1340s and one of the Russian Orthodox Church's four *lavras*, has again become a thriving religious center. The patriarch of the Russian Orthodox Church, also known as the Metropolitan, resided here until 1988, when he moved to Moscow's Danilov Monastery (see **Religious Sights,** p. 679).

Each church is exquisite, but few moments match the serene calm of standing in **Trinity Cathedral** (Ероицкий Собор; Troitskiy Sobor), surrounded in dim light by walls of gilded Andrei Rublyov icons. Nearby, the magnificently frescoed **refectory** (Трапезная; Trapeznaya) houses some of the most beautiful paintings in any church. The **Chapel-at-the-Well** (Надкладезная Часовня; Nadkladeznaya Chasovnya) has a miraculous history: allegedly, it was established after a spring with magical healing powers appeared here. *Babushki* still bring vessels to the well to carry the holy water home. Next door, in the center of the courtyard, the **Assumption Cathedral** (Успенский Собор; Uspenskiy Sobor), modeled after the cathedral in Moscow's Kremlin (see **Sights,** p. 674), proves itself as beautiful as any larger house of worship. On your left as you enter, the **grave of Boris Godunov** and his family (see **History,** p. 652) lie under the modest white tomb. The fortress wall at the far end of the monastery gives access to the 55m **Pilgrim's Tower** at the far wall of the monastery for a panorama of the surrounding sights (20R).

THE GOLDEN RING
(ЗОЛОТОЕ КОЛЬЦО)

North and east of Moscow lies the Golden Ring (Zolotoye Koltso), a string of towns with some of the most beautiful and beloved churches and kremlins in Russia. Many of the towns reached their zenith in the 12th century, when the Russian empire's center of power shifted from Kyiv to Moscow. The slower, calmer pace of these towns provides a much-needed break from the chaos of Moscow.

YAROSLAVL (ЯРОСЛАВЛЬ)　　　☎(8)0852

Yaroslavl (yi-ra-SLAH-vl; pop. 630,000) is one of the most touristed cities in Russia, earning it the nickname "The Florence of Russia." Yaroslavl's numerous churches, pleasant riverside promenades, and proximity to Moscow have made it a regular stop on the tour bus circuit. This has pushed up prices, so true budget travelers might want to make their visit a daytrip from Moscow.

RUSSIA

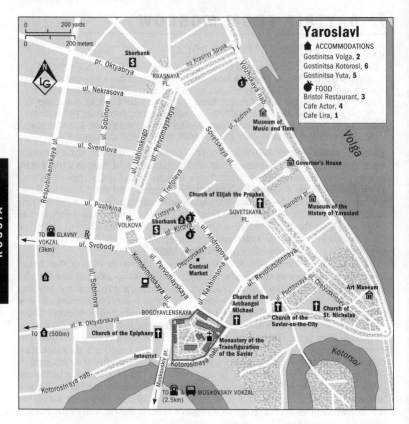

Yaroslavl

▲ ACCOMMODATIONS
Gostinitsa Volga, **2**
Gostinitsa Kotorosl, **6**
Gostinitsa Yuta, **5**

● FOOD
Bristol Restaurant, **3**
Cafe Actor, **4**
Cafe Lira, **1**

TRANSPORTATION

Trains: Glavnyy Vokzal (☎ 79 21 12). To: **Moscow** (4½hr., 19 per day, 170R); **St. Petersburg** (12hr., 4 per day, 320R); **Vologda** (4hr., 1 per day, 112R). *Kassa* #4 open 24hr.

Buses: Avtovokzal (☎ 44 18 37), in the same building as Moskovskiy Vokzal. To **Vladimir** (6hr., 4 per wk., 160R) and **Vologda** (5hr., 1 per day, 104R).

Public Transportation: Buy **tickets** (5R) at the blue kiosks next to main stops labeled "Яргортранс" or on board. On board, hand your ticket or money to the person with the black waist pouch. 10R fine for riding ticketless.

ORIENTATION AND PRACTICAL INFORMATION

Yaroslavl lies at the confluence of the **Volga** and **Kotorosl Rivers** (Волга, Которосль), 280km northeast of Moscow. The center is defined to the south and northeast by the two rivers and on the west by **Pervomayskaya ul.** (Первомайская). Pervomayskaya runs from **Krasnaya pl.** (Красная) to **Bogoyavlenskaya pl.** (Богоявленская), home to Yaroslavl's main monastery and the beginning of **Mosk-**

ovskiy pr. (Московский), which runs south across the Kotorosl to **Moskovskiy Vokzal,** the main bus station. From the bus station, cross Moskovskiy pr. and take trolley #5 or 9 three stops to **pl. Volkova** (Волкова). From the main train station, **Glavnyy Vokzal** (Главный Вокзал; Main Station), **ul. Svobody** (Свободы) hits the center at pl. Volkova, from which **ul. Kirova** (Кирова), a pedestrian walkway, runs east toward the Volga and Sovetskaya pl. To get to the center from Glavny Vokzal, take trolley #1 six stops to pl. Volkova. Many streets are marked with both their current and former names. For travelers navigating the city, only the topmost name is useful. Cyrillic **maps** (35R) are sold at the House of War Books (Дом Военной Лниги; Dom Voyennoy Knigi), Pervomaiskaya 39.

Currency Exchange: Sberbank, ul. Kirova 16, cashes AmEx/Thomas Cook/V **traveler's checks** for 3% commission. Open M-Sa 8:30am-1pm and 2-6:30pm, Su 9am-1pm and 2-4pm; closed last day of each month.

Luggage Storage: Available at Glavny Vokzal for 15R per day. Open 24hr.

24hr. Pharmacy: Ul. Svobody 8 (☎32 95 61). Ring buzzer 8pm-8am. MC/V.

Internet access: Punkt internet dostupa, Komsomolskaya ul. 14, 1st floor, room 5 (☎30 80 55; idostup@yandex.ru). Through the arch with Internet written over it. Follow the signs upstairs. 30R per hr. Offers a variety of other services. Open daily 9am-9pm.

Post Office: Komsomolskaya ul. 22 (Комсомольская; ☎32 90 71), across the square from the monastery. Open M-Sa 8am-8pm, Su 8am-6pm. **Postal Code:** 150 000.

ACCOMMODATIONS

Yaroslavl's hotel prices are high due to the city's popularity, and rooms are scarce in summer. Add 25-50% to the first night's bill if you reserve in advance.

Gostinitsa Kotorosl, ul. Bolshaya Oktyabrskaya 87 (☎21 24 15; www.kotorosl.yaroslavl.ru). Walk up ul. Bolshaya Oktyabrskaya 10-15min. from pl. Bogoayavlenskaya. The hotel is on the left. Although it's a little far, the sauna, tennis courts, and decent prices should make your stay worthwhile. Singles 900-1100R; doubles 1600-1800R. ❸

Gostinitsa Yuta (Юта), Respublikanskaya ul. 79 (Республиканская; ☎21 87 93). Walk down ul. Svobody, take a left on Respublikanskaya, and walk 2 blocks. Old, spacious rooms with TVs, phones, and private baths. Staff runs a restaurant, casino, and tourist agency. Singles 900R; doubles 1100R, lux double 1300-1500; lux suites 2300R. ❸

Gostinitsa Volga (Волга), ul. Kirova 10 (☎30 81 31; fax 72 82 76). Clean, comfortable rooms in a prime location. Check-out noon. Singles 1500R; doubles 1600R. ❺

FOOD

Sidewalk cafes sell beer, ice cream, and sweet rolls. Stock up on produce at the **tsentralnyy rynok** (центральный рынок; central market), ul. Deputatskaya 5 (Депутатская; open M-Sa 8am-6pm, Su 8am-4pm). The **tsentralnyy gastronom** (central grocery store), ul. Kirova 13, has a huge selection. (Open daily 8am-10pm.)

▨ **Cafe Actor** (Актёр; Akytor), ul. Kirova 5 (☎72 75 43). Go up the courtyard stairs. Decorated with theater posters. Full meals 110-180R. Open daily 8am-11pm. ❷

▨ **Bristol Restaurant,** ul. Kirova 10 (☎72 94 08). Russian and Georgian cuisine in the elegance of a silver-age ballroom. Entrees 100-350R. Open daily noon-midnight. ❸

Cafe Lira (Лира), Volzhskaya nab. 43 (Волжская; ☎72 79 38). Basic Russian fare along the Volga. Entrees 50-150R. Open daily noon-11pm. ❷

👁 SIGHTS

■ **MUSEUM OF MUSIC AND TIME.** Step inside Russia's first private museum (Музей Музыки и Времени; Muzey Muzyki i Vremeni) to enter a magical world of ticking, ringing, and chiming. Exhibits include John Mastoslavsky's collection of clocks, gramophones, and bells. Don't miss the "symphonarium" music box. *(Volzhskaya nab. 33a. ☎32 86 37. Open daily 10am-7pm. As you enter the courtyard, walk up the path and turn left. You'll have to ring the bell to be let in. 25R, students 20R. Admission includes a guided tour in Russian.)*

■ **CHURCH OF ELIJAH THE PROPHET.** Yaroslavl's most beautiful sight, this white-and-green church (Церковь Ильи Пророка; Tserkov Ili Proroka) is the centerpiece of Sovetskaya pl. (Советская). The elaborate iconostasis and frescoes flood this 17th-century church with color. *(At the end of ul. Kirova. Open M-Tu and Th-Su 10am-1pm and 2-6pm. 50R, students 10R. Cameras 35R, video 20R.)*

MONASTERY OF THE TRANSFIGURATION OF THE SAVIOR. Since the 12th century, this fortified monastery (Спасо-Преображенский Монастырь; Spaso-Preobrazhenskiy Monastyr) has guarded the banks of the Kotorosl. The monastery's high white walls enclose a number of buildings. Enter the grounds through the **Holy Gate** (Святые Ворота; Svyatyye Vorota), which faces the Kotorosl. Climb the **bell tower** (звонница; zvonnitsa) for a breathtaking view of the city. Behind the tower is the **Cathedral of the Transfiguration of the Savior** (Спасо-Преображенский Собор; Spaso-Preobrazhenskiy Sobor), built during the reign of Ivan the Terrible. The monastery houses nine exhibits of art, folk crafts, and natural history. Most captions are in Russian only. *(Bogoyavlenskaya pl. 25. Monastery open daily 8am-8pm. Admission to monastery grounds 6R, students 4R; free with museum tickets. Bell tower open daily 8am-7pm. 30R, students 10R. Exhibits open Tu-Su 10am-6pm; kassa closes at 5:30pm. Each exhibit 15-50R, students 5-25R; 80R combined. Cameras 30R, video 75R.)*

ART MUSEUM (ХУДОЖЕСТВЕННЫЙ МУЗЕЙ; KHUDOZHESTVENNYY MUZEY). The Art Museum has two branches. The **Icon Museum,** housed in the Metropolitan Palace (Метрополичьи Палаты; Metropolichi Palaty), displays the best of Yaroslavl's icons. View the life story of St. George, the dragon-slayer. *(Volzhskaya nab. 1. ☎72 92 87. Open Sa-Th 10am-5pm; kassa closes 4:30pm. 25R. Camera or video 50R).* The **modern branch,** in the former governor's house, displays 18th- to 20th-century Russian paintings and sculpture. *(Volzhskaya nab. 23. ☎30 35 04; www.artmuseum.yar.ru. Open Tu-Su 10am-5:30pm; kassa closes 5pm. 30R, students 10R. Cameras 20R, video 50R.)*

CHURCH OF THE EPIPHANY. Opposite the monastery, the red-brick Church of the Epiphany (Церковь Богоявления; Tserkov Bogoyavleniya) has an ornately carved Baroque iconostasis and several beautiful frescoes. The church's museum is currently closed for restoration. *(Bogoyavlenskaya pl. ☎72 56 23. Open W-Su 10am-5pm. Knock if the church seems closed. 15R, students 6R. Cameras 30R, video 75R.)*

SUZDAL (СУЗДАЛЬ)   ☎(8)09231

Set amid lazy streams, dirt roads, and cucumber fields, Suzdal (SOOZ-duhl; pop. 12,000) looks much as it always has. In the 12th century, the powerful Rostov-Suzdal principality ruled Moscow and even collected tribute from Byzantium. Nine centuries later, this quiet town, largely unscathed by Soviet construction, still brims with old-world charm and medieval spirit.

To reach the **kremlin,** the town's main tourist destination, turn left onto ul. Vasilevskaya as you exit the bus station. When you reach the end of the road, turn left on ul. Lenina, then make a right on ul. Kremlya. Time has softened the profile of the mighty fortress, but the faded star-studded blue domes of the **Nativity Cathedral** (Рождественский Собор; Rozhdestvenskiy Sobor) still dazzle. Its bright frescoes and ornate arches are closed to visitors until 2006, but Suzdal's most famous icons are on display in the 15th-century **Archbishop's Palace.** (Open M and W-Su 10am-6pm; closed last F of each month. 4 exhibits, 20-25R each, 80R combined. Cameras 25R.) Cross the river, turn left, and head to the **Museum of Wooden Architecture** (Музей Деревянного Зодчества; Muzey Derevyannogo Zodchestva), an outdoor museum with windmills, a well, and several houses dating from the 17th to 19th centuries. (Open M and W-Su 9:30am-4:30pm; closed last F of each month. 20R. Cameras 10R, video 20R.)

North of the kremlin lie several serene **monasteries** and convents. The **Convent of the Deposition of the Robe** (Ризоположенский Монастырь; Rizopolozhenskiy Monastyr) has a classical, picturesque bell tower. The cathedral and the Holy Gate date from the 16th and 17th centuries. (Grounds open 24hr. Free.) Farther down ul. Lenina, the **Spaso-Yevfimiyev Monastery** (Спасо-Евфимиев Монастырь) is surrounded by a stone wall and holds eight exhibits. (Open Tu-Su 10am-6pm; closed last Th of each month. 20R per exhibit, 150R combined.) The green-domed **Cathedral of the Transfiguration** boasts incredible murals and houses a **museum** that exhibits 13th- to 20th-century decorative arts and 11th- to 12th-century books, including **Russia's oldest book** (1056) and a huge 17th-century Gospel, which has attained the much-sought-after title of **Russia's largest book.** Behind the monastery and across the river stands the beautifully kept **Convent of the Intercession.** This pearl-white complex served as a prison for women of the highest class: Peter the Great, Ivan the Terrible, his son, and Basil III each exiled at least one wife here. (Open 24hr. Free.)

The **bus station,** *avtovokzal* (автовокзал; ☎2 13 43), Vasilevskaya ul. 44 (Васильевская), sends buses to **Ivanovo** (1½hr., 22 per day, 50R) and **Vladimir** (50min., every 40-70min., 18.50R). Departure times are listed at the *kassy.* (Open 5am-8pm.) **Taxis** (☎ 2 06 34) charge 10R per km. Exchange currency at **Sberbank,** ul. Lounskaya 1a (Лоунская; ☎2 19 18), off ul. Lenina, opposite the bell tower of the Convent of the Deposition of the Robe. The bank has an **ATM** (2% commission) and cashes **traveler's checks** for 2.4% commission. (Open M-F 8am-1pm and 2pm-6pm.) For a small town, Suzdal has plenty of accommodations, but all of them are expensive. The most convenient and affordable option is luxurious **Gostinitsa Sokol ❹,** Torgoboya pl. 2. The hotel is on your left immediately after the turnoff to the Kremlin from ul. Lenina. (☎2 09 87; ooosokol@online.ru. Singles 1300R; doubles 2000R.) Find cabbage soup (щи; shchi) and other satisfying Russian meals (60-150R) at **Kharchevnya ❷** (Харчевня), ul. Lenina 73. (☎2 07 22. Open M-Su 9am-11pm.) For fancier fare, try **Trapeznaya ❸** (Трапезная), behind the museum in the Kremlin. It claims a 300-year-old culinary tradition. (☎217 63. Entrees 150-300R. Open daily 11am-11pm.)

VLADIMIR (ВЛАДИМИР) ☎(8)0922

Once the capital of Russia and the headquarters of the Russian Orthodox Church, Vladimir (vlah-DEE-mihr; pop. 380,000) suffered at the hands of the Tatars and eventually fell to Moscow in the early 14th century. Since then, Vladimir has moved forward at a much slower pace. Still, the city is no medieval relic: past the 12th-century white stone monuments and cathedrals, the Soviet industrial buildings serve as a reminder of how far Vladimir has come.

▐ TRANSPORTATION. Trains (☎29 23 00) run from Vokzalnaya pl. (Вокзальная) to **Moscow's Kurskiy Vokzal** (3hr., 15-20 per day, 40R) and **Nizhniy Novgorod** (4hr., 10-15 per day, 104R). Trips to Moscow can be made cheaply on a *prigorodnyy* (пригородный; suburban) train. Opposite the train station, **buses** (☎32 37 90) go to **Ivanovo** (2½hr., 7 per day, 135R); **Moscow** (3½hr.; 18-20 per day, last departure 6:45pm; 100R); **Suzdal** (50min.; every 30min., last departure 9:40pm; 22R); **Yaroslavl** (5hr., M and F-Su 7:15am and 4:30pm, 160R).

■ ■ **ORIENTATION AND PRACTICAL INFORMATION.** A 5min. walk uphill from the train station will bring you to the Old City; its main street is **Bolshaya Moskovskaya ul.** (Большая Московская), sometimes called by its former name, ul. III-yevo Internatsionala (III-его Интернационала). Nearly everything is on or near this thoroughfare. Trolley #5 (4R) starts at the train station and runs down the street, stopping at both of the hotels listed below. **Sberbank,** B. Moskovskaya ul. 27, offers MC/V **cash advances** and has an **ATM.** (Open M-F 8:30am-12:30pm and 1:30-6:30pm, Sa 8am-12:30pm and 1:30-4:30pm.) There is a **pharmacy** at ul. Gogolya 2. (☎27 22 15. Open daily 9am-9pm.) The train station houses a **24hr. telephone office,** which sells prepaid international calling time (about 30R per min.) and 54R telephone cards. **Internet access** is available at @ **Internet Salon,** on ul. Gagarina just around the corner from B. Moskovskaya 23. It has fast connections. (48R per hr. Open daily 9am-9pm.) The **post office** is at ul. Podbelskogo 2. Head down Muzeynaya ul., and turn left on Podbelskogo. (☎32 44 60. Open M-F 8am-8pm, Sa-Su 8am-6pm.) **Postal Code:** 600 000.

■ ■ **ACCOMMODATIONS AND FOOD. Gostinitsa Vladimir ❶** (Гостиница Владимир), B. Moskovskaya ul. 74, offers clean, comfortable rooms. Head uphill on the far left path from the train station. There's a restaurant, an **ATM,** and a telephone office on the first floor and a well-stocked **grocery** next door. (☎32 30 42; tour@gtk.elcom.ru. Singles with sink 350R, with shower 800R; doubles 700R/1100R. Ask floor manager for a key to shower. 25% added to 1st night for reservation.) **Gostinitsa Zarya ❶** (Заря; Dawn), Studyonaya Gora 36a (Студюная), is 10min. past the Golden Gate on the main street. (☎32 79 60. Business center 8am-1am. Flexible check-out. Singles 300-900R; doubles 460-1000R. MC/V.) ■**Cafe Ivan-tea ❶** (Иван-Чай; Ivan-Chai), at B. Moskovskaya ul. 19, is a great, brand-new cafe. Enter from Denicheskaya ul. Try one of 20 types of Chinese tea (10R per cup), with *pelmeni.* (☎32 57 28. Snacks 10-40R. Open 10am-11pm.) ■**U Zolotykh Vorot ❸** (У Золотых Ворот; By the Golden Gates), on the second floor of B. Moskovskaya ul. 15, makes an elegant setting for fine Russian dining. (☎32 31 16; golden-gate@vtsnet.ru. Menu in English. Open daily noon-midnight. 100-300R. MC/V.)

■ **SIGHTS.** The 12th-century **St. Dmitry's Cathedral** (Дмитриевский Собор; Dmitrievskiy Sobor), is the only surviving building of Prince Vsevelod III's former palace. Walk left on B. Moskovskaya ul. from Gostinitsa Vladimir (see **Accommodations** above). The church is through a wooded park on the left. Restoration work has kept the cathedral's Byzantine interior closed to visitors, but the beautifully carved relief frescoes on the outer walls warrant a visit. The **Vladimir-Suzdal Historical, Archaeological, and Artistic Museum,** B. Moskovskaya ul. 5, is to the right of the cathedral. The highlights are the Picture Gallery, which features paintings from the 15th to 20th centuries, and a display on the lifestyles of the nobility. Each exhibit has its own admission price, but you can see everything on the first and second floors for 100R. (☎32 42 63. Open Tu-W 10am-4pm, Th-Su 10am-5pm; closed last Th of each month.) Up the hill, to the right of the museum, is the 12th-century **Assumption Cathedral** (Успенский Собор; Uspenskiy Sobor) and its 19th-century **bell tower.** (Open Tu-Su 1:30pm-4:45pm. 25R.) In front of Assumption Cathedral lies **Cathedral Square** (Соборная Площадь; Sobornaya Ploshchad).

The 12th-century **Golden Gate** (Золотые Ворота; Zolotyye Vorota), just down B. Moskovskaya ul., which is an entrance to the Old City, has been designated a UNESCO world heritage site. Climb to the top for exhibits in Russian on the involvement of the city and its citizens in various conflicts. There is a brief sound and light show, available in English, about the Tartar conquest. (Open W-M 10am-6pm; closed last F of each month. 8R, Students 5R.) Facing Cathedral Square, a path to the right leads to the **Exhibit of Old Vladimir** (Выставка Старого Владимира; Vystavka Starogo Vladimira), housed in an old water tower. It displays assorted items from 19th-century Vladimir and offers a view of the city. (☎32 54 51. Open Tu, Th, Sa-Su 10am-5pm, W and F 10am-4pm; closed last Th of each month. 20R. Cameras 20R, video 60R.) The red-brick, early 20th-century **Trinity Church,** on the left past the gate, displays crystal, lacquer crafts, and embroidery. (☎32 48 72. Open M and W-Su 10am-6pm; closed last F of each month. 20R.) The **Bogolyubov Monastery** (Боголюбов Монастырь), the city's most beautiful religious complex, is a short ride from the center. Grand Prince Andrey Bogolyubsky (literally "Andrey the God-loving") sacked Kyiv in 1169 and moved the Russian capital to Vladimir, establishing a monastery that still boasts an excellent choir. (Open daily 6:30am-10pm. Free.) From outside Gostinitsa Vladimir or the center, wait (patiently) to take bus #52 or a van headed for "Сокол." Look for the sign reading "Боголюбов" and get off when you see the blue domes (20-25min., 4R).

NIZHNIY NOVGOROD ☎(7)8312

According to a Russian proverb, St. Petersburg is Russia's head, Moscow its heart, and Nizhniy Novgorod (NEEZH-ne NOHV-guh-rud; Нижний Новгород; pop. 1,400,000) its pocket. Russia's fourth-largest city was founded in 1221 as a military outpost and grew into a key trading post between Europe and Asia. It maintained its important economic status even during the Soviet period as a manufacturing center. In 1932, its name was changed to Gorky to honor its most famous resident. The city reassumed the name Nizhniy Novgorod in 1990 and has transitioned with relative ease into free trade, which has always come naturally to the city.

▐ TRANSPORTATION

Airport: ☎54 74 36. Located 30km from the city, the airport offers flights within Russia and to **Frankfurt, GER.** To reach the airport take the metro to the Avtozavodskaya stop, and take bus #33 to its terminus at ul. Druzhaeva. From there you can take either bus #32 or *marshruta* #111 to the airport.

Trains: ☎48 28 00. **Moscovy Vokzal** (Московский Вокзал), across the river from the kremlin. Trains to: **Kazan** (9hr., 1 per day, 400R) and **Moscow** (8hr.; 6 per day, 3 of which are night trains; 450R), via **Vladimir** (4hr., 15 per day, 200R).

Buses: From the train station, the bus station (Kanavinskaya abtostantsiya; ☎44 20 21) is a 5min. walk to the left. To **Moscow** (9hr., 7 per day, 400R) and **Vladimir** (5hr., 2 per day, 200R). Open daily 6am-10:30pm.

Public Transportation: Nizhniy Novgorod, like most Russian cities, offers a slew of public transport options. **Buses, trams, trolleys,** and various brands of chartered taxi (маршрутке такси; mashrutie taksi) operate throughout the city center and the suburbs (6-10R). Unfortunately, a bus, tram, or chartered taxi with the same route number does not necessarily follow the same route, so be sure to check that your destination is serviced. A sign in Cyrillic in the window will list all the principal destinations.

Metro: Although Nizhniy Novgorod has a fine subway system, it mainly services the suburbs. It is not very useful for most tourists, except those staying at the Gostinitsa Zarechnaya. 8R. Open 5:25am-midnight.

Taxis: Taxis (☎75 11 11, 004, 30 20 40, 008) are meter-less. Negotiate price before entering the cab. Generally, 100-200R is fair for rides within the center of town.

ORIENTATION AND PRACTICAL INFORMATION

The city is bounded on one side by the **Volga** river and divided in two by the **Oka** river. The eastern bank is the oldest part of the city and centers around the krem-lin, which sits on the pl. Minina at the top of a hill. **Ul. B. Pokrovskaya,** which is closed to cars daily 9am-6am, is the city's main shopping street and connects **pl. Minina** to the city's other principal square, **pl. Gorkogo.** On the other side of the Oka sits the more recently developed lower part of the city, dominated by manufactur-ing. Both the **train station,** Moskovskiy Vokzal, and the intercity **bus station,** Kanavinskaya avtostantsiya, are on **pl. Revolutsii.** Ul. Sovetskaya runs down the side of the city's former fair grounds, connecting pl. Revolutsii to pl. Lenina.

Tourist Office: Nizhegorodskiy Tsentr Gostepriimstva (Нижненовгородский Центр Гостеприимства), ul. B. Pokrovskaya 15, 4th fl., office 5 (☎19 60 96; www.wel-comenn.ru). Fortunately for visitors, the city has a friendly tourist office, which gives advice on everything from restaurants to tour guides. The website offers information on major upcoming events. Open M-F 9am-6pm.

Currency Exchange: Uralsibbank, ul. B. Pokrovskaya 22 (☎78 42 32; www.uralsib-bank.ru), offers a full range of currency exchange services. Open M-Th 9am-1pm and 2-5pm, F 9am-1pm and 2-4:30pm.

ATMs: Can be found in train stations, hotel lobbies, and large shops, and on most major streets. Try **Sberbank,** ul. B. Pokrovskaya 3, or **Uralsibbank** (see above).

Luggage Storage: Downstairs from the entrance to the train station, to the left. 30R for 24hr. No lockers.

Pharmacy: Ay Bolit, Gorkogo ul. 142 (☎19 62 23). Open M-Su 9am-9pm.

Internet Access: Volgatelecom, 56 B. Pokrovskaya ul., 20R per 30 min. Also offers international calling services. Open 24hr. **Pauteena,** 1 Sergievskaya ul. (☎34 37 75). Combination bar-restaurant-pool hall offers excellent Internet connections. Prices depend on time of day, but you can expect to pay less than 50R per hr. Open 24hr.

Post Office: ul. Bolshaya Pokrovskaya 56, at pl. Gorkogo, on the left and up the stairs as you walk toward pl. Gorkogo. Open daily 8am-8pm. **Postal Code:** 603 000.

ACCOMMODATIONS

Otel Tsentralniy, ul. Sovetskaya 12 (☎77 55 00; www.hotel-central.ru). Turn left out of Moskovskiy Vokzal onto the main road, and follow it for about 10min. The hotel will be on your left. A Soviet megalith, the rooms of the Otel Tsentralniy are in various degrees of renovation but all are clean and come with TV and fridge. Singles economy (ekonom) 900R, standard (standart) 1300R, business class (biznes klass) 1900; doubles 1300R/1800R/2300R, economy with telephone 1400R. MC/V. ❹

Nizhegorodskiy gostinichniy kompleks, ul. Zalomova 2 (☎30 53 87; www.hotel.r52.ru). From Moskovskiy Vokzal take marshrutka #143 and get off when it goes up the hill after the river. Turn left down ul. Golgolya, then take the 1st left onto ul. Nizhegorodskaya, then the next right onto Zalomova. The hotel offers a wide range of clean rooms with a slew of options and views. Singles 750-1800R; doubles 700-2300R. MC/V. ❸

Volzhskiy Otkos, Nizhe-Volzhskaya nab. 16 (☎39 16 41; fax 19 48 94). From pl. Men-ina, walk uphill 2 blocks and turn right. The hotel is on the left. Excellent location and reasonable prices make these sparkling rooms a fine choice. Singles 300-1800R; dou-bles 600-2500R. AmEX/MC/V. ❷

Gostinitsa Oka, Pr. Gagarina 27 (☎75 94 49; www.hoteloka.ru). *Marshrutka* #T4 runs from pl. Minina to the hotel. Even the cheapest rooms in the hotel Oka have satellite TV and a mini-bar. Singles 1500R; doubles 2800R. ❹

Zarechnaya, Pr. Lenina 36 (☎52 49 40). M: Zarechnaya. Bright, clean rooms and quick quick access to the metro make up for the hotel's distance from the center. Singles 500R; doubles 900R. ❷

🍴 FOOD

Most of the city's best restaurants are either on or close to ul. B. Pokrovskaya, as are numerous stalls selling ice cream, baked goods, *shawarma* (35R), and whole grilled chickens (100-150R). If you don't like to snack from the streets, look for the ubiquitous *produkty* signs or try **Torzhok** grocery store, ul. B. Pokrovskaya. (Open 24hr.) Alternatively, there's the **Mytny rynok,** between 2 and 4 ul. B. Pokrovskaya, which sells everything from toiletries to food. (☎39 13 87. Open daily 7am-7pm.)

Vitalich, ul. B. Pokrovskaya 35 (☎33 16 91; fax 33 04 24). Vitalich offers 5 different dining halls, each with a unique ambiance. Perhaps the most interesting for tourists is the Russian *Izba* dining hall, which celebrates traditional Russian cuisine and decor. Entrees 100-550R. Open daily noon-midnight. MC/V. ❹

U Shakaskova, ul. Piskunova 10 (☎19 82 64). A perennial favorite among locals, who skip the theatric interior for the sun-drenched outdoor seating. Entrees 100-300R. Open daily noon-midnight. ❸

Cafe Dionis, ul. B. Pokrovskaya 20. Hang out and watch the locals play billiards (120R per hr.) while enjoying simple Russian food. Entrees 33-95R. Open daily noon-1am. ❶

Shankhai (Shanghai), ul. Zvezdinki 10 (☎34 38 95). Find refuge from potato-heavy fare at the aquarium-filled world of Shankhai, which serves delicious Chinese dumplings (*pelmeni*). Entrees 85-600R. Open daily noon-midnight. MC/V. ❸

🎯 SIGHTS

Those who prefer to see the sights from the water should consider a cruises on the Volga or Oka Rivers. The **Teplokhode "Oka"** offers 2hr. cruises (daily 11am, 3, 7pm). Cruises leave downstream from Otel Tsentralniy. (☎46 44 34. 100-150R.)

KREMLIN (КРЕМЛЬ; KREML). The fortress's position atop one of the few hills in the Volga region made it a good defensive outpost. Although construction was begun in 1365, the present kremlin dates to the beginning of the 16th century. The kremlin consists of 13 towers connected by over 2km of 3.5-4.5m-thick walls with a height of 15-18m. Located inside the Dmitriyevskaya tower is the **Art Museum** (Khudozhestvennyy Muzey). Its exhibits includes a collection of icons and the death mask of Tsar Nicolas I. Inside the courtyard is a display of Russian military hardware draped with tourists waiting to have their pictures taken. (☎39 08 58; www.museum.nnov.ru/art. Open Tu-Su 10am-5pm; kassa closes 4:30pm. 50R, students 15R.)

A.M. GORKY STATE MEDAL OF HONOR MUSEUMS. Although the city is no longer named after its favorite literary son, residents do not appreciate him any less. The city still has three museums dedicated to the memory of Arshile Gorky (1904-1948). The largest and most impressive is the **A.M. Gorky Literary Museum,** which features numerous displays on the achievements of Gorky, his personal possessions, and his involvement in Soviet politics and with other members of the Russian artistic community. The museum even has a life preserver from the Russian Navy ship *Gorky*. *(Ul. Minina 26. ☎ 36 65 83. Open W-Su 9am-5pm. 20R, students 10R. Admission price includes an enthusiastic and rather lengthy Russian language tour.)* Just a few blocks away is the **A. M. Gorky Apartment Museum,** Ul. Semashko 19, which preserves the interior of Gorky's last apartment in Nizhniy Novgorod almost exactly as he left it. *(☎ 36 16 51. Open Tu-W and F-Su 9am-1pm and 2-5pm; closed last F of each month. 30R, students 20R.)* The third museum is the **house of Gorky's grandfather,** Pochtovy syezd 21. Gorky's grandpa, V. Kashirin, a foreman at a local dyer's shop took in him and his mother; however, when Gorky's mother died three years later, Gorky's grandfather kicked his 9-year-old grandson out of the house. The museum details not only Gorky's childhood but also the life of a craftsman at the end of the 19th century. *(☎ 34 06 70. 20R, students 10R. Open M-Th and Sa-Su 9am-5pm.)*

A.D. SAKHAROV APARTMENT MUSEUM. Although Andrei Sakharaov was the father of the Soviet H-bomb, he later won the Nobel Peace Prize for his staunch opposition to the arms race. He was moved to the first floor of this typical Soviet apartment building and placed under house arrest from 1980 to 1986 as punishment for his outspoken opposition to Russia's war against Afghanistan. Deprived of visitors and telephone access, he was forced to live in this four-bedroom apartment with only his wife for company. The museum has preserved his apartment and details his incarceration. *(Pr. Gagarina 214. ☎ 66 86 23. Take trolley #13 from pl. Minina or bus #43 from pl. Lenina. Open Sa-Th 10am-4pm.)*

ECONOMIC HISTORY. As a consequence of Nizhniy Novgorod's key industrial role in Russia over the last 500 years, some of its most interesting sights are economic in nature. Established in 1671, the **Markayev Trade Fair,** a two-month trade extravaganza, started around July 15th and attracted merchants from across Europe and Asia to trade silks, tea, spices, sugar, paints, furs, and more. The site of the fair was moved next to pl. Lenina in 1817, and, at its peak, the fair covered over 8km sq. Little remains at the site, as most of the structures were wooden and temporary. The 1890 **main building,** however, has survived and remains impressive. The planned economy of the Soviet period finally did away with the fair in its traditional form in 1927. Since 1991 the grounds have been used to house specialized exhibitions. Visitors are welcome to walk around. The flagship of the city's industrial economy during the Soviet period was **GAZ Automotive Works,** established over 70 years ago. The **GAZ History Museum** commemorates automotive history by displaying over 25 GAZ cars. *(Pr. Lenina 95. ☎ 56 14 38. M: Komsomolskaya. Open M-F 8am-4pm.)* The **Sokol Aircraft Plant** has long been an integral part of Soviet aviation. The **museum** within the factory details aviation history from 1932 to the present. *(Ul. Chaadaeva 1. ☎ 29 37 29; sokol@attnn.ru. Trolley #15 runs from Moskovskiy Vokzal to the Sokol plant. Open M-Th 8am-5pm.)*

THE NORTHWEST

The Northwest once held the lion's share of Russia's political power and Europe's riches, as the former glory of the Orthodox Church and the tsars testify. The kremlins and monasteries of Novgorod and Pskov, along with St. Petersburg's opulent palaces, reflect the region's historical prominence, both sacred and secular. Closer to Europe than to the heart of Russia, the Northwest is the geographical and symbolic point convergence between the European East and the Asian West.

ST. PETERSBURG

☎ (8)812

(САНКТ-ПЕТЕРБУРГ)

A city so great they named it three times—St. Petersburg, Petrograd, and Leningrad. Regardless of what you call the city on the Neva, once the home of such literati as Pushkin and Dostoevsky, it is the cultural capital of Russia. Peter the Great founded the city as the new capital of Russia in 1703 on a Finnish swamp, hoping it would offer largely landlocked Russia a chance at a navy and serve as Russia's "window on Europe." In 1917, in a nationalistic rejection of Peter's europhile tendencies, the city's name was changed to the more Russian-sounding Petrograd. Not long after, Vladimir Lenin launched his Marxist revolution here, and the city was renamed Leningrad in 1924 in his honor. While the Soviets robbed St. Petersburg of its status as Russia's capital, its beautiful buildings were left untouched while Moscow's were replaced by concrete monstrosities. In 1991, after the fall of communism, the citizens voted to restore the city's original name—St. Petersburg.

✈ INTERCITY TRANSPORTATION

Flights: The main airport, **Pulkovo** (Пулково), has 2 terminals: Pulkovo-1 (☎ 104 38 22) for domestic flights and Pulkovo-2 (☎ 104 34 44) for international flights. M2: Moskovskaya (Московская). From the Metro, take bus #39 for Pulkovo-1 (25min.) or bus #13 for Pulkovo-2 (20min.). Hostels can arrange a taxi (usually US$30-35), but taking a little initiative might save a good deal of money. Call and request to be picked up (about 30min. wait), or learn the Russian name of your destination street or hotel and you should be able to negotiate a fare of around US$20 at the airport. **Taxi Millionnaya** (Такси Миллионная, ☎ 100 00 00) offers reliable, reasonably priced service and an English-speaking operator. Fare from the center out (including booking and collection) is 500R (non-negotiated fare around US$17) and from the airport to the center 600R (US$20). Millionnaya also runs within the city center (see **Local Transportation**, p. 704).

Air France, Bolshaya Morskaya ul. 35 (Большая Морская; ☎ 325 82 52; fax 325 82 53). M3: Gostinyy Dvor. Open M-F 9:30am-5:30pm.

British Airways, Malaya Konyushennaya ul. 1/3 (Малая Конюшенная; ☎ 380 06 26). M2: Gostinyy. Open M-F 9am-5:30pm.

Delta Airlines, Bolshaya Morskaya ul. 36 (Большая Морская; ☎ 311 58 20; fax 325 62 28). M2: Nevskiy Prospekt. Open M-F 9am-5:30pm.

Finnair, Kazanskaya ul. 44 (Казанская; ☎ 326 18 70). M4: Sadovaya. Open M-F 9am-6pm.

Lufthansa, Nevskiy pr. 32, 3rd fl. (Невский; ☎ 320 10 00 or 320 10 03). M2: Nevskiy Prospekt. Open M-F 9am-5:30pm.

SAS, Nevskiy pr. 25 (Невский; ☎ 326 26 00; fax 326 26 01),in the Sheraton Nevskiy Palace Hotel. M2: Nevskiy Prospekt. Open M-F 9am-5pm.

Swissair, Malaya Konyushennaya ul. 11/3 (Малая Конюшенная; ☎ 329 25 25). M2: Nevskiy Prospekt. Enter on Shvedskiy per. (Шведский). Open M-F 9am-5pm.

Trains: Tsentralnye Zheleznodorozhnyye Kassy (Центральные Железнодорожные Кассы; Central Ticket Offices), Canal Griboyedova 24 (Грибоедова; ☎ 067 or 314 35 25). Open M-Sa 8am-8pm, Su 8am-6pm. Buy international tickets at windows #4-6. If you don't speak Russian, the aid of a travel agent or hotel staffer may be necessary to make a reservation. Many trains sell out a day in advance. Check your ticket for the station your train departs from; have your passport ready for inspection.

Baltiysky Vokzal (Балтийский Вокзал; Baltic station; ☎ 168 28 59). M1: Baltiyskaya. Serves a selection of Russian destinations.

RUSSIA

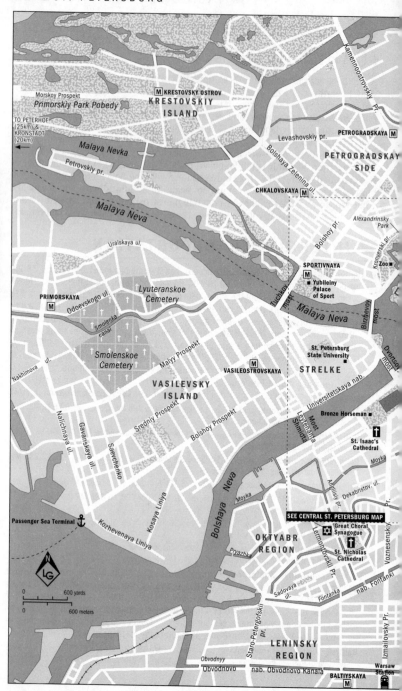

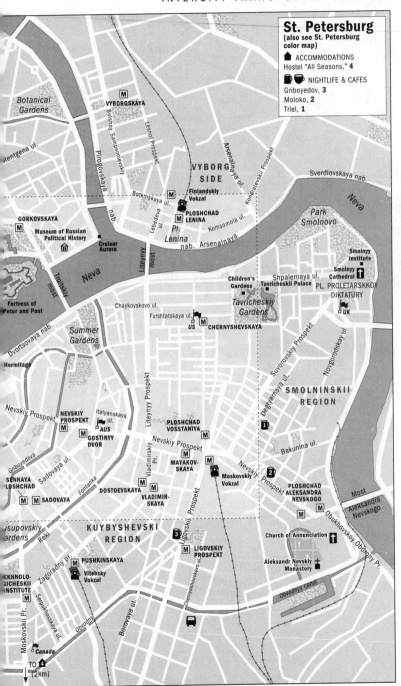

St. Petersburg
(also see St. Petersburg color map)

🛏 ACCOMMODATIONS
Hostel "All Seasons," 4

☕ NIGHTLIFE & CAFES
Griboyedov, 3
Moloko, 2
Triel, 1

RUSSIA

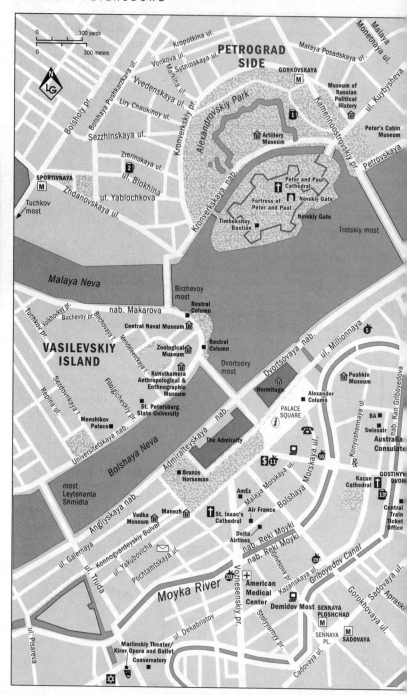

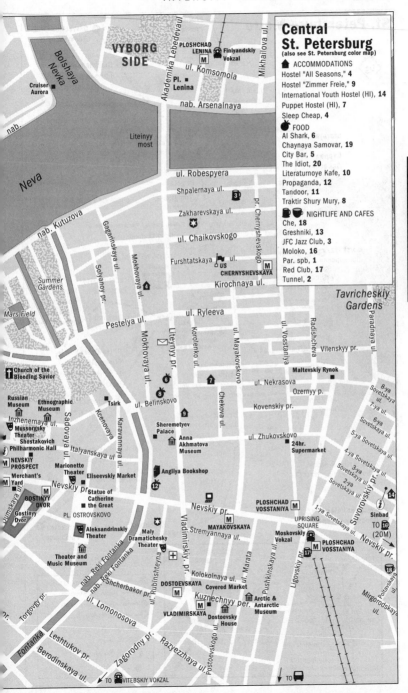

Central St. Petersburg
(also see St. Petersburg color map)

⌂ **ACCOMMODATIONS**
Hostel "All Seasons," 4
Hostel "Zimmer Freie," 9
International Youth Hostel (HI), 14
Puppet Hostel (HI), 7
Sleep Cheap, 4

🍎 **FOOD**
Al Shark, 6
Chaynaya Samovar, 19
City Bar, 5
The Idiot, 20
Literaturnoye Kafe, 10
Propaganda, 12
Tandoor, 11
Traktir Shury Mury, 8

☕ **NIGHTLIFE AND CAFES**
Che, 18
Greshniki, 13
JFC Jazz Club, 3
Moloko, 16
Par. spb, 1
Red Club, 17
Tunnel, 2

RUSSIA

St. Petersburg Metro

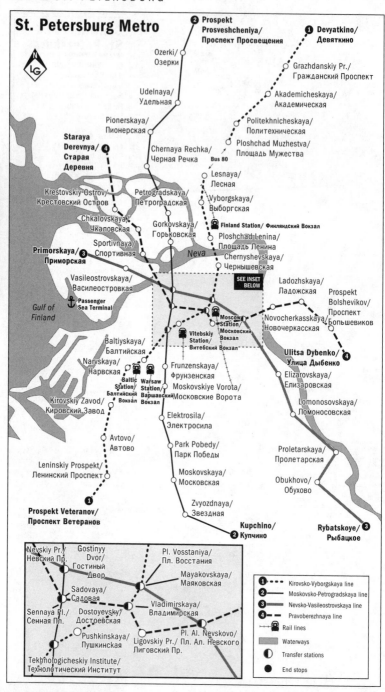

Finlyandskiy Vokzal (Финляндский Вокзал; Finland Station; ☎168 76 87). M1: Pl. Lenina (Ленина). To: **Helsinki, FIN** (6hr., 2 per day, 1375R).

Ladozhsky Vokzal (Ладожский Вокзал; ☎055). M4: Ladozhskaya. Serves destinations in Russia and Finland.

Moskovskiy Vokzal (Московский Вокзал; Moscow Station; ☎168 45 97). M1: Pl. Vosstaniya (Восстания). To: **Moscow** (5-8hr., 12-15 per day, 300-1300R); **Novgorod** (3-4hr., 2 per day, 66R); **Sevastopol, UKR** (35hr., 1 per day, 754-1186R).

Vitebskiy Vokzal (Витебский Вокзал; Vitebskiy Station; ☎168 58 07). M1: Pushkinskaya (Пушкинская). To: **Kaliningrad** (26hr., 550-3300R, 1 per day); **Kyiv, UKR** (25hr., 2 every 2 days, 506-637R); **Odessa, UKR** (36hr., 1 per day, 654R); **Rīga, LAT** (13hr., 1 per day, 887R); **Tallinn, EST** (9hr., 1 per day, 350R); **Vilnius, LIT** (14hr., every 2 days, 647R).

Buses: Nab. Obvodnogo Kanala 36 (Обводного Канала; ☎166 57 77). M4: Ligovsky pr. Take tram #19, 25, 44, or 49 or trolley #42 to the stop just across the canal. Facing the canal, turn right and walk 2 long blocks alongside it. The station will be on your right, behind the abandoned building. Surcharge for advance tickets. Open daily 6am-8pm. To: **Minsk, BLR** (18hr., daily at 6pm, 470R); **Rīga, LAT** (12hr., daily at 7am and 8:30pm, 450R); **Tallinn, EST** (7hr., daily at 8am and 11pm, 280R). **Eurolines,** Nab. Obvodnogo Kanala 120 (Обводного Канала; ☎168 28 59), is located up the street and offers similar prices and destinations. The long-distance counter is on your left as you enter. The central ticket office deals mostly with plane tickets, but bus service information is available. (Open M-Sa 8am-8pm and Su 8am-6pm.)

◩ ORIENTATION

St. Petersburg sits at the mouth of the **Neva River** (Нева) on the **Gulf of Finland** (Финский Залив; Finskiy Zaliv), occupying 44 islands among 50 canals. The heart of the city lies on the mainland, in the **Admiralteyskiy District** between the south bank of the Neva and the **Fontanka River.** Many of St. Petersburg's major sights—including the Hermitage and the three main cathedrals—are on or near **Nevskiy Prospekt** (Невский Проспект), the city's main street, which extends from the **Admiralty** (from where Peter is said to have overseen the city's early construction) to the **Alexander Nevsky Monastery** and the center's newer quarters, developed primarily in the late 19th century. In this area, east of the Fontanka, the **Smolnyy Institute** and most of the **train** and **bus stations** are found. **Moskovskiy Vokzal** (Московский Вокзал; Moscow Train Station) on **Ploshchad Vosstaniya** (Восстания Площадь; Uprising Square) is at the kink midway down Nevskiy Prospekt, marking the change

BRIDGE THE GAP

Inspired by his experiences in Holland, Peter designed a canal-crossed city to house his new Russian navy. In St. Petersburg's 300-year history, about 400 bridges have been built.

Between April and November, when the ice has melted, the bridges crossing the city's major waterways open to allow ships to pass. During White Nights (May-June), when St. Petersburg enjoys near-continuous daylight, the bridge raising is particularly fun to watch. Yet if you plan to party into the wee hours of the morning, be sure to keep these little overpasses in mind. Raised bridges have left many tourists, residents, and literary characters on the wrong side of the river. Petersburg's bridges are raised during the following times:

Volodarskiy: 2:00-3:45am and 4:14-5:45am

Finlyandskiy: 2:30-5:10am

A. Nevskovo: 1:30-5:05am

Bolsheokhtinskiy: 2-5am

Lityenyy: 1:50-4:40am

Troitskiy: 1:50-4:50am

Dvortsovyy: 1:35-2:55am and 3:15-4:50am

Letyenanta Shmidta: 1:40-4:55am

Birzhevoy: 2:10-4:50am

Tuchkov: 2:10-3:05am and 3:35-4:45am

Sampsonievskiy: 2:10-2:45am and 3:20-4:25am

Grenaderskiy: 2:45-3:45am and 4:20-4:50am

Kantemirovskiy: 2:45-3:45am and 4:20-4:50am

from what is oddly called Old Nevskiy (Старый Невский; Staryy Nevskiy) to the thoroughfare's more central section, simply called "Nevskiy." North of the center and across the Neva lies **Vasilevskiy Island** (Василевский Остров; Vasilevskiy Ostrov), the city's largest island. Most of the island's sights, which are among St. Petersburg's oldest, sit on its eastern edge in the **Strelka** (Стрелка) neighborhood. Here the rectangular grid of streets recalls early plans for a network of canals on the island that was originally intended to be the base for Peter the Great's dream city, later relocated to what is now known as Admiralteyskiy. The city's **Sea Terminal,** the ferry port, is at the island's southwestern edge on the Gulf of Finland. On the north side of the Neva, across from the **Winter Palace,** is the small **Petrograd Side** archipelago, which houses the Peter and Paul Fortress, quiet residential neighborhoods, and the wealthy **Kirov Island** trio. Outside the city center on the mainland are the southern suburbs and the northern **Vyborg Side** neighborhoods; both are vast expanses of tenements and factories with few sights for tourists, though if you make a friend or two in the city, they might invite you out here to experience Petersburg domesticity.

RUSSIA

The pipes and drainage system in St. Petersburg have not been changed since the city was founded. There is no effective water purification system, so exposure to *giardia* is very likely. Always boil tap water for at least 10min., dry your washed veggies, and drink bottled water. See **Essentials: Health,** p. 664.

⊏ LOCAL TRANSPORTATION

Public Transportation: The **Metro** (Метро), the deepest in the world, runs daily 5:45am-12:15am and is generally busy; avoid peak hours (8-9am and 5-6pm) if possible. A Metro **token** (жетон; zheton) costs 8R; stock up, as lines are often long and cutting is common. Consider investing in a multiple-journey ticket valid for 7, 15, or 30 days. **Buses, trams,** and **trolleys** (6R) run fairly frequently. Licensed private minibuses (маршрутки; **marshrutki**), which display their routes in their windows, cost more (7-20R) and are used more by commuters than by tourists, but they move much more quickly through traffic and will stop on request. Read the destination of each numbered line on the signs at the bus stop or check the list of stops posted on the outside of the bus. Trolleys #1, 5, and 22 run from Uprising Square to the bottom of Nevskiy pr., near the Hermitage. Buses, trams, and trolleys run 6am-midnight. Tickets (7R) should be purchased from the driver. A **monthly transportation card** (360R) is good for unlimited public transportation for a given calendar month; purchase one at any Metro station.

Taxis: Both marked and private cabs operate in St. Petersburg. Marked cabs have a metered rate of 11R per km; add 35R if you call ahead (☎068). Many locals get around by "catching a car:" they flag down a car on the street, determine where it's going, agree on a price, and hop a ride. This practice is usually cheaper than taking marked cabs. *Let's Go* does not recommend hitchhiking. If you choose to flag down a car, keep in mind that it's a good idea to have some facility in Russian and a degree of familiarity with the streets along your route. Never get in a car with more than 1 person in it.

BRIDGE OUT. The bridges over the Neva go up at night to allow boats to pass. It's beautiful to watch, as long as you don't get caught on the wrong side of the river. See the sidebar, p. 703, for the schedule of bridge openings.

⚡ PRACTICAL INFORMATION

TOURIST AND FINANCIAL SERVICES

Tourist Office: City Tourist Information Center, ul. Sadovaya 14/52 (☎310 82 62 or 310 22 31; www.ctic.spb.ru). M: Gostinyy Dvor. In addition to offering English-language advice and free brochures, the info center sells postcards and souvenir books. Open M-F 10am-7pm. There is also a smaller office, pl. Dvortsovaya 12, between the Hermitage and the Admiralty, which has fewer free pamphlets but more souvenirs. Open M-Su 10am-7pm. Also helpful are the free English-language publications the *Neva News* and the *St. Petersburg Times,* which are available in hostel, hotels, and some restaurants. The two publications offer a comprehensive list of services and important information for travelers.

Tours: Russian **bus tours** (80min.; 100R, students 80R) leave from the corner of Nevskiy pr. and the Griboyedov Canal (Грибоедов), in front of the Kazan Cathedral, and cover the main sights. The "intercity service," Nevskiy Prospekt 30 (☎318 92 89), at the corner with Griboyedov Canal, offers daily (10am and 2pm) guided tours in English of St. Petersburg, Peter and Paul Fortress, Pushkin, the cathedrals, the Hermitage, Pavlovsk, and Peterhof. M2: Nevskiy Prospekt. 400-1800R per tour. **Boat cruises** (1hr.) leave from the Neva, in front of the Bronze Horseman. (Daily noon-10pm about every hr.; June-Aug. 1:20am to see the raising of the bridges. 150R.) Cruises also leave 11am-8pm every 30-40min. from the Fontanka, at the corner of Nevskiy pr 160R, under 12 80R), and from the Griboyedov Canal, at the corner of Nevskiy pr. (every hr.; 300R, children 150R). **Russkie Kruzy** cruises leave every hr. from nab. Dvortsovaya, behind the Hermitage, and last 1-2hr. Cruise price (300-600R) includes a meal. (☎/fax 325 61 20; www.russian-cruises.ru. Cruises leave noon-10pm.)

Peter's Walking Tours, 3-ya Sovyetskaya ul. 28 (3-я Советская; www.peterswalk.com), in the International Hostel. Offers a range of enjoyable, informative 3-6hr. English-language excursions centered around particular themes. Especially popular is Peter's Big Night Out Tour, during which your guide takes you to the best party spots in town, then makes sure you get back in the morning. Tours cost between 400-500R. Tours can be booked online or in person, but those who simply turn up at the pre-arranged departure points are more than welcome. Details on tours and meeting places can be found in their widely available pamphlet.

Budget Travel: Sindbad Travel (FIYTO), ul. 3-ya Sovetskaya 28 (☎327 83 84; www.sindbad.ru), in the International Hostel. Books plane, train, and bus tickets. Student discounts on airplane tickets 10-80%. English spoken. Open M-F 9am-10pm, Sa-Su 10am-6pm. 2nd location, Universitetskaya nab. 11 (Университетская; ☎/fax 324 08 80). Open M-F 10am-6pm.

Consulates: Citizens of **Ireland** and **New Zealand** should contact their embassies in Moscow but can use the UK consulate in an emergency. **Australia:** Italyanskaya ul. 1 (☎325 73 33; www.australianembassy.ru). M2: Nevskiy Pr. Open M-F 9am-6pm. **Canada:** Malodetskoselskiy pr. 32 (Малодетскосельский; ☎325 84 48; fax 325 83 93). M2: Frunzenskaya. Open M-F 9am-1pm, 2-5pm. **UK:** Pl. Proletarskoy Diktatury 5 (Пролетарской Диктатуры; ☎320 32 00; www.britain.spb.ru). M1: Chernyshevskaya. Open M-F 9:30am-1pm, 2-5:30pm. **US:** Furshtatskaya ul. 15 (Фурштатская; 24hr. line ☎331 26 00; www.stpetersburg-usconsulate.ru). M1: Chernyshevskaya. Services for US citizens open M-Tu and Th-F 2-5pm and W 10am-1pm. Phone inquiries from citizens accepted M, Tu, Th, F 10am-1pm and W 3-5pm.

Currency Exchange: Look for "обмен валюты" (obmen valyuty) signs everywhere. **Sberbank** (☎329 87 87), Dumskaya ul. 1 (M2: Nevskiy pr.), Nevskiy pr. 82/99.

American Express: Malaya Morskaya ul. 23 (☎326 45 00; fax 326 45 01). Open M-F 9am-5pm.

English-Language Bookstore: Angliya British Bookshop (Англия), nab. Reki Fontanki 38 (Реки Фонтанки; ☎279 8284; www.anglophile.ru). Enter number 38, and the bookstore will be on the right. Stocks a variety of titles, including the Russian masters in translation. Open daily 10am-7pm.

COMMUNICATION AND EMERGENCY SERVICES

Police Services for foreigners: ☎ 164 97 87 or 278 30 14.

Pharmacy: Throughout the city center. **PetroFarm,** Nevskiy pr. 22 (☎ 314 54 01), stocks Western medicines and toiletries. Open 24hr. Pharmacist daily 8am-10pm. MC/V.

Medical Assistance: American Medical Clinic, nab. Reki Moyki 78, #78 (Реки Мойки; ☎ 140 20 90; fax 310 46 64). M2/4: Sennaya Pl./Sadovaya. Follow per. Grivtsova across Griboyedov Canal and along to the Moyka river. English-speaking doctors provide comprehensive services, including house calls. Consultation US$50. Open 24hr. AmEx/MC/V. **British-American Family Clinic,** Grafsky per. 7 (Графски; ☎ 327 60 30; fax 327 60 40), on the corner of Vladmirskiy pr. Expat staff offers primary care services. Consultation with a Western doctor €90, Russian doctor €60. 25% discount with ISIC if you pay in cash. Open 24hr. **Euromed Clinic,** Suvorovsky pr. 60 (☎ 327 03 01; www.euromed.ru). M1: pl. Vosstaniya. 24hr. emergency and evaluation services, dental care, and billing services for major European and Asian insurance policies. Consultation $100. 25% student discount with ISIC.

Internet and Telephones: Cafemax, Nevskiy pr. 90-92 (☎ 273 66 55; spb@e-max.ru). M3/1; Mayakovskaya. Massive, modern Internet cafe. 70R per hr. All night for only 120R (11pm-7am). Open 24hr. **Red Fog Internet Cafe,** Kazanskaya ul. 30-32 (☎ 595 41 38). M2: Nevskiy pr. 40R per hr., nights (11:30pm-8:30am) 100R. Open 24 hr. **Quo Vadis,** Nevskiy pr. 24 (☎ 311 80 11; www.quovadis.ru). Internet 80R per hr., with ISIC 70R. Long-distance calls to the US 12R per min. Open 24hr.

Post Office: Pochtamtskaya ul. 9 (Почтамтская; ☎ 312 83 02). From Nevskiy pr., go west on ul. Malaya Morskaya, which becomes Pochtamtskaya ul. It's about 2 blocks past St. Isaac's Cathedral. **Currency exchange** and **telephone** service. International mail at windows #24-30. **Poste Restante** held up to 1 month at windows #1 and 2. Open M-Sa 9am-7:45pm, Su 10am-5:45pm. **Postal Code:** 190 000.

▌ ACCOMMODATIONS

Travelers can choose from a variety of **hostels** and **private apartments.** The *St. Petersburg Times,* an English-language newspaper, lists apartments for rent; free copies are available at the City Tourist Information Center.

Sleep Cheap, Mokhovaya ul. 18/32 (☎ 115 13 04; www.sleepcheap.spb.ru). M1: Chernyshevskaya. When you reach Mokhovaya 18, head into the courtyard. Go down about 30m, and you'll find #32 on the left, with a sign above the door saying "Sleep Cheap." Light pine floors and immaculate modern furnishings define St. Petersburg's newest hostel. The English-speaking staff is more than happy to help you book tickets. A/C. Internet 50R. Breakfast included. Laundry 150R. Airport and train transfer available. Dorms 700R. ❷

Hostel "Zimmer Freie," Lityenniy pr. 46/23 (☎ 273 08 67 or 973 37 57; www.zimmer.ru). To check in, talk to the English-speaking building manager who sits in the front hall. Not the fanciest of hostels, but the rooms are clean, and prices are sensational for the location. Showers, bathrooms, TV, refrigerator, kitchen, and free laundry. Check out noon. May 1-Sept. 30 dorms US$15, singles US$30; Oct. 1-Apr. 30 US$10/US$20. 5% discount with YIHA or ISIC cards. ❶

International Youth Hostel (HI), 3-ya Sovetskaya ul. 28 (☎ 329 80 18; www.ryh.ru). M1: Pl. Vosstaniya. Walk along Suvorovskiy pr. (Суворовский) for 3 blocks, then turn right on 3-ya Sovetskaya ul. TV and English movies in common room. Internet 1R per min. Breakfast included (8-10am). Friendly English-speaking staff. Communal showers 8am-1am. Laundry US$4 for 5kg. Reception 8am-1am. Check-out 11am. 3- to 5-bed dorms US$21; doubles $26. US$2 discount with HI, US$1 with ISIC. ❷

Puppet Hostel (HI), ul. Nekrasova 12. (Некрасова; ☎272 54 01; www.hostel-pup-pet.ru), on the 4th fl. M3: Mayakovskaya. Walk up ul. Mayakovskaya (Маяковская) and take the 2nd left on Nekrasova. Friendly, English-speaking staff. Spotless rooms. Breakfast included. Reception 8am-midnight. Check-out noon. Mar.1-Nov. 1 dorms (3-5 beds) US$19; doubles US$48; Nov. 1-Dec. 15 US$15/US$38; Dec. 15-Jan. 15 US$16/US $42. US$1 discount with HI membership or ISIC. ❷

Hostel "All Seasons" (HI), Yakovlevskiy per. 11 (☎327 10 70; www.hostel.ru). M2: Park Pobedy. Walking along ul. Moskovskaya, turn right. When you reach the end of the park turn right on Kuznetsovskaya ul. There will be signs pointing to the hostel. Clean but basic rooms. Low prices compensate for the remote location. English spoken. Open 24hr. TV and kitchen available. Nov. 11-Dec. 28 and Jan. 11-Jan. 31 dorms (5-8 beds) €4.5, singles €17.5; Feb. 1-Apr. 30, May 11-31, and Sept. 1-Nov. 10 €5.5/€19.5; May 1-May 10 and June 1-Aug. 31 €8.5/€26.5. 4-bed dorms €1 more. €0.5 discount with HI membership or ISIC. MC/V. ❷

🗒 FOOD

Market vendors offer fresh produce, meat, bread, pastries, and honey. The biggest **markets** are the **covered market,** Kuznechnyy per. 3 (Кузнечный; open M-Sa 8am-8pm, Su 8am-7pm), just around the corner from M1: Vladimirskaya, and the **Maltsevskiy Rynok** (Мальцевский Рынок), ul. Nekrasova 52 (M1: Pl. Vosstaniya), at the top of Ligovskiy pr. (Лиговский). It's open daily 9am-8pm. There is a **24hr. supermarket,** ul. Zhukovskogo (Жуковского; M3: Pl. Vosstaniya; ☎279 14 27). **Yeliseyevskiy** (Елисеевский), Nevskiy pr. 56, stocks groceries, confections, liquors, and caviar amidst stained glass and chandeliers. (M2: Nevskiy Prospekt. Open M-F 10am-10pm, Sa-Su 11am-10pm.)

RUSSIAN RESTAURANTS

Literaturnoye Kafe (Литературное Кафе), 18 Nevskiy pr. (☎312 60 57). M2: Gostinyy Dvor. In its former incarnation as a confectioner's shop, this cafe boasted a clientele of luminaries from Dostoevsky to Pushkin, who came here the night before his fatal duel. Sumptuously decorated, the cafe boasts an excellent menu with reasonable prices. Live classical music during the day and Russian romances at night. *Bliny* with mushrooms 100R. Beef Stroganoff 250R. Black Caviar 450R. Cover 20R. Menu in Russian and English. Open daily 11am-11pm. ❸

Chaynaya Samovar (Чайная Самовар), Gorokovaya ul. 27 (☎314 39 45). M2: Sennaya Pl. Perhaps the best place in St. Petersburg to go for *bliny*. The rustic decor is offset by the pop music, likely chosen by the young waitstaff. Menu in Russian. Блины мяслом (*bliny s myaslom*; pancakes with butter) 16R. Open M-Su 10am-9pm. ❶

Propaganda (Пропаганда), nab. Reki Fontanka 40 (Реки Фонтанка; ☎275 35 58). M2: Gostinyy Dvor. Walk toward pl. Vosstaniya on Nevskiy pr. Cross the Fontanka and turn left on nab. Reki Fontanka. Serves American and Russian food in a Soviet-themed interior. Entrees 150-350R. Menu in English and Russian. Open daily 1pm-3am. ❸

Traktir Shury Mury (Трактир Шуры Муры), ul. Belinskogo 8 (Белинского; ☎279 85 50). M2: Gostinyy Dvor or M1: Vladimirskaya. From Vladimirskaya, walk toward the Admiralty and take a right on nab. Reki Fontanka. At next bridge, go right on Belinskogo. Russian and European cuisine served in a *dacha*-like setting. Entrees 100-200R. Menu in Russian. Open 11am-last customer. MC/V. ❷

The Idiot (Идиот), nab. Reki Moyki 82 (Реки Мойки; ☎315 16 75). M2: Sennaya pl. Turn right on Grivtsova per. and walk toward the Admiralty, then left on nab. Reki Moyki. Named for the Dostoevsky classic, this restaurant has salon-like decor and a variety of Russian vegetarian options, all served with a free shot of vodka. Inconsistent service. Entrees 120-250R, plus 10% tip. Happy hour 6:30-7:30pm offers 2-for-1 beer and wine and 1 vodka on the house. Menu in Russian and English. Open daily 11am-1am. ❸

INTERNATIONAL RESTAURANTS

City Bar, Millionnaya ul. 10 (☎314 10 37; www.citybar.ru). Owned and staffed largely by Americans, the City Bar is a popular expat hangout offering standard American food. Cheeseburgers 150-280R. Breakfast 90-150R. *Amerikanskiy* business lunch 150R. Open M-Su noon-last customer. MC/V. ❸

Tandoor (Тандур), Voznesenskiy pr. 2 (Вознесенский; ☎312 38 86), on the corner of Admiralteyskiy pr. (Адмиралтейский), at the end of Nevskiy pr. M2: Nevskiy Prospekt. With refined Indian decor and the English conversation, Tandoor makes it easy to forget that you're in Russia. Vegetarian dishes available. Lunch special M-F noon-5pm US$10. Dinner US$15-18. Open daily noon-11pm. AmEx/DC/MC. ❹

Al Shark (Ал Шарк), Lityennyy pr. 67 (☎272 90 73). The 24hr. *shawarma* joint has became a fixture on the St. Petersburg dining scene. A variety of Middle Eastern-inspired cuisine. *Shvarma v pite* (spiced meat in pita) 50R. Open 24hr. ❶

◎ SIGHTS

St. Petersburg is a city steeped in its past. Citizens speak of the time "before the Revolution" as though it were only a few years ago, and of dear old Peter and Catherine as if they were good friends. Signs such as the one at Nevskiy pr. 14 recall the harder times of WWII: "Citizens! During artillery bombardments this side of the street is more dangerous." The worst effects of those bombings were mitigated by Soviet-era reconstruction, and a more recent wave of projects restored the best sights in preparation for the city's 300th anniversary in 2003.

▨ THE HERMITAGE

Dvortsovaya nab. 34 (Дворцовая; ☎311 34 20; www.hermitagemuseum.ru). M2: Nevskiy Prospekt. Exiting the Metro, turn left and walk down Nevskiy pr. to its end at the Admiralty. Head right across Dvortsovaya pl. The kassa is located on the river side of the building. Going early may help avoid long lines. Allow at least 3hr. to see the museum. Open Su 10:30am-5pm and Tu-Sa 10:30am-6pm; cashier and upper floors close 1hr. earlier. 350R, students free. Cameras 100R, video 350R. 90min. English tours 120R. English audio guide 250R. Ticket includes access to all 5 Hermitage buildings. AmEx/MC/V.

Originally a collection of 225 paintings bought by **Catherine the Great** in 1764, the **State Hermitage Museum** (Эрмитаж; Ermitazh), the world's largest art collection, rivals the Louvre in architectural, historical, and artistic significance. The tsars lived with their collection in the Winter Palace and Hermitage until 1917, when both the palace and the collection were nationalized. Catherine II once wrote of the treasures, "The only ones to admire all this are the mice and me." Fortunately, since 1852 the five buildings have been open to all. Ask for an indispensable English floor guide at the info desk. The rooms are numbered, and the museum is organized chronologically by floor, starting with **prehistoric artifacts** in the Winter Palace and **Egyptian, Greek, and Roman art** on the ground floor of the Small and Great Hermitages. On the second floors of the Hermitages are collections of 15th- to 19th-century **European art**. It is impossible to absorb the museum's entire collection in a day or even a week—only 5% of the three-million-piece collection is on display at any one time. If you're running late, visit the upper floors first—the museum's higher floors close earliest.

WINTER PALACE (ЗИМНИЙ ДВОРЕЦ; ZIMNIY DVORETS). Commissioned in 1762, the majestic architecture of the Winter Palace reflects the extravagant rococo tastes of Empress Elizabeth and the architect Rastrelli. Rooms 190-198 on the second floor are the palace **state rooms.** The rest of the floor houses 15th- to 18th-century **French art** (Rooms 273-297) and 10th- to 20th-century **Russian art** (Rooms 151-187). The third floor exhibits **Impressionist, Post-Impressionist,** and **20th-century European art.** The famous **Malachite Hall** (Room 189) contains six tons of malachite columns, boxes, and urns, each painstakingly constructed from thousands of matched stones to give the illusion of having been carved from one massive rock.

OTHER BUILDINGS. By the end of the 1760s, the collection amassed by the Empress had become too large for the Winter Palace, and Catherine appointed Vallin de la Mothe to build the **Small Hermitage** (Малый Эрмитаж; Malyy Ermitazh), a retreat for herself and her lovers. The **Large Hermitage** (Большой Эрмитаж; Bolshoy Ermitazh) was completed in the 1780s and displays excellent **Italian** (Rooms 207-238) and **Dutch art** (Rooms 248-254). In Rooms 226-227, an exact copy of Raphael's *Loggia*, commissioned by Catherine the Great, covers the walls just as in the Vatican. In 1851, Stasov, a famous imperial Russian architect, built the **New Hermitage** (Новый Эрмитаж; Novyy Ermitazh).

NEAR THE HERMITAGE

DVORTSOVAYA PLOSHCHAD (ДВОРЦОВАЯ ПЛОЩАДЬ). This wind-swept site has witnessed much of Russian history's milestones. Catherine was crowned here in Palace Square and, years later, Nicholas II's guards fired into a crowd of peaceful demonstrators on "Bloody Sunday," precipitating the 1905 revolution. In October 1917, Lenin's Bolsheviks seized power from Kerensky's provisional government here during the storming of the Winter Palace. Today, vendors peddle ice cream and souvenirs beneath the angel at the top of the Alexander Column (Александрийская Колонна; Aleksandriyskaya Kolonna), which commemorates Russia's 1812 victory over Napoleon. The column weighs 700 tons and took two years to cut from a cliff in Karelia. When the column arrived in St. Petersburg, it was raised in just 40min. by 2000 war veterans using a complex pulley system.

THE ADMIRALTY (АДМИРАЛТЕЙСТВО; ADMIRALTEYSTVO). The only way into the Admiralty is to become an officer in the Russian Navy, but tourists can admire its impressive exterior and

A WHITE RUSSIAN

During St. Petersburg's beloved White Nights, held May 25-June 17, the city barely sleeps, partl[y] because of summer's hard-core partying, but also in large par[t] because of the 22½hr. of dayligh[t] per day that induce a kind o[f] wakeful indifference to the body'[s] normal sleeping pattern.

If you arrive in the city at the beginning of the summer, you can go out for a White Nights Festiva[l] show in the Mariinskiy, and enjo[y] what may well be one of the mos[t] beautiful spectacles of your life. Afterward, allow yourself the plea-sure of strolling the streets of a[ ]sleepless city cloaked in a seduc[-]tive shroud of silky twilight.

The natural festival peaks i[n] mid-June with the shortest nigh[t] (1½hr. of diminished twilight) o[n] the 22nd. Municipal festivitie[s] consist mostly of expensive ba[l]lets, operas, and concerts in th[e] city's most renowned theaters like the Mariinskiy and Shostakov[-]ich Philharmonia. Thankfully, how[-]ever, simply by extending bedtime just a few hours, everyone ca[n] afford to enjoy the early-morning spectacle of the Neva's bridges rising high to allow the passage o[f] cruisers, liners, and other vessels that glide beneath during the opened window of opportunity. It's a great time to meet people a[t] the banks of the river, drink bee[r] chat with fellow expats an[d] friendly Russians, and enjoy th[e] show.

gleaming golden spire, visible throughout St. Petersburg. The spire was painted black during WWII to hide it from German artillery bombers. Peter supposedly supervised the construction of St. Petersburg from the tower, one of the oldest buildings in the city. The gardens, initially designed as a firing range, now hold statues of important Russian literary figures. The Admiralty is home to young Russian men who spend five years here studying engineering in preparation for military careers. *(M2: Nevskiy Prospekt.)*

BRONZE HORSEMAN. This hulking statue of Peter the Great astride a rearing horse terrorized the protagonists in works by Alexander Pushkin and Andrey Bely by coming to life and chasing them through the streets. In real life, the statue hasn't moved from the site on which Catherine the Great had it set in 1782. *(M2: Nevskiy Prospekt. On the river, in the park left of the Admiralty.)*

VASILEYVSKIY ISLAND (ВАСИЛЬЕВСКИЙ ОСТРОВ; VASILYEVSKIY OSTROV). Just across the bridge from the Hermitage, the Strelka (Стрелка; arrow or promontory) section of the city's biggest island juts into the river, dividing it in two and providing a spectacular view of both sides. The former Stock Exchange (now the Naval Museum) dominates the square on the island's east end, and the ships' prows and anchors sticking out of the two red rostral columns proclaim the glory of Peter's modern navy. St. Petersburg State University and the Academy of Arts, as well as some of its most interesting museums (see **Museums,** p. 716), are housed on the embankment facing the Admiralty. *(Take bus #10 from Nevskiy pr.)*

ST. ISAAC'S CATHEDRAL

Isaakievskaya pl. between Admiralteyskiy pr. and ul. Malaya Morskaya. M2: Nevskiy Prospekt. Exit the Metro, turn left and go almost to the end of Nevskiy pr. Turn left on Malaya Morskaya. ☎ 315 97 32. Cathedral open summer Su-Tu and Th-Sa 10am-8pm; winter Su-Tu and Th-Sa 11am-7pm; kassa closes 1hr. earlier. 250R, students 125R. Cameras 50R, video 100R. Colonade summer Su-Tu and Th-Sa 10am-7pm; winter Th-Tu 11am-3pm. 100R, students 50R. Cameras 25R, video 50R. Enter on the south side (from Malaya Morskaya). A kassa is right of the entrance, but foreigners buy tickets inside.

Intricately carved masterpieces of iconography find the home they deserve in the awesome **St. Isaac's Cathedral** (Исаакиевский Собор; Isaakiyevskiy Sobor), a 19th-century megalith built under the reign of Alexander I. On a sunny day, the 100kg of pure gold coating the dome can be seen for miles. The cost of this opulent cathedral was well over five times that of the Winter Palace, and 60 laborers died from mercury inhalation during the gilding process. Due in part to architect Auguste de Montferrand's lack of experience, construction took 40 years; the superstition that the Romanov dynasty would fall with the cathedral's completion didn't speed things up. The cathedral was completed in 1858. Some of Russia's greatest artists worked on the 150 murals and mosaics inside. Although officially designated a museum in 1931, the cathedral still holds religious services on major holidays. The breathtaking 360-degree view of St. Petersburg is worth the 260-stair climb to the top of the **colonnade.**

FORTRESS OF PETER AND PAUL

M2: Gorkovskaya. Exiting the Metro, bear right on Kamennoostrovskiy pr. (Каменноостровский), the unmarked street in front of you. Follow it to the river and cross the wooden bridge to the island fortress. ☎ 238 07 61. Open M and W-Su 11am-6pm, Tu 11am-5pm; closed last Tu of each month. Purchase a single ticket for most sights (120R, students 60R) at the kassa in the "boathouse" in the middle of the fortress or in the smaller kassa to the right just inside the main entrance. English tours about 300R (call ahead). Fortress wall 50R, children under 10 30R.

Across the river from the Hermitage, the walls and golden spire of the Fortress of Peter and Paul (Петропавловская Крепость; Petropavlovskaya Krepost) beckon. Construction of the fortress, supervised by Peter the Great himself, began on May 27, 1703; the date is now considered to mark the birthday of St. Petersburg. Although it was intended as a defense against the Swedes, Peter I defeated the invaders before the bulwarks were finished and converted the fortress into a prison for political dissidents. Inmates' graffiti is still legible on the citadel's stone walls. Arrive early to set your watch by the boom of the cannon that's fired from the spire of the cathedral every day at noon.

CRUISER AURORA (АВРОРА; AVRORA). Deployed in the 1905 Russo-Japanese war, this ship later played a critical role in the 1917 Revolution when it fired a blank by the Winter Palace, scaring the pants off Kerensky and his provisional government. Cannons and exhibits await on board. *(5min. down the river past Peter's Cabin, on the Bolshaya Nevka River. ☎ 230 84 40. Open Tu-Th and Sa-Su 10:30am-4pm. Free.)*

PETER AND PAUL CATHEDRAL. The main attraction within the fortress, the cathedral (Петропавловский Собор; Petropavlovskiy Sobor) glows with walls of rose and aquamarine marble. At 122.5m, it's the tallest building in the city. From the ceiling, cherubs keep watch over breathtaking Baroque iconostasis and the ornate coffins of Peter the Great and his successors. Before the main vault sits the recently restored **Chapel of St. Catherine the Martyr.** The bodies of Nicholas II and his family were entombed here on July 17, 1998, the 80th anniversary of their murder at the hands of the Bolsheviks. Outside the church, Mikhail Shemyakin's controversial bronze **statue** of Peter the Great at once fascinates and offends Russian visitors with its tiny head and elongated body. *(Open M-Sa 10am-7pm.)*

NEVSKIY GATE AND TRUBETSKOY BASTION. To the right of the statue, the **Nevskiy gate** (Невский Ворота; Nevskiye Vorota) was the site of numerous executions. The condemned awaited their fate in the fortress's southwest corner at the **Trubetskoy Bastion** (Труецкой Бастон) prison, where Peter the Great tortured his first son, Aleksey. Dostoevsky, Gorky, and Trotsky spent time here as well.

PETER'S CABIN (ДОМИК ПЕТРА ПЕРВОГО; DOMIK PETRA PERVOGO). Peter the Great supervised the construction of his city while living in this cabin, the oldest building in St. Petersburg. The museum contains many of his personal effects and describes his victories in the Northern War of 1700-1721. *(A small brick house along the river outside the Petrograd/east side of the fortress. Open M and W-Su 10am-6pm; kassa closes at 5pm; closed last M of each month. 60R, students 40R. Cameras 20R, video 50R.)*

ALONG NEVSKIY PROSPEKT

The easternmost boulevard of central St. Petersburg, Nevskiy Prospekt is the main thoroughfare. In accordance with Peter's vision, the wide avenue is epic, running 4.5km from the Neva in the west to the Alexander Nevsky Monastery in the east.

▧ CHURCH OF SAVIOR ON THE BLOOD (СПАС НА КРОВИ; SPAS NA KROVI). This colorful forest of elaborate "Russian style" domes was built from 1883 to 1907 over the site of Tsar Alexander II's 1881 assassination. The church, also known as the Church of Christ's Resurrection and the Church of the Bleeding Savior, has been beautifully renovated according to the original artists' designs after 20 years of Soviet neglect. The interior walls are covered with mosaics of Jesus's life. In the adjacent chapel is an exhibit on the life and death of reformist Tsar Alexander II. *(2 Nab. Kanala Gibdoeva; 3 blocks off Nevskiy pr. up Canal Griboyedova from Dom Knigi. ☎315 16 36. M2: Nevskiy Prospekt. Open winter Th-Tu 11am-7pm; summer Th-Tu 10am-8pm; kassa closes 1hr. earlier. Church 250R, students 125R, under 7 free. Cameras 50R, video 100R. Alexander II exhibit 20R, students 10R.)*

BLAST IN THE BANYA

f your trip to Russia is rushed,
and you don't have time to do
everything you'd hoped, remember this: if you see just one
museum, explore a palace of a
sar; if you've got money for only
one meal, eat a bowl of *borscht*;
and if you only get to wash once,
go to a *banya*.

The *banya* is the real Russian
bathing experience—it has been a
part of Slavic culture since long
before there was a Russia to
claim it as Russian. To the novice
t may seem bizarre or unappeal-
ng, but there's no person who
doesn't appreciate the vigorous
delight of the *banya*.

Historically, and in the more
remote regions of modern Russia,
the *banya* was a simple wooden
hut down by the river or lake closest to a village. A stove (печь;
pech) burned wood to heat water
with which locals could wash
before plunging into the adjacent
body of water, even breaking a
hole in the ice to pursue the prac-
ice during bitterly cold winters.

A modern *banya* is usually single-sex and involves several
stages. During the first stage, you
enter the *parilka* (парилка), a
steam room that reaches temperatures upward of 70°C. The idea
s to stay in the *parilka* as long as
you can stand it, then cool down
under a shower before going out
nto the open air. This is repeated
several times in order to accli-
mate the body into cardiac workout, before a plunge into the icy

**KAZAN CATHEDRAL (КАЗАНСКИЙ СОБОР;
KAZANSKIY SOBOR).** This colossal edifice on the
corner of Nevskiy pr. and the Griboyedov Canal was
modeled after St. Peter's Basilica in Rome. Completed in 1811, the cathedral was originally created
to house the icon Our Lady of Kazan, to whom the
Russian general Mikhail Golenshokov Kutuzov
prayed before embarking on the military campaign.
After the Franco-Prussian conflict, Russian soldiers
placed the keys of captured French cities and military standards above Kutuzov's tomb in the cathedral, where they (and he) remain. *(Kazanskaya pl. 2.
M2: Nevskiy Prospekt. ☎318 45 28; www.kazansky.ru. Open
daily 8:30am-7:30pm. Free. Tours daily 11:30am-5:30pm.
Services daily 10am and 6pm.)*

**MERCHANTS' YARD (ГОСТИНЫЙ ДВОР; GOSTINYY
DVOR).** Completed under Catherine the Great, this
large yellow 18th-century complex near the Metro is
one of the oldest indoor shopping malls in the world.
The two-floored ring of stores is like an open-air market—with vodka, electronics, pipes, etc.—taken
inside and made far more upscale. *(M3: Gostinyy Dvor.
Open M-Sa 10am-10pm, Su 10am-9pm.)*

**OSTROVSKOGO SQUARE (ОСТРОВСКОГО;
OSTROVSKOGO).** Ostrovskogo Square is home to a
monument of Catherine the Great surrounded by the
principal political and cultural figures of her reign:
Potemkin, Marshall Suvorov, Princess Dashkova, the
poet Derzhavin, and others. To the right (with the **Aleksandrinskiy** at your back) is St. Petersburg's main
public library, decorated with sculptures of ancient
philosophers. The oldest Russian theater, the Aleksandrinskiy (Александрийский), built by the architect Rossi in 1828, is behind Catherine's monument.
On ul. Zodchevo Rossii (Зодчево России), behind
the theater, is the **Vaganova School of Choreography,**
whose graduates include Vatslav Nizhinskiy, Anna
Pavlova, Rudolf Nureyev, and Mikhail Baryshnikov.
Also located on the plaza is a small theater museum
featuring props, playbills, and some theatrical history. Signs in Russian. *(M3: Gostinyy Dvor. Exit the Metro
and head toward pl. Vosstaniya on Nevskiy pr. The square is on
the right. Museum at Ostrovskogo pl. 1, 3rd fl. ☎311 21 95.
Open M and Th-Su 11am-6pm, W 11am-9pm; closed last F of
each month. 50R, students 25R.)*

SHEREMETYEV PALACE. Constructed in the early
1700s as a residence for Peter the Great's marshal,
Boris Sheremetyev, this restored palace (Дворец
Шереметьевых; Dvorets Sheremetevykh) houses a
music museum which contains a collection of 300

antique instruments, including the pianos of Rubenstein, Glinka, and Shostakovich and the violin of Antonio Stradivarius. The palace's mirrored hall hosts concerts on weekends, sometimes played with instruments from the museum's collection. During the summer, afternoon concerts from guest orchestras are held every week. *(Nab. Reki Fontanki 34. M3: Gostinyy Dvor. From the Metro, cross the Fontanka and turn left. The palace is about 2 blocks down on your right. ☎272 44 41. Open W-Su noon-5pm; closed last W of each month. 8OR, students 25R. Cameras 50R, video 100R. Concerts (10-100R) Oct.-May F 6:30pm, Sa-Su 4pm.)*

UPRISING SQUARE (ПЛОЩАДЬ ВОССТАНИЯ; PLOSHCHAD VOSSTANIYA).

Some of the bloodiest confrontations of the February Revolution, including the Cossack attack on police, took place here. The obelisk, erected in 1985, replaced a statue of Tsar Alexander III that was removed in 1937. Across from the train station, the green Oktyabrskaya Hotel bears the words "Город-герой Ленинград" (Leningrad, the Hero-City), recalling the tremendous suffering during the German WWI siege. *(M1: Ploshchad Vosstaniya. Near Moskovskiy Vokzal.)*

ALEXANDER NEVSKY MONASTERY

Pl. Aleksandra Nevskogo 1. M3 or 4: Pl. Aleksandra Nevskogo. The 18th-century Necropolis lies behind and to the left of the entrance archway. The Artists' Necropolis is behind and to the right. ☎274 04 09; www.lavra.spb.ru. Grounds open daily 6am-10pm; cathedral daily 6am-8pm; Annunciation Church Su, Tu-W, and F-Sa 11am-5pm; 18th-century Necropolis daily 9:30am–5:45pm; Artists' Necropolis daily 9:30am-6pm; kassa closes 4:30pm. Services daily 5:45, 6, 6:20, 7, 10am, 5pm. Donations requested for upkeep of church and grounds. Admission to both necropolises 6OR, students 30R. Camera 30R, video 6OR. Museum of Sculpture 50R, students 25R. Camera 30R, video 6OR.

A major pilgrimage destination, Alexander Nevsky Monastery (Александро-невская Лавра; Aleksandro-Nevskaya Lavra) derives its name and importance from St. Alexander of Novgorod, a 13th-century Russian prince who defeated the Swedes and appeased the Mongol overlords without betraying his faith. His body was moved here by Peter the Great in 1724. In 1797, the monastery was promoted to *lavra*, a distinguished status bestowed on only four Russian Orthodox monasteries. A cobblestone path connects the cathedral and the two cemeteries. English maps (7R) in both cemeteries indicate the graves of the famous.

cold pool (холодный бассейн) is added to the cycle. At this point, it is also customary to offer and receive a beating.

Switches of birch-tree (веники; *veniki*) are doused in water and brought into the *parilka*. The oils of the birch branches are secreted and channeled to the skin with lethal accuracy when someone uses a *venik* to give you a good thrashing. It actually feels like a pleasant massage, once you're comfortable in the heat, and the leafy *veniki* can also be used for a gentler brush-massaging of the body which imparts the oils and exfoliates without the breaking skin.

Bring sandals and a sheet if you have them, or rent them upon arrival. Also bring shampoo and soap for a Western-style shower to wrap things up. Birch switches can be bought for 40-50R. **The extreme heat and cold are dangerous for anyone who is pregnant or has a heart condition.** If you have qualms about baring all before complete strangers, you can buy exclusive use of a *banya* for a group of friends.

There is a public banya at 11 Bolshoy Kazachiy per. (☎315 07 34). M1: Pushkinskaya. Enter the banya through the courtyard of Dom 11. Open M and W noon-10pm, Tu and F-Su 9am-10pm, Th (women's day) 10am-10pm. 50R. A private banya is at Gagarinskaya ul. (☎272 96 82), in Dom 32. M1: Chernashevskaya. Call ahead to book for a group. Open 11am-2am. 450R. per hr.

ARTISTS' NECROPOLIS (ТИХВИНСКОЕ КЛАДБИЩЕ; TIKHVINSKOYE KLADBISHCHE).
Also known as the Tikhvin Cemetery, the Artists' Necropolis (Некрапол Мастеров Искусств; Nekrapol Masterov Iskusstv) is the resting place of many famous Russians. Fyodor Dostoyevsky could only afford to be buried here thanks to support from the Russian Orthodox Church. His grave, along the wall to the right, is always strewn with flowers. Mikhail Glinka, composer of the first Russian opera, and Mikhail Balakirev, who taught Nikolai Rimskiy-Korsakov, also rest here. Alexander Borodin's grave is graced with a gold mosaic of a composition sheet from his famous *String Quartet no. 1*. The magnificent tombs of Modest Mussorgsky, Anton Rubinstein, and Peter Tchaikovsky are next to Borodin's.

OTHER SIGHTS. Next to the Artists' Necropolis is the **18th-century necropolis**, St. Petersburg's oldest cemetery. Farther along the central path on the left is the **Church of the Annunciation** (Благовещенская Церков; Blagoveshchenskaya Tserkov), the original burial place of the Romanovs, who were moved to Peter and Paul Cathedral in 1998 (see p. 711). The church now houses the graves of military heroes, including **Suvorov** and minor members of the royal family. The **Holy Trinity Cathedral** (Свято-Тротский Собор; Svyato-Troitskiy Sobor), at the end of the path, is a functioning church, teeming with priests and devout *babushki*.

SUMMER GARDENS AND PALACE

M2: Nevskiy Prospekt. Turn right on nab. Kanala Griboyedova (Канала Грибоедова), pass the Church of the Bleeding Savior, cross the Moyka, and turn right on ul. Pestelya (Пестеля). The palace and gardens will be on your left. ☎ 314 03 74. Garden open daily May-Oct. 10am-9:30pm; Nov.-Apr. 10am-8pm. Free. Palace open Tu-Su 11am-6pm; closed last Tu of each month. Palace signs in English. 270R, students 135R; free 3rd Th of each month. Camera 30R, video 70R. Tours of 15-20 people; 50R per person; call ahead.

The Summer Gardens and Palace (Летний Сад и Дворец; Letniy Sad i Dvorets) are lovely places to rest and cool off. Both the northern and southern entrances lead to long, shady paths lined with replicas of classical Roman sculptures, crafted in the 1720s. In the northeast corner of the Garden sits Peter's **Summer Palace**, which seems like more of a *dacha* (summer home) than a palace. The decor reflects Peter's diverse tastes: Spanish chairs, German clocks, and Japanese paintings fill the rooms. The **Coffee House** (Кофейный Домик; Kofeynyy Domik) and the **Tea House** (Чайный Домик; Chainyy Domik), in the garden near the palace, sell paintings and souvenirs, respectively. Though neither of these serves its original 19th-century purpose of offering refreshment, the cafe/bar behind the Tea House sells beer, non-alcoholic drinks, and simple snacks. **Mars Field** (Марсого Поле; Marsogo Pole), named after military parades held here in the 19th century, extends to the **Summer Gardens.** The broad, open park is now a memorial to the victims of the Revolution and the Civil War (1917-19). A round monument in the center holds an eternal flame.

SMOLNYY INSTITUTE AND CATHEDRAL

From M2: Nevskiy Prospekt, take bus #22 away from the Admiralty. Or, from the stop across Kirochnaya ul. from M1: Chernyshevskaya, take bus #46 or 136. Get off at the blue towers with gray domes (10-15min.). ☎ 271 76 32. Open M-W and Th-Su 11am-6pm; kassa closes 5:15pm; tower closes 4pm. 150R, students 75R. Cameras 20R, video 50R.

Once a prestigious school for aristocratic girls, the **Smolnyy Institute** (Смольный Институт) earned its place in history in 1917 when Trotsky and Lenin set up the headquarters of the **Bolshevik Central Committee** here, and they planned the Revolution from behind its yellow walls. In front of the institute stand busts of Engels, Marx, and Lenin, who lived here 1917-18. Next door, the blue and white

Smolnyy Cathedral (Смолный Собор; Smolnyy Sobor), designed by Rastrelli, combines Baroque and Orthodox Russian styles. Climb to the top of the 68m bell tower and survey Lenin's—er, Peter's—city.

OCTOBER REGION

In the October Region (Октябрьский Район; Oktyabrskiy Raion), the Griboyedov Canal meanders through quiet neighborhoods.

ST. NICHOLAS CATHEDRAL (НИКОЛЬСКИЙ СОБОР; NIKOLSKIY SOBOR). A striking blue and gold structure, St. Nicholas Cathedral was constructed in 18th century Baroque style. Inside, candles illuminate gold-plated icons. *(M4: Sadovaya. Cross the square, head down ul. Sadovaya (Садовая), and fork right onto ul. Rimskogo-Korsakogo (Римского-Корсакого). The cathedral is on the left, across the canal. Enter through the gate on the right side. Lower church open daily 6:30am-7:30pm; upper church M-F 9:30am-noon, Sa 9:30am-noon and 6pm-vespers end. Services daily 7, 10am, 6pm.)*

YUSUPOVSKIY GARDENS (ЮСУПОВСКИЙ САД; YUSUPOVSKIY SAD). On the borders of the October Region, the Yusupovsky Gardens—named after the prince who succeeded in killing Rasputin only after poisoning, shooting, and ultimately drowning him—provide a patch of green in the middle of the urban expanse. Locals come here to relax beside the pond. The palace's original interior has been maintained. *(M4: Sadovaya. At the intersection of ul. Sadovaya and ul. Rimskogo-Korsakogo. Palace open noon-4pm.)*

THEATER SQUARE (ТЕАТРАЛНАЯ ПЛОЩАДЬ; TEATRALNAYA PLOSHCHAD). The area between the Griboyedov and Kryukov (Крюков) Canals is dominated by two imposing turquoise buildings. The larger is the **Mariinskiy Theater,** home to the world-famous **Kirov Ballet.** Across the street stands the **Conservatory,** flanked by statues of composers Glinka and Rimsky-Korsakov (see **Entertainment,** p. 718). *(M2: Sennaya Ploshchad. From the western corner of Sennaya pl., follow the Griboyedov Canal left for 5-7min. until you reach the square.)*

GREAT CHORAL SYNAGOGUE. Two blocks west of Theater Square lies Europe's second-largest synagogue (Большцая Хоралная Синагога; Bolshchaya Khoralnaya Sinagoga). Built in 1893 with the permission of Tsar Alexander II, its main dome covers a two-tiered worship space. Upon its completion, the city outlawed all other Jewish meeting houses, forcing St. Petersburg's 15,000 Jews to meet in a space intended for 2000. Although the moorish exterior pays tribute to the architectural trends of the time, the interior is more traditional. The large synagogue holds services only on Shabbat (Saturday) and holidays. The small, adjacent synagogue holds regular services. *(Lermontovskiy (Лермонтовский) pr. 2. M4: Sadovaya. Turn right off ul. Sadovaya and cross the canal onto ul. Rimskogo-Korsakogo. Continue to Lermontovskiy pr. and turn right. Open daily 9am-9pm. Services daily 9am.)*

OTHER SIGHTS

MENSHIKOV PALACE (МЕНШИКОВСКИЙ ДВОРЕЦ; MENSHIKOVSKIY DVORETS).
Peter entertained guests here before he built the Summer Palace. He then gave it to Alexander Menshikov, his good friend and governor of St. Petersburg. The museum displays an exhibition on "Russian Culture of Peter's Time." To join an English tour on your visit, call ahead. Otherwise, ask for printed English info. *(Universitetskaya nab. 15 (Университетская). M3: Vasileostrovskaya or bus #10. Cross the bridge north of the Admiralty and walk left. ☎ 323 11 12. Open Su 10:30am-5pm and Tu-Sa 10:30am-6pm; kassa closes 1hr. earlier. 200R; free 1st Th of each month. English tours 200R, students 100R. Cameras 100R, video 350R.)*

RUSSIA

🏛 MUSEUMS

St. Petersburg's museums are famous worldwide, and with good reason. The city caters to all tastes: you'll be awed by the opulent extravagance of palatial residences and institutional buildings, but if you also explore more specialized collections, you'll likely be rewarded.

ART AND LITERATURE

■ **RUSSIAN MUSEUM (РУССКИЙ МУЗЕЙ; RUSSKIY MUZEY).** Inside this museum is the world's largest collection of Russian art after Moscow's Tretyakov Gallery. A world-class collection of masterpieces, 12th- to 17th-century icons, 18th- to 19th-century paintings and sculpture, and Russian folk art are arranged chronologically. The Benois Wing shows 20th-century avant-garde art and includes works by Kandinsky and Chagall. *(Inzhenernaya 2. M3: Gostinyy Dvor. In the yellow 1825 Mikhailov Palace (Михайловский Дворец; Mikhailovskiy Dvorets), behind the Pushkin monument. From the Metro, go down ul. Mikhailovskaya past the Grand Hotel Europe. Enter through the basement in the courtyard's right corner; go downstairs and turn left. ☎314 34 48; www.rusmuseum.ru. Wheelchair accessible. English signs. Open M 10am-5pm, W-Su 10am-6pm; kassa closes 1hr. earlier. 270R, students 135R. No cameras.)*

ALEXANDER PUSHKIN APARTMENT MUSEUM. Visiting this former residence of Russia's most revered literary figure is a sort of pilgrimage for poetry lovers. The museum (Музей Квартира Пушкина; Muzey Kvartira Pushkina) displays his personal effects and tells the tragic story of his last days. In the library where he died, all the furniture is original and the clock is stopped at the time of his death. *(Nab. Reki Moyki 12. M2: Nevskiy Prospekt. Walk toward the Admiralty; turn right on nab. Reki Moyki and follow the canal to the yellow building on the right. Enter through the courtyard; the kassa is on the left. ☎117 35 31; www.museumpushkin.ru. Open M and W-Su 10:30am-5pm; closed the last F of each month. 200R, students 50R.)*

DOSTOEVSKY HOUSE (ДОМ ДОСТОЕВСКОГО; DOM DOSTOYEVSKOGO). The great Fyodor Dostoevsky wrote *The Brothers Karamazov* in this house. He was surrounded—unlike most of his troubled characters—by a supportive wife and beloved children, two things he declared constituted 75% of a man's happiness in life. This worthwhile museum exhibits the author's work while providing moving insight into the writer's domestic and literary existence. *Crime and Punishment* junkies should consider taking one of Peter's Walking Tours (see p. 705; W and F 4pm; 320R; meet at Cafe Max, Nevskiy pr. 90) devoted to the artist's literature. *(Kuznechnyy per. 5/2 (Кузнечный). M1: Vladimirskaya. On the corner of ul. Dostoyevskogo (Достоевского), just past the market. ☎311 40 31. Open Tu-Su 11am-6pm; closed last W of each month; kassa closes 5pm. 90R, students 45R. English audio guide 70R.)*

HISTORY AND SCIENCE

KUNSTKAMERA ANTHROPOLOGICAL AND ETHNOGRAPHIC MUSEUM. This is Russia's oldest and perhaps most bizarre museum (Музей Антропологии и тнографииᴨКунцкамера; Muzey Antropologii i Etnografii—Kunstkamera). After exploring the "Lives and Habits" of various indigenous peoples, wander wide-eyed through Peter the Great's grisly anatomical collection. He indulged in a fetish peculiarly widespread among Europe's 18th-century ruling class: the meek may want to skip the display of such formaldehyde-bathed curiosities as a severed head and deformed babies. Still, the collection of teeth extracted by Peter from various courtiers and the display's former label do give a a degree of insight into the man's nature: "Peter the Great was an enthusiastic amateur dentist." *(Universitetskaya nab. 3 (Университетская). The museum faces the Admiralty from across the river; enter on the left, on Tamozhennyy per. (Таможенный).* ☎ *328 14 12. Open Tu-Su 11am-5:45pm; closed last Th of each month; kassa closes 4:45pm. English tour 520R; call ahead. Museum 100R, students 50R. Cameras 20R, video 50R.)*

ETHNOGRAPHIC MUSEUM (МУЗЕЙ ЭТНОГРАФИИ; MUZEY ETNOGRAFII). This museum exhibits the art, traditions, and cultures of Russia's 159 ethnic groups. Particularly noteworthy is the magnificent **Marble Hall,** which boasts a collection of fine art and a skylight of ornate crystal. An ambitious tableau in relief on the wall depicts the ethnic makeup of old Russia. *(Inzhenernaya ul. 4, bldg. 1 (Инженерная).* ☎ *313 43 20. Captions in Russian only. Open Tu-Su 11am-6pm, and last F of each month 11am-6pm; kassa closes 5pm. Museum closes 1hr. earlier on holidays. 200R, students 100R.)*

ST. PETERSBURG BOTANIC GARDEN. In 1714 Peter I established the Drugstore garden (Aptekarskiy ogorod), a plantation of rare plants and medicinal herbs, which became the Emperor's garden in 1823. The botanical garden (С-Петербург-ский Ботакичский Сад, S-Peterbyrgskiy Botanichiskiy Sad) currently houses about 6500 varieties of plants in over a hectare of greenhouses. Late in the 18th century the 16.5 hectare Den Park was added. *(Prof Popov ul. 2.* ☎ *346 36 39. Greenhouses open Th-Su 11am-5pm; park May 9th-Oct. 10am-9pm. 100R, students 50R).*

ZOO (ЗООПАРК; ZOOPARK). Founded in 1865, the zoo holds over 2000 animals comprising some 410 species including lizards, snakes, and a variety of lively monkeys. The zoo's mascot, the polar bear has bred particularly well in captivity. *(Aleksandrovskiy park, 1. M2: Gorkovskaya.* ☎ *232 82 60. Open summer 10am-7pm; winter Tu-Su 10am-5pm; kassa closes 1hr. earlier. 100R, students 50R.)*

ZOOLOGICAL MUSEUM (ЗООЛОГИЧЕСКИЙ МУЗЕЙ; ZOOLOGICHESKIY MUZEY). This museum contains 30,000 specimens of animals, fish, and insects, including a fully preserved mammoth and a blue whale skeleton. *(Universitetskaya nab. 1. Take bus #10. Next to the Kunstkamera Museum (see p. 716), across the bridge from the Admiralty. Open M-Th and Sa-Su 11am-6pm; kassa closes 4:50pm. Museum and live insect zoo each 35R, students 15R; Th free.)*

MUSEUM OF RUSSIAN POLITICAL HISTORY. You don't need to be an academic to appreciate the vast collection of historical artifacts and propaganda posters at this museum (Музей Политической Исории России; Muzey Politicheskoy Istorii Rossii). Before the Bolsheviks set up shop here, this building housed Matilda Kshesinskaya, prima ballerina of the Mariinskiy Theater and a lover of Nicholas II's nephew. Today the museum displays an exhibit about Kshesinskaya, a memorial to Lenin and his revolution, and a museum of general Russian political history. The east wing displays a range of **Soviet propaganda,** as well as artifacts from WWII. *(Ul. Kuybysheva 2 (Куйбышева). M2: Gorkovskaya. Go down Kamennoostrosky toward the mosque and turn left on Kuybysheva.* ☎ *233 70 52; www.museum.ru/museum/ polit_hist. Open M-W and F-Su 10am-6pm. 80R, students 40R. Cameras 30R, video 150R. Tour in English 5-25 people 3600R total, up to 4 people 500R each.)*

CENTRAL NAVAL MUSEUM. The old Stock Exchange building houses the boat that inspired Peter I to create the Russian navy. The museum (Централный Военно-Морское Музей; Tsentralnyy Voyenno-Morskoy Muzey) displays submarines, weapons, artwork, and model ships chronicling the development of Russia's modern fleet. *(Birzhevaya pl. 4 (Биржевая). Take bus #10 across the bridge to Vasilevskiy Island and get off at the first stop. Walk toward the Peter and Paul fortress; the museum will be* *past the zoological museums, on your left. ☎328 25 02. Open W-Su 11am-6pm; last entry 5:15pm. Closed July 3 and last Th of each month. 100R, students 35R. Cameras 20R, video 60R. Tour in English 400R, students 200R. Book tours 5 days in advance.)*

MILITARY HISTORY MUSEUM. Military hardware from 15th-century armor to 20th-century tanks is showcased at this museum (Центральный Военно-Исторический Музей; Voenno-Istoricheskiy Muzey). Here's your chance to see genuine AK-47s and medium range missiles up close. On display are exhibits on all of the Russian wars in the 19th and 20th centuries. *(Aleksandrovskiy Park 7 (Александровский Парк). M2: Gorkovskaya. Exit the Metro and walk toward the river, then bear right on Kronverskaya nab.; the museum is on the right. ☎232 02 96. Open W-Su 11am-6pm; kassa closes 1hr. earlier. 150R, students 75R.)*

RUSSIAN VODKA MUSEUM (МУЗЕЙ ВОДКИ; MUZEY VODKI). This museum chronicles the history of Russia's favorite pastime. The quaint cafe in the back offers a hands-on vodka education. Indulge in the delectable three-shot tasting menu (US$15). *(Konnogvardeyskiy bul. 5 (Конногвардейский). Walk 1 block toward the river from the Manezh and turn left on Konnogvardeyskiy bul. Continue 1 block down on the right. ☎312 34 16; russianvodkamuseum@hotmail.com. Open daily 11am-10pm. 25R. Free shot at the bar with admission. Displays in Russian. Call ahead for English tour. Vodka shots 20R-60R. MC/V.)*

ARCTIC AND ANTARCTIC MUSEUM. Everyone who likes stuffed animals or has a penguin fetish should check out this quirky little museum (Музей Артики и Антартики; Muzey Arktiki i Antarktiki) of Russia's conquests in the polar regions. The museum features ship models and nautical accoutrements, such as a life-size seaplane, an explorer's hut, and a polar bear. *(Marata ul. 24. M1: Vladimirskaya. From the Metro, walk down Kuznechnyy per. 2 blocks from Vladimirskaya Metro. On the corner of Kuznechnyy per. and ul. Marata (Марата). ☎311 25 49; www.museum.ru/m132. Signs in Russian. Open W-Su 10am-6pm; kassa closes 5pm. Museum 100R, students 30R, children under 7 free.)*

🎭 🎫 FESTIVALS AND ENTERTAINMENT

Throughout June, when the evening sun barely touches the horizon, the city holds the famed **White Nights Festival** (see sidebar). All year long, the former home of Tchaikovsky, Prokofiev, and Stravinsky lives up to its reputation as a mecca for the performing arts. It is fairly easy to get tickets to world-class performances for as little as 100R. *Yarus* (ярус) are the cheapest seats. The **theater season** ends in June and begins again in September. The **ticket office** is at Nevskiy pr. 42, opposite Gostinyy Dvor. (☎310 42 40. Schedule 20R.) The Friday issue of the *St. Petersburg Times* has comprehensive listings of entertainment and nightlife and lists what performances are in English. If this is all too high-brow, head to the movies. Most films are dubbed in Russian but it is increasingly common to for movies to be shown in their original language. **Dom Kino,** Karavannaya ul, 12 (☎314 80 36), plays some movies in English. M3: Gostinyy Dvor. Movie tickets generally cost 30-100R.

BALLET AND OPERA

Mariinskiy Teatr (Мариинский), also called **Kirov Teatr,** Teatralnaya pl. 1 (Театральная; ☎114 43 44, group bookings 314 17 44). M4: Sadovaya. Walk along Griboyedov Canal, then go right into the square. Bus #3, 22, or 27. This large aqua building premiered Tchaikovsky's *Nutcracker* and launched the careers of Pavlova and

Baryshnikov. Performances 7pm, matinees Sept.-June 11:30am. *Kassa* open Tu-Su 11am-3pm and 4-9pm. Tickets (160-3200R) go on sale 20 days in advance. It is illegal but common for people to sell tickets at the entrance 15-30min. before shows. MC/V.

Mussorgsky Opera and Ballet Theater (Театр Имени Муссоргского; Teatr Imeni Mussorgskogo), also called the **Maly Theater** (the little "Theater of Opera and Ballet"), pl. Iskusstv 1 (Искусств; ☎595 42 82). Hosts excellent performances of Russian ballet and opera. Bring your passport; documents are checked at the door. Open July-Aug. when the Mariinskiy is closed. Performances 7pm, matinees noon. *Kassa* open M and W-Su 11am-3pm and 4-7pm, Tu 11am-3pm and 4-6pm. Tickets 240-1800R.

Konservatoriya (Консерватория), Teatralnaya pl. 3 (☎117 85 74), across from Mariinskiy Teatr. M4: Sadovaya. Bus #3, 22, or 27. Ballets and operas performed by students of the elite St. Petersburg Academy. Performances 6:30pm, matinees noon. *Kassa* open daily 11am-7pm. Tickets 450R.

CIRCUS

Tsirk (Цирк; Circus), nab. Fontanki 3 (☎313 44 11; www.uraldrama.ru). M3: Gostinyy Dvor. From the Metro turn away from the Admiralty on Nevskiy pr. Go left on Sadovaya and bear right on Inzheneraya ul., continuing until you reach the Fontanka. Russia's oldest traditional circus features the usual assortment of animal and human acts, all performed to a live orchestra. Open Nov.-June. Several shows per week 11am, 3 and 7pm. *Kassa* open daily 11am-7pm. Tickets 30-200R.

CLASSICAL MUSIC

Shostakovich Philharmonic Hall, ul. Mikhailovskaya 2 (Михайловская; ☎110 42 57), across the square from the Russian Museum. M3: Gostinyy Dvor. Classical and modern performances by resident and visiting orchestras. During the summer, when the Philharmonic is on tour, other groups perform daily at 4 and 7pm. *Kassa* open daily 11am-3pm and 4-7:30pm. Tickets 480-800R.

Akademicheskaya Kapella (Академическая Капелла), nab. Reki Moyki 20 (☎314 10 58). M2: Nevskiy Prospekt. The venue is a small hall for the Emperor Court Choir Capella, a professional choir that dates back to 1437 and was transferred from Moscow to St. Petersburg in 1703.Performances 7pm. *Kassa* open daily noon-3pm and 4-7pm.

THEATER

Aleksandrinskiy Teatr (Александринский Театр), pl. Ostrovskogo 2 (Островского; ☎311 15 33). M3: Gostinyy Dvor. Turn right on Nevskiy pr., then right at the park with Catherine's statue. Ballet and theater shows of mostly Western classics like *Hamlet* and *Cyrano de Bergerac*. In summer, the theater features performances by St. Petersburg Ballet Company. Performances 7pm. *Kassa* open daily noon-6pm. Tickets 70-680R.

◪ NIGHTLIFE

St. Petersburg's club scene got started only in the mid-90s. Pre-*glasnost*, there was only one Party-run club. Yet Petersburg has more than made up for lost time. Whether you seek a quiet drink, a rave, or a chance to show off your designer clothes, the city has a nighttime hangout for you. Check the Friday issues of the *St. Petersburg Times* and *Pulse* for current events and special promotions. For those who tire of the smoky basements and pulsating club music, the city offers a range of cafes, from relaxed to vibrant.

▨ **JFC Jazz Club,** Shpalernaya ul. 33 (Шпалерная; ☎272 98 50; www.jfc.sp.ru). M1: Chernyshevskaya. Go right on pr. Chernyshevskogo (Чернышевского), continue 4 blocks. Take a left on Shpalernaya and go into courtyard 33. The club offers a wide variety of quality jazz in a relaxed atmosphere, and it holds occasional classical and folk concerts. Beer 50R, hard liquor 40-150R. Live music 8-10pm. Cover 60-100R. Arrive early or call ahead for a table. Open daily 7-11pm.

Par.spb, 5B Aleksandrovskiy Park (☎233 33 74; www.par.spb.ru). M2: Gorkovskaya. Exit the Metro and bear right, walk through the park in the direction of the Peter and Paul Fortress, and look for the red brick building. Popular with the cosmopolitan set, this establishment spins European house music. Be prepared for prolonged queuing while the door staff exercises its right to identify and privilege "the beautiful people." Beer and vodka from 30R. Cover 100-500R. Open F-Su 11pm-late.

Tunnel, ul. Blokhina 16 (Блохина; ☎233 40 15; www.tunnelclub.ru). M2: Gorkovskaya. Exit the Metro and bear left, walking along the circular Kronverskiy pr. (Кронверский) in Alexandrinskiy Park toward Vasilevskiy Island. Turn right on ul. Blokina; bear right at the fork. Russia's pioneering techno club, located inside a camouflaged bomb shelter, offers live DJs spinning cutting-edge jungle and house over an excellent sound system. Beer and vodka 40R. Cover 150-300R. Open Th-Sa midnight-6am.

Moloko (Молоко; Milk), Perekupnoy per. 12 (Перекупной; ☎274 94 67; www.moloko-club.ru). Off Nevskiy pr., halfway between M1: Pl. Vosstaniya and M3/4: Pl. Aleksandra Nevskogo. Catch the best Petersburg bands or mingle with the mostly student crowd. Beer 25R. Cover 60-80R. Music starts at 8pm. Open W-Su 7pm-midnight.

Griboyedov (Грибоедов), Voronezhskaya ul. 2A (Воронежская; ☎164 43 55; www.mfiles.spb.ru/griboyedov). M4: Ligovskiy Prospekt. Go left exiting the underpass from the Metro. With your back to the station, go left at the intersection onto Konstantina Zaslonova (Константина Заслонова) and walk 2 blocks; take a left on Voronezhskaya. Look for a big mound. This house and techno club also invites alternative acts. Beer and wine 30R, vodka 20-50R. M house night, Tu reggae, W disco, Th trance, F techno, Sa garage/house, Su acid jazz/funk. 21+. Live DJ daily 11pm-1am. Cover 60-80R, free before 8pm. Open daily 5pm-6am.

Red Club, Poltavskaya ul. 7 (☎277 13 66; www.redclubonline.com). M1: Vosstaniya. Located in a former feed storage house behind Moscow Station. 2 stages attract top club bands, both local and international. Th-Su concerts at 8pm with DJs following at midnight. Cover 70-350R. Open daily 6pm-6am.

Che, Poltavskaya ul. 3 (Полтавская; ☎277 76 00; www.cafeclubche.ru). M1: Vosstaniya. Walk down Nevskiy pr. toward pl. Aleksandra Nevskogo 2-3 blocks, then make a right on Poltavskaya. Although named for a fiery revolutionary, Che is a place to chill among the young, trendy, and well-to-do. Drinks 100-500R. Live latino/jazz music 10pm-2am. Open 24hr. AmEx/MC/V.

GLBT NIGHTLIFE

Those interested in finding out more about the gay life of St. Petersburg should pick up a copy of *GAYP*, which lists gay services, from clubs to saunas. The website www.xsgay.com is another good resource.

Greshniki (Грешники; Sinners), nab. Kanala Griboyedova 28 (☎318 42 91; www.greshinki.ru), 2 blocks off Nevskiy pr., past Kazan Cathedral. M2: Nevskiy Prospekt. Unassuming 4-fl. gay club, primarily for men. Plays disco, techno, and Europop. Drinks 40-250R. Drag shows W-Su 1 and 2am. Male strip shows daily midnight-4am. 18+. Cover for men 50-150R, women 300-500R. Open daily 10pm-6am.

Triel, 5-ya Sovetskaya ul, 45 (☎110 20 16; www.triel.hotmail.ru). M1: Vosstaniya. St. Petersburg's only lesbian club plays a mix of Russian and European pop. Pool M-F 80R per hr. Women only except Th-F. M-Tu 5pm-midnight, W and F-Sa 9pm-6am, Th 7pm-midnight. W-Sa 50-150R.

◪ DAYTRIPS FROM ST. PETERSBURG

Many residents of the city retreat to a family *dacha* (дача; summer cottage) outside the city to harvest private produce or relax for the weekend. Undoubtedly in order to identify with their subjects' lifestyle, the tsars built country houses of their own just outside the city, though "house" hardly evokes the awesome grandeur of these palatial megaliths. The imperial residences at Peterhof, Pushkin, and Pavlovsk were all torched during the Nazi retreat, but Soviet authorities provided staggering sums of money to return these proud monuments to a glorious Russian state. The famous collection of fountains is in operation from May to October.

PETERHOF (ПЕТЕРГОф)

In summer, the hydrofoils (Damarov ☎ 311 86 94, Meteor 325 6120) leave from the quay on Dvortsovaya nab. (Дворцовая) in front of the Hermitage (30-35min.; 9:30am-6pm every 20min.; 200R, roundtrip 360R, children 100R/180R). The less-glamorous train runs year-round from Baltiyskiy Vokzal (Балтийский; M1: Baltiyskaya; 35min., every 10-50min., 12R). Buy tickets from the suburban ticket office (Пригородная касса; Prigorodnaya kassa) and ask for "NOH-vee Peter-GOFF" (Новый Петергоф; New Peterhof).For a round-trip ticket (24R), add "too-DAH ee oh-BRAHT-nah" (туда и обратно; round-trip). Any train to Oranienbaum (Ораниенбаум), Kalishche (Калище), or Krasnoflotsk (Краснофлотск) will get you there. Get off at Novy Peterhof, the 11th stop (sit at the front or you might not see the sign), or when you hear the driver declare something about Staryy Peterhof (Старый Петергоф). From the station, take any bus (10min., 7R) or van (5min., 10R) bound for Petrodvorets (Петродворец; Peter's Palace.); get off when you see the palace. Bus routes #348, 350, 351, 352, and 356 will take you there.

UPPER AND LOWER GARDENS. Through the gates of the grounds lie the **Upper Gardens.** As you make this relatively modest approach you get a teasing taste of what's to come inside. Go right or left of the palace to find a *kassa* where you can pay for entrance to the **Lower Gardens.** Most of the fountains are reconstructions, as post-war Germany misplaced the stolen originals. *(Gardens open daily 10:30am-6pm. 280R, students 140R. Fountains operate May-Oct. 10:30am-5pm.)*

GRAND PALACE (ВОЛЬШОЙ ДВОРЕЦ; BOLSHOY DVORETS). In an attempt to create his own Versailles, Peter started building a residence here in 1714. Empresses Elizabeth and Catherine the Great greatly expanded and remodeled it. The rooms reflect the contrary tastes of the various tsars and changing fashions in the architecture of their respective ages. Ascend the exquisite main staircase to the second-floor rooms, including the great **Chesme Gallery,** in which artwork depicts the 1770 Russian victory over the Turks. When its German painter, Philip Gackert, refused to compose the final scene in the series for want of honest knowledge of an explosion's appearance, Catherine obligingly had her own fleet's *St. Barbara* blown to pieces to satisfy the artist's integrity. See the result to the left above the door. Farther along are the **Chinese rooms**, which contain panels restored by Russian artists after WWII, but the vases and one lacquer panel in each room are originals from the tsars' trade and diplomatic intercourse with the East. Finally, through the silk-lined luxury of the women's quarters lies the last room on the tour—**Peter's study,** lined with elegantly carved wood panels. *(☎ 420 00 73. Open Tu-Su 10am-6pm; kassa closes 5pm; closed last Tu of each month. Buy tickets inside. Russian tours 150R. Palace 420R, students 210R. Camera 100R, video 200R. Mandatory bag check 2R.)*

GRAND CASCADE. The 64 elegant, gravity-powered fountains of the Grand Cascade direct their waters to the Grand Canal. The largest of 37 shining gold statues (originally from the early 18th century but mostly recast after WWII), *Samson Tearing Open the Jaws of a Lion* is a vivid symbol of Peter's victory over Sweden. To enter the impressive **stone grotto** underneath the fountains, buy tickets just outside the palace and join the inevitably long line coming up the steps from its entrance. *(Grotto open daily 11am-5pm, kassa open 10:30am-noon and 2pm-4:15pm. 100R, students 50R.)*

HERMITAGE PAVILION AND MARLY. Russia's first hermitage initially served as a setting for the amusement of the palace residents. Fans of 17th- and 18th-century European art might enjoy the second-floor room filled floor-to-ceiling with the paintings of various lesser-known Belgian, Dutch, French, and German artists. Farther along the path leading to Catherine's hermitage pavilion lies Peter the Great's personal retreat and a collection of his belongings. *(Open Tu-Su 10:30am-6pm; kassa closes at 5pm. 100R, students 50R. Cameras 60R, video 150R.)*

OTHER BUILDINGS. On the right side of the path facing the quay is **Monplaisir**, the modest Dutch-style building where Peter actually lived—the large palace was only used for special occasions. *(Open M-Tu and Th-Su 10:30am-6pm; kassa closes 5pm. Closed 3rd Tu of each month. 190R, students 95R. Cameras 60R, video 150R.)* Next door to Monplaisir are the **Bath House** (Баный Корпус; Bannyy Korpus), which served Empress Maria Aleksandrovna as a private health center, and the **Catherine Building** (Екатерининский Корпус; Yekaterininskiy Korpus), where Catherine the Great reposed herself while her orders to depose her husband were being carried out. In the courtyard between the three buildings, the sound of children's happy shrieks can be heard at the **"joke fountains."** *(Bath House open M-Tu and Th-Su 10am-6pm; kassa closes 5pm. Closed during rain. 140R, students 70R. Cameras 60R, video 150R. Catherine Building open Tu-Su 10:30am-6pm; kassa closes 1hr. earlier. 100R, students 50R. Cameras 60R, video 150R.)* Near the end of the central path is a **wax museum** containing likenesses of historical figures. Guides will conduct a brief history lesson on a guided tour (included in price) if you happen to arrive on a day when tours occur. *(Open daily 11am-7pm. 80R. Cameras 50R, video 100R.)*

TSARSKOYE SELO (ЦАРСКОЕ СЕЛО)

From Pobedy pl. (M2: Moskovskaya) take bus #287 or one of the numerous marshrutki, such as #20, that go to Tsarskoye Selo or Pushkin. Alternatively, the elektrichka runs from Vitebskiy Vokzal (M1: Pushkinskaya; 30min., 12R). Buy tickets upstairs at the kassa before the rightmost platforms (ground level kassy are for longer journeys). Ask for a round-trip to Pushkin (Пушкин, туда и обратно; POOSH-kin, too-DAH ee oh-BRAHT-nah). Don't worry that none of the signs say Pushkin; all trains leaving from platforms 1-3 stop there. Get off at Detskoye Selo (Детское Село), the 1st stop outside Petersburg that actually looks like a station, with a large number of people. From the station, take bus #371 or 382 to the last stop (10min., 5R). Knowing where to get off is tricky; ask the conductor or get off after spotting the blue and white palace through the trees to the right.

About 25km south of St. Petersburg, Tsarskoye Selo (Tsar's Village) surrounds Catherine the Great's summer residence, a gorgeous azure, white, and gold Baroque palace overlooking extensive, English-style parks. The area was renamed "Pushkin" during the Soviet era, although the train station, Detskoye Selo (Детское Село; Children's Village) kept its old name. Built in 1756 by the architect Rastrelli in Baroque style, **Catherine's Palace** (Екатерининский Дворец; Yekaterininskiy Dvorets) was remodeled by Charles Cameron on Catherine's orders. She had the gilding removed from the facade, desiring a modest "cottage" where she could relax. This residence of unbridled opulence was devastated by the Nazis, but since then it has been restored. The Amber Room suffered the most; its walls were stripped and it was only for St. Petersburg's tricentennial celebrations in 2003 that it was finally ready. The "golden" suites—named for their lavish Baroque ornamentation—hold original furnishings that survived WWII. Latch onto one of the many tours in English. (☎465 53 08. *Open W-M 10am-6pm; kassa closes 1hr. earlier; closed last M of each month. June-Aug. 10am-noon and 2:30pm-4pm the museum is only open to private tour groups who have reserved well in advance. English tours free. Palace 500R, students 250R.*) Rastrelli's **parks** combine the liberating feel of unfenced natural space with well-tended precision of design. Here Catherine would ramble with her dogs—showing affection some believed in excess of that accorded to her children. The dogs now rest in peace beneath the **Pyramid** facing the **Island Pavilion**, which can be reached by ferry during summer. The **Cold Bath Pavilion** stands in front of the palace to the left. Designed by Charles Cameron, it contains the famous Agate Rooms. Across the street from Catherine's Palace, outside the park, is the **lycée** that Pushkin attended from age 12 to 18. (*A ferry goes to the island on Great Pond. Daily in summer noon-6pm every 40min. Round-trip 200R, students 100R. Price includes 30min. Russian tour of island. Parks open daily May-Sept. 9am-11pm; Oct.-Apr. 10am-11pm. 70R, students 35R; after 6pm free. All buildings open May-Sept. Bath Pavilion open W-Su 10am-5pm; closed last W of each month. 160R, students 80R. Lycée ☎476 64 11. Open W-M 11am-6pm; kassa closes 5pm; closed last F of each month. 200R, students 100R. Cameras 50R, video 150R.*)

PAVLOVSK (ПАВЛОВСК)

Get off the train at Pavlovsk, the stop after Pushkin. To get to the palace from the train station, take bus #370, 383, 383A, or 493. If you have time, cross the street in front of the station and walk the 2km through the park. To go to Pushkin from Pavlovsk, take bus #370 or 383 from the Great Palace or bus #473 from Pavlovsk Station (7R). Gardens open Sa-Su 10am-5pm. 60R, students 30R. Palace ☎470 21 56. Open M-Th and Sa-Su 10am-5pm, closed 1st M of each month. 350R, students 175R. Cameras 100R, video 200R. English tours 200R.

Catherine the Great gave the 600-hectare park and gardens at Pavlovsk to her son Paul in 1777. The first residence, two-story **Marienthal**, was built in 1779, and construction of the palace began in 1780. Not wanting to be in the house during construction, Paul took an extended European vacation from 1781 to 1782 to visit the workshops of some of the most respected artists of the period, buying or ordering all the silks, furniture, china, and paintings a palace could need. The **Three Graces Pavilion,** in the small garden behind the palace, is renowned for the beauty of its central sculpture, carved by Paolo Triscorni in 1802 from a single piece of white marble. A few hundred meters before the palace stands the **Monument to Maria Fyodorovna**, the widow of Paul I. Paul's **Great Palace** is not as lavish (or garish, depending on your architectural taste) as his mother's at Tsarskoye Selo, but is worth a visit. The faux-marble columns and sculpted ceilings of the **Greek Hall** are particularly noteworthy. **Maria Fyodorovna's apartments** (30R, students 15R), are among the few examples in Russia of modest royal taste.

NOVGOROD (НОВГОРОД) ☎(8)8162(2)

Founded in the 9th century by Prince Ryurik, Novgorod (pop. 235,000) blossomed during the Middle Ages. In its medieval heyday, it housed twice its current population, triumphed over the Mongols, and challenged Moscow and Kyiv for Slavic supremacy. Close to St. Petersburg and larger, prettier, and better-restored than Pskov, Novgorod offers visitors a picturesque introduction to early Russia.

 Novgorod uses both 5- and 6-digit phone numbers. When dialing 6-digit numbers from out of town, drop the last digit (2) from the city code.

▭ TRANSPORTATION

Trains: ☎ 13 93 80. To: **Moscow** (8½hr., 1 per day, 275R) and **St. Petersburg** (3-4hr., 3 per day, 108R). *Kassa* open 24hr.

Buses: To the left as you face the train station, in a building labeled "Автостанция." (Avtostantsiya; ☎ 7 73 00). Open 5am-10pm. To: **Moscow** (10hr., 1 per day, 320R); **Pskov** (4½hr., 2 per day, 150R); **St. Petersburg** (3hr., 8 per day, 135R).

■◼◪ ORIENTATION AND PRACTICAL INFORMATION

Novgorod's heart is its **kremlin**, from which a web of streets spins outward on the **west side** of the river. The **train** and **bus station** lie on **ul. Oktyabrskaya** (Октябрьская). **Pr. Karla Marksa** (Карла Маркса) runs from the train station to what remains of the earthen walls that surrounded old Novgorod. Follow **Lyudog-oshchaya ul.** (Людогоща) from the walls, through **Sofiyskaya pl.** (Софийская) to the kremlin. The east side of the river is home to most of the churches as well as Yaroslav's court, and the streets form a rectangular grid. Purchase a **map** (65R) from a kiosk in the train station, at any major hotel, or at the tourist office.

Tourist Office: ▓**Krasnaya Izba** (Красная Изба; Red Wooden Hut), pl. Sennaya 5 (Сенная; ☎ 17 30 74; http://tourism.velikiynovgorod.ru), 1 block down ul. Meretskogo (Мерецкого) from pl. Sophiyskaya. Delightfully helpful staff offers **free maps** and info on everything from clubs to hospitals. English-speaking staff. Wheelchair accessible. Open daily 10am-5pm. Call in advance to arrange for an English-language tour of the kremlin (1hr., €5-7) and the city (2½hr., €8-10).

Currency Exchange: At any "обмен валюты" (obmen valyuty) sign and in all the major banks; there's one on Bolshaya Moskovskaya ul.

ATMs: In the train station, in the telephone office, and at major banks.

Luggage Storage: In the **train station**. 29-46R per day. Open 24hr.; talk to the station manager if the door is locked. In the **bus station**. 20R per bag. Open daily 7am-7pm.

Laundromat: Ul. Germana 23, in the same building as a *banya*. Open W-Th 3-8pm, F 4-7:30pm, Sa-Su noon-8:30pm.

Pharmacy: Panacea N, B. Sankt Peterburgskaya 7/2 (Санкт Петербургская; ☎ 13 82 66). Open daily 8am-10pm.

Telephones: Novgorod Telecom, at the corner Lyudogoshchaya ul. and ul. Gazon (Газон), on Sophiyskaya pl. Pre-pay for intercity or international calls.

Internet: Ventilator, ul. Meritskogo 13 (Меритского; ☎ 7 71 82). Good connections. 30R per hr. Open noon-11pm. **Technotron,** ul. Velikaya 3 (Великая; ☎ 7 63 62). Scanner available. Internet 40R per hr. Open M-F 9am-7pm, Sa 10am-4pm.

Post Office: B. Sankt Peterburgskaya 9 (☎ 7 42 74). Open M-F 9am-2pm and 3-7pm, Sa 10am-4pm. **Postal Code:** 173 001.

▮ ACCOMMODATIONS

Gostinitsa Volkhov, ul. Predtechenskaya 23 (☎ 11 55 05 or 11 55 07; www.nov-tour.com). Totally remodeled 3-star hotel offers TVs, telephones, and private bath. The friendly and professional English-speaking staff, combined with the great location, makes this a deal. Sauna 1000R per hr. regardless of the size of the group. Breakfast included. Check-out is at noon but is flexible. Singles 1200R; doubles 1800R. ❹

Gostinitsa Intourist, ul. Velikaya 16 (☎ 17 50 89). 3-star hotel, but not centrally located. Basic amenities at a modest price. Singles 820R; doubles 1040R. ❸

Novgorod

▲ ACCOMMODATIONS
Gostinitsa Novgorodskaya, 4
Gostinitsa Sadko, 5

🍎 FOOD
Detinets, 7
Ilmyen Complex, 3
Kafe Lux, 6
Pri Dvore, 2
Zolotoy Kovsh, 1

Gostinitsa Sadko (Гостиница Садко), ul. Fyodorovskiy Ruchey 16 (Фёдоровский Ручей; ☎66 09 73; root@sadko.vnov.ru). From the train station, buses #4 and 20 (6R) cross the river and stop at the corner of Bolshaya Moskovskaya. Quiet but in a rather far location. Private baths. Breakfast included. Singles 690R; doubles 1100R. MC/V. ❷

Gostinitsa Novgorodskaya (Новгородская), Desyatinnaya ul. 6a (Десятинная; ☎/fax 7 22 60). From the train station, go down pr. Karla Marksa past the rotary and turn right on Desyatinnaya. Good location. Simple rooms with TVs, phones, and private baths. Singles 700R; doubles 700-900R. MC/V. ❷

🍴 FOOD

The well-stocked **grocery store** Vavilon (Вавилон), ul. Lyudogoshchaya 10 (Людогощая), is an alternative to fancy dining. (Open daily 8am-11pm.) There's a **market** on ul. Fyodorovskiy Ruchei. (Open daily 8am-8pm.)

🍴 **Zolotoy Kovsh** (Золотой Ковш; Golden Ladle), Nogoluchanskaya ul. 14 (Новолучянская; ☎7 60 15). Excellent traditional Russian cuisine, plus a large selection of vegetarian options. Entrees 50-200R. Open daily 11am-11pm. ❷

■ **Detinets** (Детинец; ☎ 7 46 24), in the west wall of the kremlin. Novgorod's most popular restaurant serves authentic Russian food in a medieval atmosphere. Call ahead. Entrees 80-170R. Open M noon-9pm, Tu-Su noon-5pm and 7-11pm. ❷

Ilmyen Gastronomic Complex (Ильмень; ☎ 7 24 96), ul. Gazon 2 (Газон). Whatever kind of food you're looking for, Ilmyen has it. Inside the complex is a deli offering baked goods and other snacks, a bistro for more substantial meals, and an upscale restaurant, called Holmgard, offering viking paraphernalia alongside Russian and Scandinavian food cooked over an open flame. **Deli** ❶ open daily 10am-9pm. **Bistro** ❸ open daily 10am-10pm. **Holmgard** ❸ open daily 10am-midnight.

Pri Dvore (При Дворе), in the park outside the kremlin. Shashlyki (25-47R) are grilled outside while sandwiches (10-18R) are served inside. **Grill** ❷ open daily 1pm-1am. For heartier, classier fare go to their **restaurant** ❷, ul. Lyudogoshchaya 3 (☎ 7 43 43), a block past Sophiyskaya pl. Entrees 60-200R. Open daily 10am-9pm.

Kafe Lux (Люкс), Vlasyevskaya 6 (☎ 7 24 15), just up and across Vlasyevskaya from Ventilator (see above). Offers traditional foods as cheap as they come. Sandwiches 10-20R, salads 9-28R, entrees 12-45R. Open daily 7-5am. ❶

◉ SIGHTS

KREMLIN (КРЕМЛЬ; KREML). Although known as a *detinets* (детинец; small kremlin), Novgorod's pride and joy is nonetheless impressive. Its walls, 3m thick and 11m high, and nine spiraling towers protect most of the city's sights. *(Open M-Sa 6am-midnight. Free.)* Bells are at the base of the belfry by the riverside entrance. The clock tower (часовня; chasovnya) stands at the west gate. *(Belfry open W-Su 10-5:30pm. Free.)* The golden-spired Byzantine **St. Sophia's Cathedral** (Софийский Собор; Sofiyskiy Sobor), the oldest stone structure in Russia, built in the 11th century, dominates the complex. *(Open daily 8am-1pm and 2-8pm. Services 10am and 6pm. Free.)* Between the cathedral and the clock tower sits the **Faceted Chamber** (Грановитая Палата; Granovitaya Palata), with its elaborate golden artifacts and textiles. *(Enter between the small, lion statues. Open M-Tu and Th-Sa 10am-6pm; closed last F of each month. 70R, students 30R. Cameras 30R, video 100R.)* In the center of the kremlin, directly in front of the museum, stands the **Russian Millennium** (Тысячелетие России; Tysyacheletiye Rossii). It was built in 1852 as one of three identical, bell-shaped monuments; its sisters stand in St. Petersburg and Kyiv. Just inside the west entrance, the **Philharmonic Concert Hall** hosts a variety of theatrical and musical performances. *(☎ 7 27 77. Kassa open M-F noon-7pm, Sa-Su noon-5pm. 20-50R)* Behind the museum stands the tallest tower in the kremlin walls, the Kokui tower, from whose summit you can see most of the town. *(Open Tu-W and F-Su 11am-2pm and 3pm-7pm. 40R, students 22R.)* Outside the kremlin walls, at the southern edge of the park, the **Novgorod Horseman** commemorates the city's longevity, but only by default: designed for Moscow after WWII, the statue was sent to Novgorod after the capital rejected it. In front of it stretches a clean beach. The **Novgorod United Museum** leads visitors through the city's history. Exhibits range from architectural finds to tsarist-era uniforms. *(Open M and W-Su 10am-6pm; closed last Th of each month. Exhibit captions in English. Kassa open M and W-Su 10am-1pm and 1:30-5:15pm. 60R, students 30R. Cameras 30R, video 100R.)*

YAROSLAV'S COURT (ЯРОСЛАВОВО ДВОРИЩЕ; YAROSLAVOGO DVORISHCHE). Across the footbridge from the kremlin lies Yaroslav's Court, the old market center and original site of the Novgorod princes' palace. It contains what's left of the 17th-century waterfront arcade, several medieval churches, and the market gate house, now a fresco museum. *(Grounds open 24hr. Free. Museum open W-Su 10am-4:30pm; closed last F of each month. 35R, students 17R. Cameras 30R, video 50R.)*

MUSEUM OF FINE ARTS (МУЗЕЙ ИСКУССТВА; MUZEY ISKUSSTVA). A fine collection of 18th- to 20th-century Russian art is in this museum. Upstairs, one hall exhibits local art; another houses works on loan from the Hermitage. *(Sophiyskaya pl. 2, in the white-columned building next to ul. Meretskogo. Open Tu-Su 10am-6pm; kassa closes 5:20pm; closed first Th of each month. 28R, students 15R. Cameras 30R, video 100R.)*

YURIEV MONASTERY (ЮРЬЕВ МОНАСТЫРЬ; YURYEV MONASTYR). Dating from 1030, Yuriev is one of three monasteries around the city. From here you can see Lake Ilmen, the site of Ryurik's 9th-century court, where the state of Russia first took shape. The twin-domed St. George's Cathedral (Георгиевский Собор; Georgievskiy Sobor), founded in 1119, houses icons from the 12th century, as well as a *kafedra* (кафедра), a unique round pulpit. To get to the monastery, take bus #7 or 7a (5min., every 20-30min., 6R) from the stop on Meritskogo (Меритского) between Chudintseva (Чудинцева) and Prusskaya, on the side opposite the park. Go well past the airport and get off when you see the gold dome of the monastery on your right. *(Open daily 7am-7pm. Services at 6:30, 9am, and 6pm. Free. Cameras 10R, video 30R.)*

PSKOV (ПСКОВ) ☎(8)8112

Pskov (pop. 230,000) was established in AD 903 (800 years earlier than neighboring St. Petersburg) as a key regional trading post. Pskov was so successful that by the Middle Ages, Father Piotrowski, the chronicler of the Polish king Stephen Bathori, likened the city to Paris. This comparison is no longer accurate, however, as capitalism was not kind to Pskov. Stuck between St. Petersburg and Moscow, the city has found itself unable to attract much-needed investment. While many of Russia's neighboring countries have recently joined the ranks of the EU, having met the higher agricultural and industrial standards that entails, Pskov represents the challenges still facing Russia as it strives to catch up with its increasingly Westernized counterparts.

▰ TRANSPORTATION

Trains: ☎ 16 00 00. It was in this station that Tsar Nicholas II officially abdicated from the throne on March 2, 1917 at 3pm. *Kassa* open 24hr. To: **Kaliningrad** (13hr., 1 per day, 625R); **Moscow** (12hr., 1-2 per day, 275R); **St. Petersburg** (6hr., 2-3 per day, 165R); **Minsk, BLR** (15hr., 2 per week, 370R); **Rīga, LAT** (7hr., 1 per day, 787R); **Vilnius, LIT** (7hr., every 2 days, 500R).

Buses: ☎ 15 81 37. To: **Novgorod** (4hr., 2 per day, 154R) and **St. Petersburg** (7hr., 5 per day, 205R). Each *kassa* sells tickets for a different destination, indicated to the right of the window. Advance sales *kassa* #5. Open daily 5am-8pm.

Public Transportation: Bus #17 departs from the front of the train station and stops in front of Gostinitsa Oktyabrskaya (see **Accommodations,** p. 728), between Gostinitsa Turist and Gostinitsa Rizhskaya, and at the kremlin. Buy tickets (6R) on board.

◼✚🛈 ORIENTATION AND PRACTICAL INFORMATION

The **bus** and **train stations** are next to each other on **ul. Vokzalnaya** (Вокзальная). This street intersects **Oktyabrskiy pr.** (Октябрьский пр.), Pskov's main axis, a couple blocks to the right as you exit either station. Oktayabrskiy pr. intersects **Sovetskaya ul.** (Советская), which runs north to the kremlin. The **Velikaya** (Великая) and **Pskova** (Пскова) **rivers** meet at the northernmost corner of the kremlin. On pleasant afternoons, sunbathers gather on the west (non-kremlin) bank of the Velikaya near the **Mirozhskiy Monastery.** The outer **town walls** surround the Old City and run 9km around the heart of modern Pskov.

Tourist Offices: Oktyabrskaya Tourist Bureau (☎ 16 42 27), in Gostinitsa Oktyabr-skaya. Provides maps and brochures and arranges English tours of the city (3hr., 600-700R) and nearby sights. Call ahead. Open daily 9am-6pm. The **tourist bureau** (☎ 72 25 63; fax 72 32 57), on the left after the kremlin entrance, arranges English tours of the city and kremlin (2hr., 850R for group of 10 or fewer). Open M-Su 11am-6pm.

Currency Exchange: The office at Oktyabrskiy pr. 23/25 (☎ 16 19 83), next to Sberbank (Сбербанк), cashes **traveler's checks** for 3% commission. Open M-F 9am-2pm and 3-8pm, Sa 9am-3pm. You can find better exchange rates at most "обмен валюты" (obmen valyuty) signs.

ATM: ATMs at the train station, at the currency exchange, in the telephone office, in Gostinitsa Oktyabrskaya, and in Gostinitsa Rizhskaya.

Luggage Storage: At the train station (29R for a large locker until midnight. Open 24hr.) and at the bus station (10R per bag. Open daily 7am-6:40pm).

Laundromat: Pl. Lenina 2 (☎ 2 32 06). Next-day service 20R per item. Open 8am-8pm.

Pharmacy: Oktyabrskiy pr. 16 (☎ 72 32 51), near Oktyabrskaya pl.

Telephones: Ul. Nekrasova 17 (Некрасова), in a large gray building with its entrance on Oktyabrskiy pr. Pre-pay for intercity and international calls. **Faxes** at *kassy* 4 and 5. Open 24hr.; faxes 8am-10pm.

Internet Access: Inside the telephone office. 35R per hr. Pre-pay at *kassa* 4 or 5 in the main hall. Open M-F 8am-10pm, Sa 11am-9pm.

Post Office: Sovetskaya ul. 20 (Советская; ☎ 2 27 19), obscured by trees on north side of Oktyabrskaya pl. Open M-F 9am-2pm and 3-7pm, Sa-Su 9am-2pm, last Tu of each month 2-7pm. **Postal Code:** 180 000.

ACCOMMODATIONS

Gostinitsa Oktyabrskaya (Октябрьская), Oktyabrskiy pr. 36 (☎ 16 42 46; fax 16 42 54). Take bus #1, 11, 14, or 17 from the train station. The hotel is on the right, just before the Summer Gardens. Friendly reception and comfortable rooms with TVs and sinks. Tourist office and telephone center downstairs. Dorms 100R; singles 305R, with bath from 600R; doubles 400R. Add 25% to the 1st night's reservation. ❶

Gostinitsa Rizhskaya (Рижская), Rizhskiy pr. 25 (☎ 46 22 23; hotelr@com.psc.ru). Take bus #17 from the train station (6R) to the first stop across the bridge. Walk down Rizhskiy pr. away from the bridge. Rooms have private baths, TVs, phones, and fridges. Laundry (34R for collared shirts, 4hr. service; available to non-guests), beauty center, and solarium. Singles 510-630R; doubles 900-1100R. ❷

Gostinitsa Turist (Турист), Paromenskaya ul. 4 (Пароменская; ☎ 44 51 51), tucked between Uspeniya Paromenya and Velikaya. Bus #17 stops just past the bridge. Unspectacular but decent hotel close to the kremlin. Singles 170R, with amenities 450R; doubles 340R/660R. ❶

FOOD

Restaurant fare in Pskov is almost invariably Russian with slight European influences. If you need a break from *pelmeni*, then find refuge at the **Central Market** (Центральный Рынок; Tsentralny Rynok), on ul. Karla Marksa (Карла Маркса) at the top of ul. Pushkina (Пушкина). Vendors there sell fresh produce and even rotisserie chicken (150R). Look for the entrance gate, labeled "РЫНОК" in huge letters. (Open daily 8am-4pm.) There is a **grocery store**, Oktyabrskiy pr. 22. (Open daily 8am-9pm. MC/V.) In summer you can do like the locals and head to one of the beer gardens by the river and order *shashlyk* (100R), basically a barbecue kebab.

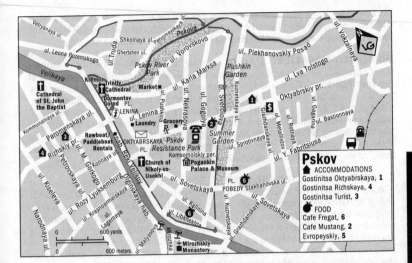

Pskov

🔺 ACCOMMODATIONS
Gostinitsa Oktyabrskaya, **1**
Gostinitsa Rizhskaya, **4**
Gostinitsa Turist, **3**

🍴 FOOD
Cafe Fregat, **6**
Cafe Mustang, **2**
Evropeyskiy, **5**

RUSSIA

🍴 **Evropeyskiy Kafe,** pl. Pobedy 1 (☎ 16 55 80), inside the large green and white cultural center. It is on the left after the 2nd set of doors. Blue velvet seats and gentle classical music set the scene for relaxed, European-inspired cuisine. Veal Cordon Bleu 154R. Menu available in English. Open M-Su noon-1am. ❸

Cafe Mustang, Oktyabrskiy pr. 15 (☎ 72 32 33), toward the Summer Gardens from the telephone office. Standard Russian and European food, including several vegetarian options. Menu available in English. Entrees 45R-200R. Live music F-Sa 7:30-11pm. Open Su-Th noon-1am, F-Sa noon-2am. MC/V. ❷

Cafe Fregat, ul. Libknekhta 9 (Либкнехта; ☎ 12 13 17). Walk away from the kremlin on Sovyetskaya. Take a right on ul. Ouritskogo, toward the river. At the end of Ouritskogo, go left on Libknekhta. This nautical-themed cafe is on is on the 2nd fl. of a boathouse. The balcony affords a great view of the river, with rowers from the club downstairs often on the water. Serves salads (53-180R), cheap *bliny* (from 12R, available until 7pm), and traditional entrees (60-150R). Live music F-Sa 8pm-midnight. Open 24hr. ❷

🔘 **SIGHTS**

If you need a break from medieval Russian art and architecture, spend the afternoon on the beach near Mirozhskiy Monastery. Paddleboats and rowboats are available for rent (30R per 30min.) at the stand by the river on the opposite side of the Rizhskiy pr. bridge from the kremlin.

KREMLIN (КРЕМЛЬ; KREML). With its thick stone walls topped by authentic wooden roofs and spires, this 9th-century kremlin keeps modernity well outside its arched portals. In the courtyard stand the ruins of **Dovmont's City** (Довмонтов Город; Dovmontov Gorod), named for Prince Dovmont, who ruled here from 1266 to 1299. A small **museum** displays icons and other relics. The tall, golden-domed **Trinity Cathedral** (Троицкий Собор; Troitskiy Sobor), built in the 17th century, boasts an elaborate iconostasis and frescoes, which exemplify the Pskovian school of icon painting. An archway at the far end of the grounds accesses the **kremlin wall,** between the courtyard and the Pskov River. (*From the train station, take* *bus #17 or any bus to pl. Lenina; get off when you spot the kremlin walls. Kremlin open daily 6am-10pm. Museum Tu-Su 11am-6pm. Museum 15R, students 10R. Cameras 40R, video 90R. Church open daily 8am-9pm. Services daily 9-11am and 6-8pm. Donations appreciated.)*

MIROZHSKIY MONASTERY. Up-river from the kremlin, the walls of the monastery (Мирожский Монастырь; Mirozhshkiy Monastyr) enclose the **Cathedral of the Transfiguration** (Спасо-Преображенский Собор; Spaso-Preobrazhenskiy Sobor), which dates from 1156 and features frescoes typical of the Pskov region. *(Take bus #2 down ul. M. Gorkogo for 5min.; get off at Krasnoarmeyskaya ul. (Красноармейская) and walk down ul. M. Gorkogo until you reach a fork; make a hard left on ul. Malyaso (Малясо), following it to the beach. Cross the bridge to your right. Enter on the far side of the monastery. ☎ 46 73 02. Open Tu-Su 11am-6pm. 100R, students 80R. Cameras 100R per 5min., no video. Cathedral closed during rain and fog.)*

CATHEDRAL OF ST. JOHN THE BAPTIST. The white, 12th-century cathedral (Собор Иоанна Предтечи; Sobor Ioanna Predtechi) stands calmly at the north end of ul. Gorkogo overlooking the west bank of the Velikaya River. First a convent and later a KGB garage, the cathedral has been restored to its Byzantine splendor. It now houses a respected **school of icon painting.** All the students use ancient icon-painting techniques, and since 1993 the superior and his students have been painting the cathedral's white walls with frescoes in an effort to restore the ancient iconographic scheme. *(Ring the doorbell of the peach-colored house, ul. Gorkogo 5a, across the path, or call ahead to notify them of your intended visit. ☎ 44 50 01. Services usually Su 9:30am, Sa 6pm, W 6pm. This is not a museum, but the friendly local curators will give free tours, some in English. Donations appreciated.)*

POGANKIN PALACE AND MUSEUM. The wealth and heritage of Pskov rest in Pogankin Palace and Museum (Поганкины Палаты и Музей; Pogankiny Palaty i Muzey), originally the home of a 17th-century merchant. The second floor of the old building is often populated by students meticulously copying the 16th-century icons on display. Vaulted ceilings and well-lit cases of coins and jewelry await visitors on the first floor. The newer wing houses a picture gallery and an exhibit on Pskov's role in WWII. *(Nekrasova 7. Enter through the new wing door on Komsomolskiy pr. (Комсомольский), buy your ticket, and go down the stairs and out through the courtyard to the main house. ☎ 16 33 11. Open Tu-Su 11am-6pm; kassa closes 5:15pm; closed last Tu of each month. Palace and museum 100R, students 80R. Cameras 40R, video 80R. For tours in English call Lydia at ☎ 295 08. 300R.)*

⚑ DAYTRIPS FROM PSKOV

PECHORY MONASTERY (ПЕЧОРЫ МОНАСТЫРЬ). Founded in 1473, **Pechory Monastery** (Pechory Monastyr) sheltered more than 200 monks in the 16th century, when it doubled as a fortress. It is a *lavra*, one of four monasteries of higher rank designated by the Russian Orthodox Church. The other *lavras* are at St. Petersburg, Moscow, and Kyiv. Today the complex is home to 60-70 monks. The golden-domed 1827 **St. Michael Church** (Михайловская Церковь; Mikhaylovskaya Tserkov), straight ahead from the main gate, stands beyond the "no entrance" (нет входа) sign. Through the archway to the left and down the hill is the yellow and white **Assumption Cathedral** (Успенский Собор; Uspenskiy Sobor), crowned with gold-starred blue domes. *(Services daily 6am and 6pm.)* A whitewashed **belfry** stands near the cathedral, and a beautiful **flower garden** surrounds the **sacred water fountain,** the destination of many pilgrims. The water is pure and potable, and many pilgrims travel far to partake of it. *(Take a bus to Pechory that goes through Old Izborsk (Старый Изборск; Staryy Izborsk). 1½hr., 6 per day, 35R. Other routes take much longer.)*

Tickets often sell out, so buy a return ticket upon arrival. Schedules vary, but the last bus back to Pskov usually leaves M-Th 5:50pm, F-Su 7:40pm. From the station, cross the square and go down Yurevskaya ul. (Юрьевская) past the red tower. Take a right; the monastery is on the left after 5min. Dress appropriately. Open daily 6am-10pm. Free. Pay the gatekeeper for permission to use a camera. Russian tours from 100R.)

OLD IZBORSK (СТАРЫЙ ИЗБОРСК; STARYY ISBORSK). Not to be confused with New Izborsk (Новый Изборск; Novyy Isborsk), Old Isborsk makes a great stop on the way to or from Pechory. The 8th-century town is older, smaller, and much less modernized than Pskov. Its secluded **fortress** stands proudly on its own hill, surrounded by trees, and provides a scenic view across the nearby **lake.** The fortress walls are not as fully restored as those of Pskov's kremlin, but the quiet 14th-century **Cathedral of St. Nicholas** is in excellent condition. You can tour the grounds on horseback (100R per 30min.). On your way back down, take a moment to peruse the collection of 11th-century ironwork and the model of the fortress as it looked long ago, on display in the small **museum,** which costs 60R. *(Buses run from Pskov—1hr., 6 per day, 17R—and go to Pechory—30min., 6 per day, 13R. Last bus to Pskov M-Th 5:25pm, F-Su 7:40pm. On the way back, wait at the road side; not all buses pull into the station. If the bus kassa is closed, pay on board. From the bus station, cross the street and take the small road, past the museum on the left. Take the 1st right and walk 10-15min. Open 24hr. Free.)*

THE KALININGRAD REGION (КАЛИНИНГРАДСКАЯ ОБЛАСТЬ)

Kaliningrad, formerly known as East Prussia, flourished under seven centuries of German rule. The Soviet Union, which gained control of the region after WWII, sealed the area and made it a base for the Red Navy's Baltic Fleet. The modern region borders Poland and Lithuania and is separate from the rest of Russia. Germans are returning to Kaliningrad—this time as tourists flocking to the bustling city of Kaliningrad and the picturesque resort town of Svetlogorsk. The Russian section of the Curonian Spit, a narrow sandbar that con-

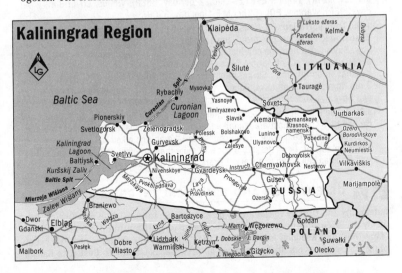

nects the region with western Lithuania—remains relatively untouched by tourists, but the intrepid travelers who trek through its pine forests and luscious sand dunes are sure to be satisfied.

KALININGRAD (КАЛИНИНГРАД) ☎(8)0112

Birthplace of philosopher Immanuel Kant, the former Königsberg (King's Mountain) was nearly destroyed during WWII. What little remained was either demolished or "converted" by the Soviets. When Stalin's henchman Mikhail Ivanovich Kalinin—who had never set foot in the city—died in 1946, Königsberg became Kaliningrad. For 50 years, it was home to the USSR's powerful Baltic fleet and was closed to the outside world. In the early days of post-Soviet Russia, it gained a reputation for high AIDS rates and rampant drug trade. But as it rebuilds the old Königsberg Cathedral and restores other monuments razed by the USSR, Kaliningrad is recasting itself as a cultural center.

⌸ TRANSPORTATION

Trains: Kaliningrad has 2 stations:

Yuzhnyy Vokzal (Южный Вокзал; South Station), Zheleznodorozhnaya ul. 15-23 (Железнодорожная ул.; ☎58 46 06), next to the bus station and behind the statue of Kalinin. Open daily 4am-10pm; info booths daily 8am-1pm and 2-8pm. To: **Moscow** (23-24hr., 2 per day, 530-1400R); **St. Petersburg** (25½hr., 1 every other day, 960R); **Svetlogorsk** (1hr., every 2hr., 30R); **Gdynia, POL** (3hr., 1 per day, 480R) via **Gdańsk, POL** and **Malbork, POL; Odessa, UKR** (18hr., 1 every other day, 900-1320R).

Severnyy Vokzal (Северный Вокзал; North Station), near pl. Pobedy (пл. Победы; ☎58 64 02), behind the large gray building immediately near the Lenin statue. Sends trains to cities within the Kaliningrad region. Electric trains run to **Svetlogorsk** (1½hr., every 2hr., 25R).

Buses: Avtobusnyy Vokzal (Автобусный Вокзал), Zheleznodorozhnaya ul. 15-23 (☎44 36 35, international reservations 44 65 00; fax 44 65 00), next to Yuzhnyy Vokzal. Open daily 5am-11pm. To: **Gdańsk, POL** (3½hr., 2 per day, 184R); **Kaunas, LIT** (4-6hr., 2 per day, 211R); **Klaipėda, LIT** (3-6hr., 5 per day, 114-180R); **Rīga, LAT** (9-12hr., 3 per day, 314R); **Tallinn, EST** (14-18hr., 1 per day, 568R); **Vilnius, LIT** (7-8hr., 2 per day, 296R); **Warsaw, POL** (6½hr., M-F 1 per day, 320R).

Public Transportation: The transportation system in Kaliningrad has been overhauled. **Buses**, which are now privatized, are speedy. Prices (7R) are posted in the bus window. Buy a ticket from the conductor if there is one. If there isn't a conductor, pay the driver when you get off. Some buses lack numbers, so you may have to check the destination on the front. Slower public **trams** (7R) still cross the city. Trams #2 and 3 run from pl. Kalinina to pl. Pobedy via Tsentralnaya pl., connecting Yuzhnyy Vokzal and Severnyy Vokzal. Tram #1 runs east-west from the zoo toward the market.

Taxis: At the train stations, Gostinitsa Kaliningrad, the zoo, and pl. Pobedy. Almost any car can be a "taxi" (most are unmarked, and almost none have meters). Let's Go does not recommend hitchhiking. If you choose to take an unmarked car, agree on a price before setting off. Don't get into a car with more than 1 person in it. If you speak Russian, you can call a cab in advance; **Express Taxi** (☎39 33 33).

✵ ⑦ ORIENTATION AND PRACTICAL INFORMATION

Autobusnyy and **Yuzhnyy Vokzal** are by **pl. Kalinina** (Калинина). The main artery, **Leninskiy pr.** (Ленинский), runs perpendicular to pl. Kalinina opposite **Pregolya** (Преголя) and **Kneiphof Island,** site of the cathedral. It continues past the crumbling House of Soviets to **Tsentralnaya pl.** (Театралая), home to **Gostinitsa Kalinin-**

RUSSIA

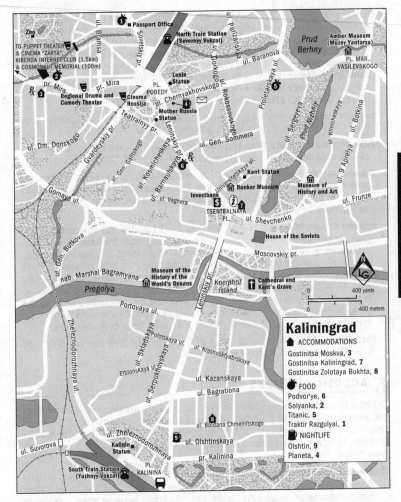

Kaliningrad

🏠 ACCOMMODATIONS

Gostinitsa Moskva, **3**
Gostinitsa Kaliningrad, **7**
Gostinitsa Zolotaya Bukhta, **8**

🍎 FOOD

Podvor'ye, **6**
Solyanka, **2**
Titanic, **5**
Traktir Razgulyai, **1**

🍸 NIGHTLIFE

Olshtin, **9**
Planeta, **4**

grad (Гостиница Калининград; Hotel Kaliningrad). Finally, it heads toward a park dedicated to Mother Russia—see the wind-swept lady holding the hammer-and-sickle—before veering left to its end, **pl. Pobedy** (пл. Победы; Victory Square). Just before the square, **Teatralnyy pr.** (Театралий) branches off from Leninskiy, becoming **pr. Mira** (Мира). **Ul. Chernyakhovskogo** (Черняховского) lies to the right, perpendicular to Leninskiy as you enter pl. Pobedy coming from the stations, and travels east to the market.

Visa Registration: Most hotels will register your visa for you. If you have a dual or multiple-entry visa, or are not staying in a hotel, you must register in person at the **Office of Passport and Visa Service** (ОВИР; OVIR), 13 Sovetskiy pr. (☎21 73 21), parallel to Severny Vokzal and just before Traktir Rasgulai. Note that this is 1 block past the larger government building at 7 Sovetskiy pr. Be ready to show all your original documents.

Currency Exchange: Exchange **kiosks,** "обмен валюты" (obmen valyuty), are at major intersections. Banks offer better rates but take longer and require a passport. **Transcredit Bank,** inside Yuzhnyy Vokzal, offers some of the best exchange rates in Kaliningrad (☎587 734). The **24hr. exchange** inside Gostinitsa Kaliningrad (see **Accommodations,** p. 734) charges higher rates but has a MC/V **ATM** outside. **Investbank** (Инвестбанк), Leninskiy pr. 28 (☎/fax 35 14 40), is across the street to the right. Accepts **AmEx Traveler's Cheques** and gives MC/V **cash advances** for 2% commission. **24hr.** (MC) **ATM** outside. Open M-Sa 9:30am-1pm and 2-4pm.

Luggage Storage: Lockers are at the bus station and Yuzhnyy Vokzal. 30R per day, large bags 47R. Open daily 7:30am-1pm, 1:30-4pm, 4:30-9pm.

24hr. Pharmacy: Apteka Gippokrat (Аптека Гиппократ), Leninskiy pr. 43 (☎54 11 11). **Formula Zdarova** (Формула Здарова), pr. Mira 27 (☎77 70 03).

Telephones: Ul. Leonova 20 (☎21 94 10), next to the post office. **Faxes** and **Internet access** (30R per hr.). Open daily 8am-9pm. **International Telephone Center** (☎45 15 15; fax 46 95 90), inside Gostinitsa Kaliningrad (see **Accommodations,** p. 734), on the left. Open 24hr.

Internet Access: Internet Zal E-Type, Sovetsky 1 (☎21 24 42), has slow connections at (30R per hr., students 24R) but is conveniently located inside the **Kaliningrad Technical University.** Facing the Lenin statue, head right to the faded pink building. The computer center is on the 1st fl., down a hallway to the right of the main entrance. Open M-F 9am-2pm and 3-7pm, Sa 10am-2pm and 3-6pm. **Kiberda Internet Club** (Киберда; ☎51 18 30), Komsomolskaya ul. 87 (Комсомольская) offers lightening-fast connections and a well-stocked bar. Follow pr. Mira west from the city center; after crossing a bridge in front of Gostinitsa Moskva, take the 3rd right onto Komsomolskaya. Kiberda is in the basement of a villa 1.5km to the left. 36R per hr. Open daily noon-11pm.

Post Office: Cheryakhovskoyo 32 (☎53 67 31). Open M-F 9am-2pm and 3-7pm; Sa 10am-2pm and 3-6pm. **Postal Code:** 236 040.

ACCOMMODATIONS

Seeking to attract German tourists and the growing numbers of international businessmen, hotels in Kaliningrad have undergone renovations in hopes of reaching Western standards. Still, many hotels are cheap enough for the budget traveler. Most accommodations charge a 20R visa registration fee, unless otherwise noted.

Gostinitsa Kaliningrad (Гостиница Калининград), Leninskiy pr. 81 (Ленинский; ☎46 94 40; www.hotel.kaliningrad.ru), at Tsentralnaya pl. (Центральная). This blue and gray structure greets travelers crossing the Leninskiy pr. bridge from Knelphof Island. This friendly hotel frequently has vacancies. Rooms have private baths, TVs, and phones; many have views of the Cathedral. Singles 900-1550R; doubles 1100-2200R; suites 1600-2100R; apartments 3400R. MC/V. ❸

Gostinitsa Zolotaya Bukhta (Гостиница Золотая Бухта; Golden Cake Hotel), ul. Khmelnitskogo 53 (ул. Хмельницкого; ☎/fax 44 62 21). From the bus station, turn left on Leninskiy and take the 3rd right on Khmelnitskogo. Pleasant hotel run by the Ministry of Defense. Many rooms have TVs, phones, and fridges. Call ahead. Singles 170-420R, with bath 650-900R; doubles 660-900R/1000-1200R. ❶

Gostinista Moskva, pr. Mira 19 (☎ 35 23 00), just 500m west of Victory Square. A microcosm of rapidly changing Kaliningrad. A renovated **modern wing** ❹ with baths, TV, and phones in all rooms (singles 1800R) shares a building with a crumbling, **Soviet-era section** ❷ with shared baths (singles 450R). English-speaking concierge. MC/V.

█ FOOD

For fresh produce, head to the indoor **central market** (центральный рынок; tsentralnyy rynok), at the intersection of ul. Chernyakhovskogo and ul. Gorkogo. (Open daily 8am-6pm.) **Vester** (Вестер) supermarkets around town stock groceries. One is at Leninskiy pr. 16. (Open daily 9am-11pm.)

 Traktir Razgulyai (Трактир Разгуляй), Sovetskiy pr. 13 (Советский пр.; ☎/fax 21 48 97), off pl. Pobedy. English-speaking waiters dressed as Cossacks serve hearty Russian fare. Inside, meat roasts over a fire. English menu available. Entrees 70-240R. Live music and traditional Russian dancing Tu-Su 9pm-1am. Open daily 1pm-2am. MC/V. ❷

Podvor'ye (Подвор'ье), Leninskiy pr. 16 (Ленинский пр.; ☎53 68 33). Boasts tremendous decor, complete with bear skins and Russian folk art. For a terrific meal, try *bliny* (pancakes) or splurge on lobster. English menu. Entrees 64-320R. Live music Th-Sa 9pm. Open daily noon-2am. MC/V. ❷

Titanic (Титаник), pr. Chernyakhovskogo 74 (☎53 67 68). No longer propelled by the once-popular film of the same name, this 2-story replica of the unfortunate ocean-liner is still sailing strong thanks to its excellent seafood specialties. Entrees 120-400R. Open daily 11am-midnight. MC/V. ❷

Solyanka, pr. Mira 24, (☎27 92 03). A Soviet-style cafeteria where friendly ladies in funny red-and-blue hats heap mounds of meat and fish onto your plate. You pick and choose your food here, so vegetarians can easily make a meal. Entrees 40-70R. ❶

◉ SIGHTS

CATHEDRAL. During the city's 700-year stint as Königsberg, the cathedral was its pride and joy. On Kneiphof Island in the middle of the Pregolya River, the cathedral and the surrounding residential neighborhood were severely damaged by British aerial assaults in 1944. The cathedral has recently got a facelift, complete with a new roof and renovated towers. Restoration experts have made headway on the interior, which will serve as a concert hall. The project is slated to be done by 2005. Prussian kings were once crowned here, and the steps made famous by German Romantic writer E.T.A. Hoffmann. The cathedral houses an expansive **City Museum.** A tapestry depicting Königsbergunder German rule offers a glimpse of the town's charm in the years before Allied bombs and Soviet architecture left lasting scars. The top two floors pay homage to Kant; don't miss the macabre copy of his death mask. The professional cathedral choir meets most days around 4pm on the second floor and delivers a free concert. (*☎44 68 68. Open daily 9am-4:30pm. 60R, students 30R. Tours in German or Russian 300R. Cameras 15R.*)

KANT'S GRAVE AND STATUE. Walk outside to the back of the cathedral to find the grave of Immanuel Kant (1724-1804), which is enclosed by a pink marble colonnade. The German philosopher, author of *Perpetual Peace* and father of the categorical imperative, spent his entire life in Königsberg, where he taught at the local university. In 1945, the Soviets razed Christian Daniel Ruach's 1857 **statue of Kant.** Hoping to lure German tourists after the fall of communism, Kaliningrad erected a new statue, a 1992 work by Ernst Thalmann, but it has not garnered the same acclaim as its predecessor. (*Statue at Universitetskaya ul., near Leninskiy pr.*)

JULIUS RUPP MEMORIAL. Behind the cathedral stands a monument, erected in 1991, to Julius Rupp (1809-1884), an ordained Lutheran minister, whose house once stood on this spot. Rupp founded a new, unofficial religious order called *Druzya Sveta* (Друзья Света; Friends of the World), which stood for harmony among all peoples and religions. Though Rupp was frequently chastised for his views, he remained one of Königsberg's most influential thinkers and passed on many beliefs to his niece, famed artist Käthe Kollwitz.

MONUMENTS TO SOVIET GLORY. A castle has guarded the hill east of Tsentralnaya pl. since 1255, when Teutonic knights first arrived. As part of the effort to turn Königsberg into a Soviet city, the castle was blown up in 1962 and replaced by the **House of Soviets** (Дом Советов; Dom Sovetov), an H-shaped monstrosity, which is vacant, despite occupying prime real estate. In the middle of **pl. Pobedy** (Victory Square), a 7m **statue of Lenin** is a popular gathering spot. Lenin faces a park in which rows of red flowerbeds lead up to a statue of **Mother Russia**, which faces bustling Leninskiy pr. Down pr. Mira, past Gostinitsa Moskva, the **Cosmonaut Memorial** honors Alexei Leonov, who in 1965 completed the first space walk. On the other end of town, don't miss the genial figure of **Mikhail Ivanovich Kalinin,** the city's namesake, who waves to travelers outside Yuzhnyy Vokzal.

🏛 MUSEUMS

MUSEUM OF THE HISTORY OF THE WORLD'S OCEANS. If you're not claustrophobic, wander through exhibits on the Soviet diesel submarine B-413, visible from the Leninskiy Bridge. Learn how a submarine works and examine Kaliningrad through the periscope (10R). On board, a memorial to the seamen who died aboard the *Kursk*, the Russian nuclear submarine lost in the Arctic Ocean in 2000, reminds visitors of the perils of seafaring life. Also part of the museum (Музей Истории Мирового Океана; Muzei Istorii Mirogogo Okeana.) is the *Vityaz*, a large expeditional ship, which once belonged to Germany and helped thousands of Germans flee the Red Army. Today, it contains a laboratories and cabins that present the secrets of the underwater world. Captions are primarily in Russian with some German. *(Bagramyana 1 (Баграмяна), on the Pregolya River, near Hotel Ademi. ☎ 34 02 44; fax 34 02 11. Open Apr.-Oct. W-Su 11am-6pm; Nov.-Mar. W-Su 10am-5pm. 30R.)*

AMBER MUSEUM (МУЗЕЙ ЯНТАРЬЯ; MUZEY YANTARYA). This museum showcases some of the best amber specimens, from chessboards to jewelry to uncut pieces, including the largest single piece of amber in Russia, weighing 4.28kg. Especially notable are the **inclusions,** pieces of amber with prehistoric insects and flora trapped inside. The museum has fragments from the legendary Amber Room of St. Petersburg, which the Germans stole during WWII. When the Russians invaded in 1945, the Germans destroyed the room and dumped the fragments into the sea. A 2003 replica of the room is in Catherine's Palace near St. Petersburg (see p. 722). Captions in Russian. *(Pl. Vasilevskogo 1 (Васильевского). ☎ 46 12 40. Open Tu-Su 10am-6pm; kassa closes 5:30pm. 50R, students 30R.)*

BUNKER MUSEUM (МУЗЕЙ БЛИНДАЖ; MUZEY BLINDAZH). Nazi commanders gathered here to hide from Allied bombers, so, unsurprisingly, it's not easy to find. Look 50m to the left of the Kant statue for a blue staircase that leads underground. The museum details the Soviet 3rd Belorusian Front's three-day siege and subsequent capture of the city, with photos and models. Room 13 has been left exactly as it was when Nazi General Otto von Lasch signed the city over to the Red Army. *(Universitetskaya ul. 2 (Университетская), off Leninskiy pr. ☎ 53 65 93. Open daily 10am-5pm. Some English captions. 50R, students 30R. Tours in German and Russian.)*

MUSEUM OF HISTORY AND ART. The first floor of the museum (Историко-Художественный Музей; Istoriko-Khudozhestvennyy Muzey) details Kaliningrad's natural history, with stuffed seals peering at passing tourists. The second floor seems to have missed Krushchev's "de-Stalinization" order: a Stalin statue still salutes visitors. Captions primarily in Russian. *(Klinicheskaya 21 (Клиническая). From Tsentralnaya pl., walk up ul. Shevchenko, which becomes ul. Klinicheskaya and snakes around Nizhniy Lake. The museum is halfway around the lake. ☎45 38 44. Open Tu-Su 10am-6pm; kassa closes 5pm. 30R, students 20R.)*

🎵 📷 ENTERTAINMENT AND NIGHTLIFE

The beautiful **Kaliningrad Regional Drama Theatre,** pr. Mira 4, is housed in a Weimar-era residence. Ask friendly director Anatoly Kravtsov for a tour. (☎21 24 22. *Kassa* open daily 10am-7pm. Shows Sa 7pm, Su 6pm. Tickets 30-100R.) The **stadium,** opposite the zoo, on pr. Mira near Gostinitsa Moskva, is home to Kaliningrad's beloved soccer team, Baltika. **Cinema Zarya** (Заря; Dawn), pr. Mira 41, has comfortable seats and surround sound. Some late-night showings are in the original language. Open daily 10am-3am. (☎21 45 88. Tickets 100R, night shows 150R.)

If you go out alone at night, catch a cab home—walking alone is dangerous. Most nightclubs in Kaliningrad are combined with a casino-entertainment complex. Be prepared for tight security, often involving a complete pat-down. Two of the best are **Olshtin** (Ольштин), Olshtinskaya 1, a popular nightclub and casino; it is on the right as you walking south down Leninskiy pr. toward Yuzney Vozka, just after ul. Olshtinskaya. (☎44 46 35. Open daily noon-6am, dance floor and nightclub 11pm-6am.) Another option is **Planeta** (Планета), ul. Chernyakhovskogo, which combines a pizza parlor, arcade, casino, nightclub, and restaurant. (☎43 38 09. Open daily noon-6am, nightclub 11pm-7am.)

🔲 DAYTRIP FROM KALININGRAD

SVETLOGORSK (СВЕТЛОГОРСК)

Reach this costal vacation town from Kaliningrad by bus (from Autobusnyy Vokzal or along Sovetskiy pr. near Severnyy Vokzal). Purchase tickets (30R) on board. If taking the train (1½hr.; about 12 per day; 25R from Severnyy Vokzal, 30R from Yuzhnyy Vokzal), get off at Svetlogorsk 2, which is steps away from the town center. Trains sometimes leave Severnyy Vokzal up to 10min. earlier than scheduled.

Formerly the German town of Rauschen, this seaside resort was used by Soviet officials for rest and relaxation. Today, some Germans have returned as tourists to Svetlogorsk. The old charm of the town's shady, tree-lined streets stands in contrast to the massive ultra-modern complexes sprouting up along Kaliningradskiy pr. The primary reason to make the trek here is for the long, pleasant **beach,** which is excellent for swimming and sunbathing. A half-kilometer **promenade** leads to a neglected **sundial.** Turn left from the train station and continue 1km. A small **chapel,** ul. Lenina 5, stands in memory of the 34 people who died—among them 23 children—when a Soviet military aircraft crashed into a kindergarten on May 16, 1972. Authorities covered up the incident until 1991, when the Russian Orthodox Church built the chapel. The **House-Museum of Hermann Brachert** (Дом-Музей Германа Брахерта; Dom-Muzey Germana Brakherta), ul. Tokareva 7, lies just outside Svetlogorsk proper. From the train station, turn right on ul. Lenina and follow it across the train tracks. Continue straight for about 2km and then turn right after the "Отрадное" sign. Brachert, a German sculptor, lived in the house from 1933 and 1944. His work is inside the museum and in the garden. He also crafted the nymph statue at the beach in Svetlogorsk. If you speak Russian or German, ask the curator to show you around. (☎211 66. Open daily summer 10am-5pm; low season Tu-Su 10am-4pm. 50R.) Several small grocery stores line ul. Lenina. Dine on the promenade at **Seestern** ❸, which serves up wiener schnitzel (292R) and gourmet fare. (Open M-F and Su 11am-10pm, Sa 11am-11pm.) **Hotel Rauschen** ❸ (☎253 215 64), across from the train tracks on ul. Lenina, is a massive complex complete with an indoor swimming pool. (Singles from 700R. Make summer reservations months in advance.) The town is quiet at night except on Saturday, when youngsters groove to live DJs at **Max Disco Club** (☎253 220 40. Open Sa 11pm-6am.)

CURONIAN SPIT (КУРШСКАЯ КОСА)

Nearly 80km long and never more than 4km wide, the Curonian Spit (Kurshskaya Kosa) is a giant sandbar. Beautiful pine forests cover all but the western side, which is covered in sand dunes. The east side faces the calmer waters of the Curonian Lagoon (Куршиский Залив; Kurshiskiy Zaliv), and has a few villages, including Rybachiy (Рыбачий; fishing village), the best base for exploring the Russian portion of the Spit. (For more about the Lithuanian section of the Spit, see p. 474).

TRANSPORTATION AND PRACTICAL INFORMATION. The city of **Zelenogradsk** (Зеленоградск), 35km north of Kaliningrad, is the gateway to the Spit. To reach Zelenogradsk from **Kaliningrad**, take the **train** from either Yuzhnyy or Severnyy Vozkal (40-45min., about 1 per hr., 24Lt.). To get back, catch the train or a **bus** (about 1 per hr.; last bus around 11:30pm). Buses (4-5 per day) and licensed shuttle-vans run frequently from Zelenogradsk to Rybachiy (40min., about 1 per hr., 34Lt). The last bus from Rybachiy to Zelenogradsk usually leaves at 5:30pm. The shuttles also link Rybachiy, **Lesnoye** (Лесное; forest village) and **Morskoye** (Морское; sea village). From Rybachiy station, ul. Pobedy, take a right on ul. Pobedy (Победы), which ends at the main road. Down 100m to the left is a large **map** of the area. Rybachiy's **post office** and **telephone office** are at ul. Pobedy 29. (Open M-F 9am-1:30pm and 2:30-4:30pm, Sa 9am-3:30pm.) **Postal Code:** 238 535.

ACCOMMODATIONS AND FOOD. Since the Spit is a national park, there are restrictions on hotel development. **Gostinitsa Postoyali Dvor** ❹ (Гостиница Постояли Двор), at the intersection of the main road and ul. Pobedy, has small, pleasant rooms with hardwood floors and TVs, phones, and baths. Reserve two weeks in advance in summer. (☎504 12 90. Singles €44, with meals €52; doubles €54/€70.) Rooms with meals include dinner and breakfast in the adjoining restaurant, **Traktir U Dorogi** ❶ (Трактирь У Дороги), famous for its fish dishes (90-460R). Otherwise, seek out a **private room** in Rybachiy; call ahead for availability. **Usadba Tronnikovoy** ❶ (Усадьба Тронниковой; Tronnikovoy Estate), Pogranichnaya ul. 4 (Пограничная), is a yellow house. From the bus station, turn right on ul. Pobedy and take the first right onto a narrow paved road. (☎504 12 04. Rooms 200-300R.) Small grocery stores along ul. Pobedy sell essential items. The closest thing to a **supermarket** is **Kooperator,** ul. Pobedy 14; it has an outdoor cafe. (☎504 12 61. Open 9am-9pm.) Rybachiy has no **ATMs**; stock up before heading to the Spit.

SIGHTS. Tourist infrastructure ranges from minimal to nonexistent. Scores of unpaved roads and unmarked footpaths crisscross the forest. Most are formed by grazing cattle and lead to private homes or nowhere at all. Before you hit the trails, visit Rybachiy's **Biological Station**, ul. Pobedy 32, which tracks wildlife on the Spit and contains a small museum explaining its research activities. Local students can direct visitors to the bird-catching site, 12km south of Rybachiy. (☎412 51; www.zin.ru/rybachy. Open daily 9am-6pm. Museum open daily Apr.-Oct. 10am-4pm.) There are two natural sights worth visiting in Rybachiy. About 1km down the main road toward Klaipėda, and past Gostinitsa Postoyali Dvor, take a left at the sign for **Zolotyye Dyuny** (Золотые Дюны; Golden Dunes). Follow the path, which leads to a beautiful **park** among sand dunes. The area's **hikinhg trail,** a gentle 3.5km loop, shouldn't be missed. Take the main road 1km from Rybachiy toward Zelenogradsk. The trailhead is on the right just after the lake on the left. Follow the wooden arrows—in doubt, follow the bigger path—to the top of **Müller's Hill,** the highest point on the Spit. Frank Müller was the German naturalist who discovered how to grow vegetation on the Spit's sands, which used to blow wildly and bury entire villages. The two observation towers offer astonishing views of the Spit. From there, the trail descends into a windy **pine forest,** where trees slant to one side. This part of the trail is poorly maintained: take care not to get lost.

THE TRANS-SIBERIAN RAILROAD

The Trans-Siberian Railroad (or TSR) is the link that connects Russia's gilded domes and Moscow's tinted windshields to the rest of her proud but crumbling empire. Over the course of six and a half days, the train rolls across 9289km, two continents, and seven time zones. Begun in 1891, construction of the railway took over 25 years and US$320 million. Ruggedly picturesque farmlands and never-ending birch forests are punctuated by occasional concrete stations, presenting an authentic experience of a Russia that few foreigners venture to enjoy. Even more memorable than the view is what goes on inside the train. Whether you find yourself riding with a nightgowned *babushka* and her bucket of berries or with a middle-aged man who drinks vodka before bed and beer for breakfast, a Trans-Siberian journey is the ultimate crash course in Russian culture. Coverage of the Trans-Siberian Railroad was last updated in July of 2003.

LOGISTICS. The term "Trans-Siberian" doesn't refer to a single train but to three distinct sets of tracks. The Trans-Siberian line links Moscow and Vladivostok; the **Trans-Mongolian** connects Moscow to Beijing via Ulaanbaatar, MON; and the **Trans-Manchurian** loops through Manchuria en route to Beijing. *Let's Go* covers the Trans-Siberian and Trans-Mongolian routes in detail. Russian Railways has yet to develop a flexible ticket that allows multiple stops; if you plan to make any stops, you'll need to purchase individual tickets for each leg of the trip. When purchasing a ticket for a multi-day journey, plan at least three days in advance. Service centers in train stations and hotel lobbies can help you bypass the maddening ticket booths for a 50-200R fee. You'll need visas to enter China, Russia, and possibly Mongolia; Chinese and Mongolian visas are best obtained in Moscow (see p. 670); a Mongolian visa can also be picked up either in Irkutsk (see p. 753) or in Ulan Ude (see p. 759). For more info concerning Mongolian visas, see p. 766.

COSTS. The cost of a Trans-Siberian ticket depends on several factors, the most important being where and when you buy it, how far you're going, and what class you want. The most popular class among foreigners is *coupé* (купе), a four-bed berth with adequate and reasonably clean facilities. *Lux* (люкс) cabins are roughly twice as expensive and sleep two. Most budget travelers take *coupé* tickets, and all *Let's Go* prices are for *coupé* berths. Purchasing all your tickets in Moscow is expensive, but generally cheaper than buying a string of tickets from town to town. Prices are always higher in summer than in winter. If you're only making a few stops, Moscow's **G&R Hostel** (see p. 672) offers several packages and can arrange tickets for US$20-50 commission. More importantly, they can explain in excellent English how the railroad works and can help you choose the ticket best suited to your itinerary. Allow at least five days for processing in high season. The website (www.hostels.ru) is a helpful resource, consolidating information on pricing and schedules. The hostel offers prearranged tickets for TSR routes, including the following from Moscow: **Beijing** via **Mongolia** (€232); **Beijing** via **Manchuria** (€243); **Vladivostok** (€275); **Ulaanbaatar** (€184); **Irkutsk** (€184). All prices are for high-season *coupé* tickets. If you speak Russian, or can fake it with a written itinerary, you can save nearly 30% by buying directly from the **Moscovskoye Zheleznodorozhnoye Agenstvo** (Московское Железнодорожное Агенство; Moscow Train Agency) in Moscow (see p. 666).

> **TRAIN TIME.** The Trans-Siberian traverses 7 time zones, but arrivals and departures are always listed in **Moscow time** at stations as well as in *Let's Go.*

TRAINS TO BEIJING (DEPARTURES IN MOSCOW TIME)

TRAIN	MOSCOW	YEKATER-INBURG	NOVOSI-BIRSK	KRASNO-YARSK	IRKUTSK	ULAN UDE	ULAAN-BAATAR	BEIJING
4	Tu 10:03pm	Th 12:19am	Th 7:35pm	F 7:40am	Sa 1:44am	Sa 9:14am	Su 2:35am	
6	W 10:03pm	F 12:19am	F and Sa 7:35pm	Su and M 10:10am	Su and M 8:46am	Su 9:14am		
10*	odd days 11:30pm	odd days 2:02am	odd days 7:35pm	odd days 9:43am				
20*	F 11:58pm	Su 2:10am	Su 7:45pm	M 9:56am	Tu 3:54am	Tu 11:15am		F 5:30am

*firmennyy trains

TRAINS TO VLADIVOSTOK (DEPARTURES IN MOSCOW TIME)

TRAIN	MOSCOW	YEKATER-INBURG	NOVOSI-BIRSK	KRASNO-YARSK	IRKUTSK	ULAN UDE	VLADIVOSTOK
2*	odd days 3:26pm	odd days 7:33pm	odd days 3:19pm	even days 4:04am	even days 1:36pm	odd days 5:57am	
10*	odd days 9:29pm		odd days 9:35pm	even days 9:29am			
904	daily 5:30am						

*firmennyy trains

DEPARTING. All outbound TSR trains depart from Moscow's **Yaroslavskiy Vokzal** (see p. 666). There is also one train (#16) that departs for Yekaterinburg from Kazanskiy Vokzal (see p. 666). The better long-distance trains, called *firmennyy* (фирменный; quality), offer cleaner facilities but can also cost twice as much as the regular *skoryy* (скорый; rapid) trains. Local color aboard *skoryy* makes for an entertaining short trip, but occasional drunks and offensive odors make the *firmennyy* worth the money for trips longer than 24hr. From Moscow, the *firmennyy* trains are: train **#2** (Россия; Rossiya; Russia) to **Vladivostok;** train **#10** (Байкал; Baikal) to **Irkutsk** and **Lake Baikal;** train **#20** (Русский Поезд; Russkiy Poyezd; the Russian Train) to **Beijing** via **Manchuria;** train **#16** (Урал; Ural) to **Yekaterinburg;** train **#26** to **Novosibirsk;** and train **#56** to **Krasnoyarsk.** Other trains include train **#4** (Китайский Поезд; Kitaiskiy Poyezd; the Chinese Train) to **Beijing** via **Ulaanbaatar;** train **#6** to **Ulaanbaatar;** train **#44** to **Khabarovsk;** train **#68** to **Abakan;** and train **#904** to **Vladivostok.** Check the train schedule above for more info. Smaller and more frequent trains serve these cities with varying availability. *Firmennyy* trains usually have a plaque on the side of each car stating the train's name. In all cases, "odd" (нечётный) and "even" (чётный) refer to calendar days and ежедневный means daily.

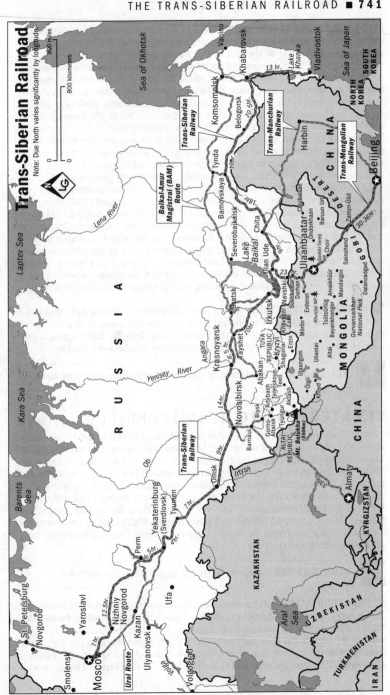

Trans-Siberian Railroad

Note: Due North varies significantly by longitude.

Trans-Siberian Railway

Trans-Manchurian Railway

Trans-Mongolian Railway

Baikal-Amur Magistral (BAM) Route

Trans-Siberian Railway

Ural Route

RUSSIA

LIFE ABOARD THE TRAIN. Two attendants—*provodnik* (male) or *provodnitsa* (female)—sit in each wagon to make sure all goes smoothly; they offer tea (2R) and tend the *samovar* at the end of the wagon, which is your source for free boiled water. On most *firmennyy* trains they also collect the linen fee (usually under 50R), and offer mini-bar service (there is a charge if you use the provided china rather than your own mug). When purchasing your ticket, try to avoid the first or last *coupé* in the wagon; these neighbor the toilets and, especially on non-*firmennyy* trains, the stench can become unbearable (on *firmennyy* trains they're cleaned often). Always carry your own toilet paper. Toilets are locked 5min. before each stop and will only reopen once in the countryside: no amount of pleading with the *provodnik* will do you any good. Cabin-mates tend to be gregarious and willing to engage in a game of cards, chess, or backgammon. You'll likely find the opportunity to share family photos or a meal with curious companions. Your compartment-mates will probably come aboard with lots of sausage and veggies to share; you will make friends if you do the same. A posted schedule in each wagon lists arrival times for each *stoyanka* (стоянка; stop). When the train stops for longer than a few minutes, locals come out to sell food, beer, water, cigarettes, and trinkets to passengers. Although harassment in the *coupé* wagons is uncommon, **female travelers** on non-*firmennyy* trains should be prepared to wade through droves of drunks and field unprovoked niceties. If you have problems with men in your compartment, ask to be transferred elsewhere. In serious cases the *provodnitsa* will summon the military official who accompanies each train.

 DISTANT DESTINATIONS. While the TSR provides ample adventure for savvy travelers, certain areas beyond the tracks are too amazing to miss. These regions are designated by the "Off the Beaten Track" icon . Each region is preceded by a major TSR stop with detailed connection info between the two.

> **ALL ABOARD!** Yekatarinburg is **Sverdlovsk** (Свердловск) in train lingo.

YEKATERINBURG (ЕКАТЕРИНБУРГ) ☎(8)3432

The stolid serenity of the Soviet cosmopolitan dream can still be felt in this pleasantly calm city on the banks of the river Iset and at the edge of the Ural Mountains. Yekaterinburg's educational institutions were political springboards for many Soviet and Russian leaders, including former president Boris Yeltsin; however, the influence of a younger Russian generation is pervasive, lending a college-town atmosphere to the streets. In Yekaterinburg (formerly known as Sverdlovsk in honor of Bolshevik revolutionary Yakov Sverdlov), classic Soviet architecture and fast-food joints fuse into a rejuvenated urban setting. With plenty of theaters, small museums, and great streets for strolling, this is the perfect place to take some time off from the train and recharge.

> **TIME CHANGE.** Yekatarinburg is 2hr. ahead of Moscow: GMT +5

TRANSPORTATION. Yekaterinberg is the major stop between Moscow and Novosibirsk. Dozens of trains in both directions leave ultra-modern **Sverdlovskiy Station** (Свердловский Вокзал) daily. Purchase **tickets** on the 3rd floor in the west wing of the station (to your right as you exit); foreigners should go to counter 5. **Luggage storage** is also available here; ask at a ticket counter for "kamera khraneniya" (камера хранения). Yekaterinburg is full of **trolleys** and **buses,** as well as a small **metro**. All public transportation costs 5R. From the station, take bus #1, 13, 21, 23, or 31 or trolley #1, 3, 5, 9, or 12 or just walk 10min. up **ul. Yakova Sverdlova** (Якова Свердлова), which bears left and then straightens as it runs into **ul. Karla Libknekhta** (Карла Либкнета), until you reach the main street **pr. Lenina** (Ленина).

■ ⑦ ORIENTATION AND PRACTICAL INFORMATION. The town center is the bridge where the main street, **pr. Lenina** (Ленина), crosses the **River Iset**, 10min. south of the train station. **Ul. Karla Libknekhta** (Карла Либкнеха) forms a T with pr. Lenina on its way to ul. Yakova Sverdlova (Якова Свердлова) and the train station. The **Opera and Ballet Theater** (see p. 744) lies to the east of this intersection on pr. Lenina. Grab a **map** of the city at the **Knigi** (Книги; Books) bookstore in the complex to the right of the pedestrian underpass in front of the train station, or at one of the bookstores along pr. Lenina. The **US Consulate** is at ul. Gogolya 15. (Гоголя; ☎ 56 46 19; after-hours 8290 51 506. Open M-F 8am-6pm.) Next door is the **UK Consulate** (☎ 56 49 31. Open M-F 11am-7pm, Sa 11am-5pm.) Yekaterinburg's many cafes are rivaled only by its ubiquitous banks: (MC/V) **ATMs** dot the downtown area. The big **pharmacy** at ul. Yakova Sverdlova 11 is well stocked. (☎ 53 28 63. Open daily 8am-9pm.) The best **Internet** access can be found at ▧**Coffee, IN,** on the 2nd floor of the Mitnyy Dvor (Митный Дворь) shopping complex at ul. 8 Marta (Марта). Head west on pr. Lenina and take a left after the river. (50R per hr. Cafe open M-Sa 10am-10pm, Su 10am-8pm. Internet 24hr.) The **post office**, pr. Lenina 51, offers international telephone calls, fax, photocopying, **currency exchange,** and Internet access for 50R per hr. (Office open M-F 8am-8pm, Sa-Su 8am-6pm. Postal counter open M-F 8am-7pm, Sa 8am-5:30pm.) **Postal Code:** 620 000.

⑦ ⑦ ACCOMMODATIONS AND FOOD. By far the best deal in town, **Gostinitsa Eurasia ❸** (Гостиница Евразия), pr. Lenina 40 (Ленина), offers comfortable and spacious singles and doubles with roomy bathrooms with showers. (☎ 71 57 58; fax 71 51 45. Breakfast included. Singles 740R; doubles 1100R.) If you're willing to forego a private bath, save a lot of rubles at **Gostinitsa Bolshoy Ural ❶** (Гостиница Большой Узал), Krasnoarmeyskaya ul. (Красноа-змейская), behind the Opera and Ballet Theater. The spartan but spotless rooms are bright and airy, which together with Bolshoy Ural's tucked-away location makes for a relaxing stay. (☎ 50 68 96. Single with sink and shared bath 327R, with full bath 1120R; doubles from 1120R.)

Yekaterinburg has a more cosmopolitan feel than most Russian cities, the result of which is a shortage of restaurants serving specifically Russian cuisine. This is especially apparent at the cheaper end of the dining spectrum, where American-style fast food is hard to avoid. Providing a comfortable compromise, **Dinamo Bar ❸** (Динамо Бар), ul. Lenina 53 (Ленина; heading away from the river on pr. Lenina, it's on the first block to the right of ul. Lenina), is a subterranean haven for cheap Russian and American eats and beer. (Pork *shashlyk* and beef stroganoff each 170R. Beer 100R. Open daily noon-midnight.) There's nothing quite like Chinese food cooked by Russians; **Peking ❸** (Пекин), overlooking the river on ul. Malysheva (Малышева), serves up surprisingly well-prepared dishes for slightly exorbitant prices in a kitschy yet glamorous Euro-chic interior. The **patio bar** facing the river has a cheaper but limited menu. (Entrees from 200-300R; patio menu 55-180R. Open daily noon-midnight.) Get cheap American-style fast food at one of the several chain restaurant **Oridey** (Оридей) locations around downtown. A tastier option is to grab a "khot dog" (хот дог) from one of the many **street kiosks;** they put their baseball stadium counterparts to shame. The **24hr. bakery** kiosk at Sverdlova 8 (Свердлова) is a local favorite serving up fresh bread and pastries.

SIGHTS AND ENTERTAINMENT. The most prominent sights in Yekaterinburg are the burnished gold domes of the new **church**, under construction in summer 2003, which overshadow the small white cross marking the spot where **Ipatiev House** stood until the Soviets bulldozed it. This was the location of the Romanovs' final incarceration and execution. Make sure to visit the ◪**Afghan War Memorial**, located between ul. Mamina-Sibiryaka (Мамина-Сибиряка) and Vasentsovskaya ul. (Васенцовская) a block from the river on pr. Lenina. The emotional weight of this monument to the men who died during the controversial campaign of 1979-1989 and in the years since is hammered home by the startlingly young women often heard grieving for lost brothers, husbands, and fathers. One block farther on pr. Lenina is the **Military History Museum** (Военно-исторический Музей; Voyenno-istoricheskyy Musey)—the authentic Soviet tank, surface-to-air missile, and mobile rocket launcher out front are hard to miss. Remnants of Gary Powers's **U2 spy plane**, which was shot down near Yekaterinburg in 1960, are on display along with Russian military memorabilia. (☎55 17 42. Open Tu-Sa 9am-4pm. 15R.) The **Opera and Ballet Theater,** pr. Lenina 46, is considered the third most important in Russia. (☎55 80 57. Shows rotate nightly.) Out front in pr. Lenina stands the macabre **Sverdlov Statue;** you can almost hear a villainous chuckle as he points down at the Romanovs. There is often **live music** on the riverbanks during summer months, as the student population comes out to relax.

NOVOSIBIRSK (НОВОСИБИРСК) ☎(8)3832

Novosibirsk's bland appearance hides an intriguing history. Resulting from the construction of the Trans-Siberian and Stalin's industrial build-up during WWII, Novosibirsk's population soared from virtually zero to 1.6 million in under a century, making it Siberia's most populous city. During the Cold War this was the center of Soviet military science, with nuclear experiments and the precursors to genetic engineering taking place at nearby Akademgorodok (the Soviet Union's Los Alamos). While funding stopped nearly 15 years ago, traces of Novosibirsk's mad-scientist history remain (just walk into one of the technical bookstores on Krasnyy prospekt). Novosibirsk isn't set up for budget travelers, but if you do stay here you'll find some great cheap restaurants and a dazzlingly beautiful church.

> **TIME CHANGE.** Novosibirsk is 3hr. ahead of Moscow: GMT +6

TRANSPORTATION. The **train station,** on ul. Shamshurina (Шамшузина) at the end of Vokzalnaya Magistral (Вокзальная Магистраль), sends trains to: **Krasnoyarsk** (13hr., 5-6 per day, 450R); **Moscow** (48-52hr., 5-6 per day, 1800R); and **Yekaterinburg** (22hr., 7-8 per day, 759R). There are also several trains daily to **Barnaul** and **Biysk** in the Altaiskiy Krai (5-6hr., 200R). Novosibirsk is a gateway to Central Asia. The main route, the Turkistan-Siberian railway, goes to **Almaty, KAZ** (35-40hr., 1 per day daily 2pm, 1100R); less frequent trains run to **Tashkent** and **Samarkand, UZB.** For a schedule of Trans-Siberian trains, see p. 740.

ORIENTATION AND PRACTICAL INFORMATION. The **Metro** (6R) connects the city center, **pl. Lenina** (Ленина), to the **train station** at Garina-Mikhailovskogo (Гарина-Михайловского). Exit the station and then head underground at the "M." Take the Metro one stop to **Sibirskaya** (Сибирская), then walk upstairs to change stations; one more stop takes you to pl. Lenina. The Sibirskaya Metro is close to the circus, the Ascension Church, the market, and the stadium, but most other sights are near pl. Lenina. **Krasnyy pr.** (Красный), Novosibirsk's main drag, runs north-south through pl. Lenina and between the two main Metro stops. Directly opposite Lenin's statue, ul. Lenina (Ленина) runs out of the square. Next to ul. Lenina, at the corner of the square, **Vokzalnaya Magistral** (Вокзальная Магистраль) runs down a few blocks to **pr. Dmitrova** (Дмитрова) and eventually hits the train station. **Alfa Bank** (Альфа Банк), Dimitrova 1, **exchanges currency** and **traveler's checks** for no commission. It also offers **cash advances, Western Union** services, and an **ATM**. (Open M-Sa 8:30-7:30pm, Su 9am-3pm.) **Store luggage** in the basement of the train station; look for "Камера Кранения." (24R for 24hr. from midnight to midnight. Pay for the first period when you drop your bag off, and then the rest when you reclaim it.) Buy a **city map** at **Dom Knigi** bookshop (Дом Книги), Krasnyy pr. 33. They also have a substantial selection of maps of Altaiskiy Krai, the Altai Republic, Abakan, and Kyzyl. (Open daily 10am-8pm. Novosibirsk map 45R.) There is a **24hr. pharmacy** at **City Hospital #1** (поликлиника; poliklinika), in the gray building with green awnings at ul. Serebrennikovskaya 42 (Серебренниковская), one block south to the right of the Opera and Ballet House behind the Lenin statue. The hospital will see foreigners at window #13. (☎23 59 22. Doctor's visit 115R. Open daily 24hr.) The **telephone office** is down ul. Sovetskaya before the post office (see below), and offers **international calls** to North America (27R per min.) and Europe (22R per min.). Access the **Internet** at ul. Lenina 5, past the post office—don't be confused by the large sign for international phone calls above the door. (30R per hr. Open daily 24hr.) The **post office** sits at ul. Lenina 5 at the corner of Sovetskaya. (Советская; ☎10 07 22. Open M-F 8am-7pm, Sa-Su 8am-6pm; 4th M of each month 8am-1pm.) **Postal Code:** 630 099.

⌂⌂ ACCOMMODATIONS AND FOOD. The bad news—Novosibirsk currently offers only one feasible and affordable accommodation to travelers. The good news—it is one of the best values on the TSR. The well starched and impeccably maintained ⊠**Gostinitsa ❶** (Гостиница), on the second floor of the train station, rents spotless 3-person dorms that overlook the main waiting hall for periods from a few hours to 24hr. The safest and cheapest option is to get a bed for 12hr. (300R), and in the morning put your backpack luggage in storage before heading out to explore the town. The pleasant female voice of the station PA system is audible at night, but the muffled announcements are actually rather soothing. (☎29 23 76. Singles 300-400R; super lux double suites 1300R. Incoming or outgoing train ticket required.) All other accommodation options will cost you an arm and a leg. **Hotel Novosibirsk ❹**, right across from the station at Vokzalry Magistral 1, offers singles with shower from 1800R (☎20 11 20). Heading down to ul. Lenina 21, **Hotel Sibir ❺** (Сибирь; 10min. from the pl. Lenina Metro station) caters to Western business-people. (☎23 12 15; fax 23 87 66. Some English spoken. Singles US$62.40.)

For a dose of Russian nostalgia and some delicious traditional treats, head upstairs at ul. Lenina 1 to ⊠**Zhili Byli ❶** (Жили Были; "The way we lived"). Fake cattails, chirping birds, a waterwheel, and a gigantic fiberglass oak tree turn this multi-level eatery into a rustic log cabin. Favorites like *borshch* (75R) and pelmeni go well with a big mug of *kvas* (30R). (☎22 57 31. English menu available. Open daily noon-10pm.) If you have a hankering for something more substantial than *Baltika 3*, you can get all your favorite Irish brews at **St. Patrick's Corner ❸**, ul. Lenina 8. Russian takes on Irish dishes (boiled tongue appetizer 195R) are served in a friendly atmosphere at slightly expensive prices. (☎22 44 77. Appetizers 70-210R. Entrees 150-410R. Guiness 175R. English menu. Open daily noon-2am.) The **Sickle and Hammer ❷** (Серп и Молот; Serp i Molot), in the basement of St. Patrick's Corner (see above), is covered in Soviet memorabilia, Khrushchev kitsch, and Cold War collectibles. The restaurant also features live music, pool (40R), and 40R karaoke (☎22 44 77. Entrees 125-300R. Open daily 4pm-2am.) The **open-air market** on ul. Krylova (Крылова) covers nearly as much area as the sta-

RUSSIA

dium next door. From Metro station Krasnyy pr., go left along ul. Krylova for two blocks. (Open daily 8am-7pm.) Grab some *kolbasa* for the train at **Kooperator** (Кооператор), a **24hr. meat shop** at Krasnyy pr. 39.

◉♫ SIGHTS AND ENTERTAINMENT. Novosibirsk Art Gallery (Новосибирская Картинная Галерея; Novosibirskaya Kartinnaya Galereya), Krasnyy pr. 5, features a varied collection with works by Surikov and Roerich. (☎22 20 42. Open Tu-F 10am-6pm, Sa-Su 11am-6pm. 100R, students 50R.) In the middle of Krasnyy pr., 500m south of pl. Lenina, the gold-domed **St. Nicholas's Chapel** (Часовня во имя Святитуля Николая; Chasovnya vo imya Svyatitelya Nikolaya) supposedly sits in the exact center of Russia. (Open Tu-Su noon-5pm.) The larger and much more impressive **Ascension Church** (Храм Вознесения Господня; Khram Vozneseniya Gospodnya), at the intersection of ul. Gogolya (Гоголя) and Sovetskaya ul. (Советская), has gorgeous blue and gold domes and a dazzling white and gold iconostasis. The interior is stunningly beautiful. As in all Russian chapels and churches, **women** should cover their heads. The largest **Opera House** in Russia stands at Krasnyy pr. 36 behind the Lenin Statue. Built largely by women and the elderly during WWII, the building is modeled after the Bolshoy in Moscow. (see **Moscow Entertainment**, p. 684. ☎22 59 90. Season runs Sept.-May. Tickets from 50R.) Swing by the **Wedding Palace**, Krasnyy pr. 68, to witness a Vegas-style public wedding ceremony. The nuptials take around 20min., as one couple after another piles through, smiles, and smooches. (Metro: Krasnyy. Services daily June-Aug.)

▨ ALTAI TERRITORY (АЛТАЙСКИЙ КРАЙ)

A distinct region from the Altai Republic (see p. 747), Altaiskiy Krai is situated to the northwest of the Republic and shares a border with Kazakhstan. Its only draw is as a gateway to the Altai Republic; the road from Novosibirsk passes through the Krai. The two main transportation hubs, Barnaul and Biysk, are accessible by both train and bus (the railway not going to Kazakhstan terminates in Biysk).

> **TIME CHANGE.** The Altaiskiy Krai is 3hr. ahead of Moscow: GMT +6

▨ BARNAUL (БАРНАУЛ) ☎(8)3882

The larger of the two hubs, as well as the region's capital, Barnaul is a friendly city on the banks of the Ob River (Обь). It's a better choice than Biysk if you plan on spending a night in the Altaiskiy Krai. The **bus** and **train stations** are side by side, 1km west of the center. Several trains run daily to: **Biysk** (2hr., 200R) and **Novosibirsk** (5-8hr., 200-400R). Buses depart daily to: **Biysk** (2hr., 15 per day, 100R); **Gorno-Altaisk** (6hr., 8 per day, 180R); and **Novosibirsk** (4-5hr., 14 per day, 180R) . Be careful around the *militsia* post in front of the stations—foreigners have been known to mysteriously lose hundreds of dollars during routine baggage checks. Barnaul's main street is **pr. Lenina** (Ленина) which runs to the town center, **pl. Sovetov** (Советов). From the train or bus station, head straight until you come to an intersection with **Molodezhnaya ul.** (Молодежная)ю There will be a ferris wheel in front of you (20R; open daily 10am-9pm). Turn left; Lenina and pl. Sovetov are a block ahead. There is a **24hr. ATM** at Gostinitsa Tsentralnaya on pl. Sovetov.

You'll likely spend the night in Barnaul en route to the Altai Republic. The rooms at **Gostinitsa Barnaul ❷** are comfortable and clean, despite the kitschy countryside decor. The floor-drain sinks and showers are functional but drain slowly. Head straight from the station and take a right on pr. Stroiteley (Строителей) for one block. (☎62 62 22; fax 62 62 66. Singles from 600R; doubles from 1200R.) Cafes dominate the food scene. **Kafe U Arki ❶** (Кафе у Арки) is an outdoor cafe several blocks northeast of the center on pr. Lenina and serves delicious *pelmeni* with butter (26R). (Open daily 11am-midnight.) **Bar Tolstyak ❶** (Толстяк), pr. Lenina 63, serves sandwiches (15R) and beer. (☎38 08 78. Open daily noon-midnight.)

＆ ALTAI REPUBLIC (РЕСПУБЛИКА АЛТАЙ)

The fundamental backpacker paradox: everyone wants to find a place that's heartbreakingly beautiful, yet free from the circus atmosphere of the standard tourist circuit. A solution presents itself in the Altai Republic (Respublika Altai), a small, semi-autonomous region bordering China, Kazakhstan, and Mongolia. Quite simply, this is one of the most beautiful places on earth. The muscular geography gives rise to a diverse range of ecosystems: arid deserts, dense forests, churning river canyons, open steppe, mountain glaciers, and high-altitude tundra. The indigenous Altai people revered the region around 4500m Mt. Belukha, the tallest mountain in Siberia, as Shambala, the paradise from which a new civilization will spring once our present one destroys itself. The Altai Republic is home to world-class trekking routes, beautiful lakes, and white-water rafting. While it's possible to travel here alone, those seeking any sort of trekking should arrange a visit through an agency. Try contacting **Plot** (☎385 236 7349; www.plot-altai.ru/engl/eindex.htm), a reputable Barnaul-based agency, or St. Petersburg-based **Wild Russia** (☎812 273 6514, US office 1 973 509-2416; www.wildrussia.spb.ru), which caters to Westerners.

＆ GORNO-ALTAISK (ГОРНО-АЛТАЙСК)   ☎(8)3882

The capital of the Altai Republic isn't big or attractive. A frontier-town vibe pervades this city, and there is little of interest within the town itself. Gorno-Altaisk is primarily a transport hub for destinations in the Republic. Visit the wonderful museum, but then move on to more scenic destinations.

 TIME CHANGE. The Altai Republic is 3hr. ahead of Moscow: GMT +6

There is no train service to the Altai Republic. The **bus station** is located a few kilometers from the town center on Kommunisticheskiy pr. (Коммунистический), with daily buses to: **Barnaul** (6-7hr., 4 per day, 500R); **Biysk** (4-5hr., 8 per day, 600R); and **Novosibirsk** (12-14hr., daily 8:30am, 800R). Within the Altai Republic, there are buses to: **Artybash** (5-6hr., daily 11:05am); **Kosh-Agach** (12hr.; Tu, Th, Su 7:10am); **Ust-Kan** (9hr., daily 1:05pm); **Ust-Koksa** (13hr., daily 7:20am). All buses within the Republic cost less than 500R. All times are given in **local time.** Gorno-Altaisk consists of two parallel streets which run one block apart from west to east. **Kommunisticheskiy pr.** is the principal road, with **ul. Choros Gurkina** (Чорос Гуркина) one block to the south. The bus station is at the west end of town; the main shopping district is the east end of Kommunisticheskiy pr. past the **Lenin statue.** There is a bank with **currency exchange** (open M-F 8am-5pm) and a **pharmacy** (☎276 88; open M-F 8am-7pm, Sa 9am-4pm) on ul. Erkemena Palkina (Эркемена Палкина), a short distance south of Gostinitsa Gornyy Altai (see below). There are **no ATMs** in the Altai Republic; bring enough cash to get yourself out. **Postal Code:** 649 000.

The only accommodation is **Gostinitsa Gornyy Altai ❶** (Готиница Горный Алтай) between Kommunisticheskiy pr. and ul. Choros Gurkina, if you're facing the Lenin statue. Walk from the station (20min.) or hail a cab (30R). The rooms are very basic with shared toilets and no showers. Be sure that Gorno-Altaisk is on your visa if you plan to stay here. (☎950 86. Singles 330R; 2-bed dorm 180R; 3-bed dorm 126R.) The best choice for regional cuisine is the small basement establishment **Kafe Ursul** ❶ (Урсул), at the corner of Choros Gurkina and per. Gromovoy (Громовой), east of the bus station. Choose from an assortment of local cuisine (Entrees 30-60R. Open daily 10am-midnight.)

SIGHTS AND OUTDOOR ACTIVITIES. Gorno-Altaisk's rough and unkempt atmosphere may not seem like a likely setting for a museum, but the **National Museum** (Национальный Музей; Natsionalnyy Muzey), four blocks east of the bus station on Choros Gurkina, is wonderful and reason enough to spend a day in Gorno-Altaisk. The museum has two floors of fascinating displays ranging from beautiful art by Chebalkov, Royehrich, and others depicting the Altai Republic to archaeological finds from the ancient Pazyryk culture. There is also a room full of stuffed local wildlife, including a Siberian tiger. (☎278 75. Open W-Su 10am-5pm. 30R, students 20R.) About a 15min. drive from town, picturesque **Lake Aya** (Озеро Ая; Ozero Aya) makes a nice daytrip. This small lake is surrounded by green hills and has a tiny island with a wooden cupola and paddleboat rental (50R). Either take a local bus (ask for help at the hotel) or arrange for a taxi (no more than 150R one-way). Make sure you arrange return transport before you go; accommodation options at the lake are overpriced.

KRASNOYARSK (КРАСНОЯРСК)   ☎(8)3912

Founded as a Cossack fort in 1628, Krasnoyarsk attracted a rough crowd: by the end of the 19th century, one-fourth of the city's population were ex-cons. Straddling the 2km wide Yenisey River, Krasnoyarsk (pop. 930,000) is Siberia's third-largest city. During WWII, Stalin pushed much of Russia's defense industry to Krasnoyarsk on the backs of Japanese POWs. When Krasnoyarsk opened to foreigners in 1991, the world discovered an industrial quagmire and a river too polluted to freeze. The city has been cleaning up, however, and now has beautiful fountains and a glamorous social scene. The work of painter V.I. Surikov and the amazing day-hike mecca of the Stolbi Reserve are the best of the city's attractions.

TIME CHANGE. Krasnoyarsk is 4hr. ahead of Moscow: GMT +7

TRANSPORTATION. The **train station,** on ul. Tridsatogo Iyulya (30-го Июля; ☎29 34 34), on the north bank of the **Yenisey** river, 2km west of the city center, has trains to: **Abakan** (11hr., 2 per day, 680R); **Irkutsk** (19hr., 1-5 per day, 700R); **Novosibirsk** (14hr., 2-6 per day, 550R); and **Vladivostok** (3 days, 1-3 per day, 1300R). Purchase **international tickets** at the downtown ticket office, between pr. Mira and ul. Karla Marksa at ul. Robespiera 29. (Робеспьера; ☎23 04 94. Open M-F 8am-10pm, Sa-Su 9am-6pm.) For a schedule of **Trans-Siberian** trains, see p. 740.

ORIENTATION AND PRACTICAL INFORMATION. With the exception of the Stolbi Nature Reserve, everything of interest lies on the north bank. From the train station's parking lot on the right, take bus #6 or 55 to the central Hotel Krasnoyarsk (4 stops). The bus makes a right turn immediately before the correct stop, which is the **Opera and Ballet Theater** (5R). To return, catch northbound #36, 50a, or 81 on the opposite side of the pedestrian bridge by the hotel. Krasnoyarsk's three main streets, **ul. Lenina** (Ленина), **pr. Mira** (Мира), and **ul. Karla Marksa** (Карла Маркса), all run west-east from the **train station,** parallel to the river. There's no tourist office, but the **Service-Center Trans-Sib** (Сервис-Центр Транс-Сиб), in the downtown ticket office at ul. Robespiera 29, reserves domestic train tickets and provides international **telephone** and **fax** service. (☎29 26 92; fax 21 65 71. Open M-F 8am-10pm, Sa-Su 9am-6pm.) Buy a **map** (35R) at **Akademknigi** (Академкниги), ul.

Lenina 60, at the intersection with ul. Surikova. (Сурикова. Open Su-F 10am-7pm, Sa 10am-6pm.) There's a **24hr.** (MC/V) **ATM** outside Gostinitsa Krasnoyarsk. **Exchange currency** at the hotel, or at any of dozens of bureaus on the main streets. **Luggage storage** (камера хранения; kamera khraneniya) is in the train station basement. (25R per bag. Open 24hr.) For an **ambulance**, call ☎45 39 04 or 45 39 75. The **24hr. pharmacy** at pr. Mira 37 is well stocked. An international **telephone office** is at ul. Lenina 49, slightly east of Hotel Krasnoyarsk. (☎22 18 01. Open daily 7am-midnight.) Access the **Internet** at **MaxSoft**, ul. Uritskogo 61 (Урицкого), across the footbridge from the hotel, on the fourth floor. (☎65 13 85. 30R per hr. Open M-F 9am-8pm.) The **post office** is next to the telephone office at ul. Lenina 49. (☎27 07 48. Open M-Sa 8am-7pm.) **Postal Code:** 660 049.

⌂ ACCOMMODATIONS AND FOOD. Gostinitsa Krasnoyarsk ❸, ul. Uritskogo 94 (Урицкого), on the corner of ul. Venbauma and ul. Karla Marksa facing the Opera and Ballet Theater, is a convenient option. Take bus #6 or 55 from the train station. (☎27 37 69; http://tlcom.kts.ru/hotelkrs/. Breakfast buffet 100R. Singles 800R; doubles 1200R.) **Hotel Ogni Eniseya ❶** (Гостиница Огни Енисея), ul. Dubrovinskogo 80 (Добровинского), faces the water one block east of Gostinitsa Krasnoyarsk. Its clean, spartan rooms are pleasantly quiet. (☎27 52 62. Singles 280-1300R; doubles 400-1500R.) **Gostinitsa Locomotiv ❷**, under the Locomotiv Rugby Stadium at ul. Lenina 40 (see **Sights**, p. 749), is a fun option, especially if there is a match going on. While not easily accessible from the train station, the basic rooms in this small establishment are similar to lux rooms elsewhere. (☎27 69 78. Singles 650R.) If you plan on spending more than two nights in Krasnoyarsk, contact **Alyans Agency** (Альянс) ul. Surikova 56; they can set you up in a huge and superbly furnished apartment for as low as 500R per night (☎23 90 47).

Budget travelers in Krasnoyarsk face a dining dilemma: either live it up and splurge or settle for cheaper Western-style food. Those who opt for the former should try **Kafein ❹** (Кафеин), about 200m west of Hotel Ogni Enseya at ul. Dubrovinskogo 80. American restaurant prices will get you some of the finest cuisine in Siberia as you rub elbows with Krasnoyarsk's elite. (Salmon *pelmeni* 60R, entrees 300-1300R. Open daily noon-midnight.) **Rosso Pizza ❶**, pr. Mira 111 and ul. Lenina 121, is an American-style pizza joint. The salmon (сёмга; syomga) pizza stands out. (Slices 28-60R. Open daily 11am-midnight.) A great option is to serve yourself at the 24hr. **Gastronom Krasnyy Yar** (Красный Яр), pr. Mira 50a, which also features a succulent selection of cooked takeout.

◎ ⚄ SIGHTS AND OUTDOOR ACTIVITIES. The ▧**Krasnoyarsk Regional Museum of Local Lore** (Краеведческий Музей; Kraevedcheskiy Muzey), ul. Dubrovinskogo 84, is puzzlingly housed in something resembling an Egyptian temple. Despite the strange architecture, this is far and away the most impressive museum on the TSR. Three floors of displays range from life-sized exhibits of many indigenous peoples of Northern Siberia to a large replica of a Cossack explorer's ship. (Open Tu-Su 11am-7pm. 20R, students 15R.) Although he studied in St. Petersburg, 19th-century Russian painter Vasily Ivanovich Surikov (1848-1916) was born and raised in Krasnoyarsk. His estate has now been turned into the **V. I. Surikov Museum-Estate** (Музей-усадьба В. И. Сурикова; Muzey-usadba V. I. Surikova), ul. Lenina 98. Inside the elegant house, 10 rooms on two floors showcase his life and work. (☎27 08 15. Open Tu-Su 11am-7pm. 20R.) Farther east, the **Krasnoyarsk Art Museum** (Художественный Музей; Khudozhestvennyy Muzey), ul. Parizhskoy Kommuny 20 (Парижской Коммуны), at ul. Karla Marksa, displays works by Surikov, Shishkin, and others. (☎27 55 81. Open Tu-Su 11am-7pm. 20R, students 10R.) The **Museum-ship St. Nicholas** (Музей-пароход Св. Николай; Muzey-parokhod Sv. Nikolai) sits at the east end of ul. Dubrovinskogo, near the Philharmonic Hall. In

1897, the ship carried Lenin up the Yenisey to his exile in Shushensk; it later transported Tsar Nicholas II to a similar fate. The now decaying museum features wax figures of both men. The museum guide gives Russian tours. (☎ 23 94 03. Open Tu-Su 10am-6pm. 5R, students 2R.) The **Locomotiv Rugby Stadium** (Стадион Локомотив), ul. Lenina 90, is home to one of Russia's best professional teams. Ask at the *gostinitsa* downstairs to find out when matches are scheduled. (Tickets 50R.) **Stolbi Nature Reserve,** a nearby haven for day-hikes and rock-climbing, features surreal, vertical rock pillars (столбьц; stolbts) and other formations amid acres of beautiful forests and streams. Catch southbound buses #50 or 50a to Turbaza (30min., 5R) from the Opera and Ballet bus stop. Keep walking and cross a small stream—the turn is immediately to your left. It's a 30min. walk to the station Kordon Laletino; another hr. up the road takes you to the path to the first pillar, which is worth the effort. Locals warn of ticks, so wear insect repellant.

▨ ABAKAN (АБАКАН)   ☎ (8)3492

Set amid grassy fields and small villages, the shady, tree-lined capital of the Republic of Khakassia (Чакасия) is the easiest point of access for Tuva. Although it's little more than a transport hub, Abakan is home to a fantastic ▨zoopark. Take bus #2, 11, or 21 from the station and ask the ticket collector to tell you when to get off (10min.); the zoo is after a big right-hand turn and can be spotted by the large sailboat fountain out front. The zoo features an impressive array of species ranging from Tuvan camels to endangered Siberian tigers. A kangaroo currently shares space with the craziest-looking chickens in Siberia. Though it may be unsettling to learn that the zoo is owned and operated by the meat processing plant next door, this actually provides an easy supply of meat for the big cats. (Open daily 9am-4pm, low season 10am-4pm.) Khakassia is full of **archaeological sites** that are only accessible by tour operators. **Abakan Tours,** in the Park-Hotel (see below), runs programs in Khakassia, Krasnoyarsk, and Tuva. Contact operator Sergei Metchtonov. (☎ 60 33; parkotel@khakasnet.ru. English spoken. US$25-200 per day.) On the first Sunday in June, the Khakass people gather near Abakan for the festival of **Tun Pairam,** which celebrates the opening of the summer livestock pastures.

The **train station,** off ul. Pushkina (Пушкина), a 10min. walk west of the town center, has service to: **Krasnoyarsk** (11-17hr., 3 per day, 700R) and **Moscow** (74hr., 14 per day). The **bus station,** a 20min. walk east of the train station, has service to **Krasnoyarsk** (6-10hr., 15 per day, 280R). The **bus** to **Kyzyl** (10hr., 3 per day, 240R), the only way to access Tuva, operates out of the train station. Purchase tickets upstairs. **Ul. Pushkina** runs east-west at the southern edge of town. It intersects **ul. Shchetinkina** (Щетинкина), which runs north through the town center at the intersection with **pr. Lenina** (Ленина). There is a **24hr. ATM** in the lobby of Gostinitsa Khakassia at the intersection. The several banks just west of the train station at ul. Pushkina 165 **exchange currency,** have **ATMs,** and give **MC/V cash advances. Luggage storage** is in a small building to the right of the train station as you exit; look for **Kamera Khraneniya** (Камера Хранения; 30R per day). The affable staff at **Gostinitsa Abakan ❶** (Гостиница Абакан), pr. Lenina 59, near the intersection with ul. Shchetinkina, offers bright, modern rooms a mere 10min. from the train station. (☎ 630 26. Singles from 385R; doubles from 750R). **Park-Hotel ❸** (Парк-Отель) is wonderful and luxurious but pricey. Walk 1½ blocks past ul. Shchetinkina on ul. Pushkina from the train station; go down the wide path in the small park on your left. The hotel is on the right, halfway down the path, surrounded by a black fence. (☎ 674 42. Double suite 945R.) Aside from hotel restaurants, the best food option is **Kafe Lakomka ❶** (Кафе Лакомка), on pr. Lenina across the street from Gostinitsa Abakan. It serves the favorite Khakassian dish, *lagman* (лагман, fried noodles with mutton), and other cheap, filling eats. (Open daily 9am-10pm.)

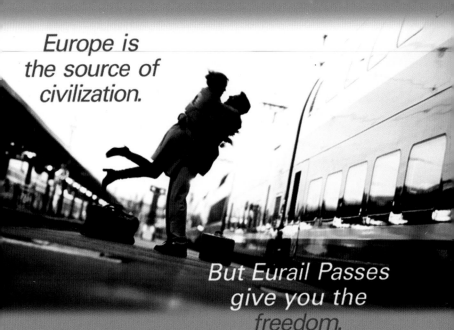

Europe is the source of civilization.

But Eurail Passes give you the freedom.

Let yourself go in Europe with a flexible and fun Eurail Pass! Feel the excitement as the train whisks you from country to country and the ever-changing landscape passes your window. Trains criss-cross the entire continent allowing you to see Europe your way. Meet new friends, take in the nightlife, explore a famous city, and soon you'll be on your way to another adventure.

There's a Eurail Pass for every budget and taste, from the classic 17-country Eurailpass, to the Eurail Selectpass that focuses on fewer countries and saves you money, to the new and highly targeted 2-country pass.

Welcome to Eurail Pass. It truly is *Europe without borders*.

TUVA (ТЫВА)

The beauty of the Tuvan landscape can be described in one word—otherworldly. The surrounding taiga forests and wildflower-dotted fields melt away, uncovering an instant and fundamental change in scenery at the Tuvan border. Snow-covered peaks and glaciers encircle this strange pocket of land, but isolated geography hasn't prevented its neighbors from invading. A brief stab at autonomy beginning in 1921 was cut short in 1944 when Tuva became a part of the Soviet Union. The collapse of communism fueled racial tensions and a desire for complete independence from Russia. Unfortunately, economic ties are stronger than nationalist sentiment, and Tuva relies heavily on economic assistance from Moscow.

> **!** To avoid problems with police at the border and within Tuva, be sure to list Kyzyl on your visa and register there if you plan on traveling anywhere in Tuva.

⚡ KYZYL (КЫЗЫЛ) ☎ (8)39542

The capital of the Republic of Tuva, Kyzyl (pop. 101,000) lies at the confluence of the Bolshoy and Malyy Yenisey rivers (Biy-Khem and Ka-Khem in Tuvan), which join to form the Verkhniy Yenisey (Upper Yenisey; known in Tuvan as Ulug-Khem), which flows north past Abakan and Krasnoyarsk and spills into the Karskoe Sea. This junction is so significant that its pattern is mimicked in the Tuvan flag. The city was called Belotsarsk (White Tsar's City), but the communists changed it to Kyzyl, a Turkic word meaning "red." The center of the Asian continent, Kyzyl has few man-made sights. Luckily, its appeal is found not in its monuments but as a base for exploring the ethereal beauty of the rest of Tuva.

TRANSPORTATION. There is **no train service** to Kyzyl. The **bus station** is at ul. Druzhby 57 (Дружбы), east of the town center, and sends buses to: **Abakan** (4hr., 3 per day, 240R); **Ak-Dovurak** (7-8hr., 2 per day most odd-numbered days); **Shagonar** (2hr., 3 per wk. 10:30am); **Teeli** (10½hr., daily 9am). A speedy alternative for Tuvan destinations is to grab a spot in one of the **private vans** that leave daily for just about anywhere; there is a different meeting spot for vans going in each of the four cardinal directions; inquire at your hotel. Most vans leave in the morning and cost anywhere from 100R to 300R; fluent Russian will get you a much better deal.

ORIENTATION AND PRACTICAL INFORMATION. Everything is situated on the south bank of the Ulug-Klem. The main street is **ul. Kochetova** (Кочетова), which runs parallel to the river from near the bus station in the east through downtown, ending in the west with **pl. Arata** (Арата) at the Musical and Dramatic Theater. One block north of ul. Kochetova, **ul. Lenina** (Ленина) is the site of many government buildings and the museum. **Ul. Tuvinskikh Dobrovoltsev** (Тувинских Добровольцев) runs from the river through these two streets just east of the theater. You can purchase a 1960s-era **map** of Tuva at one of the several bookstores on ul. Kochetova; maps of Kyzyl itself are best found in Novosibirsk or Krasnoyarsk. **Sibirskoye Bank** (Сибирское), in the purple building one block north of the theater on ul. T. Dobrovoltsev, offers **currency exchange,** MC/V **credit card advances,** and a **24hr. ATM.** (Open M-Sa 4am-5pm.) The **pharmacy** at ul. Lenina 24 is well stocked. (Open M-F 8am-7pm, Sa-Su 9am-3pm.) The **post office,** ul. Kochetova 53 opposite pl. Arata, also provides **Internet** access. (63R per hr. Open daily 8am-midnight.) The adjoining service center offers international **telephone** and fax services. (Post office open M-F 8am-6pm, Sa 8am-4pm.) **Postal Code:** 667 000.

⌐⌐ ACCOMMODATIONS AND FOOD. One of the cheapest accommodations in Kyzyl, **Gostinitsa Mongulek** ❶ (Гостиница Монгулек), is about 500m from the bus station at the intersection of ul. Kaa-Khem (Каа-Хем) and ul. Kochetova (Кочетова). Even the most luxurious rooms are cheaper than basic singles elsewhere in Russia. Comfort increases greatly with small price increases, so shell out a few extra bucks and upgrade. (☎312 53. Singles 230-503R; doubles 280-550R.) Many rooms at **Gostinitsa Oguden** ❷ (Гостиница Огуден), ul. Krasnikh Parizan 36, have views of the Yenisey. Oguden is very modern and a good value. Call ahead, as they are usually full. (☎325 18. Singles with bath from 500R; doubles from 720R.) The fanciest place in town is **Gostinitsa Cottage** ❸ (Гостиница Коттедж), next door to Odugen at ul. Krasnikh Partizan 38. Views of the river and a very upscale clientele draw most of Kyzyl's rich visitors, but it's still within the reach of the budget traveler. (☎305 03. Singles from 1000R; doubles from 1200R.)

Delicious meals and a pleasant atmosphere await you at **Kafe Shekpeer** ❶ (Кафе Шекпеер), ul. Druzhby 151 (Дружбы), at the intersection with ul. T. Dobrovoltsev. The owner is married to the current Tuvan president's daughter, and Shekpeer is the name of the president's home village. Delicious chicken dinner (70R) and fresh *pelmeni* (40R) are the best choices. (☎133 19. Open daily 10am-2am.) The best food, and the highest prices in town, can be found at **Restoran Kyzyl** ❷ (Ресторан Кызыл), under Gostinitsa Kyzyl. This upscale eatery serves mouth-watering gourmet dishes featuring meat, veggies, and fish in a swank dining room. (☎316 59. Entrees 60-200R. Open daily 8am-1am.) If you're just looking to grab a beer (20R) and something fried (under 15R), **Kafe Azas** ❶ (Кафе Азас) is a local favorite, a block down ul. T. Dobrovoltsev from ul. Kochetova. (Open daily 11am-late.) Serve yourself at any of the many **grocery stores** along ul. Kochetova or grab some fresh produce at the **market** at the southern end of ul. T. Dobrovoltsev.

◨ SIGHTS. Kyzyl's most popular sight is the **Center of Asia** monument, overlooking the river at the north end of ul. Komsomolskaya (Комсомольская). The **Tuvan National Museum "Aldan-Maadyr"** (Алдан-Маадыр; 60 Heroes), ul. Lenina 7, has mangy-looking stuffed animals alongside fantastic displays of contemporary local art and archaeological finds. There are also interesting exhibits on ancient metalwork and the art of incarceration. (☎300 96; museum@tuva.ru. US$2, students US$1. Open Tu-Su 11am-5pm.) The peninsula at the confluence of the Yenisey rivers is a pleasantly forested public **park**. Local kids splash noisily in the water, while deeper in the park you'll find **Buddhist statues** and the Tuvan wrestling **stadium**, Khuresh (Хуреш).

◪ OUTSIDE KYZYL

Every region of Tuva is painfully gorgeous. Unfortunately, it is very difficult for independent travelers to access most of the sights outside of Kyzyl. Unless you have Tuvan friends and speak fluent Russian, it is advisable and not prohibitively expensive to sign up with a tour operator or an independent guide. No matter what you choose to do, make contact well in advance of your arrival.

TOUR OPERATORS AND GUIDES. By far the best tour operator within Tuva, **Tsentr Azii** is based in the first floor of Gostinitsa Oguden (see p. 752). It offers several standard tour packages and also plans customized trips. (☎323 26; Asiatur@tuva.ru. US$90-110 per day. Office generally open M-F evenings.) **Abakan Tours** (see **Sights**, p. 750) can organize trips in Tuva, though its specialty is Khakassia. A cheaper and less touristy option is to find an independent guide in Kyzyl to organize a trip via taxi or bus—a cost-effective option for groups of two to three. One of the best guides in town, **◪Eres Salchak** is also an author, and speaks perfect

English. He is currently finishing a guidebook of Tuva which you can order from his website. Call ahead to arrange a tour. (☎133 10; www.tuvanbooks.com.) Those interested in serious mountain expeditions should contact **Aidash Lopson-Seren**. He has worked extensively in the Kyzyl-Mazhalyk government and can help arrange trekking and ice-climbing trips. He speaks very little English, so have a translator help you, or contact him through Eres, who is a distant relative (☎395 42).

■ **THE WEST. Shagonar** (Шагонар), Tuva's second-largest settlement, lies about 120km west of the capital. Another 180km takes you to **Ak-Dovurak** (Ак-Довурак) and the nearby town of **Kyzyl-Mazhalyk** (Кызыл-Мажалык), which together are the starting point for most activities and sights. Nearby **Kyzyl-Dag** (Кызыл-Даг), named for its red rock formations, is the site of the first Buddhist temple reconstructed after the fall of the Soviet Union. A local stonecutter secretly constructed his studio in accordance with the proscriptions for temples—as soon as news reached town of the fall of communism, he converted the building. Many of the world's best ice climbers visit the area each year to scale the vertical glacier walls cascading from 3487m **Mt. Mongulek** (Монгулек), considered among the best and most difficult near-vertical climbs in the world. Another popular peak is 3976m **Mt. Mongun-Taiga** (Монгун-Тайга), the highest mountain in Tuva, accessible via the nearby town **Mugur-Aksy** (Мугур-Аксы). Other sights include the **stone man** near Ak-Dovurak, an ancient statue dating from the first millennium BC. Locals parked a ring of tractors around it when scientists attempted to remove it. Nearby, the name of the village of **Bizhiktig-Khaya** (Бижиктиг-Хая) means "Rock with Drawings." The picturesque cliffs just outside of town are home to many petroglyphs representing animals, hunting scenes, and a large eagle dating from the Bronze Age. **Utug-Khaya** (Утуг-Хая; "Holed Rock") is a curious rock formation near the summit of a small mountain alongside the Kyzyl-Ak-Dovurak highway. A natural 23m tunnel through the mountain is accessible by a steep 30min. hike. On sunny days, you can see sunlight shining through the hole. About 77km east of Ak-Dovurak, the temple at **Chadaana** (Чадаана), also known as Chadan (Чадан), was once the proud center of Tuvan Buddhism and the richest and largest temple in the country. In 1937, during the height of the communist purges of Buddhism, the temple was destroyed. Parts of the thick walls remain standing despite the demolition—a sobering reminder of the suffering and violence experienced by Tuvan Buddhists in the last century. The Russian government has agreed to reconstruct the temple, but until funding comes through, the project is stalled indefinitely.

■ **THE NORTHEAST, SOUTHEAST, AND SOUTH.** Northeastern Tuva is riddled with lakes, rivers, and pine-covered mountains. Reindeer herders live in the forests of the far northeast. A popular tourist destination, the shores lining the cool, clean waters of **Lake Azas** (Азас), also known as Todzha (Тоджа), are the site of some good fishing. The lake was once accessible via Kyzyl, but since the ferry service has stopped it is difficult to reach. Within easy range of the capital, the Russian **Old Believers Village** of Erzha is a stop on most organized tours. The south and southeast are dusty steppe and semi-desert interrupted by lakes and mineral springs. Far in the southeast, near the eastern border with Mongolia, the islands in the middle of **Lake Tere-Khol** (Тере-Холь) are home to the ruins of an ancient **Oighur fortress**—unfortunately, the lake's remoteness keeps most visitors away.

IRKUTSK (ИРКУТСК)   ☎(8)3952

A vibrant riverfront and a grand lot of old houses, museums, theaters, and cafes have led this one-time Cossack fur-trading post to call itself the "Paris of Siberia." When the Trans-Siberian steamed into town in 1898, however, it found a lawless bazaar of fur-traders, ex-cons, gamblers, and prospectors where nearly one in every hundred citizens died of unnatural causes, such as a pick-axe in the skull. Like the rest of Siberia, the city's pre-Soviet infrastructure and culture took a hit under socialism. Nonetheless, Irkutsk's cultural heritage and proximity to Lake Baikal have made it the most popular Trans-Siberian stop.

 TIME CHANGE. Irkutsk is 5hr. ahead of Moscow: GMT +8.

⛏ TRANSPORTATION. The **train station,** on Vokzalnaya ul. (Вокзальная; ☎43 17 17 or 28 28 20), sends trains to: **Krasnoyarsk** (19hr., 3-4 per day, 700R); **Moscow** (3½ days, 1-3 per day, 2500R); **Ulan Ude** (8hr., 3 per day, 350R); **Yekaterinburg** (53hr., 1-3 per day, 1500R). Foreigners purchase tickets from the *mezhdunarodnaya kassa* (международная касса; international ticket booth) in the waiting room left of the restaurant when facing the station. English spoken. Open daily 24hr. except 5-6am, 7:30-9am, 1-2pm, and 8-9pm. For a **TSR schedule,** see p. 740. The **bus station,** near the Decembrists' houses (see **Sights and Entertainment,** p. 756) at ul. Oktyabrskoy Revolyutsii 11 (Октябрьской Революции; ☎27 24 11), has service to **Listvyanka** (1½hr., 3 per day, 66R) and **Khuzhir** (5-8hr., every other day, 290R).

⚔🛈 ORIENTATION AND PRACTICAL INFORMATION. The **Angara River** (Река Ангара) bisects the town. The old city center and all the sights lie on the right bank, while the train station is on the residential left bank. From the station, buses #16 and 20 and trams #1 and 2 run to **ul. Lenina** (Ленина) in the city center (4R). To get from the train station to the bus station, take tram #1 or 2 to the Centrov Market (Рынок; Rynok) and then tram #4. **Lida Scclocchini** at Amerikanskiy Dom (see **Accommodations,** p. 754) arranges **tours** (2hr. car tour US$20) and sells train tickets for US$3 commission. Bookstore **Yemaniye** (Емание), ul. Lenina 15, sells good city **maps** for 16R. (Open M-F 10am-7pm, Sa 10am-8pm.) The **Mongolian consulate,** ul. Lapina 11, arranges visas. (☎/fax 34 21 43. Passport photos required. Tourist visa: 3- to 4-day processing US$15, 48hr. US$30. Transit visa: US$15/US$30. Open M-W and F 9:30am-noon and 2:30-5pm.) **Vneshtorg-Bank** (Внешторг-Банк), ul. Sverdlova 40 #201 (Свердлова) exchanges currency, cashes **traveler's checks** for 2% commission (plus US$0.50 per check), and offers MC/V **cash advances** for 2% commission. (☎24 39 16. Open M-F 9:30am-7pm.) There's an **ATM** outside Alfabank, at bul. Gagarina 34. **Store Luggage** downstairs at the train station below the room adjoining the main waiting hall; look for the "камера кранения" (kamera khraneniya) sign. (40-60R.) The **24hr. pharmacy, Apteka Eskular-5** (Аптека Эскулар-5), is at ul. Lenina 20. If you need **medical assistance,** English-speaking Dr. George Bilikh (☎34 36 10) will perform basic medical services or get you someone who can help. The **telephone office,** ul. Proletarskaya 12 (Пролетарская), opposite the circus, at ul. Sverdlova, offers 24hr. international **telephone** and fax service. Surf the web at **Internet Klub 38 Net,** ul. Marata 38 (Марата; ☎24 23 52). 38R per hr. Open daily 24hr.) The **post office,** ul. Stepana Razina 23 (Степана Разина), has **Poste Restante** at window #6. (Open M-F 8am-8pm, Sa 9am-6pm, Su 9am-2pm.) **Postal Code:** 664 025.

🛏 ACCOMMODATIONS. Most places in Irkutsk are overpriced and fill up quickly, especially in summer. **Amerikanskiy Dom ❷,** ul. Ostrovskogo 19 (Островского), is a 30min. walk from the train station and is nearly impossible to find; take a cab at night. With your back to the northernmost part of the station, cross the street, climb the stairs, and take a left at the top. Turn right and walk between the blue and green buildings, following the path as it curves behind the next house. At the road, turn left and take an immediate right on Kaiskaya ul. (Кайская) where it intersects with ul. Profsyuznaya (Профсюзная). Follow Kai-

Irkutsk

🏠 ACCOMMODATIONS
Amerikanskiy Dom, **3**
Hotel Arena, **2**
Hotel Gornyak, **5**

🍴 FOOD
Bagira, **6**
Restoran Khunyan, **1**

🎭 NIGHTLIFE
Klub Stratosfera, **4**

skaya through several intersections and up a hill. Ul. Ostrovsko is the third right after the aqua-colored fire station; look for a house with a brick fence at the intersection. Owner Lida Sclocchini is the Russian widow of a man from Philadelphia. Their early-80s love affair broke Cold War barriers and attracted attention from *People* magazine. (☎ 43 26 89; slida@irk.ru or molga@irk.ru. Breakfast US$3. Laundry US$3. Call at least 4 days ahead. US$17-22.) **Hotel Arena ❶** (Арена), ul. Sverdlova 39 (Свердлова), behind the circus, is the best deal near downtown. Most rooms are part of larger suites with shared baths; spartan for sure but quite comfortable. (☎ 34 46 42. Singles 200-500R; doubles from 720R.) **Hotel Gornyak ❷** (Горняк), ul. Lenina 21, at ul. Dzerzhinskogo (Дзержинского), offers a convenient location with small, shared baths. (☎ 24 37 54. Singles 700R; doubles 800R.)

🍴 **FOOD.** Irkutsk has outstanding dining options. **Bagira ❷** (Багира), in the stadium off ul. Karla Marska, complements its incredible decor with incredibly fresh and creative Russian cuisine. (Entrees 100-200R. 3-course business lunch 180R. Open daily 11am-11pm.) Upscale **Restoran Seul ❸** (Ресторан Сэул), ul. Dekabrskikh Sobytiy 63 (Декабрьских Событий), in the back and upstairs, serves Korean and Chinese favorites and is one of the few spots with spicy food in Siberia. (*Bibimbap* 90R. Entrees US$5-8. Open daily 11am-2am.) **Restoran Khunyan ❷** (Ресторан Хунян), at the end of the bridge over the river on the upper street level, on the right bank, offers Russian and Chinese food, minus the spices. (Large noodle bowl 90R. Open daily 11am-2am.) Gastronom **Amurskiye Vorota** (Амурские Ворота), ul. Lenina 24, is a small but adequate grocery store. The **central market** (рынок; rynok) hawks fresh produce, cheese, and meat. From the station, walk 10min. along ul. Dzerzhinskogo and take a right on ul. Chekhova (Чехова). Any form of transport that reads "рынок" will suffice. (Open daily 8am-8pm.)

🎦 🎵 **SIGHTS AND ENTERTAINMENT.** Chandeliers brighten the gold-columned iconostasis in ⬛**Znamensky Monastery** (Знаменский Монастырь), near the river north of the town center on ul. Angarskaya (Ангарская). Several Decembrists are buried in the gardens of this very active monastery. Take trolley #3 or bus #8, 13, or 31 north to the first stop after the bridge. Walk back toward the bridge for about 100m to the large blue domes on your right. To get here on foot, take ul. Franka Kamenetskogo (Франка Каменецкого) north across the bridge and bear left for several hundred meters. (Open daily 8:30am-5pm. Services 8:30 and 11am. Free.)

Irkutsk's most illustrious residents, the **Decembrists** (see **History,** p. 652), arrived as exiles in the 19th century. Two of their houses are now museums. **Muzey-Dekabrista Volkonskogo** (Музей-Декабриста Волконского), ul. Volkonskogo 10, is a pleasant old house on a dusty side street off ul. Timiryazeva (Тимирязева). Take trams #1-4 to Dekabrskikh Sobytiy (Декабрьских Событий), and go to the right of the church. If you had the stamina to read *War and Peace*, this one should be a real treat. (☎27 57 73. Open Tu-Su 10am-6pm; last entry at 5:30pm. 50R, students 30R.) If you have the time, head to the **Prince Sergei Trubetskoy House-Museum** (Музей Трубецкого; Muzey Trubetskogo), a block away at ul. Dzerzhinskogo 64. It exhibits the books, tapestried icons, and photos of this prominent Decembrist's jail cell. (Open M and Th-Su 10am-6pm; last entry 5:30pm. 50R, students 30R.) Near the river, the **Regional Museum** (Краеведческий Музей; Kraevedcheskiy Muzey), in a Victorian building at ul. Karla Marksa 2, exhibits furs, Buddhist masks, and pipes of local Siberian tribes. It also documents the city's Slavic history and years as a frontier town in the Wild East and features a large selection of Chinese and Japanese clothing, artifacts, and weapons. (☎33 34 49. Open Tu-Su 10am-6pm. 150R, students 100R.) The **Sukachev Art Museum** (Художественный Музей Имени Сукачева; Khudozhestvennyy Muzey Imeni Sukacheva), ul. Lenina 5, houses Chinese vases, Mongolian Buddhist *thanka*, and Russian paintings from the 16th to 20th centuries. (☎34 42 30. Open M and W-Su 10am-6pm. 90R, students 60R.)

On sunny days and warm nights, locals head to the end of ul. Karla Marksa to drink and make out. When it gets dark, the crowd heads across the cove to **Youth Island** (Остров Юности; Ostrov Yunosty) to drink more and rock until dawn. **Klub Stratosfera,** ul. Karla Marksa 15, at the corner of ul. Gryaznova (Грязнова), is Irkutsk's premier disco/bowling alley. Its teen crowd dolls up to meet the strict dress code and doesn't show up until midnight. (☎24 30 33. Bowling 500R per hr. Cover Th and Su 40R; F-Sa 250R. Open Th and Su 6pm-4am, F-Sa 6pm-6am. MC/V.) During the annual (Dec. 25 to Jan. 5) **Russian Winter Festival** (Русский Зимский фестиваль; Russkiy Zimskiy Festival), which also takes place in 11 other cities, Irkutsk celebrates with troika-rides, *khorovod* performances (traditional round dancing), and *bliny* with salmon roe.

LAKE BAIKAL (ОЗЕРО БАЙКАЛ)

Lake Baikal—**the deepest body of fresh water in the world** at 1637m—contains one-fifth of the Earth's liquid fresh water. Its surface (23,000 sq. km) is twice as large as North America's Lake Superior, and it is older than any other lake in the world (25 million years). Surrounded by snow-capped peaks that edge the shore, its waters teem with 450 aquatic species found nowhere else, including **translucent shrimp, oversized sturgeon,** and **deepwater fish** that explode when brought to the surface. One such type of fish has evolved into a gelatinous blob of fat—so fatty, in fact, that locals stick wicks in its libidinous lumps and use them as candles. The local *nerpa,* the world's only freshwater seal, lives 3000km from its closest relative, the Arctic seal; scientists don't know how it came to inhabit the lake. The waters are a stunning bright blue; in places it's so clear you can see as deep as 38m from the surface.

Baikal's shores are no less fascinating than its waters. **Reindeer, polar foxes, wild horses, brown bears, wild boars,** and nefarious **Siberian weasels** hide in the surrounding mountains. Small glacial lakes melt into ice-cold waterfalls. Buryat *ger* (yurts) border the edges, while the Buryat region to the northeast holds 45 Buddhist monasteries. Deserted gulags near Severobaikal, where many Buddhist lamas and shamans spent their last days under the atheist Soviet regime, pepper the outskirts. While the southern end of the lake is heavily touristed, the rest is quite remote and undeveloped; visit in March, when the picturesque ice retains its splendor.

LISTVYANKA (ЛИСТВЯНКА) ☎(8)3952

The most popular destination for daytrippers and Baikal over-nighters is this lakeside hamlet of 2500. Meandering cows battle visitors for control of the main street, ul. Gorkogo (Горького), which runs 5km along the shore north from Hotel Baikal to the center of town at the docks. The wooden **St. Nicholas Church,** ul. Kylekova 88 (Кылукова), built in gratitude for a miraculous sea rescue, sits in a small valley away from the lake. The walk is a charming stroll through local neighborhoods. Facing away from the docks, go left, and turn right at the "Bard-Folk-Rock-Retro" music sign. Cross the footbridge when you see the spire. Detailed, golden-framed icons adorn the fragrant interior. (Open M-F 9am-7pm. Services M-F 1-3pm.)

Unfortunately, heavy tourism is changing the feel of this rural village—hotel construction is taking place all along ul. Gorkogo, replacing the local charm with garish commercialism. A **hydrofoil** runs between Irkutsk and Listvyanka, June through September. (70min. Departs Tu-Th 8:30am, F-Sa 8:30am and 2pm, Su 8:30am, noon, 2pm; returns Tu-Th noon, F-Sa noon and 4:30pm, Su 8:30am, noon, 4, 4:30pm; schedule is likely to change. 210R.) Hydrofoils depart from Irkutsk's **ferry terminal** (☎35 88 60), Solnechnaya ul. (Солнечная), south of town. From ul. Lenina in Irkutsk, take bus #16 or trolleybus #5; ask for the "raketa" stop (ракета; rocket) and walk upstream along the river. **Buses** run daily from Irkutsk to Listvyanka; buy return tickets at the bus stop in the blue shack at the boat dock. (1½hr. To Listvyanka 9am, 2:30, 4:30, 7pm; to Irkutsk 7, 11am, 4:45, 6pm. 68R.)

The upscale **Hotel Baikal,** in Listvyanka, houses an **exchange office** that gives MC/V **cash advances** for 1.5% commission, and has a **24hr. ATM.** The bus from Irkutsk stops at the hotel (Baikalskiy Muzey; Байкалский Музей) 5min. before reaching the docks. (☎25 03 91. Open daily 8am-2pm and 6pm-midnight.) Take a left out of the boat dock to get to the **post office,** ul. Gorkogo 49, just past the white WWII obelisk on the right. (Open M-F 8:30am-1pm and 3-5:30pm, Sa 8:30am-noon; closed last Th of each month.) **Postal Code:** 664 420.

Past the white obelisk on ul. Chapayeva (Чапаева, the first road leading from the water as you go left facing away from the dock), the **Art Gallery ❶** (Картинная Галерея; Kartinnaya Galereya) was built by an architect extremely enthusiastic about Siberian art. (Breakfast US$5. Comfortable housing US$10.) There are numerous **B&Bs ❷** on ul. Chapaeva; the going rate is US$15 with breakfast. One of the best is ◪**Devyatiy Val ❷,** behind the red fence at ul. Chapaeva 24. Proprietor Irina Katrych offers comfortable beds in double rooms; unlike many other homes, hers boasts a large shower and 24hr. hot water. (☎11 21 14. Beds from US$15 with breakfast.) A 25min. walk south on ul. Gorkogo from the docks is a fine seafood restaurant, **Proshlyy Vek** ❷ (Прошлый Век), the best dining in town. (Lake fish 180R. Open daily noon-11pm.) More casual, more touristy, but still delicious, **Kafe-Bar Shury Mury** ❶ (Шуры Муры), in the glitzy two-story building by the bus stop, offers fresh meals at reasonable prices. (Lake fish 130R, *ukhra* (ухра; fish soup) 50R. Open daily 10am-midnight.)

OLKHON ISLAND (ОСТРОВ ОЛЬХОН)

This large (2400 sq. km) island off the western shore of Lake Baikal is a beautiful choice for experiencing the natural wonders of the region. The sparsely settled northwestern section was the site of child labor camps from Irkutsk during WWII; today, small fishing villages and faint traces of a tourist industry are all that remain from the failed Soviet program to settle and modernize the island. **Khuzhir** (Чужир), the main town on Olkhon, has as many telephones as paved roads and as many flush toilets as restaurants (pick a number and multiply it by zero). Locals are extremely friendly and curious about visitors, however, and there are some great options for a surprisingly comfortable stay.

Khuzhir is accessible by **bus** from Irkutsk, but only starting in June, when the ferry service starts and in winter once the ice is thick enough to support the bus. Bus tickets sell like hotcakes in the summer; try to buy one in advance. The bus schedule is vicious and changes unpredictably, so give yourself a few extra days to get there and back. (June Tu-W and F 8:10am; return Th and Sa 9am despite the printed departure time of 7am on tickets purchased in Irkutsk—locals advise stopping by the "bus station" house the afternoon before you leave to remind them that you have a seat the following morning; 283R.) If your travel dates are definite, it may be worth the effort to contact one of the **tour operators** in Irkutsk. To reach the small **post office** on ul. Lenina, head left from the *gastronom* for several blocks and then take a left. (Open M-F 9am-noon and 2-5pm.) **Postal Code:** 666 137.

Green Express ❶, ul. Chelnokova 46, makes private runs to Olkhon and can arrange accommodations on the island. (☎38 01 11; www.greenexpress.ru. Leaves Irkutsk Tu and Th-F 9am; returns from Olkhon M, W, F 8am. Round-trip US$25. Bed in a shared yurt outside Khuzhir US$10, with 3 meals US$15.) Lida Sclocchini at **Amerikanskiy Dom** (see **Accommodations,** p. 754) assists with bus tickets and homestays from US$15 with meals. You can also just show up at the **guest home** ❷, ul. Lesnaya 37, of local librarian **Luba Kirilchuk** and her husband, and hope that there's space in their extremely comfortable guest wing. With your back to the "bus station," walk left for several hundred meters. (US$15 per day with meals.) If you want to meet other travelers, Khuzhir's tourist options are monopolized by the affable Nikita Bercharov. ▧**Nikita's "place where you can stay"** ❷ (he doesn't want to call it a hotel), Kirpichnaya ul. 8 (Кирпичная), is full of friendly faces and blessed with a nightly campfire. For US$15-20 you will get a cozy bed, three meals a day, and a 20min. *banya* session. Nikita works with many locals to organize a variety of excursions, from boat tours to horse treks (US$3-20). With your back to the *gastronom* in the town center, walk left for half a block, then take the first right. Ul. Kirpichnaya is the last right before town. Nikita's place is the large, new complex with a wooden fence; you can't miss the turrets. (nikita@olkhon.irkutsk.ru. Private hour in the *banya* US$5.) It's possible to **camp** for free on the beaches just north of town. There is a **gastronom** in the center of town. (Open daily 8am-midnight.) To get to the better-stocked **Khoroshiy Magazin** (Хороший Магазин; Good Store), start with your back to the *gastronom* and head right, past the WWII memorial. (Open daily 8am-midnight; low season 8am-10pm.)

On the shores north of Khuzhir, picturesque rocky cliffs give way to sandy beaches. **Shaman Rock,** behind Nikita's, was a sacred site for the indigenous population until local Russians co-opted it for **recreational climbing.** One of the most interesting ways to get a feel for the island is to take a **private taxi tour.** You can arrange this at Nikita's (see above), where drivers congregate in the morning, or Luba Kirilchuk can arrange a trip with her friend **Sergei,** who does an informative 5-7hr. circuit of the southern end of the island with stops at the ruins of an ancient walled settlement, a sulphur lake, and many gorgeous panoramas. (Displays in Russian. 300-500R per person, min. 2 people.)

ULAN UDE (УЛАН УДЭ) ☎(8)3012

When Stalin suppressed Russia's ethnic minorities, he made a few exceptions for Ulan Ude. The result is an odd, laid-back city that feels much less Russian than any other major stop on the Trans-Siberian. Long a haven for political and religious dissidents, Ulan Ude also served as Russia's customs port for the tea trade with China. But rather than develop closer ties to Asia, the capital of the Buryat Republic saw itself cemented to the Russian Empire when the Trans-Siberian appeared in 1900. Today, the Buryat comprise less than a quarter of the region's population. The city's main landmark is its gargantuan bust of Lenin. It overlooks the city center, where its ominous stare might still set the tone if the whir of cafes, kiosks, and Buddhist *datsans* was not so strong.

 TIME CHANGE. Ulan Ude is 5hr. ahead of Moscow: GMT +8

TRANSPORTATION. Ulan Ude is the last Russian city on the Trans-Mongolian line. Trains run to: **Irkutsk** (8hr., 4-6 per day, 600R); **Moscow** (4-8 per day, 2575R); **Vladivostok** (63hr., 3-5 per day, 2200R); **Beijing, CHI** (47hr., 1-2 per day, 3600R); **Ulaanbaatar, MON** (24hr., 1-2 per day, 1050R). For a TSR schedule, see p. 740. Foreigners should purchase tickets from the *kassa* in the corner of the station's first floor, at the "Международные Кассы" sign. (Open daily 9am-noon and 1-11pm.)

ORIENTATION AND PRACTICAL INFORMATION. Ulan Ude's main square, **pl. Sovetov** (Советов), lies 500m south of the **train station** (☎34 25 31), off Revolyutsii 1905-go goda (Революции 1905-го года). Cross the tracks on the pedestrian bridge; then, with your back to the station, walk left for one long block along ul. Borsoyeva (Борсоева), and take the first full right at ul. Sukhe-Batora (Сухэ-Батора). Most essential services in Ulan Ude are located either in **Hotel Buryatiya** (Бурятия), Kommunisticheskaya ul. 47a (Коммунистическая) south of pl. Sovetov, or in the **post office,** at the northwest corner of pl. Sovetov.

Baikal Naran Tour, room 105 of Hotel Buryatiya, offers tour packages and arranges train tickets for 120R. (☎21 50 97; baikalnarantour@mail.ru. Buryat visits US$60. City tours US$10. Open M-F 9am-8pm.) The **Mongolian Consulate** is hard to miss in an orange-pink building 100m west of ul. Lenina, south of the Opera House and pl. Sovetov. (☎21 05 07. Visa processing 1wk. US$25, 1-day US$50. Open M, W, F 10am-1pm.) **Exchange currency** in the lobby of Hotel Buryatiya, which also has a **24hr. ATM.** (Open M-F 9am-5pm.) **Luggage storage** is at platform 1 of the train station (30-60R). A **24hr. pharmacy** sits at ul. Lenina 29, three blocks south of pl. Sovetov at the intersection with ul. Kalandaritsvila (Каландарицвила; ☎21 37 70. Open M-Th 9am-4pm, F-Sa 9am-8pm, Su 4-7pm. Ring bell after hours.) The **hospital,** at the corner of bul. Karla Marksa (Карла Маркса) and ul. Navsova (Навсова),

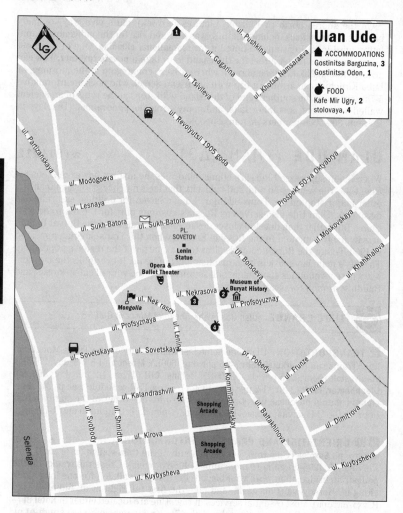

sees foreigners. Take the tram south from the east side of Hotel Buryatiya and ask
for the "Sayany" stop. Ascend the slope to your right, make a left at the arcade, and
walk to the complex of pink buildings on your right. (☎33 15 05, emergency ☎03.)
International phone service and **Internet** access (30R per hr.) are available at the
post office. (Open M-F 8am-7pm, Sa-Su 9am-5pm.) **Postal Code:** 670 000.

■■ **ACCOMMODATIONS AND FOOD.** Hotels fill quickly in the summer, so
call ahead. **Gostinitsa Odon ❷** (Гостиница Одон), ul. Gagarina 43 (Гагарина), one
block north of the train station, is in a no-frills, aging building, but its cheerful staff
and proximity to the station make it the best choice in town. (☎44 34 80. Singles
with baths 400R; doubles 661R.) **Gostinitsa Barguzina ❶** (Гостиница Баргузина),
Sovetskaya ul. 28, has spartan rooms, but is located a little closer to town. Take

bus #36 from the train station and ask the driver for the hotel. Or, from pl. Sovetov, walk two blocks down ul. Lenina and go right on Sovetskaya ul. (☎21 57 46. Singles with baths 330R; doubles 560R.)

Dining options in Ulan Ude are limited. Your best bet for a tasty meal is to head to one of the many **beer gardens** ❶ south of Sovetov. The best is behind a white fence behind casino **Mir Ugry** (Мир Угры), ul. Kommunisticheskaya 41a, just south of the Museum of Buryat History. Beautiful fountains, colorful umbrellas, and huge portions of sizzling *shashlyk* (70R) and a cold *Stella Artois* (30R) make for a pleasant, lazy afternoon. (30R; open daily 11am-midnight.) In the forest suburbs of Ulan Ude sits the inimitable **Baatarai Ürgöö** ❷ (БаатарайУргоо), which serves meaty specialities in a lavishly decorated *ger* (traditional Buryat yurt). From the bus stop, at the turn-off for the Ethnographic Museum (see below), walk away from the city center; the colorful *ger* is 1km down the road. (Sheep and horse stomach salad 75R. Lamb heart salad 75R. Meat dumplings 60R. Cover 15R. Open daily noon-11pm.) Treat yourself to cheap eats at the **stolovaya** (столовая; cafeteria) across the street from the southeast corner of the department store.

◖ **SIGHTS.** A freakishly large **Lenin head** dominates Ulan Ude's main square, **pl. Sovetov.** Forty-two tons and 18m high, this bronze behemoth was designed by the Neroda brothers in 1972. At the southwest corner of the square on the corner of ul. Lenina stands the majestic **Buryat State Academic Theater of Opera and Ballet** (Бурятский Государственный Академический Театр Оперы и Балета; Buryatskiy Gosudarstvennyy Akademicheskiy Teatr Opery i Baleta), a gorgeous castle-like building with two horsemen guarding the entrance. (Tickets 40-60R.)

The **Museum of Buryat History** (Музей Истории Бурятии; Muzey Istorii Buryatii), Profsoyuznaya ul. 29 (Профсоюзная), off Kommunisticheskaya ul. opposite Hotel Buryatiya, details the history of the city and the БАМ (BAM), the costly second Trans-Siberian railway. The third floor houses a wonderful collection of Buddhist treasures saved from local monasteries and temples just before they were destroyed under Stalin's rule. (☎21 65 87. Open Tu-Su 10am-6pm. Each floor 80R.) Follow the tram tracks down Kommunisticheskaya ul. away from pl. Sovetova and take a right at the bottom of the hill, past some kiosks and umbrellas, to reach the local **Buddhist shrine** (ламрим; lamrim), 100m down on the left. Walk past the black gate and ask to take a peek. Visit in the early morning or early afternoon.

The largest sights lie outside the city limits. The **Ethnographic Museum** (Этнографический Музей; Etnograficheskiy Muzey), north of the city, can be reached via bus #8 (every 30min., 5R) from the south end of pl. Sovetov; if you're looking into Lenin's left ear, you're in the right place. Get off at the first stop after the stadium (about 15min.). Walk 1km down the road veering left from the bus stop. The museum is on the right, sprawled over a quiet patch of Siberian countryside. It features traditional Buryat dwellings, a shamanist compound, examples of Cossack and Old Believer settlements, and an unfortunately unkempt zoo. (☎33 57 54. Open M-F 9am-5pm, Sa-Su 10am-6pm. 45R.)

Perhaps the most fascinating spot in the region is the hamlet of **Ivolga** (Иволга), about 30km west of Ulan Ude. Amid the hills stands **Datsan-Ivolga,** a Buddhist monastery complete with a yellow curved roof and Mongolian-trained lamas. Built in 1942, the shrine served as the Buddhist center of the Soviet Union. In the main building next to the temple are rare Buddhist scriptures handwritten in Tibetan, Pali, and Sanskrit. Around the complex sit 120 prayer drums, and in the greenhouse is a reputed relative of India's *bodhi* tree, under which Buddha attained enlightenment. The **lamas' houses** *(datsan)* are behind the complex. Arrive before 9am to hear the monks chanting. To reach the houses, take bus #130 from the station on Sovetskaya ul.; when you reach Ivolga, either keep following the road 5km out of town or catch a taxi. The temple is closed in the evening. (15R.)

KHABAROVSK (ХАБАРОВСК) ☎(8)4212

If you're ever exiled to Siberia, hope that you're sent to Khabarovsk (pop. 700,000). The last major Trans-Siberian city before Vladivostok, Khabarovsk blooms during the summer: wide boulevards sprout cafes, the banks of the Amur River fill with sunbathers, and ice-cream vendors make out like bandits. The city's rough past—as a garrison and fur-trading post—seems like a myth during the months when Khabarovsk's tan and taut youth lounge in the sun for hours on end in sophisticated Lenin Square before drinking the night away. Today, Khabarovsk remains a vital trade center for Russian and Chinese goods, slightly seedy but bustling with both commerce and leisure.

 TIME CHANGE. Khabarovsk is 7hr. ahead of Moscow: GMT +10

TRANSPORTATION. Trains run to: **Ulan Ude** (50hr., 1-2 per day, 1700R) and **Vladivostok** (14hr., 2 per day, 950R). The overnight #5/6 *Okean* to Vladivostok is one of the best services in Russia. It's also possible to take a **boat** into China. Agencies around the boat terminal (речной вокзал; rechnoy vokzal) sell tickets to **Fuyuan, CHI** (9am, about 1200R); from there you can catch a bus to **Harbin, CHI.**

ORIENTATION AND PRACTICAL INFORMATION. The **train station** is east of the city; the **Amur River** runs southeast to northwest and forms the western edge. **Ul. Leningradskaya** (Ленинградская) follows the tracks parallel to the river. From the train station, **Amurskiy bulvar** (Амурский бульвар) runs perpendicular to the river. **Ul. Karla Marksa** (Карла Маркса) and **ul. Lenina Muravyova Amurskogo** (Ленина Муравьёва Амурского) join at **Lenin Square** (pl. Lenina; Ленина), forming the next major street running between the tracks and river. Parallel to these streets, **ul. Lenina** (Ленина) is the town's southern edge.

The **Chinese Consulate,** in the southwest corner of the stadium just north of the museums and the waterfront, issues visas in five days. Look for the blue sign, behind a green fence, reading Визовый Отдел. (Open M, W, F 10am-1pm.) The most convenient **ATM** and **currency exchange** facilities are near Gostinitsa Sapporo, close to the river at the end of ul. Muravyova Amurskogo: there is also a **24hr. ATM** just east of Lenin Sq. **Store luggage** on the ground floor of the train station (30R per day). There are **24hr. pharmacies** in the University building on Lenin Sq. (the side with the road) and across ul. Muravyova Amurskogo from Gostinitsa Sapporo. The **international telephone office** is in the southwest corner of Lenin Square, under the big television screen. (Open daily 8am-10:30pm.) The **Internet Center** at ul. Muravyova Amurskogo 44, one block west of Lenin Sq., charges more during peak hours. (31-42R per hr. Open daily 8am-10:30pm.) For blindingly fast connections and sweet, sweet air conditioning, **Internet Kafe P@RTY,** in the cell-phone store at ul. Karla Marksa 55, charges a justifiable 60R per hr. The **post office,** ul. Muravyova Amurskogo 28, several blocks from Lenin Square, offers **Poste Restante** at *kassa* 11. (Open M-F 8am-8pm, Sa-Su 9am-6pm.) **Postal Code:** 680 000.

ACCOMMODATIONS AND FOOD. Khabarovsk's upscale aspirations are reflected in its lack of quality budget accommodations. The Soviet-style **Gostinitsa Turist ❷** (Гостиница Турист), on Leningradskaya ul., 1km south of the train station, is as cheap as you'll get. (☎31 04 17. Singles 400R; doubles 700R; triples 850R.) A more luxurious option is **Gostinitsa Amur ❸** (Гостиница Амур), ul. Lenina 29, at the corner of ul. Dzerzhinskogo (Дзержинского), which has a friendly staff and big rooms. Catch a cab; it's a long walk from the train station. (☎22 12 23. Singles 800R; doubles 1000R.)

RUSSIA

A number of tourist-oriented restaurants on ul. Muravyova Amurskogo serve good food, but in general the city has slim pickings. For easy and cheap food, try one of the vendors along the beach (delicious *shawarma* 50R), or grab some staples at the **24hr. grocery** one block east of Lenin Square on ul. Karla Marksa. **Kafe Bermudy ❶** (Кафе Бермуды), a small subterranean joint at ul. Muravyova Amurskogo 25, serves up *plov*, *pelmeni*, and other pub grub for under 30R. The scantily clad heroines of the giant murals on the walls don't seem to have a lot to do with Bermuda, but at these prices, who's complaining? (☎23 61 21. Open daily 11am-midnight.) Teenyboppers and Russian tourists fill **Tur-kafe Kasam ❷** (Тур-Кафе Касам), a combination fast-food joint and tourist agency at ul. Muravyova Amurskogo 50. Reasonable prices and delicious, made-to-order *bliny* (you can watch the chef pour the batter) make this a great stop for a quick bite.

◙ SIGHTS. The city's appeal lies in its riverfront, which varies from sandy beach to rocky gravel. On rainy days, take a trip to the trio of museums set 50m back from the river, a short walk north of ul. Muravyova Amurskogo. Facing the water at the end of the street, head to your right. The **Khabarovsk Lore Museum** combines exhibits on natural- and prehistory. The taxidermy leaves something to be desired, but the ethnographic department has a good showcase of aboriginal artifacts. (Open Tu-Su 10am-6pm. 84R.) The adjacent **Art Museum** displays Russian and indigenous art plus some interesting European pieces. Donning **protective dust booties** is an added bonus. (Open Tu-Su 10am-5pm. US$3, students US$1.50.) The colorful **Military Museum** across the street commemorates Khabarovsk's beginnings as a garrison and is surrounded by a spectacular graveyard of decommissioned tanks, missiles, and artillery guns. (Open Tu-Su 10am-5pm. 60R.) The **Oriental Trader's Market** outside of town provides a diversion if you don't mind wading through stalls of cheap clothes and gadgets from across the border. Take minibus #42 (6R). (Open daily 9am-early afternoon. Cover 1R.)

VLADIVOSTOK (ВЛАДИВОСТОК) ☎(8)4232

The Trans-Siberian's eastern terminus lies on a small crook of land in Russia's southeastern corner. Nearby land borders with China and North Korea provide trade routes for East Asian goods, and ferries cross the Sea of Japan regularly. Nevertheless, Vladivostok (vlah-de-VOSS-tok; pop. 630,000), whose name means "Ruler of the East," is a distinctly Russian city where European faces vastly outnumber those with Asiatic features. This Slavic domination would please Vladivostok's founders, who were proud that their hilly city represented the farthest reach of Russian culture. As the strategic home of the Russian Navy's Pacific Fleet, Vladivostok was closed to foreigners until the early 1990s; today, however, the city's picturesque vistas are increasingly popular attractions. Vladivostok has eagerly embraced the new attention, transforming into an enchanting metropolis.

 TIME CHANGE. Vladivostok is 7hr. ahead of Moscow: GMT +10

▐ TRANSPORTATION. Flights leave daily for Moscow, but the train is much cheaper and more popular. **Trains** to: **Khabarovsk** (14hr., 2-3 per day, 950R); **Moscow** (1wk., every other day, 5400R); **Harbin, CHI** (20hr., 3-4 per wk., 300R). Buy tickets at the train station on Aleutskaya ul. **Ferries** leave for **Niigata, JPN** (2-3 per wk.). Prices vary by port, class, and season, but expect to pay at least US$300.

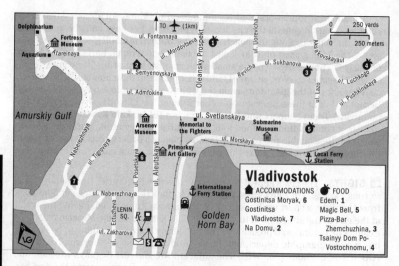

Vladivostok

ACCOMMODATIONS	FOOD
Gostinitsa Moryak, 6	Edem, 1
Gostinitsa	Magic Bell, 5
Vladivostok, 7	Pizza-Bar
Na Domu, 2	Zhemchuzhina, 3
	Tsainyy Dom Po-
	Vostochnomu, 4

RUSSIA

■ ✦ ORIENTATION AND PRACTICAL INFORMATION. Vladivostok's curving coastline and rolling landscape make it a challenge to navigate beyond the city center. The **airport** is several km north of the city; a taxi to town should run under 300R. Bus #205 (22R) runs every hour toward the city; at the end of the line, hop into any minibus marked "центр" (tsentr; center) or "вокзал" (vokzal; train station) to continue into the city center (6R). The center is easily walkable. The main drags are **Aleutskaya ul.** (Алеутская), running north-south, and **Svetlanskaya ul.** (Светланская), running east-west. West of the center is **Amurskiy Gulf** (Амурский Залив), and southeast of it is **Golden Horn Bay** (Бухта Золотой Рог; Bukhta Zolotoy Rog). The **train station** and international **ferry station** are on Aleutskaya ul.

A **24hr.** (MC/V) **ATM** sits across Aleutskaya ul. from the station in a square with (surprise!) a statue of Lenin. There is **24hr. luggage storage** (30-50R) at the south end of the station. There is a **24hr. pharmacy** at Svetlanskaya ul. 33 (Светланская), just east of the large statues. The main square also has a well-stocked pharmacy (☎51 57 54; open daily 8am-8pm), as well as a **phone** and **Internet** center (45R per hr.; open daily 8am-9pm). The **post office** is also in the square and offers **Poste Restante** upstairs at window 1. (Open daily 8am-8pm.) **Postal Code:** 690 090.

■ ✦ ACCOMMODATIONS AND FOOD. Vladivostok's hotels are hard on budget travelers: cheaper ones fill quickly, while better ones cater to wealthier visitors. The best option is the small but central **Na Domu ②** (На Дому). Head north from the train station on Aleutskaya ul. and take the third left onto Semyonovskaya ul. (Семёновская). Na Domu is on the right above a Korean restaurant. It's cozy, but passing trains may give you headaches. (☎26 51 38. Singles 550R; doubles 1000R.) **Gostinitsa Moryak ②** (Гостиница Моряк), Posetskaya ul. 38 (Посетская), offers clean, spacious dorms near the train station. (☎49 54 35. 2- to 4-person dorms 550R; singles 800R.) A favorite among Chinese tourists and North Korean delegates, **Gostinitsa Vladivostok ④** (Гостиница Владивосток) boasts the best views of Amurskiy Gulf. Walk toward the gulf on Morskaya ul. (Морская) from the ferry terminal. Follow the road uphill and right. (☎41 28 08; www.vladhotel.vl.ru. Call ahead. Singles from 1500R; 2nd fl. doubles from 1200R. MC/V.)

High-quality Asian restaurants are the stars of Vladivostok's culinary scene. If your wallet isn't up to the task, head to the waterfront near the aquarium where dozens of *shashlyk* and *shawarma* vendors set up shop. Near the Lenin statue, **Phoenix ❸** (Феникс) cooks fried rice and noodles alongside Russian standards. (Entrees from 200R. Open daily noon-2am.) Hidden underground is a fine sushi bar, **Edem ❸** (Эдем). Walk east on Svetlanskaya ul. from Aleutskaya ul. until you reach Oleansky Prospekt, opposite the statues. Go one block uphill and turn right. The chefs are Russian, the wasabi is Japanese, and the atmosphere is a cross between Tokyo business-lunch and medieval dungeon. (Sushi with red caviar 120R. Open Su-Th 11am-midnight, F-Sa 11am-2am.) A long uphill climb will be rewarded with a cup of aromatic tea and delicious Chinese cuisine at **Tsainyy Dom Po-Vostochnomu ❸** (Цайный Дом По-Восточному; Eastern Tea House), ul. Vsevoloda Sibirtseva 15 (Всеволода Сибирцева; ☎822 21 65. Entrees 120-300R. Open daily noon-2am.) The freshly prepared gourmet pizzas at **Pizza-Bar Zhemchuzhina ❷** (Жемчужина), ul. Sukhanova 51A (Суханова), are a great value if you have irresistible cheese cravings. "Jamaican" pizza with chicken, mushrooms, garlic, and sweet peppers is 130R. (Open daily 10am-9pm.) For something a little different, head to **Magic Bell ❶**, ul. Fadeeva 53, (Фадеева) at the intersection with Svetlanskaya ul. While going south of the border will take you into North Korea, this cheap joint manages to serve up credible takes on Mexican fast food for next to nothing. (☎23 83 67. Flautas 20R, chimichangas 30R. Open daily 10am-10pm.)

◪ SIGHTS. Three huge statues overlooking Golden Horn Bay comprise the **Memorial to the Fighters for the Soviet Power in the Far East,** south of Svetlanskaya ul. The figures' rough attire and scruffy appearance reflect the frontiersman-ship inherent in the conquest of the East. The square around the memorial is Vladivostok's premier site for public gatherings, street performances, and weekend vendors. Facing the central statue, turn left and walk down Svetlanskaya ul. to reach the **Arsenev Regional Museum** (Музей Арсенева; Muzey Arseneva), which showcases the history and ethnography of the Russian Far East. Pieces were donated from Moscow's Tretyakov Museum (see p. 681) and St. Petersburg's Hermitage (see p. 708) to start the collection of Vladivostok's excellent **Primorskaya Art Gallery** (Приморская Картинная Галерея; Primorskaya Kartinnaya Galereya), 200m south of the Arsenev Museum on Aleutskaya ul. The Titian in the first gallery is a fake, but nearly all the others are genuine—and impressive. (Open W-Su 10am-6:30pm. 50R.) On the waterfront east of the monument is a **Soviet submarine** that has been gutted and converted to a submarine warfare museum. Claustrophobics beware. (Open daily 10am-8pm. 50R.) Vladivostok's coastline teems with diverse aquatic life, some of which has been trapped in glass boxes at the local **aquarium** (Океанариум; Okeanarium). Follow the coast of Amurskiy Gulf north for 20min. from Hotel Vladivostok. (Open M 11am-8pm, Tu-Su 10am-8pm. 60R.) Farther up the coast is the **dolphinarium** with a handful of well behaved dolphins and sea lions. (Shows Tu-Su noon, 2, and 4pm. Open M-F 10:30am-8:30pm, Sa-Su 10:30am-9pm. 70R.) Overlooking the waterfront behind the aquarium, the **◪Vladivostok Fortress Museum** (Музей Владивостокая Крепост; Muzey Vladivostokaya Krepost), Batareynaya ul. 4A (Батарейная), was once a functioning military battery; now it's one of the most fascinating military museums in Russia, with displays on the history of hill forts as well as dozens of missiles, torpedoes, deck guns and anti-aircraft turrets. Crank the turrets on any moving gun for a hands-on experience. If you dislike crowds, don't visit around noon, when a large gun is fired daily amid swarms of organized Japanese tour groups. (Open daily 10am-6pm. 70R.)

MONGOLIA (МОНГОЛ УЛС)

The view from the train window changes as you enter Mongolia. Russian birches disappear, leaving a vast expanse dotted with the occasional *ger* (yurt). Stop over to experience the vibrant capital, Ulaanbaatar, before pressing onward to Beijing, China (p. 937). Coverage of Mongolia was last updated in July of 2003.

TÖGRÖG	
AUS$1 = 724.81MNT	1000MNT = AUS$1.38
CDN$1 = 815.88MNT	1000MNT = CDN$1.23
EUR€1 = 1231.84MNT	1000MNT = EUR€0.81
NZ$1 = 648.80MNT	1000MNT = NZ$1.54
RUR1 = 36.89MNT	1000MNT = RUR27.11
UK£1 = 1767.71MNT	1000MNT = UK£0.57
US$1 = 1126MNT	1000MNT = US$0.89
ZAR1 = 152.37MNT	1000MNT = ZAR6.56

LANGUAGE AND CULTURE

Mongolian is in the Altaic family and is distantly related to Turkish. It was originally written in a vertical Vighur script that was adopted during the reign of Chinggis (Ghengis) Khan. The classical Mongolian script was supplanted by Cyrillic in 1941 at Stalin's behest. Since the fall of the USSR, efforts have been made to reintroduce the classical script. Few people speak **English,** though many older Mongolians can speak and understand **Russian.** Mongolian Cyrillic is pronounced the same as Russian Cyrillic with a few exceptions. "Ж" is pronounced "j" (not "zh"), "З" is "dz" (not "z"), and "Л" is pronounced like the Welsh double l (hissing air is expelled from the sides of the tongue while making an "l" sound). Two vowels unique to Mongolian Cyrillic are "Θ," pronounced "œ," and "Y," pronounced "oo."

Tipping is uncommon in most establishments, but **rounding up** the bill is usually necessary, as making change is often difficult or impossible. **Bargaining** is common at open-air markets and when organizing tours, but bargaining with food vendors is not done. When meeting someone, remove your gloves before shaking hands. When you enter a *ger*, move counter-clockwise around the stove and avoid leaning against walls or furniture. When offering food or drink, your host will most likely offer it with either his right hand or both hands—you should receive it likewise. Squatting or kneeling on the floor of the *ger* is common, but if seated on a stool, tuck your legs beneath you.

DOCUMENTS AND FORMALITIES

Most international embassies can be found in Ulaanbaatar. Mongolia's embassies abroad include: **Canada,** 151 Slater St. Ste. 503, Ottawa, ON K1P 5H3 (☎613-569-3830; www.mongolembassy.org); **UK,** 7 Kensington Ct., London W8 5DL (☎020 7937 0150; www.embassyofmongolia.co.uk); **US,** 2833 M St. NW, Washington D.C. 20007 (☎202-333-7117; www.mongolianembassy.us).

US citizens can travel to Mongolia **visa-free** for up to 90 days. Citizens of Australia, Canada, Ireland, New Zealand, and the UK require visas. Visitors must register with the police if staying for more than 30 days. Single-entry visas (valid for 30 days) cost US$65; double-entry visas US$90; if you just can't get enough, multiple-entry visas cost US$105; 2-day transit visas (issued with visa of destination country) US$55. A visa application requires a passport valid at least six months after the visa expiration date, one photograph, payment by check or money order, and a self-addressed stamped envelope. Regular service takes up to two weeks; same-day service costs an additional US$25.

TRANSPORTATION

As the name might suggest, the **Trans-Mongolian** branch of the **TSR** is the best way to reach the capital, offering cheaper rates and better views than the average flight cabin. Although **buses** are becoming more common, flights are still the best way to get to major Mongolian cities. Entering Mongolia by bus is illegal. Although **driving** is permitted with an **International Driving Permit**, it is not recommended in Mongolia unless coupled with a death wish. Road conditions are extremely poor, especially outside Ulaanbaatar where malfunctioning traffic equipment and inexperienced drivers pose a constant threat. All travelers wishing to drive in Mongolia must first register with the Department of Transportation. **Taxis** are prevalent in Ulaanbaatar; however, the industry is unregulated and meters are rarely used. A typical ride will cost about 250T per km. **Hitchhiking** is common and most drivers will expect payment at least equivalent to a cab ride. *Let's Go* does not recommend hitchhiking.

TOURIST SERVICES AND MONEY

The unit of currency is the tögrög (төгрөг). Tourist centers in Ulaanbaatar sell **maps** and can organize **tours** for a fee. Exchanging money in Mongolia can be difficult. It's advisable to bring all the cash you'll need and exchange it while in Ulaanbaatar. There are no exchange services outside the capital. There is only one convenient **ATM** in the city—it offers terrible exchange rates and only accepts Visa.

HEALTH AND SAFETY

 EMERGENCY NUMBERS: Police: ☎ 102 **Fire: ☎** 101 **Emergency:** 103

Medical facilities lack basic drugs and equipment, and treatment usually requires upfront **cash** payments. **Medical evacuation** may be necessary in an emergency and travelers are advised to update their insurance policies. **Rabies** has a higher rate of occurrence in Mongolia than in most western nations, but only those coming in contact with wild and some domestic animals are at risk. In an emergency, contact your embassy. **Pharmacies** in Ulaanbaatar are usually well stocked; however, bring a supply of medicines, tampons, and condoms if leaving the city. Crime rates are generally low, though **pickpocketing** is a growing concern. Women traveling in Mongolia will likely encounter more curiosity than harassment. Females are advised not to venture into the rural areas or even the city alone after dark. Wearing shorts is acceptable unless entering museums and temples.

 THE BLACK DEATH. Some things never die, and the Bubonic Plague is one of them. Several cases are reported in Mongolia each year, mostly among those who deal with marmots. The bacterial infection is transmitted through rodent flea bites or close contact with an infected person. Travelers are at low risk of contracting the plague. Luckily, avoiding rodents is already a good idea and is the most effective means of prevention. Symptoms include painfully swollen lymph nodes in the armpit, groin, and neck which may be accompanied by fever, chills, exhaustion, and delirium. If you suspect you've contracted the plague, antibiotics are usually swift and effective. Unfortunately, these drugs may not be available in Mongolia. The plague is fatal if left untreated.

RUSSIA

ANS-SIBERIAN TREATS

While trips on the TSR yield amazing experiences, some of the most curious sights won't be outside the window—they'll be on your plate. Here are some dishes guaranteed to test, if not tantalize, your taste buds.

The Altai delicacy *karta* (карта), a boiled dish consisting of rings of horse rectum or large intestine, might be a little strong for most Western palates. First, the innards are washed and turned inside-out, so that the outer wall and the fat surrounding it are on the inside. Then, they're washed up to six times. The ends of the tube are tied shut, and the organ is boiled in salted water for about 2hr. The entrails are sliced into thin rings, like large calamari, and mixed with fried onions and cabbage. The finished dish smells wonderful and has an extremely chewy consistency and unique flavor. If you want to give *karta* a try, you can enjoy it in Gorno-Altaisk at Kafe Ursul (see p. 747).

When visiting Mongolia, you may be lucky enough to try *airag* (айраг), a moderately alcoholic drink made from fermented mare's milk. The process of preparing *airag* is simple and ancient: brewing techniques today are identical to those used during the reign of the great Ghengis Khan. To the left of the entrance within most *ger* is a large leather sack containing fresh mare's milk. The sack is never washed and contains the

ACCOMMODATIONS AND FOOD

MONGOLIA	❶	❷	❸
ACCOM.	under 4000T	4000-6000T	6001-8000T
FOOD	under 500T	500-1000T	1001-1500T

MONGOLIA	❹	❺
ACCOM.	8001-10,000T	over 10,000T
FOOD	1501-2000T	over 2000T

Hostels do not exist in Mongolia and **hotels** are often overpriced and offer few amenities. **Guesthouses** abound in Ulaanbaatar and are popular among backpackers. Rooms in a dorm with cooking facilities and a hot shower generally cost US$4 per night. Bringing a **sleeping bag** is advisable as some guesthouses **do not provide beds** (only mats on the floor). Sleeping bags are necessary if exploring outside the city. Most tour operators provide tents for clients venturing into the country, though you may need to provide your own tent. Accommodations outside the city include commercial *ger* camps and private homes.

Virtually all Mongolian dishes contain healthy doses of **mutton.** Some favorites include *buuz* (бууз; steamed mutton dumplings), *khuushuur* (хуушуур; fried mutton pancakes), and *tsuyvan* (цуйван; a fried mix of noodles, veggies, and mutton). The cheapest and most popular Mongolian beverage is *süütey tsai* (сүүтэй чай; literally **"tea with milk"**)— half tea, half milk, lots of salt, and often grains or pieces of mutton fat.

KEEPING IN TOUCH

Although Mongolia is moving toward westernization, communications services are unreliable. **Mail** outside of Ulaanbaatar is questionable. There are no payphones in Mongolia, but public mobile phones are ubiquitous. Local calls generally cost 220T per min. You can also make international calls from international phone offices. **Internet access** is readily available in Ulaanbaatar.

ULAANBAATAR ☎ 1

The only break in the Mongolian emptiness is Ulaanbaatar, a city so hip that it earned the nickname "UB." It's a big, noisy mess that throws together folk in traditional garb, young up-and-comers, expats, and enough alcoholics to make a Moscow vodka bar look like a Mormon picnic (government figures report that over half of 19- to 35-year-old Mongolians drink excessively). UB has some of the best sights and nightlife between Moscow and Beijing, but the city's main attraction is as a base for getting out into the stunning countryside.

 TIME CHANGE. Ulaanbaatar is 5hr. ahead of Moscow: GMT +8

 VISAS. Mongolian tourist visas can be arranged at the Mongolian embassies in **Moscow** (see **Embassies & Consulates,** p. 660) and **Beijing**, CHI (see p. 670), or at the consulates in **Irkutsk** (p. 753) and **Ulan Ude** (p. 759). For stays of up to 90 days, US citizens do not require a visa.

ORIENTATION AND PRACTICAL INFORMATION.
Map labels and street names are in Mongolian Cyrillic. The center of town is **Sükhbaatar Square** (Сухбаатарын Талбах), named for the patron saint of Mongolian communism. **Enkh Taivanii Örgön Chölöö** (Энх Тайваны; Peace Avenue), UB's main east-west artery, borders the square to the south; **Baga Toiruu Gudamj** (Бага Тойруу; Little Ring) and **Ikh Toiruu Gudamj** (Их Тойруу; Great Ring) form semi-circles enclosing the square, intersecting Enkh Taivan at both ends. The **train station** is on **Teeverchidiin Gudamj** (Тээвэрчидийн), southwest of Sükhbaatar Sq. (☎94 194). The easiest way to reach the square from the train station is by taxi (1000T). **International tickets** must be bought in room #212 on the second floor of the **International Railway Ticketing Office.** (Open M-F 9am-1pm and 2-5pm, Sa-Su 9am-2pm.) Exit the train station, turn left, and walk 2min. to the yellow building set back from the road on the right. Schedules are in UB time, not Moscow time.

The **Chinese embassy**, Zaluuchuudiin Örgön Chölöö 5 (Залуучуудын), is one block from the northeast corner of the square. (30-day tourist visa 7-day processing US$50, same-day US$100. ☎32 09 55. Open M, W, F 9:30am-noon.) The **Russian embassy** is at 6A Enkh Taivanii Örgön Chölöö. From the south side of Sükhbaatar Sq. facing the statue, walk left along Enkh Taivan for three blocks; it's on the left. (☎32 70 71. Open daily 2-3pm.) The **US embassy**, 59/1 Ikh Toiruu Gudamj, is behind the Laotian embassy, northeast of the square. (☎32 90 95, emergency 991 141 68; www.us-mongolia.com. Consular section open M, W, F 2-4pm.)

The best place to **exchange currency** is with the licensed moneychangers on the ground floor of the Ard Cinema on Baga Toiruu (open daily). You can

residue of last year's batch, which acts as a starter culture and begins the fermenting process. A long churn protrudes from the top of the bag, and, as the brew requires constant stirring, it is customary for anyone who enters the *ger* to give it a few turns. After about a week, the *airag* is ready to enjoy. Many Westerners consider *airag*, which has a flavor somewhere between yogurt, sawdust, and horse sweat, an acquired taste. Be warned that for bellies unused to it, 1L is enough to upset the strongest stomach.

For some hearty Mongolian fare, try *taruaga*, or marmot, which is traditionally prepared by men. The hunter first removes the head and takes out the entrails through the neck. Heated stones are stuffed in the hole and the marmot is sealed up like a furry balloon.

Traditionally, the stone-filled carcass would then be placed in the fire, cooking the meat from the in- and outside. Technology has altered this technique, and most marmot hunters now use gas-powered blowtorches to get the job done quickly. Torching the marmot in this way ralso removes the fur and kills any fleas that carry the bubonic plague.

After this flame treatment, the marmot closely resembles a bloated sewer rat. The carcass is split open, and the juice is collected and passed around for consumption. Meanwhile, the burning hot and now very greasy rocks are passed from hand to hand to promote good health.

purchase a **map** of the city at the **State Department Store** (Монгол Улсын Их Дэлгүүр; Mongol Ulsiin Ikh Delgüür). Head to the bookstores on the upper floors, or the small kiosk on the western edge of the ground floor. (☎32 03 11. Open daily 9am-8pm.) There are only a few **ATMs** in town, all of which are run by the same bank and offer terrible exchange rates. The most convenient is the **24hr. ATM** (V) in the **Bayangol Hotel**, a 5min. walk down Chingisiin Örgön Chölöö (Чингисийн) from Sükhbaatar Sq. **Mongol Bank** can wire cash via **Western Union** for 10% commission. Facing the grayish government building with your back to the statue in Sükhbaatar Sq., make a left at the yellow building on the corner to your left and proceed for two blocks. (☎31 15 30. Open M-F 9am-4pm.) **Scrolls English Bookstore**, Khu-daldaany Gudamii 22 (Худалдааны Гудамж), next to the Wrangler Jeans store, has a limited selection and will buy your dog-eared leftovers. (Open M and Sa-Su 11am-5pm, Tu-F 11am-7pm.) The **Yongsei Hospital** (☎31 09 45) in the Medical Academy, will care for foreigners. From the square, walk east along Enkh Tayran for one block; make the first right into the Academy. A **24hr. pharmacy, Tavin-Us Apteka 24** (☎31 77 59), is on Enkh Taivanii, opposite the Centerpoint shopping complex. From the south edge of the square facing the statue, walk left along Enkh Taivanii for about 5min. **Internet** access is available in Internet clubs all over the city. (600-1000T per hr.) The **post office** (Төв Шуудан) is in the southwest corner of Sükhbaatar Sq. on Enkh Taivanii. **Poste Restante** is at counter #2 inside the main entrance to the left. (Open M-F 7:30am-9pm, Sa 8am-8pm.) The post office is also a convenient, if harrowingly difficult, place to make **international calls** (open 24hr.). A less stressful option is to head to any of the private international phone centers springing up around town, where most attendants speak English; also, most upscale hotels offer international calls for a hefty sum. **Postal Code:** 210 613.

⌐ ACCOMMODATIONS. The last 10 years have seen an explosion of new options for budget travelers, as UB's citizens rush to cash in on the tourist industry. Dozens of **private rooms** operate around the city center (US$4) and friendly English-speaking runners will most likely accost you at the train station. ◤ **Nassan's Guesthouse ❷**, one block west of Sükhbaatar Sq., is a longtime backpacker favorite run by a savvy Mongolian woman and her English-speaking son. Call or email ahead for free pick-up from the train station. Nassan will donate used clothing to orphanages, provides laundry service (US$3-4), rents bicycles ($4 per day) and camping equipment, and arranges train tickets and visas for a small commission. (☎32 10 78; nassan2037@yahoo.com. Dorms US$4; doubles US$12.) The amenities are a little rough around the edges (i.e. there are no beds), but owner Bolod of **Bolod's Guesthouse ❶**, inside the apartment complex across from the post office, makes up for it with genuine warmth and hospitality, as well as fluency in English, French, Italian, and Russian. (☎99 19 24 07; u_borchy@hotmail.com. Comfortable mat in dorm US$4.) A reputable and experienced outfit, **Idre's Guesthouse ❶** is walkable from the train station, located on the third floor in entrance 2 of Building 23 (the tall apartment building) just southeast of the bus station. (☎31 67 49; www.idrehouse.url.mn. Mattress on the floor in a dorm US$4.)

◖ FOOD. Ulaanbaatar is without question the best city for dining out between Moscow and Beijing. Many expats from all corners of the globe have opened restaurants, providing a varied cuisine which is out of character for a population that subsists on mutton and dairy products. To the delight of travelers on a tight budget, even the most upscale spots are quite affordable by western (or even Russian) standards. The small and elegant ◤ **El Latino Restaurant ❸**, two blocks west of Sükhbaatar Sq. on Enkh Taivan, features delicious Cuban favorites in a refined atmosphere. (Omelettes 1200T. Open daily noon-10pm.) For the best Chinese in the city, head to the **Wen Zhou Pub ❹**, just south of the mirrored Ulaanbaatar Bank

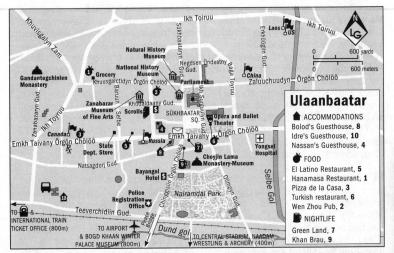

Ulaanbaatar

♠ ACCOMMODATIONS
Bolod's Guesthouse, 8
Idre's Guesthouse, 10
Nassan's Guesthouse, 4

🍴 FOOD
El Latino Restaurant, 5
Hanamasa Restaurant, 1
Pizza de la Casa, 3
Turkish restaurant, 6
Wen Zhou Pub, 2

🍸 NIGHTLIFE
Green Land, 7
Khan Brau, 9

on Baga Toiruu. The chicken dishes are superb (2000T), and the portions are enormous. One of the best values among UB's more touristed spots, **Pizza de la Casa ❺**, west of the State Department Store on Enkh Taivan, is the brainchild of two Indian brothers who serve up the best pizzas in Mongolia (2500-3800T), as well as a variety of sophisticated pasta dishes. (Open daily 11am-late.) The **Turkish restaurant ❻** on the steps of the Opera and Ballet theater overlooking Sükhbaatar is a great place for a quick, freshly carved *döner kebab* (1500T) and delicious Turkish ice cream. (Open daily noon-8pm.) A popular spot with Asian tourists, **Hanamasa Restaurant ❶**, in a shopping center at the intersection of Ikh Toiruu and Khuusgaletidiin Örgön Chölöö, boasts a huge buffet and gigantic portions of Japanese and Korean dishes. (Entrees from 3000T. Open daily 11am-late.) A convenient option for **groceries** is the supermarket in the **State Department Store**; however, you'll find much cheaper prices and a much better selection at **Minii Zakh II** (Миний Зах II), located in the same complex as the Hanamasa Restaurant.

🟢 **SIGHTS.** The elegant, overgrown home of Mongolia's eccentric last king, the 🏯**Bogd Khaan Winter Palace Museum,** exhibits religious and cultural artifacts from the 17th to 20th centuries, as well as a collection of preserved rare animals. Most displays have English captions. From the Bayangol Hotel on Chinggisiin Örgön Chölöö, take bus #7 (200T) or any bus marked "зайсан" (zaisan) two stops, or just walk south from the square for 15min. (Open daily 4:30am-5:40pm. 2500T.) South of Sükhbaatar Sq., between Chinggisiin Örgön Chölöö and Olimpiin Gudamj, stands the fantastic **Choyjin Lama Monastery-Museum** (Чойжин Ламынжийд-Музей), a complex of five temples converted into a museum. It is crammed with colorful treasures, including 108 masks used in ceremonial Tsam dancing, and a handful of Tantric sculptures worthy of careful study. (Open May-Sept. daily 9am-8pm; Oct.-Apr. W-Su 10am-6pm. 2200T.) The **Gandantegchinlen Khiyd Monastery** (Гандантэгчинлэн Хийд) is the center of Mongolian Buddhism. Built in the mid-1800s, the monastery was partially destroyed by the communists in the 1930s and restored in 1990. The main temple houses a colossal 25m golden statue of Janraisig, the Buddha of compassion and mercy. The busiest and most visually stunning time to visit is late Sunday morning. From the western intersection of Enkh Taivan and Ikh Toiruu, head north up the hill toward the visible temples. (Main temple open daily 9am-4pm. Voluntary admission 1000T.) The **National Museum of Mongolian History** (Монголын Нндэсний Түүхийн Музей) displays remnants from the Khunu Empire, Khalkh marriage headdresses, and an exhibit on Ghengis Khan. The museum also catalogues Mongolia's socialist and aerospace histories. The museum is left of the government building, at the north edge of the square. Ask for the free English brochure. (☎32 56 56; nmmh@mongol.net. Open daily in summer 10am-6pm, last entrance 5:15pm; low season daily 10am-5pm. 2000T, students 500T.) The **Zanabazar Museum of Fine Arts,** on Khudaldaany Gudamii, two blocks west of the square, is named for the enigmatic king, painter, linguist, and architect. It exhibits his works and prehistoric and folk-art masterpieces. (☎32 60 60. Open summer daily 9am-6pm; low season 10am-5pm. 2400T, students 1000T.) The popular **Naadam Festival** (July 11-13) features national competitions in wrestling, archery, and horsemanship. Book accommodations well in advance.

NIGHTLIFE. Raid your rucksack for those hotpants, iron them out, and ask any cab driver to take you to the "disco"—he'll bring you to whichever one is currently hip among UB's night crowd. Or try **UB Palace,** a huge disco on the outskirts of the city. (Cover 3000T. Open Th-Su 8pm-3am.) A perennial favorite with foreigners, **Ikra** adjoins the Drama Theater on Chinggisiin Örgön Chölöö. (Cover 5000T.) If you just want to kick back with a cold beer in the evening, the outdoor patio at **Khan Brau Restaurant and Pub,** a block south of the square on Chinggisiin Örgön Chölöö, is always packed and features locally brewed *Khan Brau* draft beer (2000T), Mongolia's best-tasting brew. More spacious and less zoo-like, **Green Land,** under a huge tent opposite the square on Enkh Taivan, is an increasingly frequented alternative more popular with Mongolians. (Draft *Chinggis* 1800T.)

OUTSIDE OF ULAANBAATAR

Mongolia's real attraction is its countryside, or Khödöö (Хөдөө), which closes tightly around the capital. All traces of civilization disappear after a 30min. drive. There are desert dunes in the Gobi, forested mountains and crystal lakes in the northwest, and rolling steppe between. The ancient way of life is unaffected by the cosmopolitan fever of the capital. Adventurous travelers quickly fall in love with rural Mongolia's charms, and they find it difficult to return to the bustle of the city.

Mongolian highways are basically dirt tracks through the steppe which appear and disappear along with the nomadic population that uses them. The easiest and most comfortable way to see the countryside is to hire a 4WD Jeep or minivan in UB and camp along the way. A driver is absolutely necessary, and, as most drivers speak no English, a translator-guide is a good idea (about $10-15 per day). While it is possible to hire a driver on your own, it is much easier to have a tourist company organize your trip, especially if your schedule is tight. Most guesthouses organize trips, and prices range from US$60-100 per day for the entire package. The cheapest method is to get together with other travelers to fill a minivan and split the costs. **Nassan's** (see **Accommodations,** p. 770) offers the best value, arranging Jeeps for $60 per day including tents, cooking equipment, and bottled water. You are expected to provide your own food, and generally the driver and translator-guide expect to be fed as well. Establish these logistics before you set out. Pack warm clothing and a sleeping bag, and prepare for the bumpiest ride of your life.

KHÖVSGÖL NUUR (ХӨВСГӨЛ НУУР)

This 2800 sq. km lake near the Siberian border in northwestern Mongolia is the most popular long-distance destination. The clear blue waters teem with fish and the shores are frequented by the many animals that call the large **Khövsgöl Nuur**

National Park home. The lake contains almost 2% of the world's liquid fresh water. The surrounding countryside, overrun by lush forests, is ideal for hiking. Most Mongolians say that the lake is most beautiful in late spring, when ice still covers much of the surface; in winter the ice is as clear as glass in many places.

▨ SOUTH GOBI (ӨМН ГОВЬ)

A trip to the Gobi Desert is unforgettable. Camel rides, towering sand dunes, and ethereal desert sunsets are just some of the highlights. Most trips head to **Gurvan-saikhan National Park,** west of the South Gobi regional capital of Dalanzadgad. The name, meaning "Three Beauties," refers to mountain ridges; top attractions include the **sand dunes** of Khongoriin Els, some of the most spectacular in Mongolia, and Yoliin Am, literally "Vulture's Mouth," an ice-filled valley amid the desert sands. Northeast of the park, the famous, spectacularly beautiful Flaming Cliffs at Bayanzag are rife with **dinosaur fossils** and eggs.

▨ KHUSTAI NATIONAL PARK (ХУСТАЙНУРУУ)

An ideal destination if you're strapped for time but want to see the countryside, Khustai is also a common stop on longer trips to the west and northwest. The park is a renowned reserve for the rare **takhi** (тахи), known as Przewalski's horse, the only species of wild horse in the world. "Discovered" in Mongolia in the late 1800s, the *takhi* became extinct in the wild during the last century. An intensive captive-breeding program undertaken by zoos around the world brought the species back from just three remaining horses, and a herd of well over a hundred now inhabits the park. An impressive sight, *takhi* have zebra-striped flanks and short bristly manes—a far cry from domestic horses. The best times for seeing the *takhi* are early evening and morning, when the horses come down from the hills to drink.

▨ TERELJ (ТЭРЭЛЖ)

Gorkhi-Terelj National Park is a popular weekend getaway for both city dwellers and foreign tourists and is easily accessible by public transportation from Ulaanbaatar (1 per day, 4pm, 1300T). Purchase your ticket on board. Buses return around 8am. The park is full of rocky gorges, grassy hills, and meandering rivers, all of which are best experienced on horseback. On the way into the park, the bus stops at all the major tourist camps, which charge US$15-35 per day for room and board in a cushy tourist *ger* and can provide **horses** ($15 per day). If you feel really rugged, pitch a tent near the village of Terelj and approach one of the young men tending horses in the morning; a horse and guide cost about $15 per day.

RUSSIA

SERBIA AND MONTENEGRO
(СРБИЈА И ЦРНА ГОРА)

Serbia and Montenegro is a land of struggles, both epic and modern. From the white city (Belgrade) to the black mountains (Montenegro), these diverse lands have been conquered numerous times, and over the past century, the region was again wracked by civil war and ethnic conflict. Troubled Yugoslavia seems to have finally died, and there is now hope that peace may prevail. Coverage of Serbia and Montenegro was last updated in July of 2003.

HISTORY

CROSSROADS. Serbia and Montenegro's turbulence is not a modern phenomenon. Long before the Slavic tribes, the land passed from the Illyrians to the Celts in the early centuries BC, and finally to the Romans. In AD 395, what is now Serbia was incorporated into the **Byzantine Empire,** while areas to the west went to the **Western Roman Empire.** Serbia broke away from Byzantium in 969, but was reincorporated in the 11th century. The Serbian Orthodox Church was established in 1217. Under ruler **Stefan Dušan,** Serbia conquered Belgrade in 1248.

FACTS AND FIGURES

OFFICIAL NAME: Serbia and Montenegro

CAPITAL: Belgrade (pop. 1.6 million)

POPULATION: 10.8 million (63% Serb, 17% Albanian, 5% Montenegrin, 3% Hungarian, 13% other)

LANGUAGE: Serbian, Albanian

CURRENCY: 1 dinar (dn) = 100 para; Montenegro uses the euro (€)

RELIGION: 65% Orthodox, 19% Muslim, 4% Catholic, 12% other

LAND AREA: 102,136km²

CLIMATE: Continental inland, Adriatic along the coast

GEOGRAPHY: Plains in the north, mountainous to the south, 199km of coast

BORDERS: Albania, Bosnia and Herzegovina, Bulgaria, Croatia, Hungary, Macedonia, Romania

ECONOMY: 38% Services, 36% Industry, 26% Agriculture

GDP: US$2300 per capita

COUNTRY CODE: 381

INTERNATIONAL DIALING PREFIX: 99

Serbia and Montenegro

CHARGE THE TURKS AND CRUSH THEIR ARMY! Serbian history came to a head on June 28, 1389, in a battle at **Kosovo Polje** (Field of Blackbirds). The Ottoman Turks wiped out a mighty Serbian army led by **Knez Lazar,** the last Serbian prince, ushering in 500 years of Ottoman domination. The Turks, however, had more trouble securing **Montenegro,** and they ruled **Vojvodina** only briefly before it fell to the Austro-Hungarian empire. The Serbs' long-standing resentment of Ottoman rule formed the basis for an **1804 revolt.** Led by **Prince Mihailo Obrenović,** the Serbs drove out the Turks in 1815, but full independence was not achieved until the **Congress of Berlin** in 1878.

YUGOSLAVIA. Led by newly independent Serbia, the Yugoslavs (South Slavs) of the Balkans united in the late 19th and early 20th centuries. In 1912, the **First Balkan War** pitted Serbia against Ottoman Turks for control of Macedonia and Kosovo. The Serbs eventually won. In 1913, Bulgaria contested the Serbs and Greeks for control of Macedonia in **Second Balkan War,** which ended also triumphantly for Serbia, after Romania came to its aid. In 1914, **Gavrilo Princip,** an ethnically Serbian student from Belgrade and member of the nationalist Young Bosnians, assassinated Austrian **Archduke Franz Ferdinand** in Sarajevo (see **Bosnia and Herzegovina: History,** p. 95). Austria-Hungary declared war on Serbia one month later, beginning **WWI.** The **Kingdom of Serbs, Croats, and Slovenes,** created in 1918, was ruled by the Serbian **Karadjordjević** dynasty. In an attempt to appease the other Slavic groups, the state was renamed **Yugoslavia** in 1929.

TITO-TALITARIAN RULE. On April 6, 1941, Hitler's troops bombed Belgrade, making way for the **Axis** occupation of Yugoslavia during **WWII.** Italy took control of Montenegro, while Serbia remained a Nazi puppet state. Yugoslavia erupted in factional fighting between the Axis supporters and the pro-communist Partisans, led by **Josip Broz Tito,** who was half-Croat, half-Slovene. Yugoslavia emerged after WWII in the form of a federation of six republics (with Kosovo and Vojvodina as autonomous provinces of Serbia). Tito ruled this unwieldy pot of nationalities with an iron hand. Unwilling to let Yugoslavia become a Soviet satellite, Tito practiced his own brand of **communism** and quickly earned the enmity of Soviet leader Joseph Stalin, who expelled Yugoslavia from the Comintern in 1948. Not until 1974 did Yugoslavia officially establish its constitution, which gave autonomy to each of the six republics and limited autonomy to Kosovo and Vojvodina.

BREAKING UP IS HARD TO DO. When Tito died in 1980, his carefully balanced state began to fall apart due to **ethnic tensions** and **inflation.** In the late 80s, former communist **Slobodan Milošević** became president of **Serbia.** Milošević's "Greater Serbia" plan for consolidating power alarmed other ethnic groups and had a detrimental effect upon Yugoslav unity. Riots broke out in Kosovo in 1989 (the 600th anniversary of the Battle of Kosovo Polje), when the Yugoslav government passed a resolution severely restricting Kosovo's autonomy. Finally, on June 25, 1991, **Slovenia** and **Croatia** declared **independence** from Yugoslavia. The **Yugoslav National Army (JNA)** promptly invaded Slovenia, but fighting only lasted 10 days before Yugoslavia was forced to recognize the nation's independence. **Macedonia** declared independence in December 1991. After **Bosnia and Herzegovina** followed suit by declaring its independence in April 1992, the war shifted. Backed by Milošević, the Bosnian Serbs began a savage albeit ultimately unsuccessful four-year siege of Sarajevo. Meanwhile, conflict escalated between Serbia and the **Kosovo Liberation Army (KLA).** In 1998, Serbia invaded Kosovo and began **"ethnic cleansing"** of Kosovo's 90% Albanian majority. **NATO** intervened with a 78-day **bombing** campaign against Serbia in 1999. Milošević was arrested in 2001 and extradited to the **UN International Criminal Tribunal** in The Hague. He was charged with genocide, crimes against humanity, and war crimes. His trial was still ongoing in August 2004.

TODAY. On February 4, 2003, Yugoslavia was officially renamed **Serbia and Montenegro.** The government is a weak federation of two republics. The president of the union parliament of Serbia and Montenegro is **Svetozvar Marovic,** who was elected in March 2003. Each republic also has its own government; **Vojislav Kostunica** and **Milo Djukanovic** are the prime ministers of Serbia and Montenegro, respectively. A notable provision of the February 2003 agreement is that, after three years, the two republics may vote to become independent, breaking one of the last Yugoslav unions.

PEOPLE AND CULTURE

DEMOGRAPHICS AND RELIGION

Serbians (62.6%), who are **Orthodox Christians,** are the largest ethnic group in Serbia and Montenegro's population. Most of the country's **Albanians** (16.5%), who are generally Muslim, reside in **Kosovo. Montenegrins** (5%), also Orthodox Christians, inhabit **Montenegro. Catholic Hungarians** (3.3%) live in **Vojvodina.**

LANGUAGE

Serbian, the dominant language in Serbia and Montenegro, is written in both Cyrillic and Latin script, as opposed to **Croatian** and **Bosnian,** which use only Latin characters. **Serbian Cyrillic** is similar to Russian Cyrillic (see **The Cyrillic Alphabet,** p. 53), though "ц" is transliterated c (still pronounced "ts"), "ж" is $\check{z}$, and "ч" is $\check{c}$. There are also additional letters, including "j," pronounced "y" (as in "yellow"), "џ" (dž), "s" (dz), "љ" (lj), "њ" (nj), and "ђ" ($\acute{c}$). Newspapers are published in both scripts. Serbian, Croatian, and Bosnian are quite similar. Certain words may vary; for example, bread is *hleb* in Serbian, *hljeb* in Bosnian, and *kruh* in Croatian. See the **guidelines for pronouncing Croatian** (p. 160) for further instruction. **English** will get you farther in Serbia than in Montenegro; **German** and **Russian** may help as well. For a phrasebook and glossary, see **Glossary: Croatian,** p. 947.

FOOD AND DRINK

FOOD	❶	❷	❸	❹	❺
SERBIA	under 150dn	150-200dn	201-300dn	301-450dn	over 450dn
MONTENEGRO	under €5	€5-10	€11-20	€21-30	over €30

Food in Serbia and Montenegro includes the usual Balkan specialties: *čevapčić* (grilled lamb rolls), *ražnjići* (skewered pork and veal, grilled with peppers and onions), *pljeskavica* (hamburger steak), *punjena tikvica* (zucchini stuffed with minced meat and rice), *muškalica* (a thick stew), *gulaš* (goulash), and other *meso-* (meat-) laden foods. **Vegetarians** find eating out challenging; ask for *nešto bez mesa* (something without meat), or make picnics with *hleb* (bread) and *sir* (cheese). *Kajmak* is a creamy Balkan cheese. Seafood, such as fried carp *(šaran)*, is readily available, particularly along the Montenegrin coast. *Kafa* (Turkish coffee) is a staple of *kafanas* (cafes), as is *pivo* (beer); look for *Jelen Pivo* (deer beer) near Belgrade and *Nikšičko* beer in Montenegro. *Dingac* and *Postup* wines are also Montenegrin specialities. Any Balkan dining experience ends with a shot of *šljivovica* (plum brandy).

CUSTOMS AND ETIQUETTE

Most shops and offices take a rest day on **Sunday.** As in the rest of the Balkans, Serbians and Montenegrins dress stylishly. Serbian **women** are "Balkan chic," dressed to the nines just to go to the market. **Jeans** are common, but **shorts** are not. **Tipping** is not generally expected, but always appreciated. Women don't **smoke** unless seated. It is considered impolite to turn down invitations, especially to coffee. Both women and men greet each other with three kisses on the cheeks.

THE ARTS

HISTORY. The Ottoman Empire produced scant written literature; instead **oral epics** dominated. Today, bards still spin tales of past national glory, accompanied by *guslar* instruments. The story of the **Battle of Kosovo,** the most famous of these epics, recounts the 1389 defeat of the Serbs in about 2000 lines. When **Romanticism** swept through Europe in the 19th century, it found expression in Serbian poetry and coincided with rising Balkan nationalism. **Petar II Petrović Njegoš,** a Montenegrin prince acclaimed as Serbia's greatest poet, is known for *Gorski Vijenac (The Mountain Wreath)*, a chronicle of Montenegro's struggle against the Ottoman Empire. Linguist **Vuk Karadžić** developed the modern Serbian grammar and language in the 19th century. During Yugoslavia's communist years, **Milovan Djilaš's** *Besuda Zemlja (Without Justice)*, a critique of the communist regime, predictably earned him a prison sentence. The most famous Yugoslav writer is Bosnian Serb **Ivo Andrić** (see **Bosnia and Herzegovina: The Arts,** p. 778). Of the postwar Serbian authors who explored the dark images of religion, **Danilo Kiš** and poet **Vasko Popa** made strong impressions on Western readers.

CURRENT SCENE. Since the disintegration of Yugoslavia, **Dobrica Cosič** and **Novica Tadić** have emerged as preeminent writers. Cosič explores nationalism in his political novels, while acclaimed poet Tadić deals with the implications of Serbian folklore. In the past two decades, Serbian and Montenegrin **film** has come into its own. Director **Emir Kusturica** and musician **Goran Bregović** have teamed up on numerous occasions to produce such notable pictures as *Time of the Gypsies* (1989) and *Underground* (1995).

HOLIDAYS AND FESTIVALS

NATIONAL HOLIDAYS IN 2005	
January 1 New Year's Day	**April 27** Statehood Day
January 7 Orthodox Christmas	**May 1** Labor Day
January 14 Orthodox New Year	**May 9** Victory Day
March 27-28 Easter Holiday	**November 26** Republic Day

Sabor Trubaca (Golden Brass Summit) is a Roma (gypsy) brass band competition in Guča on the second weekend in August. **Belef,** Belgrade's summer festival, fills July and August with performances (see p. 786)

ADDITIONAL RESOURCES

Balkan Ghosts: A Journey Through History, by Robert Kaplan (1994). A travel journal dealing with the political complexities of Serbia and Montenegro and its neighbors.

The Balkans, by Misha Glenny (2000). An engaging survey of the history of the Balkans over the past century, with an emphasis on the recent fall of Yugoslavia.

Underground, directed by Emir Kusturica (1995). This colorful film, which won the *Palme d'Or* at Cannes, sets its narrative against a turbulent half-century of Yugoslav history.

SERBIA AND MONTENEGRO ESSENTIALS

ENTRANCE REQUIREMENTS
Passport: Required of all travelers.
Visa: Not required for stays under 90 days for citizens of Australia, Canada, Ireland, New Zealand, the UK, and the US.
Letter of Invitation: Not required.
Inoculations: Recommended up-to-date on DTaP (diphtheria, tetanus, and pertussis), Hepatitis A, Hepatitis B, MMR (measles, mumps, and rubella), Polio booster, and Typhoid.
Work Permit: Required for foreigners.
International Driving Permit: Required of all those planning to drive.

DOCUMENTS AND FORMALITIES

EMBASSIES AND CONSULATES

Embassies of other countries in Serbia and Montenegro are in **Belgrade** (see p. 782). Serbia and Montenegro's embassies abroad include:

Australia: 4 Bulwarra Close, O'Malley, ACT 2606, Canberra (☎ 61 2 6290 2630; yuembau@ozemail.com.au).

Canada: 17 Blackburn Ave., Ottawa, ON K1N 8A2 (☎ 1 613 233-6289; ottambyu@capitalnet.com).

UK: 28 Belgrave Sq., London SW1X 8QB (☎ 44 207 235 9049; www.yugoslavembassy.org.uk).

US: 2134 Kalorama Rd., NW, Washington, D.C. 20008 (☎ 1 202 332 0333; www.yuembusa.org).

VISA AND ENTRY INFORMATION

Citizens of Australia, Canada, Ireland, New Zealand, the UK, and the US may visit Serbia and Montenegro visa-free for up to 90 days. A valid passport is required to enter and exit. There is no fee for crossing the border into Serbia and Montenegro.

GETTING AROUND

Jugoslav Airlines flies to Podogorica and Tivat, and internationally to Skopje, MAC, Tirana, ALB, Paris, and Zurich. **Lufthansa** flies daily from Munich and Frankfurt, GER. **Ferries** run from Bar to Bari, ITA. **Trains** from Belgrade run south to Skopje, MAC and Sofia, BUL and on to Istanbul and Thessaloniki, GCE via Niš; west to Zagreb, CRO; north to Budapest, HUN via Novi Sad; and east to Timişoara, ROM. **Buses** are cheaper and more convenient than trains and serve more destinations.

TOURIST SERVICES AND MONEY

Each city has an extremely helpful **tourist office**. English is usually spoken. **Putnik** is a popular travel agency. Serbia uses the **dinar (dn)** and Montenegro the **euro (€)**. **ATMs** are all over Belgrade but are less common elsewhere. **Komercijalna Banka** is the best place to **exchange currency. Credit cards** are accepted in shops but less so in restaurants and hotels. **Inflation** in Serbia and Montenegro is down to 8% but is still large enough to make prices increase significantly over a year. Normal **business hours** are Monday through Friday 8am-4:30pm.

HEALTH AND SAFETY

> **EMERGENCY NUMBERS: Police:** ☎92 **Fire:** ☎93 **Ambulance:** ☎94
> **Roadside Assistance:** ☎987

Serbia and Montenegro lack well-equipped **medical facilities.** You will probably need to pay any hospital bills with cash. UK citizens receive free medical care with a valid passport. **Pharmacies** are generally well stocked with basic medical supplies and hygiene products. If you choose to travel to **Kosovo** or immediately bordering areas, beware of **landmines, unexploded ordnance,** and **localized violence.** Stay on **paved roads** in these areas. **Avoid areas of military activity,** and note that taking photos of military personnel and instillations may lead to problems with the authorities. **Women** should take the usual precautions, but most likely will not encounter difficulties. **Minority** travelers will get stares but generally are not harassed. **Homosexuality** is still treated with hostility, particularly outside Belgrade. Serbia and Montenegro's first gay-rights parade in 2001 was severely marred by anti-gay violence.

ACCOMMODATIONS

ACCOM.	❶	❷	❸	❹	❺
SERBIA	under 1000dn	1000-1300dn	1301-1600dn	1601-1900dn	over 1900dn
MONTENEGRO	under €20	€21-35	€36-50	€51-75	over €75

Hostels are sparse and currently only open in summer, but efforts are underway to convert some hotels into hostels. **Pensions** are your best bet in Novi Sad and Montenegro, while **hotels** are often the only option in Belgrade and Niš. Economic sanctions and a dearth of tourists keep hotels cheap but run-down; they are a better option in Belgrade than in Niš. **Private rooms** are less common in Serbia than in Montenegro, where they are occasionally the only viable option. **Camping** facilities are generally run-down.

KEEPING IN TOUCH

Postcards to North America cost 40.50dn, letters 53dn. Mail can be received via **Poste Restante.** Address envelope as follows: Seth (First name) ROBINSON (LAST NAME), POSTE RESTANTE, Таковска 2 (post office address), 11101 (postal code) Београд (city), SERBIA AND MONTENEGRO. **Internet** cafes and card-based public **phones** are ubiquitous. International calls may be difficult, because there are **no international access numbers** in Serbia and Montenegro.

BELGRADE (БЕОГРАД)   ☎(0)11

Visitors to Belgrade (pop. 2 million) will be surprised to discover a bustling metropolis that sleeps *less* than New York. English is ubiquitous on the tongues and t-shirts of fashion-conscious locals. At every turn, Belgrade's denizens succeed in shattering the Western stereotype of the eternally bellicose Serbian and in distancing themselves from the unfortunate legacy of Milošević's infamous regime. While a militarist past is inextricably linked with Serbian identity, Belgrade shows visitors it does not define everyday life. Tourists are welcomed with small-town hospitality, world-class artistic institutions, and great nightlife.

✈ INTERCITY TRANSPORTATION

Flights: Aerodrom Beograd (☎605 555; info ☎601 964; www.airport-belgrade.co.yu), 25km west of Belgrade. Airport buses leave from train station every hr. **British Airways,** Knez Mihailova 30/IV (☎3281 303); **JAT Airlines** (see **Budget Travel,** p. 782); **KLM,** Knez Mihailova 30/III (☎3282 747); **Lufthansa,** Terazije 3/VII (☎3224 974); **Qantas,** Sremska 4a/I (☎639 166).

Trains: Glavna Železnička Stanica (Main Train Station; ☎645 822). Open 24hr. To: **Niš** (4hr., 9 per day, 550dn); **Novi Sad** (2hr., 3 per day, 300dn); **Bucharest, ROM** (13½hr., 1 per day, 1900dn); **Budapest, HUN** (7hr., 1 per day, 1950dn); **Istanbul, TUR** (12½hr., 1 per day, 2860dn); **Skopje, MAC** (10hr., 2 per day, 1300dn); **Sofia, BUL** (11hr., 1 per day, 800dn); **Thessaloniki, GCE** (16hr., 2 per day, 1930dn); **Zagreb, CRO** (7hr., 2 per day, 1110dn).

Buses: Autobuska Stanica "Beograd," Železnička 4. For international buses, see the **Basturist Office** (Бастурист; ☎658 759; fax 627 146); to the left of the toilets. Open M-Sa 7am-8pm, Su 7am-3pm. To: **Budapest, HUN** (6½hr., 1 per day, 1000dn); **Thessaloniki, GCE** (14½hr., 1 per day, 2600dn); **Vienna, AUT** (10hr., 1 per day, 2750dn).

⊞ ORIENTATION

Belgrade sprawls across the confluence of the **Sava** and **Danube** Rivers. **Stari Grad,** the Old Town, lies to the east in the corner formed by the two rivers. **Novi Beograd** lies across the Sava to the west. The main **train** and **bus stations** are next to each other on the Stari Grad side, near the Sava and close to the city center.

To reach the center from the train station, stand with your back to the station's main entrance—look for the Roman numerals above the door—and walk straight ahead; after two blocks, turn left at Hotel Beograd, onto Balkanska, and walk straight uphill for 500m. Catch your breath at the fountain atop the hill. In front of you, covered with office buildings and running northwest to southeast, is Belgrade's main street, which has three different names: 100m to the left and right it is **Terazije;** farther to the left it becomes **Knez Mihailova,** Belgrade's main pedestrian zone; farther right it becomes **Kralja Milana.** Make a beeline for the **Tourist Information Center (TIC)** in the underground shopping area where Terazije ends and Knez Mihailova begins, and pick up a map (see **Tourist and Financial Services,** p. 782). A good point from which to make your way around Belgrade is **Trg Republike** (Republic Square), farther up Knez Mihailova on the right. **The National Museum** and **National Theater** outline the square, in the center of which is a **statue of Knez Mihailo.**

⊞ LOCAL TRANSPORTATION

Public Transportation: An extremely comprehensive bus system runs throughout the city. Tickets (50dn) are valid for 6 rides on trams, trolleys, and public buses, available at kiosks next to bus stops. Buying on board (15dn per ride) from the driver or the attendant who walks through the buses is easiest. Validate tickets by punching them in yellow boxes on board. Controllers are rare, but the fine for riding ticketless is 500dn. After 11pm, all schedules are reduced, and some lines stop running altogether.

Taxis: Metered taxi rates are reasonable, but the vultures outside the train will try to cheat you. Ask for the meter first. Generally, the price should be 25dn base fare plus and 25-40dn per km, depending on the region in which you are traveling. **Maksis** (☎581 111); **Pink** (☎9803); **Plavi** (☎555 999); **Zeleni** (☎3246 088); **Žuti** (☎9802).

✷ PRACTICAL INFORMATION

TOURIST AND FINANCIAL SERVICES

Tourist Offices: The tourist organization of Belgrade, Dečanska 1 (☎3248 404; www.tob.co.yu) operates 6 TICs with info on accommodations and events and **maps** (60-100dn). The **Tourist Map of Belgrade** (60dn) includes a bus map, explanations of attractions, and lists of restaurants and clubs. The most convenient locations are **Terazije** (☎635 343; open M-F 9am-8pm, Sa 9am-4pm), in the pedestrian tunnel at the end of Terazije near Knez Mihailova, with a helpful, English-speaking staff, and **Central Railway Station** (☎3612 732 or 3612 645; open M-Sa 7am-11pm, Su 10am-6pm), inside the entrance on the bus station side of the building.

Budget Travel: JAT Airlines, Kralja Aleksandra 17 (☎3232 372 or 3245 005), just around the corner from the post office. Offers 10% discounts on flights for students with ISIC. Open M-F 8am-8pm, Sa 8am-3pm. MC/V. **PUTNIK,** Dragoslava Jovanovicá 1 (☎3232 911; fax 3234 461), on the corner at the south end of Terazije, books flights and sightseeing tours. Open M-F 8am-8pm, Sa 8am-3pm. MC/V.

Embassies and Consulates: Citizens of Ireland and New Zealand should contact the **Ministry of Internal Affairs Secretariat,** 29 Novembra 107 (☎764 236). Open M-F 7am-10pm. **Australia,** Čika Ljubina 13 (☎624 655; after hours ☎624 247; www.australia.org.yu). Open M-Th 8:45am-4:30pm, F 8:45am-4:05pm. **Bosnia and Herzegovina,** Milana Tankosića 8 (☎3291 277). **Canada,** Kneza Miloša 75 (☎3063 000 ext. 3341, after hours ☎3063 000; www.canada.org.yu. Open M-Th 8am-6pm). **Croatia,** Kneza Miloša 62 (☎3610 535; croambg@EUnet.yu). Open M-F 8am-4pm. Hungary, Krunska (Proleterskih Brigada) 72 (☎4440 472; hunemblg@Eunet.yu). **Macedonia,** Gospodar Jevremova 34, (☎3284 924; macemb@eunet.yu). **UK,** Resavska 46 (☎645 055; ukembg@eunet.yu). Open M-Th 8am-4:30pm, F 8am-1pm. **US,** Kneza Miloša 50 (☎3619 344; http://belgrade.usembassy.gov). Open M-F 9am-5pm.

Currency Exchange: Banks have the best exchange rates, while premiums are steep at the airport, train stations, and *menjačnica* (мењачница; exchange booths). **Komercijalna Banka AD** has **24hr.** (MC/V) **ATMs,** exchanges currency for 0.5% commission, cashes **traveler's checks** for 2% commission (min. 600dn), and offers V **cash advances** and **Western Union** services. The most convenient location is at Mačvanska 3 (☎3229 876), at the intersection of Terazije and Kralja Aleksandra. Open M-F 8am-8pm, Sa 8am-2pm. 2nd location (☎330 8034) Kraja Petra 19, near Kalemegdan. Open M-F 8am-8pm, Sa 8am-2pm. Other MC/V ATMs are along Knez Mihailova.

LOCAL SERVICES

Luggage Storage: *Garderoba.* A passport is required. At the train station 60dn per day. Open 24hr. At the bus station 55dn per day. Open daily 6am-10pm.

English-Language Bookstore: Plato Bookstore, Knez Mihailova 48 (☎625 834; books@plato.co.yu), toward the Kalemegdan end of the pedestrian zone on the right, stocks a comprehensive selection. Open M-Sa 9am-midnight. MC/V.

EMERGENCY AND COMMUNICATIONS

Police: ☎92.

24hr. Pharmacy: Pharmacy "Prvi May," Kralja Milana 9 (☎3240 533).

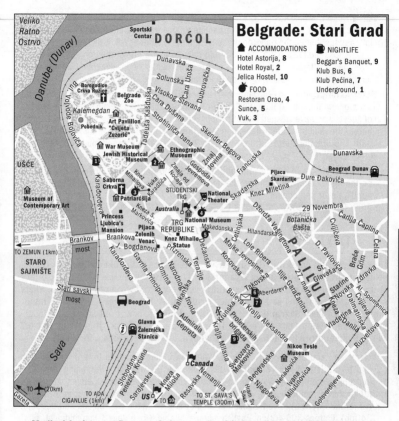

Belgrade: Stari Grad

🏠 ACCOMMODATIONS
Hotel Astorija, **8**
Hotel Royal, **2**
Jelica Hostel, **10**

🍴 FOOD
Restoran Orao, **4**
Sunce, **5**
Vuk, **3**

🌙 NIGHTLIFE
Beggar's Banquet, **9**
Klub Bus, **6**
Klub Pećina, **7**
Underground, **1**

Medical Assistance: For an **ambulance**, call ☎94. **On-call health clinic,** Klinički Centar Srbije, Pasterova 2 (☎3618 444).

Telephones: International operator ☎901. **Domestic information** ☎988. All phones use **phone cards** (300dn), available at the post office and newsstands.

Internet Access: IPS Internet Café, Makedonska 4 (☎3233 344), offers a well-lit surfing experience. From Trg Republike, turn onto Dečanska and take the first right into the alley. 50dn per 30min., 90dn per hr. Open 24hr. **Platonet Cyberclub,** Akademski Plato 1 (☎3030 630; www.plato4yu.net), around the corner from Plato Cafe, is a dim basement with over 50 computers. 25dn per 30min., 45dn per hr. Open 24hr.

Post Office: Takovska 2 (☎3230 143, www.posta.co.yu). **Poste Restante** is available at counter 2 (open M-Sa 9am-6:30pm). Houses a **telephone office** with international **fax service** (fax 3230 143; 172dn). Post office open M-Sa 8am-7pm. **Postal Code:** 11101.

🏠 ACCOMMODATIONS

Recently, a dearth of tourists combined with a surplus of decent hotel rooms has kept room prices in Belgrade remarkably low. A plan to convert some hotels to hostels is in the works; for now the only hostel in town is in a local high school.

Jelica Hostel, Krunska 8 (☎3231 272). With your back to the Roman-numeral side of the train station, walk straight on Nemanjina to Kneza Miloša and turn left. Walk up the hill, and just before the park (on the left), turn right. Enter at #8, walk through the doorway, across the large patio, turn left, and then go right through the iron gate. Huge pillows, new mattresses, 2m windows, and a great night's sleep. Reception 24hr. Checkout noon. Open late June-Aug. Beds in a triple or quad €11. ❶

Hotel Astorija, Milovan Milovanovića 1a (☎645 422; www.astoria.co.yu), across the square from the train station. Slightly threadbare red carpets give a sense of the legions of guests who have crashed here. Spotless rooms. The apartment has Victorian-style furniture. Breakfast included. Reception 24hr. Reserve 2-3 days in advance. Singles with bath 1360dn; doubles 1680dn, with bath 2260dn; 4-person apartments 4860dn. ❷

Hotel Royal, Kralja Petra 56 (☎634 222; www.hotelroyal.co.yu). Walk down Knez Mihailova almost to Kalemegdan and turn right onto Kralja Petra. Royal is 2 blocks up on the right. Garrulous locals at the bar and a funky wall mosaic evince the neighborhood's flavor and contrast with the simple rooms. A/C. Breakfast included. Reception 24hr. Reserve in advance. Singles €16-21; doubles €20-30; triples €38-43. MC/V. ❶

🖸 FOOD

Restaurants and cafes line the storefronts and patios along **Skadarlija,** the cobblestoned pedestrian area along Skadarska. The city center has no large grocery stores, but small **C markets** lurk around every corner. Two large **open-air markets** (www.bgpijace.co.yu) sell vegetables, fruit, meat, fish, cheese, eggs, and handmade pasta. **Pijaca Skadarlije,** Džordže Vašingtona bb, is at the bottom of Skadarska. **Pijaca Zelenih Venac** is where Brankova and Prizrenska join. Bear left off Terazije just before it reaches Knez Mihailova. Follow Prizrenska for 300m.

Vuk, Vuka Karadžića 12 (☎629 761). Walk down Knez Mihailova toward Kalemegdan and take a left on Vuka Karadžića; it is 50m down on the right. The dining room that looks like it could be in Vienna. Tree-shaded courtyard. Delectable Serbian specialties make Vuk a local favorite. Try the *mućalica sa pilećim mesom* (мећкалица са пилећим месом), diced chicken in a spicy sauce loaded with onions and peppers; 340dn). Entrees 300-400dn. English menu available. Open daily 10am-midnight. ❹

Sunce, Dečanska 1 (☎3248 474), just off Makedonska near Trg Republike. Feast your eyes and your stomach on a sprawling all-you-can-eat vegetarian lunch buffet (300dn) with over 20 epicurean delights, including pastas, falafels, and grilled and fried vegetables. Carnivores can order grilled meat dishes (200-400dn). Open daily 11am-5pm. ❸

Restoran Orao, 29 Novembra 28 (☎3228 836). Few restaurants in the city center are as crowded as this one at dinnertime. Locals tout it as the best pizza in Belgrade. Pasta 200dn. Fish 290-390dn. Vegetarian options. Open daily 11am-1am. ❹ The adjacent **pizza stand** is open 24hr. Pizza 30dn. Calzones 35dn. ❶

🄖 SIGHTS

🏛**KALEMEGDAN.** At the northern edge of the Old City is a beautifully lush park that overlooks the confluence of the Sava and Danube rivers. The name comes from the Turkish words *kale* (field) and *megdan* (battle), and the park is centered around the **Belgrade Fortress,** built from the 1st to the 18th century. The current layout of the park dates back to the end of the 18th century, but the concept of the architecture of an Upper Town and Lower Town is a result of the influence of the 15th-century despot Stefan Lazarević. The more-interesting Upper Town contains a lush, manicured garden dotted with monuments and statues, the **Military Museum** and the **Art Pavilion "Cvijeta Zuzorić,"** tennis courts, a basketball center, the Belgrade Zoo, and numerous cafes and restaurants.

KNEZ MIHAILOVA. Belgrade's main pedestrian zone is lined by a series of impressive buildings built in the late 1880s and filled night and day with remarkably dressed locals browsing the shops or checking out the scene from the many outdoor cafes. The first square that opens to the left is **Studentski trg** (Students' Square), the hangout of students from the Philosophy Faculty whose buildings define the square. Farther down on the left is **Trg Republike** (Republic Square), dominated by the 1882 **statue of Prince Mihailo Obrenović** (Knez Mihailo; see p. 774) and surrounded by the **National Theater** and the **National Museum.**

ZEMUN. The old town of Zemun, northwest along the Danube and now part of the city of Belgrade, is divided by a busy main street (Glavna), but the rest of the town is an idyllic escape from the surrounding city. The houses were built in the Austro-Hungarian style, and many of the narrow cobblestone streets are impassable by car. *(Buses #15 and 84 from Stari Grad.)* The **Church of St. Bogorodica** (Pokrov Presvete Bogorodice), Zemun's main Orthodox church, built in 1772, is an interesting blend of Austro-Hungarian architecture and Eastern Orthodox accents. *(Cvetosavska 15. Turn left onto Radiceva from Glavna. ☎ 613 154. Open daily 7am-9pm.)* The **Church of St. Nikolas** is Zemun's oldest church, built in 1731. Among this church's treasures are the relics of St. Andrew (the first apostle), an exquisite iconostasis fashioned by Dimitrije Baćević in 1762, and the original frescoes. *(Turn right off Glavna when the road curves left after Radiceva and bear left onto Nješeva when the road splits. Open daily 8am-7pm.)*

SABORNA CRKVA (ORTHODOX CATHEDRAL). The head church of the Serbian Orthodox faith, built from 1837 to 1840, exhibits the sublime interior details that one expects in a national cathedral. The iconostasis was honed by master goldsmiths, and it is highlighted by a backdrop of rich, charcoal-colored marble. Look up to see remarkable ceiling frescoes depicting Biblical events. *(Kneza Sime Markovića 3. ☎ 635 832. Open daily 7am-8pm. No shorts, cell phones, or cameras allowed.)*

BELGRADE ZOO (ЗООЛОШКИ ВРТ; ZOOLOŠKI VRT). Sprawling over six hectares in the northeast corner of Kalemegdan, the Belgrade Zoo's impressive collection of over 2000 animals in their natural habitats will educate and entertain visitors. Don't miss the pythons, Madeleine Albright and Warren Christopher—named during the 1999 NATO bombings. *(Mali Kalemegdan 8. ☎ 624 526; www.beozoovrt.co.yu. Open summer 8am-8:30pm, winter 8am-5pm. 150dn, children 100dn.)*

▥ MUSEUMS

▧ WAR MUSEUM (VOJNI MUZEJ). Located in the flag-crested stucco building that dominates Kalemegdan's Upper Town, this museum is perhaps the best place to learn about Serbian history. A near-obsessive collection of artifacts tells the tale of invasions by Romans, Celts, Turks, Austro-Hungarians, Russians, and Germans. One winding route runs through the entire building. On display are graphic depictions of Ivan the Impaler's favorite torture technique and a life-sized bronze statue of Tito. In the last room, just off the lobby, is a disturbingly recent exhibit from the last decade, including a paralyzing display of an American POW's uniform from the 1999 NATO involvement in Kosovo. *(Kalemegdan bb. ☎ 3343 441. Open Tu-Su 10am-5pm. 30dn, children 15dn. Invaluable 30dn English guide available at entrance.)*

ETHNOGRAPHIC MUSEUM (ETNOGRAFSKI MUZEJ). Three floors of rich anthropological exhibits explaining the cultural nuances of Balkan societies from different regions. The first floor displays traditional 19th- and 20th-century costumes and shows how features identify urban or rural society, social status, ethnicity, and religion. The other two floors focus on economic growth and adaptation in the Balkans. *(Studentski trg 13. ☎3281 888. English labels on all exhibits. Open Tu-F 10am-5pm, Sa 9am-5pm, Su 9am-1pm. 60dn, students 30dn, children under 8 free.)*

MUSEUM OF THE SERBIAN ORTHODOX CHURCH. Enter on Kralja Petra, walk up one flight, turn left, take the first left and another left at the end of the hallway to get to the museum (Muzej Srpske Pravoslavne Crkve). Housed in the Patriarćšija (Patriarchate of the Serbian Orthodox Church), the relics here still breathe incense through the glass cases. The most noteworthy items are the first printed book in Belgrade (a 1552 gospel), the serpent-headed staffs of 17th-century bishops, and the cape of 13th-century Serbian king Milutin. *(Kneza Sime Markovića 6. ☎3282 589. Open M-F 8am-3pm, Sa 9am-noon, Su 11am-1pm. 50dn, students 20dn.)*

PRINCESS LJUBICA'S MANSION. Dating from 1831, the princess's residence (Конак Књегиње Љубце; Konak Knjeginje Ljubice) is in Kosančicev venac, the preserved old section of the city. Erected on the orders of Prince Miloš, the *konak* is typically Balkan with touches of Western Baroque. Inside is an eclectic mix of traditional Bosnian and 19th-century Victorian furnishings. The basement houses a Turkish bath added after the princess lived here. It is used as a concert hall for the BELEF festival. *(Kneza Sime Markovića 8. ☎638 264. Open Tu-F 10am-5pm, Sa-Su 10am-4pm. 50dn, students 20dn. English guide with floor plan 12dn.)*

MUSEUM OF CONTEMPORARY ART (MUZEJ SAVREMENE UMETNOSTI). This five-level, concrete, crystal-shaped building houses an impressive permanent exhibit encompassing the entire 20th century and rotating exhibitions by local artists. Recent guests included painter Petar Dobrović and sculptor Olga Tevrić. *(Ušce Save bb, just across the Sava River in Novi Beograd. Bus #60 stops directly in front. ☎3115 771; www.msub.org.yu. Open Jan.-June and Sept.-Dec. M and W-Su 10am-4pm. Free.)*

◪ ◪ ENTERTAINMENT AND FESTIVALS

Belgrade Youth Cultural Center (Dom Omlandine Beograda), Makedonska 22, just off Trg Republike, brings together Belgrade youth and promotes the arts. The three-story building houses an Internet cafe, concert hall, cinema, and billiards hall. (☎3248 202. Open daily noon-midnight.) The **National Theater** (Narodno Pozorište), Francuska 3, across from Trg Republike, was completed in just two years (1868-1869), and its interior was decorated by Viennese artists. It has opera, ballet, theater, and concerts. (☎620 946, group tickets ☎626 566; www.narodnopozoriste.co.yu. Box office open daily 10am-noon and 5pm-showtime.) Several **cinemas** *(bioskop)* show English movies (200-250dn) with Serbian subtitles. **Tuckwood Cineplex,** Kneza Miloša 7 (☎3236 517), is around the corner from Jelica Hostel.

Belgrade hosts world-class festivals throughout the year. From late February through early March, the Belgrade film festival, **Fest,** offers 10 days packed with screenings of local and international films. (Majke Jerrosime 20. ☎3346 946 or 3346 837; www.fest.org.yu.) In July, locals throng to Lido Beach on **Veliko Ratno Ostrvo,** the large island in the Danube before it joins the Sava, for the **ECHO Festival,** a four-day binge of contemporary music and parties. (DJ 21, Milentija Popovića 9. ☎638 888 697; www.echofest.com. 4-day entry 1500dn.) In July and August, Belgrade welcomes **BELEF,** its summer festival of theater, music, and other fine arts exhibited on open stages throughout the city. (Makedonska 22/I. ☎3221 948; www.belef.org.yu.) In September, **BITEF,** the Belgrade International Theater Festival, arrives. Founded in 1967, it gives promising artists their first opportunity for international exposure. (Terazije 29/I. ☎3243 108; www.bitef.co.yu.)

■ NIGHTLIFE

Stari Grad has clubs and bars with slightly more soul and more history, while the floating clubs of Novi Beograd offer new digs and new tunes.

■ **Beggar's Banquet,** Resavska 24 (☎3346 168). Named for the 1968 Rolling Stones album, this rocking club gives sympathy to devilish travelers in search of rock'n'roll. Monday is a must, when local band Old Spice belts out an amazing hour of Jimi Hendrix covers, followed by other classic rock, midnight-4am. Beer 60-100dn. Tu Rolling Stones, W R&B, Th and Su funk and soul, F-Sa Eurodance. Open daily 9am-4am.

Klub Bus and **Klub Pećina** (Club Bus and Club Cave), Aberdareva 1a and 1b (☎3340 671), around the corner from the main post office. 5-level **Pećina**, carved into a 10m rock wall, has 3 bars that wrap around the ground-level dance floor. **Bus** began as a double-decker English bus. Today, the bus's shell dominates the 3-story club. Both clubs begin filling at midnight. DJs spin Eurodance and house daily. Open 10am-6am.

Underground, Pariska 1a (☎625 681). Built in the walls of Kalemegdan, with an outdoor terrace that catches the breeze off the Sava, it's the place to be on Sa night (and Su morning). One of the swankier late-night hotspots. Beer 100-170dn, mixed drinks 100-120dn. F R&B, Sa house. Open Su-W 10am-4am, Th-Sa 10am-6am.

NOVI SAD (НОВИ САД)   ☎(0)21

Novi Sad (pop. 270,000) is the capital of Vojvodina, the northernmost region of Serbia and Montenegro. Novi Sad feels more like a Austro-Hungarian city than a Turkish one. Its bridges were bombed by NATO in 1999 in an attempt to sever supply lines. Memories of the bombing are fresh in the minds of citizens, but that doesn't affect the enthusiastic welcome and hospitality they offer.

⌐ TRANSPORTATION. The adjacent **bus** and **train stations** are on bul. Jaše Tomia, across from Hotel Novi Sad. Trains go to: **Belgrade** (1½hr., 11 per day, 130dn); **Budapest, HUN** (5hr., 1 per day, 2200dn); **Vienna, AUT** (9hr., 2 per day, 3400dn). Purchase international tickets at window #6 (open daily 7:30am-midnight) and domestic tickets at windows #3-5 (open daily 6:30am-11pm). **Buses** (☎444 021; open daily 4:30am-10pm) go to: **Belgrade** (1½hr., 4 per hr., 250dn); **Budapest, HUN** (5hr., 2 per day, 1080dn); **Ljubljana, SLN** (8hr., 2 per day, 1780dn); **Prague, CZR** (2 per day, 2280dn); **Skopje, MAC** (11½hr., 2 per day, 1070dn); **Vienna, AUT** (8hr., 1 per day, 3080dn). There is **luggage storage** (garderoba) in the train station. (60dn. Open 24hr.) **City buses** #3, 4, 5, 7, 10a, and 10b run to the center from the bus station (15dn on board). Find **local bus maps** (20dn) at the bus station.

▮▮ ORIENTATION AND PRACTICAL INFORMATION. To get to the center from the train station's main entrance, cross bul. Jaše Tomia, and turn left. Walk 300m along the road and turn right when it dead ends. Continue on Kisaćka, which turns into Pasićeva in 500m. When Pasićeva ends, turn right and you'll find yourself in **Trg Slobode** (Liberty Square), the city's main square. Facing the cathedral, turn right and walk 100m to get to the **Komercijalna Banka,** Trg Slobode 4 (☎613 439; open M-Sa 8am-7pm), which **exchanges currency** for 0.5% commission, cashes **traveler's checks** for 2% commission (min. 600dn), and issues Visa **cash advances.** A MC/V **ATM** is outside. Continue to bul. Mihajla Pupina, and turn left to get to the **Tourist Information Center (TIC),** bul. Mihajla Pupina 9. (☎421 811; www.novisad-tourism.com. Open M-F 9am-8pm, Sa 9am-2pm.) It has free guides (with **maps**) to hotels, museums, and cultural programs. There is a **24hr. pharmacy, Tilia Apoteka,** at bul. Oslobodenja 3a, on the corner opposite the train station (☎443 857). The **tele-**

phone office, next to the post office (see below), offers international **fax service** (170dn) and **phone cards.** (Open M-Sa 7am-8pm, Su 8am-3pm.) Exiting the phone office, turn left and left again at the intersection of Jevreska to get to the **Internet Cafe Neobee.net,** Jevreska 1/I. (☎452 754; www.neobee.net. 1dn per min., 30min. minimum. Open M-F 8am-9pm, Sa 9am-4pm.) From the TIC, turn right down the main street to get to the **post office,** Narodnih Heroja 2, 150m up on the left. (☎611 678. Open M-F 7am-7pm, Sa 7am-2pm.) **Western Union** services are available inside, and **Poste Restante** is to the right before the main doors. **Postal Code:** 21101.

⌐⌐ ACCOMMODATIONS AND FOOD. To avoid high-rise rates of high-rise hotels, visitors should try Novi Sad's two great pensions. **Pansion Rimski ❸,** Jovana Cvijića 26, is closer to the bus station and offers low-ceilinged cottage-like rooms and an incredibly helpful staff. (☎443 237 or 333 587; www.rimski.co.yu. Breakfast included. Reception 24hr. Singles 1500dn; doubles 2000dn. V.) **Hotel Fontana ❸,** Nikole Pašica 27, is more centrally located, just outside of Trg Slobode, and offers the same cottage feel with slightly larger rooms above one of Novi Sad's premiere special occasion restaurants. (☎621 779. Breakfast included. Reception 24hr. Singles 1500dn; doubles 2000dn; triples 2500dn.) One of the best restaurants in town is **Bjanki Restoran ❸,** bul. Mihajla Pupina 6. It has plush red carpets, white linens, gold-rimmed glasses, and doting waiters. The food is served with *proja,* heavenly cornbread muffins. (☎615 395. Vegetarian options. Pasta dishes 270-300dn. Grilled meat and fish 280-400dn. Open daily 9am-11pm.) For a less formal dining experience, find **Kuća Mala ❸** (Little House), Laze Telećkog 4. From Trg Slobode, walk straight on the right side of the Catholic cathedral and turn left into the first alley off Zmaj Jovina; it's 50m up on the right. The pizzas (240-340dn) taste as good as they look. (☎422 728. Vegetarian options available. Open daily 8am-1am.) There's also an **open-air market.** Continue down Zmaj Jovina from Trg Slobode and turn right on Dunavska. At the corner with the park, turn left and follow Žarka Vasiljevića to Trg Republike. (Open daily 7am-5pm.)

◙ SIGHTS. The best place to begin a tour of Novi Sad is at its premier tourist attraction, **Petrovardin.** Dating back to Roman times, this section of the city is dominated by the **Petrovardin Fortress.** Built between 1692 and 1780 by the Austrian army, the fortress is on the ruins of a 13th-century Roman fort, which also served as the center of power during Ottoman rule (1526-1686). The **Novi Sad City Museum,** on the upper plateau of the fortress in the military barracks, displays a collection of artistic works from the 18th to 20th centuries and also allows access to the **Underground Military Galleries.** (☎433 145; muzgns@evnet.yu. City Museum open Tu-Su 9am-5pm; Military Galleries Tu-Su 10am-5pm.) Exploring the fortress's 16km of paths, tunnels, and walled gates, visitors will understand why it has been called the "Gibraltar on the Danube." Crossing back over to the city-center side of the Danube, look to the left to see the **Pontonski Ili Most na Barzama** (Barge Bridge), the first provisional bridge built across the river after the 1999 NATO bombings. Continue along bul. Mihajla Pupina, turn right onto Ivalole Ribara, go past the well-groomed **Dunavska Park** on the left, and turn left. The **Vojvodina Museum** (Muzej Vojvodine), Dunavska 35-37, is the first building to your right and the best museum in town. Housed in two buildings, the museum has four permanent exhibits—archaeology, history, ethnology, and modern history. The central treasure is two 4th-century golden Roman helmets, in better condition than those in the Louvre. (☎420 566; museumv@evnet.yu. Open Tu-F 9am-2pm and 6-9pm, Sa-Su 9am-2pm. Excellent English-speaking tours on request. Museum 50dn, students 20dn.) Trg Slobode is dominated by the 1895 neo-Gothic **Katedrala** (Catholic Cathedral), with its eye-catching 76m tower richly decorated with colorful mosaic tiles. Across Trg Slobode is the monumental **Gradska Kuća** (City Hall), constructed in 1896. Walk past City Hall to the left, cross bul. Mihajla Pupina, turn left, and walk through one of the modern archways to reach **Trg Galerija** (Gallery Square), the location of three excellent art galleries. The first on the left is **Galerija Spomen Zbirka Pavla Beljanskog** (Memorial Gallery of Pavle Beljanski), Trg Galerija 2, with Serbian art from the early 20th century. (☎281 85; szpb@evnet.yu. Open W and F-Su 10am-6pm, Th 1-9pm. Free English guide. 50dn, children 15dn.) Next door is **Galerija Matice Srpska** (Matica Srpska Gallery), Trg Galerija 1, displaying Serbian art from the 16th to 20th centuries. (☎421 455; galmats@evnet.yu. Open Tu-Th and Sa 10am-6pm, F noon-8pm. 50dn, students 30dn.) Turn left and cross the street to **Galerije Likovne Umetnosti Poklon Zbirka Rajka Mamuzica** (Modern Art Gallery—Gift of Rakjo Mamuzic), Vase Stajica 1, which exhibits a small but superb collection of Serbian contemporary art. (☎204 67. Open W-Su 9am-5pm. Free.)

🎭🎵 ENTERTAINMENT AND NIGHTLIFE. For a small city, Novi Sad offers a variety of entertainment. In the center of town, off Trg Slobode, the **National Theater** (Srpsko Narodno Pozorište), Trg Pozorišni 1, has a program of drama, music, and dance. (☎451 452 or 613 957; www.snp.org.yu. Box office open M-F 10am-8pm, Sa 10am-3pm.) The **Arena Center Theater** (Repertoar Bioskop), bul. Mihajla Pupina 3, shows English-language movies. (☎615 772. Box office open daily 10am-last showing.) One of the coolest bars in town is **Martha's Pub**, Laze Telećkog 3, across from Kuća Mala. Its motto is "God save the pumpkins." You'll find cheap beer (100dn) served with a plate of apricots. (☎611 038. Open daily 8am-midnight.) For live music, check out the club upstairs at the National Theater, **Klum "Trema,"** the venue of choice for rock and jazz performers. The macabre interior is decorated with props and costumes from past theater performances. (☎451 232. Open M-Sa 10am-2am, Su 5pm-2am.) During the first weekend in July, the Petrovardin fortress closes to visitors and opens nine different music stages for the **Exit Festival** (www.exitfest.org). Two hundred thousand young people invade the city and enjoy four straight days of concerts (8pm-7am).

NIŠ (НИШ) ☎(0)18

Seldom-visited Niš is surrounded by memorials that provide insight into Serbia's war-torn past. During WWII, the Nazis occupied the city, fueling the creation of a well-organized National Liberation movement among the citizenry. In response, the Nazis built a concentration camp at a Red Cross facility and imprisoned about 30,000 activists and their families, Jews, and Roma (gypsies). **Crveni Krst** (Red Cross Concentration Camp) is located next to Beogradska 68. From the *garderoba* exit of the bus station, turn right into Beogradska; Crveni Krst is 750m up on the right. (Open Tu-Sa 9am-4pm, Su 10am-2pm.) Almost 12,000 of the prisoners were executed by firing squads on Bubanj, a hill above the city, and their bodies burned and buried in an attempt to conceal the atrocity. The **Bubanj Monument** is up the hill on the southeast edge of town; three massive concrete fists thrust defiantly skyward behind a relief depicting the executions. Bus #3 stops close by. On foot, walk to the end of the pedestrian zone and continue straight for one block. Turn right on Dušanova and follow it for 200m until it turns into Obilićev Venac, then another 200m until it turns into Vojvode Putnika. Walk 400m up the hill until a parking lot opens to the left, and follow the steps up to the top. Long before the Nazis arrived, the Turks committed their own atrocities in town. In 1809, after the battle on Čegar Hill, in which 4000 Serbs and 10,000 Turks were killed, the Turkish *pasha* ordered the heads of 959 Serbs killed in the battle to be built into a tower on the road to Constantinople. Fewer than 50 skulls are still lodged in the masonry of the **Tower of Skulls** (Челе Кула; Ćela-Kula), Braće Tasković bb, but even time and decay cannot diminish the horrific power. Bus #11 stops in front. On foot, walk past the post office on Voždova and continue on this street for 2km (it turns into Braće Tasković after 800m). Pay at the guard house, and someone will accompany you and unlock the temple that contains it. (☎322 228. Open M 9am-4pm, Tu-Su 8am-8pm. 35dn, students 25dn.) The Turks left a less gruesome monument across the river from the city center; an early 18th-century **fortress** encloses 22 hectares of overgrown parks and fascinating architectural relics. Entering through the **Stambol Gate**, visitors will view an old **Turkish bath** to the left (interior closed to the public), an imposing **amphitheater** to the right, and an **artists' studio** just ahead to the right. Farther up the path to the left is the **Beli-Beg Mosque,** now closed to the public. Check out Niš's Roman legacy at the **Archaeological Museum,** Nikola Pasiča 13, which displays artifacts from a nearby excavation site. Walk down the main pedestrian zone and turn right at the first traffic street. The museum is two blocks up. (☎322 108. Open Tu-Sa 9am-8pm, Su 10am-2pm.)

The **bus station** (☎335 177) sends buses to: **Belgrade** (4hr., 1 per 30min., 435dn); **Sarajevo, BOS** (8hr., 1 per day, 805dn); **Skopje, MAC** (5hr., 10 per day, 455dn); **Sofia, BUL** (3½hr., 2 per day, 505dn). The **train station** (☎511 333) sends trains to: **Belgrade** (4hr., 9 per day, 500dn); **Ljubljana, SLN** (15hr., 1 per day, 2600dn); **Skopje, MAC** (5hr., 3 per day, 700dn); **Sofia, BUL** (6hr., 2 per day, 400dn). The sights are spread out around town, and catching a **city bus** (15dn per ride; day passes 45dn) can be hit or miss (there are no published maps or schedules). **Taxis** cost 40dn plus 20-40dn per km. Try **Maxi Taxi** (☎336 177 or 532 187). Niš straddles the **Nišava River,** which runs east-west through the city. The center of town is just south of the river, and the main street runs north-south from the gates of the **fortress,** north of the river, through the **Oslobodjenje trg,** the main square, south of the river, before becoming a **pedestrian zone** (ul. Pobede; Победе). Voždova runs parallel to the river just south of it, and Nikola Pasiča borders the south end of the pedestrian zone. To reach the center from the bus station, exit through the turnstiles, then turn left out of the driveway. Pass the **open-air market** (open daily 8am-4pm) on your left and turn right over the bridge at the gate of the **fortress.** Exiting the train station, turn left onto Tucovića, the busy street running parallel to the tracks. Follow it 1.5km until it turns into Dušanova, and turn left when you get to the pedestrian zone. The **Tourist Information Center (TIC),** Voždova 7, has a helpful, English-speaking staff that will load you down with several free guides in English to all city sites with **maps.** With your back to McDonald's in the main square, turn left down Voždova. (☎523 118. Open M-F 8am-7pm, Sa 9am-1pm.) **24hr. luggage storage** is available at the *garderoba* in the bus station (40dn) or the train station (60dn); a passport is required. Two blocks past the TIC along Voždova, on the same side of the street, is the **post office,** Takovska 2, with **Western Union** services, **Poste Restante, Telephones,** and **Internet** access. (☎513 193. Open M-Sa 7am-8pm, Su 8am-2pm.) **Postal Code:** 18101.

Food and accommodations can be hard to find. Monstrous **Hotel Ambassador ❸** in the main square, is a corpse of a great hotel with clean sheets and bathrooms. (☎525 511. Breakfast included. Reception 24hr. Singles 1500dn; doubles 2300dn. V.) To get to **Restoran Stara Srbija ❷,** Dušanova bb (☎521 902), walk down Pobede to the huge Kalča cafe and turn left down Kopit Areva (Копит Арева). Pass the cafes and turn right at the end of the street. Waiters in folk costume serve incredible *gulaš teleći-juneći* (veal gulash; 150dn) and other Serbian dishes (180-300dn).

MONTENEGRO (ЦРНА ГОРА)

Montenegro (pop. 680,000), or Crna Gora, sits on the Adriatic, tucked between Bosnia and Herzegovina and Kosovo. The official currency is not the dinar but the euro, and here the Latin script enjoys equal legal status with Cyrillic. Montenegro was recognized as independent at the Congress of Berlin in 1878, but lost its independence during the creation of Yugoslavia. Montenegro nearly became independent again in 2001, but opted to remain united with Serbia.

PODGORICA (ПОДГОРИЦА)   ☎(0)81

Podgorica (pop. 173,000), once Titograd and now the capital of the Montenegrin Republic, does not offer the traveler much more than a transportation hub. The **train station,** in the southeast corner of town (☎633 633), sends trains to: **Bar** (1hr., 17 per day, €8); **Belgrade** (8hr.; 4 per day; €30, sleeping car €38.50); **Niš** (10hr.; 1 per day; €33, sleeping car 43€); **Novi Sad** (9hr.; 1 per day; €34, sleeping car €44). The **bus station** (☎620 430) is in front of the train station. (Open daily 4am-midnight.) Buses run to: **Belgrade** (11hr., 8 per day, €14.50); **Budva** (40min., every hr., €6); **Cetinje** (25min., every hr., €2.50); **Kotor** (45min., every hr., €6); **Niš** (14hr., 4 per day, €13.50); **Novi Sad** (13hr., 3 per day, €16); **Sarajevo, BOS** (9hr., 5 per day, €11.50); **Trebinje, BOS** (3hr., 3 per day, €6). **Luggage storage** is available at both the train station (€1; open 24hr.) and the bus station (€1; open daily 5:30am-10pm).

If you miss your connection, **Hotel Europa ❸,** Orahovačka 16, is a godsend. With your back to the bus station, walk right and take the last left before the train station; you'll see the hotel sign overhead. This immaculate 24-room hotel with A/C seems out of place just 50m from the train tracks. (☎623 444. Breakfast included. Singles €45; doubles €70; 4-person apartment €140.)

BUDVA (БУДВА)   ☎(0)86

Touted in local tourist literature as the "metropolis of Montenegrin tourism," Budva is home to the best beaches on the Montenegrin coast. In and around Budva, the clear, blue-green waters of the Adriatic lap onto a shore of coarse sand and sea-worn pebbles, while rugged, ragged mountains tower overhead. Despite the recent addition of mega dance clubs and fast-food vendors along the boardwalk, Budva is an ancient town: people have lived here for 2500 years. The Old Town, rebuilt after an earthquake in 1979, provides a glimpse of how Budva might have looked 300 years ago, with narrow, winding alleyways and artisans' shops.

🖪🖪 TRANSPORTATION AND PRACTICAL INFORMATION. The **bus station** (☎456 000), on the north side of town, sends buses to: **Belgrade** (11hr., 7 per day, €15-17); **Cetinje** (25min., every hr., €2.50); **Kotor** (25min., every hr., €2.20); **Podgorica** (40min., every hr., €4). Budva's three main streets run parallel to the coast. **Jadranski Put** is the farthest north from the sea, **Mediteranska** runs closer to the ocean on the west side of town, and **Slovanska Obala** is practically on the water and is a pedestrian zone on the east side of town. **Stari Grad** (Old Town) is at the very west end of Slovanska Obala; from the bus station, take a left as you exit and then an immediate right onto Mainski Put. At the stop sign, turn right onto Jadranski Put, then left onto Mediteranska at the streetlights. Follow the road to the post office and turn left down the pedestrian walkway. At the next street, turn right onto Slovanska Obala and follow it to the end. Within the Old Town, the main street is **Njegoševa,** which runs out to the sea from the square near Hotel Mogren.

The **Tourist Information Center (TIC),** Njegoševa 28, provides free **maps** of Stari Grad and surrounding beaches and information on tourism in Montenegro. (☎451 814. Open daily 9am-9pm.) For local **tours** visit **ATA Travel Agency,** Njegoševa 16, which offers bus excursions to Kotor (€30) and Dubrovnik, CRO. (€40. ☎452 000; ata@cg.yu. Open daily 9am-1pm and 5-9pm.) There are three **banks** clustered between Mediteranska and Slovenska Obala, just outside of Stari Grad. **Atlasmont Banka,** Slovenska Obala 13 (☎401 840), offers Visa **cash advances** and **Western Union** services. (Open M-F 8am-8pm, Sa 8am-3pm.) The best rates for cashing **traveler's** checks (1.5%) and **exchanging currency** (US$ 2%; UK£ 1.5%), as well as a **24hr.** (V) **ATM**, are at **Euromarket Banka**, Mediteranska 4. (☎455 106. Open M-F 8:30am-2:30pm, Sa 8:30am-12:30pm.) A **24hr.** (MC) **ATM** is just across the street at **Crnogroska Comercijalna Banka AD**, Mediteranska 7 (☎451 075. Open M-F 8am-4pm, Sa 8am-2pm.) **Luggage storage** (*garderoba*) is at the bus station; ask at the information booth. (€1. Open daily 5:30am-10:30pm.) There is a **pharmacy** (*apoteka*) across the side street from Max Market (Mediteranska 23; see **Food**, p. 792), at 13 Juli 1. (Open M-F 7am-midnight.) **Telephones** are along the beach in the red phone banks. Buy **phone cards** at the post office (€2-5). There is also a **telephone office** inside the post office (see below; open daily 7am-midnight). **Internet cafes** dot the boardwalk. The most convenient is right on the beach, to the left of the walkway that runs from the post office. Look for the huge white tent. (€2 per hr. Open daily 9am-midnight.) The **post office**, Mediteranska 8, has **Poste Restante** and Western Union services. Open M-Sa 7am-8pm. **Postal Code:** 85310.

⚑⌂ ACCOMMODATIONS AND FOOD. Budva's large, overpriced hotels are booked during the summer. Tourist agencies buy up rooms and resell them to tourists, so inquiring at a tourist agency is your best bet. **JAMB Travel Agency ❶**, Mediteranska 23, books hotel rooms (singles €40-50; doubles €60-70) and private rooms (singles €15; doubles €30; 2- to 5-person apartments €40-100). They also sell maps (€2-3.50) and coordinate bus, ferry, and adventure tours. (☎452 992; fax 452 451. English spoken. Open daily July-Aug. 8am-9pm; Sept.-June 8am-3pm.) The best and most convenient *pansion* in town is ◖**Vila Pinki ❷**, Trg Sunca bb, 200m from the bus station, on the right side of Mainski Put on the way to Stari Grad. Pinki's 19 small rooms have nice, new furniture and big bathrooms with sparkling showers. (☎451 344; www.vilapinki.co.yu. Breakfast included. Reception 24hr. July is the high season. Singles high season €25, low season €20; doubles €50/€40; 4-person apartment €100/€80.) The rooms upstairs at **Restoran Fontana ❹**, Slovenska Obala 23, are just 100m from the beach. The bright, airy rooms have balconies, TVs, phones and A/C. (☎452 153; fontana.lekic@cg.yu. Breakfast included. Reception 24hr. July bed in a double €56, doubles €70; low season €40/€50.)

Next door is the well-stocked supermarket, **Max Market**, Mediteranska 23. (☎451 818. Open daily 6am-11pm.) Along the boardwalk, stalls serve *čevap*, hamburgers, pizza, cotton candy, and corn on the cob. Most sit-down restaurants are located along Slovenska Obala or in the Old Town. ◖**Konoba Demižana ❷**, Slovenska Obala 3, just outside Stari Grad, brings guests to a private, shady vineyard. The *gambori na žaru* (grilled shrimp; €11) is excellent. (☎455 028. Entrees €7-11. Open daily noon-midnight.) For an incredible view to match a meal of Mediterranean-style fish dishes (€17-27), reserve a table at **Citadela ❸**, in the Citadel in Stari Grad. The only restaurant actually on the water, Citadela's terrace offers a spectacular view of Sv. Nikola Island and the Adriatic. (☎457 026. Open 5pm-midnight.)

◉⬛ SIGHTS AND ENTERTAINMENT. There are few attractions in town that merit a visit, but the **Citadel Museum** (Citadela Muzej) is one of them. It houses a maritime museum and its walls offer the best view of the Old Town. With your back to the TIC (see **Practical Information**, p. 791), turn right and right again at the dead end and walk diagonally across the square. (☎457 027. Open daily 8am-midnight. €1.) The **Modern Art Gallery**, next to Kineski Restoran Hong Kong (see **Food**, p. 792) displays rotating exhibits of modern artwork by Serbian and Montenegrin artists. (Open M-F 10am-2pm and 7-10pm, Sa 7pm-10pm. Free.)

The annual **Mediterranean Festival**, a music festival with local and international artists, comes to Budva in late June. The **Town Theater Festival** exhibits foreign and local films July 1-Aug. 20. Ask at the TIC for a program of events. The only place in town to go for live contemporary music is **Kraljevski Vrt** (Royal Garden), Mediteranska bb, around the corner from Euromarket Banka. The beer is cheap (0.5L €1.20), and the club is packed when visiting bands rock on the outdoor patio, about every 10 days in summer. (☎ 067 351 155. Open daily 7am-3am.) The **Cinema**, Mediteranska 4, between Euromarket Banka and Kraljevski Vrt, shows current English-language films with Serbian subtitles. (Movies Th-Sa 9pm. €2.)

◀ **BEACHES.** Budva is home to five beaches; pick up a free beach **map** at the TIC (see **Practical Information**, p. 791). The biggest and most popular beach *(plaža)* is **Slovenska Plaža**, just south of Slovenska Obala. It stretches the entire length of the cove. Beyond it, the farthest from Stari Grad, is quieter **Plaža Guvance**. Just outside of Stari Grad in the opposite direction is **Plaža Stari Grad**, with rockier terrain and a long pier crowded with cannonballing kids. The best choice for peace and quiet is **Plaža Mogren**, a two-part beach, just west of Stari Grad. From the Stari Grad beach, follow the winding path along the rock face. Mogren I is 3min. beyond the statue of the ballerina, and Mogren II is another 3min. beyond Mogren I. For the discriminating beach-goer, a 30min. train trip to **Bečići** is a must. The beaches there are sandier, breezier, and more peaceful. The Disney-like wheeled train leaves from outside Atlasmont Banka (see **Practical Information**, p. 791), but weary walkers can flag it down on Slovenska Obala. (30min.; every 30min.; €1.50, children €0.50). On the beaches, sunbathers can rent a chair (€1, with umbrella €2).

▶ **DAYTRIP FROM BUDVA: CETINJE.** Cetinje (Цетиње) was the seat of power in the Montenegro region beginning in 1482, when Ivan Crnojević moved the throne of the Zeta metropolis here. Cetinje is home to four wonderful **municipal museums**, devoted to Montenegrin history and culture. (☎ 86 231 682. All open Apr.-Oct. daily 9am-5pm; Nov.-Mar. M-F 9am-5pm. €2 each, combined ticket €5.) Start exploring at the far left end of Titov trg, at the **Palace of King Nikola I Petrović Njegoš**, now home to the **State Museum**. It has a collection of period furniture from China, England, and Venice, portraits of the Njegoš rulers, and a library of books made from the first printing press in the Balkans. From the State Museum, walk across the square to the left into the **Billiard House Museum** (Biljarda Muzej), the former residence of Petar II Petrović Njegoš, beloved by the Montenegrin people as their most enlightened ruler. Exit left from *Biljarda* and turn left out of the square to the **History Museum** and **Art Museum,** both in the Neoclassical **Vladin Dom** (Government House), Novice Cerović bb (☎ 86 231 682). The History Museum presents artifacts, maps, photos, and weaponry. Upstairs, the Art Museum exhibits paintings and sculpture from artists of former Yugoslavia. From the museum, turn right to walk behind *Biljarda* to the **Cetinje Monastery.** Built in 1701, ravaged in 1712 and 1785, and rebuilt in 1786, the monastery guards medieval icons, religious artifacts, and gold-embroidered vestments. (Open daily 11am-9pm. Free.)

The only choice for a hotel in Cetinje is **Hotel Grand ❸**, Njegoševa 1. Continue past Titov trg to the end of Njegoševa. (☎ 86 231 104. Singles €38.50; doubles €75.) For a **private room ❶**, stop into the house of Petar Marinović, Baje Pivljanina 19, just around the corner from Titov trg. From the bus station, follow directions to Titov trg, but turn right on Baje Pivljanina before Njegoševa. (☎ 86 231 809. Singles €10; doubles €20.) A good cafe in which to lounge after sightseeing is the **Yellow Moon Café**, Njegoševa 33, a local art student hangout. (Open daily 8am-1am.)

Reach **Cetinje** from Budva by taking the **train** (25min., every hr., €2.50), or from **Podgorica,** by taking the **bus** (25min., every hr., €2.50).

SERBIA AND MONTENEGRO

KOTOR (KOTOP)   ☎ (0)82

Kotor, the ancient maritime center of Montenegro, makes a good day trip from Budva, which is 22km southeast. Kotor's most noticeable feature is the stone wall that winds up the rocky cliff. The 16th-century **Church of Our Lady of Health** is halfway up, and the **Fortress of St. John** is at the top. The 1km hike to the top is challenging and is best in the morning, when the path is shaded. It is accessible from the northeast corner of **Stari Grad** (Old Town). Enter Kotor's main square through the second gate on the main road. A huge clock tower dominates the square. The walls contain six Romanesque churches from the 12th and 13th centuries. With your back to the main gate, walk diagonally across the square and take the first right. Follow the road until it opens to the second square to get to the **Cathedral of St. Triphon,** which was built in 1166 and renovated between 1998 and 1999. Inside are 14th-century frescoes. The **treasury** upstairs has the cathedral's gold and silver relics and the original painted stonework. (Open daily. Free; treasury €1.)

Buses run to: **Budva** (25min., every hr., €2.20); **Cetinje** (25min., every hr., €3); **Podgorica** (45min., every hr., €4). From the bus station, walk downhill and bear right at the fork. Old Town will be on the right; skip the first entrance, go past the **market** (open daily 5am-1pm), and turn into the main gate. A **tourist info** kiosk there sells maps and travel guides (€1-3) and provides info on booking private rooms. (Open M-F 9am-1pm and 6-9pm, Sa 8am-2pm.) Just inside the arch of the main gate, on the left, is **Montenegro Express,** Trg od oružja. It books buses, flights, and guided tours of the Montenegrin coast. (☎325 647; fax 325 634. Open M-Sa 8am-1pm and 5-8pm.) To the right of the arch is the **Euromarket Banka,** Trg od oružja. It cashes **traveler's checks** for 1.5% commission, **exchanges currency** (US$ 2% commission, UK£ 1.5%), has a **24hr.** (V) **ATM,** and offers **Western Union** services. (☎323 956; www.euromarket.com. Open M-F 8am-8pm, Sa 8am-4pm.) The **pharmacy, Apoteka Montefarm,** is in the first square you encounter on the way from the main square to the cathedral. (Open M-Sa 7am-8pm, Su 9am-noon.) **IDK Computers,** in the main square, has quick **Internet** connections. (€2 per hr. Open M-Sa 9am-midnight, Su noon-midnight.) A **telephone office** (open daily 7am-9:30pm) is in the Old Town post office (open daily 7:30am-10pm), on the far right wall of the main square, as you look from the gate. The main post office is at Njegoševa 213; **Poste Restante** comes here. From the bus station, walk downhill and bear left at the lights; the post office is 20m on the left. (Open daily 7am-8pm.) **Postal Code:** 85330.

Staying in Kotor is a bargain compared to Budva. **Hotel Vardar ❷,** in the main square, has small rooms and views of the square below. (☎325 086. Breakfast included. Check-out noon. Singles €23; doubles €50.) For a more peaceful stay, **Pension Pana ❶,** Sveti Eustahije 253, 4km from Stari Grad, is perfect. Eat breakfast in a balcony overlooking the bright blue bay. Call for a ride from the bus station. (☎333 306; www.voyage.co.yu. Reception 24hr. €16.80.) Heavy wooden benches and exposed ceiling beams help create a warm ambience at **Knoba Scala Santa ❸,** Pjaca od salate, in the southeast corner of Stari Grad. Try the *Riblije Scala Santa,* an overflowing seafood plate with risotto, for €14. (☎325 765. Meat and seafood dishes €7-15. Open daily 9am-midnight.) At night, **Pizzeria Pronto ❶,** in the alley left of Hotel Vardar, is packed with locals. You can buy a full-sized pizza (€2.50-5) or take out a slice (€1) wrapped in cardboard. (☎322 209. Open daily 8am-2pm and 5pm-midnight.) In Stari Grad, clubs are thumping out techno and Eurodance until 1am. The two most popular are **Caffe Maska** and **Caffe Karampana.** Walk through the alley on the left side of Hotel Vardar. For Maska, take a right at the end; it's the first club on the left and will be mobbed by teenagers. (☎322 897. DJ spins F-Sa. Open daily 8am-1am.) For Karampana, take the first left from the alley and look for the yellow awnings on the right. Karampana caters to a crowd of 20-somethings, with a DJ spinning nightly 9pm-1am. (Open daily 7am-1am.)

SLOVAK REPUBLIC
(SLOVENSKÁ REPUBLIKA)

KORUNY

AUS$1 = 23.26SK	100SK = AUS$4.29
CDN$1 = 24.79SK	100SK = CDN$4.04
EUR€1 = 39.91SK	100SK = EUR€2.50
NZ$1 = 21.26SK	100SK = NZ$4.70
UK£1 = 59.60SK	100SK = UK£1.68
US$1 = 32.63SK	100SK = US$3.07

Known for high mountain peaks, a strong folk culture, and a strong sense of hospitality, the Slovak Republic has been scarred by nomadic invasions, Hungarian domination, and Soviet industrialization. Now, emerged as an independent nation, the republic faces new challenges. Unable to muster the resources necessary for complete modernization and unwilling to return to its agricultural past, the state is characterized by a confused but intriguing mix of conservative traditionalism and easy-going youthfulness. From vibrant and growing Bratislava to tiny villages in the famous Tatras Mountains, the Slovak Republic is gradually adapting to the modern world, but its people continue to celebrate their traditions and heritage.

HISTORY

A NEW SLAV STATE. **Roman occupation** began in AD 6; after the fall of the Roman Empire, the Slovak lands were brutally contested. The **Slavs** won power, defeating the Franks in 631. A new Slav state formed in 833 under **Prince Mojmír** of Moravia. Despite unification, the Slavs could not fend off the Franks and Germans. With the 907 triumph of the Magyars, the state was made part of the Hungarian Kingdom.

FACTS AND FIGURES

OFFICIAL NAME: Slovak Republic

CAPITAL: Bratislava (pop. 430,000)

POPULATION: 5.5 million (86% Slovak, 10% Hungarian, 2% Roma, 2% other)

LANGUAGES: Slovak (official), Hungarian, Ruthenian, Ukranian

CURRENCY: 1 Krona (Sk) = 100 haliery

RELIGIONS: 69% Roman Catholic, 13% No Affiliation, 9% Protestant, 9% other

LAND AREA: 48,845km²

CLIMATE: Temperate

GEOGRAPHY: Mountainous, with lowlands in the soutwest and east

BORDERS: Austria, Czech Republic, Hungary, Poland, Ukraine

ECONOMY: 61% Services, 31% Industry, 8% Agriculture

GAP: US$5,500 per capita

COUNTRY CODE: 421

INTERNATIONAL DIALING PREFIX: 00

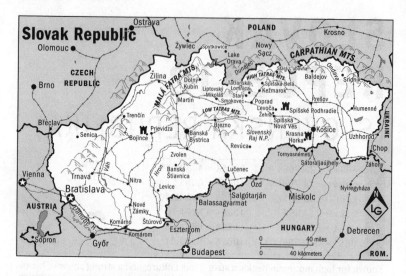

ESCAPING HUNGARY'S GRASP. The Tatar invasions of 1241-43 devastated the already weakened Hungarians, who finally fell to the Ottomans in 1526. The Empire was divided and the Slovak lands fell to the Hapsburgs, who, from their Bratislavan headquarters, wrenched all of Hungary free from Turkish hands. A Slovak nationalist movement emerged in the 18th century; however, Hungarian power continued to grow, thanks to the 1867 establishment of the **Austro-Hungarian Dual Monarchy.** The Hungarian government intensified its Magyarization policies, which only provoked the Slovak nationalist movement. On October 28, 1918, Slovakia, Bohemia, Moravia, and Ruthenia combined to form **Czechoslovakia.**

WORLD WAR II. Abandoned by Britain and France in the **Munich Agreement** of September 1938, the Slovaks clamored for their autonomy and were granted an independent unit within Czechoslovakia. When Hitler occupied Prague, Slovakia withdrew from the federation and established the first independent Slovak Republic, with **Father Jozef Tiso** as head of state. Tiso's decision to ally the new state with Nazi Germany dealt a devastating blow to the Slovaks, and over 70,000 Slovak Jews were sent to concentration camps. A partisan resistance emerged, culminating in August 1944 with the two-month **Slovak National Uprising.**

THE AFTERMATH. After WWII, the Slovaks again became a part of democratic Czechoslovakia. In February 1948, as the Popular Front government fell apart, the communists mounted a coup. Slovak **Alexander Dubček** shook the regime from Moscow's grip. In the 1968 **Prague Spring,** Dubček expanded intellectual discussion in the censored society. Soviet tanks immediately rolled into Prague to crush his "disloyal" government and reinstated totalitarian rule.

CZECHOSLOVAKIA. The communists remained in power until the 1989 **Velvet Revolution** (see p. 225), when Czech dissident **Václav Havel** was elected president; he introduced a pluralistic political system and market economy. Slovak nationalism emerged victorious with a **Declaration of Independence** on January 1, 1993. Coming out of the 1993 **Velvet Divorce** with only 25% of the industrial capacity of former Czechoslovakia, the Slovak Republic has had more trouble adjusting to the post-Eastern Bloc world. Matters were worsened by **Vladimír Mečiar**, who has been thrice elected and removed as prime minister. During his tenure he violated the constitution and failed to reform the economy.

TODAY. Rudolf Schuster became president in May 1999. His election, along with the appointment of Prime Minister **Mikuláš Dzurinda**, brought much-needed economic reforms. Reforms have attracted foreign investment, but inflation rates, though lower than they once were, are still somewhat unstable, and unemployment is fairly high. Many young Slovaks have opted to leave the country for its more prosperous neighbor, the Czech Republic. Racially motivated violence is also a problem, and **minorities**, especially the Roma (gypsies), face substantial discrimination. The Slovak Republic is politically stable, however, and entered the **EU** on May 1, 2004. **Ivan Gašparovic** was elected Slovak prime minister in 2004.

PEOPLE AND CULTURE

LANGUAGE

Closely related to **Czech**, **Slovak** is a complex Slavic language, and a traveler's attempts to speak it are appreciated. Older people will speak a little **Polish**. **English** is common among Bratislava's youth, but **German** is more useful outside the capital. **Russian** is occasionally understood but is sometimes unwelcome. The golden rules of speaking Slovak are to pronounce every letter and stress the first syllable. Accents over vowels lengthen them. See the guidelines for pronouncing Czech (p. 227). For a phrasebook and glossary, see **Glossary: Czech, p. 949.**

FOOD AND DRINK

SLOVAK	❶	❷	❸	❹	❺
FOOD	under 120Sk	121-190Sk	191-270Sk	271-330Sk	over 330Sk

The national dish *bryndzové halušky*, or **bryndza**, a creamy curd made of potato dough and sheep cheese sauce, is usually vegetarian. **Pork** is central to many traditional meals. *Knedliky* (dumplings) often accompany entrees, but it's possible to opt for *zemiaky* (potatoes) instead. For dessert, enjoy *kolačky* (pastry), baked with cheese, jam or poppy seeds, and honey. White **wines** are produced northeast of Bratislava, while *Tokaj* wines (distinct from Hungarian *Tokaji Aszú*) are produced near Košice. Enjoy them at a *vináreň* (wine hall). *Pivo* (beer) is served at a *pivnica* or *piváreň* (tavern). The favorite beer is the slightly bitter *Zlatý Bažant*.

CUSTOMS AND ETIQUETTE

Tipping is common in restaurants, though the rules are ambiguous. Most people round up to a convenient number by refusing change when they pay. **Bargaining** is unacceptable—special offense is taken when foreigners attempt the practice. Most bus and train stations and some restaurants are **non-smoking**, though most Slovaks smoke. Social mores tend to be conservative; it's wise to dress neatly and be polite. Most **museums** close Mondays, and **theaters** take a break in mid-summer.

SLOVAK REPUBLIC

THE ARTS

The nation has struggled to establish a tradition distinct from that of its neighbors. Since the local tongue only emerged as a distinct language in the 18th century, the earliest Slovak novels, like **Ignác Bajza's** *René* (1785), were written in dialects of Czech. A **literary tradition** began after 19th-century linguist **Ľudovít Štúr's** "new" language based on Central Slovak dialects inspired a string of national poets. Foremost among these was **Andrej Sládkovič**, author of the epic *Marína* (1846). **Visual artists** in the 19th century looked abroad for inspiration, but toward the end of the century, painters such as **Mikoláš Aleš** turned their attention back to Slovak soil.

In the wake of WWI, Slovak nationalism and literature matured concurrently. Cosmopolitan influences appeared alongside Romanticism: **Emil Boleslav Lukáč** introduced Symbolism while **Rudolf Fábry** championed Surrealism. The lyric began to give way to novels and short stories. Author **Janko Jesenský** savaged the linchpins of the post-war government in *The Democrats (Demokrati)*. After WWII, the Slovak literati reacted to communist rule. **Ladislav Mnačko** was among the first to criticize Stalin; he did so through his 1967 novel *The Taste of Power*. **Ján Kadar** directed *The Shop on Main Street* (1965), an Academy Award-winning **film.**

The strong artistic tradition continues today. Independence has renewed interest in **folk arts,** and many festivals feature traditional crafts, dance, and music. Classical music is popular, and both the **Bratislava Philharmonic Orchestra** and **Slovak Chamber Orchestra** have international reputations. Despite the current lack of both funding and facilities for filmmaking, Slovak directors **Martin Šulík** and **Štefan Semjan** are well-known internationally.

HOLIDAYS AND FESTIVALS

The nation is home to many of Eastern Europe's most unique celebrations. Banská Bystrica's **Festival of Ghosts and Spirits,** in late spring, is a celebration for the dead. Folk dancers gather near Poprad for the mid-summer **Vychodna Folk Festival.**

NATIONAL HOLIDAYS IN 2005

January 1 Origin of the Slovak Republic	**September 1** Constitution Day
January 6 Epiphany	**September 15** Our Lady of the 7 Sorrows
April 9 Good Friday	**November 1** All Saint's Day
April 11-12 Easter holiday	**November 17** Day of Freedom and Democracy
May 1 May Day	**December 24-26** Christmas
July 5 Sts. Cyril and Methodius Day	
August 29 Anniversary of Slovak National Uprising	

ADDITIONAL RESOURCES

GENERAL HISTORY

A History of Slovakia: The Struggle for Survival, by Stanislav Kirschbaum (1996). This comprehensive history of the Slovak Republic is well-researched, but should be read with caution: the author's views on the Holocaust are highly controversial.

Czechoslovakia: The Short Goodbye, by Abby Innes (2001). An analysis of the causes and consequences of Czechoslovakia's division into the Czech and Slovak Republics.

NONFICTION AND FILM

A History of Slovak Literature, by Peter Petro (1997). An exploration of the Slovak literary tradition with a keen eye to its political and cultural interactions.

The Shop on Main Street, directed by Jan Kadar (1965). An Academy Award-winning film about a Slovak man who befriends a Jewish woman during the Holocaust.

SLOVAK REPUBLIC ESSENTIALS

ENTRANCE REQUIREMENTS

Passport: Required of all travelers.

Visa: Not required for stays up to 90 days for citizens of Australia, Canada, Ireland, New Zealand, the UK, and the US.

Letter of Invitation: Not required for citizens of the Australia, Canada, Ireland, New Zealand, the UK, and the US.

Inoculations Recommended up-to-date on DTaP (diphtheria, tetanus, and pertussis), Hepatitis A, Hepatitis B, MMR (measles, mumps, and rubella), Polio booster, and Typhoid.

Work Permit Required of all foreigners planning to work in the Slovak Republic.

Driving Permit Required of all those planning to drive.

DOCUMENTS AND FORMALITIES

EMBASSIES AND CONSULATES

Embassies of other countries in the Slovak Republic are all in **Bratislava** (see p. 803). The Slovak Republic's embassies and consulates abroad include:

Australia: 47 Culgoa Circuit, O'Malley, **Canberra**, ACT 2606 (☎2 6290 1516; www.slovakemb-aust.org).

Canada: 50 Rideau Ter., Ottawa, ON K1M 2A1 (☎613-749-4442; www.ottowa.mfa.sk).

Ireland: 20 Clyde Rd., Ballsbridge, Dublin 4 (☎1 660 0012; fax 1 660 0008).

UK: 25 Kensington Palace Gardens, London W8 4QY (☎20 7313 6470; www.slovakembassy.co.uk).

US: 3523 International Ct. NW, Washington, D.C. 20008 (☎202-237-1054; www.slovakembassy-us.org).

VISA AND ENTRY INFORMATION

Citizens of Australia, Canada, Ireland, New Zealand, the UK, and the US can visit without a visa for up to 90 days, provided their passports are valid for at least three months after their dates of departure. Those traveling to the Slovak Republic for business, employment, study, or specific program purposes must obtain a temporary residence permit. Contact your embassy for requirements and costs.

GETTING AROUND

Flying to Bratislava may be inconvenient and expensive because many international carriers have no direct flights. Flying to **Vienna, AUT** and taking a bus or train is often much cheaper and takes comparably long. Large **train** stations operate **Wasteels** offices (www.wasteelstravel.ro), which offer discounted fares to major cities for those under 26. **EastPass** is valid in the Slovak Republic, but Eurail is not. *InterCity* or *EuroCity* fast trains cost more. A boxed R on a time-table means a *miestenka* (reservation; 7Sk) is required. There is a fine for board-ing an international train without a reservation. ŽSR is the national rail company. Master schedules, *Cestovný poriadok* (58Sk), are available for sale at info desks and are posted on boards in most stations. Reservations are recommended and often required for *expresný* (express) trains and first-class seats, but are not necessary for *rychlík* (fast), *spešný* (semi-fast), or *osobný* (local) trains. First and second class are relatively comfortable and considered safe. Buy tickets before boarding the train, except in very tiny towns. For up-to-date train info, check **www.zsr.sk.**

In hilly regions, **ČSAD** or **SAD buses** are the best and sometimes only option. Except for very long trips, buy tickets on board. The following schedule foot-notes are important: **X** (crossed hammers) means weekdays only; **a** is Saturdays and Sundays; **b** is Monday through Saturday; **n** is Sunday; and **r** and **k** mean excluding holidays. *"Premava"* means including; *"nepremava"* is except; num-bers following these words indicate dates (day is listed before month). Check **www.sad.sk** for schedules. Rambling wilds and castle ruins inspire many bike tours. **Biking** is especially popular in the Tatras, the foothills in the west, and Šariš. **VKÚ** publishes color bike maps (70-80Sk). *Let's Go* does not recommend **hitchhiking.**

TOURIST SERVICES AND MONEY

The main tourist offices form a loose conglomeration called **Asociácia Informačných Center Slovenska (AICES);** look for the green logo. To find the nearest offices, dial ☎16186 or check www.infoslovak.sk. English is often spoken, and offices can usually make accommodation bookings. **Slovakotourist,** a travel agency, helps arrange transport and accommodations. For more info, try the Slo-vak Tourist Board website at www.sacr.sk. **Credit cards** are not accepted in many Slovak Establishments, but MasterCard and Visa are the most useful. After the 1993 Czech-Slovak split, the Slovak Republic hastily designed its own currency, which is the only legal tender. One hundred **halery** make up one Slovak **koruna (Sk).** Inflation is currently around 8%, so expect price hikes. **Banks** are usually the best and may be the only place to exchange currency. Many **Slovenská Sporiteľňa** offices handle **Visa** cash advances and cash **traveler's checks** for 1% commission (min. 20Sk). **ATMs** can be found everywhere but very small towns. The **Value Added Tax** (VAT) is 19%.

HEALTH AND SAFETY

 EMERGENCY NUMBERS: Police: ☎158 **Fire:** ☎158 **Ambulance:** ☎155

In an emergency, dial ☎112 for English and German Operators. Tap water varies in quality and appearance but is generally safe. *Drogerii* (drugstores) stock Western brands. Bandages are *obväz,* aspirin *aspirena,* tampons *tampony,* and condoms *kondómy.* Petty crime is common; be wary in crowded areas and ensure that passports and valuables are secure. **Women** traveling alone will likely have few problems but may encounter stares. Dress modestly and avoid being out alone at night. **Minorities** with dark skin may encounter discrimination and should exercise caution. Homosexuality is legal but not accepted by all.

ACCOMMODATIONS AND CAMPING

SLOVAK ACCOM.	❶	❷	❸	❹	❺
	under 250Sk	251-500Sk	501-800Sk	801-1000Sk	over 1000Sk

Beware of scams and overpricing. Foreigners may be charged up to twice as much as Slovaks for the same room. It may be difficult to find cheap accommodations in Bratislava before dorms open in July. Reservations are also necessary in Slovenský Raj and the Tatras. In other regions, finding a bed is relatively easy if you call ahead. The tourist office, **SlovakoTourist**, and other agencies can usually help.

There are few **hostels** in the Slovak Republic. Most provide towels and a bar of soap. **Juniorhotels (HI)**, also uncommon, are a bit nicer than usual hostels. **Hotel** prices are dramatically lower outside Bratislava and the Tatras. **Pensions** *(penzióny)* are smaller and less expensive than hotels. **Campgrounds** are common. They are located on the outskirts of most towns and usually rent bungalows to travelers without tents. Camping in **national parks** is illegal. In the mountains, *chaty* (mountain huts/cottages) range from plush quarters around 600Sk per night to friendly bunks with outhouses (about 200Sk.)

KEEPING IN TOUCH

The nation's **mail** service is efficient. Letters abroad take two weeks. Letters to **Europe** cost 11-14Sk, to the **US** 21Sk. Those with no address can receive mail using **Poste Restante**. Address envelopes as follows: Calum (first name) DOCHERTY (LAST NAME), POSTE RESTANTE, Horná 1 (post office address), 97400 (postal code) Banská Bystrica (city), SLOVAK REPUBLIC. Most post offices *(pošta)* have **express mail**. To send packages abroad, go to a *colnice* (customs office).

Recent modernization of the **phone** system means many phone numbers are changing. Try dialing multiple times as the phone system is somewhat unreliable. **Card phones** are common and are usually better than the coin-operated ones. Purchase cards (100-500Sk) at the post office. Be sure to buy the "Global Phone" card if you plan to make international calls. **Internet access** is common in the Slovak Republic, even in smaller towns. Internet cafes usually offer cheap, fast access.

BRATISLAVA ☎ (0)2

One of only two regions in Eastern Europe with living standards above the EU average, the booming Slovak capital surprises those who take the time to discover it. A city that has come to terms with its turbulent past, modern Bratislava (pop. 500,000) manages to integrate old-world charm and chic modernity: villages, vineyards, and castles lace the outskirts, while the streets of the burgeoning downtown district are lined with shops, restaurants, and cafes.

✈ INTERCITY TRANSPORTATION

Flights: M.R. Štefánik International Airport (☎48 57 11 11), 9km northeast of town. To reach the center, take bus #61 (1hr.) to the train station and then take tram #1 to Poštová on Nám. SNP. Most airlines frequent the airport in Vienna, but the following carriers cross the Slovak border: **Austrian Airlines** (☎54 41 16 10; www.ava.com); **ČSA** (☎52 96 10 42; www.czech-airlines.com); **Delta** (☎52 92 09 40; www.delta.com); **LOT** (☎52 96 40 07; www.lot.com); **Lufthansa** (☎52 96 78 15; www.lufthansa.com).

Trains: Bratislava Hlavná Stanica. The **Wasteels** office (☎52 49 93 57; www.wasteels.host.sk) sells discounted international tickets to those under 26. Open M-F 8:30am-4:30pm. MC/V. To: **Banská Bystrica** (3-4½hr., 1 per day, 264-348Sk); **Košice** (5-6hr., 10 per day, 580Sk); **Poprad** (4¾hr., 2 per day, 412Sk); **Žilina** (2¾hr., 6 per day, 380Sk); **Prague, CZR** (4½-5½hr., 3 per day, 750-840Sk); **Warsaw, POL** (8hr., 1 per day, 1456Sk).

Buses: Mlynské nivy 31 (☎55 42 16 67; info 09 84 22 22 22). Check your ticket for the bus number (č. aut.), as several depart from the same stand. **Eurolines** offers a 10% discount for those under 26. To: **Banská Bystrica** (3-4½hr., 21-26 per day, 290-450Sk); **Poprad** (6-7¾hr., 6 per day, 228Sk); **Žilina** (3-4hr., 11-15 per day, 280Sk); **Belgrade, SMN** (12hr., 1 per day, 1200Sk); **Berlin, GER** (12hr., 1 per day, 1200Sk); **Budapest, HUN** (4hr., 1 per day, 550Sk); **Prague, CZR** (4¾hr., 5 per day, 410Sk); **Vienna, AUT** (1½hr., every 1-2hr., 380Sk); **Warsaw, POL** (13hr., 1 per day, 670Sk).

Hydrofoils: Lodná osobná doprava, Fajnorovo nábr. 2 (☎52 96 45 87; www.lod.sk), across from the **Slovak National Museum.** A scenic alternative for Danubian destinations. Open daily 9am-5pm. To: **Devín Castle** (20min., 1 per day, 90Sk); **Budapest, HUN** (4hr.; 2 per day; €68, students €59); **Vienna, AUT** (1¾hr., 1 per day, 480Sk).

■ ORIENTATION

The **Dunaj** (Danube) runs east-west across Bratislava. The city's southern half contains the shopping malls **AuPark** and **Petrzalka.** Four bridges span the Danube; the main one, **Nový Most** (New Bridge), connects **Staromestská,** the commercial district and the entertainment area on the river's southern bank. **Bratislavský Hrad** (Bratislava Castle) towers on a hill to the west, while the city center sits between the river and **Námestie Slovenského Národného Povstania (Nám. SNP;** Slovak National Uprising Square). When entering by train, make sure to get off at **Hlavná Stanica,** the central train station. From the station, take tram #2 to the sixth stop. From the **bus station,** take trolley #202 to the center, or turn right on Mlynské nivy and walk to Dunajská, which leads to **Kamenné nám.** (Stone Square) and the center of town.

☰ LOCAL TRANSPORTATION

Local Transportation: Tram and **bus** tickets (10min. 14Sk, 30min. 16Sk, 1hr. 22Sk) are sold at kiosks or at the orange **automaty** in bus stations. Use an *automat* only if its light is on. Trams and buses run 4am-11pm. **Night buses,** marked with black and orange numbers in the 500s, run midnight-4am; 2 tickets required. Stamp your ticket when you board; fine for riding ticketless 1200Sk. Some kiosks and ticket machines sell **passes** (1-day 80Sk, 2-day 150Sk, 3-day 185Sk, 1wk. 275Sk).

Taxis: BP (☎169 99); **FunTaxi** (☎167 77); **Profi Taxi** (☎162 22).

⚑ PRACTICAL INFORMATION

TOURIST AND FINANCIAL SERVICES

Tourist Office: Bratislavská Informačná Služba (BIS), Klobúčnicka 2 (☎161 86; www.bratislava.sk/bis). Books private rooms and hotels (50Sk fee); sells **maps** (60Sk), **tours** (1000Sk per hr.; max. 19 people), and a **pass** (75Sk) for 4 museums and zoo. Open June-Oct. 15 M-F 8:30am-7pm, Sa-Su 10am-6pm; Oct. 16-May M-F 8am-6pm, Sa 9am-2pm. **Branch** in train station annex open M-F 9am-6pm, Sa-Su 9am-2pm.

Budget Travel: CKM 2000 Travel, Vysoká 32 (☎52 73 10 24; www.ckm.sk). Sells ISICs. Open M-F 9am-6pm, Sa 10am-1pm.

Bratislava

⌂ ACCOMMODATIONS
Downtown Backpacker's Hostel, **4**
Družba, **24**
Orange Hostel, **23**
Pension Gremium, **17**
Slovenská Zdravotnicka Univerzita, **1**
Ubytovacie Zariadenie Zvárač, **2**

🍴 FOOD
Amsterdam Café, **20**
Bagetky, **21**
Black Rose, **10**
Café Študio Music Club, **13**

Chez David, **9**
Diétna Jadelen, **18**
El Diablo, **15**
People's Lounge Café, **19**
Prašná Bašta and Café Kút, **7**
Templars, **22**

🍷 NIGHTLIFE
Dubliner, **16**
Elam Klub, **25**
Jazz Café, **14**
KGB, **5**
Klub Apollon, **3**
Klub Laverna, **12**
Medusa Cocktail Bar, **6**

Embassies: Citizens of **Australia** and **New Zealand** should contact the UK embassy in emergency. **Canadians** should consult their embassy in **Vienna, AUT. Czech Republic,** P.O. Box 208 (☎59 20 33 03; www.czechembassy.org/wwwo/?zu=bratislava). **Hungary,** Sedlárska u. 3 (☎02 59 20 52 00; pozsony@embhung.sk). **Ireland,** Mostová 2 (☎59 30 96 11; mail@ireland-embassy.sk). Open M-F 9am-12:30pm. **Poland,** ul. Zelena 6 (☎54 43 27 44). **UK,** Panská 16 (☎59 98 20 00; www.britishembassy.sk). Visa office open M-F 9-11am. **US,** Hviezdoslavovo nám. 4 (☎54 43 08 61, emergency 09 03 70 36 66; www.usembassy.sk). Open M-F 8am-4:30pm. Visa office open M-F 8-11:30am.

Currency Exchange: Ľudová Banka, Jesenského 2 (☎54 41 89 84; www.luba.sk) cashes AmEx/V **traveler's checks** for 1% commission and offers MC/V **cash advances.** Open M-F 7am-9pm. 24hr. (MC/V) **ATMs** are at the train station and throughout the city center.

LOCAL SERVICES

Luggage Storage: Bus station 20Sk-30Sk. Open M-F 6am-noon, 12:30-7pm, 7:30-10pm; Sa-Su 6am-noon, 12:30-6pm. **Train station** 25Sk-30Sk. Open daily 6am-12am.

English-Language Bookstores: 📖 Eurobooks, Jesenského 5-9 (☎ 90 55 66 973; www.eurobooks.sk). Large selection of English-language literature and guidebooks. Open M-F 8:30am-6:30pm, Sa 9am-1pm. **Interpress Slovakia,** Sedlárska 2 (☎44 87 15 01; interpress@interpress.sk), on the corner with Ventúrska, has foreign periodicals. Open M-F 7am-11pm, Sa 9am-11pm, Su 10am-10pm. MC/V for orders over 300Sk.

EMERGENCY AND COMMUNICATIONS

24hr. Pharmacy: Lekáreň Pod Manderlom, Nám. SNP 20 (☎54 43 29 52). Open M-F 7:30am-7pm, Sa 8am-5pm, Su 9am-5pm. Ring bell after hours for emergency service.

Hospital: Milosrdni Braha, Nám. SNP 10 (☎578 87 11), on the corner of Kolárska and Treskoňova.

Internet Access: Megainet, Šancová 25, has new PCs in a relaxed cafe. 1Sk per min. Open daily 9am-10pm. **Internet Centrum,** Michalská 2, a 6-computer cafe, has a friendly staff, who serve tea (20-30Sk). M-F 10am-9pm 2Sk per min., off-peak 1Sk per min. Open daily 9am-midnight.

Post Office: Nám. SNP 34 (☎59 39 33 30). Offers **fax** service. Open M-F 7am-8pm, Sa 7am-6pm, Su 9am-2pm. **Poste Restante** and phone cards at counters #5-6. Poste restante M-F 7am-8pm, Sa 7am-2pm. **Postal Code:** 81000 Bratislava 1.

Telephones: All over town. Purchase cards (200-400Sk) at the post office and at kiosks.

⌐ ACCOMMODATIONS

Bratislava's rent laws mean most affordable accommodations lie outside the city center. In mid-summer, **university dorms** open as hostels. Buildings can be worn, but rooms are cheap and more central than many hotels. **BIS** (see **Tourist Office,** p. 802) has dorm prices and contacts; they also book comfortable, well-located **private rooms.** (Singles 1000-2000Sk; doubles 1600-1800Sk. Booking fee 50Sk.)

HOSTELS AND DORMS

▨ **Downtown Backpacker's Hostel (HI),** Panenska 31 (☎54 64 11 91; www.backpackers.sk). Chill out under the bust of Lenin in the common room or drink a pint (35Sk) on the comfy, worn sofas. The comfortable rooms, social atmosphere, and proximity to Old Town and the train station make this one of Bratislava's most popular hostels—so book ahead. Internet 2Sk per min. Laundry 100Sk per load. Reception 24hr. Check-out noon. Dorms 600Sk, HI member 530Sk; doubles 900Sk. Tax 15Sk. ❸

Orange Hostel, Dobrovicova 14 (☎902 84 29 00; www.hostelinbratislava.com). Minutes from the main square. Comfy beds and dorm rooms. Internet and laundry included. Reception 24hr. Check-out 10am. Open July 9-Aug. 25. Dorms 550Sk. AmEx/MC/V. ❸

Ubytovacie Zariadenie Zvárač, Pionierska 17 (☎49 24 67 61; www.vuz.sk). Take tram #3 from the train station or #5 or 11 from the center toward Raca-Komisárky to Pionierska. Back-track to the intersection, then turn right. An off-the-beaten-path university dorm that's open year-round with pleasant, shared baths and comfy beds. Shared kitchen and TV. Reception 24hr., ring bell after midnight. Check-in noon. Check-out 10am. Singles 600-800Sk; doubles 850-1050Sk. MC/V. ❸

Slovenská Zdravotnicka Univerzita, Limbová 12 (☎59 37 01 00; www.szu.sk). From the train station take bus #32 or the electric cable bus #204 5 stops to Nemocnica Kramárel. The hotel is to the right. It's far from the city center, but clean and comfortable. Private fridges, new baths, and shared kitchen. Breakfast 35Sk. Reception 24hr. Check-out 11am. Singles 600Sk; doubles 700Sk; apartments 1000-1200Sk. ❸

HOTELS AND PENSIONS

Pension Gremium, Gorkého 11 (☎54 13 10 26; www.gremium.sk), off Hviezdoslavovo nám. Sparkling private showers, cafe, English-speaking receptionists, and exceptional location make this a great find. TV, phone, fridge, and bath in every room ensure a comfortable stay. Shared kitchen. Breakfast €1.70-4. Check-in 2pm. Check-out 11am. Call ahead: the 5 rooms fill in advance. Singles 920Sk; doubles 1350Sk. AmEx/MC/V. ❹

Družba, Botanická 25. Take tram #1 from the train station toward Pri Kríži to Botanická Záhrada. Rooms with shared baths are open July 5-Aug. 25. Nicer rooms with radio, TV, refrigerator, and private bath are open year-round. Laundry 40Sk. **Dorms ❷ ☎** 60 29 92 61; recepcia@sdjdr.uniba.sk. Reception 24hr. 315Sk, students 130Sk. **Hotel ❸ ☎** 65 42 00 65. Reception M-Th 7am-3:30pm, F 7am-1pm. Singles 590Sk; doubles 840Sk.

🖸 FOOD

The nationwide love for good grub at better prices has shaped the food joints that line Bratislava's streets, but changing tastes mean less traditional fare and more international cuisine. If you crave that Slovak touch, feast on *bryndzové halušky* (dumplings with sheep's cheese and bacon). Head to **Tesco Potraviny,** Kamenné nám. 1, for groceries. (Open M-F 8am-9pm, Sa 8am-7pm, Su 9am-7pm. MC/V.) For a late-night snack, head to **Potraviny Nonstop,** nám. 1. Mája 15. (Open 24hr. MC/V.)

TRADITIONAL

🔳 **Black Rose Restaurant,** Jurigovo nám. 1. As you devour everything from delectable Slovak fare to fish and chips, relax outside and observe the locals and tourists on the city street. Entrees 89-250Sk. Open M-F 10am-1am, Sa 11am-1am, Su 11am-midnight. ❷

Templars, Panská 18 (☎ 0903 259 922). It's a quest to finish the hearty portions in this medieval-themed restaurant. The chivalrous staff happily points out wholesome Slovak treats, but the highlight of the menu is the delicious fish dishes. Entrees 80-200Sk. Open M-F 10am-midnight, Sa-Su noon-midnight. ❷

Diétna Jadelen, Laurinská 8. A popular lunchtime destination. Long line means you can run down the menu and choose your treat before you reach the register. The terrific food is worth the wait. English menu. Entrees 55-69Sk. Open M-F 11am-3pm. ❶

INTERNATIONAL

El Diablo, Sedlárska 8 (www.mexicana.cz). A taste of Mexico in a happening restaurant decorated with Wild West memorabilia. El Diablo is the ideal place to down a tequila and delectable fajitas or enchiladas. But beware: after the enormous portions, it might be hard to salsa. Entrees 180-280Sk. Open M-F 9am-3am, Sa-Su 11am-1am. MC/V. ❸

Bagetky, Zelená 8. A relaxed but classy sandwich bar, Bagetky is an ideal escape from the busy main streets and a great place to pick up something to go. Limited seating. Entrees 50-90Sk. Open M-Sa 9:30am-9pm, Su 2-9pm. ❶

Chez David, Zámocká 13 (☎ 54 41 38 24; fax 54 41 26 42). The only kosher restaurant in a quarter steeped in Jewish culture. Delectable cuisine is well-made. Try the chicken matzoh ball soup. Entrees 67-197Sk. Open Su-Th 11:30am-10pm, F 11:30am-3pm. ❷

Prašná Bašta, Zámočnícka 11 (☎ 54 43 49 57; www.prasnabasta.sk). Sit with the sculptures in the alcoves inside or on the leafy terrace outside. The largely 20-something crowd comes here for the generous portions of Slovak cuisine. *Bryndzové halušky* 85Sk. Entrees 85-325Sk. Open daily 11am-11pm. MC/V. ❸

🖸 CAFES

Though not as well-known, Bratislava's burgeoning cafe culture rivals those of its Danube neighbors. Would-be philosophers, eccentric 20-somethings and professionals have caught on to the java craze.

Café Kút, Zámočnícka 11 (☎ 54 43 49 57), connected to Prašná Bašta. The hidden cafe encourages visitors to plop down on the comfortable chairs and let the hours fly by. Live reggae last F of each month. Open M-F 8am-9pm, Sa-Su 4-9pm.

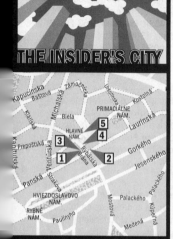

STATUES OF BRATISLAVA

Bratislava's statues have attracted attention for their colorful subject matter. They are a highlight of the capital's downtown streets.

1 **Cumil:** While some say the bronze workman emerging from a sewer is resting, others believe he is looking up the skirts of women passing by.

2 **Paparazzi:** A photographer lurks at the corner of a restaurant that shares his name.

3 **Schöne Naci (Handsome Ignatius):** A local known for his jubilant smile, Ignatius serves as a poignant reminder of the personal tragedies experienced in WWII: his wife died in a in a concentration camp.

4 **Napoleonic Solider:** Possibly weary from Waterloo, the solider leans on a bench and looks at the fountain.

5 **Roland Fountain:** This 1572 fountain is Bratislava's oldest. The man isn't Roland, but Maximillian II, the first Hungarian emperor crowned in the city.

People's Lounge Café, Gorkého 5, near the State Theatre. This fashionable cafe is the place to go to see and be seen. The soothing atmosphere and funky decor reinforce its chic popularity. Open daily 10am-11pm.

Café Štúdio Music Club, Laurinská 11 (☎09 04 95 14 52). The host of weekly jazz performances, the Music Club lives up to its name with flair. Chat with tourists and locals who come for coffee and music, or just sit and soak up the laid-back atmosphere. Espresso 30Sk. Cappuccino 35Sk. Šaris 27-45Sk. Open daily 11am-10pm.

Amsterdam Café, Prepostska 4. This relaxing coffee shop serves some of the best brews and teas in town. Open daily 10am-1pm.

⊙ SIGHTS

DEVÍN CASTLE (HRAD DEVÍN). Perched on an imposing cliff, 9km west of the center, the stunning castle ruins overlook the confluence of the mighty Danube and Morava rivers and their Austrian and Slovak banks. Though the first settlement of the grand hilltop dates back to 5000 BC, its fortress has passed through Celtic, Roman, Slavic, and Hungarian hands, undergoing destruction and reconstruction until Napoleonic armies blew it up in 1809. As communism took hold, Devín Castle grew to symbolize totalitarianism, sheltering sharpshooters who were ordered to fire at anyone trying to cross the "Iron Curtain"—the barbed-wire fence alongside the Morava. These days, visitors can walk unhindered along the paths winding through the rocks and ruins and visit the **museum,** which highlights the castle's history. (Take bus #29 from Nový Most to the last stop. ☎65 73 01 05. Open July-Aug. Tu-F 10am-5pm, Sa-Su 10am-6pm; May-June and Sept.-Oct. Tu-Su 10am-5pm; last admission 30min. before closing. English info available. Museum 60Sk, students 20Sk.)

HVIEZDOSLAVOVO NÁMESTIE. With the feel of a central square, this restored promenade is graced by a sliver of a park and surrounded by stunning 19th-century edifices, including the **Philharmonic building.** Grab a bench, head to the popular restaurants and cafes, or, in summer, frolic in the beautiful and refreshing **fountain.** In the evenings, the square fills with tourists coming to watch ballets and operas at the 1886 **Slovak National Theater** (Slovenské Národné Divadlo), by the square. (From Hlavné nám., follow Rybárska Brana until the road ends at Hviezdoslavovo nám.)

GRASALKOVICOV PALACE (GRASALKOVIČOV PALÁC). Guarded by two unyielding soldiers, the former Hungarian aristocratic residence now houses the offices of the Slovak president. The peaceful **park** remains open to the public and is a popular destination for lovers' strolls, family picnics, and friendly bocce games; it also hosts the occasional modern art display. Enter through the second gate in the back to avoid irking the presidential security staff. *(Hodžovo nám. Gardens open May-Sept. daily 8am-10pm; Oct.-Nov. 10am-7pm; Dec.-Feb. 11am-6pm; Mar.-Apr. 10am-6pm.)*

ST. MICHAEL'S TOWER (MICHALSKÁ VEŽA). The emerald green St. Michael's Tower is the only preserved gateway from the town's medieval fortifications that survived the 1775 demolitions, aimed at unifying suburbs with the inner city. Most tourists rush through the **Museum of Arms and Fortifications**, which exhibits a small display of weapons and army uniforms, to reach the real treat—the amazing view of the castle and surrounding Old Town. *(On Michalská, near Hurbranovo nám. ☎54 43 03 44. Open May-Sept. Tu-F 10am-5pm, Sa-Su 11am-6pm; Oct.-Apr. Tu-Su 9:30am-4:30pm; last admission 30min. before closing. English info available. 40Sk, students 20Sk.)*

ST. MARTIN'S CATHEDRAL (DÓM. SV. MARTINA). When war with the Ottoman empire forced the Hungarian kings to flee Budapest, this Gothic church became their coronation cathedral. Perched precariously atop the cathedral's steeple, a golden replica of St. Stephan's crown reminds church-goers of its glorious past. *(Open M-F 10-11:45am and 2-4:45pm, Sa 10am-noon and 2-4:45pm, Su 2-4:45pm. Masses daily 6:45am, noon, 5pm; Su also 3:45pm.)*

NEW BRIDGE (NOVÝ MOST). Built by the communist government in 1972, Nový Most is one of the most unusual and prominent sights in Bratislava. Its space-age design was intended to balance the antiquated presence of Bratislava Castle. The bridge is suspended from a giant flying saucer, but the viewing tower is now permanently closed. As you walk over the bridge on the way to AuPark, Bratislava's most popular shopping mall, check out the creative graffiti.

🏛 MUSEUMS

PRIMATE'S PALACE (PRIMACIÁLNÝ PALÁC). The pink Baroque palace on Primaciálne nám. houses the city magistrate and a small art gallery with intricate 17th-century tapestries. Watch the dog's head follow you around the room at the "Polovnícke zátišie" painting, or stare at yourself reflecting away to infinity in the **Hall of Mirrors** (Zrkadlová Sieň). The Peace of Pressburg between Austrian Emperor Franz I and Napoleon was signed here in 1805. Indulge in the stately grandeur of the palace rooms as you make your way to the impressive Chapel of St. Ladislaus, which is adorned with beautiful frescoes. *(Primaciálné nám. 1. Buy tickets on 2nd fl. Open Tu-Su 10am-5pm. 40Sk, students free. English pamphlets 40Sk.)*

OLD TOWN HALL (STARÁ RADNICA). The hall's **Town History Museum** has an impressive display on Bratislava's political, commercial, and social development spiced with religious undertones. The chapel, used for the obligatory council prayer, is stunning. The ceiling depicts doomsday. The dungeon chronicles **Feudal Justice** in the 12th and 13th centuries. Showcases include relics from "God trials" and mass-executioner Mestske Kat's famous red hat. *(Hlavné Nám. 1. From Primaciálne nám., head down Kostolná away from the tourist office. ☎59 20 51 30. Open Tu-F 10am-5pm, Sa-Su 11am-6pm. Museum 30Sk, students 10Sk. Ask to borrow an English guidebook.)*

BRATISLAVA CASTLE (BRATISLAVSKÝ HRAD). Visible from the Danube's banks, the four-towered Bratislava Castle is the city's defining landmark. Ruined by a fire in 1811 and finished off by WWII bombings, the castle's current form is largely a communist-era restoration that almost captures its 18th-century glory. Its **Historical Museum** (Historické Muzeum) houses a permanent collection, which focuses on the history of art from clock-making to interior design. Meanwhile, carefully designed temporary exhibits mingle art with Slovak history. The highlight of a castle visit is the spectacular view from the **Crown Tower** (Korunná Veža). Immediately noticeable is the contrast between the castle's medieval architecture and the communist block flats and high-rises, which scar the Danube's opposite bank. *(From underneath Nový Most, climb the stairs to Židovská, then turn left onto the "Castle Stairs" and climb up the steps to the hrad. Castle open daily Apr.-Sept. 9am-8pm; Oct.-Mar. 9am-6pm. Castle free. Museum ☎54 41 14 44; www.snm-hm.sk. Open Tu-Su 9am-5pm; last admission 4:15pm. Museum 60Sk, students 30Sk. 1-1½hr. tour in English 200Sk.)*

SLOVAK NATIONAL GALLERY (SLOVENSKÁ NÁRODNÁ GALÉRIA). Centered on Slovak art from the 15th- to 18th-century, the museum displays a fine collection of Gothic and Baroque sculptures, frescoes, and paintings. Modernist temporary collections contrast with the traditional Realism of the permanent displays. *(Rázusovo nábr. 2. ☎54 43 45 87; www.sng.sk. Open Tu-Su 10am-5:30pm. 80Sk, students 40Sk. English tour guide 1000Sk per hr.)*

MUSEUM OF JEWISH CULTURE (MÚZEUM ŽIDOVSKEJ KULTÚRY). Inside this new museum are exhibits on Jewish culture and valuable fragments of Bratislava's dwindling Jewish population. **Schlossberg,** Jewish quarter, was bulldozed in the 1970s in the name of "progress." *(Židovská 17. ☎54 41 85 07; mestan@snm.sk. Open Su-F 11am-5pm; last admission 4:30pm. 200Sk, students 50Sk, children 20Sk.)*

DANUBIANA-MEULENSTEEN ART MUSEUM. Established in September 2000, the gallery (Múzeum Danubiana-Meulensteen) itself is a piece of modern art. Situated on a small peninsula near the Hungarian border, the museum occupies a small park decorated with sculptures and near the Danube. The remote location prevents over-crowding, leaving patrons to admire tasteful modern-art exhibits at their leisure. *(Take bus #91, which costs 16Sk, from underneath Nový Most for 35min. to the last stop, Cunovo. Head left toward the white tower. Take the path left of the church and go through the woods to the road. Turn right, then hang a left onto the bridge. Continue past Gabčikovo Dam 3.5km to the museum. Alternatively, catch a bus from the main station toward Gabčikovo. 7-10 buses, costing 28Sk, leave per day. Ask the driver to stop at the museum, about 35min. from Bratislava's main station. ☎090 360 55 05; www.danubiana.sk. Open May-Sept. 10am-8pm; Oct.-Apr. 10am-6pm.)*

SLOVAK NATIONAL MUSEUM (SLOVENSKÉ NÁRODNÉ MÚZEUM). An archaeological exposition outlines human progress and its place in the animal world. *(Vajanského nábr. 2. ☎59 34 91 11; www.snm.sk. Open Tu-Su 9am-5pm. 20Sk, students 10Sk.)*

🎵 🎆 ENTERTAINMENT AND FESTIVALS

The monthly *Kam v Bratislave*, available at BIS (p. 802), has film, concert, and theater schedules. In summer, BIS has *Kultúrne Leto*, an all-inclusive calendar. **Slovenské Národné Divadlo** (Slovak National Theater), Hviezdoslavovo nám. 1, puts on ballets and operas that draw crowds from afar. (☎54 43 30 83; www.snd.sk. Box office open M-F 8am-5:30pm, Sa 9am-1pm. Closed July-Aug. 100-200Sk.) The **Slovenská Filharmónia** (Slovak Philharmonic), Medená 3, has two to three performances per week in fall and winter. The box office, Palackého 2, is around the corner. (☎54 43 33 51; www.filharm.sk. Open M-Tu and Th-F 1-7pm, W 8am-2pm. 100-200Sk.) Festivities usually focus on guest performances that draw large crowds; posters litter streets, billboards, and walls. The annual **Music Festival,** late September to early October, brings international performers to Bratislava to play everything from pop to house. It is followed almost immediately by the **Bratislava Jazz Days** festival. For **shopping,** try **AuPark,** next to the Nový Most Bridge.

▣ NIGHTLIFE

By day, Old Town bustles with tourists shopping and devouring *bryndza*. By night, it's filled with young people warming up for a good time on the town. Nightlife in Bratislava is relatively subdued, but there is no shortage of places to party. For info on **GLBT nightlife,** pick up a copy of *Atribut* at any kiosk.

▣ **Klub Laverna,** Laurinská 19. Expect a floor packed with a young crowd at this dance-centric nightspot. A slide transports drunken clubbers from the upper level to the floor. Cover 100Sk. Open daily 8pm-6am.

Medusa Cocktail Bar, Michalská 89, just after St. Michael's Tower. This happening cocktail bar defines chic. Posh decor and huge selection of delicious drinks (109-139Sk). Open M-Th 11am-1am, Sa 11am-3am, Su 11am-midnight.

Krčma Gurmánov Bratislavy (KGB), Obchodná 52 (☎52 73 12 79; www.kgb.sk). Stashed in a red-brick basement, KGB is where hip locals go to enjoy a healthy mix of rock and beer (20-60Sk) under pictures of Lenin. Kitchen closes 11:30pm. Open M-Th 11am-1:30am, F 11am-3:30am, Sa 3:30pm-1:30am, Su 3:30-11pm.

Jazz Café, Ventúrska 5 (☎54 43 46 61; www.jazz-cafe.sk), in Old Town. Praised mixed drinks and live jazz draw tourists and local sophisticates. Beer 40Sk. Jazz Th-Sa 9pm-1am. Cafe open daily 10am-2am; club open daily 2pm-2am. MC/V.

Klub Apollon, Panenská 24 (☎54 41 93 43; www.apollon-gay-club.sk). Go through the archway and turn left. This gay pub entertains laid-back, chatting crowds until the disco starts. Plays everything from Europop to trance. Beer 45Sk. Disco W-Sa 10pm. Cover F-Sa 50Sk. Open M-Tu and Th 6pm-3am, W and F-Sa 6pm-5am, Su 6pm-1am.

Elam Klub, Staré Grunty 53 (☎65 42 63 04; www.elam.sk). Take bus #31 or 39 from Nám. 1. Mája to the last stop. Go up the stairs and head left into the building. Elam is next door to Club 39 and near other student clubs. Good music and a lively atmosphere keep the university crowd dancing until dawn on the huge floor. Liveliest during term time. Drinks 30-100Sk. Cover 39-100Sk. Open daily 9pm-6am.

Dubliner, Sedlárska 6 (☎54 41 07 06; www.irishpub.sk). Bratislava's original Irish pub is hugely popular after dinner, when adult patrons spill onto the street. Guinness 95Sk. Occasional live music. Karaoke Sa 9pm-3am. Open M-Sa 9am-3am, Su 11am-1am.

CENTRAL SLOVAK REPUBLIC

It may be tempting to speed through the Central Slovak Republic on the way to the Tatras, but think twice. The area, rarely visited by tourists, has well-preserved folk traditions and endless opportunities to hike and bike.

BANSKÁ BYSTRICA   ☎(0)88

Banská Bystrica (BAHN-skah bis-TREE-tsah; pop. 84,280) has a perfect mix of cosmopolitan flair and rural scenery. The lively Old Town is packed with terraced cafes, shops, and folk art boutiques, while its outskirts are covered with forested hills that serve as an ideal playground for bikers, hikers, and tourists.

▣ TRANSPORTATION. Transportation to Banská Bystrice is often scarce. The **train** and **bus stations** lie next to each other on c. K. Smrečine. **Trains** (☎436 14 73) run to: **Bratislava** (3-4hr., 2 per day, 500Sk); **Košice** (4-5hr., 1 per day, 264Sk); **Budapest, HUN** (5-7hr., 1 per day, 800Sk). **Buses** (☎422 22 22) go to: **Bratislava** (3½-4hr., 15-

30 per day, 260-280Sk); **Košice** (4-5hr., 3-5 per day, 260Sk); **Liptovsky-Mikuláš** (2hr., 4 per day, 110Sk); **Prešov** (5hr., 5 per day, 250Sk); **Žilina** (2hr., 6-7 per day, 120Sk). For cabs, try **Fun Taxi** (☎167 77) or **BB Taxi** (☎411 57 57).

■ 🗹 ORIENTATION AND PRACTICAL INFORMATION. The **Hron River** cradles the city's southeastern edge. The train and bus stations lie east of the square, and suburban neighborhoods sprawl in all directions. To reach the center, head out behind the bus station and cross **Cesta K. Smrečine** into the gardens. Take the pedestrian underpass under the highway and continue along **Kukučinova**. A left on Horná at the bookstore brings you to **Námestí SNP**, the town center (15min.). Or, hop on the bus and get off at **Nám. Š. Moyzesa** (5min., 12Sk).

Kultúrne a Informačné Stredisko (KIS), Nám. Š. Moyzesa 26, between Horná and Nám. SNP, has **maps** (18Sk) and accommodations info. The staff organizes city tours and books **private rooms**. (☎415 22 72; www.banskabystrica.sk. Open May 15-Sept. 15 M-F 8am-7pm, Sa 9am-1pm; Sept. 16-May 14 9am-5pm.) **Exchange currency** and cash **traveler's checks** for 1% commission at **OTP Bank**, Nám. SNP 15. (☎430 12 47. Open 8am-6pm, Sa 8am-1pm.) MC/V **ATMs** pervade the town; there is one outside the tourist office. **Luggage storage** is available at the train station. (Open daily 7am-7pm. 10Sk, heavy bags 40Sk, bicycles 30Sk.) **Interpress Slovakia**, Dolná 19, sells English-language newspapers. (☎412 30 75. Open M-F 7am-6pm, Sa 8am-1pm.) **British Council**, Dolna 7, offers a small variety of British newspapers for free. (Open Tu and Th 12:30-6:30pm, W 10am-6:30pm, F 12:30-5pm, Sa 9am-1pm.) **Albion Books**, Dolná 23, sells English-language classics. (☎412 30 03; www.albion-books.sk. Open July-Aug. M-F 9am-4pm, Sa 9am-noon; Sept.-June M-F 8am-5pm, Sa 9:30am-noon.) The **pharmacy, Lekaren Nádej**, Dolná 5, posts open pharmacies after closing time. (☎412 62 03. Open M-F 7:30am-5:30pm, Sa 8am-noon.) Find **Internet access** at **Internet Centrum**, Nám. SNP 3., through the arch. (☎415 65 97. 20Sk per hr. Save your coupon; it is valid for a week. Open M-F 9am-10pm, Sa-Su 1-10pm.) There are phonecard-operated **phones** outside the **post office**, Horná 1, across from the **TIC. Poste Restante** is upstairs at window #24. Packages are at window #1. (☎432 62 11. Open M-F 8am-7pm, Sa 8am-noon.) **Postal Code:** 97401.

🛏 🍴 ACCOMMODATIONS AND FOOD. KIS (see **Orientation and Practical Information**, p. 810) books **private rooms** (singles 300-350Sk; doubles 500-600Sk) for 25Sk and has accommodations info on hotels, hostels, and dorms. **Montravel**, nám. Š. Moyzesa 25, books rooms in student dorms for a fee. (☎415 37 95; www.mon-travel.sk. Open M-F 9am-5pm. Dorms 250-400Sk.) **Hotel Milvar ❷**, Školská 9, rents spartan, hostel-style rooms with clean baths. Follow the directions to Domov Mládeže (see p. 810), but turn right on J.G. Tajovského and follow it under the highway. Take the first right and the first left on Školská. Alternatively, hop on bus #3 or 34, which run to J.G. Tajovského. Be careful at night, as the street is poorly lit. (☎413 87 73; www.milvar.host.sk. Reception 24hr. Check-in 2pm. Check-out 10am. Rooms 220Sk.) Popular **Študencké Domovy 4 ❶**, Trieda SNP 53, is located near the center and stations. From the stations, head straight on ul. 29 Augusta and go right on Trieda SNP. Walk straight; the dorm is on the left. Rooms are simple but pleasant and full of light. (☎471 15 16. Check-out noon. Open July-Aug. 2- to 3-bed rooms 150Sk, with ISIC 100Sk.) The older, comfortable rooms of **Domov Mládeže ❶**, J.G. Tajovského 30, are popular with youth groups. From Nám. SNP, turn right through the arch to Horná Strieborná and follow the road as it angles left to become Strieborná. Once over the river, take a left on J.G. Tajovského and continue until you spot the dorm on your right (20min.). Alternatively, take train #1 or bus #34 from the train station and get off at "Tajovského sous." (☎434 15 10. Reception 24hr. Check-out noon. Call ahead. Dorm 200-250Sk.)

In this landlocked country, locals and tourists can still find excellent seafood at **Restaurant Fishman ❸**, ul. Limbová 7, just before the main square reaches Dolna. The fountain and tasteful decor downstairs are matched with an aquarium full of tropical beauties. (Entrees 80-200Sk. Open M-Sa 10am-11pm, Su 11am-10pm.) **Rieltivora Pivnica ❶**, Lazovná 18 off Nám. SNP, serves up traditional Slovak food like its famed *bryndza*. (☎415 43 00. Entrees 50-140Sk. Open M-Sa 11am-10pm.) If you just cannot decide what to eat, sit down at **Červený Rak ❷**, Nám. SNP 13, which boasts an extensive menu. Enjoy the hustle and bustle of the main square as you sit back in the canopied outdoor eating area. (☎415 38 82; www.cervenyrak.sk. Entrees 89-160Sk. Open M-Th 10am-10:30pm, F 10am-midnight, Sa noon-11pm.) Look for groceries at **Prior**, on the corner of Horná and c. K. Smrečine. (Open M-F 8am-7pm, Sa 8am-3pm. MC/V.) You can also head to **Billa Supermarket**, just across from the bus station. (Open Su-Th 8am-8pm, F 8am-9pm, Sa 7am-9pm. MC/V.) Get fresh veggies and fruits at the **open-air market** in the courtyard of the Prior building.

◘ SIGHTS. A cluster of the town's oldest buildings stands on Nám. Š. Moyzesa. The restored **Pretórium**, now the **Štátna Galéria**, Nám. Š. Moyzesa 25, hosts a new Slovak avant-garde exhibit every two months. (☎412 48 64. Open Tu-F 10am-5pm, Sa-Su 10am-4pm. Ask for the free English pamphlet. 40Sk, students 10Sk.) Behind the Galéria is the Romanesque **Church of the Virgin Mary** (Kostol Panny Márie). Breathtaking frescoes adorn the Baroque ceiling, but the real attraction is the Gothic altarpiece, by Master Pavol of Levoča, which is housed in the church's **Chapel of St. Barbora.** (See **Levoča**, p. 817. Church only open for services. Services Su 7, 8:30, 11am, 4:30pm). Walk toward the square from the Galéria to find the **Museum of Central Slovakia** (Stredoslovenské Múzeum), Nám. SNP 4. Housed in the historic **Thurzov Dom,** the sparse collection leads you through the Stone Age to the Gothic and Renaissance periods and showcases noteworthy furniture and a folk costume exhibit. (☎412 58 97. Open June 15-Sept. 15 Su-F 9am-6pm; Sept. 16-June 14 Su-F 8am-4pm. 20Sk, students 10Sk.) The restored 18th-century villa of local artist Dominik Skutecký (1848-1921), **Skuteckého Dom,** Horná 55, now displays his work. Head left from the tourist office on Horná to reach it. A dogged Realist in the age of Impressionism, Skutecký focused on social and folk scenes, but the house is also graced with many beautiful portraits. (☎412 54 50. Open Tu-Su 10am-4pm. 40Sk, students 10Sk.) View miles of countryside and urban bustle from the city's enormous yellow **clock tower,** Nám. SNP 29. (Open daily 10am-6pm. 20Sk. Cameras 50Sk.) Turn right out of the tourist office and take the immediate left onto Kapitulská to reach the ◪**Museum of the Slovak National Uprising** (Múzeum Slovenského Národného Povstania), which chronicles the country's struggles during WWII. Banská Bystrica was home to the underground resistance after the Nazis breached the Slovak border on August 29, 1944 (see **History,** p. 795). Stark photographs show the grim reality of the Nazi occupation. Exposition #34 introduces the faces of four men who managed to escape Auschwitz on April 7, 1944 and lived to write about it. (☎412 32 58; www.muzeumsnp.sk. Open May-Sept. Tu-Su 9am-6pm; Oct.-Apr. Tu-Su 9am-4pm. 50Sk, students 10Sk. 1hr. tours in English by request, 200Sk.)

⚠ OUTDOOR ACTIVITIES. Banská Bystrica offers ample outdoor adventures, including biking, horseback riding, and bathing in geysers. Visit the tourist office for current info or purchase the handy guide to Banská Bystrica and its environs. **Mr. Spedik-Jahn,** a travel agent in the village Tajov, arranges six-day **whitewater rafting** trips on the Hron River. (☎419 76 03; www.spedik.host.sk. 2700Sk, including accommodation.) To get to Tajov, hop on a city bus from the station (20-25min., 15 per day, 25Sk). Popular hiking trails run from **Donovaly,** the ski area accessible by bus (40min., 50Sk). The trails, few in number, wind through tree-lined valleys and hills. Their tranquil beauty is hardly as dramatic as that of the Tatras, yet still manages to ensure their popularity. **Pegas Škola Paragliding,** Mistriky 230 (☎419 98 89), will teach you to fly for around 3500Sk. Call a week in advance. **Pony Farma-Suchý Urch,** Jazdiareň Uhlisko (☎410 48 58), offers horseback riding for all levels.

▣ **NIGHTLIFE.** Banska's nightlife draws tourists and locals to the Old Town each night. The poster pub for timeless grunge, the ▣**Irish Pub,** Horná 45, draws rebels of all ages, from angsty teens to Rolling Stones-fans. (0.5L Pilsner 25Sk, Guinness 35Sk. Live rock Sa 8pm. Open M-F 11am-2am, Sa 2pm-2am.) Escape at ▣**Jazz Club U Marcela,** Dolná 20, a popular local stop with a laid-back crowd. (Beer 20Sk. Parties Sa 10pm-2am. Open M-F 10am-2am, Sa-Su 2pm-2am.) Another great refuge for relaxation and a good pint is **Kapitol Pub,** Kapitulska 10. The lively courtyard beckons locals and tourists alike who unwind and chat the night away. (Beer 22-35Sk. Open M-Th 10am-2am, F 10am-4am, Sa noon-4am, Su 6pm-midnight.) Banská Bystrica's dance central, **Arcade,** Nám. ŠMP 5, draws a more mature crowd looking to let loose and get down. (Cover 40Sk. 18+. Open M-Tu and Th 1pm-midnight, W and F 1pm-4am, Sa 6pm-4am.) If you're starved for hip-hop, join a younger crowd at the **Kaktus Bar,** Horná 12, at 9pm on Thursdays. (Beer 18-20Sk. Open daily 7pm-6am.) To escape the bar scene, watch a Hollywood film at **Kino Korzo,** in Dome Kultúry on c. K. Smrečine. (☎415 24 66. Open 30min. before showtime. M 60Sk, Tu-Su 10-75Sk. Shows daily 6:30 and 9pm.)

▶ DAYTRIP FROM BANSKÀ BYSTRICA

BONJINCE ☎(0)46

Take the bus to Prievidza from Banská Bystrica (1-2hr., 7-8 per day, 106-110Sk). With the station to your right, walk to the stop on the right. Take bus #3 to the "Bojnice" stop and get off at the narrow park next to a stretch of small shops and restaurants (7min., 12Sk). Follow the departing bus to the castle gates. ☎543 06 24; www.bojnicecastle.sk. Open May-Sept. Tu-Sa 9am-5pm; Oct.-Apr. Tu-Su 10am-3pm. Mandatory 1¼hr. tours; call ahead for tours in English, min. 10 people. Day tours: Grand Tour 130Sk, students with ISIC or Euro26 70Sk; Little Tour 80Sk/50Sk. Night tours: July-Aug. F-Sa 9 and 9:30pm, otherwise call 3 days ahead. Night tours 150Sk, students 80Sk. Cameras 100Sk, video 150Sk.

Many Slovak castles survive as only ruins or reconstructions, but ▣**Bonjince Castle** remains a real-life fairytale (*sans* dragon) that revels in splendor and opulence. Originally a 12th-century wooden fortress for a Benedictine monastery, the castle was later bestowed upon loyal lords. Its last noble occupant, Jan Pálffy, spent his life (1829-1908) renovating the palace in the Romantic style. As a result, the castle evokes France's majestic Loire Valley more than rural Slovakia. See the imprint of Pálffy's efforts through the guided tour, which traverses galleries, gardens, hunting rooms, and bedrooms; mounts a citadel; descends into a crypt; and leaves visitors breathless in the depths of a 26m underground natural **cave.** The most memorable stops are the intricate **Oriental Saloon,** which boasts magnificent 17th-century Turkish architecture; the **Music Room,** where cherubs stare down from the golden ceiling; and the **chapel,** where magnificent frescoes adorn the walls. Although you can take a Little Tour, the Grand Tour is worth the extra cash, as it visits the chapel and unique bedrooms and state rooms that the Little Tour passes up. The fairytale is complete with mannequins and guides dressed in medieval attire. Ghost enthusiasts can attend the nightly tour or visit the castle in early May for the **International Festival of Ghosts and Spirits** (180Sk, students 90Sk), when evening festivities include a candlelight ceremony for the Rising of the Dead. The castle hosts six other festivals, including the **Days of Knight,** the second weekend in September, which features sword fighting. (110Sk, students with ISIC 60Sk.)

MALÁ FATRA MOUNTAINS

The Malá Fatra range is an exhilarating medley of alpine meadows, steep ravines, and limestone peaks. The mountains boast hikes for all abilities. Some travelers visit for the day, while others stay overnight in *chaty* (mountain huts).

ŽILINA   ☎(0)41

Žilina (ZHI-li-na; pop. 87,000), the country's third-largest city, is a convenient headquarters for exploring the nearby Malá Fatras. The picturesque setting and fountain-rich town square make it an inviting place for an extended, hiking-filled stay.

Across from the train station, **Hotel Polom ❷**, Hviezdoslava 22, has comfortable rooms with private showers. (☎562 11 51; fax 562 17 43. Reception 24hr. Check-in and check-out noon. Budget singles 390Sk; doubles 590Sk; triples 890Sk. Renovated singles with private bath and TV M-F 820Sk, Sa-Su 700Sk; doubles 1200Sk/1083Sk; triples 1500Sk/1383Sk. MC/V.) **Block V** at **Domov Mládeže ❶**, Hlinská ul. 1, offers clean, comfy beds in small triples and doubles, while **Block III** sports new bunk-beds in remodeled rooms. Take tram #4 or 7 from the train station to "Billa." Dorms have kitchens and shared showers with locks but no curtains. (Block III ☎723 39 12, Block V 723 39 14. Reception 24hr. Check-out 10am. July-Aug. reserve in advance. Singles 200Sk; doubles 400Sk; triples 600Sk.) Buy the freshest and cheapest vegetables at the enormous **Tesco** in nám. Andreja Hlinku. (Open M-F 8am-8pm, Sa 8am-4pm, Su 8am-1pm. MC/V.) While tourists eat in the square, locals prefer the calmer **Restaurácia a Vináreň na Bráne ❶**, Botová 16, which serves some of the town's finest Slovak food. (Restaurant entrees 48-79Sk. Tavern entrees 79-120Sk. Open M-F 8:30am-10pm, Sa 9am-10pm.) Visit the popular **Bageteria ❶**, Hlinkovo nám. 5, for simple, wholesome sandwiches. (Open M-Sa 7am-9pm, Su 9am-9pm).

The **train station,** ul. Hviezdoslava 7, is northeast of center. (☎562 22 26. MC/V.) Trains run to: **Bratislava** (2-3hr., 18 per day, 300Sk); **Košice** (3¼hr., 11 per day, 268Sk); **Poprad** (2hr., 13 per day, 180Sk); **Budapest, HUN** (4¼-7hr., 2 per day, 1360Sk); **Prague, CZR** (7hr., 5 per day, 860Sk). The **bus station,** Jana Milca 23, is on the corner of ul. Hviezdoslava and ul. 1. Mája. (☎565 19 41.) Buses run to: **Banská Bystrica** (2hr., 10 per day, 148Sk); **Bratislava** (3-4hr., 9-13 per day, 246Sk); **Liptovský Mikuláš** (1¾-2hr., 15 per day, 116Sk); **Prague, CZR** (6-7hr., 12 per day, 550Sk). For **local transportation,** buy train or bus tickets at kiosks or orange vending machines.

The bus and train stations lie northeast of the center; budget accommodations are in the southwest. From the bus station, go left on **Hviezdoslava** to reach the train station. Take the underpass to **ul. Narodná**, which runs into **nám. Andreja Hlinku,** the new town square. Cross the square and take the stairs to the right of the church to **Farská ul.,** which opens onto **Mariánske nám.,** the lively and touristy Old Town square. The tourist office **Selinan,** Jantárova 4, is on a street parallel to Farská, on the left. Buy hiking (89Sk) or town (20-89Sk) **maps** or ask about accommodations in Žilina or nearby Terhová, where many beautiful hikes start. (☎562 07 89; www.selinan.sk. Open M-F 8am-6pm, Sa 8am-noon.) **Exchange currency** and cash AmEx/MC/V **traveler's checks** for 1% commission at **OTP Banka,** Sládkovičova 9. (☎562 09 40. Open M-F 8am-6pm, Sa 8am-1pm.) **Luggage storage** is in the underpass in front of the train station. (24Sk, bags over 15kg 35Sk. Open 24hr.) **Lekáreň na Bráne,** ul. Bottova 7, posts hours of nearby pharmacies. With your back to the church in Mariánske nám., go to the far right corner and take the street to your right, ul. Bottova. (Open M-F 8:30am-noon and 12:30-5pm.) Public **telephones** are at the post office. Calling-card phones are in the underpass between the train station and ul. Narodná. Try the ▓**Internet Cafe,** Kálov 3. (8Sk per 15min. Open Su-Th 9am-10pm, F-Sa 9am-midnight.) The **post office,** Sládkovičova 14, has phone cards and **Poste Restante.** Facing the church in nám. A. Hlinku, go right and veer right with the street. (☎512 62 59. **Poste Restante** M-F 8am-noon and 12:30-6pm. Open M-F 8am-7pm, Sa 8-11am.)

HIKING IN THE MALÁ FATRAS

The wind is cold and gusty, so bring gloves. Pack food and be prepared for fickle rain that turns dirt roads into mudslides. Check conditions at the tourist office. **Emergency rescue** (☎569 52 32) is available. Trail-markings are generally accurate but not perfectly maintained. VKÚ **map** #110, sold at tourist agencies, is vital.

MOUNT VEĽKÝ ROZSUTEC. Though not the highest mountain in the range, steep **Veľký Rozsutec** (1609m) boasts some of the most exciting and challenging slopes. The **Štefanová** trail is possibly the best hike in the region. Though ladders and chains make several vertical ascents possible, the thrilling hike is tricky and should not be attempted by amateurs. Take the Terchova-Vrátna bus from platform #10 in Žilina to Štefanová (45-60min., 43Sk) and follow the trail to **Sedlo Vrochpodžiar** (30min.). Take a right on the blue trail to climb a slippery mass of tumbling waterfalls and rapids known as **Horne Diery** (Upper Hole). Continue on the blue trail to **Sedlo Medzirozsutce** (1½hr.) Take a right on the red trail to reach the **summit** (1¼hr.). To descend, follow the red trail to its intersection with the green trail near **Sedlo Medziholie** (1hr.). Turn right onto the rocky green trail to reach **Štefanová** (1¼hr.; total trip 5½hr.). For a less vigorous hike, follow the blue trail from Sedlo Medzirozsutce around the summit to its intersection with the green trail near Sedlo Medziholie (1hr.). A right here leads across a field and back to Štefanová.

MOUNT VEĽKÝ KRIVÁN. At 1709m, **Veľký Kriván** is the highest peak in the range. Take the bus from platform #10 in Žilina to **Terchová, Vrátna** (43Sk), and get off at Chata Vrátna at the end of the road. The taxing hike begins with the green trail, which heads straight up to **Snilovské Sedlo** (1¾hr.); from there, turn right on the red trail to reach the **summit** (3hr. total). To save your strength, take the **Lanová Dráha Vrátna Chleb** chairlift to the red trail and enjoy the splendor of the tree-lined peaks. (☎569 56 42. Open June-Aug. daily 8:15am-7pm; Sept. 8:15am-4pm; Oct. and May Sa-Su 8:15am-4pm. 120Sk, round-trip 160Sk.) The red trail runs along 4km of beautiful vistas on the ridge to **Poludňový Grúň** (1460m). From Poludňový Grúň, turn left onto the slightly easier yellow trail to return to Chata Vrátna (round-trip 6½hr.).

LOW TATRAS (NÍZKE TATRY)

While not as imposing as the High Tatras, the slopes of the Low Tatras (Nízke Tatry) have fewer tourists. The majestic mountains and peaceful valleys boast an extensive trail system with caves and mountain streams. Hikers indulge in colorful promenades and unparalleled views after exerting themselves in arduous climbs.

LIPTOVSKÝ MIKULÁŠ   ☎(0)44

Liptovský Mikuláš (LIP-tohv-skee mee-koo-LASH; pop. 33,000) is a quiet hiking base town surrounded by magnificent mountains. On a rainy day, explore the charming square and cafes that crowd the center. Go down Štúrova and cross nám. Osloboditeľov to reach a passage that leads to the **Galéria Petra Michala Bohuna,** Transovského 2. Founded in 1955, this gallery displays about 4500 works, most of them regional. (☎552 27 58. Open Tu-Su 10am-5pm. Combined ticket 50Sk, students 30Sk; each exposition hall 15Sk/10Sk.) **Múzeum Janka Kráľa,** nám. Osloboditeľov 31, offers a look at the city's past. (☎552 25 54; www.lmikulas.sk. Open July-Aug. Tu-Su 10am-5pm; Sept.-June Tu-F 9am-4pm, Sa 10am-5pm. Entrance every 30min. 30Sk, students 25Sk. Cameras 20Sk, video 50Sk.)

Though private rooms fill quickly during the high seasons, hotels usually have a few vacancies. The central **Hotel Kriváň ❷**, Štúrova 5, opposite the tourist office, offers small and worn but peaceful rooms. (☎552 24 14; fax 551 47 48. Reception 24hr., knock after midnight. Check-in 2pm. Check-out 10am. Singles 300Sk, with bath 400Sk; doubles 480Sk/600Sk; quads with bath 880Sk.) Twenty-five minutes from the center, **Hotel Garni ❶**, ul. M. Népora 12, offers big rooms, comfy beds, and shared showers at an unbeatable price. From the train station, take bus #2, 7, 8, 9, or 11 to ul. 1. Mája, at the Maytex bus stop (10Sk). Backtrack and take the first left, then the first right. (☎562 56 59. Reception 24hr. Check-out noon. Shared bathrooms. Singles 147Sk; doubles 294Sk.) Restaurants are limited, though some options are clustered along nám. Osloboditeľov. Stock up on supplies at **Supermarket Delvita**, Štúrova 1968, in the Prior Building on nám. Mieru. (Open M-F 7am-8pm, Sa 7am-7pm, Su 8am-5pm. MC/V.) **Liptovská Izba Reštaurácia ❶**, nám. Osloboditeľov 22, serves delicious local dishes amid pleasant wooden decor. (☎551 48 53. Entrees 55-115Sk. *Halušky* 60Sk. Open daily 10am-10pm.)

The **train station** (☎551 24 84) is at Štefánikova 2, with the **bus station** (☎551 81 21) just outside. For info, see the dispatcher in the small white tower. **Trains** run to: **Bratislava** (4hr., 12 per day, 330Sk); **Košice** (2hr., 15 per day, 212Sk); **Poprad** (30min., 5 per day, 78Sk); **Žilina** (1hr., 7 per day, 138Sk); **Prague, CZR** (8½hr., 4 per day, 1128Sk). **Buses** run to: **Bratislava** (4½hr., 7 per day, 426Sk); **Košice** (3½hr., 2 per day, 262Sk); **Poprad** (1hr., 14 per day, 71Sk); **Žilina** (1½-2hr., 13-14 per day, 116Sk). To reach the center, turn left out of the train station on **Štefánikova**. Turn right onto **M.M. Hodžu**, which crosses **Štúrova** at **nám. Mieru**. Turn left to reach **nám. Osloboditeľov**, the main square. The friendly staff at **Informačné Centrum**, nám. Mieru 1, in the Dom Služieb complex, books **private rooms** (250-400Sk) and sells hiking **maps**, including VKÚ maps (102-112Sk). Ask for the *Orava Litpov Horehronie*, a hiking and cycling map (103Sk). They also organize guided excursions (half-day 2000Sk, full-day 2500Sk) in the Low Tatras. (☎552 24 18; www.lmikulas.sk. Open June 15-Sept. 15 and Dec. 15-Mar. 31 M-F 8am-7pm, Sa 8am-2pm, Su noon-6pm; Sept. 16-Dec. 14 and Apr. 1-June 14 M-F 9am-6pm, Sa 8am-noon.) To **rent bikes,** take bus #3 to Demanovska Dolina and get off at the last stop (20-23Sk). **Exchange currency** for no commission and cash **traveler's checks** for 1% commission at **Slovenska-Sporiteľňa**, Štúrova 1. (☎551 32 03. Open M-F 8am-5pm.) **Store luggage** at the train station. (12Sk, bags over 15kg 46Sk. Open daily 7:15-11am, 11:30am-3pm, and 3:15-5:15pm.) To use the **lockers** (5Sk) next to the window, write down the combination, drop in a coin, and lock the door. A **pharmacy** is at **Lekáreň Sabadilla,** nám. Mieru 1, in Dom Služieb. (☎552 13 18. Open M-F 8am-5pm. MC/V.) **Z@vinác Internet Bar,** nám. Osloboditeľov 21, has **Internet access** (1Sk per min.). The **post office** is on M.M. Hodžu 3, near nám. Mieru. Phone cards are at window #2; **Poste Restante** is at window #7. (☎552 26 42. Open M-F 8am-6pm, Sa 8am-11pm.) **Postal Code:** 03101.

HIKING IN THE LOW TATRAS

MOUNT ĎUMBIER AND CHOPOK. To conquer Mt. Ďumbier (2043m), catch an early bus from platform #11 in Liptovský Mikuláš to **Liptovský Ján** (25-30min., every hr., 13-16Sk). The gentle blue trail winds along the calm Štiavnica River until it reaches the Svidovské Sedlo by Chata generála M. R. Štefanika (5hr.). Bear left on the red trail to reach the summit (2043m, 45min.), where views await. For a strenuous hike, go right on the red trail to reach Sedlo Javorie (1½hr.). You'll pass two beautiful, oft-cloud-covered peaks, **Tanečnica** (1680m) and **Prašivá** (1667m). Head along the ridge and continue on the red trail past its intersection with the green trail to reach the range's second-highest peak, **Chopok** (2024m), where your efforts will be rewarded with views. From Chopok, walk down the blue trail to the bus stop at **Otupné**, behind Hotel Grand (1¾hr.), or negotiate a ride down on the **chairlift.** Chair lift box office open 8:20am-3:40pm in **Jasná;** follow the signs from Hotel Grand. (Open June-Sept. 8:30am-5pm, lift every 30min. 100Sk.)

DEMÄNOVSKÁ JASKYŇA SLOBODY (DEMÄNOV CAVE OF LIBERTY). For a short hike, take the bus from platform #3 in Liptovský Mikuláš to "Demänovská jaskyňa slobody" (20-35min., every hr. 6:25am-5pm, 13-16Sk) and walk past the cave on the blue trail to Pusté Sedlo Machnate (1½hr.). Named for its role in WWII, this cave stored supplies for the Slovak Uprising. The short tour of the two-million-year-old cave covers 1.5km and passes through breathtaking underground chambers, lakes, and a magnificent stone waterfall, all created by water falling at a rate of one drop per day. The long tour includes 2km of additional corridors. Bring a sweater. (☎ 559 16 73; www.ssj.sk. Admission every 30min. Open June-Aug. Tu-Su 9am-4pm; Sept.-Nov. 15 and Dec. 15-May 9:30am-2pm. 45min. tour 120Sk, students with ISIC 100Sk. 2hr. tour 240Sk/200Sk. Cameras 100Sk, video 200Sk.)

DEMÄNOVSKÁ L'ADOVÁ JASKYŇA. This ice cave rests midway between Liptovský Mikuláš and Jasná. Take the bus from Liptovský Mikuláš to Jasná, get off at "Kamenná chata" (20-30min., every hr., 13-16Sk), and follow the signs to the cave entrance (15min.). The cave was probably inhabited in the Stone Age, but the first tourists visited when rumors of a ▨dragon circulated in the 18th century. The 25km cave contains a wall signed by the 18th-century visitors and a frozen waterfall, which drapes over bleached stone. (☎554 81 70; www.ssj.sk. Open Tu-Su June-Aug. 9am-4pm, entrance every hr.; May and Sept. 9:30am-2pm, entrance every 1½hr. 110Sk, students 90Sk. Cameras 100Sk, video 200Sk.)

SPIŠ

For centuries, Spiš was an autonomous province of Hungary with a large Saxon population. It was later absorbed into Czechoslovakia and, after the Velvet Revolution in 1993, into the new Slovak Republic. Its eastern flatlands are dotted with quiet towns where scythes are still in style and time moves slowly as villagers walk their cows. Meanwhile, Kežmarok seduces visitors with its vigor, while Levoča and the sprawling ruins of Spišský Castle recall the region's rich past.

KEŽMAROK ☎(0)52

In 1269, King Belo IV granted Kežmarok (KEZH-ma-rok; pop. 18,000) commercial rights that made that brought prosperity. The modern town boasts colorful buildings, friendly locals, a storied history, and a vibrant atmosphere. From Hlavné nám., go down Hviezdoslavova to reach Kežmarok's highlight, the ▨**Wooden Articulated Church** (Drevený Atikulárny Kostol). Constructed in the shape of a Greek cross, the church bursts with imagination—the porthole-shaped windows bear the mark of the Swedish sailors who helped build it, while the fairy-tale clouds on the ceiling are the mark of daydreaming painters. The clay exterior was painted white to resemble cement. Though the church is active, most attend services at the colossal **New Evangelical Church** (Nový Evanjelický Kostol), which blends Romanesque, Byzantine, Renaissance, and Middle Eastern styles. (Both open daily June-Sept. 9am-noon and 2-5pm; Oct.-May Tu and F 10am-noon and 2-4pm. Buy a ticket for both at the old church. 30Sk.) Farther down the road, Kežmarok's **Historical Cemetery** honors some of the town's greatest citizens. (Open daily Apr. 16-Oct.

15 7am-8pm; Oct. 16-Apr. 15 7am-6pm. Free). Down Hlavné nám. is the impressive **Kežmarok Castle**, Hradné nám. 42. Once owned by the Hapsburgs, the castle rarely stayed in one family's possession for over a generation. Renaissance decor hangs from its stocky Gothic frame. The courtyard contains the foundations of a 13th-century Saxon church, while a Soviet-era tank sits outside the walls. (☎452 26 18; www.muzeum.sk. Open Tu-F 9am-noon and 1-4:30pm, Sa-Su 9am-4pm. 1hr. tours every 30-60min. 60Sk, students 30Sk. English pamphlet 5Sk, guidebook 20-35Sk.)

Book ahead if you plan to arrive mid-July during the **European Folk Arts Festival.** The tourist office (see above) books **private rooms** (200-250Sk). **Pension Max ❸,** Starý trh 9, is a family-run pension with a friendly and multilingual staff, spacious rooms, and spectacular baths. (☎421 52 45; duchon@sinet.sk. Reception 24hr. Check-out 10am. Singles and doubles 780Sk; triples 930Sk; quads 1200Sk.) Popular among Slovaks and tourists alike is the underground **Cellar Classica Restaurant ❷,** Hviezdoslavova 2. Locals cram in to enjoy delightful Italian food and cheap drinks. (☎52 36 93. Entrees 50-150Sk. Open daily 11am-11pm). There's a **grocery store** at Alexandra 35. (Open M-Sa 7am-10pm, Su 8am-10pm.) The **Admiral Club,** near the castle on Starý str, has livened up the quiet town with blasting pop and dance music. (Open M-Sa 9pm-6am.) Or, try one of the **beer gardens** in the city center.

Trains (☎452 32 98) run to **Poprad** (25min., 12 per day, 17Sk) from the hilltop at the junction of Toporcerova and Michalská. **Buses** leave from the canopies opposite the trains; destinations include: **Banská Bystrica** (7-10 per day, 278Sk); **Levoča** (1hr., 2 per day, 40Sk); **Poprad** (20-30min., every 10-40min., 20Sk). Buy bus tickets on board and train tickets at the station. To reach the center, take the pedestrian bridge to the left and follow **Alexandra** to **Hlavné nám. Kežmarská Informačná,** Hlavné nám. 46, in an alcove, offers tips, arranges private rooms, and sells **maps.** (☎52 452 40 47; www.kezmarok.net. Open M-F 8:30am-5pm, Sa 9am-2pm; also July-Aug. Su 9am-2pm.) **Slovenská Sporteľňa,** Baštová 28, **exchanges currency** (min. 30Sk) and cashes AmEx/MC/V **traveler's checks** (min. 20Sk) for 1% commission. (☎452 30 41; www.slsp.sk. Open M and F 7:30am-4pm, Tu 7:30am-1pm, W 7:30am-5pm, Th 7:30am-2pm.) A MC/V **ATM** stands outside. The **post office,** Mučeníkov 2, sits where Hviezdoslavova becomes Mučeníkov, just past the hospital. (☎452 20 21; www.slposta.sk. Open M-F 8am-noon and 1-7pm, Sa 8-10am.) **Postal Code:** 06001.

LEVOČA   ☎(0)53

Levoča (LEH-vo-cha; pop. 14,000), the current administrative hub and former capital of Spiš, gained fame through the 16th-century "Law of Storage," which forced merchants to remain in town until they sold all their goods. The new wealth fostered craft guilds, many of which were led by the renowned sculptor Master Pavol, responsible for the detailed works that adorn Spiš's churches, including Levoča's Gothic altar. The city expresses its religious tradition through the Festival of Marian Devotion, which attracts countless pilgrims in July. A perfect escape for those seeking a relaxed atmosphere, Levoča maintains its idyllic cobblestone character.

⚏⚏ TRANSPORTATION AND PRACTICAL INFORMATION. The best way to reach Levoča is by bus. **Buses** run to: **Košice** (2½hr., 7 per day, 120Sk); **Poprad** (50min., 15 per day, 40Sk); **Prešov** (2hr., M-F 8 per day, Sa-Su 4 per day, 53Sk); **Starý Smokovec** (1-1½hr., M-F 4 per day, Sa-Su 1-3 per day, 54Sk).

To reach the center, take a right out of the station and walk down the footpath until it intersects **Zeleznicný Riadok.** Turn left and continue straight until you hit the main road, **Probstnerová Cesta.** Turn right and continue on the road until just after the graveyard, where you can cross the street and go through the **Menhard Gate,** one of the three original city gates still standing. From there, walk up ul. Hermana until you reach the main square, Nám. Majstra Pavla (15min.). Turn left out of the train station and follow the road to the red and white **Zastavka** sign, where you can catch the infrequent local bus. The **tourist office,** nám. Majstra Pavla 58, sells maps of the city center and recommends **private rooms,** which start at 400Sk. (☎161 88; www.levoca.sk. Open May-Sept. M-Sa 9am-5pm, Su 10am-2pm; Oct.-Apr. M-F 9am-4:30pm.) **Slovenská Sporiteľňa,** nám. Majstra Pavla 56, gives MC/V **cash advances** and cashes AmEx/V **traveler's checks** (min. 20Sk) for 1% commission. (☎451 01 21; fax 451 01 34. Open M-Tu and Th-F 8am-3pm, W 8am-4pm.) A MC/V **ATM** stands outside. The **pharmacy, Lekáren K Hadovi,** nám. Majstra Pavla 13, sometimes posts the hours of other pharmacies. (☎451 24 56. Open M-F 7:30am-5pm, Sa 8am-noon.) For a western-style **Internet** cafe hit **Cafe,** nám. Majstra Pavla 38, where you can buy Internet passes. Keep your password, as unused minutes have a 15-day lifetime. (15Sk for 5min., 50Sk for 65 min., 100Sk for 2½hr, 500Sk for 15hr. Open daily 10am-10pm.) The best weekend deal is across the street at the **Internet Cafe** on Nová 79. (Su-F 1.5Sk per min., Sa 0.5Sk per min. Open daily 9am-5pm.) The **post office** is at Nám. Majstra Pavla 42. (☎451 24 89. Open M-F 8am-noon and 1-4:30pm, Sa 8-10:30am.) **Poste Restante** at window #1. **Postal Code:** 05401.

ⒾⒸ ACCOMMODATIONS AND FOOD. Though choices are limited, finding accommodations is usually not difficult. During the first weekend in July, when the city hosts a festival, your best bet is to stay in Poprad and travel to Levoča. Those looking to spend the night can inquire at the tourist office (see **Orientation and Practical Information,** above), where the friendly English-speaking staff is more than willing to help book **pensions** and nearby **campsites.** The inviting, family-run **⬛Penzión Šuňavský ❶,** Nová 59, has an idyllic garden in a central location and offers clean, comfortable rooms. Follow the directions above to the town center; the pension is on the left side of Nová. (☎451 45 26. Breakfast 50Sk. Laundry 100Sk per load. Call 2 days ahead in Aug. Triples and quads with shared baths 400Sk; 2-person apartments 1500Sk.) The more luxurious **Penzión U Leva ❸,** Nám. Majstra Pavla 24, is in the heart of the main square and offers elegant rooms with TV, kitchenettes, and access to a fitness center and sauna. (☎450 23 11; www.uleva.szm.sk. Singles 1000Sk; doubles 2000Sk.)

U 3 Apoštolov ❷, Nám. Majstra Pavla 11, serves hearty portions of traditional dishes and vegetarian cuisine. Patrons can relax on a beautiful terrace or find refuge from the summer sun indoors. (☎/fax 451 23 02. Entrees 56-220Sk. Open daily 9am-10pm. AmEx/MC/V.) Popular with locals for special occasions, **Restaurant Janusa ❶,** Kláštorská 22, dishes up hearty fare. The house specialty is *pierogi* with a side of spicy sausage. (☎451 45 92; www.slovakiaguide.sk. Entrees 45-110Sk. Open M-F 10am-10pm, Sa-Su with reservations only.) **Billa Supermarket** is next to the bus station and has a huge selection of food and drinks for do-it-yourselfers. (Open M-F 7am-8pm, Sa-Su 8am-8pm. MC/V.)

Ⓖ SIGHTS. Levoča's star attraction is the 14th-century **St. Jacob's Church** (Chrám sv. Jakuba), home to the world's tallest Gothic altar (a staggering 18.62m), beautifully carved by Master Pavol between 1507 and 1517. Almost as dramatic as the altar are the frescoes on the left wall, depicting the seven heavenly virtues and the seven deadly sins. (☎090 752 16 73; www.chramsvjakuba.sk. Visitors' clothing must cover shoulders. Buy tickets at the booth across the street. Entrance every 30min.; Sept.-June every hr. after 1pm. Open July-Aug. M 11am-5pm, Tu-F 9am-5pm, Sa 9am-noon, Su 1-2:30pm; Sept.-June Tu-Sa 9am-4pm. 50Sk, students 30Sk.)

Three branches of the **Spišské Museum** dot Nám. Majstra Pavla. In addition to exhibits, each museum features a worthwhile video about Levoča's history (20min., available in English). **Dom Majstra Pavla,** Nám. Majstra Pavla 20 (☎451 34 96), displays high-quality facsimiles of Master Pavol's greatest works. The second branch is housed in the beautiful **Town Hall** *(radnica),* which provides a candid look at Levoča's past and displays everything from regal chandeliers to basic torture instruments. While the main entrance leads to wineries and small stores, the stairs on the right take visitors into Levoča's most interesting museum. Some guides speak English. Next to the town hall stands the **Cage of Shame** (Klietka Hanby), in which accused "ladies of the night" were humiliated in the 16th century. The **five frescoes** of women on the Town Hall display Levoča's commitment to its civic values. The Spišské Museum's third branch (☎451 27 86), at #40, has a small collection of masterful portraits and statues. (www.snm.sk. All branches open daily May-Oct. 9am-5pm; Nov.-Apr. 8am-4pm. 30Sk, students 15Sk. One ticket per museum. English brochure 20Sk.) The neo-Gothic **Basilica of the Virgin Mary** (Bazilika Panny Marie), separated from Levoča by 3km of wheat fields but visible from town, towers forebodingly atop Mariánská hora. Fields and hills did not stop the 750,000 pilgrims who flocked to the site when Pope John Paul II visited.

⚡ DAYTRIP FROM LEVOČA

SPIŠSKÉ PODHRADIE AND ŽEHRA

Buses come from Levoča (30min., 1 per hr., 22Sk); Poprad (1hr., 9 per day, 53 Sk); Prešov (1½hr., 1 per hr. until 6pm, 57Sk). Many uphill paths lead to the castle (check the info map at the castle end of the main square), but the most scenic—albeit strenuous— trek is the 1km walk past the town's cemetery. Facing the bus departure board, head to the main square through the wide street to the left of the garden. Turn left onto the bridge leading out of town and take the steep narrow road that passes the cemetery to your right. When you reach the castle walls, climb uphill into the castle heart.

If you only visit one Slovak castle, make it ⚑**Spišské Castle** (Spišský hrad), Central Europe's largest and possibly most interesting, in Spišské Podhradie (SPISH-skay POD-hra-dyeh). The area has been home to fortified settlements for two millennia, but the ruins crowning the hilltop today are remnants of a Hungarian castle that was abandoned in the 17th century. When a fire broke out in 1780, flames swallowed the castle, leaving it deserted and unclaimed until it became national property in 1945 and a national treasure in 1961. The view of the surrounding villages from the castle is well worth the climb, and the free museum housed in the castle exhibits war relics like musket balls, cannons, suits of armor and grisly torture devices. In 1993, it was made a **UNESCO World Heritage Sight.** (☎454 13 36. Entrance with an English-speaking guide every 30min., min. 10 people. Open daily May-Oct. 8:30am-6pm. 60Sk, students 30Sk. Cameras 10Sk, video 50Sk.)

West of town stands the region's religious capital **Spišské Kapitula.** Its walls enclose a seminary, bishop's quarters, and **St. Martin's Cathedral** (Katedrála sv. Martina). The church was sacked in 1241 by the invading Tatar army, destroying much of its beauty. More impressive for its historical and cultural significance than for its visual appeal, the cathedral was used as a police academy under Soviet rule but has returned to its original purpose and has even hosted the Pope. Facing the bus station departure board, veer right and walk through the gardens and over the river. The main road winds up and around to the cathedral (15min.). Get tickets at the souvenir shop, 50m from the church. (☎090 838 84 11; www.spiskap.sk. Visitors' clothing should cover their knees and shoulders. Tours every hr. on the hr. Open May-Sept. M-Sa 9am-4pm, Su 10am-4pm; Oct.-Apr. M-Sa 9am-4:30pm, Su 11am-3pm. 30Sk, students 20Sk.) To escape the beer gardens and touristy restaurants, head uphill to **Spišský Salaš ❷**, Levočská cesta 11. This traditional restaurant is a favorite among locals. The English translations on the menu are dubious: try the "Domestic Slaughter" (150Sk), a mix of pork entrees and a godsend for hungry carnivores. (☎454 12 02. Entrees 60-250Sk. Beer 28Sk.)

SLOVAK REPUBLIC

A long and tranquil walk from the castle brings you to the ancient village of **Žehra,** home of the **Church of the Holy Spirit** (Kostol Svätého Ducha). Built in a late Romanesque to early Gothic style, it's not to be missed if you have the strength to trek to its doors (2hr.). Though faded and in need of restoration, its UNESCO-protected murals have made the church famous. The interior is decorated with remarkable frescoes painted in five stages during the 12th to 15th centuries and uncovered in the 1950s. From the castle entrance, descend to the closer parking lot and take the yellow trail—it is only recognizable by its closely cut grass. Continue past the limestone crags and bear left into the valley below. The church's brown, onion-domed tower is easy to spot. (Open M-F 9:30-11:30am with entrance every 30min. and 1-4pm with entrance every hr.; Su 2-4pm. 20Sk, students 10Sk.)

SLOVENSKÝ RAJ NATIONAL PARK ☎(0)53

The peaks of Slovenský Raj National Park, southeast of the Low Tatras, don't match their neighbors in height, but they make up for it in pizzazz. Dazzling forests, dramatic waterfalls and deep limestone ravines await hikers and lovers of the outdoors. The subdued natural beauty of these mountains earns them their title: Slovenský Raj means Slovak Paradise. Life moves slowly in the tiny mountain villages, even as hikers and skiers speed by on the nearby trails.

⊑ TRANSPORTATION. Reaching the park is difficult. Nestled by the shores of Lake Palčmanská Maša, **Dedinky** (pop. 400) is the largest town on Slovenský Raj's southern border. Its sublime location and efficient transportation system make it a favorite among hikers. Catch a train to **Spisska Nová Ves** (1¾-2¼hr., 5:50 and 11:30am, 60Sk) from where buses head to paradise. Alternatively, go straight from Poprad by catching the **bus** toward **Rožňava** (1hr., 4 per day, 65 Sk). The bus stops first at the Dobšinská ľadová jaskyňa (where you can catch the infrequent train to Dedinky; 15 Sk), then at the village Stratená, and finally at a junction 2km south of Dedinky. The fastest way to get to Dedinky is to follow the yellow trail that branches off to the right about 150m from the bus stop. When you reach the road at the bottom, turn left, and the dam will be on your right.

⊞☑ ORIENTATION AND PRACTICAL INFORMATION. The best trail guide is the **VKÚ Sheet #4.** Pick up a copy at **Delika** (see **Accommodations and Food,** p. 820). To find the **Sedačková Lanová Dráha tourist office,** head to **Mlynky,** a town neighboring Dedinky. From the train station, head toward the dam (see **Transportation,** p. 820) but don't cross it. Follow the road and veer left as it descends to Mlynky. Signs point to Penzión Salamander at the bottom of the hill to the right. In Salamander's reception room, the tourist office staff sells VKÚ #4 (120Sk) and has info on 200-400Sk **private rooms.** (☎449 35 45. Open daily 8am-10pm. AmEx/MC/V.) Behind Hotel Priehrada, a **chairlift** runs to Chata Geravy. (☎058 798 12 12. 90Sk, round-trip 200Sk; under 10 people 1000Sk. Open July-Aug. M 9am-1pm, Tu 9am-4pm; May-June M 9am-1pm, Tu-Su 9am-4pm, 1 per hr.; Sept. daily 9am-2pm.) **Tókóly Tours,** 200m from Hotel Priehrada, rents **boats.** (☎905 592 30 11. Rowboats 50Sk per hr., paddle boats and canoes 100Sk per hr. Open daily July-Aug. 9am-6pm; June 15-30 and Sept. 1-15 1-6pm.) Dedinky's **post office** is behind the wooden tower near the bus stop. **Poste Restante** available. (☎058 798 11 34. Open M-F 8-10am, 12:30-1:30pm, and 2-3pm.) **Postal Code:** 04973.

⌐⌐ ACCOMMODATIONS AND FOOD. Book rooms at least two weeks ahead in January, July, and August, though **private rooms** (200-350Sk), the cheapest and often best option, rarely fill up: look for *"privat," "ubytowanie,"* or *"Zimmer frei"* signs. **Penzión Pastierňa ❷,** Dedinky 42, offers spacious, well-decorated rooms with shared baths. Facing Hotel Priehrada, turn left and take the second right, just after Delika. Follow the signs to the end of the street. (☎798 11 75. Breakfast 40-60Sk. Reception 8:30am-9:30pm. Check-out 11am. 2- to 4-bed rooms 300Sk.) **Hotel Priehrada ❷**, Dedinky 107, rents older rooms with well-kept bathrooms. It also runs a cheap **campground** by the lake. (☎798 12 12; fax 788 16 82. Reception 24hr. Strict check-in 2pm. Check-out 10am. Rooms 290Sk, with bath 400Sk; extra bed 190Sk/270Sk. Camping 40Sk per person, 40Sk per tent, 20Sk per car.) Also check out accommodations in nearby **Mlynky**. From the Dedinky train stop, cross the dam and turn right. When the road splits, veer to the left toward Mlynky. For cheap sleeps and a pleasant staff, head to **Turisticka Ubytovna NITA ❶**, Pakmanslá Maša 295. Its simple but comfortable rooms have shared baths. (☎/fax 449 32 79. Check-in 2pm. Check-out 10am. Call ahead. 2- to 4-bed rooms 180Sk, with breakfast and dinner 350Sk.)

The restaurant selection is very limited and most hikers prefer to stock up on trail food before heading off. In Dedinky, the restaurant in **Penzión Pastierňa ❷** serves Slovak standards and vegetarian options. (Entrees 60-170Sk. Open daily 8am-9:30pm.) Plan to eat in Dedinky if heading to the caves, where the **restaurant** serves simple but somewhat overpriced food (entrees 79-290Sk). Stock up at **Dotraviny,** across from the bus stop. (☎798 11 21. Open M-F 8am-noon and 2-6pm, Sa 7-11am.) There is also a small selection of *potraviny* (groceries) at the base of the trail. (Open M, W, F 7-10am and 1-4pm, Tu and Th 8am-1pm, Sa 8-11am.)

◙ SIGHTS. Discovered in 1870, the ▨**Dobšinská Ice Caves** (Dobšinská ľadová jaskyňa) contain over 110,000 cubic meters of beautifully held frozen water from as long ago as the last Ice Age. An awe-inspiring sight, with hall after hall of frozen columns, gigantic ice walls, and hardened waterfalls, the ice caves are a tribute to Nature's fondness of Slovakia. Dress in layers—the cave temperature hovers between -6°C and +0.5°C year round. To get here from Dedinky, take the 10am **bus** from the bus stop to the parking lot (20min., 20Sk). Alternatively, take the 7:07, 11:14am, or 2:27pm **train** toward **Červana Skala** for two stops (15min., 11Sk.) Follow the road leading from the station to the main road. Turn left and then right after you pass the restaurant; the parking lot is up ahead. From here, the blue trail leads up the steep incline to the cave, 15-20min away. (☎788 14 70; www.ssj.sk. Open June-Aug. Tu-Su 9am-4pm. 120Sk, students with ISIC 100Sk. Cameras 150Sk, video 300Sk. Tours every hr., min. 4 people. May 15-June and Sept. tours 9:30, 11am, 12:30, 2pm. English tours available.)

◪ HIKING. Camping and fires are prohibited in all Slovak national parks except at registered campsites and some *chaty*. Tourists must stick to the clearly marked trails. Having a map is advisable, as cascade trails are one-way—you can go up, but not down. All cascade trails are closed from November to June except when accompanied by a certified guides. Guides can be hired from nearby resorts, *chatas*, and the travel agencies. (3000-4000Sk).

Biele vody (White Waters; 45min.-1¾hr.). A moderately difficult cascade hike up a series of rapids. Watch your footing on slippery and loose rocks, ladders, and bridges. From the parking lot to the right of Hotel Priehrada, take the red trail to **Biele vody** (788m), which begins in **Mlynky.** A memorable view of the surrounding peaks and forested hills rewards those who venture to the top, where **Chata Geravy** and a chairlift await the weary and the green trail leads the energetic back down.

Veľký sokol (Big Falcon; 6½hr.). A demanding hike into the heart of Slovenský Raj and up its deepest gorge. Follow the road west from Stratená or east from the ice caves (with your back to the caves, take a right). At the U-bend, follow the green trail until it meets the road and the red path. From the parking lot, the yellow trail crosses the bridge and stream. From the top (971m), a right onto the red path returns to **Chata Geravy** and the chair-lift to **Dedinky**. A tougher ascent begins at Chata Geravy and traverses the cascades of Sokolia Dolina. From the bottom of the cascade, take a right onto the green trail and continue to the yellow trail all the way to **Glac** (20-30min.). Make a left onto the blue path and head to **Malá Polana** (10min.). Make sure to go right and follow the red trail to **Sokol** and **Diablova Polka** (1½hr.), not Geravy. When you reach the parking lot, head onto the yellow trail to Veľky Sokol (2-2½hr.).

Sokolia Dolina (Falcon Valley; 7hr.). An intense trek through Slovenský Raj, this hike mounts the highest of the park's waterfalls (70m). From Chata Geravy, take the red trail to the green trail and turn right (1¼hr.). After 20min., hang a right onto the yellow trail at **Pod Bykárkou.** Continue until you meet the green trail (1hr.) and head left toward Sokolia and Kamenná dolina. At Sokolia dolina (45min.) begin the arduous ascent up to the cascade (2hr.) where your efforts are rewarded with a dazzling view of the waterfall. When you reach the bottom, go left on the green trail to **Pod Bikárkou** (20min.) and retrace your steps back to Chata Geravy.

HIGH TATRAS (VYSOKÉ TATRY)

Spanning the border between Slovak Republic and Poland, the High Tatras are the highest peaks in the Carpathian range (2650m) and create mesmerizing valleys beneath. Despite its popularity with hikers and tourists, the High Tatras region retains Slovak small-town charm, with affordable accommodations and welcoming locals. Starý Smokovec is a popular base for excursions and short hikes, but the most hardcore hikers seek shelter in mountain huts *(chaty)*.

POPRAD ☎(0)92

Poprad (pop. 56,000) is one of the Slovak Republic's major tourist centers and transportation hubs. While Poprad provides amusement for a few hours, travelers may find it more pleasant to simply pass through en route to their final destination.

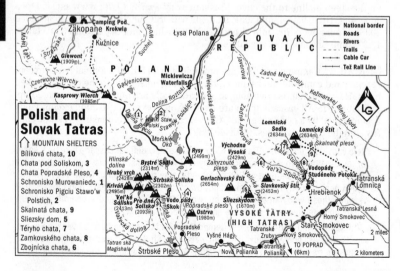

Polish and Slovak Tatras

↑ MOUNTAIN SHELTERS

Bilíková chata, **10**
Chata pod Soliskom, **3**
Chata Popradské Pleso, **4**
Schronisko Murowaniedc, **1**
Schronisko Pigciu Stawo'w
  Polstich, **2**
Skalnatá chata, **9**
Sliezsky dom, **5**
Téryho chata, **7**
Zamkovského chata, **8**
Zbojnícka chata, **6**

TRANSPORTATION. Trains run to: **Bratislava** (4¾hr., 12 per day, 384Sk); **Košice** (1-2hr., 21 per day, 138Sk); **Žilina** (2-3hr., 21 per day, 180Sk). The clean and efficient *Tatranská elektrická železnica (TEŽ)* takes longer, but runs more often between Poprad and the **Tatran resorts** (every 20min., up to 35Sk). **Buses** (☎776 25 55) stop at the corner of Wolkerova and Alžbetina on the way to: **Banská Bystrica** (2½hr., 3 per day, 220Sk); **Bratislava** (7hr., 12 per day, 350Sk); **Košice** (2½hr., 7 per day, 130Sk); **Žilina** (3hr., 13-14 per day, 170Sk); **Frankfurt, GER** (18hr., 2 per day, 2100Sk); **Prague, CZR** (11hr., 9 per day, 350Sk); **Vienna, AUT** (8hr., 2 per day, 1000Sk). Or just hail a **Rádio Taxi** (☎776 87 68).

ORIENTATION AND PRACTICAL INFORMATION. To reach the center, take a left from the **train station** as you face the bus parking lot and follow **Alžbetina** away from the **bus station.** Turn left on **Hviezdoslavova** and then right on **Mnoheľova,** which leads to **Nám. sv. Egídia.** To reach the old square from the train station, walk up Alžbetina, then turn left on **Štefánikova.** Continue about 2km and turn left onto **Kežmarská.** Keep right as the road forks and head up into **Sobotské nám.** At **Poprad-ská Informačná Agentúra (PIA),** Nám. sv. Egídia 114, the English-speaking staff sells **maps, rents bikes** (150Sk per half-day, 200Sk per day; 3000Sk deposit), and offers accommodations and recreation info. (☎772 13 94; www.poprad-online.sk. Open July-Aug. M-F 8am-6pm, Sa 9am-1pm; Sept.-June M-F 9am-5pm, Sa 9am-noon. Private rooms 200Sk.) **VÚB,** Mnoheľova 9, cashes AmEx/V **traveler's checks** and provides **cash advances** for 1% commission. (☎713 11 11. Open M-W and F 8am-5pm.) 24hr. (MC/V) **ATMs** are all over town. There's a **24hr. currency exchange** desk in the lobby of **Hotel Satel,** Mnoheľ'ova 825 (☎527 16 11; www.satel-slovakia.sk). **Store luggage** (55Sk per day) at the train station in lockers across the room from the ticket window. For **Internet access,** stop by the cafe on Nám. sv. Egidia 27. (10Sk per 15min. Open M-Sa 9am-9pm, Su 1pm-9pm.) **Postal Code:** 05801

> In winter, a guide is necessary for hiking in the Tatras. To hire one, check with the local tourist information office in your town. Snowfall is very high and avalanches are common. Dozens of winter hikers die each year, often on "easy" trails. Even in summer, many hikes are extremely demanding and require experience. Before you begin, obtain a map and info about the trail. Updated information on trail and weather conditions is available at www.tanap.sk, but at the highest elevations, weather changes frequently and abruptly. Check with a mountain rescue team, a local outdoors store, or a tourist office before going anywhere without an escort. Always inform the receptionist at your hostel or hotel of your hiking route and the estimated time of your return.

ACCOMMODATIONS AND FOOD. A student dorm during the year, **Domov Mladeze ❷,** ul. Karpatská 9, offers a great location at an affordable price. Walk down Alžbetina from the train station, keeping the bus station on your right, and turn right on Karpatská. (☎776 34 14. Reception 6am-10pm. Call ahead. Open July-Aug. 2- and 3-bed dorms 250Sk; singles 300Sk.) Those who prefer affordability over comfort should head to **Hotel Europa ❶,** Wolkierowa 1. Rooms are worn but comfortable. (☎772 18 97. 24hr. reception. Check-out 11am. Singles 370Sk; doubles 600Sk; 15Sk tourist tax.) Another accommodation option is the grand **Hotel Satel ❺,** Mnoheľova 5 opposite Egidius Restaurant, which has comfortable rooms in a relaxing atmosphere and friendly staff (☎716 11 11. Singles 1330Sk; doubles 1960Sk. AmEx/MC/V.) Pizza places and traditional restaurants populate the center square. An appetizing option is **Slovenska Restauracia ❶,** ul. 1 Mája 216, which serves both Slovak and international dishes. (☎772 28 70. Entrees 35-230Sk. Open

SLOVAK REPUBLIC

A MAP MADE IN HEAVEN

A splatter of red. A dash of green. A yellow line criss-crossing the page. Standing in the middle of nowhere, I glanced down at the paper and realized it looked more like a piece of abstract art than my only hope to emerge from the trail before nightfall. I kept walking. About 500m ahead, I saw my salvation—a tiny green mark painted faintly on the tree. I looked down at the artwork and studied it—at least I was going the right way.

Slovak trail signals are not as easy as they seem. A yellow line signals a short path connecting major trails. Blue means long—and generally easier—trails that connect sights, like caves or lakes. Green marks connect larger trails but, unlike yellow, tend to lead to famous natural sights or historical attractions. A red mark signifies the trail will be challenging and steep, with ledges and slippery slopes.

Be aware, as the marks are often infrequent. The standard trail mark shows the color (red, green, yellow, or blue), bordered by two white stripes. A colored arrow will help you when the trail forks or looks uncertain, and a colored square with the top corner missing means that you have reached a tourist attraction. A white square or circle with a colored square inside means that the trail has been completed.

Congratulations. Modern art made simple.

daily 10am-11pm. AmEx/MC/V) Or visit **Egídius ❷**, Mnoheľova 18, across the river from the town center, near the bus and train stations. Enjoy *knedle* (dumplings with plums) served with hearty helpings of meat. (☎ 772 28 98. Entrees 40-300Sk. Open daily 9.30am-11:30pm.) **Súdok,** in the center at Nám. sv. Egídia 44, serves up excellent local and Western meals at low prices. (Entrees 40-175Sk. Open M-Th 1pm-midnight, F 1pm-2am, Sa 4pm-2am, Su 4pm-2am.) Buy groceries at the **Billa Supermarket,** across from the bus station parking lot. (Open M-Sa 7am-9pm, Su 8am-8pm. MC/V.)

STARÝ SMOKOVEC ☎(0)52

Starý Smokovec (STAH-ree SMOH-koh-vets), founded in the 17th century, is the High Tatras' oldest and most central base resort. Hiking paths originate at the town's summit and connect it with the mountains. While signposts with a dozen arrows and nameless streets may seem daunting, it's difficult to get lost—Starý Smokovec was developed with tourism in mind and is easy to navigate.

🚆 TRANSPORTATION. TEŽ trains go to: **Poprad** (30min., 1 per hr., 20Sk); **Štrbské Pleso** (45min., every 30-50min., 23Sk); **Tatranská Lomnica** (15min., every 25-40min., 13Sk). **Buses** go to **Bratislava** (6hr., 2 per day, 409Sk); **Košice** (3hr., 2-3 per day, 132Sk); **Levoča** (20-50min., 2-4 per day, 67Sk); **Poprad** (30min., every 30min.-1hr., 35Sk); **Štrbské Pleso** (30-40min., 4-13 per day, 20Sk); **Tatranská Lomnica** (10-20min., every 30-50min., 9Sk). A **funicular** runs to **Hrebienok** (see p. 826; every 30-40min. 7:30am-7pm; 80Sk, round-trip 100Sk). For **taxis,** call **Rigo** (☎ 442 25 25).

🏢🛈 ORIENTATION AND PRACTICAL INFORMATION. Starý Smokovec's essential services are mostly along the main road that leads to **Horný Smokovec** to the east and **Nový Smokovec** to the west. To get to the center from the train station, walk uphill to the main road and turn left. Cross the road past the strip mall and head into the white building that emerges from behind a map-board. Signs point to hotels, restaurants, and services. The **hiking trails** lie to the north, farther uphill.

The helpful staff of **Tatranská Informačná Kancelária (TIK),** in Dom Služieb, provides weather and hiking info and **free town maps;** sells hiking guides and the crucial **VKÚ sheet #113** (89Sk); and points visitors to hotels, pensions, and private rooms. (☎442 34 40; www.zcrvt.szm.sk. Open daily July-Aug. 8am-6pm; Sept.-Dec. 26 and Jan. 12-June M-F 9am-noon and 12:30-4pm, Sa 9am-1pm; Dec. 27-Jan. 11 daily 8am-

5pm. Hotel rooms 600Sk; pensions 400Sk; private rooms 200-250Sk.) **Slovenská Sporiteľňa**, located in the commercial strip on the way to Dom Služieb, cashes **traveler's checks** and gives MC/V **cash advances** for 1% commission (min. 30Sk). A 24hr. (MC/V) **ATM** is outside. (☎244 224 70; www.slsp.sk. Open M-F 8am-noon and 12:30-3:30pm.) A **pharmacy**, **Lekáreň U Zlatej Sovy**, is on the first floor of Dom Služieb. (☎442 21 65. Open M-F 8am-noon and 12:30-4:30pm, Sa 9am-noon.)

Internet access is available in the **Rogalo** restaurant to the left of the main entrance of Dom Služieb (☎442 50 43. 1Sk per min. Open daily 9am-10pm.) Another Internet cafe, **Inteka**, offers a selection of drinks and is located on the second floor of the shopping complex opposite the bus station. (1Sk per min. Open 9am-midnight.) The **post office** is uphill to the left to the train station before the main road. **Poste Restante** is at the first window to the left. (☎442 24 71. Open M-F 7:30am-noon and 1-4pm, Sa 8-10am.) **Telephones** are located outside. **Postal Code:** 06201.

⌂ ACCOMMODATIONS AND FOOD. Uphill from the train station on the way to Dom Služieb, an electronic **InfoPanel** lists current vacancies in the greater Smokovec area. The **TIK** (see above) lists **private rooms** (200-250Sk) available to tourists. Many budget options lie in the hamlet of **Horný Smokovec**. From the bus or train station, turn right onto the main road and keep left to reach the **Hotel Šport ❷**, which has compact rooms and shared baths. Book one month in advance July through August. It shares facilities with the nearby Hotel Bellevue, including a sauna (100Sk for 2hr.), swimming pool (100Sk for 2hr.), and massage parlor. (☎442 23 61. Breakfast 80Sk. English-speaking reception 24hr. Check-out 10am. Jan. 2-Feb. 28, Apr. 8-10 and June 19-Sept. 30 singles 430Sk; doubles 750Sk. Dec. 26-Jan. 1. 770Sk/1240Sk. Mar. 1-Apr. 7, Apr. 11-June 18, and Oct. 1-Dec. 25 310Sk/550Sk. 15Sk tourist tax). Another good bargain, but farther away from the main hub of trails, is **Hotel Junior ❷** (☎442 26 61), in Horný Smokovec. The rooms offer the essentials at enticing prices (From the Horný Smokovec TEŽ station, away from the main road and turn left at the Hotel Junior sign. Reception 7am-10pm. Checkout 10am. Singles 280Sk; doubles 360Sk.) To reach family-run **Penzión Gerlach ❸**, turn left out of the TEŽ station onto the main road, and continue past the church with the tracks on your left. The pension is near the street on the right. Central, fabulously furnished rooms ensure comfort in style. (☎442 32 80; www.penziongerlach.sk. Breakfast included. Reception 10am-6pm. Call ahead in high season. Singles 600-800Sk; doubles 800-1000Sk; triples 1200-1500Sk; low season 300-400Sk/400-500Sk/500Sk.) Just behind Penzión Gerlach lies the equally pleasant **Villa Dr Szontagh ❸**, which feels like a cottage nestled in the trees and hills. (☎421 44 33; szontagh@isternet.sk. Singles 1100Sk; doubles 1200Sk.) If you plan to stay in Starý Smokovec itself, **Hotel Smokovec ❺**, uphill from the train station, has a multilingual staff and offers beautiful rooms, a swimming pool (50Sk per hr.), weight room (50Sk per hr.), sauna (350Sk for 2 people for 2hr.), and restaurant. (☎442 51 91; www.hotelsmokovec.sk. Reception 24hr. Check-out 10am. Doubles 2380Sk; triples 3420Sk. Mid-season 1980Sk/2820Sk. Low season 1580Sk/2370Sk. Restaurant open daily 7am-10pm.)

Vendors are easy to find along the streets of Starý Smokovec. The largest is in the shopping block above the bus station. (Open M-F 7:45am-6pm, Sa-Su 8am-12:30pm.) Most restaurants are homogeneous and serve up typical Slovak dishes like *bryndza* or cabbage and sausage soup. For an excellent blend of Slovak and international fare, as well as fast and friendly service, try the **Restaurant Tatra ❶**, just above the bus station. The *pastiersky syr* (fried cheese) excellent. Entrees 70-150Sk. Beer 25Sk. Open daily 11:30am-8pm. Popular with tourists and locals alike, **Restaurant Pizzeria La Montanara ❷** offers huge portions at appetizing prices. From the train station, turn right and keep right for about 40m; the restaurant is behind a wooden row of shops. (Entrees 110-170Sk. Open daily 11am-9pm.) **Res-**

taurant **Koliba ❸** is exceptional. Facing downhill, head through the parking lot to the right of the train station and across the tracks. Try the *Tatranský čaj* (Tatran tea; 40Sk), which is spiked with pure grain alcohol. (☎442 22 04. Entrees 90-280Sk. Open daily 5pm-midnight.) Hikers can stock up on supplies at the **Supermarket** just above the train station. (Open M-F 7:45am-6pm, Sa-Su noon-6pm.) Another supermarket, located in the shopping complex just opposite the bus station, carries slightly cheaper food and drinks. (Open M-F 7:45am-5:45pm, Sa-Su 8am-12:30pm.)

🏔 OUTDOOR ACTIVITIES. **T-ski,** in the funicular station behind **Grand Hotel,** offers everything from ski classes to Dunajec river-rafting expeditions (690Sk; see **Daytrip from Zakopane, POL,** p. 551), and rents sleds and snowboards. (☎442 32 65. Sleds 90Sk per day, skis 250-390Sk, snowboards 500Sk. Individual classes 600-900Sk for 2hr., groups 200-300Sk per person; guides from 490Sk per day. Open daily 8am-6pm. MC/V.) Budget-conscious travelers should bring along a stash of food and drinks when staying at the *chaty* or hiking through the great outdoors. Just beyond the funicular station, the green trail continues to **Bilikova Chata ❷** (5min.), which is more a hotel than a mountain shelter. (☎442 24 39; www.slovaki-aguide.sk. Breakfast 130Sk, breakfast and dinner 300Sk. Reception 7-8pm. Call at least one month ahead in high season. 480Sk.) Another 20min. down the green trail leads to the **Volopády studeného potoka** (Cold Stream Waterfalls). **Tatrasport,** uphill from the bus lot, rents **mountain bikes.** (☎442 52 41; www.tatry.net/tatrasport. 299Sk per day. Open daily 8am-6pm. MC/V.)

The funicular to **Hrebienok** (1285m) carries people daily to the crossroads of numerous hiking trails. (June 28-Sept. 12 90Sk up, 40Sk down, 100Sk round-trip; Sept. 13-June 27 70Sk/40Sk/80Sk.) The six skiing trails vary in difficulty. Lengths range from 100m to 530m. (Morning 440Sk, afternoon 540Sk, full day 690Sk; children 350Sk/440Sk/560Sk). Alternatively, hike the somewhat uninspiring first leg of the **green trail** behind **Hotel Grand** to reach Hrebienok. Follow the **red trail** past Rainerova Chata, then head right on the eastward **blue trail** to gradually descend through towering pines to Tatranská Lomnica (1¾hr.). The **yellow trail,** a more subdued but tranquil route, meanders along the river to Tatranská Lesná (1¾hr.). To reach the cable car and spectacular view of **Skalnaté Pleso** and **Skalnatá Chata,** keep on the red trail and head toward the lake (2½hr., see **Hiking** in **Tatranská Lomnica,** p. 820) and one of the ends of the *magistrála*. To reach the long, tame **Tatranská magistrála** at Hrebienok, head on the red trail toward **Sliezký dom** (1670m, 2½hr.; ☎442 52 61; 3000Sk) and zig-zag down through the valley to reach the sharp ascent (3hr.) to **Chata Popradské Pleso ❸,** which sits on the calm, stunning lake front. (☎449 27 65; www.horskyhotel.sk. 380-680Sk; low season 290-550Sk.) Continue on the red trail for a pine tree-lined descent to **Štrbské Pleso** (1355m, 1-1½hr.) from where the *magistrála* winds on through the Slovak Tatras. Weary hikers can hop off the wandering *magistrála* on one of the many trails that descend to the Tatran resort towns below. From **Sliezský dom,** the green trail leads back to **Tatranská Polianka** (2hr.), while the yellow descends to **Vyšné Hágy** (2hr.); both lead back to the TEŽ. A more difficult path branches off the *magistrála* 20min. west of Hrebienok to one of the highest peaks, **Slavkovský Štít.** (2452m, 8hr. round-trip from Hrebienok. Do not attempt unless you have a full day and good weather.)

The hike to **Malá studená dolina** (Little Cold Valley) is fairly relaxed; take the red trail from Hrebienok to **Zamkovského Chata ❶** (☎442 26 36; 1475m, 40min.; 290Sk), and then take the green trail to **Téryho Chata ❶** (☎442 52 45; 2015m; 2hr.; 280Sk, with breakfast 390Sk) for a spectacular view of nearby Lomnický Štít. A popular route goes along the red trail from **Hrebienok** to **Zbojnícká Chata** (3hr.; ☎090 361 90 00) and continues on the blue trail, turning more daunting as it mounts **Sedlo Prielom** (2290m, 1¼hr.). It leads to Zamrznuly kotol (30min.) and turns onto the green trail with a quick ascent of **Sliezsky dom** (1670m, 1½hr.).

⚡ DAYTRIPS FROM STARÝ SMOKOVEC

ŠTRBSKÉ PLESO

Take the train (30min., 2 per hr., 30Sk). Several beautiful hikes originate in town. In the summer, a lift carries visitors to Chata pod Soliskom, which overlooks the lake and the expansive valleys that spread behind 1840m Štrbské Pleso. (☎449 22 21. 130Sk, children 90Sk; round-trip 190Sk/130Sk. Open 8:30am-4pm, last lift up 3:30pm.) To reach the lift, take the road from the trains and follow the signs or take the yellow trail. Once at the top, hike the red trail to the peak Predné Solisko (2093m) and begin your descent to Štrbské Pleso via the steep blue trail (1hr.). If you prefer a more scenic trip down, turn right on the blue trail from the chata and head left when you reach the yellow trail. When you hit the red path hang a left to get back to town (2¾hr.).

Hotels, ski jumps towers, and souvenir stands clutter placid **Štrbské Pleso** (SHTERB-skay PLEH-soh; Štrbské Lake), which offers some of the most cherished hikes and views in the Tatras. Peaceful trails expose Štrbské Pleso's natural beauty among awe-inspiring mountains.

Two magnificent day hikes loop out from Štrbské Pleso. Bring layers for both as well as food and water. From the **Informačné Stredisko Tanapu** (Information Center; open M-Sa 11-11:30am and noon-5:30pm) and the bus station, walk past the souvenir lot and head left at the junction. Continue uphill on the challenging **yellow trail** and along **Mlynická dolina** past several enchanting mountain lakes and the dramatic **Vodopády Skok** waterfalls. The path (7-8hr.) involves some strenuous ascents, mounting **Bystré Sedlo** (2314m) and **Veľké Solisko** (2412m) and taking you above the tree line before returning to Štrbské Pleso. The scenery justifies the effort.

The second hike takes you to the top of **Rysy** (2499m), on the Polish-Slovak border. Poland's highest peak and the highest Tatra scalable without a guide. From Štrbské Pleso, follow the *magistrála* to experience the awe-inspiring views and the imposing grandeur of the Tatran peaks. The **green trail** branches off the *magistrála* and rolls by the **Hincov potok** (stream) to an intersection where you can continue up on the **blue trail** or take a 2min. detour to **Chata Popradské Pleso ❷** (☎449 21 77; www.horskyhotel.sk. High season 7- to 10-bed dorms 270-350Sk; rooms 350-680Sk). Continue on the blue trail, which branches off after 40min. Take the red branch to tackle Rysy (30-40min.). Walk past the lake **Zabie Plesá** to **Chata pod Rysmi ❶** (2250m) where hot soups (40Sk) are available. (Rooms 200Sk). Allow 8-9hr. for the round-trip. This hike is for advanced hikers and should be attempted in good weather only. (☎524 46 76 76; www.tatry.sk.)

From the Chata pod Rysmi, head south 20min. on the yellow trail to the **Symbolic Cemetery** (Symbolický cintorín; 1525m). Built between 1936 and 1940 by painter Otakar Štafl, the field of wooden crosses, metal plaques, and broken propeller blades serves as a memorial to the dead hikers who have attempted the great Tatras. (Cemetery open July-Oct.) The trail ends at a paved blue path that the weary can descend to reach the Popradské Pleso TE stop (45min.). Those hardy souls looking to hike back to Štrbské Pleso will be rewarded with striking views from the steep descent. The *magistrála* continues from the *chata* for over 5hr. along scenic ridges to **Hrebienok** (see **Starý Smokovec: Hiking**, p. 826).

The stunning region is also popular among skiers of all abilities; the slopes of Štrbské Pleso boast excellent ridges and heavy snow. The six downhill trails range from 80m to 2300m. (Morning 440Sk, afternoon 540Sk, full day 690Sk; children 350Sk/440Sk/560Sk.) Many other slopes are accessible from this region, including a fairly gentle ski from Chata Solisko on Predné Solisko, where a lift awaits. For a more challenging ride, take a cable car from the base and ski down a red trail.

SLOVAK REPUBLIC

Most people choose to stay in **Starý Smokovec** or **Tatranská Lomnica**. However, those intent on staying out late on the trails can find affordable beds with private baths at **Obchodny Dom Toliar** ❸ on the first floor of the shopping center across from the train station. (Breakfast included. Reception 24hr. Check-out 10am. One-night stays only. Singles 600Sk; doubles and triples 970Sk.) Some private rooms are available; watch for *Zimmer frei* signs. Before starting a hike, stock up at the **grocery store** across from the train station. (Open daily 7am-7pm. MC/V.)

TATRANSKÁ LOMNICA

Take the train (15min., 16 per day, 20 Sk). Uphill from the station, behind Uni banka, get help from the attentive and well informed staff at Tatranská Informačná Kancelária. ☎ 442 52 30; www.tatry.sk. Open July-Aug. M-F 8am-6pm, Sa-Su 9am-2pm; Sept.-June M and W-F 9am-3pm, Tu 10am-3pm, Sa 8am-1pm. Just left of the large white complex across from the train station, Centrum Obchodu a služieb has the best-priced maps.

Though often dwarfed by the more lively and central Starý Smokovec, Tatranská Lomnica (TA-tran-ska LOM-nee-tsa) has the charming serenity of the entire Tatran region. The town is little more than a scattering of buildings that dot the perimeter of a lush park. Buy tickets a few hours in advance for the frequently sold-out lift ride to **Lomnický Štít** (2634m), the Tatras' second-highest peak. From Penzión Bělín (see below), follow the signs to the lanová draha **lifts,** which ride up to the glacial lake of **Skalnaté Pleso** (1751m). This lift runs frequently, but the four-person lift from Skalnaté Pleso to Lomnický Štít runs every hour, and tickets for the unparalleled view sell out fast. (July 3-Sept. one-way 240Sk, round-trip 380Sk; Sept. 2-July 2 200Sk/320Sk. Open 8am-4:30pm; last ascent 4pm.) From the lake, a large cabin (June 28-Sept. 12 500Sk; Sept. 13-June 27 450Sk) ascends to the summit of Lomnický Štít while a chairlift (160Sk/140Sk) plows on to **Lomnické Sedlo.** Alternatively, hike down the **green trail,** which offers somewhat lackluster views, back to Tatranská Lomnica. Purchase a 550Sk day ticket to **ski** the excellent trails from Skalnatá Chata to Tatranská Lomnica. On a clear day, the peak offers a staggering view of the mountains and valleys, and makes for a fabulous picnic spot. At **Skalnaté Pleso,** the *chata* (☎ 446 70 75) is a great spot to begin or end an adventure on the *Tatranská magistrála* (see below). Hardcore hikers can follow the green trail from Tatranská Lomnica to mount the hill to Skalnaté Pleso (3hr.). Hiking is generally better and the views more memorable from Starý Smokovec or Štrbské Pleso, but a few full-day hikes are accessible from Tatranská Lomnica's lift. The *magistrála* **red trail,** heading southwest from Skalnaté Pleso toward **Lomnická vyhliadka** (1524m, 50min.) and then to **Zamkovského Chata** (1¼hr.), is challenging to say the least, but remarkable views reward your efforts (see **Hiking: Starý Smokovec,** p. 826). The **blue trail** leads to a gentler hike; follow it from the InfoPanel, located at the base of the hill leading to the cable cars, to **Vodopády studeného potoka** (cold stream waterfalls) and back to Tatranská Lesná (4½hr.). The terrain here is flat enough to make this trip by bike.

Many of the hotels and pensions in Tatranská Lomnica are cheaper than what you would find in Starý Smokovec, and you can book private rooms from the tourist information office or look for *Zimmer Frei* signs. **Penzión Bělín** ❷, in the center of town, is one of the best. From the InfoPanel (see above), take the path across the street straight into the park. Take the first left and then a right onto the street ahead. Penzión Bělín lies to the right. (☎ 446 77 78; belin@tatry.sk. Check-out 9am. July-Aug. 2- and 4-person rooms 250Sk; Sept.-June 200Sk.) One of the few restaurants that offers authentic Slovak cuisine, ◙**Reštaurácia Júlia** ❷ (go left out of the train station and down the road) transcends the town's ubiquitous kitsch with its specialty dishes. (☎ 446 79 47. Entrees 70-190Sk. Open M-F noon-8pm, Sa-Su noon-10pm.) Stock up on snack food for the trails at **Supermarket Sintra,** just down the

hill behind the train station. (Open M-F 7:45am-6pm, Sa 7:45am-1pr
The **Sports Shop,** just before the cable cars, sells last-minute hikin
supplies. (Open daily 8:30am-4:30pm. MC/V.)

ŠARIŠ

More than home to Slovakia's most popular beer, Šariš is a gem of n
and cosmopolitan flair. Hidden away in the green hills of the eastern Slovak
Republic, Šariš spent the last century keeping to itself. Before that, it was forced to
act as a buffer against Turkish invasions. Though Šariš's cities are largely industrial, its Old Towns are beloved by locals and pleasantly surprising for tourists.

KOŠICE   ☎(0)55

Lying only 20km north of Hungary, Košice (KO-shih-tseh; pop. 236,000) is the Slovak Republic's second-largest city. The city's cultural and architectural development date back to the 19th century, when it was an important industrial center.
Hungarian nobles settled here and pumped money into the city's artistic institutions, laying the foundations for an enchanting Old Town. A journey outside Old
Town will remind visitors of Košice's communist past, as concrete bloc architecture scars the city's otherwise beautiful landscape. While the sun shines, crowds
stream through the Old Town's restaurants and shops. As night falls, locals and
visitors emerge from surrounding high-rises and party until dawn.

▐▘ TRANSPORTATION

Trains: ☎613 21 75. Predstaničné nám. To: **Banská Bystrica** (3½-5hr., 264Sk); **Bratislava** (6hr., 13 per day, 550Sk); **Poprad** (1¼hr., 1 per day, 138Sk); **Prešov** (50min.,
10 per day, 53Sk); **Rožňava** (1½hr., 12 per day, 88Sk); **Budapest, HUN** (5hr., 3 per
day, 827Sk); **Kraków, POL** (6-7hr., 3 per day, 901Sk); **Prague, CZR** (10-11hr., 4 per
day, 1200Sk).

Buses: ☎625 16 19. To the left of the train station. Bus prices, which fluctuate annually,
are based on the number of km traveled. Destinations include: **Banská Bystrica**
(4½hr., 1 per day); **Bardejov** (2-3hr., 12-20 per day); **Bratislava** (8hr., 12 per day);
Levoča (3hr., 10 per day); **Poprad** (2½hr., 5 per day); **Prešov** (50min., 30 per day);
Rožňava (1¼hr., 37 per day); **Prague, CZR** (9hr., 3 per day). **SAD** (Slovenská autobus-
ová doprava; ☎680 73 06; www.sad-kds.sk), on the 2nd fl. of the train station, also
sends buses to **Berlin, GER** (19hr., 2 per day, 2400Sk) and **Budapest, HUN** (6hr., 1
per day, 520Sk). Open M-F 8am-noon and 12:30-3:30pm.

Public Transportation: Trams and **buses** cross the city and suburbs. Tickets from kiosks
and yellow boxes at bus stops (12Sk) or from driver (14Sk). Extra charge for large backpacks (6Sk). Punch ticket upon boarding. Fines for riding ticketless up to 1000Sk.

Taxis: Taxis await on almost every corner. **Classic Taxi** (☎622 22 44), **CTC** (☎43 34
33), and **Radio Taxi** (☎163 33).

▚▟ ORIENTATION AND PRACTICAL INFORMATION

To get to the heart of Košice's **Staré Mesto** (Old Town), exit the train station and
follow the "Centrum" signs across the park. Walk down **Mlynská** to reach the main
square, **Hlavná nám.** To find the tourist office, turn right.

Tourist Office: Informačna Centrum Mesta Kosiče, Hlavná 58 (☎625 88 88;
www.kosice.sk/icmk), provides helpful information on accommodations and cultural
attractions. **Maps** free and 45Sk. Open M-F 9am-6pm, Sa 9am-1pm.

SLOVAK REPUBLIC

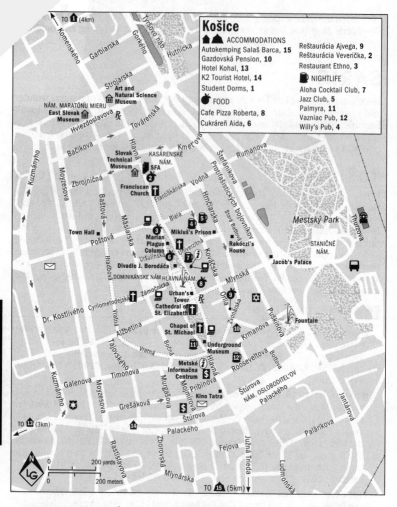

Košice

🏠🏔 ACCOMMODATIONS
Autokemping Salaš Barca, **15**
Gazdovská Pension, **10**
Hotel Kohal, **13**
K2 Tourist Hotel, **14**
Student Dorms, **1**

🍴 FOOD
Cafe Pizza Roberta, **8**
Cukráreň Aida, **6**

Reštaurácia Ajvega, **9**
Reštaurácia Veverička, **2**
Restaurant Ethno, **3**

🍺 NIGHTLIFE
Aloha Cocktail Club, **7**
Jazz Club, **5**
Palmyra, **11**
Vazniac Pub, **12**
Willy's Pub, **4**

SLOVAK REPUBLIC

Currency Exchange: VÚB branches are everywhere; the one at Hlavná 8 (☎622 62 50) **exchanges currency** for no commission and cashes **traveler's checks** for 1% commission and a hefty 200Sk min. Gives MC **cash advances.** Open M-Tu and F 7:30am-5pm, W 8am-7pm, Th 8am-noon, Sa 9am-1pm. 24hr. (MC/V) **ATMs** are in front of many VÚB branches. **OTP Banka Slovenska,** Alžbetina 2 (☎681 12 67), cashes AmEx/V checks for 1%. Open M-F 8am-6pm.

Luggage Storage: At the train station. 24Sk per bag per day, 14Sk each additional day; bags over 15kg 35Sk/20Sk. Small lockers 5Sk. Open 24hr.

English-Language Bookstore: SFA, Hlavná 97 (☎623 36 76), through the arch and up the stairs. Small selection of English language classics (97Sk) and a variety of popular and classic literature (300-800Sk). Open M-F 9am-6pm, Sa 10am-1pm. **Knihkupec-tuo,** Mlynská 14, also sells some English books. Open M-F 9am-7pm; Sa 9am-1pm.

Pharmacy: Lekáreň Pri Dóme, Mlynská 1. Open M-F 7:30am-6:30pm, Sa 8am-noon.

Telephones: Scattered around Hlavná and outside the post office (see below).

Internet Access: At the central **tourist office** (see above), 40Sk per hr. **Net Internet Cafe,** Poštová 3. Ring the bell to be let in. 29Sk per hr., after 4pm 20Sk per hr. Open daily 10am-10pm. **Internet Centrum,** Hlavná 27 (www.kosez.sk). 0.58Sk per min., 30Sk per hr. Open daily 9am-10pm.

Post Office: Poštová 20 (☎617 14 01). Open M-F 7am-7pm, Sa 8am-noon. **Poste Restante** at window #16. **Postal Code:** 04001.

ACCOMMODATIONS

Keep in mind that some larger hotels can be cheaper, cleaner, and closer to the center than *penzióny*, which often overcharge and fail to impress. There are limited budget accommodations in the center of town, so it may be a commute if you want to save the money. **Student dorms** (☎643 94 84; 200-400Sk per night), are the cheapest option in July and August but are far from the center.

K2 Tourist Hotel, Štúrova 32 (☎625 59 48). Take tram #6 or bus #16, 21, or 30 from the train/bus station to the "Dom Umenia" stop, or follow Hlavná from the main square and turn right on Štúrova. The best bargain within walking distance from town, this hostel provides clean, yet poorly lit, rooms in a cheerful environment. Shared showers lack curtains. Restaurant open M-Sa 10am-10pm, Su noon-10pm. Reception 24hr. Check-in and check-out noon. Beds in triples and quads 300Sk. 15Sk city tax per day. ❶

Gazdovská Pension, Ćajkovského 4, (☎625 01 43). The friendly staff at this central hostel helps visitors navigate the city. Clean, comfortable rooms with well-kept baths. Call 2 days ahead. Singles 800Sk; doubles 1000Sk. 15Sk tax per day. ❸

Hotel Kohal, Trieda SNP 61 (☎/fax 642 55 72). Take tram #6 from the train/bus station to a roundabout at Toryská and Trieda SNP. Get off at the 5th stop, "Ferrocentrum." Hotel rooms have TVs, radios, and renovated baths. Singles and doubles share showers; apartments have private baths. The hotel hosts a hostel with plain singles and doubles. The hostel is welcoming, but it's a long walk back from the town center after the trams stop at night. Breakfast 90Sk. Laundry 5-60Sk per item. Reception 24hr. Check-out 11am. Hostel singles 330Sk; doubles 610Sk. Hotel singles 580Sk; doubles 1120Sk; apartments 1300Sk. 15Sk city tax per day. AmEx/MC/V. ❷

Autokemping Salaš Barca (☎623 33 97; www.eurocampings.net). From the station, take tram #6 to "Ferrocentrum" and switch to tram #9. Get off at "Autokemping" and backtrack 100m; turn left at sign. Simple, clean, 2-bedroom bungalows with well-kept baths. Badminton, volleyball, soccer, and ping-pong available. Reception 24hr. Check-in and check-out noon. Reserve 3 days ahead. 70Sk per person, 60Sk per tent, 80Sk per car. 2-bed bungalows 500Sk; 3-bed 750SK. 15Sk tax per day. AmEx/MC/V. ❶

FOOD

With restaurants on rooftop terraces, under arches, and on the central square itself, Košice is a culinary paradise. For **groceries,** try the **Tesco,** at Hlavná 109, next to Pizza Hut. (☎670 48 10. Open M-F 8am-8pm, Sa-Su 8am-4:30pm. MC/V.)

Restaurant Ethno, Hlavná 102, boasts an array of international foods, but specializes in delectable Slovak cuisine. Relax in the outdoor beer garden or enjoy the quiet, laid-back atmosphere inside. Entrees 89-140. Open daily noon-10pm. ❷

Reštaurácia Veverička (Squirrel Restaurant), Hlavná 97 (☎622 33 60). Look for the pair of rodents carved out of dark wood. Enjoy a variety of local dishes on the sun-drenched patio (don't worry, squirrel isn't on the menu). English menu. Entrees 56-208Sk. Open daily 9am-10pm. ❷

Cafe Pizza Roberta, Hlavná 45 (☎0905 678 231). Delight in the spectacular views from this popular pizzeria, located near the base of St. Elizabeth's Cathedral and Urban's Tower. The friendly waitresses are happy to help decipher the Slovak menu. The food is worth the wait. Entrees 53-155Sk. Open daily 10am-midnight.

Reštaurácia Ajvega, Orlia 10 (☎622 04 52; www.ajvega.sk). Vegetarians praise this organic food restaurant, which adds a touch of Spanish spice to traditionally straightforward dishes. Large vegetable and tortilla portions add flavor to this corner of Eastern Europe. Soups 20-25Sk. Entrees 89Sk. Daily special (soup and an entree) 59Sk. Open Su-Th 11am-11pm, F-Sa 11am-midnight. ❶

Cukráreň Aida, Hlavná 77. Indulge your sweet tooth at Košice's most popular ice-cream parlor, which offers an array of flavors (5Sk per scoop) and bakery sweets (15-80Sk). Open daily 8am-10pm. ❶

👁 SIGHTS

▒ CATHEDRAL OF ST. ELIZABETH (DOM SV. ALŽBETY). Dominating much of Old Town, this gigantic cathedral practically spans the width of Hlavná. Begun in 1378 as a high-Gothic monument, the cathedral has undergone repeated renovations. It is now a unique mixture of Western styles, from Baroque to Rococo. Inside the Cathedral, pay special attention to the impressive **altar,** complemented by majestic stained-glass windows on all sides. In 1900, renovators built a crypt under the cathedral's north nave, where Košice's revolutionary hero Ferenc Rakóczi II now rests—*sans* heart. His body was transported from Turkey, where he lived in exile, and his heart was taken to Grosbois. The church's North Tower offers a stunning view of the Old Town and a spectacular look at the detailed cathedral roof. The roof's intricate pattern provides a stark contract to the drab Soviet architecture that overwhelms the visible distance. (☎090 866 70 83. Crypt open all year M-F 9:30am-4:30pm; tower open Apr.-Nov. M-F 9:30am-4:30pm. Admission to exhibit 20Sk, students 15Sk; both 30Sk/20Sk. Cathedral tours 35Sk/20Sk.) On the other side of the cathedral, the barren facade of **Urban's Tower** (Urbanova veža) melts from sight next to the grandeur of St. Elizabeth's Cathedral. Though it now hosts a wax museum, the tower is not without historical significance of its own. A closer look reveals 34 tombstones ringing the exterior, one of which dates from the 4th century. The fountain in front dazzles crowds with musical water dances to the likes of Simon and Garfunkle. Across the park from the Cathedral of St. Michael, follow the stairs to the ruins of the **town fortifications.**

EAST SLOVAK MUSEUM (VÝCHODNOSLOVENSKÉ MÚZEUM). As you walk up, Hlavná, take a right at the **State Theater** onto Univerzitná to arrive at two branches of the East Slovak Museum: **Mikluš's Prison** (Miklušova väznica) and **Rakóczi's House.** Housed in the former city jail, Mikluš's prison details life behind bars from the 17th to 19th century, exhibiting prisoner graffiti and torture instruments. Haunting descriptions of brutal deaths can be found in the photo collection in the reconstructed chambers—one woman, who killed her illegitimate baby, was thrown into her grave before a stake was driven into her heart. (*Hrnčiarska 7. Ticket office behind the gate at Hrnčiarska. Open Su 9am-1pm, Tu-Sa 9am-5pm. English info sheet available. Mandatory tours every hr. 30Sk, students 10Sk.*) At Nám. Mieru Maratónu, in the ornate building closest to the runner's statue, stands the **archaeological branch** of the East Slovak Museum, which displays tools, bones, and black-and-white photos that detail the history of the Šariš region. The museum's best exhibit, in tı vault downstairs, is a copper bowl filled with 2920 gold *tholars*, discovered in 1935 while workers were laying foundations for new finance headquarters at Hlavná 68. *(Hviezdoslavova 2. ☎622 05 71. Open Su 9am-1pm, Tu-Sa 9am-5pm. 30Sk, students 10Sk. Temporary exhibits 30Sk/10Sk. English guide book 30Sk.)* Across the street, the **Art and Natural Science Museum**, Hviezdoslavova 3, is housed in a Baroque-inspired building. Lined with stars and geological finds, this museum is popular with families and young children. The large taxidermy exhibit could make stomachs churn, but provides a fascinating detail of the **natural splendor of the Carpathians** (Priroda Karpat). Upstairs chronicles a century of art, from Rome to the Middle Ages. *(☎622 01 81. Open Su 9am-1pm, Tu-Sa 9am-5pm. 30Sk, students 10Sk.)*

AROUND JACOB'S PALACE (JAKUBOV PALÁC). Walking down Mlynská from the cathedral toward the train station leads to the 19th-century Jacob's Palace, built of stones discarded from the cathedral in a dazzling style described as "pseudo-Gothic." Behind the cathedral on Hlavná, on the far side of the fountain, is the neo-Baroque **State Theater** (Štátne divadlo), built at the end of the 19th century. Past the theater on Hlavná, the **Marian Plague Column** (Morový Sloup), decorated with cherubs, commemorates the devastating plague of 1711.

🎵 🎭 ENTERTAINMENT AND NIGHTLIFE

Fans of high and low culture alike won't be disappointed by Košice. Info about its **philharmonic orchestra** and four **theaters** is available at the tourist office (see **Orientation and Practical Information,** p. 829). **Štatne Divadlo Košice,** Hlavná 58, performs Su 2:30pm, W and F-Sa 7pm, Tu 10am. Consult the website and notice board outside for more specific info on shows offered. The season runs Sept.-June. (☎622 12 33; www.sdke.box.sk. Open M-F 9am-5pm, Sa 10am-1pm. Tickets 100-180Sk. 50Sk discount with ISIC.) On the first Sunday of October, the annual **Košice Peace Marathon** keeps runners on their toes from Turňa nad Bodvov to the bronze runner statue on Hlavná. The event, which first took place in 1924, is the **second-oldest modern marathon** (after Boston's). At night, the Old Town booms with live music as locals pack into the clubs and bars, which line the main streets and hide on side streets. For those looking to make their own fun, purchase wine (89-300Sk) or beer (25Sk) at **Diskont Luis Lawrence,** Biela 1 (open M-F 7am-1am, Sa-Su 8am-1pm).

▨ **Jazz Club,** Kováčska 39 (☎622 42 37). Disco dominates Tu, Th, and Sa, drawing in a younger crowd looking to dance. Jazz and funk draw an older, sophisticated crowd during the week, and classical piano fills the Su-M gap. Beer 25-35Sk. Concert/disco cover 30Sk. Open daily 4pm-2am, disco nights until 3am.

Willy's Pub, Kováčska 49, opposite the Jazz Club. The homey atmosphere of this underground bar ensures its popularity with a mixed crowd. An excellent choice for cheap pints. The jukebox (5Sk) equipped with modern songs of all genres. Beer 19Sk-30Sk. Open M-F 10am-midnight, Sa-Su 4pm-midnight.

Aloha Cocktail Club, Hlavná 69, attracts a younger crowd to a loud mix of R&B, rap, and pop. Party until dawn on the cavernous dance floor with the help of Aloha's exhaustive cocktail selection. Open Su-Th 2pm-11pm, F 2pm-3am, Sa 5pm-3am.

Palmyra, Hlavná 24. Relaxed 20-somethings swing to the beats of salsa, reggae, and pop under a disco ball. If dancing isn't your thing, enjoy the pounding music from comfy booths. Beer 40Sk. 18+. Open Su-Tu 3pm-2am, W-Th 3pm-3am, F-Sa 3pm-3am.

Vazniac Pub, Roosweltova 12. This prison-style bar morbidly features its very own electric chair. The friendly waiters, dressed in inmate uniforms, bring your drinks quickly. Open M-Th 11am-10pm, F 11am-1am, Sa 3pm-1am, Su 3pm-3am.

DOMICA ☎ (0)58

to Rožňava (1½hr., 12 per day, 125Sk). Then take the train (17Sk) or bus
5, 6, or 14 to Plešivec (30min., 23Sk). Get off at bus stop at the parking lot. Catch the
connecting bus (3Sk) to Jaskyňa Domica. Check the timetable across from the cave
entrance for return buses. Be prepared to wait; it may be 1-2hr. between buses. If you
think you missed the bus, run to the friendly, English-speaking TIC staff, which has info
about buses that make the trip to Plešivec and the caves. ☎ 788 20 10; www.domica.sk.
June-Aug. Tu-Su 9, 10:30am, 12:30, 2, 3, 4pm; Feb.-May and Sept.-Dec. 9:30, 11am,
12:30pm, 2pm. Mandatory 45min. tours (min. 4 people) 80Sk, students 60Sk, children
40Sk. 1½hr. tours 110Sk/90Sk/60Sk. Cameras 100Sk, video 200Sk.

🌋Jaskyňa Domica is a challenge to reach, but the breathtaking caverns are worth
the effort. Dazzling stalactites and stalagmites jut from three-million-year-old
UNESCO-protected cave walls, creating complex patterns in the spacious chambers, the largest of which measures 48,000 cubic meters. When underground water
levels permit, a 1½hr. tour includes a boat ride covering 1.5km of the cave. A shortened version during droughts lasts 40-45min. and allows a peek at 780m of the
grand expanse. Only 5km of the 23km cave lie on the Slovak side—the rest is
accessible from across the Hungarian border. If you want to see more, travel 1km
(10min. on foot, above ground) to the border and find the Hungarian entrance (see
Baradla Caves, HUN, p. 371), only 2km away from the Slovak entrance.

KRASNA HORKA CASTLE

Take the train (1½hr., 12 per day, 125Sk) or bus (1hr., 10 per day, 120Sk) to Rožňava.
From there, take bus from platforms #7 or 12 to Krásnohorské Podhradie (20min.,
20Sk). Check the timetable for return buses and walk up the path toward the castle.
☎ 732 47 69. Open May-Oct. M-F 8:30am-4:30pm. Mandatory 1hr. tours 9:30, 11am,
12:30, 2pm. 80Sk, students 40Sk. Cameras 100Sk.

The beautifully restored Krasna Horka Castle is located just outside the picturesque village of Rožňava. Known as one of the Slovak Republic's most amazing
castles, Krasna Horka's history stretches far back beyond its host country. Built
in the 14th century, its exterior is a tribute to the popular Gothic style and dominates the surrounding countryside for miles. Once inside, feel like a nobleman
while traversing through the magnificent state rooms. The 1hr. tour takes you
through over 30 rooms. Of particular interest is the music room, a tribute to the
oft-forgotten artisans who added merriment to castle life. In contrast, downstairs, torture instruments, including clamps and a rack, reveal the hidden brutal-
ity of this one-time war fortress. The imposing castle tells a story not only of
gallant deeds but also of gruesome punishment.

PREŠOV ☎ (0)51

Encircled by cosmopolitan commercial centers and communist-era residential
blocks, Prešov's (preh-SHOV; pop. 92,600) colorful Old Town reflects its rural
roots. The town moves slowly, allowing peaceful promenades around the square
and relaxing drinks in one of the town's many popular beer gardens and pubs.

🚆 **TRANSPORTATION. Trains** (☎773 01 43) travel to **Bardejov** (1½hr., 5 per day,
50Sk); **Bratislava** (5-7hr., 2 per day, 476Sk); **Košice** (45min., 14 per day, 38Sk);
Budapest, HUN (5hr., 4:25am, 948Sk); **Kraków, POL** (5½-7hr., 2 per day, 859Sk). **Buses**
(☎773 13 47), across the street from the train station, travel to **Banská Bystrica**

(4hr., 9 per day, 360Sk); **Bardejov** (1hr., 12 per day, 53Sk); **Bratislava** (9hr., 4-16 per day, 550Sk); **Kežmarok** (5hr., 4 per day, 116Sk); **Košice** (1hr., every 15-55min., 43Sk); **Poprad** (1¼hr., 20-29 per day, 116Sk). The ticket window is open M-F 6am-5:30pm, Sa-Su 7am-2:30pm. **AB Taxi** (☎773 37 33). **EuroTaxi** (☎771 62 16).

■ ⁊ **ORIENTATION AND PRACTICAL INFORMATION.** Prešov's major artery, **Košická**, passes between the train and bus stations, becoming **Masarykova**, then **Hlavná**, where the city's heart lies. To get to the town center, take the walkway under Masarykova, purchase a ticket (8Sk, exact change required) from the kiosk, and hop on any **tram** or **bus** (except #19 or 31) heading toward the center. You can also turn right out of the bus stop and head straight up until you hit Hlavná (20min.) or take a taxi (90Sk). The **tourist office, Mestské Informačné Centrum,** Hlavná 67, provides info on the town and hotels, as well as a great pocket **map** (15Sk) and **info guide** (5Sk) of the city. (☎773 11 13; www.pis.sk. Open May-Oct. M-F 10am-6pm, Sa 9am-1pm; Nov.-Apr. M-F 9am-5pm.) **Istrobanka**, Hlavná 75, which has good rates for **currency exchange**s and a 24hr. (MC/V) **ATM** outside. The bank also cashes **traveler's checks** for 1% commission. (☎758 04 18; fax 772 31 65. Open M-F 8am-5pm.) **Tatra Banka**, Nám. Legionároy 1, cashes **traveler's checks** for 1% commission (min. 30Sk) and gives **cash advances**. There's an MC/V ATM outside. (☎772 04 85; www.tatrabanka.sk. Open M-F 8am-6pm, Sa 8am-noon.) **Store luggage** at the train station. (10Sk, over 15kg 20Sk. Open daily 6am-noon, 12:30-5:30pm, and 6-10pm.) There is a **24hr. pharmacy** called **Amuletum**, Sabinovská 15 (☎771 94 05). Walk up Hlavná away from the train station and past the town center; Sabinovská is to the left. Find **Internet access** at **Slovanet Internet Klub**, Hlavná 42, 2nd fl. (www.presov.viapvt.sk/club.htm. M-F 30Sk 1st hr., 20Sk each additional hr.; Sa-Su 20Sk/10Sk. 10% ISIC discount. Open M-F 8am-8pm, Sa-Su 8am-3pm.) For access later at night, wander to **Internet Palinet**, Jarkova 63. (☎775 15 29. 5Sk per 10min., 25Sk per hr. Open M-Sa 10am-10pm, Su 3-10pm.) The tourist office also has **Internet access** (2Sk per min.). **Phones** are outside the **post office**, Masarykova 2, which sits where Masarykova becomes Hlavná. (☎777 62 73. **Poste Restante** at window #1. **Western Union** services. Open M-F 8am-7pm, Sa 8am-noon.) **Postal Code:** 08001.

◗◖ **ACCOMMODATIONS AND FOOD. Penzión Lineas** ❷, Budovateľská 14, is closer to the train station than to the center, which lies a 10min. walk away. From the station, walk toward the center, take the first left on Skultétyho and then your second left on Budovateľská. You'll come upon nine floors of comfortable doubles with private baths and balconies. Snacks are available 24hr. at reception, and the coffee shop is open daily 7:30-10am. (☎772 33 25; www.presov.sk. Check-in 2pm. Check-out 11am. Doubles 550Sk, with TV 700Sk.) To get to **Turistická Ubytovňa Sen** ❷, Vajanského 65, take a bus toward the center. Get off at "Na Hlavnéj," at the entrance to the main square. Follow the departing bus and take the first right on Metodova. Walk toward the tower and take the first left past Konštantinova to reach the unmarked Vajanského. The location next to the town center makes up for the spartan rooms.(☎772 06 28; www.presov.sk. Breakfast and dinner 100Sk. Reception 24hr. Check-out 10am. 1- to 4-person dorms 250Sk.) **Penzión Antonio** ❸, on Jarková 22, boasts an incredible location right in the thick of things and comfortable, well-decorated rooms with TVs and showers for weary travelers. Follow the bus directions for Turistická Ubytovňa Sen, taking a left onto Florianova rather than right on Metodova. Hang another left on Jarková. You can reach reception at the pension's pizza restaurant by walking through the archway to the left of the **tourist office.** (☎/fax 772 32 25. Reception M-F 10am-10pm, Sa-Su 1-10pm. Check-out noon. Call ahead. Doubles 1000Sk; triples 1300Sk.)

What it lacks in accommodations, Prešov makes up for in food. **Restaurant u Richtára ❷**, ul.Hlavná 71, boasts fine dining at excellent prices. The friendly staff and varied menu woo locals and tourists alike in an elegant and relaxing atmosphere. (☎772 32 36. Entrees 160-250Sk. Open M-F 11am-11pm, Sa-Su noon-11pm.) For a delightful taste of the Far East, head to **Čínska Reštaurácia ❶**, Hlavná 41. You'll be aided by a picture menu and helpful waiters. (Entrees 88-139Sk. Open M-Su 10:30am-11pm.) **Góvinda ❶**, Hlavná 70 under an orange banner, serves up cheap options for weary vegetarians seeking tasty alternatives to meaty Slovak fare. The restaurant boasts a shaded checker-board courtyard with a fountain. (☎772 28 19. Open noon-7pm.) **Veliovič Cukráreň ❷**, Hlavná 28, is heavenly. Indulge your sweet tooth with sinful banana splits (50Sk), homemade ice cream (5Sk per scoop), and a 26Sk frothy cappuccino. (☎772 51 68. Open M-F 8am-9pm, Sa-Su 9am-9pm.) There's a **Tesco supermarket**, Nám. Legionarova 1, where Hlavná becomes Masarykova. (☎772 22 41. Open M-F 7am-8pm, Sa 7am-3pm, Su 8am-1pm. MC/V.)

◖ SIGHTS. The colossal **St. Nicholas's Church** (Kostol sv. Mikuláša) dominates Prešov's main square. Built in 1347, the Gothic church's distinctive turrets attest to Saxon influence during the late Middle Ages. The gold-laden altar, considered to be among the best works crafted by Master Pavol (see **Levoča**, p. 817), lies under a late-Gothic tower. (Open M-F 8am-4pm. Su Service 10am. Visitors' clothing should cover their shoulders and knees.). To the right of the church stands the 16th-century **Rákoczi Palace**, Hlavná 86, home of the **Regional Museum** (Krajské múzeum). The fire exhibit includes a display on fire's discovery in the Stone Age and an illuminating history of botched attempts to control it and concludes with old fire trucks parked out back. True to its name, the museum features local folk costumes, craftsmanship, and handmade instruments. (☎773 47 08. Open Tu-F 8am-noon and 12:30-5pm, Su 1-6pm. 40Sk, students 20Sk.)

To reach the **Wine Museum**, Floriánova ul., head left before hitting St. Nicholas's Church. The subterranean cellar showcases more than 3000 varieties of wines, many of which you can sample for 100-200Sk. Ask for a recommendation. The museum focuses on the region's wine making, which dates back to the 17th century, and sells common local vintages for 42-100Sk. However, a few rare bottles are more expensive: a 1942 Argentine wine, the pride of their international collection, is 35,000Sk. (☎773 31 08; muzeumvin@stonline.sk. Open M-F 9am-6pm, Sa 8am-noon. 40Sk.) The **town hall**, still in use today, is in the same building as the wine museum. A luxurious home that dates back to the Middle Ages, the hall was restored to its Early Baroque style after a great fire in 1887. On the west side of Hlavná, the restored Gothic **Šarišská Gallery**, Hlavná 51, features local art and provides a taste of regional mythology. (☎772 54 23; fax 773 40 38. Open Tu-W and F 9am-5pm, Th 9am-6pm, Su 2-6pm. 20Sk, students 10Sk; Su free.) Heading left from the town hall on Hlavná, the narrow, medieval Floriánova ul. leads to **St. Florian's Gate** (Brána sv. Floriána), a remnant of Prešov's early Renaissance fortifications and a tribute to the town's patron saint. Walking up Hlavná away from the train station, take a left near its end onto Ku Kumštu, which will lead to Švermova and a courtyard at #56. Inside is a **synagogue** and a monument to Prešov's 6000 Holocaust victims. If the doors are closed, you can still see the interior via the **Judaica Museum**, on the upper balcony. (☎773 16 38. Open Tu-W 11am-4pm, Th 3-6pm, F 10am-1pm, Su 1-5pm. 60Sk, students 10Sk.)

◖ NIGHTLIFE. This placid town has a reasonably active nightlife. The most popular spots are the canopied beer gardens along the west side of Hlavná. **Club 54**, Hlavná 72, is a disco and bar where a younger crowd gyrates to hip-hop. (www.club54.szm.sk. *Šaris* 30Sk. Open M-Th 10am-midnight, F 10am-3am, Sa

4pm-3am, Su 4pm-midnight.) Next door, at **Pizzeria La Cucharacha**, Hlavná 72, locals finish off food with a few drinks or a game of pool. This pub hosts a relaxed crowd. (☎773 17 18. Beer 25Sk. Open M-Th 11am-1am, F 11am-2am, Sa 6pm-2am, Su 6pm-midnight.) **Vináreň Neptun**, Hlavná 64, draws a mature crowd. Sprawling through seven rooms, this winery, restaurant, and pub has space for all. Head through the arch and hang a right. (☎773 25 38. *Šaris* 30Sk. Disco F-Sa 8pm-3am. Open M-Th 11am-10pm, F 11am-3am, Sa 6pm-3am.) If you're starved for English films, hit up **Kino Panorama**, ul. Masarykova 7, across from the post office, to see the latest Hollywood movies to reach Slovakia. (☎773 34 66. Ticket window open 4-10pm. Showings at 5 and 7:30pm. M 50Sk, Tu-W 60Sk, Th-Su 70Sk.)

BARDEJOV ☎(0)54

A favorite destination for Slovak newlyweds, life in scenic Bardejov (bahr-day-YOW; pop. 38,000) hasn't always been a honeymoon. Having endured earthquakes, fires, and the occasional Turkish army, this former trade center underwent a complete reconstruction in 1986—a feat that earned it the UNESCO Heritage Gold Medal. Relaxing Bardejov attracts those who wish to sidestep the hectic pace of modern metropolises and delight in the town's main attraction, its soothing baths.

⌁ TRANSPORTATION. Trains, Slovenská 18 (☎472 36 05) go to: **Košice** (1¾-2¼hr., 3 per day, 102Sk); **Prešov** (1¼hr., 5 per day, 58Sk); **Kraków, POL** (7hr., 2 per day, 900Sk). The best way to Bardejov is by **bus** (☎723 353). To: **Banská Bystrica** (4hr., M-F 5 per day, 285Sk); **Bratislava** (11hr., 4 per day, 460Sk); **Košice** (1¾hr., 5 per day, 106Sk); **Poprad** (2-2½hr., M-F 9 per day, 130Sk); **Prešov** (1hr.; M-F 10 per day, Sa-Su 3 per day; 50-53Sk); **Rožňava** (4hr., 3 per day, 176Sk).

▉⚡ ORIENTATION AND PRACTICAL INFORMATION. From the **train and bus station**, cross the parking lot, go left, and continue until you see a cobblestone path leading to the ruined lower gate of **Staré Mesto** (Old Town). Continue onto the unmarked Stöclova around to the left. Turn right on **Paštová** to reach **Radničné námestie**, the main square. The **tourist office, Globtour Bratislava**, Radničné nám. 21, sells **maps** (10Sk) and provides useful info on accommodations and attractions. (☎/fax 472 62 73. Open June 15-Sept. 15 M-F 9am-6pm, Sa-Su 10am-noon and 1:30-4pm; Sept. 16-June 14 M-F 9am-4:30pm.) Get MC/V **cash advances** or cash AmEx/V **traveler's checks** (min. 200Sk) for 1% commission at **VÚB**, Kellerova 1. A 24hr. (MC/V) **ATM** stands outside. (☎472 26 71. Open M-W and F 8am-5pm, Th 8am-noon.) A **pharmacy, Lekaren Sv. Egidia**, Radničné nám. 43, posts the locations of after-hours pharmacies. (☎472 75 62. Open M-F 7:30am-5pm.) Access the **Internet** at **Internetový Klub**, Radničné nám. 12, 3rd fl. (Open M-F 10am-10pm, Sa-Su 2pm-10pm. 5Sk per 15min.) The **post office**, Dlný rad 14, sells phone cards; **telephones** are outside. (☎472 40 62. Open M-F 7:30am-6pm, Sa 7:30-11:30am.) **Postal Code:** 08501.

⌂▢ ACCOMMODATIONS AND FOOD. Accommodations are limited in Bardejov. Book rooms in advance June through September. More **private rooms** and **pensions** (200-300Sk) lie outside of town but are poorly connected. The tourist office can help book rooms. Vladimír Kaminsky and his wife run ◙**Penzión Semafór ❸**, Kellerova 13, and welcome visitors with unmatched hospitality. Spacious rooms have TV, private bath, and a shared kitchen. From the train station, cross the parking lot and go left on Slovenská; go right on Nový sad. Walk 200m and turn right on Kellerova; the pension is right ahead. (☎474 44 33; www.slovenska.infoglos.sk/semaford. Free tea, coffee, and breakfast. Singles 700Sk; doubles 900Sk; apartment with kitchens 1100Sk; extra beds 200Sk.) **SOU Pod Vinbargom ❶**, with balconies, comfy beds, and well-kept baths, is a comfortable base near the train station. Turn left from the bus stop and follow the road as it curves. The hotel is on the left past the supermarket. (☎472 40 10. Reception 24hr. Check-in noon. Check-out 10am. Call ahead. Singles 162Sk; doubles 324Sk; triples 486Sk; quads 548Sk.)

Though restaurants have besieged Radičné nám., few are more than snack bars and pubs. The classy and romantic **Roland ❷**, Radičné nám. 12, fuses Italian and Slovak flavors by day but becomes pub-like at night. Go through the arch and to the back to reach the patio, or sit amid the medieval decor in the underground restaurant and pub. (☎472 92 20. Entrees 75-129Sk. Open M-F 10am-10pm, Sa-Su 11am-10pm.) **Cafe Restaurant Hubert ❷**, Radničné nám. 6, serves delicious grilled beef and fish. (☎474 26 03. Entrees 89-142Sk. Open M-Th 10am-11pm, F-Sa 10am-1am, Su 11am-11pm. MC/V.) Locals satisfy their sweet tooth with ice cream (6Sk per scoop) and desserts (15-18Sk) at **Oaza ❶**. (☎474 64 70. Open daily 8:30am-10pm.) **Billa Supermarket**, next to the train station, offers a huge selection of food and drinks. (Open M-Sa 8am-9pm. Su 9am-8pm.)

◎ SIGHTS. Visiting Bardejov and scoping out the **Bardejov Baths** (Bardejovské Kúpele) could be good for your health. The waters are rumored to have curative powers—powers so great the acidic taste doesn't deter the crowds who fill bottles here. Tsar Alexander I of Russia, Joseph II of Austria-Hungary, Napoleon, and Austrian Emperor Franz Josef's wives frequented the baths. For a dip in 28°C spring waters, head to the *kupalisko* (swimming pool) at the end of the park. (☎477 44 21. Open May 10-Sept. 22 M 1-7pm, Tu-F noon-7pm, Sa-Su 8am-7pm. Tu-F 8am-noon patients with prescription only. M-F 30Sk, students 20Sk; Sa-Su 45Sk/35Sk.) Or, drop into any of the hotels for various **spa treatments**, including massages and manicures. To reach the baths, which lie just outside the Bardejov city center, take bus #1, 6, or 12 from the station to the end of the line (20min., 7Sk).

Back in town, the **Church of St. Egidius** (Kostol sv. Egídia), Radničné nám. 47, contains 11 Gothic wing altars crafted between 1450 and 1510 by Master Pavol. The largest of these, the detailed 15th-century **Nativity Altar**, was consecrated by St. Gilles, patron saint of the town and church. When examining the equally spectacular main altar, look up at the crucifixes for a painfully detailed depiction of Christ's death on the cross. (English info. Open M-F 10am-4:30pm, Sa 10am-2:30pm, Su open for services and visits 11:30am-2pm. 25Sk, students 15Sk. Tower 40Sk/20Sk.) Head out of the main square on Františkǎnov and turn right onto Mlynská to reach Bardejov's **Jewish quarter**, where there is a closed **synagogue** and a moving memorial plaque to the more than 7000 Jews of Bardejov who perished during the Holocaust. Twelve **bastions** mark the perimeter of the Old Town. Ul. Veterna ends at one of the remaining bastions, which served as a crossroads beacon and, later, as the local beheading stock. The **icon exhibit**, Radničné nám. 27 (☎472 20 09), boasts a small collection of miniature religious figures and models of nearby wooden churches, striking for their detail. The collection's treasure is the gorgeous original **iconostasis** from the altar of a wooden church that stood in Zboy. (Open M-F 10am-4pm. 40Sk).The **town hall** *(radnica)*, Radničné nám. 48 (☎474 60 38), now serves as a **museum**, displaying historic trinkets. Among them is the key to the city, which the treacherous mayor's wife lent to her Turkish lover in 1697. The aptly named "Nature of Northeastern Slovakia" display, in the **Prirodopisne Museum**, Rhodýho 4, across from the entrance to the icon exhibit, will tickle the taxidermist in you. (☎472 26 30. Museums open daily May-Sept. 15 8:30am-noon and 12:30-5pm; Oct.-Apr. Tu-Su 8am-noon and 12:30-4pm. 25Sk, students 10Sk. Cameras 50Sk, video 100Sk.) Take note of the **maple trees** at the uphill end, a gift from the US, brought by former Vice President Dan Quayle in 1991.

The **Museum of Svidník,** Bardejovska 14, gives an overview of the bloody WWII Battle for the Dukla Pass. The adjacent **abandoned battlefield** is littered with tanks, artillery, and other vestiges of the brutal battle. Visitors may walk on the dirt paths but should not stray as some landmines remain. A bus runs from Bardejov to Svidník (30min., 60Sk); a connecting bus runs to Dukla (20Sk). From behind the station, turn left and walk 10min. (☎054 742 13 98. Open Tu-F 8am-3:30pm, Sa-Su 10am-2pm. 20Sk; students, children, soldiers 8Sk. Camera 50Sk, video 100Sk.)

■ **NIGHTLIFE.** Evenings in Bardejov are subdued. Nightlife is based around the beer gardens that dot the main square. For those determined to party late, head to **Morca Cafe,** Radničné nám. 37, where a mixed crowd chatters over drinks under neon lights. (☎090 897 68 81. Open M-F noon-2am, Sa 6pm-3am, Su 3pm-2am.) The shamrock-lined **Irish Pub,** Radničné nám. 32, is a hip yet easy-going place to enjoy a Guinness. (☎377 18 30. Guinness 35-65Sk. Themed parties F 9pm-midnight. Open Su-Th 10am-10pm, F-Sa 10am-midnight.)

SLOVAK REPUBLIC

SLOVENIA
(SLOVENIJA)

TOLARS		
AUS$1 = 140.21SIT	100SIT = AUS$0.71
CDN$1 = 151.15SIT	100SIT = CDN$0.66
EUR€1 = 240.22SIT	100SIT = EUR€0.42
NZ$1 = 128.39SIT	100SIT = NZ$0.78
UK£1 = 363.67SIT	100SIT = UK£0.27
US$1 = 199.14SIT	100SIT = US$0.50

Slovenia, the most prosperous of Yugoslavia's breakaway republics, revels in its newfound independence and has quickly separated itself from its neighbors. With a hungry eye turned toward the West, Slovenia has used liberal politics and a high GDP to gain entrance into the European Union. Fortunately, modernization has not adversely affected the tiny country's natural beauty and diversity: you can still have breakfast on an Alpine peak, lunch under the Mediterranean sun, and dinner in a Pannonian vineyard, all in one day.

HISTORY

THE EARLY YEARS. The **Alpine Slavs,** predecessors of the Slovenes, migrated to the eastern Alps in the 6th century AD, absorbing the existing cultures. The Slovenes converted to **Catholicism** during the 10th and 11th centuries. Between 1278 and 1335 all but Istria (nabbed by Venice) fell to the **Austrian Hapsburgs.** In the early 1800s some of the Slovenian lands were overrun by **Napoleon,** triggering the development of Slovenian **nationalism** in the 19th century.

PARTISANS AND PARTITIONS. After the collapse of Austria-Hungary (see **Hungary: History,** p. 336) following **World War I,** Slovenia agreed to join the newly formed **Kingdom of Serbs, Croats, and Slovenes** (renamed **Yugoslavia** in 1929). The new state was too weak, however, to withstand **Hitler's** forces during WWII. When

FACTS AND FIGURES

OFFICIAL NAME: Republic of Slovenia

CAPITAL: Ljubljana (pop. 330,000)

POPULATION: 2 million (88% Slovene, 3% Croat, 2% Serb, 7% other)

LANGUAGE: Slovenian

CURRENCY: 1 tolar (SIT) = 100 stotini

RELIGION: 71% Catholic, 5% atheist, 24% other

LAND AREA: 20,151km²

CLIMATE: Mediterranean on the coast, Continental inland

GEOGRAPHY: Mountains and plateaus, 47km of coast

BORDERS: Austria, Croatia, Hungary, Italy

ECONOMY: 61% Services, 35% Industry, 4% Agriculture

GDP: US$18,000 per capita

COUNTRY CODE: 386

INTERNATIONAL DIALING PREFIX: 00

Slovenia

Yugoslavia fell in 1941, Slovenia was partitioned among Germany, Italy, and Hungary. Slovenian resistance groups formed and united under the **Slovenian National Liberation Front,** which soon joined the Yugoslav Partisan Army of **Josip Brož Tito.**

WILD WILD WESTERNIZATION. After WWII, a unified state once again emerged, this time as the communist **Federal People's Republic of Yugoslavia,** with Slovenia as a republic. Tito liquidated Slovenian politicians and leaders who failed to cooperate; tens of thousands of Slovenian patriots were murdered at **Kočevje.** After a rift between Tito and Stalin in 1948, Yugoslavia followed its own brand of communism for half a century. In 1990, Slovenia held the first contested elections in Yugoslavia since before the war, empowering a rightist coalition. The new government adopted a Western-style constitution, and on June 25, 1991, Slovenia seceded from Yugoslavia. Its **independence** was recognized by the European Community in 1992.

TODAY. In December 2002, newly elected president **Janez Drnovšek,** of the **Liberal Democratic Party,** took the reins from **Milan Kučan,** who had been president since independence. In April 2000, Drnovšek, of the **Liberal Democratic Party,** lost the majority in a confidence vote after his conservative coalition partner, the **People's Party,** left the government. The country was without a government until June 7, when parliament approved the center-right cabinet proposed by Prime Minister-designate **Andrej Bajukin.** Slovenia was invited to join both the **EU** and **NATO,** and eagerly accepted both of these invitations in a referendum in March 2003.

PEOPLE AND CULTURE
LANGUAGE

Slovenian is a south Slavic language written in the Latin alphabet. Most young Slovenes speak at least some **English,** but the older generation is more likely to understand **German** or **Italian.** The tourist industry is generally geared toward Germans, but most tourist office employees speak English. When speaking Slovenian, *č* is pronounced "ch," and *š* is "sh," and *ž* is "zh." *R* is rolled and is sometimes a vowel

S L O V E N I A

THE WORLD'S BIGGEST DANCE PARTY

After beautiful but quiet snow-filled winters, Slovenia literally bounces back to life each spring. As the country's hillsides bloom with tulips and lavender, its residents take to the streets in celebration. Villagers throughout the region participate in festive costume carnivals, while high school students welcome spring in their own youthful way—by holding the world's largest dance party.

Unlike the typical Ljubljana raves, where you're likely to find Slovenian youth at night, this party isn't held in a disco or warehouse and is not set to the beat of thumping drum-and-bass. On the last day of school each May, students transform city streets across the nation into their own dance floor for a few hours in broad daylight.

At the cue of the famous Slovenian tune "Gaudeamus," thousands of upper-classmen begin the *quadrille*, a traditional dance. Thousands of others follow, accompanied by live, festive folk music. With tens of thousands of students spinning and gyrating simultaneously, the Graduation Parade, as the lively event has become known, has been listed in the *Guinness Book of World Records* as the largest synchronized dance in the world.

(pronounced "er"). *L* and *v* are tricky: they are usually pronounced as in English, but are "w" at the end of a word or before a consonant; also, *v* is "oo" when no vowel is near. For a phrasebook and glossary, see **Glossary: Slovenian, p. 960.**

FOOD AND DRINK

SLOVENIA	❶	❷	❸
FOOD	under 600Sit	600-1000Sit	1001-1400Sit
SLOVENIA	❹		❺
FOOD	1401-1800Sit		over 1800Sit

For home-style cooking, try a *gostilna* or *gostišče* (country-style inn or restaurant). Traditional meals begin with *jota*, a soup with potatoes, beans and sauerkraut. **Pork** is the basis for many dishes, such as *Svinjska pečenka* (roast pork) or Karst ham. The country's **winemaking** tradition dates from antiquity. *Renski, Rizling,* and *Šipon* are popular whites; *Cviček* and *Teran* are favorite reds. Brewing is centuries old as well; good **beers** include *Laško* and *Union.* For something stronger, try *žganje*, a fruit **brandy,** or *Viljamovka*, distilled by monks who know the secret of getting a whole pear inside the bottle.

CUSTOMS AND ETIQUETTE

A **tip** is usually included in the bill, which it is considered rude to split. 10% is sufficient for good service. Slovenes don't **bargain,** and attempts may cause offense. **Hiking** trails are marked with a white circle inside a red one. Hikers greet each other on the path. The ascending hiker should speak first, for they consider it proper to show respect to those who have already summited. **Shorts** are rare in cities, but common in the countryside. **Jeans** are worn everywhere.

THE ARTS

In the 19th century, Slovenian literature emerged as an important secular art form with the codification of the language by **Jernej Kopitar** in 1843 and the writings of the Romantic poet **France Prešeren** (see **Ljubljana: Sights,** p. 851). Throughout the later **Realist** period (1848-1899), writers such as **Fran Erjavec** focused on folkloric themes with a patriotic flavor; the first Slovenian novel, *The Tenth Brother (Deseti brat)*, by **Josip Jurčič,** was published in 1866. **Modernist** prose flowered in **Ivan Cankar's** 1904 *The Ward of Our Lady of Mercy (Hisa Marije pomocnice)*, while

Expressionist poetry showed the social and spiritual tensions brought on by WWI in the works of **Tone Seliskar, Miran Jarc,** and **Anton Vodnik.** Soviet **Socialist Realism** crushed many of the avant-garde impulses of the Slovenian literature.

Coincident with the Modernist and Expressionist movements in Slovenian literature, architect **Jože Plečnik** was a major figure in the development of **Art Deco.** His masterpiece was the transformation of his hometown, Ljubljana to a cosmopolitan capital (see **Ljubljana: Sights,** p. 849). Musically, Slovenia experienced a **folk** revival after WWII, which was followed by an explosion of punk sounds led by **Laibach.**

Slovenia has slowly but surely become a player in the **contemporary** art scene thanks to the artistic cooperative **IRWIN.** Founded in the 1980s, this group continues to exhibit eclectic paintings and sculpture. Postmodern literary trends emerged in the **Young Slovenian Prose** movement, which has its strongest representation in short prose pieces. Current authors with international reputations include poet **Tomaž Šalamun** and cultural critic and essayist **Slavoj Žižek.**

HOLIDAYS AND FESTIVALS

NATIONAL HOLIDAYS IN 2005	
January 1 New Year's Day	**June 25** National Day
February 8 Culture Day (Prešeren Day)	**October 31** Reformation Day
March 27-28 Easter Holiday	**November 1** Remembrance Day
April 27 National Resistance Day (WWII)	**December 25** Christmas
May 1 Labor Day	**December 26** Independence Day

Hitting Ljubljana in July and August, the **International Summer Festival** is the nation's largest, featuring ballet, theater, and music. The **Peasant's Wedding Day** is a presentation of ancient wedding customs, involving a real ceremony in which local couples tie the knot (end of July).

ADDITIONAL RESOURCES

Independent Slovenia: Origins, Movements, Prospects, edited by Jill Benderly (1996). Essays by economic theorists, Slovenia's foreign minister, and punk sociologists.

Slovenia and the Slovenes: A Small State and the New Europe, by James Gow and Cathie Carmichael (2001). A critical assessment of the modern Slovenian experience through examinations of Slovenian language, literature, culture, and geography.

SLOVENIA ESSENTIALS

ENTRANCE REQUIREMENTS
Passport: Required of all travelers.
Visa: Not required for stays under 90 days for citizens of the Australia, Canada, Ireland, New Zealand, the UK, and the US.
Letter of Invitation: Not required.
Inoculations: Recommended up-to-date on DTaP (diphtheria, tetanus, and pertussis), Hepatitis A, Hepatitis B, MMR (measles, mumps, and rubella), Polio booster, and Typhoid.
Work Permit: Required of all foreigners planning to work.
International Driving Permit: Required of all those planning to drive.

DOCUMENTS AND FORMALITIES

EMBASSIES AND CONSULATES

Embassies of other countries in Slovenia are all in **Ljubljana** (see p. 845). Slovenia's embassies and consulates abroad include:

Austria: Nibelungeng. 13/3, A-1010 Vienna (☎1 586 13 09; vdu@mzz-dkp.gov.si).

Australia: Level 6, 60 Marcus Clarke St., Canberra, ACT 2601 (☎2 6243 4830; vca@mzz-dkp.gov.si).

Canada: 150 Metcalfe St., Ste. 2101 Ottawa, ON K2P 1P1 (☎1 613-565-5781; vot@mzz-dkp.sigov.si).

Ireland: Morrison Chambers, 2nd fl., 32 Nassau St., Dublin 2 (☎1 670 5240; vdb@mzz-dkp.gov.si).

New Zealand Consulate: 201-221 Eastern Hutt Rd., Pomare, Lower Hutt Wellington (☎4 567 0027; fax 567 0024). Mail to: P.O. Box 30-247

UK: 11-15 Wigmore Street London W1U 1AN (☎20 7495 7775; vlo@mzz-dkp.gov.si).

US: 1525 New Hampshire Ave. NW, Washington, D.C. 20036 (☎1 202-667-5363; www.embassy.org/slovenia).

VISA AND ENTRY INFORMATION

Citizens of Australia, Canada, Ireland, New Zealand, the UK, and the US can visit Slovenia visa-free for up to 90 days. For more info, consult the website of the Slovenian Ministry of the Foreign Affairs at www.sigov.si/mzz/ang.

GETTING AROUND

Commercial **flights** all arrive at **Ljubljana Airport.** Most major airlines offer connections to the national carrier **Adria Airways.** Traveling to Vienna by plane and then to Ljubljana by train saves money but not time.

First and second class do not differ much on Slovenian **trains;** save your money and opt for the latter. Travelers under 26 can get a 20% discount on most international train fares. ISIC holders get 30% off domestic tickets; ask for a *popust* (discount). Schedules usually list trains by direction. *Prihodi vlakov* means arrivals; *odhodi vlakov* departures; *dnevno* daily. Though usually more expensive than trains, **buses** are often the only option in mountainous regions. Buy tickets at the station or on board. Large backpacks cost 300Sit extra.

Car rental agencies in Ljubljana offer reasonable rates, and Slovenia's roads are in good condition. Nearly every town has a **bike** rental office; renting costs 2000-3000Sit per day. In the summer, a **hydrofoil** runs between Venice and Portorož.

TOURIST SERVICES AND MONEY

There are **tourist offices** in most major cities and tourist destinations. Staffs generally speak **English** or **German** and, on the coast, perfect **Italian.** They can usually find accommodations. **Kompas** is the main tourist organization. **Inflation** hovers around 8%, so expect some change in prices. **SKB Banka, Ljubljanska Banka** and **Gorenjska Banka** are common banks. AmEx **Traveler's Cheques** and **Eurocheques** are accepted almost everywhere. Major **credit cards** are not consistently accepted, but MC/V **ATMs** are everywhere. Normal **business hours** are Monday through Friday 8am-4pm; **banks** and **exchange offices** Monday through Friday 7:30am-6pm, Saturday 7:30am-noon; **shops** Monday through Friday 8am-7pm, Saturday 7:30am-1pm.

HEALTH AND SAFETY

EMERGENCY NUMBERS: Police: ☎ 112 Ambulance and Fire: ☎ 113

Medical facilities are of high quality, and most have English-speaking doctors. UK citizens receive free medical care with a valid passport; other foreigners must pay cash. **Pharmacies** are stocked with Western standards. *Obliž* means band-aids; *tamponi* tampons; *vložki* sanitary pads. **Crime** is rare in Slovenia. Even in the largest cities, only overly friendly drunks and bad drivers are a public menace. **Female travelers** should, as always, exercise caution and avoid being out alone after dark. There are few **minorities** in Slovenia, but minority travelers shouldn't have any trouble, just curious glances. **Homosexuality** is legal, but may elicit unfriendly reactions outside urban areas.

ACCOMMODATIONS AND CAMPING

SLOVENIA	❶	❷	❸	❹	❺
ACCOM.	under 2800Sit	2800-4400Sit	4401-6000Sit	6001-7600Sit	over 7600Sit

All establishments charge per night **tourist tax. Youth hostels** and **student dormitories** are cheap (2500-3500Sit) and fun, but generally open only in summer (June 25-Aug. 30). **Hotels** tend to be expensive. **Pensions** are the most common form of accommodation; usually they have private singles as well as inexpensive dorms. **Private rooms** are the only cheap option on the coast and at Lake Bohinj. Prices vary, but rarely exceed US$30. Inquire at the tourist office or look for *Zimmer frei* or *Sobe* signs. **Campgrounds** can be crowded, but are in excellent condition. Camp in designated areas to avoid fines.

KEEPING IN TOUCH

For **airmail,** ask for *letalsko;* it takes 1-2 weeks to reach North America, Australia, and New Zealand. Letters to the US cost 107Sit and postcards cost 100Sit; to the UK 100Sit/83Sit; to Australia and New Zealand 110Sit/100Sit. Mail can be received through **Poste Restante.** Address envelopes as follows: Lauren (first name) RIVERA (LAST NAME), Poste Restante, Slovenska 32 (post office address), 1000 (postal code) Ljubljana (city), SLOVENIA.

All phones now take **phone cards,** which are sold at post offices, kiosks, and gas stations (750Sit per 50 impulses, which yields 1½min. to the US). Only **MCI World-Phone** (☎ 080 88 08) has an international access number in Slovenia. Dial ☎ 115 for English-speaking operator-assisted collect calls. Dial ☎ 1180 for the **international operator.** Calling abroad tends to be expensive. If you must, try the phones at the post office and pay when you're finished. **Internet access** is very fast and common.

LJUBLJANA ☎ (0)1

Though the city itself is small, Ljubljana (loob-lee-AH-na; pop. 280,000) possesses a mysteriously complex character woven through the layers of its colorful past. According to legend, Ljubljana was founded when Jason sailed onto the Ljubljanica River while fleeing King Aites, and slew the horrible Ljubljana dragon. Today, Dragon Bridge is surrounded by a mix of Baroque monuments, Art Nouveau facades, and high-rises.

SLOVENIA

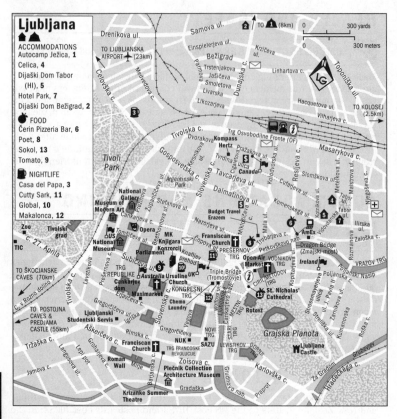

Ljubljana

ACCOMMODATIONS
Autocamp Ježica, **1**
Celica, **4**
Dijaški Dom Tabor
    (HI), **5**
Hotel Park, **7**
Dijaški Dom Bežigrad, **2**

🍎 **FOOD**
Čerin Pizzeria Bar, **6**
Poet, **8**
Sokol, **13**
Tomato, **9**

📕 **NIGHTLIFE**
Casa del Papa, **3**
Cutty Sark, **11**
Global, **10**
Makalonca, **12**

✈ INTERCITY TRANSPORTATION

Flights: Aerodrom Ljubljana, (☎4 206 10 00; www.lju-airport.si). The **Super Shuttle** (☎070 887 766; info@shuttlenet.com), available to all, runs from major hotels to the **airport.** Reservations required. **Adria Airways** and **EasyJet** run a joint airport minibus to and from the main bus terminal (30min., 6 per day, 1000Sit). The slower but slightly cheaper **local bus #28** runs from the main bus station (1hr.; M-F every hr. 6am-8pm, Sa-Su every hr. 6am-9am and odd hours until 7pm; 850Sit). **Adria Airways,** Gosposvetska 6 (☎231 33 12; fax 232 16 68); **Aeroflot,** Dunajska 21 (☎436 85 66; fax 436 85 93); **Austrian Airlines,** Dunajska 58 (☎436 12 83; fax 436 12 82); **British Airways,** Trg Republike 3 (☎241 40 00); **Lufthansa,** Gosposvetska 6 (☎434 72 46; fax 232 66 72); **Swissair,** Dunajska 156.

Trains: Trg OF 6 (☎291 33 32). To: **Bled** (1hr., 11 per day, 890Sit); **Koper** (2¼hr., 4 per day, 1660Sit); **Maribor** (1½hr., 4 per day, 1660Sit); **Belgrade, SMN** (8-9hr., 5 per day, 9500Sit); **Budapest, HUN** (9hr., 1 per day, 14,836Sit); **Munich, GER** (6-7hr., 3 per day, 15,200Sit); **Sarajevo, BOS** (11hr., 1 per day, 8315Sit) via **Zagreb, CRO** (2hr., 9 per day, 2700Sit); **Skopje, MAC** (23hr., 1 per day, 15,767Sit); **Trieste, ITA** (3hr., 2-3 per day, 4836Sit); **Venice, ITA** (6hr., 3 per day, 7900Sit); **Vienna, AUT** (5-6hr., 2 per day, 12,800Sit).

Buses: Trg OF 4 (☎090 42 30; www.ap-ljubljana.si). To: **Bled** (1½hr., 14 per day, 1400Sit); **Koper** (2½hr., 13 per day, 2460-2540Sit); **Maribor** (2½-3hr., 10 per day, 2670-2760Sit); **Rijeka, CRO** (2½hr., 1 per day, 3430-4090Sit); **Sarajevo, BOS** (9¾hr., 1 per day, 9230Sit); **Skopje, MAC** (19-23hr., 2 per day, 10,650Sit); **Zagreb, CRO** (3hr., 3 per day, 3310Sit).

⬛ ORIENTATION

The curvy **Ljubljanica River** (loob-lee-AH-neet-sa) divides central Ljubljana, with the picturesque **Stare Miasto** (Old Town) on one bank and 19th- and 20th-century buildings on the other. About a half-mile from either bank, the historic area turns into a concrete business district. The train and bus stations are on **Trg Osvobodilne Fronte** (Trg OF). To get to the center from them, turn right and then left on Miklošičeva cesta and take it to **Prešernov trg**, the main square. After crossing the **Tromostovje** (Triple Bridge), you'll see Stare Miasto at the base of castle hill. The tourist office is on the left at the corner of Stritarjeva and Adamič-Lundrovo nab. To reach **Slovenska c.**, Ljubljana's main artery, walk up Čopova from Prešernov trg.

⬛ LOCAL TRANSPORTATION

Buses: Run daily until midnight. Drop 300Sit in the box (drivers don't have change) beside the driver or buy 190Sit tokens *(žetoni)* at post offices kiosks, or the main bus terminal. Daily passes (900Sit) sold at **Ljubljanski Potniški Promet,** Trdinova 3. Open M-F 6:45am-7pm, Sa 6:45am-1pm. Pick up a bus map at the TIC.

Taxis: ☎97 00 through 97 09. 150Sit base fee plus 100Sit per km.

Car Rental: Avis Rent-a-Car, Cufarjeva 2, in Grand Hotel Union (☎430 80 10). **Budget Car Rental,** Miklošičeva 3 (☎421 73 40). **Kompas Hertz,** Trdinova 9 (☎434 01 47).

Bike Rental: Tir Bar, in the train station. Contact "Bajk Oglasevanje" (☎527 31 47). 200Sit per 2hr., 700Sit per day. Open daily 8am-8pm.

⬛ PRACTICAL INFORMATION

TOURIST AND FINANCIAL SERVICES

Tourist Office: Tourist Information Center (TIC), Stritarjeva 1 (☎306 12 15; 24hr. English info 090 939 881; www.ljubljana.si). Distributes **free maps** and the useful, free *Ljubljana from A to Z.* Also arranges accommodations. Open daily June-Sept. 8am-9pm; Oct.-May 8am-7pm. **Branch,** Trg OF 6, at the train station (☎/fax 433 94 75). Open daily June-Sept. 8am-10pm; Oct.-May 10am-7pm.

Budget Travel: Erazem, Trubarjeva c. 7 (☎433 10 76). Helpful, student-oriented staff. Open June-Aug. M-F 10am-5pm, Sa 10am-1pm; Sept.-May M-F noon-5pm. **Wasteels,** Trg OF 6, on the train station platform books discounted train tickets for students and those under 26 (☎/fax 611 339 281. Open M-F 9:15am-5pm. AmEx/MC/V).

Embassies: Australia, Trg Republike 3 (☎425 42 52; fax 426 47 21). Open M-F 9am-1pm. **Bosnia and Herzegovina,** Kolarjeva 26 (☎432 40 42; fax 432 22 30). Open M-F 8:30am-noon. **Canada,** Miklošičeva 19 (☎430 35 70; fax 430 35 77). Open M-F 9am-1pm. **Croatia,** Gruberjevo nab. 6 (☎425 62 20, consular department 425 72 87; hrvaske@siol.net). **Hungary,** ul. Konrada Babnika 5 (☎512 18 82; www.hu-embassy.si). **Ireland,** Poljanski nasip 6 (☎300 89 70; fax 282 10 96). Open M-F 9am-noon. **Macedonia,** Dunjaska c. 104 (☎568 44 54; makamb@siol.net). Open M-F 9am-noon. **Serbia and Montenegro,** Slomškova 1 (☎438 01 10). Open M-F 9am-noon. **UK,** Trg Republike 3 (☎200 39 10; fax 425 01 74). Open M-F 9am-noon. **US,** Prešernova 31 (☎200 55 00; fax 200 55 55). Open M-F 9am-noon and 2-4pm.

Currency Exchange: *Menjalnice* booths abound. **Ljubljanska banka** has branches all over that exchange currency for no commission and cash **traveler's checks** for 1.5% commission. Open M-F 9am-noon and 2-7pm, Sa 9am-noon.

24hr. ATMs: MC/V ATMs are found throughout the city.

American Express: Trubarjeva 50 (☎433 20 24; amex@siol.net). Ring the doorbell outside to be let upstairs. Open M-F 8am-7pm.

Work Opportunities: Ljubljanski Studentski Servis, Borstnikov trg 2 (☎200 88 00). Open M-F 10am-6pm. **MB Studentski Servis,** Slovenska 27 (☎421 45 50). Open M-Sa 11am-4pm. Both agencies help students find jobs. Open to foreigners.

LOCAL SERVICES AND COMMUNICATIONS

Luggage Storage: Lockers *(garderoba)* at train station. 400Sit per day. Open 24hr.

English-Language Bookstore: MK-Knjigarna Konzorcij, Slovenska 29 (☎252 40 57). A wide variety of English-language books (1200-5000Sit) and international press. Open M-F 9am-7:30pm, Sa 9am-1pm.

Laundromat: TIC (Student Campus), 27 Aprila 31, bldg. 9 (☎251 44 04). Self-service. Open M-F 8am-8pm, Sa 8am-2pm. **Chemo Express,** Wolfova 12 (☎231 07 82). 1200Sit per kg. Open daily 7am-9pm.

Medical Services: Bohoričeva Medical Center, Bohoričeva 4 (☎232 30 60). Open daily 5am-8pm. **Klinični Center,** Zaloška 2-7 (☎522 50 50). Take bus #2, 9, 10, 11, or 20 to the "Bolnica" stop. Open 24hr.

24hr. Pharmacy: Lekarna Miklošič, Miklošičeva 24 (☎231 45 58).

Telephones: Outside the post office and all over town. Buy magnetic phone cards at the post office and at newsstands (1700Sit).

Internet Access: Free 10min. with purchase of a drink at **Čerin Kavarna,** above **Čerin Pizzeria Bar** (see **Food,** p. 849). Open M-F 11am-5pm. **Cyber Cafe Xplorer,** Petkovško nab. 23 (☎430 19 91; www.sisky.com), has fast connections. 530Sit per 30min, students 477Sit. 20% discount 10am-noon. Open M-F 10am-10pm, Sa-Su 2-10pm.

Post Office: Trg OF 5 (☎433 06 05). Open M-F 7am-midnight, Sa 7am-6pm, Su 9am-noon. Various smaller branches are located throughout the city. **Poste Restante,** Slovenska 32 (☎426 46 68), at the *izročitev pošiljk* counter. Open M-F 7am-8pm, Sa 7am-1pm. **Postal Code:** 1000.

⌂ ACCOMMODATIONS

Finding cheap accommodations in Ljubljana is easier in July and August, when university dorms open to travelers. The **Hostelling International Slovenia** (PZS; ☎231 21 56) provides info about hostels throughout Slovenia. The **TIC** (see **Tourist and Financial Services,** p. 847) can help you find **private rooms** (singles 4000-10,000Sit; doubles 5000-15,000Sit). There is a nightly 240Sit **tourist tax** at all establishments.

■ **Celica,** Metelkova 8 (☎430 18 90; www.souhostel.si). With your back to the train station, go left down Masarykova, then right on Metelkova. Look for the red and yellow building on your left. Each room of this former prison has been designed by a different artist, transforming it into a creative living space. Bar, cafe, free Internet, live music performances, and mediation room. Breakfast included. Laundry 1200Sit. Reception 24hr. Call 1-2 weeks ahead in summer. Dorms 3500Sit; doubles 5250Sit. MC/V. ❷

Dijaški Dom Tabor (HI), Vidovdanska 7 (☎234 88 40; ssljddta1s@guest.arnes.si), 1km from the bus and train stations. Turn left down Masarykova c. from stations, then right on Kotnikova ul. Walk down almost to the end of the street. Tabor is on the left. Alternatively, take bus #5 to the Illirska stop. Clean rooms, communal bathrooms, and proximity to nightlife. Free Internet. Breakfast included. Laundry 1700Sit. Reception 24hr. Check-out 11am. Open June 25-Aug. 25. Dorms 2500-3700Sit. 200Sit HI discount. ❶

Dijaški Dom Bežigrad (HI), Kardeljeva pl. 28 (☎534 00 61; www2.arnes.si). Take bus #6 (Črnuče) or #8 (Ježica) and get off at Stadion (5min.). Cross the road, walk 1 block, turn right on Dimiceva, then left at the HI sign on Mariborska. Though not in the center, this student complex offers a deal. Clean, quiet, comfortable rooms. Free Internet. Flexible check-out. Open June 25-Aug. 25. Singles 3600Sit; with shower 4800Sit; doubles 4800Sit/7200Sit; triples 7200Sit/8400Sit. No HI discount. ❷

Hotel Park, Tabor 9 (☎232 13 98; hotel.park@siol.et). Choose from tidy, budget-oriented rooms or more luxurious rooms, which are equipped with modern furnishings and have TVs. All with private bath. Knowledgeable, helpful staff. Singles 11,520-12,480Sit; doubles 14,640-16,320Sit. 10% ISIC discount. AmEx/MC/V. ❺

Autocamp Ježica, Dunajska 270 (☎568 39 13; ac.jezica@gpl.si). Take bus #6 or 8 to Ježica's wooded campgrounds. The peaceful atmosphere offers a respite for the weary traveler. Offers both camping and spacious, impeccably clean rooms with TV and private showers. Reception 24hr. Flexible check-out 1pm. Reservations recommended. June 20-Aug. 20 camping 2160Sit per person; Aug. 21-June 19 1680Sit. Electricity tax 480Sit. Tourist tax 162Sit. Bungalow singles 11,000Sit; doubles 15,000Sit. MC/V. ❶

▣ FOOD

The largest **grocery store** is in the basement of the **Maximarket**, Trg Republike 1. (Open M-Th 9am-8pm, F 9am-10pm, Sa 8am-3pm.) Buy fresh produce at the large **open-air market** next to St. Nicholas's Cathedral. (See **Sights**, p. 850. Open June-Aug. M-Sa 6am-6pm; Sept.-May 6am-4pm). Fast-food stands feature Slovenian favorites such as *burek*—fried dough filled with meat *(mesni)* or cheese *(sirov)*.

▨ Sokol, Ciril Metodov trg 18 (☎439 68 55), just off Prešernov trg. Walk or take bus #2, 11, or 20 to Metodov. Discover the meaning of "Slovenian food" in Sokol's home-style atmosphere. Hearty dishes include grilled squid and deer medallions with cherry sauce. Entrees 1290-2590Sit. Open M-Sa 9am-11pm, Su 10am-11pm. AmEx/MC/V. ❸

Čerin Pizzeria Bar, Trubarjeva 52 (☎232 09 90). Entrance on the small alleyway to the right of the building. Watch your pizza cook in the Italian-style kitchen before sinking your teeth into the delicious final product. Salad bar (550-950Sit), pastas (1130-1560Sit), and fabulous desserts (440-650Sit). Pizzeria open Sept.-June M-F 10am-11pm, Sa noon-10pm; July-Aug. M-F 10am-9pm, Sa noon-9pm. AmEx/MC/V. ❸

Tomato, Šubičeva ul. 1. (☎252 75 55). Tomato is great for a quick, tasty meal. Enormous hot and cold sandwiches (390-820Sit), salads (1050-1150Sit), and entrees (1150-1500Sit). Vegetarian options. Eat in or take out. Open M-F 7am-10pm, Sa 9am-4pm. ❷

Poet, Petkovško nab., next to the Triple Bridge. With courteous service and a view of the river, Poet has perfected the art of ice cream concoctions (700-1400Sit) and sandwich creation (550-750Sit). Open daily Apr. 15-Oct. 10 9am-midnight. ❶

◙ SIGHTS

One way to see the sights is to meet in front of the city hall *(rotovž)*, Mestni trg 1, for a 2hr. **walking tour**, given in English and Slovenian. (Daily June-Sept. 10am and 6pm; July-Aug. also Su 11am. Oct.-Apr. F-Su only 11am. 1500Sit, students 700Sit. Buy tickets at the tour or at the TIC.)

■ **LJUBLJANA CASTLE (LJUBLJANSKI GRAD).** While the castle's existence was first documented in 1144, most of the present buildings are 16th- and 17th-century renovations, which followed the 1511 earthquake. The castle has served as a prison for high profile captives, such as Slovenia's most famous author, nationalist Ivan Cankar (see **The Arts**, p. 842). The panorama of the city from the tower is breathtaking, and the castle is rapidly becoming a new cultural center, hosting various exhibitions and performances throughout the year. The newly renovated **Virtual Museum** inside the castle uses computerized presentations to illuminate the story of Ljubljana's past. *(Take 1 of several paths up the hill: from Gornji trg along ul. na Grad, or from Vodnikov trg following Študenska ul. Tower and Virtual Museum ☎ 232 99 94; www.festival-lj.si/virtualnimuzej. Open daily June-Sept. 10am-dusk; Oct.-May 10am-5pm. 790Sit, students 490Sit. Castle open daily May-Oct. 10am-9pm; Nov.-Apr. 10am-7pm. English tours 1100Sit, students 790Sit; 3 people min.)*

■ **ST. NICHOLAS'S CATHEDRAL (STOLNICA).** St. Nicholas's is so exquisite that it would take weeks to absorb its beauty. The dazzlingly ornate cathedral occupies the site of a 13th-century Romanesque church. According to local legend, townsfolk once threw garbage into the Ljubljanica from this spot. When a law forced the litterers to live on the banks they had defiled, they built a small chapel dedicated to their patron, St. Nicholas. The current building dates from the early 18th century. Aside from the 15th-century Gothic Pietà, little original artwork remains, yet nearly every centimeter contains something marvelous. *(On the Stare Miasto side of the river, walk left to see the gorgeous arcades, also designed by Plečnik, that form part of the nearby market. The Cathedral is to the right. Open daily 6:45am-12:30pm and 3-8pm.)*

PREŠEREN SQUARE (PREŠERNOV TRG). Nestled between Miklošičeva cesta and the gorgeous Triple Bridge, Prešernov trg lies at the true heart of Ljubljana and is one of the city's liveliest spots. The large cobblestone square was named for famed Slovenian poet France Prešeren (see **The Arts**, p. 842), whose **statue** watches over the crowds. The enormous, pink 17th-century **Franciscan church** (Frančiškanska cerkev) dominates the square. Its beautiful interior and stunning ceiling frescoes resemble that of neighboring St. Nicholas's Cathedral; local master Francesco Robba crafted the impressive altar inside. *(A short walk from City Hall down Stritarjeva and across the Triple Bridge. Church open daily 6:45am-12:30pm and 3-8pm. Free.)*

TRIPLE BRIDGE (TROMOSTOVJE). The ornate Triple Bridge provides a majestic entrance to the Old Town. The current structure was created in the 1930s, when architect Jože Plečnik (see **The Arts**, p. 842) modernized the old Špitalski bridge by supplementing the original stone construction with two parallel footbridges.

FRENCH REVOLUTION SQUARE (TRG FRANCOSKE REVOLUCIJE). Inhabited by the Teutonic Knights during the 13th century, this quiet square was formally created in 1793 and received its current name in 1952. The surrounding area of Križanke gained its present appearance between the two World Wars through restorations led by the masterful Plečnik. The highlight of the square is the beautiful, stone **Križanke Summer Theater,** which hosts open-air music, dance, and theater performances from June to September. *(☎ 241 60 26. Tickets 2000-5000Sit. Box office open M-F 10am-1:30pm and 4-8pm, Sa 10am-1pm; also 1hr. before each performance.)*

OTHER SIGHTS. Walk down Zoisova past French Revolution Sq. and take a left on Barjanska c. to see the ruins of a **Roman wall** preserved from the previous settlement of Emona. Head back up Barjanska to reach Slovenska c., Ljubljana's main artery, which hosts the city's best shopping. Behind the **Ursuline Church** on the left is Trg Republike, home to the **Parliament** and **Cankarjev dom,** the city's cultural center. **Kongresni trg**, on the other side of Slovenska c., is a shady park just above **Ljubl-**

Jana University that has vibrant nightlife. One block below the University stands the **Slovenian Academy of Arts and Sciences** (Slovenska Akademija Znanosti in Umetnosti; SAZU), a former Baroque palace; the **National Library** (Narodna in Univerzitetna Knjiznica; NUK), another of Plečnik's creations, is diagonally across the street. In front of **City Hall** (Rotovž) sits a **fountain** embellished with allegorical representations of three rivers—the Ljubljanica, the Sava, and the Krka.

🏛 MUSEUMS

NATIONAL MUSEUM (NARODNI MUZEJ). Slovenia's oldest museum features exhibits on archaeology, culture, and Slovenian history from the prehistoric era to the present. Upstairs, the **Natural History Museum** showcases a small paleontology exhibit and geological and mineral collections from around Slovenia. *(Muzejska 1. ☎ 241 44 04. Open Tu-W, F, Su 10am-6pm. Both museums 1000Sit, students 700Sit. One museum 700Sit/500Sit. 1st Su of each month free.)*

PLEČNIK COLLECTION ARCHITECTURE MUSEUM (PLEČNIKOVA ZBRIKA). This small museum chronicles the modest life and marvelous work of Plečnik, Slovenia's premier architect, in a house built by the master himself. The informative guided tour takes you through Plečnik's living and working quarters. Its highlight is the artist's well-preserved studio, which features mind-bogglingly intricate furniture made by Plečnik's own hand as well as stunning models of ambitious architectural projects that were never brought to fruition. *(Karunova 4. Walk toward the center on Slovenska, turn left on Zoisova, then right on Emonska. Cross the bridge and head behind the church. ☎ 280 16 00; fax 283 50 66. Open Tu and Th 10am-2pm. 1000Sit, students 800Sit. Mandatory tour available in English.)*

NATIONAL GALLERY (NARODNA GALERIJA). This handsome Austro-Hungarian building houses works by Slovenian and lesser-known European painters and sculptors from the Romantic through Impressionist periods and religious icons dating from 1270. *(Prešernova 24. ☎ 241 54 34. Open Tu-Su 10am-6pm. 800Sit, students 600Sit; Sa afternoons free.)*

🔲 🌺 ENTERTAINMENT AND FESTIVALS

Pick up a free *Where To?* events listing from the TIC (see **Tourist and Financial Services,** p. 847). **Cankarjev dom,** Prešernov trg 10 (☎ 241 17 64), hosts the **Slovenian Philharmonic.** (Performances Oct.-June. Box office in the basement of Maximarket. Open M-F 11am-1pm and 3-8pm, Sa 11am-1pm and 1hr. before performance. Tickets 2000-7000Sit.) The **opera house,** Župančičeva 1, also houses the **ballet.** (☎ 241 17 64. Tickets 2000-9600Sit. Box office open M-F 1-5pm, Sa 11am-1pm, and 1hr. before each performance.) In December, the city center and Old Town come alive with church concerts, street fairs, and New Year's Eve celebrations. **Tivoli Hall,** an arena in Tivoli Park, hosts sports events and rock concerts. A new cinema, **Kolosej,** Šmartinska c. 152 (☎ 520 55 00; www.kolosej.si), shows English-language movies (1000Sit). Buses #2, 7, and 17 run from the town center to the multiplex.

The festival season kicks off with a celebration of Ljubljana's standing in the **International Viticulture and Wine Fair** held at the **Fairgrounds** in April. Throughout June, the **Festival of Street Theater** (Ana Desetnica) transforms the city streets and squares into impromptu stages. In late June, the alternative arts scene hosts the international **Break 22 Festival,** which blends urban technology with the avant-garde. The 46th annual **International Jazz Festival** grooves in Cankarjev dom and

Križanke in late June; inquire at the TIC for a free schedule. The vaguely titled **International Summer Festival**, from mid-June to mid-September, is a conglomeration of musical, operatic, and theatrical performances held at Cankarjev dom and other local venues. The **Ljubljana International Film Festival** plays in early November.

🔉 NIGHTLIFE

At night, Ljubljana trades its daytime majesty for a kind of moody enchantment. Cafes and bars line the waterfront, Trubarjeva ul., Stari trg, and Mestni trg.

▨ **Makalonca**, Hribarjevo nab., just past the Triple Bridge. Hidden on a terrace below the waterfront's main drag, this hip cavern bar has gorgeous views of the river and is a local favorite. Fewer crowds and more attitude than its neighbors above. Mixed drinks 500-900Sit, sangria 350Sit. Open M-Sa 10-1am, Su 10am-3pm.

▨ **Global,** Tomsiceva ul. 2 (☎426 90 20; www.global.si). Take the glass elevator to the 6th fl. This rooftop hotspot draws the city's trendsters with its chic ambience, extensive cocktail menu, and magnificent views of the castle. On weekend nights, the action gets going around midnight, when it transforms into one of the Ljubljana's most popular dance spots. Mixed drinks 900-1400Sit. Cover 1000Sit after 9pm; July-Aug. no cover. Open Sept.-June M-Th and F-Sa. Bar open M-Sa 8am-9pm. Disco Th-Sa 9pm-5am.

Casa del Papa, Celovška 54a (☎434 31 58). This island-themed bar on the outskirts of the center draws 20- and 30-somethings seeking a change from the packed waterfront nightlife. The decor pays homage to Hemingway, and the downstairs club throbs with Latin beats and sells Cuban cigars. Beer 280-550Sit per 0.25L. Mixed drinks 1000-1300Sit. Open M-Sa noon-midnight, Su noon-11pm.

Cutty Sark, Knafljev prehod 1 (☎425 14 77). From Prešernov trg, take the 1st right into the arched entrance; it is on the left. Outside garden terrace and a dim interior make it both pub and outdoor cafe. *Union* 350Sit. Open M-Sa 9am-1am, Su 5pm-1am.

🔉 DAYTRIPS FROM LJUBLJANA

ŠKOCJANSKE CAVES   ☎(0)5

Trains run to Divača en route to the coast (1¾hr., 10 per day, 1340Sit). Buses also pass through Divača (1hr., 5 per day, 1740Sit). Signs from the station lead to the ticket booth, a 40min. walk over the highway, through the village, and onto a very narrow path through the woods. Ask for a free trail map at the booth. ☎763 28 40; www.gov.si/parkskj. Tours daily June-Sept. 10am-5pm; Oct.-May 10am, 1, and 3:30pm. 2200Sit, students 1200Sit, ages 6-12 800Sit, under 6 free.

The UNESCO-protected ▨**Škocjanske Caves** are an amazing system of caverns said to have inspired literary great Dante Alighieri. The **Silent Cave** features enormous limestone formations including stalactites, stalagmites, and rock curtains. The cavern's highlight is the breathtaking Reka River **underground gorge,** the biggest of its kind in Europe. This spelunking trip is more physically demanding but considerably less touristy than Postojna Caves. Tours are given in English, German, Italian, and Slovenian. Bring a jacket to keep warm.

POSTOJNA CAVES AND PREDJAMA CASTLE   ☎(0)5

Trains (1¼hr., 10 per day, 1250Sit) and buses (1hr., every 30min., 1320Sit) go to Postojna on the way to Koper. With your back to the bus station, go left on Ljubljanska c., then left at the 1st light. Follow signs to the cave (25min.). ☎700 01 00; www.postojna-cave.com. Mandatory 1½hr. tours leave May-Sept. daily every hr. 10am-6pm; April and

Oct. daily every even hr. 10am-noon; Nov.-Mar. M-F every even hr. 10am-noon, Sa-Su 10am-4pm. 3390Sit, students 2190Sit. From Postojna, taxis run to Predjama (☎ 031 406 446, 5000-6000Sit). During the school year, school buses go to Bukovje, 2km from the castle (15min., M-F 2 per day, 400Sit). ☎ 756 82 60. Open May-Sept. daily 9am-7pm; April and Oct. daily 10am-5pm; Nov.-Mar. M-F 10am-3pm, Sa-Su 10am-5pm. 1200Sit, students 700Sit. Call ahead to arrange a visit to the cave below Predjama Castle. If you plan to visit both the caves and the castle as a single daytrip from Ljubljana, it may be more economical and convenient to rent a car (see p. 847 for information).

Stunning in its breadth and beauty, **Postojna Cave** (Postojnska Jama) is one of Slovenia's greatest and most popular natural treasures. Although its fame and the subsequent flow of tourists have turned the caverns into a kind of amusement park ride, once you're inside, the crowds all but disappear against the array of multicolored rock formations. The tour covers only 20% of the two-million-year-old cave's 20km; part is on foot and part by train. Bring a jacket or rent a cloak (500Sit); the temperature in the cave is a constant 8°C.

Though challenging and costly to reach, **Predjama Castle** (Predjamski Grad), 9km from Postojna, is worth the hassle. Carved into the face of an enormous cliff, the Gothic castle is a labyrinth of rooms and passageways that sits above a karst cave. Predjama's most famous inhabitant was robber-baron Erasmus, a German knight who brazenly supported the Hungarian crown in its wars against the Austrian emperor Friedrich III. Friedrich III sent his entire army after the errant knight, but Erasmus had a secret supply tunnel and the siege lasted over a year. Yet just as the besiegers were running low on supplies, Erasmus's servant turned the tides by betraying his master. The servant promised to light a candle when his lord went to the outhouse. With a single catapult round, Friedrich won his revenge on the rebel knight, who died in the least honorable of positions.

THE JULIAN ALPS (JULIJSKE ALPE)

Stretching across northwest Slovenia, the Julian Alps are no less stunning than their Austrian or Swiss cousins. The serene wilderness of Lake Bohinj, the alpine culture of Kranjska Gora, and the waters of Lake Bled all lie within a short bus ride of each other. Whether hiking, rafting, or simply relaxing in the fresh air, the Julian Alps are an absolute playground for all who relish the outdoors.

BLED ☎ (0)4

Bled (pop. 6000) captivates visitors with its beauty and tranquility. For centuries, its green alpine hills, snow-covered peaks, turquoise lake dotted with Slovenia's only island, and stately castle have drawn people to this internationally renowned resort to swim, to hike, or just to breathe.

▐▛ TRANSPORTATION AND PRACTICAL INFORMATION. Trains leave to **Ljubljana** (1hr., 11 per day, 1150Sit) from the Lesce-Bled station (☎ 294 23 63), 4km from Bled proper. To reach Bled from the station, take one of the frequent **commuter buses** (10min., 300Sit), which stop on Ljubljanska and at the bus station, c. Svobode 4 (☎ 578 04 20). **Buses** from Bled go to: **Ljubljana** (1½hr., 1 per hr. 7am-9pm, 1400Sit) and **Bohinjsko Jezero** (35min., 5-13 per day, 790Sit) and from Lesce to **Kranjska Gora** (40min., 1 per hr., 1130Sit).

The town spreads around **Lake Bled,** and most buildings cluster on the eastern shore. **Ljubljanska,** the main street, leads to the water, where it meets c. Svobode. To get to the center, with your back to the bus station, turn right on c. Svobode, follow the road as it curves uphill, and turn left on Ljubljanska. **Generalturist,** c.

SLOVENIA

Svobode 11, sells **maps** (1000-1600Sit) of Bled and of nearby hiking trails. (☎578 05 00; fax 578 05 01. Open M-Sa June-Sept. 8am-7pm; Nov.-Feb. 9am-5pm; Mar.-May 9am-7pm.) **Nova Ljubljanska Banka**, Ljubljanska c. 11, **exchanges currency** for no commission, cashes **traveler's checks** (500Sit per check), gives MC/V **cash advances**, provides **Western Union** services and a has a MC/V **ATM** outside. (☎757 12 00. Open M-F 9am-4pm.) There's a **pharmacy** at Prešernova 36. (☎578 07 70. Open M-F 7am-7:30pm, Sa 7am-1pm.) **Internet access** is available at the **library**, Ljubljanska 10. (☎575 16 00. 1000Sit per hr. Use is limited to once per day per person. Passport or other ID document needed. Open M 8am-7pm, Tu-F 8am-2pm, Sa 8am-noon.) The **post office** is at Ljubljanska 4. (☎575 02 00. Open M-F 7am-7pm, Sa 7am-1pm.) **Postal Code:** 4260.

🖩🛏 ACCOMMODATIONS AND FOOD. Globtour, Ljubljanska 7, arranges **private rooms.** (☎574 18 21; www.globtour-bled.com. Open M-Sa 8am-8pm, Su 9am-noon and 4-7pm. June-Sept. 15 and Dec. 21-Jan. 4 singles 3500-4800Sit; doubles 4200-7000Sit. Tourist tax 162Sit. Stays under 3 nights 30% more.) To find a room on your own, look for *"Sobe"* signs, or request a brochure of listings at Globtour. A rare find in the countryside, ⬛**Bledec Youth Hostel (HI) ❷**, Grajska c. 17, is conveniently located just down the hill from Bled Castle. Facing away from the bus station, turn left and walk to the top of the steep hill, bearing left at the fork. Bledec feels more like a pension than a hostel, with comfortable beds, spotless private bathrooms, and a homestyle atmosphere. (☎574 52 50; bledec@mlino.si. Breakfast and tourist tax included. Internet access 500Sit per 30min. Laundry 2000Sit. Reception 24hr. Check-out 10am. Reservations recommended. Apr. 27-Oct. and Dec. 21-Jan. 4 4560Sit, HI members 4080Sit.) **Hotel Vila Bojana ❷**, Ljubljanska c. 12, boasts bright, luxurious rooms and a central location with a view of the lake. (☎576 81 70; fax 576 83 60. Breakfast included. May-Oct. and Dec. 24-Jan. Singles 17,520-19,920Sit; doubles 21,600-24,000Sit. Jan.-Apr. 20 and Nov.-Dec. 23 12,720-15,120Sit/16,800-19,200Sit. Rooms 4000-23,000Sit.) **Camping Bled ❶**, Kidrieva 10c, sits in a beautiful valley on the opposite side of the lake. Walk around the bus station, follow c. Svobode downhill, turn left at the lake, and walk 25min. The campground has a store, restaurant, beach, and laundry facilities. (☎575 20 00; info@camping.bled.si. Internet access 590Sit per 15min. Laundry 1000Sit. Reception 24hr. Check-out 3pm. July 10-Aug. 20 2400Sit per person; June-July 9 and Aug. 21-Oct. 15 2000Sit per person; Apr.-May and Sept. 16-Oct. 15 1600Sit per person. Tourist tax 81Sit.)

Okarina ❹, Riklijiva 9, just up the hill from the bus station, specializes in Indian-inspired and vegetarian foods, but has something for everyone. The food is served on the elegant garden terrace. (☎574 14 58. Entrees 1200-2950Sit. Open M-F 6pm-midnight, Sa-Su noon-midnight.) Huge portions of high-quality food and excellent service distinguish **Gostilna pri Planincu ❸**, Grajska c. 8, near the bus station. (☎574 16 13. Entrees 900-1700Sit. Pizza 790-950Sit; crepes 400Sit. Open daily 9am-11pm.) **Franci Šmon ❶**, Grajska c. 3, offers coffee and seductive desserts. Their torte arsenal (350-400Sit) includes the *grmada*, a chocolate biscuit with vanilla cream, nuts, raisins, or rum. (☎574 22 80. Pizza 300Sit. Sandwiches 280Sit. Open daily 7:30am-10pm.) For **groceries**, head to **Mercator**, in the shopping complex at Ljubljanska c. 13. (Open M-Sa 7am-8pm, Su 8am-noon.)

◩ SIGHTS. The **island** in the center of Lake Bled is home to the **Church of the Assumption** (Cerkev Marijinega Vnebovzetja). There are several ways to reach the it. The supervised swimming area below the castle rents row boats, as does Janez Palak, Koritenska 27. (☎578 05 28. 3-seaters 2400Sit 1st hr., each additional hr. 1200Sit; 5-seaters 2880Sit/1440Sit. 1000Sit deposit.) You can also cross the lake on the gondola-style *plentas*, stationed at the Rowing Center and in Mlino under Hotel Park. (Round-trip 1½hr., 2400Sit.) In the summer, swimming to the island is permitted; dive in from the well-kept **Castle Swimming Grounds** (Grajsko Kopališoe) under Bled Castle. (Day ticket 1200Sit, students 840Sit; afternoon 960Sit/720Sit.) The lake becomes an ice-skating rink in winter. (Open June-Sept. daily 7am-7pm. Lockers 720Sit.) Built in 1004, Slovenia's oldest citadel, **Bled Castle** (Blejski grad), rises 100m above the lake offering a view of the Alps. The official path to the castle is on Grajska c., but there are several pleasant hikes through the forest. One runs uphill from ornate **St. Martin's Church** (Cerkev sv. Martin), on Kidričeva c. near the lake. Another route begins behind the swimming area; follow blazes marked with a "1" up the hill. Castle tickets include admission to the compelling **History Museum**, stocked with furniture, weapons, and Roman coins. Poke your head into the small printing studio opposite the museum to watch a artist in traditional dress produce medieval, Gutenberg-style prints. (Castle open daily 8am-8pm. Museum ☎578 05 25. Open daily May-Sept. 8am-8pm; Oct.-Apr. 9am-5pm. 1000Sit, students 800Sit.)

🎭 🎲 **ENTERTAINMENT AND NIGHTLIFE.** The tourist office distributes a free brochure listing local events. The second weekend in July draws together orchestral musicians for **Bled Days** (www.festivalbled.com), which features concerts, arts and crafts, and fireworks on the lake. The folk music extravaganza **No Borders Music Festival** (☎574 14 58) is held each August. Nightlife in Bled centers on gambling and hotel lounges. The ingeniously named **Pub,** c. Svobode 8a, draws a vivacious local crowd. With outdoor seating right above the lake, memorable exploits will surely not go unnoticed. (☎574 22 17. 0.3L *Union* 400Sit. Open M-Su 7-1am.)

🎿 **OUTDOOR ACTIVITIES. Humanfish** (www.humanfish.com), below Hotel Park, has info on **trekking, tobogganing, skiing,** and **hiking,** and leads excursions ranging from several hours to a full week. The **Kompas agency,** also in the shopping center, rents **bikes** and offers **white-water rafting** trips. (☎574 15 15; www.kompas-bled.si. Bikes 700Sit per hr., 1500Sit per half-day, 2200Sit per day. Rafting 4800Sit. Open daily 8am-7pm.) Many hiking paths snake from the lake into the hills, each marked with a name and trail number. The **tourist office** (see p. 862) sells **trail maps. Promontana Outdoor Agency,** Ljubljanska 1, offers guided **hiking, climbing, cycling, rafting, spelunking, snowshoeing, ice climbing,** and **paragliding** excursions around Bled and Triglav National Park and also rents **bikes.** (☎578 06 60; www.sigov.si/ trip. Hiking 4800-8400Sit; climbing 4800-24,000Sit; spelunking 2160Sit; rafting 4800Sit, paragliding 13,200-16,800Sit. Bikes 700Sit per hr., 1500Sit per half-day, 2200Sit per day. Open M-Sa 8am-4pm.) 🏞**Blejski Vintgar,** a 1.6km gorge traced by the waterfalls and rapids of the Radovna River, carves through the rocks of the nearby **Triglav National Park** (Triglavski Narodni Park). The park info office is at Kidričeva c. 2. (☎574 11 88; fax 574 35 68. 600Sit, students 500Sit) Several bridges wind through the gorge to the 16m high **Šum Waterfall.** Go over the hill on Grajska c., away from Bled town center, and go right at the bottom. Turn left after 100m and follow signs for Vintgar. Alternatively, hop on one of the frequent buses to Podhom (10min., M-Sa 10 per day, 280Sit) and follow the 1.5km route. From mid-June to September, **Alpetour** (☎532 04 40) runs a bus to the trailhead (15min., 9:30am, 390Sit).

LAKE BOHINJ (BOHINJSKO JEZERO) ☎(0)4

Bohinjsko Jezero (BOH-heen-skoh YEH-zeh-roh), 30km southwest of Lake Bled, may surpass even its neighbor in natural beauty. Three farming villages dot its shoreline, all of which have preserved a traditional Slovenian atmosphere. Protected by the borders of Triglav National Park, this glacial lake is a portrait of serenity and one of the best spots for alpine adventures. Some travel here for the water sports, but most come to scale the local summits.

S L O V E N I A

▉ ▊ TRANSPORTATION AND PRACTICAL INFORMATION. Trains do not run to or from the three villages around Lake Bohinj, but you can catch a bus to **Bohinjska Bistrica** and take a train from there to **Ljubljana** (2½hr., 8 per day, 1250Sit) via Jesenice. **Buses** run from Hotel Zlatorog in Ukanc to Lake Bohinj (10min., 1 per hr., 300Sit) and from Ribčev Laz to: **Bled** (35min., 16 per day, 740Sit); **Bohinjska Bistrica** (15min., 1 per hr., 380Sit); **Ljubljana** (2hr., 1 per hr., 1950Sit). Buses going to Bohinjsko Jezero stop at Hotel Jezero in Ribčev Laz or at Hotel Zlatorog in Ukanc.

The town nearest to the lake is **Bohinjska Bistrica**, 6km to the east. The lake is surrounded by three villages: Ribčev Laz, Stara Fužina, and Ukanc. **Ribčev Laz,** where the bus arrives, has most things you need. The **tourist bureau,** Ribčev Laz 48, provides maps and transportation info, issues fishing permits, books private rooms, and arranges guided excursions. (☎574 60 10; www.bohinj.si. Open July-Aug. M-Sa 8am-8pm, Su 8am-7pm; Sept.-June M-Sa 8am-6pm, Su 9am-3pm.) **Alpinsport,** Ribčev Laz 53, rents **mountain bikes, kayaks,** and **canoes** and organizes **mountaineering** guides and **canyoning** trips in nearby gorges. (☎572 34 86; www.alpinsport.si. Bikes 950Sit per hr., 2100Sit per 3hr., 3200Sit per day; kayaks 950Sit/2200Sit/3400Sit; canoes 1100Sit/2700Sit/4800-26,400Sit per day. Open daily July-Aug. 9am-7pm; Sept.-June 10am-5pm.) The nearest bank, **Gorenjska Banka,** Trg Svobode 2B, in Bohinjska Bistrica, **exchanges currency** and cashes **traveler's checks** for no commission. (☎572 16 10. Open July-Aug. M-F 8am-6pm, Sa 8am-noon; Sept.-June M-F 9-11:30am and 2-5pm, Sa 8am-11am.) The closest **pharmacy** is also in Bohinjska Bistrica, at Triglavska 15. (☎572 16 30. Open M-F 8am-7:30pm, Sa 8am-1pm.) **Internet access** is at Pansion Rožic, Ribčev Laz 42. (☎572 33 95. 20Sit per min.) The **post office,** Ribčev Laz 47, has a MC/V **ATM** outside. (Open July-Aug. M-F 8am-7pm, Sa 8am-noon; Sept.-June M-F 8am-6pm, Sa 8am-noon.) **Postal Code:** 4265.

▉ ▊ ACCOMMODATIONS AND FOOD. The tourist bureau (see above) arranges **private rooms** and other accommodations in all three villages year-round. (Breakfast 1000Sit. July 5-Aug. 23 2300-2800Sit; Apr. 26-July 4 and Aug. 24-Dec. 24 1900-2300Sit; tourist tax 162Sit. 30% more for stays under 3 nights. Singles 20% more.) **AutoCamp Zlatorog ❶,** Ukanc 2, is on the lake's west side, near the Savica Waterfall and many trailheads. The complex, run by Alpinum Tourist Agency (see p. 856), has sports facilities, showers, bathrooms, and a restaurant. Take a bus to Hotel Zlatorog in Ukranc and then backtrack. (☎572 34 82; fax 572 34 46. Reception July-Aug. 24hr.; Sept.-May 8am-noon and 4-8pm. Check-out noon. July-Aug. 1800-2300Sit per day; May-June and Sept. 1300-1700Sit. Tourist tax 81Sit.) On the way, check out the Mount Vogel **gondola** (10min., 1 per 30min. 7am-7pm, 1400Sit one-way, 2000Sit round-trip) that takes you 1535m up for an outstanding view of the mountains and lake. **Camping Danica ❶,** Bohinjska Bistrica 4264, is just outside town in a quiet area below the mountains. Get off the bus in Bohinjska Bistrica and backtrack about 75m; the site is on the right. Tennis courts, a restaurant, and showers compensate for a lack of shade. (☎572 10 55; www.bohinj.si/campingdanica. Camping July 18-Aug. 21 1750Sit; June 13-July 17 and Aug. 22-Sept. 4 1500Sit; May-June 12 and Sept. 5-30 1200Sit. Electricity 500Sit. 10% off stays longer than 1 week. Tourist tax 100Sit, children 50Sit. AmEx/MC/V.)

On the shores of Bohinj, **Gostišče Kramar ❶,** Stara Fužina 3, has a view of the lake. The menu is limited to pizza (200-1200Sit), hot dogs, and other fast food (350-900Sit). From Ribčev Laz, walk over the stone bridge and follow the first path on your left through the woods for 7min. (☎572 36 97. 0.5L *Union* 400Sit. Open Su-Th 11am-midnight, F-Sa 11-1am.) **Restavracija Center ❸,** Ribčev Laz 50, also has pizzas (1100-1450Sit) and a fairly good "tourist menu" (1400-1600Sit) including soup, salad, and entree. The menu always features a fish and meatless options. (☎572 31 70. Open daily 8am-11pm.) **Mercator Supermarket,** Ribčev Laz 49, by the tourist office, has **groceries.** (☎572 95 34. Open M-F 7am-8pm, Sa 7am-8pm, Su 7am-5pm.)

⚠ OUTDOOR ACTIVITIES. The shores of Bohinj are a gateway to a wide range of outdoor adventures. Good **hiking maps** are available at the tourist office (1500Sit). The most popular destination is **Savica Waterfall** (Slap Savica), which cascades into the Sava Bohinjka River. Take the local bus from **Ribčev Laz** toward "Bohinj-Zlatorog" and get off at Hotel Zlatorog (15min., 1 per hr., 290Sit). Follow the signs uphill to Savica Waterfall for 1hr. to the trailhead, Dom Savica, where visitors must pay 400Sit before heading up to the waterfall (20min. from the trailhead). In July and August, a bus runs to the trailhead from Ribčev Laz (20min., 4 per day 9am-6pm, 380Sit). If you forego the bus, turn left at the lake in Ribčev Laz and follow the road along the lake past **Ukanc** (1½hr.). If the hiking spirit compels you to continue on after the waterfall, follow the signs up the mountain toward **Black Lake** (Črno Jezero) at the base of the Julian Alps' highest peaks (1½hr.). The hiking is extremely steep; avoid going alone. Facing the small lake's shore, a trail to the right (Dol Pod Stadorjem) leads to **Mt. Viševnik,** a grassy hillside that overlooks the small peaks. Facing the valley below, veer left and follow the signs and trailblazes to reach **Pršivec** (1761m; 1½hr.). Return the way you came or follow the trail east for a quicker and easier return (1hr.) along the ridge through Vogar. When you hit the highway at the base, turn right and proceed via **Stara Fužina** and Ribčev Laz (2½hr.). In winter, Bohinj becomes an enormous **ski** resort with five main ski centers: **Soriška Planina, Kobla, Senožeta, Pokljuka,** and **Vogel.** The season tends to run from late December to mid-April, depending on weather conditions. Vogel, the most popular area, appeals to intermediate and expert skiers and is reputed to have some of the best **skiing** in Slovenia. (Morning or afternoon lift pass 3400Sit. 1 day 4900Sit, 2 days 9500Sit, 3 days 13,800Sit.) Nearby Kobla offers gentler slopes for beginners. During the winter, **Alpinsport** (see p. 856) rents skis and snowboards and also holds group and private ski lessons. (Skis and ski boot set rental 3910Sit per day. Snowboard set 4140Sit per day. Private ski lessons 5200Sit per hr.). For more info, contact Vogel, Ukanc 6 (☎574 60 60; vogel@bohinj.si), or Kobla, c. na Ravne 7 (☎574 71 00; kobla@siol.net). For more info on outdoor activities, check out **www.bohinj.si.**

KRANJSKA GORA ☎0(4)

The mountain village of Kranjska Gora (pop. 1500) mixes small town, alpine culture with a solid outdoors-adventure infrastructure. This portion of the Alps appeals to serious mountaineers, while less-experienced climbers enjoy the Karavanke ridge to the north, which provides gentler inclines.

🖪🔁 TRANSPORTATION AND PRACTICAL INFORMATION. The nearest **train station** is in Jesenice (20km). **Buses** run to: **Bled-Lesce** (40min., 1 per hr., 1130Sit); **Jesenice** (15min., 2 per hr., 700Sit); **Ljubljana** (2¼hr., 1 per hr., 2150Sit). The village is spread along **Borovška cesta.** With your back to the **bus stop** on **Koroška c.,** turn right and take the first left on **Kolodvorska cesta.** Turn right at the end of the street on Borovška and follow it past the church. The **tourist office, Turistično društvo Kranjska Gora,** Tičarjeva 2, in the town center on the corner of Tičarjeva and Borovška, arranges **private rooms.** It also sells hiking and walking **maps** (1300Sit) and has a free list of guides for hire. (☎588 17 68. Open July-Sept. M-Sa 8am-8pm, Su 9am-6pm; Oct.-June M-F 8am-3pm, Sa 9am-6pm, Su 9am-1pm.) **Globtour,** Borovška c. 92, in the same shopping complex as the post office, arranges mountain excursions and runs daytrips to Bled, Venice, Škojanske and the Postojna Caves, and the Adriatic coast. (☎582 02 00; www.globtour.si. Daytrips 5500-15,000Sit. Open June M-F 9am-4pm, Sa 9am-noon; July-Sept. M-Sa 8:30am-8pm, Su 9am-noon.) **SKB Banka,** Borovška c. 99a, cashes **AmEx Traveler's Cheques** for 1000Sit commission, **exchanges currency** for no commission, has a **24hr. ATM,** and gives MC/V **cash advances.** (☎588 20 06. Open M-F 8:30am-noon and 2-5pm.) The **pharmacy,** Lekarna Kranjska Gora, is at Naselje Slavka Černeta 34. With your back to the bus station, walk left down Koroška ul., just past the intersection with Vrišiška c. The pharmacy is in the basement of the shopping complex. (☎588 47 60. Open M-W and F 7:30am-3pm, Th noon-7pm, Sa 8am-1pm.) **Internet access** is available at Gostilna Frida, Koroška 14a. (☎588 19 31. First 10min. 200Sit, then 12Sit per min. Open daily 10am-11pm.) Closer to the center, Hotel Larix, Borovška 99, has one terminal for 400Sit per 20min. **Telephones** are inside and outside the **post office,** Borovška 92. (☎588 17 70; fax 588 14 67. Open M-F 8am-7pm, Sa 8am-noon.) **Postal Code:** 4280.

⌨🖳 ACCOMMODATIONS AND FOOD. Your best budget option is a **private room**—there are plenty available in town, marked by *sobe* signs. The **tourist office,** on Tičarjeva, arranges rooms for no additional fee and has a comprehensive price list of all hotels and pensions in the city. (Breakfast 1100Sit. July 26-Aug. 23 2640-4320Sit; Apr.-July 25 and Aug. 24-Nov. 2400-3360Sit. 20% more for stays under 3 days. Singles 1100Sit extra. Tax 168Sit.) Though pricier than most HI establishments, **HI Pension and Youth Hostel Borka ❸,** Borovška 71, has 2- to 4-bed suites with private bath for 6000Sit per person. (☎587 91 00. Breakfast included.) For a splurge, **Hotel Kotnik ❺,** Borovška 75, offers spotless, beautifully decorated rooms with TV, phone, and private bath. (☎588 15 64; kotnik@siol.net. Breakfast included. June 19-Aug. and Aug. 18-Sept. 11 singles 10,230; doubles 18,240Sit; July 31-Aug. 21 8800Sit/14,880Sit; Apr. 4-17, May 15-June 19, and Sept. 11-Oct. 2 9600Sit/16,800Sit; Apr. 1-7, Apr. 17-May 15, and Oct. 2-Nov. 30 7920Sit/13,440Sit. AmEx/MC/V.) The traditionally clad servers at **Gostilna pri Martinu ❸,** Borovška 61, deliver huge portions of Slovenian fare like goulash and polenta for 800-2200Sit. (☎582 03 00. Vegetarian plates 1000-1200Sit. Open daily 10am-11pm.) **Papa Joe Razor ❸,** Borovška 83, serves Slovenian-style meals (1600Sit for 4 courses), pizza (1100-1300Sit), and fast food. (☎588 15 26. Open daily 8am-midnight.) **Mercator,** Borovška 92, is a sure bet for **groceries.** (Open June 15-Sept. 15 M-F 7am-8pm, Sa 7am-7pm, Su 7am-noon; Sept. 16-June 14 M-F 7am-7pm, Sa 7am-6pm, Su 8am-noon.)

🚶 OUTDOOR ACTIVITIES. Kranjska Gora's agencies can help you milk the natural surroundings for all they're worth. **Agencija Julijana,** Borovška 93, next to the Prišavik Hotel, arranges **hiking** and **skiing** excursions, and also leads **rafting, biking, sledding,** and **tobogganing** trips. (☎588 13 25; www.sednjek.si. Bike rentals 700Sit per hr., 1500Sit per half-day, and 2000Sit per day. Rafting trips 7200Sit. Open daily 8am-noon and 3-8pm.) **InterSport Bernik,** Borovška 88a, rents **mountain bikes** and **skis** and offers **ski and snowboarding lessons.** (☎588 14 70; sport@S5.net. Mountain bikes 800Sit per hr., 1650Sit per half-day, 2400Sit per day. Skis and poles 3000Sit per day, boots 1320Sit. Snowboards with boots 4320Sit per day. Individual ski and snowboard lessons 5760-6000Sit per hr. Open daily 8am-10pm. AmEx/MC/V.) There are 17 marked footpaths around the vicinity, ranging in difficulty and from 30min. to 3½hr. in duration one-way. The wooden pillar in front of the tourist office lists all the different footpaths and points you in the right direction; signs with trail numbers provide further guidance along the way. For a relatively short hike, take trail #3 (40min., 2.2km) or more difficult #4 (1½hr., 3.5km) to **Podkoren,** 3km from Kranjska Gora toward the Austrian border, known for its well preserved folk architecture. From there, you can pick up trail #12 toward **Rateče,** a small village 7km from Kranjska Gora that sits below **Pec** (1510m), a peak on the border with Austria and Italy. One of the best hikes runs through the **Planica Valley** to the **Mount Tamar**. From town, take trail #9 to Planica (2hr., 5km), where you'll see impressive ski runs and enjoy an amazing view of the **Mojstrovka, Travnik,** and **Šit Mountains.** Continue on the trail past the ski ramps for 45min. to reach the mountain home **Tamar,** from which the beautiful peak Jalovec can be seen. Another popular, more strenuous hike is to **Vršič** (1611m), the highest mountain pass in the eastern Julian Alps. From town, take trail #7 (3½hr., 12.5km).

ISTRIA

Slovenia claims only 40km of the Adriatic coast, but its remarkable stretch of green bays and vineyards have a palpable Italian flavor. Reminiscent of the French Riviera or Dalmatian coast, Slovenian Istria is the site of bustling coastal villages.

PORTOROŽ   ☎ (0)5

The "Port of Roses" (pohrt-oh-ROHZH; pop. 9,000) is the party town of Slovenian Istria. Streams of visitors have washed away the distinctly Slovenian flavor retained by neighboring coastal towns, but the grassy beach, seaside restaurants, and deep blue tide of Portorož remain undiminished.

▐▀ TRANSPORTATION. Buses go to **Koper** (30min., every 20min. 5am-10:30pm, 680Sit) and **Ljubljana** (2¾hr., 9 per day, 2950Sit). A **minibus** runs the length of **Obala,** from Lucija through Portorož and on to **Piran** (every 15min. until 11pm, 240Sit). A **catamaran** speeds to **Venice, ITA** (2½hr.; Apr.-Nov. 2-4 per week; June-Aug. 15,600Sit, Sept.-May 14,500. Buy tickets at any local tourist agency). **Atlas Express,** Obala 55, has **AmEx travel services** and rents **bikes** and **scooters.** (☎674 88 21; Bikes 1900Sit per 2hr., 2900Sit per 6hr., 4300Sit per day. Scooters 4600Sit/8100Sit/9200Sit. Open July-Sept. M-F 9am-8pm, Sa 9am-7pm, Su 10am-1pm and 6-8pm; Oct.-June M-Sa 8am-7pm.) **Maestral,** Obala 123, rents **boats.** (☎677 92 80; www.maestral.si. July-Aug. 24,000Sit per 4hr., 43,200Sit per day; June and Sept. 21,600/36,000Sit.) For **sailboats,** find **Marina Portorož,** c. Solinarjev 8 (☎676 11 00; www.marinap.si).

▐▚ ORIENTATION AND PRACTICAL INFORMATION. Most streets start at **Obala,** the waterfront boulevard. The main bus stop is across from the **tourist office,** Obala 16. (☎674 02 31; www.portoroz.si. Open daily July-Aug. 9am-1:30pm and 3-9pm; Sept.-June M-Tu and Th-Su 10am-5pm, W 10am-3pm.) Commission-free **exchange offices** line Obala, and a 24hr. (MC/V) **ATM** is at Obala 32, by Banka Koper. A **pharmacy, Lekarna Potorož,** is at Obala 41. Walk down Obala in the direction of Piran, turn right into the Hotel Palace Courtyard, and follow the sign. (☎674 86 70. Open M-F 8am-8pm, Sa 8am-1pm, Su 9-1pm. AmEx/V.) **Telephones** line Obala and are inside and outside the post office. **Internet access** is available at **Pub Planet,** Obala 14, next door to restaurant Paco. (250Sit per 15min. Open daily 9am-2am.) The **post office,** Stari cesti 1, off Obala just past the old Palace Hotel, beside the pharmacy, cashes all major **traveler's checks** for 2% commission and holds **Poste Restante.** (☎674 60 40. Open M-F 8am-7pm, Sa 8am-noon.) **Postal Code:** 6322.

▐▛ ACCOMMODATIONS AND FOOD. Maona Portorož, Obala 14b, arranges **private rooms.** (☎674 03 63; www.maona.si. July-Aug. doubles 7900Sit; triples 10,200Sit; Sept.-June 6200Sit/8600Sit.) **Tourist Service Portorož,** Postajališka 2, right next to the bus station, is another reliable option. (☎674 03 60; fax 674 03 61. July-Aug. singles 3400-4200Sit, doubles 5200-7600Sit, triples 7300-10,600Sit; Sept.-June

2900-4100Sit/4400-6400Sit/6200-9000Sit. 50% more for 1 night, 30% more for 2 nights. Registration 500Sit; tax 126-154Sit.) **Kamp Lucija ❶**, Seča 204, just beyond the Marina Portovož, is a mid-sized campground along the seaside, with showers, toilets, and a restaurant and supermarket nearby. Hop on a minibus from any point along Obala and ride it away from Piran to the stop "Lucija." Continue walking away from Piran and turn right at the sign on c. Solinarjev. Follow the street as it curves left into Seča. (☎690 60 00; camp@metropolgroup.si. Reception 6am-10pm. Guarded 24hr. Camping July-Aug. 2200-2800Sit; May-June and Sept. 1700-2000Sit. Electricity 500Sit, tourist tax 81Sit.) ▧**News Cafe ❷** serves everything from breakfast all day (omelettes 590-1040Sit) to pasta, fajitas, salads, and burgers. By night it is one of the best bars in town. You can kick back to live music and enjoy wild mixed drinks (570-1390Sit) or beer (290-780Sit). The tastefully decadent, 1920s-style interior makes it a local favorite—take a glance at the ceiling. (☎674 10 04. Open daily 8am-midnight. Entrees 990-2000Sit; bring a doggie bag.) Beachside **Paco 2 ❸**, Obala 18a, delights patrons with excellent food at reasonable prices. Choose from pizza (1000-1600Sit), Slovenian entrees, and seafood (1400-3800Sit) under the shade of the tropical thatched roof. (☎674 10 20. Open daily 9am-12:30am.) **Supermarket Mercator,** on Obala 53 next to the bus station, is a more wallet-friendly option and convenient for beachside picnics. (Open M-Sa 7am-8pm, Su 8-11am.)

🖪🖥 **ENTERTAINMENT AND NIGHTLIFE.** For some fun in the sun, head to the manmade sand **beach.** (Open 8am-8pm. Entrance 8am-1pm 600Sit; 1-5pm 500Sit; 5-8pm free. Lockers 700Sit, deposit 1100Sit.) When darkness falls, Obala's main stretch melds into one mammoth beach party. Local favorite **The Club,** at Hotel Belvedere in nearby Izola, is one of the hottest nightclubs in Istria. Take the intercity bus from the station in the direction of Koper (15min., every 20min., 360Sit). Stay until closing to catch an early bus back to Portorož; otherwise a taxi is the only way home. (☎153 93 11. Beer 400Sit. Open daily 11pm-6am.) Also in Izolia is the nightclub **Ambaceda Gavioli,** internationally famous for its wild parties. The club is not open regularly, so keep your eyes out for flyers advertising an event, or inquire at the tourist office for info. In February, Portorož hosts the **Pust,** a carnival that attracts visitors from all along the coast with its crazy costumes and performances. Portorož also participates in events based in its neighbor Piran, such as the theater-oriented Primorska Summer Festival in July.

PIRAN ☎(0)5

In contrast to its modern neighbor Portorož, Piran retains an old-world charm and distinctly Venetian feel. Dubbed "the pearl of Istria," Piran's beautiful churches, crumbling medieval architecture, and budding artistic scene have made the small fishing village a Mediterranean favorite for centuries.

🖪🖅 **TRANSPORTATION AND PRACTICAL INFORMATION.** Buses go to **Ljubljana** (2¾hr., 9 per day, 2950Sit). A minibus runs the length of Obala, from Lucija through Portorož and on to **Piran** (every 15min. until 11pm, 240Sit). Alternatively, a 25min. walk takes you from Piran to Portorož; facing the sea, head left.

The streets of Piran radiate from two main squares. **Tartinijev trg,** named for the native born violinist and composer Giuseppe Tartini, is the city's commercial heart and home to most of its shops and services. From the bus stop, face the sea, turn right and continue for 5min. The square is on the right. Following Verdijeva from Tartinijev trg takes you to the smaller and quieter **Trg 1 Maya.** The center of medieval Piran, the square serves as an open-air stage for theater and dance performances during the **Primorska Summer Festival** (see p. 861). The **tourist**

office, Tartinijev trg 2, in the far left corner of the square, offers **free maps** and bus schedule info. (☎673 02 20. Open daily 9am-1pm and 3-9pm.). **Banka Koper,** on the opposite corner of the square, **exchanges currency** for no commission, gives MC **cash advances,** and has a 24hr. **ATM** outside. (☎673 32 00. Open M-F 8:30am-noon and 3-5pm, Sa 8:30am-noon.) The **pharmacy, Obalne Lekarne Koper,** is at Tartinijev trg 4. (☎611 00 00. Open M-F 7:30am-8pm, Sa 7:30am-1pm. AmEx/MC/V). **Internet access** (240Sit per hr.) is available at **Youth Hostel Val** (see p. 861). **Telephones** are behind the tourist office on the right corner of Zelenjavni trg. The **post office,** Leninova ulica 1, exchanges currency, cashes **traveler's checks** for 2% commission, and gives MC **cash advances.** (☎673 26 88. Open M-F 8am-7pm, Sa 8am-noon.) **Postal Code:** 6330.

⌐⌐ ACCOMMODATIONS AND FOOD. Accommodations tend to be pricey. The staff at **Maona Travel Agency,** Cankarjevo nabrezje 7, on the waterfront before Tartinijev trg, find **private rooms.** (☎673 45 20; www.maona.si. Open daily 8am-8pm. Singles 4300-5500Sit; doubles 6900-8000Sit.) More like a pension than a hostel, ◨**Youth Hostel Val** ❸, Gregorčičeva 38a, offers spotless 2- 4-bed suites. To get there from the bus station, follow the waterfront past Tartinijev trg as it curves around and away from the harbor. Look for the sign three blocks up on the right-hand side. (☎673 25 55; www.hostel-val.com. Breakfast included. Reception 8am-10pm. May 15-Sept. 15 5760Sit per person; Sept. 16-May 14 4800Sit per person. 240Sit/ 480Sit discount for HI members. 480Sit additional for stays less than 2 nights in high season.) Many similar waterfront cafes are on Prešemovo nab. **Tri Vdove** ❹, Prešemovo nab. 4, stands out for its large portions of delicious seafood, meat, and pasta dishes at decent prices. (☎673 02 90. Entrees 1300-3600Sit. Open daily 10am-midnight.) A cheaper but less elegant option is the local favorite **Gostiše Pirat** ❸, Župančičeva 26, in between Tartinijev trg and the bus station. (☎673 14 81. Entrees 900-1800Sit. Open M-Sa 10am-10pm, Su noon-10pm.) There is an open-air **produce market** directly behind the tourist office at Zelenjavni trg. (Open daily 7am-8pm.) A small but well-stocked **Mercator supermarket,** Levstikova 5, stands one block behind. (Open M-F 7am-8pm, Sa 7am-1pm, Su 8am-11am. AmEx/MC/V.)

◙ SIGHTS. The sea is Piran's primary attraction. The coastal waters support Slovenia's sole national marine preserve and offer **scuba diving** opportunities. **Sub-net,** Prešemovo nab. 24, gives certification classes and guided dives. (☎673 22 18; www.sub-net.si. 6000-8400Sit plus equipment. Open M-F 10am-noon and 2-6pm, Sa 10am-noon and 2-7pm.) A short walk uphill from Tartinijev trg leads to the Gothic **Church of St. George** (Crkva sv. Jurja) and the nearby **St. George's Tower,** constructed in 1608, which commands a spectacular view of Piran and the Adriatic. (Church and tower open daily 10am-10pm. Church free. Tower 100Sit.) From the tower, head uphill away from the church and continue parallel to the shoreline and to the right to the old **city walls.** Discover the secrets of Piran's seaside past at the **Maritime Museum** (Pomorski Muzej), just off Tartinijev trg on Cankarjevo nab. The three-story building has exhibits on marine archaeology and seamanship, and an impressive collection of ship replicas. (☎671 00 4; muzej@pommuz-pi.si. Open Tu-Su 9am-noon and 6-9pm. 600Sit, students 500Sit.) Meet the ocean critters themselves at the **aquarium,** Tomažičeva 4, on the opposite side of the marina. (Open daily 9am-5pm. 500Sit, students 400Sit.)

⊿◙ ENTERTAINMENT AND NIGHTLIFE. Piran lacks beaches, but paved swimming and sunning areas line the peninsula. Best of all, unlike neighboring Portorož, they are free. Nightlife in Piran tends to be extremely tame. Perched above the old city stage, the beautiful terrace cafe **Theater** is a perfect place to sit back and watch the sunset. (Mixed drinks 600-1000Sit. Open daily 8am-midnight.)

Da Noi, Prešemovo nab. 1, draws a younger crowd with its nightly drink specials and prime-people watching location. (Sangria 450Sit, 0.5L *Laško Pivo* 420Sit. Open daily 9am-midnight.) July welcomes **Primoska Summer Festival,** which features outdoor plays, ballets, and concerts. Inquire at the tourist office for event schedules. In September, the cultural life of the city peaks with the **International Painting Reunion Ex tempore.** Some of Europe's most promising young painters set up shop on the city's streets and squares, and selected works are displayed in Mestna Galerija (the Town Gallery) and Tartinijev trg.

ŠTAJERSKA

Štajerska's green hills and rolling farmland lie in sharp contrast to the alpine peaks to the west. To Slovenes, the name evokes vineyards, natural springs, and delicious cuisine. The region preserves a strong local character and it doesn't hesitate to welcome visitors with open arms and maybe even a bottle of wine.

MARIBOR
☎(0)2

Stretched between the wine-growing Piramida Hill and the slow Drava River, Maribor (MAHR-ee-bohr; pop. 106,000) possesses a youthful vibrance which belies its deep history. Although second in size to Ljubljana, this 700-year-old university town exudes a charmingly provincial feel. Maribor is more than meets the eye.

▤ TRANSPORTATION. From the **train station,** Partizanska c. 50 (info ☎292 21 00; tickets 292 21 64), trains run to **Ljubljana** (1½hr., 4 per day, 1660Sit) and **Ptuj** (1hr., 5 per day, 650Sit). The **bus station,** Mlinska ul. 1 (☎251 13 33), sends buses to **Ljubljana** (2½-3hr., 10 per day, 2670-2760Sit) and **Ptuj** (50min., 6 per day, 790Sit).

▤▨ ORIENTATION AND PRACTICAL INFORMATION. The majority of Maribor's sights lie in the city center on the north shore of the **Drava River,** which invites exploration by foot. From the train station, turn left and follow Partizanska past the large Franciscan **Church of St. Mary** to **Grajski trg,** where you'll see the **Florian Column.** Turn left down **Vetrinska ul.,** follow it past the shopping complex on the right, and turn right on **Koroška cesta** to reach **Glavni trg.** From the main bus station, turn right on Mlinska ul., follow it until you hit Partizanska, and take a left. **Maribor Tourist Information Center "Matic,"** Partizanska c. 47, just across from the train station, is stocked with **maps** and brochures and can book **private rooms.** (☎234 66 11; www.maribor-tourism.si. 2hr. city tours 7200Sit. Open M-F 9am-6pm, Sa 9am-1pm.) **Nova KBM,** ul. Vita Kraigherja 4 (☎062 229 229) **exchanges currency** for no commission, **traveler's checks** for 1.5% commission, and has **Western Union** and **American Express** services. (Open M-F 8-11:30am and 2-5pm.) A **24hr. ATM** is at **A-Banka,** Glavni trg 18, perpendicular to Gosposka ul. A 24hr. **pharmacy, Lekarna Glavni trg,** is at Glavni trg 20. Use side window for night service. A **hospital** is at Ljubljanska ul. 5 (☎321 10 00). For free **Internet access,** head to **Kibela Multimedia Center,** ul. Kneza Koclja 9. It also has a lively bar and modern art gallery, and it stocks the free English-language newspaper the *Slovenian Times.* Enter Narodni Dom and go through the large art space on the left. (☎229 40 12; www.kibla.org. Open M-F 9am-10pm, Sa 4-10pm. Closed July 15-Aug. 15.) In the summer months, similarly named **Kibala Multimedia,** Glavni trg, next to Benetton, has fast connections for 200Sit per hr. **Telephones** are located inside both **post offices,** Partizanska c. 1 (open M-F 8am-7pm, Sa 8am-noon) and Partizanska c. 54 (open 24hr.; exchange desk open M-F 7am-7pm, Sa 8am-noon). **Postal Code:** 2000.

ACCOMMODATIONS AND FOOD. "Matic" (see **Orientation and Practical Information,** p. 862) can arrange **private rooms** (singles 3500-9000Sit; doubles 7000-12,000Sit). **HI Dijaški Dom 26 Junij ❷,** ul. Železnikova 12, is a 15min. walk from the center. From the local bus station, take bus #3 (Brezje) to the "Pokopališče" stop. Cross the street and walk a few paces to the right, then take the first left and follow the road as it curves. Past the Mercator supermarket, you'll see a building with "12" painted on the side. Its tidy rooms and quiet environs are the best deal in town. Time your arrival carefully, however, because check-in is only from 7-10am and 7-11pm. (☎480 17 10. Open June 25-Aug. 25. Singles 3500Sit; doubles 4800Sit. 20% HI discount.) **Toti Rotovž ❸,** Glavni trg 14, has savory set meals (1600Sit) and a variety of international dishes. (☎228 76 50. Open M-Th 8am-midnight, F-Sa 8am-2am.) A favorite among locals and one of the only restaurants in town open on Sundays, **Ancora ❸,** Beblerjeva 12, off Juriciceva, offers large portions of delicious seafood, pastas, and brick-oven pizzas. (☎628 11 40. Seafood 1030-1650Sit, pizza 590-1360Sit. Open M-Th 9am-midnight, F-Sa 9am-1am, Su 10:30am-10:30pm.) **TAKOS ❸,** Mesarski prehod 3 in a small alley off Glavni trg, serves the biggest, freshest salads in town, along with excellent Mexican fare. (Entrees 900-2600Sit. Open M-W 11am-midnight, Th-Sa 11am-2am, Su noon-5pm.) For groceries in the center, head to **Mercator,** Partizanska 7 (open M-F 7am-7pm, Sa 7am-1pm) or Mlinska 1, near the bus station (open daily 6am-midnight, both MC/V). Closer to the hostel, **Interspar,** Pobreska 18, in the **Europark** shopping mall on the river, has the largest selection in the city. (Open M-F 8am-9pm, Sa 9am-9pm, Su 9am-1pm.)

SIGHTS. Maribor's historical neighborhood, **Lent,** runs along the Drava River and is flanked by three old towers: **Sodni stolp** (Law Court Tower), built in 1310; **Vodni stolp** (Water Tower); and **Židovski stolp** (Jewish Tower), home to a small art gallery. Cross Koroška c. from Glavni trg and take the stairs next to Stari Most down to the river. Face the water and go left to reach **Vodni stolp,** which used to be the city's major wine cellar. Just up from Vodni stolp is Židovski trg. The **synagogue** dates from the 14th century. (Open M-F 7:30am-2:30pm. Free.) Facing the river down Dravška ul. hangs the **Stara Trta,** a 400-year-old vine that still produces a red wine called Žametna Črnina (Black Velvet), which is only distributed in small bottles as gifts for special visitors to Maribor. Glavni trg centers around the elaborate **Plague Memorial,** built in 1743 to commemorate the

THE BIG SPLURGE

ROGAŠKA SLATINA

Nestled on the Croatian border, the ancient, sap-producing town of Rogaška Slatina is an oasis of mental and physical relaxation. According to local legend, the town's natural thermal springs were created when the winged, mythical horse Pegasus dug his hoof into the ground and magical healing waters spewed forth.

Today, Rogaška is one of Slovenia's premiere spa towns, drawing thousands of visitors seeking the town's magnesium-rich, curative waters. Its lush main square is lined by posh health resorts. The most famous is the sprawling Grand Hotel Sava, known for its extensive list of massage treatments, ranging from Indian reflexology to hot herbal rubs. At the more medically oriented Rogaška Medical Clinic, you can sample the region's famed, pungent Donag Mg., one of the world's richest magnesium drinking waters, believed to remedy an array of ailments.

As there are only three buses per day from Rogaška to Maribor, the best way to take full advantage of the town is to stay a night or two.

For more info, visit the tourist office at Zdravilski trg 1 (☎03 581 4414). Open M-F 9am-7pm, Sa-Su 9am-noon and 3-7pm. Spas fill up fast, so be sure to book at least 1-2 weeks ahead end 3 weeks ahead in Aug. Buses run daily from Maribor (3 per day M-Sa, 1½hr., 1320Sit.).

1679 epidemic. Up from Grajski trg on ul. Heroja Tomšiča 5, the **Maribor National Liberation Museum** (Muzej Narodne Osvoboditve Maribor) commemorates the city's struggle against Nazi occupation during WWII. (☎221 16 71. Open M-F 8am-6pm, Sa 9am-noon. 300Sit, students 200Sit.) To sample some of the Štajerska region's best wines, head to **Vinag**, Trg Sobode 3, a wine cellar with a very knowledgeable staff. (☎220 81 11. Open M-F 7:30am-7pm, Sa 8am-1pm. Call ahead for cellar tours. AmEx/MC/V.)

▓▓ **NIGHTLIFE AND FESTIVALS.** Most nightlife is concentrated in the old Lent neighborhood, where lively cafes line the waterfront. **Bongo's Latin Club**, next door to TAKOS (see **Accommodations and Food**, p. 863) puts a little fire into the evening with music, salsa, and a lot of tequila. (Sangria 400Sit, mixed drinks 400-1000Sit. Open M-W 11am-midnight, Th-Sa 11am-2am.) Cuban-themed **Cantente**, Ul. Pariške Komune 37, pours the best mixed drinks in town in a red-lit underground cafe. (☎331 29 89; www.cantante.net. Cocktails 550-1250Sit. Open M-F 8am-1:30am, Sa 8am-2am, Su noon-1am.) Hang out with the university crowd at **Štuk**, Gosposvetska c. 83, Maribor's most popular disco. (☎228 56 30; www.gaudeamus.si/stuk. *Union* 300Sit. Open M-Tu 8am-2am, W-F 8am-4am, Sa 4:30pm-4am, Su 4:30pm-midnight.) **Kino Kolosej**, on the river at Blagana, shows English-language Hollywood films. (☎230 14 40; www.kolosej.si. 900Sit.) From late June to early July, Maribor's historical waterfront neighborhood explodes during the **Lent Festival**. Theater, dance, and outdoor jazz and folk music concerts take place virtually non-stop for 17 days (info and tickets ☎229 40 01). The mid-September **International Chamber Music Festival** features classical music concerts in Narodni Dom Maribor, ul. Kneza Koclja 9. (Info ☎229 40 07; www.nd-mb.si.)

▶ **DAYTRIP FROM MARIBOR: PTUJ.** From its beginnings as the Roman town of Poetovio, the rich winemaking industry of Ptuj (puh-TOO-ee; pop. 19,000) has kept it thriving through the centuries. Reach Ptuj from Maribor by taking the **bus** (50min., 12 per day, 790Sit). The heart of Ptuj lies at Slovenski trg. To get there from the bus station, turn right into the Mercator shopping complex, go straight through the parking lot, and turn left onto Trstenjakova ul. Turn right onto Ulica h. Lacka, which opens out into the main square. The **tourist office**, Slovenski trg 3, offers **free maps** of the town. (☎779 60 11. Open M-F 8am-5pm, Sa 8am-noon.) To reach the beautiful ▓**Ptuj Castle**, head up the hill from Slovenski trg along Grajska. The current fortress dates from 1549, but settlers have occupied its hillsides since 3000 BC. The exquisite structure is one of the best preserved in Slovenia and contains an impressive collection of Gothic and Baroque art, armaments, musical instruments, and festive **Kurent** (carnival spirit) costumes. (☎748 03 60. Open May-Oct. 15 M-F 9am-6pm, Sa-Su 9am-8pm; Oct. 16-April M-F 9am-5pm. 700Sit, students 400Sit. Guide 200Sit/150Sit.) Down the hill, on the opposite side of the castle lies the 13th-century **Dominican Monastery**, Muzejski trg 1, which holds prehistoric and Roman finds from the Ptuj area. (☎787 92 30. Open Apr. 15-Dec. 1 M-F 10am-5pm. 600Sit, students 300Sit.) ▓**Gostilna Amadeus** ❷, Prešernova 36, across from the library, offers a traditional Slovenian entrees. The *štruklji* (dumplings with meat or cheese filling; 700-800Sit) are phenomenal. (☎771 70 51. Entrees 700-2000Sit. Open M-F 11am-11pm, Sa noon-11pm, Su noon-3pm.) Ptuj's most famous celebration is the **Kurent Carnival**, which takes place over 10 days in early February, from Candlemas to Ash Wednesday. Dancing along the streets among other masked figures, the Kurents don sheepskins and headpieces in their mission to chase away the evil spirits of winter and invite spring.

MARIBORSKO POHORJE   ☎(0)2

Just a 20min. bus and stunning cable car ride from the center of Maribor, the Pohorje hills are an outdoor adventurer's haven. Lively year-round, the steep mountains host intense skiing during the winter, and its numerous trails and footpaths make for excellent biking and trekking during the warmer months. Whether you're passing through on a short hike or enjoying a full ski weekend, Pohorje is a peaceful respite from the urban bustle of Maribor. **Bolfenk,** Pohorje's gateway into the wilderness, centers around picturesque stucco **Bolfenk Church.** To fully take advantage of the footpaths that criss-cross the mountains, pick up a **free trail map** at the church. For a short but scenic **hike** (2.5km), turn right out of the Bolfenk Church and follow the gravel road. The trail winds around to the **lookout tower** Razelinski Stolp, which provides a panoramic view of the Štajerska valley, before leading to the **waterfall** Slap Skalca, whose mysterious black waters are a regional treasure. In the summer, you can also explore the hills by **horseback** (2200Sit per hr.), **bicycle** (rentals 550-1400Sit per hr.), or **summer toboggan** (1500Sit per hr.), a contraption which resembles a seated skateboard. All are available at kiosks directly below the gondola terminal at Hotel Bellevue. From December to March, Pohorje boasts some of Štajerska's most popular **skiing.** The best slopes are just above Bolfenk, accessible by **chairlift** from the village center. For information, contact Sportni Center Pohorje, Mladinska ul. 29. (☎220 88 25. Daily pass 4500Sit; skis 1800-3000Sit per day; snowboards 4000Sit per day.) Bolfenk also houses the area's only **museum,** which features exhibits on the history of Pohorje and a small archaeological collection.(☎603 42 11; www.pohorje.org. Open W-F 10:30am-4:30pm, Sa-Su 9:30am-4:30pm. Free.)

To reach Pohorje, take local bus #6 from the main station in Maribor to the last stop, Vzpenjača. Aa free **bus map** is available at the Maribor tourist office. From the terminus, a **gondola** takes you up the mountain to the tiny village of Bolfenk. (Gondola open daily 8am-10pm. Round-trip 1500Sit, students 1200Sit.) To get to Pohojre's church from the bottom of the gondola, start with your back to the Hotel Bellevue, then turn left and follow the signs downhill. The church serves as the cultural center of Pohojre, and has **tourist information,** free summer choral **concerts** (Sa-Su at 11:30am), and **food fairs** featuring local produce and wines. Most services, like **pharmacies** and **Internet access,** are only available in nearby Maribor.

Because food and accommodations in Pohorje are extremely limited and other tourist services are virtually nonexistent, the most comfortable and economical way to experience the hills is to commute from Maribor, where restaurants, rooms, and bars abound (see p. 863). If proximity to the slopes is your top priority, there are a small number of **private apartments** (from 4000Sit per person) on the hill. The **tourist office** can help you track one down. *Sobe* signs also cluster around the base of the gondola. Although most of Pohorje's food offerings are limited to fast food, **Hotel Bellevue ❹** has a decent selection of set meals for 1600Sit.

UKRAINE (УКРАЇНА)

HRYVNY	AUS$1 = 3.78HV	1HV = AUS$0.26
	CDN$1 = 4.02HV	1HV = CDN$0.25
	EUR€1 = 6.49HV	1HV = EUR€0.15
	NZ$1 = 3.46HV	1HV = NZ$0.29
	UK£1 = 9.69HV	1HV = UK£0.10
	US$1 = 5.31HV	1HV = US$0.19

Translated literally, the word "Ukrayina" means "borderland," and it is this precarious position that the country has occupied for most of its history. Ukraine still oscillates between nostalgic, overbearing Russia on one side, and a bloc of newly prosperous countries on the other. Traveling through Ukraine's landscape is a unique experience. With no beaten path, the challenges of exploration reward travelers with a genuine and intriguing look into Ukrainian life.

HISTORY

KYIVAN RUS. Recorded Ukrainian history dates from the **Kyivan Rus** dynasty that sprang from the Viking (Varangian) warrior-traders visiting the Dnieper River region in AD 882. **Prince Volodymyr the Great** welcomed missionaries from Constantinople and was baptized in 988. With Christianity came the Cyrillic alphabet and a flow of Byzantine thought and culture; Kyivan Rus grew so enamored that it tried to conquer its southern neighbors three times. Volodymyr's son **Yaroslav** promoted architecture, music, and the development of Old Church Slavonic (see p. 883).

HOW TO SURVIVE FOUR CONQUERING EMPIRES. In the 1230s **Genghis Khan** invaded Ukraine; his grandson Batu sacked Kyiv in 1240. By the mid-14th century, Ukraine proper was ruled by the Mongols and the Grand Duchy of Lithuania. Mongolian rule persisted as late as 1783 in the Crimea. Eastern Ukrainian **Cossack** bands came under the employment of the Polish-Lithuanian government as sol-

FACTS AND FIGURES

OFFICIAL NAME: Ukraine

CAPITAL: Kyiv (pop. 2.6 million)

POPULATION: 48.4 million (78% Ukrainian, 17% Russian, 0.5% Belarusian, 0.5% Crimean Tatar, 3.5% other)

LANGUAGE: Ukrainian, Russian, Romanian, Polish, Hungarian

CURRENCY: 1 hryvnya = 100 kopiykas

RELIGION: 85% Orthodox, 10% Uniate Catholic, 3% Protestant, 1% Jewish

LAND AREA: 603,700km²

CLIMATE: Temperate continental; hot in the south

GEOGRAPHY: Mostly plains; mountains in the west and extreme south

BORDERS: Belarus, Hungary, Moldova, Poland, Romania, Russia, Slovak Republic

ECONOMY: 45% Services, 40% Industry, 15% Agriculture

GDP: US$4200 per capita

COUNTRY CODE: 380

INTERNATIONAL DIALING PREFIX: 8-10

Ukraine

diers against Constantinople and Muscovy. A rebellion led by Cossack commander **Bohdan Khmelnitsky** in 1648 led to a war with Poland, but a tenuous treaty with Russia eventually led to what is known as **"the Ruin."** By 1667, Ukraine had been divided along the Dnieper River. Russia won the east (Left Bank), including Kyiv and Odessa, while the west went to Poland. Jews were restricted to the Polish-controlled Right Bank, which became known as the **Pale of Settlement.** Local culture was given more freedom in Western Ukraine. In 1772, its capital city, Lviv, fell into Austro-Hungarian hands after the **First Partition of Poland.**

MODERN UKRAINE. Ukrainian nationalism resurfaced in the 19th century, led by the poet-painter **Taras Shevchenko,** who sought to revitalize the Ukrainian language and establish a democratic state. For his efforts, Shevchenko was arrested and exiled to Central Asia. Ukraine declared its independence in 1918, but the **Bolsheviks** set up a rival government in Kharkiv and seized complete power during the **Civil War** (1918-20). Meanwhile the Poles retook Lviv and Western Ukraine only to lose them again in 1940. The next 70 years saw one tragedy after another, as this "bread basket of Russia" bore the brunt of Stalin's murderous collectivization of agriculture, Nazi invasion, a long-standing ban against the Ukrainian language, and the 1986 meltdown at the **Chernobyl** nuclear power plant.

SHIPPING OUT. Ukraine pulled out of the Soviet Union on December 1, 1991, following a vote by 93% of its population for complete **independence.** The Soviet legacy, however, was not easily shed: the **Black Sea Fleet** at Sevastopol was in dispute, as was the status of the Crimea. On May 28, 1997, after nearly five years of conflict, Prime Ministers Lazarenko and Chernomyrdin agreed to divide the fleet and to lease key port facilities to the Russian Navy.

TODAY. President **Leonid Kuchma** won a second five-year term in October 1999, despite his dismal record of economic stagnation and political repression. Though Kuchma is eligible for a third term in October 2004, he has said that he will not seek re-election. Widespread public outcry erupted after allegations surfaced suggesting that Kuchma was involved in the September 2001 murder of journalist Grigory Gongadze; Kuchma has steadfastly denied any involvement. Thirty-eight Ukrainian journalists have been murdered since 1991. In May 2002 Ukraine declared its desire to join **NATO,** but accepted that widespread corruption and economic turmoil would have to be confronted before admittance. Ukraine did, however, station more than 1000 troops in Iraq in contribution to NATO's peacekeeping force. Russia and Ukraine reached a diplomatic breakthrough in August 2002, when ownership disputes concerning 10 former Soviet properties were resolved after nearly seven years of negotiations.

PEOPLE AND CULTURE
LANGUAGE

It's much easier to travel in Ukraine if you know some **Ukrainian** or **Russian.** In Kyiv, Odessa, and Crimea, Russian is more common than Ukrainian (although all official signs are in Ukrainian). If you're trying to get by with Russian in Western Ukraine, you may run into some difficulty: everyone understands Russian, but some people will answer in Ukrainian out of habit or nationalist sentiment. Try to preface your inquiry by saying, "I'm sorry, I don't speak Ukrainian." Acknowledging that Ukrainian is the preferred language and explaining that you can't speak it, rather than simply launching into Russian, will likely improve communication. All city names are in Ukrainian. *Let's Go* uses Ukrainian street names in Kyiv and Western Ukraine, and primarily Russian street names in Crimea, Odessa, and Eastern Ukraine. The Ukrainian alphabet resembles the Russian one (see **The Cyrillic Alphabet,** p. 52), with a few differences. The most notable additions are "і" (i; pronounced "ee") and "ї" (yi; "yee"). The "и" is pronounced like Russian ы (y; "і" as in "s*i*lver"), and "г" is transliterated as "h." For a phrasebook and glossary, see **Glossary: Russian,** p. 958.

FOOD AND DRINK

UKRAINE	❶	❷	❸	❹	❺
FOOD	under 11hv	11-27hv	28-54hv	55-105hv	over 105hv

New, elegant restaurants accommodate tourists and the few Ukrainians who can afford them, while *stolovayas* (столовая; cafeterias), dying bastions of the Soviet era, serve cheap, hot food. Ravioli-like dumplings with various fillings, called *vareniki*, are quite good. *Kvas* is a fermented bread drink. **Vegetarians** will have to create their own meals from potatoes, mushrooms, and cabbage. Produce is sold at **markets;** bring your own bag. **State food stores** are classified by content: *gastronom* (гастроном) packaged goods; *moloko* (молоко) milk products; *ovochi-frukty* (щвочі-фрукты) fruits and vegetables; *myaso* (мясо) meat; *hlib* (чліб) bread; *kolbasy* (колбаси) sausage; and *ryba* (риба) fish. Grocery stores are often simply labeled *magazin* (магазин; store).

CUSTOMS AND ETIQUETTE

When buying flowers for hosts, purchase an odd number, as an even number is only bought for funerals. Several gestures that are considered positive in other cultures have a different significance in Ukraine. The "OK" sign, with the thumb and forefinger touching each other and forming a circle, can be considered crude. The same goes to a shaken fist and pointing your index finger. At the Ukrainian dinner table, hands are usually kept on the table. Dinners can last long into the evening; leaving early may offend your hosts. **Tipping** in restaurants is minimal, never more than 10%. When taking a taxi, bargain the price down and do not give a tip. Don't shake hands across a threshold; doing so is believed to bring bad luck. When in a theater or any other seated public arena, always face seated patrons when entering or exiting a row; passing with your back to them is considered offensive. When on trains, give up seats to women with children and the elderly. In **churches,** men should wear long pants, and women should cover their heads and shoulders.

THE ARTS

Ukraine's **literary tradition** shares roots with Russia and Belarus in the histories and sermons of Kyivan Rus. Religious works in Old Church Slavonic gave way to original works, such as the 12th-century epic *Song of Igor's Campaign (Slavo o polku Ihorevi)*. Ukrainian literature re-emerged in the 17th and 18th centuries. The most accomplished author of the period, **Ivan Kotliarevsky**, established the Ukrainian vernacular with his comic travesty of Virgil's *Aeneid*, the *Eneïda*. In 1830s Kyiv, **Mykola Kostomarov, Panteleymon Kulish,** and **Taras Shevchenko** (see **Kyiv: Sights,** p. 881) joined the **Brotherhood of St. Cyril and Methodius**, devoted to increasing Ukrainian national consciousness. The early 20th century saw a dramatic outburst of artistic activity. Major literary movements overtook one another rapidly: the **Modernism** of **Lesya Ukrainka** gave way to decadent **Realism** in prose and **Symbolism** in verse. Another newly developed movement, **Futurism,** created one of Ukraine's greatest poets, **Mykola Bazhan.** Communist-imposed **Socialist Realism** rained on the artistic parade, with censorship and Stalinist purges of dissenting writers. The result was a coma, from which the arts are just beginning to awaken.

Iconic art lies at the heart of Ukrainian **painting;** as books began to be printed, the art of engraving quickly ensued. In the visual arts, **Monumentalism** dominated painting while a **Neo-Baroque** style dominated in the graphic arts. Under communism, creativity lay dormant until the thaw of the early 1960s allowed it to burst forth in expressionistic paintings depicting communist horrors. In addition to a history of church **choral music,** Ukrainian music also features a rich **folkloric tradition,** typically featuring a trio of violin, *slure,* and *tsymbaly* (hammered dulcimer). In classical music, Ukraine boasts pianists **Benno Moisivitsch** and **Sbiatoslav Richter.**

HOLIDAYS AND FESTIVALS

One of the most widely celebrated festivals is the **Donetsk Jazz Festival,** usually held in March. The conclusion of the 20th century brought the **Chervona Ruta Festival,** which celebrates both modern Ukrainian pop and more traditional music. The **Molodist Kyiv International Film Festival,** held in the last week of October, sets the stage for student films and film debuts.

UKRAINE

NATIONAL HOLIDAYS IN 2005	
January 1 New Year's Day	**May 1** Labor Day
January 7 Orthodox Christmas	**May 9** Victory Day
January 14 Orthodox New Year	**June 19** Holy Trinity Day
March 8 International Women's Day	**June 28** Constitution Day
May 1 Easter	**August 24** Independence Day

ADDITIONAL RESOURCES

Borderland: A Journey Through the History of Ukraine, by Anna Reid (2000). Provides a general overview of Ukrainian history.

Execution by Hunger: The Hidden Holocaust, by Miron Dolot (1987). A riveting memoir of Stalin's forced collectivization of agriculture.

Journey to Chernobyl: Encounters in a Radioactive Zone, by Glenn Cheney (1995). A depiction of Ukraine's most recent national tragedy.

Everything Is Illuminated, by Jonathan Safran Foer (2002). The creatively-written, best-selling novel about a young Jewish man who travels to the Ukraine in an attempt to find the young woman who saved his grandfather from the Holocaust.

UKRAINE ESSENTIALS

ENTRANCE REQUIREMENTS
Passport: Required of all travelers.
Visa: Required of all travelers.
Letter of Invitation: Required of citizens of Australia and New Zealand.
Inoculations: Recommended up-to-date on DTaP (diphtheria, tetanus, and pertussis), Hepatitis A, Hepatitis B, MMR (measles, mumps, and rubella), Polio booster, and Typhoid.
Work Permit: Required of all foreigners planning to work.
International Driving Permit: Required of all those planning to drive.

DOCUMENTS AND FORMALITIES

EMBASSIES AND CONSULATES

Embassies of other countries in Ukraine are all located in **Kyiv** (see p. 878). Ukraine's embassies and consulates abroad include:

Australia: Ste. 12:1, St. George Centre, 60 Marcus Clarke St., Canberra ACT 2601 (☎02 6230 5789; www.ukremb.info).

Canada: 331 Metcalfe St. Ottawa, ON K2P 1S3 (☎613-230-8015; www.infoukes.com/ukremb).

UK: Ground Floor, 78 Kensington Park Rd. London W11 2PL (☎020 7243 8923, information 090 0188 7749; www.ukremb.org.uk).

US: 3350 M St. NW, Washington, D.C. 20007 (☎202-333-0606; www.ukremb.com). **Consulate:** 240 East 49th St., New York, NY 10017 (☎212-371-5691; www.ukrconsul.org).

VISA AND ENTRY INFORMATION

A **visa** is required of all travelers to Ukraine. Citizens of Australia and New Zealand require a **letter of invitation.** All visas are valid for three months. Single-entry visas cost US$100, double-entry US$110, multiple-entry US$165. Transit visas cost US$10, plus the US$100 processing fee. Three business-day rush service costs US$200; double-entry US$220; multiple-entry US$320. There is no next-day service. The visa fee is waived for children under 16 years of age and American students with proper documents. Submit a completed visa application, your passport, one passport-size photo, and payment by money order or cashier's check. It is possible to extend your visa while in Ukraine at the OVIR office in Kyiv. If you need an invitation, there are organizations that arrange visas and invitations. **Diane Sadovnikov,** a former missionary living and working in Ukraine, arranges invitations (US$30). **Janna Belousova,** (☎380 182 21 85 83; www.eugeniatravel.com), of Eugenia Travel's Odessa office, can help with invitations. Janna can arrange for you to obtain a two-week visa upon arrival at Kyiv's Borispil airport, Odessa airport, or Simferopol airport.

When proceeding through **customs** you will be required to declare all jewelry and foreign currency (including traveler's checks) regardless of value. It is difficult to bring Ukrainian currency into Ukraine; you must have a customs declaration stating that the amount you are bringing into the country is no more than you originally brought out. **Do not lose the paper given to you when entering the country to supplement your visas.** The **Office of Visas and Registration** (OVIR; ОВИР), in Kyiv at bul. Tarasa Shevchenka 34 (Тараса Шевченка), or at police stations in smaller cities, extends visas. Make sure to carry your passport and visa at all times.

GETTING AROUND

Air Ukraine flies to **Kyiv, Lviv,** and **Odessa** from many European capitals. Aerosvit, Air France, ČSA, Delta, Lufthansa, LOT, Malév, and SAS fly to **Kyiv.**

Trains run frequently from all of Ukraine's neighbors, and are the best way to travel. They usually run overnight and are timed to arrive in the morning. When coming from a non-ex-Soviet country, expect a 2hr. stop at the border. When purchasing train tickets, you must present a passport, even for travel within the country. Once on board, you must present both your ticket and ID to the *konduktor.* Be sure to store your luggage securely. If you're on the bottom bunk, lift up your seat and put your luggage in the storage space below. Top bunk storage is above the bed. Remember to bring exact change for renting sheets (6-10hv) on overnight trains. On most Ukrainian trains, there are **three classes:** *platzkart,* where you'll be crammed in with *babushki* and baskets of strawberries; *coupé,* a clean, more private four-person compartment; and first class, referred to as *SV,* which is twice as roomy and expensive as *coupé.* Unless you're determined to live like a local, pay the extra two dollars for *coupé.* The *kasa* will sell you a *coupé* seat unless you say otherwise. Except in larger cities, where platform numbers are posted on the electronic board, the only way to figure out which platform your train leaves from is by listening to the distorted announcement. In large cities, trains arrive well before they are scheduled to depart, so you'll have a few minutes to show your ticket to cashiers or fellow passengers and ask "plaht-FORM-ah?"

Buses cost about the same as trains, but are often much shabbier. For long distances, the train is usually more comfortable. One exception is **AutoLux** (АвтоЛюкс), which runs buses with A/C, snacks, and movies, and is located at bus stations. Bus schedules are generally reliable, but low demand sometimes causes cancellations. Buy tickets at the *kasa* (ticket office); if they're sold out, try going directly to the driver who might just magically find a seat and pocket the money.

UKRAINE

Taxi drivers love to rip off foreigners, so negotiate the price beforehand. In major urban areas road conditions are fair; in rural areas roads are poor and are not well lit. *Let's Go* does not recommend **hitchhiking**. Hitchhiking is uncommon in Ukraine, but those who do hold a sign with their desired destination.

TOURIST SERVICES AND MONEY

The **official tourist offices** in Lviv and Uzhgorod are extremely helpful. There is no state-run tourist office. The remains of the Soviet giant **Intourist** have offices in hotels, but usually don't speak English. They mainly deal with groups and organize excursions. There are many **private travel agencies** in Kyiv, Odessa, and Crimea.

The Ukrainian unit of currency is the **hryvnya** (hv), and **inflation** is around 6%. If you're looking to **exchange currency**, *obmin valyut* (обмiн валют) kiosks in the center of most cities offer the best rates. **Traveler's checks** can be changed into US dollars for small commissions in many cities. **Western Union** and **ATMs** are everywhere. Most banks will give MasterCard and Visa cash advances for a high commission. The lobbies of fancier hotels usually exchange US dollars at lousy rates. **Private money changers** lurk near kiosks, ready with brilliant schemes for ripping you off. **Do not exchange money with them**; it's illegal. The Ukrainian **work week** is eight hours Monday through Friday, with a lunch break from 1-2pm. Banks are open Monday through Friday from 9am-1pm.

HEALTH AND SAFETY

 EMERGENCY NUMBERS: Police: ☎02 **Fire:** ☎01 **Emergency:** ☎03

Hospital facilities in Ukraine are limited and don't meet Western standards. Often basic supplies are lacking and patients may be required to provide their own medical supplies (bandages, etc.). Foreigners must have medical insurance to receive health care, but be prepared to front the bill yourself. When in doubt, get to your embassy, and they will find you adequate care or fly you out of the country. Medical evacuations to Western Europe cost US$25,000 and upward of US$50,000 to the US.

Boil all **water** before drinking. Peel or wash **fruits and vegetables** from markets. Meat purchased at markets should be checked very carefully and cooked thoroughly; refrigeration is a foreign concept and insects run rampant. Don't trust the tasty-looking hunks of meat for sale out of buckets on the Kyiv subway—they are not safe. Embassy officials declare that Chernobyl-related **radiation** poses minimal risk to short-term travelers, but the region should be given a wide berth. Public restrooms range from disgusting to frightening. Pay **toilets** (платнiй; platnyiy) are cleaner and might provide toilet paper, but bring your own anyway. **Pharmacies** are common and carry basic Western products. Aspirin is the only painkiller on hand, but plenty of cold remedies and bandages are available. Anything more complicated should be brought from home. **Sanitary napkins** (гiгiєнiчнi пакети; hihienchni paketi), **condoms** (презервативи; prezervativi), and **tampons** (прокладки; prokladki) are intermittently sold at kiosks.

While Ukraine is neither violent nor politically volatile, it is poor. **Pickpocketing** and wallet scams are the most common crimes. Do not exchange money on the street, and beware of con artists. Do not accept drinks from strangers, as this could result in your being drugged and robbed. Be careful when crossing the street—drivers do not stop for pedestrians. It's wise to **register** with your embassy once you get to Ukraine. For more information, see **Safety and Security,** p. 18.

UKRAINE

Women traveling alone will be addressed by men on the street, in restaurants, and pretty much anywhere they go, but are usually fairly safe. Ukrainian women rarely go to restaurants alone, so expect to feel conspicuous if you do. Women may request to ride in female-only compartments during long train rides, though most do not. Although non-Caucasians may experience **discrimination** and some stares, the biggest problems stem from the militia, which frequently stops people whom it suspects to be non-Slavic. **Homosexuality** is not yet accepted in Ukraine; discretion is advised.

ACCOMMODATIONS AND CAMPING

UKRAINE	❶	❷	❸	❹	❺
ACCOM.	under 55hv	55-105hv	106-266hv	267-480hv	over 480hv

Though room prices in Kyiv are astronomical, singles run anywhere from 5-90hv in the rest of the country. Youth **hostels** are practically non-existent in Ukraine though a few can be found in Lviv and Yalta. Budget accommodations are usually in unrenovated Soviet-era buildings. The phrase "*samoe deshyovoe mesto*" (самое дешёвое место) means "the cheapest place." More expensive hotels aren't necessarily nicer. In some hotels **women** lodging alone may be mistaken for prostitutes. Standard hotel rooms include TVs, phones, and refrigerators. You will be given a *vizitka* (визитка; hotel card) to show to the hall monitor (дежурная; dezhurnaya) to get a key; surrender it upon leaving. **Hot water** is rare—ask before checking in. **Private rooms** are the best bargain and run 15-60hv. They can be arranged in through overseas agencies or bargained for at the train station. Most cities have **camping** facilities—usually a remote spot with trailers. Camping outside designated areas is illegal, and enforcement is merciless.

KEEPING IN TOUCH

Mail is cheap and reliable, taking about 10-14 days to reach North America. Sending a letter internationally costs about 2-3hv. Mail can be received through **Poste Restante** (До Запитание). Address envelopes as follows: Aaron (first name), LITVIN (LAST NAME), До Запитание, Хрещатик 22 (post office address), 01 001 (postal code) Київ (city), UKRAINE. **Telephones** are modernizing. The easiest way to make international call is with **Utel**. Buy a Utel phonecard (sold at most Utel phone locations) and dial the number of your international operator (counted as a local call; see the back cover). International access codes include: **AT&T Direct** (☎8 100 11); **Canada Direct** (☎8 100 17); and **MCI WorldPhone** (☎8 100 13). **Internet** cafes can be found in every major city. Alternatively, make a call at the central telephone office: estimate how long your call will take, pay at the counter, and they'll direct you to a booth. Calling can be expensive, but you can purchase a 30min. Ukrainian international calling card for 15hv. Local calls from payphones are very inexpensive. For an English-speaking operator, dial ☎8192.

KYIV (КИЇВ) ☎(80)44

Originally a dynamic center of social and economic life, Kyiv was destroyed under Nazi occupation during WWII, and then rebuilt with extravagant Stalinist pomp during the Soviet era. Since Ukraine gained its independence from the USSR in 1991, Kyiv has recovered its pre-Soviet role as a cultural hub, while also emerging as a proud, modern European capital.

UKRAINE

KIEV, KYYIV, OR KYIV? The spelling Kiev reflects both the old Ukrainian language and the modern Russian language. After the fall of the USSR, some felt that the spelling Kiev was a transliteration of the Russian Киев rather than the Ukrainian Київ. Although a direct transliteration of the Ukrainian would yield Kyyiv, the Ukrainian Language Institute declared in 1995 that Kyiv would be the official transliteration. *Let's Go* uses the official spelling: Kyiv.

■ INTERCITY TRANSPORTATION

Flights: Boryspil International Airport (Бориспіль; ☎296 72 43), 30km southeast of the capital. **Polit** (Політ; ☎296 73 67) sends buses from Boryspil to Ploscha Peremohi and the train station. Buy tickets on the bus (every 30min.-1hr., 10hv). A taxi to the center costs 70-100hv. **Kyiv-Zhulyany Airport** (Київ-Жуляни; ☎242 23 08 or 242 23 09), a smaller hub located on pr. Povitroflotskyy (пр. Повітрофлотський), handles flights to most major Ukrainian cities, **Warsaw, POL** and **Bratislava, SLK.**

Aeroflot, vul. Saksahanskoho 112a (☎245 43 59). Open M-Th 9am-1pm and 2-5:30pm, F 9am-1pm and 2-4:30pm.

Austrian Airlines, vul. Velyka Vasylkivska 9/2 (☎244 35 40). Open M-F 9am-5:30pm.

British Airways, vul. Yaroslaviv Val. 5 (☎490 60 60). Open M-F 9am-5:30pm, Sa 10am-2pm.

ČSA, vul. Ivana Franka 36 (☎246 56 27; fax 246 5627). Open M-F 10am-4:30pm.

Delta Airlines, bul. Tarasa Shevchenka 10 (☎246 56 56). Open M-F 9:30am-5pm.

KLM, vul. Ivana Franka 34/33, 2nd fl. (☎490 24 90; www.klm.com.ua). Open M-F 9:30am-5pm.

LOT, vul. Ivana Franka 36 (☎246 56 20), next to ČSA. Open M-F 9am-5pm.

Lufthansa, vul. B. Khmelnytskoho 52 (☎490 38 00; fax 490 38 01). Open M-Sa 9am-8pm.

Malév, vul. Pushkinska 45/2 (☎490 73 42; fax 490 59 75). Open M-Th 9am-6pm, F 9am-5pm.

Ukraine International Airlines, Peremohi Pr. 14 (☎461 50 50). Open daily 8am-8pm.

Trains: Kyiv-Pasazhyrskyy (Київ-Пасажирський), Vokzalna pl. (☎005). MR: Vokzalna (Вокзальна). Purchase tickets in the main hall. A passport is required. An info kiosk (довідка; dovidka) is in the center of the main hall. Open daily 6:30am-11pm. There is an **Advance-Ticket Office,** bul. Shevchenka 38, next to Hotel Express. Many travel agencies also book train tickets. Trains to: **Lviv** (10hr., 20 per day, 50hv); **Odessa** (11hr., 5 per day, 40hv); **Sevastopol** (20hr., 2 per day, 60hv); **Bratislava, SLK** (18hr., 1 per day, 453hv); **Budapest, HUN** (24hr., 1 per day, 586hv); **Minsk, BLR** (12-13hr., 1 per day, 104hv); **Moscow, RUS** (15-17hr., 20 per day, 195hv); **Prague, CZR** (35hr., 1 per day, 832hv); **Warsaw, POL** (17hr., 2 per day, 305hv).

Buses: Tsentralnyy Avtovokzal (Центральний Автовокзал), Moskovska pl. 3 (Московська; ☎265 04 30), 10min. from MB: Libidska. **Avtolyuks** (Автолюкс; ☎265 05 23), left of the main entrance, provides more comfortable buses at a slightly higher price. To: **Lviv** (8hr., 2 per day, 52hv); **Odessa** (10hr., 4 per day, 57hv). Window #12 sells international tickets to: **Minsk, BLR** (12hr., 1 per day, 47hv) and **Moscow, RUS** (21hr., 2 per day, 75hv).

■ ORIENTATION

Most of Kyiv's attractions and services lie on the west bank of the **Dniper River** (Дніпро; Dnipro). The **train station,** at MR: Vokzalna (Вокзальна) on the western edge of the city center, is three metro stops from **vulitsa Khreshchatyk** (Хрещатик), Kyiv's main avenue. Khreshchatyk runs from **Bessarabska Square** (Бессарабська плю) to **Evropeyska Ploshchad** (Європейська площадь; European Square) through

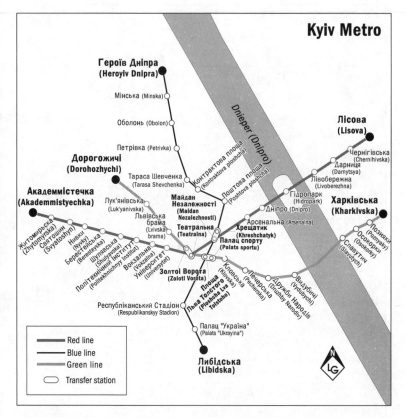

Kyiv Metro

Героїв Дніпра
(Heroyiv Dnipra)

Мінська (Minska)

Оболонь (Obolon)

Петрівка (Petrivka)

Dnieper (Dnipro)

Лісова
(Lisova)

Дорогожичі
(Dorohozhychi)

Тараса Шевченка
(Tarasa Shevchenka)

Контрактова площа
(Kontraktova ploshcha)

Поштова площа
(Poshtova ploshcha)

Чернігівська
(Chernihivska)
Дарниця
(Darnytsya)
Лівобережна
(Livoberezhna)

Академмістечка
(Akademmistyechka)

Лук'янівська
(Luk'yanivska)
Львівська
брама
(Lvivska
brama)

Майдан
Незалежності
**(Maidan
Nezalezhnosti)**

Театральна
(Teatralna)

Гідропарк
(Hidropark)

Дніпро (Dnipro)

Харківська
(Kharkivska)

Арсенальна (Arsenalna)

Крещатик
(Khreshchatyk)
Палац спорту
(Palats sportu)

Познаки
(Poznaki)
Осокорки
(Osokorki)
Славутич
(Slavutych)

Житомирська
(Zhytomyrska)
Святошин
(Svyatoshyn)
Нивки
(Nyvky)
Берестейська
(Beresteyska)
Шулявська
(Shulyavska)
Політехнічний Інститут
(Politekhnichny Instytut)
Вокзальна
(Vokzalna)
Університет
(Universytet)

Золоті Ворота
(Zoloti Vorota)

Контрактова... Кловська
(Klovska)
Печерська
(Pecherska)
Дружби Народів
(Druzhby Narodiv)
Видубичі
(Vydubychi)

Республіканський Стадіон
(Respublikanskyy Stadion)

Площа
Льва Толстого
(Ploshcha Lva
Tolstoho)

Палац "Україна"
(Palats "Ukrayina")

Либідська
(Libidska)

─── Red line
─── Blue line
─── Green line
⬭ Transfer station

N
LG

Maidan Nezalezhnosti (Майдан Незалежності; Independence Square), the city's social and patriotic center. Three blocks up the hill from vul. Khreshchatyk is **Volodymyrska vul.** (Володимирська), which runs past the Ukrainian National Opera, Zoloti Vorota (the city's ancient gate), and the St. Sophia Monastery in **Sofiiska Square.** The area surrounding the square, known as the **Upper City,** was the first site of ancient settlement in Kyiv. At the end of Volodymyrska vul. is St. Andrew's Church and the top of the winding **Andreyevskyy Spusk,** Kyiv's famous historical street, which leads down to the **Podil** district, full of monuments and home to the first tram line in the Russian empire. Along the west bank of the Dniper, **Khreshchatyk Park** covers the slope that runs from the city center to the water's edge. The **Kyiv-Pecherska Monastery,** full of churches and museums, is a 10min. walk from MR: Arsenalna. The territory across the river, around MR: Livoberezhna (left bank), became a part of Kyiv in 1927 and is now a major residential area.

▐ LOCAL TRANSPORTATION

Public Transportation: The Kyiv **Metro's** 3 intersecting lines—blue (MB), green (MG), and red (MR)—cover the city center, but stops are spaced far apart and the Metro does not reach most residential areas. A token (жигон; zhyton) costs 0.50hv and can be purchased either at the windows (каса; *kassa*) or from the machines, which accept only

UKRAINE

PODIM

Lukianivska vul.

Olehivska vul.

vul. Nyzhnii Val
vul. Verkhnii Var

Mezhyhirska

Kostiantynivska vul.

Hlybochytska vul.

Kosohirnyi prov.

Petrivska vul.

Vozdvyzhens'ka vul.

Andriivs'ky

Kudriavsky uziz

Kudriavska vul.

Kudriavska vul.

Museum
of History

Desiatynn
prov.

vul. Mykoly Pyrmonenka

US (Consular Section)

TO AMERICAN
MEDICAL CENTER

vul. Artema

Velyka Zhitomirska vul.

UPPE
CITY

LVIVSKA
PLOSHCHA

Canada

SOFIYS
PLOSHCH

vul. Yuriya Kotsyubinskoho

Observatorna vul.

Strilletska vul.

St. Sophia
Monastery

Central
Indoor
Market

vul. Yaroslaviv Val

vul. Reytarska

Heorhievsky prov.

Pavlovska vul.

Gogolivska vul.

vul. Vorovskoho

Chekhovsky prov.

TO BABYN YAR

Turhenevska vul.

British
Airways

Volodymyrska vul.

Dmytrivska vul.

vul. Olesya Gonchara

vul. Chapaeva

Golden Gate
Museum

ZOLOTI
VOROTA
3

Kyiv Youth
Theater

TO 4 5
& UKRANIAN AIRLINES

Circus

Lufthansa

vul. Ivana Franka

Shevchenko Opera
and Ballet

Science and Natu
History Museum

Prosp. Peremohy

PLOSHCHA
PEREMOHY

6

Aeroflot

Advanced Ticket
Sales (Kassy) 8

vul. Mikhaila Kotsyubinskoho

KLM, LOT, CSA

vul. Bohdana Khmelnytskoho

US

Starovokzalna vul.

7

Australia

vul. Salsahanskoho

Volodymyrskyy
Cathedral

bul. Tarasa Shevchenka

Shevchenko
Museum

Delta
Airline

UNIVERSITET

VOKZALNA

vul. Kominternu

Botanical Gardens

University

Monument
to Taras
Shevchenko

12
Russian Art
Museum

VOKZALNA
PLOSHCHA

Train
Station

vul. Lva Tolstoho

vul. Lva Tolstoho

vul. Pankivska

Tarasivska vul.

Tereshchenkivska vul.

Khanenk
Museum

Malév

PLOSHCHA
LVA
TOLSTOH

TO ZHULYANY AIRPORT &
RUSSIAN EMBASSY

TO YANA (i) (100m)

UKRAINE

Central Kyiv

ACCOMMODATIONS
Hotel Druzhba, 15
Hotel Express, 8
Hotel St. Petersburg, 11
Instytut Tsyvilnoyi
  Aviatsiyi Student
  Hotel, 4

FOOD
Dva Gusya, 9
Fruktopia, 13
Osteria Pantagruel, 3
Taras, 12
Za Dvoma Zaytsyamy, 1

NIGHTLIFE
Androhyn, 5
Artclub 44, 10
Caribbean Club, 7
Chaikovsky, 14
Cocktailbar "111", 6
O'Brien's Pub, 2

Chernobyl Museum

Voloska vul.

Illinska vul.

KONTRAKTOVA PLOSHCHA

Borysohilbska vul.

Museum of One Street

Andriivska vul.

Ihorivska vul.

Borychiv Tik

uzviz

Desatynna

Volodymyrska Hirka Park

River Station

Dniper (Dnipro)

Funicular Station

UK

Pishokhidny mist

St. Mikhail's Monastery

Prince Volodymyr Statue

MYKHAYLIVSKA PLOSHCHA Princess Olga Statue

Naberezhne shosse

Ilodymyrskyy proizd

vul. Mykhaylivska

Khreshchatyk Park

Volodymyrsky uzviz

Sofievska vul.

Friendship of the Peoples Arch

Mikhailivsky prov.

Ukrainian National Philharmonic

MAIDAN NEZALEZHNOSTI

Palace of Culture

National Bank of Ukraine

Petrivska Aleya

Parkova Doroha

Monument to Independence

Central Recreation Park

Telephone-Telefax

MAIDAN NEZALEZHNOSTI

Bukva

Prorizna vul.

vul. Arkhitektora Horodetskoho

Passage

KHRESHCHATYK

Dinternal Books

Museum of Ukranian Art

Dynamo Stadium

Pushkinskaya vul.

vul. Khreshchatyk

Instytutska vul.

vul. Mykhaila Hrushevskoho

Maryinsky Palace

Maryinsky Park

TSUM Department Store

TEATRALNA

Lyuteranska vul.

Druzhba Theater

Museum of Ukrainian Literature

Bankivska vul.

Shovkovychna vul.

Lipska vul.

ARSENALNA

Kruty uzvyz

BESSARABSKA PLOSHCHA

Bessarabskyy Rynok

Baseyna vul.

South Africa

Russia
Moldova

TO BORYSPIL INTL. AIRPORT & VOLODYMYRSKKY-KOLHOSPNYY RYNOK

PALATS SPORTA

TO LAVRA, CAVES & KYIV-PECHERY MONASTERY

0   300 yards
0   300 meters

N

UKRAINE

1hv or 2hv notes and dispense 2 or 4 tokens, respectively. Monthly passes are available and cost 25hv for the Metro or 57hv for all forms of public transport (except *marshrutki*). "Перехід" *(perekhid)* indicates a walkway to another station; "вихід у місто" *(vykhid u misto)* an exit onto the street; and "вхід" *(vkhid)* an entrance to the Metro. **Buses** stop at each station. Bus tickets (0.50hv) can be purchased at kiosks or from conductors on board. Remember to punch your ticket on the bus to avoid the 10hv fine for riding without a ticket. Numbered vans known as **marshrutki** follow bus routes, usually pulling over a few meters behind corresponding bus stops. *Marshrutki* tickets cost 0.60-1hv and are purchased on board; request stops from the drivers. **Trolleys** and buses with identical numbers may have very different routes; it's best to buy a route map. Public transport runs 6am-midnight, but some buses continue to run later.

Taxis: ☎058. Taxis are everywhere. Always negotiate the price before getting in. Write down your destination if you don't know the name in Ukrainian or Russian. A ride within the city center should be 10hv or less. Owners of **private cars** often act as taxi drivers. Locals hold an arm down at a 45° angle to hail a ride. It is unsafe to get in a private car with more than 1 person already in it. *Let's Go* does not recommend hitchhiking.

GETTING A RIDE IN KYIV. The cheapest and most reliable way to get a taxi is to call one of the taxi companies, especially if you are at the train station, bus station, or airport. If you see a taxi on the street and call the number written on it, you will likely get the same ride for less money than if you had just gotten in. If you do hail a taxi, open the passenger door and tell the driver your destination and a price; the driver will either invite you in or scowl and drive off. It's not unusual for Kyiv residents to stop several cabs before agreeing on a price. Avoid taking taxis from directly outside nightclubs, as prices tend to be inflated.

PRACTICAL INFORMATION

TOURIST AND FINANCIAL SERVICES

Tourist Offices: Kyiv lacks official tourist services. Representatives of various agencies at the airport offer vouchers, excursion packages, hotel arrangements, and other services. Travel agencies also organize tours. **Carlson Wagonlit Travel,** vul. Ivana Franka 34/33, 2nd fl. (☎238 61 56). Open M-F 9am-6pm. **Yana Travel Group,** vul. Saksahanskoho 42 (Саксаганського; ☎246 62 13; www.yana.kiev.ua). Open M-F 9am-7pm, Sa 10am-5pm, Su 10am-3pm. Students and youths should check out **STI Ukraine,** vul. Priorizna 18/1 #11. (☎490 59 60; www.sticom.ua). Open M-F 9am-9pm, Sa 10am-4pm.

Embassies: Australia, vul. Kominternu 18/137 (Комінтерну; ☎/fax 235 75 86). Open M-Th 10am-1pm. **Belarus,** vul. Sichnevoho Povstannya 6 (Січневого Повстання; ☎254 43 48; fax 290 34 13). MR: Arsenalna. Open M and F 9:30am-12:30pm, Tu and Th 2:30-5pm. **Canada,** vul. Yaroslaviv Val 31 (Ярославів Вал; ☎464 11 44; fax 464 11 33). Open M-F 8:30am-noon. **Hungary,** ul. Reytarskaya 33 (☎238 63 84; attrkev@hunemb.com.ua). **Poland,** vul. Yaroslaviv Val 12 (☎230 07 00; www.polska.com.ua). **Romania,** ul. Mihaila Kotziubinskogo 8 (☎234 52 61; fax 235 20 25; romania@iptelecom.net.ua). **Russia,** Povitroflotskyy pr. 27 (Повітрофлотський; ☎244 09 63; www.embrus.org.ua). Open M-Th 9am-6pm, F 9am-5pm. **Visa section** at vul. Kutuzova 8 (Кутузова; ☎294 67 01; fax 294 79 36). Open M-Th 9am-1pm and 3-6pm, F 9am-1pm and 3-5pm. **UK,** vul. Desyatynna 9 (Десятинна; ☎462 00 11; fax 462 00 13). Consular section at vul. Glybochytska 6 (Глибочицька; ☎494 34 00; fax 494 34 18). Open M-F 9am-noon. **US,** vul. Yu. Kotsyubynskoho 10 (Ю. Коцюбинського; ☎490 40 00; www.usinfo.usemb.kiev.ua). Consular section on vul. Pymonenka (Пимоненка; ☎490 44 22; fax 216 33 93). From the corner of Maidan

Nezalezhnosti and Sofievska (Софіевска), take trolley #16 or 18 for 4 stops. Continue on vul. Artema (Артема) until it curves to the right, then take the 1st right, vul. Pymonenka. Call ahead for an appointment. Open M-Th 9am-6pm.

Currency Exchange: *Obmin valut* (обмін валют) windows are everywhere, but often only take US dollars and euros. Try **Lehbank** (Легбанк), vul. Shota Rustaveli 12 (Шота Руставелі). From MB/G: Palats Sportu (Палац Спорту), go northwest on vul. Rohnidynska (Рогнідинська) and turn right on Rustaveli. Cashes **traveler's checks** for a US$5 fee; 2% commission on transactions over US$250. Gives MC/V **cash advances** for 3% commission. Open M-F 10am-4pm, Sa 10am-3pm. The **National Bank of Ukraine,** on the corner of Instytutska and Khreshchatyk, charges 3.5% commission for all services. It also offers **Western Union** services. Open daily 9am-1pm and 2-8pm.

ATMs: MC/V machines are all along Khreshchatyk, at the post office, and at various banks and upscale hotels. Look for банкомат (bankomat) signs.

LOCAL SERVICES, EMERGENCY AND COMMUNICATIONS

Luggage Storage: At the train station. Look for *kamery skhovu* (камери схову; luggage storage), downstairs outside the main entrance. Open daily 8am-noon, 1-7:30pm, 8pm-midnight, 1-7:30am. 4.4hv per bag. **Hotel Rus,** Hospitalna 4, MB: Palats Sporta. 4.30hv per bag per night. Open 24hr.

General Information: ☎067. The **Kyiv Business Directory** (Союзпечать or пресса; 10hv), available in many *Soyuzpechats* or press kiosks, lists useful information about dining, shopping, and travel in parallel English and Ukrainian. The website www.uazone.net is an excellent resource for information on Kyiv and all of Ukraine. Several of the major hotels sell **foreign-language newspapers.**

English-Language Bookstores: Bukva (Буква), Instytutska vul. 2A, in the Globus mall behind the statue in Maidan Nezalezhnosti. ☎238 83 07; www.bookva.com.ua. Sells English-language maps of Kyiv (6.34hv) and the indispensable guidebook *Touring Kiev* (74hv). Open daily 10am-10pm. MC/V.

Laundromat: Vul. Komiterna 8 (Комітерна). MR: Vokzalna (Вокзальна). Exit the Metro, walk straight, then turn left, and walk downhill. In Budynok Pobutu Stolichnyy (Будинок Побуту Столичний), off Victory Square. Self-service laundromat (прачечная; prachechnaya or хімчистка; khimchystka). 25.25hv. per load. Open Tu-Su 8am-7:30pm.

WHERE HAVE ALL THE BUSES GONE?

In Kyiv, you can't help noticing the thousands of *marshrutki* minivans zipping recklessly through the streets. Where, exactly, did they all come from, and where are all the buses?

In the poverty that followed the fall of communism, people began to travel only a few essential routes. The crowds that packed into the remaining public transportation made the travel experience nearly unbearable. The old, accordion-style Soviet buses eventually caved under the pressure, and with no money to repair them, the future looked grim.

Enter enterprising government deputies. After conveniently easing tax laws, they began selling the dilapidated machines to themselves, which they proceeded to run privately in direct competition with the public bus lines they were supposed to be overseeing.

They were successful enough to upgrade to newer mini-vans. *Marshrutki,* or "route taxis" as they are sometimes known, have succeeded by offering faster, more frequent service, sometimes even undercutting the prices of the surviving public transit by a few cents. They typically copy bus and trolley routes exactly, oftentimes so closely that they drive directly on trolley tracks. The phenomenon isn't limited to Kyiv or Ukraine—it's common throughout the former USSR, one more example of capitalism run rampant.

24hr. Pharmacy: Apteka, vul. Khreshatyk 24 (Аптека; ☎229 47 89), next to the post office. Ring the bell for service 8pm-8am.

Medical Assistance: Ambulance: ☎03. The **American Medical Center,** vul. Berdycherska 1 (Бердичерска; ☎490 76 00; www.amcenters.com), has English-speaking doctors. Open 24hr. AmEx/MC/V. The **Center of European Medicine** (Шовксвична), vul. Shovkovychna 18-a, #2 (☎253 82 19; sokrnta@ln.ua), will take patients without documents or insurance. Open M-F 8am-8pm, Sa 9am-2pm.

Telephones: Myzhmiskyy Perehovornyy Punkt (Мижміський Переговорний Пункт), at the post office, or **Telefon-Telefaks** (Телефон-Телефакс), around the corner (enter on Khreshchatyk). Both open 24hr. Buy cards for **public telephones** (Таксофон; taksofon) at any post office. **English operator** ☎81 92. Less widespread than Taksofon, **Utel phones** are in the post office, train station, hotels, and nice restaurants. Buy Utel phone cards (10hv, 20hv, or 40hv) at the post office and upscale hotels.

Internet Access: Orbita (Орбіта), vul. Khreshchatyk 46, 2nd fl. (☎234 16 93). 6hv. per hr., unlimited use at night (11pm-8am) for 10hv. Ring bell after 11pm. Open 24hr. The main **post office** (see below) houses 2 Internet cafes. 10hv per hr. Pay in advance. Open M-Sa 8am-9pm, Su 9am-7pm.

Post Office: vul. Khreshchatyk 22 (☎228 11 67). **Poste Restante** at counters #29-30. To pick up packages, enter on the Maidan Nezalezhnosti side. Copy, fax, and photo services available. Open M-Sa 8am-9pm, Su 9am-7pm. **Postal Code:** 01 001.

■ ACCOMMODATIONS

Hotels in Kyiv tend to be expensive. It's worth looking into short-term apartment rentals, which are listed in the *Kyiv Post* (www.kyivpost.com). People at the train station offer **private rooms** (US$5 and up). The telephone service **Okean-9** (Океан; ☎443 61 67) helps find budget lodgings. Tell them your price and preferred location, and they'll reserve you a room for free. (Open M-F 9am-5pm, Sa 9am-3pm.)

Hotel St. Petersburg (Санкт-Петербург), bul. T. Shevchenka 4 (☎229 73 64; s-peter@i.kiev.ua). MR: Teatralnaya. The hotel has an ideal location, just up the street from Bessarabska Square. Be sure to reserve 1 month in advance. Shared bathrooms. Breakfast included. Singles 129hv; doubles 182hv; triples 213hv. MC/V. ❸ The hotel owns a **second location,** Volodymyrska vul. 36, with cheaper rooms, also without baths. Singles 73hv; doubles 130-178hv; triples 150hv; quads 172hv. ❷

Hotel Express (Експрес), bul. Shevchenka 38/40 (☎239 89 95; www.railwayukr.com), up vul. Kominternu from the train station or MR: Universytet (Університет). Clean rooms with telephones, TVs, fridges, and toilets. The rooms without showers are more reasonably priced. Internet 4hv per 30min. Train tickets sold next door. Shower 5hv. Singles 145hv; doubles 230hv. ❸

Hotel Druzhba, bul. Druzhby Narodiv 5 (Дружби Народів; ☎268 34 06; fax 268 33 87). From MB: Lybidska (Либідська), take a left on bul. Druzhby Narodiv, and walk 200m; hotel is on the left. Clean, spacious rooms with private shower, phone, TV, and fridge. Singles 190hv; doubles 342hv. ❸

Instytut Tsyvilnoyi Aviatsiyi Student Hotel (Інститут Цувільної Авіації), vul. Nizhinska 29E (Ніжінська; ☎404 90 59). Take tram #1K or 3 from MR: Politekhnichna and exit at the 3rd stop (Harmatna). Cross the street and walk back. Turn right at Bank Narda and follow the road to the traffic circle, then take a left. Hotel behind the store with the large sign "Серго" on top. Rooms are clean. Singles 50hv, with private bath, TV, and fridge 110hv; doubles 85hv/180hv. ❶

◘ FOOD

Kyiv has a large selection of restaurants and **markets,** as well as an army of **street vendors** selling cheap snacks. Cafes in the city center tend to cost more than similar establishments in outlying areas. For complete Kyiv restaurant listings, check out *What's On* magazine (www.whatson-kiev.com). Those brave enough to cook for themselves will find high-quality fare at the open-air **Bessarabskyy Rynok** (Бессарабський Ринок), at the intersection of vul. Khreshchatyk and bul. Shevchenka. (Open daily 8:30am-7pm.) For more urban grocery shopping, head to 24hr. **Furshet** (фуршет), vul. Yaroslavska 57 (Ярославська).

Taras (Тарас; ☎235 21 32), Tereshchenkivska vul. 10, in the Taras Shevchenko Park. A beautifully decorated restaurant, Taras serves outstanding meals and commendable tea (9-25hv) and dessert. A booth outside sells pancakes (2-4hv) in the summer. Entrees 30-50hv. Open Sept.-May 10am-1am, Jun.-Aug. 10am-2am. MC/V. ❸

Osteria Pantagruel, vul. Lysenko 1 (☎228 81 42). MG: Zoloti Vorota. The Italian chef prepares an array of pasta dishes, fish, and meat entrees (29-179hv). Open daily 11am-11pm. Also open for breakfast M-F 7-11am. MC/V. ❹ During the sumemr months, stop by the Pantagruel affiliated **Osteria Pantagruel Cafe,** down the street, which serves slightly less expensive options on its terrace cafe. Open 10am-11pm. ❸

Fruktopia Fashion Cafe, bul. Shevchenka 2 (☎235 83 47). MR: Teatralna. Just up the street from Bessarabska Sq. on the right side, before Hotel St. Petersburg. Downstairs are a hip bookstore and a colorful cafe; upstairs is a restaurant serving European cuisine. Menus in English. Business lunch 25hv. Salads 23-35hv; entrees 35-90hv. Live piano Tu and Sa 8-10pm. Open daily 9am-last customer. ❸

Za Dvoma Zaytsyamy (За Двома Зайцями), Andriyivskyy Uzviz 34 (☎416 35 16). Named after the famous 1962 Ukrainian film, this restaurant serves dishes prepared from 19th-century recipes. Try the home-brewed cranberry vodka, *klyukovka* (клюковка). Vegetarian menu. Entrees about 50hv. Open daily 11am-11pm. MC/V. ❹

Dva Gusya (Два Гуся) vul. Khreshchatyk 42 (☎229 76 83), upstairs in the Gastronom. The hall on the left is a cafe, serving omelettes and other light food; the larger hall on the right has cafeteria-style Ukrainian dishes. Go through the line and point out what you want to the servers. Quick and cheap, but the prices add up fast. Entrees 3-8hv. 7% discount with ISIC. Cafe open daily 8am-10pm; cafeteria daily 10am-10pm. ❷

◎ SIGHTS

Kyiv bursts with museums that await discovering and parks that invite relaxation. First-time visitors usually devote a few days to wandering along vul. Khreshchatyk and Volodymyrska vul., enjoying the city's monuments, parks, museums, and historic buildings. More seasoned or permanent travelers spend time exploring the hidden avenues and monasteries that bestow such charm on the ancient city.

CENTRAL KYIV

INDEPENDENCE SQUARE. This is a popular meeting place, and it hosts speeches and concerts on national holidays. Independence Square (Майдан Незалежності; Maidan Nezalezhnosti), often called simply "Maidan," is considered the official center of Kyiv and has been renamed and redesigned many times over the past century. It now features the Monument to Independence, a 12m bronze statue of a woman atop a 50m column, inaugurated in 2001 on the 10th anniversary of Ukraine's independence. On the other side of the square, across vul. Khreshchatyk, is a large fountain and the post office building. *(MB: Maidan Nezalezhnosti.)*

UKRAINE

KHRESHCHATYK STREET. Kyiv centers around this broad commercial avenue. The houses along Khreshchatyk were destroyed during the Nazi occupation in 1941. After the city was liberated, war criminals were publicly hanged on the street. The road was rebuilt in the Soviet style after the war. It is now a popular place for strolling and relaxing, and is closed to traffic on weekends and holidays. Students often play guitar on the sidewalks of Khreshchatyk in the evenings. An archway from Khreshchatyk leads to the **Passage,** Kyiv's most fashionable area, with several high-priced cafes and bars. *(MR: Khreshchatyk; Хрещатик.)*

TARAS SHEVCHENKO BOULEVARD. This boulevard (бул. Тараса Шевченка; bul. Tarasa Shevchenka) is named for Taras Shevchenko, whose poetry reinvented the Ukrainian language in the mid-19th century (see **The Arts,** p. 869). On the boulevard is bright-red **Taras Shevchenko University,** which still promotes independent thought in Ukraine. The many-domed **Volodymyrskyy Cathedral,** 20 bul. Tarasa Shevchenka, commemorates 900 years of Christianity in Kyiv; its interior is decked with Art Nouveau saints and seraphim. *(At the intersection with vul. Khreshchatyk. MR: Universytet. Cathedral open daily 9am-9pm.)*

KHRESHCHATY PARK

Vul. Khreshchatyk continues up to Evropeyska Pl. (Європейська пл.; European Sq.) and meets Volodymyrska uzviz, which runs along Kyiv's Khreshchatyk Park. In the large park is the Friendship of the Peoples Arch and smaller monuments.

FRIENDSHIP OF THE PEOPLES ARCH. Called the "Yoke" by locals, this monument was built to commemorate the 1654 Russian-Ukrainian Pereyaslav Union (see **History,** p. 866). It consists of a metal arch 30m in diameter, a sculpture of the participants of the Pereyaslavskaya Rada, and bronze statues of a Russian and a Ukrainian worker. The arch provides a romantic view of the Dnieper.

MONUMENT TO KYIV'S SOCCER PLAYERS. This is a monument to Kyiv pride. In 1941, the Nazis invaded and took thousands of Ukrainians as prisoners. Having discovered that one prisoner was a player for the Dynamo Kyiv soccer team, Nazi officers rounded up the other players and arranged a "death match" against the German army team. Despite the Dynamo players' weakened condition and a Gestapo referee, Ukraine won, 3-0. Shortly thereafter the entire team was thrown into a concentration camp, where most of them perished before a firing squad. Recent scholars suggest, however, that such a match never happened, and that Soviet propagandists created the story. *(Go right at the arch and into the park.)*

MARIYINSKY PALACE. Built by Francesco Rastrelli, who also designed Kyiv's St. Andrew's Church and helped his father design much of St. Petersburg, the palace was built for Tsaritsa Elizabeth's visit in the 1750s. It was first called Mariyinsky in honor of Maria Alexandrovna, consort of Russian Tsar Aleksandr II. Today the palace is used for formal state receptions. *(From European Sq., walk down vul. Hrushevskoho. The palace is on your left, about 500m after the entrance to Dynamo Stadium.)*

ST. SOFIA AND ENVIRONS

Take trolley #16 from Maidan Nezalezhnosti or get off at MG: Zoloti Vorota.

ST. SOFIA MONASTERY COMPLEX. The monastery, established in the 17th century, served as the religious and cultural center of Kyivan Rus. The site became a national reserve in 1934, and includes a historical museum and an architectural museum. The **St. Sofia Cathedral** is notable for its golden domes and its 260 square meters of mosaics; some additional mosaics, along with drawings and design plans, are on display in the **architectural museum.** The St. Sofia **bell tower,** located above the entrance gate, is 76m tall and dates back to the late 17th century. A **statue of Bohdan Khmelnytsky** (see **History,** p. 866) stands near the entrance of St. Sofia. *(Vul. Volodymyrska 24. ☎228 61 52. Monastery grounds open daily 9am-7pm. 1hv. Museums open daily Apr.-Oct. and Nov.-Mar. M-W and F-Su 10am-6pm. Ticket kiosk on the left after entering the main gate. Ticket for both museums 11hv, students and children under 7 4hv. Cameras 20hv, video 50hv. Special exhibits 3hv. 45min. English tour 40hv.)*

ST. MICHAEL'S MONASTERY. This 11th century monastery (Михайлівський Золотоверхий Монастир; Myhaylivskyy Zolotoverkhyy Monastyr) was destroyed in 1934 to make way for a government square. Plans never materialized, and instead, a sports center occupied the sacred territory for over 60 years. Before the monastery was destroyed, some of the original mosaics and frescoes were moved to St. Sofia, where many are on display today. The current blue-and-gold-domed monastery was reconstructed in the 1990s. *(At the top of Mykhaylivska pl. Open daily 9am-9pm. Free.)* A **museum** in the bell tower with detailed English captions leads to the chamber of the bells. The bells ring every 15min., and the carillon plays every hour during the day. *(☎28 70 68. Open Tu-Su 10am-6pm. Ticket office closes 5pm. 6hv.)* To the right of the monastery, vul. Tryokhsvyatytelska passes a series of smaller churches as it winds down to the **Volodymyrska Hirka Park** (Володимирська Гірка), which is full of tiny pavilions and sculptures by folk artists.

GOLDEN GATE (ЗОЛОТІ ВОРОТА; ZOLOTI VOROTA). The wood and stone gate has marked the entrance to the city since 1037. As legend has it, the gate's strength saved Kyiv from the Tatars during the reign of Yaroslav the Wise, whose statue stands nearby (see **History,** p. 866). Inside, a museum devoted to the gate is closed for restoration. *(300m down vul. Volodymyrska from St. Sofia.)*

ANDRIYIVSKYY PATH AND THE PODIL DISTRICT

The cobblestone **Andriyivskyy path** (Андріївский узвіз; Andriyivskyy uzviz), is Kyiv's most touristy area. The steep, winding street is lined with historic buildings, souvenir vendors, and cafes. From Mykhaylivska Sq., walk down Desyatynna vul. to get to the top of Andriyivskyy path. There is **St. Andrew's Church,** conceived by Empress Elizabeth Petrovna in the 18th century and designed by her favorite architect, Italian Bartolomeo Rastrelli. The church was renovated in the 1970s according to Rastrelli's original plans, which were discovered in Vienna in 1963. *(☎228 58 61. Open M-Tu and Th-Su 10am-5pm. Free before 2pm; 2-5pm 4hv, students 1hv. Camera 20hv, video 50hv. Call in advance for a tour (45hv) in English. Church is open for services M-Tu and Th-Su 5-7:30pm.)* Down Andriyivskyy 100m, you'll see steep wooden stairs. Climb up for a great view of Podil, Kyiv's oldest district. Farther down are writer **Mikhail Bulgakov's house** (Andriyivskyy uzviz 13) and the **Museum of One Street** (see p. 885). Andriyivsky path ends at **Kontraktova Sq.** (Контрактова пл.), the center of **Podil.**

TITHE CHURCH (ДЕСЯТИННА ЦЕРКВА; DESYATINNA TSERKVA). Ruins are the only remnant of Kyivan Rus's oldest stone church, which converted pagan Kyivans to Christianity in the 10th century. It was destroyed under the Soviet "Socialist Reconstruction" program in 1937. *(Walk up the gray steps at the corner of Andriyivskyy uzviz, Desyatinna, and Volodymyrska. Next to the National Museum of Ukrainian History.)*

BABYN YAR (БАБИН ЯР). The monument at Babyn Yar marks the graves of the first Holocaust victims in Ukraine, buried in September 1941. Although plaques state that 100,000 Kyivans died here, current estimates double that figure. Many of the victims—most of them Jews—were buried alive. Above the grass-covered pit,

UKRAINE

a statue shows the victims falling to their deaths. In June 2001, Pope John Paul II visited the site and prayed for the victims. *(MG: Dorohozhychi (Дорогожичі). In the park near the TV tower, at the intersection of vul. Oleny Telihy and vul. Melnykova.)*

KYIV-PECHERY MONASTERY

Kyiv's oldest and holiest religious site, the Kyiv-Pechery Monastery (Киево-Печерська Лавра; Kyivo-Pecherska Lavra) merits a full day of exploration. Take the metro to MR: Arsenalna (Арсенальна). Turn left as you exit the metro, and walk 10min. down vul. Sichnevoho Povstaniya, or take trolleybus #20.

MONASTERY. The ▇monastery, first mentioned in chronicles in 1051, was the Russian Empire's major pilgrimage site (the Russian proverb "your tongue will lead you to Kyiv" derives from the long journey of the pilgrims). The 12th-century **Holy Trinity Gate Church** (Троїцка надбрамна церква; Troyitska Nadbramna Tserkva) contains some beautiful frescoes, a 600kg censer, and the ruins of an ancient church. Step into the functioning **Refectory Church,** home to one of the largest and most decorated domes in the complex. The exhibits inside have capitions in English. The 18th-century **Great Lavra Bell Tower** (Велика Лаврська Дзвінниця; Velyka Lavrska Dzvinnytsya) offers fantastic views of the river and the golden domes. *(☎ 290 30 71. Buy tickets at the white kiosks on beside main entrance. Open daily May-Aug. 9am-7pm; Sept.-Apr. 9:30am-6pm. Monastery 10hv, students 5hv. Bell tower 5hv/3hv. Camera and video 12hv. The office on the left past the main entrance arranges English tours for up to 10 people; 160hv, students 80hv.)*

MONASTERY MUSEUMS. The nearby **Museum of Historical Treasures of Ukraine** (Музей Історичних Коштовностей України; Muzey Istorychnykh Koshtovnostey Ukrayiny) displays precious stones and metals. *(Open M and W-Su 10am-5pm.)* The **Micro-Miniature Exhibit** contains the world's smallest book and other amazingly small things. *(Open daily 10am-1:30pm and 2:30-6:30pm. 5hv, students 3hv. Closes in heavy rain or snow.)*

CAVES. The Kyiv-Pechery Monastery is named for its caves *(pechery)*, located at the bottom of the hill on the monastery grounds. Some monks lived in isolation in these caves, receiving only food and water from the outside world. When they died, they were mummified, sometimes with one or both hands exposed. Without a guided tour you may only view a 15m section of the caves. All visitors must buy a candle (1hv) and carry it with them in the caves. The tours have a religious tone. Women must wear headscarves (provided free for use during tour) and long skirts or pants; men must wear long pants and remove hats. *(☎ 254 33 90. Open daily May-Sept. 9am-5:30pm; Oct.-Apr. 9am-4:30pm. 50min. Tours in Russian every 15min.; 7hv, students 5hv. Tours in English 1 person 60hv, 3 people 80hv, 5 people 100hv.)*

🏛 MUSEUMS

MUSEUM OF FOLK ARCHITECTURE AND RURAL LIFE. Over 100 Ukrainian huts and wooden churches representing seven cultural regions of Ukraine cover the grounds of this open-air museum (Музей народнщі архітектури та побуту України; Muzey narodnoyi arkhitektury ta pobutu Ukrayiny), which is ideal for children. Traditional performances occur during the 20 folk festivals held throughout the year. *(Just outside Kyiv in the Pirohiv village. MB: Libidska. Take trolleybus #11 outside the Metro station to the park's entrance. 10min. walk to museum. Alternatively, take marshrutka #156 from outside MB: Respublykanskyy Stadion (Республіканський Стадіон); ask the driver to stop at the museum. ☎ 266 24 16. Open daily 10am-6pm. 10hv, students 5hv. 1½hr. tour in English 120hv. Map 2.50hv. Camera 5hv, video 10hv.)*

MUSEUM OF ONE STREET. This small museum at the bottom of Andriyivskyy Path recounts the colorful history of the famous street with a creatively arranged collection of photos and old documents. *(Andriyivskyy uzviz 2b. ☎416 03 98; mus1str@ua.fm. Open Tu-Su noon-6pm. 5hv. 45min. English tour 50hv.)*

CHERNOBYL MUSEUM. An excellent multimedia tour (5hv) details the explosion, clean-up, and evacuation of the area, but it is not available in English. *(Provulok Kho-ryva 1 (Провулок Хорива). MB: Kontraktova. At the lower end of Andriyivskyy uzviz. ☎417 54 22. Open M-F 10am-6pm, Sa 10am-5pm; closed last M of each month. 5hv, students 1hv.)*

NATIONAL MUSEUM OF UKRAINIAN HISTORY. This museum (Національний музей історії України; Natsionalnyy muzey istoriyi Ukrayiny) glorifies Ukraine's ancient past and its most recent achievements. *(Vul. Volodymyrska 2, up the stairway at the crossroad with Andriyivskyy uzviz. ☎228 29 24. Open M-Tu and Th-Su 10am-5pm. 4.20hv, additional exhibits 1.20hv each.)*

RUSSIAN ART MUSEUM. A lavish interior and works by Russian greats, like Shishkin and Repin attract visitors to this museum. *(Vul. Tereschenkivksa 9, near the Tarasa Shevchenka Park. MR: Teatralna. ☎234 62 18. Open M 11am-6pm, Tu-Su 10am-6pm. 3hv, students 1hv. Booklet with short English summary 6hv.)*

MUSEUM IN HONOR OF BOHDAN AND VAVRAVA KHANENKO. The dark wood interior of this museum (Музей мистецтва ім. Богдана та Варвара Ханенків; Muzey Mystetstva ym. Bohdana ta Varvara Khanenkiv) houses a small collection of Renaissance art. *(Vul. Tereschenkivska 15. MR: Teatralna. ☎235 32 90. Open W-Su 10:30am-5:30pm. Call ahead to arrange an English tour for 120hv. 5hv, students 2hv.)*

TARAS SHEVCHENKO MUSEUM. This museum, dedicated to the exiled artist, contains a huge collection of sketches, paintings, and prints. Housed in a 19th-century mansion, which looks like it's straight out of a Russian novel. *(Bul. Tarasa Shevchenka 12. MR: Universytet (Університет). ☎224 25 56. Open Tu-Su 10am-5pm; closed last F of each month. English tours 60hv. 3hv, students 1hv.)*

MUSEUM OF UKRAINIAN LITERATURE. The nationalistic museum (Музей літератури України; Muzey literatury Ukrayiny) traces Ukrainian literature from its inception to the present. A wax museum on the second floor features full-size figures of Lenin, Kuchma, and other leaders. *(Vul. Khmelnytskoho 11, 3rd fl. MG: Zoloti Vorota. ☎225 13 15. Open M-Sa 9am-5pm. 2hv, students 1hv; W free. Wax museum 6hv.)*

🎭 🎪 ENTERTAINMENT AND FESTIVALS

In May, a two-week theater festival leads up to **Kyiv Days,** when drama, folklore, jazz, and rock music performances are staged all over town. The famed **Kyiv International Film Festival** comes to town in July. If you're there between late spring and fall, don't miss **Dynamo Kyiv,** one of Europe's top soccer teams. (Ticket office in front of the stadium. Tickets 5-30hv.) Hot summer days are perfect for a boat ride down the Dniper or a trip to **Hydropark** (Гідропарк), which is an **amusement park** (rides 8-16hv) and **beach** on an island on the river (MR: Hidropark). The beach has showers, toilets, and changing booths. The **National Philharmonic,** Volodymyrsky uzviz 2, holds regular concerts. (☎228 16 97. *Kassa* open Tu-Su noon-3pm and 4-7pm.) **Shevchenko Opera and Ballet Theater,** vul. Volodymyrska, puts on several shows each week. (MR: Teatralna. ☎224 71 65. Shows at noon and 7pm. Ticket office open M 11am-3pm, Tu-Su 11am-3pm and 4:30-7pm.) **Koleso Theater** (Колесо; ☎416 05 27), Andriyivskyy uzviz 8, gives avant-garde performances.

ᗏ NIGHTLIFE

Kyiv's nightlife scene has developed considerably in the past decade, with lots of new bars and discos, many of them owned and run by expats. Check out *What's On* (www.whatson-kiev.com), *Kyiv Weekly*, and the *Kyiv Post* (www.kyiv-post.com), for the latest hot spots in town. The websites www.clubs.kiev.ua and www.afisha.org.ua also have info on nightclubs and events.

O'Brien's Pub, vul. Mykhaylivska 17a (Михайлівська; ☎229 15 84; www.obriens.kiev.ua). Up the street from Maidan Nezalezhnosti. The original Irish pub in Kyiv and the most popular expat bar in the city. Offers satellite TV, darts, billiards, and a good variety of food (14-45hv). Beer 6-22hv. Happy hour daily 5-7pm. Live music 9:30pm-12:30am. Open daily 8am-2am. AmEx/MC/V.

Artclub 44, Khreshchatyk pr. 44 (☎229 41 37), in the basement. Walk into the court-yard; it's through an unmarked brown door on the left. Kyiv's most popular jazz club. Live music daily 10pm-midnight. Cover Th-Sa 10-40hv. Open daily 10am-2am.

Caribbean Club (☎244 42 90), vul. Kominternu 4 (Комінтерну), is jam-packed with Latin guests, and the rest blend in just fine: the crowd here really knows how to salsa. The DJ sits in a red classic car with a Rio plate. Th is free and more relaxed. Mixed drinks 30-50hv, beer 9-20hv. Cover F-Sa women 30hv, men 50hv. W striptease (cover 30hv for men). 1½hr. dance lessons (M, W, Su6pm; 20hv). Open 6pm-6am.

Cocktailbar "111," Peremohy pl. 1 (☎238 02 86), in Hotel Lybid. MR: Universytet (Університет). Once the prime nightspot in Kyiv, 111 is still going strong as its round bar rotates. Founded by a German expat who owns several bars and clubs in Kyiv. Cover Su 20hv. W 20hv, age 30+ free. Th 8-11pm women only; after 11pm men 30hv, women 20hv. F-Sa men 40hv, women 20hv. Open daily 10am-2am or later.

Chaikovsky, Bessarabskyy pl. 2 (☎229 56 66), on the 3rd fl. of the market building. This posh club is popular among wealthy young Ukrainians. An occasional destination for models. Beer 10-20hv, cocktails 30-60hv. Th R&B night. Cover W-Th 30hv, F-Sa 50hv; no cover for women before 1am. Open W-Sa 10pm-6am.

GLBT

In summer, the gay scene centers around the **Hydropark;** follow the mob to **Youth Beach** (Molodizhny Plyazh). Buy a 1hr boat ride to the opposite beach, where the crowd is mixed. **Androhyn,** vul. Harmatna 26/2 (☎443 65 56; MR: Shulyavska), is one of the few gay clubs in town. (Cover 20-30hv. Open Th-Su 8pm-8am.)

ᗏ DAYTRIP FROM KYIV

CHERNIHIV (ЧЕРНІГІВ) ☎(80)46

Trains run daily to Chernihiv from Kyiv (3hr., 5 per day, 23-35hv.); also, an elektrichka (commuter rail) departs daily from the Kyiv train station (8am, 6.45hv). Alternatively, from MR: Lisova, exit to the right and take a bus or marshrutka (2.5hr., 10-20hv).

Near the Russian and Belarusian borders, Chernihiv has many of the churches and monuments of Kyivan Rus. At the end of Prospekt Mira, the 18th-century **St. Catherine's Church** is now a museum (open M-Tu and F 9am-5pm, Sa-Su 10am-6pm). Across the street and off to the left, the **Cathedral of the Saviour and Transfiguration** (Сиаский Собор) dates from 1036. To the left of the cathedral, the 12th-century **Cathedral of Boris and Bleb** houses artifacts from archeological digs of the grounds. Off to its left, the 16th-century **Collegium** building hosts exhibits. To its right is the **Chernihiv History Museum,** which contains a copy of the 1581 Osfroh Bible. (2hv. Open Tu-Su 9am-5pm.) To get to the **Yeletsky Convent** and its imposing 12th-century

Durmition Cathedral, cross back over Pr. Mira past the area in front of St. Catherine's and catch trolleybus #8 just after the corner on the road's right side; it stops at the foot of the hill leading to the convent. The next stop down the road brings you to the 17th-century **Monastery of the Holy Trinity.** For a fine view of the town, climb the rickety stairs of the monastery's late 18th-century bell tower (1hv, students 0.50hv). Backtracking down in the direction of the town, stroll through the park off to the right to the 12th-century **Church of St. Elijah** beside which open the enigmatic **Antoniyevy Caves.** Inside, 318m of labyrinthine paths lead you into the Church of St. Theodosis, past burial grounds and their red-lit bones. Legend has it these are the bones of monks killed during the Mongol sacking here in 1239. Walking on Pr. Mira away from St. Catherine's, you'll arrive at the little red-brick **Friday Church,** tucked away in the park behind the white-columned Drama Theater.

Options for accommodations and food in Chernihiv are very limited, but you can find everything you need at the central **Gradetsky Hotel ❷,** vul. Lenina 68. Rates are reasonable, and with a capacity of 500 people, there are always rooms available. (☎224 50 25. Singles 69hv; doubles 100hv.) Gradetsky's **restaurant ❸** is the main dining option in the city center. (Entrees 15-60hv. Open 11am-10pm.) There is another restaurant down the street at the **Slavyansky Hotel ❷,** vul. Lenina 33. (Entrees 10-40hv. Open 11am-11pm.)

KAM'YANETS-PODILSKYY ☎(80)3849

In Kam'yanets-Podilskyy (Кам'янець-Подільський; pop. 105,000), visitors can see historic buildings against a beautiful river and a modern town center. Though the town is somewhat difficult to reach, its famous landmarks, pleasant atmosphere, and friendly residents make it a choice stop on the way from Lviv to Odessa.

TRANSPORTATION AND PRACTICAL INFORMATION. Kam'yanets-Podilskyy is divided into two parts by the canyon of the **Smotrych River.** On one side is quiet **Old Town,** where the fortress and many churches are located. Across the bridge is the **New Town,** with most of the hotels, restaurants, and businesses. **Vul. Knyaziv Koriatovychiv** starts from the bridge and runs through the center of the New Town. The **bus station** is located in the very center of the New Town, next to the large central market. Buses go to: **Chernivtsi** (2hr., hourly 7am-8pm, 10hv); **Lviv** (12hr., 1 per day, 30hv); **Kyiv** (12hr., 2 per day, 40hv); and **Odessa** (14hr., 2 per day, 50hv). The **train station** (☎3 07 32) is a short ride from the city center; to get to the center from the station, take bus #15 or *marshrutka* #127. Trains leave for **Kyiv** (11hr., 7:45pm, 30hv) and **Odessa** (14hr., even-numbered days at 7:45pm, 23hv). For most other destinations, it's best to take a bus to **Khmelnitska** (2hr., hourly, 10hv) and catch a bus or train from there. To reach the Old Town from the central market square, go down **vul. Soborna** and take a left on vul. Lesy Ukrainy in front of Hotel Ukraina, then take a right onto vul. Knyaziv Koriatovychiv and cross the bridge over the Smotrych River.

Many agencies offer tours of the town and surrounding areas. **Daniloe & Co.,** vul. Zarvanska 3, has comprehensive tours led by a local historian. They also organize bungee jumping (200hv per jump). The office is in the first building on the left after crossing the bridge into the Old Town; enter through the door on the left side of the building, climb to the 2nd floor, and go through the unmarked door on the right. English spoken. (☎/fax 2 54 50; danko@kp.km.ua. Tours 50-120hv. Open daily 9am-6pm.) **Internet access** is available at **Internet-Center,** vul. K. Koriatovychiv 9a. It's a bit removed from the street, in the back of the green area. (☎9 11 71. 4hv per hr. Open daily 10am-2pm and 3-9pm.) For **currency exchange** and cash advances, use **Bank Aval.** (☎/fax 3 18 40. Open M-F 8:30am-5:30pm.) The **post office** (M-F 9am-6pm, Sa 9am-3pm) and a **telephone office** (open 24hr.) are in pl. Saborna near Hotel Ukrayina. **Postal Code:** 32 300.

⛌⛊ ACCOMMODATIONS AND FOOD. The town's hotels are not especially impressive or comfortable, but they're friendly and well-located. **Hotel Smotrich ❷**, vul. Soborna 4, is in a tall concrete building two blocks from the central market square. It has decent rooms, though the beds are hard. Most rooms have private baths. The cheap rooms without hot water are a great deal; ask the staff on the 7th floor to let you use the hot showers. (☎3 03 92; fax 3 03 22. Singles 50hv, without hot water 20hv; doubles 80hv/40hv. MC/V.) Two blocks farther down the street is **Hotel Ukrayina ❶**, vul. Lesi Ukrainky 32, on the corner of vul. Soborna. The hotel is old and some of its mattresses sag, but the rooms are clean and the prices are low. Only doubles have bath. (☎3 23 00; fax 3 98 56. Singles 30hv; doubles 44hv, with bath 100-180hv; triples 66hv.) For those seeking more comfort or privacy, short-term **apartment rental** is a worthwhile accommodation option. (☎3 39 93 or 8067 803 45 49. Apartment for up to 3 people, 60hv per night.)

There are several good restaurants and cafes in town. For a tasty meal and a memorable evening of dancing, visit ⛊**Oskar ❷**, vul. Danyla Halytskoho 13. The *myaso oskar* (meat with olives and cheese; 15hv) is a good option. (☎3 15 07. Entrees 3-16hv. Live music and dancing M-Tu and Th-Su 7-11pm. Open daily 10am-midnight. MC/V.) **Ukrayina ❶**, next to the hotel at the same address, has a majestic dining room and live music daily after 7pm. The *myaso ukrayina* (steak topped with egg, mushroom, onion, and cheese; 11hv) is marvelous. (☎3 95 27. Entrees 6-11hv. Music cover 1.50-3hv. Open daily noon-midnight.) If you need a lunch break in the Old Town, try **Cafe Nika ❶**, vul. Staro Bulvarna 4, where *zharkoe z myasom* (meat stew; 6.50hv) is excellent. (☎2 32 52. Entrees 3-7hv. Open daily 8am-6pm.)

◉ ⛲ SIGHTS AND FESTIVALS. The town is famous for its **fortress**, originally constructed out of wood in the 11th century and rebuilt in the 1400s. It has been occupied 3 times: first in 1393, then in 1672 by the Turkish army, and finally during WWII by the Nazis, who turned the Old Town into a Jewish ghetto. The fortress is located at the far end of the Old Town, across another bridge. Some of the old fortress walls can be climbed; use caution on the steep ladders and shoddy wooden boards. (☎2 15 00. 3.50hv, students 2hv. Open M 9am-6pm, Tu-Su 9am-7pm.) The **Cathedral of St. Peter and St. Paul** was first built out of wood in 1360 and was rebuilt using stone in 1430. It was used as a mosque during the Turkish occupation from 1672 to 1699; the Turks added the 36.5m minaret that stands outside. In 1756, after the Polish took over, a 4.5m golden statue of the Virgin Mary was placed atop the minaret so that the whole town could see it. Brochures, postcards, and maps of the cathedral and the Old Town are sold at the entrance. (Vul. Tatarska 20. Open daily 10am-6pm.) **Festivals** include the mid-May **Cossack Amusements,** an international cultural festival that features hot-air balloons, and the mid-September **Knight's Tournament,** a medieval-style celebration held at the fortress.

ODESSA (ОДЕСА) ☎(80)482

Since its 1794 founding by Catherine the Great, Odessa (pop. 1,100,000) has been blessed by prosperity but cursed with corruption. Due to many foreign influences, life in the port town has always been exciting. Attractive to intellectuals, thieves and mafiosi, Odessa has served as a background for writers from Alexander Pushkin to Isaac Babel, who wrote about Odessa's Jewish mafia in his *Odessa Tales*. The recent reopening of the famous and painstakingly restored opera house has boosted local pride and given tourists yet another reason to visit.

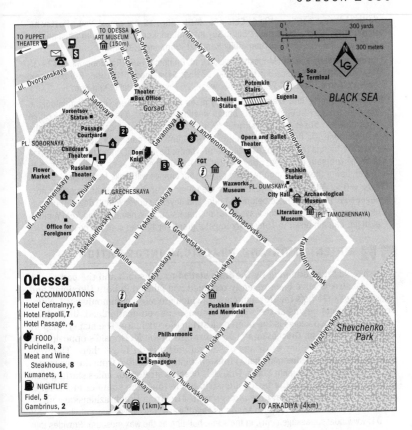

Odessa

🏠 ACCOMMODATIONS
Hotel Centralnyy, **6**
Hotel Frapolli, **7**
Hotel Passage, **4**

🍴 FOOD
Pulcinella, **3**
Meat and Wine
Steakhouse, **8**
Kumanets, **1**

🎵 NIGHTLIFE
Fidel, **5**
Gambrinus, **2**

▣ TRANSPORTATION

Flights: Ovidiopolskaya Doroga (Овидиопольская Дорога; ☎006 or 21 35 49), southwest of the center. *Marshrutka* #129 goes from the airport to the train station; #101 goes to the city center (Grecheskaya).

Trains: Zheleznodorozhnyy Vokzal (Железнодорожный Вокзал), pl. Privokzalnaya 2 (Привокзальная; tickets ☎005). International and advance tickets must be purchased at the **service center**; after going through the main entrance, enter the hall on the right, then take a left and go through the doors into the back room. To: **Kyiv** (10hr., 6 per day, 59hv); **Lviv** (12hr.; 1 per day, June 16-Aug. 30 even-numbered days 2 per day; 52hv); **Simferopol** (12hr.; 1 per day, June 18-Sept. 18 even days 2 per day; 43hv); **Chişinău, MOL** (5hr.; June 19-Aug. 19 2 per day, Aug. 20-June 18 odd days; 13hv); **Moscow, RUS** (25hr., 2-3 per day, 210hv); **Warsaw, POL** (24hr., even days, 340hv).

Buses: Avtovokzal (Автовокзал), Kolontayevskaya ul. 58 (Колонтаевская; ☎004). From the train station, cross the road behind the McDonald's and take tram #5 to the last stop. From there, walk straight down one block. To: **Kyiv** (8-10hr., 11 per day, 36hv); **Simferopol** (12hr., 2 per day, 40hv); **Sevastopol** (13½hr., 1 per day, 45hv);

Yalta (14hr., 3 per day, 48hv); **Chişinău, MOL** (5hr., 15 per day, 19hv).; **Rostov-na-Donu, RUS** (18hr., 2 per day, 95hv). Buy international tickets (except to Chişinău) on the 2nd fl. (☎732 66 67). Open daily 8am-12:30pm and 1:30-4pm.

Ferries: Morskoy Vokzal (Морской Вокзал), ul. Primorskaya 6 (Приморская; ☎729 38 03). To: **Yalta** (10-15hr., 3-5 per week, 171hv); **Sevastopol** (10-15hr., 3-5 per week, 139hv); **Varna, BUL** (20-25hr., 4-5 per week, 267hv). Open daily 9am-6pm.

Public Transportation: Trams and **trolleybuses** run almost everywhere 7am-midnight. Buy your tickets (0.50hv) from the badge-wearing *konduktor*. It is hard to tell the difference between **buses** and **marshrutki** (0.60hv/1-1.50hv), but locals can point to the one you need. On buses, pay as you exit. When entering *marshrutki*, look for a sticker that says "обплата при входе" (obplata pri vhode; payment at entry) or "обплата при выходе" (obplata pri vihode; payment at exit). If payment is at entry, it's common to first sit down, then pass money to the driver; your change will make its way back to you.

Taxis: ☎070, 345, 077. The yellow taxis are rather expensive, and their prices are non-negotiable. Check the price before you ride, and have the driver write it down. Don't pay more than 10hv from Grecheskaya pl. to the train station. When returning from Arcadia at night, bargain down to 15hv or try to get a group together to split the cost.

■✳ 🛈 ORIENTATION AND PRACTICAL INFORMATION

Odessa's center is bounded by the **train station** to the south and the **port** to the north. All streets have been recently renamed and labeled in both Ukrainian and Russian; *Let's Go* lists the Russian names, which are more commonly used. Numbering of streets begins at the sea and increases as you head inland. **Ul. Deribasovskaya** (Дерибасовская) is the main pedestrian thoroughfare. The main transport hub is right off of **pl. Grecheskaya** (Греческая); from the McDonald's opposite the train station, take trolley #1 or any of several *marshrutki* to get there. The treelined promenade of **Primorskyy bul.** (Приморский) is separated from the sea terminal by the famous **Potemkin Stairs.** Odessa's **beaches** stretch for miles starting east of the center. **Arkadiya**, the beachside strip home to all the summer nightlife, is southeast of the city center; take *marshrutka* #195 from Preobrazhenskaya ul.

Tourist Offices: FGT Travel (also known as Fagot; Фагот) Rishelyevskaya ul. 4 (☎37 52 01; www.odessapassage.com), in the same building as the wax museum. Provides info about accommodations and runs a variety of excursions, including city tours and catacomb tours (each 75hv per person, 2.5hr.), wine-tasting tours (95hv), and hunting trips. Open daily 8:30am-8pm. **Office for Foreigners** (Канцелярия для иностранцев; Kantselyariya dlya inostrantsev), ul. Bunina 37, 2nd fl. (☎28 28 46). Visa assistance. Open Tu-Th 10am-12:30pm and 2-4:30pm.

Currency Exchange: An *obmen valyut* (обмен валют) is on every corner. Rates vary, so check several. **Bank Aval** (Аваль), Sadovaya ul. 9 (Садовая; ☎777 31 70) cashes **traveler's checks** for 2% commission, gives **cash advances** for 2% commission, and provides **Western Union** services. Open M-F 9am-1pm and 2-3pm.

Luggage Storage: Kamera Zberiganniya (Камера Збериганния), outside the **train station,** 50m along the far right track on the right-hand side. 3hv per bag, 4hv per large bag. Open 24hr. Downstairs in the **bus station.** 1hv. Open 24hr. Downstairs in **sea terminal.** 1.5hv per bag per day, 3hv per night. Open daily 8am-8pm.

English-Language bookstore: Dom Knigi (Дом Книги), Deribasovskaya ul. 27 (☎22 34 73). Good city maps (7hv) and a few books in English. Open daily 10am-7pm.

Pharmacy: Apteka #32, Deribasovskaya 16 (☎22 49 06). Open M-F 8am-8pm, Sa-Su 10am-6pm. 24hr. pharmacies in the train station.

Telephones: At the post office, to the left. Pay in advance. Open 8am-1pm and 2-5pm.

Internet Access: Tech-21, Sadovaya ul. 5 (☎728 64 79), opposite the post office. 3hv per hr. Open 24hr. **VIP Bar,** Preobrazhenskaya ul. 34 (☎715 50 09; vipbar_odessa81@mail.ru), in the back of Hotel Passage's lobby, has 2 computers with fast connection. (7hv per hr.). Has a phone center with cheap international calls.

Post Office: Sadovaya ul.10 (☎26 74 93). **Poste Restante** (До Востребования; Do Vostrebovaniya) at counters #15 and 16. Open daily 8am-8pm. **Fax** service at #22 (☎26 64 50). Open daily 8am-1pm and 1:45-5pm. **Photocopy** at window #21. Open M-Sa 8am-8pm, Su 8am-6pm. **Postal Code:** 65 001.

ACCOMMODATIONS

Comfort isn't cheap in Odessa, especially in the summer when only the best hotels have hot water. The city's rundown budget hotels are located in the center, and **Private rooms** are cheap but not necessarily safe; you'll be lucky to get anything near the center. Train station hawkers hold signs reading "Сдаю комнату" (Sdayu komnatu; I'm renting a room). Ask "Skolko?" (Сколько?; how much?). The asking price is usually 25-50hv; bargain down, and don't pay until you see the room.

Hotel Passage (Пассаж), ul. Preobrazhenskaya 34 (☎22 48 49; fax 22 41 50), near the corner of ul. Deribasovskaya. The best budget option, though the building has seen grander days, and there's no hot water in summer. The rooms differ, so look before checking in. Shared bathrooms may have no toilet seats. Reservations, when accepted, add 50% to the price of the 1st night; it's best to just show up at noon. Luggage storage 1hv. Singles 41hv, with bath 75hv; doubles 60hv/96hv; triples 83hv/122hv. ❶

Hotel Centralnyy (Центральний), ul. Preobrazhenskaya 40 (☎26 84 06; fax 26 86 89), 1 block down from Hotel Passage. A bit more expensive than other options, but Centralnyy's rooms are better and the rates include breakfast. No hot water in summer. Singles 92hv, with bath 100hv; doubles 92hv/150-300hv. ❷

Hotel Frapolli, ul. Deribasovskaya 13 (☎35 68 01; frapolli@te.net.ua), next to Mick O'Neill's Pub. Perfect location. Summer in Odessa is the time and place to consider splurging on a room, and, despite being "economy class," these rooms have private baths with hot water year-round, Internet access, TV, mini-bar, and A/C. Breakfast included. Reservations recommended. Singles $60; doubles $90. MC/V. ❹

FOOD

The central streets of Odessa are lined with cafes and restaurants, though most of them are expensive. For the budget traveler, Odessa is *shawarma* (шаурма) town: **Top Sandwich** has all but taken over ul. Deribasovskaya, while Egyptian immigrants run their own competing stands. **Privoz** (Привоз), ul. Privoznaya (Привозная), to the right of the train station, sells food. (Open daily 6am-6pm.)

■ **Pulcinella,** ul. Lanzheronovskaya 17 (☎777 30 10), between ul. Gavannaya and ul. Yekaterinskaya. This beautiful, authentic Italian pizzeria serves excellent brick-oven Italian and Ukranian dishes in a charming dining room. English menu. Live music Th-Su 7:30-11pm, piano or Latin guitar. Open daily 11am-last customer. MC/V. ❷

Kumanets, (Куманець) ul. Gavanna 7 (Гаванна; ☎37 69 46). A good place to try traditional Ukrainian dishes. The decor has a country theme, and servers wear folk outfits. 11 kinds of *vareniki* (dumplings; 10-19hv). Red or green *borshch* (15hv). Entrees include fish and meat dishes (15-54hv). English menu. Open 11am-midnight. ❷

Meat and Wine Steakhouse, ul. Deribasovskaya 20 (☎34 87 82). This classy steakhouse serves up exquisite dishes in an almost-pretentious atmosphere. International wine list. New Zealand lamb 112hv. Steaks (34-70hv). Open daily 9am-midnight. ❹

◉ SIGHTS

CATACOMBS. When Catherine the Great decided to build Odessa, the limestone used for its construction was mined from below, leaving the longest catacombs in the world. During WWII, Odessa's resistance fighters *(partizany)*, hid in these dark, intertwining tunnels, surfacing only for raids against the Nazis. The accessible portion of the catacombs lies under the village of Neribaiskoye, where the city has set up an outstanding subterranean **museum.** You can enter the catacombs through one entrance only and you must have a guide. At the recreated resistance camp, rocks with graffiti have been transported from the original site. One rock declares "Blood for blood; death for death." *(30min. by car from Odessa. Many tour agencies provide rides and tours. FGT offers 2hr. English tours for 75hv per person, including transportation. Russian tours leave in front of the train station, 15hv. Dress warmly.)*

411TH BATTALION MONUMENT. Far from the busy commercial center lies the Memorial Complex of the 411th Battalion, one of Odessa's more entertaining monuments. The typical armaments of the Soviet forces are here, spread throughout a large park. You'll think the guns and torpedoes are impressive until you see the tanks, bomber, and submarine. There is a small museum by the battleship. The cliffs along the rocky coast are a short walk from behind the bus stop to the left. *(From the train station, take marshrutka #127 30-40min. to the last stop. Walk straight and take a right at the concrete "411." Museum open Sa-Th 10am-6pm. 2hv.)*

PUSHKINSKAYA STREET. Formerly ul. Italianskyy, this street was named after the Russian poet. During his exile, Pushkin lived at the house at #13, which at the time was a hotel. The building is now a museum dedicated to the poet and his time in Odessa. At #15, on the corner of ul. Bunina (Бунина), is the **Philharmonic building** (Филармония; Filarmoniya), built between 1894 and 1899. A block farther down is the **Brodskiy Synagogue,** which was once the center of Odessa's Jewish community.

SHEVCHENKO PARK. This large park separates the city center from the sea. At the entrance is a **monument** to the poet Taras Shevchenko (see **The Arts,** p. 869). Within are the ruins of the **Khadzhibey Fortress** and monuments to the dead of the Great Patriotic War and the Afghanistan War. An eternal flame burns in memory of an unknown soldier.

DERIBASOVSKAYA STREET. Odessa's most popular street, lined with cafes and full of vendors and performers. Don't be surprised by all the snakes, monkeys, and exotic lizards—some residents make a living by photographing tourists with their odd pets. On the east end of the street is the **Gorsad** (Горсад), where artists sell jewelry, landscape paintings, and *matryoshka* dolls.

PRIMORSKYY BOULEVARD. Primorskiy bul. is a shaded promenade with some of the finest buildings in Odessa. The **statue of Alexander Pushkin** turns its back to the City Hall, which refused to help fund its construction. On either side of the hall are Odessa's two symbols: **Fortuna,** goddess of fate; and **Mercury,** god of trade. From Primorskyy bul., descend the **Potemkin Stairs** (Потшмкинская Лестница; Potomkinskaya Lestnitsa) to reach ul. Primorskaya and the Sea Terminal. Past the bridge to the left is the long, white **Mother-in-Law Bridge,** supposedly built so that an elderly lady could more easily visit her son-in-law, a high-ranking Communist official.

🏛 MUSEUMS

▨WAX MUSEUM. This small, private museum (Музей Восковых Скульптур; Muzey Voskovykh Skulptur) displays wax figures of the city's most famous inhabitants, from Spanish city governor De Ribas to Russian poet Pushkin. The figures were created by experts in St. Petersburg. *(Rishelyevskaya ul. 4, in same building as the FGT travel agency. ☎22 34 36. English placards. Open daily 8:30am–10pm. 11hv, students 5hv. Even for students, the adult ticket is a good deal—it includes a photo and 7hv credit at the bar.)*

ART MUSEUM (ХУДОЖНИЙ МУЗЕЙ; KHUDOZHNIY MUZEY). A great collection of 19th-century art, including works by Kandinsky, Ayvazovski, and Levitskyy, is displayed in the former palace of Polish magnate Felix Potoski's daughter Olga. One of the rooms, containing golden religious icons, requires an additional ticket. The most exciting part of the museum is the grotto underneath. It is rumored that Olga used the underground passageways leading from the palace to conduct secret trysts with Count Vorontsov. Entrance is permitted only with a guide. The museum is a bit chilly, so dress warmly. *(Sofiyevskaya ul. 5a (Софиевская). ☎23 82 72, tours 23 84 62. Open W-M 10:30am–6pm; ticket office closes 5pm. Closed last F of each month. Museum 2hv, students, children and seniors 0.50hv; icon room 2hv/0.50hv; grotto 2hv/0.50hv.)*

ARCHAEOLOGICAL MUSEUM. The museum (Археологический Музей; Arkheologicheskiy muzey) displays ancient Greek and Roman artifacts found in the Black Sea region, including gold coins stored in the basement vault. Its Egyptian collection is the only one in Ukraine. *(Lanzheronovskaya 4. ☎22 01 71. Open Tu-Su 10am–5pm. 5hv; students, children, and seniors 2hv. Call ahead to arrange an English tour, 10hv per person.)*

PUSHKIN MUSEUM AND MEMORIAL. This 1821 building was Pushkin's residence during his exile from St. Petersburg from 1823 to 1824 (see **The Arts**, p. 869). The fascinating museum (Литературно-мемориальный Музей Пушкина; Literaturno-memorialnyy Muzey Pushkina) displays his manuscripts and possessions, as well as portraits of his family. The guided tour is informative but is rarely offered in English; Russian and French tours are available. *(Pushkinskaya ul. 13. Enter through the courtyard. ☎25 10 34. Open Tu-Su 10am–5pm; last admission 4:30pm. 3.50hv, students 1.50hv. Tours in Russian 15hv, French 52hv. Call ahead for English tours, ☎22 74 53.)*

LITERATURE MUSEUM (ЛИТЕРАТУРНЫЙ МУЗЕЙ; LITERATURNYY MUZEY). In the beautiful, 19th-century summer residence of Prince Gagarin, this museum provides a fascinating look at the city's intellectual and cultural heritage, with emphasis on Pushkin and Gogol. The collection includes the famous letter from Vorontsov to the tsar, requesting that Pushkin be sent out of Odessa "for his own development," because he "is getting the notion into his head that he's a great writer." The museum exhibits are in Russian. *(Lanzheronovskaya 2. ☎22 00 02. Open Tu-Su 10am–5pm. 3.50hv, students 1.50hv. Sculpture courtyard 2hv.)*

🏖 BEACHES

Arkadiya (Аркадия), the city's most popular beach, is the last stop on trolley or tram #5; *marshrutka* #195 stops here as well. The shoreline from Shevchenko Park up to Arkadiya makes a good path for an early-morning jog. **Zolotoy Bereg** (Золотой Берег; Golden Shore) is farther away but boasts the most impressive shoreline. Take tram #18 or *marshrutka* #215 or 223 (runs May-Aug.) to the end. Tram #18 also goes to **Riviera** (Ривиера) and **Kurortnyy** (Курортный). Tram #17 heads out to **Chaika** (Чайка). Tram #4 stops at **Lanzheron** (Ланжерон), the beach closest to central Odessa, and at **Otrada** (Отрада). Some beaches are free, but others charge up to 15hv admission and offer beach chairs, umbrellas, and waiter service.

ENTERTAINMENT

Buy tickets for all shows in town at the **theater box office,** ul. Preobrazhenskaya 28. Same-day tickets are available until 2pm. (☎22 02 45. Open daily 10am-5pm.) Odessa's most colorful festival, the **Holiday of Humor** (Юморіна), occurs on April 1.

Theater of Opera and Ballet (Театр Опери и Балета; Teatr Opery i Baleta; ☎29 13 29), pr. Chaikovskovo 1 (Чайковского), at the end of ul. Rishelyevskaya. Recently renovated theater hosts performances Tu-Su 6 or 7pm. Tickets 10-50hv; check with the box office for the schedule. Theater tours in Russian (2hv) often occur 30min. before curtain.

Odessa Russian Drama Theater, ul. Grecheskaya 48 (☎24 07 06), has several performances each week. Schedule is posted outside the entrance. Shows start at 7pm. Tickets 5-20hv; the 10hv tickets are the best value.

Philharmonic (Филармония; filarmoniya), ul. Bunina 15 (☎21 78 95), on the corner of ul. Pushkinskaya, has great concerts conducted by American Hobart Earle. Box office open daily 10am-6pm. Tickets 3-20hv.

NIGHTLIFE

From May to September, almost all the nightlife is at the beach clubs of **Arkadiya.** To get there, take tram #5 or *marshrutka* #195. A taxi back to the city center costs about 20hv per person if you form a group. The glitziest Arkadiya club is **Ibiza,** with its curvy whitewashed walls and enormous dance floor. (☎777 02 05. Th-Sa live music, 40hv. Cover Su-W after 10pm 20hv. Open noon-6am.) Also bumping is **Luxor,** located near the beginning of the strip, where revelers party hard year-round. (☎715 33 33. Shows Th-Su. Open 9pm-late. Cover after 10:30pm M-Th and Su 15hv, F-Sa 20hv.) Toward the end of the strip is **Pago,** a student-oriented club that plays lots of Russian pop. Only women may enter on Wednesday from 9pm to midnight. (☎715 38 30. Cover M-Th and Su 15hv; F-Sa 25hv, students 10hv. Open 9pm-6am.) For house/trance and big-name DJs from Moscow and London, check out **Stereo.** (☎37 42 37. Cover M-Th and Su 20hv, F-Sa 30hv. Open 10pm-6am.)

If you want to stay in town, start your night at **Gambrinus** (Гамбринус), ul. Deribasovskaya 31, at the corner of ul. Zhukova (Жукова). It was the center of Odessa's cultural scene before the Revolution. (☎26 36 57. Beer 5-18hv. Live folk music M and Th-Su 6-11pm. Tu-W live modern music. Open daily 10am-midnight.) **Fidel** (Фидел), ul. Deribasovskaya 23, at the corner of Aleksandrovsky pr., is also known as "Havana Club." It has a tacky interior, but it has live Latin guitar on the sidewalk most nights. Avoid the unauthentic Cuban food. (☎22 71 16. Beer 12-20hv. F-Sa band 11:30pm-2:30am, DJ 2:30-4am. Cover 20hv. Open 24hr. MC/V.)

CRIMEA (КРЫМ)

An important trading thoroughfare on the Black Sea Coast, the Crimean peninsula has a 2500-year history of Greek, Turkish, Mongol, and Russian rule. Though bequeathed to Ukraine in 1991, it remains Russian at heart—Crimeans are Russian-speaking, call Ukrainian currency "rubles," and feel closer to Moscow than Kyiv. In summer, hordes of vacationers mean scarce hotel rooms and high prices. It is best to visit in September, when the crowds have left but the sea is still warm.

UKRAINE

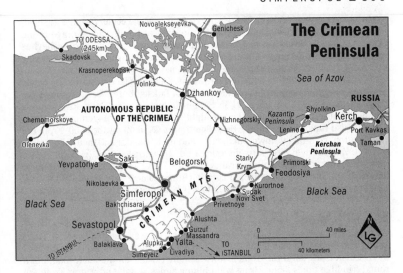

The Crimean Peninsula

SIMFEROPOL (СІМФЕРОПОЛЬ)   ☎(80)652

Simferopol is the capital of the Autonomous Republic of Crimea and the transport hub of the peninsula. Most pass through en route to more pleasant destinations. The **train station** (вокзал; vokzal) at Vokzalnaya pl. (Вокзальная; ☎005), sends trains to: **Kyiv** (19hr., 3 per day, 80hv); **Lviv** (27 hr., 1 per day, 75hv); **Odessa** (13½hr., 1 per day, 40hv); **St. Petersburg, RUS** (20hr., 1 per day, 270hv). The **information desk** charges 1hv per question. Tickets for the **elektrichka** (commuter rail) are sold behind the main station at the window marked "пригородный кассы" (prigorod-nyy kassy). These head to **Sevastopol** (2-2½hr., 7 per day, 3.23hv) via **Bakhchisarai** (1hr., 2.44hv). **Buses** and **marshrutki** vans to various Crimean destinations leave from the square next to the McDonald's. Buses (☎25 25 60) run to: **Feodosiya** (2hr., 11 per day, 15hv); **Sevastopol** (2hr., 2-3 per hr., 15hv); **Yalta** (2hr., 4-5 per hr., 12hv). The 2-3 hr. **trolleybus** #52 ride to Yalta costs 2.30hv. Buses to more distant destinations leave from the central station, across town at ul. Kiyevskaya 4. Take trolleybus #6 from the train station to get there. Destinations include: **Kyiv** (14½hr., 1 per day, 100hv); **Odessa** (12hr., 4 per day, 40-60hv); **Rostov-na-Donu, RUS** (13½hr., 2 per day, 90hv). *Marshrutki* are usually faster than buses but charge a bit more.

Currency exchange offices are everywhere, but look beyond the train and bus stations for the best rates. **ATMs** are at the post office and train station, and along ul. Pushkina. **Store luggage** at the train station in the building next to track #1, through the door marked with "камера хранения" (kamera khraneniya; guarded 2-3hv, lockers 2.50hv). There are **24hr. pharmacies** (аптека; apteka) at the train station inside the luggage storage room (☎24 92 86 or 29 95 41), and in the same building

PHONE CALLS. Crimea is an autonomous republic within Ukraine, and its phone system mirrors the political situation. Dialing from one Crimean town to another requires special Crimean area codes; the area codes listed in *Let's Go* for each Crimean town work only when calling from outside the peninsula. The intra-Crimean area codes (all preceded by 8) are: Simferopol 22, Bakhchisarai 254, Feodosiya 262, Kerch 261, Yalta 24, Sevastopol 0692.

as Hotel Ukraina (☎54 56 82). There's also a **24hr. medical center** (медпункт; medpunkt; ☎24 21 03) at the train station, to the right of the luggage storage room. *Babushki* peddle **private rooms ❶** at the train station and the next-door trolleybus station; most are offering rooms in Yalta or other coastal towns. If you need to stay overnight, try **Hotel Moskva ❷**, ul. Kievskaya 3, in the city center. (☎23 97 95. Singles 57hv, with bath 284hv; doubles 97hv/340hv.) A nicer place to stay is the newly renovated **Hotel Ukraina ❸** (Україна), ul. Roza Luksemburg 7-9. All rooms have private baths. (☎51 01 65; fax 27 84 95. Singles 162hv; doubles 204hv. Reservations add 50% of the room price to the 1st night's stay.) The management of Hotel Ukraina also runs a budget hotel, **Hotel Sportivnaya ❷**, ul. Zhelyabova 50. From the train station, go straight down bul. Lenina and ul. Karla Marksa, then take a right onto ul. Zhelyabova; alternatively, take a bus or *marshrutka*. (☎27 23 11. To reserve by fax, contact Hotel Ukraina. Singles 70hv, with bath 140hv; doubles 86hv/170hv.) The cafe **Vinogradnaya Loza ❶** (Виноградная Лоза), ul. Pushkina 4, has large seafood salads. (☎27 85 63. Salads 9-11hv. Open daily 8am-11pm.)

BAKHCHISARAI (БАХЧИСАРАЙ)   ☎(80)6554

Bakhchisarai, meaning "palace garden" in Turkish, was once the seat of Tatar power and home of the Crimean Khanate; later, it became a favorite destination of the Russian tsars. All three of its historic landmarks are on the main road, but a round-trip hike takes 3-5hr. Bring good hiking shoes, a hat, and water. From the train station, take a *marshrutka* (0.60hv) or a taxi (7hv) to the ◪**Khan's Palace** (Ханський Дворец; Khanskiy Dvorets). The palace was built in 1952 by Adil-Sahib-Guirey (the fourth Khan), who was inspired by the lush gardens and grapevines of Bakhchisarai. Its buildings and garden, with roses and tulips, maintain the traditional design and planting of the Khans. The palace was home to 45 Khans before the Russian empire took over in 1783. The palace is famous for its Fountain Courtyard, which contains the 1733 **Golden Fountain.** Its 1764 **Fountain of Tears,** supposedly built by a disconsolate Khan who loved a dying Polish slave, was immortalized in Pushkin's great poem "Bakhchisarai Fountain." The intricately decorated **Aleviz Portal** predates the rest of the palace: it was commissioned by second Khan Mengli-Guirei as part of the Khan palace in Ashlama-Dere. Official matters were discussed in the 16th-century **Divan Chamber.** The **Harem** retains much of its original furnishings, and the **Drawing Room** has stained-glass windows and Arabic verse on the ceiling. Fifty-six members of the Guirey Khan dynasty are buried in the unusual **cemetery.** The palace also has an **ethnographic museum,** which describes Tatar culture and displays hand-written books dating from the 13th century. (☎47 640. Open May-Sept. daily 9am-5:45pm; Oct.-Apr. M and Th-Su 9am-4pm. 14hv, students and children 7hv. English tours June-Aug., 35hv per group.)

From the Khan's Palace, walk 20min. up to the end of the road. At the parking area, take the pathway up the hill on the right, which leads out to the **Holy Assumption Cave Monastery.** Alternatively, take a *marshrutka* or taxi from the palace. Carved out of a cliff in the 15th century, the monastery commands one of the best views in the central steppes. From the 8th to the 18th century, the monastery was a refuge for an Orthodox religious minority, which faced persecution from Byzantium and later from the Tatars. Empty for most of the last 200 years, it recently reopened as a working monastery, hence the rather modern-looking buildings.

Continue on the pathway that leads past the monastery for about 25min. At the very top of the hill, overlooking the town, is **Chufut-Kale** (Чуфут-Кале; Jews' Fortress). Once a densely populated settlement, it received its current name when the capital of the Crimean Khanate was moved from Bakhchisarai in the 16th century, leaving only Turkish Karaite Jews and Armenians to occupy the old fort. As you enter the complex, climb up through the caves to reach the main road of the settlement. Inside the fortress are two *kenassi* (кенасси; prayer houses); the one to the left was built in the 14th century from the cliff stones, while the red-pillared *kenassa* on the right dates to the 18th century. (Open Mar.-Nov. Tu-Su 9am-8pm; Dec.-Feb. Tu-Su 9am-5pm. 8hv, students 4hv.) Up the road lie the ruins of a 1346 **mosque** and, farther along, the 1437 domed **mausoleum** built for Dzhanike Khan. Nearby is a small **wishing-tree,** where you can add your piece of cloth to the others hanging in the wind. Beyond the Byzantine wall stands a 15th-century **cave complex** with hollows for wine production and storage. Nearby, you can explore a recently discovered 16 story-deep **well.** A smaller cave city, **Tepe-Kermen,** is 2km from the fortress.

Bakhchisarai's **train station,** ul. Rakytskovo (☎426 37), sends trains to **Simferopol** (45min.-1¼hr., 7 per day, 2.50-3hv). **Buses** and **marshrutki** stop in the square in front. They are faster than the train, but operate out of the inconveniently located **Simferopol bus station** (30-40min., 1-2 per hr., 3.50hv). Within town, *marshrutki* run from the train station to the Old City (Старый Город; Staryy Gorod). The **tourist agency** at Hotel Prival, ul. Shmidta 43, offers guided tours. (☎478 46; prival@tavria.net. Singles with bath 90hv; doubles with bath 120hv.)

MANGUP-KALE (МАНГУП-КАЛЕ)

Stunning rock formations, including four connected plateaus—which jut like four fingers into the sky—greet hiking and camping enthusiasts. Hidden within is the region's largest **cave city.** Hikers will pass the ruins of defensive **walls, a fortress,** and a **Jewish cemetery** on the way up the first finger. Hewn into the side of the mountain atop the plateau, a prison, various dwellings, and a **church** beg to be explored. You can hit all the major sites on a focused 3hr. hike.

Mangup-Kale makes an excellent daytrip. **Buses** run from **Simferopol** (1¼hr., 2 per day, 5hv) and **Yalta** (2-3hr., 2 per day, 10hv). Buses and *marshrutki* leave from **Bakhchisarai** in the morning. A **taxi** out to the base should cost around US$10. A nearby camp sells **maps** (3-10hv) and gives tours. (Open May 1-Oct. 1. Solar-heated shower. Meals under 15hv; camping 4hv; sleeping bag in 6-person tent 18hv.) Another cave city, **Eski-Kermen** (Эски-Лузмун), lies 5km from the camp.

FEODOSIYA (ФЕОДОСИЯ)   ☎(8)06562

Founded as a slave-trading town over 2500 ago, Feodosiya, which rests atop a 16km stretch of sand, is one of the most popular Crimean vacation spots.

TRANSPORTATION AND PRACTICAL INFORMATION. The **train station,** pr. Lenina 5, sells advance tickets to the left of the main door. (☎005, advance tickets 3 02 91. Ticket office open daily 7am-noon and 12:30-6pm.) **Trains** run to: **Kerch** (2½hr., even-numbered days, 3hv); **Kyiv** (18hr., 1 per day, 55hv); **Moscow, RUS** (24hr., 3 per day, 210hv). The **bus station,** ul. Engelsa 28 (Энгельса; ☎54 56 76; open 5:30am-9:30pm), connects Feodosiya with: **Kerch** (2hr., 1-2 per hr., 20hv); **Odessa** (13hr., 1 per day, 70hv); **Sevastopol** (5hr., 5 per day, 20hv); **Simferopol** (2hr., 1-5 per hr., 15hv); **Yalta** (4hr., 4 per day, 17hv). Tickets for large bags cost 1-4hv.

Feodosiya is currently changing some of its street names. Both the old and new names will be posted on street signs for the next several years. **City buses** #2 and 4 run along ul. Fedko and ul. Karla Marksa (Карла Маркса) and connect the bus station with the city center (0.60hv). Get off after the bus makes a left on **pr. Lenina,** the main thoroughfare along the waterfront. Ul. Galereynaya and ul. Nazukina (Назукина) run inland from pr. Lenina, and ul. K. Libknekhta (К. Либкнехта) connects the two. As you head away from the station, pr. Lenina becomes **ul. Gorkovo;** follow it uphill and turn left into a residential area to see the 1348 **Genoese fortress** and its three 13th-century **churches.** Bus #1 runs from the market to the fortress.

UKRAINE

Oshchadbank (Ощадбанк), at the corner of ul. K. Libknekhta and ul. Kirova (Кирова), gives MC/V **cash advances** for 2% commission, cashes AmEx/MC/V **traveler's checks** for 2% commission, offers **Western Union** services, and gives one of the best exchange rates. (☎3 04 51. Open M-F 8am-1pm and 2-6pm, Sa 8am-5pm, Su 8am-2pm. Closed last day of each month.) **ATMs** are along ul. Galereynaya and ul. Libknekhta. **Maps** are sold at the kiosks along ul. Galereynaya. **Luggage storage** is available at the train or bus stations for 2hv. A **pharmacy** (аптека; apteka) is at ul. K. Libknekhta 16. (Open daily 8am-2pm and 2:30-7pm.) For **Internet,** try **PingWin,** ul. Galereynaya 14, across from the post office. (☎4 37 05; www.feodosia.net. 7am-2pm 1.50hv per hr.; 2pm-midnight 2hv per hr.; midnight-7am 0.50hv per hour. Additional 0.50hv per megabyte of traffic. Open 24hr.) The main **telephone office** is **Ukrtelecom,** ul. Lyuksemburg 1. There is a branch at ul. Galereynaya 9. (☎3 04 33. Open daily May-Sept. 24hr.; Oct.-Apr. 7am-9pm.) Next door is the **post office.** (☎3 24 97. Open M-F 8am-7pm, Sa 8am-6pm, Su 8am-3pm.) **Postal Code:** 981 00.

▶◁ ACCOMMODATIONS AND FOOD. *Babushki* at the train and bus stations offer **private rooms** which cost from 20-60hv. **Gostinitsa Astoriya ❷** (Гостиница Астория), pr. Lenina 9, is just across the railroad tracks from the beach. The four types of rooms range from "3rd class" to "lux." (☎/fax 3 23 43; hotel@astoria.crimea.ua. Hot water M-Sa 5-8pm. Shower 3hv. Call ahead in summer. Singles 43-59hv, with bath 90-117hv; doubles 64-96hv/138-234hv.) **Gostinitsa Lidiya ❹** (Гостиница Лидия), ul. K. Libknekhta 13, offers more comfort and constant hot water. It boasts a gym, swimming pool, sauna, business center, banking facilities, restaurant, and bar. (☎3 09 01 or 2 11 11; www.lidiya-hotel.com. Breakfast included. Singles 167-217hv; doubles 237-932hv. MC/V.) The **Greenwich ❷** (Гринвич) entertainment complex, ul. Galereynaya 7, has a terrace restaurant in summer. (☎3 09 52. Pizza 12-21hv; entrees 8-45hv. Open May-Sept. 9am-last customer. MC/V.) Indoors, its year-round **bistro ❶** offers cafeteria-style food. (Entrees 2.50-10hv. Open daily May-Sept. 9am-10pm; Oct.-Apr. 10am-8pm. MC/V.) For fresh fruits and vegetables, head to the central **market.** (Open June-Sept. M 6am-3pm, Tu-Su 6am-9pm; Oct.-May M 7am-2pm, Tu-Su 7am-5pm.) At night, the cafes, bars, and discos that line pr. Lenina have live music and dancing well into the morning.

◙ SIGHTS. In addition to its beaches, the town is famous for the legacy of landscape artist **Ayvazovsky** and his 1854 ▓**picture gallery** (картинная галерея; kartinnaya galereya). The gallery, ul. Galereynaya 4, contains paintings by Ayvazovsky and other local artists. (☎3 02 79. 15hv, students and children 7.50hv. Open M and Th-Su 9am-8pm, Tu 9am-1pm; ticket office closes 45min. earlier; closed last Tu of each month.) Feodosiya also has the oldest museum in Ukraine, the **Museum of Local Lore,** pr. Lenina 11. The collection focuses on the nature and medieval history of the region. (☎3 43 55. 5hv, students and children 2hv. English brochure available. Open daily June-Aug. 10am-5pm; Sept.-May M and W-Su 10am-5pm.) To get to the **beach** from the **bus station,** go past the small church, turn right on ul. Fedko (Федко), and cross the bridge over the tracks. Beaches with toilets and showers cost 1-2hv; free beaches (without amenities) are farther to your left.

▶ DAYTRIP FROM FEODOSIYA: SUDAK. Sudak (Судак) is famous for its ▓**Genoese Fortress,** the best-preserved medieval landmark on the peninsula. The fortress was taken over by the Turks in 1475 in spite of a valiant defense by the Genoese. Its walls enclose a large green area, which is now the site of frequent medieval-themed festivals and gladiator contests. The round tower rewards climbers with a view of the shoreline. Just 7km down the coast, the glorified town of **Novi Svet** (New World) has some of Crimea's most beautiful scenery. It is also home to Ukraine's most famous **champagne distillery,** founded by L. Golotsin in

1878. The distillery offers tours (15lv) with tastings. *(Buses make the 1hr. trip from Feodosiya 3 times per day and cost 9hv. Marshrutki run from the Sudak bus station to Novi Svet every 10-15min. They cost 2hv for the 15-20min. trip. Fortress open daily June-Oct. 9am-9pm; Nov.-May 9am-6pm. 5hv. Camera 5hv, video 10hv. Champagne distillery open daily 9am-3pm.)*

YALTA (ЯЛТА)   ☎(8)0654

Known by every high school student as the location of the 1945 conference in which in which the "Big Three" decided the fate of post-war Europe, Yalta today draws Ukrainian and international tourists with its clean air and natural beauty. The city has also beckoned such famous writers and artists as author Anton Chekhov, poet Lesya Ukrayinka, and composer Sergei Rachmaninov.

⌨ TRANSPORTATION

Trains: Yalta is **not accessible by train,** but the city has an Advance Booking office, ul. Ignatenko 14 (☎32 43 47), where you can get tickets to depart from Simferopol or Sevastopol. Purchase tickets in advance (3 week min. in summer). From pl. Lenina, walk up ul. Ignatenko and look for the "Железнодорожные Кассы" sign. Open daily 8am-7pm.

Buses: On ul. Moskovskaya (☎34 20 92). To: **Bakhchisarai** (3hr., 2 per day, 20hv); **Feodosiya** (5hr., 2 per day, 17hv); **Kerch** (7hr., 1 per day, 27hv); **Kyiv** (17½hr., 1 per day, 110hv); **Odessa** (14½hr., 1 per day, 110hv); **Sevastopol** (2hr., 2-3 per hr., 14hv); **Simferopol** (2hr., 1-6 per hr., 14hv). **Intourist, LTD.** (see **Orientation and Practical Information,** p. 899) arranges bus trips to Kyiv during the summer.

Ferries: To: **Alupka** (1¼hr., July-Aug. 16 per day, 12hv) via **Livadiya** (15min., 5hv) and **Lastochkino Gnezdo** (45min., 10hv). Buy tickets at the waterfront past the Gastronom store with the "Orbit" window shades (☎32 42 74). Ferry tickets to **Istanbul, TUR** (33hr.; Tu-W 1 per day; US$90, round-trip US$190-250) are available at the Omega window in the front right-hand corner of the Sea Terminal, ul. Rusvelta 5 (Рузевелта; ☎34 30 64, after-hours 34 64 02). Open daily 9am-1pm.

Public Transportation: Buses run throughout the city (0.50hv). #1 covers most of the central area; it travels from the bus station to pl. Sovetskaya. From the stop "Kinoteatr Spartak," bus #8 goes to Polyana Skazok and Chekhov's house; bus #24 goes from Chekhov's house to Polyana Skazok. Private **marshrutki** depart from the square at the corner of ul. Moskovskaya and ul. Karla Marksa. They run the same routes as buses, are faster, and make fewer stops, but cost 3-5hv more.

◼⍰ ORIENTATION AND PRACTICAL INFORMATION

Stretched along the Black Sea, Yalta centers around the pedestrian **nab. Lenina** (Ленина), which runs along the waterfront *(naberezhnaya)* from **pl. Lenina.** From the **bus** and **trolley stations,** take trolley #1 toward the center. It runs down ul. Moskovskaya (Московская) past the circus and market to **pl. Sovetskaya** (Советская), where ul. Moskovskaya converges with **ul. Kievskaya** (Киевская). You can get off there and walk two blocks to **pl. Lenina.** There, nab. Lenina begins to the right, while a left turn leads to the **Old Quarter.** At the other end of nab. Lenina, both pedestrian **ul. Pushkinskaya** (Пушкинская) and parallel **ul. Gogolya** (Гоголя) run inland to **Kinoteatr Spartak.** Trolley #1 and many *marshrutki* stop there.

Tourist Offices: Eugenia Travel, ul. Rusvelta 12 (☎27 18 29; www.eugenia-tours.com.ua). English-speaking office helps arrange apartment rental and provides tours and info. Open M-F 9am-6pm. **Intourist, LTD.,** ul. Rusvelta 5 (☎/fax 32 76 04; intour@yalta.crimea.ua), across from Eugenia Travel, next to the sea terminal, helps book hotel rooms and arrange tours. Its luxury buses run to Kyiv June 15-Sept. 10 (60-

UKRAINE

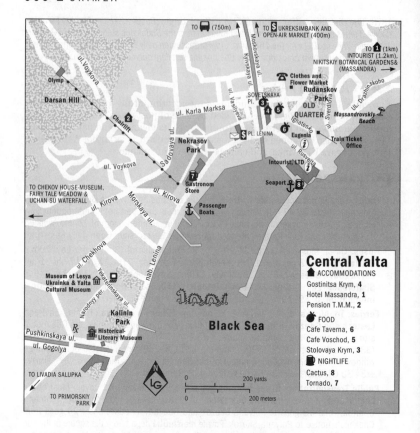

TO 🚌 (750m)
TO 💲 UKREKSIMBANK AND OPEN-AIR MARKET (400m)
TO 🛈 (1km) INTOURIST (1.2km), NIKITSKIY BOTANICAL GARDENS& (MASSANDRA) →

ul. Voykova
Olymp
Darsan Hill
Chairlift
Moskovskaya ul.
Kyivskaya ul.
Clothes and Flower Market
Rudanskov Park
SOVETSKAYA Pl.
ul. Karla Marksa
ul. Vasilyeva
OLD QUARTER
Massandrovskiy Beach
ul. Drazhinskoho
ul. Sverdlova
Ignatenko
Nekrasov Park
Sadovaya ul.
PL. LENINA
Eugenia
Train Ticket Office
ul. Voykova
ul. Rusvelta
Intourist, LTD
TO CHEKOV HOUSE-MUSEUM, FAIRY TALE MEADOW & UCHAN SU WATERFALL
ul. Kirova
Gastronom Store
Seaport
ul. Kirova
Morskaya ul.
Passenger Boats
ul. Chekhova
nab. Lenina
Museum of Lesya Ukrainka & Yalta Cultural Museum
Yekaterininskaya ul.
Narodnyy per.
Kalinin Park
Pushkinskaya ul.
Historical-Literary Museum
ul. Gogolya
TO LIVADIA SALUPKA
TO PRIMORSKIY PARK
N LG

Black Sea

Central Yalta

🏠 ACCOMMODATIONS
Gostinitsa Krym, 4
Hotel Massandra, 1
Pension T.M.M., 2

🍎 FOOD
Cafe Taverna, 6
Cafe Voschod, 5
Stolovaya Krym, 3

🍸 NIGHTLIFE
Cactus, 8
Tornado, 7

0   200 yards
0   200 meters

135hv; price rises until Sept.). They plan to open an info center by summer 2005. Open M-F 10am-5pm. **Intourist,** ul. Drazhinskogo 50 (☎27 01 32; fax 35 30 93), in Hotel Yalta, uphill from Hotel Massandra (see **Accommodations,** p. 901), books flights and organizes excursions with English-speaking guides. Open daily 8am-7pm. MC/V.

Currency Exchange: Exchange booths and banks are everywhere, but offer the worst rates in the country. It's better to exchange money before arriving in Yalta. **Ukreksimbank,** ul. Moskovskaya 31a (☎32 79 35), to the left of the Tsirk (Цирк; Circus) stop, cashes **traveler's checks** for 2% commission. Open M-Th 9am-1pm and 2-4pm, Sa 9am-3pm. **Avalbank** (☎32 03 35), in the central post office (see below), offers **Western Union** services, gives MC/V **cash advances** for 2.5% commission, and cashes traveler's checks for 2% commission. Open daily 9am-1pm and 2-7pm.

ATM: At the bus station, the post office (see below) and along nab. Lenina.

Luggage Storage: At the bus station. Look for "Камера-Хранения" (Kamera-Khraneniya) at the bottom of the stairs, in back of the building. 3hv per day. Open daily 8am-7pm.

Pharmacy: Apteka #6, ul. Botkinskaya 1 (Боткинская; ☎32 30 42). From nab. Lenina, walk up ul. Pushkinskaya and turn right. Open daily June-Sept. 8am-9pm; Feb.-May and Oct. 8am-8pm; Nov.-Jan. 8am-7pm. For after-hours service, walk through the next set of doors in the same building and ring the bell at the little window to the left. Open 24hr.

Telephones: Ukrtelecom, ul. Moskovskaya 9 (☎32 43 02), down the alley, across from the flower and clothing market. Internet access. Open 24hr. Fax available 9am-5pm.

Internet Access: Internet Center, ul. Yekaterinskaya 3 (☎32 30 72). From nab. Lenina, go up ul. Yekaterinskaya, then take a right down the steps marked with a sign. Decent connections, though often crowded. 4.5hv per hr. Open 24hr.

Post Office: Pl. Lenina. **Poste Restante** at window #4. Packages held for 30 days. Fax at #19. Open M-F 8am-7pm, Sa 8am-6pm, Su 9am-4pm. **Postal Code:** 98 600.

■ ACCOMMODATIONS

If you plan to stay in a hotel in Yalta during June or August, reserve at least two months in advance and be prepared to pay the hefty price. If you arrive in town in summer without a reservation, you may have to negotiate with bus station middlemen for **private rooms** (25-50hv per person) or contact Eugenia Travel for **apartment rentals** (150hv per person). During other seasons, hotels become much cheaper and availability is not a problem.

Gostinitsa Krym (Крым), ul. Moskovskaya 1/6 (☎27 17 10, reservations 27 17 03). The 4th stop on trolley #1 from the bus station, between pl. Lenina and pl. Sovetskaya. Clean rooms in a convenient, central location. Hot water M-F 4pm-9am, Sa-Su 24hr. All singles have shared bath. Singles 20-50hv; doubles 50-90hv, with bath 110-350hv. ❶

Pension T.M.M., ul. Lesi Ukrayinki 16 (☎/fax 23 09 50). From the bus station, take trolley #1 to Sadovaya (Садовая). Backtrack to the left, heading uphill, then turn left at the intersection. The entrance is an unmarked black fence on the left. Peaceful, stately mansion with views of the sea and its own courtyard. The airy rooms have balconies, TV, and private showers. Singles 160hv; doubles 300-415hv. Includes 3 meals daily. 25hv less without meals; see the manager to arrange this. ❸

Hotel Massandra (Массандра), ul. Drazhinskovo 46 (Дражинского; ☎27 24 27; fax 27 24 01). Near the beach and 20min. from the town center. Go up ul. Drazhinskovo and left at Avalon Cafe (Авалон), or take *marshrutka* #34 up the hill. Expensive but comfy rooms with private baths, TV, and fridges. Doubles 150hv-600hv. ❹

■ FOOD

Most of the cafes and restaurants on and near nab. Lenina are expensive, especially in the summer. Read the menus carefully: some places sneak in large surcharges for service and live music. Soviet-style **cafeterias** (столовая; stolovaya) in the city center offer a cheap, quick alternative (10-20hv), though they are often crowded at lunch and have few selections at dinner. The **Gastronom** (Гастроном) supermarket at nab. Lenina 15 sells cheap, fresh bread. The **open-air market,** opposite the circus, has a large selection of fruits and vegetables. To get there, take trolley #1, or walk up ul. Moskovskaya. (Open daily 8am-7pm.)

Cafe Voschod (Восход), ul. Ignatenko 2 (Игнатенко; ☎32 75 46), near pl. Sovetskaya. Serves Turkish cuisine and some Russian and European dishes. Try the baked fish (25-45hv) or the meat (13-20hv), grilled right in the dining room. Entrees 10-45hv. English menu does not list all entrees. Open daily June-Sept. 24hr.; Oct.-May 8am-midnight. ❷

Cafe Taverna (☎32 38 62), ul. Rusvelta 3, near pl. Lenina. This popular cafe near the seaport has tasty food and an unusual schedule: it is nocturnal in non-summer months. Entrees 9-22hv. Open daily June-Aug. 9am-2am; Sept.-May 5pm-6am. ❷

Stolovaya Krym (Столовая), ul. Moskovskaya 1/6, next to Gostinitsa Krym. One of the best self-service cafeterias in town, with a decent selection of classic Russian (Soviet) food at lunchtime. The *solyanka* (meat soup; 4hv) is phenomenal. Entrees 2-10hv. Open daily 9am-9pm. ❶

👁 🏛 SIGHTS AND MUSEUMS

Most of Yalta's impressive sights are located outside town. The most efficient way to see the main attractions is to divide them into three days: one day for the museums and beaches in town, one day for Massandra and the Nikitskiy Botanical Garden, and another day for Livadiya, Swallow's Nest, and Alupka. The must-see sights are the Chekhov House-Museum and the Livadiya and Massandra palaces.

■ **ANTON CHEKHOV HOUSE-MUSEUM.** The famous Russian author Anton Chekhov (see **Russia: The Arts,** p. 658) lived in Yalta for the final five years of his life. In 1899, he built a house (known as the "white dacha") on the hill. In 1921, after he died of tuberculosis, his sister established the property as a museum (Дом Музей А. Р. Чехова; Dom Muzey A. P. Chekhova). A recently constructed building displays photos, letters, and manuscripts, as well as the desk at which Chekhov wrote *Three Sisters, The Cherry Orchard,* and *Lady with a Lapdog.* Chekhov's **garden** represents "eternal spring"—at any time of year, some plants are in bloom. The house retains its original furnishings. From the center, take *marshrutka* #8 from Kinoteatr Spartak (at the end of ul. Pushkinskaya). Alternatively, take trolleybus #1 to ul. Pionerskaya (Пионерская), cross the street, turn left, then right into the walkway, and left at the top of the stairs. *(Ul. Kirova 112. ☎39 49 47. Open June-Sept. Tu-Su 10am-5:15pm; Oct.-May W-Su 10am-4pm. 10hv, students 5hv. Photo 3hv, video 5hv. English booklet 10hv, brochure 3hv. English video upon request.)*

OTHER SIGHTS. For a great view of the city, take the **chairlift** (канатная дорога; kanatnaya doroga) up to **Olymp,** a mock Greek temple atop the hill. The lift starts on nab. Lenina, to the right of the Gastronom. *(☎32 81 62. Open daily June-Sept. 10am-9pm; Oct.-May 10am-5pm. 5hv, children 3hv.)* The **Museum of Lesya Ukrayinka,** ul. Yekaterinskaya 8, honors the famous Ukrainian writer who lived here briefly in 1897 (see **The Arts,** p. 869) and pays tribute to the Ukrainian cultural heritage of Crimea. *(☎32 55 25. Call ahead for English tours, 10hv. Open June-Aug. Tu-Su 11am-7pm; Sept.-May Tu-Su 10am-5pm. 2hv.)* The **Yalta Cultural Museum,** in the same building, highlights aspects of local life from the 19th and 20th centuries. The entrance is to the left as you enter the building. *(Open Sept.-May Tu-Su 11am-6pm. 2hv.)* From June to August, **"The World of Dolls"** exhibit takes over the Cultural Museum's space. *(☎32 16 34. Open daily June-Aug. 11am-6:30pm. 6hv, students and children 3hv.)* A great place for children and the young-at-heart is the **Fairy Tale Meadow** (Поляна Сказок; Polyana Skazok), dotted with wooden sculptures of Snow White and characters from Russian and Ukrainian fairy tales. To get there, take bus #24 from Kinoteatr Spartak. *(☎39 64 02. Open daily July-Sept. 8am-7pm; Oct.-June 9am-5pm. 8hv, children 4hv.)*

🎵 🎭 ENTERTAINMENT AND NIGHTLIFE

Follow the seashore either way from the harbor to reach one of Yalta's many **beaches.** (Entrance to most city beaches 1.50hv, commercial beaches 2-5hv.) Many are crowded, and all lack sand. The **amusement park** *(lunapark)* on nab. Lenina has a roller coaster (10hv) and bumper cars (15hv). **Organ concerts** take place in the Roman Catholic church, ul. Pushkinskaya 25. *(☎23 00 65. Open July-Sept. M-Sa 8pm, Su 5pm; May-June and Oct. M-Sa 7:30pm, Su 5pm. Buy tickets on site.)*

Overlooking the waterfront is the pricey but popular nightclub **Tornado,** nab. Lenina 11, up the stairs through the arch and to the left. House music and nightly laser shows. *(☎32 20 36. Beer 8hv. Cover 50-100hv; free for women until 11pm. Open June-Sept. daily 10pm-5am; Oct.-Nov. Th-Sa 10pm-5am; Dec.-May F-Sa*

10pm-5am.) **Cactus** (Кактус), ul. Rusvelta 5, above the Sea Terminal, has Tex-Mex food, disco music, theme nights, billiards, and a sea view. (☎32 16 14. Beer 5-15hv. Cover 30hv after 10pm; women free until 11pm. Open daily 11am-5am.)

▶ DAYTRIPS FROM YALTA

MASSANDRA (МАССАНДРА)

To get to Massandra Palace, take trolleybus #2 from Yalta, cross the street, and go uphill until you see the "Дворец" sign and arrow on the street pointing to a forest path on the left. The path is poorly marked—when in doubt head up and left. ☎32 17 28. Open July-Aug. Tu-Su 9am-6pm; May-June and Sept.-Oct. Tu-Su 9am-5pm; Nov.-Apr. W-Su 9am-4pm. 15hv, students and children 7hv. English booklet 10hv. Massandra Winery is at ul. Vinodela Egorova 9 (Винодела Егорова). From Yalta, take marshrutka #40 from the downtown station, by the clothing market, to "Vinzavod" (Винзавод). ☎23 26 62. Admission with tour only. 1hr. tours daily every 2hr. starting at 11am; last tour May-Oct. 7pm, Nov.-Apr. 5pm. 25hv, with wine tasting and cellar admission 40hv.

Overlooking Massandra from atop the hill, the elegant ◪ **Massandra Palace** has a fascinating past that reflects the major historical developments in Crimea during the last century. In the mid-1800s, the house of Count Vorontsov was located at the site. In 1881, after the house was wrecked by a storm, Vorontsov's son commissioned a French architect to build a palace here; the design was modeled after a castle in the Loire Valley. Work was left unfinished due to the son's death, but construction resumed in 1892 by order of Aleksander III, who hired a Russian architect to complete the structure in a decorative Baroque style. The building served as the tsar's palace until 1920, and later was used as a base for the Crimean cadet corp (1920-1929), a tuberculosis sanatorium (1929-1941), a German officers' hospital (1941-1944), a Soviet hospital (1944-1946), Stalin's summer residence (1948), and a favorite vacation spot for Soviet officials. The palace was opened to the public as a museum in 1992. The first floor contains impressive dining and billiard rooms. The second floor is divided into "his" and "hers" rooms, and contains a unique chocolate-colored fireplace. The Russian-language guided tour is excellent.

Founded in 1894, the **Massandra Winery** holds in its cellars the largest wine collection in the world—about 1 million bottles, including a rare 1775 "Jerez de la Frontera" vintage. The collection was hidden under floorboards during WWI, and thousands of bottles were shipped abroad during WWII; thanks to this foresight, much of the collection escaped the German pillagers. Guided tours and tasting is available, and there's a store inside.

NIKITSKIY BOTANICAL GARDEN

From Yalta, take bus #34 or trolley #2 past Massandra. Ask the driver to let you off at "Nikitskiy Sad." ☎33 35 30. Open daily June-Aug. 8am-8pm; Sept.-May 9am-4pm. 6hv, students and children 3.50hv. Cactus orangerie 2hv/1hv.

Founded in 1812, the **Nikitskiy Botanical Garden** (Никитский Сад; Nikitskiy Sad) has over 15,000 species of native and foreign flora, including 1000 varieties of roses and many kinds of trees from around the world. Russian tour groups fill the territory in summer. A walking path runs between the upper and lower entrances to the garden; follow the blue signs if you're going up, or the green signs if you're going down. Below the lower entrance is a ◪ **cactus orangerie,** with a greenhouse and a garden. A stand in the garden sells cactuses—pretty, but hard to pack.

LIVADIYA (ЛІВАДИЯ)

Take bus or marshrutki #11 or 45 from the train station or from "Kinoteatr Spartak." Bus #13 (1hr) also leaves from "Spartak." Ferries (15min., 2 per hr., 5hv) stop at the dock; from there, hike 150m up the hill. Alternatively, a 1hr. hike along the beach from Yalta will get you to Livadiya. Palace ☎31 55 81. Open May-Nov. Th-Tu 10am-5pm; Dec.-Apr. Tu and Th-Su 10am-5pm. 15hv, children 7hv. Photo 5hv, video 15hv. English booklet 10hv.

The ■ **Great Livadiya Palace,** built in 1911 as a summer residence for Tsar Nicholas II, is famous for hosting the **Yalta Conference** at the end of WWII. At this historic meeting, held February 4-11, 1945, Winston Churchill, Franklin Roosevelt, and Josef Stalin negotiated post-war claims. Stalin joined the war against Japan after the German defeat, while Roosevelt and Churchill promised to return all Soviet prisoners of war. On the first floor is the majestic **White Hall,** where the talks took place. The round table at which the three leaders sat is just outside the hall. The **billiard room,** where the final agreement was signed, looks out onto the **Italian court-yard,** where the famous photo of the "Big Three" was taken. The American delegation resided at the Livadiya Palace during the conference. The second floor of the palace houses the **Nicholas II Museum,** which displays the imperial family's living quarters, photographs (they enjoyed Kodak cameras), and possessions.

ALUPKA (АЛУПКА)

In summer, take a ferry (1½hr.; 16 per day; 12hv, children 6hv) or marshrutka #27 (every 20min.-1hr., 3hv) from Yalta, or the ferry from Livadiya (9hv). Palace ☎72 29 51. Open July-Aug. daily 8am-7:30pm; Apr.-June and Sept.-Nov. 15 daily 9am-5pm; Nov. 16-Mar. Tu-Su 9am-4pm. 15hv, students and children 7hv. To avoid waiting hours in line in July and Aug., show up before 10am or after 6pm. Miskhor (Мисхор) cable car ☎72 28 94. 15hv, children 8hv. Runs every 10min. May-Sept. 9am-7pm; Oct.-Apr. 10am-4pm.

The village of Alupka is the site of the **Vorontsov Palace** (Воронцовский Дворец; Vorontsovskiy Dvorets), built for Count Mikhail Vorontsov (see **History,** p. 866) during the first half of the 19th century. The palace, designed by a pair of English architects, has the grandeur and elegance of an English castle; when the British delegation stayed here during the Yalta Conference, Winston Churchill remarked that he felt at home. The interior includes a majestic entrance hall, a large dining room (with a balcony for musicians), a billiard room, and an indoor winter garden with a fountain and rare plants. English landscapes and portraits of renowned figures (including Catherine the Great) decorate the walls. The palace **gardens,** designed by an expert German landscaper, extend down toward the sea. The Lion Staircase, with three pairs of lions in different poses, is a favorite photo spot among visitors.For a view of the area, go to the nearby village of Miskhor and take the **cable car** (канатная дорога) 1234m up to the top of **Ay-Petri Mountain** (Ай-Петри). To get there from the palace exit, take a left and walk 1km through the park up the coast. From the top of Ay-Petri, you can take a *marshrutka* to Yalta.

On the coast between Yalta and Alupka is **Swallow's Nest** (Ласточкино Гнездо; Lastochkino Gnezdo), a castle overhanging a cliff. Built for a German businessman in 1912, it is now a popular symbol of the Crimea and is one of the peninsula's most-photographed sites. There is an Italian **restaurant** inside the castle. The ferry between Yalta and Alupka stops at the dock below Swallow's Nest. You can get off and climb up to the castle, but the view from below is more spectacular.

SEVASTOPOL (СЕВАСТОПОЛЬ)　　☎(80)692

Sevastopol (pop. 400,000) first gained international attention in the Crimean War (1854-55). In WWII, it was named one of the Soviet "Hero Cities" due to its tragic losses. Sevastopol is not part of the Autonomous Republic of the Crimea, and is governed directly by Kyiv. Both Russia and Ukraine use Sevastopol as a naval base. Some tourists come here to visit the historical museums and the naval port, others relax on the beach, and take boat rides in the city's many bays.

☐ TRANSPORTATION

Trains: Privokzalnaya pl. 3 (Привокзальная; ☎54 30 77). To: **Kyiv** (18hr., 2 per day, 57hv); **Moscow, RUS** (26hr., 2 per day, 220hv); **St. Petersburg, RUS** (35hr., 1 per day, 280hv). Purchase tickets for non-Crimean destinations several weeks in advance for travel during July and Aug. Advance ticket office across the street from the bus station (open daily 7am-6pm). All Crimean *elektrichka* (commuter rail) connect through **Simferopol** (2-2½ hr., 7 per day, 3hv). Tickets are sold to the right of the train station. All trolleybuses at the train station go to the center; #17 and 20 run to the very start of Bolshaya Morskaya ul.; and all others head to pl. Lazaryova (0.40hv).

Buses: Pl. Revyakina 2 (Ревякина; ☎46 16 32). To: **Feodosiya** (4-5hr., 3 per day, 20hv); **Kerch** (13hr., 2 per day, 32hv); **Odessa** (13hr., 1 per day, 14hv); **Simferopol** (2hr.; 1-2 per hr. 6am-6pm; 12hv) via **Bakhchisarai**; **Yalta** (2hr., 1-3 per hr., 12hv) via **Alupka**; **Yevpatoriya** (3½hr., 1 per day, 14hv); **Krasnodar, RUS** (16hr., 1 per day, 47hv); **Rostov-na-Donu, RUS** (16hr., 1 per day, 84hv). Luggage fee 0.50-4.50hv.

Ferries: Leave from Artilleriyskaya Bay behind Gostinitsa Sevastopol and from Grafskaya Pristan (Графская Пристань) for the north shore (Северная Сторона; Severnaya Storona), landing near pl. Zakharova (Захарова; 20min., every hr., 1hv). If you are headed to the north shore, take the ferry from Artilleriyskaya to Radiogorka (10-15min., 1 per hr., 1hv). **Taxis** ☎050.

Other Public Transportation: Less crowded *marshrutki* (1hv) run the same routes as **buses** (0.60hv). *Marshrutki* leave from pl. Zakharova to popular Uchkuyuvka Beach (Учкуювка). **Trolleybuses** (0.40hv; pay on board) are efficient and convenient. #12 runs up ul. Bolshaya Morskaya. #7 and 9 circle the center, stopping at the train station. #5 goes up ul. Admirala Oktyabrskova to the west of the peninsula.

☒ ☑ ORIENTATION AND PRACTICAL INFORMATION

The town center is on a peninsula below the Sevastopol harbor. **Pl. Lazaryova** (Лазарёва), up the street from Gostinitsa Sevastopol (see **Accommodations,** p. 906), is a good starting point for exploring the city center. **Ul. Generala Petrova** (Генерала Петрова) delves inland, while **pr. Nakhimova** (Нахимова) circles from here along the peninsula, where it meets **ul. Lenina** (Ленина) at pl. Nakhimova. Ul. Lenina runs parallel to the sea until **pl. Ushakova** (Ушакова). **Ul. Bolshaya Morskaya** (Большая Морская) heads back to pl. Lazaryova to finish off the circle. Vendors sell **maps** all along nab. Kornilova and Primorskiy bul.

Tourist Offices: Kiosks along Primorskiy bul. offer city tours (50-80hv). Those near the seaport (Morskoy Vokzal) advertise boat tours of the harbor (30min., 15hv). **Sanmarin** (Санмарин; ☎45 57 10; tur@stel.sevastopol.ua), in Gostinitsa Sevastopol, provides walking tours of the city (75hv) and other excursions. Open M-Sa 9am-7pm.

Currency Exchange: Exchange booths are everywhere. **Oshchadbank** (Ощадбанк; ☎54 12 16), at ul. Bolshaya Morskaya 41, cashes AmEx/Thomas Cooke **traveler's checks,** and gives MC/V **cash advances,** all for 2% commission. **Western Union** services are available here and at the post office. Open M-F 8am-1pm and 2-6pm, Sa 8am-4pm.

Luggage Storage: Lockers in **bus station.** 2hv for 24hr. Open daily 6am-6pm. Guarded luggage storage in the **train station,** to the far right of the *elektrichka* ticket office. 2hv until 8pm the next day. Open daily 8am-1pm and 2-8pm; desk closes 6pm.

UKRAINE

Pharmacy: (Аптека; Apteka), ul. Bolshaya Morskaya 48 (☎55 41 75). Has an English "pharmacy" sign. Large selection. Open 24hr.; closed 2nd W of each month. MC/V.

Telephones: ☎55 02 66. To the left of the post office. Open 24hr.

Internet Access: Absolutnaya Realnost (Абсолутняя Реальность; ☎54 40 79), on ul. Bolshaya Morskaya on the 2nd fl. of Kinoteatr Pobeda (Кинотеатр Победа). 5hv per hr. Open 24hr. **Soyuz** (Союз), pr. Nakhimova 4 (☎45 59 90), in the basement of Pioneer's House (Дом Пионира), around to the right and down the stairs through the metal fence. 6hv per hr. Open 24hr.

Post Office: Ul. Bolshaya Morskaya 21. **Western Union.** Open June-Aug. M-F 8am-7pm, Sa-Su 8am-6pm; Sept.-May M-F 8am-6pm, Sa-Su 8am-5pm. **Postal Code:** 99 011.

▮ ◖ ACCOMMODATIONS AND FOOD

Private rooms and short-term **apartments** are inexpensive and easy to arrange in summer. A desk at the entrance of the bus station sets up accommodations for a 25hv service fee. Rooms fill up quickly in July and August; the safest option is to reserve a hotel well in advance. At **Gostinitsa Sevastopol ❷**, pr. Nakhimova 8, elegant pre-Soviet architecture meets bland Soviet interior design. It has an ideal central location, just five stops from the bus station on trolleybus #1, 3, 7, or 9. Many rooms have sea views, and the hotel entrance is grand. The cheapest rooms lack hot water. Breakfast (21hv) is required for those staying in rooms with hot water. (☎46 64 00; fax 46 64 09. Hot showers 2.50hv. Singles 75-280hv; doubles 65-180hv. MC/V.) **Gostinitsa Krym ❷** (Крым), Shestaya Bastionnaya ul. 46 (Бастионная), is up ul. Admirala Oktyabrskova from ul. Bolshaya Morskaya. To get there, take trolleybus lines #5, 6, or 10, or hop on any 100-numbered *marshrutka* from the train and bus stations. All rooms have balconies and private baths; most have sea views. (☎55 71 54. Breakfast included. Hot water 7-9am and 7-9pm. Singles 109hv; doubles 158hv.) The **central market** is downhill from pl. Lazaryova at the intersection of Partizanskaya ul. (Партизанская) and Odesskaya ul. (Одесская; open Tu-Su 6am-8pm.) A local favorite is ▨**Traktir ❷** (Трактир), ul. Bolshaya Morskaya 8. Waitresses in sailor uniforms serve excellent Ukrainian food and drinks, including wonderful *solyanka* (meat soup; 9hv small, 15hv large) and *kulebyaka* (pie with meat and cabbage; 6hv). The outdoor terrace (May-Sept.) is pleasant in summer. (☎54 47 60. Entrees 15-40hv. English menu available. Open daily 10am-11pm.) **Cafe Zdorovye ❶** (Здоровье; Health), Partizanskaya ul. 3, is at the end of the road leading off to the left at the start of the central market. (☎55 05 07. Chicken cutlets with soy 0.75hv. *Piroshki* with soy filling 0.30hv. Open daily 8am-7pm.)

◉ ♫ SIGHTS AND ENTERTAINMENT

▨**PANORAMA "DEFENSE OF SEVASTOPOL 1854-1855".** One of the most impressive sights in Ukraine, the panorama (Панорама Оборона Севастопола; Panorama Oborona Sevastopola) was built by Franz Roubaud in 1905 to commemorate the heroic defense of the city during the Crimean War against Britain and France. Though destroyed during WWII, it was recreated by a team of Moscow artists and reopened in 1954. The panorama artfully blends the painted backdrop with a realistic 3D scene in front. The 360° canvas is 14m high and has a circumference of 115m. English descriptions are posted in the lower viewing area. The panorama's 100th anniversary will be celebrated on May 14, 2005. *(Enter the park at pl. Ushakova and continue to the end of Istoricheskiy bul. (Исторический). It is the round building, opposite the fountain. ☎49 97 38. Open May-June daily 9:30am-5pm; July-Sept. daily 9am-7pm; Oct.-Apr. Tu-Su 9:30am-5pm; ticket office closes 30min. earlier. 12hv, students 8hv, children 6hv. Photo 5hv, video 15hv. English tours 14hv. English brochure 4hv.)*

RUINS AT CHERSONESUS. The 2500-year-old Chersonesus (Херсонес; Khersones) ruins include an ancient amphitheater, acres of foundation, and the remains of several basilicas. In the middle stands the modern **St. Vladimir's Cathedral** (Владимирский Собор; Vladimirskiy Sobor), originally built during the late 19th century and reconstructed in 2001. The nearby new **pavilion** marks the supposed spot where Prince Vladimir was baptized, thus bringing Kyivan Rus into the Orthodox faith. *(Take the marshrutka labeled "Херсонес" from pl. Lazaryova. ☎24 13 01. Open daily June-Aug. 8am-8:15pm; Sept.-May 9am-5pm. 7hv, students 5hv, children 4hv. With Russian tour 10hv/6hv/5hv. With English tour 16hv. Photo 3hv, video 7hv.)*

MUSEUM OF THE BLACK SEA FLEET. This museum (Музей Чёрноморского Флота; Muzey Chyornomorskovo Flota) tells the military history of the Black Sea with documents, models, and original weapons. The lower floor displays maps and items recovered from ships. The upper floor has Soviet flags and decorated uniforms. Exhibit captions in Russian only. Even if you don't enter the museum, check out the cannons and rockets displayed behind the museum building. *(☎54 22 89 or 54 03 92. Open W-Su 10am-5pm; closed last F of each month. 4hv, students and children 2hv. English tour 12hv, min. 6 people. Russian tour 5hv, children 3hv.)*

OTHER SIGHTS. Impressive monuments to Sevastopol's naval heroes decorate the streets and the harbor. In the bay near pl. Nakhimova is the **monument** to the sunken ships. During the Crimean War, the Black Sea Fleet sunk many of its own ships in order to prevent the enemy from entering the bay. The **obelisk** that marks Sevastopol's status as a Soviet hero-city is visible from nab. Kornilova; the nearby **Monument to the Black Sea Submariners** can also be seen from there. **Omega Beach** (Пляж Омега; Plyazh Omega) is packed day and night in summer; its bars and discos thump until dawn. *(Take trolleybus #10 to the Plyazh Omega stop.)*

KERCH (КЕРЧЬ) ☎(80)6561

Near the eastern tip of the peninsula, just 5km from Russia, Kerch has been ruled by Greeks, Tatars, and Genoese. Modern Kerch is known for industry and fishing, but also has some of Crimea's best beaches and most ancient treasures.

TRANSPORTATION. Flights to Kyiv operate during the summer months (3 per week, under 300hv). The **train station** lies quite far from the city center on pl. Privokzalnaya 3 (Привокзальная; ☎211 26). Take bus #6 to the city center. Trains go to: **Kyiv** (23hr., even days, 60hv); **Lviv** (33hr., odd days, 90hv); **Simferopol** (7¼hr., 22hv); **Moscow, RUS** (27hr., 1 per day, 220hv). You can buy advance tickets in town at the *kassa* (касса) across the street from the bus station at the corner of ul. Gaidara (Гайдара) and ul. Gorkovo (Горкого). The **bus station** (☎5 35 72 or 1 05 72) is on ul. Marshala Yeryomenko (Ерїменко), 1.5km from the center. Buses go to: **Feodosiya** (2hr., 1-2 per hr., 20hv); **Odessa** (15hr., 1 per day, 90hv); **Sevastopol** (7hr., 2 per day, 27hv); **Simferopol** (3hr., 7 per day, 25hv); **Yalta** (6hr., 2 per day, 27hv); **Krasnodar, RUS** (10hr., 6 per day, 14-18hv). Many buses with Crimean destinations run through Simferopol. To get to the center from the bus station, take bus #5 or 19. To reach the beach from the center, take bus #6 or 10 to the last stop, "Institut."

ORIENTATION AND PRACTICAL INFORMATION. Kerch clusters around **pl. Lenina** (Ленина) and its large **griffin** statue. To the left of the griffin, the **Mithridates staircase** leads up to the WWII obelisk (see **Sights**, p. 908). Behind the plaza, lies the sea and the **Esplanade** (Naberezhnaya; Набережная). Kerch's main pedestrian zone is along **ul. Lenina,** which intersects **ul. Volodi Dubina** (Володи Дубина). Two main roads cup the center: **ul. Sverdlova** (Свердлова) runs along the coast and changes names twice—first to Admiralteyskiy Prezd (Адмиралтейский Презд), then to ul. Kirova—before intersecting **ul. Karla Marksa** (Карла Маркса). Another street, located farther down off ul. Sverdlova, starts there from the dock and the permanently anchored ship with a crane and leads to the **bus station.**

On the Esplanade, the NGO **Bospur Foundation,** Haberezhnaya 2, last door on the 2nd fl., can refer you to travel agencies and accommodations, and organizes tours. (☎2 82 51; bosportour@kerch.krid.net. Open M-F 9am-5pm.) The **tourist agency** "Prestige" (Престиж), ul. Eryimenko 30 (Ерïменко), is to the right of the bus station, inside the building marked "Швейнная Фабрика." It is in right corridor, on the first floor. The staff does not speak English, but can set up tours, accommodations, and flights, and can help interested individuals contact local archaeologists. (☎/fax 2 39 78; prestizh_tour@bosportele.com.ua. Open June-Aug. daily 9am-5pm, Sept.-May M-Sa 9am-5pm.) **Privat Bank,** ul. Lenina 44 (☎2 02 51), cashes **traveler's checks** for 2% commission and gives V **cash advances** for 3% commission. There are **ATMs** along ul. Lenina. **Store luggage** at the bus station (0.15hv per day) or at the train station (1hv). A **24hr. pharmacy** (Аптека #19) is at ul. Lenina 43 (☎2 12 71. Ring the bell under the sign closest to pl. Lenina for service 8pm-8am.) **Internet access** is available at **Aironet Jump,** ul. Dubinina 20. (☎2 02 60. 7hv per hr. Open 9am-6pm.) Facing the griffin in pl. Lenina with the sea behind you, the large building straight ahead is the **telephone office** (☎2 14 99; open daily 8am-8pm) and **post office** (☎2 02 09; open M-Sa 8am-6pm, Su 8am-2pm). **Postal Code:** 98300.

ⓘⓘ ACCOMMODATIONS AND FOOD. As usual in the Crimea, bus station *babushki* offer good deals on **private rooms** (20-40hv). In the center on ul. Kirova, the 1938 **Hotel Kerch ❶** offers cramped, Soviet-style rooms with shared bathrooms and showers. The lux rooms feature private baths with hot water, fridges, TVs, and telephones. Take bus #5 from the bus station and get off at the second stop or take bus #6 from the train station and exit at the seventh stop. (☎2 12 04 or 2 11 55. Singles 33hv, lux 125hv; doubles 55hv/230hv.) Luxurious **Hotel Klassik ❸** (Классик), near the beach at ul. Kurortnaya 9/2 (Курортная), has spacious two-room suites with hot water, private shower, A/C, fridge, TV, and telephone. The hotel restaurant serves delicious traditional dishes. (☎3 30 71; www.kerch.info. Breakfast included. Singles 125-225hv; doubles 225-255hv.) If you want to live simply near sand beaches, the little suburb of Geroyevskoye (Героевское), also called "Eltigen" (Эльтиген), is lined with bungalow-style accommodations in what are called **"tour bases"** (тубразд; tubrazd). Bases offer old showers and shared bathrooms, but beds are low as 10hv in a triple. From the bus station, take bus #5 to the stop "ZhRK" (ЖРК); from the train station, take a *marshrutka* marked "ЖРК." From there, *marshrutki* go to Geroyevskoye. The ride takes 30-40min.

The open-air **market** (рынок), across the square from the bus station, has fresh produce in July and August. (Open daily 7:30am-6pm.) Restaurants line ul. Lenina. **Uyut ❶** (Уют), Lenina 41, serves consistently enjoyable food. (☎2 00 84. Entrees 6-35hv. Salads 4-8hv. Open daily 9am-midnight.) Little cafes are along ul. Sverdlova.

ⓖ SIGHTS. The 4th-century BC **Tsar's Burial Mound** has an entrance lined with ancient Greek tombstones. Take *marshrutka* or bus #4 from the bus station to the final stop, "Muzey" (Музей), then walk past the catacombs to the entrance on the left. The tombstone in English to the right of the entrance was brought from Sevastopol and marked an 1854-55 common grave of English, French, and Russian soldiers. (☎5 47 13. Open daily 9am-5pm. English booklet 10hv. 3hv, students and children 1.50hv.) Near the Tsar's Burial Mound are the **Bospor Catacombs,** miles and miles of man-made underground passages, where 10,000 soldiers and 5000 civilians hid in 1942. The museum shows only 30m of the cave system. Dress warmly, as the interior blasts cold, sub-10°C air. (☎5 40 01. Open Tu-Su 9am-5pm. Closed last Th of each month. Mandatory tour free. Catacombs 5hv, children 3hv.)

Built in the 8th century, the **Church of St. John the Baptist,** located behind pl. Lenina, is among the oldest surviving Christian churches in the world. It is said that the apostle Andrew visited Kerch and that the present-day church was built by his followers. Off pl. Lenina lie the ruins of **Pauticpaeum,** the capital of the Bospor kingdom in the 6th century BC. Climb the 402 stairs to **Mithridate Mount,** which contains a memorial **obelisk** and an **eternal flame** in memory of local soldiers who fell in WWII. The hill offers a spectacular view of the city and the Strait of Bosporus. To the right lies a **fortress** so well integrated into the landscape that the Mongol-Tatar invaders never knew its exact location. (Open 24hr. Free.) Founded in 1826, the **Museum of Antiquities,** ul. Sverdlova 22, displays a small fraction of what has been found in archaeological digs near Kerch, including 3rd-century BC black lacquered vases depicting the Amazons, a 4th-century BC skeleton of an athlete, and artifacts left behind by the city's various foreign invaders. (☎2 18 60 or 2 17 13. Open Tu-Su 9am-5pm. Closed last Th of each month in winter. 10hv.)

■■ **ENTERTAINMENT AND NIGHTLIFE.** To **spelunk** through local catacombs and caves, call **Hotel Klassic** (see **Accommodations and Food,** p. 908) and ask for Sergei Husselnov. **Lake Chokrak's** famous curative **mud bath** is a 7km hike from the last outpost served by *marshrutki,* in the suburb Kurortnoye (Курортное). The colorful **Bosporan Agons Festival,** featuring music and dance performed by troupes from around the world, is held annually from late June to early July. The little cafes along ul. Sverdlova near the water turn into bars and discos at night.

WESTERN UKRAINE

Proud residents of Western Ukraine will tell you that their region is "the most Ukrainian" part of the country. It has stubbornly maintained its unique identity. During WWII, some Western Ukrainians fought against both the Nazis and the Soviets, aiming instead for independence. Since the fall of the USSR, the western region has earned a reputation as the core of Ukrainian nationalism. Lviv is the cultural center, with a large proportion of the country's historic monuments, while the beautiful Carpathian Mountains are home to traditional peasant communities.

LVIV (ЛЬВІВ)   ☎(80)32[2]

While Kyiv is the political and economic capital of Ukraine, Lviv (pop. 830,000) is widely considered to be the cultural and patriotic center of the country. The city was at the crossroads of international trade during medieval times and experienced Austrian and Polish rule before the rise of the Soviet Union. Modern Lviv, which stretches far beyond the historic center, is a bustling, cafe-centric city; visitors who've had their fill of history and patriotism will happily move on to the nearby Carpathian mountains.

All phone numbers in Lviv that used to begin with "9" now have a "2" added in front when dialed locally. But when dialed from a different area code, the number remains the same as before, as the "2" added in front for local calls is actually the last digit of the area code. For example, a phone number that used to be 90 00 00 is now dialed 290 00 00 from within Lviv, but is still dialed 80 32 290 00 00 from elsewhere. Numbers that do not begin with 9, like 70 00 00, remain as before, and are still dialed 80 322 70 00 00 from elsewhere.

⌐ TRANSPORTATION

Flights: Lviv Airport, vul. Lyubinska (Любінська; ☎69 21 12). **Traident** (Траидент), vul. Kopernika 18 (☎/fax 297 14 93 or 297 13 32), books tickets for most major airlines.

Trains: Pl. Vokzalna (Вокзальна; ☎748 20 68, info 005). Buy tickets at the railway ticket office, Hnatyuka 20 (Гнатюка; ☎35 25 79 or 39 00 53), marked by the big "каси" sign. Open M-Sa 8am-2pm and 3-8pm, Su 8am-2pm and 3-6pm. Bring your passport or ISIC. You may have to go to the train station for same-day tickets. To: **Kyiv** (9hr., 9 per day, 46hv); **Odessa** (12½hr., 2 per day, 45hv); **Simferopol** (23hr., 1 per day, 69hv); **Bratislava, SLK** (18hr., 1 per day, 355hv); **Budapest, HUN** (13½hr., 1 per day, 405hv); **Kraków, POL** (7½hr., 1 per day, 136hv); **Minsk, BLR** (14hr., 1 per day, 95hv); **Moscow, RUS** (24½hr., 2 per day, 185hv); **Prague, CZR** (24hr., 1 per day, 390hv); **Warsaw, POL** (12hr., 1 per day, 220).

Buses: Main station, vul. Stryyska 189 (Стрийська; ☎63 24 93). From pl. Galytzka take trolley #5 or *marshrutka* #71. The ticket offices are on the 2nd fl. To: **Kraków, POL** (8-9hr., 1 per day, 75hv); **Przemyśl, POL** (4hr., 11 per day, 30hv); **Warsaw, POL** (10hr., 4 per day, 90hv). Lviv also has a series of smaller **regional stations.** The one at vul. Khmelnytskoho 225 (Хмельницького; ☎52 04 89) can be reached by tram #4 from vul. Shevchenka (Шевченка). Buses to **Brest, BLR** leave from here and from the **train station** (9hr., 1 per day, 32hv).

Public Transportation: Maps, available at the English-language bookstore (see **Orientation and Practical Information**), include public transit lines for **trams, trolleys,** and **buses.** Buy tickets (0.50hv for trams and trolleys, 0.80hv for *marshrutki*) on board from the fanny-pack-wearing conductor. 10hv fine for riding ticketless. In Old Town, pl. Halytska (Галицька) is a hub for buses.

Taxis: ☎39 34 34. Taxis cost 7-12hv. Agree on the price before you get in.

✈ 🛈 ORIENTATION AND PRACTICAL INFORMATION

The center of town is **pl. Rynok** (Ринок), the old market square. Around it, a grid of streets forms **Old Town,** where most of the sights are located. Toward the train station, broad **pr. Svobody** (Свободи) runs from the **Opera House** to **pl. Mitskevycha** (Міцкевича), Old Town's center of commerce. **Pr. Shevchenko** (Шувченко) extends to the right of pl. Mitskevycha. Trams #1, 9, and *marshrutka* #68 run from the main train station to Old Town's center; tram #6 to the north end of pr. Svobody, behind the Opera. Tram #9 goes from Old Town to the station.

Tourist Office: Lviv Tourist Information Center, vul. Pyidvalna 3 (Підвальна; ☎297 57 51 or 297 57 67; www.tourism.lviv.ua). Enter the building and turn right; it's the door at the end of the hall. English-speaking staff provides info on hotels, restaurants, and sights, but not for free: they charge a negotiable 3hv. for each question. **Maps** 2-10hv. City tour 50hv. per hr. Open M-F 10am-1pm and 2-6pm.

Consulate: Canada, vul. Bohomolska, 2/4 (Богомольська; ☎97 17 72).

Currency Exchange: The **UkrExim** exchange in **Hotel George** (see **Accommodations,** p. 912) cashes AmEx/V **traveler's checks** at 2% commission and gives MC/V **cash advances** for 3% commission. Open daily 9am-7pm. **Western Union** services (M-F 9am-1pm and 1:30-6:30pm, Sa 9am-1pm) available at the **post office's** window #10, on the 2nd fl. **Availabank,** at #12, cashes traveler's checks (3% commission) and gives MC/V cash advances. (☎93 46 77. Open M-F 9am-1pm, 2-4pm). Open M-F 9:30am-1pm, 2-6pm, Sa 10am-2pm. Storefronts along pr. Svobody **exchange currency.**

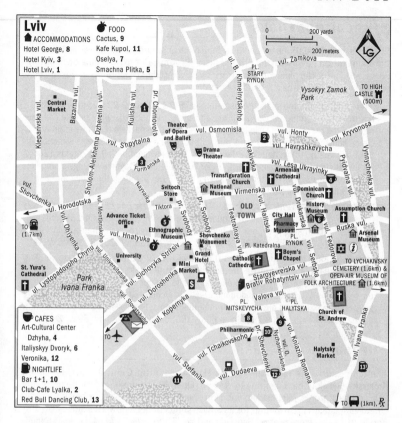

Lviv

ACCOMMODATIONS
Hotel George, 8
Hotel Kyiv, 3
Hotel Lviv, 1

FOOD
Cactus, 9
Kafe Kupol, 11
Oselya, 7
Smachna Plitka, 5

CAFES
Art-Cultural Center
Dzhyha, 4
Italiyskyy Dvoryk, 6
Veronika, 12

NIGHTLIFE
Bar 1+1, 10
Club-Cafe Lyalka, 2
Red Bull Dancing Club, 13

ATMs: Located throughout the city center and advertised by giant banners.

Luggage Storage: At the train station. 6hv. Open 24hr.

English-Language Bookstore: Budinok Knigi, Pl. Mitskevycha 8 (☎ 74 41 64). Sells city **guidebooks** and **maps** (6hv). Open Aug.-May M-F 10am-6pm, Sa 10am-4pm; June-July M-F 10am-7pm, Sa 10am-4pm.

24hr. Pharmacy: Apteka #28 (Аптека), vul. Zelena 33 (Зелена; ☎ 75 37 63).

Emergency: Ambulance ☎ 03. **City-wide information number:** ☎ 09.

Telephones: Vul. Doroshenka 39 (Дорошенка; ☎ 72 90 12), around the corner from the post office. Open daily 7am-11pm.

Internet Access: Internet Club, vul. Dudaeva 12 (Дудаева; ☎ 72 27 38; www.ic.lviv.ua). Walk into the alley; the door is on the right. High-speed Internet access on 25 computers. 8am-midnight 4hv per hr., midnight-8am 2hv per hr.; 15min. minimum. Printing 0.25hv per page. Open 24hr.

Post Office: Vul. Slovatskoho 1 (Словатского; ☎ 74 40 62), 1 block from Park Ivana Franka, to the left if facing the park from the front of the university. **Poste Restante** at window #3, 2nd fl. Take claim slip window #3, 1st fl., to collect packages. ID required. Open M-F 8am-8pm, Sa 8am-4pm. Lower fl. open Su 9am-3pm. **Postal Code:** 79 000.

ACCOMMODATIONS

Budget accommodations in Lviv are limited and generally unpleasant. Ladies at the train station hawk apartments and private rooms. Before agreeing on anything, be sure to check the place out: there are many dilapidated buildings in the city center, and water only runs a few hours per day.

Hotel Lviv, vul. Chornovola 7 (Чорновола; ☎79 22 70 or 79 22 72; fax 72 86 51), down the street from the Opera off the end of pr. Svobody. Despite its ugly concrete exterior and dreary Soviet-style lobby, many foreign backpackers tend to end up at this clean, convenient hotel. The rooms without baths are a good deal. Singles without bath 50hv, with bath 100hv; doubles 80hv/140hv; triples without bath 90hv; quads 120hv/240hv. The disco downstairs is loud; upper floors are best. Daytime luggage storage for departing guests 5hv; ask the staff on your floor. Utel phone in the lobby for international calls; reception staff sells cards (25-48hv). ❶

Hotel George (Готель Жорж), pl. Mitskevycha 1 (☎74 21 82 or 72 59 52; info@georgehotel.com.ua), in the square where pr. Svobody meets pr. Shevchenko. Rooms with bath are pricey, but the budget rooms are reasonable. Breakfast included. Singles 149-161hv, with bath 357-455hv; doubles 26-138hv/333-432hv. MC/V. ❸

Hotel Kyiv (Київ), vul. Horodotska 15 (Городоцка; ☎72 85 71). Entrance on vul. Furmanska, near the corner of vul. Horodotska. From the train station, take *marshrutka* #66 and ask to be let off at the hotel. A bargain for groups of 3-4, if you don't mind that the building is 101 years old and running water is limited (6am-9am and 6pm-9pm). All singles have baths and are nicer than the other rooms. Singles 75-78hv; doubles without bath 50hv, with bath 90hv; triples 60hv/105; quads without bath 80hv. ❶

FOOD

The main market is **Tsentralnyy Rynok** (Центральний; Central Market), called **Krakivskyy Rynok** (Краківський) by locals. (Open M-Sa 9am-6pm.) There are many 24hr. grocery stores. **Mini Market,** vul. Doroshenka 6 (☎72 35 44), is a block from the Grand Hotel. Lviv is also famous for its **Svitoch** confectionery, now a subsidiary of Kraft Foods. The main store is at pr. Svobody and vul. Tiktora. (☎72 76 84. Open M-F 9am-9pm, Sa 9am-8pm, Su 11am-6pm. MC/V.)

Smachna Plitka (Смачна Плітка), vul. Kurbasa 3 (Курбаса; ☎40 33 37), just off pr. Svobody, between vul. Tiktora and vul. Hnatyuka. A popular, inexpensive restaurant serving Ukrainian cuisine. Try the *pechenya* (печеня), a local meat specialty (13.30hv). Entrees 5-12hv. Coffee 2-4hv. Open daily 11am-11pm. ❶

Oselya, vul. Hnatyuka 11 (Оселя; ☎72 16 01). Authentic Ukrainian cuisine served by staff in traditional outfits. Try the vegetarian *borshct* (5.70hv). Entrees 7-70hv. Live folk music Sa-Su (and sometimes other nights) 7pm. Open daily 11am-11pm. MC/V. ❷

Cactus (Кактус), vul. O. Nyzhankivskoho 18 (Нижанківського; ☎74 50 61). Funky decor and a creative menu, which is available in English. The 3-course business lunch (M-F noon-3pm; soup, salad, and an entree) is a good deal (22hv). Try the "kangaroo dressed with figs and almonds" (120hv), or the "Ukrainian narcotic" (lard marinated in garlic; 7hv). Entrees 22-150hv. Open Su-Th 7am-11pm, F-Sa 7am-2am. MC/V. ❷

Kafe Kupol (Кафе Купол), vul. Chaykovskoho 37 (Чайковского; ☎74 42 54; kupollviv@ukr.net). From Hotel George walk down pr. Shevchenka, turn right on the 2nd street (across from the McDonald's) and continue to a hill; it will be on the left. Specializes in Polish cuisine. Located in the former home of a Polish poet. Free tours on request. Dine on the patio or in the 1920s-style dining room. Entrees 15-30hv. Open daily 11am-11pm. MC/V. ❷

☕ CAFES

▓ **Veronika** (Вероніка), pr. Shevchenko 21 (☎297 81 28). Famous for its delicious cakes (4.50-7hv per slice), pastries (2-3hv), and truffles (2.30hv). A menu is available in English, but most people choose from the tantalizing display case. Outdoor tables in summer. Coffee or tea 3-15hv. The iced coffee (7.50-9.50hv) is excellent. Pricey European restaurant downstairs (entrees 26-88hv). Open daily 10am-11pm. MC/V.

Italiyskyy Dvoryk (Італійський Дворик), pl. Rynok 6, in the courtyard of the building that houses the History Museum. Walk through the museum entrance to reach the cafe. Once privately owned by a wealthy 16th-century merchant, the building is now one of Lviv's most pleasant spots for coffee (3hv). The courtyard opens for spring and summer, and a classical violinist plays Sa-Su 3-5pm. In winter, the cafe moves to a room inside the building. Open M-F 10am-8pm, Sa-Su 10am-7pm; in winter closes 1hr. earlier.

Art-Cultural Center Dzhyha (Джига), vul. Virmenska 35 (Вірменська; ☎75 21 01; www.li.org.ua). Inside a free art gallery, this small cafe boats unique coffee concoctions with a touch of artistic pretense. Order a flaming coffee (3.50-5.20hv) and become the center of attention as the lights dim. Unique vodka cocktails (3hv). Bizarre "lard in chocolate" dish (4hv). English menu. Open daily 10am-10pm.

🏛 SIGHTS

The Old Town is full of churches, squares, and old buildings that show the influence of various nations that have shaped Lviv over the centuries. Most of the sights and museums are located in or near pl. Rynok. The best time to visit churches is 5-7pm, when the doors are open for services.

PLOSCHAD RYNOK. This historic market square lies in the heart of the city, surrounded by richly decorated merchants' homes dating from the 16th to 18th centuries. The **town hall** (ратуша; ratusha) is a 19th-century addition. For a wonderful view of the Old Town, climb the wooden staircase of the ▓**tower** in the middle of the square. (Ticket office is downstairs, to the left of the main entrance. ☎297 57 73. Open Tu-F 10am-5pm, Sa-Su 11am-7pm. 10hv, children 2.50hv, ask about student discounts.)

ARMENIAN CATHEDRAL. The cathedral was built by the Lviv's Armenian community in the 14th century. The complex has a convent, printing press, and cemetery. (Vul. Virmenska 7-9. Open M-F 9am-5pm.) If medieval Armenian inscriptions intrigue you, go see the collection at the Inner Courtyard. (1b vul. Lesa Ukrayinky.)

GOLDEN ROSE SYNAGOGUE. For centuries, Lviv was an important center of Jewish culture. Today, little remains of the synagogue, which was built in the late 16th century and destroyed by the Nazis in 1942. (Walk up vul. Staroyevreiska, or Old Jewish Road; it's on the left before the Arsenal Museum.) Call the tourist office to arrange a guided tour (50hv per hr.) of the city's Jewish heritage sites.

BOYM'S CHAPEL (КАПЛИЦЯ БОЇМІВ; KAPLYTSYA BOYIMIV). This small chapel was commissioned in the early 17th century by a rich Hungarian merchant, Gregory Boym, and contains the remains of 14 of his family members. The walls are covered with intricate sculptures. (Pl. Katedralna 1. ☎74 40 47 or 75 22 77. Open daily 11am-5pm; Nov.-Apr. call ahead. 2hv.)

OTHER OLD TOWN SIGHTS. The massive **Assumption Church** (Успенська Церква; Uspenska Tserkva) lies just up vul. Pidvalna (Підвальна); enter through the archway. Next to the church, **Kornyakt's Tower** (Башта Корнякта; Bashta Kornyakta) hoists a bell 60m above ground. The Baroque **Dominican Church** is on pl. Muzeyna

(Музейна); look for the high elliptical dome. The **Church of the Transfiguration** (Преображенська Церква; Preobrazhenska Tserkva), vul. Krakivska 21 (Краківська), has beautiful side altars.

HIGH CASTLE HILL (ВИСОКИЙ ЗАМОК; VYSOKYY ZAMOK). For a great workout and an even better view of the city, climb up High Castle Hill, the former site of the Galician king's palace. A Ukrainian flag and a cross, the two most potent symbols of Lviv in the age of Ukrainian independence, sit high atop the hill. *(Follow vul. Krivonosa (Кривоноса) from its intersection with Hotny and Halytskono. Go until you pass #39, then take a left down the dirt road and wind your way up around the hill counter-clockwise.)*

LICHAKIVSKY CEMETERY. Entering through the main gate of the cemetery (Личаківський Цвинтар; Lychakivskyy Tsvyntar) and follow the path to the right to visit the graves of famous Ukrainian artists. On the left, a hammer-armed Stakhanovite decorates the eternal bed of Ivan Franko (Іван Франко), poet, socialist activist, and celebrated national hero. *(Take tram #4 or 7 from the beginning of vul. Lichakivska (Личаківська), and get off at the 1st stop after the sharp right turn. ☎ 75 54 15. Open daily 9am-6pm. 3hv. English tours 40hv. Call 2 days in advance.)*

IVAN FRANKO PARK. Walk uphill through Ivan Franko Park (Парк ім. Ивана Франка; Park im. Ivana Franka) to **St. Yura's Cathedral** (Собор св. Юра; Sobor sv. Yura). The interior boasts an elaborate altar, while the equestrian dragon-slayer Yura (George) guards the outside entrance. *(Open daily 7am-1pm and 3-8pm.)* Toward the train off vul. Horodetska is **St. Elizabeth's Cathedral,** constructed the Poles who settled in Lviv. *(From pr. Svobody, head down Hnatyuka, then take a left on Sichovka Stritsiv to the park, which faces the columned facade of Lviv University.)*

▥ MUSEUMS

▨ OPEN-AIR MUSEUM OF FOLK ARCHITECTURE AND RURAL LIFE. This outdoor museum (Музей Народної Архітектури та Побуту у Львові; Muzey Narodnoi Arkhitektury ta Pobutu u Lvovi) at Shevchenkivskyy Hay (Шевченківський Гай) features a collection of wooden houses (скансен; skansen) from all around Western Ukraine. Don't miss the 18th-century wooden church. *(From vul. Doroshenka, take tram #2 or 7 to Mechnykova. Cross the street and follow vul. Krupyarska all the way up the hill, bearing right at the top. Tours ☎ 71 23 60. Open Tu-Su 10am-6pm. 1.50hv, children and students 0.75hv. English map with museum description 2hv.)*

▨ PHARMACY MUSEUM (АПТЕКА-МУЗЕЙ; АРТЕКА-MUZEY). This fascinating museum, located in one of Lviv's old pharmacies, shows the history of the pharmaceutical business. There are vials of chemicals, the earliest written prescriptions, and an old wine bar in the basement. Don't miss the spooky alchemist's room. A modern pharmacy is located in the front of the building. *(Vul. Drukarska 2. ☎ 72 00 41. Open Su-F 10am-5pm, Sa 10am-4pm; sometimes open later. 1hv, children 0.50hv.)*

HISTORY MUSEUM (ІСТОРИЧНИЙ МУЗЕЙ; ISTORYCHNYY MUZEY). A complex of three museums on pl. Rynok. The main building, at #6, has the King's Chambers (Короловські Зали; Korolivski Zaly), which house the treasures of the Italian *mascalzone* (rascals) who lived here in the 16th century. The building was the 17th-century home of Polish King Jan III Sobieski. It was here that the "eternal peace" of 1686 was signed. The agreement split Ukraine in two—the Western half went to the Polish empire and the Eastern to the Russian empire. The museum at #4 recounts the horrors of WWII and Soviet occupation. The museum at #24 traces the history of the region from Kyivan Rus to its incorporation into the Polish empire in 1686. *(Pl. Rynok #4, 6, and 24. ☎ 72 06 71. Open M-Tu and Th-Su 10am-5:30pm. English tours, 10-15hv, when guides are available. Each museum 3hv. Camera/video 10hv.)*

NATIONAL MUSEUM. This museum holds the world's most important collection of Ukrainian icons, most of which were created by village amateur artists. They are unique in that they are painted in the Orthodox style but depict Catholic subjects. The rotating art exhibit is worth a look. *(Vul. Drahomanova 42. ☎ 72 57 45. English tours 25hv. Open Tu, Th, Sa-Su 10am-6pm; W noon-8pm. 2hv, children 0.50hv.)*

ARSENAL MUSEUM. Housed in a stone fortress, this museum has a neatly presented collection of cannons, swords, daggers, guns and armor gathered from over 30 countries. Artifacts date from the 11th- to the 20th centuries. *(Vul. Pidvalna 5. ☎ 72 19 01. Open M-Tu, Th-Su 10am-5:30pm. 3hv; students, children, and seniors 1.50hv.)*

MUSEUM OF ETHNOGRAPHY AND CRAFTS. The three-floor museum (Музей Етнографиії та Художнього Промислу; Muzey Etnotrafyiyi ta Khudozhnoho Promyslu) displays tools, art, crafts, pottery, and weaving. *(Pr. Svobody 15. ☎ 72 78 08. Open W-Su 11am-5pm. 2hv, students 1hv. Camera 3hv, video 6hv.)*

🎵 ENTERTAINMENT

After lunch, Pr. Svobody fills with colorful characters singing tunes to accordion accompaniment. On summer evenings, the sounds of light jazz from sidewalk cafes permeates the avenue. Purchase tickets at the box offices (театральни касси; *tea*tralny kassy), pr. Svobody 37. (Open M-Sa 10am-1pm and 2-5pm.) Concerts, theater performances, and competitions are at various venues during the **Lviv City Days** (☎ 97 59 13), held around May 6. Easter is celebrated at the **Museum of Folk Architecture** (☎ 71 80 17) with folk and religious traditions and games for children. In September of even-numbered years, the **Golden Lion Theater Festival** takes to the streets with free performances by local and international troupes.

Theater of Opera and Ballet (Театр Опери Та Балету; Teatr Opery Ta Baletu), pr. Svobody 1 (☎ 72 88 60). Many of the world's foremost artists have patronized this beautiful theater, which still hosts several performances per week. Schedule posted in front of entrance. Ticket office open daily 11am-7pm, but often closed on days without shows.

Philarmonic (Філармонія, Filarmoniya), vul. Tchaikovskoho 7 (☎ 72 10 42), around the corner from Hotel George. Classical music performances by renowned guest performers. Ticket office open daily Sept.-May 11am-2pm and 3-6pm. 3-20hv, children's show 2hv.

Organ and Chamber Music (Будинок органної і камерної музики; Budynok ophannoi i kamernoi muzyky), S. Bandery 8 (Бандери; ☎ 39 88 42). Take tram #2 or 9 down S. Bandery to the Lviv Polytechnic stop. Concerts Sa-Su 5pm. Tickets (1hv) at the door.

🌙 NIGHTLIFE

Club-Cafe Lyalka (Клуб-Кафе Лялька), vul. Halytskoho 1 (Галицького; ☎ 298 08 09), below the Teatr Lyalok (Театр Лялок; Puppet Theater), in the basement. A young crowd fills this lively club, where locals jam to disco and live performances while surveying the decorative art installations; call ahead for schedule. Cheap food (2-20hv) and drinks (wine 4hv, beer 2-13hv). English menu. Cover 7-25hv. Open daily 1pm-7am.

Red Bull Dancing Club, vul. Ivana Franka 15 (☎ 296 51 51). Full of red bikes and trucks, Red Bull's emulation of the standard American club is unparalleled in Western Ukraine. Dancing every night 9pm-4am. Min. order 20-40hv., depending on night and gender. Check out the "war room" downstairs. Beer 3-14hv. Open 24hr.

Bar 1+1, pr. Shevchenka 11 (☎ 74 37 47), downstairs. A cozy, well-decorated bar with wood, stone, and stained glass. Heineken (6hv) on tap. Entrees 10-25hv. Open 24hr.

UZHGOROD (УЖГОРОД) ☎(80)312[2]

The calm border town of Uzhgorod (pop. 125,000) is located at the foot of the Carpathian Mountains along both banks of the Uzh River, only 1km from the Slovak Republic and 21km from Hungary. "Uzh" means "snake," and the river was named after its many (non-poisonous) reptiles. During the peaceful evenings, residents stroll along the river and central pedestrian thoroughfare sipping beer or Italian espresso. The charming town is best used as a base for trips into the nearby mountains, and several agencies in town arrange excursions.

When calling Uzhgorod from outside the city, the area code you should dial depends on the number. For 6-digit phone numbers, use the area code 80 312. For 5-digit numbers, use area code 80 3122.

☰ TRANSPORTATION. The **train station,** vul. Stantsiyna 9 (Станційна; ☎3 23 002) sends trains to Lviv (8hr., 2 per day, 23hv). Trains to **Kyiv** (12hr., 2 per day, 52hv), **Hungary,** and the **Slovak Republic** leave from the border hub of **Chop**; to get there, take a **marshrutka** (30min., every 15-30 min., 2hv) from behind the bus station. Buy train tickets at the **advance ticket office,** vul. Lva Tolstoho 33. (Льва Тольстого; ☎3 23 33. Open M-Sa 8am-1pm and 2-7pm, Su and holidays 8am-noon and 1-3pm.) The **bus station,** vul. Stantsiyna 2 (☎3 21 27), sends buses and *marshrutki* via **Mukachevo** (1hr., 2-4 per hr., 4hv) to **Budapest, HUN; Košice, SLK;** and **Prague, CZR. City buses** and *marshrutki* within the city cost 0.65hv. **Taxis** cost 5-6hv for rides within the city.

◼◪ ORIENTATION AND PRACTICAL INFORMATION. The town is split between the two sides of the **Uzh River.** The Old Town, which includes the castle and museum, and the bus and train stations are on one side of the river, while the broad vul. Lva Tolstoho runs on the other side. The bus and train stations are close together on the south side of town. To get to the center, follow **pr. Svobody** (Свободи) or take a *marshrutka* or taxi. For tourist information and brochures, visit the **Regional Office for Tourism and Resorts,** pl. Narodna 4 (Народна), on the sixth floor in room 612 or 610. The friendly staff has info about Uzhgorod and excursions in the Transcarpathian Region. The office runs the **English-language website www.transcarpathia.org,** which lists festivals, news, and events, and offers printable maps of the region. (☎61 28 39 or 61 28 17; turizm@uzhgorod.ukrsat.com. Open M-F 8am-5pm.)

Eximbank (Ексимбанк), in Hotel Uzhhorod, cashes **traveler's checks** for 1.5% commission. (☎3 58 62. Open daily 9am-1pm, 2-3pm, 3:30-7pm.) Its **branch,** pl. Petefi 19, provides the same services. (☎61 22 62. Open M-F 9am-1pm and 2-5pm). The lobby of Hotel Zakarpattya has an **ATM** and offers **currency exchange** and **Western Union** services. (☎61 23 57. Open M-F 9am-6pm, Sa-Su 10am-2pm.) **Store luggage** at the train station or at Hotel Zakarpattya (4hv per day). There is a **24hr. pharmacy,** pr. Svobody 40, near Hotel Zakarpattya. (☎2 56 02.) The telephone office, **Ukrtelekom** (Укртелеком) is in the same building as the post office. (☎61 37 65. Open 24hr.) **Utel** phones can be found inside Hotels Zakarpattya and Uzhgorod. **Internet access** is available at **Polyus** (Полюс), vul. Korzo 11 (Корзо), in the center of town, though you may have to wait for a computer. Enter the alley from the main street; it's through the door on the right. (☎61 64 52. 4hv. per hr. Open daily 7:30am-11pm.) The **post office** is at Pochtova pl. 3 (☎3 22 15. Open M-F 8am-1:30pm and 2:30-6pm, Su 8am-2pm). **Postal Code:** 88 000.

⚠🏠 ACCOMMODATIONS AND FOOD. The most pleasant place to stay is **Hotel Atlant ❷** (Атлант), pl. Koryatovycha 27 (Корятовича), in the Old Town. The hotel is best for couples: except for the one single (89hv), all rooms have private baths and only one bed. In any case, you won't be alone, as mosquitoes visit from the nearby river. The hotel staff provides Raid: unwrap the block of Raid, insert it into the colored bulb, and plug it into an outlet. Call ahead to reserve, especially for the single, as the small hotel fills up quickly. (☎61 40 95 or 61 49 88; www.hotel-atlant.com. 139-259hv.) Two Soviet-style hotels vie for second place. Both offer views of the far-off mountains from their east-facing upper rooms. The drawback of more conveniently located **Hotel Zakarpattya ❷** (Закарпаття), pl. Kyryla i Mefo-diya 5 (Кизила и Мефодшя), is limited hot water (daily 6-10am and 9pm-midnight). Check out the patriotic metal map of the USSR at the far left end of the lobby. Old-style phones and TVs. (☎9 75 10. Singles 90hv; doubles 120hv. Ask for discounts.) **Hotel Uzhgorod ❷**, pl. Bohdana Khmelnytskoho 2 (Богдана Хмельницького), provides more comforts, with fridges in every room and constant hot water, but is less central. (☎3 50 60. Singles 90hv; doubles 140hv.) There are several pizza joints in Old Town and a string of cafe-bars with outdoor seating along the river, on the right as you approach the pedestrian bridge.

The ▓**Atlant restaurant ❷**, on the first floor of Hotel Atlant, has good food and friendly service. Try the house special "appetizing meat Atlant" (12hv), a tantalizing meal of pork stuffed with cheese and mushrooms. (☎61 40 95. English menu. Entrees 3-14hv. Open daily 8am-11pm. MC/V.) At **Pizza Prima ❶**, pl. Koryatovycha 17 (Корятовича), try the *Primo*, which has salami and mushrooms. (All pizzas 10hv or 2.50hv. per ¼ pizza. Open daily 7am-8pm.) There is a large **market** on pl. Koryatovycha, near Hotel Atlant. The indoor hall has bread, vegetables, and meat; the space out back has drinks and non-edible items. (Open inside daily 6am-7pm, outside 5am-8pm.)

🏛🎭 SIGHTS AND FESTIVALS. The three main attractions are all conveniently located to the east of the city center. Take vul. Kapitulna (Капітульна) to its end, away from the intersection with vul. Voloshyna (Волошина). At the top of the hill is the 1644 twin-spired **Catholic Cathedral.** Farther down the hill, at vul. Kapitulna 33, the town's **15th-century castle** (замок; zamok) contains a quaint museum that showcases local musical instruments, including 2m mountain longhorns. (☎3 44 42. Open Tu-Su 10am-6pm. 3hv.) Next door, at vul. Kapitulna 33a, the open-air ▓**Transcarpathian Museum of Folk Architecture and Daily Life** (Закарпатський Музей Народної Архітектури та Побуту; Zakarpatskyy Muzey Narodnoyi Arkhitektury ta Pobutu) displays examples of houses from the region, with textiles and pottery inside. The museum features the **1777 St. Michael's Church,** a nail-less, wooden basilica. (☎3 73 92. Open M and W-Su 10am-6pm. 2hv, children 0.50hv.) Info booklets in English are available at the entrances of the three sites for 5hv each.

The Transcarpathian region is full of religious, musical, and cultural **festivals** held throughout the year, including January's **Dark Wine Festival,** May's **Blacksmith Festival,** June's **Sheep-pasturing Festival,** and September's **Local Sheep Cheese** (бринзи; brynzy) **Festival.** The festivals take place in Uzhgorod and in smaller towns in the mountains. Exact dates are released about a month in advance, so check at the tourist office or log onto their website, www.transcarpathia.org.

🪂 OUTDOOR ACTIVITIES. Zakarpatturyst (Закарпаттурист), vul. Koshytska 30 (Кошицька), in Turbaza Svitanok, runs 12 resorts throughout the region. They also organize hiking and sightseeing tours. (☎3 43 17; www.zaktur.karpat.org.

UKRAINE

Open M-F 8am-noon and 1-5pm.) **Turkul** (Туркул) organizes active tours, including **hiking** and **mountain biking.** Contact them at least two weeks in advance. (☎3 41 75; www.turkul.com.) **Busol Voyazh** (Бусоль Вояж), vul. Vysoka 8 (Висока), runs tours to the **Valley of the Narcissus** (blooms at the start of May), the **Salt Lake,** and various local **castles** (☎61 66 47). **Kameliya-Tur** (Камелія-Тур) has **horseback riding** and opportunities for experiencing traditional **peasant life.** (☎5 07 26.) For a short **day-trip** from Uzhgorod, visit the **Nevitskyy Castle,** 12km from town near Kamyanitsya village. Take *marshrutka* #115 from pl. Koryatovycha in the center of Uzhgorod and ask the driver to let you off near the castle. Cross the bridge and walk up the trail for 15min. The castle was built during medieval times and underwent several transformations before a Transylvanian prince destroyed it in 1644. It was restored in the 1970s and is a popular tourist attraction.

GATEWAY CITIES

BERLIN, GERMANY

Berlin is dizzying, electric, and dynamic—currently nearing the end of a transition from a reunited metropolis to the epicenter of the European Union. Everything in this city of 3.5 million is changing, from the demographics of the diverse population, to which *Bezirk* (neighborhood) has become the newest hotspot of nightlife and culture. Germany is the industrial leader of the continent, and when the Lehrter *Stadtbahnhof* (soon to be Europe's largest train station) opens in 2006, Berlin will essentially become its capital too. In 1999, 10 years after the fall of the Wall, the German government moved from Bonn to Berlin, throwing the new capital back into chaos. Amid the turmoil, spectacular and ambitious plans for the city's renovation are speeding toward completion.

TRANSPORTATION

Flights: The city is currently transitioning from 3 airports to 1 (Schönefeld), but until 2008, **Flughafen Tegel** will remain Western Berlin's main international airport. Take express bus X9 from Bahnhof Zoo, bus #109 from "Jakob-Kaiser-Pl." on U7, bus #128 from "Kurt-Schumacher-Pl." on U6, or bus TXL from Potsdamer Pl. **Flughafen Schönefeld** is used for intercontinental flights and travel to developing countries. The S9 or 45 to *Flughafen Berlin Schönefeld* (Schönefeld Express Train) runs every 30min. through most train stations, including Bahnhof Zoo and Ostbahnhof. **Flughafen Tempelhof**, Berlin's smallest airport, was slated to close in 2003 but remains open for flights within Europe. Take U6 to "Pl. der Luftbrücke."

Train Stations: During construction on the mega-station **Lehrter Hauptbahnhof**, trains (☎0180 599 66 33; www.bahn.de.) to and from Berlin will keep using **Zoologischer Garten** (usually called **Bahnhof Zoo**) in the West and **Ostbahnhof** in the East. Most trains go to both stations, but some connections to cities in former East Germany stop only at **Ostbahnhof**. Trains run every hour to: **Cologne** (4¼hr., €95); **Frankfurt** (4hr., €92); **Hamburg** (2½hr., €49); **Leipzig** (2hr., €33); **Munich** (6½-7hr., €111). 1 per 2hr. to: **Dresden** (2¼hr., €30); **Rostock** (2¾hr., €29). **International connections** to: **Amsterdam, NED** (6½hr.); **Brussels, BLG** (7½hr.); **Budapest, HUN** (12hr.); **Copenhagen, DEN** (7½hr.); **Kraków, POL** (8½-11hr.); **Moscow, RUS** (27-33hr.); **Paris, FRA** (9hr.); **Prague, CZR** (5hr.); **Rome, ITA** (17½-21hr.); **Stockholm, SWE** (13-16hr.); **Vienna, AUT** (9½hr.); **Warsaw, POL** (6hr.); **Zurich, SWI** (8½hr.).

Public Transportation: The **BVG** *(Berliner Verkehrsbetriebe)* includes **Straßenbahn** (streetcar or tram), **U-Bahn** (subway), and **S-Bahn** (surface rail). Buy tickets from vending machines, ticket windows, or on the bus. Berlin is divided into 3 transit zones: **Zone A** encompasses central Berlin, the rest of Berlin is in **Zone B**, and **Zone C** is the outlying

areas, including Potsdam. A single ticket *(Einzelfahrschein)* is good for 2hr. after validation. (Zones AB €2.20, BC €2.25, ABC €2.60.) A **Tageskarte** (AB €5.60, BC €5.70,
ABC €6) is good from the time of validation until 3am the next day. The **WelcomeCard**
(€19) is valid on all lines for 72hr. and includes discounts on tours and sites. Within
the validation period, the ticket may be used on any S-Bahn, U-Bahn, bus, or streetcar.
You must time-stamp your ticket as you board or risk a €40 fine.

Night Transport: U- and S-Bahn lines shut down 1-4am on weeknights (with final runs
around 12:15am), but **night buses** (with numbers preceded by the letter N) run every
20-30min. Pick up the *Nachtliniennetz* map at a *Fahrscheine und Mehr* office.

Taxis: (☎26 10 26 or 21 02 02.) Call at least 15min. in advance. Women may request
a female driver. Trips within the city cost up to €21.

▚ ORIENTATION

Berlin is a huge city, covering an area eight times the size of Paris. The former
West, including **Charlottenberg** and **Schöneberg**, is still the commercial heart of
united Berlin, though more businesses and embassies are moving to **Potsdamer
Platz** and **Mitte.** The former East contains the happening neighborhoods of Mitte,
Prenzlauer Berg, and **Friedrichshain.** Counter-culture **Kreuzberg** was part of West Ber-
lin, but falls geographically in the east.

▐ PRACTICAL INFORMATION

PHONE CODES:	Country code: ☎49. Berlin city code: ☎030 within Ger-many, 30 abroad. International dialing code: ☎00.

TOURIST AND FINANCIAL SERVICES

EurAide, in the Bahnhof Zoo *Reisezentrum,* sells rail tickets, maps, phone cards, and walking tour tickets, gives general help in English and German, and recommends hostels.
Open daily June-Oct. 8am-noon and 1-6pm, Nov.-May M-F 8am-noon and 1-4:45pm.

Europa-Center, entrance on Budapester Str. From Bahnhof Zoo, walk along Budapester
Str.; the office is on the right after about 2 blocks. The English-speaking staff answers
questions and reserves rooms for a €3 fee. Free lists of campgrounds and budget pensions and transit maps. City **maps** (€0.50). Open M-Sa 10am-7pm, Su 10am-6pm.

Embassies: Australia, Wallstr. 76-79 (☎880 08 80; www.australian-embassy.de). U2 to
"Märkisches Museum." Open M-F 8:30am-1pm and 2-5pm, F closes at 4:15pm. **Canada,** Friedrichstr. 95 (☎20 31 20; www.canada.de), on the 12th fl. of the Intl. Trade
Center. S1, 3 or U6 to "Friedrichstr." Open M-F 8:30am-12:30pm and 1:30-5pm. **Ireland,** Friedrichstr. 200 (☎22 07 20; www.botschaft-irland.de). U2 or 6 to "Stadtmitte."
Open M-F 9:30am-12:30pm and 2:30-4:45pm. **New Zealand,** Friedrichstr. 60 (☎20
62 10; www.nzembassy.com). U2 or U6 to "Stadtmitte." Open M-F 9am-1pm and 2-
5:30pm, F closes at 4:30pm. **UK,** Wilhelmstr. 70-71 (☎20 18 40; www.britische-
botschaft.de). S1-3, 5, 7, 9, 25, or 75, or U6 to "Friedrichstr." Open M-F 9am-4pm. **US
Citizens Service/US Consulate,** Clayallee 170 (☎832 92 33; fax 83 05 12 15). U1 to
"Oskar-Helene-Heim." Open M-F 8:30am-noon. Telephone advice available M-F 2-4pm;
after hours, call ☎830 50 for emergency advice.

Bank and ATM: Berliner Sparkasse and **Deutsche Bank** are everywhere and have MC/V
ATMs. Citibank has 23 branches in Berlin with 24hr. **ATMs,** including Tegel Airport.

American Express: Main Office, Bayreuther Str. 37-38 (☎21 47 62 92). U1, 2, or 15 to
"Wittenbergpl." Holds mail and offers banking services. No commission for cashing AmEx
travelers cheques. Expect out-the-door lines F-Sa. Open M-F 9am-7pm, Sa 10am-1pm.

Central Berlin

⛺ ACCOMMODATIONS
Circus, 4
Die Fabrik, 17
Honigmond, 1
Hotel-Pension München, 10
Lette'm Sleep Hostel, 3
Mitte's Backpacker Hostel, 2
Pension Knesebeck, 6

Die Feinbeckerei, 12
Schwarzes Café, 7

🎵 NIGHTLIFE
Astro-Bar, 5
Die Busche, 8
Freischwimmer, 18
Hafen, 11
Rose's, 13
SO36, 14
Tresor/Globus, 9

🍴 FOOD
Abendmahl, 16
Café V, 15

500 meters
500 yards
0

MITTE

TIERGARTEN

Tiergarten

River Spree
River Spree

Unter den Linden
Friedrichstr.
Wilhelmstr.

Reichstag
Soviet Army Memorial
Brandenburger Tor
PARISER PLATZ
POTSDAMER PLATZ

Berliner Dom
Marienkirche
Fernsehturm
ALEXANDER PLATZ
HACKESCHER MARKT
Pergamon Museum
Bode-museum
Alte Synagoge
Zeughaus
Humboldt Universität
Staatsoper
BEBEL PLATZ
GENDARMEN-MARKT
Haus am Checkpoint Charlie
former Berlin Wall
Martin-Gropius-Bau
Philharmonie
Neue Nationalgalerie
Kunstgewerbemuseum
Kongresshalle

ORANIENBURGER TOR
ORANIENBURGER STR.
FRIEDRICHSTR.
Bahnhof Friedrichstr.
LEHRTER STADTBAHNHOF
WEINMEISTER STR.
ROSA-LUXEMBURG-PL.
SPITTELMARKT
HAUSVOGTEIPL.
STADTMITTE
FRANZÖSISCHE STR.
MOHRENSTR.
KOCHSTR.
POTSDAMER PLATZ
MÄRK. MUS.

TO ÄGYPTISCHES MUSEUM (3.2km)
TO ZOOLOGISCHER GARTEN, KUDAMM

GATEWAY CITIES

EMERGENCY AND COMMUNICATIONS

Police ☎110. **Ambulance and Fire** ☎112.

Medical Assistance: The American and British embassies list English-speaking doctors. **Emergency doctor** (☎31 00 31); **Emergency dentist** (☎89 00 43 33). Both 24hr.

Internet Access: Netlounge, Auguststr. 89 (☎24 34 25 97). U-Bahn to Oranienburger Str. €1.50 per hr. Open noon-midnight. **Easy Everything** is at Karl-Marx-Str. 78, Kurfürstendamm 224, Schloßstr. 102, Sony Center, and Rathausstr. 5. **Wireless Internet** can be found throughout Berlin, sometimes for free.

Post Offices: Joachimstaler Str. 7 (☎88 70 86 11), down Joachimstaler Str. from Bahnhof Zoo. **Poste Restante** should be addressed: NAME, Postlagernde Briefe, Postamt in der Joachimstaler Str. 7, 10706 Berlin. Open M-Sa 8am-midnight, Su 10am-midnight.

BERLIN	❶	❷	❸	❹	❺
ACCOM.	under €12	€12-20	€21-30	€31-50	over €50
FOOD	under €4	€4-8	€9-12	€13-20	over €20

ACCOMMODATIONS

Same-day accommodations in Berlin aren't impossible to find, but advance reservations are recommended. During the Love Parade (which will be held mid-July 2005, if it finds funding), reserve at least two weeks in advance

HOSTELS

▨ **Mitte's Backpacker Hostel,** Chausseestr. 102 (☎2839 09 65). U6 to "Zinnowitzer Str." The apex of hostel hipness, Mitte's gregarious English-speaking staff and themed rooms make it the perfect place to end long days and wild nights. Kitchen and laundry available. Reception 24hr. Dorms €15-18; singles €20-30; doubles €40-60. ❷

▨ **Circus,** Rosa-Luxemburg-Str. 39-41 (☎28 39 14 33). U2 to "Rosa-Luxemburg-Pl." Staff gives nightlife info in English. Laundry available. Internet €0.60 per 10min. A 2nd **Circus,** at Rosenthaler Pl. on Weinbergersweg 1a, has similar facilities and prices, and rents bikes for €12 per day. Sheets €2. 24hr. reception and bar. 4- to 8-bed dorms €15-18; singles €32, with shower €45; doubles €48/€60; triples €60. ❷

Jugendgästehaus am Zoo, Hardenbergstr. 9a (☎312 94 10; www.jgh-zoo.de), opposite the Technical University Mensa. Bus #145 to Steinpl., or a short walk from *Bahnhof Zoo* down Hardenbergstr. Reception 9am-midnight. Check-in 10am. Check-out 9am. Lockout 10am-2pm. Dorms €20, under 27 €17; singles €28/25; doubles €47/44. ❷

Lette'm Sleep Hostel, Lettestr. 7 (☎44 73 36 23; www.backpackers.de). U2 to "Eberswalder Str." A street-level common room, laid back staff, and a big kitchen make this cozy hostel social. Free Internet access. Wheelchair accessible. Sheets €3. Dorms €15-16; doubles €48; triples €57. 10% off (15% in winter) for stays over 3 nights. ❷

Heart of Gold Hostel, Johannisstr. 11 (☎29 00 33 00; www.heartofgold-hostel.de). S1, 2, or 25 to Oranienburger Str. or U6 to Oranienburger Tor. Designed after *The Hitchhiker's Guide to the Galaxy.* Internet €0.50 per 10min. Breakfast €3. Laundry €3. 24hr. Reception and bar. 3- to 6-bed dorms €17-21; singles €24-28; doubles €48-56. ❷

Die Fabrik, Schlesische Str. 18 (☎611 71 16; www.diefabrik.com). U1 to "Schlesisches Tor." A classy former factory offers spacious rooms and easy access to nightlife. Reception 24hr. Dorms €18; singles €38; doubles €52-64; triples €69; quads €84. ❷

HOTELS

Pension Knesebeck, Knesebeckstr. 86 (☎312 72 55; fax 313 95 07). S3, 5, 7, or 9 to "Savignypl." Follow Kantstr. to Savignypl.; go clockwise around the green until Knesebeckstr. appears on your left. Friendly owners. Breakfast included. Laundry €4. Reception 24hr. Singles €35-45; doubles €55-72; quads and up €25-30 per person. ❸

Hotel-Pension München, Güntzelstr. 62 (☎857 91 20; www.hotel-pension-muenchen-in-berlin.de). U9: Güntzelstr. Charming rooms with cable TV and phones. Breakfast included. Singles €40, with bath €55; doubles with bath €70-80; triples €95; quads €105. ❹

Hotel Transit, Hagelberger Str. 53-54 (☎789 04 70; fax 78 90 47 77). U6 or 7, or night bus #N19 to Mehringdamm. Modern rooms with bath overlooking a courtyard in this friendly (and gay-friendly) hotel. Internet €6 per hr. Breakfast included. Reception 24hr. 3- to 6-bed dorms €15; singles €52; doubles €60; triples €78; quads €104. ❷

Honigmond, Tieckstr. 12 (☎284 45 50; www.honigmond-berlin.de). U6 to "Zinnowitzer Str." Old-style rooms with canopy beds. Reception 9am-6pm. Check-in 3pm-1am; call ahead if arriving after 8pm. Singles €49-89; doubles €69-89, with bath €89-119. ❺

FOOD

Döner Kebap—shaved roast lamb or chicken stuffed into a toasted flatbread and topped with vegetables and garlic sauce—has cornered Berlin's fast-food market, with falafel running a close second (both run €1.50-3). Schöneberg and Prenzlauer Berg are famous for their relaxed cafes and lengthy Sunday brunches.

▨ **Cafe Berio,** Maaßenstr. 7 (☎216 19 46). U1, 2, 4, or 15 to "Nollendorfpl." A Viennese cafe with a great breakfast menu (€3.50-8.50) and special business lunch (€4.50). Open daily 8am-1am. ❷

▨ **Die Feinbeckerei,** Vorbergstr. 2 (☎784 51 58). U7 to "Kleistpark." Swabian cuisine as unassuming and cost-effective as the restaurant's interior. The *Spätzle* (noodles) with cheese or herbs (€6.50) and the weekday lunch special (M-F noon-5pm, any entree €4.90) cannot be beat. Open daily noon-midnight. ❷

Damas Falafel, Goethestr. 4 (☎37 59 14 50). A vegetarian haven in a city of carnivores. The falafel (€2.50) and *makali* (mixed grilled vegetables, €3) are popular and tasty. Don't forget to load up on free *Zimttee* (cinnamon tea). Open daily 11am-10pm. ❶

Zab Thai Cuisine, Leibnizstr. 43 (☎324 35 16). Bus #149 or 349 from Zoologischer Garten to "Kantstr/Leibnizstr." or #145 to "Otto-Suhr-Allee/Leibnizstr." Scrumptious fruit cocktails (€4.50) and main courses (€12-20), served in a romantic setting with friendly service. Open M-F noon-3pm and 6pm-midnight, Sa 5pm-midnight. ❹

Mario Pasta Bar, Leibnizstr. 43 (☎324 35 16), in the same building as Zab (see above). No real menu—the cook helps guests decide what to eat. Handmade pasta (€6.50-7.50) and meat dishes (€10.50-11.50) rotate weekly. Open M-Sa noon-3pm, 6:30-11pm. ❸

Schwarzes Café, Kantstr. 148 (☎313 80 38). S3, 5, 7, 9, or 75 to "Savignypl." The ground floor bathrooms at this popular bohemian cafe must be seen to be believed. Breakfast (€6-8) served around the clock. Open 24hr.; closed Tu 3am-10am. ❸

Zur Henne, Leuschnerdamm 25 (☎614 77 30). U1 or 15 to "Kottbusser Tor." Other dishes are €2.50-6, but everyone orders the *Brathänchen* (fried chicken), arguably the best in Berlin. Always packed, so reserve a table in advance. Open Tu-Su 7pm-late. ❷

Café V, Lausitzer Pl. 12 (☎612 45 05). U1 or 15 to "Görlitzer Bahnhof." In Berlin's oldest vegetarian cafe, vegan and fish entrees are served in a romantic interior. Try spinach balls in cheese sauce (€8.80) or tasty specials (€6-8). Open daily 10am-late. ❸

Abendmahl, Muskauer Str. 9 (☎612 51 70; www.abendmahl-berlin.de). U1 or 15 to "Görlitzer Bahnhof." Vegetarian and fish entrees and fabulously macabre desserts—"Last Date" is coffin-shaped ice cream petit-fours (€8.50). Open daily from 6pm. ❹

☉ SIGHTS

Most of central Berlin's major sights are along the route of **bus #100,** which travels from Bahnhof Zoo to Prenzlauer Berg, passing the Siegessäule, Brandenburg Gate, Unter den Linden, the Berliner Dom, and Alexanderpl. along the way. Tickets for individual bus rides quickly add up, so consider investing in a day pass.

▩ **THE REICHSTAG.** Home to Germany's parliament, the Reichstag draws throngs of tourists, who spiral up the inside of the dome for views of Berlin. Recently, a glass dome, built around the upside-down solar cone that powers the building, was added to the top . *(☎ 22 73 21 52. Open daily 8am-midnight. Free. Last admission 10pm.)*

▩ **BRANDENBURGER TOR.** Friedrich Wilhelm II had this monumental arch built as an image of peace during the 18th century. While it once was the enduring symbol of the Cold War East-West division, today the Brandenburg gate is the most powerful emblem of a reunited Germany and Berlin.

▩ **EAST SIDE GALLERY.** The longest piece of the Wall, this 1.3km stretch of cement and asbestos slabs also serves as the world's largest open-air art gallery, unsupervised and open at all hours. The murals are the efforts of an international group of artists who gathered here in 1989 to celebrate the end of the city's division. It was expected that the wall would be destroyed soon after, but in 2000, with the wall still standing, many of the same artists repainted their work. Sadly, the paintings are once again being covered by graffiti. *(Along Mühlenstr. Take U1 or 15 or S3, 5, 6, 7, 9, or 75 to "Warschauer Str." or S5, 7, 9, or 75 to "Ostbahnhof" and walk to the river.)*

POTSDAMER PLATZ. After reunification, Potsdamer Pl. became the new commercial center of united Berlin, and quickly achieved infamy as the city's largest construction site. Today the cutting-edge, wildly ambitious architecture makes for spectacular sightseeing. The central complex of buildings overlooking Potsdamer Str., includes the towering **Deutsche Bahn headquarters,** the glossy ▩**Sony Center,** and an off-kilter glass recreation of Mt. Fuji. *(S1, 2, or 25 or U2 to "Potsdamer Pl.")*

SIEGESSÄULE. The slender 70m victory column, in the heart of the Tiergarten, commemorates Prussia's crushing victory over France in 1870. The statue at the top—the **goddess of victory**—is made of melted French cannons. In an obvious affront to the French, the Nazis moved the monument here in 1938 to increase its height and visibility. Climb the monument's 285 steps for a panorama of the city. *(Großer Stern. Take bus #100 or 187 to "Großer Stern" or S5, 7, or 9 to "Tiergarten" and walk 5min. down Straße des 17. Juni. ☎ 391 29 61. Open Apr.-Nov. M-F 9:30am-6:30pm, Sa-Su 9:30am-7pm; Nov.-Mar. M-F 10am-5pm, Sa-Su 10am-5:30pm. €2.20, students €1.50.)*

🏛 MUSEUMS

▩ **HAUS AM CHECKPOINT CHARLIE.** From its beginnings as a 2½-bedroom apartment, this eccentric museum at the famous border-crossing point has become one of Berlin's most popular attractions. The museum is a wonderfully cluttered morass of artwork, newspaper clippings, and photographs mixed in with all types of devices used to get over, under, or through the wall. *(Friedrichstr. 43-45. U6 to "Kochstr." ☎ 253 72 50; www.mauer-museum.com. Museum open daily 9am-10pm. German films every 2hr. from 9:30am. €9.50, students €5.50.)*

▩ **JÜDISCHES MUSEUM BERLIN.** Built from Daniel Libeskind's winning design, the zinc-plated museum is a fascinating architectural experience. None of the walls are parallel, and the jagged hallways end in windows overlooking "the void."

Wander through the labyrinthine "Garden of Exile" or experience the chill of being shut in the "Holocaust Tower," a giant concrete room virtually devoid of light and sound. Exhibits feature work by modern artists, Holocaust memorials, and a history of Jews in Germany. *(Lindenstr. 9-14. U6 to "Kochstr." or U1, 6, or 15 "Hallescher Tor."* ☎ *308 78 56 81; www.jmberlin.de. Open daily 10am-8pm, M until 10pm. €5, students €2.50.)*

■ **ÄGYPTISCHES MUSEUM.** This stern Neoclassical building holds a huge array of ancient Egyptian art, dramatically lit for the full Indiana Jones effect. The most popular item on display is the famous limestone bust of **Queen Nefertiti** (1340 BC) sculpted by Tuthmosis. The Sammlung Berggruen across the street has a huge collection of paintings by Picasso, Paul Klee, and French Impressionists. *(Schloßstr. 70.* ☎ *34 35 73 11. Open M-Su 10am-6pm. Audio guide included. €6, students €3; Th 2-6pm free.)*

■ **MUSEUMSINSEL: PERGAMONMUSEUM.** The "Museum Island" complex, one of the world's great ancient history museums, is named for Pergamon, the city in present-day Turkey from which the enormous **Altar of Zeus** (180 BC) was taken. The museum features gargantuan chunks of ancient Near Eastern history. The colossal blue **Ishtar Gate** of Babylon (575 BC) and the Roman **Market Gate of Miletus** are just two more massive pieces in an amazing collection. *(Bodestr. 1-3.* ☎ *20 90 55 77. Last entry 30min. before closing.)*

■ **KULTURFORUM: GEMÄLDEGALERIE.** Enormous collection of works by Italian, German, Dutch, and Flemish masters, including pieces by Dürer, Rembrandt, Rubens, Vermeer, Raphael, Titian, and Botticelli. For more modern art, visit the neighboring Kulturforum museums. *(Stauffenbergstr. 40.* ☎ *266 29 51.)*

♫ ENTERTAINMENT

■ **Berliner Philharmonisches Orchester,** Herbert Von Karajanstr. 1 (☎ 25 48 81 32; www.berlin-philharmonic.com). S1, 2, or 25 or U2 to "Potsdamer Pl." and walk up Potsdamer Str. It may look bizarre, but this yellow building, designed by Scharoun in 1963, is acoustically perfect. The *Berliner Philharmonike* is one of the world's finest. To get a seat, check 1hr. before shows or write in advance. Closed late June to early Sept. Box office open M-F 3-6pm, Sa-Su 11am-2pm. Tickets start at €7 for standing, €15 for seats.

■ **Deutsches Theater,** Schumannstr. 13a (☎ 28 44 12 25; www.deutsches-theater.berlin.net). U6 to "Friedrichstr." Go north on Friedrichstr., left on Reinhardtstr., and then right on Albrechtstr. Even residents of western Berlin will admit that this is the best theater in Germany. Tickets €4-42. Box office open M-Sa 11am-6:30pm, Su 3-6:30pm.

Deutsche Oper Berlin, Bismarckstr. 35 (tickets ☎ 343 84 01; www.deutscheoperberlin.de). U2 to "Deutsche Oper." Berlin's best and youngest opera. Box office open M-Sa 11am until 1hr. before performance, Su 10am-2pm. Evening tickets available 1hr. before performances. Closed July-Aug. Tickets €10-112. 25% student discounts.

◙ NIGHTLIFE

The best sources of information about bands and dance venues are the bi-weekly magazines *Tip* (€2.50) and the superior *Zitty* (€2.30), available at all newsstands, or the free and comprehensive *030*, distributed in hostels, cafes, and bars. In eastern Berlin, Kreuzberg's reputation as dance capital of Germany is challenged nightly as clubs sprout up in **Mitte, Prenzlauer Berg,** southern **Friedrichshain,** and near **Potsdamer Platz.** Prenzlauer Berg, originally the edgy alternative to the trendy Mitte repertoire, has become more expensive and established, especially around Kollwitzplatz and Kastanianallee. Still, areas around Schönhauser Allee and Danziger Str. keep the dream alive, such as the "LSD" zone of Lychener Str., Schlie-mannstr., and Dunckerstr. Friedrichshain, despite increasing gentrification, boasts edgier venues farther east, as well as a lively bar scene along Simon-Dach-Str. and Gabriel-Max-Str. Raging dance venues aimed at young Berlin are scattered between the car dealerships and empty lots of Mühlenstr. If at all possible, try to hit (or, if you're prone to claustrophobia, avoid) Berlin during the **Love Parade,** usually held in the third weekend of July, which draws over 750,000 techno-lovers from all over Europe.

■ **SO36,** Oranienstr. 190 (www.SO36.de). U1, 12, or 15 to "Görlitzer Bahnhof" or night bus #N29 to "Heinrichpl." Berlin's best mixed club, with a hip clientele. A massive dance floor packs in a friendly crowd for techno, hip-hop, and ska—often live. Last Sa of every month is gay night. Cover for parties €4-8, concerts €7-18. Open from 11pm.

■ **Freischwimmer,** vor dem Schlesischen Tor 2. U1 or 15 to "Schlesisches Tor" or night bus #N65 to "Heckmannufer." Patrons gather at waterside tables with roses, on sofas, or in boats. Food until midnight, F-Sa until 1am. F a roll of the die dictates cover (€1-6). M poetry reading then a party. Open M-F from noon, Sa-Su from 11am.

■ **Tresor/Globus,** Leipziger Str. 126a. U2 or S1, 2, or 25 or night bus N5, N29, or N52 to "Potsdamer Pl." One of the best techno venues in Berlin. Downstairs former bank vaults flicker in strobe light as ravers sweat to hard-core techno; upstairs the music is slower. Cover W €3, F €7, Sa €4. Open W and F-Sa 11pm-6am.

Astro-Bar, Simon-Dach-Str. 40 (www.astro-bar.de). The rough edges of this retro-space locale are obscured by plenty of 70s plastic robots. Back room with many mod things to sit on and many mod things sitting on them. DJs spin anything from R&B to reggae and loud electronica. Cocktails €4.50-5.50. Open daily from 6pm.

Insel der Jugend (Island of Youth), Alt-Treptow 6 (www.insel-berlin.com). S4, 6, 8, or 9 to "Treptower Park," then bus #265 or N65 to "Rathaus Treptow." The club, located on an island in the Spree River, is a tower of 3 winding stories crammed with gyrating bodies, multiple bars, river-side couches, an open-air movie theater, and a sweet little cafe. Depending on the night, the top 2 floors spin reggae, hip-hop, ska, and house (sometimes all at once), while the techno scene in the basement is generally as frantic as can be. Club cover Th-Sa €4-6. Club open W from 7pm, F-Sa from 10pm, sometimes Th from 9pm. Cafe open Sa-Su from 2pm. Movies M-Tu, Th, Su; €5-8.

▼ **GLBT NIGHTLIFE**

All of Nollendorfpl. is gay-friendly, but the main streets, including Goltzstr., Akazienstr., and Winterfeldtstr., have mixed bars and cafes, while the locally dubbed "Bermuda Triangle" of Motzstr., Fuggerstr., and Eisenacherstr. is more purely gay. *(U1, 2, 4 or 15 to "Nollendorfpl.")*

■ **Rose's,** Oranienstr. 187 (☎615 65 70). U1, 12, or 15 to "Görlitzer Bahnhof." Marked only by "Bar" over the door. A friendly, mixed clientele packs this claustrophobic party spot at all hours. The voluptuous dark-red interior is accessorized with hearts, glowing lips, furry ceilings, feathers, and glitter. Margaritas €4. Open daily 10pm-6am.

■ **Hafen,** Motzstr. 19 (www.hafen-berlin.de). U1, 2, 4, or 15 to "Nollendorfpl." All art was made by one of the owners, who take turns at the bar. Mostly male but not restricted. The pub quiz (at 10pm) is in English the first M of each month. Open daily 8pm-late.

Die Busche, Mühlenstr. 12. U1, 12, or 15, or S3, 5-7, 9, or 75 to "Warschauer Str." East Berlin's most famous disco in the DDR days is still a color-saturated haven of dance, spinning an incongruous rotation of techno, top 40, and German *Schlager* to a mixed crowd. Cover €3.50-5. Open W and F-Su from 10pm-5am, F-Sa until 6am.

VIENNA, AUSTRIA   ☎ 1/01

PHONE CODES	Country code: 43. **Vienna city code:** ☎ 01 within Austria, ☎ 011 43 1 abroad. **International dialing prefix:** 00.

Occupying a pivotal position between Eastern and Western Europe, Vienna is a living monument to nearly two millennia of rich history. From its humble origins as a Roman camp, to its Baroque glory days under the Hapsburg dynasty and the gas-lit "merry apocalypse" of its bohemian *fin-de-siecle* cafe culture, Vienna has rivaled Paris, London, and Berlin in cultural and political significance. Here, Freud grappled with the human psyche, Mozart found inspiration for his symphonies, and Maximilian I and Maria Theresia altered the shape of European politics. The darker ghosts of Austria's past still lurk in the Judenplatz, location of a WWII ghetto, but the Museums Quartier, an ultra-modern venue for the arts, proves that Vienna is a city still writing an evolving and dynamic brand of history.

◾ INTERCITY TRANSPORTATION

Flights: Wien-Schwechat Flughafen (VIE; ☎ 700 70). Serviced by **Austrian Airlines** (☎ 051 1789; www.aua.com). To reach the city center (18km), take S7 Flughafen/Wolfsthal, which stops at **Wien Mitte** (every 30min. 5am-10:40pm, €3), a short ride on U3 from downtown **Stephansplatz. Buses** connect the airport to the train stations (every 30min. 6:20am-12:20am; €6, round-trip €11).

Trains: Info ☎ 05 17 17; www.oebb.at. Vienna has 2 international train stations.

Westbahnhof, XV, Mariahilferstr. 132 (☎ 892 33 92). Trains run primarily **west. Info counter** open M-F 7:30am-9:20pm, Sa 7:30am-8:50pm, Su and holidays 8am-8:50pm. To: **Amsterdam, NED** (14hr., 8:28pm, €153); **Berlin, GER** (11hr., 9:28pm, €108); **Budapest, HUN** (3-4hr., 6 per day, €38); **Hamburg, GER** (9hr., 2 per day, €125); **Munich, GER** (4hr., 5 per day, €64); **Paris, FRA** (14hr., 8:34pm, €156); **Zurich, SWI** (9hr., 3 per day, €78).

Südbahnhof, X, Wiener Gürtel 1a. Trains run **south** and **east.** To: **Berlin, GER** (9hr., 10:34am, €88); **Bratislava, SLK** (1hr., 19 per day, €16); **Kraków, POL** (7-8hr., 4 per day, €46); **Prague, CZR** (4hr., 5 per day, €41); **Venice, ITA** (9-10hr., 2 per day, €72).

Buses: Terminals at Wien Mitte/Landstr., Hütteldorf, Heiligenstadt, Floridsdorf, Kagran, Erdberg, and Reumannpl. Ticket office open daily 7am-10pm. International bus info, call BundesBus (☎ 711 01).

◾ ORIENTATION

Vienna is divided into 23 **Districts** *(Bezirke)*. The first is the *Innenstadt* (city center), defined by the **Ringstraße** on three sides and the *Donaukanal* (Danube Canal) on the fourth. The Ringstraße (or "Ring") consists of many different segments, each with its own name, such as Opernring or Kärntner Ring. Districts II-IX spread out clockwise from the city center. The remaining districts expand from another ring, the **Gürtel** ("belt"). *Let's Go* includes district numbers for establishments in Roman numerals before the street address.

◾ LOCAL TRANSPORTATION

Public transportation: Info ☎ 790 91 00. The **subway** (U-Bahn), **tram** (Straßenbahn), **elevated train** (S-Bahn), and **bus** lines operate under one ticket system. A **single fare** (on board €2; from machine, ticket office, or kiosk €1.50) allows changes between forms of transportation, as long as your travel is uninterrupted. Punch ticket upon entering the first vehicle. Otherwise, inspectors may fine you €60. 24hr. pass €5, 3 days €12. Free travel with **Vienna Card** (3 days, €16.90). When daytime routes end, **Night-Line** buses run every 30min.; "N" signs designate night stops. (€1.50; passes invalid.)

Taxis: ☎313 00, ☎401 00, ☎601 60, or ☎814 00. Stands at Westbahnhof, Südbahnhof, Karlspl., and Bermuda Dreiecke.

Car Rental: Avis, I, Opernring 3-5 (☎587 62 41). Open M-F 7am-8pm, Sa 8am-2pm, Su 8am-1pm. **Hertz** (☎700 73 26 61), at the airport. Open M-F 7am-11pm, Sa 8am-8pm, Su 8am-11pm.

🛈 PRACTICAL INFORMATION

TOURIST AND FINANCIAL SERVICES

Tourist Office: I, Albertinapl. (☎21 11 40, www.info.wien.at), 1 block up Operng. from the Opera House. Dispenses brochures, including *Youth Scene,* and **free maps.** Books rooms, €3 fee plus 1-night deposit. Open 9am-7pm.

Embassies: Australia, IV, Mattiellistr. 2-4 (☎506 74); **Canada,** I, Laurenzerberg 2 (☎531 38 30 00); **Ireland,** I, Rotenturmstr. 16-18, 5th fl. (☎715 42 46); **New Zealand,** XIX, Karl-Tornay-G. 34 (☎318 85 05); **UK,** III, Jauresg. 10 (☎716 13 51 51); **US,** IX, Boltzmanng. 16 (☎313 39 0).

Currency Exchange: ATMs are your best bet. **Banks** and **airport exchanges** use the same official rate.

American Express: I, Kärntnerstr. 21-23 (☎515 40), near Stephanspl. Cashes AmEx and Thomas Cook traveler's checks for €7 commission and holds mail for 4 weeks. Open M-F 9am-5:30pm, Sa 9am-noon.

Laundromat: In most hostels. **Schnell und Sauber,** VII, Westbahnhofstr. 60 (☎524 64 60). Wash €4.50, dry €1 per 20min. Soap included. Open 24hr.

EMERGENCY AND COMMUNICATIONS

Police: ☎133. **Ambulance:** ☎144. **Fire:** ☎122. **Emergency:** ☎141.

Medical Assistance: Allgemeines Krankenhaus, IX, Währinger Gürtel 18-20 (☎404 00 0). Your embassy will help you find an English-speaking doctor.

24hr. Pharmacy: ☎15 50.

Internet Access: bigNET.internet.cafe, I, Kärntnerstr. 61 or I, Hoher Markt 8-9. €3.70 per 30min. **Cafe Stein,** IX, Wahringerstr. 6-8. €4 per 30min.

Post Offices: Hauptpostamt, I, Fleischmarkt 19. Open 24hr. Branches throughout the city; look for yellow signs with trumpet logo. Address **Poste Restante:** SURNAME, Firstname, *Postlagernde Briefe,* Hauptpostamt, Fleischmarkt 19, A-1010 Wien, AUSTRIA. **Postal codes:** 1st district A-1010, 2nd A-1020, 3rd A-1030, etc., to 23rd A-1230.

VIENNA	❶	❷	❸	❹	❺
ACCOM.	under €9	€9-15	€16-30	€31-70	over €70
FOOD	under €5	€5-10	€11-16	€17-25	over €25

🏠 ACCOMMODATIONS

Cheap rooms can be hard to find during peak season (June-Sept.); call five days ahead. Otherwise, call between 6 and 9am to put your name on a waiting list

Central Vienna

▲ ACCOMMODATIONS
Hostel Panda, 7
Hostel Ruthensteiner (HI), 10
Westend City Hostel, 9
Wombats City Hostel, 12

● FOOD
Nikala, 5
Sato Café-Restaurant, 11
Trzesniewski, 4

☕ CAFES & NIGHTLIFE
Café Central, 2
Das Möbel, 8
Demel, 3
Kleines Café, 6
Mapitom der Bierlokal, 1

GATEWAY CITIES

▨ **Hostel Ruthensteiner (HI),** XV, Robert-Hamerlingg. 24 (☎893 42 02). Exit *Westbahnhof*, turn right on Mariahilferstr., and continue until Haidmannsg. Turn left, then right on Robert-Hamerlingg. Knowledgeable staff, spotless rooms, and rose-filled courtyard. Internet €2 per 25min. Breakfast €2.50. 4-night max. stay. Reception 24hr. Dorms €11.50-13; singles, doubles, and triples €14-25. AmEx/MC/V. ❷

Wombats City Hostel, XIV, Grang. 6 (☎897 23 36). Exit Westbahnhof, turn right on Mariahilferstr., right on Rosinag., and left on Grang. Compensates for location with a pub. Internet €1 per 12min. Bike or skate rental €8-13 per day. Dorms €16-42. ❷

Westend City Hostel, VI, Fügerg. 3. Near Westbahnhof. Exit on Äussere Mariahilferstr., cross the large intersection, go right on Mullerg., and left on Fügerg. Comfy beds and ideal location. Internet €2.60 per 30min. Breakfast included. Reception 24hr. Checkout 10:30am. Dorms €16.80; singles €40.50; doubles €48.60. ❷

Hostel Panda, VII, Kaiserstr. 77 (☎522 25 55). U6: Burgg. Small, old-fashioned, *Jugendstil*, co-ed rooms. Kitchen and TV. Check-in by 11pm. Dorms €13. ❷

☐ FOOD

The restaurants near Kärntnerstr. can be expensive—cheaper areas are north of the university (U2: Schottentor) and near Naschmarkt (U4: Kettenbrückeg).

▨ **Nikala,** I, Grünangerg. 10. Off Singerstr. near Stephanspl. Sensual decor complements sumptuous crepes (€4-15). Try the *Himbeer* (raspberry) soda (€2). Open M-F 4pm-midnight, Sa-Su 11am-midnight. AmEx/MC/V. ❸

Trzesniewski, I, Dorotheerg. 1, 3 blocks down the Graben from Stephansdom. Has served petite open-faced sandwiches for over 80 years. Kafka's favorite place to eat. 6 sandwiches and mini-beer €6. Open M-F 8:30am-7:30pm, Sa 9am-5pm. ❷

Sato Café-Restaurant, XV, Mariahilferstr. 151 (☎897 54 97). U3: Westbahnhof. Family-run. Offers some of the best Turkish fare in the city. Veggie options available. Excellent breakfast omelettes €3-4. Entrees €5-9. English menu. Open daily 8am-midnight. ❶

☐ CAFES

For years Vienna's coffeehouses were havens for many of the world's most influential artists, writers, and thinkers. The original literary cafe was **Café Griensteidl,** but after it was demolished in 1897 the torch passed to **Café Central.** Today, only Café Central looks as it did in imperial times.

▨ **Kleines Café,** I, Franziskanerpl. 3, in the courtyard of the Franziskanerkirche. Turn off Kärntnerstr. onto Weihburg. Low, vaulted ceiling and a few tables in the courtyard. Salads (€6.50) are veritable works of art. Open daily 10am-2am.

Café Central, I (☎533 37 63 24), inside Palais Fers at the corner of Herreng. and Strauchg. Has surrendered to tourists because of its fame, but is definitely worth a visit. Occasional live music. Open M-Sa 8am-10pm, Su 10am-6pm. AmEx/MC/V.

Demel, I, Kohlmarkt 14 (☎535 17 17; www.demel.at), down Graben from the Stephansdom. Confectioner to the imperial court until the Empire dissolved. All chocolate made fresh every morning. Mirrored rooms, cream walls, and legendary desserts. Divine confections (*Mélange* €3). Don't miss the *crème-du-jour*. Also serves small sandwiches and antipasti. Open daily 10am-7pm. AmEx/MC/V.

☉ SIGHTS

Most of Vienna's sights are in District I, the city center. Pick up *Vienna from A to Z* (€3.60 with Vienna Card) and *Walks in Vienna* (free) at the tourist office.

STEPHANSDOM. St. Stephen's Cathedral is Vienna's most treasured symbol. Take the elevator up the North Tower or climb the 343 steps of the South Tower. Downstairs, skeletons of thousands of plague victims fill the **catacombs.** The **Gruft** (vault) stores all of the Hapsburg innards. *(U1 or U3: Stephanspl. Tours M-Sa 10:30am and 3pm, Su and holidays 3pm. €4. North Tower open daily July-Aug. 9am-6:30pm, Apr.-June and Sept.-Oct. 9am-6:30pm, €3.50. South Tower open M-Sa 6am-10pm, Su 7am-10pm. Free.)*

HOFBURG. A reminder of the Hapsburgs' 700-year reign, sprawling **Hofburg** was the family's winter residence. **In der Burg** includes the Imperial apartments and the Hapsburgs' collection of gold and silver. The **Alte Burg** contains a Gothic chapel and the Imperial jewels. The **Österreichische Nationalbibliothek** is housed in the **Neue Burg,** along with three branches of the Kunsthistorisches Museum (see p. 931). Attached to Hofburg is the **Stallburg** (Palace Stables, with the famous Lipizzaner Stallions); the **Augustinerkirche,** a 14th-century Gothic church; and the **Albertina,** a former Augustinian monastery now home to an impressive art collection. *(Tram #1 or 2 to Heldenpl., or enter from Michaelerpl. Each wing with its own prices; some are free.)*

SCHLOß SCHÖNBRUNN. This Rococo palace was Empress Maria Theresa's favorite residence. In the lavish **Great Gallery,** the Congress of Vienna danced the night away after a day of dividing up the continent, and six-year-old Mozart once performed in the **Hall of Mirrors.** Outside are the immense **Imperial Gardens,** which include the massive stone **Neptunbrunnen** (Neptune Fountain), a maze, a greenhouse and butterfly house, and a zoo. *(U4: Schönbrunn. www.schoenbrunn.at. Apartments open daily July-Aug. 8:30am-6pm; Apr.-June and Sept.-Oct. 8:30am-5pm; Nov.-Mar. 8:30am-4:30pm. Gardens open daily 6am-dusk. English audio guide free. Imperial tour €8, students €7.40. Grand tour €10.50/€8.60. Gardens free.)*

🏛 MUSEUMS

All museums run by the city are free Friday before noon (except on public holidays).

🖾 ÖSTERREICHISCHE GALERIE (AUSTRIAN GALLERY). In Schloß Belvedere, the collection is in two parts. The **Upper Belvedere** (built 1721-22) houses European art of the 19th and 20th centuries, including Klimt's masterpiece *The Kiss.* The **Lower Belvedere** contains the **Austrian Museum of Baroque Art** and the **Museum of Medieval Austrian Art.** *(III, Prinz-Eugen-Str. 27. Tram D: Schloß Belvedere, or tram #71: Unteres Belvedere. ☎ 79 55 71 34; www.belvedere.at. Open Tu-Su 10am-6pm. €7.50, students €5.)*

🖾 HAUS DER MUSIK. Near the Opera House, this new, interactive science-meets-music museum allows you to experience the physics of sound, learn about Viennese composers, and play with a neat invention called the Brain Opera. *(I, Seilerstatte 30. ☎516 48; www.hdm.at. Open daily 10am-10pm. €10, students €8.50.)*

KUNSTHISTORISCHES MUSEUM (MUSEUM OF FINE ARTS). The world's fourth-largest art collection, it has vast collections of 15th- to 18th-century Venetian and Flemish paintings. Also part of the complex are the **Hofjagd- und Rustkammer** (the world's second-largest arms and armor collection) and the **Sammlung alter Musikinstrumente,** which includes Beethoven's harpsichord and Mozart's piano. *(I, U2: Museumsquartier. ☎ 52 52 40; www.khm.at. Open Tu-Su 10am-6pm, Th 10am-9pm.)*

MUSEUMSQUARTIER. It includes **Leopold Museum** *(☎52 57 00; www.leopoldmuseum.org),* with the world's largest Schiele collection; **Kunsthalle Wien** *(☎521 89 33; www.kunsthallewien.at),* with themed exhibits of international contemporary artists; and **Museum Moderner Kunst** *(Museum of Modern Art; ☎525 00; www.mumok.at),* which holds a large collection of modern art in a brand-new building made from lava. *(U2: Museumsquartier, or U2/U3 or tram 1, 2, D, or J: Volkstheater. ☎523 58 51; www.mqw.at.)*

HISTORISCHES MUSEUM DER STADT WIEN (VIENNA HISTORICAL MUSEUM).
This collection of historical artifacts and paintings documents Vienna's history, from the Roman era through 640 years of Hapsburg rule. *(IV, Karlspl. ☎ 50 58 74 70; www.museum.vienna.at. Open Tu-Su 9am-6pm. €4.50, students €2. Su free.)*

Staatsoper, I, Opernring 2 (www.wiener-staatsoper.at). Vienna's premiere opera performs nearly every night Sept.-June. 500 standing-room tickets available for each performance (€2-3.50), but plan on getting there 2hr. early. Box office around the corner sells advance tickets (€5-254). Open M-F 8am-6pm, Sa-Su 9am-noon.

Wiener Philharmoniker (Vienna Philharmonic Orchestra) plays in the **Musikverein,** Austria's best concert hall. Visit box office well in advance, even for standing-room tickets. (Bösendorferstr. 12, www.wienerphilharmoniker.at).

Wiener Sängerknaben (Vienna Boys' Choir) sings during mass every Su 9:15am (mid-Sept. to late June) in the Hofburgkapelle (U3: Herreng.). Standing room free; arrive by 8am.

Vienna is magical during Christmas. **Christmas markets** *(Christkindlmärkte)* open around the city, including the **Rathausplatz Christkindlmarkt** (open daily 9am-9pm) and **Schloß Schönbrunn's** *Weihnachtsmarkt* (open M-F noon-8pm, Sa-Su 10am-8pm). February brings **Fasching** (Carnival season), weeks of Viennese balls, as well as a **parade.** The **Vienna Festival** (mid-May to mid-June) features plays and concerts. (☎ 58 92 20; www.festwochen.or.at.) The **Danube Island Festival** comes in late June along the Donauinsel. July and August see the **Wiener Film Festival,** with showings in front of the Neues Rathaus. The first weekend of July is the **Regenbogenparade,** a predominantly gay and lesbian celebration of free love.

■ NIGHTLIFE

Popular party areas include the **Bermuda Dreieck** (Bermuda Triangle) near Schwedenpl., the streets off Burgg. and Stiftg. in District VII, the university quarter (XIII and IX), and the **Donauinsel** along the Danube. Vienna's kinetic club scene rages all week, especially once the bars close—don't arrive before 11pm. For the scoop on raves, concerts, and parties, pick up a copy of the indispensable **Falter** (€2). Make sure to bring a copy of the **Nightline** bus schedule to get back to your hostel.

☒ Das Möbel, VII, Burgg. 10 (☎524 94 97; www.dasmoebel.at). U2/U3: Volkstheater. Cafe functions as a showcase for furniture designers. Metal couches, car-seat chairs, and Swiss-army tables rotate every 6 weeks and are well used (and purchased) by an artsy crowd. *Mélange* €2.25. Open M-F noon-1am, Sa-Su 10am-1am.

Mapitom der Bierlokal, I, Seitenstetteng. 1 (☎535 43 13). Located right in the center of the Bermuda Triangle, this cozy bar has large tables with candles. Beer on tap (0.3L €2.40, 1.5L €9.20). A great place to chat after work on F nights. Open daily 5pm-3am, F-Sa 5pm-4am.

HELSINKI, FINLAND   ☎ 09

PHONE CODES	Country code: **358.** International dialing prefix: **00.**

With all the appeal of a big city but none of the grime, Helsinki's (pop. 560,000) broad avenues, grand architecture, and green parks make it a model of successful urban planning. The city distinguishes itself with a decidedly multicultural flair: Lutheran and Russian Orthodox cathedrals stand almost face-to-face, and youthful energy mingles with old-world charm. Baltic Sea fish fill the marketplaces and restaurants, while St. Petersburg and Tallinn are only a short cruise away.

VISAS. EU citizens do not require visas to visit, study, or work in Finland. Citizens of Australia, Canada, New Zealand, and the US can visit for up to 90 days without a visa, although the 90-day period begins upon entering any of the 20 countries in the EU's **freedom of movement zone.**

⬛ TRANSPORTATION

Flights: Helsinki-Vantaa Airport (HEL; ☎020 01 46 36). **Buses** #615 and 617 run between the airport and the train station (35min., every 20min. 5:20am-12:20am, €3). A **Finnair bus** (☎0600 14 01 40; www.finnair.com) runs between the airport and the Finnair building next to the train station (35min., every 15min. 5am-midnight, €5).

Trains: ☎030 072 09 00. Reserve ahead for all long-distance routes. To **Moscow** (14hr., daily 5:40pm, €85) and **St. Petersburg** (5hr., 2 per day, €50).

Buses: ☎020 040 00. The station is between Salomonk. and Simonk.; from the train station, take Postik. past the statue of Mannerheim. Cross Mannerheimintie onto Salomonk. and the station is on the left.

Ferries: Viking Line, Mannerheimintie 14 (☎12 35 77), sails to **Stockholm** (16hr., daily 5:30pm, from €40). Take tram #2 or bus #13 to Katajanokka terminal. **Tallink,** Erottajank. 19 (☎22 83 11), sails to **Tallinn** (3¼hr., 2-3 per day, from €20). Take bus #15 to West terminal.

Local Transportation: ☎010 01 11; www.ytv.fi. **Buses, trams,** and the **metro** run 5:30am-11pm; major bus and tram lines, including tram #3T, run until 1:30am. There is 1 metro line (running approximately east-west), 10 tram lines, and many more bus lines. **Night buses,** marked with an "N," run after 1:30am. A single-fare ticket on the tram without transfers is €1.80. Single-fare tickets with 1hr. of transfers to buses, trams, and the metro are €2. The **City Transport Office** is in the Rautatientori metro station, below the train station. (Open summer M-Th 7:30am-6pm, F 7:30am-4pm, Sa 10am-3pm; low season M-Th 7:30am-7pm, F 7:30am-5pm, Sa 10am-3pm). The office sells the **tourist ticket,** a good investment for unlimited bus, tram, metro, and local trains during the period of validity. (1-day €5.40, 3-day €10.80, 5-day €16.20.)

⬛⬛ ORIENTATION AND PRACTICAL INFORMATION

Sea surrounds Helsinki on the south, east, and west, and the city center is bordered on the north by two lakes. Water shapes everything in the Finnish capital, from relaxing city beaches to gorgeous lakeside parks. Helsinki's main street, **Mannerheimintie,** passes between the bus and train stations on its way south to the city center, eventually crossing **Esplanadi.** This tree-lined promenade leads east to **Kauppatori** (Market Square) and the beautiful South Harbor. Both Finnish and Swedish are used on all street signs and maps; *Let's Go* uses the Finnish names.

Tourist Offices: City Tourist Office, Pohjoisesplanadi 19 (☎169 37 57; www.hel.fi/tourism). From the train station, walk 2 blocks down Keskusk. and turn left on Pohjoisesplanadi; from the ferry terminals, head left on Pohjoisesplanadi. Open May-Sept. M-F 9am-8pm, Sa-Su 9am-6pm; Oct.-Apr. M-F 9am-6pm, Sa-Su 10am-4pm. The **Finnish Tourist Board,** Eteläesplanadi 4 (☎41 76 93 00; www.mek.fi), has info covering all of Finland. Open May-Sept. M-F 9am-5pm, Sa-Su 11am-3pm; Oct.-Apr. M-F 9am-5pm.

Embassies: Canada, Pohjoisesplanadi 25B (☎22 80 30; www.canada.fi). Open M-F 8:30am-noon and 1-4:30pm. **Ireland,** Erottajank. 7A (☎64 60 06). Open M-F 9am-5pm. **UK,** Itäinen Puistotie 17 (☎22 86 51 00; www.ukembassy.fi). Also handles diplomatic matters for **Australians** and **New Zealanders.** Open M-F 8:30am-5pm. **US,** Itäinen Puistotie 14A (☎61 62 50; www.usembassy.fi). Open M-F 8:30am-5pm.

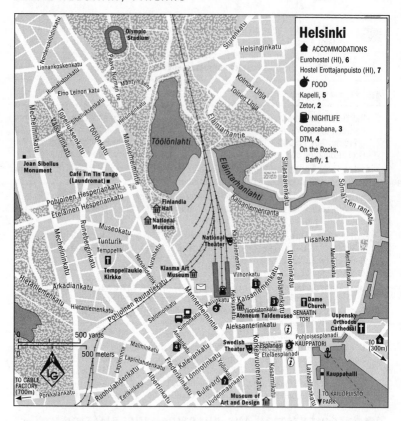

Helsinki

⚓ ACCOMMODATIONS
Eurohostel (HI), **6**
Hostel Erottajanpuisto (HI), **7**

🍎 FOOD
Kapelli, **5**
Zetor, **2**

🍷 NIGHTLIFE
Copacabana, **3**
DTM, **4**
On the Rocks,
Barfly, **1**

Currency Exchange: Forex has 5 locations and the best rates in the city. Hours vary; the branch in the train station is open daily 8am-9pm.

Laundromat: 🧺**Café Tin Tin Tango** (☎27 09 09 72), Töölöntorink. 7, has a bar, cafe, laundromat, and sauna. Laundry €3.50. Sandwiches €4.50-5.50. Sauna €20. Open M-F 7am-2am, Sa-Su 10am-2am. MC/V.

Emergency: ☎112. **Police** ☎100 22.

Pharmacy: Yliopiston Apteekki, Mannerheimintie 96 (☎41 78 03 00). Open 24hr.

Medical Assistance: 24hr. **hotline** (☎100 23). 24hr. medical clinic **Mehilainen,** Runebergink. 47A (☎010 414 44 44).

Internet Access: Cable Book Library, Mannerheimintie 22-24, in the mall across from the bus station. Free 30min. slots. Open M-Th 10am-8pm, Sa-Su noon-6pm.

Post Office: Mannerheiminaukio 1A (☎98 00 71 00). Open M-F 9am-6pm. Address mail to be held in the following format: First name SURNAME, *Poste Restante,* Mannerheiminaukio 1A, 00100 Helsinki, Finland. Open M-F 9am-6pm.

HELSINKI	❶	❷	❸	❹	❺
ACCOM.	under €10	€11-20	€21-45	€46-70	over €70
FOOD	under €8	€8-15	€16-20	€21-30	over €30

ACCOMMODATIONS

Helsinki's hotels tend to be expensive, but budget hostels are often quite nice. In June and July, it's wise to make reservations a few weeks in advance.

Hostel Erottanjanpuisto (HI), Uudenmaank. 9 (☎64 21 69). Head right from the train station, turn left on Mannerheimintie, bear right onto Erottajank., and turn right on Uudenmaank. Friendly staff tends well-kept rooms in a beautiful 19th-century building in the heart of the city. Internet €1 per 10min. Breakfast €5. Kitchen available. Lockers €1. Reception 24hr. In summer, dorms €20; singles €44; doubles €58. Low season singles €42; doubles €56. Non-members add €2.50. AmEx/MC/V. ❷

Eurohostel (HI), Linnank. 9, Katajanokka (☎622 04 70; www.eurohostel.fi). 200m from the ferry terminal. From the train station, head right to Mannerheimintie and take tram #2 or 4 to Katajanokka. From Uspensky Cathedral, head down Kanavank., turn left on Pikku Satamank. (not the same as Satamank.), and then bear right on Linnank. Bright rooms, a cafe, and a sauna with great views of the harbor. Internet €1 per 10min. Breakfast €5. Kitchen and sauna available. Sheets included. Reception 24hr. Dorms €20; singles €34. Non-members add €2.50. MC/V. ❷

Stadion Hostel (HI), Pohj. Stadiontie 3B (☎49 60 71). Take tram #7A or 3 to Auroran Sairaala. Walk down Pohj. Stadiontie toward the white tower for 250m, following the signs. The hostel, on the far side of the Olympic stadium, looks like a minimalist high-school locker room and brims with social life. Breakfast and sheets €5.50. Kitchen available. Internet €1 for 15min. Lockers €1. Laundry €2.50. Lockout noon-4pm. Reception June to early Sept. 7am-3am; mid-Sept. to May 8-10am and 4pm-2am. Dorms €13; singles €25; doubles €36. Non-members add €2.50. AmEx/MC/V. ❷

FOOD

Restaurants and cafes are easy to find on **Esplanadi** and the streets branching off from **Mannerheimintie** and **Uudenmaankatu.** A large **supermarket** is under the train station. (Open M-F 7:30am-10pm, Sa 9am-10pm, Su 10am-10pm.) Get lunch at the open-air market of **Kauppatori,** by the harbor, where stalls sell a variety of fried fish and farm-fresh produce; it's not hard to assemble a satisfying meal for €6-8. (Open June-Aug. M-Sa 6:30am-5pm, Sept.-May M-F 7am-2pm.)

Zetor, Kaivok. 10 (☎66 69 66), in Kaivopiha, the mall opposite the train station. The dishes' names are cheeky and the farm-inspired decor is cheekier, but the authentic Finnish fare is absolutely delicious. Homemade beer €4. Entrees €9-16. After 9pm 22+. Open Su-M 3pm-1am, Tu-Th 3pm-3am, F 3pm-4am, Sa 1pm-4am. ❷

Kapeli, Eteläesplanadi 1 (☎681 24 40), at the Unionk. end of Esplanadi park. Frequented by well-heeled Bohemians since 1837, this lovely outdoor cafe serves salads and sandwiches (€6-9); head inside to the left. The restaurant to the right is pricier. Open daily 9am-2am; kitchen closes at 1am. AmEx/MC/V. ❶

Zucchini, Fabianink. 4 (☎622 29 07), just south of the tourist office. A casual vegetarian restaurant featuring organic produce as well as vegan and gluten-free options. Daily lunch specials €8, with soup €9. Open Aug.-June M-F 11am-4pm. MC/V. ❶

SIGHTS

Most of Helsinki's major sights are packed into the compact center of the city, making it ideal for walking tours; pick up *See Helsinki on Foot* from the tourist office for suggested routes. Trams #3T and 3B loop around the major sights in roughly 1hr., providing a cheap alternative to sightseeing buses.

GATEWAY CITIES

■**SUOMENLINNA.** Five beautiful, interconnected islands are home to this 18th-century military fortification, erected for fear of a Russian invasion. The old fortress's dark passageways are great to explore, while the **Suomenlinna Museum** and **Coastal Artillery Museum** add historical perspective. Sunbathers and swimmers take to the smooth rocks on the southern island. *(Website www.suomenlinna.fi. Museums open daily May-Aug. 10am-6pm; Apr. and Sept. 11am-4pm; Mar. Sa-Su 11am-4pm. €5.50, students €2.50. Ferries depart from Market Sq. every 20min. 8am-11pm, round-trip €3.60.)*

SENAATIN TORI (SENATE SQUARE). The square and its gleaming white **Tuomiokirkko** (Dome Church) exemplify the splendor of Finland's 19th-century Russian period. *(At Aleksanterink. and Unionink. in the city center. Church open June-Aug. M-Sa 9am-midnight, Su noon-midnight; Sept.-May M-Sa 9am-6pm, Su noon-6pm.)* On a dramatic hill to the east, the onion domes of the red-brick **Uspenskinkatedraadi** (Uspensky Orthodox Cathedral) cap the largest Orthodox church in Western Europe. *(Open M and W-Sa 9:30am-4pm, Tu 9:30am-6pm, Su 9:30am-3pm.)*

ESPLANADI AND MANNERHEIMINTIE. A lush boulevard spangled by statues and fountains, Esplanadi is an ideal place to stroll or people-watch on a sunny day. At the western end, turn right onto Mannerheimintie and right again onto Kaivok. past the train station to reach the **Ateneum Taidemuseo,** Finland's largest art museum, with comprehensive exhibitions of Finnish art since the 1700s. Don't miss Aksel Gallen-Kallela's work illustrating episodes from the Kalevala. *(☎17 33 64 01; www.ateneum.fi. Kaivok. 2, opposite the train station. Open Tu and F 9am-6pm, W-Th 9am-8pm, Sa-Su 11am-5pm. €5.50, during temporary exhibits €7.50.)* Continue on Mannerheimintie past the post office to ■**Kiasma,** a stark, silvery warehouse that houses top-flight modern art and calibrates the width of its doors to Fibonacci's golden ratio. The cafe and surrounding lawn are popular hangouts for artsy 20-somethings. *(☎17 33 65 01; www.kiasma.fi. Mannerheiminaukio 2. Open Tu 9am-5pm, W-Su 10am-8:30pm. €5.50, students €4.)* Backtrack toward the post office, turn right onto Arkadiank. and right again onto Fredrikink. to reach the stunning **Temppeliaukio Church.** Hewn out of a hill of rock with only the roof visible from the outside, the huge domed ceiling inside appears to be supported only by rays of sunshine. *(Lutherink. 3. Usually open M-F 10am-8pm, Sa 10am-6pm, Su noon-1:45pm and 3:15-5:45pm. English services Su 2pm.)*

🎵 📷 ENTERTAINMENT AND NIGHTLIFE

Helsinki's parks are always animated; jazz fills the **Esplanadi** park all summer Monday through Thursday at 4:30pm (www.kulttuuri.hel.fi/espanlava), while concerts rock **Kaivopuisto** (on the corner of Puistok. and Ehrenstromintie, in the southern part of town) and **Hietaniemi Beach** (down Hesperiank. on the western shore). The free English-language papers *Helsinki This Week, Helsinki Happens,* and *City* list popular cafes, bars, nightclubs, and events; pick up copies at the tourist office.

Bars and beer terraces start filling up in the late afternoon; most clubs don't get going until midnight and stay hopping until 4am. With the exception of licensed restaurants and bars, only the state-run liquor store **Alko** can sell alcohol more potent than light beer. (Branch at Mannerheimintie 1, in Kaivopiha across from the train station. Open M-F 9am-8pm, Sa 9am-6pm.) Bars and clubs, ranging from laid-back neighborhood pubs to sleek discos, line **Mannerheimintie, Uudenmaankatu,** and **Iso Roobertinkatu.** One of the hottest spots in town is **DTM (Don't Tell Mama),** Iso Roobertink. 28, a huge, popular gay club that draws a mixed crowd to foam parties and drag bingo. *(☎67 63 14; www.dtm.fi. After 11pm 22+. F-Sa cover €6-8. Open M-Sa 9am-4am, Su noon-4am.)* On Mikonk. across from the station, the edgy bar **On the Rocks** (23+, cover €6-7, open 8pm-4am) and chic club **Barfly** (F-Sa cover €7, open daily 8pm-4am) share a broad terrace. Nearby **Copacabana**, Yliopistonk. 5, has salsa dancing each Sunday. (☎278 18 55. F-Sa cover €8-10. Open daily 8pm-4am.) A student crowd gathers at **Vanha**, Mannerheimintie 3, in the historic Old Students' House, which features club nights every other weekend. (☎13 11 43 46. F-Sa cover €2-4. Beer €4-5. Open M-Th 11am-1am, F 11am-2am, Sa 11am-4am.) **Mother Bar**, Eerikink. 2, is a relaxed lounge with techno. (☎612 39 90; www.mother.to. Open M-Th 11:30am-midnight, F-Sa 2pm-3am.)

BEIJING, CHINA ☎(0)10

Beijing is a city built for giants. From the gargantuan boulevards to the sprawling Forbidden City, everything seems to aspire to greatness. As China's political, economic, and cultural nucleus for nearly 700 years, Beijing is the hope, future, future hope, and hopeful future of China. Whether the nation's capital is your first or last stop on a Trans-Siberian itinerary, take a moment to enjoy Beijing, the enigmatic gateway to the people's Republic of China.

VISAS Visas are required of all travelers to China. Those arriving on the Trans-Siberian railroad should get a visa from the Chinese embassy in **Moscow** (p. 670) before their departure.

YUAN		
AUS$1 = Y6.00		Y10 = AUS$1.66
CDN$1 = Y6.38		Y10 = CDN$1.57
EUR€1 = Y10.24		Y10 = EUR€0.98
NZ$1 = Y5.56		Y10 = NZ$1.80
UK£1 = Y15.17		Y10 = UK£0.66
US$1 = Y8.26		Y10 = US$1.21

PHONE CODE	**Country code: 86. International dialing prefix: 00.**

▐ TRANSPORTATION

Flights: Capital Airport (☎962 580), 1hr. outside the city by taxi (at least Y80-100, tolls Y15). **Civil Aviation Administration of China (CAAC;** zhōngguó mínháng) in the Aviation Bldg., 15 Xi Chang'an Dajie (every 30min. 5am-8pm) or at the **Beijing International Hotel,** near the main train station (every 30min. 6:30am-6:30pm). Travelers flying internationally must pay Y90 departure tax; domestic flights Y50.

Trains: Foreigners enter and exit through the **Beijing Main Station** (bēijīng huôchē zhàn; ☎6512 8931 or 6232 0025) or **Beijing West Station** (bēijīng xī zhàn; ☎6321 6253), on Lianhuachi Dong Lu near Lianhuachi Park (accessible by buses #5, 48, 52, 320, and 845). Beijing is the endpoint of the Trans-Manchurian and Trans-Mongolian branches of the Russian Trans-Siberian Railroad. For ticket and route info, see p. 740. Beijing is 7hr. ahead of Moscow (GMT+8).

▐ ORIENTATION

Beijing is vast. Everything in Beijing is far away from everything else, and most of the budget accommodations are littered around the city's perimeters. But for all its size, Beijing is surprisingly symmetrical, with **five ring roads** radiating out from the city's geographic center of **Tiananmen Square** and the **Forbidden City.** They are on either side of **Changan Jie,** the main downtown east-west thoroughfare. **Dazhalan** and **Wangfujing,** southwest and northeast of Tiananmen Square, respectively, are full of shopping options. To the northeast is **Gongren Tiyuchang Bei Lu,** commonly known as Gongti Bei Lu, which leads to **Sanlitun,** one of the city's embassy compounds. Many older neighborhoods and *hutongs* (Beijing alleyways) are preserved in the Drum Tower and Lama Temple sectors to the north. Beijing and **Qinghua Universities,** the **Summer Palace,** and the **Old Summer Palace** are in the far northwest, just beyond the fourth ring road in the northern district of **Haidian.**

🔢 PRACTICAL INFORMATION

Travel Agencies: There is a **tourist information service** in Beijing (☎6513 0828), but no actual tourist bureau. **China International Travel Service (CITS)** 9 Jianguomennei Nei Dajie, in the west lobby of the Beijing International Hotel (☎6512 1368; fax 6512 0503). **Branch,** 1 Jianguomen Wai Dajie, Rm. 301 i (☎6505 3775 or 6505 3776; fax 6505 3105), in the World Trade Tower #2. Both open M-F 8:30am-noon and 1-5pm, Sa 9am-noon and 1:30-4pm. **Hualong International Travel Service** (huálóng guójì lǚxíng shè) 9 Jianguomen Nei Dajie, 1st fl. (☎6522 9444 or 6512 1486; beijinghualong@163.com), at the Beijing International Hotel, at what looks like a reception desk. Arranges Mongolian and Russian **visas,** and railway tickets. Open daily 8:30am-8pm.

Embassies: Beijing has 2 huge embassy compounds. One is at **Jianguomenwai,** near the Friendship Store, and the other is at **Sanlitun,** home to dozens of expat bars. **Australia,** 21 Dongzhimenwai Dajie, Sanlitun (☎6532 2331; fax 6532 4605). **Canada,** 19 Dongzhimenwai Dajie, Chaoyang District (☎6532 3536; fax 6532 5544). **Ireland,** 3 Ritan Dong Lu, Jianguomenwai, (☎6532 2691; fax 6532 6857). **Mongolian Consulate,** 2 Xiushui Bei Jie, Jianguomenwai (☎6532 1203; fax 6532 5045). **New Zealand,** 1 Donger Jie, Ritan Lu (☎6532 2731; fax 6532 3424). **Russia,** 4 Dongzhimennei, Beizhong Jie (☎6532 2051, visa section 6532 1267; fax 6532 4853), near, but not in, Sanlitun. **UK,** 11 Guanghua Lu, Jianguomenwai (☎6532 1961; fax 6532 1937). **US,** 3 Xiushui Dong Jie, Jianguomenwai (☎6532 3431; fax 6532 6057).

Currency Exchange: The **Bank of China** and almost every hotel or hostel can exchange **traveler's checks** and US dollars. To cash traveler's checks into US dollars, head to **CITS** or the **Bank of China Head Office** (☎6601 6688) 410 Fuchengmen Nei Dajie, 2nd fl., counter #1 or 2 (☎6601 6688). Open M-F 9am-noon and 1-5pm.

Emergency: Police ☎110. **Fire** ☎119. **Ambulance** ☎120.

Police: Public Security Bureau (gōngān jú), 9 Qianmen Dong Daji (☎6524 2063, foreigners' section 8401 5292, visa extensions 6532 3861).

Telephones: Almost all accommodations have telephones for international (IDD) calls. **Directory Assistance:** ☎114. **International Directory Assistance:** ☎115.

Internet Access: Qianyi Internet Cafe (qiányì wǎngluò kāfeīwü; ☎6705 1722), Station Shopping Mall, 3rd fl., opposite the southeast corner of Tiananmen Square. Y10 per 30min. Open daily 9am-midnight.

Post Office: International Post Office (guójì yóujú; ☎6512 8120), on the west side of Jianguomen Bei Dajie. EMS, IDD service, and **Poste Restante.** Open daily 8am-6:30pm.

BEIJING:	❶	❷	❸	❹	❺
ACCOM.	Y1-80	Y81-180	Y181-250	Y250-350	Y351+
FOOD	Y1-8	Y9-30	Y31-60	Y61-100	Y101+

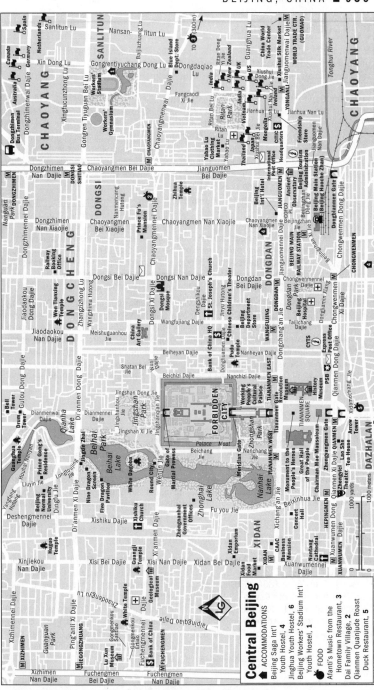

Central Beijing

♠ ACCOMMODATIONS

Beijing Saga Int'l Youth Hostel, 4
Jinghua Youth Hostel, 6
Beijing Workers' Stadium Int'l Youth Hostel, 1

🍴 FOOD

Afanti's Music from the Hometown Restaurant, 3
Dai Family Village, 2
Qianmen Quanjude Roast Duck Restaurant, 5

ACCOMMODATIONS

In Beijing, "budget" typically means a poor location around the city's southern periphery. The hostels and hotels along the mid-stretch of **Nansanhuan Lu**, between the **Yangqiao** and **Muxiyuan** exits, teem with backpackers.

■ **Beijing Saga International Youth Hostel (HI)** (běijīng shíjiā guójì qīngnián lǚshè), 9 Shijia Hutong, Dongcheng (☎6527 2773; fax 6524 9098), behind the Beijing International Hotel. Accessible by bus (#1, 4, 20, 808) or subway to Beijing Zhan. Neat rooms, wooden bunk beds, and A/C. Table football, energetic lounge, and chatty backpackers keep the place buzzing. Friendly, English-speaking staff. Bike rental (Y10 for 4hr., Y20 per day; deposit Y300), Internet (Y4 for 30min., Y10 per hr.), and laundry facilities (Y10). Book ahead. 8-bed dorms Y60, members Y50; 4- and 5-bed Y80/Y70; doubles Y200/Y180; triples Y230/Y210. ❶

■ **Beijing Workers' Stadium International Youth Hostel (HI)** (běijīng gōngtǐ guójì qīngnián lǎeshè), 9 Tai (Platform), Workers' Stadium, East Gate, Chaoyang (☎6552 4800; gongti@hotmail.com). Take buses #110, 113, 115, 118, 120, 403, 813, or 834 to Tiyuchang (stadium). Spacious and airy rooms, with clean, Western-style common bath, inside the stadium. Hot water, A/C, and Internet on the 1st fl. Free laundry, kitchen, luggage storage, and safe deposit box. They're reluctant to accept reservations; best way to secure a room is to appear in person. Deposit room rate plus Y100. 4-bed dorms Y60, members Y50; 2-bed dorms Y80/Y70; singles Y100-120. ❶

Jinghua Youth Hostel (jīnghuá fàndiàn), Xiluoyuan Nanli, Yongdingmen Wai Dajie, Fengtai (☎6722 2211; fax 6721 1455), off Nan Sanhuan Zhong Lu. Take bus #66 from Qianmen or 14 from Hepingmen to Yangqiao. With co-ed dorms, a pool, and an unending flow of travelers, the Jinghua is a cauldron of carousal and arousal. Cheaper dorms downstairs are basic; newer ones feel more like home, with spacious compartments and cleaner pillows. Better bring your own bedsheets and towel. Internet Y10 per hr. 20-bed dorm Y25; 11-bed Y30; 6-bed Y35-40; standard doubles Y240-300; triples Y230; suites with A/C Y480. ❶

FOOD

The streets of Beijing burst with food options. The *hutongs* (alleyways) overflow with stalls that vary in quality but are consistently low in price; special attention should be paid to the areas around **Qianmen** and **Wangfujing,** and **Tiantan, Ritan,** and **Beihai Parks.** Great restaurants can be found around **Liangmaqiao.** An absolute must-see, the night food market at **Donganmen,** off Wangfujing Dajie, serves treats like fried ice cream and more exotic fare like whole-sparrows-on-a-stick nightly from dusk to 9:30pm. For an easy sit-down meal, just head into any restaurant that advertises *jiachangcai* (everyday family food). **Beijing duck** is as intrinsic to the capital's history as *jingiu* (proposing toasts) and the Forbidden City.

■ **Qianmen Quanjude Roast Duck Restaurant** (qiánmén quánjùdé kǎoyā diàn), 32 Qianmen Dajie (☎6511 2418 or 6701 1379). Take a bus or subway to Qianmen; walk south. Founded in 1864, the Qianmen location is the oldest of 25 branches and cooks 2000 quackers per day to fill the bellies of demanding patrons. If you're going to splurge on a duck, do it with style—head through the archway to the fancier section. A duck can feed 3 people (Y168; with sauce, scallions, and pancakes Y184; carving extra). Make reservations. The fast-food area in front serves the same delicious duck (Y68 per person), but with less panache. Meals Y75-100. "Fancier" part open daily 11am-1:30pm and 4:45-8pm; "less fancy" part 10am-9pm. ❹

▨ **Dai Family Village** (dăijiā cūn), Guandongdian Nan Jie, Chaoyang (☎6585 8709), near Sanhuan Lu, about a block north of the Kerry Center Hotel. Also at 80 Tiantan Dong Lu (☎6714 0145 or 6711 1616). In the style of the Dai minority tribe of Yunnan, meals of mushroom, turtle, snake, and other treats are complemented by booze served in bamboo trunks and dance performances in the aisles. Most dishes Y30-70. More expensive, more bizarre entrees also available: crispy scorpions (Y80), sauna bullfrogs (Y48), eels stuck in bamboo pipes (Y38), and smoked young pigeons (Y18). Delectable pineapple porridge with 8 essences Y25. Performances at 11:30am, 6:30, 7:30pm. Open daily 10:30am-2:30pm and 4:30-9:30pm. Reservations recommended. ❸

Afanti's Music from the Hometown Restaurant (āfántí jiāxiāng yīnyuè cāntīng), Chaoyangmen Nei Dajie ("Chao Nei"), 2A Houguaibang Hutong, Dongcheng (☎6525 1071 or 6527 2288; www.afunti.com), in an alley just south of the (Chaonei) Xiaojie stop. Take bus #101, 109, 110, or 112. This Uighur funhouse serves up delectable Xinjiang fare, like melt-in-your-mouth "fried mutton with toothpick" (kebabs; from Y32). A wild song-and-dance troupe performs daily 7:30-8pm, accompanied by women in Uighur dress and enthusiastic *lǎowài* trying to dance on tabletops. Entrees Y30-90. 40% off lunch options. Open daily 10am-10:30pm. ❹

👁 SIGHTS

TIANANMEN SQUARE (TIĀN'ĀNMÉN GUĀNGCHĂNG). China's equivalent of Red Square, Tiananmen Square, one of the world's largest public meeting spaces, has created enough historical and political fodder to last a lifetime. The political epicenter of popular protest in modern China, the square has witnessed May 4th anti-imperialist demonstrations, anti-Japanese protests, Mao Zedong's proclamation of the People's Republic of China, the Red Guard rallies of the Cultural Revolution, politically charged outpourings of grief for Zhou Enlai, and pro-democracy protests. For most Chinese, Tiananmen Square is an ideological mecca, a place to pay tribute to the heroes and victims of China's tumultuous history. Despite its complicated past, the square seems rooted in an eternally celebratory atmosphere, a prime site for kite-flying and picture-taking. On special occasions, when crowds fill this vast expanse of cement, as they did after the announcement of Beijing's victorious Olympic bid, nationalistic fervor and contagious enthusiasm will rouse even the most skeptical. *(Between Chang'an Dajie and Qianmen Dajie. Take the blue line of the subway to Qianmen or the red line to Tiananmen East (red line). Buses #1, 4, 10, and 20 stop along Chang'an Jie to the north, while #5, 9, 17, 22, 47, 53, 54, 59, and 307 reach Qianmen to the south. Bus #116 runs along the side of the square.)*

FORBIDDEN CITY (ZĬJÌN CHÉNG). During the palace's 500-year history, only 24 emperors and their most intimate attendants could have known every part of its 800 buildings and 9000 chambers. Because common folk could not enter its gates, the palace was named the Forbidden City. Now known as the **Former Palace** (gù gōng), the complex opened to the public in 1949, and is the largest and most impressive example of traditional architecture in China. Construction of the Forbidden City began in 1406, the fourth year of Ming Emperor Yongle's reign. The palaces have seen so many face-lifts that it is hard to tell what is original anymore, but no amount of fresh paint can diminish the epic weight they carry.Within these ceremonial halls, the Son of Heaven conducted his stately affairs, often seated atop his imperial throne at the **Hall of Supreme Harmony.** The first hall contains the imperial throne. Peek through blackened windows (from too much tourist paw-

GATEWAY CITIES

ing) at the silk-flowered beds of the wedding chamber in the **Empress' Palace of Earthly Tranquility.** In the **Imperial Garden** out back, visitors linger in the once quiet beautiful and shady grounds. *(Take any bus to Tiananmen Square. From there, go under Tiananmen Gate to the ticket booths for the Palace Museum. ☎6525 0614. English captions; English tour guides Y200. Open daily summer 8:30am-4pm; winter 8:30am-3:30pm; last admission 1hr. before closing. Palace Y60, students Y20, children under 1.2m free. Additional halls around the palace extra Y5-10.)*

SUMMER PALACE (YÌHÉ YUÁN). First constructed by Qianlong in 1750, the magnificent **Summer Palace** contains over 3000 halls, pavilions, towers, courtyards, and most eye-catching of all, a sweeping lake. Within **Suzhou Jie** cool green water laps the sidewalks, stylized gondolas idle beside dumpling restaurants, and stone walkways wind between water on one side and shops, snack stands, and street artists on the other. With all the picture-taking, backpack-sporting, sunglass-wearing daytrippers, this remade town is more like a modern carnival. Other sights include Empress Dowager Ci Xi's infamous **Marble Boat,** a stationary edifice built courtesy of embezzled funds, the **Seventeen-Arch Bridge** topped with 544 stone lions, the **Pavilion for Listening to Orioles,** and the **Porcelain Pagoda.** A stroll along the stunning 728m **Long Corridor** (cháng láng) winds past 8000 paintings and most of the sights. *(The quickest way to the Summer Palace is to take minibus #375 from Xizhimen station. Open daily Apr.-Oct. 6:30am-6pm; Nov.-Mar. 7am-5pm. All halls close 1hr. earlier. Park Apr.-Oct. Y30, students Y15, through ticket Y50. Nov.-Mar. Y20/ Y10/Y40. English maps Y5.)*

BADALING GREAT WALL (BĀDÁLÍNG CHÁNG CHÉNG). Badaling is the part of the wall to visit if you want to take pictures that look like "official" photos and documentary stills. Getting that elusive shot without souvenir shops and other tourists, however, is a whole other feat. The government has taken great pains to restore Badaling to its "original" condition. Every tower and turret stands just as it did when the Mongols overran the country 700 years ago, give or take a few massive shops and gaudy pastel flags. Guard rails and cable cars make Badaling the safe—almost easy—way to see the Great Wall. A **museum** displays a brief history of the Wall alongside a bare-bones collection of artifacts. *(Take **bus** #5 or 44 from Qianmen or 800 to Deshengmen; hop on bus #919 in front of the Watchtower to Badaling (1½hr., approx. every 10min. 6am-6pm). Official tourist buses #1-4 (round-trip Y50) leave daily for Badaling Great Wall and the Ming Tombs from bus #1 station at Qianmen (6-10am), northeast corner of Qianmen (6:30-9am), Beijing Train Station in the 103 bus station (6-10am), and the zoo (6-10am). Hotel services and tour guides are the most expensive way of getting there. ☎6912 1988. Open daily summer 7:30am-5pm; winter 8am-5pm. Admission including museum and film Y45, students and seniors Y25.*

▤ NIGHTLIFE

Welcome to China, Beijing Journal offers an insider's look at fun stuff to do, from bungee-jumping to bar-hopping. In the decadent embassy district of **Sanlitun** (sānlǐtún) in northeast Beijing, every bar and street is bursting at the seams with foreigners and yuppie businessmen. The south gate of **Chaoyang Park** is a veritable mini-Las Vegas, but the new favorite place is a few minutes away by foot, near the **west gate** of Chaoyang Park. There, restaurants and bars wrestle for space and the spotlight—just don't expect to find the "real China." For a much more intimate, relaxed feel, go to the streets that line the north and south sides of **Houhai Lake,** near the Bell and Drum Towers behind **Beihai Park.**

The World of Suzie Wong (☎6593 6049), at the west gate of Chaoyang Park, in the same building as The Phoenix; look for the sign. Arguably the most popular haunt to be seen and heard for expats and affluent locals alike. Strong techno beats inside, more ventilation outside on the rooftop terrace. Arrive before 9pm for an intimate tète-a-tète; after 10pm, forget about personal space. Drinks Y20-60. Open daily 7pm-2am.

The Den (dūnhuáng xī cāntīng), 4A Gongti Dong Lu, Chaoyang (☎6592 6290; www.the-Den.com.cn), next to the City Hotel in Sanlitun. Go before midnight and you'll be sorely disappointed. On weekends, arrive fashionably late (past 1am) to a packed dance floor upstairs. Gravitate downstairs to a smoky chamber decorated with Eurocup jerseys for drinks, sustenance (Y20-50), and breathing space. Cover Y30. Open Su-Th 10:30am-3am, F-Sa 10:30am-7am.

GLOSSARY

PHONETIC TRANSCRIPTION

	PRONOUNCE		PRONOUNCE		PRONOUNCE
p	Poland	b	Bosnia	m	Macedonia
t	tank	d	dictatorship	n	Non-Aggression Pact
k	Kremlin	g	*glasnost*	ng	protesting
f	Former USSR	v	Volga	w	workers of the world
th	theft	th	those capitalist pigs	r	October Revolution
s	Serbia	z	Communism	kh	fricative, Ger. *Bach*
ts	🔳 Let's Go	dz	comrades	h	President Havel
sh	dictatorship	zh	mirage	l	Lenin
ch	China	j	Joseph Stalin	y	Yalta
ee	Eastern Europe	ih	Independence	ew	rounded, Ger. *über*
ay	Romania	eh	Estonia	oe	rounded, Fr. *sœur*
a	Battle of Stalingrad	ah	Prague	uh	Russia
oh	Croatia	oo	Budapest	y	unrounded, sIlver; Ru. ы, Ro. â or î
ai	Iron Curtain	oy	Oy	ey	vey!
au	Wow	yoo	Ukraine		

ALBANIAN (SHQIP)

ENGLISH	ALBANIAN	PRONOUNCE	ENGLISH	ALBANIAN	PRONOUNCE
Hello	Mirëdita, allo	meer-dee-TAH	one	një	nyuh
Yes/no	Po/jo	poh/yoh	two	dy	dew
Please	Ju lutem	yoo loo-TEHM	three	tre	treh
Thank you	Faleminderit	fah-leh-meen-deh-REET	four	katër	KAH-tuhr
Goodbye	Mirupafshim	mee-roo-pahf-SHIHM	five	pesë	pehs
Sorry/excuse me	Më falni	muh-fahl-NEE	six	gjashtë	jyasht
Help!	Ndihmë!	NDEEM	seven	shtatë	shtaht
ticket	biletë	bee-LET	eight	tetë	teht
train/bus	treni/autobusi	TREH-nee/au-toh-BOO-see	nine	nëntë	nuhnt
toilets	nevojtorja	neh-voy-TOR-ya	ten	dhjetë	thyeht

ENGLISH	ALBANIAN	PRONOUNCE
Where is...?	Ku është...?	koo UHSHT
How do I get to...?	Si mund të vete te...?	see moond tveht TEH
How much does this cost?	Sa kushton	sah koosh-TOHN
Do you speak English?	A flisni Anglisht?	ah flees-nee ahn-GLEESHT
Cheers!	Gëzuar!	guh-zoo-AHR
I love you.	Të dua.	tuh doo-AH

BULGARIAN (БЪЛГАРСКИ)

ENGLISH	BULGARIAN	PRONOUNCE
Hello	Добър ден	DOH-buhr dehn
Yes/no	Да/Не	dah/neh
Please/you're welcome	Моля	MO-lyah
Thank you	Благодаря	blahg-oh-dahr-YAH
Goodbye	Добиждане	doh-VIZH-dan-eh
Good morning	Добро утро	doh-BROH OO-troh
Good evening	Добър Вечер	DOH-buhr VEH-cher
Good night	Лека Нощ	LEH-kah nohsht
Sorry/excuse me	Извинете	iz-vi-NEE-teh
Help!	Помощ!	POH-mohsht
Where is...	Къде е...	kuh-DEH eh
...the bathroom?	...тоалетната?	toh-ah-LYEHT-nah-tah
... the nearest telephone booth?	...най-близкия телефон?	nai-bleez-kee-yah teh-leh-FOHN
...center of town?	...центъра на града?	TSEHNT-ur-a nah grahd-AH
How do I get to...?	Как да стигна...?	kahk dah STEEG-nah
How much does this cost?	Колко Струва?	KOHL-koh STROO-vah
When?	Кога?	koh-GAH
Do you speak English?	Говорите ли Английски?	goh-VOH-ree-teh lee ahn-GLEEY-skee
I don't understand	Не разбирам.	neh rahz-BEE-rahm
I don't speak Bulgarian.	Не говоря по-български.	neh gah-var-YA po-buhl-GAHR-skee
Speak a little slower, please.	Малко по-бавно, ако обичате.	MAHL-koh poh-BAHV-noh, AH-ko ohb-ee-CHAT-eh
Please write it down.	Може лида ми го запишете.	MOH-zhe LEE-dah mee goh za-pee-SHEE-teh
Do you have a vacancy?	Имате ли свободна стая?	ee-MAH-te lee svoh-BOHD-nah STAH-ya
I'd like a room.	Искам стая.	EES-kahm STAH-yah
I'd like to order...	Искам да поръчам...	EES-kahm dah por-RUH-cham
Check, please.	Бих искал да платя сметката.	beekh ees-kahl dah plaht-YAH SMEHT-kah-tah
I want a ticket to...	Искам билет да...	ees-KAHM bee-LEHT dah
Go away.	Махнете се.	makh-NEH-teh seh
Cheers!	Наздаве!	nahz-DRAHV-eh
I love you.	Ас те обичам.	ahs tay OHB-ee-chahm

ENGLISH	BULGARIAN	PRONOUNCE	ENGLISH	BULGARIAN	PRONOUNCE
one	едно	ehd-NOH	single room	единична	ye-din-EECH-nah
two	две	dveh	double room	двойна	dvoy-NAH
three	три	tree	reservation	резевация	re-zer-VAH-tsee-yah
four	четири	CHEN-tee-ree	departure	заминаващи	zaminavashti
five	пет	peht	arrival	пристигащи	pristigashti

ENGLISH	BULGARIAN	PRONOUNCE
six	шест	shest
seven	седем	SEH-dehm
eight	осем	O-sehm
nine	девет	DEH-veht
ten	десет	DEH-seht
twenty	двадесет	DVAH-DEH-seht
thirty	тридесет	TREE-deh-seht
forty	четиридесет	CHEH-TEE-REE-deh-seht
fifty	петдесет	peht-deh-SEHT
sixty	шестдесет	shest-deh-SEHT
seventy	седемдесет	se-dem-deh-SEHT
eighty	осем	OH-sehm
ninety	деветдесет	deh-veht-deh-SEHT
one hundred	сто	stoh
one thousand	хиляда	hee-LYA-dah
Monday	понеделник	poh-neh-DEHL-neek
Tuesday	вторник	FTOHR-neek
Wednesday	сряда	SRYA-dah
Thursday	четвъртък	cheht-VUHR-tuhk
Friday	петък	peh-TUHK
Saturday	събота	suh-BOH-tah
Sunday	неделя	neh-DEHL-yah
today	днес	dnehs
tomorrow	утре	OO-treh
day	ден	dehn
week	семица	seh-MEE-tsah
morning	сутрин	SOO-treen
afternoon	следобед	SLEH-doh-behd
evening	вечер	VEH-chehr
spring	пролет	pro-LEHT
summer	лято	LYA-toh
fall	есен	EH-sehn
winter	зима	zee-MAH
hot	топло	toh-PLOH
cold	студено	stoo-DEHN-oh
open	отварят	ot-VAHR-yaht
closed	затварят	zaht-VAHR-yaht
left	ляво	LYAH-voh

ENGLISH	BULGARIAN	PRONOUNCE
one-way	отиване	o-TEE-vahn-eh
round-trip	отиване и Връщане	oh-TEE-vahn-eh ee VRUH-shtah-neh
ticket	билет	bee-LEHT
train	влак	vlahk
bus	автобус	ahv-toh-BOOS
airport	летище	LEHT-ee-shteh
train station	гара	gahrah
bus station	автогарата	AHV-toh-gah-rah-tah
luggage	багаж	bah-GAHZH
bank	банка	BAHN-kah
police	полиция	poh-LEE-tsee-yah
exchange	обменно бюро	OHB-mehn-noh byoo-ROH
passport	паспорт	pahs-POHRT
market	пазар	pah-ZAHR
grocery	бакалия	bah-kah-LEE-yah
breakfast	закуска	za-KOO-ska
lunch	обяд	oh-BYAHD
dinner	вечеря	veh-cher-YAH
menu	меню	mehn-YOO
bread	хляб	hlyahb
vegetables	зеленчуци	ZEH-lehn-choot-zee
beef	говеждо месо	goh-VEHZH-doh meh-SOH
chicken	пиле	PEE-leh
pork	свинско	SVIN-ska
fish	риба	REE-bah
coffee	кафе	kah-FEH
milk	мляко	MLYAH-koh
beer	бира	BEE-rah
sugar	захар	ZAH-khar
eggs	яйца	yai-TSAH
toilet	тоалетна	toh-ah-LEHT-nah
square	площад	PLOH-shad
monastery	манастир	mah-nah-STEER
church	църква	TSUHRK-vah
post office	поща	POH-shtah
stamp	марка	MAHR-kah
airmail	въздушна поща	vuhz-DOOSH-nah POH-shtah
right	дясно	DYAHS-noh

CROATIAN (HRVATSKI)

ENGLISH	CROATIAN	PRONOUNCE
Hello/hi	Dobar dan/bog	doh-bahr DAHN/bohg
Yes/no	Da/ne	Dah/Neh
Please/you're welcome	Molim	MOH-leem
Thank you	Hvala lijepa/hvala	HVAH-la lee-ye-pah/hvah-lah
Goodbye	Bog	Bog
Good morning	Dobro jutro	DOH-broh YOO-tro
Good evening	Dobro večer	DOH-broh VEH-chehr
Good night	Laku noć	LAH-koo nohch
Sorry/excuse me	Oprostite	oh-PROH-stee-teh
Help!	U pomoć!	OO pohmohch
Where is...?	Gdje je...?	GDYEH yeh
...the bathroom?	...zahod?	ZAH-hod
...the nearest telephone booth?	...nalazi najbliža telefonska govornica?	NAH-lah-zee nai-BLEE-zhah teh-leh-FOHN-skah goh-vohr-NEE-tsah
...center of town?	...centar grada?	TSEHN-tahr GRAH-dah
How do I get to...?	Kako mogu doći do...?	KAH-koh MOH-goo DOH-chee doh...
How much does this cost?	Koliko to košta?	KOH-lee-koh toh KOH-shtah
When?	Kada?	KAH-dah
Do you speak English?	Govorite li engleski?	goh-VOHR-ee-teh lee ehng-LEH-skee
I don't understand.	Ne razumijem.	neh rah-ZOO-mee-yehm
I don't speak Croatian.	Ne govorim hrvatski.	neh goh-VOH-reem KHR-va-tskee
Speak a little slower, please.	Govorite polako, molim.	go-VOR-iteh PO-la-koh MOH-leem
Please write it down.	Napišajte mi, molim vas.	nah-PEE-shai-teh mee MOH-leem
Do you have a vacancy?	Imate li slobodne sobe?	ee-MAH-teh lee SLOH-boh-dneh SOH-beh?
I'd like a room.	Želio bih sobu.	ZHEL-ee-oh beeh SOH-boo
I'd like to order...	Želio bih naručiti...	Jeh-ee-oh beeh na-ROO-chiti
Check, please.	Račun, molim.	ra-CHOON moh-leem
I want a ticket to...	Htio bih kartu za...	HTEE-oh beeh KAHR-too zah...
Go away.	Bježi	BYEH-zhee
Cheers!	Živjeli!	ZHIV-yehl-ee
I love you.	Volim te.	VOH-leem teh.

ENGLISH	CROATIAN	PRONOUNCE
one	jedan	YEHD-ahn/noh
two	dva	dvah/DVEE-jeh
three	tri	tree
four	četiri	CHEH-tee-ree
five	pet	peht

ENGLISH	CROATIAN	PRONOUNCE
single room	jedno-krevetnu sobu	YEHD-noh-kreh-VEHT-noo SOH-boo
double room	dvokrevetnu sobu	DVOH-kreh-VEHT-noo SOH-boo
reservation	rezervacija	reh-zehr-VAH-tsee-yah
departure	odlazak	OHD-lahz-ahk
arrival	polazak	POH-lahz-ahk

GLOSSARY

ENGLISH	CROATIAN	PRONOUNCE
six	šest	shehsht
seven	sedam	SEH-dahm
eight	osam	OH-sahm
nine	devet	DEH-veht
ten	deset	DEH-seht
twenty	dvadeset	DVAH-deseht
thirty	trideset	TREE-deseht
forty	četrdeset	CHETR-deseht
fifty	pedeset	peh-DEH-seht
sixty	šesdeset	shehs-DEH-seht
seventy	sedamdeset	sedam-DEH-seht
eighty	osamdeset	osam-DEH-seht
ninety	devedeset	de-vet-DEH-seht
one hundred	sto	stoh
one thousand	tisuća	TEE-soo-chah
Monday	ponedeljak	POH-neh-djehl-yahk
Tuesday	utorak	OO-toh-rahk
Wednesday	srijeda	SREE-yehdah
Thursday	četvrtak	CHEHT-vehr-tahk
Friday	petak	PEH-tahk
Saturday	subota	SOO-boh-tah
Sunday	nedjelja	NEH-dyehl-yah
today	danas	DAH-nahs
tomorrow	sutra	SOO-trah
day	dan	dahn
week	tjedna	TYEHD-nah
morning	ujutro	oo-YOO-troh
afternoon	popodne	poh-POH-dneh
evening	večer	VEH-chehr
spring	proljeće	proh-LYE-cheh
summer	ljeto	LYEH-toh
fall	jesen	YEH-sehn
winter	zima	ZEE-mah
hot	vruće	VROO-cheh
cold	hladno	HLAHD-noh
open	otvoreno	OHT-voh-reh-noh
closed	zatvoreno	ZAHT-voh-reh-noh
left	lijevo	lee-YEH-voh

ENGLISH	CROATIAN	PRONOUNCE
one-way	u jednom smjeru	oo YEH-dnohm smee-YEH-roo
round-trip	povratna karta	POHV-raht-nah KAHR-tah
ticket	kartu	KAHR-too
train	vlak	VLAHK
bus	autobus	au-TOH-bus
airport	zračna luka	ZRAH-chnah loo-kah
train station	kolodvor	KOH-loh-dvohr
bus station	autobusni kolodvor	AU-toh-boos-nee KOH-loh-dvohr
luggage	prtljaga	PEHRT-lyah-gah
bank	banka	BAHN-kah
police	policija	poh-LEE-tsee-yah
exchange	mjenjačnica	myehn-YAHCH-nee-tsah
passport	putovnica	POO-toh-vnee-tsah
market	trgovina	TER-goh-vee-nah
grocery	trgovina	TER-goh-vee-na
breakfast	doručak	doh-ROO-chahk
lunch	ručak	ROO-chahk
dinner	večera	VEH-cheh-rah
menu	karta	KAR-ta
bread	kruh	krooh
vegetables	povrće	POH-vehr-chay
beef	piletina	PEE-leh-tee-nah
chicken	koka	koh-kah
pork	svinja	SVEE-nyah
fish	riba	REE-bah
coffee	kava	KAH-vah
milk	mlijeko	mlee-YEH-koh
beer	pivo	PEE-voh
sugar	šečer	SHEH-chehr
eggs	jaje	YAH-yeh
toilet	WC	vay-tsay
square	trg	terg
monastery	samostan	SAM-oh-stahn
church	crkva	TSERK-vah
post office	pošta	POSH-tah
stamp	markica	MAHR-kee-tsah
airmail	zrakoplovom	ZRAH-koh-ploh-vohm
right	desno	DEHS-noh

CZECH (ČESKY)

ENGLISH	CZECH	PRONOUNCE
Hello	Dobrý den (formal)	DOH-bree dehn
Yes/no	Ano/ne	AH-noh/neh
Please/you're welcome	Prosím	proh-SEEM
Thank you	Děkuji	DYEH-koo-yee
Goodbye	Nashedanou	NAH sleh-dah-noh-oo
Good morning	Dobré ráno	DOH-breh RAH-noh
Good evening	Dobrý večer	DOH-breh VEH-chehr
Good night	Dobrou noc	DOH-broh NOHTS
Sorry/excuse me	Promiňte	PROH-meen-teh
Help!	Pomoc!	POH-mohts
Where is...?	Kde je...?	kdeh yeh
...the bathroom?	...kúpelňa?	KOO-pehl-nyah
...the nearest telephone booth?	...nejbližší telefonní budka?	NEY-bleezh-shnee TEH-leh-foh-nee BOOT-kah
...center of town?	...centrum města?	TSEN-troom MYEHST-steh
How do I get to...?	Jak se dostanu do...?	YAHK seh dohs-TAH-noo doh
How much does this cost?	Kolik to stojí?	KOH-leek STOH-yee
When?	Kdy?	kdee
Do you speak English?	Mluvíte anglicky?	MLOO-veet-eh ahng-GLEET-skee
I don't understand.	Nerozumím.	NEH-rohz-oo-meem
I don't speak Czech.	Nemluvím Česky.	NEH-mloo-veem CHESS-kee
Speak a little slower, please.	Mluvte pomaleji, prosím.	MLOOV-teh POH-mah-le-yee proh-SEEM
Please write it down.	Prosím napište.	proh-SEEM nah-PEESH-tye
Do you have a vacancy?	Máte volný pokoj?	MAA-teh VOHL-nee POH-koy
I'd like a room.	Prosím pokoj.	proh-SEEM PO-koy
I'd like to order...	Prosím...	khtyel bikh
Check, please.	Paragon, prosím.	PAH-rah-gohn proh-SEEM
I want a ticket to...	Prosím jízdenku do...	khtyel a bikh YEEZ-denkoo DO
How long does the trip take?	Jak dlouho trvá ta cesta?	YAHK DLOH-oo-hoh TER-vah tah TSE-stah
Go away.	Prosím odejděte.	pro-SEEM ODEY-dyeh-teh
Cheers!	Na zdraví!	nah ZDRAH-vee
I love you.	Miluji tě.	MEE-loo-yee tyeh.

ENGLISH	CZECH	PRONOUNCE
one	jeden	YEH-dehn
two	dva	DVAH
three	tři	trzhee
four	čtyři	SHTEER-zhee
five	pět	pyeht
six	šest	shehst
seven	sedm	SEH-duhm

ENGLISH	CZECH	PRONOUNCE
single room	jednolůžkový pokoj	YEHD-noh-loozh-koh-vee POH-koy
double room	dvoulůžkový pokoj	DVOH-oo-loozh-ko-vee POH-koy
reservation	rezervace	REH-zehr-vah-tseh
departure	odjezd	OHD-yezd
arrival	příjezd	PREE-yehzd
one-way	jen tam	yehn tahm
round-trip	zpáteční	SPAH-tehch-nyee

ENGLISH	CZECH	PRONOUNCE
eight	osm	OHS-uhm
nine	devět	dehv-YEHT
ten	deset	dehs-SEHT
twenty	dvacet	dvah-TSEHT
thirty	třicet	trzhee-TSEHT
forty	čtyřicet	SHTEE-rzhee-TSEHT
fifty	padesát	PAH-dehs-aht
sixty	šedesát	she-des-aht
seventy	sedmdesát	SEH-duhm-dehs-aht
eighty	osmdesát	OHS-uhm-dehs-aht
ninety	devadesát	DEH-vah-des-aht
one hundred	sto	stoh
one thousand	tisíc	TEE-seets
Monday	pondělí	POHN-dyeh-lee
Tuesday	úterý	OO-te-ree
Wednesday	středa	STRZHEH-dah
Thursday	čtvrtek	CHTVER-tehk
Friday	pátek	Pah-tehk
Saturday	sobota	SOH-boh-tah
Sunday	neděle	NEH-dyeh-leh
today	dnes	dnehs
tomorrow	zítra	ZEE-trah
day	den	dehn
week	týden	tee-dehn
morning	ráno	RAH-noh
afternoon	odpoledne	OHD-pohl-ehd-neh
evening	večer	VEH-chehr
spring	jaro	YAH-roh
summer	léto	LEE-toh
fall	podzim	POHD-zeem
winter	zima	ZEE-mah
hot	teplý	TEHP-leeh
cold	studený	STOO-deh-nee
open	otevřeno	O-teh-zheno
closed	zavřeno	ZAV-rzhen-oh
left	vlevo	VLE-voh

ENGLISH	CZECH	PRONOUNCE
ticket	lístek	LEES-tehk
train	vlak	vlahk
bus	autobus	AU-toh-boos
airport	letiště	LEH-teesh-tyeh
station	nádraží	NAH-drah-zhee
bus station	autobusové nádražé	AU-toh-boo-sohv-eh NAH-drazh-eh
luggage	zavadla	ZAH-vahd-lah
bank	banka	BAHN-kah
police	policie	POH-leets-ee-yeh
exchange	směnárna	smyeh-NAHR-nah
passport	cestovní pas	TSEH-stohv-nee pahs
market	trh	terh
grocery	potraviny	POH-trah-vee-nee
breakfast	snídaně	SNEE-dahn-yeh
lunch	oběd	OHB-yehd
dinner	večeře	VEH-cher-zheh
menu	listek	LEES-tehk
bread	chléb	khleb
vegetables	zelenina	ZEH-leh-nee-nah
beef	hovězí	HOH-vyeh-zee
chicken	kuře	KOO-rzheh
pork	vep	VEPRZH
fish	ryba	RY-bah
coffee	káva	KAH-vah
milk	mléko	MLEH-koh
beer	pivo	PEE-voh
sugar	cukr	TSOO-ker
eggs	vejce	VEY-tseh
toilet	WC	VEE-TSEE
square	náměstí	NAH-myeh-stee
monastery	klašter	KLAHSH-tehr
church	kostel	KOH-stehl
post office	pošta	POSH-tah
stamp	známka	ZNAHM-kah
airmail	letecky	LEH-tehts-kee
right	vpravo	VPRAH-voh

ESTONIAN (ESTI KEEL)

ENGLISH	ESTONIAN	PRONOUNCE	ENGLISH	ESTONIAN	PRONOUNCE
Hello	Tere	TEH-reh	one	üks	euwks
Yes/no	Jaa/ei	jah/ay	two	kaks	kahks
Please	Palun	PAH-loon	three	kolm	kohlm
Thank you	Tänan	TAH-nahn	four	neli	NEH-lee
Goodbye	Head aega	heh-ahd EYE-gah	five	viis	vees
Sorry/Excuse me	Vabandage	vah-bahn-DAHG-eh	six	kuus	koos
Help!	Appi!	AHP-pee	seven	seitse	SAYT-seh
ticket	pilet	PEE-leht	eight	kaheksa	KAH-heks-ah
train/bus	rong/buss	rohng/boos	nine	üheksa	EUW-eks-ah
toilet	tualett	twah-LEHT	ten	kümme	KEUW-meh

ENGLISH	ESTONIAN	PRONOUNCE
Where is...?	Kus on...?	koos ohn
How much does this cost?	Kui palju?	kwee PAHL-yoo
Do you speak English?	Kas te räägite inglise keelt?	kahs teh raa-GEE-teh een-GLEE-seh kehlt
Cheers!	Proosit!	PROH-seet

HUNGARIAN (MAGYAR)

ENGLISH	HUNGARIAN	PRONOUNCE
Hello	Szervusz/Szia/Hello	SAYHR-voose/See-ya/Hello
Yes/no	Igen/nem	EE-gehn/nehm
Please	Kérem	KAY-rehm
Thank you	Köszönöm	KUH-suh-nuhm
Goodbye	Viszontlátásra	Vi-sohnt-lah-tah-shraw
Good morning	Jó reggelt	YOH raig-gailt
Good evening	Jó estét	YOH ehsh-teht
Good night	Jó éjszakát	YOH ay-soh-kaht
Sorry/excuse me	Elnézést	EHL-nay-zaysht
Where is...?	Hol van...?	hawl vohn
...the bathroom?	...a WC?	a WC
...the nearest telephone booth?	...a legközelebbi telefonfülke?	a lehg-kohz-ELL-EBEE teh-leh-FOHN-FEWL-keh
...center of town?	...a városközpont?	a vahrosh-kohz-pont
How do I get to...?	Hogy jutok...?	hawdj YOO-tawk
How much does this cost?	Mennyibe kerül?	MEHN-yee-beh KEH-rewl
When?	Mikor?	MI-kor
Do you speak English?	Beszél angolul?	BESS-ayl ON-goal-ool
I don't understand.	Nem értem.	nem AYR-tem
I don't speak Hungarian.	Nem tudok magyarul.	Nehm TOO-dawk MAH-dyah-rool
Speak a little slower, please.	Kérem, beszéljen lassan.	KAY-rem, BESS-ayl-yen LUSH-shun
Please write it down.	Kérem, írja fel.	KAY-rem, EER-yuh fell.
Do you have a vacancy?	Van üres szoba?	vahn ew-REHSH SAH-bah
I'd like a room.	Szeretnék egy szobát.	seh-reht-naik ehdj SOW-baht.
I'd like to order...	...kérek.	KAY-rehk

ENGLISH	HUNGARIAN	PRONOUNCE
Check, please.	A számlát, kérem.	uh SAHM-lot KAY-rehm
I want a ticket.	Szeretnékegy jegyet.	sehr-eht-nayk-ehj yehdg-at
Go away.	Távozzék.	TAH-vawz-zayk
Cheers!	Egészségedre	ehg-eh-SHEHG-eh-dreh
I love you.	Szeretleu	sehr-EHT-lyuh

ENGLISH	HUNGARIAN	PRONOUNCE
one	egy	ehdge
two	kettő	ket-tuuh
three	három	hah-rohm
four	négy	naydj
five	öt	uh-t
six	hat	huht
seven	hét	hayte
eight	nyolc	nyoltz
nine	kilenc	kih-lentz
ten	tíz	teehz
twenty	húsz	hoohz
thirty	harminc	hahr-mihntz
forty	negyven	nehdj-vehn
fifty	ötven	ut-vehn
sixty	hatvan	huht-vohn
seventy	hetven	heht-vehn
eighty	nyolcvan	nyoltz-vahn
ninety	kilencven	kih-lehntz-vehn
one hundred	száz	saaz
one thousand	ezer	eh-zehr
Monday	hétfő	hayte-phuuh
Tuesday	kedd	kehd
Wednesday	szerda	sayr-dah
Thursday	csütörtök	chew-ter-tek
Friday	péntek	paine-tek
Saturday	szombat	SAWM-baht
Sunday	vasárnap	VAHSH-ahr-nahp
today	ma	mah
tomorrow	holnap	HAWL-nahp
day	nap	nahp
week	hét	hayht
morning	reggel	regh-ghel
afternoon	délután	deh-lu-taan

ENGLISH	HUNGARIAN	PRONOUNCE
single room	egyágyas	ehdge-AGAS
double room	kétágyas szoba	keht-AHGAHS soh-bah
reservation	helyfoglalás	HEY-fohg-lah-DASH
departure	indulás	IN-dool-ahsh
arrival	érkezés	ayr-keh-zaysh
one-way	csak oda	chohk AW-doh
round-trip	oda-vissza	AW-doh-VEES-soh
ticket	jegyet	YEHD-eht
train	vonat	VAW-noht
bus	autóbusz	ow-toh-boos
airport	repülőtér	rehp-ewlu-TAYR
train station	pályaudvar	pah-yoh-OOT-vahr
bus station	buszmegálló	boos-mehg-AH-loh
luggage	csomag	CHOH-mahg
bank	bank	bohnk
police	rendőrség	rehn-doer-SHEGH
exchange	pénzaváltó	pehn-zah-VAHL-toh
passport	az útlevelemet	ahz oot-leh-veh-leh-meht
market	piac	PEE-ohts
grocery	élelmiszerbolt	Ay-lel-meser-balt
breakfast	reggeli	REG-gehl-ee
lunch	ebéd	EB-ayhd
dinner	vacsora	VOTCH-oh-rah
menu	étlap	ATE-lohp
bread	kenyér	KEHN-yair
vegetables	zöldségek	ZULD-sehgek
beef	marhahús	MOHR-hoh-hoosh
chicken	csirke	CHEER-keh
pork	disznóhús	dihsnow-hoosh
fish	hal	huhl
coffee	kávé	KAA-vay
milk	tej	tay
beer	sör	shurr

ENGLISH	HUNGARIAN	PRONOUNCE	ENGLISH	HUNGARIAN	PRONOUNCE
evening	este	ES-te	sugar	cukor	TSU-kor
spring	tavasz	TO-vos	eggs	tojást	to-yaasht
summer	nyár	njaar	toilet	WC	veh-tseh
fall	ősz	öss	square	tér	tehr
winter	tél	tail	monastery	kolostor	KEH-lohsh-tor
hot	meleg	me-legh	church	templom	TEHM-plohm
cold	hideg	hi-degh	post office	posta	pawsh-tuh
open	nyitva	NYEET-vah	stamp	bélyeg	BAY-yeg
closed	zárva	ZAHR-vuh	airmail	légiposta	LAY-ghee-pawsh-tah
left	bal	bol	right	jobb	yowb

LATVIAN (LATIVSKA)

ENGLISH	LATVIAN	PRONOUNCE	ENGLISH	LATVIAN	PRONOUNCE
Hello	Labdien	LAHB-dyen	one	viens	vee-yenz
Yes/no	Jā/nē	yah/ney	two	divi	DIH-vih
Please/ you're welcome	Lūdzu	LOOD-zuh	three	trīs	treese
Thank you	Paldies	PAHL-dee-yes	four	četri	CHEH-trih
Goodbye	Uz redzēšanos	ooz RE-dzeh-shan-was	five	pieci	PYET-sih
Sorry/excuse me	Atvainojiet	AHT-vain-oy-iet	six	seši	SEH-shee
Help!	Palīgā!	PAH-lee-gah	seven	septini	SEHP-tih-nyih
ticket	biļete	BEE-leh-teh	eight	astoņi	AHS-toh-nyih
train/bus	vilciens/autobuss	VEEL-tsee-ehns/AU-to-boos	nine	devini	DEH-vih-nyih
toilet	tualete	TWA-leh-teh	ten	desmit	DEZ-miht

ENGLISH	LATVIAN	PRONOUNCE
Where is...?	Kur ir...?	koohr ihr
How do I get to...?	Kā es varu nokļūt uz...?	kah ess VA-roo NOkly-oot ooz
How much does this cost?	Cik maksā?	sikh MAHK-sah
Do you speak English?	Vai jū runājat Angliski?	vai YOO roo-nai-yat ahn-GLEE-skee

LITHUANIAN (LIETUVIŠKAI)

ENGLISH	LITHUANIAN	PRONOUNCE	ENGLISH	LITHUANIAN	PRONOUNCE
Hello	Labas	LAH-bahss	one	vienas	VYEH-nahss
Yes/no	Taip/ne	TAYE-p/NEH	two	du	doo
Please	Prašau	prah-SHAU	three	trys	treese
Thank you	Ačiū	AH-chyoo	four	keturi	keh-TUH-rih
Goodbye	Viso gero	VEE-soh GEh-roh	five	penki	PEHN-kih
Sorry/excuse me	Atsiprašau	aHT-sih-prh-SHAU	six	šeši	SHEH-shih
Help!	Gelbėkite!	GYEL-behk-ite	seven	septyni	sehp-TEE-nih
ticket	bilietas	BEE-lee-tahs	eight	aštuoni	ahsh-too-OH-ni

ENGLISH	LITHUANIAN	PRONOUNCE
Where is...?	Kur yra...?	Koor ee-RAH
How do I get to...?	Kaip nueti į...?	KYE-p nuh-EH-tih ee
How much does this cost?	Kiek kainuoja?	KEE-yek KYE-new-oh-yah
Do you speak English?	Ar kalbate angliškai?	AHR KULL-buh-teh AHN-gleesh-kye

MACEDONIAN

ENGLISH	MACEDONIAN	PRONOUNCE
Hello	Добар ден	DAW-bahr-den
Yes/no	Да/не	dah/neh
Please	Повелете	poh-VEL-et-ey
Thank you	Фала	FAH-lah
Goodbye	Довидуванье	DAW-ve-DOO-va-ne
Sorry/excuse me	Дозволете	dohz-VOH-leh-teh
Help!	Помош!	POH-mohsh
ticket	билет	BEE-leht
train/bus	возот/автобусот	VOH-zoht/av-toh-BOO-soht
toilet	тоалетот	toh-ah-LEH-toht

ENGLISH	MACEDONIAN	PRONOUNCE
one	едно	ehd-NO
two	две	dveh
three	три	tree
four	четири	CHEH-tee-ree
five	пет	peht
six	шест	SHEST
seven	седем	
eight	осем	O-sehm
nine	девет	DEH-veht
ten	десет	DEH-seht

ENGLISH	MACEDONIAN	PRONOUNCE
Where is...?	Каде?	kah-DEY
How do I get to...?	Како да стигнам...?	KAH-koh dah STIG-nahm doh
Do you speak English?	Зборивате ли англиски?	ZVOR-oo-va-te li an-GLEE-ski

POLISH (POLSKI)

ENGLISH	POLISH	PRONOUNCE
one	jeden	YEH-den
two	dwa	dvah
three	trzy	tshih
four	cztery	ch-TEH-rih
five	pięć	pyainch
six	sześć	sheshch
seven	siedem	SHEH-dehm
eight	osiem	OH-shehm
nine	dziewięć	JYEH-vyainch
ten	dziesięć	JYEH-shainch
twenty	dwadzieścia	dva-JEHSH-cha
thirty	trzydzieści	tshi-JEHSH-chee
forty	czterdzieści	chter-JEHSH-chee

ENGLISH	POLISH	PRONOUNCE
single room	jednoosobowy	YEHD-noh-oh-soh-BOH-vih
double room	dwuosobowy	DVOO-oh-soh-BOH-vih
reservation	miejscówka	myay-STSOOF-ka
departure	odjazd	OHD-yazd
arrival	przyjazd	PSHIH-yazd
one-way	w jedną stronę	VYEHD-nowm STROH-neh
round-trip	tam i z powrotem	tahm ee spoh-VROH-tehm
ticket	bilet	BEE-leht
train	pociąg	POH-chawng
bus	autobus	ow-TOH-booss
airport	lotnisko	loht-NEE-skoh
train station	dworzec	DVOH-zhets
bus station	dworzec autobusowy	DVOH-zhets ow-toh-boo-SOH-vih

ENGLISH	POLISH	PRONOUNCE	ENGLISH	POLISH	PRONOUNCE
fifty	pięćdziesiąt	pyench-JEHSH-ont	luggage	bagaż	BAH-gahzh
sixty	sześćdziesiąt	sheshch-JEHSH-ont	bank	bank	bahnk
seventy	siedemdziesiąt	shed-ehm-JEHSH-ont	police	policja	poh-LEETS-yah
eighty	osiemdziesiąt	ohsh-ehm-JEHSH-nt	exchange	kantor	KAHN-tor
ninety	dziewięćdziesiąt	JYEH-vyehnch-JYEH-shont	passport	paszport	PAHSH-port
one hundred	sto	stoh	market	rynek	RIH-nehk
one thousand	tysiąc	TIH-shonts	grocery	sklep spożywczy	sklehp spoh-ZHIV-chih
Monday	poniedziałek	poh-nyeh-JAW-ehk	breakfast	śniadanie	shnyah-DAHN-yeh
Tuesday	wtorek	FTOH-rehk	lunch	obiad	OH-byahd
Wednesday	środa	SHROH-dah	dinner	kolacja	koh-LAH-tsyah
Thursday	czwartek	CHVAHR-tehk	menu	menu	MEH-noo
Friday	piątek	PYOHN-tehk	bread	chleb	khlehp
Saturday	sobota	soh-BOH-tah	vegetables	jarzyny	yah-ZHIH-nih
Sunday	niedziela	nyeh-JEHH-lah	beef	wołowina	vo-wo-VEEN-ah
today	dzisiaj	JEESH-ai	chicken	kurczak	KOOR-chahk
tomorrow	jutro	YOO-troh	pork	wieprzowina	vye-psho-VEE-nah
day	dzień	JAYN	fish	ryba	RIH-bah
week	tydzień	TIH-jayn	coffee	kawa	KAH-vah
morning	rano	RAH-no	milk	mleko	MLEH-koh
afternoon	popołudnie	poh-poh-WOOD-nyeh	beer	piwo	PEE-voh
evening	wieczór	VYEH-choor	sugar	cukier	TSOOK-yehr
spring	wiosna	VYOH-snah	eggs	jajka	YAI-kah
summer	lato	LAH-toh	toilet	toaleta	toh-ah-LEH-tah
fall	jesień	YEH-shayn	square	rynek	RIH-nehk
winter	zima	ZHEE-mah	monastery	klasztor	KLAH-shtohr
hot	gorący	goh-ROHN-tsih	church	kościół	KOSH-choow
cold	zimny	ZHIH-mnih	post office	poczta	POHCH-tah
open	otwarty	ot-FAHR-tih	stamp	znaczki	ZNAHCH-kee
closed	zamknięty	zahmk-NYENT-ih	airmail	lotniczą	loht-NEE-chawm
left	lewo	LEH-voh	right	prawo	PRAH-voh

ENGLISH	POLISH	PRONOUNCE
Hello	Cześć	cheshch
Yes/no	Tak/nie	tahk/nyeh
Please/you're welcome	Proszę	PROH-sheh
Thank you	Dziękuję	jen-KOO-yeh
Goodbye	Do widzenia	doh veed-ZEHN-yah
Good morning	Dzień dobry	jayn DOH-brih
Good evening	Dobry wieczór	doh-brih VYEH-choor
Good night	Dobranoc	doh-BRAH-nohts
Sorry/excuse me	Przepraszam	psheh-PRAH-shahm

ENGLISH	POLISH	PRONOUNCE
Help!	Pomocy!	poh-MOH-tsih!
Where is...?	Gdzie jest...?	GJEH yest
...the bathroom?	...łazienka?	wahzh-EHN-ka
...the nearest telephone booth?	...najbliziej budka telefoniczna?	nai-BLEEZH-ay BOOT-kah teh-leh-foh-NEE-chnah
...center of town?	...centrum miasta?	tsehn-troom MYAH-stah
How do I get to...?	Którędy do...?	ktoo-REHN-dih doh
How much does this cost?	Ile to kosztuje?	EE-leh toh kohsh-TOO-yeh
When?	Kiedy?	KYEH-dih
Do you (male/female) speak English?	Czy pan(i) mówi po angielsku?	chih pahn(-ee) MOO-vee poh ahn-GYEHL-skoo
I don't understand.	Nie rozumiem.	nyeh roh-ZOOM-yem
I don't speak Polish.	Nie mowię po polsku.	nyeh MOO-vyeh poh POHL-skoo
Speak a little slower, please.	Proszę mówić wolniej.	PROH-sheh MOO-veech VOHL-nyay.
Please write it down.	Proszę napisać.	PROH-sheh nah-PEE-sahch
Do you have a vacancy?	Czy są jakieś wolne pokoje?	chih SAWM yah-kyesh VOHL-neh poh-KOY-eh
I (male/female) would like a room.	Chciał(a)bym pokój.	kh-CHOW-(ah)-bihm POH-kooy
I'd like to order...	Chciałbym zamówić...	kh-CHOW-bihm za-MOOV-eech
Check, please.	Proszę rachunek	PROH-sheh ra-HOON-ehk
I want a ticket to...	Poproszę bilet do...	poh-PROH-sheh BEE-leht do...
Go away.	Spadaj.	SPAHD-ai.
Cheers!	Stolat/na zdrowie	STOH-laht/nah ZDROH-wyeh
I love you.	Kocham cię	KOH-ham chewn.

ROMANIAN (ROMÂNA)

ENGLISH	ROMANIAN	PRONOUNCE
Hello	Bună ziua	BOO-nuh zee wah
Yes/no	Da/nu	dah/noo
Please/you're welcome	Vă rog/cu plăcere	vuh rohg/coo pluh-CHEH-reh
Thank you	Mulţumesc	mool-tsoo-MESK
Goodbye	La revedere	lah reh-veh-DEH-reh
Good morning	Bună dimineaţa	BOO-nuh dee-mee-NYAH-tsah
Good evening	Bună seara	BOO-nuh seh-AH-rah
Good night	Noapte bună	NWAP-teh BOO-nuh
Sorry/excuse me	Îmi pare rău/Scuzaţi-mă	ym PA-reh ruh-oo/skoo-ZAH-tz muh
Help!	Ajutor!	AH-zhoot-or
Where is...?	Unde e...?	OON-deh YEH?
...the bathroom?	...toaleta?	to-ah-LEH-ta
...the nearest telephone booth?	...un telefon prin apropiere?	oon teh-leh-FOHN preen ah-proh-PYEH-reh
...center of town?	...centrul oraşului?	CHEHN-trool oh-RAHSH-oo-loo-ee
How do I get to...?	Cum se ajunge la...?	koom seh-ah-ZHOON-jeh lah
How much does this cost?	Cât costă?	kyt KOH-stuh

ENGLISH	ROMANIAN	PRONOUNCE
When?	Când?	kynd
Do you speak English?	Vorbiţi englezeşte?	vor-BEETS ehng-leh-ZESH-te
I don't understand.	Nu înţeleg.	noo-ihn-TZEH-lehg
I don't speak Romanian.	Nu vorbesc Româneşte.	noo vohr-BEHSK roh-myn-EHS-HTE
Speak a little slower, please.	Vorbiţi mai rar vă rog.	vohr-BEETS mai rahr vuh rohg
Please write it down.	Vă rog să scrieţi.	vuh rog suh SCREE-ehts
Do you have a vacancy?	Aveţi camere libere?	a-VETS KUH-mer-eh LEE-ber-e
I'd like a room.	Aş vrea o cameră.	ahsh VREH-ah oh KAH-mehr-ahr
I'd like to order...	Aş vrea nişte...	ash vreh-A NEESH-teh
Check, please.	Nota, vă rog.	NO-tah VUH rohg
I want a ticket to...	Vreau un bilet pentru...	vrah-oo oon bee-LEHT PEHN-troo
Go away.	Du-te.	doo-TEH
Cheers!	Noroc!	noh-ROHK
I love you.	Te iubesc.	TEH YOO-behsk

ENGLISH	ROMANIAN	PRONOUNCE	ENGLISH	ROMANIAN	PRONOUNCE
one	unu	OO-noo	single room	cu un pat	koo oon paht
two	doi	doy	double room	o cameră dublă	oh KAH-meh-rah DOO-blah
three	trei	tray	reservation	rezervarea	re-zer-VAR-eh-a
four	patru	PAH-tru	departures	plecări	pleh-CUHR
five	cinci	CHEEN-ch	arrivals	sosiri	so-SEER
six	şase	SHAH-seh	one-way	dus	doos
seven	şapte	SHAHP-teh	round-trip	dus-intors	doos-in-TORS
eight	opt	ohpt	ticket	bilet	bee-LET
nine	nouă	NO-uh	train	trenul	TREH-null
ten	zece	ZEH-cheh	bus	autobuz	AHU-toh-booz
twenty	douăzeci	doh-wah-ZECH	airport	aeroportul	air-oh-POR-tool
thirty	treizeci	tray-ZEHCH	station	gară	GAH-ruh
forty	patruzeci	pa-TROO-zech	luggage	bagajul	bah-GAHZH-ool
fifty	cincizeci	chin-ZECH	bus station	autogară	AU-toh-gah-rah
sixty	şaizeci	shay-ZECH	bank	banca	BAHN-cah
seventy	şaptezeci	shap-teh-ZECH	police	poliţia	poh-LEE-tsee-ah
eighty	optzeci	ohpt-ZECH	exchange	un birou de de schimb	oon bee-RO deh skeemb
ninety	nouăzeci	noah-ZECH	passport	paşaport	pah-shah-POHRT
one hundred	o sută	o SOO-tuh	market	piaţa	piazza
one thousand	o mie	oh MIH-eh	grocery	o alimentară	a-lee-men-TA-ra
Monday	luni	loon	breakfast	micul dejun	MIK-ul DEH-zhoon
Tuesday	marţi	marts	lunch	prânz	preunz
Wednesday	miercuri	MEER-kur	dinner	cină	CHEE-nuh
Thursday	joi	zhoy	menu	meniu	menEE-oo
Friday	vineri	VEE-ner	bread	pâine	PUH-yih-nay
Saturday	sâmbătă	SIM-buh-tuh	vegetables	legume	LEH-goom-eh

ENGLISH	ROMANIAN	PRONOUNCE
Sunday	duminică	duh-MIH-ni-kuh
today	azi	az
tomorrow	mâine	MUH-yih-neh
day	zi	ZEE
week	săptămână	septa-mOOnch
morning	dimineaţa	dee-mee-NYAH-tsah
afternoon	după-amiază	DOO-pah-MYAH-zuh
evening	seara	seh-AH-rah
spring	primăvară	PREE-mehr-vahr-ehr
summer	vară	VAH-ruh
fall	toamnă	TWAM-nuh
winter	iarnă	YAHR-nuh
hot	cald	kahld
cold	rece	REH-cheh
open	deschis	DESS-kees
closed	închis	un-KEES
left	stânga	STYN-gah

ENGLISH	ROMANIAN	PRONOUNCE
beef	carne de vacă	CAHR-neh deh VAH-cuh
chicken	carne de pui	poo-EE
pork	carne de porc	CAR-neh deh pork
fish	peşte	PESH-teh
coffee	cafea	kah-FEAH
milk	lapte	LAHP-teh
beer	bere	BE-reh
sugar	zahăr	ZAH-hahr
eggs	ouă	OH-oo-uh
toilets	toaleta	toh-AHL-eh-tah
square	piaţa	pee-AHTZ
monastery	mănăstire	my-nuh-STEE-REH
church	biserică	bee-SEH-ree-cuh
post office	poşta	POH-shta
stamps	timbru	TEEM-broo
airmail	avion	ahv-ee-OHN
right	dreapta	drahp-TAH

RUSSIAN (РУССКИЙ)

ENGLISH	RUSSIAN	PRONOUNCE
Hello	Добрый день	DOH-bryy DEHN
Yes/no	Да/нет	Dah/Nyet
Please/you're welcome	Пожалуйста	pa-ZHAL-u-sta
Thank you	Спасибо	spa-SEE-bah
Goodbye	До свидания	da svee-DAHN-yah
Good morning	Доброе утро	DOH-breh OO-tra
Good evening	Добрый вечер	DOH-bryy VEH-cher
Good night	Спокойной ночи	spa-KOI-noy NOHCH-ee
Sorry/excuse me	Извините	iz-vi-NEET-yeh
Help!	Помогите!	pah-mah-GEE-tyeh
Where is...?	Где...?	gdyeh
...the bathroom?	...туалет?	TOO-ah-lyet
...the nearest telephone booth?	...ближайший телефон-автомат?	blee-ZHAI-shiy teh-leh-FOHN-ahf-tah-MAHT
...center of town?	...центр города?	TSEHN-ter GOHR-rah-dah
How do I get to...?	Как пройти...?	kak prai-TEE
How much does this cost?	Сколько это стоит?	SKOHL-ka EH-tah STOH-it
When?	Когда?	kahg-DAH
Do you speak English?	Вы говорите по-английски?	vy ga-va-REE-tye pah ahn-GLEE-skee
I don't understand.	Я не понимаю.	yah neh pah-nee-MAH-yoo

ENGLISH	RUSSIAN	PRONOUNCE
I don't speak Russian.	Я не говорю по-русски.	yah neh gah-vah-RYOO pah ROO-skee
Speak a little slower, please.	Медленее, пожалуйста	MEHD-leh-neh-yeh, pah-ZHAHL-oo-stah
Please write it down.	Напишите пожалуйста	nah-pee-SHEET-yeh pah-ZHAHL-uy-stah
Do you have a vacancy?	У вас есть свободный номер?	oo vahs yehst svah-BOHD-neey NOH-mehr
I'd like a room.	Я бы хотел(а) номер.	yah by khah-TYEHL(ah) NO-mehr
I'd like to order...	Я хотел(а) бы...	ya khah-TYEHL(a) by
Check, please.	Счёт, пожалуйста.	SHYOHT pah-ZHAHL-oo-stah
I want a ticket to...	Один билет до...	ah-DEEN bee-LYET dah
Go away.	Уходите.	oo-khah-DEE-tye
Cheers!	Ваше здоровье!	vahsh-yeh zdah-ROH-vyeh
I love you.	Я люблю тебя.	yah lyoob-LYO teh-BYAH

ENGLISH	RUSSIAN	PRONOUNCE
one	один	ah-DEEN
two	два	dvah
three	три	tree
four	четыре	chi-TIH-rih
five	пять	pyat
six	шесть	shest
seven	семь	syehm
eight	восемь	VOH-syehm'
nine	девять	DYEV-it
ten	десять	DYES-it
twenty	двадцать	DVAHD-tsat
thirty	тридцать	TREE-dtsat
forty	сорок	SOHR-ahk
fifty	пятьдесят	pyaht-dyeh-SYAHT
sixty	шестьдесят	shehs-dyeh-SYAHT
seventy	семьдесят	sehm-dyeh-SYAHT
eighty	восемьдесят	Vahsehm-dyeh-SYAHT
ninety	девяносто	dyeh-vyah-NOH-sta
one hundred	сто	stoh
one thousand	тысяча	TY-sya-cha
Monday	понедельник	pah-nyeh-DYEHL-neek
Tuesday	вторник	FTOR-neek
Wednesday	среда	sryeh-DAH

ENGLISH	RUSSIAN	PRONOUNCE
single room	одноместный номер	ahd-nah-MYEHS-nyy NOH-myehr
double room	двухместный номер	dvookh-MYEHS-nyy NOH-myehr
reservation	предваритель-ный заказ	prehd-vah-REE-tyehl-ny zah-KAHZ
departure	отъезд	aht-YEHZD
arrival	приезд	pree-YEHZD
one-way	в один конец	v ah-DEEN kah-NYETS
round-trip	туда и обратно	too-DAH ee ah-BRAHT-nah
ticket	билет	beel-YEHT
train	поезд	POH-yehzd
bus	автобус	af-TOH-boos
airport	аэропорт	ah-ehro-PORT
station	вокзал	VOHK-zahl
luggage	багаж	bah-GAZH
bus station	автовокзал	ahv-toh-VAHK-zahl
bank	банк	bahnk
police	милиция	mee-LEE-tsee-yah
exchange	обмен валюты	ahb-MYEHN vahl-YOO-ty
passport	паспорт	PAHS-pahrt
market	рынок	RYN-nahk
grocery	гастроном	gah-stra-NOM
breakfast	завтрак	ZAHF-trahk
lunch	обед	ah-BYED
dinner	ужин	OO-zheen

ENGLISH	RUSSIAN	PRONOUNCE
Thursday	четверг	chyeht-VYEHRK
Friday	пятница	PYAHT-nit-sah
Saturday	суббота	soo-BOT-tah
Sunday	воскресенье	vahs-kryeh-SYEH-nye
today	сегодня	see-VOHD-nya
tomorrow	завтра	ZAHF-trah
day	день	dyen
week	неделя	nyeh-DYEL-yah
morning	утром	OO-trahm
afternoon	днём	dnyom
evening	вечером	VYEH-cher-ahm
spring	весна	vyehs-NAH
summer	лето	LYEH-tah
fall	осень	OHS-syehn'
winter	зима	zee-MAH
hot	жаркий	ZHAHR-keey
cold	холодный	kha-LOD-nyy
open	открыт	oht-KRYT
closed	закрыт	za-KRYT
left	налево	nah-LYEH-vah

ENGLISH	RUSSIAN	PRONOUNCE
menu	меню	mehn-YOO
bread	хлеб	khlyehp
vegetables	овощи	OH-vah-shee
beef	говядина	gah-VYAH-dee-nah
chicken	курица	KOO-ree-tsah
pork	свинина	svee-NEE-nah
fish	рыба	REE-bah
coffee	кофе	KOH-fyeh
milk	молоко	mah-lah-KOH
beer	пиво	PEE-vah
sugar	сахар	SAH-khahr
eggs	яйца	yai-TSAH
toilet	туалет	too-ah-LYET
square	площадь	PLOH-shahd'
monastery	монастырь	mohn-ahs-TYR
church	церковь	TSEHR-kahf
post office	почта	POCH-tah
stamp	марка	MAHR-kah
airmail	авиа	AH-vee-ah
right	направо	nah-PRAH-vah

SLOVENIAN (SLOVENSKO)

ENGLISH	SLOVENIAN	PRONOUNCE
Hello	Dober dan	DOH-behr dahn
Yes/no	Ja/ne	yah/nay
Please	Prosim	proh-SEEM
Thank you	Hvala	HVAHL-ah
Goodbye	Nasvidenje	nah-SVEE-dehn-yay
Sorry/excuse me	Oprostite	oh proh-STEE-tei
Help!	Na pomoč!	nah POH-moch
ticket	karta	KAHR-tah
bus	avtobus	ow-TOH-boos
toilet	Toaleta	toh-ah-LEH-tah

ENGLISH	SLOVENIAN	PRONOUNCE
one	eden/eno	EH-dehn/EH-noh
two	dva	dvah
three	tri	tree
four	štiri	SHTIHR-ee
five	pet	peyt
six	šest	SHEYST
seven	sedem	SEH-dehm
eight	osem	OH-sehm
nine	devet	DEH-veht
ten	deset	DEH-seht

ENGLISH	SLOVENIAN	PRONOUNCE
Where is...?	Kje...?	kyay
How much does this cost?	Koliko to stane?	KOH-lee-koh toh STAH-nay
Do you speak English?	Ali govorite angleski?	AH-lee goh-VOHR-ee-tay AHNG-lesh-kee
Cheers!	Na zdravje!	nah zh-DRAHV-yay
I love you.	Ljubim te.	LYOO-bihm tay

INDEX

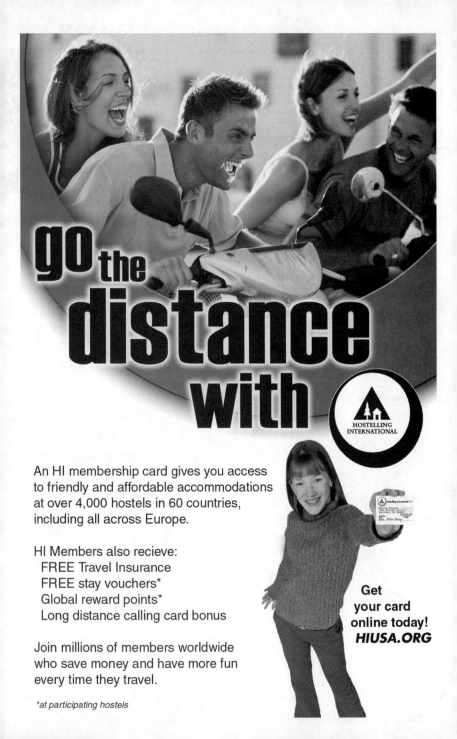

LONG ON WEEKEND. SHORT ON CASH.

ABOUT LET'S GO

GUIDES FOR THE INDEPENDENT TRAVELER

At Let's Go, we see every trip as the chance of a lifetime. If your dream is to grab a machete and forge through the jungles of Brazil, we can take you there. If you'd rather bask in the Riviera sun at a beachside cafe, we'll set you a table. We write for readers who know that there's more to travel than sharing double deckers with tourists and who believe that travel can change both themselves and the world— whether they plan to spend six days in London or six months in Latin America. We'll show you just how far your money can go, and prove that the greatest limitation on your adventures is not your wallet, but your imagination. After all, traveling close to the ground lets you interact more directly with the places and people you've gone to see, making for the most authentic experience.

BEYOND THE TOURIST EXPERIENCE

To help you gain a deeper connection with the places you travel, our researchers give you the heads-up on both world-renowned and off-the-beaten-track attractions, sights, and destinations. They engage with the local culture, writing features on regional cuisine, local festivals, and hot political issues. We've also opened our pages to respected writers and scholars to hear their takes on the countries and regions we cover, and asked travelers who have worked, studied, or volunteered abroad to contribute first-person accounts of their experiences. We've also increased our coverage of responsible travel and expanded each guide's Alternatives to Tourism chapter to share more ideas about how to give back to local communities and learn about the places you travel.

FORTY-FIVE YEARS OF WISDOM

Let's Go got its start in 1960, when a group of creative and well-traveled students compiled their experience and advice into a 20-page mimeographed pamphlet, which they gave to travelers on charter flights to Europe. Four and a half decades later, we've expanded to cover six continents and all kinds of travel—while retaining our founders' adventurous attitude toward the world. Our guides are still researched and written entirely by students on shoestring budgets, experienced travelers who know that train strikes, stolen luggage, food poisoning, and marriage proposals are all part of a day's work. This year, we're expanding our coverage of South America and Southeast Asia, with brand-new *Let's Go: Ecuador*, *Let's Go: Peru*, and *Let's Go: Vietnam*. Our adventure guide series is growing, too, with the addition of *Let's Go: Pacific Northwest Adventure* and *Let's Go: New Zealand Adventure*. And we're immensely excited about our new *Let's Go: Roadtripping USA*—two years, eight routes, and sixteen researchers and editors have put together a travel guide like none other.

THE LET'S GO COMMUNITY

More than just a travel guide company, Let's Go is a community. Our small staff comes together because of our shared passion for travel and our desire to help other travelers see the world. We love it when our readers become part of the Let's Go community as well—when you travel, drop us a postcard (67 Mt. Auburn St., Cambridge, MA 02138, USA) or send us an e-mail (feedback@letsgo.com) to tell us about your adventures and discoveries.

For more information, visit us online: www.letsgo.com.

MAP INDEX

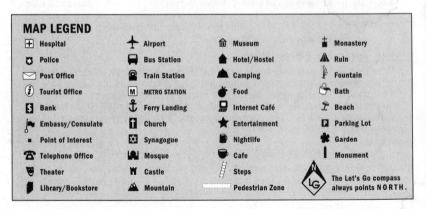

MAP LEGEND

- ✚ Hospital
- ✪ Police
- ✉ Post Office
- (i) Tourist Office
- $ Bank
- ◢ Embassy/Consulate
- ▪ Point of Interest
- ☎ Telephone Office
- ♥ Theater
- ▮ Library/Bookstore

- ✈ Airport
- 🚌 Bus Station
- 🚆 Train Station
- M METRO STATION
- ⚓ Ferry Landing
- ✝ Church
- ✡ Synagogue
- 🕌 Mosque
- ♜ Castle
- ⛰ Mountain

- 🏛 Museum
- ⌂ Hotel/Hostel
- ▲ Camping
- ❀ Food
- 💻 Internet Café
- ★ Entertainment
- 🍷 Nightlife
- ☕ Cafe
- ⫽ Steps
- ⣿ Pedestrian Zone

- ✝ Monastery
- ⛰ Ruin
- ⚐ Fountain
- ♨ Bath
- ☂ Beach
- P Parking Lot
- ✿ Garden
- | Monument

The Let's Go compass always points NORTH.